The New York Times
CROSSWORD PUZZLE
DICTIONARY

The New York Times
CROSSWORD PUZZLE
DICTIONARY

By

Thomas Pulliam and Clare Grundman

A HUDSON GROUP BOOK

 QUADRANGLE/THE NEW YORK TIMES BOOK COMPANY

Produced in association with Morningside Associates.

Second printing December 1974

Library of Congress Catalog Card Number: 73-79912

International Standard Book Number: 0-8129-0382-x

PREFACE

THE NEW YORK TIMES CROSSWORD PUZZLE DICTIONARY exceeds in completeness and scope all other puzzle dictionaries. No useful word has been omitted. Not only have puzzles themselves been combed for synonyms that are used over and over, but also a word-for-word reading of major unabridged dictionaries, both current and old, produced a thoroughly complete and extensive checklist.

Each of us has been solving and compiling puzzles for many years, and our chief purpose has been to design a practical and easy-to-use dictionary, in the belief that your needs and requirements for such a volume closely reflect our own. For example, the synonyms are arranged by the number of letters, and then alphabetized so you can quickly find the very word that fills the spaces in the puzzle. Another feature, one that seems obvious for a crossword puzzle dictionary but is not found in most of them, is that all words are printed in easy-to-read capital letters. The type has been chosen with great care for its legibility, and the three-column format not only provides a short line of type to scan, but also enables us to get a very large number of words on each page.

Synonyms of great length have been omitted to give room for the shorter, more useful words. The puzzler can always "fill in" the very long words provided he has a good supply of short common synonyms. We have placed, therefore, an arbitrary ceiling of eight-letter word-lengths, knowing this will satisfy almost all needs. Here and there, however, you will find occasional exceptions to this rule. These are synonyms of such frequent, interesting and normal usage that their omission might handicap the puzzler.

The "shaded boxes" scattered through the book are a notable and unique feature of THE NEW YORK TIMES CROSSWORD PUZZLE DICTIONARY. They collect under one heading a variety of categories and synonyms that you would have a hard time finding in other dictionaries. For example, when you are confronted by the clue "Brazilian river" merely turn to the shaded area marked BRAZIL, where you will find several excellent possibilities. Similarly, look for a "Philippine native" under PHILIPPINES, or a "Scottish measure" under SCOTLAND.

Another useful feature is the lavish listing of phrases. For instance, instead of being confronted by the simple clue "Sword," you may run up against "Double-edged sword." Under the entry word SWORD in this dictionary you will find ample phrases that qualify the entry word or more sharply specify its meaning. Also, given the definition "Turn aside," simply look under TURN and find that phrase, along with many others.

THE NEW YORK TIMES CROSSWORD PUZZLE DICTIONARY is a versatile reference book which you will want to keep on your desk or next to your chair for help, not only with crossword puzzles, but also for a large variety of other puzzles and contests. In addition, it will be invaluable for writers, speakers, and the like, for (with more than ½ million words) it is one of the largest books of synonyms ever published. Its simple arrangement makes it far easier to use than the standard thesauri.

Our hope is that you will come to use this new word book as we might. Get to know it and be adventuresome! If the first entry you consult does not corner the exact word you are seeking, let any listing at that spot lead you to a cross-reference. Follow this track until you have the right word "treed."

A project of this scope may well have been beyond the ability of only two to accomplish. We have required and welcomed top-flight support during our work. Although many might be named, special note must be given to the efforts of Richard Martz and David House of Dartmouth College, who were responsible for much of the computerization; also, to Gorton Carruth and Robert O'Brien of Morningside Associates. Each made his individual contributions, which we gratefully acknowledge.

Happy word hunting!

Tom Pulliam
Clare Grundman

The New York Times

CROSSWORD PUZZLE
DICTIONARY

A AN AY HA AIR ARY PER ALFA EACH
ALPHA
(EVER —) ARROW
AA LAVA
AAL AL MULBERRY
AARDVARK ANTEATER EDENTATE
AARDWOLF HYAENID
AARON (BROTHER OF —) MOSES
(BURIAL PLACE OF —) HOR
(FATHER OF —) AMRAM
(SISTER OF —) MIRIAM
(SON OF —) ABIHU NADAB ELEAZAR
AARONIC LEVITIC LEVITICAL
AB HATI
ABA ABAYAH
ABACA HEMP FIBER LUPIS LINAGA
MANILA
ABACK SHORT
ABACUS SOROBAN
ABADDON PIT HELL ABYSS SATAN
APOLLYON
ABAFT AFT BACK BAFT ABAFF
ASTERN BEHIND REARWARD
(— THE BEAM) LARGE
ABALONE EAR PAUA AWABI NACRE
ORMER UHLLO ASSEIR MOLLUSK
ABANDON EGO CAST DROP FLEE
JUNK QUIT SINK ALLAY DITCH
EXPEL LEAVE PLANT REMIT SCRAP
WAIVE YIELD ABJURE BANISH
BETRAY DESERT DEVEST DISUSE
DIVEST EXPOSE FOREGO FORHOO
FORLET MAROON RECANT REFUSE
REJECT RELENT RESIGN SLOUGH
VACATE DEPLORE DISCARD FORLEIT
FORSAKE SCUTTLE ABDICATE
FORHOOIE FORSWEAR JETTISON
RASHNESS RENOUNCE SURCEASE
(WITH —) DESPERATELY
ABANDONED BAD LEFT LORN LOST
WICKED CORRUPT FORLORN
PROJECT DEPRAVED DERELICT
DESERTED DESOLATE FLAGRANT
FORSAKEN
ABANDONMENT BURIAL APOSTASY
(— OF RESTRAINT) LETUP
ABASE SINK VAIL AVALE AVILE
BLAME DEMIT DIMIT LOWER SHAME
ABJECT BEMEAN DEBASE DEFAME
DEJECT DEMEAN DEPOSE GROVEL
HUMBLE LESSEN MEEKEN REDUCE
DEGRADE DEPRESS MORTIFY
DIMINISH DISGRACE DISHONOR
ABASED ABAISSE DEJECTED
ABASH AWE COW BASH BAZE DASH
AVALE ESBAY SHAME HUMBLE
CONFUSE MORTIFY BEWILDER
BROWBEAT CONFOUND
ABASHED BLANK CHEAP SHAMED
ASHAMED FOOLISH SHEEPISH
ABASHMENT VERGOYNE
ABATE EBB END LOW CALM CURB
FAIK FALL MEND OMIT SLOW SOFT
VOID WANE ALLAY ANNUL BREAK
CHECK LOWER QUASH RELAX REMIT
SLAKE SWAGE ASLAKE DEDUCT
LESSEN PACIFY REBATE REDUCE
RELENT ABOLISH ASSUAGE
CASSARE CHANCER NULLIFY

QUALIFY SLACKEN SUBSIDE
DECREASE DIMINISH MITIGATE
MODERATE OVERBLOW PALLIATE
ABATEMENT DELF FALL ALLAY
DELFT DELPH LETUP GUSSET
MIOSIS DECREASE DISCOUNT
ABATIS OBSTACLE SLASHING
ABAXIAL DORSAL
ABBA FATHER
ABBE MONK CLERIC CURATE PRIEST
ABBESS AMMA VICARESS
ABBEY ABADIA ABBAYE PRIORY
CONVENT NUNNERY CLOISTER
ABBOT ABBAS COARB
(— OF MISRULE) BISHOP
ABBREVIATE CUT CLIP DOCK PRUNE
DIGEST ABRIDGE BOBTAIL CURTAIL
SHORTEN CONDENSE CONTRACT
TRUNCATE
ABBREVIATED SHORT BOBTAIL
CRYPTIC MUTILATE
ABBREVIATION LAPSE SIGLUM
SYMBOL
(PL.) SIGLA
ABC ALPHABET
ABDICATE CEDE QUIT DEMIT EXPEL
LEAVE REMIT DEPOSE DISOWN
FOREGO RESIGN RETIRE VACATE
ABANDON DISCLAIM RENOUNCE
ABDICATION DRIFT
ABDOMEN BOUK WOMB ALVUS
APRON BELLY MELON MIRAC PLEON
THARM PAUNCH VENTER STOMACH
ABDOMINAL HEMAL CELIAC
COELIAC VENTRAL VISCERAL
ABDUCT LURE TAKE STEAL ABDUCE
KIDNAP RAVISH SPIRIT CAPTURE
ABDUCTION APAGOGE RAPTURE
ABDUCTOR SPIRIT
ABEAM ABREAST
ABECEDARIAN TYRO NOVICE
LEARNER BEGINNER
ABECEDARIUS ABC
ABED SICK RESTING RETIRED
SLEEPING
ABEL (BROTHER OF —) CAIN SETH
(PARENT OF —) EVE ADAM
ABELMOSK MUSK MALLOW
ABERDEEN ANGUS BLACK DODDY
DODDIE
ABERRANT WILD CLAMMY DEVIANT
ABNORMAL STRAYING VARIABLE
ABERRATION SLIP WARP ERROR
FAULT LAPSE MANIA DELIRIUM
DELUSION INSANITY
ABESSIVE CARITIVE
ABET AID EGG BACK HELP BOOST
COACH ASSIST FOMENT INCITE
SECOND SUCCOR UPHOLD
COMFORT CONNIVE ESPOUSE
FORWARD FURTHER SUPPORT
SUSTAIN ADVOCATE BEFRIEND
ABETTING CONFEDERATE
ABETTOR FAUTOR ADVOCATE
PROMOTER
ABETO ACXOYATL
ABEYANCE ABEYANCY DORMANCY
ABEYANT LATENT
ABHOR UG IRK HATE SHUN AGRISE

DETEST LOATHE DESPISE DISLIKE
EXECRATE
ABHORRENCE HATE ODIUM HATRED
HORROR DISGUST DISLIKE
AVERSION LOATHING
ABHORRENT UGSOM HATEFUL
INFAMOUS
ABIDE BE WIN WON BEAR BIDE KEEP
LAST LEND LENG LIVE REST STAY
WAIT ABEAR AWAIT DELAY EXIST
HABIT PAUSE STAND SWELL TARRY
ENDURE HARBOR LINGER REMAIN
RESIDE SUBMIT INHABIT SOJOURN
SUBSIST SUSTAIN CONTINUE
TOLERATE
(— BY) HOLD
ABIDING FAST STABLE LASTING
ABIDINGNESS PERMANENCE
ABIES FIRS CONIFERS
ABIETATE SYLVATE
ABIGAIL MAID
(HUSBAND OF —) DAVID NABAL
ABIGEUS ABACTOR
ABIJAH (FATHER OF —) DAVID
(SON OF —) ASA
ABILITY G CAN MAY CLAY EASE
FORM HAND CLASS FLAIR FORCE
MIGHT POWER SKILL STUFF VERVE
ENERGY ENGINE MAUGHT STROKE
TALENT CALIBER CUNNING FACULTY
POTENCY APTITUDE CAPACITY
STRENGTH
(— TO ENTER) ACCESS
(— TO THROW) ARM
(BATTING —) STICKWORK
(CREATIVE —) IMAGINATION
(INVENTIVE —) CONTRIVANCE
(MENTAL —) INGENY BRAINPOWER
ABIPON CORONADO
ABJECT LOW BASE MEAN POOR
SUNK VILE HELOT PALTRY SORDID
SUPINE FAWNING FORLORN
IGNOBLE SERVILE SLAVISH
BEGGARLY CRINGING DEGRADED
DOWNCAST LISTLESS WRETCHED
ABJOINT ABSTRICT
ABJURE DENY NITTE SPURN ESCHEW
RECALL RECANT REJECT RESIGN
REVOKE ABANDON DISAVOW
EJURATE RETRACT ABNEGATE
DISCLAIM FORSWEAR RENOUNCE
ABLAUT APOPHONY
ABLAZE ALOW AFIRE ALOWE
ABLEEZE BURNING GLOWING
RADIANT GLEAMING INFLAMED
ABLE APT BIG CAN FIT FERE ADEPT
HABIL SMART THERE CLEVER
EXPERT FACILE FITTED HABILE
POTENT STRONG BASTANT
CAPABLE DOUGHTY DEXTROUS
POSSIBLE POWERFUL SKILLFUL
SUITABLE TALENTED VIGOROUS
(— TO WALK) FEERIE FEIRIE
ABLE-BODIED YAL YALD YAULD
ABLUTION BATH WIDU WUDU WUZU
LOTION BAPTISM BATHING WASHING
ABNAKI WABANAKI
ABNEGATE DENY ABJURE FOREGO
REFUSE REJECT DISAVOW DISCLAIM

FORSWEAR IMMOLATE RENOUNCE
ABNORMAL ENORM QUEER UTTER
ERRATIC UNUSUAL VICIOUS
ABERRANT ATYPICAL FREAKISH
ABNORMALITY ATAXY ATAXIA
LETHAL BROWNING DEMENTIA
ENORMITY
(CATTLE —) SAWDUST
ABOARD ON ONTO ACROSS
ATHWART
ABODE COT DAR HUT INN WON
BODE CELL FLAT HALL HOME NEST
OMEN REST SEAT TENT WOON
BEING BOWER DELAY HAUNT HOUSE
MANOR PITCH RESET SIEGE SUITE
ABIDAL BIDING ESTATE ADDRESS
COTTAGE HABITAT LODGING
MANSION SITTING CUNABULA
DOMICILE DWELLING RESIANCE
TENEMENT
(— OF DEAD) DAR AARU HELL
ARALU HADES ORCUS SHEOL
HEAVEN SHADES XIBALBA
(— OF DELIGHT) ELYSIUM
(— OF EVIL POWERS) ABYSS
(— OF GODS) MERU ASGARD
OLYMPUS
(— OF LOST SOULS) ABADDON
(— OF SOULS) LIMBO
(ANIMAL —) ZOO MENAGERIE
(CELESTIAL —) HEAVEN
(FILTHY —) STY STYE
(MISERABLE —) DOGHOLE
(SHELTERED —) SHADE
ABOLISH END BLOT KILL ABATE
ANNUL ERASE FORDO QUASH
CANCEL EFFACE FOREDO RECALL
REPEAL REVOKE VACATE DESTROY
NULLIFY RESCIND REVERSE
ABROGATE
ABOLITION EXTINCTION
ABOMA BOA BOM BOMA
ABOMASUM READ REED
ABOMINABLE VILE RUSTY ODIOUS
ROTTEN BEASTLY HATEFUL
HEINOUS MALEDICT
ABOMINABLY BEASTLY
ABOMINATE HATE ABHOR DETEST
LOATHE EXECRATE
ABOMINATION EVIL CRIME CURSE
HORROR PLAGUE DISGUST
AVERSION
ABONGO BABONGO
ABORAL DORSAL
ABORIGINAL ABO YAO FIRST NATAL
BINGHI NATIVE SAVAGE NATURAL
PRIMARY ORIGINAL
(— WOMAN) GIN
ABORIGINE KA KHA TODA ALFUR
BAIGA BLACK BOONG DASYU MAORI
MYALL ALFURO ARANDA ARANTA
ARUNTA BINGHI INDIAN KIPPER
KODAGA NATIVE SAVAGE ADIBASI
CHINHWAN WARRAGAL WARRIGAL
ABORT SLIP
ABORTION SLIP ABORT FAILURE
CASTLING FETICIDE MISBIRTH
ABORTIVE IDLE VAIN BLIND FUTILE
ABOUND SNY FLOW SNEE TEEM

COVER FLEET SWARM REDOUND
OVERFLOW
ABOUNDING RIFE FLUSH ROUTH
COPIOUS REPLETE TEEMING
ABUNDANT
ABOUT BY IN OF ON RE SAY AWAY
NEAR SOME UMBE UPON ANENT
ASTIR CIRCA ABROAD ACTIVE
ALMOST ANENST AROUND CIRCUM
TOWARD ENVIRON CIRCITER
ABOUT-FACE FLOP
ABOVE ON UP OER SUP ATOP OVER
PAST UPON ABEEN ABOON ABUNE
ALOFT SUPRA BEFORE BEYOND
HIGHER THEREUP OVERHEAD
SUPERIOR
(— GENERAL LEVEL) APART
ABRADE RAW RUB BARK FILE FRET
GALL RASP SAND WEAR CHAFE
ERASE GRATE GRAZE GRIND SCORE
TOUCH SCRAPE IRRITATE
ABRADER FILE RASP EMERY
SANDER ABRASER GRINDER
SCRAPER
ABRAHAM (BIRTHPLACE OF —) UR
(BROTHER OF —) HARAN NAHOR
(CONCUBINE OF —) HAGAR
(FATHER OF —) TERAH
(GRANDFATHER OF —) NAHOR
(GRANDSON OF —) ESAU
(NEPHEW OF —) LOT
(SON OF —) ISAAC MEDAN SHUAH
MIDIAN ZIMRAN ISHMAEL JOKSHAN
(WIFE OF —) SARAH KETURAH
ABRASION BURN GALL OUCH SCAR
SORE GRAZE BRUISE BLASTING
ABRASIVE SAND EMERY PUMICE
QUARTZ SILICA ALUNDUM ERODENT
ABRADANT CORUNDUM SCRUBBER
ABRAXAS GEM STONE AMULET
ABRASAX
ABREAST EVEN AFRONT BESIDE
HANGING
ABRET BREAD WAFER
ABRI SHED COVER DUGOUT SHELTER
ABRIDGE CUT DOCK LASK BRIEF
ELIDE LIMIT RASEE RAZEE BRIDGE
REDUCE SHRINK CURTAIL DEPRIVE
REWRITE SHORTEN ABSTRACT
BREVIATE COMPRESS CONDENSE
CONTRACT DIMINISH RETRENCH
SIMPLIFY
ABRIDGED TAIL
ABRIDGEMENT TAIL BRIEF DIGEST
PRECIS RESUME SKETCH COMPEND
EPITOME PANDECT SUMMARY
SUMMULA ABSTRACT BOILDOWN
BREVIARY SYNOPSIS
ABROAD OFF ASEA AWAY ABOUT
ASTIR FORTH ABREED AFIELD
ASTRAY WIDELY DISTANT OUTWARD
OVERSEA OFFSHORE
ABROGATE ANNUL QUASH REMIT
CANCEL REPEAL REVOKE VACATE
ABOLISH NULLIFY RESCIND
DISSOLVE OVERRULE
ABRUPT BOLD CURT DEAD FAST
RUDE BLUFF BLUNT BRIEF BRUSK
HASTY ICTIC QUICK ROUGH SHARP

SHEER SHORT STEEP STUNT SURLY
TERSE TOTAL CHOPPY CRAGGY
CRUSTY PROMPT RUGGED SUDDEN
ANGULAR BRUSQUE PRERUPT
VIOLENT HEADLONG VERTICAL
(NOT —) SOFT
ABRUPTLY BANG SHARP SHORT
STEEPLY SUDDENLY
ABSALOM (FATHER OF —) DAVID
(SLAYER OF —) JOAB
ABSAROKA CROW
ABSCESS BOIL MORO SORE ULCER
FESTER INCOME LESION QUINSY
VOMICA EXITURE GUMBOIL PARULIS
APOSTEME SQUINACY
ABSCISSA X COSINE
ABSCISSION APOCOPE
ABSCOND GO FLY RUN BOLT FLEE
HIDE QUIT ELOPE SCRAM SMOKE
DECAMP DEPART DESERT ELOINE
ESCAPE LEVANT WITHDRAW
ABSENCE CUT LACK VOID WANT
BLANK LEAVE DEFECT REMOVE
VACUUM DEFAULT FAILURE
VACANCY FURLOUGH
(— FROM DUTY) LIBERTY
(— FROM ONE'S COUNTRY) EXILE
(— OF AN ORGAN) AGENESIA
AGENESIS
(— OF BIAS) DETACHMENT
(— OF CEREMONY) FAMILIARITY
(— OF FAMILIARITY) DISTANCE
(— OF FEELING) APATHY
(— OF FEVER) APYREXY APYREXIA
(— OF FORM) ENTROPY
(— OF GOVERNMENT) ANARCHY
(— OF INHIBITIONS) ANIMALITY
(— OF LIGHT) BLACK DARKNESS
(— OF MARRIAGE) AGAMY
(— OF MIND) ABSTRACTION
(— OF NAILS) ANONYCHIA
(— OF PAIN) ANODYNIA
(— OF PIGMENTATION) ACHROMA
ACHROMIA
(— OF SKULL) ACRANIA
(— OF TAIL) ANURY
(— OF TASTE) AGEUSIA
(— OF TRUMPS) CHICANE
(— OF TRUTH) FALSEHOOD
ABSENT CUT OFF OUT AWAY AWOL
GONE LOST WANE DESERT MUSING
LACKING MISSING WANTING
ABSORBED DREAMING
(— IN MIND) ABSTRACT
ABSENTMINDED MUSING DISTRAIT
DREAMING
ABSENTMINDEDNESS STARGAZING
ABSINTHE AJENJO GENIPI
ABSOLUTE GOD ONE TAO TAT DEAD
DOWN FAIR FINE FREE MEAR MEER
MERE PLAT PLUM PURE RANK REAL
SELF TRUE VERY BLANK CLEAR
FIXED PLUMB SHEER STARK TOTAL
UTTER WHOLE ENTIRE SEVERE
SIMPLE SQUARE CERTAIN PERFECT
PLENARY ABSTRACT COMPLETE
DESPOTIC EVENDOWN EXPLICIT
IMPLICIT POSITIVE
(— TEMPERATURE) T

(NOT —) FINITE CONDITIONAL

ABSOLUTELY YEA YES AMEN BONE COLD DEAD FAIR JUST PLAT SLAP PLAIN PLUMB STARK BARELY FAIRLY FLATLY SIMPLY WHOLLY SHEERLY ENTIRELY EVENDOWN

ABSOLUTION EXCUSE PARDON SHRIFT LOOSING SHRIVING

ABSOLUTISM CAESARISM DESPOTISM

ABSOLVE FREE QUIT CLEAR LOOSE REMIT ACQUIT ASSOIL EXCUSE EXEMPT FINISH PARDON SHRIVE UNBIND CLEANSE FORGIVE JUSTIFY RELEASE DISPENSE LIBERATE OVERLOOK

ABSORB EAT FIX SOP SUP SOAK SUCK TAKE AMUSE DRINK MERGE RIVET UNITE DEVOUR ENGAGE ENGULF ENWRAP IMBIBE INGEST INSORB INWRAP OCCUPY SPONGE STIFLE COMBINE CONSUME ENGROSS IMMERSE INVOLVE OCCLUDE SWALLOW

ABSORBED DEEP GONE LOST RAPT SUNK FIXED ABSENT BURIED ENRAPT HIPPED INTENT PLUNGED RIVETED WRAPPED IMMERSED
(— BY) ALL

ABSORBENT BASE FOMES SPONGY ANTACID SORBENT ANTIACID DRINKING

ABSORBER SNUBBER
(— OF MONEY) LICKPENNY
(SHOCK —) BUFFER DAMPER

ABSORBING

ABSORPTION AUTISM
(— UNIT) SABIN

ABSTAIN DENY FAST KEEP STAY AVOID CEASE SPARE SPURN WAIVE DESIST DISUSE ESCHEW FOREGO REFUSE REJECT FORBEAR REFRAIN RESTRAIN TEETOTAL WITHHOLD
(— FROM) FAST FORGO LEAVE ABJURE ESCHEW FOREGO REFRAIN

ABSTAINER TOTE RECHABITE

ABSTEMIOUS SOBER ACETIC SLENDER MODERATE

ABSTENTION CELIBACY CHASTITY

ABSTERGE WIPE BATHE CLEAN PURGE RINSE

ABSTINENCE ENCRATY

ABSTINENT SOBER ABSTEMIOUS

ABSTRACT CULL DEED DRAW NOTE PART PURE TAKE BRIEF IDEAL STEAL ABSORB DEDUCT DETACH DIVERT DOCKET PRECIS REMOVE ABRIDGE COMPEND EXCERPT ISOLATE PURLOIN SECRETE SUMMARY VIDIMUS ABSTRUSE ACADEMIC ARGUMENT BREVIATE DISCRETE SEPARATE SYLLABUS SYNOPSIS TABLEITY WITHDRAW
(NOT —) CONCRETE
(PL.) PARATITLA PARATITLES

ABSTRACTED REMOTE

ABSTRACTION STUDY ENTITY ABSTRACT QUODDITY

ABSTRUSE DARK DEEP HIGH HIDDEN MYSTIC REMOTE SECRET SUBTLE CURIOUS OBSCURE RETIRED ABSTRACT ACROATIC ESOTERIC PROFOUND

ABSURD HOT RICH WILD DOTTY DROLL FALSE INANE INEPT SILLY SCREWY STUPID ASININE FATUOUS FOOLISH LAPUTAN DOGGEREL FABULOUS

ABSURDITY FATUITY FOOLERY FOPPERY WALTROT MAGGOTRY NONSENSE UNREASON

ABUNA METRAN

ABUNDANCE WON COPY FLOW MORT SONS WONE CHEAP DEPTH FOUTH POWER RIVER ROUTH ROWTH SCADS SONSE STORE WRECK BOUNTY FOISON GALORE LAVISH OODLES PLENTY POWDER RICHES TALENT UBERTY WEALTH FLUENCY LASHINS SATIETY BELLYFUL FULLNESS LASHINGS OPULENCE PLEURISY RIMPTION
(IN —) APLENTY

ABUNDANT FAT OLD FREE LUSH MUCH RANK RICH RIFE AMPLE FLUSH HEFTY LARGE OPIME ROUTH ROWTH STORE DEMOID GALORE HEARTY ROUTHY APLENTY COPIOUS FERTILE FULSOME LIBERAL PROFUSE REPLETE TEEMING UBERANT UBEROUS WEALTHY AFFLUENT FRUITFUL GENEROUS NUMEROUS
(NOT —) LIGHT SPARE

ABUNDANTLY RIFE WELL FREELY LARGELY HEARTILY

ABUSE MAR MOB TAX BUSE CALL DRUB FLAY GAFF HARM HURT LACK MAUL RAIL RUIN SLAM TEEN VAIN CRIME CURSE FAULT GRIEF SCOLD SLANG SNASH SPOIL BERATE DEFILE INJURE INSULT MALIGN MISUSE MUMBLE PUNISH RAVISH REVILE TANCEL TANSEL VILIFY YATTER AFFRONT BACKJAW BEDEVIL DECEIVE DESPITE FALSIFY MISBEDE MISCALL MISNAME OBLOQUY OUTRAGE PERVERT PROFANE SLANDER TRADUCE UPBRAID VIOLATE BALLARAG BUSINESS DISHONOR FRUMPERY LANGUAGE MALTREAT MISAPPLY MISTREAT REPROACH SLAPDASH

ABUSED DOWNTROD DOWNTRODDEN

ABUSIVE FOUL DIRTY SHREWD CORRUPT SATIRIC CHEATING INSOLENT LIBELOUS

ABUT BUTT JOIN REST TOUCH ADJOIN BORDER BUTTAL PROJECT

ABUTILON MALLOW

ABUTMENT CRIB PIER ALETTE BUTTRESS

ABUTTING FLUSH ADJACENT

ABYSM ABIME BISME DOWNFALL

ABYSMAL DEEP DREARY PROFOUND UNENDING WRETCHED

ABYSS PIT POT DEEP GULF HELL VOID ABYSM CHAOS CHASM DEPTH GORGE BOTTOM VORAGO ABADDON GEHENNA SWALLOW DOWNFALL INTERVAL

ABYSSAL ABYSMAL BASSALIAN

ABYSSINIA AXUM ETHIOPIA

ABYSSINIAN SIDI ABASSIN
(— BANANA) ENSETE

ACACIA GUM JAM BABUL GIDYA MULGA MYALL SIRIS THORN TIMBE VEREK ARABIC BABLAH BINDER GIDGEA GIDGEE GIDYEA HASHAB LEGUME LOCUST MIMOSA WATTLE YARRAN BLUEBUSH BRIGALOW CHAPPARO IRONWOOD ROSEWOOD

ACADEMIC IVY RIGID FORMAL CLASSIC DONNISH ERUDITE LEARNED POMPIER

ACADEMY LYCEE CRUSCA LYCEUM MANEGE SCHOOL COLLEGE SOCIETY YESHIVA SEMINARY
(RIDING —) MANAGE MANEGE

ACADIAN CAJUN

ACAJOU CAJU CAJOO CAJOU

ACALEPH MEDUSA MEDUSAN

ACANA ALMIQUE

ACANTHA FIN SPINE THORN PRICKLE ACANTHON

ACAPU WALNUT WACAPOU CHAPERNO

ACARID NYMPH NYMPHA OCTOPOD DIBRANCH

ACAUDAL BOBBED ANUROUS ECAUDATE TAILLESS

ACAULESCENT STEMLESS

ACCEDE LET AGREE ALLOW ENTER GRANT YIELD ACCORD ASSENT ATTAIN COMPLY CONCUR CONCEDE CONFORM CONSENT

ACCELERATE GUN REV RUN HYPO JAZZ RACE URGE DRIVE FAVOR FORCE HURRY SPEED HASTEN ADVANCE FORWARD FURTHER QUICKEN ANTEDATE DISPATCH EXPEDITE INCREASE THROTTLE

ACCELERATION SPEEDUP
(— OF REACTION) CATALYSIS
(— UNIT) STAPP

ACCELERATOR GAS SPEEDER BETATRON THROTTLE

ACCENT BEAT BLAS BURR MARK TONE ACUTE GRAVE ICTUS PITCH PULSE SOUND THROB VERGE BROGUE LENGTH RHYTHM STRESS THESIS EMPHASIS
(DORIC —) PLATEASM
(IRISH —) BROGUE
(MUSICAL —) BEAT
(WITHOUT AN —) ATONIC

ACCENTED FZ SFZ TONIC STRONG MARCATO MARCANDO SFORZATO

ACCENTUATE ACCENT

ACCENTUATION DECLAMATION ENHANCEMENT

ACCEPT BUY EAT BEAR FANG HAVE HOLD JUMP TAKE ADMIT ADOPT AGREE ALLOW HONOR INFER MARRY ASSENT ASSUME AVOUCH POCKET APPROVE BELIEVE CONCEDE EMBRACE ESPOUSE RECEIVE

(— **AS ONE'S OWN**) NOSTRIFICATE
(— **AT RANDOM**) DRAW
(— **BETS**) BOOK
(— **EAGERLY**) LEAP
(— **INHERITANCE**) ADIATE
(— **READILY**) SWALLOW
(— **WITHOUT QUESTION**) ABIDE
ACCEPTABLE LIEF SIGHTLY
WELCOME GRACIOUS PASSABLE
PLEASANT
ACCEPTANCE PASS SNAFF ADITIO
TAQLID PASSAGE CREDENCE
CURRENCY
(— **OF INHERITANCE**) CERNITURE
(— **OF ORDER**) ALLOTMENT
ACCEPTED GOING VULGAR
POPULAR APPROVED CREDITED
ORTHODOX STANDARD
(**WIDELY** —) INVETERATE
ACCEPTOR BASE
ACCESS FIT WAY ADIT DOOR GATE
PATH ROAD ENTRY GOING ROUTE
ACCOST AVENUE COMING ENTREE
PORTAL STREET ADVANCE
APPROACH ENTRANCE PAROXYSM
RECOURSE
(— **OF DISEASE**) ATTACK
ACCESSIBILITY EXPOSURE
ACCESSIBLE NEAR OPEN HANDY
PATENT AFFABLE PRESENT
FAMILIAR PERVIOUS SOCIABLE
ACCESSION ENTER ALLUVIO
ILLAPSE ADDITION ALLUVION
ENTRANCE INCREASE
ACCESSORY HAT AIDE ALLY DOME
TOOL EXTRA SCARF HELPER
ABETTOR ADJUNCT ANCILLA
ENCLAVE FITTING FIXTURE ADDITIVE
HATSTAND
(PL.) ADDENDA FIXINGS STAFFAGE
ACCIACCATURA MORDENT
ACCIDENT HAP CASE LUCK EVENT
GRIEF CHANCE HAZARD INJURY
MISHAP FORTUNE QUALITY
CALAMITY CASUALTY DISASTER
FORTUITY INCIDENT
(**EUCHARISTIC** —**S**) SPECIES
ACCIDENTAL ODD CASUAL CHANCE
RANDOM EXTERNAL
ACCIPITER HAWK
ACCLAIM CRY CLAP FAME HAIL
LAUD ROOT CHEER CLAIM ECLAT
EXTOL SHOUT PRAISE APPLAUD
HOSANNA OVATION PLAUDIT
WELCOME APPLAUSE
(**NOISY** —) RIOT
ACCLAMATION CRY VOTE CHEER
SHOUT HOSANNA PLAUDIT
APPLAUSE
ACCLIMATE INURE HARDEN SEASON
ACCUSTOM
ACCLIMATIZE ADAPT HARDEN
SEASON
ACCLIVITY BANK BROW HILL RISE
GRADE PITCH SLANT SLOPE TALUS
ASCENT HEIGHT INCLINE
ACCOLADE EMMY KISS RITE SIGN
AWARD HONOR KUDOS MEDAL
OSCAR TOKEN SYMBOL EMBRACE

GARLAND CEREMONY
ACCOMMODATE AID BED BOW FIT
CAMP GIVE HELP HOLD LEND SORT
SUIT ADAPT BOARD DEFER FAVOR
HOUSE LODGE SERVE YIELD
ADJUST COMPLY FAVOUR OBLIGE
SETTLE CONFORM CONTAIN
FASHION ATTEMPER GARRISON
ACCOMMODATION LOAN BERTH
BERTHAGE GIFFGAFF
(— **BILL**) KITE
ACCOMPANIED FRAUGHT
ACCOMPANIMENT SON ALBA
BURDEN EXCORT OOMPAH ADJUNCT
DESCANT SUPPORT OBLIGATO
(PL.) FIXINGS
ACCOMPANIST JONGLEUR
ACCOMPANY SEE FARE FERE JOIN
LEAD TEND WAIT BRING PILOT
ASSIST ATTEND CONCUR CONVEY
CONVOY ESCORT FOLLOW SECOND
SQUIRE COEXIST CONDUCT
CONSORT SUPPORT CHAPERON
ACCOMPANYING FELLOW ADJUNCT
ACCOMPLICE PAL AIDE ALLY CHUM
BUDDY CRONY LOUKE SHILL TILER
BONNET COHORT FELLOW HELPER
ABETTOR FEODARY FEUDARY
HUSTLER PARTNER STEERER
ACCOMPLISH DO GO END WIN FILL
WORK ENACT EQUIP FETCH FORTH
SWING AFFORD ATTAIN EFFECT
FINISH FULFIL MANAGE ABSOLVE
ACHIEVE CHEVISE COMPASS
EXECUTE EXPLETE FULFILL FURNISH
OPERATE PERFECT PERFORM
REALIZE SUCCEED COMPLETE
CONTRIVE DISPATCH ENGINEER
OUTCARRY
ACCOMPLISHED APT ABLE DONE
ADEPT ENDED GREAT TERSE
BESEEN EXPERT HANDSOME
TALENTED
ACCOMPLISHMENT ART END DEED
FEAT PASS CRAFT SKILL EFFECT
TALENT EARNING QUALITY FRUITION
LEARNING
(**PRIOR** —) ANTICIPATION
ACCORD GIVE JIBE JUMP SUIT UNIT
AGREE ALLOW ATONE AWARD BEFIT
CHIME CHORD CORDE GRANT LEVEL
STAND TALLY UNITY ACCEDE
ADJUST ASSENT BESTOW BETEEM
COMPLY CONCUR SETTLE UNISON
COMPORT COMPOSE CONCEDE
CONCERT CONCORD CONSENT
CONSORT HARMONY RAPPORT
RESPOND UNANIME DIAPASON
SYMPATHY
(— **WITH**) SUIT
(**IN** —) ALONG
ACCORDANCE CONCERT CONSENT
(**IN** —) ALONG
ACCORDANT EVEN ATTUNED
AGREEING COHERENT SUITABLE
ACCORDING (— **TO ART**) SA
(— **TO LAW**) SL
(— **TO**) AD BY SEC EMFORTH
ENFORTH PURSUANT SECUNDUM

ACCORDINGLY SO THEN THUS
HENCE IGITUR
ACCORDION LANTUM FLUTINA
FLAUTINO
ACCOST BAIL HAIL MASH MEET
ABORD BOARD GREET SPEAK
ACCESS BROACH HALLOO SALUTE
ACCOAST ADDRESS SOLICIT
APPROACH GREETING
ACCOUCHEUR OBSTETRICIAN
ACCOUCHEUSE MIDWIFE
ACCOUNT TAB BILL BOOK DEEM
DRAW ITEM NICK NOTE RATE REDE
SAKE TAIL TALE TELL TEXT WORD
AUDIT BLAME CHALK COUNT JUDGE
SCORE STATE STORY VALUE
WORTH BATTEL CREDIT DETAIL
ESTEEM HORARY LEGEND PROFIT
REASON RECKON RECORD REGARD
RELATE RENDER REPORT REPUTE
TREATY ACCOMPT COMPOST
COMPUTE EXPLAIN JOURNAL
LEXICON NARRATE PROCESS
RECITAL TAILZIE BREVIARY
CONSIDER ESTIMATE TREATISE
(— **FOR**) SAVE EXPLAIN
(**ACCURATE** —) GRIFF GRIFFIN
(**CREDIT** —) TICK
(**LONG** —) ILIAD
(**TRAVEL** —) ITINERARY
ACCOUNTABILITY DETAIL LIABILITY
ACCOUNTABLE LIABLE AMENABLE
ACCOUNTANT CLERK SIRCAR
SIRKAR AUDITOR PESHKAR
PUTWARI KULKARNI MUTSUDDY
RECKONER
ACCOUNTANT-GENERAL DAFTARDAR
DEFTERDAR
ACCOUNTING TASK REASON
COSTING
ACCOUTER ARM RIG GIRD ARRAY
DRESS EQUIP ATTIRE CLOTHE
OUTFIT BEDIGHT FURNISH HARNESS
PROVIDE
ACCOUTERMENTS GEAR TIRE
DRESS ATTIRE GRAITH
ACCREDIT ALLOT VOUCH CREDIT
DEPUTE APPOINT APPROVE ASCRIBE
BELIEVE CERTIFY CONFIRM
ENDORSE LICENSE SANCTION
ACCRETION SUM GAIN GROWTH
DEPOSIT EXUDATE ADDITION
ADHESION INCREASE
(**INJURIOUS** —) RUST
ACCRUAL ACCRUE DEMERIT
ACCRUE ADD WIN EARN GAIN GROW
PILE ARISE ENSUE ENURE INCUR
INURE ISSUE MATURE RESULT
SPRING ACQUIRE COLLECT
REDOUND ACCRESCE CUMULATE
INCREASE
ACCUMULATE DRAW FUND GROW
HEAP HIVE MASS PILE SAVE AMASS
DRIFT HOARD STACK STORE TOTAL
ACCRUE GARNER GATHER MUSTER
SCRAPE COLLECT HARVEST
INCREASE
ACCUMULATION DRIP DUMP FUND
GAIN HEAP MASS PILE STACK

STORE ANLAGE BACKUP BUDGET
COLUMN DEBRIS GARNER BACKLOG
CUMULUS DEPOSIT DOSSIER
MORAINE DIVIDEND INTEREST
(— OF FLUID) EDEMA OEDEMA
ASCITES
(— OF FORCE) CHARGE
(— OF SNOW) ALIMENTATION
(— OF TRIFLES) FLOTSAM
(— ON CONCRETE) LAITANCE
ACCURACY NICETY FIDELITY
JUSTNESS
(HISTORICAL —) SYNCHRONISM
ACCURATE JUST LEAL NICE TRUE
CLOSE EXACT FLUSH RIGHT
NARROW PROPER SEVERE STRICT
CAREFUL CORRECT PRECISE
FAITHFUL PERQUEER PUNCTUAL
TRUTHFUL
(NOT —) IMPURE
(UNPLEASANTLY —) BRUTAL
ACCURATELY JUST FAIRLY JUSTLY
CLOSELY EXACTLY INSOOTH
ACCURSED FEY CURSED DAMNED
DOOMED FORBID SACRED WARIED
BLASTED MALEDICT
ACCUSATION BEEF WITE BLAME
CAUSE CRIME POINT WHITE APPEAL
ATTACK CHARGE THREAP THREEP
ACCUSAL SCANDAL DELATION
(FALSE —) SUGGESTION
ACCUSATORY WRAYFUL
ACCUSE TAX WRY CALL FILE NOTE
SHOW SLUR TASK WITE WRAY
ACOUP ARGUE BLAME PEACH TAINT
TOUCH WHITE APPEAL ATTACH
ATTACK BECALL BEWRAY CHARGE
DEFAME DELATE DETECT INDICT
INTENT MURMUR APPEACH ARRAIGN
ATTAINT CENSURE IMPEACH
IMPLEAD TRADUCE CHASTISE
DENOUNCE QUESTION REDARGUE
REPROACH
(— UNJUSTLY) SLANDER
ACCUSER CHARGER DELATOR
LIBELANT
ACCUSING CULPATORY
DENUNCIATORY
ACCUSTOM URE USE WIN WON
HAFT WONT ADAPT BREAK DRILL
ENURE FLESH HABIT HAUNT INURE
TRAIN ADDICT ADJUST CUSTOM
INDUCE SEASON CONSORT
EDUCATE TOUGHEN ACQUAINT
(— HORSE TO BIT) MOUTH
(— TO PASTURE) HAFT
ACCUSTOMED TAME USED WONE
WONT USANT USUAL INURED
CHRONIC CURRENT HABITED
CONSUETE
ACE AS ALS JOT ONE PIP TIB ATOM
CARD HERO MARK TOPS UNIT
ADEPT BASTO FLYER POINT BULLET
EXPERT AVIATOR BRISQUE
PARTICLE
(— OF CLUBS) BASTA BASTO
(— OF SPADES) SPADILLE SPADILLO
(— OF TRUMPS) TIB HONOR PUNTO
(THREE —S) GLEEK

ACEDIA SLOTH ACCIDIA ACCIDIE
ACEPHALOUS HEADLESS
ACER NEGUNDO
ACERB ACID HARD SOUR TART
ACRID HARSH SHARP BITTER
SEVERE
ACERBATE EMBITTER IRRITATE
ACERBITY ACRIMONY ASPERITY
SEVERITY TARTNESS
ACETABULUM PAN PYXIS CUPULE
ACETABLE HOLDFAST
ACETAL KETAL FORMAL KETATE
BUTYRAL
ACETALDEHYDE ETHYL ETHANAL
ALDEHYDE
ACETIC SOUR SHARP ZOONIC
ACETYLENE TOLAN ALKINE ALKYNE
ETHINE ETHYNE TOLANE
ACHE AKE NAG NIP ECHE GELL
HURT LONG PAIN PANG PINE RACK
WARK WERK HACHE SMART STANG
STOUN THROB THROE WARCH
DESIRE MISERY STITCH STOUND
TWINGE TWITCH ANGUISH EARACHE
SORENESS
ACHENE CYPSELA UTRICLE
ACHIEVE DO END GET WIN EARN
GAIN HACK HAVE MAKE FETCH
FORCE REACH SCORE AFFORD
ARRIVE ATTAIN EFFECT FINISH
OBTAIN CHEVISE COMPASS EXPLOIT
FULFILL PRODUCE REALIZE
SUCCEED TRIUMPH COMPLETE
CONCLUDE CONTRIVE
(— HARMONY) AGREE
(— ORIENTATION) ADJUST
ACHIEVEMENT ACT JOB DEED FEAT
WORK ACTION CAREER RESULT
EXPLOIT HARVEST FELICITY
ACHILLEA PTARMICA
ACHILLES PELIDES
(FATHER OF —) PELEUS
(FRIEND OF —) PATROCLUS
(HORSE OF —) XANTHUS
(MOTHER OF —) THETIS
(SLAYER OF —) PARIS
ACHIOTE OLEANA ACHUETE
ANNATTO ARNATTA ARNATTO
ACHRAS SAPOTA
ACHROMACYTE SHADOW
ACHROMATIC GRAY GREY NEUTRAL
ACICULAR SPLINTERY
ACID DRY YAR DIAL DOPA KEEN
PABA SOUR TART ACERB ACRID
ALGIN AMINO CERIN EAGER HARSH
LYSIN RHEIN SHARP ULMIC ABRINE
ALLIIN BITING BITTER GLYCIN
LYSINE PROLIN SERINE TWEAKY
VALINE ACERBIC ACETOSE CERASIN
FILICIN GLYCINE PROLINE STEARIN
VINEGAR
(NITRIC —) AQUAFORTIS
ACIDITY ACOR VERDURE ACERBITY
SOURNESS VERJUICE
ACKNOWLEDGE NOD OWN AVER
AVOW SIGN ADMIT ADOPT ALLOW
GRANT KITHE KYTHE THANK YIELD
ACCEDE ACCEPT AGNIZE ANSWER
ASSENT AVOUCH BEKNOW COUTHE

FATHER REWARD CONCEDE
CONFESS DECLARE OBSERVE
PROFESS DISCLOSE
ACKNOWLEDGEMENT GRANT
THANK AVOWAL CREDIT SHRIFT
APOLOGY AGNITION
ACLE AKLE IRUL JAMBA IRONWOOD
PYENGADU
ACLYS HURLBAT
ACME IT ACE CAP TOP APEX CULM
HIGH PEAK CREST PITCH POINT
STATE APOGEE CLIMAX COMBLE
CRISIS CULMEN HEIGHT HEYDAY
SUMMIT ZENITH CUMULUS SUBLIME
CAPSHEAF CAPSTONE PINNACLE
ACNE WHELK
ACOLYTE BOY HELPER NOVICE
SERVER LEARNER PATENER
ACOMIA BALDNESS
ACONITE BIKH ACONITUM NAPELLUS
ACORN NUT MAST GLAND OVEST
BELLOTA BELLOTE
(— CUPS) VALONIA
(PL.) MAST CAMATA PANNAGE
CAMATINA
ACORN-SHAPED BALANOID
ACOUSTICS SONICS PHONICS
ACQUAINT KNOW TELL TEACH
VERSE ADVISE INFORM NOTIFY
SCHOOL APPRISE APPRIZE POSSESS
RESOLVE
ACQUAINTANCE KITH HABIT
COUSIN FRIEND GOSSIP AFFINITY
FAMILIAR INTIMATE
(CLOSE —) HABIT INWARDNESS
(PRACTICAL —) PRACTICE PRACTISE
(PL.) KITH SOCIETY
ACQUAINTED ACQUENT VERSANT
ACQUIESCE BOW ABIDE AGREE
CHIME YIELD ACCEDE ACCEPT
ASSENT COMPLY CONCUR SUBMIT
CONCEDE CONFIRM CONFORM
CONSENT
ACQUIRE ADD BAG BUY GET WIN
EARN FORM GAIN GRAB HAVE MAKE
REAP ADOPT AMASS ANNEX BEGET
CHEVY CHIVY GLEAN LEARN REACH
SEIZE STEAL ATTAIN CHIVEY CHIVVY
DERIVE EFFECT GARNER OBTAIN
SECURE SNATCH COLLECT
CONQUER DEVELOP PROCURE
RECEIVE CONTRACT
(— DESIRABLE QUALITY) AGE
(— KNOWLEDGE) LERE
ACQUISITION WIN GAIN LUCRE
ACQUEST ACQUIST GETTING
CONQUEST
(DISHONEST —) GRAFT
ACQUIT PAY FREE QUIT CLEAR
QUIET ASSOIL BEHAVE BESTOW
EXCUSE PARDON ABSOLVE
COMPORT CONDUCT RELEASE
REQUITE LIBERATE OVERLOOK
UNCHARGE
ACQUITTAL EXCUSE
ACQUITTANCE QUIETUS RELEASE
ACRE AKER LAND ACKER FIELD
STANG ARPENT COLLOP FARMHOLD
(120 —S) HIDE

(2-3RDS —) COVER
(QUARTER —) ROOD
(PL.) ACREAGE
ACREMAN CARUCARIUS
ACRID HOT ACID BASK KEEN SOUR
HARSH ROUGH SHARP SURLY
BITING BITTER CAUSTIC PUNGENT
REEKING UNSAVORY VIRULENT
ACRIMONIOUS MAD ACID KEEN
ACRID ANGRY GRUFF HARSH IRATE
SHARP SNELL SURLY BITTER
CAUSTIC STINGING
ACRIMONY VIRUS PUNGENCY
SOURNESS
ACRISIUS (DAUGHTER OF —) DANAE
ACROBAT ZANY KINKER GYMNAST
TOPPLER TUMBLER BALANCER
ACROPOLIS FORT HILL POLIS
CADMEA CITADEL LARISSA
ACROSOME IDIOSOME IDIOZOME
ACROSS OVER SPAN YOND CROSS
ABOARD THWART ATHWART
OPPOSITE TRAVERSE
(CLEAN —) SHORT
ACROSTIC ABC AGLA DORA GAME
POEM TANAK PHRASE PUZZLE
TANACH
ACRYLIC PROPENOIC
ACT BE DO GO APE LAW LET ACTU
BILL COME DEAL DEED DORA FACT
FEAT HOCK JEST MAKE MOVE PART
PASS PLAY SKIT SLIM TAKE TURN
WORK ACTUS DRAMA EDICT EMOTE
ENTRY EXERT FEIGN GRACE KARMA
MODEL SCENE SHIFT STUNT ACTION
BEHAVE BESTIR DECREE DEMEAN
FACTUM MANAGE RAGMAN
COMPORT EXECUTE EXPLOIT
PERFORM PORTRAY PRETEND
STATUTE FUNCTION PRETENSE
SIMULATE
(— AFFECTEDLY) MIMP
(— AS WANTON) RIG
(— AWKWARDLY) HOCKER
(— BEFORE) ANTICIPATE
(— BLUNDERINGLY) BULL
(— DECEITFULLY) DOUBLE
(— DISHONESTLY) FUDGE
(— FOOLISHLY) FON FONNE FOLEYE
FOOTER FOOTLE
(— FRIVOLOUSLY) FRIVOL FRIBBLE
(— IN THEATER) GAFF
(— INDECISIVELY) DITHER
(— INDEPENDENTLY) SEVER
(— OF APPROVAL) EUGE
(— OF BEGGING) CADGE
(— OF CIVILITY) CURTSY DEVOIR
CURTSEY
(— OF KINDNESS) CARESS BENEFIT
(— OF LABOR) DILIGENCE
(— OF PRAYER) DEVOTION
(— OF STUPIDITY) BETISE
(— OF TRICKERY) COG
(— OUT) ENACT DRAMATIZE
(— PLAYFULLY) DALLY BANTER
(— QUICKLY) GIRD
(— RASHLY) RACKLE
(— SPORTIVELY) DAFF
(— SUDDENLY) FLASH

(— TIMIDLY) NESH
(— TOGETHER) AGREE COACT
CONCUR CONCORD
(— TRIFLINGLY) JANK
(— UP TO) EVEN
(— UPON) AFFECT HANDLE
(COMICAL —) JIG
(CONVENTIONAL —) AMENITY
(CORRUPT —) DEPRAVITY
(CRIMINAL —) INFAMY
(DARING —) ESCAPADE
(DECEITFUL —) ABUSE
(DECEPTIVE —) FEINT
(FAULTY —) PARAPRAXIS
(FOOLISH —) DIDO IDIOTISM
(FORBIDDEN —) CRIME
(FORMAL —) CEREMONY
(HABITUAL—) EXERCISE
(HASTY —) FLING
(HOSTILE —) BLOW
(INJURIOUS —) SPOIL
(LAUDATORY —) COUP
(LITURGICAL —) LAVABO
(LIVELY —) JIG
(MISCHIEVOUS —) DIDO CANTRAP
CANTRIP
(OFFENSIVE —) AFFRONT
(OFFICIAL —S) ACTA
(PLAYFUL —) RALLERY RAILLERY
(PRAISEWORTHY —) DEMERIT
(RUDE —) INCIVILITY
(SUDDEN VIOLENT —) BENSEL
BENSIL
(THOUGHTLESS —) FOLLY
(UNMANNERLY —) SOLECISM
(UNUSUAL —) STUNT
(VALOROUS —) WORSHIP
(VARIETY —) SKETCH
(WRONG —) DERELICT DERELICTUM
(PL.) DOINGS
ACTINAL ORAL
ACTING AGENT SERVING
(— AGAINST) ADVERSE
(— BY TURN) ALTERN
(— ODDLY) HAYWIRE
(— RAPIDLY) DRASTIC
(UNSKILLFUL —) BUNGLING
ACTINIAN OPELET VESTLET
ACTINOST RADIAL RADIALE
ACTINOZOAN SEAFLOWER
ACTION ACT AIR DAP JOB ACTO
CASE DEED FACT FRAY GEST PLAY
PLOY PUSH SHOW STEP SUIT WORK
ACTIO DOING EDICT FIGHT FLING
GESTE ISSUE THING TREAD VENUE
AFFAIR AGENCY BATTLE BEFOOT
COMBAT PRAXIS CONDUCT FACTION
GESTURE PROCESS TANQUAM
ACTIVITY BEHAVIOR BUSINESS
CONFLICT FUNCTION PRACTICE
PRACTISE
(— OF WIND) EOLATION
(ABSURD —S) BOSH
(ANTAGONISTIC —) ATOMISM
(BLAMEWORTHY —) WITE
(CAPRICIOUS —) FREAK
(COARSE —) HARLOTRY
(COOPERATIVE —) SYNERGISM
(COURT —) LAW SUIT ASSIZE

LAWSUIT QUERELA QUERELE
(CRUEL —) RUTH
(CUSTOMARY —) COURSE
(EXTEMPORE —) SCHEDIASM
(FINAL —) CATASTROPHE
(FOOLISH —) FOPPERY INEPTITUDE
(FRISKY —) FRISKIN
(FRIVOLOUS —) DALLIANCE
(IMPULSIVE —) STAMPEDE
(INITIAL —) LEADOFF INDUCTION
(JOINT —) COACTION
(LEGAL —) DEBT SUIT ACCOUNT
DETINET DETINUE
(MEAN —S) DOGGERY
(MILITARY —) SWEEP
(ODD —S) JIMJAMS
(PLAYFUL —) FUN FROLIC
(RASH —) HASTE
(REPEATED —) DRUM DOUBLE
(SUDDEN —) FLISK
(SYMBOLIC —) CHARADE
(TACTLESS —) GAUCHERIE
(UNAVOIDABLE —) FORCEPUT
(UNINTERMITTED —) HEAT
(VIOLENT —) HEAT AFFRAY
(WHIMSICAL —S) HUMORS
HUMOURS
(WILY —) WRINKLE
ACTIVATE SPARK ACTIFY ELICIT
ACTIVE UP YAL YAP YEP BUSY GAIN
LISH LIST PERT RASH SPRY TRIG
WHAT YALD YARE YEPE YERN
ABOUT AGILE ALERT ALIVE ASTIR
BRISK DEEDY FRESH LIGHT LINGY
LUSTY NIPPY PEART QUICK READY
SMART SNELL SPICY SPRIG STOUT
SWANK VIVID WIGHT YAULD YERNE
ACTUAL CLEVER DIRECT FEERIE
FEIRIE FIERCE HEARTY LIVELY
LIVING MOVING NIMBLE PROMPT
QUIVER SEMMIT SPEEDY SPRACK
SPROIL SPRUCE SPRUNT SWANKY
WIMBLE DASHING DEEDFUL DELIVER
DYNAMIC HOPPING HUMMING
KINETIC STHENIC THRODDY
YANKING ANIMATED ATHLETIC
BRAWLING DILIGENT SPIRITED
VIGOROUS
(NORMALLY —) ABOUT
ACTIVELY DOWN BUSILY DEEDILY
HEARTILY
ACTIVITY ACT ADO GOG VIR FIZZ
LIFE PLAY STIR BLAST CAPER
EVENT HEART RAJAS RALLY TRADE
VIGOR ACTION AGENCY BUSTLE
ENERGY HUSTLE SATTVA SPROIL
AGILITY CALLING BUSINESS
EXERCISE FUNCTION MOVEMENT
PARERGON STIRRING
(FUNCTIONAL —) SHOP
(MENTAL —) CONCEIT BRAINWORK
(SHARED —) COMMUNITY
(TROUBLESOME —) COIL
ACTON HOGTON HAQUETON
ACTOR HAM DOER HERO LEAD MIME
STAR AGENT COMIC DROLL EXTRA
HEAVY MIMIC PLANT SERIO SUPER
ARTIST COWBOY DISEUR FEEDER
FIDDLE MUMMER PLAYER PUPPET

STAGER TOMMER ARTISTE CABOTIN
DISEUSE HISTRIO PRIMOMO
ROSCIUS STORMER TROUPER
AISTEOIR COMEDIAN HISTRION
JUVENILE STROLLER THESPIAN
(INEPT —) HAM
(INFERIOR —) SHINE
ACTRESS DIVA STAR INGENUE
STARLET FARCEUSE THESPIAN
ACTUAL GOOD HARD REAL TRUE
VERY POSIT RIGHT BODILY FACTUAL
GENUINE CONCRETE DEFINITE
EXISTING MATERIAL POSITIVE
TANGIBLE
ACTUALITY FACT BEING VERITY
REALITY ENERGEIA REALNESS
ACTUALLY BUT DONE TRULY FAIRLY
ITSELF REALLY
ACTUATE ACT EGG RUN DRAW
MOVE URGE ENACT IMPEL ROUSE
START AROUSE COMPEL EXCITE
INCITE INDUCE AGITATE ANIMATE
ENLIVEN INSPIRE POINTED SHARPEN
MOTIVATE PERSUADE
ACUITY FINENESS
ACUMEN WIT INSIGHT CAPACITY
KEENNESS SAGACITY
ACUTE ACID FINE HIGH KEEN TART
HEAVY QUICK SHARP SMART SNACK
SNELL ARGUTE ASTUTE CRYING
SHREWD SHRILL SUBTLE TRELBE
URGENT CRUCIAL FEELING INTENSE
POINTED VIOLENT CRITICAL INCISIVE
POIGNANT
(MOST —) DIRE
(NOT —) SLOW GRAVE CHRONIC
ACUTENESS DEPTH SENSE ACUITY
ACUMEN NOSTRIL INCISION
SAGACITY SUBTLETY
(— OF SMELL) HYPEROSMIA
ACYCLIC SPIRAL ALIPHATIC
ADAD RAMMAN
ADAGE SAW DICT REDE TEXT WORD
AXIOM MAXIM MOTTO HOMILY
SAYING TRUISM WHEEZE BROMIDE
PRECEPT PROVERB APHORISM
APOTHEGM
ADAGIO ADAGE ADAGIETTO
ADAM ADE EDIE ADKIN
(GRANDSON OF —) ENOS ENOCH
(SON OF —) ABEL CAIN SETH
(TEACHER OF —) RAISEL
(WIFE OF —) EVE LILITH
ADAM-AND-EVE CRAWFOOT
ADAMANT FIRM GRIM HARD SOLID
STONY ADAMAS DIAMOND UNMOVED
OBDURATE SOLIDITY STUBBORN
ADAMANTINE FIRM BORON STONE
VAJRA ADAMANT
ADAMITE PICARD
ADAM'S APPLE GUZZLE
THROATBOLL
ADAM'S NEEDLE YUCCA
ADAPT APT FIT PLY PUT EDIT MOLD
SORT SUIT AGREE HUMOR INURE
SHAPE ADJUST CHANGE COMPLY
DERIVE DOCTOR HUMOUR TEMPER
ARRANGE CONFORM CONVERT
PREPARE QUALIFY ATTEMPER

CONTRIVE EQUALIZE REGULATE
ADAPTABILITY FLUIDITY ELASTICITY
ADAPTABLE LABILE ELASTIC
PLIABLE FLEXUOUS
ADAPTED FIT FOR FITTED SUITED
ADAPTER KIT ARRANGER
ADAXIAL SUPERIOR
ADD AD EIK EKE SAY SUM TOT CAST
FOOT GAIN JOIN LEND PLUS TOTE
AFFIX ANNEX GIVEN TOTAL UNITE
ACCRUE ADJECT APPEND ATTACH
CONFER FIGURE RECKON SUPPLY
ACCRETE AUGMENT COMBINE
COMPILE COMPUTE ENLARGE
SUBJOIN SUMMATE INCREASE
(— ALCOHOL) SPIKE
(— FUEL) BEET
(— IN WRITING) ASCRIBE
(— TO) ADORN ENRICH AUGMENT
(— UP) SUM TOT COUNT TOTAL
AMOUNT
(— WORT TO BEER) KRAUSEN
ADDA SCINK SKINK LIZARD
ADDAX PYGARG PYGARGUS
ADDED AND EKE PLUS ADJUNCT
(— SOMETHING) TILLY
ADDEND SUMMAND
ADDER ATHER KRAIT VIPER ELAPID
NADDER NEDDER ELAPOID
HAGWORM HYPNALE
ADDER'S-TONGUE LILY LILIUM
COXCOMB ROOSTERS
ADDICT FAN BUFF DOPE DOPY HYPE
USER COKEY COKIE FIEND HOPPY
HOUND JUNKY SLAVE BOTARY
DEVOTE JUNKER JUNKIE DELIVER
DEVOTEE HABITUE HOPHEAD
SNIFTER ACCUSTOM DOPEHEAD
SNOWBIRD
ADDICTED GIVEN PRONE HOOKED
BIBULOUS
ADDICTION HABIT MONKEY
BIBACITY
ADDITION AND EIK EKE ELL TAB
TOO ALSO ELSE GAIN PLUS AFFIX
RIDER ACCRUE AUGEND ENCORE
GANSEL INCOME PREFIX ADJUNCT
ADVANCE AUCTARY CODICIL
JOINING PENDANT UNITING
ADDENDUM INCREASE MANTISSA
(— TO ARTICLE) SHIRTTAIL
(— TO BEEHIVE) IMP
(— TO MASS) FARCE FARSE
(— TO PRICE) ADVANCE
(TRIVIAL —) FILIP FILLIP
ADDITIONAL NEW ELSE MORE
ADDED EXTRA FRESH OTHER
TIDDER TOTHER ANOTHER BESIDES
FURTHER
ADDITIVE CUMOL CUMENE
ADDLE EARN HOME IDLE MIRE
AMAZE FILTH RIPEN SPOIL CURDLE
MUDDLE THRIVE AGITATE CONFUSE
BEFUDDLE BEWILDER
ADDLED ASEA EMPTY PUTRID
MUDDLED UNSOUND
ADDRA DAMA NANGER
ADDRESS AIM SUE WOO BACK CALL
EASE HAIL HOME MINT PRAY TACT

TALK TULK TURN ABODE APPLY
BOARD COURT DRESS ELOGE
GREET POISE SKILL SPEAK TREAT
ACCOST ADJUST APPEAL BOUNCE
CHARGE DEVOTE DIRECT EULOGY
MANNER PARLEY SALUTE SERMON
SPEECH BEHIGHT CONDUCT
CONSIGN ENTRUST LECTURE
ORATION TUTOYER APPROACH
DEDICATE DELIVERY DISPATCH
FACILITY HARANGUE INSCRIBE
PETITION
(— FAMILIARLY) TOM TUTOYER
(— SAUCILY) CHYAK CHYACK
(METHOD OF —) TONE
(PULPIT —) KHUTBA KHUTBAH
ADDUCE BEAR CITE GIVE NAME
ALLAY ARGUE BRING INFER OFFER
QUOTE ALLEGE ASSIGN OBJECT
ADVANCE COUNTER MENTION
PRESENT
ADE SQUASH
ADEPS FAT LARD
ADEPT ACE APT ABLE HANDY
ADROIT ARTIST CRAFTY DEACON
EXPERT MASTER VERSED ANCIENT
CAPABLE DABSTER MAHATMA
DEXTROUS SKILLFUL
ADEQUATE DUE FIT ABLE FAIR FULL
GOOD MEET WELL AMPLE DIGNE
EQUAL COMMON DECENT ENOUGH
PROPER CONDIGN SUITABLE
ADHERE HEW HUG CLAG CLAM GLUE
HOLD JOIN KEEP LINK AFFIX APPLY
CLEAM CLING STICK UNITE ATTACH
CEMENT CLEAVE COHERE FREEZE
ACCRETE ANNERRE PERSIST
ADHERENCE CLING ADHESION
ARIANISM FIDELITY
ADHERENT IST ITE AIDE ALLY JAIN
SIKH ADEPT BAHAI BLACK BONPA
DEIST JAINA SIDER SPIKE STOOP
FACTOR KIRKER VOTARY APRISTA
BAHAIST CHANIST FASCIST FLACIAN
GNOSTIC NICAEAN OWENIAN
SECTARY SEQUELA THOMIST
AGATHIST BELIEVER BUDDHIST
CABALIST DISCIPLE FAITHFUL
FATALIST FOLLOWER HUMANIST
HYLICIST IMPERIAL PARTISAN
RETAINER SERVITOR SOCINIAN
UPHOLDER
(PL.) FOLD FOLLOWING
ADHESION BLOCKING STICKAGE
SYNECHIA
ADHESIVE GUM WAX BOND CLAM
GLUE SIZE TAPE DABBY DAUBY
PASTE TACKY BINDER CEMENT
CLINGY GLUTEN MASTIC PLUCKY
SMEARY STICKY HOTMELT
MUCILAGE
ADHIBIT USE ADMIT AFFIX APPLY
ATTACH
ADIANTUM MAIDENHAIR
ADIEU ADEW ADDIO ADIOS LEAVE
FAREWELL
ADIPOSE FAT HARD SUET FATTY
OBESE PURSY SQUAT TALLOW
ADIT DOOR ENTRY SOUGH STULM

ACCESS TUNNEL PASSAGE
APPROACH ENTRANCE

ADJACENT NEAR NIGH CLOSE
FLUSH HANDY BESIDE NEARBY
MEETING VICINAL ABUTTING
TOUCHING

ADJECTIVE ADNOUN DIPTOTE
EPITHET MONINAL MODIFIER

ADJOIN ADD ABUT BUTT JOIN LINE
TACK COAST MARCH TOUCH UNITE
ACCOST APPEND ATTACH BORDER
CONTACT

ADJOURN END MOVE RISE STAY
ARISE CLOSE DEFER DELAY RECESS
SUSPEND DISSOLVE POSTPONE
PROROGUE

ADJUDGE TRY DEEM FIND GIVE
HOLD RATE ALLOT AREAD AREED
AWARD GRANT JUDGE ORDER
ADDEEM ADDICT ASSIGN DECERN
DECIDE DECREE ORDAIN REGARD
BEHIGHT CONDEMN SENTENCE

(— GUILTY) DAMN

(— NOT GUILTY) ABSOLVE

ADJUDICATE ACT TRY HEAR PASS
RULE JUDGE DECIDE ESTEEM
RECKON REGARD SETTLE ADJUDGE
CONSIDER SENTENCE

ADJUNCT AID HELP PART WORD
ANNEX DEVICE PHRASE ADJOINT
ANCILLA EPITHET FITTING GARNISH
PERTAIN TEACHER ADDITION
ADDITIVE APPANAGE APPENDIX
ORNAMENT

ADJURATION OATH APPEAL
SWEARING

ADJURE ASK BEG BID BIND ETHE
PRAY CRAVE PLEAD SWEAR APPEAL
CHARGE BESEECH COMMAND
CONJURE CONTEST ENTREAT
REQUEST UNSWEAR

ADJUST FIT FIX SET CAST EASE
FORM FREE GEAR JUST LINE PARE
RATE SIZE SORT SUIT TRAM TRIM
TRUE ADAPT ADMIT ALIGN ALINE
ANGLE EQUAL FRAME PATCH
RANGE RIGHT SHAPE ACCORD
ATTUNE HAMMER JUSTEN SETTLE
SQUARE TEMPER WANGLE ADDRESS
ARRANGE BALANCE CHANCER
COMPOSE CONCERT CONFORM
CORRECT DISPOSE JUSTIFY
PREPARE RECTIFY COMPOUND
REGULATE

(— A LOOM) GATE

(— SAIL) FLATTEN

ADJUSTED KEYED

ADJUSTER FIXER FITTER ASSESSOR

ADJUSTMENT FIT GEAR TRIM
FITNESS FITTING CHANCERY

ADJUTANT AIDE ALLY STORK
ARGALA HELPER HURGILA
MARABOU OFFICER

ADJUVANT AIDE HELPER ADJUNCT
HELPFUL

AD-LIB FAKE

ADMAN HUCKSTER

ADMEASURE METE

ADMETUS (WIFE OF —) ALCESTIS

ADMINISTER DO RUN DEAL DEEM
DOSE GIVE MOVE RULE APPLY
SERVE TREAT DIRECT GOVERN
MANAGE SETTLE SUPPLY TENDER
ADHIBIT CONDUCE CONDUCT
CONTROL EXECUTE EXHIBIT
FURNISH HUSBAND DISPENSE
MINISTER

(— FORCIBLY) HAND

(— SACRAMENT) BISHOP HOUSEL

ADMINISTRATION HELM RULE
SWAY POLICY TAHSIL CONDUCT
DIOCESE ECONOMY RECTORY
REGIMEN CARRIAGE DISPOSAL
MINISTRY

(— OF OATH) JURATION

(REVENUE —) HACIENDA

ADMINISTRATOR CAID HELM QAID
GABBAI MANAGER TRUSTEE
DIRECTOR EXECUTOR MINISTER
PROVICAR

(INCA —) CURACA

(MORMON —) APOSTLE

ADMIRABLE FINE GOOD HIGH
GRAND GREAT LUMMY PROUD
DIVINE AMIABLE CAPITAL ELEGANT
MIRANDA RIPPING

ADMIRAL FLAG AMREL AMRELLE
FLAGMAN GENERAL

ADMIRATION FUROR GLORY
ESTEEM LIKING WONDER CONCEIT
WORSHIP

(— FOR BIGNESS) JUMBOISM

ADMIRE DIG LIKE LOVE ADORE
EXTOL HONOR PRIZE VALUE
ESTEEM MARVEL REGARD REVERE
WONDER ADULATE APPROVE
DELIGHT IDOLIZE RESPECT
VENERATE

ADMIRER FAN BEAU LOVER SWAIN
AMATEUR DEVOTEE FOLLOWER
IDOLATOR

(PL.) FOLLOWING

ADMISSION FEE ADIT CALL ENTRY
ACCESS CHARGE ENTREE TICKET
APOLOGY CONSENT INGRESS
ENTRANCE

(— TO BAR) CALL

ADMIT KEN LET OWN AVER AVOW
BEAR TAKE AGREE ALLOW ENTER
GRANT IMMIT INLET ACCEDE
ACCEPT ADJUST ASSENT AVOUCH
ENROLL INCUCT PERMIT SUFFER
ADHIBIT CONCEDE CONFESS
INCLUDE PROFESS RECEIVE SUFFICE
INITIATE

(— AS MEMBER) INDUCT

(— AS VALID) SUSTAIN

ADMITTANCE ACCESS ADMITTY
ENTRANCE

ADMIX DALLOP DOLLOP

ADMIXTURE DASH ALLOY BLEND
SHADE SPICE TINGE DALLOP
DOLLOP FLAVOR LEAVEN STREAK
MIXTURE SOUPCON COMPOUND
INFUSION

ADMONISH WARN CHIDE SCOLD
ADVISE ENJOIN EXHORT NOTIFY
REBUKE REMIND SCHOOL CAUTION

COUNSEL MONITOR REPROVE

ADMONITION ITEM ADVICE CAVEAT
HOMILY CAUTION LECTURE
REPROOF WARNING DOCUMENT
REMINDER

ADNATE ADHERENT EPIGYNOUS

(— TO CALYX) INFERIOR

ADO DO COIL DEED FUSS ROUT STIR
WORK HURRY TOUSE TOWSE
BOTHER BUSTLE EFFORT FLURRY
HUBBUB POTHER RUCKUS BLATHER
BLETHER SPUTTER TROUBLE
TURMOIL BUSINESS

ADOBE MUD CLAY DOBE DOBY SILT
BRICK DOBIE TAPIA MUDCAP

ADOLESCENCE TEENS YOUTH
NONAGE PUBERTY MINORITY

ADOLESCENT LAD YOUNG YOUTH
IMMATURE TEENAGER

ADONIS ADON

(MOTHER OF —) MYRRH MYRRHA

ADOPT TAKE STEAL ACCEPT
ASSUME ATTACH BORROW CHOOSE
FATHER FOLLOW FOSTER MOTHER
ACQUIRE EMBRACE ESPOUSE
RECEIVE WELCOME ADVOCATE
ARROGATE MAINTAIN

ADOPTION ESPOUSAL

(— OF DEBTS) ASSUMPTION

ADORABLE LOVELY LOVABLE
CHARMING

ADORATION HOMAGE WORSHIP
DEVOTION

(— OF GOD) LOVE

ADORE DOTE LAUD LOVE EXALT
EXTOL HONOR WURTH ADMIRE
ESTEEM PRAISE REVERE GLORIFY
IDOLIZE WORSHIP VENERATE

ADORN DUB FIG GEM ORN SET BEAD
BUSK DECK DILL DINK FOIL GAUD
GILD LACE OUCH PICK PINK STUD
SWAG TRIM ADORE ANORN ARRAY
BEDUB BEGEM BELAY BRAVE
CROWN DIGHT DRAPE DRESS
FRONT GRACE HIGHT INLAY JEWEL
MENSK PRANK PRICK PRIDE PRIMP
PRINK ROUGE SPLAY SPRIG TRICK
ATTIRE ATTRAP BECOME BEDECK
BETRIM BLAZON BROOCH CLOTHE
COLLAR DAMASK DIADEM EMBOSS
ENAMEL ENRICH ENROBE FIGURE
FINIFY FRIEZE FRINGE GRAITH
INSTAL INVEST ORNIFY POUNCE
QUAINT STATUE SUBORN TASSEL
APPAREL BEDIGHT BEDIZEN
COMMEND CORONET DEPAINT
DIGNIFY EMPEARL FEATHER
FOLIAGE FURNISH GARNISH
GLORIFY GRATIFY IMPLUME
SPANGLE VARNISH BEAUTIFY
DECORATE EMBLAZON FLOURISH
ORNAMENT SPLENDOR

ADORNED CLAD BESEEN DAEDAL
ORNATE PICKED BRAIDED CLOTHED
COLORED DAISIED FIGURED

(SHOWILY —) BEPRANKED

ADORNMENT TIRE ADORN DRESS
PRIDE BEAUTY DECORE TAHALI
TINSEL DECKING OUNDING

PRANKING TIREMENT

ADRIFT ASEA LOST AWAFT LIGAN LOOSE AFLOAT DERELICT FLOATING UNMOORED

ADROIT DEFT EASY FEAT GOOD NEAT SLIM ADEPT HANDY READY SMART SNACK TIGHT TRICK ARTFUL CLEVER EXPERT HABILE NIMBLE CUNNING DEXTROUS HANDSOME SKILLFUL

ADROITNESS ART EASE TACT KNACK SKILL ADDRESS FACILITY

ADSORBENT BASE EARTH SILICA

ADULATE FAWN LAUD GLOSS GLOZE PRAISE FLATTER

ADULATION GLOSE GLOZE PRAISE FLATTERY

ADULT MAN FULL MANLY MATURE EPHEBIC GROWNUP THRIVEN

ADULTERANT DOPE ALMEIDINA

ADULTERATE CUT MIX CARD DASH LOAD ABUSE ALLOY HOCUS TAINT DEACON DEBASE DEFILE DILUTE EXTEND MANAGE WEAKEN BASTARD CORRUPT FALSIFY VITIATE DENATURE IMPURIFY SPURIOUS

ADULTERATED CUT SHAM IMPURE CORRUPT SPURIOUS

ADULTEROUS ERRING

ADULTERY AVOUTRY CUCKOLDOM

ADUMBRATE IMAGE SHADE VAGUE OBSCURE SUGGEST INTIMATE

ADUMBRATION SHADE SHADOW PHANTASM

ADUNCOUS BENT HOOKED

ADUST BURNT FIERY GLOOMY SALLOW PARCHED SCORCHED SUNBURNT

ADVANCE GO AID PAY SOP WAY BULL CITE COME DASH GAIN HELP INCH LAUD LEND LIFT LOAN MARK MOVE NEAR NOSE PASS PUSH RISE SHOW STEP WORM AVANT BOOST BRING CREEP ENTER EXALT EXTOL FAVOR FORGE MARCH OFFER PLACE RAISE SERVE SPEED STAIR STAKE THROW ADDUCE ADMOVE ALLEGE AMOUNT ASSIGN ASSIST AVAUNT BETTER DEGREE EXTEND FAVOUR GROWTH HASTEN INCEDE INROAD PREFER PREPAY SCHOOL STRIDE STRIKE THRIVE VAUNCE BENEFIT DEVELOP ELEVATE ENHANCE FORTHGO FORWARD FURTHER HEADWAY IMPREST IMPROVE PROCEED PROCESS PROMOTE PROMOVE PROPOSE PROSPER PROVECT SUCCEED ADDITION DEVELOPE HEIGHTEN INCREASE PROGRESS

(— **BY CUTTING**) DRIVE

(— **BY LEAPS**) SALTATION

(— **IN LIFE**) WAY

(— **LABORIOUSLY**) STRIVE

(— **OBLIQUELY**) SIDLE

(— **ONE'S POINT**) TAKE

(— **SLOWLY**) INCH WORM CRAWL CREEP

(— **WAVERINGLY**) HOBBLE

(— **WITH EFFORT**) DRAG

(**DIFFICULT** —) SLOG

(**GRADUAL** —) ILLAPSE

(**STEADY** —) SWING

(**SUDDEN** —) SHOOT

(**VIGOROUS** —) SWING

(PL.) APPROACHES

ADVANCED FAR DEEP GONE HIGH LATE AHEAD OUTER FORWARD IMPREST LIBERAL VANWARD FOREMOST

(— **IN AGE**) DEEP ANTIQUATED

(— **IN YEARS**) SENIOR AGEABLE ELDERLY

(**MOST** —) EXTREME FARTHEST FOREMOST HEADMOST

(**WELL** —) AGED

ADVANCEMENT UP GOOD ASCENT INCREASE

ADVANTAGE AD BOT USE VAN BEST BOOT BOTE DRAW DROP EDGE GAIN GOOD HANK JUMP MEND NOTE ODDS PULL SAKE VAIL AVAIL BULGE BUNCE FAVOR FRAME FRUIT KINCH LAUGH SPEED START STEAD USAGE BEHALF BEHOOF BETTER CARROT EFFECT PROFIT ACCOUNT BENEFIT EXPLOIT FORDEAL FURTHER PROMOTE UTILITY VANTAGE HANDICAP INTEREST LEVERAGE OVERHAND OVERPLUS

(**ACCIDENTAL** —) FLUKE

ADVANTAGEOUS GOOD JOLI WELL JOLIE GOLDEN PLUMMY SPEEDY USEFUL ELIGIBLE

ADVENT COMING INCOME ARRIVAL APPROACH PAROUSIA

ADVENTITIOUS CASUAL FOREIGN STRANGE ACQUIRED EPISODIC

ADVENTURE GEST LARK RISK SEEK WAGE EVENT GESTE PERIL QUEST AUNTER AUNTRE CHANCE DANGER HAZARD EMPRISE EMPRIZE FORTUNE VENTURE ESCAPADE JEOPARDY

ADVENTURER ROUTIER ARGONAUT

ADVENTURESS DEMIREP DEMIMONDAINE

ADVENTUROUS RASH DARING ERRANT AUNTROUS RECKLESS

ADVERSARY FOE ENEMY RIVAL SATAN FOEMAN OPPONENT

(— **OF GOD**) DEVIL

ADVERSE FOE ILL EVIL CROSS LOATH THRAW AVERSE INFEST WITHER AWKWARD COUNTER DIVERSE FROWARD HOSTILE OPPOSED CONTRARY INIMICAL OPPOSING OPPOSITE OVERWART THRAWART

ADVERSITY ILL WOE DECAY NIGHT MISERY SORROW WITHER ILLNESS TROUBLE CALAMITY DISTRESS

ADVERT HEED AVERT RECUR REFER ALLUDE ATTEND RETURN REVERT OBSERVE CONSIDER

ADVERTISE CRY BARK BILL CALL PLUG PUFF STAR WARN BLURB INFORM NOTIFY PARADE DECLARE

DISPLAY OBSERVE PLACARD PUBLISH ANNOUNCE PROCLAIM

ADVERTISED AFFICHE

ADVERTISEMENT AD BILL SIGN BLURB CHANT ADVERT CACHET DODGER NOTICE POSTER TEASER AFFICHE PLACARD STUFFER CIRCULAR HANDBILL

ADVERTISING BUSH BILLING PUFFERY

ADVICE AVIS AVYS LORE NEWS REDE AVYSE STEER ADVISO DEVICE NOTICE CAUTION COUNSEL OPINION TIDINGS GUIDANCE MONITION

(PL.) INFORMATION

ADVISABLE BOOK PROPER PRUDENT

ADVISE SAY READ REDE TELL VISE WARN WISE AREAD AREED COACH GUIDE WEISE WEIZE ADJURE ADVISO BEREDE CONFER DEVISE EXHORT INFORM PONDER REVEAL APPRISE APPRIZE COUNSEL ACQUAINT ADMONISH CONSIDER

(— **AGAINST**) DISSUADE

ADVISED DELIBERATE

ADVISER AIDE TOUT COACH COMES TUTOR DOCTOR EGERIA LAWYER NESTOR ADVISOR MONITOR STARETS TEACHER ATTORNEY CROUPIER DIRECTOR FIELDMAN PREACHER

ADVISORY URGING PRUDENT

ADVOCACY BOOM FAVOR AVOWRY FAVOUR ARIANISM

ADVOCATE PRO ABET BACK URGE VOGT ACTOR ADOPT FAVOR PLEAD ASSERT AVOWRY BACKER DEFEND IDEIST LAWYER PATRON SYNDIC ABETTOR APOSTLE DECLAIM ENDORSE ESPOUSE EXPOUND FASCIST GOLDBUG PATRIOT PLEADER PROCTOR SCHOLAR SUPPORT ATTORNEY CHAMPION CLUBBIST DEFENSOR HUMANIST PARTISAN PREACHER

(— **OF REVOLT**) ANARCH

ADVOWSON ADVOCACY TENEMENT

ADZ AX AXE ADZE EDGE ADDIS ADDICE EATCHE THIXLE HATCHET

AEACUS (**FATHER OF** —) ZEUS

(**SON OF** —) PELEUS TELAMON

AECIUM CAEOMA

AEETES (**DAUGHTER OF** —) MEDEA

AEGEAN SEA (**ANCIENT PEOPLE OF** —) PSARA PSYRA SAMIAN LELEGES SAMIOTE

(**GULF OF** —) SAROS

(**ISLAND OF** —) COS IOS KEOS NIOS RODI SCIO CHIOS LEROS MELOS NAXOS PAROS PATMO SAMOS SIROS TENOS THERA ANDROS IKARIA IMBROS LEMNOS LESBOS RHODES SKYROS

(**RIVER INTO** —) STRUMA VARDAR MARISTA

(**TOWN ON** —) CHIOS VATHY MYTILENE

AEGEON (**WIFE OF** —) AEMILIA

AEGIR HLER GYMIR

(WIFE OF —) RAN
AEGIRITE ACMITE
AEGIS EGIS SHIELD AUSPICE
DEFENCE DEFENSE
AEGISTHUS (FATHER OF —)
THYESTES
AEGYPTUS (BROTHER OF —)
DANAUS
(FATHER OF —) BELUS
AENEAS (COMPANION OF —)
ACHATES
(FATHER OF —) ANCHISES
(GREAT-GRANDSON OF —) BRUT
(MOTHER OF —) VENUS APHRODITE
(SON OF —) IULUS ASCANIUS
(WIFE OF —) CREUSA LAVINIA
AENGUS (MOTHER OF —) BOANN
AEOLUS (DAUGHTER OF —) CANACE
ALCYONE HALCYONE
(FATHER OF —) HIPPOTES
(SON OF —) SISYPHUS
AEON AGE EON ERA AION AEVUM
CYCLE KALPA PERIOD
(PAIR OF —S) SYZYGY
AEPYTUS (FATHER OF —)
CRESPHONTES
(MOTHER OF —) MEROPE
AERATE AERIFY CHARGE INFLATE
AERIAL AERY AIRY TWIN AERIE
LOFTY UNREAL ANTENNA ETHEREAL
AERIALIST FLIER FLYER
AERIE AERY AIRE AYRE EYRY NEST
AIERY BROOD EYRIE
AERIFORM UNREAL GASEOUS
AEROBE BACTERIUM
AERODROME AIRPORT AIRFIELD
AEROEMBOLISM BENDS
AEROLITE AEROLITH
AERONAUT PILOT SKYMAN
AERONAUTICS AVIATION
AEROSE BRASSY
AEROSTAT AIRSHIP BALLOON
AIRCRAFT
AERUGO RUST PATINA
AESON (BROTHER OF —) PELIAS
(FATHER OF —) CRETHEUS
(SON OF —) JASON
(WIFE OF —) ALCIMEDA
AESTHETIC ARTISTIC ESTHETIC
TASTEFUL
AETA ITA
AETOLUS (FATHER OF —) ENDYMION
(SON OF —) CALYDON PLEURON
(WIFE OF—) PRONOE
AFAR OFF AWAY SAHO FERNE
FERREN REMOTE YFERRE DANAKIL
DANKALI DISTANT
AFARA LIMBA
AFFABLE FAIR OPEN CIVIL FRANK
SUAVE BENIGN FACILE FORTHY
GENIAL URBANE AMIABLE CORDIAL
GENERAL LIKABLE CHARMING
FAMILIAR FRIENDLY GRACIOUS
PLEASANT SOCIABLE TOWARDLY
AFFAIR DO JOB PIE BLOW CASE
DUEL GEAR PLOY BRAWL CAUSE
EVENT FIGHT LEVEE PARTY THING
ACTION BATTLE BEHALF DOMENT
EFFEIR MATTER SETOUT SHAURI

BLOWOUT CONCERN FUNERAL
HOEDOWN JOURNEY LIAISON
PALAVER SHEBANG BUSINESS
COMETHER ENDEAVOR HYPOTHEC
INTRIGUE OCCASION
(CONFUSED —) SCHEMOZZLE
(CRITICAL —) KANKEDORT
(LOVE —) LOVE AMOUR INTRIGUE
(SOCIAL —) FORMAL JUNKET
SUPPER
(STATE —S) ESTATE
(PL.) SQUARES
AFFECT AIL AIR HIT BEAR MELT
MOVE POSE RINE SHAM STIR SWAY
ALLOT ALTER ANNOY COLOR DRIVE
FANCY FEIGN HAUNT IMPEL MINCE
SHOCK TOUCH ASPIRE ASSIGN
ASSUME CHANGE DESIRE MOLEST
SOFTEN STRIKE THRILL ATTAINT
ATTINGE BEWITCH CONCERN
EMOTION FEELING IMPRESS
OPERATE PASSION PRETEND
PROFESS ALLOCATE DISPOSED
FREQUENT INTEREST SIMULATE
(— BY HANDLING) TOUCH
(— FAVORABLY) LIKE
(— INJURIOUSLY) INTERESS
(— STRONGLY) HIT HOLD SURPRISE
AFFECTATION AIR POSE SHAM
FRILL GRACE MINCE CHICHI
DISPLAY FOPPERY FROUNCE
GRIMACE PIETISM FONDNESS
PRETENSE PUPPYISM
(PL.) LUGS
AFFECTED MOY AIRY FEAT AILED
APISH MOVED POSEY CHICHI
FALLAL FEISTY FORMAL QUAINT
SEIZED FEIGNED MINIKIN MISSISH
REACHED SMITTEN STILTED
TAFFETA TAFFETY TOUCHED
INVOLVED PRECIEUX
(— BY DECAY) DOTY
AFFECTING AIRIFIED POIGNANT
TOUCHING
AFFECTION LOVE WAFF ALOHA
AMOUR FLAME HEART CHERTE
DOTAGE ESTEEM HYDROA MALADY
REGARD THRUSH AILMENT CHARITY
EMOTION FEELING SYMPTOM
CHLOASMA DEARNESS DEVOTION
FONDNESS KINDNESS MELICERA
TENDENCY
(PARENTAL —) STORGE
(PL.) HEART HEARTSTRINGS
AFFECTIONATE DEAR FOND WARM
ARDENT DOTING LOVING TENDER
AMOROUS DEVOTED EARNEST
ZEALOUS ATTACHED PARENTAL
SISTERLY
AFFECTIVE SENSIBLE
AFFERENT BEAR ESODIC SENSORY
ADVEHENT INFERENT
AFFIANCE AFFY FAITH TRUST
ASSURE ENGAGE ENSURE FIANCE
PLEDGE PLIGHT SPOUSE BETROTH
PROMISE CONTRACT RELIANCE
AFFIANCED INTENDED
AFFIANT DEPONENT AFFIDAVIT
AFFIDAVIT DAVY OATH AFFIANT

AFFIDAVY AFFYDAVY
AFFILIATE ALLY UNIT ADOPT MERGE
UNITE ATTACH BRANCH RELATE
ASCRIBE CHAPTER CONNECT
FILIATE
AFFINITY KIN TELE FAMILY LIKING
AVIDITY CHEMISM KINDRED KINSHIP
RAPPORT ALLIANCE GOSSIPRY
HOMOLOGY RELATION SYMPATHY
AFFIRM PUT AFFY AVER AVOW TAKE
POSIT STATE SWEAR TRUTH VOUCH
ALLEGE ASSERT ATTEST AVOUCH
DEPOSE RATIFY SUBMIT THREAP
THREEP VERIFY ASSEVER CONFIRM
DECLARE PROFESS PROTEST
TESTIFY MAINTAIN
AFFIRMATION SAY VOW YES AMEN
OATH WORD DIXIT PONENT THESIS
AVERRAL AVERMENT
AFFIRMATIVE AY AYE NOD YAH YEA
YEP YES AMEN ATEN YEAH
DOGMATIC POSITIVE
AFFIX ADD FIX PEN PIN SET CASE
CLIP FAST JOIN NAIL SEAL SIGN
ANNEX INFIX STAMP UNITE ANCHOR
APPEND ATTACH FASTEN SETTLE
STAPLE ADHIBIT CONNECT ENTITLE
FORMANT IMPRESS PLASTER
SUBJOIN
AFFLATUS FURY FUROR FRENZY
VISION IMPULSE
AFFLICT AIL RUE TRY VEX COMB
FIRE HOLD HURT PAIN PINE RACK
TUKE ARRAY BESET CURSE GRILL
GRIPE HARRY PINCH PRESS SEIZE
SMITE TRYST VISIT WOUND BURDEN
GRIEVE HARASS HUMBLE INFECT
MOLEST PESTER REMORD SCORCH
STRAIN STRESS STRIKE CHASTEN
INFLICT OPPRESS SCOURGE
TORMENT TROUBLE DISTRESS
LACERATE STRAITEN
AFFLICTED JOB SAD SORRY AILING
WOEFUL GRIEVED HAUNTED
SMITTEN IMPAIRED STRICKEN
TROUBLED
AFFLICTION WOE EVIL LOSS PAIN
SORE TEEN TRAY ASSAY CROSS
GRIEF PRESS SMART STOUR
BUFFET DURESS MISERY PATHOS
PLAGUE SORROW STRESS THRONG
AILMENT DISEASE ILLNESS PASSION
PURSUIT SCOURGE TORTURE
TROUBLE CALAMITY DISTRESS
HARDSHIP SEVERITY SICKNESS
VEXATION
AFFLICTIVE SAD DIRE SORE SOUR
HEAVY SEVERE
AFFLUENCE EASE AFFLUX INFLUX
PLENTY RICHES WEALTH FORTUNE
OPULENCE
AFFLUENT FAT RICH FLUSH RIVER
STEAM BRANCH SPRUIT COPIOUS
FLOWING HALCYON OPULENT
WEALTHY ABUNDANT INFLUENT
AFFORD GO BEAR GIVE LEND GRANT
INCUR OFFER STAND THOLE YIELD
CONFER ENDURE MANAGE SUPPLY
ACHIEVE FORWARD FURNISH

FURTHER PRODUCE PROVIDE
MINISTER

AFFRAY FEUD FRAY RIOT ALARM
BRAWL BROIL CLASH FIGHT MELEE
SCARE SPURN ATTACK BATTLE
COMBAT EFFRAY ENFRAI FRIGHT
STRIFE TERROR TUMULT ASSAULT
CONTEST QUARREL SCUFFLE
STARTLE FRIGHTEN STRUGGLE

AFFRIGHT COW FEAR AGAST ALARM
DAUNT DOUBT DREAD SCARE
AGRISE APPALL DISMAY CONFUSE
STARTLE TERRIFY FRIGHTEN

AFFRONT CUT DEFY SLAP ABUSE
BEARD PEEVE HARASS INJURE
INSULT NETTLE OFFEND SLIGHT
STRUNT ASSAULT OFFENCE
OFFENSE OUTRAGE PROVOKE
CONFRONT DISGRACE ILLTREAT
IRRITATE

AFFUSION POURING INFUSION

AFGHAN RUG GHAN COVER DURANI
HASARA HAZARA BLANKET
PAKHTON PAKHTUN PUKHTUN
ACHAKZAI COVERLET

AFGHAN FOX CORSAC CORSAK

AFGHANISTAN

CAPITAL: KABUL
COIN: PUL ABBASI AMANIA
AFGHANI
LANGUAGE: DARI PASHTO PUSHTU
BALOCHI BALUCHI
MEASURE: JERIB KAROH
MOUNTAIN: KOH SAFEO CHAGAI
PAMIRS SULAIMAN HIMALAYAS
NATIVE: SISTANI
PARLIAMENT: SHURA
PROVINCE: GHOR FARAH HERAT
KABUL KUNAR KUNUZ LOGAR
ZABUL GHAZNI KAPISA PARWAN
WARDAK
RIVER: LORA OXUS CABUL FARAH
HARUT INDUS KABUL KHASH
KUNAR KOKCHA KUNDUZ
HELMUND MURGHAB
SEA: DARYA
TOWN: RUI JURM NANI WAMA
ASMAR BALKH DOSHI KABUL
KUNAR MARUF MATUN MUKUR
PAHRA TULAK URGAN CHAMAN
KUNDUZ NAUZAD PANJAO
RUSTAK SANGAN SAROBI
TUKZAR WASHIR BAGHLAN
BAMIYAN DILARAM
TRIBE: SAFI TURK ULUS KAFIR
TAJIK UZBEK BALOCH BALUCH
HAZARA KIRGIZ PATHAN
WEIGHT: PAU PAW SER SIR
KARWAR KHURDS

AFICIONADO FAN AMATEUR
DEVOTEE FOLLOWER

AFIELD ABROAD ASTRAY

AFIRE ALOW ALOWE EAGER ABLAZE
AFLAME ARDENT BURNING FLAMING

A-FLAT AS AIS

AFLOAT ASEA AWAFT AWASH
ADRIFT BUOYED NATANT FLOODED

UNFIXED FLOATING

AFOOT ABOUT ASTIR ABROAD
TOWARD WALKING

AFOREMENTIONED SAID SUCH

AFORESAID DITTO NAMED PRIOR
PREVIOUS

AFORETIME ERE FORMER
FORMERLY

AFRAID RAD REDE ADRAD FRAID
REDDE TIMID AGHAST CRAVEN
FEARED SCARED WROTHE AFEARED
ALARMED ANXIOUS ASCARED
FEARFUL GASTFUL COWARDLY
GHASTFUL TIMOROUS

AFREET JINN AFRIT DEMON GIANT
IFRIT JINNI AFRITE EFREET

AFRESH ANEW ANON OVER AGAIN
NEWLY DENOVO ENCORE REPEATED

AFRICAN BOER AFRIC

AFRICAN MARIGOLD KHAKIBOS

AFRIKAANS TAAL DUTCH

AFT BACK REAR ABAFT AFTER
ASTERN BEHIND
(FARTHEST —) AFTERMOST

AFTER A AB BY TO AFT EFT FOR SIN
ANON NEXT PAST POST SYNE
ABAFT APRES ARTER EFTER INFRA
LATER SINCE ASTERN BEHIND
BEYOND FOLLOW HINDER
(— MEALS) PC

AFTERBIRTH HEAM SOOTERKIN

AFTERBODY TONNEAU

AFTEREFFECT SEQUEL SEQUELA
(PL.) HANGOVER

AFTERGRASS FOG AFTERFEED

AFTERIMAGE SPECTRUM SENSATION
(KIND OF —) PURKINJE

AFTERMATH FOG ETCH LOSS ISSUE
ROWEN ROWET TRAIL TRAIN
ARRISH EDDISH EDGREW EDGROW
EFFECT PROFIT RESULT ROWETT
SEQUEL UPSHOT EAGRASS STUBBLE
BACKWASH

AFTERMOST LAST HINDMOST

AFTERNOON AFTER TARDE UNDERN
EVENING TEATIME

AFTERPIECE EPODE EXODE
EXODIUM POSTLUDE

AFTERSONG EPODE

AFTERSWARM CAST SPEW SPUE
CASTLING

AFTERTASTE FAREWELL

AFTERTHOUGHT FOOTNOTE

AFTERWARD EFT POST SITH THEN
APRES LATER EFTSOON EFTSOONS

AGA AGHA LORD CHIEF
(WIFE OF —) BEGUM

AGAIN OR TO BIS EFT YET AGIN
ANEW ANON AYEN AYIN BACK
MORE OVER NEWLY AFRESH
DENOVO ENCORE ITERUM EFTSOON
FRESHLY FURTHER EFTSOONS
MOREOVER
(— AND AGAIN) AND

AGAINST BY IN UP CON GIN NON
AGIN ANTI GAIN INTO WITH AGAIN
ANENT AYENS UNTIL ANENST
AVERSE AYENST CONTRA GAINST
UPTILL VERSUS FERNENT FORNENT
OPPOSED ADVERSUS CONTRAIR

FORENENT FORNENST FORNINST
(— HOPE) AGLEE AGLEY

AGAL HEADROPE

AGALLOCH AGGUR ALOES GAROO
GARROO GARROW TAMBAC LINALOE
AGALWOOD CALAMBAC

AGAMA AGA AGHA GUANA AGAMID
IGUANA LIZARD AGAMIAN

AGAMEMNON (BROTHER OF —)
MENELAUS
(DAUGHTER OF —) ELECTRA
IPHIGENIA
(FATHER OF —) PLISTHENES
(GRANDFATHER OF —) ATREUS
(SON OF —) ORESTES
(WIFE OF —) CLYTEMNESTRA

AGAMID AGA AGHA BALETE BALITI

AGAPANTHUS TULBAGHIA
LOVEFLOWER

AGAPE LOVE OPEN FEAST GAPING
YAWNING

AGAR MOSS GELOSE KANTEN
GELOSIN GELOSINE

AGARIC BLEWITS BLUSHER FLYBANE
LEPIOTA

AGASP EAGER GASPING

AGATE TAW ONYX RUBY ACHATE
GAGATE MARBLE PEBBLE QUARTZ

AGATI SESBANIA

AGAVE ALOE LILY AGAUE AMOLE
DATIL SISAL LILIUM MAGUEY
MESCAL PULQUE ZAPUPE CANTALA
KARATTO KERATTO TEQUILA
HENEQUEN HENIQUEN JINIQUEN
SOAPWEED
(BROTHER OF —) POLYDORUS
(FATHER OF —) CADMUS
(HUSBAND OF —) ECHION
(MOTHER OF —) HARMONIA
(SISTER OF —) INO SEMELE
AUTONOE
(SON OF —) PENTHEUS

AGE ALD BIN DAY ELD EON ERA
AEON EDGE OLAM TIME YUGA
AETAT CYCLE EPOCH OLDEN RIPEN
SECLE WORLD YEARS MATURE
MELLOW PERIOD SIECLE WITHER
CENTURY DEVELOP GLACIAL
OLDNESS SECULUM SENESCE
VORHAND ANCIENTY DURATION
ETERNITY LIFETIME MAJORITY
MATURITY
(— OF 100 YEARS) CENTENARY
(— OF MOON) EPACT
(ADVANCED —) DOTAGE
(EARLY MIDDLE —) SUMMER
(GREAT —) ANTIQUITY GRANDEVITY
(OLD —) CRUTCH SENIUM VETUSTY
SENILITY

AGED AE AET AGY OLD RIPE ANILE
HOARY OLDEN PASSE FEEBLE
INFIRM MATURE OGYIAN SENILE
WINTRY YEARED ANCIENT ELDERLY
WINTERED
(NOT —) GREEN
(WELL —) STALE

AGEE AJEE AWRY AGLEY ASKEW

AGELESS ETERNAL TIMELESS

AGELONG SECULAR SAECULAR

AGENCY DINT HAND CHECK FORCE

LEVER MEANS MOYEN ORGAN
PROXY ACTION BUREAU MEDIUM
OFFICE ARBITER BENEFIT BROKERY
FACULTY LIBRARY MACHINE
ACTIVITY COMPTOIR COURTESY
MINISTRY
(PUBLIC —) AUTHORITY
(RESTORATIVE —) BALM
(SUPPOSITITIOUS —) ENTELECHY
AGENDUM SLATE DOCKET RECORD
RITUAL PROGRAM
AGENOR (BROTHER OF —) BELUS
(DAUGHTER OF —) EUROPA
(FATHER —) ANTENOR NEPTUNE
(MOTHER —) LIBYA
(SON OF —) CILIX CADMUS PHOENIX
(WIFE OF —) TELEPHASSA
AGENT SPY AMIN DOER ETCH GENE
ACTOR AMEEN BUYER CAUSE
ENVOY MEANS ORGAN PROXY
REEVE RIDER VAKIL WALLA ADUROL
ASSIGN ATOPEN BROKER BURSAR
COMMIS DEALER DEPUTY ENGINE
FACTOR FITTER KEHAYA LEDGER
MEDIUM MINION MUKTAR PESKAR
SELLER SYNDIC VAKEEL WALLAH
BAILIFF BLISTER CHANNEL
COUCHER DRASTIC FACIENT
FEDERAL HUSBAND LEAGUER
MOOKTAR MOUNTAR MUKTEAR
MUTAGEN OFFICER PESHKAR
PROCTOR SCALPER APPROVER
ATTORNEY AUMILDAR CATALYST
EMISSARY EXECUTOR GOMASHTA
GOMASTAH IMPROVER INCITANT
INSTITOR MINISTER MOOKHTAR
OPERATOR PROMOTER QUAESTOR
RESIDENT SALESMAN VIRUCIDE
(— OF CROMWELL) AGITATOR
(ANTIKNOCK —) ADDITIVE
ALKYLATE
(CLEANSING —) SOAP
(CONFIDENTIAL —) AMIN AMEEN
(DESTRUCTIVE —) DEVOURER
(EMPLOYMENT —) PADRONE
(ENFORCEMENT —) LAW
(ESPIONAGE —) COURIER
(FISCAL —) STEWARD
(MEDICINAL —) DRASTIC
(NARCOTIC —) GAZER
(PRESS —) FLACK
(PUBLICITY —) BEATER
(PURCHASING —) CIRCAR SIRCAR
SIRKAR
(STIMULATING —) FILIP FILLIP
(SUBVERSIVE —) STOOGE
(SWEETENING —) DULCIN
(VOLATILE —) SPIRIT
(WETTING —) SPREADER
AGGLOMERATE HEAP LUMP MASS
PILE SELF SLAG WIND CHAOS
GATHER CLUSTER COLLECT
AGGLOMERATION HORDE
CONGERY FAVELLA CONGERIE
AGGRANDIZE LIFT BOOST EXALT
RAISE ADVANCE AUGMENT DIGNIFY
ELEVATE ENLARGE MAGNIFY
PROMOTE INCREASE
AGGRAVATE IRK NAG VEX FEED

LOAD TWIT ANGER ANNOY TAUNT
TEASE BURDEN PESTER WORSEN
AGGREGE BEDEVIL ENHANCE
ENLARGE MAGNIFY PROVOKE
AGGRIEVE HEIGHTEN INCREASE
IRRITATE
AGGRAVATED ACUTE
AGGREGATE ADD ALL SET SUM
AUGE BAND BULK CLON CLUB
COMB DEME FLOC GOUT LATH
MASS BLOCK BUNCH CLASS CLONE
COVER CROWD FIELD GROSS
SHOOT TOTAL UNITE WHOLE
AMOUNT BALLAS DOMAIN PLUREL
VOLUME ASBOLAN COLLECT
ARCULITE ASBOLANE ASBOLITE
AXIOLITE COMPOUND COVERAGE
CUMULITE ENSEMBLE MANIFOLD
MULTEITY TOTALITY
(— OF MICA) BOOK
(— OF MINERALS) EYE
(— OF ORE) KIDNEY
(— OF POINTS) CELL
(— OF STATEMENTS) AUTHORITY
(— OF TISSUES) BODY
(MATHEMATICAL —) FIELD
SEQUENCE
AGGREGATION HEAD HERD CLUMP
CUTIN FLOCK GORGE GROUP LURRY
SWARM COLONY FAMILY NATION
SYSTEM CLUSTER CONGERY
GALLERY SORITES CONGERIE
EUMERISM
AGGRESSION WAR RAID ATTACK
INJURY ASSAULT OFFENSE
INVASION
AGGRESSIVE PUSHING
AGGRESSIVENESS CRUST
BELLICOSITY
AGGRIEVE TRY HARM HURT PAIN
HARRY WRONG INJURE AFFLICT
OPPRESS TROUBLE DISTRESS
AGGRIEVED SORE OFFENDED
AGHAST AGAST AFRAID
AGILAWOOD AGALLOCH
AGALLOCHUM
AGILE DEFT FAST LISH SPRY WIRY
ADEPT ALERT BRISK CATTY ELFIN
FLEET LITHE QUICK WANLE WITHY
ACTIVE ADROIT FEERIE FEIRIE
LIMBER LISSOM LITHER LIVELY
LUTHER NIMBLE QUIVER SUPPLE
WANDLE LISSOME SALIENT SPRINGE
SPRINGY ATHLETIC
AGILITY LEVITY SPROIL SLEIGHT
ACTIVITY LEGERITY SALIENCE
AGING BINNING
(PREMATURE —) GERODERMA
GERODERMIA
AGIO BATTA DISAGIO PREMIUM
DISCOUNT EXCHANGE
AGIST TAX FEED RATE GRAZE
PASTURE
AGITATE FAN IRK JAR VEX WEY
FRET FUSS MOVE PLOT RILE ROCK
SEEK STIR TEEM ALARM ALTER
BREAK BROIL CHURN DRIVE HARRY
IMPEL QUAKE ROUSE SHAKE
AROUSE BETOSS BUSKLE DEBATE

DEVISE EXCITE FOMENT HARASS
INCITE JABBLE JOSTLE JUMBLE
JUSTLE LATHER MANAGE RATTLE
RUFFLE SEETHE ACTUATE CANVASS
COMMOVE CONCUSS DISCUSS
DISTURB PERTURB REVOLVE
TEMPEST TROUBLE ACTIVATE
CONTRIVE CONVULSE DISQUIET
DISTRACT TRANSACT
(— A LIQUID) SPARGE
AGITATED STEWED STORMY YEASTY
AGITATO ESTUOUS UNQUIET
AESTUOUS FEVERISH FLURRIED
SEETHING
AGITATION GOG JAR JOG BOIL
FEAR FRET FURY GUST HEAT ITCH
JERK JOLT ALARM DANCE HURRY
QUAKE SHAKE STORM STOUR
TWEAK YEAST BUSTLE DITHER
ENERGY FIZZLE FLIGHT FLURRY
FRENZY JABBLE MOTION PUCKER
QUIVER RIPPLE SHAKES TREMOR
TUMULT EMOTION FERMENT
FLUSTER FLUTTER MADNESS
RAMPAGE STICKLE SWITHER
TEMPEST TURMOIL DISQUIET
PAROXYSM UPHEAVAL
(— AND PROPAGANDA) AGITPROP
AGITATOR HOG TREATER
AGLAIA (FATHER OF —) JUPITER
(MOTHER OF —) EURYNOME
(SISTER OF —) THALIA
EUPHROSYNE
AGLET TAB TAG LACE STUD PLATE
AIGLET PENDANT SPANGLE
HAWTHORN STAYLACE
AGLEY AWRY AGLEE ASIDE ASKEW
WRONG
AGLYCON GENIN NONSUGAR
AGNATE AKIN ALLIED COGNATE
KINDRED
AGNEL MOUTON
AGNOETE THEMISTIAN
AGNOMEN NAME ALIAS EPITHET
SURNAME COGNOMEN NICKNAME
AGNOSTIC ATHEIST DOUBTER
SKEPTIC NESCIENT
AGO BY SIN BACK ERST GONE PAST
SENS SYNE YGOE YORE ABACK
AGONE SINCE YGONE SINSYNE
BACKWARD
(LONG —) ANCIENTLY
AGOG AVID KEEN ASTIR EAGER
LIVELY EXCITED VIGILANT
AGONIZE BEAR RACK STRAIN
WRITHE
AGONIZING GRINDING HARROWING
AGONY ACHE PAIN PANG DOLOR
GRIEF GRIPE PANIC STOUR THRAW
THROE TRIAL ACHING ANGUISH
ANXIETY EMOTION TORMENT
TORTURE TRAVAIL DISTRESS
PAROXYSM
AGOUTI CAPA CAVY PACA ACUCHI
AGOUTY ACOUCHI
AGRARIAN RURAL PASTORAL
AGREE FAY FIT GEE HIT PAN YES
GIBE GREE JIBE JUMP MEET SIDE
SORT SUIT ADMIT ALLOW ATONE

BLEND CHECK CLICK CLOSE FADGE
GRANT HITCH JUTTY LEVEL MATCH
PIECE STAND TALLY UNITE YIELD
ACCEDE ACCORD ASSENT ASSORT
COMPLY CONCUR CONDOG COTTON
ENGAGE REWARD SETTLE SQUARE
SUBMIT ARRANGE BARGAIN
COMPORT CONCEDE CONFORM
CONGREE CONGRUE CONSENT
CONSIGN DARESAY PACTION
PROMISE COINCIDE COMPOUND
CONTRACT COVENANT QUADRATE
(— **MUTUALLY**) STIPULATE
(— **TO JOIN**) ADHERE
(— **TO**) ACCEPT
(— **UPON**) TAILYE TAILZEE TAILZIE
(— **WITH**) SIT LIKE SIDE TAIL
ANSWER
AGREEABLE AMEN EASY FAIR FINE
GOOD KIND LIEF NICE SOFT WEME
AMENE CANNY DULCE GRATE JOLIE
JOLLY LITHE LUSTY QUEME READY
SAPID SMIRK SUANT SUAVE SUENT
SWEET COMELY COWDIE DAINTY
DULCET KINDLY LIKELY SAVORY
SMOOTH SUITED ADAPTED AMABILE
AMIABLE COUTHIE DOUCEUR
TUNABLE WELCOME WILLING
WINSOME AMENABLE CHARMING
DELICATE GRATEFUL LIKESOME
LOVESOME OBLIGING PLACABLE
PLAUSIVE PLEASANT PLEASING
PURSUANT SOCIABLE SUITABLE
THANKFUL
(**NOT** —) ABHORRENT
(**UNPLEASANTLY** —) SACCHARINE
AGREEING CONNATE CONTENT
AGREEMENT GO FIT NOD AXIS
BOND DEAL FINE LINE MISE PACT
TACK TAIL TRUE ATONE COVIN
LEASE MATCH TERMS TOUCH
TRUTH TRYST UNITY ACCORD
ACTION ASSENT CARTEL CAUTIO
COMITY COVINE DICKER LEAGUE
PACTUM PLEDGE TREATY UNISON
BARGAIN CLOSURE COMPACT
CONCERT CONSENT CONSULT
ENTENTE HARMONY ONENESS
PACTION RAPPORT CONTRACT
DIAPASON SANCTION SORTANCE
SYMPATHY
(— **TO JOIN**) ADHESION
(**GRAMMATICAL** —) ATTRACTION
(**SECRET** —) CAHOOT CAHOOTS
AGRICULTURAL GEOPONIC
GEOPONICAL
AGRICULTURE FARMING GAINAGE
TILLAGE AGRONOMY
(— **SYSTEM**) KOLKHOZ
AGRICULTURIST THO FARMER
GROWER SANTAL PLANTER
RANCHER
AGRIMONY CLIVE BORWORT
HEMPWEED
AGRITO AGARITA MAHONIA
ALGERITO ASHBERRY
AGROUND SEWED ASHORE
BEACHED STRANDED
AGRYPHA LOGION
AGRYPNIA INSOMNIA

SLEEPLESSNESS
AGUACATE AHUACA AVOCADO
AGUAMAS PINGUIN
AGUE CHILL FEVER MALARIA
SHAKING SHIVERS
AGUE TREE SASSAFRAS
AGUEWEED BONESET
AH ACH
AHARTALAV YARROW MILFOIL
AHEAD ON UP ALEE FORE AFORE
ALONG DORMY BEFORE DORMIE
ONWARD ALREADY ENDWAYS
ENDWISE FORWARD LEADING
ADELANTE ADVANCED ANTERIOR
(— **OF TIME**) FAST
(**STRAIGHT** —) FORERIGHT
AHEM HUM
AHOY AVAST
AHUEHUETE CEDAR SABINO
CYPRESS
AID KEY ABET BACK BEET HAND
HELP PONY REDE ALLAY BOOST
COACH FAVOR GRANT SERVE
SPEED TREAT ASSIST FAVOUR
FRIEND PROFIT RELIEF REMEDY
RESCUE SECOND SUCCOR SUPPLY
UPHOLD ADVANCE AIDANCE
ANCILLA BACKING BENEFIT
COMFORT ENDORSE FORWARD
FURTHER INDORSE RELIEVE
SECOURS SERVICE SUBSIDY
SUPPORT ADJUVATE AUXILIUM
BEFRIEND SUFFRAGE
(— **A VESSEL**) HOVEL
(— **SECRETLY**) SUBAID
(**COMPLEXION** —) FUCUS
(**MORMON** —) COUNSELOR
COUNSELLOR
AIDE AID BEAGLE DEPUTY SECOND
OFFICER ORDERLY ADJUTANT
GALLOPER
(**BULLFIGHTER'S** —) CAPEADOR
AIGRETTE EGRET HERON PLUME
SPRAY AIGRET FEATHERS
AIL ILE AILD EILE EYLE FAIL PAIN
PINE AFFECT BOTHER FALTER
SUFFER AFFLICT DECLINE TROUBLE
COMPLAIN DISTRESS
AILANTHUS SUMAC SUMACH
AILING SICK CRAZY CRONK DONCY
DONSY SOBER DONSIE SICKLY
UNWELL CRAICHY CREACHY
AILMENT AIL ILL COUGH MALADY
DISEASE ILLNESS DISORDER
SICKNESS WEAKNESS
AIM END LAY TRY BEAD BEAM BENT
BUTT FINE GLEE GOAL HEAD HOLD
LEAD MARK MINT PLAN SEEK TEMP
VIEW VIZY WINK ACIES BLANK
DRIVE ESSAY ETTLE GUESS LEVEL
POINT PRICK SCOPE SIGHT TRAIN
VISIE VIZZY ASPIRE DESIGN DIRECT
ESTEEM INTEND INTENT OBJECT
SCHEME STRIVE ADDRESS ATTEMPT
CHIMERA MEANING PRETEND
PURPOSE RESPECT STAGGER
CHIMAERA CONSIDER ENDEAVOR
ESTIMATE PRETENSE STEERING
TENTAMEN
(— **A KICK**) FLING

(— **AT**) EYE AFFECT
(— **FURTIVELY**) STEAL
(— **INDIRECTLY**) GLANCE
AIMED FAST
(— **AT**) AFFECTED
AIMING LEVEL GUNLAYING
AIMLESS IDLE BLIND CHANCE
RANDOM DRIFTING
AIMLESSNESS FLANERIE
AIR AER PEW SKY AERE ARIA AURA
AYRE BROW DIRT FEEL LILT LOFT
MIEN PORT POSE SONG TELL TUNE
VENT WIND ETHER FRILL OZONE
UTTER VOICE AERATE AETHER
ALLURE ASPECT BROACH CACHET
MANNER MELODY OSTENT PIAFFE
REGARD REGION STRAIN VANITY
WELKIN WITHER BEARING DISPLAY
EXHIBIT EXPRESS FANFARE
MALARIA NEPHELE PIAFFER
ATTITUDE BEHAVIOR CARRIAGE
PRESENCE
(— **COOLED**) WATERLESS
(— **EXHALED**) BLAST
(— **IN MOTION**) BREATH
(— **PLANT**) LIFELEAF
(**BOASTFUL** —) PARADO
(**CONFIDENT** —) BRAVURA
(**COOL** —) FRESCO
(**COQUETTISH** —) MINAUDERIE
(**FETID** —) REEK
(**FOUL** —) DIRT
(**HAUGHTY** —**S**) ALTITUDES
(**MUSICAL** —) ARIA SOLO TUNE
BRAWL MELODY ARIETTA ARIETTE
MUSETTE
(**POMPOUS** —) SWELL
(**PUT ON** —**S**) PROSS
(**STALE** —) STEAM
(**STIFLING** —) SMORE
(**THE** —) GATE
(**WARM** —) OAM
(PL.) LUGS FRONT
AIRCRAFT KITE ABORT BLIMP CRAFT
FLYER PLANE GLIDER AEROBUS
AERONEF AIRSHIP BALLOON
AEROBOAT AERODYNE AEROSTAT
AIRLINER AIRPLANE AUTOGIRO
AUTOGYRO GYRODYNE
(**UNIDENTIFIED** —) UFO BOGY
BOGEY BOGIE
AIRCRAFTSMAN ERK
AIRCREWMAN KICKER AIREDALE
AIRFIELD AERODROME SATELLITE
AIRFOIL FIN FLAP SLAT BLADE
SURFACE AEROFOIL ELEVATOR
AIRILY JAUNTILY
AIRLINE FEEDER SKYWAY
AIRMAN FLIER FLYER BIRDMAN
WARBIRD WASTEMAN
AIRPLANE BUS CUB JET MIG BAKA
GYRO KILL KITE SHIP ZERO AVION
CRATE FLIER FLYER FRITZ GOTHA
HEINE JENNY LINER PLANE SCOUT
SNOOP BOMBER CANARD CHASER
COPTER FERRET FESSEL FOKKER
GLIDER JENNIE SMOKER TANDEM
VESSEL AERONEF AVIATIK BIPLANE
CLIPPER FIGHTER FLIVVER FLYAWAY
HOTSHOT PENGUIN SNOOPER

SPOTTER TRACTOR WARBIRD
AEROSTAT ALBATROS KAMIKAZE
SEAPLANE SKYCOACH SKYCRAFT
SOCIABLE STRUTTER TRIPLANE
TURBOJET WARPLANE
(REMOTE-CONTROLLED —) DRONE
AIR PLANT LIFELEAF LIVELEAF
AIRPORT DROME AIRPARK JETPORT
SCUTTLE AIRDROME AIRFIELD
AIRSHIP (SEE ALSO AIRPLANE AND
AIRCRAFT) SHIP BLIMP GASBAG
AERONAT AEROSTAT PARSEVAL
ZEPPELIN
AIRSTREAM PEW DOWNWASH
AIRSTRIP LILY
AIRTIGHT SEALED AIRPROOF
HERMETIC
AIRWAY MONKEY RETURN SKYWAY
AIRWAVE WINDWAY WINDROAD
AIRY GAY COOL RARE THIN EMPTY
HUFFY LIGHT MERRY WINDY AERIAL
BREZZY FLUFFY JAUNTY JOCUND
LIVELY STARRY AIRLIKE AIRSOME
HAUGHTY JOCULAR SFOGATO
AFFECTED ANIMATED DEBONAIR
DELICATE ETHEREAL FLIPPANT
GRACEFUL SPARKISH TRIFLING
VOLATILE
AISLE ILE WAY YLE AILE LANE NAVE
WALK ALLEE ALLEY FEEDWAY
GANGWAY PASSAGE CORRIDOR
AIT OAT EYOT HOLM ISLE EIGHT
ISLET
AITCHBONE ICEBONE EDGEBONE
AJAR OPEN DISCORDANT
AJAX AIAS
(FATHER OF —) OILEUS TELAMON
(MOTHER OF —) ERIBOEA PERIBOEA
AJONJOLI SESAME
AJOWAN AJAVA AIWAIN
AKALI SHAHIDI
AKEAKE AKE HOPBUSH IRONWOOD
AKHA KAW
AKIMBO ANGLED AKEMBOLL
AKENBOLD
AKIN SIB LIKE NEAR NIGH ALIKE
CLOSE AGNATE ALLIED COUSIN
SIBBED TENDER COGNATE CONNATE
GERMANE RELATED SIMILAR
(— ON MALE SIDE) AGNATIC
(NOT —) UNSIB
AKRA ACCRA INKRA
AKU VICTORFISH
AL AAL AWL MULBERRY
ALA AXIL DRUM WING AXILLA
RECESS NOSEWING

ALABAMA
CAPITAL: MONTGOMERY
COUNTY: LEE BIBB CLAY DALE
PIKE COOSA HENRY LAMAR
MACON PERRY BLOUNT BUTLER
COFFEE DALLAS ELMORE
ETOWAH GENEVA GREENE
MARION MONROE MORGAN
SHELBY SUMTER WILCOX
CHILTON
MOUNTAIN: CHEAHA

NATIVE: LIZARD
RIVER: PEA COOSA CAHABA
MOBILE SIPSEY TENSAW
CONECUH SEPULGA TOMBIGBEE
STATE BIRD: YELLOWHAMMER
STATE FISH: TARPON
STATE FLOWER: CAMELLIA
STATE TREE: PINE LONGLEAF
TOWN: OPP PIPER SELMA ATHENS
CORONA LINDEN MARION
MOBILE SAMSON FLORALA
GADSDEN ANNISTON

ALABASTER GYPSUM TECALI
ONYCHITE
ALACK ALAS ALAKE
ALACRITY HASTE SPEED CELERITY
RAPIDITY
ALAMEDA MALL WALK
ALAN ALAND ALANT ALAUNT
ALANG-ALANG COGON KOGON
ALANS GHUZ OGHUZ
ALANTIN INULIN
ALAR PTERIC WINGED AXILLARY
WINGLIKE
ALARM COW DIN BELL FEAR FRAY
GAST LARM ALERT BROIL CLOCK
DAUNT FEEZE LARUM NOISE PANIC
ROUSE SCARE SIREN START STILL
UPSET AFFRAY ALARUM APPALL
AROUSE ATTACK BUZZER DISMAY
EXCITE FRIGHT OUTCRY SIGNAL
TERROR TOCSIN DISTURB GLOPPEN
GLOPPEN MOUNTEE STARTLE
TERRIFY TORPEDO WARNING
AFFRIGHT DISQUIET FRIGHTEN
SURPRISE
(FIRE —) STILL FIREBOX
ALARMED SCARY SCAREY FEARFUL
GASTFUL GHASTFUL SCAREFUL
STREAKED
ALARMER HUER
ALARMING SCARY SCAREY FEARFUL
SCAREFUL
ALAS AY ACH HEU LAS OCH VAE
WOE EHEU HECH OIME ALACK
HALAS HELAS OIMEE OCHONE
OTOTOI WAESUCK ULLAGONE
WAESUCKS WELLADAY WELLAWAY

ALASKA
CAPITAL: JUNEAU
ISLAND: ADAK ATKA ATTU UMNAK
KODIAK UNIMAK DIOMEDE
NUNIVAK
ISLAND GROUP: RAT ALEUTIAN
PRIBILOF ANDREANOF
LAKE: NAKNEK ILIAMNA
MOUNTAIN: BONA VETA SPURR
KATMAI PAVLOF FORAKER
MCKINLEY
MOUNTAIN RANGE: CRAZY
BROOKS KAIYUH CHUGACH
KILBUCK WRANGELL
NATIVE: ALEUT AHTENA ESKIMO
INGALIK KOYUKON TLINGIT
PENINSULA: KENAI SEWARD

RIVER: CHENA KOBUK YUKON
COPPER NOATAK TANANA
KOYUKUK SUSITNA CHULITNA
COLVILLE
STATE BIRD: PTARMIGAN
STATE FLOWER: FORGETMENOT
STATE TREE: SPRUCE
TOWN: EEK NOME KENAI SITKA
BARROW KODIAK NENANA
SKAGWAY KOTZEBUE
ANCHORAGE FAIRBANKS

ALASTRIM AMAAS
ALB ALBE AUBE CAMISIA CHRISOM
VESTMENT
ALBACORE TUNA TUNNY GERMAN
GERMON LONGFIN ALALONGA
ALALUNGA MACKEREL SCOMBRID

ALBANIA
ANCIENT PEOPLE: ILLYRIAN
CAPITAL: TIRANA TIRANE
COIN: LEK FRANC GUINTAR
KING: ZOG
LAKE: ULZE OHRIDSKO
MOUNTAIN: KORAB SHALA PINDUS
KORITNJK
REGION: EPIRUS
RIVER: MAT DRIN OSUM ERZEN
SEMAN VIJOSE SHKUMBI
TOWN: LIN FIER KLOS BERAT
DUKAT KORCE KRUJE PECIN
PEQIN QUKES RUBIC SPASH
VLONE VLORE ARLONA BITSAN
DARDHE DURRES PRESHE
VALONA DURAZZO KORITZA
SCUTARI SHKODER
TRIBE: GEG CHAM GHEG TOSK

ALBANIAN GEG GHEG GUEG
ARNAUT SKIPETAR
ALBATROSS GONY GOON GONEY
GOONY NELLY FABRIC GOONEY
GOONIE QUAKER SEABIRD
BLUEBIRD STINKPOT
ALBEIT ALL ALBE ALBEE ALLBE
THOUGH HOWBEIT
ALBINO LEUCAETHIOP
ALBIZZIA SIRIS
ALBUM ALBE BOOK RECORD
VOLUME REGISTER
ALBUMEN WHITE
ALBUMIN ALBUMEN PHASELIN
SYNTONIN
ALBUMINOID ELASTIN FIBROIN
KERATIN PROTEIN SERICIN
COLLAGEN GORGONIN
ALBURNUM SAP BLEA SPLINT
SAPWOOD
ALBUS BLANCO
ALCAEUS (FATHER OF —) PERSEUS
(SON OF —) AMPHITRYON
ALCAIDE CADE CAID QAID JUDGE
ALCADE
ALCESTIS (FATHER OF —) PELIAS
(HUSBAND OF —) ADMETUS
ALCHEMIST ADEPT ARTIST CHEMIC

CHEMICK CHEMIST HERMETIC
ALCHEMY ART MAGIC ALCUMY
CHYMIA SPAGYRIC
(GOD OF —) HERMES
ALCHORNEA DOVEWOOD
ALCINOUS (DAUGHTER OF —)
NAUSICAA
(FATHER OF —) NAUSITHOUS
(MOTHER OF —) PERIBOEA
(WIFE OF —) ARETE
ALCMAEON (FATHER OF —)
AMPHIARAUS
(MOTHER OF —) ERIPHYLE
(WIFE OF —) CALLIRHOE
ALPHESIBOEA
ALCMENE (FATHER OF —)
ELECTRYON
(HUSBAND OF —) AMPHITRYON
(SON OF —) HERCULES IPHICLES
ALCOHOL ALKY ETHAL ETHYL IDITE
LEDOL VINYL AMYROL ANDROL
CEDROL ELEMOL GLYCOL GUAIOL
HYDROL IDITOL LUPEOL LUTEIN
METHYL PHYTOL SPIRIT STERIN
STERNO STEROL TALITE ACRITOL
ADONITE ALDITOL ALKANOL ANISOIN
BORNEOL BUTANOL CAROTOL
DECANOL ETHANOL FENCHOL
HEPTITE HEXITOL INOSITE MENTHOL
PULEGOL QUINITE SCOPINE
SORBITE STETHAL STYRONE
TAGETOL TALITOL TROPINE XYLITOL
LINALOOL METHANOL
ALCOHOLATE SPIRIT ESSENCE
ALCOHOLIC ALKY
(NOT —) SOFT
ALCOHOLOMETER GENOMETER
VINOMETER
ALCOVE BAY NOOK BOWER NICHE
ORIEL STALL CARREL RECESS
CARRELL CUBICLE DINETTE
RETREAT SERVERY ALHACENA
SNUGGERY TABLINUM
ALDEHYDE ALDOL CITRAL ALKANAL
CHLORAL COGENER DECANAL
GLYOXAL HEXANAL ACROLEIN
CONGENER FURFURAL
ALDER ARN OLER ALNUS ELDER
OWLER SAGEROSE
ALDERMAN BAILIE SENIOR
HEADMAN
ALE MUM NOG BEER BOCK BREW
FLIP MILD NOGG PURL SCUD YELL
AUDIT CLINK DARBY JOUGH LAGER
NAPPY STOUT ALEGAR PORTER
STINGO SWANKY BITTERS
MOROCCO OCTOBER PHARAOH
HUGMATEE
**(— BREWED WITH BRACKISH
WATER)** TIPPER
(— MIXED WITH SWEETENER)
BRAGGET
(INFERIOR —) SWANKY SWANKEY
(NEW —) SWATS
(SOUR —) ALEGAR
(SPICED —) SWIG
(STRONG —) MUM HUFF BURTON
STINGO HUFFCAP
(WEAK —) TWOPENNY

ALEATORY HAZARDOUS
ALECOST COSTMARY
ALECTRYON TITOKI
ALEE AHEAD LEEWARD
ALEHOUSE PUB TAVERN BARROOM
MUGHOUSE POTHOUSE
ALEMBIC LIMBEC LIMBECK
CUCURBIT
ALERT APT GAY HEP HIP YAL YEP
FOXY GLEG KEEN LIVE PERT SNAP
WAKE WARN WARY YALD YEPE
ACUTE AGILE ALARM ALIVE AWAKE
AWARE BREME BRISK EAGER ERECT
LEERY MERRY PEART PEERT QUICK
READY SHACK SHARP SIREN SLICK
SWIFT TIGHT WAKER YAULD ACTIVE
ALARUM ARRECT BRIGHT DAPPER
LIVELY NIMBLE PROMPT SLIPPY
SPRACK SUDDEN TIPTOE TOCSIN
WACKER CAREFUL KNOWING
WAKEFUL WORKING PREPARED
THOUGHTY VIGILANT WAKERIFE
WATCHFUL
ALERTNESS NOUS SNAP APTNESS
APTITUDE
(MENTAL —) WIT
ALETTE WING ABUTMENT
ALEUT ATKA ORARIAN UNALASKA
**ALEUTIANS (ISLANDS AND ISLAND
GROUPS OF —)** FOX RAT ADAK
ATTU NEAR KISKA UMNAK KODIAK
(TOWN OF —) UNALASKA
(VOLCANO ON —) SHISHALDIN
ALEWIFE BANG ALLICE ALOOFE
BUCKIE ALEWHAP HERRING
OLDWIFE POMPANO WALLEYE
GRAYBACK GREYBACK SAWBELLY
SKIPJACK
ALEXANDER ALEX PARIS SAWNY
ELLICK SAWNEY SAWNIE ISKANDER
(BIRTHPLACE OF —) PELLA
(HORSE OF —) BUCEPHALUS
ALFA HALFA ESPARTO
ALFALFA HAY MEDIC FODDER
LEGUME LUCERN LUCERNE
ALFILARIA ERODIUM FILAREE
FILARIA PINWEED
ALFORJA BAG POUCH WALLET
ALFARGA ALFORGE
ALGA NORI ALGAL BROWN FUCUS
JELLY SLAKE SLOAK SLOKE DESMID
DIATOM FUNORI NOSTOC AMANORI
GULAMAN HAITSAI OARWEED
SEAWEED ANABAENA FERNLEAF
GELIDIUM HAIRWEED ROCKWEED
SEABEARD SILKWEED SPOROGEN
WHIPCORD ZOOGLOEA
ALGARROBA CAROB CALDEN
ALGEBRA LOGISTIC
ALGEBRAIC COSSIC
ALGENIB MIRFAK

ALGERIA

BERBER: KABYLE SHAWIA TUAREG
BERBER DIALECT: ZENATA
SENHAJA
CAPITAL: ALGIERS
CAVALRYMAN: SPAHI SPAHEE

DEPARTMENT: ORAN ALGIERS
GRASS: ESPARTO
HILL: TELL
HOLY MAN: MARABOUT
MEASURE: PIK REBIS TARRI
TERMIN
MONASTERY: RIBAT
MOUNTAIN: AISSA ATLAS AURES
DAHRA TAHAT CHELIA AHAGGAR
MOUYDIR DJURJURA
NAME: ALGERIE NUMIDIA
NATIVE: BERBER KABYLE
PIRATE: CORSAIR
RIVER: SHELIF CHELIFF MEDJERDA
RULER: BEY DEY BEVLERBEY
SECT: SUNNITE
SETTLER: COLON PIEDNOIR
SHIP: XEBEC
TOWN: BONE ORAN AFLOU ARZEW
BATNA BLIDA MEDEA SAIDA
SETIF TENES ABADLA ANNABA
AUMALE BARIKA BECHAR BEJAIA
BENOUD BISKRA BOUGIE
DELLYS DJANET DJELFA DZIOUA
FRENDA GUELMA SKIKDA
BOGHARI MASCARA MILIANA
NEGRINE NEMOURS OUARGLA
TEBESSA TLEMCEN
WEIGHT: ROTL

ALGERINE COOLOOLY KOOLOOLY
ALGID COLD COOL CHILLY CLAMMY
ALGOLOGY VERATRIN
ALGONKIAN EOZOIC
(— ROCKS) UNKAR
ALIAS ELSE OTHER AYLESS
ASSUMED EPITHET
ALIBI PLEA EXCUSE APOLOGY
PRETEXT
ALIDADE INDEX DIOPTER
ALIEN GER DEED FREMD METIC
ALAUNT ALLTUD AUBAIN CONVEY
EXOTIC INMATE REMOTE ADVERSE
DENIZEN FOREIGN FRAMMIT
INVADER OUTLAND STRANGE
DETAINEE STRANGER TRANSFER
ALIENATE PART WEAN ALIEN AVERT
ANNALY CONVEY DEMISE DEVEST
FREEZE FORFEIT SUBVERT
AMORTIZE DISUNITE ESTRANGE
MORTMAIN SEPARATE STRANGER
TRANSFER WITHDRAW
ALIENATION GIFT DISTASTE
DISUNION DISUNITY DIVISION
DONATION INSANITY
ALIENIST PSYCHOPATH
PSYCHIATRIST
ALIGHT DROP LAND LEND REST
STOP LATCH LIGHT LODGE PERCH
ROOST STOOP SWOOP ARRIVE
SETTLE BURNING DESCEND
ALIGN LINE TRAM TRUE ALINE
ARRAY DRESS RANGE ADJUST
ARRANGE MARSHAL
(— PAPER) JOG
ALIGNED FAIR COLORED
ALIGNMENT KELTER KILTER
GROUPING

ALII ARIKI
ALIKE AKIN LIKE SAME EQUAL INLIKE
SQUARE YLICHE EQUALLY SIMILAR
UNIFORM
ALIMENT PAP FOOD FUEL BROMA
MANNA VIANDS ALIMONY PABULUM
RATIONS
ALIMONY ALIMENT
ALIPHATIC FATTY
ALIVE VIF BUSY KEEN SPRY VIVE
AGILE ALERT ALIFE ASTIR AWARE
BEING BRISK FRESH GREEN QUICK
VITAL AROUND EXTANT LIVING
SLIPPY ANIMATE VIBRANT ANIMATED
EXISTENT SENSIBLE SWARMING
ALKALI LYE REH BASE BRAK KALI
SALT SODA USAR BRACK CAUSTIC
ALKALOID BASE ERGOT ESERE
ARICIN BRUCIN CEVINE CODEIN
CONINE CURINE ESERIN QUINIA
QUININ ACONINE ARABINE ARICINE
ATROPIA BOGAINE BOLDINE
BRUCINE CAFFEIN COCAINE
CODEINE CONIINE EMETINE
HARMINE HYGRINE JERVINE KAIRINE
NARCEIN NEOPINE PTOMAIN
QUININE SCOPINE SINAPIN SOLANIN
SOPHORA VIOLINE PIPERINE
ALKANE PARAFFIN
ALKANET BUGLOSS REDROOT
ALKANNIN ORCANET ANCHUSIN
ORCHANET
ALKYD GLYPTAL
ALL A AL ANY SUM EACH FULL TOTE
AUGHT EVERY GROSS OMNES
OUGHT QUITE TOTAL TOTUM TUTTA
TUTTO WHOLE ENTIRE SOLELY
WHOLLY PLENARY ENTIRELY
EVERYONE TOTALITY
(**— BUT ABSOLUTELY**) ALMOST
(**— IN**) ALTOGETHER
(**— TOGETHER**) COLLECTEDLY
(**AND —**) ANA
(**AT —**) AVA ANYWISE ANYTHING
ANYWHERE
(**OF —**) AVA
ALLANITE CERINE CERITE ORTHITE
ALLAY AID LAY CALM CITE COOL
EASE HELP HUSH STAY ABATE
AGATE ALLOY CHARM CHECK
DELAY QUELL QUIET SALVE SLAKE
STILL ADDUCE LESSEN PACIFY
QUENCH REDUCE SOFTEN SOLACE
SOOTHE STANCH SUBDUE TEMPER
APPEASE ASSUAGE COMFORT
COMPOSE LIGHTEN MOLLIFY
RELIEVE REPRESS STAUNCH
MITIGATE PALLIATE
ALLAYED DEFERRED
ALLEGATION PLEA COUNT VOUCH
CHARGE ESSOIN AVERRAL FICTION
PROFERT SCANDAL SURMISE
AVERMENT SCIENTER
ALLEGE LAY SAY AVER AVOW CITE
SHOW URGE ALLAY CLAIM FEIGN
INFER LEDGE OFFER PLEAD QUOTE
STATE SWEAR VOUCH ADDUCE
AFFIRM ASSERT ASSIGN CHARGE
DEPOSE ESSOIN RECITE ADVANCE

ASCRIBE DECLARE LIGHTEN
PRESENT PROFESS PROPOSE
MAINTAIN
ALLEGED SUPPOSED SURMISED
ALLEGIANCE TIE DUTY FAITH
HONOR FEALTY HOMAGE LYANCE
LOYALTY SERVAGE SERVICE
TRIBUTE CIVILITY DEVOTION
FIDELITY LIGEANCE
ALLEGORICAL PARABOLIC
SYMBOLICAL
ALLEGORICALLY SECRETLY
ALLEGORIZE TALMUDIZE
ALLEGORY MYTH TALE FABLE
STORY EMBLEM PARABLE
APOLOGUE METAPHOR
ALLELUIA AEVIA LAUDS
ALL-EMBRACING INFINITE
SWEEPING
ALLERGEN INHALANT
ALLERGY ATOPY IDIOBLAPSIS
ALLEVIATE AID BALM CALM CURE
EASE HELP ABATE ALLAY QUIET
ALIGHT ALLEGE LENIFY LESSEN
PACIFY SOFTEN SOLACE SOOTHE
SUCCOR SUPPLE TEMPER ASSUAGE
COMPOSE CONSOLE CORRECT
LENIATE LIGHTEN MOLLIFY RELEASE
RELIEVE DIMINISH MITIGATE
MODERATE PALLIATE
ALLEVIATION ALAY SOLACE
ALLEY MIG ROW WAY CHAR LANE
LEAD MALL MEWS PASS PATH VENT
WALK WENT WIND WYND AISLE
ALLEE BLIND BYWAY CHARE ENTRY
TEWER WEENT PEEWEE TRANCE
VENNEL PASSAGE
(**BLIND —**) LOKE STOP POCKET
IMPASSE
ALLHALLOWTIDE HOLLANTIDE
ALLHEAL PANACEA WOUNWORT
ALLIANCE AXIS PACT UNION
ACCORD FUSION LEAGUE LYANCE
TREATY COMPACT ENTENTE
SOCIETY AFFINITY AGNATION
CACTALES COVENANT DREIBUND
FEDERACY FUNGALES LILIALES
TRIPLICE
(**— IN WAR**) SYMMACHY
ALLICE SHAD ALEWIFE POMPANO
ALLIED SIB AKIN AGNATE COUSIN
JOINED LINKED UNITED COGNATE
CONNATE FEDERAL GERMANE
KINDRED RELATED SIMILAR
RELATIVE
ALLIGATOR GATOR NIGER CAIMAN
CAYMAN CROTCH JACARE LIZARD
TRAVOY YACARE CRAWLER
CREEPER LAGARTO TRAVOIS
ALAGARTO LORICATE
(**— PEAR**) ZABOCA AVOCADO
AGUACATE
(**— TURTLE**) LOGGERHEAD
(**MALE —**) BULL
ALLIGATORING WEBBING
ALL-INCLUSIVE GLOBAL
ALLITERATION LETTER
ALLITERATIVE LITERAL
ALLIUM LILY ONION GARLIC

ALLNESS OMNEITY OMNITUDE
ALLOCATE DEAL DOLE METE RATE
ALLOT AWARD SHARE AFFECT
ASSIGN OUTPLACE
ALLOCATION DRAW DESIGNATION
ALLOT FIX SET BILL CAST DEAL
DOLE GIVE MARK METE PART RATE
SORT ALLOW AWARD CAVEL GRANT
SHARE ACCORD AFFECT ASSIGN
BESTOW DEPUTE DESIGN DIRECT
INTEND ORDAIN RATION ACCOUNT
APPOINT DESTINE PRORATE
QUARTER SPECIFY TRIBUTE
ALLOCATE
(**— QUARTERS**) CANTON
ALLOTMENT CUT LOT DOLE CAVEL
SHARE RATION SIZING LOTMENT
LOTTERY PORTION DIVISION
PITTANCE
ALLOW LET LOW BEAR GIVE HAVE
LEND LOAN ADMIT DEFER GRANT
LEAVE STAND THOLE YIELD ACCEPT
ACCORD ASSIGN BESTOW BETEEM
ENABLE ENDURE PERMIT SUFFER
APPROVE CONCEDE CONFESS
LICENCE LICENSE SUFFICE SUPPOSE
SUSTAIN CONSIDER DISPENSE
SANCTION TOLERATE
ALLOWABLE FREE LICIT LAWFUL
ALLOWANCE BOT FEE ICE AGIO
BOTE DOLE EASE EDGE GIFT HIRE
ODDS RATE SALT SIZE ARRAS
BATTA CLOFF GRANT LEAVE SHARE
STENT STINT BOUCHE BOUNTY
CORODY FODDER MARGIN RATING
REGAIN SALARY SEQUEL TANTUM
ALIMENT ALIMONY CORRODY
DIETARY DIOBELY LEAKAGE
LOWANCE PENSION PORTION
PREBEND SCALAGE STIPENT
TEARAGE APPENAGE APPROVAL
BREAKAGE DISCOUNT DRAFTAGE
ORDINARY QUANTITY SANCTION
SOLATIUM VIATICUM
(**— FOR EXPENSES**) DIET
(**— FOR MAINTENANCE**) ALIMENT
(**— FOR THICKNESS**) BOXING
(**— FOR WASTE**) TRET
(**— FOR WEIGHT**) BUG TARE DRAFT
DRAUGHT
(**— OF ARROWS**) SHEAF
(**— OF FOOD**) DIET BOUCHE
DIETARY
(**— OF TIME OR DISTANCE**) LAW
(**— TO COMPETITOR**) LAW
(**CLOTHING —**) INLAY
(**CORRECTIVE —**) SALT
(**NEGATIVE —**) INTERFERENCE
ALLOWED VENIAL LICENTIATE
(**NOT —**) ILLICIT FORBIDDEN
ALLOY LAY LOY MIX AICH ASEM
ALPAX BIDRI BIDRY BRASS CALIN
DURAL FLINT INVAR MOKUM MONEL
TERNE ALBATA ALNICO ALUMEL
BIDREE BILLON BRONZE CERMET
GARBLE ILLIUM LATTEN LEAVEN
NIELLO OCCAMY OREIDE OROIDE
PEWTER SOLDER TAMBAC TOMBAC
TOMBAK ACIERAL ALCHEMY

AMALGAM BABBITT BIDDERY
ELINVAR INCONEL MIXTURE
PAKTONG RHEOTAN RHODITE
SEMILOR SIMILOR TAENITE TUTANIA
TUTENAG ALFENIDE ARGENTON
ARSEDINE AWARUITE CALAMINE
CARACOLI DORALIUM ELECTRUM
EUTECTIC GUNMETAL HARDENER
KAMACITE METALINE ROMANIUM
STELLITE
ALL-PERVADING UNIVERSAL
ALL RIGHT OK YES OKAY AGREED
OKEYDOKE
ALLSEED FLAXSEED BURSTWORT
ALL SOULS' DAY SOULMASS
ALLSPICE BUBBY PIMENTO
ALLTHORN JUNCO
ALLUDE HINT IMPLY POINT REFER
ADVERT GLANCE RELATE CONNOTE
MENTION SUGGEST INDICATE
INTIMATE
ALLURE IT AIR COY WIN WOO BAIT
DRAW LEAD LURE MOVE SWAY WILE
ANGLE BRIBE CHARM COURT
DECOY SNARE TEMPT ALLECT
ENTICE ENTRAP ILLURE INDUCE
INVITE SEDUCE ATTRACT BEGUILE
ENSNARE BLANDISH INESCATE
INVEIGLE PERSUADE SIRENING
ALLUREMENT BAIT CORD LURE
ALLURE GLAMOR GUDGEON
ALLURING GREEN TAKING SIRENIC
SUGARED TAKEFUL CATCHING
ENTICING FETCHING
ALLUSION HINT TWIT TOUCH
GLANCE REFLEX INKLING MENTION
INNUENDO INSTANCE
ALLUSIVE CANTING
ALLUVIUM WASH
ALLY PAL AIDE JOIN RANGE UNION
UNITE BACKER COXCOX FRIEND
HELPER LEAGUE ALLIANT CONNECT
PARTNER ADHERENT CONFEDER
FEDERATE
(PL.) FOEDERATI
ALMANAC ORDO PADDY CALENDAR
ALMEMAR BEMA BIMA BIMAH
ALMIGHTY GOD GREAT CREATOR
EXTREME JEHOVAH INFINITE
POWERFUL PUISSANT
ALMOND DOE PILI BADAM CHUFA
JORDAN KAMANI KANARI AMYGDAL
BISCUIT TALISAY ALMANDER
ALMENDRO AMYGDALA ROSACEAN
VALENCIA
(— BROWN) WOOD
(— SHAPED OBJECT) MANDORLA
ALMONRY AMBRY
ALMOST JUST LIKE MOST MUCH
NEAR NIGH ABOUT ANEAR CLOSE
AMAIST FECKLY MOSTLY NEARLY
NIGHLY MUCHWHAT WELLMOST
WELLNEAR
ALMS DOLE GIFT ALMOIN AUMOUS
AWMOUS BOUNTY CORBAN MAUNDY
RELIEF ALMOIGN CHARITY HANDOUT
PASSADE DEVOTION DONATION
GRATUITY OFFERING PITTANCE
ALMSHOUSE POORHOUSE
WORKHOUSE

ALMUCE HOOD AMICE VAGAS TIPPET
VAKASS VARKAS
ALODIUM ODAL ODEL ODHAL
ESTATE PROPERTY
ALOE PITA AGAVE
ALOEUS (FATHER OF —) NEPTUNE
(SON OF —) OTUS EPHIALTES
(WIFE OF —) IPHIMEDIA
ALOFT UP HIGH ABOVE AHIGH
UPWARD AHEIGHT SKYWARD
OVERHEAD
ALONE ALL ONE BARE LANE LORN
ONLY SOLE SOLO ALOOF APART
SOLUS SIMPLY SINGLE SOLEIN
SOLELY SULLEN UNIQUE ALONELY
FORLORN UNAIDED DESOLATE
DETACHED ISOLATED SEPARATE
SOLITARY
(ALL —) LEELANE LEELONE
ALONG ON UP VIA AWAY LANG WITH
YOND AHEAD LONGS BESIDE
FORBYE FOREBY ONWARD ALONGST
ENDLONG FORWARD PARALLEL
TOGETHER
(— THE MARGIN) DOWN
(— WITH) AND
(WELL —) ENDWAYS ENDWISE
ALONGSIDE AT BY ASIDE CLOSE
ABOARD BESIDE ABREAST FORNENT
SIDLINS FORNENST PARALLEL
ALONSOA MASKFLOWER
ALOOF DRY SHY COLD COOL ABACK
ALONE APART PROUD ABEIGH
FROSTY OTIOSE REMOTE SILENT
DISTANT REMOVED RESERVED
ALOPECIA PELADE ATRICHIA
BALDNESS
ALOPECURUS FOXTAIL
ALPACA PACO
ALPENGLOW AFTERGLOW
ALPENSTOCK STOCK BERGSTOCK
ALPHABET ABC CUFIC KUFIC LATIN
ONMUN ORDER BISAYA BRAHMI
CIPHER GLAGOL HANGUL HANKUL
KAITHI NAGARI PRIMER ROMAJI
SARADA SCRIPT TAGALA VISAYA
ALJAMIA FUTHARK KALEKAH
LETTERS PESHITO ALJAMIAH
CROSSROW GUJARATI GURMUKHI
(— SQUARE) TABLEAU
ALREADY EEN NOW DONE EVEN
SINCE BEFORE
ALSACE-LORRAINE REICHSLAND
ALSINE ALLBONE
ALSO SO ALS AND EKE TOO YET
ERST ITEM MORE PLUS ALONG
DITTO BESIDES FURTHER THERETO
LIKEWISE MOREOVER
ALTAR ARA BEMA BOMOS TABLE
WEVED ACERRA AUTERE HAIKAL
SHRINE TRIPOD VEDIKA CHANCEL
CHANTRY ESCHARA SCROBIS
THYMELE OMPHALOS REPOSOIR
(— BACK) TABLE
(— TOP) MENSA
ALTARPIECE ANCONA DIPTYCH
TRIPTYCH
ALTAZIMUTH ABA
ALTER COOK DRAW EDIT GELD

MOVE RASE TURN VARY VEER
WEND ADAPT AMEND BREAK ELIDE
EMEND FORGE RESET SHAPE SHIFT
ADJUST BUSHEL CENSOR CHANGE
DEFORM IMMUTE JIGGER MODIFY
MUTATE NEUTER REVISE TEMPER
UNSAME CHAFFER COMMUTE
CONVERT CORRECT CORRUPT
DISTORT FASHION QUALIFY
STRANGE ACTIVATE EXCHANGE
(— APPEARANCE) WRY
(— BOUNDARIES) DEACON
(— DIRECTION) BREAK
(— STANCE) CLOSE
ALTERATION DOWN CROSS ACTION
CHANGE JANGLE DISEASE HEMIOLA
MUTATION UPHEAVAL
(— OF BOUNDARY) ERUB ERUV
ALTERATIVE LAPPA FUMARIA
ALTERCATE JANGLE STICKLE
WRANGLE
ALTERCATION SPAT TIFF TILT
BRAWL BROIL CROSS FIGHT
BARNEY BICKER FRACAS JANGLE
STRIFE BRABBLE CONTEST DISPUTE
PASSAGE QUARREL WRANGLE
SQUABBLE
ALTERED BURNT BROKEN VARIED
ANOTHER FEIGNED ADJUSTED
ALTERNATE ELSE SWAY VARY
OTHER RECUR SHIFT ALTERN
CHANGE RINGER ROTATE SECOND
SEESAW SPIRAL EXCHANGE
INTERMIT TRAVERSE
(— LEAPS AND DIVES) GREYHOUND
ALTERNATELY ABOUT
RECIPROCALLY
ALTERNATION ADDITION
ALTERNATIVE OR FORK HORN
CHOICE EITHER OPTION DISJUNCT
ELECTION
ALTHAEA MALLOW
(FATHER OF —) THESTIUS
(HUSBAND OF —) OENEUS
(SON OF —) MELEAGER
ALTHORN SAX ALTO ALTUS
SAXHORN
ALTHOUGH ALL EEN SET ALBE ALIF
EVEN THAT WHEN WHILE ALBEIT
THOUGH WHENAS DESPITE HOWBEIT
WHEREAS
ALTITUDE APEX PEAK HIGHT LEVEL
PITCH HEIGHT STATURE
ALTO MEAN ALTUS ALTHORN
SAXHORN
ALTOGETHER ALL NUDE QUITE
SHEER STICK AGREAT BODILY
FREELY WHOLLY EXACTLY TOTALLY
UTTERLY ALLTHING ENTIRELY
ALTRUISM OTHERISM
ALTRUISTIC HEROIC HEROICAL
ALUDEL POT LUDEL UDELL
ALULA LOBE WING ALULET SQUAMA
TEGULA LOBULUS WINGLET
CALYPTER
ALULIM ALOROS
ALUM AUM ALME ALUMEN MIGITE
TSCHER STYPTIC HARDENER
KALINITE

(FEATHER —) ALUNOGEN
ALUMINA ARGIL ALOXITE
ALUMNUS GRAD PUPIL GRADUATE
ALUMROOT HEUCHERA
ALUR LUR LURI
ALVEARY HIVE BEEHIVE
ALVEOLA FAVEOLUS
ALVEOLAR SPUMOID GINGIVAL
ALVEOLATE FAVOSE FAVOUS PITTED
ALWAYS O AY AYE EEN EER EVER
 SIMLE STILL ALWISE SEMPRE
 ALGATES FOREVER EVERMORE
ALYSSUM ALISON
AM M AME HAM
 (— NOT) NAM AINT AMNT
 (I —) CHAM CHYM
AMA CUP AMULA CRUET DIVER
 VESSEL CHALICE
AMABILE GENTLE TENDER
AMADAVAT WAXBILL TIGERBIRD
AMADOU PUNK TINDER
AMAH NURSE SERVANT
AMAIN GREATLY FORCIBLY
AMALA AMLAH
AMALGAM ALLOY MAGNESIA
AMALGAMATE MIX FUSE JOIN
 ALLOY BLEND MARRY MERGE UNITE
 BLUNGE MINGLE COMBINE
 COALESCE COMPOUND
AMALGAMATION MERGER ADDITION
AMALGAMATOR PLATEMAN
AMANORI NORI LAVER
AMANUENSIS PENMAN SCRIBE
 TYPIST RECORDER
AMARANTH JATACO FLORAMOR
 (PL.) LIGHTHOUSES
AMARILLO FUSTIC
AMARYLLIS LILY AGAVE CRINUM
AMASS HEAP HILL MASS PILE SAVE
 GROSS HOARD STACK STORE
 GATHER COLLECT COMPILE
 CONGEST ENGROSS ASSEMBLE
 OVERHEAP
AMATA (DAUGHTER OF —) LAVINIA
 (HUSBAND OF —) LATINUS
AMATEUR HAM TIRO TYRO NOVICE
 SUNDAY VOTARY ADMIRER
 DABBLER DEVOTEE FANCIER
 JACKLEG PATRIOT VARMENT
 VARMINT BEGINNER
AMATEURISH TYRONIC
AMATORY EROTIC LOVING TENDER
 AMOROUS GALLANT
AMAZE AWE MAZE STAM STUN
 ALARM FERLY ASTONY AWHAPE
 WONDER ASTOUND CONFUSE
 IMPRESS PERPLEX STAGGER
 STUPEFY ASTONISH BEWILDER
 CONFOUND DUMFOUND FRIGHTEN
 SURPRISE
AMAZED AGAZED BUSHED ASTONIED
AMAZEMENT STAM AMAZE FERLY
 GHAST FERLIE FRENZY WONDER
 MADNESS SURPRISE
AMBARI KANAF KENAF KANAFF
AMBASSADOR AGENT ELCHI ENVOY
 VAKIL DEPUTY ELCHEE LEDGER
 LEGATE NUNCIO VAKEEL EMBASSY
 LEAGUER CAPUCIUS DIPLOMAT
 MINISTER

AMBER GRIS LIME AUMER AWMER
 RESIN FUSTIC LAMMER SUCCIN
 YELLOW BURMITE AMBEROID
 ELECTRUM SUNSTONE
AMBERFISH JUREL CARANX KAHALA
 RUNNER CARANGID CARANGIN
 KINGFISH MACKEREL MEDREGAL
AMBERGRIS AMBER AMBRACAN
AMBERJACK ALMICORE CORONADO
AMBIENCE MILIEU AMBIANCE
AMBIGUITY AMBAGE PARADOX
AMBIGUOUS DARK VAGUE DOUBLE
 FORKED CRYPTIC DUBIOUS
 DOUBTFUL SLIPPERY SPURIOUS
 (NOT —) EXPRESS
AMBIT LIMIT SCOPE SPACE BOUNDS
 EXTENT SPHERE CIRCUIT COMPASS
 BOUNDARY PRECINCT
AMBITION ATE GOAL HOPE WISH
 GLORY DESIRE PURPOSE
AMBITIONLESS DRIFTING
AMBITIOUS AVID BOLD HIGH KEEN
 EAGER ETTLE SHOWY EMULOUS
 ASPIRING
AMBITUS TENOR
AMBIVALENCE BIPOLARITY
AMBIVALENT EQUIVOCAL
AMBLE FOOL GAIT MOOCH PADNAG
 MEANDER SAUNTER TRIPPLE
AMBLING TOLUTATION
AMBO DESK PULPIT
AMBOCEPTOR COPULA MEDIATOR
AMBOYNA LINGOA KIABOOCA
AMBROSIA AMBROSE KINGWEED
AMBROSIAL DIVINE FRAGRANT
AMBRY SAFE CHEST NICHE AUMRIE
 CLOSET PANTRY RECESS ALMONRY
 ARMOIRE ARMARIUM CUPBOARD
AMBULANCE AUXILIUM
AMBULATE GAD HIKE MOVE WALK
AMBULATORY WALK ALURE
 GALLERY PORTICO CLOISTER
 PERAMBLE
AMBUSCADE WATCH WAYLAY
 BUSHMENT
AMBUSH NAB LURE LURK TRAP
 WAIT AWAIT BLIND BUSSE CATCH
 COVER SHOMA SNARE STALE TRAIN
 WATCH INBUSH THREAT WAYLAY
 FORELAY SCUPPER DISGUISE
 ENBUSSHE
AMCHOOR AMHAR
AMELIORATE EASE HELP MEND
 AMEND EMEND BETTER REFORM
 IMPROVE PROMOTE
AMEN YEA TRULY ASSENT SOBEIT
 VERILY APPROVAL SANCTION
AMENABLE OPEN LIABLE PLIANT
 SUBJECT
AMEND END BEET HEAL MEND
 ALTER ATONE BEETE EMEND REDUB
 BETTER CHANGE DOCTOR REFORM
 REMEDY REPAIR REPEAL REVISE
 CONVERT CORRECT ENLARGE
 IMPROVE RECOVER RECTIFY
 REDRESS RESTORE CHASTISE
AMENDING COMPENSATION
AMENDMENT RIDER AMENDS
 SLEEPER

AMENDS BOOT MEND ASSETH
 ASSYTH REWARD APOLOGY
 REDRESS
AMENITY JOY COMITY FEATURE
 SUAVITY CIVILITY COURTESY
 MILDNESS
 (PL.) AGREMENS FROUFROU
 NICETIES
AMENT JUL CHAT IDIOT IULUS
 MORON CATKIN CACHRYS CATTAIL
 GOSLING IMBECILE NUCAMENT
AMERCE FINE MERCE MULCT TREAT
 AFFEER PUNISH SCONCE CONDEMN
 FORFEIT
AMERCEMENT MULCT UNLAW
 BLOODWIT
AMERICA INDIA
AMERICAN YANK GRINGO YANKEE
 YANQUI AMERICA WESTERN
 JONATHAN
AMERICANISM HECKERISM
AMETHYST ONEGITE CORUNDUM
AMIABILITY DOUCEUR
AMIABLE GOOD KIND WARM SWEET
 CLEVER GENIAL GENTLE LOVING
 MELLOW SMOOTH TENDER AFFABLE
 LOVABLE WINSOME CHARMING
 ENGAGING FRIENDLY PLEASING
AMICABLE KIND FRIENDLY
AMICE AMIT AMYS CAPE COWL
 HOOD EPHOD ALMUCE DOMINO
 TIPPET VAKASS AMICTUS VESTMENT
AMID IN OMEL AMELL AMONG
 AMIDST DURING IMELLE AMONGST
 BETWEEN
AMIDE LACTAM SULTAM ANILIDE
 ARYLIDE
AMINE ANILIN ANILINE
AMISS ILL MIS AWRY BIAS AGATE
 AGLEY ASKEW WRONG ACROSS
 AGRIEF ASTRAY FAULTY MISTAKE
 IMPROPER
AMITY PEACE ACCORD CONCORD
 HARMONY
AMMA ABBESS MOTHER
AMMONIA HARTSHORN
AMMONITE POLYPOD AMMONOID
 BACULITE CACULOID CERATITE
 SALIGRAM
AMMONIUM CARBONATE
 HARTSHORN
AMMUNITION AMMO AMMU ARMS
 SHOT BOMBS FODDER POWDER
 SHELLS BULLETS GRENADES
 MATERIAL MATERIEL ORDNANCE
 SHRAPNEL
AMNESIA LAPSE FORGETFULNESS
AMNESTY COWLE PARDON OBLIVION
AMNION SAC CAUL SEROSA
 INDUSIUM MEMBRANE
AMOBARBITAL AMYTAL
AMOEBA AMEBA AMEBULA AMOBULA
 PROTEUS RHIZOPOD
AMOK MAD AMUCK CRAZY CRAZED
 VIOLENT FRENZIED
AMOLE EMOL AMOULI AMOLILLA
 MANFREDA
AMONG IN MID AMID INTO MANG
 MONG OMEL WITH AMANG AMELL

MIDST AMIDST BIMONG IMELLE
WITHIN BETWEEN
(— **OTHER THINGS**) IA
AMOR EROS LOVE CUPID AMOROSO
AMORAL NEUTRAL NONMORAL
AMORITE CANAANITE
AMOROUS FOND GAMY SOFT WARM
CADGY JOLLY NUTTY ARDENT
COQUET EROTIC LOVELY LOVING
TENDER AMATIVE AMATORY
AMIABLE FERVENT GALLANT
JEALOUS SMICKER LOVESOME
VENEREAN
AMORPHOUS VAGUE HYALINE
DEFORMED FORMLESS RESINOUS
AMORT ALAMORT DEJECTED
LIFELESS
AMORTIZE DESTROY MORTISE
ALIENATE
AMOUNT GO GOB LOT SUM SUP TOT
ANTE BODY COME DOSE DRAW
FECK KIND LEVY MESS REAM RISE
SOUD SOWD UNIT WARE CHUNK
COUNT GROSS MOUNT PRICE
REACH STACK STORE STUFF TOTAL
WHOLE BUDGET DEGREE DOSAGE
EFFECT EXTENT FIGURE MATTER
NUMBER SUPPLY ADVANCE
FOOTING QUANTUM SCRUPLE
SIGNIFY SLATHER TODDICK
INCREASE QUANTITY SPOONFUL
SURMOUNT VALLIDOM
(— **BORNE BY BEAST**) SEAM
(— **CARRIED AT ONE TIME**) GANG
(— **DUE**) BILL SCORE
(— **HELD**) CAPACITY
(— **OF BASS**) BOOMINESS
(— **OF CONCRETE**) LIFT
(— **OF DYE**) STRIKE
(— **OF FLOW**) STRENGTH
(— **OF FREIGHT**) CARLOAD
(— **OF GAS**) BREATH
(— **OF HERRINGS**) CRANNAGE
(— **OF LEAKAGE**) SLIP
(— **OF LIQUOR**) SLUG
(— **OF MEDICINE**) DOSAGE
(— **OF MONEY**) BEAN BOND CASH
SCOT
(— **OF OIL**) ALLOWABLE
(— **OF PAYMENT**) FOOTAGE
(— **OF POWDER**) INCREMENT
(— **OF SOIL**) INTHROW
(— **OF WATER**) CATCHMENT
(— **OF WORK**) ASSIGNMENT
(— **OWED**) LIABILITY
(— **PAID**) COST
(— **TURNED BY SPADE**) GRAFT
(**APPRECIABLE** —) BEANS
(**COMPLETE** —) FULL
(**CONSIDERABLE** —) MIGHT HANTLE
HATFUL
(**EXACT** —) NICK
(**EXTRA** —) BONUS
(**GREAT** —) MICKLE INFINITY
MOUNTAIN
(**GROSS** —) SLUMP
(**INADEQUATE** —) DEFICIENCY
(**INDEFINITE** —) BAIT SNAG SOME
(**INFINITESIMAL** —) IOTA

(**INSIGNIFICANT** —) SCRAT
(**LARGE** —) GOB LOB JUNT LUMP
MINT SNAG SWAG SIEGE SLASH
SPATE BOODLE SOMDEL BONANZA
SOMDIEL CARTLOAD MUCHNESS
SOMEDEAL
(**LAVISH** —) SLATHER
(**LEAST POSSIBLE** —) GRAIN
(**LIMITED** —) SPRINKLING
(**MINUTE** —) HAIR FLEABITE
(**RENT** —) GALE
(**SIZABLE** —) CHUNK SMART
(**SLIGHT** —) ADDED SNACK TILLY
(**SMALL** —) ACE BIT DAB DITE DOIT
DRAM DRIB FLOW HINT HOOT INCH
LICK SNAP SONG SPOT SPECK
SPURT TRACE DRAPPY PICKLE
SMIDGE TICKET CAPSULE DRAPPIE
GLIMMER KENNING SMIDGEN
SMIDGIN
(**SMALLEST** —) JOT STIVER
STEEVER STUIVER
(**TENFOLD** —) DECUPLE
(**USUAL** —) GRIST
(**WHOLE** —) ALL SUBSTANCE
(**YEARLY** —) ANNUITY
AMOUR DRURY DRUERY AMOURET
INTRIGUE PARAMOUR
AMPERSAND AND ALSO PLUS
AMPASSY IPSEAND
AMPHETAMINE BENZEDRINE
AMPHIBIA BATRACHIA
AMPHIBIAN EFT OLM FROG HYLA
NEWT RANA TOAD ANURA SIREN
SNAKE AMPHIB CAUDATE ERYOPID
PROTEUS TADPOLE AISTOPOD
AMPHIBOLE EDENITE ORALITE
URALITE ASBESTOS CROSSITE
AMPHICARPA FALCATA
AMPHIGASTRIUM UNDERLEAF
AMPHION (**BROTHER OF** —) ZETHUS
(**FATHER OF** —) ZEUS IASUS
JUPITER
(**MOTHER OF** —) ANTIOPE
(**WIFE OF** —) NIOBE
AMPHIPOD SHRIMP
AMPHITHEA (**DAUGHTER OF** —)
ANTICLEA
(**HUSBAND OF** —) AUTOLYCUS
AMPHITHEATER BOWL OVAL ARENA
CAVEA CIRCUS STADIUM THEATER
AMPHITRITE (**FATHER OF** —)
NEREUS OCEANUS
(**HUSBAND OF** —) NEPTUNE
POSEIDON
(**MOTHER OF** —) TETHYS
(**SON OF** —) TRITON
AMPHORA JUG URN VASE CADUS
DIOTA PELIKE
AMPLE BIG FAIR FULL GOOD MUCH
RICH SIDE WIDE BROAD GREAT
LARGE LUCKY PLUMP ROOMY
ROUND WALLY ENOUGH HEARTY
PLENTY PROLIX COPIOUS LIBERAL
OPULENT WEALTHY ABUNDANT
ADEQUATE BARONIAL GENEROUS
HANDSOME SPACIOUS
AMPLIFICATION GAIN
AMPLIFIED EXTENDED

AMPLIFIER BOOSTER REPEATER
AMPLIFY PAD FARCE FARSE SWELL
WIDEN DILATE EXPAND EXTEND
STRESS AUGMENT ENLARGE
STRETCH AMPLIATE HEIGHTEN
INCREASE LENGTHEN MULTIPLY
AMPLITUDE LATITUDE OPULENCE
AMPLY LARGE
AMPUTATE CUT LOP PRUNE SEVER
CURTAIL
AMPUTATION APOCOPE
AMRITA RASA
AMULA AMA VESSEL
AMULET GEM MET HAND JUJU MOJO
PLUM CHARM IMAGE MENAT SAFFI
SAFIE TOKEN FETISH GRIGRI
MASCOT SAPHIE SCROLL TABLET
AMALETT ICHTHUS ICHTHYS
PERIAPT GREEGREE HAGSTONE
LIGATURE ORNAMENT TALISMAN
AMULIUS (**BROTHER OF** —) NUMITOR
(**FATHER OF** —) PROCAS
(**NEPHEW OF** —) LAUSUS
AMURRU MARTU
AMUSE GAME LAKE ENJOY MIRTH
SHORT SPORT ABSORB DELUDE
DIVERT ENGAGE FROLIC PLEASE
POPJOY SOLACE TICKLE BEGUILE
DISPORT GRATIFY PASTIME
BEWILDER DISTRACT RECREATE
AMUSEMENT FAD FUN JEU GAME
JEST LAKE PLAY MIRTH SPORT
LAKING MUSERY PASTIME
COTTABUS LAUGHTER PLEASURE
(**PL.**) MIDWAY
AMUSING COMIC DROLL FUNNY
MERRY COMICAL FOOLISH KILLING
RISIBLE FARCICAL HUMOROUS
PLEASANT SPORTFUL
AMYGDALA TONSIL
AMYL AMYDON PENTYL ISOAMYL
AMYLASE PTYALIN DIASTASE
AMYMONE (**FATHER OF** —) DANAUS
(**HUSBAND OF** —) ENCELADUS
(**SON OF** —) NAUPLIUS
AMYTHAON (**BROTHER OF** —)
AESON PHERES
(**FATHER OF** —) CRETHEUS
(**MOTHER OF** —) TYRO
(**SON OF** —) BIAS MELAMPUS
(**WIFE OF** —) IDOMENE
AN ONE ARTICLE
ANA EVENTS OMNIANA SAYINGS
ANABAPTIST DIPPER ABECEDARIAN
ANABAS MARTINICO
ANABATIC DESCENDING
ANABO NABO ANABONG
ANABRANCH BRANCH TALLYWALKA
ANACHRONISM SOLECISM
ANACONDA BOA ABOLLA SUCURI
SUCURY CAMOUDIE SUCURUJU
ANACREONTIC TEIAN
ANACRUSIS UPBEAT
ANADEM CROWN DIADEM FILLET
WREATH CHAPLET CORONET
GARLAND
ANAGNOST LECTOR READER
ANAGOGICAL MYSTICAL
ANAGRAM REBUS PUZZLE
METAGRAM

(PL.) VERBARIUM
ANAGUA KNACKAWAY KNOCKAWAY
ANAL PODICAL
ANALABOS CLOAK
ANALGESIC ANTIPYRIN PHENALGIN
ANALOGICAL NORMAL
ANALOGOUS LIKE SIMILAR
ANALOGUE DFDT ANALOG
ANALOGY QIYAS
(CLOSE —) PARITY
ANALYSIS TEST INDEX STUDY
ANATOMY AUTOPSY SCANSION
SOLUTION
(ECONOMIC —) DYNAMICS
(LOGICAL —) SYLLOGISM
ANALYTIC SUBTLE REGULAR
(NOT —) SYNTHETIC SYNTHETICAL
ANALYTICAL CLINICAL DIVISIVE
ANALYZE RUN PART ASSAY BREAK
PARSE SENSE STUDY WEIGH
ASSESS DIVIDE REDUCE DISSECT
EXAMINE ITEMIZE RESOLVE TITRATE
UNPIECE APPRAISE CONSTRUE
DIAGNOSE SEPARATE
(— ACCOUNT) AGE
(— VERSE) SCAN
ANAMITE TWINE
ANANAS ANANA PINGUIN
ANANIAS LIAR SIDRACH
ANANSI NANCY
ANAPEST ANTIDACTYL
ANARCHIST RED REBEL ANARCH
NIHILIST REDSHIRT
ANARCHY RIOT CHAOS REVOLT
LICENSE MISRULE DISORDER
ANASARCA DROPSY
ANASAZI PUEBLO PLATEAU
ANASCHISTIC EUMITOTIC
ANASTOMOSIS GLOMUS
ANASTROPHE INVERSION
ANATHEMA WO BAN MUD WOE
OATH CURSE CENSURE
ANATHEMATIZE CURSE ACCURSE
EXECRATE
ANATOMIZE ANALYZE DISSECT
ANATOMY TOPOLOGY
(— OF HORSE) HIPPOTOMY
(MICROSCOPIC —) HISTOLOGY
(VEGETABLE —) PHYTOTOMY
ANAXIBIA (DAUGHTER OF —)
PELOPEA ALCESTIS PISIDICE
(FATHER OF —) BIAS
(HUSBAND OF —) PELIAS
(SON OF —) ACASTUS
ANCESTOR ION MIL ADAM EBER
HETH ROOT SIRE DORUS ELDER
STOCK APETUS ATAVUS AUTHOR
BELDAM EPONYM FATHER MANNUS
MILEDH PARENT STIPES ANCIENT
BELDAME BELSIRE EPAPHUS
FLEANCE FORBEAR IAPETUS
ISHMAEL SAKULYA DARDANUS
FOREBEAR FOREGOER MILESIUS
MYRMIDON RELATIVE
(— CULT) MANISM
(—S OF GOTLANDERS) GEAT
(MAORI —) TIKI TUPUNA
(PL.) OLDERS ANCESTRY
ANCESTRAL AVAL AVITAL AVITIC

LINEAL FAMILIAL
ANCESTRY KIN RACE SEED ATHEL
FAMILY ORIGIN PEOPLE SOURCE
STRAIN DESCENT KINDRED LINEAGE
BREEDING PEDIGREE
ANCHISES (FATHER OF —) CAPYS
(MOTHER OF —) THEMIS
(SON OF —) AENEAS
ANCHOR FIX BIND DRAG DRUG
HOOK MOOR REST SLUG SPUD
STOP AFFIX BERTH BOWER KEDGE
RIVET SHEET STOCK ATTACH
DROGUE FASTEN HERMIT KEDGER
KELLEG SECURE STREAM CHAPLET
CONNECT DEADMAN GRAPNEL
GROUSER KILLICK MUDHOOK
SUPPORT COCKBILL
(— IN PLACE) ACOCKBILL
(— RING) TORUS
(AT —) ASTAY
(BEAM —) WALL
ANCHORAGE DOCK STAY HARBOR
REFUGE RIDING MOORAGE
ABUTMENT BERTHAGE ROOTHOLD
ANCHORITE MONK HERMIT
ACHORET ASCETIC EREMITE
RECLUSE STYLITE
ANCHOVY NEHU BOCON SPRAT
HERRING SARDINE
(PL.) ALICI
ANCHUSA OXTONGUE
ANCIENT ELD OLD AGED AULD FERN
HIGH HOAR IAGO YORE EARLY
ELDER HOARY OLDEN BYGONE
ENSIGN FORMER NOETIC PISTOL
PRIMAL VETUST ANTIENT ANTIQUE
ARCHAIC ARCHEAN CLASSIC
OGYGEAN OGYGIAN HISTORIC
NOACHIAN OBSOLETE PRIMEVAL
PRISTINE
(MOST —) ELDEST
ANCIENTLY OLD HIGH
ANCILLA HELPER ADJUNCT SERVANT
ANCON ELBOW CORBEL CONSOLE
AND N U AN ET SO ANT TOO ALSO
PLUS BESIDES FURTHER MOREOVER
(— SO FORTH) ETC USW
ANDAMAN MINCOPI MINKOPI
MINCOPIE
ANDESITE BONINITE TIMAZITE
ANDIRON DOG CHENET COBIRON
FIREDOG HESSIAN HANDIRON
LANDIRON
ANDORRA (LANGUAGE OF —)
CATALAN
(NATIVE OF —) ANDOSIAN
(RIVER OF —) VALIRA
ANDRADITE APLOME GARNET
ANDROCONIUM STIGMA PLUMULE
ANDROID ROBOT AUTOMATON
ANDROMACHE (FATHER OF —)
EETION
(HUSBAND OF —) HECTOR HELENUS
(SON OF —) PIELUS ASTYANAX
MOLOSSUS PERGAMUS
ANDROMEDA (FATHER OF —)
CEPHEUS
(MOTHER OF —) CASSIOPEA
(RESCUER OF —) PERSEUS

ANDROMEDE BIELID
ANECDOTE GAG TOY JOKE TALE
YARN EVENT STORY SKETCH
HAGGADA EXEMPLUM HAGGADAH
ANECDOTAL LITERARY
ANECHOIC DEAD
ANEMIA SURRA SURRAH ANAEMIA
HYPAEMA HYPHEMA HYPHEMIA
ISCHEMIA SPANEMIA
ANEMIC LOW PALE WEAK WATERY
LIFELESS
ANEMONE LILY CRASS EMONY
OPELET BOWBELLS SNOWDROP
ANENT ON RE ABOUT ANENST
BESIDE TOWARD AGAINST OPPOSITE
ANESTHESIA BLOCK CORYL SPINAL
ANESTHETIC GAS ETHER ACOINE
OBTUSE OPIATE COCAINE DULLING
MENTHOL PARAFORM SEDATIVE
ANESTHETIZE FREEZE ETHERIZE
ANEW OVER AGAIN NEWLY AFRESH
ITERUM NEWLINS NEWLINGS
RECENTLY
ANFRACTUOUS SPIRAL BENDING
SINUOUS WINDING TORTUOUS
ANGEL MAH DEVA EBUS ANGLE
ARDOR ARIEL DAEVA DULIA NAKIR
YAKSA ABDIEL ARIOCH BACKER
BELIAL CHERUB MONKIR MUNKAR
NEKKAR SERAPH SPIRIT UZZIEL
YAKSHA ANGELET EGREGOR
ISRAFEL RAPHAEL SPONSOR
WATCHER ZADKIEL ZOPHIEL
APOLLYON GUARDIAN ITHURIEL
SUPERNAL
(— OF DEATH) AZRAEL SAMMAEL
(FALLEN —S) HELL
(GUARDIAN —) YAKSA YAKSHA
YAKSHI
(RECORDING —) SIJIL SIJILL
(PL.) HOST FRAVASHI SERAPHIM
ANGELFISH MONK MUNK ANGEL
QUOTT SQUAT MONACH FLATFISH
KINGSTON MONKFISH SQUATINA
ANGELIC SAINTLY BEATIFIC
CHERUBIC HEAVENLY SERAPHIC
ANGELICA JELLICA
ANGELIN PACAY ANGELEEN
ANGER ARR IRE IRK VEX BILE BURN
CRAB FELL FUME FURY GALL GRIM
HUFF MOOD RAGE RILE ROIL RUFF
TEEN TIFF ANNOY BIRSE GRAME
GRIPE HATEL IRISH PIQUE SPONK
SPUNK THRAW WRATH BOTHER
CHOLER DANDER ENRAGE EXCITE
GRIEVE MONKEY NETTLE OFFEND
RANCOR SPLEEN TALENT TEMPER
WARMTH BURNING DESPITE
DUDGEON EMOTION INCENSE
INFLAME PASSION PROVOKE
STOMACH ACRIMONY DISTRESS
EBENEZER IRRITATE VEXATION
ANGERED SORE AGRAMED PELTISH
INCENSED
ANGICO CURUPAY
ANGINA PRUNELLA
ANGIOSPERM HARDWOOD
METASPERM
ANGLE IN BOB DIP ELL OUT TEE

WRO CANT COIN COOK DRAW FISH
FORK HADE KEEN KNEE LEAD NOOK
PEAK SITE WICK ANCON ARRIS
AXIAL BEVEL BIGHT CHOIL COIGN
DRAFT DRIFT ELBOW FLEAM GROIN
GUISE INGLE PHASE POINT QUOIN
SLANT ALLURE ANGULE ASPECT
CANTON CORNEL CORNER DIRECT
ENGHLE EPAULE HADING LAGGEN
LAGGIN OCTANT SCHEME SQUARE
TORNUS ANGLIAN ANGULUS
AZIMUTH BASTION DRAUGHT
GIMMICK KNUCKLE PERIGON
RAVELIN SALIENT ARGUMENT
DECALAGE DIHEDRAL FISHHOOK
INTRIGUE SHOULDER
(— OF BEVEL) FLEAM FLEEM
(— OF BOWSPRIT) STEEVE
STEEVING
(— OF CLUB HEAD) LIE
(— OF EYELIDS) CANTHUS
(— OF HAT BRIM) BREAK
(— OF HIPBONE) HOOK
(— OF LEAF) AXIL
(— OF RAFTER) HEEL
(— OF TIMBER KNEE) BREECH
(DRIFT —) LEEWAY
(OBTUSE —) HEEL BULLNOSE
(ROOF —) HIP FASTIGIUM
(ROUND —) PERIGON
(SALIENT —) ARIS ARRIS
ANGLED CANTED NOOKED
ANGULATE
ANGLER MONK FRIAR THIEF SLIMER
LOPHLID RODSTER SPINNER
WIDEGAB WIDEGAP ALLMOUTH
FROGFISH MONKFISH PISCATOR
TOADFISH
ANGLESMITH SLABMAN
ANGLEWORM ESS WORM
FISHWORM
ANGLICAN EPISCOPAL
ANGLO CAUCASIAN

ANGOLA

CAPITAL: LUANDA
COIN: MACUTA MACUTE
DISTRICT: CABINDA
KINGDOM: BAKONGO
LANGUAGE: BANTU KIMBUNDU
MOUNTAIN: LOVITI
PLATEAU: PLANALTO
PORT: LOBITO LUANDA
RIVER: CONGO CUITO COANZA
CUNENE KUNENE KWANGO
KWANZA
TOWN: LOBITO LUANDA
BENGUELA MOSSAMEDES
TRIBE: BANTU KIKONGO

ANGORA CAT GOAT ANGOLA RABBIT
ANGRILY ANGERLY IRATELY
FUMINGLY
ANGRY MAD ASHY EVIL GRIM GRUM
HIGH RILY ROID ROSY SORE WARM
WAXY WILD WRAW CROOK CROSS
GRAME HUFFY IRATE IROUS MOODY
RATTY RILEY SNAKY STUNT VEXED
WEMOD WROTH BIRSIT CHAFED

CROUSE FRENZY FUMING FUMOUS
HEATED IREFUL LOADED SHIRTY
SNAKEY STUFFY FRETFUL FURIOUS
HOPPING IRACUND PAINFUL
SNAKISH SPLEENY CHOLERIC
INFLAMED RIGOROUS SPITFIRE
TEMPERED VEHEMENT WREAKFUL
(BE —) STEAM
ANGRY-LOOKING THUNDERY
ANGUISH WOE ACHE HARM HURT
PAIN PANG RACK TRAY AGONY
ANGST ANGUS DOLOR GRIEF THROE
MISERY REGRET SORROW ANGOISE
ANGWICH REMORSE TORMENT
TORTURE DISTRESS
ANGUISHED GRIEFFUL
ANGULAR BONE BONY EDGY LEAN
SLIM THIN GAUNT SHARP ABRUPT
POINTED SCRAWNY CORNERED
(NOT —) SOFT
ANGULARITY EDGINESS
ANGUS FORFAR FORFARSHIRE
ANHYDRIDE LACTAM SULTAM
FULGIDE LACTIDE SULTONE
GLUCOSAN MANNITAN SORBITAN
ANHYDROUS DRY DESICCATED
ANI WITCH CUCKOO JEWBIRD
KEELBILL KEELBIRD TICKBIRD
ANIMADVERSION BLAME REMARK
CENSURE COMMENT REPROOF
WARNING MONITION REPROACH
ANIMAL (LOOK ALSO UNDER
SPECIFIC HEADINGS) DEER BEAST
BIPED BLACK BRUTE GRADE GROSS
LUSTY STORE STRAY BRUTAL
CARNAL DAPPLE DESPOT FLESHY
KICKER MAMMAL RODENT SILVAN
SORREL SPONGE SYLVAN BEASTIE
BREEDER CARRION CRITTER
SENSUAL BURROWER CREATURE
EMIGRANT ORGANISM
(— COLLECTION) LARDER
(— FOR MARKET) STOCKER
(— INHABITED BY SPIRIT) GUACA
HUACA
(— OF LITTLE VALUE) SCALAWAG
SKALAWAG
(— RESEMBLING MAN) HOMINOID
(— SHOT) KILL
(— WITH BLACK COAT AND
MARKINGS) PARSON
(— WITH DOCKED TAIL) CURTAL
(—S AS RENT) CAIN
(2-HORNED —) BICORN BICORNE
(BEEF —) BONER GRASSER
(BOVINE —) BOSS BRUTE
(BROKEN-DOWN —) CROCK
(CARNIVOROUS —) SARCOPHILE
(CASTRATED —) SEG SEGG SPAY
SPADO GELDING
(COLD-BLOODED —) ECTOTHERM
(CREATED —) BARAMIN
(DOMESTIC —) DOER SCRUB
BESTIAL FOLLOWER SCRUBBER
(DRAFT --) AVER AIVER
(EMACIATED —) FRAME SKELETON
(FABULOUS —) KYLIN BUNYIP
DRAGON ACEPHAL GRIFFIN GRIFFON
GRYPHON UNICORN SEMITAUR
(FEMALE —) HEN SHE LADY JENNY
SHEDER

(FERAL —) CIMAROON CIMARRON
CIMMARON
(FLEA-RIDDEN —) FLEABAG
(FOOTLESS —) APOD APODE
(FREAKISH —) FERLY FERLIE
(GRASSHOPPER-EATING —)
WHANGAM
(GRAY —) GRIZZLE
(GRAZING —) HERBAGER
(GREEDY —) GORB
(HORNED —) HORN REEM
(HYPOTHETICAL —) PROAVIS
(IMAGINARY —) CATAWAMPUS
(LOWER —) BEAST CREATURE
(LUSTY OR PLUMP —) BILCH BILSH
(MALE —) HE TOM BUCK BULL JACK
STAG JOHNNY BACHELOR
(MARINE —) LANCELET
(MATURE —) SENIOR
(MEAT —) CHOPPER
(MISCHIEVOUS —) ELF
(MYTHICAL —) HODAG KYLIN
MOONACK
(ODD —) SPLACKNUCK
(PACK —) HUNIA SUMPTER
(PET —) CADE
(PURSUED —S) GAME
(ROASTED —) BARBECUE
BARBEQUE
(SADDLE —) LOPER
(SCRAWNY —) SCRAG
(SHORN —) SHEAR
(SKINNY —) SCRAE
(SLUGGISH —) DRUMBLE
(SPOTTED —) CALICO
(STOCKY —) BLOCK
(STUNTED —) SHARGAR SHARGER
(THICKSET —) NUGGET
(TOTEM —) EPONYM
(UNBRANDED —) SLICK
(UNCASTRATED —) ENTIRE
(UNDERSIZED —) DURGAN DURGEN
(UNHOUSED —) OUTLER OUTLIER
(UNWEANED —) SUCKER
(WANDERING —) STRAY ESTRAY
(WARM-BLOODED —) ENDOTHERM
HAEMATHERM
(WATER —) AQUATIC AQUATILE
(WEAK —) DRAG DOWNER
(WILD —) SAVAGE WILDLING
(WORNOUT —) KANCKER
(WORTHLESS —) CARRION
(YOUNG —) HOG BIRD HOGG JOEY
SHOT STORE JUNIOR PULLUS
FATLING LITTLIN KINDLING LITTLING
SUCKLING YOUNGLET
(PL.) ZOA FAUNA NECTON NEKTON
ANIMALCULISM SPERMISM
ANIMALITY HOGGERY
ANIMA MUNDI WELTGEIST
ANIMATE ACT PEP FIRE MOVE PERK
STIR URGE ALIVE BRISK CHEER
DRIVE FLUSH IMBUE IMPEL LIGHT
LIVEN QUICK ROUSE VITAL AROUSE
BRIGHT ENSOUL EXCITE INCITE
INDUCE INFORM KINDLE LIVING
PROMPT SPIRIT VIVIFY ACTUATE
COMFORT ENLIVEN INSPIRE
QUICKEN ACTIVATE ENERGIZE
INSPIRIT VITALIZE

(NOT —) BRUTE

ANIMATED UP GAY VIF GLAD VIVE ALIVE ANIME BRISK QUICK VITAL VIVID ACTIVE ARDENT BLITHE BRISKY LIVELY LIVING SPARKY SPUNKY BUOYANT JOCULAR STHENIC BOUNCING LIFESOME SPIRITED VIGOROUS

ANIME COPAL ELEMI RESIN ROSIN ANIMATO

ANIMIKEAN LAWSON

ANIMISM NATURISM

ANIMOSITY HATE PIQUE SPITE ANIMUS ENMITY HATRED MALICE RANCOR DISLIKE

ANIMUS MIND ONDE WILL EFFORT ENMITY SPIRIT TEMPER ATTITUDE

ANISE ANET DILL CUMEN UMBEL FENNEL SIKIMI SHIKIMI

ANKH TAU

ANKLE COOT CUIT HOCK QUIT ANCLE QUEET TALUS WRIST TARSUS SHACKLE

(COCKED —S) KNUCKLING

ANKLEBONE TALUS ASTRAGAL

ANKLET SHOE SOCK BANGLE FETTER SHACKLE

ANLAGE INCEPT PROTON INITIAL BLASTEMA

ANNALIST WRITER RECORDER

ANNALS NIHONGI REGISTER

ANNAM (ALSO SEE VIETNAM) VIETNAM

(BOAT OF —) GAYYOU GAYDIANG

(MEASURE OF —) LY GON NGU QUO SAO TAT PHAN THAT SHITA THUOC TRUONG

(TOWN OF —) HUE VINH TOURANE QUANGTRI

(WEIGHT OF —) CAN BINH DONG

ANNATTO OTTER URUCU ORLEAN SALMON ACHIOTE ACHUETE ANNOTTO ARNATTO ORLEANS

ANNEAL BAKE FUSE HEAT SMELT TEMPER INFLAME TOUGHEN GRAPHITE

ANNEALER TUBER HEATER

ANNEALING LIGHTING

ANNELID NAID WORM LUGWORM SERPULA ANNULATE SANDWORM SERPULAN

ANNEX ADD ELL LAY JOIN AFFIX SEIZE UNITE ADJECT ANNECT APPEND ATTACH FASTEN ACQUIRE CONNECT FIXTURE POSTFIX SUBJOIN ADDITION ANNEXURE DOCUMENT

ANNIHILATE END OUT KILL RAZE RUIN SLAY ABATE ANNUL ERASE WRECK DELETE DEVOUR NOUGHT QUENCH REDUCE ABOLISH DESTROY EXPUNGE DECIMATE DISCREAT UNCREATE

ANNIHILATION FANA NEGATION

ANNIVERSARY FETE MASS EMBER FEAST ANNUAL JUBILEE YEARDAY BIRTHDAY FESTIVAL YAHRZEIT

(100TH —) CENTENNIAL

(150TH —) SESQUICENTENNIAL

(200TH —) BIMILLENARY BIMILLENIUM

(25TH —) SEMIJUBILEE

(50TH —) JUBILEE SEMICENTENNIAL

ANNONA ATIS ATTA ATEES

ANNOTATE EDIT NOTE STET GLOSS BENOTE NOTIFY POSTIL REMARK APOSTIL COMMENT EXPLAIN FOOTNOTE

ANNOTATION APOSTIL COMMENT SCHOLION SCHOLIUM

ANNOTATOR NOTIST

ANNOUNCE BID CRY BODE CALL DEEM MAKE SHOW SING TELL BRUIT CLAIM KNELL STATE VOICE ASSERT BLAZON BROACH DENOTE HERALD INFORM PREACH REPORT REVEAL SIGNAL SPRING STEVEN DECLARE DIVULGE FORERUN GAZETTE PUBLISH SIGNIFY DENOUNCE FORETELL INTIMATE PROCLAIM RENOUNCE SENTENCE

ANNOUNCEMENT BID CRY HAT BILL CALL LEAD ALARM BANCO BANNS BLURB EDICT ALARUM DECREE DICTUM NOTICE GAZETTE SENSING BULLETIN CIRCULAR DECISION

ANNOUNCER NEBO PAGE CRIER EMCEE CALLER HERALD NUNCIO GONGMAN GRINDER SPIELER NUNCIATE SPRUIKER

ANNOY ARR BUG DUN EAT EGG GET GIG HOX IRE IRK NAG NOY NYE TRY VEX BAIT BORE BURN FASH FRET FUSS GALL GRIG HALE HARM HAZE HUFF NARK PAIN RILE ROIL CHAFE CHASE CHEVY CHIVY DEVIL GRAMY GRATE HARRY PEEVE PIQUE SPITE STURT TEASE THORN UPSET WEARY WORRY BADGER BOTHER CADDLE CHIVEY CHIVVY EARWIG ENRAGE GRAVEL HAGGLE HARASS HECKLE HECTOR INFEST INJURE MOLEST NEEDLE NETTLE OFFEND PESTER POTTER RATTLE REHETE RUFFLE TICKLE BEDEVIL DISTURB HOTFOOT JACKSON TERRIFY TROUBLE DISTRESS IRRITATE

ANNOYANCE VEX FASH PEST WEED CROSS GRIEF LOATH SPITE STALL THORN INSECT PESTER DISGUST FASHERY NOYANCE TROUBLE UMBRAGE FASHERIE FLEABITE NOISANCE NUISANCE PINPRICK

ANNOYED SORE INSULTED

ANNOYING TARE NOYOUS DISEASY HATEFUL IRKSOME NOISOME TARSOME FASHIOUS FRETSOME SPITEFUL TIRESOME

ANNOYINGLY CONFOUNDED CONFOUNDEDLY

ANNUAL BOOK BUGLE PLANT FLOWER YEARLY ANNUARY BUGSEED BUGWEED ETESIAN GIFTBOOK PERIODIC YEARBOOK

(OLD WORLD —) WELD

ANNUITY CENSO CONSOL INCOME PENSION TONTINE

ANNUL TOL CASS NULL TOLL UNDO VOID ADNUL AVOID BLANK ELIDE ERASE QUASH REMIT RETEX UNLAW CANCEL FRIVOL NEGATE RECALL REPEAL REVERT REVOKE UNLIVE VACATE ABOLISH CASHIER CASSARE CASSATE DESTROY NULLIFY RESCIND RETRACT REVERSE ABROGATE ARROGATE DEROGATE DISANNUL DISSOLVE IMBECILE OVERRULE

ANNULAR BANDED CYCLIC RINGED ANNULATE CINGULAR CIRCULAR

ANNULARLY RINGWISE

ANNULET RING RIDGE FILLET ANNULUS MOLDING

ANNULMENT UNDOING

ANNULUS RING ANNULE COLLAR GYROMA INDUSIUM

ANNUNCIATION MARYMASS

ANNUNCIATOR TELLER INDICATOR

ANOA BUFFALO SAPIUTAN

ANODE PLATE ZINCOID

ANODIC ASCENDING

ANODYNE BALM ACOPON OPIATE REMEDY EUGENOL SOOTHER NARCOTIC SEDATIVE

ANOINT FAT OIL RUB BALM BEAT CERE NARD ANELE ANOIL CREAM CROWN ENOIL LATCH NUNCT PRUNE SALVE SMEAR SMERL CHRISM GREASE INUNCT SPREAD THRASH MOISTEN UNGUENT

ANOINTMENT CHRISMATORY

ANOMALOUS ODD DIFFORM STRANGE UNUSUAL ABERRANT ABNORMAL ATYPICAL PECULIAR

ANOMALY CREEPER CYCLOPY EPILOIA CYCLOPIA

ANON NAN ANEW ONCE SOON AGAIN LATER AFRESH BEDEEN BEDENE THENCE SHORTLY

ANONYMITY NOBODYNESS

ANONYMOUS UNKNOWN NAMELESS UNAVOWED UNSIGNED

ANOPLURA PARASITA PEDICULINA

ANOTHER NEW THAT ALIAS FRESH SECOND TIDDER TOTHER ANITHER FURTHER

ANOXIA ASPHYXIA

ANSWER DO IT SAY SIT ECHO MEET PLEA SUIT ATONE AVAIL COMES COVER JAWAB REACT REPLY SERVE LETTER REJOIN RESULT RETORT RETURN RIPOST COUNTER DEFENCE DEFENSE FULFILL RESPOND SATISFY ANTIPHON COMEBACK PLEADING REBUTTAL REPARTEE RESPONSE SOLUTION

(— BACK) CHOP

(— FOR) FORM VANG

(— IN FUGUE) COMES

(— THE PURPOSE) DO FIT SUIT AVAIL SERVE

(DECISIVE —) SOCKDOLAGER SOCKDOLGER

(LEGAL —) DUPLY

ANSWERABLE EQUAL LIABLE FITTING ADEQUATE AMENABLE

ANSWERER USHABTI
ANT ANAI ANAY ANER ATTA GYNE
MIRE AMPTE EMMET KELEP MAXIM
MINIM NURSE SIAFU SLAVE AMAZON
DRIVER ERGATE NEUTER WORKER
BULLDOG FORAGER FORMICE
OUVRIER PISMIRE PISSANT PONERID
REPLETE SOLDIER TERMITE
ACULEATA DORYLINE FORMICID
GYNECOID HONEYPOT MICRANER
MYRMICID TAPINOMA
(— LION) DOODLEBUG
(— SHRIKE) BATARA
(— STUDY) MYRMECOLOGY
(— THRUSH) PITTA
(— TREE) WORMIGO
(WORKER —) ERGATE
ANTA PIER PARASTAS PEDESTAL
PILASTER
ANTACID SATURANT
ANTAGONISM WAR ANIMUS ENMITY
QUARREL AVERSION CONFLICT
(IN —) COUNTER
ANTAGONIST FOE ENEMY PARTY
RIVAL FOEMAN BATTLER WARRIOR
COPEMATE OPPONENT OPPOSITE
WRANGLER
ANTAGONISTIC ADVERSE COUNTER
HOSTILE ANTERGIC CONTRARY
INIMICAL OPPONENT OPPOSITE
(— TO GROWTH) ANTIBLASTIC
(NOT —) SYMPATHETIC
ANTAGONIZE CONTEST
ANT BEAR BEAR ERDVARK
AARDVARK ANTEATER EDENTATE
TAMANOIR
ANTE PAY STAKE
ANTEATER TAPIR NUMBAT ECHIDNA
TAMANDU AARDVARK AARDWOLF
DASYURID EDENTATE PANGOLIN
TAMANDUA TAMANOIR
ANTEBRACHIUM CUBIT CUBITAL
CUBITUS FOREARM
ANTECEDENT FORE CAUSE PRIOR
FORMER REASON WHENCE PREMISE
ANTERIOR PREVIOUS
(— OF CANON) GUIDA
ANTECHAMBER LIWAN
ANTEDATE PRECEDE PREDATE
FOREDATE
ANTEDATED FORETIMED
ANTELOPE GNU KID KOB RAM SUS
ASTE BISA BUCK DODA DUST GUIB
IBEX KOBA KUDU ORYX PUKU ROAN
SUNI TOPI TORA ADDAX BAIRA
BEIRA BEISA BEKRA BOHOR BONGO
BOVID BUBAL CHIRU ELAND GORAL
GUIBA IPETE LICHI NAGOR NYALA
ORIBI PEELE PERON SABLE SAIGA
SASIN SEROW TAKIN YAKIN
BAGWYN BHOKRA BUBALE CABREE
CABRET CABRIE CABRIT CHOUKA
DUIKER DUYKER DZERAN DZEREN
DZERIN DZERON GOORAL GRIMME
HEROLA IMPALA INYALA KOODOO
LECHWE LELWEL NAKONG NILGAI
NILGAU PALLAH POOKOO RHEBOK
ALGAZEL BLAUBOK BLESBOK
BUBALIS CHAMOIS CHIKARA

DEFASSA GAZELLE GEMSBOK
GERENUK GREENUK GRYSBOK
MADOQUA REDBUCK RHEEBOK
SASSABY STEMBOK AGACELLA
BLEEKBOK BLESBUCK BONTEBOK
BOSCHBOK BUSHBUCK KORRIGUM
LEUCORYX REEDBUCK STEENBOK
(YOUNG —) KID LAMB
ANTENNA DISH HORN LOOP PALP
TIER YAGI AERIAL DIPOLE FEELER
TACTOR DOUBLET WHISKER
PARABOLA RADIATOR
ANTENNATA INSECTA
ANTERIOR FORNE FRONT PRIOR
ATLOID BEFORE FORMER ANTICUS
PRORSAL VENTRAL ATLANTAL
INFERIOR PREVIOUS
ANTEROOM HALL FOYER LOBBY
ENTRANCE
ANTEWAR PREBELLUM
ANTHELION HALO NIMBUS ANTISUN
AUREOLE
ANTHELMINTIC CUNIC BRAYERA
EMBELIN
ANTHEM HYMN SONG AGNUS MOTET
PSALM INTROIT RESPOND
ASPERGES
(JAPANESE —) KIMIGAYO
ANTHER TIP CHIVE THECA
ANTHESIS BLOOM BLOSSOM
ANTHILL BANK TUMP
ANTHOCYANIN BETANIN PUNICIN
VIOLANIN
ANTHOLOGIST RHAPSODE
RHAPSODIST
ANTHOLOGY ANA POSY ALBUM
SYLVA CORPUS READER GARLAND
SYNTAGMA
ANTHOZOAN CORAL POLYP
ANEMONE GULINULA
ANTHRACONITE STINKSTONE
SWINESTONE
ANTHRAX CHARBON BLACKLEG
ANTHROPOLOGIST TOTEMIST
CULTURALIST
ANTHROPOPHAGITE CANNIBAL
ANTIAIRCRAFT ARCHIE
ANTIBALLOONER SEPARATOR
ANTIBIOTIC BIOTIC ABIOTIC
HUMULON CIRCULIN CITRININ
CLAVACIN CLAVATIN FRADICIN
HUMULONE NYSTATIN SUBTILIN
ANTIBODY REAGIN BLOCKER
GLUTININ
ANTIC TOY DIDO FOOL WILD CAPER
CLOWN COMIC DROLL MERRY
PRANK STUNT GAMBOL BUFFOON
CAPRICE GAMBADE GAMBADO
ANTICIPATE BALK BEAT HOPE JUMP
WISH ALLOT AUGUR AWAIT DREAD
SENSE STALL DIVINE EXPECT
THWART DEVANCE FORERUN
FORESEE OBVIATE PORTEND
PREPARE PREVENE PREVENT
PROPOSE RESPECT SUPPOSE
ANTEDATE FORECAST FOREFEEL
FORETAKE PROSPECT
ANTICIPATION ODIUM AUGURY
OPINION PROSPECT

ANTICLIMAX BATHOS
ANTICLINE ARCH DOME ISOCLINE
OVERFOLD
ANTICYCLONE HIGH
ANTIDOTE GUACO BEZOAR EMETIC
GALENA REMEDY THERIAC
DELETERY THERIACA
ANTIGEN N LYSOGEN BIOLOGIC
ANTIGONE (BROTHER OF —)
POLYNICES
(FATHER OF —) OEDIPUS
(MOTHER OF —) JOCASTA
ANTIGORITE SERPENTINE
ANTIMASK ANTIC ANTICK
ANTIMONIAL STIBIAL
ANTIMONY SB KOHL STIBIUM
ANTIMONY SULFIDE SURMA
SOORMA
ANTINOMIAN FIDUCIARY
ANTIOXIDANT SESAMOL
ANTIPATHY HATE ODIUM ENMITY
NAUSEA RANCOR DISGUST DISLIKE
AVERSION DISTASTE DYSPATHY
LOATHING
ANTIPHON GRADUAL GRADUALE
ANTIPHONALLY CHOIRWISE
ANTHEMWISE
ANTIPHONARY LEDGER
ANTIPODAL ANTARCTIC
ANTIPYRETIC SALOL MALARIN
THALLIN THALLINE
ANTIQUARY ARCHAIST ANTIQUARIAN
ANTIQUATED OLD AGED FUSTY
MOSSY PASSE FOSSIL VOIDED
ANCIENT ARCHAIC FOGYISH
NOACHIAN OBSOLETE OUTDATED
OUTMODED TIMEWORN
ANTIQUE ANTIC RELIC SIRUP SYRUP
VIRTU ANTICK NOETIC ANCIENT
NOACHIC NOACHIAN OUTMODED
ANTIQUITY ELD OLD PAST YORE
RELIC OLDNESS ANCIENCE
ANCIENCY
(PL.) ARCHEOLOGY ARCHAEOLOGY
ANTIRED WHITE
ANTI-SEMITISM JUDOPHOBIA
ANTISEPTIC CAVA EGOL KAVA SALT
AMIDO AMINE EUPAD EUSOL IODOL
SALOL AMADOL IATROL IODINE
KRELOS PHENOL PICROL ALCOHOL
ALUMNOL ARBUTIN ASEPTIC
COLYTIC LORETIN STERILE TACHIOL
TEUCRIN THALLIN CREOSOTE
ICHTHYOL KAVAKAVA METAPHEN
TEREBENE THALLINE
ANTISOCIAL HOSTILE ANARCHIST
ANTISPASMODIC KELLIN SAMBUL
SUMBAL SUMBUL KHELLIN
ANTISTROPHE REVERT
COUNTERTURN
ANTITHESIS AND CONTRAST
ANTITOXIN SERUM BIOLOGIC
ANTIVIVISECTIONIST BESTIARIAN
ANTLER DAG HORN KNOB RIAL TRAY
DAGUE RIGHT ROYAL SHOOT SPIKE
BOSSET SHOVEL TROCHE SPELLER
DEERHORN TROCHING
(— POINT) TROCHING
(PL.) HEAD ATTIRE

ANT LION DOODLEBUG
ANTSHRIKE BATARA
ANT THRUSH PITTA
ANT TREE HORMIGO
ANUS ASS ARSE BUNG VENT SIEGE
ANVIL BLOCK INCUS SNARL STAKE
STITH TEEST STETHY STITHY
ANFEELD BICKERN BEAKIRON
(— **SUPPORT**) STOCK
(**MINIATURE** —) STAKE STUMP
ANXIETY HOW CARE FEAR FRAY
PAIN ALARM ANGOR DOUBT DREAD
PANIC WORRY KIAUGH PUCKER
ANGUISH CAUTION CHAGRIN
CONCERN SCRUPLE TENSION
THOUGHT TROUBLE DISQUIET
SUSPENSE
ANXIOUS AGOG BUSY FOND TOEY
EAGER FIRST UPSET AFRAID
UNEASY CARKING EARNFUL
FORWARD TIDIOSE UNQUIET
DESIROUS RESTLESS THOUGHTY
WATCHFUL
ANY A AN AY AIR ALL ARY ONI ONY
AIRY EVER PART SOME WHAT
(— **WHATEVER**) ALL
ANYBODY ANY ONE ANYONE
SOMEONE
ANYHOW HOW NOWAY ALWAYS
ANYWAY
ANYTHING THAT AUGHT OUGHT
ANYONE HE MAN ANYBODY
ANYWAY NOHOW ALWAYS
ANYWHERE EINWER OWHERE
UBIQUE ANYPLACE
ANYWISE ANYHOW ANYWAY
ANYWAYS
AOUDAD ARUI UDAD AUDAD SHEEP
CHAMOIS
APACE FAST QUICK QUICKLY
RAPIDLY SPEEDILY
APACHE YUMA PADUCA CIBECUE
VAQUERO QUERECHO
APAGOGE ABDUCTION
APAP EPIPHI
APAR APARA BOLITA MATACO
APART BY OFF AWAY BOUT ELSE
ALONE ALOOF AROOM ASIDE RIVEN
SOLUS SPLIT YTWYN ABREID
ATWAIN LONELY SUNDRY ASUNDER
ENISLED REMOVED SEVERAL
SEVERED SEPARATE
(**WIDE** —) ASPAR
(**WIDELY** —) ABROAD
APARTMENT BUT WON DIGS FLAT
HALL ROOM STEW WENE WONE
WOON ABODE BOWER OECUS ORIEL
ROOMS SALON SOLAR SUITE
ANDRON CLOSET DECKER DINGLE
DUPLEX GROTTO LYCEUM SALOON
SINGLE SOLLAR SPENCE STANZA
BUTTERY CHAMBER COCKPIT
GALLERY MANSION PRIVACY
BUILDING EPHEBEUM SHOWROOM
SOLARIUM TENEMENT THALAMUS
(— **FOR IDOL**) TING
(— **IN CASTLE**) BOWER
(— **OF WARSHIP**) COCKPIT
(**OUTER** —) BUT

(**PRIVATE** —) MAHAL
(**RENTED** —) LET
(PL.) GYNAECEUM
APATHETIC CALM COLD COOL DEAD
DOWF DULL BLASE DOWFF INERT
STOIC GLASSY SUPINE TORPID
ADENOID PASSIVE UNMOVED
LISTLESS SLUGGISH
APATHY SLOTH ACEDIA CAFARD
PHLEGM TORPOR LANGUOR
DOLDRUMS DULLNESS LETHARGY
OMISSION STOICISM
APATITE IJOLITE MOROXITE
APAYAO ISNEG
APE KRA LAR PAN BOOR COPY DUPE
FOOL MAHA MIME MOCK SHAM
BEROK CLOWN MAGOT MIMIC
ORANG PONGO PYGMY APELET
BABOON GELADA GIBBON LANGUR
MARTEN MARTIN MONKEY OURANG
PARROT PONGID SIMIAN SIMIID
BUFFOON COPYCAT EMULATE
GORILLA IMITATE PORTRAY
PRIMATE SIAMANG DURUKULI
IMITATOR MANTEGAR SIMULATE
(— **STUDY**) PITHECOLOGY
APEAK VERTICAL
APEIRON MATTER
APER BOAR MIME SNOB CLOWN
MOCKER BUFFOON COPYCAT
APERCU DIGEST GLANCE PRECIS
SKETCH INSIGHT OUTLINE
APERIENT LAX OPENER
APERIODIC DEADBEAT
APERITIF WHET CONZANO
DUBONNET
APERTURE F EYE GAP OPE VUE
BOLE BORE HOLE LEAK PASS PORE
RIMA SLIT SLOT VENT BREAK
CHASM CLEFT CRACK LIGHT MOUTH
PUPIL STOMA CUTOUT HIATUS
KEYWAY LOUVER WINDOW FISSURE
KEYHOLE OPENING ORIFICE
OSTIOLE PINHOLE SWALLOW
TROMPIL APERTION FENESTRA
LOOPHOLE OVERTURE SPIRACLE
APEX EPI PIN TIP TOP ACME AUGE
CONE CUSP NOON PEAK RUFF
CREST HIGHT PITCH POINT SPIRE
APOGEE CLIMAX CRISIS CUPULA
GENION HEIGHT SUMMIT TITTLE
VERTEX ZENITH CACUMEN EVEREST
PAPILLA PUNCTUM PINNACLE
(— **OF HELMET**) CREST
APHAREUS (**FATHER OF** —)
PERIERES
(**SON OF** —) IDAS LYNCEUS
APHASIA ALALIA ALEXIA JARGON
APHEMIA
APHID APHIS LOUSE APTERA BLIGHT
COLLIER DIMERAN MIGRANS
PUCERON BLACKFLY GREENFLY
GYNOPARA HOMOPTER
APHORISM SAW ADAGE AXIOM
GNOME MAXIM MOTTO SUTRA
SUTTA DICTUM SAYING WISDOM
EPIGRAM PRECEPT PROVERB
APOTHEGM PISHOGUE
APHORISTIC GNOMIC

APHRODISIAC DEWTRY DAMIANA
VENEREAL
APHRODITE VENUS CYPRIS URANIA
ANTHEIA MYLITTA CYTHEREA
PANDEMOS
(**FATHER OF** —) JUPITER
(**HUSBAND OF** —) VULCAN
(**MOTHER OF** —) DIONE
(**SON OF** —) EROS CUPID AENEAS
APIARIST SKEPPIST
APIARY HIVE SKEP BEEYARD
BEEHOUSE
APICULTURE BEEKEEPING
APIECE UP ALL PER EACH SERIATIM
APIKORES BECORESH
APIO ARRACACH ARRACACHA
APIOS SOIA SOJA GLYCINE
APIS HAPI
APISH SILLY FOPPISH AFFECTED
APITONG BAGAC HAPITON KERUING
APIUM UMBEL
APLITE HAPLITE
APLOMB TACT NERVE POISE SURETY
COOLNESS
APOCALYPSE SHOWING
REVELATION
APOCRISIARY RESPONSAL
APOCRYPHAL SHAM FALSE UNREAL
DOUBTFUL FABULOUS FICTIOUS
APODAL FOOTLESS
APOGEE ACME APEX AUGE PEAK
CLIMAX ZENITH
APOGON AMIA CARDINAL
APOLLO SUN DELIUS AGYIEUS
APOLLON LYKEIOS PATROUS
PHOEBUS PYTHIUS CYNTHIUS
PYTHAEUS
(**FATHER OF** —) ZEUS JUPITER
(**MOTHER OF** —) LETO LATONA
(**SISTER OF** —) DIANA ARTEMIS
APOLLYON DEVIL SATAN ABADDON
APOLOGETIC SORRY
APOLOGUE MYTH FABLE STORY
APOLOGY PARABLE ALLEGORY
APOLOGY PLEA ALIBI AMENDS
EXCUSE PARDON REGRET SCRUPLE
APOLOGIA
APOPHYGE SCAPE ESCAPE
APOPLEXY ESCA SHOCK STROKE
POPLESIE
APOSTASY FALL LAPSE
APOSTATE RAT LAPSED CONVERT
HERETIC PERVERT SECEDER
DESERTER DISLOYAL RECREANT ⟩
RENEGADE TURNCOAT ⟩
APOSTLE ESCAPE TEACHER
DISCIPLE FOLLOWER PREACHER
(**BIBLICAL** —) JOHN JUDE LEVI PAUL
DENIS JAMES JUDAS PETER SIMON
ANDREW PHILIP THOMAS DIDYMUS
MATTHEW BARNABAS MATTHIAS
APOSTLE BIRD CATBIRD
APOSTROPHE TURNWAY TURNTALE
APOTHECARY CHEMIC SPICER
CHEMICK DRUGGIST
APOTHECIUM CUP PELTA TRICA
SHIELD ARDELLA LIRELLA PATELLA
APOTHEGM SAW DICT ADAGE AXIOM
GNOME MAXIM SUTRA DICTUM

SAYING SUTTAH PROVERB
APHORISM SENTENCE
APOTHEOSIS DEIFICATION
CONSECRATION
APOTHEOSIZE DEIFY EXALT
ELEVATE GLORIFY CANONIZE
APPALL STUN APPAL DAUNT SHOCK
DISMAY REDUCE REVOLT WEAKEN
ASTOUND DEPRESS DISGUST
DISMISS HORRIFY TERRIFY
AFFRIGHT ASTONISH ENFEEBLE
FRIGHTEN OVERCOME
APPALLING AWFUL AWESOME
FEARFUL TERRIBLE TERRIFIC
APPANAGE GRANT ADJUNCT
APANAGE
APPARATUS BOX GUN LOG SET
ADON DRAG ETNA FAKE GEAR GRIP
HECK HELM LAMP LIFT STOW TIRE
TOOL BURET GANCH HOIST HORSE
LEECH RELAY SCUBA SHEAR SIREN
SONAR STILL STOVE SWING BUDDLE
BUFFER COILER COOKER DEVICE
DINGUS ENGINE FEEDER FILTER
FOGGER GADGET GEYSER GRAITH
LADDER LIFTER MILKER ORRERY
OUTFIT REFLUX SEESAW SHEARS
SMOKER SMUDGE TACKLE TIPPLE
TREMIE TROMPE AERATOR ALEMBIC
APPAREL AUTOMAT BAGGAGE
BALANCE BASCULE BURETTE
COVEYER DERRICK ECHELON
FURNACE GASOGEN GRILLER
HOISTER INHALER ISOTRON
MACHINE MEGAFOG PINCERS
PRESSER SOXHLET SPRAYER
STIRRER TELEPIX TREMOLO
TRIMMER UTENSIL AGITATOR
AQUALUNG BLOWDOWN CALUTRON
CONVEYOR CRYOSTAT DIALYZER
DIAPHOTE DIGESTER DRENCHER
DUMBBELL EOLIPILE EQUIPAGE
ERGOSTAT GASIFIER GAZOGENE
INJECTOR ISOSCOPE JACQUARD
OSMOGENE OZONISER PULMOTOR
PURIFIER RECORDER REDUCTOR
REHEATER SCRUBBER SOFTENER
STRIPPER
(— IN STOMACH OF LOBSTER) LADY
(SEGMENTAL —) BRAINSTEM
APPAREL DECK FARE GARB GEAR
ROBE SECT TIRE WEAR WEDE
ADORN ARRAY CLOTH DRESS EQUIP
HABIT TUNIC ATTIRE CLOTHE
GRAITH OUTFIT PARURE ROBING
CLOBBER COSTUME FURNISH
GARMENT HARNESS PREPARE
RAIMENT VESTURE CLOTHING
FOOTWEAR HEADWEAR WARDROBE
(MILITARY —) WARENTMENT
(RICH —) ARRAY
APPARENT OPEN BREEM BREME
CLEAR OVERT PLAIN FORMAL
PARENT PATENT PHANIC CERTAIN
EVIDENT GLARING OBVIOUS
SEEMING SHALLOW VISIBLE
DISTINCT ILLUSORY MANIFEST
PALPABLE PROBABLE SEMBLANT
APPARITION HUE HANT SHOW

DREAM FANCY FETCH GHOST
HAUNT IMAGE LARVA PHASM SHADE
SHAPE SPOOK ASPECT DOUBLE
IDOLUM SOWLTH SPIRIT SPRITE
STOUND SWARTH TAISCH THURSE
VISION WRAITH DISPLAY EIDOLON
FANTASY FEATURE PHANTOM
SPECTER SPECTRE EPIPHANY
ILLUSION PHANTASM PRESENCE
REVENANT SPECTRUM
APPARITOR BEADLE PARURE
PARITOR SUMMONER
APPEAL ASK BEG BID CRY CALL
CASE PLEA SEEK SUIT APPLY
CHARM CLEPE REFER SPEAK
ACCUSE ADJURE AVOUCH INVOKE
PRAYER SUMMON ADDRESS
CONJURE ENTREAT IMPLORE
REQUEST SOLICIT APPROACH
ENTREATY PETITION
(— TO) APPLY AVOUCH INVOKE
ARRAIGN
(SEX —) IT
APPEALING CUTE NICE CATCHY
CLEVER CUNNING SUGARED
PLEASANT
APPEAR BID CAR EYE GET COME
DAWN FARE LOOK LOOM MAKE
MEET PEER REAR RISE SEEM WALK
ARISE ENTER ISSUE KITHE KYTHE
OCCUR SOUND THINK ARRIVE
BESEEM EMERGE INFORM REGARD
SPRING BLOSSOM COMPEAR
DEVELOP RESEMBLE
(— AND DISAPPEAR) COOK
(— BRIEFLY) GLINT
(— DIRECTLY BEFORE) AFFRONT
(— SUDDENLY) BURST
(— UNEXPECTEDLY) BLOOM IRRUPT
APPEARANCE AIR CUT HUE CAST
FARE FORM GARB IDEA LATE LEEN
LOOK MIEN SHOW VIEW BLUSH
COLOR EIDOS FAVOR FRONT GUISE
HABIT PHASE PHASM SHAPE SIGHT
SOUND SPICE ASPECT EFFECT
FACIES FAVOUR MANNER OBJECT
OSTENT REGARD VISAGE ARRIVAL
DISPLAY FARRAND FASHION
FEATURE GLIMPSE RESPECT
SHOWING SPECIES ARTEFACT
ARTIFACT EPIPHANY ILLUSION
LIKENESS PRESENCE PRETENSE
(— LIGHT ON HAIR) HAG
(CLOUDED —) HAZE CHILL
(CONSPICUOUS —) FIGURE
(DISTINCTIVE —) AURA
(FIRST —) DAWN DEBUT SPRING
(IMPOVERISHED —) BEGGARY
(MERE —) INTENTIONAL
(MOCK —) SIMULACRUM
(MOTTLED —) ROE DAPPLE
(MOTTLED SKY —) BLINK
(OUTWARD —) FACE SEEM SHOW
APPAREL BALLOON SEEMING
SURFACE
(PERSONAL —) PRESENCE
(STRIPED —) ROE
(SUPERNATURAL —) APPARITION
(SURFACE —) TOUR BLOOM

(UNGAINLY —) ANGULARITY
(VAGUE —) BLUR
APPEASE LAY PAY CALM EASE
HUSH SATE ALLAY ALONE ATONE
MEASE PEACE PEASE QUIET SLAKE
STILL DEFRAY GENTLE MEEKEN
MODIFY PACIFY PLEASE SOFTEN
SOOTHE ASSUAGE CONTENT
DULCIFY GRATIFY MOLLIFY PLACATE
SATISFY STICKLE SUFFICE SWEETEN
MITIGATE
(— APPETITE) STAY
APPEASEMENT MUNICHISM
APPELLATION NAME TERM GODDY
STYLE TITLE APPEAL CALLING
EPITHET GOODMAN SURNAME
COGNOMEN METRONYM NICKNAME
APPEND ADD PIN TAG CLIP HANG
JOIN TACK AFFIX ANNEX ADJOIN
ATTACH FASTEN AUGMENT SUBJOIN
APPENDAGE ARM AWN FIN LEG TAB
TAG ARIL BARB CAUD FLAP HOOK
HORN LIMB LOBE SPUR TAIL AFFIX
BEARD CAUDA CERAS EXITE RIDER
SCALE TROLL WHISK CERCUS
CIRRUS CORONA ELATER ENDITE
LAGENA LIGULE PALPUS PAPPUS
STIPEL STYLET SUFFIX UROPOD
ADJUNCT ANTENNA AURICLE
CODICIL EARLOBE EMBLAST
FIXTURE FURCULA GONOPOD
HOUSING MALELLA PENDANT
STIPULE SWIMMER THIMBLE
TRAILER ADDITION ADHERENT
ASCIDIUM BRACHIUM EMPODIUM
FILAMENT GNATHITE PEDIPALP
PENDICLE PHYLLOID PREDELLA
RHABDITE SYNTROPE
(— ON MOCCASIN) TRAILER
(EAR-SHAPED —) AURICLE
(PL.) ADNEXA ANNEXA FORCEPS
APPENDIX EKE ANNEX LABEL
APPEND VERMIX AURICLE CODICIL
PENDANT ADDENDUM AURICULA
EPILOGUE
APPERTAIN LIE FALL REFER
BELONG RELATE CONCERN PERTAIN
APPETITE MAW YEN LUST PICA
TUCK URGE WILL ZEST BELLY
BLOOD GORGE GREED GUSTO
TASTE TWIST BULIMY DESIRE
FAMINE GENIUS GODOWN HUNGER
LIKING OREXIS RELISH STROKE
TALENT BULIMIA CRAVING EDACITY
LONGING PASSION STOMACH
SWALLOW WANTING CUPIDITY
FONDNESS GULOSITY TENDENCY
(— LOSS) ANOREXIA
(ANIMAL —) BLOOD
(CANINE —) PHAGEDENA
(EXCESSIVE —) GULOSITY
POLYPHAGIA
APPETIZER WET WHET SAUCE
CANAPE RELISH SAVORY CEVICHE
SASHIMI APERITIF COCKTAIL
DUBONNET
APPETIZING NICE GUSTY SAVORY
GUSTFUL GUSTABLE
APPLAUD CLAP LAUD ROOT RUFF

CHEER EXTOL HUZZA PRAISE
ACCLAIM APPROVE COMMENT
ENDORSE HOSANNA PLAUDIT
APPLAUSE CLAP HAND BRAVO
CHEER ECLAT HUZZA SALVO
HURRAH PRAISE ACCLAIM OVATION
CLAPPING
APPLE PIP CRAB OHIA POME COPEI
JAMBO BEEFIN BIFFIN CODLIN
DOUCIN ESOPUS GOLDIN KARELA
KAVIKA MACUPA MAKOPA PIPPIN
PUFFIN RENNET RUSSET BALDWIN
BEAUFIN CODLING COSTARD
FAMEUSE GOLDING PEELING
POMEROY RAMBURE RIBSTON
WAGENER WEALTHY WINESAP
AMPALAYA COCCAGEE CORTLAND
GREENING JONATHAN MCINTOSH
NONESUCH PARADISE PEARMAIN
POMANDER POROPORO QUEENING
REINETTE ROSACEAN WHITSOUR
(— OF PERU) JIMSON JIMPSON
SHOOFLY
(BITTER —) COLOCYNTH
(CRAB —) CRAB SCRAB WHARRE
POWITCH
(EMU —) COLANE
(GOLDEN —) BEL BAEL
(LIKE AN —) POMACEOUS
(PEELED —) DUMPLING
(SHRIVELED —) CRUMPLING
(SLICED DRIED —S) SNITS SNITZ
SCHNITZ
(SMALL —) CODLIN CODLING
(SMALL —S) GRIGGLES
(THORN —) MAD METEL
APPLEBERRY DUMPLING
APPLEJOHN DEUSAN DEUZAN
APPLE-POLISH BROWNNOSE
APPLIANCE GEAR GRAB IRON TOOL
BRACE CLAMP DEVIL FLIER FLYER
GLODE SHADE BONNET BREWER
DEVICE ENGINE FABRIC GADGET
GAITER JUICER SPLINT CHARGER
MACHINE SCRAPER STOPPER
UTENSIL BALANCER DEVIATOR
APPLICABLE APT FIT MEET PROPER
USEFUL FITTING PLIABLE APPOSITE
RELATIVE RELEVANT SUITABLE
(UNIVERSALLY —) CATHOLIC
(WIDELY —) BROAD
APPLICANT PROSPECT
APPLICATION USE DAUB FORM
BLANK TOPIC APPEAL EFFORT
ADDRESS EPITHEM REQUEST
EPITHEME LENITIVE PETITION
PRACTICE SEDULITY
(— OF KNOWLEDGE) PRACTICE
PRACTISE
(— TO WRONG PURPOSE) ABUSE
(MEDICINAL —) PLASTER DRESSING
FRONTING LENITIVE
(MENTAL —) INTENTION
APPLICATOR COLPOSTAT
APPLIED (CLOSELY —) ACCUMBENT
APPLIQUE DAG DAGGE ATTACH
DESIGN ORNAMENT
APPLY ASK LAY PLY PUT RUB SET
USE BEAR BEND CLAP DAUB GIVE

HOLD MOVE SEEK TOIL TURN WORK
ADAPT GRIND IMPLY LABOR LIKEN
REFER SMEAR ADDICT APPEAL
APPOSE BESTOW BETAKE BUCKLE
COMPLY DEVOTE DIRECT EMPLOY
EXTEND RESORT ADHIBIT COMPARE
CONFORM IMPRESS OVERLAY
PERTAIN REQUEST SOLICIT UTILIZE
DEDICATE DISPENSE MINISTER
PETITION
(— BRAKE) BUR
(— COSMETICS) DO POP
(— GRAPHITE) BLACKLEAD
(— GREASE) ARM
(— HOT CLOTHS) FOMENT
(— IMPROPERLY) ABUSE
(— ONESELF) ATTEND INTEND
MUCKLE
(— PIGMENT) DRAG
(— TO) CONSULT CONTACT
APPOGGIATURA BACKFALL
ACCIACCATURA
(DOUBLE —) FALL
APPOINT ARM FIX SET CALL DECK
GIVE MAKE NAME ALLOT ARRAY
AWARD CREST DIGHT ELECT ENACT
EQUIP INSET PITCH PLACE POINT
SHAPE SLATE ASSIGN ASSIZE
ATTACH CREATE DECREE DEPUTE
DETAIL DEVISE DIRECT ENTAIL
ORDAIN OUTFIT SETTLE STEVEN
TAILYE ARRAIGN CONFIRM DESTINE
DISPOSE FURNISH GAZETTE
RESOLVE TAILZIE DELEGATE
DEPUTIZE INDICATE NOMINATE
ORDINATE
(— A CLERIC) COLLATE
(— BEFOREHAND) STALL
APPOINTEE PLACEMAN
APPOINTMENT SET DATE BERTH
ORDER TRYST BILLET OFFICE
STEVEN COMMAND STATION
CREATION DELEGACY POSITION
(— OF HEIR) INSTITUTION
APPORTION LOT DEAL DOLE MARK
METE PART RATE ALLOT AWARD
CAVEL GRANT PARAL SHARE SHIFT
WEIGH APPLOT ASSESS ASSIGN
DIVIDE PARCEL RATION TAVERN
ARRANGE BALANCE QUARTER
ALLOCATE DESCRIBE
APPORTIONMENT DIVISION
APPOSITE APT PAT COGENT TIMELY
GERMANE INCIDENT RELATIVE
RELEVANT SUITABLE
APPRAISAL APPRIZAL
APPRAISE GAGE LOVE METE RATE
ASSAY GAUGE JUDGE PRICE PRIZE
VALUE ASSESS ESTEEM EVALUE
PONDER PRAISE SURVEY ADJUDGE
ANALYZE COMMEND ESTIMATE
EVALUATE
APPRECIABLE ANY SENSIBLE
APPRECIATE DIG FEEL LOVE JUDGE
PRIZE RAISE SAVOR TASTE VALUE
ADMIRE ESTEEM SAVOUR ADVANCE
APPRIZE APPROVE CHERISH
REALIZE INCREASE TREASURE
APPRECIATION EYE GUSTO SENSE
CONCEIT

APPRECIATIVE AWAKE GRATEFUL
(— OF BEAUTY) ESTHETIC
AESTHETIC
APPREHEND COP GET LAG NAB SEE
FEAR HEAR KNOW NOTE SCAN
TAKE VIEW CATCH DREAD GRASP
GRIPE INTUE SEIZE ARREST BEHOLD
DETAIN INTEND INTUIT BELIEVE
CAPTURE CONCEIT ENDOUTE
FORESEE IMAGINE REALIZE RECEIVE
SENSATE SUPPOSE CONCEIVE
DISCOVER OVERTAKE PERCEIVE
APPREHENDED GRIPPIT
APPREHENSIBLE NOETIC SENSATE
SENSIBLE
APPREHENSION FEAR FRAY PAIN
PANG SCAN WERE ALARM DOUBT
DREAD FANCY WORRY ARREST
DISMAY NOESIS ANXIETY CAPTURE
CONCERN PRESAGE SUSPECT
DISTRUST MISTRUST SUSPENSE
APPREHENSIVE APT JUMPY FEARED
MORBID ANXIOUS FEARFUL
JEALOUS NERVOUS STREAKY
DOUBTFUL
APPRENTICE CUB BIND BOOT SNOB
TYRO CADET DEVIL BURSCH
HELPER JOCKEY NOVICE BANKMAN
GROMMET LEARNER TRAINEE
WAISTER APRENDIZ BEGINNER
JACKAROO SERVITOR TURNOVER
APPRENTICESHIP SERVITUDE
APPRISE WARN LEARN TEACH
ADVISE INFORM NOTIFY REVEAL
APPRIZE ACQUAINT DISCLOSE
INSTRUCT
APPROACH TRY ADIT BUMP BURN
CHAT COME DRAW NEAR NERE
NIGH ROAD ABORD BOARD CLOSE
COAST ESSAY STALK VERGE
ACCEDE ACCESS ACCOST ADVENT
ANIMUS APPEAL BORDER BREAST
BROACH COMING GATHER IMPEND
PROACH TRENCH ADVANCE
AGGRESS APPULSE CONTACT
SEAGATE SUCCEED CONVERGE
NEIGHBOR ONCOMING
(— FROM WINDWARD) BEAR
(— GAME) DRAW
(— HOSTILELY) SWAY
(— NEAR) TOUCH
(— OF NIGHT) FALL
(— TENDENCY) ADIENCE
APPROACHABLE COMMON
APPROACHING LIKE COMING
TOWARD ONCOMING
APPROBATION TEST FAVOR PROOF
TRIAL ASSENT FAVOUR LOANGE
PRAISE REGARD REPUTE PLAUDIT
APPLAUSE APPROVAL SANCTION
APPROPRIATE ADD APT DUE FIT
LAY PAT AKIN CRIB FEAT GOOD
GRAB GRIP HELP JUST MEET SINK
SUIT TAKE ALLOT ANNEX FITTY
HAPPY RIGHT STEAL USURP ASSELF
ASSIGN ASSUME BORROW DECENT
DEVOTE DEVOUR DIGEST GATHER
GENTIL KINDLY PILFER PIRATE
PROPER TIMELY WORTHY APPROVE

APROPOS CABBAGE CONDIGN
CONVERT FITTING GERMANE
GRABBLE GRADELY IMPOUND
PREEMPT PURLOIN RELATED
SECRETE SWALLOW ACCROACH
APPOSITE ARROGATE BECOMING
DESERVED EMBEZZLE GRACEFUL
HANDSOME IDONEOUS PROPERTY
RELEVANT RIGHTFUL SUITABLE
(— **UNLAWFULLY**) HEIST STEAL
(**MOST** —) CHOICE
APPROPRIATENESS APTNESS
DECENCY FITNESS APTITUDE
(**NICE** —) ELEGANCE
APPROPRIATION FUND VOTE
DEVOTION
(**FRAUDULENT** —) CON
EMBEZZLEMENT
APPROVAL AMEN ECLAT ASSENT
ESTEEM APPROOF CONSENT
PLAUDIT SUPPORT APPLAUSE
BLESSING SANCTION SUFFRAGE
APPROVE DO OK BUY TRY HAVE
LIKE OKAY OKEH PASS TEST VOTE
ALLOW BLESS CLEAR FAVOR PROVE
VALUE ACCEPT ADMIRE BISHOP
CONCUR RATIFY APPLAUD CERTIFY
COMMEND CONFIRM CONSENT
ENDORSE EXHIBIT INDORSE
SUPPORT ACCREDIT MANIFEST
SANCTION
APPROVED TRYE EXPERT PROBAL
ACCEPTED ORTHODOX
APPROVING HEARTY
APPROXIMATE NEAR ABOUT CIRCA
CLOSE COAST ROUGH COARSE
GENERAL APPROACH ESTIMATE
APPROXIMATELY SAY AWAY GAIN
MUCH NIGH ABOUT ALMOST
AROUND NEARLY TOWARD
CRUDELY ROUGHLY
APPROXIMATING COMPARATIVE
APPROXIMATION CIRCA
COUNTERFEIT
APPURTENANCE GEAR ANNEX
ASSIGN EFFEIR ADJUNCT COMFORT
APPANAGE PENDICLE
(**PL.**) ADDENDA
APRICOT COT UME ANSU MUME
BLENHEIM
(**DRIED** —**S**) MEBOS MEEBOS
A PRIORI PURE
APRON BIB CAP BASE BOOT BRAT
DICK RAMP SLOP TAYO TIER COVER
EPHOD BARVEL BISHOP CANVAS
DAIDLE DICKEY NAPRON RUNWAY
SHIELD TARMAC TOUSER BRATTLE
CANVASS DAIDLIE GREMIAL TABLIER
LAMBSKIN PINAFORE PRASKEEN
(— **OF FURNITURE**) PETTICOAT
(— **OF SEAT**) FALL
(**CHILD'S** —) TIER BISWOP SLIPPER
(**LEATHER** —) DICK DICKY BARVEL
DICKEY BARMFEL BARVELL
BARMSKIN
(**MASON'S** —) LAMBSKIN
(**SILKEN** —) GREMIAL
(**PL.**) ARMITAS
APROPOS APT FIT PAT MEET TIMELY

RELEVANT SUITABLE
APSE APSIS NICHE CONCHA RECESS
APSIS APSE AUGE
APT FIT PAT YAP ABLE DEFT FAIN
FEAT KEEN VAIN WONT ADEPT
ALERT HAPPY PRONE QUICK READY
ASPERT CLEVER DOCILE KITTLE
LIABLE LIKELY SUITED TOWARD
APROPOS CAPABLE FITTING
IDONEAL WILLING APPOSITE
DEXTROUS DISPOSED HANDSOME
IDONEOUS INCLINED PRACTIVE
PREPARED SKILLFUL SUITABLE
(— **TO TURN**) WALT
APTERYX KIWI RATITE KIVIKIVI
KIWIKIWI
APTITUDE ART BENT GIFT HEAD
TURN CRAFT FLAIR HABIT KNACK
SKILL VERVE GENIUS TALENT
ABILITY CONDUCT FACULTY FITNESS
LEANING CAPACITY INSTINCT
TENDENCY
APTNESS GIFT KNACK SKILL
APTITUDE FELICITY
APUS CYPSELUS MICROPUS
AQUARIUS SKINKER
AQUEDUCT AQUA DUCT CANAL
AQUAGE SPECUS CHANNEL
CONDUIT PASSAGE
(— **OF SILVIUS**) ITER
AQUEOUS HYDATOID WATERISH
ARA MACAW
ARAB AHL AUS IBAD OMAN SLEB
WAIF ARABY GAMIN NOMAD SAUDI
TATAR SEMITE SLUBBI URCHIN
ARABIAN BEDOUIN SARACEN
SOLUBBI AZZAZAME KABABISH
LARRIKIN SLOUBBIE YEMENITE

ARABIA

COIN: LARI CARAT DINAR KABIK
RIYAL
DESERT: NYD ANKAF DEHNA
NAFUD NEFUD
GODDESS: ALLAT
GARMENT: ABA HAIK CABAAN
BURNOUS
HOLY CITY: MECCA MEDINA
HOLY LAND: HEJAZ
ISLAND: SOCOTRA
JUDGE: CADI
KINGDOM: NEJD
MEASURE: DEN SAA FERK KIST
ACHIR BARID CABDA CAFIZ
COVID CUDDY MAKUK QASAB
TEMAN WOIBE ZUDDA ARTABA
ASSBAA COVIDO FEDDAN
GARIBA GHALVA CAPHITE
FARSAKH FARSANG KILADJA
MARHALE NUSFIAH
MOUNTAIN: NEBO HOREB SINAI
PORT: ADEN
RULER: AMIR EMIR AMEER EMEER
STATE: ASIR OMAN YEMEN
KUWAIT
TOWN: ABHA ADEN BEDA BERA
HAIL RIAD SANA TAIF DUBAI
HAUTA HOFUF JIDDA MECCA

MOCHA QATIF TAIZZ YENBO
ANAIZA MANAMA MATRAH
MEDINA RIVADH SALALA
SHAQRA BURAIDA HODEIDA
MUKALLA ONEIZAH SHARJAH
TRIBE: AUS ASIR IRAD TEMA
KEDAR DIENDEL SHUKRIA
WEIGHT: ROTL BAHAR CHEKI
KELLA MAUND NASCH NEVAT
OCQUE OUKIA RATEL TOMAN
VAKIA BOKARD DIRHEM MISKAL
FARSALAH

ARABIC CARSHUNI GARSHUNI
KARSHUNI THAMUDIC
(— **ALPHABET**) BA FA HA RA TA YA
ZA AYN DAD DAL JIM KAF KHA LAM
MIM NUN QAF SAD SIN THA WAW
ZAY ALIF DHAL SHIN GHAYN
ARABLE FERTILE PLOWABLE
TILLABLE
ARACHNID CRAB MITE TICK TAINT
ACARUS CARTER SPIDER CARTARE
OCTOPOD PEDIPALP SCORPION
SOLPUGID
ARAGONITE ALABASTER
ARAIN ARRAND
ARAKANESE MAGHI
ARAMAIC SYRIAC MANDAEAN
(— **TRANSLATION**) TARGUM
ARANEA EPEIRA
ARAPONGA BELLBIRD
ARAROBA ZEBRAWOOD
ARAUCANIAN AUCA PAMPA
MAPOCHE MOLUCHE PAMPERO
PICUNCHE
ARAWA AOTEA MATATUA
ARAWAK ARUA BARE URAN ARAUA
BAURE CAMPA CHANE GUANA INERI
SIUSI BAINOA BANIVA GUINAU
IGNERI GOAJIRO IPURINA CAQUETIO
CUSTENAU
ARBITER JUDGE CRITIC ODDMAN
UMPIRE ADVISER DAYSMAN
ODDSMAN OVERMAN REFEREE
DICTATOR STICKLER
ARBITRAGE SHUNTING
ARBITRARY SEVERE THETIC
WILLFUL ABSOLUTE DESPOTIC
MASTERLY
(**NOT** —) FREE
ARBITRATE DECIDE MEDIATE
ARBITRATION DAYMENT
ARBITRATOR REF JUDGE UMPIRE
ARBITER MUNSIFF REFEREE
MEDIATOR
ARBOR BAR AXLE BEAM ABODE
BOWER SHAFT STAFF STALK TRAIL
ARBOUR BOWERY GARDEN HERBER
PANDAL RAMADA VOIDER BERCEAU
HARBOUR MANDREL MANDRIL
ORCHARD PERGOLA RETREAT
SPINDLE TRELLIS FRESCADE
TONNELLE
ARBORVITAE AKEKI
ARBUTUS IVY
ARC BOW ARCH BEND FOIL HALO
CURVE HANCE ORBIT SPARK SWING

FOGBOW FOLIUM OCTANT RADIAN
COMPASS RAINBOW FROSTBOW
(— OF HORIZON) AZIMUTH
AMPLITUDE
(ELECTRIC —) SPARK
ARCA BOX CHEST PATEN ARCULA
ARCADE ORB AVENUE LOGGIA
STREET GALLERY PORTICO
ARCATURE CLOISTER
ARCANE HIDDEN SECRET
ARCH ARC BOW COY SET SLY BACK
BEND COPE COVE DOME HARP
HOOP IRIS LEER OGEE PASS PEND
PERT SPAN ARCUS CHIEF CURVE
FAULD GREAT HANCE HUNCH
INBOW JOWEL OGIVE PAUKY PAWKY
POKEY PRIME ROACH SAUCY
SWEEP VAULT ARCADE BRIDGE
CALCAR CAMBER CLEVER DIADEM
FOGBOW FORNIX GIRDLE IMPISH
INVERT LANCET MANTEL SPRING
SUNBOW WICKET ZYGOMA
ARCHWAY CUNNING EMINENT
GATEWAY ROGUISH SEGMENT
SQUINCH SUPPORT TESTUDO
TRIUMPH WAGGISH ALVEOLAR
FOGEATER OVERCAST
(— OF SKY) FIRMAMENT
(DENTAL —) ARCADE
(LOGGING —) SULKY
(PL.) SUBARCUATION
ARCHAEOCYTE SORITE
ARCHAEOLOGIST POTHUNTER
ARCHAIC OLD ANCIENT ANTIQUE
HISTORIC OBSOLETE
ARCHANGEL SATAN URIEL GABRIEL
MICHAEL RAPHAEL
ARCHBISHOP HATTO PRELATE
PRIMATE ORDINARY
ARCHDEMON BELFAGOR BELFAZOR
ARCHDIOCESE EPARCHY
ARCHDUKE ERZHERZOG
ARCHED ARCHY CONVEX EMBOWED
VAULTED HOOPLIKE
(— IN) CONCAVE
ARCHEGONIUM CALYPTRA
OOANGIUM
ARCHEMORUS (FATHER OF —)
LYCURGUS
(MOTHER OF —) EURYDICE
(NURSE OF —) HYPSIPYLE
ARCHER BOW CLIM CLYM BOWER
BUTTY CUPID ROVER BOWBOY
BOWMAN BOWYER SHOOTER
(EQUIPMENT OF —) TACKLE
ARCHERY TOXOLOGY ARTILLERY
(— SPACE) PETTICOAT
ARCHETYPE IDEA MODEL FIGURE
SAMPLE ESSENCE EXAMPLE
PARAGON PATTERN EXEMPLAR
FRAVASHI ORIGINAL
ARCHIL CORKE CORCIR CORKER
PERSIS CUDBEAR LECANORA
ORCHILLA ORSEILLE
ARCHING CAMBER
ARCHITECT MAKER ARTIST ARTISAN
BUILDER CREATOR PLANNER
BEZALEEL DESIGNER SURVEYOR
ARCHITECTURAL TECTONIC
OECODOMIC

ARCHITECTURE DRAVIDA
ARCHITRAVE EPISTYLE PLATBAND
ARCHIVES TABULARY TABULARIUM
ARCHIVOLT RING ARCHBAND
HEADBAND
ARCHLUTE THEORBO
ARCHON RULER DIRECTOR OFFICIAL
ARCHWAY ARCH PEND ARCUS
PAILOO PAILOU
ARC LAMP MONOPHOTE
ARCOGRAPH BOW
ARCO SALTANDO SPICCATO
ARCTIC ICY COLD COOL GELID
POLAR BOREAL CHILLY FRIGID
GALOSH NORTHERN OVERSHOE
ARCTIUM LAPPA
ARCTOID URSINE
ARDENT HOT AVID FOND KEEN LIVE
WARM EAGER FIERY GLEDY RETHE
SHARP ABLAZE FERVID FIERCE
IGNITE STRONG TORRID AMOROUS
BURNING CORDIAL DEVOTED
EARNEST FEELING FERVENT
FLAMING FORWARD GLOWING
INTENSE SHINING ZEALOUS
DESIROUS EMPRESSE FEVERISH
FLAGRANT SANGUINE SCALDING
SPORTIVE VEHEMENT
ARDOR DASH EDGE ELAN FIRE
GLOW HEAT LOVE ZEST ESTRO
FLAME GUSTO HEART TAPAS VERVE
WRATH DESIRE FERVOR FOUGUE
METTLE SPIRIT SPLEEN WARMTH
ARDENCY EARNEST ENTRAIN
PASSION DEVOTION FEROCITY
VIOLENCE VIVACITY
ARDUOUS HARD LOFTY STEEP STIFF
SEVERE TRYING ONEROUS
EXACTING TIRESOME TOILSOME
ARE MU RE AIR ARN ARUN HARE
AREA BELT SIZE TREF ZONE BASIN
COAST COURT FIELD RANGE REALM
SCENE SCOPE SPACE TRACT
ACCENT AREOLA EXTENT GROUND
LOCALE MOARIA REGION SECTOR
SPHERE SPREAD VOLUME ACREAGE
AMENITY AREAWAY CIRCUIT
COMPASS COUNTRY ENVIRON
EXPANSE KINGDOM PURLIEU
SURFACE CAPACITY DISTRICT
ENCEINTE PROVINCE
(— AT INTERSECTION) CIRCUS
(— BETWEEN FILLETS) CANALIS
(— IN CARTOON) BALLOON
(— IN HOSTILE TERRITORY)
AIRHEAD
(— OF EXPERIENCE) BOOK
(— OF FLAG) CANTON
(— OF OLDER LAND) KIPUKA
(— OF RIDGES) BILO
(— OF TIMBERLAND) CHENA
(— ON MOON) MARE WANE
(— UNIT) TAN YOKE LABOR
VIRGATE PLETHRON PLOWGANG
PLOWGATE
(BLANK —) BITE HOLE
(COMBAT —) GLACIS
(CULTURAL —) HORIZON
(CURLING —) PARISH

(DENUDED —) BURN
(DIKED —) SLUSHPIT
(ELONGATED —) BELT
(ENCLOSED —) FOLD SEPT
(FENCED —) CAGE COMPOUND
(FERTILE —) HAMMOCK
(FLOORING —) SQUARE
(FORTIFIED —) BASTION ENCIENTE
(GATHERING —) MANDAPA
(HUNTING —) SURROUND
(INFESTED —) FLYBELT
(LOW-LYING —) GLADE SWALE
COULEE COULIE GUTTER
(LUMINOUS —) AUREOLA AUREOLE
(MINE —) SQUEEZE
(NUCLEAR —) HEARTH ECUMENE
(OPEN —) COURT LAUND CAMPUS
SQUARE HAGGARD
(OVERGROWN —) COGONAL
(PASTURE —) SOUM
(PAVED —) CAUSEY
(PLOWED —) BREAK
(RESIDENTIAL —) BANLIEU
BANLIEUE
(SLUM —) STEW
(SMALL —) AREOLA
(SMOKING —) BULLPEN
(STERN —) AFTERPART
(SUBURBAN —) ADDITION
FAUBOURG
(SUNKEN —) SAG
(SWAMPY —) SLASH
(TEST —) MILACRE
(TIDAL —) CLAMFLAT
(TRANSITION —) ECOTONE
(TREELESS —) SLICK
(TUMID —) CERE
(UNCLEARED —) BUSH
(VOLCANIC —) SOLFATARA
(WASTE —) FOREST
(WOODED —) HAG BOSK BOSQUE
ARECA ARAK ARCHA BETEL
ARENA AREA LIST OVAL RING RINK
COURT FIELD SCENE SCOPE SPACE
STAGE CIRCUS REGION SPHERE
COCKPIT STADIUM TERRAIN
THEATER BULLRING
ARENACEOUS SANDY GRITTY
SABULOUS
AREOLA PIT AREA RING SPOT SPACE
ARES MARS ENYALIUS GRADIVUS
QUIRINUS
(FATHER OF —) ZEUS JUPITER
(MOTHER OF —) ENYO HERA JUNO
(SON OF —) REMUS CYENUS
ROMULUS
ARGALA STORK MARABOU
ARGALI AMMON ARKAR AOUDAD
ARGAN IRONWOOD
ARGENT LUNA MOON PEARL WHITE
BLANCH SILVER CRYSTAL SHINING
SILVERY

ARGENTINA
CAPITAL: BUENOSAIRES
COIN: PESO CENTAVO ARGENTINO
DANCE: TANGO CUANDO GAUCHO
FALLS: GRANDE IGUAZU

INDIAN: LULE GUARANI
LAKE: VIEDMA CARDIEL FAGNANO
  MUSTERS
MEASURE: SINO VARA LEGUA
  CUADRA FANEGA LASTRE
  MANZANA
MOUNTAIN: TORO ANDES CHATO
  LAUDO POTRO CONICO PISSIS
  RINCON FAMATINA MURALLON
  OLIVARES TRONADOR ZAPALERI
  ACONCAGUA
PLAIN: PAMPA PAMPAS
PORT: ROSARIO
PROVINCE: CHACO JUJUY SALTA
  CHUBUT CORDOBA FORMOSA
  LARIOJA MENDOZA NEUQUEN
  TUCUMAN MISIONES PATAGONIA
REGION: CHACO PATAGONIA
RIVER: SALI ATUEL CHICO COYLE
  DULCE LIMAY NEGRO PLATA
  TEUCO BLANCO CHUBUT
  CUARTO FLORES GRANDE
  PARANA QUINTO SALADO
  BERMEJO DESEADO MENDOZA
  TERCERO TUNUYAN SENGUERR
TOWN: AZUL GOYA ORAN PUAN
  BAHIA JUNIN LANUS LUJAN
  METAN SALTA PARANA RUFINO
  ZARATE BOLIVAR CORDOBA
  DOLORES FORMOSA LABANDA
  MENDOZA POSADAS RAFAELA
  ROSARIO TUCUMAN
VOLCANO: LANIN MAIPO DOMUYO
  PETEROA
WEIGHT: LAST GRANO LIBRA
  QUINTAL TONELADA

ARGIL CLAY ALUMINA
ARGOL TARTAR
ARGOSY SHIP GALLEON RAGUSYE
ARGOT CANT FLASH LINGO SLANG
  JARGON PATOIS DIALECT
ARGUE JAW ARGY CHOP FUSS MEAN
  MOOT MOVE SPAR WORD ARGIE
  CAVIL ORATE PLEAD PROVE TREAT
  ACCUSE ADDUCE CAFFLE DEBATE
  EVINCE HASSLE REASON ARRAIGN
  CONTEND CONTEST COUNTER
  DISCUSS DISPUTE WRANGLE
  ERGOTIZE INDICATE MAINTAIN
  PERSUADE QUESTION TRAVERSE
  (— **DEDUCTIVELY)** SYLLOGIZE
  (— **SUBTLY)** DISTINGUISH
ARGUER JAW
ARGUMENT ROW AGON BEEF BLUE
  CASE FUSS MOOT PLEA SPAR TEXT
  CLASH DEBAT INDEX KNIFE LEMMA
  PROOF THEME TOPIC BARNEY
  COMBAT DEBATE DUSTUP ELENCH
  HASSLE MATTER TUSSLE APAGOGE
  CLAMPER DEFENCE DEFENSE
  DILEMMA DISPUTE ESSENCE
  FLUBDUB POLEMIC RHUBARB
  SOPHISM SUMMARY ABSTRACT
  CLINCHER COURSING EVIDENCE
  SPARRING TRILEMMA
  (**INVALID —)** SOPHISM
ARGUMENTATION DEBATE DISPUTE
  ERGOTISM

ARGUMENTATIVE ERISTIC FRATCHY
  FORENSIC
ARGUSFISH SCAT
ARHAT MONK LOHAN RAKAN SAINT
  ARAHANT
ARIA AIR SOLO SONG TUNE MELODY
  SORTIE ARIETTA ARIETTE SORTITA
ARIADNE (FATHER OF —) MINOS
  (**HUSBAND OF —)** THESEUS
  (**MOTHER OF —)** PASIPHAE
ARIAN AGNOETE AGNOITE HOMOEAN
  ANOMOIAN EUSEBIAN
ARID DRY BALD BARE DULL LEAN
  BARREN DESERT JEJUNE MEAGER
  DROUTHY PARCHED STERILE
  THIRSTY DROUGHTY WITHERED
ARIDITY DROUTH DROUGHT SICCITY
ARIKARA REE
ARIL POD ARILLUS COATING
  ARILLODE
ARISE WAX COME FLOW FORM
  GROW LIFT REAR RISE SOAR STEM
  AWAKE BEGIN BUILD EXIST ISSUE
  MOUNT RAISE SPRAY STAND START
  SURGE TOWER WAKEN ACCRUE
  AMOUNT APPEAR ASCEND ATTAIN
  DERIVE EMERGE HAPPEN KITTLE
  SPRING DEVELOP EMANATE
  EXSURGE PROCEED REDOUND
  SOURDRE
ARISING LEVEE EMERGENT
ARISTOCRACY CLASS ELITE
  GENTRY ARISTOI SAMURAI NOBILITY
  OPTIMACY
ARISTOCRAT LORD NOBLE ARISTO
  GRANDEE PARVENU EUPATRID
  OPTIMATE
  (**PL.)** ARISTOI
ARISTOCRATIC HIGH TONY NOBLE
  QUALITY CAVALIER
ARISTOTELIAN PERIPATETIC
ARITHMETIC SUM AUGRIM
  ALGORISM
ARITHMOMETER MULTIPLIER

ARIZONA
CAPITAL: PHOENIX
COUNTY: GILA PIMA YUMA PINAL
  APACHE MOHAVE NAVAJO
  COCHISE COCONINO MARICOPA
INDIAN: HOPI PIMA YUMA NAVAHO
  NAVAJO PAPAGO HUALAPAI
MOUNTAIN: BANGS GROOM
  LEMMON TURRET PASTORA
  HUALAPAI MERIDIAN
MOUNTAIN RANGE: GILA KOFA
  MOHAWK GALIURO AQUARIUS
  BUCKSKIN HUALAPAI
STATE BIRD: CACTUSWREN
STATE FLOWER: SAGUARO
STATE NICKNAME: OCOTILLO
STATE TREE: PALOVERDE
RIVER: GILA SALT ZUNI VERDE
  PUERCO COLORADO
TOWN: AJO ELOY MESA NACO
  YUMA GLOBE LEUPP TEMPE
  BISBEE MCNARY SALOME
  TOLTEC TUCSON CORTARO

KINGMAN MORENCI NOGALES
SAFFORD FREDONIA

ARJUN KUMBUK
ARK BIN BOX BOAT SHIP BARGE
  CHEST HUTCH BASKET COFFER
  REFUGE WANGAN RETREAT
  SHELTER WANIGAN FLATBOAT
ARKANSAN ARKANSAWYER

ARKANSAS
CAPITAL: LITTLEROCK
COUNTY: CLAY DREW PIKE POLK
  POPE YELL CROSS DESHA
  IZARD SHARP STONE BAXTER
INDIAN: CADDO OSAGE QUAPAW
  CHOCTAW CHEROKEE
LAKE: CONWAY NIMROD GREESON
  NORFORK OUACHITA
MOUNTAIN: GAYLOR MAGAZINE
MOUNTAIN RANGE: OZARK
  OUACHITA
NATIVE: TOOTHPICK
RIVER: WHITE SALINE BUFFALO
  CURRENT COSSATOT OUACHITA
STATE BIRD: MOCKINGBIRD
STATE FLOWER: APPLEBLOSSOM
STATE TREE: SHORTLEAFPINE
TOWN: COY CUY KEO OLA ROE
  ULM ALMA BONO CASA DELL
  DIAZ MORO ENOLA PERLA
  RONDO ALICIA

ARKOSE ARENITE SANDSTONE
ARM FIN OAR TOE BOOM HEEL LIMB
  WING BLADE BOUGH CRANE EQUIP
  FENCE FIORD FIRTH FJORD FORCE
  GARDY INLET MIGHT OXTER POWER
  RIFLE SNORD STOCK BRANCH
  CRUTCH ENERGY FRETUM GIBBET
  MEMBER OUTFIT PINION RADIAL
  SLEEVE TAPPET WEAPON CATCHER
  DERRICK DRAWARM FLIPPER
  FOREARM FORTIFY FURNISH
  GARNISH HARNESS OCKSTER
  PREPARE PROTECT PROVIDE
  QUILLON SUPPORT ARMORIAL
  CROSSARM FOLLOWER FORELIMB
  PULLDOWN SOUPBONE STRENGTH
  TRANSEPT
  (— **HOLDING FLINT)** HAMMER
  (— **OF BARNACLE)** CIRRUS CIRRHUS
  (— **OF CHAIR)** ELBOW
  (— **OF CRANE)** JIB GIBBET
  RAMHEAD
  (— **OF GIN)** START
  (— **OF PROPELLER)** BLADE
  (— **OF SEA)** COVE FLOW MEER
  MERE BRACE CANAL FIRTH FRITH
  GRAIN FRETUM ESTUARY
  (— **OF SPINNING MULE)** SICKLE
  (— **OF WINDMILL)** VANE WHIP
  (— **WITH GAFF)** HEEL
  (**IRON —)** CRANE
  (**LEVER —)** SWEEP NIGGER
  (**PITCHING —)** SOUPBONE
  (**PL.)** ARMORY ARMAMENT

ARMADA NAVY FLEET FLOTILLA

ARMADILLO APAR PEBA TATU
APARA POYOU TATOU BOLITA
MATACO MATICO MULITA PELUDO
TATOUAY TATUASU EDENTATE
KABASSOU LORICATE PANGOLIN

ARMAMENT ARMADA BATTERY

ARMATURE ARMING KEEPER LIFTER

ARMBAND BRASSARD

ARMCHAIR BERGERE FAUTEUIL

ARMED FLUTE HEELED DAGGERED
WEAPONED

ARMENIA

ANCIENT CAPITAL: ANI ARTASHAT
ARTAXATA
CAPITAL: ERIVAN
FORTRESS: EREBUNI
HERO: ARA ARAM HAIK ARAME
VARTAN
KING: ASHOT GAGIK TRDAT
ZAREH DIKRAN ARTAKIAS
ARTASHES TIGRANES ZARIADES
KINGDOM: URARTU VANNIC
CILICIA SOPHENE ARDSRUNI
LAKE: VAN SEVAN URMIA
MOUNTAIN: ARA ALAGEZ ARARAT
TAURUS ALADAGH ARAGATS
KARABAKH
NATIVE: ARMEN GOMER
RIVER: KUR ARAS KURA ARAKS
CYRUS HALYS ZANGA ARAXES
RAZDAN TIGRIS EUPHRATES
SAINT: SAHAK MESROP
TOWN: VAN SIVAS BITLIS EREVAN
ERIVAN ERZURUM TRABZON
YEREVAN

ARMENIAN ERMYN HADJI

ARMFUL LOCK YAFFLE

ARMHOLE MAIL SCYE OXTER
ARMSCYE ARMSEYE ARMSIZE

ARMISTICE LULL PEACE TRUCE
INDUCIAE

ARMLET TABLET TORQUE ARMHOOP

ARMOR (AND SPECIFIC PIECES
THEREOF) ARMS BACK BOOT EGIS
JAMB MAIL TACE WEED ACTON
AMURE BARDS BRACE CUISH CULET
DORON GUARD GUIGE JAMBE PIECE
PLATE PROOF SCALE STEEL TAPUL
TASSE TRUSS ARMLET ARMOUR
BEAVER BRINIE BRUNIE BYRNIE
CAMAIL CORIUM COUTER CRANET
CUISSE GORGET GRAITH GREAVE
JAMBER POLEYN RONDEL SECRET
SHIELD TASSET THORAX TONLET
TUILLE VOIDER AILETTE ARMHOOP
BESAGNE BROIGNE CORSLET
CUIRASS DEFENSE EPAULET
HARNESS HAUBERK JAZERAN
KNEELET LAMBOYS PANOPLY
PAUDRON PLACATE POITREL
REREDOS ROUNDEL SABATON
VENTAIL RAMENTUM VAMBRACE
(— **ON TREE**) TROPHY
(— **PLATE**) TUILLE
(**ELBOW** —) CUBITIERE

(**FOOT** —) SABATON SABBATON
SOLLERET
(**HEAD** —) CASQUE HELMET PALLET
SCONCE
(**HORSE** —) BARB BARD BARDE
CRINET CRINIERE
(**LEATHER** —) CORIUM
(**LEG** —) BOOT JAMB CUISH JAMBE
CUISSE GREAVE JAMBER TUILLE
JAMBEAU
(**NECK** —) COLLAR GORGET
(**PADDED** —) GAMBESON
(**SUIT OF** —) CAST STAND

ARMOR-BEARER SQUIRE ARMIGER
CUSTREL

ARMORED PANZER

ARMORER GUNSMITH ARTIFICER

ARMORICAN BRETON

ARMORY HERALDRY

ARMPIT ALA OXTER AXILLA
ARMHOLE

ARMS TACKLE

ARMY FERD HERE HOST IMPI LEVY
MAIN ARRAY CROWD FORCE HERSE
HORDE POWER RANKS ZOMBI
COHORT HONVED LEGION NUMBER
THRONG TROOPS MILITIA CHIVALRY
MILITARY
(**HOSTILE** —) FOE
(**PL.**) SABAOTH

ARMYWORM GRASSWORM

AROID APII ARAD TARO APIUM KRUBI
TANIA KONJAK TANIER YAUTIA
PINUELA CALADIUM CUNJEVOI
MOCOMOCO

AROMA NOSE ODOR NIDOR SAVOR
SCENT SMELL SNUFF SPICE FLAVOR
BOUQUET PERFUME
(— **OF WINE**) BLOOM

AROMATIC BALMY SPICY SWEET
MASTIC ODOROUS PIQUANT
PUNGENT FRAGRANT REDOLENT
SPICEFUL

AROUND NEAR UMBE ABOUT CIRCA
CIRCUM ENVIRON

AROUSAL INDUCTION

AROUSE SOW CALL CITE FIRE GAIN
HEAT MOVE REAR SPUR STIR WAKE
WHET ADAWE ALARM ALERT AWAKE
EVOKE FLESH PIQUE RAISE RALLY
ROUSE ROUST SHAKE STEER
WAKEN ABRAID AWAKEN ELICIT
EXCITE FOMENT INCITE INDUCE
KINDLE REVIVE SUMMON THRILL
ACTUATE AGITATE CONNOTE
INCENSE INFLAME INSPIRE
PROVOKE SUGGEST INSPIRIT
(— **DISPLEASURE**) AGGRAVATE
(— **ENMITY**) ESTRANGE
(— **WRATH**) SPLEEN

ARPEGGIO SWEEP ROULADE
FLOURISH
(— **EFFECT**) RASGADO

ARRACACHA APIO ARRA

ARRACK ARAK RACK ARAKI
RACKAPEE

ARRAIGN TRY CITE ARGUE PEACH
ACCUSE CHARGE IMPUTE INDICT
INDITE SUMMON APPOINT IMPEACH
DENOUNCE

ARRANGE DO FIX LAY RAY SET
CAST COMB EDIT FILE FORM PLAN
PLAT RAIL RULE SIDE SIZE SORT
TIER TIFT WORK ADAPT AGREE
ALIGN ALINE ARRAY BESEE CURRY
DRAPE DRESS ETTLE FANCY FRAME
GRADE RANGE SCORE SHAPE SHIFT
SPACE STALL TRICK ADJUST
BRANCH CODIFY DAIKER DESIGN
DEVISE FETTLE INFORM ORDAIN
SETTLE SOLUTE TAILYE ADDRESS
APPOINT BESPEAK CATALOG
COLLATE COMPONE COMPOSE
CONCERT DISPOSE ENRANGE
GRADATE MARSHAL PERMUTE
PREPARE REDRESS SERIATE
TAILZEE TAILZIE ALPHABET
CLASSIFY CONCLUDE ORGANIZE
REGULATE TABULATE
(— **BEFOREHAND**) FORLAY FORELAY
(— **FANTASTICALLY**) HARLEQUINIZE
(— **FASTIDIOUSLY**) PREEN
(— **HAIR**) SET TED COIF TRUSS
COIFFE
(— **HARMONIOUSLY**) GRADATE
(— **IN FLOCKS**) HIRSEL HIRSLE
(— **IN FOLDS**) DRAPE
(— **IN LAYERS**) DESS TIER
(— **IN ROW**) RACE
(— **STRAW**) HAULM
(— **SYSTEMATICALLY**) DIGEST
(— **WITH BEST AT TOP**) DEACON

ARRANGEMENT FIX FLY LAY RAY
DEAL FLOW PLAT RANK TIFF ARRAY
BUILD DRAPE INDEX ORDER SETUP
BORDER DESIGN HOOKUP LAYOUT
SCHEME SETOUT SYNTAX SYSTEM
TREATY BLEEDER INTERIM POSTURE
TONTINE ATTITUDE CONTRACT
DISPOSAL GROUPING POSITURE
SEQUENCE
(— **IN LOCK**) DETECTOR
(— **OF BRISTLES**) CHAETOTAXY
(— **OF CHESS PAWNS**) CHAIN
(— **OF DRAPERIES**) CAST
(— **OF FLOWERS**) CASCADE
CORSAGE
(— **OF GRADES**) CURVE
(— **OF GUNS**) ARMADA
(— **OF HAIRDO**) FORETOP
(— **OF HAIRS**) SCOPA
(— **OF HOOKS**) GIG
(— **OF LOOM BARS**) GRIFF GRIFFE
(— **OF ROCKS**) BEDDING
(— **OF TACKLE**) BURTON
(— **OF TIMBER**) ANCHOR
(— **OF TROOPS**) ECHELON
(**CIRCULAR** —) CYCLE
(**DISHONEST** —) CROSS
(**GEOMETRICAL** —) LATTICE
(**TRADITIONAL** —) AKOLUTHIA
AKOLOUTHIA

ARRANGING ORDONNANT

ARRANT BAD THIEF OUTLAW
ROBBER VAGRANT PRECIOUS
RASCALLY

ARRAS ORRIS ARISTE DRAPERY
TAPESTRY

ARRASTRA TAHONA

ARRAU JURARA
ARRAY DON DUB FIG ARMY BUSK
DECK DOLL FYRD GALA GARB HOST
POMP RAIL RANK ROBE VEST
ADORN ALIGN ALINE ATOUR DRESS
EQUIP HABIT HARKA HEDGE ORDER
ADIGHT AGUISE ATTIRE ATTRAP
BEDECK CLOTHE DEVISE FETTLE
FINERY GRAITH INVEST MUSTER
PLIGHT SERIES SETOUT SHROUD
ADDRESS AFFAITE AFFLICT
APPAREL ARRANGE BATTERY
BEDIGHT COMPANY DISPLAY
DISPOSE ENVELOP FURNISH
FYRDUNG MARSHAL PANOPLY
REPAREL ACCOUTER
(— **OF CHEMICALS**) ARA
(— **OF GUNS**) BROADSIDE
(— **OF TROOPS**) PAREL
(— **OF WEAPONS**) ARMORY
(— **TASTELESSLY**) DAUB
(**BATTLE** —) ACIES HERSE BATTALIA
ARRAYED HABITED ABULYEIT
ARREAR DEBT BEHIND UNPAID
ARRIERE
(**IN** —**S**) BACK BEHIND
ARREST CAP COP FIX FOB LAG NAB
NIP VAG BALK CURB FALL GLOM
GRAB HALT HOLD JAIL KEEP NAIL
NICK PULL REST SHOP SIST STAY
STOP ARRET CATCH CHECK DELAY
PINCH REEST SEIZE STILL STUNT
ATTACH BRIDLE COLLAR DECREE
DETAIN ENGAGE FINGER HINDER
PLEDGE RETARD SLOUGH SNEEZE
THWART CAPTION CAPTURE
CUSTODY SUSPEND IMPRISON
OBSTRUCT RESTRAIN
(— **OF BLEEDING**) HEMOSTASIS
(— **OF DEVELOPMENT**) ABORTION
ARRESTER (**SPARK** —) BONNET
ARRESTING BOLD SEIZING
MAGNETIC PLEASING STRIKING
ARRET EDICT ARREST DECREE
DECISION JUDGMENT
ARRHA HANDGELD
ARRIS PIEN ANGLE PIEND ARRIDGE
ARRIVAL COMER IKBAL VENUE
ADVENT COMING INCOMING
REACHING
(— **TIME RECORD**) OS
ARRIVE GO SEY COME FALL FLOW
GAIN LAND LEND RIVE LIGHT
OCCUR REACH WORTH APPEAR
ATTAIN HAPPEN OBTAIN UPCOME
COMPASS
(— **AT**) GET HIT FIND GAIN HENT
MAKE BRING EDUCE FETCH GUESS
SEIZE ATTAIN DERIVE ESTIMATE
ARRIVED-IN DONE
ARROBA ROVE
ARROGANCE PRIDE SWANK TUMOR
BOWWOW HUBRIS BOBANCE
CONCEIT DISDAIN EGOTISM
HAUTEUR STOMACH BOLDNESS
SUCCUDRY SURQUIDY
ARROGANT BOLD COXY HIGH MOOD
COCKY GREAT HUFFY JOLLY LOFTY
PROUD STOUT SURLY WLONK

ASSUME FIERCE LORDLY UPPISH
UPPITY WANTON FORWARD
FROSTED HAUGHTY HAUTAIN
HUFFISH STATELY TOPPING
AFFECTED ASSUMING CAVALIER
FASTUOUS IMPUDENT SNUFFING
SUPERIOR TUMOROUS
ARROGATE GRAB TAKE CLAIM SEIZE
USURP ASSUME ADROGATE
ARROW FLO PIN ROD SEL BOLT
DART REED SELF SELL SHOT VIRE
BLUNT DEATH FLANE ROVER SHAFT
ARCHER FLIGHT GANYLE GARROT
QUARRY SPRITE TACKLE WEAPON
BOBTAIL DOGBOLT MISSILE
POINTER PROJECT QUARREL
SAGITTA SPINNER FISHTAIL
FORKHEAD
(— **ARUM**) TUCKAHOE
(— **IN GRASS**) GREEN SNAKE
(— **IN LEG OF STAND**) FOOT
(**FIRE** —) MALLEOLUS
(**POISONED** —) DERRID SUMPIT
(**WOBBLING** —) FISHTAIL
ARROWHEAD BUNT FORK HEAD
PILE FLUKE POINT NEOLITH
ARTIFACT CROWBILL FORKHEAD
SPICULUM
ARROWROOT PIA ARUM MUSA SAGU
ARARU CANNA TACCA TIKOR
ARARAO CURCUMA
ARROWWORM SAGITTA
CHAETOGNATH
ARROYO DRAW BROOK CREEK
GULCH GULLY HONDO ZANJA
RAVINE STREAM CHANNEL
BARRANCA BARRANCO
ARSENAL ARMORY SUPPLY
MAGAZINE
ARSHIN ARCHIN ALTSCHIN
(**ONE-24TH OF** —) PARMAK
PARMACK
ARSIS BEAT ICTUS ACCENT RHYTHM
UPBEAT DOWNBEAT
ARSON FIRE CRIME FELONY
BURNING
ARSONIST ARSONITE
ARSPHENAMINE SIX SALVARSAN
ART WILE CRAFT KNACK KUNST
MAGIC SKILL TRADE MISTER
TECHNE ARTWORK CALLING
CUNNING DESCANT DISCANT
FACULTY FINESSE MYSTERY
SCIENCE APTITUDE ARTIFICE
BUSINESS LEARNING PRACTICE
PRACTISE
(— **OF APPLYING TESTS**) DOCIMASY
(— **OF BLAZONING**) ARMORY
(— **OF CALCULATING**) ALGORISM
ALGORITHM
(— **OF DEFENSE**) SKIRMISH
(— **OF HEALING**) LEECHCRAFT
(— **OF HORSEMANSHIP**) MANEGE
(— **OF SPEECH**) RHETORIC
(**DIABOLIC** —) DEVILRY DEVILTRY
(**DRAMATIC** —) STAGE
(**LEG** —) CHEESECAKE
(**MAGIC** —) WITHERCRAFT
(**MYSTERIOUS** —) CABALA KABALA

CABBALA KABBALA QABBALA
CABBALAH KABBALAH QABBALAH
(**OCCULT** —) THEURGY
(**SHODDY** —) BONDIEUSERIE
ARTEMIS UPIS DELIA DIANA PHOEBE
CYNTHIA AMARYSIA
ARTERY WAY PATH ROAD AORTA
PULSE ROUTE COURSE DENTAL
FACIAL RADIAL STREET VESSEL
ANONYMA CAROTID COELIAC
CONDUIT HIGHWAY SCIATIC
VAGINAL CEREBRAL CERVICAL
CORONARY DORSALIS EMULGENT
PROFUNDA
ARTFUL APT FLY SLY FOXY WILY
AGILE CRATY DOWNY SUAVE
ADROIT CLEVER FACILE QUAINT
SCHEMY SHREWD SMOOTH TRICKY
CROOKED CUNNING KNOWING
PLAITED POLITIC PRACTIC SUBTILE
VULPINE DEXTROUS SCHEMING
STEALTHY
ARTFULNESS ARTIFICE SUBTLETY
ARTHRITIS GOUT CARPITIS
ARTHROPOD GOLACH GOLOCH
SPIDER CHILOPOD DIPLOPOD
ARTICHOKE BUR CANADA CYNARA
CHOROGI CROSNES KNOTROOT
ARTICLE AN YE LOT ONE THE BOOK
ITEM TERM BRIEF CHEAT ESSAY
GEANE PAPER PIECE PLANK POINT
STORY THEME THING CLAUSE
DETAIL LEADER NOTICE OBJECT
REPORT FEATURE BROCHURE
CAUSERIE DOCTRINE POSTFACE
TREATISE
(— **OF CLOTHING**) DUD DIDO APRON
CLOUT DICKY FANCY THING CASUAL
DICKEY GARMENT COINTISE
CREATION
(— **OF FOOD**) CATE KNACK
(— **OF FURNITURE**) STICK
(— **OF LITTLE WORTH**) DIDO
(— **OF SILK**) SQUEEZE
(— **OF TRADE**) PADNAG
(— **OF UNUSUAL SIZE**) IMPERIAL
(—**S OF FAITH**) CREDENDA
(—**S OF MERCHANDISE**) CHAFFER
(**CAST-IRON** —**S**) KENTLEDGE
(**CHEAP** —) CAMELOT
(**DECORATIVE** —) LACKER LAQUER
(**FANCY** —) CONCEIT
(**FIVE** —**S**) HAND
(**GENUINE** —) GOODS
(**HANDICRAFT** —) BOONDOGGLE
(**INFERIOR** —**S**) SHODDY
(**METAL** —**S**) BATTERY
(**MISCELLANEOUS** —**S**) SUNDRIES
(**NONDESCRIPT** —) DODAD DOODAB
DOODAD
(**SECONDHAND** —) JUNK
(**SHOWY** —) FRIPPERY
(**VALUABLE** —**S**) SWAG
(**WORTHLESS** —) TRANGAM
ARTICULATE BACK JOIN CLEAR
FRAME JOINT SPEAK UNITE UTTER
VOCAL ACCENT FLUENT VERBAL
EXPRESS JOINTED DISTINCT
ARTICULATED BACK BLADE DENTAL

DORSAL LABIAL JOINTED ALVEOLAR
CEREBRAL
ARTICULATION JOINT VOICE
SUTURE ARTHRON JUNCTURE
SYNTAXIS
(DEFECTIVE —) LALLATION
LAMDACISM
ARTIFACT CELT DISC DISK BATON
GUACA HUACA AMGARN BRONZE
EOLITH FABRIC GORGET REJECT
RONDEL SAGAIE SKEWER ABRADER
ARTEFAC DISCOID RACLOIR
SCRAPER ARTEFACT DATEMARK
RONDELLE TRANCHET
(PL.) CACHE CERAUNIA
ARTIFICE ART GIN JET GAUD HOAX
JOUK PLAN PLOT RUSE TURN WILE
BLIND CHEAT COVIN CRAFT CROCK
CROOK DODGE DRAFT FEINT FETCH
FRAUD GUILE SHIFT SKILL STALL
TRAIN TRICK CAUTEL DECEIT
DEVICE DOUBLE ENGINE COMPASS
CUNNING DODGERY DRAUGHT
EVASION FINESSE SHUFFLE SLEIGHT
COZENAGE DISGUISE DOUBLING
INTRIGUE MANAGERY MANEUVER
PRACTICE PRACTISE PRETENSE
STRATEGY TRICKERY WINDLASS
(PL.) CABAL CRANS
ARTIFICER WRIGHT ARTIFEX
WORKMAN DAEDALUS LAPIDARY
MECHANIC OPIFICER TVASHTAR
TVASHTRI
ARTIFICIAL CUTE SHAM BOGUS
DUMMY FAKED FALSE ARTFUL
ERSATZ FORCED FORGED UNREAL
ASSUMED BASTARD FEIGNED
AFFECTED FABULOUS FALSETTO
POSTICHE POSTIQUE SPURIOUS
(NOT —) REAL NATURAL
(OVERLY —) ALEXANDRIAN
ARTILLERY (OR PIECE THEREOF)
ARMS GUNS DRAKE SAKER CANNON
MINION HEAVIES LANTACA LANTAKA
CANNONRY ORDNANCE
(— FIRE) STONK RAFALE
ARTILLERYMAN GUN GUNNER
LASCAR REDLEG LASHKAR
ENGINEER TOPECHEE
ARTISAN FEVER SMITH ARTIST
COOPER ARTIFEX TARKHAN
WORKMAN KAMMALAN LETTERER
MECHANIC OPIFICER
ARTISANSHIP FOLKCRAFT
ARTIST DAB NABI ACTOR ADEPT
BRUSH HILDA RAPIN DANCER
ETCHER EXPERT FICTOR MASTER
SINGER WIZARD ARTISAN ARTISTE
ARTSMAN FAUVIST OPERANT
PAINTER PONTIST SCHEMER
COLORIST FUSINIST IDEALIST
LADISLAW LETTERER MAGICIAN
MUSICIAN SCULPTOR SKETCHER
STIPPLER
(— SCHOOL) LUMINISM
(SIDEWALK —) SCREEVER
(PL.) SCHOOL
ARTISTIC ARTLY DAEDAL EXPERT
ESTHETIC

(— MATERIAL) KITSCH
(— QUALITY) VERTU VIRTU
ARTISTRY FOLKCRAFT
ARTLESS NAIF OPEN FRANK NAIVE
PLAIN SEELY CANDID RUSTIC
SIMPLE GIRLISH NATURAL
INNOCENT
ARTS TRIVIUM
ARTY CHICHI
ARUM ARAD TARO AROID CALALU
DRAGON TAWKEE WAMPEE
MANDRAKE TUCKAHOE
ARVIRAGUS CADWAL
ARYAN MEDE SLAV NORDIC
(NOT —) ANARYA
AS S SO ALS FOR HOW QUA ALSO
INTO LIKE SOME THAT THUS TILL
WHEN EQUAL QUOAD SINCE WHILE
BRONZE WHENAS BECAUSE
EQUALLY SIMILAR QUATENUS
(— FAR AS) TO INTO QUATENAS
(— IT WERE) FAIRLY
(— LONG AS) SOBEIT
(— MUCH) ALSMEKILL
(— SOON) ALSOON ASTITE ALSWITH
DIRECTLY
(— TO) QUOAD
(— WELL AS) FORBY FORBYE
(— WELL) EVEN
(— YET) HITHERTO
ASAFETIDA HING LASER FERULA
ASARABACCA HAZEL FOALFOOT
ASBESTOS ABBEST XYLITE AMIANTH
ABSISTOS ALBESTON AMIANTUS
WOODROCK
ASCEND UP STY RISE SOAR STYE
UPGO ARISE CLIMB MOUNT SCALE
STAIR TOWER AMOUNT ASPIRE
BREAST CLIMAX UPRISE CLAMBER
UPCLIMB ESCALATE PROGRESS
ASCENDANCY SWAY POWER
CONTROL MASTERY SUCCESS
DOMINION OWERANCE PRESTIGE
ASCENDANT MOUNTANT
ASSURGENT
ASCENDING ANODAL ANODIC
UPHILL UPWARD ANABATIC
ASPIRANT SUBERECT
(— WITHOUT A TURN) FLYING
ASCENSION APOTHEOSIS
ASCENT STY HILL RAMP RISE RIST
UPGO CLIMB GLORY GRADE MOUNT
SCEND SLOPE STEEP STEPS STILL
UPWAY SOURCE STAIRS UPCOME
UPGANG UPHILL UPRISE UPWITH
INCLINE SCALING UPGRADE
UPSWING EMINENCE GRADIENT
ASCERTAIN GET SEE SET TRY FEEL
FIND COUNT GLEAN LEARN PITCH
PROVE ASSURE ATTAIN FIGURE
ANALYSE ANALYZE APPRISE
APPRIZE COMPUTE MEASURE
UNEARTH DISCOVER
ASCETIC NUN MONK SOFI SUFI YATI
YOGI DANDY FAKIR FRIAR SADHU
SOFEE STOIC YOGIN CHASTE
ESSENE HERMIT SADDHU SEVERE
SOOFEE STRICT ADAMITE AUSTERE
BHIKSHU DEVOTEE EREMITE

RECLUSE SRAMANA STYLITE
TAPASVI AVADHUTA MARABOUT
SANNYASI
(PL.) THERAPEUTAE
ASCIDIAN POLYP CUNGEBOI
CUNGEVOI TETHYDAN TUNICATE
ASCIDIUM PITCHER VASCULUM
ASCOCARP ASCOMA
ASCOMA CUPULE
ASCRIBABLE DUE
ASCRIBE LAY ARET EVEN GIVE
BLAME COUNT GUESS IMPLY INFER
PLACE REFER TITLE ACCUSE
ALLEGE ARETTE ASSIGN ATTACH
CHARGE CREDIT IMPUTE PREFER
RECKON RELATE ASCRIVE ENTITLE
ACCREDIT ARROGATE DEDICATE
INSCRIBE INTITULE
ASCRIPTION LAUD CREDIT ADDITION
ASCUS BAG SAC THECA ASCELLUS
ASEA LOST ADDLED ADRIFT
PUZZLED SAILING CONFUSED
ASEXUAL AGAMIC
ASH AS ALS ASE ASS FIG RON COKE
SORB ARTAR ASHEN EMBER FRAIN
ROWAN CINDER CORPSE DOTTEL
DOTTLE WICKEN CLINKER RESIDUE
DOGBERRY FRAXINUS HOOPWOOD
WINETREE
(SILKY —) CEDAR
(PL.) ASE AXAN KELP SOIL ASHEN
VAREC WASTE BREEZE CINDERS
PULVERIN
ASHAMED MEAN NACE NAIS
ABASHED HANGDOG HONTOUS
ASH-COLORED CINEREAL
CINEREOUS
ASHEN WAN GRAY GREY PALE
WAXEN WHITE PALLID GHASTLY
BLANCHED CINEREAL
ASHKOKO CONY DAMAN HYRAX
ASHLAR ASELAR RANGEWORK
ASHORE ACOST ALAND AGROUND
BEACHED STRANDED
ASHTRAY SPITKID SPITKIT
ASHWEED GOUTWEED
ASHUR FEROHER
ASIDE BY BYE OFF AWAY GONE
NEAR PAST AGLEY ALOOF APART
FORBY ASLANT ASTRAY BESIDE
BEYOND BYHAND FORBYE FORTHBY
LATERAL PRIVATE WHISPER
OVERHAND RESERVED SECRETLY
SEPARATE SIDEWISE
ASININE DULL CRASS DENSE INEPT
SILLY ABSURD ASSISH OBTUSE
SIMPLE STUPID DOLTISH FATUOUS
FOOLISH IDIOTIC
ASK BEG SPY SUE FAND PRAY QUIZ
CLAIM CRAVE EXACT FRAYN PLEAD
QUERY SPEAK SPEER SPEIR SPELL
SPERE ADJURE DEMAND DESIRE
EXAMIN EXPECT FRAIST FRAYNE
INVITE BESEECH BESPEAK CONSULT
ENTREAT IMPLORE INQUIRE
REQUEST REQUIRE SOLICIT
PETITION QUESTION
(— ALMS) CANT THIG
(— FOR) BEG BID CRY DUN LAIT

SEEK BESPEAK INQUIRE REQUEST
(— **PAYMENT)** CHARGE
ASKANCE AWRY ASKEW ASKILE
CROOKED SIDEWAYS
ASKEW CAM AGEE ALOP AWRY
AZEW AGLEY AMISS ATILT CRAZY
GLEED ASKANT ASLANT ATWIST
FLOOEY SKEWED ASQUINT
CROOKED OBLIQUE BIASWISE
COCKEYED SIDELING
ASLANT ASIDE SLOPE
ASLEEP DEAD FAST IDLE LATENT
NUMBED DORMANT NAPPING
ASOCIAL EGREGIOUS
ASP ESP ASPIC ASPIDE URAEUS
ASPARAGUS LILY GRASS SPRUE
ASPERGE SPARAGE SPERAGE
(— **GARNISH)** PRINCESS
ASPECT AIR HUE WAY AURA FACE
HAND KIND LEER LOOK MIEN SIDE
VIEW VULT ANGLE COLOR DECIL
FACET GUISE IMAGE NORMA PHASE
SIGHT STAGE TRINE VISOR VIZOR
DECILE FACIES FIGURE GLANCE
MANNER PHASIS REGARD VISAGE
APPAREL BEARING ESSENCE
FEATURE MALEFIC OUTLOOK
RESPECT SEXTILE SHOWING
SPECIES CARRIAGE CONSPECT
FOREHEAD OUTSIGHT PROSPECT
QUINTILE
(— **OF CURVE)** INSIDE
(— **OF EMOTION)** AFFECT
(— **OF MOON)** CRESCENT
(— **OF MUSICAL NUANCES)**
AGOGICS
(**BALEFUL** —) DISASTER
(**CULTURAL** —) EMANATION
(**DETERMINING** —) HEART
(**FACIAL** —) EXPRESSION
(**LANGUAGE** —) DURATIVE
(**PRIMARY** —) HIGHWAY
(**QUARTILE** —) SQUARE
(**SECONDARY** —) BYWAY
ASPEN APS ASP ALAMO NITHER
POPLAR POPPLE QUAKER QUAKING
TREMBLE
ASPER AKCHA AKCHEH OTHMANY
ASPERGILLUM HYSSOP SPRINKLE
STRINKLE
ASPERITY IRE RIGOR ACERBITY
ACRIMONY TARTNESS
ASPERSE SKIT SLUR SPOT ABUSE
DECRY LIBEL SPRAY DEFAME
DEFILE MALIGN REVILE SHOWER
APPEACH BLACKEN DETRACT
LAMPOON SLANDER TARNISH
TRADUCE BESMIRCH FORSPEAK
SPRINKLE
ASPERSION SLUR BAPTISM
CALUMNY INNUENDO
ASPHALT BREA SLIME FILLER
MANJAK BITUMEN CUTBACK
MANJACK BYERLITE UINTAITE
ASPHALTUM CONGO
ASPHODEL KNAVERY AFFODILL
ASPHYXIA APNEA APNOEA
ACROTISM
ASPIC JELLY GELATIN GELATINE
LAVENDER

ASPIRATION GOAL IDEAL DESIRE
RECOIL SIGHTS AMBITION
ASPIRE AIM STY HOPE LONG MINT
RISE SEEK SOAR WISH ETTLE
MOUNT TOWER YEARN ASCEND
ATTAIN DESIRE PRETEND
ASPIRIN FEBRIFUGE
ASPIRING ASPIRANT
ASS DOLT FOOL JADE KHUR MOKE
BURRO CHUMP CUDDY DUNCE
EQUID GUDDA HINNY CUDDIE
DAPPLE DONKEY ONAGER ASINEGO
ASSHEAD JACKASS LONGEAR
MALTESE SOLIPED IMBECILE
(**FEMALE** —) JENNY JENNET
(**MALE** —**S)** JACKSTOCK
(**WILD** —) KIANG KULAN KYANG
KIYAND KOULAN ONAGER HEMIPPE
CHIGETAI GHORKHAR
(**PL.)** JACKSTOCK
ASSAI MANICOLE
ASSAIL WOO BEAT FRAY HOOT JUMP
PELT SAIL ASSAY BESET SHOCK
STONE WHACK WHANG ACCUSE
ATTACK BATTER BICKER BULLET
HURTLE IMPUGN INFEST INSULT
INVADE MALIGN MOLEST OFFEND
RATTLE SAILYE SCATHE STRIKE
ASSAULT ATTEMPT BELABOR
BESEIGE BOMBARD CATCALL
ENFORCE ASSEMBLE TOMAHAWK
ASSAILANT ONSETTER
ASSAM (MOUNTAIN OF —) JAPVO
(**STATE OF** —) KHASI MANIPUR
(**TOWN OF** —) IMPHAL SADIYA
GAUHATI SHILLONG
(**TRIBE OF** —) AO AKA AOR AHOM
GARO NAGA
ASSARACUS (FATHER OF —) TROS
(**SON OF** —) CAPYS
ASSART SART THWAITE
ASSASSIN THAG THUG BRAVE
BRAVO FEDAI FIDAI CUTTLE FIDAWI
KILLER SLAYER RUFFIAN STABBER
TORPEDO HACKSTER MURDERER
SICARIUS
ASSASSINATE KILL SLAY MURDER
REMOVE
ASSASSINATION THUGGEE
ASSAULT BEAT BLOW COSH FRAY
RAID SLUG ABUSE ALARM ASSAY
BRUNT HARRY ONSET POISE POUND
SHOCK SMITE STORM STOUR VENUE
AFFRAY ALARUM ASSAIL ATTACK
BREACH BUFFET CHARGE ENGINE
EXTENT HOLDUP INSULT INVADE
ONFALL STOUND STOUSH THRUST
YOKING ATTEMPT BOMBARD
DESCENT LAMBAST PURSUIT
RUNNING VIOLATE INVASION
OUTBURST
ASSAY RUN SAY TRY TEST ESSAY
PROOF PROVE TOUCH TRIAL ASSAIL
ATTACK EFFORT ANALYZE ATTEMPT
EXAMINE TASTING ANALYSIS
APPRAISE ENDEAVOR ESTIMATE
HARDSHIP
ASSAYER POTDAR TESTER
ASSEMBLAGE ARMY BODY CAMP

CLOT COMA CREW HERD HOST
MASS PACK RUCK BUNCH CHOIR
CROWD DRIFT DROVE FLOCK
GROUP LEVEE POSSE QUIRE SALON
SHOCK SWARM CONVOY GALAXY
HOOKUP RESORT SPREAD SYSTEM
THRONG CIRCUIT CLUSTER
COLLEGE COMPANY COMPLEX
CONVENT CULTURE SOCIETY
STATION STATUTE TABAGIE
ASSEMBLY AUDITORY CONGRESS
MULTIPLE
(— **OF FOSSILS)** COLONY
(— **OF INTEGERS)** IDEAL
(**CONFUSED** —) FARRAGO
ASSEMBLE FIT LAY POD SAM BULK
CALL HERD HOST KNOT MASS MEET
ROUT SAMM AMASS ASAME FLOCK
PIECE RALLY TROOP UNITE COUPLE
GATHER HUDDLE MUSTER SUMMON
COLLATE COLLECT COMPILE
CONVENE CONVOKE RECRUIT
CONGRESS
(— **CARDS)** BUNCH
ASSEMBLER BONDER
ASSEMBLY HUI SUM BAUD BEVY
BOGY DIET DRUM DUMA FEIS HOEY
MALL MOOT RAAD ROUT SEJM
SEYM TING AGORA BOGEY COURT
COVEN CURIA DOUMA FORUM
GROUP JUNTA LEVEE PARTY PRESS
SABHA SETUP SOBOR SYNOD THING
TROOP AENACH AONACH ASSIZE
BOBBIN BUSING CHAPEL COETUS
COVINE GEMOTE MAJLIS PARADE
PLENUM POWWOW SEIMAS SENATE
STEVEN CHAMBER CHAPTER
COLLEGE COMITIA COMMAND
COMPANY CONCION CONSORT
CONVENT COUNCIL DIETINE
EOTATES FOLKMOT HUSTING
LANDTAG MEETING PENSION
SERVICE SESSION SOCIETY
SYNAGOG SYNAXIS TEMPEST
TYNWALD ZEMSTVO AUDIENCE
CONCLAVE CONGRESS ECCLESIA
FOLKMOOT PLACITUM PORTMOTE
PRESENCE SEDERUNT SOBRANJE
TINEWALD TRIBUNAL VOLKSTAG
WARDMOTE
(— **HOUSE)** KASHIM
(— **OF BLESSED)** HEAVEN
(— **OF CONDUCTORS)** BUS
(— **OF WITCHES)** COVEN SABBAT
SABBATH
(**AFTERNOON** —) LEVEE
(**BOY SCOUT** —) JAMBOREE
(**CLOSED** —) CONCLAVE
(**FASTENER** —) SEMS
(**GRENADE** —) BOUCHON
ASSENT AYE BOW NOD YEA YES
AMEN SEAL SENT ADMIT AGREE
GRANT YIELD ACCEDE ACCEPT
ACCORD BELIEF CHORUS COMPLY
CONCUR SUBMIT UNISON APPROVE
CONCEDE CONFESS CONFORM
CONSENT ADHESION SANCTION
SUFFRAGE
ASSERT LAY BRAG SHOW VOICE

AFFIRM ALLEGE ASSURE AVOUCH
DEFEND DEPONE DEPOSE INTEND
INTENT THREAP UPHOLD ADVANCE
BETOKEN CONFIRM CONTEND
DECLARE PROTEST SUPPORT
ADVOCATE CHAMPION CONSTATE
MAINTAIN OUTSTAND POSITIVE
ASSERTION VOW FACT HOTI CLAIM
VOUCH AVERMENT
(BOASTFUL —) JACTATION
(DUBIOUS —) PLINYISM
ASSERTIVE BRASH DOGMATIC
POSITIVE
ASSESS LAY TAX CESS DOOM LEVY
MISE RATE SCOT TOLL CENSE
PRICE TEIND VALUE AFFEER ASSIZE
CHARGE EXTEND IMPOSE SAMPLE
MEASURE APPRAISE ESTIMATE
ASSESSMENT FEE LUG TAX CESS
DUTY LEVY SCOT TOLL CULET
JUMMA PRICE RATAL TITHE WORTH
EXTENT IMPOST PURVEY SURTAX
TARIFF SCUTAGE BRIGBOTE
TAXATION
ASSESSOR JUDGE MUFTI RATER
CESSOR LISTER TASKER AUDITOR
STENTOR TAXATOR
(PL.) FINTADORES
ASSET HONOR GETPENNY PROPERTY
RESOURCE STRENGTH
ASSETS GOODS MEANS MONEY
STOCK CREDIT WEALTH CAPITAL
EFFECTS ACCOUNTS PROPERTY
RESOURCE
ASSEVERATE SAY VOW AVER AVOW
STATE SWEAR AFFIRM ALLEGE
ASSERT ASSURE DECLARE PROTEST
ASSEVERATION VOW OATH
ASSIDUOUS BUSY GREAT ACTIVE
DEVOTED PENIBLE STUDIED
DILIGENT FREQUENT SEDULOUS
STUDIOUS
ASSIGN FIX LET SET CAST CEDE
DEAL DOLE DRAW GIVE METE RATE
SEAL SHOW SIGN ALLOT ALLOW
AWARD DIGHT ENDOW REFER SHIFT
TITLE ADDUCE AFFECT ALLEGE
CHARGE CONVEY DESIGN DIRECT
ENTAIL ORDAIN ACCOUNT APPOINT
ASCRIBE CONSIGN DISPOSE ENTITLE
SPECIFY STATION TRIBUTE
ALLOCATE ANTEDATE DELEGATE
INSCRIBE TRANSFER
(— QUARTERS) BILLET
(— TASK) STINT
ASSIGNATION DATE MEET TRYST
MEETING
ASSIGNMENT DECK DUTY TASK
GRIND STENT STINT TUNCA CESSIO
LESSON CESSION BUSINESS
HOMEWORK
ASSIGNOR CEDOR CEDENS CEDENT
ASSIMILATE MIX ONE FUSE ADAPT
ALTER BLEND LEARN MERGE
ABSORB DIGEST IMBIBE COMPARE
CONCOCT RESEMBLE
ASSIMILATION ECHOISM HOMEOSIS
(— OF FOOD) CONCOCTION
ASSINIBOIN HOHE

ASSIST AID ABET BACK HELP JOIN
AVAIL BOOST COACH FAVOR NURSE
SERVE SPEED STEAD ATTEND
ESCORT PROMPT SECOND SQUIRE
SUCCOR BENEFIT COMFORT
FURTHER RELIEVE SUPPORT
SUSTAIN ADJUVATE BEFRIEND
(— A READER) FESCUE
(— AT) STAY
ASSISTANCE AID ALMS CAST GIFT
HAND HELP LIFT BOOST FAVOR
HEEZE RELIEF REMEDY SUCCOR
SUPPLY ADJUTOR COMFORT
SECOURS SUBSIDY SUPPORT
AUXILIUM EASEMENT GIFFGAFF
LARGESSE
ASSISTANT CAD AIDE ALLY HAND
HELP MAID MATE PUNK SOUS ZANY
CLERK GROOM USHER VALET
AIDANT BUMPER COMMIS CURATE
DEPUTY FLUNKY HELPER LEGATE
SECOND TULTUL YEOMAN ABETTOR
ACOLYTE ADJOINT DOORMAN
DRESSER HOGGLER PADRINO
PARTNER PROVOST RUBBLER
SHIFTER STRIKER SWAMPER
ADJUTANT ADJUVANT FELDSHER
GOMASHTA LECTURER MINISTER
OFFSIDER PARASITE SERVITOR
SIDESMAN SUBPRIOR
(— TO ANIMAL SHOW JUDGE)
STEWARD
(AUCTIONEER'S —) SPOTTER
(DYEING —) CARRIER
(MASON'S —) GOUJAT
(MATADOR'S —) CHULO
(POLICE —) CORPORAL
(SURVEYOR'S —) CHAINMAN
(WAITER'S —) BUSBOY
ASSOCIATE MIX PAL AIDE ALLY
BAND CHUM HERD JOIN LINK MATE
MOOP MOUP PEER WALK WIFE
YOKE BLEND BUDDY CRONY HABER
MATCH TRAIN TROOP ASSORT
ATTACH ATTEND CHABER COHORT
COUSIN FASTEN FELLOW FRIEND
HELPER HOBNOB MARROW MEDDLE
MEMBER MINGLE PUISNE PUISNY
RELATE SOCIUS SPOUSE TRAVEL
ADJUNCT ASSOCIE BRACKET
COALITE COMMUNE COMPANY
COMPEER COMRADE CONNECT
CONSORT HUSBAND PARTNER
PEWMATE SOCIATE CONJOINT
CONVERSE COPEMATE FAMILIAR
FEDERATE FOLLOWER FREQUENT
GADSHILL IDENTIFY INTIMATE
PARTAKER
(— WITH) FRAT MOOP MOUP
(DEMON —) FLY
(PL.) ENTOURAGE
ASSOCIATION HUI BODY BOND
BUND CLUB GILD HONG HUNT TONG
ARTEL BOARD GUILD HANSA HANSE
SANGH TRUCK UNION CARTEL
CERCLE CHAPEL COMITY CONGER
GRANGE LEAGUE LEGION LYCEUM
PLEDGE SANGHA SCHOLA VEREIN
CIRCUIT COMPANY CONSORT

CONTACT CONVENT COUNCIL
SOCIETY SOROSIS SYNOECY
AFFINITY ALLIANCE ASSEMBLY
ATHENEUM CONVERSE HABITUDE
INTIMACY SODALITY SYNOMOSY
TAALBOND
(— OF FOSSILS) FAUNULA FAUNULE
(ANTAGONISTIC —) ANTIBIOSIS
(BOOK-SELLERS' —) CONGER
(CLOSE —) HARNESS INTIMACY
(EMPLOYERS' —) GREMIO
(FARMERS' —) GRANGE
(IN —) ALONG
(LABOR —) ARTEL UNION
(RELIGIOUS —) SAMAJ
(SECRET —) CABAL
(STUDENTS' —) CORPS
ASSOIL RID SOIL ATONE CLEAR
SOLVE ACQUIT PARDON REFUTE
ABSOLVE DELIVER EXPIATE FORGIVE
RELEASE RESOLVE
ASSONANCE PUN RHYME
PARAGRAM
ASSORT BOLT CULL SUIT WINNOW
(— COINS) SHROFF
ASSORTED CHOW CHOWCHOW
ASSORTER FEEDER LOOKER
ASSORTMENT BAG LOT SET OLIO
BATCH GROUP SUITE MIXTURE
(— OF TYPE) BILL FONT
(COMPLETE —) STANDARD
ASSUAGE CALM EASE LIOS LISS
ABATE ALLAY CHARM DELAY LISSE
SALVE SLAKE STILL SWAGE LENIFY
LESSEN MODIFY PACIFY QUENCH
REDUCE SOFTEN SOLACE SOOTHE
TEMPER APPEASE COMFORT
MOLLIFY QUALIFY RELIEVE SATISFY
DIMINISH MITIGATE MODERATE
ASSUASIVE MILD LENIENT LENITIVE
SOOTHING
ASSUME DON PUT SAY SET BEAR
DARE FANG GIVE MASK PULL SHAM
SHIP TAKE ADOPT ANNEX CLOAK
ELECT FEIGN GUESS INDUE INFER
RAISE USURP ACCEPT AFFECT
BETAKE CLOTHE FIGURE ASSUMPT
BELIEVE PREMISE PRESUME
PRETEND RECEIVE SUBSUME
SUPPOSE SURMISE ACCROACH
ARROGATE SIMULATE
(— CHARACTER) ACT AFFECT
(— FORM) ENGENDER
(— OFFICE) ACCEDE
(— PAINTING STANCE) BACK
ASSUMED ALIAS FALSE GIVEN
FEIGNED AFFECTED
ASSUMING LOFTY UPPISH UPPITY
AFFECTED ARROGANT SUPERIOR
ASSUMPTION DONNEE THESIS
BALLOON FICTION SURMISE
HOMEOSIS MARYMASS PRETENCE
PRETENSE
(BASIC —) BEGINNING
(EMPTY —) IMAGINATION
ASSURANCE FACE GALL SEAL
BRASS FAITH NERVE TRUST
APLOMB BELIEF CAUTIO CREDIT
PLEVIN SAFETY COURAGE PROMISE

WARRANT AUDACITY BOLDNESS
COOLNESS FIRMANCE FOREHEAD
SECURITY SUREMENT

ASSURE AVER SURE CINCH HIGHT
VOUCH AFFEER ASSERT AVOUCH
ENSURE INSURE PLEDGE SECURE
SEKERE SICCAR SICKER WITTER
BETROTH CERTIFY COMFIRM
DECLARE HEARTEN PROMISE
PROTEST RESOLVE WARRANT
AFFIANCE CONVINCE EMBOLDEN
PERSUADE

ASSURED BOLD CALM COLD FIRM
SURE BOUND SIKER SLUSH FACILE
PROBAL SECURE SICCAR SICKER
CERTAIN
(BLUNTLY —) KNOCKDOWN

ASSUREDLY AMEN SOON INDEED
REDELY SICCAR SICKER SURELY
VERILY HARDILY WITTERLY

ASSYRIA ASHUR ASSUR ASSHUR
(CAPITAL OF —) CALAH NINEVEH

ASSYRIAN NESTORIAN
(— PLUM) SEBESTEN

ASTER ARNICA COCASH AMELLUS
BEEWEED BONESET EUASTER
ASTROFEL COMPOSIT CYTASTER
MONASTER STARWORT STOKESIA

ASTERISK MARK STAR ASTER
ASTERISM WINDMILL
(THREE —S) ASTERISM

ASTERN AFT BAFT HIND REAR
ABAFT APOOP BEHIND OCCIPUT
BACKWARD

ASTEROID EROS HEBE IRIS JUNO
CERES DIONE FLORA IRENE METIS
VESTA ASTREA EGERIA EUROPA
HYGEIA PALLAS PLANET PSYCHE
THALIA THEMIS THETIS ELECTRA
EUNOMIA FORTUNA LUTETIA
CALLIOPE MASSALIA STARFISH
STARLIKE VICTORIA

ASTHMA PHTHISIC

ASTHMATIC POUCY PURSY POUCEY
WHEEZY PANTING PUFFING

ASTIR UP AGOG ABOUT AFOOT
AGATE ALERT GOING ACTIVE
AROUND ASTEER MOVING ROUSED
ABROACH EXCITED STIRRING
VIGILANT

ASTONISH AWE DAZE STAM AMAZE
KNOCK SHOCK DAMMER MARVEL
STOUND ASTOUND GLOPPEN
IMPRESS STARTLE AMERVEIL
BEWILDER CONFOUND SURPRISE

ASTONISHING AMAZING FABULOUS

ASTONISHMENT MUSE FERLY
DISMAY FARLEY MARVEL STOUND
WONDER SURPRISE

ASTOUND BEAT STUN AMAZE APPAL
SHOCK STOUN APPALL STOUND
STAGGER STUPEFY STUPEND
TERRIFY ASTONISH CONFOUND
SURPRISE

ASTOUNDING STUNNING

ASTRAGAL TALUS CHAPLET
CORNICE

ASTRAKHAN BOKHARA

ASTRAL REMOTE STARRY STELLAR

ASTRAEAN SIDEREAL STARLIKE

ASTRAY AWRY LOST WILL AGLEY
AMISS ASIDE GLEED WRONG
ABROAD AFIELD ERRANT ERRING
FAULTY DEPAYSE DEVIOUS
FORLORN SINNING WILSOME
MISTAKEN STRAYING

ASTRIDE ATOP ABOARD ACHEVAL
SPANNING

ASTRINGENCY ACERBITY ACRIMONY

ASTRINGENT ACID ALUM COTO
SOUR TART ACERB HARSH SAPAN
STERN CORNUS MASTIC PONTIC
SEVERE TANNIN ALUMNOL AUSTERE
BINDING CATECHU PUCKERY
RHATANY STYPTIC GERANIUM
TRILLIUM

ASTROLOGER JOTI JOSHI ARTIST
JOTISI MERLIN ZADKIEL SCHEMIST

ASTROLOGY STARCRAFT
MATHEMATICALS

ASTRONOMER JOTI JOSHI JOTISI

ASTRONOMICAL FAR HUGE GREAT
URANIC DISTANT IMMENSE URANIAN
COLOSSAL INFINITE
(— INSTRUMENT) ARMILL

ASTRONOMY WAGON WAGONER
WAGGONER

ASTUTE SLY FOXY KEEN WILY
ACUTE CANNY QUICK SHARP SMART
CLEVER CRAFTY NASUTE SHREWD
CUNNING KNOWING SKILLED

ASUNDER ATWO APART SPLIT
ATWAIN SUNDER SUNDRY DIVIDED
DIVORCED YSOWNDIR

ASURA VARUNA

ASYLUM ARK HOME JAIL ALTAR
COVER GRITH HAVEN BEDLAM
HARBOR REFUGE ALSATIA COLLEGE
HOSPICE RETREAT SHELTER
BUGHOUSE MADHOUSE

ASYMMETRIC PEDIAL

AT A AL AU BY IN TO ALS TIL TILL
UNTO ATTEN THERE HEREAT
(— ALL) ANY AVA EER EVER HALF
OUGHT SOEVER HOWEVER

ATABAL DRUM TABOR ATTABAL

ATAMAN CHIEF JUDGE HETMAN
HEADMAN

ATAVISM REVERSION

ATELIER SHOP STUDIO BOTTEGA
WORKSHOP

ATEO WAKEA

ATES SWEETSOP

ATHAMAS (DAUGHTER OF —) HELLE
(FATHER OF —) AEOLUS
(SON OF —) PHRIXUS LEARCHUS
PALAEMON
(WIFE OF —) INO NEPHELE

ATHANOR OVEN ATHENOR FURNACE

ATHAPASKAN HAW HARE HUPA
KATO KASKA AHTENA BEAVER
CHETCO GILENO LASSIK SARCEE
SEKANI CARRIER CHILULA KOYUKON
KUTCHIN

ATHEIST ZENDIK DOUBTER INFIDEL
NASTIKA AGNOSTIC APIKOROS
NETHEIST

ATHENA ALEA AUGE NIKE ALERA
AREIA ERGANE HIPPIA HYGEIA

ITONIA PALLAS POLIAS AIANTIS
MINERVA APATURIA

ATHENIAN ATTIC CHORAGUS
CHOREGUS

ATHLETE PRO BLUE KEMP STAR
BOXER COLOR CRACK CUTEY CUTIE
TURNER ACROBAT AMATEUR
GYMNAST STICKER TUMBLER
VARMINT GAMESTER REPEATER
WRESTLER

ATHLETIC AGILE BURLY LUSTY
VITAL BRAWNY GYMNIC ROBUST
SINEWY STRONG BOARDLY
BOORDLY MUSCULAR POWERFUL
VIGOROUS

ATHLETICS GAMES SPORT EXERCISE

ATHWART CROSS ABOARD ACROSS
ASLANT OBLIQUE SIDEWISE
TRAVERSE

ATLAS BOOK LIST MAPS TOME TITAN
TELAMON MAINSTAY
(DAUGHTERS OF —) ATLANTIDES
(FATHER OF —) IAPETUS
(MOTHER OF —) CLYMENE
(WIFE OF —) PLEIONE

ATLE ETHEL

ATMAN ATMA ATTA SELF

ATMOSPHERE AIR SKY AURA FEEL
LIFT MOOD TONE AROMA CLIME
DECOR ETHER SMELL FROWST
MIASMA NIMBUS SPHERE WELKIN
FEELING HYALINE QUALIFY
AMBIANCE AMBIENCE
(— OF DISCOURAGEMENT) CHILL
(NOXIOUS —) MIASMA
(SECTION OF —) SOLENOID
(STALE —) FROUST FROWST
(STUFFY —) FUG
(SUFFOCATING —) STIFLE

ATMOSPHERICS STATIC SPHERICS

ATOM ACE BIT ION JOT DIAD DYAD
HAET HATE IOTA MITE MOTE WHIT
ATOMY HENAD LABEL MONAD
SHADE SPECK TINGE ADATOM
BRIDGE CARBYL HEPTAD ISOBAR
TETRAD ATOMIZE BODIKIN IONOGEN
ISOTOPE RADICAL SPECIES
FUNCTION ISOSTERE MOLECULE
PARTICLE QUANTITY
(— TOTALITY) MATTER
(PL.) SMITHERS SMITHEREENS

ATOMIC TINY MINUTE NUCLEAR

ATOMIZER SPRAY SPARGE SCENTER
SPRAYER AIRBRUSH ODORATOR
PERFUMER

ATONE AGREE AMEND ACCORD
ANSWER ASSOIL RANSOM REDEEM
REPENT APPEASE EXPIATE
RESTORE SATISFY
(— FOR) ABY BYE ABYE MEND
ABIDE ABEGGE

ATONEMENT MEND MICHTAM
PENANCE

ATOP ACOR

ATORAI DAURI

ATRABILIOUS GLUM ADUST
GLOOMY MOROSE SULLEN

ATREUS (BROTHER OF —) THYESTES
(FATHER OF —) PELOPS
(HALF-BROTHER OF —) THYESTES

(MOTHER OF —) HIPPODAMIA
(SON OF —) MENELAUS
(WIFE OF —) AEROPE
ATRIP AWEIGH
ATRIUM HALL ATRIO COURT CAVITY
AURICLE CHAMBER PASSAGE
ATROCIOUS BAD DARK RANK VILE
AWFUL BLACK CRUEL GROSS
ATROCE BRUTAL ODIOUS SAVAGE
WICKED HEINOUS UNGODLY
VIOLENT FLAGRANT GRIEVOUS
HORRIBLE TERRIBLE
ATROPHIC AUANTIC
ATROPHY RUST STUNT TABES
MACIES SHRINK STARVE SWEENY
WITHER SWINNEY WASTING
STULTIFY
ATTACH ADD FIX SET SEW TAG TIE
BIND BOLT GLUE HANG JOIN LINK
SPAN TAKE VEST WELD ADOPT
AFFIX ANNEX BEWED FOUND HINGE
HITCH LATCH PASTE SCREW SEIZE
SPEND STICK TACHE TATCH UNITE
ACCUSE ADDICT ADHERE ADJOIN
APPEND ARREST CEMENT DEVOTE
ENGAGE ENTAIL ENTIRE FASTEN
FATHER INDICT SPLINE ADHIBIT
APPOINT ASCRIBE CONNECT
ESPOUSE SUBJOIN
(— TEMPORARILY) SECOND
ATTACHED FAST FOND DOTING
ADJUNCT BIGOTED SESSILE
ADSCRIPT INSERTED
ATTACHING INCIDENT ALLIGATION
ATTACHMENT ARM GAG BAIL BALE
DRUM FLAY HEAD HECK LOVE MOTE
SHIM SHOE AMOUR CHUCK CRUSH
DOBBY DODAD FENCE GUARD STRIG
AFFAIR BEATER BINDER BUMPER
DAMSEL DOBBIE DOCTOR DOODAD
DREDGE FELLER FETICH FETISH
HEMMER HILLER LAPPET LAYBOY
MARKER PACKER PICKUP SECTOR
SHIELD SIDING ADAPTOR AFFAIRE
BIGOTRY BRAIDER CREASER
DROPPER FAGOTER FITTING
GIGBACK HEADSET HOLDING
JOINTER KNOCKUP LEVELER
SPANNER SPRAYER DEVOTION
DINGDONG FASTNESS FIXATION
FONDNESS GOVERNOR HEADREST
ATTACK FIT HIT HOP SIC BAIT BOMB
BOUT CLAW COSH DINT FANG FORK
FRAY GANG GIVE HOOK JUMP PAIL
PANG RAID RISE RUSH SAIL SICK
SLOW TACK TURN WADE YOKE
ABUSE ALARM ASSAY BEGIN BESET
BLAST BLITZ BRASH BRUNT CATCH
CHECK DRIVE FIGHT FLUSH FORAY
FORCE GLIDE HARRY ICTUS ONSET
POISE PULSE SALLY SCUFF SMITE
SOUSE SPASM SPELL STORM
ACCESS ACCUSE ACTION AFFRAY
AFFRET ASSAIL ATTAME BATTLE
BICKER CHARGE CRISIS DOUBLE
ENVAYE EXPUGN EXTENT GRUDGE
INDICT INFEST INSULT INVADE
OFFEND ONFALL ONRUSH POUNCE
RUFFLE SAVAGE SHOWER SORTIE

STOUND STRIKE STROKE TACKLE
TAKING THRUST AGGRESS ASPERSE
ASSAULT ATTEMPT BARRAGE
BELABOR BELIBEL BESEIGE
BOMBARD CENSURE CRUSADE
DESCENT OFFENSE PICKOUT
POTSHOT RUNNING SCALING
SEIZURE STACKER CAMISADO
ENDEAVOR ESCALADE PAROXYSM
SKIRMISH SURPRISE TOMAHAWK
(— IN COCKFIGHT) SHUFFLE
(— OF ILLNESS) GO DWAM DWALM
(— OF SICKNESS) WHIP SEIZURE
(— TO ROB) THUG
(— WITH SHOUTS) HUE
(— WITH WORDS) STOUSH
(— ZEALOUSLY) CRUSADE
(CHESS —) FORK
(CRITICAL —) SLATING
(FENCING —) GLIDE
(LIGHT —) TOUCH
(SLIGHT —) WAFF
(SUDDEN —) ICTUS RAPTUS
SURPRISE
(SUICIDAL —) KAMIKAZE
(SURPRISE —) ALARM ALARUM
(VERBAL —) FIRE BLUDGEON
ATTACKER AGGRESSOR OFFENDANT
ATTAIN GO GET HIT WIN BUMP
COME EARN GAIN RISE SORT ARISE
CATCH COVER CROSS FETCH
PROVE REACH TOUCH ACCEDE
AMOUNT ARRIVE ASPIRE EFFECT
OBTAIN SECURE STRIKE ACHIEVE
ACQUIRE COMPASS PROCURE
SUCCEED OVERTAKE
(— TO ACCOMPLISH) FIND FORCE
ATTAINMENT ARRIVAL ADEPTION
ENERGEIA PURCHASE
(— OF NIRVANA) MOKSHA
(SCHOLARLY —) LETTERS
ATTAR ITR OIL ATAR OTTO ATHAK
OTTAR ESSENCE PERFUME
ATTEMPT GO PUT SAY SHY TRY
BOUT BURL DARE DASH FAND FIST
FOND HACK JUMP MIND MINT MIRD
OSSE SEEK SHOT SLAP STAB WAGE
WORK ASSAY BEGIN ESSAY ETTLE
FLING FRAME OFFER ONSET PRESS
PROOF PROVE START TEMPT TRIAL
WHACK ASSAIL ATTACK EFFORT
FRAIST STRIVE ENFORCE IMITATE
PRETEND PROFFER STAGGER
VENTURE CONATION ENDEAVOR
EXERTION PURCHASE TENTAMEN
(— TO AROUSE) AGITATE
(— TO BRIBE) APPROACH
(— TO INFLUENCE) AGITATION
(ABORTIVE —) FUTILITY
ATTEND GO HO HOA HOO SEE HEAR
HEED LIST MIND OYES OYEZ STAY
TEND WAIT WALK APPLY AUDIT
AWAIT GUARD LAKEY NURSE SERVE
TREAT VISIT WATCH ASSIST
CONVEY ESCORT FOLLOW HARKEN
INTEND LISTEN SECOND SHADOW
SQUIRE CONDUCT CONSORT
ESQUIRE HEARKEN LACQUEY
PERPEND RETINUE

(— A LADY) WAIT
(— FUNERAL) FOLLOW
(— REGULARLY) KEEP
(— TO) MIND TREAT FETTLE INTEND
(— UPON) TENT CHASE CHAPERON
ATTENDANCE GATE SUIT CHAPEL
NUMBER OFFICE REGARD SERVICE
PRESENCE
ATTENDANT BOY FLY LAD JACK
MAID MUTE PAGE PEON SYCE ZANY
CADDY COMES GILLY GROOM GUIDE
JAGER USHER VALET ALEXAS
CADDIE DACTYL DAMSEL EMILIA
ESCORT FRIEND GESITH HAIDUK
HOGMAN JAEGER MINION PORTER
SQUIRE STOCAH TUBMAN VARLET
VERGER WAITER YEOMAN ALIPTES
ARMORER BULLDOG CHOBDAR
COURIER CROSSER DAMOSEL
FAMULUS FENELLA FOOTBOY
GHILLIE HALLMAN HOSTESS
JACKMAN LINKMAN MYRIDON
ORDERLY PAGEBOY PIQUEUR
PRESSER SEQUENT SERVANT
SHIPBOY SPOUTER TRABANT
TRESSEL ATTENDEE BEACHBOY
CHASSEUR CORYBANT CRUTCHER
FEWTERER FOLLOWER GATHERER
HANDMAID HENCHBOY HENCHMAN
HOUSEMAN MINISTER OBSERVER
ROSALINE SERGEANT SERJEANT
STAFFIER TIPSTAFF WATERMAN
(— OF CYBELE) CORYBANT
(CROSSING —) GATEMAN
(KNIGHT'S —) SWAIN ESQUIRE
(PROCTOR'S —) BULLDOG
(YOUNG —) BOY LAD JACK PAGE
KNIGHT
(PL.) STAFF CORTEGE RETINUE
ATTENDED FRAUGHT
ATTENTION EAR CARE GAUM HEED
HIST MARK MIND NOTE RUSH SHUN
TENT FLOOR GUARD STUDY TASTE
DETAIL FAVORS NOTICE REGARD
ACCOUNT ACHTUNG ADDRESS
EARNEST HEARING RESPECT
THOUGHT AUDIENCE
(— FROM SUPERIOR) TASHRIF
TASHREEF
(— TO PETTY ITEMS) MICROLOGY
(AMOROUS —) GALLANTRY
(FIXED —) DHARANA
(FLATTERING —) HOMAGE
(PLEASING —) INCENSE
(SPECIAL —) ACCENT
ATTENTIVE WARY ALERT AWAKE
CIVIL CLOSE SHARP TENTY ARRECT
INTENT POLITE CAREFUL GALLANT
HEEDFUL LISTFUL MINDFUL
PRESENT DILIGENT OBEDIENT
STUDIOUS THOUGHTY VIGILANT
WATCHFUL
(— TO) IMMINENT
ATTENUATE SAP DRAW FINE THIN
WATER DILUTE LESSEN RAREFY
REDUCE WEAKEN SLENDER
AVIANIZE DECREASE DIMINISH
EMACIATE ENFEEBLE TAPERING
ATTENUATED GAUNT AERIAL

DILUTED SPINDLY FINESPUN
SMORZATO

ATTENUATION LOSS

ATTENUATOR PAD

ATTEST CHOP SEAL SIGN PROVE
STATE SWEAR VOUCH ADJURE
AFFIRM INVOKE RECORD WITTEN
CERTIFY CONFESS CONFIRM
CONSIGN TESTIFY WARRANT
WITNESS EVIDENCE INDICATE
MANIFEST

ATTESTATION DOCKET RECORD

ATTESTED SWORN CERTIFIED

ATTIC LOFT CELER SOLAR SOLER
GARRET TALLET GRENIER
COCKLOFT
(— SIDE) SKEELING

ATTIRE (ALSO SEE DRESS) BEGO
SUIT TIRE ADORN ARRAY BIGAN
DRESS HABIT AGUISE ENROBE
PLIGHT REVEST TOILET ADDRESS
APPAREL DUBBING PANOPLY
ACCOUTER CLEADING EQUIPAGE
FEATHERS
(FORMAL —) BALLDRESS
(SHINING —) SHEEN

ATTIRED TRICKSY

ATTITUDE AIR CUE SET BIAS MIEN
MOOD POSE SIDE ANGLE FRAME
HEART PHASE SHAPE SHELL SIGHT
SLANT STAND ACTION ANIMUS
ASPECT MANNER SPIRIT STANCE
BEARING FEELING GESTURE
POSTURE STATION STOMACH
BEHAVIOR CARAPACE CROTCHET
HABITUDE POSITION
(PREVAILING —) STREAM

ATTORNEY DOER AGENT PROXY
VAKIL DEPUTY FACTOR FISCAL
LAWYER LEGIST MUKTAR SYNDIC
VAKEEL PROCTOR ADVOCATE

ATTRACT BAIT CALL DRAW LURE
PULL TILL WIND BRING CATCH
CHARM COURT FETCH TEMPT
ALLURE ENGAGE ENLIST ENTICE
GATHER INVITE SEDUCE STRIKE
BEWITCH PROCURE INTEREST
(— FISH) CHUM

ATTRACTION BAIT CALL CARD
CLOU DRAW PULL CHARM DRAFT
SPELL TRACT APPEAL DESIRE
MAGNET BLOWOFF COITION
DRAUGHT GRAVITY INDRAFT
ADHESION AFFINITY COHESION
CONTRACT PENCHANT SIDESHOW
WITCHERY

ATTRACTIVE BRAW CHIC CUTE FAIR
GOOD BONNY FATAL JOLLY QUEME
SWEET COMELY FLASHY FRUITY
HEPPEN LOVELY PRETTY SAVORY
SNAZZY TAKING TRICKY AMIABLE
CIRCEAN CUNNING EYEABLE
EYESOME GRADELY WINNING
WINSOME ALLURING CHARMING
ENGAGING ENTICING FEATURED
FETCHING GRACEFUL GRACIOUS
HANDSOME INVITING SPECIOUS
VENEREAN
(NOT —) FOUL INCURIOUS

ATTRACTIVENESS CHARM GRACE
BEAUTY GLAMOR AMENITY GLITTER
AFFINITY HARLOTRY

ATTRIBUTABLE DUE

ATTRIBUTE FOX OWE GIVE MARK
SIGN TYPE ALLOT BADGE BLAME
CHARM PLACE POWER REFER
ALLEGE ALLUDE ASSERT ASSIGN
BESTOW CHARGE CREDIT IMPUTE
PREFER REPUTE SYMBOL ADJUNCT
ASCRIBE COUNTER ESSENCE
PERTAIN QUALITY ACCREDIT
GRANDITY INTITULE PROPERTY
PROPRIUM STRENGTH
(— WRONGFULLY) FOIST
(—S OF ROCKS) GEOLOGY
(PL.) SARIRA SHARIRA

ATTRIBUTION ACCENT THEORY
ANIMISM ETIOLOGY

ATTRITION WEAR GRIEF REGRET
SORROW ANGUISH ABRASION
BLASTING FRICTION

ATTUNE KEY TUNE ADAPT AGREE
ACCORD ADJUST TEMPER PREPARE

ATUA AKUA DEMON SPIRIT

ATYPICAL BIZARRE GROTESQUE

AUBERGE INN ALBERGO

AUBERGINE EGGPLANT

AUBURN ABRAM BLOND CACHA
CUTCH BLONDE CACHOU CATECHU
GOREVAN

AU COURANT CONTEMPORARY

AUCTION CANT ROUP SALE SELL
VEND COKER TRADE BARTER
BRIDGE HAMMER OUTCRY VENDUE
OUTROOP UNCTION DISPOSAL
KNOCKOUT PORTSALE

AUCTIONEER CRIER CRYER
OUTCRIER

AUDACIOUS BOLD BRASH BRAVE
FRACK HARDY SAUCY AUDACE
BRAZEN CHEEKY DARING FORWARD
ARROGANT FEARLESS IMPUDENT
INSOLENT INTREPID SPIRITED
(NOT —) CIVIL

AUDACITY CHEEK NERVE COURAGE
BOLDNESS TEMERITY

AUDIBLE RIFE ALOUD CLEAR HEARD

AUDIENCE EAR PIT FANS AUDIT
COURT FLOOR HOUSE PUBLIC
GALLERY HEARING ASSEMBLY
AUDITORY TRIBUNAL

AUDIT SCAN CHECK PROBE APPOSE
RECKON VERIFY ACCOUNT EXAMINE
INQUIRE INSPECT ESTIMATE

AUDITION HEARING

AUDITOR CENSOR HEARER APPOSER
AUDIENT PITTITE COUNTOUR
DISCIPLE LISTENER

AUDITORIUM HALL ROOM CAVEA
FRONT ODEUM THEATER AUDITORY

AUDITORY ORAL OTIC AURAL
AUDILE ACOUSTIC AUDITIVE

AUGER BIT BORE BORAL BORER
GRILL BORING GIMLET NAUGER
WIMBLE PIERCER TEREBRA

AUGHT ACHT EAWT AUCHT OWNED
CIPHER NAUGHT WORTHY NOTHING
VALIANT ANYTHING

AUGMENT ADD EKE FEED GROW
HELP URGE BOOST EXALT SWELL
APPEND DILATE EXPAND EXTEND
AMPLIFY BALLOON ENHANCE
ENLARGE IMPROVE INFLAME
MAGNIFY COMPOUND HEIGHTEN
INCREASE MAJORATE MULTIPLY
(— IN STRENGTH) INGROSS

AUGMENTATION RISE EKING SWELL
GROWTH AUCTARY ADDITION

AUGMENTED SHARP EXTREME

AUGUR BODE OMEN SEER SPEAK
AUSPEX DIVINE BETOKEN CONJECT
FORESEE OMINATE PORTEND
PREDICT PRESAGE PROMISE
PROPHET SIGNIFY DENOUNCE
FOREBODE FORESHOW FORETELL
FOREWARN INDICATE PROPHESY

AUGURY ORE OMEN RITE SIGN
SOOTH TOKEN HANSEL RITUAL
HANDSEL PRESAGE CEREMONY

AUGUST AWFUL GRAND NOBLE
KINGLY SERENE SOLEMN EXALTED
STATELY IMPOSING MAJESTIC
(FIRST DAY OF —) LAMMAS LUGNAS
LUGHNAS LUGNASAD

AUGUSTINIAN AUSTIN
ASSUMPTIONIST

AUHUHU HOLA

AUK FALK LOOM ARRIE DIVER LEMOT
MURRE NODDY SCOOT SCOUT
SKOUT MARROT PUFFIN ROTCHE
STARIK TINKER DOVEKEY DOVEKIE
PENGUIN PYGOPOD SEAFOWL
WILLOCK GAIRFOWL GAREFOWL
ROCKBIRD

AULA HALL COURT EMBLIC

AUNT TIA BAWD AUNTY NAUNT
TANTA TANTE AUNTIE GOSSIP
(— SALLY) STICKS

AURA AIR HALO ODOR AROMA
SAVOR SMELL BREEZE BUZZARD
ESSENCE FEELING

AUREATE GOLDEN ORNATE ROCOCO
YELLOW

AUREOLE HALO CROWN GLORY
LIGHT AREOLA CORONA GLORIA
NIMBUS VESICA GLORIOLE
MANDORLA

AUREUS (HALF —) SEMIS

AURICLE EAR PINNA ATRIUM EARLET
TRUMPET PAVILION

AURIGA WAGONER WAGGONER

AURIST OTOLOGIST

AUROCHS TUR UROX URUS BISON
WISENT BONASUS

AURORA EOS DAWN DRAPERY
MORNING

AURORA BOREALIS DANCERS

AUSPICE CARE OMEN SIGN AUGURY
PORTENT GUIDANCE
(PL.) EGIS AEGIS

AUSPICIOUS FAIR GOOD TWINE
WHITE BRIGHT CHANCY DEXTER
CHANCEY FAVORING

AUSTERE BARE COLD HARD SOUR
BLEAK BUDGE GRAVE GRUFF
HARSH RIGID ROUGH SHARP STERN
STIFF STOUR BITTER CHASTE

FORMAL RUGGED SEVERE SIMPLE
SOMBER STRICT SULLEN TETRIC
ASCETIC EARNEST SERIOUS
GRANITIC RIGOROUS TETRICAL
AUSTERITY RIGOR CATOISM
AUSTRAL SOUTHERN

AUSTRALIA

ABORIGINE: MYALL
CAPE: HOWE
CAPITAL: CANBERRA
COIN: DUMP POUND SHILLING
DESERT: STURT GIBSON TANAMI
SIMPSON
ISLAND: CATO COCOS KOOLAN
CORINGA LACEPEDE ROTTNEST
TASMANIA
LAKE: EYRE COWAN FROME
BARLEE BULLOO AMADEUS
BLANCHE EVERARD TORRENS
GAIRDNER
LANGUAGE: YABBER
MEASURE: SAUM
MOUNTAIN: OLGA BRUCE LEGGE
CRADLE GARNET GAWLER
MAGNET STUART BONGONG
GREGORY CUTHBERT JUSGRAVE
MULLIGAN KOSCIUSKO
MOUNTAIN RANGE: DARLING
FLINDERS
NATIVE: MARA BINGE AUSSIE
DIGGER BILLIJIM KANGAROO
WARRAGAL WARRIGAL
JINDYWOROBAK
PENINSULA: EYRE
RIVER: DALY BULLO COMET ISAAC
PAROO ROPER SNOWY YARRA
BARCOO BARWON CULGOA
DAWSON DEGREY DARLING
FITZROY LACHLAN STAATEN
GEORGINA VICTORIA
SEA: CORAL TIMOR TASMAN
ARAFURA
SOLDIER: DIGGER SWADDY
BILLIJIM
STATE: TASMANIA VICTORIA
QUEENSLAND
TOWN: AYR YASS DUBBO PERTH
WAGGA ALBURY AUBURN
CAIRNS CASINO COBURG
DARWIN HOBART MACKAY
SYDNEY BENDIGO GEELONG
KOGARAH MILDURA MITCHAM
ADELAIDE BRISBANE ESSENDON
RANDWICK RINGWOOD
MELBOURNE TOOWOOMBA
VALLEY: GROSE JAMIESON
MEGALONG
WATER HOLE BILLABONG
WOMAN: LUBRA

AUSTRALIAN ANZAC AUSSIE DIGGER
AUSTRAL CURRENCY KANGAROO
WARRAGAL WARRIGAL
(— GIRL) LUBRA

AUSTRIA

ANCIENT PEOPLE: HUNS AVARS
RAETIANS SLOVENES
BAVARIANS
CAPITAL: WIEN VIENNA
CELTIC KINGDOM: NORICUM
COIN: DUCAT KRONE FLORIN
HELLER ZEHNER GROSCHEN
SCHILLING
DUCHY: STYRIA CARNIOLA
CARINTHIA
EMPEROR: CHARLES FRANCIS
FERDINAND
LAKE: ALMSEE FERTOTO
MONDSEE BODENSEE TRAUNSEE
CONSTANCE
MEASURE: FASS FUSS JOCH MASS
MUTH YOKE HALBE LINIE MEILE
METZE PFIFF PUNKT ACHTEL
BECHER SEIDEL DLAFTER
VIERTEL DREILING
MOUNTAIN: STUBAI EISENERZ
RHATIKON KITZBUHEL
NATIVE: STYRIAN TYROLEAN
NOBILITY: RITTER
PASS: LOIBL ARLBERG BRENNER
PLOCKEN
PROVINCE: TIROL TYROL STYRIA
VIENNA SALZBURG CARINTHIA
VORARLBERG
RIVER: INN MUR DRAU ENNS
KAMP LECH MURZ RAAB DONAU
MARCH SALZA THAYA TRAUN
DANUBE SALZACH
RIVER PORT: LINZ KREMS VIENNA
ROMAN PROVINCE: RAETIA
NORICUM PANNONIA
TOWN: ENNS GRAZ LECH LINZ
RIED WELS WIEN GMUND LIENZ
STEYR TRAUN LEOBEN VIENNA
BREGENZ MODLING SPITTAL
VILLACH DORNBIRN SALZBURG
INNSBRUCK
WEIGHT: MARC SAUM UNZE
DENAT KARCH PFUND STEIN
CENTNER PFENNIG VIERLING

AUTACOID HORMONE INCRETION
AUTARCHIC FREE
AUTHENTIC ECHT PURE REAL SURE
TRUE EXACT PUCCA PUCKA PUKKA
RIGHT VALID ACTUAL DINKUM
PROPER CORRECT CURRENT
GENUINE SINCERE CREDIBLE
OFFICIAL ORIGINAL RELIABLE
AUTHENTICATE SEAL PROVE
VOUCH ATTEST SIGNET VERIFY
APPROVE CONFIRM LEGALIZE
AUTHOR DOER JUDE SIRE JUDAS
MAKER RULER AUCTOR FACTOR
FORGER LOKMAN PARENT PENMAN
SCRIBE SOURCE WRITER ANCIENT
CLASSIC CREATOR ELOHIST
FOUNDER LOLLIUS ANCESTOR
BEGETTER COMPILER COMPOSER
IDEALIST IMMORTAL INVENTOR

JEHOVIST ORIGINAL PAYYETAN
PRODUCER
(PL.) SS
AUTHORITATIVE GRAVE CLASSIC
OFFICIAL ORACULAR POSITIVE
TEXTUARY
AUTHORITY LAW ROD SEE BALL
RULE SWAY ADEPT BOARD FAITH
POWER RICHE RIGHT STAMP SWING
TITLE ARTIST AUTHOR CREDIT
DANGER EMPERY EXPERT FASCES
REGENT REGIME SWINGE WEIGHT
AMITATE COMMAND CONTROL
DYNASTY FACULTY LEADING
LICENCE LICENSE SCEPTER
WARRANT DISPOSAL DOMINION
DOMINIUM HEGEMONY LORDSHIP
PRESTIGE SANCTION STRENGTH
(— OF SWITZERLAND) BUNDESRAT
(ARBITRARY —) ABOVE
(ROYAL —) SCEPTRE SOVRANTY
(SPIRITUAL —) KEYS KHILAFAT
(SUPREME —) SAY SIRCAR SIRKAR
(UNLIMITED —) AUTOCRACY
(PL.) ISNAD
AUTHORIZATION BARAT BERAT
PASSPORT SANCTION WARRANTY
AUTHORIZE LET LEAL VEST ALLOW
CLEAR CLOTHE PERMIT RATIFY
APPROVE EMPOWER ENDORSE
ENTITLE INDORSE JUSTIFY LICENSE
WARRANT ACCREDIT DELEGATE
LEGALIZE SANCTION
AUTHORIZED LEGAL OFFICIAL
AUTHORSHIP PENCRAFT PATERNITY
AUTO (ALSO SEE AUTOMOBILE)
CRATE CHUMMY LIZZIE
AUTOBIOGRAPHY VITA MEMOIR
AUTOCHTHONOUS NATIVE EDAPHIC
ENDEMIC
AUTOCLAVE DIGESTER DIGESTOR
AUTOCRACY MONARCHY
AUTOCRAT CZAR TSAR TZAR
MOGUL CAESAR DESPOT AUTARCH
MONARCH DICTATOR MONOCRAT
AUTOCRATIC ABSOLUTE
AUTO-DA-FE AUTO SERMO
AUTOGRAPH NAME SIGN MANUAL
INSCRIBE
AUTOMATIC MACHINE
AUTOMATON GOLEM ROBOT
AUTOMA ANDROID MACHINE
AUTOMOBILE BUG BUS CAR SIX
AUTO FOUR HEAP JEEP PONY TRAP
BUGGY COACH COUPE CRATE
EIGHT PONEY RACER SEDAN
BUCKET CHUMMY CUSTOM JALOPY
JUNKER SALOON AUTOCAR
COMPACT FLIVVER HACKNEY
HARDTOP MACHINE PHAETON
STEAMER TORPEDO VOITURE
CARRYALL DRAGSTER ELECTRIC
ROADSTER SQUADROL SUBURBAN
VICTORIA
(CONVERTIBLE —) DROPHEAD
(MIDGET —) DOODLEBUG
AUTONOMOUS FREE SEPARATE
AUTONOMY SOVEREIGNTY
SEPARATENESS

(— **OF GOD**) ASEITY ASEITAS
AUTOPSY NECROPSY
AUTUMN FALL KHARIF AUTOMPNE
FALLTIME MATURITY
AUXILIARY AID SUB AIDE ALLY
AIDING BRANCH DONKEY HELPER
ABETTER ABETTOR ADJUNCT
HELPING PARTNER ADJUTANT
(PL.) FOEDERATI
AVAIL DO AID DOW USE BOOT HELP
FADGE SERVE SKILL STEAD VALUE
MOMENT PROFIT BENEFIT BESTEAD
PREVAIL SERVICE SUCCEED SUFFICE
UTILIZE SUBSERVE
(— **ONESELF**) EMBRACE IMPROVE
SUBSERVE
AVAILABLE FIT FREE OPEN FLUSH
HANDY READY PATENT USABLE
PRESENT VISIBLE
AVALANCHE SLIDE LAWINE
VOLLENGE
AVANT-COURIER HERALD SCURRIER
AVANT-GARDE LITERATI
AVARICE GREED MISERY AVIDITY
CUPIDITY RAPACITY
AVARICIOUS CLOSE SLOAN GREEDY
HAVING HUNGRY SORDID STINGY
GRIPING GRIPPLE ITCHING MISERLY
COVETOUS GRASPING
AVATAR BALARAMA EPIPHANY
AVELLANEOUS HAZEL
AVENGE REPAY RIGHT VISIT WRACK
AWREAK PUNISH BEWREAK REQUITE
REVENGE SATISFY CHASTISE
AVENGER KANAIMA NEMESIS
WREAKER
AVENS GEUM BENNET BAREFOOT
AVENTURINE SUNSTONE
GOLDSTONE
AVENUE RUE WAY GATE MALL PIKE
ROAD ALLEE ALLEY DRIVE ENTRY
ACCESS ARCADE ARTERY RIDING
STREET AVENIDA OPENING
PASSAGE
AVER SAY AIVER CLAIM PROVE
STATE SWEAR AFFIRM ALLEGE
ASSERT ASSURE AVOUCH DEPOSE
VERIFY DECLARE JUSTIFY PROTEST
AVERAGE PAR SUM DUTY FAIR
MEAN NORM RULE RATIO USUAL
VALUE CHARGE MEDIAL MEDIAN
MEDIUM MIDDLE NORMAL TARIFF
ARRIAGE ESTIMATE MEDIOCRE
MIDDLING MODERATE ORDINARY
OVERHEAD QUANTITY STANDARD
(**NOT** —) BORDERLINE
AVERSE LOTH BALKY LOATH AFRAID
ADVERSE AGAINST OPPOSED
BACKWARD INIMICAL OPPOSITE
PERVERSE
(— **TO**) ABOVE
AVERSION TOY HATE DERRY ODIUM
ENMITY HATRED HORROR REGRET
DESPITE DISDAIN DISGUST DISLIKE
MISLIKE DISTASTE
(— **TO FOOD**) APOSITIA
(— **TO WORK**) ERGOPHOBIA
AVERT WRY BEND FEND MOVE SHUN
TURN WARD AVOID DETER DODGE

EVADE PARRY SHEER TWIST
DEFRAY DIVERT RETARD SHIELD
DECLINE DEFLECT EXPIATE
PREVENT ALIENATE ESTRANGE
FOREFEND WITHTURN
AVIARY CAGE HOUSE VOLARY
ORNITHON
AVIATOR ACE FLIER FLYER PILOT
AIRMAN FLYING ICARUS BIRDMAN
LOOPIST LUFBERY MANBIRD
SOLOIST
AVID AGOG KEEN WARM EAGER
ARDENT GREEDY HUNGRY JEJUNE
ANXIOUS ATHIRST CRAVING
LONGING THIRSTY DESIROUS
GRASPING
AVIDITY AVARICE CUPIDITY
AVIFAUNA BIRDS ORNIS BIRDLIFE
AVIKOM JACKS
AVOCADO COYO PEAR PALTA
AHUACA CHININ MARROW PERSEA
ZABOCA ABACATE ABBOGADA
AGUACATE ALLIGATO
AVOCET BARKER TILTER YELPER
SCOOPER
AVOID FLY SHY BALK FLEE HELP
MISS PASS QUIT SAVE SHUN VOID
WARE ABHOR ANNUL AVERT BURKE
DITCH DODGE ELUDE EVADE FEIGN
HEDGE PARRY SHIFT SHIRK SKIRT
SKULK SLACK SPAIR SPARE START
WANDE WONDE ABJURE BLENCH
BYPASS DETOUR ESCAPE ESCHEW
REFUTE REMOVE VACATE ABSTAIN
DECLINE EVITATE FORBEAR
FORSAKE REFRAIN
(— **A PUNCH**) SLIP
(— **COMMITMENT**) FUDGE
(— **EXPENSE**) HELP MISS SKIVE
(— **OVERWORKING**) FAVOR
(— **RESPONSIBILITY**) BLUDGE
AVOIDANCE DODGE OUTLET
EVASION ESCHEWAL
(— **OF RISK**) CAUTION
AVOUCH AVER ASSERT
AVOW OWN BIND WARE ADMIT
STATE AFFIRM ASSERT AVOUCH
DEPONE DEPOSE DEVOTE CONFESS
DECLARE JUSTIFY PROFESS
MAINTAIN
AVOWAL OATH WORD AVOURE
PROTEST
AVOWED FRANK SWORN STATED
DECLARED
AWAIT BIDE HEED KEEP PEND STAY
TEND WAIT ABIDE TARRY WATCH
ATTEND EXPECT IMPEND REMAIN
WAYLAY
(— **PAYMENT**) CARRY
AWAITING BEFORE BIDING
AWAKE DAW STIR WAKE ADAWE
ALERT ALIVE AWARE ROUSE ABRAID
ACTIVE AROUSE AWAKEN EXCITE
CAREFUL HEEDFUL STARTLE
VIGILANT
AWAKEN DAW STIR ALERT AROUSE
EXCITE KINDLE
AWAKENING REVIVAL WAKEFUL
AWARD LAW GIVE MARK MEED METE

WARD ALLOT GRANT MEDAL PRICE
PRIZE ACCORD ACTION ADDEEM
ASSIGN BESTOW BOUNTY CONFER
DECIDE MODIFY ADJUDGE APPOINT
CONSIGN CUSTODY KEEPING
ACCOLADE SENTENCE
(PL.) DESERTS
AWARE HEP RECK SURE WARE
WARY WISE ALERT ALIVE AWAKE
JERRY BEWARE KNOWING MINDFUL
APPRISED INFORMED SENSIBLE
SENTIENT VIGILANT WATCHFUL
AWARENESS EAR FEEL SENSE
FEELING INSIGHT
(— **OF WORTH**) APPRECIATION
AWAY BY TO AWA FRO OFF OUT VIA
WAY AFAR GONE PAST SCAT YOND
ALONG APART ASIDE FORTH HENCE
ABROAD ABSENT BEGONE ONWARD
THENCE DISTANT FROWARD
FAREWELL
(— **FROM HOME**) AFIELD OUTLAND
(— **FROM PORT**) AFLOAT
(— **FROM**) DOWN WITH ALONE
ALOOF APART BESIDE
(**FARTHER** —) BEYOND
AWE COW FEAR AMAZE DAUNT
DREAD SCARE FRIGHT HORROR
REGARD TERROR WONDER BUFFALO
RESPECT ASTONISH BEWILDER
OVERCOME RELIGION
AWE-INSPIRING GODFUL SOLEMN
AWESOME RELIGIO FEARSOME
OLYMPIAN
AWESOME EERY FELL HOLY AWFUL
EERIE WEIRD SOLEMN DREADED
GHOSTLY
AWESTRUCK SILENT
AWETO WERI
AWFUL DIRE FINE UGLY DREAD
GHAST AUGUST HORRID AWESOME
FEARFUL HIDEOUS SATANIC
DREADFUL SHOCKING TERRIBLE
AWFULLY AWFUL FIERCE
AWKWARD AWK CAR GAUM UNCO
CRANK FALSE FUDGY GAUMY
GAWKY GOATY INAPT INEPT SPLAY
STIFF UNCOW UNKED UNKID
CLUMSY GAUCHE RUSTIC STICKY
THUMBY UNEASY WOODEN
ADVERSE BOORISH CUBBISH
FROWARD HALTING LOUTISH
LUMPISH STILTED UNCANNY
UNCOUTH UNHANDY UNREADY
BUNGLING CLOWNISH FECKLESS
LUBBERLY PERVERSE UNGAINLY
UNTOWARD UNWIELDY
(— **PERSON**) TAWPY TUMFIE
(**NOT** —) FACILE
AWL BROD BROG NAIL NALL PROD
PROG BRODE ELSEN NALLE
BROACH DRIVER ELSHIN FIBULA
GIMLET BRADAWL SCRIBER
STABBER
AWN AIL EAR JAG BARB BEAK JAGG
PILE ARISTA BRISTLE
(— **OF BARLEY**) HORN
(— **OF OATS**) JAG JAGG
(PL.) BEARD

AWNING TILT BLIND SHADE VELUM CANOPY SEMIAN SHADER TIENDA TENTORY SEMIANNA SUNBLIND SUNSHADE VELARIUM

AWNLESS NOT NOTT HUMBLE HUMMEL POLLARD

AWRY CAM WRY AGEE BIAS SKEW AGLEY AMISS ASKEW GLEED GLEYD SNAFU WONKY WRONG ACROSS ASIDEN BLOOEY BLOOIE CAMMED FLOOEY ASKANCE ASQUINT ATHWART CROOKED OBLIQUE PERVERSE

AX ADZ AXE ADZE EAWT HACHE MATAX BIFACE PICKEL PIOLET POLEAX THIXLE TWIBIL BESAGUE BOUCHER BROADAX CHOPPER CLEAVER HATCHET JEDDING PULASKI TWIBILL FRANCISC

SUNDERER TOMAHAWK
(DOUBLE —) LABRYS
(HEADSMAN'S —) MANNAIA
(MASON'S —) CAVEL
(WOODEN —) MACANA

AXHAMMER CAVEL CAVIL KEVEL KNAPPER

AXIAL VENTRAL

AXIL ALA

AXILLA ALA AXIS ARMPIT SHOULDER

AXIOM SAW ADAGE MAXIM MOTTO BYWORD DICTUM SAYING TRUISM DIGNITY PRECEPT PROVERB APHORISM APOTHEGM DIGNITAS PETITION SENTENCE

AXIS AXE NUT AXLE STEM ARBOR HINGE STALK ARBOUR CAUDEX CENTER CHITRA RACHIS CAULOME

CORNCOB DENTATA POLAXIS SPINDLE SUCCULA SYMPODE TENDRIL AXLETREE MONOPODE

AXLE EX BAR COD PIN AXIS BOGY ARBOR BOGEY BOGIE EXTRE SHAFT AXTREE SLEEVE MANDREL SPINDLE SUCCULA

AYAH IYA CHAY EYAH MAID NURSE

AYE I AY EY EYE PRO YEA YES EVER ALWAYS ASSENT FOREVER

AYU AI SWEETFISH

AZALEA ERICA MINERVA CARDINAL

AZAZEL EBLIS

AZIMUTH ZN BEARING

AZTEC AZTECA MEXICA MEXICAN TENOCHCA

AZURE BICE BLUE HURT JOVE COBALT JOVIAL JUPITER CERULEAN SAPPHIRE

B SI BEE BAKER BRAVO
  (— **FLAT**) ZA BEMOL
BA TRIPOS
BAA MAA MAE BLEAT
BABBAR UTU UTUO
BABBLE CHAT GASH KNAP TOVE
  BABIL BLATE CLACK CLYDE GLOCK
  HAVER PRATE TAVER WLAFF
  CACKLE DITHER GABBLE GAGGLE
  GLAVER GOSSIP JANGLE MURMUR
  PALTER RABBLE TAIVER TUMULT
  BLABBER BLATHER BLUSTER
  CHATTER CHIPPER CLATTER
  PRATTLE SMATTER TWADDLE
  GLAISTER
BABBLER CACKLER BLATEROON
  STIPITURE
BABEL DIN MEDLEY TUMULT
  CHARIVARI CONFUSION
BABESIA APIOSOMA NUTTALIA
BABOON APE PAP PAPA DRILL
  SPHINX BAVIAN CHACMA GIRRIT
  PAPION BABUINA MANDRILL
  HAMADRYAD
BABUL SANT SUNT ACACIA BABOOT
  GARRAT GONAKE NEBNEB ATTALEH
  GONAKIE
BABUSHKA SCARF KERCHIEF
BABY MOP BABA BABE CHAP DOLL
  JOEY TOTO WEAN BAIRN CHILD
  HUMOR SPOIL WAYNE CHRISM
  CODDLE FONDLE INFANT MOPPET
  PAMPER PUPPET SQUALL WEANIE
  BAMBINO CHRISOM INDULGE
  PAPOOSE WADDLER
BABY CARRIAGE PRAM BUGGY
  WAGON GOCART STROLLER
BABYISH TIDDY PULING SIMPLE
  PUERILE CHILDISH
BABYLONIAN (— **CYCLE**) SAROS
BABY'S BREATH GYP GYPSOPHILA
BACALAO MURRE SCAMP ABADEJO
  CODFISH GROUPER GUILLEMOT
BACCATE BERRIED
BACCHANAL DEVOTEE REVELER
  CAROUSER
BACCHANTE FROW MAENAD
BACCHUS LIBER LYAENS BROMIUS
  DIONYSUS
  (**AUNT OF** —) INO
  (**FATHER OF** —) JUPITER
  (**MOTHER OF** —) SEMELE
BACHELOR BACH SEAL BATCH
  GARCON WANTER BACULERE
  BENEDICT CELIBATE
BACILLUS GERM VIRUS MICROBE
BACK AID FRO TUB VAT ABET BAKE
  BECK FULL HIND HINT NAPE NATA
  REAR TAIL ABACK AGAIN ANGEL
  BROAD CHINE DORSE NOTUM SPINE
  SPLAT STERN VOUCH ASSIST
  DORSUM HINDER SECOND SOOTHE
  TERGUM TROUGH UPHOLD VERIFY
  CISTERN ENDORSE FINANCE
  RIGGING SPONSOR SUPPORT
  SUSTAIN BACKWARD FULLBACK
  HALFBACK MAINTAIN
  (— **A ROWBOAT**) STERN
  (— **OF ANIMAL**) RIG TERGUM

(— **OF ARCHERY TARGET**) BOSS
(— **OF AWNING**) RIDGEROPE
(— **OF BOOK**) DORSE SPINE
(— **OF BULL**) ROOF
(— **OF HAND**) OPISTHENAR
(— **OF HEAD**) NODDLE NIDDICK
OCCIPUT
(— **OF INSECT**) NOTUM
(— **OF NECK**) NAPE NUQUE SCRUFF
(— **OF PAGE**) FV
(— **OUT**) BEG JIB DUCK FLUNK
CRAWFISH
(— **TO BACK**) ADDORSED
(— **WATER**) STERN SHEAVE
(**SHOWING** —) TERGANT
BACKBITING DETRACTION
BACKBOARD BANK MONITOR
BACKBONE BACK GRIT GUTS CHINE
  NERVE PLUCK RIDGE SPINA SPINE
  LADDER METTLE SPIRIT GRISTLE
  RIGBANE SPINULE STAMINA
  VERTEBRA
  (— **OF FISH**) GRATE
BACKCOUNTRY BUSH STICKS
  BACKLAND BACKVELD BOONDOCKS
BACKDROP OLEO
BACKFIELD SECONDARY
BACKFIRE BOOMERANG
BACKFLASH GUTTER
BACKGAMMON IRISH LURCH TABLE
  FAYLES GAMMON TABLES
  BACKGAME TICKTACK
  (— **MAN**) BLOT TABLEMAN
BACKGROUND FOND REAR GROUND
  OFFING LINEAGE SETTING
  BACKDROP DISTANCE EXTERIOR
  OFFSCAPE TRAINING EDUCATION
  (**MUSICAL** —) SUPPORT
BACKHANDED AWKWARD
BACKHOE PULLSHOVEL
BACKHOUSE PRIVY OUTHOUSE
BACKING AID EGIS AEGIS BACKUP
  BEHIND LINING MUSLIN REFUSE
  SUPPORT HEARTING FINANCING
  (**LEGAL** —) STRENGTH
BACKLASH LASH SHAKE SLACK
BACKLOG RESERVE SURPLUS
  BACKBRAND
BACKPIECE DOSSIERE
BACKPLATE REREDOS
BACKREST LAZYBACK
BACKROPE GOBLINE
BACKSEY SEY SIRLOIN
BACKSLIDE FALL LAPSE DESERT
  REVERT RELAPSE
BACKSPIN DRAG UNDERCUT
  UNDERSPIN
BACKSTITCH PURL PEARL
BACKSTOP BUTT
BACKWARD FRO JAY LAX YON
  BACK CRAB DARK DULL LOTH
  ABACK AREAR BLATE INAPT LOATH
  THRAW UNAPT ARREAR ASTERN
  AVERSE BYGONE POSTIC RETRAD
  RETRAL STUPID BASHFUL LAGGARD
  LAGGING REVERSE UPSTAGE
  DILATORY IGNORANT LATEWARD
  PERVERSE REARWARD TAILFIRST
BACKWARDNESS DARKNESS
  BARBARISM

BACKWARDS YON AROUND
BACKWATER EBB COVE SLEW SLUE
  BAYOU SHEAVE SLOUGH RETRACT
  RETREAT BACKWASH BILLABONG
BACKWOODSMAN HICK WOODSY
  BUCKSKIN HILLBILLY
BACKWORT COMFREY
BACON PIG BARD MEAT PORK
  BARDE JAMON PRIZE SPECK FLITCH
  GAMMON RUSTIC SAWNEY
  GAMBONE SOWBELLY
BACOPA BRAMIA
BACTERIUM ROD COLI GERM
  AEROBE CYTODE ANTHRAX
  CHOLERA MICROBE PROTEUS
  SARCINA VIBRION BACILLUS
  LISTERIA BOTULINUS CYTOPHAGA
  HEMOPHILE INFECTANT INFECTION
BAD BIG DUD ILL SAD EVIL FULL
  HARD LEWD POOR PUNK QUED SICK
  SOUR VILE WICK GAMMY NASTY
  SORRY WEARY WORST WRONG
  ARRANT FAULTY LITHER LUTHER
  NOUGHT ROTTEN SEVERE SHREWD
  SINFUL UNGOOD UNKIND WICKED
  BALEFUL BANEFUL CORRUPT
  FEARFUL HARMFUL HEINOUS
  HURTFUL IMMORAL INUTILE
  NAUGHTY SPOILED TAINTED
  UNLUCKY UNMORAL UNSOUND
  VICIOUS ANNOYING CRIMINAL
  DEPRAVED DOGGEREL FIENDISH
  FLAGRANT INFERIOR PRECIOUS
  SINISTER UNSUITED
  (— **MANNERS**) TROLLOPE
  (**OUTRAGEOUSLY** —) GRIEVOUS
  (**OUTSTANDINGLY** —) ARRANT
  (**RATHER** —) INDIFFERENT
  (**VERY** —) ALMIGHTY EXECRABLE
BADDERLOCKS MURLIN PURSES
  HENWARE SEAWEED HONEYWARE
BADGE PIN MARK SIGN STAR COLOR
  CREST CROSS FAVOR HONOR
  ORDER PATCH TOKEN BUTTON
  BUZZER COLLAR EMBLEM ENSIGN
  FASCES GARTER GIGLIO PLAQUE
  SHIELD SYMBOL TIPONI WEEPER
  CHEVRON EPAULET FEATHER
  BRASSARD INSIGNIA SCAPULAR
  EPAULETTE
  (**JAPANESE** —) MON KIRIMON
  (**RUSSIAN** —) ZNAK
BADGER NAG PAT BAIT GRAY GREY
  GRIS MELE PATE ANNOY BRACE
  BROCK BRUSH CHEVY CHIVY
  HURON MELES PAHMI RATED RATEL
  TAXEL TAXUS TEASE WORRY
  BAUSON BOTHER BRAROW CHIVVY
  HAGGLE HARASS HAWKER HECKLE
  KIDDER MELINE PESTER TELEDU
  WOMBAT GRISARD TORMENT
  BRAIREAU BULLYRAG CARCAJOU
  HUCKSTER IRRITATE STINKARD
  MISTONUSK
  (— **STATE**) WISCONSIN
  (**AUSTRALIAN** —) WOMBAT
  (**COMPANY OF** —S) CETE
  (**LIKE A** —) MELINE
BADINAGE FOOL JOKER BANTER

RAILLERY TRIFLING
BADLANDS MALPAIS
BADLY BAD ILL EVIL HARD ILLY SICK
SADLY EVILLY HARDLY POORLY
UNWELL FAULTILY WICKEDLY
VICIOUSLY
BADMINTON POONA
BADNESS MALICE PRAVITY UNVALUE
EVILNESS
BAD-TEMPERED FOUL ANGRY
STINGY GROUCHY
BAFFLE FOX GET BALK BEAT FOIL
LICK MATE POSE STOP UNDO
CHEAT CHECK ELUDE EVADE FLING
STICK STUMP BLENCH BOGGLE
DEFEAT DELUDE FICKLE INFAMY
OUTWIT PUZZLE RESIST THWART
BUFFALO CONFUSE DECEIVE
QUIBBLE STONKER BEWILDER
CONFOUND DISGRACE JUGGLING
BAFFLING SHREWD ELUSIVE
BAG COD KIT MAT NET PAD POD POT
SAC CELL DRAG GRIP LOBE MAIL
POCK POKE SACK TOOT TRAP
WOMB BELLY BOUGE BULSE CATCH
DILLI DILLY EMERY FLOAT HUSSY
PETER POUCH PURSE SCRIP SEIZE
SNARE STEAL BLOUSE BUDGET
CAVITY ENTRAP FOLLIS GASBAG
MATAPI PAGGLE POCKET POUNCE
SACHET SEABAG VALISE WALLET
ALFORJA BALLOON BEANBAG
BLISTER BUCKRAM CANTINA
CAPCASE CAPTURE CUSHION
GAMEBAG GOMUKHI HANDBAG
HOLDALL RETICLE SANDBAG
SARPIER SATCHEL TRAVOIS
CARRYALL CORNSACK ENTRAILS
ENVELOPE FOLLICLE KNAPSACK
MONEYBAG OVERSLIP RETICULE
RUCKSACK SUITCASE WINESKIN
MULTIWALL WEEKENDER
(— BULGING) SWAG
(— FOR LETTERS) MAIL POUCH
KAREETA MAILBAG POSTBAG
(— FOR TOOLS) WALLET
(— OF ANISEED) DRAG
(— WITH POCKETS) TIDE TIDY
(AUSTRALIAN —) SWAG DILLI SHIRT
SHAMMY
(GAS —) CELL
(GRAB —) FISHPOND
(HAWSE —) JACKASS
(LEATHER —) JAG JAGG ASKOS
BUDGE BOUGET MUSSUK
(NET —) SNOOD GARLAND
(SEWING —) HUSSY
(SLEEPING —) FUMBA FLEABAG
SLEEPER
(WATER —) CHAGAL CHAGEN
CHAGUL
BAGASSE BEGASS LINAGA MEGASS
BAGATELLE CANON TRUNK VERSE
CANNON TRIFLE
BAGGAGE ARMS GEAR MINX SWAG
CUTTY HUZZY NASTY SAMAN STUFF
TENTS TRASH WENCH HARLOT
REFUSE TRASHY TRUNKS CLOTHES
DUNNAGE EFFECTS FARDAGE

PLUNDER RUBBISH SALMARY
SUMPTER VALISES CARRIAGE
HARLOTRY RUBBISHY UTENSILS
BAGGAGE CAR WAGON FOURGON
BAGGER SACKER BATCHER
BAGGING SOUTAGE
BAGGY LOOSE POCKY PURSY
FLABBY PUFFED PURSIVE
BAGNIO BAIN BATH BAGNE PRISON
BROTHEL HOTHOUSE
BAGPIPE MUSE PIPE PIVA DRONE
TITTY BIGNOU BINIOU CHORUS
GEWGAW MUSETTE SAMBUKE
DULCIMER SYMPHONY ZAMPOGNA
CORNAMUTE CORNEMUSE
SYMPHONIA
BAGUETTE CHAPLET
BAH PO FOH PAH POH ROT RATS
FAUGH PSHAW NONSENSE
BAHAMAS (CAPITAL OF —) NASSAU
(ISLAND OF —) ABACO EXUMA
ANDROS BIMINI
BAHRAIN (CAPITAL OF —) MANAMA
(MONEY OF —) FILS DINAR
(TOWN OF —) RIFAA JIDHAFS
BAIL BOW DIP ANDI BALE BOND
HOOP LADE LAVE RING RYND YOKE
LADLE SCOOP THROW VOUCH
BUCKET HANDLE PLEDGE SECURE
SURETY VADIUM CUSTODY DELIVER
RELEASE REPLEVY BAILSMAN
BULWARKS SECURITY GUARANTEE
(— OUT) ABANDON
BAILEE LESSEE POSITOR
CONDUCTOR
BAILER SPOUCHER
BAILIFF GRAB HIND AGENT REEVE
SAFFO SCULT STAFF BAILIE BAILLI
BEADLE DEPUTY FACTOR GRIEVE
LOOKER OFFICE PORTER PREVOT
SCHOUT VARLET BUMTRAP GRIPPER
PROVOST PUTTOCK SHERIFF
STEWARD APPROVER HUISSIER
OVERSEER TIPSTAFF CONSTABLE
HUNDREDER PORTREEVE
SENESCHAL WAPENTAKE
BAILIWICK AREA FIELD DOMAIN
OFFICE PROVINCE
BAILOR LESSOR
BAIN NEAR LITHE READY SHORT
DIRECT LIMBER SUPPLE FORWARD
WILLING
BAIT BAD BOB COG DAP LUG BITE
CAST CHUM FEED HALT HANK LURE
PLUG TAIL DECOY HOUND LEGER
SHACK SLATE SQUID TEMPT TRAIN
WORRY ALLURE APPAST ATTACK
BADGER BERLEY ENTICE HARASS
HECKLE HECTOR KILLER LEDGER
REPAST SHRAPE SLIVER FULCRUM
GUDGEON PROVOKE TAGTAIL
TOLLING TORMENT CUNGEBOI
(— FOR BIRDS) SHRAP SHRAPE
(— FOR COD) CAPELIN
(GREASY —) ROGUE
(GROUND —) BERLEY
(MAGGOT —) GENTLE
(SCENTED —) DRAG
BAITING HANK

BAIZE BAY BAYES BAYETA DOMETT
BAKE DRY BURN COCT COOK FIRE
BATCH BROIL GRILL PARCH ROAST
ANNEAL HARDEN BISCUIT PISTATE
SCALLOP CLAMBAKE ESCALLOP
(— EGGS) SHIRR
(— THOROUGHLY) SOAK
BAKED (— IN EARTH OVEN) KALUA
(— PRODUCT) KICHEL
BAKER OVEN FIRER BAXTER BURNER
FURNER PISTOR FURNACE
OVENMAN ROASTER
BAKER BIRD HORNERO
BAKING CUIT BATCH COCTION
FURNAGE ASSATION
BAKONGO FIOT
BALACHONG NGAPI
BALANCE BEAM EVEN PEIS REST
SWAY TRIM COVER ERASE PEISE
POISE SCALE TRONE WEIGH WEIHE
ADJUST AUNCEL CANCEL EMBLEM
EQUATE KELTER KELVIN KILTER
LAUNCE OFFSET SANITY SQUARE
STRIKE DESEMER LIBRATE
OVERRUN RESIDUE TRABUSH
TRUTINE EQUALITY EQUALIZE
EQUATION SERENITY WESTPHAL
TREBUCHET
(— DUE) ARREAR
(— IN ACCOUNT) CREDIT
(— OF SAILS) ATRY
(MENTAL —) HEAD
BALANCED EVEN EQUAL LEVEL
APOISE KITTLE WEIGHED COMPLETE
QUADRATE
BALANCER HALTER ACROBAT
GYMNAST HALTERE
BALATA ICICA BULLACE BEEFWOOD
BORRACHA
BALCONY POY ORIEL PORCH STOOP
CIRCLE GAZEBO PIAZZA PODIUM
SOLLAR BALAGAN GALLERY
MIRADOR PERGOLA TERRACE
BRATTICE CANTORIA VERANDAH
BALD RAW BARE BASE BOLD CRUDE
DODDY NAKED PLAIN CALLOW
PALTRY PEELED PILLED SIMPLE
CALVOUS EPILOSE LITERAL
GLABROUS HAIRLESS
(— HEAD) PILGARLIC
(— SPOT) TONSURE
BALDACHIN CANOPY CIBORIUM
BALDER BALDR BALDUR BAELDAEG
(CHILD OF —) FORSETE FORSETI
(FATHER OF —) ODIN
(SLAYER OF —) HOTH LOKE HOTHR
(WIFE OF —) NANNA
BALDERDASH ROT GUFF TRASH
DRIVEL JARGON FLUBDUB
NONSENSE BALDUCTUM RIGMAROLE
BALDNESS ACOMIA CALVITY
ALOPECIA ATRICHIA OPHIASIS
BALDPATE ZUISIN POACHER
BALDRIC BELT LACE GIRDLE ZODIAC
BALTEUS SUPPORT NECKLACE
BALE NO GIB NOT WOE EVIL FIRE
HARM PACK PYRE BLOCK CRATE
DEATH FARDO SERON BALLOT
BUNDLE EMBALE SEROON SORROW

PACKAGE SARPLER

BALEARIC ISLANDS (ISLAND OF —)
IBIZA CABRERA MAJORCA MINORCA
CONEJERA
(MEASURE OF —) PALMO MISURA
QUARTA QUARTIN BARCELLA
(TOWN OF —) IBIZA MAHON PALMA
(WEIGHT OF —) CARGO CORTA
QUARTANO

BALEEN WHALEBONE

BALEFUL BAD EVIL DEADLY MALIGN
SACRED SULLEN MALEFIC NOXIOUS
RUINOUS SIDERAL SINISTER
WRETCHED

BALI (DANCE OF —) ARDJA BARIS
KRISS BARONG KETJAK MONKEY
DJANGER
(MOUNTAIN OF —) AGOENG
(MUSICAL INSTRUMENT OF —)
GAMELAN
(RICE FIELD OF —) SAWAII
(STRAIT OF —) LOMBOK
(TOWN OF —) SINGARADJA

BALINGHASAY ANAM ANAN

BALK GAG HUE JUB SHY BEAM BILK
BUCK BULL COND FOIL GORM HADE
HEAP LICK LOFT MISS OMIT PROP
SHUN SKIP SLIP STAY STOP AVOID
BAULK BLOCK CHECK CLAMP
DEMUR HUNCH MOUND REBEL
REEST RIDGE STAKE STICK WAVER
BAFFLE DEFEAT FALTER HINDER
IMPEDE OUTWIT RAFTER REFUSE
STRAIN THWART BLUNDER CODLING
GALLOWS ISTHMUS MISTAKE
(— IN FISHING) HUE COND
(HALF —) FLITCH
(PL.) MIDDLES

BALKAN (— COIN) NOVCIC
(— COUNTRY) GREECE SERBIA
ALBANIA RUMANIA BULGARIA
(— INSTRUMENT) GUSLA
(— RIVER) JIU OLT IBAR JIUL SAVA
TISA OLTUL DANUBE MORAVA
(— SEA) BLACK AEGEAN IONIAN
ADRIATIC

BALKER HUER CONNER

BALKY NAPPY STICK MULISH REESTY
RESTIVE CONTRARY STUBBORN
OBSTINATE

BALL IN BAL BOB FLY HOP NOB ORB
PEA TOY BEAD BOWL CLEW CLUE
KNOB KNOP KNUR PICK PILL POME
TRAP DANCE EDGER FAULT FLOAT
GLOBE GLOME HURLY ORBIT PEARL
PUPPY SHAPE SNACK SPORT TRUCK
BULLET BUTTON HOOKER HURLEY
MOONIE MUDDLE PEELEE PELLET
PELOTA POMMEL POMPON RONDEL
RUNDLE SPHERE SQUASH BALLOON
CONFUSE FLOATER GLOBULE
INCURVE INSHOOT KNAPPAN
LEATHER MANDREL PELOTON
RIDOTTO SLITTER BASEBALL
BISCAYEN FANDANGO FOOTBALL
GROUNDER HANDBALL QUENELLE
SOFTBALL SPHEROID TRAPBALL
(— AS SHIP'S SIGNAL) SHAPE
(— FOR MUSKET) GOLI SLUG

(— OF CLAY) KNICKER
(— OF RICE OR MEAT) PINDA
(— OF THREAD) CLEW CLUE GOME
BOTTOM WHARROW
(— OF THUMB) THENAR CUSHION
(— OF WASTE IRON) COBBLE
(— USED IN SHINTY) PEG
(—S OF MEDICI FAMILY) PALLE
(BILLIARD —) SPOT IVORY
SNOOKER
(BOWLED —) TICE CURVE SKYER
BAILER BUMPER FIZZER GOOGLY
KICKER POODLE YORKER CREEPER
SNORTER SPINNER BREAKBACK
CROSSOVER INSWINGER
(BOWLING —) DODO JACK
(CRICKET —) SNICK SHOOTER
(FIVES —) SNACK
(GOLF —) PUTTY
(HARD —) SNUG
(HOCKEY —) NUN NUR ORR
(INK —) PUMPET
(SKITTLE —) CHEESE
(TENNIS —) PALM
(WOODEN —) KNUR

BALLAD JIG LAI LAY LILT MELE
POEM SONG CAROL DERRY FANCY
BALLET BYLINA CARVAL SONNET
BALLANT CANZONE CORRIDO
GWERZIOU SINGSONG

BALLAST BED CRIB LOAD TRIM
METAL POISE STONE BOTTOM
BURDEN GRAVEL WEIGHT BALANCE
LASTAGE SANDBAG DRAGROPE
KENTLEDGE SABURRATE

BALLET BALLAD MASQUE BOURREE
PANTOMIME
(— MOVEMENT) VOLE TEMPS
APLOMB OUVERT POINTE RELEVE
RETIRE ALLONGE ARRONDI
ASSEMBLE ATTITUDE ARABESQUE

BALLHOOTER BRUTTER

BALLISTA SWEEP MANGONEL

BALLOON BAG BALL BLIMP EXPAND
GASBAG AIRSHIP DISTEND DRACHEN
INFLATE SAUSAGE SKYHOOK
AEROSTAT ENVELOPE DIRIGIBLE
(TRIAL —) KITE

BALLOONING BOSOMY

BALLOON VINE FAROLITO
HEARTPEA HEARTSEED

BALLOT BALE POLL PROX VOTE
ELECT PROXY VOICE BILLET CHOICE
POLICY TICKET SUFFRAGE

BALLROOM SALOON

BALLYHOO BALLY HOOPLA

BALM OIL BEEB BITO DAUB SALVE
ANOINT BALSAM EMBALM LOTION
RELIEF SOLACE SOOTHE ANODYNE
BESMEAR COMFORT PERFUME
UNGUENT OINTMENT
(— OF GILEAD) CANADA
OPOBALSAM

BALMY MILD SOFT BLAND DAFFY
MOONY SPICY SUNNY SWEET
GENTLE INSANE SERENE HEALING
LENIENT AROMATIC BALSAMIC
DRESSING FRAGRANT SOOTHING

BALONEY BUNK HOOEY BUSHWA
BUSHWAH

BALSA RAFT FLOAT GUANO POLAK
POLACK BOBWOOD CORKWOOD

BALSAM BALM RIGA TOLU UMIRI
COPALM GURJAN GURJUN STORAX
AMPALEA COPAIBA CREEPER
AMPALAYA BDELLIUM BENJAMIN
OINTMENT

BALSAM APPLE KARELA AMARGOSA
AMPALAYA BALSAMINE

BALSAM FIR SAPIN BAUMIER

BALSAM POPLAR BAUMIER
TACAMAHAC

BALSAMROOT SUNFLOWER

BALSAMWEED MOONSHINE
FEATHERWEED

BALT YOD ESTH LETT ESTONIAN

BALTIC (— GULF) RIGA DANZIG
BOTHNIA FINLAND
(— ISLAND) DAGO FARO OSEL
ALAND ALSEN OESEL OLAND
GOTLAND HIIUMAA BORNHOLM
(— PORT) KIEL RIGA MEMEL REVAL
DANZIG GDANSK TALINN LEIPAJA
(— RIVER) ODER ODRA DVINA
VIADUA
(— TOWN) MEMEL DANZIG GDANSK
LEIPAJA

BALUCHISTAN (— CULTURE)
QUETTA

BALUSTER SPOKE COLUMEL
BANISTER COLUMELLA

BALUSTRADE BARRER PARAPET
RAILING BALCONET BANISTER

BAMBOO DHA CANE REED BATAK
GLUMAL GUADUA TONKIN BATAKAN
WANGHEE WHANGEE
(SACRED —) NANDIN
(WOVEN —) SAWALI

BAMBOOZLE DUPE HAVE CHEAT
COZEN GRILL CAJOLE HUMBUG
BUFFALO DECEIVE DEFRAUD
MYSTIFY PERPLEX

BAN BAR WOE TABU VETO BANAL
BANUS BLOCK CURSE EDICT ORDER
TABOO BANISH CENSOR ENJOIN
FORBID HINDER INVOKE NOTICE
OUTLAW CONDEMN EXCLUDE
ANATHEMA DENOUNCE EXECRATE
PROHIBIT

BANAK UCUUBA

BANAL FLAT CORNY INANE SILLY
STALE TRITE VAPID JEJUNE INSIPID
TRIVIAL

BANANA FEI FIG MUSA SABA BERRY
ENSETE FINGER SAGING LACATAN
PLATANO SAGUING SUNBEAM
PLANTAIN

BAND BAR GAD HUB TIE TUB ZON
BEAD BELT BEND BOND CAME CASH
CORD CREW CUFF FALL FERD FESS
GANG GATE GIRT HOOD HOOP
KNOT LACE LIST RING SASH SHOE
TAPE WISP ZONA ZONE AMPYX
BANDY BRAID CHOIR CLAMP CORSE
COVEY COVIN CRAPE CROWN
FEMUR FLOCK FRAME GIRTH GORGE
GUARD JATHA LABEL MEINY NOISE
PANEL PATTE PRIDE QUIRE SABOT
SNOOD STRAP STRIP STROP TAPIS

TORSE TRACK TRIBE UNITE WERED
WITHE ARMLET BENDEL BINDER
BORDER BOYANG BRIDGE BUNDLE
CIMBIA CLAVUS COHORT COLLAR
COLLET COPULA COVINE CRANCE
CRAVAT DECKLE FASCIA FETTER
FILLET FRIEZE FRINGE FUNNEL
GAMMON GARTER GASKET GIRDLE
HYPHEN LEGLET MATRIX NIPPER
NORSEL PLEDGE RADULA REGULA
ROLLER SCREED STRAKE STRING
STRIPE SWATHE TAENIA TETHER
TISSUE WEEPER BINDING BLANKET
CHAMBUL CIRCLET COMPANY
ENOMOTY FERRULE FRONTAL
GARLAND HATBAND HEADING
NECKTIE ORPHREY PALLIUM PIGTAIL
PROMISE SEQUELA SHACKLE
SHOEING SWADDLE VINCULUM
(— **ACROSS SUNSPOT**) BRIDGE
(— **IN BRAIN**) LIGULA FRENULUM
FUNICULUS
(— **OF 13 WITCHES**) COVEN
(— **OF CLAY**) COTTLE
(— **OF COLOR**) SOCK SLASH STRIA
LACING
(— **OF CRAPE**) WEED SCARF
(— **OF INDIANS**) SHIVWITS
(— **OF PILLAGERS**) SKINNERS
(— **OF PURPLE**) CLAVUS
(— **OF STRAW**) GAD SIMMON
(— **TOGETHER**) BANDY
(**ARMED** —) JATHA POSSE
(**ARMOR** —) TONLET
(**CIRCULAR** —) HOOP RING ANNULE
WREATH
(**DANCE** —) CHORO
(**DECORATIVE** —) PATTE LEGLET
CORNICE
(**IRON** —) FRET GATE TRUSS
FUNNEL STRAKE
(**LACE** —) SCALLOP
(**MUSICIANS** —) CONCERT
(**RADIO** —) CHANNEL
(**RESONANCE** —) FORMANT
(**TRIBAL** —) AIMAK
(PL.) GRIPES INTERLACERY
BANDAGE BAND BELT BIND TAPE
BLIND BRACE CLOUT DRESS GALEA
LINEN SLING SPICA SWARF SWATH
TRUSS BINDER COLLAR CRAVAT
FASCIA FETTLE FILLET LIGATE
NIPPER ROLLER SWARTH SWATHE
SWEATH REVERSE ROLLING
SWADDLE TRUSSER ACCIPTER
CAPELINE CINCTURE GAUNTLET
LIGAMENT LIGATURE SCAPULAR
STOCKING
(**EYE** —) MUFFLER
(**FINGER** —) HOVEL
(**JAW** —) FUNDA
(PL.) SWADDLING
BANDALORE QUIZ
BANDANNA WEB TURBAN BANDANA
PULICAT PULICATE PULLICAT
BANDEAU BAND STRIP FILLET
BRASSIERE
BANDICOOT RAT MARL BILBI BILBY
BADGER BIELBY PINKIE QUENDA

BANDIT CACA TORY BRAVO THIEF
BANISH HAIDUK HEYDUK OUTLAW
ROBBER BANDIDO BRIGAND
LADRONE TULISAN BUSHWACK
MARAUDER MIQUELET PICAROON
(PL.) MANZAS
BANDLEADER MASTER MAESTRO
CHORAGUS CONDUCTOR
BANDORE PANDURA
BANDSMAN WINDJAMMER
BANDSTAND KIOSK STAND
BANDY VIE BAND CART CHOP SWAP
TRADE LEAGUE RACKET STRIVE
CHAFFER CONTEND DISCUSS
CARRIAGE EXCHANGE
(— **WORDS**) REVIE GIFFGAFF
BANE BAN WOE BONE EVIL HARM
KILL PEST RUIN CURSE DEATH
VENOM INJURY MURDER POISON
SLAYER NEMESIS SCOURGE
MISCHIEF MURDERER NUISANCE
BANEBERRY COHOSH REDBERRY
TOADROOT GRAPEWORT
BANEFUL BAD ILL EVIL VILE SWART
HARMFUL HURTFUL NOXIOUS
RUINOUS VENOMOUS SINISTRAL
BANG POM RAP BAFF BEAT BLOW
BOOT DASH DOCK DRUB POUF
SCAT SLAM SWAP SWOP TANK
BLAFF CLASH CRACK DRIVE EXCEL
FORCE IMPEL POUND SLAKE SLUMP
SOUND SPANG STRAM THUMP
WHACK WHANG WHUMP BOUNCE
CUDGEL ENERGY FRINGE STRIKE
THRASH THUNGE THWACK SARDINE
SURPASS THUNDER FORELOCK
(— **ON HEAD**) BRAIN
BANGLADESH (**CAPITAL OF** —)
DACCA
(**MONEY OF** —) TAKA
(**NATIVE OF** —) BENGALI
(**RIVER OF** —) GANGES
BANG-UP SLAP CRACK TIPTOP
BANISH BAN FREE ABAND EJECT
EXILE EXPEL FLEME WAIVE WREAK
BANDIT DEPORT DISPEL DISTER
FORSAY OUTLAW ABANDON
CONDEMN CONFINE DISMISS
DIVORCE EXCLUDE DISPLACE
RELEGATE
BANISHED FUGITIVE
BANISHMENT EXILE BANNIMUS
OUTLAWRY XENELASY OSTRACISM
XENELASIA
BANISTER RAILING BALUSTER
BANJO BOX BANJORE BANJORINE
BANK BAR BAY COP JUG RIM ROW
BINK BRAE BREW BUTT CAJA DIKE
DUNE DYKE EDGE HEAD HILL LINK
MASS PILE RAKE RAMP RIPA RIVE
SAND SEAT SIDE TIER WEIR BANCO
BENCH BLUFF BRINK COAST DITCH
EARTH FENCE HOVER HURST LEVEE
MARGE MOUND MOUNT RIDGE
SAVER SHARE SHELF SHOAL SHORE
SLOPE STACK STAGE TRUST
BANQUE BORROW CAISSE CAUSEY
CRADGE DEGREE DEPEND DOUBLE
MARGIN RANDOM RECKON RIVAGE

STRAND ANTHILL BANKING CUSHION
DEPOSIT LOMBARD POTTERY
SANDBAG SHALLOW WINDROW
BARRANCA PLATFORM TRAVERSE
(— **A FIRE**) REST
(— **OF CANAL**) BERM BERME
HEELPATH
(— **OF EARTH**) COP DAM DITCH
(— **OF RIVER**) WHARF STRAND
(— **OF SAND OR MUD**) BAR SCALP
(— **OF SNOW**) WREATH SNOWDRIFT
(— **OF TURF**) SUNK
(**OVERHANGING** —) BREW HOVER
(**RUSSIAN** —) CRAPETTE
(**STEEP** —) HEUCH HEUGH WOUGH
BARRANCA BARRANCO
BANKER BOOK SETH SETT FACTOR
FINDER SAHKAR SHROFF SOUCAR
SOWCAR LOMBARD MARWARI
MONEYER SPONSOR TAILLEUR
BANQUETER FINANCIER
BANKNOTE CRISP FLIMSY SCREEN
BANKRUPT SAP BUNG BUST RUMP
BREAK BROKE DRAIN SMASH STRIP
BROKEN BUSTED DYVOUR QUISBY
CRACKED DEPLETE
BANKRUPTCY SMASH FAILURE
SMASHUP
BANKSMAN LANDER HILLMAN
BANLIEUE LOWY ENVIRONS
BANNER FANE FLAG JACK SIGN
COLOR ENSIGN FANNON PENNON
LABARUM LEADING PENNANT
SALIENT BANDEROL BRATTACH
FOREMOST GONFALON ORIFLAMB
STANDARD STREAMER VEXILLUM
BEAUSEANT ORIFLAMME
(**FUNERAL** —) BANNEROL
GUMPHEON GUMPHION
(PL.) ENSIGNRY
BANNOCK PANAK DIGGER JANNOCK
BANNS CRY BANS CRIES NOTICE
SIBRET SIBRIT SIBREDE SPURRINGS
BANQUET FETE MEAL DIFFA FEAST
DINNER JUNKET MANGER REGALE
REGALO REPAST SEUDAH SPREAD
AHAAINA CONVITO CONVIVE
NAMGERY REGALIO CAROUSAL
FESTIVAL SYMPOSIUM SYSSITION
BANQUETER CONVIVE SYMPOSIAST
BANQUETING EPULATION
TRENCHERING
BANSHEE BOW SIDHE
BANTAM COCK GRIG BANTY DANDY
SAUCY CHICKEN SEBRIGHT
COMBATIVE
BANTENG OX TSINE BANTIN
TEMADAU
BANTER COD KID RAG ROT CHIP
FOOL JEST JOKE JOSH MOCK QUIZ
RAIL RAZZ BORAK CHAFF DRAPE
JOLLY QUEER RALLY ROAST TAUNT
TRICK DELUDE DERIDE HAGGLE
SATIRE BADINER STASHIE BADINAGE
CHAFFING GIFFGAFF RAILLERY
RIDICULE
BANTU ILA BULU GOGO GUHA HEHE
YAKA ZULU DUALA KAFIR KAMBA
KIOKO KONDE KONGO LAMBA

SHONA SWAZI BANYAI BASUTO
DAMARA HERERO KAFFIR NATIVE
THONGA WAGUHA YAKALA CABINDA
MASHONA SWAHILI WACHANGA
(— LANGUAGE) ILA RONGA THONGA
NYANAJA NYAMWEZI
BANYAN BUR BURR BANIYA BUNNIA
JAGUEY
BAOBAB MOWANA IMBONDO TEBELDI
CALABASH
BAPTISM CLEANSING IMMERSION
PALINGENY PERFUSION
BAPTISMAL FONTAL
BAPTIST DIPPER DIDAPPER
SEPARATE TRASKITE
BAPTIZE DIP DEPE FULL NAME
HEAVE VOLOW PLUNGE PURIFY
ASPERSE CLEANSE IMMERSE
CHRISTEN SPRINKLE
BAPTIZED ILLUMINATE
BAR BAN DAM FID FOX GAD LAW LEG
RIB ROD TAP AXLE BALK BAND
BANK BAUR BEAM BOLT BOOM
BULL CAKE CHAR CORE CROW
DRAG FLAT GATE HIDE JOKE LOCK
MAKE OUST POLE RACK RAIL REEF
SAVE SETT SHUT SKID SLAB SLAT
SLIP SLOT SNIB STOP TREE YARD
ARBOR BENCH BETTY BILBO BILCO
BLOCK BLOOM BRACE CATCH
CLASP CLOSE COURT CRAMP
CREEL DEBAR DETER DOLLY EASER
EMBAR ESTOP FENCE FORCE
GEMEL HEDGE HORSE HUMET
LEVER PERCH PILOT PINCH PITCH
RATCH SHADE SHAFT SHAPE SIGHT
SLOTE SNEEK SPELL SPOON SPRAG
STAFF STANG STAVE STRAP STRIP
STRUT SWIPE TRACE YAIRD
ANCONY BARRET BATTEN BILLET
BISTRO BODEGA BROOCH BUMPER
CRUTCH DOFFER DOLLEY DOLLIE
EVENER EXCEPT EYEBAR FASTEN
FORBAR FORBID FORCER FORSET
GRILLE HEAVER HINDER LADDER
MEAGRE NORMAN PEELER RABBLE
RADIAL RETURN RIFFLE SALOON
SHADES SHANTY STOWER STRIPE
TABLET TANGLE TILLER TOGGLE
BARRACE BARRAGE BARRIER
BOBSTAY BOLSTER BUVETTE
CHANNEL CHARIOT CONFINE
COUNTER DRAWBAR EXCLUDE
GALLOWS MANDREL MANDRIL
OVERARM PREVENT SCRATCH
SIDEBAR SNIBBLE SPINDLE
STEMMER TOMBOLO TOPRAIL
TRUNDLE WIREBAR ASTRAGAL
KNIFEWAY MURDERER PESSULUS
(— FOR TAPPING FURNACE) LANCET
(— IN FABRIC) BARRE
(— IN RIVER) CHAR SANDBAR
(— IN SEA) SWASH
(— OF CULTIVATOR) ARCH
(— OF DOOR) SLOT STANG
(— OF ELECTRIC SWITCH) BLADE
(— OF GATE) SPAR LEDGE
(— OF HARROW) BULL
(— OF LOOM) EASER SWORD

BATTEN BACKSTAY
(— OF RAYS) SHOOT
(— OF STEEL) BLOOM STIRRUP
(— OF WAGON) SHETH
(— ON SIDE OF BOWSPRIT)
WHISKER
(— ON WINDMILL) UPLONG
(— WITH SPIKES) HERISSON
(HERALDIC —) FESS FESSE HUMET
LABEL
(JOINTED —) CHILL
(MINING —) MOIL
(NOTCHED —) RISP SKEY
(PAIR OF —S) GEMEL GEMMEL
(REFRESHMENT —) CANTEEN
(SOAP FRAME —) SESS
(STIRRING —) CRUTCH
(TAMPING —) STEMMER
(TYPEWRITER —) BAIL BALE
SPACER SHUTTLE
(WEAVING —) TEMPLE
(WHEEL —) AXLE SPOKE
BARANI BRANDY
BARB AWN BUR JAG MOW BURR
CLIP FILE FLUE HAIR HERL HOOK
JAGG BEARD HORSE POINT RIDGE
SHAFT SPEAR PIGEON STRAIN
TIPPET WITTER BARBARY BARBULE
BRISTLE FILAMENT KINGFISH
(— OF ARROW) HOOK WING BEARD
WITTER
(— OF FEATHER) HARL HERL
RAMUS PINNULA FILAMENT
(— OF HARPOON) FLUE FLUKE
BARBADOS (CAPITAL OF —)
BRIDGETOWN
(MOUNTAIN OF —) HILLABY
(NATIVE OF —) BIM
BARBADOS CHERRY ACEROLA
BARBAREA CAMPE
BARBARIAN HUN BOOR GOTH RUDE
WILD ALIEN BRUTE SAVAGE VANDAL
RUFFIAN FOREIGNER UNTUTORED
BARBARIC GROSS ATROCIOUS
BARBARISM CANT DATISM
SAVAGISM SOLECISM
BARBARITY FERITY CRUELTY
FELLNESS FEROCITY RUDENESS
SAVAGERY BRUTALITY
BARBAROUS FELL RUDE WILD
CRUEL BRUTAL FIERCE GOTHIC
BESTIAL FOREIGN HUNNISH
INHUMAN SLAVISH UNCIVIL
IGNORANT CUTTHROAT FEROCIOUS
PRIMITIVE
BARBARY MAGOT MAGHRIB
MOGHRIB
(— STATE) TUNIS ALGIERS
MOROCCO TRIPOLI
BARBASCO CUBE JOEWOOD
BARBECUE ASADO BOCAN BUCCAN
BARBEL BEARD CIRRUS WATTLE
BARBLET CYPRINID
BARBER NAI FIGARO POLLER
SHAVER TONSOR SCRAPER
TONSURE
(— FISH) TANG
BARBET BARBION BARMKIN
DREAMER BARBICAN PUFFBIRD

WATERRUG IRONSMITH PEARLBIRD
THICKHEAD TIGERBIRD
BARBITAL VERONAL
BARD BHAT MUSE POET SCOP SWAN
DRUID OVATE RUNER SCALD SKALD
OSSIAN SHAPER SINGER BARDING
PENBARD MINSTREL MUSICIAN
TALIESEN DEMODOCUS
BARE DRY BALD LEAN MERE NUDE
POOR ALONE CRUDE EMPTY NAKED
PLAIN PLUME STARK STRIP WASTE
BARISH BARREN CALLOW DENUDE
DIVERT DIVEST EXPOSE HISTIE
MARGIN MEAGER MEAGRE PALTRY
PILLED REVEAL SCARRY SIMPLE
DIVULGE EXPOSED UNARMED
UNCOVER DENUDATE DESOLATE
DISCLOSE STRIPPED DESTITUTE
(— TEETH) TUCK
(NOT —) COOL
BAREFACED GLARING IMPUDENT
AUDACIOUS SHAMELESS
BARELY JIMP JUST ONLY FANIT
HARDLY MERELY POORLY SIMPLY
UNEATH UNNETH NAKEDLY
UNNETHE EDGEWAYS SCANTILY
SCARCELY SLIGHTLY
BARER NAVVY DELVER FEIGHER
MUCKMAN CALLOWER
BARFISH DORAB
BARGAIN GO BUY RUG WOD COPE
DEAL HUCK KOOP MART MISE PACT
PICK RUGG SALE SELL SNIP TROG
WHIZ CHEAP FIGHT PRICE STEAL
TROKE TRUCK WHACK WHIZZ
BARTER DICKER HAGGLE HIGGLE
NIFFER PALTER CHAFFER CHEAPEN
COMPACT CONTEND CONTEST
DISPOSE PACTION TRAFFIC
CONTRACT COVENANT PENNORTH
PURCHASE STRUGGLE WANWORTH
(— HARD) PRIG
(— IN MINING) STURT
BARGAINER NIP KITE COPER
COWPER CHAFFERER
(SHARP —) SCREW
BARGAINING MART ACHATE
CHAFFER CHEAPING HUCKSTERY
BARGE ARK BOX BOY HOY TOW TUB
BARK BOAT FUST LUMP PRAM RAFT
SCOW TROW BARCA CASCO DUMMY
FOIST LUNGE LURCH PRAAM SCOLD
SHREW VIXEN BARQUE BERATE
BUGERO DREDGE GALLEY GYASSA
PRAHAM REBUKE STUMPY TENDER
THRUST WHERRY BALLOON BIRLING
CHALANA DROGHER GABBARD
GABBART GONDOLA LIGHTER
OMNIBUS TOWBOAT TUMBLER
TUMBRIL BUDGEROW CARRIAGE
MOORPUNKY
(COAL —) KEEL
BARGEMAN PUG BARGEE BARGER
HOYMAN HUFFLER
BARGHEST PADFOOT
BARITE CAUK CAWK TIFF CAULK
BARYTES BARYTINE HEPATITE
BARK AGO BAG BAY OUF RUB TAN
WAP YAP YIP BAFF BOAT BOOF

COAT COTO DITA HOWL HUSK OPEN
PEEL PELT PILL REND RIND ROSS
SKIN SNAP TAPA WAFF YAFF YAWP
YELP AABEC BALAT BARCA BARGE
COUGH MOCHA NIEPA SHELL SHOUT
SPEAK STRIP TIMBE YABBA YAMPH
YOUFF ABRADE AGAMID AVARAM
BARKEY BOWWOW CASSIA CORNUS
CORTEX GIRDLE MASSOY SINTOC
TRANKY WAFFLE YAFFLE MALAMBO
MESENNA PERIERA PHLOEUM
SOLICIT TANBARK DOUNDAKE
EUONYMUS FRANGULA GRANATUM
MEZEREUM WOODSKIN
(AROMATIC —) CANELLA
CULILAWAN
(EXTERIOR OF —) ROSS
(LAVER OF —) HAT
BARKER BUFFER DOORMAN
GRINDER SPIELER SPUDDER
SPRUIKER CHARLATAN
BARKING BAY SPUD QUEST
LATRANT LATRATION
BARLEY BIG BEAR BENT BIGG GRAIN
SPRAT LICORN HORDEUM
WHITECORN
(AWN OF —) HORN
(GROUND —) TSAMBA
(HULLED —) PTISAN
(REFUSE —) SHAG FLINTS
BARN BYRE AMBAR LATHE STALL
GRANGE STABLE SKIPPER
COWHOUSE
(— OWL) LULU MADGE
(COW —) SAUR SHIPPON
BARNACLE BRAY BREY ACORN
LEPAS CYPRIS ANATIFA BALANID
LEPADID CIRRIPED GNATHOPOD
SACCULINA
BARNBURNER SOFT
BARNSTORM TOUR
BARNYARD PIGHTLE BACKSIDE
FARMYARD STRAWYARD
BAROMETER GLASS ANEROID
OROMETER
BARON DAIMIO BARONET FREEMAN
FREIHERR
(COURT —) HALLMOOT
BARONY HAN DOMAIN
BAROQUE GOTHIC ORNATE ROCOCO
GROTESQUE IRREGULAR
BAROTO VINTA
BARRACK CAMP BOTHY CASERN
CANNABA CUARTEL
BARRACUDA CUDA KAKU SPET
BARRY PELON SNAKE SNOEK
SNOOK BECUNA PICUDA SCOOTS
SENNET VICUDA KATONKEL
SCOOTERS
BARRAGE BAR ATTACK VOLLEY
BARRIER DRUMFIRE UMBRELLA
CANNONADE FUSILLADE
BARRAMUNDA SALMON CYCLOID
DIPNOAN FLATHEAD CERATODUS
BARRED CUCKOO RIBBED STRIPED
BARREL FAT HUB KEG TUN VAT
BUTT CADE CASK DRUM KANG TREE
BOWIE QUILL SHELL STAND UNION
FESSEL GIRNAL GIRNEL HOGGET

RUMBLE RUNLET TIERCE TUMBLE
VESSEL CALAMUS CISTERN
PACKAGE RATTLER RUNDLET
TUMBLER CYLINDER HOGSHEAD
KILDERKIN
(— OF FEATHER) CALAMUS
(— OF REVOLVER) CHAMBER
(— ROW) LONGER
(— WITH CRANKS) VANGEE
(CAPSTAN —) SPOOL
(CORE —) LANTERN
(HERRING —) CADE CRAN
(SMALL —) KEG KIT CADE KNAG
RUNLET BARRICO RUNDLET
BARRELHOUSE GUTBUCKET
BARREN DRY ARID BARE BOWY
DEAD DEAF DOUR DULL EILD GAST
GELD LEAN NUDE POOR SALT SECK
YELD YELL BLEAK BLUNT BOWEY
DRAPE DUSTY EMPTY GAUNT
GHAST GUESS NAKED STARK STERN
WASTE YEILD DESERT EFFETE
FALLOW HISTIE HUNGRY JEJUNE
MEAGER STUPID SAPLESS STERILE
DESOLATE IMPOTENT TEEMLESS
TREELESS
(NOT —) FACILE FECUND
(PL.) LANDES
BARRENNESS VACANCY EMPTINESS
BARRICADE BAR STOP BLOCK
CLOSE FENCE ABATIS PRISON
BARRAGE BARRIER DEFENSE
FORTIFY OBSTRUCT RAMFORCE
ROADBLOCK
(— OF TREES) ABATIS
BARRIER ALP BAR DAM BOMA CRIB
CROY DIKE DOOR DYKE FOSS GATE
LINE LOCK PALE STOP WALL WEIR
BOUND CHAIN FENCE FOSSE GRILL
HEDGE LIMIT STILE STUMP CORDON
GLACIS GRILLE HURDLE SCREEN
TREBLE BARRAGE CEILING CURTAIN
GALLERY PARAPET RAILING
RAMPART BOUNDARY FORTRESS
FRONTIER STOCKADE STRENGTH
TRAVERSE
(— ACROSS RIVER) STILL KIDDLE
(— IN TRUCK) HEADER
(ARTIFICIAL —) FOSS FOSSE
(TRAFFIC —) SEPARATOR
(PL.) BAIL
BARRING BUT SAVE CLOSED
BARRISTER COLT BARMAN JUNIOR
LAWYER TUBMAN COUNSEL
POSTMAN TEMPLAR ADVOCATE
ATTORNEY SERJEANT
BARROOM PUB CAFE HOUSE
SALOON CANTINA DOGGERY
GROCERY TAPROOM DRAMSHOP
DRINKERY EXCHANGE GROGGERY
GROGSHOP
BARROW HOD HOG BANK BIER DUNE
GALT HILL MOTE TUMP CARRY
GRAVE GURRY HURLY MOUND
BURROW GALGAL KURGAN NAVETA
HILLOCK TROLLEY TUMULUS
MOUNTAIN PUSHCART
BARRULET VIVRE
BARTENDER MIXER BARMAN

BARMAID SKINKER TAPSTER
BARTER CHAP CHOP COPE COUP
HAWK MANG MONG SELL SWAP
TROG VEND CORSE TRADE TROKE
TRUCK DICKER NIFFER SCORSE
BARGAIN CAMBIUM CHAFFER
PERMUTE TRAFFIC TRUCKLE
COMMERCE EXCHANGE
BARTERER COPER COWPER
TRUCKER
BASAL BASIC BASILAR RADICAL
BASALT MARBLE NAVITE DIABASE
GHIZITE KULAITE POTTERY
AUGANITE BANDAITE DOLERITE
ANAMESITE ARAPAHITE MELAPHYRE
SUDBURITE
BASE BED DEN HUB LOW TUT ANIL
CLAM EVIL FOOT FOUL HUBB LEWD
MEAN POOR RELY REST ROOT
SACK STAY STEM STEP VILE BASIS
BLOCK CHEAP DIRTY FIRST FLOOR
FOUND LACHE MUDDY PETTY SNIDE
SOCLE STAND STOOL WORSE
ABJECT BOTTOM BRASSY COARSE
COMMON DEMISS GROUND GRUBBY
HARLOT HUMBLE MENIAL NOUGHT
PALTRY PATAND PATTEN PERRON
PODIUM RASCAL SECOND SHABBY
SORDID VULGAR BASTARD CAITIFF
COMICAL CURRISH DEBASED
FOOTING HANGDOG HILDING
HOUSING IGNOBLE PEASANT
ROINISH SERVILE SLAVISH STADDLE
STANDER SUBBASE SUPPORT
CHURLISH COISTREL COISTRIL
DEGRADED DRAWHEAD HARLOTRY
HOLDFAST INFAMOUS INFERIOR
MECHANIC MESCHANT PEDESTAL
PEDIMENT RASCALLY SCULLION
SHAMEFUL STANDARD STEPPING
SUBSTRAT UNWORTHY WRETCHED
NIDDERING
(— IN QUALITY) LEADEN
(— OF CANNON) SOUL
(— OF OPERATIONS) BOOK HOME
(— OF PETAL) CLAW
(— OF PLANT) CAUDEX
(— OF POLLINIUM) DISC DISK
(— OF TUBER) HEEL
(CHEMICAL —) ACRIDAN ADENINE
ANSERIN CHOLINE GUANINE
ACRIDANE ACTININE AGMATINE
ALDIMINE ALKALOID ANSERINE
CONYRINE GALEGINE KETIMINE
LEPIDINE SEMIDINE
(HIDDEN —) LAIR
(HOME —) DEN
(LEAF —) FOVEA
(LOGARITHM —) E
(SECOND —) KEYSTONE
(STALKLIKE —) CNIDOPOD
BASEBALL PILL APPLE DUSTER
FLOATER INSHOOT LEATHER
BEANBALL HARDBALL HORSEHIDE
STICKBALL
(— PLAYER) YANNIGAN
BASEBOARD GRIN SKIRT PLINTH
EASEMENT MOPBOARD SKIRTING
WASHBOARD

BASE-DEALING BROKING
BASELESS IDLE UNFOUNDED
BASEMAN SACKER
BASEMENT BASE CELLAR
  TAHKHANA
BASENESS FELONY VILITY BEGGARY
  SQUALOR TURPITUDE
BASH BAT LAM BEAT BLOW DENT
  MASH SWAT WHAM WHOP ABASH
  SLOSH SMASH BRUISE STRIKE
BASHFUL COY SHY HELO SHAN
  BLATE HELOE TIMID MODEST
  PUDENT ASHAMED DAUNTED
  BACKWARD BLUSHING DAPHNEAN
  DISMAYED LOATHFUL PUDIBUND
  RETIRING SACKLESS SHAMEFUL
  SHEEPISH SKITTISH VERECUND
BASHFULNESS PUDOR SHYNESS
BASIC BASE BASAL VITAL BOTTOM
  BEDROCK CANONIC CENTRAL
  CLASSIC ZINCOUS CARDINAL
  ULTIMATE ELEMENTAL ESSENTIAL
  SUBSTRATE
BASIL TULASI
BASIN DOP PAN BOWL COMB COVE
  DISH DOCK EWER FLOW FONT GULF
  LAKE PARK SINK SLAD TALA TANK
  COMBE LAVER SLAKE STOUP
  BASSON BULLAN CHAFER CIRQUE
  HOLLOW LAVABO LEKANE LOUTER
  MARINA VALLEY VESSEL CUVETTE
  PISCINA RECEIPT URCEOLE
  CESSPOOL LAVATORY RECEPTOR
  VANITORY WASHBOWL GEMELLION
  (**MOUNTAIN** —) HOYA
  (**ROCK** —) KEEVE KIEVE
BASIS BASE FOND FOOT FORM FUND
  ROOT SILL AXIOM STOCK ANLAGE
  BOTTOM GROUND ACCOUNT
  BEDROCK FOOTING PREMISE
  SUPPORT GRAVAMEN STRENGTH
  AUTHORITY CRITERION FUNDAMENT
  GROUNDSEL SUBSTANCE
BASK SUN BEEK WARM ACRID BATHE
  ENJOY REVEL BITTER REJOICE
  APRICATE
BASKET IE ARK COB FAN HOT KIT
  LUG PAD PED PEG POT TAP TOP
  BUCK CAUL COBB COOP CORB
  CORF CRIB FLAT GOAL HOTT IEIE
  KIPE KISH KIST KITT LEAP MAND
  MAUN SKEP TAPE TILL TOUR TRUG
  WEEL CABAS CASSY CESTA CHEST
  CRAIL CRASH CRATE CREEL DEVIL
  DILLI DILLY FRAIL GRATE MAUND
  MOLLY NATTE RUSKY SCULL SWILL
  WILLY BEACON BOKARK CASSIE
  CLEAVE COFFIN COURGE CRADLE
  DORSEL DORSER DOSSER FANNER
  FASCET GABION HAMPER HOBBET
  HOBBIT HOPPET JICARA JUNKET
  KIBSEY KIPSEY MOCOCK MOLLIE
  MURLIN PANIER PEGALL PETARA
  POTTLE PUNNET SEQUIN TAPPET
  TEANAL TOPNET VOIDER WINDEL
  WINDLE WISKET ZEQUIN CANASTA
  CORBEIL CRESSET FLASKET
  HANAPER PANNIER PATTARA
  PITARAH PRICKLE SCUTTLE SEEDLIP

  SHALLOW SKEOUGH SKIPPET
  WATTAPE WHISKET CALATHUS
  CANISTER CHEQUEEN ZECCHINO
  (— **BOTTOM**) SLATH
  (— **FOR CRUMBS**) VOIDER
  (— **FOR EELS**) BUCK COURGE
  (— **FOR FIGS**) TAP CABAS FRAIL
  TAPNET
  (— **FOR FRUIT**) MOLLY CALATHOS
  CALA
BASKET MAKER ANASAZI
BASKETRY UPSET
BASKETWORK TEE SLEW WALE
  SLATH STAKE SLATHE STROKE
  SLEWING
BASQUE VASCON EUSCARA
  EUSCARO IBERIAN BISCAYAN
  (— **DIALECT**) LABOURDIN
  (**PL.**) VASCONA VASCONES
BAS-RELIEF PLAQUETTE
BASS LOW PES CHUB DEEP DRUM
  FOOT ROCK BASSO DRONE HURON
  ROCHE SWEGO VOICE BORDUN
  BRASSE BURDEN CHERNA GROUND
  JUMPER REDEYE SINGER STRIPE
  ACHIGAN BARFISH BOURDON
  BROWNIE GROWLER JEWFISH
  STRIPER BACHELOR BIGMOUTH
  BLUEFISH CABRILLA ROCKFISH
  SPOTTAIL STREAKER CONTINUO
  TALLYWAG WELSHMAN LINESIDES
  (— **DRUM**) TAMBURONE
  (— **PART**) ALBERTI
  (**GROUND** —) OSTINATO
  (**THOROUGH** —) BC
BASSOON CURTAL FAGOTT
  FAGOTTE FAGOTTO
BASSWOOD LIN BASS WAHOO
  LINDEN WICOPY DADDYNUT
  WHITEWOOD
BAST LIBER RAMIE PHLOEM
  NOSEBURN
BASTARD GET SOB BASE FALSE
  CANNON COWSON GALLEY HYBRID
  IMPURE MAMZER BYSPELL GETLING
  LOWBRED MONGREL WOSBIRD
  BANTLING BASEBORN MISBEGET
  NAMELESS SPURIOUS WHORESON
BASTE SEW BEAT CANE COOK DRUB
  LARD TACK FLAMB SAUCE CUDGEL
  JIPPER PUNISH STITCH THRASH
BASTION JETTY MOINEAU
BAT CAT HIT WAD BACK BAKE BATE
  BEAT CLUB FOWL GAIT JACK LUMP
  MASS SWAT TRAP WINK BANDY
  BATON BRICK CHUCK FUNGO HARPY
  PIECE SPREE STICK ALIPED BACKIE
  BASTON BEETLE CUDGEL DRIVER
  KALONG POMMEL RACKET STRIKE
  STROKE WILLOW BAUCKIE FLUTTER
  JAVELIN NOCTULE VAMPIRE
  BLUDGEON SEROTINE REREMOUSE
BATAK (— **DIALECT**) TOBA
BATCH LOT BAKE BREW CAST CROP
  FINE MASS MESS SORT FLOOR
  GROUP BAKING CHEESE MAKING
  BOILING BREWING FORMULA
  MIXTURE RAISING QUANTITY
  (— **OF EGGS**) SETTING

  (— **OF GRAIN**) GRIST
  (— **OF MAIL**) SEPARATION
BATCHER BAGGER
BATE BAIT BEET PUER PURE GRAIN
BATELEUR BERGHAAN
BATEMAN DRENCHER
BATFISH ANGLER DIABLO MALTHE
  DEVILFISH
BATH DIP TUB BAIN BATE PERT
  TOSH BATHE LAVER STEEP THERM
  DOUCHE LIQUOR MIKVAH PICKLE
  PLUNGE SHOWER SPONGE
  BALNEUM LAVACRE ABLUTION
  BALNEARY
  (**FOOT** —) PEDILUVIUM
  (**HOT** —) STEW SCALD STUFE
  THERM STUPHE THERME
  (**MUD** —) ILLUTATION
  (**PHOTOGRAPHIC** —) FIXER
  (**SITZ** —) BIDET SITZBAD SEMICUPE
  INSESSION
  (**SPINNING** —) DOPE
  (**STEAM** —) SAUNA
  (**TANNING** —) BATE SOAK
  (**TURKISH** —) HUMMUM HOTHOUSE
BATHE BAY TUB BAIN BASK DOOK
  LAVE STEW WASH CLEAN DOUSE
  DOWSE EMBAY SOUSE STEEP
  ENWRAP FOMENT SHOWER SPLASH
  EMBATHE IMMERSE PERVADE
  SUFFUSE PERMEATE
BATHHOUSE SEW STEW SAUNA
  STUFE CABANA HAMMAM STUPHE
  BALNEARY
BATHING LAVACRE LAVEMENT
  (— **SUIT**) SLIP TOGS MAILLOT
BATHSHEBA (**HUSBAND OF** —)
  DAVID URIAH
  (**SON OF** —) SOLOMON
BATHTUB TUB TOSH LAVACRE
BATON ROD BEND BURN WAND
  STAFF STICK BAGUET BASTON
  CUDGEL BOURDON SCEPTER
  SCEPTRE BAGUETTE CROSSBAR
  TRUNCHEON
BATSMAN BAT BATTER HITTER
  SLOGGER SLUGGER STRIKER
BATTALION WARD CONREY
BATTEN END LAY RIB SLEY CLEAT
  LEDGE BATTON BEATER ENRICH
  FATTEN REEPER THRIVE FERTILIZE
  (**PL.**) SPARRING
BATTER RAM BEAT DENT MAIM
  CLOUR DINGE FRUSH PASTE POUND
  SMASH BALLER BRUISE BUFFET
  HAMMER HATTER HITTER PUMMEL
  THRING TUMBLE BATSMAN
  BOMBARD CRIPPLE DESTROY
  FRITTER SHATTER SLUGGER
  STRIKER DEMOLISH
BATTERCAKE WAFFLE
BATTERING BLAST LACING
BATTERY PILE SINK TIRE TROOP
  RADEAU EXCITER SINKBOX
  SINKBOAT
  (**GUN** —) SWINGER
BATTLE WAR CAMP DUEL FEUD
  FRAY MART MEET TILT TOIL UNDO
  BRUSH FIELD FIGHT JOUST STOUR

ACTION AFFRAY CAMLAN COMBAT
SHOWER STRIVE CONTEND
CONTEST HOSTING JOURNAL
JOURNEY WARFARE CONFLICT
SKIRMISH STRUGGLE ENCOUNTER
NAUMACHIA THEOMACHY
BATTLE-AX WIFLE POLEAX SPARTH
TWIBIL BROADAX HALBERD TWIBILL
WHIFFLE FAUCHARD FRANCISC
BATTLE CRY CRY ENSIGN
GERONIMO BEAUSEANT
BATTLEFIELD BLAIR CHAMP TAHUA
CHAMPAIGN
BATTLEMENT KERNEL MERION
PINION CORNELLE
BATTLESHIP MAINE CARRIER
BATTY BATS BUGGY CRAZY SILLY
BATLIKE FOOLISH
BAUBLE BOW TOY BEAD GAUD
BUTTON GEWGAW TRIFLE MAROTTE
TRINKET GIMCRACK PLAYTHING
BAWD AUNT HARE DIRTY MADAM
DEFILE MADAME PANDER COMMODE
MACKEREL PROCURER PURVEYOR
BAWDY DIRTY SCARLET
BAWL CRY HOWL ROUT YAUP YAWP
BLORE GOLLY SHOUT BELLOW
BOOHOO OUTCRY GLAISTER
(— OUT) JUMP CRACK SCOLD
BAY ARM COD DAM RIA VOE BANK
BARK CHOP COVE GULF HOLE HOPE
HOWL LOCH ROAN TREE WICK
YAUP YAWP BAHIA BASIN BAYOU
BERRY BIGHT COLOR CREEK FIORD
FJORD FLEET HAVEN HORSE INLET
LOUGH MOUTH ORIEL QUEST SINUS
SPEAK TRAVE BABBLE HARBOR
LAUREL RECESS SEVERY WINDOW
BADIOUS BAYGALL ENCLOSE
ESTUARY MALABAR SILANGA
ULULATE BREWSTER CHESTNUT
(— OF BARN) GOAF SKEELING
SKILLING SKILLION
(— STATE) MASSACHUSETTS
(SWEET —) BREWSTER
BEAVERWOOD
BAYBERRY AUSU PIMIENTA
WAXBERRY
BAYOU SLEW SLOO SLUE BROOK
CREEK INLET RIVER OUTLET
SLOUGH STREAM RIVULET
BACKWATER
BAY WINDOW ORIEL MIRADOR
BAZAAR FAIR FETE SALE AGORA
BURSE CHAWK CHOWK MARKET
CANTEEN BOOKFAIR EMPORIUM
BEZESTEEN
BDELLIUM GUGAL GUGUL GOOGUL
BE ABE ARE BES BEEN BETH BIST
LIVE ABIDE EXIST OCCUR WORTH
REMAIN BREATHE CONSIST SUBSIST
CONTINUE
BEACH AIR BANK CHIP MOOR NARD
RIPA SAND SLIP COAST PLAGE
PLAYA PRAYA SHORE GROUND
SHILLA STRAND HARDWAY SEASIDE
SHINGLE LAKESHORE
(— RIDGE) FULL
(PROJECTING —) CUSP

BEACH APPLE CANAJONG
BEACHCOMBER SEASONER
STRANDLOOPER
BEACH FLEA SCUD SCREW
SANDBOY
BEACH GRASS STAR SPIRE
MARRAM BENTSTAR
BEACON MARK PIKE SIGN BAKEN
FANAL GUIDE PHARE RACON
ENSIGN PHAROS RAMARK SIGNAL
CRESSET SEAMARK WARNING
NEEDFIRE SIGNPOST STANDARD
BEAD NIB POT DROP FOAM GAUD
AGGRI AGGRY BUGLE FILET GRAIN
KNURL PEARL QUIRK SIGHT STAFF
ARANGO BAGUET BAUBLE BICUNE
BUBBLE CORNET FILLET PELLET
PIPPER PRAYER RONDEL WAMPUM
DEWDROP GLOBULE MOLDING
SPARKLE TRINKET AVEMARIA
CABOCHON
(ROSARY —) GAUD PATERNOSTER
(SHELL —S) SEWAN
BEADING VEINING
(PL.) TASBIH
BEADLE CRIER MACER POKER
USHER BEDRAL BUMBLE HARMAN
HERALD BAILIFF NUTHOOK OFFICER
SERVITOR SUMMONER APPARITOR
MESSENGER
BEADSMAN BEGGAR HERMIT
BLUEGOWN GOWNSMAN
BEAK NEB NIB BECK BILL CLAP
NOSE PIKE PROW LORUM SNOUT
SWORD TUTEL MASTER NOZZLE
SPERON WEAPON EMBOLON
EMBOLUM FOREBOW MOLDING
ROSTRUM BEAKHEAD MANDIBLE
CAPITULUM
(— OF SHELL) UMBO
(— OF SHIP) SPERON
(— OF SWORDFISH) SWORD
BEAKER CUP HORN TASS BIKER
BOCAL BOUSE GLASS BARECA
BEAM BAR LEG RAY TIE BALK BEAK
BOOM EMIT GLOW PLAT SILE SILL
SKID SPAR STUD ARBOR CABER
FLASH GLEAM GLEED JOIST LIGHT
RAYON SHAPE SHINE SHOOT SMILE
SPEAR STANG STOCK TRAVE
BINDER CAMBER CHEESE COLLAR
FLITCH GIRDER GLANCE HEADER
MANTEL NEEDLE RAFTER SUMMER
TIMBER TRABES TREVIS WALKER
BALANCE BUMPKIN CHANNEL
CHEVRON DORMANT DRAWBAR
FRIJOLE MADRIER PINRAIL RADIATE
SLEEPER SUPPORT TRANSOM
TRIMMER TYNDALL AXLETREE
BROWPOST HERISSON PADSTONE
PLOWHEAD ROOFTREE STENTREL
TEMPLATE
(— OF LIGHT) CHINK GLEED RAYON
SHAFT SIGNAL STREAM SUNBEAM
STRICTURE
(HIGH —) BRIGHTS
(LARGE —) BALK LACE BAULK
SUMMER
(LOW —) DIM

(SANIO'S —) CRASSULA
(WEAVER'S —) TRAM TAVIL
(PL.) CRANEWAY
BEAMER SCUDDER
BEAMING GAY ROSY BRIGHT
LUCENT MASSIVE RADIANT SHINING
BEAMY BROAD BRIGHT JOYOUS
LUCENT MASSIVE RADIANT
MIRTHFUL
BEAN BON NIB URD CHAP FABA
FAVA GRAM HABA HEAD LIMA POLE
SNAP TEKE TICK BRAIN CARAT
PULSE SIEVA SKULL CACOON
CASTER COLLAR FELLOW KIDNEY
LABLAB LENTIL NIPPLE NOGGIN
RUNNER RUTTEE SEEWEE STRIKE
TEPARY THRASH TRIFLE CALABAR
FRIJOLE PHASEMY SNAPPER
WINDSOR BONAVIST BONNYVIS
TICKBEAN TORNILLO
(— CURD) TOFU
(LOCUST —) CAROB
(MESCAL —) SOPHORA
(PL.) NIBS FASELS FESELS PODDER
PODWARE
BEANIE DINK
BEAN-SHAPED FABIFORM
BEANSHOOTER TRUNK
PEASHOOTER
BEAN TREE BOGUM
BEAN TREFOIL LABURNUM
BEAR GO CUB LUG BALU BERN
BORN CAST DREE DUBB FURE GEST
GIVE HAVE HOLD LIFT TEEM TOTE
URSA WEAR ABIDE ALLOW BALOO
BEGET BHALU BREED BRING BROOK
BROWN BRUIN CARRY DREIE DRIVE
GESTE ISSUE KOALA POLAR PRESS
SPARE STAND STICK THOLE THROW
WEIGH WIELD YIELD AFFORD
BEHAVE BRUANG CONVEY ENDURE
IMPORT INFANT KADIAK KINDLE
KODIAK PIERCE RENDER SUFFER
THRUST UPHOLD URSULA WOMBAT
WOOBUT ARCTOID BROWNIE
COMPORT CONDUCT EPHRAIM
FORBEAR GRIZZLY MUSQUAW
PRODUCE STOMACH SUPPORT
SUSTAIN UNDERGO FISSIPED
(— EXPENSES) DEFRAY
(— FLOWERS) FLOURISH
(— FRUIT) FRUCTIFY
(— INVESTIGATION) WASH
(— ON) CONCERN
(— OUT) PROPORT
(— PATIENTLY) DIGEST
(— UP) CAPE ENDURE SUSTAIN
(— WITH CREDIT) BROOK
(— WITNESS) TEEM SPEAK ATTEST
DEPOSE
(— YOUNG) FIND CALVE CHILD
(MALE —) BOAR
(SLOTH —) ASWAIL
BEARBERRY LARB WHORTLE
BILBERRY DOGBERRY FOXBERRY
CREASHAKS
BEARD ANE AWN AVEL BARB DEFY
FACE FUZZ NECK NOSE PEAK TUFT
ZIFFS ARISTA BEAVER GOATEE

TASSEL AFFRONT BARBULE
CHARLEY CHARLIE VANDYKE
IMPERIAL STILETTO WHISKERS
(— OF GRAIN) AIL AWN
(— TREATISE) POGONOLOGY
(SMALL —) BARBET
BEARDED AWNIE HAIRY BARBED
BARBATE HIRSUTE POGONIATE
WHISKERED
BEARDLESS NOT NOTT IMBERBE
POLLARD
BEARER NEWS HAMAL MACER
BEADLE HAMMAL HOLDER PACKER
PORTER ANCIENT CARRIER JAMPANI
PINCERN CHAPRASI ESCUDERO
PORTATOR STANDARD SUPPORTER
(— OF GREAT BURDEN) ATLAS
(ARMOR —) ESQUIRE
(BURDEN —) HAMAL HAMMAL
(CROZIER —) CROCIARY
(CUP —) SAKI COPPER
(PALANQUIN —) BOY SIRDAR
MUSAHAR
(SHIELD —) SQUIRE ESCUDERO
(STANDARD —) ANCIENT
(STRETCHER —) BRANCARDIER
(SWORD —) PORTGLAVE
PORTGLAIVE
BEARING AIM AIR COD BALL DUCT
GEST MIEN ORLE PORT RUBY BIRTH
FRONT GESTE HABIT JEWEL POISE
SETUP TENUE TREND ALLURE
APPORT ASPECT BILLET CHARGE
COURSE DEPORT GERENT GIGLIO
MANNER ORIENT SADDLE THRUST
VOIDER ADDRESS AZIMUTH
CONDUCT FASHION GESTURE
MEANING POSTURE PURPORT
RHODING SUPPORT AMENANCE
ATTITUDE BEHAVIOR BIRTHING
CARRIAGE DELIVERY DEMEANOR
FOOTSTEP PEDESTAL PRESENCE
PRESSURE RELATION STANDARD
TENDENCY TOURNURE YIELDING
(— FRUIT) FRUCTED
(— OUTWARD) EFFERENT
(ARROGANT —) HUFF
(HERALDIC —) GAD DELF ENTE
GORE MARK ORLE CROWN DELFT
DELPH FUSIL LAVER PHEON BILLET
DEVICE ENSIGN GOUTTE CHAPLET
CLARION DEMIVOL PLASQUE
QUARTER ORDINARY QUENTISE
(PERSONAL —) GARB
BEARLIKE URSINE
BEAR'S-EAR AURICULA
BEAR'S-FOOT OXHEAL PEGROOTS
BEARSKIN BUSBY
BEAR STATE ARKANSAS
BEAST BETE HOOF BRUTE VACHE
ANIMAL JUMENT MONSTER
MUSIMON VENISON BLIGHTER
OPINICUS
(— OF BURDEN) JUMENT SUMPTER
(3-HORNED —) TRICORN
(CASTRATED —) SPADO
(DEAD —) MORKIN
(FABULOUS —) YALE THRIS
BAGWYN TRICORN DINGMAUL

EPIMACUS GYASCUTUS
(HORNED —) RETHER ROTHER
(STURDY —) NUGGET
(WILD —) FERIN FERINE OUTLAW
UNBEAST
(WILD —S) ZIIM
BEASTLY GROSS PRONE ANIMAL
BRUTAL WICKED BESTIAL BRUTISH
INHUMAN SWINISH OFFENSIVE
BEAT BAT BUM COB DAD FAN FIB
LAM PIP PLY PUN RUN TAN TAP
TAW TEW TIE WAX BAFF BAIT BANG
BASH BATE BELT BEST BLOW BOLT
BRAY BUFF CANE CAST CHAP CLAP
CLUB COIL COLT COMB CRAB DAUD
DING DINT DRUB DUMP DUNT FELL
FIRK FLAP FLAX FLOG FRAM FRAP
FRAT GROW HAZE KILL LACE LAMP
LASH LICK LOUK LUMP LUSH MAUL
MELL MEND MILL PAIK PALE PANT
PELT POSS PRAT ROUT SCAT SLAM
SLAT SLOG SOCK SOLE SOWL STUB
SWAP SWOP TACK TAKD TICK TRIM
TUND TWIG WALK WARP WELT WHIP
WHOP WIPE BASTE BATON BERRY
BIRCH CHURN CLINK CREAM CURRY
DOUSE DRASH DRESS DRIVE FEEZE
FIGHT FILCH FLAIL FLANK FORGE
ICTUS INLAY KNOCK LABOR NEVEL
NOINT POUND PULSE ROUND SCATT
SCOOP SCOUR SKELP STAMP
STRAP SWACK SWING TARGE
THREP THROB THUMP TREAD
TRUMP UPEND WADDY WHACK
WHANG WORST ACCENT ANOINT
BAMBOO BATTER BENSEL BETTLE
BOUNCE BUFFET COTTON CUDGEL
DEFEAT DOWSEL FEAGUE FETTLE
HAMMER HAMPER JACKET KNEVEL
LARRUP LATHER NEAVIL NODDLE
OUTRUN PUMMEL RADDLE REBUKE
REESLE RHYTHM SCUTCH SQUASH
STOUND STOUSH STRIKE STRIPE
STROKE SUGGIL SWINGE SWITCH
TANSEL TEWTAW TEWTER THRASH
THREAP THREIP THREPE THRESH
TICKLE WAGGLE WALLOP WATTLE
ASSAULT BATTUTA BELABOR
BLATTER BLISTER CADENCE
CANVASS CONQUER CONTUSE
EXHAUST FATIGUE FLYFLAP
KNUCKLE LAMBACK LAMBAST
LOBTAIL LOUNDER PULSATE
REESHIE SHELLAC SURPASS
SWABBLE SWADDLE TROLLOP
TROUNCE VIBRATE
(— ABOUT) BUSK BANGLE
(— AGAINST THE WIND) LAVEER
(— AGAINST) BLAD
(— BARLEY) PAIL WARM
(— CLOTHES) BATTLE
(— COVERT) TUFT
(— DOWN) LAY FELL FULL ABATE
FLASH
(— EGGS) CAST
(— FIBERS) BRUSH
(— HIGH) LEAP
(— IT) LAM
(— OF HEART) DUNT STROKE

(— ON BUTTOCKS) COB
(— SEVERELY) DRUB LUMP SOAK
BASTE SOUSE LATHER
(— SMALL) CHAP
(— WINGS) BATE FLAP
(— WOODS) TUSK
(MUSICAL —) BOUNCE BATTUTA
BEATEN BEAT BETE BATTU PARTY
TRITE TRADED
BEATER RAB MAUL SEAL CANER
LACER STOCK DASHER DRIVER
MALLET TRIMMER THRESHER
SCUTCHER
BEATIFIC DEIFIC ELYSIAN
BEATIFY SAINT HALLOW HEAVEN
ENCHANT GLORIFY SANCTIFY
BEATING COB COBB LICK TUND
BEANS DOUSE JESSE PULSE STICK
HAZING HIDING ROPAND TATTOO
BASHING BATTERY BELTING
CLANKER DASHING DUSTING
LICKING SKELPIN WELTING WHALING
BIRCHING DRESSING DRUBBING
RIBROAST WHIPPING JACKETING
STRAPPADO
BEATITUDE JOY BLISS BENISON
MACARISM HAPPINESS
BEAU BEW BOY CHAP BLADE DANDY
FLAME LOVER SPARK SWELL
ESCORT FELLOW GARCON STEADY
SUITOR TATTLE ADMIRER AIMWELL
BRAVERY COURTER COXCOMB
CUPIDON GALLANT SPARKER
FOLLOWER
BEAU GREGORY COCKEYE
BEAUTIFUL FAIR FINE GLAD GOOD
MEAR MEER MERE WALY BELLE
BONNY KALON LUSTY SHEEN WLITY
WLONK BLITHE BONNIE COMELY
DECORE FREELY LOVELY POETIC
PRETTY VENUST ELEGANT
FORMOSE FORMOUS TEMPEAN
TOKALON CHARMING DELICATE
ESTHETIC FAIRSOME GORGEOUS
GRACEFUL HANDSOME LUCULENT
SPECIOUS
BEAUTIFY FAIR GILD ADORN GRACE
HIGHT PREEN PRIMP PRUNE BEAUTY
BEDECK DECORE ENAMEL QUAINT
ADONIZE ENHANCE GARNISH
GLORIFY DECORATE FAIRHEAD
EMBELLISH PULCHRIFY
BEAUTY FACE FAIR FORM GLEE
BEAUT BELLE CHARM FAVOR GLORY
GRACE PRIDE WLITE FINERY
LOOKER LOVELY POLISH DECORUM
FEATURE TOKALON SPLENDOR
FORMOSITY
(— OF FORM) SYMMETRY
(— OF STYLE) ELEGANCE
BEAVER BOOMER CASTOR RODENT
PRALINE MUSHROOM SEWELLEL
STARLING
(— SKIN) PLEW
(— STATE) OREGON
(DARK —) NUTMEG
BEBEERINE CURINE
BEBEERU SWEETWOOD
GREENHEART

BECAUSE AS SO FOR THAT BEING CAUSE SINCE THERE FORWHY THROUGH INASMUCH
BECCAFICO FIGEATER FIGPECKER
BECHE-DE-MER PIDGIN TREPANG
BECK RUN VAT BECON BROOK
(— **AND CALL**) DEVOTION
BECKEN CYMBALS
BECKET SQUILGEE SQUILLGEE
BECKON BOW NOD WAG BECK WAFT WAVE CURTSY SUMMON BIDDING COMMAND CURTSEY GESTURE
BECKONING WAFTURE
BECLOUD HIDE MASK BEDIM DARKEN MUDDLE MYSTIFY OBSCURE
BECLOUDED FOGGY
BECOME GO FIT GET RAX SET SIT WAX COME FALL GROW LIKE PASS SUIT TAKE TILL WEAR ADORN BEFIT GRACE PROVE WORTH ACCORD BEFALL BESEEM BETIDE CHANGE IWORTH BEHOOVE FLATTER PROCEED
(— **A PARTY**) ACCEDE
(— **AUDIBLE**) ARISE
(— **DAMP**) EVE
(— **DAZED**) DWAM DWALM
(— **DIM**) DASWEN
(— **DROWSY**) DOW
(— **FAT**) GRAZE
(— **FLUID**) FLOW FLUX LEACH
(— **KNOWN**) GO KITHE KYTHE SPUNK
(— **MOLDY**) FUST MOUL FINEW
(— **MOROSE**) SOUR
(— **ROUND**) GLOBE
(— **SOUR**) FOX BLINK CARVE
BECOMING FIT FEAT GOOD BHAVA FITTY RIGHT COMELY DUEFUL GAINLY DECORUM FARRAND FARRANT DECOROUS HANDSOME SUITABLE WISELIKE
BECOMINGLY TALLY
BED COT HAY KIP PAD PAN TYE BAND BASE BODY BUNK DOSS DOWN FLOP FORM LAIR PLOT SACK VEIN WADI WADY BERTH BOIST COUCH FLASK FLOCK GRATE GROVE LAYER THORE BORDER BOTTOM COUCHE CRADLE GIRDLE HOTBED LIBKEN LIBKIN LITTER MATRIX OSIERY PALLET STRATA CHANNEL CHARPOY FLEABAG HAMMOCK LODGING QUARTER REPOSAL SEEDBED SETTING STRATUM SUBSOIL TRUCKLE TRUNDLE BASSINET CAPSTONE LENTICLE PLANCHER
(— **DOWN**) DOSS
(— **IN WAGON**) KATEL
(— **OF ANIMAL**) LAIR KENNEL
(— **OF COAL**) BRAT DELF SEAM
(— **OF EMBERS**) GRIESHOCH
(— **OF FURNACE**) HEARTH
(— **OF GUN-CARRIAGE**) FLASK
(— **OF HAND PRESS**) COFFIN
(— **OF REFUSE**) NITRIARY
(— **OF ROCK**) CAP PLUM

(— **OF ROSES**) ROSARY
(— **OF SEDIMENT**) WARP
(— **OF STREAM**) DRAW WASH BILLABONG STREAMWAY
(**CREEK** —) COULEE COULIE
(**DRIED LAKE** —) CHOTT SHOTT
(**FEATHER** —) TIE TYE
(**FOLDING** —) SLAWBANK
(**LOW** —) LOWBOY
(**OYSTER** —) STEW LAYER SCALP CLAIRE LAYING OYSTERAGE
(**RUBBLE** —) CALLOW
(**SEED** —) SEMINARY
(**WATER-BEARING** —) AQUAFER AQUIFER
BEDAUB CLAG CLAT DAUB SOIL SLAKE SMEAR SLAISTER
BEDBUG BUG CHINK CIMEX CHINCH CHINTZ COREID PUNESE VERMIN CIMICID PUNAISE REDCOAT CONENOSE HEMIPTER HOUSEBUG
BEDCHAMBER BEDROOM CUBICLE
BEDCLOTHES COVER BEDDING CLOTHES
BEDCOVER COMFORTER PALAMPORE
BEDDING BEDROLL DOMESTICS
BEDECK GEM BEDO LARD TRAP ADORN ARRAY DIGHT GRACE PRINK ORNAMENT EMBELLISH
BEDECKED PRINKY
BEDEVIL ABUSE ANNOY BESET WORRY HARASS MUDDLE PESTER BEWITCH CONFUSE TORMENT
BEDEW DEW SHOWER IRRORATE
BEDIZEN DAUB ADORN ARRAY DIZEN BEDAUB
BEDLAM RIOT NOISE RUDAS ASYLUM TUMULT UPROAR MADNESS MADHOUSE BETHLEHEM
BEDOUIN ABSI ARAB BEDU MOOR NOMAD BADAWI BEDAWEE SHAMMAR HOWEITAT
BEDQUILT POURPOINT
BEDRAGGLE TRACHLE
BEDRAGGLED FORLORN SHOPWORN
BEDRAIL RAVE RATHE
BEDRIDDEN ILL AILING BEDFAST
(**NOT** —) AFOOT
BEDROCK LEDGE NADIR SHELF BOTTOM HARDPAN STONEHEAD
BEDROLL BINDLE
BEDROOM FLAT BERTH CABIN BEDDER DORMER BOUDOIR CHAMBER CUBICULO WARDROBE GARDEROBE
BEDSORE DECUBITUS
BEDSPREAD ALEZE STRAIL BEDCOVER COVERLET COVERLID
BEDSTEAD BED COT CRIB HATCH STEAD STAPLE ANGAREP CHARPOY
BEDSTRAW CRUDWORT CURDWORT FLEAWEED BEDFLOWER CROSSWORT SCRAMBLER
BED TESTER SPARVER
BEDWARMER CURATE
BEE DOR FLY APIS BEVY KING RING KARBI MASON NOMIA NURSE PARTY DINGAR DRONEL DRONER FROLIC

INSECT NOTION TORQUE TSETSE WORKER ANDRENA DEBORAH KOOTCHA MELISSA RAISING SERPENT STINGER SWERVER TRIGONA ANDRENID ANGELITO HONEYBEE QUILTING SCOPIPED SHUCKING WAXMAKER GATHERING
(**QUEEN** —) KING
(**PL.**) BEEN BONE HIVE SPEW SOCIALES
BEEBREAD CERAGO AMBROSIA
BEECH BUCK BIRCH MYRTLE FLINDOSA FLINDOSY
BEECHNUT SPLITNUT
(**PL.**) BUCK MAST PANNAGE
BEEF JERK BEEVE BULLY GRIPE JERKY VIFDA VIVDA CASSON CUTTER CHARQUI TOPSIDE COMPLAIN COMPOUND PASTRAMI PIPIKAULA
(— **FOR SLAUGHTER**) MART
(**BOILED** —) BOUILLI
(**BROILED** —) CHURRASCO
(**CORN** —) BULLY
(**CUT OF** —) SEY LOIN RUMP SIDE BARON CHINE CHUCK FLANK ROAST ROUND SHANK STEAK ALOYAU CUTLET SADDLE BRISKET KNUCKLE QUARTER SIRLOIN EDGEBONE SHOULDER AITCHBONE NINEHOLES RATTLERAN
(**GROUND** —) HAMBURGER
(**INFERIOR** —) COMPOUND
(**JERKED** —) TASAJO BILTONG CHARQUE CHARQUI
(**LEAN** —) LIRE
(**SALTED** —) JUNK VIFDA
BEEF BREAD SWEETBREAD
BEEFEATER OXBIRD OXBITER OXPECKER TICKBIRD
BEEFWOOD TOA BELAH BELAR FILAO
BEEFY HEAVY HEFTY SOLID BRAWNY FLESHY
BEE GLUE PROPOLIS
BEEHIVE GUM BUTT GUME HIVE SKEP PYCHE STAND STATE STOCK SWARM APIARY HOPPET ALVEARY SWARMER BEEHOUSE PRAESEPE
(— **STATE**) UTAH
(— **TOMB**) TREASURY
BEEKEEPER HIVER BEEMAN BEEHERD APIARIST SKEPPIST
BEELZEBUB DEVIL
BEEN BE BON SEE BONE
BEE PLANT GUACO STINKWEED
BEER ALE MUM BIER BOCK BREW FARO GAIL GROG GYLE HOPS KVAS MALT MILD QUAS SCUD SUDS BELCH CHANG CHICA GROUT KVASS LAGER POMBE QUASS SCUDS STOUT WEISS CHICHA DOUBLE GATTER LIQUOR PORTER SPRUCE STINGO SWANKY SWIPES WALLOP ZYTHUM PANGASI PHARAOH PILSNER TANKARD TAPLASH TAPWORT CERVISIA
(**ADD TO** —) KRAUSEN
(**BAD** —) TACK TAPLASH

(HOT — AND GIN) PURL
(INFERIOR —) BELCH SWANKY
(SMALL —) TIFF GROUT
(SOUR —) BEEREGAR
(STRONG —) HUFF DOUBLE STINGO
(THIN —) PRITCH SWIPES
(TIBETAN —) CHANG
(WARM — AND OATMEAL) STORRY
(WEAK —) BEVERAGE
BEERHOUSE TIDDLYWINK
BEESWAX CAPPING
BEET CHARD MANGEL MANGOLD
STECHLING
(SUGAR —) BOLTER
BEETLE BAT BOB BUG JUT RAM
BEAT BUZZ FLEA FOWL GOGA
GOGO IPID MAUL MELL STAG TROX
TURK UANG AMARA ATLAS BORER
BULGE CAROB CHUCK DRIVE FIDIA
GOGGA HISPA LYCID MELOE SAGRA
TIGER CHAFER CLERID CUCOYO
CUCUYO ELATER GOLACH GOLOCH
HISTER JUTOUT KHAPRA LICTUS
MALLET MELOID PESTLE PRUNER
PTINID SAWYER SCARAB WEAVER
WEEVIL ADELOPS BRUCHID
BUZZARD CADELLE CARABID
CARABUS CUCUJID FIDDLER
FIREFLY GIRDLER GOLDBUG
LADYBUG LUCANID PAUSSID
PRIONID PROJECT SILPHID SKIPPER
SNAPPER SOLDIER TANBARK
TICKLER ATEUCHUS CALOSOMA
CETONIAN COCKTAIL CURCULIO
DYTISCID ENGRAVER EROTYLID
FIGEATER GLOWWORM HARDBACK
LADYBIRD LAMPYRID LOWERING
OVERHANG RUTELIAN SCOLYTID
SEARCHER SHARNBUD SHARNBUG
SKIPJACK SPHINDID SQUASHER
SQUEAKER SYMPHILE TOKTOKJE
WHIRLWIG DEDEMERID LONGICORN
OSTOMATID TUMBLEBUG TWIRLIGIG
WHIRLIGIG
(PL.) XYLOPHAGA
BEEWEED TONGUE
BEFALL HAP COME LIMP SORT TIDE
TIME CHEFE CHIVE OCCUR SHAPE
ASTART BECOME BETIDE HAPPEN
PERTAIN
BEFIT DOW SIT COME LONG SEEM
SORT SUIT BESET SERVE BECOME
BEHOVE BESEEM BETIDE BEHOOVE
BEFITTING FIT AFTER DECENT
PROPER WORTHY SEEMING THRIFTY
BECOMING DECOROUS SORTABLE
(PROFESSIONALLY —) ETHICAL
BEFOG GAUM CLOUD OBSANE
CONFUSE MYSTIFY
BEFOOL FON SOT BURN COLT CRAP
DOLT DUPE FODE JADE ASSOT
ELUDE FONNE DIDDLE TRIFLE
FOOLIFY
BEFORE OR TO AIR BUT ERE FOR
GIN TIL ANTE FORE SAID TILL YORE
AFORE AHEAD ANENT AVANT
CORAM FIRST FORBY FORNE FRONT
PRIOR SOPRA UNTIL FORBYE
FORMER RATHER SOONER TOFORE

WITHIN AGAINST ALREADY EARLIER
FORTHBY FORWARD
(— LONG) SOON ERELONG
(JUST —) TOWARD FORMERLY
BEFOUL FILE SLUT SOIL BERAY
DIRTY GRUFT BEMIRE DAGGLE
DARKEN DEFILE DRABBLE FEWMAND
POLLUTE SLUTTER BESQUIRT
ENTANGLE
BEFOULED SHARNY
BEFRIEND AID ABET HELP FAVOR
ASSIST BENFIT FOSTER FRIEND
SUCCOR SUPPORT SUSTAIN
BEFUDDLE BOX GAS ADDLE BESOT
MUDDLE BECLOUD CONFUSE
FLUSTER MYSTIFY STUPEFY
BEFUDDLED REE
BEG ASK BID CRY SUE WOO CANT
COAX KICK MUMP PRAY PRIG SEEK
SORN SUIT THIG TRAM CADGE
CRAVE MAUND MOOCH PLEAD
SCAFF TEASE YEARN ADJURE
BESEECH ENTREAT IMPLORE
MAUNDER REQUEST SKELDER
SOLICIT PETITION OBSECRATE
BEGET GET WIN BEAR HAVE KIND
SIRE BREED YIELD BIGATE CREATE
FATHER ACQUIRE ENGRAFF
CONCEIVE ENGENDER GENERATE
BEGETTER SIRE AUTHOR FATHER
MOTHER PARENT
BEGGAR BLOB RUIN ASKER HALFY
LAZAR RANDY ROGUE THRUM
TRAMP ARMINE BACACH BIDDER
CANTER DYVOUR MUMPER PARIAH
PAUPER SORNER WRETCH
ABRAHAM ALMSMAN BAIRAGI
BEGSTER JARKMAN LAZARUS
MAUNDER PARDHAN PROCTOR
RUFFLER SCAFFER SORNARI
STEMMER THIGGER ABRAMMAN
BADGEMAN BEADSMAN DUMMERER
GLASSMAN PALLIARD STROLLER
WHIPJACK SCHNORRER
(— DESCRIPTION) PASS
(PL.) GUEUX
BEGGARED PEELED
BEGGARLY MEAN POOR CHEAP
PETTY SORRY ABJECT PALTRY
PILLED PEGRALL BANKRUPT
INDIGENT HUNGARIAN
BEGGAR'S-LICE STICKWEED
BEGGAR-TICK CUCKOLD
(PL.) BOOTJACKS
BEGGARY THIG WANT INDIGENCE
PAUPERISM
BEGGING MAUND CRAVING
MENDICANT THOMASING
(— FOR FOOD) SCRANNING
(FRAUDULENT —) TRUANDISE
BEGHARD PICARD
BEGIN GIN GYN HIT FALL FANG
HEAD JUMP LEAD OPEN RISE TAME
YOKE ARISE ENTER FRONT START
ATTACK ATTAME INCEPT SPRING
STREAK COMMENCE INCHOATE
INITIATE
BEGINNER BOOT PUNK TIRO TYRO
ROOKY SOFTA GINNER NOVICE

ROOKIE SOPHTA AMATEUR
ENTRANT RECRUIT RUBBLER
STUDENT TRAINEE FRESHMAN
INCEPTOR NEOPHYTE NOVELIST
BEGINNING EGG DAWN EDGE GERM
HEAD RISE ROOT SEED ALPHA
BIRTH DEBUT ENTRY FIRST FRONT
ONSET START VAUNT AURORA
INCOME INSTIL ONCOME ORIGIN
OUTSET SETOUT SOURCE SPRING
CALENDS DAWNING GENESIS INCIPIT
INFANCY INITIAL INITION KALENDS
NASCENT OPENING SUNRISE
ENTRANCE EXORDIUM INCHOATE
OUTSTART RUDIMENT
(NEW —) EPOCH
(PL.) INCUNABULA
BEGONE OFF OUT VIA AWAY SCAT
SHOO SCOOT SCRAM AROINT
AVAUNT DEPART SKIDDO SKIDDOO
VAMOOSE
BEGONIA GAIETY GAYETY
BEGRIME COOM SOIL COLLY DITCH
GRIME BECOOM SMIRCH SMUDGE
BRUCKLE
BEGRIMED DIRTY GRIMY SMUDGY
CINDERY SMIRCHY
BEGRUDGE ENVY GRUDGE MALIGN
JALOUSE
BEGTI NAIR COCKUP
BEGUILE FOX COAX FODE FOIL
FOND GULL LURE VAMP WILE WISE
AMUSE CHARM CHEAT COZEN
ELUDE EVADE GUILE TRICK TROLL
TRYST WEIZE BRIGUE BUTTER
DELUDE DIVERT ENTRAP JUGGLE
VAMPEY DECEIVE ENSNARE
FLATTER FLUMMER MISLEAD
BEHALF HALF PART SAKE SIDE
FAVOR SCORE STEAD AFFAIR
MATTER PROFIT BENEFIT DEFENCE
SUPPORT INTEREST
BEHAVE DO ACT LET BEAR FARE
HAVE KEEP MAKE PLAY WALK
WORK CARRY REACT TREAT ACQUIT
DEMEAN DEPORT HANDLE COMPORT
CONDUCT CONTAIN DISPORT
GESTURE MANAGER FUNCTION
REGULATE RESTRAIN
(— AFFECTEDLY) MOP
(— AWKWARDLY) GAUM HOCKER
(— BOLDLY) GAUSTER
(— BRASHLY) HOOK
(— CHURLISHLY) CARL
(— EVASIVELY) DODGE
(— FOOLISHLY) DOLT
(— MISCHIEVOUSLY) LARK
(— NOISILY) HELL REHAYTE
(— OSTENTATIOUSLY) SWANK
(— VULGARLY) RAMP
BEHAVIOR AIR MIEN PORT RULE
THEW WALK FRONT GUISE HABIT
LATES USAGE ACTION COURSE
GOINGS MANNER ACTIONS BEARING
BIGOTRY COMPORT CONDUCT
DECORUM ERGASIA FACTION
FASHION HAVANCE HAVINGS
AMENANCE ATTITUDE BLINDISM
BREEDING BYRONICS CARRIAGE

FUNCTION MAINTAIN
(ARROGANT —) SIDE SWAGGER
(COURTEOUS —) COMITY
COURTESY
(DECENT —) CIVILITY
(FOOLISH —) SIMPLES SOTTISE
(LIVELY —) TITTUP
(LOUTISH —) BUFFOONRY
(RIOTOUS —) RAMPAGE
(SILLY —) SPOONISM
(STUDIED —) ART
BEHEAD NECK
BEHEST BID LAW HEST RULE ORDER
DEMAND BIDDING COMMAND
MANDATE
BEHIND AFT HINT PAST RUMP
ABACK ABAFF ABAFT AFTER AHIND
AREAR LATER PASSE TARDY
ARREAR ASTERN DERERE
BACKWARD DILATORY
BEHINDHAND TARDY LAGGARD
DILATORY HINDERLY
BEHOLD LA LO EYE SEE SPY ECCE
ESPY GAZE HOLD KEEP LOOK SCAN
STOP TOOT VIEW WAIT HOLDE
OCULE SIGHT VOILA WATCH ASPECT
DESCRY MIRROR REGARD RETAIN
DISCERN OBSERVE SURVISE
WITNESS
BEHOLDEN OWING BOUNDEN
OBLIGED INDEBTED
BEHOOVE DOW FIT NEED SUIT THAR
BEFIT OUGHT THARF BELONG
PROPER REQUIRE
BEIGE HOP TAN ECRU HOPI GREGE
DORADO GREIGE STRING SUNBURN
BEING ENS ESSE FEAL SELF ENTIA
GNOME HUMAN SHAPE TROLL
ANIMAL ENTITY EXTANT LIVING
MORTAL PERSON SYSTEM ESSENCE
PRESENT REALITY VIVENCY
CREATURE EXISTENT ONTOLOGY
PRESENCE STANDING
(ANIMATE —) LIFE JAGAT
(CELESTIAL —) ANGEL CHERUB
SERAPH WATCHER DIVINITY
(DIMINUTIVE —) ELF GNOME
(DIVINE —) DEV DEVA DEMIGOD
(ESSENCE OF —) SAT
(ETERNAL —) EON AEON
(EVIL —) DEVIL GHOUL
(FABULOUS —) TENGU TORNIT
(HUMAN —) BODY BUCK JACK SOUL
BLADE HUMAN SLIME ANIMAL
ADAMITE CREATURE RATIONAL
CHRISTIAN
(IDEAL —) IMMORTAL
(ILL-FAVORED —) BLASTIE
(IMAGINARY —) SYLPH TERMAGANT
(INNER —) INWARD SPRITE INBEING
(INNERMOST —) HEART
(INTRINSIC —) ESSENCE
(LEGENDARY —) GIANT
(LIVING —) BLOOD WIGHT
(MATERIAL —) HYLIC
(PERFECT —) GOD
(PHYSICAL —) FLESH
(SEMIDIVINE —) SHEDU LAMASSU
(SMALL —) INCHLING

(SO —) SAEBEINS
(SUPERNATURAL —) DEV MAN AKUA
ATUA DEVA JANN ZEMI ADARO
BALAM DAEVA DEMON FAIRY TROLL
DAEMON GARUDA GODKIN SPIRIT
GODLING FOLLETTO HAMINGJA
(SUPREME —) DEITY MONAD
NYAMBE NZAMBI CREATOR
(TRUE —) OUSIA
BELABOR PLY BEAT DRUB LASH
WORK ASSAIL BOUNCE CUDGEL
HAMMER HAMPER THRASH THWACK
BELAY BESET BELAGE INVEST
WAYLAY BESEIGE
BELCH BOKE BOLK BURP GALP
RASP RIFT ERUCT FRUCT REBOKE
ERUCTATE
BELDAM HAG FURY CRONE RUDAS
ALECTO ERINYS RUDOUS VIRAGO
BELDAME JEZEBEL TISIPHONE
BELEAGUER BELAY BESET INVEST
ASSAULT BESEIGE LEAGUER
BLOCKADE SURROUND
BELEM PARA
BELEMNITE ARTIFACT KERAUNION
BELFRY SHED TOWER BEFFROY
CLOCHER CLOGHEAD BELLHOUSE

BELGIUM
CAPITAL: BRUSSELS BRUXELLES
CANAL: UNION ALBERT CAMPINE
GAUL TRIBE: REMI BELGAE NERVII
MEASURE: VAT AUNE LAST PIED
CARAT PERCHE BOISSEAU
MOUNTAIN: BOTRANGE
NAME: BELGIE BELGIQUE
PLATEAU: ARDENNES HOHEVENN
PORT: OSTEND ANTWERP
PROVINCE: LIEGE NAMUR
ANTWERP BRABANT HAINAUT
LIMBURG FLANDERS HAINAULT
RIVER: LYS DYLE LEIE MAAS
MARK YSER BOUCQ DEMER
LESSE MEUSE NETHE RUPEL
SENNE DENDER ESCAUT MANJEL
OURTHE SAMBRE SEMOIS
VESDRE WARCHE AMBLEVE
SCHELDT
TOWN: AS AAT ANS ATH HAL HUY
MOL SPA AATH AMAY ASSE
BOOM BREE DOEL GAND GEEL
GENK GENT HOEI LIER LOOZ
MONS VISE WAHA ZELE AALST
ALOST ARLON CINEY EEKLO
ESSEN EUPEN EVERE GENCK
GHENT HEIST IEPER JETTE
JUMET LIEGE NAMUR RONSE
TIELT UCCLE VORST WEZET
YNOIR YPRES AARLEN ANVERS
BERGEN BILZEN BRUGES
DEURNE IZEGEM LEUVEN LIERRE
MERXEM OPWIJK OSTEND
ANTWERP ARDOOIE BERCHEM
DOORWIK HERSTAL HOBOKEN
IXELLES LOUVAIN MECHLIN
ROULERS SERAING TOURNAI
BRUSSELS COURTRAI KORTRIJK
MOUSCRON TURNHOUT

VERVIERS WATERLOO
WEIGHT: LAST CARAT LIVRE
POUND CHARGE CHARIOT
ESTERLIN

BELIE BELONG DEFAME BESEIGE
FALSIFY PERTAIN SLANDER
TRADUCE DISGUISE STRUMPET
SURROUND
BELIEF CRY FAY ISM LEVE MIND
SECT TALE TROW VIEW VOTE WEEN
CAUSE CREDO CREED DOGMA FAITH
OBEAH TENET TROTH TRUST
CREDIT GROUND CRIANCE FEELING
HOLDING OPINION TROWING
ARYANISM BITHEISM CREDENCE
DOCTRINE FINALISM HUMANISM
RELIANCE
(— IN DEVILS) DIABOLISM
(— IN GHOSTS) EIDOLISM
(FALSE —) DELUSION
(GROUNDLESS —) CANARD
(MORTAL —) HALL
(SHALLOW —) BALLOON
(SUPERSTITIOUS —) FREET
(TRADITIONAL —) ICON IKON EIKON
(UNFOUNDED —) FICTON
BELIEVE BUY WIS DEEM FEEL HOLD
TAKE TREW TROW WEEN CREED
FAITH FANCY GUESS JUDGE SEPAD
THINK TRUST ACCEPT CREDIT
ESTEEM EXPECT DARESAY SUPPOSE
ACCREDIT CONSIDER CREDENCE
(— ERRONEOUSLY) FEIGN
(— NAIVELY) SWALLOW
(— UNCRITICALLY) EAT
BELIEVER IST LEVER BOTARY KITABI
CREDENS ADHERENT ARMINIAN
BELITTLE DECRY DWARF SNEER
MINISH SLIGHT DETRACT DIMINUE
LIGHTLY MINIMIZE VILIPEND
DENIGRATE DISCREDIT DISPARAGE
BELITTLER ZOILUS
BELL HUB TOM CALL FAIR GONG
HUBB RING ROAR CHIME CLOAK
CLOCK CODON FLARE KNELL SWELL
TENOR BASKET BELLOW BUBBLE
CLOCHE CROTAL CURFEW PHONIC
SOCKET TAPPER TOCSIN TOLLER
TREBLE TRIPLE VESPER ANGELUS
BLOSSOM CAMPANA CAMPANE
COROLLA COWBELL JANGLER
JINGLER LOWBELL SKELLAT
SKILLET TAMBOUR TANTONY
TINKLER CASCABEL COCKBELL
DINGDONG DOORBELL HANDBELL
HAWKBELL MORTBELL PAVILLON
STARTLER TINGTANG
(ALARM —) TOCSIN
(CLOSED —) CROTAL
(EVENING —) CURFEW
(FUNERAL —) TELLER
(HAND —) CLAG
(LARGE —) SIGNUM
(LOWEST —) BORDON BOURDON
(PASSING —) KNELL
(SACRING —) SQUILLA
(SLEIGH —) GRELOT

BELLABELLA HAELTZUK HEILTSUK
BELLADONNA DWALE MANICON
  BANEWORT DAFTBERRY
  DWAYBERRY MYDRIATIC
BELLARMINE GRAYBEARD
  GREYBEARD LONGBEARD
BELLBIRD MAKO SHRIKE COTINGA
  ARAPUNGA KORIMAKO MAKOMAKO
  CAMPANERO
BELLBOY BUTTONS
BELLE SPARK TOAST
  (SPANISH —) MAJA
BELLEEK POTTERY CHAMPAGNE
BELLEROPHON (FATHER OF —)
  GLAUCUS
  (MOTHER OF —) EURYMEDE
BELLFLOWER RAMPION BELLWORT
  HASKWORT IVYBELLS MILKWORT
BELLHOP BELLBOY HALLBOY
  CHASSEUR
BELLICOSE MAD IRATE WARFUL
  HOSTILE WARLIKE MILITANT
BELLIGERENT BRISTLY HOSTILE
  WARLIKE CHOLERIC FIGHTING
  JINGOIST COMBATIVE IRASCIBLE
  LITIGIOUS WRANGLING
BELLOW CRY LOW MOO YAP BAWL
  BEAL BELL GAPE ROAR ROME ROUT
  YAUP YAWP BELVE BLART BLORE
  CROON ROUST SHOUT BULLER
  CLAMOR RUMMES BLUSTER
  RUMMISH ULULATE
BELLOWING ROUT ROUST BELLING
  BOATION MUGIENT
BELLOWS BELY LUNGS BULIES
  FEEDER SANDER WINKER SYLPHON
  WINDBAG EXPELLER
  (SMALL —) PLUFF
  (STORAGE —) RESERVOIR
BELLOWS FISH BUGLER SNIPEFISH
BELL RINGER TOLL YOUTH TOLLER
  CLINKUM
BELLWETHER MASTER
BELLY BAG COD GIE GUT MAW POD
  BOUK FILL KYTE MARY WAME WEAM
  WOMB BINGY BOSOM BULGE FRONT
  GORGE PLEON TABLE THARM
  THERM TRIPE BAGGIE BINGEE
  HUNGER PAUNCH VENTER ABDOMEN
  BALLOON STOMACH TUMBREL
  APPETITE
BELLYACHE COMPLAIN
  COLLYWOBBLES
BELLYBAND WANTY
BELLYING BUNTING PREGNANT
BELONG BE GO FIT LIE BEAR FALL
  RELY APPLY BELIE GROUP AFFEIR
  INHERE RELATE RETAIN BEHOOVE
  PERTAIN APPERTAIN SUBSCRIBE
BELONGINGS ALLS DUDS FARE
  GEAR GOODS TRAPS ASSETS
  DUFFEL DUFFLE ESTATE USINGS
  BAGGAGE EFFECTS CHATTELS
  PROPERTY PURPRISE FURNITURE
  HOUSEHOLD
BELOVED DEAR IDOL LIEF AIMEE
  BOSOM CHERI SWEET ADORED
  CHERIE MINION DARLING PRECIOUS
  (MOST —) ALDERLIEFEST

BELOW ALOW BAJO DOWN ABLOW
  AFTER INFRA NEATH SOTTO UNDER
  BEHIND BENEATH
BELT LAS AREA BAND BEAT BLOW
  CEST FELT GIRD LACE LIST MARK
  RING SASH ZONE GIRTH MITER
  MITRE PATTE STRAP STRIP SWATH
  TRACT WAIST WHACK ZONAR ZONIC
  BODICE CESTUS CINGLE FETTLE
  GIRDLE INVEST LUNGER REGION
  STRAIT STRIPE SWATHE ZONNAR
  ZONULE BALDRIC CIRCUIT PASSAGE
  BALTHEUS CEINTURE CINCTURE
  ELEVATOR ENCIRCLE MECHANIC
  SURROUND
  (ASTROLOGICAL —) CLIMATE
  (CONVEYOR —) HAUL
  (ENDLESS —) APRON CREEPER
  (GREEK —) ZOSTER
  (HINDU SWAMP —) TERAI
  (MACHINE —) SWIFTER
  (MINERAL —) RANGE
  (TREE —) BERM BERME
BELTED ZONATE GIRDLED
  CINCTURED
  (— WITH WHITE) SHEETED
BELUGA HUSE HUSO HAUSEN
  MARSOON WHITEFISH
BELVEDERE GAZEBO LOOKOUT
BEMIRE DAG SOIL JARBLE
BEMOAN MEAN MOAN SIGH MOURN
  PLAIN BEWAIL LAMENT DEPLORE
BEMUSE SOT BULL DAZE AMUSE
BEMUSED DOPY DOPEY
BENCH PEW BANC BANK BENK BERM
  BINK DAIS DEAS FORM MESA SEAT
  SILL STEP TRAM BASIN BASON
  BERME BREAK CABIN CHAIR FORME
  JUDGE PLANK STALL STOOL
  BANCUS BANKER SCONCE SEDILE
  SETTEE SETTLE SITTER COUNTER
  DRESSER REPOSAL SHAMBLE
  SITTING TRESTLE TRIBUNE
  ALEBENCH
  (— FOR DAIRY TUBS) TRAM
  (— FOR KNEADING DOUGH) BREAK
  (OUTDOOR —) EXEDRA EXHEDRA
  (PLAYER'S —) WOOD
  (ROWER'S —) BANK THOFT ZYGON
  THWART
  (SHOEMAKER'S —) FORME
  (WORKMAN'S —) SIEGE
BEND BOW NID NIP PLY SAG SET
  WIN WRY ABOW ARCH BENT BOOL
  BUCK COPE CURB DOME FAUD FLEX
  FOLD GENU HOOK KINK LEAN LOUT
  PLOY RUMP TURN VERT WEEP
  ANGLE BATON BIGHT BREAK COUDE
  COURB CRANK CRIMP CRINK CROOK
  CULGE CURVE DROOP FLECT FRESE
  HINGE HUNCH INBOW KNEEL PLICA
  QUIRL ROUND SCRAG SKELP SLANT
  STOOP TREND TWINE TWIST
  BOUGHT BUCKLE CAMBER CONVEX
  COTICE
BENDER BUM JAG LEG BUST DRUNK
  SPREE BRIDGE WHOPPER GUZZLING
  SIXPENCE BRANNIGAN INFLECTOR
BENDING BOW SAG KNEE KNOT

  CROOK CURVE LITHE TWIST PLIANT
  SUPPLE TWISTY ANFRACT FLEXION
  HOGGING SINUOUS BUCKLING
  FLECTION
  (— OF ROCK) DRAG
BENDY TREE MIRO MAHOE
BENEATH ALOW ANETH BELOW
  LOWER UNDER ANEATH
BENEDICITE BENISON CANTICLE
BENEDICTINE CLUNIAC
  CAMALDOLESE
BENEDICTION ABOT AMEN ABOTH
  NANDI AMIDAH BROCHO PRAYER
  BENISON BERAKAH BLESSING
BENEFACTION ALMS BOON GIFT
  PRESENT DONATION GRATUITY
BENEFACTOR AGENT ANGEL
  DONOR FRIEND HELPER PATRON
  SAVIOR MAECENAS PROMOTER
BENEFICE FEE FEU FEUD FIEF
  FAVOR SCARF CURACY LIVING
  BENEFIT PRELACY RECTORY
  TOTQUOT DONATIVE KINDNESS
  SINECURE VICARAGE
BENEFICENCE BOON GIFT GRACE
  BOUNTY CHARITY GOODNESS
  KINDNESS
BENEFICENT KINDLY AMIABLE
  GRACIOUS
BENEFICIAL GOOD USEFUL
  HEALTHY HELPFUL BONITARY
  SALUTARY SANATIVE SINGULAR
  AVAILABLE BENIGNANT DESIRABLE
  ENJOYABLE HEALTHFUL LUCRATIVE
  REWARDING WHOLESOME
BENEFICIARY HEIR USER DONEE
  CESTUI CESTUY USUARY VASSAL
  LEGATEE FEUDATORY
BENEFIT AID USE BOON BOOT GAIN
  GIFT GOOD HELP PROW SAKE AVAIL
  BOOST FRUIT SELTH STEAD VISIT
  ASSIST BEHALF BEHOOF BETTER
  FRINGE PROFIT SALUTE USANCE
  ADVANCE BESPEAK CONCERT
  DESERVE IMPROVE SERVICE UTILITY
  BEFRIEND INTEREST
BENEVOLENCE JEN GOODNESS
  GOODWILL HUMANITY
BENEVOLENT GOOD KING BENIGN
  KINDLY LOVING AMIABLE LIBERAL
  GENEROUS AVUNCULAR BENIGNANT
BENIGN BOON GOOD KIND MILD
  BLAND SWEET GENIAL GENTLE
  AFFABLE BENEDICT GRACIOUS
  INNOCENT SALUTARY FAVORABLE
  WHOLESOME
BENIGNANT KIND BLAND GENIAL
  LIBERAL GRACIOUS MERCIFUL
BENJAMIN (FATHER OF —) JACOB
  (MOTHER OF —) RACHEL
  (SON OF —) ARD EHI BELA GERA
  ROSH ASHBEL BECHER HUPPIM
  MUPPIM NAAMAN
BENNET CLOVEWORT
BENNISEED SESAME
BENO TUBA
BENT AIM BOW SET BIAS CAST GIFT
  TURN BOUND BOWED BOWLY
  COUDE CRANK CRUMP FLAIR

HUMOR KNACK LURCH PRONE
SQUAT SWING TASTE TREND
AKIMBO ANLAGE BENNET BIASED
BRACED COURBE COURSE CURVED
DOGLEG ENERGH GENIUS HOOKED
INTENT LIKING NECKED SQUINT
SWAYED TALENT BUCKLED
CROOKED CURVANT EMBOWED
FLEXION FLEXURE IMPETUS INTENSE
LEANING LEVELED PRONATE
PURPOSE STOOPED TENSION
APTITUDE ARCUATED CRUMPLED
DECLINED FLECTION IMMINENT
INFLEXED PENCHANT REFLEXED
TENDENCY
(— AT THE END) HAMATE HOGGED
GRYPANIAN
(— DOWNWARD) BOWED DECURVED
INCUMBENT RECLINATE
(— IN) INCAVATE
(— OF MIND) GEME AFFECTION
(EASILY —) LITHY
(NATURAL —) SWING
BEN-TEAK NANDI NANAWOOD
BENUMB NIP DAZE DUNT NUMB
STUN DAVER DOZEN SCRAM SHRAM
CUMBER DEADEN STOUND BINOMEN
FRETISH FRETIZE STIFFEN STUPEFY
TORPEDO
BENUMBED CHILL SCRAM CLUMSE
CLUMSY FROZEN TORPID CLUMPST
SHRAMMED
BENUMBING LEADEN
BENZENE PHENE BENZIN BENZOL
PHENENE
BENZOIN BENJOIN LINDERA
BENJAMIN FIXATIVE
BEQUEATH GIVE WILL ENDOW
LEAVE OFFER BESTOW COMMIT
DEMISE DEVISE LEGATE QUETHE
BEQUEST COMMEND TRANSMIT
BEQUEST GIFT WILL LEGACY
BEQUEATH HERITAGE PITTANCE
ENDOWMENT
BERATE JAW NAG DRUB LASH RAIL
ABUSE BASTE CHIDE SCOLD SCORE
SLATE REVILE CENSURE REPROVE
UPBRAID CHASTISE
BERBER RIF RIFF KABYL SHLUH
KABYLE SHILHA HARATIN MZABITE
SHILLUH HARRATIN MOZABITE
(— CHIEF) CAID
BERCEUSE CRADLESONG
WIEGENLIED
BEREAVE ROB STRIP WIDOW DIVEST
SADDEN DEPRIVE DESPOIL
BEREAVED BEREFT VIDUOUS
WIDOWED DESOLATE
BEREAVEMENT ORBITY ORBITUDE
VIDUATION
BEREFT ORB LORN LOST POOR QUIT
WIDOW ORBATE FORLORN
FORFAIRN DESTITUTE
BERG FLOE BARROW ICEBERG
FLOEBERG
BERGAMOT BOSE BERGAMA
BURGAMOT
BERIBERI KAKKE
BERITH BRIS BRISS BRITH

BERM BERME LISIERE HEELPATH
BERRY BAY DEW HAW ALEY BEAT
CRAN POHA RASP BACCA BLACK
FRUIT GRAIN GRAPE LANSA MOUND
SALAL SAVIN BURROW LANSAT
LANSEH SABINE THRESH CURRANT
ETAERIO HILLOCK ACROSARC
ALLSPICE COWBERRY DEWBERRY
HAWEBAKE
(ACID —) CURRANT
(COFFEE —) CHERRY
(DRIED —) PASA
(JUMPER —) ABHAL
(LAUREL —) BAY
(POISONOUS —) BANEBERRY
BERTH BED JOB BUNK DOCK SLIP
SOPT CABIN PLACE UPPER BILLET
OFFICE SECURE LODGING MOORING
SLIPWAY POSITION ANCHORAGE
BERYL EMERALD AEROIDES
HELIODOR GOSHENITE
BERYLLIA GLUCINA GLUCINE
BESEECH ASK BEG BID CRY SUE
WOO PRAY CRAVE HALSE PLEAD
ADJURE APPEAL OBTEST CONJURE
ENTREAT IMPLORE SOLICIT
IMPETRATE OBSECRATE
BESET PLY SET SIT BEGO SAIL STUD
ALLOT BELAY BIGAN HARRY PRESS
SIEGE SPEND STEAD ASSAIL
ATTACK HARASS INFEST OBSESS
WAYLAY ARRANGE BESIEGE
OVERSET PERPLEX BLOCKADE
ENCUMBER ENTHRONG OBSTRUCT
SURROUND BELEAGUER
BESHOW SKIL CUDDY CUDDEN
CUDDIE BADDOCK COALFISH
SKILFISH
BESIDE BY HEAR INBY ALONG
ANENT ASIDE FORBY ABREAST
AGAINST FORNENT ADJACENT
FORNENST
(— ONE ANOTHER) ABREAST
(— ONESELF) FEY
BESIDES BY TO AND BUT TOO YET
ALSO ELSE MORE OVER THEN UNTO
WITH ABOVE AGAIN FORBY SUPRA
BESIDE BEYOND EXCEPT FORBYE
WITHAL THERETO WITHOUT
LIKEWISE MOREOVER
BESIEGE GIRD GIRT BELAY BELIE
BESET SIEGE STORM ATTACK
OBSESS OBSIDE PESTER PLAGUE
COMPASS SOLICIT SURROUND
BELEAGUER
BESMEAR RAY BALM DAUB SOIL
APPLY COVER GRIME GRUFT MUDDY
SLAKE SMEAR SULLY TAINT BEDAUB
PLATCH BESLIME SMOTHER
BESMIRCH BESLUBBER
BESMIRCH DASH SLUR SOIL SMEAR
SULLY SLURRY SMIRCH ASPERSE
BLACKEN DRAGGLE TURPIFY
DISCOLOR
BESOM COW MAP DRAB BISME
BROOM SWEEP SLOVEN HEATHER
BESOT DULL ASOTE ASSOT MUDDLE
STUPID STUPEFY BEFUDDLE
BESPANGLE DOT STAR STUD

ADORN JEWEL SPRINKLE
BESPATTER BLOT DASH JAUP SOIL
SPOT MUDDY PLASH STAIN SULLY
BEGARY SPARGE ASPERSE
SCATTER SMOTTER REPROACH
SPRINKLE
BESPEAK CITE HINT SHOW ARGUE
IMPLY ORDER SPEAK TRYST
ACCOST ATTEST ENGAGE STEVEN
ADDRESS ARRANGE BENEFIT
BETOKEN DISCUSS EXCLAIM
RESERVE FORETELL INDICATE
BESPECKLE DASH
BESPRINKLE DROP POWDER
ASPERSE BESTREW BESPRING
SPRINKLE BEQUIRTLE
BEST O ACE BEAT GOOD LACE MOST
PICK TOPS WALE ELITE EXCEL
WORST CHOICE DEFEAT FINEST
FLOWER OUTWIT SUNDAY TIPTOP
UTMOST ARISTOS CONQUER
GARLAND LARGEST OPTIMUM
DAMNDEST GREATEST KOHINOOR
OUTMATCH OUTSTRIP POSSIBLE
VANQUISH
BESTIAL LOW VILE WILD BRUTE
FERAL PRONE BRUTAL FILTHY
BEASTLY BRUTISH INHUMAN
SENSUAL BELLUINE DEPRAVED
BESTIR STIR AWAKE SHIFT STEER
AROUSE HUSTLE
(— ONESELF) LEG
BEST MAN PARANYMPH
BESTOW ADD PUT USE CAST DEAL
DOTE GIVE SEND STOW TAKE WARE
ALLOT ALLOW APPLY AWARD BESET
GRANT INFER LODGE PLACE SPEND
THOLE WREAK ACCORD BETEEM
CONFER DEMISE DEVOTE DIVIDE
DONATE DOTATE EMPLOY ENTAIL
ESTATE EXTEND IMPART IMPOSE
RENDER SHOWER COLLATE
COMMEND DISPOSE ENLARGE
EROGATE INDULGE INSTATE
PARTAKE PRESENT QUARTER
TRIBUTE BEQUEATH
(— LAVISHLY) HEAP
(— UPON) GIFT
BESTOWAL DOLE DISPOSAL
COLLATION LARGITION
(— OF PRAISE) ACCOLADE
BESTRIDE HORSE STRIDE STRADDLE
BET GO UP BAS BOX LAY SET VIE
WAD ANTE BACK BRAG CHIP GAGE
HOLD JACK NOIR PAIR PLAY PLOT
PUNT RISK WAGE BOUND CARRE
HEDGE ROUGE SAVER SPORT
STAKE WAGER GAMBLE HAZARD
IMPAIR MANQUE MILIEU PLEDGE
DERNIER PREMIER
(— AGAINST) MILK COPPER
(— AT LONG ODDS) SKINNER
(— BOLDLY) BLUFF
(— CHIP) CHECK
(FARO —) SLEEPER
(HEDGING —) SAVER
(POKER —) BLIND
BETA AND GAMMA GUARDS
BETAKE GO GET HIE MOVE TAKE

APPLY CATCH GRANT ASSUME
COMMIT REMOVE REPAIR RESORT
COMMEND JOURNEY WITHDRAW
(— **ONESELF TO MILL**) SUE
(— **ONESELF**) BUN HIT BOUN MARK
PIKE TEEM AVOID FOUND HAUNT
REFER TRUSS YIELD
BETEL IKMO ITMO SERI SIRI SIRIH
PUPULO
BETEL LEAF PAN BUYO PAUN
PAWNE
BETEL NUT BONGA BONYA BUNGA
SUPARI
BETHABARA NOIBWOOD
GREENHEART
BETHEL BETHESDA
BETHINK TAKE THINK ADVISE
DEVISE RECALL REFLECT CONSIDER
REMEMBER RECOLLECT
(— **ONE'S SELF**) MIN MINE
UMBETHINK
BETHLEHEM BEDLAM
BETHROOT TRILLIUM
BETIDE HAP TIDE BEFIT OCCUR
TRITE WORTH BECOME BEFALL
CHANCE HAPPEN BETOKEN
PRESAGE
BETIMES ANON RATH SOON EARLY
RATHE TIMEOUS SPEEDILY
FORTHWITH
BETOKEN MARK NOTE SHOW SIGN
AUGUR TOKEN ASSERT BETIDE
DENOTE EVINCE IMPORT SHADOW
BESPEAK EXPRESS OBLIQUE
PORTEND PRESAGE SIGNIFY
FOREBODE FORESHOW INDICATE
BETONY BROOMWORT
BETRAY BLAB BLOW BOIL GULL
SELL SHOP SILE SING SPOT TELL
TRAY UNDO WRAY CROSS FALSE
PEACH ROUND SPILL SPLIT SWICK
SWIKE ACCUSE BEWRAY DELUDE
DESCRY DESERT QUATCH REVEAL
SEDUCE SNITCH SQUEAL BEGUILE
DECEIVE FALSIFY MISLEAD
PROMOTE TRAITOR DISCLOSE
DISCOVER
(— **CONFIDENCES**) SPILL
BETRAYAL RAP ACCUSE TREASON
GIVEAWAY PRODITION
BETRAYER RAT JUDAS SKUNK
SEDUCER TRAITOR DERELICT
RECREANT SQUEALER
BETRAYING TELLTALE
BETROTH AFFY EARL TOKEN TROTH
TRUTH ASSURE ENGAGE ENSURE
PLEDGE PLIGHT ESPOUSE PROMISE
AFFIANCE CONTRACT DESPOUSE
HANDFAST
BETROTHED SURE VOWED ASSURED
ENGAGED HANDFAST INTENDED
COMBINATE
BETTA PLAKAT
BETTER AID TOP BEET MEND AMEND
EMEND EXCEL SAFER WISER
BIGGER EXCEED REFORM ADVANCE
CHOICER CORRECT GREATER
IMPROVE PROMOTE RECTIFY
RELIEVE SUPPORT SURPASS

EMINENCE INCREASE SUPERIOR
(— **A SCORE**) BREAK
(— **THAN ORDINARY**) EXTRA
BETTING ACTION GAMBLING
(— **SYSTEM**) PAROLI ALEMBERT
BETTOR ORALER
BETTY JENNY COTBETTY JOCRISSE
MOLLYCOT WIFECARL
BETWEEN AMID EMEL AMELL
AMONG ENTRE TWEEN YTWYN
ATWEEN ATWIXT TWEESH AVERAGE
BETWIXT
BEUDANITE CORKITE
BEVEL BLOW CANT CONE EDGE
PUSH REAM ANGLE BEARD BEZEL
MITER MITRE SLANT SLOPE SNAPE
SPLAY ASLANT CIPHER RHYMER
CHAMFER INCLINE OBLIQUE
(— **EDGES**) BEARD
(**WITHOUT** —) FLAT
BEVERAGE ADE ALE CUP NOG POP
RUM SAP TEA BEER BREW CHIA
GROG MABI MATE MEAD MILK NIPA
SODA WHIG WINE CHOCA CIDER
CLARY COCOA DRAFT DRINK JULEP
LAGER LEBAN MORAT MULSE
NEGUS PUNCH SHRUB SMASH
TREAT TWIST WATER BISHOP
COFFEE EGGNOG LIQUID LIQUOR
NECTAR PORTER SPRUCE TISWIN
BUNNELL CASSINA LIMEADE
OENOMEL POTABLE STEPONY
TULAPAI ALEBERRY COCKTAIL
LEMONADE PIQUETTE POTATION
CALIBOGUS CHOCOLATE
GINGERADE POMPERKIN SOMETHING
SWITCHELL
(— **FROM COW'S MILK**) KEFIR
KEPHIR
(— **FROM PEPPERS**) KAVA
KAVAKAVA
(— **FROM SAP**) TUBA
(— **OF BUTTERMILK AND WATER**)
BLAND
(— **OF CHAMPAGNE**) POPE
(— **OF HOT MILK**) POSSET
(— **OF PORT WINE**) BISHOP
(— **OF VINEGAR AND WATER**)
POSCA
(**ALCOHOLIC** —) DEW ARAK SAKE
SAKI ARRAK BASIG SHRUB SNAPS
STUFF ARRACK FIREWATER
STIMULANT
(**COLA** —) DOPE
(**EFFERVESCENT** —) FIZZ
(**FERMENTED** —) BASI KUMYS
KUMISS
(**FRUIT** —) BEVERAGE
(**INSIPID** —) WASH
(**MEXICAN** —) TEPACHE
(**WEAK** —) LAP
(**PL.**) WAIPIRO
BEVY HERD PACK COVEY DROVE
FLOCK GROUP SWARM FLIGHT
SCHOOL COMPANY
BEWAIL CRY RUE WEY KEEN MOAN
RAME SIGH WAIL WEEP MOURN
PLAIN BEMOAN GRIEVE LAMENT
PLAINT SORROW THROPE DEPLORE
COMPLAIN

BEWARE WAR CAVE GARE HEED
SHUN TENT WARD AVOID SPEND
ESCHEW WARNING
BEWILDER FOG FOX MAR BEAT
DAZE FOIL GAUM MAZE STUN
ABASH ADDLE AMAZE AMUSE
DEAVE DIZZY BAFFLE BEMIST
BEMUSE BOTHER DAZZLE DUDDER
MOIDER MOMBLE MUDDLE PUZZLE
WANDER WILDER BUFFALO
BUMBAZE CONFUSE FLASKER
MYSTIFY PERPLEX STAGGER
STUPEFY ASTONISH CONFOUND
DISTRACT ENTANGLE OVERMUSE
SQUATTER SURPRISE
BEWILDERED MAR ASEA LOST
MANG WILL AGAPE DAZED MAZED
BUSHED MAPPED STUPENT
WILSOME CONFUSED HELPLESS
WILLYARD PERPLEXED
BEWILDERMENT AWE FOG DAZE
MISMAZE STICKLE AMAZEMENT
CONFUSION
BEWITCH HEX WISH BLINK CHARM
MAGIC OBEAH SPELL WITCH
ENAMOR ENTICE GLAMOR GRIGRI
HOODOO STRIKE THRILL ATTRACT
BEDEVIL DELIGHT ENCHANT
GLAMOUR ENSORCEL FORSPEAK
GREEGREE OVERLOOK
BEWITCHED HAGGED
BEWITCHING SIREN
BEYOND BY FREE OVER YOND
ABOVE ASIDE AYOND FORBY ULTRA
BEHIND BEYANT YONDER BENEATH
BESIDES FORTHBY FURTHER
OUTGATE PASSING WITHOUT
OVERMORE SUPERIOR HEREAFTER
(— **DOUBT**) ASSURED
(— **ORDINARY METHODS**) AFIELD
(— **THE MARK**) GONE
(— **THE SEA**) ULTRAMARINE
(— **THIS**) STILL
BEZEL RIM TOP EDGE OUCH SEAL
BEVIL BEZIL CROWN FACET CHATON
FLANGE MARQUISE TEMPLATE
BEZIQUE PENCHANT
BEZOAR GOATSTONE HIPPOLITH
B-GIRL SITTER
BHAKTA BHAGAVATA
BHANG BANG BENG BENJ HASHISH
BHARAL TUR HALL NAHOOR
BURRHEL
BHIKSHU GELONG
BHUTAN (**ASSEMBLY OF** —)
TSONGDU
(**CAPITAL OF** —) THIMPHU
(**CURRENCY OF** —) PAISA RUPEE
(**LANGUAGE OF** —) DZONGKHA
(**RIVER OF** —) MACHU MANAS
AMOCHU
BHUTAN PINE KAIL
BIANNUAL BIYEARLY
BIAS PLY WRY AWRY BENT CANT
SWAY WARP AMISS COLOR FAVOR
POISE SLANT SLOPE SWING TWIST
BIGOTRY INCLINE OBLIQUE
SUGGEST CLINAMEN COLORING
DIAGONAL TENDENCY PREJUDICE

PROCEDURE SPECTACLE
BIASED SLANT COLORED PARTIAL
BIB SIP BRAT POUT APRON DRINK
FEEDER TIPPLE TUCKER BAVETTE
(CHILD'S —) BISHOP
(LEATHER —) DICK
BIBLE BOOK VULGATE SCRIPTURE
(— TEXT) MIKRA MIQRA
BIBLE LEAF COSTMARY
BIBULOUS DRINKING BIBACIOUS
BICKER JAR WAR BOWL SPAR TIFF
ARGUE BRAWL CAVIL FIGHT ASSAIL
ATTACK BATTLE CONTEND DISPUTE
PICKEER QUARREL WRANGLE
PETTIFOG SKIRMISH SQUABBLE
BICKERN ANVIL BEAKIRON
BICYCLE BIKE QUAD CYCLE HOBBY
MOUNT STEED WHEEL JIGGER
ORNARY SAFETY TANDEM ORDINAR
TRIPLET ORDINARY ROADSTER
BID GO BEG NAP BEDE BODE CALL
GIVE HEST HIST PRAY WISH CHEAP
CLEPE FRAGE OFFER ORDER
ADJURE CHARGE DIRECT ENJOIN
INVITE REVEAL SIMPLE SUMMON
TENDER BALANCE CHEAPEN
COMMAND DECLARE DROPVIE
ENTREAT PROFFER ANNOUNCE
PROCLAIM PROPOSAL
(— ADIEU) TEACH
(— AT AUCTION) CRY
(— IN CARDS) CUE FROG JUMP
SOLO FRAGE GRAND SHIFT BOSTON
DEFEND DEMAND DENIAL SMUDGE
BLUCHER COMMAND SHUTOUT
SUPPORT CONTRACT SCHMEISS
(SEALED —) TICKET
BIDDING AUCTION BIDDANCE
DIRECTIVE
BIDE FACE STAY WAIT ABIDE AWAIT
DWELL TARRY WATCH ENDURE
REMAIN SUFFER SOJOURN
CONTINUE TOLERATE
BIDENS CUCKOLD MANZANILLA
BIDET SITZBAD INSESSION
BIDRI VIDRY BIDDERY TUTENAG
BIER BEAR PYRE FRAME GRAVE
HANDY HORSE TABUT COFFIN
HEARSE LITTER SUPPORT
FERETORY FERETRUM
BIFURCATION WYE FORK SPLIT
BRANCH CROTCH FORKING DIVISION
DICHOTOMY
BIG FAT BARO BOLD HUGE MUCH
VAST BULKY CHIEF GAUCY GRAND
GREAT GROSS HUSKY LARGE
GAUCIE MIGHTY BIGGISH BUMPING
EMINENT HUMMING LEADING
MASSIVE POMPOUS UPRIGHT
VIOLENT BOASTFUL BOUNCING
ENORMOUS GENEROUS GIGANTIC
IMPOSING PLUMPING PREGNANT
SLAPPING SWANKING SWAPPING
THUMPING
(— WITH YOUNG) FULL GRAVID
(MARVELOUSLY —) TREMENDOUS
BIGHORN ARGAL AOUDAD ARGALI
CIMARRON
BIGHT BAY BEND BITE COIL GULF

LOOP ROVE ANGLE CURVE INLET
NOOSE CORNER HOLLOW POCKET
BIGOT CAFARD ZEALOT FANATIC
MUMPSIMUS
BIGOTED BIASED NARROW
HIDEBOUND ILLIBERAL SECTARIAN
BIGOTRY INTOLERANCE
BIGROOT MANROOT BITTERROOT
BIG SHOT MUCKAMUCK
BIG SKY COUNTRY MONTANA
BILE BOIL GALL HUMP VENOM
CHOLER GROWTH ATRABILE
BILGE PUMP SCUM BOUGE BULGE
BILLAGE THURROCK
BILIMBI CAMIAS KAMIAS CUCUMBER
BILINGUAL DIGLOT
BILIOUS GALLISH
BILIOUSNESS LIVER CHOLER
BILK DO GYP BALK HOAX CHEAT
COZEN TRICK DELUDE FLEECE
SWEDGE DECEIVE DEFRAUD
SWINDLE
BILL ACT DUN GET LAW NEB NIB TAB
BEAK CHIT CLAP GETT KITE NOTE
PECK SHOT CHECK ENTRY LIBEL
SCORE CARESS CHARGE DOCKET
INDICT LAWING PECKER PICKAX
POSTER STRIKE DERTRUM INVOICE
LAMPOON MATTOCK PLACARD
PROGRAM REMANET STATUTE
BILLHOOK DOCUMENT HEADLAND
INNOCENT PETITION TREASURY
(— OF ANCHOR) PEE PEAK
(— OF COMPLAINT) QUERELA
(— OF CREDIT) ANGEL
(— OF DIVORCE) GET GETT
(— OF EXCHANGE) SOLA HUNDI
DEVISE
(— OF FARE) MENU CARTE
(— OF PARCELS) FACTURE
(10-DOLLAR —) TEN TENNER
SAWBUCK
(100-DOLLAR —) CENTURY
(2-DOLLAR —) DEUCE
(5-DOLLAR —) FIN VEE FIVE FIVER
(COUNTERFEIT —S) STIFF
(DOLLAR —) BUCK SPOT SINGLE
FROGSKIN
(REVOLUTIONARY —) ASSIGNAT
BILLET BAR GAD HUT LAY LOG
LOOP NOTE PASS POST SPOT
BERTH ENROL HOUSE LODGE
ORDER SHIDE SPRAG STICK STRAP
BALLOT BULLET ENROLL HARBOR
LETTER LIBBET NOTICE TICKET
BEARING EPISTLE MISSIVE POLLACK
COALFISH DOCUMENT FIREWOOD
ORNAMENT POSITION QUARTERS
(— SOLDIERS) CESS
BILLET-DOUX CAPON
BILLETING LIVERY
BILLFISH GAR LONGJAWS SAILFISH
SPEARFISH
BILLHOOK BILL DHAW HOOK
PAWPAW SLASHER SNAGGER
SCIMITAR
BILLIARD BALL IVORY
BILLIARD CUE MACE MAST
(TIP OF —) LEATHER

BILLIARDS PILLS TRUCKS
(LAWN —) TROCO
BILLINGSGATE ABUSE SLAPDASH
BILLION MILLIARD
BILLON BAIOC VELLON BAJOCCO
BILLOW SEA BLOW WAVE BULGE
CLOUD FLOAT SURGE SWELL
RESACA RIPPLE ROLLER WALLOW
BREAKER UNDULATE
BILLY CAW CHAP CLUB GOAT MACE
MATE BATON FANNY NEDDY
CUDGEL FANNIE FELLOW BROTHER
COMRADE BILLIKIN BILLYCAN
BLUDGEON JACKSHAY BLACKJACK
TRUNCHEON
BIMAH ALMEMAR ALMEMOR
BIN ARK BOX CUB GUM BING BONE
CART CRIB VINA FRAME HUTCH
KENCH PUNGI STALL STORE WAGON
BASKET BUNKER GARNER HAMPER
MANGER POCKET TROUGH WITHIN
BLEACHER
(— FOR CEMENT) SILO
(— FOR FISH) KENCH
(— FOR GRAIN) ARK
BINARY HYDRIDE
BINATE DUAL DOUBLE PAIRED
COUPLED TWOFOLD GEMINATE
BINAURAL DIOTIC
BIND JAM LAP TIE WAP EARL FAST
FRAP GIRD GYVE HOLD HOOP KNIT
KNOT LASH MAIL NAIL TAPE YERK
BRACE CADGE CHAIN CINCH EDDER
GIRTH SNAKE STICK STRAP TRUSS
ATTACH BUNDLE COMMIT EMBIND
ENGAGE FETTER FREEZE GARTER
GIRDLE LIGATE OBLIGE STRAIN
SWATHE TETHER WRITHE ARTICLE
ASTRAIN BANDAGE CONFINE
EMBOUND ENCHAIN GRAPPLE
SHACKLE SWADDLE ASTRINGE
CONCLUDE FLIGHTER HANDFAST
INNODATE LIGATURE OBLIGATE
RESTRAIN
(— A FALCON) MAIL
(— BY LEASE) THIRL
(— BY PLEDGE) GAGE SWEAR
(— IN BUNDLE) KID BAVIN
(— INTO SHEAVES) GAVEL THRAVE
(— ONESELF) ADHERE
(— TO SECRECY) TILE
(— TOGETHER) LIME FAGOT SEIZE
CEMENT FAGGOT ASTRINGE
RELIGATE
(— UP) KILT BAVIN TRUSS UPBAND
ASTRICT REVOLVE
(— WITH THREAD) OOP
BINDER BAND BEAM BOND CORD
ROPE BALER COVER FRAME LEVER
FILLET FOLDER GIRDER HEADER
LIGNIN TARMAC HAYBAND
BONDSTONE BOOKMAKER
BINDING TAG BAND CORD GARD
HARD LEAR ROPE TAPE YAPP
COVER VALID CADDIS EDGING
RIBBON BOUNDEN CADDICE
GALLOON LAPPING MOUSING
WEBBING FAITHFUL LIGATIVE
LIGATORY STRINGENT

(— **FAST**) IRON
(— **OF BOOK**) FACE
(— **OF GOLD**) BISSET
(— **ON DRESS**) FENT
BINDWEED BINE WIRE CREEPER
TIEVINE BEARBIND BEARBINE
BELLBINE BINEWEED CORNBINE
HELLWEED MILKMAID WOODBINE
WITHYWIND
BINE WIRE
BINGE BAT BOW HIT BLOW BUST
SOAK BEANO PARTY SOUSE SPRAY
SPREE CRINGE BLOWOFF
CAROUSAL
BINGO KENO BEANO LOTTO BRANDY
SCREENO
BINNACLE PYX BITTACLE
BINOCULARS GLASS
BINOMIAL DIONYM BINOMEN
BIOGEOGRAPHY CHOROLOGY
BIOGRAPHER PLUTARCH
BIOGRAPHY BIO LIFE VITA MEMOIR
ACCOUNT HISTORY RECOUNT
(— **OF SAINTS**) HAGIOGRAPHA
HAGIOGRAPHY
BIOPHORE BIOGEN PLASOME
BIOPLAST MICELLA MICELLE
BIOTITE MICA ANOMITE MEROXENE
BIOTOPE STATION
BIPED DIPODE HINDQUARTERS
BIRCH COW BIRK CANE FLOG WHIP
ALDER ALNUS CANOE SWISH
BETULA BIRKEN TAWHAI HICKORY
BIRD ANI DAW DOG JAY NUN PIE TIT
COOT CROW DOVE FOWL IBIS JACK
KAGU KITE KNOT LARK QUIT RUFF
TERN TODY WING WREN BAKER
BRANT CHUCK CLEAR COVEY
EGRET FINCH FLIER FLYER GOOSE
HOBBY JUNCO LARID LIVER PEWEE
PEWIT RAVEN ROBIN SNIPE STILT
SWIFT TEREK TURCO TWITE VIREO
BULBUL DICKEY DIPPER DRIVER
DRONGO DUCKER DUNLIN FALCON
GROUSE GUINEA HOOPOE HOOTER
JACANA JAEGER LINNET MARTEN
MOCKER NESTER ORIOLE OSCINE
PHOEBE PLOVER SHRIKE SILVAN
SINGER SITTER SYLVAN THRUSH
TROGON TURNIX VERDIN WAYBUG
YAWPER ANTBIRD BABBLER
BLUEJAY BUNTING BUSTARD
BUZZARD CATBIRD CHIRPER
FEATHER FLAPPER FLICKER
FLIGGER FLOPPER GRACKLE
HALCYON HORNERO HURGILA
INCOMER IRRISOR JACAMAR
JACKDAW KINGLET MINIVET
MOULTER ORTOLAN PEACOCK
PERCHER QUILLER REDWING
SCRAPER SKINNER SKYLARK
SPARROW SUNBIRD SWALLOW
TANAGER TINAMOU TITLARK
TOMFOOL WARBLER WAXWING
ACCENTOR AIRPLANE AMADAVAT
ANNOTINE BLACKCAP BLACKNEB
BLUEBIRD BOATBILL BOBOLINK
BOBWHITE BUBBLING CAGELING
CARINATE COCKBIRD COCORICO

COTTINGA DREPANID FERNBIRD
FIREBIRD FIRETAIL GROSBEAK
GRUIFORM IBISBILL JUVENILE
KILLDEER KINGBIRD LOBEFOOT
OXPECKER PHEASANT PLUMIPED
POORWILL PREACHER REDSTART
SALTATOR SONGBIRD STARLING
SURFBIRD SWAMPHEN TAPACOLO
THRASHER THROSTLE TITMOUSE
TREMBLER UMBRETTE WHINCHAT
WOODCHAT WOODCOCK YEARBIRD
(— **OF BRILLIANT PLUMAGE**) TODY
JALAP ORIOLE TROGON JACAMAR
KIROMBO MINIVET TANAGER
(— **OF INDIA**) BAYA KALA SHAMA
(— **OF OMEN**) WAYBIRD
(— **OF PREY**) OWL HAWK KITE
EAGLE ELANT GLEAD GLEDE STOOP
EAGLET ELANET BUZZARD
GOSHAWK STOOPER VULTURE
(**AFRICAN** —) TAHA QUELEA
TOURACO UMBRETTE NAPECREST
(**AUSTRALIAN** —) EMU ROA LORY
ARARA LEIPOA BOOBOOK BUSTARD
FIGBIRD WAYBUNG BELLBIRD
LORIKEET LYREBIRD MANUCODE
(**BIG-BEAKED** —) BECARD HORNBILL
(**CRESTED** —) KAGU COPPY
HOATZIN TOPKNOT
(**CROCODILE** —) TROCHIL
(**DECOY** —) CALL STOOL
(**DIVING** —) AUK LOON GREBE
DOPPER DUCKER GRAYLING
PLUNGEON
(**EUROPEAN** —) ANI DAW MEW QUA
CIRL DARR KITE MALL MORO QUIS
ROOK STAG WHIM YITE AMSEL
BOONK GLEDE MAVIS MERLE OUSEL
OUZEL SACER SAKER SERIN TARIN
TEREK TERIN WHAUP AVOCET
COCKOO CUSHAT GAYLAG GODWIT
MARTEN MERLIN MISSEL REDCAP
WHEWER WINDLE WINNEL WRANNY
BITTERN BUSTARD HAYBIRD
KESTREL MOTACIL ORTOLAN
SAKERET STARNEL WHISKEY
WINNARD WITWALL BARGOOSE
CHEPSTER DOTTEREL GARGANEY
REDSTART WHEATEAR WHEYBIRD
WHIMBREL WRANNOCK YOLDRING
(**EXTINCT** —) MOA DODO JIBI KIWI
MAMO RUKH OFFBIRD
(**FABULOUS** —) ROC HALCYON
OOFBIRD
(**FEMALE** —) HEN JENNY
(**FICTITIOUS** —) JAYHAWK PHOENIX
(**FISH-CATCHING** —) OSPREY
CRABIER
(**FLEDGLING** —) SQUAB
(**FLIGHTLESS** —) EMU GOR MOA
DODO EYAS GORB GULL KAGU KIWI
CALLOW GORLIN APTERYX GORLING
NESTLER OSTRICH PENGUIN
BUBBLING NESTLING
(**FRIGATE** —) IOA IWA
(**FRUIT-EATING** —) COLY
(**GALLOWS** —) HEMPY HEMPIE
(**GAME** —) QUAIL SNIPE COLIMA
GROUSE INCOME FLAPPER INCOMER

(**HAWAIIAN** —) IO OO AVA IOA IWA
OOA IIWI JIBI KOAE MAMO MOHO
OMAO OOAA KAMAO PALILA
(**HORN-HEADED** —) KAMICHI
(**INJURED** —) CRIPPLE
(**LARGEST** —) LAMMERGEIER
(**MADAGASCAR** —) KIROMBO
(**MECHANICAL** —) ORTHOPTER
(**MYTHICAL** —) FUM ROC GANZA
SIMURG SIMURGH
(**NEW ZEALAND** —) KEA MOA OII
ROA HUIA KAKA KIWI KOKO KUKU
KULU PEHO RURU TITI WEKA
KAKAPO KOKAKO KUKUPA APTERYX
KORIMAKO MOREPORK NOTORNIS
(**PASSERINE** —) QUIT FINCH
SPARROW STARNEL SWALLOW
SYLVIID DREPANID FALCONET
FERNBIRD GRALLINA JACKBIRD
(**PERTAINING TO** —**S**) OSCINE
(**RAPACIOUS** —) JAEGER
(**RASORIAL** —) SCRATCHER
(**RUNNING** —) COURSER
(**SAMOAN** —) IAO
(**SEA** —) AUK ERN ERNE GONY
GULL SMEW TERN EIDER SOLAN
FULMAR GANNET HAGDON OSPREY
PETREL PUFFIN PELICAN SEAFOWL
MURRELET
(**SHORE** —) REE RAIL SORA SNIPE
STILT WADER AVOCET CURLEW
PLOVER WILLET WRYBILL
(**SHORT-TAILED** —) BREVE
(**SINGING** —) LARK WREN PIPIT
ROBIN VEERY VIREO CANARY
LINNET MOCKER ORIOLE OSCINE
SINGER THRUSH WARBLER
FAUVETTE REDSTART
(**SMALL** —) TIT TODY WREN DICKY
PEGGY PIPIT TYDIE VIREO DICKEY
LINNET SISKIN TOMTIT CREEPER
SPARROW TITLARK COCORICO
GNATSNAP STARLING WHEATEAR
(**SOUTH AMERICAN** —) GUAN MINA
MYNA RARA TOCA BAKER CHAJA
JOPIN TURCO BARBET BECARD
CHUNGA TOUCAN CARIAMA OILBIRD
BELLBIRD BOATBILL CARACARA
GUACHARO HOACTZIN PUFFBIRD
SCREAMER TAPACOLO TAPACULO
TERUTERO
(**STYLIZED** —) DISTELFINK
(**TROPICAL** —) ANI GUAN KOAE
TODY BOS'N BOSUN JALAP BARBET
BECARD MOTMOT TROGON
JACAMAR WIGTAIL LONGTAIL
SALTATOR
(**WADING** —) HERN IBIS RAIL SORA
CRANE HERON SNIPE STILT STORK
AVOCET GODWIT JACANA BOATBILL
FLAMINGO SHOEBILL SHOEBIRD
(**WILD** —**S**) GALLINAE
(**YOUNG** —) EYA GULL PIPER
FLAPPER NESTLER BIRDIKIN
NESTLING
(PL.) AVIFAUNA POLYMYODI
PRAECOCES
BIRD BOLT BURBOLT QUARREL
BIRD CAGE AVIARY PINJRA VOLARY

VOLERY PADDOCK
BIRDCATCHER FOWLER
BIRD CHERRY DOGWOOD
EGGBERRY HACKWOOD HAGBERRY
BIRDLIFE ORNIS
BIRDLIME GLUE LIME BELIME
VISCUM BIRDGLUE
BIRD OF PARADISE APUS
MANUCODE RIFLEBIRD
BIRD'S-FOOT FOWLFOOT
SERRADELLA
BIRD'S KNEE SUFFRAGO
BIRD'S MANTLE STRAGULUM
BIRI BIDI
BIRTH KIN BEAR FALL BLOOD
BURDEN GENTRY ORIGIN BEARING
BORNING DESCENT GENESIS
LINEAGE DELIVERY GENITURE
NASCENCY NATALITY NATIVITY
(FALSE —) SOOTERKIN
(GENTLE —) GENTILITY
(HONORABLE —) BLOOD
(OF LOW —) CRESTLESS
(OF NOBLE —) CORONETED
BIRTHMARK MOLE IMAGE NAEVE
NEVUS BLEMISH SPILOMA
SIGNATURE
BIRTHRATE NATALITY FERTILITY
BIRTHRIGHT KIND HERITAGE
BIRTHROOT BATHROOT BATHWORT
DEATHROOT DISHCLOTH
SQUAWROOT
BIRTHWORT GUACO ASARUM
BATHROOT
BISAYAN AKLAN CEBUAN AKLANON
CEBUANO
BISCUIT BUN NUT BAKE ROLL RUSK
SNAP WOOD BREAD SCONE WAFER
BISQUE COOKIE DODGER MUFFIN
SIMNEL CRACKER GALETTE PENTILE
PRETZEL RATAFIA RATIFIA
CRACKNEL HARDTACK ZWÍEBACK
(BROKEN —S) DUNDERFUNK
(COLOR —) DOE PAWNEE
BISECT FORK CROSS HALVE SPLIT
CLEAVE DIVIDE MIDDLE SEPARATE
BISECTION MEDIATION
BISHOP EP ABBA EPUS LAWN PAPA
POPE ANGEL DENIS ARCHER
BUSTLE DESPOT EPARCH EXARCH
MAGPIE PRESUL PRIEST ROCHET
ROCKAT PONTIFF PRELATE PRIMATE
TULCHAN ANTISTES DIOCESAN
DIRECTOR ORDINARY OVERSEER
PONTIFEX
(— AND MARTYR) EM
(CHESS —) ALFIN ALPHYN ARCHER
BISHOP'S-WEED AMMI AMMEOS
KHELLA WILLIAM BOLEWORT
BULLWORT GOUTWEED TOOTHPICK
BISKOP BRUSHER STEENBRAS
BISMARK KRAPFE KRAPFEN
BISMUTH WISMUTH TINGLASS
BISON BUGLE BOVINE MITHAN
WISENT AUROCHS BONASUS
BUFFALO
BISTORT PATIENCE ADDERWORT
ASTROLOGE SNAKEWEED
SNAKEWORT

BISTRO BAR CAFE TAVERN
WINESHOP ESTAMINET NIGHTCLUB
BIT ACE FID FIP GAG JOT NIP ORT
PIP WEE ATOM BITE BITT CHIP
CROP CURB DITE DOIT DRIB FLAW
FOOD GRUE HAET HATE HOOT IOTA
ITEM LEVY MITE MOTE PART SLUT
SNAP SNIP SPOT TOOL WHIT AUGER
BLADE CHECK CRUMB DRILL GROAT
PATCH PEZZO PIECE POINT SCRAP
SHRED SMACK SNACK SPECK STEEK
TASTE THRUM WIGHT BITTIE BRIDLE
CANNON EATING MORSEL PELHAM
PICKLE SIPPET SMIDGE SPLICE
STITCH STIVER THOGHT TITTLE
TRIFLE BRADOON BRIDOON
CHILENO GLIMMER MORCEAU
PALLION PORTION SCATCHE
SMIDGEN SMIDGIN SMIGEON
SNAFFLE TRANEEN FISHTAIL
FRACTION FRAGMENT QUANTITY
SMITCHIN TWOPENNY
(— OF GOSSIP) HEARING
(— OF INFORMATION) GRIFF
GRIFFIN WRINKLE
(— OF KEY) WEB
(— OF LAND) CROOK
(— OF METAL) FLITTER
(— OF TOAST) SNIPPET
(— TO EAT) MUNGEY
(—S AND PIECES) GUBBINS
GUBBINGS
(—S OF COKE) BREEZE
(—S OF WRITING) EXCERPTA
(ONE-QUARTER —) GILL
(CUTTING —) CHASER
(DRILL —) CROWN
(FANCIFUL —) FLAM
(FIPPENY —) SIXPENCE
(FLORID —) FLOURISH
(HORSE'S —) KEVEL SNODE
CANNON PELHAM SCATCH SNAFFLE
BASTONET
(LEAST —) FIG JOT RAP HANG LICK
GHOST GROAT RIZZOM STITCH
(LITTLE —) PICK TOUCH BITTOCK
REMNANT SOUPCON
(SMALL —) BLEB GLIM SPUNK
(SMALL —S) SMATTER
(TINY —) SPECK DRIBBLE SCRINCH
TODDICK
(PL.) SMITHERS SMITHEREENS
BITCH DO GYP BICK LAMP SLUT
BRACH BROOD CHEAT GROUSE
COMPLAIN
BITE BIT CUT EAT JAW NIP BAIT
CHAM CHEW ETCH FOOD GASH
GNAP GNAW HOLD KNAP MEAL RIVE
SNAP TAKE CHACK CHAMM CHAMP
CHEAT GNASH PINCH SEIZE SMART
SNACK STING TOOTH TRICK
CRUNCH MORSEL NIBBLE PIERCE
SAVAGE BUGBITE CHEATER
CORRODE FORBITE IMPRESS
MORSURE MUNCHET PARTAKE
SHARPER SLANDER
(— AT) HIT
(— GREEDILY) HANCH
(— REPEATEDLY) CHAMP

BITING BIT HOT ACID HOAR KEEN
ACRID NIPPY QUICK SHARP SNELL
BITTER RODENT SEVERE SHREWD
STINGY TEETHY TWEAKY CAUSTIC
CUTTING MORDANT MORSURE
NIPPING PUNGENT SUBACID
DRILLING INCISIVE POIGNANT
SCALDING SCATHING STINGING
BITIS ECHIDNA
BITO BALM HAJILIJ
BITT BLOCK KNIGHT BOLLARD
(PL.) RANGEHEADS
BITTER AWA GAL ACID ACRE ASIM
BASK KEEN MARA RUDE SALT SORE
SOUR TART ACERB ACRID AMARA
ASPER BLEAK HARSH IRATE SHARP
BITING PICRIC SEVERE AUSTERE
CAUSTIC CRABBED CUTTING
FERVENT GALLING GALLISH PAINFUL
PUNGENT SATIRIC POIGNANT
STINGING SUBAMARE VIRULENT
BITTER APPLE COLOCYNTH
BITTER BIT SMALLPOX
BITTERBUSH SNAKEROOT
BITTER CLOVER YELLOWTOP
BITTERLY SOUR FELLY BITTER
ROUNDLY CURSEDLY
BITTERN BUMP SOCO BOONK BUTOR
HERON BITORE BUMBLE BUMMLE
BUTTAL KAKKAK BLITTER BUMMLER
ERICIUS DUNKADOO GRUIFORM
LONGNECK
(FLOCK OF —) SEDGE SIEGE
BITTERNESS RUE ACOR BILE FELL
GALL ATTER ENMITY MALICE
RANCOR AMARITY ACERBITY
ACRIDITY ACRIMONY FERVENCY
SEVERITY WORMWOOD
(EXTREME —) VIRULENCE
(WITH —) AMAREVOLE
BITTER PIT STIPPEN
BITTERROOT LEWISIA
TOBACCOROOT
BITTERS AMER
BITTER SPAR DOLOMITE
BITTERSWEET FELLEN DOGWOOD
LOBSTER SOLANUM WAXWORK
DULCAMARA FELONWOOD
FELONWORT FEVERTWIG
WITHYWIND WOLFBERRY
BITTER VETCH ERS
BITTERWEED RAGWEED
HORSEWEED
BITTERWORT FELWORT DANDELION
BITUMEN TAR CONGO PITCH SLIME
ASPHALT CARBENE ALKITRAN
ALCHITRAN ELATERITE
BIVALVE HEN CLAM SPAT PINNA
COCKLE DIATOM MUSSEL OYSTER
MOLLUSK NUCULID PANDORA
SCALLOP TOHEROA
BIVOUAC CAMP ETAPE WATCH
ENCAMP SHELTER
BIZARRE ODD ANTIC DEDAL OUTRE
QUEER QUAINT ANTICAL CURIOUS
FANCIFUL ECCENTRIC FANTASTIC
GROTESQUE
BLAB LAB CHAT BLART BLATE
CHEEP CLACK PEACH BABBLE

BETRAY GOSSIP REVEAL SQUEAL
TATTLE BLABBER CHATTER
CLATTER
BLACK DHU JET WAN CALO CROW
DARK EBON FOUL INKY NOIR PIKY
SOOT BUGLE COLLY DUSKY MURKY
NEGRO NOIRE RAVEN SABLE SOOTY
TARRY THICK ATROUS BRUNET
DISMAL ETHIOP GLOOMY MURREY
PITCHY SULLEN ABAISER AFRICAN
BLACKEN DIAMOND MELANIC
NEGRITO NIGRINE NIGROUS
PICEOUS SWARTHY UNCLEAN
MOURNFUL
(— **AND BLUE**) LIVID
(— **OUT**) CONK
(**BONE** —) SPODIUM
(**BROWNISH** —) LAVA
(**GREENISH** —) CORBEAU
(**IVORY** —) ABAISER
(**LIGHT-SKINNED** —) BROWN
(**RATHER** —) DUSKISH
(**VIOLET** —) CROW
BLACKAMOOR BLECK NEGRO
MORIAN NEGRESS ETHIOPIAN
BLACK ASH HOOPWOOD
BLACKBALL PIP PILL BALLOT
EXCLUDE HEEBALL OSTRACIZE
BLACK BASS HURON TROUT
ACHIGAN GROWLER OCHIGAN
BLACKBERRY AGAWAM LAWTON
DEWBERRY MULBERRY ROSACEAN
(— **BUSH**) MORE
BLACKBIRD ANI DAW PIE CROW
AMSEL COLLY MERLE OUSEL OUZEL
RAVEN BLACKY COLLEY MAIZER
BLACKIE COWBIRD GRACKLE
JACKDAW REDWING WOOFELL
TROOPIAL
BLACKBOARD CHALKBOARD
GREENBOARD
BLACKBREAM TARWHINE
BLACK-BROWED GLOOMY
BLACK BRYONY LILY LILIUM
OXBERRY BINDWEED MANDRAKE
BLACK BUCK SASIN
BLACKCAP GULL JACK PEGGY
HAYBIRD WARBLER MOCKBIRD
TITMOUSE JACKSTRAW RASPBERRY
BLACKDAMP STYTH STYTHE
CHOKEDAMP
BLACKDRINK YAPON YAUPON
BLACKEN INK TAR CHAR CORK SOIL
SOOT BLECK CLOUD COLLY JAPAN
SMOKE SULLY BEFOUL BLATCH
DARKEN DEFAME MALIGN SMEETH
SMIRCH VILIFY ASPERSE BENEGRO
NIGRIFY SLANDER SMOLDER
TRADUCE BESMIRCH
BLACKENED REECHY
BLACKEYE COWPEA
BLACKFELLOW BLACKBOY
YAMMADJI
BLACKFIN CISCO SESIS
BLACKFISH GRIND TAUTOG
BORLASE DOGFISH GRAMPUS
POTHEAD HARDHEAD
BLACKFLY GNAT SIMULIID
BLACKFOOT BLOOD KAINAH PIEGAN

SIKSIKA SIHASAPA
BLACK GROUPER MERO AGUAJI
WARSAW GARRUPA
BLACKGUARD SHAG BLECK CATSO
GAMIN GUARD SNUFF SWEEP
ROTTER LADRONE VAGRANT
BLAGGARD CRIMINAL LARRIKIN
VAGABOND SCOUNDREL
BLACK GUILLEMOT CUTTY TYSTE
SCRABE DOVEKEY DOVEKIE
SCRABER PUFFINET
BLACK GUM TUPELO HORNPIPE
STINKWOOD
BLACK HAW SLOE BOOTS ALISIER
STAGBUSH VIBURNUM
BLACKHEAD COMEDO
BLACK HOREHOUND HENBIT
ARCHANGEL
BLACK HORSE SUCKER SUCKEREL
BLACKING LINK BLECK BLATCH
BLEACH ATRAMENT
BLACK IRONWOOD AXMASTER
AXEMASTER
BLACKISH DUSKY MOREL SWART
BLACKY
BLACKJACK OAK SAP CLUB COSH
DUCK FLAG JACK BETLE BILLY
JERKIN NATURAL BLUDGEON
BLACKLEG LEG FIRE SCAB SNOB
ANTHRAX GAMBLER JACKLEG
APOSTATE BLACKNEB BLACKNOB
SWINDLER KNOBSTICK
BLACK LETTER GOTHIC
BLACKLY SABLY
BLACK MAGIC DIABLERIE
BLACKMAIL BRIBE CHOUT COERCE
EXTORT TRIBUTE CHANTAGE
BLACKMAILER GHOUL BRIBER
LEECHER
BLACK MANGROVE COURIDA
BLACK MEDIC HOP TREFOIL
NONESUCH SHAMROCK
BLACKNESS GRIME DARKNESS
NIGRITUDE
BLACK NIGHTSHADE MOREL
DUSCLE SOLANUM BLUEBERRY
MOONSHADE TROMPILLO
BLACK OLIVE OXHORN
BLACK PEPPER PIMENTA
BLACK PINE MATAI
BLACK POISON WALNUT
BLACK RHINOCEROS BORELE
KEITLOA UPEYGAN
BLACK SALLY SALLEE
MUZZLEWOOD
BLACK SANICLE LUNGWORT
MASTERWORT
BLACK SHANK LANAS
BLACK SKIMMER CUTWATER
SHEARBILL
BLACKSMITH GOW SMUG LOHAR
SHOER SMITH PLOVER SMITHY
VULCAN BROOKIE FARRIER STRIKER
BURNEWIN IRONSMITH
BLACKSNAKE WHIP QUIRT RACER
ELAPID RUNNER COLUBRID
BLACK SPECK DARTROSE
BLACK SPURGE FLUXWEED
BLACKTAIL DASSY DASSIE

BLACK TERN DARR STARN
BLACKTHORN HAW SLOE SNAG
SCROG GRIBBLE SLOEBUSH
SLOETREE SNAGBUSH
BLACK-VARNISH TREE THEETSEE
BLACK VULTURE URUBU CORBIE
ZOPILOTE
BLACK WALNUT NOGAL
BLACKWATER STATE NEBRASKA
BLACK WIDOW POKOMOO
BLACK WOLF KARAKURT
BLACKWOOD BITI LIGHTWOOD
BLACKWORT COMFREY
BLADDER SAC VES VESICA AMPULLA
BLATHER BLISTER INFLATE
UROCYST UTRICLE VESICLE
(**AIR** —) POKE SWIM SOUND
SINGALLY
BLADDER-AND-STRING BUMBASS
BLADDER CAMPION BEHN BEHEN
SILENE COWBELL SNAPPER
RATTLEBOX
BLADDER KETMIE MODESTY
BLADDERNUT BAGNUT
BLADDERWORT POPWEED
BLADDER WRACK CUTWEED
KELPWARE
BLADE BIT FIN FOP OAR SAW WEB
BLOW BONE BOWL EDGE FLAG
HEAD LEAF LIMB TANG WEAK
BLOOD BRAND DANDY FLUKE GRAIN
GUIDE KNIFE LANCE SHEAR SPARK
SPEAR SPIRE SWORD BLUNGE
BUCKET BUSTER CUTTER DOCTOR
FOIBLE HEDDLE LAMINA PAGINA
RIPPER ROARER SCYTHE SICKLE
TOLEDO BAYONET CHIPPER
GALLANT POLESAW SCALPEL
SCAPULA SCRAPER SPINNER
MOLDBOARD PROPELLER
(— **OF FAN**) VANE
(— **OF GRASS**) PILE CHIRE SPEAR
SPIRE STRAP TRANEEN
(— **OF KNIFE**) TANG GRAIN
(— **OF LEAF**) LIMB LAMINA
(— **OF MORION**) COMB
(— **OF OAR**) PALM PELL WASH
(— **OF SCISSORS**) BILL
(— **OF YOUNG GRAIN**) SORAGE
(**CULTIVATOR** —) SWEEP DUCKFOOT
(**SKATE** —) RUNNER
(**SURGICAL** —) LEUCOTOME
BLAFFERT PLAPPERT
BLAIN RUBY SORE BULLA BLISTER
INFLAME PUSTULE
BLAKE MCKAY
BLAMABLE FAULTY CULPABLE
BLAME CALL CHOP HURT LACK
ONUS SAKE SPOT TWIT WITE CHIDE
FAULT GUILT ODIUM PINCH SHEND
SNAPE SWICK SWIKE TOUCH WHITE
ACCUSE ATTASK BUMBLE BURDEN
CHARGE DIRDUM PLIGHT REBUKE
REVILE SCANCE ASCRIBE CENSURE
CONDEMN CULPATE OBLOQUY
REPROOF REPROVE SLANDER
UPBRAID WITHNIM REPROACH
BLAMED BLINDING BLISTERING
BLAMELESS ENTIRE PERFECT

INNOCENT SACKLESS SPOTLESS
WITELESS RIGHTEOUS

BLAMEWORTHY GUILTY CRIMINAL
CULPABLE REPROBATE

BLANCH FADE PALE BLENK CHALK
SCALD WHITE APPALL ARGENT
BIANCA BLEACH BLENCH FALLOW
WHITEN ETIOLATE

BLANCHED ASHEN ETIOLATE
BLOODLESS COLORLESS

BLANCMANGE FLUMMERY

BLAND COLD KIND MILD OILY OPEN
SOFT SLEEK SUAVE BENIGN BREEZY
GENIAL GENTLE SMOOTH URBANE
AFFABLE AMIABLE LENIENT
FAVONIAN GRACIOUS UNCTUOUS

BLANDISH COAX CHARM ALLURE
BLANCH CAJOLE FONDLE SMOOTH
FLATTER WHEEDLE HONEYFUG

BLANDLY CREAMILY

BLANK BARE BURR FLAN FORM
SHOT VOID ANNUL BLIND BREAK
CHASM CLEAN EMPTY FALSE RANGE
SPACE WASTE WHITE COUPON
VACANT ANTIQUE BRINDLE
NONPLUS UNMIXED VACUOUS
UNFILLED

BLANKED BLIND

BLANKET RUG BROT MAUD WRAP
BLUEY COTTA COVER CUMLY LAYER
MANTA PATTU QUILT SHEET SUGAN
THROW AFGHAN COOLER CUMBLY
GLOBAL KAMBAL MANTLE PALLET
PONCHO PUTTOO SERAPE SOOGAN
STIFLE STROUD TILPAH CHIRIPA
DOUBLER SMOTHER WHITTLE
COVERLET MACKINAW
(— A VESSEL) WRONG
(— WITH BOMBS) SATURATE
(BUSHMAN'S —) BLUEY
(QUILTED —) BROT
(SADDLE —) CORONA

BLANKETING DUFFEL DUFFLE

BLANKNESS VACUITY NEGATION

BLARE PEAL BLEAR BLART BLAST
NOISE BLAZON SCREAM FANFARE
TANTARA TRUMPET

BLARNEY CON BUTTER FLATTER
WHEEDLE

BLASPHEME ABUSE CURSE DEFAME
REVILE PROFANE

BLASPHEMOUS BAD RIBALD
IMPIOUS PROFANE

BLASPHEMY CALUMNY CURSING
IMPIETY ANATHEMA SWEARING

BLAST BUB NIP WAP BANG BLOW
FRAP GALE GUST RUIN RUST SHOT
TOOT WIND BLAME BLIST BLORE
SPLIT STUNT ATTACK BLIGHT
BUGGER FORBID NIDDER NITHER
REBUFF VOLLEY WITHER BLUSTER
DESPOIL EXPLODE SHATTER
SHRIVEL DYNAMITE OUTBURST
PROCLAIM WHIRLPUFF
(— OF WIND) GUST RISE PERRY
PIRRIE VENTOSITY
(— ON HORN) TOOT PRYSE
(— WITH COLD) SNEAP
(FURIOUS —) SNIFTER

BLASTED BLAME BLAMED BLIGHTED
BLINDING BLINKING

BLASTER FROSTER SHOOTER
SHOTMAN

BLASTING SHOOTING STELLATION
(— METHOD) MUDCAP

BLASTULA PLACULA PLANULA
PLANULAN

BLATANT GLIB LOUD BRASH GROSS
NOISY SILLY VOCAL COARSE
GARISH TONANT VULGAR BRAWLING
STRIDENT

BLATHER STIR BLEAT BABBLE
WAFFLE BLITHER PRATTLE
NONSENSE

BLAUBOK ETAAC BLUEBUCK

BLAZE LOW BURN FIRE GLOW HACK
LEAM LOWE MARK SHOT SPOT
FLAME FLARE FLASH GLARE GLEAM
GLORY INGLE RATCH SHINE STARE
STEAM TORCH BLAZON BLEEZE
BONFIRE PIONEER SPLENDOR
(— OUT) FLAP

BLAZING AFIRE FIERY FLAMY LIGHT
FLAMING FLARING

BLAZING STAR LIATRIS GRUBROOT
SNAKEROOT

BLAZON DECK SHOW ADORN BLARE
BLAZE BOAST DEPICT SHIELD
DECLARE DISPLAY EXHIBIT PUBLISH
EMBLAZON INSCRIBE

BLAZONED ARMED BANNERED

BLEACH SUN WASH BLEAK CHALK
CROFT POACH BLANCH BLENCH
CHLORE PURIFY WHITEN DECOLOR
LIGHTEN BLONDINE ETIOLATE
PEROXIDE
(— PULP) POTCH

BLEACHER WHISTER

BLEACHERS SCAFFOLD

BLEAK DIM RAW BLAE BLAY COLD
DOUR GRAY PALE SPRAT STARK
SWALE ALBURN BITTER BLEACH
DISMAL DREARY FRIGID PALLID
CUTTING DESOLATE CHEERLESS

BLEAT BAA BLAT BLEA YARM BLART
BLATE BLATHER BLUSTER WHICKER

BLEATING BALANT

BLEB BLOB BULLA BUBBLE BLISTER
PUSTULE VESICLE SWELLING

BLEED FLUX MILK WEEP BLOOD
LEECH MULCT SWEAT SWINDLE
TEICHER

BLEEDER STICKER

BLEEDING BLOODY SANGLANT

BLEEDING HEART EARDROP
DICENTRA

BLEMISH MAR BLOT BLUR DENT
FLAW GALL LACK MAIM MARK MOIL
MOLE RIFT SAKE SCAR SLUR SPOT
TASH VICE WANT AMPER BLAME
BOTCH BRECK CLOUD CRACK
FAULT FLECK MULCT NAEVE SPECK
STAIN SULLY TACHE TAINT TOUCH
BLOTCH BREACH DEFAME DEFECT
IMPAIR INJURE MACULA MACULE
MAYHEM SMIRCH STIGMA BUBUKLE
CATFACE DEFAULT FAILING FISSURE
SUNSPOT

(— IN CLOTH) AMPER SULLY
(— IN PAPER) FISHEYE

BLEMISHED BAD WEMMY

BLENCH FOIL SHUN WILE AVOID
ELUDE EVADE QUAIL SHAKE SHIRK
TRICK BAFFLE BLANCH BLEACH
FLINCH RECOIL SHRINK DECEIVE

BLEND MIX RUN BLOT FADE FUSE
JOIN MELT MENG MOLD ADMIX
BLIND CREAM GRADE MERGE
MOULD SHADE SMEAR SPOIL STAIN
TINGE UNITE BLUNGE COMMIX
CRASIS DAZZLE MINGLE TEMPER
COMBINE CONFUSE CORRUPT
DECEIVE GRADATE MIXTURE
POLLUTE COALESCE CONCRETE
IMMINGLE TINCTURE
(— OF NOISES) CHARM
(— OF SHERRY) SOLERA
(— OF WINES) CUVEE

BLENDE JACK SPHALERITE

BLENDED FONDU FUSED MIXED
MERGED MINGLED CONFLATE
CONFLUENT

BLENDING FUSION HOTCHPOT

BLENNY GUNNEL SHANNY EELPOUT
JUGULAR KELPFISH SENORITA
WOLFFISH WRYMOUTH QUILLFISH

BLESBOK NUNNI BLESBUCK

BLESS KEEP SAIN WAVE ADORE
ANELE BENSH CROSS EXTOL FAVOR
GUARD THANK VISIT WOUND
CROUCH FAVOUR HALLOW PRAISE
THRASH APPROVE BEATIFY EMBLISS
GLORIFY PROTECT MACARIZE
PRESERVE SANCTIFY

BLESSED HOLY BLEST HAPPY SEELY
DIVINE JOYFUL SACRED SEELFUL
BENEDICT BHAGAVAT BLISSFUL
BLOOMING HALLOWED HEAVENLY

BLESSEDNESS BLISS FELICITY
BEATITUDE HAPPINESS

BLESSING BOON GIFT SAIN BLISS
DUKAN GRACE SORRA BARAKA
DUCHAN PRAISE BENISON DARSHAN
WORSHIP BERACHAH FELICITY
BEATITUDE

BLEU DE ROI SEVRES

BLIGHT NIP FIRE RUIN RUST SMUT
SOKA BLAST BRANT FROST SNEAP
MILDEW NITHER TAKING WITHER
DESTROY

BLIND BET POT ANTE BOMA DARK
DEAD DULL HIDE HOOD SEEL BISME
BLANK BLEND DUNCH SHADE STAKE
STALL WAGER AMBUSH BISSON
BLENDE DARKEN DAZZLE SCREEN
SECRET AIMLESS ANTIQUE
BANDAGE BATTERY BENIGHT
ECLIPSE EYELESS OBSCURE
PRETEXT RAYLESS SHUTTER
ABORTIVE ARTIFICE BAYARDLY
BLINDING EXCECATE HOODWINK
IGNORANT INVOLVED JALOUSIE
OUTSHINE PURBLIND UMBRELLA
VENETIAN
(— IN ONE EYE) PEED GLEED
GLEYD
(— MAN) MOLE

(HALF —) STARBLIND
(PL.) PERSIENNES
BLIND ALLEY LOKE STOP POCKET
IMPASSE
BLINDER FLAP HOOD BLIND BLUFF
LUNET WINKER BLINKER EYEFLAP
LUNETTE HOODWINK BLINDFOLD
BLINDFOLD MOP DARK BLINK BLUFF
SCARF MUFFLE BANDAGE BLINDER
OBSCURE ENCLOSER HEEDLESS
HOODWINK RECKLESS CONCEALED
BLINDING BISME BISSON
BLINDMAN'S BLUFF POST
HOODWINK
BLINDNESS BISSON CECITY
ABLEPSY ANOPSIA MEROPIA
ABLEPSIA DARKNESS IGNORANCE
(— TO TRUTH) AVIDYA AVIJJA
(COLOR —) ACHROBIA
(DAY —) HEMERALOPIA
(NIGHT —) NYCTALOPIA
(PARTIAL —) MEROPIA HEMIOPSIA
(RED-GREEN —) DALTONISM
(SNOW —) CHIONABLEPSIA
(STUDY OF —) TYPHLOLOGY
(TEMPORARY —) MOONBLINK
BLINDSTITCH FELL
BLINDWORM SLOW ORVET ANGUID
HAGWORM SLOWWORM
BLIND-YOUR-EYES GANGWA
ALIPATA
BLINK BAT PINK SHUN WINK BLUSH
CHEAT FLASH GLEAM SHINE TRICK
GLANCE IGNORE OBTUSE WAPPER
BLINTER CONDONE GLIMMER
GLIMPSE NEGLECT NICTATE
SPARKLE TWINKLE
BLINKER EYE BLINK BLUFF LIGHT
SIGNAL WINKER BLINDER FLASHER
GOGGLES COQUETTE HOODWINK
MACKEREL
BLINTZE BLIN BLINTZ PANCAKE
BLIP ECHO
BLISS JOY EDEN KAIF SEIL BLESS
GLORY ANANDA HEAVEN DELIGHT
ECSTASY GLADDEN RAPTURE
FELICITY GLADNESS PARADISE
PLEASURE
BLISSFUL HOLY SEELY BLITHE
BLESSED ELYSIAN UTOPIAN
BEATIFIED GLORIFIED
BLISTER BEAT BLEB BLOB BLOW
BOIL BURN LASH QUAT APTHA
BLAIN BLIBE BULGE BULLA TOPIC
VESIC APHTHA BUBBLE CUPOLA
SCORCH SOTTER TETTER BLADDER
BLUSTER SCALDER SKELLER
VESICLE VESICATE
BLITHE GAY GLAD BONNY BUXOM
HAPPY JOLLY MERRY BONNIE
JOVIAL JOYOUS LIVELY GAYSOME
JOCULAR WINSOME CHEERFUL
GLADSOME SPRIGHTLY
BLIZZARD BLOW GALE WIND BURAN
PURGA RETORT SNIFTER
SQUELCHER
(— STATE) SD SDAK
BLOAT BLOW BLAST BLOWN FLOAT
HOOVE HOVEN PUFFY SWELL

BOWDEN EXPAND TUMEFY DISTEND
FERMENT INFLATE
BLOATED FOZY BLOAT BROSY
CURED FOGGY HOVEN TUMID
GOTCHY SODDEN TURGID POMPOUS
REPLETE
BLOATER MOONEYE
BLOB LIP WEN BEAD BLEB BLOT
BOIL CLOT DAUB DROP GLOB GOUT
LUMP MARK MASS BUBBLE DALLOP
DOLLOP PIMPLE SPLASH BLEMISH
BLISTER BLOSSOM GLOBULE
PUSTULE SPLOTCH
BLOC RING BLOCK CABAL PARTY
UNION CLIQUE FACTION
BLOCK AME BAR COB COG DAM DIE
DOG FID HOB HUB JAM KEY NOG
ROW TOP VOL BALK BASE BEAR
BILK BLOC BUCK BUNT CAKE CLOG
CUBE DRUM FOIL FOUL FROG GLUT
HEAD JAMB LEAD MASK MASS
MOCK QUAR STAY STEP STOP TRIG
BAULK BRICK CHAIR CHECK CHEEK
CHUMP CLAMP CLEAT CLOSE
COVER DETER DOLLY DUMMY
EMBAR FLOAT HEART HORST
JUMBO NUDGE PARRY PATCH
SHAPE SPIKE SPOKE STOCK STUFF
STUMP ASSIZE DENTIL DOLLEY
DOMINO FIPPLE FORMER HAMPER
HINDER IMPEDE KIBOSH MONKEY
MUFFLE MUTULE OPPOSE OUTWIT
QUERRE RIPPER SADDLE SCOTCH
SNATCH SQUARE STREET STYMIE
TAPLET THWART TROLLY WAYLAY
BOLLOCK BOLSTER BUCKLER
CONDEMN DEADEYE ERRATIC
INHIBIT OUTLINE PREVENT QUADREL
RAMHEAD STONKER TRIGGER
TROLLEY BLOCKADE DEADHEAD
ELECTRET FOLLOWER KEYSTONE
MONOLITH OBSTACLE OBSTRUCT
STOPPAGE WITHSPAR
(— A WHEEL) SCOTE
(— AT SPAR END) STEEVE
(— FOR SKIDDING LOGS) BICYCLE
(— IN SPEAKING) STAMMER
(— OF COAL) JUD JUDD
(— OF EARTH'S CRUST) HORST
(— OF GRANITE) SET
(— OF ICE) SERAC
(— OF LAND) FORTY
(— OF SEATS) CUNEUS
(— OF TIMBER) BOLT JUGGLE
(— SUPPORTING MAST) STEP
(— UP) BAR DAM QUIRT CONDEMN
FORECLOSE
(— WITH HOLE IN IT) WAPP
EUPHROE
(— WITH PROJECTING CORE)
SETTLE
(—S OF STONE) DIMENSION
(ARCHITECTURAL —) DRUM STONE
DENTIL IMPOST MUTULE PLINTH
DOSSERET
(CHOPPING —) HACKLOG
(CLAY —) DRAWBAR
(FAULT —) MASSIF
(FELTED —) DAMPER

(FULCRUM —) GLUT
(FUSE —) CUTOUT
(IRON —) USE VOL BITT ANVIL
CHAIR
(LOGGING —) LEAD JUMBO
(NAUTICAL —) CHOCK HEART
STOCK SADDLE DEADEYE FAIRLEAD
(ORNAMENTAL —) BOSS
(PAVING —) SET CUBE SETT STONE
WHEELER
(PLASTER —) BATTER
(POLISHING —) BUFF FLOAT
(PRINTING —) CUT QUAD RISER
QUADRAT
(PULLEY —) CRAWL
(SANDSTONE —) SARSEN
(SQUARED —) MITCHEL
(STUMBLING —) HURTING
(TACKLE —) CALO TONGUE
(VAULTING —) BUCK HORSE
BLOCKADE DAM FERM BESET
BLOCK EMBAR SIEGE WHISKY
EMBARGO BLOCKAGE OBSTRUCT
BARRICADE BELEAGUER
BLOCKAGE LOGJAM
BLOCKER CASER BRACER
BLOCKHEAD ASS LUG OAF BUST
CLOT COOF COOT DAFF DOLT FOOL
MOME NOWT STUB BLOCK CHUMP
CUDDY GOLEM GOOSY IDIOT NINNY
DIMWIT DISARD NOODLE TURNIP
ASSHEAD DIZZARD DULBERT
JACKASS LACKWIT MUDHEAD
NOGHEAD TOMFOOL BEEFHEAD
BONEHEAD CLODPATE CODSHEAD
DULLHEAD DULLPATE DUMBHEAD
DUMMKOPF GAMPHREL HARDHEAD
JOLTHEAD LUNKHEAD
BLOCKHOUSE SPUR PUNTAL
GARRISON
BLOCKING JAM JAMB DUNNAGE
BLOCKADE CROSSING
BLOKE MAN CHAP COVE TOFF
BLOAK JOKER FELLOW
BLOLLY BEEFWOOD CORKWOOD
PORKWOOD
BLOND BAN FAIR LIGHT BLONDE
FLAXEN GOLDEN YELLOW LEUCOUS
BLONDINE
(AUTUMN —) FAWN
BLOOD KIN SAP GORE LIFE MASS
MOOD RACE SANG SANK BLADE
BLUDE BLUID CRUOR FLESH FLUID
SERUM STOCK CLARET INDRED
KAINAH SLUDGE GALLANT KINSHIP
KINSMAN LINEAGE RELATION
TROPHEMA
(CORRUPT —) YOUSTIR
(HALF —) DEMISANG
BLOODCURDLING GORY HORROR
BLOODFLOWER HIPPO REDHEAD
BLOODWEED
BLOODHOUND LYM LYAM LYME
HOUND LIMER SLOTH BANDOG
LEAMER SLEUTH TIEDOG
LYAMHOUND
BLOODIED BEBLED
BLOODLESS DEAD ANEMIC ANAEMIC
INHUMAN TURNIPY LIFELESS
UNFEELING

BLOODLETTER BLEEDER

BLOOD PHEASANT ITHAGINE

BLOODROOT PUCCOON REDROOT BOLOROOT COONROOT CORNROOT TURMERIC

BLOODSHED DEATH CARNAGE VIOLENCE SLAUGHTER

BLOODSHOT RED INFLAMED

BLOODSTAINED GORY

BLOODSTONE SANGUINE HEMACHATE

BLOODSUCKER LEECH SPONGER VAMPIRE

BLOODTHIRSTY BLOODY CARNAL TIGERISH FEROCIOUS MURDEROUS

BLOOD VESSEL VEIN COMES HEMAD ARTERY CAPILLARY

BLOODWOOD AJHAR JAROOL

BLOODY GORY RUDE BLODE CRUEL RUDDY BLUGGY CRUENT PLUCKY CRIMSON BLEEDING DEATHFUL HEMATOSE INFAMOUS SANGLANT BUTCHERLY CRUENTOUS FEROCIOUS MERCILESS MURDEROUS

BLOODY BARK LANCEPOD

BLOOM DEW BLOW CAST HAZE KNOT BLURT BLUSH CHILL BLOOTH BLOWTH BLOSSOM BLOWING ANTHESIS BLOOMING FLOREATE FLOURISH
(— **OF WILLOW**) GULL
(— **ON SHELL**) CUTICLE
(— **ON TREE**) GOSLING
(**METAL** —**S**) HEAT

BLOOMER ERROR BLOWER BLUNDER FAILURE

BLOOMERS KNICKERS PANTALETS

BLOOMERY FORGE HEARTH FURNACE

BLOOMING PERT ROSY FLUSH FRESH GREEN PRIME ABLOOM FLORID BLOWING FLAMING ROSEATE BLINKING

BLOOPER BLOOMER

BLOSSOM BUD BELL BLOB BLOW CHIP SILK BLOOM LEHUA FLOWER BLOWING BURGEON PROSPER BOURGEON FLOURISH
(**BLIGHTED** —) BLAST
(**HERALDIC** —) FRASE FRAISE
(PL.) SET BLOSSOMRY

BLOSSOMING BLOWTH FLORAISON FLORULENT
(— **AFTER NOON**) POMERIDIAN

BLOT MAR BLOB BLUR DAUB SOIL SPOT BLACK BLANK BLEND BLOTE ERASE SMEAR SPECK STAIN SULLY BLOTCH CANCEL DAMAGE EFFACE IMPAIR MACULA SHADOW SMIRCH SMOUCH SMUDGE SMUTCH STIGMA BLEMISH ECLIPSE EXPUNGE INKBLOT OBSCURE SPLOTCH TARNISH DISGRACE REPROACH
(— **OUT**) OUT ANNUL ERASE CANCEL DELETE EXPUNGE

BLOTCH DAB BLOT DASH GOUT MONK SPOT AMPER PATCH SMEAR SPLAT STAIN MACULA MOTTLE PLOTCH PURPLE SMIRCH SPLASH STIGMA BLEMISH PUSTULE SPLOTCH ERUPTION MACULATE
(PL.) BLIBE

BLOTCHED SCABBY MACULATE SCABROUS SPLASHED

BLOTCHY SCOVY

BLOTTER BLAD

BLOUSE SHIRT SMOCK TUNIC CAMISA GUIMPE JUMPER CASAQUE VAREUSE CAMISOLE CASAQUIN JIRKINET
(**BUSHMAN'S** —) BLUEY

BLOW BOB COB COP CUT DAB DAD DUB FAN FIB HIT JAB JAR NAP ONE PAT PEG POP RAP TAP TIP TIT WAP ANDE BAFF BANG BASH BEAT BELT BIFF BIRR BLAD BLAW BRAG BUFF BULL BUMP BUTT CHAP CHOP CONK COUP CRIG CUFF DASH DAUD DENT DING DINT DIRD DOLE DRAW DRUB DUNT DUSH FLAP FLEG FLIG FUFF FUNK GALE GOWF GUST HACK HUFF HURT JOLT KNAP KNEE LASH LEAD LEFT LICK LOUK LUSH MINT ONER PAIK PALT PANT PASS PICK PIRR PLUG POLT PUCK PUFF PUSH SCUD SLAM SLAP SLAT SLUG SOCK SPAT STOP SWAP SWAW SWOP SWOT THUD WELT WIND WIPE YANK BINGE BLADE BLAST BLIZZ BLOOM BOAST BRUNT BURST CLINK CLOUR CLOUT CLUMP CLUNK CRUMP CRUNT CURSE DEVEL DOUSE DOWSE DUNCH FACER FILIP FLACK FLICK FLIRT GOWFF ICTUS IMPEL KNOCK OUTER PALMY PANDY PASTE PEISE PLUNK PUNCH RIGHT SHAKE SHOCK SKELP SKIRL SKITE SLASH SLIPE SLOSH SMACK SMASH SMITE SNICK SOUND SOUSE SPANK SPEND STORM STRIP SURGE SWACK SWEEP SWIPE THROW THUMP TRICE WHACK WHANG WHIFF WHOOF WHUFF BELTER BENSEL BENSIL BETRAY BOUNCE BUFFET CONKER DEPART DIRDUM DUNDER EXPAND FILLIP FISTER FLOWER FROLIC HANDER HUFFLE LARRUP REBUKE SIFFLE STOUSH STRIPE STROKE SWITCH THUNGE THWACK WALLOP AFFLATE ASSAULT ATTAINT BELLOWS BENSAIL BLOSSOM BLOWOUT BLUSTER BOASTER COUNTER CRUSHER DESTROY INFLATE KNOCKER LAMBACK LOUNDER MOUTHER PUBLISH SHATTER SMACKER SPANKER SQUELCH WHAMPLE WHIFFLE WHITHER CALAMITY DISASTER KNOCKOUT SASARARA SICKENER
(— **ABRASIVES**) BLAST
(— **CEMENT**) KIBOSH
(— **GUSTILY**) FLAW TUCK WINNOW
(— **IN PUFFS**) FAFF
(— **NOSE**) SNITE
(— **OFF STEAM**) SNIFT
(— **ON HEAD**) NOB CONK CLOUR CONKER NOBBER TOPPER NOBBLER
(— **ON NOSE**) NOSER CANKER NOZZLER SMELLER
(— **SMOKE**) NOSE
(— **SOFTLY**) BREATHE
(— **UP**) BOMB BLAST DYNAMITE SUFFLATE
(— **VIOLENTLY**) STORM
(— **WITH CUDGEL**) DUB DRUB CRUNT
(— **WITH FIST**) BOP BOX PEG BELT HOOK CLOUT BUFFET
(— **WITH FOOT**) BOOT KICK SPURN
(**GLANCING** —) SCUFF
(**HARD** —) SLOG STOT YANK BEVEL SWACK TWITCHER
(**HEAVY** —) DAD DONG DRUB DUNT ONER SLAM SLUG CLOUT KNOCK POISE SOUSE SQUAT STAVE SWASH STOUND PLUMPER REEMISH
(**MOCK** —) FEINT
(**NOISY** —) DUNDER DUNNER
(**RESOUNDING** —) CLAP CRACK
(**SHARP** —) BAT NAP KNAP SLAP SPAT CLICK FLICK FLEWIT STINGER
(**SLIGHT** —) SCLAFF
(**SMART** —) FLIP SKELP SKITE YANKER

BLOWCASE EGG

BLOWER PAN DRIER DRYER WHALE FANNER PUFFER BELLOWS BLOOMER BOOSTER MUMBLER BRAGGART OUTBURST
(**GLASS** —) GAFFER

BLOWGUN SUMPIT SUMPITAN SARBACANE

BLOWHOLE BLOW GLOUP SPOUT SPIRACLE

BLOWING ABLOW BLAST BLORE GUSTY BLUSTER BLUSTERY
(— **AT LOW SPEED**) SLACK
(— **AT RIGHT ANGLES**) SIDE
(— **OF WHALE**) SPOUT

BLOWN STALE TIRED OPENED WINDED BLOSSOM SWOLLEN TAINTED BETRAYED FLYBLOWN INFLATED

BLOWOUT BLOW FEED MEAL BURST VALLEY FLAMEOUT

BLOWSY DOWDY BLOUSY BLOWZY FROWZY

BLOWY DUSTY

BLUBBER CRY FAT BLUB FOAM WAIL WEEP BIBLE MELON PIECE SPECK SPICK SWELL THICK WHINE BUBBLE FLITCH LIPPER LUBBER MEDUSA NETTLE SEETHE BLABBER BLUSTER SLOBBER SWOLLEN WHIMPER
(— **AT WHALE'S NECK**) CANT
(**REFUSE** —) FENKS FOOTING FRITTERS

BLUDGEON BAT HIT SAP CLUB MACE BILLY STICK TOWEL COERCE COURSE TRUNCHEON

BLUE HAW LOW SAD SKY AQUA BICE BLAE GLUM TEAL WOAD AZURE BERYL LIVID NIKKO PERSE SMALL WAGET COBALT GLOOMY INDIGO LUPINE ORIENT PEWTER SEVERE TRYPAN CELESTE CYANINE GENTIAN

GOBELIN HYPPISH LEARNED
LIBERTY LOBELIA MATELOT
MISTBLU MURILLO PEACOCK
QUIMPER REGATTA WATCHET
CERULEAN DEJECTED LABRADOR
LARKSPUR LITERARY MAZARINE
MIDNIGHT NATIONAL SAPPHIRE
WEDGWOOD POMPADOUR
(BLACKISH —) BLO BLOO
(DULL —) HAW
(ROYAL —) HATHOR
BLUEBELL CROWBELL HAREBELL
BLUEBERRY OHELO STONER
PALBERRY RABBITEYE VACCINIUM
BLUEBIRD (— GUIDE) LEADER
BLUE-BLACK BLO
BLUEBLOSSOM LILAC
BLUEBONNET CAP SCOT BLUECAP
BLUEBOTTLE BLUET BLAVER
BARBEAU BLAWORT BLOWFLY
BLUECAP BLUECUP BRUSHES
HARDOCK BLUEBLAW HYACINTH
CORNBINKS
BLUE CREEPER LOVE
BLUE CURLS FLEASEED FLEAWEED
BLUE-EYED GRASS PIGROOT
SATINFLOWER
BLUEFIN TUNNY
BLUEFISH ELF BASS ELFT SHAD
TUNA HORSE SAURY DARZEE
TAILER TAILOR FATBACK SKIPJACK
WEAKFISH
(YOUNG OF —) SNAPPER WHITEFISH
BLUEGILL BREAM SUNFISH
PONDFISH
BLUE GOOSE BALDHEAD
BLUEGRASS STATE KENTUCKY
BLUE GREEN VENICE
BLUE GUM FEVERGUM EUCALYPTUS
BLUE HEN STATE DELAWARE
BLUE HERON CRANE NAILROD
BLUEJACKET SAILOR DRAGMAN
BLUEJOINT REDTOP BLUETOPS
BLUE PETER ASK
BLUE PINE LIM
BLUE POINTER MAKO
BLUEPRINT MAP PLAN PLOT DRAFT
TRACE SKETCH DIAGRAM PROJECT
CYANOTYPE
BLUE RUNNER JUREL
BLUES MARE DUMPS CAFARD
DISMAL GLOOMS DISMALS
HORRORS HUMDRUM MEGRIMS
SADNESS DOLDRUMS DOLEFULS
BLUE SLATE SKAILLIE
BLUE SUCCORY CATNACHE
CUPIDONE
BLUET PISSABED EYEBRIGHT
INNOCENCE
BLUE TIT NUN STONECHAT
BLUE TITMOUSE YAUP TYDIE
TIDIFE BLUECAP
BLUETONGUE THICKHEAD
BLUE VERVAIN IRONWEED
BLUE VINNY DORSET
BLUEWEED ECHIUM IRONWEED
ADDERWORT
BLUFF ALTO BANK BRAG CURT FOOL
RUDE BLUNT BRAVE BURLY CLIFF

FRANK GRUFF SHORT SURLY WINDY
ABRUPT BOUNCE CRUSTY BLINDER
BLINKER BLUFTER BRUSQUE
DECEIVE UNCIVIL BARRANCA
BARRANCO CHURLISH HOODWINK
IMPOLITE
BLUISH-GRAY MERLE
BLUMEA PLACUS
BLUNDER ERR MIX BALK BONE
BUBU BULL DOLT FLUB GAFF ROIL
SKEW SLIP STIR BONER BOTCH
BREAK ERROR FAULT FLUFF GAFFE
LAPSE MISDO BOGGLE BUMBLE
BUNGLE ESCAPE FUMBLE GAZEBO
HOWLER MAFFLE MINGLE MUDDLE
BLOOMER BLOOPER CONFUSE
DERANGE FAILURE FLOATER
MISTAKE OVERSEE SOTTISE
STUMBLE SOLECISM
(— IN LANGUAGE) BULL
(— IN SPEECH) SOLECISM
(VERBAL —) SLIPSLAP SLIPSLOP
BLUNDERBUSS TRABU TRABUCO
TRABUCHO TROMBONE ESPINGOLE
BLUNDERER BUMBLER BUMMLER
KNOTHEAD LUMBERER
BLUNDERING AWKWARD BUMBLING
BLUNT BALD BATE BULL CURT DAMP
DULL FLAT MULL SNUB ABATE
BLATE BLUFF BRUSK DUBBY INERT
MORNE PLAIN PLUMP STUNT
CANDID CLUMSY DEADEN DIRECT
OBTUND OBTUSE REBATE RETUND
SHEATH STUBBY STUPID BRUSQUE
DISEDGE HACKNEY SHEATHE
SNUBBED SPADISH STUBBED
STUPEFY HEBETATE
BLUNTLY PLAT FLATLY CRUDELY
FRANKLY
BLUR DIM FOG HUM BLOB BLOT
FADE FUZZ MIST SLUR SOIL SPOT
BLEAR CLOUD FUDGE SHAKE
SMEAR STAIN SULLY MACKLE
MACULE SMUDGE STIGMA BLEMISH
CONFUSE FEATHER OBSCURE
TAILING
BLURB AD BOLT PUFF RAVE BRIEF
NOTICE
BLURRED FAINT FUZZY MUZZY
BLURRY SMUDGY SWIMMY WOOLLY
CLOUDED COMATIC EDGELESS
FLANNELLY
BLURT BLAT BOLT BLUNDER
EXCLAIM
BLUSH BLUE GLOW BLINK COLOR
FLUSH GLEAM PAINT ROUGE TINGE
CHANGE GLANCE MANTLE REDDEN
CRIMSON FLICKER LIKENESS
JOSEPHINE
BLUSHING RED ROSY ABLUSH
ROSEATE FLUSHING ROSACEOUS
BLUSTER BEEF BLOW DING HUFF
RAGE RANT BLAST BLEAT BLORE
BOAST BRACE BULLY NOISE STORM
SWANK BABBLE BELLOW BOUNCE
FRAPLE HECTOR HUFFLE TUMULT
WUTHER BLUBBER BRAVADO
FLUSTER GAUSTER ROISTER
SWAGGER WHITHER BOASTING

BULLYING THREATEN
BLUSTERER SWAG FLASH HECTOR
HUFFER FRAPLER HUFFCAP
TEARCAT
BLUSTERING BOG LOUD BRASH
VAPORS HUFFCAP VAPOURS
BULLYING
BOA BOM BOID BOMA ABOMA JIBOA
SCARF THROW ABOLLA ADJIGA
GIBOIA JOBOYA PYTHON ADJIGER
CAMOODI EMPEROR PEROPOD
ANACONDA CORALLUS
BOAR HOG APER SUID BRAWN SWINE
BARROW HOGGET TUSKER
BRAWNER SOUNDER SUIDIAN
VENISON WILRONE BRISTLER
SANGLIER HOGGASTER
(— CRY) FREAM
(— HEAD) HURE
(— IN 2ND YEAR) HOGGET
(— IN 3RD YEAR) HOGSTEER
HOGGASTER
(— STY) FRANK
(YOUNG —) GRISE SOUNDER
BOARD EAT LAG PAX TOE DAIL DEAL
DECK DIET EATS FARE FLIP HACK
JOIN KEEP LATH MEAT SHIP SIGN
SLAT TRAY TRIP BUIRD CHESE
CLEAR COARD COUCH COURT
ENTER FOUND HOUSE LODGE
MEALS PANEL PLANK RATCH SHIDE
STAGE STALL SWALE TABLE THEAL
ABACUS ACCOST COMMON PALLET
PLANCH RANDOM RIBBON SHIELD
SIDING TUCKER CABINET CHAMBER
COUNCIL CRIMPER DUOVIRI
ENPLANE ENTRAIN KNEELER
PALETTE PLANCHE SCRAPER
TABLING TRANSOM WHATMAN
APPROACH ASSEMBLY BOXBOARD
CUPBOARD EXCLUDER FETIALES
KEYBOARD LAPBOARD PEGBOARD
TRIBUNAL
(— FOR FALCON'S MEAT) HACK
(— OF BRIDGE) CHESS
(— OF LOOM) CARD
(— OF MILL WHEEL) AWE
(— ON CALF'S NOSE) BLAB
(— OVER) BERTH
(— WITH GROOVE) COULISSE
(— WITH HANDLE) CLAPPER
(— WITH NUMBER) SLATE
(— WITH PINS) RIDDLE
(— WITH TEETH) HACKLE RUFFER
(BLOCKHEAD —) DOLL
(CHANNEL —) PAN
(CHESS —) TABLER
(DRAWING —) COQUILLE
(EXHIBITION —) FRAME
(FLOOR —) KEY
(GAME —) HALMA
(HEART-SHAPED —) PLANCHET
(MORTAR —) HAWK
(NOTCHED —) HORSE
(OTTER —) DOOR
(POLING —) RUNNER
(PRESSED —S) FELT
(PULP-PRESSING —) COUCH
(RABBETED —S) SHIPLAP

(SHEATHING —S) SARKING
(STRIKE —) SCREED
(TANNING —) BEAM
(THIN —) SHIDE SARKING
(THIN —S) SLITWORK
(WARPING —) BARTREE
BOARDER MEALER TABLER GRAINER
PENSIONER SOJOURNER TRANSIENT
BOARDING LIVERY
BOARDINGHOUSE FONDA HOUSE
PENSION
BOARDWALK MARINA DUCKBOARD
BOARWOOD CHEWSTICK
BOAST BOG GAB JET BEEF BLAW
BLOW BRAG CROW POMP PUFF
RAVE VANT WIND WOST YELP
BLAST BRAVE CRACK CRAKE EXTOL
EXULT GLORY PRATE QUACK
ROOSE SCOLD SKITE VAPOR VAUNT
VOUST YOLPE AVAUNT BLAZON
BLEEZE BOUNCE CLAMOR FLAUNT
INSULT MENACE OUTCRY SPLORE
BLUSTER BRAVING CLAMOUR
DEVAUNT DISPLAY GLORIFY
SWAGGER FLOURISH THREATEN
VANTERIE VAUNTERY
BOASTER BLOW HUFF SKITE
CROWER GASCON PEDANT PRATER
SHAKER BOUNCER BRAGGER
BRAVADO CRACKER RUFFLER
BLOWHARD BRAGGART CACAFUGO
FANFARON GLORIOSO JINGOIST
RODOMONT TARTARIN WOUSTOUR
BOASTFUL BIG BRAG HIGH LARGE
BRAGGY PARADO JACTANT VAUNTIE
FANFARON GLORIOUS GASCONADE
THRASONIC
BOASTFULLY SIDE LARGE
BOASTFULNESS GLORY EGOTISM
WINDINESS
BOASTING BLOW HUFF YELP BOAST
CRACK PRATE ROOSE QUACKY
BOBANCE GASSING JACTANCE
JACTANCY QUACKISH VAUNTAGE
VENTOSITY
(EMPTY —) GAS
BOAT ARK BUM BUN CAT COG COT
DOW GIG MON TUB ACON BAIT
BARK BOOT BRIG CARV CHOP COCK
DHOW DINK DORY DUMP FLAT FOUZ
JUNK PAIR PLAT PRAM PUNT RAFT
SCOW SHIP SKAG TACK TODE TOPO
TROW WAKA YAWL YOLE ACCON
AVISO BANCA BARCA BARGE BARIS
BATEL BIDAR BOLIA BOYER BULLY
BUYER CANOE COBLE CRAFT DHONI
DINGY FERRY FOIST FORTY FUNNY
JOLLY KETCH LAKER LINER NADIR
OOLAK PIECE PILOT PRAAM RACER
SHELL SHOUT SIKAR SKIFF SKIFT
SMACK TOPPO UMIAK WAAPA WHIFF
XEBEC ZEBEC BAIDAK BANGKA
BATEAU BAWLEY BELLUM BILALO
BORLEY BOTTOM BOUTRE CAIQUE
CARVEL CAYUCO CHEBEC COCKLE
CRUISE CUTTER DINGHY DREDGE
DRIVER DROVER DUGOUT FLATTY
GALLEY GARVEY GAYYOU GLIDER
HOOKER JAGGER JIGGER KEELER

KICKER KUPHAR LERRET MAILER
NAGGAR NUGGAR PACKET PEAPOD
PEDULE PICARD PINKIE PLAYTE
PULWAR RANDAN ROCKER SANDAL
SCAPHE SCHOUW SCHUYT SETTEE
SINGLE SKERRY STRUSE TANKER
TENDER TIMBER TOGGER TORPID
TRANKY TROUGH VESSEL WAFTER
WHERRY ZEBECK AIRBOAT ALMADIA
ANGEYOK BALLOEN BALLOON
BAULEAH BUMBOAT CAISSON
CARRIER CATCHER CORACLE
CRUISER DOGBODY DRIFTER
DROGHER FLATTIE FLEETER
FLYBOAT FOYBOAT FRIGATE
GAIASSA GASBOAT GONDOLA
HOVELER HUFFLER KELLECK
LIGHTER MACHINE MASOOLA
NACELLE PEARLER PEDIWAK
PINNACE PIRAGUA POOKAWN
PUTELEE SCOOTER SCULLER
SHALLOP SHARPIE SHIKARA
SIKHARA SKAFFLE SKIPPET
SPONGER SPYBOAT STEAMER
TRAWLER TUCKNER TUMBREL
TUMBRIL VEDETTE WHIRREY
BALANGAY BARANGAY BILLYBOY
BOOMBOAT BULLBOAT BUMBARGE
CANALLER CHALOUPE CHEBACCO
CHELINGA CHELINGO COCKBOAT
DAHABEAH DUCKBOAT FIREBOAT
FLAGBOAT KEELBOAT LIFEBOAT
MACKINAW MONOXYLE NEWSBOAT
OYSTERER PALANDER PANCHWAY
PESSONER PESSULUS PULLBOAT
SAILBOAT SCHOKKER SCHOONER
SURFBOAT TONGKANG TRANSFER
(— OF MALTA) DGHAISA
(— WITH SAILS AND OARS)
LYMPHIAD
(3-OAR —) RANDAN
(6-OAR —) SEXERN
(8-OAR —) SHIP
(ABANDONED —) DERELICT
(CHEMICAL —) CAPSULE
(CHINESE —) JUNK SAMPAN
(CLUMSY —) HOOKER DROGHER
(DISPATCH —) AVISO PACKET
(ESKIMO —) KAMIK UMIAK OOMIAC
UMIACK
(FERRY —) BAC CUTT
(FISHING —) COG BOVO BUSS DONI
CANOA COBLE DHONI NOBBY
PYKAR SMACK VINTA BALDIE
BAWLEY DOGGER DROVER FISHER
KUPHAR NICKEY SANDAL SCAFFY
SEINER SEXERN TOSHER VOLYER
CARAVEL CRABBER DRAGGER
FOLLYER POOKAUN SHARPIE
SKAFFIE TRAWLER DRAGBOAT
GAROOKUH SHRIMPER
(FLAT-BOTTOM —) ARK BAC DORY
FLAT PLAT PRAM PUNT SCOW
BARGE COBLE DOREY FLOAT
MOSES PRAAM SHOUT BATEAU
BUGEYE GAYYOU PUTELI GONDOLA
LIGHTER FLATBOAT GUNDELOW
JOHNBOAT
(FLY —) BUSS FLUTE FLIGHT

(INCENSE —) NEF SHIP NAVICULA
(MORTAR —) PALANDER
(OPEN —) WHIFF LERRET SHALLOP
(PATROL —) SPITKID SPITKIT
(RACING —) SIX FOUR EIGHT SCULL
SHELL SINGLE TORPID SCULLER
(SHIP'S —) GIG MOSES DINGEY
DINGHY LAUNCH TENDER PINNACE
(SKIN —) BIDAR BAIDAR ANGEYOK
BIDARKA BULLBOAT
(WICKER —) KUFA GOOFA GOOFAH
CORACLE
(PL.) LIGHTERAGE
BOATBUILDING SETWORK
BOATHOOK STOWER HITCHER
BOATMAN DANDI DANDY PHAON
BARGER BOWMAN CHARON YAWLER
HOBBLER HOVELER HUFFLER
COBLEMAN VOYAGEUR WATERMAN
GONDOLIER
BOAT SEAT TAFT
BOAT SHELL YET SWEETMEAT
BOATSWAIN BOSN BOSUN SERANG
TINDAL
BOAZ (FATHER OF —) SALMA
SALMON
(SON OF —) OBED
(WIFE OF —) RUTH
BOB BAB BOW CUT DAB DIP HOD
JOG POP RAP TAP BALL BLOW
BUFF CALF CLIP CLOD COIN CORK
DUCK GRUB JEER JERK JEST KNOB
MOCK WORM BUNCH CHEAT DANCE
FILCH FLOAT FLOUT SHAKE TAUNT
TRICK JINGLE BOBBER BOBBLE
BUFFET CURTSY DELUDE HOBBLE
POMMEL POPPLE STRIKE WEIGHT
BOBSLED BOBTAIL CLUSTER
HAIRCUT PAGEBOY PENDANT
PLUMMET REFRAIN SHINGLE
SHILLING
(— UP) LOLLOP
BOBAC PAHMI TARBAGAN
BOBBER CORK DUCK FLOAT BOBFLY
BOBBIN PIN CONE CORD PIRN REEL
BRAID QUILL SPOOL BROCHE
HANGER SKREEL TAVELL WORKER
RATCHET SPINDLE TARELLE
TORCHON
(PL.) BONES
BOBBINET ILLUSION
BOBBLE ERROR
BOBOLINK DEER REED SUCKER
BUNTING MAYBIRD ORTOLAN
REEDBIRD RICEBIRD
BOBSLED BOB DRAY BOBLET
RIPPER TRAVERSE
BOBWHITE COLIN QUAIL PARTRIDGE
BOCACCIO TOMCOD
BOCCACCIO JACK TRECENTIST
BOCCARELLA NOSEHOLE
BOCE BOGUE OXEYE
BODE OMEN SIGN STOP AUGUR
OFFER HERALD MESSAGE PORTEND
PRESAGE FOREBODE FORECAST
FORESHOW FORETELL INDICATE
BODHISATTVA KWANNON MAITREYA
AVALOKITA PADMAPANI
BODICE JUPE CHOLI GILET JUMPS

WAIST BASQUE CORSET JELICK
LYFKIE CORSAGE OVERBODY
SLIPBODY
BODIERON BOREGAT
BODILY SOLID SOMAL ACTUAL
CARNAL FLESHLY SOMATIC
CORPORAL ENTIRELY EXTERNAL
MATERIAL PERSONAL PHYSICAL
SARKICAL VISCERAL CORPOREAL
(NOT —) INTERIOR
BODKIN AWL PIN POINT BROACH
DAGGER NEEDLE POPPER HAIRPIN
PONIARD STILETTO EYELETEER
BODO CACHARI
BODY BAND BELL BOLE BOOK BOUK
BUCK BULK CREW DEHA FORM
HEAD LICH MASS MOLD NAVE RIND
RUPA SOMA STEM ATOMY FLESH
FRAME HABIT MOULD SHANK STIFF
TORSO TRUNK CORPSE CORPUS
CUERPO EXTENT FUSEAU LICHAM
PERSON SARIRA AIRFOIL ANATOMY
CADAVER CARCASS COMPANY
ECONOMY QUANTUM SKINFUL
SUPTION TEXTURE CORSAINT
DEMARCHY EXTENSUM MAJORITY
QUARROME TENEMENT
(— OF 12 MEN) DOUZAINE
(— OF ARROW) SHAFT STELE
(— OF BELIEVERS) FAITH
(— OF CANONS) CHAPTER
(— OF CARDINALS) CONCLAVE
(— OF CHILDREN) INFANTRY
(— OF CHRISTIANS) KOINONIA
COMMUNION
(— OF DOCTRINES) DOGMA
(— OF ECHINODERM) DISC DISK
(— OF EVIDENCE) CASE CORPUS
(— OF FIBERS) FORNIX
(— OF HELMET) BELL
(— OF ISLAMIC CUSTOM) SUNNA
SUNNAH
(— OF KNOWLEDGE) STUFF
(— OF LAW) CODE SHAR HALAKA
SHARIA SHARIAT HALACHAH
(— OF MANKIND) HERD
(— OF MUSCLE) BELLY
(— OF NOTIONS) FOLKLORE
(— OF OFFICERS) BUREAU
(— OF ORE) BUNCH MANTO
(— OF PIGMENT) EYESPOT IMPASTO
(— OF POETRY) EPOS
(— OF ROCK) DIKE DYKE HORSE
STOCK BIOHERM MUDFLOW
INTRUSION
(— OF SINGERS) CHORUS
(— OF STUDENTS) CLASS
(— OF TEN) DECURY
(— OF TENANTS) GAVEL HOMAGE
(— OF THIEVES) SCHOOL
(— OF TRADITIONS) HADIT HADITH
(— OF TROOPS) FORCE AMBUSH
BATTLE CONREY SCREEN SQUARE
BRIGADE SUPPORT BATTALIA
GARRISON
(— OF TYPE) SHANK
(— OF VASSALS) BAN
(— OF WATER) BAY RIP SEA BAHR
FORD HEAD LAKE LAVE POND POOL

WAVE ABYSS BAYOU DRINK FLOOD
OCEAN SHARD SHERD SWASH
LAGOON NYANZA STREAM
FLOWAGE SWALLOW
(— OF WELLBORN MEN) COMITATUS
(— OF WRITINGS) SMRTI SMRITI
(— POLITIC) ESTATE
(— RIDDLED BY BULLETS) SIEVE
(CAROTID —) GLOMUS
(CART —) SIRPEA
(CELESTIAL —) SUN BALL COMET
PLANET SPHERE ELEMENT
ASTEROID SATELLITE
(COMPACT —) GLOBE
(CONDUCTING —) GROUND
(CORPORATE —) SOCIETY
(DEAD —) LICH MORT CADAVER
CARCASS CARRION SUBJECT
(ECCLESIASTICAL —) CLASSIS
(ELASTIC —) CUSHION
(EXTENDED —) LENGTH
(FAT —) EPIPLOON
(FRUITING —) CONK CLAVA
ASCOCARP
(GLOBULAR —) NOB KNOB
(GOVERNING —) KAHAL SYNOD
DURBAR SENATE DECARCHY
DIRECTORY
(HAT —) HOOD
(HEAVENLY —) SUN LAMP STAR
COMET LIGHT CANDLE
(HYALINE —) DRUSE
(IMMUNE —) DESMON
(JUDICIAL —) FORUM
(LEGISLATIVE —) CHAMBER
ASSEMBLY CONGRESS LAGTHING
(MAIN — OF ARMY) BATTLE
(MATHEMATICAL —) FILAMENT
(MORMON —) BISHOPRIC
(MORTAL —) KHET
(PRESBYTERIAN —) SESSION
JUDICATORY
(RELIGIOUS —) SECT CONVENT
(REPRODUCTIVE —) EGG GEMMA
SPORE GEMMULA
(SONOROUS —) PHONIC
(SPIRITUAL —) SAHU
(SWELLING —) BOSS
(WAGON —) BED BUCK PUNT
BODYGUARD THANE ESCORT
INWARD HUSCARL RETINUE
TRABANT THINGMAN WARDCORS
BOER TAKHAAR AFRIKANER
BOG BUG CAR DUB FEN GOG HAG
BOLD CARR CESS FLOW MIRE
MOOR MOSS OOZE SINK SLEW SLUE
SPEW STOG SUDS SYRT WASH
LETCH MARSH MIZZY SAUCY SLADE
SLOCK SWAMP MORASS MUSKEG
SLOUGH CRIPPLE FORWARD
PEATERY TURBARY QUAGMIRE
(PEAT —) CESS MOSS YARPHA
BOG ASPHODEL KNAVERY
BOGEY BUG COW HAG BOGIE BOGLE
DEVIL GNOME BOGGLE BOOGER
GOBLIN BOGGARD BOGGART
BUGABOO BUGBEAR SPECTER
SPECTRE
BOGGLE JIB SHY BALK FOIL STOP

ALARM BOTCH DEMUR SCARE
START STICK BAFFLE BUNGLE
GOBLIN SHRINK BAUCHLE BLUNDER
PERPLEX SCRUPLE STUMBLE
FRIGHTEN HESITATE
BOGGY WET DEEP MIRY SOFT
FENNY FOGGY GOUTY HAGGY
MOSSY SNAPY SPEWY MARSHY
QUAGGY SLOBBY SWAMPY WAUGHY
BOGGISH QUEACHY SQUASHY
BOGIER RIDER GEARMAN
BOGLAND SLADE
BOG MANGANESE WAD LAMPADITE
BOGO ABILO ABILAO
BOGOMILE PATARIN PATARINE
BOGUS FAKE SHAM FALSE PHONY
SPURIOUS
BOHEMIAN ARTY PICARD PICARO
ARTISTIC
(— RIVER) ELBE VLTAVA LUZNICE
BEROUNKA
(— TOWN) PISEK PLZEN PRAHA
TABOR PILSEN PRAGUE
BOHOR REEDBUCK
BOIL FRY PET STY BILE BLOB BOLL
BRAN BUCK BUMP COCT COOK
COWL LEEP PLAY PUSH QUAT RAGE
SEED SORE STEW STYE TEEM WALL
WALM WELL BOTCH BREDE STEAM
BETRAY BUBBLE BULDER BULLER
BURBLE DECOCT GALLOP PIMPLE
RISING SEETHE SIMMER TOTTLE
WABBLE WOBBLE ANTHRAX
BEALING BREEDER CATHAIR
ELIXATE ESTUATE INFLAME
AESTUATE EBULLATE FURUNCLE
PHLEGMON
(— IN LYE) BUCK
(— SYRUP) PEARL
(SAND —) BLOWOUT
BOILED SOD SODDEN
(— WITHOUT SAUCE) ANGLAISE
BOILER YET REEF STILL COPPER
KETTLE RETORT TEACHE ALEMBIC
CALDRON FURNACE
(SALT —) WELLER
BOILING WALM ABOIL FERVID
COCTION FERVENT SCALDING
SEETHING ELIXATION
BOISTEROUS GURL HIGH LOUD
RUDE WILD BURLY GURLY NOISY
ROUGH WINDY COARSE SHANDY
STOCKY STORMY STRONG UNRULY
FURIOUS MASSIVE ROARING
VIOLENT BIGMOUTH CUMBROUS
LARRIKIN STRIDENT VEHEMENT
BOLD BIG BOG YEP DERF HARD
KEEN PERT RASH RUDE TALL WHAT
YEPE APERT BARDY BIELD BRASH
BRAVE BRENT FRACK FREAK FRECK
GALLY HARDY JOLLY LARGE MANLY
NERVY PAWKY PEART POKEY
SAUCY STEEP STOUT WLONK
ABRUPT AUDACE BRASSY BRAZEN
CROUSE DARING FIERCE HEROIC
PLUCKY STRONG ASSURED
DASHING DEFIANT FORWARD
GRIVOIS HAUGHTY MASSIVE
VALIANT ARROGANT FAMILIAR

FEARLESS IMMODEST IMPUDENT
INTREPID MALAPERT POWERFUL
RESOLUTE TEMEROUS
(NOT —) GENTEEL
BOLDFACE BOLD BLACK FULLFACE
BOLDLY CRANK CROUSE HARDLY
HARDILY ROUNDLY STRONGLY
BOLDNESS BROW DARE FACE GALL
BIELD CHEEK NERVE PLUCK VIGOR
DARING BRAVERY COURAGE
FREEDOM AUDACITY TEMERITY
(— OF SPEECH) PARRHESIA
BOLDO NUTMEG
BOLE CLAY DOSE STEM BOLUS
CRYPT TRUNK RUDDLE TIMBER
BOLETUS CEPE
BOLIVIA PILE

BOLIVIA
CAPITAL: LAPAZ SUCRE
COIN: TOMIN CENTAVO
DEPARTMENT: LAPAZ ORURO
PANDO ELBENI POTOSI TARIJA
INDIAN: URO INCA ITEN MOXO
URAN ARAWAK AYMARA
CHARCA CHICHA IXIAMA
TACANA PUQUINA QUECHUA
SIRIONE TUMUPASA
LAKE: POOPO COIPASA ROGAGUA
AULLAGAS TITICACA
MEASURE: LEAGUE CELEMIN
MOUNTAIN: JARA CUSCO CUZCO
PUPUYA SAJAMA SORATA
ILLAMPU ANCOHUMA ILLIMANI
ZAPALERI
MOUNTAINS: ANDES SUNSAS
SANSIMON SANTIAGO
PANPIPE: SICU SIKU
PLATEAU: ALTIPLANO
RIVER: BENI YATA ABUNA APERE
BOOPI LAUCA ORTON BAURES
GRANDE ICHILO ITENEZ MADIDI
MAMORE MIZQUE TARIJA
YACUMA GUAPORE ITONAMA
MACHUPO BENECITO INAMBARI
PARAGUAY PARAPETI
SALT DEPOSIT: UYUNI EMPEXA
SWAMP: IZOZOG
TOWN: IVO ICLA ITAU MOJO POJO
SAYA YACO YATA YURA CLIZA
LAPAZ LLICA ORURO QUIME
SUCRE UNCIA UYUNI ZONGO
GUAQUI POTOSI TARIJA
VOLCANO: OLLAGUE
WEIGHT: LIBRA MARCO

BOLL BOW POD BULB KNOB SNAP
ONION BUBBLE CAPSULE
BOLLARD BITT KEVEL DOLPHIN
DEADHEAD
(—S AND BITTS) APOSTLES
BOLLER STRIPPER
BOLL WEEVIL PICUDO
BOLO MACHETE SUNDANG
BOLSHEVIST BOLO
BOLSHEVISM COMMUNISM
SOVIETISM
BOLSTER AID PAD JACK PILLOW
CUSHION HEADING STIFFEN

SUPPORT BACKSTOP BALUSTER
COMPRESS MAINTAIN
BOLT BAR JAG KEY LUE PEN PIN
ROD RUN BEAT BURR CRAM DART
DUMP FLEE GULP LOCK PAWL SHUT
SIFT SLOT SNIB SPAR STUD ARROW
BILBO CLOSE ELOPE FLASH FLOUR
GORGE LATCH RIVET SETUP SHAFT
STOCK ASSORT DECAMP DESERT
FASTEN FLIGHT GANYIE GARBLE
MOOTER PINTLE PURIFY QUARRY
REFINE SAFETY SEARCE SECURE
SNIBEL STREAK STRONG TOGGLE
WINNOW BAYBOLT DOGBOLT
EYEBOLT MISSILE QUARREL
SETBOLT SHACKLE SLABBER
THUNDER DRAWBOLT FASTENER
FISHBOLT FLATHEAD KINGBOLT
RINGBOLT SEPARATE STAMPEDE
(DOOR —) DRAWBOLT
(FIERY —) RESHEPH
(LIGHTNING —) SHAFT
(THUNDER —) FULMEN
BOLTER BOLT DRESSER MUGWUMP
BOMB DUD EGG ROC AZON BOOM
FRAG BLARE CRUMP RAZON SHELL
SQUIB ASHCAN SALUTE BALLOON
BOMBARD GRENADE MARMITE
FIREBALL WHIZBANG PINEAPPLE
(— RELEASE) TOGGLE
(TRENCH —) MINNIE
(PL.) STICK
BOMBARD BOMB CRUMP SHELL
ATTACK BATTER BOTTLE STRAFE
BOMBARDON TUBA NICOLO
POMMER BRUMMER
BOMBARDMENT BLITZ SIEGE
ATTACK RAFALE STRAFE BATTERY
SHELLING
BOMBAST GAS PAD PUFF RAGE
RANT RAVE STUFF TUMOR BLUSTER
FUSTIAN TYMPANY BOASTING
TURGIDITY
BOMBASTIC PUFFY TUMID VOCAL
WINDY FLUENT HEROIC MOUTHY
TURGID BOMBAST FLOWERY
FUSTIAN OROTUND POMPOUS
RANTING STILTED SWOLLEN
INFLATED SWELLING
(— STYLE) TYMPANY
BONACE TREE NOSEBURN
BONACI AGUAJI
BONA FIDE LEVEL GENUINE
AUTHENTIC
BONANZA STATE MONTANA
BONBON CANDY CREAM GOODY
DAINTY CARAMEL SNAPPER
CONFETTO
(PL.) CONFETTI
BOND BON DOG TIE VOW ANDI BAIL
BAND DUTY FIVE FOUR GLUE GYVE
HOLD KNOT LINK NOTE YOKE
BOUND CHAIN NEXUS SWATH
BINDER CEMENT CONNEX COUPLE
ENGAGE ESCROW FETTER LEAGUE
PLEDGE SOLDER SWATHE FOREIGN
HUSBAND LIAISON LIBERTY LINKAGE
MANACLE SHACKLE STATUTE
ADHESIVE CONTRACT COVENANT

LIGAMENT LIGATION LIGATURE
MORTGAGE SECURITY VADIMONY
VINCULUM
(PL.) IRON KHAKIS SHORTS
BONDAGE YOKE THRALL HELOTRY
SERFDOM SLAVERY BONDSHIP
THIRLING CAPTIVITY
BONDED CATTED ENGAGED
BONDMAN CARL ESNE PEON SERF
CHURL HELOT SLAVE STOOGE
SURETY THRALL VASSAL CHATTEL
PEASANT SERVANT VILLEIN
BONDSMAN
BONDSTONE BINDER BONDER
KEYSTONE
BONE OS DIB HIP RIB BANE ULNA
BLADE FEMUR HYOID ILIUM INCUS
JUGAL SLATE STONE TALUS TIBIA
UNION VOMER CANNON COCCYX
CONCHA COPULA CUBOID EPURAL
FIBULA NUCHAL PECTEN RADIAL
SPLINT STAPES TRIPOD UNGUIS
ZYGOMA
(ANKLE —) TALUS
(HIP —) HUGGIN
(SHIN —) CNEMIS
(THIGH —) FEMUR
BONEFISH OIO MACABI GRUBBER
BONYFISH LADYFISH
BONER BUBU FLUB ROCK ERROR
BRODIE STAYER STUMER BLOOMER
BLUNDER MISTAKE STEELER
STUMOUR
BONESET COMFREY AGUEWEED
EUPATORY HEMPWEEK
BONEYARD STOCK
BONFIRE BLAZE TANDLE TAWNIE
BALEFIRE BURNFIRE NEEDFIRE
BONGO DOR
BONING SAP
BONITO AKU ATU NICE COBIA
SARDA BONITA ROBALO ALBACORE
KATONKEL MACKEREL SCOMBRID
SKIPJACK
BONNET CAP HAT HOOD POKE POXY
SCON COVER DECOY SCONE SHAPE
TOQUE CAPOTE MOBCAP SLOUCH
CHAPEAU COMMODE CORONET
LEGHORN SOWBACK VOLUPER
BONGRACE HEADGEAR
BONNET MONKEY ZATI MUNGA
TOQUE MACACO RILAWA MACAQUE
BONNY GAY FINE MERRY PLUMP
BLITHE BONNIE PRETTY STRONG
HEALTHY BUDGEREE HANDSOME
BEAUTIFUL
BONTOK IGOROT
BONUS GIN TIP GIFT MEED AWARD
BRIBE BUNCE BUNTS PILON PRIZE
SPIFF REGALO REWARD CUMSHAW
DOUCEUR PREMIUM SUBSIDY
BOUNTIH DIVIDEND TANTIEME
LAGNIAPPE
BON VIVANT SPORT EPICURE
BON VIVEUR FLANEUR
BONY HARD LANK THIN LANKY STIFF
TOUGH OSTEAL SKINNY OSSEOUS
SCRAGGY SKELETAL
BONYFISH MENHADEN

BOOB ASS FOOL GOON GOOP
DUNCE GOONY NEDDY NITWIT
BOOBOOK OWL PEHO RURU
CUCKOO MOPOKE MOPEHAWK
MOREPORK
BOOBY GAWK GONY SULA DUNCE
IDIOT LOSER PRIZE SLEIGH STUPID
CAMANAY PIQUERO GOOSECAP
BOOBYALLA DOGWOOD
WATERBUSH
BOODLE SWAG CROWD GRAFT
BUDDLE NOODLE PLUNDER
CABOODLE
BOOGEYMAN PADFOOT
TANKERABOGUS
BOOJUM SNARK
BOOK MO LIL LOG CHAP CODE
FORM HEFT OPUS PAGE TEXT TOME
ALBUM ALDUS BIBLE CANON CANTO
CODEX DETUR DIARY DIVAN ENTER
FLETA FOLIO FROST GUIDE KITAB
LIBEL LIBER QUAIR QUIRE RAZEE
ZOHAR ALDINE ANONYM BODONI
CURSUS DOCKET HERBAL LEDGER
MAHZOR MANUAL MISSAL NUMBER
REBIND RECORD RITUAL SCHOOL
TICKET TROPER VOLUME BLOTTER
CATALOG COUCHER DIETARY
DISCARD FEODARY GARLAND
GRAMMAR JOURNAL LAWBOOK
LEXICON MANDALA OCTAPLA
OMNIBUS ORDINAL OUTBOOK
PEERAGE RECITER SAMHITA
SERVICE SLEEPER SPEAKER
SPELLER SYNAXAR TERRIER
TICKLER TRAVAIL TRIGLOT TYPICON
TYPICUM VESPERA WRITING
BANKBOOK BROCHURE CALCULUS
CASEBOOK CASHBOOK CHAPBOOK
COOKBOOK COPYBOOK DOCUMENT
FESTIVAL GIFTBOOK GOSPELER
HANDBOOK HARDBACK HERDBOOK
JESTBOOK JUVENILE LIBRETTO
PASTORAL POMANDER POSTBOOK
REGISTER SONGBOOK STUDBOOK
SYNAXARY TALEBOOK TRIODION
TWENTYMO
(**— BACK**) DORSE
(**— FOR HARVARD GRADUATE**)
DETUR
(**— OF CHARTS**) WAGONER
(**— OF HERALDRY**) ARMORY
ARMORIAL
(**— OF MAPS**) ATLAS
(**— OF PSALMS**) PSALTER TEHILLIM
(**— OF RULES**) HOYLE
(**— OF SOLUTIONS**) KEY
(**—S KEPT IN PRINT**) BACKLIST
(**CHEAP —**) BLOOD
(**CHINESE —**) CHING
(**COMMONPLACE —**) ADVERSARIA
(**ELEMENTARY —**) PRIMER
(**FOLDED —**) ORIHON
(**JOKE —**) JOE JESTBOOK
(**MEMORANDUM —**) AGENDA JOTTER
TICKLER
(**MINIATURE —**) BIBELOT
(**PRAYER —**) PORTAS SIDDUR
PORTASS PORTHORS

(**RECORD —**) LIBER TICKLER
(**RELIGIOUS —**) KITAB KORAN
QURAN GOSPEL HORARY KYRIAL
PROSAR GRADUAL KYRIALE
BREVIARY MEGILLAH ORDINARY
SYNAXARY
(**SERVICE —**) COMES GRAIL TEXTUS
(**SLOW-SELLING —**) PLUG
(**STRANGE —S**) CURIOSA
(**UNBOUND —**) CAHIER
(**PL.**) SHELF STUDY EROTICA
SCRIPTURE
BOOKBINDING STUB YAPP STRING
BOOKCASE DESK STAGE STALL
SCRINE PLUTEUS CREDENZA
BOOK COVER LID SIDE FOREL
RECTO VERSO FORREL REVERSE
REVERSO
BOOKISH BOOKY ERUDITE STUDIOUS
BOOKLET FOLDER NOVELET
BROCHURE
BOOKMAKER LAYER BOOKER
BOOKIE
BOOKMARK MARKER TASSEL
REGISTER
BOOK PALM TARA TALIERA
BOOKSHELF DESK PLUTEUS
(**PL.**) CLASSIS
BOOM JIB BEAM BOMB BUMP CRIB
POLE ROAR SPAR BRAIL CHAIN
CRANE CROON PROBE BUMPKIN
CATHEAD CURTAIN RESOUND
SUPPORT BOWSPRIT FLOURISH
(**CRANE —**) ARM GIB JIB
BOOMERANG KALIE KILEY KYLIE
WANGO ATLATL BOUNCE RECOIL
LEEWILL REBOUND WOMERAH
WOOMERA BACKFIRE HORNERAH
LEEANGLE RICOCHET TROMBASH
BOOMING HUMMING
BOOM IRON WITHE CRANCE
BOON GAY BENE GIFT GOOD KIND
BOUND FAVOR GRANT MERRY
ORDER BENIGN BOUNTY GOODLY
JOVIAL PRAYER BENEFIT COMMAND
PRESENT BLESSING INTIMATE
PETITION
BOOR CAD OAF BOER BORE CARL
HICK JACK KERN LOUT PILL RUNT
SLOB CHUFF CHURL CLOWN KERNE
SLAVE BUMKIN CARLOT CLUNCH
HOBLOB JOBSON JOSKIN LUBBER
LUMMOX RUSTIC BUMPKIN
CAUBOGE GROBIAN PEASANT
VILLAIN BOEOTIAN BOSTHOON
BOORISH ILL RUDE GAWKY ROUGH
RUNTY SURLY CLUMSY RUSTIC
SAVAGE SULLEN VULGAR WOOLEN
AWKWARD CRABBED HIRSUTE
HOBLIKE KERNISH LOUTISH PEAKISH
ROISTER UNCOUTH VILLAIN
WOOLLEN CARTERLY CHURLISH
CLODDISH CLOWNISH LUBBERLY
SWAINISH UNGAINLY
BOORISHNESS VILLAINY
GROBIANISM
BOOST AID LEG ABET BACK BOOM
HELP LIFT PLUG PUSH COACH
EXALT HOIST HOOSH RAISE ASSIST

ADVANCE COMMEND ELEVATE
ENDORSE PROMOTE INCREASE
BOOT PAC PAD USE CURE GAIN
HALF HELP HOOF KICK SHOE SOCK
AVAIL BOOTY EJECT JEMMY KAMIK
PEWEE SPOIL BOOTEE BUDGET
BUSKIN CASING CHUKKA CRAKOW
ENRICH FUMBLE GAITER GALOSH
INSHOE JOCKEY MUKLUK PEDULE
SHEATH BENEFIT BOTTINE COTHURN
COWHIDE CRUISER HESSIAN
HIGHLOW SEABOOT SHOEPAC
VANTAGE BALMORAL BOTTEKIN
CHASSURE COVERING FINNESKO
JACKBOOT LARRIGAN NAPOLEON
(**— OF CARRIAGE**) FOREBOOT
(**— ON SADDLE**) GAMBADE
GAMBADO
(**HALF —**) PAC BUSKIN COCKER
SKILTY
(**HOB-NAILED —**) BAT
(**HORSE'S —**) SCALPER
(**LUMBERMAN'S —**) CRUISER
(**MARINE —**) SKINHEAD
(**RIDING —**) JEMMY JIMMY JODHPUR
(**SEALSKIN —**) KAMIK
(**STOUT —**) STOGA STOGY
(**TORTURE —**) SQUEEZER
(**PL.**) OVERS HESSIANS
BOOTBLACK SHINER BLACKER
SHOEBOY
BOOTED OCREATE
BOOTES WAINMAN HERDSMAN
BOOTH BOX COOP DESK LOGE SHED
SHOP SOOK BOTHY CABIN CRAME
HOUSE KIOSK LIWAN LODGE PITCH
STALL STAND PAGODA PANDAL
PAYBOX SUCCAH SUKKAH TIENDA
BALAGAN COCKSHY TABERNA
BOOTLACE LACET
BOOTLEG SHY SLY ILLEGAL ILLICIT
BOOTY BOOT FANG GAIN LOOT PELF
PREY SWAG BUTIN CHEAT FORAY
GRAFT PRIZE CREAGH FLEECE
SPOILS DESPOIL PILLAGE PLUNDER
SPREATH STEALTH PURCHASE
SPUILZIE STEALAGE
BOOZE BOLL BOUT BUDGE DRINK
SPREE FUDDLE LIQUOR
BOOZY LIQUORY
BORAGE ANCHUSA
BORAX FLUX TINCAL
(**— SOURCE**) KERNITE
BORDER CUT HEM RIM TAB ABUT
BRIM CURB DADO EAVE EDGE LIMB
LINE LIST LOVE MARK NARK ORLE
RAND ROON RUND SIDE TRIM WELL
WELT BOARD BOUND BRAID BRINK
CHEEK COAST COSTA DRAFT FILET
FLANK FOREL FRAME FRILL GUARD
LIMIT MARCH MARGE MARLI PLAIT
SHORE SKIRT STRIP SWAGE TOUCH
VERGE ADJOIN EDGING FILLET
FORREL FRINGE IMPALE LACING
LIMBUS LISERE MARGIN ORFRAY
PURFLE QUADRA STRIPE TANIKO
WEEPER CONFINE DRAUGHT
FIMBRIA FLOROON MARGENT
SELVAGE VALANCE BOUNDARY

DOUBLING FRONTIER MARCHESE
NEIGHBOR OUTSKIRT PLATBAND
SKIRTING SURROUND TERMINUS
TRESSOUR TRESSURE
(— OF EXTERNAL EAR) HELIX
(— OF LACE) PICOT
(— OF ROCK) SALBAND
(— OF SAIL) DOUBLING
(— OF SHIELD) BORDURE
(— OF STREAM) ROND
(— ON) ABUT ACCOST AFFRONT
NEIGHBOR
(FLOWERED —) FLOROON
(ORNAMENTAL —) WAGE FRAME
FRINGE MATTING TRESSURE
(RIBBON —) FRILAL
(PL.) CONFINE CONFINES
BORDERED ORLE LIMBATE
BORDERING MARGENT FRONTIER
BORE BIT CUT EAT IRK JET TAP
DRAG FLAT HOLE JUMP PALL POKE
REAM RUSH SINK SIZE TIDE TIRE
TOOL ANNOY CHINK DRILL EAGRE
ENNUI GAUGE GOUGE OUGHT
PLONK PRICK PUNCH SUGUR TEWEL
TRICK VAPOR WEARY BEFOOL
CANNON GIMLET PIERCE THRILL
THRUST TUNNEL WIMBLE BROMIDE
CALIBER CALIBRE CONCAVE
CREVICE HUMDRUM NUDNICK
OPENING AIGUILLE CAPILLUS
DIAMETER DRAWBORE GRATIANO
POROROCA
(— OF CANNON) SOUL CHASE
BOREAS AQUILO AQUILON
(DAUGHTER OF —) CLEOPATRA
(FATHER OF —) ASTRAEUS
(MOTHER OF —) AURORA
(SON OF —) ZETES CALAIS
BORED WEARY ENNUYEE TEDIOUS
SATIATED
BOREDOM YAWN ENNUI TEDIUM
BORELE KEITLOA UPEYGAN
BORER MOLE BARDEE WIMBLE
HAGFISH TANBARK TERMITE
TERRIER FLATHEAD SHIPWORM
WOODWORM
BORING DIM DRY FLAT SLOW
BROACH STODGY STUPID TIRING
LUMPISH TEDIOUS PIERCING
TIRESOME
(— TOOL) AIGUILLE
BORN N NEE NATE INNATE NASCENT
NATURAL UTERINE ORIGINAL
(PREMATURELY —) SLINK ABORTIVE
(WELL —) FREE EUGENIC
BORNE RODE NARROW CARRIED
ENDURED
(— AFFRONTEE) CABOCHED
(— LOWER THAN USUAL) ABASED
(— ON WATER) AFLOAT

BORNEO
BAY: ADANG KUMAI SAMPIT
CAPE: ARU DATU LOJAR PUTING
SAMBAR SELATAN
MOUNTAIN: RAJA SARAN NIJAAN
TEBANG

MOUNTAINS: IRAN MULLER
SCHWANER
NAME: KALIMANTAN
NATIVE: DYAK DAJAK
RIVER: ARUT IWAN BAHAU BERAU
KAJAN PADAS PAWAN BARITO
KAPUAS SEBUKU KAHAJAN
MAHAKAM MENDAWI PEMBUANG
TOWN: KUMAI SAMBAS SAMPIT
MALINAU PAGATAN SANGGAU
SINTANG TARAKAN KETAPANG
TREE: KAPOR KAPUR
WEIGHT: PARA CHAPAH

BORO MARIANA
BORON BORAX ULEXITE
BORORO COROADO
BOROUGH BURG CITY TOWN WICK
BRUSH BURGH CASTLE COUNTY
CITADEL FORTRESS VILLAGE
TOWNSHIP
BORROW BOT BITE COPY HIRE KICK
LOAN SHIN TAKE THIG ADOPT
STEAL TOUCH DESUME DUPLEX
PLEDGE STRIKE SURETY CHEVISE
HOSTAGE MUTUATE TITHING
BORROWER BOT CRIB MUTUARY
BOS OX NEAT TAURUS
BOSH END ROT JOKE SHOW TALK
TOSH TRASH BUSHWA FIGURE
FLAUNT HUMBUG TRIVIA TOSHERY
GALBANUM NONSENSE POPPYCOCK
BOSKY BUSHY TIPSY WOODY
FUDDLED
BOSNIA-HERZEGOVINA (RIVER OF
—) BOSNA DRINA NERETVA
(TOWN OF —) TUZLA MAGLAJ
MOSTAR VISOKO SARAJEVO
BOSOM LAP BARM CLOSE DICKY
HEART SINUS BREAST CAVITY
DESIRE DICKEY RECESS BELOVED
EMBRACE GREMIAL INCLOSE
INTIMATE
(— OF DRESS) SQUARE
(FALSE —) PLUMPER
BOSS BUR HUB MOP NOB ORB PAD
POP BAAS BEAD BOCE BUHR BURR
COCK CZAR KNOB KNOP KNOT NAIL
NULL STUD TSAR BULLA BULLY
BWANA CHIEF EMPTY JEWEL KNOSP
ORDER OWNER PEARL ANCHOR
BROOCH BUCKRA BUTTON CHEESE
DIRECT HOLLOW MANAGE MASTER
OCULUS PATERA PELLET SHIELD
BULLION CACIQUE CAPATAZ
CAPTAIN CUSHION FOREMAN
HASSOCK HEADMAN HOBNAIL
MANAGER PADRONE PHALERA
SPANGLE SPONSON DIRECTOR
DOMINEER MISERERE OMPHALOS
OVERSEER UMBILICUS
(— OF LOGGING CAMP) BULLY
(— OF SHIELD) UMBO
(FIRE —) GASMAN
(LEATHER —) BUTTON
(MINE —) SHIFTER SHIFTMAN
(POLITICAL —) CACIQUE CAUDILLO
(STRAW —) BULL LEADER

BOSTONIAN HUBBITE
BOTANY HERBARISM PHYTOLOGY
BOTCH MAR MUX BOIL BOSS MEND
MESS MULL SORE BITCH BODGE
BUTCH FLUFF FUDGE SPOIL STICK
BOGGLE BOLLIX BUMBLE BUNGLE
COBBLE JUMBLE MUCKER REPAIR
TINKER BLUNDER BUTCHER
SCAMBLE SCLATCH SLUBBER
SWELLING
BOTCHER GRILSE SALMON TINKER
BUNGLER BUTCHER CLOUTER
COBBLER
BOTCHERY PATCHERY
BOTE KINBOT MAGBOTE CARTBOTE
FRITHBOT PLOWBOTE WAINBOTE
BOTFLY BOTT GADBEE GADFLY
NITTER CANOPID OESTRID TORSALO
DIPTERAN OESTRIAN
BOTH BO ALL TWO BAITH EQUALLY
BOTHER ADO AIL BUG NAG VEX
FASH FAZE FUSS JADE WORK
ANNOY DEAVE KNOCK PHASE TEASE
TRADE WORRY BADGER BUSTLE
CUMBER DITHER FLURRY GRAVEL
HARASS MEDDLE MITHER MOIDER
MOLEST MUCKLE PESTER POTHER
POTTER PUTTER PUZZLE TAMPER
CONFUSE DISTURB FASHERY
GRIZZLE PERPLEX TERRIFY
TRACHLE TROUBLE BEWILDER
DISTRESS IRRITATE NUISANCE
BOTOCUDO BORUN AIMORE
AYMORO
BOTONEE TREFLEE FLEURONE
BO TREE PIPAL

BOTSWANA
CAPITAL: GABORONE GABERONES
COIN: RAND
DESERT: KALAHARI
LAKE: DOW NGAMI
LANGUAGE: BANTU CLICK
KHOISAN SETSWANA
MOUNTAIN: TSODILO
NATIVE: BANTU TSWANA
BUSHMAN
RIVER: NATA OKWA CHOBE
NOSOB CUANDO MOLOPO
SHASHI CUBANGO LIMPOPO
OKAVANGO
TOWN: KANYE ORAPA TSANE
SEROWE LOBOTSI MOCHUDI
PALAPYE THAMAGA
GABERONES

BOTTLE JUG BOSS SKIN VIAL VIOL
AMPUL ASKOS BETTY BOCAL BUIRE
BURET CADUS COOJA CROFT
CRUET CRUSE FIFTH FLASK GIRBA
GLASS GOURD HOUSE PHIAL SPLIT
VERRE ALUDEL BACBUC BUNDLE
CARAFE CARBOY CASTER CASTOR
CHAGUL CHATTY CREWET DORUCK
DUBBER FESSEL FIASCO FLACON
FLAGON GOGLET GUTTUS JORDAN
LAGENA MAGNUM MARINE MATARA
NURSER PACKER SIPHON VESSEL
WOULFF BALLOON BIBERON

BOMBARD BOMBOLA BURETTE
CANTEEN CARAFON COSTREL
DEADMAN FLACKET FLOATER
GRENADE INKHORN BOMBONNE
BORACHIO BUILDING CALABASH
DECANTER DEMIJOHN GARDEVIN
JEROBOAM MARIOTTE PRESERVE
REHOBOAM
(— IN WICKER) CARBOY DEMIJOHN
(18 —S OF WINE) RIDDLE
(EGYPTIAN —) DORUK DORUCK
(EMPTY —) MARINE
(HOT-WATER —) PIG
(LARGE —) KIT JEROBOAM
(LEATHER —) BOOT DUBBA BUDGET
DUBBER DUPPER MATARA BOMBARD
WHINNOCK WINESKIN
(OVERSIZED —) BALTHAZAR
(PAIR OF —S) GEMEL GEMMEL
(SMALL —) VIAL AMPUL PHIAL SPLIT
FLACON AMPOULE TICKLER
BOTTLE CAP CAPSULE
BOTTLE CARRIER FASCET
BOTTLE CASE CELLAR
BOTTLEHEAD DOEGLING
BOTTLER COOPER
BOTTOM ASS BED ARSE BASE DALE
DOUP FLAT FOND FOOT FUND HOLM
LEES ROOT ABYSS BASIS DREGS
FLOOR LAIGH NADIR BATHOS
FOUNCE FUNDUS GROUND GUTTER
LAAGTE LEEGTE BEDROCK
LOWLAND SUPPORT SURFACE
BUTTOCKS INTERVAL SEDIMENT
TETRAPOD
(— OF BENCH) TOE
(— OF CUPOLA) HEARTH
(— OF FURROW) SOLE
(— OF PAGE) TAIL
(— OF PISTOL GRIP) BUTT
(— OF POT) POTSTONE
(— OF PRINTER'S GALLEY) SLICE
(— OF PULLEY BLOCK) BREECH
(— OF SEA) GROUND BENTHOS
(— OF SOLE) NAUMK NAUMKEAG
(MARSHY —) SIKE
(ROCK —) HARDPAN
(PL.) HOLM HOLME
BOTTOM-DWELLING DEMERSAL
BOTTOMER FOOTMAN STATIONMAN
BOTTOMLAND STRATH
BOTTOMLESS ABYSMAL
BOTULISM LAMSIEKTE LAMZIEKTE
BOUDOIR ROOM CABIN BEDROOM
CABINET
BOUGH ARM LEG LIMB TWIG CHUCK
SHOOT SPRAY SPRIG BRANCH
RAMAGE SHROUD GALLOWS
PHYLLIS OFFSHOOT SHOULDER
(— ON TAVERN) BUSH
(PL.) RAMAGE DUNNAGE RAMMAGE
BOUGHT KEFT STORE ZEBINA
BOUGIE CANDLE COLLYRIE FILIFORM
BOULDER NOB KELK KNOB ROCK
STONE GIBBER BOOTHER DORNICK
ERRATIC GRAYBACK HARDHEAD
MEGALITH POTSTONE
BOULE BIRNE
BOULEVARD DRIVE PRADO AVENUE

STREET HIGHWAY TERRACE
BOULTER TRAWL SPILLER SPILLET
BOUNCE DAP HOP BANG BLOW
BRAG BUMP DING DIRD FIRE GATE
JUMP LEAP SACK STOT BOAST
BOUND BULLY CAROM CHUCK
EJECT KNOCK SCOLD THUMP VERVE
SPIRIT SPRING STRIKE ADDRESS
BLUSTER CHOUNCE DISMISS
REBOUND SWAGGER PROCLAIM
RICOCHET
BOUNCER CHUCKER SCROUGER
BOUNCING BIG BUXOM LUSTY
STOUT BOUNCY HEALTHY
(— OF TONGUE) FLAP
BOUND DAP END HOP LOP BENT
BIND BOND BONE BROW BUTT DART
GIRT JUMP LEAP LIST MERE RAMP
RISE SCUD SKIP STEM STOT SURE
TERM WALL AMBIT BOURN FIXED
GOING LIMIT READY SALLY START
STEND STING TILED VAULT VERGE
BORDER BOUNCE BOURNE BUTTAL
CAVORT CURVET DEFINE DOMAIN
FINISH GAMBOL GIRDED HURDLE
JETTED LIABLE LOLLOP OBLIGE
PRANCE SPRING BARRIER CERTAIN
CHAINED CLOSURE CONFINE
CONTAIN COSTIVE DELIMIT
DRESSED GAMBADO INCLUDE
REBOUND SALTATE SECURED
SUBSULT TERMINE TRUSSED
BOUNDARY CONFINED DESTINED
ENCLOSED FASCIATE FRONTIER
HANDFAST LANDMARK LIMITATE
OBLIGATE PINIONED PRECINCT
PREPARED RESTRICT SHACKLED
(— BY OATH) SWORN
(— BY OBLIGATION) AFFINED
(NOT —) SOLUTE
(RIGIDLY —) STATIC STATICAL
(PL.) AMBIT MOUND CLOSURE
COMPASS CONFINE PURLIEUS
BOUNDARY AHU END RIM DOLE
DOOL EDGE FINE FORM LINE LIST
MARK MEAR MEER MERE META
METE PALE SURF TERM TRIG WALL
AMBIT BOURN CLOSE FENCE FRAME
FRONT HEDGE LIMES LIMIT MARCH
MOUND SHORE VERGE BORDER
COLLET DEFINE OCTROI OCTROY
TROPIC BARRIER BOUNDER BUTTING
COMPASS FURLONG CURBLINE
FRONTIER LANDLINE LIMITARY
PRECINCT TERMINUS UMSTROKE
(PL.) ABUTTALS ENVIRONS
BOUNDLESS VAST UNTOLD
ENDLESS ETERNAL INFINITE
UNLIMITED
BOUNTEOUS BOON CROWNED
LIBERAL PLENTEOUS
BOUNTIFUL GOOD LUSH RICH
AMPLE FREELY LAVISH LIBERAL
PROFUSE ABUNDANT GENEROUS
BOUNTY BOON GIFT MEED AWARD
BONUS GRANT LARGE VALOR
WORTH BONTEE REWARD VIRTUE
LARGESS PREMIUM PRESENT
PROWESS SUBSIDY DONATIVE

GOODNESS GRATUITY KINDNESS
BOUQUET BOB AURA ODOR POSY
AROMA BLOOM CIGAR POSEY
SHEAF SPRAY BOWPOT BUSKET
SHOWER CORSAGE NOSEGAY
BOUGHPOT
(— GARNI) FAGOT FAGGOT
BOURGEOIS ORGON COMMON
STUPID BOORISH BURGHER
BOURSE BOLSA BORSE CAMBIO
BOURTREE ELDER
BOUT GO JOB BOOT FALL PULL
TURN BOOZE BRASH CRASH ESSAY
FIGHT MATCH PLUCK ROUND TRIAL
VENNY VENUE ATTACK COURSE
FRACAS YOKING ASSAULT ATTEMPT
CAROUSE CIRCUIT CONTEST
DEBAUCH OUTSIDE WITHOUT
CONFLICT
(DRINKING —) BAT BUST TIRL
BOOZE SPRAY SPREE SCREED
SPLORE CAROUSE GAEDOWN
WASSAIL POTATION
BOUTONNIERE BOUQUET
BUTTONHOLE
BOUW BAHU BAHOE
BOVATE OSKEN OXGANG OXGATE
OXLAND
(TWO —S) HUSBANDLAND
BOVINE OX BOS COW BOSS BULL
CALF DULL NEAT SLOW ZEBU
BEAST BISON STEER ANIMAL
COWISH HUMLIE HUMMEL OXLIKE
ROTHER BULLOCK TAURINE
BANGTAIL LEPTOBOS
BOW ARC LEG LUG NOD SAW TIE
YEW ARCH BAIL BECK BEND BENT
CURB DUCK FOLD FORE GORA
JOUK KNEE KNOT LATH LOUT MOVE
PROW SELF STEM SWIM TRUE TURN
WEND BINGE CLINE CONGE COQUE
COUCH CROOK CRUSH CURVE
DEFER GOURA HONOR KNEEL
NOEUD SHIKO STICK STOOP VENIE
YIELD ARCHER ASSENT BAUBLE
BUCKLE CONGEE CRINGE CROUCH
CURTSY FIDDLE FOGBOW RIBBON
SALAAM SALUTE SCRAPE SUBMIT
SWERVE TOURTE WEAPON DEPRESS
FOREBOW FORMBOW HANDBOW
INCLINE INFLECT LONGBOW
NECKTIE RAINBOW ARBALEST
COURTESY CRESCENT ENTRANCE
FOGEATER GREETING STONEBOW
TRUELOVE
(— DOWN) ALOUT HUMBLE
(— IN ONE PIECE) SELF
(— LOW) BINGE
(— OF VESSEL) HEAD PROW STEM
ENTRANCE
(— ON SCRAPER) BAIL BALE
(— ON SEA) ATRY
(— OUTWARD) CONVEX
(— SLIGHTLY) ADDRESS
(OVERHANGING —) SWIM
(VIOLIN —) STICK
BOWED ARCO BENT BANDY KNEED
ARCATE ARCATO CURVED BULGING
CURVANT SHAMBLE DOWNBENT

BOWELS GUT GUTS WOMB BELLY COLON ROPES VISCERA ENTRAILS

BOWER RUN BOOR JACK NOOK SALE ABODE ARBOR JOKER KNAVE ANCHOR BOWERY LEFSEL PANDAL BERCEAU CABINET CHAMBER COTTAGE EMBOWER ENCLOSE LEVESEL PERGOLA RETREAT SHELTER TRELLIS THALAMUS
(— **FOR SNAKES**) KISI
(**GARDEN** —) ALCOVE

BOWERBIRD CATBIRD COLLARBIRD

BOWFIN AMIA GANOID LAWYER MORGAY SAWYER CHOUPIC DOGFISH GRINDAL GRINDLE GRINNEL MUDFISH

BOWIE STATE ARKANSAS

BOWING FEATHERING

BOWL CAP CUP PAN TUN COUP ROLL TASS TRAY WOOD ARENA BASIN BOWIE DEPAS GUARD JORUM KITTY LAVER MAZER PHIAL PITCH ROGAN SCALE TANOA TAZZA TREEN TROLL BEAKER BICKER CHAWAN CLOSET COOTIE CRATER FESSEL JICARA KETTLE LEKANE MAZARD MORTAR TROUGH TUREEN VESSEL BRIMMER DITCHER DOUBLER DUGGLER SCYPHUS SKYPHOS SPILLER STADIUM TOUCHER TRINDLE TRUNDLE WHISKIN AQUARIUM BRIDECUP FISHBOWL LAVATORY MONTEITH REHOBOAM
(— **ILLEGALLY**) JERK
(— **OF PIPE**) STUMMEL
(— **ON PEDESTAL**) TAZZA SALVER
(— **OUT**) YORK
(— **THAT TOUCHED JACK**) TOUCHER
(— **WITH TWO HANDLES**) CAP DEPAS
(**DRINKING** —) TUN TASS
(**OBLONG** —) PITCHI
(**PUNCH** —) SNEAKER
(**SHALLOW** —) CAP COUPE WHISKIN
(**SMALL** —) JACK
(**SOUP** —) ECUELLE
(**SUGAR** —) SUGAR SUCRIER
(**TOILET** —) HOPPER
(**WOODEN** —) CAP BOWIE KITTY ROGAN BASSIE COOTIE

BOWLEG OUTKNEE

BOWLEGGED BANDY VALGUS

BOWLER POT DERBY KEGLER PINMAN SPINNER TRUNDLER
(**CRICKET** —**S**) ATTACK

BOWLINE BOWLIN FARGOOD

BOWLING BOWLS ATTACK KEGLING TENPINS

BOWLS RINK BOCCE BOCCIE

BOW-SHAPED ARCATE

BOWSTRING SERVING

BOWYER BOWER ARTILLER

BOX BED BIN CAR EAR FUR GIG KIT LOB LUG PIX PYX TYE ARCA BARK BODY BOOT CAGE CAJA CASE CIST CRIB CUFF CYST DRAB FLAT HEAD LOGE MILL PACK PUNG SCOB SEAT SLAP SLUG SPAR STOW TILL TRAY ARBOR BARGE BOIST BUXUS CADDY CAPSA CHEST CLOUT CRATE FIGHT FRAME HUTCH LADLE POUCH PUNCH SHRUB STALL TRUNK ASCHAM BUFFET BUNKER CARTON CASKET COFFER COFFIN DRAWER GRILLE HAMPER HATBOX HAYBOX HOPPER ICEBOX MAROON MOCUCK PATRON PETARA PILLAR SAGGER SHRINE STRIKE TARBOX VANITY ARCANUM BANDBOX BATTERY BOXTREE BOXWOOD CABINET CAISSON CARRIER CASHBOX CASQUET CASSONE CONFINE COREBOX DICEBOX DREDGER DUSTBOX ENCLOSE EXHAUST FOSTELL FREEZER HANAPER JACKBOX PACKAGE PILLBOX PITARAH PRINTER SANDBOX SCATULA SHELTER TRUMMEL WHERRET BOXTHORN DOVECOTE DRAGEOIR JUNCTION LAVARIUM MATCHBOX POMANDER SHOWCASE SLIPCASE SOLANDER SWEATBOX
(— **FOR CUTLERY**) CANTEEN
(— **FOR FISH**) CAR NID
(— **FOR MONEY OFFERING**) ARCA LADLE
(— **FOR SALT**) DRAB
(— **FOR SEAL**) SKIPPET
(— **FOR SEED**) LEAP
(— **FOR TOBACCO**) BUTT DOSS CADDY SARATOGA
(— **IN TIMEPIECE**) BARREL
(— **IN WHEEL HUB**) FUR
(— **OF BIRCHBARK**) MOCUCK
(— **OF FIRE CLAY**) SAGGAR SAGGER
(— **OF ORGAN**) BOOT SWELL
(— **TO SHELTER BELL**) SCONCE
(— **USED AS DARKROOM**) TENT
(**BERRY** —) HALLOCK
(**BREAD** —) BARGE
(**CANDLE** —) BARK
(**CIRCULAR** —) THIMBLE
(**COMPASS** —) KETTLE BINNACLE
(**FANCY** —) ETUI ETWEE
(**FLOATING** —) CAISSON
(**FOUNDRY** —) FRAME
(**IRON** —) HANGER
(**JUGGLER'S** —) TRANKA
(**MONEY** —) CASH SAFE PIRLIE
(**PIVOTING** —) TOUR
(**PRINTING** —) TURTLE
(**REFRIGERATOR** —) COOLER
(**SHALLOW** —) FLAT BACKET HARBOR
(**SNUFF** —) MILL MULL
(**TEA** —) CADDY
(**TIN** —) TRUMMEL VASCULUM

BOX BRIER INDIGO INKBERRY

BOXCAR LOWRY STOCKCAR

BOX ELDER MAPLE NEGUNDO

BOXER CHAMP DARES BANTAM MILLER NOBBER TANKER WELTER BRUISER CRUISER FIGHTER SLUGGER SPARRER BUFFETER PUGILIST SOUTHPAW

BOXFISH CHAPIN COWFISH SHELLFISH TRUNKFISH

BOXING PLUG SAVATE PARINGS SCIENCE SPARRING
(— **GLOVE**) MUFFLE

BOX TORTOISE COOTER

BOXWOOD KNYSNA DUDGEON

BOXY BLOCKY

BOY BO BUB FAG GUY HIM LAD PUR TAD BOYO CHAP LOON NINO PAGE PUER BILLY BUBBY BUDDY CHABO CHILD CRACK GAMIN GILPY GROOM KNAVE PUTTO ROGUE SWAIN VALET YOUTH BIRKIE BUTTON CALLAN CHOKRA GAFFER GARCON MANNIE MASTER NIPPER RASCAL SHAVER STIRRA UMFAAN URCHIN BOUCHAL CALLANT DRAWBOY GLEANER GOSSOON GRUMMET JACKBOY RUBBLER SERVANT SPADGER TRAPPER CLERGION HENCHBOY MUCHACHO SPALPEEN
(— **DRESSED AS WOMAN**) MALINCHE
(— **OF FREE BIRTH**) CAMILLUS
(**ALTAR** —) ACOLYTE THURIFER
(**AWKWARD** —) CUB CALF GRUMMET
(**BOLD** —) SPALPEEN
(**CHOIR** —) CHILD
(**CLEANING** —) BUSBOY
(**COLLIER'S** —) HODDER
(**EFFEMINATE** —) SISSY
(**HEAD** —) SENIOR CAPTAIN
(**ILL-MANNERED** —) CUB
(**MY** —) AVICK
(**NATIVE** —) MOWGLI
(**NON-JEWISH** —) SHEGETZ
(**OFFICE** —) DUFTRY DUFTERY
(**PERT** —) CRACK
(**POOR** —) HERO
(**ROGUISH** —) CRACK GAMIN URCHIN
(**SAUCY** —) NACKET
(**SERVING** —) KNAVE PEDEE CHOKRA MOUSSE FOOTBOY GOSSOON
(**SILLY** —) CALF
(**SMALL** —) BO BUDDY UMFAAN SPADGER
(**SPRIGHTLY** —) CRACK
(**STABLE** —) MAFU MAFOO MEHTAR
(**TOWN** —) CAD
(**YOUNG** —) LAD SONNY YOUTH NIPPER
(**PL.**) BOYHOOD

BOYCOTT MITE SHUN AVOID DEBAR BLACKBALL

BOYFRIEND BEAU STEADY

BRACE LEG MAN TIE TWO BEND BIND CASE FRAP GIRD JACK KNEE LACE MARK PAIR PROP SPUR STAY STEM STUD CLAMP CRANK DWANG GIRTH HOUND NERVE POISE RIDER SHORE STOCK STRUT ANKLET BINDER BRACHE CLENCH COLLAR COUPLE CRUTCH FASTEN FATHOM HURTER SPLINT STRING WIMBLE BOTTINE BRACKET EMBRACE REFRESH SPANNER STIFFEN SUPPORT ACCOLADE BITBRACE BITSTALK BITSTOCK BUTTRESS CROSSBAR ENCIRCLE
(— **ACROSS CABLE**) STUD
(— **AND HALF**) LEASH

(— BETWEEN FRAMES) TOM
(— FOR POST) SPUR
(— UP) ACCINGE SHARPEN
(PL.) BRIDGING
BRACED BENT
  (— ABACK) ABOX
BRACELET BAND RING ARMIL CHAIN
  ARMLET BANGLE GRIVNA ARMILLA
  CURCLET MANACLE POIGNET
  RACETTE WRISTER HANDCUFF
  MUFFETEE WRISTLET
  (SHELL —) SANKHA
BRACER TONIC SHORER BLOCKER
  ARMGUARD STIFFENER STIMULANT
BRACHIAL HUMERAL
BRACHIOPOD ATREMATE ATRYPOID
  SPIRIFER
BRACHIUM ARM
BRACING CRISP QUICK TONIC
  DUNNAGE
BRACKEN FERN BRAKE PLAID
BRACKET BIBB COCK CONK FORK
  GATE PUNK ANCON BELOW BRACE
  CLASS CONCH COUCH CRANE
  CRANK CROOK LEVEL SHELF STRUT
  TRUSS ANCONE BECKET BRIDGE
  CORBEL COUPLE GUSSET HANGER
  LADDER SADDLE SCONCE BECKETT
  CONSOLE DERRICK FEATHER
  FIXTURE GATELEG LOOKOUT
  POTENCE SPONSON SPOTTED
  BRAGWORT CATEGORY CROTCHET
  MISERERE SPECKLED STRADDLE
  (PL.) HOOKS CROOKS
BRACKISH YAR FOIST SALTY
  BRACKY SALINE BREACHY SALTISH
  NAUSEOUS
BRACT HUSK LEAF GLUME LEMMA
  PALEA PALET SCALE SPADIX
  SPATHE BRACTLET PHYLLARY
BRAD PIN NAIL PRIG RIVET SPRIG
BRAE BANK BRAY BROW HILL CLEVE
  SLOPE WOUGH CLEEVE VALLEY
BRAG JET BLAW BLOW CROW DEFY
  FACE HUFF PUFF WIND WOST YELP
  BLUFF BOAST CRACK FLIRD PREEN
  SKITE STRUT VAUNT BLEEZE
  BOUNCE INSULT SPLORE SPROSE
  SQUIRT DISPLAY GAUSTER ROISTER
  SWAGGER BRAGGART FLOURISH
  PRETENSE THREATEN
BRAGGART BRAG PUFF BOAST
  FACER BLOWER CROWER GASCON
  HECTOR POTGUN SKITER THRASO
  BLOWOFF BOASTER BOBADIL
  CRACKER RUFFLER SHALLOW
  VAPORER BANGSTER BLOWHARD
  CACAFUGO FANFARON PAROLLES
  PUCKFIST RENOWNER RODOMONT
  SKIPJACK
BRAGGARTISM COCKALORUM
BRAGGING ROOSE JACTANCE
  RODOMONT THRASONIC
BRAHMA KA SELF BRAMAH
BRAHMAN ARYAN HINDU PUNDIT
  SMARTA BRAHMIN
BRAID CUE BRAY GIMP JERK LACE
  PLAT TAIL TRIM BREDE FANCY
  FREAK JIFFY LACET MILAN ONSET

ORRIS PLAIT PLEAT QUEUE START
TAGAL TRACE TRADE TRESS TRICK
TWINE VOMIT WEAVE BOBBIN
BORDER CORDON EDGING GALLON
LACING MOMENT PLIGHT RIBBON
SENNET SNATCH STRING BANDING
BULLION CAPRICE ENTWINE
UPBRAID BRANDISH ORNAMENT
REPROACH SOUTACHE TRIMMING
(— FOR HATS) SENNET SINNET
(— OF WIG) SNAKE
(LINEN —) INKLE
BRAIDER RATCHER
BRAIDING FROG BREDE
BRAIN MAD BEAN HARN MIND PATE
  UTAC WITS AXION HAIRN HAURN
  SKULL NODDLE PSYCHE FURIOUS
  SENSORY THINKER CEREBRUM
  (PL.) HARN PATE SCONCE HEADPICE
BRAINLESS SILLY STUPID FOOLISH
  WITLESS
BRAINPAN PAN HARNPAN PANNICLE
BRAIN SAND SABULUM
BRAIZE BECKER
BRAKE COW BULL BURR CAGE CLOG
  CURB DRAG FERN LOCK RACK SKID
  SLOW STAY TARA TRAP BLOCK
  CHECK COPSE DELAY DETER GRIPE
  SNARE SPOKE SPRAG VOMIT BRIDLE
  CONVOY HARROW HINDER REMORA
  RETARD STAYER WARABI BRACKEN
  DEADMAN DILEMMA SLIPPER
  STOPPER THICKET TRIGGER
  DRAGROPE RETARDER
BRAKEMAN GUARD SHACK SHAKE
  BRAKIE NIPPER DILLIER SNAPPER
  SWAMPER DILLYMAN INCLINER
  TRAINMAN
BRAMBLE WHIN BRIER RHAMN THIEF
  THORN BUMBLE JAGGER LAWYER
  STICKER DEWBERRY MAYBERRY
  NESSBERRY
BRAMBLE BUSH TUTU GRANJENO
BRAMBLING KATE SNOWHAMMER
BRAMBLY DUMAL SPINY THORNY
  PRICKLY
BRAN GRIT SEED DARAK TREAT
  CEREAL CHISEL POLLARD TOPPING
  BEESWING
  (— AND MEAL) SHORTS
  (CORNMEAL —) HUSK
  (FINE —) POLLEN
  (UNSORTED —) RUBBLES
BRANCH ARM BOW LAP LEG LOP
  RAY RUN BARB BROG BUSH CHAT
  FANG FORK LIMB PALM PART RAME
  RICE RISE SNAG SNUG SPUR STEM
  STUD TANG TWIG YARD AXITE
  BAYOU BOUGH BREAK BRIAR BRIER
  CREEK DRUPA GRAIN LAYER LULOV
  PLASH PRONG RAMUS REISE SCROG
  SHOOT SHRAG SPRAY SPRIG STICK
  TWIST VIMEN WITHE BUREAU
  CLADUS DIVIDE DRUKPA EXOPOD
  GERMEN GREAVE GROWTH LEADER
  MEMBER OFFSET OUTLET PHYLUM
  PORTIO RADDLE RAMAGE RAMIFY
  RUNNER SHROUD SPRANG STOLON
  STREAM TAPOUN CHAPTER DIALECT

DIVERGE ENDOPOD FURCATE
LATERAL PHYLLIS RAMULUS
TENDRIL TORRENT ANAPHYTE
BRONCHUS DISTRICT EFFLUENT
OFFSHOOT PEASTICK SCAFFOLD
SPRANGLE TRAILING
(— OF ANTLER) SPELLER
ADVANCER
(— OF COLONY) STIPE
(— OF CRAFT) INDUSTRY
(— OF FAMILY) SEPT
(— OF FEATHER) BARB
(— OF HORN) RIAL ANTLER
(— OF IVY) BUSH
(— OF LEARNING) ART STUDY
FACULTY KNOWLEDGE
(— OF MATHEMATICS) ALGEBRA
CALCULUS
(— OF THALLUS) STICHID
(— OF TREASURY) FISCUS
(DEAD —) FLAG
(EVERGREEN —S) GREENS
(LOCAL —) COURT
(MINE —) LEADER
(PALM —) LULAB
(SMALL —) RICE
(YOUNGER —) CADET
(PL.) LOFT RAMI SKIRT SPRAY
RAMAGE CYPRESS DEADWOOD
BRANCHED FORKY FORKED RAMATE
RAMOSE CLADOSE TROCHED
BRANCHIA GILL
BRANCHING ARMY RAMOSE
FURCATE DICHOTOMY
BRANCHIOPOD SHRIMP
BRANCHLET RAMULUS SPILLER
BRAND BIRN BLOT BURN CHOP
FLAW KIND MARK NOTE SEAR SMIT
SMOT SORT VENT WIPE BUIST
INURE LABEL SCEAR STAIN STAMP
SWORD TAINT TORCH BARREL
MARQUE STIGMA FLAMBEAU
BRANDING IRON BRAND CAUTER
SEARER CAUTERY
BRANDISH WAG DART STIR WAVE
WIND BLESS BRAID SHAKE SWING
WIELD FLAUNT HURTLE QUAVER
RUFFLE STRAIN WINNOW FLUTTER
GLITTER SWAGGER VIBRATE
FLOURISH VAMBRASH
BRANDY DOP BOOF FINE JACK
MARC BINGO MOBBY NANTS PEACH
RAKIA CINDER COGNAC GRAPPA
KIRSCH PUPELO RAKIJA VISNEY
ANISADO AQUAVIT QUETSCH
ARMAGNAC CALVADOS SLIVOVIC
BRANK MUMPS BRIDLE PILLORY
BRANLE BRAWL
BRANT ROUT ERECT PROUD QUINK
SHEER STEEP ROUGHT
BRASH GAY BOLD FACY RASH
HASTY SAUCY STORM ATTACK
RUBBLE BRITTLE FORWARD
IMPUDENT TACTLESS
BRASQUE STEEP
BRASS CASH ALLOY MONEY NERVE
BRAZEN BRONZE MASLIN ORMOLU
OFFICER ORICHALC
(— PLAYER) WINDJAMMER

BRASSIERE BANDEAU
BRAT BIB GET IMP BROT FILM SCUM
APRON BAIRN BILSH BROLL CHILD
CLOAK GAITT INFANT MANTLE
TERROR URCHIN GARMENT
BRATTICER AIRMAN CANVASMAN
BRAVADO POMP BRAVE PRIDE
STORM HECTOR BLUSTER BOMBAST
BRAVERY SWAGGER VAUNTERY
GASCONISM
BRAVE BOLD BRAW DARE DEFY
FACE FINE GAME GOOD PROW TALL
WILD ADORN BOAST BRAVO BULLY
FELON HARDY JOLLY MANLY
MOODY ORPED ROMAN STIFF
STOUT VAUNT WIGHT BRAWLY
BREAST DARING HEROIC MANFUL
PLUCKY STURDY BRAVADO
DOUGHTY GALLANT HAUTAIN
SOLDIER SWAGGER VALIANT
VENTURE WARRIOR CAVALIER
DEFIANCE EMBOLDEN FEARLESS
INTREPID LIONLIKE STALWART
SUPERIOR VALOROUS VIRTUOUS
BRAVELY BIG FINELY
BRAVERY GRIT VALOR SPIRIT
VIRTUE BRAVADO BRAVURA
COURAGE HEROISM JOLLITY
MANHEAD MANHOOD PROWESS
BOLDNESS
BRAVO OLE RAH EUGE THUG BRAVE
BULLY BANDIT CUTTER BRAVADO
SHABASH VILLAIN APPLAUSE
ASSASSIN
BRAWL DIN ROW BEEF CLEM FRAY
RIOT BLIND BROIL CHIDE CLASH
FIGHT MELEE REVEL SCOLD SCRAP
AFFRAY BICKER FRACAS HABBLE
REVILE RUFFLE RUMPUS SHINDY
STOUSH STRIFE TUMULT UPROAR
YATTER BOBBERY BRABBLE
DISCORD DISPUTE QUARREL
SCUFFLE WRANGLE COMPLAIN
SQUABBLE STRAMASH
BRAWLER FRATCH NICKER SQUARER
FRAMPLER NIGHTCAP OUTCRIER
BRAWLING NOISY BLATANT FLITING
SCAMBLING
BRAWN BEEF BOAR LIRE FLESH
FATTEN MUSCLE STRENGTH
(MOCK —) HEADCHEESE
BRAWNY BEEFY FLESHY ROBUST
SINEWY SQUARE STRONG STURDY
CALLOUS MUSCULAR POWERFUL
STALWART
BRAXY BRADSOT
BRAY CRY MIX RUB BEAT ROUT
TOOL CRUSH GRIND NOISE POUND
STAMP BRUISE HEEHAW OUTCRY
PESTLE THRASH WHINNY
BRAYERA KOSO CUSSO KOSSO
BRAZEN BOLD CALM HARD PERT
BRASS HARDY HARSH SASSY
AENEAN BRASSY BLATANT CALLOUS
FORWARD IMMODEST IMPUDENT
INSOLENT METALLIC
BRAZENFACED CHEEKY
BRAZIER HEARTH HIBACHI REREDOS
SCALDINO
BRAZIL ROSET

BRAZIL
BAY: MARAJO IGRANDE SEPETIBA
GUANABARA
BIRD: MITU MITUA
CAPE: FRIO BLANCO BUZIOS
GURUPY ORANGE SAOTOME
SAOROQUE
CAPITAL: BRASILIA
COIN: JOE REIS CONTO DOBRA
HALFJOE MILREIS CRUZEIRO
DAM: FURNAS PEIXOTO
DANCE: SAMBA MAXIXE
ESTUARY: PARA
FALLS: IGUAZU IGUASSU
INDIAN: ANTA ACROA ARARA
ARAUA BRAVO CARIB GUANA
ARAWAK CARAJA CARAYAN
JAVAHAI TARIANA BOTOCUDO
CHAMBIOA
ISLAND: MARACA MARAJO
BANANAL CARDOSO CAVIANA
MEXIANA COMPRIDA
LAKE: AIMA FEIA MIRIM
MEASURE: PE MOIO PIPA SACK
VARA BRACA FANGA LEGOA
MILHA PALMO PASSO TONEL
CANADA COVADO CUARTA
LEAGUE QUARTO TAREFA
ALQUIER GARRAFA ALQUEIRE
MOUNTAIN: URUCUM BANDEIRA
ITATIAIA
MOUNTAINS: MAR GERAL ORGAN
PIAUI ACARAI GURUPI ORGAOS
PARIMA AMAMBAI CARAJAS
GRADAUS RONCADOR
TOMBADOR
NATIVE: CABOCLO CURIBOCA
MAMELUCO PAULISTA
PORT: RIO PARA BAHIA BELEM
NATAL SANTOS PELOTAS
SALVADOR
STATE: ACRE PARA AMAPA BAHIA
CEARA GOIAS GOYAZ PIAUI
PARANA PIAUHY ALAGOAS
GUAPORE PARAIBA RORAIMA
SERGIPE AMAZONAS MARANHAO
PARAHIBA PARAHYBA RONDONIA
SAOPAULO
RIVER: APA ICA DOCE GEIO IVAI
JARI PARA PARU SONO TEFE
ABUNA ANAUA APORE CAPIM
CLARO CORUA ICANA IRIRI ITAPI
JURUA JUTAI MANSO NEGRO
PARDO PIAUI PRETO TIETE
TURVO URUBU VERDE XINGU
AJUANA AMAZON ARINOS
BALSAS BRANCO CANUMA
CONTAS CUIABA DEMINI GRAJAU
GRANDE GURUPI IBICUI IGUACU
JAPURA JAVARI MEARIM
MORTES MUCURI PARANA
PURPUS RONURO SANGUE
TACUTU TIBAGI UATUMA
UAUPES VELHAS CORUMBA
IGUASSU MADEIRA PARAIBA
SUCURIU TAPAJOS TAQUARI
TEODORO URUGUAI ARAGUAIA

PADAUIRI PARACATU PARAGUAI
PARNAIBA SOLIMOES TARAUACA
TOWN: ACU EXU ICO IPU ITU JAU
LUZ RIO UBA BAGE FARO IBIA
IJUI ITAI LAPA LINS PARA PIUI
TUPA UNAI BAHIA BAIAO BAURU
BELEM CEARA NATAL NEVES
CAMPOS CUIABA ILHEUS
MACEIO MANAOS MANAUS
OLINDA RECIFE SANTOS
ARACAJU CARUARU CITORIA
GOIANIA ITABUNA JUNDIAI
NITEROI PELOTAS TAUBATE
UBERABA ANAPOLIS BRASILIA
CAMPINAS CURITIBA LONDRINA
SALVADOR SOROCABA
TERESINA
TREE: ICICA UCUUBA ARARIBA
WEIGHT: BAG ONCA LIBRA
ARROBA OITAVA ARRATEL
QUILATE QUINTAL TONELADA

BRAZIL NUT JUVIA CASTANA
BRAZILWOOD VERZINO HYPERNIO
PEACHWOOD
BREACH GAP CHAP FLAW GOOL
RENT RIFT SLAP BRACK BRECK
BURST CHASM CLEFT CRACK PAUSE
SPLIT WOUND BRUISE HARBOR
HERNIA HIATUS INROAD SCHISM
SCREED SLUICE ASSAULT BLEMISH
DISPUTE FISSURE OPENING
QUARREL RUPTURE BREAKING
CREVASSE FRACTION FRACTURE
INTERVAL OUTBREAK SOLUTION
TRESPASS
(— IN DIKE) GOOL
(— IN SEAWAY) GOOL
(— OF DUTY) BARRATRY
(— OF ETIQUETTE) SOLECISM
(— OF FAITH) TREASON
(— OF MORALITY) SCAPE VAGARY
(— OF PEACE) FRACTION
(— OF UNITY) SOHISM
BREAD BAP BUN BODY BRAD DIET
FARE FOOD LOAF PAIN PONE RIMA
ROLL RUSH RUSK TOKE AZYME
BATCH BATON BOXTY CAPER CHEAT
KISRA LIMPA MICHE ROOTY TOMMY
CHAPON COCKET DAMPER DODGER
ENZYME HALLAH KANKIE MASLIN
MATZOS PANNAM SIMNEL TAMMIE
WASTEL YANNAM ALIMENT
BANNOCK EULOGIA MANCHET
POPOVER STOLLEN TOASTER
CORNCAKE HARDTACK SOFTTACK
ZWIEBACK
(— AND MILK) POBS PANADA
POBBIES
(— BOX) PANETIERE
(— QUALITY) PANEITY
(BATCH OF —) CAST
(BUTTERED —) CAPER
(DRY —) TOKE
(EUCHARISTIC —) BODY HOST
AZYME
(FANCY —) BRAID
(MAIZE —) PIKI

(OATMEAL —) ANACK JANNOCK
(POTATO —) FADGE
(QUICK —) SCONE
(S. AFRICAN —) DIKA
(SLICE OF —) TARTINE TRENCHER
(SMALL LOAF OF —) COB
(SMALL PIECE OF —) SIPPET
MEALOCK
(SOPPED —) MISER BREWIS BROWIS
(SWEET —) BUN BROWNIE STOLLEN
(TOASTED —) SIPPET
(UNLEAVENED —) AZYM AZYME
BANNOCK CHAPATTI
(WHEAT —) CHEAT HOVIS COCKET
MANCHET
BREADBOARD PANEL
BREADED ANGLAISE
BREADFRUIT MASI RIMA RIMAS
DUGDUG NANGCA CAMANSI
CASTANA ANTIPOLO BREADNUT
CHESTNUT
BREADNUT RAM
BREADWINNING GAP BOON BUST
DASH HINT KNAP PICK PLOW REND
RENT RIFT RIVE
BREAK GO CUT JAR LOP TEN ABRA
BUST CHIP DRAG FALL FLAW PART
RUIN RUSH SLIP SNAP STEP STOP
TEAR TURN UNDO WASH WORK
ALTER BLANK BURST CHECK CHINK
CLEFT COMMA CRACK CRAZE
DAUNT FALSE FRUSH LAPSE PAUSE
PLUCK ROUGH SEVER SMASH
SOLVE SPAWN SPELT STAVE SWING
WOUND BRUISE CABBLE CHANGE
CLEAVE CRANNY CUTOUT DEFEAT
HIATUS IMPAIR LACUNA PIERCE
SALTUS SHREND SPRING TEWTAW
TEWTER BLUNDER CAESURA
CRACKLE CRANKLE CREVICE
CRUMBLE DESTROY DISABLE
DISPART DISRUPT EXHAUST
FISSURE GRITTLE INFRACT INTERIM
OPENING RESPITE RUPTURE
SHATTER TAILING VARIATE
BREATHER CREVASSE DIERESIS
DIFFRACT FRACTION FRACTURE
FRAGMENT INFRINGE INTERVAL
SEPARATE SOLUTION STRAMASH
(— APART) SUNDER DISRUPT
SHATTER
(— AWAY) BOLT ESCAPE
(— BOULDERS) BULLDOZE
(— DOWN) CONK FAIL GIVE CRAZE
CROCK TRAIK BRUISE TUMBLE
ANALYZE FOUNDER REFRACT
COLLAPSE INFRINGE
(— FORCE) BAFFLE
(— FORTH) BOIL ERUPT EVENT
FLASH EXPLODE
(— FROM ICE MASS) CALVE
(— GLASS) SHREND DRAGADE
(— IN PIECES) CHAP DICE KNAP
CRASH CRAZE SMASH SMOKE
SHIVER CRUMBLE FRITTER SMATTER
DEMOLISH DIFFRACT DISJOINT
SPLINTER STRAMASH
(— IN WAVES) JABBLE
(— IN YARN) SMASH

(— IN) ENTER
(— INTO FOAM) COMB
(— INTO) BROACH IRRUPT
(— INWARD) STAVE
(— LANCE) TAINT
(— OF CONTINUITY) SALTUS
(— OFF) NUB DROP SNAP CEASE
LRAVE ABRUPT DIREMPT
(— OFF END) SNUB
(— OPEN) BUST CHOP FORCE
(— ORE) COB SPALL SPAWL
(— OUT) ERUPT START ASSURD
STRIKE
(— RANKS) DISMISS
(— SHARPLY) KNACK
(— SILENCE) QUATCH QUETCH
(— SKIN) GALL
(— SLATE) SCULP
(— STONE) CAVIL KEVEL
(— THE BACK) CHINE
(— THROUGH SHELL) PIP
(— THROUGH) BEAT FORCE
(— UP EARTH) HACK FALLOW
(— UP SIEGE) LEVY
(— UP) BUCK FALL MELT FLOUR
SEVER SPALE SPLIT STASH INCIDE
DEGRADE DIFFUSE DISBAND
DISSECT DISTURB REFRACT
SCARIFY SCATTER CROSSCUT
DISJOINT DISPERSE DISSOLVE
DISUNIFY FRAGMENT
(— WATER) FIN
(— WINDOWS) NICK
(STEM —) BROWNING
BREAKABLE BRITTLE BRUCKLE
FRIABLE DELICATE FRANGIBLE
BREAKAGE GRIEF
BREAKAX IRONWOOD
BREAKDOWN EDGER BURNOUT
DEBACLE HOEDOWN COLLAPSE
DILUTION
(— OF RIND) ADUSTIOSIS
(ELECTRIC —) AVALANCHE
BREAKER JUMP SURF WAVE BARECA
BEAKER BILLOW COMBER ROLLER
CRACKER SLEDGER LEDGEMAN
SCRAPPER
(— OF WORD) WARLOCK
(CIRCUIT —) CUTOUT
(ROCK —) ALLIGATOR
(PL.) BREACH
BREAKFAST BRUNCH DISJUNE
DISJEUNE
BREAKING BREACH BREAKUP
FRACTION FRACTURE SOLUTION
(— FORTH) ERUPTIVE
(— OFF) CHIPPING ABRUPTION
(— UP) DEBACLE ANALYSIS
BREAKSTONE SAXIFRAGE
BREAKWATER COB DAM COBB
CROY DIKE MOLE PIER PILE QUAY
JETTY GROYNE REFUGE BULWARK
STOCKADE
BREAM TAI BRIM CARP CHAD SCUP
SHAD ZOPE BROOM ROMAN BALEEN
BARWIN BRAISE SARGUS OLDWIFE
SUNFISH WAREHOU CYPRINID
FLATFISH STEENJIE TARWHINE
BREAST DUG BUMP CROP FACE

BOOBY BOSOM BRAVE BUBBY
CHEST HEART PETTO STALL
PECTUS POMMEL THORAX BRISKET
COUNTER KNOCKER FOREBOWS
(— OF HORSE) COUNTER
(PL.) BUST
BREASTBAND HORSE
BREASTBONE BREAST STERNUM
XIPHOID
BREASTHOOK CRUTCH FOREHOOK
BREASTPIECE RABAT RABBI
BREASTPLATE EGIS URIM AEGIS
BREAST GORGET LORICA ORACLE
SHIELD THORAX CUIRASS PALETTE
POITREL PECTORAL PLASTRON
BREASTWORK FORT REDAN
SANGAR SCHANZ SCHERM SUNGAR
BRATTLE PARAPET PLUTEUS
RAMPART BRATTICE
BREATH AIR ANDE GASP HUFF LIFE
ONDE PANT PECH PUFF SIGH WAFT
WIND BLAST PAUSE SCENT SMELL
VAPOR WHIFF BREEZE FLATUS
PNEUMA HALITUS INSTANT RESPITE
SPIRACLE
(— OF WIND) SPIRIT
(BAD —) OZOSTOMIA
(DIVINE —) NEPHESH
(LIFE —) PRANA SPIRIT
BREATHE ANDE LIVE ONDE PANT
PECH PUFF SIGH VENT EXIST EXUDE
SPEAK SPIRE UTTER ASPIRE
EXHALE INHALE WHEEZE AFFLATE
EMANATE RESPIRE SUSPIRE
(— HEAVILY) FOB PECH FNESE
SOUGH THROTTLE
(— LABORIOUSLY) GASP
(— NOISILY) SOUGH SNOTTER
(— UPON) FAN
BREATHING AIR ALIVE PNEUMA
SPIRIT GASPING SPIRITUS
SPIRATION
(— HEAVILY) SUSPIRIOUS
(LABORED —) ASTHMA
(SMOOTH —) LENE LENIS
BREATHLESSNESS TIFT
BREATHY HOLLOW ADENOID
BRED (WELL —-) FREE
BREECH BORE BUTT DOUP BLOCK
BRICK CULOTTE DRODDUM
BUTTOCKS CYLINDER DERRIERE
BREECHBLOCK BLOCK VENTPIECE
BREECHCLOTH HIPPEN HIPPING
BREECHES HOSE CHAPS JEANS
LEVIS SLOPS STOCK TREWS
BRACAE BRAGAS BREEKS GASKIN
SMALLS TIGHTS TROUSE BOMBARDS
BREEKUMS JODHPURS KICKSIES
KNICKERS LEATHERS TROUSERS
PANTALOON
BREED GET ILK BEAR KIND RACE
REAR SORT BEGET BROOD CASTE
CAUSE CLASS FANCY HATCH ISSUE
RAISE STOCK STORE TRAIN CREATE
GENDER STRAIN EDUCATE NOURISH
PRODUCE PROGENY SPECIES
VARIETY ENGENDER GENERATE
INSTRUCT MULTIPLY
BREEDER RANCHER AURELIAN

HERDSMAN HORSEMAN
(FISH —) MILTER
BREEDING ORIGIN DESCENT
NURTURE TUPPING BEHAVIOR
CIVILITY PREGNANT TRAINING
(GOOD —) GENTRY
BREEZE AIR AURA BLOW FLAW GALE
GUST PIRR STIR WIND BLAST
RUMOR SLANT WALTZ BREATH
DOCTOR REPORT SLATCH SPIRIT
ZEPHYR FRESHEN MUZZLER
QUARREL VIRASON WHISPER
(COOL —) DOCTOR
(GENTLE —) AIR AURA ZEPHYR
(LAND —) TERRAL
(STIFF —) STOUR TIFTER
BREEZE FLY WHAME
BREEZY AIRY BRISK FRESH WINDY
AIRISH
BRETHREN IKHWAN
BRETON ARMORICAN
BREVE NOTE WRIT BRIEF MINIM
ORDER SHORT PRECEPT
BREVIARY ORDO CURSUS DIGEST
LEDGER PORTAS COUCHER
EPITOME SUMMARY ABSTRACT
PORTESSE PORTHORS
BREVITY SYNTOMY LACONISM
UNLENGTH BRIEFNESS SHORTNESS
TERSENESS
BREW ALE MIX BEER BOIL MAKE
PLOT POUR DRINK HATCH STOUT
BROWST DEVISE DILUTE FOMENT
GATHER LIQUOR SEETHE CONCOCT
INCLINE PREPARE CONTRIVE
(HOME —) SAMOGON
BREWER TUNNER
BREWING GAIL GYLE BROWST
BRIBE BUD FEE FIX OIL ROB SOP TIP
BAIT GIFT HAVE HIRE MEED MOIL
PALM VAIL WAGE BONUS CUDDY
GRAFT OFFER STEAL SUGAR TEMPT
TOUCH EXTORT GREASE NOBBLE
PAYOLA SQUARE SUBORN CORRUPT
DOUCEUR SWEETEN TICKLER
GRATUITY VENALIZE
BRIBERY MEED
BRIC-A-BRAC CURIO VERTU VIRTU
BIBELOT TROCKERY TRUMPERY
BRICK BAT GLUT MARL PAVE TILE
BLOCK QUARL SPLIT STOCK STONE
TOOTH CUTTER FELLOW HEADER
PAMENT PAVIOR BACKING CLINKER
FLETTON GRIZZLE PERPEND
SOLDIER BURNOVER
(— WALL) NECK
(CRACKED —) CHUFF SHUFF
(FINAL HALF —) JACK
(IMPERFECT —) BURNOVER
(PILE OF —S) HACK CLAMP
(PULVERIZED —) SOORKY SOORKEE
(SECOND-RATE —) GRIZZLE
(SOFT —) CUTTER RUBBER PICKING
(SQUARE —) QUADREL
(STACK OF —) LIFT
(SUN-DRIED —) BAT ADOBE
(UNBURNT —) ADOBE
(WOODEN —) DOOK
(PL.) CLAYWARE

BRICKLAYER BRICKY MASONER
BRICKMAKER MOLDER
BRICKWORK HOB BRICKING
BRIDAL NUPTIAL BRIDALTY
BRIDE KALLAH SPOUSE SHULAMITE
BRIDE-PRICE LOBOLA LOBOLD
BRIDESMAID PARANYMPH
BRIDEWELL MILLDOLL
BRIDGE WAY BRIG LINK NOSE PONS
PONT REST SPAN WIEN CROSS
SIRAT TOWIE GANTRY ISLAND
JIGGER RUNWAY SANGAR AUCTION
BASCULE BIFROST CONNECT
CULVERT EXOSTRA PASSAGE
PASSING PINNOCK PONCEAU
PONTOON PROPONS TRAJECT
TRESTLE VIADUCT CONTRACT
TRAVERSE DUPLICATE
(— OF MUSICAL INSTRUMENT)
MAGAS CHEVALET
(ARCADED —) RIALTO
(CONTRACT —) GHOULIE PLAFOND
(FLUE —) ALTAR
(GATEWAY —) GOUT
(HOSE —) JUMPER
(IMPEDANCE —) DIPLEXER
(NATURAL —) ARCH
(ROPE SUSPENSION —) JOOLA
BRIDGEMAKER PONTIFEX
BRIDGEMAN EBBMAN
BRIDGING ASTRIDE STRUTTING
BRIDLE BIT CURB REIN RULE BRAKE
BRANK BRIDE CHECK GUARD GUIDE
STRUT DIRECT GOVERN HALTER
MASTER SIMPER SUBDUE BLINDER
CONTROL LORMERY REPRESS
SNAFFLE SWAGGER CAVESSON
RESTRAIN SUPPRESS
BRIDLE PATH SPURWAY
BRIEF FEW CURT LIST RIFE WRIT
BLURB BREVE CHARM PITHY QUICK
SHORT TERSE ABRUPT COMMON
CURTAL FLYING HOURLY LETTER
LITTLE SNIPPY SUDDEN ABRIDGE
CAPSULE COMPACT COMPOSE
CONCISE CRYPTIC INVOICE LACONIC
MANDATE OUTLINE PRECEPT
SUMMARY BREVIATE CONDENSE
FLEETING FLITTING SNATCHED
SNIPPETY SUCCINCT SYLLABUS
BRIEF CASE FOLIO TASHIE
BRIEFLY BRIEF ENFIN SHORTLY
BRIER BARB PIPE BRIAR THORN
SMILAX BRUYERE INKBERRY
BRIER TREE PIPER
BRIG RIG JAIL PRISON GEORDIE
BRIGADE TERZO CAMPOO
BRIGAND THIEF USKOK BANDIT
LATRON PIRATE ROBBER CATERAN
KETTRIN LADRONE ROUTIER
SOLDIER PICAROON
(PL.) TCHETNITSI
BRIGANDINE PLACCATE
BRIGHT APT GAY NET FINE GILD
GLAD GLEG HIGH LIVE ROSY ACUTE
AGLOW ALERT ANIME BEAMY BRAVE
CLEAR CRISP EAGLE FLARY FRESH
GEMMY JOLLY LIGHT LUCID NITID
PRINT QUICK RIANT SHARP SHEEN

SHEER SHINY SMART SMOLT STEEP
SUNNY TINNY VIVID WHITE WITTY
BERTHA CHEERY CLEVER FLASHY
FLORID GARISH LIMPID LIVELY
LUCENT ORIENT SHRILL SILVER
BEAMISH DIAMOND DILUCID
FORWARD FULGENT LAMBENT
RADIANT RINGING SHINING
ANIMATED CHEERFUL FLASHING
GLEAMING LIGHTFUL LUMINOUS
LUSTROUS SPLENDID SPLENDOR
STARLIKE SUNSHINY
(BLINDINGLY —) GLARING
(NOT —) SOFT
(OFFENSIVELY —) GARISH
(SOFTLY —) LAMBENT
BRIGHTEN GILD LAMP BLOOM
CHEER CLEAR FLAME GLOZE LIGHT
LIVEN SHINE SNUFF CANTLE ENGILD
POLISH ANIMATE BURNISH EMBRAVE
ENLIVEN FURBISH LIGHTEN
SMARTEN ILLUMINE
BRIGHTENER FLUOROL
BRIGHTLY GAY CLEAR LIGHT SHEEN
BRIGHT FRESHLY SHEENLY
BRIGHTNESS SUN BLAZE BLOOM
ECLAT FLAME GLARE GLEAM GLINT
GLORY GLOSS LIGHT NITOR SHEEN
SHINE ACUMEN BRIGHT CANDOR
FULGOR LUSTER CLARITY GLISTEN
GLITTER LAMBENT NITENCY
SPARKLE RADIANCE SPLENDOR
(— OF TOBACCO) FLASH
(— UNIT) STILB
BRILLIANCE FAME BLARE BLAZE
ECLAT FLAME GLARE GLORY SHINE
VALUE KEENNESS RADIANCE
SPLENDOR VIVACITY
BRILLIANCY FIRE BLARE ECLAT
GLORY REFLET CLARITY GLITTER
ORIENCY RADIANCE SPLENDOR
BRILLIANT GAY GOOD KEEN SAGE
WISE BREME QUICK VIVID BRIGHT
CLEVER LIVELY PURPLE SIGNAL
BRITTLE EMINENT FLAMING
GLARING LAMBENT LAMPING
LOZENGE PRISMAL RADIANT
SHINING BLINDING DAZZLING
DIZZYING GLORIOUS INSPIRED
LUCULENT LUMINOUS SLASHING
SPLENDID
(TRANSIENTLY —) METEORIC
BRIM LIP RIM RUT SEA EDGE TURF
BLUFF BRINK MARGE OCEAN VERGE
WATER BORDER MARGIN TURNUP
COPULATE STRUMPET
(— OF HAT) FLAP LEAF POKE BRINK
TARFE
BRIMFUL TIPFUL TOPFUL CROWNED
BRIMMING BIG FULL ABRIM
BRIMSTONE SULFUR VIRAGO
SULPHUR BRINSTON SPITFIRE
BRINDLED TAWNY BRANDED
FLECKED STREAKED
BRINE SEA MAIN SALT BRACK LEACH
OCEAN TEARS PICKLE MARINADE
BRINER COBBERER
BRING DO LAY TEE WIN BEAR BUCK
CALL FIRK LEAD STOP TAKE TEEM

CARRY DRIVE ENDUE FETCH INCUR
APPORT ARRIVE CONVEY DEDUCE
CONDUCE CONDUCT EXHIBIT
PROCURE PRODUCE
(— FORTH YOUNG) EAN KID YEAN
(— ABOUT CAPTURE) ACCOUNT
(— ABOUT) DO SEE BREW MAKE
STAY TEEM CAUSE DIGHT FRAME
INFER MOVEN SHAPE SWING
CREATE EFFECT INVOKE SECURE
SPIRIT COMPASS CONDUCE INSPIRE
OPERATE PRODUCE CATALYZE
OCCASION TRANSACT
(— BACK) REFER EFFECT RECALL
REDUCE REDUCT RELATE RETURN
REVIVE REVOKE PRODUCE RESTORE
OCCASION RETRIEVE TRANSACT
(— BEFORE) HAUL
(— CHARGE) APPEACH
(— DOWN STEER) HOOLIHAN
(— DOWN) LAY DROP FALL FELL
STOP ABATE COUCH SOFTEN
DECLINE DESCEND DISMOUNT
(— FORTH) CAST FOAL GIVE MAKE
TEEM EDUCE HATCH ISSUE SPAWN
THROW PROFER DELIVER TRADUCE
ENGENDER
(— FORWARD) CITE LEAD INFER
ADDUCE ALLEGE ADJOUST
ADVANCE PROPOSE
(— IN) EARN INFER USHER IMPORT
INDUCE INVECT REPORT RETURN
ADHIBIT
(— INTO BATTLE) COMMIT
(— INTO COURT) SIST
(— INTO DISGRACE) FOUL
(— LOW) AVALE DEGRADE
SUPPLANT
(— ON) INFER INDUCE
(— ONESELF) GET
(— OUT) DRAW ACCENT ELICIT
DISINTER HEIGHTEN
(— OVER) CONVERT
(— TO A HALT) STICK
(— TO AN END) DO END FIT DOCK
DRAW REDD CEASE FORDO DECIDE
EXPIRE FINISH FOREDO FULFIL
DISJOIN INCLUDE COMPLETE
CONCLUDE DISSOLVE SURCEASE
(— TO BAY) CORNER
(— TO BEAR) EXERT
(— TO HEEL) FACE
(— TO LIFE) EVOKE ANIMATE
(— TO LIGHT) GRUB REAP DREDGE
ELICIT EXPOSE REVEAL UNEARTH
DISCLOSE DISCOVER
(— TO NAUGHT) DASH FOIL UNDO
NEGATE CONFUTE DESTROY
(— TO PERFECTION) RIPEN
(— TO STOP) CURB HALT ARREST
(— TO THE GROUND) GRASS
(— TOGETHER) JOIN AMASS RAISE
UNITE ADDUCT CONFER CORRAL
ENGAGE ENLINK GATHER SUMMON
COLLATE COLLECT COMPILE
COMPORT ASSEMBLE CONFLATE
ENSEMBLE
(— UP) REAR BREED NURSE RAISE
TRAIN NURSLE UPREAR EDUCATE
NOURISH

BRINGING-UP BREEDING EDUCATION
BRINJAL EGGPLANT
BRINK END EVE LIP RIM SEA BANK
BRIM EDGE FOSS MARGE SHORE
VERGE BORDER MARGIN MARGENT
BRINY BRACK SALTY SALINE
MURIATED
BRIOCHE ROLL STICH SAVARIN
BRISE-SOLEIL BLIND SUNBREAK
SUNSHADE
BRISK GAY BRAG BUSY FAST KEEN
PERK PERT RACY RASH SPRY TRIG
VIVE YERN AGILE ALERT ALIVE
BUDGE CANTY CRISP FRESH FRISK
KEDGE NIPPY PEART PERKY QUICK
ROUND ZIPPY ACTIVE BREEZY
COCKET CROUSE DAPPER FLICKY
LIVELY NIMBLE SNAPPY SPRUNT
TROTTY VIVACE ALLEGRO HUMMING
ANIMATED BRUSHING FRISKFUL
RATTLING SMACKING SPANKING
SPIRITED
BRISKLY YERN SHARP YERNE
BUSILY CROUSE ALLEGRO ROUNDLY
BRISKNESS ALACRITY VIRITOOT
BRISTLE AWN JAG RIB BARB HAIR
JAGG SETA TELA BIRSE BRUSH
PARCH PREEN STARE STRUT STYLE
TOAST CHAETA PALPUS RUFFLE
SETULA STIVER STRIGA STYLET
GLOCHIS SMELLER STUBBLE
WHISKER ACICULUM FRENULUM
SPICULUM VIBRISSA
BRISTLED HORRENT
BRISTLE-SHAPED STYLOID
BRISTLING ROUGH HISPID HORRID
SETOSE THORNY HORRENT
SCRUBBY SPINOUS
BRISTLY BIRSY PENNY SETOSE
STUBBY SCRUBBY STICKLE
BRITISH ENGLISH BRITANNIC
WHITEHALL
BRITISH HONDURAS (BAY OF —)
CHETUMAL
(CAPITAL OF —) BELMOPAN
(FORMER CAPITAL OF —) BELIZE
(MOUNTAIN RANGE OF —) MAYA
(TOWN OF —) CAYO STANN
COROZAL
BRITOMARTIS (FATHER OF —)
JUPITER
(MOTHER OF —) CARME
BRITON CELT SCOT BRYTHON
BRITTANY (NATIVE OF —) BRETON
BRITTLE DRY FROW WEAK BRASH
CANDY CRISP CRUMP EAGER FRAIL
FROWY FRUSH SHORT SPALT
CRISPY CRUMPY FEEBLE FICKLE
FROUGH GINGER IMFIRM SLIGHT
BRICKLE BRUCKLE CRACKLY
FRAGILE FRIABLE REDSEAR
SHIVERY SMOPPLE BRITCHEL
DELICATE SNAPPISH
BRITTLEBUSH ENCELIA
BROACH AIR AWL CUT PIN ROD TAP
OPEN OUCH SHED SPIT SPUR STAB
TAME VEER VENT BEGIN DRESS
DRIFT PRICK RIMER SPOOL START
VOICE ATTAME BORING BROOCH

DRIVER FIBULA LAUNCH PIERCE
REAMER RHYMER STRIKE ENLARGE
EXPRESS PUBLISH SPINDLE
SQUARER VIOLATE WIDENER
APPROACH DEFLOWER DRIFTPIN
INCISION PORPOISE
BROAD DEEP FREE VAST WIDE
AMPLE BEAMY DORIC GROSS LARGE
LARGO PLAIN ROOMY SPLAY SQUAB
STOUT THICK WOMAN COARSE
GLOBAL BELCHER EVIDENT
GENERAL GRIVOIS LIBERAL
OBVIOUS PLATOID SPACIOUS
TOLERANT
(— AND FLAT) PLATOID
(NOT —) STRAIT
BROADBILL GAYA RAYA GAPER
SCAUP BOATBILL SHOVELER
SWORDFISH
BROADCAST AIR SOW SEED SEND
CARRY RADIO STREW AIRING
SPREAD DECLARE DIFFUSE PUBLISH
SCATTER ANNOUNCE TELEVISE
TRANSMIT
BROADCLOTH CASTOR SUCLAT
TAUNTON
BROADEN BREDE WIDEN DILATE
EXPAND EXTEND SPREAD ENNOBLE
BROADHORN ARK
BROADNESS BIGNESS LIBERALITY
BROADSIDE BROAD GARLAND
BROADSWORD BILL KRIS GLAIVE
HANGER SPATHA CUTLASS
FERRARA CLAYMORE MONTANTO
SCIMITAR
BROBDINAGIAN HUGE
BROCADE ACCA BROCHE KINCOB
KINKHAB NISHIKI BAUDEKIN
DAMASSIN
BROCCOLI ASPARAGUS
BROCHURE TRACT BOOKLET
PAMPHLET TREATISE
BROCKET PITA STAG BROCK
SPITTER
BRODIAEA GRASSNUT
BROGAN STOGA STOGY BROGUE
STOGIE
BROIL ROW BURN CHAR FEUD FRAY
GRID HEAT TOIL ALARM BRAWL
GRILL MELEE SCRAP SWELT
AFFRAY BIRSLE BRAISE GRILLY
SPLORE SQUEAL TUMULT BRANDER
BRULYIE CARBONE CONTEST
DISCORD DISPUTE EMBROIL FRIZZLE
GARBOIL QUARREL SIMULTY
BARBECUE BLOODWIT CONFLICT
GRILLADE STRAMASH
BROILER GRILL SEARER CHICKEN
POUSSIN
BROKE HOG BUST STONY STONEY
CHICANE BANKRUPT
BROKEN DOWN RENT RUDE TORN
BLOWN BROKE BURST FRACT
GAPPY HAIRY ROMPU ROUGH
TAMED BRASHY HACKLY RUINED
SHAKEN CRACKED CRUSHED
FRACTED REDUCED SUBDUED
VICIOUS WHIPPED BANKRUPT
CONTRITE OUTLAWED RUPTURED

TATTERED WEAKENED
(— **BUT NOT TRAINED**) GREEN
(— **IN HEALTH**) CRAZY
(— **IN**) STOVEN
(— **OFF**) ABRUPT
(**EASILY** —) GINGER
BROKEN-DOWN HAYWIRE
DISJASKED DISJASKIT
BROKER AGENT CRIMP CORSER
DEALER FACTOR JOBBER BROGGER
CHANGER COURSER PEDDLER
REALTOR SCALPER HUCKSTER
INSTITOR MERCHANT
BROMATIUM KOHLRABI
BROME CHEAT
BROMEGRASS CHESS
BROMO ACID EOSIN EOSINE
BROMUS DRAWK
BRONCHITIS HUSK HOOSE HOOZE
BRONCO PONY PONEY CAYUSE
BRONCHO MUSTANG
BRONCOBUSTER BUSTER GINETE
BUCKAROO
BRONZE AES TAN BUST ALLOY
BROWN COWBOY ORMOLU STATUE
ASIATIC GUNMETAL
(— **AGE CULTURE**) UBAID
(**ANTIQUE** —) CACAO
(**GILDED** —) VERMEIL
(**MEDAL** —) CALABASH
BRONZEWING SQUATTER
BROOCH BAR PIN BOSS LACE OUCH
PRIN PROP CAMEO CLASP MORSE
PREEN SLIDE SPRAY SPRIG FIBULA
NOUCHE PLAQUE SHIELD FERMAIL
PETALON CROTCHET ORNAMENT
SUNBURST
BROOD EYE FRY NYE SET SIT MOPE
NEST NIDE RACE TEAM TRIP WEEP
AERIE BREED CLOCK COVER COVEY
FLOCK GLOOM GROUP HATCH
HOVER ISSUE SEDGE STOCK
WORRY YOUNG CLETCH CLUTCH
FAMILY KINDLE LITTER PONDER
PROGENY SPECIES COGITATE
INCUBATE KINDLING MEDITATE
(— **OF BIRDS**) AERY AERIE COVEY
EYRIE SEDGE SIEGE
(— **OF PHEASANTS**) EYE NID NYE
NIDE
BROODER HOVER MOTHER NURSERY
BROOK RUN BEAR BECK BURN GHYL
GILL LAKE RILL RUSH SIKE ABIDE
BAYOU BOURN CREEK GLIDE STAND
STELL TCHAI ARROYO CANADA
DIGEST ENDURE GUTTER RINDLE
RIVOSE RUNLET RUNNEL SICKET
STREAM SUFFER COMPORT
CONCOCT STOMACH QUEBRADA
TOLERATE
(**RIPPLING** —) PURL
(**SALT** —) LICK
BROOKLET BECK DOKE RILL RILLET
RUNNEL RILLOCK RIVULET
BROOM COW MOP FRAY SWAB
BESOM BISME BREAM BRUSH
SCRUB SPART SWEEP UALIS WHISK
GENISTA HAGWEED WHISKER
HACKWEED SPLINTER

(**DYER'S** —) GENET DYEWOOD
(**NATIVE** —) DOGWOOD
(**TOPS OF** —) SCOPARIUS
BROOMCORN HURL
BROOMCORN MILLET HIRSE PANIC
PANICLE KADIKANE
BROOMRAPE HELLROOT HERBBANE
BROOMROOT SACATON ZACATON
BROSE ATHOLE
BROTH SEW BREE BROO FOND KAIL
KALE SOUP GLAZE STOCK BREWIS
CULLIS JUSSAL JUSSEL LIQUOR
SKILLY CALDERA POTTAGE SOUCHIE
SUPPING BOUILLON CONSOMME
PISHPASH POSSODIE POWSOWDY
BROTHEL KIP CRIB STEW BAGNE
HOUSE BAGNIO BORDEL LUPANAR
BORDELLO CATHOUSE HOOKSHOP
HOTHOUSE JOYHOUSE SERAGLIO
BROTHER FR BUB FRA KIN PAL SIB
BHAI BRER EGIL FRAY MATE MONK
PEER BILLY BUBBY BUDDY CADET
FRERE FRIAR FELLOW FRAILE
FRATER GERMAN COMRADE SIBLING
FOSTERER
(**HUSBAND'S** —) LEVIR
(**LAY** —) SCOLOG
(**WIFE'S** —) AFFINE
(**YOUNGER** —) CADET
(PL.) FF BRETHREN CURIATII
HARLUNGEN
BROTHERHOOD GILD GUILD LODGE
ORDER PAPEY FRIARY BRATSVO
CHISHTI THIASOS THIASUS
BRODHULL SODALITY
(— **OF FREEMASONS**) CRAFT
(**LITERARY** —) FELIBRIGE
BROTHER-IN-LAW MAUGH
BROUGHAM PILLBOX CARRIAGE
BROUGHT BROCHT
(— **FROM ELSEWHERE**) DERIVED
(— **TO BAY**) CORNERED
(— **TOGETHER**) CONFLATE
(— **UP BY HAND**) CADE
BROW TOP BRAE EDGE MIEN SNAB
BOUND BRINK CREST EAVES FRONT
RIDGE SLOPE BOLDNESS FOREHEAD
BROWBEAT FACE ABASH BULLY
BOUNCE HECTOR DEPRESS
DUMBCOW OUTFACE SWAGGER
BROWBEATEN HACKED
BROWN (ALSO SEE COLOR) ART DUN
TAN ARAB COIN COOK DARK GOAT
LION SEAR ABRAM ACORN ARGUS
BRUNO DUSKY HAZEL KAFFA
MOSUL PABLO PENNY QUAIL SEDGE
SEPIA TAWNY TENNE TOAST UMBER
APACHE BEAVER BRUNET GLOOMY
MALAGA MANILA MASTIC MOHAWK
PALOMA PLOYER PONGEE RABBIT
RUSSET SENNET TANNED TURTLE
WIGWAM ASPHALT HARVEST
LIBERIA MUSCADE OAKWOOD
OXBLOOD POMPEII PRAIRIE
REDWOOD TANBARK TOBACCO
VESUVIN BRUNETTE MOCCASIN
MUSHROOM PHEASANT PERSIMMON
PYGMALION
(**CONDOR** —) TIFFIN

(**DARK** —) BURNET
(**GRAYISH** —) DUN
(**HAIR** —) ARGALI
(**LIGHT** —) ALOMA ALESAN STRING
(**OLIVE** —) BARK AUTUMN
(**REDDISH** —) BAY SORE SEPIA
AUBURN CROTAL GINGER RUSSET
SORREL AMBROSIA
(**YELLOWISH** —) AZTEC ALMOND
BAMBOO BLONDE BEESWAX
ALDERNEY
BROWNBACK DOWITCH DOWITCHER
BROWN HEART RAAN
BROWNIE ELK NIS COOKY DOBBY
NISSE URISK DOBBIE GOBLIN
URUISG
BROWNING SCALD SCORCH SUNTAN
BROWNISH UMBER BURNET
(— **BLACK**) LAVA
BROWNSTONE CHESTNUT
BROWSE BRUT CROP FEED GRAZE
FORAGE NIBBLE PASTURE
BRUISE JAM BASH BRAY BUBU DENT
DUNT HURT JAMB MAIM MAUL SORE
STUN TUND BLACK BREAK BRIZZ
CRUSH CURRY DELVE DINGE POUND
SQUAT BATTER BREACH HATTER
INJURY INTUSE MANGLE POUNCE
SHINER STOUND SUGGIL BATTERY
CONTUND CROWNER DAMMISH
DISABLE
BRUISED HURT LIVID FROISSE
BRUIT DIN FAME RALE ROAR TELL
NOISE RUMOR SOUND BLAZON
CLAMOR REPORT DECLARE
HEARSAY
BRUNEI (— **WEIGHT**) PARA CHAPAH
(**TOWN OF** —) SERIA
BRUNET DARK BLACK BROWN GIPSY
GYPSY MORENA SWARTHY
BRUNETTE MORENITA
BRUNT JAR BLOW JOLT CLASH
FORCE ONSET SHOCK ATTACK
EFFORT IMPACT STRAIN STRESS
ASSAULT OUTBURST VIOLENCE
BRUSH DIP DUB PIG TIP CARD COMB
DUST FLAP FLAT FRAY KIYI SKIM
SWAB BROOM CHAPE CLEAN COPSE
FIGHT FITCH GRAZE LINER SABLE
SCOPA SCRUB SCUFF SWEEP
SWOOP WHISK BADGER BATTLE
BRIGHT BROSSE DABBER DAUBER
DUSTER MOGOTE PALLET PENCIL
PICKUP PUTOIS RIGGER RUBBER
SPONGE STROKE TEASEL CLEANSE
FOXTAIL GRAINER GROOMER
MOTTLER STIPPLE STRIPER THICKET
SCRUBBER SIFTENER SKIRMISH
STIPPLER TARBRUSH
(— **ASIDE**) SCUFF
(— **IN DANCING**) SCUFFLE
(— **OF TWIGS**) COW
(— **TO CLEAN SHIP BOTTOM**) HOG
(**BLUNT** —) BLENDER
(**DENSE** —) BUNDOCKS BOONDOCKS
(**ELECTRIC** —) DOCTOR
(**EMPHASIZED** —) SLAP
(**FLESH** —) SCRAPER STRIGIL
(**GROWTH OF** —) SYLVAGE

(POLLEN —) SCOPA SAROTHRUM
(SMALL —) TOOL FITCH FITCHEW
BRUSHER LIMBER LIPPER
BRUSH MAKER FLIRTY FLICKER
BRUSH SHUNT PIGTAIL
BRUSHWOOD HAG RICE RONE RUSH
BRAKE BRUSH COPSE FRITH REISE
SCROG SCRUB SPRAY COPPET
GARSIL MALLEE RAMMEL SCRUNT
SHROGS TINNET TINSEL COPPICE
ROUGHIE TEENAGE THICKET
WOODRIS BUSHWOOD
BRUSQUE CURT RUDE BLUFF BLUNT
GRUFF HASTY ROUGH SHORT
ABRUPT VIOLENT CAVALIER
IMPOLITE
BRUTAL CRUEL FERAL GROSS
CARNAL COARSE SAVAGE BEASTLY
BESTIAL BRUTISH CADDISH
INHUMAN BELLUINE INHUMANE
INSOLENT RUTHLESS
BRUTE BEAST GROSS YAHOO
ANIMAL BRUTAL SAVAGE BEASTLY
BESTIAL BRUTISH GORILLA RUFFIAN
BRUTISH FELL CRUEL BRUTAL
CARNAL FIERCE SAVAGE STUPID
BESTIAL INHUMAN SENSUAL
GADARENE
BRYONY HOP NEP ALRAUN COWBIND
MANDRAKE
(— FRUIT) OXBERRY
BRYOPHYTE ANOPHYTE LIVERWORT
BRYTHONIC CYMRIC KYMRIC
BRITTONIC
BUBBLE AIR BUB BEAD BELL BLEB
BLOB BOIL BOLL DUPE FOAM GLOB
SCUM SEED CAPER CHEAT EMPTY
VAPOR BURBLE DELUDE HOTTER
POPPLE SEETHE SOTTER TRIFLE
BLISTER BLUBBER DECEIVE
GLOBULE DELUSIVE
(— IN GLASS) BOIL REAM SEED
BLISTER
(PL.) SUDS
BUBBLING GAY BURBLY BOILING
GASSING EFFUSIVE
BUBINGA KEVAZINGO
BUBO EMEROD
BUCCANEER PIRATE RIFLER
ROBBER VIKING CORSAIR MARINER
SPOILER MAROONER PICAROON
BUCHMANITE GROUPER
BUCHU BUKA DIOSMA
BUCK FOB RAM BOIL BUTT DEER
DUDE MALE PRIG REAR SOAK STAG
TOFF WASH BLOOD DANDY PITCH
SASIN STEEP BASKET DOLLAR
OPPOSE RESIST STRIVE SAWBUCK
BUCKJUMP BUCKWASH
(— IN 1ST YEAR) FAWN
(— IN 2ND YEAR) PRICKET
(— IN 3RD YEAR) SORREL
(— IN 4TH YEAR) SORE
(— STEADILY) SUNFISH
(— UP) BRACE
BUCKBEAN BOGBEAN THREEFOLD
BUCKER DOLLYMAN
BUCKET SAY TUB BAIL BOOT BOWK
CAGE GRAB MEAL PAIL SKIP BOWIE

CHEAT SCOOP SKEEL STOOP STOUP
BAILER DIPPER DRENCH HOPPET
KIBBLE SITULA SUCKER VESSEL
FERMAIL GRAPPLE SNAPPER
SWINDLE CANNIKIN HEDGEHOG
PAINTPOT
(— ON MILL WHEEL) AW AWE EIE
(— ON WHEELS) SKIP
(GLASS-MAKING —) CUVETTE
(GRAVEL —) GRAB
(HOISTING —) HUDGE
(TWO —S OF WATER) GAIT
BUCKEYE STATE OHIO
BUCKLAW HAYSTON
BUCKLE BOW BEND CURL KINK
OUCH TACH TACK WARP BRACE
CLASP MARRY STRAP TACHE TWIST
FIBULA CONTEND FERMAIL GRAPPLE
FASTENER STRUGGLE
BUCKLER CRAB BLOCK SCUTE
TARGE SHIELD TAIRGE TARGET
BUCKLUM BUCKRAM ROTELLA
ROUNDEL SHUTTER
BUCKLING KINK UPSET
BUCK RAKE SWEEP
BUCKRAM STIFFENER
BUCKTHORN COMA RHAMN SCROG
WAHOO ALATERN CASCARA
BEARWOOD FRANGULA LOTEBUSH
WAYTHORN STINKWOOD
BUCKWHEAT BUCK CRAP BRANK
WRIGHT SARRAZIN
(PL.) FAGOPYRUM
BUCOLIC IDYL LOCAL NAIVE RURAL
FARMER RUSTIC SIMPLE COWHERD
ECLOGUE AGRESTIC HERDSMAN
PASTORAL
BUD BUR EYE GEM IMP PIP BULB
BURR CION FORM GERM GIRL
GROW KNOP KNOT WORK CAPOT
CHILD CLOVE GEMMA GRAFT SCION
SHOOT SPRIT SPURT YOUTH
BUDLET BUTTON FLOWER GERMIN
OCULUS OILLET SPROUT BLOSSOM
BROTHER CABBAGE GEMMULE
PLUMULE ROSEBUD TENDRON
BOURGEON BULBILLA
(BLIGHTED —) BLAST
(BROOD —) SOREDIUM
(UNDEVELOPED —) EYE
(PL.) CAPERS
BUDDHA FO FOH BUTSU JATAKA
GAUTAMA SRAMANA DAIBUTSU
(— STORY) JATAKA
BUDDHISM DAIJO FOISM KEGON
CHANISM LAMAISM HINAYANA
(— CODE) VINAYA
BUDDHIST (— DOCTRINE) ANATTA
TRIKAYA
(— FESTIVAL) WESAK
(— PATH) VEHICLE
(— SCHOOL) RITSU
(— SECT) SHIN TENDAI
BUDDLE TYE FRAME BODDLE SLIMER
STRIPE TROUGH
BUDDY BO BOY BUD PAL JACK MATE
DIGGER BROTHER COMRADE
COMPADRE TENTMATE
BUDGE FUR JEE BOGY MOVE STIR

BOOZE BRISK MUDGE STIFF THIEF
JOCUND LIQUOR SOLEMN AUSTERE
POMPOUS MOVEMENT
BUDGET BAG BOGY BOOT PACK
PLAN ROLL BATCH BOGEY BOGIE
BUNCH STOCK STORE BOTTLE
BUNDLE PARCEL SOCKET WALLET
PROGRAM
BUFF ASH BOB FAN TAN BLOW COAT
CURT FIRM SHINE SNUFF SPARK
BUFFET POLISH STURDY STAMMER
STUTTER NAUMKEAG
(TILLEUL —) ALABASTER
BUFFALO OX ANOA ARNA ARNI BUFF
STAG ARNEE BISON BUGLE BUFFLE
HAMPER KERBAU MURRAH WUNTEE
CARIBAO CARIBOU GAZELLE
OVERAWE TIMARAU ZAMOUSE
BEWILDER SAPIUTAN SELADANG
BUFFALO CHIPS BODEWASH
BUFFALO FISH SUCKER BUFFALO
BIGMOUTH GOURDHEAD
BUFFER DOG PAD FROG RACK
BUMPER FENDER HURTER PISTOL
CUSHION
BUFFET BAR BOB BOX BEAT BLAD
BLOW BUFF CUFF GOWF PLAT SCAT
SLAP TOSS FILIP KNOCK SCUFF
SCUFT SMITE STOOL ABACUS
BATTER FILLIP FLEWIT SERVER
SETOUT STRIKE STRIVE THRASH
COLPHEG CONTEND COUNTER
HASSOCK SMACKER SQUELCH
CREDENCE CREDENZA CUPBOARD
SPANGHEW
BUFFETING DIRD SKITE DUSTING
BUFFLEHEAD DUCK FOOL CLOWN
BUFFLE DIPPER DOPPER MARIONET
WOOLHEAD MERRYWING
BUFFOON DOR WAG WIT APER FOOL
JAPE MIME MOME VICE ZANY
ACTOR ANTIC BUFFO CLOWN COMIC
DROLE DROLL HARLOT JESTER
MUMMER STOOGE ANTIQUE
BOUFFON JUGGLER PLAYBOY
TOMFOOL BALATRON GRACIOSO
HUMORIST MACAROON MERRYMAN
OWLGLASS PLEASANT RIDICULE
PANTALOON
BUFFOONERY JAPERY ZANYISM
CLOWNERY
BUG (ALSO SEE INSECT) DOR FLAW
GERM IDEA MITE BOGEY BULGE
FIEND LYGUS ROACH ARADID
BEDBUG BEETLE BUGGER CAPSID
CHINCH COREID CORUCO ELATER
INSECT SALDID SCHEME TINGID
BELLIED BOATMAN BUGBEAR
CIMICID CORSAIR FORWARD
POMPOUS STRIDER BARBEIRO
CONENOSE HEMIPTER HOBBYIST
NAUCORID VINCHUCA
(RED —) CHIGGA CHIGGER
(SOW —) SLATER
BUGABOO BOGY FEAR GOGA GOGO
OGRE TURK ALARM BOGEY BOGIE
GOGGA BODACH GOBLIN BUGBEAR
SPECTER SPECTRE WORRICOW
BUGANDA (— KING) KABAKA

BUGBANE COHOSH BUGWORT RICHWEED HELLEBORE
BUGBEAR BUG COW BOGY BOGEY BOGIE CADDY MORMO POKER BOGGLE BOGGART BUGABOO FEARBABE SCAREBUG
BUGGER SOD CHAP BOOGER FELLOW PERSON RASCAL HERETIC
BUGGY CART SHAY TRAP NUTTY CALESA CABOOSE CALESIN FOOLISH VEHICLE DEMENTED INFESTED STANHOPE
BUGLE BEAD HORN BLACK BUFFALO BULLOCK CLARION HUTCHET TRUMPET
(— **CALL**) WARISON
(**YELLOW** —) IVA
BUGLER WINDJAMMER
BUGLOSS ALKANET ANCHUSA BLUEWEED OXTONGUE
BUILD BIG SET FORM LEVY MAKE REAR TELD CREAT DRIVE EDIFY ERECT FOUND FRAME HOUSE RAISE SHAPE THROW FABRIC GRAITH TAILLE TIMBER COMPILE EXTRUCT FASHION ASSEMBLE
(— **FIRE**) CHUNK
(— **HASTILY**) CLAP
(— **NEST**) AERIE NIDIFY
(— **UP**) AGGRADE
(**BODY** —) HABITUS
BUILDER EPEUS MAKER EPEIUS HANGER ERECTOR ENGINEER TECTONIC
(**DAM** —) DAMMER
BUILDING GIN CASA CRIB DOME FLAT HALL IGLU JAIL LAND PILE SHED SHOP SLAB SPOT TELD AEDES ARENA BLOCK COURT FOLLY FRAME HOTEL HOUSE IGLOO JAWAB STORE STUDY ARMORY BIGGIN BOTTLE CASING CHAPEL FABRIC GARAGE HAMMAM INSULA PALACE SCHOOL SUCCOR BREWERY BROODER CARBARN COLLEGE DIORAMA EDIFICE FACTORY FLATTOP FOUNDRY MANSION SALTERN STATION SYNAGOG ATHENEUM BAGHOUSE BASILICA BROCETTO CHANCERY DIPTEROS DRYHOUSE DWELLING DYEHOUSE ELEVATOR EPHEBEUM FIRETRAP GASHOUSE GINHOUSE HOTHOUSE ICEHOUSE MAGAZINE NYMPHEUM PANORAMA SERAPEUM STEMMERY TAXPAYER TENEMENT VELODROME
(— **FOR AIRCRAFT**) DOCK
(— **GROUPS**) HAM
(— **OF STONE**) KAABA CASHEL TRUDDO TRULLO
(— **ON POSTS**) PATAKA
(**BUDDHIST** —) TOPE
(**CIRCULAR** —) THOLE THOLOS ROTUNDA
(**CRUDE** —) SHANTY
(**DILAPIDATED** —) ROOKERY FIRETRAP
(**EXHIBITION** —) MUSEUM
(**FARM** —) BARN STABLE HACIENDA

(**FORTIFIED** —) CASTLE
(**GRAIN** —) GARNER
(**JAI ALAI** —) FRONTON
(**MOVABLE** —) TURRET
(**ORNAMENTAL** —) ALCOVE
(**PUBLIC** —) CASINO THEATER THEATRE COLISEUM
(**QUADRANGULAR** —) TETRAGON
(**QUARANTINE** —) LAZARET
(**SACRED** —) CHURCH MOSQUE TEMPLE SACRARY PANTHEON SARAPEUM
(**SERIES OF** —**S**) SWEEP
(**SLIGHT** —) SHED
(**SMALL** —) HUT COOP HOCK EDICULE
(**SPORTS** —) CAGE
(**STATELY** —) DOME
(**STORAGE** —) BARN HORREUM
(**SUBSIDIARY** —) ANNEX
(**TRADE** —) HALL
(**UNCOMFORTABLE** —) ARK
(PL.) FUNDUS
BUILT SET BOUKIT STACKED TIMBERED
(**COMPACTLY** —) CORKY
(**HEAVILY** —) BLOCKY
(**LOOSELY** —) GANGLING
(**STRONGLY** —) BURLY GROSS QUARRY
(**WELL** —) BUIRDLY
BUKIDNON MONTES BINOKID
BULB BUD SET BLUB CORM IXIA KNOB LAMP ROOT SEED SEGO CLOVE FLOAT GLOBE ONION SWELL TUBER BULBIL BULBUS CROCUS GARLIC SCILLA BABIANA GALTONIA SPARAXIS TRITONIA
(— **OF PERCUSSION**) CONCHOID
(**LIGHT** —) HELION
(**ONION** —) BUTTON
(PL.) SQUILL
BULBIL CHIVE BULBLET
(PL.) SPAWN
BULBLET CHIVE CORMEL BULBULE NUCLEUS PROPAGO
BULBUL KALA BUHLBUHL GREENBUL LEAFBIRD

BULGARIAN POMAK
BULGE BAG BUG JUT SAG BUMP CASK HUMP KNOB LUMP PANT BILGE BLOAT BOUGE FLASK POUCH START STRUT SWELL BEETLE BILLOW COCKLE EXTEND PUCKER WALLET BLISTER PROJECT OVERHANG PROTRUDE SWELLING
(— **OUT**) TUT BELLY BOWDEN STRUNT
(**OFFENSIVE** —) SALIENT
BULGING FULL BOMBE BOWED BUGGY GOUTY PUDGY TUMID BAGGED CONVEX GOOGLY TOROSE GIBBOUS GOUTISH SWOLLEN BOUFFANT
BULK BODY BOUK HEAP HEFT HOLD HULK HULL LUMP MASS MOLE PILE SIZE BURLY CARGO GROSS MIGHT POWER SLUMP STALL SWELL CORPSE EXPAND EXTENT FIGURE VOLUME BIGNESS MAJORITY QUANTITY
BULKHEAD CHECK BATTERY PARTITION
BULKY BIG MAIN BURLY GROSS LARGE PUDGY STOUT CLUMSY STODGY HULKING LUMPING MASSIVE WEIGHTY UNWIELDY
BULL COP SEG APIS BEEF BILL JEST MALE ROAN SEAL SEGG SLIP STOT TORO ZEBU BACIS BEEVE BOBBY BONER BOVID BRUTE DRINK EDICT ERROR ANIMAL BOVINE BUSHWA LETTER PEELER TAURUS BULLOCK BUSHWAH CRITTER CRUSADE NOVILLO TAURINE CAJOLERY DOCUMENT FLATTERY
(— **AREA**) QUERENCIA
(— **KILLING**) VOLAPIE
(**HORNLESS** —) DODDY DODDIE
(**HUMAN-HEADED** —) SHEDU CAMASSU
(**YOUNG** —) STOT BUGLE MICKY STIRK STOTT BULLOCK
(PL.) BATTERY
BULLA BLEB BULL SEAL BLAIN BLISTER VESICLE
BULL CELL TORIL
BULLDOG BULL BULLER BULLDOZE
BULLDOZE COW RAM BULLY FORCE SCOOP COERCE BROWBEAT BULLYRAG RESTRAIN
BULLET GUN BALL LEAD PILL SHOT SLUG TOWEL CONOID DUMDUM PELLET PICKET SINKER TRACER DINGBAT MISSILE PELLOCK

PROJECT SPITZER MUSHROOM WADCUTTER
(PL.) BALL LEAD STUFF
BULLETIN ITEM MEMO NOTICE POSTER REPORT SERIAL PROGRAM NEWSBILL
BULLFIGHT CORRIDA NOVILLADA
BULLFIGHTER TORERO MATADOR PICADOR CAPEADOR TOREADOR
BULLFIGHTING REJONEO
BULLFINCH ALP OLP HOOP MAWP MONK NOPE OLPH POPE HEDGE TANNY TAWNY MONACH REDBIRD REDHOOP SHIRLEY BLOODALP TONYHOOP
BULLHEAD CUR POUT
BULLIMONG FARRAGE
BULLION BILLOT
BULLISH STIFF
BULLOCK HOG HOGG NEAT NOWT STOT BUGLE KNOUT STEER STIRK BOVINE
(DECOY —) COACH
BULL-ROARER BUZZ BUMMER BUZZER ROARER TUNDUN TURNDUN WHIZZER
BULL'S-EYE EYE BULL DUMP GOLD BLANK OXEYE WHITE TARGET ROUNDEL
BULL SNAKE GOPHER
BULL TROUT TRUFF
BULLY NUT BOAT BOSS FACE FINE GOOD HUFF MATE BRAVE BRAVO GREAT JOLLY SNOOL TIGER VAPOR BOUNCE CUTTER CUTTLE HARASS HECTOR HUFFER JOVIAL RUFFLE TYRANT BLUSTER BOUNCER BULLOCK DARLING DASHING GALLANT GAUSTER HUFFCAP ROISTER RUFFIAN RUFFLER SLASHER SOLDIER SWAGGER BANGSTER BARRATER BLUDGEON BROWBEAT BULLDOZE DOMINEER FRAMPLER NIGHTCAP RABIATOR
(MASTIC —) ACOMA
BULLY TREE BALATA BULLACE GAUSTER BEEFWOOD
BULRUSH REED RISP RUSH TULE SEDGE BUMBLE GLUMAL AKAAKAI CATTAIL PAPYRUS SCIRPUS TUSSOCK
BULWARK BAIL FORT WALL FENCE JETTY MANTA MOUND TOWER WARDER BASTION DEFENCE DEFENSE PARAPET PROTECT RAMPART WEREWALL
BUM BEG DIN BOMB BOOM HOBO DRINK DRONE IDLER MOOCH SHACK STIFF TRAMP FROLIC GUZZLE SPONGE SQUEEF GUZZLER VAGABOND
BUMBLEBEE DOR CLOCK BUMBEE BUMBLE CARDER BUMBLER
BUMMER SKIDDER
BUMP CRY HIP HIT NOB BANG BLOW BOOM BUNK DIRD JOLT KNOB LUMP WHAP WHOP BULGE CLASH CLOUR CLOUT DUNCH KNOCK ORGAN THUMP BOUNCE CANNON IMPACT

JOUNCE NODULE STRIKE BITTERN COLLIDE CONFLICT SWELLING
(— ON WHALE'S HEAD) HOVEL
BUMPER BOWL FINE GOOD FACER GLASS ROUSE BUFFER CASABE FENDER GOBLET HURTER KELTIE BRIMMER DINGMAN CARANGID
(— GUARD) OVERRIDER
BUMPKIN JAY YAP BEAM BOOM BOOR CHAW CLOD GAWK HICK LOUT RUBE SWAB SWAD TIKE TYKE CHURL CLOWN ROBIN YAHOO YOKEL FARMER JOSKIN LUMMOX BUCOLIC CAUBOGE HAWBUCK
BUNCH BOB SET BALE BOSS CHOU CLEW CLUB CLUE COMA KICK KNOB KNOT PACK SWAD TUFT WISP BREAK CLUMP FAGOT FLOCK KNOLL PAHIL THUMP CLUTCH GAGGLE HUDDLE
(— OF BANANAS) HAND STEM
(— OF FLAX) HEAD STRICK
(— OF FRUIT) HOG STRAP
(— OF GRASS) WHISK
(— OF GRAIN) RIP
(— OF GRAPES) RAISIN
(— OF HAIR) COB
(— OF HERBS) BOUQUET
(— OF IVY) BUSH
(— OF TOBACCO LEAVES) HAND BREAK
(— UP) SHRUG
(SMALL —) WISP
BUNCHER BINDER
BUNCHY TRUSS
BUNCOMBE HOOEY BUNKUM
BUND BAND QUAY PRAYA LEAGUE SOCIETY
BUNDLE KID LOT PAD TOD WAD WAP BALE BAND BEAT BOLT BOOK BUNG DRUG DRUM GARB HANK HAUL HEAD KNOT LOCK PACK ROLL SWAG BLUEY BULTO BUNCH FADGE FAGOT GAVEL GLEAN GROUP LITCH NICKY PETER SHEAF SKEIN TARRY TRACE TRUSS TURSE WADGE BARSOM BATTEN BINDLE BOTTLE BUDGET DRIVER DUFTER FAGGOT FARDEL FASCES FUMBLE GATHER KNITCH LOGGIN NUMBER PACKET PARCEL SCROLL THRAVE DORLACH FASCINE GARBAGE MATILDA PACKAGE FASCICLE
(— OF 60 SKINS) TURN
(— OF BOARDS) BOLT
(— OF FASCINES) ROULEAU
(— OF FIBRILS) AXONEME
(— OF FLAX) BEET HEAD
(— OF HAIR) LEECH
(— OF HAY, STRAW, ETC.) WAP WASE WISP GAVEL SHEAF BATTEN BOLTIN BOTTLE TIPPLE WINDLING
(— OF HEATH) KID
(— OF HIDES) KIP
(— OF NERVE FIBERS) TRACT COLUMN
(— OF PAPERS) SPUR DUFTER
(— OF RODS) FASCES
(— OF SACKS) BADGER

(— OF SACRED TWIGS) BARSOM
(— OF THONGS) KNOUT
(— OF TOBACCO) CARROT
(— OF TWIGS) BIRCH BROOM FAGGOT
(— OF WOOD) PIMP BAVIN FAGOT
(— OF YARN) HAUL SLIP
(BUSHMAN'S —) DRUM BLUEY
BUNG CORK PLUG SHIVE SPILE STOPPER
BUNGEY KIT
BUNGI-BUNGI STAVEWOOD
BUNGLE ERR GOOF MESS MUCK MUFF BLUNK BOTCH FAULT FLUFF FUDGE SPOIL STICK BOGGLE BOLLIX BUMBLE FOOZLE FUMBLE MOMBLE MUCKER MUDDLE TAILOR TOGGLE BAUCHLE BLUNDER BUTCHERY SHAMMOCK
BUNGLER LUMMOX PUDDLE TINKER BUMBLER BUMMLER FOOZLER DAUBSTER
BUNGLING FLUFF FUDGY INERT CLUMSY AWKWARD TINKERLY
BUNG START FLOGGER
BUNION ONION WYROCK
BUNJI-BUNJI CUDGERIE
BUNK BED CAR BLAA BLAH CASE JUNK SACK ABIDE BERTH BUNKO FRAME HOKUM HOOEY LEAVE LODGE SLEEP TRUCK BUNKUM TIMBER BALONEY BOLSTER CHICORY HEMLOCK TWADDLE BUNCOMBE NONSENSE
BUNKHOUSE BULLPEN
BUNKUM BLAH BUNK FUDGE HOKUM HOOPLA BALONEY BUNCOMBE
BUNTAL BURI BANGKOK
BUNTING EBB POP FLAG PAPE POPE CHINK DUMPY FINCH PLUMP COTTON STOCKY TOWHEE UNTIDY COWBIRD ETAMINE GARMENT OATFOWL ORTOLAN ROUNDED BELLYING BOBOLINK PRUSIANO RICEBIRD RINGBIRD SLOVENLY NONPAREIL
BUNTON DIVIDER
BUOY DAN WAFT BAKEN ELATE FLOAT LAGAN RAISE MARKER DOLPHIN SUSTAIN DEADHEAD LEVITATE MAKEFAST SONOBUOY
BUOYANCY BALON BALLON LEVITY SPRING ELATION
BUOYANT GAY CORKY HAPPY LIGHT BLITHE BOUNCY FLOATY LIVELY ELASTIC HOPEFUL JOCULAR LILTING SPRINGY ANIMATED CHEERFUL SANGUINE SPIRITED VOLATILE
BUR BUZZ TEAZEL STICKER
BURBARK AKONGE BOXBUSH BURRBARK
BURBOT COD CONY CUSK LING LOTA CONEY LOCHE LAWYER MORGAY DOGFISH EELPOUT GUDGEON BIRDBOLT
BURDEN TAX VEX BIRN CARE CARK CLAG CLOG DRAG DUTY FARE FOOT GANG LADE LOAD MUCK ONUS PORT SEAM TACK BIRTH CARGO

CROWD CRUSH DRONE HEAVY
LABOR MIDST CHARGE CUMBER
ENTAIL FARDEL HAMPER IMPOSE
LADING SADDLE THRACK WEIGHT
BALLAST BURTHEN CONVETH
FRAUGHT FREIGHT HAGRIDE
ONERATE OPPRESS REFRAIN
SUMPTER TROUBLE CAPACITY
CARRIAGE ENCUMBER ENGREGGE
HANDICAP OVERCOME QUANTITY
RUMBELOW MILLSTONE
(— **OF SONG**) WHEEL HOLDING
OVERTURN OVERWORD
(**FINANCIAL** —) EXPENSE
BURDENED HEAVY LADEN GRAVID
FRAUGHT HARASSED
BURDENER INCUBUS
BURDENSOME HEAVY IRKSOME
ONEROUS WEIGHTY CUMBROUS
GRIEVOUS GRINDING LOADSOME
BURDOCK DOCK GOBO CLITE CLOTS
DRAIN LAPPA BARDANE BURWEED
BUZZIES CADILLO CLOTBUR
HARDOCK HAREBUR CLEAVERS
HAULBACK
BUREAU DESK CHEST AGENCY
EXCISE OFFICE CENTRAL DRESSER
AGITPROP
BUREAUCRAT MANDARIN
BURFISH ATINGA
BURGEON BUD GROW ERUPT
SHOOT SPROUT
BURGESS CITIZEN FREEMAN
PORTMAN COMMONER GORGIBUS
(PL.) BURGWARE
BURG GRASS SANDBUR COCKSPUR
SANDSPUR
BURGLAR YEGG CRACK THIEF
GOPHER ROBBER RAFFLES
YEGGMAN PETERMAN PICKLOCK
BURGLARY BREAK CRACK THEFT
LARCENY ROBBERY STEALAGE
BURGUNDY POMMARD VOUGEOT
TONNERRE
BURIAL FUNERARY INTERMENT
(— **MOUND**) TOLA HUACA
BURIAL PLACE AHU TOMB GRAVE
BURIAL GIGUNU LAYSTOW PYRAMID
CATACOMB CEMETERY GOLGOTHA
LAYSTALL
BURIED HIDDEN HUMATE SEPULT
ABSORBED IMBEDDED
(**NOT** —) UNRESTED
(**RECENTLY** —) GREEN
BURIN GRAVER PLASTIC
BURL BURR KNAR KNOT LUMP
KNAUR PIMPLE PUSTULE
BURLAP GUNNY CROCUS BAGGING
HESSIAN SACKING WRAPPING
BURLER LECKER SPILER
BURLESQUE APE ODD COPY JEST
MIME BURLY DROLL FARCE REVUE
COMEDY OVERDO PARODY
BUFFOON JOCULAR MIMICRY
MOCKERY OVERACT DOGGEREL
RIDICULE TRAVESTY
BURLY FAT BLUFF BULKY GROSS
HEAVY HUSKY LARGE LUSTY NOBLE
OBESE STOUT THICK TRAMP

BOWERLY MASTIFF STATELY
IMPOSING

BURMA
BAY: BENGAL HUNTER HEANZAY
CAPITAL: RANGOON
GULF: MARTABAN
MEASURE: LY DHA GON LAN MAU
NGU SAO TAO TAT BYEE DAIN
PHAN SEIT TAUN TENG THAT
SALAY SHITA THUOC LAMANY
PALGAT TRUONG CHAIVAI
OKTHABAH
MONEY: KYAT
MOUNTAIN: POPA NATTAUNG
SARAMATI VICTORIA
MOUNTAINS: CHIN NAGA DAWNA
KACHIN KARENNI PEGUYOMA
NATIVE: AO VU WA LAI LAO MON
PYU TAI CHIN KADU KUKI LOLO
MIAO NAGA SEMA SHAN THAI
KAREN KHMER LHOTA BIRMAN
BURMAN KACHIN RENGMA
PALAUNG ARAKANESE
PORT: AKYAB BASSEIN HENZADA
MOULMEIN
SEA: ANDAMAN
TOWN: YE AVA PEGU AKYAB
BHAMO KATHA MINBU PAPUN
PROME TAVOY HSENWI HSIPAW
LASHIO MAYMYO MONYWA
SHWEBO BASSEIN HENZADA
PAKOKKU RANGOON MANDALAY
MOULMEIN
RIVER: HKA NMAI PEGU SALWIN
SHWELI KALADAN MALIKHA
MYITNGE SALWEEN SITTANG
CHINDWIN INDAWGYI
IRRAWADDY
WEIGHT: TA CAN MAT MOO PAI
VIS BINH DONG KYAT RUAY VISS
BAHAR BEHAR CANDY TICAL
TICUL ABUCCO PEIKTHA

BUR MARIGOLD BACLIN CUCKOLD
BURMESE KADU BIRMAN
ARAKANESE
BURN BREN BREW CHAR FIRE GLOW
PLOT RAZE RILL SEAR SERE TEND
TIND ADUST BLAZE BROIL BROOK
CENSE CHARK CLAMP FLAME FLARE
PARCH PLOUT QUICK ROAST SCALD
SCAUM SINGE SWEAL WASTE
WATER CROZLE IGNIFY NIGGER
SCORCH SIZZLE STREAM CHARPIT
COMBURE COMBUST CONSUME
CREMATE CROZZLE FLICKER
FRIZZLE INCENSE OXIDIZE RIVULET
SCOWDER SMOLDER FLAGRATE
SQUANDER
(— **FEEBLY**) GUTTER
(— **FITFULLY**) FLICKER
(— **IN**) INURE
(— **MIDNIGHT OIL**) LUCUBRATE
(— **OUT**) GUT
(— **UP**) ADUST EXUST
(— **WITH LITTLE FLAME**) SMUDGE
(**LET** —) BISHOP

BURNED ADUST
BURNER BEAK KORO BAKER PILOT
ARGAND BUNSEN CENSER
BATSWING CALCINER GASLIGHT
THURIBLE WELSBACH
BURNET SELFHEAL BLOODWORT
BURNING HOT FIRE LIVE AFIRE
ANGRY BLAZE CALID EAGER FIERY
FLAME GLEDY QUICK SCALD URENT
ABLAZE ARDENT FERVID FIRING
LIVING TORRID USTION ADURENT
CAUSTIC CAUTERY FERVENT
FLAMING GLARING GLOWING
MORDANT SCOWDER SHINING
ARDUROUS EXCITING FLAGRANT
INUSTION MUIRBURN PARCHING
SCOUTHER
(— **BRIGHTLY**) LIGHT
(— **OF FORESTS IN INDIA**) JHOOM
(**MALICIOUS** —) ARSON
(**NO LONGER** —) EXTINCT
BURNING BUSH WAHOO
BURNISH RUB GLAZE GLOSS INLAY
POLISH FURBISH
BURNISHER AGATE BUFFER GLAZER
FROTTON POLISHER
BURP BOKE BELCH BUBBLE
BURR NUT PAD RIB BARB BIRR BOSS
BUZZ HALO KNOB PILE RING ROVE
SLUG WHIR BRIAR BURGH WHARL
WHIRR BANYAN CIRCLE CORONA
TEASEL TUNNEL WASHER CORONET
STICKER PARASITE
(— **IN WOOD**) GNAR KNAR
(— **OF ANTLER**) CORONET
(— **ON TYPE**) RAG
BURRO ASS DONKEY
BURROW BED DEN DIG SET BURY
HEAP HOLE MINE MOLE PIPE ROOT
TUBE BERRY COUCH EARTH MOUND
FURROW ROOTLE TUNNEL CLAPPER
GALLERY PASSAGE SHELTER
EXCAVATE WORMHOLE
(— **AS EEL**) MUD
(— **IN**) MOIL
(— **OF BADGER**) SET
(— **OF OTTER**) COUCH
(**FOSSIL** —) SCOLITE
BURROWS TOWN
BURSA SAC SACK POUCH CAVITY
BURSULA
BURSAR BOWSER PURSER TERRAR
BOUCHER CASHIER
BURSE CASE SHOP FOREL BAZAAR
BOURSE POCKET
BURST FIT FLY POP BLOW BUST
DASH GUSH GUST LOSS REND SCAT
TILT BLAST BLOUT BREAK CRACK
ERUPT FLAFF FLASH GRAZE REAVE
SALVO SCATT SHOUT SPASM SPLIT
START STAVE BROKEN DAMAGE
INJURY SPROUT EXPLODE IMPLODE
RUPTURE SHATTER AIRBURST
OUTBREAK SUNDERED
(— **ASUNDER**) OUTRIVE
(— **FORTH**) ERUPT SALLY EXPIRE
BALLOON
(— **IN**) IRRUPT IMPLODE
(— **INTO FRAGMENTS**) FLITTER

(— INTO LAUGHTER) BUFF
(— OF ACTIVITY) BRASH SPURT
SPRINT SPLURGE
(— OF ARTILLERY) GRAZE RAFALE
(— OF CHEERS) SALVO
(— OF ENERGY) BANG
(— OF FIRING) COUGH
(— OF HARMONIOUS SOUND)
DIAPASON
(— OF LIGHT) FLASH GLORY
(— OF SPEED) KICK FLUTTER
(— OF TEARS) BLURT
(— OF TEMPER) BOUTADE
(— OF WIND) FLAW
(— OPEN) UPBRAST
(— OUT) PRORUMP
(— THE HEART) RIVE
BURSTER GALE LUGGER CRACKER
BURSTING TUMID ABURST BLOWOUT
RUPTION ERUPTING

BURUNDI
CAPITAL: BUJUMBURA
COIN: FRANC
LAKE: RUGWERO TSHOHOHA
NATIVE: HUTU BANTU PYGMY
TUTSI WATUSI
RIVER: KAGERA RUVUVU RUZIZI
AKANYARU
TOWN: NGOZI BURURI KITEGA
MUYINGA BUJUMBURA

BURY URN CAMP HIDE MOOL RAKE
TURF VEIL CLOAK COVER EARTH
GRAVE INTER INURN VAULT WHELM
ENTOMB ENWOMB HEARSE INHUME
SEPULT SHROUD BEDELVE
CONCEAL ENGROSS IMMERSE
PITHOLE REPRESS SECRETE
FUNERATE SUBMERGE
BUS CAMION JITNEY JEEPNEY
BUSBOY OMNIBUS PICCOLO
BUSH TOD BUTT BOSCH BURSE
CLUMP GROVE PLASH SCRAY
SHRUB BRANCH TAVERN BOSCAGE
BOUCHON CLUSTER OUTBACK
THICKET BUSHLAND
(— SICKNESS) TAURANGA
(BLACKBERRY —) BRAMBLE
(STUNTED —) SCROG
(PL.) RUFFMANS
BUSH CLOVER HAGI
BUSH COW ZAMOUSE
BUSHEL FOO FOU GOB LOT MET
BUCKET STRICK
(1–4TH —) PECK
(1–HALF —) TOVET
(1–HALF TO 3–4THS —) CABOT
(1.6 —) FANEGA
(3 TO 5 —S) SACK
(3–4THS —) SKIPPLE
(41.28 —) WEY
(8 —S) SEAM
BUSHER SWAMPER
BUSHGRASS WOODREED
BUSHING BUSH COAK DRILL LINER
BOUCHE COLLET LINING SLEEVE
BOUCHON FERRULE GROMMET
PADDING

(HALF —) STEP
BUSHMAN GUNG BUSHY KHUAI
ABATOA ABATWA WHALER
BUSHBOY SWAGMAN NEGRILLO
(PL.) SAN SAAN
BUSHMASTER CURUCUCU
SURUCUCU
BUSHWHACKER PAPAW PAWPAW
BUSHY BOSKY SHOCK DUMOSE
DUMOUS BUSHMAN QUEACHY
BUSILY THRANG
BUSINESS ADO ART BIZ FAT JOB
PIE CARE FEAT FIRM FUSS GAME
GEAR LINE NOTE TASK WORK
CAUSE CRAFT TRADE TRUCK
AFFAIR CUSTOM EMPLOY ERRAND
MATTER METIER NEGOCE OFFICE
PIDGIN RACKET TURKEY ACCOUNT
CALLING CONCERN JOURNEY
PALAVER TRADING TRAFFIC
ACTIVITY AGIOTAGE BESOIGNE
COMMERCE FOLLOWER INDUSTRY
INTEREST VOCATION
(COMIC —) LAZZO
(MONKEY —) JOUKERY PAWKERY
(STAGE —) BYPLAY
BUSINESSMAN TYCOON POACHER
BOURGEOIS CONVERTER
BUSKIN BOOT SHOE CALIGA
BOTTINE COTHURN BRODEKIN
BUSSU UBUSSU TROOLIE
BUST BUMP FAIL RUIN TAME BOSOM
BREAK BURST BUSTO CHEST EDGAR
FLUNK SPREE BRONZE DEMOTE
REDUCE STATUE DEGRADE DISMISS
FAILURE PROTOME
(— SHAPE) TAILLE
BUSTARD KORI OTIS WATO PAAUW
TURKEY BEBILYA HOUBARA
KORHAAN FLORICAN GOMPAAUM
BUSTIC AUSUBO CASSADA
BUSTLE ADO BUZZ FIKE FRAY FUSS
JUMP STIR WHEW WHIR FRISK
HASTE HYPER KNOCK PAVIE STEER
WHIRL WHIRR BISHOP BUMBLE
ENERGY FISSLE FISTLE FLURRY
FUSTLE HUDDLE HUSTLE POTHER
RACKET TATTER THRONG TUMULT
UNREST UPROAR CLATTER CLUTTER
CONTEND LOUSTER SCOWDER
SCUFFLE SCUFTER SPUFFLE
ACTIVITY IMPROVER SPLUTTER
STRUGGLE TOURNURE
BUSTLING ADO BUSY FUSSY
SPOFFISH STIRRING
BUSY FAST FELL APPLY BRISK QUICK
AETIVE EIDENT EMPLOY INTENT
LIVELY OCCUPY STEERY THRONG
UNIDLE ENGAGED HOPPING
HUMMING OPEROSE TROUBLE
WORKING DILIGENT EMPLOYED
EXERCISE OCCUPIED SEDULOUS
TIRELESS UNTIRING
(— ONESELF) STRAP
(NOT —) SLACK
BUSYBODY BUSY SNOOP EARWIG
SPOFFY ARDELIO MARPLOT
MEDDLER SNOOPER FACTOTUM
QUIDNUNC PRAGMATIC

BUT AC LO MA BIT SED YEA YET
MERE ONLY SAVE ARRAH STILL
ALWAYS EXCEPT UNLESS BESIDES
HOWBEIT HOWEVER
BUTCHER KILL SLAY BUTCH SPOIL
BUNGLE KIDDER LEGGER LEMMER
MURDER VENDOR BOTCHER
BRAINER BRITTEN FLESHER
MEATMAN PORKMAN KILLCALF
PIGSTICK SLAUGHTER
BUTCHERBIRD SHRIKE MATAGASSE
BUTCHER'S-BROOM RUSCUS
BRUSCUS
BUTCHERY MURDER CARNAGE
MASSACRE SHAMBLES SLAUGHTER
BUTEO BUZZARD
BUTLER SOMLER YEOMAN BOTELER
SERVANT SPENCER STEWARD
CELLARER CONSUMAH KHANSAMA
STEPHANO MAJORDOMO
BUTT JUR JUT MOT PIT PUT RAM
RUN TOY TUP BUCK BUNT BURT
BUSH CART CASK DISH DOSS FOOL
GOAD GOAL GOAT HORN JOLT
JURR POLL PUCK PUSH STUB TANG
TOPE TURR BOUND HINGE JOINT
MOUND ROACH SCOPE STOCK
STUMP BREECH TARGET THRUST
BEEHIVE BUTTOCK PARAPET
PROJECT REVERSE STUMMEL
ARIETATE FLATFISH FLOUNDER
RIDICULE SACKBUTT
(— FOR RIDICULE) GAME SPORT
STALE COCKSHY
(— OF CIGAR) DOCK SNIPE
(— OF HORSEHIDE) SHELL
(— OF JOKE) JEST SCOGGIN
JESTWORD
(CIGARETTE —) BUMPER
(HALF —) BEND
BUTTE HILL PICACHO
BUTTER SHEA CLART COCUM
BAMBUK BEURRE CAJOLE SPREAD
BLARNEY FLATTER
(— MEASURE) SPAN
(ARTIFICIAL —) BOSH OLEO BOSCH
MARGARINE
(BROWNED IN —) NOISETTE
(SEMIFLUID —) GHI GHEE
BUTTER-AND-EGGS RANSTEAD
TOADFLAX
BUTTERBUR CLEAT CLOTE ELDIN
GALON GALLON OXWORT GILTCUP
FLEADOCK
BUTTERCUP BOLT CYME CRAZY
ANEMONE CRAISEY CROWTOE
GILTCUP GOLDCUP KINGCOB
KINGCUP CRAWFOOT CROWFOOT
FROGWORT
BUTTERFISH GUNNEL POMPANO
WHITING PALOMETA SKIPJACK
BUTTERFLY IO BLUE ARGUS ELFIN
GHOST NYMPH QUEEN SATYR SWIFT
WHITE ZEBRA ALPINE APOLLO
CALIGO COPPER DANAID HOPPER
IDALIA JUGATE MORPHO PIERID
PROGNE SULFUR THECLA URSULA
VIOLET YELLOW ADMIRAL BUCKEYE
DIURNAL DOLPHIN EMPEROR

FRENATE MONARCH PIERINE
SATYRID SKIPPER SULPHUR
TUSSOCK VANESSA VICEROY
ARTHEMIS CECROPIA CRESCENT
GRAYLING HESPERID ITHOMIID
WANDERER
(— BREEDER) AURELIAN
BUTTERFLY FISH MOJARRA
FLATFISH
BUTTERFLY WEED FLUXROOT
MILKWEED WINDROOT
BUTTERMILK WHIG JOCOQUE
SOURDOOK
BUTTERSCOTCH TOFFY
BUTTERWORT BEANWEED
SHEEPWEED
BUTTERY BOTRY LARDER SPENCE
BUTLERY SPICERY
BUTTOCKS ASS BUM CAN FUD HAM
ARSE BUTT CULE DOCK DOUP DUFF
LEND POOP SEAT TAIL TOBY CROUP
FANNY NATES SLATS STERN TOUTE
BEHIND BOTTOM BREECH CURPIN
HEINIE HINDER CROUPON CRUPPER
DRODDUM HURDIES KEISTER
BACKSIDE DERRIERE NATIFORM
BUTTON BUD ZIP BOSS CHIN DOME
HOOK KNOB KNOP SPUR TUFT
BADGE CATCH GLIDE OLIVE PEARL
PRILL BAUBLE BUCKLE GLIDER
SHINER TOGGLE TROCHE DEWDROP
HORNTIP KNICKER PRESSEL
REGULUS DOORBELL FASTENER
OLIVETTE
BUTTONBUSH BUCKBRUSH
SWAMPWOOD
BUTTONHOLE EYE LOOP SLIT
BUTTON SNAKEROOT LIATRIS
SAWWORT

BUTTONWOOD COTONIER
BUTTRESS NOSE PIER PILE PROP
SPUR STAY BRACE BRICK OUTCAST
OUTSHOT SUPPORT TAMBOUR
ABUTMENT
(— MEMBER) TIRE
BUTYL TETRYL
BUXOM MILD AMPLE JOLLY PLUMP
PRONE SONSY BLITHE CRUMBY
CRUMMY FLORID FODGEL HUMBLE
PLIANT SONSIE BOWERLY
BOUNCING FLEXIBLE OBEDIENT
OBLIGING YIELDING JUNOESQUE
BUY CHAP COFF COUP GAIN HAVE
SHOP SNIP TAKE BRIBE CLAIM
TRADE ABEGGE MARKET RANSOM
REDEEM SECURE ACQUIRE CHAFFER
PURCHASE
(— BACK) REPRISE
(— OFF) APPEASE
(— UP STOCKS) COVER
BUYER CHAP AGENT CATER BEGGER
EMPTOR PATRON VENDEE CHAPMAN
SHOPPER ACHATOUR CUSTOMER
PROSPECT
(— OF CLOTH) REDUBBER
BUYING ACATE ACHATE EMPTION
(— MANIA) ONIOMANIA
BUZZ HUM BURR CALL DASH HISS
HUSS HUZZ RING WHIR FANCY
FLING PHONE RUMOR BUMBLE
NOTION WHISPER
BUZZARD AURA FOOL HAWK PERN
BUTEO GLADE GLEDE HARPY
STOOP BEETLE CURLEW PREYER
STUPID PUDDOCK PUTTOCK
VULTURE BROMVOEL
BUZZER BEE BELL ALARM HOWLER
SIGNAL WHIZZER

BY A P X AB AT OF TO AGO BYE GIN
PAR PER TIL ABUT ANON INTO
NEAR PAST TILL APART ASIDE
CLOSE FORBY BESIDE TOWARD
BESIDES THROUGH
(— AND BY) BELIVE BIMEBY
(— FAR) EASILY
(— HEART) PERQUEIR
(— HOOK OR CROOK) HABNAB
(— MEANS OF) PER MOYENANT
(— NO MEANS) NA
(— REASON OF THIS) HEREAT
(— STEALTH) STOWLINS
(— SURPRISE) ABACK
(— THE DAY) PD
(— THE ORDER OF) O
(— THE WAY) APROPOS
(— THIS TIME) ALREADY
(— WAY OF) VIA
(GONE —) AGO PAST
(NEAR —) GIN
BY-BIDDER FUNK CAPPER PUFFER
BY-CHANNEL BAYOU BRANCH
BYCOKET ABACOT ABOCOCKET
BYGONE PAST YORE OLDEN BYPAST
FORMER ANCIENT ELAPSED
BACKWARD DEPARTED FOREPAST
PRETERIT
BYPASS JUMP SHUN AVOID BURKE
EVADE SHUNT CUTOFF DETOUR
CIRCUIT OUTFLANK
BYPATH LANE BYWAY UNDERWALK
BY-PRODUCT SCRAP SHORTS
EFFLUVIUM
BYWAY LANE PATH ALLEY BYPATH
BYWALK OUTWAY SIDEWAY
BYWORD AXIOM MOTTO BYNAME
DIVERB PHRASE SAYING NAYWORD
PROVERB NICKNAME REPROACH

C DO CEE DOH COCA CHARLIE
HUNDRED
CAAMA FOX ASSE SILVER
CAB FLY KAB TAXI ARABA ARANA
CABIN GHARRI CRAWLER HACKNEY
SHOWFUL TAXICAB COUPELET
MOTORCAB
(2-PONY —) KOSONG
(4-WHEELED —) BOUNDE BOUNDER
GROWLER
(HINDU —) JUDKA
(LOW-HUNG —) HERDIC
CABAL PLOT RING JUNTA PARTY
BRIGUE CLIQUE SCHEME SECRET
CHATTER CONSULT COUNCIL
DISPUTE FACTION TALKING
INTRIGUE
CABALISTIC MYSTIC
CABARET CAFE TAVERN
CABASSOU XENURUS
CABBAGE CAB CHOU CRIB KALE
WORT CROUT FILCH SAVOY STEAL
STOCK PECHAY PILFER TAILOR
BOWKAIL OXHEART PAKCHOI
PALMITO PURLOIN BORECOLE
COLEWORT CRUCIFER CULTIGEN
DRUMHEAD KOHLRABI KERGUELEN
(STUFFED —) HOLISHKES
(PL.) — WORTS
CABBAGE BARK ANGELIM ANGELIN
CABBAGE SOUP SHCHI STCHI
SHTCHEE
CABBAGE STALK CASTOCK
CABDRIVER HACK MUSH CABBY
CABMAN COCHER MUSHER
COCHERO HACKMAN
CABIN BOX CAB COT DEN HUT CAVE
CELL CREW SHED TILT BOOTH
CHOZA COACH CUDDY FELZE
HOVEL LODGE SHACK BOHAWN
CABANA CASITA LITTER REFUGE
SALOON SHANTY WIGWAM
BEDROOM BOUDOIR COTTAGE
HUDDOCK MUDSILL
(— ON SHIP'S DECK) TEXAS
(DOUBLE —) SADDLEBAG
(RUSS. LOG —) IZBA
CABINET BOX BUHL CASE FILE SINK
AMBRY BAHUT BOARD CABIN CHEST
BAFFLE BUREAU CLOSET ICEBOX
ALMIRAH BOUDOIR COMMODE
CONSOLE COUNCIL ETAGERE
FREEZER JUKEBOX WHATNOT
CELLARET CUPBOARD MINISTRY
SHOWCASE VARGUENO MONOCLEID
(FILING —) MORGUE
CABLE GUY TOW BOOM COAX CORD
FAST JUNK LINK ROPE STAY WIRE
CABLET GANGER STRAND TETHER
COAXIAL GUNLINE SKYLINE
CATENARY HIGHLINE TELEGRAM
(— WITH EYE AT EACH END) STRAP
(— WOUND) KECKLING
(CHAIN —) BOOM
(DERRICK —) BACKSTAY
(SPLICED —) SHOT
(SUSPENDED —) ROPEWAY
CABLE CAR TELFER TELPHER
CABLED RUDENTED

CABMAN IZVOZCHIK
CABOCHON CAB SHELL CARBUNCLE
CABOODLE KIT LOT CALABASH
CABOOSE CAB CAR VAN CRIB HACK
BUGGY CRUMMY GALLEY PALACE
BOUNCER COOKROOM DOGHOUSE
CABRILLA CONY GAPER GROUPER
CABSTAND HASARD HAZARD
CABUYA PITEIRA
CACAO BROMA COCOA ARRIBA
COCKER CRIOLLO FORASTERO
CACHARI BODA
CACHE BURY HIDE DEPOT STASH
STORE SCREEN CONCEAL DEPOSIT
TREASURE
CACHET SEAL STAMP WAFER
ESSENCE KONSEAL
CACIQUE BUNYAH CASSICAN
HANGNEST
CACKEREL MENDOLE
CACKLE CANK CONK CLACK LAUGH
BABBLE GABBLE GAGGLE GIGGLE
GOSSIP KECKLE TITTER CHACKLE
CHATTER SNICKER TWADDLE
LAUGHTER
CACKLING GOOSE GREASER
CACOMISTLE CIVET ARCTOID
RINGTAIL BASSARISK
CACOON SEGRA SEQUA
CACOPHONOUS HARSH RAUCOUS
JANGLING STRIDENT
CACTUS BLEO DILDO NOPAL
BAVOSO CARDON CEREUS CHAUTE
CHENDE CHINOA CHOLLA COCHAL
MESCAL PEYOTE PEYOTL TASAJO
AIRAMPO BISAGRE BISNAGA
SAGUARO ALICOCHE CHICHIPE
PITAHAYA XEROPHIL
(— FRUIT) MUYUSA
CAD CUR BOOR CHUM HEEL CHURL
MUCKER RASCAL ROTTER BOUNDER
DASTARD ASSISTANT
CADASTRAL UNIT YOKE
CADAVER BODY STIFF CORPSE
CARCASS SUBJECT SKELETON
CADAVEROUS PALE GAUNT LIVID
PALLID GHASTLY HAGGARD
CADDIE NACKET
CADDIS FLY DUN CADEW SEDGE
CADBIT
CADDISWORM PIPER
CADDO ADAI TEXAS EYEISH HAINAI
KICHAI HASINAI
CADE LAMB SOCK
CADENCE BEAT FALL IAMB LILT
PACE TONE CLOSE METER METRE
SOUND SWING THROB DACTYL
IAMBUS JINGLE RHYTHM BACCHIC
ANAPAEST CLAUSULA MOVEMENT
MEDIATION
CADENZA MELISMA BARIOLAGE
CADET SON DODO GOAT PLEBE
YOUTH EMBRYO JUNIOR SERGEANT
CADGE BEG BOT BUM TIE BIND
HAWK CARRY MOOCH PEDDLE
SPONGE SCROUNGE
CADGER BOT DEALER HAWKER
CARRIER PACKMAN SPONGER
HUCKSTER

CADGY KEDGY MERRY WANTON
AMOROUS LUSTFUL CHEERFUL
MIRTHFUL
CADMUS (DAUGHTER OF —) INO
AGAVE SEMELE AUTONOE
(FATHER OF —) AGENOR
(MOTHER OF —) TELEPHASSA
(SISTER OF —) EUROPA
(SON OF —) POLYDORUS
(WIFE OF —) HARMONIA
CADRE CORE FRAME
CADUCEUS WAND STAFF SCEPTER
SCEPTRE KERYKEION
CAECUM TYPHLON
CAESURA REST STOP BREAK PAUSE
INTERVAL DIAERESIS
CAFE BARROOM CABARET
ESTAMINET
(— AU LAIT) ALESAN
CAFE CREME SUEDE
CAFETERIA AUTOMAT
CAFFEINE THEIN THEINE
CAGAYAN IBANAG
CAGE BOX CAR GIG MEW PEN COOP
CORF CRIB GOAL BRAKE CAVEA
GRATE HUTCH AVIARY BASKET
BUCKET CHAPEL ENCAGE FLIGHT
PRISON CHANTRY CONFINE
ENCLOSE LANTERN SHELTER
TUMBREL TUMBRIL CARRIAGE
ELEVATOR IMPRISON LAVARIUM
RETAINER SCAFFOLD STRAINER
(— FOR HAWKS) MEW
(— FOR HENS) CAVEY CAVIE
(— OF MINE SHAFT) GIG
(— OF TRAM) CABIN
(BIRD —) AVIARY PINJRA VOLARY
BIRDCAGE
(FIRE —) CRESSET
(LOBSTER —) CORF CREEL
CAGED PENT CAPTIVE
CAGER ONSETTER
CAGEY CAGY WARY COONY
CAGMAG KEGMEG
CAGOT AGOTE
CAHITA YAQUI
CAHOT PITCHHOLE
CAIMAN CAYMAN JACARE
ALLIGATOR
CAINGANG COROADO AWEIKOMA
CORONADO
CAIRN MAN PIKE MOUND RAISE
GALGAL CATSTONE STONEMAN
CAIRNGORM MORION SMOKESTONE
CAISSON BOX PONT CAMEL CHEST
WAGON COFFER PONTON SAUCER
CAMAILE CHAMBER LACUNAR
PONTOON
CAITIFF BASE MEAN VILE COWARD
WICKED CAPTIVE COWARDLY
PRISONER WRETCHED
CAJOLE COG CON JIG COAX FLAM
FLUM PALP WORD CARNY CHEAT
CURRY DECOY FRAIK INGLE JOLLY
TEASE CARNEY DELUDE ENTICE
FRAISE HUMBUG WHILLY BEGUILE
FLATTER PALAVER SOOTHER
TWEEDLE WHEEDLE BLANDISH
CAJOLERY FRAIK SOOTH TAFFY

BUTTER FRAISE DAUBERY FLATTERY
CAKE BAR BUN NUT WIG BAKE BALL
FLAE FOOL LUMP MASS MOLE TART
ARVAL BATTY BLOCK BOXTY COOKY
CRUST CUPID FADGE KYAAK SCONE
SHIVE TORTE WAFER WEDGE
BARKLE CIMBAL COOKIE DAMPER
ECLAIR GATEAU HALLAH HARDEN
KICHEL KUCHEN NACKET PARKIN
PASTRY POPLIN SIMNEL TABLET
WASTEL ASHCAKE BANNOCK
BROWNIE CAKETTE CARAWAY
CROZZLE CRUMPET CUPCAKE
FAIRING GALETTE HOECAKE
MANCHET NUTCAKE OATCAKE
PANCAKE PLASTER POPADAM
CHRIMSEL CLAPCAKE KUGELHOF
MADELINE MARZIPAN SEEDCAKE
SOLIDIFY SOULCAKE TORTILLA
TURNPIKE
(— OF CLAY) PLATTEN
(— OF MEAL) DODGER
(— OF RUBBER) BISCUIT
(CREOLE RICE —) CALA
(FANCY —) SUNKET
(FLAT —) PLATE BUNUELO GALETTE
PLACENT CHRIMSEL
(FOURTH PART OF —) FARL FARLE
(FRIED —) WONDER CRULLER
DOUGHNUT
(GINGER —) BOLIVAR
(GRIDDLE —) LATKE FLIPPER
FRITTER FLAPJACK
(HOLIDAY —) SIMNEL
(HONEY —) LEKACH
(LAMB AND WHEAT —) KIBBE
KIBBEH
(LEAVENED —) BAP
(NEW YEAR'S —) HAGMENA
HOGMANAY
(OIL —) GRIT POONAC
(POTATO —) FADGE
(PRESS —) CACHAZA
(RUM —) BABA
(SEED —) WIG SEEDCAKE
(TEA —) LUNN SCONE
(THIN —) WAFER JUMBLE BANNOCK
TORTILLA
(YEAST —) KOJI
(PL.) AMSATH COLYBA
CAKED CLIT
CAKE PULLER KNOCKER
CALABA BIRMA GALBA
CALABASH GOURD CURUBA JICARA
CALABASH TREE JICARA HIGUERO
CALABOOSE JUG BRIG JAIL PRISON
CABOOSE BASTILLE
CALABUR TREE CAPULI CAPULIN
SILKWOOD
CALAMANCO MANKIE
CALAMINE CADMIA
CALAMITOUS BAD SAD DIRE EVIL
BLACK FATAL BITTER DISMAL
TRAGIC WOEFUL ADVERSE BALEFUL
DIREFUL HAPLESS RUINOUS
UNHAPPY UNLUCKY GRIEVOUS
TRAGICAL WRETCHED
CALAMITY ILL WOE BLOW DOOM
EVIL RUIN SLAP HYDRA STORM

WRACK MISERY ONCOME SORROW
EXTREME ACCIDENT DISASTER
DISTRESS FATALITY JUDGMENT
MISCHIEF
CALAMONDIN ORANGE CALAMANSI
CALAMUS PEN CANE REED QUILL
ACORUS RATTAN ROTANG
CALANGAY ABACAY COCKATOO
CALASH CALESA GALECHE
CALCANEUM FIBULARE
HYPOTARSUS
CALCAR OVEN SPUR FURNACE
CALCARIUM PREHALLUX
CALCEOLARIA FAGELIA IONIDIUM
CALCIFY CRETIFY
CALCINING BURNING
CALCINO MUSCADINE
CALCITE APHRITE CALCSPAR
ALABASTER ARGENTINE HISLOPITE
CALCIUM LIME
CALCIUM CARBONATE WHITING
DRIPSTONE
CALCULATE AIM SUM CALK CAST
PLAN RATE TELL COUNT FRAME
THINK CIPHER DESIGN EXPECT
FIGURE NUMBER RECKON ACCOUNT
AVERAGE CALLATE COMPUTE
PREPARE CONSIDER FORECAST
ESTIMATE
(— BY ASTROLOGY) ERECT
CALCULATED COLD
CALCULATING COLD WISE BRITTLE
CAUTIOUS
CALCULATION CARE SHARE
CALCUL ACCOUNT CAUTION
WORKING CALCULUS FORECAST
HINDCAST PRUDENCE
(PL.) FIGURES
CALCULATOR TABLE ABACUS
ABACIST SOROBAN CALCULER
COMPUTER ISOGRAPH
CALCULUS STONE UROLITH
ANALYSIS
CALDRON POT RED VAT LEAD
ALFET BOILER KELDER KETTLE
TRIPOD VESSEL CALDERA
CAULDRON
CALENDAR DIARY ALMANAC
CALENDS JOURNAL KALENDS
REGISTER SCHEDULE
(PL.) FASTI
CALENDER TABBY SCHREINER
CALENDERER CANROYER
SMOOTHER
CALENDS K KAL
CALF CA BOB BOX BOY LEG BUSS
DOLT VEAL VEAU BOBBY BOSSY
BUNCH DOGIE MOGGY PODDY
RANNY SOOKY YOUTH MUSCLE
VEALER WEANER BULCHIN FATLING
SLEEPER CALFLING
(LIKE A —) VITULINE
(PREMATURE —) SLINK
(UNBRANDED —) LONGEAR
SLEEPER
(YEARLING —) BUD DAIRT
(YOUNG —) DEACON
(PL.) CAURE
CALF'S-FOOT JELLY SULZE
FISNOGA

CALFSKIN COROVA VELLUM
GRASSER TULCHAN VEALSKIN
CALIBER BORE RANK DEGREE
TALENT ABILITY BREADTH COMPASS
QUALITY CAPACITY DIAMETER
(HIGH —) STATURE
CALIBRATED BRIX BEAUME BALLING
CALICHE CALCRETE TEPETATE
NITRATINE
CALICO BLAY PINTO SALLO CHINTZ
SALLOO CROYDON SPOTTED
GOLDFISH
CALICO ASTER WISEWEED
CALICOBACK STINKBUG
CALICO BASS CRAPPIE BACHELOR
CALICUT KOZHIKODE

CALIFORNIA
CAPITAL: SACRAMENTO
COLLEGE: MILLS POMONA
WHITTIER
COUNTY: INYO KERN MONO NAPA
YOLO YUBA MARIN MODOC
COLUSA LASSEN MERCED
PLACER PLUMAS SHASTA
SOLANO SONOMA SUTTER
TEHAMA TULARE ALAMEDA
VENTURA SISKIYOU CALAVERAS
INDIAN: HUPA POMO YANA YUKI
KAROK MAIDU MIWOK WAPPO
WIYOT YUROK PATWIN SHASTA
TOLOWA YOKUTS CHUMASH
LUISENO SALINAN SERRANO
DIEGUENO
LAKE: MONO SODA EAGLE OWENS
TAHOE SALTON TULARE
ALMANOR BERRYESSA
MOUNTAIN: MUIR LASSEN SHASTA
WHITNEY
NAME: ELDORADO
PARK: LASSEN SEQUOIA
YOSEMITE
PRESIDENT: NIXON
PRISON: ALCATRAZ
RIVER: EEL MAD PIT KERN OWENS
PUTAH STONY FEATHER
KLAMATH RUBICON TRINITY
SACRAMENTO
STATE BIRD: QUAIL
STATE FLOWER: POPPY
STATE NICKNAME: GOLDEN
STATE TREE: REDWOOD
TOWN: LODI AZUSA CHICO CHINO
INDIO BLYTHE CARMEL COVINA
EUREKA FRESNO LOMPOC
MERCED OXNARD POMONA
SONOMA TULARE ALAMEDA
BURBANK GARDENA NEEDLES
SALINAS VALLEJO VISALIA
ALTADENA BERKELEY
PASADENA REDLANDS
CUCAMONGA
UNIVERSITY: USC UCLA CALTECH
STANFORD

CALIPER JENNY ODDLEGS CALIPERS
CALIPH ABU ALI BEKR IMAM OMAR
CALIF OTHMAN ABBASID UMAYYAD
CALK JAG NAP COPY CORK FILL

STOP CAULK CLOSE HORSE ROUGH
CAREEN CALTROP CHINTZE
OCCLUDE SILENCE
CALKING OAKUM
CALL HO KA BAN BID CRY CUP DUB
HOY SAY SEE CITE COOP HAIL JERK
NAME NOTE PAGE PIST ROUP STOP
TERM TOOT YELL BEDUB CLAIM
CLEPE CLOCK ELECT HALLO HIGHT
HOLLA PHONE ROUSE SHOUT
SPEAK STYLE UTTER VISIT VOUCH
WAKEN YODEL ACCUSE APPEAL
AROUSE BECALL CHANGE DEMAND
HALLOA HALLOO INVITE INVOKE
MUSTER QUETHE SUMMON TEKIAH
TERUAH YELPER ACCLAIM ADDRESS
APPOINT BEHIGHT BETITLE COLLECT
COMMAND CONVENE CONVOKE
DECLARE ENTITLE IMPEACH INQUIRE
INSTYLE MOUNTEE WHISTLE
ANNOUNCE APPELATE ASSEMBLE
NOMINATE PROCLAIM VOCATION
(— A BET) STAY
(— ALOUD) COUNT
(— BACK) RECALL REVOKE
(— COARSELY) ROOP ROUP
(— DOWN) BRAWL DEVOCATE
IMPRECATE
(— FOR HELP) SOS
(— FOR HOGS) SOOK SOOEY
(— FOR) CRY TAKE CLAIM EXACT
DEMAND DESIRE COLLECT SOLICIT
(— FORTH) STIR EVOKE ELICIT
INDUCE INVOKE ATTRACT SUGGEST
(— HOUNDS) LIFT
(— IN ANGER) GREET
(— IN CHILDRENS' GAMES) FAN FEN
FIN VENTS
(— IN MARBLES) DUBS
(— INTO QUESTION) IMPUGN
(— LOUDLY) CRY HAIL ACCLAIM
(— MAN BY MAN) ARRAY
(— ON TELEPHONE) BUZZ
(— OUT) HAIL LURE ASCRY EVOKE
HALLO GOLLAR GOLLER HOLLER
HULLOO
(— TO ACCOUNT) AREASON
CONTROL
(— TO ARMS) ALARM ALARUM
RAPPEL
(— TO BELLBOY) FRONT
(— TO CAT) CHEET
(— TO COURT) ARRAIGN
(— TO COWS) SOOK COBOSS
SOOKIE
(— TO FOOD) SOSS
(— TO HORSE) HIE HUP WAY PROO
(— TO MIND) CITE MING RECORD
BETHINK REDOLLECT
(— TO PRAYER) AZAN
(— TO READINESS) ALERT
(— TO SPARROW) PHIPE PHIPPE
(— TO WITNESS) APPEAL
(— UPON) ASK SEE CITE GREDE
HALSE BECALL DEPOSE ENGAGE
SUMMON ADDRESS BESEECH
IMPLORE
(BIRD'S —) WEET
(BOATSWAIN'S —) WINDING

(BRIDGE —) DOUBLE
(BUGLE —) POST HALLALI STABLES
(CLOSE —) TOUCH
(DUCK —) SQUAWKER
(FRIENDLY —) CEILIDH
(HUNTING —) RECHATE RECHEAT
(MORNING —) MATIN
(NAUTICAL —) AHOY
(SHEPHERD'S —) OVEY
(SPORTSMAN'S —) HOICKS YOICKS
HALLALI
(SQUARE DANCE —) GEE HAW
(STAGE TRUMPET —) SENNET
SINNET
(TRUMPET —) BERLOQUE
CALLA LILY DRAGON MAYFLOWER
CALLBOY FRONT CALLER HALLBOY
CALLER FLOORMAN
CALLIGRAPHER PENMAN WRITER
COPYIST ENGROSSER
CALLIGRAPHY LETTERING
CHIROGRAPHY
CALLING ART JOB WAY CALL HAIL
RANK TRADE CAREER METIER
NAMING OUTCRY MISSION MYSTERY
PURSUIT STATION SUMMONS
WARNING BUSINESS FUNCTION
POSITION SHOUTING VOCATION
CALLIOPE (FATHER OF —) JUPITER
(MOTHER OF —) MNEMOSYNE
(SON OF —) ORPHEUS
CALLIRRHOE (FATHER OF —)
OCEANUS
(HUSBAND OF —) TROS ALCMEON
(SON OF —) ILUS GANYMEDE
ASSARACUS
CALLISTO (FATHER OF —) LYCAON
(SON OF —) ARCAS
CALLITHRIX HAPALE JACCHUS
CALLOP YELLOWBELLY
CALLOSAL TRABAL
CALLOSITY SEG CALLUS SITFAST
TYLOSIS CHESTNUT
CALLOUS HARD HORNY TOUGH
BRAWNY OBTUSE SEARED TORPID
WAUKIT DEDOLENT OBDURATE
CALLOUSED BRAWNY
CALLOW BALD BARE CRUDE GREEN
SQUAB MARSHY IMMATURE
UNFORMED YOUTHFUL
CALLUS SEG POROMA TYLOMA
CALLOUS
CALM LAY LEE COOL DILL EASY
EVEN FAIR FLAT HUSH LOWN LULL
MEES MILD REST SOFT STAY ABATE
ALLAY CHARM LEVEL LITHE LOUND
MEASE PEACE QUELL QUIET SMOLT
SOBER STILL STOIC STREW DOCILE
GENTLE GLASSY IRENIC PACIFY
PLACID SEDATE SERENE SETTLE
SLATCH SLIGHT SMOOTH SOOTHE
STEADY APPEASE ASSUAGE
CALMATO COMPOSE GLACIAL
HALCYON MOLLIFY PACIFIC PATIENT
PLACATE QUALIFY QUIETEN
RESTFUL UNMOVED CALMNESS
COMPOSED DECOROUS PEACEFUL
PLACABLE RESTRAIN SERENITY
TRANQUIL UNRUFFLE

(INTERNAL —) HARMONY
(NOT —) BOISTEROUS
CALMLY COOLY COOLLY STILLY
CALMNESS CALM LULL POISE
PHLEGM REPOSE SERENE ATARAXY
COOLNESS SERENITY STILLNESS
CALNO KULLANI
CALOMEL TURPETH
CALORIC THERMOGEN
CALORIE THERM THERME
CALQUE LOANSHIFT
CALTROP CROWTOE GALTRAP
BULLHEAD CROWFOOT
CALUMNIATE BLOT SLUR TEEN
BELIE LIBEL ACCUSE ATTACK
BEFOUL DEFAME MALIGN REVILE
VILIFY ASPERSE BLACKEN SLANDER
TRADUCE
CALUMNIATION SATIRE ASPERSION
CALUMNY SLUR DEPRAVE OBLOQUY
CALVA CALOTTE SINCIPUT
CALVARIA SKULLCAP
CALVARY GOLGOTHA
CALVE FRESHEN
CALVINIST GENEVAN GOMARIAN
CALYCULUS CELL CALYX
CALYPTER ALULA SQUAMA
CALYPTRA CAP VEIL EPIGONIUM
CALYX CUP POP HULL HUSK LEAF
CULOT SEPAL SHUCK
CAM COG AWRY LOBE TRIG ASKEW
CATCH SNAIL WIPER LIFTER TAPPET
CROOKED TRIPPET KNOCKOFF
PERVERSE ROLLBACK
CAMACHILE INGA HUAMUCHIL
CAMAGON MABOLO
CAMAS LOBELIA
CAMBER SET ARCH SWEEP
ROUNDUP CROSSFALL

CAMBODIA

CAPE: SAMIT
CAPITAL: PNOMPENH PHNOMPENH
COIN: RIEL PUTTAN PIASTER
GULF: SIAM
LAKE: TONLESAP
MOUNTAIN: PAN AURAL
MOUNTAINS: DANGREK
CARDAMOM ELEPHANT
NAME: CAMBOJA CAMBODGE
NATIVE: CHAM KHMER
RIVER: SAN SEN BASSAC MEKONG
PORONG SREPOK SEKHONG
TONLESAP
RUINS: ANGKORWAT
TOWN: REAM TAKEO KAMPOT
KRATIE PURSAT KOHNIEH
KRACHEH ROVIENG SAMRONG
PNOMPENH SISOPHON
WEIGHT: MACE TAEL

CAME BAND CALM
CAMEL COLT OONT DELOUL
DROMED FENDER HAGEEN MEHARI
CAISSON TYLOPOD BACTRIAN
RUMINANT DROMEDARY
CAMEL GRASS SCHOENANTH
CAMELLIA JAPONICA
CAMEL LIP CHILOMA

CAMELOPARD GIRAFFE
CAMEO GEM GAMAHE CAMAIEU
 CARVING PHALERA RELIEVO
 ANAGLYPH
CAMERA KINO KODAK CHAMBER
 MINICAM PANORAM ENLARGER
 MINIATURE VERASCOPE
 (— TUBE) VIDICON
CAMERAMAN LENSMAN
CAMEROON (CAPITAL OF —)
 YAOUNDE
 (RIVER OF —) DJA NYONG SANAGA
 (TOWN OF —) POLI YOKO BAFIA
 DOUALA
CAMISOLE WAISTCOAT
CAMLET MOHAIR BARRACAN
CAMOMILE OXEYE MORGAN
CAMOUFLAGE FAKE HIDE DAZZLE
 MUFFLE SCREEN CONCEAL
 DISGUISE
CAMOUFLET STIFLER
CAMP TAN PEST TENT DOUAR ETAPE
 HORDE SIEGE TABOR CASTLE
 LAAGER SUGARY BIVOUAC
 HUTMENT LODGING MAHALLA
 PALANKA ZAREEBA QUARTERS
 (— OUT) MAROON OUTLIE
 (HOBO —) JUNGLE
 (LUMBER —) CHANTIER
CAMPA ANDA ANDI ANTI
CAMPAIGN BLITZ DRIVE PLAIN
 WHOOP CANVASS CRUSADE
 JOURNEY SERVICE SOLICIT
 WARFARE
CAMPANA GUTTA
CAMPANERO COTINGA ARAPUNGA
 BELLBIRD COTINGID
CAMPANILE TOWER BELFRY
 CLOCHER STEEPLE CARILLON
CAMPESTRAL AGRARIAN
CAMPHOR ASARONE BORNEOL
 MENTHOL
 (ANISE —) ANETHOLE
CAMPHOR TREE KADUR KAPOR
CAMPING BIVOUAC
CAMPION ROBIN COWBELL
CAMPUS GATE QUAD YARD FIELD
CAN CUP JUG MAY MOW POT TIN
 ABLE FIRE JAIL BILLY CADDY
 COULD ESHIN OILER SHALL SKILL
 BOTTLE VESSEL ABILITY BOMBARD
 CANIKIN CAPABLE CREAMER
 DISMISS GROWLER PIPETTE
 BILLYCAN CONSERVE PRESERVE
 (— FOR LIQUOR) JACK
 (— ON WHEELS) DANDY
 (BULGED —) SWELL FLIPPER
 (DEFECTIVE —) SPRINGER
 (LEAKY —) LEAKER
 (MILK —) CHURN
 (TIN —) DESTROYER
 (TRASH —) DUSTBIN
CANAANITE ARKITE HIVITE AMORITE
 HIVVITE JEBUSITE
CANACE (BROTHER OF —)
 MACAREUS
 (FATHER OF —) AEOLUS
 (MOTHER OF —) ENARETE
 (SON OF —) TRIOPAS

CANADA
BAY: JAMES HUDSON UNGAVA
 GEORGIAN
CAPITAL: OTTAWA
INDIAN: CREE COMOX HAIDA
 NISKA SARSI STALO MICMAC
 NAHANE NOOTKA SARCEE
 CARRIER NANAIMO SEKANEE
 SHUSWAP SONGISH TAHLTAN
 ALGONKIN COWICHON LILLOOET
 MALECITE SQUAMISH TSATTINE
ISLAND: READ BANKS BYLOT
 COATS DEVON SABLE BAFFIN
 MANSEL VICTORIA ANTICOSTI
 VANCOUVER
ISLANDS: PARRY BELCHER
 BATHURST MAGDALEN
LAKE: BEAR CREE GARRY RAINY
 SLAVE LOUISE SIMCOE ABITIBI
 DUBAWNT NIPIGON KOOTENAY
 OKANAGAN NIPISSING
MEASURE: MINOT PERCH ARPENT
 CHAINON
MOUNTAIN: LOGAN ROYAL
 ROBSON TREMBLANT
MOUNTAIN RANGE: SKEENA
 CARIBOO STELIAS COLUMBIA
 LAURENTIAN
NATIVE: CANUCK
PARK: YOHO BANFF ACADIA
 JASPER
PENINSULA: GASPE BOOTHIA
 MELVILLE
PROVINCE: QUEBEC ALBERTA
 ONTARIO MANITOBA
 NOVASCOTIA NEWFOUNDLAND
 NEWBRUNSWICK SASKATCHEWAN
PROVINCIAL CAPITAL: QUEBEC
 REGINA STJOHN HALIFAX
 TORONTO EDMONTON VICTORIA
 WINNIPEG CHARLOTTETOWN
RIVER: HAY RED BACK PEEL
 PEACE SLAVE YUKON FRASER
 NELSON OTTAWA SKEENA
 THELON PETAWAWA SAGUENAY
 MACKENZIE RICHELIEU
STRAIT: CABOT DEASE HECATE
 HUDSON GEORGIA
SYMBOL: MAPLELEAF
TERRITORY: YUKON
TOWN: HULL BANFF LAVAL
 GUELPH OSHAWA REGINA
 SARNIA CALGARY HALIFAX
 MONCTON NANAIMO SUDBURY
 TORONTO WELLAND WINDSOR
 KINGSTON MONTREAL VICTORIA
 WINNIPEG SASKATOON
 VANCOUVER
UNIVERSITY: MCGILL DALHOUSIE

CANADA BLUEBERRY SOURTOP
CANADA GOOSE HONKER BUSTARD
 OUTARDE
CANADA JAY MEATBIRD MOOSEBIRD
CANADA LYNX PISHU LUCIVEE
CANADA PLUM CHENEY
CANADA VIOLET JUNEFLOWER

CANADIAN CANUCK
CANAILLE MOB FLOUR RABBLE
 DOGGERY RIFFRAFF
CANAL CUT CANO DUCT LODE PIPE
 SHAT TUBE BAYOU DITCH DRAIN
 FOSSA GRAFF KLONG SCALA ZANJA
 ESTERO GROOVE KENNEL STRAIT
 TRENCH VAGINA ACEQUIA APHODUS
 CHANNEL CONDUIT FOREBAY
 RACEWAY SHIPWAY TOWPATH
 AQUEDUCT EMISSARY IRRIGANT
 MILLRACE PROSODUS VOLKMANN
 (— LABORER) NAVIGATOR
 (ALIMENTARY —) GUT ENTERON
 INTESTINE
 (ANATOMICAL —) SCALA MEATUS
 (CARINAL —) LACUNA
CANARD DUCK HOAX RUMOR
 GRAPEVINE
CANARY DICKY FRILL LIZARD
 ROLLER CAYENNE CHOPPER
 JONQUIL SQUEALER
 (— HYBRID) MULE

CANARY ISLANDS
CAPITAL: SANTACRUZ
ISLAND: ROCA CLARA FERRO
 LOBOS PALMA ROCCA GOMERA
 HIERRO INFERNO GRACIOSA
 TENERIFE LANZAROTTE
MEASURE: FANEGADA
MOUNTAIN: TEYDE LACRUZ
 ELCUMBRE TENERIFE
PROVINCE: LASPALMAS
TOWN: LAGUNA ARRECIFE
 VALVERDE

CANARY MOSS CORKIR
CANASTA SAMBA BOLIVIA
CANCEL BLOT DASH DELE OMIT
 UNDO VENT WIPE ANNUL BELAY
 CROSS ERASE QUASH REMIT SCORE
 SCRUB DELETE EFFACE KILLER
 RECALL REMOVE REVOKE STROKE
 ABOLISH DESTROY EXPUNGE
 NULLIFY RESCIND RETRACT
 SCRATCH SUBLATE UNWRITE
 ABROGATE
CANCELER BUMPER STAMPER
CANCELLATION GRID CANCEL
 REVOKE SURRENDER
CANCER WOLF KASHYAPA
CANCERWORT FLUELLIN
CANDAREEN FAN FEN
CANDELABRUM PHAROS MENORAH
 GIRANDOLE
CANDID FAIR JUST OPEN PURE
 BLUNT CLEAR FRANK NAIVE PLAIN
 HONEST ARTLESS JANNOCK
 SINCERE EVENDOWN INNOCENT
 SPLENDID STRAIGHT
CANDIDATE LEGACY ESQUIRE
 NOMINEE ASPIRANT GRADUAND
 PROSPECT
CANDIED GLACE
CANDLE DIP WAX GLIM SIZE SLUT
 LIGHT SPERM TAPER TOLLY BOUGIE
 CIERGE MORTAR PLANET SHAMUS

SLUSHY TALLOW TORTIS CANDELA
PERCHER PRICKET
(IMITATION —) JUDAS
(SQUARE —) QUARRIER
CANDLEFISH SKIL EULACHON
HOOLAKIN OOLACHAN SKILFISH
SABLEFISH
CANDLEHOLDER SPIDER
CANDLEMAKER CHANDLER
TALLOWER
CANDLEMAS TERM MARYMASS
CANDLENUT AMA LAMA BIABO
KUKUI IGUAPE KEMIRI LUMBANG
ABURAGIRI
CANDLESNUFFER DOUTER
CANDLESTAND TORCHERE
CANDLESTICK BUGIA DYKER JESSE
STICK CRUSIE LAMPAD MORTAR
SCONCE PASCHAL PRICKET
CHANDLER DICERION FLAMBEAU
STANDARD TRIKERION
CANDLEWICK MATCH SNAST
SHROUD
(CHARRED PART OF —) SNOT
SNUFF SNUFFING
CANDLEWOOD CIRIO OCOTILLO
TABANUCO
CANDOR PURITY FAIRNESS
KINDNESS INTEGRITY
CANDY DROP DUMP KISS PIPE ROCK
CREAM CRISP DULCE FUDGE GLACE
GUNDY LOLLY SPICE SQUIB SWEET
TAFFY BONBON COMFIT HUMBUG
NOGADA NOUGAT PATTIE PENIDE
BRITTLE CANDIEL CARAMEL
CONGEAL FLATTER FONDATE
GUMDROP SWEETEN SWEETIE
TORRONE ALPHENIG LOLLIPOP
STICKJAW
(PL.) CUTS CONFETTI
CANDYTUFT CRUCIFER
(PL.) IBERIS
CANE ROD BEAT CRAB DART FLOG
PIPE REED STEM TUBE WAND WHIP
BIRCH GIBBY GUNDY LANCE STAFF
STICK SWISH TOLLY WADDY
BAMBOO JAMBEE KEBBIE PUNISH
RATTAN CALAMUS HICKORY
KIPPEEN MALACCA SCOURGE
STADDLE TICKLER WHANGEE
GIBSTAFF
(BLACK —) JAPAN
(END OF —) FRAZE
(SPLIT —) CANEWORK
CANELLA WHITEWOOD
CANELO CIXO
CANESCENT HOARY
CANFIELD KLONDIKE
CANICULA SIRIUS
CANINE CUR DOG FOX PUP FISC
TUSH WOLF DOGLY DOGLIKE
LANIARY
CANING RATTAN BIRCHING
CANISTEL TIES EGGFRUIT
CANNA ACHIRA GOLDBIRD
CANNABIS BHANG GANJA GUAZA
GUNJA HEMPWORT
(— TOPS) TAKROURI
CANNEL BONE FURCULE

CANNEL COAL AMPELITE
CANNER CANMAN TINNER
CANNIBAL WINDIGO LESTRIGON
THYESTEAN
CANNON BIT EAR GUN BASE SHOT
TUBE ASPIC CRACK MOYEN PIECE
SACRE SACRI SAKER SHANK SLING
THIEF BICORN CURTAL FALCON
FOWLER JINGAL LICORN MORTAR
POTGUN BASTARD BOMBARD
BULLDOG CHAMBER HANDGUN
LOMBARD MOYENNE ROBINET
SERPENT STINGER UNICORN
BASILISK CULVERIN HOWITZER
MURDERER OERLIKON ORDNANCE
SPITFIRE ZUMBOORUK
(— OF BELL) EAR
(CARRIAGE OF —) NADRIER
(DISCHARGE OF —) TIRE
(DUMMY —) QUAKER
CANNONBALL GUN PILL BULLET
GUNSTONE
CANNON BOSS TRUNNION
CANNON PLUG TAMPION
CANNOT CANT CANNA DONNA
DOWNA UNABLE
CANNY SLY COZY SNUG WARY WILY
WISE COONY LUCKY PAWKY QUIET
CLEVER FRUGAL GENTLE SHREWD
STEADY CAREFUL CUNNING
KNOWING PRUDENT QUIETLY
THRIFTY CAUTIOUS SKILLFUL
WATCHFUL
CANOE AMA KIAK LISI PAHI PROA
WAKA AOTEA ARAWA BANCA BIRCH
BONGO BUNGO CANKA KAYAK
KOLEK PRAHU SKIFF TONEE UMIAK
VINTA WAAPA BAIDAR BALLAM
BAROTO CORIAL CUNNER DUGOUT
OOMIAK PAOPAO PITPAN PUNGEY
TAINUI TROUGH ALMADIA BIDARKA
BUCKEYE CANADER CASCARA
CORACLE CURIARA CURRANE
HOROUTA LAKATOI PIRAGUA
PIROGUE BALANGAY BARANGAY
FALTBOAT FOLDBOAT MONOXYLE
TAKITUMU THAMAKAU TSUKUPIN
WOODSKIN
CANON FEN LAW CODE FUGA HYMN
LAUD LIST RULE SONG AXIOM
GORGE GULCH MODEL NODUS
TABLE TENET ACTION DECREE
GNOMON LIBRARY PRECEPT
STATUTE DECISION STAGIARY
STANDARD
(BODY OF —S) CHAPTER
CANONICAL CANONIC ACCEPTED
ORTHODOX
(NOT —) APOCHRYPHAL
CANOPY SKY CEIL COPE DAIS HOOD
TILT CHUPA CROWN HOVEL SHADE
STATE VAULT AWNING BUBBLE
CELURE ESTATE FINIAL GABLET
HUPPAH SHADOW TESTER CEILING
HEAVENS MARQUEE SHELTER
SPARVER BASILICA CIBORIUM
COVERING OVERWOOD PAVILION
SEMIANNA
(— ABOVE THRONE) STATE

(— FOR LIVESTOCK) HOVEL
(— OF ALTAR) CIBORIUM
(— OF HEAVEN) VAULT
(— OVER BROODER) HOVER
(BED —) TESTER SPARVER
(HEARSE —) MAJESTY
CANT TIP COAX HEEL LEAN LIST
NOOK SING TILT TURN ARGOT
BEVEL CHANT DRIFT FLASH HIELD
LINGO LUSTY MERRY NICHE PITCH
SHARE SLANG SLANT SLOPE WHINE
CAREEN CASTER CORNER INTONE
JARGON LIVELY PATOIS PATTER
SNIVEL AUCTION DIALECT INCLINE
PORTION SINGING WHEEDLE
CHEERFUL PRETENSE VIGOROUS
CANTABRIGIAN CANTAB
CAMBRIDGE
CANTALA MAGUEY
CANTANKEROUS ILL CURSED
CUSSED ORNERY KICKISH
CANKERED CONTRARY PERVERSE
CANTATA SERENATA VILLANCICO
CANTEEN BAR FLASK BAZAAR
CANTINA
CANTER JOG RUN GAIT LOPE PACE
RACK AUBIN ROGUE BEGGAR
WHINER SNUFFLER VAGABOND
CANTERBURY BELL MILKWORT
CAMPANULA
CANTICLE ODE HYMN LAUD SONG
CANTO ANTHEM CANTIC HIRMOS
BRAVURA
CANTILEVER LOOKOUT SEMIBEAM
CARTOUCHE
CANTING CANT PIOUS SNUFFLING
CANTO AIR FIT BOOK DUAN PACE
SONG VERSE MELODY PASSUS
CANTON ANGLE UNION CORNER
VOLOST PORTION QUARTER
SECTION DISTRICT DIVISION
(HALF —) ESQUIRE
CANTOR HAZAN HAZZAN SINGER
CHANTER CHAZZAN SOLOIST
PSALMIST
CANVAS FLY PAT DUCK GLUT PATA
SAIL TARP TENT TEWK CLOTH
COAST SCRIM TOILE VITRY BURLAP
LINING MUSLIN PICTURE POLDAVY
SCUTAGE DRABBLER PAINTING
VANDELAS
(— FOR CONVEYING GRAIN) APRON
(OLD CONDEMNED —) RUMBOWLINE
(RUBBERIZED —) TOSH
(STUFFED —) BOLSTER
(TARRED —) COAT
CANVASBACK CAN DIVER CHEVAL
DUCKER POCHARD BULLNECK
CANVASS BEAT CASE DRUM HAWK
POLL SIFT RANDY STUDY DEBATE
PEDDLE SEARCH AGITATE DISCUSS
EXAMINE SOLICIT TROUNCE
CAMPAIGN CONSIDER
CANVASSER AGENT POLLER
ROADMAN
CANYON CAJON CHASM GORGE
GULCH ARROYO CANADA RAVINE
CAOUTCHOUC RUBBER ELATERITE
CAP CUP FEZ HAT LID PAD POT TAJ

TAM TIP TOP ACME COIF CORK
COWL DINK DOME DOWD ETON
GAGE HOOD HURE JOAN KEEP KEPI
MATE SHOE SHOW TOPI BERET
BOINA BUSBY CHIEF COVER CROWN
EXCEL FANON GALEA HOUVE KULAH
MATCH MUTCH OUTDO PHANO
PUNCH SEIZE SHAKO TOPEE TRUMP
ARREST BARRAD BARRET BEANIE
BIGGIN BIRRUS BONNET CALPAC
CLIMAX COCKUP CORNET GALERA
HELMET HUBCAP JINNAH MOBCAP
PILEUS PINNER PRIMER PUZZLE
SUMMIT TABARD TURBAN ALOPEKE
BIRETTA CALOTTE CAMAURO
CAPITAL CEREVIS CHAPEAU
CHECHIA CLOSURE COMMODE
FERRULE FLATCAP FORAGER
HEADCAP OVERLIE OVERTOP
PERPLEX PETASOS PILLBOX PILLION
SOWBACK SURPASS THIMBLE
TURNCAP ACROSOME BALMORAL
BEARSKIN BYCOCKET CAPELINE
COONSKIN ELECTRIC FOLLOWER
HEADGEAR PHRYGIUM SKEWBACK
SKULLCAP SURPRISE TARBOOSH
(— FOR PILEDRIVER) PUNCH
(— OF FLAGSTAFF) TRUCK
(— OF FOAM) HOOD
(— OF PYXIDIUM) LID
(— OF WATCH) DOME CROWN
(BISHOP'S —) HURA HURE
(HUNTER'S —) MONTERA MONTERO
(ICE —) BRAE CALOTTE
(JESTER'S —) COXCOMB FOOLSCAP
(MILITARY —) KEPI BUSBY SHAKO
(MOUNTAIN —) SCALP
(PERCUSSION —) CAPSULE
(PERUVIAN —) CHULLO
(POPE'S —) CAMAURO
(ROOT —) CALYPTRA
(WOMAN'S —) CAUL DOWD JOAN
KELL MUTCH COMMODE VOLUPER
BIGGONET
(WOOLEN —) BOINA TOQUE TUQUE
CAPABILITY STROIL ABILITY
CONDUCT FACULTY POTENCY
CAPACITY
CAPABLE APT CAN FIT ABLE GOOD
ADEPT CAPAX FENDY TIGHT EXPERT
SKILLED POWERFUL
(— OF BEING DEFENDED) TENABLE
(— OF BEING DRAWN OUT) DUCTILE
(— OF BEING SEVERED) SEVTILE
(— OF BEING THROWN) MISSILE
(— OF BEING UTTERED) EFFABLE
(— OF FLYING) VOLANT
(— OF SUBMISSION) AMENABLE
(NORMALLY —) ABOUT
CAPACIOUS FULL SIDE WIDE AMPLE
BROAD LARGE ROOMY GOODLY
ROOMFUL CAPTIOUS ROOMSOME
SPACIOUS
CAPACITOR CONDENSER
CAPACITY BACK BENT BIND DISH
GIFT GIVE SIZE TURN BLAST FLAIR
FORCE KNACK MODEL POWER SKILL
SPACE AGENCY BOTTOM BURDEN
ENERGY ENGINE EXTENT GENIUS

MODULE SPREAD TALENT VOLUME
ABILITY CALIBER CALIBRE CONTENT
FACULTY FITNESS QUALITY
APTITUDE INSTINCT STRENGTH
INFLUENCE
(— FOR EATING) STROKE
(— FOR ENDURANCE) STAY
(— FOR HIGHER KNOWLEDGE)
INTELLECT
(— OF LATHE) SWING
(— OF SHIP) BURDEN
(CIVIL —) CAPUT
(INNATE —S) STAMINA
(INTELLECTUAL —) BROW
(LOAD-PULLING —) DRAFT DRAUGHT
(MENTAL —S) BELFRY
(SPECIAL —) KNACK
(UNIT OF —) MUD MUID LAGEN
KISHEN MEDIMNUS KILDERKIN
(UNLIMITED —) INFINITY
CAPANEUS (FATHER OF —)
HIPPONOUS BELLEROPHON
(SLAYER OF —) JUPITER
(WIFE OF —) EVADNE
CAPARISON DECK TRAP HOUSE
COVERING TRAPPING
CAPE RAS COPE GAPE HEAD HOOK
LOOK NECK NESS TANG WRIT
AMICE CAPPA CLOAK FICHU ORALE
POINT SAGUM STARE STOLE TALMA
BERTHA BYRRUS CABAAN CHAPEL
DOLMAN MANTLE SONTAG TABARD
TIPPET LEATHER MANTEEL
MOZETTA SALIENT TANJONG
VANDYKE CIRCULAR COLLARET
HEADLAND LAMBSKIN MANTILLA
PELERINE SEALSKIN RAINPROOF
(— OF STRAW) MINO
(BULLFIGHTER'S —) CAPA
(DRESSING —) TOILET
(FEATHER —) AHUULA
(HOODED —) HUKE DOMINO
(LACE OR SILK —) VISITE
(LOW —) TANG
(PAPAL —) FANO FANON FANUM
ORALE PHANO
(RAIN —) CAPOTE
CAPE ANTEATER AARDVARK
CAPE ARMADILLO PANGOLIN
CAPE GOOSEBERRY POHA
CAPE HEN STINKER STINKPOT
CAPELIN SMELT ICEFISH
CAPE PIGEON PINTADO
CAPE POLECAT ZORIL MUISHOND
CAPER HOP JET DIDO HOIT JUMP
LEAP ROMP SKIP SKIT ANTIC BRANK
DANCE FLING FLISK FRISK PRANK
SAUCE SHRUB CAVORT CURVET
FRISCO FROLIC GAMBOL GAMOND
PRANCE SPRING TITTUP VAGARY
CORSAIR COURANT FRISCAL
GAMBADO PRANKLE CAPRIOLE
MARIGOLD
(— ABOUT) FLING CAVORT
(SILLY —) SHINE
CAPER SPURGE CATEPUCE
CAPE TOWN BOVENLAND
CAPHITE KIST
CAPITAL CAP CASH CITY FUND

GOOD LIMA MAIN RARE SEAT BASIC
CHIEF FATAL GREAT MAJOR MONEY
MUANG STOCK VITAL DEADLY
HEADLY IMPOST LETTER LISBON
MORTAL PRIMAL UNCIAL WEALTH
CENTRAL CHATTEL DRESDEN
LEADING RADICAL SERIOUS
WEIGHTY CABECERA CATALLUM
CHAPITER DOSSERET SWINGING
(— OF HEAVEN) AMARAVATI
(— OF HELL) PANDEMONIUM
(GAMBLER'S —) STAKE
(INADEQUATE —) SHOESTRING
CAPITATUM MAGNUM
CAPITELLUM KNOP
CAPITOL STATEHOUSE
CAPITOLINE SATURNIAN
CAPITULATION MUNICH TREATY
CAPITULUM HEAD KNOP
ANTHODIUM
CAPOTE HOOD CAPPO CLOAK
BONNET MANTLE TOPPER
CAPPER CORKER SEALER STEERER
CAPPY TALLOWY
CAPRICE FAD TOY KINK MOOD WHIM
ANTIC BRAID CRANK FANCY FREAK
HUMOR QUIRK CHANGE MAGGOT
NOTION SPLEEN TEMPER VAGARY
WHIMSY BOUTADE CONCEIT
CROCHET IMPULSE TANTRUM
WHIMSEY
CAPRICIOUS DIZZY DODDY FLUKY
MOODY CHANCY FICKLE FITFUL
KITTLE PLATTY WANTON COMICAL
ERRATIC FLIGHTY MAGGOTY
MOONISH PEEVISH VAGRANT
WAYWARD EPISODAL FANCIFUL
FREAKISH HUMOROUS SKITTISH
UNSTEADY VARIABLE VOLATILE
CROTCHETY FANTASTIC VAGARIOUS
CAPRICIOUSNESS FREAK
CAPRICORN GOAT
CAPRIPEDE SATYR
CAPRYL RUTYL DECANOYL
CAPSHEAF CAP HOOD
CAPSICUM AJI PEPPER
(— SAUCE) TABASCO
CAPSID MIRID
CAPSIZE COUP KEEL PURL UPSET
WRONG OVERTURN
CAPSTAN CRAB DRUM DANDY HOIST
LEVER NIGGER CYLINDER WINDLASS
CAPSTONE LECH TOPSTONE
CAPSULE CAP POD URN BOLL CASE
CYST PILL SEED PEARL PERLE
SHELL THECA WAFER AMPULE
BARROW CACHET OOCYST SHEATH
AMPOULE EYEBALL OTOCYST
SEEDBOX SILIQUE VANILLA
PERICARP PYXIDIUM
CAPTAIN BO BOH BAAS HEAD JOAB
RAIS REIS BARAK CHIEF LEADER
MASTER NAAMAN SOTNIK CAPITAN
FOREMAN HEADMAN MANAGER
PATROON SKIPPER FLUELLEN
GOVERNOR
(— OF CAVALRY) RITMASTER
(— OF CRICKET TEAM) SKIPPER
(— OF CURLING TEAM) SKIP

(— OF PRIVATEER) CAPER
(— OF SHIP) WAFTER
(STRICT —) SUNDOWNER
CAPTION TITLE LEADER LEGEND
CUTLINE HEADING SUBHEAD
CITATION HEADLINE SUBTITLE
CAPTIOUS CRAFY TESTY CRAFTY
SEVERE CARPING CYNICAL FRETFUL
PEEVISH TETTISH ALLURING
CATCHING CAVILING CONTRARY
CRITICAL
CAPTIOUSLY TUTLY
CAPTIVATE WIN TAKE CATCH
CHARM ALLURE ENAMOR PLEASE
RAVISH SUBDUE ATTRACT BEWITCH
CAPTIVE CAPTURE ENCHANT
ENTHRALL OVERTAKE SURPRISE
CAPTIVATED EPRIS EPRISE CAPTIVE
CAPTIVATING TAKING KILLING
WINNING WINSOME CATCHING
CAPTIVE SLAVE DANIEL ENAMOR
THRALL BRISEIS CAITIFF PRISONER
CAPTIVITY BOND IRON CHAINS
DURESS BONDAGE SERFDOM
SLAVERY
CAPTOR TAKER VICTOR CATCHER
CAPTURE BAG COP FIX GET NAB
NET WIN FALL FANG GRAB HOOK
LAND PREY SNIB TAKE TRAP TREE
CARRY CATCH FORCE PRIZE PURSE
RAVEN SEIZE SWOOP ARREST
COLLAR CORRAL ENTRAP GOBBLE
OBTAIN PIRACY REDUCE TAKING
CAPTIVE LOWBELL SEIZURE
WINNING EXCHANGE SURPRISE
UNDERNIM
(— BACKGAMMON PIECE) HIT
(— BIRDS) TOODLE
(— GAME) SATCHEL
(— OF ALL PRIZES) SWEEP
(— TROUT) TICKLE
CAPUCHIN MONKEY CAY SAI
CEPID SAJOU WEEPER SAPAJOU
CAPULIN CEREZA
CAPYBARA CAVY CARPINCHO
CAR BOX BUS PIG AUTO BOGY BUNK
DOLL DRAG DUMP GRIP JEEP RATH
TRAM ZULU BOGEY COACH DINER
DUMMY GURRY HUTCH JIMMY
RATHA SEDAN STOCK TRAIN TRUCK
WRONG BASKET BOXCAR BUFFET
CHIPPY DINGEY DINGHY DUPLEX
HOPPER JIGGER JINGLE SALOON
SETOFF SMOKER TOURER
AWKWARD CARROCH CHARIOT
COMBINE FLATCAR FREEZER
GIRAFFE GONDOLA HANDCAR
SIDECAR TELPHER TRAILER
TROLLEY VEHICLE HORSECAR
OUTSIDER QUADRIGA ROADSTER
SINISTER
(— FOR TRAIN CREW) CABOOSE
(— ON RAIL) TROLLEY
(BAGGAGE —) BLIND
(COAL —) HUTCH JIMMY WAGON
WAGGON
(ELECTRIC —) TELFER TELPHER
(ELEVATOR —) CAB CAGE
(EMPTY —) EMPTY IDLER

(JAUNTING —) SIDECAR
(LOG —) BUNK
(LOW-WHEELED —) HUTCH TRUCKLE
(MINE —) SKIP LARRY BARNEY
GIRAFFE GUNBOAT
(MONORAIL —) GYROCAR
(OBSERVATION —) BUGGY
(POLICE —) CRUISER
(TROLLEY —) SHORT
(USED —) DOG
CARABAO BUFF BUFFALO
CARACAL GORKUN SYAGUSH
CARACARA HAWK CARANCHA
CHIMANGO
CARACOLE FRISK CAREER
CARADOC BALA CRADOCK
CARAFE CROFT BOTTLE
CARAGUATA CHAGUAR
CARAJURA CHICA
CARAMBOLA BLIMBING BALIMBING
CARAMEL BLACKJACK
CARAPA CRAB CRAPPO CRABWOOD
CARAPACE CRUST SHELL LORICA
SHIELD CALAPASH
CARAVAN VAN TREK TRIP FLEET
TRAIN CAFILA COFFLE CONVOY
SAFARI TRAVEL JOURNEY VEHICLE
CONDUCTA
CARAVANSARY INN CHAN KHAN
HOTEL SERAI ZAYAT HOSTEL
IMARET CHOULTRY HOSTELRY
SERAGLIO
CARAWAY CARVY UMBEL
CARBINE STEN DRAGON MUSKET
DRAGOON ESCOPET
CARBOHYDRATE SUGAR AMYLAN
GELOSE STARCH FUCOSAN GLUCIDE
CELLULIN DEXTRINE DEXTROSE
GLYCOGEN GRAMININ PENTOSAN
TRITICIN CELLULOSE
CARBON COAL COKE COPY SOOT
NORIT CRAYON DIAMOND REPLICA
CHARCOAL GRAPHITE SCHUNGITE
CARBONADO BORT BOART BOORT
CARBON
CARBONATE BURN CHAR FIZZ
AERATE ALKALI ENLIVEN ENERGIZER
CARBONER GASMAN
CARBONIZER PICKLER
CARBORUNDUM EMERY ABRASIVE
CARBUNCLE RUBY PYROPE
ANTHRAX CHARBOCLE
CARBURETOR CARB DIFFUSER
VAPORIZER
CARCASS BEEF BODY BOUK CASE
CULL BLOCK MUMMY CORPSE
CARRION
(— OF WHALE) CRANG KRANG
KRENG
CARD ACE MAP PAM WAG CLUB
COMB DRAW FACE FIVE FOUR JACK
KING MENU PLAN STOP BALOP
BLANK CARTE CHART CHECK DEUCE
DUMMY EIGHT ENTRY EQUAL FICHE
FLATS GREEN HEART JOKER LOSER
PIECE QUEEN SPADE STAMP STIFF
TAROT TEASE BENDER CARTEL
CONVEX FILLER KICKER KNIGHT
PIGEON READER SECOND TICKET

TOWSER BRAGGER BRISQUE
DIAMOND PROGRAM RELEASE
STARTER STOPPER TAROCCO
TRIUMPH BOOKMARK COMOQUER
DECKHEAD DRAWCARD SCHEDULE
SCRIBBLE SQUEEZER STRIPPER
TIMECARD
(— LAST IN BOX) HOCK HOCKELTY
(— WOOL) TUM ROVE
(3 —S IN SEQUENCE) TIERCE
FOURCHETTE
(3 ACE —S) CORONA
(3 FACE —S) GLEEK
(3 —S OF KIND) TRIO TRICON
PAIRIAL TRIPLET
(4 OF TRUMPS —) TIDDY
(5 FACE —S) BLAZE
(7, 8 AND 9 —S) VOIDS
(ACE OF CLUBS —) BASTA BASTO
MATADOR PUPPYFOOT
(ACE OF SPADES —) MATADOR
SPADILLE
(ACE OF TRUMPS —) TIB
(AVIATOR'S —) CARNET
(CLUB —) OAK
(COMPASS —) FLY ROSE
(DEAD —) SLEEPER
(DIAMOND —) PICK CARREAU
(DISCARDED —S) CRIB
(DRAWING —) BLOWOFF
(FARO —) SODA
(FOUR —) CATER QUATRE
(FOURTH —) CASE
(HIGHEST UNPAID —) COMMAND
(JOKER —) BRAGGER MISTIGRIS
(KING, QUEEN OR KNAVE —) COST
FACE
(KNAVE —) PAM TOM JACK BOWER
EQUES MAKER NODDY COQUIN
KNIGHT PICARO VARLET WENZEL
CUSTREL PEASANT VILLAIN
VARLETTO
(LAYOUT OF —S) TABLEAU
(LOW —) GUARD
(MARKED —) STAMP
(POSTAL —) COVER
(PULLING —S) TIRE
(QUEEN AND KNAVE —S) INTRIGO
INTRIGUE
(RUN OF —S) SEQUENCE
(SPADE —) PICK DIGGER
(STOCK —) TALON
(THIRD HIGHEST TRUMP —) BASTA
(THREE —) TREY THREE
(WILD —) FREAK
CARDAMOM KNOBWOOD
CARDBOARD CARD PALL BLANK
BOGUS CARTON BRISTOL
TAGBOARD
(TWO —S) SPHEROGRAPH
CARDER TOZER TEASER TUMMER
CARDIALGIA HEARTBURN
CARDIGAN CORGI FABRIC JACKET
WAMPUS SWEATER
CARDINAL MAIN BASIC CHIEF CLOAK
VITAL ALEPHA CLERIC DATARY
PRINCE RADICAL ALEFNULL
ALEFZERO CAMPEIUS
CARDINALATE PURPLE

CARDINAL BIRD CARNAL REDBIRD
REDLEGS GROSBEAK REDSHANK
CARDINAL FISH FUCINITA
ALFONCINO
CARDSHARP TRAMPOSO
CARDSHARPER GREEK SHARPER
SPIELER
CARE DO DOW HOW CARK CURE
DUTY FASH FRET HEED KEEP KEPE
MIND PASS RECK SOIN TEND TENT
WISH YEME COUNT GRIEF GUARD
NURSE PAINS SORGE TRUST
WORRY BURDEN CARIEN CHARGE
CUMBER DESIRE GRIEVE LAMENT
REGARD SORROW ANXIETY AUSPICE
CAUTION CHERISH CONCERN
CULTURE CUSTODY KEEPING
RESPECT RUNNING SCRUPLE
THOUGHT TUITION BUSINESS
PERIERGY TENDMENT
(— FOR ONESELF) BACH
(— FOR) KNOW MIND RECK TEND
WARD FORCE NURSE SAVOR
FATHER MATTER REGARD CHERISH
PROCURE
(— OF HOUSEHOLD) HUSBANDRY
(— OF LIVESTOCK) CHORE
(JUDICIOUS —) LEISURE
(WATCHFUL —) TENDANCE
CAREEN GIP CANT HEEL KEEL LIST
TILT VEER LURCH SLOPE SWIFT
INCLINE
CAREER RUN WAY LIFE ROAD
TRADE CHARGE COURSE GALLOP
CALLING PURSUIT
(MILITARY —) ARMS SERVICE
CAREFREE EASY FRANK HAPPY
DEGAGE HOLIDAY DEBONAIR
CAREFUL BUSY WARY CANNY
CHARY CLOSE EXACT HOOLY TENTY
CHOICE DAINTY EIDENT EYEFUL
FRUGAL NARROW TENDER ANXIOUS
CURIOUS ENVIOUS GUARDED
HEEDFUL PAINFUL PRUDENT
THRIFTY ACCURATE CAUTIOUS
CRITICAL DILIGENT DISCREET
DREADFUL GINGERLY MOURNFUL
PUNCTUAL TROUBLED VIGILANT
WATCHFUL
CAREFULLY HOOLY NARROW
CANNILY CHARILY TENTILY
CHOICELY GINGERLY
CARELESS LAX COOL EASY LASH
RASH SLACK CASUAL OVERLY
RAKISH REMISS SECURE SLOPPY
SUPINE UNTIDY UNWARY LANGUID
SLIGHTY UNCANNY HEEDLESS
LISTLESS MINDLESS RECKLESS
SLATTERN SLIPSHOD SLOVENLY
YEMELESS
CARELESSLY SLACK OVERLY
SLACKLY SLIGHTLY
CARELESSNESS LACHES LAXITY
INCAUTION
CARESS COY HUG PAT PET BILL
CLAP DAUT DAWT KISS MUCH NECK
INGLE NURSE CODDLE COSSET
FONDLE PAMPER STROKE CHERISH
EMBRACE FLATTER CANOODLE

CARETAKER KEEPER WARDER
JANITOR
CARGO BULK LAST LOAD BURDEN
LADING FREIGHT PACKAGE
PORTAGE CARGASON PROPERTY
SHIPLOAD SHIPMENT TRAFFICS
CARIAMA CHUNGA SERIEMA
CARIB GALIBI CALINAGO
CARIBBEAN (— GULF) DARIEN
HONDURAS
(— ISLAND GROUP) LEEWARD
ANTILLES WINDWARD
(— ISLAND) CUBA HAITI NASSAU
TOBAGO CURACAO GRENADA
JAMAICA DOMINICA
CARIBE PIRAI PIRANHA CHARACINE
CARIBOU STAG RANGIFER REINDEER
CARICATURE APE COPY MOCK SKIT
FARCE LIBEL MIMIC SQUIB OVERDO
PARODY SATIRE CARTOON
TRAVESTY BURLESQUE
CARILLONNEUR CAMPANIST
BELLMASTER
CARINA KEEL
CARMELITE EXTERN TERESIAN
CARMINATIVE GINGER CALAMUS
CAMPHOR VALERIAN
CARMINE RED LAKE CRIMSON
SCARLET
CARNAGE WAL MURDER POGROM
STRAGE BUTCHERY MASSACRE
BLOODSHED
CARNAL CROW LEWD GROSS
ANIMAL BODILY SEXUAL BESTIAL
BRUTISH EARTHLY FLESHLY
SECULAR SENSUAL WORLDLY
MATERILA PANDEMIC TEMPORAL
CARNATION JACK PINK FLAKE
BIZARRE PICOTEE DAYBREAK
DIANTHUS GRENADINE MALMAISON
CARNELIAN SARD COPPER
(BEAD OF —) ARANGO
CARNIVAL FETE SHOW CARNY
CANVAS APOKREA CANVASS
REVELRY FESTIVAL
CARNIVORE CAT DOG FOX BEAR
COON LION LYNX MINK PUMA SEAL
WOLF CIVET GENET HYENA OTTER
PANDA PEKAN RATEL SABLE STOAT
TIGER BADGER COUGAR ERMINE
FELINE FERRET FISHER FOUSSA
JACKAL JAGUAR MARTEN OCELOT
POSSUM SERVAL WEASEL DASYURE
GLUTTON LEOPARD MEERKAT
POLECAT RACCOON TIGRESS
MONGOOSE OPPOSSUM PREDACEAN
ZOOPHAGAN
CAROB HUSK LOCUST ALGAROBA
CAROL LAY NOEL SING SONG DITTY
YODEL WARBLE WASSAIL MADRIGAL
AGUINALDO
CAROLINA ALLSPICE SHRUB
**CAROLINE ISLANDS (— ISLAND
GROUP)** PALAU
(ISLAND OF —) YAP HALL PALU
TRUK PELEW PULAP OROLUK
PONAPE WOLEAI PELELIU
(TOWN OF —) LOT NIF RUNU
KOROR MUTOK TOMIL PONAPE

MALAKAL GARUSUUN
CAROLINGIAN KARLING
CAROM SHOT BOUNCE CANNON
GLANCE STRIKE REBOUND BILLIARD
CARAMBOLE
CAROUSAL GELL LARK ORGY RIOT
ROMP TOOT BINGE FEAST RANDY
REVEL ROUSE SPRAY SPREE
FROLIC SHINDY SPLORE BANQUET
CAROUSE REVELRY WASSAIL
DRINKING FESTIVAL JAMBOREE
CAROUSE JET BOUT HELL RANT
TOOT BIRLE BOUSE DRINK QUAFF
RANDY REVEL ROUSE SPREE TOAST
COURANT JOLLIFY WASSAIL
CAROUSAL
CAROUSER BACCHANAL
CAROUSING REVEL RAFFING
CARP KOI NAG BITE DRUM SING
SNAG TALK YERK CAVIL PINCH
PRATE SCOLD SPEAK CENSOR
NIBBLE RECITE CENSURE CHATTER
QUIBBLE COMPLAIN CYPRINID
GOLDFISH
(CRUCIAN —) GIBEL
(LAKE —) DRUM LAKER
CARPAL ACTINOST
CARPEL CARPID COCCUS MERICARP
CARPOPHYL
(PL.) CORE
CARPENTER ANT LOHAR FITTER
FRAMER HOUSER JOINER PINNER
WRIGHT BUILDER HOWSOUR
WOODMAN INDENTER TECTONIC
TIMBERER PITWRIGHT
(SHIP'S —) CHIPS
CARPENTRY WOODWORK WRIGHTRY
CARPER CRITIC
CARPET MAT RUG AGRA KALI KUBA
HERAT KILIM SARUK SCOLD SUMAK
TAPET TAPIS TEKKE USHAK AFGHAN
FLOSSA FRIEZE KASHAN KIDDER
KIRMAN LAVEHR NAMMAD RUNNER
SAROUK SAXONY SELJUK SMYRNA
TABRIZ VELVET WILTON DHURRIE
GIORDES HAMADAN INGRAIN
ISFAHAN ISPAHAN SHEMAKA
TEHERAN AKHISSAR AMRITSAR
BRUSSELS COVERING FOOTPACE
KARABAGH MOQUETTE TAPESTRY
TURCOMAN VENETIAN AXMINSTER
(HOLY —) KISWA
(PILELESS —) KILIM GELEEM
CARPETING FILLING
CARPET SHARK WOBBEGONG
CARPET SHELL EEROCK PULLET
CARPETWEED FICOID FICOIDAL
CARPING CRAB CAPTIOUS CAVILING
CRITICAL
CARPSUCKER QUILLBACK
CARPUS WRIST CARPOPODITE
CARRAGEEN KILLEEN
CARREL STALL CUBICLE
CARRIAGE AIR CAB CAR FLY GIG
RIG RUT SET VIS ARBA BIGA CART
CHAR DUKE EKKA GAIT GARB HACK
LOAD MIEN PORT RUTH SHAY TEAM
TRAP WYNN ARABA BANDY BRAKE
BREAK BRETT BUGGY CHAIR COACH

COUPE ESSED FRONT JUTKA MIDGE
PANEL POISE SADOO SETUP SULKY
TENUE TONGA TRUCK WAGON
BURDEN CALASH CHAISE CHARET
CISIUM CONVOY DENNET FIACRE
GHARRY GOCART HANSOM KOSONG
LANDAU MANNER MOTION PORTER
REMISE SADDLE SPIDER SURREY
TANDEM TELEGA TROIKA BAGGAGE
BEARING BERLINE BOUNDER
BRITSKA CALECHE CALESIN
CARAVAN CARIOLE CAROCHE
CHARIOT COACHEE CONDUCT
CROYDON DOGGART DOSADOS
DROSHKY FORECAR GESTURE
HACKMAN HACKNEY MINIBUS
PHAETON POSCHAY SHANDRY
SKYHOOK TALLYHO TARTANA
TILBURY TRANSIT TROLLEY
UNICORN VECTURE VEHICLE
VETTURA VOITURE VOLANTE
WAFTAGE BAROUCHE BEHAVIOR
BROUGHAM CARRYALL CLARENCE
CURRICLE DEARBORN DEMEANOR
DORMEUSE EQUIPAGE PORTANCE
PRESENCE ROCKAWAY SOCIABLE
STANHOPE TARANTAS TOURNURE
VICTORIA
(— OF HANDPRESS) COFFIN
(— OF HORSE) AIR
(AMMUNITION —) CAISSON
(ELEVATED —) LIFT
(INDIAN —) RUT EKKA BANDY
GHARRI GHARRY
(JAVANESE —) SADO SADOO
(LIVERY —) REMISE
(LOG —) DRAG
(PUBLIC —) FLY OMNIBUS
CARRIAGE HOUSE REMISE
CARRIER HOD BASE JEEP SHIP
TRAM BUGGY HAMAL KAHAR MACER
PLANE SABOT TAMEN TIGER BARKIS
BEARER CADGER COOLIE HAMMAL
HODMAN JAGGER PACKER PORTER
RUNNER TAILER WEASEL DRAYMAN
DROGHER FLATTOP POSTMAN
REMOVER TACULLI TROTTER
VEHICLE CARGADOR CARRYALL
PORTATOR RAILROAD TEAMSTER
SUBSTRATE
(COAL —) FLATIRON
(COLOR —) LUFIRIER
(ENDLESS —) TAILER
(FIRE —) PORTFIRE
(MAIL —) COURIER POSTMAN
(WATER —) BHISTI BHEESTY
CARRION KET VILE OFFAL CORPSE
HOODIE REFUSE ROTTEN CARCASS
CORRUPT DOGMEAT CROWBAIT
CARRION BIRD SCAVENGER
CARRION CROW DOWP HOODY
URUBU CORBIE HOODIE GERCROW
CARROT UMBEL CONIUM DAUCUS
CACHRYS SECRETE BUPLEVER
HILLTROT
(DEADLY —) DRIAS
(PERUVIAN —) ARRACACH
(PREPARED WITH —S) CRECY
CARROTING SECRETAGE

CARROUSEL RIDE WHIRLGIG
QUADRILLE
CARRY CAR HUG JAG LUG BEAR
BUCK CART DRAY FARE GEST HAVE
HOLD HUMP LEAD PACK PORT
SHOW TAKE TOTE TUMP BRING
BROOK CADGE CROSS FERRY
GESTE GUIDE POISE WALTZ WEIGH
BEHAVE CONVEY CONVOY DELATE
DEPORT DERIVE EXTEND COMPORT
CONDUCT CONTAIN ENTRAIN
PORTAGE PRODUCE SUPPORT
SUSTAIN UNDERGO BAJULATE
CONTINUE TRANSFER TRANSMIT
(— AWAY) FIRK DRAIN REAVE
SWEEP TRUSS ABLATE ASPORT
(— EFFIGY) GUY
(— FORWARD) EXTEND
(— IN OXCART) KURVEY
(— LIQUOR) BOOTLEG
(— OFF) HENT LIFE SACK FETCH
HEAVE RIFLE SCOUR SWOOP
ABDUCT ASPORT BRAZEN KIDNAP
SPIRIT
(— ON) DO RUN WAR HAVE LEAD
LEVY WAGE APPLY DRIVE ENSUE
FIGHT TRAIN CREATE DEMEAN
FOLLOW MANAGE OCCUPY
CONDUCT EXERCISE MAINTAIN
TRANSACT
(— ONESELF) HOLD
(— ONWARD) CONTINUE
(— OUT) DO ACT END GIVE LAST
HONOR AFFORD EFFECT ACHIEVE
EXECUTE FULFILL PERFORM
SATISFY
(— UPWARD) RAP ESCALATE
CARRYALL BUS CASE WAGON
CARRIAGE
CARRYING BURDEN GERENT
FRAUGHT
(— ON) GESTION
(— WEIGHT) EFFECTIVE
CART CAR POT RUT BUTT CHAR
COOP COUP DRAY HAUL JANG LEAD
LOAD PLOW PUTT RUTH TOTE WAIN
ARABA BANDY BOGEY BOGIE CADDY
CARRY DANDY DILLY DOLLY SULKY
TONGA TRUCK WAGON BARROW
CADDIE CHAISE CHARET CISIUM
CONVEY DOLLIE DUMPER GHARRI
GHARRY JIGGER JINKER KURUMA
LIMBER PLOUGH SPIDER CARRETA
CHARIOT DOGCART GUJERAT
HACKERY MORFREY SHALLOW
TROLLEY TRUNDLE TUMBLER
TUMBREL TUMBRIL VEHICLE
DUMPCART HANDCART PUSHCART
(— WITH TANK) TUMBLER
(2-PONY —) KOSONG
(2-WHEELED —) BANDY BUGGY
SULKY CARRETA TUMBREL
(3-WHEELED —) PORTER
(BULLOCK —) BANDY HACKERY
(COSTER'S —) TROLL
(COVERED —) JINGLE CARIOLE
(FARMER'S —) PUTT GAMBO
MORPHREY
(FREIGHT —) CARRETON

(LOG —) BUNK
(LUMBER —) GILL BUMMER
(MILKMAN'S —) PRAM
(OX —) RECKLA
(PARCELS —) FLY
(TIMBER —) CUTS
(TIP —) COOP COUP COUPE
(UNDERSLUNG —) FLOAT
CARTE MAP CARD LIST MENU CHART
CHARTER DIAGRAM
CARTE BLANCHE BLANK
CARTEL CARD DEFY PACT POOL
SHIP PAPER TRUST CORNER LETTER
TREATY CONTRACT SYNDICATE
CARTER CARMAN JAGGER LEADER
DRAYMAN LADEMAN TRUCKER
HORSEMAN TEAMSTER
CARTILAGE COPULA TISSUE
CRICOID EPIURAL GRISTLE RADIALE
STERNUM TARSALE THYROID
EPIPUBIS HYPOHYAL SESAMOID
TURBINAL
CARTILAGINOUS CHONDRIC
CARTOGRAPH MAP PLAT CHART
CARTOGRAPHER CHARTIST
CARTON BOX CASE SHELL
CARTOON EPURE ANIMATION
CARTOUCHE MESA OVAL DURANGO
CARTRIDGE
CARTRIDGE BAG CASE HULL BLANK
SHELL SHORT BULLET MAGNUM
PATRON CAPSULE TORPEDO
HANDLOAD SHOTSHELL
CARTULARY COUCHER
CARTWHEEL CLOGWHEEL
CARUCATE CARVE PLOWLAND
CARUNCLE COMB STROPHIOLE
CARVE CUT ALAY SIDE BEHEW
BREAK GRAVE KIRVE MINCE SHEAR
SPLAY SPOIL THIGH INCISE QUINSE
SCULPT THWITE TRENCH UNLACE
ENCHASE ENGRAIL ENGRAVE
DISJOINT MALAHACK SCULLION
(— A BIRD) WING
(— CHICKEN) FRUSH
(— GOOSE) REAR
(— HEN) SPOIL
(— PEACOCK) DISFIGURE
(— PLOVER) MINCE
(— SWAN) LIFT
CARVED CARVEN GLYPHIC INCISED
CARVER BODGER KIRVER CROPPER
FROSTER IVORIST CICELEUR
TRENCHER
CARVING CAMEO GLYPH IVORY
ENTAIL SCRIVE GLYPTIC MASKOID
NICKING INTAGLIO TRIPTYCH
CARYA HICORIA
CARYATID TELAMON CANEPHORA
(PART OF —) GAINE
CARYOCAR SOUARI
CARYOPHYLLUS JAMBOSA
CARYOPSIS SEED
CASCABEL POMMEL POMMELION
CASCADE LIN FALL LINN FORCE
SPOUT CATARACT
CASCARA BUCKTHORN WAHOO
SHITTIM

CASCARILLA CROTON GOATWEED SWEETWOOD

CASE BAG BOX CUP HAP LEG POD POT PYX BIND BOOT BUNK BURR CASK COPE DEED DESK DOCK DOME FILE PACK PAIR ROLL SUIT TICK BRACE BRIEF BULLA BURSE CADDY CASUS CAUSE CHAPE COVER CRATE EVENT FOLIO FOREL HUSSY HUTCH PRESS PYXIS SHELL STATE THECA THING TRIAL ACTION AFFAIR APPEAL BARREL BINDER BOXING CARTON CASING CELLAR CHANCE COFFIN COUPLE LOCKET LORICA MATTER PATRON PENNER PETARD POPPET QUIVER RIDDLE SHEATH SHRINE STATOR SURVEY TASHIE TWEEZE VALISE VANITY CABINET CAMISIA CAPCASE CAPSULE COUNTER CUSHION DIECASE ENCLOSE ENVELOP EXAMPLE GEARBOX HOLDALL HOLSTER HOUSING HUMIDOR INCLOSE LAWSUIT LUNETTE PACKAGE REMANET SATCHEL SHIPPER WARDIAN ACCIDENT ARGUMENT BOOKCASE CARRYALL CUPBOARD ENVELOPE EQUIPAGE EXEMPLAR GARDEVIN INSTANCE KNAPSACK PACKSACK PORTFIRE SHOWCASE SITUATED SOLANDER TANTALUS

(WICKER —) HASK BARROW HANAPER

(— CONTAINING ELEVATOR BELT) LEG

(— ENCLOSING CLOCK DIAL) HOOD

(— FOR CARDS) SHOE

(— FOR COMPASS) BINNACLE

(— FOR EXPLOSIVES) TRUNK

(— FOR JEWELS) TYE

(— FOR MOLD) COPE CHAPE

(— FOR MUMMY) SLEDGE

(— FOR PISTOL) HOLSTER

(— FOR PULLEY) BLOCK

(— FOR RIFLE) BOOT

(— FOR SEWING ITEMS) HUSSY

(— FOR TOOLS) TROUSSE

(— FOR TWEEZERS) BUBBLEBOW

(— FOR WRITING MATERIALS) STANDISH

(— IN WATCH) DOME BARREL

(— OF FLOUR BOLTER) HUTCH

(— OF VENETIAN BLIND) HEADBOX

(— OF) A

(— WITH COMPARTMENTS) RIDDLE

(BONY —) CARAPACE

(COSMETIC —) COMPACT

(COURT —) LAWSUIT

(EGG —) OVISAC OOTHECA

(FIREWORKS —) LANCE

(GRAMMATICAL —) DATIVE ESSIVE LATIVE ELATIVE FACTIVE ABLATIVE EQUATIVE ERGATIVE GENITIVE ILLATIVE LOCATIVE VOCATIVE

(HOPELESS —) GONER

(LUGGAGE —) IMPERIAL

(ORNAMENTAL —) ETUI

(PAPER —) COFFIN

(PILLOW —) SLIP

CASED BOUND

CASEMENT SASH LUKET WINDOW

CASHIER CASS CAST BREAK DEALER POTDAR PURSER CHECKER DISMISS

CASHIERED BROKEN DEGOMME

CASHMERE KASHMIR PRUNELL

CASH REGISTER DAMPER REGEST GREFFIER RECORDER REGISTER

CASING BODY BOOT BUNG CASE CURB HULL SHOE SKIN TIRE APRON BELLY DERMA EPHOD GAINE LINER ROUND STOCK TRUNK BOXING COFFIN COLLET JACKET KISHKE LINING SCROLL SHEATH VOLUTE FEEDBOX HOUSING MANHEAD OUTCASE STAVING THIMBLE CACHEPOT COVERING PLOWSHOE SHIRTING WHEELBOX

(— FOR BRAIN) HARNPAN

CASK KEG TUB TUN VAT BOSS BUTT CADE COWL DRUM KNAG PIPE RAPE RIER SLIP TREE WOOD ANKER BOWIE BULGE FOIST STAND UNION BARECA BARREL CARDEL CASQUE DOLIUM FIRKIN FOODER LONGER OCTAVE TIERCE WINGER BARRICO BREAKER FOSTELL RUNDLET SACKBUT CASSETTE HOGSHEAD PUNCHEON QUARDEEL ROUNDLET

(BREWING —) UNION

(LOCKED —) TANTALUS

(PERFORATED —) POT

(SMALL —) KEG TUB KNAG STOOP STOUP

(WINE —) FAT TUN BOSS BUTT PIPE TIERCE HOGSHEAD

(PL.) COOPERAGE

CASKET BOX PIX TYE CASE CASK CIST TILL TOME BUIST CHEST ACERRA CHASSE COFFER COFFIN SHRINE FOSTELL CASSETTE

CASQUE CASK HORN GALEA HELMET

CASSABANANA CURUBA

CASSANDRA (FATHER OF —) PRIAM

(HUSBAND OF —) AGAMEMNON

(MOTHER OF —) HECUBA

CASSAREEP CAXIRI

CASSAVA AIPI AIPIM YUCCA CASIRI CAZIBI MANIOC TAPIOCA

CASSEROLE TUREEN COCOTTE MARMITE TERRINE TZIMMES

CASSIA KEZIA SENNA SICKLEPOD

CASSIA FISTULA AMALTAS

CASSIMERE ZEPHYR

CASSITERITE TINSTONE

CASSITES KUSHSHU

CASSOCK GOWN SLOP VEST GIPPO PRIEST PELISSE SOUTANE ZIMARRA

CASSOWARY EMU MURUP MOORUP RATITE

CAST MEW PUT SET BILL DART HURL MOLD MOLT PICK SHED SLAT SLIP SPEW SWAK TINT TOSS TREE TURN WHAP WHOP WURP BLOCK BRAID CHUCK DEUCE DRIVE EJECT ERECT FLING FLIRT FOUND FUSIL HEAVE IMAGE KEIST PITCH SHADE SHOOT SLING STAMP THROW TINGE

COLLAR INJECT NOSING STRIKE STRIND THRILL AGARWAL CASHIER DEPOSIT DISCARD VIBRATE CASTLING CONSPECT OUTSLING POLYTYPE TINCTURE

(— A SPELL) TAKE HOODOO BESPELL BEWITCH FORSPEAK

(— ASIDE) DICE FLING

(— ASPERSIONS) SLUR SKLENT APPEACH

(— AWAY) DUMP SHOVE DEJECT REJECT

(— DICE) WHIRL

(— DISCREDIT) GLANCE

(— DOWN) DASH DUMP HURL SINK ABASE AMATE AMORT AWARP STREW ABJECT DECAST DEJECT DEMISS THRING ECLIPSE RUINATE DEJECTED

(— FORTH) SPEW SPUE WARP BELCH BRAID LAUNCH

(— GLOOM) DUSK CLOUD DARKEN DEPRESS

(— IN A MOLD) STRIKE

(— LOTS) CAVEL

(— METAL) YET

(— OF DICE) COUP DEUCE

(— OF HERRINGS) WARP

(— OF LANGUAGE) IDIOM

(— OF NET) SHOT SHOOT

(— OFF) DAFF JILT MOLT SHED DITCH LOSSE SHAKE SLUFF WAIVE CASTEN DEVEST REFUSE REJECT SLOUGH ABDICATE RENOUNCE

(— ON GROUND) TERRE

(— OUT) EGEST EJECT EXPEL BANISH ABANDON EXTRUDE OSTRACIZE

(— SHADOW) ADUMBRATE

(— UP) SUM LEVY UPBRAID

(FRESHLY —) GREEN

(PLASTER —) CUIRASS

CASTANET KNACKER KNOCKER SNAPPER TCHAPAN CROTALUM

CASTAWAY WAIF TRAMP CRUSOE REJECT OUTCAST DERELICT STRANDED

CASTE (OR CASTE MEMBER) DOM MEO AHIR BHAR BHAT GOLA JATI KOLI KORI MALI MINA PASI TELI BAGDI BANIA DHOBY GOALA IRAVA KAHAR KUMNI KUNBI KURMI LADHA LOHAR MAHAR PALLI PUGGI SAMAR SANSI SINGH SONAR SUDRA TANTI VARNA ARORAS BAIDYA BALIJA BANIAN BHANGI CHAMAR CHETTY CHUHRA DHANUK DHOBIE DOSADH DURZEE HOLEVA HOLIYA ILAVAN JAJMAN KALWAR KAMBOH KHATRI KUMHAR KURUBA LOHANA MADIGA NATION PALLAR PRABHU PULAYA PULIAN PURVOE RAJPUT VAISYA AGARWAL BRAHMAN BRAHMIN DHANGAR GADARIA HARIJAN KAYASTH KOMATRI KURUMBA NISHADA VELLALA KAMMALAN KHANDAIT PARAIYAN POVINDAH RAJBANSI VAKKALIGA

(LOWER —S) PANCHAMA

CASTER VIAL CRUET CRUSE PHIAL
CASTOR HORRAL HURLER MASTER
ROLLER FOUNDER PITCHER
TRUCKLE TRUNDLE
(SURF —) SQUIDDER

CASTIGATE LASH EMEND SCARE
SCORE BERATE PUNISH REVISE
STRAFE SUBDUE CANVASS
CENSURE CHASTEN CORRECT
LEATHER REPROVE CHASTISE
LAMBASTE FUSTIGATE

CASTIGATION HELL LASHING
DRESSING

CASTING DIE PIG CAST FONT KEEP
MOLD TYMP BLOCK CHOCK CHUCK
FOUND MOULD BILLET BUMPER
MATRIX MISRUN SPIDER COULAGE
DARTING SEGMENT SEPARATOR
(— LOTS) SORTITION
(— OF HOROSCOPE) APOTELESM
(— OVERBOARD) JETTISON
(PL.) SPRAY FOUNDRY

CAST IRON YETLING

CASTLE BURY FORT HALL KEEP
ROCK ROOK ABODE COURT MORRO
PIECE CASBAH BASTILE BOROUGH
CHATEAU CITADEL SCHLOSS
UDOLPHO BASTILLE CASTELET
CASTILLO FASTNESS FORTRESS
STAROSTY TINTAGEL
(— IN CHESS) JUEZ ROOK TOUR
JUDGE TOWER
(SMALL —) PEEL TOWER CASTLET
CHATELET

CASTOR BEAVER LEATHER TRUCKLE
TRUNDLE BARKSTONE
(— AND POLLUX) TWINS GEMINI
DIOSCURI

CASTOR-OIL PLANT KIKI MAMONA
PALMCRIST

CASTRATE CUT FIX GIB LIB GELD
GLIB SPAY SWIG TRIM ALTER
CAPON DESEX PRUNE STEER
CHANGE EUNUCH NEUTER EVIRATE
CAPONIZE MUTILATE SATURNIZE

CASTRATED CUT GIBBED UNPAVED

CASTRATO EUNUCH EVIRATO
TENORINO

CASUAL GLIB STRAY BLITHE
BYHAND CHANCE FOLKSY RANDOM
CASALTY CURSORY LEISURE
NATURAL OFFHAND RUNNING
GLANCING INFORMAL

CASUALTY LOSS DEATH CADUAC
CHANCE HAZARD INJURY MISHAP
ACCIDENT DISASTER

CASUARINA BEEFWOOD

CASUIST JESUIT

CAT GIB RAT SOW TAB CHAT EYRA
FLOG LION LYNX MISS PARD PUMA
PUSS CHAUS CIVET FELID GATOL
KITTY MANUL MEWER MOGGY
OUNCE PUSSY SMOKE TABBY TIGER
TILER WHITE ZIBET ANGORA
COUGAR FELINE JAGUAR KITTEN
KODKOD MALKIN MARGAY MAWKIN
MIAUER MOUSER MUSION NEUTER
OCELOT PAJERO PURRER SERVAL
TIBERT TORTIE BURMESE CARACAL

CATHEAD CATLING CHEETAH
KITLING KUICHUA LEOPARD
LINSANG PANTHER PERSIAN
SIAMESE TIGRESS WILDCAT
WRAWLER BAUDRONS DASYURID
FISSIPED PUSSYCAT RINGTAIL
(— CRY) WAW
(— GROUP) CLOWDER
(FEMALE —) QUEEN WHEENCAT
(MALE —) GIB TOM TOMCAT
(ROOF-PROWLING —) TILER

CATACHRESIS ABUSION

CATACLYSM FLOOD DELUGE
DEBACLE DISASTER UPHEAVAL

CATACOMB TOMB CRYPT VAULT
CEMETERY HYPOGEUM
(PL.) ARENARIAE

CATADROMOUS SEAGOING

CATALECTIC HEMIAMB TRUNCATED

CATALEPSY TRANCE SEIZURE
CATATONY

CATALOG PIE PYE BILL BOOK LIST
ROLL ROTA BRIEF CANON FLIER
FLYER INDEX PINAX AUTHOR
RAGGER RAGMAN RECORD ROSTER
ARRANGE BEADROW DIPTYCH
BEADROLL BULLETIN CALENDAR
CLASSIFY REGISTER SCHEDULE
CATALOGUE DIDASCALY INVENTORY

CATALUFA SCAD TORO BIGEYE

CATALYST CARRIER SAUSAGE
ZIEGLER CATALYTE HOPCALITE
(NEGATIVE —) INHIBITER

CATAMARAN RAFT TROW BALSA
FLOAT GUNBOAT JANGADA
MONITOR AUNTSARY

CATAMITE INGLE GUNSEL NINGLE
PATHIC BARDASH GANYMEDE

CATAMOUNT LYNX PUMA COUGAR

CATAPLASM POULTICE

CATAPULT GUN BIBLE SLING SWEEP
THROW HURTLE LAUNCH ONAGER
TREPAN ALACRAN BRICOLE
PEDRERO TORMENT TRABUCH
WARWOLF BALLISTA CROSSBOW
DONDAINE LAUNCHER MANGONEL
MARTINET SCORPION SPRINGAL
STONEBOW

CATARACT LIN FALL LINN FALLS
FLOOD PEARL DELUGE CASCADE
NIAGARA CATADUPE OVERFALL
VICTORIA

CATARRH MUR COLD MURR POSE
RHEUM CORYZA

CATASTROPHE ACCIDENT CALAMITY
DISASTER

CATCH BAG COB COP GET GIN KEP
NAB NET DRAW FANG GLOM HASP
HAUL HAWK HENT HOLD HOOK
LAND MAKE MEET MESS NAIL PAWL
SAVE SEAR SNAG SNAP SNIB STOP
TAKE TRAP TREE VANG CLASP
CLEEK CREEL FETCH GLOVE GRASP
HITCH KETCH KNACK LASSO LATCH
PLANT SEIZE SNARE SNICK SWOOP
TRICK TROLL ARREST ATTAIN
BUTTON CLUTCH CORNER CORRAL
DETECT DETENT ENGAGE ENMESH
ENTRAP IMMESH LOCKET NOBBLE

NOODLE SNATCH SPRENT TAIGLE
TAKING TURNEL ATTRACT CAPTURE
ENSNARE GIMMICK GRAPNEL
RELEASE SPRINGE TRIGGER
CONTRACT CRANNAGE ENTANGLE
FASTNESS HOLDBACK HOLDFAST
OVERTAKE SNAPHAAN SURPRISE
(— AT PROPER TIME) NICK
(— ATTENTION) FLAG
(— BIRDS) BATFOWL BIRDLIME
(— EELS) SNIGGLE
(— FIRE) SPUNK IGNITE KINDLE
(— FISH WITH HANDS) GUDDLE
GRABBLE HANDFAST
(— FISH) JAB JIG GILL HANG
GILLNET
(— IN VOICE) FETCH
(— OF DOOR) LATCH SNECK SNICK
(— OF FISH) FARE HAUL SHOT
TACK TRIP·SHACK
(— ONE'S BREATH) GASP CHINK
(— SIGHT OF) SPY ESPY SPOT
DESCRY
(RATCHET —) CLICK
(SAFETY —) CLEVIS

CATCHER TAKER BIRDER FANGER
LARKER RECEIVER

CATCHFLY SILENE FLYBANE

CATCHING CATCHY TAKING
ALLURING ARRESTING

CATCHPOLE BAILIFF PUTTOCK

CATCHWEED CLEAVERS

CATCHWORD CUE TAG MOTTO
BYWORD PHRASE SLOGAN STARTER
CATCHCRY

CATCHY CATCHING APPEALING

CATECHISM GUIDE MANUAL
CARRITCH QUESTIONS

CATECHU COTCH CUTCH KHAIR
GAMBIER

CATECHUMEN PUPIL AUDIENT
AUDITOR CONVERT BEGINNER
NEOPHYTE COMPETENT

CATEGORICAL DIRECT ABSOLUTE
EXPLICIT KNOCKDOWN

CATEGORIZE CODE HAVE

CATEGORY WAY KING RANK TALE
CLASS FIELD GENRE GENUS ORDER
STYLE FAMILY LEAGUE NUMBER
RUBRIC SERIES SPECIES DIVISION
(— OF TENSES) INFECTUM
(HIGHEST —) IDEA
(PRIMARY —) SUBSTANCE
(TAXONOMIC —) FORM FORMA
GENUS COHORT LEGION SUBCLASS
SUBGENUS SUBFAMILY

CATER CUT FEED HUMOR SERVE
TREAT PANDER PURVEY SUPPLY
PROVIDE

CATERER ACATER

CATERPILLAR CAT MUGA AWETO
ERUCA CANKER LOOPER PALMER
PORINA RISPER TAILOR WOUBIT
CUTWORM TRACTOR WEBWORM
HANGWORM HORNWORM SILKWORM
SKINWORM WORTWORM

CATERWAUL CRY WAIL MIAUL

CATFACE ARR SCAR

CATFISH MUD CUSK ELOD POUT

RAAD SHAL BAGRE DORAD RAASH
BARBER DOCMAC GLANIS GOONCH
GOUJON HASSAR MADTOM
BARBUDO CANDIRU COBBLER
FIDDLER PYGIDID SILURID WALLAGO
BULLHEAD BULLPOUT CORYDORA
FLATHEAD MATHEMEG PLOTOSID
SQUEAKER STONECAT

CATGUT THARM THAIRM CATLING
WHIPCORD

CATHARI BULGARI PATARINE

CATHARTIC ALOIN BRYONY PHYSIC
CALOMEL SCOURER EUONYMUS
EVACUANT HYDRAGOG KALADANA
LAPACTIC LAXATIVE SCAMMONY
SOLUTIVE SOLUTORY

CATHAYAN KITAN

CATHEDRA SEE

CATHEDRAL DOM SEE DUOMO
SOBOR MARTYRY MEMORIA
MINSTER BASILICA

CATHEXIS CHARGE

CATHODE K KA FILAMENT
ELECTRODE HYDROGODE

CATHOLIC BROAD GENERAL
LIBERAL TOLERANT

CATHOLICISM PAPISM POPERY

CATHOLICON PANACEA

CATKIN RAG TAG CHAT GULL AGLET
AMENT IULUS PUSSY CACHRYS
CATTAIL GOSLING

CATNIP NEP CATARIA CATMINT
CATWORT

CAT'S-CLAW LONGPOD ESCAMBRON

CAT'S CRADLE HEI

CAT'S-EAR GOSMORE CAPEWEED
FLATWEED

CAT'S EYE CHATOYANT

CAT'S-FOOT PUSSYTOE

CATTAIL DOD DODD FLAG MUSK
RUSH TULE AMENT BAYON BLECK
CLOUD RAUPO REREE WONGA
CATKIN GLADEN TOTORA BULRUSH
GLADDON MATREED BLACKCAP
CARBUNGI FLAXTAIL

CAT THYME HULWORT

CATTLE ZO BOW FEE GIR DHAN
GAUR KINE NEAT NOWT OXEN ZEBU
ZOBO DEVON STOCK ANKOLI
DURHAM GALYAK ONGOLE ROTHER
SINDHI SUSSEX BESTIAL NELLORE
REDPOLL COMPOUND OUTSIGHT
TUBICORN
(— CARRIED OFF) SPREATH
(BREED OF —) ANGUS BORAN
DEVON FJALL KERRY SANGA SANGU
ANGONI ANKOLI DEXTER DURHAM
FULANI JERSEY SUSSEX BAROTSE
BRAFORD BRAHMAN COASTER
CRIOLLA GUZERAT HARIANA
SAHIWAL ALDERNEY AYRSHIRE
CHARBRAY FRIBOURG FRIESIAN
GALLOWAY GUERNSEY HEREFORD
HOLSTEIN KANGAYAM LONGHORN
(DWARF —) NATA NIATA
(WILD YOUNG —) KANGAROO

CATTLE-BREEDER AHIR ALUR

CATTLE DEALER DROVER

CATTLEHIDE BUFF CROUPON

CATTLEMAN FAZENDEIRO

CATTLE MARKET SALEYARD

CATTLE PEN KRAAL

CATTLE RAID SPRAITH SPREAGH

CATTLE RUN STATION

CATTLE STEALER ABACTOR
ABIGEUS

CATTLE YARD CANCHA

CATTY KIN KATI

CAUCASIAN WHITE IRANIAN
EUROPEAN JAPHETIC PALEFACE
(— LANGUAGE) UDI UDIC UDIN
(PL.) MELANOI

CAUCHO ULE RUBBER

CAUDATA URODELA

CAUDEX STIPE

CAUGHT GRIPPIT ENTANGLED

CAUL HOW WEB KEEL KELL TRUG
VEIL GALEA HOUVE DORLOT
CREPINE KERCHER NETWORK
OMENTUM MEMBRANE SILLYHOW
TRESSOUR TRESSURE

CAULDRON KOHUA CALDRON

CAULICLE SCAPEL ROSTELLUM

CAULIFLOWER BROCCOLI
SNOWBALL CHOUFLEUR

CAULK CALK CORK FILL FLAG
CHINSE

CAUSAL GENETIC

CAUSE DO AIM GAR ISM KEY LET
WAY CASE CHAT FATE HOTI LEAD
MAKE MOVE ROOT SPUR SUIT
AGENT ARCHE BASIS BREED CAUSA
FRAME PARTY SKILL SLAKE WREAK
YIELD ADDICT CREATE EFFECT
ELICIT GOSSIP GROUND INDUCE
INVOKE MALADY MANNER MATTER
MOTIVE OBJECT ORIGIN PARENT
REASON RESORT SOURCE SPEECH
SPRING CHESOUN CONCERN
DISEASE LAWSUIT PROCURE
PRODUCE PROVOKE QUARREL
SUBJECT BUSINESS ENGENDER
GENERATE INSTANCE MOVEMENT
OCCASION WHEREFORE
(— A SORE) RANKLE
(— DAMAGE) DAMNIFY
(— FOR COMPLAINT) COMEBACK
(— OF RUIN) BANE
(— OF TERROR) AFFRIGHT
(— OF TROUBLE) TRACHLE
(— PAIN) URN
(— TO ARCH) ROACH
(— TO CONTRACT) PUCKER
(— TO CROUCH) COUCH
(— TO DESERT) DEFECT
(— TO END) ACHIEVE
(— TO MOVE RAPIDLY) GIG
(— TO PROJECT) JET
(— TO RESULT) ISSUE
(— TO STICK) MIRE
(— TO SWELL) BINGE EMBOSS
(— TO THICKEN) CURD
(FINAL —) END
(FORM-GIVING —) IDEA
(IMMEDIATE —) SIGNAL
(PRIMAL —) URGRUND

CAUSEWAY WAY DIKE ROAD
CHAUSSE HIGHWAY

CAUSTIC LYE ACID TART ACRID
QUICK SALTY SHARP SNELL BITING
BITTER SEVERE BURNING CAUTERY
CUTTING ERODENT MORDANT
NIPPING PUNGENT PYROTIC SATIRIC
ALKALINE DIERETIC SCATHING
SNAPPISH STINGING

CAUSTICITY ACRIMONY

CAUTERIZATION USTION INUSTION

CAUTERIZE BURN CHAR FIRE SEAR
BRAND INUST SINGE

CAUTION CARE FEAR HEED WARN
GUARD ADVICE CAUTEL CAVEAT
EXHORT ANXIETY COUNSEL
PRECEPT PROVISO WARNING
ADMONISH FORECAST FOREWARN
MONITION PRUDENCE WARINESS

CAUTIOUS SHY SAFE WARE WARY
ALERT CANNY CHARY SIKER FABIAN
HOOLIE SICKER TENDER TIPTOE
CAREFUL CURIOUS ENVIOUS
FEARFUL FERDFUL GUARDED
PRUDENT DISCREET SUSPENSE
VIGILANT

CAUTIOUSLY CANNY CANNILY
CHARILY EASYLIKE GINGERLY
TENDERLY

CAVALCADE RAID RIDE MARCH
TRAIN PARADE SAFARI COMPANY
JOURNEY PAGEANT

CAVALIER GAY CAVY CURT EASY
FINE BRAVE FRANK MOUNT RIDER
ESCORT KNIGHT BRUSQUE GALLANT
HAUGHTY OFFHAND SOLDIER
CAVALERO ROYALIST CHAMBERER
CHEVALIER COMMANDER

CAVALLA CERO JACK TORO ULUA
JUREL CARANX CARANGID
CREVALLE SCOMBRID

CAVALRY HORSE HEAVIES CHIVALRY
HORSEMEN YEOMANRY

CAVALRYMAN SOWAR SPAHI
SUWAR HUSSAR JINETE LANCER
ARGOLET COURIER DRAGOON
PLUNGER SABREUR TROOPER
GENDARME HORSEMAN STRADIOT
(PL.) FORAGERS

CAVE DEN TIP COVE HOLE LAIR MINE
REAR SINK TOSS WEEM ANTRE
CABIN CACHE CALVE CAVEA CRYPT
DELVE FOGOU SLADE SPEOS STORE
UPSET BEWARE CAVERN CAVITY
CELLAR DUGOUT GROTTO HOLLOW
LARDER LUSTER PANTRY PLUNGE
SHROUD MANSION RESERVE
SPELUNK CASTILLO COLLAPSE
OVERTURN MITHRAGUM
(— IN) COLT

CAVEAT BEWARE NOTICE CAUTION
WARNING

CAVE-DWELLER HORITE
TROGLODYTE

CAVE-DWELLING NATUFIAN

CAVEMAN NEANDERTHAL

CAVER SPELUNKER

CAVERN DEN CAVE COVE GROT
HOLE LAIR WEEM CROFT VAULT
ANTRUM CAVITY GROTTO HOLLOW
SPELUNK

CAVERNOUS ERECTILE

CAVESSON CHAIN

CAVETTO GULA GORGE

CAVIAR OVA ROE IKRA GARUM
IKARY

CAVIL CARK CARP HAFT HAGGLE
CAPTION CHICANE QUARREL
QUIBBLE PETTIFOG QUIDDITY
FORMALIZE

CAVILER CRITIC GIRDER HAFTER
ZOILUS

CAVILING CAPTIOUS CRITICAL
PICAYUNE

CAVITY BAG CUP PIT SAC ABRI AXIL
CASE CAVE CELL DALK DENT DUCT
HOLE MIND MINE VEIN VOID ABYSS
BOSOM BURSA CRYPT DRUSE
FOSSA GEODE GOUGE LUMEN
MOUTH ORBIT SCOOP SINUS
ANTRUM AREOLE ATRIUM AXILLA
BORING CAECUM CAMERA CAVERN
COELIA COELOM COTYLE CRATER
DEBLAI GROTTO HOLLOW LACUNA
POCKET SOCKET VACUUM VOMICA
ABDOMEN CHAMBER CISTERN
CYATHUS DIOCOEL KYATHOS
LOCULUS MORTISE VACUITY
VACUOLE VESICLE ALVEOLUS
BROODSAC EPICOELE FOLLICLE
WELLHOLE

(— IN BONE) LACUNA

(— IN CASTING) PIPE

(— IN HEAD OF WHALE) CASE

(— IN HILLSIDE) ABRI

(— IN MINE) BAG

(— MADE BY SEALS) IGLOO

(— OF SEA-SHELL) FLUE

(ALTAR —) TOMB

(BODY —) GUT BELLY THORAX
ABDOMEN STOMACH

(CHEST —) THORAX

(CRYSTAL-LINED —) VUGG DRUSE
GEODE

(GUN —) BORE

(NASAL —) CAVUM

CAVORT PLAY BOUND CAPER
CURVET GAMBOL PRANCE

CAVY PACA PONY AGOUTI APEREA
CAYUSE CAPYBARA

(FEMALE —) SOW

CAW KA CRY CALL CROAK QUARK
QUAWK

CAYMAN JACARE

CAYUSE CAVY PONY BRONCO
MUSTANG

CEASE HO BOW CUT DIE END LIN
BALK BLIN DROP FINE HALT HOLD
LIFT LISS QUIT REST SACE SHUT
STAY STOP STOW AVAST CLOSE
DOWSE LEAVE PAUSE PETER STINT
SWICK WAIVE DESIST DEVALL
EXPIRE FINISH FORGET ABSTAIN
OUTGIVE REFRAIN SUSPEND
INTERMIT OVERGIVE SURCEASE

(— MILKING COW) SINE

(— TEMPORARILY) LIFT

(— TO ASSERT) ABANDON

CEASELESS EVER ENDLESS
ETERNAL IMMORTAL UNENDING

CEASING CESSER CESSATION

CEBUS SAI

CECILIA SIS SISSU

CECROPS (DAUGHTER OF —) HERSE
AGLAUROS PANDROSOS

(WIFE OF —) AGLAURUS

CEDAR SUGI TOON SAVIN DEODAR
SABINA TUMION CYPRESS JUNIPER
WAXWING CALANTAS PAHAUTEA

CEDAR SWAMP GREENING

CEDAR WAXWING RECOLLET

CEDE CESS GIVE AWARD GRANT
LEAVE WAIVE YIELD ASSIGN RESIGN
SUBMIT CONCEDE RENOUNCE
TRANSFER

CEDILLA TITTLE

CEIBA KAPOK BENTANG POCHOTE

CEIL LINE SYLE OVERLAY WAINSCOT

CEILING TOP DOME LACE LOFT
CHUTT CUPOLA LINING SCREEN
SOFFIT SYLING CURTAIN LACUNAR
PLAFOND TESTUDO COVERING
DECKHAND PANELING PLANCHER
SEMIDOME

CELANDINE FICARY KILLWORT
WARTWEED WARTWORT
FELONWORT JEWELWEED

CELEBES (GULF OF —) BONE TOLO
TOMINI

(ISLAND OF —) MUNA BUTUNG
PELENG SULAWESI

(PEOPLE OF —) TORAJA

(TOWN OF —) BUOL LUWUK
MANADO MAKASAR

CELEBRATE FETE KEEP SING CHANT
DITTY EXTOL HONOR REVEL SACRE
SPEAK BESING CHAUNT EXTOLL
PRAISE ELEGIZE EXECUTE GLORIFY
MAFFICK OBSERVE EMBLAZON
EULOGIZE PROCLAIM

(— 2 MASSES) BINATE DUPLICATE

CELEBRATED KEPT FAMED NOTED
FAMOUS EMINENT FEASTED
RENOMME STORIED FABULOUS
GLORIOUS NOTIFIED OBSERVED
RENOWNED

CELEBRATION EED FETE GALA
POPE RITE FESTA REVEL COOLIN
CUSTOM DOMENT EASTER FIESTA
POWWOW RENOWN SIMHAH
BLOWOUT HOGMENA HOLIDAY
JUBILEE PASCHAL SHINDIG SIMCHAH
BINATION BIRTHDAY HOGMANAY
MAKAHIKI OLYMPIAD POTLATCH
SHIVAREE FESTIVITY HOOLAULEA
JUNKETING

CELEBRATOR JUBILIST

CELEBRITY FAME LION NAME STAR
CELEB ECLAT RENOWN REPUTE

CELERITY HASTE HURRY SPEED
DISPATCH RAPIDITY VELOCITY
SWIFTNESS

CELERY SIT ACHE STICK UMBEL
KARPAS SALARY SMALLAGE

CELESTIAL HOLY DIVINE HEAVEN
URANIC ANGELIC CHINESE ETHERED
EMPYREAL ETHEREAL HEAVENLY
OLYMPIAN

CELESTITE APOTOME

CELIBACY CHASTITY VIRGINITY

CELIBATE CLERK CHASTE SINGLE
BACHELOR SPINSTER

CELL BOX EGG BAND BOOT CAGE
CYTE DISC DISK GERM GONE HOLE
JAIL KILL CABIN CAROL CLINK
CRYPT CYTON FIBER FIBRE GHOST
GLAND GROUP OOTID TMEMA TORIL
VAULT ZOOID ANAXON CEPTOR
COCCUS COOLER CYTODE GAMETE
GONIUM INAXON PRISON SHIELD
SIPHON SYPHON WESTON ZYGOTE
AGAMETE AMEBULA APOCYTE
CELLULE CHAMBER CLOCHAN
CLOSTER COCCOID CUBICLE
DIPLOID DUNGEON ELEMENT
EPICYTE EUPLOID HAPLOID HEMATID
INITIAL LOCULUS MYOCYTE
OOBLAST PAPILLA PLASTID
RENETTE SEGMENT SPORONT
STEREID TRISOME UTRICLE VESICLE
AMACRINE BASOCYTE BASOPHIL
BIFORINE BIOPLAST CLOGHAUN
DIKARYON FAVEOLUS GLIOCYTE
GONIDIUM GONOCYTE HEMOCYTE
HOLDOVER IDIOSOME LOCELLUS
ORGANULE PROSORUS RECEPTOR
SCLEREID SPERMULE SYNERGID
TRACHEID TRIPLOID ZOOBLAST

(— OF LEADERS) CADRE

(BEE —) PIPE

(DETENTION —) BULLPEN

(PHOTOELECTRIC —) EYE

(PRISON —) BING HOLE CABIN
CLINK COOLER JIGGER

(STAB —) BAND

(THIN-WALLED —S) STOMIUM

(VOLTAIC —) BATTERY

(PL.) LAURA POTLINE SWEATBOX

CELLA NAOS

CELLAR CAVE VAULT BODEGA
PALACE FAVISSA HYPOGEE
BASEMENT HYPOGEUM MATAMORO
VAULTAGE

CELLARET TANTALUS

CELLARMAN SOMMELIER

CELLULOID XYLONITE

CELLULOSE CRUMB AMYLOID
LIGNOSE TAMIDINE

CELT GAEL GAUL KELT MANX IRISH
WELSH BRETON BRITON EOLITH
GOIDEL BRYTHON CORNISH
PALSTAFF PALSTAVE

(PL.) CYMRY KYMRY

CELTIC ERSE GAEL SCOTCH

CEMBALO DULCIMER ZIMBALON

CEMENT FIX KIT TIE GLUE HEAL
JOIN KNIT LIME LUTE SLIP GROUT
IMBED PASTE PUTTY SIMON STICK
TABBY UNITE BINDER CHUNAM
COHERE FASTEN FILLER GULGUL
KIBOSH MALTHA MASTIC MORTAR
OOGLEA SOLDER ASPHALT MIXTION
ADHESIVE ALBOLITE ALBOLITH
CEMENTUM HADIGEON SOLIDIFY
SOLUTION

CEMENTER GLUER GLUEMAN
SMEARER

CEMENT MIXER TEMPERER

CEMETERY HOWF KILL LAIR LITTEN CHARNEL BONEYARD CATACOMB GOLGOTHA URNFIELD

CENOBITE NUN MONK FRIAR ESSENE RECLUSE MONASTIC SYNODITE

CENOTAPH TOMB

CENSE THURIFY

CENSER INCENSER THURIBLE

CENSOR CRITIC SCREEN SYNDIC LAUNDER RESTRICT SUPPRESS

CENSORIOUS SEVERE BLAMING CARPING BLAMEFUL CAPTIOUS CRITICAL CULPABLE SLASHING

CENSORSHIP WRAPS ASSIZE CENSURE

CENSURABLE TAXABLE BLAMABLE CULPABLE

CENSURE BAN HIT NIP RAP TAP TAX WIG CALL CARP DEEM DRUB FLAY RATE SLAP TASK WITE BEANS BLAME CHIDE CURSE DECRY FAULT HOKER JUDGE PINCH SCOLD SLANG SLASH SLATE TAUNT TOUCH WHITE ACCUSE ATTACK BERATE CHARGE REBUFF REBUKE REFORM REMORD STRAFE TARGUE TIRADE BLISTER CHASTEN CONDEMN CONTROL DECRIAL DYSLOGY IMPEACH IMPROVE INVEIGH REPROOF REPROVE SCARIFY TRADUCE TROUNCE UPBRAID BACKBITE CHASTISE DISALLOW JUDGMENT LANGUAGE REPROACH SATIRIZE SENTENCE

CENSUS LIST POLL CENSE COUNT LUSTER LUSTRUM

CENT RED DUIT SANT BROWNIE CENTAVO STUIVER
(12 1-2 —S) LEVY
(ODD —S) BREAKAGE

CENTAUR CHIRON NESSUS HORSEMAN BUCENTAUR

CENTAURY BEHN BEHEN SABBATIA EARTHGALL

CENTENNIAL STATE COLORADO

CENTER COR EYE GIG HUB MID AXIS CORE NAVE SEAT SNAP YOLK FOCUS FOYER GLOME HEART MIDST PIVOT SPINE BOTTOM CENTRE MIDDLE PIPPER STAPLE TEMPLE CENTRUM ESSENCE LINEMAN NUCLEUS UMBILIC INCENTER OMPHALOS SNAPBACK
(— FOR SPINDLE) GIG
(— FOR TARGET) EYE PIN PINHOLE
(— OF ACTIVITY) HUB HIVE
(— OF ARCH) COOM
(— OF ASSURANCE) FORTRESS
(— OF ATTRACTION) FOCUS STAGE CYNOSURE
(— OF BASKET) SLATHER
(— OF CITY) DOWNTOWN
(— OF CULTIVATION) HOME
(— OF CULTURE) ATHENS
(— OF DIAMOND) WELL
(— OF FIGURE) CENTROID
(— OF FISHING NET) BUNT
(— OF FLOWER) EYE

(— OF HURRICANE) EYE
(— OF OPERATIONS) SHOP
(— OF POPULATION) CITY
(— OF POWER) SEE SIEGE
(— OF STAGE) LIMELIGHT
(— OF STRENGTH) GANGLION
(COLLECTION —) ENTREPOT
(COMMERCIAL —) MACHI EMPORIUM
(HARD —) KNOT
(INTIMATE —) BOSOM
(LATHE —) PIKE
(NERVOUS —) BRAIN
(NEURAL —) APPESTAT
(PROPAGANDA —) AGITPUNKT
(REHABILITATION —) HOSTEL
(TRADING —) BEACH EXCHANGE
(VITAL —) HEARTH HEARTBEAT

CENTERING COOM COOMB CENTRY FANTAIL

CENTERPIECE ROSACE DORMANT EPERGNE

CENTETES TENREC

CENTIARE LI

CENTIGRADE CELSIUS

CENTIME RAPPEN

CENTIMETER GAL

CENTIPEDE VEI VERI EARWIG GOLACH GOLOCH POLYPOD CHILOPOD MULTIPED MYRIAPOD SANTAPEE SCUTIGER

CENTRAL MID AXIAL BASIC CHIEF FOCAL MIXED PRIME MEDIAN MIDDLE CAPITAL CENTRIC LEADING NUCLEAR PIVOTAL PRIMARY CARDINAL DOMINANT

CENTRAL AFRICAN REPUBLIC
CAPITAL: BANGUI
COIN: FRANC
NATIVE: BAYA SARA BANDA BWAKA SANGO YAKOMA BANZIRI MANDJIA
RIVER: BOMU NANA CHARI KOTTO MBARI MPOKO OUAKA CHINKO LOBAYE UBANGI
TOWN: OBO IPPY BIRAO BOUAR KEMBE NDELE NGOTO PAOUA RAFAI ZEMIO BABOUA BAKALA BANGUI BOZOUM BAMBARI GRIMARI ZEMONGO

CENTRAL AMERICAN LADINO
(— TREE) TUNO TUNU

CENTRANTH SPURFLOWER

CENTRIFUGAL EFFERENT RADIATING

CENTRIFUGE CYCLONE SEPARATOR

CENTRIPETAL AFFERENT

CENTROSOME CENTRUM CENTRIOLE

CENTRUM CORE

CENTURIED SECULAR

CENTURY AGE SECLE SIECLE

CENTURY PLANT ALOE AGAVE MAGUEY CANTALA TEQUILA MONOCARP

CEPHALALGIA SODA HEADACHE

CEPHALIC CRANIAL ATLANTAL CEREBRAL

CEPHALOPOD SQUID CUTTLE INKFISH OCTOPUS SPIRULA DIBRANCH SCAPHITE

CEPHALUS (FATHER OF —) DEION
(MOTHER OF —) DIOMEDE
(WIFE OF —) PROCRIS

CERAMICS TILES POTTERY

CERATE WAX LARD SALVE UNGUENT OINTMENT

CERATOBRANCHIAL APOHYAL

CEREAL RYE BEAN BRAN CORN MUSH OATS RICE SAMP TEFF ARZUN GRAIN MAIZE SPELT WHEAT BARLEY BINDER FARINA HOMINY PABLUM OATMEAL SOYBEAN PORRIDGE

CEREAL LEAF FLAG

CEREBRAL CEPHALIC INVERTED

CEREBRATION THOUGHT

CEREBROSIDE KERASIN

CEREMENT SHROUD

CEREMONIAL FORM PRIM STIFF FORMAL RIALTY RITUAL SOLEMN PRECISE STUDIED TRIUMPH UPANAYA AVERSION SPLENDOR

CEREMONIOUS GRAND LOFTY STIFF FORMAL PROPER SOLEMN PRECISE STATELY STUDIED

CEREMONY BRIS FETE FORM GAUD HAKO ORGY POMP RITE SEAL SHOW SIGN SING BERIT DANCE STATE ACTION AUGURY BERITH BRIDAL BURIAL EXEQUY GOMBAY HOMAGE KERIAH MALKAH MAUNDY NIPTER OFFICE PARADE POWWOW REVIEW RITUAL SALUTE BAPTISM DISPLAY KIDDUSH MELAVEH OVATION PAGEANT PANAGIA PORTENT PRODIGY TAHARAH ACCOLADE APOLUSIS ASPERGES COEMPTIO CRIOBOLY ENCAENIA EXERCISE FUNCTION HABDALAH HAKAFOTH HERALDRY MARRIAGE OCCASION SKEYTING INAUGURAL INDUCTION
(HAZING —) CREELING
(MARRIAGE —) ESPOUSAL
(TEA —) CHANOYU
(PL.) DEGREE HOLIES AGENDUM FERALIA JUSTMENTS

CERES DEMETER
(DAUGHTER OF —) PROSERPINE PHERREPHATTA
(FATHER OF —) SATURN
(MOTHER OF —) VESTA

CERINTHE HONEYWORT

CERO SEARER SIERRA CAVALLA PINTADO KINGFISH

CERTAIN COLD COOL DEAD FAST FIRM FREE REAL SEAL SURE TRUE BOUND CLEAR EXACT FIXED PLAIN SIKER ACTUAL MEMORY SECURE SICKER STATED WITTER ASSURED PERFECT PRECISE SETTLED SRADDHA ABSOLUTE APPARENT CONSTANT OFFICIAL POSITIVE RELIABLE RESOLVED UNERRING CONFIDENT

CERTAINLY AY AYE WIS AMEN IWIS SOON SURE WHAT YWIS TRULY

CERTES INDEED PERDIE SICCAR
SICKER SURELY VERILY HARDILY
EVERMORE FORSOOTH SECURELY
(MOST —) SO
CERTAINTY YEA CERT PIPE CINCH
POLICY SURETY SURENESS
CONSTANCY
(LACK OF —) SCRUPLE
CERTIFICATE BOND CHIT CHECK
DEMIT JURAT LIBEL SCRIP TALON
TITLE AMPARO ATTEST CEDULA
COUPON INDENT PATENT POTTAH
RETURN TICKET VERIFY CERTIFY
CONSTAT DIPLOMA VOUCHER
WARRANT WAYBILL AEGROTAT
JUDGMENT KABBALAH NAVICERT
REGISTER REGISTRY SECURITY
TESCARIA TESTAMUR TEZKIRAH
(MARRIAGE —) LINES
(MINER'S —) LICENCE LICENSE
(PILOT'S —) BRANCH
(SERVANT'S —) CHIT
CERTIFICATION PASS STAMP
APPROVAL HECHSHER CLEARANCE
DISCHARGE
CERTIFIED SWORN
CERTIFY AVOW VISE SWEAR AFFIRM
ASSURE ATTEST DEPOSE EVINCE
VERIFY WITTER APPROVE ENDORSE
LICENSE TESTIFY
CERTITUDE CERTAIN CONFIDENCE
CERULEAN BLUE AZURE COELIN
CYANEAN CYANEOUS
CERUMEN WAX EARWAX
CESS BOG TAX CEDE DUTY LEVY
LUCK RATE ABWAB SLOPE YIELD
IMPOST MEASURE SURRENDER
(BAD —) SORRA
CESSATION HO END HOO BLIN HALT
HUSH LISS LULL REST STAY STOP
BREAK CEASE CLOSE DEVAL LETUP
LISSE PAUSE SLACK STINT TRUCE
CUTOFF DEMISE DISUSE OFFSET
PERIOD RECESS CEASING CLOSURE
RESPITE ABEYANCE BLACKOUT
DESITION INTERVAL SHUTDOWN
STOPPAGE SURCEASE SUSPENSE
(— OF HOSTILITIES) TRUCE
INDUCIAE ARMISTICE
(— OF LIFE) DEATH
(— OF RESPIRATION) APNEA
APNOEA
(— OF WORK) HARTAL
CESSPOOL SINK SUMP SINKER
CISTERN JAWHOLE SINKHOLE
SUSPIRAL
CESTRUM POISONBERRY
CESTUS CEST CESTON HURLBAT
GAUNTLET WHIRLBAT
CETACEAN ORC CETE ORCA SUSU
WHALE BELUGA COWFISH DOLPHIN
GRAMPUS NARWHAL MUTILATE
PORPOISE
CEYLON SERENDIP TAPROBANE

CEYLON
CAPITAL: COLOMBO
COIN: CENT

GULF: MANNAR
MEASURE: PARA PARAH AMUNAM
PARRAH
POINT: PEDRO
STRAIT: PALK
TOWN: GALLE KANDY JAFFNA
MANNAR MATARA BADULLA
COLOMBO PUTTALAM
TREE: HORA PALU

CEYLONESE CEYLON BURGHER
CEYLON MOSS GULAMAN
CGS UNIT STILB STOKE
CHA TSIA CHAIS
CHACMA BAVIAN BOBBEJAAN

CHAD
CAPITAL: FORTLAMY
COIN: FRANC FRANCCFA
LAKE: CHAD
NATIVE: ARAB SARA KREDA
MASSA TOUBOU KAMADJA
MOUNDAN
PLATEAU: ENNEDI
RIVER: CHARI LOGONE BAHRAOUK
TOWN: ATI BOL LAI MAO FADA
FAYA MONGO ARECHE
BONGOR LARGEAU MOUNDOU
MOUSSORO

CHADOR PHULKARI
CHAETOCHLOA SETARIA
CHAETOPOD SCALEBACK
CHAFE IRK RUB VEX FRET FRIG
FROT FUME GALD GALL HEAT JOSH
RAGE WARM WEAR ANGER ANNOY
CHAFF GRIND SCOLD SNUFF WORRY
WRING ABRADE BANTER EXCITE
FRIDGE HARASS INJURY NETTLE
RANKLE INCENSE INFLAME SNUFFLE
FRICTION IRRITATE RAILLERY
CHAFER CRESSET
CHAFF GUY HAY PUG ROT BRAN
CAFF CHIP GRIT GUFF JOSH PULU
QUIZ RAZZ BORAK CHYAK DROSS
GLUME HULLS HUSKS JOLLY SLACK
STOUR STRAW TEASE TRASH
BANTER BHOOSA REFUSE CAVINGS
TAILING RAILLERY RIDICULE
SHELLING
CHAFFER BANDY SIEVE WARES
BUYING DICKER HAGGLE HIGGLE
MARKET PALTER BARGAIN CHATTER
SELLING TRAFFIC EXCHANGE
CHAFFINCH PINK CHINK SPINK
TWINK ROBERD SCOBBY SHILFA
SKELLY ROBINET SNABBIE WETBIRD
CHAFFY SCALY ACEROSE ACEROUS
PALEATE
CHAFING GALLING IMPATIENCE
CHAGRIN ENVY SPITE VEXATION
CHAGRINED SICK ASHAMED
CHAIN FOB GUY NET ROW SET TEW
TIE TOE TOW TUG TYE BIND BOND
CURB FALL FAST FILE GYVE JOIN
LINE LINK SEAL SOAM TEAM BRAIL
CABLE GROUP GUARD LEASH

SHANK SHEET SLANG SLING SUITE
TRACE TRAIN WRASE CARCAN
CATENA COLLAR CORDON FASTEN
FETTER GANGER HANGER HOBBLE
JACKER JIGGER LINKER RACKAN
SECURE SERIES STRING TETHER
TOGGLE BOBSTAY CATFALL
CHIGNON CONNECT EMBRACE
ENSLAVE LASHING MANACLE
NETWORK PAINTER PENDANT
SAUTOIR SHACKLE TACKLER
BACKROPE BRACELET CARCANET
GLEIPNIR LINKWORK NECKLACE
RECEPTOR RESTRAIN RIGWIDDY
STROBILA WOOLDING
(— FOR ANCHOR) CATFALL PAINTER
(— FOR BINDING) JACKER TACKLER
(— FOR WRAPPING MAST)
WOOLDING
(— OF AUTHORITIES) ISNAD
(— OF DUNES) SAIF SEIF
(— OF MOUNTAINS) RANGE
(— OF ROCKS) REEF
(— ON CONVICT'S LEG) SLANG
(— TO BIND CATTLE) SEAL
(DECORATIVE —) FESTOON
(ENDLESS —) CREEPER
(MAGIC —) GLEIPNIR
(SHORT —) SHANK
(SUSPENDED —) CATENARY
(WATCH —) FOB ALBERT
(PL.) IRONS CONVEYOR
CHAIN LINK SHUT COPULA SWIVEL
CHAINMAN CLASHY CLASHEE
LINEMAN TAPEMAN
CHAIN-SHAPED CATENOID
CHAIR KEEP SEAT SHOP HORSE
SEDAN STOOL ESTATE OFFICE
PULPIT ROCKER SADDLE SITTER
TONJON CACOLET COMMODE
FANBACK GONDOLA SITTING
VOYEUSE WINDSOR ARMCHAIR
CARRIAGE CATHEDRA FAUTEUIL
KANGAROO SGABELLO VOLTAIRE
(— OF STATE) THRONE
(— SLUNG FROM POLE) KAGO
TALABON
(— WITH CANOPY) STATE
(BISHOP'S —) CATHEDRA
FALDSTOOL
(EASY —) COGSWELL
(GREEK —) KLISMOS
(MINING —) DOG
(PORTABLE —) SEDAN
(SPRING —) PERCH
(THRONE —) SHINZA
CHAIRMAN HEAD CHAIR EMCEE
PRESES SPEAKER CONVENER
DIRECTOR
CHAISE GIG SHAY CHAIR CALESIN
CARRIAGE
CHAISE LONGUE DAYBED
DUCHESSE
CHALAZA TREAD TREADLE
GALLATURE
CHALCEDONY ONYX OPAL SARD
AGATE PRASE CATEYE JASPER
QUARTZ CARNEOL ENHYROS
OPALINE SARDINE SARDIUS

CHALCOPYRITE RUN
CHALDEAN KALDANI BABYLONIAN
  (— **MEASURE**) CANE FOOT MAKUK
  QASAB ARTABA GARIBA GHALVA
  MANSION
  (— **RIVER**) TIGRIS EUPHRATES
  (— **TOWN**) UR
CHALICE AMA CUP BOWL CALIX
  GRAIL REGAL GOBLET KRASIS
CHALK CAUK CORK PALE SCAR
  TALC TICK CRETA FLOUR SCORE
  BLANCH BLEACH CRAYON CREDIT
  RUBBLE WHITEN ACCOUNT WHITING
  (**GREEN** —) PRASINE
  (**HARD** —) HURLOCK
  (**RED** —) RUBRIC
  (**SURVEYOR'S** —) KEEL
CHALKBOARD GREENBOARD
CHALKY CRETACIC
CHALLENGE VIE BRAG CALL DARE
  DEFY FACE GAGE BANCO BLAME
  BRAVE CLAIM QUERY STUMP
  ACCUSE APPEAL BANTER CARTEL
  CHARGE DACKER DAIKER DEMAND
  DESCRY FORBID IMPUGN INFIRM
  INVITE RECUSE SERDAB ARRAIGN
  CENSURE IMPEACH PROVOKE
  REPROVE SOLICIT SUMMONS
  CHAMPION DEFIANCE GAUNTLET
  QUESTION REPROACH
  (— **A BULL**) CITE
CHALLENGING PIQUANT
  BLOODSHOT
CHALYBEATE MARTIAL
CHAMBER ODA AGER CELL CIST
  DOME FLAT FOLD HALL IWAN KIVA
  ROOM SALE TOMB BOWER CAVUM
  COURT GOMER HOUSE SENAT
  SHAFT SOLAR SOLER STOVE
  ATRIUM CAMARA CAMERA COFFER
  HEADER HOLLOW MIHRAB SENADO
  SENATE SOLLAR SPRING STANZA
  WILSON BEDROOM CAISSON
  CHALMAR CHANNEL CHAUMER
  CONCAVE CUBICLE FAVISSA
  FIREBOX GALLERY GEHENNA
  MANSION RECEIPT CASEMATE
  CYLINDER DIFFUSER FOUNTAIN
  GROSSRAT SMOKEBOX SNEMOVNA
  THALAMUS
  (— **FOR MOLTEN GLASS**) FONT
  (— **IN FURNACE**) SHAFT DOGHOUSE
  (— **OF EAR**) SACCULE
  (— **POT**) JORDAN JEROBOAM
  (**AIR** —) SPONSON
  (**BOMBPROOF** —) CASEMATE
  (**FIRE** —) ARCH STOVE COCKLE
  FIREBOX
  (**FORTIFICATION** —) BUNKER
  (**OPEN** —) LANTERN
  (**ORGAN** —) SWELL
  (**PRIVATE** —) CLOSET CONCLAVE
  (**PUEBLO** —) KIVA ESTUFA
  (**SLEEPING** —) BEDROOM
  WARDROBE
  (**SMALL** —) LOCULUS
  (**SUPPLY** —) MAGAZINE
  (**UNDERGROUND** —) CAVE CRYPT
  CAVERN HYPOGEE

(**WATERTIGHT** —) CAISSON
CHAMBERLAIN EUNUCH FACTOR
  SERVANT STEWARD PALATINE
  POLONIUS
CHAMELEON ANOLE ANOLI LACERT
  SAURIAN
CHAMFER BEVEL CHIMB CHIME
  CHINE FLUTE CIPHER FURROW
  GROOVE
CHAMOIS GEMS IZARD AOUDAD
  SHAMMY
CHAMOMILE MAYWEED
CHAMP BITE CHAW FIRM HARD
  MASH CHANK CHOMP FIELD GNASH
  TRAMPLE
CHAMPAGNE AY BUBBLY SIMKIN
  BELLEEK SILLERY
CHAMPION ACE AID FAN ABET BACK
  BOSS DEFY HERO KEMP GHAZI
  ASSERT ATTEND DEFEND KNIGHT
  PATRON SQUIRE VICTOR ESPOUSE
  FIGHTER PALADIN PROTECT
  ADVOCATE DEFENDER PALMERIN
CHAMPIONSHIP TITLE LAURELS
  ADVOCACY
CHAMPLEVE INLAID
CHANCE DIE HAP LOT CASE CAST
  DINT DRAW FATE LINE LUCK ODDS
  RISK SHOT SHOW TIDE BREAK
  ETTLE STAKE WHACK BETIDE
  CASUAL GAMBLE HAPPEN HAZARD
  MISHAP RANDOM SQUEAK AIMLESS
  FORTUNE STUMBLE VANTAGE
  VENTURE ACCIDENT CASUALTY
  EVENTUAL FORTUITY
  (**ADVERSE** —) HAZARD
  (**EVEN** —) TOSSUP
CHANCELLOR LOGOTHETE
CHANDELIER LUSTER PHAROS
  PENDANT CHANDLER GASELIER
CHANDLER TALLOWER
CHANE OREJON
CHANGE MEW CHOP FLOP MOLT
  MOVE ODDS PEAL TURN VARY VEER
  WARP WEND ADAPT ALTER AMEND
  BREAK COINS EMEND MOULT SHIFT
  THROW ADJUST BECOME DIFFER
  DIGEST IMMUTE MODIFY MUANCE
  MUTATE REMOVE REVAMP REVISE
  SWITCH WISSEL WRIXLE COMMUTE
  CONVERT CUTOVER DEVIATE
  FLUXION MORTIFY BECOMING
  DENATURE EXCHANGE INNOVATE
  LENITION REVISION TRANSFER
  TRANSUME VARIANCE
  (— **APPEARANCE**) DISGUISE
  (— **COLOR**) TURN
  (— **COURSE**) GYBE JIBE
  (— **DIRECTION**) CUT CANT CHOP
  HAUL KNEE VEER ANGLE BREAK
  SHIFT
  (— **FOR BETTER**) HELP
  (— **FOR WORSE**) BEDEVIL
  (— **FORM**) DEVELOP
  (— **GAIT**) BREAK
  (— **GRADUALLY**) PASS GRADUATE
  (— **IN COURSE**) SHEER
  (— **IN DIRECTION**) JOG KNEE STEP
  (— **IN ELEVATION**) FORK

(— **IN SIZE**) ASTOGENY
(— **INTO VAPOR**) FLASH
(— **MONEY**) WISSEL
(— **OF FORM**) SET
(— **OF GEAR**) KICKDOWN
(— **OF MIND**) CAPRICE
(— **OF MOOD**) VARY
(— **OF PITCH**) MOTION INFLECT
(— **OF SEA LEVEL**) EUSTACY
(— **OF SOUND**) BREAKING
(— **OF WORD**) ANAGRAM
(— **ONE'S HEART**) REPENT
(— **POSITION**) STIR FLEET HOTCH
(— **QUICKLY**) FLY
(— **SHAPE**) DRAW CREEP DEFORM
(— **RESIDENCE**) FLIT
(**ABRUPT** —) DOGLEG SALTATION
(**ABNORMAL** —) LESION
(**GEAR** —) KICKDOWN
(**GRADUAL** —) DRIFT
(**PRESSURE** —) ALLOBAR
(**SHORT** —) FLUFF
(**SMALL** —) GROCERY
(**UNEXPECTED** —) SWITCH
(**PL.**) DOUBLES PLASTIQUE
CHANGEABLE EEMIS GIDDY IMMIS
  LIGHT WINDY CHOPPY FICKLE
  FITFUL GERFUL KETCHY LABILE
  MOBILE MOTLEY MUABLE SHIFTY
  BRUCKLE ERRATIC MUTABLE
  PROTEAN UNSTAID VARIANT
  VARIOUS VOLUBLE AMENABLE
  CATCHING GLIBBERY MOVEABLE
  TICKLISH UNSTABLE VARIABLE
  VEERABLE VOLATILE WEATHERY
CHANGEABLENESS LEVITY
  VIBRATION
CHANGED VARIED ANOTHER
CHANGEFUL FICKLE SHIFTY
  MUTABLE RESTLESS
CHANGELESS CONSISTENT
CHANGELING AUF AWF OAF DOLT
  FOOL CHILD DUNCE IDIOT WAVERER
  IMBECILE KILLCROP RENEGADE
  TURNCOAT
CHANGING FLUXIBLE ALTERNATE
  (— **MONEY**) AGIO
  (**CONTINUALLY** —) FLOATING
CHANK SANK CONCH
CHANNEL CUT GAT POD REE RUT
  SOW CANO CAVA DEEP DIKE DUCT
  DYKE FLUE GATE GOOL GOTE GOUT
  GURT KILL KYLE LAKE LANE PACE
  PIPE RACE SLEW SLOO VEIN WADI
  WADY BAYOU CANAL CARRY CHASE
  COWAL DITCH DRAIN DRILL FLUME
  FLUTE GLYPH GUIDE INSET QUIRK
  RIVER SINUS SLIDE STOOL STOVE
  STRIA SWASH AIRWAY ALVEUS
  ARROYO ARTERY BRANCH COURSE
  CUTOFF ESTERO FURROW GROOVE
  GULLET GUTTER HOLLOW KENNEL
  KEYWAY LAGOON MEDIUM OFFLET
  OILWAY RABBET RESACA RIVOSE
  RUNWAY SLOUGH SLUICE SPECUS
  STRAIT STRAND STREAM THROAT
  TROUGH CHAMFER CONDUCT
  CONDUIT CULVERT CUNETTE
  EURIPUS OFFTAKE PASSAGE

RACEWAY RIVULET SHIPWAY
SILANGA STRIGIL THALWEG
TIDEWAY WASHOUT AQUEDUCT
FLOODWAY GUIDEWAY GUNKHOLE
RACELINE SCOURWAY SPILLWAY
(— FOR MOLTEN METAL) SOW GATE
RUNNER
(— IN CLOTH) FLUTE
(— IN ICE FIELD) LEAD
(— IN MOLD) SPRAY
(— OF AQUEDUCT) SPECUS
(— ON WHALE) SCARF
(ARTIFICAL —) GAT GOUT
(DRAINAGE —) GAW
(ENGLISH —) SLEEVE
(INCLINED —) SHOOT
(IRRIGATION —) AUWAI DROVE
(LYMPH —) CISTERNA
(SECONDARY —) BINNACLE
(SLOPING —) CHUTE SHUTE
CHANNELBILL RAINFOWL
CHANNELED FLUTED
CHANT CANT MELE SING SONG
TONE CAROL PSALM SOUGH
ANTHEM CANTUS INTONE LITANY
WARBLE CHORTLE INTROIT
PROSODE REQUIEM WORSHIP
ALLELUIA ANTIPHON SINGSONG
CHANTER STICK CANTOR SINGER
BAGPIPE SONGSTER CHALUMEAU
(— OF BAGPIPE) OBOE
CHANTERELLE CANTINO
CHANTING CHARM HAZANUT
ANTIPHONY CHAZZANUT
CHANTLATE SPROCKET
CHANTRY CAGE
CHAOS NU NUN PIE APSU GULF
HYLE MESS VOID ABYSS BABEL
CHASM JUMBLE MATTER TOPHET
ANARCHY MIXTURE DISORDER
SHAMBLES TAILSPIN TOHUBOHU
CHAOTIC MUDDLED CONFUSED
FORMLESS
CHAP BOY BUY DOG LAD MAN RAP
WAG BEAN BEAT BIRD BLOW CHIP
CHOP COVE DICK DUCK HIND JOHN
KIBE MASH MATE NABS SNAP BILLY
BLOKE BUCKO BULLY BUYER CHAFT
CHINK CLEFT CRACK FRUIT KNOCK
LOVER RUMMY SCOUT SPLIT SPORT
SPRAY SWIPE TRADE YOUTH
BARTER BOHUNK BREACH BUGGER
CALLAN CHOOSE CODGER CUFFIN
FELLOW FOUTER FOUTRA GAFFER
GEEZER JOSSER KIPPER SHAVER
STRIKE STROKE TURNIP BROTHER
CALLANT FISSURE HUSBAND
ROUGHEN BLIGHTER CUSTOMER
DIVISION MERCHANT
(— HANDS) RACK SPRAY
(— IN SKIN) KIN KIBE
(FINE —) BULLY
(OLD —) GEEZER
(QUEER —) GALOOT
(S.AFRICAN —) KEREL
(YOUNG —) GAFFER
(PL.) CHOPS
CHAPARRAL MONTE CHAMISAL
BUCKTHORN

CHAPARRO YAYA
CHAPBOOK CHAP GARLAND
CHAPE CRAMPET MORDANT
CHAPEL CAGE CAPE COPE COWL
HOOD CLOAK PORCH BETHEL
CHARRE CHURCH HAIKAL MORADA
SHRINE CAPELLA CHANTRY
CHARNEL CHHATRI GALILEE
MARTYRY MEETING MEMORIA
ORATORY SACRARY SERVICE
BETHESDA DEACONRY DIACONIA
FERETORY FERETRUM SACELLUM
SODALITY
(UNDERGROUND —) SHROUDS
CHAPERON HOOD ATTEND DUENNA
ESCORT MATRON GRIFFIN PROTECT
GUARDIAN TRAPPING
CHAPLAIN PADRE LEVITE CONDUCT
ALTARIST ORDINARY
CHAPLET BEAD ORLE STUD CROWN
ANADEM ANCHOR CIRCLE FILLET
JAMBER JAMMER ROSARY STAPLE
TROPHY WREATH CORONAL
CORONET GARLAND MOULDING
NECKLACE ORNAMENT
CHAPMAN CHAP BUYER DEALER
HAWKER TRADER COPEMAN
PEDDLER CUSTOMER MERCHANT
CHAPPIE JOCKEY
CHAPS FLEWS BREECHES LEGGINGS
OVERALLS
CHAPTER BODY CELL PACE POST
CAPUT COURT LODGE BRANCH
CABILDO CAPITAL CORRECT
COUNCIL MEETING SECTION
ASSEMBLY
(— OF BOOK) CAPITAL
(— OF KORAN) SURA SURAH
(— OF SOCIETY) CAMP CIRCLE
CHAR BURN CART COAL SEAR BROIL
CHARK CHORE SHARD SINGE TROUT
SCORCH BLACKEN CHARIOT
REDBELLY SAIBLING SALMONID
SANDBANK
CHARA MUSKGRASS
CHARACIN DORADO DOURADE
BLOODFIN
CHARACTER BALL BENT CARD CASE
CLAY CLEF DASH ECAD FLAT FOND
FORM HAIR KIND MAKE MARK MOLD
NOTE PART ROLE RUNE SIGN SORT
TONE TRIM TYPE BRAND COLOR
ETHIC ETHOS FIBER HABIT HEART
HUMOR INDEX SAVOR STAMP
TENOR TOKEN TRAIT WRITE
CARACT CIPHER COCKUP DAGGER
DIRECT EMBLEM FIGURE GENIUS
HANGER LETTER MANNER METTLE
NATURE REPUTE SIGLUM SPIRIT
STRIPE SYMBOL CLOTHES EDITION
ENGRAVE ESSENCE IMPRESS
QUALITY FRACTION IDENTITY
INFERIOR INSCRIBE LIGATURE
SELFHOOD SYLLABIC DESCENDER
(— IN DRAMA) CHORUS
(— IN PLAY) DAME BESSY
(— OF SOIL) LAIR
(ASSUMED —) ROLE FIGURE
INCOGNITO

(BAD —) DROLE BUDMASH
(BASIC —) BOTTOM
(CHINESE —) SHOU RADICAL
(COMMON —) COMMUNITY
(ESSENTIAL —) ALLOY
(FIRM —) BACKBONE
(GIVE — TO) TONE
(JAPANESE —S) HIBUNCI
(MENDELIAN —) ALLEL ALLELE
(PHYSICAL —) ARMENOID
(PRIME —) ESSENCE
(SHIFTLESS —) BEAT
(STOCK —) MACCUS
(TESTED —) ASSAY
(TRIED —) TOUCH
(VULGAR —S) ONMUN
(PL.) MANA
CHARACTERISTIC CAST COST
MARK MIEN ANGLE AROMA GRACE
POINT TACHE TOKEN TRAIT ACCENT
BEAUTY NATURE STIGMA STROKE
ADJUNCT AMENITY FEATURE
IMPRESS QUALITY SPECIES TYPICAL
ACTIVITY PECULIAR PROPERTY
SYMBOLIC
(— OF ANTIBODIES) AVIDITY
(ADVENTITIOUS —) ACCIDENT
(DISTINGUISHING —) SPECIES
HALLMARK BIRTHMARK
(PECULIAR —) IDIOPATHY
(PL.) CORNERS FACULTY
CHARACTERIZATION ELOGY
ELOGIUM
CHARACTERIZE MARK STYLE
DEFINE DEPICT TITULE ENGRAVE
ENTITLE IMPRINT PORTRAY
DESCRIBE INDICATE INSCRIBE
CHARADES GAME
CHARCOAL COAL CARBO CHARK
CARBON FUSAIN PENCIL BLACKEN
SPODIUM SCRIBBET
CHARGE FEE LAP LAY RAP TAX
BEEF BILL BUCK CALL CARE CARK
CAST COST CURE DUES DUTY FILL
GIBE KEEP LADE LIEN LOAD NICK
NOTE ONUS RACK RARE REST RUSH
SHOT SIZE SOAK SPAR TASK TOLL
WARD WIKE BLAME CAUSE CHALK
COUNT CRIME DEBIT EXTRA GYRON
ONSET ORDER PRICE REFER SCORE
SHOCK STICK STING THING TRUST
ACCUSE ADJURE ALLEGE APPEAL
ASSESS ATTACK BURDEN CAREER
CENSUS COURSE CREDIT DAMAGE
DEFAME DEMAND ENJOIN ENURNY
EXCESS IMPOSE IMPUTE METAGE
OFFICE PIPAGE REATUS SURMIT
SURTAX TARIFF TOWAGE WEIGHT
ACIDIZE ANNULET ARRAIGN ARTICLE
ASCRIBE ASSAULT AVERAGE
BOATAGE CARTAGE CENSURE
CHEVRON CLAMPER COMMAND
CONCERN CONJURE CORKAGE
CORNAGE CUSTODY DOCKAGE
DRAYAGE EMBASSY EXPENSE
FLOTAGE HAULAGE IGNITER
IMPEACH KEEPING MANDATE
MILEAGE MISSION MIXTURE
MOORAGE PANNAGE QUAYAGE

REPRISE SIDEAGE SLANDER
SLIDAGE SURMISE WARPAGE
BILLBACK BRASSAGE CASUALTY
CHASTISE CRESCENT DELAYAGE
DENOUNCE LEGATION ORDINARY
OVERLOAD PLANKAGE POUNDAGE
PROVINCE QUESTION SLINGING
SPENDING STANDAGE TUTORAGE
VIGORISH COMPLAINT
(— AGAINST) TILT
(— BATTERY) SOAK BOOST
(— EXCESSIVELY) FLEECE
(— FALSELY) SURMISE
(— OF FIREARM) LOAD
(— OF METAL) HEAT
(— OF ORE) POST
(— TO BE PAID) LAW
(— UPON PROPERTY) LIEN
(— WITH CRIME) ACCUSE INDICT
ARTICLE ATTAINT IMPEACH
(— WITH GAS) AERATE
(AGGREGATE —S) BOOK
(CANNON —) GRAPE
(COVER —) COUVERT
(DEPTH —) CAN
(EXPLOSIVE —) CAP BLAST SNAKE
SQUIB TULIP BOOSTER BURSTER
IGNITER
(FALSE —) CALUMNY
(HERALDIC —) DROP GIRON GYRON
LABEL DRAGON GURGES BEARING
ESQUIRE
(MAILING —) FRANKAGE
(POWDER —) GRAIN
(SHAPED —) BEEHIVE
(SPIRITUAL —) CURE
(TEMPORARY —) CARE
(WINE —) CORKAGE
CHARGED UP HOT LADEN BELAST
BILLETY BILLETTE ELECTRIC
INSTINCT
(— WITH EMOTION) SWOLLEN
CHARGEHAND CLICKER
CHARGEMAN BLASTER
CHARGER DISH HORSE MOUNT
STEED ACCUSER COURSER
PLATTER
CHARILY FRUGALLY GINGERLY
CHARIOT CAR BIGA CART CHAR
RATH WAIN BUGGY CHAIR ESSED
RATHA TRIGA WAGON CHARET
QUADRIGA
CHARIOTEER AURIGA CARTER
DRIVER IOLAUS LEADER CARTARE
WAGONER MYRTILUS AUTOMEDON
CHARITABLE KIND BENIGN HUMANE
LENIENT LIBERAL GENEROUS
CHARITY ALMS DOLE GIFT LOVE
PITY RUTH MERCY BASKET BOUNTY
CARITAS HANDOUT LARGESS
LENIENCE TZEDAKAH
CHARIVARI BABEL SHALLAL
SERENADE SHIVAREE
CHARLATAN FAKE CHEAT FAKER
FRAUD QUACK CABOTIN EMPIRIC
IMPOSTER MAGICIAN SYCOPHANT
CHARLES II DAVID
CHARLIE MCCARTHY STOOGE
CHARLOCK KRAUT RUNCH HARLOCK

KEDLOCK KERLOCK MUSTARD
SINAPIS YELLOWS CHARDOCK
CHEDLOCK SKEDLOCK SKELLOCH
CHARM IT GBO KEY OBI CALM CHIC
HAND JINX JUJU JYNX LUCK MOJO
PLAY RUNE SNOW SONG TAKE TILL
ZOGO ALLAY BRIEF CATCH FAVOR
FREET FREIT GRACE LAMIN MAGIC
OBEAH SAFFI SAFIE SPELL VENUS
WANGA WEIRD ALLURE AMULET
BEAUTY CARACT DEASIL ENAMOR
ENGAGE ENTICE FETISH GLAMOR
GRIGRI INCANT MANTRA MELODY
PLEASE SAPHIE SCARAB SOOTHE
SUBDUE SUMMON VOODOO
ABRAXAS ASSUAGE ATTRACT
BEGUILE BEWITCH CANTION
CANTRIP CONJURE CONTROL
DELIGHT ENCHANT ENTHRAL
FLATTER HEITIKI PERIAPT PHILTER
PHILTRE SINGING SORCERY
BLESSING BRELOQUE COQUETRY
ENTHRALL ENTRANCE GLAUMRIE
GREEGREE PISHOGUE PRACTICE
TALISMAN
CHARMED CAPTIVE
CHARMER SIREN EXORCIST
MAGICIAN SORCERER ENCHANTER
CHARMING LEPID SWEET GOLDEN
WIZARD AMIABLE DARLING
EYESOME TEMPEAN WINNING
WINSOME ADORABLE DELICATE
GRACEFUL LOVESOME
CHARNEL GHASTLY CEMETERY
GOLGOTHA
CHARON (FATHER OF —) EREBUS
(MOTHER OF —) NOX
CHARPOY COT
CHARQUI JERKY XARQUE
CHART MAP BILL CARD PLAN PLAT
PLOT ROSE CARTE GRAPH STILL
RECORD SCHEME DIAGRAM
EMAGRAM EXPLORE ISOTYPE
OUTLINE PROJECT DOCUMENT
DOPEBOOK MERCATOR PLATFORM
(— BOOK) WAGONER
(— FROM AIR) AEROVIEW
(— MARK) VIGIA
(— OF A COURSE) RUTTER
(MARINER'S —) ROSE
(WEATHER —) ANALOGUE
CHARTER FIX LET BOND BOOK DEED
HIRE RENT CARTE CHART FUERO
GRANT LEASE SANAD CHARTA
PERMIT SUNNUD DIPLOMA
CONTRACT GRUNDLOV HEIRLOOM
LANDBOOK MONOPOLY PANCHART
CHARWOMAN CHARER CHARLADY
PORTRESS JANITRESS
CHARY SHY DEAR WARY CHERE
SCANT SPARE DAINTY FRUGAL
PRIZED SKIMPY CAREFUL CURIOUS
SPARING CAUTIOUS HESITANT
PRECIOUS RESERVED SPAREFUL
VIGILANT
CHASE FOG SIC SUE FALL HUNT
JERL SHAG SHOO SICK ANNOY
CATCH CHEVY CHIVY DRIVE HARRY
HOUND SCORE SHACK CACCIA

CHIVVY CHOUSE EMBOSS FOLLOW
FRIEZE FURROW GALLOP GROOVE
HALLOO HARASS HOLLOW INDENT
PURSUE QUARRY SCORSE TRENCH
CHANNEL ENGRAVE HUNTING
PURSUIT ORNAMENT PURCHASE
(— GAME) COURSE
(— HARD) RATTLE
CHASER RAM DRINK HOUND
FROGGER
(WOMAN —) SHEEPBITER
CHASM GAP KIN PIT GULF RIFT
YAWN ABYSS BLANK CANON CHAOS
CLEFT GORGE BREACH CANYON
HIATUS FISSURE MEGARON
SWALLOW VACANCY APERTURE
CREVASSE INTERVAL VACATION
CHASSE SLIP GLIDE SASHAY
CHASSEUR HUNTER BELLBOY
DOORMAN FOOTMAN HUNTSMAN
CHASSIS SASH FRAME FIGURE
CHASTE CAST PURE CLEAN ZONED
DECENT HONEST MODEST PROPER
SEVERE VESTAL VIRGIN CLEANLY
PUDICAL REFINED CELIBATE
INNOCENT VIRGINLY VIRTUOUS
CHASTEN RATE ABASE SMITE
SMOTE SNEAP SOBER HUMBLE
PUNISH REFINE SUBDUE TEMPER
AFFLICT CENSURE CORRECT
NURTURE CHASTISE MODERATE
RESTRAIN
CHASTISE BEAT FIRK FLOG LASH
SLAP TRIM WHIP AMEND BLAME
FEEZE SCOLD SPANK SPILL STRAP
TAUNT ACCUSE ANOINT BERATE
CHARGE PUNISH PURIFY REBUKE
REFINE SWINGE TEMPER THRASH
TICKLE CHASTEN CORRECT
REPROVE SCOURGE SHINGLE
SUSPECT
CHASTISEMENT ROD TOCO TOKO
CENSURE PAYMENT FLOGGING
(DIVINE —) WRATH
CHASTITY HONOR PURITY VIRTUE
HONESTY MODESTY CELIBACY
GOODNESS PUDICITY INNOCENCE
CHASUBLE CASULA DEACON INFULA
PLANET PAENULA PIANETA
VESTMENT
CHAT GAS JAW MAG BIRD CHIN
CONE COZE DISH GIST TALK TELL
TOVE TWIG YARN AMENT CAUSE
COOSE CRACK DALLY PITCH POINT
PRATE PROSE PROSS SPEAK SPIKE
VISIT BABBLE BRANCH CATKIN
CONFAB COURSE DEVICE GABBLE
GIBBER GOSSIP GOSTER HOBNOB
JABBER NATTER POTATO POTTER
SAMARA CHAFFER CHATTER
CAUSERIE CHATTERY CONVERSE
SPIKELET STROBILE
CHATEAU HOUSE TOWER CASTLE
MANSION SCHLOSS CHATELET
FORTRESS
CHATON BASIL BEZEL BEZIL STONE
COATING SETTING
CHATTEL CATTLE PLEDGE FIXTURE
CATALLUM PERSONAL

(DISTRAINT OF —S) NAAM
(PL.) STUFF FARLEU FARLEY
COMODATO HOUSEHOLD
CHATTER GAB JAW MAG YAP BLAB
CARP CHAT CHIN CLAP CLAT DISH
GASH HACK KNAP RICK TALK TEAR
YIRR CABAL CLACK GARRE HAVER
PRATE SHAKE BABBLE BRUDGE
CACKLE CLAVER GABBLE GIBBER
GOSSIP JABBER JANGLE JARGON
PALTER RATTLE SHIVER TATTER
TATTLE TINKLE YAMMER YATTER
BLABBER BRABBLE CHACKLE
CHAFFER CHIPPER CHITTER
CLACKET CLATTER CLITTER
NASHGOB PALAVER PRABBLE
PRATING PRATTLE SHATTER
SMATTER TRATTLE TWATTLE
TWITTER TWITTLE WHITTER
BABBLING LOLLYGAG SCHMOOSE
VERBIAGE
CHATTERBOX JAY MAG PIET BUCCO
CLACK CRYSTE GOSSIP MAGPIE
CHATTERER JAY CHUET CHEWET
GABBER MAGPIE RATTLE HAVERER
CHATTERING PIET BABBLY CHAVISH
POPPING TWITTER BABBLING
CHATTY CHIRRUPY GARRULOUS
CHAUFFEUR DRIVER SHOVER
TESTER
CHAUVINISM JINGOISM
CHAUVINIST JINGO JINGOIST
CHAW JAW VEX CHEW ENVY MULL
GRIND PONDER
CHAYOTE CHOCHO TALLOTE
HUISQUIL MIRLITON
CHEAP LOW BASE GAIN POOR VILE
BORAX CLOSE FLASH GAUDY
GROSS KITCH LIGHT MUCKY NASTY
PRICE SNIDE TATTY TIGHT TINNY
VALUE ABJECT BRUMMY CHEESY
COMMON CRUMBY CRUMMY LEADEN
PLENTY SHODDY SORDID STINGY
TAWDRY TRASHY UNDEAR BARGAIN
CHINTZY POPULAR TINHORN
BRUMMAGE INFERIOR PENNORTH
SIXPENNY TWOPENNY
(— ITEM) TWOFER
CHEAPEN DOCK STALE VILIFY
SMALLEN
CHEAP SKATE STIFF
CHEAT DO BAM BOB COG CON FOB
FOP FUB GIP GUM GYP JEW JIG NIP
TOP BEAT BILK BITE BULL BURN
CLIP COLT CRIB DISH DUFF DUPE
FAKE FIRK FLAM FLUM GECK GULL
HAVE HOAX JILT JINK JOUK KNAP
LIAR MACE MUMP NAIL NICK NOSE
POOP PULL REAM ROOK SELL SHAM
SILE SKIN SLUR SNAP SWAP SWOP
TRIM WEED WIPE BITCH BLINK
BOOTY BUNCO BUNKO COZEN
CROOK CULLY DODGE FAKER FLING
FOIST FOURB FRAUD FUDGE GLEEK
GOUGE GREEK GUILE HOCUS KNAVE
LURCH MULCT PINCH PLOAT ROGUE
SCAMP SCREW SHARP SHORT
SLANG SPOIL STICK STIFF STING
SWICK SWIKE TOUCH TRICK VERSE

WELSH WRINK BAFFLE BLANCH
BUBBLE BUCKET CHIAUS CHISEL
CHOUSE CLOYNE COGGER DADDLE
DECEIT DELUDE DERIDE DIDDLE
DOODLE DUFFER EMUNGE EUCHRE
FIDDLE FLEECE GREASE HUMBUG
HUMMER HUSTLE ILLUDE JOCKEY
NIGGLE NOBBLE NUZZLE OUTWIT
RADDLE RENEGE SHAVER SHICER
SNUDGE SUCKER TWICER ABUSION
BEGUILE CHICANE DECEIVE
DEFRAUD ESCHEAT FAITOUR
FINAGLE FINESSE FOISTER
GUDGEON JUGGLER MISLEAD
PLUNDER QUIBBLE SHARPER
SHIFTER SKELDER SLICKER
SWINDLE VERNEUK ARTIFICE
BEJUGGLE CHALDESE CHISELER
DELUSION HOODWINK IMPOSTOR
INTRIGUE OUTREACH OVERTAKE
SHAMMOCK SWINDLER
CHEATED SOLD
CHEATER BITE GULL KNAVE BILKER
TOPPER SHARPER FINAGLER
TREACHER
CHEATING HOCUS BARRAT ODLING
ABUSIVE FUBBERY MICHERY
ROGUERY CHEATERY JUGGLING
TRICKERY
CHECK BIT DAM HAP LID NAB NIP
SAY SET TAB BAIL BALK BEAT BILK
BILL CHIP CHIT COOK CRIB CURB
DAMP FACE FOIL GAGE HURT ITEM
KITE PAWL REIN SKID SNEB SNIB
SNIP SNUB STAY STEM STOP STUB
TAKE TEST TICK TURN TWIT WERE
ABORT ALLAY ANNUL BLOCK BRAKE
CATCH CHIDE CHILL CHING CHOKE
CRACK CROOK DAUNT DELAY
DETER DRAFT EMBAR FACER FAULT
GAUGE LIMIT MODER PAUSE QUELL
REPEL SNAPE SPOKE STALL STILL
STUNT TALLY TAUNT THROW TOKEN
WAVER ARAYNE ARREST ATTACK
BAFFLE BOTTLE BRIDLE CHEQUE
COUPON DAMPEN DEFEAT DETAIN
DETENT DURESS GRAVEL HAFFET
HAFFIT HINDER IMPEDE OPPOSE
OUTWIT QUENCH RABBET REBATE
REBUFF REBUKE RETURN SCOTCH
STANCH STAYER STIFLE STYMIE
TICKET VERIFY ANSTOSS AWEBAND
BACKSET BECLOUD COMMAND
CONTAIN CONTROL COUNTER
CURTAIN DRAUGHT INHIBIT
MONITOR REFRAIN REPRESS
REPROOF REPROVE REPULSE
REVERSE SETBACK SNAFFLE
STAUNCH STOPPER TRAMMEL
TROUBLE BULKHEAD ENCUMBER
HOLDBACK OBSTRUCT PULLBACK
RESTRAIN WITHHOLD
(— ENTHUSIASM) DISMAY
(— GRADUALLY) CUSHION
(— GROWTH) BLAST STINT STUNT
(— IN GLASS) SPLIT
(— IN TIMBER) STARSHAKE
(— MOTION) SPRAG
(— OF HORSE) SACCADE

(— PASSER) PAPERHANGER
(— PROGRESS) DEFEAT
(FORGED —) STIFF STUMER
(HOLD IN —) COMPESCE
(RESTAURANT —) LAWING
(WORTHLESS —) DUD
CHECKED CHECK BEATEN CLOSED
CAPTIVE STOPPED
CHECKER DAM DICE FRET KING
CHECK FREAK FRECK PIECE WHITE
DAMPER DRAUGHT
CHECKERBERRY JINKS DRUNKARD
TEABERRY
CHECKERBOARD TABLE DAMBROD
DAMBOARD
CHECKERED PIED VAIR DICED PLAID
CHECKY MOTLEY
CHECKERS DRAFTS CHEQUERS
DRAUGHTS
CHECKERWORK TESSEL CHECKER
TESSERA
CHECKING REST BLOCK SETBACK
EBRILLADE
CHECKMATE LICK MATE STOP
UNDO BAFFLE CORNER DEFEAT
OUTWIT STYMIE THWART SUIMATE
CHECKSTONE CHUCK
CHEDDAR CHEESE
CHEEK CHAP CHOP GALL GENA
JAMB JOLE JOWL LEER SASS WANG
WANK BUCCA CHOKE CHYAK NERVE
SAUCE SHICK CHYACK HAFFET
HAFFIT OXCHEEK AUDACITY
TEMERITY
(— OF SPUR) SHANK
(— OF VISE) CHAP
CHEEKBONE MALAR ZYGOMA
CHEEP PIP YAP YIP CHIP HINT PEEP
PULE CHIRP CREAK TWEET SQUEAK
TATTLE
CHEER OLE RAH FARE FOOD MIND
ROOT VIVA YELL BRAVO CHIRK
ELATE ERECT FEAST HEART HUZZA
JOLLY MIRTH SHOUT SPORT TIGER
WHOOP CANTLE GAIETY HOORAY
HURRAH HUZZAH REHETE SOLACE
VIANDS ACCLAIM ANIMATE APPLAUD
CHERISH COMFORT CONSOLE
ENCHEER GLADDEN HEARTEN
JOLLITY LIGHTEN REFRESH REJOICE
SUPPORT UPRAISE APPLAUSE
BRIGHTEN HILARITY INSPIRIT
RECREATE VIVACITY
(BURST OF —S) SALVO
(GOOD —) WELFARE
(JAPANESE —) BANZAI
(SORRY —) PENANCE
CHEERFUL GAY CANT GLAD GLEG
GOOD HIGH ROSY CADGY CANTY
CHIRK DOUCE HAPPY JOLLY LIGHT
MERRY PEART READY SAPPY
SUNNY VAUDY BLITHE BRIGHT
CHEERY CHIRPY CROUSE GAWSIE
GENIAL HEARTY HILARY JOCUND
LIVELY BUOYANT CHERRLY CHIPPER
JOCULAR WINSOME CHEERING
CHIRRUPY EUPEPTIC FRIENDLY
GLADSOME HOMELIKE SANGUINE
SUNBEAMY SUNSHINE

CHEERFULLY GLADLY CANTILY
CHEERLY JOLLILY CHEERILY
GENIALLY
CHEERFULNESS JOY GLEE TAIT
CHEER CHERTE GAIETY GAYETY
LEVITY SPIRIT JOLLITY FESTIVAL
GLADNESS HILARITY
CHEERING GLAD CORDIAL
CHEERFUL CHIRPING
CHEERLESS SAD BLAE COLD DIRE
DRAB GLUM GRAY BLEAK DREAR
ELYNG WASTE DISMAL DREARY
GLOOMY WINTRY DOLEFUL
FORLORN JOYLESS SUNLESS
DEJECTED DESOLATE LITHLESS
CHEER PINE CHIL
CHEERY BRIGHT GAYSOME
CHEESE OKA BLUE BRIE EDAM FETA
HAND JACK TRIP APPLE BRICK
COLBY CREAM DAISY DERBY
GOUDA GRANA KENNO SWISS
WHEEL ZIEGA ZIGER ASIAGO
BARRIE BONDON BRYNZA CANTAL
CASSAN DUNLOP GLARUS JUNKET
MYSOST SAANEN SBRINZ TILSIT
ZIEGER ANGELOT CHEDDAR
CHEVRET COTTAGE FONTINA
FROMAGE GJEDOST GRUYERE
KEBBUCK PRIMOST PROVOLA
SAPSAGO STILTON TRUCKLE
AMERICAN CHESHIRE EMMENTAL
LONGHORN MUENSTER PARMESAN
PECORINO SLIPCOAT LEICESTER
MOUSETRAP WILTSHIRE
(— **FANCIER**) TUROPHILE
(**INFERIOR** —) DICK
(**LARGE** —) KEBBOC
CHEESEPARING STINGY
CHEESE VAT CHESSEL CHESSART
CHEESEWOOD BONEWOOD
WHITEWOOD
CHEETAH CAT YOUSE YOUZE
GUEPARD
CHEF COOK SAUCIER CUISINIER
CHEFOO YENTAI
CHELA HAND MANUS PINCER
CHELATE COMPLEX
CHELICERA FALX FANG FALCER
MANDIBLE
CHEMICAL (ALSO SEE SPECIFIC
HEADINGS) ACID BASE SALT ALKALI
BLEACH CHEMIC DODGER SAFENER
ADDITIVE ALGICIDE CATALYST
DEHORNER
CHEMIN-DE-FER SHIMMY
CHEMISE SHIFT SHIRT SIMAR
SMOCK CAMISA SHIMMY LINGERIE
CHEMISETTE SHAM GUIMPE TUCKER
PARTLET
CHEMIST ANALYST ASSAYER
CHEMICK BENCHMAN COLORIST
DRUGGIST
CHENDE CHINOA
CHENFISH KINGFISH
CHENILLE SNAIL
CHEQUEEN BASKET SEQUIN ZEQUIN
CECCHINE ZECCHINO
CHERAW SARA
CHEREMIS MARI

CHERISH AID HUG PET BEAR DOTE
HAVE HOPE LIKE LOVE SAVE ADORE
BOSOM BROOD CHEER CLING
COWER ENJOY NURSE PRIZE VALUE
CARESS ESTEEM FADDLE FONDLE
FOSTER GRUDGE HARBOR NESTLE
NUZZLE PAMPER PETTLE REVERE
COMFORT EMBOSOM EMBRACE
INDULGE NOURISH NURTURE
PROTECT SUPPORT SUSTAIN
ENSHRINE INSPIRIT PRESERVE
TREASURE
CHERISHED DEAR BOSOM DANDILY
AFFECTED
CHEROOT TRICHI TRICHY
CHERRY BING CHOP DUKE FUJI
GEAN MERRY MOREL CORNEL
MAZARD BURBANK CAPULIN
CHAPMAN LAMBERT MAHALEB
MARASCA MAYDUKE MORELLO
OXHEART PITANGA WINDSOR
AMARELLE DURACINE EGGBERRY
LUKEWARD NAPOLEON ROSACEAN
CHERRY-COLORED CERISE
CHERRY PLUM MYROBALAN
CHERRY STONE PAIP
CHERT BOONE WHINSTONE
CHERUB AMOR EROS ANGEL CUPID
SERAPH SPIRIT AMORINO
AMORETTO CHERUBIM
CHERVIL BUN KECK ARFOIL CERFOIL
COWWEED HONEWORT MILKWEED
RATSBANE
CHESS CHEAT SHOGI CHECKER
SKITTLES
(— **MOVE**) ZUGZWANG
CHESSBOARD CHESS TABLE
CHECKER
CHESSMAN PIN KING PIECE
CHECKER CHEQUER
(— **SET**) MEINY MEINIE
(**ANY** — **BUT PAWN**) OFFICER
(**BISHOP** —) ALFIN ALPHIN ARCHER
(**CASTLE** —) JUEZ ROOK TOUR
UDGE JUDGE LEDGE TOWER
(**KNIGHT** —) HORSE CHEVALIER
(**PAWN** —) PON POUNE
(**QUEEN** —) FERS FIERS PHEARSE
CHEST ARK BOX FIX KIT PIX PYX
ARCA BUST CAJA CASH CIST CYST
FUND KIST SAFE SCOB AMBRY
BAHUT BUIST CADDY FRONT HOARD
HUTCH RAZEE SISTA TRUNK ALMOIN
BASKET BREAST BUNKER BUREAU
CAISSE CAJETA CASKET COFFER
COFFIN FORCER GIRNAL GIRNEL
HAMPER JORDAN LARNAX LOCKER
SCRINE SHRINE SPRUCE STRIPE
THORAX WANGAN BRAZIER BRISKET
CAISSON CAPCASE CASSONE
COMMODE DEPOSIT DRAWERS
DRESSER ENCLOSE HIGHBOY
TOOLBOX WANIGAN WINDBAG
CISTVAEN CUPBOARD FORCELET
MANIFOLD STANDARD TREASURE
TREASURY
(— **FOR CUTLERY**) CANTEEN
(— **OF ORES**) CAXON
(**FRONT OF** —) BREAST

CHESTNUT JOKE LING RATA BROWN
HORSE CASTOR MARRON SATIVA
CRENATA DENTATA
(**HORSE** —) CONKER
(**POLYNESIAN** —) RATA
(**WATER** —) LING
CHESTNUT-COLORED BAY ROAN
CHEVAL-DE-FRISE TURNPIKE
CHEVAL GLASS PSYCHE
CHEVALIER CADET NOBLE KNIGHT
GALLANT CAVALIER HORSEMAN
CHEVIN CHUB CHEVESNE
CHEVRON BEAM MARK WOUND
RAFTER STRIPE ZIGZAG
CHEVROTAIN MUSK NAPU DEERLET
KANCHIL MEMINNA PLANDOK
TRAGULE BOOMORAH PEESOREH
RUMINANT
CHEW CUD EAT GUM TAW BITE
CHAM CHAW GNAW QUID CHAMP
CHONK GRIND MUNCH RUMEN
CRUNCH MUMBLE CHUMBLE
MEDITATE RUMINATE
(— **UP NOISILY**) CHANK GROUZE
CHEWINK FINCH JOREE TOWHEE
GRASSET
CHEYENNE DOG
CHIAN SCIAN
CHIANTI FLORENCE
CHIASTOLITE MACLE ANDALUSITE
CHIBCHA MUISCA
CHIC PERT POSH TRIG TRIM KIPPY
NATTY NIFTY SMART CHICHI
DAPPER GIGOLO MODISH ELEGANT
STYLISH
CHICAGO PORKOPOLIS
CHICANE DECEPTION
CHICANERY DIRT RUSE WILE FEINT
TRICK ARTIFICE INTRIGUE TRICKERY
DECEPTION
CHICK BIRD GIRL PEEP TICK CHILD
NATTY POULET SCREEN SEQUIN
SPROUT CHICKEN CHUCKIE
CHICKADEE BLACKCAP TITMOUSE
CHICKEN HEN KIP COCK FOWL
BIDDY CAPON CHICK CHILD CHOOK
CHUCK DEEDY FRYER LAYER
MANOC POULT SILKY CHICKY
PULLET SULTAN SUSSEX TURKEN
ANCOBAR BOARDER BROILER
DIBBLER POUSSIN ROASTER
ROOSTER SCRATCH ARAUCANA
COCKEREL PHASANID SPRINGER
(— **SHELTER**) MOTHER
CHICKEN COOP CAVY CAVIE
CHICKEN POX SOREHEAD
VARICELLA
CHICK-PEA CHIT GRAM CHICH CICER
COWGRAM SOWGRAM GARBANZO
GARVANCE
(**PL.**) FASELS
CHICKWEED BLINK BLINKS SPURRY
ALLBONE STARWORT
CHICO SAPODILLA
CHICORY BUNK CREPIS ENDIVE
SUCCORY WITLOOF BLUEWEED
COMPOSIT
CHIDE FUSS RAIL RATE BLAME
CHECK FLITE FLYTE SCOLD SNEAP

BERATE REBUFF REBUKE SCHOOL
THREAP THREAT THREEP TONGUE
CENSURE REPROVE UPBRAID
WRANGLE ADMONISH LAMBASTE
REPROACH

CHIEF (ALSO SEE CHIEFTAIN) BO
AGA BIG BOH CAP CID COB DUX
MIR MOI TOP AGHA ALII ARCH ARII
BOSS CAID CHEF COCK DATO DEAN
DOEG DUCE DUKE HEAD HIER HIGH
INCA JARL JEFE KAID KHAN KING
MAIN MICO MOST NAIK ONLY QAID
RAIS RAJA REIS TYEE ALDER ALPHA
ARIKI DATTO ELDER FIRST GREAT
MAJOR MATAI NAYAK PRIMA PRIME
PRIMO RAJAH RULER THANE TITAN
VITAL ZAQUE ZIPPA ADALID CABEZA
DEPUTY FLAITH HEADLY INKOSI
KEHAYA KUBERA KUVERA LEADER
LULUAI MASTER MIRDHA NAIQUE
PENLOP PRABHU PRIMAL RECTOR
SACHEM SAYYID SHAYKH SHEIKH
SHERIF STAPLE SUDDER TOPMAN
TURNUS CAPITAL CAPTAIN CENTRAL
EMINENT FOREMAN GENERAL
HEADMAN INGOMAR LEADING
LEMPIRA MUGWUMP OVERMAN
PADRONE PALMARY POLYGAR
PRELATE PREMIER PRIMARY
SHEREEF STELLAR SUPREME
TOPSMAN TRIBUNE CABOCEER
CAPITANO CARDINAL DECURION
DIRECTOR DOMINANT ELDORADO
ESPECIAL FOREMOST GOVERNOR
HEADSMAN HIERARCH INTIMATE
MOKADDAM SAGAMORE SUBCHIEF
(— IN INDIA) PRABHU SIRDAR
(— OF 10 MEN) DEAN
(— OF ADVOCATES) BATONNIER
(— OF RELIGIOUS ORDER) GENERAL
(CHINOOK —) TYEE
(CLAN —) TOISECH
(INDIAN —) SUNCK SACHEM
SUNCKE CACIQUE SAGAMORE
(MOHAMMEDAN —) DATO DATTO
SAYID SAYYID
(SCHOOL —) DUX
(TIBETAN —) POMBO
(TURKISH —) AGA AGHA
CHIEFTAIN BEG CHAM EMIR HEAD
JARL KHAN ASTUR CHIEF EMEER
LEADER SIRDAR CAUDILLO
HIAWATHA
CHIEFTAINCY STOOL CHIEFRY
CHIEFTAINESS QUEEN
CHIFFCHAFF PEGGY CHIPCHAP
CHIPCHOP
CHIFFON SHEER
CHIFFONIER BUREAU CABINET
COMMODE
CHIGGER BICHO PIQUE CHIGGA
CHIGOE GIGGER JIGGER LEPTUS
WHEELWORM
CHIGNON COB KNOT COBBE TWIST
CHIGOE SIKA BICHO NIGUA PIQUE
SCREW CHIGGA ENIGUA JIGGER
SANDBOY SANDWORM
CHIH FU PREFECT
CHILBLAIN KIBE MULE BLAIN MOOLS

MOULS PERNIO
CHILD BEN BOY BUD ELF GET IMP
KID LAD SON SOT TAD TOT WAY
BABA BABE BABY BATA BIRD BRAT
CHIT CION FOOD GIRL GYTE PAGE
PUSS TIKE TINY TOTO TROT TYKE
WEAN BAIRN BIRTH BROLL BROWL
CHICK CHIEL COOKY ELFIN GAMIN
ISSUE KEIKI OLIVE POULT SCION
TIDDY TRICK WAYNE WENCH WHELP
CHERUB COOKIE ENFANT FILIUS
FOSTER INFANT MOPPET NIPPER
PLEDGE PROLES STUMPY TACKER
TODDLE URCHIN BAMBINO CHOOKIE
CHOPPER CHRISOM COCKNEY
DICKENS GANGREL GYTLING
KINCHIN KITLING LAMBKIN PAPOOSE
PROGENY STICHEL SUBTEEN
TIDDLER TODDLER TROTTIE
WRAWLER YOUNKER BANTLING
CHISELER DAUGHTER EPIGONUS
JUVENILE LITTLING NURSLING
PRATTLER RUNABOUT WEANLING
WHIMLING
(— OF THE WORLD) WELTKIND
(— UNDER 7 YEARS) INFANS
(BAD-MANNERED —) GOOP
(CHUBBY —) CHUNK
(ELF'S —) OAF CHANGELING
(FOSTER —) DAULT NORRY NURRY
FOSTER REARLING
(ILLEGITIMATE —) MISHAP BASTARD
(INNOCENT —) CHRISOM
(LAST-BORN —) DILLING
(LOVED —) JOY
(MERRY —) SUNBEAM
(MISCHIEVOUS —) IMP LIMB TIKE
DICKENS
(NAKED —) SCUDDY
(NEWBORN —) STRANGER
(PAUPER —) MINDER
(PLAYFUL —) ELF WANTON
(PLUMP —) FOB FUB
(PRECOCIOUS —) PRODIGY
(PURE —) DOVE
(ROWDY —) HOODLUM
(SMALL —) TAD TOT SPUD GAITT
KIDDY TIDDY TOTUM KIDLET
PEEWEE TACKER BAIRNIE
(SPOILED —) CADE COCKNEY
(STUNTED —) URF
(TROUBLESOME —) STICHEL
(UNMANNERLY —) SMATCHET
(YOUNG —) BABY JOEY INFANT
SQUIRT GANGREL NESTLER
TODDLER BANTLING INNOCENT
LITTLING SUCKLING
(YOUNGEST —) WRIG DILLING
CHILDBED JIZZEN
CHILDBIRTH LABOR CRYING INLYING
TRAVAIL OXYTOCIA
(— WOMAN) PUERPERA
CHILDHOOD INFANCY CHILDAGE
(2ND —) DOTAGE TWICHILD
CHILDISH TID WEAK DANSY NAIVE
PETTY SILLY YOUNG CHITTY PULING
SIMPLE WEANLY ASININE BABYISH
CHILDLY FOOLISH KIDDISH PEEVISH
PROGENY PUERILE UNMANLY

BAIRNISH BRATTISH IMMATURE
TOOTLING
CHILDLESS ORBATE
CHILDREN ISSUE PROLES STRAIN
PROGENY OFFSPRING
(NUMBER OF —) PARITY

CHILE

BAY: COOK EYRE NENA TARN
LOMAS OTWAY SARCO DARWIN
INUTIL MORENO STOKES
TONGOY DYNELEY INGLESA
SKYRING DESOLATE
CAPE: DYER HORN CHOROS
HORNOS QUILAN TABLAS
DESEADO BASCUNAN CARRANZA
CAPITAL: SANTIAGO
CHANNEL: ANCHO CHEAP BEAGLE
COCKBURN MORALEDA
COIN: PESO LIBRA CONDOR
ESCUDO
DESERT: ATACAMA
GULF: ANCUD GUAFO PENAS
ARAUCO
INDIAN: ONA AUCA INCA ONAN
ARAUCA CHANGO YAHGAN
MAPUCHE MOLUCHE PAMPEAN
PATAGON PUEGIAN RANQUEL
ALIKULUF PICUNCHE TSONECAN
ISLAND: LUZ PRAT BYRON GUAFO
HOSTE MOCHA NUEVA NUNEZ
VIDAL CHILOE DAWSON EASTER
LENNOX PIAZZI PICTON QUILAN
RIESCO STOSCH TALCAN
ANGAMOS CAMPANA HANOVER
REFUGIO TRANQUI CLARENCE
HUAMBLIN NALCAYEC NAVARINO
TRAIGUEN
ISLANDS: CHONOS HERMITE
PAJAROS CHAUQUES
ISTHMUS: OFQUI
LAKE: TORO RANCO YELCHO
PUYEHUE RUPANCO
MEASURE: VARA LEGUA LINEA
CUADRA FANEGA
MOUNTAIN: MACA TORO CHATO
MAIPO PAINE POTRO PULAR
TORRE YOGAN APIWAN BURNEY
CONICO JERVIS POQUIS RINCON
CHALTEL COPIAPO FITZROY
PALPANA VELLUDA COCHRANE
TRONADOR YANTELES
MOUNTAINS: ANDES DARWIN
ALMEIDA DOMEYKO
NATIVE: PATAGONIAN
PENINSULA: HARDY LACUY TAITAO
TUMBES
POINT: TORO GALLO LILES LOBOS
LOROS MORRO TALCA TETAS
VIEJA CACHOS GALERA MOLLES
ANGAMOS LAVAPIE
PORT: LOTA TOME ARICA
COQUIMBA
PROVINCE: AISEN ARICA AYSEN
MAULE NUBLE TALCA ARAUCO
BIOBIO CAUTIN CHILOE CURICO
OSORNO ATACAMA LINARES
MALLECO COQUIMBO OHIGGINS

SANTIAGO TARAPACA VALDIVIA
RIVER: LOA LAJA YALI ALHUE
AZAPA BRAVO BUENO ELQUI
ITATA LAUCA LLUTA MAIPO
MAULE PUELO RAHUE RAPEL
VITOR BIOBIO CAMINA CHOAPA
CHOROS CISNES COLINA
HUASCO LIMARI MORADO
PALENA POSCUA TOLTEN
COPIAPO VALDIVIA
SHRUB: LITRE
STRAIT: NELSON MAGELLAN
TOWN: BOCO CUYA LEBU LOTA
OCOA TOCO TOME ARICA TALCA
ARAUCO CURICO GATICO
OSORNO SERENA TEMUCO
VICUNA YUMBEL YUNGAY
CALDERA CHILLAN COPIAPO
COQUIMBO RANCAGUA
SANTIAGO VALDIVIA
TREE: RAULI
VOLCANO: LANIN MAIPO ANTUCO
LLAIMA OYAHUE TACORA
PETEROA SOCOMAP
WEIGHT: GRANO LIBRA QUINTAL
WIND: SURES

CHILE-BELLS COPIHUE LAPAGERIA
CHI-LIN KYLIN UNICORN
CHILL ICE RAW AGUE COLD COOL
DAZY ALGID ALGOR DAVER GELID
RIGOR SCHEL SHAKE FRAPPE
FREEZE FRIGID FROSTY SHIVER
SNELLY DEPRESS FRETISH FRISSON
MALARIA COLDNESS
CHILLED ACOLD CHILL FROZEN
STARVEN
CHILLING ICY COLD EERY BLEAK
EERIE CHILLY WINTRY GLACIAL
SHIVERY
CHILLY RAW COLD COOL LASH
ALGID BLEAK HUNCH AGUISH AIRISH
ARCTIC CRIMMY FROSTY FROZEN
LEEPIT
CHIMAERA BELUE DRAGON CATFISH
PLACOID RATFISH RATTAIL
DOODSKOP
CHIME DIN RIM BELL EDGE PEAL
RING SUIT TING AGREE CHIMB
CHINE PRATE ACCORD CLOCHE
CYMBAL JINGLE MELODY CONCORD
HARMONY SINGSONG
(PL.) BELL
CHIMER CYMAR SIMAR CHIMAR
TABARD
CHIMERA FANCY MIRAGE MOSAIC
POMATO ILLUSION
CHIMERICAL VAIN WILD INSANE
UTOPIAN DELUSIVE FANCIFUL
ROMANTIC IMAGINARY
CHIMNEY BAG LUM TUN FLUE LUMM
PIPE TUBE VENT GULLY STACK
TEWEL CHIMLA FUNNEL LOUVER
SMOKER TUNNEL FISSURE OPENING
ORIFICE FUMIDUCT
CHIMNEY CAP TURNCAP
CHIMNEY CORNER FIRESIDE
INGLENOOK

CHIMNEY COWL COW
CHIMNEY HOOD JACK
CHIMNEY PIECE PAREL
CHIMNEY PIPE TALLBOY
CHIMNEY POST SPEER
CHIMNEY SEAT SCONCE
CHIMNEY SWEEP SWEEP CHUMMY
FLUEMAN RAMONEUR
CHIMPANZEE APE CHIMP JACKO
JOCKO PIGMY PYGMY NCHEGA
PIGMEW PYGMEAN
CHIN JAW CHAT TSIN MENTUM
CHOLLER
(— **POINT**) MENTON POGONION
(**DOUBLE** —) BUCCULA CHOLLER
CHINA WARE JAPAN LENOX SPODE
CATHAY PARIAN SEVRES CERAMIC
CHEENEY DRESDEN LIMOGES
MEISSEN POTTERY CINCHONA
CROCKERY EGGSHELL

CHINA
ABORIGINE: YAO MANS MIAO
MANTZU YAOMIN MIAOTSE
AREA UNIT: MU MOU MOW
BAY: LAICHOW HANGCHOW
BUDDHA: FO
CAPE: OLWANPI
CAPITAL: PEKING TAIPEI PEIPING
CHANNEL: BASHI
COIN: PU CASH CENT MACE TAEL
TIAO YUAN SYCEE DOLLAR
DEPRESSION: TURFAN
DESERT: GOBI ORDOS SHAMO
ALASHAN TAKLAMAKAN
DIALECT: WU MIN AMOY HAKKA
CANTON HSIANG SWATOW
FOOCHOW WENCHOW
KANHAKKA MANDARIN
DRY LAKE: LOPNOR
DYNASTY: WU HAN SHU SUI WEI
YIN CHIN CHOU HSIA HSIN MING
SUNG TANG YUAN CHING
SHANG
GULF: POHAI CHIHLI TONKIN
PECHILI LIAOTUNG
ISLAND: AMOY FLAT MACAO
MATSU NAMKI CHUSAN HAINAN
PRATAS QUEMOY TAIWAN
YUHWAN FORMOSA HUNGTOW
TUNGSHA CHOUCHAN
KULANGSU STAUNTON
ISLANDS: PENGHU TACHEN
CHUSHAN MIAOTAO
LAKE: TAI CHAO KAOYU OLING
TELLI BAMTSO BORNOR EBINOR
ERHHAI KHANKA LOPNOR
NAMTSO POYANG CHALING
HUNGTSE KARANOR KOKONOR
HULUNNOR MONTCALM
TAROKTSO TELLINOR TIENCHIH
TSINGHAI TUNGTING
MEASURE: HO HU KO LI MU PU TO
TU FAN FEN PAU TOU TUN YIN
CHIH FANG KISH PARA QUEI
SHIH TSUN CHANG CHING
SHENG SHING CHUPAK KUNGHO
KUNGLI KUNGMU KUNGFEN

KUNGYIN KUNGCHIH
MOUNTAIN: OMI OMEI SUNG
KAILAS POBEDA EVEREST
MUZTABH SUNGSHAN
MOUNTAINS: ALTAY KUNLUN
ALASHAN KUENLUN MEILING
MINSHAN NANLING NANSHAN
TANGLHA BOGDOULA HIMALAYA
TAPASHAN TAYULING TIENSHAN
WUYLISHAN
NAME: CATHAY
NATIVE: PAT
PENINSULA: LEICHU LUICHOW
LIAOTUNG
PORT: AMOY WUHU AIGUN SHASI
ANTUNG CANTON CHEFOO
DAIREN ICHANG NINGPO PAKHOI
SWATOW SZEMAO WUCHOW
YOCHOW FOOCHOW HUNCHUN
MENGTSZ NANKING SAMSHUI
SANTUAO SOOCHOW WENCHOW
CHANGSHA HANGCHOW
KIUKIANG KONGMOON
LUNGCHOW SHANGHAI
TENGYUEH TIENTSIN TSINGTAO
WANHSIEN
PROVINCE: HONAN HOPEI HUNAN
HUPEI HUPEN JEHOL KANSU
KIRIN TIBET ANHWEI FUKIEN
SHANSI SHENSI TAIWAN YUNNAN
KIANGSI KWANGSI NGANHUI
CHEKIANG KWEICHOW LIAONING
MONGOLIA SHANTUNG
SZECHWAN TSINGHAI
MANCHURIA
RELIGION: JU SHINTO TAOISM
BUDDHISM
RESERVOIR: SUNGARI
RIVER: SI HAN ILI MIN NEN PEI
WEI AMUR HUAI LOHO TUNG
YALU YUAN YUEN ARGUN
FENHO MACHU PEIHO TARIM
TUMEN WEIHO CHUMAR DRECHU
DZACHU KHOTAN KUMARA
LIAOHO MANASS MEKONG
OCHINA URUNGU YELLOW
HOANGHO HWANGHO KERULEN
KIALING SALWEEN SIKIANG
SUNGARI TSANGPO WUKIANG
YANGTZE YARKAND YUKIANG
CHERCHEN HANKIANG
HUNGSHUI MINKIANG
RULER: WANG
SEA: ECHINA SCHINA YELLOW
STRAIT: HAINAN TAIWAN
FORMOSA
TOWN: BAI NOH AHPA AMOY ANSI
ANTA AQSU FUYU GUMA HAMI
HUMA IPIN KIAN KISI LINI LOHO
LUTA MOHO MOYU MULI NIYA
NOHO NURA OMIN OWPU RIMA
SAKA SIAN TALI TAYU WUHU
WUSU WUTU YAAN CHIAI FUSIN
HOFEI ICHUN JEHOL KIRIN
KOKLU LHASA MACAO PENKI
SHASI TAIAN TALAI TUTZE
TUYUN TZEPO WUHAN WUSIH

YENKI YULIN YUMEN ANSHAN
ANTUNG CANTON DAIREN
FUCHAU FUSHUN HANKOW
HANTAN HARBIN HOIHOW
KALGAN LOYANG LUSHUN
MUKDEN NINGPO PAOTOW
PEKING PENGPU SUCHOW
SWATOW TAINAN TAIPEI TALIEN
TSINAN YUNNAN CHUNGTU
FATSHAN FOOCHOW HANYANG
HUHEHOOT KAIFENG KUNMING
KWEISUI LANCHOW NANKING
PAOTING PEIPING SOOCHOW
TAIYUAN TZEKUNG URUMCHI
WUCHANG YENPING CHANGSHA
CHAOCHOW CHENGTEH
CHINCHOW HANGCHOW
KIAOCHOW KWEIYANG
NANCHANG QARAQASH
SHANGHAI SHENYANG SIANGTAN
TANGSHAN TENGCHOW TIENTSIN
TSINGTAO TUNGCHOW
CHUNGKING
WEIGHT: LI TA FAN FEN HAO KIN
SSU TAN YIN CHEE CHIN DONG
MACE SHIH TAEL CATTY CHIEN
LIANG PICUL TCHIN HAIKWAN
KUNGFEN KUNGSSU KUNGCHIN

CHINABERRY LILAC AZEDARACH
CHINABALL SOAPBERRY
CHINA BLUE NIKKO
CHINA HAT HAELTZUK HEILTSUK
CHINAMAN CHOW JOHN JOHNNY
(PL.) TANKA
CHINA ROSE MANETTI HIBISCUS
CHINA STONE PETUNSE
CHINA TREE LILAC HAGBUSH
CHINCHILLA ABROCOME VIZCACHA
CHINE BACK IKAT CHINK CRACK
CREST GORGE RIDGE SPINE CLEAVE
RAVINE SPROUT CREVICE
CHINESE PAT BABA CHOW CERAI
CHINK SERES SERIC SINIC MANZAS
MONGOL ASIATIC CATAIAN CHINOIS
PIGTAIL SANGLEY
CHINESE ARTICHOKE CROSNE
CHOROGI CROSNES STACHYS
KNOTROOT
CHINESE CABBAGE PECHAY
PAKCHOI
CHINESE DATE JUJUBE
CHING TSING
CHINGPAW KACHIN SINGPHO
YAWYINS
CHINIOFON YATREN
CHINK GAP BORE CASH CHAP COIN
JINK KINK RENT RIFT RIME SCAR
BOORE CHECK CHINE CHUNK CLEFT
CRACK GRIKE KNACK MONEY
CRANNY SPRAIN CHINKLE CREVICE
FISSURE APERTURE
CHINPIECE BARBEL
CHINQUAPIN OAK BONNET
BONNETS CANDOCK CHESTNUT
WANKAPIN YOCKERNUT
CHINTZ PINTADO SALAMPORE
CHIONE (FATHER OF —) BOREAS

(HUSBAND OF —) NEPTUNE
(MOTHER OF —) ORITHYIA
DAEDALION
(SLAYER OF —) DIANA
(SON —) EUMOLPUS AUTOLYCUS
PHILAMMON
CHIOT SCIOT
CHIP BIT CUT DIB GAG HEW NIG
BONE CHAP CLIP HACK KNAP KNOP
NICK PARE SAND SKIN SNIP SNUB
BEACH CHECK CRACK FLAKE PIECE
SCRAP SKELF SLICE SPALE SPALL
SPALT SPAWL SPELL SPOON WASTE
BORING CHISEL GALLET MARKER
NOODLE COUNTER SHAVING
CHIPPING COSSETTE FRAGMENT
SPLINTER WHITLING
(— OF SOLDER) LINK
(— OF WOOD) SPOON
(— OUT) DESEAM
(BUFFALO —S) BODEWASH
(CORN —S) FRITOS
(POTATO —) CRISP
(SUPPLY OF —S) STACK
CHIPMAN SCRAPMAN
CHIPMUNK CHIPPY GOPHER GRINNY
HACKEE GRINNIE SQUIRREL
CHIPPENDALE AFGHAN
CHIPPER GAY SPRY CHIRP PERKY
BABBLE COCKEY FIERCE HACKER
KIPPER LIVELY CHATTER CHEERFUL
CHIRRUP TWITTER
CHIPPINGS SWARF
CHIRO BONYFISH FRANCESCA
CHIROGRAPHY WRITING
CHIRON (— AS CONSTELLATION)
SAGITTARIUS
(FATHER OF —) SATURN
(MOTHER OF —) PHILYRA
CHIROPODIST PEDICURE
CORNCUTTER
CHIRP PEW PIP PEEK PEEP PIPE
TWIT WEAK CHEEP CHELP CHIRK
CHIRL CHIRM CHIRT TWEET TWINK
CHIPPER CHIRRUP CHITTER REJOICE
SHATTER TWEEDLE TWITTER
WHEETLE WHITTER
CHIRR PITTER
CHIRU SUS
CHISEL BUR CUT GAD CHIP ETCH
FORM MOIL PARE SEAT SETT TANG
TOOL BRUZZ BURIN CARVE CHEAT
DROVE GOUGE HARDY POINT
SCOOP SLICK STIFF BROACH
CHESIL FIRMER FORMER GRAVEL
HAGGLE POMMEL QUARRY REAMER
TOOLER BARGAIN BOASTER
CHIPPER ENGRAVE GRADINE
GRUBBER POINTER QUARREL
SCOOPER SCORPER SHINGLE
CROSSCUT SPLITTER
(BLACKSMITH'S —) HARDY HARDIE
(FLINT —) TRANCHET
(ICE —) SPUD
(JEWELER'S —) SCAUPER SCORPER
(PREHISTORIC —) CELT
(STONEMASON'S —) TOOL DROVE
POMMEL TOOLER SPLITTER
(TOOTHED —) GRADINE

(TRIANGULAR —) BUR BURR
(WHEELWRIGHT'S —) BRUZZ
CHISELER CHEAT CROOK COYOTE
GOUGER
CHIT DAB BILL NOTE DRAFT LETTER
VOUCHER
CHITARRONE ARCHLUTE
CHITCHAT GASH GUFF TALK
BANTER GOSSIP GOSSIPRY
BAVARDAGE
CHITINOUS SHELLY
CHITON EXOMIS DIPLOIS EXOMION
CHITTAMWOOD IRONWOOD
CHIVALROUS BRAVE CIVIL NOBLE
PREUX GENTLE POLITE GALLANT
GENTEEL VALIANT WARLIKE
KNIGHTLY
CHIVE CIVE SIVE CIVET SITHE
ALLIUM
CHIVY RUN VEX BAIT HUNT RACE
CHASE CHEVY TEASE BADGER
CHIVVY FLIGHT HARASS PURSUE
PURSUIT SCAMPER TORMENT
MANEUVER
CHLOASMA MOTH
CHLOR LEMON
CHLORIDE BUTTER CALOMEL
MURIATE ALEMBROTH
CHLORINE OXYGEN
CHLORION SPHEX
CHLORIS (FATHER OF —) AMPHION
(HUSBAND OF —) NELEUS
(MOTHER OF —) NIOBE
(SON OF —) NESTOR
CHLORITE AMESITE
CHOANA COLLAR
CHOBDAR USHER CHOPDAR
CHOCK COG PAD BLOCK BRACE
CHUCK CLEAT SPOKE SPRAG
WEDGE SCOTCH
(PL.) STOWWOOD
CHOCOLATE BUD CANDY COCOA
NORFOLK JACOLATT
CHOGAK SHOQ
CHOICE BET ODD TRY BEST FINE
FORE GOOD MIND PICK RARE WALE
WEAL WILL CREAM ELITE PRIME
VOICE CHOSEN DAINTY DESIRE
FLOWER OPTION PICKED PLUMMY
SELECT DILEMMA ELEGANT
EXCERPT PERMISS DELICATE
ELECTION EXIMIOUS UNCOMMON
VOLITION
(FAVORITE —) STANDBY
(FREE —) SWING DRUTHERS
CHOIR KERE QUIRE CHAPEL CHORUS
CHORALE CONCERT KAPELLE
PSALMODY
CHOIRBOY CLERGEON CHORISTER
CHOIR LEADER CANTOR CHORAGUS
CHORISTER PRECENTOR
CHOKE DAM GAG GOB CLOG DAMP
PLUG QUAR STOP WARP CHECK
CHOCK CLOSE GRAIN GRANE
SCRAG WORRY HINDER IMPEDE
STIFLE SWARVE CONGEST QUACKLE
QUEAZEN QUERKEN REPRESS
SILENCE SMOLDER SMOTHER
OBSTRUCT QUEASOME SCUMFISH

STOPPAGE STRANGLE SUPPRESS
THROTTLE
(— OFF) BESET
(— UP) CLOY GORGE STUFF
CHOKEBERRY DOGBERRY
SOAPBERRY
CHOKED FOUL WOOLY WOOLLY
CLOTTED
CHOKEDAMP STYTHE BLACKDAMP
CHOKERMAN CHAINER CHAINMAN
CHOKWE KIOKO
CHOLER IRE BILE FURY RAGE
ANGER WRATH SPLEEN TEMPER
DISTEMPER
CHOLERIC MAD ANGRY CROSS
FIERY HUFFY TESTY FUMISH IREFUL
TOUCHY BILIOUS ENRAGED
IRACUND PEEVISH PEPPERY
WASPISH WRATHFUL IMPATIENT
CHOLIAMB SCAZON
CHONDRIOME CYTOME
CHOOSE OPT TRY CHAP CULL LIKE
LIST LOVE LUST PICK TAKE VOTE
WALE WEAL ADOPT ELECT PRICK
ANOINT DECIDE PLEASE PREFER
SELECT EMBRACE ESPOUSE
EXTRACT SEPARATE
CHOOSY CHOICY FINICAL
CHOP AX AXE CUT HAG HEW JAW
LOP CHAP CHIP DICE GASH HACK
HASH HOWL RIVE SLIT CARVE
CLEFT CRACK KNOCK MINCE NOTCH
SLASH STAMP TRADE TRUCK
WHANG BARTER CHANGE CLEAVE
INCISE EXCHANGE
(— OFF) SNIG
(— SMALL) DEVIL MINCE
(— UP) HACKLE
(— WITH DULL AX) BUTTE
(PORK —) GRISKIN
CHOPINE CIOPPINO PANTOFLE
CHOPPED CUT CHAPPED
CHOPPER MINCER SLASHER
TRANCHET
CHOPPINESS CHOP JABBLE
CHOPPING BLOCK HACKLOG
CHOPPING TOOL (— CULTURE)
SOAN SOHAN
CHOPPY BUMPY LOPPY LUMPY
PECKY ROUGH SHORT POPPLY
CHORAL (— SOCIETY) ORPHEON
CHORD CORD DYAD ROLL TONE
CORDE NERVE TRIAD TRINE
ACCORD STRING TENDON TETRAD
CADENCE CONCORD HARMONY
ARPEGGIO DIAMETER FILAMENT
CHORDATA VERTEBRA
CHORE JOB JOT CHAR DUTY TASK
CHARE KNACK STINT ERRAND
BUSINESS
CHOREA JUMP JERKS
CHOREOGRAPHY TERPSICHORE
CHORION SEROSA
CHORISTER SINGER CHANTER
CHOIRBOY
CHORUS SONG CHOIR DRONE QUIRE
ACCORD ASSENT BURDEN UNISON
CHORALE HOLDING REFRAIN
RESPONSE THYMELICI

(— IN PLAY) GREX
CHOSEN ELECT ELITE SORTED
ELECTED FANCIED AFFECTED
SELECTED
CHOUGH COW CHANK CHEWET
CORBIE CHOCARD
CHOWRY COWTAIL
CHRISM CREAM CREME MURON
MYRON
CHRIST X KING LORD TRUE JUDGE
RANSOM VERITY MESSIAH SAVIOUR
DRIGHTEN PARAMOUR
(INFANT —) BAMBINO
CHRISTEN NAME KIRSEN BAPTIZE
CHRISTENING GOSSIPING
CHRISTIAN XN XT XTIAN UNIATE
GENTILE THOMEAN CHRISTEN
GALILEAN MELCHITE NAZARENE
ORIENTAL STONEITE TRADITOR
COLOSSIAN
(JEWISH —) JUDAIZER
(PL.) FLOCK LAPSED ACEPHALI
FAITHFUL
CHRISTIANIA CRISTY
CHRISTIANITY WAY XTY XNTY
CHRISTMAS NOEL YULE HOLIDAY
NATIVITY YULETIDE MIDWINTER
CHRISTMAS ROSE BEARFOOT
LUNGWORT MELAMPOD PEDELION
CHRIST'S-THORN NABK JUJUBE
ZIZYPHUS
CHROMA COLOR QUALITY
CHROMATIC HUEFUL FLAMING
SEMITONAL
CHROMATOPHORE ALLOPHORE
LIPOPHORE UNIVALENT
CHROMOSOME DIAD DYAD
HOMOLOG ALLOSOME AUTOSOME
IDIOSOME KARYOMERE LEPTONEMA
PLANOSOME
(PL.) GEMINI
CHROMOSPHERE SIERRA
CHRONIC FIXED SEVERE INTENSE
CONSTANT STUBBORN
CHRONICLE BRUT ANNAL DIARY
ENACT RECORD ACCOUNT HISTORY
RECITAL CORNICLE REGISTER
(PL.) ANNALS ARCHIVE
CHRONICLER WRITER CHRONIST
COMPILER RECORDER HISTORIAN
CHRONOLOGICAL TEMPORAL
CHRONOMETER DIAL HACK CLOCK
TIMER WATCH
CHRYSAL FRET
CHRYSALIS KELL PUPA AURELIA
CHRYSANTHEMUM MUM KIKU
SPOON BRUTUS POMPON KIKUMON
KIRIMON AZALEAMUM
CHRYSIN FLAVONE
CHRYSOBERYL CATEYE CHRYSOPAL
CYMOPHANE
CHRYSOLITE OLIVINE PERIDOT
CHRYSOPAL
CHTHONIAN INFERNAL
CHUB DACE DOLT FOOL KIYI LOUT
POLL CHOPA CHEVIN SHINER
CYPRINID FALLFISH MACKEREL
HORNYHEAD
CHUBBY FAT CHUFF FUBSY PLUMP

CHOATY CHUFFY PLUMPY ROTUND
ROLYPOLY
CHUB MACKEREL TINK TINKER
HARDHEAD SCOMBRID
CHUCK HEN LOG PIG CHUG GRUB
HURL JERK LUMP TOSS CHOCK
CLUCK PITCH THROW BOUNCE
CHUCKY COLLET CHUCKLE DISCARD
CHUCK-A-LUCK SWEAT HAZARD
BIRDCAGE
CHUCKER CROZER
CHUCK-FARTHING CHUCK KNICKER
CHUCKHOLE CAHOT CHUGHOLE
CHUCKLE CHUCK CLUCK EXULT
LAUGH GIGGLE GIZZEN KECKLE
SMUDGE TITTER CHORTLE
CHUD VEPS VEPSE
CHUDDAR PHULKARI
CHUFA SEDGE GLUMAL CYPRESS
EARTHNUT GALANGAL TIGERNUT
GROUNDNUT
CHUM CAD PAL BAIT MATE PARD
TOLE TOLL BUDDY BUTTY CRONY
AIKANE CHUMMY COBBER COPAIN
FRIEND PARDNER ROOMMATE
(— AROUND) HOBNOB
CHUMMY GREAT PALLY FAMILIAR
CHUMP ASS DOLT HEAD BLOCK
PUMPKIN ENDPIECE
CHUNCHO CHAMA
CHUNK DAB DAD FID GOB PAT WAD
JUNK JUNT SLUG CHOCK CHUCK
CLAUT PIECE THROW WHANG
WHANK DORNICK KNUCKLE
LUNCHEON
CHUNKY LUMPY PLUMP SQUAT
STOUT THICK TRUSS BLOCKY
CHUBBY STOCKY CHUNKED
CHURCH DOM SEE DOME FANE
FOLD HIGH KILL KIRK KURK TERA
ABBEY AUTEM FAITH FLOCK KOVIL
SAMAJ TITLE CHAPEL CHARGE
HIERON SPOUSE TEMPLE EDIFICE
FANACLE IGLESIA LATERAN
MEMORIA MINSTER RECTORY
STATION TEMPLET BASILICA
EBENEZER ECCLESIA PECULIAR
(— BOOK) TRIODION
(CHRISTIAN —) BODY ISRAEL
HERITAGE
CHURCHMAN KIRKMAN
(HIGH —) PUSEYIST PRELATIST
(LOW —) SIM LOWBOY SIMEONITE
CHURCH SERVICE HEARING
TENEBRAE
CHURCHWARDEN STRAW WARDEN
WARNER
CHURCHYARD HAW LITTEN
CEMETERY KIRKYARD
CHURL CAD MAN BOOR CARL GNOF
HIND LOUT SERF CARLE CEORL
CHUFF GNOFF KNAVE MISER
BODACH CARLOT HARLOT LUBBER
RUSTIC VASSAL YEOMAN BONDMAN
FREEMAN HASKARD HUSBAND
NIGGARD PEASANT VILLAIN VILLEIN
CHURLISH MEAN BLUFF GRUFF
ROUGH RUNTY SURLY URSAL
CRABBY RUSTIC SORDID SULLEN

VULGAR BOORISH CARLAGE
CARLISH CRABBED INCIVIL PEEVISH
VIOLENT
CHURN BEAT BOIL KIRN MOIL STIR
DRILL SHAKE BUBBLE SEETHE
AGITATE BARATTE TRUNDLE
CHUTE RUSH SLIP TUBE FLUME
HURRY RAPID SHOOT SLIDE
HOPPER TROUGH DECLINE DESCENT
DOWNFALL STAMPEDE TELEGRAPH
(MINING —) PASS TELEGRAPH
CIBOL SYBO ONION SYBOW SHALLOT
CIBORIUM PIX PYX CANOPY CIVORY
COFFER CIMBORIS
CICADA CAD CIGALE JARFLY
LOCUST TETTIX LYREMAN
HOMOPTER
CICATRICE FESTER
CICATRICLE TREAD GALLATURE
CICATRIX EYE MARK SCAB SCAR
SEAM
CICATRIZE FESTER SCARIFY
CICELY MYRRH
CICERO TULLY
CICERONE GUIDE PILOT MENTOR
ORATOR COURIER SIGHTSMAN
CICERONIAN TULLIAN
CID HERO CAMPEADOR
CIDER PERRY PERKIN SWANKY
SYDDIR POMMAGE BEVERAGE
COCCAGEE
(HARD —) APPLEJACK
(INFERIOR —) SWANKY
CIGAR PURO TOBY WEED BREVA
CLARO SEGAR SHUCK SMOKE
CONCHA CORONA HAVANA MADURA
MADURO MANILA STOGIE TWOFER
BOUQUET CHEROOT CULEBRA
LONDRES REGALIA TRABUCO
COLORADO LOCOFOCO PANATELA
PERFECTO PICKWICK PURITANO
CIGARETTE CIG FAG BIRI BUTT KING
PILL SKAG CUBEB JOINT SHUCK
SMOKE GASPER REEFER CIGARITO
(— BUTT) ROACH
(MARIHUANA —) STICK
CIGARFISH SCAD QUIAQUIA
CILIUM HAIR LASH EYELASH
UNCINUS BARBICEL CILIOLUM
CILLOSIS LIFEBLOOD
CIMBALOM CEMBALON DULCIMER
CIMEX BEDBUG ACANTHIA
CINCH BELT GIRD GRIP PIPE SNAP
GIRTH GRAVY BREEZE CINCHA
FASTEN PIANOLA SINECURE
CINCHONA CHINA QUINA
CINCINNATI PORKOPOLIS
CINCTURE BAND BELT GIRD HALO
LIST RING ZONE GIRTH CENTER
CESTUS COLLAR FILLET GIRDLE
BALDRIC COMPASS ENCIRCLE
SURCINGLE
CINDER ASH TAP COAL GRAY SCAR
SLAG CHARK DROSS EMBER
DANDER SCORIA CLINKER FOXTAIL
RESIDUE
(REFUSE —) BREEZE
(VOLCANIC —) LAPILLUS
(PL.) GLEEDS

CINEMATIZE FILMIZE
CINEMATOGRAPH KINO VERISCOPE
VITAGRAPH
CINERARIA SENECIO
CINGULUM BAND RIDGE GIRDLE
CINNAMON CANEL SPICE CASSIA
SANELA STACTE BARBASCO
(WILD —) BAYBERRY
CINNAMONROOT FLYBANE
FLEAWORT
CINNAMON STONE GARNET
ESSONITE
CINQUEFOIL FRASIER COWBERRY
HARDHACK ROSACEAN QUINTFOIL
CINYRAS (DAUGHTER OF —)
MYRRHA
(FATHER OF —) APOLLO
(SON OF —) ADONIS
CION BUD IMP SECT SLIP GRAFT
SCION SHOOT UVULA SARMENT
GRAFTING
CIPHER KEY NIL CODE NULL ZERO
ALBAM AUGHT OUGHT DECODE
DEVICE FIGURE LETTER NAUGHT
NOUGHT NUMBER SYMBOL
ATHBASH NULLITY MONOGRAM
VIGENERE NOTHINGLY
CIRCASSIAN ADIGHE KABARD
CHERKESS KABARDIN
CIRCE SIREN TEMPTER
(BROTHER OF —) AEETES
(FATHER OF —) SOL
(LOVER OF —) ULYSSES
(MOTHER OF —) PERSE
(SON OF —) TELEGONUS
CIRCLE DOT LAP ORB RED SET
CLUE CULT DISK GYRE HALO HOOP
IRIS LOOP MARU ORBE RING RINK
ROLL TOUR TURN ZONE BLACK
CAROL CLASS CROWN CYCLE
FETCH FRAME GROUP KREIS MONDE
PEARL REALM RHOMB RIGOL
ROUND ROWEL SWIRL TWIRL
BEZANT BROUGH CIRCUS CIRQUE
CLIQUE COLLET COLURE CORDON
CORONA DIADEM EQUANT GIRDLE
RONDEL ROTATE RUNDLE SPIRAL
SYSTEM TROPIC AZIMUTH CHUKKAR
CHUKKER CIRCLET CIRCUIT
COMPANY COMPASS CORONET
COTERIE ENCLOSE HORIZON
MONTHON REVOLVE RINGLET
DEFERENT ECLIPTIC FROSTBOW
SURROUND
(— AROUND ORGAN) ANNULET
(— IN BULL'S-EYE) CARTON
(— OF HELL) MALEBOLGE
(— OF MONOLITHS) CROMLECH
(— TRACED BY HORSE) VOLT
(ASTRONOMICAL —) EQUANT
EPICYCLE
(DANCE —) GALLEY
(FAIRY —) RINGLET
(GREAT —) EQUATOR ECLIPTIC
MERIDIAN
(IMAGINARY —) CYCLE DEFERENT
(INNER —) BOSOM
(PARHELIC —) FROSTBOW
(QUARTER —) ARC

(STONE —) CAROL HURLER
GORSEDD
(TRAVERSE —) RACER
(TWO —S) CACHET
CIRCLET BAND HALO HOOP RING
CROWN VERGE BANGLE CIRQUE
CORONA CIRCUIT CORONET
VALLARY BRACELET HEADBAND
CIRCUIT LAP AREA BOUT EYRE ITER
LOOP TOUR WEND ZONE AMBIT
CHAIN CYCLE ORBIT ROUND ROUTE
VIRON AMBAGE BUFFER DETOUR
DOUBLE SPHERE UMGANG ZODIAC
ADAPTER ADDRESS COMARCA
COMPASS COUNTER DIOCESE
ACCEPTER DIPLEXER DISTRICT
PERIPLUS PROGRESS
(BRANCH —) LEG
(ELECTRIC —) LEG LOOP DOUBLER
SQUELCH SECONDARY
(ELECTRONIC —) GATE
CIRCUITOUS MAZY CURVED
CROOKED DEVIOUS OBLIQUE
SINUOUS TWISTED VAGRANT
WINDING FLEXUOUS INDIRECT
RAMBLING TORTUOUS DECEITFUL
DEVIATING WANDERING
(— METHOD) WINDLASS
CIRCULAR O BILL FLIER FLYER
LIBEL ORBAL ORBED ROUND
DODGER FOLDER RINGED WHEELY
ANNULAR COMPASS CYCLOID
DISCOID DISLIKE HANDOUT PERFECT
COMPLETE DOPEBOOK ENCYCLIC
GLOBULAR INFINITE PAMPHLET
DOPESHEET
CIRCULAR-KNIT SEAMLESS
CIRCULATE GO AIR MIX MOVE PASS
RISE TURN WALK WIND TROLL
CANARD ROTATE SCURRY SPHERE
SPREAD WANDER CANVASS
CONVECT DIFFUSE PUBLISH
CONVOLVE
CIRCULATING WAIF AFLOAT
CURRENT
CIRCULATION ISSUE COURSE
COVERAGE CURRENCY
CIRCUMCISER MOHEL
CIRCUMCISION BRITH PERITOMY
CIRCUMFERENCE ARC AUGE AMBIT
APSIS GIRTH VERGE BORDER
BOUNDS CIRCLE LIMITS COMPASS
BOUNDARY SURROUND
(— OF SHELL) LIMBUS
CIRCUMFERENTOR PLANCHETTE
CIRCUMFLEX DOGHOUSE
(INVERTED —) HACEK
CIRCUMLOCUTION AMBAGE
CIRCUIT WINDING VERBIAGE
CIRCUMSCRIBE BOUND FENCE
LIMIT DEFINE CAPTURE CONFINE
ENCLOSE ENVIRON ENCIRCLE
RESTRAIN RESTRICT SURROUND
CONSCRIBE
CIRCUMSCRIBED NARROW INSULAR
LIMITED
CIRCUMSPECT SHY WARY WISE
ALERT CHARY CAREFUL GUARDED
PRUDENT CAUTIOUS DISCREET

VIGILANT WATCHFUL
CIRCUMSPECTION RESPECT
PRUDENCE WARINESS
CIRCUMSTANCE GO FIX CASE FACT
ITEM NOTE EVENT PHASE POINT
START STATE THING AFFAIR DETAIL
FACTOR PICKLE CALLING ELEMENT
EPISODE INCIDENT INSTANCE
POSITION
(CRITICAL —S) EXTREMES
(EXECRABLE —) ATROCITY
(LUDICROUS —) JEST
(PL.) CIRCS STATE TERMS ESTATE
FORTUNE
CIRCUMSTANTIAL EXACT FORMAL
MINUTE PRECISE DETAILED
ITEMIZED
CIRCUMSTANTIATE SUPPORT
EVIDENCE
CIRCUMVENT BALK BEAT DUPE
FOIL CHEAT CHECK COZEN EVADE
OUTGO TRICK BAFFLE DELUDE
ENTRAP NOBBLE OUTWIT THWART
CAPTURE DECEIVE DEFRAUD
ENSNARE PREVENT SURROUND
UNDERFONG
CIRCUS RING SHOW ARENA CANVAS
CIRCLE CIRQUE CARNIVAL
(— LOT) TOBER
(— RING) TAN
CIRQUE CWM CIRC BASIN CIRCLE
CIRCUS CORRIE RECESS CIRCLET
EROSION
CIS SYN NERAL NORMAL
CISCO KIYI BLOAT BLOATER BLUEFIN
LONGJAW MOONEYE BLACKFIN
GRAYBACK TULLIBEE WHITEFIN
CISSA SIRGANG
CISSUS TREEBINE
CIST BOX KIST TOMB CHEST CISTA
QUOIT CASKET CHAMBER KISTVAEN
CISTERN BAC FAT SAC TUB URN
VAT BACK PANT SUMP TANK URNA
WELL LAVER CAVITY CAISSON
CHULTUN CUVETTE STEEPER
FEEDHEAD
CITADEL ARX FORT HALL ALAMO
BURSA BYRSA TOWER CASTLE
BOROUGH CHESTER KREMLIN
FASTNESS FORTRESS TOOTHILL
CITATION CITAL NOTICE MENTION
SUMMONS MONITION AUTHORITY
EVOCATION
CITE CALL NAME SIST TELL ALLAY
EVOKE QUOTE REFER ACCITE
ACCUSE ADDUCE ALLEGE AROUSE
AVOUCH EXCITE INVOKE NOTIFY
RECITE REPEAT SUMMON ADVANCE
ARRAIGN BESPEAK CONVENT
EXCERPT EXTRACT IMPEACH
MENTION INDICATE INSTANCE
REHEARSE
CITHARA CITHER PHORMINX
CITHERN ZITTERN
CITIZEN CIT ALLY VOTER NATIVE
BURGESS BURGHER CITOYEN
CLERUCH DENIZEN ELECTOR
FLATCAP FREEMAN OPPIDAN
SUBJECT TOWNMAN AMERICAN

CIVILIAN COMMONER CONSCIVE
DOMESTIC NATIONAL OCCUPANT
RESIDENT
(— OF SECOND CLASS) KNIGHT
HIPPEUS
(—S OF MEDINA) ANSAR
(FOREIGN-BORN —) ALIEN
(PL.) SUBJECT PERIOECI CITIZENRY
CITIZENRY COUNTRY SUBJECT
CITRAL GERANIAL
CITRON LIME CEDRA LEMON
CEDRAT ETHROG YELLOW
CITTERN LAUD CITHERN PENORCON
CITY FU WON BURG DORP TOWN
URBS WOON ZION BURGH CALNO
EKRON JEBUS LILLE MANOA PIECE
PLACE POLIS SETTE STEAD VILLE
CALNEH CENTER CIUDAD CUTHAH
GILEAD JAMNIA JEBUSI LAGADO
NAGARA PITHOM STAPLE BABYLON
CAMBALU CHESTER ELLASAR
FREEDOM JABNEEL MECHLIN
CABECERA ELDORADO MAGAZINE
PALENQUE
(— LIFE) ASHCAN
(ANCIENT —) PERGAMUM
(CHIEF —) CAPITAL CABECERA
MEGAPOLIS
(RICH —) MAGAZINE
(TREASURE —) RAAMSES
(WICKED —) BABYLON
CITY-STATE POLIS CIVITAS
CIVET CAT CIT GENET RASSE ZIBET
BONDAR FOUSSA MUSANG PAGUMA
ZIBETH CIVETTA FOSSANE LINSANG
NANDINE POLECAT ZIBETUM
ZINSANG FANALOKA MONGOOSE
TANGALUNG
CIVIC LAY CIVIL SUAVE URBAN
POLITE URBANE CIVICAL SECULAR
CIVIL FAIR HEND HENDE SUAVE
POLITE URBANE AFFABLE AMIABLE
COURTLY ELEGANT GALLANT
POLITIC REFINED SECULAR
DISCREET GRACIOUS OBLIGING
POLISHED WELLBRED
CIVILIAN CIT CIVIE CIVIL CIVVY
PEKIN MOHAIR CITIZEN TEACHER
CIVILIST GOWNSMAN
(— ENTERTAINING SOLDIER) PYKE
CIVILITY BONTE COMITY NOTICE
AMENITY COURTESY URBANITY
GENTILITY
(PL.) HONORS HONOURS
CIVILIZATION ISLAM KULTUR
POLICE CULTURE ECUMENE CIVICITY
(GREEK —) HELLENISM
CIVILIZE TAME TEACH TRAIN POLISH
REFINE EDUCATE HUMANIZE
URBANIZE
CIVILIZED CHRISTIAN
CLABBER LOP MUD MIRE CURDLE
LOPPER CLAUBER
CLACKDISH CLICKET
CLAD DREST ROBED BESEEN
CLEDDE DECKED ADORNED
ARRAYED ATTIRED CLOTHED
COVERED DRESSED SHEATHED
(— IN PURPLE) PORPORATE

(SCANTILY —) SINGLY
CLADOSE RAMOSE CLADINE
BRANCHED
CLAIM ASK DUE AVER AVOW CALL
CASE DIBS LIEN MINE NAME PLEA
COLOR DRAFT EXACT PLEAD RIGHT
SHOUT TITLE ASSERT DEMAND
DESIRE ELICIT EQUITY INTEND
RECKON ACCLAIM COLLECT
DERECHO DRAUGHT PRETEND
PRETEXT PROFESS RECLAIM
REQUIRE SOLICIT ARROGATE
INTEREST MAINTAIN PRETENCE
PRETENSE PROCLAIM SUBCLAIM
(— IN BUSINESS) CAPITAL
(— TO BE BELIEVED) AUTHORITY
(FALSE —) JACTATION
(INDIAN LEGAL —) HAK HAKH
CLAIMANT CLAIMER USURPER
PRETENDER
CLAIRE PARK
CLAIRVOYANCE INSIGHT VOYANCE
LUCIDITY SAGACITY TELOPSIS
CLAIRVOYANT FEY SEER OMENER
PROPHET SEERESS
CLAM MYA BASE CLOG DAUB GLAM
HUSH MEAN BLUNT CLAMP CRASH
GAPER GLAUM GRASP GROPE
PAHUA RAZOR SHELL SMEAR SOLEN
SPOUT STICK VENUS ADHERE
CLUTCH GWEDUC QUAHOG STICKY
BIVALVE CLANGOR COQUINA
MOLLUSK STEAMER ADHESIVE
BULLNOSE SHIPWORM NANNINOSE
CLAMBAKE BAKE RALLY CLAMAROO
SQUANTUM
CLAMBER CLIMB SCALE CLAVER
SCRAWM SPRAWL RAMMACK
SCRABBLE SCRAMBLE SPRACHLE
STRUGGLE
CLAMMY DAMP DANK SOFT WACK
MOIST SAMMY STICKY WAUGHY
SQUIDGY CLAMMISH
CLAMOR CRY DIN HUE BERE BUNK
GAFF RANE RERD ROAR ROUP
ROUT SONG UTAS WAIL BLARE
BOAST BRUIT CHIDE CHIRM NOISE
OUTAS RERDE RUMOR SHOUT
BELLOW BOWWOW HUBBUB
OUTCRY QUETHE RACKET TUMULT
UPROAR YATTER CLAMOUR
EXCLAIM ORATION STASHIE
NORATION PILILLOO PULLALUE
SHOUTING
(— AGAINST) DECRY
CLAMOROUS NIP LOUD NOISY
VOCAL BLATANT CLAMANT DINSOME
YELLING BRAWLING DECRYING
CLAMP DOG HOG LUG NIP PIN SET
BAIL BALE BEND BOLT BURY CLAM
GLAM GRIP JACK MUTE NAIL VISE
YOKE BLOCK BRACE CLASP CRAMP
GLAND GLAUM HORSE CLINCH
FASTEN MOPHEAD STIRRUP
FASTENER HOLDFAST
(— FOR BASS DRUM) SPUR
(— FOR CORK) AGRAFE AGRAFFE
(— FOR FLASK) GLAND
(STORAGE —) GRAVE

CLAMSHELL CLAM GRAB SHUCK
CLAN ATI HAN KIN SET SIB CULT
GENS HAPU NAME RACE SECT SEPT
SIOL UNIT AIMAK AYLLU CLASS
GENOS GROUP HORDE PARTY TRIBE
ABUSUA CLIQUE FAMILY SENAAH
ABIEZER KINDRED PHRATRY
SATSUMA SOCIETY ZADRUGA
CALPULLI DIVISION
(— **SUBDIVISION**) OBE
CLANDESTINE BYE SLY FOXY
HEDGE PRIVY QUIET SNEAK COVERT
HIDDEN SECRET BOOTLEG FURTIVE
ILLICIT BACKDOOR HIDLINGS
STEALTHY
CLANG DIN DING PEAL RING TONK
CLANK CLASH NOISE JANGLE
TIMBRE
CLANGOR DIN CLAM ROAR CLANG
HUBBUB UPROAR
CLANGOROUS BRAZEN PLANGENT
CLANGULA HARELDA
CLANK RING RACKLE
CLAP BANG FLAP PEAL SLAP SPAT
TACK CHEER CLINK CRACK SMITE
POSTER STRIKE STROKE APPLAUD
CHATTER CLAPPER PLAUDIT
HANDCLAP
(— **OF THUNDER**) DINT
(— **ON**) CRACK
CLAPBOARD KNAPPLE CLAPHOLT
CLAPNET DAYNET
CLAPPER CLAP CLACK RATTLE
TONGUE JINGLET KNACKER
KNOCKER
(— **OF BELL**) TONGUE
(PL.) BONES
CLAPTRAP TRASH BLAGUE BUNKUM
DEVICE EYEWASH FUSTIAN
BUNCOMBE NONSENSE TRICKERY
CLARE MINORESS
CLARENCE GROWLER
CLARET TERSE LAFITTE BORDEAUX
BADMINTON
CLARIAS HARMOOT KARMOUTH
CLARIFIED PURED LAUTER
CLARIFY CLAY FINE CLEAN CLEAR
PURGE SNUFF PURIFY REFINE
RENDER SERENE SETTLE CLEANSE
DESPUME EXPLAIN GLORIFY
DEFECATE DEPURATE ELIQUATE
SIMPLIFY
CLARIN ACOCOTL
CLARINET BEN BIN BON BEEN BONE
REED AULOS CLARY PUNGI
CLARONE LAUNEDDAS
CLARION REST CLARE CLARY CLEAR
CLARINO SUFFLUE TRUMPET
CLARITY GLORY SPLENDOR
STRENGTH CLEARNESS
CLARY CLARRE SALVIA
CLASH JAR BANG BOLT BUMP DASH
FRAY NEWS SLAM BRAWL BRUNT
CHECK CRASH FIGHT FRUSH KNOCK
OCCUR PRATE SHOCK AFFRAY
DIFFER GOSSIP HURTLE IMPACT
JOSTLE STRIFE STRIKE TATTLE
THRUST THWART COLLIDE DISCORD
SCANDAL ARGUMENT CONFLICT

CLASHING HARSH CONFLICT
FRICTION COLLISION
CLASP HUG PIN CLIP DOME FOLD
GRAB GRIP HASP HOLD HOOK HOOP
KEEP OUCH STAY TACH BRACE
CATCH CLING GRASP MORSE PREEN
SEIZE SLIDE SPANG TACHE ACCOLL
AGRAFE AMPLEX BECLIP BROOCH
BUCKLE CLENCH CLUTCH ENFOLD
ENWRAP FASTEN FIBULA GIMMER
GIMMOR INCLIP INFOLD JIMMER
STRAIN TASSEL AGRAFFE AMPLECT
EMBRACE ENTWINE FERMAIL
HOLDING MOUSING TENDRIL
BARRETTE CORSELET FASTENER
SURROUND
(— **HANDS**) SHAKE WRING
CLASS ILK BRAN CHOP FORM KIND
RACE RANK RATE SECT SORT SUIT
TYPE YEAR BREED CASTE GENRE
GENUS GRADE GROUP ORDER
RANGE TRIBE VARNA VERGE
ASSORT CIRCLE CLINIC DECURY
FAMILY GENDER LEAGUE MISTER
NATION PHYLUM RATING RECKON
REMOVE RUBRIC STRAIN STRIPE
CATALOG FACTION LECTURE
REGIMEN SEMINAR SPECIES
VARIETY CATEGORY DESCRIBE
DIVISION GENOTYPE GEOMOROI
(— **OF BARDS**) THULIR
(— **OF GOODS**) BRAND
(— **OF OUTCASTS**) ETA
(— **OF PEOPLE**) FOLK SALARIAT
(— **OF SECURITIES**) LEGAL
(— **OF SHASTRAS**) SRUTI SHRUTI
(— **OF SOUNDS**) ENDING
(— **OF TEASELS**) KINGS
(**ARISTOCRATIC** —) ARISTOI
(**CHOICEST** —) ROBUR
(**DEPRESSED** —) PANCHAMA
(**FIRST** —) GAY
(**HEREDITARY** —) CASTE
(**JAPANESE** —) HEIMIN KWAZOKU
(**LABORING** —) PARAIYAN
(**LEARNED** —) VATES CLERISY
(**LOWER** —) BELOW GENTE
(**LOWEST** —) LAG SCUM
(**PEASANT** —) JACQUERIE
(**SLAVEHOLDING** —) CHIVALRY
(**SOCIAL** —) ESTATE SHIZOKU
(**WORKING** —) TOIL
CLASSIC VINTAGE
CLASSICAL PURE ATTIC GREEK
LATIN ROMAN CHASTE CLASSIC
ACADEMIC HELLENIC MASTERLY
(**NOT** —) BASE
CLASSICALLY IDEALLY
CLASSIFICATION FILE RANK RATE
SORT CODEN GENRE GENUS GRADE
ORDER TAXIS RATING SYSTEM
ANALYSIS CATEGORY DIVISION
TAXONOMY BREAKDOWN
CLASSIFIED SECRET
CLASSIFIER COUNTER SEPARATOR
CLASSIFY CODE LIST RANK RATE
SIZE SORT SUIT TAPE TYPE BREAK
CLASS DRAFT GRADE GROUP LABEL
RANGE TRIBE ASSORT CODIFY

DIGEST DIVIDE IMPOST TICKET
ACCOUNT ARRANGE BRACKET
BRIGADE CATALOG DISPOSE
DRAUGHT GRAMMAR MARSHAL
SUBSUME REGISTER
(— **TOGETHER**) SLUMP
CLASSIS CONFERENCE
CLATHRATE LATTICED
CLATTER DIN JAR CLACK NOISE
RUMOR BABBLE GABBLE GOSSIP
HURTLE RACKLE RATTLE TATTLE
BLATTER CHATTER CLUNTER
CLUTTER PRATTLE REESHLE
SHATTER SLAMBANG
CLATTERING CLATTERY SLITHERING
CLAUSE ITEM PART CLOSE COMMA
JOKER PLANK RIDER TROPE
MEMBER PHRASE ARTICLE
COMMATA PASSAGE PROVISO
SLEEPER PETITION REDDENDO
SENTENCE TENENDAS TENENDUM
NOVODAMUS
(— **IN WRIT**) TESTE
(— **OF WILL**) DEVISE
(**ADDITIONAL** —) RIDER
CLAVACIN PATULIN
CLAVER PRATE CLOVER GOSSIP
CHATTER CLABBER CLAIVER
CLAMBER
CLAVICHORD CLAVIER MANICORD
UNICHORD CLARIGOLD MONOCHORD
CLAVICLE FURCULE COLLARBONE
CLAVIER MANUAL KLAVIER
CLAVUS CORN BUNION HELOMA
CLAW DIG PEG CLEE CRAB FANG
FAWN HAND HOOK NAIL PULL SERE
TEAR UNCE CHELA CLOOF CLUFE
COURT GRASP GRIFF ONGLE SCLAW
SEIZE TALON UNCUS CLUNCH
CLUTCH CRATCH NIPPER POUNCE
SCRAPE SINGLE UNGUAL UNGUIS
UNGULA WEAPON CRUBEEN
FALCULA FLATTER SCRATCH
SHUTTLE WHEEDLE SCRABBLE
(PL.) CLUTCH
CLAY BAT COB PUG WAD WAX BASS
BEND BODY BOLE BOTT GALT GLEY
LOAM LUTE MARL MIRE PAPA SMIT
TILL ARGIL BRICK CLOAM EARTH
GAULT LOESS OCHRE PASTE RABAT
TASCO BINDER CLEDGE CLUNCH
KAOLIN PUDDLE SAGGER DAUBING
MOULDER RASHING CAMSTANE
FIRECLAY GUMBOTIL LATERITE
LIFELESS SINOPITE
(— **FOR MELTING POTS**) TASCO
(— **IN GLASS**) TEAR
(— **IRON**) BULL
(— **LAYER**) VARVE
(**3-ARMED, HARD-FIRED** —) STILT
(**COVERED WITH** —) LUTOSE
(**HARD** —) BEND
(**HARDENED** —) METAL
(**INDURATED** —) BASS CLUNCH
(**PIECE OF FIRED** —) TILE
(**PIPE** —) CAMSTANE CAMSTONE
(**POTTER'S** —) SLIP ARGIL
(**REMOVE** —) UNLUTE
(**SURPLUS** —) SPARE

(TOUGH —) LECK
CLAYEY BOLAR HEAVY MALMY
MARLY CLEDGY LUTOSE ARGILLIC
CLAYMORE FERRARA
CLAY PIGEON BIRD CLAY
CLAYSTONE LECK
CLAYWARE GLOST
CLEADING CLOTHING
CLEAN DO FAY FEY HOE MOP NET
DRUM DUST FAIR NEAT PURE REDD
RIPE SIDE SMUG SWAB TRIM WASH
WIPE CLEAR CURRY EMPTY FEIGH
GRAVE SCOUR SCRUB SMART
SWEEP TERSE TOSHY BARREL
CHASTE CLEVER KOSHER PURIFY
SPANDY APINOID BANDBOX
CHAMOIS CLEANLY CLEANSE
CLEARLY FURBISH PERFECT
SWINGLE ABSTERGE BACKWASH
BRIGHTLY DEXTROUS ENTIRELY
RENOVATE SCAVENGE SPOTLESS
UNSOILED
(— A FUR) DRUM
(— A QUILL) DUTCH
(— BOAT) CAREEN
(— BY SCRAPING) GRAVE
(— BY SMOKE) SMEEK
(— CANNON) SCALE
(— FIREARM) WORM
(— FLAX) SWINGLE
(— IN ACID) BLANCH
(— OUT) USH SPEAR
(— SHIP'S BOTTOM) HOG BREAM
GRAVE
(— UP) DISPATCH
(RITUALLY —) KOSHER
CLEAN-CUT CRISP
CLEANED BRIGHT
CLEANER SOAP BORAX PURER
FOLDER GUMMER RAMROD
FLUEMAN SPOTTER CLEANSER
(AIR —) CAN
(GRAIN —) KICKER
CLEAN-LIMBED CLEVER
CLEAN-LINED SPRUCE
CLEANLY PURE CLEAN ADROIT
ARTFUL CHASTE FAIRLY SPANDY
CORRECT ELEGANT INNOCENT
SKILLFUL
CLEANNESS PURITY
CLEANSE FAY BRAN CARD COMB
FARM HEAL PICK SOAP WASH
BROOM BRUSH CLEAN CLEAR DIGHT
DRESS FEIGH FLAME FLUSH PURGE
RINSE SCOUR SCRUB SNUFF
BOTTOM CAREEN EMUNGE PICKLE
PURIFY REFINE SPONGE WILLOW
BAPTIZE CLARIFY DEBRIDE
DETERGE EXPIATE LAUNDER
MUNDIFY SWEETEN ABSTERGE
DEPURATE OFFSCOUR RENOVATE
SCAVENGE SPRINKLE
CLEANSER LYE SOAP CLEANER
PURIFIER DETERGENT DETERSIVE
CLEANSING BATH FLUSH ABLUENT
CLYSMIC WASHING ABLUTION
CLEANING LAVATION DETERGENT
(CEREMONIAL —) LAVABO
PURGATION

CLEANUP KILLING SWEEPUP
CLEAR HOT JAM NET RID WAY CAST
EASY FAIR FINE FLAT FREE GAIN
GRUB JUMP NEAT OPEN OVER PURE
PUTE QUIT REDD RIFE SHUT SLAM
VOID ACUTE ATRIP AZURE BREAK
BREME BRENT BROAD CHUCK
CLEAN CRISP DRIVE LIGHT LUCID
NAKED PLAIN PRINT PRUNE SCOUR
SHARP SMOLT SUNNY SUTEL
SWEEP UNTIE VIVID ACQUIT AERIAL
ASSOIL BRIGHT CANDID CLEVER
EXCUSE EXEMPT FLUTED LAUTER
LIMPID LIQUID LUCENT PATENT
PURIFY SERENE SETTLE SHRILL
SMOOTH UNSTOP ABSOLVE CAPITAL
CLARIFY CLARION CRYSTAL
DELIVER DILUCID EVIDENT EXPLAIN
EXPRESS GLARING GRAPHIC
LIGHTEN OBVIOUS PERVIAL
RELEASE SILVERY ACCREDIT
APPARENT BRIGHTEN BULLDOZE
DEFINITE DISTINCT EXPLICIT
LUCULENT LUMINOUS MANIFEST
PELLUCID REVELANT
(— AWAY) FAY FEY FEIGH BANISH
DISPEL DISCUSS
(— FROM) ALOOF
(— LAND) CURE BRUSH SLASH
DEADEN
(— OF GROUND) ATRIP AWEIGH
(— OF MUD) SLUTCH
(— OF SCUM) SKIM
(— OF TUFTS) HOB
(— OUT) BLOW HOOK SWAMP
SKIDDOO HIGHTAIL DISCHARGE
(— PATH) FRAY HACK BUSHWACK
(— THROAT) HOICK HOUGH
(— UP) SOLVE ASSOIL RESOLVE
DISSOLVE UNSHADOW
(NOT —) DULL DUSKY FOGGY
INEVIDENT
CLEARANCE CHOP ROOM RUNBY
BACKLASH ALLOWANCE
CLEAR-CUT LUCID SHARP DIRECT
CONCISE DECIDED CHISELED
DEFINITE DISTINCT INCISIVE
TRENCHANT
CLEARING FIELD FRITH GLADE
SHADE TRACT ALCOVE ASSART
RIDING RIDDING SLASHING
CLEARLY FAIR CLEAR LIGHT REDLY
FAIRLY FRANKLY WITTERLY
CLEAR-MINDEDNESS LUCIDITY
CLEARNESS CLARITY FINESSE
EVIDENCE FINENESS
CLEARWEED RICHWEED
CLEAT BITT STUD BLOCK CHOCK
KEVEL LEDGE RANGE WEDGE
BATTEN RIFFLE BOLLARD COXCOMB
GROUSER SIRMARK SUPPORT
SURMARK
CLEAVAGE RIFT CLEFT WASSIE
FISSION FISSURE WEDGING DIVISION
SCISSION
CLEAVE CUT RIP CHOP HANG HOLD
JOIN LINK PART RELY REND RIFT
RIVE SLIT TEAR BREAK CARVE
CHAWN CHINE CLAVE CLEFT CLING

CLOVE CRACK SEVER SHALE SHARE
SHEAR SLIVE SPLAT STICK ADHERE
BISECT COHERE DIVIDE FURROW
PIERCE SLEAVE SUNDER DISPART
FISSURE SEPARATE
(— OFF) SCIND
CLEAVER CLIVE CLEAVE FROWER
CHOPPER PARANGI
CLEAVERS GRIP CLOTE CLOTS
CLITHE HAIRIF HAIRUP BURHEAD
LOVEMAN PIGTAIL BIRDLIME
CLEAVING DYSTOME FISSION
DYSTOMIC
(— READILY) EUTOMOUS
CLECHE URDE URDY URDEE
CLEF KEY CLIVE CHIAVETTA
CLEFT CUT GAP CHAP CHOP FENT
FLAW GASH NOCK REFT RIFT RILL
RIMA RIVE SLIT BREAK CHASM
CHAWN CHINK CLOVE CRACK
CREEK CRENA GULCH RILLE RIVEN
SINUS SPLIT BREACH CHAPPY
CLEAVE CLOUGH CLOVEN CRANNY
CROTCH DIVIDE LISSOM PARTED
RECESS RICTUS STIGMA BLASTED
CHIMNEY CREVICE DIVIDED FISSURE
OPENING SLIFTER APERTURE
FRACTURE INCISION INCISURA
MULTIFID SCISSURA SCISSURE
(— IN HOOF) SEAM
(— IN THE POSTERIORS) NOCK
(— CF BUTTOCKS) CREASE
CLEMATIS PIPESTEM CURLYHEAD
CLEMENCY ORE PITY GRACE
MERCY LENITY QUARTER KINDNESS
LENIENCY MILDNESS
CLEMENT MILD SOFT WARM GENTLE
LENIENT MERCIFUL
CLENCH FIST GRIP GRIT HOLD NAIL
BRACE CLASP CLENK CLINT CLOSE
GRASP CLINCH CLUTCH DOUBLE
(— FIST) GRIPE
CLEPE CLUPIEN
CLEPSYDRA GURRY GHURRY
CLERGY CLOTH CRAPE CHURCH
CLERISY MINISTRY
(BODY OF —) PULPIT
CLERGYMAN ABBA ABBE DEAN
PAPA CANON CLERK FROCK PADRE
PILOT PRIOR RABBI VICAR BISHOP
CLERIC CURATE DEACON DIVINE
DOMINE PAROCH PARSON PASTOR
PRIEST RECTOR SUPPLY CASSOCK
PRELATE CARDINAL CHAPLAIN
CLERICAL DIOCESAN EMERITUS
LECTURER MINISTER ORDINARY
PREACHER REVEREND SQUARSON
PRESBYTER
CLERIC ABBE CLERK FROCK
DEACON GALLAH LEVITE PRIEST
ACOLYTE ANAGNOST
CLERICAL BLACK CLERIC CLERKISH
PARSONIC PARSONLY
CLERK NUN BABU MONK AGENT
AWARD BABOO CLARK FILER RALPH
WRITE BILLER CHASER CLERIC
COMMIS GRADER HERMIT KITMAN
LAYMAN MAPPER MASTER MUNSHI
PANDIT PENMAN PRIEST PUNDIT

RALPHO SCRIBE TELLER WRITER
YEOMAN ACOLYTE ACTUARY
BOOKMAN CARCOON COMPOSE
DOPSTER GOMASTA PIARIST
SCHOLAR SHIPPER SHOPMAN
STUFFER CLERGEON CLERGION
CLERKESS EMPLOYEE GREFFIER
MUTSUDDY PENCLERK RECORDER
SALESMAN
(— OF ST PAUL) BARNABITE
(HOTEL —) DESKMAN
CLERKLY LEARNED SCRIBAL
CLERGIAL SCHOLARLY
CLEVE BRAE CLIFF CLEEVE HILLSIDE
CLEVER APT SLY ABLE CUTE DEFT
FEAT FELL FINE FOXY GNIB GOOD
HEND KEEN SLIM SPRY AGILE
ALERT CANNY CLEAN CLEAR CUNNY
FALSE FEATY FENDY HANDY HEADY
HENDE LITHE QUICK SHARP SLICK
SMART SNACK WITTY ACTIVE
ADROIT ARTFUL ASTUTE BRIGHT
CRAFTY EXPERT HABILE HEPPEN
KITTLE KNACKY NEATLY NIMBLE
PRETTY SHREWD SPIFFY STALKY
SUBTLE AMIABLE CUNNING GNOSTIC
PARLISH PARLOUS VARMENT
VARMINT DEXTROUS HANDSOME
OBLIGING SKILLFUL TALENTED
CLEVERLY SLICK FEATLY TIDELY
SMARTLY ASTUTELY
CLEVERNESS CAN CHIC NOUS TACT
SKILL ESPRIT INDUSTRY DEXTERITY
CLEVIS COP DEE HAKE CLEVY
COPSE BRIDGE BRIDLE MUZZLE
SHACKLE PLOWHEAD
CLEW BALL CLUE HINT GLOBE
GLOME SKEIN BOTTOM HURDLE
THREAD
CLICHE COMMONPLACE
CLICK DOG DOT DASH PAWL SLAP
TICK AGREE CATCH FORGE SNECK
SNICK DETENT PALLET RATCHET
(HEEL —S) BELLS
(TELEGRAPH —) DASH
CLICK BEETLE ELATER
CLIENT CEILE JAJMAN PATRON
PATIENT CUSTOMER HENCHMAN
RETAINER
CLIENTELE PUBLIC CLIENTRY
CLIFF HOE NIP CRAG HILL KLIP
ROCK SCAR BLUFF CLEVE CLINT
HEUCH HEUGH KRANS SCARP
SHORE SLOPE STEEP CLEEVE
HEIGHT KRANTZ PISKUN CLOGWYN
HILLSIDE PALISADE TRAVERSE
(BROKEN —) CRAG
(ICE —) ICEBLINK
(LINE OF —S) PALISADE
CLIFFY SCARRY
CLIMATE SKY SUN MOOD CLIME
HEAVEN REGION TEMPER ATTITUDE
(SCIENCE OF —) PHENOLOGY
CLIMAX CAP TOP ACME APEX HEAD
NEAR PEAK SHUT CREST CROWN
MOUNT SCALE TIGHT APOGEE
ASCEND FINISH HEIGHT SHINNY
SUMMIT ZENITH BLOWOFF EVEREST
CAPSHEAF CAPSTONE EPIPLOCE

CLIMB GAD STY COON RAMP RISE
SHIN SKIN SOAR STYE CREEP
GRIMP MOUNT SCALE SKLIM SPEED
SPEEL SWARM TWINE ASCEND
ASCENT BREAST SCLIMB SCRAWM
SHINNY SWARVE SWERVE CLAMBER
SCRAMBLE TRAVERSE
(— ABOARD) HOP
(— DOWN) LIGHT UNSCALE
(— IN MOUNTAINEERING) CHIMNEY
(— OVER) SURMOUNT
CLIMBER CUBE AKALA AKELA KAIWI
RIGGER SCALER CRAMPON
CREEPER
(MOUNTAIN —) ALPINIST
CLIMBING SCANDENT
(MOUNTAIN —) ALPINISM
CLIMBING FERN NITO AGSAM
CLIMBING IRON SPUR PRICK
CRAMPET CRAMPIT CRAMPON
CREEPER PRICKER CRAMPBIT
CLIMBING PALM RATTAN
CLIMBING PEPPER BETEL
CLIMBING ROSE SCRAMBLE
CLINCH FIX GET HUG TOE BIND GRIP
LOCK NAIL SEAL CLAMP CLING
CLINK CLINT GRASP RIVET SEIZE
CLENCH CLUTCH FASTEN SECURE
SNATCH CONFIRM EMBRACE
GRAPPLE SCUFFLE COMPLETE
CONCLUDE HOLDFAST
CLING HUG BANK HANG HOLD RELY
CLASP HITCH STICK TRUST ADHERE
CLEAVE CLINCH COHERE DEPEND
FASTEN SHRINK WITHER CHERISH
EMBRACE SHRIVEL CONTRACT
CLINGER LIMPET
CLINGFISH SUCKER TESTAR TETARD
SUCKFISH
CLINGING CLUNG HUGGING
ADHAMANT ADHERENT OSCULANT
CLINK ALE JUG PUT RAP BEAT
BLOW BRIG CASH CLAP COIN JAIL
MOVE RING SLAP KLINK LATCH
MONEY RHYME SEIZE CLINCH
JINGLE LOCKUP MOMENT PRISON
STRIKE TINKLE INSTANT JINGLING
CLINKER BUR BUHR BURR SCAR
SLAG WASTE HOLLANDER
CLINKER-BUILT SHINGLED
LAPSTRAKE
CLINOMETER TRIMMER
CLINTONIA BLUEBEAD DOGBERRY
COWTONGUE
CLIP BAT BOB CUT DOD HUG LIP
LOP MOW NIG NIP BARB BEAK CHIP
COLL CROP DOCK DODD FLAG
HOLD PACE PARE POLL SNIP TRIM
BRUSH CLASP DRESS FORCE LUNET
MINCE PRUNE SHAVE SHEAR SHRIP
STEEK CLUPPE CLUTCH CRUTCH
FASTEN GADGET HINDER HOLDER
LACING CALIPER CURTAIL CURTAIN
EMBRACE HICKORY LUNETTE
SCISSOR SHORTEN DIMINISH
ENCIRCLE RETAINER
(— A COIN) SHORTEN
(— WOOL) CRUTCH
(CARTRIDGE —) CHARGER

(HAIR —) BARRETTE
(SPRING —) JACK
CLIPPED TONSURED
CLIPPER BOAT SHIP DOCKER SLICER
CHAINER CLAMMER CLEANER
GRABMAN GRIPPER SHEARER
SNAPPER
CLIPPING BOB SCROW CUTTING
SNIPPING
(—S OF METAL) SCISSEL
(PL.) BRASH SHORTS EXCERPTA
CLIQUE COT MOB SET BLOC CLAN
CLUB GANG KNOT RING CABAL
CROWD GROUP JUNTO WRITE
CIRCLE CLETCH SCHISM COTERIE
FACTION CONCLAVE SODALITY
CLITELLUM GIRDLE SADDLE
CINGULUM
CLOAK ABA HAP BRAT CAPA CAPE
COPE HIDE HUKE IZAR MANT MASK
PALL RAIL ROBE VEIL WRAP BURKA
CAPOT CHOGA COVER GREGO
GUISE JELAB MANTA MANTO SAGUM
SHUBA TILMA ABOLLA AHUULA
ASSUME BAUTTA CAMAIL CAPOTE
CASTER CHAMMA CHAPEL CHIMER
DOLMAN JOSEPH MANTLE MANTUA
PHAROS PONCHO RHASON SCREEN
SERAPE SHIELD SHROUD TABARD
VISITE ALICULA BAVAROY CASSOCK
CHLAMYS CONCEAL COURTBY
GARMENT MANTEAU PAENULA
PELISSE PELLARD PRETEXT
SHELTER SURCOAT ZIMARRA
ALBORNOZ BURNOOSE CAPUCHIN
DISGUISE INTRIGUE MANTILLA
PALLIATE
(— OF FEATHERS) MAMO AHUULA
(— WITH CROSSES) ANALABOS
(HOODED —) HUKE CAPOT BAUTTA
BIRRUS BAVAROY CARDINAL
(RED —) CAPE
(SOLDIER'S —) SAGUM
(WATERPROOF —) GOSSAMER
CLOAKED PALLIATE
CLOAKROOM VESTIARY
CLOAM DAUB CLOMB CROCKERY
CLOCHE BELL
CLOCK NEF BELL CALL DIAL GOER
GONG TIME WRAP BUNDY CLUCK
GURRY HATCH HURRY KNOCK
METER QUIRK STYLE VERGE WATCH
BEETLE CROUCH GHURRY ORLAGE
TICKER SKELPER STRIKER TATTLER
HOROLOGE INCUBATE ORNAMENT
RECORDER SOLARIUM TELLTALE
(— IN FORM OF SHIP) NEF
(— ON STOCKING) QUIRK GUSHET
GUSSET
(— WITH PENDULUM) PENDULE
(TIME —) BUNDY
(WATER —) GURRY GHURRY
SOLARIUM CLEPSYDRA
CLOCKER SIZER TIMER RAILBIRD
CLOCKWISE DEASIL DESSIL
SUNWISE POSITIVE
CLOD SOD CLAT CLOT DOLT DULL
LOUT LUMP SLOB TURF CLOUT
CLOWN DIVOT EARTH GLEBE GROSS

KNOLL YOKEL CLATCH GROUND
STUPID BUMPKIN
CLODDISH GROSS STUPID BOORISH
CLODHOPPER BOOR CLOD SHOE
RUSTIC HOBNAIL PLOWMAN
CLODIA LESBIA
CLODPATE CLOT DOLT FOOL
RAMHEAD CLODPOLE CLODPOLL
IMBECILE
CLOG FUR GUM JAM LOG BALL
CLAG CLAM CLOY CURB DRAG
GLUB LEAD LOAD LUMP SHOE SKID
STOP BLIND BLOCK CHECK CHOKE
DANCE SABOT SPOKE TRASH
ADHERE BURDEN CHOPIN COBCAB
DAGGLE ENCLOG FETTER FREEZE
GALOSH HAMPER HOBBLE IMPEDE
PATINE PATTEN REMORA SANDAL
SECQUE WEIGHT CONGEST
CREEPER ENGLEIM FETLOCK
PERPLEX SHACKLE SPANCEL
TRAMMEL TRIGGER BEDAGGLE
COALESCE ENCUMBER OBSTRUCT
OVERSHOE RESTRAIN
(— A FILE) PIN
(WOODEN —S) GETA GETAS
CLOG ALMANAC STAFF
CLOGGED FOUL FURRY PINNY
FROZEN CLOTTED BEGUMMED
CLOGGING CLOGGY FOULING
CUMBROUS
CLOGGY DULL HEAVY LUMPY
STICKY
CLOISONNE SHIPPO
CLOISTER HALL STOA ABBEY AISLE
ARCADE FRIARY IMMURE PIAZZA
PRIORY CLOSTER CONVENT
NUNNERY MONASTERY
CLOISTERED RECLUSE
CLOSE BY IN CAP END GUM HAW
HOT TYE AKIN BUNG CHOP CLAP
CLIT DAUB FAST FILL FINE FIRM
GRIP HARD HIDE LOUK MEET NEAR
NIGH QUIT SEAL SHUT SLAM SNUG
SPAR STOP TINE WINK WYND ZERO
ANEAR BLOCK BREAK CEASE CHEAP
CHIEF COAPT DENSE FENCE FINIS
FLIRT GARTH GROSS ISSUE MUGGY
SNECK SOLID STEEK STICK STIVY
THICK TIGHT BUCKLE BUTTON
CLAUSE CLENCH CLUTCH DOUBLE
EFFECT EXPIRY FINALE FINISH
INSTOP INWARD NARROW NEARBY
PERIOD SECRET SETTLE SILENT
STANCH STINGY STITCH STRAIT
STRICT STUFFY THRONG ADJOURN
BOROUGH CLOSING CLOSISH
COMPACT CONDEMN CONTEXT
COSTIVE EXTREME GRAPPLE
MISERLY OCCLUDE POCKETY
PUTHERY RAMPIRE RECLUDE
SHUTTER SIMILAR STAUNCH
STOPPER ACCURATE ADJACENT
BLOCKADE CLAUSULA COMPLETE
COMPRESS CONCLUDE ENCEINTE
ESPECIAL FAMILIAR FINALIZE
HAIRLINE IMMINENT INTIMATE
PARCLOSE PRECLUDE
(— BY) FORBY AROUND BESIDE

FOREBY HEREBY FORTHBY
SISTERING
(— EYES OF HAWK) SEEL
(— IN ON) TAKE
(— IN) BESET ENCLOSE INCLOSE
(— THE MOUTH) STOPPLE
(— TO BATSMAN) SILLY
(— TO COMMUNICATION) CORDON
(— TO QUARRY) HOT
(— TO THE HEART) DEAR
(— TO THE WIND) SHARP
(— TO) BY INBY NEAR NIGH ANEAR
INBYE ALMOST AGAINST
(— TOGETHER) COLLAPSE
(— UP) DIT CORK DITT FILL FOLD
STOP SERRY UPCLOSE
(— WITH A CLICK) SNECK
(— WITH) BIND
(PARTIALLY —) HOOD
(VERY —) CHIEF STINGY
CLOSE-COUPLED COMPACT
CLOSED DARK DOWN SHUT CLOSE
LUCKEN UNOPEN BLOCKED
COVERED
(— AT ONE END) BLIND
CLOSEFISTED MEAN NEAR FISTY
TIGHT SNIPPY STINGY MISERLY
HANDFAST
CLOSE-FITTING FIT HARD MEET
SNUG THEAT THEET TIGHT THIGHT
SUCCINCT
CLOSE-KNIT TRUSSED
CLOSE-LIPPED SILENT
CLOSELY FAST JUST NEAR WELL
SADLY ALMOST BARELY HARDLY
NARROW NEARLY JUNCTLY
STRICTLY
CLOSEMOUTHED SECRET SILENT
(NOT —) LEAKY
CLOSENESS DENSITY SECRECY
FIDELITY INTIMACY NEARNESS
PARSIMONY
CLOSER VAMPER CLOSURE
CLOSEST NEXT NEAREST
CLOSESTOOL STOLE
CLOSET ARK EWRY ROOM SAFE
AMBRY CUBBY CUDDY PRESS
LOCKER PANTRY SECRET CABINET
CONCEAL PRIVATE CONCLAVE
CUPBOARD GARDEVIN WARDROBE
CLOSING FLY SLAM SNAP CLOSURE
CLOTURE CLAUDENT BUTTONING
CLOSURE END GAG BOLT SEAL
BOUND LIMIT ATRESIA CLOTURE
FERRULE TENSION CLAUSURE
FINALITY KANGAROO
CLOT DOT GEL CLAG CLAT GOUT
JELL LUMP MASS MOLE SHED
CLART GRUME BALTER COTTER
LAPPER LOPPER CLODDER
EMBOLUS THICKEN CLODPATE
COAGULUM CONCRETE SOLIDIFY
CLOTH DAB RAG BLUE COAT DRAB
DRAP ECRU FELT FILE PALL SEAM
WARE WOOF BEIGE BLUET CABAN
CLOUT DITTO FOULE GOODS GREEN
LODEN LUNGI MOORY PRINT STUPE
TAMMY TAWNY TIBET TOILE TWEED
TWILL ALPACA AWNING BENGAL

BYSSUS CANAMO CANVAS CHADOR
CLAITH CLERGY COVERT DORSEL
DOSSAL DOSSER DRAPET DUSTER
FABRIC LIVERY LONGYI LOWELL
MELLAY MULETA NAPKIN RENGUE
REXINE SARONG SURNAP TILLOT
WITNEY ACETATE BOULTEL
CHADDAR CHRISOM COATING
CRIMSON DRAPERY DUSTRAG
FALDING GARMENT JACONET
ORLEANS PANUELO RAIMENT
SACKING SURNAPE TEXTILE
WATCHET WORSTED BATSWING
CHRISMAL COMPRESS CORPORAL
CRAMOISY DWELLING FROCKING
HOMESPUN LAMBSKIN MATERIAL
PHULKARI RADEVORE SHAATNEZ
SHEETING THICKSET TOILINET
(— OF GOLD) SONERI
(— FOR BELT) SHROUD
(— FOR WIPING TABLE) FILE
(— FOR WRAPPING FABRICS) TILLET
(— FOR WRAPPING THE DEAD)
CEREMENT
(— HANGING FROM WAISTBAND)
LANGOOTY
(— OF SINGLE WIDTH) STRAITS
(— REMAINING AFTER CUTTING)
CABBAGE
(— WORN LIKE KILT) LAVALAVA
(ALTAR —) TOWEL PENDLE PALLIUM
VESPERAL CATASARKA
(ARABIAN —) HAIK CABAN CABAAN
(BARK —) TAPA TAPPA
(BED —) COVER SPREAD
(BLACK —) KISWA KISWAH
(COARSE —) DOZEN DUROY
CANGAN DOWLAS DOZENS FORFAR
FRIEZE HODDEN KERSEY KHARVA
KHARWA STAMIN STROUD TAPALO
CAMBAYE COTONIA DRUGGET
FORFARS RAPLOCH RUGGING
SARPLER SOUTAGE FLUSHING
RADEVORE SARCILIS
(COMMUNION —) FANON SINDON
CORPORAL
(COTTON —) JEAN TOBE ADATI
BLUET CAFFA CRASH DURRY JEANS
KHADI KHAKI SURAT BEAVER
CALICO CANGAN DOWLAS DURRIE
GANZIE HUMHUM KALMUK NANKIN
PENANG CAMBAYE FUSTIAN
GALATEA GINGHAM JACONET
KHADDAR LASTING NANKEEN
REGATTA BOGOTANA DOMESTIC
MUSLINET
(CRIMSON —) CRAMASIE CRAMOISY
(DECORATIVE —) SCARF
(EMBROIDERED —) SAMPLER
(GLASS —) DORON
(GOAT-WOOL —) SLING
(GREEN —) KENDAL
(GUNNY —) TAT
(HAIR —) ABA ABBA CILICE
(HEMP —) PINAYUSA
(HOMESPUN —) KELT KHADI PATTU
PUTTOO HEADING KHADDAR
(LAP —) GREMIAL
(LINEN —) BRIN LINE GULIX

DOWLAS FORFAR BRABANT
LOCKRAM SILESIA BLANCARD
CORPORAL GAMBROON GHENTING
LINCLOTH
(LONG —) LUNGI WHITE LUNGEE
(ORNAMENTAL —) TRAP DOSSAL
DOSSEL
(PACK —) MANTA
(PACKING —) SOUTAGE
(PIECE OF —) APRON CLOUT
GODET LANGOOTY
(RICH —) SCARLET
(SADDLE —) PANEL
(SILK —) CAFFA BENGAL PATOLA
(SOAKED —) BUCK
(SOFT —) RUGINE
(STAGE —) BACKDROP
(STARCHED —) GUIMPE
(STRIPED —) RAY
(STRONG —) CANVAS DURANCE
(TWILLED —) JANE JEAN
GAMBROON
(UNDYED —) HODDEN
(WASHING —) SHAMMY CHAMOIS
(WAX —) MUMJUMA
(WET —) DAB
(WOOL —) SAY DRAB PUKE BEIGE
BUREL DOZEN DUROY LAINE STARA
TAMIS TAMMY DOZENS DUFFEL
HODDEN KENDAL KERSEY MEDLEY
MELTON MUSTER SAXONY STAMIN
TAMINY TARTAN BASTARD BLANKET
DUNSTER FLANNEL RAPLOCH
ROPLOCH RUGGING BEARSKIN
BUCKSKIN FLORENCE SARCILIS
VENETIAN
(WORSTED —) RASH SHAG
BOMBAZET
CLOTHE DON DUB HAP LAP RIG TOG
DECK GARB GIRD GOWN ROBE VEST
ADORN ARRAY CLEAD CLEED
DRESS ENDOW ENDUE FLESH
FROCK HABIT INDUE ATTIRE
BEWRAP SHRIDE SHROUD SWATHE
ADDRESS APPAREL FEATHER
RAIMENT VESTURE ACCOUTER
ACCOUTRE
CLOTHED CLAD BECLAD HABITED
CLOTHES CASE DUDS GARB GEAR
GORE KAPA SUIT TACK TOGS WEAR
BRAWS DUCKS HABIT ATTIRE
FARDEL SHROUD TROGGS APPAREL
BAGGAGE COSTUME IRONING
RAIMENT REGALIA TOGGERY
VESTURE WEARING CLOTHING
FEATHERS FRIPPERY GARMENTS
INDUMENT
(CASTOFF —) FRIPPERY
(DRESS —) WAMPUM
(FINE —) BRAWS
(HANDSOME —) BRAVERY
(MOURNING —) DOLE
(SHOWY —) LUGS
(SOAKED —) BUCK
CLOTHES DRYER AIRER TUMBLER
CLOTHESPIN PEG
CLOTHESPRESS ARMOIRE TALLBOY
WARDROBE
CLOTH FOLDER CUTTLER

CLOTHING (ALSO SEE CLOTHES)
BACK BLUE BRAT COAT GARB GEAR
SEAM WEAR ARRAY BUREL CLOTH
DRESS GREEN HABIT JABOT STUFF
ATTIRE FARDEL ROBING VESTRY
APPAREL CLOBBER CLOTHES
CRIMSON DRAPERY OUTWALL
RAIMENT VESTURE WEEDERY
INDUMENT KNITWEAR ORNAMENT
SLOPWORK VESTIARY VESTMENT
(BLACK —) SABLE
(COARSE —) BUREL
(LOWER —) LAP
(MUSLIM —) IHRAM
(NAUTICAL —) SLOPS
(SHEER —) FLIMSIES
(SHOWY —) SHEEN FINERY
(WOMEN'S —) FRILLIES
(WORK —) FATIGUES
CLOTHING DEALER HOSIER
CLOTHWORKER FULLER
CLOTTED GORY CLOTTY CLOUTED
GARGETY GRUMOUS LIVERED
CLOTURE GAG CLOSURE
CLOUD DOG FOG NUE SKY BLUR
DAMP DARK DUST FOOL HAZE HELM
HIDE MIST REEK SMUR ARCUS
BEDIM BEFOG BLOOM DRIFT GLOOM
MUDDY NUBIA OXEYE SHADE STAIN
SULLY SWARM TAINT VAPOR
CIRRUS DAMAGE DARKEN DEEPEN
DEFAME FUNNEL MUDDLE NEBULA
NIMBUS PILEUS POTHER SCREEN
SHADOW STIGMA BLACKEN
CONFUSE CUMULUS ECLIPSE
FUMULUS GRANULE OBSCURE
POOTHER STRATUS SUNSPOT
TARNISH CLOUDCAP CLOUDLET
COCKTAIL NIGHTCAP NUBILATE
OVERCAST WOOLPACK
(— OF DUST OR VAPOR) STEW
SMOTHER
(— OF MIST) SOP
(— OVER MOUNTAIN) HELM
(HIGH —) CIRRUS
(HORIZONTAL —) STRATUS
(MASS OF HIGH —S) RACK
(MASSY —) CUMULUS
(NUCLEAR —) FIREBALL
(RAIN —) NIMBUS
(PL.) SCUD SOUP CARRY GASHES
CLOUDBERRY AKPEK MOLKA
AVERIN
(FRUIT OF —) NOOP
CLOUDED HAZY DIRTY DUSTY FILMY
JASPE MUCKY SHADY ACLOUD
GLOOMY TURBID INFUMATE
NEBULOUS
CLOUDINESS FAIR HAZE GLOOM
MUDDLE
CLOUDING DAPPLE
(— OF EYE) CATARACT
CLOUDLESS AZURE CLEAR BRIGHT
CLOUDY DIM DARK DULL HAZY
BLEAR FILMY FOGGY MISTY MURKY
SHADY GLOOMY LOWERY OPAQUE
SMURRY VEILED BLURRED CLOUDED
NEBULAR OBSCURE CONFUSED
NUBILOUS OVERCAST VAPOROUS

CLOUGH CLUF CLEFT CLOES
CLEUCH CLEUGH RAVINE VALLEY
CLOUT BAT BOX DAB HIT BEAT
BLOW BUMP CLOD CLUB CUFF JOIN
MEND NAIL SLAP SLUG SWAT
PATCH SMITE KLOWET STRIKE
TARGET THRASH WASHER BANDAGE
BOSTHOON
CLOVE GAP NAIL CHIVE CLEFT GILLY
BUTTON CLEAVE RAVINE SHERRY
GILLIVER
CLOVEN CLEFT SPLIT DIVIDED
BISULCATE
CLOVEN-FOOTED SLIT FISSIPED
CLOVE PINK GELOFER GRENADIN
CLOVER RED HAGI SEED HUBAM
LOTUS MEDIC NARDU PUSSY ALSIKE
BERSIM LADINO LEGUME LUXURY
NARDOO ALFALFA BERSEEM
BERSINE CLAIVER COMFORT
LUCERNE MELILOT SAPLING
TREFOIL TRIFOLY COWGRASS
HAREFOOT NAPOLEON PUSSYCAT
SHAMROCK SUCKLING YELLOWTOP
CLOVER DODDER AILWEED
EPITHYME HAILWEED HAIRWEED
HALEWEED
CLOWN HOB OAF PUT APER BOOR
FOOL GAUM GOFF JOEY LOUT MIME
MOME SWAD ZANY ANTIC BUFFO
CHURL COMIC FESTE IDIOT MIMER
PATCH PUNCH WAMBA ZANNI
AUGUST BODACH HOBBIL JESTER
LUBBER RUSTIC STOOGE AUGUSTE
BODDAGH BUFFOON BUMPKIN
CHARLEY COSTARD KOSHARE
LAVACHE LOBSTER MUDHEAD
PEASANT PIERROT PLAYBOY
SCOFFER TOMFOOL COVIELLO
KOYEMSHI MERRYMAN WHITEFACE
CLOWNISH RAW RUDE ZANY GAWKY
ROUGH CLUMSY COARSE RUSTIC
AWKWARD BOORISH HOBLIKE
KERNISH LOBBISH LOUTISH UNCIVIL
VILLAIN CLUBBISH SWADDISH
UNGAINLY
CLOY CLOG GLUT NAIL PALL SATE
GORGE PRICK ACCLOY PIERCE
SATIATE SATISFY SURFEIT
SATURATE
CLOYER SNAP
CLOYING GOOEY SWEET VANILLA
CLOYSOME LUSCIOUS
CLUB BAT DOG HIT HUI SET BEAT
CANE JOIN MACE MALL MAUL MERE
POLT TEAM BAFFY BANDY BATON
BILLY BUNCH CLOUT HURLY KEBBY
LODGE MASHY ORDER STAFF STICK
TOWEL UNITE YOKEL ZONTA
BULGER CERCLE CLIQUE CUDGEL
HURLEY KEBBIE LIBBET MACANA
MASHIE MENAGE MUCKLE NULLAH
PRIEST STRIKE TAIAHA VEREIN
WEAPON WHITES CAMBUCA
COLLEGE COUNCIL HETAERY
HETAIRY SOROSIS ATHENEUM
BLUDGEON CATSTICK SODALITY
SORORITY SPONTOON TERTULIA
KNOBKERRY

(— **IN PLAYING CARDS**) OAK
(— **OF ANTENNA**) CLAVUS
(**BASEBALL** —) FARM
(**GOLF** —) IRON WOOD BAFFY
CLEEK MASHY SPOON STICK
BRASSY BULGER DRIVER JIGGER
LOFTER MASHIE PUTTER BLASTER
MIDIRON NIBLICK PITCHER
(**MAORI** —) MERE MERAI MARREE
(**POLICEMAN'S** —) SAP BILLY
PANTOON SPONTON SPONTOON
(**POLITICAL** —) ROTA HETAERY
HETAIRY
(**WAR** —) WADDY
(**WOMEN'S** —) SOROSIS SORORITY
CLUB CARRIER CLAVIGER
CLUBFOOT TALUS VARUS TALIPES
CYLLOSIS POLTFOOT
CLUB MOSS MOSS FOFEET
LYCOPOD PILIGAN CROWFOOT
FERNWORT
CLUBROOT CLUB ANBURY HANBURY
CLUBBING CLUBFOOT
CLUB RUSH RUSH SEDGE GLUMAL
DEERHAIR
CLUCK HEN FUSS CHUCK CLACK
CLICK CLOCK CLOOK
CLUE KEY TIP BALL CLEW HINT IDEA
LEAD GUIDE TWINE BOTTOM
THREAD INNUENDO
CLUMP SOP TOD BLOW BUSH CLOT
HEAP KNOT LUMP MASS MOSS
MOTT TOPE TUFT TURB BLUFF
BUNCH CLAMP GROUP GROVE
HOUSE PATCH PLUMP STUMP
TREAD WUDGE CLUNCH DOLLOP
LUMPER CLUMPER CLUSTER
THICKET
(— **OF BRIERS OR ROSES**) ROAN
RONE
(— **OF CELLS**) SLUDGE
(— **OF SHRUBS**) BUSH
(— **OF SPORANGIA**) SORUS
(— **OF TREES**) BLUFF HOUSE HURST
HYRST BOSQUE
CLUMSILY SOUSE GREENLY
GAUCHELY
CLUMSY AWK FLOB LEWD NUMB
RUDE BLUNT BULKY GAUMY GAWKY
HOGGY HULKY INAPT INEPT SCRAM
SPLAY STIFF STOGY GAUCHE
LUBBER NOGGEN THUMBY
AWKWARD BOORISH CHOCKLE
CHUCKLE UNHANDY UNREADY
BENUMBED BUNGLING CLOWNISH
FOOTLESS HANDLESS LUMBERLY
TACTLESS UNGAINLY UNWIELDY
(**NOT** —) FINE
CLUSTER BOB BOG BUSH CLOT
COMA CONE CYME KNOT LUMP
TUFT BUNCH CLUMP DRUSE GROUP
PLUMP SHEAF CENTER COLONY
GATHER MORULA PLEIAD REGIME
BOUROCK CLUTHER DOLPHIN
ENVIRON FOLIAGE FASCICLE
NUCLEATE SURROUND
(— **AS BEES**) BALL KNIT
(— **OF BANANAS**) HAND
(— **OF BRANCHES**) SPRAY

(— **OF CRYSTALS**) DRUSE
(— **OF FEATHERS**) MUFF
(— **OF FIBERS**) NEP
(— **OF FLOWERS**) CYME CORYMB
ANTHEMY
(— **OF HAIRS**) MYSTAX
(— **OF METAL BALLS**) GRAPE
(— **OF NODULES**) GRAPES
(— **OF PILES**) DOLPHIN
(— **OF PLANTS**) BED
(— **OF RAYS**) AIGRETTE
(— **OF SPORES**) SORUS
(— **OF STARS**) PRAESEPE
(— **OF TINES**) TROCHE
(**CONFUSED** —) SPLATTER
(**SUSPENDED** —) SWAG
CLUSTER BEAN GUAR
CLUSTERED TUFTED RACEMOSE
AGGREGATE
CLUTCH HUG NAB SET CLAM CLAW
CLEM CLIP FIST GLAM GRAB GRIP
NEST BROOD CATCH CLASP CLAUT
CLEEK CLICK GLAUM GRASP GRIPE
GRISP HATCH LEVER POWER SEIZE
TALON CLEACH CLENCH CLETCH
CLINCH CUTOUT FASTEN RETAIN
SNATCH CONTROL CRAMPON
COUPLING
(— **OF EGGS**) SET LAWTER LAYING
SETTING SITTING LAUGHTER
CLUTCHING GRIP GRIPING
CLUTTER MESS STUFF BUSTLE
CUMBER CLATTER DISORDER
CONFUSION
CLUTTERED CLATTY CLOTTED
CLYMENE (**FATHER OF** —) OCEANUS
(**HUSBAND OF** —) IAPETUS
(**MOTHER OF** —) TETHYS
(**SON OF** —) ATLAS PHAETHON
MENOETIUS
CLYPEUS NASUS EPISTOME
PRELABRUM
CLYSTER LAVEMENT INJECTION
CLYTEMNESTRA (**FATHER OF** —)
TYNDAREUS
(**HUSBAND OF** —) AGAMEMNON
(**MOTHER OF** —) LEDA
(**SON OF** —) ORESTES
COACH BUS CAR FLY DRAG HACK
HELP ARABA BRIEF CABIN FLIER
FLYER PILOT PRIME STAGE TEACH
TRAIN TUTOR ADVISE DIRECT
FIACRE JARVEY SALOON ADVISER
CHARIOT COACHER CONCORD
GONDOLA PREPARE RATTLER
TALLYHO CARRIAGE DORMEUSE
PUPILIZE
(**3-WHEELED** —) TRICYCLE
(**FAST** —) FLIER FLYER
(**HACKNEY** —) FIACRE JARVEY
(**HEAVY** —) DRAG
(**SLOW** —) SLOWPOKE
COACHMAN FLY FISH JEHU WHIP
PILOT COACHY DRIVER COACHEE
COACHER YAMSHIK YEMSCHIK
COACTION EXPLOITATION
COADJUTOR PRIOR
COAGULANT CURD RENNET
STYPTIC COAGULUM GELATINE

COAGULATE GEL SET CAKE CLOD
CLOT CURD JELL QUAIL YEARN
COTTER CURDLE LAPPER LOBBER
LOPPER POSSET CLABBER CLOTTER
CONGEAL PECTIZE THICKEN
COAGULUM CONCRETE SOLIDIFY
COAGULATED CRUDY CURDY
LIVERED
COAGULATION GOUT CLOTTER
COAGULUM CLOT THROMBUS
COAL RIB BASS DUFF FUEL SWAD
BLOCK CHARK EMBER GHOST
GLEED STOKE BARING BRAZIL
BURGEE CANNEL CARBON CINDER
FIRING SPLINT BACKING BOGHEAD
BRIGHTS BYERITE COBBLES LIGNITE
RATTLER VITRAIN AMPELITE
LANDSALE
(— **IN PLACE**) SOLID
(— **PILLAR**) STOOK
(— **SLAB**) SKIP
(**BAD** —) SMUT
(**DIRTY** —) RASH
(**FINE** —) DUFF SCREENINGS
(**IMPURE** —) SWAD
(**LARGE BLOCK OF** —) JUD JUDD
(**LIVE OR GLOWING** —) GLEED
GLEYD
(**REFUSE** —) BREEZE
(**SIZE OF** —) EGG NUT PEA LUMP
RICE SLACK STOVE BARLEY
BROKEN CHESTNUT WALLSEND
BUCKWHEAT
(**SLATY** —) BASS BONE BONY
(**SMALL LUMP OF** —) NUBBLING
(**SMALL PORTION OF UNCUT** —)
PANEL
COAL BED SEAM
COALBIN BUNKER
COAL BROKER CRIMP
COAL CAR JIMMY
COAL CHUTE DOCK
COAL DUST COOM CULM SMUT
COOMB
COALESCE MIX CLOG FUSE JOIN
BLEND MERGE UNITE EMBODY
MINGLE COMBINE
COALESCENCE UNION FUSION
LEAGUE CAPTURE SYNANTHY
COALFISH SEY PARR CUDDY SEITH
BESHOW BILLET CUDDEN PODLER
SAITHE BADDOCK GLASHAN
GLASSIN PILTOCK POLLACK
(**YOUNG** —) PODLER PODLEY
COMAMIE POODLER SILLOCK
GRAYFISH
COALITION FRONT TRUST UNION
FUSION LEAGUE MERGER ENTENTE
ALLIANCE
COAL OIL KEROSENE
COALRAKE HOE FREGGIN FRUGGAN
SCRAPPLE
COAL WORKER GEORDIE HURRIER
COAL YARD REE
COAMING CURB LEDGE COMBING
COARSE FAT LOW RAW BASE BULL
DANK FOUL HARD HASK LEWD
LOUD RANK RUDE SOUR VILE
BAWDY BRASH BROAD CRASS

CRUDE DIRTY GREAT GROFF GROSS
HARSH HASKY HEAVY LARGE
LOOSE PLAIN RANDY ROUGH ROUTH
ROWTY STOGY STOUR THICK
UNORN BLOWSY BRAZEN BRUTAL
CALLOW COMMON DUDGEN EARTHY
IMPURE INCULT RANDIE RIBALD
ROUDAS RUDOUS RUSSET RUSTIC
SULTRY UNFELE VULGAR BLATANT
CARLAGE CARLISH FULSOME
GOATISH LOUTISH OBSCENE
RAPLOCH RAUCOUS ROINISH
SENSUAL CLOWNISH HOMESPUN
IMMODEST INDECENT PLEBEIAN
STUBBORN UNCHASTE

COARSE-FIBERED STRONG
COARSE-GRAINED DRY GRUFF
COARSELY BROADLY HARSHLY
COARSEN HACKNEY
COAST BANK LAND RIPA BEACH
CLIFF SHORE SLIDE WARTH ADJOIN
BORDER RIVAGE STRAND BOBSLED
SEASIDE APPROACH SEABOARD
SEASHORE

COASTER MAT SLED DOLLY TROUT
CRADLE CREEPER TOBOGGAN

COASTLAND MAREMMA

COAT FUR LAY PEE SAC TOG BARK
BLUE BUFF CONY DAUB FOIL FOLD
HIDE HUSK JACK JAMA JUPE PINK
RIND SACK SCAB SEAL TOGE ZINC
BENNY CLOTH CONEY COVER
CRUST FLASH FROCK GLACE GLAZE
HABIT JAMAH JEMMY LAYER OILER
PAINT PLATE QUYTE SAQUE SHELL
TERVE ALPACA BYRNIE COATEE
DUSTER ENAMEL EXTIMA GROUND
HACKLE INTIMA INVEST JACKET
JOSEPH KIRTLE LACKER MANTLE
MELOTE PARGET PELAGE RABBIT
REEFER SEALER SILVER SLOUGH
STUCCO TABARD VENEER BEESWAX
BOBTAIL CASSOCK COATING
COURTBY CRISPIN CUTAWAY
GARMENT GROGRAM INCRUST
KARAKUL LACQUER OILCOAT
OVERLAY PALETOT PELISSE
PLASTER SHELLAC SHOOTER
SPENCER STRATUM SUBCOAT
SURCOAT SURTOUT SWAGGER
TOGEMAN TOPCOAT VESTURE
BENJAMIN COURTEPY GRAPHITE
INTONACO MACKINAW MEMBRANE
ROCKELAY SEALSKIN SHERWANI
SILICATE TEGUMENT TRENCHER
(— **FOOD**) DREDGE
(— **LENS**) BLOOM
(— **OF ARMS**) CREST BLAZON
BEARINGS
(— **OF BIRD SKINS**) TEMIAK
(— **OF CARIBOU SKINS**) KOOLETAH
(— **OF DEFENSE**) JACK
(— **OF EYE**) CHOROID
(— **OF EYEBALL**) SCLERA
(— **OF GRAVEL**) BLOTTER
(— **OF MAIL**) FROCK BRINIE BYRNIE
SECRET HAUBERK
(— **OF ORGAN**) INTIMA
(— **OF PLASTER**) SET ARRICCIO

BROWNING INTONACO
(— **OF SEED**) BRAN
(— **OF WOOL**) FLEECE
(— **WITH ALLOY**) TERNE
(— **WITH PITCH**) PAY
(**DEER'S WINTER** —) BLUE
(**FIRST** — **OF TIN**) LIST
(**HAIR** —) MELOTE
(**HOODED** —) GREGO CAPOTE
(**LONG** —) JIBBA JIBBAH KAPOTE
DJIBBAH
(**LOOSE** —) CASSOCK PALETOT
INVERNESS
(**MILITARY** —) TUNIC BLOUSE
BUFFCOAT
(**RIDING** —) JOSEPH
(**SEALSKIN** —) NETCHA
(**SHEEPSKIN** —) ZAMARRA
ZAMARRO
(**SHORT** —) PEA SACK JERKIN
REEFER PEACOAT
(**THREE-QUARTER LENGTH** —)
ACHKAN
(**WATERPROOF** —) BURSATI SLICKER
(**WOMAN'S** —) CARACO DOLMAN

COATED GLACE BACKED FURRED
LOADED CANDIED

COAT HANGER SHOULDER

COATI NASUA TEJON NARICA PISOTE
ARCTOID

COATING (ALSO SEE COAT) FUR
GUM ARIL DOPE DRAB FILM FLOR
HAIR HOAR SKIN BLOOM FLASH
GLACE GLAZE ICING SCALE BEAVER
CHATON COVERT FINISH JACKET
PATINA VENEER BACKING DIPCOAT
FURRING GILDING LACQUER
PLATING TINNING ACIERAGE
CAMBOUIS CLADDING EMULSION
FLOODING MUCILAGE PERIDIUM
(— **OF BACTERIA**) SLIME
(— **OF GLASS**) MOILES FOLIATION
(— **OF GLUE**) ENAMEL
(— **OF ICE**) GLAZE
(— **OF SEED**) TESTA
(— **OF TONGUE**) ATTER
(**CORROSION** —) RUST
(**POWDERY** —) DOWN
(**PRUINOUS** —) FARINA
(**WALL** —) GROUT

COATTAIL LABIE LAPPET

COAX BEG COY PET CANT DUPE
FAGE FAWN LURE URGE JOLLY
TEASE BANTER CAJOLE CUITLE
CUTTER ENTICE FLEECH SEDUCE
BEGUILE CROODLE CROWDLE
CRUDDLE FLATTER IMPLORE
SOOTHER WHEEDLE BLANDISH
COLLOGUE INVEIGLE PERSUADE

COAXIAL CONCENTRIC

COB EAR LOB MEW COBB

COBBERER ROARER ROUSER

COBBLE DARN MEND PAVE BOTCH
PATCH BUNGLE COGGLE REPAIR

COBBLER PIE SNOB SHEEP SOLER
SUTOR ARTIST COZIER SOUTER
BOTCHER CATFISH CRISPIN
POMPANO SADDLER CHUCKLER
SCORPION SNOBSCAT

COBBLERFISH COBBLER SUNFISH
SHOEMAKER

COBBY STOUT HEARTY LIVELY
STOCKY COMPACT

COBLE MULE KOBIL

COBNUT COB OUABE HOGNUT
PIGNUT

COBRA ASP NAG HAJE NAGA NAJA
KRAIT VIPER ELAPID URAEUS

COBWEB NET TRAP SNARE WEVET
GOSSAMER

COCA CUCA KHOKA TRUXILLO

COCAINE COKE SNOW
(— **MIXED WITH HEROIN**)
SPEEDBALL

COCASH ASTER SWANWEED

COCCOID BERRYLIKE

COCCULUS CEBATHA FISHBERRY

COCHE MOCOA

COCHINEAL GRAIN BLANCO
COCCUS GRANILLA

COCHINEAL FIG NOPAL

COCHINEAL INSECT VERMIL
VERMEIL VERMILION

COCK COX TAP BANK BOOT COIL
FOWL HEAP KORA PILE RICK SPAN
COCKY COQUE FIGHT FUGIE GALLO
SHOCK STACK STRUT VALVE YOWLE
CRAVEN FAUCET HAMMER HEELER
LEADER CONTEND GORCOCK
PETCOCK ROOSTER SWAGGER
ASTROLOG COCKBIRD COCKEREL
COXBONES GAMECOCK JERMONAL
STOPCOCK
(— **GUNLOCK**) NAB
(— **OF HAY**) HIPPLE
(— **OF THE WALK**) KINGFISH
(— **WITHOUT COURAGE**) CRAVEN
(— **WITHOUT SPURS**) MUCKNA
(**FIGHTING** —) FUGIE HEELER
TURNPOKE
(**TURKEY** —) STAG
(**WATER** —) KORA
(**WEATHER** —) FANE VANE

COCKADE KNOT BADGE COCKARD
ROSETTE

COCKATIEL QUARRION

COCKATOO ARA ARARA COCKY
GALAH MACAW ABACAY COCKIE
PARROT CORELLA JACATOO
CALANGAY GANGGANG

COCKATOO BUSH BLUEBERRY

COCKBOAT COG COCK COGBOAT

COCKCHAFER OAKWEB BUZZARD
HUMBUZZ

COCKED HAT SCRAPER RAMILLIE

COCKER CODDLE COGGER QUIVER
SPANIEL

COCKEREL COCK SLIP BANTAM

COCKINESS SWAGGER

COCKLE COCK GALL GITH KILN
OAST BULGE KAKEL SHELL STOVE
DARNEL NUCULA PALOUR PUCKER
RIPPLE WABBLE ZIZANY CUCKOLD
WRINKLE HARDHEAD

COCKLEBUR COTS CLOTE COCKLE
BURDOCK BURWEED CADILLO
CLOTBUR CUCKOLD CLOTWEED
DITCHBUR

COCKNEY ORTHERIS LONDONESE
COCKPIT PIT RING RINK WELL
ARENA CABIN FIELD GALLERA
COCKROACH BUG DRUM ROACH
BEETLE BLATTID DRUMMER
KNOCKER
COCKSCOMB CREST COXCOMB
COCKSPUR FINGRIGO GARABATO
COCKTAIL SOUR ZOOM BRONX
CRUSTA GIBSON MARTINI SAZERAC
SIDECAR STINGER SWIZZLE
APERITIF DAIQUIRI
COCKY PERK PERT CRANK CROUSE
FARMER JAUNTY COCKING
ARROGANT
COCO KOKO BROMA COCOA COKER
YUNTIA
COCOA MAHAL PATASHTE
COCONUT COCO COCKER NARGIL
COCOANUT
COCONUT FIBER COIR KAIR KYAR
CAYAR
COCONUT MEAT COPRA
COCONUT PALM KOKO NIOG
COCOON POD CLEW CLUE KELL
SCAB SHED SHELL BOTTOM
DOUPION FOLLICLE
COCO PLUM ICACO HICACO
COCOWOOD KOKRA
COCUSWOOD KOKRA
COD BAG BIB COR KID POD AXLE
BANK CUSK FOOL GADE HOAX
HUSK POOR ROCK BELLY DROUD
GADID POUCH SCROD SHALE SHAUP
TORSK BURBOT CODGER CULTUS
ESCROD FELLOW MULVEL PILLOW
POCKET TOMCOD WACHNA
BACALAO CODFISH CODLING
CUSHION KEELING KILLING MILWELL
SCROTUM CABELIAU DOLEFISH
KABBELOW KLIPFISH
(BUFFALO —) LING
(CURED —) DUNFISH
(DRIED —) STOCK
(PILE OF DRIED —) YAFFLE
(SALTED —) COR KLIPFISH
HABERDINE
(YOUNG —) SPRAG
CODA CAUDA RONDO EPILOG FINALE
CODETTA EPILOGUE
CODDLE PET BABY CADE COOK
MUCH HUMOR NURSE SMALM SPOIL
CARESS COCKER COSSET COTTON
FONDLE PAMPER PTISAN QUADLE
PARBOIL
CODE LAW FLAG CANON CODEX
DOGMA FUERO CIPHER DIGEST
SECRET SIGNAL MULTEKA PRECEPT
DOOMBOOK
(— OF CHIVALRY) BUSHIDO
(— OF LAWS) ADA ADAT PANDECT
DOOMBOOK
(— OF RULES) VINAYA
(— OF WHAT IS FITTING) DECORUM
CODETTA CONDUIT
CODEX ALEF CODE ALEPH ANNAL
CODFISH POOR SPRAG TORSK
KEELING
CODGER COD CUFF CHURL CRANK

MISER FELLOW NIGGARD
CODICIL ANNEX LABEL SCRIPT
CODIFY INDEX DIGEST CLASSIFY
CODLING HAKE
CODOL RETINOL
COEFFICIENT CUMULANT
AUSTAUSCH
COELENTERATE POLYP MEDUSA
ACALEPH RADIATE ACALEPHE
COENOBIUM COLONY
COENOCYTE SYMPLASM SYMPLAST
SYNCYTIUM
COENZYME COFACTOR
COERCE COW CURB MAKE BULLY
CHECK DRIVE FORCE ORDER
COHERT COMPEL HIJACK CONCUSS
ENFORCE REPRESS SANDBAG
BLUDGEON BULLDOZE DISTRAIN
RESTRAIN RESTRICT
COERCION HEAT FORCE DURESS
COMMAND
COEUR D'ALENE SKITSWISH
COFFEE JO JOE RIO CAFE COHO
COHU JAVA MILD MOCHA BOGOTA
BRAZIL CAUFLE CHAOUA JAMOKE
SANTOS TRIAGE ARABICA BOURBON
MELANGE SUMATRA ESPRESSO
MAZAGRAN MEDELLIN TRILLADO
COFFEE BEAN QUAKER
COFFEEBERRY JOJOBA CASCARA
SOYBEAN PEABERRY
COFFEE CAKE KUCHEN
COFFEEHOUSE INN CAFE CAFENER
CAFENET
COFFEEMAKER SILEX
COFFEE TREE BONDUC CHICOT
VIRGILIA
COFFER ARK BOX DAM PYX CHEST
HUTCH TRUNK CASKET FORCER
FORCET SPRUCE TRENCH CAISSON
CASHBOX CASSOON COFFRET
LACUNAR LAQUEAR CIBORIUM
STANDARD
COFFIN BIER CASE CIST KIST MOLD
PALL SHELL BASKET CASING
CASKET COFFER HEARSE TROUGH
THROUGH
(LEADEN —) COPE
COG CAM LIE CAUK COCK GEAR
JEST CATCH CHEAT CHOCK CHUCK
COGUE COZEN TENON TOOTH
TRICK WEDGE WHEEL CAJOLE
COGGING DECEIVE PRODUCE
QUIBBLE WHEEDLE
COGENT GOOD PITHY VALID POTENT
STRONG TELLING FORCIBLE
POWERFUL
COGITATE MULL MUSE PLAN THINK
PONDER CONNATE MEDIATE
REFLECT CONSIDER
COGNATE KIN AKIN ALIKE ALLIED
COGENER KINDRED RELATED
SIMILAR BANDHAVA RELATIVE
APOPHONIC
COGNITION GNOSIS NOESIS
KENNING KNOWLEDGE
COGNITIVE KNOWING EPISTEMIC
COGNIZANCE KEN WIT HEED MARK
BADGE CREST EMBLEM NOTICE

BEARING COCKADE KNOWING
PRIVITY WITTING
COGNIZANT WARE WISE AWAKE
AWARE GUILTY KNOWING SENSIBLE
(BE —) DEEM
COGNOMEN NAME BYNAME
AGNOMEN SURNAME NICKNAME
PATRONYM
COGON ILLUK KUNAI LALANG
COGWOOD CERILLO
COHABIT LIVE DWELL ADHERE
OCCUPY COMPANY ACCUSTOM
COHERE FIT BOND GLUE SUIT
AGREE CLING SEIZE STICK UNITE
ADHERE CEMENT CLEAVE CONNECT
COINCIDE
COHERENCE UNION CONSENT
CONTEXT COHESION STRENGTH
COHERENT SERRIED
COHESION BOND ADHESION
HARDNESS STRENGTH
COHESIVE FATTY TENACIOUS
COHESIVENESS TENACITY
COHOBA PARICA
COHOSH SQUAWROOT
PAPOOSEROOT
COHUNE COROJO COROZO
COIF CAP HOW HOOD HOUVE
BEGGIN BURLET HAIRDO QUAIFE
ARRANGE CALOTTE BIGGONET
COIFFURE SKULLCAP
COIFFURE COIF HEAD HAIRDO
TUTULUS TRESSURE
COIL ADO WIN WIP ANSA CLEW
CURL FAKE FANK FURL FUSS HANK
LINK LOOP ROLL TUFT WIND ENROL
FLAKE HELIX QUERL QUILE ROUND
SPIRE TENSE TESLA TWINE TWIRL
TWIST WHORL WRING BOBBIN
BOTTOM BOUGHT DIMMER ENROLL
GLOMUS HEATER RENDER RUNDLE
SPIRAL TEASER TUMULT UPWIND
VOLUME WINDUP WREATH ENTRAIL
HAYCOCK INVOLVE PRIMARY
RINGLET SNAKING TICKLER
TROUBLE WREATHE COFUSION
ENCIRCLE INDUCTOR OVERCOIL
(— IN STILL) SCROLL
(— INTO BALL) WIRE
(— OF CAPILLARIES) TUFT
(— OF HAIR) BUN PUG
(— OF SNAKE) FOLD
(— OF WIRE) BOBBIN SOLENOID
(INDUCTION —) JIGGER
COILED GYRATE TORTILE WRITHEN
COILER FLARER
COILING SPIRY
COIN AS BU PU AVO BAN BIT BOO
COB DAM DIE DUB ECU FIL JOE KIP
LAT LEK LEU LEV LEY ORI PUL SEN
SOL TRA WEN WON ABAS ANNA
ATTE BAHT BATZ BESA CASH CENT
CHIP CHON DEMY DIME DOIT DONG
DOTT DUMP DURO FELS FILS GILL
GROS GROT HARP HOON HWAN
JACK JANE KRAN KYAT LEVY LION
MAIL MAKE MILL MINT MITE MULE
OBAN ONZA OORD PARA PAUL
PESA PESO PICE POND POUL QUAN

RAND RIAL ROCK RYAL SCAD SENT
SINK SIZE SLUG TAEL TARA TARE
TARI TARO TIAO TREY TYPE UNIT
ACKEY AGNEL AKCHA ALBUS ALTIN
ALTUN AMANI ANGEL ANGLE ASPER
BAIOC BAIZA BATTE BEKAR BELGA
BETSO BEZZO BISTI BLANC BLANK
BODLE BROAD BROWN CHINK CLINK
COIGN CONTO COROA CROSS
CROWN CUNYE DARIC DINAR DISME
DOBLA DUCAT EAGLE EYRIR FANAM
FANON FODDA FRANC GAZET
GRANO GROAT GROSZ HALER
HECTE JACOB JULIO JUSTO KOBAN
KRONA KRONE KROON LIARD LIBRA
LITRA LOUIS MEDAL MEDIN MEDIO
MILAN MOHUR MOPUS NOBLE
NOMOS OBANG ORKEY ORKYN
PAISA PAOLO PARDO PENNY PERAU
PESSA PIECE PLACK PLATE POALI
POALO PROOF QUART QUINE RAPPE
REBIA RIDER RIYAL ROYAL RUBLE
RUPIA SAIGA SAPEK SCEAT SCUDO
SCUTE SEMIS SHAHI SICCA SMASH
SOLDO STAMP STYCA SUCRE TALER
TANGA TANKA TEMPO THRIP TICAL
TRIME UNCIA UNITE WHITE ABASSI
ABBASI AFGHAN AHMADI ARGENT
ASSARY AUREUS AZTECA BALBOA
BAUBEE BAWBEE BEAVER BEZANT
BIANCO BLANCO BOGACH BRONZE
CARLIN CENTAS CHAISE COBANG
CONDOR COPPER CORONA CUARTO
CUNZIE DECIME DENARY DENIER
DERHAM DINDER DIOBOL DIRHAM
DIXAIN DIZAIN DOBLON DODKIN
DOLLAR DOPPIA DOUBLE ESCUDO
FILLER FLORIN FOLLIS FORINT
GEORGE GIULIO GOURDE GRIVNA
GROSSO GUINEA GULDEN HARPER
HELLER ICHIBU ITZEBU JUSLIK
KLIPPE KOPECK KORONA KORUNA
LAUREL LEPTON MACUTA MAHBUB
MAIDEN MANCUS MEDINO MISKAL
NICKEL NORKYN OCHAVO OCTAVE
ONGARO PADUAN PAGODA PARDAO
PATACA PATART PHILIP QUEZAL
ROSARY SALUNG SALUTE SATANG
SEQUIN SESKIN SHEKEL SHIELD
SIGLOS SINKER SIXAIN SOMALO
SOVRAN STATER STELLA STIVER
TALENT TARGET TESTAO TESTER
TESTON THALER THOMAN TOSTON
TRIENS TUMAIN TUNGAH TURNER
TURNEY TURTLE UNGARO VINTEM
XERIFF YUZLIK ZECHIN ZEHNER
ZEQUIN ALFONSO ALTILIK ANGELET
ANGELOT ANGOLAR ANGSTER
BAIOCCO BAJOCCO BARBONE
BOLIVAR CARDECU CARLINE
CARLINO CAROLIN CAROLUS
CENTAVO CHALCUS CHALKOS
CORDOBA COUNTER CRUSADO
DAMPANG DRACHMA DUCATON
DUPLONE ESCALAN JACOBUS
JOANNES KASBEKE KREUZER
LEMPIRA LEONINE LEOPARD
LUIGINO MANGOUR MARENGO
MOIDORE MONARCH MUZOONA

NOUMMOS ONCETTA PAHLAVI
PARISIS PATACAO PATAGON
PATAQUE PENNING PFENNIG
PISTOLE QUADRIN QUARTER
QUATTIE QUETZAL QUINYIE
REDDOCK RUDDOCK RUSPONE
SANTIMS SCRUPLE SEXTANS
SILIQUA SIZEINE SOLIDUS SPECIES
STAMPEE STOOTER STUIVER
SULTANE TALLERO TEECALL
THRYMSA TORNESE TRIOBOL
UNICORN XERAFIN ALBERTIN
AMBROSIN AQUILINO AUGUSTAL
AUKSINAS BAETZNER BAGATINE
BECHTLER BLAFFERT BLANKEEL
BLANKILO BROCKAGE CAVALIER
CHINKERS CHUCKRAM COLONIAL
COURONNE CROCKARD CRUZEIRO
DECUSSIS DENARIUS DIDRACHM
DIOBOLON DOUBLOON EQUIPAGA
FARTHING FILIPPIC FREDERIK
GAZZETTA GENOVINO GIGLIATO
GIUSTINA GROSCHEN HARDHEAD
HYPERPER IMPERIAL ISABELLA
JOHANNES KREUTZER LUSHBURG
MACARONI MAJIDIEH MARCELLO
METALLIK MILESIMA PATACOON
PAVILION PICAYUNE PIEDFORT
PISTOLET PLAPPERT PORTAGUE
QUADRANS QUADRINE QUARTINE
QUINCUNX RESTRIKE RIGMAREE
RISDALER RIXDALER SCUDDICK
SEMUNCIA SESTERCE SHILLING
SIXPENCE SKILLING SLEEPING
SOLIDARE STERLING STOTINKA
SULTANIN TENPENNY TETROBOL
THIRTEEN TWOPENCE ZECCHINO
(— **AROUND NECK)** TALI
(— **IMPERFECTLY MINTED)**
BROCKAGE
(— **OF TRIFLING VALUE)** RAP
(**BASE** —) SHAND SHEEN SINKER
(**COUNTERFEIT** —) GRAY GREY SLIP
SHEEN SHOFUL STUMER STUMOR
(**PLUGGED** —) PLUG
(**SMALL THICK** —) DUMP
(PL.) CHANGE CHINKS SERIES
COINAGE
COINAGE FICTION GALUMPH
MINTAGE
COINCIDE FIT GEE JIBE JUMP
AGREE TALLY CONCUR
COINCIDENT EVEN TOGETHER
COINCIDING CONGRUENT
COINER MONIER MONEYER
COITION SOIL VENERY MEETING
CONGRESS
COKE ASK COAL COLK CORE DOPE
CHARK COCAINE
COL GAP HALS JOCH PASS HALSE
SWIRE SADDLE
COLANDER SIEVE STRAINER
COLCOTHAR SAFFRON TUSCANY
COLD FLU ICY MUR NIP COOL DEAD
DULL HARD HASK HOAR MURR
ROUP SOUR ACALE ACOLD ALGID
BLEAK CHILL CRISP FISHY FRORE
GELID GLACE GLARE OORIE OURIE
PARKY POOSE RHEUM SHARP

STONY VIRUS ARCTIC BITTER
BOREAL CHILLY CLAMMY CRIMMY
FREDDO FRIGID FRIGOR FROSTY
GLASSY MARBLY STECKY WAIRCH
WINTRY BRITTLE CATARRH CHILLED
COLDISH COSTIVE DISTANT
FROSTED GLACIAL INHUMAN
MORFOND SHIVERY STRANGE
FREEZING MORFOUND PIERCING
RESERVED RHIGOSIS STANDOFF
UNHEATED
(— **IN HEAD)** POSE POOSE CORYZA
CATARRH GRAVEDO SNIVELS
SNIFFLES SNIFTERS
(**BITTER** —) ARCTIC
(**VERY** —) FRIGID PEEVISH
COLD-BLOODED BRUTAL LEEPIT
COLD CUTS ASSIETTE
COLD-HEARTED COLD FROZEN
BLOODLESS
COLDLY DRILY DRYLY
COLDNESS COLD FROST STEEL
PHLEGM DISTANCE FROIDEUR
COLDONG FRIARBIRD
COLE CALE KAIL KALE COLZA
FRIGOR COLEWORT
COLEUS KOORKA
COLEWORT COLE KALE RIBE STOCK
CABBAGE
(**SPROUT OF** —) STOVEN
COLIC BATS FRET BATTS GUTTIE
BELLYACHE
COLICROOT UNICORN ALOEROOT
HUSKROOT HUSKWORT STARWORT
COLIMA TAPA IRONWOOD
COLISEUM HALL STADIUM THEATER
COLOSSEUM
COLL HUG CLIP CULL POLL PRUNE
EMBRACE
COLLABORATE AID ASSIST
COOPERATE
COLLAPSE CAVE FALL FLOP FOLD
GIVE SINK CRASH SLUMP WRECK
BUCKLE SHRINK TUMBLE CAPSIZE
CROPPER CRUMBLE CRUMPLE
DEBACLE DEFLATE FAILURE
FLUMMOX FOUNDER SMASHUP
CONTRACT DOWNFALL TAILSPIN
COLLAPSED QUAT CLUNG
COLLAPSIBLE FOLDING
COLLAPSING FAILURE COLLABENT
COLLAR CAP FUR NAB BAND ETON
FALL FANO GILL GRAB POKE RING
RUFF CHAIN DICKY FANON FANUM
FICHU PHANO RUCHE SEIZE STOCK
TRASH WHISK BERTHA CARCAN
CHOKER COLLET COLLUM DICKEY
GORGET PARRAL PARREL RABATO
REBATO SADDLE SLEEVE TACKLE
TORQUE TUCKER TURNUP BOBACHE
BOBECHE CAPTURE CHIGNON
CIRCLET PANUELO PARTLET
POTHOOK REBATER SHACKLE
STICKUP VANDYKE CARCANET
CINCTURE NECKBAND NECKLACE
RABATINE STARCHER TURNDOWN
(— **FOR HORSE)** BARGHAM
BRECHAM
(**HIGH** —) GILLS

(IRON —) JOUG JOUGS CARCAN
POTHOOKS
(LACE —) SCALLOP
(MAGISTRATE'S —) GOLILLA
(ROMAN —) RABAT
(WHEEL-SHAPED —) RUFF
(WOODEN —) CANG CANGUE
COLLAR BEAM SPANNER
SPANPIECE
COLLARBONE CLAVICLE
COLL'ARCO ARCATO
COLLARED ACCOLLE ACCOLLEE
TORQUATE
COLLAR PAD AFTERWALE
COLLATE BESTOW CONFER VERIFY
COMPARE
COLLATERAL SIDE MARGIN OBLIQUE
INDIRECT PARALLEL SECURITY
COLLATION TEA MEAL LUNCH
REPAST SERMON ADDRESS
READING DEJEUNER HOTCHPOT
TREATISE
COLLEAGUE AIDE ALLY UNITE
DEPUTY SOCIUS ADJUNCT COLLEGE
COMPEER CONSORT PARTNER
CONFRERE CONSPIRE
COLLECT JUG SAM TAX CALL CARD
CULL DRAW HEAP LEVY LIFT PICK
PILE POOL REAR SAMM SAVE
AMASS CROWD GLEAN GROUP
HOARD RAISE STORE SWEEP
ACCOIL ACCRUE CENTER CONFER
GARNER GATHER MUSTER PRAYER
SEMBLE SHEAVE UPTAKE ARCHIVE
CLUSTER COMPILE CONGEST
ENGROSS IMPOUND RAMMASS
RECUEIL SCAMBLE SYNAPTE
ASSEMBLE CONFLATE CONTRACT
CUPBOARD INGATHER RESEMBLE
SCRAMBLE SCROUNGE
(— AND DRIVE INTO ENCLOSURE)
WEAR
(— FOOD) FORAGE
(— GRAIN) GAVEL
(— INTO COVEY) JUG
(— MONEY) NOB
(— WAGES) UPLIFT
COLLECTED CALM COOL SOBER
SERENE PRESENT COMPOSED
COLLECTION ANA BAG KIT SET
BAND BEVY BOOK CLAN CROP FILE
HEAD HEAP KNOT LEVY OLIO RAFT
SORT ALBUM ANNEX BATCH BUDGE
DEPOT FLOCK GLEAN GROUP
HOARD KITTY SHEAF STORE SUITE
SWATH BUNDLE CONGER CORPUS
FARDEL MISHNA PARCEL RAGBAG
RECULE SORITE SPRING SWATHE
TUMBLE ACCOUNT COLLECT
CONGERY EXHIBIT FERNERY
FISTFUL FLUTTER GALLERY
QUOTITY RECUEIL SAMHITA
SMATTER SMYTRIE SYLLOGE
TERRIER ASSEMBLY CABOODLE
CONGERIE COSTOMAL FASCICLE
GATHERUM GLOSSARY ROMESCOT
ROMESHOT SYNTAGMA
(— AT FOX HUNT) CAP
(— OF 24 SHEETS) QUIRE

(— OF ANIMALS) ZOO HEAD
(— OF BOOKCASES) STACK
(— OF BOOKS) SET BIBLE CANON
LIBRARY
(— OF CONIFERS) PINETUM
(— OF DATA) GROUND
(— OF FORMULAS) CODEX
(— OF FOUR) TETRAD
(— OF LAWS) CODE
(— OF MAPS) ATLAS
(— OF OBJECTS) AFFAIR
(— OF OPINIONS) SYMPOSIUM
(— OF PERSONS) BOODLE
(— OF PLANTS) SERTULE
(— OF POEMS) DIVAN DIWAN SYLVA
ANTHOLOGY
(— OF PUS) HYPOPYON
(— OF REVENUES) TAMSIL TEHSIL
(— OF ROCKS) SUITE
(— OF RULES) SUTRA SUTTA
(— OF SAMPLES) SWATCH
(— OF SAYINGS) ANA
(— OF SPECIMENS) CABINET
(— OF STAFFS) SYSTEM
(— OF STORIES) LEGEND
(— OF TOOLS) LAYOUT
(— OF TREES) SERINGAL
(— OF UNWANTED ANIMALS)
LARDER
(CONFUSED —) CLUTTER
(MISCELLANEOUS —) OLIO FARDEL
SMYTRIE
(VAST —) CLOUD
COLLECTIVE GROUP AGGREGATE
COLLECTIVIST COMMUNIST
SOCIALIST
COLLECTOR COMB CAMEIST
CURIOSO DUSTMAN FURIOSO
UPTAKER ANTIQUER COUNTOUR
GATHERER STAMPMAN VIRTUOSO
ZAMINDAR
(— ITEMS) RARIORA
(— OF BUTTERFLIES) AURELIAN
(— OF HERBS) SIMPLER
(— OF REVENUE) AUMIL AUMILDAR
TALUKDAR ZAMINDAR
(CUSTOMS —) HOPPO CUSTOMER
(TAX —) CAID QAID GABBAI
TAHSILDAR
COLLECTORATE TALUK
COLLEEN GIRL LASS MISS BELLE
CAILIN DAMSEL
COLLEGE TOL HALL AGGIE HOUSE
LYCEE CAMPUS COLAGE SCHOOL
SIWASH ACADEMY MADRASA
SEMINARY
COLLEGER TUG
COLLET BAND NECK RING CHUCK
CULET CASING CIRCLE COLLAR
COLLUM FLANGE BUSHING
COLLIDE HIT RAM BUMP DASH FRAY
HURT CLASH CRASH KNOCK SHOCK
SMITE WRECK HURTLE STRIKE
THRUST
(— WITH) IMPINGE
COLLIE BEARDIE
COLLIER MINER PLOVER GEORDIE
COILYEAR FLATIRON SCUTCHER
COLLIQUATION SYNTEXIS

COLLISION HIT FOUL CLASH CRASH
SHOCK HURTLE IMPACT JOSTLE
SMASHUP CLASHING CONFLICT
COLLOCATE SET PLACE ARRANGE
COLLOID GEL
COLLOQUIAL FAMILIAR INFORMAL
COLLOQUIUM INDUCEMENT
COLLOQUY CHAT TALK PARLEY
DIALOGUE
COLLOTYPE ARTOTYPE HELIOTYPE
COLLUDE PLOT SCHEME CONNIVE
COLLOGUE CONSPIRE
COLLUM NECK
COLLUSION DECEIT CAHOOTS
SECRECY PRACTICE PRACTISE
COLLUSIVE COVINOUS COLLUSORY

COLOMBIA

CAPE: VELA AGUJA MARZO
AUGUSTA
CAPITAL: BOGOTA
CAY: VELA VIGIA RONCADOR
COIN: PESO REAL CONDOR
PESETA CENTAVO
FORMER NAME: DARIEN
NEWGRANADA
GULF: URABA CUPICA DARIEN
TIBUGA TORTUGAS
INDIAN: BORO CUNA HOKA MACU
MUZO PAEZ CARIB CATIO
CHOCO COFAN COGUI CUBEO
GUANE PIJAO SEONA ARAWAK
BETOYA CALIMA INGANO SALIVA
TAHAMI TUCANO TUNEBO
YAHUNA ACHAGUA ANDAQUI
CHIBCHA CHIMILA GUAHIBO
GUAJIRO PANCHES PUINAVE
PUITOTO QUECHUA TAIRONA
GUARAUNO MOTILONE
INLET: TUMACO
ISLAND: BARU NAIPO FUERTE
GORGONA CUSACHON
MEASURE: VARA AZUMBRE
CELEMIN
MOUNTAIN: CHITA HUILA PURACE
TOLIMA
MOUNTAINS: ABIBE ANDES BAUDO
COCUY AYAPEL PERIJA TUNAHI
CHAMUSA ORIENGAL
PLAINS: LLANOS
POINT: CRUCES LACRUZ SOLANO
CARIBANA GALLINAS
PORT: LORICA CARTAGENA
PROVINCE: META CAUCA CHOCO
HUILA VALLE ARAUCA BOYACA
CALDAS NARINO TOLIMA
VAUPES BOLIVAR CAQUETA
GUAJIRE VICHADA AMAZONAS
PUTUMAYO
RIVER: UVA BITA META MUCO
SINU TOMO UPIA YARI BAUDO
CAUCA CESAR ISANA MESAI
NECHI PATIA PAUTO SUCIO
AMAZON ARAUCA ARIARI
ATRATO CAGUAN VAUPES
YAPURA APAPOIS CAQUETA
GUAINIA INIRIDA TRUANDO
VICHADA CASANARE GUAVIARE

PUTUMAYO MAGDALENA
TOWN: TEN ANZA BUGA CALI MITU
MUZO PAEZ SIPI TADO TOLU
YARI BELLO CHINU GUAPI NEIVA
PASTO TUNJA BOGOTA CUCUTA
IBAGUE QUIBDO SANGIL
CARTAGO LETICIA PALMIRA
PEREIRA POPAYAN GIRARDOT
MEDELLIN MONTERIA
CARTAGENA
TREE: ARBOLOCO
VOLCANO: PURACE
WEIGHT: BAG SACO CARGA LIBRA
QUILATE QUINTAL

COLON CROWN POINT HEMISTICH
MESYMNION
COLONIAL OVERSEA OVERSEAS
COLONIST BOOR COLON FATHER
CUTHEAN PIONEER PLANTER
SETTLER EMIGRANT
(AUSTRALIAN —) STERLING
(PL.) DEHAITES DEHAVITES
COLONIZE ECIZE FOUND PLANT
GATHER SETTLE MIGRATE
COLONIZER OECIST OEKIST
COLONNADE ROW STOA PORCH
PARVIS PIAZZA GALLERY PERGOLA
PORTICO TERRACE CHOULTRY
COLONNETTE COLUMELLA
COLONY STATE STOCK SWARM
CENOBE CORMUS APOIKIA COLONIA
CENOBIUM GANNETRY
(— OF BEES) HIVE SKEP SWARM
(BRYOZOAN —) ESCHARA
COLOR DIP DYE HUE BLEE CAST
FAKE FLAG PUKE SUIT TINT TONE
BADGE BLUSH GLAZE GLOSS GRAIN
PAINT SHADE STAIN TAINT TASTE
TENNE TINCT TINGE BANNER
BLEACH BOTTOM BRIDGE CHROMA
ENSIGN INFECT LOCKET MANTLE
RADDLE REDDEN STREAK TEMPER
COULEUR DEPAINT DISTORT
ENGRAIN PENNANT PIGMENT
SPECKLE COLORING STANDARD
TERTIARY TINCTURE
(— IMPARTED TO HERRINGS)
GILDING
(— LOSS) POLIOSIS
(— OF BIRD) SMUT
(— OF BODY) HEAT
(— OF EYES OF FOWLS) DAW
(— OF HUMAN FLESH) CARNATION
(— OF ROCK) STONE
(BLUE —) FOG JAY SKY WAD AQUA
BICE CIEL CYAN DELF DELP DUSK
IRIS NAVY PAON SAXE WADE WOAD
ZINC AZURE BERYL BLUET CADET
CAPRI CHING COPEN DELFT DIANA
DRAKE EMAIL GRAPE METAL NIKKO
ORION PEARL ROYAL SLATE SMALT
SMOKE VANDA CANTON CENDRE
COELIN ENSIGN GROTTO HATHOR
INDIGO LUPINE MARINE MASCOT
MIGNON ORIENT PENSEE ROMANY
SEVRES VENICE ZENITH CELESTE
CERAMIC CHICORY DUSTBLU

GOBELIN HORIZON LIBERTY LOBELIA
LOGWOOD MATELOT PEACOCK
PETUNIA RAMESES SISTINE SIXTINE
ABSINTHE BLUEBIRD BLUEWOOD
BRITTANY CAESIOUS CATTLEYA
CERULEAN CERULEUM DUCKLING
ELECTRIC GENDARME HYACINTH
INFANTRY LABRADOR LARKSPUR
MASCOTTE MAZARINE MIDNIGHT
MOONBEAM NATIONAL SAPPHIRE
TWILIGHT WEDGWOOD
(BROWN —) BAY ELK FOX OAK TAN
ARAB BARK BOLE BRAN BURE CAIN
CLAY CORK CUBA DATE DEER DRAB
DUST ECRU FAON FAWN GOAT
GOLD HOPI IRON LAMA LION MAST
MESA MUSK SEAL SIAM TEAK
ACORN ADUST ALOMA AZTEC BEIGE
BISON BLOND BLUSH BOLUS BRIAR
BRICK BRIER BROWN BUNNY CACAO
CAMEL CANNA CLOVE COCOA
CONGO EAGLE FRIAR FUDGE GIPSY
GRAIN GYPSY HAZEL HENNA KAFFA
KHAKI LIVER MAHAL MALAY MECCA
MINIM MUMMY NEGRO OTTER
PABLO QUAIL SABEL SEDGE SEPIA
SIENA SIRUP SNUFF SUDAN SUEDE
SUMAC SYRUP TABAC TAFFY TENNE
TOAST TOPAZ AFGHAN ALESAN
ALMOND APACHE ARGALI AUBURN
BAMBOO BEAVER BISQUE BISTER
BISTRE BLONDE BRONCO BRONZE
BURNET COCHIN COFFEE CONDOR
COOKIE COWBOY CROTAL DORADO
ESKIMO FALLOW GINGER GRAVEL
GROUSE HAVANA ISABEL LOUTRE
MAROON MERIDA MOHAWK MUFFIN
NUTMEG ORIOLE PAWNEE PLOVER
PUEBLO RABBIT RACKET RUDDLE
RUSSET SAHARA SANTOS SHERRY
SORREL SPHINX SPONGE STRING
STUCCO SUMACH SUNTAN THRUSH
TIFFIN TURTLE ASPHALT BADIOUS
BEESWAX BITUMEN BRACKEN
BRONCHO CALDRON CATTAIL
CIGARET COCONUT COTRINE
CRACKER DOGWOOD DURANGO
FEUILLE FILBERT GAZELLE
GOREVAN HARVEST LEATHER
LIBERIA MALABAR MIRADOR
MORDORE MOROCCO MUSCADE
MUSTANG NORFOLK OAKWOOD
PERIQUE PRALINE RACQUET
ROSARIO SABELLA SUNBURN
SUNDOWN TALLYHO TANBARK
TOBACCO TUSCANY ALDERNEY
ALGERIAN AMBROSIA BISMARCK
BOBOLINK CALABASH CARTOUCH
CAULDRON CINNAMON CLAYBANK
CORDOVAN DOUBLOON ETRUSCAN
EUCHROME HAZELNUT ISABELLA
KOLINSKY LEAFMOLD MANDALAY
MOCCASIN MOLESKIN MOROCCAN
MUSHROOM NOISETTE PHEASANT
SAUTERNE SHAGBARK STARLING
TAMARACK TEAKWOOD TERRAPIN
TORTOISE WOODBARK
(DEEP —) DARK
(FAST —) GRAIN

(GREEN —) BOA FIR IVY ALOE BICE
FERN JADE LEEK MOSS NILE SAGE
ALOES CEDRE CHLOR DRAKE FAIRY
HOLLY KELLY LOVAT OLIVE SPRAY
CANNON EMPIRE HUNTER JASPER
LAUREL LIERRE LIZARD MEADOW
MOUSSE MYRTLE SPRUCE VERDET
CELADON CITRINE CORBEAU
CRESSON CYPRESS EMERALD
INGENUE JADEITE JUNIPER
MESANGE NEPTUNE OLIVINE
PERIDOT SEAFOAM SERPENT
TILLEUL VERDURE BAYBERRY
CHASSEUR COPPERAS EMERAUDE
GLAUCOUS GLOWWORM PARAKEET
PERRUCHE PISTACHE POPINJAY
SHAMROCK TARRAGON VIRIDIAN
WOODLAND
(GRIZZLED —) AGOUTI AGOUTY
(OTHER —S) OR ASH BAT DOE DUN
JET TEA CHIP CORN CROW DAWN
DOVE GRAY GREY GULL HEMP LAVA
LEAD MODE MOLE NICE NUDE PLUM
PORT ROAN RUST SAND SOOT
WOOD AMBER BEACH BLACK
CAMEO CERES CHILE CHILI COPRA
CRANE CRASH CREAM DWALE
EBONY FLESH GRAPE GREBE
GREGE MAUVE MOUSE PANSY
PHLOX PLOMB PRAWN PRUNE
PUTTY RIFLE SABLE SPICE STEEL
THYME TWINE ANATTO AURORA
AUTUMN CASTOR CINDER COLLIE
CORCIR DAHLIA DAMSON DENVER
EVEQUE FIESTA FUSTIC GAMBIA
GRIEGE KASPER MALLOW MODENA
NAVAHO NAVAJO NIMBUS NUTRIA
ONDINE ORCHID OXFORD OYSTER
PEANUT PEBBLE PIGEON QUAKER
RAISIN RESEDA ROUCOU SEASAN
SILVER TUSCAN VANITY VESTAL
VIOLET WALNUT ADMIRAL ANNATTO
ARBUTUS ARDOISE ARNATTA
BEGONIA BERMUDA BLOSSOM
BRINDLE CARAIBE CARAMEL
COTRINE COWSLIP CRACKER
CRUISER MORELLO MURILLO
NATURAL OPHELIA PELICAN
PONTIFF POPCORN PRELATE
PUMPKIN QUIMPER REGATTA
ROSEBUD SAKKARA SANDUST
SPARROW SUNBEAM THISTLE
TUSSORE VERVAIN VIOLINE
WEIGELA WHEATEN ALUMINUM
AMETHYST BLONDINE CARMETTA
CHARCOAL CLEMATIS COCOBOLO
COQUETTE CREVETTE CYCLAMEN
EGGPLANT EMINENCE FELDGRAU
FLAMINGO GILLIVER GRAPHITE
GUNMETAL HONEYDEW IMPERIAL
JACINTHE LAVENDER MARATHON
MORILLON MULBERRY PALMETTO
ROSEWOOD SAUTERNE SQUIRREL
SUNBURST WIRELESS WISTARIA
WISTERIA CARNELIAN
(RED —) DAWN FLEA GOLF GOYA
HEBE LAKE MIST PUCE RUBY TULY
WINE AGATE BRASS BRICK CANNA
CANON CEDAR CORAL CUTCH

EMBER FLAME FLASH GULES LILAC
MELON NYMPH PEACH PEONY
POPPY ROSET SIENA SPARK TOTEM
ACAJOU ARCHIL AURORE AUTUMN
AZALEA BRAZIL CANYON CARROT
CATSUP CERISE CHERRY CHERUB
CLARET COGNAC DAMASK FRAISE
GAIETY GARNET GAYETY GRANET
JOCKEY KERMES MADDER MALAGA
MIKADO MURREY NECTAR ORCHIL
PATISE SALMON SANDIX SHRIMP
SIERRA SULTAN TITIAN TOMATO
AFRICAN ANAMITE ANEMONE
BEGONIA BISCUIT BOKHARA
CARMINE CATAWBA CATCHUP
CATECHU CRIMSON CURRANT
FIREFLY FUCHSIA FUCHSIN
GRANATE GRANITE HEATHER
INDIANA KETCHUP LACQUER
LOBSTER MAGENTA MASCARA
NACARAT OXBLOOD PAPRIKA
POMPEII PONCEAU REDWOOD
ROSETAN ROSETTE RUBELLE
SAFFLOR SARAVAN SCARLET
SINOPLE STAMMEL SULTANA
VERMEIL ALKERMES AMARANTH
ARCHILLA BISMARCK BORDEAUX
BURGUNDY CAMELLIA CARDINAL
CHAUDRON CHEROKEE CHERUBIM
CHESTNUT COCOANUT CONFETTI
DAMONICO DIANTHUS DUBONNET
EVENGLOW GERANIUM GRENADIN
GRIDELIN MAHOGANY MANDARIN
MAROCAIN NACARINE TOREADOR
(SOLID —) SOLID
(TONE —) TIMBRE
(YELLOW —) HAY RAT WAX BEAR
BUFF CLAY CORN CUIR ECRU FLAX
GOLD LARK LIME MOTH WELD
WOLD ACIER ALOMA AZTEC BEIGE
BLAKE BRASS CRASH CREAM GRAIN
HONEY IVORY LEMON MAIZE MAPLE
SHELL STRAW TAUPE WOULD
ACACIA ALMOND BANANA CANARY
CATHAY CHROME CITRON CITRUS
CROCUS DORADO FALLOW MANILA
MASTIC MIMOSA NANKIN NUGGET
OXGALL SULFUR SUNRAY SUNSET
ANTIQUE APRICOT BISCUIT CAVALRY
CHAMOIS GAMBOGE JASMINE
JONQUIL LEGHORN MEXICAN
NANKEEN PRAIRIE RHUBARB
SAFFRON SULPHUR SUNGLOW
ANTELOPE CALABASH CAPUCINE
COCKATOO DAFFODIL EGGSHELL
GENERALL GOLDMIST MARIGOLD
ORPIMENT PRIMROSE SNOWSHOE
(PL.) FLAG
COLORABLE SPECIOUS

COLORATION BLEE PILE FLASH
CLOUDING COLORISM SCHILLER
COLORATURA GORGIA SOPRANO
COLOR-BLINDNESS DALTONISM
COLORED FAW HUED MALE BIASED
DEPAINT STAINED
(— IN RED) RUBRIC
(— LIKE PIPE BOWL) TROUSERED
(BRILLIANTLY —) SUPERB FLAMING
(HIGHLY —) CHROMATIC
(PARTI —) PIED PIEBALD
(UNIFORMLY —) HARD
COLORFUL GAY BRAVE JUICY VIVID
COLORY GOLDEN FREAKED
GORGEOUS
COLORING BLEE TINT PAINT TINGE
TINGENT BRONZING PAINTING
TINCTURE
(— MATTER) TINCTION
COLORLESS WAN DRAB DULL PALE
ASHEN BLAKE BLANK PLAIN
MOUSEY PALLID HUELESS NEUTRAL
ACHROMIC ACHROOUS BLANCHED
ETIOLATE LIFELESS
COLOSSAL BIG HUGE VAST GREAT
LARGE IMMENSE TITANIC
ENORMOUS GIGANTIC MONSTROUS
COLOSSUS GIANT TITAN STATUE
COLOSSO MONOLITH
COLOSTRUM FOREMILK AFTERINGS
COLT FOAL STAG FILLY POTRO
STAIG HOGGET POLEYN STAGGIE
EQUULEUS
COLTER LAVER COOTER COULTER
FOREIRON
COLTSFOOT DOCK CLOTE HOOFS
CLEATS FARFARA LAGWORT
SOWFOOT BULLFOOT CLAYWEED
FOALFOOT
COLUGO COBEGO
COLUMBATE NIOBATE
COLUMBIA SINKIUSE
COLUMBINE AQUILEGE BLUEBELL
CHUCKIES ROCKBELL
COLUMBITE DIANITE NIOBITE
COLUMELLA STALACE
COLUMN COG LAT ROW FILE FUST
GOAL LINE POLE POST PROP STUB
BAGUE SHAFT STELA STELE TORSO
TRUNK WURTZ ASOKAN CORNER
GNOMON PILLAR SCAPUS STAPLE
STRING TSWETT SUPPORT VIGREUX
CYLINDER PILASTER
(— IN EAR) MODIOLUS

(— OF FIGURES) SUM
(— OF FILAMENTS) SYNEMA
(BUDDHIST —) LAT
(FIGURE USED AS —) ATLAS
TELAMON
(ROCK —) HOODOO
(ROULETTE —) DERNIER
(SPINAL —) HORN SPINE BACKBONE
(STRUCTURAL —) LALLY
(TWISTED —) TORSO
COLUMNAR TERETE STELENE
COLUMNAL VERTICAL
COLUMNIST WRITER ANALYST
COLY MOUSEBIRD
COLZA SARSON
COMA TUFT BUNCH CARUS SLEEP
STUPOR SUBETH TORPOR TRANCE
SEMICOMA CHEVELURE
COMATOSE OUT DROWSY
LETHARGIC
COMB CARD GILL KAME LASH RACK
RAKE REDD REED SEEK TOZE
BREAK BRUSH CAMBE CLEAN
CREST CTENE CURRY FLISK RAVEL
TEASE HACKLE SMOOTH CUSHION
HATCHEL WRAITHE BEATILLE
CARUNCLE TORTOISE
COMBAT WAR BLOW BOUT COPE
DUEL FRAY MEEK MEET RUSH TILT
CLASH FIGHT JOUST REPEL STOUR
ACTION AFFRAY BATTLE MEDLEY
OPPOSE RESIST SHOWER STRIFE
CONTEND CONTEST COUNTER
DERAIGN DISPUTE EXPLOIT SCUFFLE
SERVICE ARGUMENT CONFLICT
STRUGGLE
(— BETWEEN KNIGHTS) JOUST
(FUTILE —) SCIAMACHY
(SINGLE —) DUOMACHY
COMBATANT DUELER BATTLER
FIGHTER CHAMPION GLADIATOR
COMBATIVE BANTAM MILITANT
BELLICOSE DEPENDENT
COMBED CRESTED
COMBER WAVE HANDER BREAKER
KEMPSTER
COMBINATION KEY BLOC GANG
PACT POOL RING CABAL COMBO
GROUP JUNTO PARTY TRUST UNION
CARTEL CLIQUE CORNER CRASIS
FUSION LEAGUE MEDLEY MERGER
AMALGAM COMBINE CONSORT
COTERIE FACTION HARMONY
JOINING MIXTURE ADDITION
ALLIANCE ENSEMBLE MONOPOLY
(— OF 10) DECUPLET
(— OF CARDS) SET BUILD FLUSH
SPREAD STRAIGHT
(— OF CIRCUMSTANCES) ACTION
(— OF COLORS) HARLEQUIN
(— OF FACES) FORM
(— OF FIRMS) TRUST
(— OF INTAGLIO FORMS) GRYLLI
(— OF NUMBERS) GIG SADDLE
(— OF TACKLES) JEERS
(— OF TONES) CHORD
(DANCE —) SEQUENCE
(HARMONIOUS —) CONCORD
(NOSE-JAW —) LAYBACK

(SCORING —) IMPERIAL

COMBINE ADD FIX MIX WED BIND
BLOC CLUB JOIN NICK POOL BLEND
GROUP JOINT MARRY MERGE TOTAL
UNITE ABSORB CONCUR LEAGUE
MEDDLE MERGER MINGLE SPLICE
ACCRETE AMALGAM COMPACT
CONJOIN CONJURE MACHINE
COALESCE COMPOUND CONCRETE
CONDENSE CONFLATE CONSTRUE
CONTRACT CUMULATE FEDERATE
(— AGAINST) BOYCOTT
(— WITH GAS) AERATE
(— WITH WATER) AQUATE

COMBINED GUM BOUND FIXED
JOINT UNITED CONJOINT

COMBUSTIBLE FUEL FIERY ARDENT
CINDER PICEOUS BURNABLE

COMBUSTION FIRE HEAT FLAME
THERM TUMULT BURNING BACKFIRE

COME BE GET LAY COOP DRAW
FALL GROW HAUL PASS WHEN
ARISE CHIVE FETCH ISSUE LIGHT
OCCUR REACH ACCRUE ADVENE
APPEAR ARRIVE BECOME BEFALL
EMERGE HAPPEN OBTAIN SPRING
ADVANCE DEVELOP EMANATE
PROCEED APPROACH PRACTICE
(— ABOUT) ARISE CHANCE
(— AFTER) SUE FOLLOW
(— APART) FRAY SHED BREAK
STAVE
(— BEFORE) FORERUN PREVENE
ANTECEDE ANTEDATE
(— DOWN) SWOOP ALIGHT
DESCEND SUCCEED DISMOUNT
(— FORTH) EMIT BREAK ISSUE
ACCEDE FORTHGO FURNACE
(— FORWARD) ACCEDE
(— IN CONTACT) ATTINGE
(— INTO BLOOM) BURST BLOSSOM
(— INTO COLLISION) MEET CLASH
COLLIDE
(— INTO EXISTENCE) FORM BEGIN
ACCRUE HAPPEN SPRING
(— INTO POSSESSION) ACQUIRE
INHERIT
(— OF AGE) MAJORIZE
(— OFF) HARL
(— OUT) ISSUE APPEAR EMERGE
EMANATE
(— TO BELIEVE IN) ADOPT
(— TO CONCLUSION) DECIDE
(— TO DIE) DO DIE SET DROP
EXPIRE FINISH SURCEASE
(— TO GRIEF) FOUNDER
(— TO HAND) OFFER
(— TO LIGHT) SPUNK DEVELOP
(— TO MIND) OCCUR STRIKE
(— TO PASS) SORT BREAK LIGHT
BEFALL BETIDE HAPPEN
(— TO PERFECTION) RIPEN
(— TO TERMS) AGREE TRYST
ACCORD BARGAIN COMPOSE
COMPOUND
(— TO) TOUCH ADVENE STRIKE
RECOVER REVERSE
(— TOGETHER) ADD HERD JOIN
MEET AMASS CONCUR COUPLE

GATHER COLLECT COMBINE
CONVENE ASSEMBLE
(— UNDER) SUBVENE
(— UPON) FIND CROSS INVENT
STRIKE
(FULLY —) EXPIATE

COMEBACK RALLY ANSWER
RETORT RETURN REBOUND
HAULBACK RECOVERY REPARTEE

COMECRUDO CARRIZO

COMEDIAN WAG WIT CARD ACTOR
ANTIC CLOWN COMIC GAGMAN
JESTER BUFFOON FUNSTER
COMOEDUS FUNMAKER FUNNYMAN
PATTERER

COMEDO BLACKHEAD

COMEDOWN BATHOS DESCENT
LETDOWN

COMEDY SOCK DRAMA FARCE
LAZZO REVUE COMEDIA TEMACHA
COMOEDIA TRAVESTY BACCHIDES
SLAPSTICK
(HEROIC —) NATAKA

COMELINESS GRACE DECORUM
FEATURE VENUSTY

COMELY FAIR GOOD HEND PERT
TALL TIDY WEME BONNY HENDE
QUEME SONCY SONSY TIGHT
DECENT FORMAL GOODLY LIKELY
LIKING LOVELY PRETTY PROPER
SEEMLY SONSIE VENUST FARRANT
FORMFUL SIGHTLY BECOMING
DECOROUS FEATURED GRACEFUL
HANDSOME PLEASING SUITABLE

COMET STAR METEOR XIPHIAS
(— HEAD) COMA

COMEUPPANCE REBUKE DESERTS
BUSINESS

COMFIT CANDY SUCKLE CONFECT
PRALINE CONSERVE PRESERVE

COMFORT AID EASE REST STAY
BIELD CHEER LIGHT SOOTH VISIT
ENDURE RELIEF REPOSE SOLACE
SOOTHE SUCCOR ANIMATE
ASSUAGE CHERISH CONFIRM
CONSOLE ENLIVEN GLADDEN
REFRESH RELIEVE SUPPORT
SUSTAIN INSPIRIT NEPENTHE
PLEASURE REASSURE

COMFORTABLE RUG BEIN BIEN
COSH COSY COZY EASY FEEL FEIL
LIKE SNUG TRIG CANNY COMFY
COUTH CUSHY LITHE QUEME QUILT
SCARF SONCY COUTHY HEPPEN
PENTIT SONSIE RELAXED RESTFUL
CHEERFUL DELICATE EUPHORIC
HOMELIKE WRISTLET

COMFORTABLY SWEETLY

COMFORTED CONSOLATE

COMFORTER PUFF COVER EIDER
NAHUM QUILT SCARF TIPPET
CHEERER PACIFIER

COMFORTING TOSY TOSIE
FRIENDLY

COMFORTLESS DREARY FORLORN
UNCOUTH DESOLATE EITHLESS

COMFREY DAISY BONESET
BACKWORT KNITBACK

COMIC DROLL FUNNY STRIP

BUFFONE COMIQUE THALIAN
COMEDIAN FARCICAL

COMICAL LOW BASE BUFFO DROLL
FUNNY MERRY QUEER STRIP WITTY
BOUFFE AMUSING CARTOON
JOCULAR RISIBLE STRANGE TRIVIAL
HUMOROUS TICKLISH SPLITTING

COMING DUE COME NEXT VENUE
ADVENT FUTURE TOWARD ARRIVAL
FOOTING FORWARD BECOMING
DESERVED PAROUSIA
(— AFTER) LATTER
(— AND GOING) FITFUL
(— INTO BEING) BIRTH GENESIS
(— NEAR) ACCESSION
(— OUT) ISSUE EGRESS
(— TO OFFICE) ACCESS
(— TO) ADIT
(— TOGETHER) SEANCE CONGRESS
COUPLING GATHERING

COMMA POINT VIRGULE
(SCRATCH —) DIAGONAL

COMMAND DO BID SAW SOH BECK
BODE BOON CALL COME EASY FIAT
HEST HETE MAND RATE RULE SWAY
WARN WILL WISH WORD BEKEN
CHECK COVER EDICT EXACT FORCE
HIGHT ORDER POWER SWEEP
UKASE ADJURE BEHEST CHARGE
COMPEL DEGREE DEMAND DEVICE
DIRECT ENJOIN GOVERN HOOKUM
IMPOSE MASTER ORACLE ORDAIN
STEVEN SUMMON APPOINT BEHIGHT
BIDDING CONCERN CONTROL
DICTATE JUSSION JUSSIVE LEADING
MANDATE OFFICER PRECEPT
REQUIRE SKIPPER WARRANT
BIDDANCE DOMINEER IMPERATE
INSTRUCT RESTRAIN
(— OF ARMY) CONDUCT
(— TO HORSE) GEE HAW HUP HUPP
WHOA GIDDAP HUDDUP
(— TO TURN RIGHT) GEE HUP HUPP
(MAGICIAN'S —) PRESTO

COMMANDANT GOVERNOR
KILLADAR

COMMANDED IMPERATE

COMMANDEER PRESS

COMMANDER CID CIO DUX DUKE
EMIR HEAD JEFE CHIEF EMEER
ADALID LEADER MASTER RAMMER
TARTAN ALCALDE CAPTAIN
CROWNER DECARCH DEKARCH
DRUNGAR EMPEROR GENERAL
KHALIFA MARSHAL NAVARCH
OFFICER VAIVODE HERETOGA
HIPPARCH LOCHAGER LOCHAGUS
MYRIARCH PHYLARCH RISALDAR
SERASKER TAXIARCH TETRARCH
VINTENER
(— IN CHIEF) SIRDAR TARTAN
TURTAN ADMIRAL GENERAL

COMMANDING DOMINANT
IMPERANT IMPERIAL IMPOSING

COMMANDMENT LAW RULE ORDER
COMMAND MITZVAH PRECEPT
BODEWORD
(DIVINE —) LAW
(TEN —S) DECALOG DECALOGUE

COMMANDO RAIDER RANGER
FEDAYEE
COMMELINA DEWFLOWER
COMMEMORATE FETE KEEP FEAST
REMENE EPITAPH MEMORATE
MONUMENT REMEMBER
COMMEMORATION AWARD MEDAL
COMMEM PLAQUE JUBILEE
MEMORIA MENTION SERVICE
EBENEZER MEMORIAL
COMMEMORATIVE HONORARY
COMMENCE FALL FANG FILE MOVE
OPEN ARISE BEGIN FOUND START
ARRAME EMBARK INCEPT LAUNCH
SPRING STREAK STREEK INITIATE
COMMENCEMENT ONSET ORIGIN
KICKOFF OPENING ENTRANCE
COMMENCING INITIAL NASCENT
INCIPIENT
COMMEND KEN PAT GIVE LAUD
ADORN ALOSE BEKEN BOOST
EXTOL GRACE OFFER BESTOW
BETAKE COMMIT PRAISE RESIGN
APPLAUD APPROVE BESPEAK
BETEACH DELIVER ENTRUST
INTRUSE BEQUEATH
COMMENDABLE GOOD WORTHY
LOVABLE LOWABLE LAUDABLE
COMMENDATION LAUD PRAISE
CITATION
(EFFUSIVE —) SLAVER
(MARKED —) APPLAUSE
COMMENSAL EPIZOON MESSMATE
COMMENSALISM SYNOECY
SYMPHILY COMMUNISM
COMMENSURATE EVEN EQUAL
ENOUGH ADEQUATE RELEVANT
COMMENT BARB BRAG GIBE JIBE
NOTE TALK WORD ASIDE BREAK
DUNCE GLOSS GLOZE CUTTER
DILATE GAMBIT NOTATE POSTIL
REMARK SCANCE CAPTION
DESCANT DISCUSS EXPLAIN
EXPOUND ADDENDUM SCHOLION
SCHOLIUM DISPRAISE
(— DISAPPROVINGLY) HARRUMPH
(CAUSTIC —) SATIRE
COMMENTARY GLOSS GEMARA
MEMOIR SATIRE ACCOUNT
COMMENT MEKILTA POSTILS
FOOTNOTE GLOSSARY TREATISE
COMMENTATOR CRITIC GLOZER
ANALYST GLOSSIST SCHOLIAST
COMMERCE TRADE BARTER
CHANGE TRAFFIC BUSINESS
EXCHANGE MERCATURE
COMMERCIAL STORE TRADY
TRADAL MERCHANT TRADEFUL
(— ESTABLISHMENT) HONG
COMMERCIALISM HUCKSTERISM
COMMINGLE MIX FUSE JOIN BLEND
IMMIX MERGE UNITE MINGLE
COMBINE COMINGE EMBROIL
COMEDDLE
COMMINUTE MILL CRUSH GRIND
POUND POUNCE POWDER
COMMINUTED FINE
COMMISERATE PITY
COMMISERATION PITY EMPATHY
SYMPATHY

COMMISSION PLAT SEND TASK
BOARD PRESS TRUST BRANCH
BREVET CHARGE DEMAND DEPUTE
ERRAND LEGACY OFFICE ORDAIN
PERMIT COMMAND CONSIGN
DUOVIRI EMPOWER FITTAGE
GOSPLAN MANDATE MISSION
SQUEEZE WARRANT CORNETCY
DELEGATE ENCHARGE POUNDAGE
(— AS CAPTAIN) POST
COMMISSIONAIRE CADDY CADDIE
DUBASH
COMMISSIONER ENVOY TRIER
LEDGER ARRAYER OFFICER
PRISTAW DELEGATE
COMMISSURE VINCULUM
COMMIT DO GIVE PULL STOW TAKE
ALLOT ARRET HIGHT LEAVE REFER
TEACH ARETTE ASSIGN BETAKE
ENGAGE PERMIT REMAND BEHIGHT
BETEACH COMMAND COMMEND
COMMISE CONFIDE CONSIGN
DELIVER DEPOSIT ENTRUST
INTRUSE INTRUST BEQUEATH
DEDICATE DELEGATE IMPRISON
RELEGATE
(— ERROR) SNAPPER
(— MONEY) INVEST
(— TO BATTLE) LAUNCH
(— TO JAIL) JUG
(— TO MEMORY) CON LEARN
MEMORIZE
(— VIOLENCE) TOUCH
COMMITTAL COMPROMISE
COMMITTEE BODY JURY RUMP
BOARD GROUP JUNTA TABLE
BUREAU SOVIET COUNCIL
DELEGACY SYNDICATE
COMMIXTURE MIXTURE CONFUSION
IMMISSION
COMMODE CAP CHEST STOOL
TOPKNOT CUPBOARD FONTANGE
COMMODIOUS FIT AMPLE ROOMY
PROPER USEFUL SPACIOUS
SUITABLE CAVERNOUS
COMMODITY ITEM WARE GOODS
STUFF EXPORT FUTURE STAPLE
ARTICLE SHIPMENT
(— SOLD SHORT) BEAR
(UNSALABLE —) DRUG
(PL.) KIND SPOTS CHANDLERY
COMMON LAY LOW NOA TYE BASE
MEAN TOWN VILE BANAL BRIEF
CHEAP EJIDO EXIDO GREEN GRIMY
GROSS JOINT LEASE OFTEN SLACK
STALE TRITE USUAL COARSE
DEMOID FAMOUS MODERN MUTUAL
ORNERY PROPIO PUBLIC SIMPLE
VULGAR AVERAGE CURRENT
DEMOTIC GENERAL GENERIC
IGNOBLE NATURAL POPULAR
RAFFISH REGULAR TRIVIAL
UNNOBLE VILLAIN BANAUSIC
EPIDEMIC FAMILIAR FREQUENT
HABITUAL MECHANIC MEDIOCRE
ORDINARY PANDEMIC PLEBEIAN
TRIFLING
(— OF ESTOVERS) BOT BOTE
(IN —) ALIKE

(NOT —) UNTRADED
(PL.) COMMUNE
COMMONER SNOB CEORL PLEBE
SIMPLE BURGESS CITIZEN STUDENT
ROTURIER
COMMONLY VULGO FAMILIARLY
COMMONNESS IDIOTISM
COMMUNITY VULGARITY
COMMON PEOPLE VULGUS
COMMONPLACE DULL FADE WORN
BANAL DAILY PLAIN PROSE STALE
TOPIC TRIPY TRITE USUAL COMMON
GARDEN HOMELY MODERN TRUISM
FADAISE HUMDRUM INSIPID PROSAIC
TEDIOUS TRIVIAL BANALITY
EVERYDAY ORDINARY RUMTYTOO
COMMONPLACENESS BATHOS
HUMDRUM
COMMON SENSE WIT NOUS SALT
GUMPTION
COMMONWEAL WEAL REPUBLIC
COMMONWEALTH POLIS STATE
ESTATE PUBLIC WEALTH COMONTE
COUNTRY COMMONTY
(IDEAL —) UTOPIA
COMMOTION DO ADO DIN BREE
DUST FRAY FUSS HEAT RIOT STIR
TOSS WHIR ALARM FLARE FUROR
HURRY STORM STOUR WHIRL
BUSTLE CATHRO FISSLE FISTLE
FLURRY FRACAS FURORE GARRAY
HOOPLA MOTION MUTINY PHRASE
POTHER RUFFLE SHINDY SPLORE
SQUALL STEERY TUMULT UNREST
UPSTIR WELTER BLATHER BLUSTER
CATOUSE CLATTER KIPPAGE
SHINDIG TAMASHA TEMPEST
TURMOIL DISORDER ERUPTION
REMOTION STIRRAGE STRAMASH
TIRRIVEE UPHEAVAL UPRISING
COMMUNAL EJIDAL
COMMUNE AREA DEME TALK ARGUE
REALM SHARE TREAT ADVISE
CONFER DEBATE IMPORT PARLEY
REVEAL CONSULT DISCUSS DIVULGE
COMMERCE CONVERSE DISTRICT
STANITZA TOWNSHIP
COMMUNICABLE OPEN FRANK
CATCHING SOCIABLE
COMMUNICATE SAY GIVE SHOW
SIGN TELL BREAK DRILL SPEAK
YIELD BESTOW COMMON CONVEY
IMPART INFECT INFORM REVEAL
SIGNAL ADDRESS BREATHE
DECLARE DICTATE DIVULGE
CONVERSE DESCRIBE INTIMATE
(— BY ALLUSION) IMPLY
COMMUNICATION CALL NOTE
WORD CABLE FAVOR LETTER
SPEECH ADDRESS DIVULGE
GALLERY MESSAGE COMETHER
LANGUAGE TELEGRAM
COMMUNICATIVE FREE SOCIABLE
EXPANSIVE
COMMUNION CULT HOST MASS
SECT TALK CREED FAITH SHARE
UNITY CHURCH HOMILY COMMUNE
CONCORD NAGMAAL SYNAGOG
ANTIPHON COMMERCE CONVERSE

KOINONIA VIATICUM
(— **SERVICE**) ACTION
COMMUNISM LENINISM SOVIETISM
COMMUNIST RED COMMIE SOVIET
COMRADE
COMMUNITY MIR BODY BURG CITY
CLAN DESA MARK MURA DESSA
FIRCA STATE THORP CENOBY
CLIMAX COLONY FAMILY HAMLET
MILLET NATION POLITY PUBLIC
SOCIES ANTHILL BOHEMIA
COMMUNE COMONTE CONVENT
HERONRY KINGDOM PHALANX
SOCIETY VILLAGE ZADRUGA
AUTONOMY COMMONTY DISTRICT
LIKENESS PRIORATE PROVINCE
SODALITY SWEEPDOM TOWNSHIP
(— **OF INTERESTS**) KINSHIP
(— **OF NATURE**) RACE
(— **OF ORGANISMS**) GAMODEME
(— **OF TURKS**) KIZILBASH
(**JEWISH** —) JEWRY KOLEL ALJAMA
SHTETL JUDAISM SHTETEL
SYNAGOG KEHILLAH
(**MAORI** —) KAIK KAIKA
(**PERUVIAN** —) AYLLU COMUNIDAD
(**PLANT** —) HEATH FOREST ALTERNE
ENCLAVE
(**RELIGIOUS** —) CENOBY SAMGHA
SANGHA CONVENT CENOBIUM
(**RUSSIAN** —) MIR
(**VILLAGE** —) IKHWAN
COMMUTATE COMMUTE UNDIRECT
COMMUTATOR BREAK BREAKER
RHEOTROPE
COMMUTE ALTER CHANGE TRAVEL
CONVERT EXCHANGE
COMPACT BALL BOND CASE FAST
FIRM HARD KNIT PACK PACT PLOT
SNUG TRIM TRUE BRIEF CLOSE
COVIN CROWD DENSE GROSS
HARDY HORNY MATCH PITHY SOLID
SPISS TERSE THICK TIGHT BEETLE
COMART HARDEN LEAGUE SHRINK
SPISSY STOCKY VANITY BARGAIN
CONCISE CONCORD CROWDED
NUGGETY PACTION SERRIED
ALLIANCE CONDENSE CONTRACT
COVENANT FLAPJACK HEAVYSET
SOLIDIFY SUCCINCT
COMPACTED SAD CROWDED
COMPACTNESS BODY DENSITY
FASTNESS SOLIDITY INTENSITY
COMPANION PAL SOC CHUM FERE
MAKE MATE PEER TWIN WIFE BILLY
BUDDY BULLY BUTTY CHINA COMES
CRONY CULLY DARES GREEK
MATCH MATEY MAUGH RIVAL SPORT
ATTEND BILLIE BROLGA COBBER
COHORT COMATE CUMMER DUENNA
EGERIA ESCORT FELLOW FRIEND
GESITH GOSSIP KIMMER MARROW
PANION SHADOW SPOUSE STEADY
TROJAN ACHATES COMPANY
COMPEER COMRADE CONSORT
ELPENOR HUSBAND PARTNER
SOCIATE SOCIETY SPECIAL
BEAUPERE COMPADRE CORRIVAL
EPHESIAN EPHESINE FAITHFUL

FAMILIAR HELPMATE PARALLEL
PLAYFERE SYNODITE
(**ARCHER'S** —) BUTTY
(**DRINKING** —) CUPMATE
(**POT** —) ALEKNIGHT
(**READING** —) LECTRICE
(**TABLE** —) CONVICTOR
(PL.) SOCIETY
COMPANIONABLE FERE MATEY
SOCIAL CORDIAL FELLOWLY
GRACIOUS SOCIABLE
COMPANIONSHIP FERE SHIP HAUNT
COMPANY SOCIETY AFFINITY
COMPANY CRY MOB SET BAND
BEVY BODY CORE CREW CRUE
FARE FERE FIRM GANG GEST GING
HERD HOST MANY PUSH ROUT
SORT TEAM TURM AERIE COVEN
COVEY CROWD FLOCK FLOTE
GESTE GROUP GUEST HORDE
JATHA MEINY PARTY SQUAD SUITE
TROOP TURMA CIRCLE CLIQUE
COHORT COVINE CURNEY DECURY
LOCHUS RESORT THRONG TROUPE
TWENTY VOLLEY BATTERY COLLEGE
CONDUCT CONSORT HOLDING
JIMBANG MANIPLE SOCIETE
SOCIETY THIASOS THIASUS VISITOR
ASSEMBLY FAISCEAU FOLKMOOT
JINGBANG
(— **OF BADGERS**) CETE
(— **OF DANCERS**) COMPARSA
(— **OF HERDSMEN**) BOOLY BOOLEY
(— **OF HORSEMEN**) TROOP
(— **OF MARTENS**) RICHESSE
(— **OF SINGERS**) CHOIR QUIRE
CHORUS
(— **OF THE FAITHFUL**) FOLD
(— **OF TRAVELERS**) CAFILA
CAVALCADE
(— **OF WOMEN**) GAGGLE
(**EXCLUSIVE** —) CROWD
(**FINANCIAL** —) FACTOR
(**FIRE** —) SQUAD
(**MILITARY** —) WATCH DECURY
VENLIN PELOTON VEXILLUM
(**RECORDING** —) LABEL
(**SUITABLE** —) BESORT
COMPARABLE LIKE SAME SIMILAR
COMPARE VIE EVEN LIKE SIZE
APPLY EQUAL LIKEN MATCH SCALE
TALLY ALLUDE CONFER PARIFY
RELATE SEMBLE BRACKET COLLATE
EXAMINE SENIBLE SIGNIFY
ASSEMBLE CONFRONT CONTRAST
ESTIMATE RESEMBLE SIMILIZE
(— **WITH**) TO
COMPARISON SIMILE ANALOGY
BALANCE COMPARE PARABLE
DISIMILE LIKENESS LIKENING
METAPHOR PARALLEL
COMPARTMENT BAY BIN BOX CAB
POD CELL DECK FLUE PANE PART
SLOT WELL ABODE CABIN HATCH
HUTCH PANEL STALL VOLET
ABACUS ALCOVE BUNKER GARAGE
HOPPER MUFFLE REGION SEVERY
SMOKER ALVEOLE CABINET
CAPSULE CELLULE CHAMBER

FIREBOX HOUSING KITCHEN
MANSION ROTONDE SECTION
ALVEOLUS COALHOLE DIVISION
FOREPEAK GRINTERN LOCELLUS
STEERAGE TRAVERSE
(— **FOR COAL**) BUNKER
(— **FOR TREATING ORE**) KITCHEN
(— **IN BARN**) BAY
(— **IN STOVE**) BROILER
(— **OF COACH**) IMPERIAL
(— **OF ROOF**) SEVERY
(— **OF WINDOW**) LIGHT
(— **ON GAMEBOARD**) STORE
(— **ON ROULETTE WHEEL**) EAGLE
(**CARGO** —) HOLD
(**GAS-TIGHT** —) BALLONET
(**GUNNER'S** —) BLISTER
(**REFRIGERATOR** —) CHILLER
(**SLEEPING** —) CUBICLE
(**STAGECOACH** —) COUPE
(**STORAGE**—) BOOT
COMPASS BOW AREA DIAL GAIN
ROOM ROSE SIZE TOUR AMBIT
FIELD GAMUT RANGE REACH SCOPE
SWEEP TENOR WHEEL ARRIVE
ATTAIN BOUNDS CIRCLE DEGREE
DEVICE DIACLE EFFECT EXTENT
MERIST MODULE SPHERE SPREAD
VOLUME ACHIEVE AZIMUTH CALIBER
CIRCUIT CONFINE DIVIDER EMBRACE
ENCLOSE ENVIRON HORIZON
IMAGINE PELORUS PURVIEW
TRAMMEL BOUNDARY CINCTURE
CIRCUITY DIAPASON PRACTICE
PRACTISE SURROUND
(— **IN SHIP'S CABIN**) TELLTALE
(— **NEEDLE END**) LILY
(— **OF MELODY**) AMBITUS
(— **OF TONES**) DIAPASON
(— **OF VOICE**) GAMUT SCALE
(— **POINT**) RHUMB
(**BELL-MAKING** —) CROOK
COMPASS BOX KETTLE
COMPASS CARD ROSE PEDRERO
PERRIER
COMPASSION RUE PITY RUTH
GRACE HEART MERCY PIETY SORRY
KARUNA LENITY REMORSE
STOMACH CLEMENCY HUMANITY
KINDNESS SYMPATHY
COMPASSIONATE RUTH SOFT
HUMAN GENTLE TENDER CLEMENT
PIETOSO PITEOUS PITIFUL
GRACIOUS MERCIFUL
COMPASS PLANT PILOTWEED
ROSINWEED
COMPASS QUARTER PLAGE
COMPASS SIGHT VANE
COMPATIBLE AKIN CIVIL ARTISTIC
SUITABLE
COMPATRIOT NATIVE PATRIOT
SYNETHNIC
COMPEL GAR MAKE MOVE URGE
BRING CAUSE COACT DRIVE EXACT
FORCE IMPEL PRESS SHOVE
COERCE ENJOIN EXTORT INCITE
OBLIGE THREAT ACTUATE AFFORCE
ATTRACT COMMAND DRAGOON
ENFORCE NECESSE REQUIRE
VIOLENCE

(— TO GO) HALE
(— TO PAY) STICK
COMPELLED HAS FAIN MUST BOUND
FORCED ENFORCED
COMPELLING COGENT STRONG
TELLING BRUISING FORCEFUL
COMPELLINGLY BADLY
COMPENDIOUS BRIEF SHORT
DIRECT COMPACT CONCISE
SUMMARY SUCCINCT
COMPENDIUM LIST BRIEF APERCU
DIGEST PRECIS SKETCH SURVEY
CATALOG COMPEND EPITOME
LEXICON MEDULLA OUTLINE
PANDECT SUMMARY SYLLOGE
ABSTRACT BREVIARY BREVIATE
LANDSKIP SYLLABUS SYNOPSIS
COMPENSATE PAY JIBE AGREE
ATONE COVER REPAY TALLY
OFFSET RECOUP REDEEM REWARD
SQUARE COMMUTE CORRECT
PLASTER REDRESS REPRISE
REQUITE RESTORE SATISFY
COMPENSE DISPENSE EQUALIZE
COMPENSATION BOT FEE PAY UTU
HIRE MEND TOLL BONUS LOWER
WAGES AMENDS ANGILD GERSUM
OFFSET REWARD SALARY SETOFF
DAMAGES FREIGHT PAYMENT
REDRESS SALVAGE STIPEND
BREAKAGE DONATIVE EARNINGS
INTEREST OCTOGILD PITTANCE
REQUITAL SOLATIUM
(— FOR KILLING MAN) MANBOT
MANBOTE
(MEAGER —) PITTANCE
(WORKER'S —) COMPO
COMPENSATORILY EVEN
COMPETE PIT VIE COPE KEMP TEND
CLASH MATCH RIVAL STRIVE
CONTEND CONTEST EMULATE
CORRIVAL
(— WITH) BUCK
COMPETENCE SKILL ABILITY
FACULTY CAPACITY
COMPETENCY MAY CAPACITY
COMPETENT UP APT CAN FIT ABLE
GOOD HOME MEET SANE ADEPT
CAPAX SMART SWEET TIGHT INTACT
LAWFUL WORTHY CAPABLE
ENDOWED SKILLED ADEQUATE
SUITABLE
COMPETITION VIE DRAW GAME
HEAT JUMP MATCH PRIZE TRIAL
WAGER CONTEST PARAGON
RIVALRY CONCOURS CONFLICT
(— AMONG REAPERS) KEMP
COMPETITOR FOE ENEMY MATCH
RIVAL WAGER COUSIN PLAYER
ENTRANT CORRIVAL FAVORITE
GAMESTER OPPONENT
COMPILATION ANA BOOK CODE
CENTO DIGEST CASEBOOK
DIRECTORY GATHERING
COMPILE ADD EDIT AMASS GATHER
SELECT ARRANGE COLLECT
COMPOSE PREPARE
COMPILER AUTHOR EDITOR
GATHERER GLOSSIST SCISSORER

COMPLACENT CALM SMUG
FATUOUS PRIGGISH
COMPLACENTLY FATLY
COMPLAIN AIL YIP BEEF CARP CRIB
FRET FUSS GREX KEEN KICK KREX
MEAN MOAN MOOT MUTE RULE
WAIL YELP YIRN BITCH BRAWL
CRAKE CROAK CROON GRIPE
GROWL GRUMP GRUNT PINGE PLAIN
WHINE BEWAIL CHARGE COTTER
CREATE GRIEVE GROUSE GRUTCH
HOLLER MURMUR PEENGE REPINE
SQUAWK THREAP THROPE YAMMER
CHUNNER DEPLORE GRIZZLE
GRUMBLE INVEIGH PROTEST
COMPLAINANT ACTOR ASKER
ACCUSER PLAINER QUERENT
RELATOR
COMPLAINING PULY LATRANT
QUERENT DOLEANCE
COMPLAINT RAP BEEF FUSS HOWL
MEAN MOAN WAIL BITCH GRIPE
GROWL WHINE CHESON GROUCH
GROUSE GRUDGE GRUTCH HOLLER
LAMENT MALADY PLAINT REPINE
SQUAWK AILMENT DISEASE
GRUMBLE ILLNESS PROTEST
QUARREL QUERELE RECLAMA
TRAGEDY COMPLAIN DISORDER
DOLEANCE GRAVAMEN JEREMIAD
COMPLAISANCE AMENITY SUAVITY
FACILITY URBANITY
COMPLAISANT BON ABLE EASY
KIND BUXOM CIVIL SUAVE BONAIR
POLITE SMOOTH SUPPLE URBANE
AFFABLE AMIABLE BOWABLE
LENIENT GRACIOUS OBLIGING
PLEASING
COMPLEMENT CREW GANG FORCE
TALLY ALEXIN AMOUNT COUSIN
ADJUNCT OBVERSE
(MILITARY —) STRENGTH
COMPLETE DO ALL END BLUE DASH
DEAD DEEP FAIR FILL FINE FULL
JUST PASS PURE RANK CLOSE
CROWN EVERY GROSS LARGE PLAIN
PLUMB POINT PUCCA PUKKA QUITE
RIPEN ROUND SOUND TOTAL UTTER
WHOLE CHOATE DAMPEN DEADLY
EFFECT ENTIRE FINISH GLOBAL
HOLLOW INTACT MATURE PROPER
SINGLE STRICT ACHIEVE CONFIRM
EXECUTE EXPLETE FULFILL
GERMANE PERFECT PLENARY
REALIZE REPLETE SPHERAL
ABSOLUTE BLINKING CIRCULAR
CONCLUDE FINALIZE IMPLICIT
INTEGRAL OUTRIGHT OVERCOME
PRECIOUS PROFOUND THOROUGH
BODACIOUS
(— CARELESSLY) HUDDLE
(REMARKABLY —) SPLENDID
COMPLETED PAU OVER CLOSED
SUMMED COMPLETE FINISHED
(NOT —) DURATIVE
COMPLETELY ALL JAM BARE BUCK
FAIR FLAT GOOD SLAM SLAP SPAN
BLACK CLEAN CLOSE FULLY PLUMB
QUITE SHEER SMACK SPANG STICK

STOCK UTTER BODILY ENTIRE
GAINLY HOLLOW PURELY SPANDY
WHOLLY ALGATES BLANKLY
THROUGH CLEVERLY DIRECTLY
ENTIRELY HEARTILY OUTRIGHT
COMPLETENESS DEPTH ALLNESS
FULLNESS RIPENESS INTEGRITY
COMPLETION END FINISH
COMPLEX HARD MAZY BEING ETHOS
FIELD HYOID MIXED ADDUCT
DESERT KNOTTY SYSTEM CULTURE
NETWORK SAMKARA SINUOUS
TANGLED TWISTED COMPOUND
EQUATION EXCHANGE INVOLVED
MANIFOLD SAMSKARA SYNDROME
(— OF DIALECTS) HINDI
(— OF HORMONES) CALINE
(— OF IDEAS) EGO SYSTEM
(BASEMENT —) FLOOR
(NOT —) SIMPLE
COMPLEXION HUE RUD BLEE CAST
LEER LOOK RUDD TINT COLOR
HUMOR STATE TENOR TINGE
ASPECT TEMPER COLORING
(BAD —) DYSCHROA
COMPLEXITY SCHEME INTRIGUE
COMPLIANCE TRUE ASSENT
MUNICH CESSION CONSENT
HARMONY OBSEQUY ABIDANCE
CIVILITY FACILITY FORMALITY
COMPLIANT EASY OILY SOFT
BUXOM FACILE PLIANT SUPPLE
COMMODE DUCTILE DUTIFUL
WILLING OBEDIENT TOWARDLY
YIELDING
COMPLICATE INTORT PUZZLE
TANGLE EMBROIL INVOLVE PERPLEX
BEWILDER INTRIGUE INTRICATE
COMPLICATED HARD KNOTTY
PROLIX COMPLEX GORDIAN
SNARLED TANGLED INVOLVED
PLEXIFORM
COMPLICATION KNOT NODE PLOT
NODUS SNARL INTRIGUE
COMPLIMENT GIFT LAUD EXTOL
EULOGY PRAISE SALAAM SALUTE
ADULATE APPLAUD BOUQUET
COMMEND DOUCEUR FLATTER
TRIBUTE ENCOMIUM FLUMMERY
GRATUITY GREETING
COMPLY PLY CEDE OBEY ABIDE
ADAPT AGREE APPLY YIELD ACCEDE
ACCORD ASSENT ENFOLD SUBMIT
CONFORM EMBRACE OBSERVE
(— WITH) OBEY SERVE OBSERVE
SATISFY
COMPONE GOBONE GOBONY
COMPONENT KEY DRAG FORM ITEM
PART UNIT GIVEN FACTOR MEMBER
SIMPLE ELEMENT FORMANT
CONJUNCT INTEGRAL
(— OF ARMY) CAVALRY
(— OF CELL WALLS) CALLOSE
(ELECTRIC —S) CIRCUITRY
(PRINCIPAL —) BASIS
COMPORT ACT BEAR HAVE HOLD
JIBE KEEP SUIT AGREE BROOK
CARRY TALLY ACCORD ACQUIT
BEHAVE DEMEAN ENDURE SQUARE
CONDUCT

COMPORTMENT CONDUCT DEALING
BEHAVIOR DEMEANOR
COMPOSE BAT PEN SET CALM
COMP DITE FORM LULL MAKE
ALLAY BREVE BRIEF CLERK CLINK
COUCH DIGHT DRAFT FRAME ORDER
PATCH PIECE SPELL STICK WRITE
ACCORD ADJUST CREATE DESIGN
GRAITH INDITE RECITE REDACT
SETTLE SOOTHE STEADY ARRANGE
COMPACT COMPILE COMPONE
CONCOCT CONFORM DICTATE
DISPOSE DRAUGHT FASHION
PATIENT PRODUCE TYPESET
COMPOUND COMPRISE REGULATE
(— **POETRY**) SING
COMPOSED SET CALM COOL QUIET
SOBER WROTE DEMURE DIGEST
PLACID SEDATE SERENE COMPACT
WRITTEN COMPOUND DECOROUS
TRANQUIL
(— **IN METER**) FOOTED
(ILL —) LAME
COMPOSEDNESS SOSSIEGO
COMPOSER BARD POET LYRIC
ODIST AUTHOR LYRIST PENMAN
WRITER CONTEUR ELEGIST
FANTAST MAESTRO COLORIST
ELEGIAST IDYLLIST ILIADIST
MELODIST MONODIST MUSICIAN
PHANTAST TUNESMITH
COMPOSITE HYBRID ITALIC MOTLEY
COMPLEX COMPOSED CONCRETE
INTEGRAL
COMPOSITION ANA DITE MASS
OPUS WORK CENTO DITTY DRAMA
FUGUE GETUP MURKY PIECE POESY
STUCK THEME ACCORD EULOGY
FILLER HAIKAI LESSON MAGGOT
MONODY THESIS THREAD VULGUS
ARTICLE COMPOST CONSIST
DISPLAY EBURINE EPISTLE MIXTURE
PICTURE STOPPER WRITING
ACROSTIC CAUSERIE COMPOUND
DIALOGUE DIAPENTE EXERCISE
FANTASIA FROTTAGE HEELBALL
(— **FOR BILLIARD BALLS**) COMPO
(— **TO BE ACTED**) PLAY DRAMA
(— **TO FILL LEATHER**) STUFF
(AMOROUS —) EROTIC
(ARTISTIC —) COLLAGE
(BUILDING —) STAFF
(CHORAL —) MOTET CANTATA
ORATORIO
(GUMMY —) GROUND
(HAND —) CASEWORK
(HUMOROUS —) BURLA
(INSTRUMENTAL —) AIR GATO
FANCY RONDO GROUND SKETCH
SONATA TIENTO CANZONE
BERCEUSE CONCERTO FANTASIA
RHAPSODY SYMPHONY
(IMPERFECT —) SOOTERKIN
(LITERARY —) BOOK CENTO DEBAT
ESSAY PIECE COMEDY SATIRE
SKETCH THESIS TREATISE
(MAGIC —) HELLBROTH
(MUSICAL —) DUET GLEE IDYL
OPUS SOLO SONG TRIO BURLA

CANON DANCE ELEGY ETUDE
FUGUE GAZEL IDYLL NONET SCORE
STUDY ADAGIO ARIOSO ENTREE
GHAZEL HOCKET HOQUET SEPTET
SEXTET BALLADE BOURREE
BOUTADE BRAVURA QUARTET
SCHERZO TOCCATA CAVATINA
CHACONNE CLAUSULA CONCERTO
INNOMINE SERENADE SINFONIA
STANDARD SYMPHONY ANTIPHONY
(NARRATIVE —) BALLAD
(PLASTIC —) CEMENT
(POETIC —) GLOSS KAVYA
(RAMBLING —) SATIRE
(RELIGIOUS —) MOTET ANTHEM
HYMNIC CANTATA ORATORIO
(RUBBER —) GUM
(VEDIC —) GAYATRI
(VITREOUS —) ENAMEL
(VOCAL —) ARIA SOLO SONG
CANON ANTHEM ELEVATIO
CONDUCTUS
(PL.) JUVENILIA LITERATURE
COMPOSITOR COMP TYPO ADMAN
SETTER BANKMAN CASEMAN
PRINTER STONEMAN
COMPOST PELF SOIL MINGLE
COMPOTE MIXTURE COMPOUND
DRESSING
COMPOSURE BOND MIEN QUIET
UNION REPOSE TEMPER BALANCE
POSTURE CALMNESS SERENITY
COMPOTATION SYMPOSIUM
COMPOTE BOWL COMPORT
COMPOST
COMPOUND MIX BASE FILL JOIN
MIXT SOUR ALKYL ALLOY AMIDE
AMINE BLEND ESTER FURIL UNION
ADJUST ALKIDE BORANE COPULA
IODIDE JUMBLE KETONE MEDLEY
PHENOL POLYOL PTERIN PYRONE
SETTLE TEMPER URACIL URAMIL
AGATHIN ALCOHOL ALLICIN
ALLOXAN AMALGAM AMIDATE
AMIDINE AMINATE AMMONIA
COMBINE COMPLEX COMPONE
COMPOSE COMPOST DVANDVA
KAMPONG KHELLIN PHORBIN
PREPARE SPIRANE STEROID
AGLUCONE AGLYCONE ALIZARIN
ALKOXIDE AMMONATE ANTIPODE
APIGENIN BRAZILIN CEROMIDE
COMPOSED FUCHSONE GARDENIN
GENTISIN GOSSYPOL IODOFORM
ISOLOGUE STYRACIN
(ADHESIVE —) SALVE
(POISONOUS —) KETENE CACODYL
GLYCINE HELENIN STIBINE
(SYNTHETIC —) ANDROGEN
SORBITAN
COMPOUNDED CONCRETE
COMPOSITE
COMPOUNDER TANKER
COMPOUNDING INTIMACY
COMPREHEND GET SEE KNOW
TAKE TWIG COVER GRASP IMPLY
LATCH REACH SAVVY SEIZE SENSE
SKILL SMOKE SPELL ATTAIN DIGEST
EMBODY FATHOM FOLLOW PIERCE

UPTAKE COMPASS CONTAIN
DISCERN EMBRACE ENCLOSE
IMAGINE INCLUDE INVOLVE REALIZE
RECEIVE SWALLOW COMPRISE
CONCEIVE CONCLUDE PERCEIVE
COMPREHENSIBLE EXOTERIC
INCLUDED SENSABLE SCRUTABLE
COMPREHENSION HOLD SABE
GRASP SAVVY SENSE ESPRIT
FATHOM NOESIS UPTAKE EPITOME
INSIGHT KNOWING SUMMARY
BEARINGS
COMPREHENSIVE BIG FULL WIDE
BROAD GRAND LARGE GLOBAL
SCOPIC CAPABLE CONCISE
GENERAL GENERIC CATHOLIC
ENCYCLIC SPACIOUS
COMPREHENSIVENESS SCOPE
EXTENT BREADTH WIDENESS
LARGENESS
COMPRESS NIP TIE BALE BIND FIRM
LACE WRAP CLING CRAMP CROWD
CRUSH PINCH PRESS SMASH
BUNDLE DEFORM DIGEST GATHER
SHRINK STRAIN THRONG ABRIDGE
BOLSTER CABBAGE COMPACT
CURTAIL DEFLATE EMBRACE
FLATTEN REPRESS SQUEEZE
SQUINCH ASTRINGE CONDENSE
CONTRACT LAMINATE PEMMICAN
RESTRAIN SUPPRESS
(— **WOOL**) DUMP
(MEDICAL —) BOLSTER PLEDGET
COMPRESSED STRICT CROWDED
SUCCINCT
COMPRESSION CRUSH SQUEEZE
PRESSURE THLIPSIS
COMPRESSOR PUMP ROTARY
CONDENSER
COMPRISE HOLD COVER IMPLY
SEIZE ATTACH CONFER EMBODY
EMPLOY MUSTER COMPOSE
CONTAIN EMBRACE ENCLOSE
INCLUDE INVOLVE CONCEIVE
PERCEIVE
COMPROMISE FINE TRIM COMMIT
INTERIM COMPOUND ENDANGER
PALLIATO
COMPROMISING FALSE
COMPULSION NEED URGE FORCE
PRESS DURESS STRESS IMPULSE
COACTION COERCION DISTRESS
EXACTION PERFORCE
COMPULSORY COERCIVE FORCIBLE
COMPUNCTION QUALM REGRET
SORROW REMORSE SCRUPLE
COMPURGATOR COJUROR
COSWEARER
COMPUTATION COMPOT ACCOUNT
COMPUTE CALCULUS COMPUTUS
ESTIMATE
COMPUTE ADD SUM CAST ITEM
RATE COUNT TALLY VALUE ASSESS
CIPHER FIGURE NUMBER RECKON
ACCOUNT BALANCE SUPPUTE
ESTIMATE
COMPUTER ENIAC MANIAC
COMRADE PAL ALLY CHUM MATE
PEER BILLY BUDDY CRONY HABER

HAVER TOWNY BURSCH CHABER
CHAVER COPAIN COUSIN DIGGER
ENGIDU FELLOE FRATER FRIEND
GOSSIP HEARTY BROTHER
COMPEER CONVIVE BEAUPERE
CAMARADA CAMARADE COMORADO
CONFRERE COPEMATE TOVARICH
(— AT TABLE) CONVIVE
(PL.) SOCE

CON DO RAP ANTI KNOW LEAD LOOK
PORE QUIN READ SCAN CHEAT
CUNNE GUIDE KNOCK LEARN STEER
STUDY DIRECT PERUSE REGARD
VERSUS AGAINST DECEIVE EXAMINE
INSPECT OPPOSED SWINDLE

CONCAVE CAVE VOID CAMUS MINUS
ARCHED DISHED HOLLOW SIMOUS
VAULTY VAULTED CRESCENT
INCURVED

CONCAVITY COVE CONCHA HOLLOW
VENTER KNEEPAN

CONCEAL MEW WRY BURY DERN
FEAL HIDE KEEP LENE MASK SCUG
SILE VEIL VEST WRAP BLIND BOSOM
CACHE CLOAK COUCH COVER FEIGN
LAYNE PLANT SHADE BURROW
CLOSET DOCTOR ELOIGN EMBOSS
HUDDLE HUGGER IMBOSK OCCULT
POCKET SCREEN SHADOW SHIELD
SHROUD STIFLE ABSCOND ENVELOP
OPPRESS PLASTER SECRETE
BESCREEN DISGUISE ENSCONCE
PALLIATE PRETENCE PRETENSE
WITHHOLD
(— A FUGITIVE) HARBOR
(— A TRAIL) TRASH
(— INFORMATION) LAYNE

CONCEALED DERN SCUG SNUG
BLIND PRIVY BURROW COVERT
HIDDEN LATENT OCCULT PERDUE
SECRET VEILED COVERED LARVATE
WRAPPED ABSTRUSE CRYPTOUS
HIDEAWAY
(— BY) BENEATH

CONCEALING DESIGNING
OBVELATION

CONCEALMENT MEW LAIN COVER
FRAUD NIGHT SECRECY CELATION
VELATION
(IN —) DOGGO

CONCEDE OWN CEDE GIVE ADMIT
AGREE ALLOW GRANT WAIVE YETTE
YIELD ACCORD ASSENT BETEEM
CONFESS OTTROYE BEGRUDGE
(— AS ADVANTAGE) SPOT

CONCEIT EGO TOY IDEA SIDE
CRANK FANCY KNACK PRIDE QUIRK
BABERY DEVICE NOTION VAGARY
VANITY BIGHEAD CAPRICE EGOTISM
OUTRAGE TYMPANY CONCETTO
FLIMFLAM

CONCEITED BUG BRAG COXY FESS
VAIN CHUFF COCKY FLORY HUFFY
PENSY PROUD SAUCY CLEVER
BIGGETY BIGGITY ARROGANT
DOGMATIC NOSEWISE PENSEFUL
PRIGGISH SNOBBISH

CONCEIVABLE EARTHLY POSSIBLE

CONCEIVE FORM HOLD MAKE PLAN

TEEM WEEN BEGIN BRAIN CATCH
DREAM FANCY FRAME GUESS IMAGE
THINK DESIGN DEVISE IDEATE
INTEND PONDER SETTLE GESTATE
IMAGINE REALIZE SUPPOSE
SUSPECT COMPRISE CONTRIVE
ENVISAGE

CONCENTRATE AIM FIX MASS PILE
COACT EXALT FOCUS PURSE UNIFY
ARREST ATTEND CENTER CITRIN
DECOCT DISTIL FIXATE GATHER
SINGLE COMPACT CONGEST DISTILL
ENGROSS ESSENCE EXTRACT
THICKEN ABSOLUTE APPROACH
ASSEMBLE CONDENSE CONTRACT
FOCALIZE GRADUATE
(— ORE) STRAKE

CONCENTRATED HARD DENSE
FIXED INTENT STRONG EXALTED
INTENSE
(NOT —) DIFFUSE

CONCENTRATION BRIX CENTER
BALLING SAMADHI ACTIVITY
FIXATION PELMANISM
(— OF ARTILLERY FIRE) STONK
(— OF ENERGY) EXCITON
(— OF PLANTS) BED

CONCEPT GUT GUTS IDEA FANCY
IMAGE BEGRIFF CONCEIT OPINION
THOUGHT ABSOLUTE CATEGORY

CONCEPTION ENS IDEA VIEW EIDOS
FANCY FETUS IMAGE BELIEF DESIGN
EMBRYO ENTITY NOTION CONCEIT
CONCEPT PROJECT PURPOSE
CATEGORY ESTHETIC NOTATION
RATIONAL
(— OF IDEA) HENT
(— OF ONESELF) BOVARISM
BOVARYSM
(ABSTRACT —) ARCHETYPE
(FALSE —) IDOL DELUSION
(QUICKNESS OF —) PREGNANCY

CONCEPTUAL IDEAL

CONCEPTUALISM SERMONISM

CONCERN BUG BEAR CARE FEAR
FIRM GEAR HAND PART RECK SAKE
APPLY CAUSE DRIVE EVENT GRIEF
HEART SORGE STAND TOUCH
WORRY AFFAIR AFFECT BEHOLD
CHARGE DIRECT EMPLOY FINGER
IMPORT MATTER REGARD ANXIETY
ARTICLE BOTTLER COMPANY
DISTURB FUNERAL INVOLVE
PERTAIN RESPECT SHEBANG
SOLICIT TROUBLE BUSINESS
HYPOTHEC INTEREST JEALOUSY
(— ONESELF) DEAL PASS TOUCH
INTERMIT
(INDUSTRIAL —) COLOSSUS
(PRUDISH —) COMSTOCKERY
(SPECIAL —) ACCENT
(WORLDLY —S) EARTH

CONCERNED INTENT ANXIOUS
WORRIED ATWITTER BOTHERED

CONCERNING BY OF ON RE TO FOR
TIL TILL ABOUT ANENT ANENST
APROPOS TOUCHING

CONCERT POP PLAN RECK UNITE
ACCORD DEVISE SMOKER ARRANGE

BENEFIT CONCENT CONCORD
CONSORT CONSULT HARMONY
POPULAR RECITAL

CONCERTINA ORGAN LANTUM
SQUIFFER BANDONION MELOPHONE

CONCESSION BOON FAVOR GRANT
LEASE STOOP ASSENT GAMBIT
OCTROY CESSION EPITROPE
MYNPACHT ADMISSION ALLOWANCE
PRIVILEGE

CONCESSIONAIRE GRIFTER

CONCH CONK PUNK SHELL COCKLE
MUSSEL STROMB STROMBUS

CONCIERGE PORTER SUISSE
WARDEN JANITOR

CONCILIATE GET CALM EASE GAIN
ATONE HONEY THING ADJUST
PACIFY SOFTEN ACQUIRE APPEASE
CONCILE MOLLIFY PLACATE SATISFY

CONCILIATOR ARBITRATOR

CONCILIATORY MILD SOFT GENTLE
GIVING IRENIC LENIENT PACIFIC
WINNING IRENICAL LENITIVE
TREATABLE

CONCISE CURT NEAT TRIG BRIEF
CRISP PITHY SHORT TERSE COGENT
CUTTED COMPACT LACONIC
POINTED PRECISE SERRIED
SUMMARY MUTILATE PREGNANT
SUCCINCT

CONCISELY PRESSLY ELLIPTICALLY

CONCISENESS BREVITY ECONOMY
SYNTOMY FASTNESS SYNTOMIA

CONCLAVE SOBOR CLOSET
CHAMBER MEETING AREOPAGY
ASSEMBLY

CONCLUDE BAR END FINE REST
TAKE CLOSE DRIVE ESTOP INFER
JUDGE LIMIT CLINCH DECIDE
DEDUCE EXPIRE FIGURE FINISH
GATHER INDUCE PERIOD REASON
RECKON SETTLE ACHIEVE ARRANGE
COLLECT CONFINE EMBRACE
ENCLOSE RESOLVE SUPPOSE
COMPLETE DISPATCH ESTIMATE
GRADUATE PARCLOSE RESTRAIN

CONCLUDED OVER COMPLETE

CONCLUDING LAST DESITIVE

CONCLUSION END AMEN CODA
ERGO FINE LAST TERM CLOSE
ENVOY EVENT FINIS ISSUE LOOSE
POINT ENDING FINALE FINISH
PERIOD RESULT SEQUEL THIRTY
UPSHOT CLOSURE CURTAIN FINDING
OUTCOME SEQUELA APODOSIS
DECISION EPILOGUE FINALITY
FRUITION GODSPEED ILLATION
ILLATIVE JUDGMENT PARCLOSE
SENTENCE
(— OF ARIA) CABALETTA
(FINAL —) ISSUE
(RANDOM —) SURMISE
(PL.) COLLATION

CONCLUSIVE LAST FINAL VALID
COGENT CERTAIN EVIDENT
EXTREME TELLING DECISIVE
DEFINITE ULTIMATE

CONCOCT MIX BREW COOK FAKE
PLAN PLOT VAMP FRAME HATCH

THINK DECOCT DEVISE DIGEST
INVENT MINGLE REFINE SCHEME
COMPOSE CONFECT PERFECT
PREPARE COMPOUND INTRIGUE
CONCOCTION PLAN PLOT MUMMY
DEVICE MUMMIA BREWING MIXTURE
SNEEZER BUSINESS COMPOUND
CONCOMITANT SEQUELA INCIDENT
ACCESSORY ASSOCIATE ATTENDANT
ATTENDING COMPANION CONJOINED
COOPERANT SATELLITE
CONCORD PART AGREE AMITY
PEACE TERMS UNION UNITY TREATY
UNISON COMPACT CONCENT
CONCERT HARMONY ONENESS
QUARTER COVENANT SYMPATHY
COMMUNITY
(— OF SOUNDS) SYMPHONIA
CONCORDANT UNISON TUNABLE
TUNEFUL HARMONIC UNISONAL
UNISONOUS
CONCOURSE CROWD HAUNT PLACE
POINT REPAIR RESORT THRONG
COMPANY ASSEMBLY FREQUENCE
(INFERNAL —) HELL
CONCRETE CLOT FIRM HARD REAL
BETON GROUT SOLID UNITE ACTUAL
CEMENT COMBINE CONGEAL
SPECIAL COALESCE COMPOUND
POSITIVE TANGIBLE AEROCRETE
CONCRETION CLOT KNOT MESS
FLINT FUSIL PEARL STONE BEZOAR
NODULE TOPHUS LITHITE OTOLITH
CALCULUS POTSTONE SEBOLITH
(— IN BAMBOO) TABASHIR
TABASHEER
CONCUBINAGE KARAO KAREWA
HETAERISM
CONCUBINE DASI HAGAR RIZPAH
BEDMATE ODALISK MISTRESS
CONCUPISCENCE DESIRE
CONCUPISCENT ANTSY
CONCUR HAND JIBE JOIN AGREE
CHECK CHIME UNITE ACCEDE
ACCORD ASSENT CONDOG APPROVE
COMBINE CONSENT CONVENT
COINCIDE CONSPIRE CONVERGE
(— IN) SUBSCRIBE
CONCURRENCE UNION ASSENT
BESTOW CONSENT CONSORT
MEETING ADHESION SYNDROME
ADMISSION
CONCURRENT COEVAL UNITED
MEETING COPUNCTAL
CONCUSSION BUMP SHOCK IMPACT
ICEQUAKE COMMOTION
CONDEMN BAN CAST DAMN DEEM
DOOM FILE FINE HISS BLAME BLESS
DECRY JUDGE AMERCE ATTAIN
AWREAK BANISH DETEST ADJUDGE
CENSURE CONVICT DENOUNCE
FORJUDGE REPROACH SENTENCE
CONDEMNATION DOOM BLAME
CENSURE DECRIAL BRICKBAT
CONDEMNATORY SEVERE ADVERSE
CONDEMNED FATAL DAMNED
CONDENSATION BAN STORY
DIGEST CAPSULE BOILDOWN
CONDENSE CUT JIG BRIEF UNITE

DECOCT DIGEST HARDEN LESSEN
NARROW REDUCE SHRINK ABRIDGE
CAPSULE COMBINE COMPACT
DEFLATE DENSATE DISTILL
SHORTEN SQUEEZE THICKEN
COMPRESS CONTRACT DIMINISH
PEMMICAN SOLIDIFY
CONDENSED CURT BRIEF CAPSULE
COMPACT CONCISE ABSORBED
CONDENSER A! UDEL REFLUX
BALANCER CAPACITOR
CONDER HUER
CONDESCEND DEIGN FAVOR GRANT
STOOP ASSENT OBLIGE SUBMIT
CONCEDE DESCEND
CONDESCENDING AVUNCULAR
CONDESCENSION STOOP DISDAIN
COURTESY DIGNATION
CONDIGN DUE FIT FAIR JUST
SEVERE WORTHY ADEQUATE
SUITABLE
CONDIMENT SOY HERB KARI MACE
SAGE SALT CAPER CURRY DULCE
DULSE SAUCE SPICE THYME AIWAIN
AJOWAN CATSUP CLOVES GARLIC
PEPPER RELISH SAMBAL TAMARA
CANELLA CHUTNEY KETCHUP
MUSTARD OREGANO PAPRIKA
VINEGAR ALLSPICE BALACHAN
BLATJANG DRESSING SEASONER
TURMERIC
CONDITION IF AND FIG PLY WAY
CASE FORM MODE PASS RANK
ROTE TERM TIFF TRIM ANGLE BIRTH
CAUSE CLASS COLOR COVIN ESTRE
FACET JOKER PLACE POINT SHAPE
STAGE STATE THEAT WHACK
AGENCY DEGREE DONNEE ESTATE
FETTLE GENTRY MORALE MUSCLE
PLIGHT STATUS STRING ARTICLE
CALLING FEATHER FOOTING
PREMISE PROVISO STATION
SUSPEND COVENANT OCCASION
POSITION PROTASIS STANDING
(— OF ANXIETY) CARK
(— OF BODY) HEAT AFFECTION
(— OF FATIGUE) FRAZZLE
(— OF FLUCTUATION) EURIPUS
(— STATED BEFOREHAND) PREMISE
(CHANCE —) ACCIDENT
(DEBASED —) CACHEXY CACHEXIA
(DEPRESSED —) DOWNBEAT
(DETERMINING —) GROUND
(DIRTY —) CLAT
(DISEASED —) DIEBACK
(DISGRACEFUL —) IGNOMINY
(DRUNKEN —) BUN
(FLOURISHING —) HEALTH
(GENERAL —) VOGUE
(HABITUAL —) TENOR
(MISERABLE —) SQUALOR
(MORBID —) HOLDOVER
(MOST APPROPRIATE —) CHECKER
(NECESSARY —) MEAN
(NEUROTIC —) LATAH
(ORDERLY —) DECENCY
(PAINFUL —) CRICK
(PERMANENT —) HEXIS
(PROPER —) KILTER

(PROTECTIVE —) CALLUS CALLOUS
(SCURFY —) BUCKSKIN
(STATIONARY —) JIB
(SUBLIME —) HEAVEN
(SURROUNDING —) AIR
(TRUE —) SIZE
(UNEQUAL —) ODDS
(UNPROSPEROUS —) ILLTH
(WEATHER —S) ELEMENTS
(PL.) HAND TERMS STRINGS
CONDITIONAL EVENTUAL
CONNEXIVE QUALIFIED
CONDITIONED FINITE LIMITED
CONDITIONER DEGGER
CONDITIONING EDUCATION
HYPOTHESIS
CONDOLENCE PITY RUTH EMPATHY
SYMPATHY
CONDONE BLINK REMIT ACQUIT
EXCUSE FORGET IGNORE PARDON
ABSOLVE FORGIVE OVERLOOK
CONDOR TIFFIN BUZZARD VULTURE
CONDUCE GO AID HELP HIRE LEAD
TEND BRING GUIDE CONFER EFFECT
ENGAGE ADVANCE CONDUCT
FURTHER REDOUND
CONDUCT ACT CON RUN USE WIN
BEAR CALL COND CONN DEED FACT
FARE FIRK FORM GARB GEST HAND
KEEP LEAD MIEN PLAY QUIT RULE
SHOW TAKE WAGE WALK BATON
CARRY DRESS DRIVE FETCH GESTE
GUARD GUIDE HABIT MAYNE SITHE
TRADE TRAIN USAGE USHER ACTION
ATTEND BEHAVE COLORS CONVEY
CONVOY COURSE DEDUCE DEMEAN
DEPORT DIRECT ESCORT GOVERN
INDUCT MANAGE MANNER SQUIRE
ACTIONS BEARING CHANNEL
COMPERE COMPORT CONDITE
CONDUCE CONDUIT CONTAIN
CONTROL EXECUTE GALLANT
GESTION OFFICER OPERATE
WIREWAY ARRIVISM BEHAVIOR
CARRIAGE CHAPLAIN COURTESY
DEMEANOR GUIDANCE REGULATE
SHEPHERD TRANSACT
(— ONESELF) DO ACT ACQUIT
BEHAVE BESTOW DEMEAN DEPORT
COMPORT CONTAIN DISPORT
ENTREAT MAINTAIN
(APPROPRIATE —) DHARMA
(BRASH —) FACE
(CONVENTIONAL —) PRAXIS
(DISORDERLY —) RANDAN
(DORMANT —) LATENCY
(ETHICAL —) HONOR
(PROPER —) CRICKET
(RECKLESS —) DEVILRY DEVILTRY
(RIGHT —) TE TAO
(SAFE —) KOWL COWLE
(SHOWY —) BRAVADO
(SLOPPY —) SWASH
(VAINGLORIOUS —) HEROICS
(WANTON —) RUFF
(WEAK —) FOLLY
CONDUCTANCE G
(— UNIT) MHO
CONDUCTION COURSING

CONDUCTOR CON BOND CADE
LEAD MAIN BRUSH GUARD SHUNT
SPOUT TRUNK BRIDGE BUSMAN
CARMAN CONVOY COPPER ESCORT
FEEDER LEADER OFFSET RETURN
CAPTAIN CATHODE MAESTRO
MANAGER AQUEDUCT BATONIST
CICERONE CONVEYOR DIRECTOR
EMPLOYEE FILAMENT STICKMAN
(ELECTRIC —) FILAMENT
(OMNIBUS —) CAD
(PL.) SERVICE
CONDUIT BOSS DUCT GOUT MAIN
PIPE SINK TUBE WIRE CABLE CANAL
CUNDY SEWER STACK HEADER
SLUICE TROUGH CARRIER CHANNEL
CHIMNEY CONDITE CONDUCT
CULVERT CUNDITE EXHAUST
FOGGARA LATERAL LAUNDER
PASSAGE WIREWAY AQUEDUCT
OLEODUCT PENSTOCK WASTEWAY
(PL.) LIMBERS
CONDYLOMA SYCOMA
CONE CAP YOW CHAT KING PINA
TOOT CONUS CRACK SCREW SHAPE
SPIRE YOWIE BOBBIN CONOID
MONTRE PASTIL CLUSTER CONELET
CONIOLE FISSURE FRUSTUM
PROLONG PYRAMID STROBIL
THIMBLE CANNELON DUMPLING
GALBULUS PASTILLE STROBILE
STROBILUS
(— OF CLOTH) VANE
(— OF FIR) YOW YOWIE STROBIL
STROBILE STROBILUS
(— OF GUNPOWDER) PEEOY
(— OF HOP PLANT) BUR BURR
(— OF SILVER AMALGAM) PINA
(— ON LOG END) CAP
(— ON SHOE) CLEAT
(— STRUCTURE) NURAGHE
(HALF —) FORME NAPPE
(ICE CREAM —) ICE CORNET
(INVERTED —) HOPPER
(PAPER —) SPILL COFFIN
(TOP CUT FROM —) UNGULA
(PL.) HOPS
CONENOSE BEDBUG BARBEIRO
CONESTOGA WAGON CARAVAN
CONEY CONY HYRAX HYRACID
GUATIBERO
CONFAB CHAT TALK POWWOW
CONFLAB PRATTLE
CONFECTION CHOW MOSS CANDY
DULCE MEBOS SWEET BONBON
COCKLE COMFIT DAINTY DRAGEE
HALVAH JUNKET MAJOON NOUGAT
SWEETY CARAMEL CONFECT
FONDANT MIXTURE POMFRET
PRALINE SEATRON SUCCADE
ANGELICA CHOWCHOW CODINIAC
COMPOUND CONSERVE DELICACY
MARZIPAN PRESERVE SUBTLETY
CONFECTIONERY CIMBAL
CONFISERIE
CONFEDERACY BUND COVIN CREEK
KEDAR UNION COVINE LEAGUE
COMPLOT ALLIANCE COVENANT
FEDERACY ILLINOIS BLACKFOOT

CONFEDERATE AID PAL REB ALLY
BAND PUFF REBEL STALL UNITE
LEAGUE SANTAR ABETTER ABETTOR
CONJURE FEDARIE FEDERAL
FEODARY PARTNER STEERER
CONSPIRE FEDERARY FEDERATE
(— SOLDIER) CONFED JOHNNY
GRAYBACK GRAYCOAT GREYBACK
(PICKPOCKET'S —) STALL
CONFEDERATION BODY BUND
UNION LEAGUE COMPACT HASINAI
SOCIETY ALLIANCE COVENANT
CONFER DUB GIVE MEET TALK
AWARD ENDOW FEOFF GRANT
INFER SPEND TREAT ADVISE
BESTOW COMMON CONFAB DONATE
ENTAIL HUDDLE IMPARL IMPART
INVEST PARLEY COLLATE COMMUNE
COMPARE CONDUCE CONSULT
CONTACT COUNSEL DISCUSS
INSTATE PRESENT COLLOGUE
COMPRISE CONVERGE
(— DEGREE UPON) CAP
(— KNIGHTHOOD UPON) DUB
CONFERENCE DIET TALK SYNOD
TREAT TRUST CAUCUS CONFAB
HUDDLE INDABA KORERO PARLEY
PARVIS POWWOW SUMMIT CIRCUIT
COUNCIL MEETING PALAVER
PARLING SEMINAR COLLOQUE
COLLOQUY CONCLAVE CONGRESS
PRACTICE PRACTISE TUTORIAL
CONFERRING GRANT DATION
CONFESS OWN AVOW FESS KNOW
SING ADMIT GRANT KITHE ACKNOW
ATTEST AVOUCH BEKNOW COUTHE
RENDER REVEAL SHRIFT SHRIVE
SQUEAK CONCEDE DIVULGE
PROFESS DISBOSOM DISCLOSE
DISCOVER MANIFEST
CONFESSION ALHET CREDO CREED
GRANT AVOWAL SHRIFT SHRIVE
VIDDUI ASHAMNU FORMULA
PECCAVI COGNOVIT
(MUTUAL —) SHARING
CONFESSIONAL SHRIFT MALCHUS
CONFESSOR FATHER SHRIFT
SHRIVER
CONFIDANT PRIVY FRIEND INWARD
PRIVADO INTIMATE
CONFIDE AFFY RELY TELL TRUST
COMMIT DEPEND LIPPEN BELIEVE
CONSIGN ENTRUST INTRUST
(— IN) VENTURE
CONFIDENCE FACE HARK HOPE
BIELD CHEEK FAITH STOCK TRUST
APLOMB BELIEF CREDIT FIANCE
FIDUCE METTLE MORALE SECRET
SPIRIT SURETY COUNSEL COURAGE
PRIVITY AFFIANCE BOLDNESS
CREDENCE RELIANCE SECURITY
SURENESS
CONFIDENT BOLD SMUG SURE
CRANK HARDY SIKER CROUSE
SECURE SICKER TRAIST ASSURED
CERTAIN HOPEFUL RELIANT
CONSTANT FEARLESS FIDUCIAL
IMPUDENT POSITIVE SANGUINE
TRUSTFUL

CONFIDENTIAL BOSOM PRIVY
CLOSET COVERT HUSHED INWARD
SECRET PRIVATE ESOTERIC
FAMILIAR INTIMATE
CONFIDING TRUSTY CREDENT
RELIANT TRUSTFUL CONFIDENT
CONFIGURATION FORM SHAPE
FIGURE BANDING CONTOUR
DIAMOND GESTALT OUTLINE
GEOMETRY POSITURE
(CELESTIAL —) SYZYGY
CONFINE BAR BOX CUB DAM HEM
NUN PEN PIN STY TIE BAIL BIND
BOOM CAGE COOP CRIB FOLD HASP
JAIL KEEP LACE LOCK PEND SEAL
SHUT SPAN STEW STOP STOW
BOUND CABIN CHAIN COART CRAMP
CROWD DELAY FENCE HOUSE LIMIT
MARCH PINCH POUND STICK STINT
BORDER BOTTLE COARCT CORRAL
EMBANK FETTER FORBAR HAMPER
HURDLE IMMURE IMPALE IMPARK
INTERN KENNEL PINION POCKET
PRISON STRAIN TETHER ASTRICT
CHAMBER COMPASS CONTAIN
IMPOUND INCLUDE MANACLE
PINFOLD POISTER RECLOSE
SECLUDE SHACKLE TRAMMEL
BASTILLE BOUNDARY CLOISTER
CONCLUDE DISTRAIN FOCALIZE
IMPRISON RESTRAIN STRAITEN
CONFINED ILL FAST PENT BOUND
CAGED CLOSE CRAMP BEDRID
IMPALE IMPENT PENTIT SEALED
CAPTIVE CRAMPED CRIBBED
LIMITED SQUEEZY IMPENDED
IMPLICIT INTERNED
(— TO CERTAIN AREA) ENDEMIC
(— TO SELECT GROUP) ESOTERIC
CONFINEMENT MEW BOND HOLD
JAIL WARD CRYING GATING
DURANCE INLYING JANKERS
WARDING CLAUSURE FIRMANCE
GROANING SOLITARY
CONFINING NARROW
CONFIRM FIX SET FIRM SEAL PROVE
VOUCH AFFEER AFFIRM ASSENT
ASSURE ATTEST AVOUCH BISHOP
CLINCH FASTEN HARDEN RATIFY
REABLE SECOND SETTLE STABLE
VERIFY APPROVE COMFORT
CONSIGN ENDORSE FORTIFY
JUSTIFY PROPORT SUPPORT
SUSTAIN THICKEN ACCREDIT
CONVINCE CORROBER ENTRENCH
INSTRUCT SANCTION STRENGTH
VALIDATE
CONFIRMATION PROOF SANCTION
CONFIRMED SET FIXED SWORN
ARRANT STABLE CERTAIN CHRONIC
HABITUAL HARDENED RATIFIED
CONFISCATE GRAB SEIZE USURP
CONDEMN CONFISK PUBLISH
DISTRAIN
CONFISCATION ESCHEAT
INCENSION
CONFLAGRATION FIRE BLAZE
FEVER BURNING INFERNO
CONFLICT JAR WAR BOUT BUMP

DUEL FRAY MEET MUSS RIFT
AGONY BROIL BRUSH CLASH FIGHT
GRIPS STOUR ACTION BATTLE
COMBAT MUTINY OPPOSE SCRAPE
SHOWER STRIFE CONTEND
CONTEST DISCORD SCUFFLE
WARFARE ANTIMONY DISAGREE
MILITATE SKIRMISH STRIVING
STRUGGLE
(DRAMATIC —) AGON
(FINAL —) ARMAGEDDON
CONFLICTING ADVERSE
ABHORRENT
CONFLUENCE FORK CROWD INFALL
CONFLUX MEETING JUNCTION
CONFORM DO GO FIT HEW LEAN
OBEY SORT SUIT ADAPT AGREE
APPLY SHAPE YIELD ACCEDE
ADJUST ASSENT COMPLY CONFER
SETTLE SQUARE SUBMIT COMPOSE
CONFIRM
(— TO) KEEP MEET ANSWER
BEHAVE SATISFY
CONFORMABLE DONE SUING
SUITED CONFORM PURSUANT
QUADRANT
CONFORMATION FORM BUILD
(MENTAL —) SAMSKARA
CONFORMING FAIR SAME COMELY
DECENT CORRECT CONGRUOUS
CONFORMIST BOY COMPLIER
CONFORMITY FIT ACCORD DHARMA
EQUITY HARMONY JUSTICE KEEPING
ACCURACY AFFINITY JUSTNESS
LIKENESS SYMMETRY FORMALITY
(— TO LAW) DECENCY LEGALITY
CONFOUND MIX BLOW DASH MATE
MAZE ROUT STAM STUN WHIP
ABASH ADDLE AMAZE BLAST FOUND
SHEND SPOIL STUMP WASTE
AWHAPE BAFFLE COMMIT DISMAY
DUDDER MINGLE MUDDLE RABBIT
RATTLE ASTOUND CONFUSE
CONFUTE CORRUPT DESTROY
FLUMMOX FORLESE PERPLEX
STUMBLE STUPEFY ASTONISH
BABELIZE BEWILDER DISTRACT
DUMFOUND SURPRISE
CONFOUNDED MATE BLAME
BLAMED DEUCED BLASTED MURRAIN
PEEVISH DUMMERED SWITCHED
CONSARNED
(BE —) ABAVE ABAWE
CONFRATERNITY BODY UNION
SOCIETY CONFRAIRY
CONFRONT DARE DEFY FACE MEET
NOSE BEARD BRACE BRAVE CROSS
FRONT STAND ACCOST ASSAIL
BREAST OPPOSE RESIST VISAGE
AFFRONT COMPARE PROPOSE
ENVISAGE THREATEN
CONFRONTING BEFORE ADVERSE
CONFRONT
CONFUSE BOX FOX MIX BALL DASH
DAZE DOIT DOZE DUST GAUM HARL
MAZE MUSS ROUT ABASH ADDLE
AMAZE BEFOG BITCH BLEND CLOUD
DEAVE DIZZY SHEND SHENT SNARL
STEER TWIST UPSET BAFFLE

BEDAZE BEMUSE BOTHER BURBLE
CADDLE COMMIT CORPSE DUDDER
DUDDLE FLURRY FUDDLE GRAVEL
JUMBLE MADDLE MAFFLE MAMMER
MASKER MIZZLE MOMBLE MUDDLE
PUZZLE RAFFLE RATTLE TWITCH
WIMPLE BECLOUD BEDEVIL
BLUNDER BUMBAZE DERANGE
DIFFUSE EMBROIL FLUSTER
GARBOIL GIDDIFY MYSTIFY
NONPLUS PERPLEX SCATTER
SHUFFLE STUPEFY UNRAVEL
BEFUDDLE BEWILDER CONFLATE
CONFOUND DISORDER DISTRACT
DUMFOUND ENTANGLE MISORDER
SQUATTER
(— AN ACTOR) CORPSE
(— BY NOISE) DUDDER
CONFUSED ASEA LOST ADDLE
DIZZY FOGGY FUZZY HEAVY MISTY
MUDDY MUZZY VAGUE WESTY
WOOLY BLOTTO CLOUDY DOILED
DOITED DRUMLY JUMBLY MEDLEY
MOPISH MUSHED SHAGGY TAVERT
WOOLLY BLURRED CHAOTIC
CLOUDED CONFUSE DIFFUSE
OBSCURE RATTLED STUPENT
COCKEYED DERANGED FLURRIED
INVOLVED
CONFUSING DIZZY MAZEFUL
BAFFLING BLINDING DIZZYING
CONFUSION PI DIN PIE COIL DUST
FUSS HARL MESS MOIL RIOT AMAZE
ATAXY BABEL CHAOS CHEVY CHIVY
DERAY FRASE HAVOC HURLY LARRY
SNAFU SNARL STROW ATAXIA
BABBLE BAFFLE BALLUP BEDLAM
CHIVVY FRAISE HABBLE HOBBLE
HUBBUB HUDDLE JABBLE JUMBLE
MASTIC MUCKER MUDDLE POTHER
RABBLE RUFFLE RUMPUS THRONG
TOPHET TUMULT UPROAR WELTER
ANARCHY BLUNDER BLUSTER
CLUTTER COBWEBS FARRAGE
FLUTTER GARBOIL HURLING
KIPPAGE LOUSTER MISRULE
MISMAZE ROOKERY RUMMAGE
SCADDLE SCOWDER TOPHETH
TURMOIL WHEMMEL WIDDRIM
BABELISM DISARRAY DISORDER
EQUIVOKE HOOROOSH SCOUTHER
SHAMBLES SPLUTTER TOHUBOHU
CONFUTATION DISPROOF
CONFUTE DENY EVICT REBUT
EVINCE EXPOSE REFUTE FALSIFY
IMPROVE SILENCE SUBVERT
CONCLUDE CONFOUND CONVINCE
DISPROVE INFRINGE OVERCOME
REDARGUE
CONGEAL GEL ICE SET GEAL JELL
CANDY COTTER CURDLE FREEZE
HARDEN STIFFEN STORKEN THICKEN
CONCRETE SOLIDIFY
(— INTO HOARFROST) RIME
CONGEALED FROZEN
CONGELATION FROST
CONGENER BEAVER DOTTREL
DOTTEREL
CONGENIAL SIB BOON HAPPY

NATAL NATIVE AMIABLE CONNATE
KINDRED
CONGENITAL INNATE CONNATE
CONNATAL GENETOUS
CONGERIES CALCULARY
COLLECTION
CONGEST STUFF IMPACT
CONGESTED INJECTED
CONGESTION JAM HEAP LAMPAS
LAMPERS CROWDING STOPPAGE
CONGLOMERATE HEAP MASS PILE
ROCK STACK BANKET PSEPHITE
NAGELFLUH
CONGLOMERATION HUDDLE
GLOMMOX IMBROGLIO
CONGO MUMMY ASPHALTUM

CONGO

CAPITAL: BRAZZAVILLE
COIN: FRANC FRANCCFA
LAKE: MWERU TUMBA UPEMBA
LEOPOLD
NATIVE: SUSA VILI MANTU PYGMY
BATEKE MBOCHI WABUMA
BAKONGO BANGALA
PLATEAU: BATEKE
RIVER: CONGO KWILU LULUA
NGOKO NIARI SANGA WAMBA
KWENGE LOANGE UBANGI
KOUILOU LUBILASH
TOWN: EWO EPENA HOLLE JACOB
OKOYO SEMBE MAKOUA
OUESSO ZANAGA DOLISIE
ENYELLE SOUANKE DJAMBALA
BRAZZAVILLE
TRIBUTARY: LOMAMI UBANGI
ARUWIMA LUALABA LUAPULA
ITIMBITI

CONGOU KEEMUN
CONGRATULATE HUG JOY LAUD
GREET SALUTE FLATTER MACARIZE
CONGRATULATION PARABIEN
(PL) GRATTERS
CONGREGATE HERD MASS MEET
PACK TEEM GROUP SWARM TROOP
GATHER MUSTER COLLECT
CONVENE ASSEMBLE
CONGREGATION PEW BODY FOLD
HERD HOST MASS FLOCK SAMAJ
SWARM CHURCH PARISH COMPANY
MEETING SYNAXIS ASSEMBLY
BRETHREN CHAPELRY
(— OF WITCHES) COVEN
(JEWISH —) KOLEL ALJAMA
SYNAGOG
(PL.) CHARGE
CONGRESS MOD DAIL DIET SYNOD
UYEZD OBLAST OUYEZD POWWOW
COUNCIL GORSEDD MEETING
ASSEMBLY CONCLAVE
CONGRESSMAN SENATOR
DOUGHFACE
CONGRUITY ACCORD CONCORD
FITNESS HARMONY KEEPING
SYMMETRY COHERENCE
CONGRUOUS CONGRUE HARMONIC
SUITABLE ACCORDING

CONICAL CONIC TAPER COPPED COPPLED TAPERING
CONIFER FIR YEW PINE CEDAR LARCH SPRUCE SOFTWOOD EVERGREEN
CONIFERAE PINALES
CONIUM HEMLOCK
CONJECTURE AIM CAST PLOT ROVE SHOT VIEW AUGUR ETTLE FANCY GUESS OPINE THINK BELIEF DIVINE THEORY CONJECT IMAGINE OPINION PRESUME SUPPOSE SURMISE SUSPECT HINDCAST SUPPOSAL
CONJOIN JOIN KNIT ATTEND EMPALE IMPALE
CONJOINED JOINED JUGATE LINKED JUGATED CONJUNCT TOUCHING
CONJOINTLY JUNCTLY TOGETHER
CONJUGAL SPOUSAL CONNUBIAL
CONJUGATE YOKED JOINED UNITED COUPLED INFLECT
CONJUGATION SYNGAMY ZYGOSIS CYTOGAMY ENDOGAMY SYNOPSIS
CONJUNCTION AS ET IF OR AND BUT NOR TIE THAN JOINT SINCE SYNOD UNION UNITY THOUGH COITION CONSORT JOINDER CONJUNCT RATIONAL
CONJUNCTURE SEASON
CONJURATION ART CHARM MAGIC SPELL VOODOO EXORCISM
CONJURE PRAY WISH CHARM HALSE ADJURE ENJOIN INVENT INVOKE SUMMON BESEECH COMBINE ENTREAT IMAGINE CONSPIRE CONTRIVE EXORCIZE
CONJURE MAN CUNJAH CUNJER GOOFER GUFFER
CONJURER MAGE PELLAR POWWOW SHAMAN WIZARD JUGGLER WARLOCK WIELARE JONGLEUR MAGICIAN PYTHONIC SORCERER
CONJURING JADU JADOO CONJURY VOODOOISM
CONK FAIL HEAD KONK NOSE FAINT KNOCK STALL BRACKET
CONNECT COG PUT TIE ALLY BIND BOND GEAR GLUE JOIN KNIT KNOT LINK AFFIX CHAIN MARRY NITCH UNITE ATTACH BRIDGE CEMENT COHERE COMMIT CONNEX COUPLE ENLINK FASTEN RELATE SPLICE COMBINE ENCHAIN INVOLVE APPARENT CATENATE CONTINUE DOVETAIL INTERTIE
(— **TREADLE**) CORD
CONNECTED ALLIED CONNEX AFFINED COUPLED HANGING
(**ELECTRICALLY** —) ALIVE
(**NOT** —) FOREIGN ASYNARTETE
(**SYNTACTICALLY** —) ABSOLUTE

CONNECTICUT
CAPITAL: HARTFORD
COLLEGE: TRINITY
COUNTY: TOLLAND WINDHAM
INDIAN: PEQUOT MOHEGAN NIANTIC
STATE BIRD: ROBIN
STATE FLOWER: LAUREL
STATE NICKNAME: NUTMEG
STATE TREE: OAK
TOWN: AVON BETHEL CANAAN COSCOB DARIEN MYSTIC SHARON STORRS DANBURY MERIDEN NIANTIC NORWALK NORWICH TOLLAND WINDSOR NEWHAVEN SIMSBURY WESTPORT GREENWICH
UNIVERSITY: YALE WESLEYAN

CONNECTING BETWEEN SYNDETIC
CONNECTION Y HUB TAP TIE BOND LINK HITCH NEXUS UNION BUCKLE CLEVIS FAMILY GROUND REPORT SUTURE SWIVEL BEARING BOLSTER CONTACT DESCENT FERRULE HOLDING KINSHIP LIAISON SIAMESE SIBNESS SOCIETY AFFINITY ALLIANCE COMMERCE CONNEXUS INTIMACY JUNCTION LIGATION RELATIVE SYNDETIC
(**ELECTRICAL** —) GROUND
(**FORKED** —) BRANCH
(**MECHANICAL** —S) LEADOUT
CONNECTIVE IZAFAT SUTURAL JUNCTION LIGATIVE SYNDETIC VINCULAR
CONNING TOWER SAIL
CONNIVANCE CAHOOT CAHOOTS
CONNIVE ABET PLOT WINK BLINK CABAL ASSENT FOMENT INCITE COLLUDE
(— **AT MEDICAL TREATMENT**) COVER
CONNOISSEUR JUDGE CRITIC EXPERT CAMEIST EPICURE GOURMET CIDERIST DILETANT LAPIDARY
CONNOTATION DEPTH INTENT MEANING
CONNUBIAL MARITAL CONJUGAL DOMESTIC
CONQUER GET WIN BEAT BEST DOWN FIRK GAIN LICK ROUT TAME WHIP CRUSH DAUNT DEBEL EVICT DEBELL DEFEAT EVINCE HUMBLE IMPORT MASTER REDUCE SUBDUE VICTOR ACQUIRE PREVAIL SUBJECT SURPASS TRIUMPH OVERCOME OVERGANG SURMOUNT VANQUISH
CONQUEROR HERO VICTOR WINNER TRIUMPHER
CONQUEST MASTERY SCALING TRIUMPH VICTORY WINNING
CONSANGUINEOUS AKIN CARNAL KINDRED NATURAL RELATED
CONSANGUINITY BLOOD NASAB KINSHIP AFFINITY
CONSCIENCE WORD DAENA HEART INWIT SENSE SCRUPLE THOUGHT
CONSCIENTIOUS FAIR JUST EXACT RIGID EIDENT HONEST STRICT DUTIFUL UPRIGHT FAITHFUL
CONSCIENTIOUSNESS RELIGION
CONSCIOUS KEEN WARE ALIVE AWAKE AWARE JERRY GUILTY FEELING KNOWING WITTING RATIONAL SENSIBLE SENTIENT CONSCIENT
CONSCIOUSNESS EGO HEART SENSE SPIRIT ANOESIS FEELING SENTIENT AWARENESS
CONSCRIPT LEVY CHOCO DRAFT ENROL ENLIST MUSTER DRAFTEE DRAUGHT RECRUIT JEANJEAN
CONSCRIPTION LEVY
CONSECRATE VOW FAIN HOLY SAIN SEAL BLESS DEIFY HEAVE SACRE ANOINT DEVOTE HALLOW ORDAIN SACRATE CONSACRE DEDICATE SANCTIFY
CONSECRATED BLEST OBLATE SACRED VOTARY VOTIVE BLESSED SACRATE HALLOWED HIERATIC
CONSECRATION IHRAM SACRE SACRY SACRING HOLINESS
CONSECUTIVELY TOGETHER
CONSECUTIVENESS SEQUENCE
CONSENT HEAR AGREE ALLOW GRANT YIELD ACCEDE ACCORD ASSENT BETEEM COMPLY CONCUR PERMIT APPROVE GOODWILL
CONSENTIENT UNANIMOUS
CONSEQUENCE AND END BORE EVENT FORCE FRUIT ISSUE SUITE WORTH BROWST CHARGE EFFECT ENTAIL FIGURE GROWTH IMPORT MOMENT REPUTE RESULT SEQUEL WEIGHT CONCERN OUTCOME PRODUCE SEQUELA SEQUENT AFTERING INTEREST MISCHIEF OCCASION
(**DONE IN** —) PURSUANT
(**HARMFUL** —) EVIL
(**PL.**) AFTERINGS
CONSEQUENT COMES THESIS ADJUNCT
CONSEQUENTIAL HEAVY POMPOUS COROLLARY
CONSEQUENTLY SO ERGO THEN THUS HENCE LATER PURSUANT PRESENTLY
CONSERTAL SUTURAL
CONSERVATION HUSBANDRY
CONSERVATISM BOURBONISM
CONSERVATIVE SAFE TORY FUSTY STAID FABIAN HUNKER STABLE BOURBON DIEHARD MODERATE UNIONIST
CONSERVATORY STOVE SCHOOL ACADEMY
CONSERVE CAN JAM SAVE GUARD GUMBO JELLY DEFEND SECURE SHIELD UPHOLD HUSBAND PROTECT SEATRON SUSTAIN MAINTAIN PRESERVE
(**GRAPE** —) UVATE
CONSIDER AIM BAT LET SEE CALL CAST DEEM GAUM GIVE HASH HEED HOLD MULL MUSE RATE SEEM TAKE TALE VIEW VISE WISE ALLOW BESEE COUNT ENTER ETTLE JUDGE PANSE POISE SPELL STUDY THINK VERSE VOLVE WEIGH ADVERT ADVISE

BEHOLD DEBATE DEVISE DIGEST
ESTEEM EXPEND FIGURE IMPUTE
PONDER REASON RECKON REGARD
REWARD SURVEY ACCOUNT BELIEVE
BETHINK CANVASS CONSULT
EXAMINE INSPECT PREPEND
REFLECT RESPECT REVOLVE
SUPPOSE COGITATE ESTIMATE
MEDITATE PERPENSE RUMINATE
(— **FAVORABLY**) CREDIT
(— **PROS AND CONS**) ARGUE
(— **SEPARATELY**) SPECIALIZE
CONSIDERABLE GAY GEY FAIR
GOOD CANNY GEYAN GREAT LARGE
SMART STARK GOODLY PRETTY
GOODISH HEALTHY INTENSE
NOTABLE SEVERAL HANDSOME
POWERFUL SENSIBLE UNLITTLE
CONSIDERABLY GAY GEY WELL
GEYAN PRETTY SMARTLY
CONSIDERATE KIND MILD NICE
GENTLE TENDER CAREFUL HEEDFUL
PRUDENT SERIOUS DELICATE
GRACIOUS
CONSIDERATENESS GRACE
(**MUTUAL** —) SHU
CONSIDERATION GUT GUTS SAKE
COUNT PRICE STUDY TOPIC ADVICE
ASPECT COMITY DEBATE ESTEEM
MOMENT MOTIVE NOTICE REASON
REFLEX REGARD SURVEY ACCOUNT
INSIGHT PREMIUM RESPECT
THOUGHT ALTRUISM COURTESY
DELICACY EMINENCE EMPHASIS
GRATUITY SANCTION
(**BASIC** —) BEDROCK
(**ETHICAL** —) SCRUPLE
(**THOUGHTFUL** —) THEORIA
CONSIDERED ADVISED DELIBERATE
CONSIDERING IF FOR SINCE SEEING
CONSIGN DOOM GIVE MAIL SEND
SHIP ALLOT AWARD CHECK DIGHT
REMIT SHIFT YIELD ASSIGN COMMIT
DESIGN DEVOTE REMAND RESIGN
ADDRESS BETEACH CONFIDE
DELIVER DEPOSIT ENTRUST
INTRUST BEQUEATH DELEGATE
RELEGATE TRANSFER
(— **FOR DESTRUCTION**) ACCURSE
(— **TO OBLIVION**) BURY EXPUNGE
(— **TO PERDITION**) DAMN CONDEMN
CONSIGNEE AGENT FACTOR
SHIPPER RECEIVER
CONSIGNMENT INVOICE FOREDOOM
SHIPMENT
(— **OF TEA**) BREAK
CONSIST LIE HOLD RELY REST
DWELL EXIST STAND INHERE RESIDE
CONTAIN EMBRACE COMPRISE
CONSISTENCY BODY UNION
DEGREE CONCENT CONCORD
HARMONY KEEPING COMPAGES
EVENNESS FIRMNESS SOLIDITY
SYMMETRY
CONSISTENT EVEN FIRM STEADY
DURABLE LOGICAL UNIFORM
COHERENT ENDURING SUITABLE
(— **WITH NATURE**) KIND KINDLY
(**BE** —) ACCORD

(**MAKE** —) CLEAR
CONSOLATION SOP FINE RELIEF
SOLACE COMFORT SPIRITING
CONSOLE CALM ALLAY ANCON
CHEER ORGAN TABLE SOLACE
SOOTHE BRACKET CABINET
COMFORT RELIEVE SUPPORT
SUSTAIN CARTOUCH
CONSOLER PARACLETE
CONSOLIDATE COG MIX KNIT MASS
POOL WELD BLEND CLOSE MERGE
UNIFY UNITE HARDEN MINGLE
SETTLE COMBINE COMPACT
ANKYLOSE COALESCE COMPRESS
CONDENSE ORGANIZE SOLIDIFY
CONSOLIDATED CONFLATE
CONSOLS GOSCHENS
CONSONANCE ACCORD UNISON
HARMONY DIAPASON DIAPENTE
SYMPATHY SYMPHONY
CONSONANT WAW MUTE STOP
DENTAL FORTIS LABIAL LETTER
LIQUID SONANT UNISON LATERAL
MUTABLE PALATAL SPIRANT UNIFIED
ALVEOLAR ASPIRATA ASPIRATE
BILABIAL EJECTIVE GEMINATE
HARMONIC SUITABLE
(**CONSECUTIVE** —**S**) CLUSTER
(**SMOOTH** —) LENE LENIS
(**TENSE AND STRONG** —) FORTIS
(**VOICELESS** —) SPIRATE
CONSORT COT AIDE ALLY JOIN
MATE WIFE YOKE GROUP UNITE
ACCORD ATTEND ESCORT MINGLE
SPOUSE COMPANY COMRADE
CONCERT DAMKINA EMPRESS
HUSBAND PARTNER ACCUSTOM
ASSEMBLY PRINCESS
CONSPECTUS LIST APERCU SURVEY
OUTLINE THEATER THEORIC
SPECTRUM SYNOPSIS
CONSPICUOUS BIG BOLD CLEAR
FAMED PLAIN STARY EXTANT
FAMOUS MARKED PATENT SIGNAL
BLATANT EMINENT GLARING
NOTABLE OBVIOUS POINTED
SALIENT SIGHTLY VISIBLE
APPARENT EMPHATIC FLAGRANT
KENSPECK MANIFEST STRIKING
CONSPIRACY COUP PLAN PLOT
RING CABAL COVIN JUNTO PARTY
COVINE SCHEME COMPACE
COMPACT COMPLOT INTRIGUE
CONSPIRATOR PACKER PLOTTER
SCHEMER
CONSPIRE ABET PACK PLOT UNITE
LEAGUE SCHEME COLLUDE
COMPLOT CONJURE CONNIVE
CONTRIVE
CONSTABLE COP BULL PEON SLOP
BEADLE BEAGLE HARMAN KAVASS
KEEPER WARDEN BAILIFF CORONER
DOZENER NUTHOOK OFFICER
STALLER SUBASHI ALGUAZIL
DOGBERRY TIPSTAFF
CONSTANCY ZEAL ARDOR FAITH
TRUTH FEALTY HONESTY LOYALTY
ONENESS DEVOTION FIDELITY
CONSTANT K SET EVEN FIRM JUST

LEAL TRUE FIXED LOYAL SOLID
STILL TIGHT TRIED ITHAND STABLE
STEADY CERTAIN CHRONIC
DURABLE FOREVER LASTING
REGULAR STAUNCH UNIFORM
DEFINITE ENDURING FAITHFUL
POSITIVE RESOLUTE SEDULOUS
STANDING
CONSTANTLY AWAY EVER ALWAYS
THRONG
CONSTELLATION ARA CUP FLY FOX
LEO APUS ARGO COLT CROW CRUX
DOVE GOAT GRUS HARE HARP LION
LYNX LYRA MAST PAVO PLOW SIGN
SWAN TAUR URSA VELA WAIN WOLF
ALTAR ARIES CAMEL CETUS CLOCK
CRANE DRACO EAGLE GROUP
HYDRA INDUS LEPUS LIBRA LUPUS
MALUS MENSA MUSCA NORMA
ORION PYXIS RAVEN TABLE VIRGO
WAGON WHALE ANTLIA AQUILA
AURIGA BOOTES CAELUM CANCER
CARINA CORVUS CRATER CYGNUS
DIPPER DORADO FORNAX GEMINI
HYDRUS INDIAN LIZARD OBELUS
OCTANS OKNARI PICTOR PISCES
PISCIS PLOUGH PUPPIS SCALES
SCUTUM TAURUS TIGRIS TOUCAN
TUCANA VOLANS ALGEBAR
CEPHEUS CLUSTER COLUMBA
COMPASS DOLPHIN FURNACE
GIRAFFE LACERTA MONARCH
OETAEUS PATTERN PEACOCK
PEGASUS PERSEUS PHOENIX
RHOMBUS SAGITTA SCORPIO
SERPENS SERPENT SEXTANS
SEXTANT XIPHIAS AQUARIUS
ASTERISM CHAMPION CIRCINUS
CYNOSURE EQUULEUS ERIDANUS
HERCULES HERDSMAN KASHYAPA
QUADRANS REINDEER RETICULE
SCORPION SCORPIUS SCULPTOR
TRIANGLE
CONSTERNATION FEAR ALARM
PANIC DISMAY FRIGHT HORROR
TERROR TREPIDITY
CONSTITUENCY BOROUGH
CONSTITUENT ATOM ITEM PART
PIECE VOTER DETAIL FACTOR
FUSAIN MATTER MEMBER SIMPLE
ELECTOR ELEMENT FEATURE
TAGMEME INTEGRAL
(— **OF BLOOD SERUM**) OPSONIN
(— **OF CLINKER**) ALITE CELITE
(— **OF COAL**) DURAIN FUSAIN
(— **OF DURAIN**) ATTRITUS
(—**S OF BEER**) EXTRACT
(**NECESSARY** —) ESSENCE
(**PL.**) MATTER BIOSESTON
CONSTITUTE BE FIX SET FORM
MAKE ENACT ERECT FORGE FOUND
SHAPE SPELL CREATE DEPUTE
GRAITH ORDAIN APPOINT COMPOSE
FASHION STATION COMPOUND
COMPRISE
CONSTITUTION LAW SET CODE
SETT BEING CANON FRAME HUMOR
SETUP STATE CHARTE CRASIS
CUSTOM DESIGN ESTATE HEALTH

NATURE TEMPER CHARTER HABITUS
SYNODAL GRONDWET GRUNDLOV
HABITUDE PHYSIQUE POLITEIA
(— STATE) CONNECTICUT
(BODILY —) HABIT SPIRITS
(GERMINAL —) HEREDITY
CONSTITUTIONAL WALK HECTIC
INNATE RIKKEN EXERCISE
CONSTITUTIVE FORMAL
CONSTRAIN ART PUT TIE ARCT
BEND BIND CURB DOOM FAIN HALE
HOLD LEAD URGE CHAIN CHECK
CLASP COART CRAMP DETER DRIVE
FORCE IMPEL LIMIT PRESS COERCE
COMPEL EVINCE OBLIGE RAVISH
SECURE STRAIN THRAST ASTRICT
CONFINE CONJURE ENFORCE
OPPRESS REPRESS VIOLATE
COMPRESS CONCLUDE DISTRESS
PERFORCE POUNDAGE RELIGATE
RESTRAIN
CONSTRAINED FAIN TIED VAIN
BOUND FORCED FORMAL UNEASY
COACTED
CONSTRAINING UNEASY
COMPELLENT
CONSTRAINT BOND CRAMP FORCE
DURESS STRESS RESERVE STRAINT
COERCION DISTRESS PRESSURE
CONSTRICT TIE BIND CURB GRIP
CHOKE CRAMP LIMIT STRAP
HAMPER SHRINK STRAIN STRAIT
ASTRICT DEFLATE SQUEEZE
STIFFEN TIGHTEN ASTRINGE
COMPRESS CONDENSE CONTRACT
DISTRAIN RESTRICT
CONSTRICTED STRAIT STRICT
ADENOID
CONSTRICTION KNOT CHOKE
ISTHMUS STENOSIS
CONSTRICTOR BOA ABOMA
GUAVINA
CONSTRUCT UP BIG ATOM FORM
IDEA LEVY MAKE REAR BUILD
CRAFT DIGHT EDIFY ERECT FRAME
MODEL BURROW DEDUCE DESIGN
DEVISE FABRIC ARRANGE CARPENT
COMBINE COMPILE COMPOSE
CONCEPT CONFECT CONTOUR
EXTRUCT FASHION CONSTRUE
ENGINEER PRACTISE
(— ARCH) TURN
CONSTRUCTED BUILT EDIFICATE
(CAREFULLY —) CLEVER
(HASTILY —) GIMCRACK JIMCRACK
CONSTRUCTION BOOM ALTAR
FRAME FABRIC MONSTER SYNESIS
APPROACH BUILDING DWELLING
ERECTION
(— OF NAME) ABSTRACTION
(ABSTRACT —) STABILE
(GRAMMATICAL —) SYNESIS
APPOSITION
(POINTED —) BEAK
CONSTRUCTIVE FACTIVE HELPFUL
VIRTUAL CREATIVE IMPLICIT
INFERRED
CONSTRUCTOR ENGINEER
CONSTRUE INFER PARSE STRUE

INTEND RENDER ANALYZE CONSTER
DISSECT EXPLAIN EXPOUND
RESOLVE
CONSUL SUFFECT
CONSULT LOOK SEEK TALK ADVISE
CONFER EMPARL IMPARL COUNSEL
RESOLVE
CONSULTANT EXPERT ADVISER
COUNSEL
CONSULTATION ADVICE COUNCIL
COUNSEL
CONSUME EAT SUP USE BOLT BURN
CHEW FANG FARE FEED FRET GULP
IDLE KILL RUST TAKE TUCK WEAR
DALLY DRINK FLAME LURCH RAVEN
SHIFT SPEND TOOTH WASTE
ABSORB BEZZLE BROWSE CANKER
DEVOUR ENGAGE EXPEND FINISH
IMBIBE INHALE PERISH PUNISH
VANISH CORRODE DESTROY
DWINDLE ENGROSS EXHAUST
SWALLOW CONTRIVE SQUANDER
(— TOTALLY) KILL
(— VORACIOUSLY) HOG
CONSUMED ALL PAU DOWN BURNT
SPENT COMBUST OUTWORN
CONSUMING EATING SACRED
BURNING FLAMING
CONSUMMATE END FINE FULL RIPE
CLOSE IDEAL SHEER ARRANT
EFFECT FINISH FULFIL RATIFY
ACHIEVE CONSUME CROWNED
FULFILL PERFECT PERFORM
ABSOLUTE COMPLETE MERIDIAN
THOROUGH
CONSUMMATION PERIOD UPSHOT
CONSUMPTION USE DECAY WASTE
EXPENSE WASTING PHTHISIS
SPENDING
CONSUMPTIVE LUNGY HECTIC
PREDATORY
CONTACT ABUT JOIN KISS MEET
SLED CROSS TOUCH TRUCK UNION
ARRIVE IMPACT SYZYGY EPHAPSE
HOLDING MEETING TACTION
JUNCTION TANGENCY TOUCHING
(— OF TELEGRAPH KEY) ANVIL
(3-POINT —) OSCNODE
(ELECTRICAL —) HUB HUBB
(EVIL —) CONTAGION
(FLEETING —) BRUSH
(FORCIBLE —) IMPACT
CONTAGION POX TAINT VIRUS
MIASMA POISON
CONTAGIOUS TAKING NOXIOUS
SMITTLE CATCHING EPIDEMIC
CONTAIN RUN HAVE HOLD KEEP
STOW TAKE CARRY CHECK CLOSE
COVER HOUSE EMBODY ENFOLD
ENSEAM HARBOR RETAIN COMPILE
EMBRACE ENCLOSE INCLUDE
INVOLVE RECEIVE SUBSUME
SUSTAIN COMPRISE RESTRAIN
CONTAINED IN
CONTAINER BAG BOX CAN CUP HAT
JAR JUG KEG LUG NIN PAN POD
POT TIN TUB URN VAT BAIL BOMB
CAGE CASE CASK CRIB DRUM EWER
FILE FLAT JACK SACK SALT SILO

SINK SKIP TANK TUBE VASE ALBUM
BASIN BILLY CADDY CHEST CRATE
CRUET DEWAR EMPTY FLASK GLASS
GOURD POUCH SCOOP SCRAY
STAND STOOP STOUP BARREL
BASKET BOTTLE BUCKET BUSHEL
CARBOY CARTON CASTER CASTOR
COOLER CRADLE DUSTER HAMPER
HATBOX HOLDER INKPOT PICNIC
RABBIT RIDDLE SHAKER WITJAR
AEROSOL BANDBOX BLADDER
CAPSULE COASTER COSTREL
CRISPER FEEDBOX HANAPER
HOLDALL INKWELL PACKAGE
SEEDLIP SHIPPER STEEPER
CANISTER DECANTER DEMIJOHN
ENVELOPE HOGSHEAD HONEYPOT
INHOLDER KNAPSACK PUNCHEON
SLIPCASE
(— FOR BEER) GROWLER
(— FOR COINS) BANK
(— FOR EXPLOSIVE CHARGE) CAP
(— FOR GOLD DUST) SHAMMY
(— FOR HOLY OIL) STOCK
(— FOR PLANTS) BAND
(— MADE OF HOLLOW LOG) GUM
(5-GALLON —) JERICAN JERRICAN
(COFFEE —) INSET
(EARTHENWARE —) STEAN
(FIRECLAY —) SETTER
(RAILROAD —S) BUNKER
(SHELVED —) CABIN
(SHIPPING —) KIT
(SNUFF —) WEASAND
(TOBACCO —) SARATOGA
(VENTILATED —) CHIP
(PL.) CONVEYER CONVEYOR
CONTAMINATE FOUL HARM SLUR
SMIT SOIL STAIN SULLY TAINT
BEFOUL DEBASE DEFILE INFECT
INJURE POISON ATTAINT CORRUPT
DEBAUCH FLYBLOW POLLUTE
TARNISH VITIATE DISHONOR
CONTAMINATED DIRTY DEGRADED
INFECTED
CONTAMINATION INFECTION
TAINTMENT
(— IN GLASS) STONE
CONTE TALE CRAYON
CONTEMN HATE FLOUT SCORN
SPURN REJECT SLIGHT DESPISE
DISDAIN CONTEMPT INDIGNIFY
CONTEMPLATE FACE MUSE PLAN
SCAN VIEW DEIGN STUDY THINK
WEIGH DESIGN PONDER REGARD
SURVEY CHERISH PROPOSE
REFLECT CONSIDER ENVISAGE
ENVISION MEDITATE
CONTEMPLATION MUSE STUDY
DHYANA MUSING PRAYER REGARD
THEORY INSIGHT MOONING
REQUEST THEORIA PETITION
CONTEMPLATIVE BROODY PENSIVE
THEORIC STUDIOUS
CONTEMPORANEOUS COEVAL
LIVING MODERN CURRENT EXISTING
CONTEMPORARY EQUAL COEVAL
FELLOW CURRENT PRESENT
YEALING EXISTENT

CONTEMPT PRUT SCORN SHAME
SNEER SLIGHT CONTEMN DESPECT
DESPITE DISDAIN HETHING
MOCKERY DEFIANCE DERISION
DESPISAL DISGRACE MISPRIZE
CONTEMPTIBLE LOW BASE MEAN
VILE BALLY CHEAP DIRTY DUSTY
LOUSY MANGY MUCKY PETTY
POCKY RUDDY SCALD SORRY
ABJECT BLOODY GRUBBY MEASLY
PALTRY SCABBY SCUMMY SCURVY
SHABBY SNOTTY SORDID YELLOW
BROKING LIGHTLY PEEVISH PITIFUL
SCALLED SCORNED SHITTEN
SLAVISH SQUALID BAUBLING
BEGGARLY FRIPPERY INFAMOUS
INFERIOR PITIABLE SNEAKING
UNWORTHY WRETCHED
CONTEMPTIBLENESS BEGGARY
CONTEMPTUOUS SLIGHT SNOOTY
HAUGHTY LIGHTLY SLIGHTY
SPITOUS ARROGANT FLOUTING
INSOLENT SCOFFING SCORNFUL
CONTEND TUG VIE WAR WIN CAMP
COCK COPE DEAL FRAB KEMP PLEA
RACE WAGE ARGUE BANDY BRAWL
CHIDE CLAIM FIGHT FLITE PRESS
ASSERT BATTLE BICKER BREAST
BUCKLE BUFFET BUSTLE COMBAT
DEBATE DIFFER JOSTLE JUSTLE
MEDDLE OPPOSE REASON STRIVE
BARGAIN COMPETE CONTEST
COUNTER DISPUTE PROPUGN
QUARREL SCUFFLE STICKLE
SUSTAIN WRESTLE CONFLICT
CONTRAST CONTRIVE MAINTAIN
MILITATE SQUABBLE STRUGGLE
CONTENT PAY CALM EASE GIST
GLAD PAID RATH APPAY HAPPY
HUMOR RATHE SERVE AMOUNT
CUBAGE PLEASE APPEASE
CONTENU GRATIFY REPLETE
SATIATE SATISFY SUFFICE WILLING
BLISSFUL CAPACITY CONTINEU
WILCWEME
(**—S OF STOMACH**) COOKIES
(**ENERGY —**) STRENGTH
(**HEAT —**) ENTHALPY
(**SUPERFICIAL —S**) AREA
(PL.) LINING
CONTENTED COZY FAIN VAIN QUIET
SATED CONTENT PLEASED
CHEERFUL
CONTENTION WAR BAIT BATE FEUD
PLEA RIOT TIFF TOIL BROIL CHEST
STRUT BICKER COMBAT DEBATE
ESTRIF JANGLE STRIFE CHIDING
CONTEKE CONTEST DISCORD
DISPUTE OPINION QUARREL
RIVALRY WRANGLE ARGUMENT
CONFLICT SQUABBLE STRUGGLE
VARIANCE
CONTENTIOUS CROSS BATEFUL
PEEVISH PERVERSE
CONTENTMENT EASE BLISS
HEAVEN PLEASURE
CONTERMINOUS NEXT ADJACENT
FRONTIER PROXIMAL
CONTEST GO IT BEE FIX RUN SUE

TRY VIE AGON BOUT CAMP COPE
DUEL FEUD FRAY GAME HOLD KEMP
LAKE MART PULL RACE SHOW SPAR
TIFF TILT TURN YOKE AGONY
ARGUE BROIL CLASH DERBY EVENT
FIGHT MATCH PLATE PRIZE ROLEO
SCRUB SPORT TRIAL WAGER
ACTION ADJURE AFFRAY BATTLE
BISLEY COMBAT DEBATE DEFEND
FLIGHT OPPOSE RESIST RUBBER
SEESAW STRIFE STRIVE TUSSLE
YOKING BARGAIN BRABBLE CLASSIC
COMPETE CONTECK CONTEND
DERAIGN DISPUTE GRAPPLE
PROTEST SHUTOUT TOURNEY
WARFARE ARGUMENT CONCOURS
CONFLICT DOGFIGHT HANDICAP
LITIGATE SKIRMISH SLUGFEST
STRIVING STRUGGLE WALKAWAY
WALKOVER
(**— IN WORDS**) SPAR
(**— NARROWLY WON**) SQUEAKER
(**DRAWN —**) TIE DRAW STALEMATE
(**MOCK —**) SCIAMACHY
(**RACING —**) DRAG
(**REAPING —**) KEMP
CONTESTANT VIER RIVAL WAGER
PLAYER AGONIST ENTRANT
SCRATCH FINALIST PROSPECT
CONTIGUOUS NEXT NIGH NEARBY
TANGENT ABUTTING ADJACENT
TOUCHING
CONTIGUITY ADJACENCY CONFINITY
IMMEDIACY
CONTINENT ASIA MASS SOBER
AFRICA CHASTE EUROPE CONTENT
CAPACITY MAINLAND MODERATE
ABSTINENT
CONTINGENCY BOOK CASE EVENT
CHANCE ADJUNCT CONTACT
VENTURE ACCIDENT CASUALTY
FORTUITY INCIDENT JUNCTURE
PROSPECT
CONTINGENT CASUAL CHANCE
DOUBTFUL EVENTUAL INCHOATE
TOUCHING
CONTINUAL STILL HOURLY ENDLESS
ETERNAL LASTING REGULAR
UNDYING UNIFORM CONSTANT
ENDURING UNBROKEN
CONTINUALLY AY AYE EVER STILL
ALWAYS EVERLY HOURLY STEADY
ENDLESS ETERNAL FOREVER
MINUTELY
CONTINUANCE STAY WHEN DELAY
LEASE SEQUEL DURANCE LASTING
ABIDANCE DURATION SURVIVAL
CONTINUANT OPEN LIQUID
DURATIVE
CONTINUATION SEQUEL DURATION
(**— OF DOUBLET**) BASQUE
CONTINUE BE DO ABY SUE BIDE
DURE HOLD JUMP KEEP LAST LIVE
STAY TIDE ABIDE CARRY EXIST
PERGE STICK UNITE ABEGGE
BELEVE ENDURE EXTEND PURSUE
REMAIN RESUME BELEAVE CONNECT
CONTUNE PERSIST PROCEED
PROLONG SUBSIST SURVIVE

SUSTAIN PROTRACT
(**— UNALTERED**) TARRY
CONTINUED STILL SERIAL CHRONIC
CONSTANT
CONTINUING DURABLE DURATIVE
(**— FOR LONG TIME**) CHRONIC
(**— TO BE**) YET
CONTINUITY TRACT SCRIPT
COHESION SCENARIO CONTINUUM
CONTINUOUS RUN EVEN ANEND
EIDENT ENTIRE EYDENT STEADY
CHRONIC ENDLESS RUNNING
UNBROKEN
CONTINUOUSLY AWAY EVER FAST
ANEND OUTRIGHT
CONTORT WRY BEND COIL CURL
TURN WARP GNARL SCREW TWIST
WREST CRINGE DEFORM WRITHE
DISTORT PERVERT SQUINCH
WREATHE OBVOLUTE
CONTORTED WRY WRIED KNOTTY
CRISPED KNOTTED SCREWED
WRITHEN OBVOLUTE
CONTORTION SCREW STITCH
WRITHE MURGEON WORKING
CONTOUR FORM LINE CURVE
GRAPH SHAPE SWEEP AMOEBA
FIGURE OUTLINE PROFILE
CARTOUCH CONTORNO MANDORLA
PLANFORM TOURNURE
(**— ON SHIP**) HANCE
CONTRA CONTRE AGAINST COUNTER
OPPOSED
CONTRABAND HOT GOODS ILLEGAL
ILLICIT SMUGGLED UNLAWFUL
CONTRABASS BASS OCTOBASS
CONTRACT GET BOND DRAW FARM
FORM HALE KNIT PACT SALE TACK
CATCH CLOSE COACT COUCH
CRAMP FEVER INCUR LEASE LIMIT
NEXUM PINCH SHRUG SNURP
CARTEL COCKLE COMMIT CRINGE
ENGAGE FUTURE GATHER HIRING
INDENT LESSEN MUTUUM NARROW
PLEDGE POLICY PROMPT PUCKER
REDUCE SHRIMP SHRINK SUBLET
TREATY ABRIDGE BARGAIN
BUMMERY CHARTER COMPACT
CRUMPLE CURTAIL DEFLATE
FIDUCIA MANDATE PROMISE
SCRUNCH SHORTEN SHRIVEL
SOCIETY WRINKLE ASSIENTO
BOTTOMRY CONDENSE COVENANT
HANDFAST HARDNESS LOCATION
RESTRICT STEELBOW STRAITEN
SYNGRAPH
(**— BROW**) FROWN
(**— INTO WRINKLES**) KNIT
(**BRIDGE —**) SOLO AUCTION
(**MARRIAGE —**) KETUBA AFFIANCE
HANDFAST BETROTHAL SPONSALIA
CONTRACTED BOXY CRAMP
BOOKED ASTRICT INGROWN
INSULAR SCREWED CONTRACT
CONTRACTILITY MOTILITY
CONTRACTION HM ANT NIP TIC TIS
AINT CANT ISNT KNIT MAAM WONT
CRAMP HADNT HASNT NISUS SPASM
CRASIS GATHER INTAKE MUSTNT

SHRINK TWITCH ELISION EPITOME
WOULDNT APNEUSIS TRACTION
(— OF HEART) SYSTOLE
(— OF SYLLABLES) SYNIZESIS
(PL.) TREPPE
CONTRACTOR KHOT BUTTY
BUILDER REMOVER SUPPLIER
CONTRADICT DENY BELIE CROSS
REBUT FORBID IMPUGN NEGATE
OPPOSE RECANT REFUTE COUNTER
GAINSAY REVERSE WITHSAY
CONTRARY DISPROVE DOWNFACE
NEGATIVE OUTSTAND
CONTRADICTION DENIAL PARADOX
WITHSAW ANTILOGY ANTIMONY
ANTILOQUY
CONTRADICTORY OPPOSE
ANTINOME OPPOSITE THWARTING
CONTRAPTION RIG TOOL DEVICE
GADGET JIGGER CONCERN MACHINE
CONTRARILY BACKWARD
CRISSCROSS
CONTRARIWISE CROSS CONTRA
CONTRARY
CONTRARY BALKY KICKY SNIVY
AVERSE CONTRA ORNERY SNIVEY
ADVERSE COUNTER CRABBED
FROWARD HOSTILE INVERSE
OPPOSED PEEVISH RESTIVE
REVERSE WAYWARD ABSONANT
ANTIPODE CAPTIOUS CONTRAIR
INIMICAL OPPOSITE PERVERSE
PETULANT SINGULAR
(— TO HAPPINESS) ILL
(— TO REASON) SILLY
(— TO) BESIDE AGAINST ATHWART
CONTRAST CLASH STRIFE COMPARE
CONTEND DISCORD ANTIMONY
DIVISION DYNAMICS OPPOSITE
CONTRAVENE DEFY DENY HINDER
OPPOSE THWART DISPUTE VIOLATE
INFRINGE OBSTRUCT
CONTRAVENTION SIN VICE CRIME
BREACH OFFENSE
CONTRETEMPS SLIP BONER HITCH
MISHAP SCRAPE ACCIDENT
INCIDENT
CONTRIBUTE AID ANTE FORK GIVE
HELP MAKE TEND CAUSE ENTER
GROUT SERVE ASSIST BESTOW
CONCUR CONFER DONATE PUNGLE
SUPPLY TENDER ANIMATE CONDUCE
FURNISH FURTHER PROVIDE
CONTRIBUTION BIT SUM TAX ALMS
BOON GIFT SCOT SHOT ESSAY
INPUT SHARE IMPOST SYMBOL
ARTICLE LARGESS PAYMENT
PRESENT RENEWAL WRITING
DONATION EXACTION OFFERING
ROMESHOT
CONTRITE WORN SORRY HUMBLE
RUEFUL PENITENT SORROWFUL
CONTRITION SORE SORROW
PENANCE
CONTRIVANCE (ALSO SEE DEVICE)
ART BOW FLY GIN JET JIG LEG
DROP GEAR HARP JACK KITE LURE
PLAN PLOT RASP REED TOOL
CARRY CHECK DOLLY DRAFT FLOAT

FRAME GUIDE HICKY KNACK MIXER
QUIPU SHIFT SNARE STOCK
ANCHOR DAMPER DECEIT DESIGN
DEVICE DOCTOR DOLLIE ENGINE
FABRIC FANGLE GABION GADGET
GIMBAL HANGER HARROW HEATER
HICKEY HOLDER JIGGER JINKER
MARKER MORTAR MUZZLE POLICY
RATTLE SCHEME SLUICE SPIDER
TEASEL WEIGHT WHEEZE WINDAS
WRENCH BOLSTER CLEANER
CLEARER CONCERN COUPLER
CUNNING DINGBAT DRAUGHT
FICTION FISHWAY HUMIDOR
KNOCKER MACHINE PAGEANT
PROJECT REDUCER ROASTER
SCRAPER SHEBANG SPANNER
STOPPER TOASTER TRIPPER
VOLVELL ADAPTION ARTIFICE
CROTCHET DUTCHMAN EUPYRION
FAKEMENT FORECAST GOVERNOR
INDUSTRY MOLITION OXIDATOR
REGISTER RESOURCE SCISSORS
SQUEEZER SUBTLETY WITCRAFT
CONTRIVE GET LAY BREW CAST
DRAW FIND FIRK MAKE PLAN PLOT
WORK FRAME FUDGE HATCH SHAPE
STAGE WEAVE AFFORD DESIGN
DEVISE DIVINE ENGINE FIGURE
INVENT MANAGE SCHEME WANGLE
ACHIEVE AGITATE COMMENT
COMPASS CONCOCT CONJURE
CONSULT CONTEND FASHION
IMAGINE MACHINE PROCURE
PROJECT REPAREL CONSPIRE
ENGINEER FORECAST INTRIGUE
PURCHASE
CONTRIVED SLICK STAGED
TIMBERED
CONTRIVER DAEDAL DAEDALUS
ENGINEER
CONTRIVING FASHION SCHEMERY
CONTROL BIT LAP LAW MAN POT
RUN CONN CURB EGIS GRIP HAND
HANK HAVE HOLD REDE REIN RULE
STAY SWAY WIND AEGIS BOOST
CHARM CHECK COACT DAUNT
DUMMY GRASP GUIDE LEASH
ORDER POWER STEER SWING
THEAT TREAT VERGE WIELD
BANDON BRIDLE CHARGE CLUTCH
COERCE CORNER DANGER DIRECT
EMPERY GOVERN HANDLE MANAGE
POCKET TEMPER AMENAGE
COMMAND CONDUCT CONTAIN
CUSTODY FORBEAR MASTERY
QUALIFY STRINGS COACTION
DOMINATE DOMINIUM IMPERIUM
MODERATE REGULATE SERVOTAB
(— A BULL) MANDAR
(— OF RESOURCES) HUSBANDRY
(ABSOLUTE —) BECK
(FIRE —) BLANKET
(GOVERNMENT —) SQUADRISM
(NONCLERICAL —) LAICISM LAICITY
CONTROLLED STEADY SERVILE
CONTAINED
CONTROLLER FENCER MASTER
STARTER

(SPEED —) GOVERNOR RHEOCRAT
CONTROLLING MASTER LEADING
DOMINANT HEGEMONIC
CONTROVERSIAL ERISTIC POLEMIC
CONTROVERSIALIST ERISTIC
POLEMIC DISPUTANT GLADIATOR
CONTROVERSY PLEA SPAT SUIT
CHEST FUROR BATTLE COMBAT
DEBATE FURORE HASSEL HASSLE
HOORAH HURRAH STRIFE TUSSLE
DISPUTE POLEMIC QUARREL
WRANGLE ARGUMENT TRAVERSE
(ART OF —) POLEMICS
CONTROVERT DENY FACE MOOT
ARGUE DEBATE DEFEND OPPOSE
OPPUGN REFUTE CONTEST DISPUTE
GAINSAY DISPROVE
CONTUMACIOUS UNRULY RIOTOUS
CONTUMAX INSOLENT MUTINOUS
PERVERSE STUBBORN
CONTUMELY ABUSE SCORN INSULT
CONTECK DISDAIN REPROOF
UPBRAID CONTEMPT RUDENESS
CONTUSE BEAT POUND THUMP
BRUISE INJURE SQUEEZE
CONTUSION POUND BRUISE
CONUNDRUM PUN WHIM ENIGMA
PUZZLE RIDDLE CONCEIT
CROTCHET
CONURE ARATINGA
CONVALESCE MEND GUARISH
RECOVER
CONVENANCE FORM
CONVENE SIT CALL HOLD MEET
UNITE GATHER MUSTER SUMMON
CONVENT CONVOKE ASSEMBLE
CONVERGE
CONVENIENCE GAIN URINAL
LEISURE COMMODITY
CONVENIENT FIT GAIN HEND HANDY
HENDE READY CLEVER FITTED
PROPER SUITED USEFUL ADAPTED
AVENANT COMMODE HELPFUL
BECOMING EXPEDITE SUITABLE
CONVENIENTLY HANDILY CLEVERLY
CONVENT ABBEY TEKKE TEKYA
CENOBY COVENT FRIARY PRIORY
CONVENT MEETING RECLUSE
CLOISTER LAMASERY
CONVENTION DIET FEIS FORM MISE
RULE TABU SYNOD TABOO USAGE
CARTEL CAUCUS CUSTOM TREATY
DECORUM MEETING ASSEMBLY
ASSIENTO CONCLAVE CONGRESS
CONTRACT COVENANT PRACTICE
(LONG-ESTABLISHED —) TRADITION
(STAGE —) ASIDE
(PL.) DECENCIES
CONVENTIONAL MORE NOMIC
RIGHT TRITE USUAL DECENT
FORMAL MODISH PROPER CORRECT
REGULAR ACADEMIC ACCEPTED
CUSTOMARY
CONVENTIONALITY FORM
ACADEMISM FORMALITY GRUNDYISM
CONVENTIONALIZE STYLIZE
CONVERGE JOIN MEET FOCUS
CONCUR CORNER DESCEND
APPROACH FOCALIZE

CONVERSANT ADEPT BUSIED EXPERT VERSED SKILLED FAMILIAR OCCUPIED

CONVERSATION SAY CALL CHAT CHIN RUNE TALE TALK CRACK PROSE CACKLE CONFAB DEVICE GOSSIP PARLEY POWWOW SPEECH YABBER CEILIDH COMMUNE CONDUCT PALAVER PURPOSE BACKCHAT BEHAVIOR CAUSERIE CHITCHAT COLLOGUE COLLOQUY DIALOGUE GIFFGAFF HARANGUE PARLANCE QUESTION

(— **BETWEEN WHALERS**) GAM

CONVERSATIONALIST TALKER CAUSEUR

CONVERSE CHAT CHIN LIVE MOVE TALK DWELL SPEAK CACKLE CONFER DEVISE HOMILY PARLEY REASON COMMUNE CONVERT DISCUSS OBVERSE PROPOSE REVERSE COLLOQUE EXCHANGE OPPOSITE QUESTION

CONVERSION CHANGE EXCHANGE

(— **INTO VAPOR**) FLASH

(— **OF IRON**) FINING

CONVERT TAW TURN WEND ALTER AMEND APPLY MAULA RENEW CHANGE DECODE DETECT DIRECT MAWALI NOVICE SHAIKH SOUPER COMMUTE CONCOCT RESOLVE RESTORE REVERSE ACTIVATE CONVERSE DISCIPLE NEOPHYTE PERSUADE

(— **COTTON**) LAP

(— **INTO LEATHER**) TAN TAW

(— **INTO LIQUID**) BREW

(— **INTO SOAP**) SAPONIFY

(— **INTO STEEL**) ACIERATE

(— **INTO STONE**) LAPIDIFY

(— **SOAP**) CLOSE

(— **TO CARBON**) CHAR

CONVERTER ROTARY SELECTOR

CONVERTIBLE AUTO DROPHEAD

CONVEX BOWED ARCHED CAMBER CURVED BULGING EMBOWED GIBBOUS ROUNDED

CONVEY JAG BEAR BOOK CART CEDE DEED DUCT HAVE LEAD MEAN PASS SEND SIGN TAKE TOTE WAIN WILL BRING CARRY DRIVE FETCH GRANT GUIDE HURRY STEAL ARRIVE ASSIGN CONVOY DEDUCE DELATE DEMISE DEVISE ELOIGN GIGGIT IMPART IMPORT REMOVE YMMOTE AUCTION CHANNEL CHARIOT CHARTER CONDUCT DELIVER DERRICK DISPONE DISPOSE LIGHTER RESTORE ALIENATE BEQUEATH DESCRIBE TRANSFER TRANSMIT

(— **AN ESTATE**) DEMISE

(— **BY ALLUSION**) IMPLY

(— **FORCIBLY**) HUSTLE

(— **LEGALLY**) DEED GRANT LEASE DEMISE ELOIGN DISPONE

(— **NEARER**) BRING

(— **SECRETLY**) CRIM

CONVEYANCE BUS CAR AUTO CART DEED DRAG GIFT LOAD SLED TAXI TRAM GRANT SEDAN STAGE TAUGA THEFT TRAIN WAGON DEMISE JINGLE CHARTER CONDUCT COURIER MACHINE RATTLER TRAILER TRAJECT TRANSIT TROLLEY VECTURE VEHICLE WAFTAGE CARRIAGE CARRYING CONVEYAL DELATION FERRIAGE STEALING TRANSFER

CONVEYOR LIFT WORM DRAPER LADDER SHAKER CARRIER CREEPER HURRIER SCRAPER CAROUSEL CONVEYER ELEVATOR

CONVICT LAG CAST FIND STAR ARGUE EXILE FELON LIFER PROVE TAINT ATTAIN FORCAT LAGGER TERMER TRUSTY APPROVE ATTAINT CAPTIVE CONDEMN CULPRIT EXPIREE IMPEACH REPROVE CRIMINAL JAILBIRD PRISONER REDARGUE SENTENCE

CONVICT FISH MANINI HINALEA

CONVICTION CREDO CREED DOGMA FAITH SENSE TAINT TENET BELIEF CREDIT CONCERN OPINION SENTENCE

CONVINCE EVICT FETCH ASSURE EVINCE REPROVE RESOLVE SATISFY CONCLUDE

(— **OF ERROR**) CONVICT

CONVINCED FIRM SOLD SURE CERTAIN ABSOLUTE POSITIVE

CONVINCING SOUND VALID COGENT POTENT EVIDENT TELLING FORCIBLE POWERFUL PREGNANT

CONVIVIAL GAY BOON FESTAL GENIAL JOVIAL SOCIAL FESTIVE HOLIDAY JOCULAR REVELING

CONVIVIALITY REVEL FESTIVAL

CONVOCATION DIET SYNOD CALLING COUNCIL MEETING SUMMONS ASSEMBLY CONGRESS VOCATION

CONVOKE CALL HOLD GATHER SUMMON CONVENE ASSEMBLE

CONVOLUTE COIL ROLL WIND TWIST TANGLE WRITHE CONTORT INVOLUTE OBVOLUTE

CONVOLUTED GYRATE

CONVOLUTION COIL CURL FOLD TURN WRAP GYRUS SWIRL TWINE TWIRL TWIST WHORL CUNEUS GYROMA VOLUME VOLUTION

CONVOLVE TURN WIND TWIST ENFOLD ENWRAP INFOLD WRITHE

CONVOLVULUS BINDWEED SCAMMONY

CONVOY LEAD WAFT CARRY GUARD GUIDE PILOT TRADE WATCH ATTEND CONVEY ESCORT MANAGE CONDUCT WAFTAGE

CONVULSE ROCK STIR SHAKE EXCITE AGITATE DISTURB

CONVULSION FIT SHRUG SPASM THROE ATTACK TUMULT UPROAR CONVULSE LAUGHTER PAROXYSM COMMOTION

CONVULSIVE FITFUL EPILEPTIC

CONY DAS HARE PIKA CONEY CUNNY DAMAN DASSY GANAM HUTIA HYRAX BURBOT CONEEN DASSIE GAZABO GAZEBO RABBIT WABBER ASHKOKO BOOMDAS HYRACID KLIPDAS HYRACOID KLIPDACH

COO CROO CURR WOOT CHIRR CHIZZ CROOD MURMUR CROODLE CRUDDLE

COOK DO FIX FRY BAKE BOIL CHEF COCT MAKE SEAR STEW BROIL CUSIE FRIZZ GRILL POACH ROAST SCALD SHIRR STEAM BRAISE CODDLE COOKIE COOPER DECOCT DIGEST PORTER SAUTEE SEETHE SIMMER ARTISTE BROILER FRIZZLE GRIDDLE PASTLER PERCOCT POTAGER PREPARE PROCESS SERVANT SMOTHER SWAMPER BAWARCHI BOBACHEE COCINERO CUSINERO GRILLADE MAGIRIST PASTERER

(— **UP**) BUILD

(**BULL** —) FLUNKY FLUNKEY GREASER

(**SHIP'S** —) DOCTOR SLUSHY SKILLET SLUSHER

COOKED DONE FRIED BOILED

(— **WITH SUGAR**) CANDIED

COOKEE FLUNKY HASHER FLUNKEY

COOKER CANNER HAYBOX DIGESTER

COOKERY CURY CUISINE KITCHEN MAGIRICS

COOKHOUSE GALLEY

COOKIE CAKE ROCK SNAP COOKY HERMIT KIPFEL BISCUIT BROWNIE OATCAKE PLACENT CRESCENT SEEDCAKE

COOL AIR FAN ICE CALM COLD KEEL AKELE ALGID ALLAY CHILL EVENT FRESH GELID NERVY QUEEL SOBER STAID WHOLE AIRISH CALLER CHILLY PLACID QUENCH SEDATE SERENE TEMPER UNWARM COOLISH REFROID UNMOVED CARELESS CAUTIOUS COMPOSED MITIGATE MODERATE TRANQUIL

(— **IN WATER**) SLACK SLACKEN

(— **OF EVENING**) SERENE

COOLED COLD FRAPPE

COOLER ICER JAIL KEEL OLLA SINK ICEBOX LOCKUP PRISON SINKER KEELFAT KEELYAT ALCOGENE

(**WINE** —) GLACIER

COOLIE CHANGAR MADRASI MAZDOOR

COOLNESS COOL FROST NERVE SWALE APLOMB PHLEGM SERENITY

COOM CULM GAUM SMUT SOOT COOMB GRIME SLACK

COONTIE SAGO ZAMIA COMPTIE

COOP COT CUB CUP MEW PEN POT RIP CAGE COOB COTE JAIL CRAMP HUTCH BASKET CORRAL CONFINE

(— **UP**) PEN IMMEW INCOUP

(**HEN** —) CAVEY CAVIE BARTON

COOPER BUNGS COPER COWPER HEADER HOOPER TUBBER TUBBIE TUBMAN

COOPERATE HAND TEND AGREE COACT UNITE CONCUR COMBINE CONDUCE CONNIVE COADJUTE CONSPIRE

COOPERATION SOCIETY COURTESY TEAMWORK

COOPERATIVE COOP SOCIAL SYNERGIC

COORDINATE SINE ADAPT EQUAL ADJUST ARRANGE SYNTONY ABSCISSA CLASSIFY ENSEMBLE

COORDINATION BOND SKILL HARMONY LIAISON

COORG KADAGA

COOT CUIT DUCK RAIL QUEET SMYTH BELTIE GORHEN PELICK SCOTER HENBILL LOBIPED PULLDOO LOBEFOOT RAILBIRD SWAMPHEN

COP BAG NAB ROB BANK BLOW BULL HEAD HEAP JOHN LIFT PILE TRAP TUBE CATCH CREST FILCH MOUNT QUILL SHOCK SNARE STEAL STOCK SWIPE BOBBIN COPPIN PEELER SPIDER STRIKE CAPTURE

COPA YAYA COPITA

COPAL BOEA LOBA ANIME CONGO KAURI KAURY RESIN COWRIE CHAKAZI

COPE VIE WAR CAPE DUTY FACE LIFT MEET CAPPA CLOAK COVER DRESS EQUAL FIGHT MATCH NOTCH RIVAL VAULT WIELD BARTER CANOPY CHAPEL COMBAT MANTEL MUZZLE OPPOSE SEMBLE STRIKE STRIVE ANABATA CONTEND CONTEST GRAPPLE MANDYAS PLUVIAL COMPLETE EXCHANGE FACTABLE SEMICOPE STRUGGLE VESTMENT

COPEHAN WINTUN

COPEPOD CALANID CAYENNE DIAPTOMID

COPIAPITE MISY MISSY IHLEITE

COPIER COPIST SCRIBE JOHNSONIAN

COPING CAP COPE FLUE SKEW CORDON CAPSTONE FACTABLE

COPING STONE TABLET TABLING

COPIOUS FREE FULL GOOD LUSH RANK RICH AMPLE LARGE FLUENT LAVISH DIFFUSE FLOWING FULSOME LENGTHY PROFUSE REPLETE TEEMING UBEROUS ABUNDANT AFFLUENT FRUITFUL GENEROUS NUMEROUS

COPIOUSNESS COPY PLENTY

COPPER AES COP BULL CENT BOBBY METAL PENNY VENUS CUPRUM PEELER VELLON BLISTER CARNELIAN
(GILDED —) VERMEIL
(OF —) AEN

COPPERAS COPEROSE INKSTONE

COPPERHEAD REDEYE MOCCASIN

COPPERSMITH TINKERBIRD

COPPER SULFATE BLUESTONE

COPPER SULFIDE FERRETTO COVELLINE COVELLITE

COPPERY CUPREOUS

COPPICE COP BROW WOOD COPPY

COPSE FIRTH FRITH GROVE COVERT FOREST GROWTH SPROUT THICKET ARBUSTUM

COPSE CUT HAG HASP HEWT HOLT MOTT SHAW TRIM DROKE HURST CLEVIS SPINNY COPPICE LOWWOOD SHACKLE SPINNEY ARBUSTUM COPEWOOD

COPULA BAND LINK UNION

COPY APE CALK CAST ECHO EDIT MIME MOCK NICK DITTO DUMMY GROSS IMAGE MIMIC MODEL REVIE STICK STUFF TRACE CALQUE DOUBLE ECTYPE EFFIGY FILLER FLIMSY FOLLOW MATTER RECORD REFLEX SAMPLE SHADOW EDITION EMULATE ENGROSS ESTREAT EXTRACT IMITATE PATTERN REDRAFT REPLICA REPRINT RUBBING TRACING VIDIMUS APOGRAPH EXEMPLAR EXSCRIBE EXSCRIPT LIKENESS MANIFOLD POROTYPE PORTRAIT RESEMBLE SPECIMEN
(— EDITOR) SLOT
(— OF DOCUMENT) EXTRACT PROTOCOL
(— OF DRESS) FORD
(EXACT —) TENOR
(PRINTING —) KILL BOGUS
(UNREMUNERATIVE —) LEAN
(WORTHLESS —) BALAAM

COPYING MIMICRY INSINUATION

COPYIST COPIER SCRIBE COPYCAT SCRIVENER

COPYREAD EDIT SUBEDIT

COQUET TOY COPPY DALLY FLIRT TRIFLE BLINKER CELIMENE

COQUILLE SHELL

COQUINA DONAX

CORA NAYARIT

CORACLE SCOW CURAGH CURRANE

CORAL RED PINK AKORI BLOOD POLYP ALCYON PALULE PORITE FUNGIAN OCULINA ACROPORE ASTRAEAN CORALLUM FAVOSITE POLYPITE STAGHORN TUBIPORE ZOOPHYTE

CORAL BEAN SOPHORA FRIJOLILLO

CORAL-BELLS HEUCHERA

CORALBERRY BUCKBUSH

CORALFISH DOLLFISH

CORALROOT ORCHID CRAWLEY

CORAL SNAKE ELAPID ROLLER ELAPOID

CORAL TREE GABGAB ERYTHRINA

CORBEIL PANNIER

CORBEL KNOT ANCON CORBET TIMBER BRAGGER RESPOND CARTOUCH SPRINGER

CORBELING SQUINCH

CORBIESTEP CATSTEP CROWSTEP

CORCIR CORKE ARCHIL CORKER ORCHIL ARCHILLA

CORD AEA RIB AGAL BAND BIND BOND FILE LACE LASH LINE ROPE WELT BRAID CHORD FUNIS GUARD LEASH LIGNE MATCH NERVE OLONA TWINE TWIST BINDER BOBBIN

BRIDLE BUNGEE CATGUT CHORDA CORDON FIADOR GIRDLE LASHER LISERE RACHIS SENNET STRING TENDON TOGGLE AMENTUM BOWYANG BULLION CORDING FUNICLE LANIARD LANYARD MACRAME SEAMING SEIZING SKIRREH TIEBACK URACHUS BELLPULL CHENILLE DRAWCORD HAIRLINE SHOELACE WHIPCORD
(— AROUND BOWSTRING) SERVING
(— FOR PIPING) BOBBIN
(— OF CANDLENUT BARK) AEA
(CROCHETING —) CORDE
(ELECTRIC —) FLEX
(EMBROIDERY —) ARRASENE
(FRINGED —) LLAUTU
(HAMMOCK —S) CLEW
(MASON'S —) SKIRREH
(ORNAMENTED —) AGLET AIGLET
(PARACHUTE —) SHROUD
(SACRED —) KUSTI
(SPINAL —) EON AEON NUKE
(TWISTED —) TORSADE

CORDAGE DA COIR ERUC FERU HEMP IMBE JUTE KYAR ROPE HAMBER SENNIT RIGGING
(LENGTH OF —) CATENARY

CORDATE HEARTED

CORDED TIED JETTED REPPED RIBBED WELTED TWILLED

COR-DE-NUIT PASTORITA

CORDER RUFFER

CORDIAL REAL WARM CREAM ARDENT CASSIS DEVOUT ELIXIR GENIAL HEARTY CORDATE DIAMBER LIQUEUR PERSICO ROSOLIO SINCERE ZEALOUS ANISETTE FRIENDLY GRACIOUS PERSICOT VIGOROUS
(NOT —) DISTANT STANDOFF
(PL.) SWEETS

CORDIERITE IOLITE FAHLUNITE

CORDON BLEU BENGALEE

CORDONNET CRESCENT

CORDWOOD BODYWOOD

CORE AME COB HUB NUT BONE COKE COLK GIST KNOT NAVE PITH BLOCK FOCUS HEART NOWSE RUMPF SPOOL BARREL CENTER CENTRE HEATER KERNEL MATRIX MIDDLE NODULE POCKET STAPLE CENTRUM CHEMISE COMPANY CORNCOB ESSENCE NUCLEUS FILAMENT HEARTING
(— OF COAL) STOCK
(— OF COLUMN) BELL HEART
(— OF CRICKET BALL) QUILT
(— OF LOG) PITH
(WATER —) GLASSINESS

CORE ARBOR STALK

COREE CORANINE

CORELIGIONIST BROTHER

COREMIUM SYNEMA SYNNEMA

COREOPSIS TICKSEED TICKWEED LEPTOSYNE

CORF TUB CAGE CAWF COFF CORB SKIP CREEL BASKET DOSSER

CORGI CARDIGAN PEMBROKE

CORIUM CUTIS DERMA LAYER
DERMIS
CORK PLUG FLOAT SHIVE SUBER
BOBBER BOUCHON CRINKLE
PHELLEM SOBERIN STOPPER
STOPPLE
CORKER WHIZ RAKER WHIZZ
CUTTER HUMDINGER
CORKSCREW WORMER
CORKWOOD BALSA GUANO
HAREFOOT
CORM SET BULB SEED CORMEL
CORMUS FREESIA UINTJIE
CORMEL BULBLET
(PL.) SPAWN
CORMORANT SHAG CRANE GORMA
NORIE SCARF SCART DUIKER
DUYKER GORMAW GUANAY SCARFE
SCARTH GLUTTON SHAGLET
CORN ZEA DANA DENT SALT SAMP
GRAIN MAIZE SPIKE WYROK AGNAIL
CALLUS CLAVUS HELOMA INDIAN
KERNEL MEALIE NOCAKE NUBBIN
POWDER WYROCK FORMITY
FRUMENT FRUMENTY PRESERVE
SAUTERNE
(— SPURREY) YARR
(CROW —) COLICROOT
(CRUSHED —) STAMP
(DECORATED EAR OF —) TIPONI
(EAR OF —) ICKER
(GUINEA —) DURRA DHURRA
(INDIAN —) MAIZE INDIAN NOCAKE
(PARCHED —) ROKEE NOCAKE
YOKAGE GRADDAN ROKEAGE
YOKEAGE
(STRING OF —) TRACE
(UNRIPE EAR OF —) TUCKET
CORNAGE HORNGELD
CORN BREAD PONE KANKIE
BANNOCK
CORN COCKLE GITH COCKLE
POPPLE COCKWEED HARDHEAD
MELANTHY
CORNCRACKER STATE KENTUCKY
CORNCRAKE RAIL CORNBIRD
CORN CROWFOOT JOY GOLDWEED
HELLWEED JACKWEED
CORNEL DOGWOOD REDBRUSH
CORNEOUS HORNLIKE KERASINE
CORNER IN GET OUT WRO BEND
CANT COIN HALK HERN JAMB NOOK
POOL TRAP TREE WICK ANCON
ANGLE BIGHT CATCH COIGN ELBOW
HERNE INGLE JAMBE NICHE QUOIN
TRUST BOTTLE CANTLE CANTON
COLLAR CORNEL CRANNY RECESS
SQUARE QUINYIE TURNING
MONOPOLY
(— IN A DRIFT) ARRAGE
(— OF EYE) CANTHUS
(— OF GUNSTOCK) TOE
(— OF MOLDBOARD) SHIN
(— OF SAIL) CLEW CLUE TACK
GOOSEWING
(LOWER —) CLEW CLUE
(ROUNDED —) FILET FILLET
(SECRET —) CREEK
(TIGHT —) BOX

CORNERPIECE BUMPER CANTLE
CORNERSTONE COIN BASIS COIGN
HEADSTONE
CORNET HORN ZINK TWIST ZINKE
ZINCKE CORONET CORNETTO
CORNETFISH FLUTEMOUTH
HEMIBRANCH
CORNFIELD MOW
CORN FLAG LEVERS
CORNFLOWER BLUET BLAVER
BARBEAU BLUECAP BLUECUP
BLAEWORT
CORN GROMWELL SALFERN
CORNHUSK CAP
CORNHUSKER STATE NEBRASKA
CORNHUSKING SHUCKING
CORNICE CAP BAND DRIP EAVE
JOPY ANCON CROWN JOWPY
DETAIL GEISON PELMET ANTEFIX
MOLDING SURBASE ASTRAGAL
SWANNECK
(UNDER SIDE OF —) PLANCIER
CORNICLE SIPHON SYPHON
CORNISHMAN CELT KELT
CORN MARIGOLD GOLD GOOLS
BODDLE BOODLE BUDDLE GOWLAN
GOLDING GOLLAND
CORN MEAL MASA SAMP ATOLE
HOECAKE
CORN PARSLEY UMBEL
CORN POPPY BLAVER CANKER
COCKLE COPROSE EARACHE
PONCEAU REDWEED SOLDIER
CORN SALAD FETTICUS MILKGRASS
CORN STACK HOVEL
CORNSTALKS KARBI
CORNSTARCH BINDER
CORNU HORN THYROHYAL
CORNUCOPIA HORN CORNU COFFIN
CORNUS CORNIN REDBRUSH
CORN VIOLET SPECULARIA
CORN WOUNDWORT STACHYS
CORNY BANAL STALE TRITE MICKEY
BUCKEYE
COROADO BORORO
CORODY CONRED
COROLLA CUP BELL COROL CUPULE
LIGULE PERIANTH
COROLLARY DOGMA PORISM
RESULT TRUISM ADJUNCT THEOREM
COROMANDEL COLCOTHAR
CORONA BUR BURR CIGAR CROWN
GLORY AURORA FILLET ROSARY
WREATH AUREOLE CIRCLET
CORONET GARLAND SCYPHUS
CORONAL CRONET CORONEL
CROWNAL
CORONATION ABHISEKA
CROWNMENT
CORONER ELISOR CROWNER
EXAMINER SEARCHER
CORONET BAND BURR CROWN
TIARA ANADEM CIRCLE CRONET
DIADEM TIMBRE WREATH CHAPLET
CORONAL CROWNAL CROWNET
GARLAND CROWNLET
CORONOPUS CARARA
CORPORAL NYM FANO NAIG NAIK
FANON FANUM NAYAK PHANO

BODILY EXEMPT GUNNER NAIGUE
NAIQUE SINDON TINDAL
CORPORATE UNITED COMBINED
CORPORATION BODY CITY FIRM
POUCH TRUST SCHOLA BOROUGH
COLLEGE FREEDOM GUILDRY
SOCIETY SPONSOR
CORPOREAL REAL HYLIC SOMAL
ACTUAL BODILY CARNAL FLESHLY
SOMATIC MATERIAL PHYSICAL
TANGIBLE
CORPOSANT HERMO
CORPS CORE ORDU VELITES
SERAGLIO
(— DE BALLET) ENSEMBLE
CORPSE BIER BODY DUST LICH
MORT GHOST MUMMY RELIC STIFF
TRUCK ZOMBI CORPUS DEADER
ZOMBIE ANATOMY CADAVER
CARCASS CARRION CROAKER
DEADMAN FLOATER
(— WASHING) TAHARAH
CORPSMAN BEARER
CORPULENCE FAT FATNESS
STOUTNESS
CORPULENT FAT BULKY BURLY
FATTY GROSS HUSKY OBESE PLUMP
STOUT FLESHY GREASY PORTLY
ROTUND ADIPOSE BELLIED WEIGHTY
CORPUSCLE CELL GHOST GLOBULE
HEMATID HAEMATID HEMOCYTE
CORRAL PEN STY COOP ATAJO
POUND TAMBO CONFINE ENCLOSE
STOCKAGE SURROUND
(ELEPHANT —) KRAAL
CORRECT DUE FIT FIX TIC BEET
BOOK EDIT JUST LEAL LEAN MARK
MEND NICE OKAY SMUG TRUE
AMEND CHECK CLEAN EMEND
EXACT ORDER RIGHT SOUND SPILL
ADJUST BETTER CHANGE INFORM
PROPER PUNISH REBUKE REFORM
REMEDY REPAIR REVAMP REVISE
STRICT ADDRESS CHAPTER
CHASTEN CORRIGE ELEGANT
IMPROVE PERFECT PRECISE
RECLAIM RECTIFY REDRESS
REGULAR REPROVE SINCERE
ACCURATE CHASTISE DEFINITE
EMENDATE EQUALIZE REGULATE
RIGOROUS STRAIGHT TRUTHFUL
(GRAMMATICALLY —) CONGRUE
CORRECTABLE CORRIGIBLE
CORRECTION YARD CENSURE
FLEXURE IMPRINT REDRESS
FUGACITY
CORRECTIVE SALT REMEDY
CORRECTLY JUST RIGHT ARIGHT
RIGHTLY SOUNDLY PROPERLY
CORRECTNESS TRUTH DECORUM
FITNESS JUSTICE ACCURACY
JUSTNESS VERACITY
CORRELATE HARMONIZE
CORRELATIVE OR NOR THEN
EQUAL STILL EITHER MUTUAL
NEITHER ANALOGUE CONJOINT
REDDITIVE
CORRESPOND FIT GEE JIBE SUIT
AGREE MATCH TALLY WRITE

ACCORD ANSWER CONCUR SQUARE
COMPORT RESPOND COINCIDE
PARALLEL QUADRATE
(— **IN SOUND**) ASSONATE
(— **TO**) ENSUE
CORRESPONDENCE MAIL TALLY
ANALOGY CONSENT HARMONY
KEEPING LETTERS TRAFFIC
FUNCTION HOMOGENY HOMOLOGY
SYMMETRY SYMPATHY
(**INCOMPLETE** —) ASSONANCE
CORRESPONDENT QUADRATE
RELEVANT STRINGER SUITABLE
STRINGMAN
CORRESPONDING LIKE SIMILAR
CONGRUENT
CORRESPONDINGLY SORTLY
SIMILARLY
CORRIDA BULLFIGHT
CORRIDOR HALL AISLE ORIEL VISTA
ARCADE COULOIR GALLERY
PASSAGE COULISSE HALLCIST
TRESANCE
CORRIE CIRQUE
CORRIGENDUM ERRATUM
CORROBORATE PROVE SECOND
APPROVE COMFORT CONFIRM
SUPPORT SUSTAIN ROBORATE
CORRODE EAT BITE BURN ETCH
FRET GNAW RUST DECAY ERODE
EXEDE TOUCH WASTE BEGNAW
CANKER IMPAIR CONSUME
GRAPHITE
CORRODING BITE RODENT ESURINE
CORROSION EROSION EMBAYMENT
CORROSIVE ACID ACRID ARDENT
BITING CORSIE EATING CAUSTIC
EROSIVE ESURINE FRETFUL
MORDANT DIERETIC
CORRUGATE CRIMP CRISP FURROW
RUMPLE CRINKLE CRUMPLE
WRINKLE
CORRUGATED PLAITED WRINKLY
FURROWED WRINKLED
CORRUGATION BAT FOLD GILL
REED CREASE PUCKER CRINKLE
WRINKLE
CORRUPT BAD ILL LOW ROT WEM
EVIL RANK SICK SOIL VILE BLEND
BRIBE FALSE SPOIL STAIN SULLY
TAINT VENAL VENOM WEMMY
AUGEAN CANKER DEBASE DEFILE
FESTER IMPURE INFECT PALTER
POISON PUTRID RAVISH ROTTEN
SEPTIC ABUSIVE ATTAINT BEDEVIL
BEGRIME BESHREW CARRION
CORRUMP CROOKED DEBAUCH
DEFINED DEGRADE DEPRAVE
ENVENOM FALSIFY IMMORAL
PECCANT PERVERT POLLUTE
PUTREFY SUBVERT TRADING
VIOLATE VITIATE CONFOUND
DEPRAVED EMPOISON PERVERSE
POLLUTED PRACTICE PRACTISE
SINISTER VITIATED
CORRUPTED SICK
CORRUPTION DIRT SOIL VICE
DECAY SPOIL TAINT JOBBERY
PRAVITY SQUALOR ADULTERY
INFECTION

CORSAC ADIVE KARAGAN
CORSAGE WAIST BODICE BOUQUET
CANEZOU
CORSAIR BUG CAPER PIRATE
ROBBER CURSARO PICAROON
ROCKFISH
CORSELET THORAK ALLECRET
HALECRET
CORSET BELT BUSK STAY STAYS
GIRDLE SUPPORT
CORSICA (**CAPITAL OF** —) AJACCIO
(**HARBOR OF** —) BASTIA
(**MOUNTAIN OF** —) CINTO ROTONDO
(**RIVER OF** —) GOLO TARAVO
GRAVONE
(**TOWERLIKE STRUCTURES OF** —)
TORRI
(**TOWN OF** —) CALVI CORTE ALERIA
BASTIA AJACCIO SARTENE
(**VEGETATION OF** —) MAQUIS
CORSICAN PINE LARCH
CORTEGE POMP SUITE TRAIN
PARADE RETINUE
CORTEX BARK PEEL RIND MANTLE
PALLIUM PERIBLEM PERIDIUM
CORUNDUM RUBY SAND EMERY
ADAMAS ALUMINA ABRASIVE
AMETHYST CORINDON SAPPHIRE
BARKLYITE
(**SYNTHETIC** —) EMERALD
CORUSCATE BLAZE FLASH GLEAM
SHINE GLANCE GLISTEN GLITTER
RADIATE SPARKLE BRANDISH
CORVEE POLO
CORYZA COLD
COSCET COTTAR COTARIUS
COTSETLE
COSMETIC WASH CREAM FUCUS
HENNA LINER PAINT PETER ROUGE
BLANCH CERUSE CRAYON ENAMEL
POMADE POWDER MASCARA
STIBIUM LIPSTICK STIBNITE
COSMIC VAST MUNDANE ORDERLY
CATHOLIC INFINITE
COSMOLABE PANTACOSM
COSMOPOLITAN URBAN ECUMENIC
PANDEMIC AMPHIGEAN
COSMOS EARTH GLOBE ORDER
REALM WORLD FLOWER HEAVEN
HARMONY UNIVERSE
COSSACK TURK TATAR ATAMAN
HETMAN TARTAR ZAPOROGUE
COSSET MUD PET LAMB CARESS
CODDLE CUDDLE FONDLE PAMPER
TIDDLE
COSSETTE CHIP SLICE STRIP
SCHNITZEL
COST SIT GAFF LOSS PAIN SOAK
BASIS PRICE SPEND STAND VALUE
CHARGE DAMAGE OUTLAY SCATHE
EXPENSE REPRISE ESTIMATE
SPENDING

COSTA RICA
CAPE: ELENA VELAS BLANCO
CAPITAL: SANJOSE
COIN: COLON CENTIMO
DANCE: PUNTO TORITO

GULF: DULCE NICOYA PAPAGAYO
INDIAN: BORUCA GUAYMI
ISLAND: COCO
LAKE: ARENAL
MEASURE: VARA CAFIZ CAHIZ
FANEGA TERCIA CAJUELA
CANTARO MANZANA
MOUNTAIN: BLANCO CHIRRIPO
PENINSULA: OSA NICOYA
POINT: QUEPOS CAHUITA
GALONOS LLERENA
PORT: LIMON PUNTARENAS
RIVER: POAS IRAZU MATINA
SIXAOLA TENORIA TARCOLES
TOWN: CANAS LIMON VESTA
BORUCA NICOYA BAGACES
CARTAGO GOLFITO HEREDIA
LIBERIA NEGRITA ALAJUELA
COLORADO GUAPILES
VOLCANO: POAS IRAZU
WEIGHT: BAG CAJA LIBRA

COSTERMONGER COSTER HAWKER
NIPPER PEARLY PEDDLER
BARROWMAN
COSTIVE BOUND EMPLASTIC
COSTLINESS DEARTH DEARNESS
COSTLY DEAR FINE HIGH RICH SALT
DAINTY LAVISH SILVER COSTFUL
COSTLEW GORGEOUS PLATINUM
PRECIOUS PRODIGAL SPLENDID
COSTMARY TANSY ALECOST
MAUDLIN ROSEMARY
COSTREL KEG HEAD FLASK BOTTLE
COYSTREL
COSTUME RIG GARB ROBE SARI
SUIT BURKA DRESS GETUP HABIT
SHAPE TRUSS ATTIRE DOMINO
FORMAL SETOUT TOILET APPAREL
BLOOMER CLOTHES POLLERA
RAIMENT SCARLET UNIFORM
CHARSHAF CLOTHING ENSEMBLE
TOILETTE VENETIAN
(**ACADEMIC** —) GUISE
COSTUSROOT PACHAK
COSY FEEL FEIL
COT BED HUT MAT PEN BOAT COOP
COTE FOLD ABODE BOTHY CABIN
COUCH COVER HOUSE STALL
COTEEN CRADLE GURNEY PALLET
SHEATH TANGLE CHARPAI CHARPOY
COTTAGE SHELTER BEDSTEAD
COTHOUSE DWELLING STRETCHER
COTERIE SET RING CABAL JUNTO
MONDE CIRCLE CLIQUE GALAXY
SETOUT CENACLE CIRCUIT COLLEGE
PLATOON SOCIETY
COTHURNUS BOOT BUSKIN
COTHURN
COTILLION GERMAN
COTO OREJON
COTTA KATHA STOLE MANTLE
BLANKET SURPLICE VESTMENT
COTTAGE BOX COT HUT BACH BARI
COSH CRIB SHED WALK BOWER
CABIN HOUSE HOVEL LODGE SHACK
BOHAWN CABANA CHALET SHELTER
BUNGALOW COTHOUSE SHEELING

SHIELING THALTHAN
COTTAGE CHEESE SKYR
SMEARCASE
COTTER KEY MAT PIN VEX CLOT
BOWPIN COTMAN FASTEN MAILER
POTTER PUCKER SHRINK TOGGLE
WITHER CONGEAL COTTIER
PEASANT SHRIVEL VILLEIN
COTARIUS COTTAGER COTTEREL
ENTANGLE FORELOCK LINCHPIN
COTTON SAK BEAT DRAB FLOG
PIMA AGREE BAYAL BOLLY DERRY
MATTA SAKEL SURAT BROACH
CODDLE COMBER DHURRY FABRIC
MAARAD MALLOW NANKIN PEELER
STAPLE ALGODON BENDERS
BOMBACE DHURRIE GARMENT
GINNING SILESIA SUCCEED
(— SQUARE) TZUT TZUTE
(BOLL OF —) SNAP
(NAPPED —) LAMBSKIN
(PAINTED —) INDIENNE
(PIECE OF —) SPONGE
(PRINTED —) SARONG
(RAW —) LINT BAYAL
(SILK —) FLOSS
(STRIPED —) BENGAL
(TREE —) MACO
(TWILLED —) JEAN SALLO SALLOO
(WAD OF —) TAMPON
(WASTE —) GRABBOTS
COTTON GRASS CANNA CANNACH
DRAWLING
COTTON PLANT LAMB
(— FLOWER) SQUARE
COTTON TREEE SIMAL
COTYLEDON BUTTON PICHURIM
COUCH BED COT KIP LAY LIE HIDE
LAIR LURK SOFA SUNK DIVAN INLAY
LODGE PRESS SKULK SLINK SNEAK
SNOOP SQUAB SQUAT UTTER
BURROW CLOTHE DAYBED LITTER
PALLET PLINTH SETTEE CONCEAL
EXPRESS HAMMOCK OTTOMAN
OVERLAY RECLINE TRANSOM
(NUPTIAL —) THORE
COUCH GRASS CUTCH KUTCH
QUACK QUICK TWICH QUITCH
SCOTCH SCUTCH STROIL QUICKEN
WITHVINE
COUGAR CAT PUMA PAINTER
PANTHER CARCAJOU
COUGH YEX YOX BAFF BARK HACK
HOST CROUP HOAST HOOSE HOOZE
TUSSIS
COUGH DROP PASTIL TROCHE
LOZENGE PASTILLE
COUGH SYRUP LINCTUS
COULEE DRAW GORGE GULCH
COOLEY RAVINE
COULOMB WEBER
COUMA SORVA HYAHYA
COUNCIL BODY BULE DAEL DIET
DUMA FONO RAAD REDE YUAN
BOARD BOULE BUNGA CABAL
CAPUT DIVAN DIWAN DOUMA JIRGA
JUNTA JUNTO SABHA SOBOR STATE
SYNOD THING JIRGAH LUKIKO
MAJLIS POWWOW QUORUM SENATE

SOVIET TARYBA CABILDO CABINET
CHAMBER CONSULT GERUSIA
HUSTING MEETING PENSION
WHITLEY ASSEMBLY CONCLAVE
CONGRESS FOLKMOOT FOLKMOTE
HEEMRAAD HEEMRAAT MINISTRY
PLACITOM RIGSRAAD
COUNCILLOR RAT VIZIR ENDUNA
INDUNA VIZIER FAIPULE SENATOR
WISEMAN
COUNSEL RAD LORE REDE RULE
RUNE SILK WARD WARN AREED
CHIDE DEVIL GUIDE ADVICE ADVISE
CONFER LEADER ABOGADO
CAUTION COUNCIL LECTURE
ADMONISH ADVOCATE PRUDENCE
(JUNIOR LEGAL —) DEVIL
(KING'S —) SILK
(SACRED —) TORAH
COUNSELOR RAT SAGE WITE
CONSUL LAWYER MENTOR NESTOR
ADVISER ADVISOR COUNSEL
ECHEVIN GONZALO PROCTOR
STARETS ADVOCATE ATTORNEY
REDESMAN UCALEGON
COUNT ADD GAN SUM TOT BANK
CAST EARL FOOT GANO GRAF NAME
RELY RIME SIZE TALE TELL TOTE
COMES COMPT COMTE GRAVE
JUDGE RHYME SCORE TALLY WEIGH
CENSUS CONSUL COUNTY DEPEND
ESTEEM FIGURE IMPUTE NUMBER
RECKON TOTTLE ACCOUNT ARTICLE
ASCRIBE COMPUTE GANELON
ADNUMBER NUMERATE SANCTION
(— IN BILLIARDS) DOUBLE
(— OF A FIBER) GRIST
(— OF SHEEP OR CATTLE) BREAK
(— ON) LITE RELY
(— UNIT) WARP
COUNTABLE DISCRETE
COUNTENANCE AID MUG OWN RUD
ABET BROW FACE GIZZ LEER MIEN
PUSS SHOW VULT CHEER FAVOR
FRONT GRACE ASPECT ENDURE
UPHOLD VISAGE APPROVE BEARING
CONDUCT ENDORSE FEATURE
PROFFER SUPPORT BEFRIEND
DEMEANOR FOREHEAD SANCTION
COUNTER BAR DIB LOT BANK BUCK
CENT CHIP DESK DUMP EDDY FISH
JACK KIST PAWN STOP CAROM
CHECK FORCE HATCH JETON PIECE
SHELF STALL STAND TABLE TOTER
BUFFET COMBAT GEIGER ISLAND
JETTON MARKER OPPOSE SQUAIL
ADVERSE BUTTOCK CONTEND
CURRENT FANTAIL SHAMBLE
CONTRARY MAHOGANY OPPOSITE
TELLTALE
(— TO) AGAINST
(LEADEN —) DUMP
(LUNCH —) PLACE
COUNTERACT CHECK CANCEL
OPPOSE RESIST THWART BALANCE
CORRECT DESTROY NULLIFY
ANTIDOTE NEGATIVE
COUNTERACTION DEADLOCK
COUNTERACTIVE REMEDY
ADVERSE

COUNTERBALANCE COVER WEIGH
CANCEL SETOFF BALANCE
COUNTERCLOCKWISE DIRECT
DIRECTLY
COUNTERCURRENT BACKSET
COUNTEREARTH ANTICHTHON
COUNTERFEIT ACT BASE COIN
COPY DAUB DUFF FAKE IDOL MOCK
SHAM BELIE BOGUS DUMMY FALSE
FEIGN FLASH FORGE FUDGE GAMMY
MIMIC PHONY QUEER SNIDE AFFECT
ASSUME CHEMIC ERSATZ FORGED
PSEUDO TINSEL CHEMICK DUFFING
FALSIFY FASHION FEIGNED
FORGERY IMITANT IMITATE
DEFORMED POSTICHE POSTIQUE
RESEMBLE SIMILIZE SIMULATE
SPURIOUS SUPPOSED
COUNTERFEITER COINER JACKMAN
JARKMAN SCRATCHER
COUNTERFEITING COINING FICTION
POSTICHE POSTIQUE
COUNTERFOIL FOIL STUB CHECK
COUNTERFORT SCONCE BUTTRESS
COUNTERION GEGENION
COUNTERIRRITANT MOXA GINGER
IODINE PEPPER MUSTARD
CANTHARIS
COUNTERMAND STOP ANNUL
CANCEL FORBID RECALL REVOKE
ABOLISH RESCIND REVERSE
UNORDER ABROGATE PROHIBIT
COUNTERMOVE DEMARCHE
COUNTERMOVEMENT BACKFIRE
COUNTERPANE PANE LIGGER
BEDSPREAD
COUNTERPART COPY LIKE MATE
SPIT TWIN FETCH IMAGE MATCH
MORAL SHELL TALLY COUSIN
DOUBLE SHADOW BALANCE
COUNTER OBVERSE PENDANT
SIMILAR ANTIPART PARALLEL
RESCRIPT
(SPEECH —) A
COUNTERPOINT FOIL DESCANT
CONTRAST
COUNTERPOISE POISE OFFSET
BALANCE EQUALIZE
COUNTERPOISON ORVIETAN
COUNTERSIGN BACK MARK SEAL
SIGN SIGNAL CONFIRM ENDORSE
PASSWORD SANCTION
COUNTERSINK DISH REAM BEVEL
CHAMFER
COUNTERSTATEMENT ANSWER
COUNTERSUN ANTHELION
COUNTERWEIGHT TARE
COUNTERWORD ANIMAL COUNTER
COUNTESS OLIVIA COMTESSE
CONTESSA
COUNTLESS INFINITE
COUNTIFIED JAY BUCOLIC
LOBBISH HOBNAILED
COUNTRY SOD DESH EARD HICK
HOME KITH LAND PAIS SOIL ADDLE
EARTH FAIRY FRITH MARCH PLAGE
REALM STATE TRACT WEALD
GROUND KINTRA KINTRY NATION
PEOPLE REGION STICKS UPLAND

IMAMATE KWINTRA MONKERY
MUFASAL DISTRICT DOMINION
ELDORADO LANDWARD MAGAZINE
MOFUSSIL REGALITY
(— OF ETHIOPIA) SEBA
(— OF ORIGIN) HOMELAND
(— OF PERFECTION) EUTOPIA
(— ON SEA) SEABOARD
(— STYLE) PAYSANNE
(ANCIENT —) ARAM
(CABIN —) LOBBY
(FRONTIER —) BORDER
(IMAGINARY —) LILLIPUT
(MARITIME —) MAREMMA
(MYTHICAL —) UTOPIA LEONNOYS
SVITHIOD SWITHIOD TEUTONIA
(OPEN —) BLED VELD FIELD VELDT
WEALD CAMPAIGN
(PETTY —) TOPARCHY
(ROUGH —) BOONDOCK BUNDOCKS
COUNTRYMAN HOB BOOR HIND
KERN TIKE CHURL CLOWN HODGE
KERNE SWAIN YOKEL GAFFER
GIBARO JIBARO GRANGER HAYSEED
LANDMAN PAISANO PEASANT
PLOWMAN LANDSMAN
(PL.) KITH
COUNTRYSIDE BLED BOCAGE
MOFUSSIL
COUNTY AMT LAN SEAT FYLKE
SHIRE DOMAIN PARISH BOROUGH
COMITAT NORFOLK DISTRICT
COUP BUY BLOW DEAL PLAN PLAY
COUPE FAULT SCOOP UPSET
ATTACK BARTER REFAIT STRIKE
STROKE CAPSIZE TRAFFIC
OVERTURN
COUP DE POING BOUCHER
HANDSTONE
COUPE CUT CABRIOLET LANDAULET
COUPED HUMETTY HUMETTEE
COUPLE DUO TIE TWO BOND CASE
DYAD JOIN LINK MATE PAIR SPAN
TEAM TWIN YOKE BRACE LEASH
MARRY TWAIN UNITE GEMINI SPLINE
SWINGE BRACKET CONNECT
COUPLER COUPLET DOUBLET
SHACKLE TWOSOME VOLTAIC
ACCOUPLE ASSEMBLE COPULATE
COUPLED GEMEL YOKED JOINED
WEDDED GEMELED COPULATE
GEMINATE
COUPLER LINK RING BOBBER
COPULA JANNEY LINKER SUTURE
UNITER DRAGBAR DRAWBAR
REDUCER SHACKLE SNAPPER
TIRASSE DRAGBOLT DRAWBOLT
DRAWGEAR SHACKLER
COUPLET BAIT COPLA ELEGIAC
COUPLING HUB HICKY UNION
CLUTCH HICKEY NIPPLE SHACKLE
SHACKLER
COUPON TWOFER
COURAGE BIEL FIRE GRIT GUTS
MIND MOOD PROW SAND SOUL
BIELD CREST HEART HONOR NERVE
PLUCK SPUNK VALOR DARING
DAUBER METTLE PECKER SPIRIT
VIRTUE VIRTUS BRAVERY COJONES

CORAGIO HEROISM MANHEAD
MANHOOD MANSHIP PROWESS
VENTURE AUDACITY BOLDNESS
FIRMNESS TENACITY
(— OF CONVICTION) STAMINA
(MORAL —) STRENGTH
COURAGEOUS BOLD GAME GOOD
TALL BRAVE GUTSY HARDY LUSTY
MANLY STOUT DARING HEROIC
MANFUL PLUCKY SPUNKY CORIAUS
GALLANT SPARTAN STAUNCH
VALIANT FEARLESS GENEROUS
INTREPID VALOROUS
COURAGEOUSLY BIG BRAVELY
COURANT ROMP CAPER DANCE
LETTER CORANTO CURRENT
GAZETTE RUNNING
COURBARIL JATOBA LOCUST
GUAPINOL CUAPINOLE
COURIER NEWS POST GUIDE SCOUT
KAVASS NEWING POSTER ESTAFET
ORDERLY PATAMAR POSTBOY
POSTMAN SOILAGE CICERONE
CURSITOR DRAGOMAN HORSEMAN
ORDINARY PATTAMAR
COURLAN LIMPKIN
COURONNE CROWN
COURSE FLY LAP RUN WAY BEAT
BENT FLOW GAGE GAME GANG
GATE HEAT HUNT LANE LINE LODE
MESS MODE PACE PATH RACE
RACK RAND RILL RING RINK ROAD
ROTA ROTE WENT CLASS COURS
CRUST CURRY CURVE CYCLE DRAFT
DRIFT DRIVE EMBER GAUGE GREAT
LAPSE LAYER LEDGE MARCH
MOYEN ORBIT PLATE POINT ROUTE
SENSE SITHE SPACE STEPS SWELT
SWING TENOR TRACK TRACT TRADE
TRAIL TREND WEENT ARTERY
CAREER COPING CURSUS DROMOS
FURROW GALLOP GIRDER GUTTER
HONORS MANNER METHOD MOTION
RESACA SCHOOL SERIES SPHERE
STREAM STREET SYSTEM TRIPOS
ZODIAC AZIMUTH BEELINE CHANNEL
CIRCUIT CONDUCT DIAULOS
DRAUGHT HIGHWAY LECTURE
PASSADE PASSAGE PATHWAY
PROCESS ROUTINE RUNNING
SEMINAR SERVICE STRETCH
SUBJECT SUCCESS TIDEWAY
TRAJECT TRUNDLE CURRENCY
CURRICLE DISTANCE ELECTIVE
PROGRESS RECOURSE SEQUENCE
STEERAGE TENDENCY
(— OF A ROPE) LEAD
(— OF ACTION) LARK TROD VEIN
DANCE CUSTOM ROUTINE
DEMARCHE
(— OF ACTIVITY) SIDELINE
(— OF BOAT) LEG
(— OF BRICK) BED ROWLOCK
SCINTLE CREASING
(— OF FEEDING) DIET
(— OF KNITTING) BOUT
(— OF LIFE) GOINGS
(— OF LUCK) FORTUNE
(— OF MASONRY) BAHUT STILT

COPING HEADING SKEWBACK
(— OF NATURE) TAO
(— OF PROCEDURE) RULE
(— OF PROCEEDING) FORE
(— OF PURSUIT) SCENT
(— OF ROADBED) SUBCRUST
(— OF STONES) BED PLINTH
(— OF STUDY) DEBATE COLLEGE
LECTURE SEMINAR ELECTIVE
(— OF SUN) JOURNEY
(— OF TREATMENT) CURE
(— OF WALL) CORNICE
(— WITH GREYHOUNDS) GREW
(BELL-RINGING —) HUNT
(CIRCULAR —) SWEEP CHUKKAR
CHUKKER COMPASS
(CURVING —) SWING
(CUSTOMARY —) GUISE
(DOWNWARD —) DIP DECLINE
TOBOGGAN
(EASY —) PIPE
(EXACT —) BEAM
(FIRST —) ANTEPAST
(FREE —) FORTH
(IRREGULAR —) ERROR
(LAST —) VOID
(MIDDLE —) MIDS TEMPER
(NATURAL —) RITA
(OBLIQUE —) SKEW
(OVERHANGING —) JET
(PREDETERMINED —) DESTINY
(ROUNDABOUT —) DETOUR
WINDLASS
(SETTLED —) BIAS GROOVE
(SKIING —) SCHUSS
COURSER HORSE RACER STEED
CUSSER CHARGER
COURSING CURSIVE
COURT BAR BID SEE SUE WOO AREA
BAIL BODY CLAW FUSS GATE GIRL
LEET QUAD ROTA SEAT SEEK SUIT
TOWN WALE WARD WYND YARD
ARENA BENCH BUREO CURIA CURRY
DAIRI DIVAN FAVOR FORUM FUERO
GARTH JUDGE PATIO SHIRE SPACE
SPARK SPOON SWEET TEMPT THING
THINK TOURN TRAIN YAMEN
ADALAT ALLURE ATRIUM BAILEY
COUNTY DARGAH DURBAR DURGAH
GEMOTE HOMAGE INVITE PALACE
PARVIS SPLUNT SUITOR TOLSEY
ADAWLUT ADDRESS ASSIZES
ATTRACT BARMOTE DUOVIRI
EPHETAE FOREIGN HELIAEA
HUSTING JUSTICE RETINUE SOLICIT
TEMENOS TOURNEL AUDIENCE
BURHMOOT CHANCERY FOUJDARY
LAWCOURT MARKMOOT MARKMOTE
QUARANTY SERENADE SESSIONS
SWANMOTE TRIBUNAL WOODMOTE
(— FAVOR) FAWN
(— OF A HUNDRED) MALL MALLUM
MALLUS
(— OF CIRCUIT JUDGES) EYRE
(— OF FORTRESS) PEEL
(— OF MIKADO) DAIRI
(— ORDER) VACATUR
(— THE GREAT) LEVEE
(ECCLESIASTICAL —) ROTA CURIA

SYNOD COLLOQUY AUDIENCIA
(EXERCISE —) EPHEBEUM
(FORTIFIED —) BAWN
(INNER —) PATIO
(MUSLIM —) DIVAN DIWAN
(REFORMED —) CLASIS
(SMALL —) WIND WYND
(SUPREME —) SUDDER
(TURKISH —) GATE
COURTEOUS FAIR HEND BUXOM
CIVIL GENTY SUAVE BONAIR
GENTLE POLITE SMOOTH URBANE
AFFABLE CORDIAL GALLANT
GENTEEL GENTILE REFINED
DEBONAIR FAMILIAR GRACIOUS
OBLIGING
COURTEOUSLY FAIR FAIRLY
GENTLY KINDLY AFFABLY
COURTESAN MADAM QUAIL THAIS
WHORE COURTY GEISHA LALAGE
MADAME PLOVER AMOROSA
CANIDIA PUCELLE DEVADASI
(PL.) DEMIMONDE
COURTESY MENSK COMITY EXTENT
GENTRY MANSHIP TASHRIF
CALIDORE CORTEISE ELEGANCE
GENTRICE GRATUITY URBANITY
(PL.) HONORS
COURTHOUSE CUTCHERY
COURTIER CURAN OSRIC WOOER
OSRICK COURTER IACHIMO
COURTMAN POLONIUS
COURTING SUING SPLUNT
COURTLY HEND AULIC CIVIL HENDE
POLITE AULICAL ELEGANT REFINED
STATELY POLISHED DIGNIFIED
COURT-NOUE RONCET
COURTSHIP SUIT AMOUR DRURY
SPARKING
COURTYARD AREA WYND CURIA
PATIO TRANCE CORTILE TETRAGON
COUSIN COZ KIN AKIN HERO ALLIED
NEPHEW
COVE CO BAY DEN CAVE CHAP FILE
GILL HOLE NOOK PASS SUMP BASIN
BAYOU BIGHT CREEK INLET COVING
FELLOW HOLLOW RECESS VALLEY
MOLDING CALANQUE GUNKHOLE
COVENANT BIND BOND BRIS MISE
PACT TRUE AGREE BERIT BRITH
TOUCH ACCORD BERITH CARTEL
COMART CONAND ENGAGE INDENT
LEAGUE PATISE PLEDGE TREATY
BARGAIN COMPACT CONCORD
PROMISE ALLIANCE CONTRACT
DOCUMENT HANDFAST TREATISE
COVENANTER HILLMAN
COVER DO CAP COT HAP LAP LAY
LID NAP TOP TUP WRY BIND CEIL
CLAD COAT COOM CURE DAUB
DECK FACE FADE FALL FURL GARB
GATE HEAD HEAL HEEL HIDE HILL
HOOD LATH LEAD LEAP LINE MASK
PAVE ROOF SILE SPAN TELD TICK
TIDE TILT VEIL APRON BATHE
BOARD CLOAK CLOUT COPSE
CROWN DRAPE DRESS FENCE
FLESH FLOOD GUISE HATCH KIVER
MOUNT RECTO SCARF SERVE

SHADE STREW STUDY THEAK THEEK
TOWEL TREAD VERSO WELME
WHALM AWNING BATTER BINDER
BLAZON CANOPY CHALON CLOTHE
DOUBLE EARLAP ENAMEL ENCASE
ENFOLD ENTIRE ENVEIL FOLDER
HACKLE IMMASK INVEST JACKET
KIRTLE MANTLE OVERGO POTLID
RUNNER SCONCE SCREEN SHADOW
SHEATH SHIELD SLEEVE SPREAD
SPRING SWATHE TOILET TOPPER
WHAUVE APPAREL ASPHALT
BANDAGE BESTREW BLANKET
CAPSULE CONCEAL CONTECT
COUVERT ELYTRON EMBRACE
ENCRUST FASCINE HEADCAP
HOUSING INCRUST KNEECAP
MANHEAD OBSCURE OMNIBUS
OVERLAY PRETEXT SHEATHE
SHELTER SHUTTER TAMPION
THIMBLE BEDCOVER COMPRISE
COVERCLE DEBRUISE ENCLOTHE
ENSCONCE HOODWINK IMMANTLE
OVERHAIL OVERSILE OVERWEND
PALLIATE PRETENCE PRETENSE
SLIPOVER SURPOOSE
(— A FIRE) DAMP
(— AROUND FLOWER) CYMBA
(— BRICKS) SCOVE
(— FOR ALEMBIC) HEAD
(— FOR CHALICE) PALL
(— FOR DIAPER) SOAKER
(— FOR ENGINE) COWLING
(— FOR FOOD) BELL
(— FOR GUN) TAMPION
(— FOR MILITARY CAPE) HAVELOCK
(— FOR PISTON) FOLLOWER
(— FOR POWDER PAN) HAMMER
(— FOR WIRES) BOOTLEG
(— GROUND) HEAT
(— HEARTH) FETTLE
(— OF BALL) CARCASS
(— OF BOILER) VOMIT
(— OF COFFIN) COOM
(— OF HAWSEHOLE) BUCKLER
(— OF MINE CAGE) BONNET
(— OF RIFLE MAGAZINE) GATE
(— OF SPORANGIUM) EPIGONE
(— OF VEGETATION) GROWTH
(— OPPRESSIVELY) SMOTHER
(— OVER) RAKE WELME WHELM
QUELME SHEUGH BECLOUD
OVERDECK WITHHELE
(— PLANTS) BAG
(— PROTECTIVELY) SHROUD
SHEATHE
(— ROAD) BLIND
(— SOIL WITH CLAY) GAULT
(— UP) HAP BELY FOLD BELIE
SALVE SLEEK HUDDLE
(— WITH ASHES) SOIL
(— WITH BACON) BARD
(— WITH CLAY) CLOAM
(— WITH COWL) MOB
(— WITH CRUMBS) BREAD
(— WITH DOTS) CRIBBLE
(— WITH DROPS) DAG
(— WITH EARTH) BURY HEAL INTER
(— WITH FILM) SKIM

(— WITH FLESH) INCARN
(— WITH FOAM) EMBOSS
(— WITH GOLD) GILD
(— WITH MEAL) MELVIE
(— WITH MUD) BEMUD BELUTE
(— WITH OAKUM) FOTHER
(— WITH PITCH) PAY
(— WITH PLASTER) PARGET
(— WITH SHEATH) GLOVE
(— WITH SOLDER) SPLASH
(— WITH STONE) ASHLAR
(— WITH STRAW) THATCH
(— WITH TIN) BLANCH
(— WITH TOPSOIL) KELLY
(— WITH WATER) DOUSE DOWSE
FLOOD WHELM
(— WITH WAX) CERE
(— WITH WEAVING) GRAFT
(— WITH WINGS) BROOD
(BED —S) HEALING
(BEEHIVE —) QUILT
(BOOK —) CASE SIDE
(GLASS —) STRIKE
(PACK —) MANTA
(POSTAL —) ENTIRE
(POT —) BRED
(SADDLE —) PILCH HOUSING
(SLIDING —) BRIDGE
(TABLE —) BAIZE
(WING — OF BEETLE) SHARD
COVERALL GOWN JUMPER
COVERED CLAD FULL SHOD TECT
BLIND MOSSY CLOSED COVERT
HIDDEN ENCASED OBTECTED
SCREENED
(— WITH CRYSTALS) DRUSY
(— WITH FEATHERS) HIRSUTE
(— WITH FOREST) HYLEAN
(— WITH HAIRS) COMATE VILLOUS
(— WITH PROTUBERANCES) HUMPY
(— WITH SCALES) SCUTATE
(— WITH SEAWEED) TANGLY
(THINLY —) BARISH
COVERED WAGON WHITETOP
BUCKWAGON
COVERER DECKER
COVERING (ALSO SEE COVER) BOX
COT FUR HAP KEX ARIL BARB BARK
BOOT CASE CAUL CUFF DECK FILM
HAME HEAD HOOD HULL HUSK KELL
MASK OVER PALL PUFF ROBE ROOF
SLIP SPAT TARP TILE TILT TRAP
VEIL APRON ARMOR BRAID BURSE
CRUST DRESS GLOBE GLOVE
HATCH QUILT SCALE SHELL SKIRT
STALL SWARD TESTA TUNIC TWEEL
WREIL ARMING AWNING BANCAL
BANKER CANOPY CANVAS COVERT
DRAPET EMBRYO ENAMEL FACING
FENDER GAITER GANOIN HACKLE
HATCAP HELMET JACKET MUZZLE
PELAGE SADDLE SCREEN SHEATH
SHROUD SINDON VERNIX BUFFONT
CAMISIA CAPSULE CEILING COATING
COWLING EARFLAP ENVELOP
EXCIPLE GRATING HAPPING
HEALING HEELCAP HOUSING
MUFFLER OVERLAY PURPORT
SARPLER SHADING SHELTER

SHOEING SLIPPER TECTURE
TEGMENT VESTURE WRAPPER
ARMGUARD BLAZONRY BOARDING
CASEMENT CLEADING CLOTHING
COMPRESS COVERLET EGGSHELL
EPISPORE INDUMENT INDUSIUM
MANTELET MANTLING OVERCAST
PAVILION PERICARP SETATION
UMBRELLA
(— FOR BENCH) BANKER
(— FOR BOXERS' HANDS) CESTUS
(— FOR NECK) TUCKER
(— FOR ROOF APEX) EPI
(— FOR SHOULDERS) STOLE
(— FOR SKI) SKIN
(— FOR STIRRUP) HOOD
(— OF BED) TIKE
(— OF BELL ROPE) GRIP
(— OF BIRD) INDUMENT
(— OF BOW HANDLE) ARMING
(— OF CASH SHORTAGE) LAPPING
(— OF FEATHERS) DOWN
(— OF NUTMEG) MACE
(— OF ROPE) SERVICE
(— OF VEGETATION) FLEECE
(CAST —S) EXUVIAE
(CHIMNEY —) COWL
(CLOTH —) TOILET
(COARSE —) CADDOW TILLET
(DEFENSIVE —) ARMOR KICKER
(EAR —) EARLAP EARFLAP
EARMUFF OREILET
(EYE —S) GOGGLES
(FLOOR —) RUG TILE CRASH
CARPET LINOLEUM OILCLOTH
(FOUL —) SCUM
(HEAD —) CAP HAT WIG HAIR HIVE
HOOD BONNET HELMET BIRETTA
CHAPEAU CHAPERON HAVELOCK
HEADRAIL TROTCOZY
(LEG —) BOOT HOSE STOCK GAITER
LEGGIN PEDULE KNEELET LEGGING
STOCKING
(LIGHT —) GRIMING
(LINEN —) BARB
(OUTER —) BARK HIDE HULL HUSK
CRUST TESTA JACKET CARAPACE
(PROTECTIVE —) APRON ARMOR
SHELL COCOON
(SLIGHT —) CYMAR
(STAGE —) HEAVENS
(STERILE —) DRAPE
(STICKY DAMP —) GLET
(THIN —) FILM SCRUFF WASHING
COVERLET PANE HELER HOUSE
QUILT REZAI THROW AFGHAN
CADDOW CHALON COLCHA LIGGER
SPREAD BLANKET BUFFALO
COVERLID DAGSWAIN
COVER-SHAME SAVIN SAVINE
COVERT DEN LAY LIE SLY LAIR
VERT EARTH NICHE PRIVY ASYLUM
HARBOR HIDDEN LATENT MASKED
MYSTIC REFUGE SECRET COVERED
DEFENSE PRIVATE SHELTER
TECTRIX THICKET DISGUISE
INVOLVED
(PL.) CRISSUM
COVERTLY CLOSE CLOSELY

COVET ACHE ENVY PANT WANT
WISH CRAVE YEARN YISSE DESIRE
GRUDGE HANKER
COVETOUS AVID GAIR GARE EAGER
FRUGAL GREEDY SORDID STINGY
ENVIOUS GRIPPLE MISERLY
DESIROUS GRASPING
COVETOUSNESS GREED MISERY
AVARICE YISSING COVETISE
PLEONEXIA
COVEY BEVY FALL BROOD FLOCK
HATCH COVERT COMPANY
COVIN BAND CREW FRAUD COVINE
COMPANY CONVENE ASSEMBLY
TRICKERY
COW AWE KEY NOT BEEF BOGY
BOSS COWL CUSH FAZE MOIL MULL
NOTT ROAN RUNT VACA ABASH
ALARM BEEVE BOSSY BROCK BULLY
CUSHA DAUNT DOMPT DRAPE
MOGGY QUAIL SCARE SNOOL
VACHA BOVINE BULLER COLLOP
CRUMMY GOBLIN HAWKEY HAWKIE
HEIFER MAILIE MILKER MULLEY
SUBDUE BOARDER BUGBEAR
BULLOCK CRITTER CRUMMIE
DEPRESS MESTENO MILCHER
OVERTOP SQUELCH TERRIFY
ALDERNEY AUDHUMLA BROWBEAT
COWBRUTE DISPIRIT FRIGHTEN
STRIPPER THREATEN
(— ABOUT 3 FEET HIGH) GYNEE
(— BEFORE CALVING) SPRINGER
(BARREN —) DRAPE BARRENER
(DRY —) KEY SEW
(HORNLESS —) NOT MOIL NOTT
DODDY MULEY DODDIE HUMLIE
MAILIE HUMBLIE POLLARD
MOULLEEN
(PREGNANT —) CALVER INCALVER
(WHITE-FACED —) HAWKEY HAWKIE
(YOUNG —) STIRK HEIFER
(PL.) KINE DAIRY
COWARD COW COOF DAFF FUNK
FUGIE LACHE PIKER CRAVEN
FUNKER PIGEON CAITIFF CHICKEN
COUCHER DASTARD MEACOCK
NITHING PANURGE QUITTER
NIDERING POLTROON RECREANT
TURNBACK TURNTAIL
COWARDICE DASTARDY LASHNESS
COWARDLY SHY ARGH FAINT LACHE
TIMID AFRAID COWARD COWISH
CRAVEN TURPID YELLOW CAITIFF
CHICKEN GUTLESS HILDING
FACELESS NIDERING POLTROON
RECREANT SNEAKING
COWBARN BYRE SAUR SHIPPON
VACCARY
COWBIRD BECCO BUNTING
CUCKOLD OXBITER COKEWOLD
LAZYBIRD
COWBOY HAZER RIDER ROPER
SCREW WADDI WADDY CHARRO
GAUCHO GINETE HERDER JINETE
COWHAND COWHERD COWPOKE
GRAZIER HERDBOY LLANERO
PANIOLO PUNCHER REFUGEE
VAQUERO BUCKAROO DALLYMAN

JACKAROO NEATHERD NOWTHERD
OUTRIDER PASTORAL RANCHERO
SWINGMAN WRANGLER
COWCATCHER GUARD PILOT
FENDER
COWED HANGDOG DOWNCAST
COWER HUG COUR FAWN RUCK
HOVER QUAIL SHRUG SNOOL SQUAT
STOOP TOADY WINCE COORIE
CRINGE CROUCH HURKLE SHRINK
CROODLE CRUDDLE
COWFISH TORO BECCO CUCKOLD
MANATEE SIRENIA
COWHAGE KIWACH
COWHAND PEELER FLANKER
STOCKMAN
COWHERB COCKLE SOAPWORT
COWHERD HERDSMAN NEATHERD
COWHOUSE BYRE SHIPPEN SHIPPON
COWL CAP COW LID SOE TUB COUL
HOOD MONK MITER BONNET
CUCULE CAPUCHE SCUTTLE
CAPUCHIN
COW PARSNIP MADNEP CADWEED
HOGWEED PIGWEED BEARWORT
BUNDWEED
COWPEA SITAO FRIJOL FRIJOLE
TOWCOCK BLACKEYE BLACKPEA
COWPEN CUPPEN CUPPIN
COWPOX PAPPOX KINEPOX VACCINA
VACCINIA
COWRIE COWRY VENUS ZIMBI
CYPRAEID
COWSLIP PAIGLE PRIMULA SHOOTER
AURICULA CYCLAMEN MARIGOLD
PRIMROSE
COXA HIP HAUNCH
COXCOMB FOP NOB BUCK DUDE
FOOL TOFF CLEAT DANDY HINGE
PRINCOX POPINJAY PRINCOCK
COXCOMBRY FOPPERY
COY PAL SHY ARCH COAX NICE
ALOOF CHARY DECOY QUIET SQUAB
STILL ALLURE CARESS DEMURE
MODEST PROPER BASHFUL DISTANT
PEEVISH STRANGE RESERVED
SKITTISH
COYNESS SHYNESS
COYO CHININ
COYOL COŔOJO COROZO
COYOTE VARMINT
(— STATE) SOUTHDAKOTA
COYPU DEGU NUTRIA
COZEN COG CON BILK GULL POOP
CHEAT TRICK CHISEL GREASE
BEGUILE DECEIVE DEFRAUD
SWINDLE HOODWINK
COZENER SNAP SNECKDRAW
COZENING SIMILATE
COZIER CADGER CODGER COSIER
COZY RUG BEIN BIEN COSY EASY
HOMY SAFE SNUG BIELD CANNY
CUSHY HOMEY CHATTY PENTIT
SECURE TOASTY COVERING
FAMILIAR HOMELIKE SOCIABLE
CRAB GIN UCA BOCO JUEY MAJA
ZOEA ANGER ARROW AYUYU BLUEY
MAIAN MAIID MAJID RACER SANDY
THIEF WINCH BUSTER CANCER

GROUSE HARPER HERMIT KABURI
NIPPER PARTAN PEELER PUNGAR
PUNGER RACING SPRITE BUCKLER
BUCKLUM BURSTER CABOUCA
CANCRID FIDDLER GRUMBLE
INACHID OCYPODE PANFISH
POLYPOD SHEDDER SOLDIER
SPECTER SPECTRE SURIQUE
ARACHNID CRABFISH DORIPPID
GRAPSOID HORSEMAN IRRITATE
LIMULOID LITHODID OCHIDORE
OXYSTOME PORTUNID RANINIAN
TRAVELER WINDLASS
(MATING —) DOUBLER
CRAB APPLE CRAB SCRAB SCROG
COLING
CRABBED SOUR UGLY CABBY
CROSS SURLY TESTY BITTER
COPPED CROOSE CROUSE CRUSTY
MOROSE RUGGED SULLEN TEETHY
TRYING BOORISH CANKERY
CRABBIT CRAMPED CRONISH
CROOKED FRABBIT GNARLED
KNOTTED OBSCURE PEEVISH
CHURLISH CONTRARY CRABBISH
LIVERISH PETULANT VINEGARY
CRABBEDNESS ACRIMONY
ASPERITY
CRABCATCHER CRABIER
CRABER VOLE AGOUARA
CRABGRASS DRAWK FONIO PANIC
DARNEL PANICLE CRABWEED
ELEUSINE
CRAB LOUSE CRAB MORPION
MOREPEON
CRAB PLOVER DROME
CRAB TREE GRIBBLE
CRABWOOD ANDIROBA
POISONWOOD
CRACK GAG KIN POP BANG BLOW
CHAP CHIP CHOP CLAP CONE DOKE
FENT FLAW GAIG JEST JIBE JOKE
KIBE LEAK LICK QUIP REND RIFT
RIME RIVE SCAR SLAT SNAP YERK
BRACK BREAK CHARK CHECK CHICK
CHINE CHINK CLACK CLEFT CRAKE
CRAZE FLAKE FLANK FLASH GRIKE
KNACK KNICK SCORE SHAKE SLASH
SPANG SPLIT CLEAVE CRANNY
SLITER SPIDER SPRING BLEMISH
CRACKLE CREVICE FISSURE SLIFTER
SLITHER FRACTURE HAIRLINE
STRAMASH
(— A WHIP) YERK FLANK
(— IN FLESH) KIN CHAP KIBE
(— IN FLOOR) STRAKE
(— IN INGOT) SPILL
(— IN MAST) SPRING
(— IN ROCK) GRIKE JOINT
(— IN SEA ICE) RIFTER
(— IN STEEL) CHECK SPILL
(— OPEN) SEAM
(— PETROLEUM) BURN
(— WHILE FIRING) DUNT
(PL.) CRAZE
CRACKAJACK NAILER NAILING
CRACKBRAINED CRAZY NUTTY
CRACKY ERRATIC
CRACKED FLED NECKED CHAPPED

COMICAL TOUCHED CRACKERS
CRACKER BAKE LIAR WAFER
POPPER BISCUIT BOASTER
BREAKER BURSTER COSAQUE
REDNECK SALTINE SNAPPER
(— STATE) GEORGIA
(BOILED —S) CUSH
(BROKEN —S) DUNDERFUNK
CRACKERJACK TRUMP
CRACKING CRAZE SHIVERING
(PL.) SCRAP
CRACKLE SNAP BREAK CRACK
CRISP BRUSTLE CRINKLE SPARKLE
SPUTTER
CRACKLING CRISP GREAVE SNAPPY
CRACKEL CRACKLE CREMANT
GREAVES CRACKNEL CRITLING
(PL.) SCRAPS GRIEBEN
CRACKNEL SIMNEL CRACKLING
CRACKPOT CRACK ERRATIC
LUNATIC CRANKISH
CRACKSMAN YEGG BURGLAR
PETEMAN
CRADLE BED COT CRIB REST ROCK
WOMB CRATE FRAME CRECHE
MATRIX ROCKER TROUGH BERCEAU
SHELTER BASSINET CUNABULA
(— FOR SHIP) BED SLEE
(— FOR VATS) STILLING STILLION
(— IN ARCHERY) PURSE
(CERAMICS —) CHUM
(GRAIN —) CADAR CADER
(PL.) CHOCKS
CRADLESONG BERCEUSE
CRADLING BRACK
CRAFT ART BARK BOAT SAIL FRAUD
GUILE SKILL TRADE BARQUE
BATEAU DECEIT DROGER METIER
MISTER POLICE ROADER STRUSE
TALENT VESSEL ABILITY CUNNING
DROGHER MYSTERY PANURGY
SLEIGHT APTITUDE ARTIFICE
BASKETRY VOCATION
(ANTIQUATED OR CLUMSY —)
HOOKER
CRAFTILY FOXILY
CRAFTINESS DESIGN SLEIGHT
SLYNESS
CRAFTSMAN CARL HAND CARLE
CRAFT NAVVY ARTIST WRITER
ARTISAN TOHUNGA WORKMAN
LETTERER MECHANIC
CRAFTY SLY ARCH DEEP DERN FINE
FOXY SLIM WILY WISE ADEPT
COONY SLAPE SLEEK ADROIT
ARTFUL ASTUTE CALLID QUAINT
SHREWD SOLERT SUBTLE TRICKY
CUNNING SLEEKIT SLEIGHT SUBTILE
VAFROUS VERSUTE VULPINE
CAPTIOUS DEXTROUS ENGINOUS
FETCHING JESUITIC SLEIGHTY
CRAG TOR CRAW KNEE NECK ROCK
SCAR SPUR ARETE BRACK CLIFF
CLINT CRAIG HEUCH HEUGH
THROAT
CRAGGY ROUGH ABRUPT CLIFFY
CLIFTY KNOTTY PAMPER RUGGED
CRAGGED KNAGGED
CRAKE CROW RAIL ROOK RAVEN

CORNBIRD RAILBIRD
CRAKOW BEAKER CRACOWE
POULAINE
CRAM MUG RAM WAD BONE FILL
GLUT LADE PACK PANG PORR PURR
STOW TUCK URGE CROWD CRUSH
DRIVE FARCE FORCE FRANK GORGE
GRIND LEARN PRESS SCRAM STECH
STUDY STUFF TEACH AGROTE
CROMME PESTER STEEVE THRACK
CRAMMED PANG STODGY
CHOCKFUL
CRAMMER CRAM FEEDER
CRAMMING GAVAGE
CRAMP ART ARCT COOP CRIB KINK
PAIN TUCK CRICK CRIMP CROWD
DOWEL PINCH STUNT TRAMP
AGRAFE DOGTIE HAMPER HINDER
KNOTTY PESTER CONFINE CRAMPER
CRAMPET COMPRESS CONTRACT
RESTRAIN RESTRICT
CRAMPED CRIMP CRIMPED SQUEEZY
CRAMPFISH TORPEDO
CRAMPING UNEASY
CRAMPON CRAMP CRAMPET
CRAMPOON
CRANBERRY BERRY CRANE ERICAD
BOGWORT PEMBINA ACROSARC
BILBERRY BOGBERRY COWBERRY
FENBERRY FOXBERRY
(— BUSH) PIMBINA
CRANBERRY TREE PEMBINA
SNOWBALL VIBURNUM
CRANE JOB GRUS HOOK SWAY
CYRUS DAVIT HERON HOIST JENNY
RAISE SARUS TITAN WADER
BROLGA COOLEN JIGGER KULANG
SAHRAS COOLUNG CRAWLER
DERRICK GOLIATH KAIKARA
WHOOPER GRUIFORM TRAVELER
(— FOR FIREPLACE) COTTREL
COTTEREL
CRANE ARM GIB JIB GIBBET
RAMHEAD COTTEREL
CRANESBILL ALUMROOT DOVEFOOT
FLUXWEED
CRANIUM PAN HEAD CRANE CRANY
SKULL BRAINPAN
CRANK NUT WIT BENT SICK WALT
WEAK WHIM WIND BRACE LOOSE
ROGUE SHAKY THROW WALTY
WINCH AILING BOLDLY CRANKY
EVENER GROUCH HANDLE INFIRM
AWKWARD BRACKET FANATIC
LUSTILY
(SOMEWHAT —) TENDER
CRANKCASE SUMP
CRANKINESS ANGULARITY
CRANKY UGLY CRAZY CRONK
CROSS LUSTY SHAKY TESTY AILING
CRANNY FIFISH INFIRM SICKLY
CROOKED GROUCHY PERVERSE
TORTUOUS
CRANNY HOLE NOOK CHINK CLEFT
CRACK CORNER CRANNEL CREVICE
FISSURE
CRANTARA TARIE
CRANTS WREATH CORANCE
GARLAND

CRAPE BAND CURL FRIZ CREPE CRIMP DRAPE GAUZE SHROUD MOURNING

CRAPE MYRTLE JAPONICA ASTROMEDA

CRAPPIE BACH SHAD BATCH CALICO CROPPIE BACHELOR BACULERE NEWLIGHT SACALAIT TINMOUTH CHINKAPIN

CRAPS CRAP HAZARD

CRASH BASH FAIL FALL RACK BLAST BURST CLOTH CRUSH FRUSH PRANG SHOCK SMASH SOUND FIASCO FRAGOR HURTLE FAILURE SHATTER STENTER COLLAPSE ICEQUAKE SPLINTER STRAMASH **(— OF THUNDER)** CLAP

CRASHING ROPAND SMASHING

CRASH-LAND DITCH

CRASS RAW DULL LOUD RUDE CRUDE DENSE GROSS ROUGH THICK COARSE OBTUSE STUPID

CRASSNESS SQUALOR

CRATCH CRIB RACK CRITCH MANGER GRATING

CRATE BOX CAR CASE CRIB FLAT PLANE SERON BASKET CRADLE ENCASE HAMPER HURDLE CACAXTE CANASTA CARRIER PACKAGE VEHICLE **(EMPTY —)** EMPTY

CRATER CUP PIT CONE HOLE DINOS FOVEA NICHE CELEBE HOLLOW CALDERA **(— FORMED BY STEAM)** MAAR **(LUNAR —)** LINNE

CRAUNCH CRANCH SCRANCH

CRAVAT TIE TECK ASCOT FRONT SCARF STOCK CHOKER GRAVAT BANDAGE NECKTIE OVERLAY SOUBISE CRUMPLER

CRAVE ASK BEG GAPE ITCH LONG NEED PRAY SEEK WISH COVET GREED YEARN DESIRE HANKER HUNGER LINGER THIRST YAMMER BESEECH ENTREAT IMPLORE REQUEST REQUIRE SOLICIT APPETITE

CRAVEN AFRAID COWARD SCARED DASTARD COWARDLY DEFEATED OVERCOME POLTROON RECREANT SNEAKING

CRAVING AVID ITCH WANT LETCH DESIRE HUNGER THIRST LONGING APPETITE LIKEROUS TICKLING APPETENCE **(— FOR LIQUOR)** DRY **(— FOR UNNATURAL FOOD)** PICA **(ABNORMAL —)** BULIMY BULIMIA BOULIMIA

CRAW MAW CRAG CROP STOMACH

CRAWFISH KREEF

CRAWL LAG COON DRAG FAWN INCH LOOP RAMP SHUG SWIM CREEP KRAAL SLIDE SLIME SNAKE TRAIL BUSTLE CRINGE GROVEL SCRAWL SCRIDE CLAMBER SLITHER SNIGGLE TRUDGEN INCHWORM

CRAWLY CREEPY

CRAYFISH DAD CRAB YABBY YABBIE CAMARON CRAWDAD LOBSTER CAMBARUS CRABFISH CRAWFISH

CRAYON KEEL PLAN CHALK CONTE SAUCE PASTEL PENCIL SKETCH SANGUINE

CRAZE BUG FAD FLAW MAZE MODE RAGE BREAK CRACK CRUSH FEVER FUROR MANIA VOGUE DEFECT IMPAIR MADDEN MADDLE WEAKEN WHIMSY DERANGE DESTROY FASHION SHATTER WHIMSEY DISTRACT

CRAZED MAD REE AMOK LOCO WILD WOOD WOWF ZANY BALMY BATTY DAFFY DOTTY GIDDY MANIC NUTTY POTTY WACKY COOCOO DOTTLE INSANE LOONEY BERSERK FANATIC LUNATIC DATELESS DELEERIT DEMENTED DERANGED

CRAZINESS CRAZE LUNACY DEMENTIA

CRAZY (ALSO SEE CRAZED) OFF REE WET BUGS GYTE HITE LOCO WILD ZANY BATTY BEANY DAFFY DOTTY GOOFY LOONY POTTY CRANKY CUCKOO DOTTLE FRUITY INSANE LOCKET MENTAL SCATTY SCREWY CRACKED LUNATIC PEEVISH SCRANNY BUGHOUSE COCKEYED CRACKERS DERANGED HALLICET HALUCKET MESHUGGA

CREAK GIG GEIG GIRG JARG RASP YIRR CHARK CHEEP CHIRK CRAIK CRANK CROAK GRIND GROAN FRATCH SCREAK SCRIKE SCROOP SKRAIK SQUEAK COMPLAIN

CREAKING JARG SCREAK SCRIKE

CREAKY ARTHRITIC

CREAM DIP BEAT BEST FOOL HEAD REAM CREME ELITE FROTH REAME SAUCE BONBON CHOICE TRIFLE COLOGNE FATNESS EMULSION OINTMENT

CREAMING MANTLING

CREAM PUFF PUFF DUCHESSE

CREAMY RICH REAMY ACREAM SMOOTH LUSCIOUS

CREASE GAW CLAM FOLD LINE LIRK RUCK RUGA SEAM BLOCK CRESS CRIMP PLAIT PLEAT PRESS SCARF SCORE FURROW SCARPA SUTURE WREATH CRUMPLE CRUNKLE WRIMPLE WRINKLE **(SERIES OF —S)** BREAK **(PL.)** RASCETA

CREASED CRUMPLED ACCORDION

CREATE COIN CREE FORM MAKE PLAN BUILD CAUSE ERECT FORGE IMPEL RAISE SHAPE WRITE AUTHOR DESIGN IMPOSE INVENT COMPACT COMPOSE CONJURE FASHION IMAGINE PRODUCE COMPOUND GENERATE CONSTRUCT **(— A DISTURBANCE)** RIOT **(— CONFUSION)** GARBOIL

CREATION WORLD COSMOS EFFECT NATURE POETRY EDITION FACTURE FASHION POIESIS PRODUCT SHAPING BERESHIT BUSINESS CREATURE UNIVERSE **(MENTAL —)** FANTASY PHANTASY **(VISIONARY —)** DREAM

CREATIVE FERTILE FORMFUL PLASTIC POIETIC FORGEFUL GERMINAL NATURING POMATIVE

CREATOR MAKER AUTHOR FATHER FORMER VARUNA WORKER KHEPERA TAGALOA DESIGNER INVENTOR OPERATOR PRODUCER TANGALOA

CREATURE MAN FOOD TOOL BEAST BEING DABBA JOKER SLAVE THING TRICK WIGHT ANIMAL FELLOW MINION PERSON WRETCH CRITTER GANGREL MINIKIN MINIMUS SHAPING CRAYTHUR CREATION HELLICAT **(— OF LITTLE VALUE)** SHOT **(3 —S OF A KIND)** LEASH **(CANNIBALISTIC —)** WENDIGO WINDIGO **(DISORDERLY —)** ROIT ROYT **(DWARF —)** FAIRY GNOME **(ELFLIKE —)** PERI **(EVIL —)** HELLICAT **(FABLED —)** LUNG SIREN MERMAN WIVERN ALBORAK MERMAID **(LITTLE —)** MITING **(MANGY —)** RONION RONYON **(MANLIKE —)** HOMINID HOMONID HOMINIAN **(MEAN —)** LEFT **(MECHANICAL —)** GOLEM **(MISERABLE —)** SNAKE **(NONSENSE —)** SNARK **(SILLY —)** GOOSE **(SMALL —)** ATOM GRIG BEASTIE **(SPRY —)** WHIPPET **(STUNTED —)** WIRL URLING WIRLING **(SUPERNATURAL —)** MAN DRAGON **(TINY —)** ELF ATOMY **(UNDERDEVELOPED —)** SLINK **(USELESS —)** HUSHION **(VICIOUS —)** DEVIL **(WORTHLESS —)** SCULPIN SNIPJACK **(WRETCHED —)** ARMINE **(PL.)** CREATION

CRECHE CRIB PUTZ MANGER NURSERY

CREDENCE FAITH TRUST BELIEF BUFFET CREDIT CREANCE CREDENZA

CREDENTIAL VOUCHER CREDENCE

CREDENZA NICHE SHELF TABLE BUFFET SERVER CREDENCE CUPBOARD

CREDIBILITY FAITH CREDIT

CREDIBLE LIKELY CREDENT FAITHFUL PROBABLE TROWABLE

CREDIT LOAN TICK ASSET CHALK ENDOW FAITH HONOR IZZAT MENSK MERIT STRAP TENET TRUST BELIEF CHARGE ESTEEM IMPUTE RENOWN REPUTE TICKET WEIGHT ACCOUNT ASCRIBE BELIEVE CREANCE JAWBONE OPINION WORSHIP ACCREDIT CREDENCE HEADMARK **(HOCKEY —)** ASSIST

CREDITABLE HONEST CREDIBLE
  REPUTABLE
CREDITOR DEBTEE SHYLOCK
  TRUSTER ADJUDGER APPRIZER
  CRANSIER CREANCER
  (TROUBLESOME —) DUN
CREDO FAITH
CREDULITY EASINESS
CREDULOUS FOND SIMPLE SPOONY
  SPOONEY CREDIBLE GULLIBLE
CREED ISM LAY CULT SECT CREDO
  DOGMA FAITH TENET BELIEF KELIMA
  SYMBOL CREANCE KALIMAH
  TROWING DOCTRINE SYMBOLUM
CREEK BAY CUT GEO GIO GUT RIA
  RIO RUN VLY VOE BURN COVE
  HOPE KILL PILL RILL SLEW SLUE
  VLEI VLEY WASH WICK BACHE
  BAYOU BIGHT BOGUE BROOK CRICK
  DRAFT FLEET INLET ZANJA ARROYO
  BRANCH BREACH CANADA ESTERO
  SLOUGH STREAM DRAUGHT
  ESTUARY RIVULET ZANJONA
  MUSKOGEE
  (AUSTRALIAN —) COWAL
  (TIDE —) SLAKE
CREEK SEDGE THATCH
CREEL RIP CAUL CAWL HASK JACK
  KELL RACK TRAP HARSK BASKET
  JUNKET
  (— FOR BOBBINS) BANK
CREELER TUBER LIGGER
CREEP COON FAWN INCH RAMP
  CRAWL CROPE DRIFT GLIDE PROWL
  SKULK SLINK SMOOT STEAL TRAIL
  CRINGE GROVEL SCRIDE SPRAWL
  CRAMBLE CRAMMEL SNIGGLE
  TAURANGA
  (— AS IVY) RIZZLE
  (PL.) WILLIES
CREEPER IVY JITI SHOE VINE WORM
  CREEP CROPE SNAKE COWAGE
  CRADLE IPECAC REPENT ROMPER
  TECOMA CLAMPER CLIMBER
  COWHAGE COWITCH CRAWLER
  REPTANT REPTILE RUNNING
  TRAILER FOXGLOVE GUITGUIT
  PICUCULE WOODBINE
CREEPING SLOW REPTANT REPTILE
  SERVILE
CREEPING CROWFOOT SITFAST
  CRAWFOOT
CREEPING SNOWBERRY MOXA
  TEABERRY
CREESE KRIS STAB CRESS CRISE
  SWORD DAGGER
CREMATE BURN
CRENEL LOOP CORNEL KERNEL
  CRENELT
CREOLE PATOIS CRIOLLO DIALECT
  HAITIAN MESTIZO
  (— STATE) LOUISIANA
CREON (DAUGHTER OF —) GLAUCE
  (FATHER OF —) MENOECEUS
  (SISTER OF —) JOCASTA
  HIPPONOME
CREOSOTE BUSH LARREA
CREPE CRAPE FRIZZED NACARAT
  PANCAKE CHIRIMEN CRINKLED
  WRINKLED

CREPITATE SNAP GRATE RATTLE
  CRACKLE
CRESCENT HORN LUNE MOON ROOL
  CURVE LUNAR LUNOID LUNULE
  MOONED SICKLE WAXAND LUNETTE
  DEMILUNE MENISCUS
  (END OF —) CUSP HORN
CRESCENTLIKE BICORN
CRESCENT-SHAPED MOONY
  LUNATE LUNATED
CRESOL FROTHER
CRESS EKER KERSE CUCKOO
  MADWORT CRUCIFER WHITETOP
CRESSET TORCH BASKET BEACON
  SIGNAL CRISSET FLAMBEAU
CREST COP TIP TOP ACME APEX
  COMB EDGE HOOD KNAP PEAK
  SEAL TUFT CHINE CROWN PLUME
  RIDGE COPPLE CREASE CRISTA
  CUMBRE FINIAL HEIGHT HELMET
  SUMMIT TIMBER TIMBRE BEARING
  FEATHER TOPKNOT CENTROID
  CRESTING ECTOLOPH METALOPH
  PINNACLE WHITECAP
  (— OF BREAKER) SEEGE
  (— OF HELMET) COMB
  (— OF HILL) KNAP
  (— OF MINERAL VEIN) APEX
  (— OF MOUNTAIN RANGE) ARETE
  SAWBACK
  (— OF RIDGE) EDGE
  (— ON BIRD) CROWN ECKLE
  COPPLE
  (IMPERIAL —) KIKUMON
  (WAVE —) FEATHER WHITECAP
CRESTED COMBED MUFFED TAPPET
  TAPPIT COPPLED CRISATE
  CROWNED PILEATED
CRESTED GREBE CARGOOSE
CRESTED QUAIL COPPY
CRESTFALLEN COWED DEJECTED
CRESTING CHENEAU
CRETACEOUS CHALKY
CRETAN KEFTI MINOAN CANDIOT
CRETAN SPIKENARD PHU

CRETE

BAY: SUDA KANCA KISAMO
  MESARA
CAPE: BUZA LIANO SALOME
  SIDERO SPATHA STAVROS
  LITHINON SIDHEROS
GULF: KHANIA MERABELLO
MOUNTAIN: IDA DIKTE JUKTAS
  LASITHI THEODORE
MOUNTAINS: PHINO MADARAS
TOWN: HAG LATO CANEA KHORA
  SITIA ZAKRO ANOYIA CANDIA
  KHANIA KISAMO RETIMO
  KASTELLI HERAKLION

CRETIN IDIOT
CREUSA GLAUCE GLAUKE
CREUSA (FATHER OF —) CREON
  PRIAM
  (HUSBAND OF —) AENEAS
  (KILLER OF —) MEDEA
  (SON OF —) ION ASCANIUS

CREVALLE JACK JUREL
CREVASSE CHASM SPLIT SCHRUND
  CLEAVAGE
CREVICE KIN BORE LEAK NOOK
  PEEP SEAM VEIN BREAK CHINE
  CHINK CLEFT CRACK CREEK CUNNE
  GRIKE CRANNY STRAKE CRANNEL
  FISSURE GUNNIES KRAVERS
  OPENING SLIFTER CREVASSE
  PEEPHOLE
CREW LOT MEN MOB SET BAND
  GANG GING HERD OARS SHIP TEAM
  COVIN EIGHT HANDS MEINY PARTY
  SQUAD STAFF COVINE MEINIE
  SEAMEN THRONG AIRCREW
  COMPANY FACULTY MANNING
  MEMBERS RETINUE EQUIPAGE
  (— OF SHEARERS) BOARD
CREWEL CRUEL CADDIS CADDICE
CRIB BED BIN BOX CAB COT CUB
  HUT KEY BOOM CRUB CURB DIVE
  JACK PONY RACK RAFT SKIN
  BOOSE BOOSY CHEAT CRATE
  FRAME HOVEL STALL STEAL
  BUNKER CRATCH CRECHE CRITCH
  MANGER PIGSTY PILFER CABBAGE
  ENGLISH PURLOIN BASSINET
  CORNCRIB CRIBBAGE CRIBBING
  CRIBWORK
CRIBBER SHORER STUMPSUCKER
CRICK KINK CREEK HITCH SPASM
  TWIST
CRICKET GRIG MOLE SNOB CHANGA
  SADDLE GRYLLID TWIDDLER
  (— HIT) SLOG
CRICKETER CUT COLT PLAYER
  RABBIT GENTLEMAN
CRIER HUER CRYER BEADLE HERALD
  WAILER BELLMAN MUEZZIN
  WRAWLER OUTCRIER
CRIME ACT SIN EVIL FACT LACK
  ABUSE ARSON BLAME CAPER FOLLY
  LIBEL WRONG FALSUM FELONY
  INCEST MURDER PIACLE FORFEIT
  FORGERY MISDEED OFFENCE
  OFFENSE INIQUITY SABOTAGE
  VILLAINY
  (ORGANIZED —) GANGLAND
CRIMINAL BAD SORE YEGG CROOK
  FELON APACHE BASHER DACOIT
  GUILTY GUNMAN INMATE KILLER
  NOCENT SLAYER WARGUS WICKED
  CONVICT CULPRIT HEINOUS
  HOODLUM ILLEGAL NOXIOUS
  SEVENER VAUTRIN CRIMEFUL
  CULPABLE GANGSTER GAOLBIRD
  HABITUAL HARDCASE JAILBIRD
  SCELERAT
  (PETTY —) ROUNDER
  (VIOLENT —) DESPERADO
  (PL.) AMALAITA
CRIMINATE IMPEACH
CRIMP BEND CURL FOLD FRIZ POKE
  POTE WAVE WEAK CLAMP CRISP
  FLUTE FRILL FRIZZ PINCH PLAIT
  BUCKLE GOFFER RUFFLE CRIMPER
  CRIMPLE CRINKLE FRIABLE
  GAUFFER WRINKLE OBSTACLE
CRIMSON LAC RED PINK GRAIN

BLOODY JOCKEY MAROON MODENA
CARMINE SCARLET CRAMOISY

CRIMSON CLOVER NAPOLEON

CRINED MANED

CRINGE BOW BEND CURB CURR
DUCK FAWN JOUK BINGE COWER
CRAWL CREEP QUAIL SNEAK SNOOL
STOOP WINCE YIELD BUCKLE
CROUCH GROVEL SHRINK SUBMIT
CRINKLE DISTORT SCRINGE
TRUCKLE

CRINGING ABJECT HANGDOG
SERVILE SPANIEL

CRINKLE BEND CURL KINK TURN
WIND CREPE CRISP PUCKER RIPPLE
RUMPLE RUSTLE CRACKLE
CRANKLE FRIZZLE WRINKLE

CRINKLED CRIMP CURLY BUCKLED
ENCOMIC CRISPATE

CRINKLY CREPY CREPEY

CRINOID POLYP CRINITE CAMERATE
COMATULA
(BODY OF —) CROWN

CRINOLINE CRIN HOOP

CRIPPLE MAR CRIP GIMP HARM
HURT LAME MAIM BACACH HOBBLE
IMPAIR INJURE SCOTCH WEAKEN
CRAPPLE CRUMPET DISABLE
LAMETER LAMIGER LAMITER
HANDICAP LAMESTER MUTILATE
PARALYZE
(PL.) LAMZIEKTE

CRIPPLED GIMPY COUPLED
DISABLED

CRIPPLING MAIM MAYHEM

CRISIS FIT ACME CRUX FLAP HEAD
JUMP PASS TURN CARDO CRISE
PANIC PERIL PINCH POINT STATE
STORM TRIAL STRAIT DUNKIRK
DECISION JUNCTURE MOUNTAIN

CRISP NEW COLD CURL FRIZ FROW
HARD BRISK CLEAR CRIPS CRUMP
CURLY FRESH FRIZZ NIPPY PITHY
SHARP SHORT SPALT STIFF TERSE
BITING BRIGHT CRISPY LIVELY
SNAPPY BRACING BRITTLE CONCISE
CRACKLY CRUNCHY CUTTING
FRIABLE FRIZZLE SMOPPLE INCISIVE

CRISPED FUZZY FRIZZLY CRISPATE

CRISPNESS SNAP

CRISSCROSS AWRY CROSS
NETWORK CONFUSED

CRITERION LAW NORM RULE TEST
TYPE AXIOM CANON CHECK GAUGE
MODEL PROOF TOUCH CRISIS
METRIC INDICIA MEASURE PLUMMET
STANDARD

CRITIC MOME BOOER JUDGE MOMUS
CARPER CENSOR CORNER EXPERT
PUNDIT SLATER SYNDIC ZOILUS
STYLIST COLLATOR CRITIQUE
DEBUNKER OVERSEER REVIEWER
THONGMAN

CRITICAL EDGY HIGH ACERB ACUTE
CHILLY CRITIC SEVERE URGENT
ACERBIC ADVERSE CARPING
EXIGENT NERVOUS PARLOUS
CAPTIOUS CARDINAL CAVILING
DECISIVE EXACTING JUDICIAL

SLASHING TICKLISH

CRITICISM RAP FIRE GAFF SLAM
BLAME KNOCK SLATE CRITIC
REVIEW CENSURE COMMENT
DESCANT SLASHER SLATING
ZOILISM BLUDGEON CRITIQUE
DIATRIBE JUDGMENT

CRITICIZE HIT PAN RAP RIP CARP
CRAB FLAY FLOG SKIN SLAM SLUR
TIDE YELP BLAME BLAST CAVIL
DECRY GRIPE JUDGE KNOCK ROAST
SCORE SLASH SLATE BERATE
CRITIC REBUKE REVIEW CENSURE
COMMENT CONDEMN CRITIZE
EXAMINE CRITIQUE DENOUNCE
TOMAHAWK
(— SEVERELY) FLAY JUMP
(— SLASHINGLY) SLASH SLATE

CRITIQUE CRITIC REVIEW CRITICISM

CRO CROY PAYMENT

CROAK CAW DIE GASP KILL PORK
ROUP CREAK CRONK PLUNK QUALM
QUARK SPEAK CROAPE GRUMBLE
COMPLAIN FOREBODE

CROAKER SPOT RONCO CROCUS
RONCHO TOMCOD BUBBLER
CABEZON CORBINA CORVINA
CABEZONE HARDHEAD KINGFISH
SCIAENID

CROAKING CROAKY HOARSE
RANARIAN COAXATION

CROAT CHORWAT CHROBAT
SYRMIAN
(PL.) HRVATI HERVATI

CROCARD BRABANT SCALDING
SLEEPING

CROCHET HOOK KNIT BRAID PLAIT
WEAVE CROTCHET

CROCK JAR PIG POT SMUT SOIL
SOOT STEAN STEEN STOOL CHATTY
CRITCH GOOLAH PANMUG SMUDGE
CRAGGAN TERRINE POTSHERD

CROCKERY CHINA CLOAM DISHES
PIGGERY POTWARE CLAYWARE

CROCODILE GOA CROC GATOR
CAYMAN GAVIAL JACARE LIZARD
MUGGER YACARE CRAWLER
CREEPER DIAPSID REPTILE SAURIAN
SERPENT LORICATE

CROCODILE BIRD SICSAC TROCHIL
MESSMATE

CROCUS IRID LILY SAFFRON

CROFT FARM TORP CRAFT CRYPT
FIELD GARTH VAULT BLEACH
CAVERN PARROCK

CROMLECH QUOIT CIRCLE DOLMEN
CROMMEL GORSEDD

CROMORNA CREMONA KRUMHORN

CRONE HAG AUNT CRONY WITCH
BELDAM RIBIBE BELDAME

CRONY PAL CHUM BILLY GOSSY
NETOP GIMMER GOSSIP

CROOK BEND HOOK TURN WARP
CHEAT CHINK CLEEK CRANK CROMB
CROOM CRUMP CURVE HUNCH
NIBBY PEDUM STAFF THIEF TRICK
CRUMMY INDENT TWICER CAMBUCA
CROSIER CROZIER CRUMMIE
INCURVE POTHOOK SLICKER

ARTIFICE CHISELER CRUMMOCK
SWINDLER
(— IN BRANCH) KNEE
(— OF HEAD) HEEL
(SHEPHERD'S —) CROTCH

CROOKBACKED CROUCHIE

CROOKED CAM WRY AGEE AWRY
BENT GAME WOGH AGLEY ASKEW
BOWLY CRUMP FALSE GLEED KINKY
SNIDE THRAW WRONG ACROOK
AKIMBO ARTFUL ASLANT CAMMED
CRABBY CRAFTY CRANKY CURVED
DOGLEG HURLED THRAWN TRICKY
WEEWAW WEEWOW ZIGZAG
ASKANCE ASQUINT CORRUPT
CRABBED CURVOUS OBLIQUE
TURNING TWISTED WINDING
CAMSHACH THRAWART TORTUOUS

CROOKEDNESS PRAVITY RHEBOSIS

CROOKNECK CASHAW CUSHAW

CROON HUM LOW BOOM LULL SING
WAIL CHIRM CRONY WHINE LAMENT
MURMUR TEEDLE COMPLAIN

CROP BOB COW CUT MAW SET TOP
CLIP CRAP CRAW KNAP MINE REAP
SETT STOW TRAP TRIM WHIP FRUIT
GRAZE PLANT QUIRT SHAVE SHEAR
SHIFT SWATH TILTH TRASH BURDEN
DECERP GATHER GEBBIE SILAGE
BEARING BURTHEN CRAPPIN
CURTAIL CUTTING HARVEST
MAMMONI MASHLUM TILLAGE
GLEANING PROFICHI TRASHIFY
INGLUVIES
(— CANDLEWICK) SNUFF
(— OF A HAWK) GORGE
(— OF FRUIT) HANG
(— OF GRASS) LEA LEY SWATH
SWARTH SWATHE
(— OF OYSTERS) SET
(— OF POTATOES) GARDEN
(— OUT) BASSET
(GREEN —S) SOILAGE
(INDIAN —) RABI KHARIF
(LARGE —) HIT
(RIDING —) ROP
(SECOND-GROWTH —) ROWEN
(PL.) FEED TILLAGE

CROPPED GOTCH SHAVED GOTCHED

CROPPER CARVER MUCKER PURLER
GRINDER PLUMPER

CROPPING EARMARK

CROQUET ROQUE BOMBARD

CROQUETTE CECIL OYSTER
KROMESKI KROMESKY

CROSIER BAGLE CROCE CROOK
PEDUM STAFF POTENT BACULUS
CAMBUCA CROZIER PASTORAL

CROSS GO CAM CUT MIX TAU ANKH
CRUX FORD FUNK MARK PASS
ROOD SIGN SOUR SPAN TREE
WOOD ANGRY CANGY CHUFF
CORSE GAMMY GURLY SURLY
TEATY TESTY THRAW TRAVE TRIAL
YAPPY BISECT CHUFFY CRABBY
CRANKY CROUCH DENIAL EMBLEM
GIBBET GROUTY GRUMPY HIPPED
OUTWIT PATCHY SIGNUM SNAGGY
SNASTY SULLEN SYMBOL TEETHY

THWART TOUCHY WICKED WOOLLY ATHWART BECROSS CALVARY CRABBED CROSIER CROZIER CRUSADE CRUSADO FRABOUS FRETFUL FROWARD OBLIQUE PASSAGE PATIBLE PEEVISH PETTISH POTENCE SALTIER SALTIRE CAMSHACH CRANTARA CROCIATE CROISADE CROSSLET CROTCHED CRUCIFIX DEBRUISE DEMISANG FRAMPOLD FRATCHED FRUMPISH PECTORAL PETULANT PHRAMPEL SNAPPISH SWASTIKA THUNDERY TRAVERSE VEXILLUM WINDMILL

(— **BY PLANE**) HOP
(— **ONESELF**) SAIN
(— **OVER**) SPAN TRAJECT
(**DOUBLE** —) BUSINESS
(**MALTESE** —) FIREBALL

CROSSARM WISHBONE
CROSSBAR CROWN JUGUM DRIVER TRANSOM
(— **IN GATE**) SWORD
(— **IN SHAFT**) STEMPEL STEMPLE
(— **OF BALANCE**) BEAM
(— **OF WINDOW**) LOCKET

CROSSBEAM BAR BUNK SPUR TRAVE GIRDER BOLSTER TRANSOM TRAVERSE
CROSSBEARER SPREADER
CROSSBILL FINCH
CROSSBOW PROD RODD BRAKE LATCH PIECE PRODD TILLER SLURBOW ARBALEST BALLISTA STEELBOW STOCKBOW STONEBOW
CROSSBREED HUSKY METIS SANGA SANGU HYBRID
CROSS CARRIER CRUCIFER
CROSSCURRENT SURGING
CROSSCUT DRIFT OFFSET TUNNEL COUPURE
CROSSCUT SAW BRIAR
CROSSCUTTER BUCKER
CROSSE STICK
CROSSED ACROSS SQUINT WOOFED CRUCIAL THWARTING
CROSSER STICKER
CROSSETTE EAR ANCON ELBOW ANCONE CROSET
CROSS-EYE ESOTROPIA
CROSS-EYED SQUINT
CROSS-FERTILIZATION ALLOGAMY PHYTOGAMY
CROSS FORM URDE URDY
CROSS-GRAINED UGLY NURLY GNARLED HICKORY CONTRARY
CROSSHEAD YOKE
CROSSING XG PASS CROSS LACED MIXTURE PASSAGE TRAJECT CRUCIATE OPPOSING TRAVERSE CROSSOVER
CROSSPATCH BEAR CRAB CRANK GROUCH
CROSSPIECE BAR BAIL SPAR STEP YOKE BEARD GLAND GRILL ROUND STOCK THWART TOGGEL TOGGLE BOLSTER TRANSOM CROSSARM CROWFOOT FOOTRAIL HEADRAIL TRAVERSE CHOPSTICK

(PL.) CROSSTREE
CROSS-QUESTION TARGE TAIRGE
CROSSROAD LEET VENT WENT WEENT CAREFOX CARFOUR COMPITUM CROSSWAY
(PL.) TRIVIA
CROSSRUFF SAW SEESAW
CROSS-SHAPED CRUCIAL CRUCIATE
CROSS-STAFF CROSS RADIUS CROSIER CROZIER
CROSS STROKE BIND
CROSS-TEMPERED FRUMPISH
CROSSWISE CROSS ACROSS ATHWART ACROSTIC DIAGONAL OVERWART TRAVERSE WEFTWISE CROSSWAYS
CROSSWORT MAYWORT MUGWEED MUGWORT
CROTALUM CROTAL CYMBAL
CROTCH FORK POLE POST CLEFT NOTCH STAKE CRATCH CRUTCH GRAINS CROTCHET
CROTCHET FAD HOOK KINK WHIM CRANK FANCY FREAK VAGARY CORCHAT CRANKUM
CROTCHETY KINKY CRANKY
CROUCH HUG BEND CLAP COOK CURB DARE DROP FAWN FORM ROOK RUCK COWER HOVER SQUAT STOOP COORIE CRINGE CROOCH HUDDLE HUNKER HURKLE HURTLE SCOOCH SCOUCH CROODLE CROWDLE SCROOCH SCRUNCH SQUATTER
CROUCHING SQUAT CROUCHANT
CROUD SCROUGE
CROUP CRUP HIVES CRUPPER
CROUPIER DEALER TOURNEUR
CROUTON DIABLOTIN
CROW AGA CAW CRY DAW BRAG BRAN CRAW DOWP ROOK AYLET BOAST CRAKE CROWD EXULT HOODY KELLY RAVEN VAUNT CARNAL CORBIE CORVUS HOODIE KOKAKO GORCROW GRAPNEL JACKDAW SWAGGER ABSAROKA BALDHEAD BLACKNEB GAVELOCK GRAYBACK GREYBACK
CROWBAR PRY SET CROW BETTY JEMMY JIMMY LEVER SETUP SWAPE FORCER GABLOCK PITCHER GAVELOCK HANDSPEC
CROWBERRY HEATH HEATHER
CROWD FRY HUG JAM MOB SET TIP BIKE CRAM CRUT FARE HEAP HERD HOST JOSS MONG PACK PAVE PILE PUSH ROCK ROTE ROUT RUCK SERR SLUE SORT STOW SWAD TURB WOOD BUNCH CLOUD COHUE COVEY CRAMP CRUSH CRWTH DROVE FLOCK GROUP HORDE HURRY PLUMP POSSE PRESS ROTTA SERRY SHACK SHOAL STECH STIVE STUFF SWARM THREE VOLGE WEDGE BOODLE CHORUS CLIQUE HUBBLE HUDDLE HUSTLE IMPACT JOSTLE MITHER MOIDER PESTER RABBLE RESORT SCRUZE THRAVE THREAD THRIMP THRONG THRUST

TOURBE TYMPAN VOLLEY BOUROCK CHROTTA COMPANY CONGEST IMPRESS JIMBANG SCROOGE SCROUGE SQUEEZE THICKEN THRUTCH ENTHRONG FREQUENT JINGBANG SANDWICH SATURATE VARLETRY GATHERING
(— **ABOUT**) FLOCK
(— **AROUND**) BESIEGE
(— **OUT**) DISPLACE
(— **TOGETHER**) HUG HOTTER HOWDER HUDDLE CLUTTER CONTRUDE
(**CONFUSED** —) HURRY
(**MOVING** —) DROVE
(**NOISY** —) ROUT
CROWDED CLOSE DENSE SPISS STIFF THICK FILLED SPISSY THRONG BUNCHED COMPACT OPPLETE POPULAR SERRIED STIPATE STUFFED TEEMING NUMEROUS POPULOUS
CROWFOOT JOY PAGLE EXOGEN PAIGLE EELWARE GOLDCUP GOLLAND GOWLAND BANEWORT CRAWFOOT GOLDWEED HELLWEED
CROWING COCK
CROWN CAP TAJ TIP TOP BULL COIN GULL HELM PATE PEAK POLL RIGO TIAR ADORN BASIL BEZEL BEZIL CREST MITER MITRE MURAL POLOS REGAL ROUND ROYAL TIARA ANADEM CANTLE CIRCLE CLIMAX CORONA DIADEM DOLLAR FILLET INVEST LAUREL POTONG REWARD SUMMIT TIMBER TROPHY UPWARD VALLAR VERTEX WREATH AUREOLE CHAPLET CORNICE CORONAL CORONET FORETOP GARLAND INSTALL PSCHENT STEPHEN TONSURE CORONATE CORONULE ENTHRONE PINNACLE SURMOUNT TURNPIKE
(— **OF CHICORY**) ENDIVE
(— **OF EGYPT**) ATEF PSCHENT
(— **OF HEAD**) PATE SKULL CANTLE POMMEL FORETOP
(— **OF HILL**) KNAP
(— **OF LAUREL**) BAY
(**HALF** —) GEORGE ALDERMAN
(**PIECE OF** —) BULL
(**PLANT** —) STOOL
CROWNED CORONATE LAURELED
(— **WITH ROSES**) ROSATED
CROW SHRIKE MAGPIE SQUEAKER
CROW'S NEST LOOKOUT
CROZER CHUCKER
CRUCIAL ACUTE PIVOT NEEDLE SEVERE TRYING PIVOTAL SUPREME TELLING CRITICAL DECISIVE
CRUCIAN CARP GIBEL
CRUCIBLE POT DISH ETNA SHOE TEST CRUCE FOYER CRUSET HEARTH MONKEY RETORT FURNACE CROSSLET
CRUCIFIX PAX ROOD CROSS
CRUCIFIXION CROSS RANSOM
CRUCIFY VEX HANG KILL HARRY MORTIFY TORMENT TORTURE CRUCIATE

CRUDE ILL RAW BALD BARE RUDE BRUTE CRASS GREEN GROSS HAIRY HARSH ROUGH TACKY CALLOW COARSE DOUGHY INCULT KUTCHA SAVAGE UNRIPE VULGAR ARTLESS GLARING SQUALID UNCOUTH IGNORANT IMMATURE IMPOLITE INDIGEST
(NOT —) DELICATE
CRUDELY HARSHLY GAUCHELY
CRUDITY CRASSNESS GAUCHERIE ROUGHNESS
CRUEL ILL FELL GRIL GRIM HARD BLACK BREEM BREME BRUTE FELON HARSH RETHE SADIC STERN WROTH BITTER BLOODY BRUTAL DIVERS DREARY FIERCE IMMANE SAVAGE SEVERE UNJUST UNKIND UNMEEK UNMILD UNRIDE BESTIAL BOARISH BRUTISH GRIMFUL INHUMAN NERONIC SCADDLE SPITOUS WILROUN BARBARIC DIABOLIC FELONOUS FIENDISH INHUMANE PITILESS RUTHLESS SADISTIC TYRANNIC
CRUELLY FELL HARD CRUEL FELLY HARSHLY
CRUELTY RIGOR DURESS SADISM DEVILRY DEVILTRY FELLNESS SEVERITY
CRUET AMA JAR JUG VIAL BURET CRUSE BOTTLE CASTER CREVET CREWET GUTTUS AMPULLA BURETTE URCEOLE
CRUISE SAIL TRIP JUNKET STOOGE
(— AS A PIRATE) BUSK
CRUISER SHIP VALUER VESSEL WARSHIP ESTIMATOR
CRULLER WONDER OLYCOOK OLYKOEK TWISTER DOUGHNUT
CRUMB BIT ORT MURL PIECE LITTLE MORSEL CRIMBLE CRUMBLE MEALOCK MURLACK REMNANT FRAGMENT
(PL.) PANADA PANURE MOOLINGS
CRUMBLE ROT CRIM MURL MUSH BREAK BROCK CRUSH DECAY RAVEL SLAKE SPALL SPOIL BUCKLE MOLDER MYRTLE PERISH SLOUGH CORRADE CRIMBLE MOULDER COLLAPSE
(— DOWN) GRUSH
(— UNDER OVERWEIGHT) FLUSH
CRUMBLED UNDURE
(EASILY —) CRIMP BRUCKLE CRUMBLY
CRUMBLING SAMEL SAMMEL
CRUMBLY MURLY CRUMBY CRUMMY FRIABLE
CRUMPET CAKE MUFFIN PIKELET
CRUMPLE FOLD MOOL MUSS ROOL WISP CRUSH SCREW BUCKLE CREASE FURROW RAFFLE RUCKLE RUMPLE CRIZZLE CRUNKLE FRUMPLE SCRUNCH WRINKLE COLLAPSE CONTRACT SCRUMPLE
CRUNCH BITE CHEW MUCH CHOMP CRASH CRUMP CRUSH GNASH GRIND PRESS RUNCH CRANCH

CRINCH GRANCH GROWSE CRAUNCH SCRUNCH
CRUPPER CROUP CURPEL CURPIN TAILBAND
CRUSADE WAR JEHAD JIHAD CROISEE CAMPAIGN CROCIATE
CRUSADER PILGRIM TEMPLAR EQUITIST REFORMER
(PL.) CROISES
CRUSH BOW HUG JAM BEND BORE BRAY CASE CHEW CRAM DASH MASH MILL MULL PASH RAVE STUB BRAKE BREAK BRIZZ CHAMP CRASH CRAZE CREEM CROWD FORCE FRUSH GRIND GRUSH PRESS QUASH QUELL SMASH SMUSH SQUAB SQUAT STAMP TREAD UNMAN BRUISE BURDEN CRUNCH DEFOIL DEFOUL KNATCH KNETCH SCOTCH SCRUSH SCRUZE SQUASH SQUISS SUBDUE THRING THRONG THWACK ACCABLE BECRUSH CONQUER CRACKLE CRUMPLE DEPRESS DESTROY OPPRESS OVERRUN REPRESS SCRUNCH SCRUNGE SHATTER SQUEEZE SQUELCH SUCCUMB TRAMPLE COMPRESS FORBREAK OVERCOME SQUABASH SUPPRESS
(— BEANS) NIB
(— HAT) BONNET
(— IN) STAVE
(— ROCK) DOLLY DOLLEY DOLLIE
(— SPIRIT) BREAK
CRUSHABLE QUASHY
CRUSHED TAME BROKEN ECRASE MUSHED CONTRITE
CRUSHER NIBBER
CRUSHING FIERCE BRUISING SMASHING SQUABASH
CRUST FUR CAKE HULL RIND SCAB SHELL SKULL COFFIN CRUSTA ESCHAR GRATIN HARDEN RONDLE SCRUFF ABAISSE CALICHE COATING ENCRUST INCRUST CARAPACE PELLICLE SCUTULUM WINEBALL DURICRUST
(— ON WINE) ARGAL ARGOL
(PIE —) HUFF COFFIN
(PL.) SORDES
CRUSTA PES
CRUSTACEAN BUG APUS CRAB FLEA SCUD ZOEA ALIMA CARID LOUSE PRAWN SCREW SCROW CYPRID ENDITE ISOPOD SHRIMP SLATER SQUILL ARTEMIA COPEPOD CRAYLET DAPHNID DECAPOD GRIBBLE HAYSEED LOBSTER SQUAGGA SQUILLA BARNACLE CRAYFISH GAMMARID LERNAEAN MONOCULE SQUILLID
CRUSTADE DARIOLE
CRUSTY CURT BLUFF BLUNT RUSTY TESTY MOROSE SULLEN CRABBED PEEVISH PETTISH STARCHY SNAPPISH
CRUTCH FORK STILT CLUTCH CRATCH CROTCH POTENT SADDLE SCATCH STADDLE

CRUX NUB GIST HALF PITH CROSS POINT PUZZLE RIDDLE PROBLEM
CRUX ANSATA ANKH
CRWTH ROTA ROTE CROWD CRUTH ROTTA ROTTE CROUTH CHROTTA
CRY HO BOO CAW CRI FAD HOA HUE OLE PIP SOB YIP BAWL BELL BUMP CALL COWL CROW EVOE FALL GLAM GOWL HAIL HAWK HOOT HOWL KEEN MEWL NOTE OYES OYEZ PULE RAGE RAME RANE REEM RERD SCRY SIKE TOOT WAIL WEEP YELL YELP BARLA BLART BLORE CHEVY CLEPE CRAKE CROUP CRUNK GREDE GREET GROAN QUEAK RUMOR SHOUT SOUND TROAT UTTER VOGUE WHEWL WHINE WHULE WRAWL BARLEY BELLOW BOOHOO CHIVVY CLAMOR DEMAND ENSIGN LAMENT OUTCRY QUETHE SCREAM SHRIEK SLOGAN SNIVEL SQUALL SQUAWL SQUEAL TONGUE WIMICK YAMMER EXCLAIM FASHION HOSHANA SCREECH SPRAICH GARDYLOO PROCLAIM SCRONACH
(— ALOUD) BLART GREDE
(— AT SIGHT OF WHALE) FALL
(— DOWN) DOWNCRY BERATTLE
(— FOR TRUCE) BARLA BARLY BARLEY
(— HOARSELY) CROUP
(— LIKE ELEPHANT) BARR TRUMPET
(— LIKE PIG) WRINE
(— OF A BAT) CHIP
(— OF ABORIGINES) COOEE
(— OF BACCHANALS) EVOE
(— OF BIRD) CAW COO PEW BOOM CAWK CLANG BIRDCALL
(— OF BITTERN) BILL
(— OF CAT) MEW MEWL MIAOU MIAOW MIAUL MIAUW CALLING
(— OF CONTEMPT) BOO
(— OF DEER) BELL
(— OF ENTHUSIASM) BANZAI
(— OF GOOSE) HONK YANG
(— OF GUINEA HEN) POTRACK
(— OF HOUND) MUTE MUSIC
(— OF JACKAL) PHEAL PHEALE PHEEAL
(— OF MOURNING) KEEN TANGI
(— OF NEWBORN CHILD) VAGITUS
(— OF RAVEN) QUALM
(— OF SHEEP) BAA BLAT BLEAT
(— OF SNIPE) SCAPE
(— OF SORROW) ULLAGONE
(— OF SURRENDER) KAMERAD
(— OF WATCHMAN) WATCH
(— OUT) BAY BAWL BRAY GALE GAPE HOOT HOWL JERK SCRY BLORE CHIRM CLAIM ESCRY SHOUT HALLOO HOLLER SCREAM SHRIEK THREAP THROPE BREATHE EXCLAIM RECLAIM DISCLAIM PROCLAIM
(— TO CLEAR PASSAGE) HALL
(— TO COMBATANTS) BAILE
(— UP) CRACK
(BATTLE —) CRY ENSIGN MONTJOY GERONIMO MONTJOYE

(DRINKING —) RIVO
(HOARSE —) CROAK
(HUNTING —) TIVY CHEVY CHIVY
CHEVVY STABOY YOICKS TALLYHO
PILILLOO
(PROLONGED —) RANE
(RALLYING —) SLOGAN
(RAUCOUS —) CATCALL
(SHRILL) SKIRL SQUEAK SQUEAL
SCREECH YALLOCK
(WAR —) DIN ALALA SLOGAN
(WORDLESS —) KEEN ULULU
CRYING PIPING URGING CLAMANT
HEINOUS VAGIENT PRESSING
RECREANT
(— OF HOUND) BELLING
CRYPT PIT CRAFT CROFT CROWD
VAULT CAVERN GROTTO RECESS
SHROUD CHAMBER FOLLICLE
CRYPTIC DARK VAGUE HIDDEN
OCCILT SECRET OBSCURE ELLIPTIC
MYSTICAL SIBYLLIC
CRYPTOGRAM CODE CRYPT CIPHER
CRYPTOGRAPH GEMATRIA
CRYPTOGRAPHER VIGENERE
CRYPTORCHID RIDGLING
CRYSOPHANIC RHEUMIC
CRYSTAL XL ICE DIAL DOME HARD
IRIS SEED XTAL CLEAR GLASS
GRAIN LUCID LUNET TABLE GLASSY
LIMPID MIRROR NEEDLE PEBBLE
QUARTZ TABLET ACICULA DIAMOND
DIPLOID GLASSIE LUNETTE ORTHITE
TWOLING ULEXITE YAJEINE ZOISITE
FIVELING FOURLING PELLUCID
TRICHITE TRILLING
(— FOREIGN TO ROCK) XENOCYST
(FINE —) BERYL
(ICE —S IN WATER) FRAZIL
(NEEDLE-SHAPED —S) RAPHIDES
(ROCK —) BRISTOL
(TWIN —) TWIN MACLE TWINDLE
TWOLING FOURLING
(PL.) DRUSE GRAIN
CRYSTAL GAZE SCRY
CRYSTAL GAZER SEER SCRYER
SKRYER
CRYSTALLINE PURE CRYSTAL
PELLUCID
CRYSTALLITE BELONITE TRICHITE
BACILLITE SCOPULITE
CRYSTALLIZE FIX FIRM JELL CANDY
SUGAR NEEDLE CONGEAL SOLIDIFY
CRYSTALLOGRAPHY LEPTOLOGY
C-SHAPED SIGMATE
CTENIDIUM COMB
CTENOPHORE RIB NUDA CYDIPPID
JELLYFISH
CUADRA MANZANA
CUB FRY PEN BEAR CHIT COOP
SHED TOTO STALL WHELP LIONET
NOVICE CODLING REPORTER
(— SCOUT) WEBELOS

CUBA

BAY: NIPE PIGS
CAPE: CRUZ MAISI LUCRECIA
CAPITAL: HAVANA
CIGAR: HAVANA
COIN: PESO CENTAVO CUARENTA
DANCE: CONGA RUMBA DANZON
RHUMBA GUARACHA PACHANGA
FALLS: TOA AGABAMA CABURNI
GULF: MEXICO ANAMARIA
BATABANO
INDIAN: CARIB TAINO ARAWAK
ISLAND: PINES
ISLANDS: SABANA CAMAGUEY
MEASURE: VARA BOCOY TAREA
CORDEL FANEGA
MOUNTAIN: TURQUINO
MOUNTAINS: CRISTAL MAESTRA
ORGANOS TRINIDAD
PROVINCE: HAVANA ORIENTE
CAMAGUEY MATANZAS
RIVER: ZAZA CAUTO
SWAMP: ZAPATA
TOWN: COLON MANES BAYAMO
GUINES HAVANA BARACOA
HOLGUIN PALMIRA ARTEMISA
CAMAGUEY GUAYABAL
MATANZAS SANTIAGO
TREE: JIQUE JIQUI
WEIGHT: LIBRA TERCIO

CUBAN LILY SCILLA
CUBBYHOLE NOOK CUBBY
CUBE CUT DIE NOB KNOB BLOCK
EIGHT SOLID TIMBO BABASCO
CUBELET TESSELA TESSERA
BARBASCO QUADRATE
(— OF BREAD) CROUTON
(MEAT —S) CABOB KABOB KEBOB
(PL.) DICE
CUBIC SOLID CUBOID CUBICAL
CUBICALLY DIEWISE
CUBIC CENTIMETER FLUIGRAM
CUBIC METER STERE
CUBICLE BAY CELL ROOM BOOTH
CABIN NICHE STALL ALCOVE
CARREL CARRELL
CUBIT ELL CODO HATH COVID
HASTA COUDEE
CUB SHARK LAMIA GALEID REQUIEM
CUCKING STOOL THEW TUMBLER
TUMBREL TUMBRIL
CUCKOLD TUP HORN BECCO
VULCAN WITTOL ACTAEON
CORNUTE CORNUTO HORNIFY
RAMHEAD COKEWOLD
CUCKOLDED FORKED UNICORN
CUCKOLDRY HORNWORK
CUCKOO ANI COWK CUCK FOOL
GOUK GOWK KOEL KOIL CLOCK
CRAZY KOKIL SILLY COUCAL DIDRIC
HUNTER KOBIRD BOOBOOK
CHATAKA DIEDRIC KOWBIRD
SIRKEER CHOWCHOW PICARIAN
RAINBIRD RAINFOWL
CUCKOOFLOWER HEAD PAGLE
SPINK CUCKOO PAIGLE HEADACHE
MILKMAID
CUCKOOPINT ARUM RAMP AARON
BOBBIN DRAGON BUCKRAM
OXBERRY MANDRAKE
CUCKOO SPIT WOODSERE

CUCULLATE COWLED HOODED
COVERED
CUCUMBER CUKE PEPO GOURD
CONGER CUCURB PEPINO PICKLE
GHERKIN PICKLER CUCURBIT
PEPONIDA PEPONIUM
(BITTER —) COLOCYNTH
(SHRIVELED —) CRUMPLING
(WILD —) CREEPER
CUCURBIT BODY FLASK GOURD
CUCURB ALEMBIC MATRASS
CUD CHEW QUID BOLUS QUEED
RUMEN CUDGEL
CUDBEAR CORK PERSIO PERSIS
CUDWEED
CUDDLE HUG LAP PET CARESS
COSSET FONDLE HUGGLE KIDDLE
KIUTLE NESTLE PETTLE CROODLE
CRUDDLE EMBRACE SMUGGLE
SNOOZLE SNUGGLE
CUDDLESOME HUGGABLE
CUDDY ASS LOUT BRIBE CABIN
DONKEY GALLEY PANTRY CUDEIGH
CUDGEL BAT CUD BEAT CANE CLUB
CRAB DRUB KENT MACE RACK
RUNG TREE BASTE BATON DRIVE
KEBBY KEVEL LINCH LINGE SHRUB
STAFF STAVE STICK THUMP TOWEL
ALPEEN BALLOW BASTON BILLET
GIBBET KEBBIE LIBBET THRASH
WASTER BELABOR BOURDON
DRUBBER SWADDLE SWINGLE
TROUNCE BLUDGEON SHILLALA
THWACKER
CUDWEED ENAENA CATFOOT
CUE QU NOD TAG TIP HINT MAST
TAIL WINK BRAID CLUFF PLAIT
QUEUE TWIST PROMPT SIGNAL
PIGTAIL
(BILLIARD —) MAST STICK
(SHUFFLEBOARD —) SHOVEL
(TIP OF —) LEATHER
CUFF BOX BANK BLOW GOWF SLAM
SLAP SLUG SWAT TURF CLOUT
FIGHT GOWFF MISER SCUFF SCUFT
SMITE SOUSE BUFFET CODGER
FENDER MITTEN STRIKE TURNUP
COLPHEG SCUFFLE WHERRET
GAUNTLET HANDBLOW HANDCUFF
TURNBACK
CUIR DORADO
CUIRASS CURACE CURATE CURIET
LORICA THORAX
CUIRASSIER LOBSTER
CUISINE FOOD MENU TABLE
COOKERY KITCHEN
CUITLATEC TECO
CUL-DE-SAC POCKET STRAIT
IMPASSE
CULL OPT CAST COIL DUPE GULL
PICK PIKE SIFT SORT ELECT GLEAN
PLUCK ASSORT CHOOSE GARBLE
GATHER REMOVE SELECT CULLING
SEPARATE
CULLET SCRAP
CULM COOM HAULM SLACK COOMBE
REFUSE DEPOSIT
(PL.) SIRKI SIRKY
CULMINATION END ACME APEX

AUGE CULM NOON ROOF BLOOM
CREST CROWN HIGHT POINT
APOGEE CLIMAX CULMEN CUMBLE
HEIGHT PERIOD SUMMIT VERTEX
ZENITH BLOWOFF
CULPABILITY BLAME GUILT
DEMERIT
CULPABLE FAULTY GUILTY LACHES
SINFUL IMMORAL BLAMABLE
CRIMINAL
CULPRIT FELON CONVICT CRIMINAL
OFFENDER
CULT CLAN DADA SECT CREED
KUKSU CHURCH CULTUS DOMNEI
MANISM NUDISM RITUAL SCHOOL
SHINTO AMIDISM DADAISM ICONISM
MYALISM MYSTERY WORSHIP
DEVILISM HUMANISM SATANISM
CULTCH CUTCH STOOL SCULCH
CULTIVATE EAR HOE CROP DISC
DISK FARM GROW PLOW REAR
TEND TILL WORK DRESS EARTH
LABOR NURSE RAISE STUDY TRAIN
AFFECT FOSTER FURROW HARROW
MANAGE MANURE PLOUGH RATOON
SARCLE SCHOOL ACQUIRE CHERISH
CONTOUR CULTURE EDUCATE
EMBRACE EXPLOIT HUSBAND
IMPROVE NOURISH PREPARE
SCRATCH CIVILIZE
(— FAVOR) BOOTLICK
CULTIVATED ABAD TAME CIVIL
GROWN POLITE SATIVE TOILED
POLITIC REFINED CULTURED
(ARTIFICIALLY —) HOTHOUSE
CULTIVATION CROP TILTH FINISH
GROWTH CULTURE TILLAGE
TILTURE LABORAGE MANURAGE
(— IN MANNERS) FINISH
(MENTAL —) HUMANITY
CULTIVATOR JAT KMET RYOT ILAVA
SULKY FARMER GADABA HARROW
ILAVAN MAMOTY MILLER RIDGER
TILLER FLORIST GRUBBER HUSBAND
MEADOWER ROSARIAN SCUFFLER
(— GANG) RIG
(PL.) LAETI
CULTURAL HUMANIST
CULTURE ART AGAR STAB KULLI
NASCA NAZCA SHAKE SLANT SLOPE
TAJIN TASTE TILTH JHUKAR KULTUR
POLISH STREAK WILTON ABASHEV
ANANINO AZILIAN IRANISM JHANGAR
KAYENTA SOCIETY STARTER
TILLAGE HUMANISM LEARNING
(ESKIMO —) DORSET
(MEXICAN —) MAZAPAN
CULTURED CIVIL LETTERED
CULVERIN SLING CULVER LANTACA
PELICAN SPIROLE
CULVERT FOX GOUT DRAIN SLUIT
BRIDGE CONDUIT CULBERT PINNOCK
PONCEAU OVERPASS
CUMBER BURDEN CUMMER SHACKLE
CUMBERSOME GOURD HEAVY
CLUMSY UNRIDE AWKWARD
LUGSOME ONEROUS WEIGHTY
CUMBROUS UNWIELDY
CUMMER GIRL LASS WOMAN
KIMMER

CUMMERBUND BAND BELT SASH
CUMULATE HEAP GATHER COMBINE
CUMULATIVE CHAIN SUMMATIVE
CUNA CUEVA DARIEN
CUNEIFORM ULNARE WEDGED
CUNNER CANOE NIPPER WRASSE
BURGALL CHOGSET GOLDNEY
NIBBLER BERGGYLT BLUEFISH
CORKWING GILTHEAD
CUNNING ART OLD SHY SLY WIT
ARCH CUTE DEEP FAST FINE FOXY
KEEN SLIM SNOD TRAP WILY WISE
CANNY CRAFT DOWNY FAVEL GUILE
LOOPY PAUKY PAWKY POKEY
SHARP SMART ADROIT ARTFUL
ASTUTE CALLID CLEVER CRAFTY
DAEDAL DECEIT ENGINE FOXERY
PRETTY SHREWD SUBTLE SUPPLE
TRICKY WISDOM COMPASS CRAFTLY
CURIOUS FINESSE KNOWING
PARLISH PARLOUS POLITIC PRACTIC
SLEIGHT SUBTILE VARMINT VULPINE
CONTOISE DEXTROUS MANAGERY
QUENTISE SKILLFUL SLEIGHTY
STEALTHY YEPELEIC
CUNNINGLY YEPLY YEPELY
CUP AMA BOX CAN DOP MUG NOG
POT TOT TUN TYG CELL DOPP
HORN LOTA PECE SHOE SKEW TASS
TOSS BOUSE CALIX CHARK COGUE
COPPE CRUSE CYLIX DEPAS GLASS
GODET GRAIL KITTY PHIAL SCALE
STEIN STOOP STOUP TAZZA THECA
BEAKER BICKER BUCKET BUMPER
CAPPIE CHOANA COTYLA CRATER
CUPULA DOBBIN EGGCUP EYECUP
FALSIE FESSEL FINJAN GOBLET
JICARA KOTYLE MAZARD NAGGIN
NOGGIN OXHORN POTION RUMKIN
TASSIE VESSEL BRIMMER CAPSULE
CHALICE CHEERER CYATHUS
GODDARD KYATHOS QUONIAM
SCYPHUS SHERBET STIRRUP
THIMBLE TRINKET VENTOSE
BRIDECUP GRADUATE STANDARD
TJANTING
(— FOR HOLDING DIAMOND) DOP
DOPP
(— FOR PERFUMES) CONCH
(— FOR YEAST) SKEP
(— IN SAUCER OF ALCOHOL) ETNA
(— OF FLOWER) BELL
(— OF TEA) DISH SPEED OYSTER
(— ON BULLET) GASCHECK
(— WITH COVER) HANAP
(ASSAYING —) CUPEL
(DRINKING —) CAN MUG NUT TIG
TUN TYG CANN HORN TASS TOSS
GODET BEAKER GOBLET HOLMOS
RUMMER CHALICE GODDARD
TRINKET
(FAIRY —) COOLWORT
(FILLED —) BUMPER
(IRON —) CULOT MUSHROOM
(LARGE —) FACER
(LEATHER —) WELL GISPIN
(LONG-HANDLED —) CYATH DIPPER
CYATHUS KYATHOS
(NAUTICAL —) THIEF

(ORNAMENTAL —) TAZZA
(PAPER —) DIXIE
(PASTRY —) DARIOLE
(PRIZE —) PEWTER
(SACRED —) GRAIL
(SHALLOW —) CYLIX TAZZA TASTER
CAPSULE
(SMALL —) DOP NOG TOT DOPP
TASS DOBBIN NAGGIN NOGGIN
TASSIE
(SQUARE —) MADDER METHER
(STIRRUP —) BONAILIE
(WOODEN —) COG COGUE CAPPER
CAPPIE METHER QUAICH
(PL.) VALONIA
CUPBEARER HEBE SAKI CUPPER
GANYMEDE
CUPBOARD CUB KAS BOLE CASE
COIN SAFE AMBRY CHEST CUBBY
CUDDY HUTCH PRESS ABACUS
BUFFET CLOSET LARDER LOCKER
PANTRY SPENCE ARMOIRE CABINET
DRESSER SKIBBET ALHACENA
CREDENCE CREDENZA TROSTERA
(ARCHERY —) ASCHAM
CUPEL TEST
CUPFUL CUP CAROUSE
CUP HOLDER ZARF
CUPID DAN AMOR EROS LOVE
PUTTO CHERUB AMORINO AMOURET
(PL.) PUTTI
CUPIDITY LUST GREED DESIRE
AVARICE AVIDITY LONGING
APPETITE RAPACITY
CUPOLA DOME KILN TYPE VAULT
BELFRY TURRET CALOTTE FURNACE
LANTERN LOOKOUT CIMBORIO
COCKLOFT
CUPOLAMAN HEATER
CUPPING GLASS VENTOSE
CUPSEED NUTSEED
CUP-SHAPED PEZIZOID SCYPHATE
CUPULE CUP BOLSTER CYATHUS
THUMBMARK
CUR DOG YAP FICE FIST FYCE MUTT
TIKE TYKE FEIST KEOUT MESSAN
MESSIN BOBTAIL MONGREL
WHAPPET
CURARE URARE URARI OORALI
WOORALI
CURASSOW MITU COPPY HOCCO
MITUA PAUXI
CURATE ABBE CURA AGENT VICAIRE
MINISTER
CURATIVE HEALING IATRICAL
PHYSICAL REMEDIAL SALUTARY
SANATIVE
CURATOR KEEPER STEWARD
GUARDIAN OVERSEER
CURB BIT LID CRUB FOIL KERB REIN
SKID SNIP SNUB BRAKE CHECK
CRIMP CURVE GUARD LIMIT MOUND
ARREST BRIDLE COERCE COLLAR
DECKLE GOVERN HAMPER STIFLE
STRAIN SUBDUE THWART CONTROL
CURBING INHIBIT REFRAIN REPRESS
SHACKLE ATTEMPER COMPESCE
MODERATE RESTRAIN RESTRICT
WITHHOLD

(OFFICIAL —) LID
(WELL —) PUTEAL
CURCULIO TURK WEEVIL
CURD CRUD DAHI CHEESE CURDLE
CASEINE CLABBER CONGEAL
COAGULUM
(— IN MILK) ZIEGA
(—S AND WHEY) SLIP PINJANE
(BEAN —) TOFU
(PL.) FLEETINGS
CURDLE CAP LOP RUN SAM SET
CRIM CURD EARN LEEP QUAR SAMM
SOUR TURN WHIG YERN CARVE
QUAIL QUARL SPOIL YEARN CAILLE
LAPPER LOBBER LOPPER POSSET
QUARLE CLABBER CONGEAL
CRIDDLE CRUDDLE THICKEN
CONDENSE
CURDLED CURDLY QUARRED
SHOTTEN
(NOT —) UNCRUDDED
CURE DIP DRY DUN FIX BEEF BOOT
CARE CORN HEAL HEED HELP JERK
MEND SALT SANE SAVE AMEND
BLOAT BOTEN LEECH REEST SMEEK
SMOKE CHARGE CURATE KIPPER
PHYSIC PRIEST RECURE REMEDY
SEASON SUCCOR TEMPER WARISH
BESMOKE RECOVER RESTORE
THERAPY TREACLE ANTIDOTE
BARBECUE CURATION GUERISON
PRESERVE REVOCERY
(— BY SMOKING) GAMMON SMUDGE
(— FISH) DUN ROUSE
(— GRASS) HAY
(— HAY) WIN
(— HERRINGS) BLOAT
(— IN SUN) RIZZAR
(— SKINS) DRESS
(COUGH —) SAPA SAPE
CURE-ALL BALM AVENS ELIXIR
REMEDY PANACEA THERIAC
CURED SALT BLOATED
CURIOSITY CURIO INTEREST
(— OF SMALL VALUE) GABION
(—S OF THE CITY) LIONS
(PL.) CURIOSA
CURIOUS ODD NOSY RARE SELI
QUEER SELLE SELLY PRYING
QUAINT SNOOPY CUNNING STRANGE
UNUSUAL FREAKISH MEDDLING
PECULIAR SINGULAR
CURL BOB BEND COIL FEAK FURL
KINK LOCK PURL ROLL WAVE WIND
ACKER CANON CRIMP CRISP DILDO
FRILL FRIZZ QUIRL SPIRE TRESS
TWIRE TWIST BERGER BUCKLE
CANNON CRUCHE CURDLE FROWSE
MULLET RIPPLE SPIRAL WRITHE
CRIDDLE CRIMPLE CRINKLE
CROCKET CRUDDLE EARLOCK
FLEXURE FRIZZLE FROUNCE
RINGLET SERPENT TENDRIL
WHISKER FAVORITE LOVELOCK
SQUIGGLE
(— HAIR) CROOK
(— OF WIG) SNAKE
(— ON FOREHEAD) CRUCHE
CROUCHE

(— OVER) BREAK
(— UP) CRUMP HUNCH SNIRL
HUDDLE SHRINK SNUGGLE
(FRINGE OF —S) FRISETTE
FRIZETTE
(METAL —) CHIP
(SMALL —) CROCK
CURLED CRISP FUZZY KINKY SPIRY
CIRRATE COCKLED CRISPED
FRIZZLY SAVOYED WREATHY
CRISPATE GAUFFRED GOFFERED
HELICINE SCROLLED
CURLER GOFFER TEASER CRIMPER
FRIZZER MULLETS
CURLEW FUTE JACK SPOW KIOEA
SNIPE SPOWE WHAAP WHAUP
DIKKOP MARLIN SMOKER BANKERA
BUSTARD DOEBIRD BLUELEGS
WHIMBREL
CURLICUE ESS CAPER CURVE
CASSIS PARAPH SQUIRL FLOURISH
PURLICUE SCRIGGLE SQUIGGLE
CURLING MARK TEE
CURLING MATCH SPIEL
CURLING STONE IRON STONE
LOOFIE GRANITE
(— SPIN) RAISE
CURLY WAVY CRISP CRULL OUNDY
RIPPLED CRINKLED
(— HAIR) VEDDOID
CURMUDGEON CRAB CHURL MISER
GLEYDE GROUCH NIGGARD
CURMUDGEONLY STINGY
CURRANT PASA BERRY CASSIS
RAISIN RIZZAR RIZZLE CORINTH
(PL.) RIBES SPICE
CURRANT BUN WIG WIGG
CURRAWONG SQUEAKER STREPERA
CURRENCY CASH COIN PASS BILLS
CATER MONEY SCRIP SERIES
SPECIE PASSAGE WILDCAT
(FRACTIONAL —) SPONDULIX
(SHELL —) UHLLO
CURRENT NOW WAY EDDY FLOW
FLUX FORD RACE RIFE TIDE VEIN
WAFT ALIVE DRIFT GOING RAPID
ROUST SCOUR SWIFT TENOR TESLA
TREND USUAL ACTUAL COEVAL
COMMON COURSE DOUCHE DURANT
FLUENT LIVING MOTION MOVING
OFFSET OUTSET RECENT RULING
SLUICE STRAND STREAM TONGUE
VOLANT COUNTER DRAUGHT
FLOWING FRESHET GENERAL
INDRAFT INSTANT PASSANT
PRESENT RUNNING STICKLE
THERMAL TORRENT CURRANCE
DOWNCAST FREQUENT MILLRACE
PASSABLE TIDERACE TODAYISH
UNDERTOW
(— IN SPEECH) WAIF
(AIR —) DRAFT SHEET SPLIT
BREEZE DRAUGHT DOWNCAST
DOWNFLOW
(ELECTRIC —) STRAY
(HOT —) BACK
(JAPAN —) KUROSHIO KUROSIWO
(RAPID —) SWIFT TONGUE
(SOUND —) DISTORTION

(STRONG —) GALE ROOST ROUST
CURRENTLY ANYMORE
CURRISH BASE CYNICAL DOGGISH
IGNOBLE SNARLING
CURRY COMB DRUB KARI CLEAN
DRESS GROOM BRUISE CAJOLE
CARREE POWDER PREPARE
TARKEEAN
(— FAVOR) HUG NUT QUILL COTTON
SMOOGE SMOODGE
CURSE BAN BANE BLOW CUSS DAMN
OATH PIZE WARY BLAST BLESS
CORSE SHREW SPELL SWEAR
WEARY WINZE DETEST DEVOTE
GOOFER GUFFER MAKUTU MALIGN
MAUGER MAUGRE BESHREW
MALISON ANATHEMA EXECRATE
FORSPEAK
CURSED DASH CUSSED DAMNED
DASHED ACCURSED
CURSER WARIER
CURSING BLESSING BLASPHEMY
CURSIVE RUNNING
CURSORY FAST BRIEF HASTY QUICK
SHORT FITFUL ROVING SPEEDY
PASSANT PASSING SHALLOW
CARELESS RAMBLING
CURT BUFF RUDE TART BLUFF
BLUNT BRIEF BRUSK SHORT SQUAB
TERSE ABRUPT CURTAL CUTTED
SNIPPY BRUSQUE CONCISE CRYPTIC
LACONIC CAVALIER SNAPPISH
SNIPPETY SUCCINCT
CURTAIL CUT LOP CLIP CROP DOCK
PARE STOP ABATE ELIDE SHORT
SLASH STUNT TRUNK DECURT
LESSEN REDUCE ABRIDGE BOBTAIL
CRACKLE SHORTEN DIMINISH
MINORATE RETRENCH
CURTAILED TAIL SHORT STUNT
CURTAL BOBTAIL CONCISE
ABRIDGED
CURTAIN END BOOM DROP IRIS
MASK VEIL WALL BLIND DRAPE
SCENE SHADE SHEET VELUM
COSTER HANGER PURDAH SCREEN
SHROUD CEILING CONCEAL
CORTINE DRAPERY HANGING
VITRAGE-ASBESTOS PORTIERE
TRAVERSE
(CHURCH —) RIDDEL ENDOTYS
ENDOTHYS
(THEATRE —) SCRIM TEASER
TRAVELER TORMENTER
CURTAIN ROD TRINGLE
CURTAIN STRETCHER SCRAY
STRAINER
CURTAL CRAPE COURTAL CURTLAX
CURTSY BOB BOW DIP DOP BECK
DROP JOUK KNEE CONGE HONOR
CURCHY
CURUBA CASSA BANANA
CURVATED STUNT HOOKED
CURVATURE ARC PLY ARCH BENT
BOOL CURL CURVE SHEER SINUS
CAMBER CURVITY ADUNCITY
APOPHYGE CYRTOSIS GRYPOSIS
KYPHOSIS LORDOSIS
(— OF DECK) SHEER

(— **OF LEGS**) RHEBOSIS
(— **OF SHOE SOLE**) SWING
(— **OF SPINE**) KYPHOSIS SCOLIOSIS
(— **OF STOMACH**) FUNDUS
(— **OF STRAKE**) SPILING
CURVE ARC BOW CUP ESS SAG
ARCH BEND BOUT COME CURB
FADE HOOK KNEE LINE OGEE TURN
VEER WIND AMBIT BIGHT BREAK
CONIC CROOK CRUMP CUBIC HELIX
NONIC OGIVE PEDAL POLAR QUIRK
SLICE SWEEP SWIRL TARVE TREND
TWIST WITCH BOUGHT CAMBER
CIRCLE DEFLEX JORDAN SOLVUS
SPIRAL SPRING TOROID WIMPLE
ADIABAT BRACKET CAUSTIC CIRCUIT
CISSOID COMPASS CONCAVE
CONTOUR COSEISM CURVITY
CYCLOID ELLIPSE ENVELOP
FESTOON FLEXURE INCURVE
INFLECT LIMACON PHUGOID
PROFILE SCALLOP SINUATE
SOLIDUS CARDIOID CATENARY
CONCHOID DYGOGRAM ELASTICA
EXTRADOS FADEAWAY INTRADOS
INVOLUTE LIGATURE LIQUIDUS
OPHIURID PARABOLA SINUSOIS
TONOGRAM TRACTRIX
(— **DESCRIBED BY GRAPH**) GRAM
(— **IN HANDRAIL**) KNEE
(— **IN PLANKING**) HANG
(— **OF ARCH**) INTRADOS
(— **OF BALL**) DROP
(— **OF BIT**) LIBERTY
(— **OF FINGERNAIL**) GRYPOSIS
(— **OF HORSE'S NECK**) CREST
(— **OF PLANK**) SNY
(— **OF SHIP'S BOW**) FLAIR FLARE
(— **OF TIMBER**) CUP
(— **SATISFYING EQUATION**) BRANCH
(— **SPACE**) KNOT
(— **WHEN DRAWN**) COME
(**BASEBALL** —) SNAKE
(**CRICKET** —) SWERVE
(**DOUBLE** —) CIMA CYMA
(**VERTICAL** —) RAMP
CURVED BENT SOFT ADUNC CORBE
CURVE CURVY ROUND WOUND
CONVEX CURVEY GYRATE HAMATE
TURNED ARCUATE ARRONDI
CONCAVE CROOKED CURVANT
EMBOWED FALCATE SIGMOID
ADUNCOUS ANCHORAL AQUILINE
ARCIFORM CRUMPLED CYGNEOUS
DECURVED EXCURVED SCROLLED
ARCHIFORM
CURVET HOP LEAP LOPE SKIP TURN
BOUND CAPER FRISK PRANK VAULT
CAVORT CROUPE FROLIC GAMBOL
PRANCE PANNADE CORVETTA
CROUPADE
CURVING SPIRY SIMOUS TWISTY
AQUILINE DRAWDOWN
(— **IN**) CONCAVE
(**SMOOTHLY** —) FAIR
CUSH-CUSH CARA YAMPEE
CUSHION BAG COD MAT PAD PIG
BALL BANK BOSS PUFF SEAT SUNK
TRIM GADDI GADHI PANEL SQUAB

TRUSH BUFFER INSOLE JOCKEY
MUSNUD PILLOW SACHET BOLSTER
BRIOCHE COSSHEN HASSOCK
KNEELER MUFFLER PILLION
REPOSAL ROOTCAP CUTIDURE
OREILLER PULVINAR
(**LACE-MAKERS** —) BOTT
(**PIN** —) PRINCOD
(**SEAT** —) BANKER
(**TAILOR'S** —) HAM
CUSHIONING DUNNAGE
CUSHIONLIKE PULVINAR
CUSHION PLANT POLSTER
CUSHIONY PADDY
CUSHITIC NUBIAN
CUSK TUSK TORSK BURBOT CATFISH
CUSP APEX CONE HORN PEAK
ANGLE POINT STYLE TOOTH
CORNER SPINODE ENTOCONE
HYPOCONE METACONE PARACONE
CUSPIDOR GABOON CRACHOIR
SPITTOON
CUSSO KOSO KOUSSO BRAYERA
BRAZERA
CUSTARD FLAN FOOL FLAWN
DOUCET DOWCET CHARLET PARFAIT
FLUMMERY DIABLOTIN
CUSTARD APPLE ANONA ANNONA
PAWPAW CORAZON SWEETSOP
CUSTODIAN HACK GUARD BAILEE
CUSTOS KEEPER SEXTON WARDEN
WARDER CURATOR JANITOR
CERBERUS CLAVIGER GUARDIAN
CONCIERGE
CUSTODY LAP BAIL CARE HOLD
KEEP WARD TRUST ARREST
CHARGE SAFETY YEMSEL CONTROL
DURANCE KEEPING TUITION
COMMENDA CUSTODIA HANDFAST
SECURITY
CUSTOM FAD LAW MOS PAD TAX
URE USE ASAL DUTY FORM GARB
MODE MORE RITE ROTE RULE THEW
TOLL WONE WONT FUERO GUISE
HABIT HAUNT RITUS STYLE SUNNA
TRADE TREAD TRICK USAGE VOGUE
BYRLAW DASTUR DHARMA GROOVE
IMPOST MANNER MINHAG MONTEM
PRAXIS SUNNAH USANCE COSTUME
DUSTOOR DUSTOUR FASHION
FORMULA HALAKAH TRIBUTE
USAUNCE WARNOTH BUSINESS
ENDOGAMY HABITUDE PRACTICE
(**BINDING** —) LAW
(**BUSINESS** —) TRADE GOODWILL
(**CHURCH** —) COMITY
(**CORRUPT** —) ABUSE
(**FESTIVAL** —) HOCKING
(**OUTMODED** —) ARCHAISM
(**PRIMITIVE** —) COUVADE
(**RURAL** —) HEAVING
(**SECRET** —) SANDE
(**TEMPORARY** —) FAD VOGUE
(**PL.**) MORES MOEURS HAIKWAN
FOLKLORE
CUSTOMARILY USUALLY CUSTOMLY
CUSTOMARY PER RIFE TAME USED
NOMIC USUAL COMMON SOLEMN
VULGAR WONTED CLASSIC

GENERAL USITATE EVERYDAY
FAMILIAR HABITUAL ORTHODOX
(**NOT** —) INSOLENT
CUSTOMER CHAP BUYER CLIENT
PATRON SUCKER ACCOUNT
CALLANT CHAPMAN PATIENT
SHOPPER MERCHANT PROSPECT
(**PRINTER'S** —) AUTHOR
(**TOUGH** —) HARDCASE
(**PL.**) CUSTOM CLIENTELE
CUSTOMHOUSE ADUANA DOGANA
DOUANE
CUSTOM-MADE BESPOKE
BESPOKEN
CUSTOMS OFFICER SHARK WAITER
CUT AX ADZ AXE BOB DAG DAP DIE
HAG HEW KIT LOP MOW NIP RIT
SAW SNY TAP ADZE BANG BITE
BOLO BOLT BUZZ CHIP CHOP CLIP
CROP DADO DOCK FACE FELL FILE
GASH GIRD HACK HASH HEWN JERK
KNAP LIMB MAKE MODE MUSH NICK
OCHE PARE RACE RASH RAZE REAP
SIDE SKIN SLIT SLOT SMIT SNEE
SNEG SNIP SNUB STOW SUMP SWAP
SWOP TAME TRIM VELL VIDE BEVEL
BLOCK BREAK CANAL CANCH
CARVE CHIVE CLEFT COPSE COUPE
CRIMP DRESS FLICK FRAZE FRITH
GOUGE GRAVE GRIDE GROOP
HOWEL KITTE KNIFE LANCE LATHE
MINCE NOTCH PLATE PRUNE RAZEE
SABER SABRE SCALP SCARP SCIND
SCORE SEVER SHARE SHEAR SHIVE
SHRED SKICE SKISE SLASH SLICE
SLICK SLISH SLIVE SNICK SPLIT
STAMP SWEEP SWIPE SWISH TOUCH
TWITE VOGUE WHITE ABLATE
AJOURE BARBER BISECT BROACH
CAMBER CHISEL CLEAVE CORNER
CUTTED DIVIDE EXCISE FIGURE
FLETCH FLITCH FRENCH GROOVE
GULLET HACKLE HAGGLE IGNORE
INCIDE INCISE INDENT LESSEN
MANGLE OUTPUT RASURE REDUCE
RIPPLE SCORCH SCOTCH SCRIBE
SCYTHE SLIGHT SLIVER SNATHE
STRAIT STREAK SULLET SWINGE
TAILYE THWITE TRENCH AFFRONT
CONVERT CURTAIL CUTTING
DIACOPE DISSECT DRAWCUT
ENGRAVE FASHION FRITTER
HATCHET SCALPEL SCISSOR
SCUTTLE SECTILE TAILZEE WHITTLE
DISSEVER FRACTION INCISION
INCISURE INTAGLIO LACERATE
MALAHACK RETRENCH THWITTLE
(— **A THREAD**) CHASE
(— **AN OPENING**) BREACH
(— **AT ANGLE**) CANT BEVEL
(— **AT RANDOM**) SLASH
(— **AWAY**) COPE SLIT UNDO ABATE
CONCISE
(— **BACK**) HEAD SPUR
(— **BARK**) CHIP
(— **BEAM**) KERF
(— **CARS**) LIFT
(— **CHEESE**) HARP
(— **CLAY**) SLING

(— **CORNERS**) SKIRT CHAMFER
CHAMPHER
(— **CRUST**) CHIP
(— **DEEPLY**) DIG SHANK
(— **DIAGONALLY**) CATER SLANT
(— **DOWN**) MOW FELL STAG STUB
RAZEE SCARP ABRIDGE SHORTEN
RETRENCH
(— **FANCY FIGURE**) DASH
(— **FISH**) SOLAY STEAK
(— **FOR FODDER**) CHAFF
(— **FROM STACK**) DESS
(— **GEAR TEETH**) RATCH
(— **GLASS**) SPLIT
(— **GRAIN**) BAG FAG CRADLE
SWINGE
(— **IN A TREE**) FACE
(— **IN BARREL STAVE**) HOWEL
(— **IN EXCAVATIONS**) GULLET
(— **IN RELIEF**) ENCHASE
(— **IN SOFT ROCK**) CAVATE
(— **IN SQUARES**) CHECK
(— **IN**) INSECT INCISED
(— **INTO SLIPS**) ZEST
(— **INTO STRIPS**) JERK FLETCH
FLITCH JULIENNE
(— **INTO TREE**) BOX
(— **JAGGEDLY**) HACK SNAG
(— **LEDGES**) BENCH
(— **LOGS**) LUMBER
(— **OF FISH**) JOWL
(— **OF GEM**) STAR
(— **OF GRAIN**) MELL
(— **OF MEAT**) ARM SEY CROP HOCK
SHIN SIDE CHUCK SHANK STEAK
BRISKET FORESEY ICEBONE SIRLOIN
EDGEBONE FORERIBS
(— **OF RIFLING**) GROOVE
(— **OFF BY BITS**) DRIB
(— **OFF END**) BUTT
(— **OFF WOOL**) DOD DODD
(— **OFF**) BOB LOP CLIP CROP DOCK
KILL PARE SHUT SLIT STAG BELEE
CROSS ELIDE PRUNE SCIND SEVER
SHAVE SHEAR SKIVE SLIPE SPIKE
COUPED DECIDE EXEMPT FORCUT
RESECT SHIELD STIFLE SWATCH
ABSCIND ABSCISE ABSCISS CURTAIL
EXSCIND ISOLATE PRECIDE RESCIND
AMPUTATE CLEIDOIC DESECATE
RESECATE RETRENCH TRUNCATE
(— **OPEN**) SPLAY
(— **OUT**) DESS DINK CLICK BROACH
EXCIDE EXCISE EXSECT
(— **PATH**) FRAY
(— **SALMON**) CHINE
(— **SHEEP**) TOMAHAWK
(— **SHORT**) BOB COW HOG LOP
BANG CROP DOCK JIMP SNIB
BOBBED HOGGED BOBTAIL CONCISE
SCANTLE PRESCIND
(— **TENDONS**) ENERVATE
(— **THE THROAT**) JUGULATE
(— **THE WAVES**) SNORE
(— **THINLY**) CURL
(— **TO PIECES**) CHOP DICE MINCE
BRITTLE FRITTER
(— **TO SIZE**) TAIL
(— **TURF**) VELL

(— **UNDER**) KIRVE
(— **UNEVENLY**) CHATTER
(— **UP SWAN**) LIFT
(— **UP**) TUSK CARVE CHINE JOINT
PRANK SPOIL TRAIN GOBBET
COLLOPED
(— **WHALE BLUBBER**) LEAN
(— **WITH BACKWARD SLOP**) COOT
(— **WITH DIE**) DINK BLANK
(— **WITH SHEARS**) SHIRL
(— **WITH SICKLE**) BAG REAP
(**COLD** —S) ASSIETTE
(**CREW** —) BUTCH FLATTOP
(**DEEP NARROW** —) JAD
(**FENCING** —) STRAMAZON
(**LARGE** — **OF FOOD**) DODGE
(**NOT** —) UNCORVEN
(**SHORT** —) ATAJO
(**SLIGHT** —) SNICK SCOTCH
(**THIN** —) TARGET
CUT-AND-DRIED CANNED
CUTANEOUS DERMAL
CUTCH GAMBIR CATECHU GAMBIER
CUTE COY KEEN COONY DINKY
DUCKY SHARP CLEVER PRETTY
SHREWD CUNNING DARLING
CUTICLE DERM HIDE SKIN SHUCK
THECA MEMBRANE PELLICLE
(— **OF EGGSHELL**) BLOOM
CUTLASS SWORD CURTAL DUSACK
HANGER TESACK CURTAXE
MACHETE SHABBLE CAMPILAN
CUTLASS FISH HIKU SAVOLA
KALKVIS MACHETE HAIRTAIL
CUTLET SCHNITZEL
CUTOVER COUPE
CUTPURSE THIEF HORNTHUMB
CUTTER DIE BEEF BOAT IRON MILL
PONE SLED BRAVO FACER FRAZE
SLOOP SMACK BAYMAN CHERRY
COLTER COTTER DOCKER EDITOR
FRAZER MINCER SLEIGH SLICER
CLIPPER COULTER DROMOND
INCISOR RUFFIAN KNIFEMAN
REVENUER SCHOKKER SHEPSTER
(— **OF STONES**) LAPIDARY
(**BRICK** —) RUBBER
(**PEAT** —) PINER
(**WIRE** —) SECATEUR
CUTTERHEAD WABBLER WOBBLER
CUTTHROAT BRAVO CUTTER
RUFFIAN SWORDER
CUTTHROAT TROUT MYKISS
CUTTING CUT HAG RAW SET ACID
CARF CURT KEEN KERF SETT SLIP
TART TWIG ACUTE BLEAK CHECK
CRISP EAGER EDGED GRIDE SCION
SCRAP SCROW SHARP SMART
BITING BITTER BORING ENTAIL
GODOWN GORING JAGGED PHYTON
PIPING SECANT SEVERE SNITHE
BURNING CAUSTIC GRIBBLE INCISAL
MORDANT NICKING OVERCUT
PAINFUL PIQUANT POLLING
SARMENT SATIRIC SECTION SLICING
CHILLING CLEARING INCISIVE
PIERCING POIGNANT QUICKSET
SCISSION SNAPPISH WOUNDING
(— **FOR DIRT-CAR TRACK**) GULLET

(— **FOR WATER**) TAJO
(— **FROM PLANT**) SLIP SHROUD
TRUNCHEON
(— **OF DEER**) SAY
(— **OF TREES**) HAG
(— **OFF**) AVULSION
(— **SHORT**) ABORTIVE
(**DRILL** —S) MUD
(**OBLIQUE** —) BARBING
(**SECOND** —) ROWEN
(**WASTE** —) SELVAGE SELVEDGE
CUTTLEBONE SEPIA SEPION SEPIUM
GLADIUS SEPIARY
CUTTLEFISH SEPIA SHELL SQUID
CUDDLE CUTTLE SCRIBE CATFISH
DECAPOD INKFISH MOLLUSK
OCTOPUS SCUTTLE
CUVETTE POT TUB TANK BASIN
BUCKET TRENCH CISTERN
CYANIDE NITRILE CYANURET
CYANITE SAPPARE DISTHENE
CYANOGEN PRUSSIN PRUSSINE
CYBELE RHEA KYBELE AGDISTIS
(**DAUGHTER OF** —) JUNO
(**FATHER OF** —) URANUS
(**HUSBAND OF** —) SATURN
(**MOTHER OF** —) GAEA
(**SON OF** —) JUPITER NEPTUNE
CYCAD BANGA CICAD ZAMIA
COONTIE CYCADITE
CYCLAMEN BACCHAR PRIMWORT
SOWBREAD
CYCLE AGE EON ERA AEON BIKE
EPOCH KALPA PEDAL PRIME ROUND
SAROS SECLE WHEEL BAKTUN
CIRCLE COURSE CYCLUS PERIOD
BICYCLE CIRCUIT DICYCLE
TRICYCLE
(— **OF WORK**) JOURNEY
(—S **CAUSED BY KARMA**) SAMSARA
SANSARA
(**BUSINESS** —) JUGLAR KITCHIN
(**LUNAR** —) SAROS
(**ONE** — **PER SECOND**) HERTZ
(**SECONDARY** —) EPICYCLE
CYCLIC CYCLAR ANNULAR CYCLICAL
CYCLIST CYCLER WHEELER
WHEELMAN
CYCLOLITH CROMLECH
CYCLOMETER ODOGRAPH
CYCLONE GALE GUST WIND BLAST
STORM BAGUIO TORNADO TWISTER
TYPHOON SECONDARY
CYCLOPEAN HUGE VAST STRONG
MASSIVE COLOSSAL GIGANTIC
CYCLOPS ARGES BRONTES
COPEPOD STEROPES
CYCLORAMA CYKE PANORAMA
CYCLOSIS STREAMING
CYCLOSTOME HAGFISH
CYLINDER CAN EKE GIG TIN BEAM
BOMB BURR CAGE CANE DRUM
LEAD MUFF PIPE PRIM ROLL SLUG
TUBE WELL BLOCK CORER DRAIN
FIBER FIBRE FUDGE SCREW SHELL
SPOOL STELA STELE SWIFT BARREL
BOBBIN BUTTON COLUMN COPPER
DECKER DOFFER DUSTER FILTER
GABION PISTON PLATEN ROLLER

SCREEN TIPITI TUMBLE URCHIN
WORKER CUTCHER SLEEVER
SUCCULA FOLLOWER GRADUATE
NEURAXIS SPARKLET
(— AROUND MOLD) COTTLE
(— OF STEAM WHISTLE) BELL
(— OF TISSUE) CORTEX
(— OF YARN) CAKE
(— ON LOOM) BEAM
(— WITH PERFORATIONS) FLUSHER
(—S PULLED THROUGH DUCT)
MANDREL
(ARMORED —) BARBETTE
(GLASS —) MUFF
(HOLLOW —) PIPE TUBE
(MARKING —) LEAD
(NAPPING —) GIG
(RELAY —) BATON
(REVOLVING —) BEATER ROLLER
(TOOTHED —) SPROCKET
CYLINDRICAL ROUND TERETE
TOROSE CENTRIC TUBULAR
TERETIAL
CYMA GOLA GULA OGEE DOUCINE
MOLDING CYMATIUM
CYMA REVERSA HEEL
CYMBA YET
CYMBAL ZEL CHIME TARGET
CROTALUM KYMBALON
(PL.) TAL BECKEN PIATTI
CYMBIUM MELO
CYME CYMULE BOSTRYX
CYMLING SIMNEL CYMBLIN SCALLOP
PATTYPAN
CYMOSE DEFINITE SYMPODIAL
CYMRY KYMRI WELSH
CYNIC SATYR TIMON DOUBTER
APEMANTUS

CYNICAL CYNIC SULLEN CURRISH
DOGGISH DOGLIKE CAPTIOUS
SARDONIC SNARLING JAQUESIAN
CYNOCEPHALUS AANI
CYNOSURE SHOW LODESTAR
CYPRESS CULL SABINO SIPERS
FIREBALL AHUEHUETE BELVEDERE
CYPRESS SPURGE BALSAM
NAPOLEON
CYPRIPEDIUM CYP DUCK NERVINE

CYPRUS

CAPE: GATA GRECO ANDREAS
ARNAUTI ZEVGARI
CAPITAL: NICOSIA
COIN: PARA
MEASURE: OKA OKE PIK CASS
DONUM KOUZA GOMARI KARTOS
MEDIMNO
MOUNTAIN: TROODOS
TOWN: POLIS PAPHOS KYRENIA
LARNACA MORPHOU NICOSIA
LIMASSOL
WEIGHT: OKA OKE MOOSA
KANTAR

CYRILLA TITI
CYRUS KORESH
CYST BAG SAC WEN POUCH CYSTUS
RANULA DERMOID HYDATID
HYGROMA VESICLE DACRYOPS
MUCOCELE STEATOMA
CYSTOPTERIS FILIX
CYTOME SPHEROME
CYTOPLASM MASSULA OOPLASM
DIASTEMA

CZAR CSAR IVAN TSAR TZAR PETER
NICHOLAS
CZARDAS CSARDAS
(SECTION OF —) FRISS LASSU
FRISZKA
CZECH CECH TSECH BOHUNK
TSCEKH BOHEMIA

CZECHOSLOVAKIA

BEER: PILSEN
CAPITAL: PRAHA PRAGUE
CASTLE: HRADCANY
COIN: CROWN DUCAT HALER
HELLER KORUNA
DANCE: POLKA REDOWA FURIANT
MEASURE: LAN SAH MIRA KOREC
LATRO STOPA MERICE STRYCH
MOUNTAIN: ORE TATRA SUDETEN
PROVINCE: BOHEMIA MORAVIA
SLOVAKIA
RIVER: UH MZE VAG VAH DYJE
EGER ELBE GRAU HRON IPEL
ISAR ISER LABE NISA ODER
OHRE OLSE WAAG BECVA
DUNAJ MARCH NITRA SLANA
TISZA DANUBE MOLDAU
MORAVA ONDAVA SAZAVA
TORYSA VLTAVA LABOREC
LUZNICE BEROUNKA
TOWN: AS ASCH BRNO CHEB
EGER MOST BRUNN OPAVA
PLZEN TABOR TUZLA AUSSIG
BILINA KLADUS PILSEN PRESOV
VSETIN ZVOLEN BUDWEIS
JIHLAVA OSTRAVA TEPLITZ

D DE DEE DOG DELTA
DAB DAP DOB DOT DUB HIT PAT
BLOW CHIT DAUB LICK LUMP PECK
SPOT CLOUT DHABB DIGHT SMEAR
BLOTCH EXPERT STRIKE DABSTER
PORTION SPLOTCH FLATFISH
FLOUNDER MARYSOLE SANDLING
DABBER BALL PROD TAMPON
DABBING PICKING
DABBLE DAB DIB MESS DALLY
DIBBLE MEDDLE MUDDLE PADDLE
POTTER SOSSLE SPLASH TAMPER
TRIFLE DRABBLE MOISTEN PLOUTER
PLUTTER SMATTER SPATTER
DELIBATE SPRINKLE
(— WITH BLOOD) ENGORE
DABBLER AMATEUR DABSTER
DABCHICK GREBE DIPPER DOBBER
DOPPER PUFFER HENBILL DIDAPPER
DOPCHICK
DACE CHUB DARE DART CYPRINID
GRAYLING
DACHSHUND DACHS BADGERER
DACOIT DAKU DAKOO ROBBER
CRIMINAL
DACTYLOPODITE POLLEX
DACTYLOZOOID PALPON
DACTYLUS DACTYL DIGITUS
DAD BEAT BLOW DAUD HUNK LUMP
PAPA KNOCK THUMP FATHER
STRIKE
DADDY BABBO DEDDY
DADDY LONGLEGS SPINNER
LONGLEGS PHALANGID
DADO DIE GROOVE SOLIDUM
DAEDALUS (ANCESTOR OF —)
ERECHTHEUS
(NEPHEW OF —) TALUS
(SON OF —) ICARUS
DAEMON (ALSO SEE DEMON) GHOST
DAIMON PYTHON EUDAEMON
MISTRESS
(PL.) CURETES
DAFFODIL GLEN LILY DAFFY DILLY
JONQUIL ASPHODEL BELLWORT
CROWBELL
DAFT GAY WILD BALMY CRAZY
DAFFY GIDDY LOONY POTTY SILLY
INSANE FOOLISH IDIOTIC IMBECILE
DAG JAG DAGG STAB SLASH DAGGLE
PIERCE DAGGING DAGLOCK
PRICKET
DAGAME SALAMO MADRONA
LEMONWOOD
DAGGER DAG SAX DIRK ITAC KRIS
SAEX SNEE SPUD STAB TANG CRISE
DAGUE KATAR KREES POINT PRICK
SKEAN STEEL ANLACE BODKIN
COUTEL CREESE DIESIS HANGER
KIRPAN KUTTAR PANADE PINKER
POPPER SKHIAN STYLET BALARAO
BASLARD BAYONET COUTEAU
DUDGEON HANDJAR KANDJAR
KHANJAR OBELISK PONIARD
SLASHER STABBER PUNCHEON
PUNTILLA STILETTO
(— AS CERAMICS COVER) HILLER
(— REFERENCE MARK) SPIT
(— WITH WAVY BLADE) KRIS

CREESE KREESE
(DOUBLE —) DIESIS
(SACRED —) KIRPAN
DAGOMBA DAGBANE DAGBANI
DAH DAO DOW DHAO
DAHLIA JICAMA POMPON
DAHOMEY (CAPITAL OF —)
PORTONOVO
(PEOPLE OF —) FON FONG
(RIVER OF —) NIGER OUEME
(TOWN IN —) KANDI NIKKI ABOMEY
OUIDAH COTONOU
DAILY ADAY DIARY DIURNAL
DAINCHA NARDOO
DAINTIES EST ESTE SOCK CATES
DIABLOTIN
DAINTILY CHOICELY GINGERLY
MINIONLY
DAINTINESS FLUTTER DELICACY
DAINTY CATE FINE NICE RARE TEAR
ACATE DAINT DENTY FRILL GENTY
NAISH BONBON CHOICE COSTLY
FRIAND MIGNON MINION PICKED
REGALO SCARCE SPICED SUNKET
CURIOUS ELEGANT FINICAL FINICKY
MINIKIN REGALIA TAFFETA TAFFETY
DAINTITH DAINTREL DELICACY
DELICATE ETHEREAL LIKEROUS
MIGNIARD TRYPHOSA
DAIRY TAMBO LACTARY VACCARY
CREAMERY DEYHOUSE
(— PRODUCTS) MILCHIGS
DAIRYMAID DEE DEY DEYWOMAN
MILKMAID
DAIRYMAN AHIR MILKMAN
DAIS PACE SEAT BENCH LEWAN
STAGE TABLE CANOPY ESTATE
LISSOM PODIUM PULPIT SETTLE
ESTRADE TERRACE TRIBUNE
CHABUTRA FOOTPACE HALFPACE
HATHPACE HUSTINGS PLATFORM
DAISY BULL GOLD DANDY GOWAN
OXEYE BENNET MORGAN SHASTA
BONESET BOWWORT COMFREY
DOGBLOW BACKWORT BONEWORT
COMPOSIT HEXAFOIL KNITBACK
PISSABED MOONPENNY
DAISY CUTTER GRUB
DAISY FLEABANE ERIGERON
SCABIOUS
DAKOTA SIOUX LAKOTA
DALE HAW DELL DENE GLEN VALE
SPOUT BOTTOM DINGLE TROUGH
VALLEY
DALEA PAROSELA
DALLES DELLS RAPIDS
DALLIANCE TOY CHAT PLAY TALK
SPORT GOSSIP TOUSEL TOUSLE
TRIFLE COLLING
DALLIER PINGLER
DALLY TOY CHAT DAFF FOOL IDLE
JAKE JAUK PLAY SWAN WAIT DELAY
FLIRT SPORT TARRY COQUET
DABBLE DAWDLE LINGER LOITER
TRIFLE WANTON DRINGLE SLIDDER
DALLYING COQUETRY SISSETON
DALMATIC TUNICLE
DAM BAR BAY PEN REE DAME HEAD
POND SADD SPUR STAY STEM STOP

SUDD WEIR BLOCK CAULD CHECK
CHOKE GARTH MOUND POUND
STANK ANICUT CAUSEY HINDER
MOTHER PARENT ANNICUT
BARRAGE BARRIER MILLDAM
PENHEAD RAMPIRE TAPPOON
ABOIDEAU BLOCKADE GRANDDAM
OBSTACLE OBSTRUCT RESTRAIN
DAMAGE MAR BLOT BURN COST
HARM HURT JEEL LOSS RUIN SKIN
TEEN BLITZ BURST CLOUD CRACK
HAVOC PRANG SPOIL WOUND
WRONG BATTER CHARGE DANGER
DEFACE DEFECT HINDER IMPAIR
INJURE INJURY INSULT SCATHE
SORROW AFFLICT DAMNIFY
DEGRADE DISTURB EXPENSE
FOUNDER OFFENCE OFFENSE
PAYMENT SCRATCH SCUTTLE
SHATTER ACCIDENT BUSINESS
DISSERVE FRACTURE FRETTING
MISCHIEF SABOTAGE
DAMAGED HURT CRAZY LESED
BROKEN CRACKED INJURED
DAMAGES INTEREST HAMESUCKEN
DAMAGING HARMFUL HURTFUL
DAMAN DAS CONY CONEY CUNNY
DASSY GANAM HYRAX DASSIE
WABBER ASHKOKO CHEROGRIL
DAMA PADEMELON TAMMAR
WALLABY
DAMASCENED WATERED
DAMASCENE WORK KOFTGARI
DAMASK LINEN DARNEX DORNIC
DORNICK DAMASSIN DRAWLOOM
DAME DINT LADY DAMIE WOMAN
MATRON
DAME'S VIOLET EVEWEED
DAMMARA AGATHIS
DAMN DEE DEM DOG RAT BLOW
BURN DANG DARN DASH DING DRAT
DUMB DURN BLAME BLANK BLAST
BLESS CURSE FETCH WHOOP
BEDAMN BUGGER DEMPNE DEVOTE
GODDAM CONDEMN CONSARN
DOGGONE GODDAMN GOLDARN
GOLDURN CONFOUND EXECRATE
DAMNABLE DAMNED ODIOUS
ACCURSED INFERNAL
DAMNABLY DEUCED CURSEDLY
DEUCEDLY
DAMNATION NATION PERDITION
DAMNED DEE DAMN DARN DEED
DURN LOST BALLY DOOMS BLOODY
DARNED DASHED DURNED GODDAM
GORMED TARNAL BLESSED
CONSARN DOGGONE ETERNAL
GOLDARN GOLDURN MUCKING
ACCURSED BLANKETY BLINKING
DASHEDLY INFERNAL JIGGERED
DAMP DEG FOG RAW WAK WET
CLAM DANK DEWY DULL MIST ROKY
SOFT WACK BLUNT DABBY HUMID
JUICY MALMY MOCHY MOIST
MOOTH MUGGY MUNGY MUSTY
RAFTY RAINY RAWKY SAPPY SOBBY
SOGGY THONE WAUGH WEAKY
CLAMMY DAMPEN DEADEN MUFFLE
QUENCH STUPOR BEDEWED

DAMPISH DEPRESS MOISTEN
SQUIDGY DEJECTED DISPIRIT
HUMIDIFY HUMIDITY MOISTURE
(— OF EVENING) SERENE
(CHOKE —) STYTHE
DAMPEN DEG DAMP MOIL CHILL
CRAMP FREEZE SPONGE MOISTURE
DAMPENER MULLER
DAMPER DAMP MUTE BREAD CHECK
CHECKER REGISTER
DAMPNESS DAMP HUMIDITY
DAMSEL GIRL WENCH MAIDEN
MOPPET DAMOSEL DAMOZEL
PUCELLE DONZELLA PRINCESS
DAMSELFISH PINTANO
DAMSELFLY NAIAD
DAN GI DEN
DANAKIL AFAR
DANAUS ANOSIA
DANCE BAL BOB HOP JIG MAI SON
BALL DRAG DUET DUMP FISH FOOT
FRUG HEEL HOOF HORA JAZZ JIVE
JUBA KOLO LEAP LOPE MASK MILL
MOVE PROM REEL SAIL SHAG SKIT
STEP BAILE BAMBA BONGO BRAWL
CANON CAPER CAROL CONGA
DANZA ENTRY FLING FLISK FRIKE
FRISK GOPAK LASYA MAMBO PAVAN
POLKA RINKA RUMBA SALLY SAMBA
STOMP SWING TANGO TRACE
TREAD TWIST VOLTA WALTZ
ALTHEA AREITO BALLET BALTER
BOLERO BOOGIE BOSTON BRANLE
CANARY CANCAN CEBELL CORDAX
DANZON DIDDLE DREHER FADING
FORMAL FROLIC GERMAN HORMOS
MASQUE MINUET MOBBLE MONKEY
MORRIS NRITTA PASSAY RACKET
RHUMBA SHIMMY TODDLE TRESCA
TUMBLE VALETA ANTHEMA BEGUINE
CALINDA CANTICO COURANT
CZARDAS DANSANT FADDING
FARRUCA FOOTING FOXTROT
FURLANA GAVOTTE MORISCO
PATTERN SALTATE SARDANA
SHUFFLE TEMPETE TRESCHE
TRIPPLE VOLTIZE ZIGANKA
ANGLAISE AURRESCU BAMBOUJA
BAMBOULA CACHUCHA CAKEWALK
CHACONNE COMPARSA COONJINE
COTILLON ENTRACTE ESTAMPIE
FANDANGO FANTASIA FLAMENCO
GALOPADE GUARACHA HABANERA
HEYDEGUY HORNPIPE KOLATTAM
MATELOTE
(— ART) NATYA ORCHESIS
(— ATTENDANCE) LACKEY LACQUEY
(— CLUMSILY) BALTER
(— DRAMA) NO NOH
(— FACE TO FACE) SET
(— FORM) PIVA
(— IN CIRCLE) JIGGER
(— METHOD) LABAN
(— NIMBLY) CANARY
(— RESEMBLING THE POLKA)
BERLIN
(— STEP) RIFF PICKUP
(— STYLE) ABHINAYA
(— TYPE) TANDAVA

(ACROBATIC —) ADAGIO
(AFRICAN —) SHOUT
(ARGENTINE —) CUANDO
(AUSTRIAN —) LANDLER
(BALINESE —) KEBYAR LEGONG
(BALLROOM —) SON CONGO
COTILLON
(BOHEMIAN —) REDOWA FURIANT
(CARNIVAL —) COOCH FOLIA
COOTCH
(CEREMONIAL —) AREITO CANTICO
DUTUBURI
(COQUETTISH —) PURPOSE
(COUNTRY —) HAY CONFESS
ANGLAISE
(COURTSHIP —) CUECA BATUQUE
LEZGIBKA
(DANISH —) SEXTUR
(FIESTA —S) AKRIEROS
(FLAMENCO —) ALEGRIAS
(FRENCH —) BAL BOREE BRAWL
GAVOT BRANLE BOURREE BOUTADE
BRANSLE GAVOTTE LAVOLTA
(GAY —) RANT GAILLARD GALLIARD
(GESTURE —) SIVA
(GREEK —) CORDAX KORDAX
SIKINNIS
(GYPSY —) FARRUCA
(HAITIAN —) JUBA
(HOBBYHORSE —) CALUSAR
(HOLIDAY —) PATTERN
(HUNGARIAN —) KOS
(INDIAN —) IRUSKA KATHAK
(IRISH —) FADING
(ITALIAN —) FORLANA FURLANA
(JAPANESE —) BUGAKU KAGURA
(JAVANESE —) SERIMPI
(LIVELY —) JIG REEL GALOP GIGUE
POLKA RUMBA BOLERO CANARY
RHUMBA SPRING BOURREE
FURLANA HOEDOWN GALLIARD
GALOPADE HORNPIPE
(MAORI —) HAKA
(MEXICAN —) DARABE HUAPANGO
SANDUNGA
(MOURNFUL —) DUMP
(NORWEGIAN —) HALLING
(OLD ENGLISH —) CEBELL MORRIS
ARGEERS ANGLAISE
(OLD-FASHIONED —) LOURE
(PEASANT —) JOTA DANZON
BALITAO
(PERUVIAN —) CUECA KASWA
CACHUA
(POLISH —) KUJAWIAK
(POLYNESIAN —) HULA
(PORTUGUESE —) FADO
(ROUND —) RAY BRAUL CAROL
WALTZ CAROLE MAXIXE
(RUSTIC —) HAY HEY HAYMAKER
(SPANISH —) JOTA POLO JALEO
BOLERO JARABE CHACONNE
FLAMENCO GUARACHA
(SPEAR —) BARIS
(SQUARE —) SQUARE ARGEERS
HOEDOWN LANCERS QUADRILLE
(STATELY —) PAVAN PAVANE
EMMELEIA SARABAND
(SWORD —) BACUBERT MATACHIN

(VENEZUELAN —) JOROPO
(WEDDING —) CANACUAS
DANCER PONY CLOWN PONEY
ARTIST CORNER HOOFER HOPPER
MAENAD APSARAS CLOGGER
DANSEUR DEVADAS PASCOLA
PRANCER PRANKER SAILOUR
STEPPER TODDLER BALADINE
BAYADERE DANSEUSE FIGURANT
MORRICER
(BALLET —) ETOILE SOLISTE
CORYPHEE
(EGYPTIAN —S) GHAWAZI
GHAWAZEE
(JAVANESE —) SERIMPI
(JAVANESE —S) BEDOYO
(MASKED —S) GAHE
(SQUARE —S) FLOOR
(SWORD —) MATACHIN
(ZUNI —) SHALAKO
DANCING SWING ADANCE BALLET
CHANGE FROLIC MORRIS SALTANT
SURGING STEPPING TRIPSOME
(— MANIA) TARANTISM
DANDELION BLOW BLOWER CANKER
DINDLE CHICORY HAWKBIT
BLOWBALL COMPOSIT PISSABED
DANDELION HEAD PUFF CLOCK
BUFFBALL BULLFICE BULLFIST
PUFFBALL
DANDER ANGER DUTCH SCURF
STROLL TEMPER WANDER HACKLES
PASSION SAUNTER DANDRUFF
DANDIFIED SPRUCE BUCKISH
ADONIZED
DANDIFY ADONIZE DANDYIZE
DANDLE DANCE DIDDLE FADDLE
FONDLE PAMPER
DANDRUFF SCURF DANDER FURFUR
DANDY FOP JAY ADON BEAU BUCK
DAND DUDE FINE JAKE MAJO PRIG
TOFF TRIG YAWL BLOOD DILDO
JEMMY SWELL ADONIS MIZZEN
BUCKEEN CAPSTAN COXCOMB
ELEGANT FOPPISH JESSAMY
MACARONI SAILBOAT
DANDY HORSE HOBBY DRAISINE
DANDYISM BUCKISM
DANE DANSKER LOCHLIN DUBHGALL
DANEWORT EBULUS LOCHLIN
DANEBALL DANEWEED DEADWORT
WALLWORT
DANGER FEAR RISK DOUBT PERIL
WATHE HAZARD PLIGHT EXTREME
PITFALL VENTURE DISTRESS
JEOPARDY
DANGEROUS BAD HOT ILL RUM
DEAR FOUL GRAVE NASTY RISKY
FICKLE KITTLE SCATHY SHREWD
UNSURE AWKWARD FEARFUL
PARLOUS UNCANNY DOUBTFUL
INSECURE PERILOUS UNCHANCY
DANGLE LOP HANG LOLL DROOP
SWING DANDLE SHOGGLE SHOOGLE
SUSPEND TROLLOP
DANGLIN DANLI
DANK WET DAMP DONK HUMID
MOIST CLAMMY COARSE DAMPEN

DANKISH DRIZZLE WETNESS
MOISTURE
DANSEUSE DANCER BALLERINA
DANZIG GDANSK
　(— **LIQUEUR**) RATAFIA
DAPPER NEAT TRIM NATTY SPRUCE
　FINICAL FOPPISH SPARKISH
DAPPLE COVER FLECK FRECK
DAPPLED BLOCKY DOTTED POMELY
　FLECKED MOTTLED SPOTTED
　FRECKLED
DARBHA KUSA KUSHA
DARDANUS (**FATHER OF —**) JUPITER
　(**MOTHER OF —**) ELECTRA
DARE OSS DAST DEFU FACE OSSE
　RISK BRAVE STUMP ASSUME
　BANTER DACKER ATTEMPT
　BRAVADE FASHION PRESUME
　VENTURE
　(— **NOT**) DASSNT DAURNA DASSENT
DAREDEVIL MADCAP HARDYDARDY
DARING BOLD DARE DERF PERT
　RASH WILD BRAVE HARDY MANLY
　NERVE PREST FELONY HEROIC
　COURAGE DAIROUS DAREFUL
　BOLDNESS DEVILISH FEARLESS
DARIOLE MADELINE
DARK DIM DUN MUM SAD WAN BASE
　BLAE DEEP DERK DERN DUSK EBON
　HARD MALE MIRK MURK BLACK
　BLIND BROWN CLOUD DINGY DUSKY
　FAINT MIRKY MURKY SHADY SOOTY
　SWART UMBER UNLIT VAGUE
　CLOSED CLOUDY CYPRUS DIMPSY
　DISMAL DRUMLY GLOOMY OPAQUE
　SOMBER SOMBRE SWARTH WICKED
　DARKISH DUSKISH MELANIC
　OBSCURE PITMIRK RAYLESS
　STYGIAN SUNLESS SWARTHY
　THESTER UNCLEAR ABSTRUSE
　DARKLING DARKSOME GLOOMFUL
　GLOOMING IGNORANT LOWERING
　SINISTER
DARK-COLORED SAD SWART
　SOMBER SOMBRE SWARTH
　SWARTHY
DARKEN DIM DUN BLUR DULL DUSK
　BEDIM BLIND CLOUD GLOAM GLOOM
　POCHE SHADE SULLY SWART
　UMBER DEEPEN ENDARK SHADOW
　BECLOUD BENIGHT BLACKEN
　ECLIPSE EMBROWN OBSCURE
　OPACATE PERPLEX SLUBBER
　TARNISH OVERCAST
　(— **HAIR**) BLEND
DARKENED SABLE CLOUDY BLINDED
　LAMPLESS
DARKENING SCURF
DARK HORSE MOREL
DARKISH DIM
DARKLY DARK CLOSE SABLY
　MISTILY
DARKNESS DARK DERN DUSK MIRK
　MURK BLACK GLOOM NIGHT SHADE
　TAMAS SHADOW DIMNESS PITMIRK
　PRIVACY SECRECY TENEBRA
　GLOAMING INIQUITY MIDNIGHT
　TENEBRES TWILIGHT
DARLING JO JOE PET CHOU CONY

DEAR DUCK LIFE LOVE NOBS PEAT
ROON AROON ARUIN BULLY CHERI
DEARY DUCKS LIEVE SWEET WHITE
CHERIE DAUTIE DAWTIE MINION
MOPPET OCHREE ACUSHLA
BUNTING CUSHLAM DILLING MINIKIN
PIGSNEY PINKENY QUERIDA
STOREEN DEARLING DUMPLING
FAVORITE LIEBCHEN LOVELING
MACUSHLA PRECIOUS SWEETING
DARLING PEA INDICO INDIGO
DARN DOG BLOW DERN DURN MEND
　PATCH BUGGER REPAIR DOGGONE
DARNED BLAME BLAMED DEUCED
　DURNED BLESSED BLINDING
　DOWNGONE
DARNEL RAY CRAP TARE WEED
　CHEAT CHESS DRANK DRAWK
　DRUNK EAVER GRASS IVRAY NEELE
　COCKLE EGILOPS AEGILOPS
DART JET POP BOLT BUZZ CANE
　CHOP COLP FLIT JOUK LEAP LICK
　PILE PLAN PLAY ROUT ARROW
　BOUND FLAME FLING FLIRT GLEAM
　GLINT LANCE SCAMP SCOOT SHAFT
　SHOOT SKITE SKIVE SPEAR SPEED
　SPRIT START ANCHOR BULTEN
　DARTLE ELANCE GLANCE LANCET
　LAUNCH METHOD SCHEME SPRING
　SQUIRT STRIKE SUMPIT THRUST
　JAVELIN MISSILE STRALET VERUTUM
　BRANDISH GAVELOCK JACULATE
　SPICULUM
　(— **ABOUT**) SPRINKLE
　(— **OF LIGHTNING**) STREAK
　(— **OF MOLDING**) ANCHOR
　(— **REPEATEDLY**) DARTLE
DARTER SPECK
DARTING SALLY ARROWY
DARTLIKE SPICULAR
DASH DAD DAH PEP ZIP BANG BOLT
　CAST DING DIVE ELAN GIFT HINT
　HURL LASH LINE LUSH PASH PELT
　POSS RACE RASH RUIN RULE RUSH
　SHOW SLAM SOSH TICK VEIN WHAP
　WHOP ABASH ARDOR BLANK BREAK
　CHAFE CLASH CRASH CRUSH DRIVE
　ECLAT FLASH FLING FRUSH KNOCK
　PLASH PLOUT SKITE SLASH SLOSH
　SMASH SPEED SPEND SPICE SPURN
　START STYLE SWASH SWELL TASTE
　THROW TOUCH TRICK BEDASH
　DALLOP DASHEE DOLLOP ENERGY
　HURTLE HYPHEN RELISH SHIVER
　SPIRIT SPLASH SPRINT STRAIN
　STROKE THRUST BRAVURA
　BREENGE COLLIDE DEPRESS
　DISPLAY HUNDRED IMPINGE
　SHATTER SPATTER SPLOTCH
　TANTIVY CONFOUND GRATUITY
　SPLINTER
　(— **ABOUT WILDLY**) GAD REEL
　(— **AGAINST**) BEAT
　(— **DOWN**) QUELL STRAM
　STRAMASH
　(— **IN PIECES**) CRASH
　(— **OF SPIRITS**) LACE LACING
　(— **OUT**) QUELL
　(— **TOGETHER**) COLLIDE

　(— **UP**) FLURR
　(— **WITH WATER**) JAW BLASH
　SLASH
DASHBOARD DASH FACIA DASHER
　FASCIA
DASHED SWITCHED
DASHER DASH BEATER PLUNGER
DASHING BOLD BULLY DASHY
　DOGGY SHOWY SMART SWASH
　JABBLE SPANKY SWANKY VELOCE
　DOGGISH GALLOWS LARKING
　STYLISH SWAGGER VARMINT
　SLASHING SPANKING SPIRITED
DASTARD CAD SOT DAFF SNEAK
　COWARD CRAVEN DULLARD
　WITHING POLTROON
DASTARDLY FOUL VILLAIN
　COWARDLY POLTROON SNEAKING
DASYLIRION SOTOL
DASYPUS TATU
DASYURE TIGER YABBI DAPPLE
DATA DOPE FACTS IMPUT INPUT
　MATERIAL
DATE AGE DAY ERA DRAG FARD
　FUSS DATUM EPOCH FARDH FRUIT
　SAIDI CUTOFF FRIEND HALAWI
　JUJUBE RECKON GALLANT
　ANTEDATE ASHARASI DEADLINE
　(— **FIXED UPON**) TERM
　(— **RIPENING**) KIMRI RUTAB KHALAL
DATED GIVEN PASSE OUTMODED
DATE PLUM LOTUS SAPOTE ZAPOTE
DATOLITE BAKERITE HUMBOLDTITE
DATUM FACT ITEM GIVEN
DATURA DUTRA STRAMONY
　TOGUACHA
DAUB DAB DOB MUD BALM BLOB
　BLOT CLAG CLAM CLAT CLAY COAT
　GAUM MOIL SOIL TEER CLAIK
　CLART CLEAM COVER DITCH FLICK
　PAINT SLAKE SLAUM SMEAR
　BEDAUB CLATCH GREASE LABBER
　SMUDGE SPLASH BESMEAR DRIBBLE
　PLASTER SCLATCH SLUBBER
　SPLATCH SPLOTCH SLAISTER
DAUBED GAUMY
DAUBING DUBBING MOILING
DAUBY BLOTTY
DAUGHTER ANAC BINT DAME GIRL
　CHILD FILLE FILLY KIBEI REGAN
　ALUMNA CADETTE DOCHTER
　GONERÍL CORDELIA
　(**PANTALOON'S —**) COLUMBINE
DAUNT AWE COW DAW ADAW DARE
　DAZE FAZE MATE STUN TAME
　ABASH ACCOY AMATE BREAK
　CHECK DETER DOMPT DANTON
　DISMAY SUBDUE CONQUER
　CONTROL OVERAWE REPRESS
　STUPEFY TERRIFY DISPIRIT
　OVERCOME
DAUNTLESS BOLD GOOD BRAVE
　AWELESS FEARLESS INTREPID
DAVENPORT DESK SOFA COUCH
　DIVAN
DAVID TAFFY DAWKIN
DAVIDIST JORIST
DAVIT CRANE
DAW DA DAWN DRAB DAUNT MAGPIE

DAWPATE JACKDAW SLATTERN
SLUGGARD
DAWDLE LAG IDLE JAUK MUCK MULL
POKE TOIT DALLY DELAY DRILL
KNOCK DADDLE DAIDLE DIDDLE
DOODLE DRETCH FADDLE LINGER
LOITER MUCKER PICKLE PIDDLE
PINGLE POTTER PUTTER TANTLE
TRIFLE DRIDDLE FINNICK QUIDDLE
SAUNTER LALLYGAG LOLLYGAG
SHAMMOCK SLUMMOCK
DAWDLER DAWDLE MUSARD
LOUTHER
DAWN DAW ROW EOAN MORN
BREAK CREEK LIGHT PRIME SHINE
SUNUP AURORA MORROW ORIENT
SPRING UPRISE DAWNING GREKING
MORNING SUNRISE COCKCROW
DAYBREAK
DAY DA DEI ERA SUN YOM DATE
DIEM DIES DIET TIME EPOCH LIGHT
FRIDAY MONDAY PERIOD SUNDAY
JOURNEY TUESDAY LIFETIME
SATURDAY THURSDAY WEDNESDAY
(**— AND NIGHT**) KALPA
(**— BEFORE**) EVE
(**— OF JUDGMENT**) INQUEST
DOOMSDAY
(**— OF ORIGIN**) BIRTHDAY
(**— OF REST**) SABBATH
(**— OF ROMAN MONTH**) IDES NONES
CALENDS KALENDS
(**5 NAMELESS —S**) UAYEB
(**60TH OF —**) GHURRY
(**8TH — AFTER FEAST**) UTAS
(**DOG —S**) CANICULE
(**EVERY —**) ALDAY
(**EVIL —S**) DISMAL
(**FAST —**) ASHURA FASTEN
(**FIRST — OF AUGUST**) LAMMAS
(**FIRST — OF MAY**) BELTANE
BEALTINE
(**HOLY —**) FEAST HOLIDAY
(**HOT —**) BROILER ROASTER
(**LAST — OF FESTIVAL**) APODOSIS
(**MARKET —**) NUNDINE TIANGUE
(**NO FLESH —**) MAIGRE
(**PATRON SAINT'S —**) PATTERN
(**QUARTER —**) TERM
(**TWELFTH —**) EPIPHANY
(**WEEK —**) FERIA
(**WORK —**) WARDAY
DAYAK DYAK IBAN BAHAU DUSUN
KAYAN KENYA KENYAH KELABIT
DAYBOOK BOOK DIURNAL JOURNAL
DAYBREAK DAWN MORN SUNUP
DAWNING DAYDAWN DAYLIGHT
DAYDREAM DWAM MUSE DREAM
DWALM FANCY VISION FANTASY
REVERIE PHANTASY
DAYFLOWER COHITRE
DAYLIGHT DAY LIGHT DAYSHINE
(**BROAD —**) FUIRDAYS
DAYWORKER DILKER
DAZE FOG DAMP DARE MAZE STUN
DAUNT DAZZLE DIZZY DOZEN
SWOON ASTONY BEDAZE BEMUSE
BENUMB DAZZLE DEAFEN MUDDLE
TRANCE CONFUSE PETRIFY

STUPEFY TORPIFY ASTONISH
BEWILDER DUMFOUND PARALYZE
DAZED MAD ASEA DAMP ASSOT
DIZZY DOYLT SILLY TOTTY CUCKOO
DOILED GROGGY ROTTEN BEMUSED
DONNERT SPOILED WITLESS
ASTONIED BESOTTED DITHERED
DONNERED WITHERED
DAZEDLY GROGGILY
DAZZLE DARE DAZE BLEND BLIND
DROWN GLAIK SHINE FULGOR
ECLIPSE BEWILDER OUTSHINE
SURPRISE
DAZZLED BLINDED
DAZZLING FLARE FLASH FLASHY
GARISH ADAZZLE FLARING FULGENT
GLARING RADIANT DIZZYING
GORGEOUS
DDT TDE DICOPHANE
DEACON ADEPT CLERIC DOCTOR
LAYMAN LEVITE MASTER PHILIP
MINISTER
DEACONESS WIDOW
DEAD FEY LOW AWAY BUNG COLD
DEAF DOWD DULL FLAT GONE
MORT NUMB POKY SURE TAME
ADEAD AMORT BLIND DEEDS INERT
NAPOO POKEY QUIET SLAIN STARK
VAPID ASLEEP BYGONE FALLEN
LAPSED NAPOOH REFUSE DEADISH
DEFUNCT EXACTLY EXPIRED
EXTINCT INSIPID SAINTED STERILE
TEDIOUS ABSOLUTE COMPLETE
DECEASED DEPARTED INACTIVE
LIFELESS OBSOLETE
(**— AT TOP**) RAMPICK
DEAD-ARM NECROSIS
DEAD-DRUNK BLIND
DEADEN DAMP DULL DUMB KILL
MULL MUTE NUMB SEAR STUN
BLUNT SLAKE BENUMB DAMPEN
MUFFLE OBTUND OPIATE RETARD
STIFLE WEAKEN MORTIFY PETRIFY
REPRESS SLUMBER SMOTHER
AMORTIZE ASTONISH ENFEEBLE
(**— A SCENT**) FOIL
DEAD END PLACE
DEADENED DEAD DEAF SEAR SERE
DEADENING PUGGING
DEADHEAD SINK BOBBER SINKER
DEADHOUSE MORGUE MORTUARY
DEAD LETTER NIX
DEADLINE DATELINE
DEADLINESS LETHALITY
DEADLOCK TIE LOGJAM IMPASSE
STANDOFF STOPPAGE
DEADLY WAN DIRE FELL MORT
FATAL FERAL TUANT DEATHY
LETHAL MORTAL CAPITAL DEATHLY
FATEFUL RUINOUS MORTIFIC
VENOMOUS VIRULENT
DEADLY CARROT DRIAS THAPSIA
DEAD NETTLE HENBIT
DEADS MULLOCK
DEAF SURD DUNCH DUNNY SORDA
SORDO
DEAFEN DIN DORR DEAVE DEADEN
DEAFENING DEEVEY
DEAF-MUTE FENELLA SURDOMUTE

DEAFNESS ASONIA SURDITY
ANACUSIA ANACUSIS COPHOSIS
DEAL GO END JOB DAIL DOLE LEND
PART SALE TALE WHIZ ALLOT
BOARD BROKE FETCH PLANK SERVE
SEVER SHAKE SHARE SHIFT TRADE
TREAT TROKE TRUCK WIELD YIELD
BATTEN BESTOW DIVIDE HANDLE
MEDDLE NUMBER PARCEL BARGAIN
DELIVER INFLICT PIANOLA PORTION
SCATTER TRUCKLE WRESTLE
DISPENSE SEPARATE
(**— CARDS**) DRAW TALLY
(**— CLANDESTINELY**) TRINKET
(**— IN A TRIFLING WAY**) PIDDLE
(**— IN BRIDGE**) BOARD
(**— IN GRAIN**) SWALE
(**— OF CARDS**) COUP SPOIL
GOULASH
(**— SHREWDLY**) JOCKEY
(**— WITH**) HAND COVER DIGHT
TREAT BUCKET CUSTOM DEMEAN
HANDLE ENTREAT
(**GREAT —**) MORT LOADS MIGHT
SIGHT JUGFUL SKINFUL
(**POLITICAL —**) DICKER
DEALER BANK CHAP AGENT COPER
BADGER BANKER BROKER CADGER
EGGLER GROCER JOBBER JUNIOR
MONGER SELLER TRADER BUTCHER
CHAPMAN KEELMAN YOUNGER
CHANDLER MERCHANT OCCUPIER
OPERATOR STICKMAN TAILLEUR
(**— IN CATTLE**) COUPER COWPER
DROVER
(**— IN CHEMICALS**) SALTER
DRYSALTER
(**— IN DRY GOODS**) DRAPER
(**— IN GRAIN**) SWALER
(**— IN OLD CLOTHES**) FRIPPER
(**— IN PAINTS**) COLORMAN
(**— IN TEXTILES**) MERCER
(**CARDS —**) FARMER
(**COAL —**) COLLIER
(**HORSE —**) COPER COUPER
COWPER CHANTER SCORSER
(**SLAVE —**) MANGO
(**STOCK —**) STAG JOBBER
OUTSIDER
DEALFISH VAAGMAR VAAGMAER
DEALING DOLE PRICE TRUCK
TRADING TRAFFIC EXCHANGE
(**BUSINESS —S**) TROKE
(**JUST —**) DOOM
(**TRICKY —**) BROKING
(**PL.**) DEAL TRAFFIC BUSINESS
COMMERCE PRACTICE PRACTISE
DEAN DECAN DOYEN DEANER
SENIOR VERGER PREFECT PROVOST
SUBDEAN ARCHDEAN PRAEFECT
DEAR JO GRA HON JOE PET AGRA
CARA CHER CONY FAIR FOND GOOD
HIGH LAMB LIEF LOVE NEAR NOBS
SALT BOSOM CHARY CHERE CHUCK
DEARY HONEY LOVED SWEET TIGHT
COSTLY DAUTIE DAWTIE DEARIE
DEARLY POPPET SCARCE SEVERE
SQUALL TENDER WORTHY BELOVED
DARLING LOVABLE PIGSNEY

QUERIDA SPECIAL TOOTSIE
ESPECIAL ESTEEMED GLORIOUS
PRECIOUS VALUABLE
DEARLY DEAR ALIFE DEEPLY
KEENLY RICHLY HEARTILY
DEARNESS CHERTE DEARTH
DEARTH LACK WANT CHERTE
FAMINE PAUCITY POVERTY
DEARNESS SCARCITY SOLITUDE
DEATH DEE END BALE BANE DEAD
DOOM EXIT FAIL FATE KILL MORS
MORT OBIT PASS REST WINK
ANKOU DECAY GRAVE GRUEL
LETHE NIGHT SLEEP CHAROS
CHARUS DEMISE DEPART ENDING
EXITUS EXPIRY MURDER PERIOD
REAPER WAGANG CURTAIN
DECEASE FUNERAL PARTING
PASSAGE QUIETUS SILENCE
BIOLYSIS CASUALTY FATALITY
NECROSIS RAWBONES THANATOS
(— **ANGEL**) AZRAEL
(— **BY HANGING**) HALTER
(— **OF TISSUE**) GANGRENE
DEATH ADDER ELAPID ELAPOID
DEATH CAMASS LOBELIA
DEATHLESS ETERNAL UNDYING
IMMORTAL
DEATHLIKE DEATHLY GHASTLY
MACABRE GHASTFUL MORIBUND
MORTUOUS
DEATHLY DEAD FATAL DEADLY
MORTAL GHASTLY STYGIAN
DEATHFUL MORTALLY
DEATH'S-HEAD SKULL
DEBAR DENY TABU CROSS ESTOP
REPEL TABOO DISBAR FORBID
HINDER REFUSE BOYCOTT DEPRIVE
EXCLUDE OUTSHUT PREVENT
SECLUDE SUSPEND PRECLUDE
PROHIBIT
DEBARK LAND
DEBARRED FROZEN OUTSHUT
DEBASE SINK ABASE ALLOY AVILE
DIRTY LOWER STOOP BEMEAN
DEFILE DEMEAN DILUTE EMBASE
IMPAIR NIDDER NITHER REDUCE
REVILE VILIFY CORRUPT DEBAUCH
DECLINE DEGRADE DEPRAVE
PERVERT TRADUCE VILLAIN VITIATE
DEBASED BASE VILE BASTARD
CORRUPT SQUALID CANKERED
DEGRADED DEROGATE
DEBASEMENT TARNISH
DEBASING DOWNWARD
DEBATABLE MOOT DISPUTABLE
DEBATE AGON BEAT FRAY MOOT
ARGUE FIGHT PLEAD STUDY
ARGUFY HASSEL HASSLE REASON
STRIFE AGITATE CANVASS CONTEND
CONTEST DISCEPT DISCUSS
DISPUTE EXAMINE MOOTING
PALAVER QUARREL WRANGLE
ARGUMENT CONSIDER CONTRARY
MILITATE PARLANCE QUESTION
DEBATER PICADOR
DEBAUCH BOUT FILE SPREE TAINT
WHORE DEBASE DEBOSH DEFILE
GUZZLE MISUSE SEDUCE SPLORE

VILIFY CORRUPT DEBOISE DEPRAVE
MISLEAD POLLUTE VIOLATE
DISHONOR SQUANDER STRUMPET
STUPRATE
DEBAUCHED LEWD RAKELY
DEBOIST DEBOSHED RAKEHELL
DEBAUCHEE RIP RAKE ROUE
HOLOUR LECHER RAKEHELL
DEBAUCHERY RAKERY DEBAUCH
PRIAPISM
DEBENTURE SECURITY
DEBENZOLIZE STRIP
DEBILITATE SINK
DEBILITATED WEAK SEEDY FEEBLE
INFIRM SAPPED ASTHENIC
DEBILITY ATONY ASTHENY LANGUOR
ASTHENIA WEAKNESS
DEBIT DEBT LOSS CHARGE
DEBONAIR AIRY JAUNTY POLITE
CAVALIER GRACEFUL GRACIOUS
DEBOUCH FALL MOUTH
DEBOUCHMENT INFLUX INFLUXION
DEBRIS GUCK SLAG DECAY FRUSH
TRADE TRASH WASTE REFUSE
RUBBLE RUDERA CRUMBLE ELUVIUM
RUBBISH SLIDDER DETRITUS
(— **IN WOOL**) BUR BURR
(— **OF INSECTS**) FRASS
(— **OF ROCKS**) HEAD DRIFT TALUS
ELUVIUM
(**FLUFFY** —) FLUE
(**FOREST** —) SLASH
DEBT DUE SIN POST DEBIT FAULT
STOCK ARREARS DEBITUM
JUDGMENT TRESPASS
(**PL.**) OBLATA WANIGAN ARREARAGE
DEBTOR OWER SKIP DYVOUR
DEBITOR YIELDER
DEBUT OPENING ENTRANCE
DEBUTANTE BUD DEB DEBBY
INGENUE ROSEBUD
DECADENT EFFETE DECAYED
HOTHOUSE OVERRIPE
DECAHYDRATE SODA
DECALOGUE WITNESS
DECAMP GUY PUT BOLT HIKE KITE
ELOPE MOSEY SCOOT SCOUR
VAMOS DEPART ESCAPE LEVANT
MIZZLE MORRIS POWDER VAMOSE
ABSCOND DISCAMP VAMOOSE
DECAMPING GUY
DECAN DECURION
DECANT EMIT POUR UNLOAD
TRANSFER
DECANTER CARAFE CARAFON
URCEOLE GARDEVIN INGESTER
DECAPITATE BEHEAD DECOLLATE
DECAPITATION DECOLL HEADING
DECAPOD BUSTER
DECARBONIZE DECOKE
DECATING SPONGING
DECAY EBB ROT ROX BLET CONK
DOAT DOTE DOZE FADE RUIN SEED
WANE WEAR CROCK DEATH FAILL
SHANK SLOOM SLOUM SPOIL
WASTE CARIES FADING MARCOR
MILDEW MOLDER MOSKER SICKEN
WITHER CRUMBLE DECLINE FAILURE

MORTIFY PUTREFY DECREASE
FORDWINE
(— **IN WOOD**) CONK DOZE
(**INCIPIENT** —) BLET
DECAYED BAD DEAF DOZY ROXY
FRUSH SEEDY DAISED MARCID
PUTRID ROTTEN SPAKED RUINOUS
SNAGGLED
DECAYING COLD DOTY SHABBY
CARIOUS
DECEASE DIE FAIL OBIT PASS
DEATH DEMISE PASSAGE
DECEASED DEAD PARTED DEFUNCT
EXTINCT UMWHILE DEPARTED
UMQUHILE
DECEIT GAB DOLE FLUM GAFF GULL
RUSE SHAM TRAP TRAY WILE COVIN
CRAFT DOLUS FRAUD GUILE SARAB
SWICK SWIKE CAUTEL FELONY
WOIDRE CUNNING DISSAIT FAITERY
FICTION ARTIFICE FALSEDAD
INTRIGUE SPOOFERY SUBTLETY
TRICKERY TRUMPERY WILINESS
DECEITFUL BLIND BRAID FALSE
GAUDY JANUS LOOPY SLAPE
ARTFUL COVERT CRAFTY DOUBLE
FICKLE HOLLOW TRICKY CUNNING
EVASIVE FICTIVE SIRENIC SLEEKIT
SLIDDER UNWREST WINDING
COVINOUS GUILEFUL ILLUSIVE
INDIRECT SHAMMISH TORTUOUS
DECEITFULLY DOUBLE FALSELY
DECEITFULNESS SHAM DECEIT
FALSITY
DECEIVE BOB COG CON DOR FOB
FUB GAB GAS GUM KID LIE BILK
BRAG BUNK CRAP DUPE FAKE FLAM
FOOL GAFF GULL HAVE HOAX JILT
JOUK MOCK SELL SHAM SILE SNOW
TURN WILE ABUSE AMUSE BLEAR
BLEND BLENK BLIND BLINK BLUFF
CATCH CHEAT COZEN CROSS
CULLY DODGE DORRE FEINT GLEEK
GLOZE HOCUS LURCH PATCH
SPOOF SWICK SWIKE TRICK TROIL
TRUFF TRUMP TRYST BAFFLE
BEDOTE BEFLUM BEFOOL BETRAY
BLANCH BUBBLE CAJOLE CLOINE
CLOYNE DELUDE DIVERT EUCHRE
GAMMON HUMBUG ILLUDE JUGGLE
MISUSE NIGGLE SUCKER WIMPLE
BEGUILE DEFRAUD MISLEAD
OVERSEE TRAITOR BEJUGGLE
FLIMFLAM HOODWINK OUTREACH
DECEIVER ANGLE CHEAT HOCUS
COGGER FAITOR FALSER GUILER
MOCKER TRAPAN TREPAN FALSARY
ILLUSOR JUGGLER SHARPER
SPOOFER TRUMPER WARLOCK
WERNARD IMPOSTOR LOSENGER
LOTHARIO MAGICIAN
DECELERATE SLOW
DECENCY GRACE DECORUM
HONESTY MODESTY CHASTITY
DECENNIUM DECADE
DECENT FAIR CHASTE COMELY
HONEST MODEST PROPER SEEMLY
FITTING GRADELY JANNOCK
SHAPELY SIGHTLY DECOROUS

GRAITHLY WISELIKE
DECENTLY WHITE
DECEPTION BAM COG DOR GAG LIE
DOLE FLAM FLUM GAFF GULL HOAX
MAZE RIDE RUSE SELL SHAM WILE
ABUSE BLIND CHEAT COVIN CRAFT
CURVE DOLUS DORRE FAVEL FRAUD
GLEEK GUILE MAGIC SNARE SPOOF
TRICK BARRAT CAUTEL DECEIT
DUPERY HUMBUG JUGGLE ABUSION
BLAFLUM CHICANE CUNNING
EVASION FALLACY FALSERY FICTION
GULLAGE GULLERY KNAVERY
PRETEXT SLYNESS ARTIFICE
DISGUISE FALSEDAD FLIMFLAM
ILLUSION INTRIGUE PHANTASM
PRESTIGE SUBTLETY TRICKERY
TRUMPERY WILINESS
DECEPTIVE FLAM FALSE ARTFUL
SIRENIC TRICKSY DELUSIVE
DELUSORY FLIMFLAM ILLUSORY
IMPOSING SHAMMISH UNSICKER
DECEPTIVENESS FANTASTRY
DECIBEL (10 —S) BEL
DECIDE FIX CAST DEEM HOLD RULE
TELL WILL AWARD JUDGE PATCH
PITCH DECERN DECISE DECREE
FIGURE REWARD SETTLE ADJUDGE
DERAIGN RESOLVE CONCLUDE
SENTENCE
(— UPON) SET ELECT CHOOSE
TERMINE
DECIDED FIRM FLAT MAIN FORMED
SETTLED DECISIVE RESOLUTE
DECIDEDLY DIRECTLY DISTINCTLY
DECIDUA CADUCA
DECIGRAM LI
DECIMA TENTH TITHE
DECIMAL DENARY REPEATER
(— PART) MANTISSA
DECIMATE TENTH DESTROY
DECIPHER READ SOLVE CIPHER
DECODE DETECT REVEAL DECRYPT
DISCOVER INDICATE UNPUZZLE
DECIPHERING EPIGRAPHY
DECISION ACT END CALL DOOM
FIAT GRIT ARRET AWARD CANON
FAITH ISSUE PARTY PLUCK POINT
ACTION CHOICE CRISIS DECREE
DIKTAT RULING ACUERDO CONSULT
INTERIM PRACTIC VERDICT FINALITY
JUDGMENT PLACITUM SENTENCE
SUFFRAGE UMPIRAGE
(— OF COURT) HOLDING
(EXISTENTIAL —) LEAP
(FINAL —) ISSUE
DECISIVE FINAL CRISIC PAYOFF
VIRILE CRUCIAL DECIDED CRITICAL
CRUSHING DECRETAL POSITIVE
DECISIVELY FINALLY
DECK FIG TOG BANK BUSS DAUB
DINK FLAT HEAP PINK POOP PROW
TRIG ADORN ARRAY COVER DIZEN
DRESS EQUIP FLOOR HATCH PRANK
PRINK STORE AWNING BEDECK
BLAZON CLOTHE ENRICH FETTLE
FOCSLE LAUREL APPAREL BEDIGHT
BEDIZEN FEATHER FLOUNCE
GEMMATE BEAUTIFY DECORATE

EMBLAZON PLATFORM
(— OF CARDS) BOOK
(— OUT) BARB TIFF DIZEN SPICK
BEDECK FANGLE FINIFY BEDIGHT
(HIGH —) POOP
(LOWEST —) ORLOP
DECKED CLAD BESEEN ARMORIED
LAURELED
(— OUT) SPIFFED
DECKHAND BOATMAN TRIMMER
BARGEMAN
DECKHOUSE CABOOSE CAMBOOSE
DECKLE DECKEL FEATHEREDGE
DECKMAN TRIPPER LEVERMAN
DECLAIM GALE RANT RAVE ROLL
MOUTH ORATE SPEAK SPOUT
BLEEZE RECITE ELOCUTE INVEIGH
DENOUNCE DISCLAIM HARANGUE
PERORATE SINGSONG
DECLAIMER BARD SPEECHIFIER
DECLAMATION FROTHING
HARANGUE SPOUTING
DECLARATION BILL CALL DICK
NARR TALE WORD COUNT FUERO
LIBEL PAROL AVOWAL DECEIT
MISERE ORACLE PAROLE PLACET
SAYING EXPRESS PROMISE
RESOLVE MANIFEST PLATFORM
(— IN BRIDGE) MAKE AUCTION
(— OF HOSTILITIES) DEFIANCE
(OFFICIAL —) AUTHORITY
DECLARE BID KEN LAY SAY VOW
AVER AVOW DENY MAKE READ
SHOW SNUM SWAN TROW VOTE
AREAD AREED BRUIT KEETH KITHE
KYTHE POSIT SNORE SOUND SPEAK
STATE TRUTH VOUCH AFFIRM
ALLEGE ASSERT ASSURE AUTHOR
AVOUCH BLAZON COUTHE DEPONE
DESCRY EXPONE HERALD INDICT
NOTIFY PATEFY RELATE SPRING
UPGIVE ACCLAIM BEHIGHT DISCUSS
EXPRESS OUTTELL PROFESS
PROTEST PUBLISH SIGNIFY TERMINE
TESTIFY ANNOUNCE DENOUNCE
DESCRIBE INDICATE INTIMATE
MAINTAIN MANIFEST NUNCIATE
PROCLAIM RENOUNCE
(— A SAINT) CANONIZE
(— ARBITRARILY) GAVEL
(— INVALID) ANNUL
(— PUBLICLY) CRY
(— UNTRUE) DENY
(— WAR) DEFY
(SOLEMNLY —) AFFY SWEAR
DECLARED AVOWED STATED
DECLARER LAWMAN VIVANT
DECLINATION BIAS DECAY SLOPE
REGRET DECLINE DESCENT
REFUSAL SOUTHING SWERVING
DECLINE BEG DIP EBB SAG SET
BALK BEND BUST DENY DIVE DOWN
DROP FADE FAIL FALL FLAG FLOP
HELD SINK SLIP TURN VAIL WANE
WELK BAULK CHUTE DECAY DROLL
DROOP DWINE FAINT HEALD HIELD
LAPSE LOWER QUAIL REPEL SLACK
SLOPE SLUMP SPURN STOOP STRAY
TABES WAIVE DEBASE FALTER

REFUSE REJECT RENEGE SICKEN
WEAKEN ATROPHY DESCEND
DESCENT DETRECT DEVIATE
DISAVOW DWINDLE ECLIPSE
FAILURE FALLOFF FORBEAR
INFLECT LETDOWN SINKAGE
DECREASE DOWNBEAT DOWNTURN
FOREBEAR LANGUISH TOBOGGAN
WITHDRAW
(— IN MARKET PRICE) SPILL
(— IN POPULATION) CRASH
DECLINING DOWN AWANE BEARISH
FALLING WESTERN DECADENT
DECLIVITY BENT BREW FALL HANG
SIDE SKUG CLIFF COAST DEVEX
PITCH SCARP SLENT SLOPE CALADE
HANGER DECLINE DESCENT
HANGING DOWNHILL
DECLIVOUS PRONE SLOPING
DECOCT BOIL COOK SMELT EXCITE
KINDLE REFINE EXTRACT
DECOCTION BANG OOZE SAVE
BHANG APOZEM CREMOR PTISAN
TISANE APOZEMA DECOCTUM
DECOHERER TAPPER
DECOLLETE LOW
DECOMPOSE ROT FOUL FRIT DECAY
ATTACK DIGEST DEGRADE DISSOLVE
DECOMPOSED PUTRID
DECOMPOSITION DECAY BREAKUP
BIOLYSIS EXCHANGE
DECORATE DO BIND CHIP CITE
DECK EDGE FRET GAUD PINK RAIL
RULE TIFF TIRE TRIM ADORN DRESS
FLOCK FRILL GRAIN INLAY MENSE
PANEL POKER TRAIL TRICK BEDECK
BUTTON DAIKER DAMASK DECORE
EMBOSS FLOWER FRESCO PARGET
POUNCE PURFLE SPONGE SUBORN
BECROSS CORONET ENCHASE
FESTOON FURNISH GADROON
GARNISH HISTORY IMPASTE
INWEAVE MINIATE PERFORM
BELETTER FLOURISH ORNAMENT
OVERWORK TITIVATE
DECORATED GIDDY LACED AJOURE
FLAMBE ORNATE ADORNED
DAMASSE FROGGED INCISED
WROUGHT COCKADED DISTINCT
FLORETED
DECORATING LIMNERY
DECORATION KEY BUHL FALL FUSS
IKAT BOULE DECOR DODAD HONOR
MEDAL PRIDE BOULLE DECKER
DECORE DESIGN DOODAB DOODAD
FINERY FLORET FRIEZE GOTHIC
NIELLO PLAQUE SETOFF TINSEL
ARTWORK BARBOLA DECKING
EPERGNE FLUTING GARNISH
TRACERY BAYADERE DENTELLE
DIAMANTE ESCALLOP FLOURISH
FRETTING FRETWORK INTARSIA
ORNAMENT
(— IN GUEST CHAMBER) XENIUM
(— OF LEAVES) VIGNETTE
(— OF MONKEYS) SINGERIE
(— TECHNIQUE) PLANGI
(BOOK-COVER —) DENTELLE
(CUTOUT —) APPLIQUE

(FESTIVE —) GALA
(INESSENTIAL —) SPINACH
(MURAL —) TOPIA
(MUSICAL —) GRACE
(PORCELAIN —) KAKIEMON
(POTTERY —) BRODERIE
(WALL —S) TENTURE
(PL.) COLORS BUNTING GREENERY
DECORATIVE FANCY FIKIE
DECOROUS CALM DONE GOOD NICE
PRIM DOUCE GRAVE QUIET SOBER
STAID CHASTE DECENT DEMURE
MODEST POLITE PROPER SEDATE
SEEMLY SERENE STEADY BECOMED
FITTING ORDERLY REGULAR
SETTLED BECOMING COMPOSED
MANNERLY
DECOROUSLY FITLY
DECOROUSNESS CHASTITY
POLITESSE
DECORTICATE FLAY HULL HUSK
PARE PEEL PILL SKIN STRIP
DENUDE
DECORUM DECENCY DIGNITY
FITNESS MODESTY
DECOY COY BAIT CALL GOAD LURE
TOLE TOLL CRIMP DRILL PLANT
ROPER SHILL STALE STALL STOOL
TEMPT TRAIN ALLURE BUTTON
CALLER CAPPER ENTICE ENTRAP
PIGEON SEDUCE TOLLER TREPAN
BARNARD BERNARD DECOYER
INVEIGLE SQUAWKER
(— FOR GAMBLERS) CAPPER
(— FOR SWINDLERS) BARNARD
BERNARD
(AUCTIONEER'S —) BUTTON
DECREASE EBB BATE DROP FALL
LOSS SINK WANE WELK WILK ABATE
CROCK DECAY LAPSE SWAGE
TAPER WANZE WASTE CHANGE
DECESS DECREW IMPAIR LESSEN
NARROW REDUCE SHRINK ATROPHY
CUTDOWN DECLINE DWINDLE
SHORTEN SLACKEN SUBSIDE
DECIMATE DIMINISH DOWNTURN
MODERATE RETRENCH
(— IN FORCE) LAY
(— IN VOLUME) ABLATION
(— OF EFFICIENCY) FATIGUE
(— STITCHES) FASHION
DECREE ACT DIT LAW SAW SET
DOOM FIAT REDE RULE WILL WITE
AREAD AREED ARRET CANON EDICT
ENACT FIANT GRACE HATTI IRADE
JUDGE ORDER POINT SHAPE TENET
UKASE WRITE ARREST ASSIZE
DECERN DICTUM FIRMAN INDICT
MODIFY ORDAIN PLACIT RECESS
ADJUDGE APPOINT BESLUIT
COMMAND CONSULT DECREET
DICTATE DIVORCE ESCRIPT
GEZERAH MANDATE SETNESS
STATUTE WORKING DECISION
DECRETUM JUDGMENT PLACITUM
PSEPHISM RESCRIPT ROGATION
SANCTION SENTENCE
(— BEFOREHAND) DESTINE

(ECCLESIASTICAL —) CANON
SYNODICAL
(JUDICIAL —) AUTO
(MOHAMMEDAN —) IRADE
(OFFICIAL —) RESCRIPT
DECREPIT LAME WEAK UNORN
BEDRID CREAKY FEEBLE INFIRM
SENILE FAILING INVALID FORFAIRN
DECRY BOO SLUR LOWER ROGUE
DESCRY LESSEN ASPERSE BARRACK
CENSURE CONDEMN DEBAUCH
DEGRADE DETRACT BELITTLE
DEROGATE MINIMIZE
DECRYPT BREAK DECODE
DECURRENT DEFLUENT
DECUSSATION CHIASMA
DEDANS HAZARD
DEDICATE VOW VOTE DEVOW
SACRE SACRI DEVOTE DEVOVE
DIRECT HALLOW OBLATE ASCRIBE
ENTITLE CHRISTEN INSCRIBE
INTITULE SEPARATE
DEDICATED HOLY OBLATE SACRED
VOTIVE
DEDICATION CULT WAKF DEVOTION
DEDUCE PUT DRAW LEAD TAKE
BRING DRIVE FETCH GUESS INFER
TRACE DEDUCT DERIVE ELICIT
EVOLVE GATHER COLLECT EXPLAIN
EXTRACT SUBSUME CONCLUDE
DEDUCT BATE DOCK TAKE ABATE
ALLOW SHAVE DEFALK REBATE
RECOUP REDUCT REMOVE CURTAIL
SUBDUCT TRADUCE ABSTRACT
DISCOUNT SEPARATE SUBTRACT
DEDUCTION AGIO SALT CREDIT
DEDUCT REBATE BEAMAGE
DOCKAGE IMPRESS OFFTAKE
REPRISE DISCOUNT ERGOTISM
ILLATION STOPPAGE
DEDUCTIVE DOGMATIC
DEE DUANT
DEED DO ACT BILL BOOK CASE FACT
FAIT FEAT FIAT GEST HARD JEST
TURN WORK ACTUM ACTUS BROAD
CHART DOING GESTE ISSUE SANAD
THING TITLE ACTION CONVEY
ESCROW FACTUM POTTAH REMISE
SASINE SUNNUD TAILYE CHARTER
EXPLOIT FACTION TAILZIE CHIVALRY
HEIRLOOM PARERGON PRACTICE
PRACTISE TRANSFER
(BRUTAL —) ATROCITY
(CHARITABLE —S) ALMS
(GOOD —) BENEFIT MITZVAH
(HEBREW —) STARR
(PART OF —) HABENDUM
(VALIANT —) VALIANCE
(WICKED —) ILL
(PL.) DOINGS SERVICE MUNIMENTS
DEEM LET SAY SEE GIVE HOPE RECK
SEEM TELL JUDGE OPINE THINK
ESTEEM EXPECT ORDAIN RECKON
REGARD ACCOUNT ADJUDGE
BELIEVE RECOUNT RESPECT
SURMISE ANNOUNCE CONSIDER
JUDGMENT PROCLAIM
DEEMSTER DOOMSMAN
DE-ENERGIZE KILL CLEAR

DEEP LOW SAD SEA BOLD DUAT
HOLL HOWE NEAL RAPT ABYSS
BROAD DEWAT GRAVE GREAT
GRUFF HEAVY OCEAN STIFF STOOR
STOUR HOLLOW INTENT STRONG
SULLEN ABYSMAL INTENSE SERIOUS
UNMIXED ABSORBED ABSTRUSE
COMPLETE POWERFUL PROFOUND
THOROUGH
DEEP-DYED ENGRAINED
DEEPEN CLOUD DARKEN DREDGE
ENHANCE THICKEN HEIGHTEN
DEEPEST INMOST DEEPMOST
DEEPLY DEEP ADEEP DEARLY
SOUNDLY DEVOUTLY GROUNDLY
INWARDLY
DEEP-SEA DIPSY BATHYL DIPSEY
BATHYAL
DEEP-SEATED DEEP INTIMATE
PROFOUND INGRAINED
DEEP-TONED STOUR
DEER ELK RED ROE AXIS BUCK DAIM
HART HIND MILU MUSK OLEN PARA
PUDU RUSA SHOU SIKA STAG WILD
BROCK GEMUL MARAL MOOSE
SABIR SPADE STAIG CERVID CHITAL
CHITRA FALLOW GUEMAL HANGUL
HEARST HUEMUL PARRAH RASCAL
SAMBAR SAMBUR THAMIN VENADA
BROCKET BROWZER CARIBOU
CERVINE CERVOID CHEETAL
DEERLET FANTAIL GUAZUTI
KASTURA MUNTJAC PLANDOK
SAMBHAR THAMENG VENISON
BOBOLINK ELAPHURE RUMINANT
(— IN 3RD YEAR) SPAY SOREL
SPAYAD SPAYARD
(— UNDER 1 YEAR) KID
(2-YEAR OLD —) KNOBBER
(CASTRATED —) HAVIER
(FEMALE — IN 2ND YEAR) TEG
HEARST
(FEMALE —) DOE ROE HIND
(HINDQUARTERS OF —) FOUCH
FOURCHE
(MALE — IN 2ND YEAR) PRICKET
(MALE — IN 4TH YEAR) SORE
STAGGARD STAGGART
(MALE — OVER 5 YEARS) HART
STAG
(RED —) OLEN MARAL BROCKET
(RUSINE —) AXIS
(YOUNG —) KID FAWN SPITTER
DEER BUSH SOAPBUSH
DEER FERN HARDFERN
DEERFLY TABANID
DEERHAIR SEDGE BULRUSH
DEERHOUND DEERDOG BUCKHOUND
DEERSKIN BUCK DEER
DEFACE MAR FOUL RUIN SCAR
ERASE SHAME SPOIL CANCEL
DAMAGE DAMASK DEFAME DEFOIL
DEFORM DEFOUL EFFACE INJURE
INJURY DESTROY DETRACT DISTORT
SLANDER DISGRACE DISHONOR
MALAHACK MUTILATE OUTSHINE
DEFACED FOUL
DEFACING DIMINUTION
DEFALCATE DRIB DEFALK

DEFAMATION LIBEL DEFAME
DEFAMY DEPRAVE SCANDAL
SLANDER
DEFAME FOUL ABASE BELIE CLOUD
LIBEL NOISE SMEAR ACCUSE
CHARGE DEFACE DEFOIL DEFOUL
FORGAB INFAME INJURE MALIGN
SUGGIL VILIFY ASPERSE BLACKEN
BLEMISH DEBAUCH DETRACT
DIFFAME PUBLISH SCANDAL
SLANDER SPATTER TRADUCE
DISHONOR INFAMIZE
DEFAMER SYCOPHANT
DEFAULT FAIL FLAW LOSS MORA
ERROR FAULT OFFEND BLEMISH
FAILURE MISTAKE NEGLECT
OFFENSE OMISSION
(— **ON DEBT**) LEVANT
DEFEASANCE DEFEAT UNDOING
DEFEASIBLE IMPERFECT
DEFEAT EAT PIP WIN BALK BEAT
BEST BOWL CAST DING DOWN
DRUB FOIL HAVE JINK KILL LACE
LICK LOSS ROUT RUIN RUSH SINK
SKIN STOP TOLL TOSS TRAP TRIM
UNDO WHIP AVOID BREAK CHECK
FACER FALSE FLING FLOOR OUTDO
PASTE SKUNK SWAMP THROW
WASTE WHACK WORSE WORST
WRACK BAFFLE CUMBER DEROUT
EUCHRE LARRUP MASTER MURDER
STOUSH THWACK THWART WAGGLE
WEAKEN CONQUER DEPRIVE
DESTROY LICKING OVERSET
PEREMPT REVERSE SCOMFIT
SETBACK SHELLAC SNOOKER
SUBVERT TROUNCE INFRINGE
IRRITATE OVERCOME VANQUISH
WATERLOO
(— **COMPLETELY**) SKUNK
(— **DECISIVELY**) EAT DRUB SACK
BLAST CLEAN FLATTEN SHELLAC
(— **IN BRIDGE**) SET
(— **IN LAWSUIT**) CAST
(**DECISIVE** —) CLEANUP CLEANING
(**INTO** —) DOWN
(**UTTER** —) MATE ROUT DEROUT
DEFEATED DOWN LOST KAPUT
BEATEN CRAVEN WHIPPED
DEFEATIST BOLO FATALIST
DEFECT BUG FLAW LACK MAIM TWIT
VICE WANE WANT BOTCH CLOUD
CRAZE ERROR FAULT MINUS MULCT
TOUCH DAMAGE DESERT INJURY
LACUNA MALADY MAYHEM PLIGHT
VICETY VITIUM ABSENCE BLEMISH
DEMERIT FAILING MISPICK PEELING
PINHOLE COLOBOMA CRESCENT
DRAWBACK WEAKNESS
(— **IN CRYSTAL**) HOLE
(— **IN ENAMEL**) SCAB SAGGING
SCUMMING
(— **IN FABRIC**) GOUT SCOB BARRE
BRACK SMASH
(— **IN GLASS**) KNOT TEAR STONE
THREADS
(— **IN IRON**) SEAM
(— **IN MARBLE**) TERRAS TERRACE
TERRASSE

(— **IN METAL**) SNAKE
(— **IN PRINTING PLATE**) HICKY
HICKEY
(— **IN STEEL**) LAP
(— **IN TIMBER**) LAG SHAN
COLLAPSE
(— **IN YARN**) SINGLING CORKSCREW
(— **OF CHARACTER**) HOLE SHADE
HAMARTIA
(**LINT** —) SPOT
(**SPEECH** —) CLUTTERING
(**TELEVISION** —) FLOPOVER
DEFECTION LETDOWN DESERTION
DEFECTIVE BAD ILL EVIL FOXY
LACK LAME MANK POOR SICK
BAUCH BAUGH BLIND FALSE FLAWY
PASUL COMMON FAULTY FLAWED
MANGUE MEAGER MEAGRE RAGGED
HALTING TOMFOOL VICIOUS
DISGENIC DYSGENIC MUTILOUS
VITIATED
DEFEND FEND HOLD KEEP SAVE
WARD WARN WEAR COVER GUARD
SHEND WATCH ASSERT FORBID
SCREEN SECURE SHIELD UPHOLD
WARISH BUCKLER CONTEST
DERAIGN ESPOUSE EXPOUND
FLANKER JUSTIFY PREVENT
PROPUGN PROTECT SHELTER
SUPPORT WARRANT ADVOCATE
CHAMPION CONSERVE GARRISON
MAINTAIN PRESERVE PROHIBIT
DEFENDANT REA REUS ACCUSED
AVOWANT APPELLEE
DEFENDER FENDER PATRON
ADVOCATE ASSERTER ASSERTOR
CHAMPION GUARDIAN UPHOLDER
DEFENSE EGIS FORT WALL WEAR
AEGIS ALIBI FENCE GRITH ANSWER
BEHALF COVERT FRAISE SCONCE
BARRACE BULWARK CONTEST
DEFENCE OUTWORK RAMPART
SHELTER BOUNDARY SECURITY
SEPIMENT SPOLOGIA PALE ROCK
WARD GUARD TOWER ABATIS
BARRIER COUNTER DILATOR
PARADOS WARDING WARRANT
FRONTIER GALAPAGO GARRISON
MUNITION
DEFENSELESS BARE COLD NAKED
SILLY UNARMED HELPLESS
DEFENSIBLE TENABLE JUSTIFIABLE
DEFER BOW RISE STAY WAIT DELAY
DRIVE HONOR REFER REMIT TARRY
TRACK WAIVE YIELD ESTEEM
HUMBLE RETARD REVERE SUBMIT
ADJOURN SUSPEND CONSIDER
INTERMIT POSTPONE PROROGUE
PROTRACT SUSPENSE
DEFERENCE VAIL COURT HONOR
CRINGE ESTEEM HOMAGE REGARD
RESPECT WORSHIP CIVILITY
DEFERENT ECCENTRIC
DEFERENTIAL DUTIFUL OBEISANT
DEFERMENT STAY
DEFERVESCENCE LYSIS DECLINE
DEFIANCE DARE DEFI DEFY GAGE
BRAVE DEFIAL
DEFIANT BOLD BARDY BRAVE STOUT

DARING STOCKY INSOLENT
STUBBORN
DEFICIENCY FAIL LACK WANT
ANOIA ERROR FAULT MINUS
DEARTH DEFECT INLAIK ULLAGE
ABSENCE ANOESIA BLEMISH DEFICIT
FAILING FAILURE DELETION
SCARCITY SHORTAGE
(— **OF NERVOUS ENERGY**) ANEURIA
(— **OF OXYGEN**) ASPHYXIA
(**CARBON DIOXIDE** —) ACAPNIA
(**MENTAL** —) IDIOCY AMENTIA
(**PL.**) SHORTS
DEFICIENT BAD LEAN WANE BLUNT
MINUS BARREN FEEBLE MEAGER
MEAGRE SCARCE SCRIMP SKIMPY
BOBTAIL DISGENIC DYSGENIC
INDIGENT
(— **IN TURGOR**) FLACCID
(**MENTALLY** —) SOFT
DEFICIT SHORTAGE UNDERAGE
DEFILE GUT RAY ABRA BAWD BEDO
FILE FOIL FOUL GATE GOWL HALS
LIME MOIL MUCK PACE PASS SLIP
SLUT SMUT SOIL ABUSE BERAY
CLEFT CROCK DIRTY FILTH GLACK
GORGE HALSE NOTCH SMEAR STAIN
SULLY TAINT BEWRAY DEBASE
GULLET IMBRUE INFECT RAVISH
SMOUCH SMUTCH CORRUPT
DEBAUCH DEPRAVE DISTAIN
PASSAGE POLLUTE PROFANE
SMATTER TARNISH VIOLATE
DISHONOR MACULATE
DEFILED DIRTY IMPURE SPOTTY
UNCLEAN MACULATE
DEFILEMENT MOIL SOIL SULLAGE
TAINTURE
DEFILING PIKY PITCHY
DEFINE END FIX SET MERE TERM
BOUND LIMIT DECIDE CLARIFY
DELIMIT EXPLAIN EXPOUND
DESCRIBE DISCOVER
DEFINED FORMED
(**SHARPLY** —) HARD
DEFINITE SET FIRM HARD SURE
CLEAR FINAL FIXED SHARP FINITE
FORMED LIQUID STRAIT CERTAIN
EXPRESS LIMITED POINTED PRECISE
DISTINCT EMPHATIC EXPLICIT
LIMITING POSITIVE PUNCTUAL
SPECIFIC
DEFINITELY BUT WELL FAIRLY
EVERMORE
DEFINITION GLOSS CLARITY
(— **OF FORM**) SFUMATO
DEFINITIVE LAST FINAL GRAND
ORISTIC DEFINITE
DEFLATE EMPALE IMPALE
CONTRACT
DEFLATED FLAT
DEFLATING SETDOWN
DEFLATION HANGOVER
DEFLECT CUT WRY BEND COCK
SWAY WARP PARRY WREST WRING
BAFFLE DETOUR DIVERT SWERVE
DEVIATE DIVERGE INFLECT REFLECT
REFRACT

DEFLECTION DROOP SWEEP
WINDAGE
(— **ON METER**) KICK
DEFLOWER FRAY DEFOIL DEFOUL
FORLIE RAVAGE RAVISH DEFLORE
DESPOIL VIOLATE UNMAIDEN
UNVIRGIN
DEFORM MAR FLOW WARP GNARL
DEFACE BLEMISH CONTORT
DISFORM DISTORT DIFFORME
DISGUISE DISHONOR MISSHAPE
DEFORMATION CREEP SPRING
STRAIN FLEXURE FLOWAGE
DEFORMED GAMMY WRONG INFORM
PAULIE CROOKED HIDEOUS
MISBORN FORMLESS UNMACKLY
DEFORMITY GALL VICE BLEMISH
HARELIP PRAVITY CLUBFOOT
CLUBHAND FLATFOOT WANSHAPE
DEFRAUD ROB BEAT BILK FAKE
GULL NICK ROOK TRIM WIPE CHEAT
COZEN GOUGE MULCT SLICK STICK
TRICK WRONG BOODLE CHOUSE
CHOWSE DECEIVE SWINDLE
DEFRAY PAY BEAR AVERT COVER
EXPEND PREPAY APPEASE REQUITE
SATISFY DISBURSE
DEFT GAIN NEAT TALL TRIM AGILE
HANDY QUICK SLICK ADROIT
EXPERT HEPPEN NIMBLE SPRACK
SPRUCE DELIVER DEXTROUS
SKILLFUL
DEFTEST EFTEST
DEFTLY SLICKLY DELIVERLY
DEFTNESS SLEIGHT
DEFUNCT DEAD EXTINCT DECEASED
DEPARTED FINISHED
DEFY BRAG DARE DEFI FACE MOCK
BEARD BRAVE STUMP TEMPT
CARTEL FORBID MAUGER MAUGRE
REJECT AFFRONT BRAVADE
DESPISE DISDAIN OUTDARE
OUTFACE CHAMPION DEFIANCE
OUTSCOUT RENOUNCE
DEGENERATE ROT SINK DEBADE
EFFETE UNKIND DEGENER DEGRADE
DEPRAVE DESCEND DEGENDER
(— **IN IDLENESS**) RUST
(— **TOWARD BARBARISM**) WILDER
DEGENERATION WALLER ATROPHY
ADIPOSIS
DEGRADATION FALL WOHL SHAME
DECLINE DESCENT ADULTERY
DEPOSURE IGNOMINY
DEGRADE BUST SINK ABASE BREAK
DECRY LOWER SHAME SHEND
STOOP STRIP UNMAN DEBASE
DEMEAN DEMOTE DEPOSE EMBASE
HUMBLE LESSEN REDUCE VILIFY
CORRUPT DECLINE DEPRESS
IMBRUTE REGRADE VILLAIN
DIMINISH DISGRACE DISHONOR
DISMOUNT DISPLUME SUPPLANT
DEGRADED BASE SEAMY ABJECT
DEMISS FALLEN DEBASED DEGREED
GRIECED OUTCAST
DEGRADING BASE MENIAL
SHAMEFUL
DEGRAS MOELLON

DEGREE PEG PIP POL BANK CAST
DEAL FORM GREE HEAT PEEP POLL
RANK RATE RUNG STEP TERM TIER
CLASS GRADE GRADO GRECE GRICE
HONOR LEVEL NOTCH ORDER PITCH
PLACE POINT PRICK SHADE STAGE
STAIR EXTENT GRIECE LENGTH
MEDIUM SOEVER DESCENT DIGNITY
MEASURE SAENGER STATION
ACCURACY AEGROTAT QUANTITY
STANDING STRENGTH
(— **OF CLOSENESS**) FIT
(— **OF COMBINING POWER**)
VALENCE
(— **OF CONTRAST**) GAMMA
(— **OF DEVIATION**) LEEWAY
(— **OF ELEVATION**) ASCENT
(— **OF ENGAGEMENT**) DEPTH
(— **OF FLAWLESSNESS**) CLARITY
(— **OF FORCE**) KICK
(— **OF HEIGHT**) GRADE
(— **OF IMPORTANCE**) CALIBER
CALIBRE
(— **OF INFESTATION**) BURDEN
(— **OF INTOXICATION**) EDGE
(— **OF KNOWLEDGE**) SCIENTER
(— **OF LIGHTNESS**) VALUE
(— **OF MIXTURE**) ALLOY
(— **OF OPACITY**) DENSITY
(— **OF PLENTIFULNESS**)
ABUNDANCE
(— **OF SLOPE**) SPLAY
(— **OF STREAMLINING**) FAIRNESS
(— **OF THE SOUL**) RUACH
(— **OF WATER HARDNESS**) GRAIN
(— **OF WHITENESS**) BLEACH
(10 —**S OF LONGITUDE**) FACE
(15 —**S**) HOUR
(**EXCESSIVE** —) EXTREME
(**GREATEST** —) UTMOST
(**HIGHEST** —) PINK SUMMIT
SUPREME SUBLIMITY
(**INDEFINITE** —) SEEM
(**MINUTE** —) DROP SHADE
(**MUSICAL** —) SPACE SUBTONIC
(**RABINNICAL** —) SEMICHA SEMIKAH
CEMICHAH
(**SMALL** —) ACE HAIR INCH IOTA
SHADOW GLIMMER
(**SOME** —) BIT
(**UTMOST** —) SUM ACME HEIGHT
EXTREME EXTREMITY
DEGU OCTODONT
DEGUM STRIP
(— **SILK**) SOUPLE
DEHGAN SWAT SWATI
DEHORN SNUB DISBUD
DEHWAR DEHKAN
DEHYDRATE DRY DESICCATE
DEIANIRA (**BROTHER OF** —) TYDEUS
MELEAGER
(**FATHER OF** —) OENEUS
(**HUSBAND OF** —) HERCULES
(**MOTHER OF** —) ALTHAEA
DEIDAMIA HIPPODAMIA
(**FATHER OF** —) LYCOMEDES
(**LOVER OF** —) ACHILLES
(**SON OF** —) PYRRHUS
NEOPTOLEMUS

DEIFY GOD BEGOD DIVINE GODDIZE
DIVINIFY DIVINIZE
DEIGN STOOP VOUCHSAFE
DEIPHOBUS (**BROTHER OF** —) PARIS
HECTOR
(**FATHER OF** —) PRIAM
(**MOTHER OF** —) HECUBA
(**WIFE OF** —) HELEN
DEITY (ALSO SEE GOD AND
GODDESS) EA EL KA RA RE SU ABU
BEL GAD GOD RAN SHU SOL AKAL
AMEN AMON BAAL CAGN DEVA
FAUN FURY GWYN MIND MORS
RANA SIVA SOBK ALALA ALALU
AMIDA AMITA AMMON DAGAN
DAGON HOBAL HORUS HUBAL
INUUS JANUS MIDER MITRA MONAD
SATYR SEBEK SHIVA SIRIS SURYA
ZOMBI ASHIMA ATHTAR BATALA
BUNENE CAISSA FATHER FAUNUS
IASION MARDUK MOLOCH NIBHAZ
OANNES ORISHA ORMAZD ORMUZD
RIMMON SOMNUS SUCHOS SYLVAN
VARUNA ZOMBIE ALASTOR FORSETE
FORSETI GODDESS GODHEAD
GODLING GODSHIP HERSHEF
IAPETUS KHEPERA MANITOU
NINURTA NISROCH PHORCUS
PHORKYS RESHEPH SETEBOS
SILENUS TAGALOA TARANIS VIRBIUS
BAALPEOR BEELPEOR BELFAGOR
DEVARAJA DIVINITY ELAGABAL
GOVERNOR HACHIMAN MELKARTH
MERODACH PICUMNUS PILUMNUS
SEILENOS SILVANUS TANGALOA
TUTELARY ZEPHYRUS ZOOMORPH
(**AVENGING** —) ALASTOR
(**HEATHEN** —) IDOL
(**INFERIOR** —) GODKIN GODLING
DEMIURGE PETTYGOD
(**SHINTO** —) KAMI
(**SUPREME** —) HANSA
(**TUTELARY** —) NUMEN GENIUS
(**PL.**) CABIRI
DEJECT ABASE LOWER HUMBLE
LESSEN FLATTEN DISPIRIT
DOWNCAST
DEJECTA EGESTA
DEJECTED BAD LOW SAD DAMP
DOWN GLUM POOR SUNK AMORT
MUDDY WAPED ABASED DEJECT
DEMISS DROOPY GLOOMY PINING
SOMBER SOMBRE DUMPISH
HANGDOG HANGING HUMBLED
LUMPISH UNHAPPY DOWNCAST
DOWNWARD REPINING WOBEGONE
WRETCHED
DEJECTEDLY HEAVILY
DEJECTION DAMP GLOOM SLOTH
DISMAY DISMALS HUMDRUM
SADNESS
DEJEUNER LUNCH BREAKFAST
COLAZIONE COLLATION
DEL NABLA

DELAWARE
CAPITAL: DOVER

COUNTY: KENT SUSSEX NEWCASTLE
INDIAN: LENAPE
STATE FLOWER: PEACH
STATE BIRD: BLUEHEN
STATE NICKNAME: DIAMOND
STATE TREE: HOLLY
TOWN: LEWES SMYRNA ELSMERE CLAYMONT WILMINGTON

DELAY LAG LET BLIN BODE HOLD HONE LENG LING LITE MORA SIST SLOW SLUG STAY STOP WAIT ABIDE ABODE ALLAY BLINE CHECK DALLY DEFER DEMUR DETER DRIFT DWELL FRIST REPRY SLOTH STALL STENT STICK STINT TARDY TARRY TRACT ARREST ATTEND BACKEN BELATE DAWDLE DETAIN DILATE DILUTE DRETCH ESSOIN FUTURE HINDER HOLDUP IMPEDE LINGER LOITER QUENCH REMORE RETARD TAIGLE TARROW TEMPER WEAKEN ADJOURN ASSUAGE BARRACE CONFINE DRUTTLE FORSLOW PROLONG RESPECT RESPITE SLACKEN SOJOURN DEMURRAL DILATION FORESLOW FOURCHER HANGFIRE HESITATE MACERATE MITIGATE MORATION OBSTRUCT POSTPONE REPRIEVE STOPPAGE
(— TRIAL) TRAVERSE
(LEGAL —) DILATOR INDUCIAE
(UNDUE —) LACHES
DELAYED LATE TARDY LAGGED BELATED OVERDUE
DELAYING TRAIN DILATORY
DELECTABLE TASTY DESIROUS PLEASING BEAUTIFUL EXQUISITE
DELEGATE NAME SEND ASSIGN COMMIT DELATE DEPUTE DEPUTY LEGATE NUNCIO APPOINT CONSIGN EMPOWER ENTRUST EMISSARY RELEGATE TRANSFER
DELEGATION MISSION DELEGACY
(ATHENIAN —) DELIA
DELETE DELE EDIT OMIT BLACK ERASE PURGE SLASH CANCEL CENSOR DELATE REMOVE STRIKE DESTROY EXPUNGE STONKER CASTRATE
DELETERIOUS BAD PRAVE HARMFUL HURTFUL NOXIOUS PRAVOUS DAMAGING DELETERY
DELIBERATE COOL PORE RUNE SLOW STUDY THINK ADVISE CONFER DEBATE PONDER REGARD ADVISED BALANCE BETHINK CONSULT COUNCIL COUNSEL DELIBER DELIVER REFLECT RESOLVE STUDIED WILLING CONSIDER DESIGNED MEASURED MEDITATE PERPENSE PREPENSE PROPENSE STUDIOUS
DELIBERATELY COOLY COOLLY APURPOSE ADVISEDLY
DELIBERATENESS MATURITY
DELIBERATION ADVICE COUNCIL

COUNSEL LEISURE THOUGHT VISEMENT
DELICACY BIT ROE CATE EASE NORI TACT ACATE FRILL KNACK TASTE CAVIAR DAINTY DELICE JUNKET LUXURY NICETY REGALO FINESSE REGALIA TENUITY AIRINESS DAINTITH DAINTREL DELICATE KICKSHAW LEGERETE NICENESS PLEASURE SUBTLETY
(PL.) CATES ACATES
DELICATE SLY AIRY FINE LACY NESH NICE SOFT TEAR ZART DELIE DORTY ELFIN FRAIL LIGHT SILKY TEWLY CASHIE CHOICE DAINTY FLIMSY GENTLE GINGER INCONY KITTLE MINION PASTEL PETITE PULING QUEASY SILKEN SLIGHT SUBTLE TENDER TICKLE TWIGGY ELEGANT EPICENE FINICAL FRAGILE MINIKIN REFINED SLIMMER SUBTILE SUMMERY TAFFETA TAFFETY TENUOUS TIFFANY WILLOWY ARANEOUS CHARMING ETHEREAL FEATHERY GOSSAMER GRACEFUL HOTHOUSE LUSCIOUS MIGNIARD PINDLING PLEASANT SENSIBLE SUMMERLY TICKLISH UNLUSTIE
(— IN APPEARANCE) HUNGRY
DELICATELY FINE SMALLY FAIRILY
DELICATESSEN GASTRONOME CHARCUTERIE
DELICIOUS DAINTY FRIAND DELICATE
DELIGHT JOY GLEE GUST LITE LOVE SEND TAKE BLISS CHARM EXULT FEAST GRACE GUSTO MIRTH REVEL SAVOR SMACK ADMIRE ARRIDE DELICE DIVERT LIKING PLEASE RAVISH REGALE RELISH DISPORT ECSTASY ENCHANT GLADDEN GRATIFY JOYANCE JOYANCY LECHERY RAPTURE REJOICE DELICATE ENTRANCE GLADNESS PLEASURE SAVORING
(— IN) LOVE SAVOR
(PL.) DELICIAE
DELIGHTED GLAD
DELIGHTFUL NICE GREAT JAMMY JOLLY MERRY SOOTH DREAMY SAVORY ELYSIAN LEESOME ADORABLE DELICATE DELITOUS GLORIOUS GORGEOUS HEAVENLY LUSCIOUS
DELIMER DRENCHER
DELIMIT FIX DEFINE SUBTEND
DELIMITED MERED MEERED
DELINEATE MAP DRAW ETCH LIMN LINE CHALK CHART FENCE IMAGE PAINT STELL TABLE TOUCH TRACE TRICK BLAZON CIPHER DELINE DEPICT DESIGN DEVISE SKETCH SURVEY DEPAINT EXPRESS LINEATE OUTLINE PICTURE PORTRAY DECIPHER DEFIGURE DESCRIBE TRAVERSE
DELINEATION DRAFT DESIGN SKETCH SURVEY DRAUGHT
DELINQUENCY FAULT GUILT

FAILURE MISDEED OFFENSE OMISSION
DELINQUENT CRIMINAL
(PL.) KALANG
DELIQUESCE MELT LIQUEFY DISSOLVE
DELIRIOUS FEY MAD OFF REE GYTE LIGHT MANIC INSANE RAVING FLIGHTY FRANTIC LUNATIC BRAINISH DELEERIT DELIERET DERANGED FRENETIC FRENZIED
DELIRIUM FURY MAZE MANIA FRENZY LUNACY RAVERY MADNESS DELIRACY IDLENESS INSANITY
DELIRIUM TREMENS JUMP HORRORS JIMJAMS JIMMIES POTOMANIA
DELIVER DO HIT LAY LET RID BAIL BORN DEAL FREE GIVE LEND REDD SAVE SELL SEND TAKE BEKEN BRING COUGH LIVER SERVE SPEAK UTTER ADDICT ASSIZE ASSOIL BETRAY COMMIT CONVEY EXEMPT PREACH RANSOM REDEEM RENDER RESCUE RESIGN SUCCOR UNBIND BETEACH BITECHE COMMEND CONSIGN DECLAIM DICTATE OUTTAKE PRESENT RECOVER RELEASE RELIEVE DISPATCH EXORCISE EXORCIZE LIBERATE
(— BALL) BOWL
(— BLOW) LEND SEND
(— BLOWS ON HEAD) NOB
(— CHILD) LIGHT
(— FORCEFULLY) FASTEN
(— LOGS) STOCK
(— MERCHANDISE) UTTER
(— OVER) BETAKE CONSIGN
(— RHETORICALLY) DECLAIM
(— SPEECH) ADDRESS
DELIVERANCE BOOT ESCAPE RESCUE SAVING DELIVERY RIDDANCE SOLUTION VOIDANCE SALVATION
DELIVERED LANDED
(— FREE) FRANCO
(PRECISELY —) FLUSH
DELIVERER SOTER DRAYMAN SAOSHYANT
DELIVERY FLY BAIL FLIER FLYER ISSUE RESCUE ADDRESS AIRDROP BAILMENT SHIPMENT
(— IN SPEAKING) DICTION
(— OF BALL) BOWL
(— WAGON) FLY
(MAIL —) TAPPALL TAPPAUL
DELL DEN HOW DALE DEAN DENE DILL DRAB GLEN VALE SLACK SLADE TRULL WENCH DINGLE RAVINE VALLEY
(PL.) DALLES
DELPHINIUM DAUPHIN DOLPHIN LARKSPUR
DELUDE BOB JIG BILK DUPE FOOL HOAX MOCK AMUSE CHEAT COZEN ELUDE EVADE GLAIK SPOOF TRICK BAFFLE BANTER BEFOOL BUBBLE DIDDLE ILLUDE BEGUILE DECEIVE ENCHANT MISLEAD OVERSEE

BEJUGGLE HOODWINK INVEIGLE OVERSILE

DELUGE SEA FLOW FLOOD SWAMP DILUVY CATARACT INUNDATE OVERFLOW SATURATE SUBMERGE

DELUNDUNG LINSANG ZINSANG VIVERRINE

DELUSION MAZE MOHA ABUSE DWALE FRAUD TRICK MIRAGE VISION CHIMERA FALLACY FANTASM PHANTOM WANHOPE ILLUSION NIHILISM PHANTASM

DELUSTER DULL

DELVE DEN DIG DIP PIT CAVE DINT MINE DITCH PLUMB BRUISE BURROW EXHUME FATHOM INDENT IMPRESS EXCAVATE INSCRIBE

DEMAGNETIZE DEPERM DEPOLARIZE

DEMAGOGUE CLEON LEADER ORATOR ROUSER DEMAGOG SPEAKER TRIBUNE JAWSMITH

DEMAND ASK CRY TAX USE CALL NEED RAME SALE CLAIM CRAVE DRAFT EXACT GAVEL ORDER QUERY SIGHT BEHEST CHARGE DESIRE ELICIT EXPECT SNATCH SUMMON ARRAIGN COMMAND CONSIST DRAUGHT INQUIRE MANDATE REQUEST REQUIRE SOLICIT INSTANCE QUESTION
(— PAYMENT) DUN CALL
(— RECOGNITION) CLAIM ASSERT
(PL.) EXIGENCE EXIGENCY

DEMANDABLE DUE EXIGIBLE

DEMANDED COMPULSORY

DEMANDING HEFTY EXIGENT
(— ATTENTION) ACUTE

DEMANTOID EMERALD OLIVINE

DEMARCATE DELIMIT SEPARATE

DEMARCATION CELL

DEMEAN ABASE CARRY LOWER BEHAVE DEBASE DEPORT CONTAIN DEGRADE DESCEND MALTREAT

DEMEANOR AIR GARB MIEN PORT FRONT HABIT ACTION HAVIOR BEARING CONDUCT DISPOSE FASHION CARRIAGE PORTANCE

DEMENTED MAD BUGGY CRAZY NUTTY INSANE SKEWED FATUOUS

DEMENTIA FATUITY INSANITY

DEMERIT MARK FAULT DESERT BROWNIE
(PL.) GIG

DEMESNE MANOR PLACE REALM DOMAIN ESTATE REGION DISTRICT

DEMETER CERES MISTRESS

DEMIGOD HERO YIMA ADAPA SATYR TRITON GODLING
(PL.) NEPHILIM

DEMIGODDESS URD NORN HEROINE

DEMILUNE RAVELIN

DEMISE WILL DEATH CONVEY DECEASE BEQUEATH

DEMISED LETTEN

DEMIT LOWER HUMBLE RESIGN ABDICATE

DEMOCRACY POPULACY COMMONALTY

DEMOCRAT DEMO DANITE HUNKER SNAPPER DEMOCRAW LOCOFOCO POPOCRAT
(CONSERVATIVE —) HARD

DEMODULATE DETECT

DEMOISELLE KULM CRANE COOLEN KAIKARA

DEMOLISH RASE RAZE RUIN ABATE BREAK ELIDE LEVEL WASTE WRECK BATTER SLIGHT DESTROY RUINATE SHATTER SUBVERT UNBUILD DOWNCAST STRAMASH

DEMOLITION END FALL

DEMON ALP DEV HAG IMP NAT OKI AITU ATUA BADB BALI BHUT DEVA DOOK OGRE OKEE PUCK RAHU SURT WADE ASURA DEVIL DHOUL FIEND GENIE GHOST JUMBY LAMIA LESHY LESIY OTKON SATAN SATYR SHEDU SURTR TAIPO WITCH ABIGOR AFREET ARIOCH BILWIS DAEMON DAIMON DAITYA GENIUS JUMBIE MAMMON PILWIZ PISACA THURSE VRITRA YAKSHA YAKSHI ASMADAI ASMODAY DEMONIO HARPIER PISACHA VILLAIN WARLOCK ALICHINO ASHMODAI ASMODEUS BAALPEOR BEELPEOR CURUPIRA EUDAEMON OBIDICUT SUCCUBUS WATERMAN
(— OF WOODS) LESHY LESIY LESHEY
(ARABIC —) AFRIT AFREET AFRITE EFREET
(EVIL —) SHEDU
(FEMALE —) HAG LAMIA PISACHI SUCCUBUS
(NATURE —) GENIUS
(PETTY —) IMP
(PL.) DASYUS

DEMONIAC DEMONIC LUNATIC SATANIC DEVILISH DIABOLIC FIENDISH INFERNAL

DEMONIACAL DEMONIAC INFERNAL

DEMONSTRATE GIVE SHOW CLEAR PROVE SPEAK CONVICT DISPLAY PORTRAY CONVINCE INSTANCE MANIFEST

DEMONSTRATION SHOW SIGN TIME PROOF APODIXIS BALLYHOO DARSHANA MANIFEST
(OSTENTATIOUS —) SPLURGE

DEMONSTRATIVE THAT THIS THESE THOSE EFFUSIVE EVINCIVE

DEMOPHON (FATHER OF —) CELEUS THESEUS
(MOTHER OF —) PHAEDRA METANIRA

DEMORALIZE WEAKEN CONFUSE CORRUPT DEPRAVE PERVERT

DEMORALIZING INFECTIOUS SHATTERING

DEMOTE BUMP BUST REDUCE UNRANK DEGRADE DISRATE

DEMOTIC POPULAR ENCHORIAL

DEMOTION BUMP

DEMULCENT MANNA SALEB SALEP BORAGE GINSENG EMULSION SOOTHING

DEMUR COY GIB JIB SHY BALK STAY DELAY DOUBT PAUSE STICK BOGGLE LINGER OBJECT STRAIN DEMEORE SCRUPLE STICKLE STUMBLE SUSPEND DEMURRER HESITATE SUSPENSE

DEMURE COY MIM SHY MURE PRIM GRAVE SPAKE STAID SUANT SUENT MODEST SEDATE PRENZIE PRIMSIE COMPOSED DECOROUS

DEN MEW CAVE COVE DEAN DELL DIVE GLEN HOLE HOLT HUNK LAIR LAKE NEST ROOM SHED SINK BIELD CABIN CAVEA COUCH DELVE HAUNT LODGE SLADE STUDY BURROW CAVERN COVERT GROTTO HOLLOW KENNEL RAVINE SHROUD RETREAT SPELUNK HIDEAWAY SNUGGERY WORKROOM
(— OF BEAR) WASH
(— OF INIQUITY) DOMDANIEL
(FOUL —) SPITAL
(GAMBLING —) DEADFALL

DENARIUS DENAR PENNY DINDER

DENIAL NO NAY WARN DENAY DENIER NAYSAY DEFENSE DEMENTI REFUSAL REPULSE CONTRARY TRAVERSE
(— OF AUTHORITY) ANARCHY
(— OF TRUTH) HERESY

DENIED LOST

DENIER DINERO NEGATOR DENARIUS DINHEIRO
(HALF —) MAIL MAILLE

DENIGRATE BEFOUL CRUCIFY

DENIM DUNGAREE

DENIZEN CITIZEN RESIDENT
(— BY BIRTH) NATIVE
(— OF HELL) HELLION

DENMARK
CAPITAL: COPENHAGEN
CHEESE: SAMSO
COIN: ORA ORE KRONE
COUNTY: AMT RIBE SORO VEJLE AARHUS MARIBO ODENSE TONDER VIBORG AALBORG RANDERS AABENRAA BORNHOLM
INLET: ISE LIM FJORD VEJLE NISSUM ODENSE HORSENS LOGSTOR MARIAGER
ISLAND: OE ALS FYN MON AARO AERO FANO FOHR MORS ROMO BAAGO FAERO FAROE LAESO SAMSO SANDO AMAGER SEJERO SUDERO FALSTER SEELAND ZEALAND
MEASURE: ELL FOD MIL POT ALEN FAVN RODE ALBUM KANDE LINJE PAEGL TOMME ACHTEL PAEGEL SKEPPE LANDMIL OLTONDE SKIEPPE VIERTEL FJERDING
PARLIAMENT: RIGSRAD FOLKETING LANDSTING
PENINSULA: JUTLAND

POSSESSION: FAROE ICELAND GREENLAND
RIVER: ASA HOLM OMME STOR GUDEN SKIVE SUSAA VARDE GELSAA STORAA VORGOD GUDENAA LILLEAA LONBORG
SETTLERS: OSTMEN
STRAIT: KATTEGAT SKAGERRAK
TOWN: ARS HOV HALS KOGE NIBE SORO VRAA FARUM HOBRO SKIVE AARHUS DRAGOR KORSOR NYBORG ODENSE SKAGEN STRUER VIBORG AALBORG HERNING HORSENS KOLDING RANDERS BALLERUP ELSINORE GENTOFTE GLOSTRUP ROSKILDE HELSINGOR COPENHAGEN
TRIBE: DANES JUTES ANGLES CIMBRI TEUTONS
TRIBUNAL: RIGSRAD RIGSRET
WEIGHT: ES LOD ORT VOG LAST MARK PUND UNZE CARAT KVINT POUND QUINT TONDE CENTNER LISPUND QUINTIN LISPOUND SKIPPUND

DENOMINATE CALL NAME STYLE TITLE DENOTE CHRISTEN INDICATE NOMINATE
DENOMINATION CULT NAME SECT CLASS FAITH TITLE VALUE CHURCH SCHOOL SOCIETY CATEGORY
DENOMINATIONAL SECTARIAN CONFESSIONAL
DENOTATION SIGN TOKEN EXTENT NOTION SPHERE AMBITUS BREADTH
DENOTE GIVE MARK MEAN NAME NOTE SHOW SOUND IMPORT NOTIFY BETOKEN CONNOTE EXPRESS SIGNIFY DENOTATE DESCRIBE INDICATE
DENOUEMENT END ENVOY ISSUE OUTCOME SOLITION
DENOUNCE BAN WRAY ASCRY BASTE BLAST DECRY TAUNT ACCUSE DELATE DESCRY DETEST MENACE SCATHE ARRAIGN CONDEMN DECLAIM DECLARE UPBRAID EXECRATE PROCLAIM THREATEN
DENOUNCEMENT DELATION
DENSE SAD FAST FIRM CLOSE CRASS DUNCH FOGGY GROSS HEAVY MASSY MURKY SILLY SOLID SOUND SPISS STIFF THEET THICK TIGHT WOOFY OBTUSE OPAQUE SPISSY STUPID THICKY THIGHT COMPACT CROWDED INTENSE SERRIED CONDENSE
(NOT —) TENUOUS
DENSITY FOG CANDY FASTNESS GAUSSAGE SOLIDITY
DENT BASH BURT DINT DOKE DUNT FAZE NICK CLOUR DELVE DINGE NOTCH STOVE TOOTH BATTER DUNTLE HALLOW INDENT BLEMISH DEPRESS

(— OF REED) SPLIT
(PL.) BEER
DENTAL POINT
DENTICULATE SERRATE SERRATED
DENTICULATION JAG JAGG
DENTIFRICE WASH
DENTIL DENTEL DENTELLO DENTICLE
DENTINE IVORY DENTIN
DENTIST ODONTIST OPERATOR
DENTURE PLATE BRIDGE
DENUDE BARE SCALP SHAVE STRIP DIVEST NUDATE DESPOIL DENUDATE
DENUNCIATION THREAT THUNDER ANATHEMA DIATRIBE
DENY NAY NAIT NICK NITE WARN BELIE DEBAR NITTE RENAY REPEL WERNE ABJURE DISOWN FORBID IMPUGN NEGATE REFUSE REFUTE REJECT RENEGE CONFUTE DEPRIVE DISAVOW DISPUTE FORSAKE GAINSAY PROTEST SUBLATE WITHSAY ABNEGATE DENEGATE DISALLOW DISCLAIM FORSWEAR NEGATIVE RENOUNCE TRAVERSE WITHHOLD
(— ACCESS) CLOSE
(— RECOGNITION) BLINK
DEOXIDIZE REDUCE
DEPART GO DIE MOG OFF WAG BLOW EXIT FLIT HOOK MOVE PACK PART PASS PIKE QUIT SHED STEP VADE VARY VOID WALK WEND WITE AVOID BREAK FOUND LEAVE MOSEY SEVER SHAKE SHIFT START TRUSS AVAUNT BEGONE DECAMP DECEDE DEMISE DESIST DIVIDE PERISH RECEDE REMOVE RETIRE SKIDOO SUNDER SWERVE WANDER ABSCOND DEVIATE DISCEDE FORSAKE RETREAT SKIDDOO VAMOOSE DISCOAST FAREWELL SEPARATE TRESPASS WITHDRAW
(— FROM HARBOR) SORTIE
(— FROM LIFE) DECEASE
(— IN HASTE) BREEZE
(— IN HURRY) SKIVE LAMMAS
(— SECRETLY) ABSCOND
(— SUDDENLY) FLEE DECAMP
(— WITH SPEED) VAMOOSE
DEPARTED DEAD BYGONE DEFUNCT DECEASED DECEDENT
DEPARTMENT END PART OKRUG REALM AGENCY BRANCH BUREAU EXCISE MEMBER OKROOG SPHERE FOUNDRY HANAPER PORTION REVENUE SPICERY AGITPROP CHANCERY DIVISION INDUSTRY NOMARCHY PROVINCE SCULLERY
(— IN CHINA) FU
(NEWSPAPER —) COLUMN FEATURE
(TREASURY —) CAMERA
DEPARTURE BUNK EXIT BREAK DEATH EXODE GOING LEAVE OUTGO CHANGE CONGEE DEPART EGRESS EXODUS HEGIRA SETOFF WAGANG WAYING DECEASE EASTING OUTGANG PARTING PARTURE RETREAT SAILING TRUNDLE WAYGATE DEPARTER FAREWELL

OFFGOING REMOTION
(— FROM CORRECTNESS) ATROCITY
(— FROM SUBJECT) ASIDE
(— FROM THEME) CADENZA
(— OF SHIP) SORTIE
(EMERGENCY —) BAILOUT
(GEOLOGICAL —) ANOMALY
(SECRET —) GUY SLIP
DEPEND BANK HANG LEAN PEND RELY REST RIDE STAY TURN COUNT FOUND HINGE TRUST CONFIDE
DEPENDABILITY SECURITY
DEPENDABLE GOOD SURE SIKER SOLID SOUND THERE SECURE SICCAR SICKER STANCH STEADY CERTAIN STAUNCH RELIABLE SILVENDY SUREFIRE
DEPENDENCE MAINSTAY RELIANCE SERVILITY
DEPENDENCY TALUK COLONY APANAGE APPANAGE
DEPENDENT CHILD CLIENT HANGBY MINION SPONGE VASSAL FEODARY FEUDARY PRONEUR RELIANT SERVILE SPONGER SUBJECT WRAPPED BEHOLDEN CLINGING CREATURE ENCLITIC EVENTUAL FOLLOWER RETAINER
(— ON) ILLATIVE
DEPENDING ATTENDANT
(— ON UNCERTAIN EVENTS) ALEATORY
DEPICT HUE DRAW ETCH LIMN PICT UNDO ENTER IMAGE PAINT SPEAK WRITE BLAZON SHADOW DEPAINT DISPLAY EXPRESS IMPAINT PICTURE PORTRAY DESCRIBE EMBLAZON RESEMBLE
DEPICTED DEPAINT
(— AS BROKEN) ROMPU
DEPICTION SCHEMA
DEPILATION PSILOSIS
DEPILATORY RUSMA EPILATOR PELADORE PSILATRO
DEPLETE DRAIN EMPTY PUNISH REDUCE UNLOAD EXHAUST BANKRUPT DIMINISH
DEPLETED WASTE BANKRUPT
DEPLETION DRAIN EROSION
DEPLORABLE SAD WOFUL WOEFUL DOLOROUS GRIEVOUS WAILSOME WRETCHED
DEPLORABLY SADLY
DEPLORE RUE MOAN SIGH WAIL MOURN BEMOAN BEWAIL GRIEVE LAMENT REGRET COMPLAIN
DEPLOY UNFOLD DISPLAY
DEPLOYMENT FORMATION
DEPOLYMERIZE DEGRADE
DEPONE SWEAR DEPOSE TESTIFY
DEPONENT AFFIANT DEPONER EXAMINATE
DEPOPULATE RAVAGE DESOLATE DISPEOPLE
DEPORT BEAR EXILE EXPEL BANISH BEHAVE DEMEAN BEARING CONDUCT DISPORT RELEGATE
DEPORTMENT AIR GEST MIEN PORT GESTE HABIT ACTION DEPORT

HAVING MANNER ADDRESS BEARING
COMPORT CONDUCT GESTURE
HAVANCE BREEDING CARRIAGE
DEMEANOR MAINTAIN
DEPOSE AVER ABASE PRIVE SWEAR
AFFIRM ASSERT BANISH DEPONE
DIVEST REDUCE REMOVE DEGRADE
DEPOSIT DESTOOL TESTIFY
DETHRONE DISCROWN DISPLACE
DEPOSIT FUR LAY SET ADHI BANK
CAKE CAST CRUD DROP DUMP
FUND HIDE HOCK PAWN BLOOM
CHEST COUCH COVER DEPOT
LODGE PLACE SCURF STORE TOSCA
BESTOW DEPONE DEPOSE ENTOMB
ESCROW FLYSCH GARNER IMPOSE
INHUME PLEDGE REPOSE SALINE
SCORIA SCROLL SETTLE SINTER
TOPHUS ASHFALL CONSIGN
HORIZON DILUVIUM FOULNESS
SANDBANK
(— **BALLOT**) CAST
(— **DRIFT-SAND**) SUD
(— **EGGS**) BLOW SPAWN
(— **FOR COPYRIGHT**) ENTER
(— **IN CHAMPAGNE**) GRIFFE
(— **IN EARTH**) INTER INHUME
(— **IN GUN BORE**) FOULING
(— **IN WINE CASK**) CRUST TARTAR
(— **OF DEBRIS**) BRECCIA
(— **OF LOAM**) LOESS
(— **OF ORE**) BANK FLAT
(— **OF PEBBLES AND SAND**) BEACH
CASCALHO
(— **OF SALT WATER**) SOAK
(— **ON LEATHER**) BLOOM
(— **ON LEAVES**) HONEYDEW
(— **STOLEN ARTICLES**) FENCE
(— **USED AS FERTILIZER**) FALUN
(**ALLUVIAL** —) APRON DELTA
(**ARCHAEOLOGICAL** —) LENS LENSE
(**BANK** —S) CASH
(**BLACK** —) STUPP
(**CORNEA** —) ARCUS
(**EARTHY** —) GUHR MARL
(**GEOLOGIC** —) BLANKET HORIZON
(**GLACIAL** —) TILL DRIFT ESKAR
ESKER SHEET PLACER MORAINE
(**GRAVEL** —) LEAD
(**KIDNEY** —) GRAVEL
(**MASS OF SEDIMENTARY** —S) GOBI
(**MINERAL** —) FLAT LODE CARBONA
(**MUDDY** —) SLUDGE SLUMGULLION
(**SEDIMENTARY** —) SILT
(**SHOAL-WATER** —) CULM
(**SKELETAL** —) CORAL
(**TARRY** —) GUM
(**WELDING** —) TACK
DEPOSITARY POSITOR SEQUESTER
DEPOSITION PAD BURIAL DEPOSIT
OPINION SILTING DEPOSURE
SEDIMENT
DEPOSITORY BANK DROP SAFE
ATTIC VAULT DEPOSIT OSSUARY
SENTINE DEPOSITO ESCROWEE
OSSARIUM
DEPOT BANK BASE GARE AURANG
AURUNG STAPLE STATION
MAGAZINE TERMINAL TERMINUS

DEPRAVE TAINT DEBASE DEFILE
INFECT MALIGN REVILE BESHREW
CORRUPT PERVERT VITIATE
DEPRAVED BAD EVIL UGLY VILE
PRAVE ROTTEN SHREWD WICKED
BESTIAL CORRUPT IMMORAL
PRAVOUS VICIOUS
DEPRAVITY VICE ABYSS ILLNESS
PRAVITY VILLAINY
DEPRECATE PRAY INVOKE BESEECH
DEPRECIATE FALL LACK ABASE
AVILE DECRY SLUMP DEBASE
EMBASE LESSEN MINISH REDUCE
SHRINK CHEAPEN DEBAUCH
DEGRADE DEPRAVE DEPRESS
DETRACT SLANDER SMALLEN
BELITTLE DEROGATE DISCOUNT
DISPRIZE DISVALUE MINIMIZE
PEJORATE VILIPEND
DEPRECIATION AGIO DECRIAL
DISCOUNT
DEPREDATION PREY PILLAGE
DEPRESS BOW COW HIP LOW BATE
BEAR BORE DAMP DASH DENT FALL
FLAT SINK SUMP ABASE APPAL
BREAK CHILL COUCH CRUSH FAINT
LOWER SLUMP VAPOR WEIGH
APPALL DAMPEN DEBOSS DISMAY
HUMBLE INDENT LESSEN MURDER
SADDEN SETTLE SICKEN STRIKE
WEAKEN DECLINE DEGRADE
DESTROY FLATTEN OPPRESS
REPRESS BROWBEAT DIMINISH
DISPIRIT DOWNBEAR ENFEEBLE
DEPRESSANT HELLEBORE
DEPRESSED LOW SAD BLUE DAMP
DULL FLAT SICK SUNK WROTH
BROODY DISHED GLOOMY HIPPED
HOLLOW LONELY OBLATE SOMBER
TRISTE LETDOWN DEJECTED
DOWNCAST DOWNSOME
(— **AT THE POLES**) OBLATE
(**ECONOMICALLY** —) HARD
DEPRESSING SAD BLUE COLD
BLEAK CHILL DREAR DUSKY MUZZY
OURIE DREARY GLOOMY SOMBER
SOMBRE TRISTE
DEPRESSION COL DIP EYE GAT PAN
PIT BUST CROP DAMP DELK DENT
DOKE DOWN FALL FOSS GASH GLEN
HOLL HOWE SLEW SLOT SLUE WELL
ATRIO BASIN BLUES BOSOM CANON
COWAL CRYPT DELVE DINGE FOSSA
FOSSE FOVEA GLOOM GROIN NADIR
NAVEL ORBIT POLJE SALAR SCOOP
SELLA SINUS SLUMP SWALE AMPHID
BUCKLE CAFARD CANYON CAVITY
CRATER CUPULE DIMPLE DISMAY
FURROW GROOVE GULLEY GUTTER
INDENT RAVINE SAUCER SLOUGH
SPLEEN VALLEY WALLOW ALVEOLA
BLOWOUT BOGHOLE CHAGRIN
CLAYPAN CONCAVE COUNTER
FOSSULA FOSSULE FOVEOLA
JIMMIES SADNESS SALTPAN
SINKAGE SINKING VARIOLE
BOTHRIUM DOLDRUMS DOWNBEND
FAINTING FOLLICLE FOREDEEP
FOSSETTE FOSSULET PUNCTURE

SINKHOLE SOAKAWAY EPHIPPIUM
(— **BEHIND COW'S SHOULDERS**)
CROP
(— **BETWEEN BREASTS**) CLEAVAGE
(— **BETWEEN HILLS**) SWIRE
(— **IN BOARD**) SKIP
(— **IN BOTTLE BOTTOM**) KICK
(— **IN DOG'S FACE**) STOP
(— **IN FRUITS**) EYE
(— **IN GROUND**) DALK DELK SWAG
WELL SWALE CHARCO
(— **IN MILLSTONE**) BOSOM
(— **IN NILE VALLEY**) KORE
(— **IN RANGE**) PASS
(— **IN RIDGE**) COL
(— **IN SNOW**) SITZMARK
(— **IN VELD**) COMITJE KOMMETJE
(— **OF EAR**) SCAPHA
(— **OF SPIRITS**) JAWFALL
(— **PRONE**) VAPORISH
(**ARTICULAR** —) GLENE
(**OBLONG** —) CIRCUS
(**SMALL** —) DENT DIMPLE LACUNA
FOLLICLE
DEPRIVATION COST LOSS MAIM
WANT MAYHEM AMOTION MISTURE
DEPRIVAL
(— **OF SIGHT**) DARKNESS
DEPRIVE BAR ROB BATE DENY DOCK
EASE GELD TWIN ABATE BENIM
BREAK DEBAR EMPTY EXUTE PREVE
SPOIL STRIP WRONG AMERCE
DEFEAT DENUDE DEPOSE DEVEST
DISMAY DIVEST FAMISH FORBAR
HINDER HUSTLE REMOVE ABRIDGE
BEGUILE BEREAVE CASHIER
CURTAIL DECEIVE DEFORCE
DEPRAVE DESPOIL DESTROY
DISABLE EXHAUST FOREBAR
GUDGEON PRIVATE UNDRESS
BANKRUPT DENATURE DESOLATE
DISANNUL EVACUATE
(— **BY TRICKERY**) NOSE MULCT
(— **FRAUDULENTLY**) GUDGEON
(— **OF BRILLIANCE**) DEADEN
(— **OF COURAGE**) UNNERVE
(— **OF FREEDOM**) FETTER
(— **OF INDIVIDUALITY**) FORDIZE
(— **OF LIFE**) DEADEN
(— **OF OFFICE**) DEPOSE
(— **OF POSSESSIONS**) FLAY
(— **OF REASON**) DEMENT
(— **OF SENSATION**) BENUMB
(— **OF SENSE**) INEBRIATE
(— **OF SIGHT**) SEEL
(— **OF STRENGTH**) ENERVATE
(— **OF VIRGINITY**) DEFLOWER
DEPRIVED REFT SANS BANKRUPT
DESOLATE
DEPTH DIP BURY DEEP DROP MOHO
ABYSS MIDST SIDTH FATHOM
HEIGHT ALTITUDE DEEPNESS
PROFOUND SOUNDING STRENGTH
(— **OF NIGHT OR WINTER**) HOLL
HOWE
(— **OF SAIL**) HOIST
(— **OF SHIP**) GAGE GAUGE
(— **OF SIN**) SLOUGH
(— **OF SPADE**) SPIT GRAFT

(— OF WATER) DRAFT DRAUGHT
(LOWEST —) GROUND
(MORAL —) ABYSS
(PL.) MUD HEART
DEPUTATION MISSION THEORIA
LEGATION
DEPUTE SEND ALLOT ASSIGN
DEVOTE APPOINT DELEGATE
DEPUTY AIDE AGENT ENVOY NABOB
PROXY VICAR ANGELO COMMIS
CURATE DEPUTE EXARCH FACTOR
KEHAYA LEGATE MINION ADJOINT
BAILIFF ESCALUS QAMAQAM
SUBDEAN CAIMACAM DELEGATE
ORDINARY PYLAGORE TENIENTE
VICARIAN
DERAIL TOAD DERAILER THROWOFF
DERANGE TURN CRAZE UNWIT
UPSET HAMPER RUFFLE CONFUSE
DERAIGN DISEASE DISTURB
PERTURB UNSHAPE DISORDER
DISPLACE UNSETTLE
DERANGED OUT GYTE CRAZY
CRAZED FRANTIC FURIOUS
BUGHOUSE DEMENTED DETRAQUE
INFORMAL
DERANGEMENT MANIA UPSET
FRENZY LUNACY DISEASE MADNESS
PHRENSY RUMMAGE DELIRIUM
DISORDER INSANITY
DERBY POT CADY KATY RACE
BOXER CADDY DICER KELLY SHIRE
BOWLER
DERELICT STREET FAILURE
BETRAYER CASTAWAY
DERELICTION FAILURE RELICTION
DERIDE BOO GECK GIBE HOOT JAPE
JEER JIBE LOUT MOCK TWIT DRAPE
FLEER FLOUT KNACK LAUGH RALLY
SCOFF SCORN SCOUT TAUNT
EXPOSE ILLUDE IRRIDE CATCALL
LOWBELL RIDICULE
DERIDER IRRISOR
DERISION GECK JEER MOCK HOKER
SCORN SPORT MOWING ASTEISM
MOCKERY CONTEMPT IRRISION
RIDICULE
DERISIVE JEERY SNIDE MOWING
SATANIC DERISORY IRRISORY
SARDONIC SCOFFING
DERIVATION ORIGIN DESCENT
PEDIGREE
DERIVATIVE FURAN LININ SLOPE
ACOINE ACYLAL BORANE FURANE
INDOLE PHENOL RETENE ALKYLOL
ANALGEN DERIVED ENOLATE
FLAVONE FLUXION FULGIDE
FULVENE GERMANE SUCRATE
ALBUMOSE ANALGENE FLAVONOL
FORMAZAN HEMATINE INDAZOLE
STANNANE
DERIVE GET DRAW STEM TAKE
BRING CARRY DRIVE FETCH INFER
TRACE BORROW CONVEY DEDUCE
DESUME ELICIT EVOLVE GATHER
OBTAIN SPRING DESCEND EXTRACT
PROCEED RECEIVE TRADUCE
DERMA LAYER CORIUM DERMIS
KISHKE

DERMATITIS ICH ICK CASCADO
CUTITIS
DERMIS DERM CUTIS DERMA
CORIUM
DERNIER LAST FINAL DARREIN
DERNIER CRI FASHION
DEROGATE ANNUL DECRY LESSEN
REPEAL DETRACT SLANDER
RESTRICT WITHDRAW
DEROGATORY BAD
DERRICK JIB RIG LIFT SPAR CRANE
DAVIT HOIST TACKLE ERECTER
ERECTOR GALLOWS HANGING
HANGMAN STIFFLEG JINNYWINK
DERRIS TUBA DEGUELIA
DERVISH AGIB FAKIR FAKEER
SADITE SANTON DARWESH WHIRLER
CALENDER
DESALT DEIONIZE
DESATURATE SADDEN
DESCANT SING SONG COPULA
MELODY REMARK WARBLE
COMMENT QUINIBLE
DESCEND DIP SYE DIVE DROP DUCK
FALL SHED SINK SKIN VAIL AVALE
LIGHT LOWER SQUAT STOOP
SWOOP ALIGHT DERIVE DEVALL
DEVAUL SETTLE DECLINE DELAPSE
DEVOLVE SUBSIDE SUCCEED
DISMOUNT
(— INTO HELL) HARROW
DESCENDANT SON CION GHUZ HEIR
SEED SLIP CHILD GHUZZ SCION
BRANCH LINEAL DESCENT
AARONITE ASHERITE DAUGHTER
EPIGONUS
(— OF IMMIGRANTS) BRAVA
(— OF JEW) CHUETA
(— OF MOHAMMED) EMIR
(— OF NOAH) AD
(—S OF MOHAMMED) ASHRAF
(INSIGNIFICANT —) TAG
(PL.) SEED DONMEH DUNMEH
STRAIN PROGENY OFFSPRING
POSTERITY
DESCENDING FALL CADENT
DOWNWARD
(— FROM COMMON ANCESTOR)
AKIN
DESCENT JET KIN SET DIVE DOWN
DROP FALL KIND VAIL BIRTH BLOOD
CANCH CHUTE ISSUE SCARP SHUTE
SLOPE STOCK CLEUCH CLEUGH
ESCARP RAPPEL STRAIN ASSAULT
DECLINE DISSENT EXTRACT
FALLOUT INCLINE KINDRED LINEAGE
PROGENY ANCESTRY BREEDING
COMEDOWN DOWNCOME DOWNFALL
DOWNGATE DOWNHILL GLISSADE
INVASION PEDIGREE
(— IN MOUNTAINEERING) ABSEIL
(— OF AIRPLANE) LETDOWN
APPROACH
(— OF BIRD) STOOP
(— OF DEITY) AVATAR AVATARA
(— OF LIQUID) DRIBBLE
(— OF MASS) SLIDE
(— OF RIVER) LEAP
(FAMILIAR —) HAVAGE

(OVERWHELMING —) AVALANCHE
(PARACHUTE —) JUMP BAILOUT
(PLUNGING —) SPIN
DESCHAMPIA AIRA
DESCRIBE GIVE READ TELL BLAZE
IMAGE PAINT POINT STYLE WRITE
DEFINE DENOTE DEPICT DEVISE
DILATE RELATE REPORT SKETCH
TITULE DECLARE DEPAINT DISPLAY
EXPLAIN EXPRESS NARRATE
OUTLINE PICTURE PORTRAY
PRESENT RECOUNT STORIFY
DESCRIVE INSCRIBE REHEARSE
(— A LINE) CUT
(— AS) CALL
(— BRIEFLY) KODAK
(— GRAMMATICALLY) PARSE
DESCRIPTION KIN IMAGE BLAZON
SKETCH SURVEY ACCOUNT DICTION
DISPLAY PICTURE LANDSKIP
RELATION TREATISE
(— OF A COUNTRY) FACE
(— OF VISION) AISLING
(BRIEF —) LEGEND
(RUSTIC —) IDYL IDYLL
DESCRY SEE SPY ESPY MAKE SCRY
ASCRY SIGHT BEHOLD BETRAY
DETECT REVEAL DISCERN DISPLAY
DENOUNCE DESCRIBE DISCLOSE
DISCOVER PERCEIVE
DESECRATE ABUSE DEFILE
POLLUTE PROFANE VIOLATE
TEMERATE UNHALLOW
DESERT DUE ERG RAT RUN AREG
ARID BOLT FAIL FLEE MEED SAND
SERT TURN VAST GUILT LEAVE
LURCH MERIT PLANT SERIR START
WAIVE WASTE WORTH BARREN
BETRAY DEFECT EXPOSE LONELY
RENEGE REWARD SHRINK THIRST
WESTEN ABANDON ABSCOND
CHICKEN DEMERIT FORSAKE
HORNADA OVERRUN WESTERN
WASTINE DESOLATE RENOUNCE
SOLITARY SOLITUDE WASTABLE
(PL.) GUILT
DESERTED DEAD WYSTY LONELY
FORLORN DESOLATE FORSAKEN
SOLITARY
(— WOMAN) AGUNAH
DESERTER RAT BOLTER BUGOUT
APOSTATE BUSHWACK FUGITIVE
RECREANT RENEGADE TURNTAIL
DESERTION BUGOUT RATTERY
APOSTASY
DESERT LEMON KUMQUAT
DESERVE EARN MEED RATE MERIT
REPAY SERVE ASSERVE BENEFIT
DEMERIT DISSERVE PROMERIT
DESERVED JUST COMING WORTHY
CONDIGN
DESERVING WORTHY WORTHFUL
ADMIRABLE
DESICCATE DRY ARID SEAR SERE
DRAIN DEHYDRATE
DESICCATION XERANSIS
DESIDERATUM NEED DESIRE
DESIGN AIM END MAP CAST DRAW
GOAL IDEA MARK MEAN PLAN PLAT

PLOT TREE WORK ALLOT CHECK
DECAL DECOR DODAD DRAFT DRIFT
ETTLE FANCY MODEL MOTIF NOTAN
QUILT SHAPE STAMP STUDY
BOWPOT CACHET CORNER CREATE
DEVICE DEVISE DOODAD DOODLE
EMBLEM FIGURE FLORAL FLOWER
INCUSE INTEND INTENT INVENT
LAYOUT MODULE OBJECT OBTENT
PROJET SCHEME SKETCH SYSTEM
VERVER ALLOVER BOSCAGE
CARTOON CARVING CHASING
COMPOSE COUNSEL CROQUIS
DESTINE DIAGRAM DRAUGHT
ETCHING FANTASY FASHION
OUTLINE PATTERN PRETEND
PROJECT PROPOSE PURPORT
PURPOSE REVERSE SCALLOP
SLEIGHT APPLIQUE BAYADERE
BOUGHPOT CONTRIVE CYMATION
CYMATIUM ENGINEER FILIGREE
FLOCKING FORECAST GRAFFITO
GROOVING INTAGLIO PHANTASY
PLATFORM REMARQUE SINGERIE
STRIPING SUNBURST GOFFERING
(— AS TITLE PAGE) VIGNETTE
(— ON CARPET) MEDALLION
(— ON COIN) BEADING
(— ON FABRIC) BATIK BATTIK
(BOOK —) FILET FILLET
(CUP-SHAPED —) HUSK
(EMBLEMATIC —) IMPRESS
(ESSENTIAL —) BONES
(FASHION —) FORD
(OUTLINE —) KEYSTONE
(PERFORATED —) POUNCE
(STRIPED —) STRIA STRIE
(TESSELLATED —) MOSAIC
(TEXTILE —) STRIPE HAIRLINE
DESIGNATE SET HAIL MARK MEAN
NAME SHOW ELECT LABEL SPEAK
STYLE TITLE ANOINT ASSIGN
DENOTE DESIGN FINGER INTEND
SETTLE APPOINT EARMARK ENTITLE
EXPRESS SPECIFY SURNAME
ALLOCATE DESCRIBE IDENTIFY
INDICATE NOMINATE
DESIGNATION NAME STYLE TITLE
CAPTION HOMONYM ADDITION
(— OF PLACE) ADDRESS
DESIGNED PREPENSE SUPPOSED
DESIGNER FANCIER PLANNER
PLOTTER SCHEMER COLORIST
ENGINEER MEDALIST
(PL.) COUTURE
DESIGNING ARTFUL CUNNING
JESUITIC PLANNING PLOTTING
SCHEMING
DESIRABLE FAIR GOOD KEEN
WORTH PLUMMY AMIABLE GRADELY
HEALTHY OPTABLE WELCOME
WISHFUL DESIROUS ELIGIBLE
ENVIABLE PLEASING SALUTARY
DESIRE YEN ACHE CARE ENVY EROS
FAIN HAVE HOPE ITCH KAMA KEEP
LEST LIST LOAD LUST MIND NEED
PANT URGE WANT WILL WISH WIST
ARDOR BOSOM BRAME COVET
CRAVE FANCY GIMME GREED

GROAN HEART MANGE MANIA NISUS
QUEST STUDY TANHA TASTE WILNE
YEARN YISSE AFFECT APPETE
ASPIRE BEHEST DEMAND DEVICE
HANKER HUNGER OREXIS POTHOS
PREFER TALENT THIRST UTINAM
YAMMER AVARICE AVIDITY
CONATUS COURAGE CRAVING
EROTISM FANTASY HIMEROS
INKLING LONGING PASSION
STOMACH VOLUNTY WILLING
AMBITION APPETITE COVETISE
CUPIDITY PLEASING
(— FOR LIFE) TANHA
(— WITH EAGERNESS) ASPIRE
(ARDENT —) THIRST
(IRRITATING —) ITCH
(STRONG —) CUPIDITY SLAVERING
(UNCONTROLLABLE —) CACOETHES
DESIROUS AVID FAIN FOND LIEF
VAIN EAGER FRACK FRECK LUSTY
ARDENT WILFUL ANXIOUS WILLFUL
WILLING WISHING APPETENT
COVETOUS LIKEROUS SPIRITED
DESIST HO LIN EASE HALT QUIT
REST SIST STOP WHOA CEASE
LEAVE SPARE STINT SWICK SWIKE
WONDE DEPART ABANDON
FORBEAR FORFEIT RESPITE SUBSIST
SURCEASE
(— FROM) CUT LEAVE REMIT
FORBEAR
DESK PEW AMBO SCOB BOARD
DESSE TABLE BUREAU CAISSE
PULPIT CONSOLE LECTERN
PLUTEUS COPYDESK STANDISH
VARGUENO
DESMA CLON CLONE
DESMAN MOLE SQUASH MUSKRAT
ONDATRA
DESMANTHUS ACUAN
DESOLATE SAD BARE LORN RUIN
SACK SOLE VAST WILD ALONE
BLEAK DREAR GAUNT GUBAT STARK
UNKED UNKET UNKID WASTE WASTY
WYSTY BARREN DESERT DISMAL
DREARY GLOOMY GOUSTY LONELY
RAVAGE DESTROY FORLORN
GOUSTIE HOWLING LACKING
UNCOUTH WIDOWED WILSOME
DEPRIVED DESERTED FORSAKEN
SOLITARY WASTEFUL WOBEGONE
DESOLATION WOE RUIN GLOOM
GRIEF HAVOC WASTE RAVAGE
SADNESS
DESPAIR GLOOM UNHOPE WANHOPE
DESPAIRING HOPELESS
DESPERADO BRAVO BADMAN
BANDIT RUFFIAN CRIMINAL
RESOLUTE
DESPERATE MAD DIRE RASH
DESPERT EXTREME FORLORN
FRANTIC HEADLONG HOPELESS
PERILOUS RECKLESS
DESPERATELY BONE
DESPICABLE BASE MEAN ORRA VILE
CHEAP DIRTY FOUTY SCALY ABJECT
PALTRY SHABBY SORDID CAITIFF
IGNOBLE PITIFUL REPTILE PITIABLE

UNWORTHY WRETCHED
DESPICABLY DIRTILY
DESPISE DEFY HATE SCORN SCOUT
SPISE SPURN DETEST FORHOO
LOATHE SLIGHT VILIFY CONTEMN
DESPITE DISDAIN DISPRIZE
MISPRIZE VILIPEND
DESPITE BY VEX SPITE MALGRE
DESPISE
DESPOIL ROB PELF PILL POLL RAID
RAPE RUIN SKIN BOOTY HARRY
PLUME REAVE RIFLE SPOIL STRIP
STRUB TRICE DIVEST FLEECE
HESPEL HUSPEL RAVAGE RAVISH
REMOVE BEREAVE DEPRIVE
DISROBE PILLAGE PLUNDER
UNSPOIL DEFLOWER DISARRAY
SPOLIATE SPUILZIE UNCLOTHE
DESPOINA KORE PERSEPHONE
DESPONDENCY DUMP BLUES
DUMPS GLOOM ATHYMY MISERY
ATHUMIA ATHYMIA DESPAIR
DESPOND
DESPONDENT SAD BLUE GLOOMY
FORLORN DEJECTED DOWNCAST
HOPELESS
DESPOT CZAR TSAR TZAR ANARCH
SATRAP TYRANT AUTARCH
MONARCH AUTOCRAT
DESPOTIC LORDLY ABSOLUTE
DOMINANT
DESPOTISM TYRANNY SULTANISM
DESQUAMATE PEEL
DESSERT ICE PIE CAKE FOOL SKYR
SNOW VOID BETTY BOMBE COUPE
DOLCE FRUIT GLACE GRUNT JELLY
LACTO SLUMP AFTERS ECLAIR
JUNKET MOUSSE PASTRY SPONGE
SWEETS TRIFLE BAKLAVA BANQUET
PARFAIT PUDDING SHERBET
SOUFFLE SPUMONE STRUDEL
SUPREME DUMPLING FLUMMERY
FRUMENTY NAPOLEON SILLABUB
DESTINATION END GOAL PORT
BOURN BILLET BOURNE
DESTINE DOOM EURE FATE MARK
ALLOT SHAPE SLATE WEIRD DEPUTE
DESIGN DEVOTE INTEND ORDAIN
APPOINT PURPOSE SENTENCE
DESTINY LOT DOLE DOOM EURE
FATE SORT KARMA MOIRA STARS
WEIRD KHARMA KISMET DESTINE
FORTUNE PORTION FOREDOOM
DESTITUTE BARE NACE POOR SANS
VOID CLEAN EMPTY NAKED NEEDY
WASTE BEREFT DEVOID VACANT
WASTED FORLORN LACKING
NAUGHTY VIDUATE WANTING
BANKRUPT BEGGARED DEFEATED
DEPRIVED DESOLATE FORSAKEN
HELPLESS INDIGENT INNOCENT
VIDUATED
(— OF FEATHERS) DEPLUMATE
(— OF LEAVES) APHYLLOUS
(— OF LIGHT) DARK
(— OF TEETH) EDENTATE
(— OF WATER) ANHYDROUS
(— OF) BUT
DESTITUTION NEED WANT FAMINE

PENURY BEGGARY DEFAULT
POVERTY
DESTROY BAG EAT END GUT RID
BLOW CHEW FRAP FULL KILL NULL
RASE RAZE RUIN RUSH SINK SLAY
SMIT STRY TINE UNDO VOID BREAK
CRACK CRAZE DECAY ELIDE ERASE
ERODE FORDO HAVOC MISDO
PRANG QUADE QUAIL QUELL SHEND
SHOOT SMASH SMITE SPEED SPEND
SPILL SPLIT SPOIL STROY SWAMP
WASTY WRACK WRECK BLIGHT
CANCEL CUMBER DEFACE DEFEAT
DELETE DEVOID DEVOUR EFFACE
FAMISH FOREDO MURDER PERISH
QUENCH RANKLE RAVAGE STARVE
UNMAKE UNPILE UNWORK UPROOT
UPTEAR ABOLISH CONSUME
CORRODE DEPRIVE DISTURB
ENECATE EXPUNGE FLATTEN
FORFARE FORLESE MORTIFY
NULLIFY OVERRUN PEREMPT
RUINATE SHAMASH SHATTER
SMOTHER SUBVERT TERRIFY
UNBUILD WHITTLE AMORTIZE
CONFOUND DECIMATE DEMOLISH
DESOLATE DESTRUCT DISANNUL
DISPLANT DISSOLVE FRACTURE
FRAGMENT IMMOLATE INFRINGE
MUTILATE OVERTURN SABOTAGE
STRAMASH
(— **BARK**) GIRDLE
(— **BY FIRE**) CONSUME
(— **FERTILITY**) EXHAUST
(— **SELF-POSSESSION**) ABASH
(— **TOTALLY**) SMASH SWEEP
CUMBER SCUTTLE
DESTROYED FLAT BLOWN KAPUT
KAPUTT
DESTROYER CAN HUN DEATH
TINCAN UNDOER VANDAL VICTOR
FLIVVER STROYER UNMAKER
WARSHIP DEVOURER SABOTEUR
DESTROYING FELL
DESTRUCTIBLE FRAIL
DESTRUCTION BAR END HEW BANE
DOGS DOOM FIRE LOSS RACK RUIN
STRY TALA CRUSH DEATH DECAY
GRAVE HAVOC STRIP STROY WASTE
DEFEAT DISMAY ENDING EXPIRY
WONDER ABADDON CARNAGE
EROSION UNDOING COLLAPSE
DELETION DISPOSAL DOWNFALL
EVERSION EXCISION SHAMBLES
SMASHERY
(— **OF BONES**) CARIES
(— **OF SHIP'S PAPERS**) SPOLIATION
(**CELL** —) LYSIS
(**GRADUAL** —) CORROSION
(**MALICIOUS** —) SABOTAGE
DESTRUCTIVE FELL FATAL DEADLY
MORTAL BALEFUL DEATHLY EXITIAL
FATEFUL HARMFUL HUMLIKE
HURTFUL NOISOME NOXIOUS
RUINOUS ANERETIC DEATHFUL
EXITIOUS WASTEFUL WRACKFUL
WREAKFUL ANAERETIC
DESUETUDE BREACH DISUSE
DESULTORY IDLE HASTY LOOSE

ROVING AIMLESS CURSORY
RAMBLING UNSTEADY WAVERING
IRREGULAR
DETACH CUT DRAFT LOOSE SEVER
LOOSEN UNBIND UNGLUE UNWORK
CRACKLE DISJOIN DRAUGHT
ISOLATE UNHINGE UNRIVET UNSEIZE
ABSTRACT DISSOLVE DISUNITE
PRESCIND SEPARATE UNFASTEN
WITHDRAW
DETACHABLE SLIP
DETACHED CUT COLD FREE ALONE
ALOOF DEADPAN INSULAR PORTATO
SCIOLTO ABSTRACT CLINICAL
DISCRETE ISOLATED SEPARATE
SPICCATO UNBIASED
DETACHMENT POSSE ATARAXY
OUTPOST ATARAXIA AVULSION
OUTGUARD
DETAIL CREW ITEM DODAD POINT
ACCENT ASSIGN DOODAB DOODAD
NICETY PARCEL RELATE RETAIL
ACCOUNT APPOINT ARTICLE ITEMIZE
MINUTIA NARRATE NULLING
RESPECT SEVERAL SPECIFY
INSTANCE REHEARSE SALIENCE
(—**S OF MAP**) CULTURE
(**CLIMACTIC** —) BEAUTY
(**PETTY** —) CHICKEN
(PL.) DOPE FROUFROU FURNITURE
DETAILED PROLIX CLOSEUP SPECIAL
PUNCTUAL TIRESOME
DETAIN BAIL HOLD KEEP STAY STOP
CHECK DELAY TARRY ARREST
ATHOLD COLLAR HINDER RETARD
TAIGLE IMPRISON RESTRAIN
WITHHOLD
DETECT SEE SPY ESPY FIND NOSE
SPOT CATCH SCENT SENSE SMOKE
DESCRY DIVINE EXPOSE REVEAL
DEVELOP DISCERN UNCOVER
DECIPHER DISCOVER OVERTAKE
DETECTIVE EYE TEC BULL BUSY
DICK TRAP PLANT SNOOP BEAGLE
MOUSER RUNNER SHADOW SHAMUS
SLEUTH TAILER TRACER GUMSHOE
SCENTER SNOOPER SPOTTER
TRAILER DETECTOR FLATFOOT
HAWKSHAW HOUSEMAN OPERATOR
SHERLOCK PINKERTON
DETECTOR COHERER REAGENT
SFERICS SPHERICS
DETENT DOG PALL PAWL CATCH
CLICK RATCH PALLET RATCHET
DETENTION DELAY ARREST
CAPTURE DETINUE DETAINER
STOPPAGE
DETER BAR FEAR BLOCK BLUFF
CHECK DELAY DEHORT HINDER
RETARD PREVENT TERRIFY
DISSUADE PRECLUDE RESTRAIN
DETERGE PURGE CLEANSE MUNDIFY
DETERGENT SOAP SYNDET
ABLUENT PURGING RHYPTIC
SMECTIC SOLVENT CLEANSER
GARDINOL
DETERIORATE GO FAIL GIVE SLIP
SOUR WEAR DECAY ERODE SPILL
WORST APPAIR APPERE DEBASE

IMPAIR SICKEN DECLINE PERVERT
FIREFANG
DETERIORATING DECADENT
DETERIORATION DECAY IMPAIR
MALADY DECLINE EROSION FAILURE
DOLDRUMS
DETERMINABLE FIXED DEFINITE
DEFINABLE GAUGEABLE
DETERMINANT CYTOGENE
JACOBIAN CIRCULANT WRONSKIAN
DETERMINATE CERTAIN ORISTIC
DEFINITE RESOLUTE RESOLVED
SPECIFIC
DETERMINATION ACT HEST WILL
ASSAY BLANK CAUSE ADVICE
BEARING CONSULT PURPOSE
RESOLVE ANALYSIS BACKBONE
BIOASSAY DECISION DIVISION
FIRMNESS FORECAST JUDGMENT
JUDICIAL SENTENCE VOLITION
DETERMINATIVE FINAL FORMANT
SHAPING LIMITING
(**MOST** —) DOMINANT
DETERMINE END FIT FIX GET RUN
TEST WILL ASSAY AWARD JUDGE
PITCH WIELD ADJUST ASSESS
ASSIGN DECERN DECIDE DECREE
DEFINE DESCRY DETECT DETERM
DEVISE FIGURE GOVERN PERFIX
SETTLE ACCOUNT ADJUDGE
ANALYZE APPOINT ARRANGE
COMPUTE DELIMIT DERAIGN
DISPOSE RESOLVE TERMINE
COGNOSCE CONCLUDE DISCOVER
INFLUENCE
(— **FINENESS**) SET SETT
(— **RATE**) ASSESS
(— **ROOT**) EXTRACT
DETERMINED SET BENT DERN FIRM
GRIM GIVEN STOUT UPSET BITTER
DOGGED GRITTY INTENT MULISH
STURDY DECIDED SETTLED
DECISIVE FOREGONE PERVERSE
RESOLUTE RESOLVED STUBBORN
DETERMINER GENE CHANCE
DETERMINIST JABARITE
DETEST DAMN HATE ABHOR CURSE
LOATHE CONDEMN DESPISE DISLIKE
DENOUNCE EXECRATE
DETESTABLE FOUL HORRID ODIOUS
BLASTED HATABLE HATEFUL
HELLISH HIDEOUS ACCURSED
DAMNABLE HATEABLE INFAMOUS
INFERNAL
DETESTATION ODIUM HATRED
HORROR LOATHING ANTIPATHY
DETHRONE DEPOSE DIVEST
UNCROWN
DETONATE FIRE BELCH BLAST
SHOOT EXPLODE DETONIZE
DETONATION BLAST KNOCK
AMBITUS PINGING PINKING
DETONATOR CAP FUSE FUZE FUSEE
FUZEE SQUIB TORPEDO INITIATOR
DETOUR BYPASS CIRCUIT DIVERSION
DETRACT TAKE DECRY DEDUCT
DEFAME DETRAY DIVERT VILIFY
ASPERSE TRADUCE BELITTLE
DEROGATE DIMINISH DISTRACT

MINIMIZE PROTRACT SUBTRACT
WITHDRAW
(— FROM) IMPEDE
DETRACTION CALUMNY SCANDAL
SLANDER ZOILISM
DETRIMENT COST HARM HURT LOSS
SORE WOUND DAMAGE DAMNUM
DENIAL INJURY BEATING EXPENSE
JACTURE DISFAVOR MISCHIEF
DETRIMENTAL ADVERSE CAPITAL
HARMFUL HURTFUL LOSSFUL
DAMAGING INVIDIOUS
DETRITUS OUTWASH SHINGLE
SHEETWASH
DEUCALION (FATHER OF —)
PROMETHEUS
(WIFE OF —) PYRRHA
DEUCE DIANTRE DICKENS
(WILD —) FREAK
DEUCEDLY BLAME BLAMED
DEUTERIUM H
DEUTEROGAMY DIGAMY
DEUTOMALA LABIUM
DEVA DEV DEWA SURA ANGEL DEITY
DEVASTATE EXILE HARRY HAVOC
WASTE DEVAST RAVAGE ATOMIZE
DESTROY PILLAGE PLUNDER
SCOURGE DEMOLISH
DEVASTATED WASTE
DEVASTATION RUIN EXILE HAVOC
WASTE HARASS RAVAGE SACCAGE
SACKAGE SACCADGE
DEVASTATING DEADLY LETHAL
SAVAGE CRUSHING FEROCIOUS
DEVELOP BUD RUN BOOM COOK
FORM GROW STEM TILL ARISE
BREAK BREED BUILD ERECT RIPEN
SHOOT APPEAR BRANCH DETECT
EVOLVE EXPAND FLOWER FULFIL
MATURE REVEAL UNFOLD UNFURL
BURGEON BURNISH EDUCATE
ENLARGE EVOLUTE EXPOUND
FULFILL UNCOVER DEVELOPE
DISCLOSE DISCOVER DISVELOP
ENGENDER GENERATE INCUBATE
MANIFEST
(— A HEAD) HEART
(— BULB) BOTTOM
(— COLOR) AGE
(— CRACKS) ALLIGATOR
(— WELL) COTTON
DEVELOPABLE TORSE
DEVELOPED DEEP FORWARD
(— AFTER BIRTH) ACQUIRED
(FULLY —) BOLD ADULT FLORID
FORMED SUMMED
(GREATLY —) ADVANCED
(IMPERFECTLY —) ABORTIVE
(INCOMPLETELY —) SEED
DEVELOPER ELON SOUP ORTOL
AMIDOL GLYCIN KACHIN BUILDER
GLYCINE RODINAL
DEVELOPMENT WAX DRIFT EVENT
HATCH ESTATE GROWTH DESCENT
GENESIS PROCESS STATURE
BREEDING INCREASE PEDIGREE
UPGROWTH UPSPRING
(— OF SEX) DIOECISM
(FULL —) BLOW MATURITY

(HIGHEST —) BLOOM
(NORMAL —) APHANISIA
(SUBSEQUENT —) SEQUEL
(THEMATIC —) CONTINUITY
(UNEXPECTED —) ACCIDENT
DEVI UMA KALI DURGA GAURI
CHANDI SHAKTI BHAVANI BHOWANI
HIMAVAT MAHADEVI HAIMAVATI
DEVIANT ABERRANT DIVERGENT
DEVIATE ERR RUN WRY YAW LEAN
MISS VARY VEER BEVEL BREAK
DRIFT LAPSE SHEER SPORT START
STRAY WAIVE CHANGE DEPART
DETOUR DIVERT RECEDE SQUINT
SWERVE WANDER DECLINE DEFLECT
DIGRESS DIVERGE INCLINE REFLECT
ABERRANT DEROGATE
(— FROM VERTICAL) HADE
DEVIATING SKEW DEVIANT DEVIOUS
ERRATIC SINUOUS ABERRANT
INDIRECT
DEVIATION BOW HELM JUMP SKEW
TURN DRIFT LAPSE QUIRK SHEER
TWIST ABRASH BATTER CHANGE
DETOUR FIGURE SPREAD ANOMALY
BRISURE LICENCE LICENSE
ACCURACY DRIFTAGE LATITUDE
SOLECISM VARIANCE
(— OF COLOR) ABRASH
(STANDARD —) SIGMA
DEVICE (ALSO SEE INSTRUMENT)
ARM ART DIE DOG DOP EYE FAN
FLY FOB GAG GIN GUN HOG JIG
KEY MOP MOT PEN SET TIP TUP
WAY WIT ARCH BELL BOND BOOM
BUFF COIN COMB COUP DARE DOPP
DRAG DRIP FAKE FIRE FLAG FORK
FROG FUSE FUZE GAGE GATE GOBO
GRAB GRIP GYRO HASP HAUL HEAD
HECK HORN IRIS IRON JACK KEEP
KITE LAMP LENS LOCK MOVE MULE
MUTE NAIL PACE PAGE PAWK PLOW
POKE PUMP REEL SEAL SHOE SHUT
SIGN SLAY SLEY SLUR SNAP SPUD
STOP STUD SUMP TOOL TRAP TRIP
VICE WEIR WHIM WHIP WIND WING
WOLF ALARM APRON BADGE BALUN
BITCH BLOCK BREAK BRUSH CHECK
CLAMP CODER COVIN CRAMP
CROSS DODGE DRIER DRIFT DRYER
DUMMY FADER FANCY FLAIL FLARE
FLASH FLIRT FLOAT GAUGE GLAND
GORGE GRIPE GUARD GUIDE GUILE
HICKY HINGE HOKUM IMAGE KAZOO
KEYER LADLE LASER LATCH LEVEL
MATCH OTTER PARER PLATE PUNKA
SCREW SHADE SHANK SHIFT SIEVE
SIGHT SIGIL SIREN SIZER SKATE
SLAVE SLICK SLIDE SLING SONDE
SPOOL SPOUT SQUIB STAMP STILL
STOOL STOVE SWEEP SWELL TABLE
TABUT TAMER THIEF TIMER TORCH
TRUER TUNER UNION VERGE
AGRAFE AIRWAY ALARUM ALINER
ANCHOR ARREST BAILER BASTER
BEACON BEATER BECKET BEDDER
BEEPER BINDER BLOWER BOBBIN
BOOMER BRIDLE BROOCH BUCKLE
BUFFER BULLEN BUMPER BUNGEE

BUNTER BURNER BUTTON CIPHER
COOKER DASHER DECEIT DERAIL
DESIGN DIMMER DOFFER DOTTER
DRIVER DROGUE DUMPER EMBLEM
ENGINE EVENER FABRIC FALLER
FEEDER FENDER FILLER FILTER
FINDAL FINDER FORMER GADGET
GLAZER GOFFER GOGGLE GRADER
GRATER GRISLY GUIDER HANGER
HEATER HICKEY HOLDER HOOTER
INVENT JIGGER JOGGER KEEPER
KICKER LAYBOY LETOFF LIFTER
LOOPER MARKER MIRROR MODULE
MORTAR MOTHER NIPPLE NONIUS
NOTION PACKER PEELER PLAYER
PLOUGH PORTER POTEYE PULLER
PUNKAH REROLL RINGER ROCKET
ROLLER ROOTER ROTULA ROUTER
SACKER SADDLE SAFETY SANDER
SCALER SCHEME SCREEN SEALER
SEEKER SENSOR SETTER SHAKER
SHIELD SIFTER SIGNAL SINKER
SIPPER SLEIGH SLICER SLIDER
SLIMER SLOPER SLUICE SOCKET
SOLION SORTER SPACER SPRING
STONER STYLUS SUCKER SWITCH
TACTIC TAGGER TAPPER TELLER
TEMPLE TESTER TILLER TRACER
TUCKER TUNNEL TURNER WARMER
WASHER WEANER WEEDER WHEEZE
WINDER WINNOW WORKER ADAPTER
ADJUNCT AERATOR AGRAFFE
ALIGNER BAFFLE BECKETT
BIMETAL BIMORPH BINDING
BLEEDER BLENDER BLINKER
BLOCKER BLOWOFF BLOWOUT
BOOKEND BOOSTER BREAKER
CALTROP CHIPPER CLAPPER
COMPASS DASHPOT DISHMOP
DIVISOR DRAWOFF DRESSER
DRINKER EARPICK EDUCTOR
EJECTOR EMPRESA EXCITER
FACEBOW FASHION FETLOCK
FICELLE FICTION FITMENT FIXTURE
FLASHER FLIPPER FLUSHER
FLYFLAP FRISKET GAUFFER
GIMMICK GLASSES GRAINER
GRENADE GRIDDLE GRILLER
GRINDER GRIPPER GRIZZLY
GROMMET GROOVER GROWLER
GUDGEON GUZZLER HATCHER
HELIDON IGNITER IMAGINE IMPRESA
IMPRESS INFUSER INHALER
IRONMAN KICKOFF KNOTTER
LIGHTER MACHINE MUFFLER
OOGRAPH PIGTAIL PLOTTER
POINTER PRESSER RATCHET
RATTLER RECEDER REDUCER
RELEASE ROASTER ROSETTE
SAMPLER SCALPER SCANNER
SCOGGAN SCRAPER SCUPPER
SERVANT SETBACK SETOVER
SETWORK SHACKLE SHEDDER
SHIFTER SHIPPER SHOOFLY
SHUTTER SHUTTLE SINKBOX
SKIMMER SLAPPER SLEEVER
SLINGER SLITTER SLUDGER
SLUSHER SNAPPER SNIFFER
SNIGGLE SNORKEL SNUBBER

SNUFFER SNUGGER SONOVOX
SOUNDER SPARGER SPEEDER
SPLICER SPOTTER SPRAYER
SQUEEZE STACKER STAPLER
STARTER STEMMER STENTER
STIRRER STOPPER STRIKER
STRIPER SUCTION SWATTER
SWEEPER SYRINGE TAMBOUR
TENDRIL TENSION THEORIC
THINNER TICKLER TREADLE
TRINDLE TRIPPER TRIPPET
TUMBLER TURNOUT TWISTER
WASHOUT WRINGER ABSORBER
ADJUSTER AQUASTAT BACKSTAY
BAROSTAT BIOMETER BLOCKING
BOOTJACK BRAILLER BREATHER
BRONTEUM BUSINESS BUSYBODY
CATAPULT CATHETER CONTOISE
COUPLING CROTCHET CRYOTRON
DAMPENER DEHORNER DERAILER
DIFFUSER DIRECTOR DISPOSER
DOORSTOP DROPHEAD DUPLEXER
EARPHONE ESPRESSO EXPLODER
FAIRLEAD FAKEMENT FASTENER
FLASHGUN FLYBRUSH FUELIZER
GASCHECK GATHERER GIMCRACK
GUNSTICK GYROSTAT HALLMARK
HANDTRAP HEADGEAR HOLDBACK
IMPROVER INKSTAND IRENICON
IRISCOPE ISOLATOR KNOCKOUT
LAUNCHER LEEBOARD LOXOCOSM
LUNARIUM MNEMONIC MOLITION
NEOSTYLE ODOGRAPH OVERLIFT
PACIFIER PARAVANE PENWIPER
PINWHEEL PULSATOR PYROSTAT
QUADRANT QUENTISE REFILTER
REHEATER REPEATER RETARDER
REVERSER SCORCHER SCOTCHER
SCRAWLER SCUTCHER SELECTOR
SHRINKER SILENCER SILVERER
SINKBOAT SMOOTHER SNOWPLOW
SNOWSHOE SPLITTER SPREADER
SPROUTER SQUEEGEE SQUEEZER
STOPWORK STRAINER STRINGER
STRIPPER STROPPER SURFACER
SWEATBOX TELETYPE TELLTALE
TERMINAL THROWOFF THROWOUT
TRAVELER TRAVERSE TRIANGLE
(— FOR BENDING PIPE) HICKEY
(— FOR BORING WELLS) TIGER
(— FOR CONCENTRATING ORE)
JIGGER
(— FOR PUTTING IN GEAR) STRIKER
(— IN LOOM) FEELER TEMPLE
(— ON FLAG) UNION
(— PLACED OVER CHIMNEY) JACK
(— PROTECTING DENTIST'S HAND)
THIMBLE
(— TO RETAIN COFFEE GROUNDS)
GRECQUE
(CENTRIFUGAL —) CYCLONE
(CLEVER —) COUP KNACK
(DISTINGUISHING —) SPOT
(GAMBLING —) HOLDOUT
(GLASSBLOWER'S —) DUMMY
(HAMPERING —) HOBBLES
(HEATING —) ETNA
(HERALDIC —S) ARMS
(LITERARY —) FRAME

(MAGICIAN'S —) FAKE FEKE CRAFT
(MIXING —) CRUTCHER
(POLISHING —) WAGWAG
(PYROTECHNIC —) FOUNTAIN
(SIGHTING —) ALIDADE
(SIGNALLING —) CRICKET
(SKILLFUL —) ART
(SPEECH —) ITALICS
(THEATRICAL —) SLOAT SLOTE
(TIMEKEEPING —) HOROLOGE
(WATER-RAISING —) JANTU SWEEP
CHURRUS
(WEAVING —) BOAT
(PL.) ENGINERY
DEVIL DEL IMP BENG BHUT BOGY
DEIL HAZE MAHU NICK PUCK QUED
WOLF WOND ANNOY BOBBY BOGEY
BOGIE CHORT CLOOT DEMON
DEUCE EBLIS FIEND HARRY SATAN
SCRAT SHEDU TAIPO TEASE
AMAMON DAEMON DIABLE DIABLO
HORNIE NICKIE PESTER RAGMAN
SORROW THURSE AMAIMON
ANHANGA CLOOTIE DIANTRE
DICKENS GREMLIN LUCIFER
MAHOUND RUFFIAN SERPENT
SHAITAN TORMENT WARLOCK
WENDIGO WINDIGO APOLLYON
BAALPEOR BEELPEOR BELFAGOR
CAGNAZZO CURUPIRA DEVILING
DEVILKIN DIABOLUS MEPHISTO
MISCHIEF OBIDICUT PLOTCOCK
WORRICOW
(BLUE —S) MARE
DEVILFISH RAY MANTA
DEVILISH DARING DEUCED DEVILY
RAKISH WICKED DEMONIC EXTREME
FIENDLY HELLISH INHUMAN SATANIC
DEMONIAC DIABOLIC FIENDISH
INFERNAL SATURNINE
DEVILISHLY DEUCED DEUCEDLY
DEVIL'S CLUB FATSIA
DEVIL'S COACHHORSE DARDAOL
DEVIL'S-MILK WARTWEED
WARTWORT
DEVIL'S-TREE DITA
DEVIOUS DEEP ERRING LOUCHE
ROVING SHIFTY SUBTLE TRICKY
OBLIQUE PLAITED VAGRANT
WINDING HAVERING INDIRECT
RAMBLING SCHEMING TORTUOUS
DEVISE AIM CAST COOK FIND GIVE
PLAN PLOT WARP WILL ARRAY
FANCY FRAME FUDGE IMAGE LEAVE
SHAPE WEAVE ADVISE CONVEY
DECOCT DESIGN DEVICE DIVIDE
DIVINE INVENT SCHEME AGITATE
APPOINT ARRANGE BETHINK
COMMENT COMPASS CONCERT
CONCOCT CONSULT IMAGINE
PREPARE PROJECT BEQUEATH
CONTRIVE
DEVISER FINDER ARTIFICER
DEVISING DEVICE DEVISAL FORGERY
DEVITALIZE DULL DEADEN
DEVITALIZED DEGENERATE
DEVITRIFIED AMBITTY
DEVOID FREE VOID EMPTY BARREN

EXPERT VACANT SINCERE WANTING
DESOLATE
(— OF HELP) AIDLESS
(— OF KINDNESS) CRUEL
(— OF MERCY) BRUTAL
(— OF MIND) AMENTAL
(— OF VALUE) HOLLOW
(— OF) BOUT EMPTY
DEVOLUTION DESCENT
DEVOLVE FALL PASS RESULT
BLOSSOM SUCCEED OVERTURN
TRANSFER TRANSMIT
DEVOTE VOW ALLY AVOW DOOM
GIVE LEND TAKE TURN APPLY
DEVOW ADDICT ATTACH BESTOW
DEPUTE DESIGN DEVOVE DIRECT
EMPLOY INTEND RESIGN ADDRESS
CONSIGN DESTINE DEDICATE
VENERATE
(— TIME) BOTHER
DEVOTED MAD HIGH TRUE LIEGE
LOYAL PIOUS ARDENT DEVOUT
DOOMED ENTIRE FERVID OBLATE
VOTARY VOTIVE ADORING ARDUOUS
JEALOUS SERIOUS ZEALOUS
ADDICTED ATTACHED CONSTANT
FAITHFUL
(— TO COUNTRY) PATRIOTIC
(— TO ENJOYMENT) APOLAUSTIC
(OVERLY —) SUPERSTITIOUS
DEVOTEE CAT FAN NUN BUFF MONK
YATI ADEPT JNANI ADDICT BHAGAT
BHAKTA DEVOTO DEVOUT HEPCAT
VOTARY VOTEEN ZEALOT ADMIRER
AMATEUR BOPPIST BOPSTER
CINEAST FANATIC HEPSTER HIPSTER
SHAVIAN TARTUFE AMOURIST
BURNSIAN CABALIST DEVOTARY
FOLLOWER IBSENITE PARTISAN
PRIAPIAN SAVOYARD SIMPLIST
TARTUFFE VOTARESS VOTARIST
ALLIGATOR
DEVOTION CULT ZEAL ARDOR PIETY
BHAKTI NOVENA ANGELUS ARABISM
CULTISM LOYALTY FIDELITY
IDOLATRY JEALOUSY KAVVANAH
KAWWANAH RELIGION
(— OF ONESELF) VOW
(— TO HUMAN WELFARE)
HUMANISM
(FERVENT —) ADORATION
(PARENTAL —) PROGENITY
(PL.) HOLIES
DEVOTIONAL SOLEMN
DEVOUR EAT JAW FRET GULP SWAP
SWOP VOUR GORGE RAVEN WASTE
AFRETE ENGULF CONSUME
ENGORGE FRAUNCH SWALLOW
(— GREEDILY) SWILL
DEVOURING PREY EATING GREEDY
VORANT EDACIOUS
DEVOUT GOOD HOLY WARM FROOM
GODLY GRACY PIOUS HEARTY
INWARD SOLEMN CORDIAL DEVOTED
GODLIKE PITEOUS SAINTLY SINCERE
REVERENT PIETISTIC
(NOT —) LINK
DEVOUTNESS PIETY DEVOTION
DEW DAG RIME BLOOM FROST

MOISTEN REFRESH MOISTURE
(— **METER**) PAGOSCOPE
DEWBERRY MAYES
DEWDROP PEARL
DEWLAP JOWL GULLET JOLLOP
CHOLLER WATTLES
(— **OF MALE MOOSE**) BELL
DEWY DAMP RORY MOIST RORAL
RORIC RORID GENTLE ROSCID
DEXTERITY ART CHIC CRAFT KNACK
SKILL STROIL ABILITY ADDRESS
AGILITY APTNESS CUNNING FINESSE
SLEIGHT APTITUDE DEFTNESS
FACILITY
(— **IN ARMS**) CHIVALRY
DEXTEROUS APT FLY DEFT FEAT
HEND WISE ADEPT CANNY CLEAN
FEATY HANDY HAPPY HENDE JIMMY
QUICK READY SMART TIGHT ADROIT
ARTFUL CLEVER DRAFTY CUNNING
SLEIGHT DEXTROUS HANDSOME
SKILLFUL SLEIGHTY
DEXTEROUSLY YARELY HANDILY
DEXTRAN GLUCOSAN
DEXTROROTATORY POSITIVE
DEXTRORSE EUTROPIC
DEXTROSE AME CEROLOSE
DHAK DAK PALAS PULAS
DHAVA BAKLI
DHOLE KOLSUN
DHOW BUGALA LATEEN SAMBUK
SAMBOUK LATEENER
DHYANA JHANA
DIABASE OPHITE DOLERITE
THOLEITE
DIABOLICAL CRUEL WICKED
DEMONIC HELLISH INHUMAN
SATANIC VIOLENT DEMONIAC
DEVILISH DIABOLIC FIENDISH
INFERNAL
DIABOLISM SATANISM
DIACETATE ACETIN
DIACONATE DEACONRY
DIACONICON PARABEMA
DIACRITIC HACEK TILDE UMLAUT
MODIFIER
DIAD DIGONAL TWOFOLD
DIADEM MIND CROWN TIARA
ANADEM CIRCLE EMBLEM FILLET
CORONET HEADBAND
DIAERESIS CESURA CAESURA
DIALYSIS
DIAGNOSE ANALYZE IDENTIFY
KNOWLEDGE
DIAGONAL BIAS SLANT SLASH
COUNTER SOLIDUS VIRGULE
BENDWISE DIAGONIC
DIAGONALLY BIAS BENDWAYS
BENDWISE
DIAGRAM MAP PLAN PLOT TREE
CARTE CHART EPURE GRAPH
DESIGN FIGURE SCHEMA SCHEME
SYMBOL YANTRA ISOGRAM ISOTYPE
SECTION VIAGRAM
DIAGRAMMATIC GRAPHIC
DIAGRAPH OE
DIAL NOB FACE KNOB WATCH
DIACLE JIGGER AZIMUTH CRYSTAL

DECLINER HOROLOGE INCLINER
RECLINER
DIAL BIRD DAYAL DHYAL
DIALECT (ALSO SEE LANGUAGE) HO
KA WU GEG GIZ KHA LAI SAC TWI
AMOY CANI CANT EFIK EGBA EPIC
GEEZ GHEG GONA GUEG IOWA ITZA
KORA MANX NAMA NORN OGAM
PALI SAUK SHOR SOGA TALK TCHI
TOSK TUBA ALTAI ARGOT ASURI
ATTIC CONOY DORIC FANTI GHEEZ
GHESE HAKKA IDIOM IONIC IOWAY
IRAQI KANSA KAREL KOINE LADIN
LINGO MAZUR MOPAN MUKRI
NGOKO OGHAM PARSI PUNIC SABIR
SAXON SCOTS SLANG TIGRE TSCHI
VALVE VOGUL ZMUDZ AEOLIC
AGNEAN ASANTE ATSINA AWADHI
BADAGA BROGUE CANTON CREOLE
DEBATE DUNGAN FAEROE FANTEE
FURLAN GASCON GULLAH GUTNIC
HARARI HARAYA IBANAG ISINAI
ITAVES JARGON KANSAS KHAMIR
KORANA KVITSH LADAKI LAHULI
LALLAN LIBYAN PARSEE PATOIS
PATTER PICARD SANTEE SCOTCH
SHARRA SKAGIT SPEECH SUDANI
SWATOW SYRIAC SZEKEL TAVAST
TONGUE TUSCAN YANKEE ZENAGA
ACADIAN AEOLIAN AMOYESE
ASHANTI BHOTANI BHUTANI
BUNDELI CHILULA CHUVASH
CLATSOP COCKNEY CORNISH
CUZCENO CYPRIOT FAYUMIC
FOOCHOW GEECHEE GHEGISH
GUTNISH JAIPURI KARAITE KITKSAN
KONKANI LADAKHI LALLAND
LEONESE LESBIAN MALTESE
MARSIAN MARWARI MIDLAND
MULTANI MUNDARI OLONETS
PANAYAN PRAKRIT SAHIDIC SANPOIL
SHORTZY SOKOTRI SPOKANE
SQUAXON SWABIAN SZEKLER
TIGRINA VAUDOIS ABANEEME
ACHMIMIC AKHMIMIC ALGERINE
ARCADIAN ASSYRIAN BAVARIAN
BHOJPURI BISCAYAN BOEOTIAN
BOHAIRIC CLAKAMAS COLVILLE
CORSICAN CYPRIOTE FALERIAN
FALISCAN FAROEISH FRANCIEN
FRIULIAN GARHWALI HARARESE
IZCATECO KANESIAN KARELIAN
KERMANJI KICKAPOO KINGWANA
LACANDON LANGUAGE LAWLANTS
MAGHREBI MAGHRIBI MAITHILI
MANDAEAN MANDARIN MANISIAN
MAZATECO MAZURIAN MEMPHITE
NABATEAN NEENGATU PANAYANO
PEKINESE RABBINIC SALTEAUX
SOULETIN SOUTHERN TAUNGTHU
TIGRINYA TIRHUTIA TUNISIAN
VENERIAN VIENNESE
(**STRANGE** —) GIBBERISH
(PL.) WU ANGLIAN
DIALECTIC PILPUL
DIALOGUE ION CRITO DIALOG
EPILOG PATTER PHAEDO TIMAEUS
COLLOQUY DUOLOGUE EPILOGUE
EXCHANGE PHAEDRUS

(—**S OF BUDDHA**) SUTRA SUTTA
(**COMIC** —) LAZZO
DIAMETER BORE GAGE GEAR MOOT
GAUGE WIDTH MODULE
(— **OF BULLET**) CALIBER CALIBRE
(— **OF PELVIS**) CONJUGATA
(— **OF PUPIL**) APERTURE
(— **OF WIRE**) GAGE GAUGE
DIAMOND GEM ICE BORT LASK PICK
ROCK ROSE BAHIA BOORT BORTZ
DORJE FANCY FIELD JAGER JEWEL
LOZEN MELEE POINT RHOMB RIVER
SANCY SPARK TABLE VAJRA
ADAMAS CANARY CARBON JAEGER
LASQUE ORLOFF PENCIL REGENT
RONDEL SHINER TABLET ADAMANT
BRIOLET CARREAU CRYSTAL
FISHEYE INFIELD LOZENGE PREMIER
RHOMBUS SPARKLE CORUNDUM
KOHINOOR RONDELLE SPARKLER
(— **CUT TOO THIN**) FISHEYE
(— **MOLDER**) DOP
(— **STATE**) DELAWARE
(— **USED FOR ENGRAVING**) SHARP
(**BLACK** —) CARBONADO
(**FLAT** —) LASQUE
(**GLAZIER'S** —) QUARREL
(**IMITATION** —) SCHLENTER
(**INFERIOR GRADE OF** —) FLAT
(**PERFECT** —) PARAGON
(**PURE WHITE** —) RIVER
(**SINGLE** —) SOLITAIRE
(**TRANSPARENT** —) CRYSTAL
(**YELLOW** —) CANARY
(PL.) MELANGE
DIAMOND BIRD PARDALOTE
DIAMORPHINE HEROIN
DIANA LUCINA TRIVIA ARTEMIS
(**BROTHER OF** —) APOLLO
(**FATHER OF** —) JUPITER
(**MOTHER OF** —) LATONA
DIANA MONKEY ROLOWAY
DIAPASON MONTRE DIAPASE
DIAPAUSE BLOCK
DIAPER FUR DIDY CLOUT DIDIE
NAPPY HIPPEN HIPPIN NAPKIN
NAPPIE DIAPERY
DIAPHANOUS CLEAR SHEER
FRAGILE DIAPHANE
DIAPHONY ORGANUM TRIPHONY
DIAPHORETIC BUCCO BUCHU
BUCKU BORAGE DIAPNOIC HIDROTIC
SUDATORY
DIAPHRAGM IRIS RIFF SLIT APRON
PHREN SKIRT WAFER DECKER
PLATEN MIDRIFF PHRAGMA
SKIRTING TRAVERSE TYMPANUM
DIAPHRAGMATIC PHRENIC
DIARRHEA LAX FLUX LASK GURRY
RELAX SCOUR SPRUE PURGING
SQUIRTS LIENTERY
DIARY LOG RECORD DAYBOOK
DIURNAL JOURNAL REGISTER
EPHEMERIS
DIASKEUAST EDITOR REVISER
DIASPORA GALUT GOLAH GALUTH
DIASPORE MIGRULE
DIASTASE MALT ENZYME AMYLASE

DIATOM BRITTLEWORT
ASTERIONELLA
DIATONIC ACHROMATIC
DIATRIBE SCREED HARANGUE
INVECTIVE
DIB DAP DIP DIBBLE DIBSTONE
DIBBLE DAP DIB DABBLE DIBBER
KIPPIN TRIFLE DIBBLER KIPPEEN
DIBS COCKAL
DICAST HELIAST JURYMAN
DICE CHOP CUBE DEES BONES
CRAPS FLATS LOWMEN REJECT
CHECKER IVORIES
(— GAME) SET RAPHE MUMCHANCE
(— HAVING FOUR SPOTS) QUATRE
(2, 3, OR 12 ON 1ST —) MISSOUT
(FALSE —) GOAD TATS GOURD
GRAVIERS SQUARIER STOPDICE
(HIGHEST THROW AT —) APHRODITE
(LOADED —) TOPS DOCTOR
(LOWEST THROW AT —) AMBSACE
(PAIRED NUMBERS AT —) DUPLET
DOUBLETS
DICE PLAYER THROWSTER
DICER DERBY GAMBLER GRAINER
DICERION DYKER
DICHONDRA LAWNLEAF
DICHOTOMY DUALITY
DICKENS HECK DEUCE
DICKER ICRE SWAP DAKER BARTER
HAGGLE BARGAIN CHAFFER
EXCHANGE
DICKEY POOP WEAK DICKY FRONT
GILET SHAKY DONKEY RUMBLE
VESTEE HADDOCK PLASTRON
DICKIE SHAM DICKY FRONT SQUARE
TUCKER STARCHER
DICLINOUS IMPERFECT
DICTATE SAW SAY DITE TELL UTTER
WRITE DECREE DICTUM ENJOIN
IMPOSE INDITE OCTROY ORDAIN
SCHOOL COMMAND DELIVER
REQUIRE SUGGEST WARRANT
DICTAMEN
DICTATION DICTAMEN
DICTATOR CZAR DUCE TSAR
CAESAR PENDRAGON
DICTATORIAL BOSSY LORDLY
CZARIST POMPOUS TSARIST
ARROGANT DOGMATIC ORACULAR
POSITIVE
DICTION STYLE TERMS PHRASE
IMAGERY LANGUAGE PARLANCE
VERBIAGE
(BAD —) CACOLOGY
DICTIONARY GRADUS CALEPIN
LEXICON GLOSSARY WORDBOOK
THESAURUS
DICTUN SAY ADAGE AXIOM EDICT
DECREE SAYING DICTATE EFFATUM
OPINION APOTHEGM PRINCIPLE
STATEMENT
DID D CAN DED DEDE DYDE
(— NOT) DIDNA DIDNT
DIDACTIC DRY PREACHY SERMONIC
DIDO ANTIC CAPER TRICK
(BROTHER OF —) PYGMALION
(FATHER OF —) BELUS
(HUSBAND OF —) SICHAEUS

(LOVER OF —) AENEAS
DIE GO BED DEE DOD END HOB HUB
PIP ROT SIX TAT BOSS COIN CONK
CUBE DADO DEAD DICE DROP EXIT
FADE FAIL FALL FINE FIVE FLIT KICK
MARK MOLD PART PASS PIKE PILE
SEAL TATT TINE WANE CROAK
FORCE FUDGE GHOST IVORY
NAPOO PATAY PRINT PUNCH QUAIL
SHAPE SNUFF SOUGH SPILL STALL
STAMP STOCK SWELT CHANCE
DEMISE DEPART DOCTOR EXPIRE
FAMISH FINISH FORCER FORMER
FULLAM MATRIX MULLAR PATRIX
PERISH ROLLER STARVE STRIKE
TORFEL TORFLE TRANCE VANISH
WITHER BLOCKER DECEASE
SUCCUMB TESSERA INTAGLIO
LANGUISH MISCARRY PUNCHEON
TRESPASS TRUSSELL
(— AWAY) FAIL SWOON
(— BY HANGING) SWING
(— DOWN) FLIT SINK
(— FOR DRAWING WIRE) WHIRTLE
WHORTLE
(— FOR MAKING DRAINPIPE) DOD
(— FOR MOLDING BRICK) KICK
(— FROM HUNGER) AFFAMISH
(— OF COLD) STARVE
(— WITH 4 SPOTS) QUATRE
(— WITH 6 SPOTS) CISE SICE SISE
SIZE
(COINING —) SICCA
(FRAUDULENT —) FULHAM FULLAM
FULLOM
(HOLLOW —) GOURD
(IMPROPER —) FLAT
(LOADED —) TAT DOCTOR FULHAM
HIGHMAN LANGRET
(LOWER —) BED
(REVOLVING —) DREIDEL
DIEBACK STAGHEAD EXANTHEMA
DIED DYDE WRATE
DIEHARD TORY BLIMP
DIESIS FEINT
DIET BANT FARE FAST FOOD SEIM
SEYM BOARD HOFTAG REDUCE
SEIMAS VIANDS VICTUS DIETINE
LANDTAG REGIMEN RIKSDAG
CONGRESS KREISTAG VOLKSTAG
DIETARY (— LAWS) KASHRUTH
DIETETICS SITOLOGY
DIETHER APIOL APIOLE DIOXANE
DIETING BANTING
DIFFER VARY RECEDE SQUARE
COMPARE DISCORD DISSENT
DIVERGE DISAGREE
DIFFERENCE SHED CHASM CLASH
FAVOR BREACH CHANGE DIFFER
ANOMALY BRISURE DISCORD
DISPUTE QUALITY VARIETY
DISTANCE DIVISION IMPARITY
VARIANCE
(— IN ELEVATION) HEAD
(— IN LATITUDE) SOUTHING
(— IN LONGITUDE) EASTING
(— IN PITCH) COMMA INTERVAL
(— IN PRESSURE) DRAFT DRAUGHT
(— IN WIDTH) BILGE

(— OF OPINION) DISSENT
ARGUMENT
(— OF VESSEL'S DRAFT) DRAG
(ANGULAR —) EXPLEMENT
(GRADED —) GRADIENT
(MINUTE —) SHADE
(PRICE —) BASIS
(SMALL —) HAIRLINE
DIFFERENT FAR MANY SERE FRESH
OTHER PARTY DIVERS SCREWY
SUNDRY UNLIKE ANOTHER DISTANT
DIVERSE SEVERAL STRANGE
UNALIKE UNUSUAL VARIANT
VARIOUS CONTRARY DISTINCT
MANIFOLD SEPARATE
DIFFERENTIA MARK LIMIT
DIFFERENTIAL FLUXION
DIFFERENTIATE APLITE DIFFER
DISCERN HAPLITE CONTRAST
SPECIATE
DIFFERENTIATION ANABOLY
DEVIATION DICHOTOMY
DIFFERING DIVERSE SINGULAR
DIVERGENT
DIFFICULT ILL HARD WICK CRAMP
CRANK GREAT HEAVY SPINY STIFF
AUGEAN CRABBY CRANKY KNOTTY
SEVERE STICKY STRAIT STRONG
TICKLE TRAPPY UNEASY UNEATH
UPHILL WENETH WICKED ARDUOUS
AWKWARD BRITTLE CRABBED
DIFFUSE LABORED NERVOUS
OBSCURE PAINFUL PERPLEX
PRACTIC SERIOUS STICKLE
UNNETHE ABSTRACT CUMBROUS
FIENDISH PUZZLING SCABROUS
STRUGGLE STUBBORN
(— TO BEAR) BITTER
(— TO COMPREHEND) STRANGE
(— TO FOLLOW) DIRTY
(— TO GRASP) FUGITIVE
(— TO HANDLE) SPINOUS
(— TO MANAGE) SURLY STURDY
(— TO OBTAIN) CLOSE
(— TO PLEASE) CURIOUS
(— TO RAISE) DORTY
(— TO SATISFY) CHOOSY CHOOSEY
(— TO UNDERSTAND) DEEP HIGH
SUBTLE CRABBED ABSTRACT
ABSTRUSE ESOTERIC
DIFFICULTY ADO BAR ILL JAM RUB
BUMP CLOG COIL HEAT JAMB KNOT
LOCK NODE PAIN PINE SNAG SORE
WERE CHECK DOUBT GRIEF NODUS
PRESS RIGOR STAND STOUR TRADE
APORIA BOGGLE BUNKER HABBLE
HOBBLE PLIGHT PLUNGE RUBBER
SCRAPE STRAIT TIFTER BARRIER
DICKENS GORDIAN PITFALL
PROBLEM SQUEEZE ASPERITY
HARDNESS HARDSHIP OBSTACLE
SEVERITY STRUGGLE
(UNEXPECTED —) SNAG
(WITH —) SCARCELY
DIFFIDENCE DOUBT MODESTY
RESERVE SHYNESS DISTRUST
HUMILITY TIMIDITY
DIFFIDENT SHY BLATE CHARY
MODEST BACKWARD RESERVED

RETIRING SHEEPISH
DIFFUSE FULL SHED BLEED EXUDE
LARGE STREW WORDY DEFUSE
DERIVE DILATE DIVIDE EXPAND
EXTEND OSMOSE PROLIX SPREAD
SPRING COPIOUS DIALYSE DIALYZE
DIFFUND PERPLEX PERVADE
PUBLISH RADIATE SCATTER
SPARKLE SPRAWLY SPRENGE
SUFFUSE VERBOSE CONFUSED
DIFFUSED DIOSMOSE DISPERSE
PATULENT PATULOUS SPRANGLE
(NOT —) STRICT COMPACT
DIFFUSION SPREAD OSMOSIS
BLEEDING DEFUSION
DIG HOE JOB NIP CLAW DIKE DYKE
GIRD GORE GRUB HOWK MINE
MOOT PION POKE PROD ROOT SINK
SMUG SPIT SPUD SUMP SWOT
DELVE DITCH DWELL GAULT GRAFT
GRAVE LODGE POACH PROBE
SNOUT SPADE START STOCK
BURROW DREDGE EXHUME GRAVEL
HOLLOW PLUNGE SHOVEL THRUST
TUNNEL BEDELVE COSTEAN
SPUDDLE UNEARTH EXCAVATE
(— OUT CREVICES) FOSSICK
(— OUT) SCOOP STUMP EXHUME
(— PEAT) SHEUGH
(— POTATOES) LIFT
(— TRENCHES) GRIP COSTEAN
COSTEEN
(— UP) CAST GRUB STUB SPADE
STOCK EXHUME UPGRAVE DISINTER
(— WITH NAILS) SCRAPE
(— WITH SNOUT) GROUT
DIGAMMA VAU
DIGEST COCT CODE DEFY ENDEW
ENDUE INDUE RIPEN CODIFY
DECOCT DOCKET MATURE SEETHE
CONCOCT EPITOME PANDECT
SUMMARY CONDENSE SYLLABUS
DIGESTION PEPSIS COCTION
EUPEPSY EUPEPSIA
DIGESTIVE PEPTIC DIGERENT
DIGGER DIG PAL PLOW MINER
BANKER BILDAR DRUDGE PLOUGH
COMRADE PEATMAN PIONEER
PLODDER TRENCHER
(POST HOLE —) LOY
DIGGING DIG DIKAGE DYKAGE
STRIPPING
DIGHT DAB RUB DECK DINK DITE
WIPE ADORN DICHT DRESS EQUIP
ORDER RAISE TREAT MANAGE
REPAIR WINNOW APPOINT CONSIGN
PERFORM PREPARE
DIGIT TOE UNIT DOIGT POINT THUMB
FIGURE FINGER HALLUX MEDIUS
NUMBER DEWCLAW DIGITAL
(BINARY —) BINIT
(EXTRA —) PREPOLLEX
DIGITAL KEY MANUAL
DIGITATE DIGITAL FINGERED
DIGNIFIED GRAND LOFTY MANLY
NOBLE STAID AUGUST LORDLY
SEDATE SOLEMN COURTLY EXALTED
STATELY TOGATED ELEVATED
ENNOBLED MAJESTIC

DIGNIFY DUB ADORN CROWN EXALT
GRACE HONOR RAISE ELEVATE
ENNOBLE PROMOTE
DIGNITARY DON WIG RAJA RAJAH
PRIEST SHERIF DIGNITY HUTUKTU
PRELATE SHEREEF HUTUKHTU
VESTIARY
DIGNITY DOG CHIC FACE RANK
BENCH DINES HONOR IZZAT PRIDE
STATE AFFAIR BARONY LAUREL
REPOSE BARONRY BEARING
DECORUM DUKEDOM EARLDOM
FITNESS GRAVITY MAJESTY
SHAHDOM STATION WORSHIP
CHIVALRY EARLSHIP GRANDEUR
NOBILITY
(— OF BISHOP) LAWN
(ACCIDENTAL —) JOY HAYZ
(PAPAL —) TIARA
DIGRAPH CH OE PH RH TH RRH
BIGRAM LIGATURE DIPHTHONG
DIGRESS VEER EXCUR DIVERT
SWERVE WANDER DEVIATE DIVERGE
EXCURSE DISGRESS DIVAGATE
DIGRESSION ASIDE VAGARY
DIGRESS ECBASIS EPISODE
EXCURSE PASSAGE TANGENT
DISGRESS EXCURSUS SIDESLIP
(RHETORICAL —) ECBOLE
DIKE BAR RIB BANK BUND DICE DICK
DYKE POND POOL DIGUE DITCH
LEVEE CAUSEY CRADGE CHANNEL
DIKELET POWDIKE CAUSEWAY
ESTACADE SPREADER
DIKER COWAN COWEN
DIKETONE BENZIL BIACETYL
DIMEDONE
DILACTONE LACTIDE ANEMONIN
DILAPIDATE DESTROY
DILAPIDATED BAD BEATEN CREAKY
RAGGED RUINED SHABBY WRECKY
CRAICHY CREACHY RUINOUS
DESOLATE TATTERED WOBEGONE
DILAPIDATION RUIN DECAY
DECREPITY DISREPAIR
DILATATION BULB SINUS VARIX
JARBOT SPREAD AMPULLA ECTASIA
ECTASIS ANEURISM DILATION
DILATE DELAY PLUMP SWELL WIDEN
DELATE EXPAND EXTEND SPREAD
AMPLIFY BROADEN DESCANT
DIFFUSE DISTEND ENLARGE INFLATE
PROLONG STRETCH DISPERSE
INCREASE LENGTHEN PROTRACT
DISCOURSE
DILATOR DIOPTER DIOPTRA DIOPTRY
DIVULSOR SPECULUM
DILATORY LATE SLOW SLACK
SPARE TARDY FABIAN REMISS
DILATOR LAGGARD LATREDE
TEDIOUS BACKWARD DELAYING
INACTIVE SLUGGISH
DILEMMA FIX FORK LOCK NODE
BRIKE CHOICE PLUNGE CORNUTE
SNIFTER JEOPARDY QUANDARY
DILETTANTE LOVER SUNDAY
ADMIRER AMATEUR DABBLER
DABSTER ESTHETE AESTHETE
DILIGENCE HIE CARE HEED DILLY

EFFORT CAUTION HORNING
BUSINESS INDUSTRY ASSIDUITY
DILIGENT BUSY HARD TIDY ACTIVE
EIDENT ITHAND STEADY CAREFUL
EARNEST HEEDFUL OPEROSE
PAINFUL WORKFUL CAUTIOUS
CONSTANT LABOROUS SEDULOUS
STUDIOUS
DILL ANET CALM SOYA ANISE UMBEL
PICKLE SOOTHE DILLWEED
DILLYDALLY LAG TOY LOAF DELAY
DILLY STALL LOITER TRIFLE
DILOGY ECHO
DILUENT CARRIER VEHICLE
DILUTE CUT BREW FUSE LEAN THIN
WEAK ALLAY BLUNT DELAY WATER
RAREFY REDUCE WEAKEN WHITISH
DIMINISH LENGTHEN WATERISH
(— LIQUOR) BREW SPLIT
(— WINE) GALLIZE
(VERY —) SMALL
DILUTED WASHY DILUTE REMISS
DIM DIP WAN BLUR DARK DULL FADE
GRAY HAZY MIST PALE PALL VEIL
BEDIM BLEAK BLEAR BLIND DUSKY
DUSTY FAINT FOGGY MISTY STAIN
BEMIST BLEARY CLOUDY DARKEN
DASWEN DIMPSY GLOOMY OBTUSE
SHADOW TWILIT DARKISH DISLIMN
ECLIPSE OBSCURE OPACATE
SHADOWY TARNISH DARKLING
OVERCAST
(NOT —) FRESH
DIME HOG HOGG DISME TENPENCE
TENPENNY
(HALF —) PICAYUNE
DIMEDON METHONE
DIMENHYDRINATE DRAMAMINE
DIMENSION BODY BULK SIZE SCOPE
WIDTH ASSIZE DEGREE EXTENT
HEIGHT LENGTH MOISON BREADTH
(COLOR —) CHROMA
(TYPE —) EM EN
(PL.) GAGE SIZE GAUGE GIRTH
EXTENT SIDING MEASURE
DIMIDIATE HALVED
DIMINISH GO CUT EBB SAP BATE
BURN CHOP DAMP DROP EASE
FADE FAIL FINE FRET MELT PARE
PINK SINK WANE WEAR ABATE
ALLAY BREAK CLOSE DRAFT DWARF
ELIDE ERODE LOWER MINCE PETER
SLACK SMALL TAPER DAMPEN
DEBATE DECOCT DEDUCT DILUTE
IMPAIR LESSEN MINISH REBATE
REDUCE SLOUGH VANISH WITHER
ABRIDGE ASSUAGE CORRODE
CURTAIL DEGRADE DEPLETE
DEPRESS DETRACT DIMINUE
DRAUGHT DWINDLE FRITTER INHIBIT
QUALIFY REFRACT RELIEVE
TARNISH ADMINISH AMOINDER
CONDENSE DECREASE DIMINUTE
DISCOUNT MINORATE MITIGATE
MODERATE RETRENCH
(— FRONT) PLOY

DIMINISHED SLACK GRAYED
DIMINUTE

DIMINISHING TAPER CRITICAL FLAGGING
(— IN LOUDNESS) CALANDO
DIMINUTION FALL WASTE DECREASE
DIMINUTIVE TOY WEE BABY TINY BANTY DWARF PETTY RUNTY SMALL YOUNG BANTAM LITTLE PETITE POCKET MANIKIN MIDGETY MINIKIN SHRIMPY EXIGUOUS
(— OF BAR) SCARP CLOSET SCARPE
DIMLY DULLY DARKLY FEEBLY SHADOWY
DIMMED BLEARY CLOUDY GRAYED BLEARED
DIMMING GRAYOUT
DIMNESS DIM HAZE MIST SLUR GLOOM CALIGO DARKNESS
DIMPLE DOKE AHMADI AHMEDI RIPPLE GELASIN FOSSETTE
DIM-SIGHTED PURBLIND
DIN BUM DUN RERD RIOT ALARM BABEL BRUIT CHIME CHIRM CLANG DEAVE DEEVE FRUSH NOISE RERDE ALARUM BELDER CLAMOR FRAGOR HUBBUB RACKET RATTLE STEVEN TUMULT UPROAR CLANGOR CLATTER DISCORD TURMOIL DINGDONG TINTAMAR
DINAR DENARE MARAVEDI
DINDLE RING QUIVER THRILL TINGLE TINKLE TREMOR STAGGER VIBRATE
DINE EAT SUP FARE FEAST REGALE
DINER EPICURE GOURMAND
DING DIN BEAT DANG DASH KICK PUSH RING WHIP CLANG DRIVE EXCEL FLING KNOCK PITCH POUND PUNCH THUMP STROKE THRASH THRUST
DINGE DENT DINT BATTER BRUISE TARNISH
DINGHY SKIFF DINGEY ROWBOAT SHALLOP SNOWBIRD
DINGLE DEN DALE DELL GLEN VALE DIMBLE DUMBLE HOLLOW VALLEY
DINGMAN BUMPER
DINGO WARRAGAL WARRIGAL
DINGUS GADGET DOOHICKEY
DINGY DUN DARK DIRTY DUSKY GRIMY OURIE SMOKY DINGHY SUBFUSC SMIRCHED
DINING CENATION
DINING ROOM TRICLINIUM
DINKA JANGHEY
DINNER DINE HALL KALE MEAL MEAT NOON BEANO FEAST DINING REPAST BANQUET PUCHERO FUNCTION
(CEREMONIAL —) SEDER
DINOSAUR DIAPSID SAURIAN DUCKBILL NODOSAUR SAUROPOD TROODONT
DINT BEAT BLOW DENT DUNT NICK CLOUR DELVE DINGE FORCE NOTCH ONSET POWER PRESS SHOCK ATTACK CHANCE EFFORT STRIKE STROKE IMPRINT EFFICACY STRIKING

DIOCESAN EPISCOPAL
DIOCESE SEE EPARCHY DISTRICT BISHOPRIC
DIODE KENOTRON
DIOLEFIN DIENE ALLENE HEXADIENE
DIOMEDES (FATHER OF —) MARS TYDEUS
(MOTHER OF —) CYRENE DEIPYLE
(WIFE OF —) AEGIALE
DIONYSUS BACCHUS BROMIOS BROMIUS LENAEUS LIKNITES
DIOPSIDE VIOLAN ALALITE PYROXENE
DIORITE CORSITE DIABASE ORNOITE APPINITE
DIOSCURI ALCIS ANACES ANAKES CASTORES
DIOXIDE SILICA BINOXIDE
DIP DAP DIB DOP SOP BAIL DROP DUCK DUNK LADE LAVE SINK SOAK BATHE DELVE LADLE LOWER MERSE PITCH SCOOP SLOPE SOUSE SWOOP TAINT CANDLE HOLLOW PLUNGE BAPTIZE DECLINE IMMERGE IMMERSE INCLINE MOISTEN DIPSTICK SUBMERGE
(— AND THROW) BAIL BALE
(— IN DANCING) CORTE
(— INTO) SAMPLE
(— OUT) KEACH
DIPENTENE CINENE CAJUPUTENE
DIPHTHONG BIVOCAL
DIPHTHONGIZED BROKEN
DIPLOIDIZE SPERMATIZE
DIPLOMA SANAD DEGREE SUNNUD CHARTER CODICIL
DIPLOMACY TACT POLICE TREATY
DIPLOMAT DEAN ENVOY CONSUL ATTACHE MINISTER
DIPLOMATIC SUAVE FECIAL FETIAL
DIPLOPIA POLYOBA AMBIOPIA
DIPNOAN DIPNOID MUDFISH
DIPODY METER METRE DIIAMB SYZYGY
DIPPER BAIL GAWN PIET PLOW GOURD HANDY LADLE SCOOP SPOON BUCKET DUNKER PIGGIN PLOUGH TUNKER DUNKARD PICKLER CALABASH
(ASTRONOMICAL —) WAGON WAGGON
DIPSOMANIA ENOMANIA POTOMANIA
DIPTERAN SYRPHID
DIPTERON DIPTER
DIPTEROUS BIALATE
DIRDUM BLOW BLAME DURDUM OUTCRY REBUKE TUMULT UPROAR SCOLDING
DIRE DERN EVIL FELL AWFUL FATAL DEADLY DISMAL DREARY FUNEST TRAGIC WOEFUL DIREFUL DOLEFUL DRASTIC FEARFUL DREADFUL FUNESTAL HORRIBLE TERRIBLE ULTIMATE
DIRECT AIM BID CON KEN SAY SET WIS AGYE AIRT BAIN BEAM BEND BOSS CAST DEAD EDIT EVEN FLAT FULL GAIN HEAD HELM HOLD LEAD NEAR NIGH OPEN REIN SEND SOON

SWAY TELL TURN WAFT WEND WILL WISE AIRTH APPLY AREAD AREED BLANK BOUND BURLY COACH DRESS ETTLE FLUSH FRAME FRANK GUIDA GUIDE HIGHT INDEX LEVEL ORDER PLUMP POINT REFER RIGHT SPEED STEER TEACH TRAIN UTTER WEISE WRITE ADVERT ARRECT CUSTOS DEVOTE ENJOIN ENSIGN FASTEN GOVERN GRAITH HANDLE HOMELY HONEST IMPART INDITE INFORM INTEND LINEAL MANAGE MASTER MOSTRA REFORM SQUARE STEADY STRECK TEMPER WITTER ADDRESS APPOINT COMMAND CONDUCT CONTROL CONVERT DEICTIC DESTINE EXECUTE EXPRESS FRONTAL GENERAL INSTANT MARSHAL OFFICER PRESIDE SPADISH ABSOLUTE CONVERSE DEDICATE DIRECTOR HOMESPUN IMMEDIAL INSTRUCT INTIMATE MANUDUCE MANUDUCT MINISTER OUTRIGHT REGULATE STRAIGHT
(— AGAINST) LAUNCH
(— ATTENTION) ATTEND
(— BLOW) MARK
(— DOGS) BLOW
(— FALL OF TREE) GUN
(— HELMSMAN) CON CONN
(— HORSE) HUP
(— ITSELF) TENT
(— ONE'S COURSE) HIT
(— PROCEEDINGS) PRESIDE
(— SECRETLY) STEAL
(— SIDEWAYS) SKLENT
(— TO GO) ADDRESS
(— UPWARD) MOUNT
DIRECTED FAST COMPULSORY
(— FORWARD) ANTRORSE
(— TOWARD GOAL) HORMIC
(— UPWARD) ERECT
DIRECTING AIM LEADING PRINCIPAL
DIRECTION AIM RUN WAY AIRT BENT CARE DUCT EAST EGIS GATE HAND LEFT PART ROAD RULE WEST WORD YARD AEGIS ANGLE COAST DRIFT EAVER KIBLA NORTH ORDER PARTY POINT QIBLA RANGE ROUTE SENSE SOUTH TENOR TREND ASPECT COURSE DESIGN ADDRESS BEARING BIDDING CHANNEL COMMAND CONDUCT CONTROL COUNSEL DICTATE HEADING HELMAGE MANDATE PRECEPT STRETCH BEARINGS CALENDAR DELEATUR DIAGONAL GUIDANCE STEERAGE STEERING TENDENCY
(— OF CURRENT) AXIS
(— OF FLOW) SET
(— OF ROCK CLEAVAGE) GRAIN
(— OF WIND) EYE CORNER
(— OUTWARD) BEAM
(—S FOR DELIVERY) ADDRESS
(DANCE —) CALL
(HORIZONTAL —) COURSE AZIMUTH
(OBLIQUE —) SKEW
(OPPOSITE —) EYE COUNTER
(SINGING —) GIMEL GYMEL

DIRECTIVE DICTATE CIRCULAR
DIRECTLY DUE BANG BOLT DEAD
FLAT GAIN JUST MEAN PLAT PLUM
SLAP SOON PLAIN PLUMB POINT
ROUND SHEER SOUSE SPANG
STANG ARIGHT CLEVER SIMPLY
SQUARE RIGHTLY SHEERLY
OUTRIGHT PROMPTLY SLAPDASH
STRAIGHT
DIRECTNESS CLARITY IMMEDIACY
DIRECTOR BOSS HEAD COACH
GUIDE PILOT STAFF ARCHON
BISHOP LEADER MASTER RECTOR
WARDEN CURATOR DESKMAN
MANAGER PREFECT STARETS
STERNER TRAINER ACCENTOR
DISPOSER GOVERNOR PRAEFECT
PRODUCER TETRARCH
DIRECTORY PIE BOOK
DIRGE KEEN SONG ELEGY KINAH
LINOS LINUS QINAH TANGI HEARSE
LAMENT MONODY THRENE EPICEDE
REQUIEM CORONACH THRENODY
ULLAGONE
DIRIGIBLE BLIMP AIRSHIP
DIRK SNEE SKEAN SWORD DAGGER
SKHIAN SKIVER
DIRT FEN MUD PAY DUST GORE
GUCK MUCK NAST SOIL SUMP
EARTH FILTH GRIME GROUT SEUCH
SEUGH TRASH GRAVEL GROUND
REFUSE MULLOCK MUCKMENT
DIRTINESS GRIME JAKES
DIRTY LOW BASE CLAT DIRT FOUL
MUSS SOIL WORY BAWDY BLACK
CABBY DINGY FOGGY GRIMY GUSTY
HORRY MUDDY NASTY POUSY SOILY
SULLY BEMIRE CLARTY CLATTY
DEFILE DIRTEN FILTHY FULYIE
FULZIE GREASY GRUBBY IMPURE
MUSSED POUCEY SCRIMY SLASHY
SLURRY SMUTTY SOILED SORDID
STORMY BEGRIME BROOKED
BROOKIE BRUCKLE CLOUDED
GRUFTED IMBROIN MUDDIED
ROYNOUS SLOTTER SMUTCHY
SQUALID SULLIED TARNISH
UNCLEAN SLOBBERY SLOTTERY
SOAPLESS
DISABLE OUT HOCK LAME MAIM
BREAK CHINK CROCK GRUEL UNFIT
WRECK BRUISE DISMAY UNABLE
WEAKEN CRIPPLE
(— **CANNON**) SPIKE
(— **TANK**) BELLY
DISABLED LAME INVALID
DISABLING BUM
DISACCHARIDE BIOSE LACTOSE
MALTOSE SUCROSE
DISACCUSTOM DISUSE
DISACKNOWLEDGE DISCLAIM
DISADVANTAGE HURT MISS RISK
LURCH WORRY DAMAGE DENIAL
INJURY STRIKE DICKENS PENALTY
UNSELTH UNSPEED DISAVAIL
DISFAVOR HANDICAP
DISADVANTAGEOUS HURTFUL
INCONVENIENT
DISAFFECT DEBAUCH ESTRANGE

DISAFFECTED FALSE UNTRUE
DISEASED DISLOYAL FORSWORN
PERJURED RECREANT
DISAFFECTION DECEIT MUTINY
DISEASE DISGUST DISLIKE
DISORDER HOSTILITY
DISAFFIRM DENY ANNUL REVERSE
DISCLAIM
DISAGREE VARY ARGUE DIFFER
DISCEPT DISCORD DISSENT
QUARREL CONFLICT
DISAGREEABLE BAD ILL ACID EVIL
FOUL PERT SOUR UGLY VILE AWFUL
CROSS HARSH NASTY STIFF
GREASY PUTRID ROTTEN SNUFFY
STICKY UNEASY UNGAIN CHRONIC
COMICAL GHASTLY HATEFUL
INGRATE IRKSOME NAUGHTY
UNLUSTY CHISELLY KINDLESS
TERRIBLE UNGENIAL UNLIKELY
UNLOVELY UNSAVORY
DISAGREEABLENESS ILLNESS
ASPERITY
DISAGREEABLY HARSHLY
DISAGREEING ODD DISSENTIVE
DISAGREEMENT BREE CLASH
CROSS FIGHT BREACH FRATCH
DISCORD DISGUST DISPUTE DISSENT
FISSURE MISLIKE QUARREL
WRANGLE ARGUMENT DISTANCY
DIVISION FRICTION SQUABBLE
VARIANCE
(**IN —**) APART
DISALLOW FORBID REJECT
CENSURE DISCLAIM DISPROVE
PROHIBIT
DISAPPEAR DIE FLY DROP FADE
FALL FLEE LIFT PASS SINK WEND
WHOP CLEAR FAINT LAPSE SLIDE
SNUFF REMOVE RETIRE VANISH
EVANISH IMMERGE DISSOLVE
EVANESCE
(— **GRADUALLY**) ELY FADE DRAIN
EVANESCE
(— **SUDDENLY**) COOK DUCK BURST
MIZZLE
DISAPPEARANCE ECLIPSE
FADEAWAY
DISAPPOINT BALK BILK FAIL FALL
MOCK SOUR UNDO CHEAT SNAPE
BAFFLE DEFEAT DELUDE OUTWIT
THWART BEGUILE DECEIVE
DESTROY FALSIFY NULLIFY
DISPOINT
DISAPPOINTED OUTED THROWN
SOREHEAD
DISAPPOINTING FIERCE
FALLACIOUS
DISAPPOINTMENT RUE BALK SUCK
BAULK LURCH DENIAL LETDOWN
COMEDOWN
DISAPPROBATION ODIUM DISLIKE
DISAPPROVAL BAN BOOH HISS
VETO CATCALL CENSURE DISFAVOR
DISGRACE
DISAPPROVE GROAN REJECT
RESENT CENSURE CONDEMN
DISLIKE MISTAKE PROTEST
DISALLOW DISPROVE

DISAPPROVED DISTASTED
DISAPPROVER WOWSER
DISARM SUBDUE UNSTEEL
DISARRANGE MUSS DEFORM
GARBLE RUFFLE TIFFLE UNTIDY
UNTUNE CLUTTER CONFUSE
DERANGE DISTURB RUMMAGE
SLATTER TROUBLE COCKBILL
DISHEVEL DISORDER UNSETTLE
(— **TYPE**) SQUABBLE
DISARRANGEMENT DISARRAY
DISARRAY MESS STRIP CADDLE
DISRAY FUFFLE HUDDLE DESPOIL
UNDIGHT DISHEVEL DISORDER
DISARRAYED UNKEMPT
DISASSEMBLE STRIP DEMOUNT
DISMOUNT
(— **CASK**) SHAKE
DISASSEMBLY TAKEDOWN
TEARDOWN
DISASSOCIATE SEVER SEPARATE
DISASTER ILL WOE BALE BLOW EVIL
FATE RUIN GRIEF MISHAP STROKE
REVERSE ACCIDENT CALAMITY
CASUALTY EXIGENCY FATALITY
DISASTROUS BAD ILL FATAL WEARY
SINISTER
DISAVOW DENY DEVOW ABJURE
DISOWN RECANT REFUSE DECLINE
RETRACT ABNEGATE DISCLAIM
DISVOUCH RENOUNCE
DISAVOWAL DENIAL
DISBAND BREAK REDUCE REFORM
ADJOURN CASHIER DISMISS
RELEASE SCATTER DISSOLVE
DISBAR EXCLUDE
DISBELIEF ATHEISM SCRUPLE
DISBELIEVE DOUBT REJECT
SUSPECT DISCOUNT DISCREDIT
DISBELIEVER ATHEIST HERETIC
INFIDEL
DISBURDEN RID EASE CLEAR
UNLOAD DELIVER DISLOAD RELIEVE
DISBURSE SPEND DEFRAY EXPEND
OUTLAY DEBURSE
DISC (ALSO SEE DISK) DIAL DISK
BLANK MEDAL PATEN PLATE QUOIT
COLTER RECORD RONDEL COULTER
DISCOID PLATTER TROCHUS
(— **FOR PRESSING HERRINGS**)
DAUNT
DISCANT HOCKET
DISCARD CAST DECK JILT JUNK
MOLT OMIT OUST SHED CHUCK
DITCH FLING SCRAP SHUCK SLUFF
THROW CHANGE DECARD DISUSE
DIVEST EXCUSS REJECT SLOUGH
ABANDON CASHIER DISMISS
EXPUNGE FORSAKE ABDICATE
JETTISON
(— **IN BRIDGE**) ECHO
DISCARDED DORMANT
DISCARDING DISPOSAL
DISCERN KEN SEE SPY WIT DEEM
ESPY KNOW READ SCAN JUDGE
SIGHT BEHOLD DESCRY DETECT
DEVISE NOTICE PIERCE SCERNE
DIGNOSCE DISCOVER PERCEIVE
DISCERNIBLE EVIDENT VISIBLE

APPARENT MANIFEST

DISCERNING SAGE WISE SHREWD
SAPIENT

DISCERNMENT EYE DOOM GOUT
TACT FLAIR SENSE SKILL TASTE
ACUMEN INSIGHT ELECTION
JUDGMENT SAGACITY

DISCHARGE AX DO AXE CAN GUN
LET RUN BOLT BOOT CASS DUMP
EMIT FIRE FLOW FLUX FREE GIVE
KICK PASS POUR QUIT RIFF SACK
SEND SHOT VENT VOID BLAST
BLEED BRUSH CLEAR DRAIN EJECT
EMPTY EXPEL EXUDE FRUSH GLEET
GRASS ICHOR ISSUE LOOSE OZENA
PURGE RHEUM SHOOT SPEED
START VOMIT WHIFF YIELD ACQUIT
ASSOIL BOUNCE DEFRAY EFFECT
EXCERN EXEMPT EXHALE FEEDER
LOCHIA OZAENA TICKET UNLADE
UNLOAD ABSOLVE CASHIER
DEBOUCH DEFEASE DEHISCE
DELIVER DERAIGN DISBAND DISMISS
EXCRETE EXHAUST MISSION
PAYMENT PERFORM QUIETUS
RELEASE RELIEVE SATISFY SKITTER
SOLUTIO CATAPULT COMPOUND
DEFECATE DESPATCH DISGORGE
DISPATCH DISPLACE DISPLODE
EMISSION EVACUATE MITTIMUS
OUTSHOOT PERSOLVE SEPARATE
SOLUTION STREAMER
(— **ARROW**) TWANG
(— **BULLET**) DRIVE
(— **CARGO**) STRIKE
(— **DEBT**) MEET CLEAR LOOSING
(— **DUTY**) SERVE
(— **FROM HORSE'S FOOT**) FRUSH
(— **FROM RESERVOIR**) HUSHING
(— **MATTER**) WEEP
(— **OF DEBT**) SETOFF
(— **OF GAS**) FEEDER
(— **OF STREAM**) FALL SPOUT
(— **SUDDENLY**) HIKE
(**BLOODY** —) SHOW SANIES
(**CANNON** —) TIRE CANNON
(**CONCENTRATED** —) BARRAGE
(**DISHONORABLE** —) BOBTAIL
(**ELECTRIC** —) SPARK LEADER
EFFLUVE STREAMER LIGHTNING
(**ELECTRIC** —**S**) STATIC
(**HEAVY** —) STORM
(**SIMULTANEOUS** —) SALVO
BROADSIDE FUSILLADE

DISCHARGED SPED SATISFIED
DISCHARGER EXCITATOR
DISCHARGING LABILE
DISCIPLE SON JOHN MARK CHELA
JUDAS MURID PETER PUPIL TEACH
TRAIN ANANDA DISPLE DORCAS
HEARER PUNISH APOSTLE AUDITOR
MATTHEW OVIDIAN SCHOLAR
SECTARY SRAVAKA STUDENT
ADHERENT FOLLOWER GALENIST
SECTATOR

DISCIPLINARIAN RAMROD TRAINER
MARTINET

DISCIPLINARY STRICT
DISCIPLINE THEW WHIP BREAK

DRILL INURE TEACH TRAIN CHURCH
ETHICS FERULA FERULE GOVERN
INFORM PUNISH SEASON TAIRGE
VIRTUE CHASTEN CORRECT
CULTURE EDUCATE FURNACE
NURTURE SCOURGE DISCIPLE
DOCTRINE EXERCISE INSTRUCT
LEARNING MATHESIS PEDAGOGY
REGULATE RESTRAIN TEACHING
TRAINING TUTORING
(**MENTAL** —) YOGA
(**RELIGIOUS** —) CHURCH PENANCE
SADHANA

DISCIPLINED INURED STEADY
DISCLAIM DENY DEVOW ABJURE
DISOWN REFUSE DISAVOW
ABDICATE ABNEGATE DISALLOW
RENOUNCE

DISCLOSE OPE RIP BARE BLOW
CALL KNOW OPEN TELL BREAK
COUGH UNRIP UNWRY UTTER
BETRAY BEWRAY DESCRY DIVINE
EVOLVE EXPOSE IMPART REVEAL
SHRIVE UNBURY UNCASE UNHASP
UNHIDE UNLOCK UNROLL UNSEAL
UNSHUT UNVEIL UNWRAP CONFESS
DEVELOP DISCUSS DISPLAY
DIVULGE EXHIBIT EXPLAIN UNCLOSE
UNCOVER DISCOVER INDICATE
MANIFEST UNBUNDLE UNKENNEL
UNSECRET UNTHATCH

DISCLOSED OUT
DISCLOSURE REVEAL SHRIFT
COLORING DESCRIAL DISCLOSE
OVERTURE

DISCOLOR FOX BURN FADE SPOT
BLACK SMOKE STAIN TINGE SMIRCH
STREAK DISTAIN TARNISH
BESMIRCH

DISCOLORATION CORN BLEED
SCALD SPECK STAIN TINGE FOXING
LIVEDO MILDEW ARGYRIA BURNING
MELASMA BRONZING BROWNING
CHLOASMA CYANOSIS DYSCHROA
SCALDING
(— **OF FRUIT**) SUNBURN
(— **OF TURKEYS**) BLUEBACK
(— **ON CHOCOLATE**) BLOOM
(— **ON CURED FISH**) RUST
(**SMALL** —) FRECKLE

DISCOLORED HAW FOUL DINGY
FOXED RUSTY STAINED SCORCHED
USTULATE
(— **BY DECAY**) DOTY FOXED

DISCOMFIT MATE ROIT ABASH
ABAVE AFLEY SHEND SHENT UPSET
WORST BAFFLE DEFEAT FEAGUE
SQUASH CONFUSE CONQUER
DISTURB

DISCONCERT BASH BOWL FAZE
FUSS HACK ABASH BLANK DAUNT
FEEZE PHASE UPSET WORRY
BAFFLE BLENCH MISPUT PUZZLE
RATTLE SQUASH CONFUSE DISTURB
FLUMMOX NONPLUS PERTURB
SQUELCH BROWBEAT DISORDER

DISCONCERTED BLANK ASHAMED
RATTLED CONFUSED

DISCONNECT UNDO SEVER DIVIDE

UNYOKE DISJOIN DISSOLVE
DISUNITE SEPARATE UNCOUPLE

DISCONNECTED LOOSE ABRUPT
BROKEN CHOPPY CURSORY
DECOUSU RAMBLING STACCATO

DISCONSOLATE SAD GLOOMY
WOEFUL DOLEFUL FORLORN
UNCOUTH DEJECTED DESOLATE
DOWNCAST HOPELESS

DISCONTENT ENVY DISQUIET
SOURNESS

DISCONTENTED DUMPY
DISCONTINUANCE BREAK LAPSE
DEMISE CUTBACK DISUNION
SHUTDOWN

DISCONTINUE END DROP HALT
QUIT STOP BREAK CEASE CLOSE
LETUP DESIST DISUSE SUNDER
DISRUPT SUSPEND INTERMIT
SURCEASE

DISCONTINUITY JAR BREAK
DISCONTINUOUS BROKEN
DISJUNCT SALTATORY

DISCORD DIN JAR BROIL JANGLE
SCHISM STRIFE DISLIKE FACTION
FISSURE JARRING MISTONE
CONFLICT DISTANCE DIVISION
FRACTION MISCHIEF UNSAUGHT
VARIANCE

DISCORDANT AJAR RUDE CRONK
HARSH FROWZY HOARSE JANGLY
HIDEOUS JARRING SQUAWKY
ABSONANT CONTRARY JANGLING

DISCOUNT AGIO BATTA SHAVE
REBATE REDUCE DISCOMPT

DISCOURAGE CARP DAMP CHILL
DAUNT DETER FROST DAMPEN
DEJECT DISMAY FREEZE STIFLE
DEPRESS FLATTEN INHIBIT DISPIRIT
DISSUADE

DISCOURAGEMENT COLD DAMP
DAUNT LETDOWN PUTBACK

DISCOURAGING CHILL DREARY
DISCOURSE SAW CARP RANT READ
TALE TALK TELL WORD DROOL
FABLE ORATE PAPER SPEAK SPELL
THEME TRACT TREAT COMMON
DILATE EULOGY HOMILY PARLEY
PREACH REASON SCREED SERMON
THESIS TREATY ACCOUNT ADDRESS
COMMENT CONTEXT DECLAIM
DELIVER DESCANT DIETARY
DISCANT DISCUSS DISSERT
ENTREAT EXPOUND GRAMMAR
LECTURE NARRATE ORATION
PRATING PRELECT PURPOSE
TALKING ARGUMENT COLLOQUY
CONVERSE EXERCISE LOCUTION
LOQUENCE PARLANCE SPEAKING
SPELLING TRACTATE TREATISE
(— **OF LITTLE VALUE**) STUFF
(**LAUDATORY** —) PANEGYRIC
(**LONG** —) SCREED
(**PROLONGED** —) DIATRIBE
(**SERIOUS** —) HOMILY
(**SIMPLE** —) PAP
(**UNIMAGINATIVE** —) PROSE
(**PL.**) EXOTERICS

DISCOURTEOUS RUDE SCURVY

UNCIVIL UNHENDE IMPOLITE
UNGENTLE
DISCOURTESY CUT SLIGHT
DISCOVER RIP SEE SPY WIT ESPY
FEEL FIND PICK TWIG CATCH LEARN
SPELL DEFINE DESCRY DETECT
DIVINE EXPOSE IMPART INVENT
LOCATE OVERGO REVEAL STRIKE
UNHIDE CONFESS DESCURE
DEVELOP DISCERN DISCURE
DISPLAY DIVULGE EXHIBIT EXPLORE
UNCOVER UNEARTH CONTRIVE
DECIPHER DESCRIBE DISCUREN
MANIFEST UNKENNEL
DISCOVERABLE VISIBLE
DISCOVERER SPY SCOUT
COLUMBUS EXPLORER INVENTOR
DISCOVERY FIND TROVE DESCRY
ESPIAL STRIKE DESCRIAL
DISCREDIT FOUL DECRY DOUBT
REFEL DEFACE DEFECT ASPERSE
BLEMISH DESTROY IMPEACH
SCANDAL SUSPECT BELITTLE
DISGRACE DISHONOR DISTRUST
REPROACH UNCREDIT
DISCREDITABLE BLACK UNHONEST
DISCREET WARY WISE CIVIL
HUSHED POLITE SILENT CAREFUL
GUARDED POLITIC PRUDENT
CAUTIOUS RESERVED RETICENT
DISCREETLY SENSIBLY
DISCREPANCY VARIANCE
DISCREPANT VARIANT CONTRARY
DISSONANT
DISCRETE ETERNAL DISTINCT
DISCRETION TACT WISDOM
CONDUCT RETENUE COURTESY
JUDGMENT PRUDENCE
DISCRIMINATE PART SEVER
SECERN DISCERN PERCEIVE
SEPARATE
DISCRIMINATED DISTINCT
DISCRIMINATING GOOD NICE
ACUTE SHARP ASTUTE CHOICE
SELECT CHOOSEY CRITICAL
EXPLICIT
DISCRIMINATINGLY CHOICE FINELY
DISCRIMINATION EYE DOOM TACT
TASTE ACUMEN CHOICE FINESSE
RESPECT DELICACY SAPIENCE
(SYMBOL OF —) HANSA
DISCURSIVE ROVING CURSORY
RAMBLING DESULTORY
DISCURSIVELY WIDE
DISCUS DISC DISK QUOIT DISKOS
DISCOID
DISCUSS AIR MOOT RUNE TALK
ARGUE BANDY COVER DANDY
TRACT TREAT COMMON CONFER
DEBATE DICKER EMPARL EXCUSS
IMPARL PARLEY AGITATE BESPEAK
CANVASS COMMENT CONSULT
DESCANR DESCANT DISCANT
DISCEPT DISCUTE DISPUTE DISSERT
EXAMINE NARRATE TRAVERSE
(— AT LENGTH) BAT
(— CASUALLY) MENTION
(— EXCITEDLY) AGITATE
(— LIGHTLY) BANDY

(— QUICKLY) SKIP
(— SECRETLY) ROUN
(— TERMS) CHAFFER
(— THOROUGHLY) EXHAUST
DISCUSSION MOOT DEBAT FORUM
COMMON CONFAB DEBATE HASSEL
HOMILY HUDDLE PARLEY TREATY
BARGAIN CANVASS COMMENT
COUNSEL DISCUSS DISPUTE
MOOTING PRIBBLE ARGUMENT
CAUSERIE CHINFEST COLLOQUY
DIATRIBE ENTREATY EXCURSUS
QUESTION
(CONTROVERSIAL —) DISPUTE
(DIDACTIC —) HARANGUE
DISDAIN TUT DAIN DEFY PRIDE
SCORN SDAIN SPURN SDEIGN
SLIGHT CONTEMN DESPISE
CONTEMPT
DISDAINFUL COY DIGNE SAUCY
TOSSY SCORNY SLIGHT SNIFFY
SNUFFY DAINFUL HAUGHTY
ARROGANT DEIGNOUS SCORNFUL
SNIFFISH TOPLOFTY
DISDAINFULLY SMALL SNIFFILY
DISEASE BUG FLU MAL ROT BATS
COTH CRUD EVIL FLAW GOUT GRIP
NOMA PEST PHOS SORE AGROM
BATTS BEJEL BENDS CAUSE COTHE
CROUP DECAY DOLOR FEVER GRIEF
LUPUS PHOSS PINTA PINTO SCALL
SHAKE SPRUE SURRA AINHUM
ANGINA CANCER CARATE CORYZA
COURAP DENGUE GRAVEL GRIPPE
HERPES MALADY MORBUS PALMUS
PIEDRA POPEYE SCURVY SICKEN
SURRAH UROSIS ZOOSIS AILMENT
ALASTIM CHOLERA COXALGY
DECLINE ENDEMIC ENTASIA
LANGUOR LEPROSY MALEASE
MISLIKE MYCOSIS MYIASIS PATHEMA
RAPHANY SCOURGE SEQUELA
SERPIGO SIBBENS SORANCE
SYCOSIS XERASIA ZYMOTIC
ATHEROMA BERIBERI COXALGIA
CRIPPLER CYNANCHE DIAMONDS
ENZOOTIC JAUNDICE LEUKEMIA
PALUDISM PANDEMIC PELLAGRA
RAPHANIA SCABBADO SICKNESS
SMALLPOX SORRANCE STAGGERS
SYPHILIS UNHEALTH XANTHOMA
ZOONOSIS
(— OF ANIMALS, GENERAL) ROT
CLAP CORE FIRE GOUT HUSK LICK
WEED APTHA CLEFT CLING CLOSH
COTHE CROOK DRUSE FARCY
FLAPS NENTA NOANA PAINS SPEED
SWEAT TAINT APHTHA AVIVES
BROSOT CANKER CARNEY CREEPS
FARCIN GARGET GRAPES LAMPAS
NAGANA ROUGET SPAVIN SURRAH
WOBBLE ANTHRAX BIGHEAD
CALCINO CALORIS CARCEAG
DOURING EARWORM EQUINIA
FASHION FISTULA FOUNDER
FROUNCE KETOSIS LAMPERS
MURRAIN MURRINA QUITTER
QUITTOR SLOBBER SOLDIER
TAKOSIS BULLNOSE CRATCHES

CRIPPLES FERNSICK FOOTHALT
HORSEPOX HYSTERIA MAWBOUND
SLOBBERS SNUFFLES THWARTER
VACCINIA EPIZOOTIC
(— OF APPLES) CORK BLOTCH
(— OF BANANAS) SIGATOKA
SQUIRTER
(— OF BARLEY) STRIPE
(— OF BEES) SACBROOD
(— OF BEETS) HEARTROT
(— OF BIRDS) GOUT
(— OF BLUEBERRY) BLUESTEM
(— OF CABBAGE) CLUBROOT
(— OF CATERPILLARS) WILT
FLACHERY
(— OF CATTLE) TURN BLAIN CLOSH
FARCY HOOZE COWPOX GARGET
GRAPES HAMMER HEAVES ANTHRAX
BLACKLEG
(— OF CEREALS) ERGOT
(— OF CHICKEN) PIP CORYZA
(— OF COTTON) HYBOSIS CYRTOSIS
STENOSIS
(— OF DUCKLING) KEEL
(— OF EYES) WALL GLAUCOMA
SYNECHIA TRACHOMA
(— OF FIGS) SMUT
(— OF FINGERNAILS) FLAW
(— OF FLAX) BROWNING
(— OF FOWLS) PIP CRAY ROUP
GAPES SOREHEAD
(— OF GRAIN) ILIAU ICTERUS
(— OF GRAPES) COLEUR ERINOSE
ROUGEAU ROUGEOT SHELLING
(— OF HAWKS) RYE CRAY CROAK
CROAKS FROUNCE
(— OF HORSES) HAW CLAP MOSE
MULE WEED FARCY LEUMA SCALMA
DOURINE SARCOID AZOTURIA
GLANDERS HORSEPOX STRANGLES
(— OF LAMB) SWAYBACK
(— OF LETTUCE) STUNT
(— OF NARCISSUS) SMOLDER
SMOULDER
(— OF ONION) SMUDGE
(— OF ORANGE) LEPROSIS
(— OF PALMS) KOLERUGA
(— OF PLANTS, GENERAL) POX ROT
BUNT CORK DROP FIRE GOUT KNOT
PULP SMUT BLAST DWARF EDEMA
ERGOT FLECK FLOCK GRUBS SCALD
SCALE SCURF SEREH SPIKE STUNT
TUKRA TWIST AUCUBA BLIGHT
BLOTCH BLUING BRAUNE CALICO
CANKER COLEUR GIRDLE OEDEMA
OIDIUM PETECA SMUDGE STREAK
STRIPE VIROSE BLISTER BLUEING
BRINDLE CRINKLE DIEBACK ERINOSE
EYESPOT FROGEYE HYBOSIS
MEASLES PRURIGO ROSETTE
SHATTER SMOLDER STIPPEN
TIPBURN TOMOSIS VIRUELA
WALLOON BLUESTEM BREAKING
BROWNING BUCKSKIN CLUBROOT
CYRTOSIS DARTROSE EXANTHEM
FLYSPECK GUMMOSIS KOLEROGA
LEPROSIS MELANOSE MELAXUMA
POLEBURN PSOROSIS SMOULDER

STENOSIS VIROSITY WHIPTAIL WILDFIRE
(— **OF POTATO**) CURL HAYWIRE
(— **OF RABBITS**) SNUFFLES
(— **OF RICE**) BLAST SPECK
(— **OF SHEEP**) CAW COE GID MAD ROT BANE BELT CORE HALT WIND BLAST BLOOD BRAXY GILLAR OVINIA PINING STURDY ANTHRAX BRADSOT DAISING RUBBERS SCRAPIE THWARTER WILDFIRE
(— **OF SILKWORM**) UJI CALCINO GATTINE PEBRINE FLACHERY
(— **OF SUGARCANE**) ILIAU SEREH EYESPOT
(— **OF SWINE**) GARGET
(— **OF TOBACCO**) ETCH CALICO BRINDLE FROGEYE
(— **OF TOMATO**) FERNLEAF GRAYWALL
(— **OF TREES**) KNOT
(— **OF TULIPS**) SHANKING
(— **OF UNKNOWN ORIGIN**) AINHUM ACRODYNIA
(**CAISSON** —) CHOKES
(**FOOT-AND-MOUTH** —) AFTOSA
(**FUNGUS** —) PECK
(**KIDNEY** —) RIPPLE
(**LUNG** —) CON
(**MUSHROOM** —) FLOCK
(**SKIN** —) ACNE SCAB FAVUS HIVES LEPRA MANGE PSORA SCALL TINEA ECZEMA LICHEN TETTER EXORMIA PORRIGO PURPURA SERPIGO VERRUGA IMPETIGO MILIARIA MYCETOMA SHINGLES VERRUGAS VITILIGO
(**VENEREAL** —) BURNING SYPHILIS
(**WINE** —) GRAISSE
DISEASED BAD EVIL SICKLY MORBOSE PECCANT VICIOUS MORBIFIC
DISEMBARK LAND ALIGHT DEBARK UNBARK UNBOAT DISBOARD
DISEMBARRASS EXTRICATE
DISEMBODIED SEPARATE DISBODIED FLESHLESS
DISEMBODIMENT SOUL SPIRIT
DISEMBOGUE MOUTH
DISEMBOWEL GUT HULK PAUNCH DEBOWEL EMBOWEL GARBAGE UNTRIPE GRALLOCH
DISEMIC DIMORIC DICHRONOUS
DISENCHANT DISMAY
DISENCHANTED SOUR
DISENCUMBER RID FREE REDD UNCUMBER
DISENGAGE FREE CLEAR EDUCE UNTIE DETACH EVOLVE LOOSEN CUTOVER DISGAGE RELEASE UNRAVEL LIBERATE UNCLUTCH
DISENTANGLE CARD COMB FREE REED TOSE TOZE CLEAR LOOSE RAVEL TEASE EVOLVE SCUTCH SLEAVE UNMAZE UNMESH RESOLVE UNRAVEL UNREAVE UNTWINE UNTWIST OUTTWINE UNTANGLE
DISENTANGLEMENT SOLUTION
DISESTEEM UMBRAGE DISVALUE

DISFAVOR DUTCH ODIUM DISLIKE OFFENCE OFFENSE UMBRAGE MALGRACE
DISFIGURE MAR BLUR FOUL MAIM SCAR DEFACE DEFEAT DEFORM INJURE MANGLE BLEMISH DISGRACE DISGUISE MUTILATE
DISFIGURED FOUL DEFET DEFEIT DEFORMED
DISFIGUREMENT SCAR BLEMISH CATFACE DEFORMITY
DISGORGE SPEW VENT EJECT EMPTY VOMIT
DISGRACE BLOT FOIL FOUL HISS LACK SLUR SMIT SOIL SPOT TASH ABASE CRIME ODIUM SCORN SHAME SHEND SPITE STAIN TAINT BAFFLE BEFOUL BISMER HUMBLE INFAMY REBUKE STIGMA VILIFY AFFRONT ATTAINT DEGRADE OBLOQUY OFFENCE OFFENSE REPROOF SCANDAL SLANDER UMBRAGE CONTEMPT DISHONOR IGNOMINY REPROACH SHENDING UNWORTHY VILLAINY
DISGRACEFUL MEAN SOUR FILTHY INDIGN IGNOBLE CRIMINAL DEFAMOUS INHONEST SHAMEFUL
DISGRUNTLED SORE PEEVISH
DISGUISE DAUB FACE HIDE LAIN LEAN MASK VEIL BELIE CLOAK COLOR COUCH COVER FEIGN GLOZE GUISE SHADE VISOR VIZOR COVERT DEFORM IMMASK MANTLE MASQUE VIZARD CONCEAL OBSCURE PRETEND PURPORT COLORING DISLIKEN MISGUISE PALLIATE PRETENCE PRETENSE TRAVESTY UMBRELLA
(— **INFORMATION**) LAYNE
DISGUISED COVERT FUCATE GILDED LATENT MYSTIC FEIGNED PALLIATE TRAVESTY
DISGUST IRK LOATH REPEL SHOCK STALL DEGOUT HORROR NAUSEA OFFEND REVOLT SICKEN STOMACH SURFEIT AVERSION DISTASTE KREISTLE LOATHING NAUSEATE SICKNESS
DISGUSTED IRK SICK IRKSOME
DISGUSTING FOUL PERT VILE LOUSY MUCKY NASTY FILTHY SCRIMY SICKLY BEASTLY FULSOME HATEFUL LOATHLY MAWKISH NOISOME OBSCENE SHITTEN FOULSOME LOATHFUL NAUSEOUS SHOCKING
DISH CAP CAUP CUSH DISC DISK FOOL MEAT MOLD PLAT SOLE BASIN BATEA COMAL DEVIL MOULD NAPPY PATEN PINAX PLATE SHAPE BASQUE BASSIE BICKER BLAZER BUTTER CHAFER CRITCH CUSCUS ENTREE FONDUE LUGGIE OLIVES PADDLE PANADA PATERA PATINA PHIALE RECIPE SAUCER SUNDAE TAMALE TUREEN BALANCE BOBOTEE BOBOTIE CEVICHE CHARGER COCOTTE COMPORT

COMPOTE CRESSET DORMANT DOUBLER EPERGNE PAPBOAT PATELLA PLATEAU PLATTER RAMEKIN SCUTTLE SUPREME TERRINE TIMBALE AMATORIO CIOPPINO CLAPDISH COQUILLE COUSCOUS GALATINE KEDGEREE MAZARINE POWSODDY STANDARD ENTREMETS
(— **IN PYRAMID STYLE**) BUISSON
(**BAKING** —) SCALLOP SCOLLOP
(**BRAISED** —) HASLET
(**CHAFING** —) CHAFER CHOFFER
(**FANCY** —) SURPRISE
(**FLAT** —) COMAL CHARGER
(**HIGH-FLAVORED** —) HOGO
(**JEWISH** —) CHOLENT
(**PHILIPPINE** —) BURO
(**PIE** —) COFFIN
(**PILE OF** —S) BUNG
(**ROMAN** —) LANX PATERA PATINA
(**SAILOR'S** —) SCOUSE
(**SCOTTISH** —) BROSE
(**SIDE** —) OUTWORK
(**SWEET** —) JUNKET FLUMMERY
(**TASTY** —) MORSEL
(**WOODEN** —) CUP CAUP BOWIE GOGGAN LUGGIE KICKSHAW
(**PL.**) GARNISH BAKEWARE FLATWARE ENTREMETS
DISHABILLE MOB DISARRAY DISORDER NEGLIGEE
DISHARMONY SCHISM ADHARMA FRACTION
DISHCLOTH DISHRAG
DISHCLOTH GOURD LOOFAH PATOLA DISHRAG
DISHEARTEN AMATE DAUNT FAINT DEJECT DEPRESS FLATTEN UNHEART UNNERVE DISHEART DISPIRIT
DISHEARTENED DULL GLOOMY DOWNCAST DEPRESSED
DISHEARTENING GLOOMY DESOLATE
DISHEVEL MUSS TOWZE RUFFLE TOUSEL TOUSLE TUMBLE TRACHLE DISARRAY DISORDER
DISHEVELED ROOKY BLOUSY BLOWZY FROWZY TUMBLED UNKEMPT FROWZLED SHEVELED SLIPSHOD TATTERED
DISHONEST FOUL LEWD CRONK FALSE LYING QUEER SNIDE TWISTY UNFAIR UNJUST CORRUPT CROOKED KNAVISH INDECENT INDIRECT SHAMEFUL SINISTER UNCHASTE UNHONEST
DISHONESTLY DOUBLY FALSELY
DISHONESTY IMPROBITY
DISHONOR FILE FOUL ABASE ABUSE ODIUM SHAME SPITE STAIN WRONG DEFAME DEFILE DEFORM INFAMY VILIFY DEGRADE DISTAIN OBLOQUY SLANDER VIOLATE DISGLORY DISGRACE DISPLUME IGNOMINY REPROACH VILLAINY
DISHONORABLE BASE FOUL MEAN BLACK NASTY SHABBY YELLOW

IGNOBLE SHAMEFUL UNHONEST
UNWORTHY
DISHONORED DEFAMED
DISHPAN KEELER
DISHRACK FIDDLE
DISHWASHER SWILLER
DISILLUSION SOUR DISMAY
DISINCLINATION NILL UNLUST
UNWILL DISLIKE QUARREL
AVERSION DISTASTE
DISINCLINED LOTH LOATH AFRAID
AVERSE HESITANT
(— TO) ABOVE
DISINFECT SCRUB SEASON
CLEANSE SWEETEN
DISINFECTANT IODINE PHENOL
CREOLIN EUGENOL TACHIOL
FUMIGANT HALAZONE PARAFORM
DISINGENUOUS FALSE UNFAIR
OBLIQUE
DISINHERIT DEPRIVE DISHEIR
ABDICATE DISHERIT
DISINTEGRATE BEAT DUST MELT
BREAK DECAY ERODE GRUSH
SLAKE SPLIT MOLDER CRUMBLE
DISBAND RESOLVE SHATTER
COLLAPSE DISSOLVE SEPARATE
DISINTEGRATING SCHIZOID
DISINTEGRATION DECAY BREAKUP
EROSION BIOLYSIS COLLAPSE
HEARTROT
DISINTER EXHUME UNBURY UNTOMB
UNGRAVE
DISINTERESTED FAIR CANDID
APATHETIC IMPARTIAL
DISJOIN PART UNDO SEVER DETACH
SUNDER UNTACK UNYOKE DISSOLVE
DISUNITE SEPARATE
DISJOINED SEJOINED DIAZEUTIC
DISK (ALSO SEE DISC) EYE NOB ORB
PAN SAW WAX WEB BURR CHAD
DIAL DISC FLAN FLAT KNOB PALM
PUCK STAR TUFT CAKRA DAUNT
MEDAL PATEN PLATE ROUND SABLE
SABOT SPILL TOKEN TRUCK WAFER
WHEEL WHORL BEZANT BOTTOM
BUCKET BUMPER BUTTON CACHET
CARTON CHAKRA CONCHA CONCHO
CORONA DISCUS GHURRY HARROW
PALLET PELLET RECORD RIFFLE
RONDEL SEQUIN SHEAVE SQUAIL
WASHER WEIGHT ZEQUIN ACETATE
BLOTTER BOBECHE CHECKER
CHIPPER CLIPEUS DIOPTER DISCOID
GOGGLES KNICKER MEDALET
PHALERA ROSETTE SLITTER
SPINNER SPOTTER TONDINO
DIFFUSER EYEPIECE HOLDFAST
PLANCHET RONDELLE ROUNDLET
ZECCHINO
(— FOR BARRELING HERRING)
DAUNT
(— FOR CHEESE) FOLLOWER
(— FOR STRIKING HOURS) GHURRY
(— OF JELLYFISH) BELL
(— OF WAX) AGNUS
(— ON WOODEN ROD) SPILL
(BULL'S-EYE —) CARTON
(COIN-MAKING —) FLAN PLANCHET

(ECCENTRIC —) SHEAVE
(FLESHY —) SARCOMA
(HANDLED —) RIFFLE
(MEDICATED —) LAMELLA
(METAL —) SLUG MEDAL
(ORNAMENTAL —) BANGLE
SPANGLE
(PADDED IRON —) SPINNER
(PAPER —S) CONFETTI
(POTTER'S —) BAT
(REVOLVING —) WAFTER
(ROTATING —) SCANNER
(SOLAR —) ATEN ATON
(SUN —) CAKRA CHAKRA
(TROCHAL —) CORONA
(WINGED —) FEROHER
DISLIKE DOWN HATE LOTH MIND
DERRY LOATH SPITE DETEST
REGRET SPLEEN UNLIKE DESPISE
MISLIKE QUARREL SCUNDER
SCUNNER STOMACH AVERSION
DESPISAL DISFAVOR DISTASTE
(— OF CHILDREN) MISOPEDIA
(FOOLISH —) TOY
DISLOCATE LUX SLIP BREAK SPLAY
UNSET LUXATE DISLOCK UNWREST
DISJOINT DISPLACE
DISLOCATED SHOTTEN DISLOCATE
DISLOCATION BREAK SHIFT SLIDE
THROW
(PL.) SETTLEMENTS
DISLODGE BEAT BOLT BUCK BUMP
EXPEL SHAKE SHIFT SWOOP
REMOVE DISROOT UNHORSE
UNHOUSE UNLODGE DISHABIT
(— BY BLASTING) BRUSH
DISLODGING BULLING
DISLOYAL FALSE FELON UNTRUE
DISLEAL
DISLOYALTY SWICK SWIKE
UNLEWTY UNTRUTH
DISMAL SAD WAN DARK DIRE DOWF
DREE DULL EERY GASH GLUM GRAY
GREY BLACK BLEAK DOWFF DREAR
EERIE LURID OURIE SABLE SORRY
SURLY SWART WASTE WISHT
DREARY DREICH DREIGH GLOOMY
GOUSTY SULLEN TRISTE DIREFUL
DOLEFUL FUNERAL GASHFUL
GHASTLY GOUSTIE JOYLESS
OMINOUS POCOSIN UNCOUTH
UNHAPPY DESOLATE DOLESOME
DOLOROUS FUNEREAL GROANFUL
LONESOME NOVEMBRY WEARIFUL
DISMAL-LOOKING GASH
WOBEGONE
DISMALLY DERNLY DIRELY
DISMANTLE RASE RAZE STRIP
DIVEST STRIKE DEPRIVE DESTROY
UNCLOAK DISMOUNT
DISMAY BOWL FEAR RUIN ALARM
AMATE APPAL DAUNT DREAD FLUNK
APPALL ASTONY CHASSE FRIGHT
SUBDUE TERROR DEPRESS DEPRIVE
FOUNDER HORRIFY TERRIFY
AFFRIGHT CONFOUND
DISMAYED ASTONIED
DISMAYING HIDEOUS
DISMEMBER LIMB MAIM PART REND

SEVER MANGLE UNLIMB DISCERP
DISLIMB DISSECT QUARTER
DISJOINT MUTILATE
DISMISS AX AXE CAN PUT BOOT
BUMP BUST CASH CAST DROP
DRUM FIRE KICK OUST QUIT SACK
SEND SHAB SWAP SWOP TURN VAIK
VOID AMAND AMOVE BREAK BRUSH
CHUCK DEMIT DIMIT DITCH EJECT
EXPEL FLIRT FLUNK LOOSE SCOUT
BANISH BOUNCE CONGEE DISMIT
DISOWN REJECT REMOVE SHELVE
CASHIER DISBAND DISCARD
LICENCE LICENSE DISGRACE
DISPATCH DISPOINT RELEGATE
WITHDRAW
DISMISSAL AX BOOT SACK BRUSH
CHUCK CONGE SHAKE AVAUNT
KICKAXE REMOVAL DISPATCH
MITTIMUS
(UNCEREMONIOUS —) CONGE
CONGEE
DISMISSED DEGOMME
DISMOUNT AVALE AVOID LIGHT
ALIGHT DEVOID DESCEND FLYAWAY
UNHORSE UNMOUNT DISHORSE
UNSTRIDE
DISOBEDIENCE CONTEMPT
DISOBEDIENT BAD FORWARD
FROWARD NAUGHTY UNBUXOM
UNGODLY WAYWARD MUTINOUS
DISOBEY SIT REJECT
DISOBLIGE OFFEND REFUSE
AFFRONT NEGLECT
DISOBLIGING MEAN UNBAIN
UNBANE
DISORDER ILL MUX PIE CRUD FLAW
MESS MUSS RIOT RUFF STIR TOUT
CHAOS CRACK DERAY GRIME
HAVOC REVEL SNAFU SPLIT TOUSE
TUKRA UPSET BURBLE CHOREA
DESRAY HUDDLE JUMBLE LITTER
MALADY MASTIC MUCKER MUDDLE
RUFFLE TOUSLE TROPPO TUMULT
UNTIDY WALTER AILMENT CLUTTER
COBWEBS CONFUSE DERANGE
DISEASE DISTURB EMBROIL
FERMENT FLUTTER GARBOIL
ILLNESS MISDEED MISRULE
OUTRAGE PERTURB SHATTER
TROUBLE UNRAVEL UNSHAPE
DISARRAY DISHEVEL EPILEPSY
MISORDER ROWDYISM SICKNESS
UNSETTLE
(— OF EYES) HIPPUS
(— OF VISION) DIPLOPIA
(— OF WINES) CASSE
(COMPLETE —) CHAOS
(MENTAL —) INSANITY PARANOIA
(SPEECH —) LALOPATHY
DISORDERED ILL SICK CRAZY
GAUMY LIGHT MESSY UNRID
BLOTTO FROUZY FROWSY FROWZY
INCULT INSANE MUSSED CHAOTIC
CLOUDED FORLORN TUMBLED
UNSIDED CONFUSED DERANGED
DISEASED FEVERISH FLURRIED
INCHOATE
DISORDERING CRIMP

DISORDERLY RAND RANDY RABBLE UNRULY BUNTING LAWLESS ROARING CONFUSED FAROUCHE LARRIKIN SLIPSHOD SLOVENLY SLUTTISH

DISORGANIZE SHOCK UPSET CONFUSE CONTUSE DERANGE DISBAND DISRUPT DISORDER DISSOLVE

DISOWN DENY RENAY UNOWN REJECT DISAVOW RETRACT ABDICATE DISALLOW DISCLAIM RENOUNCE

DISPARAGE LACK SLUR ABUSE DECRY LOWER DEBASE LESSEN SLIGHT BACKCAP DEBAUCH DEGRADE DEMERIT DEPRESS DETRACT DISABLE DOWNCRY IMPEACH BELITTLE DEROGATE DIMINISH DISCOUNT DISHONOR DISPRIZE MINIMIZE MISLIKEN VILIPEND

DISPARAGEMENT DIASYRM SNIDERY WASHWAY

DISPARAGING SNIDE SLIGHTING

DISPARATE UNEQUAL SEPARATE

DISPARITY DISSENT DISTANCE IMPARITY

DISPASSIONATE CALM COOL FAIR STOIC SEDATE SERENE CLINICAL COMPOSED MODERATE

DISPATCH RID FREE KILL MAIL NOTE POST SEND SLAY WING BRIEF ENVOY FLASH HASTE HURRY SHOOT SPEED DIRECT EMPLOY HASTEN ADDRESS COMMAND DELIVER DISPEED EXPRESS HATCHET BREVIATE CELERITY CONCLUDE DESPATCH EXPEDITE TELEGRAM

DISPATCH BOAT AVISO PACKET

DISPATCHER STARTER

DISPEL FRAY SHOO CHASE BANISH DISCUSS SATISFY SCATTER DISPERSE

DISPENSATION LAW LILA GRACE LIVERY ECONOMY FACULTY QUIENAL TOTQUOT DISPOSAL

DISPENSE DEAL DOLE HELP WEIGH EFFUSE EXCUSE EXEMPT FOREGO MANAGE SPREAD ABSOLVE ARRANGE DISPEND DRIBBLE MINISTER
(— WITH) MISS WANT SPARE SUSPENSE

DISPENSER BOMB MANAGER STEWARD

DISPERSE DOT SOW FRAY MELT PART ROUT SHED LOOSE SCALE SEVER SKAIL STREW BAFFLE DEFEAT DILATE DISPEL SPARSE SPERSE SPREAD UNKNIT VANISH WINNOW DIFFUSE DISBAND DISJECT DISMISS DRIBBLE FRITTER SCATTER SHATTER SPARKLE SPARPLE SPERPLE DISSOLVE DISTRACT SEPARATE SQUANDER STAMPEDE

DISPERSING SCALE
(— SHADOWS) SCIALYTIC

DISPERSION CUT FOAM STAIN

SPREAD DEBACLE SCATTER DIASPORA EMULSOID SOLUTION STAMPEDE

DISPIRIT COW DAMP MATE MULL CHILL DAUNT DEJECT DEPRESS FLATTEN

DISPIRITED DOWY DOWIE ABATTU ABATTUE LETDOWN SHOTTEN DOWNCAST DOWNSOME SACKLESS UNHEARTY WOBEGONE

DISPIRITING COLD CHILL DISMAL

DISPLACE BUMP EDGE MOVE STIR BANISH DEPOSE MISLAY REMOVE WINKLE DERANGE SWALLOW UNHINGE UNPLACE ANTEVERT DISLODGE DISPLANT MISPLACE SUPPLACE SUPPLANT UNSETTLE
(— LATERALLY) HEAVE

DISPLACED ATOPIC DEPAYSE

DISPLACEMENT BUMP SLIP HEAVE SCEND SHIFT START CUBAGE UPSLIP FALLING EVECTION

DISPLAY ACT AIR BRAG DASH GAUD ORGY POMP SHOW SIGN STAR WEAR AGONY ARRAY BINGE BLAZE BOAST DERAY ECLAT EMOTE FLASH PRIDE SCENE SHINE SIGHT SPLAY SPORT STAGE VAUNT BLAZON DEPLOY DESCRY ESTATE EVINCE EXPOSE EXTEND FLAUNT MUSTER OSTENT OUTLAY PARADE REVEAL RUFFLE SETOUT SPLASH SPRANK SPREAD UNCASE APPROVE BALLOON BRAVERY ETALAGE EXHIBIT EXPRESS FANFARE FLUTTER GAUDERY PAGEANT PRESENT SHOWING SPLURGE TRADUCE UNCOVER BEEFCAKE BLAZONRY BOOKFAIR CEREMONY DISCLOSE DISCOVER EMBLAZON EQUIPAGE EVIDENCE EXERCISE EXPOSURE FLOURISH INDICATE MANIFEST PARAFFLE SPLENDOR TINSELRY
(— EXCITEMENT) FAUNCH
(— OF EMOTION) GUSH
(— OF SKILL) APPERTISE
(BOASTFUL —) JACTATION
(EMPTY —) GAUD EYEWASH
(FLORAL —) BLOW BLANKET
(IMPRESSIVE —) SWELL
(OSTENTATIOUS —) DOG GAUDERY SWAGGER
(RADAR —) SCAN

DISPLAYED SPLAY EXPANDED

DISPLEASE VEX MIFF ANGER ANNOY PIQUE MISPAY MISSET OFFEND DISLIKE DISSUIT MISLIKE PROVOKE IRRITATE

DISPLEASED GLUM UNEASY UNFAIN

DISPLEASING BAD DRY PUTRID IRKSOME TEDIOUS UNLOVELY

DISPLEASURE IRE ANGER MUMPS PIQUE INJURY STRUNT UNLUST UNWILL DISLIKE OFFENSE TROUBLE UMBRAGE UNTHANK DISFAVOR DISGRACE DISTASTE

DISPORT PLAY AMUSE FRISK SPORT DIVERT FROLIC GAMBOL DISPLAY

DISPOSAL SALE BANDON CLEANUP PROPINE BESTOWAL DEVOTION DISPATCH
(QUICK —) WASHWAY

DISPOSE APT SET BEND CAST DUMP GIVE MIND TRIM YARK ARRAY BRUSH DIGHT ORDER PLACE POSIT ADJUST ATTIRE BESTOW DIGEST SETTLE TEMPER APPOINT ARRANGE DISPONE GESTURE INCLINE PREPARE RESOLVE DISPATCH REGULATE
(— OF) JOB SELL SCRAP FINISH HANDLE

DISPOSED APT FIT SET SIB LIEF GIVEN PRONE READY WRAST MINDED MINDFUL SUBJECT WILLING ADDICTED PROCLIVE PROTENSE TALENTED
(— AT INTERVALS) ALTERNATE
(— TO ACTION) ACTIVE
(— TO ASSOCIATE WITH ONE GROUP) CLANNISH
(— TOWARD) AFFECTED
(FAIRLY —) CANDID
(WELL —) FAIN INCLINED

DISPOSITION BENT BIAS MAKE MIND MOOD RACE SORT TRIM TURN DRIVE ETHOS FRAME GRAIN HABIT HEART HUMOR SPITE TACHE AFFECT ANIMUS DESIGN GENIUS HEALTH KIDNEY NATURE PTYXIS SPIRIT SPRITE STRIND TALENT TEMPER CONCEPT COURAGE DISPOSE FACULTY STOMACH APTITUDE ATTITUDE DISPOSAL POSITURE
(— OF DRAPERIES) CAST
(— OF PAWNS) SKELETON
(— TO ANGER) CHOLER
(— TO RESIST) DEFIANCE
(GENEROUS —) HEART
(KINDLY —) CHARITY HUMANITY
(NATURAL —) KIND GRAIN TARAGE INDOLES
(ORNAMENTAL —) DECOR
(ULTIMATE —) FATE

DISPOSSESS OUST EJECT EVICT EXPEL STRIP WRONG DEPOSE DIVEST BEREAVE CASHIER DEPRIVE DISSEIZE SEPARATE

DISPOSSESSED LUMPEN

DISPRAISE BLAME CENSURE

DISPROOF ELENCH REFUTE IMPROOF REPROOF

DISPROPORTIONATE UNEQUAL

DISPROVE BREAK REBUT REFEL NEGATE REFUTE CONFUTE EXPLODE IMPROVE REPROVE DISALLOW REDARGUE

DISPUTABLE MOOT VAGUE UNSURE DUBIOUS FALLIBLE

DISPUTANT FENCER POLEMIC WRANGLER

DISPUTATION PARVIS PILPUL POLEMIC PROBLEM WRANGLE ARGUMENT COURSING DEBATING EXERCISE

DISPUTE JAR TAX CALL CHOP DENY

FEUD FRAY FUSS HOLD MOOT ODDS
RIOT SAKE SPAR SPAT TILT ARGUE
BRAWL BROIL CABAL CHEST FLITE
FLYTE HURRY PLEAD SPUTE SQUIB
ARGUFY BARNEY BICKER CAMPLE
CANGLE DABBER DACKER DAIKER
DEBATE DIFFER FITTER FRATCH
HAGGLE HASSLE IMPUGN MATTER
NAGGLE SHARRY SQUALL SQUEAL
THREAP BRABBLE CONTEND
CONTEST DERAIGN DISCUSS
DISSERT FACTION GAINSAY PRIBBLE
QUARREL WRANGLE ARGUMENT
CATFIGHT CONTRARY POLEMIZE
QUESTION SKIRMISH SPARRING
SPLUTTER SQUABBLE
(POETICAL —) FLYTING PARTIMEN
DISQUALIFY DEBAR UNFIT OUTLAW
DISABLE
DISQUIET VEX FEAR FRET PAIN
TOSS UNRO EXCITE UNCALM
UNEASE UNREST AGITATE ANXIETY
DISREST DISTURB INQUIET SOLICIT
TROUBLE TURMOIL UNPEACE
UNQUIET
DISQUIETED UNEASY
DISQUIETUDE CHAGRIN WANREST
WANRUFE
DISRAELI DIZZY
DISREGARD BY SIT BLOW MOCK
OMIT PASS WANE BELAY FLING
WAIVE FORGET HUBRIS IGNORE
SLIGHT UNHEED CASHIER DESPISE
FORHEED LICENCE LICENSE
NEGLECT OVERSEE DISCOUNT
DISFAVOR DISPENSE DISVALUE
EASINESS OVERHALE OVERLOOK
OVERPASS UNREGARD
DISRELISH DISLIKE DISTASTE
DISREPUTABLE LOW BASE GAMY
HARD WAFF GAMEY SEAMY SHADY
SHODDY RAFFISH SHAMEFUL
UNHONEST
DISREPUTABLENESS BEGGARY
DISREPUTE DISFAME DISFAVOR
DISHONOR REPROACH
DISRESPECT AFFRONT CONTEMPT
RUDENESS
DISRESPECTFUL HARM SAUCY
UNCIVIL IMPOLITE IMPUDENT
INSOLENT
DISROBE STRIP CHANGE DIVEST
DESPOIL UNDRESS
DISRUPT GASH REND TEAR BREAK
CROSS HAMPER DISRUMP DISTRACT
DISRUPTED BROKEN DISRUPT
DISRUPTION BREACH BREAKUP
DEBACLE RUPTURE SOLUTION
DISSATISFACTION PAIN DISTASTE
VEXATION
DISSATISFIED UNEASY
DISSATISFY MISPAY
DISSECT BAR ANALYZE DISJOIN
SCALPEL UNPIECE
DISSECTED MATURE
DISSECTION ANATOMY ANALYSIS
DISSEMBLE ACT FOX HIDE MASK
CLOAK FEIGN BOGGLE SEMBLE

CONCEAL DISGUISE SIMULATE
SIMULIZE
DISSEMBLER SIMULAR
DISSEMBLING SLY IRONIC FICTION
AESOPIAN IRONICAL
DISSEMINATE SOW BEAR BLAZE
STREW EFFUSE SPREAD DIFFUSE
PUBLISH SCATTER SPARPLE
DISPERSE SEMINATE
DISSENSION JAR ODDS DEBATE
STRIFE DISCORD DISLIKE DISSENT
FACTION MISLIKE BROILERY
DISPEACE DISTANCE DISUNION
DISUNITY DIVISION FRACTION
FRICTION SEDITION
DISSENT VARY DIFFER HERESY
CONTEND PROTEST DISAGREE
DISSENTER HERETIC SECTARY
RECUSANT SEPARATE RASKOLNIK
(PL.) SEPARATION
DISSEPIMENT REPLUM SEPTUM
PHRAGMA
DISSERTATION ESSAY THEME
TRACT DEBATE MEMOIR SCREED
THESIS DESCANT LECTURE
MEMOIRS EXCURSUS EXERCISE
TRACTATE TREATISE
(— ON TEA) TSIOLOGY
DISSERVICE HARM DAMAGE INJURY
MISCHIEF
DISSIDENT FRONDEUR
DISSIMILAR UNLIKE DIFFORM
DIVERSE UNLIKEN
DISSIMILATE UNLIKEN
DISSIMULATION IRONY DECEIT
DISSIPATE BURN FRAY SPEND
WASTE BANISH DISPEL EXPEND
CONSUME DIFFUSE DISCUSS
FRITTER RESOLVE SCATTER
SHATTER SWATTLE TARNISH
DISPERSE DISSOLVE EMBEZZLE
EVANESCE SQUANDER
DISSIPATED FAST HIGH LOST
SPORTY OUTWARD RACKETY
DISSOLUTE LAX LEWD WILD LOOSE
SLACK RAKELY RAKISH SUBURB
UNTIED WANTON IMMORAL
LAWLESS VICIOUS DESOLATE
RAKEHELL RECKLESS RESOLUTE
SUBURBAN UNCURBED
DISSOLUTION END RUIN DECAY
BREAKUP DECEASE DIVORCE
DIALYSIS
DISSOLVE CUT END DEFY FADE
FUSE MELT SOLV THAW BREAK
FLEET LOOSE SOLVE UNFIX DIGEST
DISTIL RELENT SOLUTE UNBIND
UNGLUE UNKNIT ADJOURN DESTROY
DISBAND DISJOIN DISTILL DIVORCE
LIQUEFY RESOLVE DISCANDY
DISUNITE SEPARATE
(— OUT) LEACH
DISSOLVED SOLUT REMISS SOLUTE
RESOLUTE
DISSONANCE WOLF DISCORD
DIAPHONY
DISSONANT HARSH RAGGED
GRATING JARRING JANGLING
DISSUADE BLUFF DETER DEHORT

DIVERT RETIRE
DISTAFF ROCK
DISTANCE DX WAY BLUE GAIT GATE
LOOK PIPE SPAN STEP DEPTH
DRAFT RANGE SPACE GROUND
HEIGHT LENGTH SPREAD STANCE
STITCH BOWSHOT BREADTH
DRAUGHT FARNESS JOURNEY
MILEAGE MILEWAY RESERVE
STRETCH YARDAGE COLDNESS
COSECANT DIAMETER FOOTSTEP
HANDSPAN INTERVAL LATITUDE
OFFSCAPE OUTSTRIP
(SAFE —) BERTH
(— ALONG TRACK) LEAD
(— BETWEEN BATTENS) GAG
(— BETWEEN MASTS) INTERVAL
(— BETWEEN RAILS) GAGE GAUGE
(— BETWEEN RIVET-HEADS) GRIP
(— FOR PUTTING COAL) RENK
(— FROM BELLY TO BACK) BODY
(— FROM EQUATOR) HEIGHT
(— FROM LOCK FACE) BACKSET
(— FROM THE EYE) DEPTH
(— IN ADVANCE) START
(— OF ARCHERY RANGE) BUTT
(— OF BOW SHOT) CAST
(— OF HAUL) LEAD LEADAGE
(— OF TURNING SHIP) ADVANCE
(— OF VISION) KEN
(— ON FISHHOOK) BITE
(— ON GEAR WHEEL) ADDENDUM
(— OVER WHICH WIND BLOWS)
FETCH
(ANGULAR —) ANOMALY
(AT A —) LARGE
(GREAT —) INFINITY
(INTERVENING —) GAP
(PERPENDICULAR —) DROP CAMBER
ALTITUDE
(SEA —) OUTING STEAMING
(SHOOTING —) SHOOT
(SHORT — AWAY) OUTBYE
(SHORT —) INCH SPIT STEP SPELL
FOOTSTEP
(SMALL —) HAIR STEP
(UNIT OF —) LI YOJAN PARASANG
DISTANT DX COY FAR OFF AFAR
AWAY BACK COLD SIDE YOND
ALOOF CHILL FERNE HENCE FERREN
REMOTE YONDER FARAWAY
FOREIGN FROSTED REMOVED
STRANGE RESERVED
(— IN TIME) EARLY
(— PART) OFFSCAPE
(MORE —) YOND YONDER ULTERIOR
DISTASTE HATE DEGOUT UNLUST
DISGUST DISLIKE MISLIKE AVERSION
MISTASTE
DISTASTEFUL SOUR AUGEAN
BITTER BEASTLY HATEFUL
BRACKISH NAUSEOUS SHOCKING
UNSAVORY
DISTEMPER SOAK STEEP CHOLER
DILUTE GARGET GARGIL GARGLE
MALADY PANTAS AILMENT DISEASE
ILLNESS DISORDER DYSCRASE
SICKNESS UNSETTLE
(— OF COLT) STRANGLES

DISTEND BAG BLOW FILL GROW
HEFT BLOAT PLUMP STRUT SWELL
WIDEN DILATE EXPAND EXTEND
INTEND SPREAD BALLOON ENLARGE
INFLATE STRETCH
DISTENDED FULL PENT TAUT TRIG
WIDE BLOWN POOCH TUMID GRAVID
BLOATED DISTENT SWOLLEN
INFLATED PATULENT PATULOUS
DISTENTION BLOAT DISTENT
TYMPANY
DISTHENE CYANITE KYANITE
DISTICH SLOKA PROODE COUPLET
DISTILL DROP ELIX EMIT RATE STILL
DISTIL EXTILL INFUSE ALEMBIC
LIMBECK TRICKLE
DISTILLATE GUNDY ROSIN BENZIN
BENZINE
DISTILLATION RUN DESCENT
DISTILLER ABKAR STILLER
DISTILLERY STILL JIGGER STILLERY
DISTINCT HOT FAIR FREE VIVE
BREME BRISK CLEAR PLAIN SHARP
VIVID PLUCKY PROPER SECRET
SUNDRY ANOTHER ASUNDER
DIVERSE EVIDENT LEGIBLE OBVIOUS
PRECISE SEVERAL SPECIAL
APPARENT DISCRETE DIVIDUAL
PALPABLE PECULIAR SEPARATE
DISTINCTION MARK NOTE RANK
SHED TEST CLASS GLORY HONOR
FIGURE LAUREL LUSTER LUSTRE
RENOWN QUALITY QUILLET
ACCESSIT DIVISION GRANDEZA
SUBTLETY
(ACADEMIC —) HONORS HONOURS
(WITHOUT —) COMMON
DISTINCTIVE JUICY DIRECT PROPER
SIGNAL PECULIAR PHONEMIC
SEPARATE SPANKING TALENTED
DISTINCTIVENESS EMPHASIS
DISTINCTLY CLEAR REDLY FAIRLY
CLEARLY
DISTINCTNESS PLUCK CLARITY
SEVERALTY
(LACKING —) SMUDGY
DISTINGUISH DEEM KNOW MARK
SORT BADGE JUDGE LABEL SEVER
SKILL STAMP DECERN DEFINE
DESCRY DEVISE DIVIDE ENSIGN
SECERN SINGLE CONCERN DISCERN
DESCRIBE PERCEIVE SEPARATE
DISTINGUISHED CLEAR GREAT
NOTED SWELL BANNER FAMOUS
GENTLE MARKED SOLEMN EMINENT
INSIGNE NOTABLE SIGNATE SPECIAL
DISTINCT LAUREATE RENOWNED
SPLENDID
DISTINGUISHING BETWEEN
DISTORT WRY SKEW CLOUD COLOR
FUDGE SCREW TWIST WREST
WRING CRINGE DEFACE DEFORM
DETORT GARBLE SHEVEL WRITHE
BLUBBER CONTORT FALSIFY
GRIMACE PERVERT SHACHLE
SHACKLE SLANDER OUTIMAGE
WIREDRAW
DISTORTED WRY AWRY SKEW
ASKEW CRANK SKEWED WARPED

CROOKED DISTORT GNARLED
LOXOTIC WRITHEN CAMSHACH
DEFORMED DEGRADED STRAINED
TORTIOUS
DISTORTING CONVULSION
DISTORTION HOG SAG WOW WREST
STRAIN FLUTTER GRIMACE
GARBLING SKEWNESS
(— IN WOOD) DIAMONDING
DISTRACT MAD AMUSE CRAZE
STROY BEMUSE DETRAY DIVERT
HARASS INSANE MADDEN MITHER
MOIDER PUZZLE TWITCH AGITATE
CONFUSE DETRACT DISTURB
EMBROIL PERPLEX SCATTER
BEWILDER CONFOUND
DISTRACTED GYTE CRAZY STRACT
FRANTIC SCRANNY
DISTRACTION ALARM BLIND
ALARUM ESCAPE FRENZY TUMULT
ECSTASY
DISTRAIN NAM NAAM DRIVE POINT
STRAIN STRESS DISTRESS
POUNDAGE
DISTRAINT NAM NAAM POIND
DISTRAUGHT MAD CRAZED FRANTIC
DERANGED DISTRACT DISTRAIT
STRAUGHT
DISTRESS AIL ILL MAR BITE CARK
HURT MOAN NEED PAIN PORT TEEN
AGONY ANGER ANNOY DOLOR
GRATE GRIEF GRILL GRIPE LABOR
PINCH PRESS SMART TRYST TWEAK
WORRY WOUND BARRAT DANGER
DURESS GRIEVE GRUDGE HARASS
HARROW LAMENT MISERY SORROW
STRESS THRONG WORRIT AFFLICT
ANGUISH ANXIETY CHAGRIN
DAYMARE DESTROY DISEASE
EXTREME HERSHIP MISEASE
OPPRESS PASSION PENANCE
PERPLEX STURBLE TORMENT
TORTURE TROUBLE UNQUERT
AGGRIEVE CALAMITY DARKNESS
DISTASTE DISTRAIN FORHAILE
PRESSURE SORENESS STRAITEN
WANDRETH GRIEVANCE
DISTRESSED WRUNG DOWNGONE
DISTRESSFUL STRAIT
DISTRESSING BAD HOT SAD GRIM
HARD SORE BLEAK CHARY CRUEL
DIRTY SHARP BITTER SEVERE
SHREWD THORNY CARKING
FEARFUL GRIPING PAINFUL
GRIEVOUS
DISTRIBUTE DOT SOW CAST DEAL
DOLE GRID METE SEED SORT TAME
ALLOT CLASS DIVVY ISSUE SHARE
SHIFT SPEND ASSIGN ASSORT
DEPART DEVISE DIGEST DIVIDE
EXPEND IMPART PARCEL REPART
SPARSE SPREAD ARRANGE DISPEND
DISPOSE EROGATE PRORATE
SCATTER ALLOCATE CLASSIFY
DESCRIBE DISBURSE DISPENSE
DISPERSE SEPARATE SPRINKLE
(— GUNFIRE) SEARCH
(— SEED) SOW SEED DRILL
(— TYPE) THROW

DISTRIBUTED BALANCED DISPERSE
DISTRIBUTION DOLE SALE ARRAY
DIVVY DETAIL DIVIDE PARTING
DISPOSAL DIVIDEND
DISTRIBUTIVELY EACH APIECE
DISTRIBUTOR SOWER SHARER
CARRIER ZANJERO
DISTRICT DO AMT GAU LAN SOC
WON AREA COIL FARM HUNT LEET
LIWA PALE PART SIDE SLUM SOKE
TEMA WARD WENE WICK WOON
AIMAK ANNEX COILA EXURB HARSH
JAGIR JEWRY MAHAL OKRUG PAGUS
PARTY SHIRE SOKEN TALUK TEMAN
TRACT VICUS AGENCY BARRIO
BOWERY CANTON CERCLE CIRCLE
COUNTY FOREST JAGHIR MARKAZ
MEMBER MERINA OKROOG PARAMO
PARISH POLLAM REGARD REGION
SIRCAR STAPLE STREET SYSSEL
VINTRY ZILLAH CALABAR CIRCUIT
CLASSIS COMARCA COMMUNE
COUNTRY CURRAGH DEMESNE
DIOCESE ENCLAVE FREEDOM
LIBERTY MAHALLA MALACCA
MAYFAIR MELIZKI MISSION PIMLICO
PURLIEU QUARTER SEASIDE
SLUMDOM THANAGE THEBAID
UPRIVER CHAPELRY CIMARRON
DISTRITO DIVISION FAUBOURG
GILDABLE LEGATION MACASSAR
MAGAZINE MONTANAS PRECINCT
PROVINCE REGIMENT
(— BORDERING RIVER) WATER
(— OF COURT) LEET
(— OF JAPAN) DO KEN
(BROTHEL —) STEW
(BURNED —) QUEMADO
(CHINESE —) HIEN
(ECCLESIASTICAL —) SYNOD
CLASSIS DIOCESE
(HUNTING —) WALK
(ICELANDIC —) SYSSEL
(JUDICIAL —) CIRCUIT
(POOR —) SLUM SLUMS
(POSTAL —) RAYON
(RURAL —) WAYBACK
(RURAL —S) STICKS
(RUSSIAN —) STANITSA STANITZA
(TENANT —) THIRL
(TRIBAL —) GAU
(TURKISH —) ORDU SANJAK
(PL.) GAELTACHT
DISTRUST FEAR DOUBT DREAD
STRIFE DIFFIDE SUSPECT UNFAITH
UNTRUST DEFIANCE DISFAITH
MISFAITH MISTRUST WANTRUST
DISTRUSTFUL SHY LEERY JEALOUS
DISTURB VEX BUSY FAZE FRET FUSS
JOLT RILE ROIL STIR TOSS ALARM
ANNOY BRASH DROVE FEEZE
KNOCK PHASE ROUSE SHAKE STEER
UPSET BOTHER HARASS JOSTLE
MOLEST RUFFLE SQUEAK UNCALM
UNEASE AGITATE COMMOTE
COMMOVE DERANGE DISREST
DRUMBLE FRAZZLE GARBOIL
INQUIET MISMAKE PERTURB
SCUFFLE SOLICIT STURBLE

TEMPEST TROUBLE CONVULSE
DISJOINT DISORDER DISQUIET
DISTRACT DISTRESS FRIGHTEN
(— **BY HANDLING**) TOUCH
(— **SUDDENLY**) START
(— **THE PEACE**) RIOT INQUIET
DISTURBANCE VEX BOIL BREE CAIN
COIL DUST RIOT ROUT STIR WIND
WORK ALARM BRAWL BROIL DERAY
FUGUE FUROR HURRY SHINE SHOCK
STEER STORM STROW STURT
TOUSE AFFRAY BOTHER BREEZE
CATHRO DESRAY FRACAS FRAISE
FURORE HUBBUB KICKUP POTHER
RUMBLE RUMPUS SHINDY SQUALL
STATIC TUMULT TURNUP UPROAR
BLUNDER BOBBERY BRULYIE
BRULZIE CHAGRIN CLATTER
CLUTTER DISTURB EMOTION
FERMENT GRINDER MADNESS
ROOKERY TROUBLE TURMOIL
BROILERY BUSINESS DISORDER
FOOFARAW INCIDENT REELRALL
STRAMASH TRAVALLY
(— **OF OCEAN**) SEA
(**ATMOSPHERIC** —) STORM GRINDER
(**DIGESTIVE** —) BLOAT
(**MENTAL** —) FRENZY PHRENSY
DELIRIUM
(**SEISMIC** —) SEAQUAKE
DISTURBED CRACKED INQUIET
MAKADOO TROUBLE AGITATED
FLURRIED STREAKED
DISTURBING BREAK HAUNTING
DISUNION DIVORCE
DISUNITE RIP PART SEVER UNTIE
DETACH DIVIDE SUNDER UNKNIT
UNLIME DISBAND DISJOIN DISLINK
DISSENT DIVORCE UNRAVEL
ALIENATE DISSEVER DISSOLVE
ESTRANGE SEPARATE UNSOLDER
DISUNITY DISCORD DISUNION
DIVISION
DISUSE MISUSE OUTAGE ABANDON
DISCARD DISUSAGE MISAPPLY
DISUSED DEAD WASTE DESUETE
EXOLETE
DITCH GAW RUT SAP SOW DELF
DICK DIKE DYKE FOSS GOOL GOUT
GRIP GURT HOLL LEET MOAT SEEK
SICK SIKE SINK TRIG CANAL CLAUD
DELFT DELVE FENCE FLEAM FOSSA
FOSSE GRAFF GRAFT GRAVE GRIPE
GROOP GULLY PUDGE RHEEN RHINE
SEWER SHORE SLONK SLUIT SOUGH
STANK STELL ZANJA GUTTER
GUZZLE HOLLOW RELAIS SHEUCH
SHEUGH TRENCH ZANJON ABANDON
ACEQUIA CHANNEL GRINDLE
GRIPPLE LATERAL VANFOSS
ZANJONA WATERING
(**MUDDY** —) LETCH
(**NARROW** —) RELAIS
(**OPEN** —) STELL
DITCH GRASS ENALID
DITCH MILLET HUREEK PASPALUM
DITCH REED SPIRE BENNEL
DITHER SHAKE BOTHER LATHER
SHIVER TROUBLE

DITROCHEE DIPODY
DITTO SAME REPEAT LIKEWISE
DITTY DIT LAY DITE DYTE POEM
SING SONG THEME VERSE SAYING
DICTATE VINETTA
DIURETIC ZEA CAVA KAVA BUCCO
BUCHU LAPPA PICHI SABAL NASROL
DROSERA EMICTORY
DIVER AMA LOON DUCKER PEARLER
PLUNGER PLUNGEON
DIVERGE LEAVE BRANCH DIFFER
DIVIDE RAMIFY SPREAD SQUARE
SWERVE DEVIATE DIGRESS DIVERSE
DISAGREE DIVAGATE
DIVERGENCE DIP ERROR CHANGE
SPREAD VAGARY CONTRAST
DIVERGENT OFF APART REMOTE
TANGENT VARIANT
(**MORE** —) FARTHER
DIVERS EVIL MANY CRUEL SUNDRY
SEVERAL VARIOUS PERVERSE
DIFFERING
DIVERSE EVIL SERE MOTLEY
SUNDRY UNLIKE VARIED ADVERSE
SEVERAL VARIOUS DISTINCT
PERVERSE SEPARATE VARIETAL
DIVERSIFIED EXTENDED
DIVERSIFY DOT FRET VARY CHECK
FRECK BEGARIE VARIATE SPRINKLE
DIVERSION JEU GAME MASK PLAY
ALARM FEINT FRISK HOBBY SPORT
ATTACK DEDUIT DIVERT LAUGHS
SCHEME SOLACE DISPORT PASTIME
ESCAPISM PLEASURE SIDESHOW
VARIORUM
(— **OF STREAM**) CAPTURE
DIVERSITY CHANGE DISCORD
DISSENT VARIETY CONTRAST
DIVERT SWAY AMUSE BLANK RELAX
SHUNT SPORT WRING DERAIL
DERIVE DETURN SIPHON SWITCH
SYPHON TICKLE BEGUILE CELIGHT
DECEIVE DEFLECT DETRACT
DISPORT PASTIME PERVERT
REFLECT ABSTRACT DISSUADE
DISTRACT ESTRANGE RECREATE
(— **ATTENTION**) COVER
(— **HEADWATERS**) BEHEAD
(— **STREAM**) CAPTURE
(— **WATER**) FLUME
DIVERTED MERRY AMUSED
DISTRACT
DIVERTICULUM UTERUS OLEOCYST
DIVERTING DROLL AMUSING
FOOLISH PLEASANT SPORTFUL
LAUGHABLE
DIVEST BARE DOFF REFT TIRL
EMPTY EXUTE REAVE SHEAR SPOIL
STRIP DELAWN DENUDE DEPOSE
DEVEST DISMIT UNVEST BEREAVE
DEPRIVE DESPOIL DISROBE
UNCOVER UNDRESS DENATURE
DETHRONE UNCLOTHE
(— **OF ARMOR**) DEMAIL
(— **OF VALUE**) DEVALUE
(— **OF**) ABDICATE
DIVIDE CUT LOT CAST DEAL FORK
MERE PART RIFT SHED SLIP ZONE
BREAK CARVE CLASS CLEFT DIVVY

GAVEL JOINT SCALE SCIND SEVER
SHARE SHIFT SLICE SNACK SPACE
SPLIT SPRIT WHACK BEPART BISECT
BRANCH CANTLE CANTON CLEAVE
COTEAU DEPART DEVISE DIFFER
DOMIFY INDENT PARCEL RAMIFY
SECTOR SEJOIN SLEAVE SUNDER
ALIQUOT ANALYZE ATOMIZE
AVERAGE BRITTEN COMPART
DIFFUSE DIREMPT DISCIDE DISPART
DISSECT DIVERGE FISSURE FRITTER
PARTAKE PRORATE ALLOCATE
CLASSIFY CROSSCUT DISCRETE
DISSEVER DISTRACT DISUNITE
FRACTION FRAGMENT GRADUATE
HEMISECT MEDISECT SEPARATE
STRATIFY UNSEEDER
(— **BEEF**) BLOCK
(— **FILAMENTS**) SLEAVE
(— **INTO 2 PARTS**) HALVE BISECT
(— **INTO 4 PARTS**) QUARTER
(— **INTO DISTRICTS**) CANTON
(— **INTO MEASURES**) BAR
(— **INTO PIECES**) GOBBET
(— **LAND**) STINT
(— **NATURALLY**) FALL
(— **SMALL**) SCANTLE
DIVIDED ENTE REFT SIDE CLEFT
FORKY SPLIT ATOMIC CLOVEN
PRONGY FISSATE FOURCHE
GYRONNY PARTITE SEPTATE
AEROLATE CAMERATE DIVIDUAL
FOURCHEE
(— **IN TWO**) FOURCHE DIMIDIATE
(— **INTO 4 PARTS**) PALY
QUARTERED
(**NOT** —) GLOBAL
DIVIDEND BONUS SHARE
DIVIDER BUNTON MERIST SHARER
BUNTING COMPASS SEVERER
DIVIDANT
DIVI-DIVI LIBIDIBI
DIVINATION OMEN SORS SORT
AUGURY MANTIC SCRYING SORCERY
GEOMANCY TAGHAIRM
(— **SCIENCE**) MANTIC
DIVINE HOLY SORT SPAE TWIG
AREAD AREED DIVUS GUESS PIOUS
DEIFIC DETECT DEVISE GODFUL
HALSEN PRIEST SACRED BLESSED
FORESEE GODLIKE PORTEND
PREDICT PRESAGE ARIOLATE
CONTRIVE FOREBODE FOREKNOW
FORETELL HEAVENLY IMMORTAL
MINISTER PERCEIVE UBIQUIST
DIVINER SEER AUGUR SIBYL
ARUSPEX AUGURER PROPHET
HARUSPEX
DIVING BELL NAUTILUS
DIVING BOARD RISE
DIVING SUIT GANGAVA
DIVINING ROD TWIG DOWSER
DIVINITY (ALSO SEE GOD AND
GODDESS) JOSS LLEU LLEW TIEN
AHURA DEITY HYBLA NUADA NUADU
NYMPH POWER ATHTAR VEDUIS
GLAUCUS GODDESS GODHEAD
GODSHIP HYBLAEA TARANIS VIRBIUS
TEUTATES VEDIOVIS

(— **CIRCUIT BINDING**) YAPP
(PL.) ELOHIM
DIVISIBLE SECABLE DIVIDUAL
PARTIBLE
(— **BY 2**) AIM
DIVISION BAY BOX CUT DAG FIT LEG
CHAP CLAN DOLE FARM FAUN FORK
GELD GELT GORE HOLD LITH NEAT
PACE PANE PART RANK RAPE RIFT
CAPUT CHASM CLASS CLEFT CURIA
DIGOR DIVVY DULAN DULAT FIELD
FIGHT GENOS GRANT GROUP IJORE
MURUT PERES REALM SHARD
SHARE SUBAH TAXIS THEME TOMAN
WHEEN CANTON DECADE DECURY
DEGREE DIVIDE EOGAEA HAWIYA
IMAHAL JHURIA PORTIO SCHISM
SEASON SECTOR SUNDER VOLOST
ZILLAH BREAKUP COMARCA
CUSTODY DIOCESE DUALISM
ENOMOTY FISSURE FURLONG
HASHIYA KINGDOM KITSKAN
NATUARY PARTAGE PARTING
ROULADE SECTION SEGMENT
SUBRACE ARPEGGIO CATEGORY
CLEAVAGE DECANATE DIERESIS
DISTRICT FASCICLE MEROTOMY
PARGANNA PRECINCT SCISSION
SCISSORE SHEDDING SQUADRON
SUBCLASS
(— **BETWEEN PIERS**) BAY
(— **BETWEEN STALLS**) BAIL
(— **FOR TAXATION**) GELD
(— **IN DENMARK**) AMT
(— **IN HUNGARY**) COMITAT
(— **IN MINING BED**) CLEAVE
(— **OF ANGELS**) CHOIR
(— **OF ARMY**) BATTLE LOCHUS
(— **OF BEJA**) BISHARIN
(— **OF BOOK**) CHAPTER FASCICLE
(— **OF BUILDING**) STORY STOREY
(— **OF CHARIOTEERS**) FACTION
(— **OF CONTEST**) HEAT INNING
(— **OF COUNTY**) RAPE BARONY
HUNDRED
(— **OF CROPLAND**) FLAT
(— **OF DISCOURSE**) HEADING
(— **OF DRAMA**) ACT SCENE
(— **OF FAMILY**) BRANCH
(— **OF FIELD**) RIG
(— **OF FOOT**) SEMEION
(— **OF FOREST**) WARD
(— **OF GEOLOGICAL TIME**) EPOCH
(— **OF GRASS**) SPRIG
(— **OF GREAT HORDE**) DULAN
DULAT KANGLA KANGLI
(— **OF HEADLINE**) BANK DECK
(— **OF LAND**) LAINE KONOHIKI
(— **OF LEGION**) COHORT HASTATI
MANIPLE TRIARII
(— **OF LOG LINE**) KNOT
(— **OF MANCHU ARMY**) BANNER
(— **OF MANKIND**) RACE
(— **OF MEAL**) COURSE
(— **OF NIGHT**) WATCH
(— **OF ORANGE**) LITH
(— **OF POEM**) FIT DUAN CANTO
STANZA STROPHE
(— **OF PROCESS**) STAGING

(— **OF ROCKS**) SYSTEM
(— **OF ROSARY**) DECADE
(— **OF SOCIETY**) CASTE ATOMISM
(— **OF SONG**) FIT
(— **OF STOPE**) FLOOR
(— **OF STRUCTURE**) STAGE
(— **OF TREF**) RANDIR
(— **OF UTTERANCE**) COLON
(— **OF WINDOW**) DAY
(— **OF ZODIAC**) SIGN DECAN
(— **OVER ISSUE**) BREACH
(**ADMINISTRATIVE** —) FU LATHE
CHARGE CIRCLE COUNTY EYALET
CUSTODY DIOCESE TOWNSHIP
(**ANTHROPOLOGICAL** —) STOCK
(**ARMY** —) MORA
(**ASTROLOGICAL** —) FACE
(**CELL** —) AMITOSIS
(**ECCLESIASTICAL** —) SCHISM
SOCIETY PRECINCT
(**GEOLOGICAL** —) ERA LIAS MALM
LUDIAN SERIES LARAMIE ARNUSIAN
RICHMOND
(**HINGED** —) LEAF
(**ISLE OF MAN** —) SHEADING
(**MUSICAL** —) ALLEGRO
(**NUCLEAR** —) FISSION
(**PHILIPPINE** —) ATO
(**POLICE** —) TANA THANA
(**POLITICAL** —) ATO CITY LATHE
STATE COUNTY PARISH BOROUGH
HUNDRED SURPLUS DISTRICT
PURCHASE
(**POPULATION** —) STRATUM
(**SOCIAL** —) HORDE
(**TRIBAL** —) CLAN
DIVORCE GET GETT AHSAN HASAN
KHULA SEVER TALAK SUNDER
ASUNDER DISBAND DISMISS
MUBARAT UNMARRY DISSOLVE
DISUNION DISUNITE SEPARATE
DIVOT CLOD TURF
DIVULGE BARE CALL SHOW TELL
BLURT BREAK SPILL UTTER VOICE
BEWRAY EVULGE IMPART REVEAL
SPREAD UNFOLD PROPALE PUBLISH
UNCOVER DISCLOSE DISCOVER
EVULGATE PROCLAIM
DIZZINESS HILO SWIM DINUS TIEGO
MEGRIM VANITY MERLIGO SCOTOMY
VERTIGO SWIMMING WILLNESS
DIZZY DUNT CRAZY FAINT GIDDY
LIGHT TOTTY WESTY FICKLE STUPID
FOOLISH SWIMMING UNSTEADY
DO D ACT DIV FAY TRY BILK BURN
CHAR COME DEAL DOST MAKE
PASS SUIT AVAIL BITCH CHEAT
EXERT GUISE SERVE SHIFT TRICK
ANSWER COMMIT NOBBLE RENDER
ACHIEVE EXECUTE PERFORM
PRODUCE SATISFY SUFFICE
TRANSACT
(— **AWAY WITH**) BURK ABATE
BURKE FORDO BANISH FOREDO
ABOLISH AMOLISH CASHIER
CONSUME ABROGATE DEMOLISH
DISSOLVE IMBOLISH RETRENCH
(— **BUSINESS**) CHAFFER
(— **CARELESSLY**) SLIM

(— **CASUAL WORK**) GRASS
(— **FOR**) FIX GET JACK SINK FETCH
NAPOO DIDDLE
(— **IMPERFECTLY**) HUDDLE
(— **IN SLOVENLY WAY**) SLUBBER
(— **INJURY**) BANE
(— **NOT**) DONT DINNA
(— **PENANCE**) SATISFY
(— **PIECEWORK**) DACKER
(— **SMARTLY**) LINK
(— **THOROUGHLY**) FLOOR
(— **WITHOUT**) LACK SPARE
FORBEAR DISPENSE
(— **WRONG**) ERR SIN MISCARRY
(— **YE**) DEE
DOABLE AGIBLE
DOBLON ISABELLA
DOBRA JO JOE OCTAVE
DOCENT TUTOR TEACHER
LECTURER
DOCILE CALM MEEK TALL TAME
TAWIE FACILE GENTLE DOCIOUS
DUCTILE DUTIFUL BIDDABLE
TOWARDLY
DOCK BOB CUT BANG CLIP MOOR
PIER QUAY RUMP SCUT BASIN
SHORE WHARF CAMBER COFFER
DOCKEN FIDDLE HAMBLE MARINA
SORREL STRUNT BOBTAIL CURTAIL
PARELLA PARELLE SHORTEN
CANAIGRE PATIENCE SHIPSIDE
DOCKAGE BERTHAGE
DOCKMACKIE VIBURNUM
DOCKYARD ARSENAL
(— **WORKMAN**) MATEY
DOCTOR DOC COOK DOPE DOSE
FAKE BRUJO HAKIM LEECH SUGAR
TREAT CROCUS DEACON EXTERN
HAIKUN HEALER INTERN MAULVI
POWWOW CROAKER KORADJI
TEACHER MEDICATE
(— **OF CANON LAW**) JCD
(— **OF LAWS**) JD
(— **UP**) COOK FAKE EYEWASH
(**PLAY** —) FIXER
(**QUACK** —) CROCUS
(**WITCH** —) BOCOR BOKOR GOOFER
GUFFER WIZARD WITCHMAN
DOCTRINAIRE ISMY
DOCTRINE ISM DOXY LEAR RULE
CREDO CREED DOGMA LIGHT MAXIM
TABLE TENET ZOISM AHIMSA
BABISM BELIEF DHARMA EGOISM
EROTIC GOSPEL HOLISM MALISM
MONISM NOETIC THEORY ACROAMA
AMIDISM ANIMISM ARTICLE ATAVISM
ATHEISM ATOMISM BAHAISM
DUALISM EGOTISM EVANGEL
KARAISM KRYPSIS MISHNAH
NEOLOGY NOETICS OPINION
PEELISM PRECEPT PROGRAM
REALISM SENSISM TRIKAYA
ACTIVISM AGATHISM ANALYTIC
ARIANISM ARYANISM BAJANISM
CHILIASM CYNICISM DARBYISM
DEVILISM DOCETISM DYNAMISM
ENERGISM FATALISM FINALISM
GOBINISM HEDONISM HYLOLOGY
IDENTISM IDEOLOGY ISLAMISM

NIHILISM PAJONISM PAMNESIA
PEJORISM POSITION POSOLOGY
PSYCHISM REGALISM RHEMATIC
SIDERISM SOLIDISM SPHERICS
TYPOLOGY UBIQUITY VITALISM
(BUDDHIST —) ANATTA ANATMAN
(CONTRARY —) HERESY
(ESOTERIC —) CABALA QABBALA
CABALISM
(EVIL —) MOLOCH
(PL.) ESOTERY SCOTISM CREDENDA
DONATISM LABADISM SCRIBISM
DOCUMENT DOC GET BILL BOND
BOOK CALL DEED FORM GETT OLLA
SEAL WRIT CHART DEMIT DIMIT
GRIEF LEASE PAPER PROOF SCRIP
SCRIT STIFF TARGE TEACH TITLE
BILLET BREVET CADJAN CAJANG
CEDULA COCKET DOCKET PATENT
RAGMAN SCHOOL SCRIPT SOURCE
SURVEY TICKET VOLUME ARCHIVE
CONDUCT DIPLOMA ELOHIST
ESCRIPT EXHIBIT INQUEST LICENSE
MISSIVE PLACARD PRECEPT
WARRANT WAYBILL WHEREAS
WRITING CONTRACT COVENANT
FURLOUGH INSTRUCT MORTGAGE
SCHEDULE SECURITY TRANSIRE
(CONDITIONAL —) SCRIP
(COPY OF —) VIDIMUS
(PL.) BUMF ARCHIVE ARCHIVES
PALAPALA
DODDER SCAD SCALD SHAKE
DODDLE DOTHER FIDEOS TOTTER
TREMBLE FLAXDROP HAIRWEED
HALEWEED HELLWEED MULBERRY
DODDERING OLD INANE INFIRM
SENILE FOOLISH
DODDER LAUREL WOEVINE
MISTLETOE
DODDIE HUMLIE
DODECANESE (— ISLAND) KOS
SYME KASOS LEROS TELOS KHALKE
LIPSOS PATMOS NISYROS
KALYMNOS
DODGE SHY BILK DUCK GAME JINK
JOUK LURK RUSE AVOID CHEAT
ELUDE EVADE FENCE FUDGE GLOSS
LURCH PARRY SHIFT SHIRK SHUNT
STALL TRICK ESCAPE WHEEZE
DECEIVE EVASION PROFFER
ARTIFICE CROTCHET GILENYIE
MALINGER SIDESTEP
DODGER FLIER FLYER HAGGLER
HANDBILL
(DRAFT —) BUSHWACK
DODGING JINK
DOE DA ROE TEG FAUN HIND NANNY
ALMOND BISCUIT
(— IN 1ST YEAR) FAWN
(BLUE —) FLIER FLYER
DOER ACTOR AGENT MAKER
AUTHOR FACTOR FEASOR WORKER
FACIENT MANAGER ATTORNEY
EXECUTOR
(— OF ODD JOBS) JACK
DOES S DOTH DUSE
(— NOT) DONT DISNA DOESNT
DOFF OFF DAFF VAIL AVALE DOUSE

DOWSE STRIP DIVEST REMOVE
UNDRESS
DOFFER DRUM DUFFER
DOFFING CAP
DOG CUR MUT PUG PUP YAP ALAN
ALCO CHOW DANE FAUS GOER KIYI
MONG MUTT PAWL STAG TIKE TRAY
TYKE ALAND ALANT ARGOS BAWTY
BEDOG BESET BOUCH BOXER
CALEB CANID CORGI DERBY DODGE
HOUND HUSKY LIMER PELON
POOCH PUPPY RACHE RAKER
RATCH SLING SPITZ STALK WHELP
AFGHAN BANDOG BASSET BAWTIE
BEAGLE BELTON BORZOI BOSTON
BOWWOW BRIARD BUFFER CANINE
COCKER COLLIE COONER DANCER
DETENT DRIVER ESKIMO FINDER
GUNDOG HEADER HEELER HUNTER
JOWLER KELPIE KENNET MISSET
POODLE RANGER RATTER SALUKI
SEIZER SETTER SHOUGH SIRIUS
SUSSEX TALBOT TOLLER TOWSER
VIZSLA YAPPER YAUPER YELPER
BASENJI BOARDER BULLDOG
CARRIER COURSER CRAMPON
CREEPER DOGGESS DROPPER
GRIFFON HARRIER LURCHER
MALTESE MASTIFF MONGREL
OWTCHAR POINTER SCOTTIE
SKIRTER SLEUGHI SPANIEL
SPORTER STARTER TERRIER
TUMBLER WHIPPET YAPSTER
AIREDALE ALEUTANT ALSATIAN
CERBERUS CYNHYENA DEMIWOLF
DOBERMAN ELKHOUND FISSIPED
FOXHOUND KEESHOND LABRADOR
LANDSEER LONGTAIL MALEMUTE
MALINOIS PAPILLON PEKINESE
SAMOYEDE SEALYHAM SHEPHERD
SIBERIAN SPRINGER TURNSPIT
VERMINER WATCHDOG WATERRUG
(— OF LATHE) DRIVER
(— TRAINED AS DECOY) TOLLER
(BIRD —) BOLTER
(CHAINED —) BANDOG
(ESKIMO —) HUSKY SIWASH
(FARM —) KOMONDOR
(FEMALE —) GYP SLUT BITCH
DOGGESS
(FOXLIKE —) COLPEO
(HOUSE —) WAP WAPP
(HUNGARIAN —) KUVASZ
(HUNTING —) ALAN BRACH RACHE
RATCH ALAUND BASSET HUNTER
KENNET LUCERN RACCHE SALUKI
SEIZER SETTER SLOUGH COURSER
DROPPER HARRIER POINTER
STRIKER
(JAPANESE —) AKITA
(LAP —) MESSAN SHOUGH
(LARGE —) DANE TOWSER MASTIFF
KOMONDOR
(LIKE A —) CYNIC
(LONG-HAIRED —) ALCO SHOCK
(MONGREL —) CUR DEMIWOLF
(NON-BARKING —) BASENJI
(PARTI-COLORED —) PIE PYE
(PET —) MINX LAPDOG MOPPET

(PUG —) MOPS
(PUNCH'S —) TOBY
(SHAGGY —) RUG OWTCHAH
(SHEEP —) CUR COLLIE KELPIE
BEARDIE MALINOIS SHEPHERD
(SMALL —) TOY FICE FIST DOGGY
FEIST PIPER DOGGIE AMERTOY
SPANIEL PAPILLON PEKINESE
(VICIOUS —) TAEPO
(WATCH —) CUR GARM GARMR
(WILD —) ADJAG DHOLE DINGO
GUARA JACKAL AGOUARA
CIMARRON
(YELPING —) WAPPET
(PL.) DOGGERY
DOGBANE KENDIR KENDYR ECHITES
FLYTRAP ALSTONIA MILKWEED
DOGBOAT PIG
DOGCART GADDER TUMTUM
BOUNDER GADABOUT
DOG COLLAR TRASH
DOG DAYS CANICULE
DOG EAR LEATHER
DOG FENNEL HOGWEED
DOGFIGHT SCRAMBLE
DOGFISH DOG HOE HUSS TOPE
FLAKE HOUND HURSE MANGO
TOPER DAGGAR GALEID MORGAY
BONEDOG GABBACK SPURDOG
TRIAKID GRAYFISH SEAHOUND
DOGGED DOUR SULLEN DOGGISH
DOGLIKE STUBBORN
DOGGEREL NOMINY TRIVIA DIGGREL
SINGSONG
DOGGONE BLESSED DOWNGONE
DOGIE LEPPY STRAY
DOG KEEPER FEWTERER
DOGLIKE CYNIC CYNOID DOGGED
DOGMA CREED TENET DICTUM
DOCTRINE DOCUMENT
DOGMATIC POSITIVE CONFIDENT
DOGMATISM BOWWOW
DOGMATIST PHILODOX
DOG POUND GREENYARD
DOG ROSE BUCKY CANKER
BEDEGUAR DOGBERRY
DOG SALMON CHUM KETA MORGAY
DOGFISH
DOGSHORE DOG DAGGER
DOG'S MERCURY SAPWORT
DOG SNAPPER JOCU
DOGSTAIL BENT
DOGWOOD OSIER SUMAC CORNEL
CORNUS GAITER WIDBIN BARBASCO
FISHWOOD
DOILY MAT TIDE TIDY NAPKIN
DOING ACT DEED FACT STIR EVENT
ACTION FUNCTION PRACTIVE
(PL.) FARE GEAR
DOIT DODKIN
DOLE LOT ALMS DEAL DOOL GIFT
GOAL METE PART VAIL ALLOT
FRAUD GRIEF GUILE MOURN SHARE
DECEIT GRIEVE RELIEF SORROW
CHARITY DEALING DESTINY
HANDOUT PAYMENT PORTION
BOUNDARY DIMENSUM DISPENSE
DIVISION GRATUITY LANDMARK
PITTANCE

DOLEFUL SAD DOWY DOWIE DREAR
HEAVY DISMAL DOOLFU DREARY
FUNEST RUEFUL FLEBILE
DOLESOME DOLOROUS FUNESTAL
MOURNFUL TRAGICAL
DOLL TOY BABE BABY MOLL ARRAY
DOLLY PUPPE DOLLIE KEWPIE
MAIDEN MAUMET MOPPET MUNECA
POPPET POUPEE PUPPET KACHINA
KATCINA KATCHINA MISTRESS
(— UP) SWANK
(PASTEBOARD —) PANTINE
DOLLAR BALL BEAN BONE BUCK
CASE DURO FISH ROCK SCAD SKIN
SPOT ADOBE BERRY DALER EAGLE
PLONK PLUNK WHEEL GOURDE
PATACA DAALDER SMACKER
FROGSKIN PATACOON SIMOLEON
(SILVER —) SINKER
(SPANISH —) COB DURO COBBE
(THOUSAND —S) GEE THOU GRAND
DOLLARFISH SHINER MOONFISH
STARFISH
DOLLY DRAB HOBBY PEGGY PUNCH
SWAGE MAIDEN FOLLOWER
MISTRESS SLATTERN
DOLLYMAN BUCKER
DOLLYWAY DOCK
DOLMEN SENAM TOLMEN CROMMEL
CROMLECH MEGALITH
DOLOMITE ANKERITE PEARLSPAR
DOLOR CALOR GRIEF SORROW
ANGUISH SADNESS DISTRESS
MOURNING
DOLOROUS SAD DISMAL DOLEFUL
GRIEVOUS PATHETIC
DOLPHIN INIA SUSU BOUTO WHALE
DORADO KILLER PALACH TURSIO
BOLLARD COWFISH PELLOCK
PULLOCK SNUFFER CETACEAN
MAHIMAHI MUTILATE PORPOISE
DOLT ASS OAF PUT ASSE CALF
CHUB CLOD COOF DULT FOOL GOFF
MOKE PEAK STUB CHUMP DOBBY
DUMMY DUNCE FUNGE IDIOT NUMPS
PATCH THICK BEFOOL CUDDEN
DOODLE DULTIE HOBBIL OXHEAD
BLUNTIE DAWCOCK DULLARD
JACKASS SCHNOOK BONEHEAD
BOSTHOON CLODPATE DUMBBELL
IMBECILE LUNKHEAD MACAROON
MOONCALF NUMSKULL
DOLTISH DULL STUPID FOOLISH
PEAKISH SOTTISH TOMFOOL
BESOTTED BLOCKISH DOLTLIKE
DOMAIN LAND BOUND BOURN
REALM SCOPE STATE WORLD
BARONY BOURNE COUNTY DEMAIN
EMPERY EMPIRE ESTATE SPHERE
DEMESNE EARLDOM BIRTHDOM
DOMINION LORDSHIP PROVINCE
SEIGNORY STAROSTY
(— OF SULTAN) SOLDAN
(— OF THE UNCONSCIOUS)
SHADOWLAND
(MATHEMATICAL —) FIELD
(NETHER —) HELL
(TRANSCENDENT —) HEAVEN
(WOMAN'S —) DISTAFF

DOMBEYA ASSONIA
DOME CAP CIMA TYPE CROWN
VAULT COCKLE CUPOLA THOLOS
CALOTTE EDIFICE CIMBORIO
HEMIDOME
(— OVER TOMB) WELI
(BUDDHIST —) TOPE
(OBSERVATION —) BLISTER
(SNOW-CAPPED —) CALOTTE
DOMER CLASPER
DOMESTIC HIND HOME MAID MOZO
DOMAL TABBY FAMILY HAMEIL
HAMELT HEYDUC HOMELY HOMISH
HOUSAL INLAND INMATE INWARD
MENIAL NATIVE FAMILIC HEYDUCK
SCALDER SERVANT FAMILIAR
HOMEBRED HOMEMADE INTIMATE
(PL.) FOLK
DOMESTICALLY ONSHORE
DOMESTICATE TAME ENTAME
AMENAGE RECLAIM CIVILIZE
DOMESTICATED TAME GENTLE
INWARD DOMESTIC FAMILIAR
DOMICILE CRIB HOME SHED ABODE
HOUSE MENAGE DWELLING
DOMINANCE SWAY INFLUENCE
DOMINANT BOSSY CHIEF FIFTH
TENOR RULING SOVRAN CENTRAL
REGNANT SUPREME DOMINULE
SUPERIOR
DOMINATE TOP HAVE RULE CHARM
REIGN COERCE DIRECT GOVERN
VASSAL BEWITCH COMMAND
CONTROL ENVELOP BESTRIDE
DOMINEER OVERSWAY OVERTONE
DOMINATING SUPERIOR
BREATHLESS
DOMINATION EMPIRE CONTROL
STRINGS BOVARISM BOVARYSM
DOMINION
DOMINEER BOSS BRAG LORD RULE
BULLY FEAST REVEL TOWER
COMPEL COMMAND SWAGGER
DOMINATE OVERBEAR OVERLEAD
OVERLORD
(— OVER) RIDE HECTOR
DOMINEERING SURLY LORDLY
HAUGHTY ARROGANT DESPOTIC
MASTERLY
DOMINICAN JACOBIN JACOBITE
PREACHER PREDICANT

DOMINICAN REPUBLIC
BAY: OCOA YUMA NEIBA RINCON
SAMANA ISABELA CALDERAS
ESCOCESA
CAPE: BEATA FALSO CABRON
ENGANO CAUCEDO ISABELA
MACORIS
CAPITAL: SANTODOMINGO
COIN: ORO PESO
INDIAN: TAINO
ISLAND: BEATA SAONA ALTOVELO
CATALINA HISPANIOLA
LOWLAND: CIBAO
MEASURE: ONA TAREA FANEGA
MOUNTAIN: TINA GALLO DUARTE

MOUNTAINS: NEIBA BAHORUCO
ORIENTAL
RIVER: YUNA OZAMA
TOWN: AZUA BANI MOCA PENA
POLO BONAO COTUI NAGUA
NEIBA NIZAO SOSUA HIGUEY
OVIEDO SANCHEZ BARAHONA
SANTIAGO
VALLEY: REAL NEYBA

DOMINIE MASTER PASTOR
DOMINION RULE SWAY CROWN
REALM REIGN DITION DOMAIN
EMPERY EMPIRE REGNUM CONTROL
DIOCESE DYNASTY KHANATE
POUSTIE REGENCY CALIFATE
IMPERIUM LORDSHIP SEIGNORY
SIGNORIA SOVRANTY
(PL.) DUCHY
DOMINO DIE BONE CARD FIVE MASK
TILE BLANK JETON STONE DOUBLE
JETTON MATADOR VENETIAN
(FIRST — PLAYED) SET
(PL.) BONEYARD
DOM PEDRO SNOOZER
DON WEAR ARRAY DRESS ENDUE
INDUE THROW ASSUME CLOTHE
INVEST ADDRESS NOBLEMAN
DONATE GIE GIFT GIVE BESTOW
PRESENT
DONATION GIFT GRANT DONATIO
PRESENT DONATIVE
(—S RECEIVED BY SINGERS) CARL
DONE GAR DEEN OVER BAKED
ENDED GIVEN COOKED THROUGH
FINISHED
(— BY WORD OF MOUTH) PAROL
PAROLE
(— CARELESSLY) SCAMBLING
(— FOR) GONE SUNK KAPUT
KAPUTT FINISHED
(— IN FAITH) AF
(— IN PLAIN SIGHT) BRAZEN
(— POORLY) BOTCHY
(— TOGETHER) CONCERTED
(— WITH) BY
(— WITHOUT DELIBERATION) SNAP
(— WRONG WAY) AWK
(TO BE —) PASS
DONEE DONATOR HERITOR
RECEIVER
DONJON KEEP ROCCA DUNGEON
DONKEY ASS BUSS DONK FUSS
MOKE BURRO CHUMP CUDDY DICKY
EQUID GENET GUDDA HINNY HORSE
JENNY NEDDY CUDDLE DICKEY
JENNET ONAGER ASINEGO
BUSSOCK FUSSOCK JACKASS
LONGEAR
DONKEY ENGINE DOCTOR DONKEY
ROADER YARDER DOLLBEER
DONOR GIVER DONATOR
DO-NOTHING DONNOT DONOUGHT
FAINEANT
DONUM GIVER DEUNAM
DOODAD DODAD DOODAB DOFUNNY
GIMCRACK JIMCRACK
DOOM KER LAW LOT DAMN FATE

RUIN CURSE DEATH JUDGE DECREE
DEVOTE STEVEN CONDEMN DESTINE
DESTINY FORTUNE STATUTE
DECISION FOREDOOM SENTENCE
DOOMED FEY DEAD DONE FATAL
DAMNED FORLORN ACCURSED
FINISHED
DOOM PALM DOUM
DOOMSMAN LAWMAN
DOOR LID DROP EXIT FOLD GATE
HECK SHUT TRAP ENTRY HATCH
JANUA VALVE JIGGER PORTAL
RADDLE WICKET BARRIER
DOORWAY INGRESS OPENING
OUTDOOR PASSAGE POSTERN
ANTEPORT ENTRANCE FOREDOOR
POSTICUM SERVIDOR STOPPING
TRAVERSE
(— **IN MINE**) STOPPING
(— **OF ASH PIT**) ARCH
(— **OF MASONIC LODGE**) TILE
(**AIRPLANE** —) CLAMSHELL
(**HALF** —) HECK HATCH
(**ROMAN** —**S**) FORES
(**SLIDING** —) SHUT SHOJI FUSUMA
TRAVERSE
(**STORM** —) DINGLE
(**STRONG** —) OAK
(**TRAP** —) SLOT SCRUTE VAMPIRE
VAMPYRE
DOORFRAME BUCK
DOORHEAD DERNER
DOORKEEPER TILER TILIA USHER
DURWAN PORTER WARDEN
DOORMAN JANITOR OSTIARY
DOORWARD HUISSIER JANITRIX
PORTRESS WISKINKY
DOOR KNOCKER HAMMER RAPPER
DOOR LATCH SNECK HAGGADAY
DOORMAN FOOTMAN HALLMAN
DOORWARD
DOORMAT COCOMAT
DOORPOST DURN JAMB PIER POST
ALETTE POSTEL
DOORSILL SOIL
DOORSTOP BUMPER HOLDBACK
DOORWAY DOOR EXIT PORTAL
OPENING
DOPATTA UPARNA DOOPUTTY
DOPE HOP BOOB DRUG GOFF GOON
GOOP BOOBY OPIUM PASTE HEROIN
INSIDE OPIATE LOWDOWN PREDICT
STUPEFY NARCOTIC
DOPER GREASER
DOR BEE DORR JOKE MOCK BONGO
CLOCK DORRE JOKER SCOFF TRICK
BEETLE DRONER BUFFOON DECEIVE
MOCKERY
DORADO CUIR XIPHIAS GOLDFISH
DORBEETLE DOR CLOCK DRONER
BUZZARD BUMCLOCK
DORIS (**BROTHER AND HUSBAND OF**
—) NEREUS
(**FATHER OF** —) OCEANUS
(**MOTHER OF** —) TETHYS
DORMANCY TORPOR ABEYANCE
DORMANT FIXED ASLEEP LATENT
TORPID RESTING SLEEPER INACTIVE
SLEEPING CONNIVENT

DORMER WINDOW LUCOMB
MEMBER DORMANT EYEBROW
LUCARNE LUTHERN
DORMITORY DORM HALL HOUSE
DORMER DORTER HOSTEL BULLPEN
COLLEGE DORTOUR CUBATORY
QUARTERS
DORMOUSE LOIR DRYAD LEROT
GLIRID SLEEPER
DORNICK DONEY LINEN DARNEX
DONACK DONNICK
DORPER DORSIAN
DORSAL NOTAL DORSER DOSSER
TERGAL ABAXIAL HANGING
SUPERIOR
DORSUM BACK
DOSAGE (**SCIENCE OF** —)
POSOLOGY
DOSE BOLE DOST SHOT BROMO
DATIO DOSIS DRAFT STORE TREAT
DATION DOCTOR DOSAGE DRENCH
POTION BOOSTER BROMIDE
CAPSULE DRAUGHT QUANTITY
(**NARCOTIC** —) LOCUS BINDLE
LOCUST
DOSS BOW DOS KNOT TUFT BUNCH
DOSSERET PULVINO
DOT SET CLOT DOTE LUMP MOTE
PECK SPOT STAR TICK COVER
DOWER DOWRY POINT PRICK SPECK
BULLET CENTER CENTRE DOTLET
PERIOD STIGME TITTLE TOCHER
PUNCTUM PUNCTUS SPECKLE
SPOTTLE STIPPLE FLYSPECK
PARTICLE SPRINKLE
(— **IN CODE**) DIT
(— **ON FOREHEAD**) BOTTU
(— **ON PATCH OF DIFFERENT**
COLOR) ISLET
(**BLACK** —) DARTROSE
(**PL.**) LEADERS
DOTAGE DOTE FOLLY DRIVEL
SENILITY TWICHILD
DOTARD DOTER SILLY DOTANT
SENILE DOTTREL DOTTEREL
IMBECILE LIRIPIPE LIRIPOOP
DOTCHIN STEELYARD
DOTE ROT DOVE DOZE FOND LIKE
LOVE ADORE DECAY ENDOW
BESTOW DOTAGE DOTARD DRIVEL
STUPOR IMBECILE
DOTING FON FOND GAGA DOTAGE
PAWING
DOTTED SEME SEMEED TICKED
TOUCHY SPOTTED PUNCTATE
SPECKLED STIPPLED STELLATED
(— **SWISS**) LAPPET
DOTTER SPOTTER
DOTTEREL DUPE GULL WIND
PLOVER DOTTREL MORINEL
DOTTY TOTY CRAZY TOTTY FEEBLE
SPOTTY
DOUBLE KA BOW PLY DUAL FOLD
SORE TWIN CRACK DUPLE FETCH
ROUND SOSIE BIFOLD BINARY
BINATE DOPPIO DUPLEX MIDDLE
DIPLOID DOUBLET TWOFOLD
BIVALENT GEMINATE
(— **IMPRESSION**) MACKLE

(— **IN POKER**) STRADDLE
(— **MUSICAL NOTES**) AUGMENT
(— **UP**) BUCK JACKKNIFE
(**PHANTOM** —) FETCH
DOUBLE BASSOON FAGOTTONE
DOUBLE CHIN CHOLLER
DOUBLECROSS BITCH CHEAT
BETRAY DECEIVE SWINDLE
BUSINESS
DOUBLE-CROSSER RAT HEEL
DOUBLED GEMEL GEMINOUS
DOUBLE DAGGER DIESIS
DOUBLE-DEALING DECEIT
DUPLICITY
DOUBLE FLUTE DIAULOS
DOUBLENESS DUALITY PLENITUDE
DOUBLE-RIPPER BOBSLED
BOBSLEIGH
DOUBLE-RUNNER SKATE
DOUBLET SNIFF DOUBLE DUPLET
PALTOCK PLACCATE POURPOINT
DOUBLETREE EVENER SPREADER
DOUBLING LAP FOLD HEAD LOOP
(— **OF THE BLIND**) STRADDLE
DOUBLOON ONZA
DOUBT FEAR WEIR DEMUR DREAD
DWERE QUERY WAVER BALANCE
DIFFIDE DUBIATE DUBIETY SCRUPLE
SKEPSIS SUSPECT SWITHER
UMBRAGE DISTRUST DUBITATE
HESITATE MISTRUST QUESTION
STAGGERS MISLIPPEN
DOUBTER CYNIC SKEPTIC
DUBITANTE
DOUBTFUL JUBUS DOUBTY UNSURE
DUBIOUS FEARFUL JEALOUS
PERHAPS WILSOME BOGGLISH
DREADFUL JUBEROUS PERILOUS
WAVERING
DOUBTING DUBIOUS DUBITANT
DOUBTLESS WITTERLY
DOUCEUR BONUS POURBOIRE
DOUCHE RINSE EYEWASH
DOUGH CASH DUFF CRUST DAIGH
MONEY PASTE PUPPY CHANGE
HALLAH NOODLE SPONGE BRIOCHE
MANDLEN TEIGLACH
(**BISCUIT** —) CAKE
(**BREAD** —) SPONGE
(**FERMENTING** —) LEAVEN
(**FRIED** —) SPUD
(**NOODLE** —) FARFEL FERFEL
DOUGHNUT NUT SINK DONUT
CYMBAL SINKER CRULLER FATCAKE
NUTCAKE OLYCOOK OLYKOEK
SIMBALL TWISTER BISMARCK
FASNACHT
(**SHAPED LIKE** —) TOROIDAL
DOUGHTY FELL PREU TALL BRAVE
VALIANT INTREPID
DOUGHY DUNCH SODDEN
DOUR DERN GLUM GRIM HARD SOUR
ROUGH STERN GLOOMY MOROSE
SEVERE STRONG SULLEN OMINOUS
TACITURN
DOUSE BEAT BLOW DOFF DUCK
QUIT STOW CEASE DOWSE RINSE
SOUSE DRENCH PLUNGE SLUICE

STRIKE STROKE IMMERSE
DOWNPOUR
DOUZEPER ANSEIS PALADIN
DOVE DOO DOW DOZE KUKU JONAH
CULVER CUSHAT JEMIMA PIGEON
COLUMBA DOVELET LAUGHER
NAMAQUA SLUMBER DOVELING
RINGDOVE
(— **SOUND**) CURR
(**GROUND** —) ROLA
(**RING** —) TOOZOO
(**ROCK** —) SOD
(**SCALE** —) INCA
DOVECOTE DOOCOT LOUVER
DOVECOT DOWCOTE PIGEONRY
DOVEKIE AUK ALLE BULL ROTCH
ROTGE DOVEKEY BULLBIRD
DOVELIKE
DOVETAIL COG JAG JAGG TENON
DOWDINESS FRUMPERY
DOWDY POKY FRUMP POKEY TACKY
BLOWZY SHABBY STODGY UNTIDY
FRUMPISH SLOVENLY
DOWEL PEG PIN COAK STUD SPRIG
JOGGLE PINTLE DULEDGE
DOWER DOS DOWRY ENDOW
TOCHER DOARIUM PORTION
HERITAGE MARITAGE
DOWITCHER SNIPE DRIVER SLEEPER
GRAYBACK GREYBACK LONGBEAK
DOWN HUP BETE CAST DOON DOWL
FELL FLIX FLUE FUZZ HILL LINT
SOUR ADOWN BELOW DOWLE EIDER
FLOOR FLUFF BEDOWN FRIEZE
LANUGO PAPPUS HANDOUT HILLOCK
PLUMAGE DOWNLAND
(— **AND OUT**) QUISBY
(— **AT THE HEEL**) SLIPSHOD
(— **THAT WAY**) DOWNBY DOWNBYE
(— **THE LINE**) ALONG
(**FAR** —) DEEP DEEPLY
(**FARTHEST** —) BOTTOMMOST
(**STRAIGHT** —) DOWNRIGHT
DOWNBEAT THESIS
DOWNCAST BAD SAD DOWN ABJECT
GLOOMY HANGING DEJECTED
HOPELESS
DOWNFALL PIT FALL FATE RUIN
TRAP ABYSS FINISH DESCENT
ECLIPSE UNDOING COLLAPSE
DOWNCOME
DOWNFEED OVERHEAD
DOWNFLOW VAIL DEFLUX
DOWNFOLD SADDLE DOWNWARP
DOWNHILL DOWNDALE
DOWNPOUR POUR RAIN DOUSE
DOWSE FLOOD SPILL SPOUT
DELUGE TORRENT CATARACT
DOWNRIGHT FAIR FLAT PURE RANK
BLANK BLUNT PLAIN PLUMB ROUND
SHEER STARK ARRANT DIRECT
FAIRLY STURDY ABSOLUTE
EVENDOWN POSITIVE THOROUGH
DOWNSPOUT SPOUT DOWNPIPE
DOWNTAKE
DOWNSTAIRS BELOW
DOWNSTROKE DOWNBEAT
DOWNSWING DOLDRUMS
DOWNWARD ADOWN BELOW LOWER

PRONE DEORSUM DOWNWITH
(— **ON ONE SIDE**) SIDEWAYS
DOWNWIND LEEWARD
DOWNY SOFT FLUEY MOSSY NAPPY
PILAR PLUMY QUIET CALLOW
FLEDGY FLOSSY FLUFFY PILARY
PLACID COTTONY CUNNING
KNOWING SOOTHING
DOWRY DOS DOT GIFT DOWER
SULKA DOWAGE TALENT PORTION
DOWSE WITCH
DOXOLOGY GLORIA KADDISH
DOXY WENCH HARLOT
DOYEN DEAN DOYENNE
DOZE NAP NOD ROT DORM DOTE
DOVE DECAY DOVER SLEEP SLOOM
CATNAP DROWSE MUDDLE SNOOZE
MEMENTO PERPLEX SLUMBER
SNOOZLE STUPEFY
DOZEN DIZZEN DOSAIN
(**FIVE** —) TALLY
(**TWO** —) THRAVE
DOZING DOGSLEEP
DRAB BOX DAW FOX SAD DELL
DRUG DULL BESOM BLEAK DINGY
DOLLY GRAVE GRAZE HEAVY
WENCH WHORE FRUMPY MALKIN
POISON STODGY PROSAIC SUBFUSC
DOLLYMOP EVERYDAY POMPLESS
(**CHAETURA** —) BEAR
DRABBLE DRAGGLE
DRACHM DRAM
DRACO ANGUIS DRAGON
DRAFT NIP SIP CHIT DOSE DRAG
DRAM DRAW GLUT GULF GUST ITEM
LEVY PLAN PLOT SUCK SWIG TOOT
WORK BLAST CHECK DRINK EPURE
SLOCK SWILL SWIPE TAPER WRITE
DESIGN DRENCH GODOWN MINUTE
POTION REDACT RETURN SCHEME
SCROLL SKETCH WAUCHT WAUGHT
ABBOZZO DRAUGHT DRAWING
OUTLINE PATTERN PROJECT
BEVERAGE POTATION PROTOCOL
(— **OF A VESSEL**) GAGE GAUGE
(— **OF AIR**) COOKE
(— **OF COMPOSITION**) SCORE
(— **OF LAW**) BILL
(— **OF PATTERN**) STRIP
(— **OFF**) SHED
(**HEAVY** —) WHITTER
(**LARGE** —) SCOUR CAROUSE
(**MIDDAY** —) NOONING
(**ORIGINAL** —) PROTOCOL
(**ROUGH** —) BROUILLON SCANTLING
(**SLEEPING** —) DORTER
(**SMALL** —) NIP SIP SUCK TIFF TIFT
DRAFTER HORSER
DRAFTSMAN DRAWER TRACER
TIPPLER
DRAG DOG LAG DRUG HONE HOOK
KITE SHOE SKID SLUR TOLE TOLL
CREEP DEVIL DRAWL DRIFT FLOAT
LURRY NOWEL PLUCK RALLY SLIDE
SNAKE SWEEP TEASE TRAIL TRAIN
TRAWL TRICE DAGGLE DROGUE
LINGER REMORA SCHOOL TAIGLE
TRAYNE DRAGBAR DRAGGLE
GRAPNEL GRAPPLE SCHLEPP

SKIDPAN ARRASTRA DRAGSHOE
(— **ALONG**) LUG CRAWL SHOOL
TRAYNE TRACHLE TRAUCHLE
(— **CARELESSLY**) HIKE
(— **DOWN**) DEGRADE
(— **FEET**) SLODGE
(— **FORCIBLY**) SNAKE
(— **HOME CARCASS OF GAME**)
TUMP
(— **IN DEEP WATER**) CREEP
(— **JERKILY**) SNIG
(— **LOGS**) SKID
(— **OFF**) HARRY
(— **OUT**) DRAWL
(**PLANK** —) RUBBER
DRAGGING LEADEN
(— **DEAD BULL FROM RING**)
ARRASTRE
DRAGGLE LAG DRAIL DAGGLE
DRABBLE
DRAGNET FLUE TRAIN TRAWL
DRAWNET TRAINEL
DRAGON AHI LUNG WORM DRAKE
RAHAB NIDHOG VRITRA WYVERN
BASILISK DRAGONET NIDHOGGR
NITHHOGG
(— **WITH 7 HEADS**) HYDRA
(**SEA** —) QUAVIVER
DRAGONET FOX ILLECK FOXFISH
GOWDNIE GURNARD JUGULAR
SCULPIN LORICATE QUAVIVER
DRAGONFLY NAIAD SKIMMER
LIBELLULA
DRAGON TREE DRACAENA
DRAGROPE DRAG GUSS
DRAIN DRY FRY GAN GAW SAP SEW
TOP BUZZ COUP DAIL DALE DELF
DIKE DRAG DRAW GOUT GRIP GURT
LADE LODE MILK SIKE SINK SOAK
SUFF SUMP TEEM TILE BLEED
BUNNY CANAL DELFT DRAFT DREEN
DRILL DROVE EMPTY FLEET GROOP
GULLY LEECH RHINE SEUCH SEUGH
SEWER SHORE SIVER STELL
EMULGE FILTER FURROW GUZZLE
RIGGOT SHEUCH SHEUGH SIPHON
SPONGE SWOUGH SYPHON TRENCH
TROGUE TROUGH ZANJON ACEQUIA
ALBERCA CAROUSE CARRIER
CHANNEL CULVERT DEPLETE
DRAUGHT EXHAUST GRINDLE
GRIPPLE SCUPPER ZANJONA
CANALIZE CARRIAGE SINKHOLE
SUBDRAIN THURROCK
(— **DRY**) JIB
(— **IN FEN**) LEAM
(— **IN MINE**) SOUGH
(— **IN STABLE**) GROOP
(**COVERED** —) THURROCK
(**OPEN** —) SIVER STELL
(**SMALL** —) TRONE
DRAINAGE ADIT SAUR SOCK
SULLAGE SUMPAGE
DRAINAGEWAY DRAW
DRAINING SEEPAGE DRAINAGE
EMULGENT
DRAINPIPE SINK SHELL WHELM
LEADER QUELME
DRAKE STAG STAIG DRAKELET

DRAM GO NIP MITE SLUG TIFT
DRAFT DRINK SOPIE CALKER
DRACHM JIGGER CAULKER SNIFTER
MERIDIAN POTATION QUANTITY
(— **OF LIQUOR**) TOT SLUG SNIFTER
(— **OF SPIRITS**) NOBBLER
DRAMA RAS AUTO MIME PLAY LEGIT
OPERA COMEDY NATAKA SCENES
SOAPER TRAGIC ATELLAN COMEDIA
HISTORY PROVERB THEATRE
TRAGEDY DUODRAMA MONODRAM
OPERETTA PASTORAL
(**DANCE** —) KATHAKALI
(**JAPANESE** —) NO KABUKI
(**MUSICAL** —) OPERA SAYNETE
OPERETTA
DRAMATIC WILD VIVID SCENIC
THESPIAN
(— **REPRESENTATION**) WAYANG
DRAMATIST OG ACTOR IBSENITE
DRAMSHOP GROGSHOP
DRAPE HANG ADORN COVER CRAPE
WEAVE CURTAIN FESTOON HANGING
VALANCE
DRAPED BEHUNG
DRAPER TAILOR LINENMAN
DRAPERY SWAG BAIZE DRAPE
SCENE CURTAIN REREDOS VALANCE
MOURNING
(— **ON BEDSTEAD**) PAND
(**PIECE OF** —) HANGING
DRAPING BLOUSE DRAPERY
DRASTIC DIRE HARSH EXTREME
RADICAL RIGOROUS
(**NOT** —) BLAND
DRAT RABBIT DOGGONE
DRATTED BLESSED
DRAUGHT (ALSO SEE DRAFT) SLUG
OENOMEL
DRAVIDIAN GOND KOTA TODA TULU
ARAVA COORG GONDI KHOND KLING
MALTO ORAON TAMIL ANDHRA
BADAGA BIRHOR BRAHUI KODAGU
KURUKH TELEGU TELUGU COLLERY
DRAVIDA TAMILIC KANARESE
TAMILIAN
DRAW LUG TEE TIE TOW TUG DRAG
DUCT HALE HAUL LADE LIMN LINE
LURE PULL RAKE SPAN TILL TIRE
TOLL TREK VENT CATCH DRAFT
DRILL EDUCE ENDUE EXACT HEAVE
PAINT SKINK TRACE TRAIN TRECK
ALLURE BUCKET DEDUCE DEPICT
DERIVE DESIGN DEVISE ELICIT
ENGAGE ENTICE INDUCE INHALE
SELECT SKETCH STRIKE ATTRACT
BEGUILE CONTOUR DETRACT
DOGFALL DRAUGHT EXTRACT
INSPIRE PORTRAY SCUMBLE
INSCRIBE INVEIGLE OUTBRAID
STANDOFF
(— **A CARD**) CUT
(— **AIR**) BREATHE
(— **ALONG**) TRACK TRAIN
(— **APART**) REAM DIVEL DIDUCE
DIVERGE
(— **AT A PIPE**) SHOOH SHAUGH
(— **AWAY**) ARACE DRAFT ABDUCT
ARACHE DRAUGHT ENTRAIN

DISTRACT
(— **AWKWARDLY**) SCRAWL
(— **BACK FROM**) BLENCH FLINCH
TORFEL TORFLE DETRECT
(— **BACK LIPS**) GRIN
(— **BACK**) FADE REVEL START
WINCE ARREAR RETIRE REVOKE
SHRINK CRINKLE RECLAIM WITHTEE
(— **BOLT**) SLOT
(— **BY SUCTION**) ASPIRATE
(— **DEEP BREATH**) SUSPIRE
(— **DRINK**) BIRL
(— **EARTH AROUND**) HILL
(— **FORTH**) EDUCE FETCH ELICIT
DEPROME EXHAUST
(— **ON**) INDUE INDUCE SOLICIT
(— **OUT**) MILK SLUB EXACT SKINK
TRACT ELICIT EXHALE EXTEND
PRODUCE PROLONG LENGTHEN
(— **TIGHT**) FRAP THRAP STRAIN
(— **TOGETHER**) COWL LACE COART
GATHER
(— **UP**) FORM MAKE HUCKLE INKNIT
UPHALE
DRAWBACK OUT LETDOWN
TAKEOFF DISCOUNT PULLBACK
DRAWBAR DRAGBAR BULLNOSE
DRAWLINK SLIPRAIL
DRAWBRIDGE PONTLEVIS
DRAWEE ACCEPTER
DRAWER TILL LIMNER LOCKER
TILLER ENTERER INTAKER SHUTTLE
(— **OF WATER**) GIBEONITE
(**COAL** —) PUTTER
(**TYPEWRITER** —) BED
DRAWER-DOWN KNOBBLER
DRAWER-IN ENTERER HEALDER
HEDDLER
DRAWER-OFF RACKER
DRAWERS PANTS SHORTS LININGS
PANTIES SHALWAR CALSOUNS
CALZOONS SHINTYAN SHULWAURS
DRAWGATE SLACKER
DRAWING DRAW CHALK DRAFT
ENVOI EPURE SEPTA TUSHE
CRAYON DESIGN DETAIL FIGURE
FUSAIN SKETCH CARTOON CROQUIS
DIAGRAM DRAUGHT HAULING
ISOTYPE PULLING TOUSCHE
CHARCOAL CROSSING DOODLING
FREEHAND FROTTAGE HATCHING
LINEWORK SANGUINE SPECULUM
STICKMAN TRACTION TRANSFER
TRICKING
(— **IN**) INDRAFT
(— **OF LOTS**) BALLOT
(— **OUT**) BATTUE
(**COMIC** —) CARTOON DROLLERY
(**SIDEWALK** —) SCREEVE
DRAWING-IN DRAW ENTERING
DRAWKNIFE SHAVE JIGGER
DRAWL DRANT DRATE DRUNT TRAIN
LOITER PROLATE
DRAWN DRAFT STREIT DRAUGHT
GRAPHIC HAGGARD
(— **APART**) DISTRACT
(— **AWAY**) ABSTRACT
(— **CLOSE**) STRICT
(— **OFF**) DRAINED

(— **OUT**) DREE DREICH DREIGH
EXTENDED
DRAWPLATE AGATE FLATTER
DRAWSHEET TYMPAN
DRAWSTRING LATCH STRING
DRAY CART LORRY SCOOT SLOOP
WAGON CAMION JIGGER SLOVEN
WHEERY
DREAD AWE DREE FEAR FRAY FUNK
WARD WERE ANGST AWFUL DOUBT
GRISE TIMOR ADREAD AGRISE
DISMAY ESCHEW HORROR TERROR
ANXIETY DISMISS DRIDDER
REDOUBT AFFRIGHT DREDDOUR
GASTNESS MISDREAD TERRIBLE
DREADED AWESOME BEDREAD
DREADFUL DIRE AWFUL CRUEL
DISMAL GRISLY HORRID AWESOME
CAREFUL DIREFUL DRIDDER
FEARFUL GHASTLY GRIMFUL
HIDEOUS UNCOUTH DOUBTFUL
DOUBTOUS GHASTFUL HORRIBLE
HORRIFIC PERILOUS SCAREFUL
SHOCKING TERRIBLE TERRIFIC
DREADFULLY DIRELY GRISLY
ABYSMALLY
DREADNOUGHT TANK DAREALL
WARSHIP FEARLESS
DREAM METE MOON MUSE REVE
FANCY SWEVEN VISION AISLING
AVISION CHIMERA FANTASY IMAGINE
NIRVANA REVERIE ROMANCE
CHIMAERA DAYDREAM PHANTASM
SOMNIATE
DREAMER POET METER MUSARD
FANTAST IDEALIST PHANTAST
DREAMINESS LANGUOR
DREAMING ADREAM TRAUMEREI
DREAMTIME ALCHERA
DREAMY KEF SOFT MOONY VAGUE
POETIC FARAWAY LANGUID ONEIRIC
PENSIVE DREAMFUL FANCIFUL
SOOTHING
DREAR DERN DISMAL GLOOMY
DOLEFUL
DREARY SAD DIRE DOWY DREE
DULL FLAT GLUM BLEAK CRUEL
DOWIE DRURY OURIE WASTE WISHT
DISMAL ELENGE GLOOMY GOUSTY
LONELY DOLEFUL GOUSTIE
HOWLING WILSOME GRIEVOUS
WEARIFUL
DREDGE MOP DRAG DREG SIFT
SCOOP TRAIN DEEPEN DRUDGE
SCRAPE SPONGE GANGAVA
SCALLOP EXCAVATE SPRINKLE
DREDGER DUSTER HEDGEHOG
DREDGING JILLING
DREGS LAG MUD CRAP FAEX LAGS
LEES SCUT SILT SUDS TAIL DRAFF
DREST DROSS DRUGS FECES FOOTS
GROUT JAUPS MAGMA BOTTOM
DRAINS DUNDER MOTHER REFUSE
SORDES SORDOR ULLAGE DRIBBLE
GROUNDS GRUMMEL HEELTAP
OUTWALE RESIDUE RINSING
GRUMMELS REMNANTS SEDIMENT
SETTLING
(— **OF LIQUOR**) TAPLASH

(— **OF MOLTEN GLASS**) DRIBBLE
(— **OF SOCIETY**) WASH
DREIBUND TRIPLICE
DREIDEL TRENDEL
DRENCH DOSE HOSE SIND SINK
SOAK TOSH BLASH DOUSE DOWSE
DRAFT DRINK DROKE DROUK
DROWN SLOCK SLUSH SOUSE
STEEP SWILL BUCKET DELUGE
DOUCHE IMBRUE INFUSE POTION
SLUICE DRUNKEN EMBATHE
IMMERSE INDRENCH PERMEATE
SATURATE SUBMERGE
DRENCHED DRUNKEN
DRENCHER INFUSER
DRENCHING DOUSE DOWSE
DOWNPOUR
DRESS AX AXE BED DON DUB FIG
FIT HOE KIT RAG RAY RIG TOG
BARB BEGO BOWN BUSK BUSS
CLAY COAT COMB DESK DILL DINK
GALA GARB GEAR GORE GOWN
HONE HUKE KNAP MILL RAIL ROBE
SUIT TIFF TIRE TRIM TUBE TUCK
VEST WEAR ADORN ARRAY BIGAN
CLEAN CLOTH CRUMB CRUSH
CURRY DIGHT DIZEN EQUIP FLOAT
FROCK GUISE HABIT IHRAM MAGMA
PREEN PRICK PRIMP PRINK PRUNE
SHAPE THING TRICK AGUISE ATTIRE
BARBER BROACH CLOTHE ENROBE
FANGLE FETTLE FRAISE GRAITH
INVEST JELICK JUMPER KIRTLE
MAGPIE MULLET MUUMUU OUTFIT
PLIGHT REVEST SARONG SHEATH
SHROUD TOILET ADDRESS AFFAITE
APPAREL BANDAGE BEDIZEN
CHEMISE CLOTHES COSTUME
DALLACK DUBBING GARMENT
GARNISH HARNESS HATCHEL
RAIMENT TOGGERY VESTURE
ACCOUTER CLEADING CLOTHING
DECORATE FEATHERS HANDMADE
ORNAMENT SUNDRESS TAILLEUR
VESTMENT EMBELLISH
(— **A SKIN**) WHEEL
(— **DOWN**) BRACE
(— **ELEGANTLY**) DINK
(— **FISH**) CALVER
(— **FLAX**) TED
(— **FLINT**) NAP KNAP
(— **FOOD**) SAUCE
(— **FOR FELTING**) CARROT
(— **HAIR**) TIRE TRUSS BARBER
(— **HIDES**) BEAM
(— **HURRIEDLY**) HUDDLE
(— **IN FINE CLOTHES**) DIKE
(— **MEAT**) LARD SHROUD
(— **NEGLIGENTLY**) MOB
(— **ORE**) VAN
(— **OVER**) STOP
(— **SHEEPSKINS**) TAW
(— **SMARTLY**) DALLACK
(— **STONE**) DAB NIG DAUB DRAG
FACE GAGE HACK GAUGE NIDGE
POINT SCABBLE SCAPPLE
(— **TAWDRILY**) BEDIZEN
(— **UNTIDILY**) MAB
(— **UP**) BUSK DILL ADORN ARRAY

PRANK PRIMP PRINK SPICK WATER
FETTLE TOGGLE BECLOUT BEDRESS
(— **VULGARLY**) DAUB
(— **WITH CHISEL**) DROVE
(— **WITH TROWEL**) STRIKE
(— **WORN BY MAN**) DRAG
(— **WOUND**) PANSE BANDAGE
(**COAT** —) SIMAR SYMAR SIMARRE
(**EVENING** —) FORMAL
(**FESTIVE** —) GALA
(**INCOMPLETE** —) DISARRAY
(**LOOSE** —) SACK SACQUE
(**MORNING** —) PEIGNOIR
(**PECULIAR** —) LIVERY
(**POPLIN** —) TABINET TABBINET
(**RUSSIAN NATIONAL** —) SARAFAN
(**STYLE OF** —) GETUP
DRESSED CLAD DONE BOUND
BECLAD COATED COMBED HABITED
GOFFERED
(— **GAILY**) FRESH SPARKISH
(— **IN WHITE**) CANDIDATE
(**LOOSELY** —) DISCINCT
(**RICHLY** —) BROCADED
(**ROUGHLY** —) HEWN
(**SHOWILY** —) BEPRANKED
(**STYLISHLY** —) SMART
(**WELL** —) BRAW GASH
DRESSER ROBER TAWER BUREAU
FRAMER MODISTE CUPBOARD
(**LEATHER** —) LEVANTER
DRESSING CAST GRAVY BEATING
BLANKET IODOFORM RAVIGOTE
REMOLADE SCOLDING STUFFING
(— **FOR WOUNDS**) LINT SPONGE
(— **OF STONE**) SKIFFLING
(**HAIR** —) LACKER LACQUER
DRESSING ROOM SHIFT VESTRY
CAMARIN VESTUARY
DRESSMAKER SEWER SEAMER
MODISTE STITCHER COUTURIER
TIREWOMAN
DRESS RACK FRIPPERY
DRESSY SHARP
DRIBBLE DRIB DRIP DROP CARRY
DRIVEL DRIBLET DRIPPLE DRIZZLE
DRIBLET CLOT PIECE
(PL.) SMALLS
DRIED SEAR SERE ADUST GIZZEN
TORRID WIZENED GIZZENED
DRIFT FAN JET SAG DENE DUNE
FORD HERD PLOT SILT TIDE TILL
DRIVE DROVE FLEET FLOAT FLOCK
IOWAN SENSE SLIDE SLOOM SLOUM
TENOR TREND BROACH COURSE
DESIGN DEVICE DRIVER OFFSET
PODGER SCHEME STREAM TUNNEL
WINDLE CURRENT DIPHEAD DRIBBLE
GALLERY HEADING IMPETUS
IMPULSE LATERAL OUTWASH
PASTURE PROCESS PURPORT
SETBOLT DILUVIUM DRIFTPIN
TENDENCY
(— **LANGUIDLY**) SWOON
(— **OF CLOUDS**) CARRY
(— **OF SAND OR SNOW**) WREATH
(— **SIDEWISE**) CRAB
(— **WITH ANCHOR DOWN**) CLUB
(**DOWNWARD** —) DROOP

(**GLACIAL** —) CARY TILL IOWAN
(**RUBBLE** —) HEAD
DRIFTER DROVER
DRIFTING ADRIFT DRIFTAGE
DRIFT PLUG DUMMY
DRIFTWAY DROVE
DRIFTWOOD WAFTURE
DRILL GAD JAR JIG RIG SOW TAP
BORE CORE SPUD AUGER BORER
CHARK CHURN DECOY DREEL
PADDY THIRL TRAIN TUTOR TWIRL
WHIRL ALLURE BROACH ENTICE
FURROW JUMPER PIERCE SCHOOL
SEEDER SINKER STOPER THRILL
CHANNEL DRIFTER JANKERS
PLUGGER STARTER EXERCISE
INSTRUCT
(— **SYSTEM**) MARTINET
DRILLMAN STOPER
DRINK GO ADE ALE BIB BUM FIX GIN
HUM LAP MOP PEG POT RUM RYE
SIP SUP TEA TOT WET BALL BEER
BEND BENO BOLL BOSA BOZA
BREW BULL CHIA COKE COLA DRAG
DRAM FIZZ FLIP GROG HAVE HORN
JAKE LUSH MEAD NIPA NOGG PULL
PURL SHOT SIND SLUG SOAK SOMA
SOPE SPOT SWIG TIFF TOOT TOPE
WHET AIRAH BEVER BLAND BOMBO
BOOZE BOUSE BOZAH BUBUD
BUMBO CRUSH DAISY DRAFT FLOAT
GLOGG HAOMA JULEP LAGER
MORAT NEGUS PAINT POSCA PUNCH
QUAFF ROUSE SETUP SKINK SLING
SLOCK SMACK SMASH SMILE
SMOKE SNIFF SNORT SOPIE SOUSE
SWATS SWILL THING TOAST TODDY
VODKA WHIFF ZOMBI ABSORB
BEZZLE BRACER BRANDY BUMPER
CALKER CASIRI CATLAP CAUDLE
CHASER COFFEE COOPER DIBBLE
DRENCH EGGHOT EGGNOG FUDDLE
GIMLET GODOWN GUGGLE GUZZLE
HOOKER IMBIBE MESCAL POSSET
POTION PTISAN RICKEY SCREED
SHANDY SIPPLE SIRPLE SWANKY
SWINGE TACKLE TAMPOY TASTER
TIPPLE VELVET WAUCHT WAUGHT
ZOMBIE BRAGGET BRIMMER
CAROUSE CHEERER CHIRPER
COBBLER COLLINS CONSUME
CORDIAL DILUENT DRAUGHT
EXHAUST FLANNEL GUARANA
GUARAPO MORNING NOONING
PROPOMA SHERBET SIDECAR
SNEEZER SNIFTER SUCTION
SUPPAGE SWALLOW TANKARD
TRILLIL APERITIF BEVERAGE
BRIDECUP COCKTAIL HIGHBALL
LIBATION MAHOGANY POTATION
QUENCHER REFRESCO RUMBARGE
SANGAREE SPRITZER SYLLABUB
TEQUILA
(— **AT DRAFT**) TOP
(— **EXCESSIVELY**) TOPE BIBLE
SOUSE BEZZLE BIBBLE SWIZZLE
(— **FROM FERMENTED MILK**) AIRAN
(— **GREEDILY**) SLOP SWACK SWILL
GUTTLE GUZZLE

(— **HEAVILY**) TOOT SWINK
(— **INTOXICATING LIQUOR**)
IRRIGATE
(— **LIQUOR**) TIP DRAM SOAK BOOZE
PAINT
(— **NOISILY**) SLURP
(— **OF BEER**) BUTCHER
(— **OF IMMORTALITY**) SOMA
(— **OF INDIA**) SOMA SHRAB
(— **OF LIQUEUR**) FRAPPE
(— **OF LIQUOR**) WET DRAM SHOT
SPOT WHET SETUP WHIFF CALKER
JIGGER TASTER WETTING HIGHBALL
NIGHTCAP
(— **OF MOLASSES**) SWITCHEL
(— **OF THE GODS**) NECTAR
(— **OF VINEGAR AND WATER**)
POSCA
(— **OFF**) COUP
(— **SOCIALLY**) BIRL HOBNOB
(— **SPARINGLY**) BLEB
(— **TO LAST DROP**) BUZZ
(— **UP**) CRUSH EPOTE CAROUSE
EXHAUST
(**ADDITIONAL** —) EIK EKE
(**ALCOHOLIC** —) BENO BINO NIPA
BOMBO BUDGE BUMBO DRAIN
JOUGH SHRAB SLING SNORT
SNIFTER
(**BRAZILIAN** —) ASSAI ASSAHY
(**BUTTERMILK AND WATER** —)
BLAND
(**DRUGGED** —) HOCUS
(**FARINACEOUS** —) PTISAN
(**FERMENTED** —) BOSA MEAD
BALCHE MUSHLA CASSIRI GUARAPO
(**FREE** —) SHOUT
(**HALF-SIZED** —) CHOTAPEG
(**HEADY** —) HUFFCAP
(**HOT** —) COPUS SALOP TODDY
BISHOP EGGHOT PLOTTY SALOOP
CARDINAL
(**INCLINED TO** —) OUTWARD
(**INSIPID** —) SLUM
(**INTOXICATING** —) GROG SUCK
BOOZE KUMISS SCOTCH DRAPPIE
PAIWARI SWIZZLE SKOKIAAN
(**INTOXICATING** —S) SAUCE BOTTLE
(**LONG** —) SWIPE HIGHBALL
(**MEAN** —) LAP
(**MIDDAY** —) NOONING MERIDIAN
(**NON-ALCOHOLIC** —) GAZOZ
COOLER
(**PARTING** —) BONAILIE
(**POISONOUS** —) DRENCH
(**RUSSIAN** —) OBARNE OBARNI
(**SACRED** —) HOMA AMRIT HAOMA
AMRITA
(**SACRIFICIAL** —) HOMA SOMA
(**SMALL** —) PEG DRAM SOPIE
DALLOP WETTING
(**STRONG** —) BUB HUM BENO SICER
FUDDLE
(**TASTELESS** —) SLOP
(**THIN** —) SLOSH
(**WEAK** —) LAP BOOL BULL CATLAP
DRINKER SOT TANK POTER TOAST
TOPER BARFLY BENDER CUPMAN
LUSHER SOAKER SPONGE IMBIBER

INTAKER QUAFFER DRUNKARD
(**EXCESSIVE** — **OF TEA**) THEIC
(**WATER** —) HYDROPOT
DRINKING BEVER DRAFT DRINKY
GUZZLE DRAUGHT POTTING
CAROUSAL POTATION
DRIP LIP SIE SYE DROP LEAK SEGE
SILE WEEP CANAL DRILL EAVES
LABEL STILL DRIBBLE DRIPPLE
LARMIER TRICKLE TRINKLE TRINTLE
(— **WITH TINKLING SOUND**) PINK
DRIPPING ADRIP STAXIS WEEPING
DRIPSTONE BAT DING LABEL
HOODMOLD
DRIVE CA CAW COT FOG JOG AUTO
BANG BEAR BEAT BUTT CALL CRAM
DING DRUB DRUM FIRE FIRK FLOG
GOAD HACK HERD HUNT HURL
JASM JEHU KICK LASH PICK PILE
POSS PUSH RIDE SEND SERR SINK
SLOG SPUR STAB STUB TOOL TOUR
TURN URGE BRAWL CHASE CHECK
COACT CROWD DRIFT DROVE FEEZE
FLAIL FORCE HORSE HURRY IMPEL
INFER LODGE POACH PRESS PULSE
PUNCH REPEL ROUST SHOVE SLASH
SMITE SPANK SWEEP TEASE
ATTACK BATTER BEETLE BENSEL
CHARGE COMPEL CUDGEL DEDUCE
DERIVE FERRET HAMMER HASTEN
IMPACT JARVEY JOSTLE PLUNGE
PROPEL BLUSTER ENFORCE
IMPULSE OVERTAX SETDOWN
TRAVAIL CATAPULT CONATION
SHEPHERD TENDENCY
(— **A BALL**) LACE SEND
(— **A HORSE ONWARD**) WHIG
(— **AIR**) BLOW
(— **ANIMALS**) HAZE
(— **AT TOP SPEED**) CAREER
(— **AWAY**) RID FIRK HUSH SHOO
BANDY EXILE FEEZE FLEME REPEL
SMOKE SWEEP AROINT BANISH
DEFEND DISPEL ENCHASE DISPLACE
EXORCISE
(— **BACK AND FORTH**) TENNIS
(— **BACK**) RUSH REBUT REPEL
CULBUT DEFEND REBATE REBUFF
RETUND REPULSE REFRINGE
(— **BEFORE STRONG WIND**) SPOON
(— **BRISKLY**) JUNE
(— **CRAZY**) BUG
(— **DISTRACTED**) BEDEVIL
(— **FORTH**) ISH
(— **HARD**) SWEAT HACKNEY
(— **HURRIEDLY**) BUM BUCKET
(— **IN**) CRAM DINT PILE TAMP
INJECT
(— **IN A PARK**) TOUR
(— **INTO THE GROUND**) STUB
(— **INTO WATER**) ENEW
(— **LOGS**) SPLASH
(— **OFF STAGE**) EXPLODE
(— **OFF**) KEEP LIFT EXCOCT
(— **OUT**) BOLT FIRE DEPEL DROWN
EJECT EXPEL KNOCK WREAK
EXTURB ABANDON DISLODGE
EXORCISE PROPULSE
(— **RECKLESSLY**) COWBOY

(— **ROUGHLY**) CHOUSE
(— **SLANTINGLY**) TOE
(— **TO BAY**) EMBOSS
(— **TO MADNESS**) FRENZY
(— **VIOLENTLY**) THUD SMASH
HURTLE
(— **WITH BLOWS**) SKELP COURSE
(— **WITH SHOUTS**) HOY HUE
DRIVEL DOTE DRIP DROOL SLUSH
DOTAGE DRUDGE FOOTLE HUMBUG
MENIAL SLAVER DRIBBLE EYEWASH
SLABBER TWADDLE NONSENSE
SALIVATE
DRIVELING SLAVERY FOOTLING
IMBECILE SLOBBERY
DRIVEPIPE POINT
DRIVER MUG HACK JEHU MUSH WHIP
DRABI URGER CABMAN CALLER
COWBOY DROVER FLYMAN HAULER
JARVEY JOCKEY MALLET MUSHER
PONIER STAGER VANMAN WAINER
CATCHER COCHERO FLANKER
HACKMAN HOODLUM HURRIER
JITNEUR PHAETON SPANKER
SPEEDER SUMPTER TOPSMAN
TRUCKER WHIPMAN BANDYMAN
BULLOCKY CALESERO CAMELEER
COACHMAN DRAGSMAN ENGINEER
GALLOWAY GOADSMAN IMPULSOR
JITNEUSE MOTORMAN OVERSEER
TEAMSTER WHIPSTER
(— **OF ANIMALS**) DROVER SKINNER
(— **OF ELEPHANT**) MAHOUT
(— **OF OMNIBUS**) PIRATE
(**CAMEL** —) SARWAN CAMELEER
(**FAST** —) JEHU SPEEDER
(**FIELD** —) HAYWARD
(**PACK-HORSE** —) SUMPTER
(**SKILLFUL** —) REINSMAN
(**TOWPATH** —) HOGGY HOGGEE
DRIVEWAY DRIVE SWEEP AVENUE
DRIFTWAY
DRIVING PELTING COACHING
SLASHING
(— **ALONG**) SCUD
(— **OF GAME**) BATTUE
(— **OF WIND**) GUST
(— **TOGETHER**) DRIFT
(— **TOWARD**) APPULSE
DRIZZLE DEG MUG DANK DRIP
DROW HAZE LING RAIN SMUR STEW
DRISK MISLE SMURR MIZZLE
DRISSEL SCOUTHER SPRINKLE
(— **OF RAIN**) SKEW
DRIZZLY SOFT DRIPPY
DROGUE DRAG DRUG
DROLL ODD COMIC DROLE FUNNY
MERRY QUEER JESTER JOCOSE
AMUSING BUFFOON COMICAL
JOCULAR STRANGE WAGGISH
FARCICAL HUMOROUS
DROLLERY WIT JEST FARCE HUMOR
DROLERIE
DROMEDARY OONT CAMEL DELUL
DELOUL HAGEEN HAGEIN HYGEEN
MEHARI CAMAILE CAMELUS
DROMOND
DRONE BEE BUM HUM DRUM SLUG
DRANT DROLL IDLER SNAIL BUMBLE

BURDEN CHORUS DRAUNT DRONEL
DRONET LUBBER BAGPIPE
BUMBARD BUMBASS HUMMING
SHIRKER SLEEPER SOLDIER
SPEAKER LOITERER SLUGGARD
DRONE BASS FOOT
DRONING HUMMING
DRONISH SLOW INDOLENT
SLUGGISH
DRONGO FORKTAIL
DROOL FLAT DRIVEL SLAVER
DRIBBLE SLABBER SLOBBER
SALIVATE
DROOP FAG LOB LOP SAG BEND
DROP FADE FLAG HANG LAVE LOLL
PINE SINK SWAG WEEP WILT DAVER
DREEP DROWK FLACK HEALD HIELD
MOURN BANGLE BLOUSE DANGLE
DEPEND NUTATE SLOUCH CURTAIN
DECLINE FLITTER LANGUISH
DROOPING LOP DRAG FLAG LANK
LAZY LIMP GOTCH ADROOP
DROOPY FLAGGY NUTANT SLOUCH
SOPITE GOTCHED HANGING
LANGUID NODDING POPPIED
CERNUOUS TRAILING
(**— OF EARS**) LAVE
(**— OF EYELID**) PTOSIS
DROOPY DREEPY SLIMPSY
DROP DAP DIP SIE SYE BEAD BEDE
BLOB CAST DRIB DRIP DUMP FALL
GLOB GOUT OMIT SEGE SHED SILE
SINK SPOT STOP TEAR BREAK
CLOTH DROOP FLUMP GUTTA LAPSE
LOWER MINIM PEARL PLUMP PLUNK
SLUMP STILL SWOOP CANCEL
DISTIL DRAPPY EXTILL FUMBLE
GOBBET GOUTTE PLUNGE SINKER
SLOUGH SPRINK TUMBLE ABANDON
CURTAIN DESCENT DEWDROP
DISCARD DISMISS DISTILL DRAPPIE
DRIBBLE DRIBLET DROPLET
EXPUNGE FORSAKE GLOBULE
GUTTULA GUTTULE INCURVE
LETDOWN MELDROP PLUMMET
RELEASE SPATTER DECREASE
DROPLING
(**— ANCHOR**) SLIP
(**— ARGENT**) LARME
(**— AS SEEDS FROM A POD**) ROSE
(**— AWAY**) DESERT
(**— BAIT IN WATER**) DAP
(**— BY DROP**) DROPWISE GUTTATIM
(**— DOWN**) VAIL
(**— IN**) STOP HAPPEN INSTIL INSTILL
(**— OF GIN**) DAFFY
(**— OUT**) FLOUNCE
(**THEATRICAL —**) TAB SCRIM
(**UNEXPECTED —**) DOYST
(PL.) GTT GUTT
DROP-CURTAIN GREENY
DROP ELBOW PIERDROP
DROPLET GLOBULE
(PL.) DEW
DROPLIGHT PENDANT
DROPPER SINK BOBBER SINKER
PIPETTE
DROPPING FALL SCAT SKAT SHARD
COWSHARD

(**— ABRUPTLY**) BOLD
(**— SHARPLY**) ABRUPT
(PL.) SOIL SPOOR FLYINGS
DROPSICAL PUFFY EDEMIC
DROPSIED HYDROPIC
DROPSY EDEMA ANASARCA
DROPWORT HORSEBANE
DEADTONGUE
DROSS KISH LEES SCUM SLAG
CHAFF DREGS DRUSH SPRUE
WASTE GARBLE REFUSE SCORIA
SCRUFF SHRUFF SINTER CINDERS
LEAVING OFFSCUM
DROSSEL SLUT HUSSY DRAZEL
DRAZIL
DROUGHT DRYTH DROUTH THIRST
ARIDITY DRYNESS
DROVE MOB SENT ATAJO CROWD
DRIFT FLOCK MANADA BOASTER
DISTURB TROUBLE DRIFTWAY
DROVER DEALER DRIVER TOPMAN
TOPSMAN WHACKER HERDSMAN
DROWN DEAFEN DRENCH STIFLE
ADRENCH DRUNKEN INDRENCH
INUNDATE OVERTONE
DROWNED ADRENT
DROWNING NOYADE
DROWSE NOD SOG DOZE DOVER
DRONE SLEEP SNOOZE SLUMBER
DROWSINESS DULLNESS LETHARDY
DROWSING DORMANT
DROWSY DOZY DULL LOGY HEAVY
NODDY SLEEPY SNOOZY SOPITE
STUPID SUPINE SWOONY DORMANT
LULLING NODDING POPPIED
COMATOSE COMATOUS OSCITANT
SLUGGISH
DRUB TAP BANG BEAT BLOW DRUM
ARRAY CURRY STAMP THUMP
WHALE CUDGEL THRASH BELABOR
SHELLAC
DRUBBING LICKING SACKING
DRUDGE DIG FAG TUG DROY DRUG
GRUB HACK MOIL FLOD TOIL DROIL
GRIND SCRAT SCRUB SLAVE SWEAT
DIGGER DRIVEL ENDURE JACKAL
MOILER SCODGY SLAVEY SLUDGE
SUFFER GRUBBER HACKNEY
PLODDER SLAVERY SWEATER
TRACHLE
DRUDGERY FAG MOIL SLOG TOIL
WORK LABOR SWEAT SWINK
FAGGERY SLAVERY TRACHLE
TURMOIL DRUDGISM
DRUG HOP ALOE ALUM CURE DOPE
DRAB DULL HEMP LOAD NUMB SINA
HOCUS JALAP LOCUS MECON
OPIUM SALOL SENNA SPECE SULFA
TONGA TRUCK COOLER DEWTRY
FINGER HEROIN IPECAC JAMBUL
LOCUST MYOTIC NOBBLE OPIATE
PEYOTE PEYOTL PITURI POTION
SIMPLE SULPHA ANODYNE ATEBRIN
BOTANIC CUSHION DAMIANA
DILATER ECBOLIC ETHICAL HASHISH
JAMBOOL PHILTER PHILTRE
QUASSIA STUPEFY STYPTIC
SURAMIN ZEDOARY ADJUVANT
AROMATIC ASPIDIUM ATARAXIC

HYPNOTIC KOROMIKO LAXATIVE
MEDICATE MEDICINE NARCOTIC
NEPENTHE SALIVANT SEDATIVE
SPECIFIC TOXICANT ZERUMBET
ATARACTIC
(**— USER**) JOYPOPPER
(**VEGETABLE —**) FINGER
(PL.) DRUGGERY
DRUGGED POPPIED
DRUGGIST CHEMIST DRUGGER
GALLIPOT
DRUGSTORE APOTHEC PHARMACY
DRUID SARONIDE
DRUM GIN GOO BOWL CAGE DRUB
LALI ROUT SKIN SPOT TOPH TRAP
BONGO CONGA CRAWL DRONE
GUMBE GUMBY SHAPE SNARE
SWASH TABOR THRUM TOMBE
ATABAL BARREL CROCUS RIGGER
TABRET TAMBOR TIMBRE TUMBLE
TUMMER TYMPAN ANACARA
BUBBLER CROAKER FRUSTUM
GRUNTER RATTLER REDFISH
SNUBBER TABORIN TAMBOUR
TEMPEST TIMBREL TUMBLER
BAMBOULA BARBUKKA CANISTER
CYLINDER DERBUKKA DRUMFISH
HUEHUETL MOULINET TYMPANUM
(**— AS SHIP'S SIGNAL**) SHAPE
(**— FOR WINDING ROPE**) CAGE
(**— IN WINCH**) GIPSY GYPSY
(**— MADE FROM HOLLOW TREE**)
GUMBE GUMBY
(**— ON WINDLASS**) WILDCAT
(**— UP BUSINESS**) HUSTLE
(**— UP INTEREST**) BALLYHOO
(**HEATED —**) DRIER DRYER
(**IGOROT —**) GANGSA
(**REVOLVING —**) GURDY RATTLER
(**SUMERIAN —**) ALA ALAL
DRUMBEAT DUB FLAM RUFF TUCK
MARCH RUFFLE BERLOQUE
BRELOQUE
(**— SOUND**) TUCK
DRUMFISH SPOT CROCUS BUBBLER
CROAKER DRUMMER DRUMSLER
SCIAENID
DRUMLIN DRUM SOWBACK
DRUMMER DRUM TABOR STICKS
TABRET ROADMAN SWASHER
TAMBOUR TUMBLER DRUMSLER
SALESMAN
DRUM ROLL DIAN DIANA
DRUMSTICK LEG STICK BAGUET
TAMPON BAGUETTE
DRUNK CUT FOU REE WET GONE
HIGH LUSH NASE PAID RIPE SOSH
BLIND BOOZE BOSKY CLEAR DRINK
LUMPY LUSHY MALTY OILED QUEER
SHICK STIFF TIGHT TIPSY BAGGED
BLOTTO BOILED BUZZED CANNED
FLUFFY GROGGY JAGGED LOADED
LOOPED MORTAL SLOPPY SODDEN
SOSHED SOZZLY SPONGY SPRUNG
STEWED STINKO STONED TIDDLY
UPPISH UPPITY BLOTTER CROCKED
DRUNKEN JINGLED MAUDLIN
SCREWED SHICKER SLOPPED
SOZZLED SQUIFFY SWACKED

COCKEYED GLORIOUS MUCKIBUS
PLEASANT SQUIFFED STINKING
BLITHERED
DRUNKARD SOT SOAK BLOAT DIPSO
DRUNK GULCH RUMMY SOUSE
TOPER LUSHER SOAKER SPONGE
DRUNKER FUDDLER POTSHOT
SHICKER STEWBUM TIPPLER
TOSSPOT BORACHIO HABITUAL
SWILLTUB
DRUNKEN REE GONE WINY BLIND
BOUSY DROWN DRUNK BLOTTO
FLUFFY SODDEN DRUCKEN PICKLED
SOTTISH WHIPCAT DRENCHED
SATURATE SQUIFFED VINOLENT
WOODSERE
DRUNKENNESS BUN IVRESSE
POTSHOT
DRUPE TRYMA DRUPEL DRUPELET
DRUPEOLE
DRUPELET GRAIN ACINUS
DRUPE STONE NUTLET
DRY EBB KEX SEC TED WIN ADRY
ARID BAKE BLOT BRUT DULL EILD
GELD HASK KEXY KILN PINE SAVE
SERE SOUR WIPE AREFY CORKY
DRAIN FROST GUESS HASKY JUSKY
PARCH PROSY SANDY SECCO
SMEEK SWEAT VAPID WIZEN
BARKEN BARREN BIRSLE BORING
CHIPPY ENSEAR GIZZEN HISTIE
JEJUNE SCORCH STARKY AREFACT
BRUSTLE INSIPID SAPLESS SICCATE
SQUALID STERILE THIRSTY
TORREFY XEROTIC BARBECUE
DROUGHTY INFUMATE TIRESOME
WOODSERE
(— HERRINGS) DEESE
(— IN SUN) RIZZAR
(— OF MILK) SEW EILD
(— PARTLY) SAMMY
(— UP) SERE WELK WITHER
AREFACT FORWELK SKELLER
(— WOOD) BEATH SWEAT SEASON
(NOT —) SWEET
DRYAD DRYAS NYMPH CAISSA
YAKSHA YAKSHI WOODMAID
DRYER DRIER STOVE SIROCCO
DRY GOODS DRAPERY
DRYING SICCANT
DRYING RACK CRIB
DRYNESS DROUTH ARIDITY
DROUGHT SICCITY XEROSIS
XEROTES HASKNESS
DUAL TWIN BINARY DOUBLE DUALIST
TWOFOLD
DUALISM DVAITA
DUALITY DUAD TWINE TWONESS
DUANT DE DEE
DUB DIB RUB ADUB BLOW CALL
NAME POOL ADORN ARRAY DRESS
STYLE THUMP CLOTHE KNIGHT
PUDDLE SMOOTH STRIKE ENTITLE
BEGINNER DRUMBEAT ORNAMENT
DUBBIN DAUBING
DUBIOUS DICKY FISHY JUBUS
DOUBTY BEARISH DOUBTFUL
DOUBTING JUBEROUS
(NOT —) EXPRESS

DUCHY DUCATUS DUCHERY
DUKEDOM PARMESAN
DUCK AIX BOB BOW CAN DIG DIP
DOP MIG PET WIO CHAP COLK
COOT DIVE DOGS DOGY DOKE
DUKW JOUK LADY LORD PATO
ROOK SMEE SMEW TEAL TEUK
BOOBY BUNTY CRICK DILLY DODGE
DOUSE DOWSE DUCKY EIDER
HOUND MOMMY NODDY PADDY
POKER ROUEN SCAUP SHIRK SOUSE
SPIKE SPRIG STOOL BOBBER
CALLOO CALLOW CANARD CANNET
DUCKIE FELLOW GARROT PEKING
PERSON PLUNGE QUANDY RUNNER
SCOTER SMETHE BARWING BLACKIE
BOWSSEN BUMMALO CANETTE
CRACKER DABBLER DARLING
DRABBET DUCKING DUCKLET
DUNBIRD FIDDLER FLAPPER
GADWALL GEELBEC GREASER
MALLARD OLDWIFE PENTAIL
PINKEYE PINTAIL POCHARD
REDHEAD REDLEGS REDWING
SCOOTER SLEEPER SPATTER
WADDLER WIDGEON YAGUAZA
BLUEBILL BLUEWING BOATBILL
BULLNECK DUCKLING DUCKWING
GARGANEY GRAYBACK GREYBACK
HARDHEAD IRONHEAD MOONBILL
MORILLON PIKETAIL REDSHANK
RINGBILL RINGNECK SHOVELER
SHUFFLER SQUEALER WIRETAIL
(— EGGS) PIDAN
(MALE —) DRAKE
(STUFFED —) DUMPOKE
(YOUNG —) CANETON FLAPPER
FLOPPER
DUCKBILL OOTOCOID PLATYPUS
TAMBREET
DUCKWEED GLIT GRAIN LEMNAD
LENTIL DIGMEAT DUCKMEAT
FROGFOOT
DUCT VAS MAIN PIPE TUBE CANAL
ALVEUS BUSWAY DUCTUS MEATUS
URETER CHANNEL CONDUIT
DUCTULE DUCTURE LACTEAL
LEADING PASSAGE TRACHEA
AQUEDUCT CALIDUCT DOWNTAKE
EFFERENT EMISSARY EXHALANT
GONADUCT GUIDANCE OLEODUCT
DUCTILE SOFT DOCILE FACILE
PLIANT PLASTIC PLIABLE TENSILE
FLEXIBLE TRACTILE
DUD FLOP LEMON STUMER STUMOR
FAILURE
DUDE FOP DANDY DUDINE JOHNNY
COXCOMB JACKEEN
DUE HAK OWE BACK CENS DEBT
FAIR FARM FLAT HAKH JUST MEED
OWED TOLL DROIT ENDOW ENDUE
FATED MERIT OWING COMING
CUSTOM DESERT EXTENT LAWFUL
MATURE PROPER UNPAID CONDIGN
EXACTLY FALDFEE FITTING JETTAGE
TALLAGE ADEQUATE DIRECTLY
HEREGELD HEREZELD RIGHTFUL
SUITABLE TRUNCAGE
DUEL TILT FENCE FIGHT AFFAIR

COMBAT DUELLO CONTEST
MEETING CONFLICT DUELLIZE
HOLMGANG
DUELIST FIGHTER SPADASSIN
DUENNA DRAGON CHAPERON
DUES TOLLS DROITS CHIEFRY
INWARDS JETTAGE PAYMENT
PENSION QUAYAGE ALTARAGE
HAVENAGE SOUNDAGE THIRLAGE
DUET DUO TWO DUETTO TWOSOME
(BALLET —) ADAGIO
DUFF ALTER BRAND CHEAT FLOOR
PUDDING
DUFFER DUB MUFF SHAM CHEAT
BUFFER HAWKER SHICER PEDDLER
DUG (— UP) HOWKIT
DUGONG SEACOW YUNGAN
COWFISH HALICORE MUTILATE
SIRENIAN
DUGOUT ABRI BOAT BURY CAVE
BANCA BONGO BUNGO CANOE
DONGA DUNGA SHELL BAROTO
BUNKER CAYUCA CAYUCO CORIAL
TROUGH BANTING PIRAGUA
PIROGUE SHELTER BLINDAGE
LIPALIPA
DUIKER IPITI DUYKER BLAUBOK
DUKE DUC DUX KNEZ PEER AYMON
CHIEF KNIAZ HERZOG LEADER
ORSINO AUMERLE GORLOIS
SOLINUS STEENIE HERETOGA
PROSPERO
DUKEDOM DUCHY DUCATAS
DULCET SWEET DULCID SIRUPY
SYRUPY SOOTHING
DULCIAN CURTAL
DULCIMER CANUN CITOLE SANTIR
CEMBALO MAGADIS SANTOUR
CYMBALOM PANTALON ZIMBALON
DULIA ADORATION
DULL DIM DOW DRY FAT LAX MAT
SAD BLAH CLOD COLD DAMP DEAD
DILL DOWD DOWF DOWY DRAB
DREE DRUG DUMB FLAT GRAY
GREY LOGY MOPE MULL POKY
SLOW TAME THIN TURN BESOT
BLAND BLATE BLEAR BLIND BLUNT
BRUTE CRASS DENSE DINGY DOWFF
DOWIE DOWLY DREAR DUBBY
DUNCH DUNNY DUSTY FISHY FOGGY
GLAZY GRAVE GROSS HEAVY INERT
LOURD MATTE MORON MOSSY
MUDDY MUSTY MUZZY NOOSE
PLUMP POKEY PROSE PROSY
SHADE SLACK SOGGY STARY STILL
SULKY TERNE THICK UNAPT VAPID
WASTE BARREN BLEARY BOVINE
CLOUDY DAMPEN DARKEN DEADEN
DISMAL DRAGGY DREARY DRIECH
DRIEGH DROWSY EARTHY FRIGID
FRUMPY GLASSY HEBETE JEJUNE
LEADEN LOURDY MUFFLE OBTUND
OBTUSE OPAQUE REBATE SLEEPY
SLOOMY SODDEN SOMBER SOMBRE
STODGY STOLID STUFFY STUPID
SULLEN TIMBER TORPID TRISTE
TURBID URLUCH WOODEN ADENOID
BLUNTED CONFUSE DEADISH
DISEDGE DOLTISH DOWFART

DRAINED DULLISH DUMPISH HUMDRUM INSIPID IRKSOME LANGUID LUMPISH MUMPISH PEAKISH PINHEAD PROSAIC SHEATHE SOTTISH STUPEFY TEDIOUS UNLUSTY VACUOUS BACKWARD BANAUSIC BEFUDDLE BLOCKISH BOEOTIAN BROMIDIC COMATOSE COMATOUS DIDACTIC DISCOLOR DULLSOME EDGELESS FRUMPISH GAUMLESS HEBETATE INFICETE LIFELESS LISTLESS LOURDISH OVERCAST PLODDING SLOTTERY SLUGGISH STAGNANT TIRESOME

(— EDGE OF) ABATE
(— IN MOTION) LOGY
(— SCENT) FOIL
(— WITH LIQUOR) SEETHE
(BECOME —) PALL RUST
(MENTALLY —) DOPY DOPEY BARREN

DULLARD DOLT DUNCE IDIOT MORON DODUNK STUPID BROMIDE DASTARD DOLDRUM DULBERT POTHEAD DULLHEAD

DULLED EMPTY HEAVY JADED BROKEN CLOUDY GRAYED SODDEN STUPID BLEARED

DULLISH DIRTY

DULLNESS DRAB HAZE YAWN TAMAS PHLEGM DIMNESS DOLDRUM DULLITY DUNCERY FATUITY LANGUOR OPACITY DUMBNESS HEBETUDE SLOWNESS VAPIDITY

DULL-SPIRITED MUZZY

DULL-WITTED FOZY WITLESS BESOTTED
(— PERSON) MOREPORK

DULLY FLATLY HEAVILY

DULSE DILLESK DILLISK SEAWEED

DULY DUE FITLY RIGHT RITELY PROPERLY

DUMB DULL MUTE STONY SILENT STONEY STUPID

DUMBBELL DUMMY DUNCE HALTER KNOTHEAD

DUMBFOUND DAZE STUN AMAZE CONFUSE CONFOUND SURPRISE

DUMBFOUNDED STUPENT

DUMBNESS APHRASIA

DUMBWAITER LIFT DUMMY

DUMMY COPY DOLT MUTE SHAM DUMBY FAGOT EFFIGY FAGGOT PONTIC SHADOW SILENT PHANTOM DUMBBELL
(SWORDSMAN'S —) PEL

DUMP SUM TIP BEAT CASH COIN COUP FALL HOLE JAIL MUSE NAIL TOOM EMPTY HOUSE SHOOT GRIEVE PLUNGE TIPPLE UNLOAD BOGHOLE COUNTER DEPOSIT REVERIE SADNESS STORAGE
(PL.) SUDS MOPES SADNESS

DUMPCART DUMPER TUMBREL TUMBRIL

DUMPER TIPMAN

DUMPLING COB CRUST KNODEL KNAIDEL NOCKERL DOUGHBOY

QUENELLE
(PL.) KLOSSE GNOCCHI

DUMPY DUNCH GROSS PUDGY SQUAB SQUAT DUMPTY STOCKY SQUATTY

DUN BUM TAN FORT KICK URGE ANNOY BROWN CRAVE CROWD DINGY FAVEL MOUND SEPIA DUNNER LEADEN PESTER PLAGUE DUNNISH SWARTHY

DUNCE ASS DOLT DULT GABY GONY BOBBY BOOBY IDIOT NINNY DULTIE HOBBIL PEDANT DULLARD SOPHIST NUMSKULL STUNPOLL TOMNODDY WISEACRE

DUNDERHEAD OAF DOLT DUNCE

DUNE BAR DENE MEAL MOUND TOWAN TWINE BARKAN BARCHAN BARKHAN
(SAND —) DRAB SAIF SEIF

DUNG MIS CACK CHIP DOLL FIME GORE MERD MUCK MUTE SOIL TATH ARGAL ARGOL FECES FILTH FUMET MIXEN SCARN SHARN BILLET CASSON FIANTS LESSES MANURE ORDURE SCUMBER SCUMMER TREDDLE COWSHARD DROPPING STALLAGE
(— AS FUEL) ARGOL CASSON CASSONS
(— OF BEAST OF PREY) LESSES
(— OF DEER) FUMET FEWMET
(COW —) UPLA COWSHARD COWSHARN
(OTTER'S —) SPRAINTS
(SHEEP —) BUTTONS TREDDLE TROTTERS

DUNGEON PIT CELL HELL HOLE LAKE VAULT CACHOT DONJON PRISON CONFINE OUBLIET REVOLVER

DUNGHILL MIXEN MIDDEN MIXHILL

DUNGON DONGON SUNDARI

DUNK DIP SOP SOAK STEEP IMMERSE MOISTEN

DUNKER DIPPER TAUFER TUNKER DUMPLER DUNKARD TUMBLER

DUNLIN STIB OXEYE PURRE STINT DORBIE OXBIRD REDBACK LEADBACK

DUODECIMO TWELVEMO

DUPE APE FOB FOP MUG BOOB COAX CONY CULL DUST FOOL GECK GULL HOAX LAMB ROOK TOOL CHEAT CHUMP COKES CONEY CULLY HEALD MOOTH MOUTH SLANG STALE TRICK BEFOOL BUBBLE CHOUSE CHOUSE COUSIN DELUDE DERIDE MONKEY PIGEON PLOVER SQUARE SUCKER VICTIM CATSPAW CHICANE DECEIVE GUDGEON MISLEAD SAPHEAD SWINDLE YOUNKER DOTTEREL HOODWINK RODERIGO

DUPERY RAMP

DUPLE BINARY DOUBLE TWOFOLD

DUPLEX DOUBLE TWOFOLD

DUPLEXITY EQUIVOKE

DUPLICATE BIS COPY DUPE ALIKE

DITTO SPARE TALLY DOUBLE FLIMSY REPEAT COUNTER ESTREAT MISLEAD REPLICA TWOFOLD LIKENESS

DUPLICATION DISOMATY

DUPLICITY ART GUILE DECEIT TRICKERY

DUPONDIUS BRONZE

DURABILITY WEAR FIBER FIBRE STEEL DURANCE STAMINA

DURABLE FIRM HARD LASTY STOUT STABLE STAPLE LASTING SERVICE CONSTANT ENDURING LIVELONG

DURABLENESS DURATION

DURAMEN HEARTWOOD

DURANCE DURANT DURESS CUSTODY

DURANGO CARTOUCH

DURATION AGE DATE LAST LIFE SPAN TERM TIME WHEN DUREE KALPA SPACE LENGTH PERIOD DURANCE LASTING INFINITE LIFETIME STANDING
(— BREEZE) SLATCH
(BOUNDLESS —) INFINITE
(INFINITE —) ETERNITY

DURESS FORCE DANGER CRUELTY DURANCE COERCION HARDNESS PRESSURE

DURGA CHAMUNDA

DURIAN JAK JACK JAKFRUIT

DURING IN ON BIN AMID OVER TIME AMONG INTRA WHILE AMIDST WHILST WITHIN AMONGST DURANTE PENDING ENDURING

DURRA DARI DURA MILO JOWAR CHOLUM DHURRA JONDLA SORGHUM FETERITA

DUSACK TESACK

DUSK DIM EVE DARK DIMPS GLOAM GLOOM DIMMET DIMPSY DIMNESS DUCKISH DARKNESS GLOAMING OWLLIGHT TWILIGHT

DUSKY DIM SAD WAN DARK DUSK ADUSK BROWN DINGY GRIMY MOORY TAWNY GLOOMY SMUTTY SOMBER SOMBRE SWARTH DARKISH DARLING OBSCURE SUBFUSC SUBFUSK SWARTHY BLACKISH

DUST ROW COOM DIRT FOGO MUCK MULL PILM SMUT BRISS CLEAN COOMB FLOUR POUCE STIVE STOUR DREDGE FILLER KITTEN POLLEN POWDER SMEECH BEFLOUR EBURINE REMAINS SAWDUST SMEDDUM TURMOIL ANTELOPE BULLDUST PUMICITE
(— IN FLOUR MILLS) STIVE
(— IN QUARTZ MILL) SLICKENS
(BLOOD —) HEMOCONIA
(COAL —) COOM CULM COOMB
(COKE —) BREEZE
(COSMIC —) STARDUST
(DIAMOND —) SEASONING
(FIBER —) FLOCK
(FLAX —) POUCE POUSE

DUST CLOUD STEW

DUST COVER WRAPPER

DUSTER DEVIL WILLOW ZEPHYR
DUSTCOAT
DUSTY ADUST MOTTY MOTTLE
POUCEY STOURY POWDERY
UNDUSTED
DUTCH (SEE NETHERLANDS) HOGEN
HOLLAND
DUTCH FOIL ORSEDE ORSEDUE
DUTCH GOLD CLINQUANT
DUTCHMAN HANS HOGEN BLANDA
DUTCHY BELANDA DUTCHER
MYNHEER BATAVIAN
DUTCHMAN'S-BREECHES
DICENTRA
DUTIFUL DOCILE LAWFUL DEBTFUL
DUTEOUS OBEDIENT OFFICIAL
REVERENT
DUTY DO END JOB LOT TAX CALL
CARE FYRD ONUS PART PROW
ROLE TAIL TASK TOLL WIKE CHORE
DEVER ERMIN LADLE OUGHT PREST
RIGHT STINT WIKEN BLANCH
BURDEN CHARGE COCKET DEVOIR
DHARMA EXCISE EXITUS HERIOT
IMPOSE IMPOST INGATE OFFICE
RIVAGE TARIFF AVERAGE BAILAGE
BOOMAGE FOSSAGE FURDUNG
GRANAGE INDULTO KEELAGE
LASTAGE PONTAGE PRIMAGE
ROYALTY SCAVAGE SERVICE
STATION TONNAGE TRIBUTE
TROWAGE TUNNAGE BALLIAGE
BUSINESS FUNCTION MALIKANA
MALTOLTE REDDENDO WEIGHAGE
(— FOR LEAD ORE) COPE
(FEUDAL —) HERIOT
(IMPORT —) ERMIN INDULTO
(MILITARY —) STABLES
(TIRING —) FATIGUE
(PL.) CUSTOMS INGATES ACTIVITY
DUX CHIEF LEADER SUBJECT
HERETOGA
DWARF ELF PUG URF AETA CRUT
GRIG GRUB NANA RUNT CRILE
CROWL GALAR GNOME KNURL
MIDGE PIGMY PYGMY SCRUB STUNT
TROLL ABLACH ALVISS CONJON
DROICH DURGAN DURGEN MIDGET
SHRIMP ANDVARI ANDWARI BLASTIE
CONGEON MANIKIN OVERTOP
PACOLET WRATACK ALBERICH
BELITTLE HOMUNCIO HOMUNCLE
HUCKMUCK KNURLING MENEHUNE
NANANDER
(PL.) CERCOPES NIBLUNGS
NIBELUNGS
DWARF DANDELION KRIGIA
DWARFED STUNTY STUNTED
DWARFING BRACHYSM
DWARFISH ELFIN PIGMY PYGMY
GRUBBY KNURLY NANOID RUNTISH
STUNTED
DWARFISHNESS NANISM
DWARFISM ATELIOSIS
DWARF MALLOW CHEESE PELLAS
DWARF RASPBERRY PLUMBOG
DWELL BIG COT DIG SIT WIN WON
BIDE BIGG HAFT HARP LIVE STAY
TELD WINE WONT ABIDE BIELD

BOWER BROOD BUILD DELAY
HOUSE LODGE PAUSE SHACK STALL
TARRY LINGER REMAIN RESIDE
TENANT CLIMATE COHABIT INHABIT
CONVERSE
(— IN) BIG BIGG BEDWELL INHABIT
(— IRRITATINGLY) GRATE
(— ON) HARP BROOD GLOAT
DWELLER TENANT WONNER
DENIZEN PALEMAN DOWNSMAN
HABITANT OCCUPANT RESIDENT
(— BY SEA) PARALIAN
(BUSH —) HATTER
(CAVE —) CAVEMAN TROGLODYTE
(CITY —) SLICKER
(COAST —) BUFFALO ORARIAN
(LAKE —) LACUSTRIAN
(PL.) HUTHOLD
DWELLING DAR HUT INN SEE WON
CASA FARM FLAT FORT HAFT HALL
HOME NEST ROOF SLUM TENT WIKE
WONE ABODE CABIN DOMUS HOTEL
HOUSE HOVEL JOINT MANSE MOTEL
CASTLE DUGOUT DUPLEX HOMING
MALOCA SHANTY TEEPEE WIGWAM
WONING COTTAGE LODGING
MANSION SALTBOX TRAILER
TRIPLEX WONNING BUILDING
BUNGALOW DOMICILE TENEMENT
(— IN UNDERWORLD) CHTHONIC
(— PLACE) HOWF HOWFF
(— WITH ANOTHER) INMATE
(ATTRACTIVE —) BOWER
(CRUDE —) SHED SHEBANG
(LAKE —) PALAFITTE
(MEAN —) SHANTY
(MISERABLE —) BURROW
(NAVAJO —) HOGAN
(NEOLITHIC —) TERRAMARA
(ONE-ROOM —) CELL
(RAMSHACKLE —) HUMPY
(RUDE —) BOTHY BOTHIE
(SUBTERRANEAN —) WEEM
(SWISS —) CHALET
(PL.) HOUSING
DWINDLE FADE FAIL FINE MELT PINE
WANE DECAY DRAIN PETER TAPER
TRAIL WASTE MOLDER SHRINK
CONSUME DECLINE FRITTER
MOULDER DECREASE DIMINISH
FORDWINE
DWINDLING DOWN FLAGGING
DYBBUK GILGUL
DYE (ALSO SEE DYESTUFF) AAL DIP
LIT ANIL BLUE COLOR EMBUE
FUCUS IMBUE LOKAO STAIN SUDAN
TINCT VENOM ARCHIL INFECT
MADDER TINGER ENGRAIN INTINCT
LACMOID LOGWOOD ZAMBESI
AMARANTH COLORANT DYESTUFF
FUGITIVE INDIGOID TINCTURE
(— FUR) FEATHER
(— NOT FAST) FUGITIVE
(BLACK —) GUAKO
(BLUE —) RUM ROOM WOAD
CYANINE DICYANINE
(BROWN —) CACHOU
(GENERAL —S) NIL NILL AZINE
BROWN EOSIN GREEN DIANIL

EOSINE ISAMIN ORANGE PURPLE
VIOLET CYANINE FUCHSIN METANIL
PONCEAU PRIMULA ALIZARIN
AURANTIA CIBACRON DICYANIN
EURHODOL FUCHSINE HYPERNIC
INDULINE TURNSOLE VIRIDINE
SAFRANINE
(HAIR —) RASTIK
(ORANGE —) KAMALA
(PURPLE —) CASSIUS GALLEIN
(RED —) AAL AURIN EOSIN GRAIN
HENNA RUBIN AURINE CERISE
EOSINE RELBUN RUBINE CORINTH
CRIMSON MAGENTA PONCEAU
SAFFLOR ALIZARIN AMARANTH
BORDEAUX CORALLIN CROCEINE
(SCARLET —) TULY GRAIN
(VIOLET —) MAUVE ARCHIL ORCHIL
LACMOID ARCHILLA
(YELLOW —) ARUSA FLAVIN
CHRYSIN FISETIN FLAVINE LAWSONE
WONGSHY AURAMINE
DYED INGRAIN
(PERMANENTLY —) FAST
DYEING TINCTION
DYER LISTER TINGER TINTER
DYESTER FIELDER SKEINER
TAINTOR TINTIST
DYERMA ZARMA ZAREMA
DYERS' MULBERRY FUSTIC
DYERS'-WEED SOLIDAGO
DYESTUFF (ALSO SEE DYE) DYE LIT
WELD WOAD LOKAO WOULD
ANATTO LITMUS ORCEIN RELBUN
ALKANET ARNATTO CUDBEAR
DYEWARE SAFFRON
DYEWEED WOODWAX
DYEWOOD FUSTET FUSTIC
BARWOOD CAMWOOD HYPERNIC
DYING FEY DEATH MORENDO
PARTING MORIBUND
(— AWAY) CALANDO DILUENDO
MANCANDO PERDENDO SMORZATO
DYNAMIC POTENT DRIVING KINETIC
FORCEFUL
DYNAMITE BLAST DUALIN SAWDUST
RENDROCK GELIGNITE
DYNAMO EXCITER TORNADO
DYNASTY (OR MEMBER THEREOF)
KIN SUI WEI YIN CHIN CHOU HSIA
RACE SUNG TANG YUAN BUYID
CHING PIAST REALM RULER SHANG
HAFSID PRINCE SAFAVI SELJUK
ALMOHAD ARSACID ATTALID
AYUBITE AYYUBID BOUIDES FATIMID
HAFSITE IDRISID JAGELLO LAKHMID
MONARCH OMAYYAD ROMANOV
SAADIAN SAFAWID SAMANID
TULUNID AGHLABID AGLABITE
ASMONEAN BUWAIHID CAPETIAN
CHALUKYA DOMINION EDRISITE
GOVERNOR IDRISITE JAGIELLO
LORDSHIP SAFFARID SARGONID
SASANIAN SELEUCID SOFFARID
SASSANIDE
DYSENTERY FLUX SCOUR MENISON
TOXEMIA DIARRHEA
DYSPHORIA FIDGET
DYSSODIA BOEBERA

E EASY ECHO
EA HEA ENKI
EACH A EA UP ALL ILK THE UCH
ILKA UCHE EVERY APIECE EITHER
EVERYONE
EAGER HOT RAD YAN ACID AGOG
AVID EDGY FAIN FELL FOND FREE
GAIR HIGH KEEN RATH SOUR TARE
THRO VAIN WARM WAVE YARE
YERN AFIRE AGASP ANTSY BRIEF
FIRST FRACK FRECK HASTY HIGRE
ITCHY PRIME READY SHARP SNELL
YIVER ARDENT FIERCE GREEDY
HETTER INTENT STRONG TIPTOE
ANXIOUS ATHIRST BRITTLE BURNING
EXCITED FERVENT FORWARD
ITCHING PROVOKE DESIROUS
IRRITATE SPIRITED VIGOROUS
YEARNING
(— IN PURSUIT) SHARP
(WILDLY —) CRAZY
EAGERLY FAST FELL YERN HOTLY
BELIVE TIPTOE YARELY YEPELY
PRESTLY HUNGRILY INTENTLY
EAGERNESS GOG ELAN GARE ZEAL
ARDOR DESIRE FERVOR ARDENCY
AVIDITY ALACRITY CUPIDITY
DEVOTION FAINNESS FERVENCY
EAGLE AAR ERN CROW ERNE GIER
TERN HARPY AQUILA BERGUT
EAGLET FALCON FORMAL FORMEL
RAPTOR ALLERION BATALEUR
BEARCOOT BERGHAAN RINGTAIL
(SEA —) ERN ERNE PYGARG
PYGARGUS
EAGLE OWL KATOGLE
EAGLESTONE AETITES
EAGLET BIRD LAIGLON
EAGLEWOOD AGALLOCH
EAGRE BORE WAVE AEGIR HYGRE
EAR LUG NEB CLIP HEAR HEED
HOOK LIST OBEY PLOW TILL AURIS
BRACE PINNA SENSE SOUSE SOWSE
SPIKE CANNON CONCHA CROSET
EARLET LISTEN AURICLE HEARING
SENSORY AUDIENCE RECEPTOR
(— OF BELL) CANON CANNON
(— OF CORN) COB ICKER NUBBIN
CORNCOB
(— OF GRAIN) RISOM SPIKE RIZZOM
(— OF WHEAT) SPICA WHEATEAR
(—S OF GRAIN) CAPES EARHEAD
(UNRIPE — OF CORN) TUCKET
EARACHE OTALGY OTALGIA
EARCOCKLE PURPLES
EARDRUM TABOR TABOUR TYMPAN
DRUMHEAD TYMPANUM
EARFLAP LUG EARLAP EARTAB
EARMUFF
EARL EORL GRAF LORD PEER
COMES NOBLE CONSUL SIWARD
(— OF COVENTRY)
SNIPSNAPSNORUM
EARLDOM DERBY COUNTY
EARLIER ERE OLD ERST FORE
ELDER UPPER BEFORE FORMER
HITHER RATHER SOONER FIRSTER
FURTHER PIONEER PREMIER
PREVIOUS

EARLIEST ERST FIRST ELDEST
MAIDEN RATHEST FURTHEST
PRIMROSE
EAR LOBE LUG EARLAP
(— PEOPLE) OREJON
EARLY AIR ERE OLD GOOD HIGH
RARE RATH SOON FORME PRIMY
RATHE VERTY REARLY SUDDEN
TIMELY ANCIENT BETIMES ERLICHE
FORWARD YOUTHFUL
EARMARK BIT CROP SPLIT LUGMARK
OVERBIT SLEEPER ALLOCATE
OVERCROP UNDERBIT
EAR MUFF OREILET
EARN GET WIN FANG GAIN TILL
VANG ADDLE ETTLE GLEAR MERIT
GARNER HUSTLE OBTAIN ACHIEVE
ACQUIRE CHEVISE DEMERIT
DESERVE
(— BY LABOR) ADDLE SWINK
BESWINK
EARNEST ARRA DEAR DERN HARD
PAWN ARLES GRAVE SMART SOBER
STAID ARDENT ENTIRE HANSEL
HEARTY INTENT SEDATE SOLEMN
EMULOUS ENGAGED FERVENT
FORWARD HANDSEL INTENSE
SERIOUS SINCERE ZEALOUS
DILIGENT EMPHATIC STUDIOUS
(IN —) AGOOD
EARNESTLY HARD DEARLY WISHLY
EARNEST DEVOUTLY DINGDONG
ENTIRELY HEARTILY INTENTLY
INWARDLY
EARNESTNESS GLOW FERVOR
WARMTH GRAVITY DEVOTION
DILIGENCE
EARNINGS GET MAKING ADDLINS
PICKING ADDLINGS
EARPIECE BUTTON
EARPLUG STOPPLE TEMBETA
EARSPOOL
EARRING DROP GRIP EARBOB
EARLET PENDLE EARCLIP EARDROP
PENDANT EARSCREW
EAR SHELL ORMER ABALONE
EARSHOT SOUND HEARING
EARREACH
EARTH ERD ORB SET BALL BANK
BURY BYON CLAY CLOD DIRT DUST
FLAG FOLD GRIT LAND LOAM MARL
MASS MEAL MOLD MOOL MUCK
ROCK SOIL SORY STAR VALE YIRD
ADOBE CRUMB FLOSS GLEBE
GLOBE GROOT INTER LOESS MOULD
REGUR TERRA TRASS UMBER
WORLD CENTER CENTRE COARSE
GROUND YACATA KOKOWAI
MIDGARD TERRENE TIERRAS
TOPSOIL TRIPOLI MAGNESIA
MIDGARTH
(— PROVIDING OCHER) KOKOWAI
(— SUITABLE FOR CULTIVATION)
LAYER
(BLACK —) MUCK SORY KILLOW
AMPELITE
(BLUE —) KIMBERLITE
(BROWN —) UMBER
(CLAYEY —) LAME LOAM

(DRY —) MOOL GROOT
(FULLER'S —) CRETA
(GEM-BEARING —) BYON
(LOOSE —) CRUMB GEEST
(MOIST —) SLIME
(POOR —) RAMMEL
(REFUSE —) MURGEON
(RIVER-BANK —) GREWT
(SMALL —) TERRELLA
(SOAP —) SOAPROCK
(STRAW-YELLOW —) BISMITE
(SUN-DRIED —) SWISH
(VITRIFIED —) FLOSS
(VOLCANIC —) TRASS TARRASS
EARTHEN FICT DIRTEN EARTHLY
YARTHEN
EARTHENWARE POT DELF CHINA
CLOAM CROCK DELFT CLAYEN
JASPER ASTBURY BISCUIT FAIENCE
POTTERY TICKNEY BUFFWARE
CROCKERY TALAVERA
(BROKEN PIECE OF —) CROCK
EARTHINESS SALT TERREITY
EARTHKIN TERRELLA
EARTHLY LAIRY CARNAL EARTHY
MORTAL EARTHEN GLEBOUS
MUNDANE SECULAR TERRAIN
TERRENE WORLDLY SUBLUNAR
TEMPORAL
EARTHNUT ARNUT CHUFA HOGNUT
JARNUT PEANUT PIGNUT HARENUT
HAWKNUT TRUFFLE
EARTH PIG ERDVARK AARDVARK
EARTHQUAKE QUAKE SEISM SHAKE
SHOCK TEMBLOR SEAQUAKE
EARTHSTAR GEASTER
EARTHWALL TRINCHERA
EARTHWORK BANK RATH AGGER
CASTLE RAMPART TERRACE
EARTHWORM ESS MAD WORM
ANNELID DEWWORM IPOMOEA
MADDOCK ANGLEDOG BRANDLIN
EACEWORM FISHWORM RAINWORM
TWATCHEL LUMBRICID
EARTHY GROSS SALTY WORMY
VULGAR EARTHLY TERRENE
BARNYARD TERREOUS VISCERAL
EAR TICK PINOLEA
EAR TRUMPET CORNET
EARWAX CERUMEN
EARWIG GOLACH GOLOCH
TOUCHBELL
EARWORM BOLLWORM
EASE CALM COSY COZY EASY REST
ALLAY KNACK PEACE QUIET RELAX
SLAKE LOOSEN PACIFY REDUCE
RELIEF REPOSE SAUGHT SMOOTH
SOFTEN SOOTHE APPEASE
ASSUAGE COMFORT CONTENT
FACULTY FLUENCY FREEDOM
LEISURE LIBERTY LIGHTEN RELIEVE
SLACKEN SUBSIDE DIMINISH
FACILITY MITIGATE MODERATE
PALLIATE PLEASURE SECURITY
UNBURDEN
(— OF A BURDEN) LIGHT
(— OFF) FLOW CHECK START
SLOUGH
(APATHETIC —) INDOLENCE

(AT —) OTIOSE
(CAREFREE —) ABANDON
EASEL FRAME SUPPORT SCAFFOLD
EASEMENT EASE EASING RELIEF
HERBAGE TURBARY SERVITUS
WAYLEAVE
EASE-TAKING PICKTOOTH
EASIEST EFTEST
EASILY EASY EATH WELL LIGHT
EATHLY GENTLY GLIBLY HANDILY
LIGHTLY READILY SLIGHTLY
SMOOTHLY
EASINESS GRACE FACILITY
EASING DETENTE
EAST ASIA MORN LEVANT ORIENT
SUNRISE EASTWARD
(— OF) FOLLOWING
EAST AFRICA (— TREE) PODO
EASTER PT PACE PASCH EOSTRE
PASCHA PASQUE
EASTERN LEVANT ORTIVE AURORAL
ORIENTAL
EASTERNER DUDE
EAST INDIAN (— TREE) SAL TEAK
KOKAN LANSA MAHUA MOHWA
NIEPA ROHAN ROHUN SALAI SIMAL
EASTLAND ESTRICHE
EASTWARD EAST EASEL EASSEL
EASY CALM COZY CRIP EATH EITH
GAIN GLIB MILD RIFE SNAP SOFT
CUSHY JAMMY LARGE LIGHT PRONE
ROYAL SUAVE YEZZY CASUAL
COMODO FACILE FLUENT FRUITY
GENTLE GENTLY SECURE SIMPLE
SMOOTH UNHARD ARTLESS
GRADUAL LENIENT NATURAL
CAREFREE CARELESS CAVALIER
EXPEDITE FAMILIAR GRACEFUL
HOMELIKE MODERATE TRANQUIL
UNFORCED
(— IN MIND) SECURE
(— TO HANDLE) HANDSOME
(— TO USE) CLEVER
EASYGOING LAX DEGAGE
EAT FOG KAI SUP BITE CHOW DINE
FARE FEED FRET GNAW GRUB HAVE
HEYT MAKE PECK RUST TUCK
ERODE FEAST GRAZE MANGE
MUNCH SCOFF STOKE TASTE
WASTE ABSORB BEGNAW DEVOUR
INGEST NIBBLE RAVAGE CONSUME
CORRODE DESTROY SWALLOW
VICTUAL
(— A MEAL) GRUB
(— AS HOGS) SLUICE
(— AWAY) GNAW ERODE RANKLE
CORRODE
(— BIG MEAL) STOKE
(— CRUNCHINGLY) GROUZE
(— GLUTTONOUSLY) GUDGE STUFF
(— GREEDILY) GAMP GAWP SLAB
SLOP TUCK CHAUM MOOCH SCOFF
GOBBLE GOFFLE GUTTLE GUZZLE
RAUNGE GLUTTON GOURMAND
(— HEARTILY) THORN
(— IN GULPS) LAB
(— MINCINGLY) PICK PICKLE PIDDLE
(— NOISILY) SLOP GULCH SLURP
GUTTLE SLOTTER

(— OUT) EXEDE
(— RUDELY) TROUGH
(— SLOVENLY) SLUP MUMMICK
(— SPARINGLY) DIET
(— TO EXCESS) COLF BEZZLE
(— UP) DEMOLISH
(— VORACIOUSLY) CRAM WORRY
(— WITH GUSTO) SMOUSE
(— WITHOUT CHEWING) BOLT
EATABLE FOODY COOKER EDIBLE
ESCULENT
EATEN CANKERED
(HALF —) SEMESE
EATER PECKER DEVOURER
(GREEDY —) GOURMAND
EATING BIT FOOD ESURINE
(— BETWEEN MEALS) TIFFIN
(— COARSE FOOD) FOUL
(— INTO) CANKEROUS
(— OUT) EXESION
EAVES EASE EASING
EAVESDROP DARK HARKEN
HEARKEN
EAVESDROPPER EARWIG
DRAWLATCH
EAVES TROUGH CHENEAU
EBB FAIL FALL SINK WANE ABATE
DECAY RECEDE REFLOW REFLUX
RETIRE TIDING DECLINE SUBSIDE
DECREASE DIMINISH
(— AND FLOW) ESTUS AESTUS
FLUIDITY
EBBING AWANE REFLUENT
REFLUOUS
(— AND FLOWING) TIDAL
EBLIS JANN IBLIS
EBONY EBON BLACK GABON
GABOON WAMARA HEBENON
IRONWOOD
EBULLIENCE OVERFLOW ELEVATION
EBULLIENT BRASH FERVID BOILING
EBULLIOSCOPE ZEOSCOPE
EBULLITION SEETHE FERMENT
OUTBURST
ECAD ECOPHENE
ECCENTRIC ODD CARD DOER
CRANK DOTTY KINKY QUEER WIPER
CRANKY LOCOED OUTISH PSYCHO
SCREWY SHAGGY BIZARRE CURIOUS
DEVIOUS ERRATIC STRANGE
TOUCHED ABNORMAL FITIFIED
PECULIAR SINGULAR
ECCENTRICITY KINK FERLY ODDITY
CROTCHET QUIDDITY
(— OF CURVE) E
ECCLESIASTES KOHELETH
QOHELETH
ECCLESIASTIC ABBE ABBOT CLERK
VICAR ARCHON FATHER LEGATE
PRIEST KIRKMAN PRELATE SECULAR
EPISTLER SUBDEACON
ECCLESIASTICAL CHRISTIAN
SPIRITUAL
ECHEVIN SCABINE SCABINUS
ECHIDNA NODIAK ANTEATER
EDENTATE PORCUPINE
ECHINODERM CYSTID CRINOID
BLASTOID STARFISH
ECHINOPANAX FATSIA

ECHINO-SOREX GYMNURA
ECHION (FATHER OF —) MERCURY
(MOTHER OF —) ANTIANIRA
(SON OF —) PENTHEUS
(WIFE OF —) AGAVE
ECHO ECO RING SING CHORUS
REPEAT REVERB SECOND IMITATE
ITERATE RESOUND RESPEAK
RESPOND REVOICE RESPONSE
ECLAT FAME GLORY RENOWN
ACCLAIM SCANDAL APPLAUSE
FACILITY PRESTIGE SPLENDOR
ECLECTIC BROAD LIBERAL
ECLIPSE DIM BIND BLOT HIDE BLIND
CLOUD SHADE STAIN SULLY
DARKEN DAZZLE DEFECT EXCEED
OCCULT DEFAULT OBSCURE
PRODIGY TRAVAIL OUTRIVAL
ECLOGUE IDYL IDYLL BUCOLIC
ECOLOGIST BIONOMIST
ECOLOGY BIOLOGY BIONOMY
MESOLOGY
ECONOMICAL WARY CHARY FENDY
FRUGAL SAVING CAREFUL PRUDENT
SPARING THRIFTY SCREWING
ECONOMICS PLUTONOMY
ECONOMIST HUSBAND MANAGER
ECONOMIZE HAIN SAVE SKIMP
STINT SCRIMP HUSBAND UTILIZE
RETRENCH
ECONOMY SPARE SAVING SYSTEM
THRIFT MANAGERY
ECSTASY JOY BLISS POWER SWOON
TRANCE DELIGHT EMOTION
MADNESS RAPTURE
ECSTATIC HOT RAPT PYTHIAN
GLORIOUS
ECTENE IRENICON
ECTODERM EXODERM EPIBLAST
ECTOMORPHIC LINEAR ASHENIC
LEPTOSOME
ECTROPION EVERSION
ECU SCUTE SHIELD

ECUADOR

ANCIENT NAME: QUITO
CAPE: ROSA PASADO PUNTILLA
CAPITAL: QUITO
COIN: SUCRE CONDOR CENTAVO
INDIAN: CARA INCA PALTA
CANELO JIVARO
ISLAND: PUNA WOLF MOCHA
PINTA BALTRA CHAVES DARWIN
PINZON WENMAN ISABELA
ISLANDS: COLON GALAPAGOS
LANGUAGE: JIBARO QUECHUA
SPANISH
MEASURE: CUADRA FANEGA
MOUNTAIN: ANDES SANGAY
CAYAMBE ANTISANA COTOPAXI
NATIVE: MONTUVIO
PROVINCE: LOJA AZUAY CANAR
COLON ELORO CARCHI GUAYAS
MANABI BOLIVAR LOSRIOS
COTOPAXI IMBABURA
RIVER: COCA MIRA NAPO DAULE
PINDO TIGRE GUAYAS TUMBES
ZAMORA CURARAY PASTAZA

AGUARICO BOBONAZA NARANJAL PUTUMAYO
TOWN: JAMA LOJA MERA NAPO PUYO TENA CANAR GUANO MANTA PAJAN PINAS PIURA QUITO YAUPI AMBATO CUENCA IBARRA PUJILI TULCAN ZARUMA AZOGUES CAYAMBE GUAMOTE MACHALA PELILEO PILLARO SALINAS BABAHOYO GUARANDA RIOBAMBA
WEIGHT: LIBRA

ECUMENE HEARTH
ECUMENICAL LIBERAL CATHOLIC
ECZEMA TETTER EARWORM MALANDERS
EDACITY GREED APPETITE VORACITY
EDDA SAGA
EDDISH ETCH ARRISH EEGRASS
EDDO TARO COCOYAM
EDDY CURL GULF PURL WASH WEEL WELL ACKER GURGE SHIFT SWIRL TWIRL WHIRL SWOOSH VORTEX WIRBLE BACKSET WREATHE
EDDYING WALE
EDEMA BRAXY TUMOR DROPSY BIGHEAD HYDROPS ANASARCA SWELLING
EDEMATOUS BLOATED HYDROPIC
EDEN ADEN HEAVEN UTOPIA ARCADIA ELYSIUM PARADISE
EDENTATA BRUTA
EDENTATE SLOTH ANTEATER
EDGE AGE BIT HEM JAG LIP RIM BANK BERM BRIM BROW CURB DRAW FACE KANT LIMB LIST RAND SIDE TRIM WHET ARRIS BERME BEVEL BLADE BOARD BRINK CHIMB CHIME CREST EAVES FRILL KNIFE LABEL LEDGE MARGE PEARL RULER SHARP SIDLE SPLAY VERGE BORDER DECKLE FLANGE FORAGE IMPALE LABRUM MARGIN NOSING PLANGE MARGENT SELVAGE SHARPEN VANDYKE BOUNDARY EMBORDER KEENNESS MAJORITY OUTSKIRT SELVEDGE STICKING UMSTROKE
(— **FORWARD**) CREEP
(— **IN MINING DRIFT**) ARRAGE
(— **OF BASKET**) FOOT
(— **OF BED**) STOCK
(— **OF BIRD'S BILL**) TOMIUM
(— **OF BOOK COVER**) FLAP
(— **OF BOOK**) FERRULE BACKBONE
(— **OF BRILLIANT**) GIRDLE
(— **OF CASK**) CHIME CHINE
(— **OF COAL PILE**) RUN
(— **OF DAM**) CREST
(— **OF DUMP**) TOE
(— **OF FLAG**) HOIST
(— **OF MESA**) CEJA
(— **OF MINERAL VEIN**) APEX
(— **OF ROADWAY**) SHOULDER
(— **OF RUDDER**) BEARDING
(— **OF RUFFLE**) HEADING

(— **OF SAIL**) FOOT HEAD LEACH LEECH
(— **OF SAW**) SAFE
(— **OF SHELL**) HINGE
(— **OF STRATUM**) BASSET
(— **OF STREAM**) HAG
(— **OF TOOL**) BEZEL BEZIL
(— **OF TOOTH**) SCALPRUM
(— **OF TROUSERS**) CREASE
(— **OF VAULT**) GROIN
(— **OF WOOD**) WOODRIME
(—**S OF COAT**) LAP
(**BEVELED** —) CHAMFER
(**CUTTING** —) SHOE
(**DOUBLE** —) FLAT
(**EMBROIDERED** —) SURFLE SURPHUL
(**EXTERIOR** —) AMBITUS
(**FRONT** — **OF BOOK**) FACE
(**ORNAMENTAL** —) FRILL
(**RAGGED** —) RAG
(**ROUGH** —S) FASH
(**SHARP** —) ARRIS BEARD
(**UNPLOWED** — **OF FIELD**) RAND
(**UNTRIMMED** —) DECKLE
EDGED EDGY EROSE SHARP CRENATE CUTTING
(— **BY ARCS**) INVECTED
EDGER WHETTER STRANDER
EDGING HEM CURB EDGE LACE LIST FILET FRILL LEDGE PICOT BORDER FILLET FRINGE BEADING BINDING GIMPING HAMBURG COQUILLE FRILLING PUNTILLA RICKRACK SKIRTING SURROUND
EDGY EAGER SHARP ANGULAR CRITICAL SNAPPISH
EDIBLE EDULE EATABLE ESCULENT
EDICT ACT BAN LAW BULL FIAT TYPE ARRET BANDO BULLA IRADE ORDER SANAD UKASE ASSIZE DECREE DICTUM NOTICE COMMAND EMBARGO PLACARD PROCESS PROGRAM STATUTE ECTHESIS
EDIFICE DOME CHURCH TURBEH BUILDING ERECTION TETRAGON
EDIFY GROW BUILD FAVOR TEACH BENEFIT IMPROVE PROSPER CONVINCE INSTRUCT ORGANIZE
EDIFYING HIGH SAVORY ELEVATED
EDIT CUT EMEND DIRECT REDACT REVIEW REVISE ARRANGE COMPILE CORRECT PREPARE PUBLISH REWRITE COPYREAD
EDITION KIND EXTRA FINAL FIRST ISSUE PRINT STAMP ALDINE DIGLOT SOURCE AUSGABE BULLDOG HEXAPLA OCTAPLA VERSION PRINCEPS VARIORUM
(**FIRST** —) PRINCEPS
EDITOR AUTHOR OVERSEER REDACTOR
EDITORIAL LEADER
EDO BENI BINI
EDUCATE REAR BREED TEACH TRADE TRAIN EXPAND INFORM SCHOOL DEVELOP NURTURE INSTRUCT
EDUCATED BRED CIVIL TAUGHT

TRAINED INFORMED LETTERED LITERATE
EDUCATION NURTURE BREEDING LEARNING NORTELRY TRAINING
(**LIBERAL** —) HUMANITY
(**PHYSICAL** —) GYM
EDUCATOR TEACHER
EDUCE DRAW EVOKE ELICIT EVOLVE EXTORT EXTRACT
EEL ELE GRIG LING OPAH SNIG TUNA ELVER MORAY SIREN APODAN CARAPO CONGER FAUSEN MOREIA MURENE CONGRIO KWATUMA LAMPREY MURAENA SNIGGLE WRIGGLE CONGEREE GYMNOTID KINGKLIP
(**25** —S) STICK SWARM
(**YOUNG** —) ELVER OLIVER YELVER
EELGRASS DREW WRACK ENALID
EELPOUT BARD LING POUT QUAB BURBOT CONGER GUFFER YOWLER LYCODOID
EELSKIN (**10** —S) TIMBER
EELSPEAR PILGER
EELWORM EEL NEMA
EERIE EERY SCARY TIMID WEIRD WISHT CREEPY DISMAL GLOOMY GOUSTY SPOOKY AWESOME GHOSTLY GOUSTIE MACABRE STRANGE UNCANNY ELDRITCH GHOULISH POKERISH
EFFACE BLOT DASH DELE RASE RAZE WEAR ERASE CANCEL DEFACE SPONGE STRIKE DESTROY DISLIMN EXPUNGE NULLIFY UNPAINT
EFFECT DO SEE DENT DOES FECK HAVE PRAY PREY TEEM WORK CAUSE CLOSE ECLAT ENACT ETTLE EVENT FORCE FRUIT ISSUE STAMP ENERGY GROWTH INDUCE INTENT OBTAIN RESULT SECURE SEQUEL STEREO UPSHOT ACHIEVE ACQUIRE ARRANGE COMPASS CONDUCE EMOTION EXECUTE FULFILL IMPRESS IMPRINT OPERATE OUTCOME PERFORM PROCURE PRODUCE PURPORT REALIZE CAUSATUM COMPLETE CONCLUDE CONTRIVE FRUITAGE
(— **OF PAST EXPERIENCE**) MNEME
(**BLURRED** —) FUZZ
(**COUNTERBALANCING** —) STANDOFF
(**DAZZLING** —) ECLAT
(**DECORATIVE** —) CHIPPING
(**ELECTRICAL** —) STRAY
(**ESTHETIC** —) ATMOSPHERE
(**FALSE** —) FACADE
(**FINAL** —) AMOUNT
(**ILL** —) EVIL
(**INTENSE** —) STRESS
(**MOTTLED** —) SPRINKLE
(**MUSICAL** —) BEND SHADING
(**PAINFUL** —) JAR
(**PAINTING** —) STIPPLE
(**PENETRATING** —) SEARCH
(**PERNICIOUS** —) BLAST
(**PERSONAL** —S) DUNNAGE
(**SHATTERING** —) BRISANCE

(THEATRICAL —) CURTAIN
(TO HAVE —) MILITATE
(TOTAL —) ENSEMBLE
(TOXIC —S) THEISM
(TREMOLO —) BEBUNG
(VISIBLE —) TOUCH
EFFECTIVE ABLE HOME REAL ALIVE
GREAT HAPPY SIKER VALID ACTIVE
ACTUAL CAUSAL DEADLY DIRECT
FRUITY POTENT SEVERE SICKER
SOVRAN CAPABLE FECKFUL
TELLING VIRTUAL ADEQUATE
FORCEFUL POWERFUL SMASHING
STRIKING VIGOROUS
EFFECTIVELY NAITLY
EFFECTIVENESS AIM BANG EDGE
VOLTAGE EFFICACY LEVERAGE
EFFECTUAL TOOTHY ADEQUATE
POWERFUL MAGISTRAL
EFFECTUATE FULFIL FULFILL
COMPLETE
EFFEMINATE NICE MILKY SAPPY
BITCHY FEMALE LYDIAN NIMINY
SILKEN TENDER WANTON WEAKLY
CITIZEN EPICENE WOMANLY
FEMINATE FEMININE LADYLIKE
OVERSOFT WOMANISH
EFFERENT EXODIC
EFFERVESCE FIZZ HUFF KNIT
BUBBLE SPARKLE
EFFERVESCENCE FRET CRACKLE
SPARKLE
EFFERVESCENT UP BRISK FIZZY
QUICK BUBBLY ELASTIC BUBBLING
EFFERVESCING BRISK
EFFETE SERE SPENT BARREN
DECADENT ETIOLATE MORIBUND
EFFICACIOUS VALID MIGHTY
POTENT FORCIBLE POWERFUL
SINGULAR VIGOROUS VIRTUOUS
EFFICACY DINT FECK DEVIL FORCE
GRACE MIGHT POWER DEGREE
VIRTUE POTENCY
EFFICIENCY POWER SKILL AGENCY
ABILITY FACULTY DISPATCH
EFFICACY
EFFICIENT ABLE GOOD SMART
VALID POTENT CAPABLE FECKFUL
POWERFUL SPEEDFUL
EFFIGY GUY IDOL POPE SIGN
DUMMY IMAGE LIKENESS
MONUMENT
EFFLORESCE GERMINATE
EFFLORESCENCE RASH BLOOM
BLOSSOM ROSEOLA ANTHESIS
ERUPTION WHITEWASH
EFFLUENCE ISSUE EFFLUX ELAPSE
EMANATE
EFFLUVIA SCENT
EFFLUVIUM AURA MIASMA FLUXION
SPECIES APORRHEA EMISSION
OUTGOING EMANATION
EFFLUX OUTGO OUTFLOW EFFUSION
EFFORT JOB TRY TUG DINT FIST
HUMP JUMP MINT SHOT TOIL ASSAY
BRUNT BURST CRACK DRIVE ESSAY
FLING LABOR NISUS PAINS POWER
REACH STUDY THROE TRIAL ANIMUS
DEVOIR FAVORS FIZZLE FUFFLE

PINGLE STRAIN STROKE THRIFT
ATTEMPT CONATUS MOLIMEN
NITENCY SPLURGE STRETCH
TENSURE TROUBLE WORKING
ENDEAVOR EXERTION GOODWILL
INDUSTRY MOLITION REACHING
STRIVING STRUGGLE
(— FOR ONESELF) FEND
(ABORTIVE —) FIZZLE
(AGONIZED —) THROE
(ARTICULATIVE —) ACCENT
(EARNEST —) STUDY
(EFFECTIVE —) LICK
(FINAL —) CHARETTE
(INITIAL —) ASSAY
(MAXIMUM —) BEST
(SALVATIONIST —) ATTACK
(SINGLE —) HEAT TRICE
(STRENUOUS —) HASSEL HASSLE
(UNSUCCESSFUL —) ATTEMPT
(UTMOST —) DEVOIR BUSINESS
(VIOLENT —) BURST STRAIN
OUTRAGE STRUGGLE
EFFORTLESS EASY
EFFORTLESSNESS EASE
EFFRONTERY BROW FACE GALL
FRONT BRONZE AUDACITY
BOLDNESS FOREHEAD TEMERITY
EFFULGENCE BLAZE GLORY
RADIANT RADIANCE SPLENDOR
EFFULGENT BRIGHT FULGENT
RADIANT SHINING
EFFUSE GUSH SHED FLING EFFUND
EMANATE DISPENSE
EFFUSION EFFLUX FOISON SPILTH
STREAM
EFFUSIVE GOOEY GUSHY LAVISH
SLOPPY GUSHING BUBBLING
EFFUSIVENESS SLOP
EFT ASK EVET NEWT LIZARD TRITON
EGAD ADAD ECOD IGAD SGAD
EGEST VOID EXCRETE ELIMINATE
EGG AI ABET GOAD GOOG OVUM
PROD SEED SPUR URGE CHECK
OVULE SPORE DARNER INCITE
OOCYTE PEEWEE ZYGOTE ACTUATE
COKENEY OOPLAST OOSPERM
PROTOVUM
(— CASE) POD
(— CLUTCH) LAUGHTER
(— OF FISH OR LOBSTER) BERRY
(— ON) HAG EDGE GOAD URGE
(— PRODUCT) ZOON
(—S OF BEES) BROOD
(—S OF SILKWORM) GRAINE
(ACID —) SLOWCASE
(CRACKED —) CHECK CRACK
LEAKER
(DRIED —S) AHUATLE
(DUCK —S) PIDAN
(FLY'S —) BLOW FLYBLOW
(FOSSIL —) OVULITE
(GOLDEN —S) SUNCUP
(GOOSE —) BLOB
(HUNT BIRDS' —S) OOLOGIZE
(INFERTILE —) CLEAR
(SMALL —) OVULE OVULUM
(PL.) OVA ROE SEED EYREN SPAWN
CLUTCH ETTING AHUATLE

EGG AND DART ECHINUS
EGGFRUIT LUCUMA CANISTEL
EGGHEAD HIGHBROW INTELLECTUAL
EGGNOG NOG ADVOCAAT
EGGPLANT BRINJAL SOLANUM
BRINGELA EGGFRUIT
EGG-SHAPED OOID OVAL OVATE
OVOID OOIDAL OBOVOID OVALOID
OVIFORM
EGGSHELL SHARD CASCARON
EGG WHITE GLAIR ALBUMEN
EGG YOLK YELLOW VITELLUS
EGO I SELF ATMAN EGOITY FYLGJA
CONCEIT SUBJECT
EGOCENTRIC INSEEING
EGOISM PRIDE ONEISM VANITY
CONCEIT EGOTISM OWNHOOD
SELFNESS
EGOTISM EGO PRIDE EGOISM
VANITY CONCEIT EGOMANIA
EGREGIOUS FINE GROSS CAPITAL
EMINENT FLAGRANT PRECIOUS
SHOCKING
EGREGIOUSLY BEASTLY
EGRESS EXIT ISSUE OUTGO OUTLET
EXITURE OUTCOME OUTGATE
PASSAGE REGRESS OUTGOING
EGRET HERON PLUME GAULIN
KOTUKU AIGRETTE GAULDING
EGYPT MIZRAIM

EGYPT

BAY: FOUL
CALENDAR: AHET APAP TYBI
PAYNI SHEMU THOTH CHOIAK
HATHOR MECHIR MESORE
PAOPHI PACHONS
CANAL: SUEZ
CAPE: BANAS RASBANAS
CAPITAL: CAIRO ELQAHIRA
CHRISTIAN: COPT COPTIC
COIN: FILS DINAR GIRSH POUND
DIRHAM GUINEA JUNAYH
PIASTER MILLIEME
DAM: ASWAN
DESERT: LIBYAN
GOVERNORATE: SUEZ CAIRO
CANAL SINAI BAHARIYA
BAHRIYAH ALEXANDRIA
GULF: AQABA
ISTHMUS: SUEZ
KING: AY IB KA ITI ITY TUT DJER
DJET HUNY PAMI PEPI SETI
TEOS TETI UNIS ARSES BEBTI
FOUAD ITETI KEBEH KHUFU
KNIAN MENES NEBKA NECHO
NEFER UDIMU ZEMTI ZOSER
CHEOPS DARIUS FAROUK
KHAFRE NARMER RANSES
SENEDJ XERXES MENKURE
PHARAOH PTOLEMY RAMESES
SALADIN CHEPHREN THUTMOSE
LAKE: EDKU IDKU MARYUT
MOERIS MANZALA BURULLUS
MAREOTIS
LAKES: BITTER
MEASURE: APT DRA HEN PIK ROB
DRAA KHET ROUB THEB ABDAT

ARDAB CUBIT FARDE KELEH
KILAH SAHME ARTABA AURURE
FEDDAN KEDDAH ROBHAH
SCHENE CHORYOS DARIBAH
MALOUAH ROUBOUH TOUMNAH
KASSABAH KHAROUBA
MOUNTAIN: SINAI GHARIB
KATHERINA
NAME: UAR
NATIVE: ARAB COPT NILOT
BERBER MUSLIM NUBIAN
OASIS: SIWA DAKHLA KHARGA
FARAFRA BAHARIYA
PENINSULA: SINAI
PORT: TOR SUEZ ATTUR DUMYAT
QUSEIR RASHID SAFAGA
SALLUM ROSETTA DAMIETTA
HURGHADA PORTSAID
ALEXANDRIA
PROVINCE: GIZA QENA QINA
ASWAN ASYUT MINYA SOHAG
DUMYAT FAIYUM SAWHAJ
TAHRIR ALJIZAH BEHEIRA
BENISUEF DAMIETTA GHARBIYA
MINUFIYA SHARQIYA
RESERVOIR: ASWAN
RIVER: NILE
RUINS: ABYDOS SPHINX THEBES
MEMPHIS PYRAMIDS
SUN GOD: RA RE TEM ATMU
ATUM
TOWN: NO MUT DUSH GIZA IDFU
ISNA QENA SAIS SIWA SUEZ
ZOAN ASWAN ASYUT BENHA
BULAQ CAIRO ELTUR FAYID
GIRGA GIZEH LUXOR NAKHL
SALUM SOHAG TAHTA TANIS
TANTA ABYDOW AKHMIN
DUMYAT ELQASR HELWAN
KARNAK RASHID THEBES
BURSAID ROSETTA ZAGAZIG
BENISUEF DAMIETTA ISMAILIA
WEIGHT: KAT KET OKA OKE HEML
KHAR OKIA ROTL ARTAL ARTEL
DEBEN KERAT MINAE MINAS
OKIEH POUND RATEL UCKIA
HAMLAH KANTAR DRACHMA
QUINTAL
WELL: BIRTABA
WIND: KAMSIN SIROCCO
KHAMSEEN

EGYPTIAN ARAB COPT GIPPY GYPPY
TASIAN PHARIAN BADARIAN
MEMPHIAN
EIDER COLK WAMP DIVER EDDER
DUCKER SHOREYER
EIDOLON ICON GHOST IMAGE
IDOLUM PHANTOM LIKENESS
EIGHT ETA ECHT AUGHT CHETH
OCTAD OCTET OCTAVE OGDOAD
OCTONARY
EIGHTH AUGHT
EIGHTH NOTE UNCA CROMA
CHROMA QUAVER
EIRE (SEE IRELAND)
EITHER ANY EDDER ITHER OTHER
WHETHER

EJACULATE BELCH BLURT EJECT
FLING EXCLAIM EMISSION
EJACULATION HOW COADS ZOWIE
BEGORRA UTTERING
(MYSTIC —) OM
EJACULATORY SPUTTERY
EJECT OUT BLOW BOOT CAST EMIT
FIRE HOOF OUST SHED SPAT SPEW
SPIT VOID WARP AVOID BELCH
CHUCK ERUCT ERUPT EVICT EXPEL
SHAKE SHOOT SPOUT SPURT VOMIT
BANISH BOUNCE SQUIRT DEFORCE
DISMISS EXCLUDE EXTRUDE
OBTRUDE DISGORGE OUTBRAID
EJECTION BLOW OUSTER OUTING
EVICTION
EJECTOR LIFTER EDUCTOR
EKE IMP ALSO YEKE AUGMENT
ENLARGE HUSBAND STRETCH
APPENDIX INCREASE LENGTHEN
LIKEWISE UNDERLAY
ELABORATE FIKIE GREAT LABOR
DELUXE DRESSY ELABOR ORNATE
QUAINT REFINE CURIOUS DEVELOP
ENLARGE LABORED PERFECT
ELABORATED WROUGHT
ELABORATELY FANCILY
ELABORATENESS FINENESS
CURIOSITY
ELAMITE SUSIAN ANZANITE
ELAN DASH ARDOR DRIVE GUSTO
VERVE SPIRIT WARMTH POTENCY
ELAND IMPOFO
ELAN VITAL ZOISM
ELAPS MICRURUS
ELAPSE GO RUN PASS ROLL SLIP
GLIDE SPEND EXPIRE
ELAPSING CURRENT
ELASTIC QUICK GARTER RUBATO
SPONGY BUOYANT SPRINGY
STRETCH CHEVEREL CHEVERIL
FLEXIBLE STRETCHY VOLATILE
ELASTICITY GIVE LIFE ELATER
SPRING STRETCH
ELATE BYOU CHEER EXALT EXULT
FLUSH LOFTY RAISE ELATED EXCITE
PLEASE THRILL ELEVATE GLADDEN
INFLATE SUBLIME SUCCESS
ELEVATED HEIGHTEN INSPIRIT
JUBILATE
ELATED RAD HIGH RADE CHUFF
ELATE HAPPY PROUD VAUDY VOGIE
WLONK CHUFFY JOVIAL UPPISH
UPPITY EXCITED EXULTED JOCULAR
SUBLIME EXULTANT GLORIOUS
INFLATED JUBILANT PRIDEFUL
UPLIFTED
ELATER BEETLE CRINULA SKIPJACK
ELATION JOY GLEE RUFF BUOYANCY
ELBOW ELL BEND ANCON JOINT
NUDGE SHOVE CROSET ELBUCK
JOSTLE JUSTLE SPRING PIERDROP
ELCAJA MAFURA
ELDER AIN IVA AINE WITE ELLER
OLDER PRIOR MAHANT SENIOR
ANCIENT NEGUNDO STAROST
TRAMMON ANCESTOR BOUNTREE
BOURTREE CARELESS DANEWORT
ELDERMAN

ELDERLY AGED GRAY ALDER
ELDERN SENILE BADGERLY
ELDEST AYNE EIGNE OLDEST
ELECAMPANE INULA CANADA
ELFWORT SCABWORT
ELECT CALL PICK VOICE ASSUME
CHOOSE CHOSEN DECIDE ISRAEL
PREFER SELECT
ELECTION PROXY CHOICE LECTION
ELECTIONEERING HUSTINGS
ELECTIVE OPTION
ELECTOR VOTER ELISOR CHOOSER
ELIGENT INTRANT ELECTANT
ELECTORATE PEOPLE COUNTRY
ELECTRA LAODICE
(BROTHER OF —) ORESTES
(DAUGHTER OF —) IRIS
(FATHER OF —) ATLAS AGAMEMNON
(HUSBAND OF —) PYLADES
(MOTHER OF —) PLEIONE
CLYTEMNESTRA
(SON OF —) DARDANUS
ELECTRICIAN GAFFER JUICER
BOARDMAN
ELECTRICITY JUICE PYROGEN
ELECTRIC GALVANISM
ELECTRIFY EXCITE THRILL STARTLE
ELECTROCUTE BURN EXECUTE
ELECTRODE DE DEE GRID ANODE
PLATE DYNODE CATHODE IGNITER
CROWFOOT REOPHORE
(PL.) ELEMENT
ELECTRODEPOSIT STRIKE
REGULINE
ELECTROLYTE STRIKE IONOGEN
ELECTROMAGNETIC (— UNIT)
OERSTED ABAMPERE
ELECTRON ION POLARON
ELECTRONIC RADIONIC
ELECTRONOGRAPHY ONSET
ELECTRON TUBE TRIODE
ELECTROPHONE MARTENOT
ELECTROPLATE SILVER
ELECTROTYPE PATCH CLICHE
WORKER ELECTRO
ELECTRUM AMBER ELECTRE
ORICHALC
ELECTRYON (DAUGHTER OF —)
ALCMENE
(FATHER OF —) PERSEUS
(MOTHER OF —) ANDROMEDA
ELECTUARY DIASCORD LECTUARY
THERIACA
ELEGANCE CHIC GARB LUXE CLASP
GRACE STYLE SWANK TASTE
FINERY GAIETY GAYETY LUXURY
NICETY POLISH COURTESY
EUPHUISM FINENESS FRIPPERY
GRANDEUR SPLENDOR
ELEGANT CHIC DINK FAIR FEAT FINE
FIXY GENT POSH CIVIL COMPT
FANCY SHARP SLEEK SWANK
CHOICE CLASSY DAINTY DELUXE
DRESSY FACETE MINION QUAINT
SUPERB SWANKY URBANE VENUST
CAPITAL CLEANLY COURTLY
FEATISH FEATOUS GENTEEL MINIKIN
REFINED SMICKER DELICATE
GINGERLY GRACEFUL GRAZIOSO

HANDSOME POLISHED TASTEFUL
ELEGANTLY FINE TALLY FAIRLY
GENTLY GINGERLY
ELEGIAC MOURNFUL EPICEDIAL
ELEGY POEM SONG DIRGE KINAH
QINAH LAMENT MONODY EPICEDE
ELEMENT AIR ATOM DIAD DYAD
RECT WOOF BEARD ETHER FIBER
FIBRE METAL MONAD PUNCT STUFF
AETHER ARTIAD COSTAL FACTOR
HEPTAD LOSSER MATTER MOMENT
SIMPLE ACTINON ADAPTER
BUNCHER CARRIER CATCHER
ESSENCE FEATURE ACTINIDE
BACKBONE CEREBRAL EQUATION
PERISSAD RUDIMENT SELECTOR
THERBLIG
(— IN GRAPH) SPIKE
(— IN WAVE) DART
(— IN WORD GROUP) KOINON
(— OF ALCHEMIST) AIR FIRE EARTH
WATER
(— OF EXISTENCE) DHARMA
(— OF MACHINE) HORN SPIDER
(— OF WEALTH) COMMODITY
(ALIEN —) ALLOY
(ARCHITECTURAL —) SLAB
(BINDING —) CEMENT
(CHEMICAL —) TIN GOLD IRON
LEAD NEON ZINC ARGON BORON
RADON XENON BARIUM CARBON
CERIUM CESIUM COBALT COPPER
CURIUM ERBIUM HELIUM INDIUM
IODINE MURIUM NICKEL OSMIUM
OXYGEN RADIUM SILVER SODIUM
SULFUR ARSENIC BISMUTH BROMINE
CADMIUM CALCIUM FERMIUM
GALLIUM HAFNIUM HOLMIUM
IRIDIUM KRYPTON LITHIUM
MERCURY NIOBIUM RHENIUM
RHODIUM SILICON TERBIUM
THORIUM THULIUM URANIUM
WOLFRAM YTTRIUM ANTIMONY
ASTATINE CHLORINE CHROMIUM
EUROPIUM FLUORINE FRANCIUM
HYDROGEN LUTETIUM MASURIUM
NITROGEN NOBELIUM PLATINUM
POLONIUM RUBIDIUM SAMARIUM
SCANDIUM SELENIUM TANTALUM
THALLIUM TITANIUM TUNGSTEN
VANADIUM
(COMMUNION —) GIFT
(CRIMINAL —) GANGLAND
(DECORATIVE —S) ART
(DOMINANT —) CAPSHEAF
(ELECTRIC —) IMPEDOR
(ESSENTIAL —) CORPUS
(EUCHARISTIC —S) HAGIA SPECIES
(FATAL —) BANE
(FUNDAMENTAL —) STAMEN
(HEATING —) CALANDRIA
(HYPOTHETICAL —) CORONIUM
(INTERFERING —) CRIMP
(LAMP —) GLOWER
(LEADING —) HEAD
(LINGUISTIC—) SERVILE INTENSIVE
(MILITARY —) SUPPORT
(MODIFYING —) LEAVENING
(MORAL —) DAENA

(MOST IMPORTANT —) CAPSTONE
(PRIMAL —) GUNA SALT ARCHE
(PRINCIPAL —) STAPLE
(SKELETAL —) SCLERE
(STRUCTURAL —) ARCUALE
(SUPPOSED —) WELSIUM VICTORIUM
(SUSTAINING —) BREAD STAPLE
(TRANSITORY —S) SKANDHAS
(UNITING —) BOND
(PL.) DETAIL ALPHABET
ELEMENTAL PURE BASIC PRIMAL
SIMPLE PRIMARY ULTIMATE
ELEMENTARY SIMPLE INITIAL
INCHOATE ULTIMATE
ELEMI ANEMI ANIME MATTI RESIN
CONIMA
ELEPHANT COW BULL CALF HINE
PUNK HATHI HATTY JUMBO ROGUE
MUCKNA TUSKER KOOMKIE
AIRAVATA LOXODONT MASTODON
OLIPHANT
ELEPHANT FISH JOSEF JOSUP
JOSEPH
ELEPHANTIASIS TYRIASIS
ELEPHANTINE HUGE ENORMOUS
ELEPHANT'S-EAR TARO
ELEPHANT SHREW JUMPER
ELEUT KALMUK KALMYK KALMUCK
ELEVATE HAIN JUMP LIFT REAR RISE
EDIFY ELATE ENSKY ERECT EXALT
EXTOL GRIMP HEAVE HOIST MOUNT
RAISE TOWER REFINE UPLIFT
ADVANCE DIGNIFY ENHANCE
ENNOBLE GLORIFY PROMOTE
SUBLIME UPRAISE HEIGHTEN
INSPIRIT
ELEVATED EL FINE HIGH GREAT
LOFTY NOBLE RISEN STEEP
AMOTUS ELATED RAISED RISING
WINGED ELEVATO EXALTED
MOUNTED STILTED MAJESTIC
UPLIFTED
(— IN CHARACTER) HIGH
(NOT —) COMICAL
ELEVATION UP ARM BAND BANK
DOME DRUM GLEE HIGH HILL HUMP
LIFT RISE SPUR TOFT TOOT UMBO
BULLA GRADE KNOLL MOUND PITCH
RAISE RIDGE SHOAL SWELL TOWER
WHEAL CONULE CRISTA HEIGHT
PAPULE UPLIFT DIGNITY FURCULA
MAJESTY UPRIGHT ALTITUDE
EMINENCE EVECTION HIGHNESS
LEVATION MOUNTAIN SWELLING
(— OF CARTILAGE) ANTHELIX
(— OF CUTICLE) BLEB
(— OF SKIN) BLISTER
(— ON TOOTH) STYLE
(— SEPARATING CREEKS) BUGOR
(GUN —) RANDOM
(TURRET —) HOOD
ELEVATOR BIN CAGE LIFT SILO
HOIST BRIDGE LIFTER TEAGLE
HOISTER STACKER UPTAKER
UPLIFTER UPRAISER
ELEVENTH ELFT
ELF FAY HAG HOB IMP OAF PUG
DROW FANE OUPH PERI PIXY
DWARF ELFIN FAIRY GNOME OUPHE

PIGMY PIXIE ELFKIN GOBLIN SPIRIT
SPRITE URCHIN BLASTIE BROWNIE
INCUBUS SUCCUBUS
ELFIN ELF FEY CHILD ELFIC ELFISH
URCHIN
ELFISH ELFIN ELVAN ELVISH IMPISH
URCHIN ELFLIKE TRICKSY
ELICIT DRAW MILK PUMP CLAIM
EDUCE EVOKE EXACT FETCH WREST
WRING DEDUCE DEMAND ENTICE
EXTORT INDUCE EXTRACT SOLICIT
ELIDE OMIT SKIP ANNUL IGNORE
DESTROY NULLIFY DEMOLISH
SUPPRESS
ELIGIBILITY FITNESS
ELIGIBLE FIT ACTIVE WORTHY
SUITABLE
ELIMINATE FAN COMB EDIT KILL
EDUCE EXPEL SCRUB DELETE
EFFACE EXCEPT IGNORE REMOVE
SCREEN WINNOW BLANKET
BRACKET DIVULGE EXCLUDE
EXCRETE RELEASE SCISSOR
SILENCE SUBLATE SEPARATE
ELIMINATION STRIP
ELISION SYNCOPE
ELITE BEST LITE PINK CIRCLE
CHOICE FLOWER GENTRY SELECT
PERFECTI
ELIXIR AMRITA SPIRIT AMREETA
ARCANUM CORDIAL CUREALL
ESSENCE PANACEA MEDICINE
ELK ALCE DEER LAMA LOSH ALAND
ALCES ELAND LOSHE MOOSE
CERVID SAMBAR WAPITI SAMBHUR
WAMPOOSE
(— HIDE) LOSH
(YOUNG —) DEACON
ELK BARK BIGBLOOM
ELL ULNA ELBOW ALNAGE ADDITION
ELLIPSE OVAL
ELLIPSIS BRING ELLIPSE
ELLIPSOGRAPH TRAMMEL
ELLIPSOID CONOID ELLIPTIC
SPHEROID
ELLIPTICAL OVAL OVATE OBLONG
ELLOBIUM AURICULA
ELM ULME ELVEN ULMUS WAHOO
MEZCAL CHEWBARK ORHAMWOOD
ELOCUTION SPEECH DICTION
ORATORY
ELOCUTIONIST READER RECITER
ELOIGN CONVEY REMOVE ABSCOND
CONCEAL
ELONGATE EXTEND REMOVE
STRETCH LENGTHEN PROTRACT
ELONGATED LANK LONG LINEAR
OBLONG PROLATE SLENDER
HAIRLIKE PRODUCED
ELOPE DECAMP ESCAPE ABSCOND
ELOQUENCE FACUND FLUENCY
ORATORY
ELOQUENT VOCAL DISERT FACUND
FERVID FLUENT SILVER RENABLE
SPEAKING

COIN: PESO COLON CENTAVO
DANCE: PASILLO
GULF: FONSECA
INDIAN: PIPIL
LAKE: GUIJA ILOPANGO
MEASURE: VARA CAFIZ CAHIZ
  FANEGA TERCIA BOTELLA
  CAJUELA CANTARO MANZANA
POINT: REMEDIOS
PORT: CUTUCO ACAJUTLA
RIVER: JIBOA LAPAZ LEMPA
RUINS: TAZUMAL
TOWN: CUTUCO IZALCO CORINTO
  METAPAN ACAJUTLA USULUTAN
VOLCANO: IZALCO
WEIGHT: BAG CAJA LIBRA

ELSE OR ENS ENSE OTHER BESIDES
INSTEAD
ELSEWHERE ALIBI EXCEPT THENCE
(FROM —) ALIUNDE
ELUCIDATE CLEAR LUCID EXPLAIN
SIMPLIFY
ELUDE BEAT FLEE FOIL MISS MOCK
SLIP AVOID DODGE EVADE BAFFLE
BEFOOL DELUDE DOUBLE ESCAPE
BEGUILE DECEIVE HEDGEHOP
ELUSIVE EELY LUBRIC SHIFTY
SUBTLE TRICKY TWISTY EVASIVE
BAFFLING FUGITIVE SLIPPERY
ELYSIUM EDEN ANNWIN PARADISE
ELYTRON HUSK SCUTE SHARD
SHERD SHEATH
ELYTRUM SHARD TEGMEN
EM EMMA
(HALF —) EN
EMACIATED LEAN POOR EMPTY
GAUNT MEAGER PEAKED SKINNY
WASTED WASTREL SKELETAL
EMACIATING MARCID
EMACIATION NITON TABES MACIES
ATROPHY POVERTY MARASMUS
EMANATE FLOW ARISE EMANE
EXUDE ISSUE DERIVE EFFUSE
EXHALE OUTRAY SPRING BREATHE
OUTCOME PROCEED RADIATE
EMANATING EFFLUENT
EMANATION FUG AURA BEAM BLAS
GLORY NITON AZILUT BREATH
EFFLUX ELAPSE EIDOLON OUTCOME
PROCESS SEPHIRA EMISSION
(— FROM A MEDIUM) ECTOPLASM
(PL.) SCENT
EMANCIPATE FREE MANUMIT
RELEASE LIBERATE UNFETTER
EMANCIPATION FREEDOM RELEASE
(FINAL —) NIRVANA
EMASCULATE GELD SOFTEN
EVIRATE CASTRATE ENERVATE
EMBALM BALM CERE MUMMY SPICE
BALSAM SEASON CONDITE MUMMIFY
EMBANK BUND
EMBANKMENT BAY BAND BANK
BUND DIKE DYKE FILL QUAY ARGIN
DIGUE LEVEE MOUND REVET
BUNKER STAITH BACKING BANKING
PILAPIL RAMPART RAMPIRE
SEAWALL APPROACH STRENGTH

EMBARGO EDICT ORDER IMBARGE
BLOCKADE STOPPAGE
EMBARK BANK SAIL SHIP ENGAGE
ENLIST INSHIP INVEST LAUNCH
IMBARGE
EMBARRASS SET CHAW CLOG FAZE
HACK LAND ABASH ANNOY SHAME
UPSET BOGGLE CUMBER GRAVEL
HAMPER HINDER HOBBLE IMPEDE
PLUNGE PUZZLE RATTLE CONFUSE
ENTRIKE FLUMMOX INVOLVE
NONPLUS BEWILDER CONFOUND
DUMFOUND ENCUMBER ENTANGLE
HANDICAP IMPESTER OBSTRUCT
STRAITEN
EMBARRASSED FLURRIED SHEEPISH
EMBARRASSING HIDEOUS
EMBARRASSINGLY AWKWARDLY
EMBARRASSMENT FIX GENE LURCH
SHAME STAND CADDLE HOBBLE
PUZZLE
EMBASSY SAND ERRAND AMBASSY
MESSAGE MISSION INBASSAT
LEGATION
EMBATTLED BATTLED CRENELE
BRETESSE CRENELEE
EMBAY BATHE DETAIN ENCLOSE
SHELTER SUFFUSE ENCIRCLE
SURROUND
EMBAYMENT FIORD FJORD
EMBED BED SET BOND IMBED
STAMP CHARGE ENGAGE EMBOWEL
IMMERSE
EMBEDDED INNATE ENGAGED
IMMERSED
EMBELLISH GEM DECK GILD TRIM
ADORN DRESS FUDGE GRACE
BEDECK BLAZON EMBOSS ENRICH
FIGURE FLOWER APPAREL BEDRAPE
EMBLAZE GARNISH MYSTIFY
VARNISH BEAUTIFY DECORATE
FLOURISH ORNAMENT
EMBELLISHED FLORID GESTED
ORNATE COLORED FUCUSED
BROCADED SPLENDID
EMBELLISHMENT FILIP GRACE
FILLIP RELISH AGREMEN GARNISH
GILDING WINDING AGREMENT
FLOURISH MOUNTING ORNAMENT
PARERGON TRAPPING TRICKING
PASSAGGIO
(MUSICAL —) ARABESQUE
(PL.) FIXINGS
EMBER ASH COAL AIZLE GLEED
IMBER CINDER
(RED-HOT —S) BAGA
EMBEZZLE STEAL PECULATE
SQUANDER
EMBEZZLEMENT THEFT
EMBITTER SOUR BITTER CURDLE
ACIDIFY ENVENOM ACERBATE
EMPOISON VERJUICE
EMBITTERED SOURED ACERBATE
EMBLAZON LAUD ADORN EXTOL
BLAZON DISPLAY EMBLAZE EXHIBIT
GLORIFY
EMBLAZONED CLOUE CLOUEE
CRINED CRESTED BRISTLED
(— WITH ANTLERS) ATTIRED

(— WITH BEARD) BARBED
EMBLAZONMENT HERALDRY
EMBLEM BAR ANKH ATEN MACE
ORLE SEAL SIGN STAR TYPE
AWARD BADGE CREST CROSS
EAGLE FAVOR IMAGE TIARA TOKEN
DEVICE DIADEM ENSIGN FIGURE
KAHILI SABCAT SHIELD SIGNAL
SYMBOL TRISUL CHARACT IMPRESA
IMPRESE SCEPTER SCEPTRE
ALLEGORY CADUCEUS COLOPHON
INSIGNIA
(— OF CUCKOLD) HORN
(— OF IRELAND) SHAMROCK
(— OF WALES) LEEK
(PRINTING —) COLOPHON
(SACRED —) HIEROGRAM
EMBLEMATIC TYPAL FIGURAL
TYPICAL SYMBOLIC
EMBLIC AMLA AULA MYROBALAN
EMBODIMENT MAP SON SELF
AVATAR GENIUS EPITOME IMAGERY
BODIMENT
EMBODY BODY UNITE INBODY
CONTAIN EXPRESS COALESCE
ORGANIZE
EMBOLDEN BOLD BIELD BRAVE
ERECT NERVE ASSURE BOWDEN
ENHARDY HEARTEN STOMACH
EMBOLUS CLOT STYLE
EMBOSOM BOSOM FOSTER CHERISH
ENCLOSE IMBOSOM SHELTER
SURROUND
EMBOSS BOSS HIDE KNOB KNOT
ADORN BLOCK CHASE GOFFER
INDENT POUNCE ANTIQUE CONCEAL
ENCLOSE EXHAUST GAUFFER
INFLATE ORNAMENT
EMBOSSED BOSSED RAISED
ANTIQUE CHAMPED
EMBOSSING CELATURE
EMBOUCHURE LIP CHOPS LIPPING
EMBOWER BOWER
EMBOWERED ARBORED
EMBRACE ARM HUG CLIP COLL
FOLD LOVE NECK PLAT SIDE ZONE
ADOPT BOSOM BRACE CHAIN CLASP
CLING CRUSH ENARM GRASP HALCH
HALSE INARM OXTER TWINE
ABRAZO ACCEPT ACCOLL AMPLEX
BECLIP CARESS CLINCH COMPLY
CUDDLE ENFOLD FATHOM HUDDLE
INCLIP INFOLD PLIGHT SHRINE
AMPLECT CHERISH CONTAIN
ENCLOSE ESPOUSE INCLUDE
INVOLVE ACCOLADE AMPLEXUS
COMPLECT COMPRESS COMPRISE
CONCLUDE ENCIRCLE
EMBRACING COLLING OSCULANT
EMBRASURE LOOP PORT VENT
CRENEL CRENELLE PORTHOLE
EMBROCATION ARNICA EMBROCHE
LINIMENT
EMBROIDER RUN TAT DARN FRET
LACE BROUD COUCH FAGOT PANEL
SMOCK BEWORK EMBOSS FAGGOT
FRIEZE PURFLE STITCH SURFLE
TISSUE BROIDER TAMBOUR
ORNAMENT

EMBROIDERED BRODE BRODEE BROWDEN BROCADED

EMBROIDERER SPRIGGER

EMBROIDERY KANT LACE OPUS WORK BREDE ASSISI BONNAZ CREWEL EDGING HEDEBO APPAREL CHICKEN CUTWORK ORPHREY SETWORK TAMBOUR ARRASENE BRODERIE BROIDERY FAGOTING LISTWORK PHULKARI SMOCKING TAPESTRY

EMBROIL BROIL JUMBLE INVOLVE PERPLEX TROUBLE DISORDER DISTRACT ENTANGLE

EMBRYO GERM CADET FETUS OVULE FOETUS EMBRYON NEURULA ACANTHOR BLASTULA GASTRULA PRINCIPE

EMBRYONIC GERMINAL

EMCEE HOST

EME AUNT YEME UNCLE FRIEND NEIGHBOR

EMEND (ALSO SEE AMEND) EDIT MEND ALTER AMEND BETTER REFORM REPEAL REVISE CORRECT IMPROVE RECTIFY REDRESS EMENDATE

EMERALD BERYL GREEN EMRAUD EMERANT PRASINE SMARAGD

EMERALD FISH ESMERALDA

EMERGE BOB DIP BOLT LOOM PEER RISE BREAK ERUPT EXUDE ISSUE START APPEAR BECOME PLUNGE SPRING DEBOUCH EXTRUDE
(— FROM EGGSHELL) HATCH ECLOSE
(— FROM SLEEP) AWAKE

EMERGENCE NEED BIRTH EGRESS GROWTH PRICKLE BECOMING DEBOUCHE ECLOSION EMERSION ERUPTION EXIGENCE TENTACLE
(— FROM DARKNESS) BREAK

EMERGENCY NEED PEND PUSH PINCH CRISIS STRAIT SUDDEN EMERGENT EXIGENCY JUNCTURE

EMERGENT RISING

EMERGING EMANANT EMERGENT

EMERITA HIPPA

EMERY EMERIL SMIRIS ABRASIVE CORUNDUM

EMETIC ALUM PICK PUKE PUKER VOMIT EVACUANT VOMITIVE VOMITORY

EMIGRANT EMIGRE EXODIST PATARIN SETTLER COLONIST PATERINE STRANGER
(— FROM MECCA) COMPANION

EMIGRATE MOVE REMOVE MIGRATE

EMIGRATION EXODUS HEGIRA HEJIRA SWARMING

EMINENCE DUN BALL BERG CRAG KNOT MONS MOTE NOTE POLE RANK RISE SCAR TOOT CHIEF HOYLE KNOLL PERCH STATE WHEAL WORTH ASCENT HEIGHT KRANTZ RENOWN RIDEAU ALTITUDE GRANDEUR TUBERCLE
(— OF HAND) SUBVOLA

EMINENT BIG ARCH HIGH CHIEF

GRAND GREAT LOFTY NOBLE NOTED FAMOUS MARKED SIGNAL EXCELSE GLORIOUS RENOWNED SINGULAR TOWERING

EMIR AMIR AMEER NOBLE RULER LEADER PRINCE ADMIRAL GOVERNOR

EMISSARY SPY AGENT SCOUT LEGATE DELEGATE

EMISSION FUME GUST VENT

EMISSIVE EMITTENT EXHALANT

EMIT RUN BARK BEAM CAST DRIP GIVE GUSH HURL LASH MOVE OOZE PASS POUR REEK SEND SHED SPIT VENT VOID WARP AVOID BELCH EJECT ERUCT EXERT EXUDE FLASH FLING ISSUE UTTER YIELD DECANT DONATE EVOLVE EXHALE EXPIRE SPREAD BREATHE DISTILL EMANATE EXHAUST OUTSEND RADIATE REFLAIR ERUCTATE TRANSMIT
(— FOAM) SPURGE
(— FORCEFULLY) FIRE
(— IN PUFFS) PLUFF
(— LIGHT) GLOW
(— OUTCRIES) CHUNNER CHUNTER
(— PLAY OF COLORS) OPALESCE
(— RAYS) RADIATE IRRADIATE
(— SMOKE) SMEECH
(— SOUND) BUFF MOVE
(— SPARKS) SNAP
(— ODOR) REEK STEAM

EMITTING EMISSIVE SOUNDING

EMMENAGOGUE ALOE SAFFRON GROUNDSEL

EMMER SPELTZ AMELCORN

EMMET ANT ENEMY PISMIRE FORMICID

EMOLLIATE SOFTEN

EMOLLIENT LENIENT ICHTHYOL LENITIVE MALACTIC MOLLIENT SUPPLING

EMOLUMENT FEES WAGES INCOME PROFIT SALARY BENEFIT STIPEND

EMOTION IRE LOVE ONDE STIR AGONY ANGER CHORD GRIEF HEART SHAME AFFECT EFFECT MOTION RAPTUS SNIVEL SPLEEN ECSTASY FEELING PASSION VULTURE GRAMERCY MOVEMENT SURPRISE
(CONTROLLING —) LEITMOTIF LEITMOTIV
(EVIL —) DEMON DAEMON

EMOTIONAL DRIPPY EMOTIVE
(UNDULY —) SPOONY SPOONEY

EMOTIONLESS COLD

EMPATHY SYMPATHY

EMPEROR I IMP CZAR INCA KING TSAR AKBAR RULER TENNO CAESAR DESPOT KAISER SULTAN BAGINDA MONARCH VIKRAMA AUGUSTUS IMPERIAL PADISHAH

EMPERY DOMAIN EMPIRE EMPIRY DOMINION

EMPHASIS ANGLE ACCENT STRESS WEIGHT EMPIRISM SALIENCE

EMPHASIZE HIT CLICK PINCH PRESS ACCENT BETONE CHARGE STRESS

EMPHATIC STRONG EARNEST MARCATO SERIOUS ENFATICO FORCIBLE MARCANDO POSITIVE

EMPHATICALLY FLATLY STRONGLY POINTEDLY

EMPHYSEMA HEAVES

EMPIRE RULE SWAY POWER REALM REIGN STATE DIADEM DOMAIN EMPERY CONTROL KINGDOM IMPERIUM
(— STATE OF SOUTH) GEORGIA
(— STATE) NEWYORK
(SELJUK —) RUM ROUM

EMPIRIC QUACK IMPOSTOR

EMPIRICIST VIRTUOSO

EMPLACEMENT BATTERY GALLERY PLATFORM

EMPLOY FEE PAY USE BUSK BUSY HIRE PLOY TAKE WAGE WISE ADOPT APPLY BESET IMPLY SPEND BESTOW ENGAGE ENLIST INFOLD INVOKE OCCUPY SUPPLY CONCERN CONDUCT ENCLOSE IMPROVE INVOLVE SERVICE UTILIZE PRACTICE
(— FLATTERY) COLLOGUE
(— ONESELF ABOUT) TOSS
(— SHIFTS) CHICANE

EMPLOYED APPLIED ENGAGED

EMPLOYEE HAND HELP BOOTS CLERK FACTOR LEADER BELLBOY BOOTBOY CALLBOY CARRIER SERVANT CHASSEUR CIVILIAN FLOORMAN IMPROVER

EMPLOYER JOSS BLOKE GAFFER ENGAGER MANAGER GOVERNOR
(SMALL —) CORK

EMPLOYMENT FEE JOB USE CALL HIRE NOTE TASK TOIL USER WORK CRAFT TRADE TREAD USAGE MISTER THRIFT CALLING PURPOSE SERVICE USAUNCE BUSINESS EXERCISE RETAINER VOCATION
(CASUAL —) GRASS

EMPORIUM MART SHOP BAZAR STORE BAZAAR EMPORY MARKET STAPLE MONOPOLE

EMPOWER POWER ENABLE ENTITLE DELEGATE DEPUTIZE

EMPRESS IMPX EMPERESS IMPERIAL KAISERIN

EMPTIED DRAINED

EMPTILY TOOMLY

EMPTINESS VAIN VOID INANE ANEMIA VACUUM VANITY ANAEMIA INANITY VACANCY VACUITY LEERNESS
(— OF SPIRIT) ENNUI

EMPTY DRY FAT RID TIM AIRY BARE BOSS BUZZ CANT DEAF DUMP EMPT FALL FARM FREE GLIB HOWE IDLE LEER NEAR POUR ROOM TEEM TOOM VAIN VIDE VOID ADDLE AVOID BLANK BLEED CLEAN CLEAR DRAIN EQUAL EXPEL HUSKY INANE LEERY MOUTH SCOOP SHOOT STARK START STRIP SWAMP TINNY WINDY BARREN BUBBLE CHAFFY DEVOID HOLLOW JEJUNE STRIKE SWASTY UNEMPT UNLOAD VACANT VACATE

DELIVER DEPLETE EXHAUST EXPRESS UNTAKEN VACUATE VACUOUS DISGORGE EVACUATE EVANESCE NEGATION UNFILLED (— AN EGG) BLOW

EMPTY-HEADED VAIN DOLLISH

EMPTYING EVACUANT (ACT OF —) KENOSIS

EMPTY-SOUNDING TOOM

EMPUSA MONSTER SPECTER SPECTRE

EMPYREAN ETHER AETHER HEAVENS EMPYREUM

EMU EMEU RHEA RATITE

EMU APPLE COLANE

EMU BUSH BERRIGAN

EMULATE APE VIE COPY EMULE EQUAL EXCEL RIVAL COMPETE IMITATE

EMULATION STRIFE CONTEST PARAGON RIVALRY

EMULATOR RIVAL

EMULOUS EMULATE ENVIOUS

EMULOUSLY AVIE

EMULSIFIABLE SOLUBLE

EMULSION PAP LATEX

EMU WREN STIPITURE

EN NUT

ENABLE ABLE EMPOWER ENTITLE QUALIFY INHABILE

ENACT LIVE MAKE PASS ADOPT DECREE EFFECT ORDAIN ACTUATE APPOINT PERFORM PORTRAY

ENACTMENT LAW DOOM ENACT NOVEL ASSIZE DECREE MEASURE PASSAGE STATUTE ENACTION ENACTURE

ENAMEL AMEL FLUX SLIP EMAIL GLAZE GLOSS PAINT SLUSH AUMAIL SHIPPO SMALTO DENTINE LIMOGES SCHMELZ

ENAMOR LOVE CHARM SMITE CAPTIVE

ENAMORED FOND EPRIS EPRISE MASHED AMOROUS CHARMED SMITTEN (VAINLY —) FOOLISH

ENCAMP TELD TENT LODGE PITCH INCAMP LAAGER BIVOUAC LEAGUER

ENCAMPMENT CAMP DOUAR SIEGE LAAGER BIVOUAC CASTRUM HUTMENT TOLDERIA

ENCASE CASE HOUSE SHELL INCASE ENCHASE INCLOSE ENCAPSUL SURROUND

ENCELIA INCIENSO

ENCEPHALON CEREBRUM

ENCHAIN FETTER INCHAIN

ENCHANT CHARM DELUDE GLAMOR INCANT ATTRACT BESPELL BEWITCH DELIGHT GLAMOUR BEDAZZLE ENSORCEL

ENCHANTED RAPT HAGGED CAPTIVE

ENCHANTER MAUGIS CHARMER MAGICIAN MALAGIGI

ENCHANTING WIZARD HEAVENLY SPELLFUL

ENCHANTMENT HEX TAKE CHARM

FAIRY MAGIC SPELL SPOKE CARACT CHANTRY DEVILRY GRAMARY SORCERY SORTIARY WITCHERY

ENCHANTRESS CIRCE FAIRY MEDEA ACRASIA URGANDA

ENCHARGE ENJOIN ENTRUST

ENCHASE INFIX ENRICH ENGRAVE

ENCHIRIDION MANUAL HANDBOOK TREATISE

ENCHORIAL NATIVE DEMOTIC DOMESTIC

ENCIPHER CODE CIPHER ENCRYPT

ENCIRCLE ORB BAND BELT BIND CLIP COIL GIRD GIRT HALO HOOP PALE RING RINK STEM WIRE ZONE BELAY BRACE CLASP CROWN EMBAY EMBOW GIRTH HEDGE INORB ROUND TWINE TWIST BECLIP CIRCLE EMBALL ENGIRT ENLACE ENRING ENWIND FATHOM GIRDLE IMPALE SWATHE WRITHE BETREND COMPASS EMBRACE ENCLAVE ENCLOSE ENTWINE ENVIRON ENWHEEL SERPENT WREATHE CINCTURE CORSELET ENSPHERE IMMANTLE SURROUND

ENCIRCLED GIRT CINCT BELTED SUCCINCT

ENCIRCLEMENT EMBRACE

ENCIRCLING AROUND EMBRACE CORONARY ENCYCLIC

ENCLAVE INLIER

ENCLOAK MANTLE

ENCLOSE IN BAY BOX CAN HEM LAP MEW ORB PAR PEN PIN RIM BANK BUNG CAGE CASE COOP FORT GIRD HAIN HOOP PALE SPAR TINE WALL WARD YARD BOSOM BOUND BOWER BRICK CHEST CLOSE DITCH EMBAR EMBED EMBOX FENCE FRAME GRIPE HEDGE HOUSE IMBED INURN BOUGHT CARTON CASTLE CAVERN CIRCLE CORRAL EMBANK EMBOSS EMPALE EMPARK EMPLOY ENCASE ENCYST ENFOLD ENGULF ENLOCK FASTEN IMMURE IMPALE IMPARK INCASE INCLIP INHOOP INSACK INWALL JACKET PICKET POCKET TACKLE APPROVE CAPSULE COMPASS CONFIDE CONTAIN CURTAIN EMBOSOM EMBOWEL EMBOWER EMBRACE ENCHASE ENCLAVE ENGLOBE ENHEDGE ENVELOP HARNESS IMBOSOM IMMERSE IMPOUND INBOUND INCLUDE INFIELD PARROCK PINFOLD SHEATHE BULKHEAD COMPRISE COMPRIZE CONCLUDE CONVOLVE EMBORDER ENCIRCLE ENSHRINE ENSPHERE IMPRISON LANDLOCK PALISADE PARCLOSE SURROUND (— IN ARMOR) EMPANOPLY (— LOGS) CRIB

ENCLOSED BOUND CLOSED OBTECT INGROWN INTERNAL

ENCLOSING LIMITARY

ENCLOSURE HAG HAW HOK MEW PAR PEN REE STY TYE BAWN BOMA BYTH CAGE CAVE CELL COOP DOCK

FOLD HAIN HOCK KILN LIST PEEL SEPT SKIT SLOT TIGH TOWN WALL WEIR YARD ALTIS ATAJO BASIN BLIND BOOLY BOOTH BOSOM CAROL CLOSE COURT CRAWL CREEP CUBBY FENCE FRANK GARTH GOTRA HOARD KENCH KRAAL LOBBY MARAI PLECK POUND REEVE STALL STELL AVIARY BOOLEY BOXING CANCHA CARREL CORRAL COWPEN CRUIVE DRYLOT GARDEN HURDLE INTAKE KENNEL OUTSET PALING PRISON SERAIL TAMBOR TEOPAN TINING VIVARY WARREN BELLOWS BOROUGH BULLPEN CLOSURE COCKPIT EMBRACE GALLERY GONDOLA HENNERY HOUSING HUMIDOR LANTERN PADDOCK PIGHTLE PUDDOCK SEVERAL STUFFER TAMBOUR AEDICULA CASEMATE CHIPYARD CINCTURE CLAPNEST CLAUSURE CLOISTER COMPOUND DELUBRUM ENCHASER PARADISE POUNDAGE PRECINCT PURPRISE SEPIMENT SERAGLIO SKIRTING STOCKADE VIVARIUM (— ABOUT ALTAR) BEMA (— FOR BOWLING) ALLEY (— FOR COCKPIT) CANOPY (— FOR FISH) CROY YAIR YARE KENCH SPILLER SPILLET (— FOR JURY) BOX (— FOR KNIGHTLY ENCOUNTERS) BARRACE (— FOR LIGHT) LANTERN (— FOR ROASTING ORE) STALL (— OF HOUSE) BAWN (— SURROUNDED BY DITCH) COP (ELEPHANT —) KEDDAH (OBLONG —) CIRCUS (POULTRY —) HENNERY (SACRED —) SECOS SEKOS

ENCOLPION PANAGIA

ENCOMIAST EULOGIST

ENCOMIUM ELOGE ENCOMY EULOGY PRAISE PLAUDIT TRIBUTE

ENCOMPASS BEGO BELT CLIP GIRD PALE RING SPAN WALL WRAP BELIE BERUN BESET BIGAN CLOSE CROWN ROUND BEGIRD BEGIRT CIRCLE ENGIRD COMPASS EMBOWEL EMBRACE ENCLOSE ENVIRON INCLUDE SUBSUME UMBESET ENCIRCLE ENGIRDLE PURPRISE SURROUND (— WITH ARMS) FATHOM

ENCOMPASSED AMID BAYED AMIDST BEGIRT

ENCOMPASSING ROUND AMBIENT CINCTURE PROFOUND INCLUSIVE

ENCORE BIS AGAIN ANCORA RECALL REPEAT

ENCOUNTER BIDE BUMP COIL COPE FACE FIND KEEP MEET MOOT RINK BRUSH FIGHT FORCE GREET INCUR OCCUR ONSET SHOCK STOUR VENUE ACCOST AFFRAY ANSWER ASSAIL ATTACK BATTLE BREAST

CAREER COMBAT JOSTLE JUSTLE
OPPOSE ADDRESS AFFRONT
CONTEST COUNTER DISPUTE
HOSTING JOINING PASSAGE
CONFLICT CONFRONT CONGRESS
REANSWER RECONTER SKIRMISH
(— HOSTILELY) CROSS
(HOSTILE —) CLOSE
(PUGILISTIC —) MILL
ENCOURAGE DAW EGG ABET BACK
FIRM URGE BOOST CHEER ERECT
FAVOR FLUSH HEART IMPEL NERVE
SERVE STEEL ADVISE ASSURE
EXHORT FOMENT FOSTER HALLOO
HARDEN INCITE INDUCE INVITE
NUZZLE REHETE SECOND SPIRIT
UPHOLD ADVANCE ANIMATE
CHERISH COMFORT CONFIRM
CONSOLE ENFORCE ENLIVEN
FLATTER FORTIFY FORWARD
HEARTEN INSPIRE PROMOTE
STOMACH UPCHEER UPRAISE
EMBOLDEN INSPIRIT REASSURE
ENCOURAGED BUCKED CONFIRMED
ENCOURAGEMENT BOOST FLUSH
HURRAH FOMENTO IMPETUS
BLESSING SANCTION
ENCOURAGING HELPFUL FAVORING
ENCRATITE TATIAN AQUARIAN
ENCROACH JET PINCH POACH
IMPOSE INVADE TRENCH IMPINGE
INTRUDE SHINGLE ENTRENCH
INFRINGE INTRENCH TRESPASS
ENCROACHING INVASIVE
ENCROACHMENT BREACH INROAD
ENCROACH INVASION
ENCRUST CAKE CANDY BARKEN
BARKLE INCRUST
ENCRUSTED SCABROUS
ENCUMBER CLOG LOAD PACK
BESET CHECK CROWD TRASH
BEMOIL BURDEN FELTER HAMPER
HINDER IMPEDE LUMBER MITHER
MOIDER RETARD SADDLE WEIGHT
BEPAPER INVOLVE OPPRESS
ACCUMBER ENTANGLE HANDICAP
OBSTRUCT OVERCOME OVERLOAD
ENCUMBERED HEAVY CONGESTED
ENCUMBRANCE CLOG LIEN LOAD
CLAIM BURDEN CHARGE CUMBER
TROUBLE MORTGAGE
ENCYCLICAL PASCENDI
ENCYCLOPEDIA TOME
(GAME —) HOYLE
ENCYSTED CYSTIC SACCATE
SACCATED
END EN AIM DAG EAR FAG TIP BUTT
DATE DOUP FACE FATE FINE FOOT
GOAL HALT HEEL LAST MAIN MARK
SAKE STOP TAIL TERM VIEW AMEND
ARTHA BLOCK BREAK CAUSE CEASE
CLOSE DEATH ENSUE EVENT FINIS
ISSUE LIMIT LOOSE NAPOO OMEGA
POINT PRICK RAISE SCOPE SCRAP
START STASH THULE DEFINE
DESIGN EFFECT EFFLUX ENDING
EXITUS EXPIRE EXPIRY FINALE
FINISH INTENT NAPOOH OBJECT
PERIOD RESULT THIRTY UPSHOT

UTMOST WINDUP ABOLISH ACHIEVE
CLOSURE CURTAIN DESTROY
FANTAIL FINANCE LINEMAN OUTGIVE
PURPOSE REMNANT BOUNDARY
COMPLETE CONCLUDE DESITION
DISSOLVE FINALITY SURCEASE
TERMINAL TERMINUS ULTIMATE
(— DEBATE) CLOTURE
(— OF ANTENNA) CLAVA
(— OF ANVIL) BICKIRON
(— OF ARCHERY PILE) STOPPING
(— OF ARROW) NOCK
(— OF BEEF LOIN) BUTT
(— OF BLANKET) DAGON
(— OF BONE) EPIPHYSIS
(— OF BOOM) JAW
(— OF BOW) EAR
(— OF BRICK) HEADING
(— OF BRISTLE) FLAG
(— OF BUILDING) GABLE
(— OF CAN) BREAST
(— OF CANE) FRAZE
(— OF CART) TIB
(— OF CRESCENT) HORN
(— OF EGG) DOUP
(— OF EXISTENCE) DEMISE
(— OF FABRIC) FENT
(— OF FISHHOOK) SPEAR
(— OF FLAG) FLY
(— OF FROG) TOE
(— OF HALTER) CAPITULUM
(— OF HAMMER) CLAW POLL
(— OF HAMMERHEAD) PEEN
(— OF HORSE-COLLAR) GULLET
(— OF INGOT) CROP
(— OF KEEL) GRIPE
(— OF LEVER) FORK
(— OF LOAF) HEEL
(— OF MINE TUNNEL) FACE
(— OF MINING LEVEL) DEAN
(— OF MUZZLE) MUFFLE
(— OF NAIL) CLENCH
(— OF ONE'S LIFE) DOOM
(— OF PIER) CUTWATER
(— OF PIPE) TAFT SPIGOT
(— OF POCKETKNIFE HANDLE)
BOLSTER
(— OF RAILROAD CAR) BEND
(— OF ROAD) ROADHEAD
(— OF ROD) FORKHEAD
(— OF SHEEP SHEARING) CUTOUT
(— OF SHIP) STERN
(— OF SPINE) ACRUMION
(— OF TENON) HAUNCH
(— OF TOOL) BUTT
(— OF UTERUS) FUNDUS
(— OF WORLD) PRALAYA
(— OF YARD) ARM YARDARM
(— ON POND) FOREBAY
(—S OF RIBBONS) FATTRELS
(—S OF SATURN'S RINGS) ANSA
(CANDLE —) DOUP SNUFF
(DOMINO —) ACE
(FAG —) RUMP
(HANGING —) DAG DAGGE
(JAGGED —) SHRAG
(NARROWED —) NEB
(NORTH — OF COMPASS NEEDLE)
LILY

(POINTED —) APEX
(POSTERIOR —) BOTTOM
(REEF —S) DEADMAN
(ROPE'S —) FEAZE PIGTAIL
FEAZINGS
(SPECIAL —) SAKE
(TAPERING —) POINT
(TATTERED —) FRAZZLE
(ULTIMATE —) SUM TELOS
(UNPLEASANT —) GRIEF
(UPPER —) HEAD
(WARP —S) ACCIDENTAL
ENDANGER DANGER HAZARD
IMPERIL
ENDANGERED BESTED BESTEAD
FRAUGHT
ENDANGERER MARPLOT
ENDEARMENT LOVE CARESS
ENDEAVOR DO AIM PUT TRY WIN
BEST MINT SEEK WORK ASSAY
ESSAY ETTLE EXERT OFFER STUDY
TEMPT TRIAL AFFAIR ASSAIL
DEVOIR EFFORT INTEND STRIFE
STRIVE AFFORCE ATTEMPT
CONATUS CULTURE EMPRISE
EMULATE IMITATE MOLIMEN
NITENCY WORKING EXERTION
PURCHASE STRUGGLE
(— TO CONCLUSION) STUDY
(BEST —) DEVOIR
(EARNESTLY —) FEND
ENDED DONE OVER PAST FINISHED
(— BY CONSONANT) CHECKED
ENDEMIC LOCAL ENDEMIAL
ENDING END CLOSE DEATH GRAVE
FINALE BREAKUP FINANCE DESITION
(NERVE —) SPINDLE
ENDIVE CHICORY WITLOOF
ESCAROLE SCARIOLE
ENDLESS ANANTA ETERNE ETERNAL
FOREVER UNDYING UNENDED
UNENDLY DATELESS FINELESS
IMMORTAL INFINITE UNENDING
ENDMOST TIPMOST FARTHEST
REMOTEST
ENDOCARP STONE PYRENA
PUTAMEN
ENDOGENOUS INNATE AUTOGENIC
ENDOMORPHIC PYCNIC PYKNIC
ENDOPITE PETASMA
ENDOPLEURA TEGMEN
ENDORSE BACK SIGN ADOPT BOOST
DOCKET ENDOSS SECOND APPROVE
CERTIFY INDORSE SUPPORT
ADVOCATE SANCTION
ENDORSEE HOLDER
ENDORSEMENT FIAT FORM VISA
RIDER BACKING APPROVAL
HECHSHER SANCTION
ENDOSPERM FARINA ALBUMEN
ENDOSPORIUM INTINE
ENDOW DOW DUE DOTE GIFT RENT
VEST BLESS CROWN DOWER ENDUE
EQUIP FOUND INDUE SEIZE STATE
STUFF ASSIGN CLOTHE DOTATE
ENABLE ENRICH ENSOUL ESTATE
INVEST CHARTER ENLARGE FURNISH
INSTATE APPANAGE BENEFICE
BEQUEATH ENTALENT
(— WITH FORCE) DYNAMIZE

ENDOWED ABLE GIFTED FAVORED
ENDOWMENT CLAY FINE GIFT WAKF
WAQF DOWER DOWRY GRACE
CORPSE GENIUS TALENT APANAGE
CHANTRY CHARISM FACULTY
APPANAGE DOTATION
(NATURAL —S) BUMP DOTES
TALENT
(PL.) ALTARAGE
ENDPAPER FLYLEAF
ENDPIECE BRACE CHUMP
(— OF STETHOSCOPE) BELL
ENDUE DUE ENDOW INDUE TEACH
CLOTHE INVEST INSTRUCT
ENDURABLE LIVABLE BEARABLE
LIVEABLE
ENDURANCE GAME LAST TACK
PLUCK BOTTOM COMFORT
DURANCE GRANITE LASTING
STAMINA BEARANCE DURATION
GAMENESS HARDSHIP PATIENCE
STRENGTH
ENDURE GO ABY SIT VIE ABYE BEAR
BIDE DREE DURE HOLD KEEP LAST
TAKE TIDE WEAR ABEAR ABIDE
ALLOW BROOK CARRY DRIVE
POUCH SPARE STAND STICK STOUT
THOLE TOUGH WIELD ABROOK
ACCEPT DRUDGE HARDEN REMAIN
SUFFER COMFORT FORBEAR
PERSIST SUPPORT SUSTAIN
SWALLOW TOUGHEN UNDERGO
WEARING CONTINUE FOREBEAR
TOLERATE
ENDURING FAST SURE STOUT
BIDING DURING STABLE STURDY
DURABLE ETERNAL LASTING
PATIENT IMMORTAL REMANENT
STUBBORN
ENDWAYS ANEND ENDWISE
ENEMA CLYSMA CLYSTER LAVEMENT
ENEMY FOE AXIS BOYG FEID DEVIL
FIEND SATAN FOEMAN HOSTILE
CONTRARY OPPONENT
(— OF MANKIND) DEVIL FIEND
SATAN
(PERSONAL —) HATER
ENERGETIC FAST FELL HARD LIVE
RASH BRISK DASHY LUSTY STOUT
TIGHT VITAL YAULD ACTIVE HEARTY
HUSTLE LIVELY SPROIL ACTIOUS
ANIMOSO ARDUOUS DASHING
DRIVING DYNAMIC ENERGIC
FURIOUS PUSHFUL PUSHING
EMPHATIC ENERGICO FORCEFUL
FORCIBLE HUSTLING VIGOROUS
(— PERSON) TOWSER
ENERGETICALLY MANLY
FURIOUSLY
ENERGIZE EXCITE ANIMATE
ENERGIZING KINETIC VIRTUAL
ENERGY U W GO PEP VIM ZIP BANG
BENT BIRR DASH EDGE JASM LIFE
SAKT SNAP TUCK ZING ARDOR
ECLAT FORCE INPUT NERVE POWER
STEAM VIGOR EFFORT FOISON
INTAKE ORGONE OUTPUT SPIRIT
SPRAWL SPRING SPROIL STARCH
VIRTUE POTENCY SPIRITS ACTIVITY

AMBITION DYNAMISM ENERGEIA
MOTIVITY PRAKRITI STRENGTH
VIVACITY
(— PEAK) NUCLEUS
(EMOTIONAL —) LIBIDO
(LIBINAL —) CATHEXIS
(LIFE —) JIVA SAKTI SHAKTI
(LIGHT —) RAD
(MENTAL —) DOCITY PSYCHURGY
(POTENTIAL —) ERGAL
(RADIANT —) SOUND ACTINISM
EINSTEIN
(VITAL —) HORME PANZOISM
ENERVATE SAP COOK FLAG MELT
SOFTEN WEAKEN MOLLIFY UNNERVE
UNSINEW ENFEEBLE
ENERVATED BEDRID EFFETE
LANGUID BEDRIDDEN
ENERVATING DREARY
ENERVATION COLLAPSE
ENFEEBLE NUMB FAINT SHAKE
APPALL DEADEN FEEBLE IMPAIR
SOFTEN WEAKEN DEPRESS
UNSINEW AFFEEBLE ENERVATE
IMBECILE UNSTRONG
ENFEEBLED FEY NUMB
ENFOLD (ALSO SEE INFOLD) LAP
FURL WRAP CLASP COVER DRAPE
ENROL IMPLY COMPLY ENLACE
ENROLL ENWIND ENWRAP INFOLD
INWIND SHADOW SWATHE WATTLE
EMBRACE ENCLOSE ENVELOP
ENVIRON INCLUDE INVOLVE
UMBELAP CONVOLVE
ENFORCE BULL LEVY EXACT FORCE
PRESS COERCE COMPEL EFFECT
FOLLOW INVOKE EXECUTE IMPLANT
ENFORCED COMPULSORY
ENFORCER EXECUTOR MUSCLEMAN
ENFRAMEMENT CARTOUCH
ENG AGMA
ENGAGE DIP WED BOOK BUSY GAGE
HAVE HIRE JOIN LIST MESH RENT
SIGN TAKE WAGE AGREE AMUSE
CATCH ENTER LEASE PITCH TRADE
TRYST ABSORB ARREST EMBARK
EMPLOY ENLIST INDUCE OBLIGE
OCCUPY PLEDGE PLIGHT BESPEAK
BETROTH CONCERN CONDUCE
CONSUME ENGROSS IMMERSE
INVOLVE PROMISE AFFIANCE
CONTRACT COVENANT ENTANGLE
INTEREST INTRIGUE PERSUADE
(— DEEPLY) DROWN
(— IN ARGUMENT) BALK BAULK
(— IN COMBAT) DEBATE STRIKE
(— IN DEBATE) STONEWALL
(— IN DISCUSSION) CONTEND
(— IN PRANKS) LARK
(— IN TILT) JUST JOUST
(— IN) GO CUT SUE HAVE JOIN
LEAD
(— WHOLLY) ABSORB CONSUME
IMMERSE
ENGAGED BENT BUSY FAST GONE
HIRED ACTIVE BONDED BOOKED
MESHED ASSURED BESPOKE
EARNEST ENTERED PLEDGED
TOKENED VERSANT ABSORBED

ATTACHED EMBEDDED EMPLOYED
INSERTED INTEREST INVOLVED
OCCUPIED PROMISED
(— IN CONTROVERSY) DISPUTANT
(— IN) ABOUT
(MENTALLY —) VERSANT
(WARMLY —) ZEALOUS
ENGAGEMENT AVAL DATE COWLE
SPURN ACTION AFFAIR BATTLE
COMBAT ESCROW PLIGHT STANZA
SURETY BARGAIN BOOKING
DUSTING SERVICE CONFLICT
RETAINER SKIRMISH WARRANTY
(— TO MARRY) TRYST
(MILITARY —) DO SHOW
(SHORT —) SNAP
(SINGLE —) GIG
(THEATRICAL —) SHOP
(WRITTEN —) COWLE
ENGAGING SOFT SAPID SWEET
TAKING
ENGENDER BEGET BREED CAUSE
EXCITE GENDER DEVELOP PRODUCE
GENERATE INGENDER OCCASION
ENGIDU EABANI
ENGINE GAS JET SIX FOUR GOAT
TANK EIGHT JINNY MOTOR OILER
STEAM BANKER DIESEL DOCTOR
DUDLER DUDLEY INGENE JORDAN
KICKER PUFFER RADIAL ROADER
YARDER MACHINE POACHER
POTCHER SKIDDER STEAMER
TRACTOR TURBINE BULLGINE
COMPOUND DOLLBEER EXPANDER
GASOLINE IMPULSOR
(— FOR HAULING LOGS) DUDLER
DUDLEY
(— FOR THROWING MISSILES) GIN
SPRINGAL
(— OF TORTURE) GIN RACK
(— OF WAR) RAM SWEEP HELEPOLE
(DONKEY —) DOCTOR
(FIRE —) TUB
(JET —) ATHODYD
(MILITARY —) BOAR TOWER FABRIC
TREPAN DONDINE PERRIER
TORMENT WARWOLF BALLISTA
DONDAINE MANGONEL MARTINET
SCORPION
(RAILROAD —) HOG GOAT YARDER
SWITCHER
ENGINEER PLAN GUIDE DRIVER
FANNER HOGGER MANAGE SAPPER
HOGHEAD PLANNER PLOTTER
CONTRIVE DESIGNER INGENIER
INVENTOR MANEUVER
ENGINEMAN HOISTER HOISTMAN
ENGINERY TIRE
ENGIRDLED CINCT
ENGLAND HOME ALBION LOGRIA
BLIGHTY BRITAIN LOEGRIA
HOMELAND

ENGLAND

AIRFORCE: RAF
BAY: TOR LYME WASH START
MOUNTS BIGBURY BIDEFORD
CARDIGAN FALMOUTH

TREMADOC WEYMOUTH
CAPITAL: LONDON
CHANNEL: SOLENT BRISTOL
ENGLISH SPITHEAD
CHANNEL ISLAND: HERM SARK
JERSEY ALDERNEY GUERNSEY
COIN: ORA RIAL RYAL ACKEY
ANGEL CROWN GROAT NOBLE
PENCE PENNY POUND SPRAT
UNITE BAWBEE FLORIN GUINEA
SESKIN TESTON ANGELET
CAROLUS HAPENNY TUPPENY
FARTHING SHILLING SIXPENCE
TUPPENCE
CONSERVATIVE: TORY
COUNTY: KENT DEVON ESSEX
HANTS SALOP WIGHT DORSET
DURHAM LONDON SURREY
SUSSEX NORFOLK RUTLAND
SUFFOLK CHESHIRE CORNWALL
SOMERSET
DANCE: MORRIS
FIRTH: SOLWAY
FOREST: ARDEN EXMOOR
DARTMOOR SHERWOOD
HEAD: SPURN BEACHY FORMBY
LIZARD CEMMAES TREVOSE
HILLS: MENDIP BRENDON CHEVIOT
CHILTERN COTSWOLD
INVADER: DANE PICT ROMAN
SAXON NORMAN
ISLAND: MAN HOLY LUNDY WIGHT
COQUET MERSEA THANET
TRESCO WALNEY BARDSEY
HAYLING IRELAND SHEPPEY
ANGLESEA ANGLESEY
FOULNESS HOLYHEAD
ISLANDS: FARNE SCILLY CHANNEL
KING: HAL LUD BRAN BRUT CNUT
COLE KNUT LEAR HENRY JAMES
SWEYN ALFRED BLADUD
BRUTUS CANUTE EDWARD
EGBERT GEORGE ARTEGAL
ELIDURE RICHARD WILLIAM
GORBODUC
LAKE: CONISTON
LIBERAL: WHIG
MEASURE: CUT ELL LEA MIL PIN
ROD RUN TON TUN VAT ACRE
BIND BOLL BUTT CADE COMB
COOM CRAN FOOT GILL GOAD
HAND HANK HEER HIDE INCH
LAST LINE MILE NAIL PACE
PALM PECK PINT PIPE POLE
POOL ROOD ROPE SACK SEAM
SPAN TRUG TYPP WIST YARD
YOKE BODGE CABOT CHAIN
COOMB CUBIT DIGIT FLOAT
FLOOR FLUID HUTCH JUGUM
MINIM OUNCE PERCH POINT
PRIME QUART SKEIN STACK
TRUSS BARREL BOVATE BUSHEL
CRANNE FATHOM FIRKIN
GALLON HOBBET HOBBIT
LEAGUE MANENT OXGANG
POTTLE RUNLET SECOND
SQUARE STRIKE SULUNG
THREAD TIERCE AUCHLET

FURLONG KENNING QUARTER
RUNDLET SEAMILE SPINDLE
TERTIAN VIRGATE CARUCATE
CHALDRON HOGSHEAD
LANDYARD PUNCHEON
QUADRANT QUARTERN
STANDARD
MOUNTAIN: PEAK SCAFELL
SKIDDAW SNOWDON
MOUNTAINS: BLACK PENNINE
SNOWDON CAMBRIAN CUMBRIAN
NAME: ALBION BRITAIN BRITANNIA
PENINSULA: PORTLAND
POINT: NAZE LYNAS MORTE
SALES DODMAN LIZARD PRAWLE
HARTLAND LANDSEND
GIBRALTAR
POLICEMAN: BOBBY COPPER
PEELER
RACE TRACK: ASCOT
RESORT: BATH BRIGHTON
BLACKPOOL
RIVER: CAM DEE DON ESK EXE
LEA NEN URE WYE AIRE AVON
EDEN LUNE NENE NIDD OUSE
PENK TAME TEES TILL TYNE
WEAR YARE ANKER COLNE
DEBEN STOUR SWALE TAMAR
TAWAR TRENT TWEED HUMBER
KENNET MERSEY RIBBLE
ROTHER SEVERN THAMES
WENSUM WHARFE WITHAM
DERWENT PARRETT WAVENEY
WELLAND TORRIDGE
ROCKS: MANACLES
ROYAL HOUSE: YORK TUDOR
STUART HANOVER WINDSOR
LANCASTER PLANTAGENET
SCHOOL: ETON RUGBY HARROW
SEA: IRISH NORTH
SETTLER: JUTE PICT ANGLE
SAXON NORMAN
SOLDIER: TOMMY REDCOAT
FUSILEER
STRAIT: DOVER
TOWN: ELY BATH DEAL HULL
RYDE WARE YORK BLYTH
BRENT DERBY DOVER ERITH
FLINT LEEDS RIPON TRURO
WIGAN BARNET BOLTON
BOOTLE CAMDEN DURHAM
EALING EXETER HANLEY
JARROW LEYTON LONDON
OLDHAM OXFORD YEOVIL
BRISTOL BROMLEY BURNLEY
CHELSEA CROYDON ENFIELD
GRIMSBY HALIFAX HORNSEY
IPSWICH LAMBETH NEWPORT
NORWICH PRESTON SALFORD
SEAFORD WESTHAM BRADFORD
BRIGHTON CORNWALL
COVENTRY DEWSBURY
HASTINGS PLYMOUTH
ROCHDALE WALLASEY
WALLSALL GREENWICH
LIVERPOOL SHEFFIELD
BIRMINGHAM MANCHESTER
TRIBE: ICENI

UNIVERSITY: LONDON OXFORD
CAMBRIDGE
VALLEY: COOM EDEN TEES TYNE
COMBE COOMB COQUET
WEIGHT: BAG KIP TOD TON KEEL
LAST MAST MAUN BARGE
FAGOT GRAIN MAUND POUND
SCORE STAND STONE TRUSS
BUSHEL CENTAL FANGOT FIRKIN
FOTHER FOTMAL POCKET
QUARTER QUINTAL SARPLER

ENGLISH SAXON AUSTRAL BRITISH
ENGLAND SAXONISH SOUTHRON
STANDARD
(IN —) ANGLICE
ENGLISHMAN SAXON BRITON
GODDAM GRINGO JOHNNY
MACARONI SOUTHRON ENGLISHER
ENGLISHWOMAN INGLESA
ENGORGE GLUT GORGE DEVOUR
SWALLOW
ENGRAFT INSET
ENGRAM TRACE
(— PATTERN) MEANING
ENGRAVE CUT ETCH RIST CARVE
CHASE GRAVE HATCH PRINT SCULP
CHISEL INCISE SCULPT CRIBBLE
ENCHASE EXARATE IMPRESS
IMPRINT INSCULP STIPPLE INSCRIBE
ORNAMENT
ENGRAVED GRAVEN GRAPHIC
INCISED
ENGRAVER POINT CHASER ETCHER
GRAVER ARTISAN INSCULP BURINIST
MEDALIST SCULLION WRIGGLER
(— OF STONES) LAPIDARY
ENGRAVING CUT PRINT SCULP
STAMP GRAVERY GRAVING
GRAVURE WOODCUT AQUATINT
DRYPOINT HATCHING INTAGLIO
LINEWORK
ENGROSS BURY SINK SOAK AMASS
GROSS ABSORB ENGAGE ENROLL
ENWRAP OCCUPY SCROLL COLLECT
CONSUME IMMERSE INVOLVE
ENGROSSED DEEP FULL RAPT
INTENT WRAPPED ABSORBED
IMMERSED
ENGULF GULF ABYSM ABYSS SOUSE
SWAMP WHELM ABSORB DEVOUR
INVADE QUELME SLOUGH ENGORGE
SWALLOW SUBMERGE
ENHANCE FOIL LIFT BUILD ENARM
ENDOW EXALT RAISE DEEPEN
AUGMENT ELEVATE ENLARGE
EXHANCE GREATEN IMPROVE
SHARPEN HEIGHTEN INCREASE
ENHANCEMENT SAKE
ENHYDRA LATAX
ENIGMA WHY EGMA GRIPH REBUS
PUZZLE RIDDLE SPHINX GRIPHUS
MYSTERY PROBLEM PROVERB
ENIGMATIC HUMAN MYSTIC
CRYPTIC OBSCURE ELLIPTIC
MYSTICAL PUZZLING RIDDLING
ENJAMBMENT OVERFLOW
ENJOIN BID JOIN WILL ENIUN ORDER

CHARGE DECREE DIRECT FORBID
COMMAND DICTATE REQUIRE
ADMONISH PROHIBIT

ENJOY GO JOY FAIN HAVE LIKE
BROOK FANCY PROVE SAVOR
TASTE WIELD ADMIRE DEVOUR
RELISH DELIGHT
(— ONESELF) FEAST LAUGH

ENJOYABLE GOOD FRUITY AMIABLE
BLESSED CAPITAL GLORIOUS
SAVOROUS SPLENDID

ENJOYING FRUITIVE

ENJOYMENT FUN JOY USE BASK
BOOT EASE GUST KAMA PLAY ZEST
GUSTO LIKING RELISH COMFORT
DELIGHT JOLLITY JOYANCE
JOYANCY FELICITY FRUITION
PLEASURE SKITTLES

ENKINDLE WARM INCENSE INFLAME

ENLARGE ADD EKE BORE GROW
HONE HUFF OPEN REAM ROOM
BUILD FARCE LARGE SWELL WIDEN
BIGGEN BRANCH BROACH DIDUCE
DILATE EXPAND EXTEND FRAISE
GATHER LARGEN OMNIFY SPREAD
AMPLIFY AUGMENT DISTEND
ENHANCE GREATEN IMPROVE
INGREAT MAGNIFY STRETCH
AMPLIATE CUMULATE FLOURISH
INCREASE
(— COAL MINE) SNUB

ENLARGED BLOATED SWELLED
SWOLLEN AMPLIATE CAPITATE
EXPANDED EXTENDED VARICOSE

ENLARGEMENT BULB DISC DISK
KNOP CLAVA SWELL BLOWUP
BUNION GIBBER GROWTH SCYPHA
ENLARGE FOOTING SCYPHUS
STATION INCREASE SWELLING
(— IN MINE SHAFT) STATION
(— OF GLAND) GOITER GOITRE
(— OF GULLET) CROP
(— OF MOLD) RAPPAGE
(— OF NERVE FIBER) BOUTON
(— OF ORGAN) STRUMA
(BONY —) SPAVIN SPAVINE

ENLARGING EVASE SWELLING

ENLIGHTEN OPEN CLEAR EDIFY
TEACH ILLUME INFORM UNSEEL
EDUCATE LIGHTEN ENKINDLE
INSTRUCT

ENLIGHTENED WISE LUMINOUS

ENLIGHTENMENT BODHI LIGHT
SATORI WISDOM CULTURE SAMADHI

ENLIST DRUM JOIN LEVY SOUD
ENROL ENTER HITCH PREST
ENGAGE ENROLL INDUCT IMPRESS
RECRUIT REGISTER

ENLISTMENT LEVY HITCH PREST
LISTING

ENLIVEN DASH JAZZ WARM BRACE
BRISK CHEER QUICK ROUSE KITTLE
REVIVE ANIMATE COMFORT INSPIRE
REFRESH SMARTEN BRIGHTEN
INSPIRIT

ENLIVENING GENIAL LIVELY VIVIFIC
CHIRPING

ENMESH TRAP CATCH SNARL
IMMESH ENSNARE ENTANGLE

ENMITY WAR FEUD SPITE WRAKE
ANIMUS HATRED MALICE RANCOR
STRIFE FOEHOOD AVERSION

ENNOBLE LORD EXALT HONOR
NOBLE RAISE GENTLE UPLIFT
DIGNIFY ELEVATE GLORIFY
GREATEN NOBLIFY

ENNUI BORE TEDIUM BOREDOM
DOLDRUM

ENORMITY GRAVITY

ENORMOUS BIG GOB HUGE REAM
VAST ENORM GREAT HEROIC
MIGHTY UNRIDE IMMENSE
ABNORMAL COLOSSAL FLAGRANT
GIGANTIC WHAPPING WHOPPING

ENOS (FATHER OF —) SETH
(GRANDFATHER OF —) ADAM
(SON OF —) CAINAN

ENOUGH BAS ENOW WELL WHEN
AMPLE ASSAI BASTA ANEUCH
PLENTY APLENTY SUFFICE
ADEQUATE
(HARDLY —) SKIMP

ENOUNCE STATE UTTER AFFIRM
DECLARE PROCLAIM

ENRAGE RAGE ANGER GRIEVE
MADDEN INCENSE INFLAME
STOMACH

ENRAGED MAD ASHY WODE WOOD
ANGRY IRATE SAVAGE AGRAMED
BERSERK CHOLERIC INCENSED
MADDENED

ENRAPTURE RAVISH TRANCE
ECSTASY ENCHANT ENRAVISH
ENTRANCE

ENRAPTURED RAPT ENRAPT
TRANCED ECSTATIC

ENRICH FAT BOOT FEED FRET LARD
RICH ADORN CROWN ENDOW
GUANO BATTEN FATTEN INVEST
FEATHER FORTIFY FURNISH
GUANIZE INCREASE ORNAMENT
TREASURE
(— A GAS) CARBURET
(— A MINE) SALT
(— FUEL MIXTURE) CHOKE

ENRICHED FLORID

ENRICHMENT DITATION

ENROLL BEAR JOIN LIST POLL
ENROL ENTER WRITE ATTEST
BILLET ENFOLD ENLIST INDUCT
MUSTER RECORD ASCRIBE IMPANEL
INITIATE INSCRIBE REGISTER

ENROLLMENT LISTING REGISTRY

ENROOT ENRACE IMPLANT

ENSCONCE HIDE COVER SETTLE
CONCEAL SHELTER

ENSEMBLE CORPS DECOR WHOLE
COSTUME
(— OF ARMS) ARMORY

ENSHEATHE EMBOSS

ENSHRINE SAINT SHRINE ENCHASE
ENTEMPLE

ENSHROUD WRAP

ENSIFORM ENSATE XIPHOID
GLADIATE

ENSIGN FLAG IAGO SIGN BADGE
COLOR SENYE AQUILA BANNER
BEACON PENNON PISTOL SIGNAL

SYMBOL ALFEREZ ANCIENT INSIGNE
DANEBROG GONFALON ORIFLAMB
PAVILION STANDARD
(—S ARMORIAL) ARMS
(IMPERIAL —) TUT
(JAPANESE —) SUNBURST
(PL.) ENSIGNRY HERALDRY

ENSILE SILO SILAGE

ENSLAVE THEW CHAIN SLAVE THIRL
ENTHRAL NESLAVE SLAVISH
ENTHRALL

ENSLAVED SLAVE THRALL

ENSLAVEMENT DULOSIS SLAVERY

ENSNARE NET WEB GIRN LACE LIME
MESH TOIL TRAP WRAP BENET
CATCH NOOSE SNARE SNARL
ALLURE ATTRAP ENGINE ENMESH
ENTOIL ENTRAP TANGLE TREPAN
BEGUILE BIRDNET ENGLEIM SNIGGLE
SPRINGE BIRDLIME INVEIGLE
OVERTAKE SURPRISE

ENSNARL ENTANGLE

ENSPHERE INORB SPHERE

ENSUE FOLLOW RESULT SUCCEED
(— UPON) SUE

ENSUING NEXT SUING SEQUENT

ENSURE ASSURE INSURE SECURE
BETROTH ESPOUSE WARRANT
AFFIANCE

ENTADA LENS

ENTAIL TAIL INCUR IMPOSE CONTAIN
INVOLVE REQUIRE TAILZIE

ENTAILED AYNE TAIL EIGNE

ENTAMOEBA LOSCHIA

ENTANGLE ELF LAP MAT TAT WEB
CAST COLL FOUL HARL KNIT KNOT
LIME MESH MIRE TOIL WRAP BROIL
CATCH HALCH RAVEL SNAFU SNARE
SNARL TWIST BEFOUL COTTER
ENGAGE ENLACE ENMESH ENTRAP
ENWRAP FANKLE FELTER HAMPER
HANKLE HATTER INMAZE INMESH
PESTER PUZZLE RAFFLE RANGLE
TACKLE TANGLE WRAPLE CONFUSE
EMBRAKE EMBROIL ENSNARL
ENTRIKE IMBRIER INVOLVE PERPLEX
TRAMMEL BEWILDER ENCUMBER
IMPESTER INTRIGUE STRAPPLE

ENTANGLED DEEP FOUL COTTY
TANGLY COMPLEX KNOTTED
IMPLICIT

ENTANGLEMENT FOUL KNOT TWIT
HITCH BUNKER HEDGEHOG
OBSTACLE

ENTASIS SWELL

ENTENTE TREATY ALLIANCE

ENTER BOX DIP SET BEAR BOOK
JOIN POST ADMIT BEGIN BOARD
BREVE ENROL INCUR PROBE SHARE
START ACCEDE APPEAR BILLET
ENGAGE ENLIST ENROLL ENTRER
INCEPT INVADE PIERCE RECORD
SPREAD INGRESS INTRUDE
COMMENCE ENCROACH INITIATE
INSCRIBE NOMINATE REGISTER
(— BY FORCE) BREAK IRRUPT
INTRUDE
(— HASTILY) BULGE
(— IN ATTACK) FORCE

(— **IN BOOKS**) ACCRUE
(— **INTO**) JOIN INTERN
(— **SLOWLY**) SEEP
(— **UNNOTICED**) CREEP
(— **UPON CAREER**) INCEPT
(— **UPON DUTIES**) ASSUME
(— **WITHOUT RIGHT**) ABATE
ENTERING ENTRY INGOING INGRESS
INTRANT INCOMING
ENTEROTOXEMIA STRUCK
ENTERPRISE FIRM IRON PUSH TOGT
DRIVE ESSAY ACTION EMPIRE SPIRIT
VOYAGE ATTEMPT EMPRISE
HOLDING PROJECT VENTURE
BUSINESS CARNIVAL GUMPTION
VIRITOOT
(**CRIMINAL** —) JOB
(**HARD** —) DIFFICULTY
(**REMEDIAL** —) CRUSADE
(**SPECULATIVE** —) ADVENTURE
(**UNPROFITABLE** —) SINKHOLE
ENTERPRISING BOLD FORTHY
PUSHFUL PUSHING
ENTERTAIN INN BEAR BUSK EASE
FETE HAVE HOLD HOST AMUSE
ENJOY FEAST GUEST SPORT TREAT
DIVERT FROLIC GESTEN HARBOR
JUNKET RECULE REGALE RETAIN
SOLACE BEGUILE CHERISH DISPORT
KITCHEN CONSIDER INTEREST
(— **WITHOUT CHARGE**) DEFRAY
ENTERTAINED OUGHT
ENTERTAINER BHAT HOST ACTOR
AMUSER ARTIST BUSKER DANCER
FIDDLE HARLOT SINGER ACTRESS
ARTISTE GLEEMAN HETAERA
HOSTESS REGALER SPEAKER
BEACHBOY COMEDIAN HOSTELER
MAGICIAN MINSTREL
ENTERTAINING GOOD RICH TREAT
PRETTY AMUSING BEDSIDE
GUESTING SPORTFUL
ENTERTAINMENT BASH BILL FARE
FETE GALA GLEE PLAY SHOW
BOARD CHEER FEAST GAUDY
OPERA REVUE SPORT CIRCUS
DIVERT DOMENT GAIETY GAYETY
HOSTEL INFARE KERMIS NAUTCH
SETOUT SHIVVO WATTLE BANQUET
BENEFIT BUMMACK BUMMOCK
BURLESK CEILIDH CONCERT
COSHERY FESTINE FESTINO JOLLITY
KERMESS PASTIME RIDOTTO
CAKEWALK COMMORTH DROLLERY
EASEMENT ENTREATY ENTREMES
FUNCTION GESTNING GESTONIE
GUESTING HOGMANAY JONGLERY
MUSICALE WAYZGOOSE
(**FAREWELL** —) FOY
ENTHALPY H
ENTHRALL SEND CHARM THIRL
THRALL ENSLAVE ENTHRAL
ENTHRONE CROWN EXALT STALL
ENSEAT THRONE THRONIZE
ENTHUSIASM BUG ELAN FIRE FURY
ZEAL ZEST ZING ARDOR ESTRO
FEVER FLAME FUROR HEART MANIA
VERVE FERVOR HURRAH SPIRIT
WARMTH ABANDON ARDENCY

AVIDITY MADNESS MUSTARD
DEVOTION LYRICISM
(— **IN BATTLE**) EARNEST
(**CONTAGIOUS** —) FUROR FURORE
(**EXCESSIVE** —) MANIA
(**WILD** —) DELIRIUM
ENTHUSIAST BUG FAN NUT BUFF
BIGOT ROOTER VOTARY ZEALOT
DEVOTEE EUCHITE FANATIC
FANCIER FOLLOWER VOTARESS
VOTARIST
(PL.) ARDITI
ENTHUSIASTIC GAGA KEEN WARM
HAPPY NUTTY RABID ARDENT
HEARTY CRACKED FERVENT
GLOWING CRACKERS
(**EXCESSIVELY** —) FANATIC
(**VAINLY** —) FOOLISH
ENTICE COG COY PUT WIN BAIT
COAX DRAW DRIB LEAD LOCK LURE
TICE TOLE TOLL WILE CHARM
DECOY DRILL LATHE SIREN SLOCK
STEAL TEMPT TRAIN TROLL TULLE
ALLECT ALLURE ATTICE CAJOLE
ENLURE INCITE INDUCE INVITE
SEDUCE ATTRACT BEWITCH SOLICIT
SUGGEST INVEIGLE PERSUADE
ENTICEMENT BAIT CORD LURE TICE
ENTICING SIREN ALLURING
ENTIRE ALL DEAD EVEN FULL HALE
MEAR MERE SOLE CLEAN EVERY
GROSS PLAIN QUITE ROUND SOUND
STARK TOTAL TUTTO UTTER WHOLE
VERSAL PERFECT PLENARY
ABSOLUTE COMPLETE ENDURING
GLOBULAR INTEGRAL LIVELONG
OUTRIGHT TEETOTAL UNBROKEN
ENTIRELY DEAD DEIN FAIR FULL
PURE CLEAN CLEAR FULLY PLAIN
QUITE STARK WHOLE BODILY
WHOLLY EXACTLY QUITELY
THROUGH CLEVERLY
ENTIRETY WHOLE ENTIRE TOTALITY
ENTITLE DUB CALL NAME TERM
AFFIX STYLE ENABLE CAPTION
EMPOWER QUALIFY INTITULE
NOMINATE
ENTITLED APPARENT ELIGIBLE
ENTITY ENS BODY FORM UNIT BEING
HABIT OUSIA SPACE THING ENERGY
ESSENCE INTEGER TOTALITY
ENTOMB BURY TOMB INTER INURN
ENCAVE HEARSE IMMURE INHUME
SHRINE
ENTOMOLOGY BUGOLOGY
ENTOMOPHTHORA EMPUSA
ENTOTROPHI DIPLURA
ENTOURAGE TRAIN COMITES
RETINUE
ENTRACTE INTERACT INTERVAL
ENTRAIL BOWEL TRAIL INTRAIL
ENTRAILS GUT GUTS DRAFT TRIPE
FIBERS GIBLET HALLOW INWARD
JAUDIE MUGGET PAUNCH QUARRY
QUERRE UMBLES INSIDES NUMBLES
CHAWDRON GRALLOCH
ENTRANCE ADIT BOCA CUSP DOOR
GATE HALL BOCCA CHARM DEBUT
ENTER ENTRY FOYER GORGE INLET

MOUTH PORCH STULM THIRL TORAN
ACCESS ATRIUM ENTREE INFAIR
INGANG INGATE INROAD PORTAL
RAVISH TORANA TRANCE ZAGUAN
DELIGHT GATEWAY HALLWAY
INGOING INGRESS INITIAL INTRADO
INTROIT PASSAGE POSTERN
ENTRESSE FOREGATE VOMITORY
(— **TO VALLEY**) CHOPS
(**ASTROLOGICAL** —) CUSP
(**CELLAR** —) ROLLWAY
(**FORCIBLE** —) INROAD
(**FORMAL** —) DEBUT
(**HARBOR** —) BOCA
(**HOSTILE** —) INVASION
(**HURRIED** —) BOUT
(**PRIVATE** —) POSTERN
ENTRANCED RAPT CHARMED
TRANCED ECSTATIC
ENTRANCEMENT SPELL
ENTRANCING ORPHIC
ENTRANT INTRANT STARTER
BEGINNER
ENTRAP BAG EBB NET HOOK SNIB
TOIL TRAP CATCH CRIMP DECOY
NOOSE SNARE ALLURE AMBUSH
ATTRAP ENGAGE ENTOIL TAIGLE
TANGLE TREPAN BEGUILE ENSNARE
PITFALL ENTANGLE INVEIGLE
ENTRAPPED (— **IN SEDIMENT**)
CONNATE
ENTREAT ASK BEG BID SUE WOO
PRAY PRIG SEEK URGE CRAVE
HALSE PLEAD PRESS TREAT
ADJURE APPEAL DESIRE INVOKE
BESEECH CONJURE EXORATE
IMPLORE PREVAIL PROCURE
REQUEST SOLICIT PERSUADE
PETITION
ENTREATING TREAT CRAVING
ENTREATY DO CRY PLEA SUIT
APPEAL DEESIS PRAYER TREATY
BESEECH BIDDING ENTREAT
PURSUIT REQUEST URGENCY
PETITION PLEADING
ENTREE ENTRY ACCESS BOUDIN
OSTIUM ENTRADA INTRADA
SOUFFLE ENTRANCE FRICANDO
MAZARINE
ENTREMES SAINETE SAYNETE
ENTRENCH INVADE SCONCE
TRENCH ENCROACH TRESPASS
ENTRENCHMENT CLOSURE
LODGMENT
ENTROPY S
ENTRUST ARET FIDE GIVE STOW
BEKEN TRUST CHARGE COMMIT
CREDIT LIPPEN ADDRESS BEHIGHT
COMMEND CONFIDE CONSIGN
DEPOSIT INTRUST BEQUEATH
DELEGATE ENCHARGE
(— **TO DEPUTY**) DEVIL
ENTRY ADIT HALL ITEM STET BREAK
CLOSE DEBIT AUTHOR CREDIT
DOCKET ENTREE POSTEA RECORD
RINGER TRANCE ENTRADA INGRESS
INTRADO PASSAGE ENTRANCE
ENTRESSE ENTRYWAY NOTANDUM
REGISTER VOCATION

ENTWINE FOLD LACE WIND BRAID CLASP IMPLY PLASH TWINE TWIST WEAVE ENLACE INWIND ENTWIST INVOLVE SERPENT WREATHE

ENTWINED ACCOLLE BRAIDED INWOVEN ACCOLLEE

ENUMERATE POLL TELL COUNT SCORE DETAIL NUMBER RECITE RECKON RELATE COMPILE COMPUTE ITEMIZE RECOUNT ESTIMATE REHEARSE

ENUMERATION LIST TALE COUNT SCORE CENSUS ACCOUNT CATALOG RECITAL CITATION

ENUNCIATE SAY UTTER DECLARE DELIVER ENOUNCE ANNOUNCE PROCLAIM

ENUNCIATION DICTION DELIVERY (IMPERFECT —) LALLATION

ENVELOP BUR FOG LAP LOT POD WEB BURR CASE COMA FOLD HUSK MAIL BRACE CLOUD COVER KNIFE ROUND BEGIRD BEGIRT BEMIST BINDLE CLOTHE COCOON CORONA ENFOLD ENGIRT ENTIRE ENWRAP FARDEL FOLDER INFOLD INVEST JACKET MANTLE MUFFLE POCKET SHEATH SHROUD STIFLE SWATHE WRIXLE CALYMMA CAPSULE CHORION ENCLOSE ENVIRON INVOLVE SWADDLE SWALLOW VESTURE WRAPPER ENSPHERE ENVELOPE MANTLING PERIANTH PERIDIUM POCHETTE SURROUND WRAPPAGE (— IN SMOKE) ENFUME (GLASS —) BULB (LUMINOUS —) CORONA (NEBULOUS —) CHEVELURE (OPEN —) JACKET (PAY —) PACKET (STAMPED —) ENTIRE (VEGETABLE —) COD

ENVELOPED WOMPLIT

ENVELOPING AMBIENT

ENVENOM VENOM CORRUPT VITIATE EMBITTER EMPOISON

ENVIOUS YELLOW EMULOUS JEALOUS ENVIABLE

ENVIRON HEM BEGO GIRD BIGAN LIMIT VIRON ENVIRE GIRDLE SUBURB COMPASS ENVELOP INCLOSE INVOLVE PURLIEU DISTRICT ENCIRCLE SURROUND (PL.) SKIRT UMLAND BANLIEU SUBURBS PRECINCT

ENVIRONMENT HOTBED MEDIUM MILIEU AMBIENT CONTEXT ELEMENT HABITAT SETTING TERRAIN AMBIANCE CINCTURE PRECINCT (— OF NURTURE) LAP (DOMESTIC —) INTERIEUR (NORMAL —) HOME

ENVISAGE FACE CONFRONT ENVISION

ENVOY AGENT ELCHI ENVOI DEPUTY ELCHEE LEGATE LENVOY NUNCIO EMBASSY TORNADA ABLEGATE LEGATION METATRON

ENVY CHAW ONDE COVET GRUDGE EMULATE BEGRUDGE GRUDGERY JEALOUSY

ENWRAP FOLD ROLL CLASP IMPLY ENFOLD INFOLD KIRTLE ENGROSS ENVELOP OBVOLVE CONVOLVE ENVELOPE INSWATHE

ENZOOTIC RABIES

ENZU SIN

ENZYME ASE ZYM ZYMO RENIN CYTASE KINASE LIPASE LOTASE MUTASE OLEASE PAPAIN PEPSIN RENNIN UREASE ZYMASE ACYLASE ADENASE AMIDASE AMINASE AMYLASE APYRASE CASEASE DIATASE EMULSIN ENOLASE EREPSIN FERMENT GUANASE HYDRASE INULASE LACCASE LACTASE MALTASE MYROSIN OXIDASE PECTASE PEPSINE PHYTASE PRUNASE TANNASE TRYPSIN ALDOLASE ARGINASE BROMELIN CATALASE CATALYST CYTOLIST DIASTASE ELASTASE ERAPTASE ESTERASE FUMARASE INVERTIN NUCLEASE PROTEASE RACEMASE SEMINASE TRYPTASE

EOS MORNING

EPAULET KNOT SWAB SWOB WING SCALE SHELL

EPENDYTES HAPLOMA

EPHELIS FRECKLE

EPHEMERAL BRIEF VAGUE HORARY DIURNAL PASSANT PASSING EPISODAL EPISODIC FUGITIVE MUSHROOM STAYLESS

EPHEMERIS DIARY TABLE RECORD ALMANAC JOURNAL CALENDAR

EPHIPPIUM SADDLE

EPHTHALITE HAITHAL

EPI PEAK SPIRE FINIAL PINNACLE

EPIBLAST ECTODERM

EPIC EDDA EPOS SAGA GRAND ILIAD NOBLE BYLINA EPOPEE HEROIC BEOWULF EPYLLION RAMAYANA

EPICALYX CALYCLE

EPICARP HUSK RIND EXOCARP

EPICENE SEXLESS

EPICURE FRIAND FEASTER GLUTTON GOURMET GOURMAND PALATIST

EPICUREAN APICIAN SENSUOUS

EPIDEMIC FLU PLAGUE POPULAR PANDEMIA PANDEMIC

EPIDERMIS SKIN CUTICLE ECDERON VELAMEN

EPIDOTE SCORZA

EPIGLOTTIS FLAP WEEZLE

EPIGRAM POEM ENGLYN EPITAPH

EPIGRAMMATIC LACONIC POINTED

EPIGRAPH EPIGRAM IMPRINT

EPILEPTIC FITIFIED

EPILOGUE CLOSE APPENDIX

EPIMANIKION CUFF

EPINAOS POSTICUM

EPINEPHRINE ADRENINE

EPIPACTIS SERAPIAS

EPIPHANY TWELFTH

EPIPHARYNX PALATE EPIGLOTTIS

EPIPHRAGM TYMPANUM

EPIPHYTE KARO EPIPHYLL

EPIPHYTOTIC EPIDEMIC

EPIRUS (KING OF —) PYRRHUS

EPISCOPACY BISHOPRIC PRELATISM

EPISCOPAL PRELATIC

EPISODE GAG EPOCH EVENT SCENE STORY AFFAIR INCIDENT SEQUENCE (COMIC —) BURLA (MUSICAL —) COUPLET

EPISPASTIC VESICANT

EPISPERM TESTA

EPISTAXIS NOSEBLEED

EPISTLE CANON JAMES LETTER PISTLE MISSIVE WRITING DECRETAL

EPISTLER SUBDEACON

EPISTOLOGRAPHIC DEMOTIC

EPISTROPHE EPODE ABGESANG

EPISTYLE PLATBAND

EPITHELIUM ENDODERM

EPITHET AKAL GOOD NAME TERM LABEL SMEAR TITLE BYWORD MONETA PHRASE AGNOMEN JAPHETIC MULCIBER (PL.) LANGUAGE

EPITOME MAP SUM FLETA DIGEST PRECIS SCHEME COMPEND PITOMIE SUMMULA ABSTRACT BREVIARY LANDSKIP SYLLABUS SYNOPSIS

EPITOMIZE RESUME CURTAIL ABSTRACT COMPRESS CONDENSE CONTRACT DIMINISH

EPITONIUM SCALA

EPIZOA PARASITA

EPOCH AGE ERA DATE ECCA TIME DWYKA EVENT EOCENE PERIOD CLINTON

EPONYM LIMMU ANCIENT

EQUABLE EVEN JUST EQUAL SUANT SMOOTH STEADY UNIFORM TRANQUIL

EQUAL AEQ PAR TIE COPE EGAL EVEN FERE JUST LIKE MAKE MATE MEET PEEL PEER SAME ALIKE LEVEL MATCH PARTY RIVAL TOUCH DOUBLE EQUATE EVENLY FELLOW MARROW PAREIL ABREAST BALANCE COMPEER EMULATE EQUABLE IDENTIC PAREGAL UNIFORM ADEQUATE EQUALIZE EVENHAND PATCHING TRANQUIL (— IN MEANING) BE (— QUANTITY) ANA (— TO) ANOTHER (NOT —) UNMEET UNMETE

EQUALING TO

EQUALITY PAR TIE EQUITY OWELTY PARAGE PAREIL PARITY BALANCE EGALITE EGALITY ISOTELY EQUATION EVENHAND EVENNESS FAIRNESS (— BEFORE THE LAW) ISONOMY (— OF ELEVATION) ISOMETRY (— OF POWER) ISOCRACY (— STATE) WYOMING

EQUALIZATION EQUATION DISCHARGE

EQUALIZE EVEN KNOT EQUAL LEVEL EQUATE BALANCE ADEQUATE

EQUALIZER EVENER

EQUALLY AS BOTH LIKE ONCE SAME
ALIKE EGALLY EVENLY JUSTLY
EMFORTH
EQUANIMITY POISE PHLEGM
TEMPER BALANCE EGALITY
CALMNESS EVENNESS SERENITY
EQUATE EQUAL BALANCE EQUALIZE
EQUATING COMPARISON
EQUATION CUBIC IDENTITY
EQUATOR LINE GIRDLE EQUINOX
(— CROSSER) POLLIWOG
EQUES KNIGHT
EQUIDISTANT CENTRAL HALFWAY
EQUILIBRIUM POISE APLOMB
BALANCE STATION EQUATION
EVENHAND ISOSTASY
(— OF FLUID) LEVEL
EQUINE COLT FOAL MARE FILLY
HORSE ZEBRA EQUOID EQUINAL
HORSELY
EQUINIA MALLEUS
EQUIP ARM FIT IMP KIT RAY RIG
ABLE BEAM DECK FEAT FIND GEAR
GIRD GIRT HEEL REEK TRIM ARRAY
DIGHT DRESS ENARM ENDOW POINT
SPEED STUFF ATTIRE BUCKLE
ORDAIN OUTFIT SUBORN APPAREL
APPOINT BEDIGHT FORTIFY
FRAUGHT FURNISH GARNISH
HARNESS PLENISH PREPARE
QUALIFY ACCOUTER ACCOUTRE
(— FOR ACTION) ARM
EQUIPAGE RIG CREW SAMAN SUITE
TRAIN SUPPLY RETINUE TURNOUT
UNICORN CARRIAGE
EQUIPMENT KIT FARE GEAR TIRE
STOCK STUFF ATTIRE CONREY
DUFFEL DUFFLE FITOUT GRAITH
OUTFIT SETOUT TACKLE APPAREL
BAGGAGE FITMENT HARNESS
PANOPLY ARMAMENT EQUIPAGE
MATERIAL MATERIEL MOUNTING
SUPELLEX
(— FOR CATCHING FISH) CRAFT
(— FOR JOURNEY) FARE
EQUIPOISE POISE BALANCE
EQUIPOTENTIAL LEVEL
EQUIPPED ARMED BODEN THERE
EQUIPT ARMORED INSTRUCT
WEAPONED
(FULLY —) SUMMED
(INADEQUATELY —) HAYWIRE
(LIGHTLY —) EXPEDITE
EQUISETUM CANDOCK
EQUITABLE EVEN FAIR JUST EQUAL
RIGHT EVENLY HONEST EQUABLE
UPRIGHT BONITARY RIGHTFUL
EQUITY LAW EPIKY MARGIN EPIKEIA
HONESTY JUSTICE EQUALITY
EVENHAND FAIRNESS
EQUIVALENT KIND SAME EQUAL
COUSIN UNISON ANALOGUE
EVENHAND
(— IN MONEY) CHANGE
(— OF TWO BUSHELS) HUTCH
EQUIVOCAL SHADY DOUBLE
FORKED DUBIOUS EVASIVE
HALFWAY OBSCURE DOUBTFUL
HAVERING PUZZLING SIBYLLIC

EQUIVOCATE LIE DODGE EVADE
SHIFT ESCAPE PALTER TRIFLE
WEASEL QUIBBLE SHUFFLE
EQUIVOCATION QUIP QUIRK
EVASION SHUFFLE EQUIVOKE
EQUULEUS FOAL
ERA AGE AEON DATE TIME EPOCH
STAGE PERIOD CENOZOIC
(EMPEROR'S —) KIMIGAYO
(HINDU —) SAMVAT
(MUSLIM —) HEGIRA HEJIRA
ERADICATE DELE ROOT SLAY WEED
CROSS ERASE STAMP DELETE
EFFACE REMOVE UNROOT UPROOT
ABOLISH DESTROY EXPUNGE
OUTROOT SUPPLANT
(— HAIR) EPILATE
ERADICATOR ERASER
ERAL MOINE
ERASE BLOT DASH DELE RACE RASE
RASH RAZE ANNUL PLANE CANCEL
DEFACE DELETE EFFACE EXCISE
REMOVE SCRAPE SPONGE DESTROY
EXPUNGE OUTRAZE SCRATCH
UNWRITE
ERASER RASER RUBBER
ERASURE RASURE ERASION
DELETION EXCISION
ERD SHREW RANNY
ERE OR AIR SOON EARLY PRIOR
BEFORE EREWHILE FORMERLY
EREBUS (FATHER OF —) CHAOS
(SISTER OF —) NOX
(SON OF —) CHARON
ERECHTHEUS (DAUGHTER OF —)
CREUSA PROCRIS CHTHONIA
ORITHYIA
(FATHER OF —) PANDION
(SLAYER OF —) JUPITER
(SON OF —) MERION CECROPS
PANDORUS
(WIFE OF —) PRAXITHEA
ERECT BIG SET BIGG LEVY REAR
RECT STEP STEY SWAY TELD
AREAR BRANT BUILD DRESS EXALT
FRAME MOUNT RAISE SETUP STAND
ARRECT UPLIFT UPREAR ADDRESS
BRISTLE ELEVATE STATELY UPRAISE
UPRIGHT UPSTART STANDING
STRAIGHT VERTICAL
(NOT —) LAZY COUCHED
ERECTED UPSET
ERECTION DOME HARD FABRIC
CHORDEE MACHINE
ERELONG ANON SOON
EREMITE HERMIT ASCETIC RECLUSE
ANCHORET
EREWHILE ERE WHILOM
ERG REG EROGON
(PL.) AREG
ERGO SO ARGO ARGAL HENCE
ERGOT SPUR CLAVUS ECBOLIC
(STAGE OF —) SPHACELIA
ERICHTHONIUS (FATHER OF —)
VULCAN DARDANUS
(MOTHER OF —) ATTHIS
(SON OF —) PANDION
ERIDANUS (FATHER OF —) OCEANUS
(MOTHER OF —) TETHYS

ERIE WENRO
ERIGONE (FATHER OF —) ICARIUS
AEGISTHUS
(MOTHER OF —) CLYTEMNESTRA
ERINYS FURY ALECTO MEGAERA
(PL.) DIRAE FURIAE SEMNAE
EUMENIDES
ERIOPHORUM DRAWLING
ERISTIC DIALECTIC
ERMINE VAIR VARE STOAT WEASEL
ERMELIN FUTERET FUTTRAT
MINIVER CLUBSTER WHITRACK
WHITRET
ERODE EAT COMB ETCH GNAW GULL
WEAR CLIFF GULLY SCOUR ABRADE
DENUDE CORRODE DESTROY
ERODIUM HERONBILL
EROS AMOR CUPID AENGUS POTHOS
EROSE ERODED UNEVEN
EROSION PIPING CHIMNEY NIVATION
SCOURING
EROTIC LOVING AMATORY AMOROUS
CURIOUS LESBIAN THERMAL
EROTICA CURIOSA FACETIAE
ERR MAR SIN FAIL MISS SLIP ABERR
LAPSE MISGO STRAY BUNGLE
FORVAY WANDER BLUNDER DEVIATE
MISPLAY MISTAKE SCRITHE
STUMBLE MISCARRY MISJUDGE
ERRAND CHORE ENVOY JOURNEY
MISSION LEGATION
(— BOY) LOBBYGOW
ERRANT STRAY ASTRAY ERRING
DEVIOUS PRICKANT
ERRATIC WILD CRAZY HUMAN
QUEER WACKY CRANKY WHACKY
STRANGE TANGENT VAGRANT
ACROSTIC ERRABUND FITIFIED
PLANETAL PLANETIC TRAVELED
VAGABOND
ERRATUM ERROR
ERRING ASTRAY ERRANT DEVIOUS
ERRINGLY FALSE
ERRONEOUS AMISS FALSE WRONG
UNTRUE ERRATIC MISTAKEN
STRAYING WRONGFUL
ERRONEOUSNESS FALLACY
ERROR X HOB SIN BUBU BULL FLUB
HELL MUFF SLIP TRIP BEARD BEVUE
BONER DEVIL FAULT FLUFF LAPSE
SCAPE BOBBLE FUMBLE GARBLE
HOWLER LAPSUS MISCUE NAUGHT
SPHALM BLOOMER BLUNDER
DEFAULT ERRATUM FALLACY
FALSITY LITERAL MISPLAY MISSTEP
MISTAKE OFFENSE RHUBARB
SNAPPER STUMBLE DELUSION
HAMARTIA MISPRINT MISSMENT
SOLECISM
ERS VETCH KERSANNE
ERSE ERSCH IRISH CELTIC GAELIC
SCOTTISH
ERST ONCE FORMERLY RECENTLY
ERSTWHILE ONCE FORMER
FORMERLY
ERUCT RASP BELCH
ERUCTATION BELCH
ERUDITE LEARNED CLERGIAL
DIDACTIC

ERUDITION WIT LORE WISDOM
LETTERS LEARNING
ERUPT BOIL BELCH BURST EJECT
IRRUPT
ERUPTING ACTIVE
ERUPTION ITCH RASH REEF RUSH
AGRIA BURST RUPIA SALVO STORM
BLOTCH HYDROA NIRLES ACTERID
BLOWOUT ECTHYMA MORPHEA
MORPHEW PUSTULE SAWFLOM
SUDAMEN EMPYESIS ENANTHEM
OUTBREAK OUTBURST
(CUTANEOUS —) HUMOR
ERVUM LENS LENTILLA
ERYSICHTHON (FATHER OF —)
CECROPS TRIOPAS
(MOTHER OF —) AGRAULOS
(SISTER OF —) IPHIMEDIA
ERYSIPELAS POX ROSE BLAST
WILDFIRE
ERYTHROBLASTOSIS HYDROPSY
ERYX (FATHER OF —) BUTES
(MOTHER OF —) VENUS
(SLAYER OF —) HERCULES
ESAU EDOM
(FATHER OF —) ISAAC
(MOTHER OF —) REBEKAH
(SON OF —) JEUSH KORAH REUEL
JAALAM ELIPHAZ
(WIFE OF —) ADAH BASHEMATH
ESCALADE SCALE SCALADE
SCALADO ESCALADO
ESCAPADE CAPER PRANK SALLY
SCHEME RUNAWAY
ESCAPE FLY GUY LAM RUN BAIL
BALE BEAT BLOW BOLT FLEE GATE
HISS JINK JUMP LEAK MISS SHUN
SKEW SLIP VENT AVOID BREAK
CHAPE DODGE ELOPE ELUDE EVADE
FLANK ISSUE SCAPE SHIFT SKIRT
SMOKE SPILL ASTERT DECAMP
ESCHEW OUTLET POWDER SQUEAK
ABSCOND AVOLATE BLOWOUT
ELUSION EXHAUST GETAWAY
LEAKAGE MISTAKE OUTFLOW
SCRITHE SQUEEZE WILDING
BLOWBACK ESCAPADE ESCAPAGE
EXSHEATH OUTSCAPE OVERSLIP
RIDDANCE WITHSLIP
(— FROM WORK) SNIB
(— FROM) FLY SHUN ILLUDE
(— NOTICE) ELUDE
(— OF FLUID) EFFUSION
(NARROW —) SHAVE
ESCAPEMENT SCAPE CRUTCH
ESCAPE FOLIOT VIRGULE KARRUSEL
ESCARGOT SNAIL
ESCAROLE ENDIVE SCAROLA
ESCARPMENT EDGE
ESCHAR SCAB CRUST ASCHER
ESCHAROTIC CAUSTIC
ESCHEAT FALL LAPSE REVERT
EXCHEAT FORFEIT
ESCHEW SHUN AVOID FORGO
ESCAPE FOREGO ABSTAIN
ESCOLAR PALU ROVET OILFISH
ROVETTO MACKEREL
ESCORT MAN SEE SET TRY BEAR
BEAU COND LEAD SHOW TEND WAIT

BRING CARRY GUARD USHER
ATTEND CONVEY CONVOY FOLLOW
SQUIRE COLLECT CONDUCT
CONSORT ESQUIRE GALLANT
CAVALIER CHAPERON SHEPHERD
(PAID —) GIGOLO
ESCRITOIRE DESK BUREAU
LECTERN
ESCULENT EDIBLE EATABLE
ESCUTCHEON CREST SHIELD
ESKER AS OS OSE KAME ESKAR
HOGBACK
ESKIMO ITA HUSKY INUIT INNUIT
AGOMIUT AMERIND ANGAKOK
KUNMIUT OKOMIUT ORARIAN
AGLEMIUT ESQUIMAU IKOGMIUT
KIDNELIK KINIPETU MAGEMIUT
MALEMIUT NUGUMIUT SINIMIUT
(— ASSEMBLY HOUSE) KASHIM
(— CULTURE) PUNUK
(— TENT) TUPEK TUPIK
ESOPHAGUS GULLET SWALLOW
WEASAND
ESOTERIC INNER MYSTIC ORPHIC
SECRET PRIVATE ABSTRUSE
ESPADON ESPADA SPADON
SPADROON
ESPALIER CORDON LATTICE RAILING
TRELLIS PALISADE
ESPARTO ALFA HALFA SPART STIPA
ATOCHA
ESPAVE CARACOLI
ESPECIAL VERY CHIEF SPECIAL
PECULIAR UNCOMMON
ESPECIALLY SUCH EXTRA RATHER
CHIEFLY OVERALL SPECIAL
ESPIAL SPY ESPY SCOUT NOTICE
ESPINAL MONTE
ESPIONAGE SPYING
ESPLANADE WALK DRIVE MAIDAN
MARINA
ESPOUSAL CEREMONY SPOUSAGE
BETROTHAL
ESPOUSE WED AFFY MATE ADOPT
MARRY DEFEND ENSURE SPOUSE
BETROTH EMBRACE HUSBAND
SUPPORT ADVOCATE MAINTAIN
ESPUNDIA UTA
ESPY SEE ASPY SPOT ASCRY SIGHT
WATCH BEHOLD DESCRY DETECT
LOCATE NOTICE DISCERN OBSERVE
DESCRIBE DISCOVER
ESQUIRE RADMAN ARMIGER
ESCUDERO SERGEANT
ESSAY TRY SEEK ASSAY CHRIA
OFFER PAPER PROVE TASTE THEME
TRACT TRAIL CASUAL EFFORT
MEMOIR SAILYE SATIRE SCREED
THESIS ARTICLE ATTEMPT PROFFER
VENTURE WRITING ENDEAVOR
EXERCISE EXERTION TRACTATE
TREATISE TURNOVER
ESSE BEING
ESSENCE ENS NET ATAR BASE
BONE CORE CRUX DRAW ESSE GIST
GUTS KIND ODOR OTTO PITH QUID
RASA SOUL YOLK ATTAR BASIC
BASIS BEING EIDOS FIBER FIBRE
FUMET HEART JUICE OTTAR OUSIA

STUFF BOTTOM EFFECT ENTITY
FLOWER INWARD MARROW NATURE
SPRITE ALCOHOL ELEMENT
EXTRACT FUMETTE GODHEAD
INBEING MEDULLA PERFUME
BERGAMOT CONCRETE ESSENTIA
(— OF BEING) SAT
(— OF FLOWERS) CONCRETE
(— OF GOD) SPIRIT DIVINITY
(— OF MEAT) BLOND
(— OF TEA) DRAW
(— OF VITAL MATTER) GLAME
(INNERMOST —) ATMAN
(UNIVERSAL —) FORM
(VITAL —) STAMINA
ESSENE ESSEE ASCETIC
ESSENTIAL REAL BASAL BASIC
VITAL ENTIRE FORMAL INWARD
CENTRAL CRUCIAL NEEDFUL
CARDINAL CRITICAL INHERENT
MATERIAL
(— TO LIFE) BIOGENOUS
ESSENTIALLY AUFOND
ESSONITE GARNET HYACINTH
ESTABLISH BED FIX PUT SET BASE
FAST FIRM FOOT MAKE REAR REST
SEAT BUILD DEFIX EDIFY ENACT
ERECT EVICT FOUND PLANT PROVE
RAISE SEIZE SETUP START STATE
STELL ATTEST AVOUCH BOTTOM
CEMENT CLINCH CREATE ENROOT
FASTEN FICCHE GROUND INVENT
INVEST LOCATE ORDAIN RATIFY
SETTLE STABLE VERIFY ACCOUNT
APPOINT APPROVE CONFIRM
ENSTATE INSTALL INSTATE INSTORE
POSSESS PREEMPT SUSTAIN
COLONIZE CONSTATE CONTRACT
ENSCONCE ENTRENCH IDENTIFY
INITIATE INSTRUCT RADICATE
REGULATE STABLISH VALIDATE
(— FACT) APPROVE
(— FIRMLY) INDURATE
(— MORALS) ETHIZE
(— TRUMP) PITCH
ESTABLISHED SAD FAST FIRM SURE
LEGAL SEATED SICCAR STABLE
STAPLE STATED STRONG CERTAIN
SETTLED STANDING
ESTABLISHMENT HONG MILL SHOP
STAB DAIRY FORGE JOINT PLANT
SALON STORE AGENCY CAISSE
CENOBY ECESIS LAYOUT MENAGE
SALOON SCHOOL ARSENAL ATELIER
BROTHEL COENOBY CONCERN
DOUNSET DOWNSET FACTORY
FISHERY FOUNDRY FUNDUCK
SHEBANG AQUARIUM AVERMENT
BUSINESS CHEESERY CREAMERY
ERECTION HACIENDA
(— IN NEW HABITAT) ECESIS
(— OF COLONY) DEDUCTION
(DOMESTIC —) MENAGE
(DRINKING —) STUBE SALOON
BARROOM SHEBEEN
(GAMBLING —) HOUSE TRIPOT
(HORSE-BREEDING —) HARAS
(MONASTIC —) CLOISTER
ESTAFETTE COURIER STAFETTE

ESTATE FEE ALOD COPY FEOD FIEF HOME LAND POMP RANK ACRES ALLOD DAIRA DOWER DOWRY ESTER ESTRE ETHEL FINCA FUNDO HABIT HOUSE MANOR STATE TALUK ABBACY DEMISE DOMAIN ENTAIL GROUND LIVING MISTER QUINTA TALUKA ALODIUM CHATEAU COMMONS DEMESNE DIGNITY DISPLAY FORTUNE HAVINGS MAJORAT ALLODIUM BENEFICE COPYHOLD DOMINION EXECUTRY FREEHOLD HACIENDA JOINTURE LIFEHOLD LONGACRE MESNALTY POSITION PROPERTY SENASORY STANDING
(— OF REBEL) FISC FISK
(— WITH SERFS) HAM
(HINDU —) CHAK
(PORTION OF —) LEGITIM
(REAL —) FUNDUS
(PL.) AMANI

ESTEEM AIM LET USE DEEM HOLD TALE ADORE COUNT FAVOR HONOR PRICE PRIDE STEEM THINK VALUE WEIGH WORTH ADMIRE CREDIT EXTIME REGARD REPUTE REVERE TENDER WONDER ACCOUNT CONCEIT OPINION RESPECT SUSPECT APPRAISE CONSIDER ESTIMATE VENERATE

ESTEEMED DEAR

ESTER BIXIN ETHER OLEIN SARIN TABUN BORATE CAPRIN ERUCIN HUMATE LAURIN MALATE OLEATE ACETATE ADIPATE ANISATE AZELATE CINERIN ELAIDIN FORMATE FUROATE GALLATE HEPARIN INDICAN LACTATE LACTONE LAURATE MALEATE MELLATE NITRATE OCTOATE OXALATE OXAMATE PECTATE PEPSIDE PICRATE SORBATE STEARIN SULTONE ABIETATE ACRYLATE ARSENATE ARSENITE ARSONATE BEHENATE BENZOATE CAFFEATE CONGENER DIPHENAN ESTOLIDE FLUORIDE FUCOIDIN KETIPATE LINOLATE LINOLEIN MALONATE MARGARIN MYRISTIN NUCLEATE PALMITIN PIMELATE PIPERATE RACEMATE SEBACATE SELENATE SILICATE SINAPATE STEARATE SUBERATE TARTRATE

ESTIMABLE GOOD SOLID WORTH GENTLE HONEST WORTHY THRIFTY VALUABLE

ESTIMATE AIM SET CALL CAST GAGE RANK RATE READ RECK ASAAY AUDIT CARAT CENSE COUNT GAUGE GUESS JUDGE MOUNT PLACE PRIZE SCALE STOCK TALLY VALUE WEIGH ASSESS BUDGET ESTEEM RECKON REGARD SURVEY ACCOUNT AVERAGE BALANCE CENSURE COMPUTE MEASURE APPRAISE CONSIDER CRITIQUE
(— OF ONE'S SELF) OPINION
(— TOO HIGHLY) OVERRATE

ESTIMATION AIM EYE CESS FAME NAME ODOR PASS RATE COUNT HONOR PRICE SIEGE VALUE CHOICE ESTEEM REGARD REPUTE OPINION JUDGMENT
(HIGH —) CONCEIT
(LOW —) DISREPUTE

ESTIMATOR CRUISER

ESTOC STOCK SWORD

ESTOILE STAR ETOILE

ESTONIA
CAPITAL: TALLINN
COIN: SENT KROON ESTMARK
DIALECT: TARTU
ISLAND: DAGO OESEL SAARE HIIUMAA
LAKE: PEIPUS
MEASURE: TUN ELLE LIIN PANG SUND TOLL TOOP FADEN VERST SAGENE VERSTA KULIMET VERCHOC TONNLAND
NATIVE: ESTH AESTI
PROVINCE: SAARE
RIVER: EMA NARVA
TOWN: NARVA PARNU REVAL TARTU TALLINN
WEIGHT: LOOD NAEL PUUD

ESTONIAN ESTH

ESTOP BAR FILL PLUG STOP DEBAR PREVENT

ESTRANGE PART WEAN ALIEN AVERT DIVERT ALIENATE DISUNITE STRANGER

ESTRANGEMENT STANCE DISTASTE

ESTRAY STRAY WANDER

ESTREAT COPY FINE EXACT RECORD STREET EXTRACT EXTREAT

ESTREPEMENT STRIP

E STRING QUINT

ESTRIOL THEELOL

ESTRONE THEELIN

ESTRUS HEAT SEASON

ESTUARY PARA WASH CREEK FIRTH FLEET FRITH INLET LIMAN ESTERO

ETCETERA ETC KTL

ETCH BITE FROST ENGRAVE AQUATINT INSCRIBE

ETCHED FROSTED

ETCHER POINT

ETCHING ETCH AQUATINT

ETEOCLES (BROTHER OF —) POLYNICES
(FATHER OF —) OEDIPUS
(MOTHER OF —) JOCASTA

ETERNAL ETERNE TARNAL AGELESS ENDLESS LASTING UNAGING ENDURING IMMORTAL TIMELESS UNCAUSED

ETERNALLY AKE EER EVER ALWAYS ETERNE FOREVER

ETERNITY AGE EON AEON OLAM GLORY ETERNE ETERNAL EWIGKEIT INFINITY

ETESIAN ANNUAL PERIODIC

ETHANE DIMETHYL

ETHER AIR SKY APIOL ESTER PINOLE ANISOLE ASARONE EPOXIDE ETHYLIN HARMINE SAFROLE SESAMIN SESAMOL SOLVENT ACACETIN ELEMICIN EMPYREAN GUAIACOL

ETHEREAL AERY AIRY SKYEY AERIAL SKYISH AIRLIKE ETHERIC FRAGILE SLENDER DELICATE HEAVENLY SUPERNAL VAPOROUS

ETHICAL ETHIC MORAL HONORABLE

ETHICS HEDONICS

ETHIOPIA
CAPITAL: ADDISABABA
COIN: BESA AMOLE GIRSH DOLLAR TALARI ASHRAFI PIASTER
DEPRESSION: DANAKIL
FALLS: TISISAT BLUENILE
ISLANDS: DAHLAK
LAKE: ABE TANA ABAYA SHOLA ZEWAY RUDOLF STEFANIE
LANGUAGE: GEEZ TIGRE SOMALI AMHARIC GALLINYA TIGRINYA
MARRIAGE: DAMOZ QURBAN SEMANYA
MEASURE: TAT KUBA SINJER SINZER FARSAKH FARSANG
MOUNTAIN: BATU GUGE GUNA TALO
MOUNTAINS: AHMAR CHOKE
NAME: ABYSSINIA
NATIVE: AFAR GALLA ABIGAR AMHARA ANNUAK HAMITE SEMITE SOMALI TIGRAI CUSHITE DANAKIL FALASHA
PORT: ASSAB MASSAWA
PRINCE: RAS
RIVER: OMO WEB BARO DAWA GILA ABBAI AKOBO AWASH FAFAN TAKKAZE
TOWN: EDD GOBA GORE THIO ADOLA ADUWA AKSUM ASSAB AWASH DIMTU HARAR JIMMA MOJJO ASMARA DESSYE DUNKUR GONDAR MAKALE GARDULA MASSAWA NAKAMTI DIREDAWA LALIBALA MUSTAHIL
VALLEY: RIFT
WEIGHT: KASM NATR OKET ALADA NETER WAKEA WOGIET FARASULA

ETHIOPIAN SIDI HAMITE HARARI AETHIOP AFRICAN CUSHITE FALASHA

ETHIOPIC GIZ GEEZ GHEEZ

ETHNIC (— GROUP) ACHANG

ETHOS MANNER

ETHYLENE ELAYL ETHENE ETHERIN

ETIQUETTE FORM DECORUM MANNERS
(— OF DRINKING TEA) CHANOYU

ETRUSCAN TUSCAN RASENNA ETRURIAN TYRRHENE
(PL.) TURSENOI TYRRHENI

ETUDE STUDY

ETUI CASE ETWEE TWEEZE TWEEZER EQUIPAGE RETICULE

ETYMOLOGY ORIGIN DERIVATION
ETYMON RADIX
EUBOEANS ABANTES
EUCALYPT GUM YATE APPLE BIMBIL
CARBUN JARRAH MALLEE MYRTAL
CARBEEN CUTTAIL MESSMAN
IRONBARK MESSMATE WHITETOP
YERTCHUK
EUCALYPTOLE CINEOL CINEOLE
EUCALYPTUS EUCALYPT WHIPSTICK
EUCHARIST HOUSEL MAUNDY
SUPPER MYSTERY VIATICUM
EUCHARISTIC (— ELEMENTS) HAGIA
EUCHITE SATANIST ADELPHIAN
MESSALIAN
EUCHRE LOVE
(**— HAND**) JAMBONE JAMBOREE
EUDAEMONIA HAPPINESS
EUDOCIMUS GUARA
EULALIA NETI
EULENSPIEGEL OWLGLASS
EULOGIST PRAISER LAUREATE
EULOGISTIC EULOGIC EPENETIC
MAGNIFIC LAUDATORY
EULOGY PRAISE TONGUE ADDRESS
ELOGIUM ORATION ENCOMIUM
PANEGYRE
EUMOLPUS (FATHER OF —)
NEPTUNE
(**MOTHER OF —**) CHIONE
(**SON OF —**) ISMARUS
EUNUCH CAPON SPORUS WETHER
GELDING HALFMAN CASTRATE
EUPHAUSID SHRIMP
EUPHEMISM DEE FIB GEE GOR
DASH GOSH GOLES GOLLY LAWKS
DIANTRE DICKENS GRACIOUS
EUPHONIOUS TUNEFUL
EUPHORIA ELATION
EUPHROSYNE JOY
EUPHUISM GONGORISM
EURASIAN BURGHER FERINGI
EURO WALLAROO
EUROPE BELAIT CONTINENT
EUROPEAN FRANK SAHIB BOHUNK
EUROPE FRINGE INDIAN FERINGI
TOPIWALA
(**— IN INDIES**) BLIJVER
(**WESTERN —**) FRANK
EUROPEAN BARRACUDA SPET
EUROPEAN BASS BRASSE
EUROPEAN BISON AUROCHS
EUROPEAN CLOVER ALSIKE
EUROPEAN GULL MEW
EUROPEAN HERRING SPRAT
EUROPEAN JUNIPER CADE
EUROPEAN KITE GLEDE
EUROPEAN LAVENDER ASPIC
EUROPEAN LINDEN TEIL
EUROPEAN MINT HYSSOP
EUROPEAN OAK DURMAST
EUROPEAN PERCH RUFF RUFFE
EUROPEAN POLECAT FITCHEW
EUROPEAN PORGY BESUGO
EUROPEAN RABBIT CONY
EUROPEAN SHARK TOPE
EUROPEAN SPARROW WHITECAP
EUROPEAN STARLING STARNEL
EUROPEAN SWALLOW MARTIN

EUROPEAN THRUSH MAVIS OUZEL
EUROPEAN WIDGEON WHIM
WHEWER
EUROPEAN WREN STAG
EURYPTERID SERAPHIM
EURYPYLUS (FATHER OF —)
NEPTUNE TELEPHUS
(**MOTHER OF —**) ASTYOCHE
(**SLAYER OF —**) PYRRHUS
HERCULES
EURYSACES (FATHER OF —) AJAX
(**MOTHER OF —**) TECMESSA
EURYSTHEUS (FATHER OF —)
STHENELUS
(**MOTHER OF —**) NICIPPE
(**SLAYER OF —**) HYLLUS
EUTECTIC STEADITE
EUTERPE (FATHER OF —) JUPITER
(**MOTHER OF —**) MNEMOSYNE
EUXANTHONE PURRONE
EUXOA AGROTIS
EVACUATE PASS VENT VOID AVOID
EMPTY EXPEL STOOL VACATE
DEPRIVE EXCRETE EXHAUST
NULLIFY VACUATE PERSPIRE
EVACUATION OFFICE DUNKIRK
EVADE BEG GEE BILK DUCK FLEE
FOIL JOUK JUMP SHUN SLIP VOID
AVERT AVOID BLINK DALLY DODGE
ELUDE FENCE FLANK PARRY SHIRK
SKIRT BAFFLE BLENCH BYPASS
DELUDE ESCAPE ILLUDE BEGUILE
FINESSE OUTSLIP QUIBBLE
HEDGEHOP LEAPFROG SIDESTEP
(**— LEGAL PROCESS**) ABSCOND
(**— PAYMENT**) BILK
(**— WORK**) JOUK
EVADNE (FATHER OF —) NEPTUNE
(**HUSBAND OF —**) CAPANEUS
(**MOTHER OF —**) IPHIS
(**SON OF —**) IAMUS
EVALUATE RATE ASSESS PONDER
RECKON DISSECT APPRAISE
ESTIMATE
EVALUATION STOCK ESTIMATE
EVANDER (FATHER OF —) HERMES
(**MOTHER OF —**) CARMENTA
EVANESCE FADE VANISH
EVANESCENCE ANICCA
EVANESCENT FLEET EVANID
BRITTLE CURSORY EVASIVE
FRAGILE DELICATE FLEETING
FLITTING FUGITIVE STAYLESS
EVANGELICAL GOSPEL
(**— ACTIVITY**) WARFARE
EVANGELIST LUKE MARK EVANGEL
GOSPELER
EVAPORATE DRY EXHALE AVOLATE
CONDENSE VAPORIZE
EVAPORATOR BOILER EFFECT
EVASION JINK SLIP DODGE QUIRK
SALVE SHIFT ESCAPE SNATCH
ELUSION OFFCOME SHUFFLE
TWISTER ARTIFICE ESCAPISM
VOIDANCE
EVASIVE SLY EELY DODGY SHIFTY
TWISTY ELUSIVE ELUSORY TRICKSY
SLIPPERY SLIPSKIN
EVE DUSK EREB EREV EVEN VIGIL

SUNSET SUNDOWN
(**NEW YEAR'S —**) HAGMENA
HOGMANAY
EVEN ALL DEN EEN TIE YET FAIR
HUNK JUST PAIR TILL ALINE EQUAL
EVERY EXACT FLUSH GRADE HUNKY
LEVEL MATCH PLAIN RIVAL STILL
SUANT SUENT SWEET DIRECT
ITSELF PLACID SILKEN SMOOTH
SQUARE STEADY ABREAST
BALANCE EQUABLE FLATTEN
REGULAR UNIFORM UPSIDES
EQUALIZE MODERATE PARALLEL
(**— NUMBERS**) PAIR
(**— OFF**) LEVEL
(**— THOUGH**) IF ALTHO ALBEIT
ALTHOUGH
(**MAKE —**) WEIGH STEADY
EVENING DEN EVE EREB EVEN
ABEND TARDE SUNSET VESPER
EVENTIDE VESPERAL
(**AT —**) TEEN
(**YESTERDAY —**) STREEN
EVENING PRIMROSE SUNCUP
SCABIOUS
EVENING STAR VENUS HESPER
VESPER EVESTAR HESPERUS
EVENLY FAIR PLAIN FLATLY
EQUALLY
EVENNESS EQUALITY
EVENT HAP CASE FACT FATE FEAT
TILT CASUS DOING EPOCH FRAME
ISSUE THING ACTION EFFECT
FACTUM RESULT TIDING TIMING
EPISODE FIXTURE MIRACLE
PORTENT TRAGEDY INCIDENT
OCCASION
(**AMUSING —**) COMEDY
(**CHANCE —**) ACCIDENT FORTUITY
(**EXTRAORDINARY —**) MIRACLE
(**FORTUITOUS —**) HAZARD
(**GRAVE —**) CALAMITY
(**HAPPY —**) GODSEND
(**IMPORTANT —**) ACE ERA
(**PAST —S**) HISTORY
(**SET OF —S**) EPISODE
(**SIGNIFICANT —**) CRISIS
(**SKI —**) DOWNHILL
(**SOCIAL —**) BENEFIT
(**SPORTING —**) STAKE
(**THEATRICAL —**) DRAW
(**TURNING-POINT —**) LANDMARK
(**UNEXPECTED —**) STUNNER
AFTERCLAP
(**YEARLY —**) ANNUAL
EVENTFUL NOTABLE
EVENTIDE VESPER EVENING
EVENTUAL LAST FINAL ULTIMATE
EVENTUALITY EVENT
EVENTUALLY YET FINALLY
EVENTUATE GO LEAD ISSUE
RESULT SUCCEED ULTIMATE
EVENUS (DAUGHTER OF —)
MARPESSA
(**FATHER OF —**) MARS
EVER O AY SO AYE EER ONCE STILL
ALWAYS ETERNE FOREVER
EVERGLADE STATE FLORIDA
EVERGREEN BOX FIR IVY YEW ASIS

BAGO ILEX PINE TAWA BOLDO
CAROB CEDAR HEATH HOLLY
LARCH SAVIN THUYA TOYON
BAUERA COIGUE DAHOON LAUREL
MASTIC SPRUCE BANKSIA BARETTA
BEBEERU BILIMBI GOWIDDE
HEMLOCK JASMINE TARATAH
BOXTHORN CALFKILL CARAUNDA
IRONWOOD TILESEED
(PL.) CHRISTMAS
EVERLASTING ETERNE AEONIAL
AEONIAN AGELONG DURABLE
ENDLESS ETERNAL FOREVER
LASTING TEDIOUS ENDURING
IMMORTAL INFINITE TIMELESS
EVERLASTINGLY ALWAYS FOREVER
EVERSION BLOWOUT BEARINGS
EVERT UPSET EVERSE SUBVERT
OVERTURN
EVERY ALL ANY ILK THE EACH EVER
ILKA ENTIRE EVERICH COMPLETE
(— **DAY**) QD QUOTID
(— **HOUR**) QH
(— **NIGHT**) QN
EVERYBODY ALL EACH EVERYMAN
EVERYONE
EVERYDAY USUAL HOMELY PROSAIC
ORDINARY WORKADAY
EVERYTHING ALL ATHING
EVERYWHERE PASSIM UBIQUE
ALGATES AYWHERE OVERALL
ALLWHERE
EVICT OUST EJECT EXPEL
EVIDENCE MARK SHOW SIGN TEST
PROOF SCRIP SMOKE TOKEN TRACE
TRIAL ATTEST RECORD REVEAL
CHARTER EXHIBIT HEARSAY
SHOWING SUPPORT ARGUMENT
DISPROOF DOCUMENT EVICTION
INDICATE MANIFEST MONUMENT
MUNIMENT WARRANTY
(— **OF DISEASE**) SYMPTOM
(— **OF FRESHNESS**) BLOOM
(— **OF WRONGDOING**) GOODS
(**POSITIVE** —) CONSTAT
EVIDENT LOUD OPEN PERT APERT
BROAD CLEAR FRANK GROSS PLAIN
EXTANT LIQUID PATENT WITTER
EMINENT GLARING OBVIOUS
PROBATE VISIBLE APPARENT
DISTINCT FLAGRANT LUCULENT
MANIFEST PALPABLE
EVIL BAD DER ILL SIN BALE BASE
DIRE HARM LEWD PAPA POOR SORE
VICE VILE WICK YELL CRIME CURSE
DEVIL FELON FOLLY MALUM QUEDE
SORRY WATHE WRONG CANCEL
DIVERS INJURY MALIGN MENACE
NAUGHT ROTTEN SHREWD SINFUL
UNFEEL UNFELE UNGOOD UNWELL
WICKED WONDER ADVERSE
BALEFUL CORRUPT DISEASE
DIVERSE HEINOUS HURTFUL
IMMORAL MISDEED NOXIOUS
SATANIC UNHAPPY UNSOUND
VICIOUS CALAMITY DEPRAVED
DEVILISH DISASTER GANGRENE
IMPROPER INIQUITY MISCHIEF
QUEDSHIP SINISTER

(— **BEING**) MARE
(— **OF MANY PHASES**) HYDRA
(— **SPIRIT**) JUMBIE
(**IMAGINARY** —) WINDMILL
(**IMPENDING** —) MENACE IMMINENCE
(**SOCIAL** —) SCOURGE
(**SPIRITUAL** —) SCAB
EVILDOER SLASHER
EVIL EYE DROCHUIL MALOCCHIO
EVINCE SHOW ARGUE PROVE
SUBDUE BREATHE CONQUER
DISPLAY EXHIBIT EVIDENCE
INDICATE MANIFEST
EVISCERATE GUT DRAW BOWEL
PAUNCH GARBAGE
EVOCATION SADHANA
EVOKE FIT MOVE STIR EDUCE
AROUSE ELICIT SUMMON EVOCATE
SUGGEST
EVOLUTION DRIFT GROWTH
BIOGENY DIOECISM HOROTELY
MANEUVER BRADYTELY
(PL.) AEROBATICS
EVOLUTIONISM DARWINISM
EVOLVE COOK EMIT EDUCE DERIVE
UNFOLD UNROLL BLOSSOM
DEVELOP EVOLUTE CONCEIVE
UNPLIGHT
EWE KEB TEG CROCK CRONE DRAPE
SHEEP GIMMER LAMBER RACHEL
THEAVE CHILVER
(— **AND LAMB**) COUPLE
(**OLD** —) BIDDY CROCK CRONE
BIDDIE
(**YOUNG** —) THEAVE
EWER JUG CREW LAIR BASIN UDDER
PITCHER URCEOLE
EXACERBATE SOUR ENRAGE
FERMENT EMBITTER IRRITATE
EXACERBATION PAROXYSM
EXACT ASK DUE DEAD EVEN FINE
FLAT HAVE JUMP JUST LEVY NICE
TRUE VERY PRESS SCREW WREAK
WREST COMPEL DEMAND ELICIT
EVINCE EXTORT FORMAL GRAITH
MINUTE NARROW PROPER SEVERE
SQUARE STRAIT STRICT CAREFUL
CERTAIN COLLECT COMMAND
CORRECT ENFORCE ESTREAT
EXPRESS EXTRACT LITERAL
PARTILE PERFECT POINTED PRECISE
PRECISO REFINED REGULAR
REQUIRE ACCURATE CRITICAL
EXPLICIT FAITHFUL RIGOROUS
SPECIFIC
(— **BY FINE**) ESTREAT
(— **SATISFACTION**) AVENGE
(**NOT** —) PLATIC
EXACTING NICE HARSH STERN STIFF
TIGHT SCREWY SEVERE STRAIT
ARDUOUS EXIGENT FINICKY
CRITICAL IMPOSING IRONCLAD
PRESSING SCREWING
(— **EXCLUSIVE DEVOTION**) JEALOUS
EXACTION TAX MART GOUGE GRIPE
(— **OF PROVISIONS**) CESS COYNE
COIGNY
(**UNDUE** —) EXTORTION
EXACTLY DUE BANG DEAD EVEN

FLAT FLOP FULL JUMP JUST VERY
PLUMB QUITE RIGHT SHARP SPANG
TRULY ARIGHT EVENLY ITSELF
JUSTLY NICELY PERFECT SLAPDAB
DIRECTLY MINUTELY
EXACTNESS RIGOR TRUTH NICETY
ACCURACY DELICACY DISPATCH
FIDELITY IDENTITY JUSTNESS
SAPIENCE SEVERITY
(**FUSSY** —) FIKE
EXAGGERATE GAB MORE CHARGE
EXTEND OVERDO AMPLIFY ENHANCE
ENLARGE MAGNIFY OUTLASH
ROMANCE STRETCH INCREASE
OVERDRAW OVERLASH OVERTELL
(— **OPENING OF MOUTH**) CHINK
EXAGGERATED SLAB TALL
COLORED FUSTIAN FABULOUS
INFLATED OVERSHOT
EXAGGERATING ARROGANT
EXAGGERATION REACHER
HYPERBOLE
EXALT HAUT REAR AREAR BUILD
DEIFY ELATE ERECT EXTOL HEAVE
HEEZE HONOR MOUNT RAISE
TOWER ALTIFY ASCEND EXHALE
PREFER REFINE UPREAR WORTHY
ADVANCE AUGMENT DIGNIFY
ELEVATE ENHANCE ENNOBLE
FEATHER GLORIFY GREATEN
INSPIRE MAGNIFY PROMOTE
SUBLIME DIVINIZE ENTHRONE
GRADUATE HEIGHTEN INHEAVEN
PEDESTAL
EXALTATION LAUD AVATAR ELATION
RAPTURE ERECTION
EXALTED HAUT HIGH ELATE GRAND
LOFTY NOBLE SHEEN SKYEY SOARY
ASTRAL TIPTOE TOPFUL HAUGHTY
SUBLIME ELEVATED EXALTATE
EXALTING HUMAN
EXAMINATION EX MAY EXAM FACE
QUIZ TEST ASSAY AUDIT BOARD
CHECK FINAL GREAT POINT PROBE
STUDY TRIAL BIOPSY EXAMEN
REVIEW SCHOOL SEARCH SURVEY
TRIPOS AUTOPSY BEARING
CANVASS CHECKUP DIVVERS
EXAMINE HEARING INQUEST INQUIRY
MIDYEAR OPPOSAL TUGGERY
ANALYSIS CRITIQUE EXERCISE
NECROPSY RESEARCH SCANNING
SCRUTINY
(PL.) HOURS
EXAMINE ASK CON FAN SEE SPY
TRY BOLT CASE COMB FEEL LAIT
LINE LOOK OGLE QUIZ RIPE SCAN
SEEK SIFT TEST VIEW ASSAY AUDIT
CHECK ENTER GROPE PROBE
QUEST QUOTE SAMEN SENSE
SOUND STUDY VISIT APPOSE
BEHOLD CANDLE DEBATE PERUSE
PONDER REVIEW SCREEN SEARCH
SURVEY ANALYZE CANVASS
COLLATE DISCUSS EXPLORE
INQUIRE INSPECT OVERSEE
PALPATE RUMMAGE CONSIDER
OVERHAUL
(— **BY TOUCH**) PALPATE

(— **CAREFULLY**) SCAN SIFT PONDER
(— **LAND**) SOUM
EXAMINER POSER TRIER CENSOR
CONNER SABORA ANALYST
APPOSER AUDITOR CORONER
PROBATOR SEARCHER
EXAMPLE A CASE CAST COPY LEAD
NORM TYPE BEAUT BYSEN ESSAY
LIGHT MODEL PIECE EMBLEM
PRAXIS SAMPLE BOUNCER LEADING
LECTURE PATTERN PURPOSE
SAMPLER THEATER CALENDAR
ENSAMPLE EXEMPLAR EXEMPLUM
FORBYSEN FOREGOER INSTANCE
PARADIGM SPECIMEN
(**DISGRACEFUL** —) BIZEN BYSEN
BYZEN
(**EXTREME** —) CAUTION
(**INFERIOR** —) EXCUSE
(**INSTRUCTIVE** —) LESSON
(**OLDEST** —) DOYEN
(**SUPERLATIVE** —) BLINGER
EXANTHEMA DIEBACK ERUPTION
EXASPERATE IRE IRK MAD BAIT
GALL HEAT URGE ANNOY BLOOD
ENRAGE EXCITE NETTLE EXASPER
INFLAME PROVOKE ROUGHEN
ACERBATE IRRITATE
EXASPERATED SNAKY WROTH
SNAKEY SNAKISH
EXASPERATION GALL HEAT WRATH
EXCAVATE CUT DIG PIT HOLE HOWK
MINE MOLE MUCK PION SINK DELVE
DRILL DRIVE GRAVE NAVVY SCOOP
STOPE BURROW DREDGE EXCAVE
GULLET HOLLOW QUARRY
EXCAVATION CUT DIG PIT HOLE
MINE REDD SINK SUMP BERRY
DELFT DELPH DITCH GRAVE PILOT
STOPE BURROW CAVITY DUGOUT
GROOVE TRENCH BREAKUP
CUTTING PADDOCK TUTWORK
WORKING DENEHOLE SLUSHPIT
EXCAVATOR DIG BILDAR CLEOID
DIGGER DIPPER DRIFTER HATCHET
PIONEER
EXCEED COW TOP BEST PASS
EXCEL OUTDO OUTGO BETTER
OUTRUN OUTVIE OVERDO OVERGO
ECLIPSE OUTPASS OVERRUN
OVERTAX PRECEDE SURPASS
OUTRANGE OUTSTRIP OVERCOME
OVERGANG OVERSTEP OVERWEND
SURMOUNT
(— **THE RESOURCES**) BEGGAR
EXCEEDING VILE
EXCEEDINGLY ALL DONE PURE
TRES VERY AMAIN BLAME BLAMED
MASTER PURELY AWFULLY LICKING
PARLOUS PASSING HEARTILY
HEAVENLY HORRIBLE PROPERLY
EXCEL CAP COB TOP BANG BEAT
BEST DING FLOG MEND PASS
BLECK OUTDO OUTGO SHINE
BETTER EXCEED MASTER OUTRAY
OVERDO OVERGO PRECEL ECLIPSE
EMULATE OUTPEER SURPASS
OUTCLASS OUTRANGE OUTRIVAL
OUTSHINE OUTSTRIP OVERPEER
SUPERATE SURMOUNT

EXCELLENCE ARETE MERIT PRICE
VIRTU WORTH BEAUTY DESERT
HEIGHT VIRTUE DIGNITY PROWESS
GOODNESS SPLENDOR
(— **OF QUALITY**) STRIKE
(**MORAL** —) GRACE
(**PL.**) SANCTITIES
EXCELLENT GAY RUM BEST BRAW
COOL FINE GOOD HEND HIGH PURE
RARE RIAL SLAP TALL TRIM ATHEL
BONNY BONZA BRAVE BULLY BURLY
GREAT JOLLY PIOUS PRIME SOLID
SUPER SWELL TRIED WALLY BONNIE
BONZER BOSKER CHEESY CHOICE
CLASSY FAMOUS FREELY GENTLE
GOODLY PRETTY PROPER SELECT
SPIFFY WICKED WIZARD WORTHY
YANKEE BLIGHTY BOSHTER CAPITAL
CORKING CURIOUS ELEGANT
GALLANT IMMENSE QUALITY
SNIFTER STAVING TOPPING
CLIPPING EXIMIOUS GENEROUS
KNOCKOUT STUNNING SUPERIOR
VALUABLE VIRTUOUS WAUREGAN
YNGOODLY
(— **IN QUALITY**) FRANK
(**MOST** —) BEST
EXCELLENTLY BRAWLY CLEVER
FINELY FREELY PROUDLY DIVINELY
FAMOUSLY
EXCELLING BEST PASSANT
EXCEPT BAR BUT CEP NOT BATE
BOUT OMIT ONLY SAVE FORBY
SEVER EXEMPT FORBYE NOBBUT
SAVING SCUSIN UNLESS BESIDES
EXCLUDE OUTCEPT OUTTAKE
OUTWITH RESERVE WITHOUT
FORPRISE OUTTAKEN RESERVED
EXCEPTING BATING EXCEPT SAVING
UNLESS
EXCEPTION DEMUR SALVO SAVING
DISSENT OFFENSE DEMURRER
FALLENCY FORPRISE INSTANCE
EXCEPTIONAL RARE EXEMPT
STRANGE UNUSUAL ABERRANT
ABNORMAL ESPECIAL SINGULAR
UNCOMMON
EXCEPTIONALLY AMAZING
SPANKING
EXCERPT CITE PATCH QUOTE
SCRAP EXTRACT OFFPRINT
(— **FROM SONG**) SNATCH
EXCESS OVER PLUS RIOT FLOOD
INORD LUXUS PRIDE ACRASY
ACRASIA BALANCE DEBAUCH
EXTREME MISRULE NIMIETY
OUTRAGE OVERAGE OVERSET
PROFUSE RIOTISE SURFEIT
SURPLUS EXCEDENT GLUTTONY
INTEREST OVERLASH OVERMUCH
OVERPLUS PLETHORA PLEURISY
(— **OF LOGS**) BANK
(— **OF METAL**) FEEDHEAD
(— **OF SOLAR MONTH**) EPACT
EXCESSIVE TOO OVER RANK ENORM
FANCY STEEP STIFF UNDUE DEADLY
WOUNDY EXTREME FURIOUS
NIMIOUS SURFEIT ABNORMAL
CRIMINAL DEVILISH ENORMOUS
HORRIBLE INSOLENT OVERMUCH

TERRIBLE TERRIFIC
EXCESSIVELY TOO SUPER DEADLY
OVERLY STRONG UNDULY PARLISH
PARLOUS PASSING PLAGUEY
WOUNDLY DEVILISH PLAGUILY
EXCHANGE RAP SET CASH CAUP
CHOP CODE COPE COUP KULA
MART SELL SWAP SWOP BANDY
BOARD BOLSA CORSE SHIFT STORE
TRADE TROKE TRUCK BARTER
BOURSE CAMBIO CHANGE DICKER
EXCAMB MARKET NIFFER RESALE
RIALTO SCORSE SHOPPE TOLSEL
TOLZEY VALUTA WISSEL WRIXLE
BARROOM CAMBIUM CHAFFER
COMMUTE CONVERT DEALING
PERMUTE TRAFFIC COMMERCE
TRUCKAGE
(— **IN CHECKERS**) CUT SHOT
(— **OF BLOWS**) HANDPLAY
(— **OF PRISONERS**) CARTEL
(— **OF SYLLABLES**) ANACLASIS
(— **SMALL TALK**) CHAFFER
(— **THOUGHTS**) CONVERSE
(— **VISITS**) GAM
(**DANCE** —) CROSSOVER
(**FAIR** —) GIFFGAFF
(**FOREIGN** —) DEVISE
(**POETICAL** —) FLYTING
(**POST** —) CANTEEN
(**TELEPHONE** —) CENTRAL
EXCHEQUER FISC PURSE COFFER
KHALSA CHECKER FINANCE
TREASURY
EXCIPIENT OXYMEL
EXCISE TAX CROP DUTY GELD TOLL
SLASH EXCIDE EXSECT IMPOST
RESECT EXSCIND ALCABALA
RETRENCH
EXCISEMAN GAGER GAUGER
EXCISOR
EXCISION CUT ERASURE
EXCITABLE NERVOUS
EXCITATION LASH
EXCITE HOT CITE FIRE HEAT HYPO
SEND SPUR STIR URGE WAKE WHET
WORK YERK ALARM AMOVE ANGER
CHAFE ELATE ERECT FLAME FLUSH
IMPEL PIQUE RAISE ROUSE SCALD
SPOOK AROUSE AWAKEN BOTHER
DAZZLE DECOCT FLURRY FOMENT
IGNITE INCEND INCITE INVOKE
JANGLE KINDLE LATHER PROMPT
SALUTE TICKLE UPREAR WECCHE
AGITATE ANIMATE COMMOVE
ENCHAFE FERMENT INCENSE
INFLAME PHILTER PROVOKE
QUICKEN STARTLE WHITTLE
DISQUIET ENGENDER EXCITATE
IRRITATE
(— **MIRTH**) DIVERT
EXCITED UP GAY HOT AGOG GYTE
PINK CADGY EAGER RANTY SKEER
BLEEZY ELATED HEATED STEAMY
ATHRILL FEVERED HAYWIRE
SKEERED WAKENED AGITATED
ATWITTER ELEVATED FEVERISH
FLURRIED FRENETIC STARTLED
(**EASILY** —) KITTLE
EXCITEMENT ADO GOG BUZZ FUSS

GLOW HEAT KICK STIR TOSS UNCO
FEEZE FEVER FUROR LARRY MANIA
SETUP STOUR UNCOW FRENZY
SPLASH WARMTH FERMENT
FRISSON NERVISM TAMASHA
WIDDRIM BROUHAHA DELIRIUM
INTEREST RACKETRY
(FILLED WITH —) HECTIC
(GREAT —) FEVER
(MENTAL —) WIDDRIM
(PLEASANT —) SUSPENSE
(VIOLENT —) GARE
EXCITING HOT HIGH HECTIC
AGACANT BURNING RACKETY
ROUSING EXCITANT EXCITIVE
PATHETIC STIRRING TERRIFIC
(— HORROR) DIRE DIREFUL
EXCLAIM CRY HOWL BLURT ESCRY
SNORT CLAMOR OUTCRY BESPEAK
EXCLAMATION O AH AI AY BO EH
EY HA HI HO LA LO MY OH OW SO
ST YO AHA AIE BAH BAM BOO FEN
FIE FOH GEE GIP GRR GUP HAI HAW
HAY HEM HEP HEY HIC HOY HUH
NOW OCH OFF OHO OUF OUT PAH
PEW POH POX ROT SEE SUZ TCH
TCK TUT UGH VOW WEE WOW YAH
YOW AHEM ALAS AVOY BUFF DEAR
DRAT EGAD EVOE FAST GARN
GOOD HAIL HECH HECK HIST HOLA
HUFF HUNH HUSH HYKE OONS
OUGH PHEW PHOO PHUT PIFF PISH
POOH PRUT PUGH RATS RIVO SCAT
SIRS SOFT SOHO TCHU TUSH WALY
WEEK WEET WELL WHAM WHAT
WHEE WHEW WHIR WHIT WUGG
YOOP YULE ALACK BRAVO EWHOW
FAINS FANCY FAUGH FEIGH GLORY
GOODY HEIGH HELLO HOLLA HUFFA
HULLO HUMPH HUZZA JOSSA
OHONE PSHAW RIGHT SALVE SHISH
SKOAL SORRY SUGAR TEREU
WAUGH WELOO WHING WHISK
WHIST WHOOP WIRRA WOONS
CARAJO CLAMOR ENCORE HALLOO
HEYDAY HOOTAY HURRAH INDEED
OUTCRY PERFAY QUOTHA RATHER
RIGHTO SHUCKS STEADY WALKER
WHOOSH CARAMBA DOGGONE
GODSAKE HOSANNA JIGGERS
KERCHOO KERWHAM NICHEVO
PRITHEE RUBBISH SALAMAT
TANTIVY THUNDER WELCOME
WHOOPEE FAREWELL WAESUCKS
WELLAWAY
(— OF DISGUST) AUH FIE FOH PAH
UGH AUGH AVOY PHEW PISH POOT
PSHA PUGH FAUGH FEICH FEIGH
PSHAW WELOO
(— OF DISTRESS) AI AIE HARO
HARROW
(— OF DOUBT) HUM HUMPH
(— OF IMPATIENCE) GIP PHEW
(— OF INCREDULITY) AHEM INDEED
WALKER
(— OF REPUGNANCE) UGH
(— OF SURPRISE) HA OW GIP LAW
HEIN HUNH LACK LAND LAWK LORD
ODSO BABAI HEUGH LAWKS

CRIMINE CRIMINY HEAVENS JUCKIES
GORBLIMY GRAMERCY
(— OF TRIUMPH) AH IO GRIG
HEUCH HOOCH HURRAH
(PROFANE —) BAN
EXCLAMATION POINT BANG
SHOUT SCREAMER
EXCLUDE BAR SHUT SINK CLOSE
DEBAR EJECT EXPEL FENCE BANISH
DISBAR EXCEPT EXEMPT FORBAR
FORBID REJECT BLANKET DEFAULT
EXPUNGE FOREBAR FOREIGN
OUTTAKE OUTWALL REPULSE
SECLUDE SUSPEND
EXCLUDED EXEMPT FOREIGN
EXCLUDING BAR BUT LESS
BARRING
EXCLUSIVE ALL ONLY RARE SOLE
ALONE ELECT WHOLE NARROW
SELECT ENTIRELY
(— OF) BEFORE
EXCLUSIVELY ALL ALONE SINGLY
ENTIRELY
EXCOGITATE CONSIDER
EXCOMMUNICATE CURSE
UNCHURCH
EXCOMMUNICATION BAN CURSE
HEREM EXCISION
EX-CONVICT LAG LAGGER
EXCORIATE FLAY GALL SCORE
STRIP ABRADE SCORCH BLISTER
LAMBASTE
EXCREMENT LEE CRAP DIRT DREG
DUNG FRASS JAKES HOCKEY
ORDURE REFUSE VOIDING
CROTTELS
(— OF EARTHWORM) CAST
(— OF HARES) CROTTELS
(— OF INSECTS) FRASS
(PL.) DEJECTA
EXCRESCENCE NOB PIN WEN BURL
BURR GALL HORN KNOB KNOT
KNUR LUMP WART FUSEE FUZEE
KNURL THORN EXCESS HURTLE
MORULA NUBBLE PIMPLE BOLSTER
PUSTULE RATTAIL SPINACH
CARUNCLE EPITHEMA TUBERCLE
(— ON HORSE'S FOOT) FIG
(— ON WHALE'S HEAD) BONNET
EXCRETA EGESTA
EXCRETE EGEST SWEAT EXCERN
DEFECATE PERSPIRE
EXCRETION SORDES ECRISIS
EXCRUCIATE RACK GRIND AGONIZE
TORMENT TORTURE
EXCRUCIATING GRINDING
EXCULPATE FREE CLEAR REMIT
ACQUIT EXCUSE PARDON ABSOLVE
FORGIVE JUSTIFY RELEASE
PALLIATE
EXCULPATION EXCUSE
EXCURSION DIP HOP ROW DIET
RIDE SAIL SPIN TOUR TRIP ESSAY
JAUNT RANGE SALLY START TRAMP
CANTER CRUISE FLIGHT JUNKET
OUTING PASEAR RAMBLE SASHAY
VAGARY VOYAGE JOURNEY
OUTLOPE OUTRIDE OUTROAD
CAMPAIGN ESCAPADE

EXCURSIONIST TRIPPER
EXCUSABLE VENIAL
EXCUSE FAIK PLEA ALIBI COLOR
GLOSS PLANE REMIT SALVO SCUSE
ACQUIT ESSOIN EXEMPT PARDON
REFUGE SCONCE SECURE SUNYIE
ABSOLVE APARDON APOLOGY
CONDONE ESSOIGN EXCUSAL
FORGIVE OFFCOME PRETEXT
DISPENSE OCCASION OVERLOOK
PALLIATE PRETENCE
(CONSCIENTIOUSLY —) SCRUPLE
EXCUSS SHAKE DISCARD DISCUSS
EXECRABLE BAD CURST CURSED
DAMNED HEINOUS ACCURSED
DAMNABLE WRETCHED
EXECRATE BAN DAMN ABHOR
CURSE DEVOTE
EXECRATION CURSE
EXECUTE DO ACT CUT TOP BURN
DASH FILL GIVE HANG HAVE KILL
OBEY PASS PLAY SLAY FRAME
GANCH LYNCH SCRAG YIELD
DESIGN DIRECT EFFECT FINISH
FULFIL GARROT GIBBET MANAGE
CONDUCT ENFORCE FULFILL
GAROTTE PERFORM STRETCH
COMPLETE DISPATCH EXPEDITE
PRACTICE PRACTISE
(— BOW) WREATHE
(— POORLY) DUB
(— SUCCESSFULLY) COMPLETE
EXECUTED GIVEN
(— EXQUISITELY) CURIOUS
(— WITH CARE) ACCURATE
(CRUDELY —) DAUBY
EXECUTION GANCH TOUCH EFFECT
FACTURE GARROTE HANGING
TECHNIC CARRIAGE GARROTTE
PRACTICE
(— BY BURNING) STAKE
(— OF WILL) FACTUM
EXECUTIONER BURRIO HEADER
TORTOR BUTCHER HANGMAN
HEADMAN LOCKMAN CARNIFEX
EXECUTOR HEADSMAN
EXECUTIVE BOSS DEAN MAYOR
WARDEN CASHIER MANAGER
PODESTA PREMIER GOVERNOR
OFFICIAL
EXECUTOR DOER AGENT ALBACEA
SECUTOR ENFORCER MINISTER
EXEGESIS ANAGOGE ANAGOGY
MIDRASH HAGGADAH
EXEMPLAR MODEL FATHER MIRROR
MODULE EIDOLON EXAMPLE
PARABLE PATTERN
EXEMPLARY LAUDABLE
EXEMPLIFICATION SOUL EXAMPLE
EXEMPLIFY SAMPLE SATISFY
ENSAMPLE MODELIZE
EXEMPT EXON FREE EXEEM EXEME
FRANK SEVER SPARE EXPERT
FIDATE IMMUNE EXCLUDE RELEASE
DISPENSE EXCEPTED
EXEMPTION GRACE CHARTER
FREEDOM LIBERTY SWEATER
BLOODWIT IMMUNITY IMPUNITY
EXEQUATUR PLACET

EXERCISE ACT AIR DIP PLY URE USE BEAR HAVE DRILL ETUDE EXERT HALMA LATIN LONGE SWEAT AIRING BREATH CAREER EMPLOY EXERCE LESSON MANUAL PARADE PRAXIS SCHOOL AUFGABE BREATHE DISPLAY ENHAUNT PROBLEM ACTIVITY EXERTION FORENSIC PALESTRA PRACTICE PRACTISE
(— CONTROL) BOSS PRESIDE
(— HORSE) BREEZE
(ACADEMIC —) PRACTICUM
(CAVALRY —) MELEE
(MUSICAL —) ETUDE SOLFEGE VOCALISE
(STRONG —) INTENSION
(UNWARRANTED —) STRETCH
(PL.) ALLEGRO ATHLETICS

EXERT DO PLY PUT DRAW EMIT HUMP STIR DRIVE SPEND SWING EXTEND REVEAL STRAIN AFFORCE ENFORCE IMPRESS CHARETTE ENDEAVOR EXERCISE
(— A SPELL) TAKE
(— POWER) ACT BEAR
(— PRESSURE) SQUEEZE
(— TRACTION) HAUL

EXERTING (— POWER) AGENT
EXERTION HEFT BURST ESSAY LABOR TRIAL WHILE ACTION EFFORT MOTION STRESS STRIFE ATTEMPT TROUBLE ENDEAVOR EXERCISE STRUGGLE
(EXCESSIVE —) STRAIN
(STRENUOUS —) HUMP

EXFOLIATE SCALE
EXFOLIATION FURFUR
EXHALATION AURA FUME REEK STEAM BREATH EXPIRY MIASMA HALITUS MALARIA FUMOSITY MEPHITIS
EXHALE CAST EMIT REEK EXUDE STEAM WHIFF EXPIRE BREATHE FURNACE REFLAIR RESPIRE EXHALATE PERSPIRE
EXHALED SFOGATO
EXHAUST DO FAG SAP BEAT BURN COOK COWL EMIT FAIL FLAG FLOG JADE KILL MATE SOAK TIRE TUCK BLAST BREAK CLEAN DRAFT DRAIN EMPTY FORDO GRUEL LEECH PETER SHOOT SPEND SWINK WASTE WEARY ABRADE BETOIL BOTTOM BUGGER EMBOSS FINISH FOREDO HARASS HATTER OVERDO TAIGLE TUCKER BREATHE CONSUME DEPLETE DEPRIVE DRAUGHT EXTRACT FATIGUE OUTWEAR SCOURGE SURREIN DISTRESS EDUCTION EVACUATE FORSPEND FORWEARY OVERWEAR
EXHAUSTED TAM BEAT DEAD DONE DUNG GONE WEAK WORN BLOWN EMPTY JADED SPENT STANK TIRED BARREN BEATEN BUSHED EFFETE GROGGY MARCID PLAYED TOILED TRAIKY ATTAINT DRAINED EMPTIED FORDONE FORSUNG FORWORN TEDIOUS WHACKED BANKRUPT

CONSUMED FOREDONE FOREWORN FORFAIRN FORSPENT FOUGHTEN HARASSED OUTSPENT OVERWORN
(— OF AIR) HIGH
EXHAUSTING ARDUOUS IRKSOME PREYING
EXHAUSTION EXHAUST FATIGUE SELLOUT SOOREYN GONENESS
EXHAUSTIVE FULL MINUTE THOROUGH
EXHIBIT AIR PEN FAIR HAVE SHEW SHOW TURN WEAR SPORT STAGE BLAZON DEMEAN EVINCE EXPOSE OPPOSE OSTEND PARADE REVEAL APPROVE CONCENE DIORAMA DISPLAY EXPRESS MONSTER PERFORM PRESENT PRODUCE PROJECT PROPOSE TRADUCE BOOKFAIR BRANDISH CONCEIVE DISCLOSE DISCOVER EMBLAZON EVIDENCE FORTHSET MANIFEST SHOWCASE
(— ALARM) GLOFF
(— DOGS) BENCH
(— IN SNARLING) GRIN
EXHIBITION FAIR SALE SHOW DROLL ENTRY SALON SIGHT ANNUAL PARADE SALARY DISPLAY EXHIBIT PAGEANT PENSION PRESENT SHOWING STAGERY EXERCISE
(— OF DOGS) BENCH
(— ON STAGE) STAGERY
(PUBLIC —) SPECIES
(RIDING —) CAROUSEL
EXHIBITIONER SERVITOR
EXHIBITIONIST HAM HAMFATTER
EXHIBITOR SHOWER
EXHILARATE AMUSE CHEER ELATE ANIMATE ELEVATE ENLIVEN GLADDEN
EXHILARATED RAD GLAD HAPPY HEADY ELEVATED
EXHILARATION GAIETY JOLLITY GLADNESS HILARITY
EXHORT URGE WARN CHARM ADHORT ADVISE CHARGE DEHORT ENGAGE INCITE PREACH CAUTION ADMONISH DISSUADE
EXHORTATION ADVICE EXHORT HOMILY COUNSEL PROPHECY
EXHORTER HORTATOR PREACHER
EXHUME DIG DELVE UNBURY UNTOMB UNEARTH DISINTER EXHUMATE
EXIGENCY NEED WANT EXIGENT URGENCY JUNCTURE OCCASION PRESSURE
EXIGENT DIRE VITAL URGENT CRITICAL EXACTING PRESSING
EXIGUITY PAUCITY
EXILE EXUL POOR RUIN THIN EXPEL GALUT WREAK BANISH DEPORT GALUTH OUTLAW SCANTY WRETCH EXULATE GERSHOM OUTCAST PILGRIM REFUGEE SLENDER DIASPORA FUGITIVE OUTLAWRY
EXILED FOREIGN FUGITIVE
EXIST AM BE IS ARE LIE COME

GROW LIVE MOVE PASS DWELL CONSIST
(— IN FULL SUPPLY) FLOW
EXISTENCE ENS ESSE LIFE SEIN BEING DASEIN ENTITY IDEATE INESSE ESSENCE IDEATUM REALITY ENERGEIA IDENTITY SURVIVAL
(— AFTER DEATH) AFTERLIFE
(DULL —) DEATH
(ETERNAL —) SAT
(EVER-CHANGING —) SAMSARA SANSARA
(IN —) GOING AROUND EXTANT
(PERMANENT —) INHERENCE
(WAKING —) JAGRATA
EXISTENT HARD REAL ALIVE BEING ACTUAL EXTANT EXISTING
(— IN DIFFERENT FORMS) ALLOTROPIC
(CONTINUALLY —) STUBBORN
EXISTING GOING ACTUAL EXTANT EXISTENT
(— IN NAME ONLY) DUMMY
EXIT ISH DOOR GATE VENT GOING ISSUE LEAVE EGRESS EXITUS OUTLET OUTWAY EXITION OUTGATE OUTPORT PASSAGE DEBOUCHE
(HURRIED —) BOUT
EXITE BRACT
EX LIBRIS BOOKPLATE
EXOCYCLIC IRREGULAR
EXODUS EXODY EXITUS HEGIRA HEJIRA EXODIUM
EXON EXEMPT
EXONERATE FREE ALIBI CLEAR ACQUIT EXCUSE EXONER UNLOAD ABSOLVE RELIEVE
EXOPODITE EXOPOD SQUAMA
EXORABLE PRAYABLE
EXORBITANT STEEP UNDUE ABNORMAL
EXORDIUM PREFACE PRELUDE
EXOSKELETON CORSLET CORSELET
EXOSPORIUM EXINE EXTINE EXOSPERM
EXOSTOSIS POROMA SPLINT OSSELET
EXOTIC ALIEN FOREIGN STRANGE
EXOTOSPORE BLAST
EXOTROPIA WALLEYE
EXPAND OPE WAX BLOW BULK FLAN FLUE FOAM GROW HUFF OPEN FARCE FLASH RETCH SPLAY SWELL WIDEN DIDUCE DILATE EXTEND INTEND SPREAD SPROUT UNFOLD UNFURL AMPLIFY BALLOON BLOSSOM BOLSTER BROADEN BURGEON DEVELOP DIFFUSE DISPAND DISPLAY DISTEND EDUCATE ENLARGE EXPANSE EXPLAIN INFLATE STRETCH DISPREAD INCREASE LENGTHEN OUTREACH
(— AS A VESSEL) FLAN
(— FEATHERS) PRIDE
(— INTO PODS) KID
EXPANDED NOWY OPEN OVERT DILATE SPREAD DILATED SWOLLEN INFLATED PATULENT PATULOUS

EXPANDER EXTENDER
EXPANDING BOSOMY
EXPANSE AREA ROOM BURST FIELD
REACH TRACT EXTENT LENGTH
SPREAD COUNTRY STRETCH
DISTANCE EXPANSUM SEPARATE
(— OF ICE) SHEET
(— OF SEA ICE) FIELD
(BROAD —) ACRE MAIN
(IMMEASURABLE — OF TIME)
ETERNITY
(IMMENSE —) OCEAN
(INDEFINITE —) VAGUE
(VAST —) SEA
(WIDE —) BREADTH
EXPANSIBILITY ELATER
EXPANSION ALA BULB WING FLUSH
SPLAY GROWTH SPREAD ECTASIA
ECTASIS EXPANSE HASTULA
ACROCYST COQUILLE DIASTOLE
DILATION INCREASE SWELLING
(— IN SEEDS) ALA WING
(— OF RIVER) BROAD
(FOLIOSE —) LAMINA
(LITURGICAL —) EMBOLISM
EXPANSIVE FREE WIDE BROAD
GENIAL ELASTIC LIBERAL
GENEROUS SPACIOUS SWELLING
EXPATIATE DWELL DILATE EXPAND
SPREAD AMPLIFY BROADEN
DESCANT DIFFUSE ENLARGE
SATISFY
EXPATRIATE EXILE EXPEL BANISH
OUTLAW OUTCAST
EXPATRIATION EXILE
EXPECT ASK DEEM HOPE LITE LOOK
STAY TEND TROW WAIT WEEN
ABIDE AWAIT THINK ATTEND
DEMAND INTEND LIPPEN RECKON
PRESUME REQUIRE SUPPOSE
SUSPECT
EXPECTANT ATIPTOE CHARGED
HOPEFUL INCHOATE
EXPECTANTLY TIPTOE
EXPECTATION HOPE VIEW WAIT
WEEN EXPECT FUTURE ESPEIRE
OPINION SUPPOSE THOUGHT
WEENING PROSPECT
EXPECTED DUE SUPPOSED
EXPECTORANT CINEOL STORAX
CINEOLE EMETINE CREOSOTE
GUAIACOL TEREBENE
EXPECTORATE SPIT
EXPECTORATION EMPTYSIS
EXPEDIENCE ARTIFICE
EXPEDIENT FIT WISE ATAJO CRAFT
DODGE JOKER KNACK SHIFT DEVICE
RESORT STRING DODGERY POLITIC
STOPGAP ARTIFICE RESOURCE
DESIRABLE
EXPEDITATE LAW
EXPEDITATION LAWING
EXPEDITE HIE EASY FREE HURRY
SPEED EXPEDE GREASE HASTEN
QUICKEN DISPATCH
EXPEDITION CAMP FARE ROAD
TREK DRAVE HASTE HURRY RANGE
SCOUT TRADE SAFARI VOYAGE
CARAVAN CRUSADE ENTRADA

JOURNEY OUTLOPE SERVICE
WARFARE WARPATH COMMANDO
HEADHUNT PROGRESS
(FISHING —) DRAVE
(HUNTING —) SAFARI
(MILITARY —) HARKA CRUSADE
JOURNEY WARPATH
EXPEDITIOUS FAST HASTY QUICK
RAPID READY SHORT PROMPT
SPEEDY
EXPEL CAN OUT USH BLOW BOLT
DRUM DUMP FIRE OUST VOID WARP
AVOID CHASE CHECK DEPEL EJECT
ERUPT EVICT EXILE KNOCK SPURT
BANISH BOUNCE DEBOUT DEPORT
DEVOID DISBAR DISOWN OUTPUT
OUTRAY REFUSE ABANDON
EXCLUDE EXPULSE EXTRUDE
OBTRUDE SCRATCH SECLUDE
SUSPEND DISLODGE DISPLACE
EVACUATE FORJUDGE
(— AIR) COUGH
(— FROM MEMBERSHIP) HAMMER
(— GAS) BELCH
(— SUDDENLY) SLIRT
EXPEND USE LEND SPEND SPORT
WASTE WREAK DEFRAY IMPEND
OCCUPY PONDER CONSUME
DISPEND EROGATE EXHAUST
OVERUSE DISBURSE SQUANDER
EXPENDITURE COST OUTGO PENSE
CHARGE OUTLAY EXPENSE PENSION
SPENDING
(— OF ENERGY) EFFORT
EXPENSE EX COST GAFF LOSS
BATTA PRICE SUMPT CHARGE
DAMAGE GERSUM ONCOST OUTLAY
OUTSET OVERHEAD SUMPTURE
(— OF CARRYING) CARRIAGE
(— OF TREAT) SAM
(PL.) BATTA COSTS MISES
EXPENSIVE DEAR HIGH SALT STIFF
COSTLY LAVISH LIBERAL THRIFTY
EXPERIENCE SEE TRY FEEL FIND
HAVE HENT HOLD KNOW LIVE TEST
ASSAY EVENT PROOF PROVE SKILL
TASTE TRIAL USAGE BEHOLD
EXPERT FRAIST ORDEAL SAMPLE
SUFFER APPROVE CALVARY
CONTACT FEELING FURNACE
KNOWING REALIZE SUSTAIN
UNDERGO ESCAPADE
(— GOOD OR ILL FORTUNE) SPEED
(— OF INTENSE SUFFERING)
CALVARY
(— WITH BITTERNESS) BEAR
(CALAMITOUS —) ADVERSITY
(ORDINARY —) USE
(PAINFUL —) FIT
(PARTIAL —) GUST
(TRYING —) ORDEAL
EXPERIENCED HAD MET OLD USED
SALTY EXPERT SALTED TRADED
ANCIENT PRACTIC THRIVEN
VETERAN WEIGHED SEASONED
(— INTENSIVELY) ACUTE
(ACTUALLY —) SPECIOUS
EXPERIENTIAL EMPIRIC
EXPERIMENT SHY TRY TEST ASSAY

ESSAY TRIAL ATTEMPT CONTROL
EXPERIMENTAL SAMPLE
(NOT —) STANDARD
EXPERT ACE DAB DEFT FULL GOOD
PERT ADEPT FLASH READY SHARP
SWELL ADROIT ARTIST CLEVER
FACILE HABILE KAHUNA PANDIT
PERTLY QUAINT SUBTLE WIZARD
ARTISTE ATTACHE CAPABLE
DABSTER SKILLED DEXTROUS
GAINSOME SKILLFUL SPEEDFUL
VIRTUOSO
(— IN JEWISH LAW) DAYAN
(— ON DRIVING LOGS) LAKER
(BANK —) SHROFF
(GREAT —) ONER
(SCIENTIFIC —) BOFFIN
EXPERTNESS SAVVY SKILL FACILITY
HABILITY
EXPIATE ABY SKUG ATONE AVERT
ASSOIL RANSOM
EXPIATORY PIACULAR
EXPIRATION END DEATH BREATH
EFFLUX ELAPSE EXPIRE EXPIRY
(SPASMODIC —) SNEEZE
EXPIRE DIE END EMIT FALL EXPEL
GHOST LAPSE ELAPSE EXHALE
INLAIK OUTRUN PERISH
EXPIRED UP DEAD
EXPIRING DYING
EXPIRY ISH CLOSE DEATH EFFLUX
EXPLAIN OPEN REDE SAVE SCAN
UNDO WISE AREAD AREED CLEAR
GLOSS GLOZE PLANE RECHE SOLVE
SPEED TOUCH DEFINE EXPAND
EXPLAT EXPONE REMENE RIDDLE
UNFOLD ABSOLVE ACCOUNT
AMPLIFY CLARIFY COMMENT
CONTRUE DECLARE DEVELOP
DISCUSS EXHIBIT EXPOUND JUSTIFY
RESOLVE CONSTRUE DESCRIBE
MANIFEST SIMPLIFY UNPLIGHT
UNWONDER
EXPLAINER EXPONENT
EXPLAINING EXPONENT
EXPLANATION KEY NOTE GLOSS
SALVE SALVO ANSWER CAVEAT
ACCOUNT APOLOGY ADDENDUM
EXEGESIS INNUENDO NOTATION
SOLUTION
EXPLETIVE AND GEE BOSH EGAD
GOSH OATH BEGAD MODAL BEHEAR
SDEATH TUNKET DAMMISH
MORBLEU GOODYEAR GRACIOUS
EXPLICATE OPEN CLEAR EXPAND
UNFOLD ACCOUNT EXPLAIN
EXPLICATION CRIB ANALYSIS
EXPLICIT OPEN CLEAR EXACT FIXED
PLAIN EXPRESS PRECISE ABSOLUTE
DEFINITE IMPLICIT POSITIVE
PUNCTUAL SPECIFIC
EXPLICITLY DIRECT FORMALLY
EXPLODE POP BLOW FIRE BELCH
BLAST BURST CRUMP ERUPT PLUFF
SHOOT SQUIB SPRING BACKFIRE
DETONATE DISPLODE
EXPLOIT ACT DEED FEAT GEST JEST
MILK WORK GESTE GOUGE STUNT
PERFORM SUCCESS CHIVALRY

PARERGON PROPERTY
EXPLORATION SPY PROBE SEARCH
EXPLORE
EXPLORATORY FRONTIER
EXPLORE DO DIP MAP SPY DIVE
DRAG FEEL VIEW CHART COAST
DELVE RANGE SCOUT SOUND
SEARCH EXAMINE PALPATE
BOTANIZE DISCOVER
EXPLORER CAVEMAN PIONEER
COLUMBUS
EXPLOSION POP BLOW BLAST
BURST CRUMP SALVO BLOWUP
BOUNCE REPORT PLOSION INCIDENT
OUTBURST
(FUEL —) BACKFIRE
(SLIGHT —) PLUFF
EXPLOSIVE EGG TNT MINE AMVIS
AMATOL JOVITE LIMPET POWDER
TETRYL TONITE TORPEX TOUCHY
TRITON ABELITE AMMONAL AZOTINE
DUNNITE LIGNOSE LYDDITE PLOSIVE
PUDDING SHIMOSE THORITE
CHEDDITE DYNAMITE ECRASITE
ERUPTIVE GELATINE MELINITE
PYROLITE ROBURITE
(CHARGE OF —) TULIP RESPONDER
EXPOLIATE SCALE SPALL SPAWL
EXPONENT INDEX
EXPORT OUTCARRY
EXPORTATION EXPORT OUTPORT
EXPOSE AIR BARE GIVE OPEN RISK
SHOW STRIP BEWRAY DEBUNK
DETECT EXPONE GIBBET OBJECT
OPPOSE REVEAL UNHUSK UNMASK
DISPLAY EXHIBIT EXPOUND PILLORY
PROPINE PUBLISH SUBJECT
UNCOVER UNEARTH UNTRUSS
BRANDISH DISCLOSE DISCOVER
MUCKRAKE RIDICULE SATIRIZE
UNCLOTHE UNSHROUD
(— FOR BLEACHING) CROFT
(— ORE) HUSH
(— PLAYING CARD) BURN
(— SELF TO) WAGE
(— SUDDENLY) FLASH
(— TO AIR) AERATE
(— TO DANGER) JUMP COMMIT
SUBMIT
(— TO HEAT) AIR
(— TO INFAMY) GIBBET
(— TO MOISTURE) RET
(— TO SCORN) PILLORY
(— TO SULFUR DIOXIDE) STOVE
(— TO SUN AND AIR) FIELD
(— TO SUN) INSOLATE SOLARIZE
EXPOSED AIRY BARE OPEN BLEAK
LIABLE UNSAFE SUBJECT VEILLESS
(— TO DANGER) INSECURE
(— TO) AGAINST
EXPOSITION FAIR GECK SHOW
ZEND TRACT EXPOSE METHOD
SURVEY ACCOUNT EXPOSAL
MIDRASH ANALYSIS EXEGESIS
EXPOSURE EXTHESIS HAGGADAH
TREATISE
(— OF FEAST) SYNAXARY
EXPOSITORY EXEGETIC
EXPOSTULATE ARGUE DISCUSS

EXAMINE PROTEST
EXPOSTULATION PROTEST
EXPOSURE ASPECT EXPOSE
EXPOSAL FLASHING FRONTAGE
PROSPECT
(— OF CARDS) SPREAD
(— OF KING) CHECK
(— TO AIR) AERATE AIRING
(BODY —) FLASH
EXPOUND OPEN UNDO GLOZE
SENSE TREAT DEFINE EXPONE
EXPOSE DEVELOP DISCUSS EXPLAIN
EXPOSIT EXPRESS CONSTRUE
SIMPLIFY
EXPOUNDER MUFTI MULLAH
EXPRESS EXPONENT HERMETIC
EXPRESS AIR BID PUT SAY CAST
EMIT PASS POST VENT COUCH
EMOTE FRAME OPINE SPEAK STATE
UTTER VOICE WIELD BROACH
DEMEAN DENOTE DIRECT EVINCE
IMPORT PHRASE ABREACT BREATHE
DECLARE DICTATE EXPOUND
EXPREME TESTIFY DEFINITE
DESCRIBE DISPATCH EXPLICIT
INTIMATE MANIFEST
(— APPROVAL) AGREE ACCEDE
APPLAUD
(— AS LANGUAGE) LAY
(— BY GESTURE) BECK
(— BY LAUGHTER) LAUGH
(— CONCERN) CLUCK
(— DISAPPROVAL) BOO CHIDE
DECRY GROAN CATCALL
(— DISDAIN) TUT
(— EFFERVESCENTLY) CHORTLE
(— FOLLY) EXPAND
(— GRATITUDE) THANK AGGRATE
(— GRIEF) DEPLORE
(— IN WORDS) SAY DRAW SPEAK
PHRASE
(— NUMERICALLY) EVALUATE
(— ONE'S FEELINGS) FLOW
(— SORROW) LAMENT COMPLAIN
(— WILLINGNESS) CONSENT
EXPRESSION DIT HIT SAY CAST
EUGE FACE FORM POSE SHOW SIGN
TERM VULT WORD ADIEU GLIFF
IDIOM SNEER TOKEN VOICE
BYWORD DILOGY DIVERB EFFECT
FACIES ORACLE PHRASE SPEECH
SYMBOL COMMENT DESCANT
EPITHET EXPRESS GRIMACE
ALLEGORY AUSDRUCK DANICISM
FELICITY LACONISM MONOMIAL
(— IN FEW WORDS) BREVITY
(— OF ANNOYANCE) SOH
(— OF APPROVAL) EUGE PLACET
(— OF ASSENT) CONTENT
(— OF BEAUTY) ART
(— OF CHOICE) VOTE
(— OF DISPLEASURE) FROWN
(— OF DISTASTE) FACE
(— OF HOMAGE) OVATION
(— OF JOY) GREETING
(— OF OPINION) EDITORIAL
(— OF RESPECT) DUTY
(— OF SADNESS) SHADE
(— OF SCORN) GECK

(— OF SINGLE IDEA) RHEME
(APT —) FELICITY
(CHEMICAL —) EQUATION
(COMMONPLACE —) BROMIDE
(CORRECT —) SUMPSIMUS
(CURT —) LACONIC
(FACIAL —) GRIN CHEER SCOWL
SMILE
(INCONGRUOUS —) BULL
(LOUD —) CLAMOR
(MATHEMATICAL —) INDEX SERIES
BINOMIAL EQUATION FUNCTION
INTEGRAL
(MOCKING —) SCOFF
(PECULIAR —) IDIOM
(PET —) CANT
(PUERILE —) BOYISM
(SARCASTIC —) GIBE JIBE
(SERIOUS —) EARNEST
(SINCERE —) CANDOR
(SYMBOLIC —) FORMULA
(TENDER —) LANGUISH
(TRITE —) CLICHE
(UNRESTRAINED —) EFFUSION
(VERBAL —) LETTER
(WISE —) ORACLE
EXPRESSIONLESS STONY LEADEN
SODDEN VACANT WOODEN
TONELESS
EXPRESSIVE POETIC TONGUED
ELOQUENT EMPHATIC SPEAKING
EXPRESSIVENESS DICTION
DELICACY TOURNURE ELOQUENCE
EXPRESSLY NAMELY EXPRESS
PRESSLY FORMALLY
EXPRESSWAY FREEWAY SPEEDWAY
EXPROBATE CENSURE UPBRAID
EXPULSION EXILE BOUNCE
BANNIMUS EJECTION EXCISION
EXPUNGE BLOT DELE ERASE SLASH
CANCEL DELETE EFFACE EXCISE
SCRAPE DESTROY SCRATCH
DISPUNGE
EXPURGATE GELD PURGE
CASTRATE
EXPURGATION BOWDLERISM
EXQUISITE FOP DUDE FINE NICE
PERT PINK RARE DANDY EXACT
CHOICE DAINTY CAREFUL ELEGANT
GEMLIKE PERFECT REFINED
AFFECTED DELICATE ETHEREAL
MACARONI
EXQUISITELY CHOICELY
EXSCIND CUT SEVER EXCISE
EXTANT ALIVE BEING LIVING VISIBLE
EXISTING MANIFEST
EXTEMPORE SUDDEN OFFHAND
IMPROVISO
EXTEND GO EKE LIE RUN BEAR
BUSH COME DATE DRAW GROW
LAST OPEN PASS RISE ROLL SPAN
SPIN BREDE BULGE CARRY COVER
FARCE REACH RENEW RETCH SEIZE
SHOOT STENT VERGE WIDEN
AMOUNT DEEPEN DEPLOY DILATE
EXPAND INTEND OUTLIE SPREAD
SPRING STRAIN STREAK THRUST
TRENCH AMPLIFY BROADEN
DIFFUSE DISPLAY DISTEND ENLARGE

OVERLAP OVERRUN PORRECT
PORTEND PRODUCE PROFFER
PROJECT PROLONG PROMOTE
PROTEND RADIATE STRETCH
CONTINUE ELONGATE INCREASE
LENGTHEN OUTREACH PROROGUE
PROTRACT PROTRUDE
(— ACTIVITIES) BRANCH
(— AROUND) GIRTH
(— IN SPACE) DURE
(— IRREGULARLY) TRAIL
(— OVER) SPAN COVER CROSS
CONTAIN OVERLAP
(— SAIL) SHEET
(— THE FRONT) DEPLOY
(— TO) LINE REACH
EXTENDED FAT LONG OPEN BROAD
EXTENT SPREAD EXTENSE LENGTHY
PROLATE SPLAYED EXPANDED
INTENDED
EXTENDER INERT FILLER LIGNIN
EXTENDING BROAD
(— OVER) ASTRIDE
EXTENSION ARM EKE ELL AREA
CAPE SCOPE POCKET SATTVA
SPHERE SPREAD BREADTH STRETCH
ADDENDUM ADDITION DURATION
INCREASE PROTENSE
(— OF BUILDING MATERIAL) APRON
(— OF CREDIT) DATING
(— OF MINERAL VEIN) FLAT
(— OF RACE TRACK) CHUTE SHUTE
(— OF SHELL) LAPPET
(— OF TIME) RESPITE
(— OF WAGON FRAME) THRIPPLE
(BALLET —) BATTEMENT
EXTENSIVE HUGE VAST WIDE AMPLE
BROAD LARGE EXTENSE IMMENSE
EXPANDED INFINITE SWEEPING
EXTENT DUE RUN TAX AREA BODY
BULK DEAL GAGE LEVY PASS SIZE
WRIT AMBIT DEPTH FIELD GAUGE
LIMIT RANGE REACH SCOPE SPACE
STENT SWEEP TRACK AMOUNT
ASSIZE ATTACK DEGREE LENGTH
SPREAD STREEK ACREAGE ASSAULT
BREADTH COMPASS EXPANSE
SEIZURE STRETCH VARIETY
DISTANCE INCREASE LATITUDE
QUANTITY STRAIGHT
(— OF FRONT) FRONTAGE
(— OF LAND) HEIGHT CONTINENT
(— OF SPACE) ROOM
(BROAD —) SWEEP
(SOME —) BIT
(UNLIMITED —) INFINITY
(UTMOST —) FULL
(VAST —) DEEP
(VERTICAL —) ALTITUDE
EXTENUATE THIN GLOZE MINCE
EXCUSE LESSEN SOOTHE WEAKEN
DIMINISH PALLIATE
EXTERIOR CRUST ECTAD ECTAL
OUTER SHELL EXTERN OUTSIDE
OUTWARD SURFACE EXOTERIC
EXTERNAL OUTLYING
EXTERMINATE WIPE EXPEL UPROOT
ABOLISH DESTROY
EXTERNAL OUT OUTER EXTERN

OUTSIDE OUTWARD STRANGE
EXOTERIC EXTERIOR INCIDENT
EXTERNALITY OUTNESS
EXTERNALLY OUTWARD WITHOUT
EXTINCT DEAD BYGONE DEFUNCT
QUENCHED
(— MAN) KANJERA
EXTINCTION DOOM FINE DEATH
EXPIRY DELETION
EXTINGUISH OUT DAMP DOUT REDD
STUB ANNUL CHOKE CRUSH DOUSE
DOWSE DROWN QUELL REPEL
SLAKE SNUFF STAMP QUENCH
STANCH STIFLE BLANKET DESTROY
ECLIPSE EXPIATE EXTINCT OBSCURE
OPPRESS SLOCKEN STAUNCH
SUPPRESS
(— CIGARETTE) SNUB
EXTINGUISHED OUT DEAD EXTINCT
EXTINGUISHER DOUTER STAUNCH
BACKPACK QUENCHER STANCHER
EXTIRPATE DELE STUB ERASE
EXPEL STAMP STOCK EXCISE
EXTIRP UPROOT DESTROY EXSCIND
OUTROOT SUPPLANT
EXTIRPATION ROOTAGE EXCISION
EXTOL CRY FETE HYMN LAUD BLESS
CRACK EXALT KUDOS ROOSE
SPEAK EXTOLL PRAISE ADVANCE
APPLAUD COLLAUD COMMEND
ELEVATE ENHANCE GLORIFY
RESOUND UPRAISE EMBLAZON
EULOGIZE
EXTOLMENT PRECONY
EXTORT PEEL PILL BRIBE EDUCE
EXACT FORCE PINCH WREST WRING
COMPEL ELICIT SPONGE STRAIN
WRENCH WRITHE EXTRACT
OUTWREST
EXTORTION CHOUT GOUGE EXTORT
HOLDUP SCOTAL BRIBERY PILLAGE
CHANTAGE EXACTION RAPACITY
EXTORTIONATE HARD CRIMINAL
GRINDING
EXTORTIONER BRIBER POLLER
SHAVER VAMPIRE
EXTORTIONIST POLLER
EXTRA ODD MORE ORRA OVER PLUS
ADDED SPARE SPECIAL SURPLUS
SUPERIOR
EXTRACT DIG PRY CITE DRAW KINO
KOLA PULL SOAK ANIMA BLEED
CUTCH DRAFT EDUCE ELUTE EXACT
KUTCH KYPOO QUOTE RENES
RUSOT SCRAP STEEP WRING
CORTIN CURARE DECOCT DEDUCE
DERIVE DEWTRY DISTIL ELICIT
ELIXIR EVULSE EXTORT GOBBET
GUACIN MULIUM OVARIN REMOVE
RENDER RUSWUT TRIPOS UZARON
ABORTIN AMALTAS ARCANUM
CATECHU DESCENT DISTILL
DRAUGHT ERGOTIN ESSENCE
ESTREAT EXCERPT EXHAUST
FUMARIA INTRAIT LIMBECK MONESIA
PASSEWA SUMMARY VANILLA
ACETRACT AMBRETTE GINGERIN
HYPERNIC INFUSION LICORICE
PERICOPE SEPARATE TIKITIKI

TINCTURE WITHDRAW
(— BY BOILING) DECOCT ELIXATE
(— BY DIGGING) GRUB
(— FORCIBLY) EVULSE
(— FROM ACACIA) KATH CASHOO
CATECHU
(— FROM BERBERIS) RUSOT
RUSWUT
(— OF GINGER) JAKE JAKEY
(— ORE) STOPE
(TANNING —) AMALTAS
EXTRACTION KIN BIRTH STOCK
ORIGIN DESCENT EDITION ESSENCE
EXTRACT EXTREAT BREEDING
TINCTURE
(— OF ROOTS) EVOLUTION
(— OF STEAM) BLEEDING
EXTRACTIVE AGAR BANG BHANG
AMAROID CARAGEEN
EXTRADITE BANISH
EXTRANEOUS OUTER EXOTIC
FOREIGN OUTLYING SPURIOUS
EXTRAORDINARILY BYOUS
EXTRAORDINARY ODD FREM ONCO
RARE BYOUS ENORM SMASH
DAMNED EXEMPT MIGHTY RAGING
SIGNAL CORKING CURIOUS
HUMMING NOTABLE SPECIAL
STRANGE UNUSUAL ABNORMAL
EXIMIOUS FORINSEC SINGULAR
SMASHING UNCOMMON
EXTRARETINAL PAROPTIC
EXTRAVAGANCE FRILL PRIDE
WASTE LUXURY EXPENSE
RAMPANCY SQUANDER UNTHRIFT
WILDNESS
(MENTAL —) MADNESS
EXTRAVAGANT MAD HIGH WILD
FANCY FISHY FOLLE LARGE OUTRE
COSTLY GOTHIC HEROIC LAVISH
SHRILL WANTON BAROQUE BIZARRE
COSTLEW FANATIC FLAMING
FURIOUS NIMIOUS PROFUSE
RAMPANT VAGRANT INSOLENT
PRODIGAL RECKLESS ROMANTIC
UNTHRIFT WANDERER WASTEFUL
EXTRAVAGANTLY LARGE
EXTRAVAGATION VIBEX
EXTRAVASATION EFFUSION
EXTREME BLUE DEEP DIRE HIGH
LAST RANK SORE VILE ACUTE
BLACK CLOSE CRUEL DENSE DIZZY
FINAL GREAT LIMIT PITCH STEEP
ULTRA UNDUE UTTER ARDENT
ARRANT BRAZEN DEADLY FIERCE
HEROIC LENGTH MORTAL SAVAGE
SEVERE STRONG UTMOST WOUNDY
DRASTIC FEARFUL FORWARD
FRANTIC HOWLING INTENSE
OUTWARD PROFUSE RADICAL
SURFEIT VIOLENT ALMIGHTY
DEVILISH DREADFUL EGYPTIAN
ENORMOUS FABULOUS FARTHEST
GREATEST MERCIFUL SPENDFUL
TERRIBLE TERRIFIC ULTIMATE
EXQUISITE
(NOT —) SWEET
(PL.) PASO
EXTREMELY SO BIG DOG TOO WAY

BONE DEAD EVER FULL MAIN RANK
SELI THAT UNCO VERY AWFUL
BLACK BULLY BYOUS CRAZY CRUEL
EXTRA HEAPS RIGHT SELLE SOWAN
SUPER BITTER DAMNED DEADLY
DEUCED HIGHLY MIGHTY NATION
POISON SORELY SURELY UNCOLY
APLENTY AWFULLY BOILING
CRUELLY EXTREME GALLOWS
HOPPING INNERLY SOPPING
STAVING ALMIGHTY ENORMOUS
MORTALLY PRECIOUS PROPERLY
EXTREMISM JACOBINISM
EXTREMIST JACOBIN RADICAL
EXTREMITY END TIP HEAD NEED
PUSH TAIL CLOSE LIMIT SHIFT
START VERGE BORDER FINGER
EXIGENT EXTREME ACROSTIC
ALTITUDE DISASTER JUNCTURE
OUTRANCE TERMINAL
(— **OF MOON**) HORN
(— **OF TENDRIL**) HOLDFAST
(— **OF TOOTH ROOT**) APEX
(**REMOTEST** —) CORNER
EXTRICATE FREE HELP CLEAR
LOOSE RESCUE SQUIRM OUTWIND
EXPEDITE LIBERATE UNTANGLE
(— **ONESELF**) WANGLE
EXTRINSIC ALIEN EVERY FOREIGN
OUTWARD EXTERNAL OUTLYING
EXTROVERT SYNTONIC
EXTRUDE BEAR SPEW EJECT EXPEL
SHOOT PROJECT PROTRUDE
EXUBERANCE PRICE EXCESS
LUXURY PLENTY ABANDON
LAUGHTER OVERFLOW RAMPANCY
EXUBERANT BOUNCY FEISTY LAVISH
COPIOUS FERTILE GLOWING
PROFUSE RAMPANT EFFUSIVE
EXUDATE GUM SPEW SPUE MANNA
DIKAMALI GUAIACUM HONEYDEW
SARCOCOL
EXUDATION DIP GUM LAC SAP TAR

BALM COPAL PITCH RESIN ROSIN
SUDOR MASTIC SANIES GALIPOT
MOCHRAS SPEWING BLEEDING
EXUDENCE LAITANCE MOISTURE
EXUDE GUM DRIP EMIT OOZE REEK
SPEW BLEED STILL SWEAT EXTILL
STRAIN STREAM EXUDATE GUTTATE
SCREEVE SECRETE SWELTER
PERSPIRE
EXULT JOY CROW LEAP BOAST
GLOAT GLORY INSULT SPRING
REJOICE TRIUMPH
EXULTANT ELATED
EXULTATION JOY OVATION
RAPTURE
EXULTING EXULTANT JUBILANT
EYALET VILLAYET
EYAS NESTLING
EYE O EE HE ORB SPY DISC GAZE
GLIM LAMP LOOP MIEN OGLE SCAN
UVEA VIEW GLARE GLASS GLENE
NAVEL OPTIC SENSE SHANK SIGHT
TOISE WATCH BEHOLD COLLAR
EUCONE EYELET GOGGLE OCULAR
OCULUS OILLET PEEPER POPEYE
REGARD ROLLER SHINER STEMMA
VISION WINDOW WINKER BLINKER
EUCONIC EXOCONE EYEBALL
EYEHOLE OBSERVE OCELLUS
PIERCER PIGSNEY PINKANY PINKENY
SENSORY WITNESS LATCHING
NOISETTE OMMATEUM RECEPTOR
(— **AMOROUSLY**) OGLE
(— **FORMED BY ROPE**) TONGUE
(— **IN BIGHT**) COLLAR
(— **IN EGYPTIAN SYMBOLISM**) UTA
(— **OF BEAN**) HILUM
(— **OF FRUIT**) NOSE
(— **OF HINGE**) GUDGEON
(— **OF INSECT**) STEMMA
(— **OF RA**) SEKHET
(— **SORENESS**) LIPPITUDE
(**BLACK** —) SHINER

(**EVIL** —) DROCHUIL MALOCCHIO
(**METAL** —) HONDA
(PL.) EEN EES NIE YEN YES EYNE
LAMPS LIGHTS SEEING GOGGLES
KEEKERS GLAZIERS GLIMMERS
EYEBALL EYE BALL GLASS GLOBE
(— **MOVEMENT**) VERGENCE
EYEBOLT SPRIG RINGBOLT
(**INTERLOCKING** —**S**) SNIBEL
EYEBRIGHT EYEWORT EUPHRASY
EYEBROW BREE BROW EEBREE
WINBROW WRIGGLE
EYE-CATCHING BOLD
EYECUP EYEGLASS
EYEGLASS QUIZ NIPPER MONOCLE
EYEGLASSES GLIMS SPECS LENSES
GLASSES LORGNON NIPPERS
BIFOCALS
EYEHOLE EYELET EYEPIT
EYELASH BREE LASH CILIUM
WINKER EYEBREE
(**LOSS OF** —**S**) MADAROSIS
(PL.) CILIA EAVES
EYELET MAIL PINK OELET AGRAFE
OILLET POUNCE AGRAFFE CRINGLE
GROMMET PEEPHOLE
EYELID HAW LID BREE WINDOW
EYEBREE PALPEBRA
(PL.) EAVES
EYEPIECE OCULAR EYEGLASS
(— **OF TELESCOPE**) POWER
EYESHADE OPAQUE
EYESHOT RANGE REACH EYESIGHT
EYESIGHT VIEW LIGHT SIGHT
EYE SOCKET ORBIT
EYESORE DESIGHT
EYESPOT EYEDOT STIGMA EYEHOLE
OCELLUS EYEPOINT
EYESTALK STIPES
EYETOOTH CUSPID DOGTOOTH
EYEWASH COLLYRIE EYEWATER
EYOT AIT EIGHT ISLET
EYRE AIR ITER

F EF FF EFF FOX DIGAMMA FOXTROT
FABA VICIA
FABLE MYTH TALE FEIGN STORY
LEGEND TRIFLE FICTION PARABLE
POETIZE UNTRUTH ALLEGORY
APOLOGUE FABULATE FABULIZE
(— **OF GOLD COAST**) NANCY
(**MORAL** —) EMBLEM
FABRIC ACCA CORD DUCK GOLD
GROS HAIR HUCK IKAT SILK SUSI
TAPA TARS TUKE CHECK CREPE
DHOTI DOBBY DYNEL FANCY MOIRE
NINOW PRINT RUMAL SCRIM SPLIT
STUFF SUPER SURAH SURAT TABBY
TAMMY TARSE TERRY TEWKE
TWEED TWILL UNION VICHY VOILE
WEAVE AGARIC ALACHA BENGAL
BROCHE BYSSUS CAFFOY CARPET
COTTON CREPON CYPRUS DACRON
DAMASK DIAPER DOBBIE EPONGE
ESTRON FLEECE HARDEN LAPPET
LUSTER LUSTRE MARBLE MASHRU
MURREY POODLE SENNIT STRIPE
TAMINY TANJIB TARTAN TRICOT
TUSSAH VELURE VELVET WADMAL
WINCEY ZENANA ACETATE ALEPINE
ALLOVER BANDALA BANDING
BELTING BEWPERS BINDING
BUCKRAM CANILLE CHALLIS
CHEKMAK CHIFFON CYPRESS
DAMASSE DOESKIN DRABBET
EDIFICE ELASTIC EPINGLE FACONNE
FUSTIAN MIXTURE MORELLA
PAISLEY PLUMBET SAYETTE
SEGATHY SILESIA SUITING TABARET
TABINET TAFFETA TEXTILE TIFFANY
VESSETS AGABANEE BARRACAN
BOCASINE BOURETTE CAMELINE
CANNELLE CASEMENT CHAMBRAY
CRETONNE DUCHESSE HAIRLINE
HANDMADE HARATEEN JACQUARD
KNITTING LUSTRINE MATERIAL
MOLESKIN OSNABURG SHANTUNG
SHIRTING SICILIAN SKIRTING
SWANSKIN TAPESTRY TARLATAN
VALENCIA
(— **CONTAINING GOLD OR SILVER
THREAD**) ACCA TASH TASS
(— **FOR STIFFENING**) WIGAN
(— **OF TWO OR MORE MATERIALS**)
UNION
(— **RESEMBLING TOWELING**)
AGARIC
(— **WITH INWOVEN SCENES**) ARRAS
(**ABSORBENT** —) HUCK
(**BROCADED** —) LAME LAMPAS
(**COARSE** —) TAT CRASH HAIRE
DUFFEL RATINE STAMIN BAGGING
BOCKING DRABBET SACKING
STAMMEL DAGSWAIN
(**CORDED** —) REP DUCAPE POPLIN
OTTOMAN
(**COTTON** —) CREA DUCK JEAN
LENO LINO SUSI BAIZE BASIN DENIM
DRILL RUMAL SUPER SWISS VICHY
WIGAN BURRAH CALICO CANVAS
CATGUT CHILLO CHINTZ COUTIL
COVERT DIMITY MADRAS MUSLIN
PENANG SATEEN BLANKET BUSTIAN

CANTOON DAMASSE ETAMINE
FLANNEL GALATEA GINGHAM
HICKORY HOLLAND JACONET
PERCALE TICKING BUCKSKIN
COTELINE COUTILLE CRETONNE
DRILLING DUNGAREE INDIENNE
SHEETING
(**DECORATED** —) DIAMANTE
(**DELICATE** —) HUSI JUSI
(**DURABLE** —) SCRIM SERGE
(**ELASTIC** —) GORING ELASTIC
(**EMBOSSED** —) CLOKY CLOQUE
(**EMBROIDERED** —) BALDAQUIN
(**FIGURED** —) BROCADE BROCATEL
(**FINE** —) PIMA SILK SUSI LINEN
DIMITY MERINO MOHAIR PERCALE
(**GAUZELIKE** —) BAREGE GOSSAMER
(**GLAZED** —) CIRE
(**GLOSSY** —) SATIN GLORIA SATEEN
(**GOAT'S-HAIR** —) TIBET
(**HEAVY** —) GROS CRASH DENIM
DRILL BURLAP CATGUT FRIEZE
LINENE TOBINE WHITNEY
(**JUTE** —) BALINE BURLAP
(**KNITTED** —) SUEDE BOUCLE
JERSEY TRICOT CHIFFON
(**LIGHTWEIGHT** —) GLORIA BUNTING
DELAINE FORTISAN
(**LINEN** —) SINDON BEWPERS
BUCKRAM CAMBRIC DRABBET
HOLLAND CRETONNE
(**MOTTLED** —) CHINE
(**MOURNING** —) ALMA
(**MUSLIN** —) TANJIB
(**OPENWORK** —) LACE SKIPDENT
(**ORNAMENTAL** —) GIMP LACE
LAMPAS GALLOON
(**PEBBLY-SURFACED** —) ARMURE
(**PILED** —) TERRY KRIMMER
CHENILLE
(**PRINTED** —) BATIK CALICO
ALLOVER PERCALE TOURNAY
(**RIBBED** —) CORD GROS COTELE
FAILLE SOLEIL CORDUROY
MAROCAIN MOGADORE WHIPCORD
(**ROUGH** —) TERRY HOPSACK
HOMESPUN
(**SATIN** —) CAMLET ETOILE
(**SHEER** —) LAWN SHEER SWISS
DIMITY BATISTE SOUFFLE VALENCE
GOSSAMER
(**SHORT-NAPPED** —) RAS
(**SILK** —) ACCA ALMA FUGI FUJI
GROS IKAT MOFF ATLAS CARDE
PEKIN RAJAH RUMAL SATIN SHIKH
SURAH TIRAZ ARMORE BROCHE
CAMACA CHAPPE CREPON DIAPER
DUCAPE FAILLE KHAIKI MANTUA
SENDAL ALACHAH ALAMODE
BROCADE EPINGLE GROGRAM
SCHAPPE YESTING DUPPIONI
EOLIENNE IMPERIAL ORMUZINE
SHAGREEN SIAMOISE
(**SOFT SILK** —) KASHA BARATHEA
(**SOFT-NAPPED** —) PANNE DUVETYN
(**STRIPED** —) ABA STRIPE
BAYADERE MERALINE
(**THIN** —) CRISP GAUZE VOILE
PONGEE TAMISE HERNANI MARABOU

PERSIAN
(**TWILLED** —) SAY DENIM KASHA
SERGE SURAH COUTIL BOLIVIA
ESTAMIN FLANNEL ZANELLA
CAMELINE CASHMERE CORDUROY
DIAGONAL SHALLOON VENETIAN
(**UNBLEACHED** —) DRABBET
(**UNGLAZED** —) CRETONNE
(**UPHOLSTERY** —) FRIEZE BROCATEL
MOQUETTE
(**VELVETY** —) TRIPE DUVETYN
(**WOOLEN** —) REPP BAIZE DOILY
OSSET SERGE TWEED BUFFIN
BURNET COTTON DJERSA DUFFEL
FRISCA MANTLE MOREEN MOTLEY
PERPET SAXONY SHODDY STAMIN
TAMISE VICUNA WADMAL WITNEY
BATISTE BOCKING BOLIVIA CHEVIOT
CHEYNEY CRYSTAL DELAINE
DRUGGET FRISADO HEATHER
RATTEEN STAMMEL ALGERINE
BATSWING BURBERRY CASHMERE
CATALOON CHIVERET HARATEEN
LAMBSKIN PRUNELLA RATTINET
SHALLOON SHETLAND WOOLENET
ZIBELINE
(**WORSTED** —) TABBY COBURG
ESTAMIN ETAMINE SAGATHY
(**WOVEN** —) LENO TWEED TWILL
SOLBIL TISSUE GROGRAM TEXTURE
VALENCIA
FABRICATE COIN COOK FAKE FORM
MAKE MINT VAMP WARP BUILD
FORGE FRAME FRUMP WEAVE
DEVISE INVENT CONCOCT FASHION
IMAGINE PRODUCE CONTRIVE
(— **CLOTH**) DRAPE
(— **PAPER**) CONVERT
FABRICATION LIE WEB TRIFLE
CHIMERA FICTION FINGURE
FORGERY UNTRUTH BASKETRY
PRETENSE
(**PL.**) INVENTARY
FABRICATOR LIAR COINER FORGER
FABULIST LIAR AESOP FABLER
FABULOUS FEIGNED MYTHICAL
ROMANTIC
FACADE FACE FRONT FUCUS
FRONTAL FRONTLET
FACE JIB MAP MUG NEB PAN BIDE
CHIV CLAD COPE DARE DEFY DIAL
GIZZ HEAD LEER LINE MASK MEET
MOUE MUNS PHIZ PUSS SIDE ABIDE
BEARD BRAVE BRICK BRUNT CASTE
CHECK CHEER COVER FACET FAVOR
FRONT GUARD INDEX REVET STAND
STONE VISOR VIZOR BRAZEN
FACADE FACIES KISSER MAZARD
MUZZLE OPPOSE PHIZOG VENEER
VISAGE COMMAND DIGLYPH
FASHION FEATURE GRIMACE
GRUNTLE PROPOSE RESPECT
REVERSE SURFACE UPRIGHT
CONFRONT ENVISAGE EXTRADOS
FEATURES FROGFACE FRONTAGE
FRONTIER PROSPECT SEMBLANT
(— **DOWN**) DEFACE
(— **IN DEFIANCE**) AFFRONT
(— **OF ANIMAL**) MASK

(— OF CUBE) SQUARE
(— OF CUTTING TOOL) BEZEL BEZIL
(— OF GLACIER) SNOUT
(— OF STUMP) SCARF SCARPH
(— ONE'S DANCING PARTNER) SET
(— TO FACE) AFRONT BEFORE
FACIAL DIRECTLY
(— WITH MARBLE) PIN
(— WITH STONE) BATCH
(CLOCK —) DIAL TABLE WATCH
(CURVED —) EXTRADOS INTRADOS
(DIE —) ACE
(FANTASTIC —) ANTIC
(HALF DOMINO —) END
(HAVING SHORT BROAD —)
LATERAL
(INNER —) CONCAVE
(MADE-UP —) MOP
(MINING —) BANK BREAST
FOREHEAD LONGWALL
(MOCKING —) MOE MOWE
(ROCK —) CLIFF
(UPPER —) BROW
(WRY —) MOUTH GRIMACE
FACE-ARBOR KNIFE
FACE GUARD FRONTAL
FACEMAN HAGGER WINNER
FACEPLATE FRONT DOGPLATE
FACER BUMPER DRIFTER TANKARD
FACET PANE STAR BEZEL CULET
PHASE COLLET STEMMA FACETTE
LOZENGE TEMPLET
FACETIAE CURIOSA
FACETIOUS FUNNY MERRY SMART
WITTY FACETE JOCOSE JOCULAR
HUMOROUS POLISHED
FACILE ABLE EASY QUICK READY
EXPERT FLUENT GENTLE AFFABLE
DUCTILE LENIENT
FACILITATE AID EASE HELP FAVOR
SPEED ASSIST GREASE EXPEDITE
FACILITY ART EASE FEEL HELP
ECLAT KNACK SKILL ADDRESS
COMMAND FREEDOM EASINESS
(PL.) ADDITIONS
FACING DADO HARL FRONT HARLE
LAPEL LINER PANEL SKIRT BEFORE
TOWARD VENEER AGAINST
FORNENT SURFACE BLACKING
CAMPSHOT CONFRONT COVERING
FACEWORK FORNENST OPPOSITE
PITCHING
(— AGAINST GLACIER) STOSS
(— AHEAD) FULL
(— APEX) ACROSCOPIC
(— AUDIENCE OBLIQUELY) EFFACE
AFFRONTY
(— EACH OTHER) AFFRONTE
AFFRONTY
(— INWARD) INTRORSE
(— OUTWARDS) EXTRORSE
FACSIMILE COPY MODEL REPLICA
AUTOTYPE
FACT CASE DEED FAIT DATUM EVENT
SOOTH TRUTH DONNEE EFFECT
FACTUM COMPERT FORMULA
GENERAL INDICIA KEYNOTE
LOWDOWN REALITY
(CONCLUSIVE —) CRUSHER
(DECISIVE —) CLINCHER

(FUNDAMENTAL —) KEYNOTE
(TRUE —S) STRENGTH
(PL.) DATA FEAT
FACTION BLOC NERI PART SECT
SIDE WING CABAL JUNTO PARTY
BRIGUE CLIQUE SCHISM BIANCHI
DISPUTE PINFOLD QUARREL
INTRIGUE SPLINTER
(PARTY —) STASIS
FACTITIOUS SHAM WHIPPED
KRITRIMA
FACTOR GEN DOER GENE ITEM
AGENT ALLEL CAUSE MAKER
ALLELE AUTHOR CENTER DETAIL
BAILIFF CONTROL COUCHER
CUSHION ELEMENT ENTROPY
FACTRIX ISOLATE STEWARD
ADHERENT AUMILDAR COFACTOR
DOMINANT EQUATION GOMASHTA
INCIDENT INCITANT
(—S IN EVOLUTION) ANTICHANCE
(CYTOPLASMIC —) KAPPA
(DECISIVE —) CAPSTONE
(ECOLOGICAL —) INFLUENT
(ENVIRONMENTAL —) GEOGEN
(HEREDITY —) GENE INSTINCT
(INTELLIGENCE —) G
(PERSONALITY —) SURGENCY
(RESTRICTIVE —) BARRIER
FACTORY HONG MILL SHOP PLANT
USINE AURANG AURUNG FABRIC
SUGARY CANNERY HATTERY
HOSIERY OFICINA SOAPERY
BUILDING COMPTOIR FABRIQUE
FILATURE OFFICINA STAMPERY
WORKSHOP
FACTOTUM COMPRADOR
FACTUAL HARD REAL TRUE ACTUAL
BEDROCK EARTHLY EMPIRIC
LITERAL
(INSUFFICIENTLY —) ABSTRACT
FACTUALLY INSOOTH
FACULTY ART WIT BOOM EASE GIFT
WILL FANCY SENSE BREATH BUDDHI
GIFTIE SEEING TALENT ABILITY
COLLEGE COUNSEL HABITUS
APTITUDE CAPACITY FELICITY
(— OF EXPRESSION) LANGUAGE
(CRITICAL —) JUDGMENT
(MENTAL —) HEADPIECE
(POETIC OR CREATIVE —) IDEALITY
PRINCIPLE
(REASONING —) DISCOURSE
(PL.) INDULTS
FAD BUG FIKE RAGE WHIM CRAZE
FANCU HOBBY FOIBLE CROCHET
FASHION WRINKLE
FADE DIE DIM DOW FLY WAN BRIT
CAST FATE FLAT GIVE PALE PEAK
PINE PINK VADE WELK WILK WILT
BLANK DAVER DECAY FLEET PASSE
PETER QUAIL SWING SWOON
DARKLE PERISH VANISH WITHER
DECLINE INSIPID LIGHTEN DIMINISH
DISCOLOR DISSOLVE EVANESCE
LANGUISH
(— AWAY) DOW BREAK FLEET
WALLOW

FADED PASSE SHABBY EXOLETE
SHOPWORN
FADGE FAY FIT SUIT
FADING FUGITIVE SWINGING
FAG FLAG JADE TIRE TOIL DROOP
WEARY DRUDGE HARASS MENIAL
EXHAUST FATIGUE FRAZZLE
FAGGED TASKIT
FAGGOT BROSNA CHUMPA FAGALD
FAGOT KID BUNT PILE PIMP FADGE
NICKY NITCH FAGGOT KNITCH
GARBAGE
FAIL GO CUT EBB ERR BANK BUST
CONK FALL FLAG FLOP FOLD LACK
LOSE MISS SINK SKEW SPIN WANE
APPAL BREAK BURST CRACK FAULT
FLUFF FLUKE FLUNK PETER QUAIL
SLAKE SPILL VAILE APPALL BETRAY
DEFAIL DEFECT DESERT FALTER
FIZZLE REPINE WINDER DECLINE
DEFAULT EXHAUST FALSIFY FLICKER
FLUMMOX FOUNDER MISFARE
MISGIVE SCANTLE LANGUISH
(— AT) FLUB
(— IN DUTY) LAPSE
(— IN EARLY STAGES) ABORT
(— IN HEALTH) SINK BREAK
(— IN STUDIES) BILGE
(— ON RIFLE RANGE) BOLO
(— TO GROW) MISS
FAILING BAD ILL BLOT FAULT
FOIBLE BLEMISH FAILURE FRAILTY
ABORTIVE WEAKNESS
FAILURE DUD BALK BUST FAIL FLOP
FLUB FOIL LACK LOSS MISS MUFF
TRIP BAULK BILGE CRASH DECAY
ERROR FAULT FLUKE FLUNK FROST
GRIEF GUILT LAPSE LEMON PLUCK
SMASH BRODIE FIASCO FIZZLE
STUMER STUMOR BLOOMER
CROPPER DEBACLE DECLINE
DEFAULT FLIVVER FLUMMOX
NEGLECT STUMBLE ABORTION
COLLAPSE DISASTER FAILANCE
FLOPEROO OMISSION
(— OF DAM) BLOW
(— OF FIREARM) STOPPAGE
(— OF MILK SECRETION) AGALAXY
AGALAXIA
(— OF MUSCLE) ACHALASIA
(— OF PAVEMENT) BLOWUP
(— OF PRIMER) HANGFIRE
(— OF VITALITY) DELIQUIUM
(— TO RAISE OAR) CRAB
(FLAT —) DUD
(RIDICULOUS —) FIASCO
FAIN FOND GLAD LIEF EAGER
PLEASED WILLING DESIROUS
INCLINED
FAINEANT IDLE LAZY
FAINT GO DIM WAN WAW COLD
CONK COOL DARK PALE PALL SOFT
THIN WEAK LIGHT QUEAL QUEER
SHADY SWELT SWOON TIMID WAUFF
WAUGH WERSH EVANID FEEBLE
REMISS SICKLY WAMBLY FEIGNED
FORGONE LANGUID OBSCURE
SWITHER SYNCOPE WEARISH
COWARDLY DELICATE LANGUISH

LISTLESS SLUGGISH TIMOROUS
(— **FROM HEAT**) SWELTER
(— **FROM HUNGER**) LEERY
(— **OF SCENT**) COLD WAUGH
FAINTHEARTED TIMID COWARD
CRAVEN COWARDLY UNHEARTY
FAINTHEARTEDNESS QUALM
FAINTING AFAINT SYNCOPE
DELIQUIUM
(— **SPELL**) DROW DWAM DWALM
FAINTLY DIMLY FAINT SMALL
FAINTNESS TENUITY GONENESS
WEAKNESS
FAINT-VOICED INWARD
FAIR GAY GEY MOP BEAU BELL
CALM EVEN FINE GAFF GALA GOOD
HEND JUST MART PLAY TIDE TIDY
BAZAR BLOND CLEAN CLEAR EQUAL
FERIA HENDE LARGE RIGHT ROUND
SHEER TRYST WHITE AONACH
BAZAAR BLONDE CANDID COMELY
DECENT DINKUM HONEST KERMIS
PRETTY SQUARE EXHIBIT JANNOCK
KERMESS STATUTE BOOKFAIR
DISTINCT FESTIVAL HORNFAIR
MIDDLING STRAIGHT UNBIASED
(— **AND CALM**) SETTLED
(— **AND SQUARE**) DINKUM
(**HINDU** —) MELA
(**VILLAGE** —) WALK
FAIRER SHIPWRIGHT
FAIRING SPAT SPINNER FAIRLING
FAIR-LEAD WAPP
FAIRLY WELL GAILY GAYLY GEYAN
EVENLY JUSTLY MEANLY HANDILY
PLAINLY RIGHTLY PROPERLY
SUITABLY
FAIRNESS FAIR CANDOR EQUITY
HONESTY JUSTICE EQUALITY
EVENNESS FAIRHEAD FAIRHOOD
FAIRWAY HOLE WATERWAY
FAIR-WEATHER SUNSHINE
FAIRY ELF FAY HOB IMP FAIN PERI
PIXY PUCK SHEE VILA OUPHE
PECHT PIXIE SIDHE WIGHT COURIL
FAERIE HATHOR KEWPIE SPIRIT
SPRITE YAKSHA YAKSHI ARGANTE
BANSHEE ORIANDA SHEOGUE
SYLPHID URGANDA FOLLETTO
MELUSINA
(**IRISH** —) SHEE SIDHE
(**TRICKSY** —) PUCK
(**PL.**) GENTRY
FAIRY BELL FOXGLOVE
FAIRYFOLK SHEE SIDHE
FAIRYLAND ANNWN ANNWFN
ELFLAND
FAITH DIN FAY FOY LAW LAY VAY
FACK FEGS SLAM TROW CERTY
CREED HAITH STOCK TOUCH TROTH
TRUST TRUTH BELIEF CERTIE
CREDIT GOSPEL FACKINS AFFIANCE
RELIANCE RELIGION
(**BAD** —) DUPLICITY
(**RELIGIOUS** —) SRADH SRADDHA
SHRADDHA
FAITHFUL FAST FEAL FIRM GOOD
JUST LEAL LIKE REAL TRIG TRUE
FALSE HEMAN LIEGE LOYAL PIOUS

SWEER TIGHT TREST TRIED ARDENT
ENTIRE FIDELE HONEST LAWFUL
PISTIC STANCH STEADY TRUSTY
DEVOTED SINCERE STAUNCH
ACCURATE CONSTANT RESOLUTE
SPEAKING
FAITHFULNESS HSIN FEALTY
VERITY LOYALTY FIDELITY
TRUENESS
FAITHLESS FALSE PUNIC FICKLE
HOLLOW UNJUST UNTRUE ATHEIST
APOSTATE DELUSIVE DISLOYAL
SHIFTING UNSTABLE
FAITHLESSNESS FALSITY PERFIDY
UNTRUTH
FAKE DUD DUFF FEKE HOAX HOKE
SHAM BOGUS CHEAT FALSE FEIGN
FLAKE FRAUD FUDGE PHONY
WANGLE DUFFING FALSIFY FURBISH
GUNDECK PRETEND SWINDLE
SIMULATE SPURIOUS
(— **OF STOWED ROPE**) FLEET
FAKER FAKIR QUACK HUMBUG
CAMELOT PEDDLER
FAKIR FAKIH FAQUIR DERVISH
FALCHION FALX
FALCON EYAS HAWK SORE BESRA
HOBBY SAKER STOOP GENTLE
JAGGER JUGGER LANNER LUGGAR
LUGGER MERLIN MUSKET PREYER
RAPTOR SHAHIN TERCEL KESTREL
SAKERET BERIGORA BOCKEREL
FALCONET PEREGRIN SOREHAWK
(— **BOARD**) HACK
(— **IN FIRST YEAR**) SORE
SOREHAWK
(**FEMALE** —) FORMAL FORMEL
LANNER
(**MALE** —) TASSEL TERCEL SAKERET
(**SMALL** —) HOBBY MERLIN KESTREL
(**WHITE** —) ICELANDER
FALCONER HAWKER OSTREGER
FALCONRY HAWKING
FALDSTOOL ORATORY
FALL GO EBB SAG SYE TIP BACK
BAND COME COUP DIVE DRIP DROP
DUNT FLOP HANG PICK PLOP RASH
RUIN RUSE SHED SILE SINK SLIP
SWAK SWAP SWAY SWOP TILT
WHAP WHOP ABATE CHUTE CLOIT
CRASH DROOP HANCE INCUR JABOT
LAPSE LIGHT LODGE PITCH PLUMB
PLUMP RAPID SAULT SHAKE SHOOT
SKITE SLIPE SLUMP SPILL SQUAB
SQUAT THROW TRACE TWINE
ALIGHT AUTUMN BRODIE DEVALL
DOUNCE DRYSNE FOOTER HAPPEN
HEADER JOUNCE PERISH PLUNGE
RECEDE SEASON SLOUGH STREEK
STRIKE TOPPLE TUMBLE CASCADE
CROPPER CROWNER DECLINE
DEGRADE DEPRESS DESCEND
DEVOLVE DRIBBLE ESCHEAT
ILLAPSE PLUMMET RELAPSE
RETREAT SQUELCH STUMBLE
SUBSIDE CATARACT COLLAPSE
COMMENCE DECREASE DOWNCOME
(— **ABRUPTLY**) DUMP
(— **APART**) BREAK SHIVER

COLLAPSE DISUNITE
(— **AWAY**) DEFECT
(— **BACK**) RECEDE RESORT
(— **BEHIND**) LAG
(— **DIZZILY**) SPIN
(— **DOWN**) CAVE FLOP SWAP SLUMP
REVERSE SWITHER
(— **DUE**) BEFALL
(— **FAST**) HOP
(— **FLAT**) PLAT FLIVVER
(— **FORWARD**) PECK PITCH
PROLAPSE
(— **FROM A HORSE**) PURL
(— **FROM UNDERMINING**) CALVE
(— **FROM VIRTUE**) LAPSE
(— **GRADUALLY**) EBB SAG
(— **HEAVILY**) DING LUMP SOSS
CLOIT CLYTE GULCH PLOUT PLUMP
SOUSE SWACK THROW
(— **ILL**) TRAIK
(— **IN DROPS**) DRIP STILL DRIBBLE
(— **IN FLURRIES**) SPIT
(— **IN FOLDS**) BLOUSE
(— **IN RIVER**) SAULT
(— **IN WITH**) INCUR
(— **IN**) CAVE FOUNDER
(— **INTO ERROR**) SLIP STUMBLE
(— **INTO FAINT**) DWAM DWALM
(— **INTO RUIN**) DECAY
(— **INTO SLUMBER**) DROWSE
(— **INTO TRAP**) DECOY
(— **INTO WATER**) DOP
(— **INTO**) STRIKE
(— **OF DEW**) SEREIN SERENE
(— **OF RAIN**) SKIFF SKIFT SHOWER
(— **OF SNOW**) SKIFF SKIFT ONCOME
SCOUTHER SNOWFALL
(— **OF WICKETS**) ROT
(— **OFF**) BATE SLIP SLACK
(— **ON BACK**) BACKER
(— **ON SUCCESSIVE DAYS**) CONCUR
(— **ON THE NOSE**) NOSER
(— **OUT**) LIGHT FORTUNE QUARREL
(— **PRONE**) GRABBLE
(— **RAPIDLY**) SKID
(— **SHORT**) DROP FAIL FAULT
(— **SLOWLY**) SETTLE
(— **SUDDENLY**) BOLT PLOP SLUMP
(— **THROWING HORSE AND RIDER**)
CRUMPLER
(— **TO NOTHING**) DISSOLVE
(— **TO PIECES**) BUCKLE CRUMBLE
(— **UPON**) WARP
(— **VIOLENTLY**) BEAT
(**BAD** —) BUSTER
(**HEAVY** —) PASH POUR SWAG
CLOIT GULCH SKELP SOUSE SQUAT
MUCKER
(**INCOMPLETE WRESTLING** —) FOIL
(**SOFT** —) SCLAFF
(**SUDDEN** —) HANCE SQUAT SQUASH
FALLACIOUS SLY WILY ABSURD
CRAFTY UNTRUE DELUSIVE
GUILEFUL ILLUSORY
FALLACY IDOL ERROR FALLAX
IDOLUM SOPHISM EQUIVOKE
ILLUSION
FALLEN DOWN FAUN FLAT SHED
LAPSED DECLASSE

(**— IN**) SUNKEN
FALLER GILL FLATHEAD
FALLFISH CHUB DACE CORPORAL
FALL HERRING TAILOR
FALLIBLE HUMAN ERRANT ERRABLE
FALLING SIT CADENT CAVING
PROLAPSE WINDFALL
(**— BACK**) ESCHEAT
(**— DOWN**) RUIN
(**— INTO**) INFALL
(**— OF MINE ROOF**) SIT
(**— OF RAIN**) SPIT
(**— OFF**) CADUCE LEEWAY
CADUCOUS
(**— ON SOMETHING**) INCIDENT
(**— OUT**) DIFFICULTY
(**— SHORT**) DEFICIT
FALLOPIAN TUBE TUBAL
FALLOVER OSTREGER
FALLOW LEA PALE HOBBY BARREN
VALEWE
FALLOW DEER DAMINE DAPPLE
FALLOWING ARDER
FALSE DEAD FAKE FLAM SHAM
BOGUS FAUSE LYING PASTE PHONY
WRONG FICKLE HOLLOW LUTHER
PSEUDO UNTRUE ASSUMED
BASTARD CROOKED FEIGNED
DISLOYAL ILLUSIVE RECREANT
SPECTRAL SPURIOUS
FALSE BEACHDROPS PINESAP
FALSE CRAWLEY PINEDROPS
FALSE FOXGLOVE FEVERWEED
FALSE HELLEBORE EARTHGALL
FALSEHOOD COG FIB LIE BUNG
CRAM FLAM TALE CRACK ERROR
FABLE STORY FALSET UNFACT
YANKER CRAMMER CRETISM
FALSAGE FALSERY FALSITY FIBBERY
FICTION LEASING PERFIDY
PHANTOM ROMANCE UNTRUTH
FALSHEDE ROORBACK STRAPPER
FALSE MERMAID FLOERKEA
LIMNANTH
FALSENESS SHAM
FALSE WINTERGREEN PYROLA
FALSEWORK CENTERING
FALSIES CHEATERS
FALSIFIER FALSER FORGER
FALSARY
FALSIFY LIE COOK FAKE WARP
ABUSE BELIE FEINT FORGE BETRAY
DOCTOR GUNDECK VIOLATE
EMBEZZLE
FALSITY LIE ERROR VANITY
UNTRUTH INVERITY
FALTER FAIL HALT PAUSE WAVER
BOGGLE FLINCH TOTTER FRIBBLE
STAMMER STUMBLE TREMBLE
HESITATE
FALTERING HINK HALTING
FALX FALCULA
FAME BAY CRY LOSE NAME STAR
WORD BRUIT ECLAT GLORY HONOR
KUDOS PRICE RUMOR VOICE
ESTEEM LAUREL RENOWN REPORT
REPUTE TONGUE HEARSAY
WORSHIP
(**EVIL —**) INFAMY

FAMED RIFE KNOWN NOTED
EMINENT RENOMEE RENOWNED
FAMILIAR FLY BAKA BOKO BOLD
COZY EASY FREE FULL HOMY TAME
TOSH CLOSE CONNU GREAT HOMEY
KNOWN PRIVY THICK USUAL
BEATEN CHUMMY COMMON ENTIRE
FOLKSY GERMAN HOMELY INWARD
KENNED STRAIT THRONG VERSED
AFFABLE FAMULAR FOLKSEY
POPULAR FREQUENT HABITUAL
INTIMATE SOCIABLE STANDARD
(**— WITH**) KNOWING
(**MAKE —**) POST
(**PRESUMPTUOUSLY —**) INSOLENT
FAMILIARITY HABIT FREEDOM
LIBERTY PRIVACY PRIVITY TRAFFIC
HABITUDE INTIMACY
FAMILIARIZE HAFT VERSE
ACCUSTOM ACQUAINT FREQUENT
FAMILIARLY HOMELY
FAMILY ILK KIN AIGA CLAN GING
KIND LINE NAME RACE TEAM TRIP
CINEL CLASS FLESH GOTRA GROUP
HOUSE MEINY STIRP STOCK CLETCH
FAIMLY PARAGE STEMMA STIRPS
STRAIN ZEGRIS DYNASTY KINDRED
LINEAGE ORLEANS PROGENY
CATEGORY FIRESIDE
(**COSMOPOLITAN —**) FELIDAE
FABACEAE
(**FIRST —**) FF
(**LANGUAGE —**) CHON BANTU CLICK
COCHE CUNAN KADAI STOCK
AIMARA ATALAN AYMARA CHOLON
GILIAK HUARPE LENCAN SERIAN
BOTOYAN CADDOAN CATIBAN
CHINOOK CHOLONA CHUMASH
COPEHAN ESSELAN KARTHLI
KARTVEL KERESAN SHASTAN
ATAKAPAN CHANGOAN
(**LARGE —**) QUIVERFUL
(**ONE-PARAMETER —**) PENCIL
(**SUPER —**) APINA APOIDEA
FAMINE LACK PINE WOLF DEARTH
HUNGER SCARCITY
FAMISH KILL STARVE DESTROY
ENFAMISH
FAMOUS MERE BREME FAMED
GRAND NOBLE NOTED FAMOSE
NAMELY EMINENT NAMABLE
NOTABLE RENOWNED
FAMULUS WAGNER SERVANT
FAN ONE RUN VAN BEAT BUFF COOL
WASH DELTA PUNKA WHIFF BASKET
BLOWER CHAMAR COLMAR FANNER
FLABEL FLIGHT PUNKAH ROOTER
SHOVEL SPREAD VENTOY WINNOW
ADMIRER DEVOTEE FLABRUM
FLYFLAP MPANGWE PAHOUIN
WHISKER EVENTAIL FOLLOWER
(**— FOR BLOWER**) WAFTER
(**ALLUVIAL —**) CONE APRON DELTA
(**FOOTBALL —**) GRIDDER
(**WINNOWING —**) SAIL LIKNON
(**PL.**) FOLLOWING
FANALOKA FOSSA FOUSSA
FANATIC MAD BIGOT CRAZY FIEND
RABID ULTRA ZEALOT DEVOTEE

FURIOSO PHANTIC PULAHAN
PULIJAN BABAYLAN FRENETIC
FANATICAL RABID ULTRA EXTREME
FURIOUS
FANCIED UNREAL DREAMED
AFFECTED
FANCIFUL ODD IDEAL QUEER VIEWY
DREAMY QUAINT UNREAL BIZARRE
FANCIED LAPUTAN STRANGE
WHIMSIC FANCICAL FILIGREE
ROMANTIC
FANCY BEE FAD GIG IDEA ITEM LIKE
LOVE MAZE TROW WEEN WHIM
BRAID BRAIN DREAM FREAK GUESS
HUMOR SHINE AFFECT BEGUIN
FIGURE FLOSSY IDEATE LIKING
MEGRIM NOTION ORNATE SHINDY
VAGARY VISION WHIMSY CAPRICE
CHIMERA CONCEIT CONCEPT
CROCHET FANCIED FANCIFY
FANTASY PROPOSE ROMANCE
SUSPECT WRINKLE CHIMAERA
CONCEIVE CROTCHET DAYDREAM
ILLUSION PHANTASM PHANTASY
(**FOOLISH —**) CHIMERA CHIMAERA
(**PASSING —**) FIKE
(**PERVERSE —**) CROTCHET
(**WILD —**) TOY MAZE
(**PL.**) DREAMERY
FANDANGO MURCIANA
FANE FLAG BANNER FANACLE
FANFARE TUSCH HOORAY HURRAH
TUCKET TANTARA FANFARON
FLOURISH
FANFARONADE BLUSTER FANFARE
SWAGGER BOASTING
FANFLOWER TACCADA
FANG FAN EARN FALX TAKE TANG
TUSK VANG BEGIN PRONG SEIZE
SNARE TOOTH ASSUME OBTAIN
PANGWE CAPTURE PAHOUIN
PROCURE
FANON CAPE ORALE PHANO FANNEL
MANIPLE
FAN PALM YARAY ERYTHEA
FANTREE TALIPOT
FAN-SHAPED ALARY
FANTAIL COMET SHAKER WAGTAIL
FAN-TAN PARLIAMENT
FANTASIA FANTASY QUODLIBET
FANTASTIC ODD ANTIC LUCIO
QUEER ABSURD GOTHIC ROCOCO
TOYISH UNREAL ANTICAL BIZARRE
WHIMSIC FANCIFUL FREAKISH
ROMANTIC SINGULAR
(**— PERSON**) KICKSHAW
FANTASY IDEA DREAM FANCY
DESIRE VISION CAPRICE CHIMERA
PHANTOM ROMANCE CHIMAERA
PHANTASM PHANTASY
FAR AWAY LONG MUCH ROOM SIDE
WELL WIDE CLEAN SIZES WIDEN
REMOTE DISTANT FARAWAY
ROOMWARD
(**— AND AWAY**) STREETS
(**— OFF**) OUTBYE
(**— ON**) ADVANCED
FARCE MIME DROLL EXODE FORCE
STUFF COMEDY GARLIC SOTTLE

EXODIUM MOCKERY TEMACHA
DROLLERY FARCETTA
(RELATING TO —) ATELLAN
FARCEUR WAG JOKER FORCER
FARCICAL BUFFO COMIC DROLL
ATELLAN
FARCTATE STUFFED
FARCY FARCIN EQUINIA FASHION
FARE DO GO EAT TRY COME DIET
FEND FOOD PATH RATE TIME WEND
CHEER CHEFE CHIVE FRAME GOING
LIGHT PRICE SPEED TABLE TOKEN
TRACK VIAND COMMON FARING
FETTLE HAPPEN TRAVEL CARFARE
JOURNEY PASSAGE PROCEED
PROSPER WAFTAGE WAYFARE
FERRYAGE PROGRESS
(— FOR FERRY) NAULUM FERRYAGE
(— WELL) SPEED
(COARSE —) HAWEBAKE
FAREWELL AVE VALE ADIEU ADIOS
ALOHA CONGE FINAL LEAVE
CHEERO BONALLY CHEERIO
GOODBYE LEAVING PARTING
FARFETCHED FARFET FORCED
DEVIOUS STRAINED EXQUISITE
FAR-FLUNG EXTENDED
FARINA MEAL FLOUR FARINE
POLLEN STARCH
FARKLEBERRY BLUET
FARL PARLY FARREL
FARM FEU CROP TACK TILL TORP
TOWN WALK CROFT DAIRY EMPTY
FIRMA HARAS MAINS MILPA PLACE
RANCH RANGE STEAD BARTON
BOWERY CHACRA ESTATE FURROW
GRANGE RANCHO TYDDEN TYDDYN
CLEANSE HENNERY KOLKHOZ
MAILING POTRERO POULTRY
SOVKHOS VACCARY ESTANCIA
HACIENDA HATCHERY LABORING
LOCATION STEADING TOWNSHIP
(— OUT) DIMIT ARRENT
(COLLECTIVE —) KIBBUTZ KOLKHOZ
(COMMUNAL —) KVUTZA KVUTZAH
(DAIRY —) WICK
(LARGE —) RANCH BARTON
(RENTED —) MAILING
(SMALL —) CHACRA
(STOCK —) ESTANCIA
(STUD —) STUD HARAS
FARMER HOB CARL FARM HOBB
KHOT KYLE RYOT TATE AILLT AUMIL
BOWER CARLE CEILE CLOWN
COLON HODGE KISAN COCKIE
GROWER HOGMAN JIBARO TILLER
YEOMAN BUCOLIC BUSHMAN
BYWONER COTTIER CROFTER
GRANGER HAYSEED HUSBAND
LANDMAN PLANTER PLOWMAN
RANCHER SCULLOG TILLMAN
TRUCKER COCKATOO PRODUCER
PUBLICAN RURALIST SELECTOR
(AUSTRALIAN —) SELECTOR
(NORWEGIAN —) BENDER
(POOR —) PIKE
(PROSPEROUS —) KULAK
(SMALL —) BOOR
(TENANT —) AILLT GEBUR SIRDAR

COLONUS SHAREMAN
FARMHAND HAND HELP
FARMHOLD CROFT
FARMHOUSE FARM TOWN ONSET
GRANGE QUINTA CASERIO ONSTEAD
STEADING
FARMING SOIL FARMERY
HUSBANDRY
(— SYSTEM) METAYAGE
FARMLAND ACREAGE
FARMSTEAD TOWN WICK STEAD
FARMERY
FARMYARD WERF CLOSE BARTON
RICKYARD
FARO MONTE STUSS TIGER
PHARAOH
(— CARD) SODA
FARO BANK TIGER
FAR-OFF DISTANT
FAR-REACHING GREAT FARGOING
FARRIER SHOER SMITH MARSHAL
FARROW PIG ROW RAKE DRAPE
LITTER
FARSIGHTED SHREWD SIGHTY
FARTHER YOND AHEAD STILL
LONGER FURTHER REMOTER
THITHER
FARTHEST ULTIMA ENDMOST
EXTREME FARMOST LONGEST
OUTMOST DOWNMOST FURTHEST
REMOTEST ULTIMATE
FARTHING RAG GRIG JACK QUAD
FADGE FERLING QUARTER
QUADRANS QUADRANT
(HALF —) CUE
(THREE —S) GILL
FARTHINGALE FERDEGEW
VERTUGAL
FASCIA BAND SASH FACIA FILLET
BANDAGE MOLDING LIGATURE
FASCICLE BUNDLE PHALANGE
FASCICULUS HEFT BUNDLE COLUMN
TRACTUS
FASCINATE DARE CHARM SEIZE
WITCH ALLURE ENAMOR ATTRACT
BEWITCH ENCHANT ENGROSS
GLAMOUR PHILTER PHILTRE
ENSORCEL ENTRANCE INTEREST
INTRIGUE SIRENIZE
FASCINATED BESOTTED
FASCINATING NUTTY SIRENIC
CHARMING FETCHING MESMERIC
FASCINATION CHARM SPELL
WITCHERY
FASCINE FAGOT FAGGOT SAUCISSE
FASCIOLA DISTOMA DISTOMUM
FASCIOLE SEMITA
FASCIST BLACK FASCISTA
FASHION GO CRY CUT FAD LAT TON
WAY CHIC FEAT FORM GARB GATE
KICK MAKE MODE MOLD RAGE RATE
SORT TURN TWIG WEAR WISE BUILD
CRAZE FEIGN FORGE FRAME GUISE
MODEL MOULD SHAPE STYLE
VOGUE WEAVE ASSIZE BUSTLE
CAMBER CREATE CUSTOM DESIGN
FANGLE INVENT MANNER METHOD
ALAMODE COMPOSE IMAGERY
PORTRAY QUALITY CONTRIVE

(LATEST —) KICK
(PREVAILING —) CRY
(SPECIAL —) TOUCH
FASHIONABLE CHIC PINK DASHY
DOGGY DOSSY SMART SWELL
SWISH VOGUE GIGOLO JAUNTY
MODISH TIMISH TONISH DASHING
GALLANT GENTEEL STYLISH
SWAGGER
(NOT —) DEMODE
FASHIONABLY SMARTLY
FASHIONED HUED CARVED SHAPED
WROUGHT FEATURED
FASHIONING FINGENT
FASHION PLATE SWELL
FASSAITE PYRGOM
FAST HOT HUT COLD FIRM HARD
LENT SOON SURE WIDE AGILE
APACE BRISK CHEAP FIXED FLASH
FLEET HASTY QUICK RAPID ROUND
SADLY STUCK SWIFT TIGHT TOSTO
CARENE ESTHER FASTLY LIVELY
SECURE SPEEDY SPORTY STABLE
STARVE ABIDING EXPRESS
HOTSHOT HURRIED PROVISO
RASPING SETTLED SIKERLY STATION
TAANITH ENDURING FAITHFUL
SPINNING SPORTING WIKIWIKI
(— DAY) ASHURA
FAST-DYED INGRAIN
FASTEN BAR DOG FAY FIX GAD GIB
KEY LAG PEN PIN SEW TAG TIE YOT
BELT BEND BIND BOLT BRAD CLIP
FRET GIRD GIRT GLUE GRIP HANG
HANK HASP HOOK HOOP HORN KILT
KNIT KNOT LACE LASH LINK LOCK
MOOR NAIL ROPE SEAL SNIB SOUD
SPAN SPAR STAY WELD WIRE AFFIX
ANNEX BELAY BIGHT BRACE CABLE
CATCH CHAIN CINCH CLAMP CLASP
CLING COPSE DEFIX GIRTH HALSH
HITCH INFIX LATCH PASTE RIVET
SCREW SEIZE SLOUR SNECK STEEK
STICK STRAP TRUSS WITHE
ANCHOR ATTACH BATTEN BUCKLE
BUTTON CEMENT CLINCH COTTER
COUPLE ENGAGE ENTAIL FATHER
GARTER HAMPER HANKLE INKNOT
PICKET SECURE SKEWER SOLDER
STAPLE STITCH STRAIN TETHER
BRACKET CONFINE CONNECT
EMBRACE GRAPPLE GROMMET
PADLOCK BARNACLE FORELOCK
INTERTIE OBLIGATE TRANSFIX
(— A SAIL) CROSS
(— ABOUT) THRAP
(— ANCHOR) SCOW
(— AS SPURS) SPEND
(— IN) EMBAR
(— TO) TAG
(— TOGETHER) COAPT SEIZE
SPLICE CONNECT
(— WINGS ON) IMP
(— WITH A GIRTH) WARRICK
(— WITH NOTCHES) GAIN
FASTENED FAST SHUT BOUND FIXED
BOUNDEN
FASTENER BAR GIB GIN NUT PIN
AGAL BOLT DOME FAST FROG HASP

LOCK NAIL SNAP TACK CATCH
CLAMP CLASP LATCH RIVET SCREW
SPIKE STRAP TATCH THONG
BUCKLE BUTTON HATPIN STAPLE
ZIPPER FIXATOR LATCHET PADLOCK
SNAPPER TENDRIL FASTNESS
STAYLACE

FASTENING TEE TIE FROG HASP
SEAL SNAP SNIB STAY TACK
BUCKLE CLINCH LACING MUZZLE
STRIKE TINGLE BINDING CLOSURE
LATCHET MOUSING PINNING SEIZING
FORELOCK KNITTING
(— FOR HAWK'S WING) BRAIL
(— ON HARPOON IRON) HITCH
(HOOK AND LOOP —) AGRAFE
AGRAFFE
(PL.) GRIPES

FASTIDIOUS FINE NICE CHARY
DONCY FEEST FUSSY NAISH NATTY
PAWKY CHOICE CHOICY CHOOSY
DAINTY DONSIE MOROSE PICKED
QUAINT QUEASY SPRUCE CHOOSEY
CURIOUS ELEGANT FINICAL FINICKY
HAUGHTY PICKING REFINED
TAFFETA TAFFETY CRITICAL
DELICATE EXACTING GINGERLY
OVERNICE PICKSOME PRECIOUS
SCORNFUL
(NOT —) GROSS
(OVERLY —) SAUCY

FASTIDIOUSNESS DAINTY NICETY
DELICACY

FASTING RAMADAN

FAST-MOVING SUDDEN

FASTNESS FORT CASTLE CITADEL
RETREAT FORTRESS

FAST-WORKING HOTSHOT

FAT GHI OIL TUB FOZY GHEE LARD
LIPA MORT RICH SAIM SUET ADEPS
BROSY CETIN CHUFF COCUM ESTER
FLECK FLICK FOGGY GROSS JUICY
KEDGE KOKUM LARDY LIPID LIPIN
LUSTY OBESE PLUMP PODGY
PORKY PUDDY PUDGY PURSY
SAAME SPICK SQUAB STOUT SUMEN
THICK WASTY AXUNGE BLOWSY
CHOATY CHUBBY CHUFFY DEGRAS
FATTED FINISH FLESHY GREASE
LIPIDE PLUFFY PORTLY PUBBLE
PUNCHY PYKNIC ROTUND STOCKY
STUFFY TALLOW UCUUBA ADIPOSE
BLOATED BLUBBER CEROTIN
FATNESS FERTILE FLESHLY
FULSOME LANOLIN OPULENT
PINGUID PURSIVE REPLETE STEARIN
EXTENDED FRUITFUL MARROWED
MURUMURU UNCTUOUS
(— AROUND WHALE'S NECK) KENT
(— MEAT) SPECK
(— OF HIPPOPOTAMUS) SPECK
(— PERSON) SQUAB
(ANIMAL —) GLOR SAIM SUET
ADEPS GLORE GREASE TALLOW
(FLOATING —) FLOT
(LARD —) FLARE FLECK FLICK
(LUMP OF —) KEECH
(NATURAL —) ESTER
(POULTRY —) SCHMALZ SCHMALTZ

(SOLID —) LARD KIKUEL STEARIN

FATAL FEY DIRE MORT FERAL VITAL
DEADLY DISMAL DOOMED FUNEST
LETHAL MORTAL CAPITAL DEATHLY
EXITIAL FATEFUL KILLING OMINOUS
RUINOUS UNSONSY BASILISK
DESTINED EXITIOUS FUNESTAL
MORTIFIC

FATALITY DOOM ACCIDENT
CALAMITY DISASTER

FAT-BELLIED GUTTY

FATE DIE END KER LOT CAST DOLE
DOOM EURE NORN RUIN SORT STAR
CAVEL EVENT GRACE KARMA MOIRA
MORTA WEIRD WHATE WRITE
ANANKE CHANCE KISMET DESTINY
FORTUNE OUTCOME PORTION
DOWNFALL FATALITY
(INEXORABLE —) HEAVEN
(ONE OF —S) NONA PARCA CLOTHO
DECUMA ATROPOS LACHESIS

FATED DUE FEY FATAL DOOMED
DECREED DESTINED

FATEFUL FATAL FATED DEADLY
DOOMFUL OMINOUS DOOMLIKE

FATHEAD REDFISH

FATHEADED FOZY

FATHEADEDNESS FOZINESS

FATHER BU DA PA ABU AMA DAD
POP TAT ABBA ABOU AMBA ANBA
ATEF BABA BAPU DADA PAPA PERE
SIRE ADOPT BABBO BEGET DADDY
FRIAR PADRE PATER VADER
PARENT PRIEST SUBORN ELKANAH
GENITOR TATINEK BEAUPERE
GENERATE GOVERNOR
(CHURCH —) APOLOGIST
(SEMIDIVINE —) PITRI
(SIDE OF —) AGNATE
(PL.) PP

FATHERLAND KITH HOMELAND

FATHER-LASHER GUNDIE SCULPIN
BULLHEAD LORICATE

FATHERLESS ORBATE SIRELESS

FATHOM BRACE BRASS DELVE
FADME PLUMB SOLVE SOUND
TOUCH BOTTOM MEASURE
PLUMMET

FATIGUE FAG HAG TEU BEAT COOK
JADE TASH TIRE TRAY SPEND
STALL TARRY THRIE TRAIK TRASH
WEARY HARASS OVERDO TAIGLE
TUCKER EXHAUST FATIGATE
VEXATION

FATIGUED BEAT GONE JADED TIRED
WEARY TASKIT OUTWORN WEARIED
FATIGATE HARASSED TUCKERED

FATIGUING HARD IRKSOME

FATLIKE LIPOID

FATNESS BLOOM GREASE

FATTEN FAT BEEF LARD SOIL
BRAWN FARCE FLESH FRANK PROVE
SMEAR STALL BATTEN ENRICH
FINISH TALLOW THRIVE PINGUEFY
SAGINATE

FATTENING FRANK BATTEL
BATTABLE

FATTY SUETY BACONY GREASY
ADIPOSE ADIPOUS FATLIKE PINGUID

SEBIFIC LIPAROID LIPAROUS
UNCTUOUS

FATUOUS DOPY DOPEY INANE SILLY
SIMPLE STUPID UNREAL FATUATE
FOOLISH IDIOTIC WITLESS
DEMENTED ILLUSORY IMBECILE

FAUCES JAWS

FAUCET BIB TAP BIBB COCK QUILL
SPOUT VALVE CUTOFF DOSSIL
DOZZLE OFFLET SPIGOT BIBCOCK
HYDRANT PETCOCK TURNCOCK
(WOODEN —) HORSE

FAUGH BAH FOH VAH

FAUJDAR PHOUSDAR

FAULT BUG RUB SIN CLAG COUP
DEBT FAIL FLAW FLUB HOLE LACK
LAST MOLE SAKE SLIP SPOT VICE
WANT WITE ABUSE AMISS BLAME
BREAK CULPA ERROR FLUFF GUILT
LAPSE SCAPE SHIFT SLIDE SWICK
TACHE BLOTCH DEFECT FOIBLE
RUNNER THRUST VICETY VITIUM
BLEMISH BLISTER BLUNDER
DEFAULT DEMERIT EYELAST FAILING
FAILURE FRAILTY MISTAKE NEGLECT
OFFENSE FAULTING PECCANCY
WEAKNESS
(— IN BADMINTON) SLING
(MINING —) COUP LEAP CHECK
HITCH
(PL.) FAULTAGE

FAULTFINDER MOMUS CARPER
CRITIC MOMIST CAPTION KNOCKER
NAGSTER

FAULTFINDING CARPING CAPTIOUS
CRITICAL

FAULTILY BADLY

FAULTLESS PURE CLEAN RIGHT
CORRECT PERFECT PRECISE
FLAWLESS

FAULTY BAD ILL SICK AMISS UNFIT
WRONG FLAWED FAULTED PECCANT
VICIOUS BLAMABLE CULPABLE
SPURIOUS

FAUN SATYR WOODMAN WOODWOSE

FAUNA FAUNULA FAUNULE ZOOLOGY
(FOSSIL —) BIOCHRON

FAUSSEBRAIE VAMURE VAUMURE

FAUX PAS GAFF SLIP BONER ERROR
GAFFE FLOATER MISSTEP MISTAKE
SNAPPER

FAVOR AID FOR ORE PRO BOON
ESTE FACE GREE HEAR HELP LIKE
MAKE BLESS BRIBE GRACE LEAVE
MENSK SERVE SPARE SPEED THANK
TREAT ASSIST ERRAND ESTEEM
FAVOUR LETTER NOTICE PENCEL
UPHOLD ADVANCE AGGRACE
ENFAVOR FEATURE FORWARD
GRATIFY INDULGE RESPECT
SUPPORT ADVOCACY BEFRIEND
COURTESY FAVORIZE GOODWILL
KINDNESS RESEMBLE SYMPATHY

FAVORABLE HOT BOON FAIR FREE
GOOD HIGH KIND ROSY TIDY CIVIL
CLEAR HAPPY LARGE MERRY TRINE
WHITE WILLY BENIGN DEXTER
GENIAL GOLDEN KINDLY TOWARD
BENEFIC EXALTED OPTIMAL

POPULAR PRESENT FRIENDLY
GRACIOUS PLEASING PROPENSE
SPEEDFUL TOWARDLY
(— TO PURCHASER) KEEN
(NOT —) INFAUST
FAVORABLY FAIR WELL HIGHLY
FAVORED WELL FAURD HAPPY
FAURED GIFTED BLESSED
FAVOURED
FAVORER FAUTOR FRIEND FAVORITE
FAVORING FAVONIAN
FAVORITE BOY PET POT PEAT
CHALK GREAT INGLE WHITE MINION
DARLING FANCIED MINIKIN POPULAR
SPECIAL GRACIOSO WHITEBOY
FAVORITISM BIAS FAVOR NEPOTISM
FAVUS WHITECOMB
FAWN COG BUCK CLAW DEER FAON
JOUK ROOT COWER CRAWL CREEP
GLOZE HONEY TOADY WHELP
CRINGE CROUCH GROVEL KOWTOW
SHRINK SLAVER ADULATE CROODLE
CRUDDLE FLATTER FLETHER
HANGDOG SERVILE SPANIEL
TOADEAT TRUCKLE WHEATEN
BOOTLICK
(— UPON) SUCK SMOOGE ADULATE
FAWNING SLEEK CRINGE GREASE
SLEEKY SURPLE FLETHER GLOZING
HANGDOG SERVILE SPANIEL
FLATTERY
FAWNSKIN NEBRIS
FAY ELF FEY FAIRY FEIGH
FAZE DAUNT FEEZE PHASE WORRY
FEALTY FEE FEWTE HOMAGE
LOYALTY SERVICE TREWAGE
FIDELITY
FEAR UG AWE DREE FLAY FUNK
WARD ALARM DOUBT DREAD JELLY
PANIC ALARUM DANGER DISMAY
FRIGHT HORROR PHOBIA TERROR
ANXIETY SUSPECT AFFRIGHT
DISQUIET DISTRUST EERINESS
MISDOUBT VENERATE
FEARFUL ARGH DIRE AWFUL PAVID
TIMID WINDY WROTH AFRAID
COWISH FRIGHTY GHASTLY
NERVOUS PANICKY WORRIED
CAUTIOUS DOUBTFUL DREADFUL
GREWSOME GRUESOME HORRIBLE
HORRIFIC SHOCKING SKITTISH
TERRIBLE TERRIFIC TIMOROUS
FEARLESS BOLD BRAVE DARING
HEROIC AWELESS IMPAVID INTREPID
FEASIBLE FIT LIKELY POSSIBLE
PROBABLE SUITABLE
FEAST (ALSO SEE FESTIVAL) EAT
FOY SUP DINE FARM FETE LUAU
MEAL TUCK UTAS AZYME CHEER
CHOES CITUA DIRGY FESTA FESTY
GAUDY REVEL TREAT ARTHEL
AVERIL DEVOUR DINNER DOUBLE
INFARE JUNKET MAUNDY REGALE
REPAST SIMPLE SMOUSE SPREAD
AHAAINA BANQUET BRIDALE
DELIGHT FESTINO GRATIFY
GREGORY LAMBALE LEMURIA
SHEVUOS SYNAXIS ANALEPSY
CAROUSAL DOMINEER EPIPHANY

FESTIVAL GESTNING GESTONIE
HANUKKAH KOIMESIS PASSOVER
POTLATCH SHABUOTH VESTALIA
(— BEFORE JOURNEY) FOY
(— OF BOOTHS) SUCCOS SUKKOTH
(— OF LANTERNS) HON
(— OF LOTS) PURIM
(— OF WEEKS) SHEVUOS
SHABUOTH
(— PLACE) IDGAH
(DRINKING —) BANQUET
(FUNERAL —) ARVAL ARVEL DIRGY
DIRGIE DREDGIE
(HARVEST —) BUSK
(JEWISH —) SENDAH
(RELIGIOUS —) CANAO KANYAW
(VILLAGE —) TANSY
FEASTER CONVIVE
FEASTING FEAST CARNIVAL
FEAT ACT KIP DEED FATE GEST
WORK GESTE SPLIT STUNT TRICK
CRADDY CUTOFF EXPLOIT MASTERY
MIRACLE WORSHIP DEXTROUS
(CRICKETER'S —) DOUBLE
(TUMBLING —) SCISSORS
(PL.) DAGS
FEATHER BOO PEN TAB DECK DOWN
FLAG HERL SETA STUB VANE
ADORN AXIAL PENNA PINNA PLUMA
PLUME QUILL REMEX CLOTHE
COVERT CRINET FLEDGE FLETCH
FLIGHT HACKLE MANUAL PINION
SARCEL SICKLE TIPPET TONGUE
AXILLAR BRISTLE FLEMISH IMPLUME
PRIMARY RECTRIX REMICLE STIPULE
TERTIAL TOPPING AXILLARY
SCAPULAR STREAMER TERTIARY
(BRISTLELIKE —) VIBRISSA
(HAWK'S —S) BRAIL BRAILS
(HORSE —) SPEAR
(NEW —) STIPULE
(OSTRICH TAIL —) BOO
(PINION —) SARCEL
(TAIL —) SICKLE RECTRIX
(YELLOW —S) HULU
(PL.) GIG BOOT CAPE DOWN FLUE
MAIL BRAIL CRISSUM CUSHION
FLIGHTS PLUMAGE REMIGES
SPURIAE
FEATHER BED TYE
FEATHER CLOAK AHUULA TEMIAK
FEATHERED FLEDGE FLEDGY
PENNATE PINNATE FLIGHTED
FEATHERING STOCKING
FEATHER KEY FIN STOP SPLINE
FEATHER
FEATHER-LEGGED COOTY COOTIE
FEATHERLIKE PINNATE
FEATHERY PLUMY FLEDGY FLUFFY
PLUMOSE PLUMEOUS
FEATLY NEATLY FOOTINGLY
FEATURE WAY FACE ITEM NOTE
STAR BREAK FAVOR GRACE MOTIF
TOKEN TRACT TRAIT TREAT ASPECT
CACHET FAVOUR SPLASH AMENITY
OUTLINE HALLMARK SALIENCE
(— OF WORD FORM) ASPECT
(ATTRACTIVE —) AMENITY
(DETERMINING —) LIMIT

(DISTINGUISHING —) TRAIT STROKE
HALLMARK
(FATAL —) BANE
(LINGUISTIC —) ISOGLOSS
SURVIVAL
(MAIN —) CRUX
(MOST COGENT —) BEAUTY
(OBJECTIONABLE —) DISCOUNT
DRAWBACK
(SALIENT —) MOTIF
(TOPOGRAPHIC —) ARC
(TOPOGRAPHIC —S) LIE
(PL.) LAY FACE CONTOUR FASHION
GEOLOGY
FEAZE FRAY FAIZE ROUGHEN
FEBRIFUGE PEREIRA
FEBRILE PYRETIC FEVERISH
FECES DRAST HOCKEY ORDURE
FECKLESS WEAK FEEBLE
FECULENCE DREG
FECULENT DREGGY
FECUND FERTILE FRUITFUL PROLIFIC
FED FAT MEATED
FEDERATION BUND CROM UNION
LEAGUE NATION COUNCIL ALLIANCE
FEDERACY TRIALISM
FEE FEU DUES DUTY FEAL FEUL FIEF
FIER HIRE RATE WAGE CAULP
EXTRA HANSE PRICE RIGHT ALNAGE
AMOBER BARONY CHARGE DASTUR
EMPLOY EXCISE REWARD SALARY
SHEKEL BUOYAGE DASTURI
DUMPAGE DUSTOOR FIRNAGE
FURNAGE GAOLAGE GARNISH
GRATIFY GUIDAGE HALLAGE
HOUSAGE JAILAGE MULTURE
PAYMENT PINLOCK PREFINE
STIPEND STORAGE TALLAGE
TRIBUTE VANTAGE BOOTHAGE
BOUNTITH CHUMMAGE EXACTION
FAREWELL GRATUITY MALIKANA
POUNDAGE REREFIEF RETAINER
SHIPPAGE WHARFAGE
(— TO LANDOWNER) TERRAGE
(— TO TEACHER) MINERVAL
(CUSTOMARY —) DASTUR
(CUSTOMS —) LOT
(ENTRANCE —) HANSA HANSE
INCOME
(INITIATION —) FOOTING
(PHYSICIAN'S —) SOSTRUM
(UNAUTHORIZED —) GARNISH
(PL.) EXHIBITS
FEEBLE WAN FLUE LAME MEAN PALE
POOR PUNY SOFT WEAK DONCY
DOTTY FAINT SEELY SILLY SOBER
UNORN WANKY WASHY WONKY
CADUKE DEBILE DONSIE DOTAGE
FAINTY FLABBY FLIMSY FOIBLE
INFIRM PAULIE PUISNE SCANTY
SEMMIT SICKLY SIMPLE TANGLE
UNFIRM WANKLE WEANLY DWAIBLY
DWEEBLE FRAGILE INVALID LANGUID
QUEECHY RICKETY SAPLESS SHILPIT
SLENDER SLIMPSY UNWIELD
UNWREST DECREPIT DROGHLIN
FEATLESS IMBECILE IMPOTENT
INFERIOR MALADIVE RESOLUTE
THEWLESS THOWLESS UNSTRONG

UNWIELDY WATERISH YIELDING
FEEBLE-MINDED ANILE DOTTY
DOTTLE FOOLISH MORONIC
WANTING IMBECILE
FEEBLENESS DOTAGE FEEBLE
POVERTY CADUCITY DEBILITY
WEAKNESS
FEED EAT HAY BAIT BEET BRAN
CROP DIET DINE FILL FOOD GLUT
GRUB MEAL MEAT OATS SATE
AGIST FLESH FLUSH GORGE GRASS
GRAZE NURSE SERVE STOKE TABLE
BROWSE FODDER FOSTER INFEED
NOODLE REFETE REPAST SUCKLE
SUPPLY BLOWOUT FURNISH
GRATIFY HERBAGE INDULGE
KEEPING NOURISH NURTURE
PASTURE PROVENT SATIATE
SATISFY SUBSIST SURFEIT SUSTAIN
VICTUAL
(— **ABUNDANTLY**) STOKE
(— **ANIMAL**) SORT SERVE
(— **AT NIGHT**) SUP
(— **FOR CATTLE**) FODDER STOVER
TACKLE
(— **FORCIBLY**) CRAM
(— **GLUTTONOUSLY**) BATTEN
(— **GREEN FOOD TO CATTLE**) SOIL
(— **HIGH**) FRANK
(— **IN STUBBLE**) SHACK
(— **ON FLIES**) SMUT
(— **RAVENOUSLY**) FRAUNCH
(— **STOCK**) FOG SOIL SOILING
(— **TO REPLETION**) ENGORGE
(— **TO THE FULL**) SATIATE
(— **WELL**) BATTLE
(**GROUND** —) CHOP
(**POULTRY** —) SCRATCH
(**RED** —) HAYSEED
(**STOCK** —) BRAN
(**WHALE** —) GRIT
FEEDBOARD DECK
FEEDER HOGGER HOPPER PECKER
STOCKER
(**YARN** —) CARRIER
FEEDHEAD RISER FEEDER SINKHEAD
FEEDING RELIEF FOLDAGE PANNAGE
(— **GROUND FOR FISH**) MEADOW
(— **THROUGH TUBE**) GAVAGE
(**FREE-CHOICE** —) CAFETERIA
FEEL FIND PALP GROPE SENSE
THINK TOUCH FIMBLE FINGER
HANDLE RESENT EXAMINE EXPLORE
FEELING SENSATE PERCEIVE
(— **ACUTELY**) SUFFER
(— **AVERSION FOR**) HATE LOATHE
(— **CHILLY**) CREEM
(— **COMPASSION**) PITY YEARN
(— **DEJECTION**) REPINE
(— **FEAR**) UG GRUE UGGE TREMBLE
(— **GRIEF**) GRIEVE DEPLORE
(— **HAPPY OR BETTER**) LIGHT
(— **NAUSEA**) WAMBLE
(— **OF CLOTH**) HAND
(— **ONE'S WAY**) GROPE FUMBLE
GRAMMEL
(— **OUT**) SOUND
(— **PAIN**) URN
(— **REPUGNANCE**) ABHOR

(— **SHAME**) BLUSH
(— **WANT OF**) MISS
FEELER DRAW KITE PALP SNIFF
PALPUS TACTOR ANTENNA SMELLER
PROPOSAL TENTACLE
FEELING FEEL PITY TACT VIEW
CHEER HEART HUMOR SENSE
SORGE TOUCH AFFECT CEMENT
MORALE CONSENT EMOTION
OPINION PASSION VELUNGE
ATTITUDE SENTIENT
(— **ILL**) HOWISH
(— **MIRTH**) JOCUND
(— **OF ACCORD**) SYMPATHY
(— **OF AMUSEMENT**) CHARGE
(— **OF ANTIPATHY**) ALLERGY
(— **OF ANXIETY**) ANGST
(— **OF CONTEMPT**) DISDAIN
(— **OF DISGUST**) UG
(— **OF HORROR**) CREEP CREEPS
(— **OF HOSTILITY**) ANIMUS
(— **OF JOY**) GLOAT
(— **OF OPPOSITION**) KICK
(— **OF RESENTMENT**) GRUDGE
(— **OF ROMANCE**) STARDUST
(— **OF UNEASINESS**) MALAISE
(— **OF WEARINESS**) ENNUI
(— **OF WELL-BEING**) EUPHORIA
(**ANGERED** —) DUDGEON
(**BODILY** —) TABET
(**CONCEITED** —) SWELLING
(**ILL** —) HARDNESS
(**INTUITIVE** —) HUNCH
(**KINDLY** —) GOODWILL
(**REPRESSION OF** —) STOICISM
(**STRONG** —) STAB
(**PL.**) HEART WITHERS
FEET DOGS TONGS STAMPS
WALKERS GUNBOATS TRILBIES
(— **WASHING**) MAUNDY
(**BOARD** —) FOOTAGE
(**LARGE** —) GUFFINS
FEIGN ACT FAKE MINT MOCK SEEM
SHAM VEYN AVOID FABLE FALSE
FORGE PAINT SHAPE SHIRK AFFECT
ASSUME GAMMON INVENT POSSUM
CONCEAL FALSIFY FASHION IMAGINE
POETIZE PRETEND ROMANCE
DISGUISE SIMULATE
(— **ASSENT**) COLLOGUE
(— **IGNORANCE**) CONNIVE
(— **ILLNESS**) MALINGER
FEIGNED SHAM FALSE FEINT POETIC
PSEUDO ASSUMED COLORED
FICTIVE FICTIOUS SIMULATE
FEIGNING FICTION FORGERY
FEIJOA ANDRE
FEINT FAKE MINT RUSE APPEL FAINT
SHIFi SPOOF TRICK FALSIFY
FEIGNED FEINTER FINCTURE
PRETENSE REVIRADO
FELDSPAR AMBITE GNEISS CELSIAN
SYENITE ANDESINE FELSPATH
SANIDINE
FELICIA AGATHAEA
FELICITATE HUG BLESS MACARIZE
FELICITOUS FIT HAPPY
FELICITOUSLY HAPPILY
FELICITY JOY BLISS SONSE HEAVEN

FELINE CATTISH
FELL CUR FEN HEW DOWN DROP
FALL HIDE HILL MOOR PELT RUIN
SKIN VERY CRUEL EAGER FIELD
GRASS GREAT SHARP DEADLY
FIERCE FLEECE INTENT MIGHTY
SAVAGE SHREWD TUMBLE BRUTISH
CRASHED DOUGHTY HIDEOUS
INHUMAN STRETCH TUMBLED
MOUNTAIN SPIRITED VIGOROUS
(— **A TREE**) HEW LODGE
FELLER GIDEON
FELLING FALL CUTTING
FELLOE BOD FELF FALLY
FELLOW S BO BOY COD DON EGG
FOX GUY JOE LAD MAC MAN MUN
NUT WAG WAT YOB BALL BEAN
BEAU BIRD BOZO BUFF CARL CHAL
CHAP COVE CUSS DEAN DICK DUCK
DULL GENT GILL GINK HIND HUSK
JACK JAKE JOHN LOON MATE NABS
PEER PRIG SNAP BILLY BIMBO
BLOKE BROCK BUDDY BULLY CARLE
CHIEL COVEY FRUIT GROOM GUEST
JOKER MATCH PARTY SCOUT SKATE
SLAVE SPORT SPRIG SWIPE
BEGGAR BILLIE BIRKIE BOHUNK
BOOGER BUDDIE BUFFER BUGGER
BUSTER CALLAN CHIELD CODGER
CUFFIN CUTTER FELLER FOOTER
FOUTER FOUTRA GALOOT GAZABO
HOMBRE JASPER JOCKEY JOHNNY
JOSSER KIPPER PERSON SHAVER
SINNER SIRRAH SISTER SOCIUS
TURNIP BASTARD BROTHER
CALLANT CHAPPIE COMRADE
CULLIES CULLION CUSTRON
KNOCKER PARTNER SCROYLE
SNOOZER BLIGHTER CONFRERE
DOTTEREL MERCHANT NEIGHBOR
SYNODITE
(**AWKWARD** —) OAF CLUB GAWK
CLOWN LOOBY GALOOT SLOUCH
(**BASE** —) CARL CARLE CULLION
(**BASHFUL** —) SHEEP
(**BOLD** —) HEARTY
(**BRUTAL** —) CLUBFIST
(**CLOWNISH** —) COOF BAYARD
LOBLOLLY
(**CLUMSY** —) FILE CAMEL FARMER
LUBBER
(**COMMON** —) JACK LOUT
(**CONCEITED** —) JEMMY DALTEEN
(**CONTEMPTIBLE** —) DOG SCUT
SMAIL SNAKE RABBIT SMATCH
PEASANT
(**CONTENTIOUS** —) SQUARER
(**CORPULENT** —) POMPION
(**COUNTRY** —) JAKE JASPER
(**CRUDE** —) STIFF
(**DASHING** —) BUCK BLADE
(**DASTARDLY** —) HOUND
(**DESPICABLE** —) FOUTER FOUTRA
HANGDOG SMATCHET
(**DIRTY** —) SCAB BROCK
(**DISAGREEABLE** —) GLEYDE
(**DISSOLUTE** —) RAKE ROUE
RAKEHELL
(**DROLL** —) CARD

(DROWSY —) LUNGIS
(DULL —) BUFF DRIP FOGY LUNGIS HUMDRUM
(FAT —) HIND GULCH GLUTTON
(FIERCE-LOOKING —) KILLBUCK
(FINE —) BAWCOCK
(FOOLISH —) SOP GABY GOFF ZANY GANDER JACKSON WIDGEON
(GOOD —) BRICK BULLY TRUMP HEARTY
(GOOD-FOR-NOTHING —) JACKEEN
(GREEDY —) SLOTE
(IDLE —) FANION FOOTER STOCAH LOLLARD SKULKER
(IGNORANT —) GOBBIN
(ILLBRED —) LARRIKIN
(IMPERTINENT —) JACK WHISK
(INSIGNIFICANT —) SQUIB
(JOLLY —) VAVASOR VAVASOUR
(LAZY —) BUM LUSK TOOL LENTO
(LOW —) RAG WAFF SWEEP LIMMER VARLET MECHANIC WHORESON
(MEAN —) CAD DOG BOOR BOUCH BUCKO CAVEL CHURL SCURF RASCAL CULLION COISTREL SNEAKSBY SPALPEEN STINKARD
(NIGGARDLY —) SNUDGE
(NOISY —) MOUTH
(OLD —) GLYDE GAFFER GEEZER
(OLD-FASHIONED —) FOGY
(OVERBEARING —) GRIMSIR
(PROSAIC —) PRUNE
(PUNY —) SMAIK
(QUARRELSOME —) HECTOR
(QUEER OLD —) GEEZER
(RESIDENTIAL —) DON
(ROGUISH —) DOG
(RUDE —) JACK ROUGH
(SHABBY —) SHAB SQUEEF
(SHEEPISH —) SUMPH
(SHIFTLESS —) PROG SHACK PROGGER
(SHREWD —) COLT
(SILLY —) TOT GUMP ZANY SHEEP SMAIK DOTTEREL MUSHHEAD
(SIMPLE —) DOODLE
(SLOVENLY —) SLUTE
(SLY —) FOX
(SNEAKING —) SNUDGE
(SORDID —) HUNKS
(SOUTH AFRICAN —) KEREL
(SPORTY —) PLAYBOY
(STRANGE —) CODGER
(STRAPPING —) SWANKY SWANKIE
(STUPID —) ASS CLOD COOF DAFF DOLT GUMP HASH MUFF SIMP BOOBY DUNCE MORON STIRK BAYARD FARMER FOOZLE GANDER DOWFART CODSHEAD SOCKHEAD
(SULLEN —) GLUMP
(TRICKISH —) HUMBUG
(TRICKY —) ROOK GREEK KNAVE SCAMP DODGER RASCAL
(UNCIVIL —) RUDESBY
(UNCOUTH —) JAKE KEMP TIKE
(VILE —) RAT SKUNK
(VULGAR —) TIGER
(WORTHLESS —) BUM CUR DOG HASH PROG WAFF JAVEL ROGUE

SCAMP SHOAT SNAKE BROTHEL BUDMASH PROGGER VAURIEN TARTARET
(WRETCHED —) DEVIL DOGBOLT
(YOUNG —) BILLY BUCKO CADIE CADDIE
FELLOWMAN BROTHER
FELLOWSHIP GUILD HAUNT UNION FAMILY COMPANY ALLIANCE SODALITY
(CHRISTIAN —) KOINONIA
FELLY RIM FELF FELLOE KEENLY CRUELLY BITTERLY FIERCELY SAVAGELY TERRIBLY
FELO-DE-SE SUICIDE
FELON WILD CRUEL FETLOW FIERCE WICKED CONVICT CULPRIT PANARIS VILLAIN WHITLOW PHLEGMON RUNROUND
FELONY ARSON CRIME OFFENSE
FELT JIG PLAIT FILTER SENSED SOLEIL VELOUR DOUBLER FELTING PANNOSE
(— INTENSIVELY) ACUTE
(— THROUGH SENSES) SENSATE
(DEEPLY —) CORDIAL INTENSE
(PERSONALLY —) CONSCIOUS
(PL.) CLOTHING
FELTWORK NEUROPIL
FEMALE DOE EWE HER SHE SOW DAME GIRL GYNE LADY MORT ADULT JENNY SMOCK SQUAW WOMAN WAHINE WEAKLY DISTAFF FEMINAL WOMANLY DAUGHTER FEMININE GYNAECIC LADYLIKE WOMANISH
(— ANCESTOR) TAPROOT
(IMPERFECT —) FREEMARTIN
(PARTHOGENETIC —) AMAZON
FEMININE FAIR SOFT WEAK WOMAN FEMALE TENDER WAHINE FEMINAL WOMANLY WOMANISH
FEMININITY MUSLIN FEMINITY
FEMME FATALE SIREN
FEMORAL CRURAL
FEMUR THIGH
FEN BOG CARR FAIN FELL FOWL MERE MOOR WASH BROAD FAINS MARSH SNIPE SWAMP VENTS MORASS QUAGMIRE
FENCE BAR HAW HAY BANK DIKE DUEL DYKE HAHA HAIN PALE PLAY RAIL STUB WALL WEIR WIRE BEARD DODGE FRITH GUARD HEDGE MOUND PALIS STICK STUMP DETENT FENDER GLANCE HURDLE LEADER PALING PICKET RADDLE RASPER SCHERM SCRIME TIMBER BARRIER BULWARK CYCLONE DEFENSE ENCLOSE FENCING FENSURE IMPALER PASSAGE RAILING SWAGMAN BACKSTOP ENCHASER ENCLOSER GRAFFAGE HOARDING PALISADE PALISADO SEPIMENT SKIRMISH
(— AROUND BULLRING) BARRERA
(— CLOSING DITCH) WOLF
(— OF LOCK) STUB
(— OF LOGS) GLANCE

(CATTLE —) WIPE SKERM SCHERM
(FISH —) WEIR LEADER
(METAL —) RAIL RAILING
FENCER DUELIST IMPALER PARRIER PROVOST SCRIMER SWORDER FOILSMAN BACKSWORD
FENCE RAIL DRAWBAR
FENCE SECTION PANE
FENCE-SITTER MUGWUMP
FENCING WIRE FENCE PALING ESCRIME PASSAGE SCIENCE SWORDING
FEND WARD PARRY SHIRK DEFEND FORBID RESIST SUPPORT
FENDER SKID WING CAMEL GUARD SKATE BUFFER BUMPER SHIELD DOLPHIN PUDDING BOWGRACE SPLASHER
(— FOR FIREPLACE) CURB KERB
(— NEAR HOLE) TELLTALE
FENDER SKID GLANCER
FENESTRA FORAMEN
FENGHUANG FUM PHOENIX
FENKS FRITTERS
FENMAN WEBFOOT
FENNEC ZERDA
FENNEL ANIS DILL HEMP SOYA FERULE FINKEL COWBANE HOGWEED SPINGEL FINOCHIO FLORENCE CAROSELLA
FENNER ZERDA
FENSTER WINDOW
FENUGREEK BAUMIER MELLILOT
(SEEDS OF —) HELBEH
FERAL WILD BRUTAL DEADLY FERINE SAVAGE BESTIAL UNTAMED FUNEREAL UNBROKEN
FER-DE-LANCE BONETAIL JARARACA
FERMATA HOLD PAUSE TENOR CORONA
FERMENT FRY LOB ZYM BARM FRET HEAT SOUR TURN WORK ZYME FEVER SWEAT YEAST DANDER ENZYME FLOWER FOMENT SEETHE SIMMER TUMULT UPROAR AGITATE QUICKEN TURMOIL DISORDER
FERMENTATION SWEAT CUVAGE FERMENT MOWBURN WORKING ZYMOSIS
FERMENTED SOD
(IMPROPERLY —) FOXY
FERMENTING WORKING
FERN HEII NITO PULU TARA WEKI BRAKE DUGAL EKAHA FROND NARDO PITAU PONGA ULUHI WHEKI AMAMAU DOODIA NARDOO OSMUND PTERIS ACROGEN ATERACH BOGFERN BRACKEN SYNANGE WOODSIA ADIANTUM ASPIDIUM BUCKHORN BUNGWALL CETERACH DAVALLIA DENDRITE FERNWORT FILICITE GOLDBACK HARDFERN KOLOKOLO MOONWORT MULEWORT PARAREKA PILLWORT POLYPODY SPOROGEN STAGHORN
FERN LEAF FROND CROSIER
FERNLIKE FERNY PTEROID
FEROCIOUS ILL FELL GRIM RUDE

WILD CRUEL FERAL BLOODY
BRUTAL FEROCE FIERCE GOTHIC
RAGING SAVAGE ACHARNE INHUMAN
OMINOUS VIOLENT WOLFISH
PITILESS RAVENOUS RUTHLESS
TARTARLY
FEROCITY FERITY SAVAGERY
VIOLENCE
FERRARA ANDREW
FERRET HOB MONK TAPE PADOU
MONACH WEASEL POLECAT
(— OUT) FOSSICK
(FEMALE —) GIL GILL JILL BITCH
(MALE —) HOB HOBB
FERRIAGE WAFTAGE
FERRIC OXIDE CROCUS
FERROTYPE GLAZE TINTYPE
FERROUS SIDEROUS
FERRULE CAP TIP CUFF RING SHOE
VIRL COLLET PULLEY RUNNER
VERREL VIROLE ARMGARN BUSHING
CRAMPET
FERRY FORD PASS PONT SCOW
PASSAGE TRAJECT TRANSFER
FERRYBOAT BAC PONT FERRY
FERRYMAN CHARON FERRIER
WATERMAN
FERTILE FAT GOOD RANK RICH
GLEBY BATFUL BATTLE FECUND
HEARTY STRONG TEEMING
ABUNDANT BATTABLE FRUITFUL
GENEROUS PREGNANT PROLIFIC
SPAWNING
FERTILITY HEART FATNESS
(PATRON OF —) YAKSHA
FERTILIZATION ENDOGAMY
POROGAMY
FERTILIZE FAT DUNG FISH LIME
MARL CHALK BATTEN ENRICH
FRUCTIFY
FERTILIZER FAT MARL GUANO
HUMUS ALINIT FLOATS MANURE
POLLEN POTASH CARRIER
COMPOTE KAINITE NITRATE
TANKAGE AMMONITE CINEREAL
NITROGEN
FERULA NARTHEX
FERULE ROD RULER COLLET FENNEL
FERULA PALMER
FERVENCY WARMTH CANDENCY
FERVENT HOT KEEN WARM EAGER
FIERY ARDENT BITTER FERVID
FIERCE INWARD RAGING SAVAGE
BOILING BURNING GLOWING
INTENSE PECTORAL VEHEMENT
FERVID HOT ARDENT TROPIC
BOILING BURNING FERVENT
GLOWING ZEALOUS UNCTUOUS
VEHEMENT
FERVOR FIRE HEAT RAGE SOUL
ZEAL ARDOR WARMTH PASSION
CANDENCY DEVOTION STRENGTH
VIOLENCE
(— IN PRAYER) KAVVANAH
KAWWANAH
FESCUE VESTER
FESS BAR BAND PERT DANCE HUMET
FESTAL GAY GALA GAUDY FESTIVE
FESTUAL FEASTFUL

FESTER ROT BEAL RANK SCAR
RANKLE PUSTULE PUTREFY
FESTERING FRETTY
FESTIVAL (ALSO SEE FEAST) ALE
BON PWE BUSK FAIR FEIS FETE
GALA HOLI MELA TIDE UTAS WAKE
DELIA FEAST FERIA FESTA GAUDY
HALOA PURIM REVEL ROUSE SEDAR
BAIRAM BRIDAL CARNEA DEWALI
DIASIA DIPALA FIESTA HOHLEE
HUFFLE KERMIS LAMMAS LENAEA
OPALIA PONGOL POOJAH SUCCOS
AGONIUM AGRANIA BANQUET
BELTANE DASAHRA EQUIRIA
FESTIAL HILARIA KERMESS MATSURI
SUKKOTH THIASOS TOXCATL
UPHELYA VINALIA AGRIONIA
AIANTEIA APATURIA ATHENAEA
BEALTINE BRUMALIA CARNIVAL
COTYTTIA DASAHARA DIIPOLIA
DIONYSIA DUSSERAH ENCAENIA
FASNACHT FLORALIA HANUKKAH
HIGHTIDE KALENDAE MARYMASS
MATRALIA MITHRIAC MUHARRAM
MUNYCHIA NATIVITY NEOMENIA
POTLATCH STAMPEDE
(PL.) MOED VOTA
FESTIVE GAY GALA JOLLY FESTAL
GENIAL JOYOUS FEASTLY HOLIDAY
JOCULAR CONVIVAL FEASTFUL
MIRTHFUL SPORTIVE
FESTIVITY GALA UTAS UTIS FEAST
MIRTH RANDY REVEL GAIETY
GAYETY SPLORE HOLIDAY JOLLITY
JOYANCE PATTERN FESTIVAL
FUNCTION
FESTOON SWAG WREATH GARLAND
DECORATE
(PL.) ENCARPUS
FETCH FET FESH GASP GIVE SHAG
TACK TAKE TEEM WAIN BRING
SWEEP TRICK DOUBLE STROKE
WRAITH ACHIEVE ATTRACT ARTIFICE
FETCHING INTEREST
FETCHED FOSH
FETCHING SWEET CRAFTY CUNNING
ALLURING PLEASING SCHEMING
FETE FAIR GALA FEAST HONOR
BAZAAR FIESTA HOLIDAY
FETID OLID RANK MUSTY PUTID
ROTTEN VIROSE NOISOME
FETIDLY FOULLY
FETISH OBI IDOL JUJU OBIA ZEME
ZEMI ZOGO ANITO ASCON CHARM
GUACA HUACA OBEAH OBIAH
TOTEM FETICH GRIGRI NAGUAL
VOODOO SHINTAI SORCERY
FETISHRY GREEGREE TALISMAN
FETLOCK COOT FOOTLOCK
FETTER BAND BEND BOLT BOND
FIND GYVE IRON SPAN BASIL BEWET
BILBO CHAIN SWATH ANKLET
GARTER HALTER HAMPER HOBBLE
HOPPLE IMPEDE LANGEL RACKAN
SWATHE CLINKER CONFINE ENCHAIN
FETLOCK GARNISH MANACLE
SHACKLE SPANCEL TRAMMEL
RESTRAIN
(PL.) IRONS LINKS DARBIES

GARNISH GARTERS
FETTERBUSH PIPESTEM PIPEWOOD
FETTLE BEAT DECK FUSS MULL TIDY
VEIN DRESS GROOM WHACK YARAK
GIRDLE REPAIR SETTLE STRIKE
ARRANGE BANDAGE FEATHER
HARNESS
FETTLER BILLYER NOBBLER
FETTLING FIX FETTLE FIXING
FETUS BIRTH CHILD YOUNG AMELUS
BREECH EMBRYO FOETUS ABORTUS
CYCLOPS FEATURE AMORPHUS
FEUD FIEF FRAY BROIL AFFRAY
ENMITY FEODUM FEUDUM STRIFE
CONTEST DISPUTE QUARREL
VENDETTA
FEUDATORY FIEF VASSAL ZAMINDAR
ZEMINDAR
FEUILLE MORTE PHILAMOT
FEVER AGUE FIRE ARDOR CAUMA
DANDY LEUMA OCTAN CAUSUS
DENGUE FEBRIS HECTIC SEPTAN
SEXTAN SODOKU TYPHIA TYPHUS
AMAKEBE FERMENT FEVERET
HELODES MALARIA PINKEYE
PYREXIA QUARTAN TERTIAN
TYPHOID SYNOCHUS TERTIANA
TYPHINIA
(— OF HORSE) SCALMA
(BRAIN —) PHRENITIS
(MALARIAL —) TAP
(MARSH —) HELODES
(TEXAS —) TRISTEZA
FEVERED DISEASED
FEVERFEW MAYWEED MUGWORT
FEVERISH HOT FIERY FEVERY
HECTIC EXCITED FEBRILE FRANTIC
RESTLESS
FEVERLESS APYREXIA
FEVERROOT GENSON
FEVER TREE BITTERBARK
FEVERWEED FITWEED
FEW LIT CURN LESS SOME SCANT
THREE WHEEN WHONE CURRAN
PICKLE LIMITED EXIGUOUS
FEWER LESS
FEWNESS PAUCITY
FEY DEAD DYING ELFIN FATAL
UNLUCKY
FEZ TARBOOSH
FIADOR THEODORE
FIANCE TRUST SPOUSE FIANCEE
PROMISE AFFIANCE
FIASCO CRASH FLASK FROST FIZZLE
FAILURE DISASTER
FIAT EDICT ORDER DECREE
COMMAND DECISION SANCTION
FIB LIE YED FLAW WHID SLANT
STORY FITTEN PUMMEL SKLENT
FIBBER LIAR
FIBER TAL ADAD BASS BAST COIR
ERUC FERU FLAX HARL HEMP IMBE
JUTE LINE PITA SILK SUNN TULA
ABACA AGUST AZLON CAJUN
CAROA CHOEL ERIZO FIBRE GRAIN
HARLE ISOTE ISTLE IXTLE IZOTE
KENAF KITUL MURVA OAKUM RAMIE
RAPHE SIMAL SISAL STRAW TERAP
TOSSA TUCUM VIVER AMIRAY

BINDER BUNTAL BURITI CABUYA
CATENA DACRON EMBIRA FIBRIL
FIMBLE HINOKI KANAFF KENDIR
KOHEMP MUCUNA NYTRIL RAFFIA
SALAGO STAPLE STRAND STRING
SUTURE THREAD TUCUMA TURURI
VINYON YACHAN ZAPUPE ACETATE
ACRYLIC ANONANG ARAMINA
BASSINE CANTALA CASCARA
CHANDUL CHINGMA COQUITA
ESPARTO FILASSE GEBANGA
GRAVATA GUAXIMA GUMIHAN
HUARIZO KERATTO KITTOOL
MOCMAIN PALMITE PANGANE
PAUKPAN POCHOTE SABUTAN
CANAPINA CURRATOW FILAMENT
HARAKEKE HENEQUEN PIASSAVA
TOQUILLA TRONADOR
(— FROM PEACOCK FEATHERS)
MARL
(— OF PALM) DOH LIF ERUC COYOL
COROZO GOMUTI COQUITA
GEBANGA
(—S OF FLAX) HARE
(CLUSTER OF —S) NEP
(COARSE —) KEMP
(COCONUT —) COIR KYAR
(COTTON —) LINT STAPLE
(KNOT OF —) NOIL
(MANUFACTURED —) DYNEL
ESTRON SPANDEX
(MATTED —) SHAG
(MINERAL —) ASBESTOS
(MUSCLE —) RHABDIUM
(NERVE —) EFFERENT DEPRESSOR
(PULVERIZED —) FLOCK
(SILKY —) KAPOK KUMBI YACHAN
CASTULI
(TWISTED —S) STRAND
(WASTE —) FLY GOUT
(WASTE —S) FLOSS
(WOODY —) BAST GRAIN SCUTCH
(PL.) FUZZ KERATTO
FIBRIL AXONEME DESMOSE
MYONEME MYOPHAN
FIBRIN GLUTEN MYOSIN
FIBROCARTILAGE FABELLA
MENISCUS
FIBROID DESMOID
FIBROMA INOMA FIBROID
FIBROUS FIBROSE STRINGY
NEMALINE
FIBULA LACE CLASP BROOCH
BUCKLE SPLINT
FICKLE GERY DIZZY FALSE GIDDY
LIGHT UNSAD HARLOT KITTLE
MOBILE PUZZLE SHIFTY VOLAGE
WANKLE WANKLY CASALTY
CASELTY FLATTER MOVABLE
MUTABLE VAINFUL VARIANT
VOLUBLE GOSSAMER MOVEABLE
SKITTISH STIRRING UNSTABLE
UNSTEADY VARIABLE VOLATILE
WAVERING
FICKLENESS LEVITY EASINESS
FICKLETY VARIANCE
FICO FIG FIGO TANTI
FICTION TALE FABLE FALSE NOVEL
ROMAN STORY DECEIT DEVICE

FABULA FITTEN LEGEND COINAGE
FANTASY FIGMENT FORGERY
MARCHEN NOVELRY ROMANCE
ROMANZA KAILYARD PHANTASY
FICTITIOUS BOGUS DUMMY FALSE
PHONY FABLED POETIC ASSUMED
FEIGNED FABULOUS FICTIOUS
MYTHICAL ROMANTIC SIMULATE
SPURIOUS LEGENDARY
FICUS PYRULA
FID PRICK NORMAN PRICKER
SPLICER
FIDDLE BOW BOX GIG SAW VIOL
CHEAT CROWD GEIGE GIGUE
GUDOK CHORUS FITHEL POTTER
TRIFLE URHEEN VIOLIN CHROTTA
SWINDLE HUMSTRUM
(— STRING) THAIRM
(— WITH) TWIDDLE
FIDDLER CRAB VIOLER VIOLIN
CROWDER SCRAPER SIXPENCE
FIDDLER CRAB RACER FIDDLER
OCYPODE SOLDIER
FIDDLESTICKS PSHAW FIDDLE
FIDELITY TRUE ARDOR FAITH PIETY
TROTH TRUTH FEALTY HONESTY
LOYALTY ADHESION DEVOTION
RELIGION VERACITY
FIDGET MOP FIKE FIRK FUSS ROIL
FIDGE FITCH HOTCH SHRUB SHRUG
WORRY BREVIT FIGGLE FISSLE
FISTLE FRIDGE FUSSER HIRSEL
JIFFLE JIGGET NESTLE NIBBLE
NIGGLE TIDDLE TRIFLE VIGGLE
WORRIT NERVOUS RESTLESS
TWITCHET
(— ABOUT TRIFLES) SPOFFLE
(STATE OF —) FANTAD FANTOD
(PL.) JUMPS
FIDGETY FIKIE FUSSY ITEMY FEISTY
FIGENT FLISKY KITTLE UNEASY
RESTIVE TWITCHY RESTLESS
FIDUCIARY TRUSTEE TRUSTFUL
FIE SISS FAUGH
FIEF FEE HAN FEUD FEOFF TIMAR
ZIAMET SATSUMA SUBFIEF
BENEFICE
(— HOLDER) TIMARIOT
FIELD LEA LOT ACRE AGER AREA
BENT CAMP FELL FLAT HADE INAM
LAND LIST MEAD PALE PARK RAND
TOWN WONG BRECK CAMPO CHAMP
CLOUR CROFT EARTH GLEBE INNAM
LAYER MILPA NILPA PADDY RANGE
ROWEN SAWAH TILTH VELDE
ARRISH CAMPUS CAREER CHAMPE
DOMAIN FURROW GARDEN GROUND
MACHAR MATTER MEADOW PINGLE
SHIELD SPHERE CHARMEL COMPASS
CULTURE DIAMOND FERRING
GARSTON INFIELD MOWLAND
NEWTAKE PADDOCK PARROCK
PIGHTLE PURVIEW QUILLET TERRAIN
THWAITE TILLAGE CLEARING
PROVINCE
(— ADJOINING HOUSE) CROFT
(— AT CRICKET) SCOUT
(— OF ACTIVITY) GAME ARENA
BARONY SPHERE TERRAIN

(— OF BATTLE) PLAIN
(— OF BLOODSHED) ACELDAMA
AKELDAMA
(— OF CONTROL) DOMAIN
(— OF ENDEAVOR) BUSINESS
(— OF SNOW) NEVE SNOWPACK
(— OF STUDY) GROUND
(— ON WHICH GRASS IS GROWN)
MEAD MEADOW
**(— SOWN FOR TWO SUCCESSIVE
YEARS)** HOOK
(ENCLOSED —) AGER TOWN CLOSE
CROFT
(FOOTBALL —) GRIDIRON
(FRUITFUL —) CHARMEL
(GRASSY —) LEA PEN GARSTON
(HOP —) HOPYARD
(LAVA —) PEDREGAL
(LITTLE-KNOWN —) BYWAY
(NEW GOLD —) RUSH
(PLOWED —) FURROW
(RICE —) SAWAH
(SMALL —) HAW CROFT PADDOCK
GRATTEN GRATTON
(STUBBLE —) HIRSH ROWEN ARRISH
(TILTING —) LISTS
(TOBACCO —) VEGA
(UNEXPLOITED —) FRONTIER
(UNPLOWED EDGE OF —) RAND
(PL.) FIELDEN
FIELD BALM SHEEPMINT
FIELD CAMOMILE OXEYE
FIELDER GLOVEMAN
(CRICKET —) SLIP COVER FIELD
GULLY SCOUT GULLEY INFIELDER
FIELDFARE FELT JACK REDLEG
FELLFARE HILLBIRD JACKBIRD
REDSHANK SNOWBIRD VELTFARE
FIELD MADDER SPURWORT
FIELD MOUSE VOLE MIGALE
FIELDPIECE GUN AMUSETTE
GALLOPER
FIELD SCABIOUS BLUECAP
FIELDWORK LUNET REDAN LUNETTE
FIEND FEN FOE PUG FEND FYND
DEMON DEVIL ENEMY SATAN TRULL
WIZARD SHAITAN SUCCUBA TITIVIL
BARBASON SUCCUBUS
FIENDISH CRUEL WICKED DEMONIC
FIENDLY SATANIC DEMONIAC
DEVILISH DIABOLIC INFERNAL
FIERCE ILL BOLD FELL GRIM KEEN
RUDE THRO ASPER BREME CRUEL
EAGER FELON HATEL ORPED RETHE
SHARP SMART STARK STERN
STOUR STOUT WROTH ARDENT
FEROCE GOTHIC HETTER IMMANE
RAGING RUGGED SAVAGE STURDY
UNMEEK UNMILD WICKED BRUTISH
FERVENT FURIOSO FURIOUS
GRIMFUL INHUMAN MANKIND
RABIOUS RAMPANT SCADDLE
VIOLENT STERNFUL TIGERISH
FIERCE-EYED WALLEYED
FIERCELY FELL HARD FELLY FIERCE
FIERCENESS FURY FEROCITY
FIERY HOT RED ADUST FIRED QUICK
SHARP ARDENT FLASHY IGNITE
BURNING FERVENT FLAMING

FURIOUS GLOWING HOTHEAD
IGNEOUS PARCHED PEPPERY
VIOLENT ADUSTIVE CHOLERIC
FEVERISH FRAMPOLD INFLAMED
PHRAMPEL SPIRITED SPITFIRE
VEHEMENT
FIESTA FETE FERIA PARTY HOLIDAY
  (— COSTUME) POLLERA
FIFE STICK PIFERO PIFFERO
FIFTEEN FIVE
FIFTEENTH DOUBLETTE
FIFTH QUINT QUINTIN
FIFTY (— YEAR ANNIVERSARY)
  JUBILEE
FIFTY-FIFTY EVEN
FIG RIG FICO ARRAY BREBA DRESS
  ELEME ELEMI PIPAL SABRA TANTI
  BALETE BALITI FOUTER FOUTRA
  GINGER LOBFIG PEEPUL TRIFLE
  FURBISH GONDANG SICONUS
  SYCONUS WARINGIN
  (— CROP) MAMME
FIG BASKET CABAS
FIGHT BOX MIX WAP WAR WIN BEAT
  BEEF BLUE BOUT CAMP CLEM COCK
  COPE COWP CRAB CUFF DUEL FLOG
  FRAY LAKE MEET MELL MILL SHOW
  SLUG SPAR TILT WAGE YOKE
  BRAWL CLASH FIELD FLOLT HURRY
  JOUST MATCH MELEE SCRAP SHINE
  SPURN STOUR TOUSE AFFAIR
  AFFRAY BARNEY BATTLE BICKER
  COMBAT DEBATE FEUCHT FRACAS
  FRAISE HASSLE IMPUGN MEDDLE
  OPPOSE RELUCT REPUGN RESIST
  RIPPIT RUFFLE SHOWER STOUSH
  STRIFE STRIKE STRIVE TOUSEL
  TURNUP BARGAIN BRABBLE
  CONTEND CONTEST COUNTER
  JOURNEY QUARREL RUCTION
  SIMULTY TUILYIE WARFARE
  CONFLICT DOGFIGHT DUOMACHY
  FINISHER GUNFIGHT MILITATE
  SKIRMISH SQUABBLE STRUGGLE
  TIRRIVEE TIRRWIRR TRAVERSE
  (— AGAINST) BUCK
  (— BETWEEN TWO) DUEL
  DUOMACHY
  (— FOR) SERVE CHAMPION
  (— WITH CLUB) TIMBER
  (FIST —) RIPPIT TURNUP
  (SEA —) NAUMACHY
  (STREET —) HABBLE
FIGHTER PUG VAMP BOXER COCKER
  BATTLER DUELIST SLUGGER
  SOLDIER WARRIOR ANDABATA
  BARRATER BARRATOR CHAMPION
  GUERILLA PUGILIST SCRAPPER
  (FIRE —) EXEMPT HOTSHOT
FIGHTING BLOW AFFRAY DEBATE
  WARLIKE CONFLICT MILITANT
  (— WITH SHADOW) SCIAMACHY
FIGHTING FISH PLAKAT
FIG MARIGOLD SAMH MESEM
  FICOID FOXCHOP FICOIDAL
FIGMENT IDEA FICTION
FIGPECKER BECCAFICO
FIGURATE FLORID FIGURAL FIGURED
  FIGURATO

FIGURATION FORM SHAPE DESIGN
  OUTLINE
FIGURATIVE FLORID FIGURAL
  FIGURED FLOWERY TYPICAL
  ALLUSIVE TROPICAL
FIGURE HUE VOL BOSH DOLL FORM
  IDEA SIGN STAR ANGLE ANTIC
  DATUM DIGIT FLIRT FRAME IMAGE
  MAGOT MOTIF SHAPE SPADE SPRIG
  BABOON CHANGE CIPHER COCKUP
  CUTOUT DEVICE EFFIGY EMBLEM
  ENTAIL FIGGER GOOGOL INCUSE
  NUMBER PERSON SCHEME SYMBOL
  TAILLE TATTOO CHASSIS CHEVRON
  CHIFFER CHIFFRE COMPUTE
  CONTOUR DRAWING GESTALT
  IMPRESS NUMERAL OUTLINE
  STATURE DIHEDRAL FIGURATE
  GRAFFITO HEXAGRAM LIKENESS
  SEMBLANT
  **(— FORMED BY INTERSECTING
  LINES)** KNOT
  (— IN PRAYER) ORANT
  (— IN WOOD GRAIN) BURL FLAKE
  (— MADE OF 3 LINES) TRIGRAM
  TRIANGLE
  (— MADE OF CORN) KNACK
  (— OF SPEECH) IMAGE IRONY
  TROPE APORIA CLIMAX FLOWER
  SCHEME SIMILE VISION ANALOGY
  IMAGERY METAPHOR METONYMY
  (— OUT) BOTTOM
  (— UP) ITEM
  (— USED AS COLUMN) ATLAS
  TELAMON CARYATID
  (— USED AS MAGIC SYMBOL)
  PENTACLE
  (—S OF SPEECH) COLORS
  (ANATOMICAL —) ECORCHE
  (ARTIFICIAL —) GOLEM
  (BIBLICAL —) ANGEL CHERUB
  (CARVED —) GLYPH FIGURINE
  (CENTRAL —) HERO
  (CIRCULAR —) HOOP
  (COMIC —) BILLIKEN
  (CONSPICUOUS —) MARK
  (CRESCENT-SHAPED —) LUNE
  (DANCE —) SWING TRACE SQUARE
  PURPOSE ASSEMBLE
  (DOMINANT —) CAPTAIN
  (FEMALE —) ORANTE
  (GEOMETRICAL —) BODY CONE
  CUBE LUNE PRISM RHOMB SOLID
  CIRCLE GNOMON ISAGON ISOGON
  OBLONG SECTOR SQUARE DIAGRAM
  ELLIPSE LOZENGE PELCOID
  RHOMBUS SECTION HEXAFOIL
  SPHEROID
  (GREEK —) KOUROS
  (GROTESQUE —) MAGOT BABCON
  MAXIMON
  (IDEAL —) EIDOLON
  (IMAGINARY —) BOGEYMAN
  (INCISED —) INTAGLIO
  (MUMMYLIKE —) USHABTI
  (MUSICAL —) IDEA LICK
  (ODD —) MAUMET
  (OVAL —) SWASH ELLIPSE
  (PREHISTORIC —) CHACMOL

CHACMOOL
  (QUADRILLE —) POULE
  (QUEER —) GIG
  (RHYTHMIC —) SNAP
  (SHADOW —) SKIAGRAM
  (SKATING —) SPIRAL BRACKET
  COUNTER
  (SPINDLE-SHAPED —) FUSEE FUZEE
  (STUFFED —) DUMMY
  (SYLLOGISTIC —) SCHEMA
  (SYMBOLIC —) MORAL EMBLEM
  (TRIANGULAR —) TRIQUET
  (UNDRAPED —) NUDE
  (WINGED —) ANGEL EIDOLON
  (PL.) SPILING
FIGURED FIGURY FACONNE
FIGUREHEAD DUMMY FRONT
  SCROLL
FIGURINE TANAGRA CRIOPHORE
FIGWORT BARTSIA PILEWORT

FIJI
BAY: MBYA NATEWA NGALOA SAVUSAVU
CAPITAL: SUVA
EASTERN GROUP: LAU
ISLAND: ELD KIA ONO AIWA KIOA KORO MALI NGAU VIWA WAIA AGATA MANGO MOALA NAIAU RAMBI MAMOLO MATUKU MBENGA MBULIA NAIRAI NAVITI NGAMEA OVALAU TOTOYA YASAWA YENDUA KAMBARA LAKEMBA TAVEUNI VITILEVU
MOUNTAIN: NARARU MONAVATU
NIECE OR NEPHEW: VASU
POINT: VUYA
TOWN: MAU MBA MOMI REWA SUVA TUVU THUVU ETUMBA NALOTO NAMOLI NARATA NASALA NAVOLA SAGARA

FIJIAN VITIAN
FILAGO GIFOLA
FILAMENT BRIN DOWL HAIR HARL
  NEMA PILE SILK CHIVE CHORD
  FIBER FIBRE FILUM TWIRE CIRRUS
  ELATER HEATER MANTLE STRAND
  THREAD CIRRHUS FLIMMER RHIZOID
  TEXTILE PARANEMA PHACELLA
  STERIGMA
  (— OF FEATHER) DOWL DOWLE
  (— OF MINERAL) STRINGER
  (— OF SILK) BRIN
  (—S OF FLAX OR HEMP) HARL
  (TWISTED —S) STRAND
  (PL.) HACKLE
FILAMENTOUS STRINGY HAIRLIKE
FILANDERS BACKWORM
FILARIASIS MUMU
FILBERT HAZEL COBNUT HAZELNUT
  (SIEVE OF —S) PRICKLE
FILCH BOB FUB NIM ROB BEAT FAKE
  PILK PRIG SMUG SNIP FETCH LURCH
  PILCH SNAKE SNEAK STEAL CLOYNE
  PILFER SMOUCH STRIKE CABBAGE
  PURLOIN
FILE BOX ROW BARB DECK LINE LIST
  RANK RASP RATE RISP ROLL SLIP

STUB EMERY ENTER FLOAT FOUND
GRAIL INDEX LABEL RIFLE TRACK
TRAIN ACCUSE ANSWER BEFOUL
CARLET DEFILE FILACE RASCAL
RUBBER STRING TOPPER ARCHIVE
ARRANGE CHOILER CONDEMN
DOSSIER EXHIBIT GRAILLE QUANNET
TICKLER DRAWFILE
(— DOWN SAW TEETH) JOINT
(— OF SIX SOLDIERS) ROT
(— OFF) DEFILE
(— USED BY COMBMAKERS) GRAIL
TOPPER GRAILER GRAILLE
(— WITH COURT OF LAW) BOX
(COARSE —) RAPE
(CURVED —) RIFFLER
FILE BOX SOLANDER
FILEFISH LIJA UNIE TURBOT
UNICORN BALISTIS FOOLFISH
FILIAL PIUS SONLY
FILIBUSTER FLIBUTOR STONEWALL
FILING RASION LIMATION
(PL.) LEMEL LIMAIL
FILIPENDULA ULMARIA
FILIPINO KALINGA KANKANAI
FILL EKE HIT PAD BUNG CLOY CRAM
FEED GLUT HOLD LADE LINE MEET
PANG QUAR SATE STOP TEEM
BELLY BLOAT BULGE CHOKE ESTOP
FLOCK GORGE KEDGE PITCH STORE
STUFF CHARGE FULFIL INFUSE
OCCUPY QUERRE SUPPLY AGGRADE
DISTEND ENLARGE EXECUTE
FILLING FRAUGHT FULFILL IMPLETE
INFLATE INVOLVE PERFECT
PERFORM PERVADE PLENISH
SATIATE SATISFY SUFFUSE
COMPLETE COMPOUND FREQUENT
PERMEATE
(— COMPLETELY) SATURATE
(— CUP TO BRIM) BRIM CROWN
BUMPER
(— FULL) FARCE STUFF
(— IN CHINKS) LIP
(— IN WITH RUBBLE) HEART
(— IN) NOG KILL STOP SLUSH
INFILL BALLAST
(— INTERSTICES) BLIND
(— LEATHER WITH OIL) FAT
(— OUT) BUNCH SWELL
(— TO EXCESS) CROWD FLOOD
CONGEST SURFEIT
(— TO OVERFLOWING) FLOW
THWACK
(— UP HOLE) STIFLE
(— UP) STOP BRICK CHOKE CLOSE
ESTOP STOAK FULFIL IMPACT
STODGE PLENISH
(— WITH ALE) RACK
(— WITH ANXIETY) ALARM ALARUM
(— WITH CARGO) STOW
(— WITH CLAY) CAT
(— WITH FEAR) APPAL APPALL
(— WITH HORROR) ABHOR
(— WITH LIGHT) GLUT
(— WITH LIQUOR) TUN SKINK
(— WITH METAL) BACK
(— WITH MORTAR) GROUT
(— WITH ODORS) EMBALM

(— WITH RUBBISH) BASH
(— WITH TERROR) AMAZE
(— WITH) SWILL
(ONE'S —) SLITHERS
FILLED BIG ALIVE FLUSH QUICK
SATED SOLID GRAVID LOADED
CROWDED HAUNTED IMPLETE
OPPLETE REPLETE SWOLLEN
FREQUENT INSTINCT POPULOUS
(— OUT) BOLD FULL
(— TO EXCESS) FLOWN
(— WITH EXCITEMENT) ABUZZ
(— WITH FEAR) AFRAID
(— WITH INTERSTICES) AREOLAR
(— WITH MOISTURE) FAT
(— WITH PRIDE) YNPRIDID
FILLER GARA BOGUS SILEX SILKA
SQUIB BALAAM LIGNIN FILLING
LOADING WRAPPER
FILLET BAND BONE GIRT LIST ORLE
ORLO SOLE TAPE AMPYX CROWN
FACET FILET GORGE LABEL LEDGE
MITER MITRE QUIRK SCROD SNOOD
STRAP STRIA TIARA VITTA ANADEM
BENDEL BINDER CIMBIA COMBLE
CORONA DIADEM FASCIA INFULA
LISTEL NORSEL POTONG QUADRA
REGULA RIBBON ROLLER TAENIA
TURBAN TURBOT ANNULET
BANDAGE BANDEAU CLOISON
CORONET EYEBROW FACETTE
FRONTAL GARLAND LAMBEAU
MOLDING TRESSON TRINGLE
BANDELET CINCTURE FRONTLET
HAIRLACE HEADBAND PLATBAND
TRESSOUR TRESSURE UNDERCUT
FILLIFORM CATENOID
FILL-IN MODESTY
FILLING GOB FILL MODE PLUG WEFT
WOOF INLAY STUFF FILLER
STOPPING STUFFING
(— OF GAPS) CONFAB
(— UP) CLOSURE RIPIENO
(BASKET —) SLEW
(DENTAL —) INLAY
(SILK —) SHIKII
FILLIP BLOW FLIP SNAP TOSS URGE
FILIP FLASH FLIRT FLISK IMPEL
BUFFET INCITE MOMENT PROJECT
FILLY COLT FOAL GIRL
FILM H BRAT HAZE HULL KELL MIST
SCUM SKIM SKIN VEIL WEFT BLEAR
COVER FLAKE GLAZE LAYER PEARL
PLATE SCALE SHOOT SHORT
BUBBLE MOTHER PATINA SCRUFF
CUTICLE FEATURE PHILOME
TAFFETA TOPICAL TRAILER
BEESWING FIRECOAT NEGATIVE
PELLICLE
(— OF OIL) SLICK
(— OF TARTAR) SCALE
(— ON COPPER) PATINA
(— ON PORRIDGE) BRAT
(— ON WINE) BEESWING
(DISCARDED —) OUTTAKE
(X-RAY —) BITEWING
FILMY FINE HAZY GAUZY MISTY
WISPY CLOUDY CLOUDED TIFFANY
FILMLIKE GOSSAMER

FILTER CLAY RAPE SIFT SILE DRAIN
SEITZ SIEVE BOUGIE CANDLE
COLATE LAUTER MEDIUM PURIFY
REFINE STRAIN BAGHOUSE
FILTRATE INFILTER STRAINER
FILTERER CLARIFIER
FILTH FEN KET DIRT DUNG GORE
MUCK NAST SLUT SOIL SUDS ADDLE
DRECK GLEAM GLEET JAKES POUCE
SWILL DEFILE FULYIE FULZIE
IMMUND ORDURE SORDES VERMIN
SLOTTER SQUALOR SULLAGE
FOULNESS MUCKMENT SNOTTERY
WORTHING
FILTHINESS MUCOR SQUALOR
SULLAGE CENOSITY
FILTHY LOW FOUL MIRY VILE DIRTY
DROVY DUNGY GROSS LAIRY
MUCKY NASTY BAWDRY CRUMBY
CRUMMY CRUSTY DIRTEN IMMUND
IMPURE SORDID BESTIAL HOGGISH
OBSCENE PIGGISH SQUALID
UNCLEAN ORDUROUS SLUTTISH
FILTRATE MALLEIN
FILTRATION BAGGING
FIN ARM RAG RIB ANAL BURR FANG
HAND KEEL SAIL FLASH PINNA
CAUDAL FINLET ACANTHA FEATHER
FLIPPER PINNULE VENTRAL
FORELIMB PECTORAL
FINAGLE CHEAT TRICK REVOKE
DECEIVE FENAGLE
FINAL LAST UTTER FINIAL LATTER
RUNOFF ULTIMA UTMOST DARREIN
DERNIER EXTREME FINALIS
OUTMOST PARTING SUPREME
ABSOLUTE DECISIVE DECRETAL
DEFINITE EVENTUAL FAREWELL
ULTIMATE
(— STANZA) ENVOI
FINALE END CODA FINIS ENDING
CLOSING
FINALITY END ERGO
FINALLY YET LAST AFINE LASTLY
FINANCE TAX BACK BANK FUND
GOODS REVENUE TAXATION
TREASURE
FINANCIAL FISCAL MONETARY
FINANCIER MONEYMAN
FINBACK WHALE FINNER GIBBAR
FINFISH RORQUAL JUBARTAS
FINCH FINK MORO PAPE JUNCO
SERIN TERIN BURION CANARY
CITRIL LINNET PALILA SISKIN
TOWHEE BUNTING CHEWINK
PEEWEEP REDHEAD REDPOLL
SENEGAL SPARROW TANAGER
WAXBILL AMADAVAT COMBASOU
FIRETAIL GOULDIAN GROSBEAK
HAWFINCH SNOWBIRD
(— FLOCK) CHARM
FIND GET RUG MEET CATCH INVENT
LOCATE STRIKE ADJUDGE FINDING
DISCOVER SCROUNGE
(— FAULT) CARP BARGE BLAME
CAVIL GRONT KNOCK PINCH SCOLD
NATTER ARRAIGN
(— GUILTY) ATTAINT CONVICT
(— OUT) AFIND CHECK ESSAY

LEARN SPELL TROVE DETECT
CONTRIVE DECIPHER DISCOVER
(— **REFUGE**) BIEL BIELD
(— **SOLUTION**) SOLVE
(— **THE SUM**) SUMMATE
(— **TIME**) EEM
FINDER SIGHT SEEKER FOUNDER
FINDING TROVER INQUEST VERDICT
FINE CRO GAY RUM TAX BEIN BIEN
BRAW CAIN CROP DIRE ERIC FAIR
GENT GOOD HUNK JAKE LEVY NICE
PURE RARE SEPT SLAP TALL TEAR
TINE TRIM ABWAB BONNY BRAVE
BULLY CHECK DAISY DANDY DELIE
DUCKY FRAIL GAUDY GRAND GREAT
HUNKY ISSUE KELTY MULCT NOBLE
RORTY SHARP SHEER SMALL SPALE
SWEET UNLAW WALLY WHITE
AMENDE AMERCE BONNIE BRAWLY
BRIGHT CHEESY CHOICE CLEVER
COSTLY CRAFTY DAINTY FACETE
FINISH FLUTED GERSUM HUNGRY
ORNATE PRETTY PROPER RANSOM
SARAAD SCONCE SERENE SILKEN
SLIGHT SPIFFY TENDER CLARIFY
CONDEMN CORKING CUNNING
ELEGANT ESTREAT FERDWIT
FINICAL FORFEIT FRAGILE GALANAS
GALLANT GALLOWS GRADELY
IMMENSE MARCHET MERCHET
MURDRUM ORFGILD PENALTY
PERFECT REFINED SCUTAGE
STAVING TENUOUS TOPPING
VALIANT ABSOLUTE BLOODWIT
BUDGEREE CAVALIER CLINKING
DELICATE DUSTLIKE FLITWITE
FOOTGELD HANDSOME LASHLITE
MARITAGE PENALIZE PESHKASH
PLEASANT SKILLFUL SPLENDID
SUPERIOR WARDWITE WIRESPUN
(— **AGAINST SERVANTS**) CHECK
(— **FOR KILLING**) BOTE
(— **IN LIEU OF FLOGGING**) HIDE
(**BLOOD** —) ERIC WITE
(**OSTENTATIOUSLY** —) GAUDY
(**PRINTING OFFICE** —) SOLACE
(**VERY** —) BUNKUM SPLENDID
(**PL.**) SILT FLOUR
FINE-DRAW RANTER
FINE-LOOKING SPICY SPIFFY
FINELY FINE GAILY GAYLY BRAGLY
RARELY SMALLY BRAVELY SMICKLY
SWEETLY
FINENESS ALLOY GRAIN TRICK
DENIER FINERY PURITY THREAD
EXILITY FINESSE DELICACY
(— **AS RECKONED BY CARATS**)
TITLE
(— **OF FABRIC**) CUT GAGE GAUGE
(— **OF METAL**) STANDARD
(— **OF PITCH**) COUNTS
FINERY GAUD WALY ARRAY BRAWS
WALLY BAUBLE BAWDRY BEAUTY
FEGARY GAIETY GAYETY TAWDRY
BRAVERY GAUDERY REGALIA
BEAUETRY ELEGANCE FINENESS
FOFARRAW FOLDEROL FOOFARAW
FRIPPERY ORNAMENT RIBANDRY
FINESPUN HAIR THIN TWITTERY

FINESSE ART CHEAT SKILL TRICK
PURITY SERENE CUNNING ARTIFICE
DELICACY SUBTLETY THINNESS
FINFOOT SUNBIRD
FINGER TOY PAUT PLAY DIGIT INDEX
PINKY DACTYL HANDLE MEDDLE
MEDIUS PILFER PINKIE POLLEX
ANNULAR DIGITAL MINIMUM
MINIMUS PURLOIN DIGITIZE
THRIMBLE
(— **INFECTION**) FELON
(**FORE** —) INDEX
(**LITTLE** —) PINKIE PIRLIE MINIMUS
AURICULAR
(**RING** —) RINGMAN ANNULARY
(**PL.**) HOOKS
FINGERFLOWER FOXGLOVE
FINGERING DOIGTE
FINGERLING PARR TROUTLET
FINGERNAIL DIGGER
(**RELATING TO** —) ONYCHOID
FINGERPRINT ARCH LOOP WHORL
LATENT
FINGERROOT FOXGLOVE
FINIAL EPI NOB TEE TOP CROP
KNOB KNOP KNOT BUNCH CREST
CROWN FINAL POPPY PRICKET
ORNAMENT PINNACLE
FINICAL NICE FUSSY CHOOSY
DAINTY DAPPER JAUNTY PRETTY
PRISSY SPRUCE CHOOSEY FINICKY
FINIKIN FOPPISH MINCING PICKING
SMICKER DELICATE
FINICALLY SMICKLY GINGERLY
FINICKY DINKY FIKEY FIKIE PRISSY
FINICAL FINIKIN
FINISH DO DIE END CHAR EDGE
FACE FINE MILL OVER PASS SINK
SNUG STOP BLOOM BOUND CEASE
CHARE CHEVE CLOSE CROWN
FEEZE GLACE GLAZE LIMIT SPEED
UPPER BOTTOM BUSHEL FULFIL
FULLDO PLISSE SETTLE WINDUP
ABSOLVE ACHIEVE DEPETER
EXECUTE FLUTING FULFILL PERFECT
SURFACE COMPLETE CONCLUDE
DEPRETER DRESSING FINALIZE
FROSTING TERMINAL
(— **CAREFULLY**) NEATEN
(— **CLOTH**) BURL CONVERT
(— **OF FABRIC**) CIRE HOLLAND
(— **OF PAPER**) STIPPLE
(— **OFF**) DASH CRUSH
(— **STONE**) COMB BOAST DROVE
(— **WITH A SEAM**) FELL
(— **WORK**) FLOOR
(**CALENDERED** —) CHASING
(**DULL** —) MAT MATTE
(**GLAZED** —) GLACE LACKER
LACQUER
(**STUCCO** —) SPATTER
(**SUPERFICIAL** —) BLAZONRY
FINISHED BY DID OER PAU DONE
DOWN FINE GONE OVER RIPE SHOT
ENDED EXACT KAPUT NAPOO
ROUND CLOSED NAPOOH ORNATE
PERFECT REFINED ROUNDED
STOPPED BANKRUPT CLIMAXED
GOFFERED LUSTERED POLISHED

(— **IN NATURAL COLOR**) FAIR
(— **WITH NAP**) BRUSHED
(**ABSOLUTELY** —) SUNK
(**HIGHLY** —) SUAVE
(**IMPERFECTLY** —) RUDE
FINISHER EYER ENDER GAFFER
BEETLER CEMENTER ENAMELER
FINISHING CRUSHING
FINITE LIMITED

FINLAND
CAPITAL: HELSINKI HELSINGFORS
COIN: PENNI MARKKA
DIVISION: IJORE VILLIPURI
GOD: TAPIO JUMALA
ISLAND: ALAND KARLO AALAND
HAILUTO VALLGRUND
ISTHMUS: KARELIA
LAKE: JUO MUO KEMI KIVI NASI
OULU PURU PYHA SIMO ENARE
HAUKI INARI KALLA LAPPA LESTI
PUULA LENTUA SAIMAA SOUNNE
SYVARI KOITERE NILAKKA
PIELIEN
LANGUAGE: AVAR LAPP UGRIC
MAGYAR OSTYAK TARAST
SAMOYED ESTONIAN
MEASURE: KANNU TUNNA VERST
FATHOM SJOMIL OTTINGER
SKALPUND TUNNLAND
MOUNTAIN: HALTIA
NAME: SUOMI
PARLIAMENT: EDUSKUNTA
PROVINCE: HAME KYMI LAPPI
VAASA
RIVER: II KALA OULU SIMO TENO
IVALO LOTTA OUNAS SIIKA
IIJOKI LAPUAN MUONIO PASVIK
TORNIO KITINEN KOKEMAKI
TOWN: ABA ABO KEM KEMI OULU
PORI VASA ENARE ESPOO
KOTKA LAHTI TURKU VAASA
IMATRA KUOPIO MIKKELI
TAMPERE HELSINKI
TRIBE: HAME VEPS VEPSE UGRIAN
KARJALAISET SUOMALAISET

FINLET PINNULE
FINN FIOUN INGER OSTIAK OSTYAK
TAVAST INGRIAN CHEREMIS
INGERMAN SWEKOMAN
(**PL.**) SUOMI
FIORD FJORD INLET
FIORIN KNOTGRASS
FIPPLE FLUTE RECORDER
FIR VER LARCH SAPIN BAUMIER
LASHORN PINABETE
FIR CLUB MOSS FOXFEET
FIRE CAN FEU LOW AGNI APOY BALE
BRIO BURN HEAT KILN LOWE POOP
SWAP SWOP ZEAL ARDOR ARSON
BLAST BLAZE BREAK BURST EMPTY
FEVER GLEED INGLE LIGHT LOGHE
LOOSE LOUGH PLUFF SERVE SHOOT
SQUIB STOKE AROUSE ENGHLE
EXCITE FERVOR IGNITE INCITE
KINDLE SMUDGE SPIRIT SPLEEN
VULCAN ANIMATE BONFIRE BURNING

BURNOUT CHIMNEY DISMISS
EMITTER EXPLODE FURNACE
GLIMMER INFLAME INSPIRE
SMOLDER BACKFIRE BALEFIRE
CAMPFIRE DETONATE HELLFIRE
ILLUMINE IRRITATE NEEDFIRE
SMOULDER VIVACITY
(— A REVOLVER) FAN
(— ON) AFIRE
(— THE CHARGE) HIT
(— TWO ROUNDS) DOUBLE
(— UPON) GUN SPRAY
(CROSS —) GANTLET GAUNTLET
(DAMPENED —) SMOTHER
(FOREST —) BREAK
(LITTLE —) SPONK SPUNK
(MASSED —) ARTILLERY
(PEAT —) GREESAGH
(RUNNING-OUT —) DANDY
(SIGNAL —) BALE BEACON
BALEFIRE
FIRE ALARM FIREBOX
FIREARM ARM GUN IRON SHOT
TUBE FIRER ORGAN PIECE RIFLE
JEZAIL MAGNUM MAUSER MUSKET
PISTOL POPPER BOMBARD CARBINE
CURRIER DEMIHAG HANDGUN
PINFIRE SHOOTER SPANNER
ARQUEBUS BROWNING CULVERIN
EXPELLER EXPLODER PETRONEL
REVOLVER
(PL.) HARDWARE ARTILLERY
FIRE ARROW MALLEOLUS
FIREBACK REREDOS MACARTNEY
FIRE BEETLE COCUYO CUCUYO
ELATER ELATERID
FIREBOAT PALANDER
FIREBRAND BLAZE BRAND BLEERY
BOUTEFEU
FIREBRICK QUARLE
(PL.) GROG
FIREBUG BUG ARSONIST
FIRE CARRIER PORTFIRE
FIRECLAY THILL
FIRE COVER CURFEW CURPHEW
FIRECRACKER DEVIL SQUIB PETARD
SALUTE CRACKER SNAPPER
FIREWORK WHIZBANG
FIRE-CURED DARK
FIREDAMP GAS FOULNESS WILDFIRE
FIREDART PHALARICA
FIREDOG DOG
FIRE ENGINE RIG TUB MANUAL
FIRE EXTINGUISHER SQUIRT
EXTINCTOR
FIRE FIGHTER EXEMPT HOTSHOT
FIREFLY CUCUYO FIREBUG GLOWFLY
LAMPFLY FIREWORM GLOWWORM
LAMPYRID
FIREGUARD FENDER
FIRELINE GUTTER
FIRELOCK FUSEE FUZEE SPANNER
FIREMAN VAMP FIRER FUELER
STOKER TEASER TIZEUR FIREBOY
HOSEMAN BAKEHEAD FURNACER
FIREPLACE FOCUS FOGON FORGE
FOYER GRATE INGLE TISAR HEARTH
CHIMNEY CHEMINEE
(— AND CHIMNEY) STACK

(— **STONE**) MANTEL
(**PORTABLE** —) BARBECUE
BARBEQUE
FIREPLUG PLUG HYDRANT
FIRER STOKER BLASTER
FIRESIDE SMOKE HEARTH
FIRESTAND HASTER HASTENER
FIRE THORN PYRACANTH
FIREWEED FIRETOP PILEWEED
PILEWORT
FIREWOOD FIRE LENA SLAB WOOD
CHUNK FAGOT BILLET BILLOT
ELDING FIRING TALWOOD FIREBOTE
TALLWOOD TALSHIDE
FIREWORK JET SUN GERB DEVIL
GERBE PEEOY SAXON SHELL WHEEL
FIZGIG MAROON PETARD ROCKET
SALUTE SHOWER TRACER CASCADE
SERPENT SPARKER TORPEDO
FOUNTAIN SPARKLER
(PL.) FUN FIRE
FIRE WORSHIPPER PARSI GHEBER
GHEBRE PARSEE
FIRING FIRE FUEL COUGH SALVO
BURNING DRUMFIRE
FIRKIN VESSEL
FIRM HUI BUFF FAST HARD IRON
NASH SURE TAUT TRIG TRIM CHAMP
CORKY CRISP DENSE FIRMA FIXED
HARDY HOUSE LOYAL RIGID SOLID
SOUND STARK STIFF STITH STOUT
SWITH TIGHT HARDEN HEARTY
SECURE SETTLE SICCAR SICKER
SINEWY STABLE STANCH STEADY
STEEVE STOLID STRONG STURDY
ADAMANT CERTAIN COMPACT
COMPANY CONCERN CONFIRM
CONTEXT DECIDED DURABLE
STAUNCH UNMOVED CONSTANT
FAITHFUL FIDUCIAL OBDURATE
RESOLUTE SUBSTANT UNSHAKEN
(— **BUT EASILY CUT**) SEMISOFT
(**NOT** —) FUZZY
FIRMAMENT SKY DEEP POLE CARRY
CANOPY HEAVEN EXPANSE
EMPYREAN EMPYREUM EXPANSUM
FIRMLY BUFF FAST FIRM HARD
SADLY STARK TIGHT HARDLY
SQUARE SURELY SOLIDLY
SECURELY STRONGLY
FIRMNESS BODY GRIT IRON ETHAN
PROOF FIXURE COURAGE FIRMITY
GRANITE BACKBONE DECISION
FASTNESS SECURITY SOLIDITY
STRENGTH TENACITY
FIRST ERST FUST GULE HEAD HIGH
MAIN ALPHA CHIEF FORME NIEVE
PRIMA PRIME PRIMO MAIDEN
PRIMAL PRIMUS VIRGIN FIRSTLY
HIGHEST INITIAL LEADING PRIMARY
EARLIEST FOREHAND FOREMOST
FORMERLY ORIGINAL PARAVANT
PREMIERE PRINCEPS
(— **PRIZE**) BLUE
(— **SERGEANT**) TOP
(— **STATE**) DELAWARE
FIRSTBORN AYNE EIGNE ELDEST
FIRST-CLASS GAY TOP BOSS FLASH
PRIME BUNKUM STUNNING

FIRST-FRUITS ANNATES
FIRSTHAND DIRECT PRIMARY
ORIGINAL
FIRST-RATE BOSS BRAG GOOD JAKE
MAIN SLAP BULLY DANDY LUMMY
PRIME SLEEK SLICK SUPER SWELL
BONSER BONZER BOSKER CHEESY
FAMOUS TIPTOP BLIGHTY BOSHTER
CAPITAL SKOOKUM STELLAR
TOPPING CHAMPION CLINKING
CLIPPING TOPNOTCH
FIRTH KYLE FRITH INLET COPPICE
ESTUARY
FISCAL BURSAL MONETARY
FISH AU ID AKU AWA AYU BIB CAT
COD DAB DAP DIB EEL FIN GAR GIG
GOO HEN IDE IHI JIG JUG ORF RAY
SAR TAI UKU BANK BARB BASS
BOCE BOGA CARP CAST CERO
CHUB CHUG CHUM CLOD CRAB
CUSK DACE DORY DRAG DRAW
DRUM ERSE FUGU GADE GHOL
GOBY GRIG HAKE HIND HUCH HUSO
JACK JUNK LINE LING LOTE MADO
MERO MOLA OPAH PEAL PEGA PIKE
POOR POUT PRIM QUAB RAIL RUDD
RUFF SCAD SCUP SEER SHAD SOLE
SPET SPIN SPOT TILE TORO TUNA
ACARA AHOLE AKULE ANGLE ATULE
BEGTI BINNY BLEAK BOLTI BOLTY
BREAM BULLY BULTI CABIO CATLA
CHIRO CISCO COBIA CONEY DANIO
DORAB DRAIL DRIFT DRIVE ELOPS
ERIZO FLOAT FLUKE FOGAS FRIAR
GADID GRUNT HILSA HUCHO JUREL
KILLY LAKER LANCE MANTA MIDGE
MINIM MORAY OTTER PERCH PIABA
PORGY POWAN POWER REINA
ROACH SAIDE SARGO SAURY SEINE
SHARK SKATE SMELT SNOEK
SNOOK SPRAT SQUID SULEA SWEEP
TENCH TRABU TROLL TROUT TUNNY
UMBRA VIUVA VORAZ WAHOO WHIFF
AIMARA ALEVIN ANABAS ANGLER
BARBEL BARBER BENNET BISKOP
BLENNY BONITO BOWFIN BUMPER
BURBOT CALLOP CANDIL CAPLIN
CARANX CARIBE COELHO COTTID
CREOLE CUCHIA CUNNER DARTER
DASSIE DENTEX FISHET GANOID
GINNEL GULPER GUNNEL HAMLET
HAPUKU HILSAH HUSSAR INANGA
KOKOPU LAUNCE LEDGER LIGGER
LOUVAR MAIGRE MARLIN MENISE
MILTER MINNOW MOLOID MULLET
NONNAT PHOEBE PLAICE POMPON
PUFFER PUNECA REDFIN REMORA
ROBALO ROUGHY RUNNER SABALO
SALELE SALEMA SALMON SAPSAP
SARDEL SAUGER SAUREL SERRAN
SHINER SIERRA SIMARA SPARID
SUCKER TAILER TAIMEN TANDAN
TARPON TAUTOG TESTAR TETARD
TINOSA TOMCOD TURBOT VENDIS
WALLER WEAVER WIRRAH WRASSE
ZINGEL ALEWIFE ALFIONA ANCHOVY
BACALAO BARBUDO BATFISH
BEARDIE BERYCID BIRCHIR BOXFISH
BRAGGLE BUFFALO CABEZON

CANDIRU CAPELIN CAPLING CATFISH
CAVALLA CAVALLY CHIMERA
CHROMID CICHLID CLUPEID CONVICT
CORVINA COWFISH CRAPPIE
CROAKER CUTLIPS CYCLOID
DRABBLE DREPANE DRUMMER
EELPOUT ESCOLAR FATHEAD
FINFISH GALJOEN GEELBEC
GEELBEK GOBIOID GOGGLER
GOLDEYE GOURAMI GRAYSBY
GROUPER GRUNTER GUAPENA
GUAVINA GUDGEON GULARIS
GURNARD GWYNIAD HADDOCK
HAGFISH HALIBUT HARMOOT
HERRING HINALEA HOGFISH
HOUTING ICEFISH ICHTHUS INCONNU
JAWFISH JEWFISH JUGULAR
LABROID LAGARTO LONGFIN
MACHETE MAHSEER MAYFISH
MOJARRA MOONEYE MORWONG
OARFISH OLDWIFE OQUASSA
PEGASUS PIGFOOT PINTADO
PIRANHA POISSON POLLACK
POMFRET POMPANO RONQUIL
SANCORD SARDINE SAUROID
SAVELHA SAWFISH SCALARE
SCAROID SCHELLY SCULPIN
SENNETT SILURUS SLEEPER
SMUTTER SNAPPER SOLDIER
SPAWNER STERLET SUNFISH
TELEOST TOMTATE TOPKNOT
TORPEDO TUBFISH UMBRANA
UNICORN VENDACE VIAJACA
WAREHOU WAUBEEN WHAPUKA
WHAPUKU WHITING ALBACORE
ALFONSIN APOGONID ARAPAIMA
ATHERINE BAITFISH BALISTID
BIGMOUTH BILLFISH BLENNOID
BLUEBACK BLUEFISH BOARFISH
BONEFISH BRISLING BROTULID
BULLHEAD CACKEREL CANCHITO
CARANGID CARANGIN CARDINAL
CATALINA CATALUFA CHANCITO
CHIMAERA CHOANATE CHROMIDE
CORACINE CROSSOPT CYPRINID
DEALFISH DIPNEUST DITREMID
DONCELLA DRAGONET DRUMFISH
DUMBFISH ECHENEID ELEOTRID
EPISCATE FALLFISH FILEFISH
FLAGFISH FLATFISH FLATHEAD
FLOUNDER FOOLFISH FROGFISH
FUNDULUS GAMBUSIA GEELBECK
GILTHEAD GOATFISH GOLDFISH
GRAINING GRAYFISH GRAYLING
GREYSKIN HAIRFISH HALFBEAK
HANDFISH HANDLINE HAPLOMID
HARDHEAD HARDTAIL HOMOCERC
HORNFISH HORSEMAN JACKFISH
JUMPROCK KABELJOU KARMOUTH
KELPFISH KINGFISH LADYFISH
LUMPFISH MACKEREL MENHADEN
MILKFISH MOONFISH PICKEREL
PILCHARD PORKFISH QUERIMAN
ROBALITO ROCKFISH ROCKLING
ROSEFISH SAILFISH SALANGID
SANDFISH SANDGOBY SCIAENID
SCOMBRID SCOTSMAN SEERFISH
SKILFISH SKIPJACK SOAPFISH
STUDFISH STURGEON TALLYWAG

TARWHINE TERAGLIN TILEFISH
TOADFISH TREEFISH TREVALLY
WARMOUTH WEAKFISH WHISTLER
WRYMOUTH
(— BY TROLLING) DRAIL
(— FOR EELS) GRIG SNIGGLE
(— FOR SALMON) SNIGGER
(— NETTED) LIFT
(— NOT UNDERSIZED) COUNT
KEEPER
(— TAPE) SNAKE
(— THROUGH ICE) CHUG
(— UNDERWATER) GOGGLE
(25 LBS. OF —) STICK
(BLIND —) PINKFISH
(CURED —) DUNFISH
(FABLED —) MAH
(FEMALE —) RAUN SPAWNER
(FIGHTING —) PLAKAT
(HAWAIIAN —) AU
(HERALDIC —) CHABOT
(INDIAN —) ROHU
(NUMBER OF —) SCHOOL
(OLD —) MOSSBACK
(QUANTITY OF —) MAZE
(RAW —) SASHIMI
(REFUSE —) CHUM SHACK
(SALTED —) COR
(SPLIT —) KLIPFISH
(THIN —) RACER
(YOUNG —) FRY ALEVIN
FISH BASKET POT CAUL CREEL
SLATH
FISH BOX TRUNK
FISH BRINER COBBERER
FISH CLEANER GILLER
FISH DRESSER IDLER
FISHER MART EELER PEKAN SABLE
SOBOL TAIRA TAYRA MARTEN
SEINER WEJACK MARTRIX TRAWLER
TROLLER
(SPONGE —) HOOKER
FISHERMAN (ALSO SEE ANGLER)
TOTY EELER ANGLER GIGMAN
GILLER KEDGER MAIMUL SEINER
WORMER ADMIRAL DORYMAN
DRAGMAN PRAWNER RODSTER
SHANKER SMELTER STRIKER
TRAWLER TROTTER TROWMAN
PETERMAN PISCATOR SEASONER
SHRIMPER
FISHERY FISHING PISCARY SEALERY
FISHGARTH WEIR
FISHHOOK FLY GIG HOOK LARI
ANGLE DRAIL KIRBY LARIN SLEEK
ANGULE SPROAT KENDALL
ABERDEEN BARBLESS CARLISLE
LIMERICK
(PL.) PULLDEVIL
FISHING PIKING ANGLING BANKING
BASSING GRAINING SNOEKING
(— TOOL) OVERSHOT
FISHING GROUNDS HAAF
FISHING ROD GAD
FISHING TACKLE TEW LEDGER
FISHLINE GIMP TROT SNELL TRAWL
DIPSEY LIGGER BOULTER GANGION
OUTLINE SETLINE TRIMMER
HAIRLINE TROTLINE

FISH LOUSE GISLER
FISHMONGER PESSONER
FISH NEST REDD
FISHNET FLUE SEINE SETNET
FISHPOND VIVER PISCINA VIVARIUM
FISHPOUND MADRAGUE
FISH SPEAR GRANES WASTER
LEISTER
FISHTAIL UROSOME
FISHWAY PASS RACEWAY
FISHY DULL FUNNY GLASSY VACANT
FISSION BREAKING CLEAVAGE
CLEAVING GAMOGENY SCISSION
FISSURE GAP CHAP CONE FLAW
GOOL GULL LEAK LOCH LODE RENT
RIFT RIMA RIME SEAM SLIT VEIN
VENT CHASM CHINE CHINK CLEFT
CRACK FLAKE PIPER PORTA SHAKE
SPLIT ZYGON CLEAVE CRANNY
DIVIDE LESION RICTUS RIMULA
SPRING SULCUS BLEMISH CREVICE
FISSURA OPENING SWALLET
APERTURE BLOWHOLE CLEAVAGE
COLOBOMA CREVASSE INCISURE
QUEBRADA SCISSURA TRAVERSE
(— IN BUILDING STONE) DRY
(— IN HEEL) GAUG
(— IN MAST) SPRING
(— IN PLATEAU) ABRA
(PL.) RHAGADES
FISSURED RIMATE CHAPPED
CLEFTED FISSATE
FIST JOB DUKE NAVE NEIF NIEF
FOIST GRASP INDEX NIEVE CLENCH
CLUTCH DADDLE EFFORT MAULER
MAULEY PINKER STRIKE ATTEMPT
CLUBFIST FISTNOTE PUFFBALL
TIGHTWAD
FISTFIGHT TURNUP
FISTICUFF BOX NEVEL FISTIFY
FISTULA EGILOPS
FISTULOUS TUBULAR
FIT GO APT FAY GEE PAN RIG SIT
ABLE AGUE FEAT FURY GOOD HARD
KINK MEET PANG RIPE SORT SUIT
TURN WELL WHIM ADAPT ADEPT
APPLY BESIT CHINK CLICK DIGNE
EXIES FADGE FANCY FITLY FRAME
FRISK FUROR HAPPY ICTUS MATCH
PITCH QUEME QUIRK READY RIGHT
SERVE SPASM SPELL START STOUR
SWOON TALLY ACCESS ADJUST
ANSWER ATTACK BECOME BEHOVE
BESORT DUEFUL FINISH FITTEN
HABILE HEPPEN LIABLE PROPER
SEASON SEEMLY SPLEEN SQUARE
STREAK STROKE STRONG SUITED
WORTHY ADAPTED BEHOOVE
CAPABLE CONDIGN CONFORM
CORRECT DESPAIR FASHION FITTING
HEALTHY PREPARE QUALIFY
SEIZURE TANTRUM WIDDRIM
ADEQUATE BECOMING DOVETAIL
ELIGIBLE GLOOMING IDONEOUS
OUTBREAK PAROXYSM PASSABLE
SUITABLE SYNCOPES
(— CLOSELY) FAY CHOCK
(— CORNER TO CORNER) BUTT
(— FOR THE GALLOWS) WIDDIFOW

(— **IN**) GO
(— **INTO SOCKET**) FANG
(— **LOOSELY**) SLOP
(— **OF ANGER**) FRAP FUME HUFF
RAGE TIFF FLING RAVERY SPLEEN
(— **OF DEPRESSION**) HUMP
(— **OF ILL HUMOR**) TIG FUNK TOUT
GRUMPS
(— **OF ILL TEMPER**) TANTRUM
(— **OF ILLNESS**) DROW TOUT FLING
(— **OF LAUGHTER**) GIRD KINK
(— **OF NERVOUSNESS**) TWITCHET
(— **OF RESENTMENT**) PIQUE SNUFF
(— **OF SHIVERING**) AGUE GROOSE
(— **OF SULKS**) GEE STRUM
(— **OF SULLENNESS**) DOD
(— **OF TEMPER**) WAX BAIT HISSY
TETCH GROUCH SPLEEN SQUALL
BRAINGE
(— **OF WEEPING**) CRY
(— **OF YAWNING**) GAPE
(— **ONE WITHIN ANOTHER**) NEST
(— **OUT**) ARM BUSK BEFIT EQUIP
ASTORE CLOTHE OUTFIT APPAREL
APPOINT FURNISH HABILLE
ACCOUTER
(— **RIFLE BARREL**) BED
(— **TIGHTLY**) STUFF
(— **TO BE DRUNK**) SORBILE
(— **TOGETHER**) MESH COAPT JOINT
COHERE ASSEMBLE
(— **UP**) RIG
(— **WITH COMPACTNESS**) BOX
(— **WITH FETTERS**) GARNISH
(**RITUALLY** —) KOSHER
(**PL.**) LUNES
FITCH LINER
FITFUL GERY CATCHY GERFUL
GLEAMY CURSORY FLIGHTY
RESTLESS UNSTABLE VARIABLE
FITLY FIT PAT DULY FEATLY GLADLY
MEETLY TIDELY APROPOS HAPPILY
PROPERLY SUITABLY
FITNESS FORM APTNESS DECENCY
DECORUM DIGNITY APTITUDE
CAPACITY IDONEITY JUSTNESS
PROPERTY
FITTED APT ABLE ADAPT KEYED
SUITED ADAPTED ENGAGED
ADJUSTED ASSORTED ELIGIBLE
FITTER TUBER GASMAN
FITTING TO APT CAP DUE LUG PAT
BUTT FAIR FEAT FORK HARP JUMP
JUST KIND MEET CLEAT HAPPY
QUEME WORTH BECOME CLENCH
CLEVIS LEADER PROPER SADDLE
SEEMLY WASHER ADAPTER
CONGRUE PENDANT SERVING
SHACKLE SUCTION TACTFUL
CONDULET DECOROUS GRACEFUL
RIGHTFUL SUITABLE
(— **TIGHTLY**) CLOSE
(**PIPE** —) CROSS ELBOW
(**PL.**) BRASS COVER REPAREL
FITMENTS
FIVE CINQ FUNF CINQUE EPSILON
QUINQUE
(— **CENTS**) JITNEY NICKEL

(— **HUNDRED DOLLARS, POUNDS**)
MONKEY
(— **IN CRAPS**) PHOEBE
(— **OF TRUMPS**) PEDRO
(— **YEARS**) LUSTRUM
(**TWO** —**S**) QUINAS
FIVES BALL SNACK
FIVESTONES SNOBS
FIX BOX JAM PEG PIN SET FAST FIRM
GAFF GLUE HOLD HOLE JAMB LOCK
MEND MOOR NAIL PICK RELY SEAL
SPOT STAY AFFIX ALLOT DEFIX
FOUND GRAFT GRAVE IMBED INFIX
LIMIT PLACE PLANT POINT POSIT
SEIZE STATE STEEK STELL TRYST
ADJUST ANCHOR ARREST ASSIGN
ASSIZE ATTACH CEMENT CLINCH
DEFINE ENROOT ENTAIL FASTEN
FICCHE FIXATE FREEZE GROUND
IMPALE REPAIR REVAMP SETTLE
SQUARE TEMPER APPOINT
ARRANGE CALCIFY CONFIRM
DELIMIT DESTINE DILEMMA GRAPPLE
IMPLANT IMPRESS IMPRINT
PREPARE STATION RENOVATE
TRANSFIX
(— **AMOUNT**) AFFEER
(— **ATTENTION**) NAIL
(— **FIRMLY**) SEAL FREEZE IMPACT
INCUBE RAMPIRE
(— **PRICE**) ASSIZE CHARGE SETTLE
(— **UPON**) CHAP AFFIX
FIXATION FETICH FETISH
FIXATIVE FIXER SKATOLE AMBRETTE
EUDESMOL HYRACEUM LABDANUM
FIXED PAT PUT SAD SET SOT FAST
FIRM FLAT HARD GIVEN SIKER
STAID UPSET FINITE FROZEN INTENT
MENDED SICKER STABLE STATED
STEADY STRONG CERTAIN
DORMANT EMPIGHT HABITED
LIMITED SETTLED SITFAST STATARY
STATIVE STELLED ACCURATE
ARRANGED ATTACHED CONSTANT
DEFINITE EXPLICIT FASTENED
IMMOBILE IRONCLAD MOVELESS
RESIDENT RESOLUTE STANDING
STUBBORN
(**NOT** —) FLUID SHIFTY FUGITIVE
FIXEDLY SAD FAST FIRM FIXLY
INTENTLY
FIXEDNESS FASTNESS
FIXER PATCH
FIXTURE ANNEX EVENT GUARD
FAUCET SHIELD BRACKET CREEPER
KNOCKER THIMBLE
(**LIGHTING** —) SCONCE
(**STORE** —) GONDOLA
FIZZING FIZZY GASSING
FIZZLE FLOP FUSS BARNEY FAILURE
FLIVVER
FLABBINESS MYATONIA
FLABBY LAX FOZY LASH LIMP WEAK
BAGGY FLASH FOGGY FRUSH SAPPY
WOOZY CASHIE DOUGHY FEEBLE
FLAGGY FLAPPY LIMBER QUAGGY
WATERY FLACCID YIELDING
FLACCID LIMP WOOZY FLABBY

FLAGGY EMARCID FLACKED
YIELDING
FLAG FAG LAG SAG SOD FAIL FANE
FLAT HOOK JACK JADE LECK PINE
TURF WAFT WAIF WILT CREST
DROOP FAINT FLAKE SEDGE SLAKE
UNION VEXIL WHEFT WHIFF BANNER
BOUGEE BURGEE COLORS CORNET
EMBLEM ENSIGN FANION GUIDON
LEVERS PENCEL PENNON SIGNAL
TABARD WIMPLE ANCIENT BEEWORT
CALAMUS CATTAIL CURTAIN
DECLINE DRAPEAU FANACLE
LABARUM PENDANT PENNANT
SCOURGE BANDEROL BRATTACH
GONFALON HANDFLAG LANGUISH
PAVILION STANDARD STREAMER
TRICOLOR VEXILLUM WATCHMAN
(— **CORNER**) UNION
(— **OF DENMARK**) DANEBROG
(— **OF TRANSVAAL**) VIERKLEUR
(— **OF TRUCE**) KARTEL
(— **OF U.S.**) GRIDIRON
(**BLUE** — **WITH WHITE SQUARE**)
PETER
(**CAVALRY** —) STANDARD
(**KNOTTED** —) WAFT
(**PIRATE** —) ROGER
(**SERPENT-LIKE** —) DRACO ANGUIS
(**SHIP'S** —) DUSTER
(**TURKISH** —) ALEM
(**WATER** —) SAG
FLAG BEARER GUIDON ANCIENT
FLAGELLANT WHIPPER SCOURGER
(**PL.**) ALBI
FLAGELLATE MONAS
FLAGELLUM WHIP RUNNER
KONSEAL WHIPLASH
FLAGEOLET PIPE ZUFOLO BASAREE
LARIGOT SIBILUS ZUFFOLO
MONAULOS
FLAGGING WEAK LANGUID
FLAGITIOUS WICKED CORRUPT
HEINOUS CRIMINAL FLAGRANT
GRIEVOUS
FLAGON GUN STOUP BOTTLE
VESSEL FLACKET FLAGONET
REHOBOAM
FLAGRANT BAD RED RANK GROSS
ODIOUS STRONG WANTON WICKED
GLARING HATEFUL HEINOUS
SCARLET VIOLENT SHAMEFUL
FLAGSHIP FLAG ADMIRAL
FLAGSTONE FLAG LECK SLAB
FAVUS
FLAIL BEAT FLOG WHIP DRASH FRAIL
THRAIL THRASH THRESH SWINGLE
SWIPPLE STRICKLE
FLAIR RAY BENT NOSE ODOR SMELL
GENIUS LEANING
FLAKE CHIP FILM FLAG FLAW RACK
SNOW FLANK FLECK FLOCK LAMIN
SCALE SLATE SPALL SPAWL STRIP
APHTHA HURDLE LAMINA PALING
FLAUGHT SHAVING FLOCCULE
FRAGMENT
(— **OF METAL**) FLITTER
(— **OF SNOW**) FLAG
FLAKY SCALY SHIVERY

FLAMBE JUBILEE
FLAMBEAU TORCH
FLAMBOYANCE BLARE PANACHE
FLAMBOYANT FLORID GARISH
ORNATE BUCKEYE FLAMING
GORGEOUS
FLAME LOW FIRE GLOW LOWE
ARDOR BLAZE FLARE FLASH GLARE
GLEED INGLE LIGHT RESEPH
TONGUE BURNING FLAMELET
INKINDLE
(ACETYLENE —) CALCIUM
(SMALL —) SPUNK FLAMELET
FLAMMULE
(PL.) GLEED
FLAME TREE KURRAJONG
FLAMING LIVE AFIRE FIERY FLAMY
VIVID AFLARE ARDENT BLAZING
BURNING FLARING FLAGRANT
FLAN PLANCHET
FLANGE BEAD BOSS BEZEL COLLAR
COLLET FLANCH SHROUD FEATHER
DUCKBILL FOLLOWER
(WITHOUT —) BALD
FLANGER FLAYER GOUGER
FLANK LEER LISK SIDE WING CHEEK
SKIRT THIGH BORDER FLITCH
FLANNEL LANA DOMETT SAXONY
STAMIN WHITTLE MOLLETON
SWANSKIN
FLAP FAN LUG ROB TAB TAG TAP
WAP BATE BEAT BLOW CLAP FLIP
FLOG FLOP GILL LOBE LOMA SLAM
SLAT WAFF WELT ALARM APRON
FLACK FLAFF FLICK BALLUP
BANGLE LAPPET LIBBET STRIKE
TONGUE WAFFLE WINNOW AILERON
BLINDER CLICKET FLAPPET FLICKER
FLOUNCE FLUTTER SWINDLE
VALANCE AVENTAIL BACKFLAP
COATTAIL CODPIECE TURNOVER
(— OF BOOTEE) FLY
(— OF GARMENT) LAP
(— OF HAT OR CAP) VALANCE
(— OF HINGE) LEAF
(— ON HOLSTER) FLOUNCE
(— ON SADDLE) SKIRT JOCKEY
(— VIOLENTLY) FLOG SLAT
(CARDIAC —) CUSP
(FLESHY —) GILL
(TROUSERS' —) FALL
FLAPPER FLAP FLOPPER SNICKET
FLAPPING WAFF WHUTTER
FLARE BELL FLUE BLAZE FLAME
FLASH FLECK FUSEE LIGHT SPIRT
TORCH FLANCH SIGNAL SPREAD
FLICKER TRUMPET OUTBURST
(— ON SHIPBOARD) DUCK
(— UP) KINDLE
FLARING BELL FLUE EVASE GAUDY
AFLARE FLAMING GLARING
SWAGGER BOUFFANT DAZZLING
FLASH DOT BEAT DASH LAIT LAMP
LASH LEAM POOL SHOT STAB WINK
BLASH BLAZE BURST FLAME FLARE
FLOSH FLUFF GLADE GLAIK GLEAM
GLENT GLINT LEVIN MARSH SPARK
STEAM BOTTLE FILLIP GLANCE
QUIVER FLAUGHT FOULDRE

GLIMMER GLIMPSE GLISTEN
GLITTER INSTANT LIGHTEN QUICKEN
SHIMMER SPARKLE TWINKLE
SPLINTER SUNBURST
(— FORTH) OUTRAY
(HOT —) FLUSHING
(NEWS —) FUDGE
FLASHBACK THROWBACK
FLASHING CURB FLASH STEEP
BRIGHT FLASHY FORWARD LAMPING
SHINING CREASING METEORIC
SLASHING SNAPPING
FLASHLIGHT BUG GLIM FLASH
TORCH PENLITE
FLASHY GAY FLAT GAUD LOUD
BAVIN FIERY GAUDY SHOWY SLEEK
FLOSSY FROTHY GARISH SLANGY
SPORTY STUNTY INSIPID RAFFISH
TINHORN DAZZLING FLASHING
SPORTING TIGERISH VEHEMENT
FLASK BOX PIG BODY HEAD HELM
JACK OLPE SNAP BETTY BULGE
FRAME GIRBA GOURD BOTTLE
FIASCO FLACON GUTTUS HELMET
LAGENA AMPULLA BOMBOLA
CANTEEN FLASKET MATRASS
TICKLER WARBURG CHRISMAL
CUCURBIT
(POCKET —) TICKLER
FLAT DEAD DOWD DULL EVEN FADE
PLAT SLOB ABODE AFLAT BANAL
BLAND BLUNT DUSTY LEVEL MOLLE
MUSTY PLAIN PLANE PRONE ROOMS
SEBKA SLAKE VAPID WALSH
AGRUFE BORING DREARY FLASHY
JEJUNE LEADEN QUATCH SEBKHA
SILENT SIMOUS DECIDED FLIPPER
INSIPID INSULSE PLATOID PROSAIC
SHILPIT TABULAR UNIFORM
DIRECTLY LIFELESS UNBROKEN
WATERISH
(— AND CIRCULAR) DISCOID
(— AND SHORT) CAMUS CAMUSE
(— IN MUSIC) BEMOL MOLLE
(— OF SWORD) PLAT
(MUD —) SLOB CORCASS
(NOT —) BRISK
(SALT —) SALINA
(THEATRICAL —) JOG
FLATBOAT ARK SCOW PULLBOAT
FLATCAR FLAT IDLER LORRY
(ON A —) PIGGYBACK
FLATFISH DAB RAY BUTT DACE KITE
SLIP SOLE TONG BREAM BRILL
FLUKE QUIFF WHIFF ACEDIA CARTER
PLAICE TURBOT HALIBUT SUNFISH
TORPEDO FLOUNDER MARYSOLE
FLATHEAD SALISH
FLATIRON IRON GOOSE STEEL
SADIRON
FLATNESS BATHOS SILENCE
EVENNESS KURTOSIS
(— OF NOSE) SIMITY
FLATTEN BEAT COMB DECK EVEN
PLAT CRUSH LEVEL PLUSH SPLAT
BEETLE CLINCH DEJECT SMOOTH
SPREAD SQUASH DEPRESS EXPLAIN
PANCAKE SUBSIDE SURBASE
COMPRESS DISPIRIT

FLATTENED ECRASE OBLATE
DILATED PLANATE
FLATTER BULL CLAW COAX DAUB
FAGE FUME PALP SOAP WORD
CHARM FLOAT GLOZE HONEY PAINT
ROOSE SLEEK SMALM BECOME
BUTTER CAJOLE FICKLE FLEECH
FRAISE GLAVER KITTLE PEPPER
PHRASE SAWDER SLAVER SMOOGE
SOOTHE STROKE ADULATE BEGUILE
BLARNEY FLETHER FLUTTER
INCENSE PALAVER SOOTHER
SWEETEN WHEEDLE BESLAVER
BLANDISH BOOTLICK COLLOGUE
FLATTERER FLOIT COGGER DAUBER
EARWIG GLOZER JENKINS PRONEUR
SOOTHER BOOTLICK CLAWBACK
COURTIER DAMOCLES LOSENGER
SLAVERER SMOOTHER
FLATTERING SOAPY SMARMY
SMOOTH BUTTERY CANDIED
COURTLY GLAVERING
FLATTERY BULL BUNK DAUB FLUM
MUSH SOAP FRAIK GLOZE SALVE
TAFFY BUTTER CARNEY FLEECH
GREASE PHRASE SAWDER SLAVER
BLARNEY DAUBING EYEWASH
FAWNING FLETHER INCENSE
PALAVER CAJOLERY
FLATULENCE VAPOR
FLATULENT GASSY WINDY TURGID
POMPOUS VENTOSE FLATUOUS
INFLATED
FLATWARE SILVER
FLATWORM ACOEL FLUKE PLATODE
RADIATE POLYCLAD
FLAUNT BOSH SHOW WAVE BOAST
STOUT VAUNT PARADE DISPLAY
FLUTTER TRAIPSE BRANDISH
FLOURISH
FLAUNTING GAUDY PURPLE
FLAGGERY
FLAVONE CHROMONE
FLAVOR GAMY GOUT MASK ODOR
RASA SALT TANG ZEST AROMA
ASSAI CURRY DEVIL SAPID SAPOR
SAUCE SAVOR SCENT SPICE TASTE
TINGE ASARUM ASSAHY INFUSE
RANCIO RELISH SEASON TARAGE
FLAVOUR PERFUME SUPTION
HAUTGOUT PIQUANCY
(HIGH —) HOGO
(SPECIAL —) GUST
(UNPLEASANT —) TACK
FLAVORED SPICY TINCT SPICED
FLAVORFUL SAVOROUS
FLAVORING DIP ALMOND MIREPOIS
FLAVORLESS STALE SILENT
WATERISH
FLAW BUG FIB GAP LIE MAR RUB
WEM BANE BLOT FLEE GALL HOLE
RASE RIFT SPOT WIND BOTCH
BRACK BURST CHICK CLEFT CRACK
CRAZE FAULT FLAKE PLUME SPECK
BLOTCH BREACH DEFECT FOIBLE
LACUNA LESION BLEMISH BLISTER
DEFAULT EYELAST FEATHER
FISSURE NULLIFY SUNSPOT VIOLATE
WHITLOW FRACTURE FRAGMENT

GENDARME WINDFLAW
(— **IN CASTING**) BUCKLE
(— **IN CLOTH**) BRACK
(— **IN DIAMOND**) GENDARME
(— **IN MARBLE**) TERRACE
(— **IN METAL**) SNAKE
(— **IN PRECIOUS STONE**) FEATHER
(— **IN STEEL**) STAR
(— **IN STONE**) DRY
(**MORAL** —) SMIRCH
FLAWED CRACKED
FLAWLESS CLEAN SOUND PERFECT
FLAX LIN POB TOW CARD FLIX HARL
LINE LINT ROCK GRAIN HURDS
BREADS KORARI PEANUT PEBBLE
SCUTCH LINSEED FLAXWORT
HARAKEKE
(— **DISEASE**) PASMO
FLAXEN FLAXY BLONDE
FLAXWEED TOADFLAX
FLAY SKIN STRIP FLEECE UNCASE
CENSURE PILLAGE REPROVE
SCARIFY
FLEA LOP SCUD FLECH FLECK PULEX
TUNGA CHEGRE CHIGOE VERMIN
PULICID SANDBOY
(— **INFESTED**) PULICOSE
FLEABANE SKEVISH SCABIOUS
WHITETOP
FLEA BEETLE THRIPS
FLEAM BEVEL
FLEAWORT CAMMOCK FLEASEED
PSYLLIUM
FLECHE SPIRELET
FLECK FLAKE FREAK DAPPLE
FLEECE POUNCE STREAK STIPPLE
FLEDGED FLUSH FLIGGED
FLEDGLING SQUAB FLIGGER
BIRDLING
FLEE FLY LAM RUN BOLT FLEG LOUP
SCUR SHUN TURN ELOPE ELUDE
SKIRR SPEED ESCAPE VANISH
ABANDON ABSCOND FORSAKE
SCAMPER LIBERATE
FLEECE JIB KET TEG BUCK CAST
FELL GAFF MORT SKIN TEGG TEGS
FLICK PASHM PLOAT SHAVE SHEAR
SHEEP SWEAT PASHIM PIGEON
PUSHUM TOISON SHEARING
(— **OF MEDIUM GRADE**) SUPER
(**POOREST PART OF** —) ABB
FLEEING FUGIENT HOTFOOT
RUNNING FUGITIVE
FLEER GIBE JIBE LEER FLIRE FLOUT
SCOFF SNEER
FLEET BAY FAST FLIT NAVY SAIL
SKIM SWIM CREEK DRAIN DRIFT
EVAND FLOAT FLOTA HASTY INLET
POWER QUICK RAPID SWIFT
ARGOSY ARMADA FLIGHT HASTEN
NIMBLE SPEEDY CARAVAN
COMPANY FLOTILLA WARCRAFT
FLEETING BRIEF CADUCE FLYING
VOLAGE FLIGHTY PASSING POSTING
SHADOWY VOLATIC CADUCOUS
FUGITIVE VOLATILE
FLESH KIN BEEF BODY FELL GAME
LAMB LIRE MEAT RACE WEED
SLATE STOCK FAMILY MUSCLE

SEASON CARNAGE KINDRED
MANKIND NATURAL HUMANITY
MOONLIGHT
(— **ABOUT CHIN AND JAWS**) GILL
(— **OF CALF**) SLINK
(— **OF GOAT**) CHEVON
(— **OF KID**) CABRITO
(— **OF SHEEP**) TRAIK
(— **ON LOWER JAW**) CHOLLER
(— **OUT**) CLOTHE
(— **UNDER SKIN**) FELL
(**ANIMAL** —) BRAWN
(**DEAD** —) MURRAIN
(**HORSE** —) JACK
(**LIFELESS** —) MUMMY
(**PUTREFYING** —) CARRION
(**SUN-DRIED** —) TAPA
(**SUPERFLUOUS** —) LUMBER
FLESHBRUSH STRIGIL
FLESH-COLORED SARCOLINE
FLESHER LINING
FLESHINESS FULLNESS
FLESHLY CARNAL FLESHY SENSUAL
SARKICAL
FLESHY FAT BEEFY LUSTY OBESE
PLUMP PULPY STOUT ANIMAL
BODILY BRAWNY CARNAL BUNTING
CARNOSE SARCOUS
FLETCH WING FLIGHT
FLEUR-DE-LIS LIS LYS LILY LUCY
FLEUR
FLEX BEND
FLEXED PENCHE
FLEXIBILITY WHIP FLUIDITY
FLEXIBLE LIMP LUSH SOFT BUXOM
LIMSY LITHE WANDY WITHY FLOPPY
LIMBER LITHER PLIANT SUPPLE
DUCTILE ELASTIC FINGENT FLEXILE
FLEXIVE LISSOME PLIABLE SPRINGY
WILLOWY WINDING WRIGGLE
BENDSOME YIELDING
FLEXURE ARCH BEND BENT CURL
FOLD CURVE TWIST SIGMOID
WINDING
FLICK FLIP CLICK FLACK FLANK
FLECK FLIRT FLISK
FLICKER FAIL FLIT LICK WINK BLINK
FLAME FLARE FLICK FLUNK WAVER
BICKER FITTER SHIVER YUCKER
BLINTER FLIMMER FLITTER FLUTTER
SKIMMER TREMBLE TWINKLE
WHIFFLE FLICHTER HIGHHOLE
FLICKERING FLICKY FLUTTER
LAMBENT FLEXUOUS UNSTEADY
FLICKERTAIL STATE
NORTHDAKOTA
FLIER ACE KIWI FLYER PILOT
AIRMAN AVIATOR
FLIGHT FLY HOP LAM BOLT LAKE
PAIR ROUT WING CHEVY FLOCK
GLIDE GRICE SCRAP VOLEE CHIVVY
EXODUS FUGACY HEGIRA HEJIRA
JOYHOP SPIRAL BOUQUET EVASION
FLAUGHT FLYOVER MIGRATE
MISSION SCAMPER STEPWAY
REGIFUGE STAMPEDE SWARMING
(— **OF BALL**) HOOK DRIVE SLICE
(— **OF BIRDS**) VOLARY VOLERY
VOLLEY

(— **OF FANCY**) SALLY
(— **OF SNIPE**) WISP
(— **OF STEPS**) RISE TRAP GRECE
PITCH SCALE STOOP PERRON
STAIRS STEPWAY STAIRWAY
(— **OF WILD FOWL**) SKEIN
(**ABORTIVE** —) ABORT
(**HASTY** —) TIFT
(**HAWK'S** —) CAREER
(**HIGH** —) TOWER
(**IN** —) ALOFT
(**SUDDEN** —) START STAMPEDE
(**UNAUTHORIZED** —) BUGOUT
(**UPWARD** —) SOAR
FLIGHTY ANILE BARMY GIDDY LIGHT
SWIFT FITFUL GARISH UNFIRM
VOLAGE WHISKY FLYAWAY FOOLISH
GIGGISH MOONISH ROCKETY
FLEETING FREAKISH
(— **PERSON**) TRIVVET
FLIMSINESS INANITY
FLIMSY LIMP THIN VAIN WEAK FRAIL
GAUDY JERRY FEEBLE PALTRY
SLEAZY SLIGHT SLIMSY HAYWIRE
SHALLOW TENUOUS TIFFANY
GIMCRACK GOSSAMER JIMCRACK
TWITTERY
FLINCH FUNK GAME JARG BLUNK
BUDGE FEIGN SHUNT START WINCE
WONDE BLANCH BLENCH FALTER
FLENSE RECOIL SHRINK SCRINGE
SCUNNER SQUINCH
FLINCHER VELLINCH
FLINDER FLITTER SMITHERS
FLINDERSIA SILKWOOD
FLINDOSA CUDGERIE
FLING SHY BUZZ CAST DART DASH
DING EMIT FLAP FLEG GIBE HURL
KICK LASH PECK PICK SLAT TOSS
WARP BRAID CHEAT DANCE FLIRT
LANCE PITCH SHOOT SLING SNEER
SWING THROW WHANG BAFFLE
EFFUSE HURTLE LAUNCH PLUNGE
REBUFF SPIRIT ENFORCE FLOUNCE
REPULSE SARCASM SCATTER
SWINDLE SHYLANCE SPANGHEW
(— **MISSILES**) CHUNK
(— **UPWARD**) HAUNCH
(**HIGHLAND** —) WALLOCH
FLINT CORE BLANK CHERT MISER
SILEX EOLITH QUARTZ REJECT
ESLABON FURISON SCRAPER
GRATTOIR GUNFLINT
FLINTINESS HEART
FLINTLOCK FUSEE FUSIL FUZEE
MUSKET SPANNER FIRELOCK
MIQUELET SNAPHAAN
FLINTWOOD WHITETOP
FLIP SKY TAP FLAP SNAP TOSS TRIP
FLANK FLICK FLIRT SLIRT SMART
FILLIP FLITCH LIMBER NIMBLE
PLIANT PROPEL
FLIPPANT AIRY FLIP GLIB FLUENT
LIMBER NIMBLE
FLIPPER ARM FIN PAW HAND SWELL
PADDLE FLAPPER SPRINGER
FLIRT TOY FIKE FLIP MASH TICK
FLICK ROVER SLIRT JILLET MASHER

TRIFLE GALLANT PICKEER TWINKLE
COQUETTE

FLIRTATION FIKE PASSADE
COQUETRY PHILANDER

FLIT DART FLOW SCUD FLECK FLEET
FLICK FLIRT FLOAT FLURR HOVER
QUICK SCOOT SKIFF SWIFT NIMBLE
FLICKER FLUTTER

FLITCH FLICK GAMMON LONGWOOD
MIDDLING

FLOAT BOB FLY KIT SEA BOOM
BUOY CORK DRAG FLOW FLUX
HAWK HONE HOVE LIVE PONT RAFT
RIDE SAIL SCOW SOAR SWIM TILT
WAFT WAVE BALSA BLADE CAMEL
DERBY DRIFT DRIVE FLEET FLOOD
FLUSH GRAIL HOVER LADLE QUILL
SHOAD SWOON BILLOW BOBBER
BUCKET BUNGEY CANNEL DOBBER
PADDLE PONTON RADEAU STREEL
TOPPER CAISSON DRINGLE FLATTER
FLOTTER FRESHEN OROPESA
PAGEANT PLANKER PLUMMET
PONTOON SLICKER LEVITATE
PICKOVER

(— AIMLESSLY) DRIFT
(— DELIGHTFULLY) COWD
(— FOR HERRING NET) BOWL
(— FOR RING BUOY) LEMON
(— LOGS) DRIVE
(— OF REEDS) KELEK LIGGER
(— PAST) GLACE
(— PROPERLY) WATCH
(CANOE —) AMA
(FISHLINE —) BOB CORK BOBBER
DOBBER
(PLASTERER'S —) DARBY

FLOATBOARD BLADE FLOAT LADLE

FLOATER STIFF

FLOATING FREE WAFT AWASH
LOOSE ADRIFT AFLOAT FLYING
NATANT BUOYANT FLYAWAY
PENDENT DRIFTING FLUITANT
SHIFTING UNFUNDED

FLOCCILATION TILMUS

FLOCK MOB POD BAND BANK BEVY
FOLD GAME GANG HERD MANY
PACK ROUT SAIL SORT TEAM TRIP
WISP BROOD BUNCH CHARM COVEY
CROWD DRIFT DROVE FLAKE FLECK
GROUP PLUMP SEDGE SHOAL
SWARM TRIBE TROOP COVERT
FLIGHT GAGGLE HIRSEL MANADA
MEINIE RAFTER SCHOOL SCURRY
VOLERY COMPANY GOOSERY
THICKEN PADDLING

(— OF BIRDS) POD BANK HERD
TEAM WISP BROWN COVEY SEDGE
SIEGE TRIBE FLIGHT VOLERY
(— OF BITTERNS) SEDGE SIEGE
(— OF FINCHES) CHARM
(— OF GEESE) GAGGLE
(— OF HERONS) SEDGE SIEGE
(— OF LARKS) EXALTATION
(— OF LIONS) PRIDE
(— OF MALLARDS) SORD SUTE
(— OF NIGHTINGALES) WATCH
(— OF PARTRIDGE) COVEY
(— OF PEACOCKS) MUSTER

(— OF PIGEONS) KIT LOFT
(— OF ROOKS) ROOKERY
(— OF SANDPIPERS) FLING
(— OF SHEEP) FOLD HIRSEL
(— OF SWANS) BANK GAME MARK
(— OF TURTLE-DOVES) DOLE
(— OF WIDGEONS) COMPANY
(— OF WILDFOWL) SKEIN
(— TOGETHER) RAFT
(SMALL —) SPRING

FLOCKING REPAIR

FLOG CAT TAN TAW BEAT CANE
CHOP HIDE LASH LICK LUMP TOCO
WALE WARM WELK WHIP YANK
BIRCH EXCEL FIGHT FLAIL HORSE
KNOUT LINGE QUILT SAUCE SKEEG
SWISH COTTON LARRUP LATHER
STRIKE SWITCH THRASH WALLOP
WATTLE BALEISE BELABOR
COWHIDE SCOURGE SJAMBOK
TROUNCE CARTWHIP CHAWBUCK
SLAISTER URTICATE VAPULATE
(— WATER) SCRINGE

FLOGGER HORSING SWISHER

FLOGGING TOCO TOKO TANNING
BIRCHING WHIPPING

FLOOD SEA BORE BUOY FLOW FLUX
POUR TIDE EAGRE FLOAT FLUSH
SPATE SWAMP SWILL WATER
DELUGE EXCESS RAVINE SLUICE
SPLASH DEBACLE FLOTTER
FRESHET NIAGARA TORRENT
ALLUVION CATARACT INUNDATE
OVERFLOW SURROUND

FLOODED AWASH AFLOAT

FLOODGATE CLOW DRAG GOLE
HATCH SLUICE STAUNCH CATARACT
PENSTOCK

FLOODING UP PROUD FLOWAGE
DILUVIAL FLOATING

FLOODLIGHT OLIVET

FLOODPLAIN BENCH DAMBO

FLOOR BECK DROP FLAT LAND PAVE
SEAT BOARD FLOAT GRASS PIANO
PIECE SOLAR STAGE STORY BELFRY
FLIGHT GROUND SOLLAR PLANCHE
BARBECUE FLOORING HALFPACE
PAVEMENT SUBFLOOR
(— OF COAL MINE) SOLE THILL
(— OF COAL SEAM) SILL
(— OF FORGE) HEARTH
(— OF GLASS FURNACE) SIEGE
(— OF OCEAN) SEABED
(— OF SPORTS RING) CANVAS
(— OF WOOLSHED) BOARD
(FOREST —) SEEDBED
(GROUND —) TERRENO BASEMENT
(OPENWORK —S) GRATINGS
(RAISED —) LEEWAN HALFPACE
(THRESHING —) MOWSTEAD

FLOORBOARD FOOTLING

FLOORING STAGE PARQUET
TERRAZZO

FLOORMAN CALLBOY

FLOP DOG SWOP WHOP SQUAB
TURKEY TRAGEDY

FLORA FLORULA
(— AND FAUNA) BIOTA

FLORAL TREE LEAF

FLORENCE FLASK BETTY
FLORENCE IRIS ORRIS TREOS
FLORID FINE HIGH BUXOM FRESH
RUDDY ORNATE ROCOCO ASIATIC
FLOWERY TAFFETA BLOOMING
FIGURATE RUBICUND SPLENDID
VIGOROUS

FLORIDA
BAY: APALCHEE BISCAYNE
WACCASASSA
CAPITAL: TALLAHASSEE
COLLEGE: ROLLINS
COUNTY: DADE GUFF ALACHUA
BREVARD BROWARD MANATEE
OSCEOLA VOLUSIA PINELLAS
SARASOTA
INDIAN: AIS OCALE UTINA CALUSA
CHATOT POTANO TIMUCUA
SEMINOLE
ISLANDS: KEYS
KEY: WEST LARGO BISCAYNE
LAKE: DORA APOPKA HARNEY
JESSUP NEWNAN LEDWITH
ARBUCKLE KISSIMMEE
OKEECHOBEE
NATIVE: CONCH CRACKER
RIVER: BANANA INDIAN AUCILLA
MANATEE SCAMBIA SUWANEE
OCHLAWAHA
STATE BIRD: MOCKINGBIRD
STATE FLOWER: ORANGE
STATE NICKNAME: SUNSHINE
STATE TREE: PALMETTO
TOWN: TICE COCOA MIAMI OCALA
TAMPA ORLANDO PALATKA
SEBRING SARASOTA
PENSACOLA
UNIVERSITY: STETSON
WETLANDS: GLADES

FLORIDIAN CRACKER
FLOSS FLUFF SKEIN WASTE CADDIS
SLEAVE CADDICE
FLOSSER FANNER
FLOSS-SILK TREE SAMOHU
FLOTSAM JETSAM WILSAM WAFTURE
WAVESON DRIFTAGE FLOATAGE
FLOUNCE FLAP HUFF SKIT SLAM
FLING FRILL RUCHE RIPPLE ROBING
ROUNCE RUFFLE VOLANT FALBALA
FALBELO FROUNCE RUCHING
FLOUNDER FURBELOW STRUGGLE
FLOUNDER DAB GAD BUTT KEEL
POLE ROLL TOSS BREAM FLUKE
SLOSH WITCH WRELE GADOID
GROVEL MEGRIM MUDDLE PLAICE
TURBOT WALLOP WALLOW WARSLE
BLUNDER FLASKER FLOUNCE
PLOUNCE STUMBLE SUNFISH
TOPKNOT VAAGMAR ANACANTH
FLATFISH FOOLFISH PLUNTHER
SANDLING
FLOUR AMYL ATTA DUST CONES
HOVIS BINDER CLEARS FARINA
FLOWER PATENT POLLEN SICKEN
TSAMBA WHITES BOXINGS CRIBBLE
CANAILLE

(— OF MALT) SMEDDUM
(COARSE —) THIRD CHISEL
BOXINGS CRIBBLE
(FINE —) CONES SUJEE
(LOW-GRADE —) TAIL
(PARTICLE OF —) CHOP
(POTATO —) FROW
(UNSORTED —) ATTA
FLOURISH TAG WAG BOOM BRAG
FUSS GROW LICK RIOT RISE SHOW
WAVE ADORN BLOOM BOAST CHEVE
GLOSS QUIRK REIGN SHAKE SWASH
SWING TUSCH VAUNT CATTER
PARADE PARAPH QUAVER SQUIRL
THRIVE BLOSSOM BURGEON
CADENZA DISPLAY ENLARGE
FANFARE GAMBADE GAMBADO
PASSAGE PROSPER ROULADE
SUCCEED TRIUMPH ARPEGGIO
BRANDISH CURLICUE INCREASE
ORNAMENT SKIRMISH
(— OF BAGPIPE) WARBLER
(— OF TRUMPET) TUCKET
FLOURISHING FAR FRIM FRUM PERT
GREEN PALMY PEART VITAL
BLOOMY FLORID GOLDEN FLORENT
HEALTHY VERNANT THRIVING
VEGETOUS
FLOURY MEALY
FLOUT BOB GIBE JEER JERK JIBE
LOUT MOCK FLEER FLITE FRUMP
SCOFF SCOMM SCORN SCOUT
SNEER TAUNT DERIDE INSULT
BETONGUE
FLOW GO EBB ERN JET PUT RUN
SET SUE BORE COMB FLIT FLUX
FUSE GUSH HALE LAVA LAVE MELT
PASS POUR RAIL ROLL SEND SHED
SILE SLIP SOAK SWIG TAIL TEEM
TIDE WELL AVALE DRAIN DRIFT
EAGRE EXUDE FLEAM FLEET FLOAT
FLOOD FLUSH FRESH GLIDE ISSUE
QUELL RIVER SCOOT SLIDE SPEND
SPILL SPURT SWILL TRILL ABOUND
AFFLUX COURSE CURSUS DELUGE
GUGGLE GUTTER RECEDE RINDLE
SPRING STREAM CURRENT DEVOLVE
DISTILL DRIBBLE EMANATE
FLOWAGE FLUTTER FLUXION
ILLAPSE INDRAFT MEANDER
SPURTLE TRINKLE TRINTLE
ALLUVION BACKWASH CURRANCE
CURRENCY DOWNFLOW EMISSION
FOUNTAIN INUNDATE
(— AGAINST) LAP LAVE BATHE
(— BACK) EBB
(— BEYOND BANKS) DEBORD
SURROUND
(— DOWN) AVALE
(— IN RILLS) DRILL
(— IN RIVULETS) GUTTER
(— IN SPURTS) SALTATION
(— IN) INFLOW INFLOOD
(— INTERMITTENTLY) HEAD
(— OF AIR) SIDEWASH
(— OF ELECTRICITY) BOLT
(— OF METAL) CREEP
(— OF RADIO SIGNAL) BEAM
(— OF SOUNDS) CADENCE

(— OUT) EMIT ISSUE EFFUSE
SPREAD EXHAUST RESOLVE
(— OVER) BERUN
(— SLOWLY) SEEP EXUDE GLEET
(— TOGETHER) CONCUR CONFLOW
(— WITH) FLEET
(CONTINUOUS —) LAPSE
(COPIOUS —) HALE RIVER
(RHYTHMICAL —) LILT
(TIDAL —) BORE AEGIR EAGER
EAGRE
FLOWER (ALSO SEE PLANT AND
HERB) BUD GAY BEST BLOW FLAG
IRIS IXIA PINK POLE POSY ROSE
ARROW ASTER BLOOM BREAK
DAISY ELITE FANCY FLOOR GOWAN
LILAC PANSY PHLOX TRUSS TULIP
TUTTY AZALIA CHOICE CORYMB
CROCUS CYMULE DAHLIA DATURA
FLORET MAYPOP ORCHID SCILLA
SEASON SHOWER SINGLE STEVIA
UNFOLD AMELLUS ANEMONE
ARBUTUS BLETHIA BLOSSOM
BOSTRYX DEVELOP ESSENCE
FLEURET FLOSCLE GAZANIA
GENTIAN GERBERA IPOMOEA
PETUNIA PICOTEE TORENIA
BELAMOUR CAMELLIA CYCLAMEN
DAFFODIL DIANTHUS GARDENIA
GERANIUM HEPATICA HIBISCUS
HYACINTH PRIMROSE SPARAXIS
(— STATE) FLORIDA
(— WITH 6 SEGMENTS) SEXFOIL
(COTTON —) SQUARE
(DEFORMED —) BULLHEAD
(DOUBLE —) BURSTER
(DRIED —S) BRAYERA
(IMAGINARY —) AMARANTH
(STRIPED —) BIZARRE
(UNFADING —) AMARANTH
(PL.) BOUQUET
FLOWERFLY SYRPHID
FLOWERING AFLOWER FLOWERY
ANTHESIS BLOOMING
FLOWERING GLUME LEMMA
FLOWER-OF-AN-HOUR SHOOFLY
FLOWER-PECKER KAKAWAHIE
FLOWERPOT POT CACHEPOT
FLOWERY BLOWN BLOOMY FLORID
POSIED FLORENT PRIMROSE
FLOWING FAIR FLUX LAVE SIDE
AFLOW FLOAT FLUID FLUOR QUICK
TIDAL AFFLUX DEFLUX FLUENT
FUSILE LIVING COPIOUS CURRENT
CURSIVE EMANANT FLUXING
FLUXION FLUXIVE RUNNING SLIDING
DEFLUENT DILUENDO FLUVIOSE
(— AT LOW SPEED) SLACK
(— BACK) EBB
(— IN) INFLUX INFLUENT INFLUXION
(— OF GLAZE) STREAMING
(— OF TIDE) FLOOD
(— OUT) ELAPSE EFFLUENT
FLOWOFF RUNOFF
FLUCAN SELVAGE SELVEDGE
FLUCTUATE SWAY VARY VEER
FLEET SWING WAVER BALANCE
VIBRATE WAMPISH UNDULATE
UNSTEADY

FLUCTUATING WAVY HECTIC LABILE
RUBATO ERRATIC FLUXIVE
WAYWARD UNSTABLE UNSTEADY
FLUCTUATION CYCLE FADING
JIGGLE FLICKER FLUTTER VIBRATO
FLUE NET BARB DOWN OPEN PIPE
THIN VENT FLARE FLUFF FLUKE
FUNNEL TUNNEL UPTAKE CHIMNEY
PASSAGE DOWNTAKE
FLUE-CURED BRIGHT
FLUENCY SKILL
FLUENT GASH GLIB FLUID READY
FACILE LIQUID SMOOTH STREAM
COPIOUS CURRENT FLOWING
FLUIDIC RENABLE VERBOSE
VOLUBLE ELOQUENT FLIPPANT
FLUFF LINT PUFF BEARD WHEEL
FLUFFING WHEELING
FLUFFY SOFT DOWNY DRUNK FILMY
FLUEY FUZZY LIGHT LINTEN PLUFFY
FEATHERY UNSTEADY
(NOT —) CLOSE
FLUID INK SAP MASS RASA BLOOD
FLUOR HUMOR JUICE LATEX SERUM
SPERM SWEAT WATER FLUENT
LIQUID WATERY FLOWING FLUIBLE
FLUXILE GASEOUS SYNOVIA
EMULSION FLOATING FLUXIBLE
FORESHOT
(ANIMAL —) SERUM
(EGYPTIAN PRIMEVAL —) NU NUN
(ETHEREAL —) ICHOR
(LIVER —) BILE
(LUBRICATING —) SYNOVIA
(MAMMARY —) MILK
(SOLDERING —) FAKE
(THICK VISCOUS —) GRUME
(WATERY —) LYE SANIES SEROSITY
(WORKING —) AIR
FLUIDITY LENGTH
(— UNIT) RHE
FLUKE FLUE PALM BLADE GRASP
PLAICE DISTOME PLATODE
SCRATCH FLATWORM FLOUNDER
(— OF ANCHOR) HOOK
(— OF WHALE'S TAIL) BLADE
FLUME CHUTE DITCH SHUTE SLUICE
FLUMMERY SOWENS WASHBREW
FLUNK BUST FAIL SKEW SPIN
FLICKER
FLUNKY SNOB TOADY COOKEE
JEAMES LACKEY FOOTMAN
SERVANT STEWARD
FLUORESCENCE BLOOM
FLUORINE PHTOR PHTHOR
FLUORITE CAND FLUX FLUOR
FLURRY ADO FIT FACT FRET GUST
PIRR SPIT STIR TEAR HASTE SKIFF
SKIRL BOTHER BUSTLE SCURRY
SQUALL CONFUSE FLUSKER
FLUSTER FLUTTER FOOSTER
SWITHER WHITHER SPITTING
FLUSH JET EVEN GLOW HUSH JUMP
POOL ROSE BLOOM BLUSH COLOR
ELATE FLASH FLUSK FRESH KNOCK
LEVEL RAISE ROUGE START VIGOR
AFLUSH EXCITE HECTIC LAVISH
MANTLE MORASS REDDEN RUDDLE
SLUICE SPRING THRILL ANIMATE

BOBTAIL CRIMSON SUFFUSE
ABUNDANT AFFLUENT PRODIGAL
ROSINESS
(— **GAME**) SERVE
(— **IN SKY**) SUNGLOW
(**NOT** —) FLAT
FLUSHED RED ROSY BEAMY FIERY
FLOWN FLORID FLUSHY HECTIC
CRIMSON
FLUSTER PAVIE SHAKE BOTHER
FLURRY FUDDLE MUDDLE POTHER
RATTLE CONFUSE FLUSKER
FOOSTER SWITHER BEFUDDLE
FLOWSTER FLUSTRUM
FLUTE NAY FIFE FUYE PIPE AULOS
CRIMP CUENA PUNGI QUENA STICK
STYKE TIBIA TWILL CANNEL DOUCET
FLAUTO GEWGAW GOFFER POOGYE
ZUFOLO CHAMFER DIAULOS
FLAMFEW FLUTING GAUFFER
HEMIOPE MAGADIS MATALAN
PICCOLO SIBILUS SIFFLOT TONETTE
TRANGAM WHISTLE ZUFFOLO
FLAUTINO MONAULOS RECORDER
(— **OF A COLUMN**) STRIGA
CHANNEL
(— **STOP**) VENTAGE
(**CHINESE** —) TCHE
(**EAST INDIAN** —) MATALAN
(**EUNUCH** —) KAZOO
(**JAPANESE** —) FUYE
(**LYDIAN** —) MAGADIS
(**MOSLEM** —) NAY
(**PHOENICIAN** —) GINGRAS
(PL.) NEHILOTH
FLUTED QUILLED
FLUTEMOUTH CORNETFISH
FLUTE PLAYER AULETE FLUTER
FLUTIST TIBICEN TOOTLER
AULETRIS FLAUTIST
FLUTING STRIX FULLER GADROON
STRIGIL COULISSE QUILLING
FLUTTER BAT FAN BATE BLOW BUZZ
FLAP FLIT FLOW PLAY WAFF WAVE
FLACK FLAFF FLARE FLECK FLICK
FLURR HOVER SHAKE WAVER
BANGLE FLAUNT FLURRY RUFFLE
SWIVET WAFFLE WALLOP FLACKER
FLAFFER FLASKER FLATTER
FLAUGHT FLICKER FLITTER
FLUSKER SKIMMER WAGTAIL
WHIFFLE FLICHTER SQUATTER
VOLITATE
(**IN A** —) PITAPAT
FLUTTERING AWING FLITTY
WHUTTER AFLUTTER FLICKERY
FLUTTER-TONGUING GROWL
FLUX FLOW FUSE LASK MELT BORAX
FLOAT FLOOD ISSUE RESIN ROSIN
SMEAR SMELT FUSION CURRENT
EURIPUS FLOWING LEAKAGE
OUTFLOW
(— **UNIT**) WEBER MAXWELL
FLY BEE FAG FAN GAD HOP RUN
FIRK FLEA FLEE FLEG FLIT GNAT
KITE KIVU LASH LEAP MELT RACK
RAKE SAIL SCUD SMUT SOAR SOLO
WHEW WHIR WHIZ WIND WING ZIMB
AGILE ALERT EMPID FLEET FLIER

FLOAT FLURR FLUSH FLYER GLIDE
LATCH MIDGE MUSCA OXFLY PERLA
PHORA PILOT QUICK SEDGE SHARP
SKIRL SKIRR STOUR WHAME WHIRR
ZEBUB ASILID AVIATE BANGLE
BLOWER BOTFLY BREEZE DAYFLY
ESCAPE FLIGHT FLYBOY GADFLY
GORFLY JARFLY LEPTID NIMBLE
PALMER PHORID PUNKIE RANDON
ROBBER SEPSID SEROOT SPRING
TIPULA TSETSE VANISH VERMIN
WINNOW AVIGATE AVOLATE
CANOPID CHALCID CONOPID
FORMATE GRANNOM KNOWING
ORTALID PYRALIS SCIARID TYRPHID
AIRPLANE BIBIONID BRACONID
COACHMAN DIPTERAN DROPPING
EPHYDRID EULOPHID GLOSSINA
HORSEFLY HOUSEFLY RUBYTAIL
SIMULIID TACHINID TATUKIRA
VOLITATE
(— **AFTER GAME**) RAKE
(— **AIMLESSLY**) BANGLE
(— **ALOFT**) SOAR TOWER
(— **AWAY**) CARRY
(— **CLUMSILY**) FLIGHTER
(— **ERRATICALLY**) GAD
(— **INTO RAGE**) FUFF RARE
(— **LOW**) DICE DRAG HEDGEHOP
(— **OUT**) EXPIRE
(— **RAPIDLY**) SCUR SKIRR
(— **TOO HIGH**) SCUD
(— **WIDE**) MISS
(**FISHING** —) BEE DUN OAK BUZZ
GNAT HARL HERL SMUT WASP ZULU
ABBEY ALDER BAKER FAIRY NYMPH
SEDGE BADGER BOBFLY CADDIS
CAHILL CANARY CLARET DOCTOR
HACKLE MILLER ORIOLE WILLOW
BABCOCK BUTCHER CADDICE
COLONEL DROPPER DUBBING
GRANNOM HUZZARD SPINNER
WATCHED WATCHET BUCKTAIL
CATSKILL COACHMAN FERGUSON
GOVERNOR STREAMER WOODRUFF
WRENTAIL
(**MAY** —) DUN DRAKE
(**SHEEP** —) FAG KED
(**STONE** —) SALLY
FLYBLOWN BLOWN STRUCK
FLYBOAT FLUTE FLIGHT
FLYCATCHER TODY PEWEE PEWIT
CHEBEC COBWEB MILLER PEEWEE
PHOEBE PIPIRI RAFTER TYRANT
YETAPA ELEPAIO FANTAIL GRIGNET
GRINDER PITIRRI TOMFOOL TYRANNI
BEAMBIRD FIREBALL FIREBIRD
FLYEATER FORKTAIL GERYGONE
KINGBIRD KISKADEE PITANGUA
WALLBIRD
FLYING AWING FLIGHT VOLANT
WAVING FLOTANT VOLATIC
AVIATION FLOATING
(— **MANEUVER**) LUFBERY
FLYING FISH SKIPPER VOLADOR
FLYING FOX KALONG PTEROPID
FLYING GURNARD ANGLER
BATFISH LATCHET LOPHIID
VOLADOR

FLYING LEMUR COBEGO COLUGO
KUBONG
FLYING MACHINE AVIATOR
AEROSTAT
FLYING PHALANGER CUSCUS
SQUIRREL
FLYING SQUIRREL TAGUAN
ASSAPAN
FLYWHEEL FLY FLIER FLYER WHORL
WHARVE
FLYMAN LOFTMAN
FLYSCH MACIGNO
FOAL CADE COLT FILLY PODDY
SLEEPER
FOAM FOB SUD BARM BEES BOIL
FUME HEAD KNIT REAM SCUD SCUM
SUDS WORK CREAM FROST FROTH
SPUME YEAST BUBBLE FLOWER
FLURRY FREATH IMBOST LATHER
SEETHE BLUBBER DESPUME
MELDROP
FOAMING AFOAM NAPPY YEASTY
SPUMOUS MANTLING
FOAMY BARMY SPUMY SUDSY
FROTHY SPUMOSE
FOB FUB SPUNG POCKET
FOCAL POINT OMPHALOS
FOCUS FIX PUT POINT PURSE TRAIN
CENTER CLIMAX DIRECT FASTEN
FIXATE HEARTH TEMPLE NUCLEUS
CONVERGE FOCALIZE GANGLION
FODDER HAY FEED FOOD SOIL VERT
GOOMA MANGE FORAGE FOTHER
PODDER SILAGE STOVER FARRAGE
PODWARE ENSILAGE ROUGHAGE
FODDERCAGE TUMBREL
FODDERER FOGGER
FOE ENEMY FIEND RIVAL FOEMAN
HOSTILE OPPOSER OPPONENT
FOG FF DAG RAG DAMP DAZE HAAR
HAZE MIST MOKE MOSS MURK PRIG
RACK ROKE SMOG SMUR SOUP
BEDIM BRUME CLOUD GRASS
HUMOR MUDDY SMIRR SPRAY
STOUR VAPOR MUDDLE NEBULA
SALMON STUPOR FOGGAGE
OBSCURE POGONIP SMOTHER
BEWILDER MOISTURE
(— **OF THE NILE**) QOBAR
(**FROZEN** —) BARBER
(**LIGHT** —) GAUZE
(**SEA** —) HAAR HARR
FOGBOW DOG FOGDOG SEADOG
MISTBOW FOGEATER
FOGDOG DOG STUBB FOGBOW
SEADOG FOGEATER
FOGGINESS CLOUDING
FOGGY DIM DULL HAZY MIRK MOKY
MURK ROKY DENSE DIRTY GROSS
MISKY MISTY MURKY ROOKY ROUKY
SPEWY CLOUDY GREASY GROGGY
MARSHY MILKEN SMURRY BRUMOUS
MUDDLED OBSCURE CONFUSED
NUBILOUS VAPOROUS
FOGHORN SIREN TYFON RIPPER
MEGAFOG
FOGY FOGEY FOGRAM FOOZLE
STODGER MOSSBACK
FOGYISH MUSTY

FOIBLE FAULT FERLY FEEBLE
FAILING FRAILTY WEAKNESS
FOIL BACK BALK EPEE FILE FOIN
SOIL TAIN BLADE BLANK BLUNT
CHEAT ELUDE EVADE FALSE STAIN
STUMP SWORD TRACK TRAIL
BAFFLE BLENCH BOGGLE CHATON
DEFEAT DEFILE FLORET OFFSET
OUTWIT STIGMA STOOGE THWART
BEGUILE FAILURE FOILING FOLIATE
LAMETTA PAILLON POLLUTE
REPULSE STONKER TRAMPLE
DISGRACE
(— STRIPS) WINDOW
(FENCING —) EPEE BLUNT FLORET
FLEURET
(POINTED —) TANG
(TIN —) TAIN
FOIST WISH FUDGE FATHER SUBORN
FOISTER SHOEHORN
FOLD BOW FLY LAP PEN PLY SET
WAP BEND COTE CREW CRUE DART
FAIL FALX FAUN FELD FLAP FURL
HANK HOOD LOOP RUGA SWAG
TUCK WRAP BREAK CLASP CRIMP
CRISP CROZE DRAPE FAULD FLIPE
FLOCK FLYPE FRILL GROIN LAYER
PARMA PINCH PLAIT PLEAT PLICA
PRANK QUILL SINUS YIELD BOUGHT
BUCKLE COLLOP CREASE CRISTA
CUTTLE DEWLAP DIAPIR DOUBLE
ENFOLD FORNIX FRENUM FURDLE
GATHER GUSSET HURDLE INFOLD
LABIUM LAPPET MANTLE PIPING
PLIGHT PUCKER RIMPLE RUMPLE
WIMPLE CAPSIZE CRINKLE CRUMPLE
EMBRACE ENVELOP FLEXION
FLEXURE PINFOLD PLACATE
PLICATE REVERSE ROLLING
ROULEAU TURNING VALVULA
CRIMPING FLECTION FLITFOLD
QUILLING SCAPULET SPLENIUM
SURROUND
(— DOWN) COLLAPSE
(— FOR CATTLE) BAWN
(— IN HOOD) SHOVE
(— INWARD) CRIMP
(— OF SKIN) APRON DEWLAP
SHEATH FORESKIN
(— ROCKS) DEFORM
(—S OF TOGA) SINUS
(CARDIAC —) CUSP
(GEOLOGICAL —) DIAPIR CLOSURE
EXOCLINE SYNCLINE
(LOOSE —) LAPPET
(RESTRAINING —) FRENUM
FRAENUM
(SHEEP —) REEVE
FOLDAGE SOC SOKE
FOLDED SHUT DOUBLE FANLIKE
PLICATE PLICATED REFLEXED
WREATHED
(— AND WAVED) GYROSE
FOLDER KIT BOOK FILE FOLD ATLAS
COVER FOLIO BINDER CLEANER
HANDOUT LEAFLET STROKER
PAMPHLET
FOLDING KNOT
(— PAPER) ORIGAMI

FOLIAGE HERB SHADE GREENS
LEAVES SHROUD GILLERY LEAFAGE
LEAFERY UMBRAGE FRONDAGE
GREENERY
(CARVED —) KNOT
FOLIATED SPATHIC
FOLIATION SEXFOIL TREFOIL
CINQFOIL SEPTFOIL
FOLIC ACID PGA
FOLIO CASE ATLAS FOLIUM
FOLK DAIONE PEOPLE
(FAIRY —) SHEE SIDHE
(PL.) GENTRY
FOLKSONG SON TONADA
FOLKTALE DROLL FABULA MARCHEN
FOLKSY HOMY HOMEY HOMESPUN
FOLLETTO DUSIO
FOLLICLE CRYPT LACUNA OVISAC
FOLLOW GO PAD SUE TAG COME
COPY HUNT NEXT SEEK SHAG TAIL
TAKE TOUT ADOPT AFTER CHASE
DODGE ENSUE SNAKE SPOOR
TRACE TRACK TRAIL TREAD
ADHERE ATTEND FOLLER OCCUPY
PURSUE RESULT SECOND SHADOW
SUIVEZ TAGGLE HOTFOOT IMITATE
OBSERVE PROFESS REPLACE
SUCCEED VALOUWE PRACTICE
SUPPLANT
(— A POINTER'S LEAD) BACK
(— IN SUCCESSION) VARY
(— INSIDIOUSLY) DOG
(— SCENT) ROAD CARRY
(— SLOWLY) DRAGGLE
(— TRACK) SLEUTH
(— UP) SUE ATTEND
(— UPON) WAIT
FOLLOWER FAN IST SON APER
BEAU ZANY ADEPT CHELA GILLY
BILFAR COHORT DRIVEN ENSUER
GILLIE GUDGET KNIGHT LACKEY
SEQUEL SUITOR SULTER VOTARY
ACACIAN ACOLYTE CARRIER
DEVOTEE EPIGONE FLATTER
GRIFTER POLIGAR PURSUER
RETINUE SECTARY SEQUENT
SPANIEL SUPPOST TRAILER
ADHERENT DISCIPLE FAITHFUL
FAVORITE HENCHMAN MYRMIDON
OBSERVER OFFSIDER PARTISAN
RETAINER SECTATOR SERVITOR
(— OF ART) BOHEMIAN
(CAMP —) GUDGET
(CRANE —) SPOTTER
(SERVILE —) SLAVE LACKEY
(PL.) FOLK SECTA SEQUACES
FOLLOWING LAST NEXT SECT SUIT
AFTER FIRST SUANT TRACE TRAIN
BEHIND SEQUEL ENSUANT ENSUING
SEQUENT AUDIENCE BUSINESS
SEGUENDO TRAILING VOCATION
FOLLOW-UP FOLO
FOLLY ATE SIN RAGE LAPSE SOTIE
BETISE DOTAGE LUNACY NICETY
WANWIT DAFFERY DAFFING
FOOLERY FOPPERY IDIOTCY
MADNESS MISTAKE SOTTAGE
UNSKILL FONDNESS FOOLHEAD
IDLENESS LEWDNESS MOROLOGY

NONSENSE RASHNESS SURQUIDY
UNTHRIFT UNWISDOM WILLNESS
WOODNESS
FOMALHAUT DIFDA DIPHDA
FOMENT SOW ABET BREW SPUR
ROUSE STUPE AROUSE EXCITE
INCITE AGITATE FERMENT INSPIRE
FOND TID DAFT DEAR DOTE FAIN
FOOL FUND KIND VAIN WEAK CRAZY
SILLY STOCK STORE ARDENT
BEFOOL CARESS CHOICE DEARLY
DOTING FONDLE FONDLY LOVING
SIMPLE TENDER AMATORY
AMOROUS BEGUILE BROWDEN
FONDISH FOOLISH INSIPID PARTIAL
DESIROUS ENAMORED SANGUINE
TRIFLING UXORIOUS
FONDLE PET BABY CLAP COAX DAUT
DAWT FOND NECK TICK WALY
DAUNT INGLE NURSE WALLY
CARESS COCKER CODDLE COSSET
CUDDLE CUTTER DANDLE GENTLE
KIUTLE MUZZLE PAMPER SLAVER
STROKE TANTLE TIDDLE CHERISH
FLATTER SMUGGLE TWATTLE
BLANDISH CANOODLE
FONDLING NINNY NURSLING
FONDLY DEAR FOND DEARLY
FOOLISH
FONDNESS GRA LOVE FANCY FOLLY
TASTE DOTAGE NOTION FEELING
DEARNESS WEAKNESS
FONT BILL FUND PILA BASIN FOUNT
SOURCE SPRING LAVACRE PISCINA
DELUBRUM
FONTANEL MOLD MOULD FENESTRA
FOOD BIT KAI PAP BAIT BITE BUNK
CATE CHIH CHOP CHOW CRAM DIET
DISH EATS FARE FARM FUEL GEAR
GRUB HASH JOCK KAIL KALE MEAT
PECK PLAT PROG SALT SOCK STEW
TACK TOKE TUCK BREAD BROMA
CHEER CHUCK FLUFF FORAY GRILL
SCAFF SCOFF SCRAN TABLE THING
TREAT TRIPE APPAST BUTTER
DODGER DOINGS EATING FODDER
FOSTER LIVING MAIGRE MORSEL
MUKTUK REFETE STOVER SUNKET
TACKLE TUCKER VIANDS VIVERS
WRAITH ALIMENT FAUSTER
HANDOUT INGESTA KEEPING
KITCHEN NURTURE PABULUM
PASTURE PECKAGE PROVANT
PULTURE EATABLES FLUMMERY
GRUBBERY PEMMICAN PROVIANT
TRENCHER VICTUALS
(— AND DRINK) BOUGE CHEER
LOWANCE
(— AND LIQUOR) GEAR
(— AND LODGING) FOUND
EASEMENT
(— BANNED DURING PASSOVER)
HAMETZ CHAMETZ
(— EATEN AS RELISH) KITCHEN
(— EATEN BETWEEN MEALS)
BAGGING
(— FOR ANIMALS) FODDER FORAGE
(— FOR CATTLE) BROWSE TACKLE
(— FROM KELP) KOMBU

(— IN SLICES) LEACH
(— IN STOCK) LARDER
(— NOT RITUALLY CLEAN)
TEREPHAH
(— OF DUCK EGGS) BALUT
(— OF RUMINANTS) CUD
(— OF THE GODS) AMRITA
AMREETA AMBROSIA
(— OF WHALE) KRILL
(— OF WORKMEN) TOMMY
(— ON TABLE AT ONE TIME) MESS
(BEE —) CANDY
(COOKED —) CURY BAKEMEAT
(DAILY —) TUCKER
(EXTRA —) GASH
(FILLING —) STODGE
(FLAVORLESS —) HOGWASH
(GROUND —) DUST
(HAWAIIAN —) POI
(LIQUID —) LAP SLOP SOUP GRUEL
LEBAN LEBEN SUPPING
(LUXURIOUS —) CATE CATES
JUNKET
(MADE OF SEVERAL —S) PANACHE
(MIRACULOUS —) MANNA
(SEMILIQUID —) SWILL
(SOFT —) PAP
(STARCHY —) AMYLOID
(TAPIOCA-LIKE —) SALEP
(WATERY —) SLIPSLOP
FOODLESS JEJUNE VICTLESS
FOODSTUFF TRADE CEREAL
COOKABLE
FOOL APE ASS BAM BOB COD CON
DAW DOR FOP FOX FUN GIG KID
MUG NUP POT RIG SAP SOT TOY
BULL BUTT CAKE CHUB COLT DOLT
DUPE FOND GECK GOER GOFF
GOWK GYPE HARE HAVE HOIT JAPE
JEST JOKE MOME MUCK NIZY POOP
RACA RACH SIMP TONY TOOT ZANY
BLIND BLUFF BUFFO CHUMP CLOWN
DALLY FUNGE GALAH GLAIK GOOSE
GREEN HORSE IDIOT KNAVE MORON
NINNY NIZEY NODDY PATCH SAMMY
SCREW SILLY SNIPE SPOOF STICK
STIRK TOMMY TRICK BUFFLE
COUSIN CUCKOO CUDDEN DELUDE
DIMWIT DISARD DOTARD DOTTLE
FOLEYE FOOTER GAMMON JESTER
MOTLEY MUCKER MUSARD NIDGET
NIMSHI NINCOM NUPSON SAWNEY
STRING TAMPER WITTOL ASINEGO
BUFFOON COXCOMB DAGONET
DECEIVE DIZZARD FATHEAD
FOOLISH FRIBBLE GOMERAL
GOMERIL HAVERAL JACKASS
LACKWIT MADLING MISLEAD
NATURAL OMADAWN PINHEAD
PLAYBOY STOOKIE TOMFOOL
WANTWIT WITLING BADINAGE
DRIVELER FONDLING HOODWINK
IMBECILE MONUMENT OMADHAUN
TOMNODDY
(— AROUND) JIVE SKYLARK
LALLYGAG
(— AWAY) FRIBBLE
(BORN —) MOONCALF
(LEARNED —) MOROSOPH

(NATURAL —) INNOCENT
(PL.) FOOLERY
FOOLERY GAME FOLLY BARNEY
MOTLEY BAUBLERY
FOOLHARDY RASH BRASH
FOOLATUM
FOOLISH FAT SOT BETE DAFT DUMB
FOND FOOL GAGA GYPE IDLE MADE
NICE RASH SOFT VAIN VOID WEAK
ZANY BALMY BARMY BATTY BOGGY
BUGGY DILLY DIPPY DIZZY EMPTY
FONNE GAWKY GOOFY GOOSY
INANE INEPT JERKY LOONY NODDY
POTTY SAPPY SAWNY SCREW
SEELY SILLY YAPPY ABSURD
CUDDEN DOTISH DOTTLE FONDLY
GLAKED GOTHAM GOWKIT HARISH
INSANE MOMISH MOPISH SHANNY
SIMPLE SLIGHT SOFTLY SPOONY
STULTY STUPID TAWPIE UNWISE
VACANT ASININE DAMFOOL DOLTISH
FANGLED FATUOUS FLIGHTY
FOLLIAL FOPPISH GLAIKIT GOOSISH
GULLISH IDIOTIC PUERILE SOTTISH
TOMFOOL UNWITTY WANTWIT
WITLESS ABDERIAN FOOTLING
FOPPERLY HEADLESS HEEDLESS
HIGHLAND IMBECILE
FOOLISHLY IDLY FONDLY SIMPLE
SIMPLY
FOOLISHNESS JAZZ FOLLY BARNEY
BUNKUM FADDLE LEVITY LUNACY
RUBBLE VANITY FATUITY
BUNCOMBE FONDNESS INSANITY
TOMMYROT
FOOT FIT PAT PAW PEG PES BASE
COOT FUSS GOER HEEL HOOF PIED
SOLE TAIL BASIS PIECE BOTTOM
CLUTCH GAMMON PATTEN PODIUM
RHYTHM TOOTSY TRILBY WALKER
FOOTING GAMBONE MEASURE
METREME PEDICEL FOREFOOT
(— OF ANIMAL) PAD PAW HOOF
TROTTER
(— OF APE) HAND
(— OF INSECT) TARSUS
(— OF WINE GLASS) MULE
(CHINESE —) CHEK CHIH
(HALF —) SEMIPED
(LARGE AWKWARD —) CAVE
(METRIC —) IAMB BASIS DIAMB
IONIC PAEAN DACTYL DIIAMB
IAMBUS SYZYGY ANAPEST BACCHIC
PYRRHIC SPONDEE ANAPAEST
BACCHIUS CHORIAMB DOCHMIUS
EPITRITE MOLOSSUS TRIBRACH
TRIMACER
(STEWED OX —) COWHEEL
(TUBE —) SUCKER
FOOTAGE SETUP
FOOTBALL GRID HURLY ROUGE
FOOTER HURLING LEATHER PIGSKIN
KICKBALL
(KIND OF —) CAMP
FOOTBOY PAGE PEDES
FOOTBRIDGE PLANK LIGGER
FOOTLOG
FOOTED FITTIT PEDATE

FOOTFALL PAD STEP TREAD
FOOTSTEP
FOOTGEAR PATTEN FOOTWEAR
FOOTHOLD TIP HACK STEP FOOTING
TOEHOLD
FOOTING PAR FOOT BASIS EARTH
TRACK HEADING PIECING FOOTHOLD
FOOTLESS APODAL
FOOTLIGHTS FOOTS FLOATS LIGHTS
FOOTLIKE PEDATE
FOOTMAN SKIP FLUNKY JEAMES
LACKEY VARLET DOORMAN
FOOTPAD BOTTOMER CHASSEUR
HIRCARRA WAGONMAN
FOOTPACE HALFPACE PREDELLA
FOOTPAD PAD WHYO PADDER
ROBBER FOOTMAN PADFOOT
LANDRAKER
FOOTPATH LANE TROD JETTY
SENDA TRAIL FOOTWAY HIGHWAY
PARAPET RAMPIRE SIDEWALK
TROTTOIR
(— TO A PASTURE) DRUNG
FOOTPICK CASCROM
FOOTPIECE STEP
FOOTPRINT PUG STEP TROD PRICK
SPOOR TRACE TRACK TRADE
TREAD FOOTING ICHNITE PUGMARK
FOOTMARK
FOOTREST HASSOCK STIRRUP
FOOTROPE HORSE
FOOTS SEDIMENT
FOOTSCRAPING SAND
FOOTSORENESS SURBATE
FOOTSTALK STRIG PODIUM PEDICEL
PETIOLE PEDUNCLE
FOOTSTEP PAD STEP TROD CLAMP
VESTIGE FOOTBEAT FORESTEP
FOOTSTOOL TUT LOVE MORA
STOOL BUFFET SAMBLE CRICKET
HASSOCK OTTOMAN FOOTREST
FOOT-WASHING NIPTER
FOOTWAY PATH CATWALK
FOOTPATH
FOOTWEAR FEET
FOP TO ADON BUCK DUDE DUPE
FOOL KNUT PRIG TOFF DANDY
FLASH PUPPY MOPPET VANITY
COXCOMB JESSAMY GIMCRACK
MACARONI MACAROON MUSCADIN
POPINJAY SKIPJACK
FOPPISH APISH DANDY FOPPY
SAPPY SILLY DAPPER PRETTY
SPRUCE STUPID BEAUISH BUCKISH
FANGLED FINICAL FOOLISH
DANDYISH SKIPJACK
FOR P IN TO PRO TIL VER TILL SINCE
FORWHY BECAUSE FORNENT
FAVORING
(— A LONG TIME) YORE
(— CASH) SPOT
(— EXAMPLE) EG VG
(— FEAR THAT) LEST
(— INSTANCE) AS SAY
(— THE EMERGENCY) PRN
(— THE MOST PART) FECKLY
GENERALLY
(— TIME BEING) ACTUALLY
FORAGE ERS OAT RYE CORN GUAR

MAST PROG RAID FORAY BREVIT
RUSSUD ZACATE GOITCHO
BOOTHALE SCROUNGE
FORAGER OUTRIDER
FORAMEN PORE EXOSTOME
METAPORE
FORAY RAID MELEE FURROW
INROAD RAVAGE RAZZIA SORTIE
CHAPPOW HERSHIP PILLAGE
SPREAGH SPREATH
FORBEAR LET BEAR HELP HOLD
SHUN SIRE AVOID FORGO SPARE
WAIVE DEPORT DESIST ENDURE
PARENT RETAIN ABSTAIN DECLINE
REFRAIN RESPITE ANCESTOR
FOREBEAR WITHDRAW
(— **PROSECUTION)** COMPOUND
FORBEARANCE MERCY LENITY
NONACT QUARTER MILDNESS
PATIENCE
FORBEARING CLEMENT LENIENT
PATIENT MERCIFUL TOLERANT
FORBID BAN BAR DEFY DENY FEND
TABU VETO WARN DEBAR TABOO
BANISH DEFEND ENJOIN IMPEDE
OPPOSE REFUSE SHIELD FORFEND
FORWARN GAINSAY INHIBIT
WITHSAY DISALLOW FORSPEAK
PRECLUDE PROHIBIT
FORBIDDANCE BAN VETO FORBODE
FORBIDDEN TABU TABOO BANNED
DENIED VERBOTEN
FORBIDDING DOUR GRIM HARD
BLACK GAUNT STERN FIERCE
GLASSY GLOOMY GRISLY ODIOUS
STRICT FORBODE GRIZZLY
FORCE GAR GUT HAP JAM LID VIM
VIS ZIP BANG BEAR BEAT BEND
BIRR BODY CLIP CRAM DINT DOOM
DRAG EDGE FECK FOSS GRIP GUTS
HEAD JAMB JINX MAIN MAKE MANA
SOCK ABATE AGENT ARDOR BRAWL
BRING BRUSH CLAMP COACT CRAFT
CROWD CRUSH DEMON DRAFT
DRIVE EXACT EXERT FOHAT GAVEL
IMPEL KARMA MIGHT PAINT PEISE
POACH POINT POWER PRESS PRIZE
PUNCH REPEL SHEAR SHOVE SINEW
STEAM STUFF THROW WAKAN
WREST CHARGE COERCE COMPEL
CUDGEL DURESS EFFECT EFFORT
ENERGY EXTORT HIJACK HOTBED
IMPACT IMPOSE JOSTLE OBLIGE
POWDER RAVISH SHAKTI STRAIN
WRENCH ABILITY AFFORCE
BLUSTER CASCADE CONCUSS
DRAUGHT DYNAMIC IMPETUS
IMPRESS IMPULSE OPPRESS
REQUIRE SQUEEZE TORMENT
VIOLATE WAKANDA ACTIVITY
ADHESION AFFINITY BULLDOZE
COACTION COERCION DYNAMISM
EFFICACY HOTHOUSE MOMENTUM
PRESSURE STRENGTH VALIDITY
VIOLENCE VIRILITY
(— **AIR UPON)** BLOW
(— **AN ENTRANCE)** RANDOM
THRUST
(— **APART)** SUNDER DISPART

(— **BACK)** REPEL RAMBARRE
(— **BY THREAT)** SWAGGER
(— **DOWN)** CLEW CLUE DETRUDE
DISMOUNT
(— **IN)** INJECT INTRUDE
(— **OPEN)** BURST JIMMY SPORT
RANFORCE
(— **OUT)** SPEW EJECT ERUPT EVICT
EXPEL KNOCK EXTUND EXPRESS
(— **PASSAGE)** SQUEEZE
(— **WAY)** CROWD WRING
(— **WITH LEGAL AUTHORITY)** POSSE
(ALLEGED —) OD
(ARMED —) CREW HEAD CONREY
ARMAMENT
(CONCENTRATED —) PITH
(CONFINING —) LID
(CONSTRAINING —) STRESS
(COSMIC —) EVIL
(CREATIVE —) NATURE
(DRIVING —) STEAM SWINGE
(HYPOTHETICAL —) FORTUNE
(LIFE —) SHAKTI
(MAIN —) BRUNT
(MILITANT —) SWORD
(MILITARY —) FYRD LEGION WERING
(NAVAL —) FLEET
(PHYSICAL —) NERVE
(PREPONDERATING —) SWAY
(PROTECTIVE —) CONVOY
(RELIGIOUS —) SANCTITY
(SACRED —) KAMI
(SPIRITUAL —) SOUL
(UNRESTRAINED —) FURY
(UPWARD —) BUOYANCY
(PL.) ARMY WILL COLORS
FORCED LABORED ENFORCED
FALSETTO SPURIOUS STRAINED
FORCEFUL GREAT GUTSY STIFF
STOUT MIGHTY PUNCHY STRONG
VIRILE DYNAMIC VIOLENT BRUISING
ELOQUENT EMPHATIC ENFATICO
FORCIBLE VIGOROUS
FORCEFULNESS EMPHASIS
FORCEMEAT FARCE BOUDIN
GODIVEAU QUENELLE STUFFING
FORCEPS DOG FURCA TONGS
TENAIL BULLDOG CLAMMER
PINCERS PINSONS CROWBILL
DENTAGRA PINCETTE VULSELLA
FORCIBLE VIVE STOUT VALID
COGENT MIGHTY POTENT STRONG
FORCIVE NERVOUS VIOLENT
WEIGHTY EMPHATIC FORCEFUL
POWERFUL PREGNANT PUISSANT
VIGOROUS
FORCIBLY AMAIN SADLY HARDLY
MAINLY HEAVILY STRONGLY
FORD PASS RIFT WADE WATH DRIFT
STREAM CURRENT FORDING
PASSAGE PASSING CROSSING
(PAVED —) STEAN STEENING
FORE VAN WAY AFORE AHEAD
FRONT PRIOR FORMER FURTHER
FOREARM CUBIT CUBITAL CUBITUS
FOREBEAR ANCESTOR
FOREBODE BODE GIVE OMEN
ABODE AUGUR CROAK BETIDE
DIVINE BETOKEN MISBODE OMINATE

PORTEND PREDICT PRESAGE
FORETELL
FOREBODING OMEN BLACK FATAL
AUGURY BODING DISMAL GLOOMY
ANXIETY BALEFUL BANEFUL
DRUTHER OMINOUS PRESAGE
BODEMENT SINISTER
FOREBODINGLY DIRELY
FOREBRAIN CEREBRUM
FORECAST BODE CAST SCHEME
CAUTION FORESEE FORESET
PREDICT FOREDEEM FOREDOOM
FORETELL PROPHESY
FORECASTLE FOCSLE ISLAND
FOREDOOM JINX DESTINY
FOREFACE CUSHION
FOREFATHER AYEL SIRE ELDER
PITRI PARENT ANCESTOR
FOREBEAR
FOREFINGER INDEX
FOREFOOT PAW PUD GRIPE
FOREFOOTING MANGANA
FOREFRONT VAN FRONT VAWARD
FOREGO FORGO WAIVE ESCHEW
ABSTAIN NEGLECT PRECEDE
REFRAIN ABNEGATE DISPENSE
RENOUNCE
FOREGOING PAST ABOVE ANTERIOR
PREVIOUS
FOREHEAD BROW FRONS FRONT
FRONTLET SINCIPUT
(— **INDENTATION)** STOP
(— **MARK)** KUMKUM
(HIGH —) LEPTENE
FOREHEARTH SETTLER
FOREIGN UNCO ALIEN FREMD
WELSH ALANGE EXILED EXOTIC
FRENCH REMOTE UNKIND DISTANT
ECDEMIC EPIGENE EXCLUDE
FRAMMIT HEATHEN OUTBORN
OUTLAND OUTWARD STRANGE
BARBARIC EPIGENIC EXTERIOR
EXTERNAL FORINSEC OVERSEAS
PEREGRIN STRANGER
(— **TO)** DEHORS
FOREIGNER ALIEN HAOLE ALLTUD
GRINGO PAKEHA GREENER
OUTBORN OUTLAND PARDESI
OUTSIDER PEREGRIN PORTUGEE
STRANGER MLECHCHHA
FOREKNOW DIVINE FORESEE
FOREWIT
FOREKNOWLEDGE PRESAGE
FORELOCK TOP BANG QUIFF
COTTER TOUPET FORETOP TOPPING
FOREBUSH
FOREMAN BOSS BULL CORK JOSS
LUNA PUSH CHIEF DOGGY GAFFER
GANGER LEADER RAMROD SIRDAR
TENTER CAPATAZ CAPORAL
CAPTAIN FOUNDER HEADMAN
MANAGER MANDOOR OVERMAN
SHOOFLY SKIDDER STEWARD
FOREHAND GANGSMAN OVERSEER
FOREMOST TOP HEAD HIGH MAIN
CHIEF FIRST FORME FRONT GRAND
BANNER FORMER LEADING
SUPREME VANMOST CHAMPION
(— **PART)** VAWARD

FOREORDAIN FATE SLATE DESTINE
FORESAY PREDOOM FORECAST
FOREORDINATION FATE
FOREPART FRONT FOREHEAD
(— OF FACE) CHAP
(— OF SHIP) STEM FORWARD
CUTWATER ENTRANCE
FOREPOLE LATH SPILE SPILING
FORERUN HERALD OUTRUN
PRECEDE PRELUDE ANNOUNCE
FORESHOT
FORERUNNER OMEN SIGN USHER
AUGURY HERALD ANCESTOR
FOREGOER FOURRIER PRODROME
FORERUNNING PRECURSE
FORESADDLE RACK
FORESEE SEE READ DIVINE PURVEY
PREVISE PROVIDE ENVISAGE
ENVISION FORECAST FOREKNOW
PROSPECT
FORESHADOW HINT FIGURE HERALD
FORERUN PATTERN PRELUDE
UMBRATE FORETYPE
FORESHORE HARD SHORE
HARDWAY SEASHORE
FORESHOW BODE ABODE AUGUR
BETOKEN PORTEND SIGNIFY
FORETELL PROPHESY
FORESIGHT FEAR VISION FOREWIT
FORECAST FORELOOK PROSPECT
PRUDENCE
FORESIGHTED CAGY CAGEY CANNY
FOREST BUSH GAPO MATA RUKH
WOLD WOOD FIRTH GLADE GUBAT
MATTA MATTO SYLVA TAIGA WASTE
WEALD JUNGLE TIMBER BOSCAGE
CALYDON COPPICE CAATINGA
WOODLAND
(— CITY) PORTLAND SAVANNAH
CLEVELAND
(— FOR DEER) FIRTH
(IMMENSE —) MONTANA
(RAIN —) SELVA
(SIBERIAN —) URMAN
(STUNTED —) CAATINGA
KRUMMHOLZ
FORESTAGE APRON
FORESTALL BEAT HELP STALL
DEVANCE FORERUN OBVIATE
PREVENE PREVENT FORSTEAL
FORESTALLER GROSSER
FORESTAYSAIL JUMBO
FORESTER FOSTER WALKER
MONTERO TINEMAN TREEMAN
WOODMAN WOODSMAN
FORETASTE GUST HANSEL TEASER
EARNEST HANDSEL ANTEPAST
PROSPECT
FORETELL BODE ERST READ SPAE
AUGUR INSEE WEIRD DIVINE
HALSEN HERALD BESPEAK FORESAY
PORTEND PREDICT PRESAGE
ANNOUNCE FOREBODE FORECAST
FORESHOW PROPHESY SOOTHSAY
FORETELLING PROPHECY
FORETHOUGHT CAUTION FORECAST
PREPENSE PRUDENCE
FORETOKEN OMEN PORTEND

PROMISE FORECAST FORESHOW
FORESIGN
FOREVER AY AKE AYE EVER ETERN
ALWAYS ETERNE ENDLESS
ETERNITY EVERMORE
FOREWARNING HINT PORTENT
FOREWING PRIMARY
FOREWORD PROEM PREFACE
PREAMBLE
FORFEIT WED FINE LOSE TINE WITE
CRIME DEDIT FORGO LAPSE
FOREGO DEFAULT ESCHEAT
FORWORK PENALTY FORFAULT
FORFEITURE FINE BLIND MULCT
TINSEL ESCHEAT FORFEIT PENALTY
FORGE FOGE MINT TILT WELL CLICK
FALSE FEIGN SMITH STOVE HAMMER
SMITHY STEADY STITCH STITHY
SWINGE CHAFERY FALSIFY FASHION
BLOOMERY
FORGED BOGUS SPURIOUS
FORGER SMITH FALSER FALSARY
LEVERMAN
FORGERY SHAM FALSUM FICTION
BLOOMERY
FORGET LOSE OMIT WANT FLUFF
BILEVE UNKNOW UNMIND NEGLECT
OVERLOOK
FORGETFULNESS SWIM FLUFF
LETHE AMNESIA AMNESTY OBLIVION
FORGET-ME-NOT MYOSOTE
FORGING HOOP CLICK JACKET
FORGIVE REMIT SPARE ASSOIL
EXCUSE PARDON ABSOLVE
CONDONE OVERLOOK
FORGIVENESS GRACE PARDON
FORGIFT
FORGIVING GRACE HUMANE
CLEMENT MERCIFUL
FORGOTTEN DERELICT UNMINDED
FORINT FLORIN
FORK CROC EVIL HOOK TANG TINE
CLEFT CLOFF FURCA GLACK GRAIN
GRAIP PRONG TWIST BISECT
BRANCH CLITCH CROTCH DIVIDE
FEEDER GAFFLE HACKER OFFSET
TWISEL BIPRONG FOURCHE
FRUGGIN HAYFORK TOASTER
CROTCHET EQUULEUS GRAINING
(— OF BODY) SHARE
(— OF PENNON) FANON
(THATCHER'S —) GROM
(TUNING —) DIAPASON
FORKED BIFID FORKY FURCAL
PRONGY DIVIDED FURCATE LITUATE
BIFORKED BRANCHED FOURCHEE
SUBBIFID
FORKING STAR
FORLORN LORN LOST REFT ALONE
ABJECT FORFAIRN FORSAKEN
HELPLESS HOPELESS PITIABLE
WITLOSEN
FORM AME DIG FIG HEW HUE SET
BLEE BODY CASE CAST CAUL DOME
FLOW GARB IDEA KERN KITE MAKE
MODE MOLD PLAN RITE SEAT THEW
TURN BENCH BLANK BLOCK BOARD
BUILD BUNCH CHART CHECK CRUSH
DUMMY EIDOS ERECT FORGE

FORMA FORME FRAME GALBE GUISE
IMAGE MATCH MEUSE MODEL
SHAPE SPELL STAMP THROW
USAGE ADJUST COUPON CREATE
CUSTOM DEVISE DOCKET FIGURE
FILLER HANGER INVENT MANNER
REMOVE RITUAL SCHEMA SCHOOL
SPONGE STRIKE SYSTEM TAILLE
AGENDUM ARRANGE COMPOSE
CONFECT CONTOUR DEVELOP
FASHION FEATURE FORMULA
GESTALT IMPANEL INVOICE LITURGY
MAKEDOM OUTLINE PATTERN
PORTRAY PORTURE PRODUCE
PROFILE SPECIES STATURE
BILLHEAD CEREMONY COMPOUND
CONCEIVE CONTRIVE FORMWORK
INSTRUCT LIKENESS ORGANIZE
(— A HEAD) POME
(— A RING) ENVIRON
(— ASSUMED AFTER DEATH)
KAMARUPA
(— BRANCHES) BREAK
(— BY CUTTING OFF) ABJOINT
(— CONNECTION) ALLY
(— FOR BELL FOUNDING) SWEEP
(— FOR CONCRETE) BOXING
(— FOR HOLDING BARREL) SQUAW
(— FOR MOLD) JACKET
(— FOR PRESSING VENEERS) CAUL
(— FRUIT) KNIT
(— INTO A CHAIN) CATENATE
(— INTO BALL) CONGLOBE
(— INTO RINGLETS) CRISP
(— LEATHER) CRIMP
(— MOUND) TUMP
(— OF GOVERNMENT) ESTATE
KINGSHIP
(— OF PREDICATION) CATEGORY
(— POLITICAL SUCCESSION) CAVE
(— WITH PLASTER) RUN
(— YARN INTO THREAD) CABLE
(ANCESTRAL —) BLASTAEA
STEMFORM
(CONVENTIONAL —) AMENITY
(DEXTROROTATORY —) CAMPHOR
(IMPERFECT —) SEMIFORM
(ISOMETRIC —) DIPLOID
(LINGUISTIC —) FOSSIL GERUND
(LITERARY —) KNACK
(LYRICAL —) SESTINA
(MUSICAL —) SUITE
(POINTED —) ANGLE
(SCHOOL —) SHELL
(SHOE —) LAST FILLER
(SONG —) BAR
(SPECTRAL —) SHADOW
(SPEECH —) LEXEME
(SPIRAL OR CIRCULAR —) GYRE
(TOP —) GROOVE
(VERB —) FUTURE CONATIVE
DEFINITE DURATIVE
(VERSE —) EPODE BALLAD SONNET
KYRIELLE LIMERICK
(VISIBLE —) RUPA
(WILD —) AGRIOTYPE
(WORD —) ETYMON ANOMALY
FORMAL SET BOOK PRIM BUDGE
CHILL COURT EXACT STIFF SOCIAL

SOLEMN STOCKY BOOKISH LOGICAL
ORDERLY OUTWARD PRECISE
REGULAR SOLWARD STARCHY
STATELY STILTED ABSTRACT
ACADEMIC AFFECTED ELEVATED
FORMULAR OFFICIAL PUNCTUAL
STARCHED

FORMALDEHYDE FORMAL MONOSE
HARDENER METHANAL

FORMALIST PEDANT

FORMALISTIC COURT ACADEMIC

FORMALITY FORM SASINE STARCH
BUCKRAM DECENCY WIGGERY
CEREMONY

FORMALIZE STIFFEN

FORMALLY FORMLY STARCHLY

FORMAT SIZE GETUP SHAPE STYLE

FORMATION FORM RANK SPUR
BIOME FLIGHT GROWTH HARROW
MASSIF SPREAD POTENCE
BOTRYOID
(— **ENCLOSING MINE WORKING**)
GROUND
(— **ENCOUNTERED IN DRILLING**)
STRAY
(— **OF BRANCHES**) CANOPY
(— **OF CRYSTAL**) SHOOT
(— **OF JOINT**) ANKYLOSIS
(— **OF PLANES**) JAVELIN
(— **ON TOAD**) SPADE
(— **RESEMBLING ICICLE**) STIRIA
(**BATTLE** —) HERSE
(**CLOUD** —) NUBECULA
(**DANCE** —) SET
(**DIAGONAL** —) HARROW
(**DRIPSTONE** —) COLUMN
(**ECOLOGICAL** —) BIOME
(**FLIGHT** —) SQUADRON
(**GEOLOGIC** —) BOEL CULM CHICO
STRAY MARKER MEDINA CURTAIN
MANLIUS MATAWAN POTOMAC
TERRAIN AQUIFUGE FERNANDO
KOOTANIE KOOTENAI LOCKPORT
TOPATOPA YORKTOWN
(**HABIT** —) FIXATION
(**INDENTED** —) CLEFT
(**INFANTRY** —) TERTIA ECHELON
(**LAND** —) BOOTHEEL
(**MILITARY** —) SNAIL FLIGHT
(**NAVAL** —) SCREEN
(**POINTED** —) BEAK

FORMATIVE PLASTIC DEMIURGIC

FORMED BUILT BOOKIT DECIDED
MATURED SETTLED WROUGHT
TIMBERED
(— **AT BASE OF MOUNTAIN**)
PIEDMONT
(— **INTO STEPS**) GRADY
(— **ON SURFACE OF EARTH**)
EPIGENE
(**IMPERFECTLY** —) ABORTIVE
(**STURDILY** —) BUXOM

FORMEE PATE PATTEE

FORMER DIE OLD ERER ERST FERN
FORE LATE ONCE PAST ELDER
FORME GAUGE GUIDE MAKER PRIOR
BYGONE RATHER WHILOM ANCIENT
ANOTHER CREATOR EARLIER
FIRSTER FURTHER ONETIME PRIDIAN

QUONDAM TEMPLET UMWHILE
PRETERIT PREVIOUS SOMETIME
STRICKLE UMQUHILE

FORMERLY ERE NEE OLD ERST
FORE ONCE THEN YORE GRAVE
WHILOM WHILST ONETIME
QUONDAM SOMETIME UMQUHILE

FORMIDABLE MEAN FEARFUL
ALARMING DREADFUL MENACING
TERRIBLE FEROCIOUS
(— **PERSON**) TARTAR

FORMLESS ARUPA DOUGHY ANIDIAN
CHAOTIC DEFORMED INDIGEST

FORMOSA (SEE TAIWAN)

FORMULA LAW MIX DATE FIAT FORM
RULE CANON CREED DHIKR GRAPH
INDEX LURRY KEKULE MANTRA
METHOD RECIPE THEORY RECEIPT
APOLYSIS CLAUSULE DOXOLOGY
EXORCISM
(— **OF FAITH**) KELIMA
(**MAGICAL** —) CARACT
(PL.) RAKA RAKAH

FORMULARY SYMBOL

FORMULATE PUT CAST DRAW
FRAME DEVISE CAPSULE COMPOSE
FORMULE PLATFORM

FORMULATED STATED WRITTEN

FORMULATION (— **OF A TRUTH**)
COUNT CREED DOGMA APHORISM
APOTHEGM DOCTRINE

FORMWORK SHUTTERING

FORNIX VAULT PSALIS

FORSAKE DENY DROP FLEE QUIT
SHUN ABAND AVOID FORGO LEAVE
WAIVE DEFECT DEPART DESERT
FOREGO FORHOO FORLET REFUSE
REJECT ABANDON DISCARD
FORLESE DESOLATE FORHOOIE
RENOUNCE WITHDRAW

FORSAKEN LORN FORLORN
DESERTED DESOLATE LASSLORN

FORSOOTH EVEN QUOTH

FORSWEAR DENY ABJURE REJECT
ABANDON PERJURE ABNEGATE
MANSWEAR RENOUNCE

FORT PA DUN LIS PAH LISS PEEL
SHEE SPUR WORK COTTA REDAN
SIDHE CASTLE SANGAR SCHERM
SCONCE STRONG BASTION
BULWARK CITADEL CLOSURE
REDOUBT BASTILE CASTILLO
FASTHOLD FASTNESS FORTRESS
MARTELLO PRESIDIO
(**FAIRY** —) LIS LIOS LISS SHEE
SIDHE
(**RUINS OF** —) ZIMBABWE
(**SMALL** —) GURRY FORTIN BASTIDE
FORTLET FORCELET

FORTE FORT STARK STRONG
EMINENCY STRENGTH

FORTESCUE COBBLER SCORPION

FORTH OUT AWAY FURTH

FORTHRIGHT BURLY GUTTY CANDID

FORTHRIGHTLY FRANKLY

FORTHWITH NOW ANON AWAY
BEDENE DIRECT BETIMES FORTHON
DIRECTLY

FORTIFICATION BOMA FORT MOAT

WALL REDAN TOWER ABATIS
CASTLE GLACIS BASTION BULWARK
CITADEL DEFENCE DEFENSE
PARAPET PILLBOX RAMPART
RAVELIN REDOUBT FORTRESS
MUNITION RONDELLE STRENGTH
(**LINE OF** —**S**) TROCHA

FORTIFIED ARMED CONFIRMED

FORTIFY ARM MAN BANK FORT LINE
WALL WARD SPIKE STANK BATTLE
IMMURE MUNIFY MUNITE BULWARK
COMFORT DEFENSE GARNISH
RAMPIRE BASTILLE EMBATTLE
FORTRESS RAMFORCE STOCKADE

FORTITUDE GRIT GUTS SAND FIBER
FIBRE PLUCK METTLE BRAVERY
COURAGE HEROISM STAMINA
BACKBONE PATIENCE STRENGTH

FORTNIGHTLY BIWEEKLY

FORTRESS (ALSO SEE FORT) BURG
KEEP KASBA PIECE PLACE ROCCA
CASBAH CASTLE ALCAZAR BARRIER
BOROUGH CASTRUM CHATEAU
CITADEL KREMLIN ZWINGER
ALCAZAVA BASTILLE FASTNESS
STRENGTH

FORTUITOUS CASUAL CHANCE
RANDOM FORTUIT FORTUNEL

FORTUITY LUCK CHANCE

FORTUNATE EDI FAT HAP SRI GOOD
SHRI WELL CANNY FAUST HAPPY
LUCKY RIGHT WHITE DEXTER
EUROUS BLESSED FAVORED
WEIRDLY GRACIOUS

FORTUNATELY FAIR HAPPILY

FORTUNE DIE HAP LOT URE BAHI
DOOM FALL FARE FATE HAIL LUCK
PILE STAR EVENT GRACE ISSUE
LINES SONSE SPEED WEIRD WHATE
CHANCE ESTATE MISHAP RICHES
WEALTH DESTINY SUCCESS
THEEDOM VENTURE ACCIDENT
CASUALTY FELICITY STOCKING
(**GOOD** —) SELE SONSE SPEED
THRIFT FURTHER GOODHAP
BONCHIEF FELICITY
(**ILL** —) DOOM THRAW

FORTUNE-TELLER SEER SIBYL
SYBIL SPAEMAN SORTIARY
SPAEWIFE
(PL.) CHALDAEI

FORUM COURT PLATFORM TRIBUNAL

FORWARD ON TO AID BOG BUG GAY
ABET BAIN BOLD FORE FREE HELP
PERT SEND SHIP STEP AHEAD
ALONG BARDY BRASH CAGER
EAGER FAVOR FORTH FRACK FRECK
FRONT HASTY PAWKY READY
RELAY REMIT SAUCY SERVE SPACK
ULTRA AFFORD ARDENT AVAUNT
BEFORE BRIGHT COMING DEVANT
FORRIT FORTHY HASTEN NUZZLE
ONWARD PROMPT ROUDAS SECOND
TOWARD ADVANCE EARNEST
EXTREME FURTHER PROMOTE
PUSHING RADICAL SOLICIT
ADELANTE ARROGANT FROMWARD
IMMODEST IMPUDENT ONCOMING
PERVERSE PETULANT TELLSOME

TOWARDLY TRANSMIT
(MOST —) HEADMOST
FORWARDNESS IMMODESTY
FOSSA FOSS FOVEA GALET TRENCH
VALLIS FOSSULA FOSSETTE
FOSSE DITCH GRAFF
FOSSIL CYCAD CYSTID DOLITE
FUCOID ICHITE PINITE AMBRITE
BICHRON BLASTID CHAMITE CRINITE
ICHNITE JUNCITE LITUITE NEREITE
OVULITE TYLOPOD ZOOLITE
ZOOLITH AISTOPOD AMMONITE
ANCODONT ASTROITE BALANITE
BLASTOID BUFONITE CALAMITE
CERATITE CONCHITE CONODONT
ECHINITE EOHIPPUS FAVOSITE
FILICITE FUSULINA GEDANITE
GYROLITH MIMOSITE PEUCITES
POLYPITE SALIGRAM SCAPHITE
SERAPHIM SPONGOID SYNAPSID
TARSIOID
FOSTER REAR NURSE COCKER
HARBOR NUZZLE SUCKLE CHERISH
DEPOSIT EMBOSOM GRATIFY
INDULGE NOURISH NURTURE
BEFRIEND
FOSTERAGE NURSERY
FOSTERER NORRY
FOUL BAD BASE EVIL HORY RANK
ROIL VILE BAWDY BLACK DIRTY
DITCH FUNKY GRIMY GURRY HORRY
KETTY MUDDY MUSTY NASTY
RUSTY SULLY WEEDY CLARTY
DEFAME DIRTEN DREGGY FILTHY
GREASY IMPURE MALIGN ODIOUS
PUTRID ROTTEN SOILED SORDID
UNFAIR ABUSIVE DEFACED FULSOME
HATEFUL ILLEGAL IMBROIN
NOISOME OBSCENE PROFANE
SMEARED SQUALID TETROUS
UNCLEAN VICIOUS AMURCOUS
ENTANGLE FECULENT INDECENT
SLOTTERY STAGNANT STINKING
TRAUCHLE WRETCHED
(— UP) BOTCH
FOULMOUTHED ROUDAS ABUSIVE
OBSCENE PROFANE
FOULNESS FEDITY PRAVITY
(— OF MOUTH) SABURRA
FOUL-SMELLING FUNKY
FOUND FIX TRY YET BASE CAST
REST STAY BEGIN BOARD BUILD
ENDOW ERECT START ATTACH
BOTTOM DEPART GROUND INVENT
EQUIPPED PRACTICE PROVIDED
SUPPLIED
FOUNDATION BED BASE BODY FIRM
FUND GIST ROOT SILL SOLE BASIS
FOUND STOCK STOOL ANLAGE
BOTTOM CRADLE GROUND LEGACY
MATRIX PODIUM RIPRAP BEDDING
BEDROCK CHANTRY COLLEGE
MORTISE PINNING RADICAL
ROADBED SUBBASE WARRANT
BACKBONE DONATION MATTRESS
MIRAPOIX PEDESTAL PLATFORM
STANDARD UNDERLAY
(— FOR WIG) CAUL
(— OF BASKET) SLATH SLARTH

(FLOATING —) CRIB
(PRECARIOUS —) STILT
FOUNDED FUSILE
FOUNDER FAIL IMAM AUTHOR
CASTER DYNAST EPONYM HELLEN
YETTER AFOUNDE STUMBLE
BELLETER MISCARRY
FOUNT FONS FONT SOURCE
FOUNTAIN URN AQUA FOND HEAD
KELD PANT PILA SYKE WELL DIRCE
FOUNT GURGE QUELL SURGE
ORIGIN PHIALE PIRENE SOURCE
SPRING BUBBLER CONDUIT
SPRUDEL AGANIPPE SALMACIS
UPSPRING WELLHEAD
(INK —) DUCT
(SODA —) SPA
FOUNTAINHEAD ORIGIN SOURCE
FOUNTAIN PEN STICK STYLO
FOUR MESS CATER DELTA DALETH
FEOWER TETRAD QUARTET
QUATRAL MURNIVAL QUADRATE
(— OF ANYTHING) GUNDA
(— OF TRUMPS) TIDDY
(— TIMES A DAY) QD QID
(— YEAR PERIOD) PYTHIAD
FOURCHETTE FORGET SIDEWALL
WISHBONE
FOURFOLD FOURBLE QUATERN
FOURIERISM SOCIALISM
FOUR-O'CLOCK FRIARBIRD
FOURPENNY BIT JOE FLAG JOEY
GROAT
FOURTEENER SEPTENAR
FOURTH DELTA QUART FARDEL
FORPIT FERLING QUARTER
QUADRANT
(— HOUR) SEXT
(— OF BAHMIN EMPIRE) TARAF
(— OF CAKE) FARL FARLE
(— OF YEAR) RAITH
(AUGMENTED —) TRITONE
FOUSSA CIVET GALET
FOVEOLA VARIOLE
FOWL HEN RED COCK GAME GRIG
JAVA ROCK SLIP BIDDY CHUCK
CLUCK COPPY MALAY MANOC
MARAN SILKY ANCONA ASHURA
BANTAM BRAHMA CAMBAR COCHIN
HOUDAN LAMONA LEGBAR POLISH
REDCAP SULTAN SUSSEX BUFFBAR
CAMPINE CHICKEN CORNISH
DORKING FRIZZLE HAMBURG
LEGHORN MINORCA OKLABAR
POULTRY ROOSTER SPANISH
SUMATRA COCKEREL CUBALAYA
DELAWARE DUCKWING DUNGHILL
GAMECOCK LANGSHAN SHANGHAI
SHOWBIRD VOLAILLE
(5-TOED —) SILKY SILKIE
(AGGREGATION OF —) RAFT
(CASTRATED —) CAPETTE
(CRESTED —) TOPKNOT
(GUINEA —) KEEL COMEBACK
(MALE —) STAG
(STUFFED —) FARCI
(TAILLESS —) RUMKIN
FOWLER BIRDMAN
FOX DOG KIT PUG TOD ASSE FOOL

STAG WILD ADIVE CAAMA SWIFT
TRICK VIXEN ZORRO ARCTIC
BAGMAN CANDUC COLFOX CORSAC
FENNEC LOWRIE OUTWIT RENARD
BEGUILE CHARLEY CHARLIE
KARAGAN REYNARD STUPEFY
VULPINE CUSTOMER MUSKWAKI
OUTAGAMI PLATINUM
FOX-AND-GEESE MERELS
FOXGLOVE POPPY POPDOCK
THIMBLE FLAPDOCK POPGLOVE
FOX GRAPE ISABELLA LABRUSCA
FOXHOUND WALKER
FOX HUNTER PINK
FOXTAIL CAUDA CHAPE COUGH
KNEED TWITCH SETARIA GAMELOTE
FOXY SLY WILY COONY SHREWD
CUNNING VULPINE DEXTROUS
FOYER HALL LOBBY
FRACAS BOUT BRAWL MELEE MUSIC
BICKER RUMPUS SHINDY UPROAR
QUARREL SHINDIG FRACTION
INCIDENT
FRACTION BIT CUT PYO FLUX PART
BREAK PIECE SCRAP BREACH
LITTLE MOIETY DECIMAL GLUTOSE
WETNESS
(— OF RADIATION) ALBEDO
(NAPHTHA —) LIGROIN
FRACTIONAL ALIQUOT FRACTED
PARTIAL
FRACTIOUS MEAN UGLY CROSS
UNRULY CRABBED PEEVISH
WASPISH PERVERSE SNAPPISH
FRACTURE BUST FLAW REND BILGE
BREAK CLEFT CRACK FAULT JOINT
BREACH DEFORM HACKLE DIACOPE
FISSURE RUPTURE DIACLASE
FRACTION
FRACTURED SPLIT BROKEN
FRACTURING SLIP STRAIN FAILURE
FRAGILE FINE FROW WEAK FRAIL
FROWY LIGHT SWACK FEEBLE
FROUGH INFIRM SLIGHT TENDER
BRICKLE BRITTLE FROUGHY
SLENDER TIFFANY DELICATE
EGGSHELL ETHEREAL FRACTILE
SLATTERY
FRAGILITY DELICACY
FRAGMENT BIT ORT ATOM BLAD
CHIP DRIB FLAW GROT MOIT MOTE
PART RUMP SHED SNIP WISP ANGLE
BRACK BREAK BROKE CATCH
CHUNK CLOUT CRUMB FRUST
GIGOT PIECE RELIC SCRAP SHARD
SHERD SHIVE SHRED SPALL SPELL
SPLIT FARDEL FILING GOBBET
MORSEL REMAIN SCREED SHIVER
SIPPET SLIVER CANTLET EXCERPT
FLINDER FLITTER FRITTER FRUSTUM
MACERAL MAMMOCK REMANIE
REMNANT SEGMENT SHATTER
SHAVING CHIPPING DETRITUS
FRACTION POTSHERD SKERRICK
SPLINTER
(— CUT OFF) CANTLE
(— OF BONE) SEQUESTER
(— OF BRICK) BRICKBAT
(— OF DIAMOND) CLEAVAGE

(— **OF ICE**) CALF
(— **OF LAVA**) FAVILLA LAPILLUS
(— **OF MELODY**) LAY
(— **OF ROCK**) CRAG AUTOLITH
(— **OF SAIL**) HULLOCK
(— **OF SOD**) TAB
(— **OF STONE**) SCABBLING
(— **OF UNFINISHED WORK**) TORSO
(— **OF VEIN MATERIAL**) SHOAD
SHODE
(—**S OF CLOUD**) SCUD
(—**S OF SAND**) FINES
(**CAST IRON** —) POTLEG
(**JAGGED** —) BROCK
(**MASS OF** —**S**) BRASH
(**PLANT** —) SHIVE
(**SHELL** —**S**) SHRAPNEL
(**WOODY** —**S FOUND IN FOOD**) CHAD
(PL.) FRUSH SCRAPS CINDERS
FITTERS GUBBINS SMATTER
FLINDERS LEFTOVER SMITHERS
FRAGMENTARY HASHY SNIPPY
SCRAPPY DIVIDUAL
FRAGRANCE BALM ODOR AROMA
SCENT SMELL SWEET FLAVOR
FRAGOR BOUQUET INCENSE
PERFUME SUAVITY
FRAGRANT NOSY RICH BALMY
OLENT SPICY SWEET SAVORY
SPICED ODORANT ODOROUS
PERFUMY SCENTED AROMATIC
FLAGRANT NECTARED ODORIFIC
REDOLENT
FRAIL FINE PUNY WEAK CRAZY
REEDY SEELY SILLY BASKET
BROTEL CROCKY FLIMSY INFIRM
SICKLY SINGLE SLIGHT SLIMSY
SQUEAL TICKLE TOPNET BRITTLE
BRUCKLE FRAGILE SLENDER
UNHARDY DELICATE PINDLING
FRAILTY FAULT FOIBLE INVENT
FAILING DELICACY WEAKNESS
(**HUMAN** —) ADAM
FRAMBESIA PIAN YAWS BUBAS
FRAME BED BIN BOW BOX FLY GYM
MAT SET BAIL BEAM BIER BUCK
BULK BUNK CANT CASE CAUM CELL
CLAM CRIB CURB DESK DRAG FORM
FROG GATE GILL HACK HARP HECK
JACK MOLD PORT RACK SASH SLEY
SOLE STEP BANJO BLADE BLIND
BLOCK BUILD CADRE CHASE CLEAT
CRATE CROOK DRAFT EASEL FLAKE
FLASK FLEAK FLOAT GRATE HERSE
HORSE MOUNT OXBOW PERCH
SCRAY SHAPE STAND STATE STEAD
STOCK STOOL TRAIL BATTEN
BINDER BUCCAN BUCKET CASING
CHEVAL COFFIN CRADLE CRATCH
CRUTCH DECKLE DREDGE FABRIC
FENDER GANTRY GRILLE HANGER
HARROW HOTBED HURDLE PERSON
PILLAR QUADRA REDACT REEDER
SCREEN SETTLE SLEDGE SPIDER
SQUARE STAPLE TANGLE TENTER
TESTER ARMRACK BREAKER
CABINET CARRIER CASEBOX
CHASSIS COAMING COASTER
CRAMPON CRIMPER DRAUGHT

DROSSER FASHION FRAMING
FRISKET GALLOWS GARLAND
GATEWAY GIGTREE GRATING
HAYRACK HOUSING ICEBOAT
MACHINE MONTURE OXBRAKE
PORTRAY SETTING STADDLE
TRANSOM TRESTLE TRIBBLE
BARBECUE BOWGRACE CARRIAGE
CONCEIVE CONTRIVE DOORCASE
GRAFFAGE GRIDIRON GRILLAGE
HALBERDS HOGFRAME PLOWHEAD
RAILROAD RECEIVER RETAINER
SKELETON THRIPPLE TRIANGLE
TURNPIKE
(— **FOR ARCH**) COOM COOMB
(— **FOR BEEHIVE**) SECTION
(— **FOR CANDLES**) HEARSE
(— **FOR CARRYING STRAW**) KNAPE
(— **FOR CASK**) GANTRY STALDER
(— **FOR CATCHING FISH**) HATCH
(— **FOR CLOTHES DRYING**) AIRER
(— **FOR CONFINING HORSE**) TRAVE
TRAVAIL
(— **FOR COW'S HEAD**) BAIL
(— **FOR DRYING FISH**) HACK HAIK
(— **FOR DRYING SKINS**) HERSE
(— **FOR FISHING LINE**) CADAR
CADER
(— **FOR GLAZING LEATHER**) BUCK
(— **FOR HAWKS**) CADGE
(— **FOR KILLING PIGS**) CREEL
(— **FOR LENS**) BOW
(— **FOR ROLLER BEARINGS**) CAGE
(— **FOR SMOKING MEAT**) BOUCAN
BUCCAN
(— **FOR STACK**) HAYRACK STADDLE
(— **OF A VESSEL**) HULL
(— **OF MIND**) HAZE SPITE SPIRIT
FEELING
(— **OF PIER**) JETTY
(— **OF SAW**) HUSK
(— **OF SPINNING MULE**) SQUARE
(— **OF STRAW**) SIME
(— **OF TINWORK**) MARQUITO
(— **ON STAGE**) CEILING
(— **TO CATCH STARFISH**) TANGLE
(— **TO CLEAN SHIP'S BOTTOM**) HOG
(**2-WHEELED** —) GILL
(**BELL** —) SWEEP
(**CARRIAGE** —) BRAKE BREAK
(**DIVING** —) LUNET LUNETTE
(**EMBROIDERY** —) TABORET
TAMBOUR
(**FISHING** —) DREDGE
(**GLAZIER'S** —) FRAIL
(**HARNESS** —) HEALD
(**LOOM** —) SLAY SLEY SLEIGH
(**MINING** —) APRON
(**PHOTOGRAPHY** —) BUTTERFLY
(**PORTABLE** —) BIER CACAXTE
(**PRINTING** —) PRESS
(**SHIP'S** —) CANT
(**SLUBBING** —) BILLY
(**STRETCHING** —) TENT SLEDGE
TENTER
(**TANNING** —) BEAM
(**WINDOW** —) CHESS
(PL.) PROFILE
FRAMED NATE NATED ENGAGED

FRAMEWORK BED BENT BIER BONE
BUCK CAGE CRIB DURN GRID RACK
SASH BONES CADRE CHUTE COPSE
CREEL FLAKE SHELL STOCK BELFRY
BRIDGE BUSTLE CABANE CRADLE
DESIGN FABRIC GOCART GUARDS
HARROW HEARSE REBATO SHIELD
STROMA WATTLE CABINET CARCASS
CLIMBER COMMODE DERRICK
FRAMING FULCRUM JACKBOX
LATTICE PANNIER REBATER
RETABLE STADDLE TRESTLE
BARBECUE BEDSTEAD BULKHEAD
CARRIAGE CRADLING CRIBWORK
GRIDIRON GRILLAGE OSSATURE
SCAFFOLD SHELVING SHOWCASE
SKELETON
(— **FOR PEAL OF BELLS**) CAGE
(— **OF REFERENCE**) SCHEMA
(— **TO EXPAND SKIRTS**) BUSTLE
PANNIER
(**EMPTY** —) HUSK
(**SCULPTOR'S** —) ARMATURE
FRAMING CURB LEAD BELFRY
ARMATURE BEDPLATE

FRANCE
BAY: BISCAY ARACHON
CAPE: HAGUE
CAPITAL: PARIS
CHEESE: BLEU BRIE BONBEL
BOURSIN MUNSTER CAMEMBERT
MARCILLAT ROQUEFORT
COIN: ECU SOL SOU GROS AGNEL
BLANC BLANK FRANC LIARD
LIVRE LOUIS OBOLE SAIGA
SCUTE BLANCA BLANCO DENIER
DIZAIN TESTON AGNEAUX
CENTIME TESTOON CAVALIER
NAPOLEON
DANCE: GAVOT BRANLE CANARY
CANCAN BOUTADE GAVOTTE
DEPARTMENT: AIN LOT VAR AUBE
AUDE CHER EURE GARD GERS
JURA NORD OISE ORNE TARN
AISNE
DIVISION, ANCIENT: ARLES
PERCHE NEUSTRIA AQUITAINE
AQUITANIA
DYNASTY: CAPET VALOIS
BOURBON ORLEANS CAPETIAN
MEROVINGIAN
FOOD: PATE CREPE CANAPE
MOUSSE QUICHE BRIOCHE
SOUFFLE ESCARGOT PIPERADE
POTAUFEU TOURNEDO
ISLAND: RE YEU CITE CORSE
GROIX HYERE OLERON USHANT
CORSICA
KING: ODO EUDES PEPIN CLOVIS
LOTHAIR
LAKE: ANNECY CAZAUX
MEASURE: POT SAC AUNE LINE
MINE MUID PIED VELT ARPEN
CARAT LIEUE LIGNE MINOT
PERCH PINTE POINT POUCE
TOISE VELTE ARPENT HEMINE
LEAGUE QUARTE SETIER

CHOPINE HEMINEE POISSON
SEPTIER BOISSEAU QUARTAUT
ROQUILLE QUARTERON
MILITARY ACADEMY: STCYR
SAINTCYR
MOUNTAIN: PUY DORE BLANC
CINTO FOREZ PELAT COTEDOR
MOUNIER VENTOUX VIGNEMALE
CHAMBEYRON
MOUNTAIN RANGE: ALPS ECRINS
VOSGES CEVENNES PYRENEES
MARITIMES
NAME: GAUL GAULE GALLIA
NATIONAL ANTHEM: MARSEILLAISE
NATIVE: CELT GAUL FRANK
BASQUE BRETON GASCON
NORMAN PICARD CATALAN
GALLOIS LORRAIN FRANCIEN
LIGURIAN PROVENCAL
BURGUNDIAN
PORT: CAEN BREST CALAIS
TOULON LEHAVRE BORDEAUX
CHERBOURG DUNKERQUE
MARSEILLE
PROTESTANT: HUGUENOT
PROVINCE: FOIX ANJOU AUNIS
BEARN ALSACE ARTOIS COMTAT
POITOU AUVERGNE BRETAGNE
BRITTANY LIMOUSIN LORRAINE
PROVENCE TOURAINE
RACE TRACK: AUTEUIL
LONGCHAMPS
REPUBLIC CALENDAR: NIVOSE
FLOREAL VENTOSE BRUMAIRE
FERVIDOR FRIMAIRE GERMINAL
MESSIDOR PLUVIOSE PRAIRIAL
FRUCTIDOR THERMIDOR
VENDEMIAIRE
RESORT: PAU NICE CANNES
MENTON RIVIERA
RIVER: AIN LOT LUY LYS VAR
AIRE AUBE AUDE CHER DRAC
EURE GARD GERS LOIR OISE
ORNE TARN VIRE ADOUR AISNE
AULNE DROME INDRE ISERE
LOIRE MARNE MEUSE RHONE
RISLE SAONE SEINE SOMME
VIAUR YONNE ALLIER ARIEGE
ESCAUT SAMBRE SCARPE
VEZERE VIENNE DURANCE
GARONNE GIRONDE MAYENNE
MOSELLE CHARENTE
DRODOGNE
STOCK EXCHANGE: BOURSE
STRAIT: BONIFACIO
TOWN: AY EU AIX DAX GEX PAU
AGDE AGEN ALBI AUBY AUCH
BRON CAEN LAON LOOS METZ
NICE OPPY ORLY RIOM SENS
SETE STLO UZES VAUX VIMY
VIRE ARLES ARRAS BLOIS
BREST DIJON DINAN DOUAI
ERNEE LAVAL LILLE LISLE
LYONS NANCY NERAC NESLE
NIMES ORNES PARIS REIMS
ROUEN SEDAN TOURS TULLE
VICHY AMIENS ANGERS CALAIS
LEMANS LONGWY NANTES

PANTIN RENNES RHEIMS SARLAT
SENLIS SEVRES TARARE TARBES
TOULON TROYES VALOIX
VERDUN BAREGES CASTRES
LIMOGES ORLEANS ROUBAIX
VALENCE BORDEAUX CLERMONT
GRENOBLE MULHOUSE
ROCHELLE TOULOUSE
MARSEILLE STRASBOURG
TRIBE: REMI AEDUI ARVERNI
SALUVII ALLOBROGES
VERSE FORM: LAI ALBA AUBADE
RONDEL BALLADE DESCORT
RONDEAU VIRELAI VIRELAY
WEIGHT: GROS MARC ONCE
CARAT LIVRE POUND TONNE
TONNEAU ESTERLIN
WIND: MISTRAL
WINE: MACON MEDOC GRAVES
CHABLIS POMEROL BORDEAUX
BURGUNDY MUSCADET
SAUTERNE CHAMPAGNE
WINE DISTRICT: MEDOC ALSACE
BORDEAUX BURGUNDY
CHAMPAGNE

FRANCHISE SOC SOKE VOTE CHASE
FERRY HONOR INFANG CHARTER
FREEDOM LIBERTY CONTRACT
FREELAGE SUFFRAGE TENEMENT
FRANCOLIN COQUI TETUR TITAR
REDWING PHEASANT
FRANCOPHILE GALLOMAN
FRANGIPANI SHAKEWOOD
FRANK FREE OPEN RANK BLUFF
BLUNT BURLY LUSTY NAIVE PLAIN
BRAZEN CANDID DIRECT FORTHY
HONEST SALIAN ARTLESS GENUINE
LIBERAL PROFUSE SINCERE
CAREFREE CAVALIER GENEROUS
STRAIGHT VIGOROUS
FRANKINCENSE THUS OLIBAN
OLIBANUM
FRANKLY FREELY OPENLY PLAINLY
CANDIDLY
FRANKNESS CANDOR FREEDOM
OPENNESS
FRANKPLEDGE BORROW FRIBORG
FRANTIC MAD WOOD RABID INSANE
MANIAC FURIOUS LUNATIC VIOLENT
DERANGED FEVERISH FRENETIC
FRENZIED MANIACAL
FRAPPE ICE GRANITE
FRATERCULA MORMON
FRATERNAL BROTHERLY DIZYGOTIC
FRATERNITY FRAT FRARY HOUSE
ORDER FRATRY QUALITY SOCIETY
SODALITY
FRATERNIZE FRAT COTTON
FRAUD GYP DOLE FAKE GAFF GAUD
GULL JAPE JUNT LURK RUSE SHAM
SKIN WILE CHEAT COVIN CRAFT
DOLUS FAKER FAVEL GLAIK GUILE
HOCUS LURCH SHARK SHIFT SWICK
SWIKE TRICK BROGUE DECEIT
FULLAM HUMBUG INTAKE STUMER
WRENCH FLIVVER KNAVEFY
ROGUERY STUMOUR SWINDLE

BOODLING COZENAGE IMPOSTER
OPERATOR SUBTLETY TRUMPERY
FRAUDULENT SKIN WILY CRONK
COGGED CRAFTY QUACKY ABUSIVE
CROOKED CUNNING KNAVISH
CHEATING COVINOUS FRAUDFUL
GUILEFUL QUACKISH SINISTER
SPURIOUS
FRAXINELLA DITTANY RUEWORT
FRAY FRET BROIL BROOM FEAZE
MELEE RAVEL AFFRAY BUSTLE
CHAUVE FRIDGE TIFFLE CONTEST
FRAZZLE
FRAYED WORN FLAGGY RAVELED
FRAZER FINNER
FREAK FIRK FLAM WHIM FANCY
HUMOR LUSUS MOODS SCAPE
SPORT MEGRIM SPLEEN WHIMSY
CAPRICE CROTCHET ESCAPADE
FLIMFLAM WHIMWHAM
(CRAZY —S) LUNES
FREAKISH FREAKY FLIGHTY
MAGGOTY WHIMSIC CRANKISH
FRECKLE CHIT EPHELIS FRECKEN
LENTIGO SUNSPOT
FRECKLED FRECKLY FLECKLED
FREE LAX LET RID BOLD EASE LISS
OPEN REDD SHED SHUT CLEAN
CLEAR FLUID FRANK LARGE LISSE
LOOSE READY SCOUR SLAKE SPARE
ACQUIT DEGAGE DEVOID EXEMPT
FACILE FLUENT FREELY GRATIS
IMMUNE LOOSEN SOLUTE UNSLIP
VACANT VAGILE CLEANSE DELIVER
GRIVOIS INEXACT LASKING LIBERAL
MANUMIT RELEASE SCIOLTO
UNBOUND UNSLAVE UNTWIST
WILLING ABSOLUTE AUTARKIC
EASINESS EXPEDITE FACILITY
FREEHAND GRIVOISE INDIGENT
LAXATIVE LIBERATE UNBRIDLE
(— AND EASY) GLIB FAMILIAR
(— BROOK OF WEEDS) RODE
(— FROM ABIGUITY) HOMELY
DECIDED
(— FROM ACCUSATION) SACKLESS
(— FROM ACIDITY) DULCIFY
(— FROM ANXIETY) CONTENT
(— FROM ARTIFICIAL) ARTLESS
(— FROM BIAS) CANDID
(— FROM CARE) EASY CARELESS
(— FROM CHARGE) FDD PURGE
FRANCO
(— FROM CONSTRAINT) CASUAL
(— FROM DEDUCTIONS) NET
(— FROM DEFECT) HAIL HALE
SOUND
(— FROM DIRT) BRIGHT
(— FROM DOUBT) RESOLVE
(— FROM ELECTRICAL CHARGE)
DEAD
(— FROM ERROR) LEAL SOUND
CORRECT ACCURATE
(— FROM EVIL) RESCUE
(— FROM EXTREMES) EQUABLE
(— FROM FLAWS) GOOD
(— FROM FROST) FRESH
(— FROM IMPURITIES) FINE DRESS
DEFECATE DEPURATE

(— FROM KNOTS) ENODE ENODATE
(— FROM MARKS) BLANK
(— FROM MICROORGANISMS)
ASEPTIC STERILE
(— FROM OBLIGATION) ACQUIT
EXCUSE
(— FROM PENALTY) ABSOLVE
(— FROM STONES) CHESSOM
(— FROM) EX REDD DEVOID
DISPATCH
(— OF DIFFICULTIES) AFLOAT
(— OF FAT) ENSEAM
(— OF TAR) WRECK
(— ONE'S SELF) SOLVE
(— PLUNGER) ARM
(— THROW AREA) KEYHOLE
FREEBOARD QUICKSIDE
FREEBOOTER TORY RIDER THIEF
PIRATE CATERAN CORSAIR
PILLAGER RAPPAREE SNAPHANCE
FREEBORN INGENUOUS
FREEDMAN LEYSING TITYRUS
(PL.) LAET
FREEDOM RUN EASE FRITH LARGE
ACCESS STREET APATHIA BREADTH
LEISURE LIBERTY LICENCE LICENSE
RELEASE AUTONOMY FREELAGE
FREENESS IMMUNITY IMPUNITY
LARGESSE WITHGATE
(— FROM BIAS) CANDOR
(— FROM CONSTRAINT) ABANDON
(— FROM DANGER) SECURITY
(— FROM ERROR) ACCURACY
(— FROM GUILT) SHRIVE
(— OF ACCESS) ENTREE
(— OF ACTION) SWINGE LATITUDE
(— OF SPEECH) PARISIA
(— TO PROCEED) HEAD
FREEHOLD BARONY
FREEHOLDER SWAIN BONDER
YEOMAN FRANKLIN
FREEING LIVERY ACQUITAL
FREE LANCE ROUTIER
FREELY FREE LIEF LARGE LARGELY
READILY HEARTILY
FREEMAN BUR AIRE BARON CEORL
HAULD BONDER FRANKLIN
ROTURIER
FREEMASON FRATER MORGAN
NOACHITE
(ONE NOT A —) COWAN
FREESTONE HAZEL
(— STATE) CONNECTICUT
FREETHINKER INFIDEL SKEPTIC
AGNOSTIC
FREEZE ICE RIME CATCH CHILL
FROST CURDLE FRAPPE HARDEN
STARVE STEEVE CONGEAL
GLACIATE
FREEZING COLD FREEZY FRIGID
FROSTY GLACIAL GELATION
FREIGHT LOAD CARGO GOODS
ASTRAY LADING FRAUGHT HOTSHOT
PLUNDER PORTAGE TRUCKAGE
(— CAR) TRUCK
FREMD FRAIM FRAMMIT
FRENCH CREOLE FRANCO GALLIC
GALLIAN GALLICAN
FRENCH GUIANA (CAPE OF —)
ORANGE

(CAPITAL OF —) CAYENNE
(RIVER OF —) MARONI
(TOWN OF —) MANA KOUROU
FRENCH HONEYSUCKLE SULLA
FRENCH LAVENDER STECHADOS
FRENCHMAN FROG GAUL FROGGY
PICARD FRENCHY MONSIEUR
PARLEYVOO
FRENCH MULBERRY SOURBUSH
FRENCH REPUBLIC MARIANNA
MARIANNE
FRENULUM TENDON
FRENUM BRIDLE FRAENUM
FRENULUM VINCULUM
FRENZIED RABID RAMAGE BERSERK
FANATIC FRANTIC FRENETIC
FURIBUND
FRENZY AMOK FURY GERE MOON
MUST RAGE AMUCK FUROR MANIA
MUSTH FURORE MADNESS OESTRUS
SWIVVET DELIRIUM INSANITY
FREQUENCY HERTZ CREBRITY
FREQUENT USE BANG KEEP HAUNT
HOWFF OFTEN AFFECT COMMON
HOURLY INFEST RESORT ENHAUNT
OFTTIME CREBROUS FAMILIAR
PRACTICE
FREQUENTLY OFT OFTEN HOURLY
UNSELDOM
FRESH GAY HOT NEW WET FLIP
GOOD RACY SMUG WARM BRISK
CRISP GREEN MOIST QUICK RUDDY
SASSY SMART SOUND SWEET VIVID
CALLER CALVER FLORID LIVELY
MAIDEN STRONG UNUSED VIRENT
VIRGIN ANOTHER NOUVEAU
UNFADED NOUVELLE ORIGINAL
SPANKING YOUTHFUL
FRESHEN BRACE FRESH RENEW
BREEZE CALLER REVIVE CHOUNCE
PEARTEN REFRESH SWEETEN
FRENCHEN
FRESHENER BRACER
FRESHET TIDE FLOOD FRESH SPATE
TORNADO
FRESHMAN FOX BEJAN FROSH
BEJANT GREENY FRESHER
FRESHNESS VERD NOVELTY
VERDURE VIRIDITY
FRET DIK NAG ORP RUB RUX VEX
CARK FASH FRAY FUSS GALL GNAW
RAGE STEW YIRM CHAFE CRAKE
CRISP FLISK GRATE PIQUE WORRY
WREAK ABRADE CORSIE CRYSAL
HARASS MUCKLE NETTLE PLAGUE
REPINE RIPPLE RUFFLE CHRYSAL
GRECQUE GRIZZLE MEANDER
SCRUPLE SQUINNY ALIGREEK
IRRITATE
FRETFUL GIRNY ORPIT TEATY TEENY
TESTY FRETTY PENCEY SULLEN
TATCHY TWISTY FRECKET PEEVISH
PETTISH SPLEENY CAPTIOUS
CRANKOUS FRETSOME FROPPISH
PETULANT PINDLING
FRETTED FRETTY MAGGED
FRETTING FRET EATING
FREY FREYR YNGVI
FRIABLE CRIMP CRISP CRUMP FLAKY
FRUSH MEALY SHORT CRUMBY

CRUMMY FLUFFY PUTRID CHESSOM
CRUMBLY MOLDERY POWDERY
RESOLUTE ROTTENLY SHATTERY
(NOT —) SAD
FRIAR FRATE FREER MINIM MINOR
BHIKKU FRATER GELONG GOSAIN
LISTER BHIKSHU JACOBIN LIMITER
SERVITE BREVIGER CAPUCHIN
JACOBITE MINORIST MINORITE
PREACHER
FRIARBIRD COLDONG PIMLICO
MONKBIRD
FRIAR SKATE DOCTOR
FRICANDEAU GRENADINE
FRICASSEE POTPIE
FRICATIVE BUZZ HISS OPEN YOGH
DURATIVE
FRICTION BUZZ DRAG HISS CHAFE
WINDAGE
FRICTIONLESS SMOOTH
FRIED FRIT SAUTE
FRIEDCAKE WONDER CRULLER
FATCAKE DOUGHNUT
FRIEND AME AMI AMY BOR CAD EME
PAX BHAI CHUM NABS OPPO WINE
AMIGO BUDDY INGLE NETOP TROUT
AIKANE BELAMY COUSIN CUMMER
GOSSIP INWARD KIMMER PRINCE
QUAKER ACHATES COMRADE
SOCIETY COCKMATE COMPADRE
DEMOPHIL FEDERATE HICKSITE
INTIMADO INTIMATE TILLICUM
(—S NOT SPEAKING) CUTS
(CLOSE —) PRIVY COBBER
COMPADRE
(DIVINE —) SOCIUS
(FAMILIAR —) CRONY GREMIAL
SPECIAL
(GIRL —) DOXY DRAG DONEY DOXIE
STEADY
(INTIMATE FEMALE —) CUMMER
(PRIVATE —) PRIVADO
(WOMAN —) GIMMER
(PL.) FOLK KITH SOCE FOLKS
SOCIETY
FRIENDLESS FORLORN
FRIENDLINESS AMITY AFFINITY
BONHOMIE GOODWILL
FRIENDLY COSH GOOD HOLD HOMY
KIND CHIEF COUTH GREAT HOMEY
THICK AMICAL CHATTY FOLKSY
FORTHY HOMELY KINDLY SMOOTH
AMIABLE AMICOUS COUTHIE
AMICABLE HOMELIKE INTIMATE
SOCIABLE
FRIENDSHIP PAX AMITY AMOUR
FRIEZE KELT FRISE CUSHION
FALDING FRISADO FRIEZING
FRIGATE ZABRA
FRIGATE BIRD IOA IWA ALCATRAS
FRIGATE MACKEREL BONITO
TASSARD
FRIGG FREA FRIJA
FRIGHT COW BOOF FEAR FLEG FRAY
ALARM GHAST GLIFF GLOFF PANIC
SCARE AFFRAY GASTER GLIFFY
SCHRIK TERROR STARTLE SWITHER
FRIGHTEN GASTNESS GLIFFING
FRIGHTEN AWE COW FLY SHY SOB
BAZE BREE DOSS FEAR FLEG FLEY

FRAY FUNK HARE HAZE SHOO AFEAR AFLEY ALARM APPAL BLUFF GALLY GHOST GLIFF HAZEN SCARE SHORE SPOOK AFFRAY ALARUM APPALL BOGGLE BOOGER COWARD FLAITE FLIGHT FRIGHT GALLEY GALLOW AFFREUX FRECKEN SCARIFY STARTLE TERRIFY AFFRIGHT MISTRYST

(— BIRDS) KEEP

FRIGHTENED RAD EERY FRIT GAST EERIE GHAST AFRAID AGHAST SCARED SCAREY STURTIN GHASTFUL

(EASILY —) TIMID SKITTISH

FRIGHTENING EERY DREAD EERIE GOURY HAIRY FRIGHTY GHASTLY SHIVERY DREADFUL FLEYSOME

FRIGHTFUL WAN GRIM UGLY AWFUL FERLY HORRID UGSOME AFFREUX DIREFUL FEARFUL GASHFUL GHASTLY HIDEOUS ALARMING DREADFUL ELDRITCH FEARSOME GHASTFUL HORRIBLE HORRIFIC TERRIBLE TERRIFIC

FRIGID DRY ICY COLD BLEAK FISHY ARCTIC FROSTY FROZEN WINTRY GLACIAL FREEZING SIBERIAN

FRIGIDITY GLARE

FRILL DIDO PURL JABOT RUCHE RUFFLE ARMILLA FLOUNCE SPINACH SPINAGE CHITLING CRIMPING FRILLERY FURBELOW

(— OF HAIR) APRON

(PL.) PUFFERY FOOFARAW FRILLERY

FRILLINESS CHICHI

FRILLING SWEEPER

FRILLY CHICHI

FRINGE WLO EDGE GILL LOMA RUFF WELT BEARD THRUM BORDER EDGING MARGIN TASSEL BULLION CREPINE EYELASH FEATHER FIMBRIA SELVAGE TRAILER VALANCE WHISKER CILIELLA FRISETTE INDUSIUM SELVEDGE TRIMMING

(SOFT —S) THRUM

(PL.) ZIZITH

FRINGED JUBATE

FRINGEFOOT UMA

FRINGEPOD LACEPOD

FRINGETAIL VEILTAIL

FRINGE TREE SHAVINGS

FRIPPERY FLIPPERY TRINKUMS

(PL.) GAUDERY

FRISK COLT FISK PLAY ROLL SKIP WHID CAPER SKICE CAREER CAVORT FRISCO FROLIC TITTUP WANTON FRISCAL FRISKLE

FRISKY GAY PERT FRISK CROUSE FEISTY KIPPER LIVELY COLTISH JIGGISH PLAYFUL SPORTIVE

FRISON KNUB

FRIT FRETT CALCINE

FRITTER FOOL FRIT TEAR BOLLO DRILL BANGLE DRIVEL LOUNGE BEIGNET DRIBBLE FLITTER SLATTERN

FRIVOLITY LEVITY FRIBBLE INANITY

ITEMING FUTILITY NONSENSE NUGACITY

FRIVOLOUS GAY DAFT GIDDY INANE LIGHT PETTY SILLY WASHY FLIMSY FRILLY FRIVOL FROTHY FUTILE TOYISH YEASTY FATUOUS FRIBBLE LIGHTLY NIDGETY SHALLOW TRIVIAL GIMCRACK JIMCRACK SKITTISH TRIFLING

FRIVOLOUSNESS FUTILITY

FRIZZ FRIZ FRIZE FRIZZLE FROUNCE

FRIZZED CRISPY

FRIZZLY FUZZY CRIMPY FRIZZY

FRIZZY FUZZY CRIMPY FRIZZLY

FROCK DUD JAM GOWN JUMP SLIP WRAP LAMMY SMOCK TRUSS TUNIC CLERIC JERSEY LAMMIE MANTLE ROCHET SUKKENYE

FROCK COAT CRISPIN

FROG PAD POD KICK FROSH FROSK FROUD PADDO PADDY RONCO ANURAN PEEPER TOGGLE CHARLIE CRAWLER CREEPER CROAKER CUSHION FRESHER FROGLET PADDOCK PODDOCK QUILKIN BULLFROG FERREIRO FROGGING PLATANNA REPLACER

(— IN LOOM) HEATER

(— OF HORSE'S HOOF) FRUSH CUSHION

FROG CRAB RANININ

FROGFISH SLIMER TOADFISH

FROGGER CHASER TRAILER ZOOGLER

FROGGY RANARIAN

FROGHOPPER HOPPER CERCOPID

FROGMOUTH MOREPORK PODARGUE

FROLIC BUM GAY RIG BLOW COLT GAME GELL HAZE JINK LAKE LARK ORGY PLAY PLOY RANT REEK ROMP CAPER FREAK FRISK MERRY PRANK RANDY ROUSE SPORT SPREE CURVET FRATCH GAMBOL PLISKY POWWOW PRANCE ROLLIX SHINDY SPLORE VAGARY WANTON DISPORT GAMMOCK MARLOCK PLISKIE SCAMPER SKYLARK SPANIEL STASHIE WASSAIL CAROUSAL JAMBOREE

FROLICSOME GAY DAFT ROID ANTIC FRISK GILPY LARKY FRISKY LIVELY WANTON ANTICAL JOCULAR LARKING LARKISH WAGGISH ESPIEGLE FRISKFUL FROLICKY GAMESOME LARKSOME PRANKISH SPORTFUL SPORTIVE

FROLICSOMENESS HEYDAY

FROM A AB DE EX OF FAE FRA FRO VAN VON THROM AGAINST

(— A DISTANCE) ALOOF

(— BEGINNING TO END) THROUGH

(— ELSEWHERE) ALIUNDE

(— OFF) AFFA

(— SIDE TO SIDE) OVER CROSS ATHWART

(— THIS PLACE) HENCE

FROND FERN TRESS CROSIER FRONDLET

FRONT BOW VAN BROW FACE FORE HEAD PROW THIN AFORE VAUNT BEFORE DEVANT FACADE FACING FORMER OPPOSE SECTOR ADVANCE FORWARD FRONTAL FURTHER OBVERSE PREFACE RESPECT SLENDER FOREHEAD FOREMOST FOREPART FORESIDE FRONTAGE

(— OF ASTROLABE) WOMBSIDE

(— OF BARN) FOREBAY

(— OF BIRD'S NECK) GUTTUR

(— OF BODY) GROUF

(— OF HEAD) VISAGE FORETOP

(— OF HELMET) VENTAIL

(— OF WATERWHEEL BUCKET) START

(— UPON) AFFRONT

FRONTAL FRONT SINDON FRONTON METOPIC FRONTLET SUFFRONT

FRONTIER BOUND COAST FRONT MARCH BARRIER FRONTURE OUTLYING

(FORTIFIED —) LIMES

FRONTING OBVIOUS

FRONTISPIECE FRONT UNWAN FRONTIS

FRONTLET TIARA FRONTAL CHAMFRON

FRONTPIECE GORE

FROST ICE COLD HOAR RIME RIND

FROSTING ICING DIVINITY

FROSTWEED ROCKROSE

FROSTY ICY COLD RIMY CHILL CRISP FRORE GELID GLARY HUNCH BOREAL FRIGID FROREN CHILLING INIMICAL PRUINOUS

(NOT —) OPEN

FROTH FOB BARM FOAM REAM SCUM SUDS WORK CREAM SPUME YEAST FLOWER FREATH LATHER SPURGE

FROTHER CREOSOTE

FROTHING HUMMING MANTLING

FROTHY FOAMY REAMY SPEWY SPUMY SUDSY FLASHY YEASTY SPUMOSE SPUMOUS WHIPPED

FROWARD RANK CROSS AWKWARD PEEVISH WAYWARD CONTRARY FROPPISH PERVERSE PETULANT PROTERVE SHREWISH UNTOWARD

FROWN GLUM LOUR GLOOM GLOUT GLUMP LOWER SCOWL GLOWER GLUNCH FROUNCE FRONTLET

FROWNING GLUM GLUNCH

FROWZY BLOUSY BLOWSY BLOWZY RAFFISH FROWZLED SCABROUS SLOVENLY

FROZEN FAST FIXED FRORE FRORY GELID GLARY FRAPPE FROREN

FRUCTOSE ACROSE

FRUGAL EASY MILD CANNY CHARY ROMAN SCANT SPARE SAVING SCARCE SCOTCH CAREFUL PRUDENT SLENDER SPARING THRIFTY

FRUGALITY SPARE THRIFT ECONOMY PARCITY MANAGERY

FRUGALLY HARD CHARILY SAVINGLY

FRUIT BEL FIG HAW UVA BAEL COYO

DATE DIKA DROP GEAN JACK LIME NOOP PEAR PLUM POME SEED SLOE SNAP SORB AKENE ANISE APPLE BERRY CLING COUMA DRUPE GENIP GOURD GRAPE GUAVA HAZEL ILAMA LEMON LIMON MANGO MELON OLIVE PAPAW PEACH RIPER SORVA ACHENE ALMOND BANANA BUTTON CEDRON CEREZA CHERRY CITRON CITRUS COBNUT COCHAL COCONA DAMSON DURIAN EMBLIC EMBOLO GUARRI JUJUBE KEEPER LEGUME LONGAN LOQUAT MARANG MAYPOP MUYUSA ORANGE PAPAYA PAWPAW PELLAS POMATO RESULT SAPOTA SQUASH UVALHA WESTME ZAPOTE APRICOT ATEMOYA AVOCADO AZAROLE BILIMBI BLOATER CARAWAY CHAYOTE CHECKER CIRUELA COCONUT CURRANT DESSERT GEEBUNG GENIPAP GHERKIN KUMQUAT PIGFACE PRODUCT RIPENER SERVICE SHALLON SOURSOP TANGELO ACHENIUM BAYBERRY BELLERIC BILBERRY CALABASH CANISTEL CAPSICUM CARDAMUM CITRANGE CUCUMBER DEWBERRY DOGBERRY EGGFRUIT FOLLICLE FRUITAGE FRUITERY FRUITLET GOLKAKRA INKBERRY LIMEQUAT OSOBERRY PIEPRINT PODOCARP RAMBUTAN SEBESTEN SEEDBALL SHADDOCK SWEETSOP

(— OF CACTUS) SABRA
(— OF CAPER) CAPOT
(— OF CITRON) ETROG ETHROG
(— OF HEMLOCK) CONIUM
(— OF PALM) SALAK
(— OF ROSE) HEP HIP BUTTON
(— ON TREES) HANG
(—S COOKED IN SYRUP) COMPOTE
(AGGREGATE —) ETAERIO DRUPETUM HETAERIO
(ASTRINGENT —) GAB GAUB CHEBULE
(AVOCADO-LIKE —) ANAY
(CANDIED —) CONSERVE
(CARMINATIVE —) BADIAN
(COILED —) STROMBUS
(COLLECTIVE —) SYNCARP
(DRIED —) PASA CUBEB MUMMY SABAL OREJON CAPSULE EMBELIA
(EARLY —) PRIMEUR HASTINGS
(FALLEN —) SHEDDER
(FIRST —S) ANNATES BIKKURIM PRIMICES
(FLESHY —) SYCONIUM
(GOURD —) PEPO
(GRAPEFRUIT-LIKE —) SUHA
(GRAPELIKE —) WAMPEE
(HAWTHORN —) PEGGLE
(IMPERFECT —) SPECH NUBBIN
(MASHED —) FOOL
(MEDICINAL —) AIWAIN AJOWAN EMBELIA
(ONE-SEEDED —) AKENE ACHENE
(PALMYRA —) PUNATOO
(PLUMLIKE —) CARISSA CIRUELA

(PRESERVED —) SUCCADE CONFITURE
(PRICKLY —) HEDGEHOG
(SELF-FERTILIZED —) AUTOCARP
(SLICED DRIED —) SNITS SNITZ SCHNITZ
(SPURGE —) TAMPOE
(SUPERIOR —) TOPPER
(UNRIPE OAK —) CAMATA
(WINGED —) SAMARA
(WOODY —) XYLOCARP
FRUIT BAT KALONG
FRUIT-BEARING FERTILE
FRUIT DOVE KUKU
FRUITFUL FAT FOODY BATTEL FECUND FRUITY GRAVID FERTILE TEEMFUL UBEROUS ABUNDANT CHILDING FRUITIVE PREGNANT PROLIFIC
FRUITFULNESS UBERTY FATNESS
FRUITGROWER FRUITIST
FRUITLESS DRY GELD VAIN ADDLE BARREN FUTILE STERILE USELESS ABORTIVE BOOTLESS
FRUIT PIGEON KUKU LUPE KUKUPA MANUMA MANUTAGI
FRUIT STONE COB PYRENE PUTAMEN
FRUSTRATE BALK BILK DASH DISH FOIL LAME BLANK BLOCK CHECK CROSS ELUDE SMEAR THRAW WRECK BAFFLE BLIGHT DEFEAT DELUDE KIBOSH OUTWIT SCOTCH THWART ANIENTE DECEIVE FALSIFY PREVENT CONFOUND INFRINGE STULTIFY
FRUSTRATER MARPLOT
FRUSTRATING BOOTLESS
FRUSTRATION FOIL SUCK DEFEAT FIASCO
FRUSTULE TESTULE HYPOTHECA
FRY SILE BROOD FRIZZ KRILL SAUTE FRIZZLE GREYFISH
FRYER FRIER FRIZZER SPRINGER
FRYING PAN FRYPAN SPIDER CREEPER SKILLET
FUCHSIA CORREA KONINI FUCHSIN EARDROPS
FUCHSIN ROSEINE SOLFERINO
FUCHSINE RUBIN RUBINE MAGENTA
FUDDLE FUZZLE FLUSTER
FUDDLED FAP REE DOPY BOSKY DOPEY SWASH TIPSY MAUDLIN
FUDGE HUNCH SNUDGE PENUCHE DIVINITY
FUEL GAS OIL POB COAL COKE FIRE PEAT UPLA ARGOL ACETOL ELDING FIRING SHRUFF TIMBER COALITE SYNTHOL FIREBOOT FIREBOTE GASOGENE GAZOGENE
FUGITIVE HOT FLEME FLYER FUGIE SCAMP OUTLAW FLEEING LAMSTER REFUGEE RUNAWAY FLEETING RUNAGATE UNSTABLE (PL.) MANZAS
FUGUE FUGA
(— THEME) DUX
(PART OF —) STRETTA
FULA PEUL PEUHL FELLANI FELLATA

FULANI PEUL PEUHL
FULCRUM BAIT GLUT
FULFILL FILL FULL KEEP MEET HONOR ANSWER COMPLY FULFIL REDEEM SATISFY COMPLETE COMPLISH
FULFILLMENT PASS EFFECT FUNCTION
(— OF GOD'S WILL) KINGDOM
(IMAGINARY —) FANTASY
FULGURATION BLICK
FULL BAD BIG FAT FOW COOL DEEP FAIR GOOD JUST PANG RANK TRIG TUCK AMPLE AWASH BROAD CLEAR FLUSH LARGE LUCKY PIENO PLAIN PLENY ROUND SATED SOLID TIGHT TOTAL WHOLE ENTIRE GOGGLE HONEST STRONG BAPTIZE BRIMFUL COPIOUS DESTROY DIFFUSE FULFILL FULSOME LIBERAL OROTUND PERFORM PLENARY REPLETE TEEMING TRAMPLE WEALTHY ABSOLUTE ADEQUATE BOUFFANT BRIMMING CHOCKFUL COMPLETE EXTENDED FREQUENT RESONANT THOROUGH
(— CLOTH OR YARN) WALK
(— OF AIR) LIGHT
(— OF BLANKS) LACUNOSE
(— OF CHINKS) RIMOSE
(— OF DELAY) MOROSE
(— OF DEVILTRY) HEMPY HEMPIE
(— OF DIRT) FOUL
(— OF EGGS) GRAVID
(— OF ENERGY) STOUT SWANK
(— OF FLAWS) CRAZY
(— OF FUN) FROLIC
(— OF HAPPINESS) SUNSHINY
(— OF INTEREST) AGOG
(— OF IRON) SIDEROSE
(— OF LIFE) SPUNKY ANIMATE
(— OF LOOPS) KINKY
(— OF MATTER FOR THOUGHT) MEATY
(— OF RUSHES) SPRITTY
(— OF SAND) ARENOSE
(— OF SLEEP) SOPOROSE
(— OF SMALL OPENINGS) POROSE POROUS
(— OF SPIRIT) GENEROUS
(— OF VIGOR) FLUSH GREEN LUSTY ANIMATED SPIRITED
(— OF ZEST) RACY
FULL-BLOWN JUICY
FULLBODIED FAT LOFTY HEARTY
FULL-BOSOMED BUXOM
FULLER GAG HARDY HARDIE ROLLER TUCKER WALKER BLOCKER CREASER THICKER CLOTHIER
FULL-FACED AFFRONTE AFFRONTY
FULL-FLAVORED BOLD RACY
FULL-FLEDGED SUMMED
FULL-GROWN RIPE GROWN MATURE SEEDED
FULLNESS BODY FLAIR FLARE FULTH PLENUM FULNESS PLEROMA SATIETY
FULLY ALL DOWN EVEN INLY WELL AMPLY LARGE ENOUGH FAIRLY

THRICE WHOLLY CLEARLY LARGELY
UTTERLY CLEVERLY ENTIRELY
INWARDLY MATURELY
FULMAR HAG NELLY NODDY
HAGDON NELLIE MALDUCK
MALMOCK STINKER
FULMINATE BLOW FULMINE
FULSOME SUAVE FOULSOME
FUMARIC BOLETIC LICHENIC
FUMBLE BOOT MUFF MULL PIRL
BOBBLE FAFFLE MUMBLE PRODDLE
MISFIELD THRUMBLE
FUMBLER STUMER STUMOUR
FUMBLING HALTING
FUME FUFF RAGE REEK EWDER
SMOKE STIFE SNUFFLE FUMIGATE
FUMID SMOKY SMOKEY
FUMIGATE SMEEK SMOKE PASTIL
CYANIDE PASTILLE
FUMIGATION GASSING
FUMIGATOR AERATOR
FUMITORY FUMARIA FUMEROOT
FUMEWORT
FUN GIG GAME GELL JEST JOKE
LAKE PLAY BORAK BOURD HUMOR
KICKS MIRTH MUSIC SPORT FROLIC
GAIETY GAYETY DAFFERY DAFFING
GAMMOCK WHOOPEE
(UNRESTRAINED —) HELL
FUNCTION ACT JOB RUN USE DUTY
FORM ROLE WORK ACTION AGENCY
MATRIX MISTER OFFICE SQUASH
CONCEPT FACULTY ISOLATE
SERVICE WORKING ACTIVITY
BUSINESS MINISTRY PROVINCE
(— EFFECTIVELY) AVAIL
(—S OF JUDGES) ERMINE
(APPARENT —) STUDY
(ESSENTIAL —) DHARMA
(MATHEMATICAL —) DEL FORM
INVERSE
(SPECIAL —) CEREMONY
FUNCTIONAL DYNAMIC
FUNCTIONARY FLUNKY CAPTAIN
FLUNKEY CHAPRASI
FUNCTIONING AFLOAT
FUNCTIONLESS OTIOSE
FUND BOX BANK FOND MASS CHEST
KITTY MOUNT SLUSH STOCK STORE
ESCROW CHALUKA JACKPOT
RESERVE HALUKKAH PECULIUM
(PL.) CAJA COFFER
FUNDAMENT NOCK TAIL BOTTOM
FUNDUS
FUNDAMENTAL BASAL BASIC
KLANG PRIME VITAL BOTTOM
SIMPLE BASILAR BEDROCK ORGANIC
PRIMARY RADICAL ABSOLUTE
ORIGINAL RUDIMENT SUBSTRAT
FUNDAMENTALLY AUFOND
FUNDUS FORNIX
FUNERAL TANGI BURIAL EXEQUY
BURYING CORTEGE FUNEBRE
FUNERARY MORTUARY
FUNERAL DIRECTOR BLACKMAN
FUNEREAL FERAL DISMAL SOLEMN
FUNEBRE FUNERAL DIRGEFUL
EXEQUIAL MOURNFUL
FUNGICIDE NABAM ZINEB FERBAM
CALOMEL BORDEAUX DICHLONE

FUNGOID MYCOID FUNGOUS
FUNGUS MOLD SMUT BRAND ERGOT
FUNGE HYPHO MOREL MOULD
PHOMA SPUNK SWARD TRUFF
VALSA VERPI AGARIC BOLETE
FUNGAL MILDEW OIDIUM AMANITA
BOLETUS CHYTRID FUNGOID
GEASTER LEPIOTA TRUFFLE
AECIDIUM CLATHRUS CORNBELL
EUMYCETE FUSARIUM HELVELLA
MUCEDINE MUSHROOM OOMYCETE
OTOMYCES PHALLOID POLYPORE
PUFFBALL SAPROGEN SPOROGEN
TREMELLA TUCKAHOE
(UNICELLULAR —) BEES EAST
YEAST
FUNK FUNG NESH
FUNNEL CAST STACK TEWEL TRUNK
FILLER FUMMEL SIPHON SYPHON
TUNNEL TUNNER TRUMPET TUNDISH
HYPONOME WINDSAIL
FUNNY ODD GOOD COMIC DROLL
MERRY QUEER COMICAL JOCULAR
RISIBLE STRANGE HUMOROUS
(VERY —) SPLITTING
FUR FOX BEAR CALF COON FLIX FOIN
GRAY GREY GRIS MINK PEAN PELF
PELL SEAL VAIR BUDGE COYPU
CROSS FITCH FLICK GENET GRISE
OTTER PAHMI SABLE SCARF SHUBA
BADGER BEAVER COUGAR DESMAN
ERMINE FISHER GALYAC JACKET
MARTIN NUTRIA PELAGE POTENT
RABBIT SPRING SUSLIK CALABER
CARACAL FITCHET FITCHEW
FURRURE MINIVER TOPCOAT
CACOMIXL ERMINOIS KOLINSKI
(— OF LAMBSKIN AND WOOL)
BUDGE
(— RESEMBLING PERSIAN LAMB)
KRIMMER
(BEAVER —) WOOM CASTOR
(GRAY —) GRAY GREY GRIS GRISE
CRIMMER LETTICE
(NUMBER OF — SKINS) TIMBER
TIMMER
(RABBIT —) CONY SCUT CONEY
FLICK LAPIN HATTER SEALINE
ERMILINE
(SQUIRREL —) CALABAR
(SQUIRREL OR MARTIN —) AMICE
POPEL
(STONE MARTEN'S —) FOIN
(PL.) PELTRY FURRIERY
FURBEARER PLATINUM
FURBELOW DIDO FALBALA
FURBISH DO FIG RUB FAKE FINE
VAMP CLEAN SCOUR FINIFY POLISH
BURNISH VARNISH RENOVATE
FURCATE FORKY BRANCH FURCAL
FURCULA SPRING FURCULUM
FURCULUM WISHBONE
FURFOOZ GRENELLE
FURIOUS MAD GRIM WOOD ANGRY
BRAIN GIDDY IRATE RABID SHARP
FIERCE FURIAL FURIED INSANE
RENISH STORMY FRANTIC HOPPING
MADDING MANKIND PELTING
RAGEOUS REDWOOD RUSHING
TEARING VIOLENT FRENZIED

VEHEMENT VESUVIAN WRATHFUL
FURIOUSLY CRAZY ANGERLY
TEARING
FURL FOLD HAND ROLL STOW WRAP
FRESE TRUSS FARDEL FURDLE
FURLED IN
FURLONG SHOT STADE
FURLOUGH LEAVE BLIGHTY
FURNACE ARC KILN OVEN TANK
BENCH CUPEL DRIER DRYER FORGE
MOUTH TISAR BURNER CALCAR
CUPOLA HEATER ATHANOR
CHAFERY CRESSET FIREPOT
PUDDLER ROASTER BESSEMER
BLOOMERY CALCINER FIREWORK
IRONCLAD LIMEKILN PRODUCER
REFINERY TRYWORKS
(— DOOR) TWEEL
(ALMOND —) ALMAN
(ARC —) HEROULT
(GLASS-HEATING —) TISAR
(PORTABLE —) DANDY CRESSET
FURNACEMAN BUSTLER DROSSER
SMELTER IMPROVER REHEATER
FURNISH ARM SOW DECK FEAT
FEED FILL FRET FRUB GIVE LEND
TRIM VEST ARRAY ENDOW EQUIP
FRAME INDUE PITCH POINT SERVE
SPEED STOCK STORE STUFF
AFFORD GRAITH INSURE INVEST
OUTFIT RENDER SUPPLY ADVANCE
APPAREL APPOINT BRACKET
GARNISH INSTORE PERFORM
PLENISH PRESENT PRODUCE
PROVIDE SUFFICE ACCOUTER
DECORATE FRUBBISH MINISTER
(— ABUNDANTLY) FREQUENT
(— ANALYSIS) ACCOUNT
(— FULLY) CHARGE
(— REFRESHMENT) EASE
(— WITH DRINK) BIRL BYRL
(— WITH MEALS) BOARD
(— WITH STEEP SLOPE) ESCARP
(— WITH STRENGTH) MAN
(— WITH WINGS) IMP
(— WITH) BESEE
FURNISHED ARMED BODEN GARNI
(COMFORTABLY —) BEIN
FURNISHING ADVANCE FITMENT
(PL.) STUFF BAGGAGE PENATES
FURNITURE ADAM TIRE SAMAN
STOOL STUFF GRAITH FITMENT
MEUBLES MOVABLE EQUIPAGE
ORNAMENT SUPELLEX TACKLING
(CHEAP —) BORAX
(SHIP'S —) HARNESS
FURORE FUROR BROUHAHA
FURRED PURED LOADED
FURRING PACKING
FURROW FUR GAP GAW RIB RUT
FURR GRIP HINT LINE PLOW RAIN
RILL ROUT RUCK SEAM SULK
CHASE DRAIN DRILL EARTH FIELD
RIGOL SCORE SEUGH STRIA
GROOVE GUTTER INDENT SULCUS
SUTURE TRENCH BREAKER
CHAMFER CHANNEL CRUMPLE
FEERING PLOWING QUILLET
SCRATCH WINDROW WRINKLE
CARRIAGE NOTAULIX THOROUGH

FURROWED SEAMED EXARATE FURROWY SULCATE TRENCHED

FURROWING KNOT DRESS

FURRY SHAGGY

FUR SEAL URSAL

FURTHER MO AID YET HELP YOND ADDED AGAIN FRESH SPEED SUPRA BEYOND EXTEND SECOND ADVANCE DEVELOP FARTHER FORWARD PROMOTE MOREOVER REMANENT ULTERIOR

FURTHERMORE BESIDES FURTHER OVERMORE

FURTIVE SLY PRIVY CLAMMY SECRET SHIFTY SNEAKY HANGDOG MEACHING MYSTICAL SNEAKING STEALTHY

FURTIVELY SLILY SLYLY SIDELINS

FURTIVENESS STEALTH

FURUNCLE BOIL

FURY HAG IRE WAX BURN RAGE ANGER BRETH DREAD FUROR IRISH RIGOR WRATH BELDAM CHOLER FRENZY FURORE MADNESS WIDDRIM DELIRIUM FEROCITY VIOLENCE WOODNESS

FURZE FUN FUZZ LING ULEX WHIN GORSE WHINCOW

FUSE RUN CAKE FLOW FLUX FRIT FUZE MELT BLEND FOUND FUSEE FUZEE QUILL SMELT SQUIB SWAGE TRAIN UNITE MINGLE SPITTER CONCRETE CONFLATE COPULATE PORTFIRE SAUCISSE

FUSED CONNATE

FUSEE FUZEE SPINDLE VESUVIAN VESUVIUS

FUSELAGE BODY

(— **MEMBER**) LONGERON

FUSIFORM FUSATE SPINDLE

FUSIL (**DIVIDED INTO —S**) PLUMETE

FUSION ZYG FLUX FUSURE CHIASMA FLUXION CYTOGAMY MITAPSIS

FUSS DO ADO ROW TEW COIL FAFF FIKE FIRK FIZZ FRET ROUT SONG STIR TIME TOUSE TOWSE TRADE WHAUP BOTHER CADDLE DIRDUM FANTAD FETTLE FISSLE FISTLE FIZZLE FRAISE FUFFLE FUSTLE HOORAY HURRAH PHRASE POTHER SETOUT STROTH TURNUP FOOSTER FRIGGLE FUSSIFY NAUNTLE POOTHER SPUFFLE SPUTTER TAMASHA BUSINESS FOOFARAW SCRONACH

FUSSBUDGETY SPOFFISH

FUSSINESS DAINTY FADDLE FIKERY FOOSTER

FUSSING BOTHER

FUSSY FIKY FIXY FUDGY FIDFAD PROSSY SPOFFY SPRUCE STICKY FIDGETY SPOFFISH

FUSTET ZANTE FUSTIC

FUSTIAN HOLMES PILLOW BOMBAST TWADDLE MOLESKIN

FUSTIC LIME MORA FUSTET DYEWOOD AMARILLO

FUSTINESS FOIST

FUSTY FOIST MOLDY MUSTY FOISTY FROWSTY

FUTILE IDLE VAIN OTIOSE USELESS FOOTLESS FUTILOUS HELPLESS

FUTILITY VANITY NUGACITY

FUTTAH WHATA

FUTURE LATER SKULD COMING ONWARD OPTION TOCOME TOWARD LAVENIR FUTURITY

(— **TIME**) MANANA

FUZZ LINTERS

FUZZY LOUSY MUZZY WOOLY WOOLLY

G GEE GOLF GEORGE
GA AKRA ACCRA INKRA
GAB GOB YAP BLAB CHINFEST
GABBLE WAB CANK CHAT CONK
JAVER BABBLE GAGGLE HABBLE
RABBLE TATTER YABBLE CLATTER
JAUNDER TWADDLE TWITTER
SLIPSLOP
GABBRO BOJITE NORITE EUCRITE
GABION KISH KEESH BASKET
WALING CORBEIL
GABLE GAVEL GOFOL DETAIL
DORMER GABLET KENNEL MEMBER
PINION AILERON PEDIMENT
GABON (CAPITAL OF —) LIBREVILLE
(LAKE OF —) ANENGUE AZINGUO
(MOUNTAIN OF —) MPELE
(NATIVE OF —) FANG ADOUMA
ECHIRA OKANDE
(RIVER OF —) OGOUE ABANGA
IVINDA NGOUNIE
(TOWN OF —) OYEM BONGO KANGO
MITZIC OMVANE MAKOKOU
GABOON OKOUME
GABRIELINO TOBIKHAR
GAD GAR RUN GAUD JAZZ RAKE
JINKET GADLING TRAIPSE
(— ABOUT) HAIK ROLL STRAM
GALLANT TROLLOP
(FATHER OF —) JACOB
GADABOUT GAD GADDER TRAIPSE
GADFLY GAD CLEG GLEG CLEGG
STOUT WHAME BOTFLY BREEZE
GADBEE OESTRID HORSEFLY
GADGET DODAD GISMO GIZMO
HICKY DINGUS DOODAD GILGUY
HICKEY JIGGER JIMJAM WIDGET
CONCERN DOFUNNY GIMMICK
BUSINESS GIMCRACK JIMCRACK
(PL.) GIBBLES GUBBINS GADGETRY
GADUS MORRHUA
GADWALL RODGE VOLANT GADWELL
REDWING SHUTTLE
GAEL CELT KELT SCOT GOIDEL
GAEDHEAL
GAELIC ERSE IRISH
GAFF CLIP SPAR SPUR YARD GAFFLE
GABLOCK GAFFLET SLASHER
GAVELOCK
(— MACKEREL) GAMBEER
GAG BOFF GEGG JOKE PONG SCOB
HEAVE KEVEL SCOBE AGUAJI
MUZZLE WHEEZE
GAGE (ALSO SEE GAUGE) LAY PAWN
WAGE GAUGE JEDGE NORMA
WAGER FEELER PLEDGE SPIDER
SCANTLE STANDARD UDOMETER
GAIETY JOY GALA JEST CHEER
MIRTH BAWDRY FROLIC GAYETY
LEVITY BAUDERY BEGONIA DAFFERY
DAFFING GAYNESS JOLLITY
JOYANCE ROLLICK FESTIVAL
HILARITY VIVACITY
GAILY GAY GAYLY BRAVELY LIGHTLY
GAIN BAG DAP GET NET POT WIN
BEAR BOOT DRAW GROW HAVE
LAND MAKE PELF SACK TILL ADDLE
BOOTY CATCH LATCH LUCRE
REACH SCORE ARRIVE ATTAIN

CHIEVE DERIVE GATHER INCOME
OBTAIN PROFIT STRAIN CAPTURE
CONQUER EMBRACE GAYMENT
GETTING HARVEST POSSESS
PROCURE REALIZE VANTAGE
WINNING CLEANING CONQUEST
PURCHASE
(— ADMISSION) ENTER
(— ADVANTAGE) GLEEK
(— ASCENDANCY) PREVAIL
(— BY EXTORTION) SQUEEZE
(— BY FORTUNE) DRAW HAZARD
(— COMMAND OF) MASTER
(— KNOWLEDGE) EDIFY LEARN
(— OVER) ENGAGE
(— UNDERSTANDING) SMOKE
(— WITHOUT DEDUCTION) CLEAR
(DISHONEST —) MEED
(ESTIMATED —) ESTEEM
(ILL-GOTTEN —) PELF
(MATERIAL —) PUDDING
(UNEXPECTED —) BUNCE
(PL.) PICKING PLUNDER GANANCIAS
GAINFUL LUCROUS GAINSOME
GAINSAY DENY FORBID IMPUGN
OPPOSE REFUTE RESIST DISPUTE
RECLAIM WITHSAY AGAINSAY
GAIT BAT JOG GANG LOPE PACE
RACK SKIP STEP TROT VOLT WALK
AMBLE AUBIN GOING STALK TRAIN
ALLURE CANTER GALLOP LOUNGE
SLOUCH SWINGE TODDLE WADDLE
WALLOW WAMBLE WOBBLE
DOGTROT HICKORY SAUNTER
SCUTTLE SHAMBLE SHUFFLE
WALKING WAUCHLE
(— OF ILL-BROKEN HORSE) CHACK
(4-BEAT —) AMBLE
(DEFECTIVE —) WINDING
(UNSTEADY —) STAGGER
GAITER SPAT VAMP STRAD BONNET
BRAGAS COCKER GASKIN GUETRE
HOGGER HUGGER LEGGIN PUTTEE
GAMBADE GAMBADO LEGGING
STARTUP BOOTIKIN CUTTIKIN
(PL.) UPPERS GASKINS GAMASHES
GRAMOCHES
GAIZE MALMSTONE
GAJO GORGIO
GALACTITE MILKSTONE
GALACTOSIDE IDEIN IDAEIN
GALAGO LEMUR LEMUROID
GALANAS GAINES
GALATEA (FATHER OF —) NEREUS
(LOVER OF —) ACIS
(MOTHER OF —) DORIS
GALAX COLTSFOOT
GALAXY NEBULA SPIRAL
GALBANUM FERULA GALBAN
ALBETAD
GALCHA PAMIR
GALE BLOW GELL HELM WIND
GAGEL PERRY STOUR BUSTER
EASTER BAYBUSH BURSTER
GALEAGE TEMPEST FLEAWOOD
GALEWORT NORWESTER
GALEA MITRA HELMET
GALGA INGUSH
GALIBI CARIBI KALINA

GALINGALE CYPRESS WANHORN
CHINAROOT
GALIPOT BARRAS GALLIPOT
TACAMAHAC
GALJOEN BLACKFISH
GALL GA GAW BAIT FELL FRET
WRING COCKLE HARASS BEDEGAR
GALLNUT KNOPPER NUTGALL
BEDEGUAR CECIDIUM FLEASEED
IRRITATE OAKBERRY SEEDGALL
SPURGALL TACAHOUT
(SAND —) SALT NATRON SANDIVER
(PL.) PURPLES
GALLANT GAY BEAU PROW BLADE
BRAVE BULLY CIVIL JOLLY LOVER
NOBLE PREUX SHOWY SPARK
SWAIN DONZEL ESCORT HEROIC
POLITE RUTTER SPARKY SQUIRE
SUITOR AMATORY AMORIST
AMOROUS CONDUCT GALANTE
GREGORY SPARKER STATELY
TOPPING YOUNKER CAVALIER
CICISBEO FEMALIST GALLIARD
HANDSOME POLISHED
GALLANTRY GAME DRURY DRUERY
BRAVERY COURAGE PROWESS
PARAMOUR
GALLBERRY INKBERRY
GALLED RAW
GALLEON CARAC CARRACK
GALLOON
GALLERY POY SAP COOP GODS
JUBE LOFT PAWN ALURE BOYAU
ORIEL PRADO ARCADE BURROW
DEDANS NARROW PIAZZA SCHOOL
SOLLAR SUBWAY TUNNEL BALCONY
GALERIE HEADWAY TERRACE
VERANDA BRATTICE CANTORIA
CORRIDOR HOARDING PARADISE
PERAMBLE SCAFFOLD TRAVERSE
VERANDAH
(— IN BAZAAR) PAWN
(— IN HOUSE OF COMMONS)
VENTILATOR
(— MADE BY INSECT) MINE
(CHURCH —) JUBE LAFT LOFT
(MINE —) BORD BROW SLOVAN
(MINSTREL'S —) ORIEL
(OPEN —) LOGGIA
(UNDERGROUND —) HYPOGEE
HYPOGEUM
GALLEY FUST CUDDY DRAKE FOIST
STICK BIREME GALIOT HEARTH
ZYGITE BASTARD CABOOSE
DROMOND GALLIOT HEXERIS
LYMPHAD TRIREME UNIREME
CAMBOOSE COOKROOM CROMSTER
GALLEASS RAMBERGE
(— BOTTOM) SLICE
(CHIEFTAIN'S —) BIRLING BIRLINN
(PHILLIPINE —) CALAN
(VIKING —) AESC DRAKE
GALLEY SLAVE FORSADO
SFORZATO
GALLFLY CYNIPID
GALLINAE RASORES
GALLINAZO VIRU VULTURE
GALLING BITTER
GALLINULE COOT KORA MOHO RAIL

GORHEN PUKEKO SKITTY MOORHEN STANKIE SULTANA DABCHICK HYACINTH MANUALII RAILBIRD RICEBIRD SWAMPHEN

GALLIVANT KITE GALLANT

GALLON GAWN CONGIUS
(— OF ORE) DISH
(128 —S) LEAGUER
(EIGHTH —) OCTARIUS

GALLOON ORRIS

GALLOP FOG RUN AUBIN PRICK CANTER CAREER COURSE TITTUP WALLOP TANTIVY

GALLOWS NUB CRAP DROP FORK TREE BOUGH CHEAT FURCA WIDDY GIBBET DERRICK FORCHES JUSTICE POTENCE STIFLER WARYTREE

GALLOWS BIRD HEMPY WIDDY HEMPIE HEMPSEED WIDDIFOW CRACKROPE

GALOSH ARCTIC ZIPPER EXCLUDER OVERSHOE

GALUTH GOLUS GOLAHI

GALVANIC VOLTAIC

GALVANIZE ZINCIFY

GALVANOMETER DETECTOR REOMETER

GAMBESON WAMBAIS

GAMBIA (CAPITAL OF —) BANJUL
(LANGUAGE OF —) JOLA WOLOF FULANI MALINKE
(MONEY OF —) DALASI
(NATIVE OF —) JOLA PEUL WOLOF DIOLAS FULANI MANDINGO SERAHULI
(TOWN OF —) MANSA BINTANG KUNTAUR

GAMBIA POD BABLOH

GAMBIER CATECHU

GAMBIT MANEUVER

GAMBLE BET DICE GAFF GAME NICK PLAY PUNT RISK SPORT STAKE WAGER CHANCE GAMMON HAZARD PLUNGE FLUTTER
(— AGAINST) BUCK

GAMBLER PIKER SPORT CARROW DEALER PLAYER PUNTER HUSTLER PLAYMAN PLUNGER SLICKER THROWER BLACKLEG GAMESTER HAZARDER

GAMBLING GAMING HAZARDRY
(— DEVICE) PACHINKO

GAMBLING HOUSE HELL TRIPOT

GAMBO GOOSE SPURWING

GAMBOL HOP PLAY CAPER FRISK KEVEL PRANK CAREER CAVORT FROLIC GAMBADO

GAMBREL CAMMOCK SPREADER

GAME COB FUN JEU JIG GAMY LAKE MAIL PLAY DANCE GAMEY PARTY SPIEL SPORT WATHE BATTUE MORRIS QUARRY RAMSCH VENERY JENKINS KNICKER BREATHER FIGHTING FOREGAME
(— FOR FISHERMEN) SKISH
(— LIKE HANDBALL) FIVES
(— LIKE HOCKEY) DODDART
(— NARROWLY WON) SQUEAKER
(— OF CAT) BILLET

(— OF FOOTBALL) BOWL CAMP
(— OF FORFEITS) KEN
(— OF HOCKEY) BANDY SHINNY
(— OF MARBLES) TAW BOWL BONCE GULLY KEEPS KNUCKS MIGGLES
(— OF MENTAL SKILL) GO CHESS CHECKERS
(— OF NINEPINS) KAILS KAYLES
(— OF PRISONER'S BASE) CHEVY CHIVVY
(— WITH BOOMERANG) BRIST
(— WITH COUNTERS) DUMPS GOOSE
(— WITH SHUTTLECOCK) TAHYING
(BACKGAMMON —) HIT IRISH
(BALL —) CAT TUT SNOB CATCH RUGBY SOCCER SQUASH TENNIS CRICKET KNAPPAN BASEBALL FOOTBALL HANDBALL SLUGFEST SOFTBALL
(CARD —) AS HOC LOO MAW NAP PAM PIT PUT SET BRAG CENT FARO FISH FROG GRAB JASS LANT PINK POOL POPE POST RUFF SANT SKAT SLAM SNAP SOLO STUD VINT BEAST BUNCO BUNKO CARDS CARIE CHICO CINCH COMET CRIMP DECOY GILET GLEEK GRAND LEAST MONTE OMBER OMBRE PEDRO PITCH POKER PRIME RUMMY SCOPA STOPS STUSS TRUMP WHIST BASSET BIRKIE BOODLE BOSTON BRIDGE CASINO CHEMMY COMMIT ECARTE EIGHTS EUCHRE FARMER FLINCH HEARTS HOWELL LOADUM PANFIL PIQUET QUINZE RAMSCH ROUNCE SLOUGH SMUDGE SPIDER TOURNE AUCTION AUTHORS BELOTTE BEZIQUE CANASTA CASSINO CAYENNE CHICAGO COONCAN GARBAGE HUNDRED JACKPOT REVERSI RONTOON SCOPONE SETBACK TRIUMPH VINGTUN VITESSE BACCARAT BASEBALL BRISCOLA COMMERCE CONQUIAN CONTRACT CRIBBAGE FREAKPOT HANDICAP IMPERIAL NAPOLEON PATIENCE PENCHANT PENNEECH PINOCHLE SHOWDOWN SKINBALL SKINNING SLAPJACK TREDILLE TRESILLO VERQUERE VIDERUFF
(CARNIVAL —) HOOPLA
(CHILDREN'S —) TAG DIBS JACKS KICKBALL
(CONFIDENCE —) RAMP BIGMITT
(COURT —) SQUASH TENNIS HANDBALL
(DICE —) FARE BINGO CRAPS NOVUM RAPHE HAZARD BARBUDI ADDITION BARBOTTE CAMEROON HOOLIGAN
(DRAWN —) SPOIL REFAIT
(DRINKING —) HIJINKS
(EGYPTIAN —) SENT SENIT
(GAMBLING —) TAN FARO HAND PICO BOULE CRAPS MACAO MONTE POKER PROPS RONDO STUSS

BRELAN HAZARD RONDEAU ROULETTE
(GENERAL —) HEI HIT HOB TAG TIG BALL BASE BULL BUZZ CENT DIBS DUCK FARE GOLF HOLE JOWL KENO MALL POLO POOL SLAM SNOB TICK BANDY BINGO BONCE BOULE CHESS CHUBA CHUNK CLOSH DARTS DOLOS FIVES GOOSE HALMA HOUSE IRISH JACKS LOTTO LURCH NOVUM NULLO PITCH PUSSY RUGBY SALTA SALVO SCRUB TROCO WHOOP BEAVER CAROMS CHIVVY CHUNKY CLUMPS COBNUT COCKAL COOTIE CRAMBO FEEDER GOBANG GRACES HAZARD HOOPLA HUBBUB JEREED KAYLES MERELE PELOTA PLUMPS RAGMAN RINGER SEESAW SHINNY SIPPIO SKILLO STICKS TENNIS TIGTAG TIPCAT TIVOLI TRIGON TRUCKS BALLOON BEANBAG BEEBALL BOWLING COBBLER CONKERS CROQUET CURLING DIABOLO DODDART DOUBLES DREIDEL ENDBALL GOGGANS HANGMAN HURLBAT LOGGATS MAHJONG MATADOR MUGGINS NETBALL PALLONE PASSAGE PEEVERS PUSHPIN QUINTET RINGTAW SARDINE SQUAILS STATUES TENPINS TOMBOLA ANAGRAMS BALKLINE BASEBALL CHARADES CHECKERS CHOUETTE DOMINOES DOUBLETS DRAUGHTS DUCKPINS FIVEPINS FOOTBALL FORFEITS GIVEAWAY HARDHEAD KICKBALL LEAPFROG PARCHESI PEEKABOO PURPOSES PUSHBALL PYRAMIDS RINGTOSS ROULETTE ROUNDERS SCRABBLE SKITTLES STOBBALL STOWBALL TRAPBALL VERQUERE
(GUESSING —) LOVE MORA CANUTE
(INDIAN —) CHUNKY HUBBUB
(INFERIOR —) CHECK
(NUMBERS —) BUG
(OUTDOOR —) GOLF POLO HURLY ROQUE RUGBY SOCCER CROQUET HURLING BASEBALL SOCCER FOOTBALL LACROSSE
(PROGRESSIVE —) DRIVE
(REHEATED —) SALMI SALMIS
(SWISS —) JASS
(THREE BOWLING —S) SERIES
(TRAPSHOOTING —) SCOOT
(WAR —) BARRIERS
(WORD —) GHOST ANAGRAMS

GAMECOCK STAG STAIG

GAMEKEEPER GAMIE KEEPER WALKER WARNER WARRENER

GAMESTER DICER PLAYER GAMBLER PLAYMAN SHARPER HAZARDER TABLEMAN

GAMETE SPERM OOCYTE ZYGOTE GAMETOID OOGAMETE OOSPHERE

GAMETOCYTE GAMONT CRESCENT GONOCYTE

GAMETOPHYTE GERMLING

GAMIN TAD ARAB URCHIN
GAVROCHE
GAMMA AGMA
GAMUT GAMME RANGE SCALE
SERIES COMPASS DIAGRAM
GANDER STEG STAIG GANNER
(— AND GEESE) SET
GANESA GUNPUT GANAPATI
GANG MOB SET BAND BUND CORE
CREW GING PACK PAIR PUSH TEAM
GROUP HORDE SPELL CHIURM
COFFLE GAGGLE LAYOUT MOHOCK
SCHOOL COMPANY
(— MEMBER) WHYO
(— OF FISHHOOKS) PULLDEVIL
(— OF MINERS) CORE
GANGLING GAWKY GANGLY
GANGLION TUMOR CEREBRUM
GANGPLANK BROW GANGWAY
GANGRENE CANKER GANGER
SPHACEL
GANGSTER HOOD WHYO BANDIT
COWBOY CHOPPER
GANGUE MATRIX LODESTUFF
VEINSTONE
GANGWAY ROAD SLIP LOGWAY
TUNNEL CATWALK COULOIR
GATEWAY
GANJA GUNJAH CANNABIS
GANNET BOOBY GAUNT SOLAN
PIQUERO SEAFOWL
GANTRYMAN DROPMAN
GANYMEDE (BROTHER OF —) ILUS
ASSARACUS
(FATHER OF —) TROS
(MOTHER OF —) CALLIRRHOE
GAP SAG FLAW GAPE GOWL GULF
MUSE NICK SLAP SLOP WANT
BREAK BRECK CHASM CHAUM
CHAWN CLOVE FRITH MEUSE MUSET
NOTCH SHARD SHERD VUIDE
BREACH GULLET HIATUS LACUNA
SPREAD THROAT VACUUM CLOSING
OPENING VACANCY VACUITY
APERTURE DIASTEMA ENTREFER
INTERVAL MULTIGAP QUEBRADA
(— IN BANK OF STREAM) GAT
(— IN MEMORY) AMNESIA
(— SERVING AS PASS) COL
GAPE GAN GAP GANT GAUP GAWK
GAWP GAZE GOVE GRIN YAWN
CHAUN HIATE STARE RICTUS
DEHISCE INHIATE
GAPING GALP AGAPE HIANT CHAPPY
CHASMA GAWISH MOUTHED
RINGENT
GAR HOUND SNOOK AGUJON
CHERNA GARFISH GARPIKE BILLFISH
GOREFISH GURDFISH HORNFISH
HORNKECK LONGJAWS LONGNOSE
GARAGE HANGAR LOCKUP SIDING
GARRIDGE
(ROW OF —S) MEWS
GARAVANCE CARAUNA GARBANZO
GARB (ALSO SEE APPAREL AND
DRESS) COWL GEAR TOGA VEST
DRESS GUISE HABIT APPAREL
CLOTHES COSTUME RAIMENT
GARBAGE GASH SLOP OFFAL TRASH

WASTE GIBLET REFUSE SCRAPS
GARBAGEMAN DUSTMAN
GARBLE GELD JUMBLE MANGLE
DISTORT GARBLING MUTILATE
GARDANT AFFRONTE
GARDEN HAW EDEN KNOT YARD
ARBOR GARTH CIRCLE POMACY
POMARY QUINTA SHAMBA VERGER
VIHARA ACADEMY HERBARY
OLITORY ORCHARD ROCKERY
TOPIARY CHINAMPA FLORETUM
HORTYARD KALEYARD LEIGHTON
PARADISE POTAGERE ROSARIUM
(— CITY) CHICAGO
(— STATE) NEWJERSEY
GARDENER MALI PONICA CROPPER
PLANNER BOSTANGI
GARDEN HELIOTROPE VALERIAN
GARDENIA TIARA
GARDENING TOPIARY
GARDEN ROCKET EVEWEED
GARDEN WARBLER JACK HAYBIRD
BECAFICO FAUVETTE FIGEATER
GARFISH (SEE GAR)
GARGANEY TEAL CRICK
GARGANTUAN HUGE VAST GIANT
HOMERIC TITANIC ENORMOUS
GIGANTIC HOMERIAN
GARGLE GURGLE COLLUTORY
GARGOYLE BOSS
GARIBALDI GOLDFISH
GARISH GAUDY GIDDY SHOWY
CRIANT GLARING
GARISHNESS GLARE
GARLAND BAY LEI CROWN VITTA
ANADEM CORONA CRANTS ROSARY
WREATH CHAPLET CORANCE
CORONAL FESTOON
GARLIC AJO MOLY CHIVE PORET
ALLIUM PORRET RAMSON
GARMENT DUD TOG BACK BRAT
COAT GOWN PELL PELT RAIL ROBE
SARK SHAG SILK SLIP SLOP SULU
VEST WEED ABAYA BUREL CENTO
CLOAK CLOTH COTTE CYMAR
DRESS FROCK HABIT HAORI JOSEY
JUPON KHAKI MANGA NABOB
SHAWL SHIFT SHIRT SIMAR SKIRT
STOLE WRIEL ALPACA ATTIRE
BARROW BLOUSE CAFTAN CAMLET
CAPOTE CHAMMA COTTON CYCLAS
ERMINE EXOMIS FECKET HUIPIL
JACKET JERSEY JUMPER KERSEY
KIRTLE MOHAIR MOTLEY SARONG
SHORTY SHROUD STROUD TAMEIN
ZIZITH AMICTUS BROIGNE BUNTING
CAMBLET CHIRIPA CRAWLER
CUCULLA CULOTTE DOUBLET
FALDING FLOCKET GROGRAM
PALETOT PELISSE RAIMENT
SHORTIE SURCOAT SWEATER
VESTURE WRAPPER BATHROBE
CAMELINE CAPUCHIN CHAUSSES
COLOBIUM CORSELET COVERALL
DEERSKIN EPIBLEMA GAMBESON
GUERNSEY HIMATION INDUMENT
PADUASOY SCAPULAR SEALSKIN
SLIPOVER SNOWSUIT VESTMENT
WEARABLE STROUDING

(— OF HERALD) TABARD
(— OF HIGH PRIEST) EPHOD
(— OF PATCHES) CENTO
(BABY'S —) BARROW CRAWLER
CREEPER
(BADLY-MADE —) DRECK
(BLUE —) MAZARINE
(BURIAL —) SHROUD
(COARSE —) BRAT STROUD
(DEFENSIVE —) JACK BROIGNE
GAMBESON
(ECCLESIASTICAL —) STOLE
RHASON CASSOCK
(ETHIOPIAN —) CHAMMA
(HINDU —) SARI SAREE
(INFANT'S —) DIAPER BUNTING
SLEEPER
(JAPANESE —) HAORI
(LEATHER —) BUFF
(LINEN —) LINE
(LONG —) JIBBA STOLE JIBBEH
MANDYAS PELISSE HIMATION
(MEDIEVAL —) ROCHET CHAUSSES
DALMATIC GAMBESON
(MONK'S —) SCAPULAR
(MOURNING —) SABLE
(OUTER —) BRAT COAT GOWN HAIK
HYKE SLOP WRAP FROCK HAORI
NABOB PALLA PILCH SMOCK
DOLMAN ROCHET CHEMISE GALABIA
PALETOT SURCOAT SWEATER
HIMATION OVERSLOP
(PADDED —) TRUSS
(SLEEVELESS —) ABA CAPE COWL
VEST MANTLE CUCULLA GANDURAH
(SQUARE —) KAROSS
(THIN —) GOSSAMER
(TIGHT-FITTING —) HOSE COTTE
LEOTARD
(WOMAN'S —) IZAR BURKA CYMAR
NABOB SIMAR BURKHA CHITON
JOSEPH PEPLOS PEPLUM VISITE
BURNOUS
(PL.) GEAR COSTUME GARNISH
FLANNELS
GARNER REAP STORE GATHER
IMBARN COLLECT
GARNET GRENAT PYROPE ANTHRAX
GRANATE OLIVINE VERMEIL
ESSONITE MELANITE ROSOLITE
YANOLITE
GARNISH LARD TRIM ADORN DRESS
EQUIP MENSE STICK FURNISH
TOPPING CHUMMAGE DECORATE
DUXELLES ORNAMENT
GARNISHED GARNI
GARNISHEE CHECK FACTOR
GARNISH
GARRET ATTIC SOLAR SOLLAR
MANSARD COCKLOFT
GARRISON WARD STUFF PRESIDY
WARNISON
GARRULITY POLYLOGY
GARRULOUS GABBY TALKY WORDY
BABBLY TONGUY VOLUBLE
GARTER GARTEN LEGLET ELASTIC
STRAPPLE
GARTH CORTILE OUTGARTH
GARUM LIQUAMEN

GAS DAMP XENON FLATUS GENAPP LEAVEN OXYGEN PETROL EXHAUST KRYPTON YPERITE AFTERGAS ETHERION FIREDAMP HYDROGEN STANNANE VESICANT

(— CONSTANT) R

(COLORLESS —) OXAN OXANE KETENE GERMANE STIBINE

(NERVE —) SARIN

(NONCOMBUSTIBLE —) INERT

(POISONOUS —) ARSINE CYANOGEN PHOSGENE

GASCONADE BRAG CROW BOAST BLUSTER

GASEOUS AERIFORM GASIFORM VOLATILE

GASH CUT CHOP LASH BLASH CRIMP GANCH GRIDE SCORE SLASH SLISH SCOTCH SLUICE TRENCH INCISION INCISURE

(— A FISH) RIM

GASKET LUTE CASKET GASKIN GROMMET SCISSIL

GASKIN BRAGAS

GASOLINE GAS AVGAS JUICE PETROL BENZINE NATURAL

GASP FOB BLOW GAPE KINK PANK PANT CHINK CROAK FETCH THRATCH

GASTRONOME EPICURE

GASTROPOD SLUG DRILL HARPA OLIVA SNAIL BUCKIE NERITE ABALONE MOLLUSK TOXIFER UNIVALVE VELUTINA

GATE BAB BAR JET HEAD LIFT PORT SASH SLAP YETT ENTRY HATCH JANUA SALLY SPRAY STICK TORAN ENAJIM ESCAPE FENDER FUNNEL HARROW INGATE LIGGAT PADDLE PORTAL RUNNER TIMBER TORANA WICKET ZAGUAN BARRIER CLICKET FIVEBAR GATEWAY LIDGATE POSTERN SHUTTER ABOIDEAU ANTEPORT DECUMANA ENTRANCE FOREGATE GURDWARA PENSTOCK TOLLGATE TOWNGATE TRIMTRAM TURNPIKE

(— OF CASTLE) BAR

(BACK —) POSTERN

(CUSTOMS —) BARRIER

(IRRIGATION —) CHECK TAPON TAPPOON

(LICH —) SCALLAGE TRIMTRAM

(RUNNING —) FUNNEL

(SAW —) FRAME

(SAWMILL —) SASH

(SLALOM —S) HAIRPIN

(SLUICE —) HATCH VALVE

(WATER —) SLUICE

GATEADO DIOMATE

GATEHOUSE BAR LODGE

GATEKEEPER WARDEN CERBERUS GATEWARD PORTITOR STILEMAN

GATEMAN GUARD

GATEPOST DURN HARR HEEL PIER POST SHAFT POSTEL

GATEWAY DAR DOOR GATE LOKE TORU PYLON TORAN TORII BARWAY GOPURA TORANA PROPYLON

GATHER GET LEK POD WIN BAND BREW CLAN CLOT CROP CULL FURL HERD HIVE HOST PICK REAP RELY TUCK AMASS BANGE BROOM BUNCH FLOCK GLEAN GUESS INFER LEASE PLUCK RAISE SWEEP ACCRUE COMPEL CORRAL DECERP DERIVE GARNER HUDDLE HUSTLE IMBARN MUSTER RAMASS SCRAPE CLUSTER COLLATE COLLECT COMPILE CONGEST CONVENE CONVOKE HARVEST RAMMASS RECRUIT ASSEMBLE CUMULATE SHEPHERD

(— AS ARMY) HOST

(— BY SCRAPING) SCRATCH

(— GRASS SEED) STRIP

(— HEADWAY) SET

(— HERBS) SIMPLE

(— IN A HEAP) HATTER

(— IN RAGS) TAT

(— SEWING) GAGE GAUGE

(— UP) KILT

GATHERED KILTED CUMULATE

GATHERER GEDDER TUCKER RUFFLER CHICLERO PLICATOR PUCKERER

GATHERING HUI LED LEK SUM FAIR FEST KNOT SING SIVA LEVEE SHINE TRYST INDABA MUDDLE PLISSE POWWOW RUELLE SMOKER COLLECT COMMERS COMPANY FUNFEST HARVEST HOSTING HUSKING JOLLITY KLATSCH MEETING MOOTING NYMPHAL ROCKING TURNOUT ASSEMBLY CONCLAVE FUNCTION JAMBOREE PANIONIA POTATION RECOURSE SINGSONG SOCIABLE STAMPEDE

(— OF ANIMALS) DRIVE

(— OF ARMED MEN) HOSTING

(— OF CLOTH) SHIRR SHIRRING

(— OF FILM) CISSING

(— OF SCOUTS) CAMPOREE JAMBOREE

(— PLACE) LESCHE

(FORMAL —) HALL

(RELIGIOUS —) SHOUT

(SOCIAL —) BEE FRY BAKE BALL CLUB DRUM STAG WINE BAILE BINGE BINGO DANCE MIXER SHIVOO SMOKER CANTICO KLATSCH SHINDIG SQUEEZE BARBECUE CAMPFIRE CLAMBAKE TALKFEST SYMPOSIUM

GAU BANT

GAUCHE CLUMSY AWKWARD

GAUD GAY GAUDY FANGLE VANITY TRINKET

GAUDINESS GLARE GLITTER

GAUDY GAY LOUD CHEAP FLARY SHOWY VAUDY BRAZEN FLASHY FLIMSY FLORID GARISH GAWISH SKYRIN TAWDRY TINSEL BRANKIE CHINTZY FLARING GAUDISH GLARING

GAUGE (ALSO SEE GAGE) BORE GAGE MOOT PLUG SIZE TRAM GADGE NORMA RANGE DENTIN FEELER FORMER GABARI DEPTHEN TEMPLET TRAMMEL ESTIMATE INDICANT MEASURER STANDARD SURFACER TEMPLATE

(— FOR SLATES) SCANTLE

(RAIN —) UDOMETER

GAUGER SURVEYOR

GAUL GALLIA

(PL.) PICTONES

GAUNT BONY GRIM LANK LEAN SLIM THIN PINED SPARE THIRL BARREN HAGGED HOLLOW MEAGER MEAGRE SHELLY HAGGARD SLENDER DESOLATE RAWBONED

GAUNTLET TOP CUFF GLOVE GANTLET GAINPAIN GANTLOPE

GAUR BISON SELADANG

GAUZE LISSE MARLI MARLY UMPLE CYPRUS CYPRESS TIFFANY CARBASUS

GAUZY FILMY

GAVE GIN GUV YAF YAFE

GAVEL HAMMER GAVELAGE

GAVIAL NAKOO LIZARD GHARIAL LORICATE

GAVOTTE MUSETTE

GAWK GAWKY GAWNEY LUMPKIN RAMMACK

GAWKY GOWKIT AWKWARD GAWKISH

GAY MAD AIRY BOON DAFT GLAD GLEG HIGH RORY TRIM WILD BONNY GAUDY JOLLY LIGHT MERRY RORTY SUNNY VAUDY WLONK ALEGER BLITHE CHEERY FLASHY FRISKY FROLIC GARISH JOCUND JOVIAL JOYFUL JOYOUS KIPPER LIVELY SPORTY CHIPPER FESTIVE GALLANT GIOJOSO GLEEFUL LARKING RACKETY SMICKER TITTUPY WINSOME CAVALIER FROHLICH GAMESOME PLEASANT PRIMROSE SPARKISH SPLENDID SPORTIVE

GAY-FEATHER LIATRIS

GAYWINGS MAYWINGS

GAZE EYE PRY CAPE GAPE GOUK GOWK LEER LOOK MOON OGLE PEER PORE SCAN TOOT GLAIK GLARE GLOAT GLORE SIGHT STARE TWIRE VISIE WLITE ASPECT GLOWER REGARD

GAZELLE AHU GOA ADMI AOUL CORA DAMA MOHR ADDRA ARIEL KORIN DZEREN GROUSE ALGAZEL CHIKARA CORINNE DIBATAG TABITHA CHINKARA

GAZELLE HOUND SALUKI

GAZETTE COURANT JOURNAL

(— OF CRIMES) HUE

GE TAPUYAN

GEAN MERRY MURIE MURRY GUIGNE GASKINS

GEAR KIT SPUR TACK TRIM IDLER TOOTH FOURTH GRAITH HYPOID PINION TACKLE CLOBBER GEARING HARNESS REVERSE RIGGING SEGMENT TRILOBE HEADGEAR

(— OF DIVER) ARMOR

(CHAFING —) SCOTCHMAN

(DEFENSIVE —) ARMORY

(RUNNING —) CARRIAGE
(TRANSMISSION —) HIGH FIRST
  SPEED FOURTH SECOND REVERSE
GEARED GIRT
GEARWHEEL UNILOBE WABBLER
  WOBBLER
GEB KEB SEB
GECKO FANFOOT TARENTE
  GEKKONID LACERTID
GEELBEC SALMON TERAGLIN
GEEPOUND SLUG
GEESE SET
GEIGER TREE ALOEWOOD
  SEBESTEN
GEL JELL JELLY LIVER GELATE
  ALCOGEL
GELATIN GLUE COLLIN GLUTIN
  GLUTOID HAITSAI NORGINE
  ISINGLASS
GELATINOUS MUCULENT JELLYLIKE
GELD LIB GELT ALTER CASTRATE
GELDING HORSE SPADE SPADO
GEM GIM JADE ONYX OPAL RUBY
  AGATE BERYL CAMEO JAZEL JEWEL
  PEARL SPARK STONE TOPAZ ZIMME
  AMULET BAGUET CRUSTA GARNET
  JASPER PEBBLE PYROPE RONDEL
  ZIRCON CITRINE DIAMOND DOUBLET
  EMERALD JACINTH KUNZITE
  ONEGITE PERIDOT SPARKLE
  ACHROITE AMATRICE AMETHYST
  BAGUETTE HYACINTH INTAGLIO
  MARQUISE ORIENTAL RONDELLE
  SAPPHIRE SARDONYX HIDDENITE
  (— CARVED IN RELIEF) CAMEO
  INTAGLIO
  (— ENGRAVED WITH CHARM)
  ABRAXAS
  (— OF IMPERFECT BRILLIANCY)
  LOUPE
  (— REFLECTING LIGHT IN 6 RAYS)
  ASTERIA
  (— STATE) IDAHO
  (IMITATION —) PASTE
  (UNCUT —) ROUGH CABOCHON
GEMMA BUD GEMMULE SOREDIUM
GEMMULE SPORE BROODSAC
GEMMY EMERALD
GEMSBOK ORYX KOKAMA
  GEMSBUCK
GEMSTONE JADE STAR CHEVEE
  SPINEL EMERALD FISHEYE
  CROSSCUT HYALITHE
GENA CHEEK
GENDER SEX KIND CLASS FEMININE
GENE GEN ALLEL AMORPH FACTOR
  LETHAL PRIMER CYTOGENE
  MODIFIER
GENERAL MAIN MOST BROAD
  GROSS COMMON VULGAR CURRENT
  GENERIC MARSHAL SUMMARY
  AUFIDIUS CANIDIUS CATHOLIC
  ECUMENIC ENCYCLIC OVERHEAD
  PANDEMIC PUFIDIUS STRATEGE
  BRIGADIER
GENERALITY CREDO GENERALE
GENERALIZATION LAW AXIOM
  BROMIDE
GENERALIZE WIDEN EXTEND

SPREAD BROADEN
GENERALIZED GROSS GLOBAL
GENERALLY BROADLY LARGELY
  ROUNDLY MOSTWHAT
GENERATE MAKE SIRE TEEM BEGET
  BREED IMPEL SPAWN STEAM
  CREATE FATHER GENDER IMPOSE
  KITTLE DEVELOP INBREED PRODUCE
  ENGENDER
  (— PUS) DIGEST
GENERATION AGE KIND TIME
  WORLD STRAIN STRIND DESCENT
  DIPLOID GETTING KINDRED
  GAMOBIUM GENITURE SAECULUM
  THEOGONY TRIPLOID UPSPRING
  OFFSPRING
GENERATIVE GENIAL GAMETIC
  GENESIC GENETIC SEEDFUL
  PROLIFIC
GENERATOR BUZZER DYNAMO
  RULING ELEMENT DIPHASER
  GENERANT
GENEROSITY GRACE LARGE
  BOUNTY GENTRY BREADTH
  FREEDOM HONESTY COURTESY
  GOODNESS KINDNESS LARGESSE
GENEROUS BIG FREE OPEN SOFT
  FRANK HEFTY LARGE NOBLE
  LIBERAL GRACIOUS HANDSOME
  INSORDID LARGEOUS MAGNIFIC
GENEROUSLY LUCKY MANLY
  KINDLY FRANKLY
GENESIS BIRTH ORIGIN BERESHIT
  GENETICS
GENET BERBE CIVET DAPPLE
  VIVERRINE
GENIAL BEIN BIEN WARM DOUCE
  SONSY DOULCE FORTHY FURTHY
  HEARTY KINDLY MELLOW MENTAL
  CHEERFUL GRACIOUS PLEASANT
GENIALITY BONHOMIE
GENICULATE KNEED ELBOWED
GENIE GENIUS HATHOR SANDMAN
GENII XIN JANN
GENIN BUFAGIN
GENIP GINEP JAGUA IRONWOOD
GENIPAP GENIP JAGUA GUENEGE
GENISTA FURZE RETAMA
GENITAL SECRET
  (PL.) HARNESS PRIVITY GENITURE
GENIUS FIRE GIFT HAPI KALI TURN
  ANGEL BRAIN DEMON GENIO NUMEN
  DAEMON INGENY INGINE TALENT
  WIZARD DUSTMAN DUAMUTEF
  EINSTEIN FRAVASHI SILVANUS
  (— OF LANGUAGE) IDIOM
GENOA GEANE
GENOTYPE BIOTYPE LOGOTYPE
GENOUILLERE KNEELET
GENRE EPIC KIND SORT TYPE CLASS
  STYLE FABLIAU SPECIES CATEGORY
GENS HOUSE
GENTEEL NICE GENTY GENTIL
  JAUNTY POLITE STYLISH GRACEFUL
GENTIAN BIT FELWORT AGUEWEED
  GALLWEED BALDMONEY
GENTILE GOI GOY ARIAN ARYAN
  GOYISH HEATHEN
GENTILITY GENTRICE

GENTLE MOY CALM DEFT DEWY
  FAIR HEND KIND MEEK MILD MURE
  NESH SLOW SOFT SOOT TAME
  BLAND CANNY LIGHT LITHE MILKY
  QUIET SMALL SOBER SWEET
  BONAIR CADISH DOCILE FACILE
  MODEST PLACID REMISS SILKEN
  SILVER SOFTLY TENDER AMABILE
  CLEMENT GRADUAL SOAKING
  SUBDUED DEBONAIR DOVELIKE
  EGGSHELL LAMBLIKE LENITIVE
  MAIDENLY MANSUETE MODERATE
  PEACEFUL SARCENET TOWARDLY
  TRANQUIL
  (— AS OF THE WIND) LOOM
GENTLEFOLK GENTRY GENTILITY
GENTLEMAN NIB SIR BABU GENT
  BABOO CURIO DORAY SAHIB SENOR
  GEMMAN MILORD SENHOR SIGNOR
  YONKER BRAVERY GALLANT
  GENTMAN MYNHEER CAVALIER
  MIRABELL SEIGNEUR SEIGNIOR
  SQUIREEN
  (— COMMONER) HAT
  (— TRAINING FOR KNIGHTHOOD)
  DONZEL
  (COUNTRY —) SQUIRE
  (GIPSY —) RYE
  (MILITARY —) CADET
  (WOULD-BE —) SHONEEN
  (PL.) HERREN CHIVALRY
GENTLEMANLY JAUNTY
GENTLENESS FLESH LENITY
  AMENITY DOUCEUR KINDNESS
GENTLY SOFT CANNY SOAVE EASILY
  FAIRLY LIGHTLY EASYLIKE PRETTILY
  TENDERLY
GENTRY COUNTY GENTRICE
  SQUIRAGE SZLACHTA
GENUFLECTION VENIE KNEELING
GENUINE ECHT GOOD LEAL REAL
  TRUE VRAI PLAIN PUKKA SOLID
  ACTUAL ARRANT DINKUM DIRECT
  HONEST KOSHER PISTIC CURRENT
  GERMANE GRADELY SINCERE
  VERIDIC GRAITHLY STERLING
  (NOT —) TIN SHAM BOGUS
  (SEEMINGLY —) COLORABLE
GENUINENESS VERIDITY
GENUS KIND CLASS ANALOG
  GENDER GENERAL
  (— OF ALGAE) DASYA FUCUS
  BANGIA CHORDA CODIUM HYPNEA
  NOSTOC PADINA DIATOMA LEMANEA
  LIAGORA PTILOTA VALONIA
  ZYGNEMA ANABAENA BRYOPSIS
  CAULERPA CERAMIUM CHONDRUS
  CONFERVA CUTLERIA DICTYOTA
  DUMONTIA GELIDIUM GOMONTIA
  HALIMEDA LERAMIUM LESSONIA
  NEMALION OOCYSTIS PALMELLA
  PORPHYRA STRIARIA TAONURUS
  ULOTHRIX
  (— OF AMOEBA) CHAOS
  (— OF AMPHIBIAN) HYLA RANA
  SIREN PROTEUS AMPHIUMA
  NECTURUS
  (— OF ANT) ATTA ECITON LASIUS
  PONERA TERMES FORMICA

PHEIDOLE TAPINOMA
(— **OF ANTELOPE**) ORYX KOBUS
GAZELLA MADOQUA REDUNCA
ANTILOPE EGOCERUS
(— **OF APE**) PAN PONGO SIMIA
(— **OF APHID**) ADELGES CHERMES
(— **OF ARACHNID**) ACARUS
GALEODES
(— **OF ARMADILLO**) DASYPUS
XENURUS
(— **OF ASCIDIAN**) CIONA MOLGULA
BOLTENIA PYROSOMA
(— **OF ASCLEPIAD**) STAPELIA
(— **OF AUK**) ALCA ALLE
(— **OF BABOON**) PAPIO
(— **OF BACTERIA**) VIBRIO EIMERIA
ERWINIA GAFFKYA PROTEUS
SARCINA BACILLUS BRUCELLA
SERRATIA SHIGELLA
(— **OF BADGER**) MELES ARCTONYX
HELICTIS
(— **OF BARNACLE**) LEPAS BALANUS
ELMINIUS
(— **OF BASIDIOMYCETE**) BOVISTA
(— **OF BAT**) EUDERMA PETALIA
DESMODUS DIPHYLLA MOLOSSUS
MORMOOPS NOCTILIO NYCTERIS
PLECOTUS PTEROPUS VAMPYRUM
(— **OF BEAR**) URSUS EUARCTOS
MELURSUS
(— **OF BEAVER**) CASTOR
(— **OF BEE**) APIA APIS BOMBUS
ANDRENA TRIGONA COLLETES
HALICTUS MELIPONA
(— **OF BEETLE**) AMARA FIDIA HISPA
LAMIA LARIA LYTTA MELOE SAGRA
ALTICA ASILUS CLERUS ELATER
LYCTUS PTINUS SILPHA ACILIUS
ADELOPS AGRILUS ANOBIUM
ANOMALA BRUCHUS CARABUS
CASSIDA EPITRIX PRIONUS SAPERDA
SITARIS ADORETUS AGRIOTES
APHODIUS CALOSOMA CATORAMA
CYBISTER DERMETES DYNASTES
DYTISCUS EPICAUTA EUMOLPUS
HARPALUS LAMPYRIS MEGASOMA
PASSALUS POPILLIA SCOLYTUS
SPHINDUS TENEBRIO
(— **OF BIRD**) ARA ALCA APUS CRAX
CREX GYPS JYNX MIRO MITU MOHO
OTIS PICA RHEA SULA TYTO XEMA
AJAJA ANOUS ANSER ARDEA ARGUS
ASTUR BUCCO FALCO GAVIA GOURA
GUARA GYGIS IRENA JUNCO LARUS
LERWA LOXIA MIMUS MITUA MUNIA
PIPRA PITTA SITTA TODUS UPUPA
VIDUA VIREO ALAUDA ALCEDO
ANHIMA ANTHUS AQUILA BONASA
BRANTA CAPITO CIRCUS COLIUS
CORVUS DACELO ELANUS FULICA
GALLUS JACANA LANIUS LEIPOA
LIMOSA MARECA MENURA MEROPS
MILVUS MONASA NESTOR NUMIDA
PASSER PASTOR PERDIX PERNIS
PROGNE QUELEA RALLUS SAPPHO
SCOPUS SIALIA SPINUS STERNA
SYLVIA TETRAO TRERON TRINGA
TROGON TURDUS TURNIX VULTUR
ANHINGA APTERYX ARTAMUS

BUCEROS CACICUS CAPELLA
CARIAMA CERTHIA CHIONIS CICONIA
CINCLUS COLINUS COLUMBA
COLYBUS COTINGA CUCULUS
ELAENIA GALBULA GARRUPA
HALCYON HIRUNDO IBYCTER
ICTERUS KAKATOE LAGOPUS
LOPHURA LYRURUS MALURUS
MANACUS MESITES MILVAGO
MOMOTUS ORIOLUS PANDION
PAROTIA PIRANGA PITYLUS
PLAUTUS PLOCEUS PORZANA
REGULUS SEIURUS SERINUS
STURNUS TANAGRA TIMALIA
TOTANUS XENICUS ZENAIDA
ACCIPTER ACREDULA AFROPAVO
AGELAIUS AMIZILIA BOTAURUS
BUCORVUS BURHINUS CHAETURA
CORACIAS COTURNIX DELICHON
DIATRYMA DINORNIS DIOMEDEA
DREPANIS EMBERIZA EUPHONIA
EURYPYGA FULMARUS GARRULUS
GEOSPIZA GERYGONE GLAREOLA
GRALLINA GYPAETUS IONORNIS
LUSCINIA MACHETES MYCTERIA
NEOPHRON NOTORNIS NUMENIUS
OREORTYX PENELOPE PHAETHON
PITANGUS PLATALEA PLEGADIS
PODARGUS PRIONOPS PRUNELLA
PUFFINUS RUPICOLA SALTATOR
SAXICOLA SCOLOPAX SPEOTYTO
SPIZELLA STRUTHIO TRAGOPAN
TYRANNUS
(— **OF BIVALVES**) MYA PINNA
ANOMIA MACTRA NUCULA ETHERIA
MYTILUS PANDORA COLYMBUS
HINNITES PISIDIUM SAXICAVA
SPHAERUM TRIDACNA XYLOTRYA
(— **OF BOWFIN**) AMIA
(— **OF BRACHIOPOD**) ATRYPA
CRANIA ATHYRIS DISCINA SPIRIFER
(— **OF BRYOZOAN**) BUGULA
ESCHARA FLUSTRA RETEPORA
(— **OF BUG**) ANASA CIMEX EMESA
CORIXA TINGIS
(— **OF BUTTERFLY**) CALIGO COLIAS
DANAUS MORPHO PIERIS THECLA
EURYMUS JUNONIA KALLIMA
LYCAENA PAPILIO STRYMON
VANESSA ARGYNNIS HESPERIA
LEMONIAS MELITAEA SPEYERIA
(— **OF CABBAGE**) COS
(— **OF CACTUS**) CEREUS NOCALEA
OPUNTIA HARRISIA
(— **OF CAT**) FELIS ACINONYX
HEMIGALE
(— **OF CEPHALOPOD**) SEPIA
SPIRULA
(— **OF CETACEAN**) INIA
(— **OF CHINK**) LACUNA
(— **OF CHIPMUNK**) EUTAMIAS
(— **OF CILIATE**) COLPODA
CHILODON EUPLOTES
(— **OF CIVET**) FOSSA PAGUMA
(— **OF CLAM**) ENSIS GEMMA SOLEN
SPISULA
(— **OF COCKLE**) CHIONE
(— **OF COCKROACH**) BLATTA
(— **OF CORAL**) ASTREA FUNGIA

MAENDRA OCULINA PORITES
ACROPURA TUBIPORA
(— **OF CRAB**) UCA MAIA BIRGUS
CANCER GRAPSUS OCYPODE
PAGURUS LITHODES PORTUNUS
(— **OF CRANE**) GRUS
(— **OF CRAYFISH**) CAMBARUS
(— **OF CRICKET**) ACHETA GRYLLUS
(— **OF CRUSTACEAN**) APUS HIPPA
JASUS LIGIA MYSIS CYPRIS LIGYDA
SELLUS TRIOPS ARGULUS ARTEMIA
ASTACUS BOPYRUS CALAPPA
CHELURA DAPHNIA EMERITA
HOMARUS IDOTHEA LERNAEA
NEBALPA SQUILLA CAPRELLA
ESTHERIA GAMMARUS LEUCIFER
LIMNETIS LIMNORIA NEPHROPS
PHRONIMA
(— **OF CTENOPHORE**) BEROE
CESTUM
(— **OF DEER**) AXIS DAMA PUDU
RUSA CERVUS MAZAMA MOSCHUS
RUCERVUS
(— **OF DIATOM**) DIATOMA SYNEDRA
MERIDION NAVICULA
(— **OF DODO**) DIDUS
(— **OF DOG**) CUON CANIS LYCAON
(— **OF DORMOUSE**) GLIS
(— **OF DRAGONFLY**) AESCHNA
(— **OF DUCK**) AIX ANAS AYTHYA
MERGUS NYROCA NETTION
SPATULA CLANGULA FULIGULA
(— **OF EAGLE**) AQUILA
(— **OF ECHINODERM**) ASTERIAS
(— **OF EDENTATE**) MANIS
(— **OF EEL**) CONGER ECHIDNA
MURAENA ANGUILLA GYMNOTUS
MORINGUA
(— **OF FERN**) FILIX TODEA ANEMIA
AZOLLA DOODIA CYATHEA ISOETES
ONOCLEA OSMUNDA PELLAEA
WOODSIA ADIANTUM ASPIDIUM
ATHYRIUM BLECHNUM CETERACH
CIBOTIUM CLEMATIS DAVALLIA
LYGODIUM MARATTIA SALVINIA
SCHIZAEA VITTARIA
(— **OF FIREFLY**) LAMPYRIS
(— **OF FISH**) AMIA ESOX HURO
LOTA MOLA RAJA ZEUS ALOSA
BADIS BERYX BETTA DORAS ELOPS
GADUS GOBIO HUCHO LATES
MANTA MUGIL PERCA SALMO
SARDA SOLEA UMBRA ALBULA
ANABAS APOGON BAIGRE BARBUS
BELONE CARANX CLUPEA COTTUS
DIODON GERRES GOBIUS HIODON
KUHLIA LABRUS LATRIS MOBULA
MYXINE NOMEUS PAGRUS PSETTA
REMORA SCARUS SPARUS TRIGLA
TRUTTA TURSIO ABRAMIS ALOPHAS
ALOPIAS ARACANA ASPREDO
BROTULA CARAPUS CLARIAS
DREPANE ECHIDNA GARRUPA
GIRELLA GYMNORA LEPOMIS
LIMANDA LUCANIA LYCODES
OSMERUS PEGASUS PRISTIS
SCIAENA SCOMBER SEPIOLA
SERIOLA SIGANUS SILLAGO SILURUS
SPHYRNA SQUALUS SYNODUS

THUNNUS TORPEDO TOXOTES
TRIODON XIPHIAS ZOARCES
AMEIURUS ANABLEPS ANGUILLA
ARAPAIMA ASTYANAX ATHERINA
BALISTES BODIANUS CARANGUS
CHIMAERA CLADODUS CTENODUS
CYPRINUS DAPEDIUS DIPLODUS
DIPTERUS DOROSOMA ECHENEIS
ETRUMEUS FUNDULUS GADOPSIS
GALAXIAS GAMBUSIA GOBIESOX
HAEMULON ICOSTEUS KYPHOSUS
LEBISTES LUTIANUS MEGALOPS
MORMYRUS MUSTELUS NOTROPIS
OPHIDION PALOMETA PANTODON
PHOCAENA POLYODON PYGIDIUM
SERRANUS SQUATINA COREGONUS
MYCTOPHUM
(— **OF FLAGELLATE)** COCOS
GONIUM OPHION SYNURA VOLVOX
ATTALEA CARYOTA EUGLENA
GIARDIA BORASSUS CERATIUM
EUDORINA HEXAMITA HYDRURUS
(— **OF FLEA)** PULEX BOSMINA
(— **OF FLY)** DACUS MUSCA MYMAR
PERLA PHORA ASILUS CEPHUS
FANNIA PIMPLA RHYSSA SCIARA
TIPULA CALIROA CHALCIS DIOPSIS
EPHYDRA HYLEMYA MIASTOR
ORTALIS OSCINIS PANORPA
TACHINA THEREVA ACROCERA
AGROMYZA ANOMALON APHIDIUS
BORBORUS CHELONUS CHRYSOPA
CHRYSOPS GLOSSINA PSYCHODA
SCHEDIUS SIMULIUM STOMOXYS
(— **OF FLYING SQUIRREL)** BELOMYS
(— **OF FOSSIL)** AMPYX ERYON
ADAPIS ATRYPA BAIERA ERYOPS
GEIKIA HYENIA KLUKIA MAMMUT
OLENUS ORTHIS RHYNIA ANDRIAS
ANTEDON APTIANA ASAPHUS
CAYONIA DICERAS EXOGYRA
GANODUS HAMITES HYBODUS
KNORRIA LESKEYA LESLEYA
LOXOMMA MESONYX MOROPUS
MYGODON OTOZOUM PHACOPS
PHIOMIA PROAVIS PROETUS
WALCHIA AGLASPIS AGNOSTUS
AMYNODON APHELOPS ARCHELON
BIRKENIA BRONTOPS CALIPPUS
CALYMENE CERATOPS CLYMENIA
CTENODUS DAPEDIUS DEINODON
DIATRYMA DINOHYUS DIPLODUS
DIPTERUS ENCHODUS ENCRINUS
EODISCUS EOHIPPUS EOSAURUS
EUSMILUS GORDONIA GRYPHAEA
HALLOPUS HELIGMUS ILLAENUS
LANARKIA LEBACHIA LECROSIA
LEGUATIA LESTODON LITUITES
MACLUREA MARRELLA METOPIAS
OLDHAMIA PLACODUS PORTHEUS
RUTIODON SMILODON SPIRIFER
STEGODON STEGOMUS TAONURUS
THELODUS XIPHODON ZAMICRUS
CONULARIA
(— **OF FOX)** ALOPEX VULPES
UROCYON
(— **OF FROG)** RANA ANURA
HYLODES
(— **OF FUNGUS)** FOMES IRPEX

PHOMA TUBER VALSA VERPA
ALBUGO BREMIA CAEOMA EMPUSA
FUMAGO HYDNUM ISARIA OIDIUM
PEZIZA TORULA ZYTHIA ACRASIA
AMANITA BOLETUS CANDIDA
CHALARA CYATHUS ELSINOE
ERYSIBE FABRAEA GEASTER
LEPIOTA MONILIA NECTRIA OZONIUM
PACHYMA PYTHIUM RHIZINA
RUSSULA SIMBLUM STEREUM
STICTIS STILBUM TYPHULA XYLARIA
ACHORION AECIDIUM AGARICUS
BOTRYTIS CALVATIA CLATHRUS
CLAVARIA COLLYBIA COPRINUS
CORYNEUM CYPHELLA CYTTARIA
DAEDALEA DIPLODIA ENDOTHIA
ENTOLOMA ENTYLOMA ERYSIPHE
EXOASCUS FUSARIUM GEASTRUM
GNOMONIA GRAPHIUM HELOTIUM
HELVELLA LENZITES MERULIUS
MYCOGONE PAXILLUS PHOLIOTA
PUCCINIA RHIZOPUS RHYTISMA
SEPTORIA SORDARIA SPICARIA
TAPHRINA TERFEZIA TRAMETES
TREMELLA TROCHILA USTILAGO
USTULINA VENTURIA CORDICEPS
(— **OF GALLFLY)** CYNIPS
(— **OF GASTROPOD)** FICUS HARPA
LIMAX OLIVA EBURNA PATELLA
TENEBRA SCYLLAEA STROMBUS
(— **OF GEESE)** CHEN ANSER
NETTAPUS
(— **OF GNAT)** SCIARA
(— **OF GOAT)** IBEX CAPRA
OREAMNOS
(— **OF GRASS)** POA ZEA AIRA COIX
AVENA BRIZA ORYZA STIPA APLUDA
ARUNDO BROMUS ELYMUS HOLCUS
LOLIUM LYGEUM MELICA MILIUM
NARDUS PHLEUM SECALE UNIOLA
ZOYSIA BAMBUSA BUCHLOE
CHLORIS CYNODON FESTUCA
HILARIA HORDEUM LAGURUS
LEERSIA MELINIS MOLINIA PANICUM
SETARIA SORGHUM ZIZANIA
AEGILOPS AGROSTIS ARISTIDA
AXONOPUS BULBILIS CENCHRUS
DACTYLIS ELEUSINE GLYCERIA
GYNERIUM IMPERATA PASPALUM
PHALARIS SPARTINA SPINIFEX
TRISETUM TRITICUM
(— **OF GRASSHOPPER)** LOCUSTA
(— **OF GULL)** XEMA LARUS
(— **OF HAWK)** BUTEO CIRCUS
(— **OF HERB)** GYP IVA AMMI ARUM
BETA GEUM GLAX HEBE LENS MEUM
MUSA OLAX RUTA SIDA SIUM ADOXA
AJUGA APIOS APIUM CALLA CANNA
CAREX CARUM CICER DALEA DRABA
ERUCA ERVUM FEDIA GALAX GAURA
GILIA GLAUX HOSTA INULA LAPPA
LAVIA LAYIA LEMNA LINUM LOASA
LOTUS LUFFA MADIA MALVA NAPEA
PANAX PARIS PHACA PHLOX PILEA
RHEUM RHOEO RUBIA SEDUM
TACEA URENA VICIA VIGNA VINCA
VIOLA ZIZIA ACAENA ACNIDA
ACORUS ACTAEA ADONIS ALISMA
ALLIUM ALSINE AMOMUM ANOGRA

ARABIS ARALIA ARNICA ASARUM
ATROPA BACOPA BAERIA BASSIA
BELLIS BIDENS BLITUM BLUMEA
BORAGO CAKILE CALTHA CASSIA
CELSIA CICUTA CISTUS CLEOME
CNICUS COLEUS CONIUM COPTIS
COSMOS CRAMBE CREPIS CRINUM
CROCUS CROTON CUNILA CYNARA
DAHLIA DATURA DAUCUS DIODIA
DONDIA ECHIUM ELODES ELODIA
EMILIA EUCLEA FILAGO GALEGA
GALIUM GIFOLA GYNURA ISATIS
ISMENE KOCHIA KRIGIA KUHNIA
LAMIUM LECHEA LUZULA MALOPE
MENTHA MIMOSA MONTIA MUCUNA
MUILLA NERINE NERIUM NESLIA
ONONIS OTHAKE OXALIS PICRIS
PISTIA PYROLA RESEDA RESTIO
RHEXIA RIVINA RUPPIA SAGINA
SALVIA SCILLA SESBAN SESELI
STEVIA SUAEDA THALIA TULIPA
VIORNA ZINNIA ABRONIA ADLUMIA
AETHUSA ALEGRIA ALETRIS
ALKANNA ALPINIA ALTHAEA
ALYSSUM AMORPHA AMSONIA
ANCHUSA ANEMONE ANETHUM
ANYCHIA APHANES ARACHIS
ARCTIUM ARNEBIA ARUNCUS
BABIANA BARTSIA BEGONIA
BOEBERA BUTOMUS CACALIA
CAJANUS CALYPSO CARLINA
CELOSIA CHELONE CIRCAEA
CIRSIUM CLARKIA COMARUM
CROOMIA CURCUMA CUSCUTA
CYTINUS DATISCA DECODON
DERINGA DIASCIA DROSERA
ELATINE EOMECON EPISCIA
ERODIUM FELICIA FICARIA FRASERA
FREESIA FUMARIA GAZANIA
GERBERA GLECOMA GLYCINE
GUNNERA HALENIA HECHTIA
HEDEOMA HOMERIA HUGELIA
HYPOXIS IRESINE JASIONE KICKXIA
KNAUTIA KOELLIA LACTUCA
LAPPULA LAPSANA LEWISIA LIATRIS
LINARIA LINNAEA LOGANIA LOPEZIA
LUNARIA LUPINUS LYCHNIS
LYTHRUM MARANTA MEDEOLA
MIMULUS MITELLA MOLLUGO
MONESES MUSCARI NEMESIA
NIGELLA OTHONNA PAEONIA
PAPAVER PAVONIA PEGANUM
PETUNIA PLUCHEA PRIMULA
RORIPPA ROTALIA RUELLIA
SALSOLA SAMOLUS SCANDIX
SENECIO SESAMUM SHORTIA
SILYBUM SINAPIS SOLANUM
SONCHUS STACHYS STATICE
SUCCISA SWERTIA TAGETES
TALINUM TELLIMA THAPSIA THESIUM
THLASPI THURNIA TORENIA TORILIS
TOVARIA TRILISA URGINEA VALLOTA
VERBENA ZEBRINA ACALYPHA
ACANTHUS ACHILLEA ACONITUM
AGALINIS AGERATUM ALLIARIA
ALLIONIA ALOCASIA AMBROSIA
AMMODIUM ANDRYALA ANGELICA
ANTHEMIS ANTICLEA APOCYNUM
ARCTOTIS ARENARIA ARGEMONE

ARISAEMA ASPERULA ATRIPLEX
BAPTISIA BARBAREA BARTONIA
BERGENIA BERTEROA BETONICA
BISTORTA BOLTONIA BORRERIA
BRASSICA BRUNONIA BUCHNERA
CALATHEA CAMASSIA CAMELINA
CANNABIS CAPSICUM CERINTHE
CLEMATIS COCHARUS COLLOMIA
COLUMNEA COMANDRA COOPERIA
CRASSULA CUBELIUM DENTARIA
DIANTHUS DICENTRA DIPSACUS
DISPORUM DYSSODIA ECHINOPS
EPIFAGUS ERANTHIS EREMURUS
ERIGENIA ERIGERON ERYNGIUM
ERYSIMUM EUCHARIS EUTHANIA
FITTONIA FLAVERIA FLOERKEA
FRAGARIA GALACTIA GENTIANA
GERARDIA GESNERIA GILLENIA
GLAUCIUM GLECHOMA GLORIOSA
GLOXINIA GOODENIA GRATIOLA
GUZMANIA HELENIUM HELONIAS
HEPATICA HESPERIS HEUCHERA
HIBISCUS HIPPURIS HOSACKIA
HOTTONIA HUDSONIA HYDROLES
HYSSOPUS IONIDIUM ISNARDIA
JATROPHA JUSSIAEA JUSTICIA
KNEIFFIA KOHLERIA LAPORTEA
LAVATERA LEONOTIS LEONURUS
LEPIDIUM LEPTILON LIMONIUM
LOPHIOLA LYCOPSIS MACLEAYA
MANFREDA MANTISIA MEDICAGO
MEIBOMIA MYOSOTIS MYOSURUS
OBOLARIA OENANTHE OPOPANAX
ORONTIUM PAROSELA PHACELIA
PHORMIUM PHYMOSIA PHYSALIS
PHYSARIA PLANTAGO PLUMBAGO
POLYGALA POLYMNIA POTERIUM
PRUNELLA PSORALEA RAPHANUS
RHAGODIA SABBATIA SAMBUCUS
SANICULA SARCODES SAROTHRA
SATUREIA SCABIOSA SCOLYMUS
SESBANIA SESUVIUM SEYMERIA
SIDALCEA SILPHIUM SOLIDAGO
SPERGULA SPIGELIA SPINACIA
STOKESIA TAENIDIA THASPIUM
TIARELLA TRIBULUS TRILLIUM
TROLLIUS TUECRIUM UVULARIA
VACCARIA VALERIAN VANELLUS
VERATRUM VERNONIA VERONICA
VISCARIA WATSONIA XANTHIUM
(— OF HERON) ARDEA EGRETTA
(— OF HORSE) EQUUS CALIPPUS
EOHIPPUS
(— OF HYDROZOAN) DIPHYES
PHYSALIA
(— OF HYENA) HYAENA CROCUTA
(— OF INSECT) NEPA APHIS EMESA
JAPYX SIREX BOREUS CICADA
COCCUS CORIXA EMPUSA ICERYA
KERMES MANTIS PHASMA PODURA
SIALIS THRIPS CHALCIS FORMICA
FULGORA LEPISMA ORYSSUS
RANATRA STYLOPS VEDALIA
BACILLUS CAMPODEA EPHEMERA
LABIDURA LACCIFER LECANIUM
LYONETIA MACHILIS MANTISPA
NERTHRUS REDUVIUS
(— OF ISOPOD) IDOTEA IDOTHEA
CIROLANA

(— OF JAY) GARRULUS
(— OF JELLYFISH) CYANEA AURELIA
AEQUOREA
(— OF JERBOA) DIPUS
(— OF KELP) AGARUM
(— OF LANGUR) SIMIAS
(— OF LEAFHOPPER) AGALLIA
EMPOASCA
(— OF LEECH) HIRUDO HAEMOPIS
(— OF LEMUR) INDRI GALAGO
(— OF LIANA) BAUHINIA
(— OF LICE) APHIS PSYLLA
ARGULUS ONISCUS BOVICOLA
ERIOSOMA GONIODES LIPEURUS
(— OF LICHEN) CORA USNEA
STICTA EVERNIA GRAPHIS LECIDEA
LOBARIA PHYSCIA CETRARIA
CLADONIA LECANORA PARMELIA
ROCCELLA STRIGULA
(— OF LIMPET) ACMAEA
(— OF LIZARD) UTA AGAMA DRACO
GEKKO AMEIVA ANGUIS ANOLIS
IGUANA EUMECES LACERTA
PYGOPUS SCINCUS ACONTIAS
CHIROTES COLEONYX LYGOSOMA
RHINEURA
(— OF LOCUST) TETRIX TETTIX
(— OF MACAW) ARA
(— OF MAMMAL) BOS SUS HOMO
LAMA ALCES BISON CAPRA TAYRA
DUGONG FRISON AELURUS AILURUS
BUBALUS GALIDIA GYMNURA
LINSANG OTOCYON AUCHENIA
CYCLOPES CYNOGALE SURICATA
TRAGULUS
(— OF MAPLE) ACER
(— OF MARSUPIAL) DASYURUS
MACROPUS POTOROUS TARSIPES
(— OF MARTEN) MARTES MUSTELA
(— OF MEDUSA) SARSIA GERYONIA
(— OF MICROSPORIDIAN) GLUGEA
(— OF MILDEW) ERYSIPHE
UNCINULA
(— OF MILLIPEDE) JULUS
(— OF MINT) ICIMUM NEPATA
MELISSA PERILLA PHLOMIS
ORIGANUM
(— OF MITE) ACARUS ACERIA
LEPTUS DEMODEX ACARAPIS
(— OF MOLD) MUCOR FULIGO
MELIOLA
(— OF MOLE) TALPA SCALOPS
SCALOPUS
(— OF MOLLUSK) ARCA DOTO LEDA
LIMA CHAMA DONAX EOLIS FICUS
HARPA LIMAX MUREX OLIVA VENUS
AEOLIS ANOMIA BANKIA CASSIS
CHITON LEPTON LUCINA OSTREA
PECTEN PHOLAS PYRULA SEMELE
TEREDO TETHYS ACTAEON ASTARTE
ATLANTA CARDITA CARDIUM
CYPRAEA CYPRINA DOSINIA
ETHERIA EXOGYRA LINGULA
TELLINA BUCCINUM GRYPHAEA
HALIOTIS LIMACINA LUTRARIA
MODIOLUS NAUTILUS PINCTADA
SCYLLAEA STROMBUS
(— OF MONGOOSE) GALIDIA
(— OF MONKEY) AOTES AOTUS

CEBUS ATELES MACACA CACAJAO
COLOBUS NASALIS SAIMIRI PITHECIA
(— OF MOOSE) ALCES
(— OF MOSQUITO) AEDES CULEX
(— OF MOSS) BRYUM CHILO EUXOA
MNIUM SAMIA SESIA TINEA ACTIAS
ALYPIA ARCTIA BOMBYX COSSUS
DATANA HYPNUM LESKEA PLUSIA
PSYCHE SPHINX THYRIS URANIA
AGROTIS ALABAMA APATELA
ARCHIPS ATTACUS BARBULA
CRAMBUS FUNARIA GRIMMIA
PHASCUM PRONUBA PYRALIS
SESAMIA TORTRIX ZEUZERA
ZYGAENA ANDREAEA CATOCALA
DAWSONIA DIATRAEA DICRANUM
ENDROMIS EPHESTIA EUPREPIA
GALLERIA GELECHIA HEPIALUS
PLUTELLA PRODENIA PYRAUSTA
SATURNIA SPHAGNUM THUIDIUM
(— OF MOUSE) MUS APODEMUS
(— OF MUSKRAT) FIBER ONDATRA
(— OF NARWHAL) MONODON
(— OF NEMATODE) ACUARIA
ALAIMUS ANGUINA NECATOR
(— OF NUDIBRANCH) GLAUCUS
(— OF OATS) AVENA
(— OF OPOSSUM) MARMOSA
(— OF ORCHID) DISA VANDA BLETIA
LAELIA PHAJUS ACINETA AERIDES
ANGULOA BRASSIA CORDULA
EUCOSIA IBIDIUM ISOTRIA LIPARIS
LISTERA MALAXIS POGONIA VANILLA
ANGRECUM ARETHUSA BLETILLA
CALANTHA CATTLEYA CYTHEREA
FISSIPES GOODYERA MILTONIA
ONCIDIUM PERAMIUM SERAPIAS
SOBRALIA TRIPHORA
(— OF OTTER) LUTRA
(— OF OWL) BUBO NINOX STRIX
KETUPA NYCTEA AEGOLIUS
SPEOTYTO
(— OF OXEN) BIBOS
(— OF PALM) NIPA ARECA ASSAI
COCOS HOWEA SABAL ARENGA
ELAEIS INODES KENTIA RAPHIA
RHAPIS ATTALEA BACTRIS CALAMUS
CARYOTA CORYPHA ERYTHEA
EUTERPE GEONOMA LATANIA
LICUALA PHOENIX SERENOA
THRINAX BORASSUS HYPHAENE
IRIARTEA LODOICEA MAURITIA
(— OF PARASITE) STRIGA CUSCOTA
HYDNORA OLPIDIUM CASSYTHIA
(— OF PARRAKEET) ARATINGA
(— OF PARROT) AMAZONA KAKATOE
(— OF PEACOCK) PAVO
(— OF PENGUIN) EUDYPTES
(— OF PHALANGER) DROMICIA
(— OF PIGEON) GOURA DUCULA
COLUMBA
(— OF PLANT) ALOE ARUM COLA
DION FABA IRIS IXIA PUYA SOJA
ADOXA AGAVE ASTER BATIS CANNA
CHARA DIOON DRYAS INULA NAIAS
PIPER RUMEX TRAPA TYPHA XYRIS
YUCCA ZILLA ABROMA ACACIA
AIZOON ALBUCA ANANAS CACTUS
CUPHEA DATURA EXACUM FERULA

IBERIS JAMBOS JUNCUS LICHEN
LILIUM MAYACA MORAEA NUPHAR
PHRYMA RICCIA SILENE SMILAX
STRIGA URTICA VISCUM ALONSOA
ASTILBE BALLOTA CABOMBA
CUCUMIS CYPERUS DIONAEA
DROSERA ENCELIA EPACRIS
EPIGAEA EURYALE FAGELIA
GLYCINE GODETIA HELXINE
HOOKERA ISOETES ISOLOMA
KARATAS LYCOPUS MANIHOT
MONARDA NELUMBO NITELLA
RAOULIA RICINUS STEMONA
SYRINGA TRIURUS TURNERA
WOLFFIA WYETHIA ZOSTERA
ABUTILON ADIANTUM ANABASIS
ANTHYLIS BRASENIA BRODIAEA
BROMELIA CALADIUM CAPSICUM
CYCLAMEN FORCRAEA FURCRAEA
GALTONIA GASTERIA GERANIUM
LATHRAEA LATHYRUS MARSILEA
MONSTERA NYMPHAEA PANDANUS
PEDALIUM PELVETIA PERESKIA
SAURURUS SPARAXIS THEVETIA
TIGRIDIA TRITONIA VELLOZIA
VICTORIA ZINGIBER
(— OF POLYZOAN) LEPRALIA
LOXOSOMA
(— OF POPLAR) ALAMO
(— OF PORCUPINE) COENDU
HYSTRIX
(— OF PORPOISE) INIA
(— OF PRAWN) PALAEMON
(— OF PROTOZOAN) BODO HYDRA
MONAS ADELEA AMOEBA ACINETA
ARCELLA EIMERIA STENTOR
DIDINIUM EUGLYPHA ISOSPORA
UROGLENA
(— OF RABBIT) LEPUS
(— OF RAT) ANISOMYS
(— OF RHIZOPOD) AMOEBA GROMIA
LAGENA HATTERIA PELOMYXA
(— OF RODENT) MUS CAVIA DIPUS
LEPUS ZAPUS GEOMYS LEMMUS
SPALAX CYNOMYS DINOMYS
ECHIMYS LEGGADA MERINES
NESOKIA ZYZOMYS ALACTAGA
ARVICOLA CAPROMYS CITELLUS
CRICETUS HAPLODON HYDROMYS
LAGIDIUM MICROTUS MYOTALPA
ORYZOMYS
(— OF ROTIFER) HYDATINA
PEDALION
(— OF RUST) UREDO HEMILEIA
UROMYCES
(— OF SALAMANDER) ANDRIAS
EURYCEA STREDON TRITURUS
(— OF SCALE) KERMES LECANIUM
(— OF SCALLOP) HINNITES
(— OF SCORPION) BUTHUS
SCORPIO CHELIFER
(— OF SEA ANEMONE) MINYAS
ACTINIA
(— OF SEA FAN) GORGONIA
(— OF SEA OTTER) ENHYDRA
(— OF SEA SLUG) ELYSIA
(— OF SEA URCHIN) ARBACIA
CIDARIS DIADEMA ECHINUS
(— OF SEAL) PHOCA HYDRURGA

MIROUNGA ZALOPHUS
(— OF SEAWEED) ULVA ALARIA
(— OF SEDGE) FUIRENA SCIRPUS
SCLERIA SCHOENUS
(— OF SHARK) LAMNA GALEUS
ISURUS ACRODUS ALOPIAS
SPHYRNA SQUALUS CLADODUS
MENASPIS SQUATINA
(— OF SHELL) PUPA LAMBIS
EXOGYRA LATIRUS MALLEUS
TROCHUS HAMINOEA MACLUREA
OLIVELLA TRIGONIA UMBRELLA
(— OF SHREW) SOREX BLARINA
(— OF SHRIMP) CRAGO CRANGON
(— OF SHRUB) IVA ACER BIXA BRYA
HOYA ILEX INGA ITEA MABA OLEA
RHUS ROSA SIDA THEA ULEX ALNUS
ANONA BIOTA BUTEA BUXUS CATHA
DALEA DIRCA ERICA EURYA FICUS
HAKEA IXORA LEDUM MALUS
OCHNA PADUS RIBES RUBUS SABIA
SALIX TAXUS THUJA TREMA UNONA
URENA VITEX ABELIA ACAENA
ADELIA ALHAGI AMYRIS ANNONA
ARALIA ARONIA AUCUBA AZALEA
BAPHIA BAUERA BETULA BLUMEA
BYBLIS CANTUA CASSIA CELTIS
CERCIS CISTUS CITRUS CLEOME
CLUSIA COFFEA CORDIA COREMA
CORNUS CORREA CROTON DAPHNE
DATURA DERRIS DIOSMA DONDIA
DRIMYS ECHIUM EVODIA FATSIA
FEIJOA GARRYA GNETUM GREWIA
GUAREA KALMIA KERRIA LARREA
LIPPIA LITSEA LUCUMA LYCIUM
MIMOSA MYRCIA MYRICA MYRTUS
OCOTEA OLINIA OPILIA PENAEA
PERSEA PIERIS PROTEA PTELEA
PUNICA QUIINA RAMONA RANDIA
ROCHEA ROYENA RUSCUS SALVIA
SAPIUM SCHIMA SELAGO SESBAN
SORBUS STEVIA STYRAX SUÆDA
TECOMA AECULUS AMORPHA
ARBUTUS ARDISIA ARMERIA ASIMINA
ASSONIA BANKSIA BAROSMA
BENZOIN BORONIA BUMELIA
BURSERA CALLUNA CARISSA
CASASIA CERASUS CESTRUM
CLETHRA CNEORUM COLUTEA
CORYLUS COTINUS CUNONIA
CYRILLA CYTISUS DEUTZIA
DOMBEYA DURANTA EHRETIA
ENCELIA EPACRIS EPHEDRA
EUCHLEA EUGENIA EURSERA
FABIANA FUCHSIA GENISTA GMELINA
GYMINDA HAMELIA HOVENIA
KARATAS LAGETTA LANTANA
MAHONIA MERATIA MONUMIA
MORINDA MUTISIA MYRRHIS
NANDINA NEMESIA OLEARIA
OTHONNA PAVETTA PAVONIA
PENTZIA PIMELEA PISONIA PURSHIA
QUASSIA QUERCUS RAPANEA
REMIJIA RHAMNUS RHODORA
ROBINIA ROMNEYA RUELLIA
SALSOLA SENECIO SKIMMIA
SOLANUM SOPHORA SPIRAEA
SURIANA SYRINGA TAMARIX
TELOPEA VERNICA XIMENIA XYLOPIA

XYLOSMA ZELKOVA ACALYPHA
ALANGIUM ALSTONIA ANAGYRIS
ATRIPLEX BALOCHIA BAUHINIA
BERBERIS BORRERIA BUCKLEYA
BUDDLEIA CAMELLIA CAPPARIS
CAPSICUM CARAGANA CASSIOPE
CASTANEA CODIAEUM COLLETIA
CONDALIA CONNARUS COPROSMA
CORIARIA CRATAEVA DAVIESIA
DENDRIUM DILLENIA DODONAEA
DOVYALIS DRACAENA DUBOISIA
EMPETRUM EUONYMUS EUPTELEA
EXOSTEMA FRAXINUS GALACTIA
GOODENIA GORDONIA GUAIACUM
HIBISCUS HIRTELLA IONIDIUM
JASMINUM JATROPHA JUSTICIA
KNIGHTIA KRAMERIA LABURNUM
LAVATERA LAWSONIA LEONOTIS
MAGNOLIA MAYTENUS MENZIESA
MICHELIA MYOPORUM NOTELAEA
PALIURUS PAROSELA PHILESIA
PHOTINIA PHYMOSIA PLUMIERA
POLYGALA POTERIUM PROSOPIS
PSORALEA RHAGODIA ROLLINIA
RORIDULA RUSSELIA SAMBUCUS
SATUREIA SAURAUIA SESBANIA
SOLANDRA SORBARIA SPARTIUM
TABEBUIA TORRUBIA TRECULIA
VARRONIA VERNONIA VIBURNUM
VOCHYSIA WITHANIA ZIZYPHUS
(— OF SILKWORM) BOMBYX
(— OF SKUNK) MEPHITIS
(— OF SLOTH) BRADYPUS
(— OF SLUG) DOTO ARION DORIS
LIMAX ELYSIA GLAUCUS
(— OF SNAIL) HUA PILA CONUS
FUSUS /GALBA HELIX MITRA OVULA
PHYSA THAIS TURBO CERION
EULIMA NATICA NERITA RISSOA
TRITON ANCYLUS BITTIUM BULINUS
BUSYCON CYMBIUM LATIRUS
LITIOPA LYMNARA MELANIA
MODULUS PURPURA RANELLA
VALVATA VERTIGO VITRINA ZONITES
ACHATINA ALOCINMA ELLOBIUM
FOSSARIA GYRAULUS HELICINA
HELISOMA JANTHINA KATAYAMA
LITORINA NERITINA OLEACINA
SUCCINEA
(— OF SNAKE) BOA ERYX NAIA
NAJA ASPIS BITIS BOIGA ECHIS
ELAPS CAUSUS DABOIA ELAPHE
HURRIA ILYSIA LIGUUS NATRIX
PYTHON VIPERA ATHERIS BOAEDON
COLUBER ECHIDNA MEHELYA
OPHIDIA ZAMENIS BOTHROPS
BUNGARUS CERBERUS CROTALUS
DEMANSIA EUNECTES FARANCIA
LAVHESIS MICRURUS STORERIA
TYPHLOPS
(— OF SPIDER) ARANEA LYCOSA
MYGALE AGALENA ARGIOPE
ATTIDAE NEPHILA PHOLCUS
LINYPHIA ULOBORUS
(— OF SPIROCHETE) BORRELIA
(— OF SPONGE) SYCON GEODIA
SCYPHA ASCETTA CHALINA
GRANTIA SPONGIA SYCETTA
LEUCETTA

(— OF SPOROZOAN) NOSEMA
(— OF SQUID) LOLIGO SEPIOLA
(— OF SQUIRREL) SCIURUS
(— OF SUBSHRUB) LECHEA
ARMERIA ASCYRUM BEGONIA
FELICIA ATRIPLEX COLUMNEA
(— OF SWAN) OLOR CYGNUS
(— OF TAKIN) BUDORCAS
(— OF TAPEWORM) BERTIA LIGULA
DAVAINEA HARRISIA
(— OF TAYRA) GALERA GALICTIS
(— OF TELEDU) MYDAUS
(— OF TERN) GYGIS STERNA
(— OF THISTLE) CARDUUS
(— OF TICK) ARGAS ARGUS IXODES
HYALOMMA
(— OF TOAD) BUFO HYLA PIPA
ALYTES XENOPUS ASCAPHUS
(— OF TREE) ACER BIXA BRYA
COLA HURA ILEX INGA MABA OLAX
OLEA RHUS THEA ABIES AEGLE
ALNUS ANIBA BIOTA BUTEA BUXUS
CARYA CEIBA CYCAS DURIO EURYA
FAGUS FICUS HAKEA HEVEA HOPEA
IXORA KHAYA LARIX MALUS MELIA
MESUA MORUS NYSSA OCHNA
PADUS PICEA PINUS PYRUS SALIX
TAXUS THUJA TILIA TOONA TREMA
TSUGA ULMUS UNONA VITEX XYLIA
ACHRAS AKANIA AMOMIS AMYRIS
ANDIRA ANNONA ARALIA AZALEA
BAPHIA BETULA BOMBAX CANTUA
CARAPA CARICA CASSIA CEDRUS
CELTIS CERCIS CITRUS CLUSIA
COFFEA CORDIA CORNUS DATURA
DRIMYS EPERUA EPERVA EUCLEA
EVODIA FEIJOA GARRYA GENIPA
GINKGO GNETUM GREWIA GUAREA
IDESIA ILLIPE LAURUS LITCHI LITSEA
LUCUMA LYCIUM MAMMEA MIMOSA
MYRCIA MYRICA OCOTEA OLNEYA
OSTRYA OWENIA PAPPEA PARITI
PERSEA PRUNUS PTELEA QUIINA
RANDIA ROYENA SAPIUM SAPOTA
SCHIMA SENCIO SESBAN SHOREA
SIMABA SORBUS STYRAX TECOMA
AGATHIS ARBUTUS ARDISIA ASIMINA
ASSONIA BANKSIA BUMELIA
BURSERA CANELLA CASASIA
CATALPA CEDRELA CERASUS
CLETHRA COPAIVA CORYLUS
COTINUS CUNONIA CUPANIA
CYDONIA CYRILLA DOMBEYA
ECHINUS EHRETIA EPACRIS EUGENIA
FERONIA GMELINA GUAZUMA
GYMINDA HAGENIA HALESIA
HICORIA HOVENIA HUMIRIA ILLICUM
JUGLANS KADELIA KOKOONA
LAGETTA LICANIA LINGOUM
MACLURA MICONIA MORINDA
MORINGA MURRAYA OCHROMA
OLEARIA PANGIUM PIMENTA PISONIA
PLANERA POPULUS PROTIUM
PSIDIUM QUASSIA QUERCUS
RAPANEA REMIJIA RHAMNUS
ROBINIA SCHINUS SENECIO SEQUOIA
SLOANEA SOLANUM SOPHORA
SURIANA SYRINGA TAMARIX
TECTONA TELOPEA TORREYA

TROPHIS VATERIA XIMENIA XYLOPIA
XYLOSMA ZELKOVA AESCULUS
ALANGIUM ALBIZZIA ALSTONIA
ANTIARIS AVERRHOA BALANOPS
BALOGHIA BAUHINIA BRABEJUM
BROSIMUM BUDDLEIA CABRALEA
CAMELLIA CANANGIA CANARIUM
CAPPARIS CAROGANA CARPINUS
CARYOCAR CASEARIA CASTANEA
CASTILLA CECROPIA CINCHONA
CODIAEUM CONDALIA CYBISTAX
DILLENIA DIPTERYX DODONAEA
DOVYALIS DRACAENA DUBOISIA
EUCOMMIA EUONYMUS EUPTELEA
EXOSTEMA FITZROYA FRAXINUS
FUNTUMIA GARCINIA GARDENIA
GORDONIA GUAIACUM HIBISCUS
HIRTELLA HOMALIUM HYMENAEA
JATROPHA KANDELIA KNIGHTIA
LABURNUM LAPORTEA LAVATERA
LECYTHIS LEUCAENA LYSILOMA
MAGNOLIA MALLOTUS MAYTENUS
MESPILUS MICHELIA MIMUSOPS
MYOPORUM NOTELAEA PHOTINIA
PISCIDIA PISTACIA PLATANUS
PLUMIERA PONCIRUS PROSOPIS
QUILLAJA RAVENALA ROLLINIA
SAMADERA SAMBUCUS SANTALUM
SAPINDUS SAURAUIA SESBANIA
SIMARUBA SPONDIAS SWARTZIA
TABEBUIA TAXODIUM TORRUBIA
TRECULIA VARRONIA VERONICA
VIBURNUM VIRGILIA VOCHYSIA
(— OF TUNICATE) SALPA ASCIDIA
DOLIOLUM
(— OF TURTLE) EMYS AMYDA
CHELUS CHELYS CARETTA CHELONE
CLEMMYS TESTUDO TRIONYX
ARCHELON CHELONIA CHELYDRA
PELUSIOS
(— OF TWINER) STEMONA
(— OF UNIVALVE) DOLIUM
(— OF VINE) ROSA ABRUS ABUTA
PISUM TAMUS UNONA VIGNA VITIS
AKEBIA CISSUS COBAEA DERRIS
ENTADA HEDERA MUCUNA PETREA
POTHOS SICANA SICYOS SOLLYA
VIORNA ARAUJIA BASELLA
BOMAREA BRYONIA ECHITES
EMBELIA EPACRIS FALCATA
HUMULUS IPOMOEA MIKANIA
PISONIA SECHIUM UNCARIA
ZANONIA ANAMIRTA ATRAGENE
BIGNONIA CLEMATIS COCCULUS
DEGUELIA DOLICHOS EUONYMUS
JASMINUM KENNEDYA PANDOREA
PUERARIA SECAMONE SERJANIA
TACSONIA WISTARIA
(— OF WALRUS) ODOBENUS
(— OF WASP) SPHEX VESPA
BEMBEX CYNIPS SCOLIA TIPHIA
CHRYSIS EUMENES MASARIS
MUTILLA ANDRICUS CHLORION
ODYNERUS POLISTES POMPILUS
SPHECIUS
(— OF WEASEL) MUSTELA
(— OF WEED) CAPSELLA
(— OF WEEVIL) APION HYPERA
SITONA CLEONUS CALANDRA

CALENDRA CURCULIO
(— OF WHALE) CETE ARETA KOGIA
BALAENA ORCINUS ZIPHIUS
PHYSETER
(— OF WOLVERINE) GULO
(— OF WORM) DERO SPIO ALARIA
EUNICE KERRIA MERMIS NEREIS
SYLLIS ACHAETA ACHOLOE ASCARIS
DUGESIA EISENIA FILARIA GLYCERA
GORDIUS HESIONE LEODICE
POLYNOE SABELLA SAGITTA
SERPULA SETARIA SPIRURA TUBIFEX
ARABELLA ASCAROPS BIPALIUM
BONELLIA COOPERIA DOCHMIUS
ECHIURUS FASCIOLA GEOPLANA
PHORONIS SPADELLA SUBULURA
SYNGAMUS SYPHACIA
(— OF ZORIL) ICTONYX
GEODE DRUSE
GEOMETRIC CUBIST CUBISTIC
GEOMETRY EUCLID SPHERICS
GEOPHAGY PICA

GEORGIA

CAPITAL: ATLANTA
COLLEGE: SPELMAN MOREHOUSE
COUNTY: BIBB COBB TIFT RABUN
TROUP DEKALB FULTON TALBOT
LAURENS GWINNETT MUSCOGEE
INDIAN: GUALE YUCHI CHIAHA
OCONEE YAMASEE
LAKE: LANIER MARTIN HARDING
NOTTELY BANKHEAD HARTWELL
SINCLAIR
MOUNTAIN: STONE KENNESAW
NATIVE: CRACKER
RIVER: PEA FLINT ETOWAH
OCONEE PIGEON CONECUH
SATILLA ALTAMAHA OCMULGEE
STATE BIRD: THRASHER
STATE NICKNAME: PEACH
STATE TREE: LIVEOAK
TOWN: JESUP MACON AUGUSTA
CONYERS DECATUR VIDALIA
MARIETTA MOULTRIE SAVANNAH
VALDOSTA WAYCROSS
UNIVERSITY: EMORY GATECH
MERCER

GEORGIAN ADZHAR CRACKER
GEORGIA PINE LONGLEAF
GEPHYREAN STARWORM
GER STRANGER
GERANIUM DOVEFOOT FLUXWEED
SHAMEFACE
GERANIUM LAKE SPARK NACARAT
GERBIL JIRD
GERIANOL ISOLATE
GERM BUG CHIT SEED SPARK
SPAWN SPERM GERMEN GERMULE
MICROBE SEMINAL SEEDLING
SEMINARY SEMINIUM
(— CELL) GONE
GERMAN HUN BALT HANS MUFF
ALMAN BOCHE FRITZ HEINE JERRY
ALMAIN DUTCHY HEINIE TEUTON
SAUSAGE TEDESCO COTILLON
GERMANIC TUDESQUE

GERMANDER POLY BETONY
FOXTAIL SOVENEZ SCORDIUM
GERMANE GERMAN PERTINENT
GERMANIC GOTHIC GOTHONIC
TEUTONIC
GERMAN SHEPHERD ALSATIAN

GERMANY
ANCIENT: ALMAIN ALMAINE
ANCIENT TRIBESMAN: JUTE
TEUTON VISIGOTH OSTROGOTH
CANAL: KIEL WESER LUDWIG
CAPITAL: BONN BERLIN
CHEESE: MUENSTER TILSITER
LIMBURGER
COAL REGION: RUHR SAAR SARRE
COIN: MARK KRONE TALER
GULDEN KRONEN THALER
PFENNIG GROSCHEN
DIALECT: KOLSCH KOELSCH
BALTISCH HESSISCH
DYNASTY: HOHENSTAUFEN
HOHENZOLLERN
FOOD: WURST KNODEL SPATZLE
STRUDEL MARZIPAN ROULADEN
HANSEATIC CITY: KOLN LUBECK
COLOGNE HAMBURG LUEBECK
ISLAND: USEDOM WOLLIN
FEHMARN FRISIAN
LAKE: DUMMER WURMSEE
AMMERSEE BODENSEE
CHIEMSEE MURITZEE
CONSTANCE
LANGUAGE: DEUTSCH
MEASURE: AAM IMI OHM FASS
FUSS LAST RUTE SACK STAB
CARAT EIMER KANNE KETTE
LINIE MAASS METZE RUTHE
SIMRI MASSEL MORGEN OXHOFT
SEIDEL STRICH JUCHART
KLAFTER TAGWERK SCHEFFEL
SCHOPPEN STUBCHEN VIERLING
MOUNTAIN: FELDBERG WATZMANN
MOUNTAIN RANGE: ORE ALPS
HARZ RHON HARDT HUNSRUCK
NAME: REICH ASHKENAZ
GERMANIA DEUTSCHLAND
NATIVE: GOTH SAXON TEUTON
RESORT: EMS BADEN AACHEN
TRIBAL REGION: GAU GAUE GAUS
UNIVERSITY TOWN: FREIBURG
HEIDELBERG
PORT: EMDEN BREMEN HAMBURG
ROSTOCK STETTIN
RIVER: ALZ EMS INN EDER EGER
ELBE ISAR LAHN LECH MAIN
NAAB NAHE ODER OKER REMS
RUHR SAAR SIEG ALLER DONAU
EIDER FULDA HAVEL HUNTE
ILLER LEINE LIPPE MOSEL
MULDE PEENE REGEN RHEIN
RHINE SAALE SAUER SPREE
UCKER WERRA WESER DANUBE
ELSTER KOCHER NECKAR
NEISSE RANDOW TAUBER
VECHTE WARNOW ALTMUHL
JEETZEL PEGNITZ SALZACH
UNSTRUT

STATE: BADEN LIPPE BAYERN
BREMEN HESSEN SAXONY
BAVARIA HAMBURG PRUSSIA
SAARLAND BRUNSWICK
TOWN: AUE EMS HOF ULM BONN
GERA GOCH HAAR HAMM JENA
KIEL KOLN LAHR AALEN AHLEN
EMDEN ESSEN FURTH GOTHA
HAGEN HALLE HERNE MAINZ
MOLLN NEUSS PIRNA TRIER
AACHEN ALTENA ALTONA
BARMEN BERLIN BREMEN
CASSEL DACHAU DESSAU
ERFURT KASSEL LINDEN
LUBECK MUNICH PLAUEN
TREVES BAMBERG BRESLAU
COBLENZ COLOGNE CREFELD
DRESDEN GORLITZ HAMBURG
HANOVER LEIPZIG MAYENCE
MUNCHEN MUNSTER POTSDAM
ROSTOCK SPANDAU ZWICKAU
AUGSBURG CHEMNITS
DORTMUND DUISBURG
FREIBURG LIEGNITZ MANNHAIM
NURNBERG WURSELEN
WURZBURG DARMSTADT
KARLSRUHE MAGDEBURG
NUREMBERG OSNABRUCK
STUTTGART WUPPERTAL
DUSSELDORF HEIDELBERG
OBERHAUSEN
WEIGHT: LOT GRAN LOTE LOTH
UNZE LOTHE PFUND STEIN
PRUNDE DRACHMA ZENTNER
VIERLING
WINE: MOSELLE RIESLING

GERMICIDE KRELOS
GERMINABLE PREGNANT
GERMINATE BUD HIT CHIP CHIT
GERM SHOOT SPIRE SPRIT BRAIRD
SPROUT STRIKE
GERMINATION CATCH
GESAN TAPUYAN CHAVANTE
GESTATION GOING BREEDING
GESTICULATE GESTURE
GESTURE CUT FIG BECK BERE GEST
SIGN FILIP GESTE HONOR SANNA
BECKON BREATH CUTOFF FILLIP
MOTION SALUTE SIGNAL CURTSEY
FASHION FLICKER MURGEON
ACCOLADE CEREMONY
(— **OF DERISION**) SNOOK
(**AFFECTED** —) GAATCH
(**USELESS** —) FUTILITY
GET COP GIT WIN FALL GAIN GRAB
HAVE HENT TAKE TILL AFONG
ANNEX CATCH COVER FETCH LATCH
DERIVE OBTAIN SECURE ACQUIRE
CONQUER PROCURE PRODUCE
RECEIVE PERCEIVE
(— **ABOARD**) FLIP
(— **ABOUT**) BEGO
(— **ALONG**) DO GEE FARE FEND
AGREE FADGE FODGE SPEED
FETTLE
(— **AROUND**) BYPASS COMPASS
FINESSE FLUMMER

(— **AT**) ATTAIN
(— **AWAY**) LAM RYNT SLIP EVADE
CHEESE ESCAPE
(— **BACK**) REDEEM RETIRE
RECOVER
(— **BETTER OF**) WAX BEST DING
DOWN DAUNT FLING SHEND SHENT
STICK STING JOCKEY OVERGO
RECOVER SURMOUNT
(— **BY ARTIFICE**) WIND
(— **BY ASKING**) KICK
(— **BY CUNNING**) WHIZZLE
(— **BY EXTORTION**) GRATE
(— **BY FLATTERY**) COG
(— **CLEAR OF**) STRIP
(— **DISHONESTLY**) FIRK
(— **DOWN**) ALIGHT
(— **ON WELL**) LIKE
(— **ON**) FARE BOARD CHEFE CHEVE
FRAME SHIFT EXPLOIT
(— **OUT**) LEAK SCRAM CHEESE
OUTWIN VOETSAK
(— **PAST**) BEAT HURDLE
(— **POSSESSION**) CARRY
(— **READY**) GET PARE RANK BRACE
FRAME FETTLE ORDAIN APPAREL
(— **RID**) CAST DISH DUMP FREE
JUNK SHAB TOSS ERASE SHAKE
SHIFT SHOOT SLOUGH UNLOAD
DELIVER DISCARD EXTRUDE
DISPATCH DISSOLVE
(— **SURREPTITIOUSLY**) SNEAK
(— **THE POINT**) SAVVY
(— **TO BOTTOM OF**) FATHOM
(— **UNDER CONTROL**) RAIM
(— **UP**) ARISE HUDDUP UPRISE
HAIRPIN
GETA SABOT
GET-TOGETHER DO DRINK HOBNOB
BAMBOCHE POTLATCH
GETUP SETOUT
GEWGAW DIE TOY WALY KNACK
WALLY BAUBLE FANGLE FEGARY
JIGGER FLAMFEW TRANGAM
TRINKET FOLDEROL GIMCRACK
JIMCRACK TRIMTRAM
GEYSER BORE JETTER

GHANA
CAPITAL: ACCRA
DAM: AKOSOMBO
LAKE: VOLTA BOSUMTWI
LANGUAGE: GA EWE TWI FANTI
HAUSA DAGBANI DAGOMBA
MONEY: NEWCEDI
MOUNTAIN: AFADJATO
NATIVE: GA EWE AHAFO BRONG
FANTI ASHANTI DAGOMBA
MAMPRUSI
RIVER: OTI PRA DAKA TANO
AFRAM VOLTA ANKOBRA
KULPAWN
TOWN: HO WA ODA AXIM FIAN
KETA TALA TEMA ACCRA
BAWKU ENCHI LAWRA LEGON
SAMPA YAPEI DUNKWA KARAGA
KPANDU KUMASI NSAWAM
OBUASI SWEDRU TAMALE

TARKWA WASIPE ANTUBIA
DAMONGO MAMPONG PRESTEA
SEKONDI SUNYANI WINNEBA
AKOSOMBO KINTAMPO
TAKORADI
WIND: HARMATTAN

GHARRY SHIGRAM
GHASTLY WAN GRIM PALE BLATE
GHAST LURID UNKET UNKID DISMAL
GOUSTY GRISLY PALLID CHARNEL
DEATHLY FEARFUL GASHFUL
GRIZZLY GRUGOUS HIDEOUS
MACABRE DREADFUL GRUESOME
HORRIBLE SHOCKING TERRIBLE
GHAWAZI BARAMIKA
GHERKIN CUCUMBER
GHETTO JEWRY JUDAISM
GHIBELLINE WAIBLING
GHOST HAG KER BHUT HANT JUBA
WAFF BUGAN CADDY DUFFY DUPPY
FETCH GAIST GUEST HAUNT JUMBY
LARVA PRETA SHADE SPOOK
UMBRA CHUREL SOWLTH SPIRIT
SPRITE TAISCH ANTAEUS ANTAIOS
BOGGART BUGGANE GYTRASH
PHANTOM SPECTER SPECTRE
VAMPIRE BARGHEST GUYTRASH
PHANTASM REVENANT
GHOSTFISH WRYMOUTH
GHOSTLY EERY EERIE GOUSTY
SHADOWY UNCANNY WEIRDLY
CHTHONIC GHASTFUL SPECTRAL
GHOST MOTH SWIFT HEPIALID
GHOST-WRITER SPOOK
GHOULISH SATANIC
GHUZ OGHUZ
GIAI NHANG
GIANT ORC ETEN HUGE OGRE OTUS
WATE YMER YMIR AFRIT BALOR
CACUS HYMIR JOTUN MIMAS MIMER
THRYM TITAN TROLL AFREET
ALBION FAFNIR GIGANT GOEMOT
PALLAS THJAZI THURSE TITYUS
WARLOW ANTAEUS CYCLOPS
GOLIATH WARLOCK ASCOPART
BELLERUS COLBRAND GIGANTIC
GOEMAGOT GOGMAGOG MASTODON
MORGANTE ORGOGLIO TYPHOEUS
(1-EYED —) CYCLOPS
(100-HANDED —) GYGES COTTUS
BRIAREUS
(1000-ARMED —) BANA
(PL.) ANAK ANAKIM COTTUS
ALOADAE REPHAIM NEPHILIM
ZAMZUMMIM
GIANTESS NORN ARGANTE
GIANT FULMAR NELLY STINKER
STINKPOT
GIANT GRASS OTATE
GIANT HERON GOLIATH
GIANT LILY FIGUE MAGUEY
GIANT PUFFBALL FUZZ FUZZBALL
GIARDIA LAMBLIA
GIB JIB SHOE DEMUR SLIPPER
GIBBAR GIBBERT JUBARTAS
GIBBER CHAT CHATTER
GIBBERISH GREEK JABBER JARGON
CHOCTAW

GIBBET STOB TREE CROOK JEBAT
GALLOWS POTENCE EQUULEUS
GIBBON LAR WAWA UNGKA WUYEN
CAMPER HULOCK HOOLOCK
SIAMANG
GIBBOUS CONVEX HULCHY HUMPED
GIBE (ALSO SEE JIBE) BOB RUB GIRD
JAPE JEST JIBE PROG QUIB QUIP
SKIT WIPE FLEER FLING FLIRT
FRUMP GLEEK KNACK SCOFF
SCOMM SCORN SLANT SNEER
DERIDE GLANCE HECKLE BROCARD
SARCASM RIDICULE
GIBING SNASH
GID DUNT GIDDY STURDY GOGGLES
POTHERY VERTIGO
GIDDINESS LUNACY SOORAWN
GIDDY GLAKY LIGHT WESTY GIGLET
GLAKED GOWKED GOWKIT SHANNY
STURDY VOLAGE GLAIKET LARKING
HALUCKET HELLICAT
GIFT BOX FOY QUO SOP BENT BOON
DASH ENAM MEED SAND BONUS
BRIBE CAULP CUDDY DONUM
GRANT KNACK TOKEN CADEAU
DASHEE DONARY GENIUS GERSUM
GIFTIE GIVING HANSEL LEGACY
RECADO REGALO TALENT XENIUM
APTNESS BENEFIT CHARISM
CHARITY DEODATE DONATIO
DOUCEUR ETRENNE FACULTY
GIFTURE HANDSEL PRESENT
PROPINE REGALIO SUBSIDY TASHRIF
TRIBUTE AMATORIO APTITUDE
BENEFICE BESTOWAL BLESSING
COURTESY DONATION DONATIVE
GARRISON GIVEAWAY GRATUITY
MORTUARY OBLATION OFFERING
POTLATCH SPORTULA
(— FROM HUSBAND TO WIFE)
ARRAS
(— OF GOD) GRACE
(— OF MONEY) POUCH BAKSHISH
(— OF NATURE) DOWER DOWRY
(CHARITABLE —) ALMS ENAM
PITTANCE
(COMPULSORY —) SIXENIA
(LIBERAL —) LARGESSE
(NATURAL —) TALENT
(NEW YEAR'S EVE —) HAGMENA
HOGMANAY
(SPIRITUAL —) CHARISM CHARISMA
(PL.) OBLATA MISSILES
GIFTBOOK ANNUAL KEEPSAKE
GIG TUB BANDY CHAIR GIGGE
CHAISE DENNET WHISKY CALESIN
TILBURY STANHOPE
GIGANTIC HUGE GIANT MAMMOTH
TITANIC COLOSSAL ENORMOUS
GIGANTAL
GIGGER TEASELER
GIGGLE KECKLE SNICKER TWITTER
GIGLET JIG
GILD GILT BEGILD ENGILD ORFGILD
GILDED GILT AURATE INAURATE
GILDER TRACER
GILGAMESH IZDUBAR
GILL JILL QUAD GHYLL PLICA GILLIE
LAMELLA BRANCHIA QUADRANT

(—S OF BIVALVE) BEARD
(PL.) GINNERS CHOLLERS
GILLAR PITTO
GILLIE GILLY HENCHMAN
GILLYFLOWER STOCK GILVER
GELOFRE GILLIVER
GILTHEAD CONNER MELANURE
GIMBAL GEMEL JEMBLE
GIMCRACK QUIP BAUBLE GEWGAW
JIMJAM TRIFLE TRANGAM TRINKET
JIMCRACK WHIMWHAM
GIMLET SCREW WIMBLE PIERCEL
PIERCER
GIMMICK GAFF
GIMP TAR ORRIS GUIMPE GIMPING
GIN MAX CRAB GRIN LACE RUIN
TAPE CLEAN JACKY SNARE SNARL
DIDDLE GENEVA JAMBER JAMMER
SPRINGE TITTERY EYEWATER
HOLLANDS SCHIEDAM SCHNAPPS
(DROP OF —) DAFFY
GINGER PEPPER RATOON AROMATIC
ZINZIBER COLTSFOOT
GINGERBREAD SPICE PARKIN
GINGERLY GINGER WARILY CHARILY
EDGINGLY
GINGERROOT HAND RACE
(PL.) ASARUM
GINGHAM CHAMBRAY
GINKGO ICHO
GINSENG SANG FATIL PANAX
ARALIA IVYWORT REDBERRY
GIRAFFE OONT CAMEL DAPPLE
KAMEEL SERAPH CAMAILE
RUMINANT
GIRD BELT BIND GIRR GIRT HASP
YERK CLOSE SCOFF ENGIRD
FASTEN GIRDLE SECURE ACCINGE
ENVIRON CINCTURE SURROUND
GIRDER BEAM GIRD GIRT GIRTH
TABLE TRUSS BINDER SUMMER
WARREN GIRDING TWISTER
BUCKSTAY STRINGER
GIRDING CINCTURE
GIRDLE OBI ZON BARK BELT CEST
GIRD HOOP SASH ZONA ZONE
CEINT GIRTH MITER PATTE SARPE
WAIST BODICE CESTUS CINGLE
CIRCLE MOOCHA TISSUE ZODIAC
ZONULA ZOSTER BALDRIC BALTEUS
CENTRUM CENTURE COMPASS
GIRDING SHINGLE CEINTURE
CINCTURE CINGULUM SURROUND
(— FOR HELMET) TISSUE
(— OF DIATOM) HOOP
(BRIDE'S —) CEST CESTUS
(LITTLE —) COULE ZONELET
(ROYAL —) MALO
(SACRED —) KUSTI
GIRDLED RUNG
GIRL BIT GAL HER KIT POP SHE SIS
TIB TID TIT BABE BABY BINT BIRD
DAME DEEM DELL GILL JANE JILL
JUDY LASS MARY MOPS MORT PERI
SLUT WREN BEAST FILLY GUIDE
KITTY LUBRA QUEAN SISSY SKIRT
TIDDY TITTY TRULL BURDIE CALICO
CLINER CUMMER DALAGA DAMSEL
DEEMIE FEMALE FIZGIG GEISHA

GIRLIE LASSIE LOVELY MAGGIE
NUMBER PIGEON SHEILA SISTER
SUBDEB TOMATO CAMILLA COLLEEN
DAMOSEL MADCHEN MAUTHER
TENDREL BONNIBEL FARMETTE
FEMININE GRISETTE MUCHACHA
(AGILE —) YANKER
(AWKWARD —) HOIT
(BEATIFIED —) BEATA
(BEAUTIFUL —) BELLE
(BOLD —) HOIDEN HOYDEN
(CAMP FIRE —) ARTISAN
(CHORUS —) CHORINE CORYPHEE
(COUNTRY —) MEG JOAN
(DANCING —) DASI KISANG KISAENG
DEVADASI
(DANCING —S) GHAWAZI
(DEAR —) PEAT
(FLIGHTY —) GOOSECAP
(FLIRTATIOUS —) JADE JILLET
(FLOWER —) NYDIA
(FORWARD —) STRAP
(FROLICSOME —) GILPY
(GIDDY —) GIG GIGLET GIGLOT
JILLET
(GREEK —) HAIDEE
(GYPSY —) GITANA
(HIRED —) BIDDY BIDDIE
(IMPUDENT —) STRAP
(JAPANESE —) GEISHA
(LITTLE —) SIS COOKY SISSY
COOKIE LASSOCK
(MISCHIEVOUS —) CUTTY HUSSY
(MODEST —) BLUSHET
(NAIVE —) INGENUE
(NON-JEWISH —) SHIKSE SHICKSA
(PERT —) MINX HUSSY
(PRETTY —) PRIM CUTEY CUTIE
(ROMPING —) STAG TOMBOY
(SAUCY —) SNIP
(SERVANT —) SLUT
(SILLY —) SKIT
(SINGING —) ALMA ALMEH
(SLENDER —) SYLPH
(SMALL —) PINAFORE
(SPIRITED —) FILLY
(UNATTRACTIVE —) FRUMP
(UNMARRIED —) MOUSME TOWDIE
MUSUMEE
(WANTON —) GIG FILLOCK
(WILD —) BLOWZE
(WORKING —) ORISETTE
(WORTHLESS —) HUSSY
(YOUNG —) BUD MODER TITTY
MAIDEN MOTHER BAGGAGE
COLLEEN FLAPPER GIRLEEN
ROSEBUD
(PL.) GIRLERY GIRLHOOD
GIRT CINCT
GIRTH GIRD GIRT TAPE CINCH
GARTH GIRSE GRETH WANTY
CINGLE WARROK GIRDING SHINGLE
WEBBING
GIST JET NET NUB SUM CHAT CORE
GITE KNOT PITH GREAT HEART
JOIST SENSE BURDEN KERNEL
PURPORT SUMMARY STRENGTH
GITH MELANTHY
GIVE ADD GIE HOB TIP BEAR DEAL

DOLE HAND METE SELL TAKE WEVE
WHIP ALLOW AWARD COUGH GRANT
REFER YIELD ACCORD AFFORD
BESTOW CONFER DEMISE DOTATE
FASTEN IMPART IMPOSE IMPUTE
RENDER SUPPLY CONSIGN DELIVER
FORGIVE FURNISH PRESENT
BEQUEATH DISPENSE
(— A BOOST) BOLSTER
(— A PLACE TO) SITUATE
(— A REMEDY) MINISTER
(— ADHERENCE) ASSENT
(— ADMITTANCE) ACCEPT
(— ADVICE) READ ADVISE
(— AN ACCOUNT) TELL RELATE
REPORT
(— AND TAKE) GIFFGAFF
(— ANYTHING NAUSEOUS TO) DOSE
(— APPROVAL) CONSENT
(— AS CONCESSION) YETTE
(— AS EXPLANATION) ASSIGN
(— ASSURANCE) EFFRONT
(— ATTENTION TO) HEED
(— AUTHORITY) ENABLE EMPOWER
ACCREDIT
(— AWAY) PART
(— BACK) REFUND RETURN
RESTORE
(— BIRTH) KIT BEAR BORN DROP
FIND MAKE BEGET BREED ISSUE
WORLD FARROW KINDLE LITTER
DELIVER FRESHEN
(— BY WILL) DEVISE
(— CARE) NURSE
(— CLAIM TO) REMISE
(— COUNSEL) AREAD AREED
(— CREDIT FOR) FRIST
(— CURRENCY TO) PASS
(— EAR) HARK HARKEN LISTEN
HEARKEN
(— EXPRESSION TO) EMOTE FRAME
VOICE
(— FORM) CUT
(— FORTH) WARP YIELD AFFORD
CONCEIVE
(— GROUND) RETIRE
(— HEED) LOOK ATTEND
(— IN EXCHANGE) SWAP SWOP
(— IN MARRIAGE) BESTOW SPOUSE
(— IN) BOW COLLAPSE
(— INFORMATION) WARN
(— INSTRUCTION) LEAR
(— NAME TO) BAPTIZE
(— NOTICE TO APPEAR) GARNISH
(— NOTICE) WARN HERALD APPRISE
PUBLISH ANNOUNCE INTIMATE
(— OBLIQUE EDGE) CANT
(— OFF) EMIT SEND SHED FLING
DIVIDE EFFUSE EVOLVE EXHALE
EXPIRE EXCRETE SEPARATE
(— ONE'S SELF OVER TO) ADDICT
(— ONE'S WORD) PROMISE
(— OUT) BOOM LEAK EXUDE ISSUE
PETAL EVOLVE EMANATE OUTGIVE
(— PAIN) AGGRIEVE
(— PLACE) VAIL BACCARE
(— PLEDGE) GAGE
(— PROMINENCE TO) FEATURE
(— RELUCTANTLY) BEGRUDGE

(— SATISFACTION) ABY ABYE
ABEGGE
(— SPARINGLY) INCH
(— STRENGTH TO) NERVE
(— SUPPORT) ASSIST ANIMATE
(— TEMPORARILY) LEND
(— TIP) TOUT
(— TONGUE) CRY YEARN
(— UP) PUT BURY DROP PART
CHUCK DEMIT DEVOW FORGO
LEAVE REMIT SHOOT SPARE SPEND
ABJURE ADDICT BETRAY DESERT
DEVOTE FOREGO MIZZLE REFUSE
RELENT RENDER RESIGN VACATE
ABANDON DEPOSIT DESPAIR
FLUMMOX FORBEAR FORGIVE
REFRAIN RELEASE ABDICATE
RENOUNCE
(— VENT TO) EMIT ISSUE
DISCHARGE
(— VOICE) BOLT ACCENT
(— WARNING) ALERT
(— WAY) GO FAIL FOLD KEEL SINK
VAIL BREAK BUDGE BURST FAINT
SLAKE YIELD BUCKLE FALTER
RELENT SWERVE FOUNDER RECLAIM
SUCCUMB
(— WITNESS) DEPOSE
GIVEN APT DONEE NATHAN PROMPT
(— TO) ALL AFTER
GIVER DONOR
(— OF LIFE) APHETA
(NAME —) EPONYM
GIVING DOLE BOUNTY DATION
REMISE
(— HELP) ADJUTANT
(— MILK) FRESH
(— NO MILK) YELD YELL
(— TROUBLE) CUMBROUS
GIZZARD GIGERIUM
GIZZARD SHAD SKIPJACK
GLABROUS SMOOTH GLABRATE
LEVIGATE
GLACIATION MINDEL
(— STAGE) RISS WURM
GLACIER BRAE ICECAP STREAM
CALOTTE ICEBERG PIEDMONT
GLACIOLOGY CRYOLOGY
GLACIS ESPLANADE
GLAD GAY FAIN LIEF VAIN CANTY
HAPPY PROUD BLITHE FESTUS
GLADLY JOCUND JOYFUL JOYOUS
GLADFUL GLEEFUL JOCULAR
ANIMATED CHEERFUL CHEERING
FESTIVAL GLADSOME PLEASING
GLADDEN JOY GLAD BLISS CHEER
EXULT MIRTH BLITHE COMFORT
GLADIFY LIGHTEN REJOICE
GLADE LAWN LAUND SLADE SHRADD
SUNGLADE SUNSCALD
GLADIATOR THRAX RETIARY
SAMNITE SECUTOR ANDABATA
GLADIOLUS GLAD IRID LILY LEVERS
LILIUM GLADIOLA
GLADLY GLAD LIEF FAINLY LIEFLY
LOVELY HAPPILY
GLADNESS JOY GLAD GLEE BLISS
MIRTH BLITHE FAINNESS GLADSHIP
PLEASURE

GLAGA KASA KUSA TALTHIB
GLAMORIZE POT GLORIFY
GLAMOROUS EXOTIC ALLURING
CHARMING
GLANCE EYE RAY SEE BEAM CAST
GLIM LEER PEEK SCRY SKEG VIEW
WINK BLENK BLINK BLUSH CAROM
FLASH GLEEK GLENT GLIDE GLIFF
GLINT GLISK GRAZE PRINK SCREW
SIGHT SKIME SLANT SQUIZ ASPECT
CARROM GANDER REGARD SCANCE
STRIKE VISION EYEBEAM EYESHOT
EYEWINK GLIMPSE BELAMOUR
GLIFFING OEILLADE
(— OFF) GLACE
(— THROUGH) SAMPLE
(MELANCHOLY —) DOWNCAST
(SHARP —) DART
(SIDELONG —) SHEW SLENT SKLENT
(SLY —) GLEG GLIME GLOAT
GLAND MILT NOIX SETA CLYER
CRYPT GONAD LIVER MAMMA
BREAST KERNEL THYMUS ADRENAL
CRUMENA NECTARY PAROTID
PAROTIS TEARPIT THYROID
ENDOCRIN FOLLICLE FOLLOWER
GANGLION GLANDULA GLANDULE
HOOFWORM PROSTATE SCIRRHUS
SPERMARY
GLANDERS FARCY MALLEUS
GLANDULAR EARTHY INNATE
SEXUAL PHYSICAL
GLANS NUT GLAND
GLARE BEAT GAZE BLARE BLAZE
BLOOM FLAME GLAZE STARE
GLITTER ICEBLINK RADIANCE
GLARING HARD RANK GLARY
AGLARE GARISH BURNING FLARING
STARING FLAGRANT
GLASS CUP VER CALX FLAT FLUX
FRIT JENA MOIL PONY VITA CHARK
FACER FLINT GLAZE STOOP STOUP
VERRE VITRE CALGON CEMENT
CULLET SPECKS VITRUM ALEYARD
BIFOCAL BRIMMER CHIRPER
CRYSTAL PERLITE SCHMELZ
TALLBOY VITRITE FROSTING
OBSIDIAN SCHOPPEN
(— IN STATE OF FUSION) METAL
(— OF A MIRROR) STONE
(— OF BEER) BREW
(— OF BRANDY) SNEAKER
(— OF WHISKY) KELTY RUBDOWN
(— OF WINE) APERITIF
(— STICKING TO PUNTY) COLLET
(BEER —) SHELL SEIDEL
(BELL-SHAPED —) CUP CLOCHE
(BURNING —) SUNGLASS
(CHEVAL —) PSYCHE
(COLORED —) SMALT SMALTO
TINTER SCHMELZ
(COLORED —S) GOGGLES
(CUPPING —) VENTOSE
(CURVED —) LENS
(DESSERT —) COUPE
(DRINKING —) GOBLET RUMKIN
PILSNER PIMLICO SCUTTLE
TUMBLER SCHOONER
(EXAMINATION —) SLIDE
(FULL —) BUMPER

(FUSIBLE —) FLUX
(HALF —) SPLIT
(ICE CREAM —) SLIDER
(LEAD —) STRASS
(LIQUEUR —) PONY PONEY
(LIQUOR —) GUN
(MAGNIFYING —) LOUPE
(MASS OF MOLTEN —) PARISON
(OPALESCENT —) OPALINE
(OPAQUE —) HYALITHE
(PIECE OF HOT —) BIT
(PULVERIZED —) FROSTING
(REFUSE —) CALX CULLET
(RUSSIAN —) CHARK
(SHERBET —) SUPREME
(SMOKED —) SHADE
(STAINED —) VITRAIL
(TALL —) RUMMER
(VOLCANIC —) PUMICE PERLITE
(WINDOW —) PANE
(PL.) SHELLS
GLASSBLOWER MUMBLER
GLASS CRAB SPECTER SPECTRE
GLASSHOUSE STOVE HOTHOUSE
GLASS-LIKE VITRIC
GLASSWARE AGATA AURENE
BURMESE FAVRILE OPALINE
STEUBEN VITRICS AMBERINA
GLASSWORK GLAZING GLAZIERY
GLASSWORKER GANGMAN GLAZIER
SNAPPER GLASSMAN SERVITOR
GLASSWORT KALI KELPWORT
SALTWORT SAMPHIRE
GLASSY GLIB FILMY GLAZY GLAZEN
GLASSEN HYALINE HYALOID
VITREAL VITREOUS
GLAUCE (FATHER OF —) CREON
(HUSBAND OF —) JASON
GLAUCUS (FATHER OF —) MINOS
SISYPHUS
(MOTHER OF —) MEROPE PASIPHAE
GLAZE DIP LEAD SIZE SLIP GLASS
SLEET SMEAR ENAMEL QUARRY
CELADON COPERTA EELSKIN
GLASSEN GLAZING GLIDDER
COUVERTE TIGEREYE
(— OF ICE) GLARE
GLAZED FILMY GLACE GLASSEN
GLOSSED
GLAZED WARE GLOST
GLAZIER (TOOL OF —) SPRIG
LADKIN
GLEAM RAY BEAM GLOW LEAM
WAFT WINK BLENK BLINK BLUSH
FLASH GLAIK GLEEN GLENT GLINT
GLISK GLIST GLOSE SHINE SKIME
SPUNK STARE STEEM TWIRE
GLANCE SCANCE FOULDRE
GLIMMER GLITTER SHIMMER
(— FAINTLY) SHIMMER
(— OF LIGHT) LEAM PINK GLAIK
SCANCE
(FAINT —) SCAD
GLEAMING FAW GLOW CLEAR GLINT
STEEP ABLAZE BRIGHT GLEAMY
ADAZZLE SHINING GLOOMING
GLEAN CULL EARN REAP LEASE
GATHER COLLECT SCRINGE
GLEANER STIBBLER
GLEANING CROP GATHERING

(LITERARY —S) ANALECTA
ANALECTS
GLEBE SOD CLOD LAND SOIL
TERMON KIRKTOWN
GLEE GLY JOY SONG MIRTH SPORT
GAIETY DELIGHT ELATION WASSAIL
HILARITY MADRIGAL
GLEEFUL GAY MERRY JOYOUS
JOCULAR GLEESOME
GLEEMAN SONGMAN MINSTREL
GLEN DEN GILL GLYN GRIFF HEUCH
HEUGH KLOOF SLACK SLADE TEMPE
CANADA DINGLE POCKET
GLIADIN GLUTIN PROLAMIN
GLIB PAT FLIP SLICK CASUAL
GLOSSY OFFHAND RENABLE
SHALLOW VOLUBLE FLIPPANT
GLIDE GO SKI FLOW SAIL SILE SKIM
SLIP SLUR SOAR SWIM COAST
CREEP DANCE FLEET GLACE GRAZE
LAPSE MERGE SCOOP SHIRL SKATE
SKIFF SKIRR SLADE SLEEK SLICK
SLIDE SLIPE STEAL GLANCE GLIDER
SASHAY SNOOVE ILLAPSE SCRIEVE
SCRITHE SKITTER SLITHER
AIRPLANE GLISSADE VOLPLANE
(— AWAY) ELAPSE
(— BY) PASS FLEET
(— OFF) EXIT
GLIDER SCOOTER
GLIDING TRAIL SLIDING
(— OF THE VOICE) DRAG
(— OVER) LAMBENT
GLIMMER FIRE GLIM GLOW LEAM
STIM BLINK FLASH GLEAM GLOOM
STIME SIMPER BLINTER FLIMMER
GLIMPSE GLITTER SHIMMER
SPARKLE TWINKLE SUNBLINK
GLIMMERING GHOST AGLIMMER
GLOOMING
GLIMPSE IDEA WAFF WAFT BLINK
BLUSH FLASH GLIFF GLINT GLISK
SIGHT STIME TINGE TRACE WHIFF
GLANCE LUSTER SCANCE GLIMMER
INKLING
(BRIEF —) APERCU
(FLEETING —) SHIM SNATCH
GLINT PEEP FLASH GLEAM GLENT
GLANCE SPARKLE
GLIS MYOXUS
GLISSANDO GLISS SMEAR GLISSADE
GLISTEN FLASH GLISK GLISS GLIST
SHINE GLISTER GLITTER SHIMMER
SPANGLE SPARKLE
GLISTENING SHINY AGLISTEN
GLITTER FLASH GLARE GLEAM
GLEIT GLINT GLORE SHEEN SHINE
SKYRE STARE LUSTER SCANCE
GLIMMER GLISTEN GLISTER SKINKLE
SPANGLE SPARKLE TWINKLE
BRANDISH RADIANCE
(FALSE —) GILT
GLITTERING GEMMY SHEEN SHINY
STEEP FULGID SPANGLY AGLITTER
GLITTERY
GLOAMING EVE DUSK GLOAM
GLOOMING TWILIGHT
GLOAT GAZE GLUT TIRE EXULT
GLOBE ORB BALL BOWL CLEW CLUE
POME AGGER GEOID MONDE ROUND

SPHERE COMPASS GEORAMA
GLOBULE GRENADE AQUARIUM
GLOBEFISH FUGU TOBY TOADO
ATINGA BOTETE PUFFER BLAASOP
BURFISH OOPUHUE
GLOBEFLOWER BOLT GOLLAND
GOWLAND CORCHORUS
GLOBE THISTLE ECHNOPS
GLOBOSE COCCOID COCCOUS
CAPITATE GLOBULAR
GLOBULAR GLOBED GLOBATE
GLOBOSE GLOBICAL
GLOBULE BEAD BLOB DROP GLOB
PEARL BUBBLE BUTTON REGULUS
GLOBULET SPHERULE
(— OF TAPIOCA) FISHEYE
GLOBULIN MAYSIN MYOSIN VIGNIN
ARACHIN CORYCIN EDESTIN
LEGUMIN TUBERIN VICILIN
ANTIBODY BIOLOGIC EXCELSIN
GLYCININ MUSCULIN ORYZENIN
GLOCKENSPIEL BELL LYRA
CARILLON
GLOMERULE GLOME FASCICLE
GLOOM DUSK MURK CLOUD DREAR
FROWN SOMBER DESPAIR DIMNESS
GLOOMTH SADNESS DARKNESS
MIDNIGHT
GLOOMY DUN SAD WAN BLUE COLD
DARK DOUR DREE DULL EERY GLUM
MURK ADUSK ADUST BLACK BROWN
DOWFF DREAR DUSKY EERIE FERAL
GUMLY HEAVY LURID MOODY
MORNE MUDDY MUNGY MUSTY
SABLE SORRY STERN SULKY SURLY
SWART TRIST CLOUDY DREARY
DREICH DROOPY DRUMLY GLUMMY
MOROSE SOLEMN SOMBER SULLEN
TETRIC THRAWN OBSCURE STYGIAN
THESTER DESOLATE DOLESOME
DOWNBEAT DOWNCAST FUNEREAL
GLOOMING LOWERING OVERCAST
GLORIA GLORY AUREOLE
GLORIFY HERY LAUD BLESS DEIFY
EXALT EXTOL HERSE HONOR PRIDE
WURTH KUDIZE PRAISE CLARIFY
ELEVATE MAGNIFY DIVINIZE
EMBLAZON EULOGIZE STELLIFY
GLORIOUS SRI DEAR DERE MERE
SHRI GRAND BRIGHT EMINENT
RENOWNED
GLORY JOY ORE SUN FACE FAME
GLOR HALO HORN BLAZE BOAST
EXULT HONOR KUDOS PRIDE
WULDER AUREOLA CLARITY
GARLAND GLORIFY RADIANCE
SPLENDOR WORTHING
GLOSS GILL COLOR DUNCE GLASS
GLAZE GLOZE JAPAN SHEEN SHINE
BLANCH LUSTER LUSTRE POSTIL
REMARK VENEER BURNISH
EXPOUND VARNISH FLOURISH
PALLIATE POLITURE
(— OVER) FARD HUSH SALVE SLEEK
SOOTHE
GLOSSA LINGUA
GLOSSARY GLOSS CLAVIS
GLOSSIPHONIA CLEPSINE
GLOSSY GLOZE NITID SHINY SILKY
SLICK SATINY SMOOTH

GLOVE KID CUFF GAGE MITT COFFE
BERLIN MITTEN CHEVRON DANNOCK
GANTLET GOMUKHI GAUNTLET
(— FOR RUBBING SKIN) STRIGIL
(BISHOP'S —) GWANTUS
(BODY OF —) TRANK
(HEDGER'S —) DANNOCK
(HUSKING —) HUSKER
GLOVEMAKER DOMER GLOVER
CLASPER FINGERER
GLOVER TRANKER
GLOW ARC LOW AURA BURN FIRE
LEAM LOOM LOWE BLAZE BLOOM
BLUSH FLAME FLASH FLUSH GLAZE
GLEAM GLEED GLORY GLOSS
GLOZE SHINE STEAM CORONA
KINDLE WARMTH FLUSTER LIGHTEN
(— OF PASSION) ESTUS AESTUS
(— WITH INTENSE HEAT) IGNITE
GLOWER GAZE GLOW GLARE
GLOOM GLORE
GLOWING HOT LIVE WARM AGLOW
FIERY LIGHT QUICK RUDDY VIVID
ABLAZE ARDENT ORIENT BURNING
CANDENT FERVENT RADIANT
SHINING FLAGRANT
GLOWWORM FIREFLY FIREWORM
GLOWBIRD LAMPYRID
GLOZE FAWN PAINT SMOOTH
FLATTERY
GLUCOSE AME GLYCOSE DEXTROSE
GLUCOSIDE GEIN APIIN RUTIN TUTIN
ADONIN BINDER CORNIN DURRIN
FRAXIN FUSTIN IRIDIN PICEIN
UZARIN ACACIIN ARBUTIN DAPHNIN
DIOSMIN ESCULIN ESTEVIN GITALIN
GITONIN GITOXIN HEDERIN HELECIN
INDICAN LOGANIN LOTUSIN LUPININ
ONABAIN POPULIN ROBININ SALICIN
TABACIN TEUCRIN ADONIDIN
CARTHAME ERICOLIN GENISTIN
GOSSYPIN MORINDIN NARINGIN
PARIGLIN PARILLIN PRUNASIN
QUINOVIN SAPONINE SCILLAIN
SINIGRIN SYRINGIN THEVETIN
VERNONIN VIBURNIN VICIANIN
GLUE PAD MOUNT STICK BEGLEW
CEMENT FUNORE FUNORIN STICKER
TAUROCOL
GLUEY GLUISH STICKY STRINGY
VISCOUS ADHESIVE
GLUM CLUM DOUR GRUM SURLY
GLOOMY GLUMPY MOROSE SULLEN
GLUMALES POALES
GLUME PILE FLIGHT
(FLOWERING —) LEMMA
(PL.) CHAFF
GLUSIDE SACCHARIN
GLUT CLOY FILL GULP QUAT SATE
CHOKE DRAFT GORGE BATTEN
ENGLUT EXCESS MARROW PAMPER
PAUNCH ENGORGE GLUTTON
SATIATE SURFEIT SWALLOW
OVERFEED SATURATE
GLUTEAL NATAL
GLUTELIN AVENINE ORYZENIN
GLUTENIN AVENIN ZYMOME
ZYMOMIN
GLUTINOUS ROPY SIZY ROPEY
SLIMY TOUGH STICKY VISCID

GLUTTED QUAT GORGED SATIATED
GLUTTER VEER
GLUTTON PIG GLUT GORB GUTS
GULCH MIKER GLOTUM HELLUO
MACCUS EPICURE GUTLING
LURCHER MOOCHER RAVENER
SWILLER DRAFFMAN GOURMAND
GULLYGUT
(STUPID —) GRUB
GLUTTONIZE BIZLE BEZZLE
GLUTTONOUS GREEDY GLUTTON
HOGGISH GOURMAND
GLUTTONY GULE SURFEIT
GLYCERIDE BUTYRIN
GLYCINE SOJA
GLYCOL CARBOWAX
GLYCOPROTEIN MUCIN MUCOID
GLYCOSIDE APIIN CROCIN ACACIIN
CYMARIN DIGOXIN GITALIN GITOXIN
HEDERIN HYPERIN LOGANIN
LOTUSIN SAPONIN ALDESIDE
ANDROSIN ANTIARIN HOLOSIDE
KETOSIDE
GNARL NOB KNOB KNUR KNARL
KNURR SNIRL WARRE DEFORM
GNARLED GNARLY KNARRY KNOTTY
CRABBED KNOTTED KNURLED
GNASH TUSK CHAMP CRASH GANCH
GRASH GRATE KNASH
GNAT KNAW SMUT MIDGE STOUT
KNATTE SCIARA SCIARID SCINIPH
BLACKFLY DIPTERAN GNATLING
GNATCATCHER SYLVIID
GNATHION MENTON
GNAW EAT NAB BITE FRET TIRE
CHELE GNARL MOUSE SHEAR
ARRODE BEFRET BEGNAW CHAVEL
NATTLE NIGGLE ROUNGE CHIMBLE
CHUMBLE CORRODE
GNAWING EATING RODENT FRETFUL
ARROSION ROSORIAL
GNOME NIS NISSE PECHT PYGMY
KOBOLD VAKSHA YAKSHI GNOMIDE
GREMLIN HODEKEN ERDGEIST
GNOMON COCK INDEX STILE STYLE
FESCUE STYLUS
GNOSTIC CLEVER SHREWD
KNOWING PERATES EBIONITE
MANDAEAN SEVERIAN SIMONIAN
SIMONITE
GNU KOKOON BRINDLE
GO BE DO ACT GAE HOP ISH LAY
NIM PEP TEE WAG BANG BEAR BING
BOWN BUSK DRAW FAND FARE
FOND GANG HARK HAUL HUMP
MOVE QUIT ROAM ROLL SEEK SHOT
SILE SLAP SNAP STAB STEP TAKE
TEEM TOUR WADE WANE WEAR
WEND WEVE WIND WISE WORK
YEDE AMBLE BOUND CARRY CHEVE
DEMON DRESS FETCH FRAME
HAUNT KNOCK LEAVE MOSEY
PLUCK REACH SCRAM SHAKE
SLOPE SPEED TOUCH TRACE TRACK
TRENE TRINE TRUSS WHIZZ YONGE
BECOME BETAKE CHIEVE CRUISE
DEPART EXTEND QUATCH QUETCH
REPAIR RESORT RESULT RETIRE
SASHAY STRAKE STRIKE TODDLE
TRAVEL WEAKEN JOURNEY SCRITHE
DIMINISH WITHDRAW

(— **ABOUT DEJECTEDLY**) PEAK
(— **ABOUT GOSSIPING**) COURANT
(— **ABOUT**) JET BEGO BIGAN
(— **AHEAD**) HOLD
(— **AIMLESSLY**) ERR
(— **ALONG**) PATH
(— **AROUND**) SKIRT BYPASS CIRCUE
(— **ASHORE**) LAND
(— **ASTRAY**) ERR MAR WRY MANG
WILL MISGO DELIRE FORVAY
MISWEND DEROGATE MISCARRY
(— **AWAY**) AGO HOP BEAT BUNK
HIKE NASH PART SHOO VADE
CLEAR HENCE IMSHI LEAVE SCRAM
SHIFT BEGONE BUGGER DEPART
REMOVE VACATE SKIDDOO
ELONGATE
(— **BACK IN TIME**) MOUNT
(— **BAD**) SOUR
(— **BEFORE**) LEAD FOREGO
PRECEDE ANTECEDE PREAMBLE
(— **BEYOND**) SURPASS FOREPASS
(— **BRISKLY**) JUNE
(— **BROKE**) BUST
(— **COURTING**) WENCH
(— **DOWN**) SET SINK DROOP SOUND
DESCEND
(— **EASILY**) AMBLE
(— **ERRATICALLY**) KICK
(— **FAST**) HURRY SPLIT BEELINE
(— **FORTH**) AGO DEPART FORTHGO
(— **FORWARD**) HUP HUPP ADVANCE
AGGRESS PROCEED
(— **FOWLING**) AUCUPATE
(— **FURTIVELY**) SLINK SNEAK STEAL
(— **HANG**) SNICK
(— **HEAVILY**) LOB LAMPER
(— **IN HASTE**) LEN LAMMAS
(— **IN HURRY**) SCOFFLE
(— **IN PURSUIT**) SUE
(— **IN**) ENTER INGRESS
(— **INTO BUSINESS**) EMBARK
(— **LAME**) FOUNDER
(— **LEISURELY**) BUMMEL JIGGET
JIGGIT
(— **LIGHTLY**) TIPTOE
(— **MAD**) CRAZE MADDLE
(— **NEAR**) APPROACH
(— **NOISILY**) LARUM
(— **OFF**) MOG DISCHARGE
(— **ON BOARD**) BOARD EMBARK
ENTRAIN
(— **ON FOOT**) SHANK
(— **ON TO SAY**) ADD
(— **ON**) DO GARN LAST PASS
PERGE FURTHER PROCEED
(— **OUT**) EXIT ISSUE SLOCK EGRESS
EXEUNT QUENCH SORTIE
(— **OVER AGAIN**) RENEW REVISE
RETRACE
(— **OVER**) KNEE REVOLT SURPASS
OVERGANG
(— **PROSPEROUSLY**) COTTON
(— **QUICKLY**) GET HIE BUZZ LAMP
PIKE SCAT SPEED
(— **RAPIDLY**) LAMP SPLIT
(— **SHARES**) SNACK
(— **SLOWLY**) CRAWL CREEP
(— **SLUGGISHLY**) SHACK
(— **SMOOTHLY**) SLIP

(— **STEALTHILY**) SHIRK SLINK
SNEAK GUMSHOE
(— **SUDDENLY**) SCOOT
(— **SWIFTLY**) SCOOT SKISE STRIP
HIGHBALL
(— **THE ROUNDS**) PATROL
(— **THROUGH WATER**) SQUATTER
(— **THROUGH**) SUFFER
(— **THROUGHOUT**) COAST
(— **TO BED**) KIP FLOP SNUG
(— **TO EXCESS**) DEBORD
(— **TO HARBOR**) VERT
(— **TO PIECES**) SNURP
(— **TO SCHOOL**) SCOLEY
(— **TO SLEEP**) HUSHABY
(— **TO WAR**) RISE
(— **UP**) CLIMB AMOUNT ASCEND
(— **WEARILY**) HAGGLE
(— **WITH EFFORT**) HIKE
(— **WRONG**) MISS FAULT CURDLE
MISFARE
GOAD EGG GAD GIG HAG BAIT BROD
BROG DARE EDGE GAUD LASH
MOVE PROD SPUR URGE WHIP YERK
ANKUS HARRY IMPEL PIQUE PRICK
PROGG PUNGE STING VALET INCITE
OXGOAD ANKUSHA HOTFOOT
INFLAME PROVOKE IRRITATE
SLAPJACK STIMULUS
GOADMAN GADMAN GAUDSMAN
GOADSTER
GOAL BYE DEN END BASE BUTT
DOLE HAIL HALE MARK METE PORT
BOURN FINIS IDEAL SCOOP SCOPE
SCORE STING DESIGN OBJECT
SIGHTS DESTINY HORIZON
TERMINUS
(— **IN GAMES**) HUNK
(**FIELD** —) BASKET
(**REMOTE** —) THULE
(**UNATTAINABLE** —) STAR
GO-ASHORE KOHUA
GOAT TUR IBEX TAHR BEDEN BILLY
BOVID EVECK SEROW ALPINE
ANGORA AOUDAD CAPRID CHAMAL
JEMLAH MAZAME NUBIAN PASANG
SAANEN WETHER CHAMOIS
AEGAGRUS CAPRIPED MARKHOOR
(**DOMESTIC** —) HIRCUS
(**FEMALE** —) NANNY DOELING
(**MALE** —) BUCK BUCKLING
(**YOUNG** —) KID KIDDY TICCHEN
GOATLING
GOAT ANTELOPE GORAL SEROW
GOORAL
GOATEE TUFT
GOATFISH MOANO
GOATHERD DAMON
GOAT-LIKE GOATISH HIRCINE
GOAT MOTH COSSID
GOATSBEARD ROSACEAN
GOATSKIN CRUST CASTOR
CHEVRETTE
GOATSUCKER PUCK PEWKE POTOO
EVEJAR DORHAWK GRINDER
SPINNER DOORHAWK EVECHURR
NIGHTJAR PAURAQUE
GOB CLOT GOAF SWAB SWOB
WASTE GOBBET SWABBY
GOBBLE MOP BOLT SLOP GOFFLE
GORBLE

GOBBLEDYGOOK PEDAGESE
GO-BETWEEN BAWD FIXER MEANS
BROKER DEALER PANDAR CONTACT
MEDIATOR
GOBLET DINOS GLASS HANAP
POKAL SKULL STOOP STOUP
HOLMOS RUMKIN CHALICE SNIFTER
TALLBOY JEROBOAM STANDARD
STEMWARE
GOBLIN (ALSO SEE HOBGOBLIN)
COW HAG NIS BHUT BOGY MARE
BOGEY NISSE OUPHE POOKA
BODACH BOGGLE BOOGER CHUREL
FOLIOT SPRITE BOGGART BROWNIE
BUGBEAR KNOCKER PADFOOT
BARGHEST BOGEYMAN FOLLETTO
GOBY MAPO BULLY BIGHEAD
CHALACO GOBIOID GUAVINA
GUDGEON MUDFISH BULLHEAD
PINKFISH SANDGOBY
GOCART SULKY WALKER STROLLER
GOD (ALSO SEE DEITY) EA EL ER RA
VE BEL BES COG DAD DES DEV DIS
DOD EAR GAR GAW GEB GOG GOL
GOM GUM ING KEB LAR LOK MEN
MIN ODD ORO SEB SUN TEM TYR
ULL UTU VAN AITU AMEN AMON
ARES ASUR ATEO ATUA ATYS BAAL
BEER BRAN BURE CHAC COCK
DEUS DEVA DIEU ESUS FONS FREY
GAWD GOSH HAPI HOLY HOTH INTI
JOVE KANE KING LIFE LLEU LOKE
LOKI LOVE LUGH MARS MIND NABU
NEBO NUDD ODIN PTAH SHEN SOMA
SOUL TANE THOR TIKI ULLR UTUG
VAYU XIPE YAMA ZEUS ARAWN
ASHUR ASURA ATTES ATTIS COMUS
DAGDA DEITY DEOTA DUVEL DYAUS
DYLAN EBISU ELOAH FREYR GHOST
GOLES GOLLY GRAVE GUACA
HESUS HIEMS HORUS HOTHR
HUACA HYMEN INDRA JUDGE KINGU
LADON LIBER LLUDD MENTU MIDER
MOMUS NJORD NUMEN PALES SILEN
TAMUZ THOTH TINIA TRUTH TYCHE
URASH WAKEA WODIN WOTAN
ZOMBI ADITYA ADONAI ADONAY
ANSHAR ANUBIS APOLLO ASEITY
AUTHOR CHAMOS CONSUS DEVATA
DHARMA ELATHA ELOHIM FATHER
FAUNUS GANESA HEAVEN HERMES
HOENIR METZLI MILCOM MITHRA
NEREUS NERGAL OSIRIS PATRON
PENEUS PLUTUS PUSHAN SESHAT
SOCIUS SOURCE SPIRIT SUTEKH
SYLENE TAAROA TAMMUZ TARTAK
TERAPH TRITON TRIVIA VARUNA
VEDUIS VERITY VISHNU VULCAN
WISDOM YAKSHA YAKSHI ZOMBIE
ABRAXAS ADRANUS ALPHEUS
ANTEROS BELENUS CHEMOSH
DAIKOKU DELLING ETERNAL
GODHEAD HANUMAN IAPETUS
JEHOVAH JUPITER KANALOA
MERCURY MITHRAS MUTINUS
NEPTUNE NJORTHR PROTEUS
PRYDERI REMPHAN ROBIGUS
SAVITAR SERAPIS TRIGLAV VATICAN
VEJOVIS ZAGREUS ALMIGHTY
ASTRAEUS BISHAMON CAMAXTLI

DEMIURGE DEVOTION DIVINITY GUCUMATZ INFINITE JIUROJIN KUKULKAN MIXCOATL MORPHEUS POSEIDON SABAZIOS SUMMANUS TANGAROA TERMINUS TUTELARY VEDIOVIS ZEPHYRUS
(— OF AGRICULTURE) PICUS URASH FAUNUS AMAETHON NINGIRSU
(— OF ARTS) SIVA
(— OF ATMOSPHERE) HADAD
(— OF COMMERCE) MERCURY
(— OF CORN) CAT
(— OF DAY) HORUS
(— OF EARTH) BEL GEB KEB SEB DAGAN
(— OF EVIL) SET FOMOR FOMORIAN
(— OF FIRE) AGNI GIRRU NUSKU RUDRA VULCAN
(— OF FLOCKS) PAN
(— OF HAPPINESS) HOTEI JUROJIN
(— OF HEAVENS) ANU JUMALA
(— OF JUSTICE) FORSETE FORSETI
(— OF LEARNING) IMHOTEP
(— OF LOVE) AMOR ARES EROS KAMA BHAGA CUPID AENGUS
(— OF MOON) SIN ENZU NANNAR
(— OF NATURE) MARSYAS
(— OF POETRY) BRAGE BRAGI
(— OF RAIN) PARJANYA
(— OF SEA) LER VAN AEGIR DYAUS NEPTUNE PROTEUS PALAEMON POSEIDON
(— OF SKY) ANU GWYDION
(— OF SLEEP) HYPNOS HYPNUS MORPHEUS
(— OF SOUTHEAST WIND) EURUS
(— OF STORM) ZU ADAD ADDA ADDU MARUT RUDRA TESHUP
(— OF SUN) RA RE SHU SOL TEM TUM UTU AMON ATMU ATUM BAAL LLEU UTUG SAMAS SEKER SURYA APOLLO HELIOS SOKARI KHEPERA PHOEBUS SHAMASH PHAETHON TONATIUH
(— OF THUNDER) THOR DONAR PERUN PERKUN PEROUN TLALOC HURAKAN TARANIS
(— OF UNDERWORLD) DIS GWYN YAMA HADES ORCUS PLUTO
(— OF VEGETATION) ATYS ATTIS
(— OF WAR) ER IRA ORO TIU TYR ARES COEL IRRA MARS MENT ODIN THOR MONTU NINIB MEXITL SKANDA CAMULUS MEXITLI NINURTA ENYALIUS NINGIRSU QUIRINUS
(— OF WEALTH) BHAGA KUBERA KUVERA PLUTUS
(— OF WIND) ADAD ADDA ADDU VAYU MARUT AEOLUS BOREAS EECATL
(— OF WISDOM) TAT THOTH
(— WILLING) DV
(BLIND —) HOTH HOTHR
(FALSE —) BAAL IDOL MAUMET
(FEMALE —) GODDESS
(HAWAIIAN —) AUMAKUA
(PAGAN —) DEMON
(RAM-HEADED —) AMON KHNUM KHNEMU
(TUTELARY —) LAR

(UNKNOWN —) KA
(WOOD —) SILEN SILENUS
(PL.) DI DII AESIR IGIGI SUPERI PANTHEON TRIMURTI
GODDESS (ALSO SEE DEITY) AI NU ANA ANU ATE AYA DEA DON NUT OPS UNI VAC ANTA BADB BODB CACA DANA DANU ERIS ERUA FRIA HELA HERA JORD JUNO MAIA MEDB NIKE NINA NONA PELE SAGA SATI TARA UPIS ALLAT AMENT ANATH ANTUM ARURU BAUBO CERES CHLOE DEESS DIANA DIANE DIRGA DOLMA DOMNU EPONA FRIGG HYBLA IAMBE ISTAR KOTYS MAEVE NANAI NINTU PAKHT PALES PARCA SALUS SEDNA SKADI TANIT TYCHE USHAS VENUS VESTA ADEONA AESTAS ANATUM ANUKIT APHAIA ATHENA BELILI BENDIS BOOPIS BRIGIT CYRENE EOSTRE FRIGGA GEFJON HELENA HESTIA HYGEIA INNINA KISHAR LIBERA MOTHER NINGAL PEITHO PHOBOS POMONA PRORSA RUMINA SEKHET SEMELE SKATHI SOTHIS TANITH TEFNUT TRIVIA URANIA VACUNA YDGRUN ANAHITA ANAITIS ARTEMIS ASHERAH DEMETER DERCETO FERONIA FJORGYN GODHEAD LARENTA LARUNDA MAJAGGA MAJESTA MINERVA MORNING MORRIGU MYLITTA NEKHEBT NEMESIS PALATUA PARBATI PARVATI SALACIA ADRASTEA AGLAUROS ANGERONA BELISAMA CARMENTA CENTEOTL COCAMAMA DESPOINA DICTYNNA GULLVEIG MORRIGAN NEPHTHYS PARBUTTY PRAKRITI RHIANNON SEFEKHET THOUERIS VICTORIA
(— OF AGRICULTURE) BAU OPS DEMETER CENTEOTL
(— OF AIR) AURA
(— OF BEAUTY) VENUS LAKSHMI
(— OF BURIAL) LIBITINA
(— OF CHILDBIRTH) LEVANA LUCINA
(— OF DAWN) EOS USAS USHAS AURORA MATUTA
(— OF DEW) HERSE
(— OF DISCORD) ATE ERIS
(— OF EARTH) GE LUA SEB ERDA GAEA GAIA TARI ARURU DIONE JORTH TERRA SEMELE TELLUS THEMIS DAMKINA PERCHTA
(— OF FERTILITY) MA ISIS MAMA NERTHUS
(— OF FLOWERS) FLORA CHLORIS
(— OF FORTUNE) TYCHE FORTUNA
(— OF GRAIN) CERES
(— OF HEALING) EIR GULA
(— OF HEALTH) DAMIA HYGEIA VALETUDO
(— OF HEARTH) VESTA HESTIA
(— OF HISTORY) SAGA
(— OF HOPE) SPES
(— OF INFATUATION) ATE
(— OF JUSTICE) DIKE MAAT ASTRAEA NEMESIS JUSTITIA
(— OF LEGISLATION) EUNOMIA

(— OF LOVE) ATHOR FREYA VENUS FREYJA HATHOR
(— OF MAGIC) HECATE
(— OF MARRIAGE) HERA
(— OF MATERNITY) APET
(— OF MERCY) KWANNON
(— OF MOTHERHOOD) ISIS
(— OF NIGHT) NOX NYX
(— OF OCEAN) NINA
(— OF OVENS) FORNAX
(— OF PEACE) PAX IRENE NERTHUS
(— OF PLEASURE) BES
(— OF RAINBOW) IRIS
(— OF SEASONS) DIKE HORA
(— OF THE DEAD) HEL HELA
(— OF THE HUNT) DIANA VACUNA ARTEMIS
(— OF THE MOON) LUNA MOON DIANA SELENA TANITH ARTEMIS
(— OF THE SEA) INO RAN DORIS BRANWEN EURYNOME
(— OF TRUTH) MAAT
(— OF VEGETATION) OPS CERES COTYS COTYTTO
(— OF VENGEANCE) ARA NEMESIS
(— OF VICTORY) NIKE
(— OF WAR) ENYO ANATH ANATU ANUNIT BELLONA
(— OF WATER) ANAHITA
(— OF WEALTH) LAKSHMI
(— OF WISDOM) ATHENA MINERVA
(— OF YOUTH) HEBE JUVENTAS
(3-HEADED —) HECATE
(COW-HEADED —) ISIS
(ESKIMO —) SEDNA
(SUBORDINATE —) DEMIURGE
(THUNDER-SMITTEN —) SEMELE KERAUNIA
(PL.) MATRIS POINAE ASYNJUR
GO-DEVIL TRAVOIS ALLIGATOR
GODFATHER GOSSIP GODPAPA PADRINO SPONSOR GODPHERE
GODHEAD DEITY GODHOOD DIVINITY
GODLESS WICKED ATHEIST IMPIOUS PROFANE UNGODLY
GODLESSNESS ATHEISM
GODLIKE DEIFIC DIVINE IMMORTAL OLYMPIAN
GODLINESS SANCTITY
GODLING DEVATA GENIUS GODKIN GODLET PANISC DEMIGOD PANISCUS
GODLY HOLY PIOUS DEVOUT GRACIOUS
GODMOTHER CUMMER GOSSIP SPONSOR GODMAMMA MARRAINE
GODPARENT SPONSOR
GOD'S S
GODSON FILLEUL GODCHILD
GOD TREE CEIBA
GODWIT PICK PRINE BARKER MARLIN SCAMMEL YARWHIP RINGTAIL SHRIEKER SPOTRUMP YARDKEEP YARWHELP
GOFFER FULLER GAUFFER
GO-GETTER HUSTLER
GOGGLER SCAD
GOGLET COOJA SERAI MONKEY SURAHI GURGLET SURAHEE

GOING FARE GAIT BOUND AGOING
WAYING PASSADO SLEDDING
(— **ABOUT**) AROUND
(— **BEYOND OTHERS**) ULTRA
(— **IN**) INEUNT INFARE INGOING
(— **ON**) FARE AGATE TOWARD
(— **OUT**) EGRESS
(— **UP**) ANABASIS
GOITER WEN GLANS GOITRE
STRUMA
GOITERED ANTELOPE ZENU
GOITROUS STRUMOUS
GOLD OR ORO RED SOL DORE GILT
GULL ALTUN AURUM GUILD METAL
OCHER OCHRE RIDGE SHINY
GOLDEN OBRIZE ORMOLU YELLOW
BULLION SPANKER
(— **PIECE**) TALI
(**GREENISH** —) AENEUS AENEOUS
GOLDBEATER (TOOL OF —) WAGON
GOLDCREST MOON TIDLEY
MUDDLER TROCHIL
GOLDEN RED DORE GOLD BLEST
DURRY GOLDY SUNNY AUREAL
BLONDE GILDEN GILTEN AUREATE
AUREOUS HALCYON AURULENT
DEAURATE
(— **STATE**) CALIFORNIA
GOLDEN CHAIN LABURNUM
GOLDEN CLUB TAWKEE TAWKIN
TUCKAHOE
GOLDEN EAGLE RINGTAIL
GOLDENEYE CUR GARROT
COBHEAD GOWDNIE BULLHEAD
IRONHEAD MORILLON WHIFFLER
WHISTLER
GOLDEN ORIOLE PIROL WITWALL
GOLDEN PLOVER KOLEA FROGSKIN
SQUEALER WHISTLER
GOLDEN RAGWORT LIFEROOT
GOLDENROD BONEWORT SOLIDAGO
JIMMYWEED
GOLDENSEAL EYEBALM EYEROOT
ICEROOT PUCCOON
GOLDEN SHINER CHUB DACE
WINDFISH
GOLDFINCH JACK FINCH GOLDY
GOWDY CANARY REDCAP FLAXBIRD
GRAYPATE
GOLDFINNY GOLDNEY CORKWING
GOLDFISH FUNA MOOR COMET
CALICO FANTAIL CYPRINID VEILTAIL
GOLD-OF-PLEASURE FLAX
MADWORT OILSEED
GOLDSMITH SONAR AURIFEX
GOLFER TEER
GOMUTI EJOO IROK ARENG KITTUL
SAGWIRE SAGOWEER
GONAD GERMEN
GONCALO ALVES KINGWOOD
GONDOLA GON BARGE GUNDALOW
GONE AWAY LOST NAPOO
(— **BY**) AGO DONE PAST AGONE
PASSE BEHIND BYGONE
(— **OUT OF USE**) EXTINCT
(— **TO PIECES**) HAYWIRE
GONG BELL CLOCK GANGSA
DOORBELL
(**SERIES OF** —**S**) BONANG
GONGORISM CULTISM

GONOPHORE MEDUSOID SPOROSAC
GOOD BON GAY TOP TRY ABLE
BEAU BEIN BIEN BOON BRAW FINE
GAIN HEND NICE NOTE PROW SAKE
BONUM BRAVE BULLY CANNY
FRESH GWEED JELLY KAPAI PAKKA
PUKKA SEELY SOUND VALID BENIGN
BRAWLY BUCKRA DIVINE EXPERT
FACTOR FORBYE HONEST MABUTI
PRETTY PROFIT PROPER WEALTH
BENEFIT COPIOUS CORKING FAIRISH
FORTHBY GODLIKE GRADELY
HELPFUL LIBERAL SNIFTER STAVING
TRAINED UPRIGHT BUDGEREE
GRAITHLY INTEREST LAUDABLE
PLEASING SALUTARY SKILLFUL
SUITABLE
(**EXCEPTIONALLY** —) SLAMBANG
(**EXTREMELY** —) SLICK
(**HOLD** —) BEAR
(**INFINITELY** —) HOLY
(**MIGHTY** —) SKOOKUM
(**NO** —) NAPOO NAPOOH
(**PRETTY** —) FAIR TIDY
(**RELATIVELY** —) SMOOTH
(**SUPERLATIVELY** —) BRAG
BEAUTIFUL
(**SUPREMELY** —) IMMENSE
GORGEOUS
(**SURPASSINGLY** —) SUPERIOR
(**VERY** —) HOT TOP DANDY DICTY
GRAND NIFTY NAILING SPLENDID
SWINGING
GOOD-BYE BY BYE TATA ADIEU
ADIOS LULLABY FAREWELL
SAYONARA
GOOD-FOR-NAUGHT LOSEL
GOOD-FOR-NOTHING BUM ORRA
SLIM SLINK KEFFEL RIBALD
BRETHEL FUSTIAN SCROYLE
SHOTTEN SKEEZIX SKYBALD
WOSBIRD VAGABOND
GOOD-KING-HENRY BLITE
ALLGOOD MARKERY MERCURY
CHENOPOD
GOOD-LOOKING FAIR BONNY
GAWSY COMELY PRETTY SEEMLY
EYESOME GRADELY WINSOME
GOODLIKE HANDSOME STUNNING
GOODLY BOON PROPER GOODLIKE
GOOD-NATURED SONSY CLEVER
AMIABLE
GOODNESS BONTE BONUM MENSK
PROOF BONITY BOUNTY SATTVA
VIRTUE KINDNESS
GOODS FEE GEAR KIND PELF CARGO
STUFF TRADE WORLD WRACK
ADVANCE CAPITAL CHATTEL
EFFECTS FINANCE HAVINGS INSIGHT
TRAFFIC CHAFFERY HIGGLERY
PROPERTY
(— **BARTERED**) DICKER
(— **CAST OVERBOARD**) JETSAM
(— **SUNK IN SEA**) LAGAN LIGAN
LAGEND
(**DRY** —) DRAPERY
(**HOUSEHOLD** —) INSIGHT
(**IMPERFECT** —) FENT
(**INFERIOR** —) BRACK
(**PIECE** —) CUTTANEE

(**SECONDHAND** —) BROKERY
(**SLOW-SELLING** —) JOBS
(**STOLEN** — **THROWN AWAY**) WAIF
(**SURPLUS** —) OVERAGE
(**VALUABLE** —) SWAG
GOOD-SIZED HEFTY GAWSIE
GOOD-TASTING DAINTY
GOODWILL GREE
GOODY-GOODY PI
GOOEY CLARTY
GOOF BOOB GOOFER
GOOGLY BOSEY WRONGUN
GOON MUSCLEMAN
GOOSANDER JACKSAW RANTOCK
GOOSE ELK LAMA NENE BRANT
BRENT EMDEN HANSA HOBBY
ROMAN SOLAN WAVEY CAGMAG
CANADA EMBDEN GALOOT GANDER
GOSLET HISSER HONKER SOLAND
AFRICAN BLACKIE BUSTARD
GAGGLER GOSLING GRAYLAG
GREASER GREYLAG OUTARDE
WIDGEON BALDHEAD BARNACLE
BERGOOSE BERNICLE SPURWING
TOULOUSE
(**MYTHICAL** —) GANZA
GOOSEBERRY BLOB FABE FAPE
POHA BRAGAS GOBLIN GOZILL
GROZER DOWNING GASKINS
GROZART CARBERRY CATBERRY
DOGBERRY EATBERRY FEABERRY
GOOSEGOG HOUGHTON INDUSTRY
(PL.) THAPES
GOOSE EGG DUCK
GOOSEFOOT BASSIA KOCHIA
ALLSEED PIGWEED
GOOSEGIRL GOSSARD
GOOSE GRASS HERIF HARIFFE
CLEAVERS
GOOSEHERD GOZZARD GOOSEBOY
GOOSENECK ROOSTER
GOPHER TUZA GAUFFRE GEOMYID
MUNGOFA QUACHIL SALAMICH
TUCOTUCO
(— **STATE**) MINNESOTA
GOPHERMAN SWAMPER
GOPHERWOOD FUSTIC
GORE CLY CLOY GARE HIKE HIPE
HOOK HORN PICK PIKE SHOT
CRUOR GODET STICK GORING
GUSSET
GOREVAN AUBURN
GORGE GAP JAM FILL GASH GAUM
GLUT JAMB KHOR RENT BREAK
CAJON CANON CHASM CHINE CLUSE
DRAFT FARCE FLUME GULLY GURGE
KLOOF PONGO POUCH STECH STRID
STUFF TANGI CANYON DEFILE
NULLAH RAVINE STODGE STRAIT
THROAT COULOIR DATIATE
DRAUGHT ENGORGE SATIATE
SLABBER QUEBRADA
GORGED ACCOLLE
GORGEOUS VAIN GRAND SHOWY
COSTLY DAZZLING GLORIOUS
SPLENDID
GORGERIN NECK NECKING
GORGING STODGE
GORGON MEDUSA STHENO EURYALE
GORILLA APE PIGMY PYGMY

GORING CORNUPETE
GORMANDIZE STECH STEGH
GUTTLE
GORMANDIZER HELLUO GLUTTON
GORSE ULEX WHIN FURZE GORST
GORY BLOODY
GOSHAWK GOS ASTUR TERCEL
GOSLING GULL
GOSPEL SPELL DHARMA EVANGEL
KERUGMA KERYGMA SYNOPTIC
(— OF REDEMPTION) CROSS
(PL.) TEXT
GOSSAMER MOUSEWEB STARDUST
GOSSIP EME GUP PIE AUNT BUZZ
CANT CLAT CONK COZE DIRT NEWS
TALK CAUSE CLACK CLASH CLYPE
COOSE CRACK FERLY FRUMP
GOSSY SIEVE BABBLE CADDLE
CALLET CAMPER CLAVER FERLIE
JANGLE NORATE TATTLE TITTLE
CLATTER COMPERE GOSTHER
HASHGOB NASHGAB SCANDAL
TATTLER TRATTLE CHITCHAT
GOSSIPRY QUIDNUNC
GOSSIPY BUZZY
GOTH GOTHIAN SUIOGOTH VISIGOTH
GOTHIC OGIVAL
GOUGE DIG PUG BENT SCUFF
CHISEL FLUKAN GOUGER HOLLOW
SCRIBE FLOOKAN SCORPER
SELVAGE SELVEDGE STICKING
(— OUT) BULLDOZE
(V-TYPE —) VEINER
GOUGER CHISELLER
GOURD MATE PEPO LUFFA ABOBRA
JICARA PATOLA ANGURIA DISHRAG
HECHIMA CALABASH CUCURBIT
PEPONIDA PEPONIUM
GOURMAND EPICURE GLUTTON
GORMAND
GOURMET PALATE EPICURE
GOURMAND
GOUT GUT CLOT DROP SPLASH
PODAGRA PODAGRY
GOUTTE DROP ICICLE
GOUTWEED AXWEED ASHWEED
ACHEWEED AISEWEED BOLEWORT
GOATWEED GOUTWORT
GOUTY PODAGRAL PODAGRIC
GOVERN RUN WIN CURB KING LEAD
REDE REIN RULE SWAY WALD WARD
WIND YEME GUIDE JUDGE REGLE
STEER TREAT WIELD BRIDLE DIRECT
MANAGE ORDAIN POLICE POLICY
TEMPER COMMAND CONDUCT
CONTROL PRESIDE REFRAIN
DISPENSE DOMINATE IMPERATE
MODERATE OVERRULE OVERSWAY
POLICIZE REGULATE RESTRAIN
GOVERNESS ABBESS DUENNA
FRAULEIN MISTRESS
GOVERNING REGENT REGITIVE
GOVERNMENT GATE LAND RULE
KREIS POWER STATE STEER
DURBAR HAVANA POLICY RULING
CABINET CZARISM DIARCHY
DYARCHY RECTION REGENCY
REGIMEN TSARISM CIVILITY
ENDARCHY GOBIERNO HEGEMONY

ISOCRACY ISOCRYME KINGSHIP
STEERING
(— BY 10) DECARCHY
(— BY 2) DIARCHY DUARCHY
(— BY GOD) THEONOMY
(— BY WOMEN) GYNARCHY
(— OF CEYLON) DISSAVA
(— OF TURKEY) GATE PORTE
(INDIAN —) CIRCAR SIRCAR
(MALAYSIAN —) KOMPENI
(MOROCCAN —) MAGHZEN
MAKHZAN
GOVERNMENTAL ARCHICAL
GOVERNOR BAN BEY DEY EARL
KAID LORD NAIK TUTU VALI BANUS
CLEON DEWAN DIWAN HAKIM
NABOB NAZIM SHEIK SUBAH TUPAN
AUTHOR DYNAST GRIEVE LEGATE
MOODIR MYOWUN NAIGUE NAIQUE
PATESI PENLOP RECTOR REGENT
SACHEM SATRAP SHEIKH SHERIF
TUCHUN WARDEN CATAPAN
DAROGHA LEONATO PODESTA
SHEREEF TOPARCH TSUNGTU
VICEROY WIELDER AUTOCRAT
BURGRAVE ETHNARCH HOSPODAR
LANDVOGT MISTRESS RESIDENT
SUBAHDAR TETRARCH
(— OF ALGIERS) DEY DISAWA
(— OF BURMA) WUN WOON
(— OF EGYPT) MUDIR
(— OF TAMMANY) SACHEM
(BYZANTINE —) EXARCH CATAPAN
(GERMAN —) LANDVOGT
(GREEK —) ETHNARCH
(JAPANESE —) SHOGUN TYCOON
(PAPAL —) LEGATE
(ROMAN —) TETRARCH
(SELJUK —) ATABEG ATABEK
(SPARTAN —) HARMOST
(TURKISH —) BEY WALI KEHAYA
GOVERNOR-GENERAL VALI
GOWK CUCKOO
GOWN GOR SAC GITE GORE HUKE
JAMA RAIL SACK SILK TOGA BANIA
DRESS FROCK GOUND HABIT JAMAH
MANTO TABBY TOOSH BANIAN
BANIYA CAFTAN CAMISE CANDYS
CHITON JESUIT JOHNNY KIMONO
KIRTLE KITTEL LEVITE MANTUA
ARISARD CASSOCK GARMENT
JOHNNIE SULTANA SULTANE
WRAPPER GANDOURA PEIGNOIR
(HAWAIIAN —) HOLOKU
GOYA CURRANT
GOYIM GENTES
GRAB NAB NAP RAP GLAM GOPE
GLAUM SCRAB COLLAR CRATCH
DIPPER NIPPER SNATCH CRAPPLE
GRABBLE GRAPNEL GRAPPLE
NIPPERS
GRABEN TROUGH
GRACE EST ORE BEAT ESTE GARB
HELD SWAY ADORN COULE HONOR
MENSE MENSK MERCY SLIDE THANK
VENUS BEAUTY BECOME BEDECK
CHARIS POLISH RELISH THALIA
AGGRACE CHARISM COMMEND
DIGNITY FINESSE GRATIFY MELISMA
MORDENT BACKFALL BEAUTIFY

BLESSING DECORATE EASINESS
ELEGANCE FELICITY GRATUITY
LEVATION ORNAMENT
(— OF FORM) FLOW SWAY
TOURNURE
GRACEFUL AIRY FEAT GENT GENTY
GRATE COMELY FEATLY FELINE
FLUENT GAINLY QUAINT SEEMLY
SILKEN VENUST ELEGANT FITTING
GENTEEL GRACILE SYLPHID
WILLOWY CHARMING DELICATE
GRACIOUS LEGGIERO MACEVOLE
SWANLIKE SYLPHISH
GRACEFULNESS JOLLITY
ELEGANCE
GRACEFULLY FAIR FEATLY HAPPILY
LEGGIERO
GRACELESS AWKWARD
GRACES CHARITES
GRACIOUS GOOD HEND HOLD KIND
MILD CIVIL GODLY HAPPY LUCKY
SUAVE WINLY BENIGN GENIAL
GENTLE GOODLY KINDLY AFFABLE
CORDIAL WINSOME BENEDICT
DEBONAIR GENEROUS HANDSOME
MERCIFUL PLEASING SOCIABLE
GRACIOUSLY FAIR SWEETLY
GRACIOUSNESS GRACE MENSK
FACILITY GRATUITY
GRACKLE BEO JACKDAW BOATTAIL
TINKLING TROOPIAL
GRADATION HUE CLIMAX NUANCE
GEOCLINE STRENGTH
GRADE CUT BANK CHOP EVEN FORM
MARK RANK SIZE STEP GLIDE LEVEL
ORDER PLANE SCORE SIEGE STAGE
ASCENT DEGREE RATING STAPLE
TRIAGE FAILURE INCLINE INSPECT
DEMISANG GRADIENT GRADUATE
MERIDIAN STANDARD
(— DOWN) FAULT
(— LUMBER) SURVEY
(— OF BEEF) GOOD CUTTER
(— OF LUMBER) CULL
(— OF OAK) WAINSCOT
(— OF OFFICER) CORNET
(— ROAD) IMPROVE
(ABLAUT —) GUNA
(SUPERIOR —) SUPER
(THIRD —) FAIR
GRADER PLANER CLASSER SCRAPER
GRADIENT GRADE LAPSE SLOPE
ASCENT INCLINE DOWNHILL
GRADIN GRADINO PREDELLA
GRADUAL EASY FLAT SLOW GRAIL
GENTLE LENTOUS STEPWISE
GRADUALLY GENTLY EDGINGLY
GRADATIM INCHMEAL
GRADUATE GRAD GRADE ALUMNA
DIVIDE FELLOW ALUMNUS GRADATE
BACHELOR
GRADUATED SCALAR MEASURED
GRADUATION CLICK
GRAFT BUD IMP CION WORK GRAFF
GRAVY INEYE BOODLE INARCH
SPLICE ENGRAFT IMPLANT JOBBERY
SQUEEZE TOPWORK APPROACH
BOODLING GRAFTING INSITION
GRAFTED ENTE
GRAFTER BOODLER

GRAFTING GRAFTAGE INSITION
GRAIL CUP GRAAL CHALICE
SANGRAAL
GRAIN JOT RUN RYE WAY CORN
CURN DANA KERN PILE RICE SAND
SEED WALE WOOD EMMER FIBER
FIBRE FUNDI GAVEL GLEBE GRIST
PANIC SCRAP SPARK STUFF TRACE
WHEAT ANNONA BARLEY BRAINS
CEREAL CURRAN GROATS KERNEL
FRUMENT GRANULE PANICLE
VICTUAL GRAINING PARTICLE
STRAIGHT SWEEPAGE
(— FOR MUSH) KASHA
(— FROM MASH TUN) DRAINS
(— LEFT AFTER HARVEST) GAVEL
SHACK
(— MEASURE) THRAVE
(— OF BOARD) BEAT
(— OF GOLD) PIPPIN
(— OF WOOD) BATE
(CHAFF OF —) BRAN
(COARSE —) THIRD
(COARSELY GROUND —) MEAL
GRITS KIBBLE
(DAMAGED —) SALVAGE
(EAR OF —) SPIKE RISSOM RIZZON
(GERMINATED —) MALT
(GROUND —) GRIST
(HANDFUL OF —) REAP
(HULLED —) GRITS GROUT GROATS
SHELLING
(HUSKED —) SHEALING SHILLING
(MIXED —) MASLIN
(MIXED —S) DREDGE
(PARCHED —) GRADDAN
(REFUSE —) SHAG DRAFF
(SACRIFICIAL —) ADOR
(SHOCK OF —) COP
(STACK OF —) HOVEL
(PL.) PICKLES RAGGING
GRAIN BEETLE CADELLE
GRAINER DICER BOARDER
GRAINSMAN THROWER DRAFFMAN
GRAIN SORGHUM DURRA SHALLU
GRAM KHESARI
(MILLIONTH —) GAMMA
GRAMMAR SYNTAX GRAMARY
PRISCIAN
GRAMMARIAN PRISCIAN
GRAMPUS ORC COWFISH DOLPHIN
SPRINGER
GRANARY GOLA GUNJ SILO GOLAH
GUNGE LATHE GARNER GIRNEL
GRANGE HORREUM RESERVE
CORNLOFT GRAINERY
GRAND OLD AIRY EPIC MAIN TALL
CHIEF GREAT LOFTY NOBLE PROUD
SHOWY SWELL WLONK ANDEAN
AUGUST COSMIC EPICAL FAMOUS
GLOBAL KINGLY LORDLY SIGHTY
SUPERB SWANKY EXALTER
IMMENSE STATELY SUBLIME
COSMICAL FOREMOST GLORIOUS
GORGEOUS IMPOSING MAJESTIC
SPLENDID
GRAND CANYON STATE ARIZONA
GRANDCHILD OE OY OYE
(GREAT —) IEROE
GRANDDAUGHTER NIECE

GRANDEE DON GRAND OMRAH
BASHAW GRANDO MAGNATE
GRANDEUR POMP STATE ESTATE
FIGURE PARADE MAJESTY
ELEGANCE GRANDEZA HAUTESSE
SPLENDOR VASTNESS
GRANDFATHER AIEL NONO BOBBY
GRAMP ATAVUS GRAMPS BELSIRE
GRANDAD GRANDPA GRANDFER
GUIDSIRE
(GREAT —) NONO
(GREAT-GREAT-GREAT —)
QUATRAYLE
GRANDILOQUENT TALL HEROIC
TURGID BOMBAST MAGNIFIC
GRANDIOSE GRAND COSMIC TURGID
COSMICAL IMPERIAL
GRANDMOTHER GRAM GRAN
LUCKY GRANNY GUDAME LUCKIE
BELDAME NOKOMIS BABUSHKA
GRANDAME
GRANDPARENT TUTU TUPUNA
GRAND SLAM VOLE
GRANDSON NEPHEW NEPOTE
GRANITE MOYITE RUNITE GREISEN
SYENITE ALASKITE RAPAKIVI
(— STATE) NEWHAMPSHIRE
(DECOMPOSED —) GROWAN
GRANITEWARE GRAYWARE
GRANNY TUTU BABUSHKA
GRANT AID FEU BOOK BOON CEDE
ENAM GALE GIFT GIVE HEAR LEND
LOAN MISE SEND STOW YARK
ADMIT ALLOT ALLOW AWARD
BONUS CHART COWLE FLOAT
FUERO LEASE SEIZE SPARE TITHE
YETTE YIELD ACCEDE ACCORD
AFFORD ASSENT BESTOW BETAKE
BETEEM BOUNTY CONFER DESIGN
EXTEND FIRMAN IMPART JAGEER
NOVATE OCTROI PATENT PERMIT
REMISE ADJUDGE COLLATE
CONCEDE CONSENT DISPONE
INDULGE LICENSE PRESENT
PROMISE SUBSIDY TRIBUTE
APPANAGE BESTOWAL CONTRACT
DONATION EXCHANGE MONOPOLY
PITTANCE TRANSFER
(— AS PROPER) ACCORD
(— OF LAND) FEU ENAM GALE PATA
SASAN CASATE
(— PERMISSION) ALLOW DISPENSE
(— RELIEF) FORGIVE
(INDIAN —) ENAM COWLE SASAN
JAGEER JAGHIR
(PL.) PORK
GRANTING IF ALTHO REMISE
ALTHOUGH
GRANTOR LESSOR
GRANULAR OPEN GRAINY
GRANULATE CORN KERN GRAIN
SUGAR
GRANULATED CORN GRANULAR
GRANULATION SUGARING
GRANULE GRIT GRANUM LUCULE
NODULE BIOBLAST GONIDIUM
GRANULET
(ALTMANN'S —S) BIOPLAST
(ICE —S) FRAZIL
GRAPE UVA VINE BERRY GRAIN

PINOT TOKAY ACINUS AGAWAM
ISABEL MALAGA MONICA MUSCAT
RAISIN VERDEA WORDEN CATAWBA
CONCORD HAMBURG MISSION
NIAGARA SULTANA VINIFER
CABERNET DELAWARE GRAPELET
ISABELLA LABRUSCA MALVASIA
MORILLON MOUNTAIN MUSCATEL
NUCULANE RIESLING SLIPSKIN
SYLVANER THOMPSON
(PL.) RAPE
GRAPEFRUIT POMOLO POMMELO
TORONJA
GRAPE HYACINTH MUSK
GRAPE JUICE MUST SAPA STUM
GRAPENUTS TERRAPIN
GRAPEROOT BERBERIS
GRAPH CHART CURVE OGIVE TRACE
CONTOUR DIAGRAM PROFILE
ISOPLETH
GRAPHITE WAD KISH LEAD WADD
KEESH PENCIL PLUMBAGO
GRAPNEL CROW DRAG GRAB CREEP
CREEPER GRABBLE GRAPPLE
SNIGGER GRABHOOK
GRAPPLE DOG CLOSE GRASP GRIPE
LATCH BUCKLE GRABBLE GRAPNEL
GRIPPLE SNIGGER SNIGGLE
WRESTLE
(— QUARRY) BIND
GRAPPLING IRON CLIP DRAG
CLASP CRAMP CORVUS CRAMPER
CRAMPON CREEPER GRAPNEL
GRAPPLE HARPAGO
GRAPTOLITHA XYLINA
GRASP HUG NAP SEE CLAM CLAW
CLUM FAKE FANG FIST GLAM GRAB
GRIP HAND HENT HOLD SNAP SPAN
TAKE VICE CATCH CINCH CLAMP
CLASP CLAUT CLEUK GRIPE GROPE
LATCH SAVVY SEIZE SENSE SHAKE
SPEND CLINCH CLUTCH COLLAR
FATHOM GOUPEN CLAUGHT
COMPASS ENCLOSE GRAPPLE
GRIPPLE SMITTLE CONCEIVE
HANDFAST HOLDFAST
(— FULLY) SWALLOW
(— MENTALLY) ENVISAGE
(— OF REALITY) EPIPHANY
GRASPING HARD NIPPY SNACK
GRABBY GREEDY GRIPPY HAVING
TAKING BROKING PUGGING
COVETOUS HANDGRIP
GRASS BON FAG FOG POA RAY
BENT COIX DISS DOOB GAMA HERB
ICHU KANS KUSA MUNJ MUSK RAGI
TORE ANKEE BARIT BROME COGON
COUCH CROFT DRAWK DRINN
FLAWN FUNDI GARSE GIRSE GLAGA
GRAMA HARIF HAVER HICHU ILLUK
KOGON KUSHA KWEEK PANIC QUILA
REESK ROOSA SEREH SPIRE STIPA
SUDAN ZORRA BARLEY BHABAR
BHARTI DARNEL EMOLOA FESCUE
GLUMAL QUITCH RAGGEE REDTOP
RIPGUT SCUTCH TOETOE TWITCH
ZACATE AMOURET CANNACH
DOGFOOT ESPARTO EULALIA
FESTUCA FINETOP FOXTAIL
GALLETA GOLDEYE HERBAGE

HORDEUM JARAGUA MATWEED
MUSCOVY PANICLE PASTURE
PIGROOT SETARIA SORGHUM
TIMOTHY TOCUSSO TUSSOCK
VETIVER ZACATON AEGILOPS
BLUESTEM BROWNTOP CALFKILL
CAMALOTE CELERITY COCKSPUR
DOGSTAIL DRAWLING DROPSEED
EELGRASS ELEUSINE FINEBENT
GAMELOTE MANGRASS MATGRASS
PASPALUM SANDBURR SANDSPUR
SANDSTAY SPANGRASS SPARTINA
SPINIFEX SWEEPAGE TEOSINTE
WHITETOP
(— AMONG GRAIN) DRAWK
(— FOR STOCK) EATAGE
(— FOR THATCHING) BANGO
(— ON BORDER OF FIELD) RAND
(— READY FOR REAPING) SWATH
SWATHE
(AROMATIC —) KHUS CUSCUS
KHUSKHUS
(BEACH —) STAR
(BERMUDA —) DOOB SCUTCH
(COARSE —) FAG RISP TATH
COGON REESK SNIDDLE
(COUCH —) CUTCH KWEEK QUITCH
SCUTCH STROIL SQUITCH
(CURED —) HAY
(DEAD —) FOG FOGGAGE
(DITCH —) ENALID
(GOOSE —) CLIVERS CLEAVERS
(MEADOW —) POA
(NUT —) COCO COCOA
(ORCHARD —) DOGFOOT
(PASTURE —) TORE GRAMMA
(POVERTY —) HEATH
(QUAKING —) SHAKER
(REED —) CARRIZO
(REEDLIKE —) BENT DISS
(SUDAN —) GARAWI
GRASSERIE JAUNDICE
GRASSHOPPER GRIG CICADA
HOPPER QUAKER SAWYER TETTIX
ACRIDID CRICKET KATYDID SKIPPER
ACRIDIAN LANGOSTA
GRASSLAND HAM LEA RAKH VELD
VELDT BOTTOM MEADOW PATANA
LEYLAND PASTURE SAVANNA
(TRACT OF —) PRAIRIE
(PL.) SCHIH
GRASS PEA LANG KHESARI
GRASSQUIT QUAT QUIT CIVITE
GRASS TREE BLACKBOY
GRASSY HERBY
GRATE JAR FRET GRIT RASP CHARK
DANDY DEVIL GRIND RANGE STOVE
ABRADE CHAFER SCRAPE SCREAR
SCREEK SCROOP GRATING
MANGRATE
(FALSE —) DANDY
GRATEFUL KIND WELCOME
THANKFUL
GRATEFULNESS GRATUITY
GRATIFICATION GLUT GUST
LUXURY RELISH REWARD SATIETY
DELICACY GRATUITY PLEASURE
TICKLING
GRATIFIED GLAD PROUD CHARMED
CONTENT PLEASED

GRATIFY PAY BABY FEED LUST
AMUSE FEAST FLESH GRACE
HUMOR MIRTH QUEME SAVOR
SERVE STILL WREAK ARRIDE
FOSTER OBLIGE PAMPER PLEASE
SALUTE TICKLE AGGRATE CONTENT
DELIGHT FLATTER GLADDEN
INDULGE SATISFY PLEASURE
(— THE PALATE) SEASON
GRATIFYING GOOD COMELY
DELICATE GRATEFUL
GRATING GRID HACK HARP HECK
JACK RACK CRATE CRUDE GRILL
HARSH RANGE TRAIL BAFFLE
CRATCH GITTER GRILLE HOARSE
WICKET BAFFLER ECHELLE
ECHELON BABRACOT CATAPULT
GRIDIRON SCRANNEL STRIDENT
GRATIS FREE FREELY BUCKSHEE
GRATITUDE THANK THANKS
GRATUITY
GRATUITOUS FREE WANTON
BASELESS NEEDLESS
GRATUITY FEE TIP DASH VAIL PILON
SPIFF SPILL CUMSHAW DASTURI
DOUCEUR PRESENT PRIMAGE
BAKSHISH BONAMANO BUCKSHEE
COURTESY DUSTOORI GRATUITO
REAPDOLE
(PL.) LARGESSE
GRAVE BED DRY LOW PIT SAD URN
BALK BIER CELL CIST DEEP DELF
FOSS GRIT HIGH HOME KIST LAIR
LAKE MOLD MOOL RUDE SADE
SAGE TOMB URNA DELFT FOSSE
GRAFF GROVE HEAVY MOULD
SHEOL SOBER STAID STIFF SUANT
VAULT BURIAL DEMURE GRIEVE
HEARSE SEDATE SEVERE SOLEMN
SOMBER SOMBRE STEADY AUSTERE
EARNEST FUNERAL PITHOLE
SERIOSO SERIOUS SOBERLY
DECOROUS MATRONAL SERMONIC
GRAVECLOTHES LINEN
GRAVEDIGGER BURIER FOSSOR
PITMAN
GRAVEL GRIT ARENA GEEST GRAIL
CHESIL RANGLE SAMMEL SHILLA
BALLAST CALICHE CHANNEL
RATCHEL STANNER BLINDING
(— AND SAND) DOBBIN
(— DEPOSIT) LEAD
(— IN KIDNEYS) ARENA
(LOOSE —) SLITHER
(SCREENED —) HOGGINS
GRAVELLY HASKY CHISELLY
GLAREOUS
GRAVELY SADLY DEEPLY
GRAVE MOUND TUMULUS
GRAVER BURIN STYLE PLASTIC
SCORPER
GRAVESTONE BAUTA PLANK STELA
STELE STONE TABLE CIPPUS
JUMPER THROUGH
GRAVEYARD CEMETERY
GRAVID HEAVY WOMBED PREGNANT
GRAVIMETER DOODLEBUG
GRAVITATIONAL UNIT SLUG
GRAVITY WEIGHT DIGNITY EARNEST
SOBRIETY

GRAVY JUS SOP BREE FOND LEAR
BLANC BUNCE JIPPER
GRAY ASH BAT FOG ASHY BEAR
BLAE BLUE DOVE DUSK GREY GRIS
GULL HOAR IRON LEAD SALT ACIER
CAMEL CRANE HOARY LYART
MOUSE STEEL WHITE CASTOR
CINDER DENVER FROSTY FRUSTY
GREIGE GRISLY LEADEN NICKEL
NUTRIA PEWTER QUAKER STRING
BLUNKET CRUISER GRANITE
GRIZARD GRIZZLE GRIZZLY
HUELESS MURINUS NEUTRAL
PELICAN PILGRIM SARKARA
SPARROW ALUMINUM CHARCOAL
CINEREAL CINEROUS EVENGLOW
PLATINUM PLYMOUTH
(DARKEST —) BLACK
(GOOSE —) LAMA
(MOLE —) TAUPE
(MOTH —) SHEEPSKIN
GRAYBACK DOWITCH GRAYCOAT
GREYBACK
GRAY CRANE COOLEN COOLUNG
GRAYLING PINK OMBRE UMBER
HERRING UMBRANA BLUEFISH
SALMONID
GRAY PARROT JAKO
GRAYNESS CANITIES
GRAYSBY CONY CONEY
GRAY WHALE RIPSACK GRAYBACK
HARDHEAD
GRAZE BITE CROP FEED SKIM AGIST
BRUSH GRASS GRIDE RANGE
SCAMP SCUFF SHAVE SKIFF STOCK
BROWSE CREASE FODDER GLANCE
RIPPLE SCRAPE SCRASE PASTURE
GRAZIER PASTURER SQUATTER
TREKBOER
GRAZING BIT FEED GRASS COLLOP
RASANT FOLDING PASCUAGE
GREASE COOM SAIM ADEPS BLECK
COOMB SMEAR SPICK ARMING
AXUNGE CREESH ENSEAM LIQUOR
POMATE ALEMITE SAINDOUX
(— IN HARD CAKES) SEAK
(PIG'S —) MORT
(WOOL —) YOK DEGRAS LANOLIN
GREASE-HEELS GRAPES
GREASER DOPER
GREASEWOOD CHICO CHEMIZO
GREASY FAT GLET OILY RICH FATTY
PORKY YOLKY SMEARY TRAINY
CREESHY TALLOWY UNCTUOUS
GREAT BIG FAR FAT FIT OLD BARO
DEEP DREE FELL FINE GONE GURT
HUGE KEEN MAIN MUCH RIAL TALL
UNCO VAST VILE AMPLE BURRA
CHIEF FELON GRAND LARGE MEKIL
STOUR SWEET SWELL YEDER
FIERCE GAPING HEROIC MICKLE
NATION STRONG CAPITAL EMINENT
EXTREME GALLOWS HOWLING
IMMENSE INTENSE STAVING TITANIC
VIOLENT VOLUMED ALMIGHTY
CRACKING ELEVATED ENORMOUS
FAVORITE GALACTIC GALAXIAN
GIGANTIC HORRIBLE INFINITE
(— LAND) ALASKA
(IMMEASURABLY —) ABYSMAL

(VERY —) MAIN SORE AWFUL STEEP ARDENT DEADLY IMMANE INGENT MORTAL EXTREME FRANTIC GHASTLY HOWLING SUBLIME DREADFUL MOUNTAIN
GREAT AUK PENGUIN PINWING GAREFOWL
GREAT BRITAIN (SEE ENGLAND)
GREATCOAT GREGO JEMMY JOSEPH OVERCOAT
GREATER SUPERIOR
GREATER STITCHWORT HEAD SNAPPER HEADACHE SNAPJACK SNAPWORT
GREATER YELLOWLEGS YELPER
GREATEST UTMOST EXTREME MAXIMAL
(— POSSIBLE) ALL SUPREME
GREAT-GRANDCHILD IEROE
GREAT GRANDFATHER NONO BESAIEL GRANDSIR
GREAT LAKE ERIE HURON ONTARIO MICHIGAN SUPERIOR
GREATLY FAR MUY FELL MUCH AMAIN SWITH FINELY MAINLY STRONG SWYTHE SWEETLY WOUNDLY
GREAT MOLE RAT ZEMMI ZEMNI
GREATNESS FORCE GRANDEUR GRANDEZA MUCHNESS
GREAT RAGWEED KINGHEAD
GREAT TITMOUSE SHARPSAW
GREAVE JAMB JAMBE JAMBEAU (PL.) CRAP HOSE GRAVES
GREBE LEAD LOON DIVER GAUNT WITCH DIPPER DOBBER DUCKER FINFOOT HENBILL PYGOPOD ARSEFOOT CARGOOSE DABCHICK DIDAPPER GRUIFORM
GRECE GRICE DEGREE GRISSEN

GREECE

ANCIENT LOCATION: ELIS DORIS PYLOS ACHAEA ACTIUM ATTICA DELPHI EPIRUS HELLAS LOCRIS PHOCIS SPARTA THEBES TIRYNS BOEOTIA CORINTH EPEIROS LACONIA MACEDON MEGARIS MYCENAE PAESTUM
ARMY UNIT: TAXIS
BAY: ELEUSIS SALAMIS PHALERON
CAPE: KRIOS MALEA SPADA AKRITAS MATAPAN SIDEROS DREPANON GRAMBYSA TAINARON
CAPITAL: ATHENS ATHENAI
COIN: OBOL HECTE DIOBOL LEPTON STATER DRACHMA DIOBOLON
COLUMN: DORIC IONIC CORINTHIAN
DANCE: PYRRHIC ROMAIKA
DIALECT: COAN ATTIC DORIC ELEAN EOLIC IONIC AEOLIC MELIAN THERAN ACHAEAN ARCADIAN
DISTRICT: ARTA ELIS CANEA CHIOS CORFU CRETE DRAMA

EVROS KHIOS PELLA SAMOS ZANTE ACHAEA ACHAIA ATTICA EPIRUS EUBOEA KILKIS KNANIA KOZANE LARISA LESBOS LEUKAS PHOCIS PIERIA SERRAI THRACE XANTHE AETOLIA ARCADIA ARGOLIS BOEOTIA CORINTH KAVALLA LACONIA LARISSA LASETHI MTATHOS PREVEZA RHODOPE CYCLADES IOANNINA KARDITSA KASTORIA MAGNESIA MESSENIA PHLORINA RETHYMNE SALONIKA THESSALY TRIKKALA MACEDONIA
GULF: VOLOS ATHENS MESARA PATRAI PATRAS ARGOLIS CORINTH KAVALLA KNANION LACONIA MESSINI RENDINA SARONIC STRIMON LEPANTRO MESSENIA SALONIKA SINGITIC THERMAIC TORONAIC
HOME OF GODS: OLYMPUS
ISLAND: DIA IOS KEA KOS NIO CEOS KEOS MILO SYME SYRA CHIOS CORFU CRETE DELOS KASOS KHIOS LEROS MELOS MILOS NAXOS PAROS PAXOI PAXOS PSARA RODOS SAMOS SARIA SYROS TELOS TENOS THERA THIRA TINOS ZANTE ANAPHE ANDROS CANDIA CERIGO CHALKE EUBOEA EVVOIA GAVDOS IKARIA ITHACA ITHAKI LEMNOS LESBOS LEUKAS LEVKAS PATMOS RHENEA RHODES SIFNOS SKYROS THASOS AMORGOS CIMOLUS CYTHERA KERKYRA KIMOLOS KYTHERA KYTHNOS LEVITHA MYKONOS NISYROS SALAMIS SIPHNOS KALYMNOS MYTILENE SANTORIN SERIPHOS
ISLANDS: IONIAN CYCLADES SPORADES DODECANESE STROPHADES
LAKE: KARLA VOLVE COPAIS KOPAIS PRESPA TOPOLIA KASTORIA TACHINOS VISTONIS
LETTER: MU NU PI XI CHI ETA PHI PSI RHO TAU BETA IOTA ZETA ALPHA DELTA GAMMA KAPPA OMEGA SIGMA THETA LAMBDA EPSILON OMICRON UPSILON
MARKET PLACE: AGORA
MEASURE: PIK BEMA PIKI POUS BARIL CADOS CHOUS CUBIT DIGIT MARIS PEKHE PODOS PYGON XYLON ACAENA BACHEL BACILE BARILE COTULA DICHAS GRAMME HEMINA KOILON ORGYIA PALAME PECHYS SCHENE AMPHORA CHENICA CHOENIX CYATHOS DIAULOS HEKTEUS METRETA STADION STADIUM STREMMA CONDYLOS DAKTYLOS DEKAPODE DOLICHOS MEDIMNOS METRETES PALAISTE PLETHRON

PLETHRUM SPITHAME STATHMOS
MOUNTAIN: IDA IDHI OSSA ATHOS PAROS ELIKON PARNON PELION PILION WITSCH HELICON OLYMPUS VURANON KRAGNOVO SMOLIKAS TAYGETOS PARNASSUS
MOUNTAINS: OETA OTHRYS PINDUS RODOPI RHODOPE HYMETTOS TAYGETUS
NAME: ELLAS HELLAS
PENINSULA: ACTE AKTE AKTI MOREA SITHONIA PELOPONNESE
PORT: SYRA CORFU PYLOS SYROS VOLOS MEGARA PATRAI PATRAS KAVALLA KERKYRA PIRAEUS SALONIKA
RIVER: IRI ARDA ARTA AURO AXIOS DOONA EVROS LERNA ALFIOS NESTOS PENEUS PINIOS STRUMA VARDAR ALPHEUS EUROTAS EVROTAS ILISSOS PENEIOS ROUFIAS SARANTA STRIMON ACHELOUS AKHELOOS ALIAKMON KEPHISOS RHOUPHIA
RUINS: DELOS PELLA SAMOS CORINTH ELEUSIS ELEVSIS ACROPOLIS
SEA: CRETE AEGEAN IONIAN MIRTOON
STATE: PHOCIS
TOWN: IOS KEA KOS ARTA ELIS KYME PETA SYME YDRA ADREA AGYIA ARGOS CANEA CHIOS CORFU DRAMA KARYA MELOS NAXOS NEMEA PELLA POROS PSARI PYLOS PYRGI SAMOS SYROS TENOS VAMOS VATHY VOLOS VYRON ZANTE ACTIUM ATHENS CANDIA DAPHNI DELPHI EDESSA ITHACA JANINA KOZANE LARISA MEGARA NIKAIA PATRAS RHODES SERRAI SERRES SPARTA THEBES TIRYNS XANTHE ATHENAI CORINTH ELEUSIS KERKYRA LARISSA MYCENAE PIRAEUS IOANNINA KOMOTINE MARATHON PHARSALA SALONIKA TRIKKALA
VALLEY: NEMEA
VERNACULAR: DEMOTIC
WEIGHT: MNA OKA OKE MINA OBOL LITRA LIVRE MANEH POUND DIOBOL DRAMME KANTAR OBOLOS OBOLUS STATER TALENT CHALCON CHALQUE DRACHMA DIOBOLON TALANTON
WOMEN: THYIAD

GREED AVARICE AVIDITY HOGGERY CUPIDITY
GREEDINESS AVARICE AVIDITY GULOSITY
GREEDY AVID GAIR GORB YELP EAGER GUTTY YIVER GRABBY GUNDIE KITISH STINGY GLUTTON

GRIPPLE HOODOCK MISERLY
PIGGISH COVETOUS ESURIENT
GRASPING RAVENOUS
GREEK GREW ATTIC HADJI KOINE
METIC ARGIVE IONIAN KLEPHT
ACHAIAN GRECIAN GRIFFON
HELLENE GRECANIC HELLENIC
ITALIOTE SICELIOT
GREEN LEEK VERD VERT CRUDE
FRESH CALLOW VIRENT VORENT
NOUVEAU SINOPLE UNFIRED
VERDANT BAYBERRY IMMATURE
NOUVELLE VAGABOND VIRIDIAN
WEDGWOOD WOODLAND
(— MOUNTAIN STATE) VERMONT
(COOKED —S) SALAD
(NILE —) BOA
(PALE —) ALOE ALOES
(YELLOWISH —) GLAUZY ABSINTHE
GLAUCOUS
GREEN AMARANTH REDROOT
GREENBACK FROGSKIN
(PL.) GREEN LETTUCE
GREEN CORMORANT SHAG
GREENFISH BLUEFISH
GREENHEART BIBIRU BEBEERU
GREEN HERON KIALEE
GREENHORN JAY YAP JAKE IKONA
GREENY SUCKER SOFTHORN
GREENHOUSE STOVE GREENERY
HOTHOUSE ORANGERY COOLHOUSE

GREENLAND
AIR BASE: THULE
BAY: DISKO BAFFIN MELVILLE
CAPE: JAAL GRIVEL WALKER
BISMARCK BREWSTER
FAREWELL LOWENORN
CAPITAL: GODTHAAB
DISCOVERER: ERIC
MOUNTAIN: FOREL PAYER
KHARDYU
STRAIT: DAVIS DENMARK
TOWN: ETAH NORD THULE
UMANAK GODHAVN IVIGTUT
GODTHAAB

GREENLING BOREGAT BODIERON
LORICATE
GREEN MONKEY GUENON
GREENNESS VERD VERT VERDURE
VERDANCY VIRIDITY
GREEN PIKE JACK
GREENROOM FOYER
GREENSHANK TATTLER
GREENSTONE POUNAMU
GREEN SUNFISH REDEYE
GREENWEED WOODWAX
GREEN WOODPECKER ECCLE
SPRITE YOCKEL YUKKEL HEWHALL
HEWHOLE SNAPPER SPEIGHT
YAFFLER WOODHACK WOODWALL
GREET CRY JOY CROW HAIL HALSE
ACCOST HERALD SALUTE ADDRESS
RECEIVE WELCOME
GREETING HOW HIYA ALOHA GREET
HELLO HOWDY KOMBO ACCOST
CHEERO SALAAM SALUTE SHALOM
ADDRESS CHEERIO COMMEND
SLAINTE WELCOME

GREGARIOUS GREGAL SOCIAL
GREGE NUTRIA
GRENADE EGG TROMBE GRENADO
FIREBALL PINEAPPLE
GRENADIER RATTAIL WHIPTAIL
GRENADINE FLORENCE
GREY (SEE GRAY)
GREYHOUND GREW BANJARA
SAPLING WHIPPET
GRID BOOCAN BUCCAN GRIDDLE
GRIDIRON
GRIDDLE COMAL GRILL GIRDLE
GRILLE BRANDER
GRIDDLE CAKE AREPA LATKE
CHAPATTY CORNCAKE FLAPJACK
SLAPJACK
GRIDIRON GRID GRILL TRAIL
BRANDER BROILER GRIDDLE
GRIEF WOE CARE DILL DOLE DOOL
DREE HARM HURT MOAN MOOD
PAIN RUTH SORE TEEN TINE AGONY
DOLOR GRAME RUING TRIAL
WRONG BARRAT DESIRE MISHAP
REGRET SORROW STOUND WONDER
ANGUISH CHAGRIN EMOTION
FAILURE OFFENSE SADNESS
THOUGHT TROUBLE WAESUCK
WAYMENT DISASTER DISTRESS
HARDSHIP
(— STEM) KELLY
(SECRET —) CANKER
GRIESEN ZWITTER
GRIEVANCE BEEF GRIEF BURDEN
BYGONE GRAVAMEN HARDSHIP
GRIEVE CARE DOLE DUMP EARN
ERME HURT PAIN PINE SIGH WAIL
GRAME GRIPE MOURN SORRY
WOUND YEARN ATHINK CORSIE
LAMENT SORROW AFFLICT CHAGRIN
CONDOLE GRIZZLE TROUBLE
WAYMENT COMPLAIN DISTRESS
GRIEVED WOE GRAME SORRY
GRIEVING SORRY
GRIEVOUS SAD DEEP DERF HARD
SORE CHARY DIRTY GRIEF HEAVY
SORRY WEARY BITTER DREARY
SEVERE SHREWD HEINOUS WEIGHTY
DOLOROUS
GRIEVOUSLY FOULLY SORELY
HEAVILY
GRIFFE SPUR
GRIFFIN GRIPE GRYPHON EPIMACUS
GRILL REJA BRACE BROIL DEVIL
TRAIL AFFLICT BROILER GRILLADE
GRILLE FACE REJA HAZARD
GRILLROOM GROOM
GRILSE PEAL FINNAC GRAWLS
BOTCHER FORKTAIL
GRIM GASH SOUR BLEAK CRUEL
GAUNT STERN GRIMLY GRISLY
HORRID SULLEN TORVID GHASTLY
GRIZZLY HIDEOUS TORVOUS
PITILESS RUTHLESS
GRIMACE MOP MUG POT FACE GIRN
IRPE MOUE MUMP YIRN FLEER
MOUTH SNEER SNOOT GIMBLE
SHEYLE STITCH MURGEON SIMAGRE
GRIME DIRT SMUT COLLY SMOUCH
SMUTCH
GRIMME COQUETOON

GRIMNESS TORVITY
GRIMY DINGY GRUBBY SCABROUS
GRIN DRAD GIRN MUMP FLEER
SNEER SIMPER GRIZZLE
GRIND DIG SAP BONE BRAY CHEW
FILE GRUN MILL MULL MUZZ SMUG
SWOT CRUSH FLOAT FLOUR GRATE
GRIDE GRIST QUERN CRUNCH
DRUDGE POWDER EMERIZE GRISTLE
SWOTTER LEVIGATE
(— COARSELY) KIBBLE
(— SMALL) BRAY
(— TEETH) GNASH GRATE GRINT
GRISBET
GRINDER CRASH MULLER BRUISER
GRINDING BREAK MOLAR ABRASION
(— OF MEAL) BREAK GRIST
GRINDSTONE MANO PAVER STONE
GRIP BITE BURR CLIP FANG FIST
HOLD HOLT TAKE VICE CHOKE
CINCH CLAMP CLASP GRASP GRIPE
PINCH SALLY SEIZE BARREL CLINCH
CLUTCH CRADLE FREEZE EMBRACE
HANDBAG HOLDING SEIZURE
ADHESION FOOTLOCK HANDFAST
HANDGRIP HANDHOLD
(— OF A SWORD) FUSEAU
(— OF BELL ROPE) SALLY
(— TO A SPAR) DOG
GRIPE FRIB BITCH CREATE HOLLER
NATTER SNATCH GRIZZLE
COMPLAIN
GRIPER GRIZZLER
GRIPES TORMINA
GRIPING GRIPPLE PINCHING
GRIPPER KEEPER NIPPER
GRIPPING STONY STONEY
GRIQUA BASTARD BASTAARD
GRISLY GRIM GHASTLY GRIZZLY
HIDEOUS GRUESOME
GRISON HURON GALICTIS
GRIST PABULUM
GRIT SAND GRIND BOTTOM BRAVERY
DECISION GRITROCK RUBSTONE
(PL.) CUTLINGS
GRITH MUND GYRTH
GRITTY SANDY SHARP GRISTY
CHISELLY SABULINE SABULOUS
GRIVET TOTA WAAG GEUNON
NISNAS
GRIZZLED GRISLY STREAKED
GRIZZLY BEAR (— STATE)
CALIFORNIA
GROAN MOAN ROME GRANK GRUNT
STECH COMPLAIN
GROAT BIT FLAG GILL HARP
GROCER SPICER EPICIER PEPPERER
GROCERY PULPERIA
GROG RUMBO TEMPER CHAMOTTE
GROGGERY SHANTY GROGSHOP
GROGGY SHAKY UNSTEADY
WAVERING
GROGSHOP SHANTY DOGGERY
GROGGERY
GROIN LISK PIER SHARE CLITCH
INGUEN GRUNZIE
GROMMET BECKET COLLAR EYELET
CRINGLE GARLAND
GROMWELL REDROOT GRAYMILL

GROOM LAD MAFU NEAT SYCE
CURRY DRESS MAFOO STRAP SWIPE
TIGER BARBER FETTLE FOGGER
GUINEA MEHTAR OSTLER HOSTLER
MARSHAL COISTREL GROOMLET
STRAPPER
GROOVE RUT BEAD DADO GAIN
KERF LUCE PORT RAKE SLOT
CANAL CHASE CROZE FLUTE GLYPH
GORGE GOUGE GUIDE JOINT QUIRK
REGAL RIFLE RIGOL SCARF SCORE
STRIA SWAGE CREASE CULLIS
FULLER FURROW GUTTER KEYWAY
RABBET RAGGLE RAGLET REBATE
RIFFLE RUNNER SCROBE SULCUS
THROAT TRENCH CHAMFER
CHANNEL GARLAND KEYHOLE
PLOWING SULCATE BOTHRIUM
GROOVING PHILTRUM
(— IN AUGER) POD
(— IN COLUMN) FLUTE
(— IN MASONRY) RAGGLE
(— IN STAVES) CROZE
(— IN STONE) JAD
(— IN TIRE) SIPE
(— ON UPPER LIP) PHILTRUM
(— ON WEEVIL) SCROBE
(— ON WHALE) SCARF
(— UNDER COPING) GORGE
(—S ON ROCK) LAPIES
GROOVED FLUTED EXARATE
SULCATE
GROOVER FLUTER
GROPE CLAM CLAW FEEL POKE
GLAUM GRAIP FUMBLE GUDDLE
GRABBLE GRAPPLE GROPPLE
GRUBBLE SCRABBLE
GROSBEAK FINCH HAWFINCH
GROSGRAIN ROYALE
GROSS FAT DULL FOUL RANK CRASS
FOGGY GREAT GUTTY LARGE THICK
WHOLE ANIMAL COARSE EARTHY
FILTHY GREASY SORDID STRONG
BLOATED FULSOME CLODDISH
FLAGRANT INDECENT SLUTTISH
GROSSO MATAPAN
GROTESQUE ANTIC WOOZY
BIZARRE CROTESCO FANCIFUL
GROTTO CAVE GROT SPEOS
CAVERN
GROUCH SULK CRANK GROUSE
SOURBALL SOURPUSS
GROUND SEW SOD SUE BASE CLOD
DIRT FOLD FOND GIST LAND MOLD
REST ROOT SOIL STAY WOLD
EARTH FIELD FIRTH FOUND MOULD
PLACE SCORE TRAIN TUTOR VENUE
CREASE MATTER REASON SMACKED
FORELAND INITIATE
(— AT TOP OF SHAFT) BANK
(— COVERED WITH RUBBLE) TITI
(— FOR COMPLAINT) BEEF
(— OF FLAG) FIELD
(— OF LACE) FOND
(— OVERLYING TIN DEPOSIT)
BURDEN
(BOGGY —) SOG SNAPE
(BROKEN —) HAG
(BURYING —) CEMETERY

(CAMPING —) AUTOCAMP
(COLLEGE —S) CAMPUS
(DUMPING —) TIP TOOM
(FALLOW —) BRISE
(FEEDING —) HAUNT
(FIRM-HOLDING —) LANDFANG
(FISHING —) HAAF
(FROZEN —) TJAELE
(GRASSY —) LAWN CLOWRE
(HARD —) HARDPAN
(HUNTING —) CHASE
(LOW —) INCH SWALE TALAO
(MIDDLE —) LIMBO
(NEW ENCLOSED —) TINING
(ORIGINAL —) URGRUND
(PASTURE —) HIRSEL
(RECREATION —) PARK
(RISING —) HURST HYRST
(SLOPING —) CLEVE
(SOLID —) HILL
(SPONGY —) BOG
(SWAMPY —) PUXY CRIPPLE
(UNCULTIVATED —) JUNGLE
(UNUSED —) AREA
(WET WASTE —) MOOR
(PL.) GROUT STOCK
GROUND HEMLOCK SHINWOOD
GROUND HOG MARMOT
GROUND IVY GILL HEWE HOVE JILL
YARROW ALEHOOF CATFOOT
GAGROOT MILFOIL TUNHOOF
FOALFOOT
GROUNDLESS IDLE FALSE
BASELESS
GROUNDLINE SETLINE
GROUNDMAN GRUNT
GROUNDMASS PASTE CEMENT
MATRIX
GROUNDNUT GOBBE PEANUT
PIGNUT
GROUND PINE FOXTAIL STAGHORN
GROUNDSEL SIMSON DOGBUSH
SENCION SENECIO BINDWEED
BIRDSEED
GROUNDSMAN CURATOR
GROUND SQUIRREL GOPHER
GRINNY SUSLIK SCIURID SOUSLIK
SCIURINE
GROUND THRUSH PITTA
GROUNDWORK BASE FOND FUND
BASIS FUNDUS
GROUP MOB SET BAND BEVY BODY
CREW DECK FOLD GANG KNOT PAIR
RING SECT SORT STEW TREF
ARRAY BATCH BREED CLASS CLUMP
COVEY FIRCA FLOCK GENUS GLOBE
PLUMP SABHA SKULK SQUAD STACK
TALLY WHEEN CLUTCH COHORT
FAMILY GRUPPO PARCEL RUBRIC
AGGROUP BATTERY BOILING
BOUROCK BRACKET COLLEGE
COMPANY CONSORT FELLOWS
FLUTTER QUOTITY SECTION
SEVERAL SOCIETY ALLIANCE
CATEGORY CLASSIFY DIVISION
FAISCEAU FLOTILLA GROUPING
(— OF 10 NOTES) DECUPLET
(— OF 1000) CHILIAD
(— OF 12) DOZEN

(— OF 2 VOWELS) DIGRAM DIGRAPH
(— OF 40 THREADS) BEER BIER
(— OF 60 PIECES) SHOCK
(— OF ANGELS) FLIGHT
(— OF ARTIFACTS) CACHE
(— OF BADGERS) CETE
(— OF BUILDINGS) BLOCK
(— OF CASTINGS) SPRAY
(— OF CATS) CLOWDER
(— OF CELLS) GLAND ISLET
CENTER CORONA EPITHEM
SEMILUNE
(— OF DECOYS) STOOL
(— OF DEITIES) CABEIRI
(— OF DIALECTS) AEOLIC
(— OF EELS) SWARM
(— OF EIGHT) OCTAD OCTET
OCTETTE
(— OF FAMILIES) FINE
(— OF FIVE) PENTAD CINQUAIN
(— OF FOUR) MESS QUARTET
(— OF FRIENDS) BUNCH
(— OF FURNISHINGS) ENSEMBLE
(— OF HAITIANS) COMBITE
COUMBITE
(— OF HOUSES) BOROUGH
(— OF HUTS) BUSTI KRAAL BUSTEE
(— OF ISOGLOSSES) BUNDLE
(— OF KINDRED) SIOL
(— OF KINSMEN) AHL
(— OF LAYMEN) COFRADIA
(— OF LIONS) PRIDE
(— OF LISTENERS) AUDIENCE
(— OF MARTENS) RICHESSE
(— OF MILITARY VEHICLES)
DEADLINE
(— OF MOLDINGS) DANCETTE
(— OF NUCLEONS) SHELL
(— OF OFFSPRING) CLUTCH
(— OF ORGANISMS) FORM STRAIN
(— OF PARACHUTISTS) STICK
(— OF PERSONS) BAG CLUB KNOT
SWAD CROWD DROVE CIRCLE
GAGGLE KENNEL
(— OF RETORTS) BENCH SETTING
(— OF SCULPTURE) MORTORIO
(— OF SEVEN) HEPTAD SEPTET
HEBDOMAD
(— OF SIX) HEXAD SENARY
(— OF SLAVES) COFFLE
(— OF SOILS) LATERITE
(— OF SOLDIERS) DRAFT COHORT
(— OF STARS) ASTERISM
(— OF STRATIFIED BEDS) FACIES
(— OF STUDENTS) SEMINAR
(— OF SYLLABLES) FOOT
(— OF SYMBOLS) FORMULA
(— OF SYMPTOMS) SYNDROME
(— OF TEN) DECADE DENARY
(— OF TENTS) CAMP CANVAS
(— OF THEATERS) CIRCUIT
(— OF THREE) TRIO GLEEK TRIAD
TRINE
(— OF TRAITS) COMPLEX
(— OF TROUT) HOVER
(— OF VERSES) SYSTEM
(— OF WINGS) RUFFLE
(— OF WIRES) DROP
(— OF WORDS) ACCENT GENITIVE

(— ON NINE) ENNEAD NONARY
(ASSISTANCE —) AINI
(ATOMIC —) LIGAND
(AUTHORITATIVE —) CONCLAVE
(CONFUSED —) SNARL
(CORE —) CADRE
(ECOLOGICAL —) GUILD
(ETHNIC —) LI ACHANG BALAHI
BATTAK ETHNOS CHINGPAW
(ETHNOLOGICAL —) ISLAND
(EXCLUSIVE —) ELECT
(FAMILY —) GWELY
(HARMONIOUS —) DOVECOTE
(INTIMATE —) COTERIE
(KINSHIP —) SUSU
(LIVELY —) GALA
(NON-MOSLEM —) MILLET
(PAGAN —) BATAK BATANGAN
(PHILOSOPHICAL —) CENACLE
(POLITICAL —) BLOC PARTY
COMMONS
(SEGREGATED —) GHETTO
(SOCIAL —) KITH SEPT TRIBE
FAMILY INGROUP
GROUPED AGMINATE
GROUPER GAG HIND MERO GUASA
HAMEL SCAMP AGUAJI BONACI
CHERNA GROPER HAMLET WARSAW
BACALAO GARLOPA GARRUPA
GOURAMI JEWFISH REDFISH
LAPULAPU REDBELLY ROCKFISH
SCIRENGA SERRANID
(YOUNG —) SNAPPER
GROUPING KIND ARRAY BATTERY
KINDRED DIVISION GROUPAGE
SODALITY SYNTAGMA
(— OF POTTERY) SERIES
GROUSE CRAB BITCH GANGA
GORHEN GROUCH HOOTER
ATTAGEN CHEEPER GAZELLE
GORCOCK PINTAIL COMPLAIN
MOORBIRD MOORFOWL
(YOUNG —) POULT SQUEALER
GROUT GROOT LARRY SLUSH
GROUTING
GROUTER GUNITER
GROVE CAMP HEWT HOLT MOTT
SHAW TOFT TOPE WONG ALTIS
BLUFF COPSE GLADE HURST HYRST
GARDEN GREAVE GROVET ISLAND
OLIVET SPRING ACADEMY ARBORET
BOSCAGE COPPICE THICKET
WOODING SERINGAL WODELEIE
(— OF ALDERS) CARR
(— OF MANGO TREES) TOPE
(— OF OAKS) ENCINAL
(— OF OSIERS) HOLT
(— OF SUGAR MAPLES) CAMP
(SACRED —) ALTIS SARNA
(SMALL —) SHAW
GROVEL FAWN ROLL CREEP CRINGE
TUMBLE WALLOW WELTER GRABBLE
FLOUNDER
GROVELING WORMY HANGDOG
REPTILE
GROW AGE BUD GET HIT ICH WAX
BOLL COME CROP ECHE ITCH MAKE
RISE SEED THEE THRO WEAR EDIFY
ISSUE PLANT PROVE RAISE SHOOT

SWELL ACCRUE BATTEN BECOME
DOUBLE EXPAND EXTEND GATHER
SPRING SPROUT THRIVE AUGMENT
BROADEN BURGEON DEVELOP
DISTEND ENLARGE IMPROVE
NOURISH ADOLESCE FLOURISH
HEIGHTEN INCREASE THRODDEN
(— ANGRY) STIVER
(— BETTER) IMPROVE
(— DARK) GLOAM GLOOM NIGHT
DARKEN DARKLE
(— FAINT) DIE APPAL APPALL
(— FAT) FEED BATTEN
(— IN LENGTH) ELONGATE
(— IRREGULARLY) SCRAMBLE
(— LESS) SLAKE ASSUAGE
DECREASE
(— LIGHT) DAWN
(— LUXURIANTLY) THRIVE
(— MAD) WOOD
(— MILD) GIVE
(— OLD) AGE OLD SENESCE
(— OVER) INVADE
(— PLUMP) PLIM
(— RICH) FATTEN
(— SOUND) HEAL
(— SPIRITLESS) FLAG
(— STILL) HUSH
(— STRONG) FORTIFY STORKEN
(— THIN) PEAK
(— TO HEAD) CABBAGE
(— TO STALK) SPINDLE
(— TOGETHER) KNIT ACCRETE
CONCREW COOSIFY COALESCE
(— UNDER GLASS) GLASS
(— UP) STEM ACCRUE
(— WEAK) FAINT
GROWING GROWY CRESCENT
CRESCIVE
(— ANGRY) IRASCENT
(— IN CLUSTERS) RACEMOSE
(— IN GRAIN FIELDS) SEGETAL
(— IN HEAPS) ACERVATE
(— IN MEADOW) PRATAL
(— IN PAIRS) BINATE
(— IN WATER) AQUATIC
(— ON A STEM) CAULINE
(— OUT) ENATE
(— RAPIDLY) BOOMING
(— THICKLY) HOUSY
(— VIGOROUSLY) THRIFTY
(— WILD) SAVAGE AGRARIAN
AGRESTAL
GROWL YAR GNAR GURL GURR
NARR RASE ROIN ROME WIRR YARR
YIRR GARRE GNARL GNARR GROIN
SNARL GOLLAR HABBLE GRUMBLE
MAUNDER
GROWLER CLARENCE
GROWLING GROIN SURLY
GROWN THRIVEN
(— COLD) DEAD
(— HIGH) LOGGY
(— TOGETHER) ADNATE ACCRETE
(FULL —) GREAT MATURE
(WELL —) THRODDY
GROWN-UP ADULT GROWN
GROWTH FUR WAX BUSH COAT
CORN FILM GROW JUBA RISE SPUR

SUIT DUVET FLUSH GUMMA MAQUI
STAND STOCK STOOL SWELL
BUTTON CALLUS CANCER CLAVUS
EATAGE EPULIS FRINGE FUNGUS
LANUGO SCREEN SPROUT TYLOSE
UPCOME WASTME AUXESIS
BRACKEN COPPICE ERINEUM
FUNGOID MACCHIE SARCOID
STATURE TYLOSIS BEARDING
CARUNCLE ENDOGENY INCREASE
SETATION SWELLING UPSPRING
(— IN EYE) FILM
(— OF BEARD) DOWN
(— OF HAIR) SUIT
(— OF HORN) BUTTON SPIDER
(— OF TREES) BOSQUE BOSCAGE
COPPICE SHINNERY
(— ON HORSE'S LEG) FUSEE FUZEE
(— ON VESSEL'S BOTTOM) GARR
(2ND — OF GRASS) FOG
(ABUNDANT —) FLUSH
(DENSE —) BRUSH FOREST
SHINNERY
(DOWNY —) LANUGO
(GREEN —) GREENTH
(HARD —) STONE
(LUXURIANT —) FLOURISH
(ROUGH —) STUBBLE
(RUDIMENTARY —) STUB STUMP
(SIDE —) SPRIG
(SPARSE —) SCRAGGLE
(SUPERFICIAL —) MILDEW
(TRANSPARENT —) DRUSE
(VIGOROUS —) THRIFT
(WOODY —) BURL
GRUB BOB DIG EATS HUHU MOIL
MOOT STUB WORM CHUCK GROUT
MATHE SCRAN SNOUT WROTE
ASSART ESSART GRUGRU MUZZLE
ROOTLE NEASCUS PIGROOT
FLAGWORM GRUBWORM
MUCKWORM SKINWORM
GRUBROOT STARWORT
GRUDGE DOWN ENVY DERRY PEEVE
SCORE SPITE GROUCH GRUNCH
GRUTCH SPLEEN DESPITE EYELAST
SIMULTY
GRUDGING JEALOUSY
GRUEL SLOP BLEERY BURGOO
CONGEE CROWDY SOFKEE
BROCHAN CROWDIE LOBLOLLY
WANGRACE
GRUESOME UGLY GRISLY HORRID
SORDID FEARFUL GHASTLY
HIDEOUS MACABRE
GRUFF BLUFF ROUGH CLUMSE
SULLEN AUSTERE BEARING
BRUSQUE CLUMPST
(PL.) TAILINGS
GRUIFORMES GRALLAE
GRUMBLE GIRN GREX HONE KREX
ROIN BROCK CROAK DRUNT GROIN
GROWL GRUMP GRUNT MUNGE
GROUCH GROUSE GRUDGE GRUNCH
MUMBLE MUNGER MURMUR MUTTER
NOLLER PEENGE REPINE RUMBLE
SQUEAL TARROW YAMMER
CHANNER CHUNNER CHUNTER
GNATTER GRIZZLE GRUNTLE

MAUNDER MURGEON QUADDLE
SWAGGER COMPLAIN
GRUMBLER GROUCH QUADDLE
GROGNARD
GRUMBLING BITCH DRUNT GRIPE
GROIN GRUDGE MURMUR MURGEON
GRUMPY ILL CROSS GLUMPY
GLUMPISH GRUMPISH
GRUNION SMELT
GRUNT BURRO GROIN HUMPH
RONCO SARGO GRUMPH RONCHO
BURRITO CROAKER GRUNTER
GRUNTLE PIGFISH PINFISH TOMTATE
KNORHAAN KOORHAAN PORKFISH
REDMOUTH RONCADOR
GUACHARO FATBIRD OILBIRD
GUAICURU CADUVEO
GUAMA INGA PACAY
GUAN JACU ORTALIS PHEASANT
GUANA CHANE
GUANABANA SOURSOP
GUANCHE CANARIAN
GUANO OSITE
GUAPENA SERRAN SERRANA
AGUAVINA
GUARANTEE (ALSO SEE GUARANTY)
BAIL BAND SEAL CINCH COVER
AVOUCH ENGAGE ENSURE INSURE
RATIFY SECURE SURETY CAUTION
CERTIFY HOSTAGE WARRANT
AWARRANT GUARANTY PRESTATE
SECURITY WARRANTY
GUARANTEED ASSURED CERTIFIED
FOOLPROOF
GUARANTOR ENGAGER GRANTOR
GUARAND GUARANTY
GUARANTY (ALSO SEE GUARANTEE)
ANDI AVAL PAWN SEAL CAUTIO
PLEDGE WARRANT SECURITY
WARRANTY
GUARD BOW LEG NIT PAD SEE CARE
CURB HERD HOLD KEEP KNOW
LOOK REDE SAVE STOP STUB TENT
TILE WAIT WEAR WERE WITE YEME
ASKAR AWARD BLESS BLOCK
CHECK COVER FENCE FORAY
HEDGE HINGE PILOT SCREW SKIRT
TUTOR WAKEN WATCH ASKARI
BANTAY BASKET BRACER BRIDLE
BUMPER BUTTON CONVOY DEFEND
DRAGON ESCORT FENDER GHAFIR
GUNMAN JAILER KAVASS KEEPER
MIDDLE POLICE SCREEN SECURE
SENTRY SHIELD SHROUD WAITER
WARDER YEMING CHERISH
ESGUARD FRONTAL GHAFFIR
GHATWAL GUARDER KEEPING
PANDOUR PRESIDY PROTECT
SOULACK TRABANT WARDAGE
WARRANT CHAPERON GARRISON
MUDGUARD OUTGUARD PEDESTAL
PILOTMAN PRESERVE SECURITY
SENTINEL SHEPHERD SPLASHER
WARDSMAN WATCHMAN
(— ON FOIL) BUTTON
(AXLE —) HOUSING
(COACH —) SHOOTER
(CONSULAR —) KAVASS
(IMPERIAL —) BOSTANGI BOSTANJI

(KEYHOLE —) LAPPET
(MOUNTED —) SHOMER
(NECK —) CAMAIL
(ON —) AWARE
(PRISON —) HACK SCREW CHASER
JAILER
(SWORD —) BOW TSUBA
(PL.) HEAVIES
GUARDED WARY IMMUNE MANNED
GUARDEDLY GINGERLY
GUARDHOUSE BRIG CLINK BULLPEN
HOOSEGOW
GUARDIAN HERD ANGEL ARGUS
TUTOR YEMER CUSTOS KEEPER
MIMING PASTOR PATRON SHOMER
WARDEN CURATOR GARDANT
GARDEEN BARTHOLO BELLERUS
CERBERUS CREANCER DEFENDER
ECKEHART FRAVASHI GOVERNOR
GUARDIAN PROTUTOR TUTELARY
(— OF HOME) SIF
(WORLD —) LOKAPALA MAHARAJA
(PL.) SELLI SELLOI
GUARDIANSHIP WARD TUTELA
CUSTODY KEEPING TUITION
WARDAGE WARDING CUSTODIA
GUARDAGE TUTELAGE WARDENRY
WARDSHIP
GUARDROOM WARDROOM
GUARDSMAN GUARDEE
GUASA MERO

GUATEMALA
CAPITAL: GUATEMALACITY
COIN: PESO CENTAVO QUETZAL
DANCE: ELSON GUARIMBA
GULF: HONDURAS
INDIAN: MAM CHOL ITZA IXIL
MAYA XINCA CARIBE QUICHE
POCOMAM
LAKE: DULCE GUIJA PETEN IZABAL
ATITLAN
MEASURE: VARA CUARTA FANEGA
TERCIA CAJUELA MANZANA
MOUNTAIN: AGUA FUEGO PACAYA
TACANA ATITLAN TOLIMAN
TAJAMULCO
PORT: OCOS BARRIOS LIVINGSTON
RIVER: AZUL BRAVO DULCE LAPAZ
BELIZE CHIXOY NEGINO PASION
SAMALA CHIAPAS MOTAGUA
SARSTUN POLOCHIC
RUINS: TIKAL
TOWN: OCOS COBAN VIEJA
CHAHAL CHISEC CUILCO
FLORES IZTAPA JALAPA SALAMA
SOLOLA TACANA TECPAN
YALOCH ZACAPA ANTIGUA
CUILAPA JUTIAPA SANJOSE
PROGRESO
VOLCANO: AGUA FUEGO ATITLAN
WEIGHT: CAJA LIBRA

GUAVA ARACA MYRTAL GUAYABA
GUAYABO GOIABADA
GUAYCURU MBAYA
GUDDLE GUMP NOODLE HANDFISH
GUDGEON PIN QUAB CHALDER
TRUNNION

GUELDER-ROSE GAITER OPULUS
DOGWOOD WHITTEN DOGBERRY
SNOWBALL VIBURNUM
GUENON GRIVET NISNAS VERVET
TALAPOIN TALLAPOI MOUSTACHE
GUEREZA COLOBIN COLOBUS
GUERRILLA COWBOY GORILLA
JAYHAWK SKINNER BUSHWACK
FELLAGHA KOMITAJI
GUESS AIM CALL HARP REDE SHOT
WEEN AREAD COUNT ETTLE FANCY
INFER TWANG DEVISE DIVINE
RECKON IMAGINE SURMISE
SUSPECT
(— CORRECTLY) TOUCH
GUEST COME GOER HOST DINER
INVITEE VISITOR SYMPHILE VISITANT
(— AT RANCH) DUDE
(UNINVITED —) SHADOW
(PL.) LEVEE COMPANY
GUFA KUFA GOOFAH KUPHAR
GUFFAW GAFF HEEHAW
GUIDANCE AIM DUCT EGIS AEGIS
STEER CONDUCT GUIDAGE
HELMAGE LEADING WISSING
AUSPICES ENGINERY REGIMENT
STEERAGE
GUIDE GUY LAY PIR TIP AIRT BEAD
CURB GAGE GATE LEAD PASS REIN
RULE SWAY CARRY CHARM DRESS
FRAME GAUGE LIGHT MAHDI MOROC
PILOT STEER TEACH WEISE ADALID
BARKER BEACON BEDWAY CONVOY
DIRECT ESCORT FORMER GILLIE
GOVERN INFORM LEADER MANAGE
POPPET CONDUCE CONDUCT
COURIER GHILLIE INSPIRE MARSHAL
MERCURY PIONEER SHIKARI
STERNER TRACKER CALENDAR
CICERONE DIRECTOR DRAGOMAN
ENGINEER FAIRLEAD LODESMAN
PEDESTAL POLESTAR PRACTICO
REPEATER SHIKAREE SIGNPOST
(SPIRITUAL —) PIR GURU BISHOP
DIVINE
(TRAFFIC —) MUSHROOM
GUIDEBOOK ABC GUIDE WAYBOOK
BAEDEKER HANDBOOK ROADBOOK
GUIDELINE SLUG
GUIDEPOST GUIDE PARSON
WAYMARK WAYPOST SIGNPOST
GUIDEWAY SLAY SLEY SLEIGH
SLIDEWAY SWANNECK
GUIDING POLAR BEHIND HOMING
LEADING
GUILD HUI GILD HOEY HONG YELD
CRAFT HANSA HANSE GREMIO
GUIDRY SCHOLA BASOCHE
COLLEGE COMPANY MYSTERY
GUILE DOLE WILE CHEAT CRAFT
FRAUD TRAIN DECEIT HUMBUG
CUNNING FALLACY ARTIFICE
GUILELESS PLAIN CANDID HONEST
ARTLESS ONEFOLD IGNORANT
INNOCENT UNNOOKED
GUILLEMOT AUK COOT LARY LAVY
LOOM QUET TURR URIA ARRIE
CUTTY FROWL MURRE SCOUT TOIST
TYSTE GRYLLE LUNGIE MAGGIE

MARROT SCRABE TINKER DOVEKEY DOVEKIE SKIDDAW TARROCK WILLOCK PUFFINET ROCKBIRD SCUTTOCK SPRATTER

GUILT SIN SAKE WITE BLAME CULPA FAULT PIACLE PLIGHT NOCENCE OFFENSE HAMARTIA INIQUITY

GUILTLESS FREE PURE CLEAN UNSAKED INNOCENT SACKLESS

GUILTY FAULTY NOCENT WICKED CORREAL HANGDOG NOXIOUS BLAMEFUL CRIMINAL CULPABLE GUILTFUL

(— OF ERROR) LAPSED

GUINEA

CAPE: VERGA
CAPITAL: CONAKRY
COIN: SILY FRANC
ISLAND: TOMBO TRISTAO
MEASURE: JACKTAN
MOUNTAIN: TAMGUE
MOUNTAINS: LOMA NIMBA
NATIVE: SUSU TOMA KISSI FULANI
  GUERZI MALINKE KOURANKE
  LANDUMAN
RIVER: NIGER BAFING FALEME
  SENEGAL KONKOURE TINKISSO
TOWN: BOKE FRIA KADE LABE
  BENTY BEYLA COYAH KOULE
  MAMOU DABOLA DALABA
  DOUAKO FABALA KANKAN
  KINDIA BOFOSSO CONAKRY
  FARANAH KONFARA KOUMBIA
  OUASSOU SIGUIRI KEROUANE
WEIGHT: AKEY PISO UZAN BENDA
  SERON QUINTO AGUIRAGE

GUINEA MEG BEAN QUID QUEED GEORGE SHINER GEORDIE

(HALF —) SMELT

GUINEA FOWL KEEL KEET PEARL MEBACK GALEENY PINTADO COMEBACK GALLINEY

(SOUND OF —) POTRACK

GUINEA GRASS PANIC PANICLE SACATON ZACATON GAMELOTE

GUINEA PEPPER PIMENTO

GUINEA PIG CAVY

(MALE —) BOAR BUCK

GUINEA RUSH ADRUE

GUISE HUE FORM GARB COLOR COVER SHAPE MANNER PERSON APPAREL CLOTHES GUISARD LIKENESS

GUITAR BOX KIT PIPA JAMON KITAR SITAR TIPLE GIMBRI KITTAR SANCHO SATTAR CITHERN CITTERN MACHETE UKULELE CHARANGO CHITARRA

GUITARFISH RAY BATOID PURAQUE

GUITGUIT PITPIT

GULANCHA GILO GILOE

GULCH GULLY SLUIT CANYON RAVINE

GULDEN FLORIN GUILDER

(100,000 —) TUN

GULES MARS RUBY TORTEAU

GULF SINE CHAOS GULPH VORAGE VORAGO

(BOTTOMLESS —) ABYSM ABYSS

GULFWEED SARGASSO

GULL COB COX MEW COBB CONY COOT CULL DUPE FOOL GOLL LARI MALL PINT PIRR SELL SKUA XEME ALLAN ALLEN ANNET BOSUN CHEAT CHUMP COBBE COKES CROCK CULLY HOODY JAGER LARID LARUS PEWIT SCULL SMELT YAGER BONXIE BUBBLE CHOUSE COUSIN JOCKEY PIGEON SIMPLE TEASER TULIAC VICTIM WAGGEL WHILLY CROCKER DECEIVE MEDRICK PICKMAW POPELER SCAURIE SEABIRD SEAFOWL SWARBIE TARROCK TRUMPIE BLACKCAP DIRTBIRD DOTTEREL DUNGBIRD SEEDBIRD

(LIKE A —) LAROID

GULLET MAW GULE LANE GORGE GARGLE PECHAN THROAT KEACORN STOMACH SWALLOW WEASAND GURGULIO

GULLIBLE GOOFY GREEN SIMPLE CULLIBLE

GULLIVER GRILDRIG

GULLY BOX GUT DRAW GULL RAIK RAKE SICK SIKE DONGA DRAFT GOYLE GULCH SLAKE SLUIT ZANJA ARROYO GULLET GULLEY GUTTER NULLAH SHEUCH SHEUGH CHIMNEY COULOIR DRAUGHT BARRANCA

GULP BOLT GAUP GLUT GULL POOP SOPE SWIG GULCH QUILT SLOSH SWIPE ENGLUT GLUTCH GOBBLE GOLLOP PAUNCH SLABBER SWALLOW SWATTLE

(— NOISILY) SLORP

GUM AMRA BLOB FILL GOOM LOAD TUNO AMAPA BABUL CUMAY DHAVA CHICLE KARAYA TOUART TUPELO CARANNA CARAUNA GINGIVA GUMWOOD BORRACHA CARABEEN DRESSING FEVERGUM

(ACACIA —) GEDDA
(AROMATIC —) MYRRH
(ASTRINGENT —) KINO
(CHEWING —) WAX
(FRAGRANT —) BUMBO
(RED —) JARRAH
(UNGRADED —) SORTS
(WOOD —) XYLAN
(PL.) ULA

GUM ARABIC KIKAR ACACIA ACACIN

GUMBO OKRA

GUMBOIL PARULIS

GUMBO-LIMBO JOBO BIRCH GOMART MASTIC NEGRITO ALMACIGO ARCHIPIN

GUMDROP GUM JUJUBE

GUMMER BIDDY BIDDIE SCRAPER SCUFFER SCUFFLER SCUPPLER

GUMMY GLUEY CLAGGY MASTIC GUMMOUS

GUMPTION SENSE SPRAWL

GUM SUCCORY HOGBITE

GUM TREE KARI KARRI TOOART TOUART TUPELO EUCALYPT

GUMWEED GRINDELIA SUNFLOWER

GUN GAT POP BREN HAKE PIAT ROER TUBE BARIL FIFTY FIRER FUSEE FUZEE RAKER REWET RIFLE ARCHIE BERTHA CANNON CHASER CULVER DUCKER INCHER JEZAIL MINNIE QUAKER RANDOM SWIVEL TUPARA CALIVER FIREARM HACKBUT HANDGUN JINGALL LANTACA MUZZLER AMUSETTE ARQUEBUS CHAUCHAT CULVERIN FIRELOCK GALLOPER SHAGBUSH TROMBONE

(BOAT —) BASE
(LOWER-DECK —) BARKER
(MACHINE —) CHOPPER GATLING
(TOY —) SPARKLER
(PL.) FLAK CHASE ARTILLERY

GUNA RAJAS TAMAS SATTVA

GUNBOAT SKIP BARCA GONDOLA TINCLAD

GUN CARRIAGE PANEL MADRIER GALLOPER

GUNCREWMAN PLUGMAN

GUNFLINT STONE

GUNITE SHOTCRETE

GUNLOCK ROWET FIRELOCK

GUNMAN HOOD GUNSEL GUNSMAN TORPEDO ENFORCER GANGSTER

GUNNEL BLENNY SWORDICK

GUNNER GUN POPPER FIREMAN SHOOTER ENGINEER

GUNNY TAT BURLAP BAGGING SACKING

GUNNYSACK CORNSACK

GUNPOWDER SULFUR SULPHUR

GUNSIGHT VISIE HAUSSE

GUNSTOCK BLANK TIPSTOCK

GUNSTONE OGRESS PELLET

GUNWALE GUNNEL PORTOISE

GUNZ SCANIAN

GUPPY MILLIONS BELLYFISH

GUR GOOR KHAUR JAGGERY VOLTAIC

GURGLE GLOX QUARK SLOSH BURBLE GOLLER GUGGLE

GURGLINGLY TRILLIL

GURJUN YANG

GURNARD CUR TUB PIPER ELLECK ROCHET BATFISH CAPTAIN GRUNTER LATCHET SOLDIER TRIGLID TUBFISH VOLADOR HARDHEAD KNORHAAN LORICATE

GURO KWENI

GUSH JET BOIL FLOW FOAM HUSH RAIL SLOP WALM BELCH SLUSH SMALM SMARM SPIRT SPURT STOUR SWOSH BURBLE PHRASE SWOOSH WALLOW WHOOSH SLOBBER

GUSHING SLOPPY SMARMY EFFUSIVE

GUSSET GORE MITER MITRE QUIRK PIECETTE

GUST BUB FLAN GALE GUSH WAFF WAFT WIND BLAST FRESH SLANT FLURRY HUFFLE SQUALL WILLIWAW WINDFLAW

(— OF RAIN) SKIT
(— OF WIND) FLAM FLAN FUFF

GALE GUSH PIRR SCUD TIFT BERRY BLAST FLAFF THODE SQUALL WINDELAW

GUSTATION TASTE

GUSTO GUST ZEST RELISH

GUSTY DIRTY PUFFY BLASHY BLASTY FRETFUL GUSTFUL SQUALLY

GUT GIB BOWEL CECUM CLEAN CAECUM CATGUT HOLLOW STRING ELISION GRALLOCH
(FISH —) GIP GILL
(TWISTED —) THARM THERM
(PL.) BOWELS COJONES PUDDING ENTRAILS

GUTTA SOH DROP PUAN SIAK SUSU DUJAN GERIP SANGE SUNDIK CAMPANA JANGKAR SEMARUM TRENAIL TRUNNEL HANGKANG KETAPANG

GUTTER GRIP SIKE GRIPE GULLY SIVER SPOUT SWEAL BOTTOM CANNEL CULLIS GROOVE GUZZLE KENNEL RIGGOT STRAND TROUGH VENNEL CHANNEL CHENEAU GRIZZLE

(— OF STREET) KENNEL
(MINING —) BOTTOM HASSING
(ROOF —) RONE
(PL.) LIMBERS

GUTTERMAN SWAMPER

GUTTURAL GRUM BURRY HARSH THICK

GUY BOD CAT EGG JOE NUT BIRD BOZO GENT GINK HUSK JACK JOHN COOKY JOKER SCOUT SPOOF BUFFER COOKIE GAZABO GAZEBO GAZOOK GILGUY HOMBRE JASPER JIGGER MALKIN MAUMET MAWKIN KNOCKER BLIGHTER

GUY ROPE STAY VANG

GUZ GAZ GEZ ZAR ZER GUDGE

GUZERAT KANKREJ

GUZZLE BUM GUM SOT TUN BEND GULL SLOSH SWILL GOOZLE GUDDLE SWATTLE SWIZZLE

GUZZLER BENDER

GWYNIAD SCHELLY

GYASCUTUS PROCK

GYMNASIUM GYM PALESTRA TURNHALL

GYMNAST SOKOL BENDER TURNER ACROBAT TUMBLER

GYMNASTIC (— SOCIETY) SOKOL

GYNOECIUM BRUSH APOCARP

GYNOPHORE PODOGYN

GYPSUM GYP GYPS YESO GESSO LUDIAN PARGET GYPSITE SATINITE SELENITE ALABASTER

GYPSY CALO APTAL CAIRD GIPSY ROMNI BOSHAS GITANO ROMANY TINKER AZUCENA CZIGANY MOONMAN TINKLER TZIGANE ZINGARO BOHEMIAN EGYPTIAN FLAMENCO ZIGEUNER
(NON —) GORGIO
(SEA —) BAJAU
(PL.) ROMANESE

GYRATE GYRE SPIN TURN TWIRL WHIRL CURVET INGYRE ROTATE REVOLVE SQUIRREL

GYRATORY GIDDY GYRAL

GYRFALCON JERKIN

GYRON GIRON ESQUIRE

H HOW AITCH HOTEL ASPIRATE
HABERDASHERY TOGGERY
HABERGEON HAUBERK
HABILIMENT GARB HABIT APPAREL
RAIMENT CLOTHING
(PL.) CLOTHES EQUIPAGE
HABILITATE ENABLE
HABIT LAW PAD SET USE COAT
GARB GATE SUIT THEW WONT
FROCK HAUNT TACHE TRADE TRICK
USAGE CUSTOM GROOVE MANNER
PRAXIS TALENT CLOTHES FOLKWAY
HABITUS WONTING CROTCHET
HABITUDE PHYSIQUE PRACTICE
PRACTISE
(— OF GRINDING TEETH) BRUXISM
(BAD —) HANK VICE MISTETCH
(SPEECH —S) ACCENT
(PL.) DAPS
HABITABLE BIGLY
HABITAT ECE HOME RANGE PATRIA
STATION LOCALITY
HABITATION HOLD TELD TENT
ABODE BIELD HABIT HOUSE WONING
DOMICILE DWELLING PANTHEON
TENEMENT RESIDENCE
(— SITE) YACATA
(QUIET —) SHADE
(UNDERGROUND —) HOLE
HABITUAL USUAL COMMON HECTIC
CHRONIC REGULAR FREQUENT
ORDINARY
HABITUATE USE HOWF ENURE
FLESH HABIT INURE ADDICT SEASON
HACKNEY ACCUSTOM ACQUAINT
OCCASION
HABITUATED WONT SEASONED
HABITUDE HABIT SCHESIS
HABITUE DENIZEN COURTIER
HABRONEMIASIS BURSATI
BURSATTEE
HACEK WEDGE
HACK HAG HEW BOLO CHIP HAKE
DEVIL HATCH DRUDGE FIACRE
HACKLE HAGGLE HODMAN JOBBER
MANGLE HACKNEY MATTOCK
VETTURA MUTILATE
(LITERARY —) GRUB DEVIL
HACKBERRY EGGBERRY HACKTREE
HAGBERRY ONEBERRY
HACKBUT HAGBUT DEMIHAG
HACKBUSH
HACK GHARRI SHIGRAM
HACKLE COMB RUFF HECKLE
NAPPER RUFFER HATCHEL
ROUGHER
HACKNEY HACK MIDGE NODDY
HACKNEY CARRIAGE MIDGE
FIACRE JARVEY VETTURA
HACKNEYED HACK WORN HOARY
TRITE CANNED CLICHE COMMON
FOREWORN
HAD D HED HEDDE
(— NOT) HADNA HADNT
HADDOCK GADE GADID SCROD
DICKEY HADDIE
(DRIED —) CRAIL RIZZAR SPELDING
SPELDRIN
HADE UNDERLIE

HADES PIT HELL AIDES ORCUS
PLUTO SHEOL SHADES TARTAR
AIDONEUS TARTARUS
(FATHER OF —) SATURN
(WIFE OF —) PROSERPINA
HAECCITY THISNESS
HAFNIUM CELTIUM
HAFT HEFT HOVE HELVE DUDGEON
HAFTER HANDLER
HAG ATE MARE REBEC RUDAS
VECKE WITCH BELDAM HECATE
ROUDAS BELDAME HAGGARD
HELLCAT HARRIDAN
HAGAR (SON OF —) ISHMAEL
HAGBOAT HOGGET HOGGIE
HAGFISH HAG BORER VECKE
MYZONT SUCKER PLACOID
MYXINOID
HAGGARD PALE THIN GAUNT WISHT
HAGGED
HAGGLE CHOP PRIG DODGE BADGER
BANTER BOGGLE DICKER HACKER
HIGGLE HUCKLE NAGGLE PALTER
SCOTCH THREEP BARGAIN CHAFFER
HUCKSTER
HAGGLER DODGER
HAGGLING BARGAIN CHAFFER
HAGIOGRAPHA KETUBIM
HAGIOSCOPE SQUINT SQUINCH
HAIDA SKITTAGET
HAIL AVE HOY HALE GREET SALVE
SPEAK STORM ACCOST BAYETE
HAGGLE HALLOO HERALD SALUTE
(SOFT —) GRESIL GRAUPEL
HAILSTONE STONE
HAINAI IONI
HAIR FAX JAG RIB WIG BARB CROP
FLUE GLIB HEAD KEMP PELF PILE
SETA WIRE BEARD CRIMP CRINE
FRIZZ FRONT PILUS QUIFF ANGORA
BRILLS BRUTUS CRINET FIBRIL
FROWZE MERKIN SETULA THATCH
TRAGUS CULOTTE ELFLOCK
GLOCHIS TOPKNOT WHISKER
CAPILLUS COLLETER PALPOCIL
TENTACLE TRICHODE TRICHOME
VIBRISSA
(— BROWN) ARGALI
(— OF ANIMALS) FUR PELF
(— OF HORSES OR COWS) CERDA
(— OF TERRIER) FALL
(— ON LEAF) GLAND
(— ON TEMPLES) HAFFET HAFFIT
(— ON THIGHS) CULOTTE
(— OVER EYES) BROW GLIB
EYELASH
(BARBED —) GLOCHIS
(BRAID OF —) QUEUE PIGTAIL
(BUNDLE OF —) LEECH
(CAMEL'S —) DEER
(COARSE —) KEMP BRISTLE
(CURLED —) FRIZZ
(CUTDOWN —) STUMPS
(FALSE —) WIG JANE FRONT
PERUKE
(FRIZZED —) FROWZE
(GRAY —) GRIZZLE
(LOCK OF —) TUZ FEAK TATE
FLOCK TRESS

(LONG HEAVY —) MANE
(LOOSE —) COMBINGS
(MATTED —) SHAG ELFLOCK
(MOP OF —) TOUSLE
(NOSE —) VIBRISSA
(PLANT —) COLLETER
(ROOT —) FIBRIL
(SNARL OF —) TANGLE
(SOFT —) DOWN LANUGO
(STINGING —) STING STIMULUS
(STRAY LOCK OF —) TAG
(TUFT OF —) PLUME KROBYLOS
(WAVING LOCK OF —) WIMPLER
(WHITE —) SNOW SNOWS
(PL.) COWAGE COWHAGE HACKLES
HAIRBREADTH HERMELE WHISKER
HAIRBRUSH TOILETRY
HAIRCLOTH HAIR CILICE
HAIRCUT BOB CUT CROP BUTCH
SHINGLE DUCKTAIL
HAIRDO FRISURE
HAIRDRESSER WAVER FRISEUR
COIFFEUR
HAIRDRESSING FRISURE
HAIR FRAME PALISADE
HAIRINESS PILOSISM PILOSITY
HAIRLESS PELON CALLOW ATRICHIC
DEPILOUS
HAIRLIKE TRICHOID
HAIRLINE WHISKER
HAIRPIN ACUS BODKIN SKEWER
HAIRSPLITTING FINE PILPUL
HAIRWORM GORDIID GORDIOID
HAIRY FAXED MOSEY ROUGH
COMATE COMOUS PILARY PILINE
CRINOSE HIRSUTE PILEOUS VILLOUS
UNSHAVEN

HAITI

CAPE: FOUX
CAPITAL: PORTAUPRINCE
CHANNEL: SUD STMARC
COIN: GOURDE
DEITY: LOA
INDIAN: TAINO
ISLAND: VACHE GONAVE TORTUE
NAVASSA TORTUGA
ISLAND GROUP: ANTILLES
CAYMITES
LAKE: SAUMATRE
MAGIC: OBI OBEAH
MOUNTAIN: NORD CAHOS NOIRES
LAHOTTE LASELLE TROUDEAU
PLAIN: NORD CAYES JACMEL
LEOGANE ARCAHAIE CULDESAC
GONAIVES
PRIEST: BOCOR HOUNGAN
RIVER: GUAYAMOUL ARTIBONITE
SPIRIT: LOA BAKA BOKO
TOWN: AQUIN CAYES FURCY
LIMBE HINCHE JACMEL JEREMIE
LEOGANE SALTROU GONAIVES
KENSCOFF

HAKAM CACAM HAHAM CHOCHEM
KHAKHAM
HAKE GADE HAIK LING GADOID
CODLING HADDOCK WHITING

ANACANTH QUODLING
HAKENKREUZLER SWASTIKA
HALBERD BILL PIKE GLAIVE GLEAVE
POLEARM PARTISAN
HALBERDIER DRABANT
HALCYON CALM ALCYON GOLDEN
HALE YELL FRACK FRECK TRAIL
ROBUST STRONG HEALTHY
VIGOROUS
HALER HELLER
HALF M ARF ELF DEMI HAUF HOVE
SEMI SIDE MEDIO HALFEN HALFLY
MOIETY MEDIETY
(**— GALLON**) POTTLE
(**— OF DRAW**) BRACKET
(**— OF EM**) EN
(**— OF INNING**) BOTTOM
(**— OF MOLD**) VALVE
(**FRUIT —S**) SLABS
HALFBEAK GAR IHI BALAO PIPER
BALLYHOO
HALF-BLOOD DEMISANG
HALF BOOT BUSKIN
HALF-BREED BREED METIF METIS
SAMBO MUSTEE RAMONA CABOCLO
MESTIZO METISSE DEMISANG
HARRATIN MIXBLOOD
HALF-CASTE TOPAZ TOPASS
HALF-CRAZY FIFISH
HALF CROWN GEORGE ALDERMAN
HALF DENIER MAILE MAILLE
HALF DOBRA PECA
HALF-EATEN SEMESE
HALF-FARTHING CUE MITE MINUTE
HALF GAINER ISANDER
HALF-GROWN HALFLIN
HALF-GUINEA SMELT
HALF HITCH ROLLING
HALF MASK LOUP DOMINO
HALF-MOON LUNETTE DEMILUNE
HALF NOTE MINIM
HALFPENCE GROCERY
HALFPENNY OB MAG MEG DUMP
GRAY GREY MAIL MAKE MEKE OBOL
SOUSE STAMP BAUBEE MAILLE
HAPENNY STUIVER
(**COUNTERFEIT —**) RAP GRAY
(**THICK —**) DUMP
HALF-PIKE SPONTON DEMIPIKE
SPONTOON
HALF-PINT CUP JACK CUPFUL
HALF REST SOSPIRO
HALF SOLE TAP
HALF STEP CHROMA
HALFTONE DROPOUT
HALF TURN DEMIVOLT
HALF-WIT DOLT DUNCE HAVEREL
TOMFOOL STAUMREL UNDERWIT
HALF-WITTED SOFT DOTTY SIMPLE
HALUCKET IMBECILE STAUMREL
HALIBUT BUT BUTT FLITCH TURBOT
FLATFISH
HALIFAX BALLYHACK
HALIOTIS ABALONE
HALIRRHOTHIUS (**FATHER OF —**)
NEPTUNE
(**MOTHER OF —**) EURYTE
(**SLAYER OF —**) MARS
HALL HA AULA HELL IWAN SALA

AIWAN ATREO ATRIO BALAI BURSA
CURIA DIVAN ENTRY FOYER HOUSE
OECUS SALLE SALON ATRIUM
CAMERA DURBAR GARDEN LESCHE
SALOON SCHOOL SENATE TOLSEY
TRANCE APADANA CHAMBER
DANCERY GALLERY HALLWAY
KURHAUS KURSAAL MEGARON
PASSAGE VINGOLF ANTEROOM
ARCHEION ASSEMBLY CHOULTRY
COLISEUM CORRIDOR FOREHALL
HASTROND HOSPITAL RAADZAAL
TOLBOOTH VALHALLA
(**— FOR PERFORMANCES**) ODEON
ODEUM
(**— WITH STATUES**) VALHALLA
(**DINING —**) COMMON
(**LECTURE —**) SCHOLA
(**MISSION —**) CITADEL
(**MUSIC —**) GAFF
(**TOWN —**) CABILDO RATHAUS
TRIBUNAL
(**UNIVERSITY —**) BURSA
HALLMARK CROWN SHOPMARK
HALLOO HO HOO LOO ALEW LURE
WHOOP ACCOST TALLYHO
HALLOW BLESS HALWE DEDICATE
SANCTIFY
HALLOWED HOLY SACRED BLESSED
HALLUCINATION DWALE ACOASMA
ACOUASM ACOUSMA FANTASY
PHONEME DELUSION ILLUSION
PHANTASY ZOOSCOPY
HALLUX TALON
HALLWAY ENTRY FOYER TRANCE
HALMA HOPPITY
HALMALILLE PETWOOD
HALO DOG BURR GLOR NIMB GLORY
SHINE AREOLA CIRCLE CORONA
GLORIA NIMBUS SUNDOG AREOLET
AUREOLE BOROUGH CINCTURE
HALT HO HOP ALTO BAIT BALK HOLD
LIMP SKID STAY STOP TRIP WAIT
BAULK BLOCK BREAK CEASE CHECK
HILCH HITCH STAND ARREST
BARLEY SCOTCH STANCE CONTAIN
CRIPPLE STATION STOPPAGE
(**— GAME**) CALL
(**— TO DOGS**) TOHO
HALTER EVIL SOLE BRANK TRASH
WANTY WIDDY WITHE POISER
CAUSSON CAVESON JAQUIMA
POINTEL BALANCER NECKLACE
HALTING BODE LAME ZOPPA
CRIPPLE LIMPING
HALVE DIMIDIATE
(**PL.**) HALVERS
HALVING HAPLOSIS
HAM PIG GAMMON JAMBON JARRET
PESTLE GAMBONE
(**FATHER OF —**) NOAH
(**PICNIC —**) CALA CALI
(**SON OF —**) CUSH CANAAN
HAMATUM UNCIFORM
HAMESUCKEN HAMFARE
HAMITE BORAN BORANA DANAKIL
DANKALI
HAMLET KOM DORP TOWN TREF
VILL CASAL HAMEL SITIO STEAD

THORP VICUS ALDEIA BUSTEE
THORPE CLACHAN KAMPONG
KIRKTON KIRKTOWN
HAMMER AX AXE BIT DOG PEG SET
CALL COCK DROP HORN MALL
MASH MAUL MELL SETT TILT CAVIL
KEVEL KNOCK MADGE POUND SMITE
THUMP BEETLE BUCKER CLOYER
DRIVER FALLER FULLER MALLET
MARTEL NOPPER OLIVER PLEXOR
SCUTCH SLEDGE TACKER TILTER
KNAPPER KNOCKER MALLEUS
PLESSOR STRIKER CRANDALL
MALLEATE MJOLLNIR SCUTCHER
TREMBLER
(**— FOR DRESSING STONE**) KEVEL
(**— OF GUNLOCK**) DOG COCK
DOGHEAD
(**— OUT**) ANVIL
(**BRICKLAYER'S —**) SCOTCH SCUTCH
SCUTCHER
(**LEADEN —**) MADGE
(**MINER'S —**) BULLY
(**PAVING —**) REEL
(**PNEUMATIC —**) GUN BUSTER
(**STEAM —**) IMPACTER IMPACTOR
(**TUNING —**) KEY
HAMMERED BEATEN WROUGHT
HAMMERHEAD CORNUDA
HAMMERKOP UMBER UMBRETTE
HAMMERLOCK BAR ARMLOCK
HAMMERMAN STRIKER
HAMMOCK SACK HUMMOCK
(**— CARRIED BY BEARERS**) DANDY
(**— SLUNG ON POLE**) MACHILA
(**WOODEN —**) KATEL KARTEL
HAMPER BIN COT MAR PED TUB
BEAT BIND CLOG CURB FLAT HURT
LOAD SLOW TUCK BLOCK CRAMP
CRATE MAUND RUSKY SERON
BASKET BURDEN FETTER HALTER
HINDER HOBBLE HOPPLE IMPEDE
BUFFALO CONFINE HANAPER
MANACLE PANNIER PERPLEX
SHACKLE TRAMMEL ENCUMBER
ENTANGLE OBSTRUCT RESTRAIN
RESTRICT STRAITEN
HAMPERING STIFLING DIFFICULT
HAMSTER CRICETID
HAMSTRING HOX HOCK LAME
HOUGH ENERVATE
HANAPER HAMPER
HAND M CAT DAB FAM FIN HAN PAW
PUD CLAW DEAL DUKE GIVE GOLL
HALF JACK LOOF MAIN MANO MITT
PART PASS SPAN CAMAY CLAUT
CLEUK FLUSH GLAUM GRASP GRIPE
INDEX MANUS MAULY NIEVE POWER
SHARE STIFF STOCK BRIDGE
CLUNCH CLUTCH DADDLE DOUBLE
FAMBLE GOWPEN HANDLE MINNIE
STAGER WORKER CLAWKER
FAMELEN FLAPPER FLIPPER
POINTER WORKMAN GRAPPLER
MORTMAIN
(**— COUNTING ZERO**) BACCARA
BACCARAT
(**— DOWN**) DEVOLVE TRADUCE
BEQUEATH TRANSMIT

(— **GESTURES**) MUDRA
(— **IN POKER**) FULL SKIP BLAZE
FLUSH SKEET TIGER BICYCLE
JACKPOT SKIPPER IMMORTAL
STRAIGHT
(— **IN WHIST**) MORT TENACE
(— **ON**) BUCK
(— **OVER**) GIVE REACH BETEACH
BITECHE DELIVER
(— **UP STRAW**) SERVE
(— **WITH 5 HIGHEST TRUMPS**)
JAMBOREE
(**BABY'S** —) SPUD
(**BIG AND UNGAINLY** —) MAIG
(**BRIDGE** —) BID DUMMY DOUBLE
LAYDOWN
(**CLENCHED** —) FIST
(**COLD** —S) SHOWDOWN
(**CURSIVE** —) CIVILITE
(**DECK** —) HAWSEMAN
(**DUMMY** —) BOARD
(**ELDEST** —) EDGE SENIOR
(**EXTRA** — **IN LOO**) MISS
(**FRENCH** —) COULEE
(**GRASPING** —) CLAUT
(**GREEN** —) FARMER JACKEROO
(**LEFT** —) SINISTRA
(**LONE** —) JAMBONE
(**PERSIAN** —) SHIKASTA
(**POKER** —S) BOARD
(**RANCH** —) COWBOY
(**REEL** —) SPINDLER
(**RIGHT** —) DEXTER
(**ROUND** —) RONDE
(**SECTION** —) SNIPE
(**SKILLFUL** —) DAB
(**SPARE** — **IN CARDS**) CAT
JAMBOREE
(**UNSKILLED** —) DABSTER
(**UPPER** —) BULGE EMINENCE
(**WEAK CARD** —) BUST
HANDBAG BAG CABA NEIF CABAS
PURSE SATCHEL ENVELOPE
GRIPSACK POCHETTE RETICULE
HANDBALL PALM
HANDBARROW BIER HANDY TRUCK
BARROW
HANDBELL SKELLAT TANTONY
HANDBILL BILL FLIER FLYER LIBEL
DODGER
HANDBOOK VADY GRADUS MANUAL
BAEDEKER
HANDBOW STONEBOW
HANDCAR DRAG
HANDCART PRAM DANDY HURLY
TRUCK GOCART TROLLY TROLLEY
HANDCUFF CUFF STAY LINKER
NIPPER STAYER MANACLE TRAMMEL
WRISTER BRACELET HANDBOLT
HANDLOCK LIGAMENT SNITCHER
WRISTLET
(**PL.**) IRONS SNAPS DARBIES
NIPPERS
HANDER-IN INGIVER
HANDFUL M MAN GRIP LOCK WISP
YELM CLAUT GRIPE LITCH GOUPIN
GOWPEN HANTLE YAFFLE FISTFUL
MANIPLE
(— **OF GRAIN**) REAP SINGLE
SONGLE

(— **OF LEAVES**) PATRIN
(**DOUBLE** —) GOWPEN
(**LAST** — **OF HARVEST**) KIRN
HANDGRIP TUFFING
HANDGUN HAKE CALIVER HANDARM
HANDICAP START BURDEN DENIAL
HAMPER HINDER IMPEDE STRIKE
ENCUMBER PENALIZE
HANDICAPPED CRIMP CRIMPED
HANDICRAFT MYSTERY MECHANIC
HANDCRAFT
HANDICRAFTSMAN ARTISAN
HANDILY HANDY GAINLY
HANDINESS YARAGE
HANDIWORK MACHINE
HANDKERCHIEF WIPE CLOUT
FOGLE HANKY STOOK WIPER
HANKIE MADRAS NAPKIN SUDARY
TIGNON BANDANA BELCHER
FOULARD KERCHER MANIPLE
SNEEZER BANDANNA KERCHIEF
MOCKETER MONTEITH MOUCHOIR
SUDARIUM VERNACLE VERONICA
HANDLE BOW EAR FAN NIB NOB PAD
PIN PLY USE ANSA BAIL BALE BOOL
BUTT CROP FEEL FIST GAUM GRIP
HAFT HALE HAND HANK HILT KILP
KNOB LIFT RAPE RUNG STOP
GRASP GRIPE GROPE HELVE MOUNT
SHAFT SPOKE STAIL STALE START
STEAL STELE STOCK SWING TREAT
WIELD BECKET FETTLE FINGER
FUSEAU HANGER LIFTER MANAGE
MANURE POMMEL ROUNCE TILLER
CONDUCT DUDGEON WOOLDER
BEERPULL BELLPULL BITSTALK
BITSTOCK DISPENSE HANDGRIP
HANDHOLD HANDLING MOPSTICK
STAGHORN
(— **AWKWARDLY**) FUMBLE THUMBLE
(— **BADLY**) ILLGUIDE
(— **CLUMSILY**) PAW FUMBLE
(— **IMPROPERLY**) GAUM
(— **MODISHLY**) GALLANT
(— **OF AXE**) HELVE
(— **OF BENCH PLANE**) TOAT TOTE
(— **OF DAGGER**) DUDGEON
(— **OF KETTLE**) BAIL
(— **OF LADLE**) SHANK
(— **OF OAR**) GRASP
(— **OF PLOW**) HALE STAFF START
STILT PLOWTAIL
(— **OF PRINTING PRESS**) ROUNCE
(— **OF RAKE**) STALE
(— **OF SCYTHE**) TACK SNATH
SNEAD THOLE SNATHE SNEATH
(— **OF SWORD**) HAFT HILT
(— **OF WHIP**) CROP
(— **RECKLESSLY**) FOOL
(— **ROUGHLY**) MALL MAUL TOWSE
MUZZLE GRABBLE
(— **VIOLENTLY**) BOUNCE
(**CRANK** —) WINK
(**CROSSBOW** —) TILLER
(**CURVED** —) BOOL BOUL
(**DETACHABLE** —) KILP
(**LIFTING** — **OF GUN**) DOLPHIN
(**PUMP** —) BRAKE SWIPE
(**ROPE** —) SHACKLE

(**WOODEN** —) TREE
(**PL.**) HALES
HANDLED (**EASILY** —) BANTAM
HANDLER DOCKHAND
(**AIRPLANE** —) AIREDALE
HANDLING USE CONTROL
(**SKILLFUL** —) CONDUCT
(**UNSKILLFUL** —) BUNGLING
HANDMAID ANCILLA
HANDOUT DOWN
HANDRAIL BAR RAIL MANROPE
BANISTER EASEMENT MOPSTICK
TOADBACK
HANDSHAKE SHAKE SHRUG
HAND-SHAPED PALMATE
HANDSOME BRAW FAIR FINE PERT
TALL BONNY FETIS FITTY FUSOM
LUSTY ADONIC BRAWLY CLEVER
FARAND GOODLY HEPPEN LIKELY
PROPER SEEMLY ADONIAN AVENANT
ELEGANT FEATISH FEATOUS
FEWSOME GALLANT LIBERAL
SMICKER GOODLIKE STUNNING
VENEREAN WEELFARD
HANDSOMELY FAIRLY HANDSOME
HANDSTONE MANO
HAND STRAP TOGGEL TOGGLE
HANDSTROKE TALLY
HANDWORK TOOLING
HANDWRITING PAW FIST HAND
WRITE DUCTUS NIGGLE SCRIPT
SCRIVE BATARDE WRITING
BACKHAND HANDWRIT
HANDY DAB DEFT GAIN WEME
JEMMY LUSTY QUEME READY TIGHT
CLEVER HEPPEN KNACKY
DEXTROUS EXPEDITE HANDSOME
SKILLFUL
HANDYMAN MOZO JUMPER
GREASER SWAMPER
HANG NUB TOP CRAP DRAG FALL
HANK KILT PEND TREE TUCK DRAPE
DROOP HOVER KETCH NOOSE
STRAP SWING TRINE TRUSS TWIST
ANHANG APPEND DEPEND GIBBET
HALTER IMPEND SLOUCH STRING
TALTER DOGGONE HANGING
LANTERN STRETCH SUSPEND
(— **ABOUT**) DRING HOVER
(— **AROUND**) KNOCK HANKER
SLINGE
(— **BACK**) LAG BOGGLE
(— **BEHIND**) PLOD
(— **CRIMINAL**) STRAP TOTTER
(— **DOWN**) DIP LOP LAVE DROOP
DEPEND FESTOON PROPEND
(— **HEAVILY**) SWAG
(— **LOOSELY**) BAG SAG FLAG FLOW
LOLL BANGLE DANGLE PAGGLE
(— **ONE'S HEAD**) SLINK
(— **OUT**) LILL
(— **OVER**) WAUVE IMPEND WHAUVE
(— **PICTURE NEAR CEILING**) SKY
(— **SOGGILY**) TROLLOP
(— **WITH TAPESTRY**) TAPIS
HANGAR DOCK GARAGE AIRDOCK
HANGER PASSIVE SHABBLE
WHINYARD
(— **FOR CARCASSES**) STANG

(COAT —) SHOULDER
(CRANK —) BRACKET
(LACE-MAKING —) WORKER
(SWORD —) CARRIAGE
HANGER-ON BUR BURR SPIV LEECH
TOADY HANGBY HEELER LACKEY
LACQUEY PENDING PARASITE
HANGING FLAG HEMP TURN ARRAS
BAGGY DRAPE SWING CELURE
DORSEL DOSSER DERRICK DRAPERY
PENDENT PENSILE ANTEPORT
HANGMENT
(— LOOSE) LOPPY BAGGED
(— LOW) SIDE
(— THREATENINGLY) IMMINENT
(LIMPLY —) FLAGGY SLIMPSY
(WALL —) CEILING TENTURE
(PL.) TAPIT TAPPET DRAPERY
PARAMENT
HANGMAN KETCH HANGER HANGIE
TOPMAN DERRICK GREGORY
TOPSMAN VERDUGO CARNIFEX
SCRAGGER
(HALTER OF —) TOW
HANGMAN'S DAY FRIDAY
HANGNAIL AGNAIL
HANGOUT JOINT SCATTER
HANGOVER HOLDOVER RESIDUUM
HANK HASP SKEIN BOBBIN
SELVAGEE
(— OF FLAX) HEAD
(— OF TWINE) RAN
(— OF YARN) SLIP
HANKER HANK LONG LINGER
HANKERING ITCH HANKER
HANKUL ENMUN ONMUN
HANSOM CAB SHOFUL SHOWFUL
HANUMAN ENTELLUS
HAP REDE CHANCE FORTUNE
HAPPING
HAPHAZARD CASUAL CHANCE
CHANCY RANDOM BUCKEYE
SCRATCH CARELESS SCRAMBLY
SLAPDASH
HAPHAZARDLY ANYHOW
HAPLESS POOR UNLUCKY
HAPLY HAPS HAPPILY
HAPPEN BE DO GO HAP COME COOK
FALL FARE GIVE LUCK PASS TIDE
TIME BREAK EVENE EVENT LIGHT
OCCUR SHAPE ARRIVE BECOME
BEFALL BETIDE CHANCE TUMBLE
FORTUNE STUMBLE SUCCEED
BECHANCE OVERCOME
(— TOGETHER) CONCUR
HAPPENING HAP FACT EVENT THING
CHANCE TIDING TIMING INCIDENT
OCCASION
(ACTUAL —) FACT
(UNEXPECTED —) ACCIDENT
HAPPILY FAIN FITLY GLADLY
JOYOUSLY
HAPPINESS JOY WIN GLEE SELE
SONS WEAL BLISS GLORY MIRTH
SOOTH FELICE WEALTH DELIGHT
ECSTASY FELICIA RAPTURE UTILITY
FELICITY GLADNESS HILARITY
HAPPY FIT COSH FAIN GLAD GLEG
SELI WELY BONNY FAUST FELIX

LIGHT LUCKY MERRY PROUD SEELY
SONSY SUNNY WHITE BONNIE
JOYFUL COMICAL GLEEFUL
HALCYON JOCULAR PERFECT
SEELFUL WEALFUL WEIRDLY
BLISSFUL CAREFREE DISPOSED
FROHLICH GRACIOUS SUNSHINE
HARA-KIRI SEPPUKU
HARANGUE ORATE CONCIO PATTER
SERMON SPEECH ADDRESS
DECLAIM EARBASH DIATRIBE
PERORATE
HARASS FAG GIG HAG HOX MAG
NAG RAG TAW VEX BAIT CARK
FRAB FRET GALL GNAW HAKE HALE
HARE HAZE HOCK JADE PAIL RIDE
SEEK TIRE TOIL TOSS WORK ANNOY
BESET BULLY CHAFE CHASE CHEVY
CHIVY CURSE FLISK GRIND GRIPE
HARRY HURRY TARGE TEASE
WEARY WORRY BADGER BOTHER
CHOUSE CUMBER FERRET HATTER
HECKLE HECTOR HESPEL HOORAY
HURRAH INFEST MOLEST MURDER
OBSESS PESTER PLAGUE POTHER
PURSUE AFFLICT AGITATE BEDEVIL
DRAGOON HAGRIDE HARRAGE
OPPRESS PERPLEX PROVOKE
TERRIFY TORMENT TRAVAIL
TROUBLE TURMOIL BULLYRAG
DISTRACT DISTRESS EXERCISE
FORHAILE IRRITATE SPURGALL
SUPPRESS
(— MENTALLY) GRUDGE
HARASSED BESTEAD HARRIED
HAUNTED
(— BY) BEFORE
HARASSING WARM
HARBINGER ANGEL USHER HERALD
FORAGER FORAYER FURRIER
PRODROME
(— OF SUMMER) SWALLOW
HARBOR REE BEAR DOCK HOLD
PIER PORT BASIN BAYOU CHUCK
CREEK HAVEN HITHE SLADE
BREACH BUNDER COTHON FOSTER
OUTPORT PORTLET SEAPORT
SHELTER CARENAGE ENHARBOR
SHIPRADE
(— A CRIMINAL) RESET
HARBOR SEAL DOTANT DOTARD
RANGER SEALCH TANGFISH
HARD DRY FIT ILL COLD DEAR DOUR
DURE FAST FIRM IRON MEAN NASH
OPEN CHAMP CLOSE CORKY HARSH
HORNY ROCKY SMART SNELL SOLID
SOUND STERN STONY STOOR
STOUT TIGHT BOARDY BRAWNY
COARSE FLINTY GLASSY KITTLE
KNOBBY KNOTTY ROBUST RUGGED
SEVERE STARKY STINGY STRICT
STRONG UNEATH UNNETH ARDUOUS
AUSTERE CALLOUS HARDWAY
ONEROUS SUBDURE CORNEOUS
DILIGENT HARDBACK HARDENED
IRONHARD OBDURATE PETROSAL
RIGOROUS SCLEROID SCLEROSE
TOILSOME
(— BY) FORBY FORTHBY

(— TO BEAR) FIERCE
(— TO MANAGE) SALTY
(— TO PLEASE) FINICKY CONCEITY
(— TO REACH) CUMBROUS
(— TO READ) BLIND
(— TO SATISFY) EXIGENT EXIGEANT
(— TO SELL) STICKY
(— TO UNDERSTAND) DIFFUSE
HARD-BILL SEEDEATER
HARD-BITTEN GNARLED
HARDEN SET TAW BAKE BEEK CAKE
FIRM HARN KERN SEAR BRAZE
ENURE FLESH INURE STEEL STONE
ENDURE FREEZE OBDURE POTASH
SEASON TEMPER CALCIFY
EMBRAWN STIFFEN THICKEN
CONCRETE ENHARDEN INDURATE
SOLIDIFY
(— QUILL) DUTCH
(CASE —) STEEL
HARDENED DRAW HARD LOST
SALTED CALLOUS CRUSTED
FIBROUS INDURATE OBDURATE
HARDENING SET POROMA
SCLEROMA
HARDHACK SPIREA IRONBUSH
WHITECAP
HARDHEAD LION BOCHE
HARDHEARTED STERN STONY
OBDURATE
HARDIHOOD PLUCK COURAGE
AUDACITY
HARDLY ILL SCANT BARELY RARELY
SCARCE UNEATH SCARCELY
HARDNESS SEG GRAIN PROOF
RIGOR STEEL DURESS DURITY
ADAMANT HARDSHIP SEVERITY
SOLIDITY
(— OF CHARACTER) HEART
HARD-OF-HEARING DULL DUNCH
DEAFISH
HARDPAN PAN CLAYPAN MOORPAN
ORSTEIN MOORBAND ORDSTEIN
HARDSHIP HARD GRIEF RIGOR
STOUR THRONG UNWEAL SQUEEZE
ASPERITY HARDNESS
(PL.) EXTREMES
HARDTACK PANTILE
(— AND MOLASSES) BURGOO
HARDWARE TRIM IRONWARE
HARDWOOD HARD BREAKAX
LEAFWOOD
HARDWORKING EIDENT
HARDY DOUR HARD WIRY LUSTY
MANLY STOUR STOUT TOUGH
GARDEN INURED RUGGED STURDY
SPARTAN STUBBED GAILLARD
GALLIARD STUBBORN
HARE PUG WAT BAWD CONY PUSS
SCUT BAWTY CUTTY LEPUS PUSSY
MALKIN MAUKIN BELGIAN LEPORID
VENISON KLIPHAAS LEPORINE
(— IN FIRST YEAR) LEVERET
(— TRACK) PRICK
(FEMALE —) DOE
(GREAT —) MANABOZHO
(LITTLE CHIEF —) CONY PIKA
(MALE —) BUCK
(SIBERIAN —) TOLAI
(PL.) FLICK

HAREBELL THIMBLE BLAEWORT
BLUEBELL
HAREBRAINED GIDDY WINDY
HARELIP LAGOSTOMA
HAREM SERAI ZENANA ANDERUN
HAREMLIK SERAGLIO
HARE'S-EAR MODESTY
HARIJAN PANCHAMA
HARL WHIRL
HARLEQUIN DUCK SQUEALER
(FEMALE —) LADY
(MALE —) LORD
HARLOT PUG DRAB SLUT HIREN
PAGAN QUEAN RAHAB STRAP
TWEAK WHORE RIBALD TOMBOY
DELILAH MERMAID WAGTAIL
MERETRIX MISWOMAN STRUMPET
HARLOTRY PUTAGE BITCHERY
HARM NEY NOY NYE WEM ARME
BALE BANE DERE HURT SORE TEEN
WERD GRAME HERME LOATH
QUALM SHEND SPOIL TOUCH
WATHE WEMMY WOUGH WOUND
WRAKE WREAK WRONG DAMAGE
DAMNUM DANGER GRIEVE INJURE
INJURY SCATHE SORROW WONDER
DESPITE DISEASE FORFEIT IMPEACH
TROUBLE UNQUERT BUSINESS
DISAVAIL DISSERVE ENDAMAGE
MISCHIEF NOCUMENT NUISANCE
(— REPUTATION) DEFAME
(DO —) ENVY
HARMFUL BAD EVIL HARM NASTY
NOXAL NOCENT NOCIVE NOYFUL
UNSELY BANEFUL HURTFUL
NOISOME NOXIOUS DAMAGING
INIMICAL SINISTER
HARMFULNESS VICE MALICE
HARMLESS SAFE SELI TAME SEELY
WHITE DOVISH FEARLESS HURTLESS
INNOCENT SACKLESS UNHARMED
HARMONIA (DAUGHTER OF —) INO
AGAVE SEMELE AUTONOE
(FATHER OF —) MARS
(HUSBAND OF —) CADMUS
(MOTHER OF —) VENUS
(SON OF —) POLYDORUS
HARMONICA HARP SYRINX AEOLINE
PANPIPE ARMONICA ZAMPOGNA
HARMONIOUS HAPPY SWEET
COSMIC SILKEN UNITED MUSICAL
SPHERAL TUNEFUL BALANCED
CHARMING HARMONIC PEACEFUL
HARMONITE RAPPIST RAPPITE
HARMONIUM ORGAN VOCALION
HARMONIZE GO FIT GEE KEY JIBE
SORT TUNE AGREE ATONE BLEND
CHORD GROUP HITCH ACCORD
ASSORT COTTON COMPORT
CONCENT CONCORD CONSORT
ORDINATE
HARMONIZING HENOTIC
HARMONY SUIT TUNE CHIME CHORD
UNITY ACCORD ATTUNE COSMOS
HEAVEN MELODY UNISON BALANCE
CONCERT CONCORD CONSENT
CONSORT KEEPING RAPPORT
DIAPASON SYMPATHY SYMPHONY
HARNESS TUG GEAR HAME LEAF

REIN BRACE CROWN DRAFT FRONT
GEARS SLING TRACE COLLAR
FETTLE GULLET INSPAN TACKLE
DRAUGHT GEARING GIGTREE
LORMERY SIMBLOT TOGGERY
DRAWGEAR ENCLOSER HEADGEAR
TACKLING TURNBACK
(— FOR LOOM) LEAF HEALD
MOUNTING
(DECORATIVE —) CAPARISON
(WEAVING —) HEADLE HEDDLE
HARNESSED ANTELOPE GUIB
GUIBA BOSCHBOK BUSHBUCK
HARNESS MAKER KNACKER
WHITTAW
HAROLD I HAREFOOT
HARP ARPA FORK VINA NABLA
NANGA HARPER SABECA CHROTTA
DECHORD SAMBUKE AUTOHARP
CLARSACH
(CELTIC —) TELYN
(FINNISH —) KANTELA KANTELE
(ICELANDIC —) LANGSPIL
(JAPANESE —) KOTO
(JEW'S —) TRUMP
(PERSIAN —) SANG
(TRIANGULAR —) TRIGON TRIGONON
HARPOON IRON FIZGIG GRAINS
FISHGIG PARPAGO STRIKER
HARPAGON
HARPOONED FAST
HARPOONER STRIKER
HARP SEAL HARP BEATER SADDLER
HARPSICHORD SPINET CEMBALO
CLAVIER CLAVECIN HASPICOL
HARPY HAG AELLO CELAENO
OCYPETE PODARGE
HARQUEBUS HAGBUT CALIVER
HACKBUT ARQUEBUS
HARQUEBUSIER CARABIN
HARRIER HAWK KAHU FALLER
MILLER PUTTOCK HARROWER
HARROW COG CHIP DISC DISK DRAG
HARO TINE BRAKE BREAK HERSE
DREDGE DRUDGE FALLOW LADDER
SPADER CUTAWAY LACERATE
OXHARROW
HARROWED HAGGARD
HARROWING TINE TINING TEARING
HARRY HAG BRACE CHIVEY CHIVVY
FERRET HARASS CRUCIFY
HARSH ILL ACID BULL DOUR FOUL
HARD HASH HASK IRON RUDE SOUR
ACERB ACRID ASPER BRUTE CRONK
CRUDE GRILL GRUFF HEAVY HUSKY
RASPY ROUND RUVID SHARP SNELL
STARK STERN STIFF STOUR STOUT
BRUTAL COARSE FLINTY GRAVEL
GRISLY HOARSE RAGGED RASPED
RUGGED SEVERE SHREWD STURDY
SULLEN TETRIC UNKIND UNRIDE
AUSTERE RASPING RAUCOUS
SQUAWKY ACERBATE ASPERATE
ASPEROUS CATONIAN CLASHING
DRACONIC GRAVELLY GRINDING
GUTTURAL JANGLING OBDURATE
RIGOROUS SCABROUS SCRANNEL
STRIDENT STROUNGE STUBBORN
TETRICAL UNGENTLE UNKINDLY

(— OF VOICE) STEER
HARSHLY HARD HARSH SHORTLY
HARSHNESS WOLF RIGOR DURESS
CATOISM CRUDITY CRUELTY
DUREZZA ACERBITY ASPERITY
FELLNESS HARDNESS HASKNESS
SEVERITY
HART SPADE VENISON
HARTEBEEST ASSE TORA TORI
BUBAL CAAMA KAAMA KONZE
LECAMA BUBALIS CONGONI
KONGONI
HART'S-TONGUE LONGLEAF
HARUSPEX ARUSPEX ARUSPICE
EXTISPEX
HARVEST IN WIN CROP HEAP RABI
REAP SLED SNAP FOISON GATHER
HAIRST RUBBEE COMBINE GRABBLE
INGATHER SHEARING
HARVEST FISH WHITING MOONFISH
STARFISH
HARVEST HOME KIRN MELL
HOCKEY HORKEY
HARVESTING SLEDDING
HARVESTMAN CARTER CARTARE
HAS S AS HATH
(— NOT) NAS AINT
HAS-BEEN WUZZER
HASH RAPE MINCE HACHIS
HASHISH HEMP ASSIS
HASID ASSIDEAN
HASKALAH (FOLLOWER OF —)
MASKIL
HASP COP HAPS COPSE SPRENT
HASSAR DORAD
HASSOCK TUT BOSS PESS TOIT
TRUSH BUFFET TUFFET
HASTE HIE POST RACE RAGE RAPE
CHASE FEVER HASTY HURRY SPEED
BUSTLE FLURRY SWIVET DISPATCH
RAPIDITY STROTHER
(HEADLONG —) SPURN
(IN —) HOTFOOT
(IN GREAT —) AMAIN
HASTEN HIE RAP RUN BUSK DUST
FIRK PELL PLAT POST RACE RAPE
RUSH SPUR URGE CATCH CHASE
DRIVE FLEET HASTE HURRY PRESS
PREST SLATE SPEED STEER EXPEDE
SCURRY STREAK SWITHE ADVANCE
FORWARD HACKNEY HOTFOOT
PREVENT QUICKEN SLITHER
SWIFTEN WITHHIE DISPATCH
EXPEDITE
(— AWAY) FLEE SHERRY SQUIRR
HASTILY HOTLY RAPELY RASHLY
FOOTHOT HOTFOOT HYINGLY
HEADLONG
HASTY FAST RAPE RASH FLEET
QUICK FLYING RAPELY CURSORY
HOTHEAD HURRIED TEARING
HASTEFUL HEADLONG SUBITANE
(TACTLESSLY —) BRASH
HAT DIP FEZ LID NAB ATTE BAKU
COIF DISC DISK FELT FLAT HIVE
HOOD KNAB MOAB SLOP TILE TOPI
BEANY BENJY BENNY BERET BOXER
CADDI CORDY DERBY DICER GIBUS
JERRY KELLY MILAN MITER MITRE

SHELL TARAI TOPEE TOQUE TRUSH
ABACOT BEANIE BEAVER BOATER
BOWLER BRETON BUMPER CASQUE
CLAQUE CLOCHE COCKUP COIFFE
FEDORA HELMET PANAMA PILEUS
RAFFIA SAILOR SHOVEL SLOUCH
TOPPER TURBAN VIGONE BANDEAU
BANGKOK BRIMMER BYCOKET
CATSKIN CAUBEEN CHAPEAU
FANTAIL HATTING HATTOCK
HOMBURG LEGHORN PETASOS
PILLBOX PLATEAU PLATTER
SALACOT SCRAPER SHALLOW
SKIMMER SMASHER BONGRACE
CAPELINE GOSSAMER HEADGEAR
JIPIJAPA MONTABYN MUSHROOM
NABCHEAT RAMILIES REHOBOAM
ROUNDLET SOMBRERO
(— BLOCKER) ROPER
(3-CORNERED —) TRICORN
(BEAVER —) CASTOR
(CLERGYMAN'S —) SHOVEL
(COCKED —) BICORNE RAMILIE
SCRAPER
(COWBOY —) STETSON
(FABRIC —) TOQUE
(FELT —) DERBY JERRY TARAI
TERAI ALPINE BOWLER TRILBY
(HIGH —) KYL TILE TOPPER
(IRON —) GOSSAN GOZZAN
(MILITARY —) BUSBY BEARSKIN
(OILSKIN —) SQUAM
(OPERA —) GIBUS CLAQUE
(PITH —) TOPI TOPEE
(SILK —) KYL BEAVER SHINER
CATSKIN
(STIFF —) TILE DERBY KELLY
BOATER BOWLER SAILOR
(STOVEPIPE —) CAROLINE
(STRAW —) BAKU FLAT HOOD KADY
KATY BENJY BENNY CADDY STRAW
BOATER PANAMA LEGHORN
(TOP —) PLUG TOPPER
(UNBLOCKED —) CONE
(WIDE-BRIMMED —) FLAT BENJY
TARAI SUNDOWN
HATBAND BAND WEED WEEPER
HAT BRIM LEAF TARFE TURNUP
HATCH HECK BROOD CLECK CLOCK
COVEY GUICHET UNSHELL
DISCLOSE INCUBATE
HATCHERY CHICKERY
HATCHET MOGO HACHE GWEEON
THIXIE FRANCISC TOMAHAWK
HATCHING CLETCH BREEDING
ECLISION
HATCHWAY HATCH SCUTTLE
HATE FIRE TEEN ABHOR SPITE
DETEST HATRED LOATHE UNLOVE
DESPISE
HATEFUL FOUL LOTH BLACK CURST
DIRTY HATEL LOATH CURSED
ODIOUS HEINOUS HIDEOUS
FLAGRANT
HATER ULYSSES
HATH MOOLUM
HAT MONEY TAMPANG
HATRED DOSA ENVY HATE HELL

ONDE HAINE ODIUM SPITE ENMITY
RANCOR AVERSION
(— OF CHILDREN) MISOPEDIA
(— OF MARRIAGE) MISOGAMY
(— OF MEN) MISANDRY
(— OF NEW IDEAS) MISCAINEA
(— OF WOMEN) MISOGENY
HATTER GADGER HURRER
HAUBERK BYRNIE
HAUGHTILY BIGLY
HAUGHTINESS AIR PRIDE HEIGHT
MORGUE ORGUIL HAUTEUR
STOMACH HAUTESSE
HAUGHTY DAIN HIGH RANK STAY
DIGNE DORTY HUFFY LOFTY LUSTY
POTTY PROUD STOUT SURLY TAUNT
FEISTY FIERCE HAUGHT QUAINT
DISTANT HAUTAIN HONTISH
PAUGHTY STATELY SUBLIME
ARROGANT CAVALIER DEIGNOUS
FASTUOUS GLORIOUS IMPERIAL
INSOLENT ORGULOUS PRIDEFUL
SCORNFUL SNIFFISH SUPERIOR
TOPLOFTY
HAUL KEP LUG RUG TEW TOW TUG
DRAG DRAW DRAY HALE HURL
JUNK PULL SKID TAKE TOTE TRAM
BOUSE DRAVE HEAVE LIGHT ROUSE
SNAKE TRACT TRAVOY DRAUGHT
SCHLEPP CORDELLE HANDBANK
(— AFT) TALLY
(— DOWN) STRIKE
(— IN) GATHER
(— LOGS) TODE SLOOP SWAMP
SIWASH HANDBANK
(— OF FISH) TACK DRAVE
(— OF NET) LIFT
(— SAIL) BUNT CLEW CLUE
(— SHIP) SPRING
(— TO DECK) BOARD
(— UP AND FASTEN) TRICE
(— WITH TACKLE) BOUSE
HAULAGE DOOK
HAULAGEWAY GANGWAY
HAULING HALE CARTAGE
HAUNCH HIP HOOK HUCK HANCE
HUCKLE
(PL.) GRUG HUNKERS
HAUNT DEN HANT HOME HOWF KEEP
NEST WALK GHOST HOWFF SPOOK
STALK INFEST OBSESS OUTLAY
REPAIR PURLIEU FREQUENT
PRACTICE
(— OF ANIMALS) LIE HOME
(FAMILIAR —) SLAIT
HAUNTED SPOOKY
HAUNTING SPOOKY BESETTING
HAUSTELLATE GLOSSATE
HAUSTORIUM SINK SINKER SUCKER
HAUTBOY OBOE WAIT
HAUTEUR HEIGHT
HAVE A AN OF OWN HOLD BOAST
ENJOY OUGHT WIELD POSSESS
HAVEN HOPE PIER PORT HITHE
HARBOR HAVENET
HAVOC HOB HELL WASTE RAVAGE
HAW HOI HECK SLOE WIND WYND
BOOTS PEGGLE ALISIER

HAWAII

BAY: POHUE HALAWA KIHOLO
MAMALA KAMOHIO KANEOHE
WAIAGUA KAWAIHAE MAUNALUA
BEACH: WAIKIKI
CAPITAL: HONOLULU
CHANNEL: AUA KAIWI KALOHI
PAILOLO
COUNTY: MAUI KAUAI HAWAII
HONOLULU
CRATER: KILAUEA
DESERT: KAU
DISTRICT: KONA PUNA
FISH: ULUA AKULE MOANO
HARBOR: PEARL
HEAD: DIAMOND
ISLAND: MAUI OAHU KAUAI KAULA
LANAI NIIHAU MOLOKAI
MOUNTAIN: KAALA KOHALA
KAMAKOU MAUNAKEA
LANAIHALE
MOUNTAIN RANGE: KOHALA
KOOLAU WAIANAE
NATIVE: KANAKA
STATE BIRD: GOOSE *NeNe*
STATE FLOWER: HIBISCUS
STATE NICKNAME: ALOHA
STATE TREE: CANDLENUT
TOWN: EWA AIEA HANA HILO LAIE
PAIA KAPAA LIHUE MAILI KAILUA
KEKAHA KAHULUI KANEOHE
WAHIAWA WAIANAE WAILUKU
HONOLULU
TREE: KOA NAIO WILIWILI
VALLEY: MANOA
VOLCANO: MAUNALOA

HAWAIIAN KANAKA KAMAAINA
HAWFINCH KATE GROSBEAK
HAWK IO EYAS KITE ALLAN BATER
BUTEO CADGE EYESS HOICK HOUGH
REACH RIVER STOOP BAWREL
FALCON FOOTER HIGGLE MERLIN
MUSKET OSPREY PALLET PEDDLE
RAMAGE RAPTOR RIFLER SHIKRA
VERMIN BUZZARD GOSHAWK
HAGGARD HARRIER HERONER
LENTNER SWOOPER BRANCHER
CARACARA HARROWER LENTINER
PASSAGER ROUGHLEG SPARHAWK
TALENTER TARTARET
(— FIGHT) CRAB
(CROP OF —) GORGE
(FEMALE —) FORMAL FORMEL
(MALE —) JACK TASSEL TERCEL
(YOUNG —) EYAS NIAS BRANCHER
HAWKER CRIER CRYER BADGER
CADGER COSTER DUFFER JOWTER
PEDDER PETHER CAMELOT
CHAPMAN HIGGLER MERCURY
PEDDLER CRATEMAN GLASSMAN
HUCKSTER
HAWKEYE STATE IOWA
HAWKING FALCONRY
HAWK PARROT NIA
HAWKWEED DINDLE BUGLOSS
FIREWEED
HAWSE BAG JACKASS

HAWSER FAST WARP HEADLINE
HAWTHORN HAW MAY QUICK
THORN AIGLET MAYBUSH
COCKSPUR MAYBLOOM MAYTHORN
QUICKSET
(FRUIT OF —) HAZEL PEGGLE
HAY HEI RIP MATH RAKH RISP
FETTLE STOVER WINDLIN
SWEEPAGE
(— CUT FINE) CHAFF
(— PUT IN BARN) END
(BUNDLE OF —) TRUSS
(PILE OF —) TUMBLE
(ROW OF —) WINDROW
(SECOND-GROWTH —) EDDISH
(SMALL LOAD OF —) HURRY
(SMALL PIECE OF —) TATE
HAYCOCK MOW COIL HOVEL QUILE
SHOCK DOODLE HIPPLE LAPCOCK
HAYSHOCK
HAYFIELD PARK RAKH MOWING
HAYFORK PIKE PICKEL
HAYLOFT LOFT TALLET SCAFFOLD
HAYMAKER PICKMAN
HAYMOW GOAF HAYLOFT OVERDEN
OVERHEAD
HAYRACK HECK HAYRIG THRIPPLE
HAYSTACK COB PIKE RICK HOVEL
HAYRICK STACKAGE
HAYSUCK EYSOGE
HAY SWEEP BUCK
HAYWARD MEADSMAN
HAZAN CANTOR CHAZZAN
HAZARD DIE LAY LOT JUMP PAWN
RISK WAGE JENNY LOSER PERIL
CHANCE DANGER BALANCE IMPERIL
VENTURE ENDANGER JEOPARDY
HAZARDOUS RISKY CHANCY
QUEASY RISQUE UNSAFE UNSURE
PERILOUS
HAZARDOUSLY CHANCILY
HAZE FOG URE FILM GLIN MIST REEK
SMOG TRUB DEVIL GAUZE HAZLE
SMEETH
HAZEL AGLET AIGLET COBNUT
MUFFIN FILBERT HAZELNUT
NOISETTE
(— FOR THATCHING) SPRAYS
HAZEL HOE PULASKI
HAZELNUT NIT HAZEL FILBERT
HAZEL TREE AVELLANO
HAZILY DIMLY
HAZINESS HAZE GRAYOUT
HAZY DIM FOGGY MISTY SMOKY
THICK VAGUE CLOUDY DREAMY
OBSCURE SMUISTY NEBULOUS
HE A E HI HO HEH HEY HIM HYE SHE
ILLE THON CESTUI
(— DIED) OB
(— GAVE AND DEDICATED) DDD
(— MADE) F FEC
(— PAINTED IT) PNXT
(— READS) LEG
(— WAS NOT FOUND) NEI
HEAD BIT BUT COP DON FAT MIR
NAB NOB PEN POW TOP BEAN BOSS
CAPE COCO CONK COSP CROP
DATU DEAN DOME HELM JOLE JOWL
KAID KNOB LEAD MASK NOLL PASH

PATE POLL RAIS TURN YEAD ALDER
ATTIC BLADE BLOCK CHIEF CHUMP
CROWN DATTO MAZER ONION RISER
SCALP SHODE SKULL START TIBBY
TROPE BELFRY BLANCH CABEZA
CENTER CHAULE COBBRA COCKER
DAROGA EXARCH GARRET GATHER
HEADER KAISER MAHANT MAZARD
NAPPER NODDLE PALLET RUBRIC
SCONCE CAPITAL CAPTAIN
COCONUT COSTARD COSTREL
COXCOMB CRUMPET CUPHEAD
GENARCH HEADING HEGUMEN
NUCLEUS PRELATE TOPKNOT
CALABASH CEPHALON DECURION
DIRECTOR DUFFADAR FOUNTAIN
HEADLINE INITIATE PHYLARCH
POINTING TOPPIECE
(— IN PARTICULAR DIRECTION)
STEM
(— OF 10 MONKS) DEAN
(— OF ABBEY) ABBOT
(— OF ALEMBIC) MITER MITRE
(— OF BEAR, WOLF OR BOAR) HURE
(— OF CABBAGE) LOAF
(— OF CEREAL) EAR
(— OF CHAIR) MAKER
(— OF CLOVER) COB SUCKER
(— OF COMET) COMA
(— OF CONVENT) ABBESS
SUPERIOR
(— OF DRILL BRACE) CUSHION
(— OF FAMILY) ALDER GOODMAN
(— OF FISH) JOWL
(— OF GANG) TINDAL
(— OF GOVERNMENT) MUKHTAR
(— OF GRAIN) ICKER
(— OF HAIR) SUIT CRINE FLEECE
(— OF HARPOON) BOMB
(— OF HERRING) COB
(— OF JEWISH ACADEMY) GAON
(— OF LANCE) MORNE MOURNE
(— OF LOOM) JACQUARD
(— OF MONASTERY) HEGUMEN
(— OF MUSICAL INSTRUMENT)
SCROLL
(— OF NUNNERY) DAME
(— OF ORDER) MURSHID
(— OF RING) CHATON
(— OF RIVET) BULLHEAD FLATHEAD
SNAPHEAD
(— OF STATE) PRINCEPS
(— OF TAPEWORM) SCOLEX
(— OF TREE) COMA
(— ON) SQUARE
(— PREMATURELY) BUTTON
(— USED AS TARGET) SARACEN
(BAKED SHEEP'S —) JAMES JEMMY
(BALD —) PILGARLIC
(BARBED —) FLUKE
(DRAGON'S —) RAHU
(FLOWER —) DAISY ARNICA BUTTON
PINBALL
(FLOWER —S) CURD ANTHEMIS
(NAIL —) ROSEHEAD
(POPPY —) POST
(PRINTED —) BOXHEAD
(SEED — OF FLAX) HOPPE

(SHRUNKEN —) TSANTSA
(PL.) GEONIM
HEADACHE HEAD SODA BUSTHEAD
HEADWARK MIGRAINE
HEADBAND MITER MITRE VITTA
CARCAN DIADEM TAENIA CIRCLET
GARLAND CARCANET FOOTBAND
STEPHANE
HEADBOROUGH VERGES
HEADCAP SETHEAD
HEADDRESS FLY TOP TOY APEX
COIF FRET HEAD HORN PARE POUF
TETE TIRE TOUR AEGIS AMPYX
CROWN GABLE LAUTU PASTE
POLOS PSHEM SHAKO TIARA
TOWER VITTA ALMUCE ATTIRE
ATTOUR BONNET CASQUE CORNET
FAILLE HENNIN KENNEL KULLAH
MOBCAP PINNER TIRING TUINGA
BANDORE COMMODE FLANDAN
MORTIER PSCHENT STEEPLE
TABLITA THERESE TRESSON
TUTULUS BILIMENT BINNOGUE
BYCOCKET CAPRIOLE COIFFURE
HEADGEAR HEADTIRE KAFFIYEH
MASKETTE STEPHANE TRESSURE
(— OF DOGES) TOQUE
(— WITH LONG LAPPET) PINNER
(HIGH —) TOWER STEEPLE
(WIDOW'S —) BANDORE
HEADED KNOTTED
(— OUT) RIZZOMED
HEADER BINDER NOBBER SADDLE
KNOBBER HEADSMAN STRETMAN
HEADFAST HEADROPE
HEADFIRST HEADLONG
HEADFOREMOST TOPSAIL
HEADFRAME POPPET GALLOWS
HEADGEAR (ALSO SEE HEADDRESS)
HIVE PASTE BONNET BRIDLE
HEADWEAR
HEADHUNTER LAKHER TAIYAL
ATAIYAL QUIANGAN
HEADING END HEAD STOW PILOT
TROPE WICKET CAPTION DIPHEAD
HEADILY STENTON WITCHET
FOREHAND STENTING
HEADLAND KOP PEN RAS BILL HEAD
MULL NAZE NESS NOOK PEAK
SCAW THRUM FORELAND
HEADLINE HEAD LABEL BANNER
CAPTION DROPLINE SCREAMER
STREAMER
HEADLONG FULL RANK HASTY
PRONE STEEP SUDDEN RAMSTAM
TANTIVY GADARENE HEADLING
RECKLESS
HEADMAN JARL CHIEF DATTO MALIK
PATEL POMBO VIDAN ATAMAN
CABEZA HETMAN INDUNA LOWDAH
LULUAI POTAIL TOPMAN KOMARCH
ALDERMAN CABOCEER CAPITANO
HEADSMAN KONOHIKI MALGUZAR
MOKADDAM PENGHULU PRINCEPS
STAROSTA TENIENTE
HEADMASTER HEAD REGENT
HEADMOST FOREMOST
HEADNOTE SYLLABUS
HEADPIECE CAP POT BASKET

CASQUE HELMET PALLET TESTER TREMOR CASQUET CHAMFRON TESTIERE

HEADPIN KINGPIN

HEADQUARTERS DEPOT YAMEN AGENCY FONDACO EXCHANGE BATTALION

HEADROPE BALK BAULK HEADLINE

HEADSET PHONES

HEADSHIP CHIEFTY

(SPIRITUAL —) KHALIFAT

HEADSPACE OUTAGE

HEADSTALL HALTER BRADOON BRIDOON JAQUIMA

HEADSTOCK POPPET

HEADSTRONG RASH COBBY RACKLE STOCKY UNRULY HOTSPUR RAMSTAM VIOLENT WAYWARD

HEADWAITER CAPTAIN

HEADWAY WAY DENT SEAWAY WAYGATE HEADROOM

HEADWORD ENTRY

HEADY BOLD NAPPY HUFFCAP

HEAL CURE HALE MEND SAIN AMEND COVER LEECH SALVE SOUND WHOLE PHYSIC RECURE SUPPLE TEMPER WARISH CLEANSE GUARISH RECOVER REDRESS RESTORE MEDICATE

(— OVER) INCARN

HEALD CAMB DUPE HAVEL

HEALER CURER ALTHEA SHAMAN POWWOWER

HEALING IATRIC POWWOW BALSAMIC CURATION IATRICAL SANATION

HEALTH SAP HAIL HEAL SONS QUART SALEW LIKING PLEDGE SALUTE SANITY EUCRASY SLAINTE EUCRASIA TONICITY VALETUDE

(GOOD —) PLIGHT VERDURE

(ILL —) SICKNESS

(NORMAL —) USUAL

HEALTHFUL HEALTHY HYGIENIC SALUTARY SANATORY SANITARY

HEALTHY FIT FIER FIRM HALE IRON SAFE SANE TIDY WELL BONNY HODDY QUART SOUND STOUT VALID ENTIRE HEARTY ROBUST BOUNCING LAUDABLE SALUTARY SANITARY VEGETOUS VIGOROUS

HEAP COP CUB HOT MOW PIE SOW TON BALE BING BULK DECK DESS HILL HOTT LEET PILE POKE POOK REEK RUCK SESS TASS TUMP AMASS CLAMP CLUMP COUCH CROWD SHOCK STACK WOPSE BURROW HIPPLE HOTTER ISLAND MEILER OODLES QUARRY RICKLE RUCKLE SCRAPE SORITE TOORIE BOUROCK CUMULUS ENDORSE HAYCOCK HAYRICK HURROCK TOOROCK TUMMELS WINDROW BASURALE

(— HAY) UNCOCK

(— OF DEAD BODIES) CARNAGE

(— OF GAME) QUARRY

(— OF ORE) PANEL

(— OF PRODUCE) BURY CLAMP

(— OF REFUSE) BURROW BASURAL

(— OF RUBBISH) GAGING

(— OF SILVER ORE) TORTA

(— OF STONES) AHU MAN CAIRN SCRAE SCREE HURROCK MONTJOY

(— OF VEGETABLES) HOG

(— REPROACHES) KICK

(— TOGETHER) AGGEST HOWDER LUMBER CUMULATE

(— UP) HILL SACK AGGEST ACERVATE AGGERATE OVERHEAP

(COMBUSTIBLE —) PYRE

(MANURE —) HOTT MIXEN

(PROMISCUOUS —) RAFF

HEAR EAR LIST OYES OYEZ LEARN LITHE HARKEN LISTEN HEARKEN

(— DIRECTLY) IMPINGE

HEARD AUDIBLE

(EASILY —) CLEAR

HEARER AUDIENT AUDITOR

HEARING EAR LIST OYER AUDIT SOUND ASSIZE AUDIENCE AUDITION

HEARKEN HARK HEAR HEED LIST TEND LITHE ATTEND HARKEN INTEND

HEARSAY REPORT ACCOUNT

HEARSE HACK CATAFALCO

HEART AB COR CORE GIST HATI RAAN SOUL YOLK BOSOM BOWEL CHEER QUICK BREAST CENTER CENTRE DEPTHS HASLET MIDDLE TICKER VISCUS COURAGE EMOTION ESSENCE FEELING

(— OF DIXIE) ALABAMA

(DEAR —) DILIS

HEARTACHE SORROW

HEARTBEAT STROKE

HEARTBURN PYROSIS

HEART CHERRY GASKINS

HEARTEN BIELD CHEER HEART SPIRIT EMBOLDEN INSPIRIT

HEARTFELT DEAR DEEP REAL TRUE INFELT INWARD CORDIAL GENUINE SINCERE

HEARTH EARD SOLE TEST ASTRE CUPEL EARTH FOCUS FOGON FOYER SMOKE CHIMNEY

(— GODDESS) VESTA

HEARTILY INLY AGOOD DEARLY FREELY WARMLY SHEERLY DINGDONG INWARDLY STRONGLY

HEARTINESS GOODWILL

HEARTTHROB DUNT

HEARTWOOD HEART SAPAN SPINE GUAYAB BUBINGA DURAMEN TRUEWOOD

HEARTY REAL WARM COBBY FRECK HEAVY STOUT DEVOUT ENTIRE ROBUST STANCH BOBBISH CORDIAL EARNEST HEALTHY RAFFING SINCERE HEARTFUL VIGOROUS

HEAT HET HOT RUT SUN TAP BOIL FIRE GLOW SALT WARM ARDOR BROIL CALOR CAUMA CHAFE FEVER PRIDE PROUD STECH TEPOR TRIAL ACHAFE ANNEAL DEGREE DIGEST FERVOR HEATEN IGNITE SCORCH SEASON SPARGE WARMTH CALCINE CALORIC ENCHAFE FERMENT

FLUSTER INCENSE INFERNO PASSION SWELTER UPERIZE CALIDITY

(— GENTLY) SOAK

(— OF BATTLE) PRESS

(— SCRAP IRON) BUSHEL

(— SWEETEN, AND SPICE) MULL

(— TOBACCO) SAP

(SCORCHING —) EWDER

HEATED WARM FIERCE STEAMY

HEATER FIRE COCKLE SMOKER CHAFFER CHOFFER LATROBE

HEATH BENT YETH BESOM BRIAR BRIER ERICA ERICAD COMMONS HEATHER

HEATHEN AKKUM PAGAN ETHNIC GENTILE PROFANE SARACEN GENTILIC

HEATHENISM ODINISM OTHINISM PAGANISM

HEATHER BENT GRIG LING BROOM ERICA HEATH HADDER

HEATHERY LINGY

HEATH PEA CARMELE

HEATING BAKEOUT BURNING

HEATLESS ATHERMIC

HEAVE GAG BUNG HEFT HOVE KECK LIFE QUAP FETCH HOIST SCEND SURGE BUCKLE KECKLE POPPLE ESTUATE

HEAVEN SKY HIGH ABOVE BLISS DYAUS ETHER GLORY CANAAN HIMMEL SVARGE SWARGA URANUS WELKIN KINGDOM OLYMPUS DEVALOKA EMPYREAL EMPYREAN PARADISE SVARLOKA

(12TH PART OF —) HOUSE

(PL.) ARCH LIFT LANGI HEIGHT REGION SPHERE ELEMENT TENGERE EMPYREAN KAMALOKA

HEAVENLY ABOVE DIVINE ANGELIC URANIAN ETHEREAL OLYMPIAN

HEAVENWARD ZIONWARD

HEAVER COALY DANNER HEFTER

HEAVILY SOSS CLOIT CLYTE HEAVY SADLY SOUSE SWACK

HEAVINESS HEFT GLOOM POISE WEIGHT GRAVITY

HEAVY FAT HOT SAD CLIT DEEP DULL HARD BEEFY BURLY DENSE DOWFF DUNCH GRAVE GREAT GROSS HEFTY HOGGY STIFF THARF THERF WROTH CHARGE CLUMSY DOUGHY DRAGGY HEARTY LEADEN LIVERY LOGGER SODDEN STODGY STRONG STUPID INSIPID LABORED LIVERED LUMPING MASSIVE ONEROUS WEIGHTY CUMBROUS GRIEVOUS PERSANTE PREGNANT THUMPING

HEAVY-FOOTED SOGGY LEADEN INFICETE

HEBDOMADARY WEEKLY

HEBE (FATHER OF —) JUPITER

(HUSBAND OF —) HERCULES

(MOTHER OF —) JUNO

HEBREW RABBINIC

HECATE TRIVIA

(FATHER OF —) PERSES

(MOTHER OF —) ASTERIA
HECKLE BAIT GIBE HACK BADGER
HARASS HECTOR HATCHEL
HECTIC ETIK SEPTIC HECTIVE
FEVERISH FRENETIC FRENZIED
HECTOLITER VAT
(5.82 —S) LEAGUER
HECTOR BAIT HUFF BULLY HARRY
WORRY HARASS HECKLE BLUSTER
BRAVADO BROWBEAT
(FATHER OF —) PRIAM
(MOTHER OF —) HECUBA
(WIFE OF —) ANDROMACHE
HECUBA (DAUGHTER OF —)
POLYXENA
(FATHER OF —) DYMAS CISSEUS
(SON OF —) PARIS HECTOR
POLYDORUS
HEDDLE CAMB DOUP HAVEL HEALD
(PL.) CAAM
HEDGE BAR HAW HAY HYE OXER
SAVE BEARD EDDER FENCE FRITH
FUDGE HOVER MOUND QUICK
COPPER FRIGHT RADDLE ENCLOSE
QUICKSET RUFFMANS SEPIMENT
SURROUND THICKSET
HEDGE BINDWEED CREEPER
HELLWEED WOODBINE
HEDGEHOG ORCHEN URCHIN
ECHINUS ERICIUS YLESPIL
HEDGEPIG HERISSON
HEDGE LAUREL TARATA
HEDGE MUSTARD BANKWEED
FLUXWEED
HEDGE NETTLE STACHYS
HEDGE PARSLEY HOGWEED
HEDGE-PRIEST PATRICO
HEDGE SPARROW DICKY DONEY
DICKEY EYSOGE PHILIP CHANTER
DUNNOCK HAYSUCK PINNOCK
TITLING ACCENTOR
HEDGEWOOD LAYER
HEED CARK COME CURE GAUM HEAR
KEEP LOOK MIND NOTE RECK TEND
TENT VISE WARE YEME AWAIT
TASTE VALUE ATTEND INTENT
NOTICE REGARD REMARK REWARD
CAUTION OBSERVE RESPECT
SUSPECT THOUGHT
HEEDFUL WARE ATTENT DILIGENT
HEEDLESS RASH BLIND DIZZY GIDDY
BLITHE REMISS UNWARY LANGUID
UNHEEDY CARELESS LISTLESS
MINDLESS RECKLESS WISTLESS
HEEDLESSLY BLIND HEADLONG
HEEL TIP BUTT CALX FROG HIELD
SPIKE TALON DOTTLE INCLINE
BOOTHEEL
(— IN) SHOUGH
(— OF GATE) HARR
(— OF HORSESHOE) SPONGE
(— OF SWORD BLADE) TALON
RICASSO
(— OVER) SEEL TILT CAREEN
HEEL BEVEL RAND
HEEL PLATE SHOD CLEAT
HEFT WEIGHT
HEFTY HEAVY
HEIFER IO QUI QUEE QUEY QUOY

BULLER STOCKER
(— IN 2ND YEAR) STIRK
(YEARLING —) BURLING
HEIGH-HO HECH
HEIGHT SUM ACME ALTO APEX FELL
HIGH LOFT MOTE PINK TUNE CREST
HICHT STATE ALTURE INCHES
SUMMIT CEILING COMMAND
HEIGHTH STATURE SUPREME
ALTITUDE EMINENCE HAUTESSE
SIDENESS VERTICAL ACROPOLIS
(— OF FASHION) GO
(— OF PROSPERITY) GLORY
(— OF ROOM) STUD STUDDING
(— OF SAIL) HOIST
(GREATEST —) SUMMIT ZENITH
(ROCKY —) KNOT
HEIGHTEN ENDOW EXALT FORCE
RAISE ACCENT BOLSTER ENHANCE
SUBLIME
(— FLAVOR) PETUNE
HEINOUS SWART CRYING WICKED
SCARLET FLAGRANT GRIEVOUS
HEIR SCION SPRIG COHEIR HERITOR
APPARENT PARCENER
(— APPARENT) ATHELING ETHELING
(FEMALE —) DISTAFF
HEIRESS BEGUM PORTIA FORTUNE
HERITRIX
HEIRLOOM (PL.) CIMELIA
HELENUS (FATHER OF —) PRIAM
(MOTHER OF —) HECUBA
(SON OF —) CESTRINUS
(WIFE OF —) ANDROMACHE
HELIANTHEMUM SUNROSE
HELICAL SPIRAL
HELICOPTER COPTER CHOPPER
WINDMILL
HELIOPOLIS ON
HELIOS HYPERION PHAETHON
(FATHER OF —) HYPERION
(MOTHER OF —) THEIA
HELIOSIS SUNBURN
HELIOTROPE HELIO BENNET
SETWALL GIRASOLE TURNSOLE
HELIPORT SKYPORT
HELIX COIL SPIRAL
HELIXIN HEDERIN
HELL PIT POT HECK PAIN ABYSS
AVICI BLAZE DEUCE HADES SHEOL
BLAZES NARAKA TARTAR TOPHET
TUNKET ABADDON GEHENNA
HELLBOX INFERNO TARTARUS
BARATHRUM
HELLBENDER TWEEG
HELLE (FATHER OF —) ATHAMAS
(MOTHER OF —) NEPHELE
(SISTER OF —) PHRIXUS
HELLEBORE POKE BUGBANE
ITCHWEED LINGWORT LUNGWORT
NOSEWORT POKEROOT VERATRUM
EARTHGALL
HELLEN (FATHER OF —) DEUCALION
(MOTHER OF —) PYRRHA
(SON OF —) DORUS AEOLUS
XUTHUS
(WIFE OF —) ORSEIS
HELLER HALER HALERZ
HELLERI SWORDTAIL

HELLGRAMMITE DOBSON SIALID
CLIPPER CRAWLER SPRAWLER
HELLISH HELLY SATANIC STYGIAN
DEVILISH INFERNAL TOPHETIC
HELLO HALLO HILLO HULLO HILLOA
HELM KEY STEER STERN TIMON
HELMET TIMBER STEERAGE
HELMET CAP POT CASK HELM HOOD
ARMET CREST GALEA MAZER
MOUND BARBEL BEAVER CASQUE
CASTLE GALERA HEAUME MORION
PALLET SALADE SALLET TESTER
BASINET CASQUET GALERUM
GALERUS AVENTAIL BURGONET
HEADGEAR KNAPSCAP SCHAPSKA
SKULLCAP TARNHELM TESTIERE
(— PART) VENTAIL
(PITH —) TOPI TOPEE
HELMET-SHAPED GALEATE
HELMSMAN PILOT STEER GLAUCUS
TIMONEER
HELP AID BOT ABET BACK BOOT
CAST LIFT STOP AVAIL FAVOR
FRITH HEEZE RESET SPEED START
STEAD YELDE ASSIST HELPER
RELIEF REMEDY SECOND SUCCOR
UPTAKE BENEFIT BESTEAD CHEVISE
COMFORT FORWARD FURTHER
HELPING IMPROVE PRESIDY
PROMOTE REDRESS RELIEVE
SUPPORT SUSTAIN ADJUMENT
BEFRIEND SUFFRAGE
(— FORWARD) FRANK FURTHER
(— ON) ADVANCE
(— ONWARD) FORWARD
(— OUT) FIRK
(HIRED —) LABOR
HELPER AID CAD FOAL HELP MATE
PAGE ANSAR AIDANT BARBOY
COOKEE DIENER FLUNKY JUMPER
NIPPER TENTER WAITER ADJOINT
ADJUTOR ANCILLA CASHBOY
GALOPIN SUMPMAN SWAMPER
HELPMATE OFFSIDER SCULLION
TROUNCER
(— IN GLASSWORKS) SNAPPER
(BLACKSMITH'S —) STRIKER
(CHIMNEY SWEEP'S —) CHUMMY
(COOK'S —) SLUSHY
(COOPER'S —) TUBBIE
(HORSESHOER'S —) FLOORMAN
(PICKPOCKET'S —) BULKER
(YOUNG —) FOAL
HELPFUL GOOD AIDANT AIDFUL
HELPLY SECOND SPEEDY USEFUL
ADJUVANT HELPSOME OBLIGING
SINGULAR
HELPING HELP AIDANT PORTION
SERVING ADJUTORY ADJUVANT
HELPLESS NUMB SILLY ABJECT
UNABLE AIDLESS FORLORN
FECKLESS HAVELESS REDELESS
HELTER-SKELTER TAGRAG
PELLMELL
HELVE HELM SHAFT
HELVE HAMMER OLIVER
HEM HUM WLO FELL SLIP WELT
HEDGE SPLAY PURFLE TURNUP
HEMMING TURNING SURROUND

(— **AND HAW)** HAVER
(— **GLOVE)** WRIST
(— **IN FISH)** EBB
(— **IN)** BOX LAP BEBAY BESET
IMPALE BESIEGE COMPASS
ENCLOSE ENVIRON STRAITEN
SURROUND
(— **OF SAIL)** TABLING
(— **OF TROUSERS)** CUFF
HEMATITE ORE OLIGIST SANGUINE
HEMICRANIA MIGRAINE
HEMIEPES ENOPLION
HEMIMORPHITE CALAMINE
HEMIOLIC SESCUPLE
HEMISTICH SECTION
HEMLOCK BUNK CASH KELK
BENNET CICUTA COWBANE DEATHIN
SHINWOOD
HEMOPHILIAC BLEEDER
HEMORRHAGE STAXIS APOPLEXY
BLEEDING HEMOPTOE PETECHIA
HEMOSTATIC ERIGERON
HEMP IFE KEF KIF TOW BANG CARL
POOA RINE SUNN ABACA BHANG
DACHA DAGGA FIQUE GANJA HURDS
MURVA SABZI SISAL AMBARY
CABUYA FIMBLE LIAMBA NALITA
SINAWA AMYROOT CABULLA
GAGROOT NIYANDA PANGANE
PITEIRA SOSQUIL BIRDSEED
CANNABIS CHUCKING LOCOWEED
NECKWEED NEPENTHE
HEMP AGRIMONY EUPATORY
HEMPWEED
HEMPEN NOGGEN
HEMP NETTLE IRONWORT
HEMPWEED BONESET DUCKBLIND
HEN FOWL BIDDY CHUCK LAYER
BROODY MABYER PULLET HOVERER
PARTLET
(— **THAT HAS NOT LAID)** TOWDIE
(— **WITH CHICKENS)** CLUCK
(— **WITH SHORT LEGS)** GRIG
(**1-YEAR-OLD** —) YEAROCK
(**BROODY** —) SITTER
HENBANE HEBENON CHENILLE
HENCE AWAY ERGO HYNE THUS
AVAUNT HETHEN HEREOUT
HENCEFORTH YET HENCE
HENCHMAN FELLOW SATRAP
FOLLOWER
HEN COOP CAVY CAVIE
HENGEST (BROTHER OF —) HORSA
(**KINDOM FOUNDED BY** —) KENT
(**SON OF** —) AESC
HEN HARRIER FALLER KATABELLA
(**IMMATURE** —) RINGTAIL
(**MALE** —) MILLER
HENNA MENDY ALCANNA ALHENNA
CAMPHIRE
HENNIN STEEPLE
HENRY QUAD HAWKIN SECOHM
HEINRICH QUADRANT
HEP (NOT —) ICKY
HEPATICA AI TRINITY
HEPATITIS JAUNDICE
HEPHAESTUS LEMNIAN
(**FATHER OF** —) ZEUS
(**MOTHER OF** —) HERA
(**WIFE OF** —) CHARIS

HER A ARE SHE HARE HERS HURE
HERA JUNO
(**FATHER OF** —) KRONOS
(**HUSBAND OF** —) ZEUS
HERALD BODE USHER BEADLE
DECLARE FORERUN PREFACE
STENTOR BLAZONER PRECURSE
PROCLAIM ROTHESAY
HERALDIC FECIAL FETIAL
HERALDRY ARMORY
HERB ANU APE PIA RUE UDO WAD
ALOE ANET ANYU ARUM COUS DILL
HEMP IRID LEEK MINT MOLY POLY
RAPE SAGE SOLA WOAD WORT
YAMP YARB AWIWI BLITE BRUSH
CREAT CROUT DAGGA DAISY DRABA
GALAX GAURA GILIA GRASS HOSTA
LOASA LUFFA MEDIC MUNGO NANCY
SEDGE SOLAH STOCK SULLA THYME
ZIZIA ALLIUM ARALIA ARNICA
AXSEED BAGPOD BAMBAN BANANA
BLINKS BORAGE CANCER CATGUT
CATNIP CENIZO CICELY CISTUS
CLOVER COCASH COLEUS CONIUM
COWISH COWPEA ELODEA ENDIVE
ERYNGO FENNEL GALAXY GINGER
HARMEL HYSSOP KOCHIA KRIGIA
KRIGLA LOOFAH LOVAGE RAMTIL
RATTLE ROBERT SESAME SESELI
SHEVRI WASABI ABRONIA ALPINIA
ALTHAEA ALYSSUM AMORPHA
AMSONIA ANCHUSA ANEMONE
ANGELON ARACHIS BABIANA
BABROOT BARTSIA BIRDEYE
BLINKER BONESET BUGSEED
BUGWEED CHICORY CUDWEED
CULVERS DEWDROP DYEWEED
EPISCIA ERODIUM FREESIA FROGBIT
FUMMORY GERBERA GINSENG
GOITCHO GOSMORE GOUAREE
GUAYULE GUNNERA HARMALA
HEDEOMA HENBANE HERBLET
IRESINE ISOLOMA JONQUIL LABIATE
LEWISIA LINNAEA MARANTA
MIMULUS MUDWEED MUDWORT
MULLEIN MUSTARD NAILROD
NEMESIA NIEVETA PAVONIA PETUNIA
PINESAP PINWEED PUCHERA
ROSELLE SAFFLOR SALSIFY
SEEDBOX SKIRRET SOWBANE
SPIGNEL STACHYS ABELMUSK
ACANTHUS ACONITUM AGERATUM
ALOCASIA ALUMROOT AMBROSIA
AMMOBIUM ANGELICA ARGEMONE
ASPHODEL BEDSTRAW CALATHEA
CAPEWEED CARELESS CENTAURY
CHENILLE COLLOMIA COSTMARY
COWWHEAT CRASSULA CROMWELL
DANEWEED DEERWEED DROPWORT
ECHINOPS EGGPLANT EREMURUS
ERIGERON EUCHARIS FEVERFEW
FLEABANE FOWLFOOT GAYWINGS
GERARDIA GESNERAD GESNERIA
GHETCHOO GLOXINIA GOATROOT
GUZMANIA HAREBELL HEPATICA
HEUCHERA HIBISCUS HOLEWORT
HONEWORT HOROKAKA HUDSONIA
IRONWEED LICORICE LOCOWEED
MANDRAKE MANFREDA MANYROOT

MARJORAM MARTYNIA MURRNONG
PHACELIA PINKROOT PLUMBAGO
SACALINE SAINFOIN SALICORN
SAMPHIRE SANDBURR SCABIOUS
SHINLEAF SMALLAGE SNOWDROP
SOAPROOT SOAPWORT STAPELIA
SUNDROPS TETRIFOL TOCALOTE
WOODRUFF
(— **COUNTERACTING POISON)**
CANCER
(— **OTHER THAN GRASS)** FORB
(**AROMATIC** —) MINT ANISE CLARY
CATNIP CAAPEBA CHERVIL DITTANY
(**BIENNIAL** —) LEEK PARSLEY
ANGELICA
(**BULBOUS** —) LILY CANNA ALLIUM
CRINUM GARLIC NERINE SQUILL
BABIANA SHALLOT DOGTOOTH
SLANGKOP
(**FABULOUS** —) MOLY PANAX
PANACE
(**FLOATING** —) FROGBIT
(**FORAGE** —) FITCHES GOITCHO
(**POISONOUS** —) CONIUM HEMLOCK
(PL.) POTAGERIE
HERBAGE HAY BITE GRASS GRAZE
PICHI ADONIS SACATE ZACATE
GRAZING
HERB EVE IVA IVY
HERB GRACE RUE
HERBICIDE IPE
HERB IMPIOUS DOWNWEED
HOARWORT
HERB PARIS TRUE ONEBERRY
TRUELOVE
HERB ROBERT JENNY ROBIN
ROBERT
HERCULEAN HUGE
HERCULES ERCLES ALCIDES
HERSHEF OETAEUS OVILLUS
HERAKLES
(**BROTHER OF** —) IPHICLES
(**FATHER OF** —) JUPITER
(**MOTHER OF** —) ALCMENA
(**WIFE OF** —) HEBE MEGARA
DEIANIRA
HERCULES ALLHEAL OPOPANAX
HERCULES-CLUB ARALIA IVYWORT
RUEWORT SHOTBUSH
HERD BOW GAM MOB BAND CREW
GAME GANG HEAD RACE ROUT TAIL
TEAM TRIP DROVE FLOCK HEARD
TROOP CAVIYA CHOUSE HIRSEL
HUDDLE MANADA MEINIE REMUDA
SPREAD THRAVE CREAGHT
RANGALE SHEPHERD
(— **CATTLE)** TAIL WRANGLE
(— **OF CATTLE)** FLOTE
(— **OF COLTS)** RAG
(— **OF HORSES)** RACE HARAS
HARRAS
(— **OF SEALS)** PATCH
(— **OF WHALES)** GAM
(— **OF WILD SWINE)** SOUNDER
HERDBOY BOUCHAL
HERDER DROVER FEEDER HERDBOY
HERDSMAN AMOS SENN GAUCHO
HERDER LOOKER PASTOR HERDBOY
LLANERO THYRSIS VAQUERO

BEASTMAN DAMOETAS GARTHMAN
NEATHERD PASTORAL PASTURER
RANCHERO SWANHERD WRANGLER
HERE READY WHERE HEREAT HITHER
PRESENT
(— AND THERE) ABOUT ABROAD
AROUND PASSIM SPARSIM
HEREAFTER BEYOND
HEREDITAMENT LAND
HEREDITARY INBORN INNATE
KINDLY LINEAL
HEREIN WITHIN
HERESY KETZEREI MISBELIEF
HERETIC BUGGER KETZER ZINDIQ
LOLLARD PATARIN PROFANE
SECTARY JUDAIZER
HERETICAL HERETIC HETERODOX
MISCREANT
HERETO HITHER
HERETOFORE ERST BEFORE
ERENOW EREWHILE FORMERLY
HERITAGE HEIRDOM HEIRSHIP
HERMA MERCURY
HERMAPHRODITE MOPH SCRAT
HERMAPHRODITIC BISEXED
BISEXUAL
HERMAPHRODITISM GYNANDRY
HERMAPHRODITUS (FATHER OF —)
MERCURY
(MOTHER OF —) VENUS
HERMES MERCURY AGORAIOS
CYLLENIUS
(FATHER OF —) ZEUS
(MOTHER OF —) MAIA
HERMIONE (FATHER OF —)
MENELAUS
(HUSBAND OF —) PYRRHUS
(MOTHER OF —) HELEN
HERMIT ARME MUNI HANIF MINIM
ANCHOR SANTON SULLEN ASCETIC
EREMITE RECLUSE TAPASVI
ANCHORET MARABOUT SOLITARY
HERMITAGE ASHRAM ASHRAMA
RECLUSE
HERNIA BURST RAMEX BREACH
RUPTURE MEROCELE
HERO KIM RAB AJAX EGIL IDAS MAUI
NALA NATA OFFA RINK YIMA ADAPA
BERNE DEBON ETANA FAUST GHAZI
HODER HOTHR IRAYA KIPPS MARKO
ORSON TASSO TIMON VOTAN
EGMONT FIGARO GIDEON GOLIAS
HEROIC IASION IOLAUS MAUGIS
MINYAS OSSIAN PELHAM PENROD
RIENZI ROLAND RUSTAM SIGURD
TARZAN USHEEN VATHEK ALCESTE
BOGATYR DEMIGOD FAUSTUS
GLUSKAP INGOMAR JAMSHID
MACBETH MANRICO MARMION
MAZEPPA ORLANDO OTHELLO
PALADIN RAFFLES TANCRED
THALABA THESUES TROILUS
ULYSSES VOLPONE WERTHER
WIDSITH WIELAND ACADEMUS
ARGONAUT FANSHAWE FERUMBAS
FRITHJOF GAEDHEAL GILGAMES
LAMMIKIN MALAGIGI MORGANTE
OROONOKO PALMERIN PARSIFAL
PERICLES RASSELAS RODOMONT

SUPERMAN TRISTRAM WAVERLEY
(LOVER OF —) LEANDER
(TRIBAL —) JUDGE
HEROIC EPIC FELL GREAT NOBLE
EPICAL FEATLY EXTREME GALLANT
VALIANT FEARLESS HEROICAL
HOMERIAN INTREPID
HEROIN JUNK HORSE
HEROINE AIDA EMMA MIMI RUTH
JULIE MEDEA NORMA SEDNA THAIS
ESTHER FEDORA GUDRUN HELENA
JUDITH JULIET MARTHA MIGNON
PAMELA PHEDRE RAMONA ROMOLA
SALOME SILVIA TRILBY UNDINE
ERMINIA EVELINA GALATEA GINEVRA
GRAINNE HEROESS MONIMIA
SHIRLEY ZENOBIA ZULEIKA
ATALANTA ISABELLA MARGARET
PATIENCE POMPILIA ROSMUNDA
SOFRONIA
HEROISM VALOR BRAVERY
COURAGE
HERON QUA POKE SOCO CRAIG
CRANE EGRET FRANK HERNE
PADDY QUAWK YABOA AIGRET
KIALEE KOTUKU QUAKER SQUAWK
BITTERN CRABIER GOLIATH
HANDSAW QUABIRD SQUACCO
BOATBILL GAULDING HERONSEW
UMBRETTE
(— FLOCK) SIEGE
HERON'S-BILL ERODIUM
HERPES TETTER
HERPES ZOSTER ZONA SHINGLES
HERRING ALEC BRIT CHUB SILD
BLOAT CAPON CISCO DORAB HILSA
MARAY MATIE SPRAT KIPPER
TAILOR BLOATER CLUPEID NAILROD
ROLLMOP SHADINE BLUEBACK
BRISLING BUCKLING CROPSHIN
GRAYBACK QUODDIES SCUDDAWN
STRADINE
(— SEASON) DRAVE
(— UNIT) LAST MAZE
(2, 3 OR 4 —S) WARP
(FEMALE —) RAUN
(LAKE —) KIYI CISCO
(RED —) CAPON SOLDIER
(SMOKED —) BLOATER
(YOUNG —) COB BRIT SILE SILL
SOIL WILE COBBE MATIE SPRAT
SARDINE SPERLING
HERS HERN SHISN
HERSE (FATHER OF —) CECROPS
(SISTER OF —) AGLAUROS
(SON OF —) CEPHALUS
HERSELF HI HER SELF ITSELF
HERSHEF ARSAPHES
HESHVAN BUL CHESHVAN
HESIONE (FATHER OF —)
LAOMEDON
(HUSBAND OF —) TELAMON
(RESCUER OF —) HERCULES
HESITANCY HANG
HESITANT SHY CAGY CHARY
GROPING HALTING SUSPENSE
(NOT —) FACILE
HESITATE COY HEM STAY STOP
CHECK CRANE DEMUR DOUBT

FORCE PAUSE STAND STICK SUSSY
WAVER BOGGLE FALTER HANKER
LINGER MAMMER RELUCT SCOTCH
TARROW TARTLE BALANCE
PROFFER SCRUPLE STAGGER
STAMMER SWITHER THRIMBLE
(— IN SPEAKING) HACKER
HESITATING JUBUS HALTING
BACKWARD DOUBTFUL JUBEROUS
TIMOROSO
HESITATION HANG HINK WAND
PAUSE STAND STICK SUSSY
SWITHER
HESSIAN BURLAP
HESTIA (FATHER OF —) KRONOS
(MOTHER OF —) RHEA
HETAERA LAIS THAIS PHRYNE
MISTRESS
HETERODOX HERETIC SINISTRAL
HETERODOXY HERESY CACODOXY
HETEROGENEOUS MIXED MOTLEY
UNLIKE DIVERSE PIEBALD
ASSORTED
HETEROMYS SACCOMYS
HETEROTROPHIC HOLOZOIC
HETEROXENOUS INDIRECT
HETEROZYGOUS CROSS SPLIT
IMPURE
HETMAN ATAMAN
HEW CUT HAG CHIP SNAG STUB
SHRED SLICE
(— OUT) CARVE
(— STONE) CHAR
HEWER JOEY GETTER GIDEON
FACEMAN
HEX WITCH VOODOO WHAMMY
HEXAGON SEXANGLE
HEXAGONAL HEX DIMETRIC
HEXAGRAM PENTACLE
HEXAMETER MIURUS
(DACTYLIC —) EPOS HEROIC
HEXOBARBITAL EVIPAL
HEXOSAN MANNAN GLUCOSAN
MANNOSAN
HEYDAY MAY HIGHDAY
HEZEKIAH (FATHER OF —) AHAZ
HIATUS GAP BREAK CHASM BREACH
HIATAL LACUNA
HIBERNATE SHACK WINTER
SLUMBER
HIBERNATING LATITANT
HIBERNIA JUVERNA
HIBERNIAN IRISHMAN IVERNIAN
HICCUP YEX YOX HICK HOCKET
HOQUET SINGULTUS
HICK BOOR HIND JAKE BACON
BUSHMAN CORNBALL
HICKORY NOGAL PIGNUT BULLNUT
SHAGBARK
HICKORY NUT TRYMA PIGNUT
BULLNUT KISKITOM
HICKWALL ECCLE HECKLE HICKWAY
HIDDEN HID SHY DEEP DERN LOST
TECT BLIND DUSKY PERDU PRIVY
ARCANE BURIED COVERT INNATE
LATENT MASKED MYSTIC OCCULT
SECRET VEILED BOSOMED COVERED
CRYPTIC OBSCURE RECLUSE
SUBTILE ABDITIVE ABSTRUSE

CRYPTOUS HIDEAWAY PALLIATE
SCREENED SECLUDED SNEAKING
HIDE HOD WRY BUFF BURY CASE
CROP DARK DERN FELL FELT HILL
HOOD JOUK LEAN MASK PELL PELT
SCAB SKIN SKUG SNUG STOW VEIL
WELL BELIE BELLY BLIND CACHE
CLOAK CLOUD COUCH COVER
DITCH EARTH FLANK GLOSS LAYNE
LOSHE MANSE PLANT SHADE SPOIL
STASH STEER TAPIS BURROW
BUSHEL CASATE EMBOSS ENCAVE
ENWOMB FOREST HUDDLE IMBOSK
MANENT PELAGE SCREEN SHADOW
SHIELD SHROUD CONCEAL COWHIDE
EMBOWEL OBCLUDE OVERLAY
SECLUDE SECRETE SPREADY
CARUCATE DISGUISE ENSCONCE
HIDELAND HOODWINK PALLIATE
PLOWLAND SQUIRREL SUPPRESS
(— AS AN EEL) MUD
(— IN WOODS) WOOD BUSHWACK
(— UNDER) BUSHEL
(CALF'S —) DEACON
(DRESSED —S) LEATHER
(HALF OF —) BEND
(HAVING SOFT —) MELLOW
(SHEEP'S —) SLAT
(TANNED —) CROP
(THICKEST —S) BACKS
(UNDRESSED —) KIP
(PL.) KIP JUFTI JUFTS
HIDE-AND-GO-SEEK BOGLE WHOOP
BOGGLE
HIDEAWAY MEW LAIR
HIDEBOUND BORNE NARROW
BIGOTED
HIDEOUS FELL GRIM UGLY AWFUL
TOADY DEFORM GRIMLY GRISLY
HORRID ODIOUS OGRISH GHASTLY
DEFORMED DREADFUL FIENDISH
GRUESOME HORRIBLE SHOCKING
TERRIBLE
HIDEOUSLY FOULLY
HIDING MICHING SECRECY ABDITIVE
HIDEAWAY
HIEMAL WINTRY
HIERACIUM DINALE HAWKWEED
HIERARCHY SATRAPY
HIEROGLYPH CIPHER
(PL.) SIGNARY
HIGGLE HUCK HAGGLE
HIGH UP ALT AIRY DEAR HAUT MAIN
MUCH TALL ACUTE ALOFT BRENT
CHIEF CLOSE FIRST GREAT LOFTY
MERRY NOBLE SHARP STEEP
COSTLY SHRILL EMINENT EXALTED
HAUGHTY SUBLIME TOPPING
VIOLENT ELEVATED FOREMOST
PIERCING TOWERING
(— AND MIGHTY) HOGEN
(— IN CHROMA) STRONG
(— IN PITCH) ALT ACUTE
(— IN RANK) MUCH
(— PITCH) ORTHIAN
(MOST —) SERENE
(PRETTY —) STIFFISH
(VERY —) TAUNT
HIGHBORN NOBLE GENEROUS

HIGHBOY TALLBOY
HIGHBRED SOFT REFINED
HIGHBROW EGGHEAD
HIGH-CLASS CLASSY UPSTAGE
HIGH-CLIMBER TOPPER
HIGH-COLORED BLOWSY BLOWZY
HIGHER ABOVE SENIOR SUPERIOR
HIGHEST TOP HEXT FIRST EXTREME
MAXIMAL SUPREME BUNEMOST
HIGHMOST OVERMOST
(— IN DEGREE) LAST
HIGHFALUTIN PAUGHTY
HIGH-FED BEANY
HIGH-FLAVORED GAMY
HIGH-FLOWN TALL TUMID
HIGH-HANDED CAVALIER
HIGHLAND RAND CERRO
HIGHLANDER GAEL TARTAN
NAINSEL PLAIDMAN REDSHANK
TREWSMAN UPLANDER
(PL.) TREWS TARTAN
HIGHLIGHT ADORN HEIGHTEN
SALIENCE
HIGHLY THRICE
HIGH-MINDED HAUGHT
HIGHNESS ALTESSE ALTEZZA
ALTITUDE
(— OF PRICE) DEARTH
HIGH-PITCHED PROUD PIPING
TREBLE SHRIEKY
HIGH-POWERED MAGNUM
HIGH-PRICED DEAR
HIGH-RIGGER TOPPER
HIGH-SOUNDING BIG BOMBAST
MAGNIFIC SONORANT SONOROUS
SOUNDING
HIGH-SPIRITED CRANK FIERY
FIERCE LIVELY GALLANT GINGERY
RAMPANT CAVALIER VASCULAR
HIGH-SPIRITEDNESS SPLEEN
HIGH-STRUNG TENSE NERVOUS
HIGH-TONED TONY DICTY DICKTY
HIGHWAY VIA WAY BELT ITER PATH
PIKE ROAD TOBY BOLOS ARTERY
CAUSEY COURSE RUMPAD SKYWAY
STREET BELTWAY CALZADA
FREEWAY RAMPIRE ARTERIAL
BROADWAY CAUSEWAY CHAUSSEE
HIGHROAD SPEEDWAY
(— ROBBERY) TOBY
(LOCATED OFF THE —) DEVIOUS
HIGHWAYMAN PAD RIDER SCAMP
CUTTER PADDER RODMAN FOOTPAD
LADRONE PRANCER RODSMAN
TOBYMAN BIDSTAND DAMASTES
HIGHTOBY HIJACKER LANCEMAN
OUTRIDER
HIGH-WROUGHT INTENSE
HIKE MUSH MARCH TRAMP RAMBLE
HILARIOUS MAD JOVIAL JOCULAR
CHIRPING GLORIOUS
HILARITY GIG JOY GLEE LAUGH
MIRTH GAIETY GAYETY DEVILRY
JOLLITY WHOOPEE
HILL BEN DEN HOE HOW KOP LOW
PUY VAN ALTO BANK BERG BRAE
BULT BUMP COTE DAGH DENE
DOWN DRUM FELL HIGH HONE KNAP
LOMA LUMP MESA MOOR MOTE

NOUP PAHA TOFT ZION BARGH
BUTTE CERRO CLIFF COAST HEUGH
KNOCK KNOLL KOPJE MORRO
MOUND MOUNT STILL SWELL TELLE
WATCH ASCENT BARROW BEACON
COBBLE COLLIS COPPLE CUESTA
HEIGHT HEUVEL LOMITA SPRUNT
STRONE CAELIAN CAPITOL COLLINE
DRUMLIN HILLOCK NUNATAK
PICACHO SOWBACK VIMINAL
AREOPAGY CATOCTIN DRUMLOID
FOOTHILL MONTICLE QUIRINAL
(— OF SAND) DENE DUNE
(— OF STRATIFIED DRIFT) KAME
(— UP) MOLD
(BROAD-TOPPED —) LOMA
(CONICAL —) LAW
(CRAGGY —) TOR
(FORTIFIED —) RATH
(HIGH —) BEN
(ISOLATED —) HUM TOFT BARGH
BUTTE
(LAST —) STRONE
(LOW —) HOW BAND WOLD
SOWBACK
(NIPPLELIKE —) PAP
(NORTH AFRICAN —) JEBEL DJEBEL
(RESIDUAL —) CATOCTIN
(ROUNDED —) DODD HONE
(SHARP-POINTED —) KIP KIPP
(SMALL —) KNAP KNOLL KOPJE
KOPPIE HILLOCK MOLEHILL
(STEEP —) BREW BROW STILL
(STONY —) ROACH
(SUGAR-LOAF —) SPITZKOP
(WOODED —) HOLT HURST
HILLOCK HOW LOW NOB BOSS BULT
DOWN KAME KNOB TERP TUMP
BERRY HEAVE HURST KNOCK
KNOLL KOPJE MOUND TOMAN
BURROW COPPET HILLET HUMMOCK
TUMMOCK TUMULUS MOLEHILL
HILLSIDE BENT BRAE COTE EDGE
CLEVE FALDA SLADE FELLSIDE
SIDEHILL
HILLTOP PIKE KNOLL
HILLY KNOBBY
HILT HAFT POIGNET HANDGRIP
(— OF DAGGER) DUDGEON
(PART OF —) LANGUET
HILUM EYE HILUS PORTA NUCLEUS
CICATRIX
HIM A EN HE HEM HIN MUN
HIMATION PALLION PALLIUM
HIMSELF HIM IPSE SELF HISSEL
ITSELF HERSELF HISSELF
HIND ROE CONY HINE HINT CONEY
HEARST HINDER VENISON CABRILLA
HINDER BAR DAM KEP LET MAR ROB
CLOG HELP SLOW SLUG STAY STOP
TENT WARN AFTER BLOCK CHEAT
CHECK CHOKE CRAMP DEBAR
DELAY DETER EMBAR ESTOP HEDGE
SLOTH THROW TRASH ARREST
CUMBER DETAIN FORBID FORLET
HAMPER HARASS HINNER IMPEDE
IMPEND INJURE RETARD SCOTCH
TAIGLE UNHELP ABSTAIN DEPRIVE
FORELAY IMPEACH INHIBIT PREVENT

TRACHLE ENCUMBER HANDICAP
IMPEDITE OBSTRUCT PRECLUDE
PROHIBIT
HINDERED FOUL
HINDERER LETTER
HINDERMOST LAG ACHTER
(**HALF —**) LEG
(**PL.**) FOUCH CRUPPER HAUNCHES
HINDRANCE BAR LET RUB BALK
CURB REIN SLUG STAY STOP
BLOCK CHECK DELAY HITCH TRASH
ARREST CUMBER DENIAL HINDER
OBJECT UNHELP UNSPEED
DISCOUNT DRAWBACK HOLDBACK
OBSTACLE PULLBACK
HINDU BABU BABOO SUDRA BABHAN
GENTOO JAJMAN KALWAR KHATRI
NAYADI SHUDRA THAKUR VAISYA
MUSAHAR VAIRAGI
(**— ASCETIC**) SADHU
(**— ASSOCIATION**) SANGH
(**— CASTE**) TELI VARNA
(**— CUSTOM**) SATI SUTTEE
(**— ENERGY**) SAKTI SHAKTI
(**— IDOL**) SWAMI
(**— INTERJECTION**) OM AUM
(**— PHILOSOPHY**) VEDANTA
(**— PRACTICE**) PURDAH
(**— RITE**) PUJA POOJA
(**— SAGE**) RSI RISHI
(**— VARNA MEMBER**) SUDRA
(**— WORSHIPER**) SAKTA
(**— WRITINGS**) SMRTI TANTRA
(**TWICE-BORN —**) KSATRIYA
HINDUSTANI URDU HINDI OORDOO
DAKHINI
HINGE RUN BAND BUTT FLAP HARR
TRIM TURN CARDO CROOK GEMEL
JOINT MOUNT NODUS SKELL SKEWL
TWIST DEPEND GARNET GEMMEL
GIMMER HANGLE JIMMER SNIBEL
CHARNEL COXCOMB FULCRUM
HOLDBACK
(**— OF BIVALVE SHELL**) CARDO
(**— OF HELMET**) CHARNEL
(**— TOGETHER**) SCISSOR
(**HALF OF —**) FLAP
(**PHILATELIC —**) STICKER
HINGED SWING
HINNY BURDON FUNNEL JENNET
HINT CUE ASTE ITEM MINT WINK
CHEEP IMPLY INFER POINT SPELL
STEER TOUCH TRACE WHIFF
ALLUDE GLANCE OFFICE SMATCH
WHEEZE INKLING LEADING
MEMENTO SUGGEST UMBRAGE
WHISPER WRINKLE ALLUSION
INDICATE INNUENDO INTIMATE
TELLTALE
HINTERLAND BLED BACKLAND
HIP HEP COXA HUCK PITCH SHOOP
HAUNCH HUCKLE HIPBERRY
(**— JOINT**) THURL
(**— OF ROSE**) BERRY CHOOP SHOOP
(**— OF TARGET**) SPOT
HIPBONE FINBONE EDGEBONE
SIDEBONE
HIPPEUS KNIGHT

HIPPOCAMPUS ERGOT HIPPO
HIPPOCOON (BROTHER OF —)
TYNDAREUS
(**FATHER OF —**) OEBALUS
(**MOTHER OF —**) GORGOPHONE
(**SLAYER OF —**) HERCULES
HIPPODAMIA (FATHER OF —)
ADRASTUS OENOMAUS
(**HUSBAND OF —**) PELOPS
PEIRITHOUS
(**SON OF —**) ATREUS TROEZEN
PITTHEUS THYESTES
HIPPOLYTUS (FATHER OF —)
THESEUS
(**MOTHER OF —**) HIPPOLYTE
(**STEPMOTHER OF —**) PHAEDRA
HIPPONACTEAN SCAZON
HIPPOPOTAMUS HIPPO ZEEKOE
BEHEMOTH BUNODONT
HIPPOTRAGUS OZANNA EGOCERUS
HIRE FEE JOB HAVE MEED RENT
SIGN WAGE PREST WAGES EMPLOY
ENGAGE RETAIN SALARY BESPEAK
CHARTER CONDUCE CONDUCT
FREIGHT STIPEND
(**— CATTLE**) TACK
HIRED PAID TEEKA TICCA WAGED
HIRELING HACK VENAL HACKNEY
MYRMIDON WAGELING MERCENARY
HIRSUTE HAIRY SHAGGY
HIS S AS ES IS HISN
HISPID STRIGOSE STRIGOUS
HISS BLOW FUFF HISH HIZZ QUIZ
SISS SIZZ GOOSE WHISS FISSLE
FIZZLE SIFFLE WHOOSH WHISTLE
SIBILATE
(**— OF SWORD**) SOUGH
HISSING BIRD SIBILANT
HISTONE GLOBIN
HISTORIAN MORONI STORIER
ANNALIST
HISTORICAL GENETIC
HISTORIOGRAPHER SCALD SKALD
HISTORY STORY ANNALS LEGEND
SURVEY ACCOUNT ANCESTRY
PROPHECY RELATION
(**— OF EXPERIENCES**) MEMOIRS
(**— OF JAPAN**) KOJIKI
(**LIFE —**) COURSE
HISTRIONIC ACTORY ACTORISH
ACTRESSY
HIT BAT BOP BOX DOT GET HAT JOB
PEG PIP WOW BASH BEAN BEAT
BELT BLOW BOFF BUST CHOP CONK
DONG FOUR GOLD NAIL PINK PUCK
PUNT RUFF SLAM SOCK SWAT SWIP
TAKE TANK TUNK WART WIPE
ANGLE CHECK CLOUT CLUNK
CROWN FIVER FLICK GOUFF KNOCK
POTCH PRANG PUNTA PUNTO
SCORE SLASH SLOSH SMITE SNICK
SWIPE TAINT TOUCH VENUE ATTAIN
DOUBLE FOURER HURTLE SCLAFF
STRIKE VOLLEY ATTAINT BOFFOLA
CONNECT MUZZLER SANDBAG
WHERRET BLUDGEON BOUNDARY
LENGTHER STRICKEN
(**— A KEY**) STRIKE
(**— BALL**) CUR FLY DINK DRIVE

SHOOL SNICK
(**— BUNT**) DRAG
(**— GAME**) STOP
(**— GENTLY**) BABY
(**— GOLF BALL**) CAN BLAST
EXPLODE
(**— HARD**) DUMP SLOG SLUG SOUSE
STOUSH STONKER
(**— IN BOXING**) LEADOFF
(**— IN FIELD HOCKEY**) CORNER
(**— IN TILTING**) TAINT
(**— IT OFF**) CLICK
(**— LIGHTLY**) KISS
(**— ON BULL'S-EYE**) GOLD
(**— POORLY**) DUB
(**— TOGETHER**) CLASH
(**— UPON**) FIND
(**— WITH FOOT**) KICK SPURN
(**BASE —**) BINGLE DOUBLE SAFETY
SINGLE TRIPLE SCRATCH SMOTHER
(**CRICKET —**) SLOG BOUNDARY
(**EASILY —**) SITTING
(**FENCING —**) HAI HAY
(**SHARP —**) LICK
(**SMASH —**) SOCKEROO
HITCH JET TUG HALT HIKE ITCH
KNOT PULL CATCH HOTCH SPELL
TRACE HIRSLE INSPAN MAGNUS
(**NOSE —**) BOZAL
HITCHHIKE HOP THUMB
HITCHING KNOT SHRUG
HITHER HERE
HITHERTO YET BEFORE
HIT-OR-MISS CASUAL CHANCE
HOBNOB CARELESS
HITTER SWATTER
HITTING BATTING SLOGGING
HITTITE HATTI KHATTI TABALIAN
HIVE GUM BIKE SKEP PYCHE STAND
STATE STOCK SWARM APIARY
ALVEARY BEEHIVE SWARMER
(**— PLACED OVER ANOTHER**) SUPER
HLORRITHI THOR THORR
HOAR GRAY RIME HOARY
HOARD HEAM POSE SAVE AMASS
HUTCH MISER STOCK COFFER
MAGPIE MUCKER STOUTH GENIZAH
HUSBAND SQUIRREL TREASURE
HOARDER MUCKER STORER
HUSBAND
HOARFROST RAG HOAR RIME RIND
HOARINESS HOAR MUCOR
HOARSE RAW FOGGY GRUFF HEAZY
HUSKY RAWKY ROKEY ROUGH
ROUPY STOUR CROAKY RASPED
ROUPIT GRATING RAUCOUS
HOARSENESS FROG ROUP QUACK
HASKNESS
HOARY GRAY GREY HOAR WHITE
FROSTY ANCIENT HOARISH
INCANOUS
HOATZIN ANNA HANA HOACTZIN
HOAX BAM COD FUN GAG HUM KID
RAG RIG BILK DUPE FAKE GAFF
GEGG GUNK QUIZ RAMP RUSE SELL
SHAM SKIT CHEAT FRAUD GREEN
SHAVE SPOOF TRICK WINDY
CANARD DIDDLE HUMBUG STRING
BLAFLUM DECEIVE FLIVVER
ARTIFICE

HOB HUB PUNCH MATRIX
HOBBER LEANER
HOBBLE GIMP LOCK SPAN BUNCH
HILCH HITCH STILT STUMP HABBLE
HIRPLE HOPPLE LANGLE LANKET
TOLTER CRAMBLE CRAMMEL
CRIPPLE SHACKLE SHAFFLE
SPANCEL STAGGER SIDELINE
HOBBLEBUSH DOGWOOD
HOBBY BUG FAD HOBBLER
AVOCATION
HOBBYHORSE HOBBY PLAYMARE
HOBBYIST BUG
HOBGOBLIN (ALSO SEE GOBLIN)
COW HAG HOB PUG BOGY PUCK
BOGEY BUCCA BUGAN POKER
SCRAT SPOOK BOODIE BOWSIE
BUGANE EMPUSA SPOORN
BUGABOO RAWHEAD BOGGLEBO
COLTPIXY POPLEMAN PUCKEREL
WORRICOW
HOBNAIL HOB HUB PUNCH TACKET
HOBNAILED TACKETY
HOBO BO BOE BUM STIFF
HOCK HAM HOX HEEL HOUGH HUXEN
SINEW SKINK JARRET GAMBREL
HOCKSHIN SUFFRAGO
HOCKEY HURLY HORKEY HURLEY
SHINNY CAMMOCK HURLBAT
HOCKEY STICK HOOKY HURLY
STICK BULGER SHINNY CAMBUCA
CAMMOCK DODDART HURLBAT
HOCUS-POCUS HUMBUG FLIMFLAM
QUACKERY
HOD TRAY
HOD CARRIER PADDY
HODGEPODGE CHOW HASH MESS
OLIO RAFF SALAD BOLLIX JUSSEL
MAGPIE MEDLEY CHIVAREE
CHOWCHOW HOTCHPOT KEDGEREE
MISHMASH PASTICHE PORRIDGE
SCRAMPUM
HOE BROD CHIP CLAT HACK HOWE
SHIM LARRY THIRD CHONTA
HACKER PAIDLE SARCLE GRUBBER
PULASKI SCRAPER SCUFFLE
GRIFFAUN
(— **HANDLE**) STAIL
(**HORSE** —) NIDGET NIGGET
HOECAKE CORNCAKE
HOG BEN SOW BOAR GALT GILT
PORK DUROC GRUNT SHOAT
BARROW HOGGET HOGGIE PORKER
PORKET YORKER BACONER
BUTCHER GRUNTER HOGLING
MONTANA BABIRUSA BENODONT
BUNODONT HEREFORD LANDRACE
VICTORIA
HOGBACK FLATIRON HOGFRAME
HOGCHOKER SOLE
HOGFISH CAPITAN LADYFISH
LORICATE SCORPION
HOGGER HUGGER HOGHEAD
HOGGISHNESS GRILL GRYLL
HOGNOSE SNAKE ADDER
FLATHEAD
HOG PLUM AMRA JOBO
HOGSHEAD CASK CARDEL
HOG'S-MEAT TOSTON HOGWEED

HOG-TIE HAMPER
HOGWASH DRAFF SWASH SWILL
PIGWASH
HOIST FID HEFT KILT LIFT SWAY
SWIG WHIM WHIP ERECT HEAVE
HEEZE HEIST HOICK HOOSH HORSE
RAISE WEIGH JAMMER LAUNCH
LIFTER TUGGER WHIMSY DERRICK
(— **A LOG**) CANNON
(— **FISH**) BRAIL
(— **FLUKES**) FISH FANCIER
HOISTED (— **TIGHT**) ATRIP
HOISTMAN CAGEMAN
HOKUM BLAA BLAH HOKE JUNK
HOLD HOD OWN BULK DEEM FEEL
FILL GAUM GIVE GRIT HANK HAVE
HELD HEND HILT HOLE HOLT HOOK
KEEP LOCK NAIL RELY STOW
AFONG AHOLD AHOLT CARRY CINCH
CLAMP CLING GRASP GRIPE LATCH
LEASE PAUSE ROCCA STORE
WOULD ADHERE ADSORB ARREST
CLUTCH DETAIN HANDLE INTERN
MANURE OCCUPY REGARD REPUTE
RETAIN ADJUDGE CAPTURE
CONFINE CONTAIN ENCLOSE
FERMATA GRAPPLE HOLDING
RECEIVE SEIZURE SUBSIST
SUSPEND COMPRISE FOOTHOLD
FOREHOLD HANDFAST HANDHOLD
HEADLOCK HOLDFAST PURCHASE
THURROCK
(— **A BELIEF**) SUPPOSE
(— **AS PRECIOUS**) TREASURE
(— **AS TRUE**) ACCEPT
(— **AT BAY**) DOMPT
(— **BACK ON LEASH**) TRASH
(— **BACK**) STOP WELL BELAY
LAYNE BOGGLE DETAIN FLINCH
HINDER RETIRE SHRINK CONTAIN
DETRACT FORBEAR INGIBIT
RECLAIM REFRAIN SLACKEN
HESITATE SUPPRESS WITHDRAW
(— **CLOSELY**) CRADLE CUDDLE
(— **CONSULTATION**) ADVISE
(— **CORONER'S INQUEST**) CROWN
(— **DEAR**) CHERISH
(— **DOWN**) PINION CONTAIN
(— **FAST**) FIX BAIL BITE CLING
SNARL CLENCH CLINCH SECURE
STABLE
(— **FIRMLY**) INSIST
(— **FOR FOOD**) COZY COSEY
(— **GOOD**) SERVE
(— **IN CHECK**) REIN GOVERN
REPRESS COMPESCE
(— **IN CONTEMPT**) SMILE DISPRIZE
(— **IN PLACE**) ANCHOR
(— **OF PLASTER**) KEY
(— **ON COURSE**) STEM FETCH
STAND
(— **ON FINAL NOTE**) TENOR
(— **ON SHORE**) LANDFAST
(— **OUT**) DREE LAST STAY OFFER
EXTEND PROTEND STRETCH
SUSTAIN
(— **PROTECTIVELY**) LAP
(— **TIGHTLY**) CLIP STICK
(— **TOGETHER**) BOND COHERE
CONSIST

(— **UP BY LEADING STRINGS**) DADE
(— **UP TO CONTEMPT**) FLEER
(— **UP TO PUBLIC NOTICE**) GIBBET
(— **UP**) BEAR HALT STAY ERECT
HEIST IMPEDE UPHOLD RUMPADE
SUPPORT SUSTAIN TRADUCE
(**SHIP'S** —) HOLE HOLL FISHHOLD
(**WRESTLING** —) CROTCH KEYLOCK
CHANCERY HEADLOCK SCISSORS
SIDEHOLD
HOLDER WYE HAVER STOCK DIPPER
SOCKET CRACKER JAGIRDAR
(— **FOR CARRYING GLASS**) FRAIL
(— **FOR COIL**) SPOOL
(— **FOR CUP**) ZARF
(— **FOR TOOLS**) TURRET
(— **OF GRANT**) ENAMDAR
(**CANDLE** —) SPIDER GIRANDOLE
(**LAMP** —) BODY
(PL.) GRIPPERS
HOLDFAST CLINCH HAPTERON
HOLDIKEN HADDIN
HOLDING HAL COPY COTE HOLD
TAKE GRASP HONOR HADDIN
POFFLE TENANT TENURE TENANCY
COMMENDA
(— **DIFFERENT OPINIONS**) APART
(— **FAST**) IRON
(— **OF SECURITIES**) CARRY
(PL.) FLOCKS PROPERTY
HOLDUP HEIST STICKUP
HOLE CAN CUP EYE GAP PIT TAP
BORE BURY LEAK MAIL MUSE PECK
PINK POCK PUKA WANT CHINK
DITCH FLOSS FOSSE MEUSE SINUS
SLACK SPRUE SQUAT TEWEL THURL
BURROW CAVITY CENTER CENTRE
CRANNY CRATER EYELET HOLLOW
LACUNA OBTAIN OILLET PIERCE
POCKET POUNCE WEEPER
BLOWOUT BOGHOLE BOTHROS
DIBHOLE EYEHOLE KEYHOLE
MORTICE MORTISE OILHOLE
OPENING PINHOLE POTHOLE
SCUTTLE SWALLET VENTAGE
ACCEPTER APERTURE BLOWHOLE
BOREHOLE COALHOLE CRABHOLE
FUMAROLE HANDHOLE KNOCKOUT
KNOTHOLE OVERTURE PEEPHOLE
POSTHOLE PUNCTURE WELLHOLE
WINDHOLE
(— **CAUSED BY LEAK**) GIME
(— **FOR WIRE**) HUB HUBB
(— **IN BANK OF STREAM**) GAT
(— **IN GARMENT**) FRACK
(— **IN GUILLOTINE**) LUNET LUNETTE
(— **IN HEDGE**) SMEUSE
(— **IN KEEL**) RUFFLE
(— **IN KIVA**) SIPAPU
(— **IN STREAM BED**) DUMP
(— **IN WIND INSTRUMENT**) LILL
(— **INTO MOLD**) SPRUE
(**AIR** —) SPIRACLE
(**DEEP** —) POT GOURD
(**FOX** —) KENNEL
(**GOLF** —) CUP DOGLEG
(**MELON** —) GILGAI
(**SAND** —) BUNKER
(**SINK** —) SOAKAWAY

(TO —) GOBBLE HAZARD
(VOLCANIC —) FUMAROLE
(WATER —) DUB CHARCO
(WELL-LIKE —) CASCAN
HOLIDAY HOL PLAY TIDE WAKE
FERIE FESTA MERRY FIESTA JOVIAL
FESTIVE HALEDAY PLAYDAY
YEARDAY SHABUOTH WAYGOOSE
(HALF —) REMEDY
(PL.) FERIA
HOLINESS PIETY HALIDOM SANCTITY
HOLLA SOLA
HOLLAND (ALSO SEE NETHERLANDS)
FROGLAND
HOLLANDAISE GULASH GOULASH
HOLLANDER DUTCHMAN
HOLLANDS GIN GENEVA
HOLLER HALLO HOLLO HALLOO
KYOODLE
HOLLO SOLA
HOLLOW DEN DIP KEX BOSS BOWL
CAVE COMB COOM COVE DALK
DELL DENT DINT DISH DOCK DOKE
FOLD GORE HOLE HOLL HOWE
KEXY SINK SLOT THIN VOID WAME
BASIN BIGHT CAVUM CHASE CLEFT
CUPPY DELVE DOWFF EMPTY
GAUNT GOYLE GULCH GULLY
HEUCH LAIGH NOTCH SCOOP SINUS
SLOCK SWAMP WOMBY BULLAN
CAVITY CORRIE DIMPLE HOLLER
INDENT KETTLE MATRIX POCKET
SOCKET SUNKEN VACANT WALLOW
BOXLIKE CONCAVE UNSOUND
VACUITY CAVITARY CHELIDON
CRUCIBLE FISTULAR FOSSETTE
NOTCHING SPECIOUS
(— AMONG HILLS) SWAG SLOCK
(— IN COIL OF CABLE) TIER
(— IN HILL) COOM CLASH COOMB
CORRIE
(— IN TILE) KEY
(— OF ARM) LEAD ARMPIT
(— OF HANDS) GOUPEN GOWPEN
(— OF HORSE'S TOOTH) MARK
(— OF KNEE) HAM
(— OUT) CUT DIG BORE HOWK
KERF CAVERN EXCISE
(LONG —) GROOVE
(NOT —) SOLID FARCTATE
(PASSING —) CRESCENT
(SECLUDED —) GLEN
(SPRINGY —) GAW
(WOODED —) GULLY
HOLLOWED HOWKIT CONCAVE
SPOUTED
HOLLOWNESS VANITY INANITY
VACUITY
HOLLY HOLM HULL ILEX MATE
DAHOON HOLLIN HULVER TOLLON
YAUPON CATBERRY INKBERRY
MILKMAID
HOLLYHOCK HOCK ALTHEA
MALLOW
HOLOTHURIAN TREPANG
HOLY SRI SHRI HUACA SAINT SANTO
DEVOUT DIVINE SACRAL SACRED
BLESSED PERFECT SAINTLY
SINLESS BLISSFUL INNOCENT
REVEREND

(— MAN) SADHU
(— OF HOLIES) ADYT ADYTUM
(ALL —) PANAGIA
HOLY BASIL TULCE TOOLSY
HOLY STONE BEAR BIBLE
HOLY WOOD LIGNUM
HOMAGE FEE COURT HONOR YMAGE
FEALTY MANRED INCENSE LOYALTY
MANRENT MANSHIP OVATION
SERVICE TREWAGE EMINENCE
(SUPREME —) LATRIA
HOME BYE DEN HAM HAME HUNK
WIKE ABODE ASTRE BEING DOMUS
FOYER HAUNT SMOKE HEARTH
BLIGHTY SHELTER DOMICILE
FIRESIDE ROOFTREE
(— FOR THE POOR) HOSPICE
(— OF THE BLESSED) GIMLE
(FUNERAL —) CHAPEL
(HARVEST —) KERN KIRN MELL
HOCKEY
(REST —) FARM HOSTEL
HOMELAND HAVAIKI
HOMELESS ROOFLESS VAGABOND
HOMELIKE HOMEY HAMEIL HAMILT
HOMISH HOMESOME
HOMELINESS YEOMANRY
HOMELY FOUL UGLY PLAIN DUDGEN
PLAINLY EVERYDAY FAMILIAR
HOMELIKE
HOME PLATE RUBBER
HOMER KOR CHOMER
HOME RUN SWAT SWOT
HOMESICKNESS HEIMWEH
NOSTALGIA
HOMESPUN KERSEY RUSSET
HOMESTEAD TOFT TREF ONSET
PLACE WORTH TYDDYN FARMERY
ONSTEAD STEADING
HOMESTEADER NESTER
HOMETHRUST HAI HAY
HOMEWORK PREP
HOMICIDE DEATH MORTH KILLING
HOMILETIC KERYSTIC
HOMILY PRONE OMELIE POSTIL
SERMON
HOMINY SAMP NASAUMP
HOMOEOMERY GERM SEED
(PL.) SPERMATA
HOMOGENEITY SAMENESS
HOMOGENEOUS LIKE SOLID
GLOBAL SIMPLE COMPACT SIMILAR
HOMOGENOUS ENTIRE
HOMOLOGUE CYANINE HOMOTYPE
HOMOPHONY MONODY
HOMORGANIC COGNATE
HOMOZYGOUS PURE ISOGENIC

HONDURAS

CAPITAL: TEGUCIGALPA
COIN: PESO CENTAVO LEMPIRA
GULF: FONSECA
INDIAN: MAYA PAYA SUMO ULVA
CARIB LENCA PIPIL TAUIRA
JICAQUE MISKITO MOSQUITO
ISLAND: ROATAN
ISLANDS: BAY BAHIA
LAKE: CRIBA YOJOA BREWER

MEASURE: VARA MILLA MECATE
TERCIA CAJUELA MANZANA
MOUNTAINS: PIJA AGALTA
CELAQUE
PORT: LACEIBA TRUJILLO
RIVER: COCO SICO ULUA AGUAN
LEMPA NEGRO TINTO WANKS
PATUCA SULACO GUAVAPE
OLANCHO SEGOVIA SANTIAGO
RUINS: TENAMPUA
TOWN: TELA YORO COPAN LAPAZ
ROATAN GRACIAS LACEIBA
TRUJILLO YUSCARAN JUTICALPA
WEIGHT: CAJA LIBRA

HONE HO STROKE
HONEST FAIR GOOD TRUE AFALD
FRANK ROUND SOUND WHITE
CANDID DEXTER DINKUM ENTIRE
PROPER RUSTIC SINGLE SQUARE
SINCERE UPRIGHT RIGHTFUL
STRAIGHT
HONESTLY TRULY DINKUM HONEST
INDEED SINGLY SQUARE SQUARELY
HONESTY FAITH HONOR SATIN
EQUITY LUNARY REALTY VERITY
JUSTICE LUNARIA PROBITY
BOLBONAC FAIRNESS FIDELITY
MOONWORT SATINPOD YEOMANRY
HONEY MEL MELL HINNY HONEYBUN
(— BEVERAGE) MULSE
HONEYBEE (ALSO SEE BEE) BEE
GYNE KING DRANE DRONE QUEEN
DINGAR DRONER EGATES CYPRIAN
DEBORAH DESERET KOOTCHA
MELISSA STINGER ACULEATE
ANGELITO
HONEY BUZZARD PERN
HONEYCOMB COMB FRAME
WAXCOMB
HONEYCREEPER IIWI MAMO PALILA
DREPANID GUITGUIT
HONEYDEW MILDEW
HONEY EATER OO IAO TUI MOHO
MINER TENUI MANUAO MAOMAO
ROSTER BELLBIRD WURRALUH
HONEYED SWEET HYBLAN SUGARY
SUGARED HYBLAEAN LUSCIOUS
HONEY GUIDE MOROC
HONEY MESQUITE ALGAROBA
HONEYPOD
HONEY PLANT HOYA HUAJILLO
HONEYSUCKLE VINE SUCKLE
WEIGELA BINDWEED SUCKLING
WOODBINE

HONG KONG

BAY: SHEKO REPULSE
CAPITAL: VICTORIA
COIN: CENT DOLLAR
DISTRICT: WANCHAI
GARDENS: TIGERBALM
ISLAND: LANTAO
MOUNTAIN: CASTLE VICTORIA
PENINSULA: KOWLOON

HONK KONK YANG CRONK

HONOR BAY ORE FAME FETE HORN
ADORE GLORY GRACE HERRY IZZAT
MENSE MENSK SPEAK TREAT
CREDIT DECORE ENHALO ESTEEM
HOMAGE HONOUR LAUREL PRAISE
REVERE SALUTE WORTHY DIGNITY
EMBLAZE GLORIFY HONESTY
MANSHIP RESPECT WORSHIP
DECORATE GRANDEZA TASHREEF
(PL.) ACES

HONORABLE DEAR FREE GOOD
DIGNE NOBLE OPIME WHITE GENTLE
HONEST HONORA LORDLY SQUARE
UPRIGHT GENEROUS HANDSOME
HONORARY

HONORABLENESS HONESTY

HONORABLY GENTLY

HONORARIUM SALARY DOUCEUR
ALTARAGE HONORARY

HONORED GOOD FAMOUS LAUREL
LAURELED

HONORIFIC MAGNIFIC

HOOD HOW COIF COWL HEAD HUDE
JACK AMICE ALMUCE BIGGIN
BONNET BURLET CALASH CAMAIL
CANOPY CAPOTE CUTOFF DOMINO
FUNNEL MANTLE RAFFIA BANGKOK
BASHLYK CALOTTE CAPUCHE
BLINDAGE CAPUTIUM CHAPERON
CUCULLUS FOOLSCAP LIRIPIPE
LIRIPOOP MAZARINE TROTCOZY
(— AND CAPE COMBINED)
FALDETTA
(— OF BOILER) VOMIT
(— OF CARRIAGE) HEAD
(— OF MAIL) COIF CAMAIL COIFFE
(— OF VEHICLE) TOP CAPOTE
(— ON CUPBOARD) TREMOR
(— ON HORSES) BLINKER
(LENS —) SUNSHADE
(MONK'S —) COWL
(STIRRUP —) TAPADERO
(STRAW —) JAVA
(WOMAN'S —) SURTOUT VOLUPER

HOODED COWLED GALEATE

HOODED CROW HOODIE GRAYBACK
GREYBACK

HOODED MERGANSER SMEW
SNOWL SPIKE TADPOLE TOWHEAD
MOSSHEAD

HOODED SEAL WIG HOOD
HOODCAP

HOODLUM HOOD BADDY BADDIE
SKOLLY LURCHER HOOLIGAN
LARRIKIN

HOODOO JINX

HOODWINK MOP DUPE FOOL BLEAR
BLIND BLUFF CHEAT CLOYNE
DELUDE GAMMON WIMPLE AVEUGLE
BEGUILE BLINKER DECEIVE MISLEAD
INVEIGLE

HOOEY BUSHWAH

HOOF CLOOF CLOOT COFFIN UNGUIS
UNGULA CLOOTIE HOOFLET
FOREHOOF

HOOK DOG GAB JIG PEW TUG CLIP
DRAG FLAG GAFF HAKE HUCK KILP
MEAK NOCK PRIN PUGH SETT SKID
STAY TACK CATCH CLEEK CLICK

CRAMP CROME CROOK DRAIL
HAMUS ONCIN PREEN SARPE SPOON
TACHE UNCUS BECKET DETENT
HANGLE HINGLE PINTLE TENTER
AGRAFFE GAMBREL GRUNTER
HAMULUS HITCHER HOOKLET
KNUCKLE NUTHOOK PELICAN
PENNANT PINHOOK POTHOOK
RAMHEAD SNIGGLE SPERKET
UNCINUS BOATHOOK CROTCHET
GRABHOOK PORTHOOK PULLBACK
VULSELLA WEEDHOOK
(— FISH) FOUL HANG SNAG DRAIL
HITCH STRIKE SNIGGLE FISHHOOK
(— FOR BACON) COMB
(— FOR KETTLE) KILP HANGLE
TRAMMEL
(— FOR POT) DRACKEN POTHOOK
SLOWRIE
(— FOR TWISTING HEMP) WHIRL
WHIRLER
(2 —S FASTENED AT SHANKS)
DOUBLES
(BENCH —) JACK
(BOAT —) HITCHER
(BOXING —) CROSS
(COUPLING —) JIGGER
(LONG-HANDLED —) HOCK MEAK
(MUSICAL —) FLAG PENNANT
(PRUNING —) SARPE CALABOZO
(REAPING —) HINK TWIBILL
(SAFETY —) CLEVIS
(SKIDDING —S) GRAB

HOOKAH KALIAN

HOOKED ADUNC UNCOUS FALCATE
HAMATED HAMULAR ADUNCATE
AQUILINE HAMIFORM UNCINATE

HOOKEDNESS ADUNCITY

HOOKER-OUT STICKMAN

HOOK-SHAPED ANKYROID

HOOKUP CIRCUIT

HOOKWORM STRONGYL

HOOLIGAN GOONDA
(PL.) AMALAITA

HOOP RIB BAIL BAND BOND BOOL
CLIP GIRD GIRR PASS RING TIRE
GARTH GIRTH FRETTE HOOPLE
LAGGIN WICKET CIRCLET GARLAND
TRUNDLE
(— FOR A SPAR) BANGLE
(— FOR BARREL) BAND GIRD GIRTH
(— FOR LAMPSHADE) HARP
(— FOR ORE BUCKET) CLEVIS
(— FOR WINNOWING GRAIN)
WEIGHT
(— NET) TRUNK
(— TO STRENGTHEN GUN) FRETTE
(HALF —) BAIL BALE

HOOPED RUNG

HOOPOE HOOP UPUPA WHOOP
IRRISOR DUNGBIRD PICARIAN

HOOPSKIRT TUBTAIL

HOOP SNAKE WAMPUM

HOOSE HUSK

HOOSIER STATE INDIANA

HOOT CURR WHOO WHOOT EXPLODE
ULULATE

HOP HIP NIP FLIP JUMP LEAP BOUND
HITCH SWINE FLIERS GAMBOL

SPRING TITTUP CROWHOP HOPBIND
HOPVINE LUPULUS SKIPPER

HOPBUSH AKE AKEAKE

HOP CLOVER SHAMROCK SUCKLING

HOPE WON DEEM SPES TROW THINK
TRUST DESIRE EXPECT PERDUE
ESPEIRE THOUGHT SPERANZA
VELLEITY
(VAIN —) PIPE WANHOPE

HOPEFUL FOND SANGUINE
WENLICHE

HOPELESS DULL ABJECT FORLORN
DOWNCAST

HOPELESSNESS DESPAIR

HOP HORNBEAM DEERWOOD
HARDHACK IRONWOOD

HOPI MOKI MOQUI

HOP-LIKE LUPULINE

HOPPER CURB JACK CLOSET
HAPPER MACARONI

HOPPLE HOBBLE PASTERN
SIDELANG

HOPS SHATTER
(— BETWEEN 2 AND 4 YEARS) OLDS

HOPSCOTCH POTSY HOPPERS
PALLALL PEEVERS

HOP TREE RUEWORT WINGSEED

HORDE ARMY CAMP CLAN PACK
CROWD GROUP SWARM LEGION
THRONG
(INNER —) BUKEYEF

HOREHOUND HENBIT MARVEL
WONDER MARRUBE

HORIZON LAYER COMPASS FINITOR
ORTERDE SKYLINE

HORIZONTAL LEVEL LINEAR NAIANT
ACLINAL STRAIGHT

HORIZONTALLY FLATLY BARWAYS
BARWISE ENDLONG FESSWAYS
FESSWISE

HORMIGO QUIRA

HORMONE CORTIN LUTEIN EQUILIN
ESTRIOL ESTRONE GASTRIN INSULIN
RELAXIN THEELIN THEELOL
ANDROGEN ENDOCRIN ESTROGEN
FLORIGEN GALACTIN LACTOGEN
OESTRIOL SECRETIN CORTISONE

HORN BEAK BATON BUGLE CONCH
CORNO CORNU SHOOT ANTLER
CLAXON KLAXON OXHORN TOOTER
ALPHORN ALTHORN BUFFALO
CLARONE FOGHORN HELICON
HUTCHET OUTHORN PRICKET
SHOPHAR UNICORN BEAKIRON
BUCKHORN CLAVICOR CORNICLE
OLIPHANT SLUGHORN STAGHORN
WALDHORN
(— NOTE) MORT
(— OF CRESCENT MOON) CUSP
(— OF DILEMMA) PIKE
(— OF DRINK) SLOSH
(— OF YOUNG STAG) BUNCH
(BUDDING —) SHOOT
(DRINKING —) RHYTON
(ENGLISH —) CA
(FRENCH —) CORNO
(GREY —) COLUMN
(HUNTER'S —) HUTCHET
(INSECT'S —) ANTENNA

(RAM'S —) SHOPHAR
(RUDIMENTARY —) SLUG
(STUNTED —) SCUR
HORNBEAM HARDBEAM HARDHACK
HORNWOOD IRONWOOD
HORNBILL TOCK CALAO TOUCAN
HOMURAI BROMVOEL PICARIAN
YEARBIRD
HORNBLENDE SIDERITE
HORNED FORKED
HORNED DACE CHUB
HORNED POUT CATFISH
HORNED SCREAMER ANHIMA
KAMACHI UNICORN
HORNED VIPER WAMPUM
CERASTES
HORNET VESPA VESPID STINGER
HORNGELD CORNAGE
HORNLESS NAT NOT MOIL POLL
DODDY MULEY POLEY DODDED
HUMBLE HUMMEL MAILIE MULLEY
POLLED ACEROUS
HORNPIPE MATELOTE
HORN POPPY SQUATMORE
HORNSTONE KERALITE
HORNTAIL SIREX ORYSSID
UROCERID WOODWORM
HORNWORT COONTAIL HORNWEED
HORNY WAUKIT CALLOUS CERATOID
CORNEOUS KERASINE KERATOID
HORNYHEAD CHUB
HOROSCOPE SCOPE THEME FIGURE
GENESIS NATIVITY
HORRIBLE DIRE GRIM UGLY GREAT
GRISLY HORRID GEARFUL GHASTLY
HIDEOUS HORRENT UNSLOGH
DREADFUL GRUESOME HORRIFIC
SHOCKING TERRIBLE
HORRID GRIM UGLY AWFUL ROUGH
RUGGED SNUFFY UGSOME WICKED
HIDEOUS DREADFUL GRUESOME
HORRIBLE SHOCKING
HORRIFIC FEARFUL
HORRIFIED AGHAST GHASTLY
HORRENT
HORRIFY DISMAY ENHORROR
HORROR FEAR DREAD TERROR
(PL.) JIMJAMS
HORS D'OEUVRE CANAPE RELISH
OUTWORK ZAKUSKA
(PL.) ASSIETTE
HORSE BAY CUT DUN GEE GRI NAG
PAD POT RIP TIT ARAB AVER BARB
DOON GOER GROG HACK HAND
HOSS JADE MARE MOKE PRAD
PROD QUAD RACK RIDE ROAN ROIL
SKIN STUD TEAM TURK WEED YAWD
ZAIN AIVER ARION ARVAK BEAST
BIDET BLACK BROCK CAPLE CAPUL
CHUNK CREAM CROCK DUMMY
EQUID FAVEL GLYDE GRANI HAIRY
HOBBY MILER MOREL PACER PINTO
PIPER POLER PUNCH RACER ROGUE
RUNSY SCREW SHIER SHIRE SKATE
SOMER STEED STIFF TACKY WALER
WIDGE ALEZAN AMBLER BANKER
BOLTER BRONCO BRUMBY BUCKER
BUSSER CABBER CALICO CASTER
CHEVAL COLLOP CURTAL CUSSER

DAPPLE DOBBIN DRIVER ENTIRE
EQUINE FENCER FILLER GANGER
GARRON GLEYDE GRULLA HUNTER
JUMPER KEFFEL LEADER MAIDEN
MORGAN NUBIAN ORLOFF OUTLAW
PELTER PLATER POSTER PULLER
ROARER ROUNCY RUNNER SAVAGE
SORREL STAGER TARPAN TRACER
TURKEY VANNER WARPER WEAVER
ALSVINN ALSVITH ARABIAN
BARBARY BELGIAN BOARDER
CABALLO CHARGER CLICKER
CLIPPER COACHER COCOTTE
COURSER CRIBBER CRIOLLA
CRITTER DRAFTER FLEMISH
GALATHE GELDING GIGSTER
GRUNTER HACKNEY KNACKER
LEEFANG MONTURE MUSTANG
NEIGHER PACOLET PALFREY
PIEBALD PRANCER PRANKER
RATTLER REESTER REFUSER
REMOUNT RUNAWAY SADDLER
SLEDDER SLEEPER SPANKER
STAGGIE STEPPER SUFFOLK
SUMPTER TRAPPER TRESTLE
TROOPER TROTTER WHEELER
ARDENNES BATHORSE BUCKSKIN
CHESTNUT CHEVALET COCKTAIL
COLICKER CREATURE CYLLAROS
DEMISANG DESTRIER EOHIPPUS
FOOTROPE FRIPPERY GALLOPER
GALLOWAY HRIMFAXI KADISCHI
MACHINER OUTSIDER RIDGLING
ROADSTER SKEWBALD STIBBLER
TRIPPLER WHISTLER YARRAMAN
(— ACT) MANAGE
(— CERTAIN NOT TO WIN) STIFF
(— ESTABLISHMENT) HARAS
(— LOSING FIXED RACE) STUMER
STUMOUR
(— OF UNIFORM DARK COLOR) ZAIN
(— RACE) WALKOVER
(—S RUNNING BEHIND) RUCK
(2-YEAR OLD —) TWINTER
(3 —S ABREAST) TROIKA
(3 —S ONE BEHIND ANOTHER)
RANDEM
(4 —S ABREAST) QUADRIGA
(ARABIAN —) ARAB KOHL ARABIAN
(BALKY —) JIBBER
(BROKEN-DOWN —) JADE CROCK
SCREW DURGAN GARRAN
(CALICO —) PINTO
(CASTRATED —) GELDING
(CLUMSY —) STAMMEL
(DECREPIT —) SKATE GLEYDE
(DRAFT —) HAIRY PUNCH SHIRE
BEETEWK BELGIAN SUFFOLK
(DROVE OF —S) ATAJO
(EASY-PACED —) PAD
(FALLOW —) FAVEL
(FAMILY —) DOBBIN
(FAST —) GANGER
(FEMALE —) MARE FILLY
(FLEMISH —) ROIL
(GRAY —) SCHIMMEL
(HIGH-SPIRITED —) STEPPER
(IMAGINARY —) AULLAY
(IMMUNIZED —) BLEEDER

(INFERIOR —) PLUG PLATER
(JUMPING —) LEPPER
(MALE —) STALLION
(NEAR —) HAND
(OLD —) JADE PROD AIVER CROCK
(PACK —) BIDET SUMPTER
(RANGE —) FANTAIL
(SHAFT —) SHAFTER THILLER
(SHAGGY —) ALTAI
(SLUGGISH —) HOG
(SMALL —) NAG TIT BIDET GENET
HOBBY JENNET GALLOWAY
(STOCKY —) COB
(TEAM OF —S) CARTWARE
(TEAM OF 3 —S WITH LEADER)
UNICORN
(TRICK —) SIMON
(UNBROKEN —) BRONCO
(VICIOUS —) LADINO
(WILD —) FUZZY BRUMBY KUMRAH
TARPAN JUGHEAD BANGTAIL
FUZZTAIL WARRIGAL
(WINGED —) PEGASUS
(WORN-OUT —) HACK GARRAN
KNACKER CROWBAIT
(WORTHLESS —) JADE SHACK
KEFFEL
(YOUNG —) TIT COLT FOAL STAG
STOT STAGGIE
(PL.) MANADA STABLE UNICORN
HORSE BALM KNOBWEED
KNOTROOT RICHWEED
HORSE BLANKET RUG MANTA
HORSE BOY TRACER
HORSE CHESTNUT CONKER
HORSECLOTH HOUSE HOUSING
HORSE DEALER COPER CHANTER
COURSER
HORSE-EYE JACK XUREL
HORSE FENNEL SESELI
HORSEFLESH JACK
HORSEFLY BOT GAD CLEG CLEGG
STOUT BOTFLY BREEZE GADBEE
GADFLY BULLDOG DEERFLY
TABANID
HORSEHAIR SETON
HORSELAUGH GUFFAW
HORSELEECH ALUKAH
HORSELOAD SEAM
HORSE MACKEREL TUNNY SAUREL
HORSEMAN RIDER CHARRO
COWBOY HUSSAR KNIGHT RUTTER
COURIER PICADOR PRICKER
GALLOPER
(PL.) HORSE CAVALRY
HORSEMANSHIP CAVALRY
HORSEMINT RIGNUM
HORSE MUSHROOM WHITECAP
HORSE NETTLE SOLANUM
HORSEPLAY HIJINKS
HORSEPOWER SOUP
HORSEPOX GREASE
HORSE-RADISH MAROR MOROR
REDCOLL
HORSE-RADISH TREE BEHN BEHEN
HORSESHOE TIP SHOE PLATE
HOBBER LUNETTE
HORSETAIL TAIL PRELE TOADPIPE
HORSETAIL LICHEN TREEHAIR

HORSETAIL TREE AGOHO AGOJO
HORSEWEED COCASH COWTAIL
HOGWEED FIREWEED SCABIOUS
HORTATORY EMOTIVE
HORUS SEPT SOPT SEPTI
HORMAKHU
(FATHER OF —) OSIRIS
HOSACKIA ACMISPON
HOSE LINE VAMP HOSEN GASKIN
BROGUES BULLION HOSIERY
HANDLINE HOSEPIPE
HOSIERY HOSE KNITWEAR
(— WORKER) LOOPER
HOSPICE IMARET DIACONIA
HOSPITAL
HOSPITABLE DOUCE CLEVER
DOULCE SOCIAL CORDIAL FRIENDLY
HOSPITAL BEDLAM CRECHE SPITAL
COLLEGE LAZARET
HOSPITALITY SALT MENSE
XENODOCHY
HOSPODAR VOIVOD GOSPODAR
HOST SUM ARMY FYRD WARE
CROWD JASON MAKER POWER
SWARM WERED LEGION LODGER
NATION THRONG BALEBOS
COMPANY FYRDUNG SACRING
VIANDER LANDLORD PARTICLE
(— OF INVADERS) HERE
(EUCHARISTIC —) LAMB SACRING
(PL.) SABAOTH
HOSTA NIOBE FUNKIA
HOSTAGE BORROW PLEDGE SURETY
RANSOMER
HOSTEL INN ENTRY HOSTAGE
KINGDOM HOSPITAL
HOSTESS TAUPO LANDLADY
HOSTILE FOE HARD ALIEN BLACK
ENEMY FREMT HATEL STOUT
DEADLY FRIGID INFEST ADVERSE
ASOCIAL FIENDLY OPPOSED
UNQUERT WARLIKE CONTRARY
INIMICAL OPPOSITE
HOSTILITY WAR FEID FEUD HATE
ANIMUS ENMITY HATRED RANCOR
SCHISM DAGGERS RUPTURE
(PL.) WAR ARMS ARMOR WARFARE
HOSTLER NAGMAN OSTLER
HORSEBOY
HOT WARM CALID EAGER FIERY
ARDENT ESTIVE FERVID IGNITE
SULTRY TORRID ANIMOSE ANIMOUS
BOILING BURNING FERVENT
PEPPERY THERMAL CAYENNED
FEVERISH SEETHING SIZZLING
(— WATER) SOUP
HOTBED BED HOTHOUSE
HOT-BLOODED VASCULAR
HOTBOX SMOKER STINKER
HOTEL INN SPA FLOP FONDA HOUSE
HYDRO HOSTEL HOTTLE POSADA
FLEABAG FONDACO FUNDUCK
GASTHOF HOSTELRY
HOTELKEEPER HOTELIER
HOT-HEADED BRAINISH MADBRAIN
HOTHOUSE STEW STOVE PINERY
FRUITERY
HOT ROD DRAGSTER
HOT-TEMPERED PEPPERY

CHOLERIC SPITFIRE
HOTTENTOT TOTTY HOTNOT
KOKANA WITBOOI QUAEQUAE
(PL.) BALAO BALAWU
HOUND DOG PIE BAIT HARL HUNT
MUTE BRACE BRACH ENTRY HARRY
LEASH LIMER SLATE AFGHAN
BASSET BEAGLE HUNTER LEAMER
LUCERN SLEUTH TUFTER CURTISE
ENTRADA GELLERT REDBONE
SKIRTER BARUKHZY BLUETICK
BRATCHET COURSING FOXHOUND
(BITCH —) BRACH
(CRY OF —) MUSIC
(RELAY OF —S) VANLAY
(SLEUTH —) TALBOT
(SPECTRAL —) SHUCK
(PL.) RACHES
HOUND'S-TONGUE TORYWEED
HOUR URE TIDE TIME CURFEW
GHURRY
(6 —S) QUADRANT
(CANONICAL —) NONE SEXT PRIME
MATINS TIERCE VESPERS COMPLINE
EVENSONG
(HALF —) BELL
(KILOWATT —) KELVIN
(LAST —S) DEATHBED
(STUDY —) PREP
HOURLY HORAL HORARY
HOUSE BOX KEN CASA CRIB DOME
DUMP FIRM FLET HALL HELL HOLE
HOME RACE ROOF STOW ABODE
ADOBE AERIE BAHAY BANDA COVER
DACHA DOMUS HOOSE JACAL
LODGE MEESE STAGE WHARE
BIGGIN BOTTLE CAMARA CASITA
CASTLE CHEMIS CLOTHE DUPLEX
FAMILY HEARTH MAISON PALACE
PARISH SINGLE STABLE WIGWAM
BASTIDE BIGGING CABOOSE
CASSINE EUDEMON FAZENDA
HOGGERY HOUSING MESUDGE
QUARTER SHELTER AEDICULA
BARADARI BUNGALOW DOMICILE
DOVECOTE DWELLING MEDSTEAD
MESSUAGE TENEMENT
(— AND 5 ACRES) COTE
(— AND LAND) DEMESNE
(— FOR DOGS) KENNEL
(— FOR WOMEN) HAREM
(— IN BOROUGH) HAW
(— OF A MARABOUT) KOUBA
(— OF LEGISLATURE) CHAMBER
ASSEMBLY
(— OF PARLIAMENT) COMMONS
(— OF PROSTITUTION) CRIB BAGNIO
(— OF THIEVES) KEN
(— OF WORSHIP) BETHEL CHURCH
(APARTMENT —) INSULA
(ASTROLOGICAL —) ANGLE
(AUSTRALIAN —) HUMPY
(CHANGE —) DRY
(CHAPTER —) CABILDA
(CLAY —) ADOBE TEMBE
(COACH —) REMISE
(COMMUNAL —) MORONG
(COUNTRY —) PEN DACHA CASINO
GRANGE QUINTA BASTIDE CHATEAU

(COW —) VACCARY
(DAIRY —) WICK
(EATING —) COOKSHOP
(ESKIMO —) IGLU IGLOO TOPEK
KASHGA KASHIMA
(FIJI —) BURE
(FORTIFIED —) GARRISON
(GAMBLING —) BANK HELL
(GOVERNMENT —) KONAK
(GRINDING —) HULL
(HAWAIIAN —) HALE
(LODGING —) INN KIP HOST ENTRY
HOTEL HOSTEL
(LOG —) TILT
(MANOR —) HAM HALL COURT
PLACE SCHLOSS
(PLANETARY —) TOWER
(POULTRY —) ARK HENNERY
(PUBLIC —) INN HOSTEL SNUGGERY
(RANCH —) HUT
(RELIGIOUS —) CELL CONVENT
KELLION
(RENTED —) LET
(REST —) DAK KHAN SERAI
(RETREAT —) CENACLE
(ROOMING —) DOSS FLOP FLEABAG
(ROYAL —) AERIE
(SMALL —) COT HUT BACH CELL
CABIN HOVEL SHACK CASITA
COTTAGE
(SOD —) SODDY
(STILT —) CHIKEE CHICKEE
(SUMMER —) TRELLIS
(TENEMENT —) LAND CHAWL
(THATCHED —) BANDA
(TOY —) COBHOUSE
(TURKISH —) KONAK
HOUSEBOAT BARGE HOUSER
WANGAN DAHABEAH
HOUSEBREAKER MILL JACOB
MILLKEN
HOUSEBREAKING CRACK
HOUSECARL THINGMAN
HOUSECOAT DUSTER
HOUSEFINCH BURION LINNET
REDHEAD
HOUSEHOLD HIRED HOUSE FAMILY
HOUSAL MEINIE MENAGE FIRESIDE
MAINFAST
HOUSEHOLDER ASTRER GOODMAN
GUIDMAN NAUKRAR FRANKLIN
HOUSEKEEPER HUSSY MATRON
HOUSELEEK JUBARB AYEGREEN
HOMEWORT SENGREEN SILGREEN
HOUSEMATE DOMESTIC
HOUSEWARMING INFARE
HOUSEWIFE DAME FRAU FROW
WIFE HUSSY VROUW BUSHWIFE
HAUSFRAU
(MEAN —) NIP
HOUSING BOX BASE CASE DRUM
TRAP BANJO BLIMP GLOBE HOUSE
KIOSK BARREL RADOME SHIELD
HOUSAGE SHELTER DOGHOUSE
PADCLOTH PECTORAL PEDESTAL
(HORSE'S —) BASE
(RADAR —) BLISTER
(PL.) HOLSTERS
HOVA IMERINA

HOVEL COSH CREW CRIB CRUE HELM HULK HULL CHOZA HUTCH LODGE BURROW CRUIVE PONDOK

HOVELER HOBBLER HUFFLER

HOVER BAIT FLIT HANG HOVE BROOD FLUTTER HOVERER

HOW AS FOO HOO HOWE HOWEER HOWEVER QUOMODO WHEREBY

HOWDAH TOWER AMBARI AMBAREE

HOWEVER BUT THO YET HOWSO STILL THOUGH

HOWITZER HOWITZ LICORN UNICORN

HOWITZER SHELL OBUS

HOWL WAP WOW BAWL GOWL GURL HURL WAUL WAWL YAWL YOLL YOUT YOWL TIGER WHEWL WRAWL BEHOWL STEVEN ULULATE
(— **VOCIFEROUSLY**) TONGUE

HOWLER ERROR ARAGUATO

HOWLER MONKEY MONO ARABA HOWLER GUARIBA GUEREBA STENTOR ALOUATTE

HOWLING ULULANT

HOY TJALK CRUMSTER

HOYDEN MEG BLOWZE RIGSBY TOMBOY

HREIDMAR (SON OF —) REGIN FAFNER

H-SHAPED ZYGAL

HUAMUCHIL INGA

HUAVE WABI HUABI

HUB HOB BOSS NAVE STOCK CENTER CENTRE FAUCET HUBBLE SOCKET SPIDER OMPHALOS
(— **AND SPOKES**) SPEECH

HUBBLE-BUBBLE CALEAN CALAHAN

HUBBUB DIN STIR CLAMOR FRAISE HUBBLE RACKET TUMULT BOBBERY CLUTTER BROUHAHA HUBBABOO ROWDYDOW SPLATTER

HUCHEN HUSO

HUCHNOM TATU

HUCKLEBERRY HURT ERICAD CRACKERS

HUCKSTER BADGER CADGER KIDDER HAGGLER KIDDIER TRUCKER OUTCRIER

HUDDLE RUCK HUNCH CRINGE FUMBLE HOWDER HURTLE SCRUMP SHRIMP SHRINK CROODLE SCRINCH SCROOCH SCRUNCH SHUFFLE

HUE RUD BLEE BLUE COND CYAN CHLOR COLOR GREEN LEMON TAINT TINCT
(**DULL** —) DRAB
(**SOMBER** —) DARK

HUELESS GRAY GREY

HUFF DOD BLOW RUFF DRUNT SNUFF

HUFFY FUFFY SHIRTY

HUG CLIP COLL COUL MOLD CREEM CRUSH HALSE CUDDLE HUDDLE HUGGLE STRAIN CHERISH EMBRACE SQUEEZE

HUGE BIG FELL MAIN VAST ENORM GIANT GREAT JUMBO LARGE STOUR HEROIC IMMANE BANGING BUMPING DECUMAN IMMENSE MASSIVE MONSTER TITANIC COLOSSAL ENORMOUS GALACTIC GIGANTIC MOUNTAIN PYTHONIC SLASHING SWAPPING THWACKING

HUGENESS ENORMITY

HUISACHE WABI AROMO CASSIE POPINAC OPOPANAX

HULK CHOP HULL CORSE

HULL HUD POD BODY BULK HULK HUSK PILL BURSE CASCO SWELL
(— **OF COTTON BOLL**) BUR BURR
(— **OF SHIP**) BODY HULK BOTTOM

HULLABALOO DIN FLAP CLAMOR HUBBUB RACKET BROUHAHA

HUM BUM BLUR BRUM BUZZ HUSS TUNE CHIRM CROON DRONE FEIGN SOUGH SOWFF HUMBLE TEEDLE FREDDON TRUMPET

HUMAN BEING MANLY FINITE FLESHY HUMANE MORTAL MANNISH HOMININE HUMANIST

HUMAN BEING MAN WIGHT MORTAL PERSON ADAMITE CREATURE RATIONAL

HUMANE CIVIL KINDLY TENDER MERCIFUL

HUMANELY MANLY

HUMANITY FLESH MENSK WORLD MANHEAD MANHOOD MANSHIP SPECIES ADAMHOOD HUMANISM KINDNESS LENITUDE

HUMBLE LOW HOWE MEAN MILD MURE POOR TAME VAIL ABASE ABATE BUXOM DEMIT DIMIT LOWER LOWLY PLAIN SILLY SMALL SOBER WORMY ATTERR DEJECT DEMISS EMBASE HONEST MASTER MODEST REDUCE SIMPLE SLIGHT UNPUFF AFFLICT DEGRADE DEPRESS FOOLISH IGNOBLE MORTIFY OBSCURE CONTRITE DISGRACE
(— **ONESELF**) STOOP GROVEL

HUMBLED SMALL ABASED DEJECTED

HUMBLENESS HUMILITY

HUMBLER INFERIOR

HUMBLING SETDOWN

HUMBLY SIMPLE

HUMBUG GAS GUM HUM KID FLAM GAME GUFF JAZZ SHAM CHEAT FRAUD FUDGE GUILE JOLLY SPOOK TRICK BLAGUE GAMMON FLUMMER VERNEUK FLIMFLAM FLUMMERY HUCKMUCK IMPOSTER NONSENSE

HUMDINGER DOOZY DINGER HUMMER SNORTER

HUMDRUM IRKSOME PROSAIC

HUMERUS ARM

HUMID WET DAMP DANK MOIST SOGGY STICKY SULTRY WETTISH HUMOROUS

HUMILIATE ABASE ABASH SCALP SHAME NIDDER NITHER DEGRADE MORTIFY UNPLUME DISGRACE

HUMILIATED SMALL ASHAMED

HUMILIATION DUST COMEDOWN DISGRACE

HUMILITY MODESTY MEEKNESS MILDNESS

HUMIN MELANIN

HUMMEL FALTER

HUMMING AHUM BROOL SINGING

HUMMINGBIRD RUBY STAR MANGO SYLPH TENUI TOPAZ AMAZON COQUET HERMIT HUMMER ROSTER SAPPHO COLIBRI EMERALD HUMBIRD JACOBIN RAINBOW SNOWCAP TROCHIL WARRIOR CALLIOPE COQUETTE FIRETAIL FROUFROU MIMOTYPE PICARIAN SAPPHIRE WHITETIP

HUMMOCK HUMP CHENIER HAMMOCK TUSSOCK

HUMOR CUE PIN TID WIT BABY BILE CANT MOOD TIFF VEIN WHIM FRAME IRONY TUTOR MEGRIM PHLEGM SANIES SOOTHE SPLEEN SPRITE TEMPER FOOLING GRATIFY INDULGE VITREUM VITRINA ARCHNESS DISHUMOR DROLLERY EYEWATER FUMOSITY SANGUINE VITREOUS
(**BAD** —) BATS THROW
(**ILL** —) BILE DUDGEON
(**QUIET** —) DRYNESS
(**SLIMY** —) HIPPOMANES

HUMORIST JOKER FUNSTER FUNMAKER FUNNYMAN

HUMOROUS DROLL FUNNY QUEER JOCOSE COMICAL GIOCOSO PLAYFUL WAGGISH PLEASANT SARDONIC

HUMP BOSS HUNK BULGE BUNCH CROUP CRUMP HULCH HUNCH GIBBER GIBBUS HUMMIE GIBBOUS

HUMPBACK LORD CRUMP PUNCH

HUMPBACKED HUMPED HUMPTY GIBBOSE GIBBOUS

HUMPBACKED SALMON HADDO HOLIA

HUMPED HULCH HUMPY HUTCH HUMPTY HUNCHY

HUMUS MOR MOLD MULL HUMIN MOULD

HUNCH HUMP HUNK HULCH HUNCHET SCRUNCH

HUNCHBACK URCHIN HUMPBACK

HUNDRED RHO CENT CENTUM HUNDER HUNNER CANTRED CENTARY
(— **THOUSAND**) LAC LAKH
(**5** —) D

HUNDREDFOLD CENTUPLE

HUNDREDTH (— OF INCH) POINT
(— **OF RIGHT ANGLE**) GRAD GRADE

HUNDREDWEIGHT CENT CENTAL CENTENA CENTNER HUNDRED QUINTAL

HUNGARIAN HUN KUMAN MAGYAR

HUNGARY

CANAL: SIO SARVIZ
CAPITAL: BUDAPEST
COIN: GARA BALAS LENGO FILLER FORINT KORONA
DANCE: CZARDAS
DYNASTY: ARPAD ANGEVIN
FOREST: BAKONY
GYPSY: SZIGANE TZIGANI

KING: BELA GEZA IMRE ARPAD ISTVAN KALMAN MATTHIAS
LAKE: FERTO BALATON VELENCE BLATENSEE
MEASURE: AKO HOLD JOCH YOKE ANTAL ITCZE MAROK METZE HUVELYK MERFOLD
MOUNTAIN: KEKES BAKONY MECSEK BORZSONY KORISHEGY
MOUNTAIN RANGE: BUKK MATRA MECSEK CARPATHIAN
MUSICAL INSTRUMENT: TAROGATO
NATIVE: HUN SERB CROAT GYPSY MAGYAR SLOVAK UGRIAN
PLAIN: PUSZTA
REGIME: KADAR
RIVER: DUNA MURA RAAB RABA SAJO ZALA BODVA DRAVA DRAVE IPOLY KAPOS KOROS MAROS RABCA TARNA TISZA DANUBE HENRAD POPRAD SZAMOS THEISS ZAGYVA VISTULA BERRETYO
TOWN: ABA ACS OZD VAC BUDA EGER GYOR MAKO PAPA PECS PEST TATA ZIRC KOMLO CEGLED MOHACS SOPRON SZEGED DBRECEN MISKOLC SZENTES DEBRECEN SZEGEDIN
WEIGHT: VAMFONT VAMMAZSA
WINE: EGER TOKAJ TOKAY SZEKSZARD

HUNGER BELL CLEM WANT ACORIA DESIRE FAMINE CRAVING
HUNGRY YAP HOWE KEEN LEER EMPTY THIRL HOLLOW JEJUNE PECKISH YAPPISH ANHUNGRY ESURIENT
HUNK DAD DAUD JUNK MOUNTAIN
(— **OF BREAD**) TOMMY
HUNT DOG GUN JAG MOB RUN GREW JACK LARK PUMP SEAL SEEK SHOP CHASE CHEVY DRIVE HOUND REVAY TRACK TRAIL BATTUE BEAGLE BREVIT CHEVVY COURSE FALCON FERRET SEARCH SHIKAR VANLAY ENCHASE AUCUPATE PIGSTICK SCROUNGE
(— **BIG GAME**) GHOOM
(— **DEER**) FLOAT
(— **DOWN**) QUARRY
(— **DUCKS**) TOLL
(— **FOX**) CUB
(— **WITH HAWK**) FLY
(— **WITH SPEAR**) STICK
HUNTER GUN HUNT PINK JAGER BIRDER CHASER GUNNER JAEGER NIMROD THERON ACTAEON BUSHMAN CATCHER COURSER MONTERO SHIKARI SHOOTER SKIRTER STALKER TRAILER VENERER CEPHALUS CHASSEUR FIELDMAN HUNTSMAN TRAILMAN
(— **ON SNOW**) CRUSTER
(**BUFFALO** —) CIBOLERO

(**MYTHOLOGICAL** —) GWYN ORION
(**RING OF** —**S**) TINCHEL TINCHILL
HUNTING DRAG HANK AHUNT WATHE SHIKAR VENERY CUBBING GUNNING BEAGLING PURCHASE SHOOTING SURROUND VENATION
(— **SIGNAL**) SEEK
HUNTSMAN WHIP HUNTER JAEGER ACTAEON CATCHER COURSER MONTERO SCARLET VENATOR VENERER CHASSEUR
HURDLE TRAY FLAKE FRITH PANEL STALE STICK DOUBLE RADDLE SLEDGE WATTLE
HURDS TOW
HURDY-GURDY LIRA ROTA LANTUM VIELLE SAMBUKE HUMSTRUM SYMPHONY
HURL BUN CAST CLOD DASH DUST FIRE PASH PELT PICK SLAT SOAK SOCK DRIVE FLING HEAVE LANCE PITCH SLING SMITE SPANG SWING THIRL THROW WHIRL THRILL HURLBAT SWITHER WHITHER JACULATE
HURLY-BURLY HURL UPROAR
HURRAH HAIL HUZZA HOORAY HURRAY
HURRICANE PRESTER FURACANA FURICANE WILDWIND
HURRIED HASTY THRONG HASTEFUL SNATCHED
HURRY ADO FOG NIP RAP RUB RUN DUST HUMP PELL PLAT POST RAPE RESE RUSH STIR TIFT TROT URGE WHIR CHASE CROWD HASTE HYPER LURRY PRESS SESSA SKIRT SPEED STAVE STOUR WHIRL BUCKET BUNDLE BUSTLE HASTEN HUSTLE POWDER STROTH TATTER WHORRY HOTFOOT QUICKEN SCUDDLE SKELTER SLITHER WHITHER DISPATCH EXPEDITE SPLUTTER
(— **A HORSE**) SPUR
(— **ABOUT**) SCOUR
(— **AWAY**) FLEE BUNCH SCREW SKIRT
(— **CLUMSILY**) TAVE TEAVE
(— **NOISILY**) SPLUTTER
(— **OFF**) DUST
(— **UP**) BUSK
HURT CUT HOT DERE FIKE GALL HARM ABUSE BLAME GRIEF GRIPE SORRY SPITE THORN WATHE WOUND BRUISE DAMAGE GRIEVE IMPAIR INJURE INJURY LESION MIFFED MITTLE PAINED SCATHE STRAIN STROKE WINGED AFFLICT HURTING OFFENCE OFFENSE MISCHIEF NUISANCE
(— **EASILY**) FROISSE
(— **FEELINGS**) CUT TOUCH
(— **REPUTATION**) LIBEL
(— **SEVERELY**) KILL
(**EASILY** —) GINGER
HURTFUL BAD ILL EVIL MALIGN NOCENT NOCIVE NOUGHT SHREWD TAKING BANEFUL HARMFUL MALEFIC NOCUOUS NOXIOUS

UNQUERT GRIEVOUS HURTSOME SCATHFUL
HURTLE HURL FLING THIRL
HUSBAND EKE MAN WER BOND CHAP FERE KEEP LORD MAKE MATE SAVE SIRE BARON CHURL HOARD HUBBY MATCH STORE MANAGE MASTER MISTER SPOUSE CONSORT GOODMAN GUIDMAN HENPECK PARTNER CONSERVE
(— **OF ADULTRESS**) CUCKOLD
(**AFFIANCED** —) FUTURE
(**PL.**) PUNALUA
HUSBANDMAN BOND BOOR CARL CLOWN COLON TILLER ACREMAN HUSBAND PLOWMAN TILLMAN AGRICOLE
HUSBANDRY GAINER GAINOR THRIFT ECONOMY MANAGERY
HUSH SH HSH MUM PAX HESH HOOT LULL BURKE SHUSH STILL WHISH WHIST WHUSH HUDDLE HUSHABY SILENCE
HUSHED QUIET STILL GENTLE WHISHT
HUSK BUR COD HUD KEX SID BARK BURR COAT COSH HOSE HUCK HULK SEED SHIV SKIN HOOSE SCALE SHACK SHALE SHAUP SHELL SHILL SHOOD SHUCK SHUDE COLDER DEHUSK FLIGHT SLOUGH BOLSTER CARCASS CASCARA
(— **OF NUT**) SHACK BOLSTER
(— **OF OATS**) SHUD SHOOD FLIGHT
(**CORN** —) HOJA
(**PL.**) BHUSA CHAFF BHOOSA HULKAGE SHELLING
HUSKY HUSK CODDY FOGGY FURRED BUIRDLY HULKING BOUNCING SIBERIAN
HUSSITE TABORITE
HUSSY MINX SLUT BESOM CUTTY GIPSY GYPSY MADAM STRAP HIZZIE LIMMER DROSSEL
HUSTLE FAN HUMP JUMP BLITZ SKELP BUCKET BUNDLE BUSTLE JOSTLE RUSTLE SCUFTER
HUSTLECAP PINCH
HUSTLER HUSTLE PEELER BUSTLER FIREBALL
HUT COE COT BARI BUTT COSH COTE CREW CRIB HALE HULK HULL ISBA IZBA SHED SKEO TENT BASHA BENAB BOHIO BOTHY CABIN CHAWL CHOZA HOVEL HUMPY HUTCH JACAL KRAAL LODGE SCALE SETER SHACK SHIEL TOLDO TOPEK WHARE WURLY BOHAWN CANABA CHALET GUNYAH GUNYEH MIAMIA PONDOK RANCHO REFUGE SAETER SCONCE SHANTY SHELTY WIGWAM WIKIUP BALAGAN BARRACK BOUROCK CAMALIG COTTAGE GOONDIE HUDDOCK HUTMENT SHEBANG YAKUTAT BARABARA CHANTIER RONDAWEL SHIELING THOLTHAN TUGURIUM
(— **FOR TEMPORARY USE**) CORF
(— **OVER MINING SHAFT**) COE

(ABORIGINAL —) MIMI WURLY
GUNYAH MIAMIA WURLEY GOONDIE
(FISHERMAN'S —) SKEO
(HEATED —) HOTHOUSE
(HERMIT'S —) CELL
(NAVAJO —) HOGAN
(POULTRY —) IGLOO
(SAMOYED —) CHUM
(SIBERIAN —) JURT
(SOUTH AFRICAN —) STRUIS
HUTCH ARK RABBITRY
HUTIA UTIA JUTIA PILORI
HYACINTH LILY MUSK LILIUM
CROWTOE FLOATER GREGGLE
JACINTH BLUEBELL CROWFOOT
HAREBELL JACOUNCE
HYACINTH BEAN LABLAB BONAVIST
BONNYVIS DOLICHOS
HYACINTHUS (FATHER OF —)
AMYCLAS
(MOTHER OF —) DIOMEDE
HYALOGEN NEOSSIN
HYBRID DZO ZHO MULE ZOBO
CROSS GRADE HINNY LIGER
COYDOG GALYAK MOSAIC MULISH
SPLAKE TURKEN BASTARD BIGENER
CATTALO PLUMCOT ZEBRASS
ZEBRULA ZEBURRO CARIDEER
KAFERITA LIMEQUAT ZEBRINNY
HYBRIDIZE CROSS
HYDRANT CHUCK FIREPLUG
HYDRANTH SIPHON SYPHON
HYDRATE SLAKE
HYDRAZINE DIAMIDE
HYDRAZOATE AZIDE
HYDRIA KALPIS
HYDROCARBON ARENE CUMOL
FREON GUTTA IDRYL INDAN IRENE
TOLAN XYLOL ALKANE ALKYNE
ALLENE BUTANE BUTYNE CARANE
CETANE CETENE CYMENE DOCANE
ETHANE ETHENE HEXINE INDANE
INDENE MELENE NONENE OCTANE
OCTENE OCTINE PICENE PYRENE
RETENE TOLANE TOLUOL XYLENE
AMYLENE AZULENE BENZENE
CHOLANE CYCLENE DECALIN
ETHERIN FULVENE HEPTANE
HEPTENE HEPTYNE LYCOPIN
MUCKITE MYRCENE OLEFINE
PENTINE PENTYNE PROPANE
STYRENE TETROLE TOLUENE
BIPHENYL CADALENE CADINENE
CARBURAN CEROTENE CETYLENE

CHRYSENE CORONENE CUMULENE
DECYLENE DIOLEFIN DOCOSANE
DYSODILE EICOSANE ETHYLENE
EUDALENE FLUORENE HEXYLENE
ILLIPENE ISOPRENE LYCOPENE
MENTHENE NONYLENE OCTYLENE
PARAFFIN PRISTANE PYRACENE
RUTYLENE SABINENE SQUALENE
STILBENE
HYDROCYANIC PRUSSIC
HYDRODAMALIS RHYTINA
HYDROEXTRACTOR BUZZER
WHIZZER
HYDROFLUORIC PHTHORIC
HYDROGEN HYDRO
HYDROHEMATITE TURGITE
HYDROID POLYP OBELIA ACALEPH
ZOOPHYTE
HYDROLEA NAMA
HYDROMEL ALOJA
HYDROMETER SPINDLE
HYDROPERITONEUM ASCITES
HYDROPHOBIA LYSSA RABIES
HYDROPHOBIC LYSSIC
HYDROPHYLLIUM BRACT
HYDROXIDE ALKALI HYDRATE
HYDRIDE
HYDROZINCITE CALAMINE
HYENA HINE DABUH SIMIR HYAENID
HYGIENIC SANITARY
HYGRODEIK PAGOSCOPE
HYLLUS (FATHER OF —) HERCULES
(MOTHER OF —) DEIANIRA
(SLAYER OF —) ECHEMUS
(WIFE OF —) IOLE
HYLOZOIST PHYSICIST
HYMEN CHERRY BRIDEGOD
HYMENIUM THECIUM
HYMENOCALLIS ISMENE
HYMN ODE FUGE LAUD SING DIRGE
GATHA PAEAN PSALM YASHT
YMPNE ANTHEM CARVAL CHORAL
HIMENE HIRMOS MANTRA ORPHIC
THEODY VESPER CHORALE EXULTET
HEIRMOS INTROIT CANTICLE
DOXOLOGY ENCOMIUM PSALMODY
SEQUENCE
(— COLLECTION) MENAION
(MEXICAN —) ALABADO
(PL.) HYMNODY
HYMNAL HYMNARY HYMNBOOK
HYPERCORACOID RADIAL SCAPULA
HYPERCRITICAL NICE CAPTIOUS
CRITICAL

HYPERDULIA ADORATION
HYPEREMIA RUBOR
HYPEREMIC CONGESTED
HYPERICUM TUTSAN
HYPERION (DAUGHTER OF —)
AURORA
(FATHER OF —) URANUS
(MOTHER OF —) GAEA
(WIFE OF —) THEA
HYPEROPIC FARSIGHTED
HYPERSENSITIVITY ATOPY
HYPHA STOLON
HYPHEN BAND
(PL.) LEADERS
HYPNOTIC AMYTAL BARBITAL
HYPNOTISM DEVIL BRAIDISM
HYPNOSIS MESMERISM
HYPNOTIST OPERATOR SVENGALI
HYPOBLAST ENDODERM HYPODERM
HYPOCHONDRIA HIP HYP HYPO
MEGRIM
HYPOCHONDRIAC ARGAN HIPPY
HIPPIST
HYPOCOTYL RADICLE TIGELLA
TIGELLUS
HYPOCRISY SHAM POPEHOLY
HYPOCRITE CANT BIGOT CHEAT
FACER FRAUD BLIFIL CAFARD
HUMBUG MAWWORM CHADBAND
DECEIVER TARTUFFE
HYPOCRITICAL FALSE SLAPE
DOUBLE CANTING PLASTER
POPEHOLY SPECIOUS
HYPOCYCLOID ASTROID
HYPODERMIS SKIN
HYPOPHARYNX LINGUA LABIELLA
HYPOSTASIS PERSON
HYPOSTATIZE ENTIFY
HYPOTENUSE SUBTENSE
HYPOTHESIS SYSTEM THEORY
WEGENER SUPPOSAL
HYPOTHETICAL IDEAL
HYPOTRACHELIUM GORGERIN
HYPTIS OREGANO
HYRAX DAS CONY CONEY DAMAN
WABUR DASSIE WABBER ASHKOKO
KLIPDAS HYRACOID
HYSTERIA MOTHER PIBLOKTO
TARASSIS
(PRONE TO —) VAPORISH
(RELIGIOUS —) LATA
HYSTERICAL SHRIEKY

I Y HI HY ICH ISS SHE ITEM UTCH
INDIA UTCHY
(— **AM**) ISE CHAM ICHAM
(— **HAD**) CHAD
(— **WILL**) CHILL ICHULLE
(— **WOULD**) CHUD
IALEMUS (FATHER OF —) APOLLO
(**MOTHER OF** —) CALLIOPE
IAMB IAMBIC IAMBUS
(**DOUBLE** —) DIIAMB
IAPETUS (FATHER OF —) URANUS
(**MOTHER OF** —) GAEA
(**SON OF** —) ATLAS MENOETIUS
(**WIFE OF** —) ASIA CLYMENE
IAPYGIANS MESSAPII
IATROCHEMICAL SPAGYRIC
IATROCHEMISTRY SPAGYRIC
IBANAG CAGAYAN
IBEX KYL TEK TUR ZAC KAIL BEDEN
EVECK IZARD JAELA EVICKE
SAKEEN
IBIS GUARA GANNET HADADA JABIRU
TURKEY CICONIID IRONHEAD
ICARIUS (DAUGHTER OF —) ERIGONE
PENELOPE
(**FAITHFUL DOG OF** —) MOERA
(**FATHER OF** —) OEBALUS
ICE YS GEAL FROST GLACE CRYSTAL
VERGLAS
(— **IN ROUGH BLOCKS**) RUBBLE
(**ANCHOR** —) FRAZIL
(**DRIFTING FRAGMENT OF** —) PAN
CALF
(**PATCH OF** —) RONE
(**PINNACLE OF** —) SERAC
(**RIDGE OF** —) HAMMOCK HUMMOCK
(**SEA** —) GLACON SLUDGE
(**SHORE** —) FAST
(**SLUSHY** —) SISH
(**SOFT** —) SLOB LOLLY
(**THIN NEW** —) DISH PANCAKE
(**THIN OR FLOATING** —) FLOE GRUE
BRASH
(**WATER** —) SHERBET
ICEBERG BERG GROWLER
FLOEBERG
ICEBOAT SKEETER
ICE CREAM BISK CREAM GLACE
AUFAIT BISQUE NOUGAT TASTER
SPUMONI TORTONI
ICE CREAM CONE CORNET
ICED COLD GLACE FRAPPE
ICEFISH SALANGID
ICEHOUSE (— WORKER) AIRMAN

ICELAND
BALLAD: RIMUR
CAPITAL: REIKJAVIK REYKJAVIK
COIN: AURAR EYRIR KRONA
DISH: SKYR SVIO BLOOMOR
HAROFISK
EPIC: EDDA SAGA
FIRST SETTLER: ARNARSON
GEYSER: GRYLA
GIANT: ATLI
GLACIER: HOFSJOKULL
LANGJOKULL VATNAJOKULL

HERO: BELE ERIC LEIF
SIGUROSSON
LAKE: MYVATN THORISVATN
MEASURE: SET ALIN LINA ALMUD
TURMA ALMENN ALMUDE
FERFET POTTUR FATHMUR
FERALIN FERMILA OLTUNNA
SJOMILA
MOUNTAIN: JOKUL
PARLIAMENT: ALTHING
REPUBLIC: LYOVELDIO
RIVER: HVITA JOKULSA THJORSA
TOWN: AKRANES AKUREYRI
KEFLAVIK KOPAVOGUR
VOLCANIC ISLAND: SURTSEY
VOLCANO: LAKI ASKJA HEKLA
WATERFALL: GULLFOSS
DETTIFOSS
WEIGHT: PUND POUND

ICHNEUMON URVA NYMSS VANSIRE
ICHOROUS GLEETY
ICHU HICHU STIPA
ICICLE ICARY ICKLE YOKEL TANGLE
SHOGGLE SHOOGLE COCKBELL
ICINESS GLARE
ICING ICE PIPING FROSTING
MERINGUE
ICON IKON EIKON IMAGE DEESIS
ICONOCLAST DEBUNKER
ICONOSTASIS DIASTYLE
ICTEROHEMATURIA CARCEAG
ICTONYX ZORILLA
ICTUS ACCENT DOWNBEAT
ICY GELID BOREAL FRIGID WINTRY
GLACIAL
ID ES ORF GARDON SYPHILID

IDAHO
CAPITAL: BOISE
COUNTY: ADA GEM BUTTE LATAH
POWER TETON CARNAS CASSIA
BENEWAH KOOTENAI
DAM: OXBOW BROWNLEE
INDIAN: BANNOCK KALISPEL
NEZPERCE SHOSHONI
LAKE: BEAR GRAYS PRIEST
MOUNTAIN: RYAN BORAH RHODES
TAYLOR BIGBALDY BLUENOSE
MOUNTAIN RANGE: CABINET
SELKIRK
NICKNAME: GEM
RIVER: SNAKE LOCHSA SALMON
PAYETTE
SPRINGS: SODA HOOPER
LAVAHOT
STATE BIRD: BLUEBIRD
STATE FLOWER: SYRINGA
TOWN: BUHL MALAD NAMPA
MOSCOW REXBURG POCATELLO

IDAS (BROTHER OF —) LYNCEUS
(**FATHER OF** —) APHAREUS
(**WIFE OF** —) MARPESSA
IDE ORFE
IDEA EGG GIG KINK EIDOS IMAGE
THING ANONYM DHARMA ECTYPE

FIGURE INTENT NOTICE NOTION
RECEPT THREAP THROPE BEGRIFF
CONCEIT CONCEPT GIMMICK
GLIMPSE MAROTTE OPINION
PROJECT SPECIES SURMISE
THOUGHT GIMCRACK NOTIONAL
(—**S OF LITTLE VALUE**) STUFF
(**CENTRAL** —) ARGUMENT
(**CONSERVATIVE** —**S**) FOGYISM
(**DULL STUPID** —**S**) STODGE
(**FAINT** —) GLIMMER
(**FALSE** —) FALLACY
(**FANTASTIC** —) VAPOR
(**FAVORITE** —) HORSE
(**FIXED** —) TICK
(**FUNDAMENTAL** —) KEYNOTE
(**IRRATIONAL** —) FOLLY
(**MUSICAL** —) SENTENCE
(**ODD** —) FREAK
(**OVERWORKED** —) CLICHE
(**PLATONIC** —) ESSENCE
(**RECURRING** —) BURDEN
(**STALE** —**S**) BILGE
(**SUPERSTITIOUS** —) FREIT
(**TRANSCENDENT** —) FORM
(**PL.**) THOUGHT
IDEAL ISM IDEA DREAM AERIAL
BEAUTY DOMNEI DREAMY MENTAL
UNREAL PATTERN PERFECT
UTOPIAN ABSTRACT FANCIFUL
IDEALITY QUADRATE
(— **OF BEAUTY**) KALON
IDEALISM IDEOLOGY
IDEALIST IDEIST UTOPIAN FICHTEAN
UTOPIAST
IDENTICAL LIKE SAME SELF VERY
ALIKE EQUAL EVENLY PROPER
CORRECT IDENTIC NUMERIC
SELFSAME
IDENTIFICATION IDENT DOCUMENT
EQUATION
IDENTIFIED SIGNATE
IDENTIFIER BIRDER
IDENTIFY MARK NAME RANK SPOT
IDENT TALLY FINGER DISCERN
DIAGNOSE
(— **WITH**) ENTER
IDENTITY UNITY IPSEITY ONENESS
EQUALITY SAMENESS
IDEOGRAPH CHARACTER
(**PL.**) KANJI
IDEOGRAPHIC REAL
IDEOLOGICAL MENTAL
IDIOBLAST SPHERE IDIOSOME
IDIOCY ANOIA ANOESIA FATUITY
IDIOTRY MOROSIS IDIOTISM
IDIOM CANT ARGOT JUANG DORISM
IFUGAO JARGON MEDISM SPEECH
AEOLISM ANOMALY GRECISM
TURKISM DANICISM DORICISM
IDIOTISM IONICISM LANGUAGE
LOCALISM RURALISM
IDIOMORPHIC EUHEDRAL
IDIOPHONE RATTLE
IDIOSOME SPHERE
IDIOSYNCRASY WAY IDIASM
RUMNESS
IDIOT FON OAF SOT DAFF DOLT
FOOL AMENT BOOBY DUNCE FONNE

HOBBIL NIDGET NIDIOT DULLARD
NATURAL OMADAWN PINHEAD
IMBECILE INNOCENT
IDIOTIC DAFT ZANY IDIOT FATUOUS
FOOLISH WANTWIT IMBECILE
IDLE COLD DEAD HACK HAKE HANG
HULL JAUK LAKE LAZE LAZY LUSK
MUZZ SOFT SORN TICK VAIN VOID
DALLY EMPTY SHOOL SLIVE THOKE
WASTE COOTER DANDER DREAMY
FOOTER GAMMER LOUNGY OTIANT
OTIOSE SLIMSY TEETER TIDDIE
TIFFLE TRUANT UNUSED VACANT
IDLEFUL IDLESET LOAFING SAUNTER
SHACKLE SLUMBER SLUTHER
UNLUSTY VACUOUS WHIFFLE
WORLESS BASELESS FAINEANT
INACTIVE INDOLENT SHAMMOCK
SLAISTER SLOTHFUL TRIFLING
(TO BE —) SLOTH
IDLENESS LAZE RUST SLOTH IDLETY
IDLESET IDLESSE IGNAVIA VACANCY
FLANERIE IDLEHOOD INACTION
(— PERSONIFED) LAURENCE
LAWRENCE
(LIVE IN —) MAROON
IDLER BUM GAUM HAKE JAUK KERN
DRONE BADAUD BUMBLE IDLEBY
LUBBER PLAYER QUISBY RODNEY
STALKO BLELLUM BUCKEEN
DAWDLER FAITOUR FRANION
IDLESBY LOUNGER LOUTHER
LURDANE SLOUNGE TRIFLER
DOLITTLE FAINEANT IDLESHIP
LAZARONE UNWORKER WHIFFLER
IDLE WHEEL IDLER RUNNER
IDLY TOOMLY VAGUELY
IDMON (FATHER OF —) APOLLO
(MOTHER OF —) CYRENE ASTERIA
IDOCRASE EGERAN CYPRINE
VESUVIAN
IDOL GOD BAAL ICON JOSS TIKI ZEMI
ANITO BESAN EIKON GUACA HOBAL
HUACA IMAGE STOCK SWAMI
IDOLET IDOLUM MAUMET MINION
PAGODA POPPET PUPPET TERAPH
EIDOLON MAHOMET BAPHOMET
MAUMETRY PANTHEUM
(HEATHEN —) DEVIL
IDOLATER AKKUM HEATHEN IDOLIST
IDOLATROUS PAGAN IDOLISH
IDOLATRY BAALISM IMAGERY
ADULTERY MAUMETRY
IDOLIZE GOD IDOL ADORE ADMIRE
WORSHIP
IDUMAEAN EDOMITE
IDYL IDYLL BUCOLIC ECLOGUE
IDYLLIC PASTORAL
IF AN AND GIF GIN THO GEVE IFFEN
SOBEIT THOUGH PROVIDED
(— EVER) ONCE
(— NOT) BUT ELSE NISI
IGNEOUS PLUTONIC
IGNIS FATUUS WISP SPUNKIE
WILDFIRE
IGNITE FIRE TIND FLASH LIGHT
SHOOT ILLUME KINDLE CALCINE
LIGHTEN
IGNITED LIVING BURNING

IGNITER SPARKER
IGNITION FIRE LIGHTING
IGNOBLE LOW BASE MEAN VILE
ABJECT GRUBBY SORDID CURRISH
SERVILE UNNOBLE BASEBORN
SHAMEFUL
IGNOBLY BASELY
IGNOMINIOUS BASE INFAMOUS
SHAMEFUL
IGNOMINY SHAME REBUKE SCANDAL
DISGRACE DISHONOR
IGNORAMUS IDIOT IGNARO SIMPLE
AMHAAREZ
IGNORANCE IRONY TAMAS AGNOSY
AVIDYA AVIJJA BETISE NICETY
RUDITY UNSKILL DARKNESS
IDIOTISM
(FEIGNED —) IRONY
IGNORANT LAY DARK NICE RUDE
VAIN GREEN GROSS SILLY INGRAM
SIMPLE ARTLESS SECULAR
UNAWARE UNCOUTH UNKNOWN
IMPERITE INNOCENT INSCIENT
INSCIOUS NESCIENT UNTAUGHT
IGNORANTLY SIMPLY
IGNORE BALK BLOW SINK SNUB
VAIN BAULK BLINK ELIDE BYPASS
MISKEN SLIGHT DESPISE MISKNOW
CONFOUND OVERJUMP OVERLEAP
OVERLOOK
IGOROT BONTOK NABALOI KANKANAI
IGUANA GUANA GUANO LEGUAN
IJO DJO BONI BONNY
ILAIRA (FATHER OF —) LEUCIPPUS
(SISTER OF —) PHOEBE
ILEUS MISERERE
ILIA RHEA
(FATHER OF —) NUMITOR
(SON OF —) REMUS ROMULUS
ILIONE (FATHER OF —) PRIAM
(HUSBAND OF —) POLYMNESTOR
ILK KIN
ILL BAD EVIL ILLY SICK AEGER
DONCY FUNNY WISHT GROGGY
INJURY POORLY SICKLY UNWELL
SICKISH VICIOUS MISCHIEF
PHYSICAL
(— AT EASE) ASHAMED AWKWARD
ILL-ADVISED FOOLISH
ILL-BEHAVED UNTHEWED
ILL-BEING ILLTH
ILL-BODING DIRE DISMAL
ILL-BRED HOYDEN CADDISH
CHURLISH PLEBEIAN
ILL-CHOSEN UNSORTED
ILL-CONSIDERED HASTY
ILL-DEFINED BLIND VAGUE
ILLEGAL BLACK LAWLESS
UNLAWFUL WRONGOUS
(NOT —) COLD
ILLEGALITY UNLAW
ILLEGIBLE BLIND
ILLEGITIMACY BASTARDY
ILLEGITIMATE BASE BASTARD
BOOTLEG NATURAL NOTHOUS
MISBEGOT UNLAWFUL WRONGFUL
ILL-FATED UNHAPPY UNSONCY
UNCHANCY
ILL-FAVORED UGLY UNSONCY

ILL-FORMED SCRAWLY INFORMED
ILL HUMOR TID BILE DRUNT GRUMP
THRAW FANTEE SPLEEN DUDGEON
FANTIGUE
ILL-HUMORED FOUL GLUM CROOK
DUDDY GRUMPY MOROSE STUFFY
SULLEN CROOKED FRETFUL
PEEVISH
ILLIBERAL LITTLE NARROW INSULAR
GRUDGING
ILLICIT SLY BLACK ILLEGAL
UNLAWFUL
ILLIMITABLE INFINITE

ILLINOIS
CAPITAL: SPRINGFIELD
COLLEGE: AURORA EUREKA
OLIVET QUINCY SHIMER
COUNTY: BOND CASS COOK KANE
OGLE COLES MACON BUREAU
DUPAGE GRUNDY HARDIN
MASSAL PEORIA IROQUOIS
MACOUPIN SANGAMON
FRENCH SETTLEMENT: CAHOKIA
HILLS: SHAWNEE
INDIAN: FOX SAUK
LAKE: MICHIGAN
NICKNAME: PRAIRIE
RIVER: OHIO ROCK WABASH
ELKHORN MACKINAW
SANGAMON
STATE BIRD: CARDINAL
STATE FLOWER: VIOLET
STATE TREE: OAK
TOWN: PANA ALTON FLORA
OLNEY PEKIN ALBION CANTON
HERRIN JOLIET PEORIA SKOKIE
CHICAGO DECATUR GENESCO
MENDOTA NOKOMIS ROCKFORD

ILLINOISIAN SUCKER
ILLIPE BASSIA VIDORICUM
ILLITERATE UNREAD IGNORANT
MUSELESS UNTAUGHT
ILL-MADE AWKWARD
ILL-NATURED UGLY SURLY CRABBY
SNARLY SULLEN CANKERY PEEVISH
ILLNESS DROW TOUT BRASH CHILL
TRAIK MORBUS PLUNGE DISEASE
SICKNESS
(MINOR —) HURRY
(MOMENTARY —) DROW
(SUDDEN —) WEED SWEAM
ILL-NOURISHED SHELLY
ILLOGICAL SPURIOUS
ILL-OMENED DISMAL UNLUCKY
ILL-SHAPED WEEDY
ILL-SMELLING FUSTY STINKING
ILL-TEMPERED ILL FESS MEAN
PUXY CHUFF NURLY CAMMED
CHUFFY GIRNIE SHRILL SNAGGY
RAMPANT VICIOUS CAMSHACH
LUNGEOUS SHREWISH VIXENISH
ILL-TREAT FOB HOIN MISDO
AFFRONT
ILLUMINATE FIRE LIMN CLEAR
LIGHT ENLIMN ILLUME KINDLE
BESHINE CLARIFY EMBLAZE

LIGHTEN MINIATE RADIATE
EMBRIGHT FLOURISH ILLUMINE
LUMINATE
(— **FAINTLY**) TWILIGHT
ILLUMINATION E GLIM GLORY
LIGHT SHINE LIGHTING LUMINARY
(— **INCREASE**) WOMP
(— **UNIT**) PHOT
ILLUMINE SUN FIRE CLEAR LUMINE
ENLIGHT
ILL-USAGE ABUSE
ILLUSION DEATH ERROR FAIRY
FANCY FLESH TRICK MATTER
CHIMERA ELUSION FALLACY FICTION
MOCKERY PHANTOM RAINBOW
ZOLLNER DELUSION PHANTASM
PRESTIGE
ILLUSORY FALSE EVANID FATUOUS
APPARENT ILLUSIVE SPECTRAL
ILLUSTRATE INSTANCE
ILLUSTRATION CUT GAY ICON IKON
SHOW SPOT INSET FIGURE
COMPARE DISIMILE EXEMPLUM
INSTANCE VIGNETTE
ILLUSTRATIVE CLASSIC
ILLUSTRIOUS GRAND NOBLE NOTED
SHEEN BRIGHT CANDID HEROIC
EMINENT EXALTED GLORIED
SHINING GLORIOUS HEROICAL
LUCULENT MAGNIFIC PRECLARE
RENOWNED SPLENDID STARLIKE
ILL WILL SPITE ENMITY GRUDGE
MALICE MAUGER MAUGRE RANCOR
DESPITE AMBITION
ILL-WISHER FOE
ILUS (FATHER OF —) TROS
(**MOTHER OF** —) CALLIRRHOE
(**SON OF** —) LAOMEDON
ILVAITE YENITE LIEVRITE
ILYSIA TORTRIX
IMAGE DAP GOD MAP FORM ICON
IDOL IKON JOSS MAKE SEAL SIGN
SPIT TIKI AGNUS DITTO EPHOD
FANCY HERMA IMAGO MEDAL
MORAL PAINT PRINT SAMMY SANTO
SHAPE SIGIL SWAMI SWAMY TOTEM
AGALMA ALRAUN EFFIGY EMBLEM
FIGURE MAUMET MODULE POPPET
RECEPT REFLEX SHRINE SPHINX
STATUE SVAMIN TERAPH VISAGE
WEEPER EIDOLON EXPRESS
FANTASY GODLING IMAGERY
KATCINA PICTURE PROPOSE
CONCEIVE DAIBUTSU OPTOGRAM
PORTRAIT SURPRINT ZOOMORPH
(— **IN CHINESE COSTUME**)
MANDARIN
(— **OF CHRIST**) SUDARIUM
(— **OF DEITY**) SWAMI GODKIN
SVAMIN GODLING
(— **OF SAINT**) BULTO SAINT SANTO
GEORGE SANTON
(— **OF WOOD**) XOANON
(— **RECALLED BY MEMORY**) IDEA
(**CULT** —) JOSS
(**FALSE** —) GHOST
(**GOOD-LUCK** —) ALRAUN ALRUNA
(**HEAVENLY** —) FRAVASHI
(**LINGERING** —) SHADE

(**MENTAL** —) FANCY IMAGO RECEPT
CONCEPT FANTASY SPECIES
PHANTASM
(**RADAR** —) BLIP
(**REFLECTED** —) SHADOW SPECIES
(**SEQUENCE OF** —S) REVERIE
(**VAGUE** —S) FRINGE
(**PL.**) IMAGERY TERAPHIM
IMAGERY ICONISM
IMAGINARY IDEAL AERIAL FEIGNED
FICTIVE SHADOWY CHIMERAL
CHIMERIC FANCIFUL FICTIOUS
MYTHICAL NOTIONAL QUIXOTIC
ROMANTIC SCENICAL VISIONAL
IMAGINATION CHIC BRAIN FANCY
FLAME NOTION FANTASY PROJECT
THOUGHT
(**DROLL** —) HUMOR
IMAGINATIVE FORMFUL CREATIVE
FANCIFUL POETICAL
IMAGINE SEE WIS REDE WEEN
DREAM FANCY FEIGN FRAME GUESS
IMAGE THINK DEVISE FIGURE
IDEATE INVENT COMPASS CONCEIT
CONJURE FANCIFY FANTASY
FEATURE PICTURE PORTRAY
PROJECT PROPOSE SUPPOSE
SURMISE SUSPECT CONCEIVE
DAYDREAM JEALOUSE
IMAGINED FANCIED SUPPOSED
IMAGINER FANCIER
IMAGINING FICTION PHANTOM
IMAM IMAUM MAHDI
IMBALANCE DRIVE DYSCRASIA
IMBECILE MAD DOTE FOOL AMENT
DAFFY IDIOT CRANKY DOTARD
DOTING DOTISH CONGEON FATUOUS
IMBECILITY FATUITY
IMBIBE DRINK SMACK ABSORB
SPONGE INHAUST SWALLOW
IRRIGATE
IMBIBING SUCTION
IMBIBITORY SPONGY
IMBRUE EMBREW INSTEEP
IMBUE SOAK STEW COLOR CROWN
EMBUE INDUE SCENT STEEP TINCT
ENSOUL IMBIBE INFUSE LEAVEN
SEASON ANIMATE INGRAIN INSENSE
INSTILL SATURATE TINCTURE
IMBUED INSTINCT REDOLENT
IMIDE LACTIM SACCHARIN
IMITATE APE COPY ECHO MIME
MOCK ZANY ENSUE FORGE IMAGE
MIMIC ANSWER FOLLOW SEMBLE
COPYCAT EMULATE PAGEANT
PASTICHE RESEMBLE SIMULATE
IMITATION COPY FAKE SHAM
DUMMY IMAGE MIMIC ALPACA
ANSWER BUMPER ECTYPE SHADOW
CAMBLET FOULARD IMITANT
MIMESIS MOCKAGE MOCKERY
CHENILLE PARROTRY PASTICHE
POSTIQUE
(— **OF COIN**) COUNTER
(**BURLESQUE** —) TRAVESTY
(**EXAGGERATED** —) BURLESQUE
(**UNSUBSTANTIAL** —) GHOST
IMITATIVE ARTY MIMIC ARTFUL
ECHOIC SHODDY MIMETIC SIMULAR

SLAVISH APATETIC EPIGONAL
IMITATOR APE MIME ZANY MIMIC
COPIER COPYIST EPIGONE
EMULATOR EPIGONUS HOMERIST
IMMACULATE CLEAN CANDID
CHASTE BLOTLESS SPOTLESS
UNSOILED
IMMANENCE INBEING
IMMATERIAL MENTAL SLIGHT
ETHEREAL FORMLESS SEPARATE
TRIFLING
IMMATURE RAW CRUDE GREEN
SAPPY SMALL VEALY YOUNG
BOYISH CALLOW JEJUNE LARVAL
NEANIC TENDER GIRLISH HALFLIN
IMPUBIC LADDISH NOUVEAU
UNBAKED JUVENILE NEPIONIC
UNWEANED
IMMATURITY NONAGE
IMMEASURABLE UNTOLD INFINITE
IMMEDIACY HERE
IMMEDIATE DIRECT MODERN
PARATE SUDDEN INSTANT PRESENT
PROXIMAL SYNECTIC
IMMEDIATELY TIT ANON AWAY FAST
JUST ONCE SOON PLUMB RIGHT
ASTITE DIRECT PRESTO SUBITO
DIRECTLY HEREUPON OUTRIGHT
STRAIGHT
IMMEDIATENESS INSTANCY
IMMEMORIAL DATELESS
IMMENSE HUGE VAST GRAND GREAT
LARGE UNMEET UNRIDE TITANIC
ENORMOUS GIGANTIC INFINITE
SLASHING WHOOPING
IMMENSELY EVER
IMMENSITY VAST IMMANE IMMENSE
ENORMITY GRANDEUR HUGENESS
IMMERSE DIP SINK SOAK COVER
DOUSE MERGE MERSE SOUSE
STEEP DRENCH PLUNGE BAPTIZE
BOWSSEN DEMERGE EMBATHE
ENSTEEP IMMERGE DISSOLVE
IMMERSED DEEP INNATE
IMMERSION DIP DUNKING MERSION
IMMERSIONIST DIPPER
IMMIGRANT LAG BALT ISSEI JIMMY
METIC POMMY GUINEA HALUTZ
CHALUTZ INCOMER PILGRIM
COMELING
IMMINENCE INSTANCY
IMMINENT TOWARD PENDING
IMMOBILE FIXED STILL FROZEN
DORMANT GLACIAL TRANCED
MOVELESS
IMMOBILIZATION FUSION FIXATION
IMMOBILIZE FREEZE SPLINT
STIFFEN
IMMOBILIZED STIFF
IMMODERATE FREE DIZZY UNDUE
LAVISH UNMETH EXTREME
IMMODERATENESS EXCESS
IMMODEST FREE BRAZEN OBSCENE
INDECENT PETULANT UNCHASTE
IMMORAL BAD ILL EVIL IDLE LOOSE
WRONG WANTON CORRUPT VICIOUS
CULPABLE DEPRAVED INDECENT
SLIPPERY
IMMORTAL DIVINE ENDLESS

ETERNAL GODLIKE UNDYING
ENDURING UNDEADLY
IMMORTALITY ATHANASY ETERNITY
IMMOVABLE PAT SET FAST FIRM
FIXED RIGID ADAMANT SITFAST
CONSTANT IMMOBILE IMMOTIVE
OBDURATE
IMMUNE FREE SALTED
IMMUNITY SOC CHARTER FREEDOM
LIBERTY WOODGELD
IMMURE MURE WALL CONFINE
CLOISTER IMPRISON
IMMUTABILITY ONENESS
IMMUTABLE ETERNAL
IMP PUG LIMB DEVILET DEVILING
DEVILKIN FOLLETTO
IMPACT HIT JAR BEAT BITE BLOW
BUMP DASH JOLT SLAM BRUNT
CLASH FEEZE PEISE POISE PULSE
SHOCK SKITE GLANCE STROKE
CONTACT IMPULSE
IMPAIR MAR BLOT HARM HURT
MANK SOUR WEAR ALLOY CLOUD
CRACK CRAZE DECAY ERODE QUAIL
SPOIL TAINT ACRAZE DAMAGE
DEADEN DEFACE HINDER INJURE
LABEFY LESSEN REDUCE SICKEN
WEAKEN WORSEN BLEMISH DISABLE
IMPEACH REFRACT SHATTER
STRETCH VITIATE DECREASE
ENFEEBLE IMBECILE IMPERISH
INFRINGE LABEFACT
(— BY INACTIVITY) RUST
(— ESSENTIALLY) RUIN
IMPAIRED HURT STALE CROCKY
FLYBLOWN
(— BY AGE) FUSTY
(— IN TONE) BREATHY
IMPAIRMENT FAULT SPOIL DOTAGE
IMPAIR INJURY LESION BEATING
DEFICIT DISEASE EROSION WEARING
AKINESIA PAIRMENT
(— OF CONSCIOUSNESS) ABSENCE
IMPALA PALLA PALLAH REDBUCK
ROODEBOK
IMPALE BAIT SPIT GANCH GANSH
SPEAR SPIKE STAKE STICK STING
SKIVER TRANSFIX
IMPALPABLE ELUSIVE
IMPART GIVE SHED TELL BREAK
DRILL SHARE YIELD BESTOW
COMMON CONFER CONVEY DIRECT
IMPUTE INSTIL PARTEN REVEAL
DELIVER DIVULGE PURPORT
DISCOVER INSTRUCT INTIMATE
(— TONE) TONE
(— ZEST) ANIMATE
IMPARTIAL EVEN FAIR JUST EQUAL
LEVEL NEUTER UNBIASED
IMPARTIALITY CANDOR EQUITY
EQUACITY EVENNESS
IMPARTIALLY FAIRLY EQUALLY
IMPASSABLE WICKED PASSLESS
IMPASSE LOGJAM DEADLOCK
IMPASSION COMMOVE
IMPASSIONED ARDENT FERVID
FERVENT FEVERISH
IMPASSIVE FROZEN STOLID PASSIVE
STOICAL

IMPASSIVENESS APATHY MORGUE
STOICISM
IMPATIENT HOT ANTSY EAGER
HASTY SHARP TESTY FRETFUL
PEEVISH TIDIOSE CHOLERIC
PETULANT
IMPATIENTLY HASTILY
IMPEACH CALL ACCUSE CHARGE
INDICT ARRAIGN CENSURE IMPLEAD
TRAVERSE
IMPECCABLE SINLESS
IMPECUNIOUS POOR
IMPEDE BOG DAM GUM JAM LET
MAR CLOG GRAB JAMB KILL SLUG
SNAG ANNOY BLOCK CHECK CHOKE
DELAY EMBAR ESTOP HITCH SLOTH
SPOKE FETTER FORBID FORSET
HAMPER HARASS HINDER HOBBLE
PESTER RETARD STYMIE IMPEACH
PREVENT SHACKLE ENCUMBER
HANDICAP OBSTRUCT PRECLUDE
IMPEDIMENT BAR RUB CLOG SNAG
STOP BLEAR BLOCK HITCH SPOKE
STICK RUBBER SCOTCH BLINDER
EMBARGO OBSTACLE OBSTANCY
(— IN SPEECH) HAAR
IMPEDIMENTA STUFF
IMPEDING CATCH HEAVY FOULING
IMPEL PAT PUT BEAR BEAT CALL
CAST GOAD HURL MOVE SEND
URGE WHIP CARRY DRIVE FEEZE
FORCE KNOCK PRICK PULSE
COMPEL EXCITE INCITE INDUCE
PROPEL DESTINE INSPIRE INSTINCT
MOTIVATE
(— TO GREATER SPEED) GATHER
IMPELLER RUNNER
IMPEND BREW HANG DEPEND
IMPENDING PENDENT PENDING
IMMINENT MENACING
IMPENETRABLE HARD DENSE
MURKY PROOF THICK AIRTIGHT
HARDENED
IMPENITENT HARDENED OBDURATE
IMPERATIVE VITAL PRESSING
IMPERCEPTIBLE OCCULT SUBTLE
IMPERFECT ILL HALF POOR AMISS
BLIND FUZZY ROUGH FAULTY
PLATIC STICKIT UNWHOLE VICIOUS
INPARFIT MUTILOUS
IMPERFECTED INCHOATE
IMPERFECTION BUG RUB WEN
FLAW KINK MOLE SLUR VICE ERROR
FAULT BLOTCH DEFECT FOIBLE
BLEMISH CRUDITY DEFAULT
DEMERIT FAILING FRAILTY
WEAKNESS
(— IN BOTTLE) HEELTAP
(— IN GLASS) STRIA STREAK
(— IN LEATHER) FRIEZE
(— IN SILK) CORKSCREW
(— IN WICK) THIEF WASTER
IMPERFECTIVE ATELIC
IMPERFECTLY ILL HALF AMISS
IMPERFORATION ATRESIA
IMPERIAL TUFT ROYAL KINGLY
PURPLE MAJESTIC
IMPERIL RISK EXPONE EMPERIL
ENDANGER JEOPARDY

IMPERIOUS SURLY LORDLY
HAUGHTY DESPOTIC IMPERIAL
MASTERLY PRESSING
IMPERISHABLE ETERNAL UNDYING
ENDURING IMMORTAL
IMPERMANENCE ANICCA
IMPERMANENT FLEETING
IMPERSONAL COLD DEADPAN
INHUMAN ABSTRACT
IMPERSONATE ACT POSE TYPIFY
PERSONIFY
IMPERSONATION GENIUS
IMPERSONATOR ACTOR CACHINA
KACHINA KATCINA
IMPERTINENCE PAWK SNASH
AUDACITY
IMPERTINENT GAY FREE RUDE
FRESH SASSY SAUCY IMPERENT
IMPUDENT
IMPERTURBABILITY ATARAXY
ATARAXIA SANGFROID
IMPERTURBABLE COOL PLACID
GLACIAL TRANQUIL
IMPERVIOUS DEAD GASTIGHT
HARDENED HERMETIC
IMPETUOSITY FURY HASTE WRATH
FOUGUE POWDER RANDOM SPLEEN
IMPETUOUS HOT RAMP RUDE
BRASH EAGER FIERY FRECK HASTY
HEADY SHARP ARDENT BROTHE
FIERCE FLASHY LAVISH RACKLE
STRONG BUCKISH FURIOUS
HOTHEAD HOTSPUR BRAINISH
EMPRESSE HEADLONG SLAPDASH
VEHEMENT
IMPETUS BIRR FARD SEND DRIFT
GRACE SWING YMPET BENSEL
IMPACT POWDER RAVINE SWINGE
SWOUGH IMPULSE MOMENTUM
IMPINGE FALL IMPACT ASSAULT
CROSSCUT
IMPINGEMENT IMPACT
IMPIOUS UNHOLY ATHEIST ATHEOUS
GODLESS UNGODLY DOWNWEED
HOARWORT NEFANDOUS
IMPISH IMPY ELFISH WARLOCK
IMPLACABLE STOUT DEADLY
IMPLACABLY FATALLY
IMPLANT FIX IMP SOW HAFT ROOT
GRAFT INFIX INLAY ENRACE
ENROOT FASTEN INFUSE INSTIL
ENFORCE IMPRESS INSPIRE
ENTRENCH INSTINCT
IMPLANTED INBORN INSITE
IMPLEMENT (ALSO SEE TOOL) AX
AXE BAT CARD DISC DISK FORK
GRAB HACK HONE HOOK LOOM
PLOW SPUD SPUR TOOL CROOK
DRILL FLINT LANCE SCRUB SHEAR
SLICK SPADE SPOON STEEL STICK
TRIER AMGARN BEAMER BLADER
BROACH COLLAR COOLER DIBBLE
DREDGE DRIVER DUSTER EOLITH
FLAKER FLUTER HACKER HARROW
INVOKE LADDER LIPPER LUNATE
MARKER MEALER PACKER PADDLE
PALLET PESTLE PLOUGH RIMMER
SCREEN SCYTHE SEATER SEEDER
SERVER SHEARS SHOVEL SICKLE

SLICER SMOOTH BREAKER
CHOPPER CLEANER CLEAVER
ENFORCE FLESHER FLYFLAP
GAROTTE GRUBBER HARPOON
HUSTLER KNAPPER MATTOCK
NUTPICK SKIMMER SLABBER
SLASHER SLEEKER SLICKER
SPATTLE SPATULA SPITTLE
SPURTLE STAMPER STICKER
SWATHER UTENSIL AGITATOR
BUSHWACK MEASURER SCUTCHER
SEARCHER SHREDDER SKETCHER
SPLITTER SPREADER STRIPPER
TERRACER THWACKER TOLLIKER
TRANCHET TWEEZERS WARKLOOM
WORKLOOM
(— **FOR CUTTING CHEESE**) HARP
(— **FOR HANGING POT**) HALE
(— **TO PREVENT MALT FROM
OVERFLOWING**) STROM
(—**S OF HUSBANDRY**) WAINAGE
(**ANCIENT** —) POINT SLICE AMGARN
EOLITH NEOLITH RACLOIR
(**BAKER'S** —) PEEL
(**CLIMBING** —) CREEPER
(**ESKIMO** —) ULU
(**GARDENING** —) HOE RAKE SEEDER
SICKLE
(**HEDGING** —) TRAMP
(**IRRIGATION** —) CROWDER
(**LOGGING** —) TODE
(**POTTER'S** —) PALLET SPATTLE
(**PREHISTORIC** —) CELT FLAKER
(**SHOVEL-LIKE** —) SCOOP
(**SOLDERING** —) DOCTOR
(**TORTURE** —) ENGINE
(**UPROOTING** —) MAKE
(**WINNOWING** —) FAN
(PL.) GEAR CUTLERY GAINAGE
FLAUGHTS
IMPLICATE DIP ENWRAP CONCERN
EMBROIL INCLUDE INVOLVE
IMPLICATION CLAIM IMPLIAL
INNUENDO
IMPLICIT COVERT
IMPLIED TACIT IMPLICIT
IMPLORATION PETITION
IMPLORE ASK BEG CRY PRAY
CHARM CRAVE PLEAD INVOKE
BESEECH CONJURE ENTREAT
SOLICIT PETITION
IMPLY HINT ARGUE CARRY COUCH
INFER EMPLOY ENTAIL IMPORT
INDUCE CONNOTE CONTAIN
INCLUDE INVOLVE SIGNIFY SUGGEST
SUPPOSE
IMPOLITE RUDE UNCIVIL
IMPOLITENESS CRUDITY
IMPONDERABLE FRIGORIC
IMPORT SAY WIT BEAR BODY TOUR
DRIFT FORCE IMPLY MORAL SCOPE
SENSE SOUND SPELL VALOR
AMOUNT CHARGE DENOTE INGATE
INTENT MATTER BETOKEN MEANING
PRETEND SIGNIFY CARRIAGE
INDICATE
(PL.) INWARDS
IMPORTANCE BORE MARK PITH
FORCE POISE WORTH CHARGE

IMPORT MATTER MOMENT REMARK
STRESS STROKE WEIGHT ACCOUNT
ESSENCE GRAVITY VALENCY
EMPHASIS
IMPORTANT DEAR DREE HIGH MAIN
REAL GRAVE GREAT GAPING
NEEDLE STRONG URGENT VALOUR
CAPITAL CRUCIAL EMINENT
MATTERY SERIOUS EVENTFUL
MATERIAL
IMPORTER MILLINER
IMPORTUNATE URGENT INSTANT
DEVILING EXIGEANT PRESSING
IMPORTUNE BEG BEAT BONE TOUT
TEASE BESIEGE INSTANT SOLICIT
TERRIFY INSTANCE
IMPORTUNITY BRASS URGENCY
IMPOSE LAY SET TOP CLAP GIVE
LEVY MUMP POLE SORN ABUSE
APPLY INPUT STAMP TRUMP
BURDEN CHARGE ENJOIN ENTAIL
FASTEN FATHER IMPONE IMPUTE
BLAFLUM DICTATE INFLICT
IRROGATE
(— **UPON**) FOB GAG HUM LAY DUPE
SELL CULLY TRAIL BLUDGE DELUDE
EXCISE HUMBUG NUZZLE DECEIVE
HOODWINK
IMPOSED BOUNDEN
IMPOSING BIG EPIC BUDGE BURLY
GRAND HEFTY NOBLE PROUD
AUGUST EPICAL FEUDAL PORTLY
HAUGHTY POMPOUS STATELY
HANDSOME SONORANT SONOROUS
(— **UPON**) PRACTICE PRACTISE
IMPOSITION BAM COD HUM LEVY
SELL TAIL GOUGE IMPOT CHOUSE
GAMMON INTAKE TAILLE IMPOSAL
ARTIFICE IMPOSURE
(**MILITARY** —) CESS
IMPOSSIBLE HOPELESS
IMPOST LAY TAX CAST LEVY TAIL
TASK TOLL ABWAB ANNALE AVANIA
EXCISE GABELLE POUNAMU
TALLAGE TONNAGE TRIBUTE
CHAPTREL SPRINGER
(PL.) CUSTOMS
IMPOSTOR FOB FAKE GULL IDOL
CHEAT FAKER FRAUD GOUGE
QUACK BUNYIP FOURBE HUMBUG
MUMPER EMPIRIC FAITOUR
PROCTOR SHAMMER PHANTASM
IMPOSTURE GAG FAKE HOAX SHAM
CHEAT FRAUD TRICK DECEIT
HUMBUG JUGGLE ARTIFICE
DELUSION JUGGLERY
IMPOTENCE ACRATIA UNMIGHT
WEAKNESS
IMPOTENCY UNWELTH
IMPOTENT WEAK FRIGID PAULIE
UNABLE STERILE UNMIGHTY
IMPOUND FIND POUND INTERN
IMPOVERISH PILL CLOUD BEGGAR
IMPOOR SICKEN DEPLETE DEPRESS
EMPOVER BANKRUPT POVERISH
IMPOVERISHED POOR OBOLARY
BANKRUPT INDIGENT
IMPRACTICAL CRAZY FECKLESS
IMPRECATE WISH

IMPRECATION DASH OATH PIZE
WISH BLAME CURSE DAMME
DAMMIT CONSARN ANATHEMA
IMPREGNABILITY STRENGTH
IMPREGNABLE FAST PROOF
IMPREGNATE BIG HOP DOPE FILL
LIME MILT BREED IMBUE STOCK
STUFF TINCT AERATE CHARGE
INFORM INFUSE LEAVEN SEASON
ASPHALT ENVENOM IMPREGN
CHROMATE CONCEIVE CREOSOTE
FRICTION FRUCTIFY GRAPHITE
MEDICATE PERMEATE SATURATE
SILICATE TINCTURE
IMPREGNATED BRED COATED
IMPRESS FIX BITE COIN DING DINT
ETCH MARK AFFIX BRAND CLAMP
CRIMP DRIVE GRAVE GRILL INFIX
PRESS PRINT REACH SEIZE STAMP
STEAD WRITE AFFECT ENSEAL
FASTEN INCUSE INDENT SALUTE
STRIKE ANTIQUE ENGRAVE
ENSTAMP IMPLANT IMPREST
IMPRINT INSENSE INSCRIBE
NEGATIVE
(— **DEEPLY**) DELVE ENGRAVE
(— **SUDDENLY**) SMITE
(— **WITH FEAR**) AFFRIGHT
IMPRESSED BLIND ANTIQUE
INDENTED
IMPRESSIBLE WAXY
IMPRESSION CUT HIT AURA CAST
CHOP DENT DINT IDEA MARK MOLD
SEAL STEP STIR FANCY GOUGE
IMAGE MOULD STAMP STATE
ECTYPE EFFECT ENGRAM FIGURE
INCUSE OFFSET SIGNET STRIKE
EOPHYTE ETCHING FANTASY
IMPRESS MOULAGE OPINION
SEALING SQUEEZE STENCIL
TOOLING BLANKING ENGRAMMA
PRESSION PRESSURE STAMPAGE
TOOLMARK
(— **ON COIN**) CROSS
(— **WITHOUT INK**) ALBINO
(**AUDITORY** —) SOUND
(**DOUBLE** —) MACKLE MACULE
(**IMMEDIATE** —) APERCU
(**MENTAL** —) GRAVING
(**STRONG** —) HUNCH
(**VIVID** —) SPLASH
IMPRESSIONABLE SOFT WAXY
WAXEN TENDER PLASTIC PASSIBLE
IMPRESSIONIST LUMINIST
IMPRESSIVE BIG FAT EPIC AWFUL
GRAND NOBLE PROUD EPICAL
PESANTE STATELY TEARING
WEIGHTY FORCIBLE IMPOSING
SMASHING SONORANT SONOROUS
STUNNING
IMPRINT DINT ETCH SIGN STEP
PRESS STAMP CUTOFF FASTEN
STRIKE ENGRAVE ENSTAMP
IMPRESS APREYNTE EPIGRAPH
PRESSION PRESSURE STAMPAGE
(— **ON CHEEK**) FASTEN
IMPRISON JUG LAG NUN BOND
GAOL HULK JAIL SEAL SHOP WARD
CROWD EMBAR GRATE COMMIT

IMMURE JIGGER PRISON SLOUGH
CONFINE INTOWER BASTILLE
IMPRISONED FAST
IMPRISONMENT BAND BOND
ARREST CHAINS DURESS PRISON
CUSTODY DURANCE
IMPROBABLE FISHY UNLIKE
UNLIKELY
IMPROMPTU GLIB SUDDEN OFFHAND
IMPROPER BAD PAH PAW AMISS
LARGE UNDUE UNFELE UNJUST
ILLICIT INDECENT TORTIOUS
UNSEEMLY WRONGOUS
IMPROPRIETY SOLECISM
IMPROVE FIX GAIN GOOD GROW
HELP MEND AMEND EDIFY EMEND
GRADE MOISE SMART TOUCH
BETTER ENRICH PROFIT ADVANCE
BENEFIT CORRECT ELEVATE
PROMOTE RECTIFY UPSWING
(— **APPEARANCE OF HORSE**)
BISHOP
(— **APPEARANCE OF TEA**) FACE
(— **CONDUCTIVITY**) AGE
IMPROVED BETTER
IMPROVEMENT AMENDS PICKUP
POLICY PROFIT REDRESS UPSWING
IMPROVIDENT PRODIGAL WASTEFUL
(— **PERSON**) MICAWBER
IMPROVISATION THEME CALYPSO
IMPROVISE JAM COOK FAKE PONG
VAMP FANTASY
IMPRUDENCE FOLLY
IMPRUDENT FESS RASH FALSE
UNWARY FOOLISH RECKLESS
IMPUDENCE GALL BRASS CHEEK
MOUTH SLACK BRONZE PUPPYISM
IMPUDENT BOLD COXY FACY RUDE
BANTY BARDY BRASH FRESH GALLY
LIPPY SASSY SAUCY BRASSY
BRAZEN CHEEKY STOCKY BIGGETY
CHUNKED FORWARD GALLOWS
PERKING INSOLENT MALAPERT
IMPUDENTLY COOLY COOLLY
FRESHLY
IMPUGN DENY FALSE DISPUTE
IMPEACH
IMPULSE FIT BIAS RESE SEND URGE
DRIVE SPEND START DESIRE
MOTIVE SIGNAL SPLEEN YETZER
CALLING CONATUS IMPETUS
INSTINCT MOVEMENT STIRRING
(**BLIND** —) ATE
(**ELECTRICAL** —) KICK
(**SPONTANEOUS** —) ACCORD
(**SUDDEN** —) SPLEEN
(**SUPERNATURAL** —) AFFLATUS
IMPULSION SWING IMPULSE
IMPULSIVE QUICK FITFUL HEADLONG
IMPURE DRY FOUL LEWD GROSS
HORRY FILTHY TURBID UNPURE
UNCLEAN VICIOUS INDECENT
MACULATE
IMPURITY CRUD DONOR DROSS
FEDITY ACCEPTER FOULNESS
(— **IN LINT**) SHALE
(— **IN MINERAL**) GANG GANGUE
(**PL.**) SCUM GARBLE SLUMMAGE
IMPUTATION SCANDAL

IMPUTE LAY RET ARET EVEN WITE
COUNT REFER CHARGE FASTEN
IMPOSE OBJECT RECKON REPUTE
ASCRIBE ENTITLE IMPEACH
IN A I N Y AT TO BAJO INBY INTO
UPON ALONG INTIL
(— **A FAINT**) AWAY
(— **A SERIES**) SERIATIM
(— **A STATE OF ACTION**) ENERGIC
(— **ACCORDANCE**) AFTER
(— **ADDITION**) EKE TOO ALSO
ABOVE AGAIN ALONG FORBY STILL
BEYOND BESIDES FARTHER
FURTHER MOREOVER OVERPLUS
THERETIL
(— **ADVANCE**) AHEAD FORTH
BEFORE
(— **ANY CASE**) EVER HOWEVER
(— **BEHALF OF**) PRO
(— **CASE THAT**) AUNTERS
(— **CIRCULATION**) ABROAD
(— **CONNECTION WITH**) FORNENT
FERNINST
(— **EARNEST**) AGOOD
(— **EXCESS OF**) OVER
(— **FACT**) SOOTH TRULY INDEED
ITSELF MERELY VERILY ACTUALLY
VERAMENT
(— **FAITH**) IVADS EFECKS YFACKS
(— **FRONT**) FORE AFACE FORNE
AGAINST PARAVANT
(— **FULL**) ALONG
(— **GOOD SEASON**) BETIMES
(— **GOOD SPIRITS**) BOBBISH
(— **GRACEFUL MANNER**) ADAGIO
(— **JEST**) AGAME
(— **NO MANNER**) NOWISE NAEGATES
(— **ONE DIRECTION**) ANON
(— **ORDER**) FOR ATAUNT ATAUNTO
(— **PLACE OF**) FOR WITH INSTEAD
(— **POSSESSION**) WITHIN
(— **PROGRESS**) AFOOT TOWARD
(— **PROPER MANNER**) DULY
(— **RESPECT TO**) ANENT
(— **RETURN FOR**) AGAINST
(— **ROTATION**) ABOUT
(— **SO FAR AS**) AS QUA
(— **SOLE CONTROL**) ABSOLUTE
(— **SOOTH**) PARFEY PERFAY
(— **SPITE OF**) FOR ALTHO MALGRE
AGAINST DESPITE MALGRADO
(— **SUSPENSE**) PENDING
(— **THE DOING OF**) WITH
(— **THE FIRST PLACE**) IMP IMPRIMIS
(— **THE FUTURE**) HENCE
(— **THE MORNING**) MANE
(— **THE REAR**) AREAR ASTERN
(— **THE REGIONS OF UNBELIEVERS**)
IPI
(— **THE SAME PLACE**) IBID IBIDEM
(— **THE SAME WAY**) AS
(— **TOWARD**) INOWER
(— **TRUTH**) MARRY SOOTH CERTES
INDEED VERILY SOOTHLY
FORSOOTH
(— **VAIN**) WASTELY
(— **VIEW OF THE FACT THAT**)
SEEING
(— **WHAT MANNER**) HOW QUOMODO

INABILITY (— **TO FEED**) APHAGIA
(— **TO MASTICATE**) AMASESIS
(— **TO SPEAK**) ALOGIA ANEPIA
DUMBNESS
(— **TO WALK**) ABASIA
INACCESSIBLE COY REMOTE
UNGAIN WICKED SHADOWY
INACCESSIBILITY FASTNESS
INACCURATE SOUR FALSE LOOSE
FAULTY UNJUST INEXACT IMPROPER
SLIPSHOD
INACHUS (**DAUGHTER OF** —) IO
(**FATHER OF** —) OCEANUS
(**MOTHER OF** —) TETHYS
(**SON OF** —) PHORONEUS
INACTION RUST
INACTIVATE MOTHBALL
INACTIVE LAX DEAD DRUG FLAT
IDLE LAZY MESO SLOW HEAVY
INERT NOBLE SLACK SULKY ASLEEP
SUPINE CESSANT DORMANT
PASSIVE RESTIVE COMATOSE
COMATOUS DEEDLESS DILATORY
FAINEANT SLOTHFUL SLUGGISH
INACTIVITY SLOTH ANERGY
ANERGIA ABEYANCE IDLENESS
CESSATION
INADEQUACY DEFECT FRAILTY
SCARCITY
INADEQUATE BAD BARE POOR THIN
INEPT SHORT SLACK FEEBLE STRAIT
FOOLISH INVALID SLENDER
HIGHLAND INFERIOR
INADEQUATELY BADLY SLACK
SLACKLY
INADVERTENCE LAPSUS
INADVERTENT CARELESS
INAJA JAGUA
INALIENABLE INHERENT
INAMORATA AMORADO AMORETTO
INANE DIZZY EMPTY JERKY SILLY
VAPID JEJUNE VACANT FATUOUS
FOOLISH INSIPID VACUOUS IMBECILE
SLIPSLOP TRIFLING
INANGA MINNOW
INANIMATE DEAD DULL BRUTE
INERT DEADLY STOLID STUPID
LIFELESS
INANITY FATUITY VACUITY
INAPPLICABLE SPURIOUS
INAPPROPRIATE INEPT UNAPT
UNDUE FOREIGN UNHAPPY
INAPT BACKWARD FOOTLESS
INARTICULATA LYOPOMA
INARTICULATE DUMB LAME THICK
INARTISTIC ARTLESS
INATTENTION ABSENCE NEGLECT
APROSEXIA
INATTENTIVE DEAF SLACK ABSENT
REMISS SUPINE DREAMSY UNTENTY
CARELESS DISTRAIT HEEDLESS
MINDLESS
INAUDIBLE SECRET
INAUDIBLY INWARDLY SECRETLY
INAUGURATE AUGUR BEGIN
HANDSEL INITIATE
INAUSPICIOUS BAD ILL EVIL FOUL
ADVERSE OBSCENE OMINOUS
UNHAPPY UNLUCKY SINISTER

INAUTHENTIC SPURIOUS

INBORN GENIAL INBRED INNATE
NATIVE CONNATE NATURAL
HABITUAL INHERENT

INBRED INBORN INNATE

INBREED SELF

INBREEDING ENDOGAMY

INCA INGUA OREJON

INCALCULABLE UNTOLD SUMLESS
UNKNOWN

INCA MAGIC FLOWER CANTUT
CANTUTA

INCANDESCENCE GLOW

INCANDESCENT BRIGHT

INCANTATION CHARM DAWUT
SPELL CARMEN FETISH MANTRA
CANTION CHANTRY GREEGREE

INCAPABLE DEAD NUMB UNABLE
HANDLESS

INCAPACITATE NAPOO UNFIT
NOBBLE UNABLE DISABLE

INCAPACITATED FLAT DISABLED
STRICKEN

INCARCERATE IMMURE CONFINE
IMPRISON

INCARNATE BODIED EMBODY
CARNATE ENFLESH HUMANIFY

INCARNATION IMAGE ADVENT
AVATAR GENIUS MNEVIS TERTON
HUTUKTU EPIPHANY

INCAUTIOUS RASH UNWARY
UNCHARY UNTENTY CAREFREE
RECKLESS

INCENDIARY FIREBUG ARSONIST
BOUTEFEU

INCENSE CENSE INFLAME KETURAH
PROVOKE IRRITATE THYMIAMA
(— INGREDIENT) ONYCHA
(— VESSEL) SHIP

INCENSED RAW IRATE WROTH
WRATHFUL

INCENTIVE BROD GOAD SPUR PRICK
MOTIVE IMPETUS IMPULSE INCITIVE
STIMULUS

INCEPTION ORIGIN ANCESTRY

INCESSANT STEADY ENDLESS
CONSTANT

INCESSANTLY FOREVER

INCH UNCH PRIME UNCIA
(100TH OF —) POINT
(4 —S) HANDFUL
(48TH OF —) IRON
(9 —S) SPAN
(ABOUT 7 —S) FISTMELE

INCHOATE FORMLESS

INCIDENT GO EVENT LIABLE
CAUTION EPISODE PASSAGE
SUBJECT ACCIDENT CASUALTY
OCCASION
(AMUSING —) BREAK
(LITERARY —) BIT

INCIDENTAL BY BYE SIDE STRAY
CASUAL EPISODIC GLANCING
INCIDENT

INCIDENTALLY BYHAND OBITER
APROPOS

INCINERATE COMBUST CREMATE

INCINERATOR BURNER

INCIPIENCE BUD

INCIPIENT INITIAL GERMINAL
INCHOATE

INCISE CHOP RASE INCIDE CHANNEL
ENGRAVE

INCISION CUT GASH SLIT SNIP
ISSUE SCORE BROACH SCOTCH
STREAK CUTDOWN DIACOPE
APLOTOMY CECOTOMY COLOTOMY

INCISIVE ACID KEEN CRISP SHARP
BITING BRUTAL CUTTING ACULEATE

INCISOR CUTTER NIPPER GATHERER

INCITE EGG HIE HOY PUT SIC TAR
ABET BUZZ EDGE FIRE GOAD LASH
MOVE PROD SICK SNIP SPUR STIR
URGE AWAKE CHIRK IMPEL PRICK
PROKE SPARK SPURN STING TEMPT
AROUSE ENTICE EXCITE EXHORT
FOMENT HALLOO INDUCE KINDLE
NETTLE PROMPT UPSTIR ANIMATE
COMMOVE INCENSE INSPIRE
PROMOVE PROVOKE QUICKEN
SOLICIT INCITATE MOTIVATE
(— SECRETLY) SUBORN
(— TO ATTACK) SET HIRR SOOL

INCITEMENT GOAD PROD SPUR
STING MOTIVE EGGMENT STIRRING
(— OF LITIGATION) BARRATRY

INCITER FEEDER MONITOR
INCENSOR INCENTOR

INCLEMENCY RIGOR CRUELTY
TYRANNY ASPERITY HARDNESS
SEVERITY

INCLEMENT RAW HARD RUDE SOUR
GURLY STARK COARSE SEVERE
UNFINE UNKINDLY
(NOT —) OPEN CIVIL

INCLINATION DIP GEE MAW PLY
SET BENT BIAS BROO CANT CARE
DRAG DRAW EDGE FALL GUST
HANG LEAN LIKE LIST LOVE LUST
MIND SLEW TURN VEIN WILL BEVEL
BOSOM DRAFT DRIFT FANCY GRAIN
HABIT HIELD HUMOR KNACK LURCH
PITCH POISE SLANT SLOPE STUDY
SWING TASTE THEAT TREND
AFFECT ANIMUS ANLAGE ASCENT
DESIRE DEVICE GATHER GENIUS
INTENT LIKING MOTION NOTION
PONDUS RELISH SQUINT TALENT
YETZER APTNESS CONATUS
COURAGE CURRENT DESCENT
DRAUGHT FANTASY INKLING
LEANING STOMACH VERSANT
WILNING APTITUDE DEVOTION
GRADIENT PENCHANT TENDENCY
VELLEITY VERGENCY WOULDING
(— DOWNWARD) DIP DESCENT
HANGING
(— OF OARSMAN'S BODY) LAYBACK
(PREDOMINATE —) STRENGTH

INCLINE APT BOW DIP TIP WRY
BEND BIAS BREW CANT CAST DOCK
DOOK DOOR DROP GIVE HANG HEEL
HELD HILL LEAN LIKE LIST PEND
RAKE STAY SWAY TILT TURN BEVEL
CLIMB CLINE DROOP FLECT HIELD
JINNY OFFER SHAPE SLANT SLOPE
SOUND VERGE AFFECT GLACIS
INTEND SHELVE STEEVE UPBROW

DECLINE DESCEND GANGWAY
PROPEND PROCLINE PROCLIVE
(— SKI) EDGE

INCLINED APT SIB BENT CANT FAIN
RIFE VAIN ARAKE GIVEN PRONE
READY COUCHE MINDED PROMPT
SLOPED SUPINE FORWARD HANGING
OBLIQUE PRONATE STUDIED
AFFECTED DISPOSED ENCLITIC
PROPENSE SIDELING TALENTED
(— TO DRINK) BIBULOUS

INCLINING HILLY SHELVY SLOPING
CERNUOUS SIDELING

INCLUDE ADD LAP HAVE TAKE
ANNEX COUCH COVER IMPLY
EMPLOY ENSEAM RECKON BELOUKE
COLLECT CONTAIN EMBRACE
IMMERSE INVOLVE RECOUNT
SUBSUME COMPRISE CONCLUDE
(— IN LIST) ENGROSS

INCLUDING TO CUM

INCLUSIVE GRAND CAPABLE
CATHOLIC

INCLUSIVELY BROADLY

INCLUSUS RECLUSE

INCOHERENT FUZZY BROKEN
RAVING INCHOATE

INCOHERENTLY IDLY

INCOMBUSTIBLE APYROUS
ASBESTIC

INCOME GAIN PORT RENT LIVING
PEWAGE PEWING PROFIT SALARY
FACULTY INTRADO INTRATE
PRODUCE REVENUE STIPEND
INTEREST PROCEEDS
(ANNUAL —) RENTE
(UNFORESEEN —) GRAVY

INCOMMENSURATE UNEQUAL

INCOMMODE VEX ANNOY MOLEST
PLAGUE TROUBLE DISQUIET

INCOMPARABLE ALONE

INCOMPATIBILITY SOLECISM
ANTIPATHY

INCOMPETENT INEPT UNFIT
SLOUCH UNABLE UNMEET FECKLESS
HANDLESS HELPLESS SPLITTER

INCOMPLETE WANE BLIND ROUGH
BROKEN UNDONE DIVIDED LACKING
PARTIAL IMMATURE INCHOATE

INCOMPLETELY BADLY HALVES

INCOMPOSITE PRIME

INCOMPREHENSIBLE PARTIAL
COCKEYED

INCONCLUSIVE FUZZY

INCONGRUITY JAR SOLECISM

INCONGRUOUS ALIEN ABSURD

INCONNU CONY NELMA CONNIE
SHEEFISH

INCONSIDERABLE LIGHT PETTY
LITTLE

INCONSIDERATE RASH UNKIND
ASOCIAL RECKLESS

INCONSISTENCY HOLE

INCONSPICUOUS OBSCURE

INCONSTANCY CHANGE LEVITY

INCONSTANT FICKLE BRUCKLE
FLUXILE SLIDING VARIOUS FLUXIBLE
MOVEABLE VARIABLE

INCONTESTABLE SURE CLEAN
CERTAIN

INCONTINENCE ENURESIS
INCONTINENT LOOSE LAXATIVE
INCONTROVERTIBLE GRAND
INCONVENIENCE FASH BOTHER
CUMBER STRESS SQUEEZE
DISQUIET
INCONVENIENT UNKED CLUMSY
UNBANE UNGAIN AWKWARD
UNHANDY ANNOYING UNCHANCY
UNTOWARD
INCOORDINATION ASTASIA
INCORPORATE MIX FOLD FUSE JOIN
ANNEX KNEAD MERGE UNITE
ABSORB EMBODY ENGRAIN ENTRAIN
INWEAVE INCORPSE
(— IN WALL) ENGAGE
INCORPOREAL AERY BODILESS
ASOMATOUS
INCORRECT BAD ILL FALSE WRONG
PECCANT UNRIGHT UNSOUND
VICIOUS
INCORRIGIBLE HARD
INCORRUPTIBLE IMMORTAL
INCREASE UP ADD EIK EKE IMP WAX
BUMP ECHE GAIN GROW HELP HIKE
ITCH JACK JUMP MEND MORE MUCH
PLUS PUSH RISE SOAR THEE THRO
BOOST BUILD BULGE CLIMB CROWD
FLUSH FRESH HEAVE LARGE RAISE
SPURT SWELL ACCENT ACCESS
BETTER BIGGEN CHANGE CREASE
DEEPEN DOUBLE EXPAND EXTEND
EXTENT GATHER GROWTH SPREAD
SPRING ADVANCE AMPLIFY AUCTION
AUGMENT AUXESIS BALLOON
DISTEND ELEVATE ENGROSS
ENHANCE ENLARGE GREATEN
IMPROVE INFLATE MAGNIFY
STEEPEN SURCRUE ACCRESCE
ADDITION COMPOUND FLOURISH
HEIGHTEN LENGTHEN MAJORATE
MAXIMATE MAXIMIZE MULTIPLY
THRODDEN
(— AT USURY) OCKER
(— HEAT OF KILN) RUSTLE GLISTER
(— IN PAY) FOGY FOGIE
(— IN STRENGTH) FRESHEN
(— KNOWLEDGE) ENRICH
(— POWER) SOUP
(— PRICE BY BIDDING) CANT
(— SPEED) JAZZ
(— STITCHES) FASHION
(— SUDDENLY) LEAP
(PRICE —) RIST
(SHORT-TERM —) BOOMLET
INCREASING GROWING CRESCENT
CRESCIVE DILATANT SWELLING
(— RAPIDLY) BOOMING
INCREDIBLE TALL STEEP DAMNED
FABULOUS
INCREDULITY UNBELIEF
INCREDULOUS INFIDEL
INCREMENT DOSE DELTA INCREASE
INCRIMINATE ACCUSE
INCRUST FOUL
INCRUSTATION CRUD MOSS CRUST
SCALE TARTAR FOULING FURRING
INCUBATE SIT BROOD CLOCK
COVER HATCH

INCUBATOR FURNACE HATCHER
COUVEUSE ISOLETTE
INCUBUS DUSE MARE DUSIO
NIGHTMARE
INCULCATE BREED INFIX INCULK
INFUSE IMPLANT IMPRESS INSTILL
INCULCATED BRED
INCUMBENT COARB BEARER
INCUR RUN BEAR GAIN WAGE
CONTRACT
INCURABLE BOOTLESS HOPELESS
INCURRENT INHALANT
INCURSION RAID ROAD FORAY
INFALL INROAD RAZZIA DESCENT
HOSTING INBREAK INCURSE
INVASION
INCUS AMBOS ANVIL
INDEBTED DEBTFUL BEHOLDEN
INDEBTEDNESS DEBT SCORE
INDECENCY IMPURITY PRIAPISM
RIBALDRY
INDECENT PAW FOUL LEWD RANK
BAWDY GROSS NASTY SAUCY
GREASY IMPURE PAWPAW SMUTTY
GRIVOIS IMMORAL OBSCENE
IMMODEST IMPROPER SHAMEFUL
UNCOMELY
INDECISION DEMUR DOUBT MAYBE
POISE SWITHER
INDECISIVE DRAWN HALTING
INDECISIVENESS SUSPENSE
INDECOROUS RUDE COARSE
FORWARD UNCIVIL IMMODEST
IMPOLITE IMPROPER INDECENT
UNSEEMLY UNTOWARD
INDEED SO ARU WIS YEA AWAT
DEED EVEN IWIS JUST SURE QUOTH
TIENS ITSELF SURELY FAITHLY
FRANKLY FORSOOTH VERAMENT
INDEFATIGABLE TIRELESS
INDEFENSIBLE INVALID
INDEFINITE HAZY FUZZY GROSS
LOOSE VAGUE DIVERS INEXACT
AORISTIC
INDEFINITELY IN
INDELIBLE FAST FIXED
INDELICATE RAW FREE WARM
BROAD GROSS COARSE GREASY
IMPOLITE IMPROPER UNSEEMLY
INDEMNIFICATION RELIEF
INDEMNIFY PAY RECOUP SATISFY
WARRANT
INDENT JAG BRIT DENT GIMP MUSH
CHASE DELVE NOTCH STAMP
TOOTH WHEEL BRUISE ENGRAIL
GAUFFER
INDENTATION CHOP DENT DINT
DOKE FOIL KINK SCAR BOSOM
BULGE CLEFT CRENA DINGE NOTCH
SINUS DIMPLE FURROW GROOVE
INDENT IMPRESS CRENELLE
TOOTHING
(— IN BOTTLE) KICK
(— IN DOG'S FACE) STOP
(— IN SHELL) EYE
INDENTED WAVED NOTCHED
INDENTURE BIND INDENT ESCALLOP
SYNGRAPH
INDEPENDENCE AUTARKY

FREEDOM AUTARCHY
(— OF GOD) ASEITY ASEITAS
(POLITICAL —) SWARAJ
INDEPENDENT FREE PROUD
SEEKER BIGGITY DIVIDED MUGWUMP
SECTARY ABSOLUTE PECULIAR
SEPARATE
INDEPENDENTLY APART
INDESCRIBABLE TERMLESS
INEFFABLE
INDETERMINATE AORISTIC
FORMLESS INFINITE
INDEX PIE FIST HAND ARNETH
ELENCH PIGNET TONGUE POINTER
ALPHABET REGISTER

INDIA

CAPE: COMORIN
CAPITAL: NEWDELHI
CASTE: JAT MAL AHIR GOLA JATI
MALI DHOBI SANSI SUDRA
VARNA DACOIT DHANUK
LOHANA VAISYA AGARWAL
BRAHMAN DHANGAR
COAST: MALABAR
COIN: LAC PIE ANNA FELS LAKH
PICE TARA ABIDI CRORE PAISA
RUPEE
COLLEGE: TOL
DESERT: THAR
DISTRICT: SIBI NASIK PATNA
SIMLA ZILLAH MALABAR
NELLORE MOFUSSIL
GULF: KUTCH CAMBAY MANNAR
ISLAND: CHILKA
LAKE: WULAR CHILKA COLAIR
DHEBAR SAMBAHR
LANGUAGE: URDU HINDI TAMIL
TELUGU SANSKRIT
MEASURE: ADY DHA GAZ GUZ
JOW KOS LAN SER BYEE COSS
DAIN DHAN HATH JAOB KUNK
MOOT PARA RAIK RATI SEIT
TAUN TENG TOLA AMUNA BIGHA
CAHAR COVID CROSA DANDA
DRONA GARCE GIREH HASTA
PALLY PARAH RATTI SALAY
YOJAN ADHAKA ANGULA
COVIDO CUDAVA CUMBHA
GEERAH LAMANY MOOLUM
MUSHTI PALGAT PARRAH
ROPANI TIPREE UNGLEE YOJANA
ADOULIE DHANUSH GAVYUTI
KHAHOON NIRANGA PRASTHA
VITASTI OKTHABAH
MOUNTAIN: MERU GHATS KAMET
MASTUJ TANKSE KALAHOI
SIWALIK VINDHYA SULEIMAN
MOUNTAIN RANGE: SATPURA
VINDHYA ARAVALLI HIMALAYA
NATIVE: HINDU TAMIL
PROVINCE: HAR ASSAM BIHAR
ANDHRA BENGAL KERALA
MADRAS MYSORE ORISSA
PUNJAB GUJARAT HARYANA
KASHMIR MANIPUR
REGION: MALABAR
RIVER: AI DOR SON TEL KOSI KUSI

NIRA REHR SIND BETWA BHIMA
DAMOH GOGRA INDUS JAWAI
RAPTI SANKH SONAR TAPTI
TUNGA CHENAB GANGES KISTNA
PENNER SUTLEJ WARDHA
CAUVERY CHAMBAL IRAWADI
KRISHNA NARMADA NARMEDA
HEMAVATI HYDASPES MAHANADI
NERBUDDA VINDHYAS
SEAPORT: DAMAN BOMBAY
COCHIN MADRAS CALCUTTA
STRAIT: PALK
TOWN: DIU AGRA DAMA GAYA
PUNA REWA ADONI AKOLA
ALWAR ARCOT BHERA DACCA
DATIA DELHI GIROT KALPI
MYSOR PATAN PATNA POONA
SALEM SIMLA SURAT TEHRI
AJMERE AMBALA BARELI
BARODA BHOPAL BOMBAY
CHAMBA COCHIN DUMDUM
HOWRAH INDORE JAIPUR
KANPUR LAHORE MADIRA
MADRAS MADURA MEERUT
MULTAN MUSORE MUTTRA
NAGPUR RAMPUR UJJAIN
ALIGARH BENARES BIKANER
CALICUT CAWNPUR DINAPIR
GWALIOR JODHPUR KARACHI
KURNOOL LASWARI LUCKNOW
RANGOON RANGPUR AMRITSAR
BHATINDA BHATPARA CALCUTTA
DINAPORE JABALPUR KOLHAPUR
MANDALAY MIRZAPUR
PESHAWAR SHOLAPUR
SRINAGAR VARANASI
TRIBE: AO GOR BHIL BADAGA
SHERANI
WEIGHT: MOD PAI SER VIS DHAN
DRUM KONA MYAT PALA PANK
PICE RAIK RATI RUAY SEER
TANK TOLA YAVA ADPAD BAHAR
CANDY CATTY HUBBA MASHA
MAUND PALLY POUAH RATTI
RETTI RUTEE TICAL TICUL TIKAL
ABUCCO DHURRA KARSHA
CHITTAK PEIKTHA

INDIAN LO RED BUCK ROJO INJUN
TAWNY INDISH BHARATI HOSTILE
NAIKPOD REDSKIN LONGHAIR
(AMERICAN —) AIS AUK FOX HOH
KAW OTO SAC SIA UTE WEA ZIA
ADAI COOS CREE CROW DOEG ERIE
EYAK HANO HOPI HUPA IOWA KATO
KOSO MOKI MONO OTOE OTTO PIMA
PIRO SAUK TANO TAOS TEWA TIOU
TOAG UTAH WACO YUMA ZUNI
ACOMA ALSEA BANAK BIDAI CADDO
CHAUI COMOX CONOY COREE
CREEK HANIS HOOPA HUECO
HURON JEMEZ KANIA KANSA KAROK
KERES KIOWA KOROA KUSAN
LENCA LIPAN MAKAH MANSO MIAMI
MINGO MODOC MOQUI NAMBE
OMAHA OSAGE OSTIC OZARK
PECOS PINAL PIUTE PONCA SAMBO
SARSI SEWEE SIOUX SITKA SKIDI

SLAVE SNAKE SOOKE TETON TEXAS
TIGUA TONTO TWANA TYIGH UINTA
UNAMI WAPPO WASCO WASHO
WIYOT YAMEL YAZOO YUCHI YUROK
AGAWAM AHTENA APACHE ATSINA
ATUAMI AVOYEL BILOXI CALUSA
CAYUGA CAYUSE CHATOT CHERAW
CHETCO COOSUC CUPENO DAKOTA
DIGGER EYEISH FARAON GILENO
HAINAI HAISLA ISLETA KAIBAB
KAINAH KANSAS KICHAI KOSIMO
KUITSH LAGUNA LENAPE MANDAN
MAUMEE MAYEYE METOAC MICMAC
MIKMAK MOHAVE MOHAWK MUNSEE
NASHUA NATICK NAUSET NAVAHO
NAVAJO NEUTER NOOTKA OGLALA
ONEIDA OREJON OTTAWA PAIUTE
PAPAJO PATWIN PAWNEE PEORIA
PEQUOD PEQUOT PIEGAN PODUNK
PUEBLO QUAPAW QUERES RIKARI
SALISH SAMISH SANTEE SAPONI
SATSOP SENECA SHASTA SILETZ
SIOUAN SIWASH SKAGIT SOKOKI
SUMASS SUMDUM SUTAIO SYLVID
TAPOSA TENINO TOHOME TOLOWA
TONGAS TUNICA TUTELO UNPQUA
WALAPI WAPATO WATALA WAXHAW
WEANOC WIKENO WINTUN YAKIMA
YAMASI YAVAPA ZUNIAN ABENAKI
ALABAMA ALIBAMU AMERIND
ANDARKO ANDASTE ARIKARA
ATAKAPA AYAHUCA BANNOCK
CAHOKIA CAHUILA CALOOSA
CATAWBA CHILCAT CHILULA
CHINOOK CHOCTAW CHUMASH
CHUMAWI CIBECUE CLALLAM
CLATSOP COCHITI COLCINE
COWLITZ DEADOSE DHEGIHA
DWAMISH ESSELEN GOSHUTE
HELLELT HIDATSA HUCHNOM
HUICHOL INGALIK JUANENO
KANAWHA KLAMATH KOASATI
KOHUANA KOPRINO KUNESTE
KUTCHIN KUTENAI LUISENO
MASHPEE MASKOKI MOHEGAN
MOHICAN MONACAN MONSONI
MONTAUK MOUSONI NANAIMO
NASCAPI NATCHEZ NIANTIC NIMKISH
NIPMUCK OJIBWAY PACIFID
PADUCAH PAMLICO PICURUS
QUAITSO SALINAN SANETCH
SANFOIL SERRANO SHAPTAN
SHAWANO SHAWNEE SIKSIKA
SIUSLAW SONGISH SPOKANE
SQUAXON STIKINE TAMAROA
TESUQUE TIMUCUA TLINGIT
TONKAWA TUALATI TULALIP
TUTUTNI UGARONO WAILAKI
WALPAPI WAMESIT WANAPUM
WASHAKI WEWENOC WHILKUT
WICHITA WISHOSK WITUMKI
WYANDOT YANKTON YAQUINA
YOJUANE YONKALA ABSAROKA
ACHOMAWI ACHUMAWI ALGONKIN
AMERICAN AMOSKEAG APALACHI
ARIVAIPA ARKANSAS ASTAKIWI
ATFALATI ATSUGEWI CAHINNIO
CAHUILLA CANARSIE CHAWASHA
CHEHALIS CHEMAKUM CHEROKEE

CHEYENNE CHIMAKUM CHOPTANK
CHOWANOC CLACKAMA COLUMBIA
COLVILLE COMANCHE COQUILLE
COYOTERO DELAWARE DIEGUENO
ETCHIMIN FLATHEAD HITCHITI
HUNKPAPA ILLINOIS IROQUOIS
KALISPEL KAWAIISU KICKAPOO
KIKATSIK KLASKINO KLIKITAT
KONOMIHU LAMANITE MALECITE
MASKOTIN MENOMINI MIKASUKI
MINITARI MISSOURI MOGOLLON
MUSCOGEE MUSKWAKI NEHANTIC
NESPELIM NOTTOWAY OKINAGAN
ONONDAGA PAMUNKEY PANAMINT
PATUXENT PAVIOTSO PENACOOK
PISHQUOW POWHATAN PUYALLUP
QUATSINO QUERECHO QUILEUTE
QUINAULT ROCKAWAY SAHAPTIN
SAULTEUR SAVANNAH SEMINOLE
SHIVWITS SHOSHONE SIHASAPA
SINGSING SINKIUSE SINKYONE
SINTSINK SISSETON SOUHEGAN
SQUAMISH SQUEDUNK TLAKLUIT
TOBIKHAR TOPINISH TSIHALIS
TUSHEPAW TUSKEGEE UMATILLA
WABANAKI WACHUSET WAHPETON
WETUMPKA YAHUSKIN YAMACRAW
DOUSTIONI SQUAWTITS
(BRAZILIAN —) BUGRE
(CANADIAN —) DENE COMOX HAIDA
SLAVE TINNE DOGRIB HAISLA
LASSIK SARSEE BEOTHUK GOASILA
KHOTANA KOYUKON CHISEDEC
COEICHAN HEILTSUK KIMSQUIT
KWAKIUTL LILLOOET SALTEAUX
(FEMALE —) SQUAW KLOOCH
(MALE —) BUCK SANNUP
(MEXICAN —) MAM OVA CHOL CORA
JOVA MAYA MAYO ROTO SERI TECA
TECO XOVA AZTEC CHIZO CHORA
HUABI HUAVE KAMIA NAHUA OPATA
OTOMI YAQUI ZOQUE CAHITA
CHOCHO CONCHO EUDEVE KILIWI
NEVOME OTONIA PAKAWA TARASC
TOLTEC ZOTZIL ACOLHUA AKWAALA
AMISHGO CHATINO CHINCHA
CHINIPA CHONTAL COTONAM
COUHIMI GUASAVE HUASTEC
HUAXTEC MAZATEC MISTECA
MIXTECA NAYARIT SINALOA
TEGUIMA TEHUECO TEPANEC
TEPEHUA TZENTAL TZOTZIL
ZACATEC ZAPOTEC CHANABAL
CHAPANEC CHUCHONA COLOTLAN
COMANITO CONICARI GUASAPAR
HUASTECO IRRITILA JACALTEC
JANAMARE LACANDON LAGUNERO
TARUMARI TECPANEC TEXCOCAN
TEZCUCAN TOTONACO TZAPOTEC
YUCATECO
(OTHER —) GE ITE ONA URO URU
YAO AGAZ ANDE ANTA ANTI AUCA
BABU CAME CANA CARA CHUJ
COTO CUNA DENE DIAU DUIT INCA
ITEN ITZA IXIL MOJO MOXO MURA
MUSO MUZO PEBA PIRO RAMA
TAMA TAPE TATU TOBA TRIO TUPI
TUPY ULUA ULVA ACROA ARARA
ARAUA ARUAC AUETO BAURE BETOI

BRAVO BUGRE CAITE CAMPA CANCA
CARIB CHANE CHIMU CHITA CHOKO
CHOLA CHOLO CHONO COCTO
COLAN CUEVA DIRIA GUANA GUATO
HUARI JAVAH KASKA LENCA MOCOA
MOZCA OPATA OYANA PALTA
PAMPA PASSE PETEN PINTO PIOJE
PIOXE PIPIL POKAN POKOM QUITU
SENCI SIUSI SMOOS TAINO UAUPE
UMAUA VEJOZ WAURA XINCA
YAGUA YAMEO YUNCA YUNGA
AGUANO AIMARA AKAVAI AKAWAI
AMORUA ANDOKE ANTISI APANTO
APARAI APIACA ARAWAK AROACO
ATORAI AYMARA BABINE BANIVA
BETOYA BORORO BRIBRI BRUNKA
CAHETE CAIGUA CANCHI CANELO
CARAHO CARAJA CARAYA CARIRI
CAUQUI CAVINA CAYAPA CHAIMA
CHARCA CHAYMA CHICHA CHISCA
CHOCOI CHORTI COCAMA COCOMA
COCORA COFANE COLIMA COTOXO
CUCAMA CULINO CUMANA DOGROB
DORASK GALIBI GOYANA GUAIMI
GUAQUE GUAYMI HUARPE HUBABO
IGNERI INCERI IXIAMA JIVARO
JUCUNA JUMANA JURUNA KARAYA
KEKCHI KUCHIN LENGUA LUCAYO
MACUSI MAKUSI MANGUE MANIVA
MIRANA MUYSCA NAHANE NASCAN
OMAGUA OTOMAC PAPAGO
PKOMAM PURUHA QUICHE SABUJA
SACCHA SALIBA SALIVA SAMUCU
SEKANE SETIBO SIPIBO SUERRE
TACANA TAGISH TAHAMI TAMOYO
TAPAJO TAPUYA TARUMA TECUNA
TICUNA TIMOTE TOTORO TUCANO
TUNEBO UIRINA UITOTO VILELA
WAIWAI WITOTO WOOLWA YAHGAN
YAHUNA YARURO YURUNA ZAPARA
ACHAGUA ACKAWOI AKAMNIK
ANDAQUI ANGAITE APALAII APINAGE
ARECUNA ARHUACO BEOTHUK
BILQULA CACHIBO CAINGUA
CALIANA CAMACAN CARANGA
CARIBAN CARIBEE CARRIER
CASHIBO CHARRUA CHIBCHA
CHIMANE CHIMILA CHIRINO
CHONCHO CHOROTE CHUMULU
CHUNCHO CHURAPA CHUROYA
CIBONEY CJACOGO COROADO
FRENTON FUEGIAN GITKSAN
GOAHIVO GOAJIRA GUA9RAU
GUAHIVO GUARA5Y GUARANI
GUARAYO GUARUAN GUATUSO
GUETARE HUANUCO HUATUSO
ITONAMA JACUNDA JICAQUE
KALIANA KOPRINO KULIANA
LUCAYAN MAIPURE MONGOYO
MORCOTE NICARAO PAMPERO
PAYAGUA PEDRAZA PIARROA
POKOMAM PUELCHE PUQUINA
QUECHUA QUEKCHI RANQUEL
SARIGUE SATIENO SHUSWAP
SINSIGA SIRIONE TAHLTAN TALUCHE
TALUHET TAMANAC TARIANA
TARRABA TAYRONA TELEMBI
TIMBIRA TIRRIBI TSONECA UARAYCU
UCAYALE VOYAVAI WOYAWAY

YUSTAGA ZUTUHIL AGUARUNA
AHOUSAHT AKIYENIK ALACALUF
AMAHUACA APOLISTA ARAQUAJU
AWISHIRA BOTOCUDO CAINGANG
CALINAGO CANAMARY CANOEIRO
CAQUETIO CARIBISI CARIJONA
CARIPUNA CAYUBABA CHAMBOIA
CHANDALA CHAVANTE CHIQUITO
CHIRIANA COLORADO COMIAKIN
CONCHUCO CORABECA CUSTENAU
GUAYAQUI GUAYCURU JAVITERO
KANHOBAL KLASKINO LOROKOTO
MACARANI MAYORUNA MISSKITO
MOSQUITO NIQUIRAN OCHOZOMA
OROTINAN PACAVARA PALENQUE
PARUKUTU PINALENO POIGUARA
POKONCHI POPOLOCO POTYUARA
PUPULUCA QUATSINO QUERENDY
QUIMBAYA SHIRIANA SNONOWAS
SUBTIABA TADOUSAC TAPACURA
TENAKTAK TOCOBAGA TOROMONA
TSATTINE TUMUPASA UAREKENA
URUKUENA USPANTEC YURUCARE
(SPANISH-AMERICAN —) CHOLO

INDIANA
CAPITAL: INDIANAPOLIS
COLLEGE: BALL BETHEL DEPAUW
  GOSHEN MARIAN PURDUE
  WABASH
COUNTY: JAY CASS VIGO JASPER
  TIPTON DAVIESS
INDIAN: MIAMI SHAWNEE
LAKE: MONROE MANITOU
  WAWASEE MICHIGAN
NATIVE: HOOSIER
RIVER: OHIO WHITE WABASH
STATE BIRD: CARDINAL
STATE FLOWER: PEONY
STATE TREE: TULIP
TOWN: GARY PERU BRAZIL
  GOSHEN JASPER KOKOMO
  MUNCIE WABASH

INDIAN BEECH KURUNJ
INDIAN BREAD TUCKAHOE
INDIAN CORN KANGA MAIZE
  CHOLUM JAGONG MEALIES
INDIAN FIG SABRA
INDIAN FISH FLATFISH
INDIAN GOOSEBERRY EMBLIC
INDIAN HEMP KEF KIF DAGGA SABZI
  AMYROOT DOGBANE
INDIANIAN HOOSIER
INDIAN JALAP TURPETH
INDIAN LICORICE JEQUIRITY
INDIAN MADDER MUNJEET
INDIAN MALLOW SIDA DAGGA
  PIEPRINT
INDIAN MILLET JONDLA
INDIAN MULBERRY AL AAL ACH
  ALROOT
INDIAN PIPE FITROOT EYEBRIGHT
  WAXFLOWER
INDIAN SHOT ALIIPOE
INDIAN TOBACCO GAGROOT
  LOBELIA PUKEWEED SOURBUSH
INDIAN YELLOW PIOURY PURREE

INDIC (— LANGUAGE) URDU VEDIC
INDICATE RUN SAY BODY CITE HINT
  LOOK MAKE MARK READ SHOW
  ARGUE INDEX INFER POINT PROVE
  SPEAK ALLUDE ATTEST BETRAY
  DENOTE DESIGN EVINCE FINGER
  IMPORT NOTIFY REVEAL BESPEAK
  BETOKEN CONNOTE DECLARE
  DISPLAY SIGNIFY SPECIFY
  ADMONISH ANNOUNCE DECIPHER
  DISCLOSE EVIDENCE MANIFEST
  OUTPOINT REGISTER
  (— BY SOUNDING) STRIKE
  (— WILLINGNESS) AGREE
INDICATION BECK CLEW CLUE HINT
  LEAD MARK NOTE SHOW SIGN
  CURVE INDEX PROOF SCENT TOKEN
  AUGURY BEACON INDICE REMARK
  SAMPLE SIGNAL AUSPICE MENTION
  PROFFER SYMPTOM ALLUSION
  ARGUMENT EVIDENCE MONITION
  MONUMENT NOTATION SIGNANCE
  TELLTALE
  (— OF APPROVAL) CACHET
  (— OF CONTROL) COLLAR
  (— OF LIGHT) AUREOLE
  (— OF OFFICE) SEAL
  (OBSCURE —) SHADOW
  (VAGUE —) GLIMMER
  (PL.) INDICIA
INDICATOR PIN HAND SIGN FLOAT
  INDEX LITMUS SHOWER STYLUS
  TARGET LACMOID POINTER
  DETECTOR TELLTALE
  (— OF BALANCE) COCK
  (— OF HOUR) GNOMON
INDICT DITE CRIME PANEL ACCUSE
  ATTACH CHARGE INDITE ARRAIGN
  ARTICLE IMPEACH TROUNCE
  WARRANT
INDICTMENT CHARGE DITTAY
INDIFFERENCE APATHY PHLEGM
  DISDAIN COLDNESS EASINESS
  FROIDEUR
INDIFFERENT COLD COOL DEAD
  DRAM EASY SOSO ALOOF BLASE
  EQUAL SOBER CASUAL DEGAGE
  FRIGID SUPINE CALLOUS NEUTRAL
  DETACHED LISTLESS LUKEWARM
  MEDIOCRE RECKLESS SUPERIOR
  UPSITTEN
INDIFFERENTIST POLITIC
INDIFFERENTLY DRYLY HUMDRUM
INDIGENCE NEED WANT PENURY
  BEGGARY POVERTY TENUITY
INDIGENE ENDEMIC
INDIGENOUS DESI NATIVE
  DOMESTIC HOMEBORN
INDIGENT POOR BEGGARLY
INDIGESTION APEPSY APEPSIA
  DYSPEPSY
INDIGNANT ANGRY WROTH
  ANNOYED INCENSED
INDIGNATION IRE ANGER WRATH
  DESPITE DISDAIN JEALOUSY
INDIGNITY CUT SLUR SCORN INSULT
  SLIGHT AFFRONT OFFENCE
INDIGO ANIL NILL SHOOFLY
INDIRECT SIDE DEVIOUS OBLIQUE

CIRCULAR GLANCING OVERHEAD OVERWART SIDELONG SIDEWAYS SIDEWISE
(— WAY) AMBAGE
INDIRECTION CIRCUITY
INDISCREET RASH HASTY SILLY WITLESS CARELESS HEEDLESS
INDISCRETION FOLLY FREDAINE
INDISCRIMINATE MIXED MINGLED SWEEPING
INDISCRIMINATELY PELLMELL
INDISPENSABLE NEEDFUL CRITICAL
INDISPOSED ILL MEAN SICK ILLISH UNWELL
INDISPOSITION AIL MALADY AILMENT SICKNESS
(— TO MOTION) INERTIA
INDISPUTABLE SURE CERTAIN EVIDENT MANIFEST POSITIVE
INDISTINCT DIM DARK DULL HAZY FAINT FUZZY INNER LIGHT MISTY MUDDY SHADY THICK VAGUE CLOUDY DREAMY INWARD SLURRY WOOLLY BLEARED BLURRED OBSCURE SHADOWY UNCLEAR
(— IN UTTERANCE) CHOKING
INDISTINCTNESS BLUR
INDITE DITE DRAW
INDIVIDUAL GEE MAN ONE HEAD SORT UNIT BEING MONAD THING PROPER SINGLE SPIRIT APOMICT ATAVISM AZYGOTE BIONTIC DIPLOID EIDETIC ISOLATE MONADIC NUMERIC SEVERAL SPECIAL EVERYONE IDENTITY SEPARATE SINGULAR SOLITARY SPECIMEN
(COUNTRIFIED —) HOBNAIL
(DESPICABLE —) HEEL
(DULL —) BOEOTIAN
(FOOLISH —) SOP
(HAUGHTY —) POT
(IMMATURE —) ADULTOID
(IMPUDENT —) BOLDFACE
(IRRITABLE —) SNAPPER
(LEADING —) KEY
(MOSAIC —) GYNANDER
(MUTANT —) SALTANT
(PHYSIOLOGICAL —) BION
(ROUGH-LOOKING —) BOHUNK
(SKILLED —) ADEPT
(SLOVENLY —) GROBIAN
(STUPID —) HOBBIL
(TRICKY —) BILK
(UNDERSIZED —) KIT KITT
(WINGED —) ALATE
(YOUNG —) KID
(PL.) FRY
INDIVIDUALITY SEITY QUALITY SELFDOM HECCEITY IDENTITY SELFHOOD
INDIVIDUALIZE ATOMIZE
INDIVIDUALLY APART APIECE SINGLY PROPERLY
INDIVIDUATION AHANKARA
INDIVISIBLE PUNCTUAL
INDO-CHINESE SERIFORM
INDOCTRINATE BRIEF INSTRUCT
INDO-EUROPEAN ARIAN ARYAN
INDOLE KETOLE

INDOLENCE SLOTH LANGUOR IDLESHIP MUSARDRY SLUGGING
(— PERSONIFIED) LAURENCE LAWRENCE
INDOLENT IDLE LAZY FAINT INERT SWEER DROWSY OTIOSE SUPINE DRONISH LABGUID WILSOME FAINEANT INACTIVE LISTLESS LOUNGING SLOTHFUL SLUGGISH PICKTOOTH
INDO-MALAYAN (— TREE) SUPA

INDONESIA
CAPITAL: DJAKARTA
COIN: RUPIAH
GULF: BONE TOLO TOMINI
ISLAND: ALOR BALI BURU JAVA CERAM IRIAN SUMBA WETAR BANGKA BAWEAN BORNEO BUTUNG FLORES KOMODO LOMBOK MADURA PELENG CELEBES SALAJAR SUMATRA SUMBAWA BILLITON SULAWESI KALIMANTAN
ISLAND GROUP: EWAB SUNDA BANJAK NATUNA ANAMBAS MOLUCCA TABELAN SABALANA
LANGUAGE: BAHASA MALAYAN
LAKE: RANAU TOWUTI
MOUNTAIN: BULU NIUT RAJA DEMPO MURJO NIAPA LEUSER SLAMET MENJAPA OGOAMAS SAMOSIR KATOPASA KERINTJI MAHAMERU RINDJANI TALAKMAU
MOUNTAINS: MULLER BARISAN QUARLES SCHWANER
RIVER: HARI MUSI DIGUL KAJAN PAWAN BARITO KAMPAR KAPUAS MAHAKAM
SEA: JAVA BANDA CERAM TIMOR FLORES ARAFURA CELEBES
STRAIT: SUNDA LOMBOK MAKASSAR
TOWN: MEDAN MALANG MANADO BANDUNG MAKASAR SEMARANG SURABAJA
VOLCANO: SLAMET
WEIGHT: CATTY OUNCE THAIL

INDONESIAN NESIOT SADANG
INDOORS WITHIN
INDRA SAKKA SAKRA
INDUBITABLE SURE EVIDENT APPARENT MANIFEST UNIVOCAL
INDUCE GET DRAW LEAD MOVE URGE WORK ARGUE BRIBE BRING CAUSE IMPEL INFER TEMPT WEIGH ADDICT ADJURE ALLURE ENGAGE ENTICE IMPORT INCITE INVITE OBTAIN REDUCE SEDUCE SUBORN PREVAIL PROCURE SOLICIT MOTIVATE PERSUADE WIREDRAW
(— BY BRIBERY) FIX
INDUCEMENT MOTIVE REASON FEATURE
INDUCT STALL INSTAL INITIATE
INDUCTANCE HENRY
INDUCTION EPAGOGE

INDULGE PET BABY CADE CANT FEED GLUT HUMOR JOLLY SPOIL TUTOR WALLY WREAK COCKER FOSTER PAMPER PETTLE DEBAUCH GRATIFY
(— IN PRIDE) PRIDE
(— TO EXCESS) PAMPER DEBAUCH SURFEIT
INDULGED CADE
INDULGENCE LAW BINGE FAVOR FOLLY MERCY SPREE EXCESS INDULT PARDON PATENT JUBILEE QUIENAL SURFEIT COURTESY DELICACY EASINESS GLUTTONY POCULARY
(SEXUAL —) LECHERY
INDULGENT FOND GOOD MEEK MILD SPOONY LENIENT TOLERANT
INDURATE HARDEN INDURE
INDURATED SCLEROID SCLEROUS
INDURATION SCLEROMA
INDUSTRIOUS BUSY DEEDY EIDENT PAINFUL DILIGENT SEDULOUS VIRTUOUS WORKSOME
INDUSTRY TOIL LABOR SCREEN VIRTUE CERAMICS SEDULITY
INDWELLING IMMANENT INHERENT
INEBRIATE SOUSE EBRIATED
INEBRIATED DRUNK DRINKY
INEFFACEABLE INBURNT INDELIBLE
INEFFECTIVE DUD WEAK CLUMSY DREEPY FLABBY FUTILE FLACCID HALTING STERILE BUMBLING
INEFFECTIVELY ILL BADLY FEEBLY
INEFFECTUAL WAN DEAD IDLE TAME VAIN VOID JERKY FUTILE SPINDLY USELESS FAINEANT FIDDLING NUGATORY
INEFFICIENT ILL LAME POOR CLUMSY DOLESS UNABLE SLOUCHY USELESS FECKLESS HANDLESS
INELEGANT RUDE HOYDEN AWKWARD
INELOQUENT WANMOL
INEPT INAPT ABSURD AWKWARD FOOTLESS
INEQUAL ROUGH
INEQUALITY ODDS CAHOT ANOMALY EVECTION IMPARITY NUTATION
INEQUITABLE HARD
INERADICABLE LASTING IDELIBLE PERMANENT
INERT DEAD DULL LAZY SLOW HEAVY NOBLE SULKY LEADEN SODDEN STUPID SUPINE TORPID PASSIVE INACTIVE INDOLENT LIFELESS SLOTHFUL SLUGGISH STAGNANT
INERTIA TAMAS
INESCAPABLE DEAD
INESTIMABLE SUMLESS PRICELESS
INEVITABILITY FINALITY
INEVITABLE DUE DIRECT CERTAIN FATEFUL
INEXACT FREE ROUGH CLOUDY
INEXHAUSTIBLE INFINITE
INEXORABLE STERN STONY STRICT RIGOROUS
INEXPEDIENCY IMPOLICY

INEXPEDIENT UNWISE
INEXPENSIVE CHEAP
INEXPERIENCED RAW PUNY CRUDE
FRESH YOUNG UNSEEN KITLING
STRANGE INEXPERT INSOLENT
PRENTICE UNTRADED
INEXPERT ILL RUDE CRUDE GREEN
SIMPLE
INEXPLICABLE FELL
INFAMOUS BASE RUDDY BLOODY
NOTOUR ODIOUS BLEEDING
FLAGRANT NIDERING SHAMEFUL
INFAMY STAIN BAFFLE DEFAME
SHONDE DISHONOR IGNOMINY
INFANCY CRADLE BABYHOOD
INFANT BABE BABY TINY WEAN
CHILD MINOR PREMIE CHRISOM
MILKSOP BALDLING BANTLING
(NAKED —) SCUDDY
(NEWLY-BORN —) NEONATUS
(VORACIOUS -) KILLCROP
INFANTILE BABYISH
INFANTRY FOOT FANTERIE
FOOTFOLK
INFANTRYMAN ASKAR ZOUAVE
DOGFACE DRAGOON DOUGHBOY
PIOUPIOU SOREFOOT
INFATUATE FOOL ASSOT
INFATUATED MAD FOND GONE
ASSOT CRAZY DOTTY ENGOUEE
FOOLISH BESOTTED
INFATUATION ATE RAVE CRUSH
FOLLY BEGUIN
(TRANSIENT —) CRAZE
INFECT SMIT TAINT CANKER DEFILE
EMPEST ENTACH INFEST POISON
CORRUPT DISEASE POLLUTE
SMITTLE
INFECTED FUNGUSED
(NOT —) BLAND
INFECTION COLD DOSE FELON
TAINT FUNGUS
INFECTIOUS TAKING SMITTLE
CATCHING SMITABLE SMITTING
VIRULENT
INFER DRAW PICK TAKE GUESS
JUDGE DECIDE DEDUCE DEDUCT
DERIVE DIVINE GATHER INDUCE
REASON COLLECT INCLUDE
PRESUME SURMISE CONCLUDE
CONSTRUE
INFERENCE EDUCT SEQUEL
ANALOGY SEQUELA ILLATION
SEQUENCE SEQUITUR
INFERIOR BAD BUM DOG ILL LOW
SAD EVIL LESS MEAN PUNK SLIM
SOUR WAFF BASER BAUCH BELOW
DOGGY GROSS LOWER PETTY PLAIN
SCALY SCRUB WORRY BEHIND
CAGMAG COMMON CRAPPY FEEBLE
FEMALE IMPURE LESSER MEASLY
PEDARY PUISNY ROTTEN SECOND
SHABBY WOODEN BADDISH CRIPPLE
HUMBLER NAGGISH POPULAR
SCRUBBY SUBJECT ABNORMAL
ANTERIOR DEROGATE ORDINARY
INFERIORITY LESSNESS MEANNESS
INFERNAL AVERNAL ETERNAL
HELLISH SATANIC SHEOLIC STYGIAN

CHTHONIC DAMNABLE DEVILISH
PLUTONIC
INFERTILE DEAD DEAF DOUR LEAN
POOR THIN CLEAR STERILE
INFEST COE VEX BESET INFECT
PESTER PLAGUE OVERRUN
TORMENT
INFESTATION SCALE PLAGUE
STRIKE LOAIASIS
INFESTED MITY BLOWN BROOD
BUGGY FLUKY FLUKED GRUBBY
HAUNTED FLYBLOWN
INFIDEL DEIST GIAOUR PAYNIM
ATHEIST SARACEN SKEPTIC
AGNOSTIC
INFIDELITY PERFIDY ADULTERY
TRAHISON
INFIELD INTOWN DIAMOND
INFILTRATE FILTER CRETIFY
COLONIZE
INFILTRATION SEEPAGE ADIPOSIS
INFINITE CHAOS COSMIC ENDLESS
ETERNAL IMMENSE
INFINITENESS ETERNITY
INFINITESIMAL PUNCTUAL
INFINITIVE SUPINE VERBID
INFINITY OLAM ANANTA ETERNITY
INFIRM LAME WEAK ANILE CRAZY
CRONK SHAKY CRANKY FEEBLE
SICKLY UNFIRM UNSURE CASALTY
CRAICHY DOWLESS DWAIBLE
FRAGILE INVALID SAPLESS UNFEARY
DODDERED FIRMLESS INSECURE
RESOLUTE UNSTRONG
INFIRMITY WOE CRAZE DOTAGE
FOIBLE UNHEAL DISEASE FAILING
FRAILTY UNMIGHT DEBILITY
SICKNESS WEAKNESS
INFIX INLAY INSET ENGRAVE
IMPLANT INGRAIN
INFIXED INHERENT
INFLAME BURN FIRE GOAD HEAT
STIR ANGER BLAIN FLAME SCALD
SHAME AROUSE ENAMOR EXCITE
FESTER IGNITE INCEND KINDLE
MADDEN RANKLE EMBRASE
FLUSTER INCENSE ESCHAUFE
INFLAMED RED ANGRY FIERY
ABLAZE FRETTY TORRID FLAGRANT
INFLAMMABLE FIERY ARDENT
TOUCHY PICEOUS TINDERY
INFLAMMATION FIRE ANGER FELON
GLEET SCALD SEBEL AGNAIL
BLIGHT CANKER DEFLUX GREASE
IRITIS AORITIS CATARRH CECITIS
CHAFING COLITIS COXITIS FISTULA
GONITIS ILEITIS QUITTOR SUNBURN
ADENITIS ANGIITIS BURSITIS
CHILITIS CYCLITIS CYSTITIS
SHINGLES
INFLATE HOVE HUFF KITE PLIM
BLOAT BOLNE HEAVE SWELL DILATE
EMBOSS EXPAND HUFFLE INBLOW
TUMEFY BLADDER BOMBAST
DISTEND FORBLOW OUTSWELL
SUFFLATE
INFLATED BLOWN FLOWN GASSY
PUFFY TUMID TURGID BOMBAST
FUSTIAN STILTED SWOLLEN

TURGENT BLADDERY OUTBLOWN
TUMOROUS VANITOUS
INFLATION FLATUS CADENCE
TYMPANY
INFLECT COMPARE DECLINE
INFLECTION SIGN ACCENT FLEXION
LATINISM
INFLECTIONAL FORMAL
INFLEXIBILITY ACAMPSIA
INFLEXIBLE ACID DOUR FIRM HARD
IRON EAGER SOLID STERN STIFF
STONY STOUR SEVERE STRICT
STUFFY ADAMANT RESTIVE
GRANITIC IRONCLAD OBDURATE
PREFRACT RESOLUTE RIGOROUS
STIFFISH STUBBORN
INFLICT DO ADD SET GIVE SEND
INFER YIELD IMPOSE RAMROD
STRIKE
(— CHASTISEMENT) WREAK
(— HURT) BRUISE
(— INJURY) AGGRIEVE
(— PAIN) LAY CHASTISE
INFLORESCENCE CHAT CYME
AMENT ARROW BRUSH SPIKE
UMBEL CORYMB FLOWER RACEME
SPADIX TASSEL PANICLE THYRSIS
CYATHIUM FASCICLE
INFLOW INSET INCOME INFLUX
INCOURSE
INFLUENCE IN WIN BEND BIAS COAX
DRAG DRAW HANK HEFT LEAD
MOVE PULL PUSH RULE SUCK SWAY
BRIBE CHARM COLOR ENACT FORCE
GRACE IMPEL MOYEN POWER
REACH SPELL VAPOR VOGUE WEIGH
AFFECT ALLURE CREDIT EFFECT
GOVERN IMPORT INDUCE INFLOW
INFLUX MOTIVE OBSESS PONDUS
SALUTE SHADOW STROKE WEIGHT
ATTINGE ATTRACT BEARING
BEWITCH BLARNEY BOSSDOM
CAPTURE CONCUSS CONTROL
DISPUTE ENCHANT GRAVITY
IMPRINT INCLINE INSPIRE MASTERY
TENDRIL DOMINION HEGEMONY
INTEREST LEVERAGE MEDICINE
PRESTIGE SANCTION STRENGTH
CAPTIVATE
(— BY GIFTS) GREASE
(— CORRUPTLY) BRIBE
(— OF GODS) MANA
(— OF THE STARS) BLAS
(— UNREASONABLY) OBSESS
(BENIGN —) UNCTION
(CONTROLLING —) SWAY
(CORRUPTING —) SMOUCH SMUTCH
(DEPRESSING —) CHILL
(DIABOLICAL —) DEVILDOM
(DISRUPTIVE —) GREMLIN
(DOMINANT —) GENIUS STREAM
(DULLING —) DAMPER
(ELEVATING —) LIFT
(HARMFUL —) UPAS GRUDGE
(INJURIOUS —) RUST
(MALEVOLENT —) DISASTER
(MALIGN —) TAKING
(PERNICIOUS —) BALE BLAST
(SINISTER —) MALICE

(SOOTHING —) SALVE
(SURROUNDING —) AIR
INFLUENCING INFUSIVE
INFLUENTIAL GRAVE POWERFUL
INFLUENZA FLU LEUMA GRIPPE
PINKEYE
INFLUX STORM INCOME INFLOW
INRUSH ILLAPSE
(— IN A MINE) COURSE
(— OF TIDE) INSET
INFOLD WRAP IMPLY TWINE EMPLOY
INWRAP ENVELOP INVOLVE
CONVOLVE
INFORM KEN BEEF BLOW FINK NOSE
POST SHOP SHOW TELL WARN WISE
LEARN PEACH ADVISE ASSURE
DELATE DETECT NOTIFY PREACH
SNITCH WITTER APPRISE EDUCATE
IMPEACH INSENSE PARTAKE
POSSESS RESOLVE SIGNIFY
SUGGEST ACQUAINT DENOUNCE
INFORMED INSTRUCT SPARSILE
INFORMAL BREEZY CASUAL CHATTY
COMMON FOLKSY TWEEDY
INTIMATE SLIPSHOD SOCIABLE
INFORMANT AUTHOR INFORMER
SYCOPHANT
INFORMATION AIR GEN OIL WIT
CLEW CLUE DOPE INFO LORE NEWS
NOTE TALE WIRE WORD DATUM
GRIFF SCOOP SKILL ADVICE INSIDE
LIGHTS NOTICE APPRISE PEMICAN
TIDINGS WITTING BRIEFING
NOTITION PEMMICAN
(BODY OF —) DIGEST
(SECRET —) ARCANUM
INFORMED UP HEP WISE AWARE
WITTY KNOWING LEARNED
INFORMER FINK NARK NOSE PIMP
STAG RUSTY SPLIT CANARY FINGER
SETTER SNITCH TELLER DELATOR
TANQUAM APPROVER PROMOTER
SQUAWKER SQUEAKER SQUEALER
TELLTALE
INFORTUNE MARS SATURN
INFRACTION BREACH OFFENCE
TRESPASS
INFRARED ULTRARED
INFREQUENCY SELDOMCY
INFREQUENT RARE SELDOM
FUGITIVE UNCOMMON
INFRINGE IMPOSE INVADE TRENCH
IMPINGE INFRACT INTRUDE
ENCROACH REFRINGE TRESPASS
INFRINGEMENT FOUL BREACH
TRESPASS VIOLENCE
INFRINGER PIRATE
INFULA FANON LABEL LAPPET
HEADBAND
INFUNDIBULUM FUNNEL PAVILION
INFURIATE ENRAGE ENFELON
INFUSE DRAW IMBUE IMMIT SPOIL
STEEP AERATE AERIFY IMMISS
INFLOW INFORM INFUND INVEST
LEAVEN BREATHE DISTILL ENGRAIN
IMPLANT INFOUND INSPIRE INSTILL
SUFFUSE SATURATE
(— TEA) TRACK
(— WITH HATRED) TURN

INFUSED SHOT
INFUSION SHADE CARDIN INCOME
TISANE HORDEATE
(— OF MALT) WORT GROUT
INFUSORIAN LEPOCYTE
INGA GUAVA
INGATE GATE LEDGE TEDGE
INGATHERING HARVEST
INGENIOUS SLY CUTE FAST FEAT
FINE ACUTE SHARP SMART ADROIT
BRAINY CLEVER CRAFTY DAEDAL
GIFTED KNACKY PRETTY SUBTLE
CUNNING SKILLFUL
INGENUITY ART WIT ENGINE
ADDRESS COMPASS ARTIFICE
CONTOISE INDUSTRY QUENTISE
INGENUOUS FREE FRANK NAIVE
PLAIN HONEST ARTLESS SINCERE
INNOCENT
INGENUOUSNESS NAIVETE
INGEST EAT INCEPT ENGLOBE
SWALLOW
INGESTION SLURP
INGOT GAD SOW WEDGE LINGOT
NIGGOT CROPHEAD
(— OF BRASS) STRIP
(— OF SILVER) SHOE TING SCHUYT
(SILVER —S) SYCEE
(SOAKING —S) HEAT
INGRAIN GRAIN INFUSE ENFLESH
INGRAINED INWORN
INGRATE SNAKE
INGRATIATE FLATTER
INGRATIATING BLAND SILKY SLEEK
SLICK SOAPY SILKEN SMOOTH
INGRATITUDE UNTHANK
INGREDIENT FACTOR BINDING
ELEMENT ADJUVANT
(ACTIVE —) ANIMA
(FUNDAMENTAL —) BASIS
(FUSIBLE —) BOND
(MAIN —) BASE
INGRESS ENTRY ENTRANCE
INGROWTH APODEMA
INGUEN GROIN
INHABIT BIG WIN WON COVER
DWELL HABIT BEDWELL INDWELL
POSSESS
INHABITANT INMATE BURGHER
CITIZEN DENIZEN DWELLER
PEOPLER BORDERER CONFINER
DEMESMAN HABITANT INCOLANT
INHOLDER
(— OF ALASKA) SOURDOUGH
(— OF BORDER REGION) MARCHER
(— OF CITY) CIT CITIZEN
(— OF INDIA) BHARATA
(— OF JUNGLE) JUNGLI
(— OF SWISS ALPS) GRISON
(— OF TORRID ZONE) ASCIAN
(— OF VIRGINIA) COOHEE
(— OF WISCONSIN) BADGER
(PL.) SIDE WARE
INHALATION SNUFF BREATH
INHALE DRAW TAKE SMOKE SNIFF
ATTRACT BREATHE INHAUST
INSPIRE RESPIRE ASPIRATE
INHALER SNIFTER
INHARMONIOUS ABSURD

INHERE CONSIST INEXIST
INHERENCE INBEING
INHERENT KIND INBORN INNATE
INWARD NATIVE PROPER INGENIT
HABITUAL IMMANENT INTEGRAL
INTERNAL RESIDENT
INHERIT HEIR SUCCEED
INHERITANCE KIND ENTAIL
HEIRDON HEIRSHIP HEREDITY
HERITAGE LANDFALL VACANTIA
(— OF CATTLE) ERF
INHERITED INBORN INNATE
INHIBIT COOP CURB SNUB CRIMP
DETER FORBID STIFLE SUPPRESS
INHIBITED COLD
INHIBITION AKINESIS
INHIBITORY COLYTIC
INHOSPITABLE STERN DESERT
INHUMAN FELL CRUEL BRUTAL
FIERCE IMMANE SAVAGE BESTIAL
MANLESS DEVILISH KINDLESS
INHUMANE WANTON
INHUMANITY CRUELTY
INHUME BURY INTER ENTOMB
INIMICAL BAD FROSTY HOSTILE
INIQUITOUS ILL DARK WRONG
SINFUL WICKED
INIQUITY SIN EVIL VICE CRIME GUILT
DARKNESS MISCHIEF
INITIAL LETTER VIRGIN ASPIREE
(INTERWOVEN —S) CIPHER
(PL.) PERFINS
INITIATE HEAD MYST OPEN ADMIT
BEGIN BREAK ENTER EPOPT FOUND
START GROUND INDUCE INDUCT
INVENT LAUNCH MYSTES ORPHIC
BAPTIZE INSTALL INSTATE OPERATE
ORPHEAN SYMMIST COMMENCE
ESOTERIC INCHOATE
INITIATION DIKSHA OPENING
ENTRANCE
(— OF GROWTH) BUDBREAK
INITIATIVE PEP LEAD GETUP ACTION
AMBITION GUMPTION
INJECT DRIVE IMMIT
INJECTION HYPO SHOT BOOSTER
CLYSTER
INJUDICIOUS UNWISE
INJUDICIOUSNESS ACRISY
INJUNCTION HEST BEHEST CHARGE
IMPOSE BIDDING DICTATE EXPRESS
MANDATE PRECEPT
INJURE DO GAS ILL MAR BURN
CHEW ENVY GALL HARM HURT
MAUL TEEN WERD ABUSE BLAST
CRAZE DIRTY MISDO SCALD SHEND
SMITE SPOIL STEER WOUND WRONG
BRUISE DAMAGE DEFACE DEFECT
DEPAIR GRIEVE HINDER IMPAIR
INJURY MANGLE RANKLE SCATHE
SCOTCH STRAIN AFFLICT AFFRONT
CONTUSE DAMNIFY DESPITE
FORWORK MISBEDE TERRIFY
DISASTER DISSERVE IMPERISH
INTERESS MISCHIEF MISGUIDE
MUTILATE PREJUDGE SPURGALL
(— BY ASPERSION) SPATTER
(— BY FALSE REPORT) SLANDER
(— BY GLANCE OF BASILISK)
STRIKE

(— **BY TREADING UPON**) FITTER
(— **SCENT**) STAIN
(— **SERIOUSLY**) DO KILL SPOIL
(— **SLIGHTLY**) ANNOY
(— **THE BACK**) CHINK
INJURED HURT LESED BLASTED
INJURIOUS BAD ILL EVIL NOYANT
NOYFUL SHREWD ABUSIVE
HARMFUL HURTFUL NOXIOUS
DAMAGING GRIEVOUS SINISTER
TORTIOUS TORTUOUS WRACKFUL
WRONGFUL
INJURIOUSLY HEAVILY
INJURY ILL JAM MAR BANE BURN
EVIL HARM HURT JEEL LOSS RUIN
TEEN TORT WITE ABUSE BLAME
CHAFE CRUSH GRIEF SCALD SCORE
SPITE SPOIL TOUCH WATHE WRACK
WRONG BREACH BRUISE DAMAGE
DANGER IMPAIR LESION SCATHE
STRAIN STROKE TRAUMA BEATING
DESPITE EXPENSE OFFENSE
PAYMENT SCADDLE SCRATCH
SORANCE BUSINESS CASUALTY
CREPANCE INTEREST MISCHIEF
NUISANCE
(— **OF HORSES**) TREAD
(— **OF PLANTS**) SUNSCALD
(**CHIEF** —) FOCUS
(**SERIOUS** —) MAYHEM
INJUSTICE WRONG INJURY INJURIA
UNRIGHT HARDSHIP INEQUITY
(**GROSS** —) INIQUITY
INK BEAT COLOR ARNEMENT
ATRAMENT
INK-BALL DABBER PUMPET
INKER SLOSHER
INKING PAD TOMPION
INKLE SPINEL
INKLING HINT ITEM SCENT GLIMMER
GLIMPSE
INKSTAND STANDISH
INKWELL FOUNT INKSTAND
INLAID PIQUE CONTISE
(— **WORK**) KOFTGARI
INLAND MAUKA INMORE INWARD
MIDLAND INTERIOR
INLAY PICK PIKE COUCH HATCH
INLET PIQUE SPELL CRUSTA
ENAMEL IMPAVE INDENT NIELLO
TARSIA ENCHASE ENCRUST
INCRUST COMMESSO
INLAYING TARKASHI
INLET ARM BAY CUT GEO RIA VOE
COVE DOCK HOPE MERE SLEW
WICK BAYOU BRACE CHUCK CREEK
FIORD FJORD FLEET HAVEN LOGAN
LOUGH STOMA ESTERO HARBOR
INFALL SLOUGH DOGHOLE INDRAFT
SUCTION CALANQUE SEAPOOSE
(— **OF THE SEA**) EA
(**MUDDY** —) SUMP
(**TIDAL** —) GAP
INLIER WINDOW
INLYING INNERLY
INMATE FISH LODGER TENANT
BEADSMAN DOMESTIC PRISONER
INMOST SECRET RETIRED
INN PUB KHAN STOP VENT ANGEL

FONDA HOTEL MESON TAMBO
VENTA CABACK HARBOR HOSTEL
HOSTRY IMARET POSADA PUBLIC
SHANTY ALBERGE AUBERGE
BOLICHE CAFENEH CAFENET
FONDACO FONDOUK HOSTAGE
LOCANDA OSTERIA SOJOURN
SURAHEE CHOULTRY GASTHAUS
HOSTELRY ORDINARY SERAGLIO
WAYHOUSE
INNARDS GIZZARD INWARDS
STUFFING
INNATE BORN KIND INBORN INBRED
CONNATE INGRAIN NATURAL
INSTINCT
(— **QUALITY**) LARGESS
INNER BEN ENTAL INSIDE INWARD
INWITH MENTAL INTERIOR INTERNAL
PECTORAL
(— **LIGHT**) SEED
INNERMOST UPPER INMOST
INTIMATE
INNINA ISHTAR
INNING END HAND HEAD FRAME
(PL.) KNOCK
INNKEEPER HOST DUENA TAPPER
VENTER GOODMAN HOSTESS
HOSTLER PADRONE BONIFACE
(PL.) CAUPONES
INNOCENCE BLUET WHITE CANDOR
PURITY
INNOCENT SOT FREE PURE CLEAR
SEELY WHITE CHASTE DOVISH
HONEST SIMPLE CHRISOM LAMBKIN
UPRIGHT HARMLESS IGNORANT
PASTORAL PRIMROSE SACKLESS
UNGUILTY ZACCHEUS
INNOCUOUS HARMLESS INNOCENT
INNOVATE NOVELIZE
INNOVATION NOVEL NOVELTY
INNOVATOR HERETIC
INNUENDO HINT SLUR SLIPE
INNUMERABLE MYRIAD
INO (**FATHER OF** —) CADMUS
(**HUSBAND OF** —) ATHAMAS
(**MOTHER OF** —) HARMONIA
INOCULATE SEED PLANT INFUSE
ENGRAFT EQUINATE
INOCULUM STAB STREAK
INOFFENSIVE HARMLESS
INOPERATIVE OFF DEAD NUGATORY
INOPPORTUNE UNTIMELY
INORDINATE WILD UNDUE
ENORMOUS
INORGANIC MINERAL
INOSITOL DAMBOSE
INPOURING INFLUX
INQUEST CROWN QUEST ASSIZE
OFFICE INQUIRY
INQUIET UNEASY
INQUILINE GUEST
INQUIRE ASK AXE SEEK QUERY
SPERE DEMAND FRAYNE SEARCH
EXAMINE HEARKEN QUESTION
INQUIRER ASKER QUERENT
INQUIRY PROBE QUERY THANK
TRIAL DEMAND EXAMEN TRACER
DOCIMASY QUESTION RESEARCH
SCRUTINY SPEERING

INQUISITION CUSTOM INQUIRY
QUAESTIO
INQUISITIVE NOSY PEERY PRYING
CURIOUS MEDDLING
INROAD RAID BREACH INBREAK
INVASION
INSALUBRIOUS NOXIOUS
INSANE MAD WUD DAFT WOOD
BALMY BATTY BUGGY CRAZY DIPPY
QUEER WRONG CRANKY LOCOED
SCREWY FLIGHTY FRANTIC FURIOUS
LUNATIC WITLESS BUGHOUSE
DEMENTED DERANGED DISTRACT
INSANITY RAGE CRACK CRAZE
FOLIE MANIA FRENZY LUNACY
MADNESS VESANIA DELIRIUM
DEMENTIA WOODNESS PSYCHOSIS
INSATIABLE GREEDY
INSCRIBE DELVE ENTER WRITE
BLAZON DOCKET INDITE LEGEND
LETTER SCRIBE SCRIVE SCROLL
ASCRIBE ENDORSE ENGROSS
DEDICATE DESCRIBE EMBLAZON
ENSCROLL INTITULE
INSCRIBED INWRIT WRITTEN
DESCRIPT
INSCRIPTION HEAD ELOGY CACHET
LEGEND LETTER ELOGIUM EPIGRAM
EPITAPH MENTION TITULUS WRITING
COLOPHON EPIGRAPH GRAFFITO
INSCRIPT SCRIBING
(— **ON TOMBSTONE**) ELOGE
ELOGIUM
(**3-LETTER** —) TRIGRAM
INSCRUTABLE EQUIVOCAL
INSECT ANT BEE BUG DOR DUN ELF
FLY NIT ANER FLEA GNAT GOGO
GYNE MOTH PELA PEST PUPA SPIT
WASP WETA ZIMB APHID APHIS
BICHO BORER FLYER GOGGA GUEST
IMAGO LOUSE MINER ROACH SCALE
BEETLE BLIGHT CALLOW CICADA
CIXIID EARWIG EMBIID HAWKER
HOPPER INSTAR MANTIS NITTER
PODURA SAPPER SAWFLY THRIPS
VERMIN WALKER WEEVIL ATTACUS
BLATTID BOATMAN BUZZARD
CRAWLER CREEPER CRICKET
CYNIPID DEALATE DRUMMER
EARWORM FIREBUG FIREFLY
GALLFLY GIRDLER GRAYFLY
HEXAPOD JAPYGID KATYDID
SANDBOY SCINIPH SKIPPER
SPECTRE STAINER STYLOPS
TERMITE VAGRANT WEBWORM
ALDERFLY ALKERMES BLACKFLY
BRACONID FIREBRAT FULGORID
GLOWWORM HOMOPTER HORNTAIL
LACEWING LECANIUM PRONYMPH
SEMIPUPA SEXUPARA SPHECOID
STINKBUG STYLOPID SYMPHILE
INSECTICIDE DDD DDT DIP CUBE
FLIT ALDRIN DERRIS ENDRIN
CALOMEL ISODRIN LINDANE OVICIDE
CHLORDAN CULICIDE DIELDRIN
SCHRADAN
INSECTIVORE MOONRAT ALAMIQUI
INSECURE DICKY EEMIS LOOSE
SHAKY INFIRM TICKLE UNFAST

UNSAFE UNSURE CASALTY
INSEMINATE BREED
INSENSATE SURD FATUOUS
INSENSIBILITY DAMP APATHY
TORPOR
INSENSIBLE DEAR DULL LOST NUMB
BRUTE DENSE SEARED DATELESS
INSENSITIVE BLUNT STONY STUPID
BOORISH
INSEPARABLE WRAPPED
INSERT SLIP SPUD STOP BOTCH
DICKY ENROL ENTER FUDGE IMMIT
INFER INFIX INLET INSET STUFF
COLLET GUSSET INWORK INWEAVE
GATEFOLD INTROMIT SANDWICH
SLASHING SUBTRUDE THROWOUT
(— IN SHOE) CUSHION
(— SURREPTITIOUSLY) FOIST
INSERTION FLOWER BEADING
INSET GODET INSERT
INSHEATHE EMBOSS
INSIDE IN BEN ATHIN INBYE INNER
INWITH KEYHOLE INTERIOR
(— OF ANGLE BAR) BOSOM
(— OF OUTER EAR) BUR BURR
INSIDIOUS SLY SNARY COVERT
SUBTLE GUILEFUL
INSIGHT KEN SIGHT APERCU
THEORY NOSTRIL
INSIGNIA ORDER SIGNS COLLAR
GEORGE CADUCEUS COMMENDA
HERALDRY OPINICUS
INSIGNIFICANT NULL POOR PUNY
DINKY FOOTY PETIT PETTY POTTY
SMALL HUMBLE NAUGHT PALTRY
PUISNE SIMPLE SLIGHT FOOLISH
NAUGHTY NIFLING PELTING PIMPING
SCRUBBY TENUOUS TRIVIAL
BAUBLING INFERIOR PEDDLING
PITIABLE SNIPPING TRIFLING
TRIPENNY
INSINCERE FALSE DOUBLE FEIGNED
INSINCERITY ARTIFICE DISGUISE
INSINUATE HINT MINT WIND CRAWL
SCREW TWIST ALLUDE GLANCE
INFUSE INSTIL WRITHE IMPLANT
INNUATE
INSINUATING SNIDE SILKEN
SMARMY
INSINUATION HINT INKLING
INSIPID DRY WAW DEAD FADE FLAT
FOND FOZY TAME BANAL BAUCH
BLAND FLASH INANE PROSY STALE
VAPID WALSH WAUGH FLASHY
FRIGID JEJUNE SWASHY THREEP
WAIRSH WALLOW EXOLETE
FATUOUS INSULSE PROSAIC
SAPLESS SHILPIT WEARISH WEERISH
LIFELESS UNSAVORY WATERISH
INSIST AVER CONSIST
(— PEEVISHLY) CRAIK
(— UPON) SOLICIT
INSISTENCE URGENCY INSTANCY
INSISTENT ADAMANT INSTANT
EMPHATIC FRENZIED IMPOSING
INSOLE CUSHION SLIPSOLE
INSOLENCE CHEEK PRIDE SNASH
DISDAIN AUDACITY SURQUIDY
INSOLENT FACY PERT RUDE WISE

BARDY LUSTY LORDLY WANTON
ABUSIVE DEFIANT PAUGHTY
ARROGANT IMPUDENT PETULANT
SCORNFUL
INSOLUBLE HOPELESS
INSOMNIA AHYPNIA AGRYPNIA
INSOUCIANT CAVALIER
INSPECT SEE VET CASE ESPY LOOK
BRACK CHECK SIGHT VISIT INLOOK
PERUSE SURVEY EXAMINE OVERSEE
CONSIDER OVERLOOK OVERVIEW
(— CASUALLY) BROWSE
(— COINS) SHROFF
(— MERCHANDISE IN BALTIC)
BRACK
INSPECTION EYE PRY VIEW CHECK
SIGHT REVIEW SURVEY BEDIKAH
CHECKUP INSIGHT INSPECT
PERUSAL VIDIMUS OVERVIEW
SCRUTINY
INSPECTOR SAYER SNOOP BISHOP
CENSOR CONNER JUMPER LOOKER
VIEWER GRAINER MOOCHER
PERCHER SAMPLER SNOOPER
VEADORE EXAMINER SEARCHER
(— OF COAL) KEEKER
(— OF COTTON LOOMS) TACKLER
(— OF ELECTRIC LAMPS) AGER
INSPIRATION FIRE SIGH POESY
ANIMUS SPIRIT SPRITE IMPULSE
MADNESS AFFLATUS INFLATUS
INSPIRE FIRE MOVE CHEER ELATE
EXALT SPARK BEACON INBLOW
INCUSS INDUCE INFORM INFUSE
KINDLE PROMPT ACTUATE ANIMATE
EMBRAVE ENFORCE ENLIVEN
HEARTEN IMPLANT PREMOVE
QUICKEN SUGGEST CATALYZE
ENTALENT INSPIRIT MOTIVATE
SUFFLATE
INSPIRED AFFLATED ENTHEATE
VISIONED
INSPIRER SOUL
INSPIRING INFUSIVE STIRRING
INSPIRIT CHEER HEART ROUSE
SPIRIT ANIMATE CHERISH COMFORT
ENLIVEN HEARTEN INSPIRE QUICKEN
ALACRIFY
INSPISSATE STIFFEN THICKEN
INSPISSATED STIFF THICK
INSTABILITY SLIDDER FLUIDITY
INSTALL SEAT CHAIR STALL INDUCT
INVEST ENSTOOL POSSESS
ENTHRONE INITIATE
INSTALLATION INDUCTION
(— OF MINISTER) INFARE
(MILITARY —) GARRISON
INSTALLMENT KIST SERIAL
EARNEST CONTRACT
(— OF WAGES) COMPO
(— SELLER) TALLYMAN
(FIRST —) HANDSEL
(NEXT —) SEQUEL
INSTANCE CASE PINK SAMPLE
EXAMPLE PURPOSE ENSAMPLE
EXEMPLAR
(EXTREME —) CAPSHEAF
INSTANT POP HINT WHIP WINK
BLICK CLINK CRACK FLASH GLENT

GLIFF GLISK JIFFY POINT SHAKE
SOUND START TRICE WHIFF WIGHT
BREATH FLIFFY MINUTE MOMENT
SECOND PRESENT CLIFFING
(PRECISE —) TIME
INSTANTANEOUS PRESTO
DIRECTLY
INSTANTLY SLAP SWITH SWITHE
DIRECTLY MOMENTLY
INSTAR STAGE
INSTEAD EITHER
INSTEP WRIST TARSUS
INSTIGATE EGG ABET GOAD MOVE
SPUR URGE IMPEL ATTICE ENTICE
EXCITE FOMENT INCITE INDUCE
INVOKE PROMPT SPIRIT SUBORN
INCENSE INSTINCT
INSTIGATION MOTION MOTIVE
EGGMENT INSTANCE INSTINCT
INSTIGATOR AUTHOR MOTIVE
SOURCE MONITOR
INSTILL GRAFT INFIX IMPART INFUSE
INSTIL BREATHE IMPLANT
INSTINCT KIND FILLED CHARGED
IMPULSE CAPACITY TENDENCY
INSTINCTIVE INNATE NATURAL
INHERENT ORIGINAL
INSTITUTE BRING ERECT FOUND
RAISE STUDY INVENT KINDLE
ORDAIN ACTIVATE
(— MEMBER) PIARIST
INSTITUTION BANK CAMP FOLD
CLINIC FRIARY SCHOOL ACADEMY
CHARITY COLLEGE GALLERY
JUBILEE LIBRARY SHELTER STATION
VERITAS SEMINARY
(— FOR INSANE) ASYLUM
(CHARITABLE —) SPITTLE
DEACONRY HOSPITAL
(DRUIDICAL —) GORSEDD
INSTRUCT KEN REAR SHOW WISE
COACH DRILL EDIFY ENDUE GUIDE
TEACH TRAIN CHARGE DIRECT
GROUND INDUCE INFORM LESSON
PREACH REFORM SCHOOL
COMMAND EDUCATE INSENSE
POSSESS DOCUMENT
INSTRUCTED SCIENCED
INSTRUCTION LORE ADVICE ASSIZE
CHARGE LESSON COUNSEL
PRECEPT TUITION WISSING
COACHING DOCTRINE DOCUMENT
MONITION PEDAGOGY PROPHECY
TEACHING TUTELAGE
(DIVINE —) LAW
(SACRED —) TORAH
(PL.) BRIEFING
INSTRUCTIVE DOCENT DIDACTIC
INSTRUCTOR DON SOAK SCREW
TUTOR MENTOR REGENT ACHARYA
CRAMMER TEACHER BEACHBOY
CHAIRMAN ELDERMAN
INSTRUMENT (ALSO SEE MUSICAL
INSTRUMENT) DEED TOOL WRIT
AGENT SLANG THEME FACTUM
UTENSIL SYNGRAPH
(— NOT UNDER SEAL) PAROL
(— OF DESTRUCTION) SWORD
(— OF DIVINATION) EPHOD

(— **OF TORTURE**) BOOT RACK
BRAKE BRANK FURCA GADGE
WHEEL TUMBREL BARNACLE
SQUEEZER
(—**S OF WAR**) ENGINERY
(**FINANCIAL** —) ITEM
(**LEGAL** —) DEED GRANT FACTUM
SASINE SCRIPT CHARTER CODICIL
DUPLICATE
(**NEGOTIABLE** —) HUNDI HOONDEE
(**OFFICIAL** —) SLANG
(**PREHISTORIC** —) CELT
(**SCIENTIFIC OR OTHER** —) AWL FAN
HOE KEY MET RAX SAX BROG
COMB DIAL DRAG FILE FORK GAGE
HOOK PLOW RACK RING SPAR
ARMIL BEVEL BLADE BRACE BRAKE
CHAIN CLAMP DATER DOLLY DRILL
FLAIL FLOAT FLUKE GAUGE GLASS
INDEX KNIFE LADLE LEVER METER
PILOT RAZOR SCALE SCOPE SLATE
SLICE SLING SPADE SPEAR SPRAY
STAMP STEEL SWIFT THROW TONGS
TUNER WHISK ABACUS BEETLE
BODKIN BRIDGE CIRCLE DOUCHE
ENGINE ERASER FERULE FOLDER
GRATER LEAPER MORTAR NEEDLE
PESTLE PICKER PLOUGH PULLER
PUMPER RAMMER RASPER RATTLE
RUBBER SCALER SCORER SCRIBE
SCUTCH SCYTHE SHEARS SQUARE
SQUIRT STADIA STRAIK STROBE
STYLET STYLUS TACKLE TICKER
WIMBLE ALIDADE BELLOWS
BREAKER CADRANS CLEAVER
COMPASS DIOPTER DOLABRA
DOUBLER FISTUCA GRAFTER
GRAINER GRAPPLE HATCHEL
LAYOVER MASSEUR MEASURE
OOMETER OOSCOPE PAVIOUR
PELORUS PIERCER PINCERS
PRICKER PRINTER PYROPEN
QUADRAT SCRAPER SEXTANT
SHOCKER SHUTTLE SLITTER
SOUNDER SPLAYER SPRAYER
STRIGIL SUNDIAL SWINGLE
TRAMMEL TRIMMER WHISTLE
ANALEMMA ATOMIZER BIRDCALL
BLOWPIPE BUTTERIS CALLIPER
COALRAKE DECAPPER DETECTOR
DIAGRAPH DIPMETER DIVIDERS
EQUULEUS ERGMETER EXPLORER
FATHOMER GEOPHONE HOROLOGE
IMPINGER ISOGRAPH ISOSCOPE
JOVILABE MESOLABE MHOMETER
ODOMETER OHMMETER PHOTOMER
QUADRANT RECORDER RINGHEAD
RUMMAGER SCISSORS SEARCHER
SQUEEGEE STILETTO STRICKLE
TJANTING TRIANGLE VELLINCH
VIAGRAPH YAWMETER
(**SURGICAL OR MEDICAL** —) GAG
HOOK SPUD FLEAM PROBE SCOOP
SNARE SOUND STAFF STYLE BILABE
BOUGIE BROACH GORGET LANCET
SEEKER TREPAN TROCAR UNGULA
VECTIS XYSTER AIRDENT DILATER
FORCEPS HARPOON LEVATOR
LIGATOR MYOTOME PELICAN

PLUGGER RONGEUR SCALPEL
SOUNDER SYRINGE TRACTOR
TRILABE TURNKEY ANOSCOPE
AURILAVE AXOMETER BISTOURY
DIRECTOR DIVULSOR ECRASEUR
ELEVATOR EXSECTOR HEMOSTAT
KERATOME MYOGRAPH SPECULUM
TREPHINE
INSTRUMENTAL MEDIATE ORGANIC
SERVILE SERVIENT
INSTRUMENTALIST KLEZMER
SIDEMAN
INSTRUMENTALITY HAND MEANS
AGENCY MEDIUM CHANNEL COUNCIL
MINISTRY
(— **FOR ACQUISITION OF
KNOWLEDGE**) ORGANON
(**NAVAL** —**S**) BEACH
INSUBORDINATE FACTIOUS
MUTINOUS UNWIELDY
INSUBORDINATION MUTINY
INSUBSTANTIAL AIRY INANE
FROTHY SLENDER SPECTRAL
INSUBSTANTIALITY FRAILTY
INSUFFICIENCY PAUCITY
INSUFFICIENT POOR WANE SHORT
SCANTY
INSUFFICIENTLY BARELY FEEBLY
THINLY
INSULATE ISLE ISLAND ISOLATE
INSULATION LAGGING ISOLATION
INSULATOR NOB KNOB TAPLET
VITRITE MEGOHMIT
(**PL.**) STRING
INSULT CAG FIG JOEY RUMP SLAP
ABUSE CHECK FLOUT FRUMP SLANG
INJURE INJURY OFFEND OUTRAY
RUFFLE SCRAPE ABUSION AFFRONT
OFFENCE OUTRAGE BRICKBAT
DISHONOR CONTUMELY
INSULTING RUDE ARROGANT
INSOLENT
INSULTINGLY FOULLY
INSURANCE LINE CHOMAGE
COVERAGE INDEMNITY
(— **AGENT**) TWISTER
(**UNEMPLOYMENT** —) DOLE
INSURE COVER ASSURE ENSURE
FURNISH
INSURGENT REBEL RISER CHOUAN
OAKBOY TAIPING BARRABAS
CAMISARD STEELBOY
INSURRECTION RIST MUTINY
REVOLT UPROAR OUTBREAK
SEDITION UPRISING
INSURRECTO GUGU
INTACT SOUND WHOLE ENTIRE
INTAGLIO ENTAIL DIAGLYPH
(**PART OF** —) INCAVO
INTANGIBLE VAGUE SUBTLE
AERIFORM SLIPPERY
INTEGER SUM NORM TOTITIVE
INTEGRAL FLUX NEEDFUL
INTEGRANT ELEMENT
INTEGRATE FUSE PIECE COMBINE
FULFILL
INTEGRATED FUSED INTEGRAL
INTEGRATION BALANCE HARMONY
INTEGRITY HONOR TRUTH HONESTY

JUSTICE PROBITY CHASTITY
STRENGTH
INTEGUMENT KEX SKIN TESTA
TUNIC SWATHE CUTICLE ENVELOP
EPIDERM EXODERM PRIMINE
TUNICLE EPISPERM PERISARC
SCABBARD
INTELLECT MIND HEART INWIT
MAHAT SKILL BRAINS NOTICE
REASON SPIRITS THINKING
(**HIGHEST** —) NOUS
INTELLECTUAL BLUE GAON IDEAL
BOOKSY MENTAL SOPHIC BRAHMIN
EGGHEAD GNOSTIC CEREBRAL
LONGHAIR SOPHICAL DIANOETIC
INTELLIGENCE AIR CIT SAT CHIT
KNOW MIND NEWS NOTE WORD
AGIEL SENSE ADVICE BRAINS
ESPRIT INGENY NOTICE WITTING
(— **IN EGYPTIAN LORE**) CHU
(— **OF PLANET JUPITER**) JOPHIEL
(**LIVELY** —) WIT
INTELLIGENT APT GASH PERT
ACUTE ALERT SMART SPACK
AKAMAI BRAINY BRIGHT CLEVER
MENTAL SPRACK WITFUL KNOWING
INFORMED LUMINOUS RATIONAL
SKILLFUL
INTELLIGENTSIA CLERISY
INTELLIGIBLE CLEAR PLAIN
LUMINOUS PELLUCID PERVIOUS
REVELANT
INTELLIGIBLY SIMPLY
INTEMPERANCE ACRASY EXCESS
ACRASIA OUTRAGE
INTEMPERATE SHRILL SURFEIT
(**NOT** —) SWEET
INTEND GO AIM FIX CAST MEAN
MIND MINT PLAN PLOT TEND ALLOT
ALLOW ETTLE TIGHT ATTEND
DESIGN RECKON BEHIGHT DESTINE
FORELAY PRETEND PROPOSE
PURPORT PURPOSE FOREMIND
MEDITATE PRETENSE
INTENDED SUPPOSED
INTENSE HOT ACID COLD DEEP
HARD HIGH KEEN BLANK DENSE
GREAT HEAVY QUICK SHARP TENSE
VIVID ARDENT BRAZEN FIERCE
INTENT PITCHY STRONG BURNING
CHARGED CHRONIC CUTTING
EXTREME FERVENT FRANTIC
FURIOUS VIOLENT EGYPTIAN
GRIEVOUS POWERFUL SEETHING
VEHEMENT
INTENSELY STIFF HIGHLY ACUTELY
CURSEDLY FERVIDLY SHREWDLY
INTENSIFIED ACUTE
INTENSIFY RISE URGE EXALT RAISE
ACCENT DEEPEN BOLSTER
ENFORCE ENHANCE IMPROVE
INFLAME SHARPEN THICKEN
CONDENSE HEIGHTEN INCREASE
INTENSION INTENT MEANING
INTENSITY EDGE HEAT ARDOR
DEPTH DRIVE FEVER FIELD DEGREE
DOSAGE FERVOR FRENZY STRESS
CURRENT FEROCITY STRENGTH
VIOLENCE

INTENSIVE HARD HIGH EXTENDED
INTENSIVELY HARD SOLIDLY
INTENT SET DEEP DOLE FELL HENT
MIND TENT BEADY CAUSE DRIFT
ETTLE FIXED HEART PRICK SCOPE
TENOR TENSE EFFECT SPIRIT
COUNSEL INTENSE PRESENT
STUDIED WISTFUL
(CRIMINAL —) DOLE
(EVIL —) DOLUS
INTENTION AIM END GOAL HENT
MIND WILL HEART SCOPE ANIMUS
ATTENT DESIGN DEVICE EFFECT
INTENT OBJECT REGARD COUNSEL
COURAGE EARNEST FORESET
MEANING PROPOSE PURPORT
PURPOSE SUPPOSE PRETENSE
INTENTIONAL SET WILLFUL WILLING
WITTING INTENDED
INTENTLY BUSILY WISHLY EAGERLY
FIXEDLY
INTER BURY EARTH ENTER GRAVE
PLANT ENTOMB INHUME INEARTH
INTERACTION COUPLING
INTERAGENT MEDIUM MIDDLER
INTERBREED CROSS
INTERBREEDING APOGAMY
MIXTURE PANMIXY CROSSING
INTERCALATE INSERT
INTERCALATION EMBOLISM
INTERCEPT KEP HEAD KEEP STOP
CATCH NORMAL TRAMMEL
GAINCOPE INTERPEL RETRENCH
INTERCEPTION CUTOFF
INTERCESSION MOYEN DIPTYCH
PLEADING
INTERCESSOR MEANS PLEADER
ADVOCATE MEDIATOR
INTERCHANGE CHANGE ANAGRAM
COMMUTE PERMUTE COMMERCE
EXCHANGE
(— OF OPINION) COUNSEL
(— OF WORDS) SPEECH
INTERCHANGEABLE FUNGIBLE
INTERCOLUMNIATION EUSTYLE
SYSTYLE DIASTYLE
INTERCOMMUNICATION LIAISON
INTERCONNECTED SYNDETIC
INTERCONNECTION BONDING
INTERCOURSE GAM DEAL MANG
MONG TRADE TRUCK TURGY
BAWDRY HOBNOB NEGOCE COITION
DEALING MIXTURE QUARTER
SOCIETY TRAFFIC BUSINESS
COMMERCE CONVERSE RECOURSE
INTERDICT BAN TABU TABOO
FORBID UTRUBI INHIBIT PROHIBIT
SUPPRESS
INTERDICTION VETO
INTEREST BUG DIP FAD USE BENT
GOOD HAND HOLD PART CLOSE
COLOR DRIVE FAVOR FETCH GAVEL
HOBBY RIGHT STAKE STUDY USAGE
USURA USURY BEHALF ENGAGE
EQUITY ESTATE FAENUS FERVOR
FINGER INCOME USANCE ATTRACT
CONCERN RESPECT USAUNCE
CONTANGO INCREASE VIGORISH
(— OF HUSBAND) CURTESY

(— ON LAND) CLOSE
(ACTIVE —) SYMPATHY
(LEGAL —) EASEMENT
(POLITICAL —) FENCE
(SECURITY —) LIEN
(SPECIAL —) ANGLE
INTERESTED HIPPED ENGAGED
SERIOUS
INTERESTING FRUITY CURIOUS
STORIED
INTERFERE CUT MAKE ANNOY
BLOCK CHECK HITCH POACH
BAFFLE HAMPER HINDER HOBBLE
IMPEDE MEDDLE STRIKE TAMPER
INTRUDE INTROMIT
(— SLIGHTLY) BRUSH
(— WITH) AIL JOLT HECKLE
BLANKET DISTURB
INTERFERENCE BALK CHOKE
THUMP HINDER JOSTLE MEDDLE
CONFLICT FREINAGE
INTERFERING CUT
INTERFEROMETER ETALON
INTERFLUVE DOAB
INTERIM BREAK VACANCY
INTERIOR BEN BELLY BOSOM INNER
ENTIRE INLAND INWARD INWITH
MIDDLE GIZZARD ENTRAILS
INTERNAL
(— OF CUPOLA) CALOTTE
(— OF TEMPLE) CELLA
(— OF VESSEL) HOLD
(— PART) MANTLE
INTERJECT ENTER SQUIB INJECT
THRUST
INTERJECTION AW ER HA LO FIE
GEE GIP HAH HEH HEY AHEM AHOY
ALAS EGAD FORE GOSH HECH HOLA
JOVE GOODY HEIGH MAFEY SUGAR
TENEZ EUREKA HARROW OUTCRY
LACKADAY
INTERLACE LACE WARP BRAID
WEAVE ENLACE PLEACH INWEAVE
WREATHE
INTERLACED BRACED FRETTED
PLEACHED
INTERLACEMENT KNOT
INTERLACING TWINY
INTERLINING DOUBLER
INTERLOCK KNIT LOCK PITCH
ENGAGE FINGER TANGLE DOVETAIL
INTERLOPE INTRUDE
INTERLUDE JEST COMEDY VERSET
TEMACHA TRIUMPH ENTRACTE
ENTREMES RITORNEL VERSETTE
(ROMANTIC —) IDYL IDYLL
INTERMEDDLER STRANGER
INTERMEDDLING GESTION
INTERMEDIARY MEAN AGENT
MOYENER MEDIATOR TRAMPLER
INTERMEDIATE MEAN MESNE
FILLER ISATIN MEDIAL MEDIUM
MIDDLE MIDDLING
INTERMEDIATOR BROKER
INTERMENT BURIAL BURYING
DEPOSIT HUMATION
INTERMINABLE ETERNAL INFINITE
TIMELESS UNENDING
INTERMINGLE MIX BRAID IMMINGLE

INTERMIT INTERMIX
INTERMINGLED AMONG AMONGST
INTERMISSION REST WAIT BREAK
DWELL PAUSE DEVALL RECESS
NOONING RELACHE RESPITE
INTERVAL SURCEASE VACATION
(— OF PAIN) SABBATH
INTERMISSIVE CESSANT
INTERMIT CEASE DEFER DEVAUL
SUSPEND
INTERMITTENT BROKEN FITFUL
PERIODIC
INTERMIX MEDLEY MINGLE
INTERMIXTURE INTIMACY
INTERNAL INLY INNER ENTIRE
INLAND INNATE INSIDE INWARD
DOMESTIC
INTERNALLY INLY INSIDE INWARD
INWARDLY
INTERNODE ROSETTE
INTERPELLATION FLOWER
INTERPENETRATED SHOT
INTERPLAY AUSPICE
INTERPOLATE FARCE FARSE FOIST
FUDGE INSERT THRUST
INTERPOLATION GAG FARSE
INTERPOSE BAR CHOP DEMUR
OBJECT THRUST THWART MEDIATE
INTERPRET MAKE OPEN READ SCAN
TAKE AREAD AREED FANCY GLOSS
GLOZE RECHE DEFINE DIVINE
INTEND CLARIFY COMMENT
DECLARE ENGLISH EXPLAIN
EXPOUND CONSTRUE DECIPHER
SIMPLIFY
INTERPRETATION REDE GLOSS
SENSE GOSPEL STRAIN ANAGOGE
BARAITA COMMENT EPIKEIA
CABALISM EXEGESIS INNUENDO
SOLARISM SOLUTION
INTERPRETER BROKER DUBASH
UNDOER EXEGETE LATINER
MUNCHEE CABALIST DRAGOMAN
EXPONENT LINKSTER TRUCHMAN
(— OF SCRIPTURE) TROPIST
(PL.) HAHAM SELLI SELLOI
CHOCHEM HAKAMIM
INTERRELATED INTIMATE
INTERRELATIONSHIP ACCORD
LIAISON COMMERCE
INTERROGATE ASK TARGE DEBRIEF
EXAMINE INQUIRE
INTERROGATION EROTESIS
QUESTION
INTERRUPT CUT MAR NIP CHOP
STOP TAKE BREAK CHECK CRACK
EMBAR ARREST DERAIL DERANGE
DISRUPT FORBREAK INTERMIT
INTERPEL OBSTRUCT
INTERRUPTED BROKEN CHOPPY
SNATCHY
INTERRUPTER BUZZER
INTERRUPTION CESS JUMP STOP
BLOCK BREAK CHECK DWELL LAPSE
PAUSE BREACH HIATUS HOCKET
HOQUET ISLAND CAESURA CUTBACK
DIASTEM BLOCKING BREAKAGE
SOLUTION STOPOVER
(WITHOUT —) FLUSH

INTERRUPTOR TIKKER BREAKER CHOPPER RHEOTOME
INTERSECT CUT CROSS BISECT INCISE CROSSCUT
INTERSECTING CRUCIAL COMPITAL
INTERSECTION LEET CHINE CROSS CURVE CHIASMA CROSSING CROSSWAY JUNCTION
INTERSEXUAL EPICENE
INTERSEXUALITY GYNANDRY
INTERSPACE SPACE POCKET
INTERSPERSE DOT SALT SHED MEDDLE THREAD CHECKER INTERSOW SPRINKLE
INTERSTICE PORE SEAM CHINK GRATE AREOLA RIFFLE CELLULE VACUITY
(PL.) CANCELLI
INTERSTRATIFY INTERBED
INTERTWINE KNIT LACE WARP TWINE FELTER TANGLE WAMPLE WARPLE WRITHE ENSNARL COMPLECT INTERTEX
INTERTWINED INWOUND
INTERVAL GAP LAG CENT GULF REST SAND SEXT SPOT STEP BLANK BREAK COMMA CYCLE FIFTH LAPSE QUINT SIXTH SPACE SWING TENTH THIRD BREACH DECIMA DEGREE DIESIS DITONE FOURTH MERLON SECOND SYSTEM ADVANCE DIASTEM DISCORD HEADWAY HEMIOLA INTERIM PASTIME RESPITE SCHISMA SETTIMO STADIUM TRITONE DIAPASON DIAPENTE DISTANCE ELEVENTH ENTRACTE FONTANEL
(— **BETWEEN FINGERS**) SUBVOLA
(— **OF BRIGHTNESS**) FLICKER
(— **OF FAIR WEATHER**) SLATCH
(— **OF HARSH WEATHER**) SNAP
(— **OF SEMITONE**) APOTOME
(**REST** —) SOB
(**SHORT** —) STREAK
(**TIME** —) HEADWAY
INTERVALE BOTTOM
INTERVENE CHOP STEP STRIKE MEDIATE OBVIATE STICKLE INTERCUR
INTERVENING MESNE MIDDLE MEDIANT
INTERVIEW BUZZ CONTACT AUDIENCE CONGRESS
INTERWEAVE MAT PLAT CRISP PLAIT PLASH RADDLE TANGLE WATTLE ENTWINE TEXTURE TRELLIS COMPLECT ENTANGLE IMPLEACH INTERTEX
INTERWEAVING BREDE CROWN INTIMATE
INTERWOVEN INWOVEN IMPLICIT INTIMATE
INTESTINAL INNER ENTERAL ENTERIC
INTESTINE GUT ROPE BOWEL INNER THARM INWARD MIDDLE
(**PORTION OF** —) JEJUNUM
(PL.) VISCUS INGANGS CHITLINS
INTHROW RIDGE

INTIMACY LIAISON PRIVACY AFFINITY CHUMMERY GOSSIPRY INTRIGUE
(**UNDUE** —) LIBERTY
INTIMATE SIB BOON GRIT HINT HOME HOMY KIND NEAR NEXT PACK TOSH BOSOM CHIEF CLOSE GREAT PALLY PRIVY THICK ALLUDE ENTIRE FRIEND HOMELY INTIME INWARD NOTICE SECRET STRAIT STRICT THRANG THRONG CHAMBER CLOSEUP GREMIAL INNERLY INNUATE KEYHOLE PRIVADO PRIVATE SIGNIFY SPECIAL SUGGEST COCKMATE ESPECIAL FAMILIAR FREQUENT FRIENDLY INDICATE INTIMADO
(**MOST** —) MIDMOST
(PL.) FOLKS
INTIMATELY INLY TOSH WELL COZILY CLOSELY INWARDLY
INTIMATION CUE HINT ITEM WARN WIND SCENT NOTICE OFFICE GLIMMER INKLING INNUENDO MONITION
INTIMIDATE COW HAZE ABASH BULLY COWER DAUNT DETER HECTOR TERRIFY BROWBEAT BULLDOZE BULLYRAG FRIGHTEN
INTO IN INTIL WITHIN
INTOLERANCE BIGOTRY
INTOLERANT CLOSED BIGOTED
INTONATION FALL ITALICS
INTONE CANT SING TONE CHANT CHAUNT ENTUNE MODULATE
INTOXICATE FOX TIP TOX FLAW GOOF SOAK TODDY FUDDLE MUDDLE SOZZLE SPRING TIPSIFY DISGUISE OVERTAKE SPRINKLE
INTOXICATED CUT FAP LIT WET HIGH LUSH RIPE SHOT SOSH TOFT TOSY BOSKY BUFFY DRUNK FRESH FRIED FUNNY HEADY LACED NAPPY PIPED TIGHT BOILED GROGGY LOADED MELLOW PIPPED QUAINT SCREWY SKEWED SLEWED SLOPPY SODDEN SOSHED SOZZLE STEWED TANKED UPPISH UPPITY EBRIATE EXALTED FLECKED JINGLED POTSHOT SCREWED SLOPPED SMASHED SPIFFED SQUIFFY UNSOBER BESOTTED COCKEYED DELEERIT ELEVATED OVERSEEN OVERSHOT PLEASANT SQUIFFED TEMULENT TOXICATE
INTOXICATING HARD HEADY STARK HUFFCAP
INTOXICATION WINE FUDDLE IVRESSE LOCOISM DISGUISE EBRIOSITY
(— **OF ANIMALS**) DUNZIEKTE
INTRACTABLE BAD HARD SALTY STACK SURLY FIERCE SULLEN THWART UNRULY CRABBED HAGGARD RESTIVE ROPABLE WAYWARD CHURLISH INDOCILE MUTINOUS OBDURATE PERVERSE SHREWISH
INTRADOS SOFFIT

INTRANSITIVE NEUTER
INTREPID BOLD BRAVE HARDY HEROIC PRETTY SAVAGE DOUGHTY VALIANT RESOLUTE
INTREPIDITY GAME COURAGE
INTRICACY KNOT INTRIGUE
INTRICATE HARD MAZY BLIND DAEDAL IMPLEX KNOBBY KNOTTY TANGLY TRICKY COMPLEX CRABBED CURIOUS GORDIAN PERPLEX PUZZLED SINUOUS INVOLUTE INVOLVED
INTRIGUE PLOT ANGLE CABAL CLOAK STORY AFFAIR AMOUNT BRIGUE DECEIT SCHEME CONNIVE FACTION FINAGLE JOBBERY TRINKET TRINKLE ARTIFICE CHEATING COLLOGUE PRACTICE PRACTISE STRATEGY TRIPOTER
INTRIGUER JESUIT SCHEMER DESIGNER
INTRIGUING EXCITING SCHEMING
INTRINSIC REAL TRUE INBORN INBRED INNATE INWARD NATIVE GENUINE NATURAL ABSOLUTE IMMANENT INHERENT INTERNAL INTIMATE
INTRINSICALLY PROPERLY
INTRODUCE READ DEBUT ENTER FRONT IMMIT INFER PLANT START USHER BROACH HERALD INDUCE INDUCT INFUSE INJECT INSERT INVECT INVOKE LAUNCH PREFER FORERUN IMPLANT INSTILL INVEIGH PRECEDE PREFACE PRELUDE PRESENT SHUFFLE SPONSOR ACQUAINT INNOVATE INTROMIT WIREDRAW
(— **AIR INTO**) AERATE
(— **AS FIRST ACT**) INITIATE
(— **FROM WITHOUT**) IMPORT
(— **SURREPTITIOUSLY**) FOIST
INTRODUCTION LASSU PROEM PRONE INTRADA INTROIT ISAGOGE MENTION PREFACE ENTRANCE EXORDIUM PREAMBLE PROLOGUE
(— **INTO STOMACH**) GAVAGE
(— **OF DRAMA**) PROTASIS
(— **OF NOVELTY**) CHANGE
(**MUSICAL** —) INTRO INTRADA
INTRODUCTORY EXORDIAL LIMINARY PROTATIC SYSTATIC
INTROIT REQUIEM
INTRORSE ANTICAL
INTROSPECTION INLOOK REFLEX
INTRUDE JET ABATE CRASH POACH BOTHER CHISEL INGYRE INJECT INVADE IRRUPT THRUST OBTRUDE ENCROACH INFRINGE TRESPASS
INTRUDER INTRUS INCOMER INVADER STRANGER
INTRUSION INVASION
INTRUSIVE FRESH SPURIOUS
INTUITION HUNCH INSTINCT
INTUITIONIST EIDETIC
INULIN ALANTIN
INUNDATE FLOW DROWN FLOOD INUND SWAMP DELUGE OVERFLOW SUBMERGE SURROUND

INUNDATION FLOW FLOOD WATER
DELUGE ALLUVIO FRESHET
ALLUVION FLOODAGE OVERFLOW
INURE URE BREAK ENURE STEEL
HARDEN SCHOOL SEASON
ACCUSTOM INDURATE
INVADE ASSAIL INTRUDE ENCROACH
INTRENCH TRESPASS
INVADER HUN PICT
INVADING INGRUENT
INVAGINATION GULLET
INVALID BAD BUM NULL NUGATORY
INVALIDATE AVOID BREAK CANCEL
INFIRM IMPROVE INVALID VITIATE
INVALUABLE COSTLY PRECIOUS
INVARIABLE STEADY UNIFORM
CONSTANT
INVARIABLENESS ONENESS
INVARIABLY EVER ALWAYS
INVASION RAID INROAD DESCENT
INBREAK INJURIA
INVECTIVE ABUSE HOKER RAILING
DIATRIBE REPROACH
INVEIGH INVECT DECLAIM
DENOUNCE
INVEIGLE COAX ROPE CHARM
DECOY SNARE ALLURE ENTICE
SEDUCE
INVENT COIN FIND FORM MINT VAMP
FEIGN FRAME FRUMP CREATE
DESIGN DEVISE IDEATE CONCOCT
CONJURE CONTRIVE DISCOVER
INVENTION FANCY DEVICE FINDAL
NOTION FANTASY FICTION FIGMENT
FORGERY WITCRAFT
(DRAMATIC —) IBSENISM
INVENTIVE ADROIT FERTILE
CREATIVE MECHANIC ORIGINAL
PREGNANT
INVENTIVENESS WIT ARTIFICE
INVENTOR TALOS COINER FINDER
FRAMER MINTER CREATOR
MINTMAN ENGINEER
INVENTORY BILL LIST STOCK
ACCOUNT INVOICE TERRIER
ANAGRAPH REGISTER SCHEDULE
INVERSION WALDEN CHIASMUS
ENTROPION
INVERT CANT TURN REVERT
REVERSE
INVERTASE SUCRASE
INVEST DON DUB PUT BELT FUND
GARB GIFT GIRD GIRT GOWN LOCK
SINK VEST WRAP BELAY BLOCK
ENDOW ENDUE FEOFF INDUE
CLOTHE EMBODY ENROBE FORSET
OCCUPY COMPASS ENFEOFF
ENVELOP INSTATE OBSERVE
BENEFICE BLOCKADE SURROUND
(— ONESELF) COVER ASSUME
(— WITH AUTHORITY) SCEPTER
ACCREDIT
(— WITH ENERGY) CATHECT
(— WITH SOVEREIGN DIGNITY)
ENTHRONE
(— WITH) INFEFT
INVESTED GARTERED
INVESTIGATE SPY SIFT CHECK
PROBE SOUND STUDY EXCUSS

FATHOM SEARCH DISCUSS EXAMINE
EXPLORE INQUIRE INDAGATE
SCRUTATE
(— QUICKLY) SKIP
INVESTIGATION CHECK PROBE
TRIAL EXAMEN PILPUL SEARCH
DELVING INQUEST INQUIRY
LEGWORK ZETETIC ANALYSIS
QUESTION RESEARCH SCRUTINY
SOUNDING
INVESTIGATOR SNOOP TRIER
SLEUTH GUMSHOE SPOTTER
FIELDMAN
INVESTITURE VESTURE INDUMENT
INVESTMENT DOG FLIER CUTICLE
CATHEXIS
INVETERATE BLACK SWORN
ROOTED CHRONIC HARDENED
INVIDIOUS ENVIOUS HATEFUL
INVIGORATE BRACE CHEER RAISE
RENEW VIGOR VIVIFY COMFORT
ENFORCE ENLIVEN FORTIFY
INNERVE INSINEW REFRESH INSPIRIT
INVIGORATING BRISK CRISP FRESH
TONIC VITAL HEARTY BRACING
CORDIAL VEGETANT
INVIOLABILITY SANCTITY
INVIOLABLE SECURE STYGIAN
INVIOLATE SACRED
INVISIBLE HID SECRET UNSEEN
VIEWLESS
INVITATION BID CALL CARD INVITE
BIDDING CALLING
(— TO CONTEND) DARE
INVITE ASK BID WOO BEAR CALL
LURE PRAY TOLL CLEPE COURT
LATHE TRYST ALLURE DESIRE
ENTICE INDITE ATTRACT CONVITE
PROVOKE REQUEST SOLICIT
INVITING ADORABLE HOMELIKE
INVOCATION WISH DAWUT NANDI
BISMILLAH
INVOICE BILL BRIEF CHALAN
FACTURE MANIFEST
INVOKE WISH CLEPE EVOKE APPEAL
ATTEST OBTEST CONJURE ENTREAT
PROVOKE SOLICIT INVOCATE
INVOLUCRE HULL HUSK CUPULE
EPICALYX
INVOLUNTARY FORCED HELPLESS
INVOLUTE INVOLVED
INVOLUTED SCREWY
INVOLUTION ATRESIA
INVOLVE DIP LAP MIX MIRE WRAP
BROIL CARRY COUCH IMPLY RAVEL
DIRECT EMPLOY ENGAGE ENTAIL
HANKLE INWRAP TANGLE COMPORT
CONCERN CONNOTE EMBRACE
EMBROIL ENSNARE ENTWINE
ENVIRON IMMERSE INCLUDE
ENCUMBER ENTANGLE INTEREST
(— IN DIFFICULTY) STEAD
INVOLVED IN DEEP GONE BLIND
KNOTTY COMPLEX ENGAGED
PLAITED IMPLICIT INVOLUTE
INWARD ENTAD INNER INWITH
BENWARD INNERLY HOMEFELT
INWICK INRING
IO (BROTHER OF —) PHORONEUS

(FATHER OF —) INACHUS
(SON OF —) EPAPHUS
IOLE (FATHER OF —) EURYTUS
(HUSBAND OF —) HYLLUS
IOLITE IBERITE PELIOMA
ION ACID ADION ANION CATION
ISOMER KATION LIGAND AMPHION
HYDRION OXONIUM SPECIES
(— DURATION) LIFETIME
(FATHER OF —) XUTHUS
(MOTHER OF —) CREUSA
IONIZATION BURST
IOTA JOT WHIT GHOST SCRUPLE
IOU MARKER

IOWA
CAPITAL: DESMOINES
COLLEGE: COE DORDT LORAS
CORNELL PARSONS GRINNELL
WARTBURG
COUNTY: IDA SAC LINN TAMA
ADAIR KEOKUK KOSSUTH
OSCEOLA
LAKE: CLEAR STORM SPIRIT
NICKNAME: HAWKEYE
PRESIDENT: HOOVER
RIVER: CEDAR SKUNK BIGSIOUX
MISSOURI
STATE BIRD: GOLDFINCH
STATE FLOWER: WILDROSE
STATE TREE: OAK
TOWN: MASON PERRY SIOUX
ALGONA KEOKUK LEMARS
MARION ANAMOSA OTTUMWA
WATERLOO DAVENPORT

IOWAN HAWKEYE
IPECAC ITOUBOU
IPHICLUS (BROTHER OF —)
HERCULES
(FATHER OF —) PHYLACUS
AMPHITRYON
(MOTHER OF —) ALCMENA
IPHIGENIA (BROTHER OF —)
ORESTES
(FATHER OF —) AGAMEMNON
(MOTHER OF —) CLYTEMNESTRA
(SISTER OF —) ELECTRA
IPHIS (FATHER OF —) LIGDUS
(MOTHER OF —) TELETHUSA
(WIFE OF —) IANTHE
IPHITUS (FATHER OF —) EURYTUS
(SLAYER OF —) HERCULES
IPIL VESI
IPOMOEA NIL NILL BATATAS
MANROOT SCAMMONY
IPSEITY SELFHOOD
IRACUND IREFUL

IRAN
CAPE: HALILEH
CAPITAL: TEHRAN TEHERAN
COIN: PUL ASAR CRAN LARI RIAL
BISTI DARIC DINAR LARIN SHAHI
TOMAN STATER ASHRAFI
KASBEKE PAHLAVI
DESERT: KERMAN

FORMER NAME: PERSIA
LAKE: NIRIS NIRIZ TASHT TUZLU
URMIA SAHWEH SISTAN
MAHARLU NEMEKSER URUMIYEH
LANGUAGE: ZEND PAHLAVI
MEASURE: GAZ GUZ MOV ZAR
ZER CANE FOOT GAREH JERIB
KAFIZ MAKUK QASAB ARTABA
CHARAC CHEBEL GARIBA
GHALVA OUROUB CAPICHA
CHENICA FARSAKH FARSANG
MANSION MISHARA PARASANG
PIAMANEH SABBITHA STATHMOS
MOUNTAIN: CUSH KUSH HINDU
KHOSF ARARAT HAMUNT
BINALUD KHORMUJ SABALAN
DEMAVENO
MOUNTAIN RANGE: ELBURZ
SIAHAN ZAGROS JAGATAL
PEOPLE: LUR KURD MEDE SART
KAJAR MUKRI PERSE TAJIK
HADJEMI PERSIAN
PORT: JASK BUSHIRE PAHLEVI
RIVER: MAND MUND SHUR ARAKS
JAGIN KARUN RABCH SEFID
BAMPUR GORGAN HALIRI TIGRIS
KARKHEH MASHKEL SAFIDRUD
ZAYENDEH EUPHRATES
STRAIT: HORMUZ
TOWN: FAO KOM AMOL YAZD
AHVAZ KHVOY NIRIZ RESHT
ABADAN DEZFUL GORGAN
KASVIN KERMAN MASHAD
MESHED SHIRAZ TABRIZ TAURIS
HAMADAN ISFAHAN SANANDAJ
WEIGHT: SER DRAM DUNG ROTL
SANG SEER ABBAS ARTEL
MAUND PINAR RATEL BATMAN
DIRHEM GANDUM KARWAR
MISCAL NAKHOD NIMMAN
ABBASSI TCHEIREK

IRANIAN TAT SART GALCHA SHUGNI
BACTRIAN BARTANGI
(— **SOVEREIGN**) SHAH

IRAQ
CAPITAL: BAGDAD BAGHDAD
COIN: DINAR
DISTRICT: BASRA KURDISTAN
FORMER NAME: MESOPOTAMIA
MOUNTAINS: ZARGOS KURDISTAN
OASIS: MANIYA
PEOPLE: ARAB KURD
PORT: BASRA
RIVER: ZAB TIGRIS EUPHRATES
TOWN: AMARA BASRA MOSUL
NAJAF HILLAH KIRKUK KARBALA

IRASCIBILITY BILE CHOLER
IRASCIBLE WARM ANGRY CROSS
FIERY GASSY HASTY IRATE SHARP
TECHY TESTY CRANKY IREFUL
SPUNKY TETCHY TOUCHY BILIOUS
FRETFUL IRACUND PEEVISH
WASPISH CAPTIOUS CHOLERIC

PETULANT SNAPPISH STOMACHY
IRATE ANGRY HEATED CHOLERIC
WRATHFUL
IRE FURY ANGER WRATH
IREFUL ANGRY JEALOUS

IRELAND
BAY: MAL CLEW SLIGO BANTRY
DINGLE GALWAY TRALEE
DONEGAL DUNDALK KILLALA
BLACKSOD DROGHEDA
CAPE: CLEAR
CAPITAL: TARA DUBLIN
COIN: RAP REAL
COUNTY: CORK DOWN LEIX MAYO
CAVAN CLARE KERRY LOUTH
MEATH SLIGO ANTRIM ARMAGH
CARLOW GALWAY OFFALY
TYRONE ULSTER DONEGAL
KILDARE LEITRIM WEXFORD
WICKLOW KILKENNY LIMERICK
MONAGHAN
ISLAND: ARAN TORY SALTEE
RATHLIN
LAKE: DOO KEY REE TAY CONN
DERG MASK CARRA GOWNA
LEANE RAMOR BODERG COOTER
ENNELL DROMORE OUGHTER
SHEELIN
MEASURE: MILE BANDLE
MOUNTAIN: OX CAHA ANTRIM
GALTEE KEEPER MOURNE
MULREA DONEGAL ERRIGAL
KENNEDY KIPPURE WICKLOW
LEINSTER
MOUNTAIN RANGE: GALTY
STACKS COMERAGH
OTHER NAME: EIRE ERIN BANBA
IERNE IRENA ULSTER BOGLAND
HIBERNIA INISFAIL
PEOPLE: CELT ERSE GAEL CELTIC
HIBERNIAN
PERTAINING TO: CELTIC GAELIC
POINT: CAHORE CARNSORE
PROVINCE: ULSTER MUNSTER
LEINSTER CONNAUGHT
RIVER: LEE BANN DEEL ERNE
NORE SUIR BOYNE CLARE
FEALE FLESK FOYLE LAUNE
BANDON BARROW LIFFEY
KENMARE MUNSTER SHANNON
TOWN: CORK ADARE DUBLIN
LURGAN LIMERICK TIPPERARY

IRENE (**FATHER OF** —) JUPITER
(**MOTHER OF** —) THEMIS
IRENIC CALM HENOTIC PEACEFUL
IRENICA AITESIS
IRIDESCENCE LUSTER LUSTRE
IRIDESCENT SHOT IRISED IRIDINE
IRISATE PAVONINE
IRIS EYE SET FLAG LILY LUCE LUCY
SEGG AZURE IREOS ORRIS SEDGE
FLAGON LEVERS LILIAL LILIUM
SHADOW SUNBOW ALCAZAR
BABIANA FLAGGER GLADDON
FLAGLEAF

(**FATHER OF** —) THAUMAS
(**MOTHER OF** —) ELECTRA
IRISH ERSE EIRANN IRISHRY
MILESIAN
(— **KING**) RIG
(**ILLITERATE** —) KEELMAN
IRISHMAN MAC PAT CELT GAEL
HARP KELT MICK SCOT GREEK
IRISH MICKY PADDY YREIS TEAGUE
GRECIAN IRISHER MILESIAN
ORANGEMAN
(**LEARNED** —) OLLAMH
IRISH MOSS SLOKE CHONDRUS
IRISHWOMAN HARP
IRK BORE ITCH ANNOY WEARY
BOTHER
IRKSOME DULL WARM WEARY
HUMDRUM OPEROSE TEDIOUS
ANNOYING TIRESOME
IROKO ODUM ODOOM MUVULE
KAMBALA
IRON BIT DOG IRE MARS WIRE
ANGLE ANVIL BASIL BRAND DRAIL
DRIFT FLOSS HORSE NEGRO SPIKE
STEEL WAVER ANCONY BEATER
CALKER CAUTER FERRUM GAGGER
GOFFER JAGGER OSMUND CAUTERY
COBIRON CRAMPER FERRITE
FURISON GAMBREL GAUFFER
PRICKER SADIRON FLATIRON
TRICOUNI
(— **FOR CLOSING STAVES**) HORSE
(— **OF MILLSTONE**) RIND RYND
(— **ORE**) LIMNITE
(— **PIECES**) POTLEG
(— **PLATE**) TRAMP
(— **SUPPORTING SPIT**) COBIRON
(— **TO SUPPORT BEAM**) TORSEL
(**8 PIGS OF CAST** —) FODDER
(**ANGLE** —) LATH STIFFENER
(**BASKETWORK** —) BEATER
(**BOOM** —) WITHE WYTHE
(**BRANDING** —) BURN
(**CAST** —) METAL YETLIN SPIEGEL
YETLING SEMISTEEL
(**CLIMBING** —) GAFF SPUR CREEPER
(**CRUDE CASTING OF** —) PIG
(**DRIVING** —) CLEEK
(**GLASSBLOWING** —) BAIT
(**GOLF** —) JIGGER
(**GRAPPLING** —) CRAMPON
CRAMPOON
(**HATTER'S** —) SLUG
(**MASS OF WROUGHT** —) BLOOM
(**METEORIC** —) SIDERITE
(**PASTY** —) SPONGE
(**PIG** —) SPIEGEL KENTLEDGE
(**PRIMING** —) DRIFT
(**RUSSIAN** —) SABLE
(**SHEET** —) TERNE
(**SOLDERING** —) COPPER
(**SPECULAR** —) HEMATITE
(**TAILOR'S** —) GOOSE
(**TAMPING** —) DRIVER
(PL.) GARTERS
IRONBARK MUGGA
IRON BROWN NEGRO
IRONCLAD ARMORED IRONSIDE
IRON HAT GOSSAN

IRONIC ACERB ACERBIC SATIRIC
IRONICAL CRUEL
IRON-LIKE MARTIAL
IRON MAN TALUS
IRONMONGERY HARDWARE
IRONSMITH FERRER
IRONSTONE DOGGER
IRONWEED FLATTOP VERNONIA
WINGSTEM
IRONWOOD TITI COLIMA MOPANE
MOPANI PURIRI WAMARA CYRILLA
JOEWOOD AXMASTER BURNWOOD
FIREWOOD
IRONWORKER LOHAR MOSCHI
IRONWORT SIDERITE
IRONY SATIRE ASTEISM SARCASM
RIDICULE
IROQUOIS HURON MINGO CAYUGA
MENGWE
IRRADIATE XRAY ENBEAM
IRRATIONAL REE SURD WILD SILLY
RAVING STUPID BESTIAL FOOLISH
IRREDUCIBLE BASIC
IRREGULAR DUMB WILD BUMPY
EROSE FANCY MIXED WOPSY
ATYPIC CATCHY FITFUL RAGGED
RUGGED SPOTTY UNEVEN UNLIKE
WEEWAW ANAXIAL ATACTIC
BAROQUE CATERAN CRABBED
CROOKED CURSORY DEVIOUS
DIFFORM ERRATIC FRECKET
MUTABLE SCRAWLY UNEQUAL
WAYWARD ABNORMAL ATYPICAL
DOGGEREL INFORMAL PINDARIC
SCRAGGLY SCRAMBLY UNLAWFUL
UNSTABLE UNSTEADY VARIABLE
IRREGULARITY SNAG DEFECT
RUFFLE ANOMALY ACCIDENT
(— IN YARN) SNICK
IRREGULARLY UNDULY
IRRELIGIOUS PAGAN WICKED
HEATHEN IMPIOUS PROFANE
SENSUAL
IRREMEDIABLE HELPLESS
HOPELESS
IRREPROACHABLE SPOTLESS
IRRESISTIBLE MESMERIC
IRRESISTIBLY FATALLY
IRRESOLUTE FICKLE INFIRM
UNSURE WANKLE DOUBTFUL
UNSTABLE
IRRESPONSIBLE WILDCAT
CAREFREE FECKLESS SKITTISH
IRRESPONSIVE LEADEN
IRRETRIEVABLE HOPELESS
IRREVERENCE IMPIETY
IRREVERENT ATHEIST AWELESS
IMPIOUS PROFANE
IRREVOCABLE DEAD
IRREVOCABLY FATALLY FINALLY
IRRIGATE FLOAT WATER SYRINGE
IRRIGATION KAREZ
IRRIGATOR FLOATER
IRRITABILITY ERETHISM SORENESS
VAGOTONY
IRRITABLE BAD EDGY BIRSY CROOK
FIERY FUSSY HASTY HUFFY JUMPY
MUSTY NAGGY TETTY TILTY TOITY

CRANKY GROWLY NETTLY SPUNKY
STOCKY TEETHY TETCHY TOUCHY
FRATCHY FRETFUL HORNETY
HUFFISH KICKISH PECKISH PEEVISH
SPLEENY TEDIOUS TWITCHY
WASPISH PETULANT SNAPPING
SNAPPISH STOMACHY
IRRITATE BUG EAT GET IRE IRK NAG
RUB TAR TEW TRY VEX BURN CRAB
FIRE FRET GALL GOAD GRIG GRIT
ITCH NARK RILE ROIL SOUR TEEN
ANGER ANNOY CHAFE EAGER
FRUMP GRATE GRILL GRIPE PEEVE
PIQUE STING TARRY ABRADE
BOTHER FRIDGE GRAVEL HARASS
HECTOR NETTLE RUFFLE AFFRONT
INCENSE INFLAME NERVOUS
PROVOKE STOMACH ACERBATE
IRRITATED RILY SORE HUFFY
MUFFED SHIRTY EMPORTE
FRATCHED SOREHEAD
(EASILY —) TESTY
IRRITATING ACRID HARSH CORSIE
ELVISH GRAVEL FRETFUL GALLING
IRKSOME PUNGENT RASPING
ANNOYING FRETSOME GRAVELLY
NETTLING SCRATCHY SPITEFUL
STINGING TIRESOME
IRRITATION FRET TEEN BIRSE PIQUE
STEAM RUFFLE TEMPER WARMTH
ANTPRICK FLEABITE PINPRICK
VEXATION
IRRUPTION BREAK INROAD INBURST
ERUPTION INVASION
IS S YS BEES
(— NOT) NIS AINT ISNT
ISAIAH ESAY ESAIAS
ISCHEMIA ANEMIA
ISCHIAL SCIATIC
ISHPINGO CINNAMON
ISHSHAKKU PATESI
ISHTAR NINNI
ISINGLASS LEAF PIPE KANTEN
ISIS (BROTHER OF —) OSIRIS
(FATHER OF —) SATURN
(MOTHER OF —) RHEA
ISLAM ABBASID
ISLAMIC (— CUSTOM) SUNNA
ISLAND CALF CAYO HOLM INCH ISLE
JAVA POLO ENNIS MALTA MAYDA
AVALON ITHACA OGYGIA REFUGE
RIALTO CIPANGO JAMAICA MADEIRA
TOWHEAD BLEFUSCU CALAURIA
DOMINICA GUERNSEY LILLIPUT
LUGGNAGG
(— IN EVERGLADES) HAMMOCK
(— OF REIL) INSULA
(ARTIFICIAL —) CRANNOG
(CORAL —) ATOLL
(FABLED —) MERU UTOPIA
(FLOATING —) HOVER
(FLYING —) LAPUTA
(LEGENDARY —) BRAZIL OBRAZIL
(LITTLE —) AIT KAY KEY ISLET
(LOW —) KEY
(ROCKY —) SKERRY
(SANDY —) BEACH BARRIER
(SMALL —) CAY ISLE ISLET

SANDKEY
ISLANDER KANAKA ISLEMAN
INSULARY
ISLE IZLE ISLET SKERRY
ISLET OE AIT CAY KEY EYOT HAFT
HOLM ILOT MOTU ROCK ISLOT
STACK NUBBLE
ISMENE (FATHER OF —) OEDIPUS
(MOTHER OF —) JOCASTA
(SISTER OF —) ANTIGONE
ISOBAR MEIOBAR MESOBAR
PLEIOBAR
ISOLATE ISLAND DISSECT SECLUDE
COLONIZE INSULATE SEPARATE
SEQUESTER
ISOLATED POCKET UNIQUE
SOLITARY STRANDED
ISOLATION HERMITRY LONENESS
SOLITUDE
ISOMER PYRAN TOSYL XYLENE
CUMIDINE DECOSANE DODECANE
ISOMERIC ISO ALLO
ISOMETRIC CUBIC REGULAR
TESSULAR
ISOPLETH GEOTHERM
ISOPOD SLATER ASELLUS BOPYRID
GRIBBLE EPICARID
ISOTOPE IONIUM CARRIER
ISOTYPE COTYPE SYNTYPE
ISPAGHUL SPOGEL
ISPAHAN HERAT HERATI

ISRAELI SABRA
(— STUDY CENTER) ULPAN
ISRAELITE JEW SAINT HEBREW
JACOBITE
(PL.) ZION
ISSUE END ISH COME EMIT FALL
FLOW GIVE GUSH HEAD MISE REEK
TERM VENT ARISE COUNT EVENT
FRUIT LOOSE OUTGO SETON SOURD

UTTER EFFECT EFFUSE EGRESS
EMERGE ESCAPE EXITUS MUTTON
RESULT SEQUEL SETTER SPRING
UPPING BALLOON DEBOUCH
DESCENT DRIZZLE EMANATE
ESSENCE EXSURGE OUTCOME
PROCEED PROGENY REDOUND
REFLAIR SUCCESS EXPEDITE
FONTANEL INCREASE ISSUANCE
KINDLING OUTGOING
(— **AND ORDER**) BID
(— **SLOWLY**) EXUDE
(— **SPASMODICALLY**) BELCH
(— **SUDDENLY**) SALLY
(— **WITH FORCE**) SPOUT
(**BOND** —) CONSOL
(**FAVORABLE** —) SPEED FORTUNE
(**FINAL** —) UPSHOT UTMOST
(**NUMEROUS** —) SPAWN
ISSUED OUT
ISSUING EMANANT JESSANT
MANATION
ISTHMUS BALK STRAIT TARBET
ISTLE PITA IXTLE JUAMAVE
GUAPILLA
IT A HE HIT MUN TAGGER
(— **FOLLOWS**) SEQ SEQU
(— **HAS BEEN SWORN**) JURAT
ITALIAN ITIE ITALIC AUSONIAN
MACARONI
ITALITE VESBITE

ITALY

CAPE: TESTA CIRCEO LICOSA
LINARO COLONNE FALCONE
PASSERO RIZZUTO SANVITO
TEULADA VATICANO
CAPITAL: ROMA ROME
CHEESE: ROMANO FONTINA
RICOTTA BELPAESE PARMESAN
TALEGGIO
COIN: LIRA LIRE TARI GRANO
PAOLI PAOLO SCUDO SOLDO
DANARO DENARO DUCATO
SEQUIN TESTONE ZECCHINO
FOOD: PASTA PIZZA SCAMPI
GNOCCHI LASAGNE POLENTA
RAVIOLI RISOTTO SPUMONI
TORTONI CAPONATA LINGUINE
MACARONI PEPERONI
FAMILY: ASTI ESTE AMATI CENCE
DORIA BORGIA MEDICI SFORZA
GULF: GAETA GENOA OROSEI
SALERNO TARANTO CAGLIARI
ORISTANO
ISLAND: ELBA LERO CAPRI LEROS
PONZA GIGLIO ISCHIA LINOSA
SALINA SICILY USTICA ALICUDI
ASINARA CAPRAIA GORGONA
LEVANZO PANAREA PIANOSA
SICILIA VULCANO FILICUDI
SARDINIA
ISLANDS: EGADI LIPARI TUSCAN
PELAGIE PONTINE TREMITI
LAKE: COMO ISEO NEMI GARDA
ALBANO LESINA LUGANO
VARANO BOLSENA PERUGIA

MAGGIORE BRACCIANO
MEASURE: PIE ORNA CANNA
PALMA PALMO PIEDE PUNTO
SALMA STAIO STERO BARILE
MIGLIE MIGLIO MOGGIO RUBBIO
TAVOLA TOMOLO BOCCALE
BRACCIO SECCHIO GIORNATA
POLONICK QUADRATO
MOUNTAIN: ROSA VISO AMARO
BLANC CORNO SOMMA CIMONE
BERNINA VESUVIUS
MOUNTAIN RANGE: ALPS ORTLES
APENNINES MARITIMES
NATIVE: ITALO LATIN OSCAN
ROMAN SABINE TIRANO TUSCAN
LOMBARD SIENESE LIGURIAN
VENETIAN
PASS: FREJUS BERNINA BRENNER
SPLUGEN
PORT: BARI POLA ZARA GENOA
TRANI ZADAR RIMINI TRIESTE
REGION: CARSO APULIA LATIUM
MARCHE MOLISE PUGLIA SICILY
UMBRIA ABRUZZI LIGURIA
TUSCANY VENETIA CALABRIA
CAMPANIA LOMBARDY
PIEMONTE SARDINIA
RESORT: LIDO SANREMO
TAORMINA
RIVER: PO ADDA AGRI ARNO LIRI
NERA RENO SELE TARO ADIGE
CRATI MANNU OGLIO PARMA
PIAVE SALSO STURA TIBER
TIRSO ANIENE BELICE MINCIO
OFANTO PANARO RAPIDO
SANGRO SIMETO TANARO
TEVERE TICINO BIFERNO
BRADANO CHIENTI METAURO
MONTONE OMBRONE PESCARA
RUBICON SECCHIA TREBBIA
VOLTURNO
SEA: IONIAN ADRIATIC LIGURIAN
STRAIT: MESSINA OTRANTO
BONIFACIO
TOWN: BRA RHO ACRI ALBA ASTI
BARI COMO DEGO ELEA ENNA
ESTE FANO GELA IESI LODI
NARO NOLA PISA POLA ROMA
ROME ACQUI ANZIO AOSTA
ASOLA AVOLA CAPUA CUNEO
EBOLI FIUME FORLI GENOA
IMOLA LECCE LUCCA MASSA
MILAN MONZA OSTIA PADUA
PARMA PAVIA TEANO TRENT
TURIN UDINE VELIA ALCAMO
AMALFI ANCONA ANDRIA
AREZZO CEFALU FAENZA
FOGGIA GENOVA MANTUA
MESTRE MILANO MODENA
NAPLES NAPOLI NOVARA RIVOLI
SPEZIA TRENTO VENICE VERONA
BERGAMO BOLOGNA BOLZANO
BRESCIA CARRARA CASERTA
CATANIA COSENZA CREMONA
FERRARA FIRENZE GORIZIA
IMPERIA LEGHORN LIVORNO
MARSALA MESSINA PALERMO

PERUGIA PISTOIA POMPEII
RAVENNA TARANTO TRIESTE
BRINDISI CAGLIARI FLORENCE
PIACENZA SORRENTO
SYRACUSE
VOLCANO: ETNA SOMMA VULCANO
VESUVIUS STROMBOLI
WATERFALL: TOCE
WEIGHT: CARAT LIBRA ONCIA
POUND CARATO DENARO
LIBBRA OTTAVA
WINE: SOAVE CHIANTI MARSALA
ORVIETO

ITALY AUSONIA HESPERIA SATURNIA
ITCH EWK EACH REEF RIFF YEUK
YEWK TICKLE ITCHING SCABIES
VANILLISM
ITCHING ITCHY YEUKY PRURIENT
PRURITIS URTICANT
ITEM ANA JOB TOT ENTRY POINT
THING DETAIL ARTICLE SEVERAL
(— **IN SERIES**) COURSE
(— **OF PROPERTY**) CHATTEL
(— **OF VALUE**) ASSET
(**APPENDED** —) ADDENDUM
(**COLLECTOR'S** —) SPOIL
(**DECORATIVE** —) CONCEIT
(**LUXURY** —) BOUTIQUE
(**NEWS** —) DISPATCH
(**UNPUBLISHED** —S) ANECDOTE
(**VALUELESS** —) BEAN
(PL.) CHECKAGE
ITEMIZE DETAIL
ITERATION PLEONASM
ITHURIEL'S-SPEAR GRASSNUT
ITINERANT ERRANT AMBULANT
ITINERARY DIET JOURNAL WAYBILL
(— **OF ROYAL PROGRESS**) GEST
ITINERATION EYRE
ITS HIS
ITSELF IT HERSELF
ITYS (**FATHER OF** —) TEREUS
(**MOTHER OF** —) PROCNE
ITZA PETEN
IULUS ASCANIUS
IVATAN BATAN
IVORY EBURE DENTINE ELEPHANT
(**DUST OF** —) EBURINE
(**WALRUS** —) RIBZUBA RIBAZUBA
IVORY BLACK ABAISER

IVORY COAST

CAPE: PALMAS
CAPITAL: ABIDJAN
DAM: BANDAMA
LANGUAGE: DIOULA
PEOPLE: ABE AKAN ATLE KOUA
KROU MANDE ABOURE LAGOON
MALINKE VOLTAIC
RIVER: KOMOE BANDAMA
CAVALLY SASSANDRA
TOWN: TABOU BOUAKE GAGNOA
SASSANDRA

IVORY GULL SNOWBIRD

IVORY NUT ANTA TAGUA JARINA
IVORY PALM TAGUA COROJO
  COROZO
IVORY TREE PALAY
IVY TOD GILL HOVE IVIN JILL PICRY

ARALIA HEDERA HIBBIN ALEHOOF
ARALIAD IVYWORT BINDWEED
FOALFOOT
IWW WOBBLY

IXION (FATHER OF —) PHLEGYAS
  (SISTER OF —) CORONIS
  (WIFE OF —) DIA
IZMIR SMYRNA

J JAY JIG JULIETT
JAAL GOAT BEDEN JAELA
JAB GAG GIG JAG JOB POKE STAB
JABBER CHAT JAVER BURBLE
GABBER GABBLE JOBBER YABBER
CHATTER
JABIRU STORK CICONIID
JABOT RUFFLE
JACANA PARRA
JACARE CAIMAN CAYMAN
JACINTH LIGURE
JACK DIB FLAG JACA CRICK DICKY
KNAVE NANCA COLORS KATHAL
SCALET SETTER WENZEL MATADOR
BLOCKING JACKFISH POLIGNAL
SOURJACK TURNSPIT UPLIFTER
(— IN BOWLS) BABY MARK KITTY
MASTER MISTRESS
(— IN CARDS) PAM PUR TOM
BOWER CNAFE KITTY KNAPE KNAVE
MAKER KNIGHT VARLET WENZEL
VARLETTO
(— OF CLUBS) NODDY BRAGGER
MATADOR
(— OF SAME SUIT) NOB
(— OF TRUMPS) TOM JASS JASZ
BOWER HONOR PLAYBOY
(PIANO —) HOPPER STICKER
(SPINNING —) BEAT
JACKAL DIEB JACK KOLA THOS
CANID CANINE DRAGON SILVER
THOOID SIACALLE
JACKAROO RINGNECK
JACKASS JACK
JACKASS FISH MORWONG TERAKIHI
JACK BEAN OVERLOOK
JACK CREVALLE TORO
JACKDAW DAW KAE JACK SHELL
CADDOW CARDER CHOUGH KADDER
CADESSE DAWCOCK DAWPATE
GRACKLE
JACKER SLIPMAN TORCHER
JACKET SAC ETON JACK JUMP JUPE
SACK VEST ACTON COVER DICKY
JUPON POLKA SHRUG WAMUS
BIETLE BLAZER BOLERO CARACO
CORSET DOLMAN FECKET GANSEY
JERKIN JERSEY JUMPER RAILLY
REEFER SACQUE SADDLE SLEEVE
SLIVER SONTAG TABARD TEMIAK
WAMPUS WARMUS BEDGOWN
CANEZOU LOUNGER NORFOLK
PALETOT PALTOCK PEACOAT
RISTORI SPENCER SURCOAT
SWEATER CAMISOLE CARDIGAN
CHAQUETA HANSELIN JIRKINET
MACKINAW OVERSLOP PENELOPE
SEALSKIN
(— FOR TURKEY) APRON
(— LINED WITH STEEL) PLACCATE
(— OF INDIA) BANIAN BANIYA
(— UNDER ARMOR) ACTON TRUSS
(CROCHETED —) SONTAG
(HOODED —) GREGO ANORAK
GRIEKO
(MALAY —) BAJU BADJU
(UNDRESS MILITARY —) SHELL
(WORK —) BAWNEEN
JACKFRUIT JACA KATHAL
SOURJACK

JACKHAMMER SINKER PLUGGER
JACKKNIFE JACK PIKE BARLOW
JACKMAN SHELLMAN
JACK-OF-ALL-TRADES DOCTOR
TINKER GIMCRACK
JACKSCREW CRICK
JACKSMELT PEIXEREY
JACKSNIPE GID JED JACK PEERT
SCAPE SNIPE SNIGHT CHOROOK
CREAKER JUDCOCK SQUATTER
JACKSTAY JACK HORSE PARREL
JACKROD RAILWAY
JACKSTRAW SPILIKIN
JACK TREE NANGKA
JACOB ISRAEL
JACQUARD FACONNE
JADE YU DUN TIT HACK JAUD MINX
PLUG SLUT TIRE HUSSY QUEAN
TRASH BEJADE HARASS RANNEL
AXSTONE HILDING POUNAMU
(DIRTY —) SLAISTER
JADED FORGONE SHOPWORN
DISJASKIT
JAEGER LARI SKUA ALLAN BOSUN
LARID SHOOL BONXIE TEASER
TULIAC TRUMPIE DIRTBIRD
DUNGBIRD
JAG BUN JOG GIMP JAUG LOAD
SOSH TOOT SKATE TOOTH INDENT
JAGGED JAGGY HACKLY RAGGED
SCRAGGY SHAGGED SNAGGED
INDENTED SCRAGGLY TATTERED
JAGGERY GUR GOOR GOUR KHAUR
KHAJUR KITTUL
JAGUAR CAT OUNCE TIGER
PANTHER UTURUNCU
JAI ALAI PELOTA
(— COURT) FRONTON
JAIL CAN GIB JUG BOOB CAGE COOP
CRIB DUMP GAOL HELL HOLD HOLE
KEEP LAKE LOCK STIR WARD
CHOKY CLINK GRATE KITTY LIMBO
LODGE TENCH TRONK BUCKET
CARCEL COOLER ENJAIL JIGGER
LIMBUS LOCKUP TOLZEY FREEZER
FURNACE GEHENNA KIDCOTE
PINFOLD TOLLERY BASTILLE
CALABOZO HOOSEGOW IMPRISON
MILLDOLL TOLLHALL
(— TERM) JOLT
JAILBIRD LAG
JAILER ADAM GAOLER KEEPER
WARDEN TURNKEY INCLUDER
JAKE FINE HICK FELLOW
JAKES AJAX GONG
JALAP MECHOACAN
JALOPY CLUNKER
JAM DIP CRAM JAMB BLOCK CHOKE
CROWD STICK THRONG JACKPOT
JAMAICA (CAPITAL OF —) KINGSTON
(RIVER OF —) BLACK MINHO
JAMAICA COBNUT OUABE PIGNUT
JAMAICA DOGWOOD BABASCO
BARBASCO FISHWOOD
JAMAICAN RAINBIRD TOMFOOL
JAMAICA VERVAIN GERVAO
JAMB DURN ALETTE HAUNCH
REVEAL DOORPOST
JAMES JEM JIM JIMMY SEAMAS
SHAMUS

JANGLE CLAM SQUABBLE
JANGLING HARSH JANGLY AJANGLE
JANISSARY CREOLE RABIRUBIA
JANITOR DURWAN PORTER
JANIZARY SOLAK SOLACH
JANSENIST RIGORIST
JANUS IANUS BIFRONT
JAOB JOW

JAPAN

BAY: ISE MUTSU OTARU ARIAKE
ATSUMI SENDAI SURUGA
TOYAMA WAKASA UCHIURA
CAPE: TOI ESAN MINO NOMA SHIO
SOYA SUZU ERIMO KYOGA
RURUI MUROTO NOJIMA
TODOGA SHIRIYA ASHIZURI
SHAKOTAN
CAPITAL: TOKIO TOKYO
COIN: BU RIN SEN YEN OBAN
KOBAN OBANG TEMPO ICHEBU
ITZEBU KOBANG
ISLAND: IKI SADO BONIN HONDO
KURIL REBUN HONSHU KIUSHU
KURILE KYUSHU RYUKYU
CIPANGO LOOCHOO RISHIRI
SKIKOKU HOKKAIDO IKISHIMA
OKIGUNTO OKUSHIRI YAKUJIMA
LAKE: BIWA TOYA TOWADA
KUTCHAWA SHIKOTSU
MEASURE: BU JO SE BOO CHO
KEN TAN HIRO SHAKU TSUBO
MOUNTAIN: ZAO FUJI ASAHI
ASAMA YESSO ASOSAN ENASAN
HIUCHI KIUSIU YARIGA FUJISAN
HAKUSAN KUJUSAN TOKACHI
FUJIYAMA
SEA: SUO AMAKUSA
STRAIT: KII BUNGO OSUMI
NEMURO TANEGA TOKARA
TSUGARU TSUSHIMA
STREET: GINZA
TOWN: OME KOBE KURA MITO
NARA OITA UEDA AKITA ATAMI
FUKUI KIOTO KOCHI KYOTO
NIKKO OSAKA OTARU SAKAI
UJINA CHOSHI MATSUE NAGOYA
SASEBO SENDAI TAKADA
TOYAMA FUKUOKA NIIGATA
OKAYAMA OKAZAKI SAPPORO
HAKODATE KAMAKURA
KANAZAWA KAWASAKI
KUMAMOTO NAGASAKI
YOKOHAMA YOKOSUKA
VOLCANO: ASO ASAMA ASOSAN
HAKUSAN FUJIYAMA
WEIGHT: MO FUN KIN KON RIN SHI
KATI KWAN NIYO CARAT CATTY
MOMME PICUL KWAMME
HIYAKKIN

JAPAN NIPPON YAMATO CIPANGO
JAPAN CEDAR SUGI
JAPANESE JAP SKIBBY JAPONIC
JAPANESE APRICOT UME
JAPANESE CHERRY SAKURA
JAPANESE DEER SIKA
JAPANESE IRIS SHADOW

JAPANESE PERSIMMON KAKI
JAPANESE PLUM KELSEY
JAPANESE PORGIE TAI
JAPANESE QUINCE JAPONICA
JAPANESE VELVET BIRODO
JAPE GAUD JOKE
JAPONICA ASTILBE
JAR TUN CELL JANG JARG JOLT
JURR OLLA BANGA CADUS CRUSE
KADOS SHOCK DOLIUM HUSTLE
HYDRIA IMPACT JUDDER KALPIS
PANKIN PINATA PITHOS TINAJA
CANOPUS CONCUSS PSYKTER
STAMNOS TERRINE MARTABAN
STINKPOT
(2-HANDLED —) AMPHORA
(BELL —) CLOCHE
(BULGING —) OLLA
(EARTHENWARE —) CAN NAN
CROCK GAMLA PITHOS TERRINE
(POROUS —) GURGLET
(SQUAT —) KORO
(STONE —) STEEN STONE CROPPA
(WATER —) BANGA CHATTI CHATTY
GUMLAH HYDRIA
JARGON CANT JIVE RANE SLUM
ARGOT SLANG LINGUA LINSEY
PATOIS PATTER PIDGIN SHELTA
SIWASH CHINOOK CHOCTAW
DIALECT JARGOON PALAVER
BARRIKIN KEDGEREE POLYGLOT
SCHMOOZE SHOPTALK
(THIEVES' —) FLASH
JARRING JARG RUDE SOUR HARSH
ROUGH DARING
JASMINE BELA MALATI PIKAKE
JESSAMY WOODBINE
JASPER JASPIS MORLOP DIASPER
CREOLITE
JAUNDICE AURIGO GULSACH
ICTERUS JANDERS YELLOWS
JAUNDERS GRASSERIE
JAUNDICED ICTERODE
JAUNT SALLY JAUNCE VAGARY
JOURNEY
JAUNTILY AIRILY BOUNCILY
JAUNTING CAR SIDECAR OUTSIDER
JAUNTY PERK COCKY PERKY SASSY
DAPPER JANTEE SHANTY FINICAL
PERKING DEBONAIR

JAVA
ISLAND: BALI LOMBOK MADURA
MEASURE: PAAL
MOUNTAIN: GEDE MURJO RAOENG
SLAMET SEMEROE SOEMBING
PORT: BATAVIA SURABAJA
TOWN: BOGOR DESSA KEDIRI
MALANG BANDUNG BATAVIA
JAKARTA SEMARANG SURABAJA
WEIGHT: POND TALI

JAVA ALMOND PILI CANARI KANARI
TALISAY
JAVA COTTON KAPOK
JAVANESE KRAMA KROMO
JAVANESE SKUNK TELEDU
JAVA PLUM DUHAT JAMBUL
LOMBOY JAMBOOL

JAVA SPARROW MUNIA PADDY
RICEBIRD
JAVELIN COLP DART PILE ACLYS
PILUM JAREED LANCET ASSAGAI
HARPOON HURLBAT JAVELOT
ACONTIUM GAVELOCK
JAW JIB BEAK CHAP CHAW CHOP
JOWL WANG ANVIL CHAFT CHEEK
CHOKE SCOLD CHAWLE FEELER
JAWBONE MAXILLA MANDIBLE
(— OF FORCEPS) BEAK
(— OF SPIDER) FANG
(— OF VISE) CHAP
(—S OF BIRD) BILL
(FALSE —) CLAMP
**(RECEDING NOSE AND UNDERSHOT
—)** LAYBACK
(PL.) MAW BITS THROAT
JAWBONE JOWL WANG MAXILLA
CHAWBONE
JAWBREAKING CRACKJAW
JAY JAYPIET SIRGANG BLUECOAT
MEATBIRD
JAYHAWKER KANSAN
JAZERANT GESSERON
JAZZ BOP JIVE HOTCHA
JEALOUS YELLOW EMULOUS
ENVIOUS
JEALOUSY ENVY YELLOWS
EMULATION
JEAN FROCKING
JEANPAULIA BAIERA
JEEP PEEP SEEP BANTAM
JEER BOB BOO MOB GECK GIBE
GIRD JAPE JEST JIBE MOCK SKIT
WIPE FLIRT FLOUT FLUTE FLYTE
FRUMP GLAIK LAUGH SCOFF
SCOMM SNEER TAUNT CHIACK
DERIDE BARRACK RIDICULE
JEERING BIRD FLOUT DERISIVE
JEHOVAH JAH LORD JAHVE YAHWEH
(— WITNESS) PIONEER
JEJUNE DRY ARID MEAGER INSIPID
JELL COME FIRM
JELLY GEAL JEEL JELL GELEE
CULLIS JUJUBE ALCOGEL FISNOGA
GELATIN JELLIFY FLUMMERY
HYDROGEL QUIDDANY
(CALF'S-FOOT —) SULZE
(FRUIT —) ROB
(MEAT —) ASPIC
JELLYFISH JELLY QUARL CARVEL
MEDUSA ACALEPH AURELIA
MEDUSAN SLOBBER SUNFISH
SCYPHULA SEACROSS STROBILA
JELLYLIKE SLABBY
JENNY MULE JINNY
JEOPARDIZE EXPOSE HAZARD
IMPERIL ENDANGER
JEOPARDY RISK PERIL DANGER
HAZARD
JEQUIRITY BEAN EYEN RUTTEE
JERBOA GERBIL JUMPER
JEREED TZIRID
JEREMIAD TRAGEDY
JERK GAG JET NUD TIT BOUT CANT
FIRK GIRD HIKE JERT JIRT JOLT
JOUK KICK PECK SNAP SNIG YANK
YERK BRAID CHUCK FLIRT HITCH

SCHMO SNAKE SPANG SURGE
TWEAK TWICK FILLIP JIGGER
SWITCH TWITCH WRENCH FLOUNCE
SPANGHEW
JERKED MEAT TASAJO
JERKILY HITCHILY
JERKIN JACKET
JERKY NERVY SHARP CHOPPY
ELBOIC FLICKY FLINGY HITCHY
JIGGETY CHOPPING PALMODIC
RATCHETY SACCADIC
JEROBOAM REHOBOAM
JERSEY FROCK SHIRT GANSEY
TRICOT ZEPHYR MAILLOT SINGLET
CAMISOLE GUERNSEY
JERUSALEM ARIEL SOLYMA
AHOLIBAH
JERUSALEM ARTICHOKE TUBER
CANADA GIRASOL
JERUSALEM CHERRY SOLANUM
JERUSALEM OAK AMBROSIA
JERUSALEM SAGE PHLOMIS
SAGELEAF
JERUSALEM THORN CASCOL
RETAMA
JESSAMINE JASMINE WOODBINE
JEST BOG COG FUN JOE TAX BULL
GAME GAUD GIRD JAPE JOKE JOSH
PLAY QUIP QUIZ RAIL SKIT BOURD
BREAK CHAFF CLOWN DROLL FLIRT
GESTE GLEEK SPORT THING
BANTER GLANCE JAPERY RAILLY
TRIFLE DICTERY GAMMOCK JOLLITY
WAGGERY DROLLERY RAILLERY
(— SPITEFULLY) SLENT
JESTER FOOL MIME BUFFO CLOWN
DROLL IDIOT JAPER JOKER PATCH
WAMBA DISOUR MOTLEY YORICK
BADCHAN BOURDER BUFFOON
DIZZARD DROLLER JOCULAR
JUGGLER PICADOR SCOFFER
SCOGGIN TOMTRAM MERRYMAN
OWLGLASS PLEASANT RAILLEUR
TRINCULO
JESTING DROLL JAPERY WAGGISH
JESUIT PAULIST TERTIAN IGNATIAN
LOYOLITE
JESUS GEE GIS IHC IHS JHS YHS
JESU WISDOM
(SAYINGS OF —) AGRAPHA
JET BOLT TAIL TANG BREAK DUMBY
DUMMY JETTO SALLY SPOUT SPRAY
SPURT DELUGE DOUCHE GAGATE
SQUIRT FANTAIL JETTEAU SPATTER
SPURTER FOUNTAIN SOFFIONE
UPSPRING
(— OF METAL) BREAK
(— OF VOLCANIC STEAM) STUFA
(SMALL —) SQUIB
JET-BLACK BUGLE
JETTING SALIENT
JETTISON DUMP JETSAM
JETTY JET DIKE GROIN JUTTY
BRIDGE OVERHANG
JEW SAINT ESSENE JUDEAN LITVAK
SEMITE SMOUCH TOBIAD BARABAS
GRECIAN MARRANO SMOUSER
APIKOROS CONVERSO GALICIAN
JUDAHITE LANDSMAN SEPHARDI

(—S OUT OF ISRAEL) DIASPORA
(BALKAN —) LADINE
JEWEL GEM JOY DROP OUCH BIJOU
REGAL STONE BROOCH GEORGE
TRIFLE CRAPAUD GARLAND
POUNDER
(PL.) BULSE PERRIE
JEWELER GEMMARY LAPIDARY
JEWELRY ICE JUNK OUCH PARURE
COLLARET LAPIDARY
(MOCK —) LOGIE
(PIECE OF —) GAUD
JEWELWEED CEROLINE EARJEWEL
SNAPWEED
JEWFISH MERO GUASA WARSAW
PERCOID JUNEFISH MULLOWAY
SERRANID
JEWISH JUDAIC SEMITIC
(— BODY) VAAD
(— COMMUNITY) KEHILLAH
(— QUARTER) MELLAH
(— SCHOOL) ALJAMA
JEWRY GHETTO JUDAISM
JEW'S-HARP HARP TROMP TRUMP
GEWGAW FLAMFEW TRANGAM
GUIMBARD
JEW'S MALLOW DESI
JEZEBEL GILLIVER
JIB GIB DEMUR GIGUE GIBBET
SPITFIRE
JIBE (ALSO SEE GIBE) GEE KAY GAFF
GIBE JAPE JERK MOCK SKIT AGREE
FLIRD MARCH SNACK THRUST
JIFFY JIFF BRAID FLISK WHIFF
GLIFFY GLIFFING
JIG BUCK FRISK GIGUE SQUID
GARLIC JIGGER JIGGET JITTER
LOCATOR
(— FOR WASHING ORE) HUTCH
(FISHING —) PILK
JIGGER SHOT DANDY PIQUE
DOODAD GADGET JIGMAN VATMAN
CHIGGER
JIGGLE DIDDLE JUGGLE TEETER
JILT GUNK KICK SACK BEGOWK
BEGUNK MITTEN
JIMMY BETTY JAMES JEMMY
JIMSONWEED DATURA DEWTRY
JIMSON FIREWEED STRAMONY
JINGLE CHIME CLINK DINGLE RICKLE
TINKLE CHINKLE DINGDONG
JINGLING
(MEANINGLESS —) SPORT
JINGLING SMIT JANGLE RIGADIG
TINKLING
JINGO WARRIOR WARMONGER
JINKER WHIM
JINN DJIN JANN AFRIT GENIE AFREET
DJINNI SHAITAN
(PL.) JINNI
JINNI MARID AFREET ALUKAH
GENIUS YAKSHA YAKSHI JINNIVEH
JINRIKIMAN KURUMAYA
JINRIKISHA GOCART KURUMA
RICKSHAW
JINX HEX JONAH HOODOO
JIPIJAPA CHIDRA PALMILLA
TOQUILLA
JITTERBUG TRUCKING

JITTERY JUMPY SPOOKY AJITTER
JIVARO JIBARO SHUARA XIBARO
JOAN JUG JONE
(— OF ARC) PUCELLE
JOB LAY TUT CHAR FIST SHOP TURN
BERTH CHORE FIRST BILLET
HUSTLE JOBSITE SWEATER
BUSINESS
(EASY —) BLUDGE
(SMALL —) CHORE JOBBLE
JOBBER BRAGER DEALER FLUNKY
BROGGER COURSER
JOB'S TEARS COIX ADLAI ADLAY
JOCKEY JOCK ROPER WASTER
CHANTER EQUISON TURFITE
SKIPJACK
(DISC —) DEEJAY
JOCOSE JOCO LEPID JOCULAR
JOCOTE MOMBIN
JOCOTE DE MICO BARBAS
JOCULAR GAY AIRY GLAD JOKY
DROLL FUNNY HAPPY JOLLY MERRY
WITTY BLITHE ELATED JAPISH
JOCOSE JOCUND JOKISH JOVIAL
JOYFUL JOYOUS LIVELY BUOYANT
COMICAL FESTIVE GLEEFUL
PLAYFUL WAGGISH ANIMATED
CHEERFUL DEBONAIR GLADSOME
HUMOROUS JOCATORY JOKESOME
LAUGHING MIRTHFUL
JOCULARITY FUN WAGGERY
JOCUND BUDGE JOCANT JOCULAR
JOE JO
(HALF —) JOANNES JOHANNES
JOE-PYE WEED EUPATORY
JOEWOOD JOEBUSH BARBASCO
IRONWOOD
JOG BOB HOD JAG JIG JOT MOG
KICK POKE SHOG SPUD STIR TROT
WHIG DUNCH HOTCH NUDGE TWEAK
DIDDLE JITTER JOGGLE JUNDIE
(— ALONG) FADGE FODGE
(— AWKWARDLY) DODGE
(— WITH ELBOW) DUNCH
JOGGER LAYBOY
JOGGLE HOTCH JUGGLE SHOGGLE
SHOOGLE
JOHANNES JOE PECA
JOHN IAN JEAN JOCK JONE JUAN
SEAN JOHANN SEAGHAN GIOVANNI
JOHNNYCAKE CORNCAKE
JOIN ADD COP FAY MIX PAN TAG TIE
UNY ALLY COPE FAIR FUSE GAIN
GLUE KNIT LINK MEET MELL SEAM
SOUD TAIL TEAM YOKE ANNEX
BLEND BLRND ENTER FRANK GRAFT
JOINT MERGE TENON UNITE WRING
ACCEDE ADJECT ADJOIN ASSIST
ATTACH CEMENT COCKET COMMIT
CONCUR ENGAGE INDENT JOGGLE
MARROW MINGLE PIECEN RELATE
RELIDE SPLICE STITCH STRIKE
COMBINE CONJOIN CONNECT
CONTACT INJOINT JOINING SHACKLE
ACCOUPLE COALESCE COMPOUND
COPULATE DOVETAIL JUNCTION
(— BATTLE) JOUST ENGAGE
(— BY SEWING) STITCH SUTURE
(— CLOSELY) FAY AFFY WELD
GRAFT

(— IN COMBAT) BUCKLE
(— IN MARRIAGE) WED TACK HITCH
COUPLE
(— THE PARTS OF) PIECE
(— TOGETHER) CLOSE COAPT
FRANK HITCH COUPLE ENGLUE
ENJOIN ASSEMBLE COAGMENT
COALESCE
JOINED JOINT ALLIED DIRECT
SEAMED ACCOLLE ADJUNCT
APPINED EMBOITE ADJUGATE
COMBINED CONJUNCT COPULATE
INTEGRAL
JOINER SNUG JOINTER
JOINING BAR JOIN SEAM BRIDE
CLOSE SPLICE BETWEEN JOINDER
ADDITION JUNCTION JUNCTIVE
JUNCTURE SYNECTIC
JOINT BED HAR HIP BUTT COXA FISH
HEAD HELL HOCK JOIN KNEE LITH
LOCK SEAL SEAM TUCK ANKLE
BRAZE BUILD CARDO CHASE ELBOW
MITER MITRE PLACE SCAPE SCARF
SPALD UNION UNITE WRIST BOXING
COMMON HAUNCH SCARPH SPLICE
STIFLE SUTURE TOGGLE UNITER
ARTHRON ARTICLE COGGING
DIGITAL FETLOCK FLEXURE ISCHIUM
JOINING KNUCKLE SCATTER
SHIPLAP SIAMESE CONJOINT
CONJUNCT COUPLING DIACLASE
DOVETAIL FLASHING JOINTURE
JUNCTURE SUBJOINT SUFFRAGO
TROCHOID VARIATOR
(— ABOVE HOCK) STIFLE
(— OF BIRD'S WING) FLEXURE
(— OF FLAIL) CAPEL
(— OF MEAT) BARON
(— OF SHIP) CHASE
(— OF STEM) NODE
(ANKLE —) COOT
(ELBOW —) NOOP
(FLEXIBLE —) HINGE
(GROOVED —) RABBET
(HIP —) COXA THURL
(MASONRY —) JOGGLE
(MINING —) CLEAT SLINE
(SCARF —) BOXING
(UNIVERSAL —) CARDAN
(VERTICAL —) BUILD
(WHEEL-LIKE —) TROCHITE
JOINTED ARTHROUS
JOINTED CHARLOCK KRAUT
RUNCH
JOINTER JOINER SKIMMER
JOINT FIR EPHEDRA
JOINT GRASS PASPALUM
JOIST GEEST LEDGE BRIDGE RAGLIN
SLEEPER CARRIAGE
(PL.) PIGGIN JOISTING
JOJOBA PIGNUT SHEEPNUT
JOKE BAR DOR FUN GAB GAG GIG
JOE KID ROT WIT FOOL GAFF GAME
GAUD GEGG JAPE JEST JOSH LICE
NOTE QUIP QUIZ TYPE BREAK
CRACK FLIRT GLEEK GRIND LAUGH
PRANK RALLY SPORT BANTER
JAPERY PLISKY WHEEZE JOKELET
WAGGERY CHESTNUT

(PRACTICAL —) BAR FUN GAG RIG
HOAX REAK SHAVIE HOTFOOT
(STALE —) CHESTNUT
(PL.) JAPERY
JOKER BUG DOR WAG CLOWN GRIND
SLAVE FARCER FOOLER GAGGER
JOKIST FARCEUR GIMMICK
FUNNYMAN HUMORIST JOKESTER
JOKING JOSH BANTER JOCOSE
(PRACTICAL —) GAME
JOLLIFICATION RAG RANT JOLLY
JOLLITY MIRTH GAIETY HILARITY
JOLLITRY
JOLLY GAY KID BUXOM GAWSY
WALLY CROUSE JOVIAL STRING
JOCULAR DISPOSED
JOLLY BOAT YAWL DANDY
JOLT JET JIG JOG JOT JUT BELT
BUMP DIRD DIRL HIKE JOWL JUMP
KICK SHOG JAUNT HOTTER IMPACT
JOGGLE JOSTLE JOUNCE JUMBLE
JOLTING JERKY BUMPITY HOTTERY
JONAH JINX JONAS HOODOO
JONQUIL JONK LILY DAFFODIL

JORDAN
CAPITAL: AMMAN
COIN: DINAR
MOUNTAIN: BUKKA DABAB ATAIBA
MUBRAK
REGION: PEREA BASHAN PERAEA
RIVER: JORDAN YARMUK
TOWN: AQABA ARIHA IRBID KARAK
ZARQA ZERKE NABLUS

JOSEPH JOSEY GIUSEPPE
JOSEPHINE BLUSH PHENY
JOSH GUY KID RIB JOKE CHAFF
STRING
JOSHI JOTI JOTISARU
JOSHUA JESUS
JOSTLE JOG JOLT JOSS PUSH SHOG
CROWD ELBOW HUNCH JUNDY
SHOVE HURTLE HUSTLE JOGGLE
JUNDIE JUSTLE SHOULDER
JOSTLING SCRAMBLE
JOT ACE DOT ATOM IOTA MITE TARE
WHIT GRAIN MINIM POINT TWINT
WIGHT TITTLE SCRUPLE SYLLABLE
(— DOWN) NICK
JOTTING TOT
JOTUNN GEIRROTH
JOUNCE HIKE JOLT JAUNT
JOURNAL TOE BOOK DIARY PAPER
BLAZER SERIAL DAYBOOK DIURNAL
GAZETTE GUDGEON JOURNEY
CASHBOOK NOCTUARY TRUNNION
(SEA —) LOGBOOK
JOURNAL BEARING RHODING
JOURNALIST SCRIBE WRITER
BYLINER DIARIAN
JOURNEY BE GO JOG RUN WAY
DIET EYRE FARE FORE GAIT GANG
GATE HIKE JUMP RACE RIDE ROAD
STEP TOUR TREK TRIP TURN WENT
BROAD COVER DRIVE JAUNT REISE
SITHE TRAIK TRAIL TURUS WEENT
ERRAND FLIGHT HEGIRA JUNKET
TRAVEL VAGARY COMMINO

EMBASSY ENTRADA EXCURSE
JORNADA JOURNAL MEANDER
PASSAGE STRETCH TRAVAIL
TROUNCE WALKING WAYFARE
GODSPEED PROGRESS
(— BY SEA) VOYAGE
(— DOWNSTREAM) DESCEND
(DAY'S —) DIET
(DESERT —) JORNADA
(FATIGUING —) TRAIK
(LONG —) TREK
(TEDIOUS —) TRANCE
JOURNEYING CRUISE
JOURNEYMAN YEOMAN
JOUST PLAY TILT JOSTLE JUSTLE
TOURNEY
JOUSTER TILTER
JOVIAL GAY BOON JOVY BULLY
JOLLY MERRY GENIAL HEARTY
MELLOW BACCHIC HOLIDAY
JOCULAR
JOVIALITY JOLLITY ROLLICK
HILARITY
JOWL CHOW CHAULE
(PL.) CHOPS
JOY JO WIN GLEE LIST PLAY BLISS
DREAM EXULT MIRTH REVEL GAIETY
HEYDAY DELIGHT ECSTASY ELATION
JOYANCE RAPTURE REVELRY
FELICITY GLADNESS HILARITY
PLEASURE
JOYFUL GAY GLAD BEAMY JOLLY
BLITHE FESTUS JOCUND JOVIAL
JOYANT JOYOUS GAUDFUL GLADFUL
GLEEFUL JOCULAR GLADSOME
JOYFULLY FAIN FAINLY GLADLY
JOYOUSLY
JOYLESS DESOLATE LUSTLESS
UNBLITHE
JOYOUS GAY GLAD JOLLY MERRY
YOUSE BLITHE JOVIAL FESTIVE
GIOJOSO GLEEFUL JOCULAR
FROHLICH SUNSHINY
JOYOUSNESS HILARITY
JUBILANT ELATED JOYFUL
EXULTANT
JUBILATION JOY JOYANCE JUBILEE
JUDAHITE JEW
JUDAISM JEWISM HEBRAISM
JUDAS TREE CERCIS
JUDEA JEWRY
JUDEO-SPANISH LADINO
JUDGE DAN JUS SEE WIG CAID CAZY
DEEM DOOM HOLD IMAM JUEZ JURY
KAZI SCAN AWARD COUNT COURT
DAYAN GAUGE HAKIM INFER JUDEX
MINOS OPINE PUNEE TRIER WEIGH
CENSOR CRITIC DANIEL DEEMER
DICAST DOOMER INTEND JUDGER
JURIST OPINER PUISNE SAMSON
SAMUEL SETTLE SQUIRE ACCOUNT
ADJUDGE ARBITER BENCHER
BRIDOYE CENSURE FLAGMAN
FOUJDAR HELIAST JURYMAN
JUSTICE MUNSIFF PODESTA
REFEREE SCABINE SHAMGAR
SUPPOSE APPRAISE CENTENAR
CONCLUDE CONSIDER DEEMSTER
DEMPSTER DIRECTOR DOOMSMAN

DOOMSTER ESTIMATE FOREDEEM
JEPHTHAH JUDGMENT JUDICATE
LINESMAN MINISTER MITTIMUS
ORDINARY QUAESTOR RECORDER
REGICIDE SCABINUS STRADICO
JUDGMENT ACT EYE BOOK DEEM
DOME DOOM REDE VIEW ARRET
AWARD FANCY JUISE SENSE SIGHT
SKILL TASTE ADVICE ASSIZE
DECREE ESTEEM JUWISE STEVEN
ACCOUNT CENSURE CONCEIT
HOLDING OPINION VERDICT WITTING
ESTIMATE JUDICIAL JUDICIUM
SAGACITY SENTENCE THINKING
JUDICATORY SYNOD
JUDICIOUS WISE CRITICAL JUDICIAL
MODERATE SENSEFUL SENSIBLE
WISELIKE
JUDO (— EXERCISES) KATA
(— PRACTICE) RANDORI
JUG CAN EWER JACK JUST ASCUS
ASKOS BUIRE GAMLA GOTCH
JORUM JUBBE STEAN BOGGLE
CROUKE GOGLET GOMLAH HYDRIA
CREAMER PITCHER CRUISKEN
LECYTHUS LEKYTHOS OENOCHOE
PROCHOOS
(— WITH SPOUT) BUIRE DOLLIN
(ALE —) TOBY
(BULGING —) GOTCH
(LEATHER —) JACK BOMBARD
(ONE-HANDLED —) URCEUS
(SPOUTLESS —) OLPE
JUGATED BAJOIRE
JUGGLE TRICK BAFFLE FUMBLE
CONJURE SHUFFLE
JUGGLER HARLOT CONJURER
JONGLEUR
JUGLONE NUCIN
JUGULARES DERIPIA
JUGUM FIBULA JUGULUM
JUICE JUS SEW BREE BROO FOND
OOZE SUCK ANIMA BLOND BLOOD
GRAVY HUMOR MOBBY PERRY
CASIRI CREMOR JIPPER SUCCUS
CAMBIUM AGUAMIEL HYPOCIST
VERJUICE
(— OF COCONUT) MILK
(— OF TREE) SAP LYCIUM
JELUTONG
(— OF UNRIPE FRUIT) OMPHACY
(APPLE —) CIDER
(CANE —) SLING
(CONCENTRATED —) SIRUP SYRUP
(DRIED —) ALOE KINO
(FERMENTED —) SURA GRAPE
(FRUIT —) ROB ROHOB
(GRAPE —) MUST SAPA STUM
(INTOXICATING —) SOMA
(LETTUCE —) THRIDACE
(MEAT —) BLOND
(POPPY —) CHICK
(TOBACCO —) AMBEER AMBIER
(PL.) ESSENCE HUMIDITY
JUICY FAT FRIM FRUM NAISH SAPPY
FRUITY SUCCOSE WATERISH
JUJUBE BER ELB TSAO LOTEBUSH
LOTEWOOD ZIZYPHUS
JUKEBOX PICCOLO

JUMBLE PIE ROG HASH MESS MUSS RAFF BOTCH BOLLIX BUMBLE FUDDLE GARBLE HUDDLE JUMPER JUNGLE MEDLEY MOMBLE MUDDLE PALTER RAFFLE WELTER WUZZLE CLUTTER CONFUSE EMBROIL GOULASH SHUFFLE DISORDER MISHMASH RHAPSODY SMACHRIE
(— OF SOUNDS) LURRY
JUMBLED CRAZY HASHY JUMBLY HUDDLING
JUMP HOP LEP NIP DART JETE LEAP LUTZ SKIP SKIT STEN STOT TUMB BOUND CAPER FENCE HALMA SALTO SAULT SPANG SPEND START STOIT VAULT DOUBLE FOOTER HURDLE INSULT LAUNCH SPRING SPRUNT STARRE WALLOP CISEAUX CROWHOP SALTATE SKYLARK BALLONNE
(— ABOUT) SKIT CAPER
(— FROM AIRCRAFT) BAIL BALE
(— IN FENCING) BALESTRA
(— ON HORSEBACK) LARK
(— ON SKATES) AXEL SALCHOW **(PL.)** ALLEGRO
JUMPER LAMMY SWAGE BARKER LEPPER HANDYMAN
JUMPING SALIENT SALTANT
JUMPY ITCHY
JUNCO SNOWBIRD
JUNCTION HIP FROG JOIN CLOSE CROWN UNION FILLET INFALL CONTACT JOINING MEETING UNITION JUNCTURE
(— OF EARTH AND SKY) HORIZON
(— OF STREAMS) GRAINS
(— OF THREADS) FELL STOP
(— ON TOOTH) CERVIX
JUNCTURE PASS PINCH CRISIS STRAIT ARTICLE BRACKET JOINING OPHRYON EXIGENCY JOINTAGE JOINTURE OCCASION QUANDARY

JUNEBERRY SHADBLOW SHADBUSH
JUNE BUG BUZZARD DUMCLOCK
JUNGLE BUSH RUKH SHOLA BOONDOCK
JUNGLE BENDY WEENONG
JUNIOR PUNY CADET YOUNG PUISNE YOUNGER
JUNIPER CADE EZEL GORSE GORST SAVIN SABINE
JUNK CRAM GEAR GOOK TOPE DRECK REFUSE SCULCH DISCARD PLUNDER TONGKANG
(WORTHLESS —) SLUM
JUNKET TRIP KNACK JINKET SAFARI
JUNKMAN TATTER SCRAPMAN SCAVENGER
JUNO MONETA PRONUBA
JUPITER JOVE STATOR FORTUNE MUSHTARI TERMINUS
JUPITER'S BEARD JOUBARB
JUR LWO LUOH
JUREL RUNNER CREVALLE HARDTAIL
JURISDICTION SOC BAIL SOKE FUERO HONOR REALM ABBACY BANDON BEYLIK DANGER DIWANI RIDING SPHERE DEANERY DEWANEE DROSTDY EMIRATE KHANATE BAILIERY FOUJDARY LIGEANCE PASHALIC PROVINCE
(— OF BISHOP) SEE
(COERCIVE —) SWORD
(MORMON —) KEYS
JURISPRUDENCE LAW REPORTS
JURIST JUDGE MUFTI BREHON LAWYER DOTTORE
JUROR JURAT ASSIZER JURYMAN CENTUMVIR
JURY ARRAY PANEL QUEST ASSIZE JURATA COUNTRY EMPANEL INQUEST
(— COUNTY) VISNE
JURYMAN DICAST JURIST ASSIZER

JURY-RIGGED HAYWIRE
JUST ALL DUE EVEN FAIR FLOP LEAL TRUE EQUAL FIRST LEVEL NOBUT ROUND VALID ZADOC CANDID GIUSTO HONEST JUSTIN JUSTUS MERELY SQUARE EQUABLE LEESOME UPRIGHT LIEFSOME RIGHTFUL SKILLFUL UNBIASED
(— AS) AFTER
(— HOVE CLEAR) ATRIP
(— IN TIME) SONICA
(ONLY —) HARDLY SCARCELY
JUSTAUCORPS JUSTICO
JUSTICE LAW DOOM RIGHT SKILL DHARMA EQUITY REASON HONESTY SHALLOW SILENCE DEEMSTER JUDGMENT JUSTITIA JUSTNESS RECORDER
(— OF PEACE) BEAK SQUIRE
JUSTIFIABLY FAIRLY
JUSTIFICATION CALL COLOR EXCUSE APOLOGY DEFENCE WARRANT APOLOGIA
JUSTIFIED FAIR JUST
JUSTIFY AVOW CLEAR PROVE SALVE DEFEND EXCUSE HONEST EXPLAIN RECTIFY SUPPORT WARRANT MAINTAIN SANCTION UNDERPIN
JUSTLY WELL TRULY EVENLY FAIRLY EQUALLY HANDILY SQUARELY
JUSTNESS SQUARE FITNESS JUSTICE ACCURACY
JUSTUS JESUS
JUT HANG BULGE JETTY JUTTY BEETLE EXTEND IMPEND EXTRUDE
JUTE PAT DESI PAUT DAISEE ARAMINA CHINGMA
JUTTING HANGING
JUVENILE YOUNG JEJUNE PUERILE YOUTHFUL
JUXTAPOSED ADJACENT
JUXTAPOSITION BALANCE CONTACT CONTRAST NEARNESS

K KA KAY KILO KING
KAABA CAABA ALCAABA
KABAYA BADJU CABIE
KABELJOU KOB
KABISTAN KUBA
KABOB KEBOB SHASLIK
KABUKALLI CUPIUBA
KACHARI BODO
KACHIN SINGFO SINGPO CHINGPAW
KADAGA COORG
KAFFIR KATI XOSA FINGO TEMBU
CAFFRE INFIDEL TAMBUKI WAIGULI
(— BOY) UMFAAN
KAGU GRUIFORM
KAIKAWAKA CEDAR
KAINGIN SWIDDEN
KAKI TRIUMPH
KALAPOOIAN LAKMIUT
KALE COLE KAIL COLLARD SPROUTS
BORECOLE
KALMUCK ELEUT UIRAD KHOSHOT
KALUMPIT ANAGEP
KAMAHI BIRCH TOWAI
KAMALA WURRUS ROTTLERA
KAMICHI SCREAMER
KANA IROFA IROHA
KANGAROO ROO EURO BILBI FLIER
FLYER TUNGO BOOMER FOSTER
WOILIE DIDELPH POTOROO
WALLABY BETTONGA BOONGARY
FILANDER FORESTER WALLAROO
(FEMALE —) DOE GIN
(YOUNG —) JOEY
KANGAROO APPLE GUNYANG
POROPORO
KANGAROO RAT JERBOA
KANHOBAL CONOB
KANKANAI IGOROT
KANS KUSA GLAGA KUSHA GLAGAH

KANSAS
CAPITAL: TOPEKA
COLLEGE: BAKER TABOR
BETHANY STERLING WASHBURN
COUNTY: ELK GOVE NESS RENO
TREGO NEMAHA ATCHISON
FORT: RILEY SCOTT
INDIAN: KANSA KIOWA PAWNEE
WICHITA COMANCHE
LAKE: CHENEY KIRWIN NEOSHO
MILFORD
MOUNTAIN: SUNFLOWER
NATIVE: JAYHAWK
NICKNAME: SUNFLOWER
PRESIDENT: EISENHOWER
RIVER: ARKANSAS MISSOURI
STATE BIRD: MEADOWLARK
STATE FLOWER: SUNFLOWER
STATE TREE: COTTONWOOD
TOWN: HAYS IOLA COLBY DODGE
SALINA CHANUTE LIBERAL
WICHITA

KANSAN JAYHAWK
KAOLIANG SORGHUM
KAPOK CEIBO FLOSS
KARAISM ANANISM
KARAKA KOPI
KARA KIRGHIZ BURUT BOUROUT

KARATAS PITA
KAREN SGAU SGAW
KARENNI PADAUNG
KARMA (BAD —) DEMERIT
KASKA NAHANE
KAT KHAT QUAT CAFTA
KATE KAI
KAUNAS KOVNO
KAURI COWRIE BERAIROU
KAVA AVA AWA YAQONA KAVAKAVA
YANGGONA
KAW AKHA
KAZOO BAZOO GAZOO ZARAH
HEWGAG MIRLITON
KEEL FIN BACK SEEL BARGE CARINA
CRISTA SERRULA
(— OF BIRD'S MANDIBLE) GONYS
(AFTERPART OF —) SKAG SKEG
KEEN DRY FLY GAY SHY YAP ACID
DEAR FINE GAIR GLEG HIGH PERT
TART TEEN WAIL WARM WILD
ACUTE BREME BRIEF BRISK EAGER
QUICK SHARP SMART SNELL SPICY
VIVID ASTUTE BITTER CAOINE
GREEDY LIVELY SEVERE SHREWD
SHRILL CUNNING HAWKING
MORDANT PARLISH PARLOUS
PUNGENT SERIOUS THIRSTY
KEENER HOWLER
KEENLY KEEN FELLY DEARLY
ACUTELY
KEENNESS EDGE ACUITY ACUMEN
PUNGENCY
(— OF SIGHT) ACIES
KEEN-SCENTED NOSEWISE
KEEN-SIGHTED EAGLE
KEEP HUG HAVE HOLD SALT SAVE
WAIT WITE BLESS ROCCA WITIE
COFFER DETAIN CONFINE CONTAIN
DEFORCE HUSBAND KEEPING
RESERVE CONSERVE MAINTAIN
PRESERVE RESTRAIN WITHHOLD
(— A COURSE) CAPE
(— A SMALL SHOP) CRAME
(— A WOUND OPEN) TENT
(— ABREAST) FOLLOW
(— AFLOAT) BUOY
(— AN EYE ON) STAG
(— APART) DOTTLE ISOLATE
SEPARATE
(— AT A DISTANCE) ESTRANGE
(— AWAY FROM) ABHOR AVOID
(— AWAY) ABSENT
(— BACK) HAP ROB STAY ARREAR
DETAIN RETARD RESERVE
(— COMPANY WITH) GANG MOOP
CONSORT
(— FREE) ESCHEW
(— FROM BOILING OVER) KEEL
(— FROM BURNING) REDD
(— HIDDEN) HOARD SECRETE
(— IN CIRCULATION) WIND
(— IN EXCITEMENT) ALARM ALARUM
(— IN MIND) RETAIN
(— IN ORDER) TARGE
(— IN STOCK) CARRY
(— IN THE TRACK) GATHER
(— IN) CAGE
(— OFF) FEND WEAR SHIELD

(— OUT) BAR EXPEL
(— POSSESSION) HARBOR
(— SCORELESS) BLANK
(— SECRET) HUSH WHIST
(— STRAIGHT) DIRECT
(— TABS ON) FINGER
(— TIME) GO
(— TO ONESELF) BOSOM
(— UNTIL YEAR OLD) HOG
(— UP) SUBSIST SUSTAIN CONTINUE
(— WAITING) DELAY
(— WARM) STIVE STOVE FOSTER
(— WATCH) TOUT WAIT BEWAKE
KEEPER NAB KEEP SCREW TUTOR
YEMER CUSTOS GAOLER JAILER
LIFTER LOOKER PARKER PASTOR
RAHDAR RANGER WARDEN BAILIFF
CURATOR GEARMAN PIKEMAN
PROVOST BEARWARD DEERHERD
DOLLYMAN ELDERMAN FEWTERER
GUARDANT GUARDIAN HOUNDMAN
TRAITEUR WARRENER
(— OF CATTLE) HAYWARD
(— OF DOGS) FEWTERER
(— OF ELEPHANT) MAHOUT
(— OF PRISON) GAOLER JAILER
WARDEN ALCAIDE
(DOOR —) DURWAN
KEEPING CARE WARD CHARGE
CUSTODY DETAINER
KEEPSAKE DRURY TOKEN GIFTBOOK
SOUVENIR
KEEVE TUB KIEVE
KEG CAG PIN TUB CADE CASK KNAG
WOOD ANKER BARRICO COSTREL
KELP KILP LEAG VAREC WRACK
GIRDLE SEAWEED BELLWARE
KELPIE BARB
KELT SLAT
KENAF DA GOMBO MESTA AMBARI
KANAFF PAPOULA STOKROOS
KENNEL STALL VENERY VENISON
DOGHOUSE
KENO HOUSE
KENTISH (— UNIT) YOKE

KENTUCKY
CAPITAL: FRANKFORT
COLLEGE: BEREA ASBURY
CENTRE BRESCIA URSULINE
COUNTY: ADAIR ESTIL TRIGG
FAYETTE MENIFEE MAGOFFIN
INDIAN: SHAWNEE CHEROKEE
IROQUOIS
LAKE: CUMBERLAND
RIVER: DIX OHIO SALT BARREN
STATE BIRD: CARDINAL
STATE FLOWER: GOLDENROD
STATE TREE: TULIP
TOWN: BEREA CORBIN HAZARD
GLASGOW PADUCAH DANVILLE
COVINGTON LEXINGTON

KENYA
BAY: FORMOSA
CAPITAL: NAIROBI
COIN: SHILLING

LAKE: MAGADI RUDOLF NAIVASHA VICTORIA
LANGUAGE: LUO KIKUYU SWAHILI
MEASURE: WARI
MOUNTAIN: KENYA KULAL NYIRU MATIAN LOGONOT
PEOPLE: LUO MERU BANTU KAMBA KISII LUHYA MASAI NANDI KIKUYU OGADEN BALUHYA HAMITIC HILOTIC TURKANA KIPSIGIS
RIVER: LAK ATHI TANA TURKWELL
TOWN: MERU KITUI NAROK KIPINI KISUMU MOYALE NAKURU NAYUKI ELDORET MALINDI MOMBASA

KERCHIEF CURCH ROMAL RUMAL ANALAV CYPRUS MADRAS NAPKIN PEPLUM CYPRESS KERCHER PANUELO THERESE BABUSHKA BANDANNA HEADRAIL KAFFIYEH KINGSMAN
KERF CARF SKAFF GROOVE UNDERCUT
KERI QRI KERE
KERMANSHAH COCONUT
KERMES GRAIN
KERNEL NUT BUNT CORE KERN MEAT PITH BERRY GOODY GROAT ACINUS ALMOND CARNEL PICKLE NUCLEUS
(CORN —S) HOMINY
(UNHUSKED —S) CAPES
(PL.) NIXTAMAL
KEROGEN SAPROPEL
KEROSINE PARAFFIN
KERSENNEH ERS ERVIL
KERSEY WASHER ORDINARY
KESTREL FANNER KEELIE STANNEL STANCHEL WINDHOVER
KETCH SAIC
KETONE IRONE ACETOL ARMONE CARONE CARVOL COTOIN HEXONE IONONE QUINOL ACETOIN ACETONE ACYLOIN BAEKEOL BENZOIN CAMPHOR CARVONE DYPNONE FLAVONE JASMONE MUSCONE PHORONE SHOGAOL THUJONE ACRIDONE ANTHRONE BUTANONE BUTYRONE CHALCONE CHALKONE CHROMONE DEGUELIN EXALIONE FENCHONE MENTHONE PROPIONE PULEGONE ROTENONE STEARONE TAGETONE THIENONE VALERONE XANTHONE
KETTLE LEAD STEW DIXIE BOILER CANNER FESSEL MARMIT MASLIN TRIPOD VESSEL CALDRON SKILLET STEWPOT CALABASH FLAMBEAU
KETTLEDRUM NAKER ATABAL KETTLE TIMBAL TYMBAL TIMBALE TYMPANY
KEVEL CAVEL KNAPPER
KEY CAY KAY CLEW CLUE CRIB FLAT JACK KING NOTE PLUG PONY DITAL SCREW TASTO WREST BUTTON CHIAVE CIPHER CLAVIS COTTER

SAMARA SPLINE WINDER DIGITAL LANGUET PASSKEY SPEAKER LATCHKEY
(— FOR TUNING HARP) WREST
(— OF KEYBOARD INSTRUMENT) MANUAL
(— OF LIFE) ANKH
(— OF ORGAN) TASTO DIGITAL
(— OF PIANO) IVORY NATURAL
(— OF SPINET) CHIP
(— ON WOODWIND INSTRUMENT) LANGUET SPEAKER
(— UP) STRING
(—S OF CARILLON) CLAVECIN
(ARITHMETICAL —) ADDITIVE
(ASH —) PIGEON
(FALSE —) GLUT
(FEATHER —) FIN STOP SPLINE FEATHER
(SKELETON —) GILT TWIRLER
(TELEGRAPH —) BUG TAPPER
KEYBOARD CLAVIER PEDALIER
KEYHOLE KEY LOCKHOLE
KEYNOTE A B D E KEY TONIC FINALIS
KEYSTONE KEY QUOIN VERTEX SAGITTA VOUSSOIR
(— STATE) PENNSYLVANIA
KEYWAY SPLINE KEYSLOT
KEX KECKSY
KHA KA KHMU KACHE LAMET
KHALAT SEERPAW
KHAN CAN CHAM HAWN TACON KHAKAN
KHAS-KURA NEPALI PAHARI PARBATI GORKHALI
KHATTISH HATTIC
KHEDIVE QUITEVE
KHELLIN VISAMMIN
KHOTANA KOYUKON
KHUSKHUS CUSCUS VETIVER
KIANG CHIGETAI HEMIONUS
KIBBLE GIG KETTLE
KIBBLER CRACKER
KICK BOOT FICK FLEG FLIG FOOT FUNK HEEL HOOF LASH PORR POTE PUNT SHIN TURF YERK ANGLE BUNCH FLING KEVEL PAUSE PUNCH SKELP SPANG SPURN CHARGE CORNER FITTER KICKER KICKUP SPIRAL VOLLEY DROPOUT FOUETTE KICKOFF DROPKICK
(— ABOUT) SPARTLE
(— AS A HORSE) FLING WINCE
(— HEELS UP) SPURN
(— ON SHINS) HACK SHINNER
(BALLET —) BRUSH
(SOCCER —) CORNER
KICKER TEDDER WINCER
KID COD FUN POD TUB FAWN FOOL JIVE JOKE CHILD FAGOT HORSE JOLLY KIDDY SPOOF KIDLET SQUIRT DECEIVE EANLING FATLING TICCHEN YOUNGER CHEVEREL YEANLING
KIDDING JOKE SPOOFERY
KIDNAP STEAL PANYAR SPIRIT
KIDNAPER SPIRIT PLAGIARY SNATCHER SPIRITER
KIDNAPING SNATCH PLAGIUM PLAGIARY

KIDNEY NEAR NEER REIN NEPHRON
(PL.) REINS ROGNONS
KIDNEY BEAN FRIJOLE
(PL.) FASELS
KIER KEEVE PUFFER
KIESELGUHR DOPE GUHR
KILL DO BAG END GET OUT PIP BANE BOLO COOK COOL DOWN FELL MORT NECK SLAY TAME WING BLAST BRAIN CROAK CULLE FETCH FORDO GANCH MISDO NAPOO QUELL SABER SCRAG SHOOT SMITE SNUFF SPEED SPEND SPILL SPOIL STALL STICK SWELT SWORD CORPSE DEADEN DIDDLE FAMISH FINISH HANDLE IMPALE MARTYR MURDER POISON STARVE UNLIVE ACHIEVE BUTCHER DESTROY EXECUTE FLATTEN HATCHET KILLING MORTIFY SMOTHER STONKER SUICIDE DEATHIFY DISPATCH DISSOLVE IMMOLATE JUGULATE STILETTO
(— ANIMALS) CONTROL
(— BY STONING) LAPIDATE
(— BY SUBMERSION) STIFLE
(— CALF AFTER BIRTH) DEACON
(— CATTLE) PITH
(— EVERY TENTH) DECIMATE
(— GAME) SATCHEL
(— OFF) ENECATE
(— SMALL GAME) BARK
(— TIME) GOOF
KILLDEER KILLDEE DEERKILL
KILLED KILT WINGED SKITTLED
(FRESHLY —) GREEN
KILLER GUN GUNMAN SLAYER TORPEDO MURDERER THRESHER
KILLER WHALE ORCA DOLPHIN GRAMPUS
KILLIFISH KELLY KILLY MINNOW COBBLER GUDGEON MAYFISH MUDFISH PANCHAX FUNDULUS ROCKFISH SACALAIT STUDFISH SWAMPINE
KILLING FELL KILL MORT QUELL TUANT MURDER CLEANUP HANGING CLEANING DISPATCH FELICIDE HOMICIDE
KILLJOY NARK GLOOM LEMON SOURPUSS
KILN BING KEEL LEHR OAST CULLE DRIER GLAZE STOVE TILER COCKLE CUPOLA TILERY FURNACE CALCINER LIMEKILN
KILOMETER LI
KILT QUELT PIUPIU FILIBEG PHILIBEG PETTICOAT
KILTER SKEET
KIN SIB KATI KITH CUNNE FLESH FAMILY AFFINITY RELATION
KIND ILK KIN LOT BOON CAST FAIR FORM GOOD HAIR HEND LIKE MAKE MEEK MILD MODE MOLD NICE RATE SELY SOFT SORT SUIT TYPE WING BREED CLASS GENRE GENUS GESTE ORDER SPICE STAMP BENIGN BLITHE FACILE GENDER GENTLE GOODLY HUMANE KIDNEY KINDLY

MANNER MISTER NATURE SPEECE STRAIN STRIPE TENDER EDITION FASHION FEATHER FLESHLY LENIENT QUALITY REGIMEN SPECIAL SPECIES SPECKLE FRIENDLY GENEROUS MANSUETE OBLIGING INDULGENT
(— OF PEOPLE) FOLK
(— OF) A
(DIFFERENT IN —) DIVERS
(DISTINCTIVE —) BRAND
(OF EVERY —) ALKIN
KINDLE BEET FIRE LUNT MOVE TAKE TEND TIND FLAME LIGHT QUICK SPUNK ALIGHT DECOCT ENFIRE EXCITE IGNITE ILLUME EMBLAZE ESPRISE INCENSE INFLAME SOLICIT KINDLING
KINDLINESS CANDOR
KINDLING FIRE BAVIN FAGOT TINDER IGNITION
KINDLY FAIR GAIN KIND NESH AGREE COUTH HENDE NAISH BENIGN BLITHE COUTHY GENIAL HOMELY INNERLY FAVOROUS GENEROUS GRACIOUS QUEMEFUL TOWARDLY
KINDNESS LOVE ALOHA FAVOR BOUNTY CANDOR LENITY SERVICE CLEMENCY EASINESS GOODNESS HUMANITY LENITUDE MILDNESS
KINDRED KIN SIB KIND KITH BLOOD FLESH FAMILY KOBONG NATION STRIND COGNATE KINFOLK KINSMEN SIBSHIP AFFINITY
KINE KYE COWS
KINETIC ACTUAL —
(— POTENTIAL) L
KING RI SO BAN DAM LOT LUD PUL REX REY RIG ROY AGAG BALI BELI BIJA BORS BRAN BRES CRAL CZAR JEHU KRAL LEIR MARK NUDD NUMA OMRI OTTO PHUL RAJA RIAL TSAR TZAR WANG YIMA ARDRI BALOR BELUS CONOR CREON DAGDA DAHAK EGLON ETZEL GYGES HIRAM HOGNI HOSEA IPHIS IXION JOASH LAIUS LLUDD LYCUS MESHA MIDAS MINOS NADAB NEGUS NORSE NUADA PEKAH PRIAM RAJAH SAMMY SWAMI ZIMRI ZOHAK AEOLUS AGENOR AILILL ALBOIN ALONSO ALOROS ARIOCH BLADUD CODRUS DIOMED DUNCAN ELATHA FINGAL FRODHI FROTHI GOEMOT INKOSI KABAKA LEMUEL LYCAON MEMNON MINYAS NESTOR NODONS OENEUS OGYGES PELEUS PELIAS SAUGHT SHESHA SVAMIN TEUCER URIENS UZZIAH VASUKI AHAZIAH AMAIMON AMYCLAS ANGEVIN ARTEGAL ATHAMAS BAGINDA BELINUS BUSIRIS CACIQUE CEPHEUS CROESUS ELIBURE EPAPHUS EPOPEUS ETHBAAL EURYTUS GUNTHER HYGELAC INACHUS JAMSHID JEHOASH JEHORAM KINGLET LAERTES LATINUS LEONTES MENAHEM MONARCH

PANDION PHINEUS POLYBUS REGULUS ROMULUS ROYALET SMERDIS SOLOMON VOLSUNG ACRISIUS ADRASTUS AEGYPTUS ALBERICH AMRAPHEL ASNAPPER BAHMANID BRENNIUS CLAUDIUS COPHETUA ELDORADO ETEOCLES GILGAMES GOEMAGOT GOGMAGOG GORBODUC HEZEKIAH HROTHGAR JEHOAHAZ JEROBOAM KINGLING LAOMEDON LISUARTE MANASSEH MELIADUS MENELAUS ODYSSEUS ORCHAMUS OSNAPPAR OVERKING PADISHAH PEKAHIAH PENTHEUS RAMESSID REHOBOAM RODERICK RODOMONT ROITELET SARPEDON SHEPHERD SISYPHUS TANTALUS
(— AND QUEEN OF TRUMPS) BELLA
(— CHANGED TO WOLF) LYCAON
(— OF ARMS) GARTER NORROY
(— OF BEASTS) LION
(— OF DWARFS) ALBERICH
(— OF FAIRIES) OBERON
(— OF TRUMPS) HONOR
(IRISH —) RI RIG ARDRI ARDRIGH
(POLYNESIAN —) ALII ARII ARIKI
KINGBIRD PIPIRI PETCHARY
KINGBOLT KING KINGPIN MAINPIN
KING CRAB LIMULID LIMULUS PANFISH
KINGDOM WEI REALM REIGN WORLD ESTATE MONERA MORVEN REGION SAXONY MITANNI
KINGFISH BARB CERO HAKE HAKU MINK TOMCOD CHENFISH SCIAENID TOMMYCOD
KINGFISHER HALCYON PODITTI TOROTORO
KINGLET REGULI
KINGLY REGAL ROYAL BASILIC IMPERIAL MAJESTIC PRINCELY
KING PARAKEET WELLAT
KINGSHIP STOOL KINGDOM ROYALTY DEVARAJA KINGHOOD
KING'S PEACE GRITH
KING'S SCHOLAR TUG
KING VULTURE PAP PAPA
KINK NIB SNICK BUCKLE DOGLEG KINKLE
(— IN ROPE) GRIND
KINKAJOU POTTO HEYRAT APOROSO
KINKING FLUTING
KINKY ENCOMIC KINKLED
KINO BIJA BIJASAL
KINSHIP SIB BLOOD NASAB STOOL ENATION KINDRED SIBNESS SIBSHIP AFFINITY AGNATION RELATION
KINSMAN KIN SIB ALLY BLOOD AFFINE AGNATE COUSIN FRIEND BROTHER GOTRAJA KINDRED WINEMAY BANDHAVA RELATION RELATIVE
KINSWOMAN SISTER KINDRED RELATIVE
KIP SKIP GRASSER KIPSKIN UPSTART
KIRGHIZ QYRGHYZ
KIRN MELL
KISS BA LIP NEB BASS BUSS PECK

PREE MOUTH POGUE SLAKE SMACK BEKISS CARESS SLAVER SMOOCH SMOUCH OSCULATE
(— OF PEACE) PAX
(— WETLY) SLOBBER
(STOLEN —) SMOORICH
KISSING LIPWORK
KIT CHIT DUFFEL KITTEN POCHETTE
(LUMBERMAN'S —) TURKEY
(MESS —) CANTEEN
KITCHEN BUT GALLEY CUISINE KITCHIE COOKROOM
KITE LAP CHIL CYTE HAWK GLEDE CHILLA DRACHE DRAGON ELANET FALCON PREYER SENTRY MILVINE PUDDOCK PUTTOCK FORKTAIL HELLKITE
KITTEN KIT KITTY KITTLE CATLING KITLING
KITTIWAKE GULL WAEG ANNET KITTY PICKUP TARROCK TIRRLIE
KITTY CAT BADRANS BAUDRONS
KIVA ESTUFA
KIWI APTERYX
KLAMATH WEED AMBER GOATWEED
KLANG PHONE
KLIPSPRINGER KAINSI KLIPBOK
KLONDIKE CANFIELD SOLITAIRE
KNACK ART FEAT FEEL GATE GIFT HANG CATCH QUIRK TRICK SLEIGHT WRINKLE INSTINCT
KNACKER CLAPPER
(PL.) BONES
KNAPSACK WALLET MOCHILA MUSETTE SNAPBAG SNAPSACK
KNAPWEED SWEEP BLUETOP FLATTOP BALLWEED BELLWEED BOLEWEED BULLWEED BUNDWEED CENTAURY CLUBWEED CROPWEED HARDHEAD IRONHEAD IRONWEED KNOTWEED MATFELON
KNAVE BOY ELF LAD NOB PAM PUR TOM JACK BOWER CHEAT MAKER NODDY ROGUE TIGER COQUIN HARLOT KNIGHT PICARO RASCAL VARLET WENZEL CAMOOCH CUSTREL PEASANT VILLAIN SWINDLER VARLETTO
KNAVERY CATZERIE PATCHERY
KNAVISH ROGUISH SCAMPISH
KNAWEL KNOTWEED KNOTWORT
KNEAD ELT TEW MOLD POST STOCK PETRIE MASSAGE
(— HIDES) STOCK
KNEADING (— MACHINE) BRAKE
KNEE GENU HOCK CROOK KNAPPER SLEEPER SUFFRAGO
(— HOLLOW) HAM
(— OF COMPOSING STICK) SLIDE
KNEECAP CAP PATELLA
KNEEL SIT KNEE COUCH SHIKO KOWTOW
KNEELER SPRINGER
KNEELING SHIKO BENDED
KNEEPAN ROTULA PATELLA
KNELL BELL RING TOLL KNOLL STROKE
KNICKKNACK TOY KNACK TRICK

GEWGAW NOTION PRETTY
GIMCRACK

KNIFE DAH DIE PIN SAX ULU BOLO
BUCK MOON SAEX SHIM SHIV SPUD
TANG BOWIE BURIN CHIVE FACON
GULLY KNIVE KUKRI PANGA SHANK
SHAVE SKEAN SLICE BARLOW
BARONG CAMPIT CARVER COLTER
COUTEL CUTTLE DAGGER DOCTOR
JIGGER PANADE PARANG PAVADE
PORKER PULLER RIMMER SICKLE
SLICER TREVET TRIVAT WORKER
BREAKER CATLING CHOPPER
COUTEAU FIPENNY KIOTOME
MACHETE PALETTE SCALPEL
SEVERER SKINNER SLASHER
SNICKER STICKER SUNDANG
TICKLER WHITTLE BELDUQUE
BILLHOOK CALABOZO JOCTELEG
SERPETTE THWITTLE YATAGHAN
(**— FOR BREAKING FLAX**) BEATER
(**— FOR LEATHER**) PIN
(**— FOR RUBBER DOUGH**) DOCTOR
(**BURMESE —**) DAH DAO DOW
(**CURRIER'S —**) CLEANER
(**ESKIMO —**) ULU
(**MORO —**) BARONG
(**SHOEMAKER'S —**) BUTT
(**SURGICAL —**) CATLING SCALPEL
BISTOURY EXSECTOR
(**TANNER'S —**) GRAINER

KNIFE-PLEATED KILTED
KNIGHT N ELF SIR ADUB GANO TULK
EQUES EQUIS HORSE LANCE RIDER
THANE TOLKE CABALL ERRANT
PENCEL RITTER ROGERO GENILON
PALADIN YOUNKER ALMANZOR
BACHELOR BANNERET CAVALIER
COLVILLE GANELONE IRONCLAD
ISENBRAS PALMERIN RUGGIERO
(**— IN CHESS**) HORSE
(**— OF ROUND TABLE**) GAN BORS
OWEN GARETH GAWAIN MODRED
CARADOC CRADOCK GALAHAD
GANELON EGLAMORE LANCELOT
PALMERIN PERCIVAL TRISTRAM
(**CARPET —**) DAMMERET
KNIGHTHOOD CAVALRY
KNIPHOFIA TRITOMA
KNIT SET BIND KNOT PLAIT PURSE
UNITE WEAVE COMPACT CONNECT
WRINKLE CONTRACT
(**— STOCKINGS**) SHANK
KNITTED FLAT WOVEN
KNITTING LOOP STEEK
KNITTING NEEDLE WIRE
KNOB BOB BUR NOB NUB BEAD
BOSS BURR CLUB DENT HEAD HEEL
KNOP KNOT KNUB LIFT NODE PULL
SNUG STUD TORE BERRY BULLA
FORTE GEMMA KNURL NATCH
ONION PLOOK PLUKE BUTTON
CROCHE EMBOSS NOBBLE NUBBLE
PIMPLE PISTON POMMEL FERRULE
HORNTIP KNOBBLE BELLPULL
DOORKNOB DRAWSTOP OMPHALOS
(**— OF HAIR**) TOORIE
(**— OF ROCK**) BUHR BURR KNUCKLE
(**— ON BILL OF SWAN**) BERRY

(**— ON BUTT OF CANNON**) GRAPE
(**— ON CHAIR**) POMMEL
(**— ON DEER'S ANTLER**) OFFER
CROCHE
(**— ON ROPE**) MOUSE
KNOBBED NODOSE TOROSE
TUBEROUS TYLOTATE
KNOBBY GOUTY KNOTTY GOUTISH
KNOBBLY
KNOCK CON DAD HIT JOW JUT POP
PUN RAP WAP BANG BASH BEAT
BUMP CALL CHAP CHOP DASH
DAUD DING DUMP DUNT HACK JOLT
JOWL KNAP NOCK NOIT PLUG POLT
POSS PUSH ROUT SLAM SLAY SNOP
TANK TIRL WHAP WHOP CLUMP
KNOIT POUND SMITE SNOCK STAVE
STRAM THUMP BOUNCE DUNTLE
KNATCH KNETCH STOTER CANVASS
PINKING
(**— ABOUT**) RUMBLE
(**— DOWN**) DROP DUMP FELL FLOOR
GRASS LEVEL SMITE SOUSE HURTLE
RAFFLE UNPILE
(**— OFF**) SECURE
(**— ON HEAD**) MAZER MAZARD
(**— OUT**) OUT SAP CONK COOL
KAYO FLATTEN STIFFEN
(**— UNCONSCIOUS**) COLDCOCK
(**— WITH THE HORNS**) DISH
KNOCKER CROW RISP HAMMER
WHACKER
(**DOOR —**) CROW HAMMER RAPPER
KNOCK-KNEED VARUS VALGUS
KNOCKOUT KO KAYO CRUSHER
NOBBLER
(**PRETENDED —**) DIVE
KNOLL NOB HIGH KNAP KNOB KNOW
TOFT HEAVE HURST HYRST MOUND
SHOAL COPPLE BOUROCK
HUMMOCK
KNOP NOB KNOB KNOSP KNAPPE
KNOT BOB BOW BUN FAG NIB NOB
NUB PIN TIE BEND BURR CHOU
CLOD CLOT CLUB HARL KILL KNAG
KNAR KNOB NODE NOIL NURL SLUG
SNUB TRUE WAFT WALL CROWN
DUNNE GNARL GNARR HALCH
HALSH HATCH HITCH KNURL MOUSE
NODUS NOEUD SNARL SNICK SWIRL
TWIST WARRE BUTTON CLINCH
CROCHE FINIAL GRANNY MASCLE
SORTIE TANGLE BOWKNOT BOWLINE
CHIGNON COCKADE GORDIAN
MAYBIRD CICISBEO DRAWKNOT
GRAYBACK KNITTING SLIPKNOT
TRUELOVE
(**— IN CLOTH**) FAG BURL
(**— IN COTTON FIBERS**) NEP
(**— IN SIGNAL FLAG**) WAFT WEFT
WHEFT
(**— IN WOOD**) PIN BURL BURR KNAG
KNAR SNUB GNARL KNAUR KNURL
(**— IN YARN**) SLUG SNICK
(**— OF HAIR**) BUN COB PUG CLUB
KNURL CHIGNON
(**LOVE —**) AMORET
(**ORNAMENTAL —**) BOW
(**SHOULDER —**) WING

(**WALL —**) WALE
KNOTGRASS LIGNUM HOGWEED
PIGWEED BINDWEED BIRDWEED
DOORWEED KNOTWEED KNOTWORT
PINKWEED POLYGONY WIREWEED
KNOTTED KNIT NOUE TIED NOWED
NODOSE SWIRLY CRABBED
NODATED SCRAGGY
KNOTTY HARD CRAMP GOUTY
COMMON CRAGGY GNARLY KNAGGY
KNOBBY KNURRY NODOSE NODOUS
COMPLEX GNARLED GOUTISH
JOINTED KNARRED KNOTTED
SCABROUS
KNOTWEED LIGNUM ALLSEED
HOGWEED JUMPSEED POLYGONY
KNOW CAN CON KEN WIS WIT WOT
CITE HAVE SABE WEET WIST WOTH
SAVVY SKILL COGNIZE
(**— NOT**) NOOT
(**—S NOT**) NOTE
(**DID NOT —**) KENDNA
(**DO NOT —**) KENNA
KNOWABLE SENSABLE
KNOW-HOW SAVVY SKILL
KNOWING FLY HEP HIP FOXY GASH
SPRY WISE AWARE CANNY DOWNY
JERRY LEERY SPACK WITTY EXPERT
SCIENT SCIOUS SHREWD WITFUL
WITTER GNOSTIC SAPIENT
(**— SUPERFICIALLY**) SCIOLOUS
KNOWINGLY CANNILY SCIENTER
SHREWDLY WITTERLY
KNOWLEDGE CAN WIT BOOK KITH
KNOW LAIR LEAR LORE INWIT
JNANA SKILL VIDYA ADVICE AVIDYA
CLERGY GNOSIS NOESIS NOTICE
WISDOM CUNNING DIANOIA HEARING
KNOWING MEANING SCIENCE
WITTING DAYLIGHT DOCTRINE
EPISTEME LEARNING LETTRURE
NOTITION PRUDENCE SAPIENCE
SCIENTIA
(**— OF SPIRITUAL TRUTH**) GNOSIS
(**FAMILIAR —**) HANG
(**LATER —**) AFTERWIT
(**MYSTERIOUS —**) ARCANUM
(**PIECEMEAL —**) SMATTER
(**PRIVATE —**) PRIVITY
(**PUBLIC —**) LIGHT
(**SLICK —**) ANGLE
(**SLIGHT —**) INKLING
(**SUPERFICIAL —**) SCIOLISM
(**SUPREME —**) PRAJNA
(**SYSTEMATIZED —**) SCIENCE
KNOWLEDGEABLE KNOWING
SKILLED STUDIED
KNOWN EVER COUTH COMMON
(**ACTUALLY —**) SPECIOUS
(**LITTLE —**) FAMELESS
(**NOT —**) DARK SILENT
(**OTHERWISE — AS**) ALIAS
(**PUBLICLY —**) EXOTERIC
(**UNMISTAKABLY —**) STATED
(**WIDELY —**) COMMON
KNOW-NOTHING SAM
KNUCKLE KNUCK JARRET
KNUCKLEBONE DIB DOLOS TALUS
COCKAL SHACKLE

KNURL MILL NULL DWARF SNARL
KNURLING NULLING REEDING
  KNULLING
KOALA BEAR BAALU BALOO SLOTH
  KOOLAH WOMBAT CARBORA
  PHALANGER
KOBOLD NIS NISSE HODEKEN
  HUTCHEN
KOEL KOIL KOKIL RAINBIRD
KOHL COHOL ALCOHOL
KOHLRABI BROMATIUM
KOKAN LAMPATIA
KOKO LEBBEK
KOKUM GARCINIA
KOKUMIN BAN
KOLA COLA BICHY GOORANUT
KOMBU KOBU KAMBOU CHAKOBU
KOMMETJE WALLOW COMITJE
KONAK YALI
KOOKABURRA KOOKA JACKASS
KOPECK KAPEIKA
KORAKAN RAGI RAGGI RAGGY
KORAN KITAB QURAN ALCORAN
  (SECTION OF —) SURA SURAH

KORE DESPOINA
KOREA (SEE NORTH KOREA OR
  SOUTH KOREA)
KOREC MIRA
KORINA LIMBA
KOS COAN
KOSIN KOUSSIN TAENNIN BRAYERIN
KOSO PANAMINT
KOULAN GOUR
KOWHAI GOAI PELU LOCUST
  SOPHORA
KOWTOW KNEEL SHIKO
KOYUKON TENA KHOTANA
KRAAL CRAW MANYATTA ZIMBABWE
KRAIT ADDER KORAIT BUNGARUM
KRATER KELEBE
KRAUNHIA WISTARIA
KREIS CIRCLE
KRIS CREASE CREESE DAGGER
KRISHNA VASUDEVA
KRONE CROWN CORONA
KRU KROOBOY KROOMAN
KRUMMHORN CREMONA CROMORNE
KSHATRIYA THAKUR

KUA MAKUA MAKWA
KUBA BUSHONGO KABISTAN
KUDZU VINE KOHEMP
KUI KHONDI
KU KLUXER KLUXER KLUCKER
  KLANSMAN
KUKURUKU IKPERE
KULANAPAN POMO
KUMAN POLOUTZY
KUMBUK ARJAN ARJUN
KUMMEL ALLASCH
KUMQUAT NAGAMI
KURRAJONG CALOOL LACEBARK
KURUKH ORAON
KUSA DARBHA
KUSIMANSEL MANGUE
KUTCHIN LOUCHEUX
KUWAIT (TOWN OF —) AHMADI
  HAWALLI ABDULLAH FAHAHEEL
KVASS QUASH
KWENI GURO
KYPHOSIS HUMPBACK
KYURINISH LESGHIN LEZGHIAN

L EL LIMA FIFTY
LAAGER LEEGTE LEAGUER
LABDACUS (FATHER OF —)
POLYDORUS
(MOTHER OF —) NYCTEIS
(SON OF —) LAIUS
LABDANUM MYRRH
LABEL TAG BILL FILE FICHE STAMP
TALLY TITLE DIRECT DOCKET
TICKET ENDSEAL LAMBEAU STICKER
(— ON SUIT OF CLOTHES) ETIQUET
LABELLUM LIP LABEL
(PART OF —) HYPOCHIL
LABIAL ROUND
LABIATE HOREHOUND
LABIUM LIP LABRUM
LABOR FAG TUG WIN CARK MOIL
TASK TAVE TILL TOIL WORK BEGAR
DELVE GRAFT GRIND HEAVE PAINS
SWEAT SWINK TEAVE TREAD WHILE
YAKKA CORVEE DRUDGE EFFORT
HAMMER STRIVE BULLOCK FATIGUE
MANUARY OPIFICE PROCURE
SERVICE SLAVERY TRAVAIL
TROUBLE TURMOIL BUSINESS
DRUDGERY EXERTION GROANING
INDUSTRY LABORAGE STRUGGLE
(— ARDUOUSLY) BILDER
(— HARD) THRASH THRIPPLE
(— UNDER) SUFFER
(DAY'S —) DARG JOURNEY
(DIFFICULT —) DYSTOCIA
(EXCESSIVE —) STRAIN
(FORCED —) BEGAR
(HARD —) HARD BULLWORK
(HIRED —) TOGT
(IMPOSED —) TASKAGE
(MENTAL —) HEADWORK
(SEVERE —) AGON
(UNPAID —) CORVEE
LABORATORY LAB SHOP KITCHEN
OFFICINA WORKSHOP
LABORED HEAVY FORCED SWEATY
STRAINED
**LABORER (ALSO SEE WORKER AND
WORKMAN)** BOY BHAR ESNE HIND
JACK JOEY MOZO PEON TOTY
BAGDI GUASO HUNKY NAVVY PALLI
PINER STIFF BALAHI BEGARI
BOHUNK COALER COOLIE DAYMAN
DILKER DOCKER FELLAH FLUNKY
FOGGER HEAVER HOLEYA JIBARO
LUMPER RAFTER TASKER WAYMAN
WORKER BRACERO BYWONER
CREWMAN DAYSMAN DIGGORY
DIRGLER DRAINER DVORNIK
HOBBLER MANUARY MAZDOOR
PICKMAN PIONEER PIPEMAN
PLOWMAN SANDHOG SCOURER
SHIPPER SMASHER SOUGHER
SPALLER STOCKER SWINKER
TOTYMAN WORKMAN BIJWONER
CHAINMAN COTTAGER DOLLYMAN
FARMHAND FLOORMAN GANGSMAN
HOLDSMAN SPADEMAN SPALPEEN
STRAPPER TIDESMAN
(INEXPERIENCED —) GREENER
LABORIOUS HARD HEAVY STIFF
SWEATY UPHILL ARDUOUS

OPEROSE SLAVISH TOILFUL
DILIGENT LABOROUS TOILSOME
LABRADOR TEA LEDUM GOWIDDIE
LABURNUM AWBER
LABYRINTH MAZE CIRCUIT MEANDER
LABYRINTHINE TORTUOUS
LAC LACCA LACQUER
LACE BEAT BEST FOND GOTA LASH
PEAK FILET LACIS LIVEN ORRIS
POINT SCREW SPRIG WEAVE
BLONDE CORDON DEFEAT EDGING
GRILLE LACING LASHER THRASH
TUCKER VENISE ALENCON ALLOVER
BULLION CURRAGH CUTWORK
FOOTING GALLOON GUIPURE
HONITON LATCHET MACRAME
MALINES MECHLIN MELANGE
NANDUTI TAMBOUR TATTING
TORCHON TROLLEY ARGENTAN
BOBBINET BONEWORK BOOTLACE
BRUSSELS DENTELLE ILLUSION
LACEWORK LIMERICK PEARLING
STAYLACE
(— EDGING) PUNTILLA
(— IN PLACE OF COLLAR) RUCHE
(— MAKER) TWISTHAND
(— PATTERN) TOILE
(KNOTTED —) TATTING
LACEBARK LAGETTO DAGUILLA
LACEWOOD
LACE BUG TINGITID
LACERATE REND TEAR ENBORE
HARROW MANGLE SCARIFY
FRACTURE
LACERATION RIP TEAR WOUND
LACEWOOD SYCAMORE
LACEWORK DENTELLE
LACHRYMOSE SAD TEARY WEEPY
MAUDLIN
LACINARIA LIATRIS
LACING LACET LINGEL ECHELLE
LANGUET
LACK FAIL LANK LIKE LOSS MAIM
MISS NEED VOID WANE WANT
FAULT MINUS DEARTH DEFECT
INLAIK ABSENCE BLEMISH DEFAULT
FAILURE PAUCITY VACANCY
SCARCITY SOLITUDE WANTROKE
(— CONFIDENCE) DOUBT
(— FAITH) DIFFIDE
(— HARMONY) DISAGREE
(— OF APPETITE) ANOREXIA
(— OF CLARITY) DARKNESS
(— OF COORDINATION) ASYNERGY
DYSERGIA
(— OF DEVELOPMENT) AGENESIS
(— OF EARNESTNESS) ITEMING
(— OF EFFUSIVENESS) RESERVE
(— OF EMOTION) APATHY
(— OF ENERGY) ATONY ANERGY
ATONIA
(— OF FLAVOR) SILENCE
(— OF FORESIGHT) MYOPIA
(— OF HARMONY) DISCORD
DISUNITY
(— OF INTENTION) ACCIDENT
(— OF INVOLVEMENT) DISTANCE
(— OF ORDER) ATAXY ATAXIA
DISARRAY

(— OF PATRIOTISM) INCIVISM
(— OF REFINEMENT) CRUDITY
(— OF SENSE OF SMELL) ANOSMIA
(— OF SENSE) FOLLY
(— OF STEADINESS) LEVITY
(— OF SYMPATHY) DYSPATHY
(— OF VIGOR) LANGUOR
(— OF VITALITY) ANEMIA ADYNAMIA
(— OF WIND) CALM
(— OF WORTH) IMMERIT
(— STRENGTH) DROOP
LACKADAISICAL LANGUID LISTLESS
LACKEY SKIP SLAVE LACQUEY
STAFFIER
LACKING BUT SHY BARE FREE
WANT ALACK GNEDE MINUS SHORT
ABSENT BARREN DEVOID WITHIN
WANTING DESOLATE INDIGENT
LACKLUSTER DULL FISHY CLOUDY
GLASSY
LACONIC CURT SHORT CONCISE
POINTED SPARTAN SUCCINCT
LA CORUNA GROIN
LACQUER LAC DOPE DUCO JAPAN
CHATON LACKER URUSHI VARNISH
LACTATION (— PERIOD) NOTE
LACTONE CUMARIN LIMONIN
MECONIN DIKETENE
LACTOSCOPE PIOSCOPE
LACUNA GAP BREAK
LACUSTRINE LAKISH
LAD BOY BUB MAN BOYO CARL CHAP
DICK HIND JOCK LOON SNAP BILLY
BUCKO CADDY CHIEL GROOM
YOUTH BURSCH CADDIE CALLAN
FELLOW LADDIE LADKIN MANNIE
NIPPER SHAVER CALLANT
MUCHACHO SPRINGER STRIPLING
(AWKWARD —) GROMET GRUMMET
(MISCHIEVOUS —) GAMIN
(MY —) AVICK
(SERVING —) GILLIE GOSSOON
LADDER STY STEE JACOB SCALE
AERIAL BANGOR ESCAPE PULEYN
GANGWAY POLEYNE POMPIER
(FIREMAN'S —) STICK
(FISH —) FISHWAY
(JACOB'S —) CHARITY
LADDIE JOCKEY LATHIE LADDOCK
LADDIKIE
LADE BAIL LAVE LADEN TRUSS
BURDEN FRAUGHT
(— INTO COOLER) STRIKE
LADEN HEAVY BELAST LOADED
FRAUGHT FREIGHT GESTANT
LADING LOAD CARGO FREIGHT
LADINO SPANIOL
LADLE DIP JET GAWN SKEP CLATH
CYATH KEACH STOOP DIPPER
LADING CUVETTE CYATHUS
KYATHOS POTSTICK
(— OUT SOUP) SLEECH
(— WITH HANDLES) CYATH SHANK
CYATHUS KYATHOS SKIPPET
(BRINE —) LOOT
(LARGE —) SCOOP
LADRONE TULISAN LATHERIN
LADY BIBI BURD DAME RANI DONNA
HANUM BEEBEE DOMINO FEMALE

KADINE RAWNIE SAHIBA SENORA
LADYKIN MADONNA SENHORA
SINEBADA
(— OF HIGH RANK) BEGUM
(— OF HOUSE) GOODWIFE
(BEAUTIFUL —) CLEAR
(TURKISH —) KHANUM
(PL.) LADYHOOD
LADYBUG VEDALIA
LADYFISH WRASSE PUDIANO
BONEFISH BONYFISH DONCELLA
LADYLIKE FEMALE
LADYLOVE LADY DELIA MINION
MISTRESS
LADY'S-COMB NEEDLES
LADY'S-MANTLE DEWCUP PADELION
LADY'S-SLIPPER DUCK YELLOW
NERVINE YELLOWS UMBILROOT
LAERTES (FATHER OF —) ARCESIUS
(MOTHER OF —) CHALCOMEDUSA
(SON OF —) ULYSSES
(WIFE OF —) ANTICLEA
LAG DRAG DRAW SLOG DELAY TRAIL
HOCKER LAGGER LINGER LOITER
STRING DRIDDLE LAGGING
(— IN PRODUCTION) SLIPPAGE
LAGGARD SLOW TARDY LAGGER
TORTOISE
LAGGING TARDY JACKET DEADING
LAGGARD CLEADING DRAWLING
FOREPOLE
LAGNIAPPE TIP GIFT BONUS PILON
PRESENT
LAGOMORPH PIKA RABBIT
LAGOON HAFF POOL BAYOU LIMAN
LAGUNA
LAID **(— ACROSS WALL)** INBOND
(— DOWN) THETIC THETICAL
(— WASTE) BARE
LAIR DEN LAY FORM HOLD SHED
EARTH HAUNT LODGE MEUSE
SQUAT HARBOR KENNEL SPELUNK
(— OF FOX) KENNEL
(— OF OTTER) HOLT HOVER
(— OF WILD BOAR) SOUNDER
LAISSE TIRADE
LAITY FOLK LAYMEN PEOPLE
LAIUS (FATHER OF —) LABDACUS
(SON OF —) OEDIPUS
(WIFE OF —) JOCASTA
LAKE LAY SEA VLY BAHR JAIL JHIL
LAGO LLYN LOCH MERE MOAT
SHOR TANK TARN VLEI VLEY BAYOU
CHOTT JHEEL LERNA LIMAN LOUGH
SPARK TUBIG LAGOON NYANZA
STROND ANCYLUS CARMINE
LAKELET TURLOUGH
(CASHEW —) AUBURN
(FENNY —) BROAD
(MOUNTAIN —) TARN
(RELATING TO —S) LIMNAL
(SALT —) SHOT CHOTT SHOTT
SALINA SALINE
(SMALL —) GURGES
(TEMPORARY —) PINAG
LAKE CARP DRUM LAKER
LAKE HERRING KIYI CISCO
GRAYBACK
LAKE TROUT POGY TOGUE
LAKE WHITEFISH POLLAN

LAKSHMI SRI SHREE
LAMA ELK AUCHENIA
LAMB BUM PET PUR CADE DEAR
DUPE LOME SOCK YEAN AGNUS
PESAH PODDY AGNEAU COSSET
HIEDER LAMBIE LAMKIN PESACH
SUCKER WASTER WEANER CHILVER
EANLING FATLING HOGLING
PASCHAL PERSIAN RUFFIAN
TWAGGER BAAHLING LAMBLING
PASSOVER YEANLING
(— AND WHEAT) KIBBE
(SCYTHIAN —) BAROMETZ
LAMBASTE CREAM SQUABASH
LAMBENT BRIGHT RADIANT
LAMBREQUIN MANTLING
LAMBSKIN LAMB BAGDAD BAGHDAD
SALZFELLE
LAMB'S QUARTERS MUCKWEED
LAMB'S WOOL WASSAIL
LAME BUM GAME HALT LAHN GAMMY
GIMPY GRAVEL TINSEL CRIPPLE
CRIPPLY HALTING HIPHALT
GORGERIN SPAVINED
(— A HORSE) STUB
LAMELLA PLICA FOLIUM FORNIX
LAMENESS HALT
LAMENT CRY WEY CARE DOLE HONE
HOWL KEEN MEAN MOAN PINE SIGH
TEAR WAIL WALY WEEP CROON
DUMKA GREET KINAH MOURN PLAIN
QINAH BEHOWL BEMOAN BEWAIL
BEWEEP COMMOS KOMMOS PLAINT
REPINE SORROW SQUAWK THREAP
YAMMER BEMOURN CONDOLE
DEPLORE EJULATE ELEGIZE
GRIZZLE REGRATE THRENOS
WAYMENT COMPLAIN MOURNING
THRENODY ULLAGONE WELLAWAY
LAMENTABLE YEMER RUEFUL
DOLEFUL PITIFUL PITIABLE
PLAINFUL YAMMERLY
LAMENTATION KEEN MOAN WAIL
DOLOR LINOS RUING TANGI LAMENT
PLAINT REGRET SORROW THRENE
PLANGOR TRAGEDY WILLAWA
CORONACH MOURNING PATHETIC
WAILMENT WELLAWAY LAMENTING
LAMINA FILM LAME LAMP LEAF
OBEX BLADE FLAKE LAMIN PLATE
SCALE SHELL TABLE CAPSULE
LAMINATE LEAFY FLAGGY
LAMINATED BUILT FOLIATE
TABULAR
LAMINATION SLABBING
LAMINITIS FOUNDER
LAMMAS DAY GULE TERM
LAMMERGEIER AREND
LAMP ARC EYE SEE DAVY GLIM INKY
JACK SLUT ALDIS ARGAND ASTRAL
BULLET HELION LAMPAD TARGET
ILLUMER LAMPION LAMPLET
LANTERN LUCERNE LUCIGEN
SUNLAMP SUNSPOT AEOLIGHT
CIRCLINE GASLIGHT SIDELAMP
TORCHERE
(— FOR FIREPLACE) KYLE
(4-CORNERED —) CHILL
(CHIMNEYLESS —) TORCH

(IRON —) CRUSIE
(MAKESHIFT —) BITCH
(SAFETY —) DAVY GEORDIE
(PL.) CLUSTER
LAMPBLACK LINK
LAMPETIA (FATHER OF —) APOLLO
(MOTHER OF —) NEAERA
LAMP HOLDER HUSK
LAMPOON PIPE GESTE LIBEL SQUIB
IAMBIC BERHYME PASQUIN
COCKALAN RIDICULE SATIRIZE
LAMPOONER PASQUIL PASQUIN
LAMPREY PRIDE LAMPER MYZONT
RAMPER SAYNAY SUCKER LAMPERN
LAMP RING CRIC
LAMPSHADE GLOBE
LAMPWICK MATCH
LANATE WOOLY LANOSE WOOLLY
LANCE PIC CANE DART SHAFT
SPEAR STAFF BROACH ELANCE
GLAIVE GLEAVE LANCET ROCKET
LANCELET SPICULUM
(KING ARTHUR'S —) RON
LANCE GUARD VAMPLATE
LANCE HEAD MORNE SOCKET
LANCER LANCE SOWAR UHLAN
LANCE REST QUEUE FEWTER
LANCET FLEAM FLEEM LANCELET
LANCEWOOD YAYA CIGUA CANELA
YARIYARI
LAND ERD ERF NOD RIB AGER DIRT
FOLD GALE GISH GORE JODO MARK
SITE SOIL EARTH EJIDO ETHEL
FIELD GLEBE JUGER PLANT SHORE
SOLUM ALIGHT ASSART FUNDUS
GROUND COMMONS COUNTRY
DEMESNE ELLASAR HOLDING
LANDING LIBRATE QUILLET
TERRENE ALLODIAL BOOKLAND
COMMONTY FARMLAND FLEYLAND
FOLKLAND POMERIUM PRAEDIUM
(— A PLANE) GREASE
(— BETWEEN FURROWS) SELION
(— BETWEEN RIVERS) DOAB
(— CLEARING) KAINGIN
(— CONVERTED TO TILLAGE)
TWAITE THWAITE
**(— HAVING VALUE OF POUND PER
YEAR)** LIBRATE
(— IN CONACRE) MOCK
(— IN GRASS) LAYER
(— LEFT FALLOW) ARDER
(— MEASURE) RIG
(— OF BLISS) GOKURAKU
(— OF GIANTS) UTGARTHAR
(— OF MANSION) DEMESNE
(— OF OPPORTUNITY) ARKANSAS
(— OF PLENTY) GOSHEN
(— OF REGION) MOLD MOULD
(— PLOWED IN A DAY) JORNADA
(— RECOVERED FROM SEA) INTAKE
INNINGS
(— REGULARLY FLOODED) SALTING
(— SURROUNDED BY WASTE) HOPE
(— UNIT) URE KIPUKA MECATE
MORGEN MANZANA VIRGATE
(ALLUVIAL —) BATTURE
(ANCESTRAL —) ETHEL
(ARABLE —) LEA LEY LAINE

(ARID —) DESERT STEPPE
(BOTTOM —) SLASH CALLOW
STRATH
(CHURCH —) GLEBE TERMON
(CHURCH —S) CROSS
(CLEARED —) ASSART
(COMMON —) EJIDO EXIDO STRAY
(CONTINENTAL —) MAIN
(CULTIVATED —) FARM ARADA
TILTH CULTURE FEERING WAINAGE
LABORAGE METAIRIE
(ENCLOSED —) CLOSE INTAKE
(FREEHOLD —) MULK
(GRAVELLY —) GEEST GRAVES
(GRAZING —) GRASS HIRSEL HIRSLE
FEEDING
(HEATHY —) ROSLAND
(HERITABLE —) ODAL UDAL
(IMAGINARY —) FAERIE COCKAYNE
LILLIPUT
(LEASED —) TACK
(LONG STRIP OF —) SLANG SPONG
(LOW —) BOG FEN GALL INKS
CARSE BOTTOM
(LOW RICH —) CARSE
(NATIVE —) BLIGHTY BIRTHDOM
HOMELAND
(OBDURATE —) TILL
(PARCEL OF —) FEU LOT MOCK
(PASTURE —) HA ALP FEED HOGA
WALK GRASS VELDT LEASON
(PLATEAU —) HIGHVELD
(PLOWED —) ARADA FALLOW
FURROW BREAKING
(PRIVATE —) SEVERAL
(PROMISED —) CANAAN
(PURE —) JODO SUKHAVATI
(RESOWN —) HOOKLAND
(ROUGH —) BRAKE
(SAVANNAH —S) LALANG
(SCRUBBY —) SCROG SCROGS
(SMALL PARCEL OF —) SUERTE
(SWAMPY —) WOODSERE
(TIMBER —S) STICKS
(WASTE —) HEATH
(WESTERN —) HESPERIA
(WET —) SOAK SWAMP SWANG
(WOODED —S) STICKS
(PL.) ACRES SUCKEN LAENDER
NOVALIA
LANDBOOK TERRIER
LANDED PRAEDIAL
LANDFORM CUSP CUESTA
LANDHOLDER LAIRD COSCET
TALUKDAR
LANDHOLDING BARONY
LANDING BANK YARD STAITH
LANDAGE ARRIVAGE FOOTPACE
HALFPACE LANDFALL
(SMOOTH —) GREASER
LANDING PLACE GHAT HARD
SCALE PALACE ARRIVAGE
LANDING STAGE MEAR STAGE
STAIR STAITH STELLING
LANDLADY WIFE DUENA PADRONA
GOODWIFE
LANDLORD HOST GOODMAN
PADRONE ZAMINDAR
LANDSMAL MAL

LANDMARK COPA DOLE DOOL MARK
MERE BAKEN BOUND CAIRN MARCH
MEITH SENAL CIPPUS SEAMARK
LANDMASS BULGE
LANDOWNER THANE BONDER
SQUIRE CACIQUE EFFENDI FREEMAN
BHUMIDAR FRANKLIN ZAMINDAR
(PL.) GAMORI GEOMOROI
LANDSCAPE BOCAGE PAYSAGE
SCENERY LANDSKIP
LANDSLIDE SLUMP LANDFALL
LANDSLIP
LAND SPRING LAVANT
LANDVOGT BAILIFF
LANE WAY GANG LOAN LOKE PASS
RACE VEIN WIND ALLEY CHASE
DRANG DRONG ENTRY BOREEN
VENNEL LANEWAY LOANING
TWITTEN DRIFTWAY
(AIR TRAFFIC —) CORRIDOR
(NARROW —) CHAR CHARE TEWER
BOREEN
(OCEAN —) SEAWAY
LANGUAGE (ALSO SEE DIALECT) LIP
CHIB CODE LEED RUNE LEDEN
LINGO SLANG LANGUS LINGUA
SPEECH TONGUE YABBER CABLESE
DIALECT IDIOLECT LEGALESE
(SPECIFIC —) GA GE HO MO VU AIS
AKA ATA EDO EFE EPE EVE EWE
FAN FON FOX FUL GEG HET ICA IJO
ILA KAI KAU KOL KOT KRU KUI LAB
LAI LAZ MON MRU SIA TWI UDI YAO
ZIA AFAR AGAO AGAU AGNI AHOM
AINU AKAN AKIM ALUR AMBO ANDI
ANTA ARUA AVAR BARI BEJA BIAK
BODO BONI BORA BUBE BUGI BULU
CARA CHAM CHIN CHOL CHUJ COOS
CORA COTO CREE CROW CUNA
DENE DOBU DYAK EFIK EKOI ERIE
EYAK FANG FIJI FULA FUNG GARO
GHEG GOLA GOLD HARE HEHE HOPI
HOVA HULA HUPA IBAN IDJO IJAW
IXIL KADU KAFA KAMI KAVI KAWI
KELE KOCH KOMI KONO KOTA KUKI
KURI LAHU LAKH LAPP LASI LATI
LAZI LESU LETT LUBA MANX MAYA
MOLE MORO NAGA NAMA NIAS NIUE
NUBA NUPE OGOR PALA PEGU PEUL
PUME RAMA SAHO SERB SERI SGAW
SHAN SIUS SORB SULU SUMO SUMU
SUSU TAAL TIAM TIBU TINO TODA
TSHI TUPI TUPY VEPS VOTE XOSA
ZULU ALEUT ALSEA ARAUA AUETO
AZTEC BAJAU BALTI BASSA BATAK
BATTA BAURE BEMBA BHILI BICOL
BILIN BONNY CAMPA CATIB CAYUA
CHANE CHIMU CHOCO CHOPE
COFAN COIBA COMAN CUEVA
CUMAN CUNZA CZECH DAFLA
DAYAK DIERI DINKA DUALA DUTCH
DYULA EMPEO FANTI FINGO FUNJI
GAFAT GALLA GANDA GETAN GETIC
GOLDI GONDI GREBO GREEK
GUAMO GUATO GURMA GYPSY
HABAB HAIDA HAIKH HATSA HAUSA
HINDI HUABI HUARI HURON HUSKY
HYLAM IGALA ILOKO IRAYA IRISH
JAKUN JATKI JUANG JUTIC KABYL

KAMBA KAMIA KANDH KAREN
KAROK KHASI KHMER KHOND KHUZI
KIOWA KISSI KIWAI KOINE KOLIS
KONDE KONGO KORKU KORWA
KOTAR KUMUK KUMYK KUSAN
KWOMA LAMBA LAMUT LANGO
LATIN LENCA LENDU LHOKE LHOTA
LIMBA LIMBU LUIAN LUNDA MAGHI
MAHRA MAHRI MALAY MALTO
MAORI MAZUR MBUBA MEDIC MENDI
MIKIR MODOA MOSSI MUONG MURMI
MURUT NAHUA NOGAI NORSE
NYORO ORAON ORIYA OROMO
OSCAN PALAU PAMIR PELEW PEUHL
PLATT PUNIC RONGA SAKAI SAMAL
SANTO SAXON SCOTS SERER SHILH
SHINA SHONA SICEL SIKEL SLAVE
SOTHO SOYOT SUOMI SWAZI TAINO
TAMIL TELEI TONGA TURKI UDISH
UIGUR URIYA UZBEK VOGUL WAYAO
WELSH WOLOF YAKUT YUNCA
ZERMA ABIPON ABKHAS ACAWAI
ACHOLI ADIGHE ADZHAR AFGHAN
AHTENA ALTAIC ANDAKI ANDHRA
ANDOKE ANGAMI APACHE APANTO
APIACA ARABIC ARANDA ARAONA
ARAWAK ARUNTA ATAROI AVANTI
AYMARA BAGOBO BAITSI BAKELE
BANIVA BASQUE BEAVER BHOTIA
BHUMIJ BIHARI BILAAN BILOXI
BONTOC BORORO BRAHUI BRETON
BRIBRI BUKAUA BULGAR BURIAT
CAGABA CANITA CARAJA CARIAN
CARIRI CAUQUI CAVINA CAYAPA
CAYUGA CAYUSE CEBUAN CHAGGA
CHAIMA CHANGO CHOCHO CHOKWE
COCAMA CONIBO COPTIC CREOLE
DAKOTA DANISH DOGRIB DYERMA
ESKIMO EUDEVE FRENCH FULANI
FULNIO FUTUNA GADDAN GALCHA
GALIBI GATHIC GENTOO GERMAN
GILAKI GILIAK GILYAK GOTHIC
GUAIMI GUETAR GUINAU GULLAH
GURIAN HAINAN HANTIK HARARI
HATTIC HEBREW HERERO HIBITO
IBANAG IBIBIO IFUGAO IGNERI
IGOROT INDIAN INDOIS INNUIT
INUPIK ISINAI ISLETA IVATAN
KABARD KACHIN KAFFIR KAIBAL
KALMUK KAMASS KANAKA KANURI
KEKCHI KHALKA KHAMTI KHARIA
KHOWAR KIKUYU KILIWA KODAGA
KODAGU KOIARI KOIBAL KOLAMI
KOREAN KORYAK KOTIAK KPEELE
KUNAMA KURNAI KURUKH KYURIN
LADINO LAGUNA LAHNDA LAHULI
LENAPE LEPCHA LIBYAN LIUKIU
LIVIAN LUSHAI LUVIAN LYCIAN
LYDIAN MAGAHI MAGYAR MANCHU
MANOBO MBONDO MBUNDA MEDIAN
MEGREL MINOAN MISHMI MISIMA
MOHAWK MONTES MUYSCA MYSIAN
NEWARI NINGPO NUBIAN NYANJA
OORIVA OSTIAK OVAMPO PAHARI
PALAIC PAPUAN PASHTO PAZAND
POLISH PUSHTO PUSHTU QUECHA
RASHTI REJANG ROMANY SAFINE
SAKIAN SALISH SAMOAN SANGIL
SANGIR SARCEE SASSAK SAVARA

SEDANG SEKANI SELKUP SELUNG
SEMANG SENECA SENUFO SESUTO
SHARRA SHASTA SILETZ SINDHI
SLOVAK SOMALI SONRAI SUBIYA
SURHAI SUSIAN TARTAR TAVGHI
TELEGU TELEUT TETTUM THONGA
TIPURA TUNGUS VANNIC VOTYAK
YANKEE YARURA YORUBA ZAREMA
ABENAKI ACHAGUA AEQUIAN
AKWAALA AKWAPIM ALABAMA
ALTRIAN AMANAYE AMHARIC
AMORITE AMUESHA APINAYE
ARAMAIC ARAPAHO ARAUCAN
ARECUNA ARGOBBA ARICARA
ARMORIC ASHANTI ASURINI
ATACAMA ATAKAPA AUSTRAL
AVESTAN AXUMITE BAGHELI
BAGIRMI BAINING BAKONGO
BALANTE BALUCHI BAMBARA
BANGALA BANNACK BASHKIR
BENGALI BEOTHUK BERBERI
BHOTIYA BHUTANI BOSNIAN BRITISH
BULANDA BUNDELI BUNYORO
BURMESE BUSHMAN CALIANA
CALINGA CARRIER CASHIBO
CATALAN CATAWBA CAWAHIB
CHACOBO CHARRUA CHATINO
CHEBERO CHECHEN CHIBCHA
CHIMILA CHINOOK CHIRINO
CHIWERE CHONTAL CHOROTI
CHUKCHI CHUMASH CHUROYA
CHUVASH CIBONEY CLALLAM
COCHIMI CORNISH COTONAM
COWLITZ CYMRAEG DAGBANE
DAGOMBA DANAKIL DANKALI
DARGHIN DEUTSCH DHEGIHA
DRAVIDA ENGLISH ESCUARA
ESSELEN EUSKERA FINNISH FLEMISH
FOOCHOW FRIESIC FRISIAN GAULISH
GOAJIRO GUAHIBO GUARANI
GUAYAKI GURUNSI GYARUNG
HAITIAN HANUNOC HIDATSA HITTITE
HUASTEC HUCHNOM HUICHOL
HURRIAN IBERIAN ILOKANO
ILONGOT INGALIK IPURINA ITALIAN
ITELMES ITONAMA JACUNDA
JAGATAI KAKHYEN KALINGA
KAMASIN KANAUJI KANNADA
KASHUBE KASSITE KIKONGO
KIPCHAK KIRANTI KIRGHIZ KIRUNDI
KLAMATH KOASATI KONKANI
KOYUKON KUBACHI KULAMAN
KURDISH KUTCHIN KUTENAI
LAMPONG LATVIAN LESGHIN
LOATUKO LUGANDA MAGADHI
MALTESE MAPUCHE MARATHI
MASKOKI MERCIAN MEXICAN
MINAEAN MINGREL MITANNI
MOABITE MOCHICA MONUMBO
MORATTY MORISCO NAHUATL
NICOBAR OSMANLI OSSETIC
PAHLAVI PALAUNG PANJABI
PARBATE PERMIAK PERMIAN
PERSIAN PICTISH PUNJABI PUQUINA
QUERCHI SABAEAN SALINAN
SAMBALA SAMNANI SAMNITE
SAMOYED SANDAWE SANTALI
SANTANA SEMITIC SERBIAN
SHAWANO SHAWNEE SHILLUH

SHIPIBO SHUSWAP SIAMESE
SIRIONO SIUSLAW SOGDIAN
SONGHAI SONGISH SORBIAN
SPANIOL SPANISH STIKINE SUBANUN
SVANISH SWAHILI SWEDISH
TAGALOG TIBETAN TUAMOTU
TURKISH UMBRIAN UMBUNDU
VISAYAN WALLOON WENDISH
YENISEI YIDDISH ZABERMA
ZONGORA ABANEEME ACHINESE
ACHUMAWI AKKADIAN AKSUMITE
ALACALUF ALBANIAN ALFURESE
AMAHUACA AMERICAN AMMONITE
ANGOLESE ANNAMESE ANZANIAN
APALACHI ARMENIAN ASSAMESE
ASSYRIAN ATJINESE AWISHIRA
BACTRIAN BALINESE BARBACOA
BECHUANA BHOJPURI BISCAYAN
BOSNISCH BOTOCUDO CAHUILLA
CAINGANG CANARESE CANOEIRO
CAQUETIO CARELIAN CARIJONA
CAYUBABA CHALDEAN CHAMORRO
CHEHALIS CHEMAKUM CHEYENNE
CHINGPAW CHIQUITO CHITRALI
COCONUCA COLUMBIA COMANCHE
CORAVECA CROATIAN CUSTENAU
DELAWARE DIEGUENO EGYPTIAN
ELAMITIC ETHIOPIC ETRUSCAN
FALISBAN FORMOSAN FRANKISH
FULFULDE GALICIAN GALLEGAN
GEORGIAN GERMANIC GORKHALI
GUAICURU GUJARATI HADENDOA
HAWAIIAN HITCHITI ILLINOIS
ILLYRIAN IROQUOIS JAPANESE
JAVANESE KANARESE KANAWARI
KANKANAI KASHMIRI KASUBIAN
KERMANJI KIMBUNDU KOLARIAN
LANDSMAL LANUVIAN LIGURIAN
LIHYANIC LILLOOET LIVONIAN
LUSATIAN MADURESE MAHRATTI
MAKASSAR MALAGASY MANDINGA
MARSHALL MASOVIAN MAYATHAN
MAZOVIAN MONGOLIC MUSKOGEE
NUMIDIAN NYAMWEZI OSSETIAN
PAMPANGO PHRYGIAN POLABIAN
PORTUGAL PRUSSIAN RABBINIC
ROMANIAN SABELLIC SANSKRIT
SAWAIORI SCOTTISH SCYTHIAN
SEBUNDOY SEECHELT SHAMBALA
SHIRIANA SHOSHONE SICILIAN
SLAVONIC SOUTHRON SQUAMISH
SUBARIAN SUBTIABA SUMATRAN
SUMERIAN TAHITIAN TALMUDIC
TAMASHEK THRACIAN TURCOMAN
VENETIAN VOLSCIAN WOGULIAN
YUGOSLAV YUKAGHIR CANAANITE
(— **THAT CONDEMNS**) ABUSE
(**ARTIFICIAL** —) RO IDO ARULO
NOVIAL VOLAPUK ESPERANTO
(**FIGURATIVE** —) IMAGERY
(**FLORID** —) SILLABUB
(**FOOLISH** —) STUFF FLUMMERY
(**FOUL** —) SMUT ORDURE
(**GYPSY** —) CALO
(**INCOMPREHENSIBLE** —) CHOCTAW
(**INTERNATIONAL** —) ANGLIC
(**LATIN** —) GRAMMAR HUMANITY
(**NONSENSICAL** —) BANTER
(**OBSCENE** —) BAWDY BAWDRY

(**ORDINARY** —) PROSE
(**OVERPRETENTIOUS** —) BOMBAST
(**PERT** —) SAUCE
(**PIDGIN** —) SABIR CAVITENO
FANAKALO
(**PLAIN** —) CLEAR
(**SECRET** —) ARGOT
(**SHOWY** —) FLUBDUB
(**UNCLEAN** —) SEWERAGE
(**UNIVERSAL** —) PASILALY
(**WELSH** —) CYMRAEG
(PL.) BALTIC FINNIC MAHORI SEMITIC
SUDANIC ILLYRIAN
LANGUE D'OC LEMOSI LIMOSI
LANGUET LANGUID LANGUAGE
LANGUID WAN LANK DOWIE FAINT
DREAMY FEEBLE SICKLY SUPINE
TORPID CARELESS FLAGGING
HEEDLESS INDOLENT LISTLESS
SLUGGISH
LANGUISH DIE FADE FALL FLAG
PINE WILT DROOP DWINE FAINT
SWOON SICKEN WITHER DECLINE
LANGUISHING FADE SICK LANGUID
LANGUOR KEF KIF ENNUI DEBILITY
LANGUR DOUC MAHA LOTONG
LUTONG SIMPAI WANDEROO
LANK LEAN THIN GAUNT LANKY
SLANK MEAGER MEAGRE SLUNKEN
LANKY LEAN RENKY SLINK GANGLY
GANGLING
LANOLIN LANUM DEGRAS
LANSEH DUKU LANSA LANZON
LANTANA OREGANO
LANTERN (ALSO SEE LAMP) BUAT
BOUET BOWET DARKY LIGHT
CUPOLA LOUVER PHAROS SCONCE
THOLUS CIMBORIC LANTHORN
(— **ON ROOF**) FEMEREIL
(**DARK** —) DARKY ABSONSA
ABSCONCE
(**ELEVATED** —) PHAROS
(**OPTICAL** —) EPISCOPE
LANTERN FISH INIOME
LANTERN FLOUNDER MEGRIM
LANTERN FLY FULGORID
LANTERN PINION RUNDLE
TRUNDLE
LANYARD WAPP GILGUY LANIARD
BACKROPE
LAODAMIA (**FATHER OF** —) ACASTUS
(**HUSBAND OF** —) PROTESILAUS
(**MOTHER OF** —) HIPPOLYTE
LAODICE (**FATHER OF** —) PRIAM
(**HUSBAND OF** —) HELICAON
(**MOTHER OF** —) HECUBA
LAOIGHIS LEIX
LAOMEDON (**SON OF** —) PRIAM

LAOS

CAPITAL: VIENTIANE
COIN: KIP
MEASURE: BAK
MOUNTAIN: BIA LAI LOI SAN COPI
  KHAT ATWAT KHOUNG TIUBIA
PEOPLE: LU KHA LAO MEO YAO
  THAI

RIVER: NOI DONE KHONG MEKONG SEBANG
TOWN: NAPE PAKSE XIENG PAKLAY THAKHEK

LAP LEP LIP BARM FOLD GORE LICK SLAP SLOD SOSS SUCK WASH WELT LAPPER LAPPET SHOVEL INTERLAP
(— **IN STEEL**) SPILL
(— **OF STRAKES**) LAND
LAPACHOL TECOMIN
LAPBOARD PANEL
LAPDOG MESSAN MESSET SHOUGH
LAPEL LAPPET REVERE REVERS
LAPIDARY STONER GEMMARY LAPIDIST
LAPILLUS RAPILLO
(PL.) CINDER
LAPIS LAZULI AZURE
LAP-JOINTED CLINCH
LAPP LAPPISH LAPPONIC
LAPPED FOLIATED
LAPPET LAP PAN BARBE FANON LABEL CORNET INFULA PINNER
LAPSE DROP FADE FALL HALT SLIP ERROR FAULT FOLLY SPACE TRACT EFFLUX HIATUS LAPSUS DELAPSE ESCHEAT FAILURE PROCESS RELAPSE RESOLVE SLIDING ABEYANCE CADUCITY
(— **OF MEMORY**) BLACKOUT
(PL.) LACHES
LAPSED CADUCOUS
LAPSTRAKE CLINCH
LAPWING WEEP WYPE PEEWEE PLOVER TIRWIT HORNPIE PEEWEEP PIEWIPE TEUCHIT FLOPWING PEESWEEP TEEWHAAP TERUTERU
LARBOARD PORT BABURD
LARCENY THEFT FELONY ROBBERY BURGLARY STEALAGE
LARCH LARICK JUNIPER EPINETTE TAMARACK
LARD MORT SAIM ADEPS DAUBE ENARM FLARE FLECK FLICK AXUNGE ENLARD INLARD NEUTRAL SAINDOUX
LARDED PIQUE CADUCE CADUCOUS
LARDER CAVE PANTRY SPENCE BUTTERY LARDINER
LARGE BIG BULL FEAT GOOD LONG MAIN ROOM TALL AMPLE BULKY BURLY GRAND GREAT GROSS HUSKY JOLLY LARGY MACRO MAXIM RENKY ROUND SMART SPACY WALLY GAWSIE GOODLY HEROIC MAXIMA STRONG TRABAL BOWERLY CAPITAL COPIOUS FAIRISH FEARFUL HEALTHY HULKING LASKING LIBERAL MASSIVE SIZABLE CHOPPING PLUMPING SENSIBLE SWACKING
(— **AND HOLLOW**) CAVAL
(— **AND ROUND**) SIDE
(— **IN DIAMETER**) STOUT
(**APPALLINGLY** —) HIDEOUS
(**EXTREMELY** —) GIANT DECUMAN GIGANTIC

(**FAIRLY** —) SMART
(**INDEFINITELY** —) NTH INFINITE
(**MODERATELY** —) FAIR
(**UNUSUALLY** —) HEAVY SKELPIN SKELPING
(**VERY** —) HUGE ROYAL BOXCAR INGENT NATION GOLIATH INTENSE BEHEMOTH SLAPPING SWINGING WHACKING
LARGE-FOOTED MEGAPOD
LARGE-FRAMED ROOMY
LARGE-LETTERED UNCIAL
LARGELY BIG HARD BIGLY
LARGENESS MICKLE BREADTH FREEDOM GIANTISM LARGEOUR
LARGEST BEST MAXIMUS
LARIA BRUCHUS
LARIAT ROPE LASSO RIATA CABESTRO
LARK GAME FROLIC PEEWEE SCHEME LAVROCK LAYROCK SKYLARK CALANDER LAVEROCK
LARKA KOLS HO
LARKSPUR LOCOWEED
LARNITE BELITE
LARRIKIN NUT ROWDY HOODLUM
LARVA BOT BLOW BOTT CRAB GRUB HUHU SLUG TURK WOLF WORM ALIMA ASCON BARDY BRUKE ERUCA LEECH OTTER REDIA SYCON CORBIE COSSID DRAGON EPHYRA GRUGRU HOPPER LEPTUS LEUCON LOOPER MAGGOT MEASLE NIGGER PEDLAR TORCEL WABBLE WORMIL WOUBIT ATROCHA BUDWORM CADELLE CREEPER DIPORPA FIGWORM FLYBLOW GORDIAN HYPOPUS PEDDLER PLANULA PLUTEUS PREPUPA WIGGLER ACTINULA ANTIZOEA ARMYWORM BOLLWORM BOMBYCID BOOKWORM CASEWORM CERCARIA COENURUS CYRTOPIA DEUTOVUM DROPWORM EPHYRULA FIREWORM FURCILIA GEOMETER GILTTAIL GLOWWORM GNATWORM LEAFTIER LEAFWORM MUCKWORM NAUPLIUS PILIDIUM ROOTWORM SCYPHULA SEMIPUPA SILKWORM SKINWORM SPANWORM SPRAWLER STAGWORM SUBIMAGO TORNARIA VERMICLE WASPLING WIREWORM WOODGRUB WOODWORM
LARVACEA ATREMATA COPELATA
LARVAL NEPIONIC
LARYNGITIS CROUP
LASCIVIOUS LEWD NICE SALT HORNY LUBRIC WANTON BLISSOM FLESHLY GOATISH
LASCIVIOUSNESS LECHERY ASELGEIA LUXURITY
LASERWORT SILPHIUM
LASH CUT BEAT FIRK FLOG JERK LACE WELT WHIP WIRE YERK LEASE LEASH SCORE SKEEG SLASH THONG WHALE CANVAS LAINER LAUNCH STRIPE SWINGE SWITCH FLYFLAP KURBASH SCOURGE
(— **TOGETHER**) RACK
LASHER THONGMAN

LASHING YARK YERK GAMMON LISTING MOUSING SEIZING SLATING FRAPPING
(PL.) OODLES OODLINS SLITHERS
LASS TIB GILL PRIM TRULL DAMSEL KUMMER LASSIE DAMOZEL LASSIKY TENDREL MUCHACHA
LASSITUDE LANGUOR LETHARGY
LASSO LASH LAZO ROPE RIATA LARIAT CABESTRO
LAST ABY LAG DURE HOLD KEEP RIDE SAVE ABIDE FINAL SERVE ABEGGE ENDURE LATEST LATTER REMAIN ULTIMA UTMOST DARREIN DERNIER EXTREME PERDURE SUPREME CONTINUE EVENTUAL HINDMOST LATEMOST REARMOST TERMINAL ULTIMATE
(— **BUT ONE**) PENULT
(— **OUT**) SPIN STAY
(**AT** —) FINALLY
(**THE** —) OMEGA
LASTING FIXED LASTY DURANT DURING STABLE ABIDING DURABLE DUREFUL CONSTANT ENDURING LIVELONG REMANENT STANDING
(— **FOR LONG PERIOD**) AEONIC AEONIAL
(— **FOR ONE DAY**) DIARY DIURNAL
LASTINGNESS STAY DURATION
LAST SUPPER CENA COENA MAUNDY
LAT STAMBHA
LATCH FLY PIN HASP RISP CATCH CHAIR CLICK CLINK SNECK SNICK KEEPER CLICKET
LATCHET DAG TAB SANDAL LANGUET
LATCHING LASKET
LATCHKEY CLICKET PASSKEY
LATE LAG NEW DEEP RIPE SLOW TARDY TARDIVE UMWHILE ADVANCED LATEWARD SOMETIME UMQUHILE
LATELY LATE ALATE NEWLY
LA TENE MARNEAN
LATENT HIDDEN ABEYANT DORMANT LATITANT
LATER POI SIN ANON POST SYNE AFTER ELDER BEHIND FUTURE LATTER PUISNE ANOTHER INFERIOR UMQUHILE
LATERAL SIDE
LATERALLY SIDELONG
LATERITE CABOOK
LATEST LAST LATTER FARTHEST FURTHEST
LATEX GUTTA SORVA
LATH SLAT SPAIL SPALE SPELL SWALE REEPER SPLENT SPLINT STOOTH LATHING FOREPOLE LATHWORK
LATHE LAY SLEY TURN LAITH THROW BEATER WISKET
(— **FOR CYLINDERS**) BROAD
(— **OF LOOM**) LAY
(**TURNING** —) THROW
(**WATCHMAKER'S** —) TURN TURNS MANDREL

LATHER FOAM SUDS FROTH FREATH
SAPPLES
LATHERED SOAPY
LATIN ROMAN HISPERIC LATINITY
(— COMPOSITION) VULGUS
LATIN-AMERICAN LATIN LADINO
LATINO HISPANIC
LATINUS (DAUGHTER OF —) LAVINIA
(FATHER OF —) FAUNUS
(SON-IN-LAW OF —) AENEAS
(WIFE OF —) AMATA
LATITUDE SCOPE WIDTH EXTENT
HEIGHT
(HELIOCENTRIC —) LIMIT
LATONA (DAUGHTER OF —) DIANA
(FATHER OF —) COEUS
(MOTHER OF —) PHOEBE
(SON OF —) APOLLO
LATRIA ADORATION
LATRINE PRIVY TOILET BOGGARD
LATTER LAST FINAL RECENT
SECOND PRESENT
(— PORTION) AUTUMN
LATTICE GRATE HERSE TWINE
PINJRA UMBREL GRATING CANCELLI
(— OF POINTS) SATIN
(MOVING —) APRON
LATTICE PLANT LACELEAF
LATTICEWORK ARBOR GRATE
GRATING TUKUTUKU

LATVIA
CAPITAL: RIGA
COIN: LAT RUBLIS KAPEIKA
SANTIMAS
MEASURE: STOF KANNE STOFF
STOOF VERST ARSHIN KULMET
SAGENE VERCHOC KROUCHKA
POURVETE
PEOPLE: LETT
RIVER: AA OGRE GAUJA SALACA
LIELUPE
TOWN: CESIS LIBAU DVINSK
LIBAVA TUKUMS JELGAVA
REZEKNE DUNABURG VALMIERA
WEIGHT: LIESPFUND

LAUAN KALUNTI
LAUD EXTOL PRAISE ADVANCE
APPLAUD COMMEND GLORIFY
MAGNIFY EMBLAZON EULOGIZE
MACARIZE
LAUDATION EULOGY PRAISE
LAUDATORY SNEER EPENETIC
PRAISING
LAUGH GAFF CHUCK FLEER LEUGH
RISUS ARRIDE NICKER TITTER
CHORTLE GRIZZLE SNICKER
SNIGGER SNIRTLE TWITTER
LAUGHTER
(— CONTEMPTUOUSLY) SNORT
DERIDE
(— GLEEFULLY) CHECKLE
(— HYSTERICALLY) CHECKLE
(— IN AFFECTED MANNER) GIGGLE
(— IN COARSE MANNER) FLEER
GUFFAW
(— LIKE HEN) CACKLE
(— LOUDLY) GAFF GUFFAW

(— QUIETLY) GULE SMUDGE
CHUCKLE SNIRTLE
(BELLY —) BOFF BOFFOLA
(LOUD —) GAUSTER
LAUGHABLE ODD RICH COMIC
DROLL FUNNY MERRY QUEER WITTY
AMUSING COMICAL RISIBLE
STRANGE WAGGISH FARCICAL
HUMOROUS LAUGHING PLEASANT
SPORTIVE
LAUGHING RIANT RIDENT IRRISION
(— MATTER) MOWS
LAUGHING GULL PEWIT
LAUGHING OWL WEKAU WHEKAU
LAUGHINGSTOCK GUY BUTT JEST
JOKE SONG SPORT DERISION
RIDICULE
LAUGHTER JOKE MIRTH RISUS
SNIRT CACKLE LAWTER SPLEEN
HILARITY
LAUNCE LANT LANCE SMELT
AMMODYTE SANDLING
LAUNCH PUT BURST DRIVE LANCE
ELANCE STRIKE BAPTIZE PINNACE
STEAMER VIBRATE CATAPULT
(— HOSTILELY) DIRECT
LAUNCHER (ROCKET —) BAZOOKA
LAUNDER TYE WASH TRUNK SLUICE
STRAKE LAUNDRY
LAUNDRESS TRILBY LAVENDER
LAUNDRY WASH LAVATORY
LAUREL BAY IVY LAURY UNITE
WICKY DAPHNE KALMIA MALLET
MYRTLE CAJEPUT IVYWOOD
WOEVINE BREWSTER CALFKILL
(GROUND —) ARBUTUS
LAUREL OAK ACAJOU
LAURIC PICHURIC
LAURUSTINE VIBURNUM
LAUSUS (FATHER OF —) NUMITOR
MEZENTIUS
(SISTER OF —) ILIA
(SLAYER OF —) AMULIUS
LAUTVERSCHIEBUNG SHIFT
LAVA AA ASHES SPINE COULEE
LATITE SCORIA VERITE FAVILLA
LAPILLO MALPAIS ASPERITE
ORENDITE PAHOEHOE
(SCORIACEOUS —) AA SLAG
(SLAGGY —) SCORIA
LAVABO LAVATORY
LAVAGE LAVATION LAVEMENT
LAVALAVA SULU
LAVAN KALUNTI
LAVATORY BASIN LAVETTE
WASHROOM
LAVE LIP WASH BATHE SPLASH
LAVENDER BEHN ASPIC BEHEN
SPICK SPIKE INKROOT LAVANDIN
STICHADO
LAVER SION SLAKE SLOKE LOUTER
PHIALE AMANORI CISTERN
LAVINIA (FATHER OF —) LATINUS
(HUSBAND OF —) AENEAS
(MOTHER OF —) AMATA
LAVISH FREE LASH LUSH FLUSH
LARGE SPEND SPORT WASTE
COSTLY WANTON COPIOUS
OPULENT PROFUSE GENEROUS

LUCULLAN PRODIGAL SQUANDER
WASTEFUL
LAVISHNESS WASTE FINERY LAVISH
LAW ACT FAS IUS JUS LAY LEX ADAT
DOOM JURE RULE CANON DROIT
NOMOS TORAH BYELAW BYRLAW
DECREE DHARMA EQUITY DANELAW
DERECHO HALACHA HALAKAH
JUSTICE PRECEPT SETNESS
STATUTE JUDGMENT JUDICIAL
ROGATION STATEWAY TANISTRY
(—S OF MANU) SUTRA SUTTA
(BEDOUIN —) THAR
(DIETARY —S) KASHRUTH
(ISLAMIC —) ADA BAI ADAT SHERI
SHARIA SHERIAT
(MARRIAGE —) LEVIRATE
(OPPOSING —) ANTINOMY
(PROPOSED —) BILL
(UNIVERSAL —) HEAVEN
(PL.) LORS
LAW-ABIDING LAWFUL
LAWBREAKER FELON HOUGHER
LAWFUL DUE LEAL TRUE VERY
LEGAL LICIT LOYAL VALID KINDLY
LEEFUL ENNOMIC LEESOME
INNOCENT LIEFSOME RIGHTFUL
LAWGIVER MINOS MOSES SOLON
LAWYER LAWMAKER
LAWLESS LEWD UNRULY ILLEGAL
MOBBISH ANARCHIC
LAWLESSNESS ANOMY ANOMIE
LAWMAKER LEGIFER
LAWN ARBOR GRASS LINON SWARD
UMPLE CYPRUS BATISTE QUINTIN
TIFFANY
LAWSUIT LIS CASE SAKE SECTA
BRABBLE
LAWYER JET PEAT AVOUE PATCH
SHARK BREHON JURIST LAWMAN
LEGIST SQUIRE WRITER COUNSEL
TEMPLAR DEFENDER LEGISTER
TRAMPLER BARRISTER
LAX DULL FREE LASH LAZY LINK
SLOW SWAG WIDE LARGE LOOSE
RELAX SLACK TARDY REMISS
BACKWARD INACTIVE DISSOLUTE
LAXATIVE LAX LASK APERIENT
HYDROMEL LAPACTIC RELAXANT
SOLUTIVE
LAXITY LASCHETY LATITUDE
LAY LIE SET CLAP LAIC LEWD SLEY
SONG WAGE BIGHT COUCH DITTY
LATHE LEDGE QUIET STAKE STILL
COMMON HAZARD IMPOSE IMPUTE
APPEASE ASCRIBE LAYDOWN
POPULAR SECULAR
(— ASIDE) DOFF DOWN DUMP
SHUCK DEPOSE DIVEST DEPOSIT
(— AWAY) STORE
(— BARE) BARE NAKE TIRL TIRVE
DENUDE DETECT OPPOSE UNCOVER
DENUDATE
(— CLAIM) ASSERT BESPEAK
ARROGATE
(— CROSSWISE) COB
(— DOWN) ABDICATE
(— EGGS) BLOW WARP LEDGE
OVIPOSIT

(— **FLAT**) SQUAT ADPRESS
(— **HOLD OF**) FANG GRIP HENT
TAKE GRIPE LATCH ATHOLD
ATTACH COLLAR COMPRISE
(— **IN BIGHTS**) JAG
(— **IN COIL**) FLEMISH
(— **IN PLEATS**) FOLD
(— **LOW**) STREW STRIKE
(— **OF LOOM**) BEATER
(— **ON**) APPLY INFLICT
(— **OPEN**) BREAK CHINE EXPOSE
UNMASK
(— **OUT**) FRAY PLAT RANGE SPELD
SPEND BEWARE DESIGN EXTEND
SPREAD STREAK STREEK CHECKER
DEVELOP STRETCH CONTRIVE
(— **PRONE**) LEVEL
(— **RUBBLEWORK**) SNECK
(— **SIEGE**) INVEST
(— **SMOOTH**) EVEN
(— **SNARE FOR RABBITS**) HAY
(— **STONE**) PAVE
(— **STRAIGHT**) COMB
(— **TYPE**) CASE
(— **UP**) HEAP HIVE ADDLE HOARD
HUTCH STOCK TREASURE
(— **WASTE**) PEEL WEST HARRY
HAVOC HARASS RAVAGE DESTROY
DESOLATE FORWASTE
LAYBOY JOGGER
LAYDOWN LAYOUT SPREAD
LAYER BED LAY BARK CAKE COAT
DASS FACE FILM FLAP FOLD LAIR
SEAM SKIN WEFT ZONA CHESS
COUCH COVER CRUST CUTIS FLAKE
FLASH LEDGE SCALE CARPET
COURSE FASCIA FILLER FOLIUM
INTINE LAMINA LISSOM STREAK
BLANKET COATING CUTICLE
EPICARP FEATHER FLAVEDO
GANGMAN INLAYER LAMELLA
PACKING PHELLEM PROPAGO
PROVINE STRATUM SUBCOAT
SUPPORT ECTOCYST ECTOSARC
ENDOCYST ENDODERM EPIBLAST
EPIBLEMA EPISPORE EPITHECA
INTERBED MOLLISOL PERIOPLE
SUBCRUST
(— **IN FUNGI**) HYMENIUM
(— **OF BLOOD VESSEL**) EXTIMA
EXTERNA
(— **OF CELLS**) EXINE CORTEX
EXTINE CAMBIUM
(— **OF CLAY**) GLEY SELVAGE
SELVEDGE
(— **OF EARTH**) SPIT
(— **OF FAT**) LEAF FINISH
(— **OF FELT**) BAT BATT
(— **OF FIBER**) LAP
(— **OF FINE MATERIAL**) CUSHION
(— **OF FOREST GROWTH**)
SUBSTORY
(— **OF FUEL**) FIREBED
(— **OF GLASS**) CASING
(— **OF IRIS**) UVEA
(— **OF MEAT**) SPINE
(— **OF NERVE FIBERS**) ALVEUS
(— **OF ORGANIC MATTER**) FLOOR
(— **OF PLASMA**) BUFFCOAT

(— **OF ROCK**) CAP SHELF SHELL
SLATE FOLIUM SEPTUM BLISTER
SKULLCAP
(— **OF ROOTS**) SOLE
(— **OF SEDIMENT**) WARP
(— **OF SHALE**) BONE
(— **OF SHEEPSKIN**) FLESHER
(— **OF SHOE HEEL**) LIFT
(— **OF SILT**) VARVE
(— **OF SKIN**) DERM DERMA EPIDERM
(— **OF SOIL**) SOLUM CALLOW
CASING HARDPAN HORIZON
(— **OF STONES**) DASS DESS
(— **OF TANBARK**) HAT
(— **OF TISSUE**) BED DARTOS FASCIA
SEROSA ELASTICA EPIBLEMA
(— **OF TOBACCO LEAVES**) HANGER
(— **OF TURF**) FLAW
(— **OF WHITE MATTER**) CAPSULE
(— **OF WOOD**) CORE
(**BONY** —) LAMELLA CEMENTUM
(**BOTTOM** —) BEDDING
(**FLAT** —) BED FLAP FLAKE
(**GERM** —) MESODERM
(**IMPERVIOUS** —) LINING
(**OUTER** —) HUSK
LAYERING LAP GOOTEE STOOLING
LAYMAN LAIC CLERK IDIOT DEACON
SECULAR DEFENSOR EXHORTER
EXOTERIC FAMILIAR STRANGER
WORLDMAN
LAYOFF FURLOUGH
LAYOUT MISE DUMMY SETOUT
(— **OF CARDS**) TABLEAU
LAZARETTO SPITAL SPITTLE
LAZINESS LAZE SLOTH SLOUCH
OISIVITY
LAZULITE SIDERITE
LAZY ARGH IDLE LASS DOXIE DRONY
FAINT INERT LINGY LUSKY RESTY
SLOAN SLOTH CLUMSY LIMPSY
LURDAN LUTHER ORNERY SWEERT
TRAILY CLUMPST LUSKISH PEAKISH
SLIVING DROGHLIN FAINEANT
FECKLESS INDOLENT LITHERLY
OSCITANT SLOTHFUL SLUGGARD
THOWLESS TRIFLING
LEA LAY GRASS LAYER LAYLAND
LEALAND
LEACH TAP LETCH SOFTEN
LEAD GO TEE VAN WIN BEAR DADE
GIVE GROW HAVE HEAD HERD LEED
SLIP TAKE TEEM WORK BLAZE
BOUND BRING CARRY GREBE GUIDE
MAYNE PILOT PRESA SOUND START
TRAIN TREAT CONVEY DEDUCE
DIRECT ESCORT INDUCE INDUCT
LEADER SATURN BEGUILE CAPTAIN
CONDUCE CONDUCT LEADING
MARSHAL PIGTAIL PIONEER
PLUMBUM PLUMMET LEADSMAN
MANUDUCE MANUDUCT SQUIRREL
(— **A BAND**) BATON
(— **AND SUPPORT**) DADE
(— **ASIDE**) CHAR SINGLE
(— **ASTRAY**) ERR MANG TURN WARP
BEFOOL BETRAY ENTICE WANDER
WILDER DEBAUCH MISLEAD
MISWEND PERVERT SOLICIT

TRADUCE BEWILDER INVEIGLE
MISGUIDE
(— **AWAY**) CHAR ABDUCT DIVERGE
(— **BACK**) REDUCT
(— **FORCIBLY**) ESCORT
(— **IN CARD GAME**) SNEAK
(— **IN RACE**) LAP
(— **IN SINGING**) PRECENT
(— **INTO ERROR**) ABUSE DELUDE
(— **MONOXIDE**) MASSICOT
(— **ON**) TRAIL
(— **PASSIVE EXISTENCE**) VEGETATE
(— **POISONING**) PLUMBISM
(**BLACK** —) WAD WADD GRAPHITE
(**COLOR** —) PLOMB
(**DEEP-SEA** —) DIPSY DIPSEY
(**OVERLAPPING** —) DRIP
(**PLUMBING** —) BLUEY
(**SYMBOL FOR** —) PB
(**WHITE** —) KREMS CERUSE
LEAD-COLORED WAN BLAE
LEADEN HEAVY PLUMBEAN
LEADER BO BOH COB DUX HOB MIR
CAST COCK DUCE DUKE HEAD
HOBB JEFE NAIG NAIK OMDA SOUL
TYEE CHIEF DOYEN ELDER FIRST
MAHDI MOSES OMDEH PILOT SEYID
TRACE ARCHON CALIPH DESPOT
HEADER RECTOR SAYYID TYCOON
ACREMAN ADVISER CAPTAIN
CONDUCT DEMAGOG DRUNGAR
FOREMAN FUEHRER INDUCER
ACCENTOR CAUDILLO DIRECTOR
FUGLEMAN HEADSMAN HERETOGA
LODESMAN PANDARUS STRATEGE
(— **OF DACOITS**) BOH
(— **OF MUTINEERS**) ELECTO
(— **OF REVOLT**) ANARCH
(**BAND** —) BATONEER
(**CHOIR** —) CANTOR
(**CHORUS** —) CHORAGUS
(**COSSACK** —) HETMAN
(**FASCIST** —) RAS
(**INTELLECTUAL** —) BRAIN
(**MOB** —) MOBOCRAT
(**POLITICAL** —) SACHEM
(**PRAYER** —) IMAM
(**RELIGIOUS** —) AGA AGHA SHEIKH
(**SCOUT** —) AKELA SIXER
(**SPIRITUAL** —) GURU SADDIK
GUARDIAN
LEADERSHIP LEAD AEGIS MANRED
CONDUCT IMAMATE LEADING
MANRENT CHIEFDOM GUIDANCE
HEADSHIP HEGEMONY
LEADING BIG BEST COCK DUCT
HEAD LEAD MAIN CHIEF FIRST
PREMIER STELLAR GUIDANCE
(— **OUTWARD**) EMISSARY
(— **TO NOTHING**) IDLE
LEADSMAN SOUNDER
LEADWORK PLUMBAGE PLUMBING
LEADWORT CROWTOE PLUMBAGO
LEAF PAD BACK BARB BUYO FLAG
FLAP FOIL FOLD GEAR PAGE PALM
STUB BLADE BLANK FLIER FLYER
FOLIO FROND GRASS GUARD LEAVE
SCALE SEPAL SIGHT SPILL TEPAL
BONNET CADJAN COUPON FOLIUM

FRAISE FULZIE NEEDLE PEPPER
DAMIANA FOLDOUT HARNESS
LEAFLET TREFOIL WITNESS
PHYLLADE PHYLLOME
(— **FAT**) FLICK
(— **FROM AXIL**) BRACT
(— **OF BOOK**) PAGE FOLIO INSET
PLATE FLYLEAF
(— **OF CALYX**) BARB
(— **OF CORN**) HUSK
(— **OF COROLLA**) PETAL
(— **OF DOOR**) VALVE
(— **OF HEDDLES**) GEAR
(— **OF PALM**) FAN OLA CHIP OLLA
FROND LATANIER
(— **OF SPRING**) BACK
(**BETEL** —) PAN
(**BIBLE** —) COSTMARY
(**DEAD** —) FLAG
(**HOLLOW** —) PHYLLODE
(**SPRING** —) WRAPPER
(**STRAWBERRY** —) FRAISE
(**THIN** —) LAMELLA
(**TOBACCO** —) STRIP CUTTER
WRAPPER
(**WASTE GOLD** —) SKEWING
LEAFAGE FOLIAGE
LEAFHOPPER HOPPER JASSID
THRIPS HOMOPTER
LEAFLET PINNA TRACT MAILER
FOLIOLE STUFFER
(**PAIR OF** —S) JUGUM
(PL.) SENNA CATOBA
LEAFLIKE PHYLLINE
LEAFMOLD KOLINSKY
LEAFY GREEN LEAVY FOLIATE
FOLIOSE FRONDOSE
LEAGUE BOND BUND BANDY BOARD
GUEUX HANSA PARTY UNION WHEEL
CIRCUIT ALLIANCE SYSTASIS
(— **OF NATIONS**) GENEVA
(**BUSH** —S) STICKS
LEAGUED FEDERATE
LEAK BLOW SEEP WEEP GEYZE
SPUNK INLEAK SIGGER SPRING
ZIGGER LEAKAGE MELTERS
SCREEVE
(— **IN ELECTRIC CIRCUIT**) FAULT
LEAKAGE ESCAPE SEEPAGE
(— **OF ELECTRICITY**) CREEPAGE
(— **OF GAS**) SLIP
(— **OF WIND**) RUNNING
LEAKING ALEAK DRIBBLE NAILSICK
LEAKY LEAK UNTIGHT GIZZENED
LEAL FAITHFUL
LEAN BEND BONY HANG HEEL LANK
PEND POOR PRIN RACY RELY REST
STAY SWAY THIN TOOM EMPTY
GAUNT HIELD LANKY LEANY SLANK
SOUND SPARE STOOP HOLLOW
MEAGER RECUMB SKINNY SPRING
UPLEAN ANGULAR FATLESS INCLINE
SCRAGGY SCRAWNY SLUNKEN
STRINGY MACILENT SCRAGGED
SCRANNEL
(— **FOR SUPPORT**) ABUT
(— **FORWARD**) PROCLINE
(— **OVER**) WHAUVE
LEANER HOBBER

LEANING DRIFT FLAIR PENCHE
HANGING ACCLINAL ENCLITIC
FROMWARD
(— **BACKWARD**) SUPINE
(**STRONG** —) GENIUS PENCHANT
LEANNESS LANK POVERTY
SPARENESS
LEAN-TO SHED LINTER OUTSHOT
SKILLION
LEAP FLY HOP POP BEND DART DIVE
FALL GIVE JUMP LOPE LOUP RAMP
RISE SKIT WIND BOUND BREAK
CAPER DANCE EXULT FLIER FLYER
FRISK LUNGE PRIME SALTO SAULT
SCOPE SCOUP SPANG STEND VAULT
BOUNCE BREACH CURVET INSULT
LAUNCH SPRENT SPRING SPRUNT
WALLOP REBOUND SALTARY
SALTATE SUBSULT BUCKJUMP
LEAPFROG SPANGHEW UPSPRING
(— **BACK**) RESULT SPRUNT
(— **FOR JOY**) EXULT
(— **IN DANCING**) STOT
(— **LIGHTLY**) SKIP
(— **OF HORSE**) CURVET BALOTADE
CAPRIOLE
(— **OF WHALE**) BREACH
(— **OUT**) SALLY
(— **OVER**) FREE OVER SKIP CLEAR
HURDLE
(— **UPON**) ASSAIL
(**BALLET** —) JETE CABRIOLE
(**FROLICSOME** —) CAPER
(**SUICIDAL** —) BRODIE
(PL.) ALLEGRO
LEAPING GAMBOL SPRING SALIENT
SALTANT
LEARCHUS (**BROTHER OF** —)
MELICERTA
(**FATHER OF** —) ATHAMAS
(**MOTHER OF** —) INO
LEARN DO GET SEE WIT ARAL FIND
HAVE HEAR LEAR LERE EDIFY
GLEAN STUDY RECORD REALIZE
RECEIVE DISCOVER
(— **FROM EXPERIENCE**) ASSAY
LEARNED BLUE SEEN LERED LORED
DUCTUS BOOKISH CLERKLY
CUNNING ERUDITE STUDIED TUITIVE
ACADEMIC CLERGIAL LETTERED
OVERSEEN POLYMATH SCIENCED
(— **MAN**) OLLAV
(**AFFECTEDLY** —) INKHORN
(**SOMETHING TO BE** —) LIRIPIPE
LEARNEDLY CLERKLY
LEARNER PUPIL NOVICE TRAINEE
PRENTICE
(**LATE** —) OPSIMATH
LEARNING ART WIT BOOK LEIR
LERE LORE CLERGY WISDOM
APPRISE CUNNING GRAMMAR
INSIGHT LETTERS WISTING
BOOKLEAR BOOKLORE DOCTRINE
HUMANISM LETTRURE MATHESIS
PEDANTRY
LEASE FEU FEW LET SET FARM HIRE
RENT TACK COWLE DIMIT FIRMA
LISSE DEMISE POTTAH RENTAL
ASSEDAT CHARTER SETTING

BACKTACK SUBLEASE
LEASEHOLDER LIVIER
LEASH LEAD LYME SLIP LEASE
COUPLE STRING SWINGE
(— **OF HOUNDS**) HARL
(**DOG** —) SLIP TRASH TIRRET
(**HAWK'S** —) LOYN LUNE TIRRET
CREANCE
LEASING LOCATIO
LEAST LEST MINIMAL MINIMUM
MINIMUS
(**AT** —) HURE
LEAST FLYCATCHER CHEBEC
LEAST SANDPIPER PEEP OXEYE
STINT
LEATHER ELK KID BEND BOCK BUFF
CALF CAPE HIDE NAPA SEAL ADUST
ALUTA BALAT FLANK NIGER RETAN
SUEDE BULGAR CASTOR CHROME
LIZARD ORIOLE OXHIDE PEBBLE
RUSSET SKIVER TURKEY BELTING
BUFFING CANEPIN CHAMOIS
COWHIDE COWSKIN DEGRAIN
DOGSKIN DONGOLA HEADCAP
HOGSKIN KIDSKIN MURRAIN
PANCAKE PECCARY PERSIAN
SAFFIAN ANTELOPE BUCKSKIN
BULLNECK CABRETTA CALFSKIN
CAPESKIN CHEVEREL COLTSKIN
CORDOBAN CORDWAIN DEERSKIN
GOATSKIN KANGAROO LAMBSKIN
SHAGREEN
(— **FOR DRESSING FLAX**) RIBSKIN
(— **SHREDS**) MOSLINGS
(— **STRIP**) RAND
(**ARABIAN** —) MOCHA
(**ARTIFICIAL** —) KERATOL
(**BOARDED** —) BOX
(**CORDOVAN** —) CORDOBAN
CORDWAIN
(**MOROCCO** —) LEVANT MAROQUIN
(**PATCH OF** —) CLOUT
(**PRUSSIAN** —) SPRUCE
(**RUSSIAN** —) YUFT BULGAR RUSSIA
JUCHTEN
(**SHEEPSKIN** —) BOCK BUCK
(**SOFT** —) ALUTA
(**SUPERIOR** —) BUFF
(**WASH** —) LOSH LOSHE
LEATHERBACK LUTH
LEATHERFISH LIJA FOOLFISH
LEATHERJACKET FILEFISH
ZAPATERO
LEATHERLEAF CASSANDRA
LEATHERWOOD DIRCA WICOPY
BURNWOOD FIREWOOD IRONWOOD
LEADWOOD ROPEBARK
LEATHERWORKER TAWER BEDDER
CHAMAR MADIGA FLUFFER
CHUCKLER
LEAVE GO GET LET BUNK DROP
FADE FLEE HOOK LEAF PART QUIT
VADE VOID WALK AVOID FAVOR
FORGO GRACE SHOVE WAIVE
BUGGER DEPART DESERT DEVOID
FORLET PERMIT RETIRE SECEDE
STRAND VACATE FORLEIT FORLESE
FORSAKE LARGESS LIBERTY
LICENSE FAREWELL PATIENCE
UNTENANT

(**— ALONE**) FORBEAR DESOLATE
(**— BEHIND**) LET PLANT DISTANCE
(**— BRIGHT TRAIL**) STREAM
(**— BY WILL**) BEQUEATH
(**— COVER**) BREAK
(**— HASTILY**) SCUR SKIRR
(**— HURRIEDLY**) CUT BLOW FLEE
JUMP SCAT SKIP
(**— IN ISOLATION**) MAROON
(**— IN SAFEKEEPING**) CHECK
(**— NOTHING TO BE DESIRED**)
SATISFY
(**— OF ABSENCE**) ABSIT LIBERTY
FURLOUGH
(**— OFF**) CEASE DEVAL PETER
BILEVE CHEESE DESIST SURCEASE
(**— OUT**) BATE OMIT SKIP SLIP
ELIDE
(**— PORT**) CLEAR
(**— QUICKLY**) SCREW
(**— SECRETLY**) STEAL
(**— SUDDENLY**) KITE
LEAVEN ZYM ZYMO RAISE YEAST
INFUSE RAISING SOURING
LEAVENING EMPTINGS
LEAVES PATRIN FOLIAGE LEAFAGE
LEAFERY
(**— OF BAOBAB TREE**) LALO
(**— OF ORCHID**) FAHAM
(**— OF TOBACCO**) LEAF FLYINGS
SECONDS
(**— ON STEM AFTER WITHERING**)
INDUVIAE
(**— USED AS STYPTIC**) MATICO
(**BOILED — OF POTHERB**) CHARD
(**DRIED —**) LAUHALA
(**MEDICINAL —**) COCA FILE BUCCO
BUCKU FARFARA FUMARIA
(**PALM —**) ATAP ATTAP CADJAN
CAJANG
(**TEA —**) SOUCHONG
(**WITHERED —**) PININGS
LEAVE-TAKING VALE ADIEU
CONGEE PARTING WAYGANG
FAREWELL WAYGOING
LEAVING BIT
(**PL.**) RAFF SNUFF REFUSE RESIDUE
RESIDUUM

LEBANON
CAPITAL: BEIRUT BEYROUTH
COIN: LIVRE PIASTRE
MOUNTAIN: ARUBA HERMON
SANNINE KENISSEH
PLAIN: ELBIKA
RIVER: LYCOS DAMOUR LITANI
HASBANI LEONTES KASEMIEH
SEAPORT: TYRE SAIDA SIDON
BEIRUT
TOWN: SUR TYRE SAIDA SIDON
ZAHLE ZAHLHA TRIPOLI
MERJUYUN
VALLEY: BEQAA

LEBBEK KOKO KOKKO SIRIS
LEBKUCHEN LEKACH
LECHER GOAT LUXUR PALLIARD
LECHEROUS LEWD PRIME WANTON

BOARISH CODDING GOATISH
LUSTFUL LIKEROUS SCABROUS
SPORTIVE
LECHERY LUXURY
LECTERN DESK EAGLE LUTRIN
LATERAN LATTERIN
LECTION GOSPEL EPISTLE READING
PROPHECY
LECTIONARY LEGEND
LECTOR LISTER READER
LECTURE JOBE CREED FORUM
HOMILY LECTOR LESSON SERMON
ADDRESS EARBASH HEARING
PRELECT READING JOBATION
ORDINARY
LECTURER DOCENT LECTOR
READER DRYASDUST
LEDA (DAUGHTER OF —) HELEN
CLYTEMNESTRA
(**FATHER OF —**) THESTIUS
(**HUSBAND OF —**) TYNDAREUS
(**SON OF —**) CASTOR POLLUX
LEDGE BEAD BERM DESS LINE STEP
ALTAR BENCH CLINT SHELF SNOUT
BEARER OFFSET SETTLE STANCE
CHANNEL LEDGING RETABLE
LEDGEMAN BREAKER
LEDGER BOOK SLAB LIEGER
JOURNAL OVERLIER
LEDGER BOARD RIBBON
LEE LEW LEEWARD
LEECH GILL HARPY LEACH APODAN
BDELLOID HELMINTH
LEEK ALLIUM PORRET SCALLION
(**— COLORED**) PRASINE
LEER LEAR LOOK OGLE FLEER
LEERY SKIME SMIRK TWIRE
LEERFISH GARRICK
LEES LAGS ADDLE DRAFF DREGS
DROSS GROUT AMURCA BOTTOM
DUNDER MOTHER ULLAGE
GROUNDS EMPTINGS SEDIMENT
WINEDRAF
LEEWAN SOFA DIVAN
LEEWARD DOWNWIND
LEEWAY DRIFT
LEFT G CAR KAY GAWK NEAR OTHER
TOWARD DESERTED
(**— EYE**) OL OS
LEFT-HAND GAUCHE
LEFT HAND MG MS SM SIN
(**— PAGE**) VERSO
LEFTHANDED CAR GAUCHE
AWKWARD DUBIOUS OBLIQUE
KITHOGUE SOUTHPAW
LEFT-HANDER SOUTHPAW
LEFTOVER END REMNANT
(**TOBACCO —**) TOPPER
(**PL.**) SCRAN ANALECTS
LEG ARM GAM PEG PIN CRUS GAMB
JAMB LIMB TRAM BOUGH GAMBE
JAMBE REACH SHANK STICK STUMP
BENDER GAMBON GAMMON LEGLET
MOGGAN OVIGER PESTLE PLANTA
PROLEG WALKER FORELEG
TRESTLE FORELIMB
(**— OF HAWK**) ARM
(**— OF LAMB**) GIGOT WABBLER
WOBBLER

(**— OF TABLE**) BALUSTER
(**— OF WHEELBARROW**) STILT
(**— USED FOR FOOD**) PESTLE
(**—S OF ARTIFICAL FLY**) HACKLE
(**FURNITURE —**) CABRIOLE
(**MILK —**) WEED
(**TROUSER —**) SLOP
(**WIRE —S**) SLING
(**WOODEN —**) PEG STUMP TIMBER
(**PL.**) PROPS TONGS STAMPS STICKS
LEGACY ENTAIL LEGATE BEQUEST
HERITAGE WINDFALL
LEGAL LEAL LICIT SOUND VALID
LAWFUL SQUARE JURIDIC RIGHTFUL
LEGALISM NOMISM SCRIBISM
LEGALISTIC COURT
LEGATE ENVOY DEPUTY LEGATUS
CONSULAR LEGATARY PANDOLPH
LEGATION MISSION
LEGATO SMOOTH
LEGEND EDDA MYTH POSY SAGA
TALE FABLE STORY TITLE THREAP
CUTLINE HAGGADA
(**MAP —**) KEY
LEGENDARY FABLED FICTIOUS
LEGERDEMAINIST JUGGLER
LEGGING SPAT COCKER BOTTINE
GAMBADO BALATONG BOOTIKIN
CHIVARRA
(**LEATHER —**) STRAD
(**PL.**) CHAPS SHANKS BROGUES
COGGERS GAMASHES LEATHERS
OVERALLS
LEGIBLE FAIR READABLE
LEGION HOST TERZO TERZIO
LEGIONARY ANT DRIVER FORAGER
LEGISLATION DYSNOMY
LAWMAKING
LEGISLATOR SOLON LAWGIVER
LAWMAKER
LEGISLATURE DIET COURT THING
LAGTING RIKSDAG LANDRATH
RIGSRAAD
LEGITIMATE JUST TRUE VERY
LEGAL LEGIT LOYAL HONEST
KINDLY KOSHER LAWFUL REABLE
SQUARE LEGITIME
LEGITIMATELY FAIRLY MULIERLY
LEGPIECE JAMBEAU
LEGUME POD GUAR PULSE LOMENT
PODDER COCHLEA LEGUMEN
PODWARE SOYBEAN STROMBUS
LEIPOA LOWAN MEGAPOD PHEASANT
LEISHMANIASIS UTA ESPUNDIA
LEISTER SPEAR WASTER
LEISURE TIME TOOM VOID OTIUM
RESPITE VACANCY VACATION
LEISURELY SLOW SOODLY TIMELY
TOOMLY GRADUAL PICKTOOTH
LEMAN UNDERPUT
LEMMING CRICETID
LEMMUS MYODES
LEMNISCUS FILET FILLET LAQUEUS
LEMON DOG DUD CEDRA CHLOR
LEMONY CEDRATE FAILURE
KUMQUAT
LEMONADE COOLER
LEMON GRASS TANGLAD
LEMON SOLE MARYSOLE

LEMON VERBENA ALOYSIA
LEMUR MAKI VARI AVAHI INDRI
KOKAM LORIS MACAO POTTO SIFAC
ADAPID COBEGO COLUGO GALAGO
KUBONG MAHOLI MONKEY SIFAKA
NATTOCK PRIMATE SEMIAPE
TARSIER AMPONGUE BABAKOTO
MONGOOSE PRIMATAL TARSIOID
LEND OCKER PREST SECOND
IMPREST
(— **AT INTEREST**) GAVEL
(— **ITSELF**) ALLOY
LENDING (— **AGENCY**) MOUNT
LENGTH LUG DREE TOWT PITCH
SCOPE SIDTH COURSE EXTENT
TOWGHT FOOTAGE DISTANCE
LEGITUDE SIDENESS
(— **ATHWARTSHIP**) ABURTON
(— **OF BRIDGE**) BAY
(— **OF CABLE**) SCOPE SHACKLE
(— **OF CHAIN**) SHOT
(— **OF CLOTH**) CUT
(— **OF FIBER**) STAPLE
(— **OF FISHING LINE**) CAST
(— **OF GEAR TOOTH**) FACE
(— **OF HAIR IN FISHING LINE**) IMP
(— **OF HAIR**) KNOT
(— **OF LINE**) LOYN
(— **OF METAL**) SHAPE
(— **OF MOUTH**) GAPE
(— **OF NET**) LEAD
(— **OF ROPE**) DRIFT SPOKE BRIDLE
COURSE STOPPER
(— **OF SERVICE**) STANDING
(— **OF SHOEMAKER'S THREAD**) END
(— **OF THREAD**) STITCH
(— **OF TILE**) GAUGE
(— **OF TIMBER**) BALK FLITCH
(— **OF TRIP**) GATE
(— **OF WINDMILL ARM**) WHIP
(— **OF YARN**) KNOT TAPE CHASE
SKEIN
(**AT FULL** —) ALONG
(**CONTINUOUS** —) STRETCH
(**FOCAL** —) FOCUS
(**UNIT OF** —) PIC PIK ROD FOOT
INCH KILO PIKE REED VARA WRAP
YARD METER SHAKU POLLEX
FURLONG PLETHRON
(**UTMOST** —) EXTREME
LENGTHEN EKE LONG DILATE
EXPAND EXTEND LENGTH AMPLIFY
DISTEND PRODUCE PROLONG
STRETCH ELONGATE INCREASE
PROTRACT
(— **BY INTERPOLATION**) FARSE
LENGTHENING HOLD ECTASIS
DIASTOLE
LENGTHWISE ALONG ALENGTH
ENDLONG ENDWAYS ENDWISE
LENGTHY LONG LARGE PROLIX
LONGFUL EXTENDED
LENIENCY FAVOR MERCY LENITY
LENIENCE
LENIENT LAX EASY KIND MILD SOFT
FACILE GENTLE HUMANE LENITIVE
LENITIVE MILD MITIGANT SEDATIVE
LENITY MERCY HUMANITY KINDNESS
LENITUDE

LENO GAUZE
LENS EYE CROWN GLASS OPTIC
FLASER READER APLANAT BIFOCAL
CONCAVE CONTACT DOUBLET
ACHROMAT EYEGLASS EYEPIECE
HYPERGON LENTICLE LUNETTES
MENISCUS
(**WITHOUT** —) APHAKIA
LENT CAREME IMPREST
LENTICULAR PHACOID
LENTIGO FRECKLE
LENTIL LENS LINT TILL LENTILE
LENTICLE
LEONTOCEBUS MIDAS
LEOPARD PARD TIGER PARDAL
WAGATI LIBBARD PAINTER PANTHER
PARDALE
(**SNOW** —) IRBIS OUNCE
LEPCHA RONG RONGPA
LEPER LAZAR MESEL LAZARUS
LEPIDOMELANE ANNITE
LEPIDOPTERA GLOSSATA
LEPIDOSIS SCALING
LEPRECHAUN ELF LURACAN
LEPROSY LEPRA MESEL ALPHOS
LAZARY MESELRY
LEPROUS MESELY MESELED
LEPTON MITE
LEPTOSPIROSIS JAUNDICE
LERP LAAP
LESBIAN EROTIC TRIBADE SAPPHIST
LESION PIT GALL HIVE SORE
CRATER ESCHAR LEPRID ANTHRAX
CHANCRE FISSURE LEPROMA
BEESTING ERUPTION LEUKEMID
TERTIARY

LESOTHO

CAPITAL: MASERU
FORMER NAME: BASUTOLAND
LANGUAGE: SOTHO SESOTHO
PEOPLE: BASOTHO
RIVER: ORANGE CALEDON
TOWN: LERIBE QUTHING
MAFETENG

LESPEDEZA SERICEA
LESS FEW MIN MENO FEWER MINOR
LESSER SMALLER WANTING
(— **BY A COMMA**) MINOR
LESSEE FARMER TERMOR HUURDER
TACKSMAN
LESSEN EBB BATE DOCK EASE FAIK
FRET KILL LESS SINK WANE ABATE
BREAK LOWER MINCE SMALL
BUFFER DEJECT IMPAIR INLESS
MINIFY MINISH NARROW REBATE
REDUCE WEAKEN AMENUSE
ASSUAGE CURTAIL DEPLETE
DEPRESS ELEVATE LIGHTEN
RELIEVE SHORTEN CONTRACT
DECREASE DEROGATE DIMINISH
DISCOUNT EMBEZZLE MITIGATE
MODERATE PALLIATE
(— **FORCE**) GELD
(— **IN VALUE**) SHRINK CHEAPEN
(— **SENSITIVITY**) DULL
(— **STRENGTH**) WEAR

(— **TENSION**) RELAX
(— **VELOCITY**) DEADEN
LESSENING LETUP
LESSER MINUTE SMALLER INFERIOR
LESSER CELANDINE PILEWORT
LESSON TAX LEAR TASK STUDY
EXAMPLE LECTURE PRECEPT
READING DOCUMENT LIRIPOOP
(**DIFFICULT** —) SOAK
(**TORAH** —) PARASHAH
LESSOR SETTER
LEST UNLESS ANANTER ANAUNTERS
LET LAT SET HIRE ALLOW LEASE
LEAVE LETTEN PERMIT SUFFER
TENANT
(— **BAIT BOB**) DIB
(— **BECOME KNOWN**) SPILL
(— **BURN**) BISHOP
(— **CONTINUE**) DRILL
(— **DOWN**) DEMIT DIMIT LOWER
STOOP STRIKE SUBMIT
(— **FALL**) DROP VAIL AVALE AWALE
DEPOSE
(— **FLY**) PEG BOLT FIRE WING
(— **GO**) DROP FAIK QUIT DEMIT
BILEVE DEMISE DISMIT UNHAND
DISCARD UNSEIZE
(— **HIM TAKE**) SUM
(— **IN**) IMMIT INLET IMMISS ADHIBIT
(— **IT BE REPEATED**) REPET
(— **IT STAND**) STET
(— **KNOW**) ACQUAINT
(— **LAND**) GAVEL
(— **LOOSE**) FREE SLIP LIBERATE
(— **OUT**) TEAM WAGE BREAK SPILL
ARRENT
(— **SLIP**) CHECK FOREGO
LETDOWN HANGOVER
LETHAL FATAL DEADLY MORTAL
LETHARGIC INERT DROWSY SLEEPY
DORMANT COMATOSE COMATOUS
SLUGGISH SLUMBROUS
LETHARGY STUPOR TORPOR
SLUMBER HEBETUDE INACTION
LETO LATONA
LETT BALT
LETTER EF EL EM EN EX HE AIN AYN
BEE CEE CHI DEE EDH ESS ETA ETH
GEE HET JAY KAY LIL PEE SIN TEE
VEE YOD YOK ZED ZEE ALEF ALIF
AYIN BETA BETH BILL BULL CHIT
DEAD HETH IOTA KAPH SHIN SORT
YODH YOGH AITCH ALEPH BLIND
BREVE DELTA DEMIT FAVOR GAMMA
GIMEL GRAPH KAPPA KNOWN
KOPPA SIGMA STAVE STIFF ZAYIN
ACCENT ADVICE ANSWER BILLET
CADJAN CARTEL CHARTA COCKUP
DALETH FAVVER ITALIC LAMBDA
LAMEDH MEDIAL SCRIPT SIGLUM
SUNNUD SYMBOL VERSAL CODICIL
COLLINS CONTROL DIGAMMA
DIPLOMA EPISTLE EPSILON
KAREETA MISSIVE SPECIAL
AEROGRAM ASCENDER ENCYCLIC
MONITORY NUNDINAL PASTORAL
(— **OF DEFIANCE**) CARTEL
(— **OF PERMISSION**) EXEAT
(—**S DIMISSORY**) APOSTOLI

(—S OF MARQUE) MART
(ANGLO-SAXON —) EDH ETH THORN
(AUTHORIZING —) BREVE
(BEGGING —) SCREEVE
(BLACK —) GOTHIC
(BREAD AND BUTTER —) COLLINS
(CAPITAL —) CAP UNCIAL CAPITAL
FACTOTUM
(FRIENDLY —) SCREED
(LOVE —) POULET
(OFFICIAL —) BRIEF
(PAPAL —) BULL TOME ENCYCLIC
(PRIVATE —) BOOK
(SHORT —) CHIT LINE NOTE BILLET
LETTERET
(SILENT —) MUTE
(SMUGGLED —) KITE
(SUBSCRIPT —) SUBFIX
(WORD —) LOGOGRAM
(PL.) MAIL APOSTOLI
LETTER BOX APARTADO
LETTER CARRIER CORREO
MAILMAN POSTMAN
LETTERER SKETCHER
LETTERING FAC WRITE INCUSE
LETTERPRESS TEXT CAPTION
LETTING FIRMA LOCATIO
LETTING-OUT DROPPING
LETTUCE COS GRASS SALAD
KARPAS SALLET ICEBERG ROMAINE
FIREWEED MILKWEED
LEUCIPPUS (DAUGHTER OF —)
PHOEBE HILAIRA
(FATHER OF —) OENOMAUS
(WIFE OF —) PHILODICE
LEUCITE LENAD
LEUCITITE ITALITE SPERONE
ALBANITE CECILITE
LEUCOCYTE NEOCYTE HEMAMEBA
MONOCYTE OXYPHILE
LEUCOMA WALLEYE
LEUCORRHEA WHITES
LEUKEMIA CHLOROMA LEUKOSIS
LEVANT EASTERN WORMSEED
LEVEE DIKE DYKE WALL WEIR
DURBAR STOPBANK
LEVEL BONE EVEN FAIR FLAT GLAD
LUTE PLAT RAZE SHIM EQUAL
FLUSH GRADE PLAIN PLANE POINT
SLICK SOLID CHARGE DOUBLE
EVENLY FIELDY NIVEAU SLIGHT
SMOOTH STRIKE TUNNEL FLATTEN
GALLERY GANGWAY DEMOLISH
LEVELLER SUBGRADE
(— A RAFTER) EDGE
(— AFTER PLOWING) BUSH
(— AND SCATTER) GELD
(— OF SOCIETY) STRATUM
(— OF STAGE) STUDY
(— OFF) HAMMER BULLDOZE
(— PLACE) PLANILLA
(COMMON —) PAR
(ENERGY —) SINGLET
(EYE —) EYELINE
(HIGHER —S) BRASS
(HIGHEST —) SUMMIT
(LOWEST —) FLOOR BOTTOM
HARDPAN
(MINING —) HEAD GALLERY

GANGWAY
(STRATIGRAPHIC —) HORIZON
(TOP —) HIGH CEILING
LEVELED BENT
LEVELER DIGGER
LEVELING EGALITE EGALITY
LEVER KEY PRY BEAM GAUL HOOK
HORN JACK SWAY TREE FLAIL FLIRT
HELVE PEDAL PINCH PLUTO PRIZE
SPOON STANG STANK SWIPE
THROW BINDER CLUTCH COUPER
DETENT FEELER GAFFLE HAMMER
HEAVER HOPPER LOWDER PORTER
ROCKER TAPPET TILLER BALANCE
BOOTLEG POINTER RAMHEAD
SHIPPER SWINGLE TREADLE
TRIGGER TUMBLER BACKFALL
GAVELOCK SELECTOR THROTTLE
(— ARM) NIGGER
(— FOR CROSSBOW) GAFFLE
GARROT
(— FOR TURNING RUDDER) HELM
TILLER
(— IN KNITTING MACHINE) JACK
(— LIKE CANTHOOK) PEAVY PEAVIE
(— OF GIN) START
(GEARSHIFT —) STICK
(SPINNING —) BOOTLEG
(SPOKELIKE —) SWINGLE
(THROTTLE —) GUN
(WEAVING —) LAM LAMM SWELL
BINDER TIPPLER
LEVERAGE PRY PRIZE
LEVIGATE DUST
LEVITY FOLLY HUMOR GAIETY
LEVOROTATORY LAEVO LEVOGYRE
NEGATIVE
LEVY CUT TAX CESS MISE REAR
LEVEL RAISE ASSESS EXTEND
EXTENT IMPOSE IMPOST UPTAKE
IMPRESS TRIBUTE DISTRAIN
DISTRESS SHIPPAGE
(— A TAX) GELD GELT TAIL STENT
(— DISTRESS) DRIVE
(IRISH —) MART
LEVYING EXACTION
LEWD NICE BAWDY FOLLY PRIME
RANDY HARLOT IMPURE LACHES
LUBRIC RAKISH WANTON HIRCINE
LEERING LUSTFUL OBSCENE
RAMMISH SCARLET SENSUAL
WHORISH PRURIENT SLUTTISH
UNCHASTE
LEWDNESS FOLLY RAKERY
LECHERY HARLOTRY PUTANISM
LEXICON CALEPIN WORDBOOK
LIABILITY DEBT DEBIT CHARGE
TRIBUTE
LIABLE APT ABLE OPEN GUILTY
EXPOSED OBVIOUS SUBJECT
AMENABLE INCIDENT
LIAISON BOND AFFAIR LINKING
INTIMACY INTRIGUE
LIANA CIPO BEJUCO BUSHROPE
LIANG TAEL
LIAR LEAR ANANIAS BOUNCER
CRACKER CRAMMER PROCTOR
WARLOCK WERNARD FABULIST
LIBATION AMBROSIA

LIBEL DEFAME MALIGN VILIFY
SLANDER
LIBELOUS FAMOUS
LIBERAL FAIR FREE GOOD OPEN
WHIG BROAD FRANK LARGE NOBLE
SOLUTE JANNOCK PROFUSE
ADVANCED GENEROUS HANDSOME
LARGEOUS PRODIGAL SEPARATE
(CANADIAN —) GRIT
(NOT —) CHARY SPARE
LIBERAL ARTS MUSES
LIBERALITY LARGE BOUNTY
BREADTH CHARITY FREEDOM
HONESTY LARGESS
LIBERALLY LARGE BROADLY
LIBERATE FREE QUIT FRITH REMIT
UNGYVE UNWRAP DELIVER MANUMIT
RELEASE UNSLAVE UNFETTER
UNTHRALL
LIBERATION FREEDOM RELEASE
DELIVERY KAIVALYA DISCHARGE

LIBERIA

CAPITAL: MONROVIA
CUSTOM: SANDE
HILLS: BOMI
MEASURE: KUBA
MOUNTAIN: UNI NIETE NIMBA
PEOPLE: GI KRU KWA VAI VEI
GOLA KROO KROU TOMA BASSA
GIBBI GISSI GREBO KPELLE
KROOBY KRUMAN KROOBOY
MANDINGO
RIVER: CESS LOFA MANNA MORRC
DOUOBE STJOHN CAVALLA
SANPEDRO
TOWN: GRIBO REBBO HARPER
NANAKRU BUCHANAN MARSHALL

LIBERTINE PUNKER PANURGE
STRIKER LOTHARIO STRINGER
LIBERTY MAY SOC EASE LARGE
LEAVE SCOPE ACCESS STREET
FREEDOM LARGESS LICENSE
WITHGANG
(— OF ACTION) PLAY SWING
(— OF ENTRANCE) INGRESS
(— OF GOING OUT) ISH
(— OF TURNING PIGS INTO FIELDS)
SHACK
(— TO BUY AND SELL) TOLL
(— TO HUNT) CHASE
(PARTIAL — OF HAWK) HACK
(SEXUAL —) INTIMACY
(UNDUE —) HEAD
LIBERTY CAP PILLEUS
LIBIDINIZATION EGOISM
LIBIDINOUS FLESHY FLESHLY
LIBRA AS PONDUS
LIBRARY AMBRY BIBLE MUSEUM
BHANDAR BOOKERY ATHENEUM
LIBRETTO BOOK WORD TESTO
TEXTBOOK

LIBYA

ALPHABET: TIFINAGH
CAPITAL: BENGASI BENGAZI
TRIPOLI

GULF: SIDRA SIRTE
MEASURE: SAA BOZZE DONUM
   JABIA TEMAN BARILE MISURA
   MATTARO
MOUNTAIN: BETTE
OASIS: KUFRA SEBHA TAZERBO
SEAPORT: HOMS DERNA SIDRI
   TOBRUK BENGAZI
TOWN: HOMS SEBHA SIDRI ZAWIA
   ELMARJ GARIAN MURZUQ
   MISURATA
WEIGHT: KELE UCKIA GORRAF
   TERMINO KHAROUBA

LICE CREEPERS
  (FISH —) EPIZOA
LICENSE CHOP GALE HEAD EXEAT
  LEAVE SLANG SWING BANDON
  CAROON FIRMAN INDULT PATENT
  PERMIT READER CAROOME CERTIFY
  CROTTLE FACULTY FREEDOM
  INDULTO LIBERTY LICENCE
  PLACARD WARRANT ESCAMBIO
  IMMUNITY MORTMAIN PASSPORT
  TEZKIRAH
  (— FOR CART) CAROOME
  (— PLATE) NUMBER
  (PEDDLER'S —) SLANG
LICENTIOUS GAY LAX FREE LEWD
  WILD FRANK LARGE LOOSE FILTHY
  UNRULY WANTON CYPRIAN FLESHLY
  IMMORAL LAWLESS LIBERAL
  UNYOKED
LICENTIOUSNESS DIRT LICENSE
LICHEN RAG MANNA USNEA ORCHIL
  CROTTAL CROTTLE CUDBEAR
  EVERNIA OAKMOSS PARELLA
  ARCHILLA CAREWEED LECANORA
  LUNGWORT PARMELIA ROCKHAIR
  TREEHAIR WARTWORT
LICIT LEGAL LAWFUL LEEFUL
LICK LAP LIKE SUCK MOUTH SLAKE
  CONQUER
LICKER-IN TUMBLE
LICKING GRUELING
LICORICE POMFRET SWEETROOT
LICORICE PILL CACHOU
LICYMNIUS (FATHER OF —)
  ELECTRYON
  (SISTER OF —) ALCMENA
  (SLAYER OF —) TLEPOLEMUS
LID DIP BRED DECK TYMP COVER
  BRIDLE EYELID POTLID CLAPPER
  CLICKET CLOSURE SCUTTLE
  SHUTTER COVERCLE
LIE FIB GAB LAY LIG LIN SIT YED
  CRAM FALL FLAW LIGG REST RIDE
  WHID DEVIL DWELL FABLE FEIGN
  LEASE STAND STORY FITTEN
  RAPPER RESIDE SPRAWL VANITY
  BOUNCER CONSIST CRACKER
  CRAMMER CRUMPER FALSITY
  GRABBLE LEASING PLUMPER
  TWISTER UNTRUTH WHACKER
  WHISKER WHOPPER
  (— ALONGSIDE) ACCOST
  (— AROUND) COMPASS
  (— AT ANCHOR) HOVE

  (— AT FULL LENGTH) STRETCH
  (— CONCEALED) DARKLE
  (— CONTIGUOUS) CONFINE
  (— DETECTOR) POLYGRAPH
  (— DORMANT) SLEEP
  (— DOWN) LEAN COUCH CHARGE
  (— FLAT ON BELLY) GROVEL
  (— HEAD TO WIND) TRY
  (— HIDDEN) LURK MICHE TAPPISH
  (— IN AMBUSH) HUGGER
  (— IN BED) KIP THOKE
  (— IN WAIT) AWAIT LOWER AMBUSH
  FORELAY
  (— IN WATER) DOUSE DROWN
  (— NEXT TO) ADJOIN
  (— OPPOSITE TO) SUBTEND
  (— OVER) COVER
  (— PRONE) GROVEL GRABBLE
  (— PROSTRATE) STREEK
  (— QUIET) SNUDGE
  (— SNUG) CUDDLE
  (— UNEVENLY) SAG
  (— WITH SAILS FURLED) HULL
  (IMPUDENT —) BOUNCE
  (MONSTROUS —) STRAMMER

LIECHTENSTEIN
CAPITAL: VADUZ
CASTLE: VADUZ GUTEMBURG
MOUNTAIN: RHATIKON
RIVER: RHINE
ROMAN NAME: RHAETIA
TOWN: HAAG BALZER SCHAAN
  NENDELN
TRIBE: ALAMANNI

LIED BALLAD
LIEF DEAR LEAVE LEEVE LIEVE
  FREELY GLADLY BELOVED
LIEUTENANT LUFF ZANY LOUEY
  JAYGEE KEHAYA CAIMAKAM
  QAIMAQAM TENIENTE WOODVILE
LIFE IT VIE ZOE HIDE JIVA PUFF
  SNAP TUCK VALE ANIMA BEING
  BLOOD DEMON HEART LIFER QUICK
  SWEAT BIOSIS BREATH CANDLE
  COURSE ENERGY SPIRIT SPRITE
  LIFELET LIFEWAY VITALITY VIVACITY
  (— AFTER DEATH) FUTURITY
  (— IN HEAVEN) GLORY
  (— IN SOCIETY) SAMSARA SANSARA
  (— OF FURNACE LINING) CAMPAIGN
  (— OF THE SEA) HALIBIOS
  (ACADEMIC —) ACADEMIA
  (ANIMAL —) FLESH
  (ANIMAL AND PLANT —) BIOS BIOTA
  BIOLOGY EDAPHON
  (CLOISTERED —) VEIL
  (INTELLECTUAL —) JIVATMA
  (MONASTIC —) CLOISTER
  (MORAL —) DAENA
  (MOSS —) BRYOLOGY
  (PLANT —) FLORA BOTANY
  (ROBUST —) JUICE
  (SINGLE —) CELIBACY
  (TERRESTRIAL —) GEOBIOS
  (WITHOUT —) AZOIC
LIFE BELT SAFETY
LIFEBLOOD BLOOD SWEAT

LIFELESS ARID DEAD DULL FLAT
  AMORT HEAVY INERT VAPID ANEMIC
  TORPID SAPLESS DESOLATE
  GRIPLESS INACTIVE
LIFELESSLY DEADLY INERTLY
LIFELESSNESS ANEMIA
LIFELIKE VIVE QUICK EIDETIC
  ANIMATED SPEAKING
LIFE PRESERVER FLOAT NEDDY
LIFETIME AGE DAY WORLD LIVING
  LIFEDAY DURATION LIFELONG
LIFT WIN BOOM BUOY CAST COCK
  HEFT JACK REAR TOSS WEVE
  BOOST BREAK ELATE HEAVE HITCH
  HOICK HOIST HOOSH MOUNT PRESS
  RAISE SPOUT STEAL WEIGH BUCKET
  CLEECH SNATCH ELEVATE ENHANCE
  HEELTAP NAUNTLE BOOKLIFT
  CHAIRWAY ELEVATOR LEVITATE
  (— HAT) DOFF
  (— IN VEHICLE) SETDOWN
  (— OF WAVE) SCEND
  (— ONESELF) SOAR
  (— QUICKLY) PERK
  (— UP) HOVE CRANE ERECT EXALT
  EXTOL HORSE WEIGH ADVANCE
  ELEVATE NAUNTLE
  (— WITH BLOCK AND TACKLE)
  BOUSE
LIFTED ARRECT SUBLIME
LIFTER GAGGER SERVER HOISTER
  HOISTMAN
LIFTING HIKE UPTAKE
LIFT VALVE POPPET
LIGAMENT BAND BOND ARTERY
  PAXWAX STRING ZONULE ARMILLA
  LIGATURE
LIGAMENTOUS DESMOID
LIGATE BAR
LIGATURE CLAM PLICA DIGRAM
  PNEUMA STIGMA DIGRAPH
  LIGAMENT LIGATION
LIGGER TRIMMER
LIGHT BUG DAY GAY HAP LAW SHY
  SUN AIRY EASY FAIR FALL FINE
  FIRE FLUX GLIM LAMP LEET LUNT
  MILD SLUT SOFT BAVIN BLAZE
  CORKY FANAL FILMY FLAME FLEET
  FUFFY LEGER LOUGH MERRY PITCH
  QUICK SHEER SPILL WHITE BEACON
  BRIGHT CHAFFY FLOATY FLOSSY
  FLUFFY FROTHY GENTLE HAPPEN
  ILLUME KINDLE LANCET LUSTER
  LUSTRE MARKER PASTEL PHAROS
  SIGNAL SLUSHY STINGY STRIKE
  SUTTLE VOLAGE BENGOLA
  BUOYANT CRESSET FRAGILE
  GLITTER LAMBENT SFOGATO
  SMITHER SUMMERY TORTAYS
  TRIVIAL UNGRAVE BACKFIRE
  DAYLIGHT DELICATE DIAPHANE
  ELECTRIC EXPEDITE FEATHERY
  GASLIGHT GOSSAMER LEGGIERO
  LUMINARY PALOUSER SUNLIGHT
  SUNSHINE
  (— AND BRILLIANT) LAMBENT
  (— AND FIRE ON HORSE'S MANE)
  HAG
  (— AND FREE) FLYAWAY

(— **AND QUICK**) VOLANT
(— **CANDLES**) TOLLY
(— **FROM NIGHT SKY**) AIRGLOW
(— **IN WINDOW**) LANCET
(— **OF MORNING**) AURORA
(— **ON TV SCREEN**) SNOW
(— **UP**) FLASH GLOZE ILLUME
RELUME GLORIFY
(— **UPON**) STRIKE
(**BRIGHT** —) GLARE GLEAM
(**BURST OF** —) FLASH
(**CIRCLE OF** —) HALO NIMBUS
(**FAINT** —) GLIMMER SCARROW
(**FEEBLE** —) GLIMMER
(**FITFUL** —) SHIMMER
(**HARBOR** —) BUG
(**INNER** —) SEED
(**NEW** —) SEPARATE
(**NIGHT** —) MORTAR
(**PARKING** —**S**) DIMMERS
(**PERSIAN GOD OF** —) MITHRAS
(**REFLECTED** —) SKYME
(**SHIP'S** —) FANAL
(**SMALL** —) TAPER
(**TRAFFIC** —) BLINKER
(**WAVERING** —) FLICKER
LIGHT-COLORED BLONDE
LIGHTEN CLEAR LEVIN LIGHT RAISE
ALLEGE BLEACH ENCLEAR FOULDRE
MOLLIFY SWEETEN THUNDER
LEVIGATE
LIGHTENING BREAK
LIGHTER SCOW ACCON CASCO
WHERRY DROGHER GABBARD
PONTOON CHOPBOAT
LIGHTERMAN KEELER KEELMAN
LIGHT-HEADED IDLE LIGHT LIVELY
CARRIED GLAIKET
LIGHT-HEARTED GAY GLAD GIDDY
WINSOME CAREFREE DEBONAIR
VOLATILE
LIGHTHEARTEDNESS BUOYANCY
LIGHTHOUSE FANAL LIGHT BEACON
PHAROS LANTERN
LIGHTLESS APHOTIC
LIGHTLY LIGHT AIRILY FAIRILY
HOVERLY LEGGIERO SLIGHTLY
LIGHT-MINDED BLITHE
LIGHTNESS CHEER VALUE GAIETY
LEVITY AIRINESS BUOYANCY
LEGERETE LEGERITY
(— **OF MOVEMENT**) BALLON
LIGHTNING BOLT FIRE LAIT LEVIN
FULMEN METEOR FOULDRE
SULPHUR THUNDER FIREBALL
FIREBOLT WILDFIRE
LIGHT-O'-LOVE LEVERET
LIGHT-TEXTURED FOZY
LIGHTWOOD FATWOOD
LIGIA LIGYDA
LIGNEOUS WOODY XYLOID
LIGNIN LIGNOSE XYLOGEN
LIGNUM VITAE GUAYACAN
POCKWOOD
LIGROIN BENZINE CANADOL
LIGULA LANGUET
LIGULE STRAP LIGULA
LIKE AS DIG DOTE LIST LOVE ALIKE
ENJOY EQUAL FANCY SAVOR TASTE

ADMIRE AFFECT BELIKE LIKELY
MATTER PLEASE SEMBLE SIMILE
CONCEIT SIMILAR SEMBLANT
SUITABLE
(— **A GLAND**) ADEMOSE ADENOUS
(— **BETTER**) PREFER
(— **HAIR**) CRINITE
(**VERY** —) SIAMESE
LIKELIHOOD APTNESS
LIKELY APT FAIR LIKE READY LIABLE
PROOFY SEEMLY GRADELY SMITTLE
APPARENT FEASIBLE POSSIBLE
PROBABLE
(**MOST** —) BELIKE
LIKEN EVEN LIKE REMENE SEMBLE
COMPARE SMILIZE ASSEMBLE
RESEMBLE
LIKENESS DAP BLEE ICON IDOL
MAKE SECT BLUSH DUMMY GLIFF
IMAGE MORAL SHAPE EFFIGY
FIGURE STATUE KINSHIP PATTERN
PICTURE RETRAIT EQUALITY
HOMOLOGY PARALLEL PORTRAIT
(**PERFECT** —) SPIT
LIKEWISE EKE TOO ALSO ITEM
EITHER EQUALLY LIKEWAYS
(— **NOT**) NOR
LIKING GOO GRA PAY GOUT GUST
LIKE LUST FANCY FLAIR GUSTO
HEART SHINE SKILL SMACK TASTE
THEAT SWALLOW AFFINITY
APPETITE FONDNESS
(**ECCENTRIC** —) FOIBLE
LILAC LILAS MAUVE LAYLOCK
LILACIN SYRINGIN
LILY IXIA KELP SEGO AZTEC CALLA
CLOTE AUGUST LILIUM VALLEY
COCUISA MONOCOT LILYWORT
MARTAGON NENUPHAR
(**CLIMBING** —) GLORIOSA
(**PALM** —) TI
(**SEA** —) CRINOID
(**WATER** —) CANDOCK CAMALOTE
LILY OF THE VALLEY LILIUM
MUGGET MUGUET MUGWET
LILYWORT SHINLEAF
LIMA BEAN HABA LIMA
LIMB ARM LEG CLAW FOOT KNOT
LITH TRAM WING ARTUS BOUGH
SPALD SPAUL SWAMP BRANCH
MEMBER PODITE FEATURE FLIPPER
FORCEPS NECTOPOD
LIMBA AFARA FRAKE
LIMBER BAIN FLIP LIMP LUSH LINGY
LITHE LISSOM SEMMIT SUPPLE
SWANKY BRUSHER BRUTTER
KNOTTER LIMMOCK PLIABLE
FLEXIBLE FLIPPANT
LIME CALX LIMA CEDRA CEDRAT
CHUNAM CITRON FUSTIC
(— **IN BRICK**) BOND
(**WILD** —) COLIMA
LIMESTONE HUM CAUK LIAS LYAS
MALM POROS CLUNCH KUNKUR
PISOLITE
(— **REGION**) KARST
LIME TREE LIME TEIL LINDEN
LIMIT END FIX BIND BUTT FINE HOLD
LINE LIST MARK MERE TAIL BLOCK

BOUND GAUGE HEDGE STENT STINT
VERGE BORDER BOURNE DEFINE
EFFLUX EXTENT FINISH FINITE
HAMPER LENGTH MODIFY NARROW
PALING SCRIMP TROPIC UPSHOT
ASTRICT CLOSURE COMPASS
CONFINE CONTENT HORIZON
MAXIMUM MEASURE BOUNDARY
CONTRACT DEADLINE IMPRISON
LIMITARY LIMITATE OUTGOING
RESTRAIN RESTRICT SOLSTICE
TERMINUS
(— **EFFECT**) ALLAY
(— **IN A FOREST**) BAIL
(— **MOTION**) HOLD
(— **OF VISION AT SEA**) KENNING
(**EXTREME** —) HEIGHT
(**LOWER** —) FLOOR
(**UPPER** —) CEILING
(**UTTER** —) EXTREME
(**PL.**) AMBIT CANCELS ENVIRONS
LIMITATION TAIL FRAME STINT
DENIAL CLOTURE RESERVE
(**PL.**) SWADDLE
LIMITED TAIL BORNE BRIEF SHORT
SMALL FINITE NARROW STINTY
STRAIT BOUNDED SPECIAL
CONFINED DEFINITE LIMITARY
(— **IN APPEAL**) CHICHI
LIMITING DEFINITE ADJECTIVE
EXCLUSIVE
LIMMA DIESIS
LIMMU EPONYM
LIMONENE CINENE CARVENE
CITRENE
LIMONIUM STATICE
LIMOUSINE BERLIN SUBURBAN
LIMP HIP HOP CLOP GIMP HALT HIMP
HOIT SOFT THIN HENCH HILCH
HITCH LINGY LOOSE LOPPY SLAMP
STILT FLABBY FLIMSY HAMBLE
HIMPLE HIRPLE HOBBLE LENNOW
LIMBER LIMPSY FLACCID LIMMOCK
SHAFFLE UNSMART DRAGGLED
DROOPING
LIMPET CHINK OPIHI SHELL ACMAEA
LIMPIN FLIDDER
LIMPID PURE CLEAR LUCID BRIGHT
CRYSTAL PELLUCID
LIMPING LAME GIMPY LIMPY ZOPPA
HALTING
LIMPLY LANKLY
LINAGE SPACE
LINALOOL LICAREOL
LINCHPIN FORELOCK
LINCTUS LOOCH LOHOCH LOHOCK
LINDEN LIN LIME LYNE TEIL TILIA
TILLET LINWOOD BASSWOOD
DADDYNUT WOODLIND
LINE BAR BOX FIX RAY ROW TAW
BOFF CASE CEIL COLA CRIB DASH
FACE FILE GAME GAPE LACE LARD
LATH LEAD LING MAIN MARK RACE
RANK RULE STOP TAUM WHIP
AGONE FAINT FEINT FLEET HATCH
LIGNE LINEA METER RANGE SCORE
STRIA TOUCH TRACE TRAIL TRAIN
TWIST BINDER CABURN CEVIAN
CREASE DEGREE DOUBLE EARING

GASKET ISOBAR ISOHEL ISOPAG
ISOTAC METIER NETTLE SECANT
SECOND SPRING STRING STRIPE
AZIMUTH BABBITT CATLINE
CONTOUR CREANCE ENVELOP
GUNLINE HIPLINE ISOCHOR
ISOGRAM ISOHYET ISONEPH
ISORITH ISOSTER ISOTOME KNITTLE
MARLINE NACARAT SCRATCH
WINDROW BALKLINE BISECTOR
BOUNDARY BUSINESS CHAMPAIN
DATELINE DEADLINE DIAGONAL
DIAMETER DRAGLINE DRUMLINE
FISHBACK GANTLINE GEODESIC
GIRTLINE HAIRLINE HANDLINE
HEXAPODY ISOGLOSS ISOGONIC
ISOPHANE ISOPHENE ISOPLERE
ISOTHERE ISOTHERM LANDWIRE
LIFELINE MARTINET SLIPBAND
STRINGER SUBCLONE SUBSTILE
SUBSTYLE UPSTROKE
(— **AROUND STAMP**) FRAME
(— **AS CENTER FOR REVOLVING**)
AXIS
(— **HEARTH**) FIX FETTLE
(— **IN GLASS**) STRING
(— **IN HAT**) HEADLINE
(— **MINESHAFT**) TUB
(— **OF ACTION**) LAY
(— **OF BATTLE**) FRONT
(— **OF BUSINESS**) WAY
(— **OF CELLS**) ANNULUS
(— **OF CLIFFS**) SCARP BREAKS
(— **OF COLOR**) SLASH STREAK
(— **OF DANCERS**) CHAIN
(— **OF DESCENT**) SIDE STEM STIRP
STOCK STRAIN ANCESTRY
(— **OF DETERMINANT**) COLUMN
(— **OF DEVELOPMENT**) STREET
(— **OF DEVOLUTION**) ENTAIL
(— **OF FIBERS**) CHRYSAL
(— **OF FIRE HOSE**) LEAD
(— **OF FLOTATION**) BEARINGS
(— **OF FORTIFICATION**) LIMES
ENCEINTE
(— **OF HAY**) WAKE WALLOW
(— **OF HEALTH**) HEPATICA
(— **OF HIGH TIDE**) LANDWASH
(— **OF HOUSES**) BLOCK
(— **OF INTERSECTION**) GROIN
BUTTOCK
(— **OF JUNCTION**) MEET SEAM
(— **OF MERCURY**) HEPATICA
(— **OF PERSONS**) QUEUE CORDON
STICKLE
(— **OF PORES**) HATCHING
(— **OF SOLDIERS**) RAY FILE RANK
WAVE CORDON
(— **OF STITCHING**) BASTING
(— **OF TIMBERS**) BOOM STOCKADE
(— **OF TREES**) SCREEN
(— **OF TYPE**) SLUG KICKER
(— **OF UNION**) SUTURE
(— **ON A LETTER**) SERIF
(— **ON BOOK COVER**) BAND
(— **ON COAT**) GORGE
(— **ON DOLPHIN**) STOP
(— **ON HIGHWAY**) BARRIER
(— **THAT CUTS ANOTHER**) SECANT

(— **TO BIND CABLES**) CABURN
(— **TO FASTEN SAIL**) EARING
GASKET
(— **TO RAISE FLAG**) LANIARD
LANYARD
(— **TO START RACE**) TRIG
(— **TOUCHING ARC**) TANGENT
(— **UP**) LAY
(— **WITH BRICKS**) GINGE
(— **WITH PANELLING**) WAINSCOT
(— **WITH STONES**) STEEN STEYN
(— **WITH TIMBER**) CRIB
(42 —**S**) LENGTH
(**ANCHOR** —) RODING
(**BEARING** —) CUT
(**BOUNDARY** —) MERE FENCE
BORDER ISOGLOSS
(**BOUNDING** —) SIDE BOUNDARY
(**BRIEF** —) ITEM
(**COASTAL** —) SEAMARK
(**CONNECTING** —) LIGATURE
(**CONTINUOUS** —) STRETCH
(**CURVED** —) ARC SLUR SWEEP
(**DEMARCATION** —) BOMBLINE
(**DIAGONAL** —) BIAS
(**DIVIDING** —) EDGE MIDRIB DIVISION
FRONTIER
(**ELECTRIC** —) HIGHLINE
(**FACIAL** —) TRAIT
(**FINISHING** —) TAPE WIRE
(**FISHING** —) TOME TROT FLEET
SNELL SNOOD LEADER LEDGER
NORSEL BACKING BOULTER SPILLER
SPILLET TRIMMER BLOWLINE
CORKLINE FISHLINE SNAGLINE
TROTLINE
(**HORIZONTAL** —) LEVEL
(**IMAGINARY** —) AGONE HINGE
GROOVE ISOBAR ISOGAM ISOHEL
ISOPAG HORIZON ISOBASE ISOBATH
ISOGRIV ISOHYET ISOLINE ISOTACH
ISOBRONT ISOCHASM ISOCHEIM
ISOCHLOR ISOCHORE ISOCRYME
ISOPHOTE ISOPLETH ISOSTERE
ISOTHERM
(**INCLINED** —) CANT
(**LONGITUDINAL** —) MERIDIAN
(**MEDIAN** —) RAPHE
(**METRICAL** —) EIGHT STAFF STICH
DIMETER SAPPHIC STICHOS
(**MUSICAL** —) ACCOLADE
(**NAUTICAL** —) EARING LACING
GESWARP MARLINE RATLINE
DOWNHAUL
(**ONE-TENTH OF** —) GRY
(**PLOTTED** —) ADIABAT
(**RADIATING** —) BEAM
(**RAILROAD** —) STEM STUB
(**RAISED** —) RIDGE
(**SPECTRUM** —) GHOST DOUBLET
SINGLET TRIPLET
(**STARTING** —) SCRATCH
(**STRAIGHT** —) CHORD BEELINE
STRAIGHT
(**SUPPLY** —) AIRLIFT
(**SURVEYING** —) WAD BASE CHAIN
(**THEATRICAL** —**S**) FAT
(**TOW** —) CORDELLE
(**TRANSPORTATION** —) FEEDER
CARRIER

(**WAVY** —) SQUIGGLE
LINEAGE GET KIN KIND RACE TEAM
BIRTH BLOOD SPACE STIRP STOCK
FAMILY HAVAGE NATION PARAGE
SOURCE SPRING STRAIN DESCENT
KINDRED PROGENY SUCCESS
ANCESTRY PEDIGREE
LINEAL DIRECT
LINEAMENT LINE TRACT TRAIT
FEATURE
LINEAR RUNNING
LINECUT ZINCO
LINED MASONED
LINEMAN FORWARD WIREMAN
CHAINMAN
LINEN LIN LAWN IRISH TOILE
BARRAS DAMASK DIAPER RAINES
SENDAL HOLLAND LOCKRAM
TABLING BARANDOS OSNABURG
PLATILLA
(— **CLOSET**) LOCKER
(— **FOR SHIRTS**) SARKING
(**CHINESE** —) KOMPOW
(**COARSE** —) HARN BARRAS
(**FINE** —) LAKE LAWN DAMASK
DIAPER RAINES
(**HOUSEHOLD** —) NAPERY TABLING
(**SCRAPED** —) LINT
(**SPANISH** —) CREA
LINER SHIP BASKET SCRIBER
STEAMER
LINEUP SHOWUP
LING BURBOT DRIZZLE STOKVIS
LINGA DILDO
LINGCOD CULTUS
LINGER LAG HANG HOVE LING STAY
CLING DALLY DELAY DEMUR DWELL
HAUNT HOVER PAUSE TARRY
DRETCH HANKER LOITER TARROW
DRINGLE
LINGERER LUNGIS LAGGARD
LINGERIE FRILLIES PRETTIES
LINGERING SLOW DELAY MOROSE
TARDANT DRAGGING
LINGO BAT CANT LINGUA PATTER
DIALECT
LINGUA GLOSSA TONGUE
LINGUAL GLOSSAL
LINGUISTIC GLOTTIC
LINGUISTICS GRAMMAR PHILOLOGY
LINIMENT EIK EMBROCHE
OPODELDOC
LININ PLASTIN
LINING FUR BACK COAT BAIZE
BRASS FACING PANNEL BABBITT
BUSHING CEILING FURRING
FURRURE THIMBLE TINNING
TUBBING CLEADING DOUBLING
DOUBLURE FIREBACK SHEETING
UNDERLAY WAINSCOT
(— **FOR WELL**) STEENING STEYNING
(— **OF BEARING**) JEWEL
(— **OF FURNACE**) BASQUE
FIREBACK
(— **OF HAT**) TIP
LINK JAR TIE TOW JOIN KNIT LUNT
SHUT YOKE NEXUS COPULA COUPLE
FASTEN FETTER TOUGHT CODETTA
CONNECT COUPLER ENCHAIN

INVOLVE LIAISON SHACKLE
CATENATE IDENTIFY VINCULUM
(— **ARMS**) CLEEK
(— **IN NETWORK**) LEG
(**COMPOUND** —) SWIVEL
(**WOODEN** —) LAG
LINKAGE BOND CELL COUPLING
LINKWORK
LINKED CONNEX INTEGRAL
LINKING HOOKUP ANNECTANT
(— **DEVICE**) LINCHPIN
LINKMAN LINKBOY LIGHTMAN
LINNET FINCH TWITE LENARD LINTIE
REDPOLL REDFINCH
LINSANG CIVET ZINSANG
LINSEED LINGET
LINSEY-WOOLSEY WINCEY
LINT FLY FLUE FLICK CADDIS
CADDICE CHARPIE CARBASUS
(**SCRAPED** —) XYSTUS
LINTEL CAP CLAVY HANCE CLAVEL
DARNER SUMMER SQUINCH
TRANSOM
LION CAT LLEW MORNE SHEDU
SIMBA LIONEL LIONET LEOPARD
(**MOUNTAIN** —) PUMA COUGAR
LION MONKEY LEONCITO
LION-TAILED MONKEY MACACO
MACAQUE WANDEROO
LIP BLOB MASK PUSS APRON CHOPS
GROIN MOUTH SPOUT TUTEL
LABIUM LABRUM ROUTER CHILOMA
LABELLUM UNDERLIP
(— **DISEASE**) PERLECHE
(— **OF BELL**) SKIRT
(— **OF COROLLA**) GALEA
(— **OF ORCHID**) SLIPPER
(— **OF PITCHER**) BEAK
(—**S OF MOOSE**) MUFFLE
(**FLAT** —) APRON
(**LOWER** —) JIB FIPPLE
(**PL.**) LABRAS CUSHION
LIPASE PIALYN
LIPIDE CERIDE ADIPOID STERIDE
TETHELIN
LIPOCHROME LUTEIN
LIPOMA STEATOMA
LIPPED LABIATE
LIPPIA WRIGHT ALOYSIA
LIP PLUG LABRET TEMETA
LIPPY STIMPART
LIQUEFIED FUSILE POTATE REMISS
RESOLVED
LIQUEFY RUN FUSE MELT RELENT
LIQUATE DISSOLVE ELIQUATE
LIQUEUR EAU OUZO RAKI AURUM
CREME NOYAU CHASSE GENEPI
KUMMEL PERNOD STREGA ANESONE
CORDIAL CURACAO PERSICO
RATAFIA RATIFIA ABSINTHE
ALKERMES ANGELICA ANISETTE
MANDARIN PRUNELLE VESPETRO
(**PL.**) EAUX
LIQUID AQUA BLASH DRINK FLUID
LEACH MOIST ACETAL FLUENT
FURANE AEROSOL BUCKING
CINEOLE EYEWASH FLOWAGE
VINASSE BLACKING EFFLUENT
EFFUSION EXCITANT FURFURAN

LEACHATE LIBATION SOLUTION
(— **IN CELL**) EXCITANT
(— **UNIT**) TUN CHENG SHENG SHING
POTTLE MUTCHKIN PUNCHEON
(**ACID-RESISTANT** —) GROUND
(**COLORING** —) HENNA
(**COOKING** —) BREE BROO BROTH
STOCK
(**DISTILLED** —) SPIRIT
(**FILTHY** —) ADDLE
(**INSULATING** —) ASKAREL
(**OILY** —) ANILINE CHLORAL
PICAMAR CARDANOL CREOSOTE
(**PERFUMED** —) COLLEN COLOGNE
(**REFUSE** —) SCOURAGE
(**REFUSE** —**S**) SEWAGE
(**SIZING** —) GLAIK
(**STERILIZED** —) JOHNIN
(**SYRUPY** —) HONEY
(**TANNING** —) LIME
(**THICK** —) DOPE SIRUP SYRUP
(**VISCOUS** —) TAR SCHRADAN
(**VOLATILE** —) ETHER ALCOHOL
DILUENT LIGROIN
(**WEAK** —) BLASH SLIPSLOP
LIQUIDATE SINK SETTLE
LIQUIDATION CLEANUP
LIQUOR ALE BUB DEW GAS LAP OKE
PAD POT RUM SUP TAP WET BEER
BREE FIRE FIZZ GEAR GROG LUSH
PURL SUCK SWIG TAPE TIFF BOGUS
BUDGE CEBUR DRINK GLASS
HOOCH KEFIR MOBBY NAPPY PERRY
PISCO SAUCE SHRAB SHRUB SICER
SKINK STICK BOTTLE CASSIS
CHICHA DIDDLE DOCTOR FOGRAM
FUDDLE GATTER GENEVA GUZZLE
HYDROL KIRSCH MASTIC MESCAL
POTTLE ROTGUT SAMSHU STRUNT
TIPPLE WHISKY BITTERN BRACKET
BRAGGET GROCERY PHLEGMA
SPUNKIE SUCTION TAPLASH
TEQUILA WAIPIRO WHISKEY
ABSINTHE BRAGWORT EYEWATER
HYDROMEL MEDICINE OKOLEHAO
POTATION RUMBOOZE FIREWATER
(— **CABINET**) TANTALUS
(— **CASE**) GARDEVIN
(— **FROM MUST**) ARROPE
(— **FROM PEARS**) PERRY PERRIE
(— **FROM WOOL-SCOURING**) SUD
SUDS
(— **MIXED WITH WINE**) DOCTOR
(— **SALE**) ABKARI
(— **TAKEN IN SODA WATER**) CINDER
(**ACID** —) VERJUICE
(**ALCOHOLIC** —) GIN ARAK HOOCH
ARRACK BRANDY SAMSHU AQUAVIT
BITTERS SNOOTFUL
(**ALCOHOLIC** —**S**) ARDENT
(**BITTER** —) TIRE
(**CHEAP** —) SMOKE
(**COLORLESS** —) GLYCID GLYCOL
GLYCIDOL GUAIACOL
(**CRAB APPLE** —) WHERRY
(**DISTILLED** —) DEW SOTOL GRAPPA
PHLEGM SCHNAPPS
(**DRUGGED** —) HOCUS
(**HARD** —) BOOZE

(**INTOXICATING** —) GROG LOAD
LUSH TAPE BUDGE GUZZLE KUMISS
HASHISH
(**MALT** —) ALE BUB BEER STOUT
ENTIRE PORTER
(**MOTHER** —) HYDROL BITTERN
(**RICE** —) SAMSHU
(**SPIRITUOUS** —) DEW GROG MOBBY
STRUNT WAIPIRO KAOLIANG
(**STRAIGHT** —) SHORT
(**STRONG** —) RUG TUBA VINO
HOGAN RUMBO STINGO
(**TAN** —) OOZE
(**TANNING** —) LAYAWAY TAILING
(**WEAK** —) SLIPSLOP
LIRA LIRE ZWANZIGER
(**ONE-TWENTIETH** —) SOLDO
LIRIPIPE TIPPET
LISSOME LITHE LIMBER NIMBLE
SUPPLE FLEXIBLE
LIST TIP BILL FILE HEEL LEET NOTE
POLL ROLL ROTA SWAG BRIEF
CANON GISTS INDEX PANEL SCORE
SCRIP SCROW SLATE AGENDA
CENSUS COLUMN DETAIL DOCKET
ERRATA HUDDLE LEGEND PURREL
RAGGER RAGMAN ROSTER SCREED
SCROLL SERIES CATALOG CITATOR
COMPILE DIPTYCH ITEMIZE LISTING
NOTITIA WAYBILL CALENDAR
CINCTURE HANDLIST PLATBAND
REGISTER SCHEDULE SYNONYMY
TITULARY
(— **OF BOOKS**) CANON
(— **OF CANDIDATES**) LEET SLATE
TERNA
(— **OF CONTESTANTS**) DRAW
SEEDING
(— **OF JURORS**) TALES
(— **OF MAP SYMBOLS**) LEGEND
(— **OF PASSERS WITHOUT HONORS**)
GULF
(— **OF RATES**) TARIFF
(— **OF THEATRICAL PARTS**) CAST
(**GENEALOGICAL** —) BEGATS
(**IMPRESSIVE** —) ARRAY
(**LEGAL** —) TABLEAU
(**PRAYER** —) BEADROLL
(**WINE** —) CARD
(**PL.**) CAREER
LISTEL QUADRA
LISTEN HARK HEAR LIST TEND
TENEZ ATTEND HARKEN INTEND
WHISPER
(— **TO**) DIG EAR HARK HEAR CATCH
ATTEND
LISTENER AUDITOR OTACUST
LISTENING PRICK AUDIENT HEARING
LISTER SULKY RIDGER
LISTERA OPHRYS
LISTING ITEM FRAME PARADE
LASHING
(— **OF JURORS**) ARRAY
LISTLESS DOPY DULL DOWFF FAINT
DONSIE SUPINE LANGUID UNLISTY
UNLUSTY CARELESS INDOLENT
UNHEARTY
LISTLESSLY DAVIELY
LISTLESSNESS APATHY UNLUST

LITANY AITESIS ROGATION
LITERAL VERBAL
LITERALLY SIMPLY
LITERARY BLUE BOOKISH LITERATE
  (— **MATERIAL**) KITSCH
LITERATE LETTERED
LITERATI CLERISY
LITERATURE FICTION LETTERS
  CLAPTRAP
  (**SACRED** —) VEDA SRUTI
  (**WISDOM** —) CHOKMAH HOKHMAH
LITHE BAIN SWACK CLEVER LIMBER
  SILKEN SUPPLE SVELTE WANDLE
  LISSOME FLEXIBLE

LITHUANIA
CAPITAL: KOVNO KAUNAS
COIN: LIT LITAS MARKA CENTAS
  FENNIG OSTMARK AUKSINAS
  SKATIKAS
NAME: LITVA LIETUVA
PEOPLE: BALT LETT ZHMUD
  LITVAK YATVYAG
RIVER: NERIS RUSNE DUBYSA
  NEMUNAS PREGOLYA
TOWN: MEMEL VILNA JELGAVA
  VILNIUS KAPSUKAS KLAIPEDA
  SIAULIAI

LITHUANIAN BALT ZHMUD
LITIGANT SUITOR
LITIGATE LAW PLEAD CONTEST
LITIGATION LAW LIS MOOT SUIT
  LAWING PLEADING PLEASHIP
LITMUS LAKMUS TURNSOLE
LITOTES MEIOSIS
LITTER DIG PIG BIER RAFF REDD
  BREED CABIN CLECK DOOLY DRECK
  HAULM MULCH SEDAN DOOLIE
  FARROW GOCART KINDLE KITTEN
  MAHMAL REFUSE CLUTTER LETTIGA
  LOUSTER MAMMOCK NORIMON
  RUMMAGE SCAMBLE BRANCARD
  CARRIAGE KINDLING MUNCHEEL
  PAVILION STRETCHER
  (— **FOR LIVESTOCK**) BEDDING
  (— **OF PIGS**) FAR FARE FARROW
  (— **ON PACK ANIMAL**) CACOLET
  (**FOREST** —) DUFF
LITTERED FOUL
LITTLE FEW LIL WEE LITE TINY VEEN
  CHOTA CRUMB SMALL TASTE
  WHONE BITTIE DAPPER LEETLE
  MINUTE PETITE PICKLE PUSILL
  KENNING MODICUM THOUGHT
  FRACTION SNIPPING
  (— **BY LITTLE**) EDGINGLY INCHMEAL
  (— **LESS THAN**) ABOUT
  (— **MUSICALLY**) POCO
  (— **ONE**) BUTCHA POPPET
  (**A** —) SOMEWHAT
  (**INDEFINITELY** —) NTH
LITTLENESS ATOMITY
LITTORAL COAST
LITURGY FORM RITE ABODAH
  MAARIB MINHAG NEILAH MINCHAH
  MYSTERY HIERURGY SHAHARIT
LIVE BE USE WIN KEEP LEAD STAY

ALERT ALIVE DWELL EXIST GREEN
  HABIT LEEVE QUICK SHACK VITAL
  HARBOR LIVELY LIVING REMAIN
  RESIDE BREATHE INHABIT SUBSIST
  CONTINUE CONVERSE VIGOROUS
  (— **AT ANOTHER'S EXPENSE**)
  COSHER
  (— **BY BEGGING**) CADGE SKELDER
  (— **BY STRATAGEMS**) SHARK
  (— **FROM DAY TO DAY**) EKE
  (— **IN CONTINENCE**) CONTAIN
  (— **IN LUXURY**) STATE
  (— **IN PEACE**) COEXIST
  (— **IN SAME PLACE**) STALL
  (— **ON**) SURVIVE
  (— **RIOTOUSLY**) JET
  (— **TEMPORARILY**) CAMP
  (— **THROUGH**) PASS TIDE
  (— **TOGETHER**) AGREE COHABIT
LIVE-BOX CAR
LIVE-FOREVER LULANG ORPINE
LIVELIHOOD BEING BREAD LIVING
  LIFEHOOD
LIVELINESS PEP FIRE FIZZ LIFE
  SPUNK BOUNCE GAIETY SPIRIT
  SPARKLE ACTIVITY VITALITY
  VIVACITY
LIVELONG LEELANG ENDURING
LIVELY GAY TID AIRY BRAG CANT
  FAST FESS GLEG KECK LIVE PERT
  RACY TAIT TRIG VITE VIVE WARM
  YARE AGILE ALERT ALIVE BONNY
  BRISK BUXOM CANTY CHIRK COBBY
  CORKY CRISP DESTO FRESH FRISK
  KEDGE KINKY MERRY PAWKY PEART
  PEPPY POKEY RUDDY SMART VIVID
  WHICK ACTIVE BLITHE BOUNCY
  CHEERY CHIRPY COCKET CROOSE
  CROUSE DAPPER FIERCE FRISCH
  GINGER JOCUND KIPPER LIVING
  NIMBLE QUIVER SEMMIT SPARKY
  SPRACK TROTTY VEGETE WHISKY
  WIMBLE ALLEGRO ANIMATE
  ANIMOSE BUCKISH BUOYANT
  GIGGISH GIOCOSO JOCULAR
  KINETIC LEBHAFT POINTED SPIRITY
  SPRINGY TITTUMY WINCING
  ANIMATED BOUNCING CHIRRUPY
  FRISKFUL FRISKING GALLIARD
  SKITTISH SMACKING SPANKING
  SPIRITED SPORTIVE STEERING
  STIRRING TRIPSOME VEGETOUS
  VOLATILE SPARKLING
LIVEN LACE CHEER ANIMATE
LIVE OAK ENCINA
LIVER MAW FOIE HEPAR VISCUS
  PUDDING
  (— **ATROPHY**) LUPINOSIS
  (— **OF LOBSTER**) TOMALLEY
LIVERWORT HEPATICA MOSSWORT
LIVERY SUIT CLOTH LIVRE UNIFORM
  CLOTHING
LIVESTOCK FEE WARE STOCK
  STORE STUFF CHATTEL BESTIALS
  FATSTOCK
LIVE WIRE HUSTLER
LIVID HAW WAN BLAE BLUE
LIVING KEEP ALIVE BEING BREAD
  GOING QUICK VITAL WHICK AROUND

LIVELY VIABLE ZOETIC ANIMATE
  SUPPORT ANIMATED
  (— **IN THE WORLD**) SECULAR
  (— **IN WAVES**) LOTIC
  (— **NEAR THE GROUND**) EPIGEAN
  (— **ON BANKS OF STREAMS**) RIPAL
  RIPARIAN
  (— **THING**) QUICK
  (**BARE** —) CRUST
  (**ECCLESIASTICAL** —) BENEFICE
LIVRE FRANC
LIXIVIATE LEACH
LIXIVIUM LYE
LIZARD DAB EFT GOH UMA UTA
  DABB GILA IBIT SEPS TEGU TEJU
  URAN AGAMA ANOLE BLUEY DRACO
  GECKO GUANO SKINK SNAKE SWIFT
  TEIID TOKAY TWEEG VARAN AMEIVA
  ANGUID ARBALO DRAGON GOANNA
  HARDIM IGUANA LACERT LEGUAN
  MOLOCH TEIOID WORRAL ZONURE
  BUMMAJO CAUDATE CHEECHA
  DIAPSID MONITOR REPTILE SAURIAN
  SCINCID TUATARA TUCKTOO
  BASILISK KAKARIKI MOKAMOKA
  SCORPION SLOWWORM TEGUEXIN
  WHIPTAIL ZONUROID CHAMELEON
LIZARD FISH ULAE INIOME
  SOAPFISH SPEARING
LLAMA ALPACA VICUNA GUANACO
LLUDD NUDD
LO SEE ECCE
LOACH DOJO BEARDIE MUDFISH
LOAD LUG BUCK CARK CRAM DECK
  DRAW FILL HAUL LADE LAST LUMP
  PACK RAKE SEAM STEM STOW
  TOTE TURN BARTH CARGO DRAFT
  PITCH STACK TRUSS TURSE
  BURDEN CHARGE COMBLE DEMAND
  FODDER FOTHER HAMPER LADING
  LOADEN THRACK WEIGHT BALLAST
  CARLOAD DERRICK DRAUGHT
  ENDORSE FRAUGHT FREIGHT
  ONERATE OPPRESS BACKPACK
  CARRIAGE ENCUMBER HEADLOAD
  SHIPLOAD
  (— **A DIE FOR CHEATING**) COG
  (— **FABRICS**) WEIGHT
  (— **OF COAL**) KEEL
  (— **OF HAY OR CORN**) HURRY
  (— **OF LAMBS**) DECK
  (— **OF LOGS**) PEAKER BUNKLOAD
  (— **OF WOOL**) TOD
  (— **ON BACK**) ENDORSE INDORSE
  (— **SHIP**) STEM
  (— **TO CAPACITY**) SATURATE
  (— **TO EXCESS**) ENCUMBER
  (**ELECTRIC** —) DEMAND
  (**HORSE** —) SEAM SUMAGE
  (**LAST** — **OF GRAIN**) WINTER
  (**SMALL** —) JAG JAGG JOBBLE
  (PL.) BUSHEL
LOADER CHARGER
LOADING LADING MARGIN
  ARRASTRE
LOADSTONE MAGNET SIDERITE
  LODESTONE
LOAF BAP BUM COB HACK HAKE
  HULL LAKE MIKE SLIM SORN BANGE

BREAD DRING MOUCH SHOOL SLIVE
SLOSH BROGUE CADDLE DIDDLE
GEORGE HALLAH RODNEY SLINGE
WASTEL HOOSIER MANCHET
SHACKLE SLOUNGE SOLDIER
OBLATION QUARTERN SHAMMOCK
(— **AROUND**) HULL HOWFF SLOSH
RODNEY
(— **OF BREAD**) COB BATON FADGE
MICHE TOMMY HALLAH TAMMIE
(**BROWN** —) GEORGE
(**ROUND** —) BUN
(**SMALL** —) BAP COB
(**SUGAR** —) TITLER
LOAFER BUM BEAT GRUB STIFF
BUMBLE KEELIE SLOUCH SLOVEN
BLUDGER COASTER FAITOUR
HOODLUM SLINKER SOLDIER
COBERGER HOOLIGAN LARRIKIN
SEASONER
LOAFING IDLE MIKE
LOAM RAB LAME SLIP LOESS REGUR
CLEDGE
LOAMY MELLOW
LOAN DHAN LEND LENT PREST
CREDIT DONATE MUTUUM FIXTURE
IMPREST
LOANBLEND HYBRID
LOATH LOTH LAITH LEATH SWEER
DAINTY BACKWARD
LOATHE HATE SHUN ABHOR LAITH
WLATE AGRISE DETEST DESPISE
SCUNDER SCUNNER NAUSEATE
LOATHING NAUSEA REVOLT
DISGUST
LOATHLY LAIDLY
LOATHSOME FOUL UGLY VILE
POCKY LAIDLY UNLIEF HATEFUL
LOATHLY OBSCENE TETROUS
WLATFUL DEFORMED NAUSEOUS
WLATSOME
LOBBY HALL FOYER NARTHEX
TAMBOUR ANTEROOM COULISSE
LOBBYIST PROMOTER
LOBE ALA FIN LAP AXIS LIST MALA
ALULA EXITE FIBER FIBRE FLUKE
GALEA LOBUS TOOTH UVULA
EARLAP FILLET FOLIUM GLOSSA
LAPPET LIGULE LOBING MANTLE
VANNUS VERMIS AROLIUM AURICLE
HEMAPOD LOBULUS EPICHILE
GLABELLA LABELLUM PALPIFER
PHYLLOID SQUAMULE
LOBED CUT LOMATINE
LOBSTER CRAY HOMARD DECAPOD
SHEDDER CRAWFISH CRAYFISH
LANGUSTA MACRURAN
(— **ENCLOSURE**) CRAWL
(— **LESS THAN 10 INCHES LONG**)
JOE
(**FEMALE** —) HEN
(**SMALL** —) PAWK NANCY
(**UNDERSIZED** —) SHORT
LOBSTER POT COY CRAIL CREEL
TRUNK FISHPOT
LOBULARIA KONIGA
LOCAL HOME NATIVE LIMITED
VICINAL REGIONAL EPICHORIC
LOCALE SITE LOCAL PLACE SCENE

LOCALITY SPA HAND PLAT SPOT
LOCUS PLACE POINT SITIO SITUS
STEAD HABITAT LATITUDE POSITURE
(**BARREN** —) GALL
(**GUARDED** —) POST
LOCALIZE SITUATE POSITION
LOCATE SITE SPOT PITCH PLACE
BESTOW BILLET SETTLE SITUATE
(— **AT INTERVALS**) SPOT
(— **WATER**) DIVINE
LOCATED SET FIXED SEATED
SITUATED
(— **OFF THE HIGHWAY**) DEVIOUS
LOCATING SYSTEM SOFAR
LOCATION FALL HOME PLOT SEAT
PLACE SITUS WHERE UBIETY
AMENITY STATION HOMESITE
STANDING
(**ESSENTIAL** —) EYE
(**FOREST** —) CHANCE
(**GEOGRAPHIC** —) SEAT
(**MINING** —) MYNPACHT
(**NATURAL** —) HABITAT
LOCH LOUGH LOCHAN
LOCK COT KEY FEAK FRIB HOLD
TRIM YALE CLASP SASSE DUBBEH
ENLOCK LUCKEN DAGLOCK
EARLOCK KEYLOCK PINLOCK
SPANNER DEADLOCK FORELOCK
(— **IMPROPERLY**) BIND
(— **IN RIVER**) SASSE
(— **OF HAIR**) COT TAG TUZ COTT
CURL FEAK TATE FLAKE FLOCK
FLUKE TRESS TANGLE COWLICK
EARLOCK FRIZZLE SERPENT
WIMPLER FORELOCK SIDELOCK
(— **OF WOOL**) TAG COTT FRIB
FLOCK STAPLE HASLOCK
(— **UP**) JAIL STOW CABINET
(**CANAL** —) CHAMBER
(**DIRTY** —) FRIB
(**MATTED** —) COT COTT DAGLOCK
(**MUSKET** —) ROWET
(**PART OF** —) STRIKE
(**WHEEL** —) REWET
LOCKED FAST LUCKEN
LOCKER HUTCH ASCHAM
LOCKERMAN NIBBLER SCOTCHER
SNIBBLER
LOCKJAW TETANUS TRISMUS
LOCKNUT JAMNUT KEEPER
LOCKOUT SHUTOUT
LOCKSMITH LOCKYER
LOCKUP JUG GAOL JAIL LOCK LOGS
CHOKY CLINK TRONK COOLER
HOOSEGOW
LOCOMOTION FLYING LATION
LOCOMOTIVE HOG PIG BOGY GOAT
HOGG MULE SHAG TANK BOGIE
DINKY DUMMY MOGUL PILOT DIESEL
DOCTOR DOLLIE DONKEY ENGINE
LOADER PUSHER SMOKER YARDER
BOBTAIL BOOSTER SHUNTER
STEAMER CALLIOPE CHOOCHOO
COMPOUND DOLLBEER
(— **WITHOUT CARS**) WILDCAT
(**EXTRA** —) HELPER
LOCOMOTOR ATAXIA TABES
LOCOWEED LOCO LEGUME PEAVINE

LOCUS PLACE EVOLUTE SURFACE
SYNAPSE CONCHOID ENVELOPE
HOROPTER
LOCUST WETA BRUKE HONEY
ACACIA CICADA QUAKER SKIPPER
TETRIGID
LOCUST TREE CAROB ACACIA
LOCUST ROBINIA ALGAROBA
LODE LEAD REEF VEIN LEDGE
COURSE FEEDER QUARRY COUNTER
LODESTONE MAGNET
LODGE DIG HUT INN LIE BEAT CAMP
HOST KEEP ROOM STAY STOW
TENT BOWER CABIN COUCH COURT
GROVE GUEST HOGAN HOTEL
HOUSE HOWFF LAYER LOGIS STICK
TARRY ALIGHT BESTOW BILLET
BURROW COSHER GESTEN GRANGE
HOSTEL RESIDE SETTLE BARRACK
LODGING QUARTER SOJOURN
EMBOLIZE HARBINGE
(— **AND EAT**) COSHER
(— **FOR SAFEKEEPING**) DEPOSIT
(— **IN COURT**) BOX
(**LOCAL** —) COURT
(**SPORTSMAN'S** —) SHEAL
LODGEPOLE PINE TAMARACK
LODGER INMATE ROOMER TENANT
LODGING BED CRIB GIST HAFT
HOST NEST GEAST LOGIS HARBOR
HOSTEL LIVERY HOSPICE HOUSING
COUCHANT GUESTING
(— **FOR SOLDIERS**) CASERN
(— **OF MARABOUT**) KOUBA
(**PL.**) DIGS DIGGINGS
LODGINGHOUSE INN KIP GITE STOP
HOTEL LOGIA LOCANDA PENSION
HOSTELRY
LODICULE SQUAMULA SQUAMULE
LOESS LIMON
LOFT BALK FLAT GOLF LAFT ATTIC
SOLAR GARRET SOLLAR HAYLOFT
COCKLOFT SCAFFOLD TRAVERSE
(**HAY** —) TALLET TALLIT
LOFTIEST SUPREME
LOFTINESS PRIDE HEIGHT DIGNITY
MAJESTY EMINENCE GRANDEUR
HIGHNESS
LOFTSMAN LINESMAN
LOFTY AIRY HIGH LOFT TALL ELATE
GRAND GREAT NOBLE PROUD
SKYEY STEEP WINGY AERIAL
ANDEAN HAUGHT TOPFUL TOWERY
UPWARD WINGED ANDESIC
ARDUOUS EMINENT EXCELSE
HAUGHTY SUBLIME ARROGANT
ELEVATED GENEROUS MAJESTIC
OLYMPIAN TOWERING
LOG NOG BUNK CLOG DRAG SKID
CHUCK CHUNK PIECE STICK STOCK
BATTEN BILLET PEAKER PEELER
SADDLE SAWLOG BACKLOG
DAYBOOK DEADMAN DEGRADE
JOURNAL LOGBOOK DEADHEAD
(— **AS ANCHOR**) DEADMAN
(— **AS RAFTER**) VIGA
(— **BINDING A RAFT**) SWIFTER
(— **CAR**) BUNK
(— **FASTENED TO TRAP**) DRAG

(— **SUPPORTING MINE ROOF**) NOG
(— **WITH SPIKES IN END**) DEADENER
(— **WITHOUT BARK**) BUCKSKIN
(**ENCLOSED** —**S**) BOOM
(**FLOATING** —**S**) DRIVE
(**LOAD OF** —**S**) PEAKER
(**PILE OF** —**S**) DECK ROLLWAY
(**SAWED** —) BOULE
(**SLABBED** —) CANT
(**SMALL** —) LOGGET
(**SPLIT** —) PUNCHEON
(**STRIPPED** —) BATTEN
(**SUNKEN** —) DEADHEAD
LOGANIN MELIATIN
LOGARITHM DENSITY
(— **SYMBOL**) PF PH PK RH
(**NEGATIVE** —) PH
LOGBOOK LOG JOURNAL
LOGE BOX BOOTH LODGE STALL
LOGGER RIDER BOWMAN DECKER
FALLER GOPHER HOOKER LIMBER
MARKER SCORER CHOPPER
FROGGER GRABBER SPOTTER
CATTYMAN
LOGGIA LODGE BALCONY MIRADOR
LOGIC NYAYA LOGICS CANONIC
WITCRAFT
(— **OF DISCOVERY**) HEURETIC
LOGICAL SANE RAISONNE RATIONAL
LOGMAN CHASER CHOPPER
LOGOGRAM IDEOGRAM
LOGOS WORD
LOGOTYPE SIG
LOG PERCH DARTER HOGFISH
ROCKFISH
LOGROLLING BIRLING
(— **TOURNAMENT**) ROLEO
LOGWOOD BRAZIL ADMIRAL
DYEWOOD BLUEWOOD HYPERNIC
LOGY DROWSY GROGGY
LOHAN RAKAN
LOIN LEER LISK ALOYAU LUNYIE
(**2 UNCUT** —**S**) BARON
(**PORK** —) GRISKIN
(**PL.**) REINS FILLET SADDLE
LOINCLOTH IZAR MALO MARO
DHOTI LUNGI PAGNE PAREU
MOOCHA PANUNG DHOOTIE
LOITER LAG CLUG FOOL HAKE HANG
HAWM HAZE HOVE LOUT MIKE
MUCK SLUG COOSE DELAY DRAWL
KNOCK MOUCH SHOOL SIDLE
TARRY COOTER DAWDLE LAGGER
LINGER MUCKER STRAKE TAIGLE
PROJECT SHAFFLE LALLYGAG
LOLLYGAG SCOWBANK SLAMMOCK
SLUMMOCK
LOITERER DRONE IDLER LAGGER
LAGGARD LURCHER
LOITERING SLIMSY LAGGARD
LOKAPALA MAHARAJA
LOKI (**DAUGHTER OF** —) HEL
(**MOTHER OF** —) ANGRBODHA
(**WIFE OF** —) SIGYN
LOLL FUG LOUT FROWST LOLLUP
LOUNGE SOZZLE SPRAWL RECLINE
SCAMBLE SCOWBANK
LOLLIPOP LOLLY SUCKER
SUCKABOB

LOLO NOSU
LONDON SMOKE COCKAGNE
(**BRIDGE IN** —) TOWER ALBERT
PUTNEY CHELSEA WATERLOO
(**DISTRICT OF** —) SOHO ACTON
ADELPHI ALSATIA BRIXTON
CHELSEA MAYFAIR
(**MONUMENT IN** —) GOG MAGOG
NELSON CENOTAPH VICTORIA
(**RIVER OF** —) THAMES
(**STREET OF** —) BOND FLEET
CANNON SAVILE DOWNING
WARDOUR HAYMARKET
(**SUBURB OF** —) KEW FINCHLEY
LONDONER FLATCAP
LONE LANE SOLE ALONE APART
SINGLE SOLITARY
(— **STAR STATE**) TEXAS
LONELINESS ONENESS VACANCY
SOLITUDE
LONELY ONLY SOLE VAST ALONE
UNKET UNKID WISHT ALANGE
DEAFLY SULLEN DEAVELY FORLORN
LONEFUL SOLEYNE DESOLATE
SECLUDED SOLITARY
LONESOME ALONE DOLEY LONELY
LANESOME SOLITARY
LONG HO DIE FAR FIT YEN ACHE
DREE HANK HONE ITCH LANG SIDE
TALL WILN WISH YAWN CRAVE
DREAM GREEN LATHY LONGA
MOURN STARK WEARY YEARN
ARIGUE ASPIRE DESIRE DREICH
HANKER HUNGER LINGER LONGUS
PROLIX STOUND THIRST LENGTHY
TEDIOUS WEILANG GEMINATE
INFINITE
(— **AGO**) FERN LANGSYNE
(— **AND SLENDER**) REEDY SQUINNY
(— **AND UNIFORM IN WIDTH**) LINEAR
(— **FOR**) CARE HONE COVET CRAVE
TASTE ASPIRE DESIRE SUSPIRE
(— **RESTLESSLY**) ITCH
(— **SINCE**) YORE
LONG-BILLED CURLEW SMOKER
LONGBOAT SLOOP
LONG-BODIED RACY RANGY
LONGERON SPAR
LONGEVITY VIVACITY
(— **CHARACTER**) SHOU
LONGING YEN ENVY ITCH LUST PINE
WISH BRAME YEARN DESIRE
HANKER TALENT THIRST ATHIRST
CRAVING THIRSTY WILLING WISHFUL
APPETENT APPETITE CUPIDITY
HOMESICK PRURIENT
LONGITUDINALLY ENDLONG
LONG-LASTING CHRONIC
LONGLEGS STILT
LONGLINE BULTOW
LONG-LIVED LONGEVE MACROBIAN
LONGSHOREMAN DOCKER
HOBBLER WHARFIE DOCKHAND
LONG-STANDING OLD
LONG-SUFFERING MEEK PATIENT
ENDURING PATIENCE
LONG-TAILED WHIDAH REDBILL
LONG TOM SKIPPER
LONG-WINDED PROLIX PROSAIC

LOOK LA LO AIR EYE KEN SEE SPY
CAST GAWK GAZE GIVE GLOM HEED
KEEK LATE LUCK MARK POKE SEEM
SWAP VIEW WAIT ACIES BLUSH
DEKKO FAVOR FLASH GLEAM GLEER
GLIFF GLINT SCREW SIGHT SQUIZ
VIZZY WLITE APPEAR ASPECT
EYEFUL GANDER GLANCE REGARD
REWARD VISION EYESHOT EYEWINK
INSIGHT SEEMING DISCOVER
LANGUISH OEILLADE
(— **ABOUT**) BELOOK SPECTATE
(— **AFTER**) TENT ATTEND FATHER
FETTLE PROCURE
(— **ASKANCE**) GLIM LEER SKEW
BAGGE GLENT GLEDGE SKLENT
(— **AT**) DIG SEE GLOM LAMP VIEW
GLISK ADVISE BEHOLD REGARD
REWARD CONSIDER SPECTATE
(— **CLOSELY**) PRY ESPY SCAN
(— **CROSS-EYED**) SHEYLE
(— **DOWN UPON**) SNOB DESPISE
(— **DULLY**) BLEAR
(— **FIXEDLY**) GAZE KYKE GLORE
STARE
(— **FOR**) SPY FOND SEEK GROPE
EXPECT PROPOSE RESPECT
(— **FORWARD**) EXPECT FORESEE
ENVISAGE ENVISION
(— **GLANCINGLY**) BLINK
(— **IN SNEAKING MANNER**) SNOOP
(— **INTENTLY**) GLOSE VISIE GLOWER
EYEBALL
(— **INTO**) SOUND SEARCH
(— **OBLIQUELY**) GLIME GOGGLE
SQUINT
(— **OF DERISION**) FLEER
(— **OF PLANETS**) ASPECTS
(— **OUT**) FEND MIND CHEESE
JIGGERS OUTLOOK
(— **OVER**) SCAN TOISE BROWSE
SURVEY EXAMINE
(— **SEARCHINGLY**) PEER PORE
TOOT
(— **SLYLY**) PEEP GLINK
(— **SOUR**) GLUNCH
(— **STEADFASTLY**) GLOAT
(— **SULKY**) LUMP
(— **SULLEN**) LOUR LOWER
(— **UPON AS**) ACCOUNT
(— **WILDLY**) GLOP WAUL WHAWL
(— **WITH FAVOR**) SMILE
(**AMOROUS** —) SMICKER
(**BRIEF** —) GLIM GLINT GLIMPSE
(**LOVING** —) BELGARD
(**QUICK** —) SCRY GLENT
(**SEARCHING** —) SCRUTINY
(**SEVERE** —) FROWN
(**SIDELONG** —) GLEE GLIME
(**SLY** —) GLEG GLIME TWIRE
(**SULLEN** —) GLOOM GLOUT
GLUNCH
(**TENDER** —) LANGUISH
(**WANTON** —) LEER
(**PL.**) DAPS
LOOKER BEAUTY HERDSMAN
SEARCHER
LOOKER-ON BEHOLDER
LOOKOUT TOUT SCOUT WATCH

BANTAY CONNER TOOTER FUNERAL OUTLOOK ATALAYAN BANTAYAN BARTIZAN COCKATOO PROSPECT TOWERMAN WATCHOUT

LOOM BEAM BULK HULK LEEM DOBBY FRAME GLOOM BEETLE DOBBIE DRAWLOOM HANDLOOM JACQUARD OVERPICK

(— **ATTACHMENT**) LAPPET

LOOM AXLE ROCKTREE

LOOM BAR EASER DAGGER

LOOMFIXER TACKLER

LOOM HARNESS LEAF HEADLE SIMBLOT MOUNTING

LOON DIVER IMBER WABBY COBBLE DUCKER GUNNER WHABBY PYGOPOD

LOOP BOW EYE LUG NOB TAB TAG ANSA BEND COIL FAKE HANK KINK KNOB KNOP LEAF LINK LOUP PURL BIGHT BRIDE CHAPE COQUE GUIDE LACET LATCH NOOSE PEARL PICOT SHANK STRAP TERRY WITHY BECKET BILLET BUCKLE FOLIUM HANGER HOLDER KEEPER KINKLE PARRAL SPIRAL STAPLE STITCH TWITCH COCKEYE COUPURE CRINGLE CRUPPER GROMMET KNUCKLE LATCHET SEGMENT ANTINODE COURONNE

(— **AND THIMBLES**) CLEW CLUE

(— **BY ICESKATER**) SPOON

(— **IN KNITTING**) STEEK

(— **IN MINER'S ROPE**) SLUG

(— **IN NEEDLEWORK**) BRIDE

(— **OF INTESTINES**) KNUCKLE

(— **OF IRON**) OOLLY

(— **OF ROPE**) FAKE BIGHT FLAKE KINCH NOOSE ANCHOR BECKET PARRAL SNORTER SNOTTER

(— **OF SCABBARD**) FROG

(— **OF TUBING**) SCROLL

(— **ON ARMOR**) VERVELLE

(— **ON SPINNING FRAME**) BAND

(— **ON SWORD BELT**) HANGER

(**HANGING** —) FESTOON

(**HEDDLE** —) DOUP

(**ORNAMENTAL** —) PICOT

(**SHOULDER** —) EPAULET

(**SURGICAL** —) CURET CURETTE

(**TIGHT** —) KINK KINKLE

LOOPER INCHWORM SPANWORM

LOOPHOLE LOOP CHINK MEUSE EYELET OILLET WICKET PORTHOLE

LOOSE GAY LAX EMIT FREE GLAD LASH LIMP OPEN SOFT UNDO WIDE WILD BAGGY CRANK FRANK LARGE LIGHT RELAX SLACK VAGUE WASHY ADRIFT FLUFFY LIMBER SLOPPY SOLUTE SPORTY SUBURB UNBIND UNGIRT UNLASH WOBBLY CHESSOM FLYAWAY IMMORAL MOVABLE RELAXED SHOGGLY STRINGY UNBOUND UNHITCH UNTIGHT DISCINCT FLOATING INSECURE LAXATIVE SHATTERY UNSTABLE

(— **ARROW**) BOLT

(**MORALLY** —) FRANK

LOOSE-JOINTED LANKY SHACKLY

LOOSELY SLACK LARGELY SLACKLY

LOOSEN LAX BREAK SLACK UNTIE LAXATE LIMBER UNBEND RESOLVE SLACKEN UNGRIPE UNLOOSE UNSCREW DISHEVEL UNSTRING

(— **ANCHOR**) TRIP

(— **ROCK**) GAD

LOOSENESS SLACK LAXITY LATITUDE

LOOSENING START SOLUTIVE SOLUTORY

LOOSESTRIFE KILLWEED PEATWEED PEATWOOD PRIMWORT

LOOT SACK SWAG BOOTY HARRY SPOIL STEAL THEFT HERSHIP PILLAGE PLUNDER SNAFFLE

LOOTING SACK

LOP DOD LAP CLIP DODD OCHE SNED SNIG TRIM SHRAG SHRED SHRUB STUMP TRASH TWINE SHROUD SNATHE TRASHIFY TRUNCATE

(— **OFF**) COW DOD CROP DODD HEAD SNAG SNEP PRUNE SHRED TRUNK DEFALK AMPUTATE

LOPE SHAG

LOPPER CLABBER

LOQUACIOUS GABBY FUTILE

LOQUACITY PRATE PRATTLE FUTILITY

LOQUAT BIWA NISPERO

LORAL FRENAL

LORD BEL DAM DEN DON GOD HER LOR MAR SID SIR DION DOMN EROS HERR LAUK LOSH SIRE TUAN ANGUS ARAWN BARON LAFEU LIEGE LUDDY NIGEL OMRAH RABBI SAHIB SWAMI DOMINE DUMAIN KYRIOS PRABHU SAYYID SIGNOR TANIST THAKUR CAMILLO CERIMON JACQUES JEHOVAH MARCHER OGTIERN VAVASOR BHAGAVAT DESPOTES DRIGHTEN GRANDPRE LORDLING MARGRAVE OVERLORD PALATINE SEIGNEUR SEIGNIOR SUPERIOR SUZERAIN THALIARD

(— **OF DARKNESS**) HYLE

(— **OF WORLD**) LOKINDRA

(**FEUDAL** —) DAUPHIN VAVASOR SUZERAIN

LORD CHANCELLOR WOOLPACK

LORDLINESS PRIDE

LORDLY PROUD SUPERB ARROGANT DESPOTIC

LORDOSIS SWAYBACK

LORDSHIP NAVY DYNASTY ERECTION SEIGNORY SIGNORIA

LORE LEAR LORUM MASTAX LEARNING

LORGNETTE STARER

LORICA LORIC SHEATH SHIELD

LORIKEET PARROT WARRIN CORELLA WEROOLE

LORIS KOKAM LEMUR SLOTH LEMUROID

LORN ALONE

LORRY RULLY ROLLEY

LORY LOORY CORELLA LORIKEET

LOSE LET TIN AMIT DROP TINE WANT

FORGO LAPSE LEASE TRAIL GAMBLE MISLAY FORBEAR FORFEIT FORLESE SLATTER

(— **AT CARDS**) BUST

(— **BET**) WRONG

(— **BRILLIANCE**) FAINT

(— **BY DEATH**) BURY

(— **BY GAMING**) GAME

(— **BY STUPIDITY**) BLUNDER

(— **CONTROL**) BLOW CRACK

(— **COURAGE**) DREEP TAINT

(— **FLAVOR**) FOZE APPAL APPALL

(— **FORCE**) COLLAPSE

(— **FRESHNESS**) FADE WILT WITHER

(— **HEART**) JADE FAINT QUAIL

(— **HOPE**) DESPAIR DESPOND

(— **LUSTER**) TARNISH

(— **MOISTURE**) GUTTATE

(— **NERVE**) CHICKEN

(— **OFFICE**) FALL

(— **ONE'S BREATH**) CHINK

(— **ONE'S WAY**) STRAY

(— **POWER**) FAIL DISSOLVE

(— **SELF-POSSESSION**) ABASH

(— **SPIRIT**) JADE

(— **STRENGTH**) GO FADE FAIL WEAKEN LANGUISH

(— **VISION**) DAZZLE

(— **WARMTH**) COOL CONGEAL

(— **WEIGHT**) ENSEAM

LOSS ACE COST HARM LEAK LOST MISS LAPSE QUALM WASTE BURIAL DAMAGE DAMNUM DEFEAT INJURY TINSEL AVERAGE DEBACLE DEFICIT EXPENSE JACTURE LEAKAGE LEESING MISTURE REPRISE AMISSION BREAKAGE CLEANING MISSMENT

(— **BY SIFTING**) ULLAGE

(— **IN WORKING**) SLIPPAGE

(— **OF ABILITIES**) COLLAPSE

(— **OF ACTIVITY**) AKINESIA

(— **OF APPETITE**) ANOREXIA

(— **OF CONSCIOUSNESS**) SWOON ABSENCE APOPLEXY BLACKOUT FAINTING

(— **OF ELASTICITY**) SET

(— **OF ELECTRICITY**) EFFLUVE

(— **OF EXPRESSION**) AMIMIA

(— **OF HAIR**) DEFLUX ALOPECIA PTILOSIS

(— **OF HOPE**) DESPAIR

(— **OF MEMORY**) AMNESIA

(— **OF PRESTIGE**) DISHONOR

(— **OF SCENT**) CHECK

(— **OF SENSE OF SMELL**) ANOSMIA

(— **OF SIZE**) WANE

(— **OF SOUND**) APOCOPE SYNCOPE APHERESIS

(— **OF SPEECH**) ALALIA APHASIA APHONIA

(— **OF VOICE**) ANAUDIA APHONIA

(— **OF VOWEL**) APHESIS

(— **OF WILL POWER**) ABULIA

(**CONTRACT** —) LESION

LOST GONE LORN TINT WASTE ASTRAY BUSHED HIDDEN NAUGHT FORFEIT FORLORN MISSING CONFUSED OBSCURED

LOT CUT HAP PEW CHOP CROP DEAL
DOLE DOOM DRAW FALL FATE HEAP
PACK PART PILE REDE SLEW SLUE
SORS SORT BATCH BLOCK BREAK
CAVEL FIELD GRACE GRIST GROSS
LINES SHARE SHOOT SIGHT SITHE
STAND TEEMS TROOP WEIRD
AMOUNT BARREL BUNDLE CHANCE
DICKER FARDEL OODLES TICHEL
BOILING DESTINY FEEDLOT
FORTUNE PORTION SANDLOT
BACKYARD CABOODLE MOUTHFUL
RIMPTION WOODLAND
(— OF 60 PIECES) SHOCK
(— OF PERSONS) BOODLE
(— OF TEA) BREAK
(BUILDING —) ERF
(BURIAL —) LAIR
(GREAT —) SWAG
(VACANT —) COMMON COMMONS
LOTION WASH EYEWASH EYEWATER
LAVATORY
LOTS HEAPS TEEMS BUSHEL HODFUL
LOTTERY AMBO LOTTO TERNO
RAFFLE TOMBOLA
LOTTO KENO BINGO TOMBOLA
(— GAME) HOUSE
LOTUS LOTE LOTOS WANKAPIN
LOTUS TREE SADR ZYZYPHUS
LOUCHEUX KUTCHIN
LOUD HARD HIGH MAIN CRUDE
FORTE GAUDY GREAT HEAVY
SHOWY STARK STOUR WIGHT
BRASSY BRAZEN COARSE CRIANT
FLASHY HOARSE VULGAR BLATANT
CLAMANT HAUTAIN VIOLENT
BIGMOUTH FRENZIED SLAMBANG
STREPENT STRIDENT VEHEMENT
LOUDLY BOST ALOUD FORTE STARK
LOUDNESS STRESS SONORITY
(— UNIT) PHON SONE
LOUDSPEAKER WOOFER SPEAKER
TWEETER BULLHORN SQUAWKER
LOUD-SPOKEN RANDY
LOUIS LUIGI LODOWIC

LOUISIANA
CAPITAL: BATONROUGE
COLLEGE: LSU TULANE DILLARD
GRAMBLING
COUNTY: CADDO ACADIA PARISH
TENSAS LAFOURCHE
CULTURE: TCHEFUNCTE
DIALECT: CREOLE
FESTIVAL: MARDIGRAS
INDIAN: ADAI WASHA ATAKAPA
LAKE: IATT CLEAR LARTO
BORGNE SALINE DARBONNE
MAUREPAS
NATIVE: CAJUN CREOLE ACADIAN
NICKNAME: PELICAN
RIVER: AMITE TENSAS OUACHITA
STATE BIRD: PELICAN
STATE FLOWER: MAGNOLIA
STATE TREE: CYPRESS
STREAM: BAYOU
TOWN: HOUMA GRETNA MINDEN
RUSTON BASTROP BOGALUSA

LOUISIANIAN CAJUN ACADIAN
LOUNGE HAWM LOLL SORN SOSS
BANGE TRAIK FROUST FROWST
GLIDER LOLLUP LOPPET RIZZLE
SLINGE SOZZLE LAMMOCK SAUNTER
SLOUNGE
LOUNGER IDLER SLOUNGER
LOUSE BOB BUG SOW CRAB CRUMB
BOOGER BRAULA COOTIE GISLER
PALMER SISTEN VERMIN MORPION
PUCERON GRAYBACK
(FISH —) GISLER ARGULUS
(PLANT —) APHID APHIS
(WOOD —) SOW SLATER
(YOUNG —) NIT
LOUSEWORT RATTLE SNAFFLES
LOUSY SEEDY CRAPPY
LOUT HOB LOB LUG BOOR CHUB
COOF GAUM GAWK LOON NOWT
SWAB SWAD CHUMP CUDDY GNOFF
LOURD ROBIN THRUM WHAUP
YAHOO BOHUNK CLUNCH GOBBIN
HOBLOB LOURDY LUBBER LUNGIS
SLOUCH TRIPAL GROBIAN HAWBUCK
LOBCOCK LOBLOLLY
(COUNTRY —) KERN BUMPKIN
LOUTISH SWAB HULKY SLOOMY
BOORISH HULKING VILLAIN
BOEOTIAN
LOUVER SLAT LOUVRE LUFFER
DIFFUSER FEMERELL
(PL.) SHUTTER
LOVABLE AMABEL CUDDLY AMIABLE
ADORABLE DOVELIKE LOVESOME
LOVABLENESS DEARNESS
LOVAGE SMELLAGE
LOVE GRA LOO AMOR EROS KAMA
LIKE ALOHA AMOUR CUPID DRURY
FANCY HEART MINNE TENDRE
CHARITY EMBRACE FEELING
DEVOTION KINDNESS LOVEHOOD
PARAMOUR
(— IN RETURN) REDAME
(— OF MARVELOUS) TERATISM
(— TO EXCESS) IDOLIZE
(— TOWARD DEITY) BHAKTI
(CHRISTIAN —) CHARITY
(INTENSE —) FIRE
(NATURAL —) STORGE
(SELF-GIVING —) AGAPE
(UNLAWFUL —) LEMANRY
LOVED DEAR BELOVED
(MUCH —) SWEET
LOVE FEAST AGAPE
LOVE KNOT AMORET
LOVELINESS BEAUTY
LOVELOCK EARLOCK
LOVELY LOVING TENDER AMIABLE
AMOROUS ADORABLE LOVESOME
LOVEMAKING AMOUR
LOVER GRA MAN BEAU CHAP AMANT
AMOUR DRURY LEMAN ROMEO
SPARK SWAIN AMADIS AMANTE
MARROW MINION SQUIRE ADMIRER
AMORIST AMOROSO CELADON
GALLANT PATRIOT SPARKER
SPECIAL SPRUNNY BELAMOUR
CASANOVA CICISBEO PARAMOUR
STREPHON

(MODEL —) LEILAH
(SILLY —) SPOON
LOVE SEAT CAUSEUSE
LOVING DEAR FOND TENDER
AMATORY AMOROUS
LOW BAS BOO LAW MOO BASE KEEN
MEAN ORRA ROUT SLOW VILE
WEAK BLORE DIRTY GROSS LAICH
PUTID SHORT SMALL SNIDE THIRD
CALLOW EARTHY FILTHY GENTLE
GRUBBY HARLOT HUMBLE LIMMER
MENIAL RASCAL RIBALD SECRET
SILKEN TURPID VULGAR BESTIAL
IGNOBLE RAFFISH REPTILE SLAVISH
SUBMISS SOUTERLY
(— AS OF A VOWEL) OPEN
(— DOWN) SIDE
(— IN LIGHTNESS) DULL
(— IN PERCEPTION) CRUDE
(— IN PITCH) GRAVE
(— IN QUALITY) HEDGE
(— IN SATURATION) GRAYISH
(— IN SPIRITS) BLUE DOWN
GLOOMY DOWNCAST
(— IN TONE) SOFT SUBMISS
(— IN WATER) RACE
(— NUMBERS) MANQUE
(— POINT) TROUGH
(IMMEASURABLY —) ABYSMAL
LOWBORN WAFF
LOWBRED BASTARD PLEBEIAN
LOW-DOWN BUCKASS
LOWER CUT DIP LOW BASE BATE
DOWN DROP DUCK FELL SINK
ABASE ABATE ALLOY AVALE BELOW
BLAME COUCH COWER DECRY
DEMIT DOUSE FROWN GLOOM
LEVEL SCOWL STOOP BEMEAN
DEBASE DEJECT DEMEAN EMBASE
GLOWER HUMBLE JUNIOR LESSEN
MODIFY NETHER REDUCE SETTLE
STRIKE SUBDUE SUBMIT BENEATH
DECLASS DEGRADE DEPRESS
SHORTEN DIMINISH DOWNWARD
INFERIOR MODERATE
(— BANNER) VAIL
(— BY HALF STEP) FLAT
(— IN ESTEEM) CHEAPEN
DEROGATE
(— IN PITCH) FLAT SHADE
(— ONESELF) SINK BEMEAN
DESCEND
(— PRICES) BEAR
(— SAIL) AMAIN
(— THE HEAD) STOOP
LOWERING DIP DUCK DOWLY HEAVY
LAPSE BEETLE SULLEN
(— OF BODY) FONDU
(— OF LAND) ABLATION
LOWEST LAST LEAST EXTREME
LOWMOST
(— CLASS) LAG
(— POSSIBLE) KNOWDOWN
LOWING MUGIENT
LOWLAND LAICH POLDER LALLAND
DOWNLAND
(— BESIDE RIVER) INKS
(BARREN —) LANDES

LOWLANDER SAXON ZHMUD SASSENACH
LOWLIER LESS
LOWLY LOW BASE SILLY HUMBLE BASEBORN
LOW-LYING CALLOW LALLAN INFERIAL SUBJECTED
LOW-MINDED BASE MEAN
LOWNESS LOWTH
  (— OF SPIRITS) GLOOM SPLEEN MEGRIMS
LOW-PITCHED GRUFF
LOW-SPIRITED HIPPED DEJECTED
LOY SLICK
LOYAL FAST FEAL FIRM HOLD LEAL REAL TRUE LIEGE PIOUS SOUND ARDENT HEARTY LAWFUL SECRET STANCH FAITHFUL YEOMANLY
LOYALIST TORY
LOYALLY SURELY
LOYALTY ARDOR FAITH FEALTY HOMAGE LEALTY REALTY SPIRIT REALITY DEVOTION FIDELITY
LOZENGE TAB JUBE COIGN QUOIN JUJUBE MASCLE QUARRY ROTULA RUSTRE TABLET TABULE TROCHE CREMULE DIAMOND TABELLA PASTILLE ROSEDROP
  (— OF CEMENT) WAFER
LOZI ROZI BAROTSE
LUBBER SWAB LOOBY SLOUCH LOBCOCK LILBURNE
LUBBERLY AWKWARD
LUBRICANT DOPE GREASE AQUADAG UNGUENT
LUBRICATE OIL DOPE GLIB GREASE LUBRIFY
LUBRICATOR OILER OILCAN
LUCARNE LUCOMBE
LUCENT BRIGHT LUCIBLE
LUCERNE LEGUME ALFALFA
LUCID SANE CLEAR AERIAL BRIGHT LIMPID CRYSTAL DILUCID LITERATE LUCULENT LUMINOUS
LUCIDITY SANITY
LUCIFER DEVIL PHOSPHOR
LUCK HAP CESS EURE SONS SPIN GRACE ISSUE CHANCE THRIFT FORTUNE HANDSEL SUCCESS VENTURE HAMINGJA
  (BAD — TO YOU) YLAHAYLL
  (BAD —) ACE DOLE DEUCE HOODOO UNLUCK AMBSACE
  (GOOD —) HAP FORTUNE THEEDOM
  (ILL —) UNHAP DIRDUM DISGRACE
  (RELATING TO —) ALEATORY
  (UNEXPECTED —) BUNCE
LUCKILY HAPPILY
LUCKY HOT CANNY HAPPY SONSY CHANCY LUCKLY LUCKFUL GRACIOUS
LUCRATIVE FAT GOOD GAINFUL
LUCRE SWAG
LUDICROUS AWFUL COMIC DROLL ABSURD FOOLISH HIDEOUS FARCICAL
LUDO UCKERS
LUFFA LOOFAH SPONGE
LUG EAR HUG TUG WAG SNUG SPUD

ZULU PATCH WALTZ
LUGGAGE SWAG TRAPS HATBOX BAGGAGE TRUSSERY
LUGGAGE CASE IMPERIAL
LUGGAR JAGGAR JUGGER LAGGAR
LUGGER CAT TOUP ZULU FIFIE
LUGUBRIOUS DOLEFUL DOLOROUS
LUGWORM LOB LUG LOBWORM SANDWORM
LUIGINO TEMIN
LUKEWARM LEW LUKE TEPID WLACH
LULL CALM DRUG FODE HUSH ROCK CROON HUSHO SLACK STILL SOPITE HUSHABY HUSHEEN
LULLABY LULL BALOO BALOW LULLAY HUSHABY HUSHEEN ROCKABY
LULLING DROWSY CIRCEAN
LUMBER BURR DEAL RAFF NANMU STOCK STRIP FINISH FLITCH REFUSE SAMCHU SHORTS TIMBER DEGRADE DUNNAGE GUMWOOD TRUNDLE STEPPING
  (INFERIOR —) SAPS SCOOT
LUMBERING AWKWARD LUMBERLY LUMBROUS
LUMBERJACK JACK TOPPER TIMBERER
LUMBERMAN PINER DOGGER SCORER CHOPPER GIRDLER TIMBERER
LUMINANCE HELIOS
LUMINARY LIGHT CANDLE PLANET
LUMINESCENCE FLAME
LUMINOSITY FIRE GLOW LIGHT VALUE
LUMINOUS LIGHT LUCID SHINY BRIGHT LUMINANT
LUMMOX LOBSTER
LUMP BAT BOB COB CUB DAB DAD FID GOB JOB NIB NOB NUB WAD BLOB BURL CLAG CLAM CLOT COOL COWL DUNT JUNK KNOB KNOT PONE SWAD TOKE BLOOM CHUCK CHUNK CLAUT CLUMP CLUNK GLEBE HUNCH KNOLL KNURL MOUSE SLUMP STONE WEDGE WODGE CLUNCH DOLLOP GOBBET HUBBLE HUDDLE LUMPET NUBBLE NUGGET CLUMPER CLUNTER PUMPKNOT
  (— IN CLOTH) BURL
  (— IN GLASS) YOLK
  (— OF BLACK LEAD) SOP
  (— OF BLOOD) CLOD
  (— OF COAL) NUBBLING
  (— OF DOUGH) DIP
  (— OF FAT) KEECH
  (— OF GLASS) BLOOM
  (— OF IRON) OOLLY
  (— OF LAVA) BOMB
  (— OF LINT) SLUG
  (— OF METAL) MASS SLUG
  (— OF ORE) ROCK HARDHEAD
  (— OF RUBBER) THIMBLE
  (— OF SALT) SALTCAT
  (— OF YEAST) BEE
  (LARGE —) DOLL HUNK

  (LITTLE —) NODULE KNOBBLE
  (ROUNDED —) CLOT
LUMPFISH GROSS PADDLE SUCKER
LUMPISH STODGY CHUCKLE
LUMPY GOBBY CHUNKY CLUNCH COBBLY
LUNACY MOON FOLLY MADNESS DELIRIUM INSANITY
LUNARIA SATINPOD
LUNARY VOLVELLE
LUNATIC GELT LOONY BEDLAM MADMAN MANIAC FANATIC FRANTIC CRACKPOT MOONLING MOONSICK
LUNCH CUT BAIT CRIB TIFF BEVER PIECE SNACK BRUNCH NACKET TIFFIN UNDERN BAGGING ELEVENS DEJEUNER DRINKING ELEVENER LUNCHEON
  (DAIRY —) CREMERIE
  (MINER'S —) SNAP
LUNCHEON CRIB LUNCH STULL TIFFIN DINETTE NOONMEAT
LUNCHROOM EATERY
LUNETTE OUTWORK
LUNG DRAGON LONGUE
LUNGE FOIN PASS SPAR POINT VENUE CHARGE ALLONGE
LUNGFISH CYCLOID DIPNOAN MUDFISH SIRENOID
LUNGS LIGHTS VISCUS BELLOWS
  (PERTAINING TO —) PULMONIC
LUNKHEAD DOLT JUGHEAD
LUNULE ALBEDO
LUO DHOLUO
LUPINE SUNDIAL
LURCH JOLL STOT SWAG STOIT CAREEN STOITER STUMBLE SWAGGER
LURCHING DRUNKEN ROLLING
LURE CON JAY BAIT HOOK ROPE TOLL WISE DECOY DRILL FEINT SLOCK SNARE SPOON SQUID STALE TEMPT TROLL ALLURE CAPPER CLARET ENTICE ENTRAP SEDUCE TREPAN VELURE GUDGEON INVEIGH PHANTOM PITFALL WOBBLER BUCKTAIL INVEIGLE LUREMENT
  (— INTO GAMBLING) HUSTLE
  (— OF CARRION) TRAIN
  (— WILDFOWL) STOOL
LURI ALUR
LURID RED PURPLE SULTRY CRIMSON GHASTLY
LURK DARE LOUT COUCH LOWER SKULK SLINK SNEAK AMBUSH DARKLE
LURKING LURKY GRASSANT
LUSCIOUS FOND RICH SWEET CREAMY DULCET DELICATE
LUSH GREEN LUSTY MOIST SAVORY FERTILE OPULENT THRIVING
LUST HELL KAMA BLOOD PRIDE DESIRE LIBIDO LIKING LUXURY NICETY PASSION COVETISE CUPIDITY
LUSTER NAIF GLASS GLINT GLOSS SHEEN SHINE WATER LUSTRE POLISH REFLET BURNISH GLIMPSE GLISTER LUSTRUM NITENCY

FULGENCE LUSTRATE RADIANCY SPLENDOR
(— **OF FIBER**) BLOOM
(**BRONZE-LIKE** —) SCHILLER
LUSTERLESS WAN DEAD DULL FISHY STARY
LUSTFUL HOT GAMY GOLE LEWD RANK SALT CADGY LUSTY PRIME RANDY RUTTY WANTON BEASTLY CODDING FLESHLY FULSOME JEALOUS RAMMISH RUTTISH LIKEROUS
LUSTFULNESS SATYRISM
LUSTILY CRANK HOTLY
LUSTING ITCHY
LUSTRATION ABHISEKA
LUSTROUS CLEAR DOGGY NITID BRIGHT GLOSSY ORIENT SHEENY SILKEN SILVER SHINING SPLENDID
LUSTY BRAG CANT CRANK FLUSH FRACK FRANK FRECK GUTSY HARDY JUICY STIFF STOUT GAWSIE ROBUST STURDY LUSTFUL LUSTICK BOUNCING PHYSICAL SPORTIVE VIGOROUS
LUTE TAR BIWA LAUD DOMRA NABIA NABLE REBAB REBEC SAROD CITOLE ENLUTE LORICA LUTING SCREED ANGELOT BANDORE DICHORD DYPHONE MANDOLA MANDORE MINIKIN PANDORE THEORBO VIHUELA ANGELICA ARCHLUTE PENORCAN TAMBOURA TEMPLATE TRICHORD
LUTER DAUBER PASTER
LUTJANID JEWFISH

LUXEMBOURG
CAPITAL: LUXEMBOURG
HIGHEST POINT: BURGPLATZ

LOWLAND: BONPAYS GUTLAND
MEASURE: FUDER
MOUNTAIN RANGE: ARDENNES
PLATEAU: ARDENNES
RIVER: OUR SURE SAUER ALZETTE MOSELLE
TOWN: ROODT WILTZ PETANGE VIANDEN DIEKIRCH

LUXURIANT GOLE LUSH RANK RICH FRANK PROUD LAVISH WANTON OPULENT PROFUSE TEEMING PAMPERED PRODIGAL
LUXURIANTLY FATLY
LUXURIATE BASK WALLOW WANTON
LUXURIOUS HIGH LUSH NICE POSH RANK SOFT GAUDY SWANK CAPUAN DELUXE GILDED SILKEN SWANKY WANTON ELEGANT LUCULLAN PRODIGAL REGALADO SENSUOUS TRYPHENA TRYPHOSA
LUXURIOUSLY HIGH DELUXE
LUXURY FRILL FINERY OUTRAGE DELICACY ELEGANCE PLEASURE RICHNESS
LUXURY-LOVING DELICATE
LYCANTHROPE WEREWOLF
LYCAON (DAUGHTER OF —) CALLISTO
(**FATHER OF** —) PALASGUS
LYCEUM PLATFORM
LYCHNIS FIREBALL NONESUCH
LYCIUM RUSOT
LYCOPODIUM MOSS FOXTAIL CROWFOOT STAGHORN
LYDIA MAEONIA
LYE LEY BOUK BUCK STRAKE LESSIVE LIXIVIUM SOAPLEES
LYING FLAT FALSE LEASE CRETISM

LEASING MENTERY
(— **APART**) DISSITE
(— **AT BASE OF MOUNTAINS**) PIEDMONT
(— **CLOSE**) QUAT
(— **DOWN**) DOWN LODGED DORMANT COUCHANT
(— **HID**) LATITANT
(— **IDLE**) INACTIVE
(— **ON BACK**) SUPINE
(— **ON FACE**) PRONE
(— **OVER**) JACENT
(— **UNDER GRASS**) LEA
LYING-IN INLYING CHILDBED GROANING
LYMPH CHYLE VIRUS
LYMPHAD GALLEY
LYMPHANGITIS WEED FILLING
LYMPHOGRANULOMA BUBO
LYMPHOMATOSIS FISHEYE
LYNCEUS (BROTHER OF —) IDAS
(**FATHER OF** —) AEGYPTUS APHAREUS
(**WIFE OF** —) HYPERMNESTRA
LYNCH HANG DEWITT
LYNX LOSSE PISHU BOBCAT GORKUN LUCERN CARACAL LUCIVEE WILDCAT CARCAJOU
LYRE ASOR HARP LYRA SHELL CHELYS KINNOR KISSAR TRIGON CITHARA PHORMIX TESTUDO BARBITON TRICHORD TRIGONON
LYREBIRD LYRETAIL PHEASANT
LYRIC LAY LIED HOKKU MELIC GHAZEL TENSON CANCION CHANSON DESCORT MADRIGAL
(**LOVE** —) ALBA
(**PL.**) SONG
LYTTA WORM

M EM EMMA MIKE METRO
(WRONG USE OF —) MYTACISM
M-1 GARAND
MA'AM MARM MISTRESS
MAARIB ARBIT ARBITH
MACA ENIMAGA
MACABRE SICK HORRIBLE
MACACA PITHECUS
MACADAMIZE METAL
MACAO (CHINESE NAME OF —)
AOMEN
(ISLAND OF —) TAIPA COLOANE
MACAQUE KRA BROH BRUH MACAC
MACHIN RHESUS
MACARIA (FATHER OF —) HERCULES
(MOTHER OF —) DEIANIRA
MACARONI DITALI
MACARONIC SKEW
MACAW ARA ARARA PARROT
MARACAN ARACANGA COCKATOO
MACE CROC MALL MAUL VERGE
MALLET SPARTH CATTAIL
(REED —) DOD DODD
(ROYAL —) SCEPTER SCEPTRE
MACE-BEARER BEADLE VERGER
MACEMAN
MACERATE SOUR STEEP
MACHAON (BROTHER OF —)
PODALIRIUS
(FATHER OF —) AESCULAPIUS
(MOTHER OF —) CORONIS
MACHETE GULOC PARANG CURTAXE
CUTLASH CUTLASS
MACHIAVELLIAN CRAFTY CUNNING
GUILEFUL
MACHINATION ARTIFICE INTRIGUE
SCHEMERY
MACHINE (ALSO SEE DEVICE AND
ENGINE) GIN HOG JIG SAW AGER
COMB GEAR JACK LIFT MULE PUMP
RASP TRAY WHIM WINK ADDER
AWNER BALER BENCH BILLY BOARD
BRAKE BREAK COPER CRANE DEVIL
EDGER FRAME FUDGE FUGAL JENNY
JERRY JOLLY LATHE LAYER METER
MIXER MOWER NAVVY RAKER
RESAW ROVER SCREW SETUP
SHEEN SIZER STAMP SULKY TRONE
VINER WILLY BARKER BEADER
BEAMER BEATER BEETLE BENDER
BILLER BINDER BOLTER BUCKLE
BUMPER BUTTER CANTER CAPPER
CARDER CONCHE COOLER CREWER
DECKER DOFFER DONKEY DRAPER
DREDGE DUSTER ENGINE FLAKER
FOLDER FOOTER FORMER GADDER
GAPPER GLAZER GRADER GRATER
GUMMER HEADER HEMMER HOBBER
HOGGER HOOPER HULLER HUSKER
IRONER JIGGER JORDAN KICKER
LEGGER LIFTER LINTER LOGGER
MAILER MANGLE MILLER MITRER
NAPPER NETTER NIBBER NIPPER
PACKER PEGGER PINNER PLATER
PUMPER RIPPER ROSSER ROTARY
ROUTER SANDER SCUTCH SEALER
SEAMER SHAKER SHAPER SHAVER
SINGER SKIVER SLICER SORTER
SPACER STOCKS STOKER TEDDER

TENTER TWINER VANNER WASHER
WELDER WILLOW ABRADER
AUTOMAT AVIATOR BACKHOE
BATCHER BELLOWS BLENDER
BOTTLER BRANNER BREAKER
CANDROY CAPSTAN CHIPPER
COMBINE CRUSHER DIBBLER
DRESSER EMULSOR ENCODER
ENROBER ERECTOR EXOSTRA
FLANGER FLOSSER FREEZER
GARNETT GLASSER GRAINER
GRINDER GROOVER GROUTER
HUMIDOR IRONMAN JOINTER
KNITTER KNOTTER MACHINA
MANGLER MATCHER MITERER
PLODDER PLUCKER POTCHER
PRINTER QUILLER REPRESS
RIVETER ROASTER SAMMIER
SCALPER SHEARER SHEETER
SIROCCO SLABBER SLASHER
SLITTER SLOTTER SLUBBER
SLUGGER SMASHER SPALLER
SPEEDER SPINNER SPONGER
SPOOLER SPRAYER STACKER
STAMPER STAPLER STEAMER
STEMMER STICKER TENONER
TEREBRA TOOTHER TRAMPER
TREATER TRIMMER TRUSSER
TWILLER TWISTER TYPOBAR
WHIPPER WHIZZER AERIFIER
AIRCRAFT BROACHER CALENDER
CANCELER CARTONER CLINCHER
COLLATOR COMPRESS DUNGBECK
ELEPHANT EXPLODER EXTRUDER
FINISHER FLYWINCH FORKLIFT
GATHERER HARDENER HAYMAKER
HERCULES HUMMELER IMPACTER
KILLIFER MORTISER MOULINET
ODOGRAPH OROGRAPH PROFILER
PULSATOR SCHIFFLI SCUTCHER
SHREDDER SOFTENER SPLITTER
SPREADER SPRIGGER SQUEEZER
STITCHER STRANDER STRIPPER
SURFACER TEMPERER THREADER
THRESHER THROSTLE TRAVELER
TRISPAST TUNNELER UPSETTER
WINNOWER ADDRESSER
MACHINE GUN STINGER CHAUCHAT
MACHINERY MINT TOPCAP SUCCULA
APPARATUS
MACHINE SHOP TURNERY
MACHINIST FRILLER THINNER
MACHINER
MACKEREL CHAD PETO TINK BLINK
OPELU SNOEK TUNNY BONITO
SAUREL TINKER BLINKER BLOATER
TASSARD HARDHEAD SCOMBRID
SEERFISH
(— ABOUT 8 OR 9 INCHES) TINK
TINKER
(PICKLED —) SCALPEEN
(POOR BONY —) SLINK SLINKER
(YOUNG —) SPIKE
MACKLE SLUR SHAKE MACULA
MACROSCOPIC GROSS
MACROSPECIES LINNEON
MAD FEY AWAY GITE GYTE HYTE
WOOD YOND ANGRY BRAIN CRAZY
DIPPY FOLLE RABID BEDLAM

FRENZY INSANE MANIAC WOODEN
BERSERK FANATIC FRANTIC
FURIOUS LUNATIC MADDING
MADDOCK MANKIND REDWOOD
WITLESS DELIRANT DEMENTED
DISTRACT INFORMAL MANIACAL
MINDLESS RAVENING
MADAGASCAR (SEE MALAGASY
REPUBLIC)
MADAM MEM MUM BAWD MAAM PANI
DONNA MADAME SENORA SENHORA
SIGNORA GOODWIFE MISTRESS
SINEBADA
MADAR YERCUM
MADDEN ENRAGE INCENSE INFLAME
DISTRACT
MADDENED ENRAGED FRENZIED
MADDER GAMENE LIZARY ALIZARI
GARANCE MUNJEET TANAGRA
GARANCIN SPURWORT WOODRUFF
MAD-DOG SKULLCAP MADWEED
HOODWORT
MADE SET BUILT COMPACT
PREPARED TIMBERED
(— FLUID BY HEAT) FUSILE
(— OF DISSIMILAR PARTS) MIXED
(— OF FLAX) LINEN
(— OF GRAIN) OATEN CEREAL
(— OF IVORY) EBURNEAN
(— OF SILVER) ARGENT
(— OF STONE) STONEN
(— OF TWIGS) VIRGAL
(— SHORT) CURTAL
(— TART) EUCHRED
(— TO ORDER) BESPOKEN
(— TRANSLUCENT) AJOURE
(— UP) ACCRETE
(— WITH CEDAR) CEDARN
MADE-BEAVER SKIN CASTOR
MADEIRA ISLANDS (ISLAND OF —)
GRANDE DEZERTE
(TOWN OF —) FUNCHAL
(WINE OF —) BUAL TINTA MALMSEY
SERCIAL VERDELHO
MADELON POLIXENE
MADHOUSE ASYLUM BEDLAM
MADHUCA BASSIA ILLIPE
MADLY WOOD CRAZY
MADMAN BEDLAM MANIAC FURIOSO
LUNATIC WOODMAN
MADNESS MAD FURY MOON WOOD
FOLLY FUROR MANIA BEDLAM
FRENZY LUNACY DEWANEE
ECSTASY MOONERY WIDDRIM
DELIRIUM DEMENTIA PIBLOKTO
WILLNESS WOODNESS WOODSHIP
MADONNA LADY VIRGIN
MADREPORE FUNGID
MADRIGAL ENSALADA
MADRONA LAUREL MANZANITA
MADTOM TADPOLE
MADWORT BUGLOSS
MAENAD FROW BASSARID
BACCHANTE
(PL.) BACCHAE
MAFIC FEMIC
MAFURA ROKA ELCAJA
MAGANI BAGANI
MAGAZINE BOOK DRUM FLAT IGLOO

SLICK STORE RETORT ALMACEN
JOURNAL CASSETTE
(BLACKWOOD'S —) MAGA
MAGDALEN MAUDLIN
MAGGOT MAD GRUB MAWK WORM
METHE GENTLE WARBLE WORMIL
MADDOCK SKIPPER MUCKWORM
MAGIC JUJU MAYA RUNE CRAFT
FAIRY GOETY SPELL TURGY GOETIC
TREGET VOODOO ALCHEMY
CANTRIP CONJURY DEVILRY
GLAMOUR GRAMARY MAGICAL
SORCERY BRUJERIA HECATEAN
WIZARDRY
(BLACK —) GOETY GOETIC
MALEFICE
(WHITE —) TURGY
MAGICAL WIZARD WONDER
HERMETIC NUMINOUS THEURGIC
MAGICIAN MAGE BOKOR MAGUS
UTHER CUNJAH GOETIC GOOFER
GUFFER MAGIAN MERLIN WABENO
WIZARD CHARMER GWYDION
KOSCHEI WIELARE WISEMAN
CONJURER FETISHER SORCERER
THEURGIC TROLLMAN
MAGISTERIAL LOFTY PROUD
AUGUST LORDLY HAUGHTY
STATELY ARROGANT DOGMATIC
MAGISTERY MASTERY
MAGISTRACY AMT PRYTANY
MAGISTRATE BEAK FOUD EPHOR
JUDGE JURAT MAYOR PRIOR REEVE
AMTMAN ARCHON AVOYER BAILIE
CENSOR CONSUL FISCAL KOTWAL
SYNDIC BAILIFF BURGESS DUUMVIR
ECHEVIN EPHORUS JUSTICE
NOMARCH PODESTA PRAETOR
PREFECT PROVOST STEWARD
SUFFETE TRIBUNE ALABARCH
ALDERMAN CAPITOUL DEFENSOR
DEMIURGE DICTATOR GOVERNOR
MITTIMUS PHYLARCH PRYTANIS
RECORDER STRADICO STRATEGE
HUNDREDER
(— IN CHANNEL ISLANDS) JURAT
(— OF ANCIENT ROME) EDILE
(— OF VENICE AND GENOA) DOGE
(MOHAMMEDAN —) CADI CADY
(SCOTCH —) STEWARD
MAGMA ICHOR
MAGMATIC JUVENILE
MAGNANIMITY HEIGHT FREEDOM
MAGNANIMOUS BIG FREE GREAT
LARGE LOFTY NOBLE HEROIC
EXALTED GENEROUS
MAGNATE MOGUL BASHAW TYCOON
MAGNESIA PULVIL
MAGNET FIELD ADAMAS MAGNES
ADAMANT SOLENOID TERRELLA
MAGNETISM IT DEVIL
MAGNETITE LOADSTONE
LODESTONE
MAGNETIZE TOUCH SATURATE
MAGNETOMETER DOODLEBUG
MAGNIFICENCE GITE POMP FLARE
GLORY STATE PARADE JOLLITY
ROYALTY GRANDEUR SPLENDOR
MAGNIFICENT RIAL GRAND NOBLE

ROYAL AUGUST LAVISH IMMENSE
STATELY SUBLIME GLORIOUS
GORGEOUS MAGNIFIC PALATIAL
PRINCELY SPLENDID
MAGNIFY LAUD ERECT EXALT
PRAISE ADVANCE DISTEND ENLARGE
GLORIFY GREATEN INCREASE
MAXIMIZE MULTIPLY
MAGNIFYING GLASS LOUPE
READER
MAGNILOQUENT TURGID BOMBAST
MAGNITUDE BULK MASS SIZE
DATUM LEVEL SOLID EXTENT
FIGURE PERIOD EXTREME
CONSTANT FUNCTION INFINITE
MAGNOLIA YULAN BIGBLOOM
CUCUMBER MAURICIO
(— STATE) MISSISSIPPI
MAGPIE MAG PIE PIET PYAT CISSA
KOTRI MADGE NINUT MARGET
NANPIE PIANET PIEMAG SIRGANG
HAGISTER MARGARET PHEASANT
PIENANNY
MAGPIE LARK PEEWEE GRALLINA
MAGPIE ROBIN DAYAL DHYAL
MAGUEY MESCAL CANTALA
MAGYAR SZEKEL SZEKLER
MAHATMA ARHAT
MAH-JONGG WOO
MAHOE EMAJAGUA
MAHOGANY SIPO ALMON CAOBA
CEDAR ACAJOU AGUANO SAPELE
THITKA ALBARCO AVODIRE
BAYWOOD GUNNUNG MADEIRA
RATTEEN TABASCO BANGALAY
HARDTACK TANGUILE
(INDIAN —) TOON
(PHILIPPINE —) BAGTIKAN
MAHONIA ASHBERRY ODOSTEMON
MAHOUND MACON
MAHUA FULWA MOWHA MOWRA
MADHUCA PHULWARA
MAHUANG EPHEDRA
MAIA (FATHER OF —) ATLAS
(MOTHER OF —) PLEIONE
(SON OF —) MERCURY
MAID AYAH GIRL MEDE SLUT CHINA
WENCH WOMAN MAIDEN SLAVEY
TWEENY VIRGIN ANCILLA GENERAL
MAIDKIN PHYLLIS PUCELLE
WENCHEL BRANGANE HANDMAID
SUIVANTE TIREMAID
(— IN WAITING) DAMSEL DAMOZEL
(— OF HONOR) MARIE
(— OF-ALL-WORK) SLAVEY GENERAL
(KITCHEN —) SCOGIE
(LADY'S —) AYAH TIREMAID
(NURSE —) BONNE
(OLD —) TABBY SPINSTER
(WAITING —) ABIGAIL SUIVANTE
MAIDEN MAY BIRD DAME GIRL MAID
DALAGA DAMSEL FROKIN MEISJE
COLLEEN CYDIPPE DAMOZEL
MADCHEN DAUGHTER
(— WITH BASKET ON HEAD)
CANEPHOR
MAIDENHAIR GINGKO ADIANTUM
MAIDENLY VIRGIN GIRLISH VIRGINAL
MAIDEN PINK SPINK DIANTHUS

MAIDSERVANT LASS BIDDY BONNE
ANCILLA LISETTE
MAIEUTIC HEBAMIC
MAIGRE BAR SCIAENID WEAKFISH
MAIL BAG DAK HOOD POST MATTER
AIRMAIL JACKPOT MAILBAG
ORDINAR POSTAGE POSTBAG
SEAPOST TAPPALL ORDINARY
(IMPROPERLY ADDRESSED —) NIX
NIXY
MAIN LINE MOST SHEER MIGHTY
MAILBAG BAG POUCH POSTBAG
MAILBOX POST PILLAR POSTBOX
MAILLECHORT ARGENTON
MAILLOT SWIMSUIT
MAILMAN POSTMAN BREVIGER
MAIM LAME BREAK TRUNK HAMBLE
MANGLE MAYHEM CRIPPLE
MUTILATE
(— AN ANIMAL) LAW MANK
MAIMED SPAVINED
MAIN HIGH CHIEF GRAND GREAT
PRIME CAPITAL LEADING FOREMOST

MAINE

CAPITAL: AUGUSTA
COLLEGE: BATES COLBY
  BOWDOIN
COUNTY: KNOX WALDO KENNEBEC
  AROOSTOOK
INDIAN: ABNAKI
LAKE: SEBEC SEBAGO RANGELEY
  SCHOODIC MOOSEHEAD
MOUNTAIN: BIGELOW CADILLAC
  KATAHDIN
NATIVE: MANIAC
RIVER: SACO KENNEBEC
  AROOSTOOK KENNEBAGO
  PENOBSCOT
STATE BIRD: CHICKADEE
STATE FLOWER: PINECONE
STATE NICKNAME: PINETREE
STATE TREE: PINE
TOWN: ORONO BANGOR KITTERY
  BOOTHBAY OGUNQUIT
  PORTLAND

MAINLY BROADLY CHIEFLY
MAINSTAY KEY ATLAS SINEW STOOP
PILLAR BACKBONE RELIANCE
MAINTAIN BEAR FEND FIND HOLD
KEEP LAST SAVE ADOPT ARGUE
CARRY CLAIM ESCOT SALVE
ADHERE ALLEGE ASSERT AVOUCH
DEFEND INTEND RETAIN THREAP
UPHOLD UPKEEP CONFIRM
CONTEND DECLARE DISPUTE
JUSTIFY NOURISH SUBSIST
SUPPORT SUSTAIN CONTINUE
PRESERVE
(— AS TRUE) AVOUCH SOOTHE
(— POSITION) STALL
(— WITHOUT REASON) ARROGATE
MAINTAINER FOUNDER RETAINER
MAINTENANCE KEEP LIVING
UPKEEP ALIMONY CUSTODY FINDING
KEEPING PREBEND SERVICE
(— OF POPULATION) BALANCE

MAITHILI TIRHUTIA

MAIZE CORN GRAIN CEREAL INDIAN
JAGONG STAPLE MEALIES
DJAGOONG
 (— **CRUSHED WITH PESTLE**) STAMP

MAJAGUA HAU BARU BOLA MAHO
MOJO BURAO GUANA MOHOE
PURAU BALIBAGO CORKWOOD
EMAJAGUA

MAJESTIC HIGH GRAND LOFTY
REGAL ROYAL AUGUST KINGLY
SUPERB STATELY SUBLIME
ELEVATED IMPERIAL MAESTOSO
SPLENDID

MAJESTY DIGNITY AUGUSTUS
GRANDEUR KINGSHIP

MAJOON BANG BHANG

MAJOR DUR DURUM SHARP CAPITAL
GREATER MAGGIORE

MAJORITY BODY BULK FECK
CORPSE SUBSTANCE
 (ABSOLUTE —) QUORUM

MAKARAKA IDDIO

MAKARI KOTOKO

MAKE DO CUT GAR LET MAY FORM
GIVE LEVY BRAND BUILD CAUSE
COVER FETCH FORGE FRAME SEIZE
SHAPE STAMP AUTHOR COBBLE
CREATE GRAITH INDUCE RENDER
CONFECT FASHION IMAGERY
IWURCHE PERFORM PRODUCE
CONTRIVE GENERATE
 (— **A DIFFERENCE**) SKILL
 (— **A MESS OF**) PIE
 (— **A RUG**) HOOK
 (— **A VISIT**) COSHER
 (— **ACKNOWLEDGMENT**) CONFESS
 (— **ACTIVE**) ENERGIZE
 (— **AMENDS**) ABYE ATONE ABEGGE
ANSWER REDEEM EXPIATE REDRESS
 (— **ANGRY**) GRAMY WRATH
 (— **ATTRACTIVE**) GILD
 (— **AWAY WITH**) ABOLISH EMBEZZLE
 (— **BARE**) STRIP DENUDE
 (— **BELIEVE**) LET PRETEND
 (— **BETTER**) AMEND HEIGHTEN
 (— **BLUE**) HIP
 (— **BRIGHT**) ENGILD ILLUME
CLARIFY
 (— **BRISK**) PERK
 (— **BROWN**) TAN
 (— **BY STAMPING**) MINT
 (— **CANDLE**) DIP DRAW
 (— **CERTAIN**) ASSURE ENSURE
 (— **CHANNEL IN**) THROAT
 (— **CHEERFUL**) SOLACE
 (— **CHOICE**) OPT CHOOSE SELECT
 (— **CLAMMY**) ENGLEIM
 (— **CLEAR**) DECLARE DEVELOP
DISCUSS EXHIBIT EXPOUND LIGHTEN
DESCRIBE
 (— **COLD**) REFREID
 (— **COMPLETE**) SPHERE
 (— **CONSPICUOUS**) ENNOBLE
 (— **CONTENT**) SATISFY
 (— **CULTIVABLE**) EMPOLDER
 (— **CUT PRIOR TO LAYERING**)
TONGUE
 (— **DESTITUTE**) BEREAVE

 (— **DIFFERENT**) ALTER CHANGE
 (— **DIRTY**) MOIL GRIME
 (— **DISPLAY OF**) AFFECT DISCOVER
 (— **DRUNK**) FOX SOUSE FUDDLE
SOZZLE
 (— **DRY**) HAZLE HAZZLE
 (— **EARLIER**) ADVANCE
 (— **EFFERVESCENT**) AERATE
 (— **EFFIGY**) GUY
 (— **END OF**) SNIB FETCH
 (— **ENDURING**) ANNEAL
 (— **EQUAL**) WEIGH EQUATE
 (— **EVEN**) GLAZE LEVEL WEIGH
SQUARE
 (— **FACES**) GIMBLE MURGEON
 (— **FALSE PRETENSES**) SHAM
 (— **FAST**) FIX BAIL FAST GIRD KNIT
MAKE STOP BELAY HITCH BUCKLE
FASTEN SECURE
 (— **FAT**) BATTEN
 (— **FIRM**) FIX BRACE FASTEN
 (— **FIT**) APTATE STRIKE
 (— **FOOL OF**) DOR BORE DOLT
DORRE BEGOWK DOODLE
 (— **FOOLISH**) DAFF GREEN NUGIFY
STULTIFY
 (— **FOOTSORE**) SURBATE
 (— **FROTHY**) MILL
 (— **FULL**) FARCE FULFILL
 (— **FUN OF**) GUY KID GAFF JEST
JOSH DROLL GLAIK SCOUT SMOKE
 (— **FUSS OVER NOTHING**) FAFF
 (— **GLAD**) FAIN
 (— **GLASS**) FOUND
 (— **GLOSSY**) SLEEK
 (— **GLOW**) FURNACE
 (— **GOLDEN**) ENDORE
 (— **GRINDING NOISE**) GRINCH
 (— **GURGLING SOUND**) CROOL
 (— **HAPPY**) BLESS ENJOY REFORM
BEATIFY SATISFY FELICIFY
 (— **HARD**) TAW STEEL ENDURE
HORNIFY
 (— **HARDY**) FASTEN
 (— **HEADWAY**) STEM WALK
ENFORCE
 (— **HELPLESS**) STAGGER
 (— **HOLY**) BLESS SACRE HALLOW
SANCTIFY
 (— **HORSE SEEM YOUNGER**) BISHOP
 (— **ILL**) MORBIFY
 (— **IMMOBILE**) FREEZE
 (— **IMPACT**) ASSAIL
 (— **INCURSION**) HARRY
 (— **INSIGNIFICANT**) MICRIFY
 (— **INTO BUNDLE**) FARDEL
 (— **INTO LAW**) ENACT
 (— **INVALID**) DAMASK
 (— **JOINT**) SYPHER
 (— **KNOWN**) BID OUT GIVE WISE
AREAD BEKEN BREAK KITHE SOUND
SPEAK BEWRAY BROACH COUTHE
DENOTE DESCRY EXPOSE INFORM
REVEAL SPREAD CONFESS DECLARE
DELIVER DIVULGE PUBLISH SIGNIFY
UNCOVER ANNOUNCE DECIPHER
DISCLOSE DISCOVER INDICATE
PROCLAIM PROMULGE
 (— **LESS DENSE**) THIN RAREFY

 (— **LESS SEVERE**) MITIGATE
 (— **LIABLE**) DANGER
 (— **LOVE**) WOO COURT SPOON
GALLANT
 (— **LUKEWARM**) WLECCHE
 (— **LUSTERLESS**) FLATTEN
 (— **MANIFEST**) EVINCE EXPLAIN
 (— **MELANCHOLY**) HYP
 (— **MELODIOUS**) ATTUNE
 (— **MELODY**) DREAM
 (— **MENTION**) SPEAK
 (— **MERRY**) JET GAUD CHEER
SPORT FROLIC SHROVE DISPORT
REHAYTE
 (— **METALLIC SOUND**) CHINK
 (— **MISTAKE**) ERR BOOB GOOF
 (— **MONOTONOUS NOISE**) DRONE
 (— **MORAL**) ETHICIZE
 (— **MUCH OF**) DAWT DANDLE
 (— **MURMURING NOISE**) BUM
 (— **NEAT**) FEAT SMUG TIDY GROOM
 (— **NEST**) TIMBER
 (— **NONMAGNETIC**) DEGAUSS
 (— **NUMB**) DAZE ETHERIZE
 (— **OFF**) BAG BOLT HOOK ANNEX
HEIST SPIRIT SCARPER
 (— **ONE'S WAY**) AIRT BORE TRADE
 (— **ONE**) UNE
 (— **OPEN**) AIR PATEFY
 (— **OUT**) FARE FILL GLEAN SKILL
DISCERN DECIPHER
 (— **OVER**) TURN ALIEN CHANGE
RECOCT DELIVER REFORGE
 (— **PALE**) CHALK
 (— **PLEASANT**) SWEETEN
 (— **POIGNANT**) SAUCE
 (— **PREGNANT**) ENWOMB
 (— **PROGRESS**) GAIN STEM GATHER
 (— **PROUD**) WLENCH
 (— **PUBLIC**) BLOW BLAZE BREAK
BLAZON DELATE DIVULGE FANFARE
PUBLISH BULLETIN
 (— **QUIET**) ALLAY QUIET APPEASE
 (— **RATTLING NOISE**) TIRL
 (— **READY**) DO BUN GET BOWN
BUSK YARK BELAY DRESS PREST
PRIME FETTLE GRAITH ADDRESS
APPAREL DISPOSE PREPARE
 (— **RECORD OF**) REFER
 (— **REFERENCE**) MENTION
 (— **RESISTANCE**) REBEL
 (— **RESOLUTE**) STEEL
 (— **RETURN FOR**) REQUITE
 (— **RICH**) FREIGHT IMBURSE
 (— **ROSY**) FLUSH
 (— **RUSTLING SOUND**) FISSLE
FISTLE
 (— **RUTTING CRY**) FREAM
 (— **SCANTY LIVING**) EKE
 (— **SERIES OF NOTES**) TINKLE
 (— **SHIFT**) SCAMBLE
 (— **SIGN OF CROSS**) BLESS
 (— **SMALL**) MICRIFY BELITTLE
 (— **SMALLER**) MINIFY COMPRESS
 (— **SMOOTH**) SLAB GLAZE SLEEK
GENTLE HAMMER SCRAPE LEVIGATE
 (— **SOFT**) NESH GENTLE
 (— **SOGGY**) SOP
 (— **SOUR**) FOX WIND

(— SPIRITLESS) MOPE
(— SPORT OF) LARK
(— SPRUCE) PERK SMARTEN
(— STRAIGHT) ADDRESS
(— STRONG) STEEL FASTEN
FORTIFY
(— STUPID) MOIDER STULTIFY
(— SUITABLE) ADAPT
(— SURE) SEE INSURE
(— TIPSY) FLUSTER
(— TRANSITION TO) MODULATE
(— UP ACCOUNTS) BREVE
(— UP) UP COOK FORM SPELL
INDITE SETTLE ANALYZE COMPACT
COMPOSE COMPUTE CONCOCT
CONFECT FASHION COMPOUND
COMPRISE DISPENSE
(— USE OF) FEE BUSK APPLY AVAIL
BROOK SERVE SPEND EMPLOY
EXECUTE IMPROVE UTILIZE
(— VIBRANT SOUND) CHIRR
(— VOID) ABATE ANNUL
(— WAR) WARRAY
(— WET) DRAGGLE
(— WHISTLING NOISE) WHEW
(— WHITE) BLANCH BLEACH
CANDIFY
(— WORSE) IMPAIR PEJORATE
MAKE-BELIEVE BORAK DUMMY
ASSUMED
MAKER DOER JACK KNAVE SMITH
FACTOR FORGER FORMER WORKER
CREATOR DECLARER OPERATOR
(— OF ARROWS) FLETCHER
(— OF BARRELS) COOPER
(— OF POTS) POTTER
(— OF SADDLETREES) FUSTER
(— OF SONGS) BULBUL
(— OF TALLOW) CHANDLER
MAKESHIFT JURY RUDE JERRY
TOUSY BEWITH KUTCHA APOLOGY
JACKLEG STOPGAP
MAKEUP FACE BUILD GETUP HABIT
SETUP SHAPE FACIES FORMAT
ANATOMY CONSIST FEATURE
TRAVESTY
MAKING FACT
MALABAR BAY
MALABAR ALMOND KAMANI
ALMENDRO
MALACEAE POMACEAE PYRACEAE
MALADJUSTMENT SCAR
MALADROIT ILL AWKWARD
UNHANDY BUNGLING
MALADY AMOK EVIL MORB CAUSE
GRIEF ONCOME AILMENT DISEASE
ILLNESS DISORDER MISCHIEF
SICKNESS
MALAGASAY LEMURIAN

MALAGASY REPUBLIC
ALTERNATE NAME: MADAGASCAR
CAPITAL: TANANARIVE
ISLAND GROUP: ALDABRA
LAKE: ALAOTRA
MEASURE: GANTANG
NATIVE: HOVA SAKALAVA
PEOPLE: HOVA COTIER MARINA

RIVER: IKOPA MANIA SOFIA
MANGOKY MANGORO ONYLAHY
TOWN: TULEAR MAJANGA
NOSSIBE TAMATAVE ANTISIRABE

MALAPROPISM SLIPSLOP
MALAR JUGAL
MALARIA MIASMA SHAKES PALUDISM
(— PARASITE) VIVAX
MALARIAL PALUDOSE PALUDOUS

MALAWI
CAPITAL: ZOMBA
COIN: KWACHA
FORMER NAME: NYASALAND
HIGHLANDS: SHIRE
LAKE: NYASA
LANGUAGE: YAO CEWA NGONI
TONGA NYANJA TUMBUKA
MOUNTAIN: MLANJE
PEOPLE: YAO BANTU CHEWA
NGURU NYANJA
TOWN: MZUZU BLANTYRE
LILONGWE
VALLEY: RIFT

MALAY AMOK ASIL AMUCK BAJAU
ILOCO JAKUN MANOBO ILOKANO
MALAYAN (— TREE) TERAP
MALAY APPLE OHIA JAMBO KAVIKA

MALAYSIA
CAPITAL: KUALALUMPUR
COIN: TRA TRAH
ISLAND: ARU GOA KAI OBI OMA
ALOR BALI GAGA JAVA MUNA
MURU SULO AMBON BANDA
BOHOL BUTON CERAM LUZON
MISOL PANAY SANGI SUMBA
TIMOR WETAR BANGKA BOEFON
BOEROE BORNEO BUTUNG
FLORES LOMBOK MADURA
PELENG SANGIR TALAUR
WAIGEU AMBOINA CELEBES
JAMDENA MINDORO MOROTAI
PALAWAN SALAJAR SALWATI
SUMATRA SUMBAWA BELITONG
DJAILOLO TANIMBAR
ISTHMUS: KRA
LANGUAGE: TAGALOG
MOUNTAIN: BULU NIUT RAJA
MURJO NIAPA LEUSER SLAMET
BINAIJA RINDJANI
PEOPLE: ATA BAJAU SEMANG
BISAYAN TAGALOG VISAYAN
RIVER: KUTAI PERAK BARITO
PAHANG
TOWN: DAVAO ILOILO KUPANG
MANADO KUCHING MALACCA
SANDAKAN
WEIGHT: TAEL WANG TAMPANG

MALCONTENT FRONDEUR
MALE HE DOG HIM MAN BUCK BULL
COCK JACK ADULT MANLY SPEAR
JOHNNY MANFUL MASCLE VIRILE

LALAQUI MANKIND MANLIKE
MANNISH PURUSHA
(— OF ANIMALS) TOM BUCK BULL
JACK STUD STALLION
(GELDED —) GALT
(YOUNG —) GROOM
MALECITE ETCHEMIN
MALEDICTION BAN WISH CURSE
MALISON ANATHEMA
MALEFACTOR BADDY FELON
BADDIE CULPRIT CRIMINAL
EVILDOER
MALEFIC TAKING
MALEFICENT BALEFUL
MALEO MEGAPOD
MALE ORCHIS CUCKOO CROWTOE
CULLION PURPLES RAGWORT
CROWFOOT
MALEVOLENCE SPITE ENMITY
GRUDGE HATRED MALICE RANCOR
SPLEEN
MALEVOLENT ILL EVIL FELL MALIGN
HATEFUL HOSTILE SPITEFUL
MALFORMATION CURL ERROR
HEMITERY
(— OF CARNATION) TWITTER
(— OF FRUIT) CATFACE
MALFORMED SHAMBLE

MALI
ANCIENT CITY: TIMBUKTU
CAPITAL: BAMAKO
LAKE: DO DEBO GAROU KORAROU
LANGUAGE: DOGON DYULA
MANDE MARKA PEULH BAMBARA
MALINKE SENOUFO SONGHAI
MOUNTAIN: MINA MANDING
PEOPLE: MOOR PEUL TUAREG
BAMBARA MALINKE SONGHAI
SENOULFO
RIVER: BANI BAGOE BAKOY NIGER
BAOULE AZAOUAK SENEGAL
TOWN: GAO SAN KAYES MOPTI
SEGOU SIKASSO

MALICE DOLE ENVY HAIN PIQUE
SPITE VENOM VIRUS ENMITY
GRUDGE RANCOR SPLEEN DESPITE
AMBITION
MALICIOUS SHREW TEENY BITTER
DOGGED MALIGN WANTON HATEFUL
HEINOUS LEERING SPITOUS
CANKERED SINISTER SPITEFUL
VENOMOUS
MALIGN ILL FOUL ABUSE LIBEL
WRONG BEWRAY DEFAME VILIFY
ASPERSE DEPRAVE HURTFUL
SLANDER
MALIGNANCY FEROCITY
MALIGNANT EVIL ATTRY FELON
FERAL SWART ATTERY MALIGN
ENVIOUS HATEFUL HELLISH PEEVISH
REPTILE VICIOUS WARLOCK
SHREWISH SPITEFUL VENOMOUS
VIPEROUS VIRULENT WRATHFUL
MALIGNITY LIVER VENOM VIRUS
HATRED MALICE RANCOR DESPITE
MALINGER DODGE SKULK
MALINGERER SCONCER

MALL WALK ALLEE
MALLARD TWISTER
  (FLOCK OF —S) SORD SUTE
  PADDLING
MALLEABLE MILD SOFT DUCTILE
  BATTABLE
MALLEIN MORVIN
MALLEMUCK MOLLIE MALMARSH
MALLET MALL MAUL MELL GAVEL
  BEATER BEETLE DRIVER HAMMER
  DRESSER FLOGGER STRIKER
  PLOWMELL
  (— FOR BREAKING CLODS) BILDER
  (CURRIER'S —) MACE
  (HATTER'S —) BEATER
  (PAVER'S —) TUP
MALLEUS HAMMER OSSICLE
  PLECTRUM
MALLOW MAW DOCK HOCK ALTEA
  KOKIO MALVA MAUVE CHEESE
  ESCOBA GEMAUVE ABUTILON
  PIEPRINT
MALMSEY MALVASIA
MALNUTRITION CACHEXY CACHEXIA
MALODOROUS GAMY HIGH NOSY
  FETID SMELLY VIROSE VIROUS
MALT WORT
  (GROUND —) GRIST
  (REMAINS OF —) DRAFF
MALTASE GLUCASE
MALTHA BREA
MALTHOUSE MALTINO
MALTOSE AMYLON
MALTREAT ABUSE DIGHT DEFOUL
  DEMEAN HESPIL HUSPEL MISUSE
  THREAT BEDEVIL MISGUIDE
MALTREATMENT ABUSE
MALVA DOCK MALLOW
MAMAMU MU
MAMBA COBRA ELAPOID
MAMMA MA MOM MAMA WIFE
  MOMMA WOMAN MOTHER
MAMMAL OX ASS BAT CAT COW
  DOG FOX PIG YAK BEAR BOAR
  COON DEER GOAT HARE LION LYNX
  MINK MOLE PUMA SEAL ZEBU
  BEAST BISON CAMEL COATI COYPU
  GENET HORSE HYENA LEMUR
  LLAMA MOOSE OKAPI OTTER PANDA
  RATEL SABLE SHEEP SHREW SKUNK
  SLOTH SWINE TAPIR TIGER WHALE
  ZORIL ALPACA ANIMAL BADGER
  COUGAR CULPEO DESMAN DUGONG
  FISHER FOUSSA GOPHER GRISON
  JAGUAR MARTEN MONKEY OCELOT
  TENREC VICUNA WALRUS WOMBAT
  BUFFALO CARIBOU DOLPHIN
  ECHIDNA GIRAFFE GLUTTON
  GUANACO HIPPOID HUANACO
  MANATEE OPPOSUM PECCARY
  POLECAT PRIMATE RACCOON
  SUCKLER SURICAT TARSIER
  TYLOPOD WILDCAT ANTELOPE
  BANXRING CACOMIXL CREODONT
  ELEPHANT FALANAKA HEDGEHOG
  KINKAJOU MAMMIFER PANGOLIN
  REINDEER SQUIRREL
MAMMALIA MASTOZOA
MAMMEE ABRICO ABRICOT

MAMMILLA PAP TEAT NIPPLE
MAMMOTH HUGE LARGE GIGANTIC
MAN BO HE BOY GEE GUY HIM LAD
  TAO WAT WER BUCK CHAL CHAP
  COVE DICK EARL GENT GOME
  HOMO JACK JONG MALE RINK TULK
  BERNE BIMBO BIPED BLOKE CHURL
  COVEY FORCE FREKE GROOM
  GUEST HEART HOMME HORSE
  JOKER SEGGE SWAIN WIGHT
  BIMANE FELLOW HOMBRE MANTZU
  WEPMAN BIMANUS HOMONID
  KINSMAN MANKIND
  (— AFFECTING FOREIGN WAYS)
  MACARONI
  (— DRESSED AS WOMAN) MALINCHE
  (— IN DEBT) DYVOUR
  (— IN PRIVATE STATION) IDIOT
  (— IN TUG-OF-WAR) ANCHOR
  (— LEADING 12TH NIGHT) BEAN
  (— OF ALL WORK) MOZO
  (— OF AUTHORITY) AGHA SEIGNIOR
  (— OF BEAUTY) APOLLO
  (— OF BRASS) TALOS
  (— OF GREAT WEALTH) NABOB
  (— OF HIGH RANK) CHAM KHAN
  THAKUR GRANDEE
  (— OF SUBSTANCE) IDLEMAN
  (— OF THE COMMON PEOPLE) JACK
  (— OF VIGOR) WYE
  (— OF VIOLENCE) RABIATOR
  (— OF WAR) ANDREW CARAVEL
  CRUISER
  (— TO MAN) SINGLE
  (ARTIFICIAL —) GOLEM
  (BACKGAMMON —) BLOT BUILDER
  (BALD —) PILGARLIC
  (BEST —) BRIDEMAN
  (BIG —) COB BRUISER MUGWUMP
  (BRISK —) SPARK
  (CASTRATED —) SPADO EUNUCH
  (CHIEF —) FOREMAN OPTIMATE
  (CHURLISH —) NABAL BODACH
  (CLEANING —) BUSBOY
  (COMMON —) CARL STREET
  YEOMAN
  (COVETOUS —) HUNKS
  (CRAFTY —) FOX
  (CRUEL —) OGRE BRUTE
  (DISAGREEABLE —) GLEYDE
  (DISLIKED —) CUT
  (DISSOLUTE —) RAKE
  (ECCENTRIC —) GEEZER
  (EDUCATED —) EFFENDI
  (EFFEMINATE —) DILDO FAIRY SISSY
  COCKNEY MEACOCK MIDWIFE
  MILKSOP ANDROGYN
  (END —) BONES BRAKE
  (ENLISTED —) GI SNIPE AIDMAN
  AIRMAN KEEPER STORES ARMORER
  STRIKER SONARMAN
  (ENTIRE —) EGO
  (EXTINCT —) TEPEXPAN
  (FAITHFUL —) TRUEMAN
  (FANCY —) PONCE
  (FASHIONABLE —) TOUPET
  ELEGANT FOPLING GALLANT
  (FIRST —) ASK ADAM ASKR TIKI
  FOREMAN

  (FOPPISH —) BLOOD
  (FREE —) LIBER
  (GRAY-HAIRED —) GRIZZLE
  (GREAT —) VAVASOR
  (HARDHEARTED —) KNARK
  (HOLDUP —) FOOTPAD
  (HOLY —) SADHU SAINT SANNYASI
  (HONORS —) WRANGLER
  (IDEAL —) SUPERMAN
  (IMMORAL —) REP
  (INEFFECTUAL —) DUFFER
  (INSANE —) FURIOSO
  (LADY'S —) FOPLING DAMMARET
  (LAME —) BACACH
  (LEARNED —) ULEMA LAMDAN
  OLLAMH PUNDIT SAVANT SOPHIST
  (LECHEROUS —) SATYR
  (LEWD —) BROTHEL
  (LIAISON —) COURIER
  (LITERARY —) GIGADIBS
  (LITTLE —) MANNET SHRIMP
  MANNIKIN
  (LUSTFUL —) GOAT
  (MAINTENANCE —) CAMPMAN
  (MARRIED —) HUSBAND BENEDICT
  (MEDICINE —) PEAI DOCTOR
  SHAMAN ANGAKOK
  (MEEK —) MOSES
  (MIGHTY —) SAMSON
  (ODD-JOB —) JOEY
  (OLD —) HAG OLD BOOL CUFF GAFF
  CRONE DOBBY UNCLE BODACH
  DUFFER FATHER GAFFER NESTOR
  GERONTE STARETS ECKEHART
  VELYARDE
  (OLD-CLOTHES —) POCO
  (ONE-ARMED —) WINGY
  (ONE-EYED —) ARIMASP
  (OVERFASTIDIOUS —) DUDE
  (PARTY —) SIDESMAN
  (PRIMITIVE —) URMENSCH
  (PRINCIPAL —) HERO TOPARCH
  (RASH —) HOTSPUR
  (RICH —) DIVES CROESUS
  (RIGHT-HAND —) HENCHMAN
  (RIGHTEOUS —) SADDIK
  (SERVING —) GARCON
  (SOUND-EFFECTS —) CRAWK
  (STERN —) GRIMSIRE
  (STRAIGHT —) STOOGE
  (STRONG —) KWASIND
  (STRONG-ARM —) HOOD GORILLA
  (STUPID —) SUBMAN
  (THICKSET —) GRUB KNAR SPUD
  (TOUGH —) KNAR
  (UNEMPLOYED —) BATLAN
  (UTILITY —) JUMPER
  (VICIOUS —) YAHOO
  (WHITE — LIVING WITH ABORIGINE)
  COMBO
  (WHITE —) BOSTON BUCKRA
  CACHILA
  (WILD —) WOODMAN WOODWOSE
  (WISE —) NAB HAKAM SABIO SOLON
  SOPHY NESTOR WIZARD SOLOMON
  TOHUNGA
  (WIZENED —) GNOME
  (WRETCHED —) CAITIFF
  (YOUNG —) BOY LAD JONG YOUTH

BOCHUR DAMSEL EPHEBE KNIGHT
BOUCHAL BUCKEEN YOUNKER
SPRINGAL
MANABOZHO MICHABOU WINABOJO
MAN-ABOUT-TOWN FLANEUR
MANACLE BAND BOND DARBY
HAMPER TIRRET SHACKLE
HANDCUFF HANDLOCK
(PL.) IRONS CHAINS
MANAGE DO GET MAN RUN BEAR
CURB FEND HACK HOLD KEEP LEAD
MAKE RULE TEND TOOL WIND
WORK BROOK CARRY DIGHT FORTH
FRAME GUIDE MAYNE ORDER SHIFT
SPEND STEER SWING WIELD
CONVEY DEMEAN DEVISE DIRECT
FETTLE GOVERN HANDLE INTEND
MANURE TEMPER AGITATE
CONDUCT DISPOSE EXECUTE
FINAGLE HUSBAND MINSTER
OFFICER OPERATE SOLICIT
STEWARD CONTRIVE ENGINEER
(— **AWKWARDLY**) FOOZLE
(— **CLUMSILY**) KEVEL
(— **TO BEAR**) AFFORD
MANAGEABLE EASY YARE BANTAM
DOCILE WIELDY DUCTILE FLEXIBLE
YIELDING
MANAGEMENT CARE HEEL WORK
CHARGE CONDUCT CONTROL
ECONOMY GESTION RUNNING
CARRIAGE DEMEANOR ENGINERY
MANAGERY MANEUVER REGIMENT
STEERAGE STEERING
(**DOMESTIC** —) MENAGE
HUSBANDRY
(**GOOD** —) EUTAXY
(**SKILLFUL** —) PRACTICE PRACTISE
MANAGER BOSS DOER AGENT
DAROGA DEPUTY PURSER SYNDIC
CURATOR HUSBAND STEWARD
WIELDER AUMILDAR DIRECTOR
DISPOSER ENGINEER HERENACA
INSTITOR
(— **OF FARM**) HIND GRIEVE
(**ASSISTANT** —) CAPORAL
(**MINE** —) CAPTAIN
(**POLITICAL** —) FUGLEMAN
MANAKIN PIPRA
MAN-AT-ARMS KNIGHT
MANATEE COWFISH HOGFISH
MERMAID LAMANTIN MUTILATE
SIRENIAN
MANBARKLAK JARANA KAKARAL
MANCALA WARI
MANCHU SHERRY
MANDAEAN SABAEAN
MANDARIN TOWKAY CHINESE
MANDARIN ORANGE SATSUMA
MANDATE BREVE ORDER BEHEST
CHARGE DECREE FIRMAN BIDDING
COMMAND PRECEPT PROCESS
MANDAMUS MANDATUM WARRANTY
(— **OF GOD**) JUDGMENT
MANDIBLE JOWL SETA JAWBONE
GNATHITE
(— **PART**) MALA
MANDINGO MANDE WANGARA
MANDOLIN OUD MANDORA

MANDRAKE ALRAUN DUDAIM
MANDREL BALL STUD SLEEVE
CHEMISE SPINDLE TRIBLET
MANDRILL MAIMON MORMON
MANE JUBA MONE CREST PITRI
MAN-EATER REQUIN REQUIEM
MANEGE TRAIN
MANEUVER PLAY TURN WISE
GAMBIT JOCKEY MANURE PESADE
VRILLE FINAGLE FINESSE ARTIFICE
DEMARCHE ENGINEER EXERCISE
STRATEGY WINDLASS
(- **GENTLY**) EASE
(**AERIAL** —) LOOP SPIN FISHTAIL
WINGOVER
(**ILLEGAL** —) GAME
(**ROCK-CLIMBING** —) LAYBACK
(**SKIING** —) SNOWPLOW
(**WRESTLING** —) ESCAPE BUTTOCK
MANEUVERABLE YARE
MANEUVERING FINESSE FLANKING
MANGE ITCH REEF SCAB CANKER
DARTARS SCABIES
MANGER BIN BUNK CRIB HECK
STALL CRATCH
MANGLE MAR HACK MOUTH BRUISE
GARBLE HACKLE IRONER MAGGLE
MURDER MAMMOCK LACERATE
MUTILATE
MANGO DIKA AMHAR AMINI BAUNO
AMCHOOR CARABAO PAHUTAN
(**POINT OF** —) NAK
MANGOSTEEN SANTOL GARCINIA
MANGROVE BACAO GORAN MANGLE
MYRTAL BACAUAN CERIOPS
COURIDA HANGALAI LANGARAI
MANGUE CHOLUTECA CHOROTEGA
MANGY SCABBY ROINISH SCABETIC
MANHANDLE SCRAG
MANHOOD ADAMHOOD
MANIA RAGE CRAZE FUROR FRENZY
DELIRIUM HYSTERIA INSANITY
MANIAC KILLER MADMAN FANATIC
LUNATIC
MANIFEST HAVE NUDE OPEN RIFE
SENE SHOW APERT CLEAR FRANK
GROSS KITHE NAKED OVERT PLAIN
PROVE SPEAK SUTEL ATTEST
COUTHE EVINCE EXTANT GRAITH
LIQUID OSTEND PATENT PHANIC
APPROVE CONFESS DECLARE
EVIDENT EXHIBIT EXPRESS OBVIOUS
SIGNIFY VISIBLE APPARENT
DISCLOSE DISCOVER INDICATE
PALPABLE PROCLAIM
(**NOT** —) LATENT
MANIFESTATION ACT SON BEAM
COMA GLINT AVATAR COMING
EFFECT OSTENT ADVANCE DISPLAY
EXPRESS SHOWING EPIPHANY
MANIFEST
(**BARELY PERCEPTIBLE** —) SCINTIL
(**BRIEF** —) GLEAM
(**DIVINE** —) SPIRIT SHEKINAH
(**HORRIBLE** —) CHIMAERA
(**MORAL** —) SOUL
(**VAGUE** —) GLIMMER
MANIFESTLY WITTERLY
MANIFESTO PLACARD

MANIFOLD MANY TURRET VARIOUS
FELEFOLD MANYFOLD MULTIPLE
MANIKIN ECORCHE PANTINE
PHANTOM HOMUNCIO HOMUNCLE
MANNIKIN
MANIOC CATELLA
MANIPLE FANON SUDARIUM
MANIPULATE COAX COOK DIAL
FAKE HAND STIR TOOL CROOK
HUMOR KNEAD SHAPE TREAT WIELD
CHIVVY GOVERN HANDLE JOCKEY
MANAGE SHUFFLE
(— **BY DECEPTIVE MEANS**) RIG
MANIPULATION PASS JUGGLERY
MANAGERY
MANITO ORENDA POKUNT MANITOU
TAMANOAS
MANKIND MAN FLESH SHEEP
WORLD SPECIES HUMANITY
UNIVERSE
MANLIKE MALE MANLY MANNISH
HOMINOID
MANLINESS ARETE VIRTUS MANSHIP
MANLY BOLD MALE HARDY MANNY
DARING VIRILE MANLIKE
MAN-MADE CULTURAL SYNTHETIC
MANNER AIR BAT JET LAT WAY
FORM GAET GARB GATE KIND MAKE
MIEN MODE RATE SORT THEW TOUR
WISE WONE GUISE LATES STYLE
TENUE TRICK COURSE CUSTOM
METHOD ADDRESS AMENITY
FASHION QUALITY QUOMODO
CARAPACE DEMEANOR LANGUAGE
(— **OF APPROACH**) ABORD
(— **OF DOING**) ACTION
(— **OF HANDLING**) HAND
(— **OF MAKING ANYTHING**)
FACTURE
(— **OF SITTING**) ASANA
(— **OF SPEAKING**) SLUR SOUGH
ACCENT GRAMMAR
(— **OF WALKING**) STEP
(**AFFECTED** —) AIR
(**AMUSING** —) DROLLERY
(**ARROGANT** —) BRAG HAUTEUR
(**FORBIDDING** —) SHELL
(**FORMAL** —) STARCH
(**HABITUAL** —) SONG
(**OUTWARD** —) TOUR FRONT
(**SMOOTH** —) JAPAN
(**SWAGGERING** —) SIDE
(**USUAL** —) HABIT
(PL.) CORNERS HAVINGS BREEDING
MANNERED CUTE MORATE THEWED
MANNERISM TRICK IDIASM
(PL.) DAPS
MANNERLY CIVIL
MANNERS MORES HAVANCE
HAVINGS BEAUETRY BREEDING
MANNITOL MANNITE PUNICIN
MAN-OF-WAR CARAVEL
MAN-OF-WAR FISH PASTOR
MANOR HAM BURY HALL TOWN VILL
COMMOTE MANSION LORDSHIP
TOWNSHIP
MANPOWER BRAWN LABOR
MANROOT IPOMOEA
MANROPE LIMMER

MANSERVANT (ALSO SEE SERVANT)
LAD MOZO GROOM VALET ANDREW
BUTLER TEABOY

MANSION DOME HOTEL HOUSE
MANSE SIEGE TOWER CASTLE
HARBOR HOSTEL CHATEAU
(— OF THE MOON) ALNATH

MANSLAUGHTER BLOOD FELONY
HOMICIDE

MANTEL CLAVY CLAVEL

MANTELET MANTA MANTLE
MANTLET GALAPAGO

MANTELPIECE BRACE PAREL
CLAVEL MANTEL MANTLING

MANTICORE MONTEGRE

MANTIS CAGN RACER REARER
MANTOID PROPHET

MANTIS CRAB SQUILLA

MANTLE CAPA HOSE PALL ROBE
CLOAK CREAM FROCK JABUL
LAMBA PALLA TUNIC CAMAIL
CAPOTE KHIRKA SLAVIN TABARD
CHLAMYS CHRISOM CHUDDAR
FERIDJI MANTEAU PAENULA
PALLIUM SLEEVES WHITTLE
WRAPPER BARRACAN CHRYSOME
MANTELET REGOLITH RICINIUM
STOCKING

MANTLEROCK REGOLITH

MANTO (FATHER OF —) HERCULES
TIRESIAS
(SON OF —) MOPSUS

MANTRA DHARANI GAYATRI
MANTRAM SAVITRI

MANTUA MANTY SEMAR

MANTZU MIAOTZE

MANUAL VADY COACH GREAT
TUTOR PORTAS CAMBIST CEMBALO
DIDACHE MANUARY BOMBARDE
HANDBOOK KEYBOARD ORDINARY
PORTHORS SYNOPSIS
(MAGICIAN'S —) GRIMOIRE
(NAVIGATION —) BOWDITCH

MANUAO IAO

MANUBRIUM HYPOSTOME

MANUFACTURE COIN FAKE MAKE
FORGE PERFORM PRODUCE
WORKING BOOKWORK
(— OF LIQUOR OR DRUGS) ABKARI
(ILLEGAL —) COINING

MANUFACTURED STORE

MANUFACTURER BRAND MAKER
WRIGHT DISKERY SPINNER
SUPPLIER

MANUMIT FREE LIBERATE

MANURE HOT MIG DUNG LIME MUCK
SAUR SOIL TATH FECES MIXEN
FULZIE SEASON SLEECH COMPOST
FOLDING GOODING POUDRET
DRESSING WORTHING

MANURED BONED

MANUS HAND

MANUSCRIPT CODEX FLIMSY
MATTER SCRIPT UNCIAL CURSIVE
PANDECT PINTURA WITNESS
EXEMPLAR

MANX CAT RUMPY

MANX SHEARWATER CREW PUFFIN
SCRABE SCRABER

MANY TEN FELE MUCH SERE FORTY
GREAT MAINT MOULT TWENTY
ENDLESS JILLION SEVERAL VARIOUS
MANIFOLD COUNTLESS
(BEING —) NUMEROUS
(GOOD —) HANTLE
(GREAT —) MORT RAFF SWITH

MANYATTA KRAAL

MANY-HANDED BRIAREAN

MANYROOT RUELLIA

MANY-SIDED VARIOUS

MAORI (— IMAGE) TIKI
(— LAW) UTU
(— VILLAGE) PA PAH KAINGA
(NOT —) PAKEMA

MAP KEY CARD DICE PLAT PLOT
CARTE CENTO CHART DRAFT INSET
QUART STILL DRAUGHT GRAPHIC
CARTGRAM GATEFOLD PLATFORM

MAPAU MAPLE MATIPO TARATA
PIRIPIRI

MAPLE MAZER DOGWOOD
SYCAMORE WINGSEED
(GROVE OF —) SAPBUSH

MAR BLOT SCAR SNIP BLOOM BOTCH
SHEND SPILL SPOIL BLOTCH
DEFACE DEFEAT DEFORM IMPAIR
INJURE BLEMISH DISGRACE

MARABOU STORK ARGALA MORABIT

MARANAO LANAO

MARASMUS MARCOR ATHREPSIA

MARAUD RAID DACOIT PICKEER
PILLAGE

MARAUDER TORY BANDIT BUMMER
LOOTIE PIRATE CATERAN LADRONE
(PL.) BLACKS

MARAUDING BANDITRY OUTRIDING

MARBLE MIB MIG PEA POT TAW
ALLY BOOL BOWL DUCK MARL
AGATE AGGIE ALLEY BONCE COMMY
IMMIE IVORY LINER PUREY RANCE
DOGGLE MARMOR MARVEL PARIAN
PEEWEE STEELY CARRARA CIPOLIN
GLASSIE GRIOTTE KNICKER
PARAGON PITCHER SHOOTER
BROCATEL DOLOMITE KNUCKLER
(BLACK —) JET
(PL.) TAW BOWLS PLUMPS HUNDRED

MARBLED MIRLY

MARCH FILE HIKE LIDE MARK MUSH
SLOG ROUTE TRACE TRINE TROOP
WALTZ DEFILE DOUBLE PARADE
REVIEW DEBOUCH STRETCH
FOOTSLOG PROGRESS
(— BEHIND) COVER
(— IN FRONT OF) LEAD
(— OBLIQUELY) INCLINE
(PL.) FRONTIER

MARCHING (— UP) ANABASIS

MARCHIONESS MARCHESA
MARQUISE

MARCOT GOOTE

MARCOTTAGE GOOTEE

MARE SEA YAD YADE YAUD GILLIE
GILLOT GRASNI HUNTRESS

MARE'S-TAIL HIPPURID

MARGARET MEG META MARGET
MARGOT GRETCHEN

MARGATE PORGY

MARGAY TIGER

MARGIN HEM RIM VAT BANK BRIM
BROW CURB EDGE FOLD INCH LIMB
LIST RAND BRINK EAVES MARGE
VERGE BORDER FRINGE LABRUM
LACING CUSHION DRAUGHT
MARGENT SELVAGE HAIRLINE
(— OF CARAPACE) DOUBLURE
(— OF CIRCLE) LIMB
(— OF LIP) PROLABIUM
(— OF PAGE) BACK
(— OF SAFETY) LEEWAY
(— OF SHELL) LABRUM LIMBUS
(— OF SUPERIORITY) LEAD
(— OF WING) TERMEN
(—S OF HERD) SWING
(SEA —) COAST

MARGOSA NIM NEEM NEEMBA

MARGRAVE RUDIGER MARKGRAF

MARIANA SILYBUM

MARIGOLD GOLD GULL SAMH AZTEC
BOOTS GOLDE GOOLS HELIO
BACLIN BUDDLE GOLDCUP GOLDING
GOLLAND KINGCUP MARYBUD
TAGETES

MARIJUANA POT WEED MOOCAH
LOCOWEED

MARINE JOLLY GALOOT GULPIN
GYRENE TOPMAN MARINAL
HALIMOUS MARITIME NAUTICAL

MARINER MARINE SAILOR SEALER
SEAMAN BUSCARLE SEAFARER
WARRENER
(PL.) SEAFOLK

MARINHEIRO ACAJOU

MARIONETTE PUPPY POPPET
PUPPET

MARITAL INTIMATE HUSBANDLY

MARITIME MARINE HALIMOUS
NAUTICAL

MARK AIM END HOB HUB MOT POP
BELT BLOT BUOY BUTT CHOP CLIP
DELE DINT FAZE FIST GOAL KEEL
LINE MIND NOTE RIST SCAR SEAR
SIGN SMOT SMUT SPOT TEND TEXT
TICK VIRE WAND WIND BADGE
BOTTU BRAND BREVE CHANT
CHECK CLOUD DATUM DITTO DRAFT
FLECK FRANK GHOST GRADE HILUM
KNIFE LABEL MARCH MARCO MEITH
NOKTA PRINT PROOF ROVER SCART
SCOPE SCORE SCUFF SPOOR
STAMP SWIRL TOKEN TOUCH TRACE
TRACK TRACT WATCH WHITE
ACCENT ALPIEU BEACON BESPOT
BLOTCH BUTTON CARACT DAGGER
DAPPLE DENOTE DIRECT INDICE
LETTER MARKER NOTICE OBJECT
SMUTCH STREAK STRIKE STROKE
SUCKER SYMBOL TARGET UPSHOT
WICKER WITTER BETOKEN CHARBON
COCKSHY DEMERIT DIAMOND
DRAUGHT EROTEME EXCUDIT
FINMARK IMPRESS IMPRINT INSIGNE
KENMARK SCARIFY SERRATE
SIGNARY SPECKLE STRIATE
SYMPTOM VESTIGE WAYMARK
BRACELET CROWFOOT DATEMARK
DIASTOLE DISPUNCT EVIDENCE

FOOTMARK FOOTSTEP IDENTIFY
IDEOGRAM MONUMENT NOTATION
(— A BIRD) BAND
(— AFTER ASSAY) TOUCH
(— AS SPURIOUS) ATHETIZE
(— BY BURNING) CHAR
(— BY CUTTING) SCRIBE
(— BY PLOWING) STRIKE
(— CROSSWISE) CRANK
(— DENOTING CORRUPT PASSAGE)
OBELUS
(— DIRECTIONS) ADDRESS
(— IN ARCHERY) CLOUT HOYLE
ROVER WHITE
(— IN CANON) LEAD
(— IN CURLING) TEE COCK
(— IN QUOITS) MOT
(— INDICATING CONTRACTION)
CORONIS
(— INDICATING DIRECTION) ARROW
(— OF ACKNOWLEDGEMENT)
ACCOLADE
(— OF DISGRACE) STAIN STIGMA
(— OF DISTINCTION) BELT
(— OF ESTEEM) LAUREL GARLAND
(— OF OFFICE) SEAL
(— OF OWNERSHIP) SWANMARK
(— OF PURITY) HALLMARK
(— OF REFERENCE) OBELISK
(— OF SIGNATURE) CROSS
(— OF SUPERIORITY) BELL
(— OF WEAVER) KEEL
(— OFF LAND) FEER PHEER
(— OFF) SUBTEND
(— ON ANIMAL'S FACE) BLAZE
STRIPE
(— ON CHART) VIGIA
(— ON EXAM) PASS
(— ON FEATHER) BAR SPANGLE
(— ON FOREHEAD) KUMKUM
(— ON PENNSYLVANIA BARNS)
HEXAFOOS
(— ON SHEEP) SMIT
(— ON SHIP) SURMARK
(— ON SKIN) PLOT CREASE
(— ON STAMP) CONTROL
(— OUT) CANCEL DELINE AIRMARK
APPOINT COMPART DESCRIBE
(— OVER GERMAN VOWEL) UMLAUT
(— OVER LETTER N) TILDE
(— OVER LONG VOWELS) MACRON
(— SHEEP OR CATTLE) BASTE
BUIST DEWLAP
(— TIME) COUNT
(— TO BE ATTAINED) BOGEY BOGIE
(— TO GUIDE VESSELS) MYTH
(— TRANSVERSELY) LADDER
(— UNDER LETTER C) CEDILLA
(— WITH LINES) HATCH CAMLET
(— WITH POINTED ROLLER) GRILL
(— WITH RIDGES) RIB
(— WITH STRIPES) WALE STREAM
(— WITH TAR) BASTE
(ACCENT —) VERGE
(ANGULAR —) HOOK
(BALLOT —) SCRATCH
(BOUNDARY —) MEAR MERE TERM
WIKE MEITH STAKE LANDMARK
(CADENCY —) BRISURE

(CANCELLATION —) BUMPER KILLER
(DIACRITICAL —) TIL TILDE
(DIRTY —) SMIRCH
(DISTINCTIVE —) BADGE INDICIA
(DISTINGUISHING —) ITEM COCARDE
EARMARK INSIGNE
(DOUBLE-DAGGER —) DIESIS
(EASY —) YAP SMELT
(EIGHTH —) URE
(EXACT —) NICK
(EXCLAMATION —) SCREAMER
(IDENTIFICATION —) MOLE CREST
SPLIT SIGNET WATTLE EARMARK
KENMARK LUGMARK COLOPHON
(LOW-WATER —) DATUM
(MERIDIAN —) MIRE
(MUSICAL —) PRESA CORONA
(PARAGRAPH —) PILCROW
(PROOFREADER'S —) STET CARET
(PUNCTUATION —) DASH STOP
BRACE BREVE COLON COMMA
HYPHEN PERIOD BRACKET DIERESIS
ELLIPSIS DIACRITIC SEMICOLON
(SECTARIAN —) BOTTU TILAKA
(SKATE —) CUSP
(SMALL ROUND —) DOT
(TRAMP'S —) MONICA MONNIKER
(WHITE —) RACHE
(PL.) POINTING
MARKED FAR GREAT SCORED
SEVERE SPOTTY COLORED EMINENT
MARCATO POINTED SCARRED
SPECKED SPOTTED
(— BY COLORED RINGS) AREOLATE
(— BY FURROWS) RIVOSE
(— BY INTELLIGENCE) ABLE
(— BY PROSTRATION) ALGID
(— BY REFINEMENT) ELEGANT
(— BY RIDGES) SERRIED
(— BY SHREWDNESS) ADROIT
(— BY SIMILARITY) AKIN
(— BY SIMPLICITY) ATTIC
(— BY WAVY LINES) GYROSE
(— OUT) DISTINCT
(— UP) FOUL
(— WITH BANDS) ZONATE
(— WITH SMALLPOX) FRETTEN
(— WITH SPOTS OR LINES) NOTATE
(EXTREMELY —) INTENSE
MARKEDLY BYOUS
MARKER HOB HUB DOLE FLAG MARK
STUMP TYPER BUTTON GUIDON
HOBBLE HUBBLE TABBER DAYMARK
SCRIBER
MARKET CURB GUNJ MART PORT
SALE SOOK VEND VENT CHEAP
CROSS GUNGE HALLE PASAR PRICE
TRONE TRYST BAZAAR BOURSE
OUTLET PARIAN RIALTO POULTRY
CHEAPING DEBOUCHE EMPORIUM
EXCHANGE MACELLUM
(CATTLE —) TRISTE
(MEAT —) SHAMBLES
MARKETABLE SUK SUQ SOUK
STAPLE SALABLE VENDIBLE
MARKETPLACE SUK SUQ SOUK
AGORA CHAWK CHOWK HALLE
PLAZA BAZAAR EMPORIUM
MARKING EYE HOOD COLLAR

CLOUDING SCARRING SCRIBING
(— OF WOOD) CURL GRAIN
(— ON FEATHER) SPANGLE
(— ON MARS) CANAL
(—S ON STEEL) DAMASK
(ANIMAL —) SADDLE SHIELD
(CATTLE —) JINGLEBOB
(CRESCENT-SHAPED —) LUNULA
LUNULE
(DROP-SHAPED —) GUTTA
(POSTAL —) INDICIA
(RINGLIKE —) ANNULUS
(STRIPED —) STRAKE
MARKKA FINMARK
MARKSMAN SHOT MARKER PLUFFER
SHOOTER SHOTMAN SHOOTIST
MARL MALM MARLITE
MARLI MARIE
MARLIN AU AGUJA
MARLINESPIKE FID JAEGER
PRICKER STABBER
MARMALADE CHEESE SQUISH
CODINIAC
MARMALADE TREE CHICO MAMMIE
SAPOTE ZAPOTE
MARMOSET MICO TITI SAGOIN
JACCHUS QUIRCAL SAIMIRI TAMARIN
WISTITI ORABASSU
MARMOT BOBAC PAHMI GOPHER
SUSLIK SCIURID SIFFLEUR
WHISTLER
MARMOTA ARCTOMYS
MAROON AZTEC PICNIC CIMARRON
MARQUEE CANOPY MARQUISE
MARQUISE NAVETTE
MARQUISETTE LENO
MARRANOS ANUSIM
MARRED CUPPY SCABBY SPECKED
MARRIAGE MUTA DAIVA HYMEN
KARAO BRIDAL BUCKLE SPLICE
SPOUSE EXOGAMY NUPTIAL
PUNALUA SPOUSAL WEDDING
WEDLOCK CONUBIUM LEVIRATE
OPSIGAMY
(— AFTER DEATH OF FIRST
SPOUSE) DIGAMY
(— AT ADVANCED AGE) OPSIGAMY
(— BELOW POSITION) HYPOGAMY
(— CONTRACT) KETUBAH
(— OUTSIDE FAMILY) EXOGAMY
(— PORTION) TOCHER
(— WITHIN GROUP) ENDOGAMY
MARRIAGEABLE NUBILE
MARRIED COVERT WEDDED
ESPOUSED
MARROW KEEST MARIE MERCH
MERGH MEDULLA
MARRY TIE WED FAST WIFE WIVE
CLEEK MATCH BUCKLE CROTCH
ENSURE MARROW SPLICE HUSBAND
NUPTIAL WEDLOCK DESPOUSE
(— OFF) BESTOW
MARS ARES MAMERS MARMAR
MAVORS MASPITER TEUTATES
(FATHER OF —) JUPITER
(MOTHER OF —) JUNO
(SON OF —) REMUS ROMULUS
MARSH BOG FEN HAG CARR DANK
FELL FLAM FLAT HOPE JHIL MASH

MIRE OOZE SOIL SUDS TARN VLEI
VLEY WASH WHAM FLASH GLADE
JHEEL LIMAN SLACK SLASH SLUMP
SWAMP MORASS PALUDE PUDDLE
CIENAGA CORCASS POCOSIN
PONTINE QUAGMIRE STROTHER
TURLOUGH
(SALT —) SALT SALINA SALINE
MARSHAL ARRAY MUSTER PARADE
JERONIMO MERECHAL
(— FACTS) HASH
MARSH ELDER JACKO
MARSH FEVER HELODES
MARSH GAS METHANE
MARSH HARRIER PUDDOCK
PUTTOCK
MARSHMALLOW MALLOW WYMOTE
MARSH MARIGOLD BOOTS CAPER
CRAZY GOOLS DRAGON GAMOND
GOWLAN COWSLIP ELKSLIP
GOLDCUP KINGCOB KINGCUP
MATYBUD DRUNKARD
MARSH PENNYWORT PENNYROT
WATERCUP
MARSH PINK SABBATIA
MARSH TEA LEDUM
MARSH TREFOIL BUCKBEAN
MARSH WREN LONGBILL
MARSHY FOGGY MOORY MOSSY
PONDY SNAPY SPEWY CALLOW
PLASHY QUAGGY QUASHY SLUMPY
HELODES MOORISH QUEACHY
PALUDIAL PALUDINE WATERISH
MARSUPIAL KOALA CUSCUS
POSSUM WOMBAT DASYURE
OPOSSUM KANGAROO
MART STAPLE EMPORIUM
MARTEN FOIN SABLE SOBOL FISHER
MARTRIX MUSTELID MUSTELIN
(GROUP OF —S) RICHESSE
MARTENSITE SORBITE
MARTIAL BELLIC WARLIKE WARRIOR
BELLICAL MILITARY
MARTIN MARTLET SWALLOW
MARTINET
MARTINMAS TERM
MARTYR STEPHEN WITNESS
SUFFERER
MARTYRDOM MARTYRY PASSION
MARVEL MARL MUSE FERLY SELLY
ADMIRE WONDER MAGNALE
MIRACLE MONSTER PORTENT
PRODIGY SELCOUTH
MARVELOUS MIRIFIC STRANGE
FABULOUS WONDROUS
MARY MOLL POLL MAMIE MAURA
MOLLY MIRIAM MARILLA

MARYLAND
BATTLESITE: ANTIETAM
CAPITAL: ANNAPOLIS
COLLEGE: HOOD GOUCHER
STJOHNS
COUNTY: CECIL TALBOT
ALLEGANY SOMERSET
INDIAN: CONOY NANTICOKE
LAKE: PRETTYBOY
MOUNTAIN: BACKBONE

NATIVE: WESORT TERRAPIN
NICKNAME: OLDLINE
RIVER: CHESTER POTOMAC
CHOPTANK PATUXENT
STATE BIRD: ORIOLE
STATE TREE: OAK
TOWN: EASTON TOWSON
ABERDEEN BETHESDA
POCOMOKE BALTIMORE

MARYSOLE CARTER LEADER
CARTARE
MASAI WAKWAFI WAKWAVI
MASCOT BILLIKEN
MASCULINE MALE DOGGY VIRILE
LALAQUI MANLIKE
MASH BEER CHAP MASA MASK MESH
SLOP CHAMP CREEM SMASH SMUSH
MUDDLE STILLAGE
MASHED CHAPPED DAUPHINE
MASHER FLIRT BEETLE
MASJID MOSQUE
MASK FACE HIDE JEST LOUP SLUR
VEIL BLOCK BLOOP CLOAK COVER
GRILL GUISE LARVE POINT VIZOR
DOMINO GRILLE MUZZLE SCREEN
VEILER VIZARD BECLOUD CONCEAL
CURTAIN MASKOID ANTEMASK
DEFILADE DISGUISE MASCARON
(— OUT) CROP
(GAS —) CANARY
(HALF —) LOO LOUP DOMINO
(PL.) AREITO
MASKED LARVATED VIZARDED
MASKER GUISARD MASQUER
MASKING MUMMERY MUMMING
COLORING
MASLIN MESTLEN MASHLOCH
MUNGCORN MASSELGEM
MASON LAYER BUILDER MASONER
COMACINE KNOBBLER LAMMIKIN
SCUTCHER
MASONRY ASHLAR BACKING
BLOCAGE MOELLON NOGGING
ISODOMUM QUOINING ROCKWORK
MASQUE MASK COMUS DEVICE
ANTIMASK DISGUISE
MASQUER REX
MASQUERADE MASK GUISE DOMINO
MASQUE PARADE MASKERY
DISGUISE
MASQUERADER RAGSHAG
MASQUERADING CARNIVAL
MASS BAT BED GOB SOP WAD BODY
BULK GOUT HEAP HEFT KNOT LEAD
LUMP MOLE OBIT STOW SWAD
AMASS BATCH BLOOM CLAMP
CLASH CLUMP CROWD CRUST
DIRGE GLOBE GORGE GROSS
MATTE MISSA SLUMP SOLID SPIRE
STORE WODGE COMMON GOBBET
NUGGET PROPER VOLUME WEIGHT
BOUROCK CONGEST DENSITY
MASKINS MESKINS NYSTERY
REQUIEM SALOMON CALAPITE
CONGERIE ENDOSOME FLOCCULE
MOUNTAIN SOULMASS
(— IN THE WHITE NILE) SUDD

(— OF BACTERIA) SLIME SYMPLASM
(— OF BLOSSOMS) BLOW
(— OF BLUBBER) MELON
(— OF BRANCHES) SPRAY
(— OF BUBBLES) FOAM
(— OF BUSHES) SHAG
(— OF CARPELS) SOREMA
(— OF CELLS) COMB CANCER
CUMULUS STALACE
(— OF CLOUDS) BANK
(— OF COAL) JUD
(— OF COLORS) BLOB
(— OF COTTON) FUSSOCK
(— OF CURED RUBBER) LOAF
(— OF DEBRIS) SLIDE
(— OF DOUGH) DUMPLING
(— OF FIBERS) KAPOK
(— OF FILAMENTS) FLOCCUS
(— OF FILTH) GORE
(— OF FRAGMENTS) BRASH
(— OF HAIR) GLIB TOUPET
(— OF ICE) BERG CALF FLOE FLAKE
PATCH ICICLE STURIS GROWLER
ICEBERG FLOEBERG
(— OF INSECTS) CACHE
(— OF IRON) BALL BLOB CORE
BLOOM INDUCTOR
(— OF LAVA) BOMB SPINE
(— OF LEAVES) FOLIAGE
(— OF LIMESTONE) HUM
(— OF LOOSE BOULDERS) CLATTER
(— OF METAL) SOW INGOT BUTTON
(— OF MOLTEN GLASS) GOB
GATHER PARISON
(— OF MUD) CLASH
(— OF ORE) BACK SLUG BUNNY
SQUAT
(— OF PEOPLE) CROWD HORDE
(— OF POMACE) CHEESE
(— OF ROCK) DOME NECK HORSE
LEDGE NAPPE SCALP SNOUT INLIER
SARSEN BOULDER FOOTWALL
(— OF SAND) PAAR
(— OF SOAP) CURD
(— OF SPORES) SORUS
(— OF SUGAR CRYSTALS) STRIKE
(— OF SUGAR) FONDANT
(— OF TISSUE) COLLAR GANGLION
(— OF WATER) HEAD
(— OF YARN) COP BALLOON
(— OF YOLK) LATEBRA
(— OVERHANGING) CORNICE
(— TOGETHER) HUDDLE
(—S OF DRIFTWOOD) EMBARRAS
(AMORPHOUS —) JUMBLE
SYMPLASM
(BILLOWY —) CLOUD
(BUSHY —) SHOCK
(COMPACT —) BRIQUET
(CONFUSED —) COT JUMBLE
JUNGLE CLUTTER RUMMAGE
SHUFFLE
(DISORDERLY —) SCRAMBLE
(EGG —) BUNION CULTCH SPONGE
(FATTY —) BEAN HEADSKIN
(FECAL —) SCYBALUM
(FLATTISH —) DAB
(FLUID —) FLUOR
(GLASSY —) SLAG

(GLOBULAR —) MOORBALL
(INDISTINCT —) SMUDGE
(IRREGULAR —) CUB
(LIVING —) BLASTEMA
(MOIST —) PULP
(MOUNTAIN —) OROGEN
(NUCLEAR —) SHIELD
(OVERSPREADING —) PALL
(PEAR-SHAPED —) BOULE
(POROUS —) FILTER
(PROJECTING —) BOSS
(PULPY —) SQUELCH
(RECTANGULAR —) BRICK
(ROOT —) SOLE
(ROUNDED —) COB NOB KNOB
BOLUS KUGEL BULLET RONDLE
(SEDIMENTARY —) GOBI
(SHAPED —) PAT LOAF
(SHAPELESS —) JELLY
(SLIPPERY —) SIND SLUD SLUDDER
(SLUSHY —) POSH
(SOFT —) MASH MOXA MUMMY
(SWOLLEN —) CERE
(TANGLED — OF HAIR) MOP KNURL
(UNCTUOUS —) LANOLIN
(UPRIGHT —) COLUMN
(PL.) MEINY MEINIE TRENTAL

MASSACHUSETTS
CAPE: ANN COD
CAPITAL: BOSTON
COLLEGE: SMITH AMHERST
  SIMMONS WHEATON WILLIAMS
  RADCLIFFE WELLESLEY
COUNTY: DUKES BERKSHIRE
  NANTUCKET BARNSTABLE
INDIAN: NAUSET POCOMTUC
ISLAND: DUKES NANTUCKET
LAKE: ONOTA QUABBIN ROHUNTA
  WEBSTER
MOUNTAIN: BRODIE POTTER
  ALANDER EVERETT GREYLOCK
MOUNTAIN RANGE: BERKSHIRE
POND: WALDEN
RIVER: NASHUA CHARLES
  CONCORD QUABOAG TAUNTON
  CHICOPEE DEERFIELD
STATE BIRD: CHICKADEE
STATE FLOWER: MAYFLOWER
STATE NICKNAME: BAY
STATE TREE: ELM
TOWN: AYER LYNN OTIS ATHOL
  BARRE LENOX AGAWAM
  DEDHAM GROTON NAHANT
  NATICK REVERE SAUGUS
  WOBURN HOLYOKE IPSWICH
  PEABODY TAUNTON BROCKTON
  CHICOPEE COHASSET SCITUATE
  UXBRIDGE YARMOUTH
UNIVERSITY: CLARK TUFTS
  HARVARD BRANDEIS

MASSACRE SLAY POGROM
  CARNAGE SCUPPER BUTCHERY
  SLAUGHTER
MASSAGE WISP KNEAD FACIAL
  PETRIE SHAMPOO TRIPSIS LOMILOMI
MASSAGER MASSEUR VIBRATOR

MASSECUITE GUR FILLMASS
MASSED DENSE
MASSENA QUAIL COPPY
MASSIVE BIG BEAMY BULKY GROSS
  HEAVY LUSTY MASSY SOUND STERN
  STRONG HEALTHY HULKING
  VOLUMED TIMBERED
MAST BUCK MAIN POLE SPAR OVEST
  STICK STING DRIVER JIGGER
  MIZZEN ARTEMON ASHERAH
  MASTAGE SPANKER FOREMAST
  MAINMAST SHIPMAST
  (FALLEN —) SHACK
  (SIXTH —) DRIVER
MASTAX TROPHI
MASTER DON HER JOE MAS RAB
  SAB SIR ARCH BAAS BEAK BOSS
  COCK FACE HERR JOSS KING LORD
  MIAN SIRE TUAN BWANA MARSE
  MASSA RABBI SAHIB SWAMI SWAMY
  SWELL BRIDLE BUCKRA CASTER
  DEACON DOMINE HUMBLE MAITRE
  PATRON RECTOR RHETOR SIRCAR
  WAFTER CAPTAIN CONQUER
  DOMINIE DOMINUS EFFENDI
  MAESTRO NAKHODA OGTIERN
  PADRONE RABBANI RABBONI
  AMAISTER BARGEMAN BEMASTER
  KINGFISH LANDLORD MAGISTER
  OVERCOME SLOOPMAN SURMOUNT
  VANQUISH
  (— OF CEREMONIES) EMCEE
  VERGER COMPERE CHAIRMAN
  (— OF CRAFT) KAHUNA
  (— OF HOUSEHOLD) BALABOS
  GOODMAN
  (— OF REVELS) ALYTARCH
  (— OF WHALER) SPOUTER
  (FENCING —) LANISTA
  (INFERIOR —) KNIFER
MASTER-AT-ARMS JAUNTY JAUNTIE
MASTERFUL LORDLY VIRILE
  HAUGHTY ARROGANT MAGERFUL
MASTERPIECE TOPPIECE
MASTERY GREE GRIP GRIPE
  COMMAND MAISTRY OVERHAND
MASTHEAD FLAG HIGHTOP
MASTICATE GUM CHAW CHEW
MASTICATORY BUYO
MASTIC BULLY JOCUM JOCUMA
MASTIC TREE ACOMA AUSUBO
  COCUYO COCULLO
MASTIFF ALAN MASTY BANDOG
  TIEDOG
MASTIGONEME FLIMMER
MASTITIS CLAP WEED GARGET
MAST TREE ASAK
MASTURBATE ABUSE
MASTURBATION ONANISM
  FROTTAGE
MASTWOOD POON KAMANI
MAT COT RUG TOD BASS FLAT FLET
  FOOT HAIR MOSS NIPA PACE RAFT
  SHAG TAUT DOILY KILIM TATTY
  COTTER FELTER FOOTER PAUNCH
  PETATE TARGET COASTER CUSHION
  DOORMAT KAITAKA MATTING
  FOOTPACE FROSTING MATTRESS
  SPANDREL

(— BORDER) TANIKO
(BOWLING —) FOOTER
(FIBER —) IE BASS
(PALM-LEAF —) YAPA
(PICTURE-FRAME —) FLAT
(POLYNESIAN —) LAUHALA
(SCOURING —) BEAR
(TABLECLOTH —) GARDNAP
(PL.) DUNNAGE
MATACHIN BOUFFON
MATACO CORONADO
MATADOR MAT ESPADA CAPEADOR
  (— MOVEMENT) PASE
MATCH GO CAP VIE BOUT COPE
  EVEN FERE LUNT MAKE MATE MEET
  MILL MOTE PAIR PEEL PEER SIDE
  SUIT AMATE EQUAL FIRER FUSEE
  FUZEE MOUSE PARTY SPUNK TALLY
  VENUE VESTA ASSORT CANCEL
  COMMIT FELLOW KIPPIN MARROW
  QUADER RUBBER SAMPLE SWATCH
  COMPEER EXAMPLE IGNITER
  ILLUMER KINDLER KIPPEEN LIGHTER
  LUCIFER PARAGON PAREGAL
  PATTERN PENDANT SINGLES
  APPROACH BONSPIEL BREATHER
  EUPYRION FOURSOME INFLAMER
  LOCOFOCO PORTFIRE REANSWER
  VESUVIAN VESUVIUS SEMIFINAL
  (— AT DICE) MAIN
  (BOXING —) SPAR FIGHT SLUGFEST
  (CURLING —) SPIEL BONSPIEL
  (DISHONEST —) CROSS
  (GOLF —) NASSAU FOURSOME
  (SHOOTING —) TIR SHOOT
  (SLOW —) LUNT SMIFT SQUIB
  (PL.) LIGHTS
MATCHED ASSORTED
MATCHING MARROW SUITABLE
MATCHLESS ALONE UNIQUE
  NONESUCH PEERLESS
MATCHMAKER SHADCHAN
MATE CAWK FERE METE PAIR PEER
  BILLY BREED BUDDY BULLY CLASP
  CULLY DICKY MATCH PARTY TALLY
  YERBA BUNKIE FELLOW FUTURE
  MARROW PAREIL BROTHER
  COMPEER COMRADE CONSORT
  HUSBAND PARAGON NEIGHBOR
  PIRRAURA
  (BOATSWAIN'S —) BUFFER
  (GUNNER'S —) LADY
  (SECOND —) DICKY
MATERIAL FINE MOLD GAUZE
  GOUGE HYLIC METAL MOULD PASTE
  PLASS STUFF THING TRADE
  BORROW CYANUS FABRIC GRAITH
  HOGGIN MATTER PAPREG THINGY
  APPAREL FOOTING SUBJECT
  TEXTILE UNIDEAL WEIGHTY
  ADDITIVE CORPORAL ECONOMIC
  EQUIPAGE SENSIBLE SNOODING
  TANGIBLE THINGISH
  (— ELIMINATED) CULLAGE
  (— FOR FERMENTING) GUILE
  (— FOR OYSTER BEDS) CULCH
  CULTCH
  (— IN GRAIN) DOCKAGE
  (— IN MAKING CEMENT) ADDITION

(— IN NEEDLEWORK) INKLE
(— OF CORDED SILK) CRYSTAL
(— OF SCREENINGS) HOGGIN
HOGGING
(— REMOVED BY SAW CUT) KERF
(— USED IN WAXING) BALL
(— WEIGHED) DRAFT DRAUGHT
(—S FOR MAKING GLASS) FRIT
(ABSORBENT —) DOPE
(ALLUVIAL —) SHINGLE
(ANCIENT —) MURRA MURRHA
(ARTISTIC —) KITSCH
(BAGGING —) HOPSACK
(BITUMINOUS —) KEROGEN
(BONY —) COSMINE
(BUILDING —) LATH ADOBE BRICK
STAFF SWISH TABBY TAPIA SILLAR
CONCRETE
(BUILDING —S) TIGNUM
(CLAY —) TAPIA
(CLAYEY —) GOUGE
(COLORING —) TINCTION
(COMBUSTIBLE —) KINDLING
(CONSTRUCTION —) BREEZE
(CORE —) NIFE
(CUSHIONING —) AIRFOAM
(DEPOSITED —) FOOTS
(DIAMOND —) BORT
(DOWNY —) FLUE
(DRESS —) FOULE VOILE PEELING
COTILLON
(DYEING —) SUMAC SUMACH
(EMBROIDERY —) ARRASENE
(EXCAVATED —) SPOIL
(FACING —) ENAMEL
(FISSIONABLE —) STUFF
(FOUNDATION —) UNDERLAY
(GLUTINOUS —) GELATIN
(GRANULAR —) BASIS
(HARD —) CARBIDE
(HEAT-RESISTANT —) ALSIFILM
(ILLUSTRATIVE —) ART
(INSECTICIDAL —) SCABRIN
(INSULATING —) KERITE PECITE
BLANKET LAGGING OKONITE
MEGOTALC
(LEFTOVER —S) ARISINGS
(LOOSE —) SAND GRAVEL DETRITUS
(MINING REFUSE —) ATTLE
(MINUTE —) SESTON
(NUTRITIVE —) FUEL
(ORGANIC —) EXINITE
(PAPER-THIN —) FOIL
(PATCHING —) BOTCH
(PETRIFIED —) GEMSTONE
(POLISHING —) RABAT
(POWDERED —) FINES
(RAW —) STOCK STAPLE
(REFRACTORY —) GROG BULLDOG
CASTABLE
(RESIDUAL —) CEMENT
(RESOURCE —) SWIPE
(REVERSIBLE —) DAMASK
(SEDIMENTARY —) SILT
(SILK —) HONAN PEKIN FOULARD
SARCENET
(SLIMY —) SWARF
(SMOKING —) KEF KIF
(STIFF —) CANVAS

(STIFFENING —) BOXING
(TANNING —) SYNTAN
(TILE-STRENGTHENING —) WEB
(TRASHY —) SLUSH
(TWEEDY —) HOMESPUN
(TYPE-HIGH —) BEARER
(UNPUBLISHED —) INEDITA
(VOLCANIC —) EJECTA
(WATERPROOF —) KERATOL
(WORTHLESS —) GARBLE
(WOVEN —) LAPPET
(PL.) STOCK STUFF
MATERIALISM HYLISM SOMATISM
(DIALECTICAL —) DIAMAT
MATH MUTH MONASTERY
MATERIALISTIC SENSATE SENSUAL
BANAUSIC
MATERIALIZE REIFY DESCEND
MATER LECTIONIS GRAPHY
MATERNITY WARD NATUARY
MATGRASS NARD MATWEED
MATHEMATICIAN ALGORIST
GEOMETER
MATHEMATICS METHESIS
MATING NICK COUPLE DIALLEL
BREEDING HOMOGAMY PANMIXIA
MATRASS BOLTHEAD CUCURBIT
MATRIMONIAL MARITAL NUPTIAL
SPOUSAL CONJUGAL
MATRIMONY WEDLOCK MARRIAGE
MATRIMONY VINE JASMINE
JESSAMY BOXTHORN
MATRIX BED MAT SORT PLASM
SHELL SLIDE DYADIC MASTER
MOTHER STRIKE STROMA CALYMMA
FORMULA MATRICE PATTERN
PROPLASM
MATRON DAME
MATTE SLURRY REGULUS
MATTED COTTY FELTY PINNY
FELTED TAGGED TAUTED WAUKIT
STRINGY FELTLIKE
MATTER RES BONE CASE GEAR
HYLE ITEM RECK WHAT AMPER
FORCE PARTY SKILL STUFF THEME
AFFAIR ARGUFY BEHALF DITTAY
IMPORT ARTICLE CONCERN
MATERIA SIGNIFY SUBJECT
BUSINESS COMETHER MATERIAL
(— ADDED TO BOOK) APPENDIX
(— AROUND THE TEETH) TOPHUS
(— CONSTITUTING PERFUME)
ESSENCE
(— IN DISPUTE) ISSUE
(— OF BUSINESS) SHAURI
(— OF CONCERN) FUNERAL
(— OF INTEREST) GRIST
(— TO) CONCERN
(ALLUVIAL —) GEEST
(BRAIN —) ALBA
(CARTILAGINOUS —) GRISTLE
(COLORING —) DYE COLOR CROCK
EOSIN MORIN PIURI ALNEIN BUTEIN
FUSTIC INDIGO PIOURY CARMINE
CASTORY CUDBEAR LIGULIN
OENOLIN PIGMENT PUNICIN XANTHIN
ALGOCYAN FUSTERIC LAPACHOL
SCOPARIN TINCTION
(CORRUPT —) PUS ATTER

(DECAYED ORGANIC —) DUFF
(ESSENTIAL —) POINT
(EXPLANATORY —) HAGGADA
(FATTY —) SEBUM
(FECAL —) SIEGE
(FILTHY —) GUNK
(FOREIGN —) SOIL DROSS
(FOUL —) FILTH SORDES
(FRONT —) FOREWORD
(GELATINOUS —) BREAK SPAWN
(GRAY —) GLIOSA CINEREA
(INANIMATE —) AJIVA
(INFECTIOUS —) MIASMA
(MINERAL —) FLOAT FLOATS
(POTENTIAL —) PRAKRITI
(PRIMARY —) PRADHANA
(PRINTED —) BOX DISPLAY
(PULVERIZED —) ATTRITUS
(READING —) BODY
(SLIMY —) GLAIR
(SMALL —) MINUTIA
(SOFT —) PASH
(SUBJECT —) SCOPE CONTENT
(SUPPURATIVE —) PUS
(TRIVIAL —) JOKE
(TYPESET —) CHASE
(WASTE —) DIRT DRAFF DROSS
RAMMEL SEWAGE EXCRETA
(WORTHLESS —) SLAG GARBAGE
(WRITTEN —) SCRIVE
(PL.) HARNESS SQUARES
MATTER-OF-FACT DRY LITERAL
MATTER-OF-FACTNESS PROSE
MATTING MAT TAT BEAR BUMP
SIRKI TATTY SAWALI TATAMI
COCOMAT RABANNA
MATTOCK MAT BILL HACK MATAX
PICKAX TUBBAL TWIBIL GRUBBER
MATTRESS BED MAT TICK DIVAN
QUILT RESAI REZAI PALLET
MATRACE
MATURATE MATTER
MATURE AGE OLD BOLD FULL GRAY
RIPE ADULT MANCY RIPEN SHOOT
ACCRUE AUTUMN DECOCT DIGEST
MELLOW SEASON SEEDED
CONCOCT DEVELOP FURNISH
PERFECT PROVECT MATURATE
MATURED ADULT GROWN FORMED
HEADED MELLOW SEEDED
HOMOGAMY
(SEXUALLY —) HIGH
MATURING (— EARLY) RATHRIPE
MATURITY AGE RIPENESS
MATZOTH MATZOS AFIKOMEN
MAUDLIN BEERY MOIST FUDDLED
MAUDLINISM BATHOS
MAUL FAN TUG MALL MELL GAVEL
GLAUM BEATER BEETLE BEMAUL
MUZZLE
MAUND MAO MEIN MAHAN
MAUNDER HAVER
MAUNDY NIPTER MANDATE
MAUSOLEUM MOLE TOMB TURBEH
BARADARI
MAUVE PURPLE MAUVINE
MAW MAA GORGE CROPPY THROAT
MAWKISH CUTE SAPPY SOUPY
WALSH DRIPPY SICKLY VANILLA

MAXILLA SETA GNATHITE CULTELLUS

MAXILLIPED JAWFOOT GNATHITE

MAXIM SAW SAY DICT ITEM NORM RULE TEXT WORD ADAGE AXIOM GNOME LARGE MOTTO DICTUM SAYING SYMBOL BROCARD DICTATE IMPRESA PRECEPT PROVERB APHORISM APOTHEGM DOCTRINE MORALISM PROTASIS SENTENCE **(PL.)** LOGIA

MAXIMUM FULL CREST EXTREME OUTSIDE SUMMARY ULTIMATE

MAXWELL LINE WEBER

MAY CAN MUN MOWE MUST PRIME SHALL HEYDAY HAWTHORN SYCAMORE **(3D OF —)** RUDMASDAY

MAYA PRAKRITI

MAYAN COCOM **(— CALENDAR PERIOD)** UAYEB UINAL **(— GOD)** CHAC CHAAC

MAYAPPLE MANDRAKE

MAYBE MEBBE HAPPEN PERHAPS POSSIBLY

MAY DAY BELTANE

MAYFISH ROCKFISH

MAYFLOWER ARBUTUS

MAYFLY DUN DOON DRAKE NAIAD DAYFLY SPINNER EPHEMERA

MAYHEM FELONY

MAYONNAISE GOULASH DRESSING

MAYOR MAIRE BAILIFF DEMARCH PODESTA PROVOST PALATINE **(BULGARIAN —)** KMET **(SPANISH —)** ALCALDE

MAYORSHIP CHAIR

MAYPOLE SHAFT

MAYPOP MAYCOCK MARACOCK

MAYWEED BALDER COTULA MATHER HOGWEED COMPOSIT DILLWEED

MAZE JUNGLE WARREN CONFUSE BEWILDER LABYRINTH

MCCOY QUILL

ME I MA US

MEAD MEATHE HYDROMEL

MEADOW LEA ABEL MEAD VEGA WISH WONG FIELD GRASS LEASE MARSH SWALE WARTH CALLOW PARAMO SAETER SMOOTH POTRERO THWAITE CHINAMPA **(ARTIFICIAL —)** CHINAMPA **(IRISH —)** BAAN **(LOW —)** ING INGE HAUGH CALLOW

MEADOW CROWFOOT FROGWORT

MEADOW GRASS POA

MEADOWLAND ALP MOWING MOWLAND

MEADOWLARK ACORN MEDLAR

MEADOW MOUSE VOLE

MEADOW PEA COWPEA

MEADOW PIPIT WEKEEN CHEEPER TIETICK TITLING LINGBIRD TWITLARK

MEADOW SAFFRON UPSTART

MEADOW SAXIFRAGE SESELI

MEADOWSWEET SPIREA MEADWORT

MEAGER BALD BARE LANK LEAN NICE POOR GAUNT NAKED SCANT SILLY SKIMP SOBER SPARE JEJUNE LEEPIT LENTEN MEAGRE NARROW PILLED SCANTY SLIGHT SPARSE STINGY SCRAGGY SCRANNY SCRIMPY SCRUBBY SLENDER SPARING STARVED STERILE SCRATCHY

MEAGERLY BARELY SPARELY SPARINGLY

MEAGERNESS ECONOMY EXILITY TENUITY SPARENESS

MEAL AMYL ATTA BAKE CHOW FARM FEED HASH KAIL MEAT MONG TUCK COENA FLOUR MANGE SCOFF BUFFET COMIDA DINNER FARINA MANGER POLLEN REPAST SPREAD SQUARE SUPPER UNDERN BLOWOUT COOKOUT CRIBBLE NAGMAAL NOONING SETDOWN ALMUERZO CORNMEAL EVENMETE MEALTIDE ORDINARY TRENCHER **(— FROM CASSAVA ROOT)** FARINE FARINHA **(— GROUND BY HAND)** GRADDAN **(— OF FELLOWSHIP)** AGAPE **(— STIRRED WITH MILK)** STUROCH **(COARSE —)** GRIT GROUT KIBBLE GURGEONS **(COLLEGE —)** HALL **(CORN —)** MASA ATOLE **(ELABORATE —)** FEAST BANQUET **(FIRST —)** ALMUERZO **(FULL —)** GORGE **(HASTY —)** SNAP **(HEARTY —)** AIT **(IMPROMPTU —)** BITE CHECK **(LIGHT —)** BAIT CHECK FOURS **(MIDDAY —)** NOON **(MORNING —)** BRUNCH **(PURIM —)** SEUDAH **(SCANTY —)** PICK **(SMALL —)** SNAP MORSEL **(SOLITARY —)** SULLEN **(UNSORTED —)** ATTA **(PL.)** TUCKER

MEALTIDE MELTITH

MEALTIME CHOW MELTETH

MEALY FLOURY FARINOSE PERONATE

MEALYBUG COCCID

MEAN LOW BASE CLAM HARD LEAN MIDS NICE POKY SLIM VILE AGENT ARGUE DINGY DUSTY FOOTY GRIMY KETTY MANGY MESNE MEZZO MIDST MINGY MOYEN MUCKY NASTY PETIT PETTY RATTY RUNTY SCALL SCALY SCRUB SEEDY SILLY SMALL SNIDE SNIVY SORRY SOUND SPELL ABJECT BEMEAN COMMON DENOTE DESIGN DIRTEN FEEBLE FROWZY FRUGAL GRUBBY HUMBLE HUNGRY IMPORT INTEND LEADEN LITTLE MEASLY MEDIAL MEDIUM MIDDLE NARROW PALTRY PEANUT PILLED POKING RASCAL SCABBY SCREWY SCUMMY SCURVY SHABBY SLIGHT SNIFTY SNIPPY SORDID SQUALL STRAIT TEMPER YELLOW AVERAGE CAITIFF CHANNEL CHETIVE COMICAL CONNOTE HACKNEY HILDING IGNOBLE MESQUIN MISERLY MOTETUS OBSCURE PEAKING PELTING PIGGISH PITIFUL PORTEND REPTILE ROINISH SCABBED SHABBED SIGNIFY VICIOUS BEGGARLY CHURLISH DOGGEREL MEDIOCRE MIDDLING PICAYUNE PITIABLE RASCALLY RIFFRAFF SHAMEFUL SNEAKING TWOPENNY WRETCHED

MEANDER WIND STRAY TWINE CIRCLE WIMPLE WINDLE SERPENT WINDING STRAGGLE

MEANING WIT HANG DRIFT SENSE SOUND IMPORT INTENT SEMEME PURPORT PURPOSE CARRIAGE INNUENDO SENTENCE STRENGTH **(BASIC —)** EFFECT **(DOUBLE —)** WHIM EQUIVOKE **(ESSENTIAL —)** CORE CONTENT **(IMPLIED —)** EMPHASIS **(MANIFEST —)** FACE **(REAL —)** SPIRIT **(SECRET —)** HEART

MEANINGFULNESS BODY

MEANINGLESS FECKLESS **(— LETTER OR CODE)** NULL

MEANNESS BEGGARY

MEANS MIDS AGENT DRIVE MESNE MOYEN PURSE THEME AGENCY AVENUE ENGINE MATTER MIDDES POCKET STRING WRENCH BALANCE BENEFIT DEMESNE FACULTY FASHION QUOMODO COURTESY **(— OF COMMUNICATION)** CANAL COMMERCE **(— OF DEFENSE)** HORN HEDGE SHIELD BULWARK **(— OF ESCAPE)** CHINK SCAPE FLIGHT **(— OF LIVING)** ALIMONY **(— OF OFFENSE)** ARM **(— OF PROTECTION)** SAFETY **(— OF SUPPORT)** HOLD ALIMENT SUPPORT

MEANSPIRITED POOR SUPINE CURRISH RECREANT

MEANTIME MEAN WHILE WHILES INTERIM

MEANTONE TERTIAN

MEANWHILE WHILST INTERIM MEANTIME

MEASLES RUBEOLA MORBILLI **(BLACK —)** ESCA APOPLEXY

MEASURE (ALSO SEE UNIT AND WEIGHT) AR BU EM EN HO KO LI MO RI SE TU AAM ARE AUM CAB CHO DRA ELL FAT FEN FIT FOU FUN GAD GAZ GUZ HIN HOB IMI KAB KAN KIP KOR KOS LEA LOG LUG MAU MIL MOY PIK RIG RIN ROD SAA SHO TON TUN VAT VOG WEY ACRE ALMA AUNE BARN BATH BEKA BOLL BOUW BUTT CADE CENT CHIH COOM COSS DEPA DOSE DRAA DRAM DYNE EPHI FALL FANG FOOT

FULL GAGE GERA GILL GIRT GOAD
GRAM GREX HAND HATT HIDE HOOP
HOUR IMMI INCH KNOT KOKU LAST
MEAL METE MILE NAIL NOOK PACE
PINT PIPE POLL REAM RIME ROOD
ROPE ROTL SAAH SACK SALM SEAH
SEAM SIZE SKEP SPAN STEP TAKT
TAPE TIME TRAM TRUG TSUN VARA
WIST YARD ALMUD AMBER ANKER
ARDAB ARURA BEKAH BIGHA BLANK
BODGE BRASS CABAN CABLE
CABOT CANDY CARAT CARGA
CATTY CAVAN CHAIN CHANG CHING
CLOVE COOMB CRANS CUBIT
CUMAL CUNIT DENUM DEPOH DIGIT
DRAFT DUNAM DUNUM EPHAH
GAUGE GERAH GIRTH HOMER
HUTCH JUGER LABOR LAGEN LIANG
LIBRA LIGNE LITER LITRE MEITH
METER METRE MINIM MODEL OUNCE
PEISE PERCH PLANK POUND QUIRE
RASER RHYME SALMA SCALE
SCORE SHAKU SHENG SHING SIEVE
SLEEP STACK STERE STONE STOOP
STOUP THERM TOISE TOVET TRACE
VERST YOJAN APATAN ARCHIN
ARPENT ARSHIN ASSIZE BARREL
BATMAN BEMETE BOVATE BUNDLE
BUSHEL CANADA CANTAR CHOMER
CHOPIN COLLOP COUDEE COVIDO
CUERDA DAVACH DAVOCH DECARE
DEGREE DENIER DIPODY DIRHAM
DRACHM ENGLER EXTENT FANEGA
FATHOM FEDDAN FINGER FIRKIN
FIRLOT FLAGON FODDER FORPET
FOTHER GALLON GRAMME HALEBI
HIDAGE KISHEN LEAGUE MICRON
MODULE MOGGIO MORGEN NUMBER
OITAVA OUROUB OXHIDE QANTAR
REASON SETIER SQUARE STERAD
STRIKE SULUNG TERMIN THRAVE
WINDLE YOJANA ADOULIE ALQUIRE
AMPHORA ANAPEST ARSHINE
BATTUTA BRACCIO BREADTH
CADENCE CALIPER CALORIE
CENTARE CENTNER CENTRAD
CHITTAK COMPASS CONGIUS
CONTAIN DECIARE DIOPTER
DRACHMA DRAUGHT ENTROPY
FARSAKH FARSANG FRUNDEL
FURLONG HECTARE HEMINEE
KILIARE NOCKTAT QUARTAN
QUARTER SCHEPEL SCRUPLE
SECCHIO SKEPFUL SKIPPLE
SPANGLE SPINDLE STADION
STADIUM TERTIAN VIRGATE
CAPACITY CARUCATE CENTIARE
CHETVERT CRANNOCK DACTYLIC
DECAGRAM DECIGRAM DESIATIN
DIAPASON HOGSHEAD INNOCENT
LANDYARD METEWAND PLOWGANG
PLOWGATE SCHOONER SCHOPPEN
STANDARD
(— DEPTH) SOUND
(— FOR DRINKS) JIGGER
(— FOR FISH) COT VOG CRAN LAST
DRAFT HAMPER DRAUGHT
(— FOR SHELLFISH) WASH
(— OF BEER) HANDLE

(— OF BUTTER) SPAN
(— OF CHAFF) FAN
(— OF COAL) TEN CORF KEEL
CHALDER CHALDRON
(— OF DEVELOPMENT) AGE
(— OF DISCREPANCY) LEEWAY
(— OF EELS) BIND STICK
(— OF EFFICIENCY) DUTY
(— OF FURS) MANTLE
(— OF GRAIN) MOY COOP
(— OF LIQUOR) FIFTH
(— OF MERCURY) FLASK
(— OF MINING CLAIMS) MERE
(— OF PEAS) COP
(— OF RAISINS) FRAIL
(— OF ROTATION) ANGLE
(— OF SILK) DRAMMAGE
(— OF STRAW) KEMPLE
(— OF SUPERIORITY) LEAD
(— OF TIMBER) TON STANDARD
(— OF WAR) BLOCKADE
(— OF WATCHES) LIGNE
(— OF WATERCRESS) HAND
(— OF WEIGHT FOR ARROWS)
SHILLING
(— OF WOOD) CORD STACK
(— OF WOOL FINENESS) BLOOD
(— OF WORK) POOL
(— OF YARN) LEA CLEW HEER
THREAD SPANGLE SPINDLE
(— OUT) BATCH
(ANGULAR —) ARC
(COERCIVE —) SANCTION
(DANCE —) TRACE
(DUE —) MANNER
(FULL —) SATIETY
(ROAD —) SCHENE
(SANCTIONED —) STANDARD
MEASURED NUMEROUS
MEASURELESS ENDLESS INFINITE
MEASUREMENT GAGE DEPTH
GAUGE LEVEL MEITH METAGE
DIALING MEASURE SOUNDING
(— FOR TAXATION) HIDE HIDAGE
(— OF CLOTH) ALNAGE
(— OF FINENESS) SET SETT
(LUMBER —) LAST
MEASURER METER
MEAT BEEF FISH FOOD LAMB LEAN
LIFT PORK FLESH STEAK VIFDA
VIVDA BUCCAN CAGMAG FLEECE
MATTER NUTTON TARGET PECKAGE
(— AND FISH) LAULAU
(— DRIED IN SUN) JERKY CHARQUI
PEMMICAN
(— OF CONCH) SCUNGILI
(— OF KID) CAPRETTO
(— WITH VEGETABLES) STEW
MULLIGAN
(BOILED —) SOD SODDEN BOUILLI
(BROILED —) GRISKIN GRILLADE
(BUFFALO —) FLEECE
(CANNED —) SPAM
(CHOPPED —) BURGER
(COCONUT —) COPRA
(CURED —) HAM
(CUT OF —) ARM
(DRIED —) MUMMY
(FAT —) SPECK

(FROZEN —) FRIGO
(INFERIOR —) CAGMAG STICKING
(JERKED —) BILTONG CHARQUI
(LEAN —) MUSCLE
(MINCED —) CHUET JIGOTE
RISSOLE SANDERS
(POTTED —) RILLETT
(RABBIT —) LAPAN
(RAGOUT OF —) HARICOT
(ROAST —) BREDE CABOB
(ROLLED —) BIRD
(SALTED —) JUNK MART
(SIDE —) SOWBELLY
(SMOKED —) BUCCAN
MEAT CURER BATHMAN
MEAT HOOK GAMBREL
MEAT JELLY ASPIC
MEATLESS PARVE LENTEN PAREVE
MEAT PIE PASTY
MEATUS BUR BURR ALVEARY
MEATY PITHY
MECATE MCCARTY
MECHANIC JOINER WRIGHT ARTISAN
FELTMAN SHOPMAN WORKMAN
MECHANICAL FROZEN INHUMAN
METALLIC AUTOMATIC
(NOT —) HORMIC
MECHANICALLY BLINDLY
MECHANISM FAN BOND FEED GEAR
KITE LIFT MOTE APRON CATCH
CROWD FORCE ORGAN SHAKE
SLIDE SPARK STEER ACTION
BOTTOM CUTOFF INFEED MOTION
SICKLE STRIKE BUILDER CHANNEL
CONTROL EJECTOR GIGBACK
GRIPPER GUNLOCK HOLDOUT
SETTING TRIPPER ACTUATOR
ELEVATOR KINETICS RACKWORK
SELECTOR SETWORKS SIGNALER
STEERING STOPWORK THROWOUT
MECHANIZE DESKILL AUTOMATE
MECONIN OPIANYL
MEDAL STAR AWARD STAMP PLAQUE
MEDALET OSCELLA
MEDALLION CAMEO TONDO PADUAN
PATERA PANHAGIA
MEDDLE TIG FOOL MELL MESS MIRD
TOUCH DABBLE FIDDLE FINGER
HECKLE POTTER PUTTER TAMPER
TANGLE TINKER
MEDDLER SNOOP SNOOPER
BUSYBODY KIBITZER STICKLER
STIFFLER BUTTINSKY
MEDDLESOME FRESH NEBBY
MEDDLING BUSY
MEDEA (BROTHER OF —) ABSYRTUS
(FATHER OF —) AEETES
(HUSBAND OF —) JASON AEGEUS
(MOTHER OF —) IDYIA
(SISTER OF —) CHALCIOPE
MEDIA ELASTICA
MEDIAL MEDIAN MEDIUM MIDDLE
AVERGAGE
MEDIAN MEDIAL MESIAL AVERAGE
(— STRIP) MALL TERRACE
MEDIANT THIRD
MEDIATE MEAN REFEREE
MEDIATING MIDDLE MIDWAY
MEDIATOR MEANS MEDIUM

DAYSMAN MIDDLER PLACATER
STICKLER
MEDIC HOP NONESUCH
MEDICAL IATRIC PHYSIC IATRICAL
PAEONIAN
(— WORK) ALMONING
MEDICAMENT SMEGMA FRONTAL
MEDICINAL IATRIC PHYSIC MEDICAL
THERIAL PHYSICAL SALUTARY
THERICAL
MEDICINE DRUG MUTI PEAI DROPS
GRUEL STEEL STUFF TONIC TRADE
AMULET ECLEGM ELIXIR MAGUAL
PHYSIC POWDER REMEDY SIMPLE
ANODYNE CORDIAL HEPATIC
LUCHDOM MIXTURE PLACEBO
POROTIC PYROTIC SPLENIC
AROMATIC DIGESTER DRUGGERY
EARDROPS EMULGENT LAXATIVE
LEECHDOM LENITIVE LOBLOLLY
PECTORAL PHARMACY PULMONIC
RELAXANT SPECIFIC STOMATIC
(CHINESE —) SENSO
(QUACK —) NOSTRUM
(SYSTEM OF —) AYURVEDA
(UNIVERSAL —) PANACEA
(PL.) GALIANES
MEDICINE MAN PEAI DOCTOR
KAHUNA PIACHE POWWOW SHAMAN
SINGER ANGEKOK TOHUNGA
CONTRARY POWWOWER
MEDIEVAL OLD GOTHIC
MEDIOCRE HACK MEAN SUCH
MEDIUM AVERAGE INFERIOR
MIDDLING PASSABLE
MEDITATE CAST CHEW MUSE GLOAT
STUDY WEIGH PONDER RECORD
IMAGINE PREPEND REFLECT
REVOLVE COGITATE CONSIDER
PURPENSE RUMINATE
MEDITATION MOYEN STUDY THINK
DHYANA MUSING HIGGAION
MEDITATIVE MUSING MUSEFUL
PENSIVE RUMINANT
MEDITERRANEAN MIDLAND
MEDIUM BATH EVEN LENS MEAN
ETHER JUICE MIDST MOYEN ORGAN
BALIAN BISTER BISTRE DIGEST
MIDDLE MIDWAY ORACLE SLUDGE
TEMPER PSYCHIC VEHICLE
MEDIOCRE SHOWCASE CONTINUUM
(— OF EXCHANGE) CURRENCY
(— OF TRANSMISSION) AIR
AIRWAVE
(CULTURE —) AGAR STAB BROTH
HYRAX SLANT CULTURE
(ENVELOPING —) SWATH
MEDLAR MESPIL LAZAROLE
MEDLEY OLIO BABEL REVUE JUMBLE
CHIVARI CLANGOR FARRAGO
GOULASH MELANGE MIXTURE
BROUHAHA KEDGEREE MACARONI
MISHMASH RHAPSODY SLAMPAMP
VARIORUM
MEDOC WINE LAFITTE
MEDREGAL BONITO
MEDULLA PITH MARROW
MEDULLA OBLONGATA BULB
MEDUSA JELLY QUARL GORGON

BLUBBER GERYONID
(FATHER OF —) PHORCYS
(MOTHER OF —) CETO
(SLAYER OF —) PERSEUS
(PL.) BRACT
MEEK LOW DAFT MURE LOWLY
GENTLE HUMBLE PACIFIC LAMBLIKE
YIELDING
MEERSCHAUM PIPE GRAVEL
KIEFEKIL SEPIOLITE
MEET FIT KEP SEE COPE FACE FILL
HENT NOSE CLOSE CROSS FRONT
GREET INCUR OCCUR PIECE TOUCH
ANSWER BATTLE BEMEET COMBAT
CONCUR FULFIL INVENT SEMBLE
CONTACT CONVENE CONVENT
COUNCIL FULFILL SATISFY
ASSEMBLE CONFRONT CONVERGE
GAINCOPE
(— A BET) SEE
(— A NEED) SUFFICE
(— AT END) BUTT
(— FACE TO FACE) AFFRONT
(— SQUARELY) ENVISAGE
(— VIOLENTLY) CHECK HURTLE
(— WITH) GET SEE BUMP FIND
STRIKE
(ATHLETIC —) GALA GYMKHANA
MEETING MOD FEIS MOOT CLOSE
FORUM SABHA SHINE STOUR SYNOD
TRYST ACCESS AUMAGA CAUCUS
CHAPEL CLINIC HUDDLE POWWOW
SEANCE CABINET CHAPTER
COLLEGE CONTACT CONVENT
COUNCIL JOLLITY MOOTING
OCCURSE REVIVAL SEMINAR
SITTING SYNAXIS ASSEMBLY
CONGRESS DELEGACY ECCLESIA
EXERCISE JUNCTION OSCULANT
TERTULIA WARDMOTE
(— OF NEIGHBORS) HUSKING
(— OF SCHOLARS) LEVY
(— OF WORSHIPERS) SERVICE
(ANGLO-SAXON —) GEMOTE
(GENERAL —) PRIME
(POLITICAL —) CAUCUS
(PRIVATE —) CONCLAVE
(SECRET —) CABAL CONSULT
(SOCIAL —) CLUB JOLLY HOBNOB
(TOWN —) TUNMOOT
MEETINGHOUSE MORADA
MEETING PLACE AMBALAM
TINWALD
MEGAPHONE VAMPHORN
MEGAPODE MALEO LEIPOA
MEGARA (FATHER OF —) CREON
(HUSBAND OF —) HERCULES
MEGILP GUMPTION
MEHTAR BUNGY BHUNGI
MELANCHOLIA ATHYMY ATHYMIA
SADNESS
MELANCHOLIC HYPPISH
MELANCHOLY WO SAD WOE BLUE
DRAM DULL DUMP MARE BLUES
DEARN DOWIE DREAR DUSKY
GLOOM SORRY WISHT GLOOMY
SOMBER SOMBRE SORROW SPLEEN
SULLEN YELLOW CHAGRIN DOLEFUL
DUMPISH ELEGIAC SADNESS

SPLEENY THOUGHT ATRABILE
LIVERISH TRISTFUL
MELANESIAN DOBUAN KANAGA
KANAKA EFATESE
MELANGE GOMBO GUMBO
MELANISM PHAEISM
MELANTERITE INKSTONE
MELATOPE EYE
MELD SET SAMBA SPREAD BOLIVIA
DECLARE
MELEAGER (FATHER OF —) OENEUS
(MOTHER OF —) ALTHAEA
MELEE BRAWL MEDLEY DOGFIGHT
PELLMELL
MELIORATE MITIGATE
MELISMA JUBILUS
MELL KIRN
MELLIFLUOUS SUGARED HYBLAEAN
MELLOW AGE OMY HAZE LUSH
MALM PLUM RICH RIPE SOFT FRUSH
FLUTED GOLDEN MATURE
MELLOWED BEERY
MELODIOUS SOFT SOOT TUNY
SWEET TUNED ARIOSO DULCET
MELODIC MUSICAL SIRENIC
SONGFUL STRENIC TUNABLE
TUNEFUL CANOROUS CHARMING
NUMEROUS SOUNDFUL
(EXCESSIVELY —) SIRUPY SYRUPY
MELODRAMA HAM TANK
MELODY AIR HUM LAY ARIA NOTE
TUNE CANTO CHANT CHARM DREAD
MELOS MIRTH NIGUN CANTUS
CHORAL GHAZEL MONODY NIGGUN
STROKE CANZONA CANZONE
CHORALE DESCANT HARMONY
MEASURE MELISMA PLANXTY
ROSALIA CAVATINA DIAPASON
VOCALISE
(— COMPASS) AMBITUS
(MOURNFUL —) DUMP
(SYNAGOGAL —S) CHAZANUT
HAZANUTH
MELON PEPO GOURD MANGO
CASABA CITRON DUDAIM MAYCOCK
CUCURBIT HONEYDEW PEPONIDA
PEPONIUM
MELT FLY RIN RUN BLOW FADE
FLOW FLUX FUSE THAW FOUND
LEACH SMELT SWEAL SWELT
TOUCH GUTTER RELENT SOFTEN
DISTILL FORMELT RESOLVE
DISCANDY DISSOLVE ELIQUATE
(— AWAY) SWEAL
(— DOWN) RENDER
(— IRREGULARLY) DROZE
MELTED RUN FONDU FUSED FUSILE
MELTING SOFT FUSILE FUSION
MELTWATER OUTWASH
MEMBER LIMB LITH BRANCH
FELLOW FILLET GIRDER SOCIUS
AMANIST ERANIST FAIRING
ALBRIGHT AULARIAN BRIDLING
(— OF ANSAR) HELPER
(— OF BALLET) FIGURANT
(— OF BAND) SIDEMAN
(— OF BODYGUARD) HUSCARL
(— OF BROTHERHOOD) ESSENE
SENUSSI

(— **OF CLAN**) CHILD CALEBITE
(— **OF CLERGY**) DEFENSOR
(— **OF COAST GUARD**) SPAR
(— **OF COUNCIL**) CONSUL
HEEMRAAD
(— **OF COURT**) DICAST EPHETE
(— **OF CREW**) HAND IDLER LAYER
DRIVER STROKE BOWSMAN
FORETOP BRAKEMAN SHAREMAN
(— **OF CULT**) ANGEL AMIDIST
(— **OF FACULTY**) COUNSEL
LECTURER
(— **OF FAMILY**) FETII
(— **OF FRATERNAL ORDER**) ELK
SHRINER FORESTER KIWANIAN
(— **OF FRATERNITY**) GREEK
(— **OF FRENCH ACADEMY**)
IMMORTAL
(— **OF GANG**) HENCHMAN
(— **OF GENTRY**) SEIGNEUR
(— **OF GIRL SCOUTS**) BROWNIE
(— **OF GREEK ARMY**) EVZONE
(— **OF GUILD**) COMACINE
(— **OF HOUSEHOLD**) FAMILIAR
(— **OF HUNTING PARTY**) STANDER
(— **OF INN OF COURT**) ANCIENT
BENCHER
(— **OF ITALIAN ARMY**) ALPINO
(— **OF KNOW-NOTHING PARTY**) SAM
(— **OF LEGISLATURE**) SOLON
DEPUTY DELEGATE
(— **OF LITERARY GROUP**) FELIBRE
(— **OF MIDDLE CLASS**) BURGHER
(— **OF PARLIAMENT**) CONTENT
THINGMAN
(— **OF PRIMROSE LEAGUE**) KNIGHT
(— **OF RELIGIOUS ORDER**) DAME
FRIAR EUDIST FRAILE FRATER
HERMIT JESUIT SISTER ALEXIAN
BRINSER DERVISH HUSSITE
SEPARTE SERVANT CENOBITE
EXORCIST HUMANIST SALESIAN
(— **OF RETINUE**) SEQUEL SEQUENT
(— **OF RUSSIAN ARISTOCRACY**)
BOYAR BOYARD
(— **OF SAME GENUS**) CONGENER
(— **OF SECRET ORGANIZATION**)
DEMOLAY
(— **OF SECRET SOCIETY**) BOXER
(— **OF SECT**) DRUSE HASID KHOJA
AUDIAN BRAHMO CATHAR DIPPER
DOPPER IBADHI JUMPER KHLYST
SMARTA AISSAWA AJIVIKA AUDAEAN
CAINITE CHASSID DREAMER EMPIRIC
EUCHITE IBADITE ISAWIYA ISMAILI
RAPPIST SEVENER AQUARIAN
CALIXTIN EBIONITE FAMILIST
GLASSITE LABADIST SADDUCEE
SEVERIAN SIMONIAN
(— **OF STAFF**) ATTACHE
(— **OF STATE**) CITIZEN
(— **OF STOCK EXCHANGE**)
BOARDMAN
(— **OF TEAM**) SPARE BOBBER
KICKER
(— **OF TRIBE**) LEVITE JUDAHITE
LAMANITE
(— **OF UPPER CLASS**) EFFENDI
(— **OF VARNA**) SUDRA SHUDRA

(— **OF WHITE RACE**) HAOLE
(— **OF WINDOW**) APRON
(—**S OF CLASS**) FRY
(—**S OF PROFESSION**) FACULTY
(—**S OF SECT**) SKOPTSY
(—**S OF TRIBUNAL**) ACUERDO
(**ARCHITECTURAL** —) FAN ARCH
FLAT SILL SPAN GABLE SOCLE
STILE STILT CORBEL FASCIA
CONSOLE CORNICE
(**CHURCH** —) GREEK LATIN DANITE
DUNKER KIRKER TUNKER BAPTIST
BEGHARD BROTHER DUNKARD
KIRKMAN SECEDER ARMENIAN
BRYANITE CATHOLIC DISCIPLE
DOWIEITE JACOBITE
(**CHURCH** —**S**) FAITHFUL
(**EVERY** —) ALL
(**FEEBLEST** —) WRIG
(**FULL** —) GREMIAL
(**OLDEST** —) FATHER
(**OVERHANGING** —) BRACKET
(**POLITICAL** —) CADET ENDEK SHIRT
GUELPH HUNKER LEADER APRISTA
LEFTIST LIBERAL BUCKTAIL
DEMOCRAT HERODIAN LABORITE
(**PROJECTING** —) TENON
(**SENIOR** —) DOYEN
(**TENSION** —) HANGER
(**TERMINAL** —) TOE
MEMBERSHIP SEAT GARTER
GUILDRY
MEMBRANE RIM WEB CAUL COAT
DURA FELL HEAD TELA GALEA
HYMEN VELUM AMNION AMNIOS
EXTINE INTINE MENINX MOTHER
MUCOSA PLEURA RETINA SEPTUM
SEROSA TIMBAL TUNICA TYMPAN
BLANKET CAPSULE CHORION
CUTICLE EPICYTE HYALOID
OOLEMMA PUTAMEN STRATUM
VELAMEN ECTODERM ENDOCYST
ENVELOPE EPENDYMA EPISPORE
EXOLEMMA INDUSIUM INTEXINE
LABELLUM PATAGIUM PELLICLE
STRIFFEN
(— **OF ORANGE**) ZEST
(**NICTITATING** —) HAW
(**TYMPANIC** —) TYMPAN MYRINGA
DRUMHEAD DRUMSKIN
(**PL.**) ADNEXA ANNEXA MENINGES
MEMBRANOUS HUSKY SKINNY
HYMENOID SCARIOSE SCARIOUS
MEMENTO RELIC TOKEN MEMORY
TROPHY KEEPSAKE REMINDER
SOUVENIR
MEMINNA PEESOREH
MEMNON (**FATHER OF** —) TITHONUS
(**MOTHER OF** —) AURORA
(**SLAYER OF** —) ACHILLES
MEMOIR ELOGE RECORD HISTORY
MEMORIAL
MEMORABLE GRAND SIGNAL
CLASSIC NOTABLE MEMORIAL
NAMEABLE
MEMORANDA (**SET OF** —) TICKLER
MEMORANDUM BILL CHIT NOTE
SLIP BRIEF JURAT CIPHER DOCKET
MEMOIR MINUTE TICKET JOTTING

MEMORIAL NOTANDUM PROTOCOL
MEMORIAL AHU AGALMA CAHIER
FACTUM MEMOIR MEMORY RECORD
TROPHY DENKMAL MEMENTO
MENTION EBENEZER MONUMENT
MEMORIZE LEARN MANDATE
REMEMBER
MEMORY MIND HEART IMAGE STORE
RECALL RECORD MEMENTO
STORAGE MEMORIAL SOUVENIR
(**OF POOR** —) FLUFFY
(**PAINFUL** —) SCAR
MEN THEY ORANG INNUIT MANHEAD
MANHOOD MANKIND MENFOLK
HUMANITY
MENACE BOAST IMPEND THREAT
BOGEYMAN MINATORY THREATEN
MENACING STOUT SURLY FIERCE
TOWARD MINATORY
MEN-AT-ARMS CHIVALRY
MEND DO FIX BEET DARN HEAL
HELP STOP TINK AMEND CLOUT
EMEND GRAFT MOISE PALCH
COBBLE DOCTOR FETTLE RANTER
REFORM REPAIR SOLDER SPETCH
TINKLE IMPROVE INWEAVE REDRESS
RIGHTLE
(— **BY ADDING FEATHERS**) IMP
(— **CLUMSILY**) BOTCH
(— **MEN'S CLOTHES**) BUSHEL
MENDACIOUS FALSE DISHONEST
MENDACITY LYING DECEIT FALSITY
UNTRUTH
MENDER TINKER KETTLER
BEATSTER
MENDICANCY BEGGARY
MENDICANT NAGA DANDI FAKIR
FRIAR UDASI BEGGAR BHIKKU
FAKEER FRATER GOSAIN AJIVIKA
BAIRAGI EUCHITE VAIRAGI
PANDARAM SANNYASI
MENDING COBBLE
MENEL NELL
MENELAUS (**BROTHER OF** —)
AGAMEMNON
(**FATHER OF** —) PLISTHENES
(**WIFE OF** —) HELEN
MENHADEN POGY PORGY BUNKER
CHEBOG SHINER ALEWIFE BUGFISH
BUGHEAD CLUPEID ELLFISH
FATBACK OLDWIFE SAVELHA
SHADINE WHITING BONYFISH
HARDHEAD
MENHIR BOUTA GORSEDD PEULVAN
CATSTONE HAGIOLITH
MENIAL FAG BASE LOON PAGE
KNAVE DRIVEL HARLOT POTBOY
VARLET SERVILE SLAVISH BANAUSIC
SCULLION SERVITOR
MENISCOID CRESCENT
MENNONITE HOOKER AMISHMAN
AMMANITE HUTERITE
MENOETIUS (**BROTHER OF** —)
ATLAS PROMETHEUS
(**FATHER OF** —) ACTOR
(**MOTHER OF** —) AEGINA
(**SON OF** —) PATROCLUS
MENOPAUSE CLIMAX
MENSTRUATE FLOW

MENSTRUATING SICK
MENSTRUATION FLOW CURSE
  FLUOR CRAMPS PERIOD COURSES
MENSTRUUM SOLVENT
MENTAL IDEAL GENIAL INWARD
  MINDLY PHRENIC PSYCHIC
  CEREBRAL
MENTALITY MIND SENSE ACUMEN
  REASON SPIRIT PSYCHISM
MENTHA LABIATE
MENTHANE TERPANE
MENTHOL CAMPHOR
MENTION CALL CITE HINT MIND
  MING MINT NAME CHEEP CLEPE
  SPEAK TOUCH MEMBER NOTICE
  SPEECH MEANING SPECIFY
  SUGGEST CITATION INSTANCE
  MEMORATE REHEARSE REMEMBER
  (— BY NAME) NEMN NEMME
  NEMPNE
  (— CASUALLY) DROP
  (HONORABLE —) ACCESSIT
MENTOR TEACHER CICERONE
MENTUM PERULA
MENU CARD CARTE
MEPERIDINE DEMEROL
MEPHISTOPHELIAN SATANIC
MERCAPTAN THIOL
MERCEDARIAN NOLASCAN
  RANSOMER
MERCENARY HACK VENAL JACKAL
  HESSIAN PINDARI HIRELING
  WAGELING
MERCER SILKMAN
MERCERIZE SCHREINER
MERCHANDISE CARGO CHEAP
  GOODS STUFF WARES ARTWARE
  CHAFFER SHIPPER TRAFFIC
  CHAFFERY SALEWARE
  (CHEAP SHODDY —) BORAX
  (RETURNED —) COMEBACK
MERCHANT ARAB SETH SETT TELI
  WALLA BADGER FACTOR KITELY
  NEPMAN RETAIL TAIPAN TRADER
  ANTONIO CHAPMAN GOLADAR
  HANSARD HOWADJI CHANDLER
  HUCKSTER MARCHAND POVINDAH
  SOUDAGUR
  (GRAIN —) LAMBADI
  (GREAT —) TAIPAN
  (WINE —) VINTNER
MERCIFUL KIND MILD HUMANE
  RUEFUL TENDER CLEMENT LENIENT
  MILDFUL PITIFUL SPARING
  GRACIOUS QUEMEFUL
MERCILESS GRIM CRUEL SHARP
  BLOODY FIERCE SAVAGE WANTON
  PITILESS
MERCURY HG AZOCH AZOTH
  DRAGON HERMES SPIRIT CHIBRIT
  MARKERY TEUTATES
  (FATHER OF —) JUPITER
  (MOTHER OF —) MAIA
MERCY LAW ORE HORE PITY RUTH
  GRACE GRITH BLITHE LENITY
  CHARITY CLEMENCY LENIENCY
MERE BARE NUDE ONLY PURE PUTE
  SOLE VERY NAKED SHEER SINGLE
MEREL PIN

MERELY BUT JUST ONLY BARELY
  PURELY SIMPLY SINGLY SOLELY
  ALONELY UTTERLY ENTIRELY
  SCARCELY
MERETRICIOUS CHEAP GAUDY
  GILDED PUNKISH
MERGANSER SMEE SMEW HARLE
  SNOWL SPIKE HERALD SAWNEB
  WEASER BRACKET GARBILL
  JACKSAW RANTOCK SAWBILL
  TADPOLE TOWHEAD TWEEZER
  WHEEZER EARLDUCK MOSSHEAD
MERGE FUSE JOIN BLEND ENTER
  GLIDE UNIFY MINGLE COMMERGE
  CONFLATE
MERGING BLEND FUSION
MERICARP COCCUS
MERIDIAN (THOSE LIVING UNDER
  SAME —) ANTOECI
MERINGUE KISS
MERINO DELAINE
MERISTEM PERIBLEM
MERIT DUE EARN MEED PUNY
  BROOK THANK WORTH DESERT
  VIRTUE WRIHTE DEMERIT DESERVE
  PUDDING
  (— CONSIDERATION) COUNT
  (POSSESSING —) WORTHY
MERITED JUST
  (NOT —) INDIGN
MERITORIOUS CAPITAL MERITORY
  THANKFUL VALOROUS
MERL BLACKIE
MERLON COP
MERMAID NIXIE SIREN MERROW
  MERWOMAN
MERMAN SEAMAN MANFISH
MEROPE (BROTHER OF —)
  PHAETHON
  (FATHER OF —) CRESPHONTES
  (HUSBAND OF —) SISYPHUS
  (MOTHER OF —) CYPSELUS
MEROPODITE FEMUR MEROS
MEROZOITE AGAMETE
MERRILY GAILY GAMELY LUSTICK
  JOYOUSLY
MERRIMENT FUN JOY GALE GLEE
  JEST UTAS DERAY MIRTH FROLIC
  SPLEEN DAFFERY DAFFING FESTIVE
  JOLLITY WAGGERY HILARITY
MERRY GAY BOON CANT GLAD GOLE
  BONNY CADGY CRANK DROLL
  JOLLY LIGHT LUSTY MURRY SUNNY
  VOGIE VOKIE BLITHE COCKET
  FROLIC JOCANT JOCUND JOVIAL
  JOYOUS LIVELY FEASTLY GLEEFUL
  HOLIDAY JOCULAR LUSTICK
  RAFFING WINSOME CHIRPING
  DISPOSED FESTIVAL GAMESOME
  GLEESOME LAUGHING PLEASANT
  SPANKING SPORTFUL SPORTIVE
MERRY-ANDREW AIRY ZANY ANTIC
  DROLL JESTER BUFFOON
MERRY-GO-ROUND CAROUSEL
  TURNABOUT
MERRYMAKING ALE MAY RAG KIRN
  PLOY REVEL GAIETY RACKET
  SPLORE CARNIVAL
MERRYTHOUGHT WISHBONE

MERUS PALM
MESA MESILLA CARTOUCH
MESADENIA CACALIA
MESCAL PEYOTE WOKOWI MEXICAL
  CHALLOTE
MESCALERO FARAON
MESENTERY CROW RUFFLE
MESH MASK MOKE CHAIN PITCH
  SHALE ACCRUE ENGAGE MASCLE
  SCREEN SCREENING
  (— IMPROPERLY) BUTT
  (IN —) DIRECT
MESHED ENGAGED
MESOCARP FLESH
MESOMORPHIC SOMAL SOMATIC
  ATHLETIC
MESOPODIUM PETIOLE
MESOPOTAMIA (TREE OF —) HOMA
MESOTONIC TERTIAN MEANTONE
MESQUITE HONEY KEAWE PACAY
  CASHAW ALGAROBA HONEYPOD
  IRONWOOD MOSQUITO
MESS JAG JAM MIX MUX PIE SOP
  CLAT FIST HASH JAMB MUCK MULL
  MUSS SLUB SOSS STEW SUSS
  BOTCH CAUCH JAKES STREW SWILL
  BOLLIX BUNGLE CADDLE CLATCH
  JUMBLE MUCKER PICKLE PUDDLE
  SOZZLE TUMBLE MAMMOCK
  MULLOCK SCAMBLE SLOTTER
  COUSCOUS DISORDER LOBLOLLY
  SHAMBLES SLAISTER
  (— AROUND) JUKE
  (— OF FOOD) SAND
  (GREASY —) GAUM
  (SLOPPY —) SLOBBER SLAISTER
MESSAGE CHIT MODE SAND SEND
  WIRE WORD RUMOR BREVET
  CIPHER ERRAND GOSPEL LETTER
  SCROLL BLINKER BODWORD
  DEPECHE EMBASSY MISSION
  SENDING TIDINGS AEROGRAM
  CREDENCE DISPATCH
  (— BY FLAGS) HOIST
  (— FROM GOD) ANGEL
  (CHRISTIAN —) EVANGEL
  (CIPHER —) SCYTALE
  (COMPLIMENTARY —) RECADO
MESSALIAN EUCHITE
MESSENE (FATHER OF —) TRIOPAS
  (HUSBAND OF —) POLYCAON
MESSENGER BODE PEON POST
  SAND SEND TOTY VAUX ANGEL
  ENVOY MUMMU VISOR BEADLE
  BROKER BUNENE CHIAUS HERALD
  LEGATE NUNCIO PIGEON RUNNER
  APOSTLE CARRIER CASHBOY
  CONTACT COURANT COURIER
  EXPRESS FORAGER FORAYER
  MALACHI MERCURY MESSAGE
  MISSIVE NAMTARU PATAMAR
  TOTYMAN TROTTER TRUMPET
  EMISSARY FOREGOER HIRCARRA
  LOBBYGOW NUNCIATE ORDINARY
  PORTATOR
  (— OF APSU AND TIAMAT) MUMMU
  (— OF GOD) ANGEL
  (— OF SHAMASH) BUNENE

(— OF THE GODS) HERMES MERCURY
(MOUNTED —) COSSID ESTAFET
(RELIGIOUS —) APOSTLE
(UNDERWORLD —) NAMTARU
MESSIAH CHRIST WOVOKA
MESSMATE YUBA
MESSUAGE HAW TOFT MEESE MIDSTEAD
MESSY GOOEY SLOPPY SOZZLY STICKY
MESTIZO CHOLO LADINO CURIBOCA MAMELUCO
METAL ORE TIN BODY DIET GOLD IRON LEAD ZINC BARIUM CESIUM CHROME COBALT COPPER INDIUM LATTIN NICKEL OSMIUM RADIUM SILVER SODIUM BISMUTH CADMIUM CALCIUM HAFNIUM IRIDIUM LITHIUM MERCURY RHENIUM RHODIUM THORIUM URANIUM YTTRIUM ALUMINUM ANTIMONY CHROMIUM DEADHEAD PLATINUM RUBIDIUM SCANDIUM TANTALUM TINCTURE TITANIUM TUNGSTEN VANADIUM
(— IN MASS) BULLION
(— IN SHEETS) LEAF PLATE
(BABBITT —) LINING
(GROUND —) BRONZING
(HEAVIEST —) OSMIUM
(IMPURE MASS OF —) REGULUS
(LIGHTEST —) LITHIUM
(LIQUID —) MERCURY
(MASS OF —) INGOT
(MOLTEN —) TAP SQUIRT
(OLD POT —) POTIN
(PERFORATED —) STENCIL
(PIECE OF CRUDE —) SLUG
(POINTED —) NAIL
(POROUS —) SPONGE
(SEMIFINISHED —) SEMIS
(SHEET —) DOUBLES KALAMEIN
(WASTE —) GATE
METALLIC HARD TINNY
METALLOPHONE SARON
METALWARE LORMERY GRAYWARE PONTYPOOL
METALWORK ZOGAN
METALWORKER BARMAN FOONER FORKMAN FOUNDER SUDSMAN
METAMERE SOMITE SEGMENT MEROSOME
METAMORPHOSE TURN SHAPE INDENIZE TRANSMEW
METAMORPHOSIS METABOLE PETALODY PHYLLODY SEPALODY
METANIRA (HUSBAND OF —) CELEUS
(SON OF —) DEMOPHON TRIPTOLEMUS
METAPHOR IMAGE TROPE FIGURE
METAPHORICAL FIGURAL FIGURATE TROPICAL
METASTOMA LABIUM
METATE QUERL
METE DEAL GIVE AWARD SERVE
METEMPSYCHOSIS SAMSARA
METEOR STAR ARGID CETID COMID DRAKE LUPID LYRID URSID ANTLID

AUGUST BOLIDE BOOTID CORVID CYGNID DRAGON HYDRID LIBRID LYNCID LYRAID PHASMA PISCID TAURID AQUARID AQUILID ARIETID AURIGID CAMELID CANCRID CEPHEID CORONID GEMINID MEATURE ORIONID PEGASID PERSEID POLARID PRODIGY COLUMBID CRATERID DRACONID ERIDANID FIREBALL FORNAXID HERCULID LACERTID SAGITTID SCORPIID SHOTSTAR TOUCANID VIRGINID
METEORITE BAETYL BOLIDE ANDRITE ATAXITE EUCRITE AEROLITE AEROLITH BAETULUS BAETYLUS IREOLITE SIDERITE SKYSTONE
METEOROLOGY AEROLOGY
METER IONIC METRE SEVEN ALCAIC RHYTHM CADENCE GAYATRI MEASURE SUBMETER VIAMETER YAWMETER
(10,000 —S) GREX
(CUBIC —) STERE
(MILLIONTH OF —) MICRON
(NETHERLANDS —) ELL
(SQUARE —) CENTIARE
(VEDIC —) GAYATRI
METHADONE AMIDONE
METHANE FORMENE
METHANOL WOODINE CARBINOL
METHEGLIN MEAD
METHOD ART WAY DART FORM GARB GATE KINK LINE MIDS MODE REDE RULE SORT ORDER STYLE TRACK USAGE COURSE ENGINE MANNER STEREO SYSTEM FASHION PROCESS TACTICS WRINKLE ADJUVANT STANDARD
(— OF ANGLING) HARLING
(— OF APPEALING) DHARNA DHURNA
(— OF COLORING TEA) FACING
(— OF CONSTRUCTION) JACAL
(— OF CULTIVATION) JUM JOOM STUMPING
(— OF DIETING) BANTING
(— OF DISTILLATION) DESCENT
(— OF ELECTION) SCRUTINY
(— OF FATTENING POULTRY) GAVAGE
(— OF INDUCTION) CANON
(— OF MILKING) NIEVLING
(— OF MURAL DECORATION) KHASI
(— OF PROCEDURE) GAME
(— OF TRACKING) DOVAP
(— OF TREATMENT) SCOPE
(CLEVER —) KINK KINKLE
(FIXED —) FORMULA
(MEDICAL —) CUSHION
(OUTMODED —) ARCHAISM
(PAINTING —) GOUACHE
(PRINTING —) AQUATONE
(SCIENTIFIC —) BACONISM
(SURVEYING —) STADIA
(USUAL —) COURSE PRACTICE
METHODICAL TRIG EXACT FORMAL ORDERLY REGULAR ORDINARY ORDINATE

METHODIST JUMPER WESLEYAN SWADDLING
METHODIZE REGULATE
METHYLAL FORMAL
METICULOUS FUSSY STICKY CAREFUL FINICAL FINICKY
METONYM SYNONYM
METRICAL MEASURED
(— QUANTITY) MATRA
METROPOLIS CITY SEAT CAPITAL
METROPOLITAN EPARCH
METTLE SAUL PRIDE SPUNK GINGER SPIRIT COURAGE
METTLESOME FIERY PROUD SKEIGH SPUNKY STUFFY FLIGHTY GINGERY SPIRITED
MEW WOW MEWL MIAOU MIAOW INTERMEW SEEDBIRD
MEWER WRAWLER
MEWL WRAWL
MEXICAN CHOLO LEPERO WETBACK
MEXICAN-AMERICAN PACHUCO
MEXICAN ELM MEZCAL
MEXICAN ONYX TECALI
MEXICAN PERSIMMON CHAPOTE
MEXICAN POPPY ARGEMONE
MEXICAN TEA BASOTE APASOTE FISHWEED WORMSEED

MEXICO
COIN: PESO TLAC ADOBE CLACO TLACO AZTECA CENTAVO PIASTER
LAKE: CHAPALA
MEASURE: PIE VARA ALMUD BARIL JARRA LABOR LEGUA LINEA SITIO FANEGA PULGADA
MOUNTAIN: BUFA BLANCO CUPULA PEROTE ORIZABA
PENINSULA: BAJA YUCATAN
PEOPLE: MAM CORA MAYA SERI XOVA AZTEC NAHUA OPATA OTOMI ZOQUE EUDEVE MIXTEC TOLTEC NAYARIT TEPANEC TOTONAC ZACATEC ZAPOTEC TEZCUCAN TOTONACO ZACATECO
RIVER: BRAVO LERMA BALSAS GRANDE PANUCO TABASCO GRIJALVA SANTIAGO
STATE: LEON NUEVO COLIMA OAXACA SONORA CHIAPAS DURANGO HIDALGO NAYARIT SINALOA TABASCO YUCATAN CAMPECHE QUINTANA VERACRUZ
TOWN: LEON TEPIC ARIZPE COLIMA JALAPA JUAREZ MERIDA OAXACA PARRAL POTOSI PUEBLA CANANEA DURANGO GUAYMAS MORELIA ORIZABA PACHUCA TAMPICO TORREON CULIACAN MAZATLAN MONCLOVA SALTILLO VERACRUZ
VOLCANO: COLIMA TOLUCA JORULLO PARICUTIN
WEIGHT: BAG ONZA CARGA LIBRA

MARCO ADARME ARROBA OCHAVA TERCIO QUINTAL

MEZZANINE ENTRESOL
MIASMA MALARIA MAREMMA
MIB MIGGLE
MICA DAZE TALC GLIST SLUDE
BIOTITE GLIMMER ALURGITE
FUCHSITE
MICE (BREEDING PLACE FOR —)
MURARIUM
MICHAEL MIKE MICKY MICHEL
MIGUEL

MICHIGAN
BAY: SAGINAW THUNDER
KEWEENAW STURGEON
CAPITAL: LANSING
COLLEGE: ALMA WAYNE ADRIAN
ALBION CALVIN OLIVET OWOSSO
OAKLAND
COUNTY: IONIA IOSCO ALCONA
GOGEBIC OSCEOLA TUSCOLA
KALKASKA
INDIAN: OTTAWA
LAKE: BURT TORCH HOUGHTON
NATIVE: WOLVERINE
NICKNAME: WOLVERINE
RIVER: CASS HURON SAGINAW
ESCANABA
STATE BIRD: ROBIN
STATE FLOWER: APPLEBLOSSOM
STRAIT: MACKINAW
TOWN: ALMA CARO FLINT ADRIAN
ALPENA BADAXE OWOSSO
DETROIT LANSING SAGINAW
ANNARBOR CADILLAC
ESCANABA MANISTEE MUNISING
MUSKEGON CHEBOYGAN
KALAMAZOO

MICONIA TAMONEA
MICROBE GERM
MICROMETER BIFILAR
(— **CALIPER**) MIKE
MICRON MU
MICRONESIAN KANAGA NAURUAN
(— **ISLAND**) NUI GUAM ROTA TRUK
MAKIN NAURU WOTHO MAJURO
MICROORGANISM BUG GERM
AZOFIER BUTYRIC BACILLUS
MICROPHONE BUG MIKE PARABOLA
MICROPYLE FORAMEN
MICROSECOND (HUNDREDTH OF —)
SHAKE
MICROSCOPE GLASS SCOPE
MICROSCOPIC SMALL MINUTE
MICROSPECIES JORDANON
MICROSPOROPHYLL STAMEN
MICROTONE SRUTI SHRUTI
MICROTUS ARVICOLA
MIDDAY NOON UNDERN MIDNOON
NOONDAY MERIDIAN NOONTIME
MIDDEN BASURAL SAMBAQUI
MIDDLE MEDIO MESNE NAVEL
CENTER MEDIAL MEDIAN CENTRAL
MEDIATE MEDILLE

(— **OF SAIL**) BUNT
(— **OF SHIP**) WAIST
(— **OF WINTER**) HOLL HOWE
MIDDLE-AGED MIDDLING
MIDDLE EAST (— NATIVE) WOG
MIDDLEMAN BUTTY BROKER
DEALER FOGGER JOBBER LUMPER
BUMAREE BUTTYMAN HUCKSTER
REGRATER
MIDDLER PLATEMAN
MIDDLETONE HALFTONE
MIDDLING FAIR MEAN SOSO
NEUTRAL MEDIOCRE MEETERLY
(PL.) DUNST FARINA SHARPS
SIZINGS SEMOLINA WEATINGS
MIDGE GNAT SMUT MIDGET MINGIE
PUNKIE WEEVIL
MIDNIGHT NOON NOONTIDE
MIDPOINT BASION PORION STOMION
GNATHION
MIDRIB COSTA SHAFT MIDVEIN
(— **OF LEAF**) PEN
MIDRIFF APRON SKIRT
MIDSHIPMAN WART MIDDY PLEBE
REEFER SNOTTY OLDSTER
MIDST DEPTH CENTER MIDDLE
MIDWARD
MIDSUMMER DAY JOHNSMAS
MIDWAY MEDIO GAYWAY HALFWAY
MIDWIFE BABA DHAI GAMP DHOLL
HOWDY LUCKY COMMER CUMMER
GRANNY HOWDIE KIMMER LUCINA
LUCKIE GRANNIE HEBAMME
MIEN AIR BROW VULT ASPECT
DEMEAN MANNER OSTENT BEARING
DEMEANOR
MIG MIB DUCK
MIGHT ARM BULK MOTE FORCE
MOUND POWER SHOULD STRENGTH
MIGHTILY HEFTILY
MIGHTINESS (HIGH —) HOGEN
MIGHTY FELL HIGH KEEN MAIN
MUCH RANK RICH VAST FELON
GREAT HEFTY STERN STOOR
POTENT STRONG VIOLENT
ENORMOUS FORCEFUL POWERFUL
PUISSANT SAMSONIC
MIGNONETTE WOLD RESEDA
LUTEOLA
MIGRAINE MEGRIM
MIGRANT MOVER
MIGRATE RUN FLIT TREK DRIFT
FLIGHT COLONIZE
MIGRATION TREK EXODUS FLIGHT
EELFARE EMOTION PASSAGE
DIASPORA
MIKADO DAIRI
MIKIR ARLENG
MILD LEW MOY CALM COLD EASY
FAIR LENT MEEK NESH PLUM SOFT
TAME WARM BALMY BUXOM GREEN
LIGHT LITHE MELCH MELSH MILKY
NAISH QUIET BENIGN FACILE GENIAL
GENTLE HUMBLE KINDLY REMISS
SMOOTH AMIABLE CLEMENT
LENIENT VELVETY BENEDICT
DOVELIKE FAVONIAN LENITIVE
MERCIFUL SOOTHING TRANQUIL
MILDEW OIDIUM

MILDLY FEEBLY GENTLY
MILDNESS MILD LENITY SUAVITY
CLEMENCY HUMILITY KINDNESS
MILE (3 —S) HOUR LEAGUE
(**NAUTICAL** —) KNOT KAIRI
(**ONE-EIGHTH** —) FURLONG
(**SEA** —) NAUT
MILESTONE LEAGUE
MILFOIL AHARTALAV
MILIEU CLIMATE TERRAIN AMBIENCE
MILITANT WARRISH FIGHTING
MILITARY MARTIAL WARLIKE
MILITANT SOLDIERY
(— **POST**) THANA
(— **SCIENCE**) LOGISTICS
MILITIA FYRD ARRAY MILICE
MILITIAMAN CHOCO UHLAN LUMPER
TRAINER SHIRTMAN
MILK COW LAC FUZZ LAIT PAIL SKIM
BLEED JUICE MILCH MULCT BOTTLE
ELICIT RAMMEL STROKE SUCKLE
EXPLOIT
(— **DRY**) STRIP
(— **OUT**) EMULGE
(— **PAN**) LEAD
(— **PRODUCT**) KHOA
(— **SICKNESS**) TIRES
(**BREAST** —) SUCK DIDDY
(**COW'S** —) MESS
(**CURDLED** —) SKYR TYRE TAYER
LOPPER CLABBER TATMJOLK
(**FERMENTED** —) KUMISS MATZOON
(**NEW** —) RAMMEL
(**SOUR** —) SKYR WHIG BONNY
BLEEZE BLINKY CLABBER JOCOQUE
(**WATERY** —) BLASH
MILK CART KIT PRAM BUNGEY
MILKFISH AWA BANGOS SABALO
SAVOLA BANDENG SABALOTE
MILKING (— PARLOR) BAIL
(— **TIME**) MEAL
MILKLESS PARVE PAREVE
MILKMAN KITTER CHALKER
MILK PAIL TRUG LEGLEN
MILK SHAKE FRAPPE
MILK SNAKE ADDER
MILKSOP SOP MOLLY COCKNEY
MILKWOOD MELKHOUT
MILKWORT SENECA CENTAURY
GAYWINGS
MILKY MILCHY LACTARY LACTEAL
OPALOID LACTEOUS
MILL FULL MILN STAR BREAK FLOUR
KNURL QUERN CHERRY FANNER
STAMPS BLOOMER MOLINET
PUGMILL SMUTTER ARRASTRA
BUHRMILL SPINNERY TRAPICHE
WALKMILL
(**CHOCOLATE** —) MOLINET
(**FULLING** —) STOCKS
(**SHINGLING** —) FORGE
(**SUGAR** —) CENTRAL TRAPICHE
MILLBOARD TARBOARD
MILLDAM WARREN WARRANT
MILLED GRAINED
MILLENARIAN CHILIAST
MILLENIUM CHILIAD
MILLER MILLMAN STOCKER
MULTURER NILLWARD

MILLER'S-THUMB BLOB CULL CABOT CHABOT COTTOID MUDDLER BULLHEAD

MILLET BUDA KODA KOUS MOHA ARZUN BAJRA CHENA CUMBU DUKHN DURRA GRAIN HIRSE KODRA MILLY PANIC PROSO TENAI WHISK BAJREE DHURRA HUREEK JONDLA JOWARI MILIUM DAGASSA PANICLE ZABURRO BIRDSEED KADIKANE

MILLHAND CROPMAN

MILLILITER MIL

MILLIMETER LI (THOUSANDTH OF —) MICRON

MILLINER ARTISTE MODISTE

MILLING GRAINING

MILLION CONTO QUENT (10 —) CRORE

MILLIPEDE JULID POLYPOD DIPLOPOD PILLWORM RINGWORM WIREWORM

MILLISECOND SIGMA

MILLPOND DAM MILLDAM BINNACLE MILLPOOL

MILLRACE LADE LEAD LEAT FOREBAY TAILRACE

MILLRYND INK

MILLSTONE RYND STONE BEDDER LEDGER RUNNER (PL.) RUN

MILLSTREAM FLEAM

MILLWORKER DOGGER

MILO SORGHUM

MILPA LADANG

MILT MILK SEED SPLEEN

MILTONIST DIVORCER

MIMAS (FATHER OF —) THEANO (MOTHER OF —) AMYCUS (SLAYER OF —) MEZENTIUS

MIME ACTOR MIMER MIMIC (PL.) MIMIAMBI

MIMEOGRAPH RONEO

MIMIC APE HIT COPY MIME MINT MOCK MOCKER MONKEY COPYCAT IMITATE PAGEANT

MIMICRY APERY MIMESIS MOCKAGE MOCKERY

MIMOSA AROMA CASSIE ALBIZZIA HUISACHE TURMERIC

MINCE CHOP SHEAR FINICK

MINCED HACHE

MINCEMEAT GIGOT MINCE

MINCING NIMINY FINICAL MINIKIN MIGNIARD SKIPJACK

MINCINGLY FINE GINGERLY

MIND CIT CHIT HEAD HEED MOOD NOTE NOUS RECK SOUL BESEE BRAIN SENSE SKULL WATCH ANIMUS MATTER NOTICE PSYCHE REGARD COURAGE SENSORY SUBJECT THINKER THOUGHT (CONSCIOUS —) SENTIENT (INFINITE —) GOD (RIGHT FRAME OF —) TUNE (YEAR'S —) MINNING

MINDFUL HEEDY MINDLY HEEDFUL

MINE BAL PIT DELF HOLE HUEL MEUM BARGH DELFT DELPH METAL STOPE WHEAL COYOTE GOPHER GROOVE RESCUE BONANZA BORASCA COALPIT MINERAL OPENCUT TORPEDO GOLCONDA MYNPACHT PROSPECT (— BY BLASTING) SHOOT (— IRREGULARLY) GOPHER (— PASSAGE) SLUM (COAL —) ROB COALPIT COLLIERY (MILITARY —) FOUGADE FOUGASSE (OLD —) GWAG (RICH —) GOLCONDA (TIN —) STANNARY (UNPRODUCTIVE —) SHICER BORASCA

MINER PECK PICK PYKE BARER DOGGY ARTIST BUCKER CUTTER DAMMER DELVER DIGGER GANGER GETTER HAGGER JUMPER MATTER PELTER REEFER SNIPER STOPER TINNER TOPMAN VANNER COLLIER CRUTTER DIRGLER FEIGHER GEORDIE GROOVER HITCHER HUTCHER LEADMAN PICKMAN PIKEMAN PIONEER PLUGMAN ROCKMAN SNUBBER ENTRYMAN HEADSMAN STRIPPER WINZEMAN (— WHO WORKS ALONE) HATTER

MINERAL JET GEET HOST MINE SPAR BERYL BLOOM EARTH FLUOR GLEBE GUEST LENAD SQUAT TRONA ACMITE ALAITE AUGITE BARITE BARYTE BLENDE CASTOR CERITE COCKLE CURITE DAVYNE EGERAN EHLITE ERRITE GALENA GARNET GYPSUM HALITE HAUYNE HELVIN HUMITE ILLITE IOLITE LABITE MIXITE NATRON NOSEAN NOSITE PINITE RUTILE SALITE SILICA SPHENE SPINEL ADAMINE ADAMITE ADELITE ALTAITE ALUMITE ALUNITE AMOSITE APATITE ATOPITE AXINITE AZORITE AZULITE AZURITE BAUXITE BAZZITE BELLITE BISMITE BITYITE BOHMITE BOLEITE BORNITE BRUCITE CALCITE CELSIAN CYANITE DIAMOND DICKITE DUFTITE EDENITE EPIDOTE ERIKITE ERINITE EUCLASE FLOKITE GAGEITE GAHNITE GEDRITE GLADITE GOTHITE GUMMITE HELVITE HESSITE HOPEITE HOWLITE HULSITE IHLEITE ILVAITE INESITE INYOITE ISERITE JADEITE JARLITE JOSEITE KEMPITE KERNITE KOPPITE KOTOITE LANGITE LARNITE LAURITE LAUTITE LEHIITE LEIFITE LEONITE LEPTITE LEUCITE LOWEITE MARTITE MELLITE OKENITE PALAITE PENNINE PETZITE PYRITES RATHITE REALGAR RETZIAN RHAGITE RINKITE ROMEITE ROSSITE SENAITE SODDITE SVABITE SYLVITE THORITE TURGITE ULEXITE UTAHITE UVANITE VAUXITE VOGLITE VRBAITE WARBITE WIIKITE ZEOLITE ZINCITE ZOISITE ZORGITE ZUNYITE AIKINITE ALLANITE ALLUVIAL ALUNOGEN AMBONITE ANAUXITE ANCYCLITE ANDORITE ANKERITE ARIEGITE ARMENITE ARTINITE ASBOLITE AUGELITE AUTUNITE AWARUITE BADENITE BAKERITE BARARITE BARYLITE BAVENITE BETAFITE BEYERITE BILINITE BIXBYITE BLAKEITE BLOEDITE BOOTHITE BORACITE BOWENITE BRAGGITE BRAUNITE BRAVOITE BROMLITE BRONZITE BROOKITE BRUSHITE CALCSPAR CARBOCER CEROLITE CHIOLITE CHLORITE CHROMITE CIMOLITE CINNABAR COHENITE COLUSITE COOKEITE COSALITE CREEDITE CROCOITE CRYOLITE DANALITE DAPHNITE DATOLITE DELTAITE DENDRITE DIASPORE DIGENITE DIOPSIDE DIOPTASE DIXENITE DOLOMITE DYSODILE EGUEIITE ELIASITE ELPIDITE EMBOLITE ENARGITE EPSOMITE ERIONITE EUCOLITE EULYTINE EULYTITE EUXENITE EVANSITE FASSAITE FAYALITE FELDSPAR FERSMITE FIBROITE FLINKITE FLUORITE FOOTEITE FUCHSITE FUSINITE GEMSTONE GENTHITE GIBBSITE GINORITE GOETHITE GOYAZITE GRIPHITE GROTHINE GROUTITE GYROLITE HANKSITE HANUSITE HARTTITE HATCHITE HAUERITE HAUYNITE HEMATITE HOMILITE HUGELITE IDOCRASE INDERITE IODYRITE JALPAITE JAROSITE JEZEKITE KALINITE KAMACITE KASOLITE KEHOEITE KLEINITE KOKTAITE KOLSKITE KRAUSITE LAGONITE LAVENITE LAZULITE LAZURITE LEVYNITE LEWISITE LIMONITE LINARITE LOMONITE LOWIGITE MARSHITE MEIONITE MELILITE MELONITE MESITITE MESOLITE MIERSITE MIMETITE MISENITE MOLYSITE MONAZITE MONETITE MORAVITE MOSESITE NADORITE NASONITE NEPOUITE NOCERITE NOSELITE OXAMMITE PEGANITE PETALITE PIMELITE PINNOITE PISANITE PODOLITE PORODINE PRICEITE PRIORITE RINNEITE ROSELITE SAGENITE SALEEITE SALESITE SAPONITE SASSOLIN SCAWTITE SHANDITE SHARPITE SHORTITE SIDERITE SMALTITE SMITHITE SODALITE SPADAITE SPURRITE STANNITE STIBNITE STILBITE STOLZITE STRUVITE STURTITE SZMIKITE TAGILITE TANGEITE TEALLITE TENORITE TILASITE TITANITE TRIPLITE TROILITE TYROLITE TYSONITE URANOTIL VEGASITE VOLTAITE VOLTZITE WEHRLITE WEISSITE WELLSITE WILKEITE WURTZITE XENOLITE XENOTIME YENTNITE ZARATITE WILLEMITE (BLACK —) JET GEET CERINE YENITE KNOPITE NIOBITE ALLANITE GRAPHITE HIELMITE ILMENITE ONOFRITE (BRIGHT —) BLENDE (BROWN —) CERINE EGERAN

GUILDITE JAROSITE
(FIBROUS —) ASBESTOS
(GRAY-WHITE —) TRONA HOPEITE
(GREEN —) AMESITE GAHNITE
ILESITE PRASINE PREHNITE
SMECTITE
(ORANGE —) SANDIX
(RADIATED —) ASTROITE
(RADIOACTIVE —) CURITE
(RARE —) CYMRITE EUCLASE
TYCHITE BARYLITE
(RED —) GARNET
(SOFT —) TALC KERMES
(TRANSPARENT —) MICA POLLUX
SODALITE
(WHITE —) BARITE HOWLITE
STILBITE
(YELLOW —) TOPAZ PYRITES
(YELLOWISH-GREEN —) EPIDOTE
ECDEMITE
MINERAL TAR MALTHA
MINERAL WATER SELTZER
MINERVA MENFRA
MINESWEEPER ALGERINE
MINGLE MIX FUSE JOIN MELL MOLD
MONG MOOL ADMIX BLEND MERGE
TWINE COMMIX FELTER HUDDLE
JUMBLE MEDDLE MEDLEY COMBINE
COALESCE CONFOUND
MINGLED FUSED MEDLEY CONFUSED
MINIATURE SMALL LITTLE POCKET
MINIKIN
MINIMAL BASAL LIMINAL
MINIMIZE DECRY MINCE LESSEN
SMOOTH SCISSOR BELITTLE
DISCOUNT
MINIMUM BARE BEDROCK
MINING WORK MINERY SPATTER
GROOVING
MINION PEAT SATAN MIGNON
DARLING MINIKIN CREATURE
MINIONETTE EMERALD
MINISTER PRIG CLERK DEWAN
ELDER ENVOY HAMAN PADRE VIZIR
ATABEG DEACON DIVINE GALLAH
PANDER PARSON PASTOR PESHWA
PRIEST VIZIER BROTHER DOMINIE
OFFICER PESHKAR PREFECT
PALATINE PREACHER
(— OF FINANCE) DEWAN
(— TO) TEND SERVE INTEND
(— WITHOUT SETTLEMENT)
STIBBLER
(PRIME —) PADRONE
MINISTRANT(PL.) SELLI SELLOI
MINISTRATION SERVICE TENDANCE
MINISTRY SERVICE
MINIUM SANDIX
MINIVER LASSET
MINK FAG HURON NORSE VISON
JACKASH KOLINSKY MUSTELIN
PLATINUM

MINNESOTA
CAPITAL: STPAUL
COLLEGE: BETHEL STOLAF
WINONA BEMIDJI HAMLINE
AUGSBURG CARLETON

COUNTY: ANOKA ISANTI ROSEAU
WASECA WABASHA HENNEPIN
INDIAN: SIOUX OJIBWA CHIPPEWA
LAKE: LEECH ITASCA BEMIDJI
SUPERIOR
MOUNTAIN: EAGLE MISQUAH
MOUNTAIN RANGE: CUYUNA
MESABI MISQUAH
NICKNAME: GOPHER NORTHSTAR
RIVER: RAINY STCROIX
STATE BIRD: LOON
STATE TREE: REDPINE
TOWN: ADA ELY MORA AUSTIN
DULUTH NEWULM WINONA
BEMIDJI FOSSTON HIBBING
MANKATO BRAINERD

MINNESOTAN GOPHER
MINNOW PINK GUPPY HITCH MINIM
MINNY BAGGIE MENNON DOGFISH
FATHEAD GULARIS PHANTOM
PINHEAD PINKEEN BONYTAIL
CYPRINID FLATHEAD GAMBUSIA
MOONFISH SATINFIN
(PL.) MENISE
MINOR FLAT LESS MOLL WARD
PETIT PETTY INFANT LESSER
SLIGHT
MINORESS CLARE CLARISSE
MINORITY FEW NONAGE INFANCY
MINOS (FATHER OF —) JUPITER
(MOTHER OF —) EUROPA
(SLAYER OF —) COCALUS
(WIFE OF —) PASIPHAE
MINSTER CHADBAND
MINSTREL BARD BADHAN HARPER
JOCKEY BADCHAN GLEEMAN
JOCULAR PARDHAN PIERROT
SONGMAN JONGLEUR
MINSTRELSY GLEE DREAM
MINT COIN NANA SAGE AJUGA BASIL
ORGAN THYME HYSSOP SAVORY
STRIKE ALLHEAL BALLOTA CAPMINT
LABIATE OLITORY OREGANO
PERILLA PHLOMIS POTHERB
STACHYS BERGAMOT CALAMINT
IRONWORT LAMPWICK LAVENDER
MARJORAM SAGELEAF SELFHEAL
MINTER MONEYER
MINUET MINAWAY
MINUS LESS WANTING
MINUTE FINE NICE TINY CLOSE
MINIM PRIME SMALL ATOMIC
MOMENT INSTANT SCRUPLE
DETAILED
(24 —S) GHURRY
MINX JADE PEAT SLUT SNIT HUSSY
HUZZY LIMMER SNICKET
MIRACLE SIGN ANOMY MARVEL
WONDER PRODIGY THEURGY
MIRACLE PLAY GUARY
MIRAGE SERAB CHIMERA FLYAWAY
LOOMING ILLUSION TOWERING
MIRE BOG DUB CLAY GLAR LAIR
MOIL SLOB SLUB SLUE SLUR ADDLE
CLART EMBOG FANGO GLAUR
SEUGH SLAKE SLUSH SQUAD STALL
SLOUGH SLUDGE SLUTCH CLABBER

GUTTERS SLUBBER WORTHING
MIRITI PALM MORICHE
MIRLITON KAZOO
MIRO TOMTIT
MIRROR FLAT BERYL GLASS IMAGE
STEEL STONE PEEPER PSYCHE
REFLEX SHINER SHOWER CONCAVE
HORIZON REFLECT DIAGONAL
SPECULUM
MIRTH GLEE CHEER DREAM SPORT
GAIETY BAUDERY DISPORT JOLLITY
HILARITY
(CONTEMPTUOUS —) SPORT
(VIOLENT —) SPLEEN
MIRTHFUL CADGY MERRY FESTIVE
GLEEFUL JOCULAR DISPOSED
LAUGHFUL
MIRY OOZY PUXY LAIRY MUCKY
SLAKY CLAGGY CLASHY LUTOSE
MIRISH SLABBY GUTTERY SLOUGHY
MISADVENTURE GRIEF ACCIDENT
CALAMITY CASUALTY DISASTER
MISANTHROPE CYNIC TIMON
MISANTHROPIC CYNICAL
MISANTHROPY TIMONISM
MISAPPLIED ABUSIVE
MISAPPLY ABUSE CROOK WREST
DISUSE MISUSE
MISAPPREHEND MISTAKE
MISAPPREHENSION ILLUSION
MISBECOME MISSIT MISSEEM
MISBEHAVE MISUSE MISBEAR
MISFARE MISHAVE MISLEAD
MISGUIDE
MISBELIEF MISCREED
MISCALCULATE DUTCH MISCAST
MISCOUNT
MISCALL BECALL MISNAME
MISCARRIAGE FAIL MISHAP FAILURE
ABORTION
MISCARRY FAIL MISGO FOUNDER
MISFARE MISGIVE BACKFIRE
MISCARRYING ABORTIVE
MISCELLANEOUS CHOW ORRA
SUNDRY ASSORTED CHOWCHOW
MISCELLANY CHOW VARIA MEDLEY
WHATNOT CHOWCHOW GIFTBOOK
MISCHANCE CALAMITY CASUALTY
DISASTER
MISCHIEF HOB ILL BANE EVIL HARM
HURT JEEL WRACK INJURY MURCHY
SORROW WONDER DEVILRY
KNAVERY SCADDLE DEVILTRY
MISCHIEF-MAKING URCHIN
MISCHIEVOUS BAD SLY ARCH IDLE
ROYT ELFIN HEMPY ROYET ELFISH
ELVISH GALLUS HEMPIE IMPISH
NOYANT SHREWD SULLEN WICKED
GALLOWS HARMFUL KNAVISH
LARKISH MOCKING NAUGHTY
PARLISH PLISKIE PUCKISH ROGUISH
SCADDLE UNHAPPY UNLUCKY
WAGGISH LITHERLY LUNGEOUS
SPORTIVE SPRITISH VENOMOUS
WANSONSY
MISCHIEVOUSNESS ROGUERY
MISCONCEPTION DELUSION
ILLUSION
MISCONDUCT CULPA DOLUS

OFFENCE OFFENSE DISORDER
MISCONSTRUCTION STRAIN
MISCONSTRUE MISJUDGE
MISCREANT KNAVE
MISDEED ILL MISS SLIP AMISS
UNWORK DEFAULT FORFEIT
OFFENCE OFFENSE DISORDER
MISDEMEANOR SIN CRIME FAULT
OFFENCE OFFENSE DISORDER
MISDIRECT MISGUIDE
MISER CUFF SKIN CHUFF CHURL
FLINT GRIPE HAYNE HUNKS NABAL
SCRAT SCRIB CODGER HUDDLE
NIPPER PELTER SCRIMP SNUDGE
WRETCH DRYFIST GOBSECK
NIGGARD SCRAPER CHINCHER
GATHERER HAPTERON HARPAGON
HOLDFAST MUCKERER MUCKWORM
PINCHGUT
MISERABLE WOE EVIL GRAY PUNK
SOUR DAWNY DEENY DUSTY MISER
WOFUL YEMER ABJECT CHETIF
CRUMBY CRUMMY ELENGE FEEBLE
PRETTY UNSELY WOEFUL FORLORN
SCRUFFY UNHAPPY WANSOME
FORSAKEN PITIABLE UNTHENDE
WRETCHED
MISERERE SUBSELLA
MISERLINESS MISERISM SNUDGERY
TENACITY
MISERLY WOE MEAN GRIPPY KNIVEY
STINGY CHINCHE WANSITH
SCRAPING SNUDGERY
MISERY WO WOE RUTH GNEDE
GRAME WREAK THREAT ANGUISH
MISEASE TRAGEDY CALAMITY
DISTRESS WANDRETH WOWENING
MISFIRE SKIP SNAP
MISFORTUNE ILL BLOW DOLE DREE
EVIL HARM TEEN CURSE HYDRA
SCATH TRAIK DAMAGE DIRDUM
MISERY MISHAP RUBBER SCATHE
SORROW UNHEAL UNLUCK WANHAP
MALHEUR MISCARE MISFALL
MISFATE MISLUCK REVERSE
TRAGEDY TROUBLE UNSELTH
UNSPEED CALAMITY DISASTER
DISGRACE DISTRESS MISCHIEF
MISGIVING DOUBT QUALM
MISGOVERN MISRULE
MISGUIDED WET
MISHANDLE BUNGLE
MISHAP SLIP GRIEF SITHE UNHAP
WANHAP FORTUNE MISTIDE
ACCIDENT CASUALTY MISCHIEF
MISHEARING OTOSIS
MISHIT DUFF
MISHMASH BOTCH GOULASH
MISINFORM MIZZLE
MISINTERPRET WARP WRITHE
MISREAD MISCOUNT
MISJUDGE MISDEEM MISWERN
MISLAY LOSE DISPLACE MISPLACE
MISLEAD COG ERR BUNK DUPE
GULL HOAX BLUFF CHEAT FALSE
BETRAY DELUDE SEDUCE WILDER
CONFUSE DEBAUCH DECEIVE
MISLEAR INVEIGLE MISGUIDE

MISLEADING BLIND FALSE CIRCEAN
TORTIOUS
MISMANAGE BLUNK BLUNDER
MISLEAD MISRULE ILLGUIDE
MISGUIDE
MISOGYNIC CYNICAL
MISPLACE MISLAY MISPUT MISSET
DISPLACE
MISPLACED MALPOSED
MISPLAY BLOW DUFF ERROR FLUFF
FUMBLE
MISPRONOUNCE MISCALL STUMBLE
MISQUOTE GIVE
MISREPRESENT SKEW ABUSE BELIE
COLOR MISUSE FALSIFY SLANDER
MISCOLOR
MISREPRESENTATION FRAUD
CALUMNY DAUBERY GARBLING
MISS ERR HIP FAIL LACK LOSE SKIP
SLIP SNAB FORGO HANUM MISSY
PANNA SKIRT DESIRE FRAULEIN
MISTRESS SENORITA
MISSEL BIRD MAVIS SHIRL DRAINE
JAYPIE MISTLE SHRITE SYCOCK
CHERCOCK
MISSHAPE DEFORM
MISSHAPEN UGLY BLOWN DEFORM
THRAWN DEFORMED UNSHAPED
MISSILE GUN BALL BIRD BOLT DART
SHOT PLUMB SHAFT STONE BULLET
SEEKER BOMBARD GRENADE
MISSIVE OUTCAST PROJECT
(DEFECTIVE —) DUD
(PL.) MITRAILLE
MISSING LACK WANT ABSENT
WANTING
(— OF CUE) FLUFF
MISSION SAND CHARGE ERRAND
SORTIE VISITA MESSAGE BUSINESS
DEVOTION LEGATION
MISSIONARY APOSTLE COLPORTER

MISSISSIPPI
CAPITAL: JACKSON
COLLEGE: RUST ALCORN
BELHAVEN MILLSAPS TOUGALOO
COUNTY: HINDS YAZOO ATTALA
PANOLA TIPPAH NESHOBA
NOXUBEE ITAWAMBA
INDIAN: BILOXI TUNICA CHOCTAW
NATCHEZ CHICKSAW
LAKE: ENID SARDIS BARNETT
GRENADA OKATIBBEE
MOUNTAIN: WOODALL
NATIVE: MUDCAT TADPOLE
NICKNAME: MAGNOLIA
RIVER: LEAF PEARL YAZOO
BIGBLACK
STATE BIRD: MOCKINGBIRD
STATE FLOWER: MAGNOLIA
STATE TREE: MAGNOLIA
TOWN: BILOXI HELENA LAUREL
TUPELO WINONA BELZONI
CORINTH GRENADA NATCHEZ
BOGALUSA MERIDIAN
KOSCIUSKO

MISSIVE NOTE BILLET LETTER
EPISTLE MESSAGE MISSILE

MISSOURI
CAPITAL: JEFFERSONCITY
COLLEGE: AVILA DRURY TARKIO
LINCOLN WEBSTER STEPHENS
COUNTY: RAY IRON MACON
TANEY PETTIS DAVIESS
INDIAN: OSAGE
LAKE: OZARKS TABLEROCK
MOUNTAIN: TAUMSAUK
NATIVE: PUKE PIKER
NICKNAME: SHOWME
PLATEAU: OZARK
PRESIDENT: TRUMAN
RIVER: OSAGE
STATE BIRD: BLUEBIRD
STATE FLOWER: HAWTHORN
STATE TREE: DOGWOOD
TOWN: ELDON HAYTI LAMAR
MACON ROLLA BUTLER
BETHANY BOLIVAR CAMERON
LEBANON MOBERLY SEDALIA
STLOUIS HANNIBAL SIKESTON

MISSTATEMENT ERRATUM
MISSTEP TRIP
MIST DAG FOG MUG URE DAMP DRIP
DROW FILM HAAR HAZE MOKE
RACK ROKE SCUD SMUR BRUME
CLOUD DRISK GAUZE STEAM
MIZZLE NEBULE SEREIN SERENE
SMEETH
(COLD —) DROW BERBER
(DRIZZLING —) SMUR DRISK SMIRR
SMURR
(SMOKY —) SMOG
(WHITE —) HAG
(PL.) SMOKES
MISTAKE ERR BALK GAFF GOOF
MISS SLIP TRIP ERROR FAULT
GAFFE LAPSE BARNEY BOBBLE
ESCAPE MISCUE SLIPUP STUMER
BLUNDER CONFUSE DEFAULT
JEOFAIL STUMOUR WRONGER
CONFOUND MISPRINT MISPRISE
(STUPID —) BUBU BONER
MISTAKEN WRONG ASTRAY
OVERSEEN OVERSHOT TORTIOUS
MISTER DON REB HERR SENOR
SENHOR SIGNOR GOODMAN
SIGNIOR GOVERNOR
MISTFLOWER EUPATORY
MISTILY FOGGILY
MISTLETOE ALLHEAL GADBUSH
MISTREAT BANG VIOLATE
MISTRESS MRS PUG TOY AMIE BIBI
DAME DOLL DOXY LADY MISS PURE
AMIGA AMOUR DOLLY DONNA
DUENA FANCY LEMAN LUCKY
MADAM NANCY WOMAN BEEBEE
MINION MISSIS NEAERA PARNEL
SAHIBA SENORA TACKLE WAHINE
BEDMATE DELILAH HERSELF
HETAERA KITTOCK LEVERET
METREZA PADRONA SENHORA
SIGNORA SULTANA CAMPASPE
DESPOINA DULCINEA FARMWIFE
GOODWIFE GUDEWIFE HAUSFRAU
LADYLOVE LANDLADY MIGNIARD

PARAMOUR PECULIAR SINEBARA TIMANDRA

(— **OF CEREMONIES**) FEMCEE

MISTRUST MISTROW SURMISE DISTRUST JEALOUSE JEALOUSY MISDOUBT

MISTY HAZY MOKY DAGGY FILMY FOGGY MISKY MOCHY MOOTH RAWKY ROKEY BLURRY CLOUDY GREASY SMURRY STEAMY BRUMOUS OBSCURE NEBULOUS NUBILOUS VAPOROUS

MISUNDERSTAND MISKNOW MISTAKE

MISUSE ABUSE ABUSION PERVERT MALTREAT

MITE BIT ATOM CENT DITE DRAM ATOMY BICHO SPECK ACARID ACARUS CHIGOE LEPTUS MINUTE SMIDGE ACARIAN BDELLID CHIGGER DEMODEX SMIDGEN ARACHNID DIBRANCH FARTHING HANDWORM ORIBATID SANDMITE

MITER MITRE TIMBER TIMBRE

MITERWORT COOLWORT

MITIGATE BALM COOL EASE ALLAY DELAY MEASE RELAX REMIT SLAKE LENIFY LESSEN MODIFY PACIFY SOFTEN SOOTHE SUCCOR TEMPER ASSUAGE CUSHION ELEVATE QUALIFY RELEASE RELIEVE SWEETEN PALLIATE

(— **PAIN**) PLASTER

MITIGATING LENITIVE

MITTEN BOOT CUFF MITT MUFF LOOFIE MUFFLE NIPPER MUFFLER

MIX BOX BEAT CARD DASH FUSE JOIN KNIT MELL MENG STIR ADMIX ALLOY BLEND BRAID IMMIX KNEAD MISCE TWINE BLUNGE COMMIX CRUTCH GARBLE JUMBLE MEDDLE MEDLEY MINGLE MUDDLE PERMIX STODGE TEMPER WUZZLE BLUNDER SHUFFLE SWIZZLE CONFOUND LEVIGATE SCRAMBLE

(— **AND STIR WHEN WET**) PUG

(— **CONFUSEDLY**) BROIL

(— **FLOCKS**) BOX

(— **LIQUORS**) BREW

(— **PLASTER**) GAGE GAUGE

(— **TEA**) BULK

(— **WINE**) PART

(— **WITH YEAST**) BARM

(— **WOOL OF DIFFERENT COLORS**) TUM

(**CONCRETE** —) SOUP

MIXABLE MISCIBLE

MIXED CHOW IMPURE MEDLEY MOTLEY PIEBALD STREAKY CHOWCHOW

(— **BLOOD**) MESTIZO

(— **CHALICE**) KRASIS

(— **UP**) HAYWIRE

(**NOT** —) SINCERE

MIXER HOG BANBURY MUDDLER PICKLER

(**CEMENT** —) BOXMAN

(**CONCRETE** —) PAVER

MIXTURE AIR MIX BODY BREW DASH

FEED HASH MANG MULL OLIO PUER SOUP STEW ALGIN ALLOY BLEND BROMO DOUGH GUMBO SALAD STUFF FOURRE GARBLE GUNITE LIGNIN MASLIN MEDLEY MELLAY MINGLE MOTLEY TEMPER AMALGAM COMPOST CUSTARD FARRAGO FILICIN FORMULA GOULASH HEADING KOGASIN MELANGE MISTION MIXTION OLLAPOD RECEIPT TIMBALE ALKYLATE BLENDURE DRAMMOCK EMULSION POSSODIE POWSOWDY SOLUTION

(— **ADDED TO WINE**) DOSAGE

(— **ATTRACTIVE TO PIGEONS**) SALTCAT

(— **FOR CAKE**) BATTER

(— **FOR DRESSING LEATHER**) DUBBIN DUBBING

(— **OF ALE AND OATMEAL**) STOORY

(— **OF ALKALOIDS**) ADONIDIN JABORINE

(— **OF BARKS**) TONGA

(— **OF CEMENT AND STONE**) BUMICKY

(— **OF CLAY AND ROCK**) BODY

(— **OF CLAY AND SAND**) LOAM

(— **OF DRUGS**) SPECIES

(— **OF ELEMENTS**) DIDYMIUM

(— **OF FEEDS**) MASH

(— **OF IMPURE ARSENIDES**) SPEISS

(— **OF OATS AND BARLEY**) DREDGE

(— **OF PRINCIPLES**) EUONYMIN

(— **OF PROTEINS**) CROTIN

(— **OF SALTS**) SOYATE

(— **OF SAND AND STONES**) CHAD

(— **OF SHALE AND SANDSTONE**) HAZLE

(— **OF SLAG AND ORE**) BROWSE

(— **OF VITAMINS**) BIOS

(— **OF WHITE AND BLACK**) GRIZZLE

(— **OF WINE, HONEY AND SPICES**) CLARY

(— **TO ADULTERATE LIQUORS**) FLASH

(— **TO WHITEN BREAD**) HARDS

(— **USED AS A FERMENT**) BUB

(— **USED AT SEDER**) HAROSET CHAROSES

(**ACUTE** —) ACUTA

(**AERIFORM** —) GAS

(**CARVER'S** —) COMPO

(**CAULKING** —) BLARE

(**CLAY** —) COB SLIP

(**COATING** —) COLOR

(**CONFUSED** —) MESS CHAOS FUDDLE SOZZLE

(**CRUMBLY** —) STREUSEL

(**EXPLOSIVE** —) FIREDAMP

(**FOOD** —) FILLING

(**FREEZING** —) CRYOGEN

(**GILDING** —) ASSIETTE

(**HYDROCARBON** —) ABIETENE

(**ITALIAN CONDIMENT** —) TAMARA

(**JUMBLED** —) BOTCH

(**MECHANICS'** —) PUTTY

(**PLASTIC CEMENT** —) CLOY

(**PRESERVATIVE** —) STUFF

(**SEASONED** —) STUFFING

(**SMOKING** —) CHARAS CHURRUS

(**TANNING** —) PURE

(**THICKENING** —) ROUX

(**UNPALATABLE** —) DRAMMOCK

(**WATERY** —) SLURRY

(**WELDING** —) THERMIT

MIZZEN DANDY

MIZZONITE DIPYRE

MKS UNIT JOULE

MNEMONIC MEMORIAL

MOAN HONE MOON REEM WAIL CROON GROAN MOURN MUNGE QUIRK SOUGH MUNGER

MOANING SOUGH DIRGEFUL

MOAT FOSS DITCH FOSSE GRAFF RUNDEL

MOB CREW HERD ROUT COHUE CROWD HURRY PLEBE PLEBS MOBILE RABBLE TUMULT VOULGE DOGGERY CANAILLE RIFFRAFF VARLETRY

MOBILE FLUID MOVEABLE

MOBSTER HOODLUM

MOCCASIN PAC CONGO TEGUA SHOEPACK

(— **WITH LEGS**) LARRIGAN

(**PL.**) SHANKS

MOCCASIN FLOWER NERVINE

MOCHA BARK

MOCHICA YUNCA

MOCHILA MACHEER KNAPSACK

MOCK BOB DOR GAB MOW COPY DEFY GECK GIBE GIRD JAPE JEER JEST JIBE PLAY QUIZ BOURD DORRE ELUDE FLEER FLIRT FLOUT FRUMP HOKER KNACK MIMIC RALLY SCOFF SCORN SCOUT SLEER SPORT TAUNT BEMOCK DELUDE DERIDE ILLUDE NIGGLE IMITATE MURGEON RIDICULE

MOCKER MOWER GIRDER BOURDER FLOUTER SCORNER RAILLEUR

MOCKERNUT BULLNUT

MOCKERY DOR MOW GLEE JEER BOURD DORRE FARCE FLOUT GLAIK SCOFF SPORT BISMER HETHING LUDIBRY MOCKADO MOCKAGE DERISION ILLUSION RIDICULE SCOFFERY

MOCKING GAB ACID SPORT TRUMPERY

MOCKINGBIRD MIMUS MOWER MOCKER

MOCK ORANGE SYRINGA

MOCOA COCHE

MODE CUT JET TON WAY FORM GATE MOOD RAGA TONE TWIG WISE FERIO FINAL GENUS MODUS STATE STYLE ACTING BAROCO CESARE COURSE DATISI FAKOFO FANGLE FESAPO MANNER METHOD BAMALIP CALEMES CAMENES DABITIS DARAPTI DIBATIS DIMARIS DIMATIS DISAMIS FAPESMO FASHION FERISON FESTINO CELARENT DOKMAROK FELAPTON FRESISON

(— **OF BEHAVIOR**) THEW HABITUDE

(— **OF BEING**) CATEGORY

(— **OF CONDUCT**) LAW

(— OF DRESS) HABIT TENUE
(— OF DRESSING HAIR) MADONNA
(— OF EXPRESSION) IRONY
(— OF MORAL ACTION) CONDUCT
(— OF PARTITIONING) CANT
(— OF PROCEDURE) ORDER
SYSTEM
(— OF RULE) REGIME
(— OF SPEECH) LATINISM
(— OF STANDING) STANCE
(— OF STRUCTURE) BUILD
(PREVAILING —) GARB
(TEMPORARY —) VOGUE
MODEL WAX COPY FORM MOLD
NORM CANON DUMMY IDEAL LIGHT
MOULD NORMA SHAPE DESIGN
FUGLER GABARI MODULE PRAXIS
SOURCE DIORAMA EXAMPLE
GABARIT MODULET PARAGON
PATTERN PICTURE SAMPLER
CALENDAR ENSAMPLE EXEMPLAR
EXEMPLUM FORMULAR FUGLEMAN
MAQUETTE MODELLER MODULIZE
PARADIGM PROPLASM SPECIMEN
TYPORAMA
(— OF HUMAN BODY) FORM
MANIKIN
(— OF STATUE) ESQUISSE
(INFERIOR —) JALOPPY
(MATHEMATICAL —) SPACE
(PRELIMINARY —) MAQUETTE
PROPLASM
MODERATE BATE COOL CURB EASE
EASY EVEN MEEK SOFT ABATE
ALLAY ALLOY LIGHT LOWER MEZZO
MODER REMIT SLACK SLAKE SOBER
SWEET ARREST BRIDLE DECENT
GENTLE LESSEN MEANLY MIDWAY
MODEST MODIFY REMISS SEASON
SOFTEN SUBMIT TEMPER CENTRAL
CONTROL SLACKEN ATTEMPER
CENTRIST MEETERLY MIDDLING
MITIGATE MODERATO ORDINATE
PALLIATE PASSABLE
(— IN BURNING) SOFT
(— OF THE WIND) LOOM
MODERATELY GEY FAIR MEAN
MEETLY PRETTY MIDWISE
MEETERLY MIDDLING
MODERATENESS CLEMENCY
MODICITY
MODERATION MEAN STAY MINCE
SPARE MANNER MEDIUM REASON
COMPASS MEDIETY MODESTY
SOBRIETY IMMODESTY
MODERATO MASSIG
MODERN NEW LATE RECENT
NEOTERIC
MODEST SHY DEFT MURE NICE
SNUG DOUCE LOWLY QUIET SMALL
CHASTE DEMURE HUMBLE PUDENT
SIMPLE VIRGIN CLERKLY PUDICAL
DISCREET MAIDENLY PUDIBUND
RESERVED RETIRING SHAMEFUL
VERECUND VIRTUOUS
MODESTY PUDOR NICETY DECENCY
PUDENCY SHYNESS CHASTITY
FOREHEAD HUMILITY PUDICITY

MODICUM DROP BREAK SPICE
PENNORTH
MODIFICATION BOB ECAD FORM
SALT CHANGE ENGRAM FACIES
SANDHI SINGLE UMLAUT ENGRAMMA
(— OF A REMEDY) TINCTION
(GLOTTAL —) STOP
MODIFIED VARIANT
MODIFY EDIT VARY ALTER AMEND
HEDGE TOUCH BUFFER CHANGE
DOCTOR MASTER TEMPER ARABIZE
COMPARE FASHION QUALIFY
ATTEMPER DENATURE GRADUATE
MODERATE FAUCALIZE
(— ARTICULATION) COLOR
(— COLOR) TONE
MODILLION ANCON MODEL TRUSS
CARTOUCH
MODISH CHIC MODY SOIGNE TIMISH
TONISH STYLISH
MODISHNESS CHIC
MODULATE SINK INFLECT QUALIFY
MODULATION ACCENT CHANGE
CADENCE BUNCHING PASSAGIO
MOGUL PADISHAH
MOHAIR MOIRE
MOHAMMED MAHOMET MAHOUND
MUDEJAR PROPHET
MOHAMMEDAN MOSLEM PAYNIM
MAHOMET
MOHAMMEDANISM TURBAN
TURKERY MAUMETRY
MOHR MHORR GAZELLE
MOHUR MOOR AHMEDI
MOIETY MEDIETY
MOIST WET DAMP DANK DEWY NESH
UVID DABBY GIVEY GREEN HUMID
JUICY MADID MOCHY SAMMY SAPPY
SLACK SOAKY SOCKY SPEWY
SWACK WEEPY CLAMMY MOISTY
STICKY WETTISH HUMOROUS
MUCULENT
MOISTEN DIP WET DAMP MOIL
BASTE BATHE BEDEW JUICE LATCH
LEACH STEEP WOKIE DABBLE
DAMPEN HUMECT IMBRUE MADEFY
SPARGE TEMPER HUMIDIFY
IRRIGATE IRRORATE
(— LEATHER) SAM SAMMY
MOISTURE DEW WET BREE DAMP
DANK ROKE HUMOR MOIST WATER
PHLEGM AQUOSITY HUMIDITY
(— DEFICIENT) XERIC
(— IN STONE) SAP
(— ON BEARD) BARBER
(CONDENSED —) BREATH
MOJARRA SHAD PATAO
MOKI MOGUEY MOKIHI
MOKSHA MUKTI
MOLAR WANG FORMAL MOLARY
GRINDER
MOLASSES DIP LICK CLAGGUM
THERIAC TREACLE LONGLICK
MOLD DIE FEN PIG PLY SOW CALM
CAST CURB FORM MULL MUST SOIL
TRAP BLOCK CHAPE CHILL FRAME
INGOT MODEL MOULD MUCOR
PLASM PRINT SHAPE SHARE STENT
STINT VALVE COFFIN GABARI

INFORM LINGET MATRIX SQUARE
BASTARD FASHION FESTOON
MATRICE RILLETT SANDBOX SKILLET
TEMPLET COQUILLE FUMAGINE
HOODMOLD PROPLASM TEMPLATE
WHISKERS
(— FOR METAL) SOW SKILLET
(— OF ASPIC) DARIOLE
(— OF SHIP) SWEEP
(— THAT ATTACKS HOPS) FEN
MOLDAVITE TEKTITE
MOLDBOARD REEST
(— SURFACE) WREST
MOLDED FICTILE
MOLDER MURL CAPPER MANGLE
MOSKER FIGURER PLASTER PLASTIC
MOLDINESS FINEW MUCOR VINEW
MOLDING BEAD COVE CYMA DADO
GULA KEEL LIST OGEE OVAL CABLE
FILET GORGE LABEL LEDGE ROVER
STAFF BANDLE BASTON CASING
COLLAR CONGEE COVING FILLET
LISTEL MULLER REGLET SQUARE
ZIGZAG ANNULET BEADING
CHAPLET DOUCINE ECHINUS
EYEBROW FINGENT HIPMOLD
LOZENGE MOULAGE NECKING
SURBASE TONDINO TRINGLE
BAGUETTE BANDELET CASEMATE
CASEMENT CYMATION CYMATIUM
DANCETTE FUSAROLE HOODMOLD
KNURLING MOULDING NAILHEAD
NECKMOLD
(CONCAVE —) GORGE CONGEE
SCOTIA CAVETTO
(CONVEX —) REED CABLE OVOLO
THUMB TORUS BASTON REEDING
ASTRAGAL FUSAROLE
(OGEE —) TALON
(OUTSIDE —) BACKBAND
(PL.) LEDGMENT
MOLDY FUSTY HOARY MUCID
MUGGY MUSTY VINNY FOISTY
MOULDY FOUGHTY
MOLE COB UNT COBB MAIL OONT
PIER PILE TAPE WANT JUTTY
MOODY NEVUS TALPA TAUPE
ANICUT MOUDIE HYDATID TALPOID
MOLDWARP MOONCALF SORICOID
STARNOSE UROPSILE ZANDMOLE
MOLE CRICKET CHANGA
MOLECULE ACID ATOM BASE
AMMINE DIPOLE HYDROL LIGAND
HYDRONE SPECIES
MOLEHILL TUMP HOYLE WANTHILL
MOLE RAT SEMNI ZEMMI ZOKOR
SLEPEZ SPALACID ZANDMOLE
MOLEST GALL HAUNT TEASE
BOTHER HARASS HECKLE INFEST
PESTER MISLEST TROUBLE
MOLLIFY HUSH RELAX ADULCE
GENTLE PACIFY RELENT SOFTEN
SOOTHE TEMPER ASSUAGE DULCIFY
SWEETEN ATTEMPER MITIGATE
UNRUFFLE
MOLLIFYING MILD SUPPLING
MOLLUSK ARK CLAM CONE PIPI
SPAT BORER CHAMA CHANK CHINK
CLAMP CONCH COWRY DORIS DRILL

MUREX PINNA SNAIL VENUS AEOLID
BAILER BUBBLE CERION CHITON
COCKLE COURIE DOLIUM JINGLE
LEPTON LIMPET MUSSEL NERITA
OYSTER PECTEN PHOLAD PURPLE
SEMELE STROMB ABALONE
ASTARTE BIVALVE CARDITA
DECAPOD JUNONIA MOLLUSC
PIDDOCK SCALLOP TOHEROA
TREPANG TROPHON DUCKFOOT
FIGSHELL HALIOTIS NAUTILUS
PTEROPOD SAXICAVA STROMBUS
UNIVALVE VERMETUS
(— TRIBE) NAIADES
(LARVAL —) VELIGER
(YOUNG —) SPAT
MOLLYCODDLE MOLLY WANTON
INDULGE MILKSOP
MOLOSSUS (FATHER OF —)
PYRRHUS
(MOTHER OF —) ANDROMACHE
MOLT MEW CAST MUTE SHED MOULT
DISCARD EXUVIATE INTERMEW
MOLTEN FUSED
MOLTING BROKEN ECDYSIS
MOLYBDENUM (EXCESS OF —)
TEART
MOMBIN JOCOTE
MOMENT MO GIRD HINT SAND TICK
AVAIL BLINK BRAID CLINK CRACK
GLIFF GLISK JIFFY SHAKE SNIFT
SPURT STOUN TRICE VALUE FILLIP
GLIFFY MINUTE PERIOD SECOND
STOUND WEIGHT YAWING ARTICLE
INSTANT INSTANCE MOMENTUM
TWINKLING
(— FOR LEGERDEMAIN ACTION)
TEMPS
(— OF STRESS) CRISE
(CRITICAL —) BIT INCH CORNER
(DECISIVE —) CRISIS
(EXACT —) BIT POINT
(OPPORTUNE —) KAIROS
(SCHEDULED —) TIME
MOMENTARY MOMENTAL
TRANSIENT
MOMENTOUS FELL GRAVE EPOCHAL
FATEFUL WEIGHTY EVENTFUL
MOMENTOUSNESS GRAVITY
MOMENTUM WAY FORCE SPEED
IMPETUS
MON PEGUAN TALAING

MONACO

DYNASTY: GRIMALDI
LANGUAGE: FRENCH
PEOPLE: MONEGASQUES
PRINCE: LOUIS ALBERT HONORE
ANTOINE CHARLES RAINIER
FLORESTAN
RIVER: VESUBIE
SECTION: MONTECARLO
LACONDAMINE MONACOVILLE

MONAD JIVA HENAD MONAS
MONADNOCK BARABOO
MONARCH KING QUEEN DANAID

DIADEM PRINCE DANAINE EMPEROR
AUTOCRAT
MONARCHIAN PRAXEAN
MONARCHICAL KINGLY
MONARCHY KINGDOM
MONASTERY WAT ABBEY BADIA
LAURA RIBAT TEKKE TEKYA FRIARY
MANDRA VIHARA BONZERY
CERTOSA CONVENT KHANKAH
MINSTER CLOISTER LAMASERY
(ALGERIAN —) RIBAT
(BUDDHIST —) TERA KYAUNG
BONZERY LAMASERY
(CARTHUSIAN —) CERTOSA
(HINDU —) MATH
(MOSLEM —) TEKKE TEKYA
KHANKAH
MONASTIC MONKLY MONKISH
CENOBIAN MONACHAL
MONASTICISM MONKERY MONKISM
MONETARY EXPLICIT
MONEY (ALSO SEE COIN) AES BOX
DIB FEE FEI GET OOF ORO SAP TIN
WAD CASH COAT COIN COLE CRAP
CUSH DUBS DUST FUND GATE GELT
GILT GOLD HOOT JACK JAKE KALE
LOUR MINT MOSS MUCK PELF ROLL
SALT SAND SHAG SOAP SWAG
BEANS BLUNT BRASH BRASS BREAD
BUNCE BUNTS CHINK CHIPS CLINK
DARBY DIMES DOUGH DUMPS
FUNDS GREEN GRIGS IMPUT LUCRE
MOPUS OCHER PURSE RHINO
ROCKS ROWDY SCADS SHINY
SMASH SPUDS STIFF STUFF SUGAR
ARGENT BARATO BARREL BOODLE
CHANGE CUNYIE DANARO DINERO
FARLEU FARLEY FEUAGE FLIMSY
FUMAGE GRAITH HANSEL KELTER
MAZUMA POCKET SHEKEL SILVER
SPENSE SPLOSH STAMPS STEVEN
STUMPY TALENT WISSEL ADVANCE
CHATTEL CHINKER COUNTER
CRACKER CRUSADE DEPOSIT
FALDAGE GUNNAGE OOFTISH
SCRATCH SPANKER SPECIES
STOCKER CRIMPAGE CURRENCY
DEMIMARK INCOMING INTEREST
SPENDING STERLING STOCKING
XERAPHIN
(— BET) COMEBACK
(— DUE) DEVOIRS
(— FOR LIQUOR) WHIP
(— LENT) LUMBER
(— OF ACCOUNT) ORA
(— PAID TO BIND BARGAIN) ARLES
(— TAKEN IN) DRAWING
(ADDITIONAL —) BONUS
(AVAILABLE —) CAPITAL
(BAR —) BONK TANG
(BASE —) SHICE
(BRIBE —) SOAP BOODLE
(COUNTERFEIT —) BOGUS QUEER
BOODLE DUFFER SHOWFUL SLITHER
(EARNEST —) ARLES ARRHA
DEPOSIT HANDSEL HANDGELD
HANDSALE
(EXPENSE —) DIET
(FERRY —) NAULUM

(HARD —) SPECIE
(HAT —) TAMPANG
(HAVING NO —) FLYBLOWN
(INVESTED —) STOCK
(PAPER —) GREEN CABBAGE
CURRENCY FROGSKIN
(PASSAGE —) SHIPHIRE
(PRIZE —) PEWTER
(PROTECTION —) ICE
(PUSH —) SPIFF
(READY —) CASH DARBY READY
STUFF STUMPY
(REFUNDED —) DRAWBACK
(SHELL —) PEAG HAWOK WAKIKI
WAMPUM
(SILVER —) SYCEE
(SMALL SUM OF —) SPILL
(STANDARD BANK —) BANCO
(SUBSISTENCE —) BATTA
(TRAVELLING —) VIATICUM
(WIRE —) LARI LARIN LARREE
MONEYBAG FOLLIS
MONEY BELT ZONE
MONEY BOX TILL CHEST PIRLIE
MONEY-CHANGER SARAF SHROFF
ARGENTER
MONEY DRAWER TILL SHUTTLE
MONEYED RICH WEALTHY
MONEYLENDER BANYA CHETTY
USURER LOMBARD MAHAJAN
MARWARI SHYLOCK
MONEYMAKING BANAUSIC
MONEYWORT MANG MYRTLE
PRIMWORT
MONGOL HUN KALKA BALKAR
BURIAT DAGHUR SHARRA BERBERI
KALMUCK KHALKHA SILINGAL
(PL.) HU
MONGOOSE MUNG URVA CIVET
MUNGO MONGOE MEERKAT VANSIRE
MONGREL CUR DOG FICE FIST
CROSS FEIST LIMER SCRUB
BASTARD CURRISH PIEBALD
DOGGEREL
MONILIALES HYPHO
MONISM HENISM ONEISM
MONITION TUITION
MONITOR MARKER MENTOR
LANTERN PREFECT
MONITOR LIZARD IBID IBIT URAN
VARAN WARAL GOANNA WORRAL
MONITOR
MONK BO FRA COWL LAMA MARO
ARHAT BONZE CLERK FRATE FRIAR
PADRE YAHAN BHIKKU CULDEE
GALLAH GETSUL GOSAIN MONACH
VOTARY ARAHANT CALOYER
CLUNIAC GALLACH STARETS
STUDITE ATHONITE MARABOUT
MONASTIC SANNYASI TALAPOIN
TRAPPIST
(PL.) AGAPETI ACOEMETI
MONKEY APE CAY ORA PUG SAI TUP
BEGA BROH BRUH DOUC KAHA
MONA MONK MONO SAKI SIME TITI
TOTA WAAG ZATI ARABA CEBID
DIANA JACKO JOCKO KAHAU
MUNGA OATAS PATAS PUGGY
SAJOU TOQUE UNGKA BANDAR

COAITA COUXIA GRISON GRIVET
GUENON HOWLER LANGUR MACACO
MARTEN MIRIKI MONACH NISNAS
OUBARI PINCHE RILAWA SAMIRI
SIMIAN SIMPAI TEETEE VERVET
WARINE WEEPER WISTIT BHUNDAR
COLOBIN GUARIBA GUEREZA
HANUMAN KALASIE LUNGOOR
MACAQUE MEERKAT MOUSTOC
OUAKARI PRIMATE ROLOWAY
SAIMIRI SAPAJOU STENTOR
TAMARIN ARAGUATO CAIARARA
CAPUCHIN DURUKULI ENTELLUS
LEONCITO MALBROUK MANGABEY
MARMOSET MARTINET MUSTACHE
ORABASSU PRIMATAL TALAPOIN
TCHINCOU WANDEROO
(LIKE A —) PUGGISH
MONKEY BREAD BAOBAB
MONKEY FLOWER MIMULUS
MONKEYPOT LECYTH KAKARALI
LECYTHIS SAPUCAIA
MONKEY PUZZLE PINON PINION
MONKEYSHINE SINGERIE
(PL.) HORSE
MONKFISH MONK SQUATINA
MONKISH CENOBIAN MONASTIC
MONK PARROT LORO
MONKSHOOD ATIS ACONITE
ACONITUM NAPELLUS MOUSEBANE
MONO MONACHI
MONOACETATE ACETIN
MONOCARPELLARY SIMPLE
MONOCHORD MAGAS MAGADIS
UNICHORD
MONOCHROME CAMAIEU MONOTINT
MONOCLE QUIZ EYEGLASS
MONOCLINOUS PERFECT
MONOECISM SYNOECY SYNOEKY
MONOGRAM IHS JHS YHS CIPHER
HERALD CHRISMON
MONOGRAPH STUDY BULLETIN
DISCOURSE
MONOLITH MENHIR PILLAR
(CIRCLE OF —S) CROMLECH
MONOLITHIC GLOBAL
MONOLOGIST DISEUSE
MONOLOGUE MONOLOGY
SOLILOQUY
MONOPHTHONGAL PURE
MONOPHTHONGIZE SMOOTH
MONOPHYSITE AGNOETE AGNOITE
JACOBITE
(PL.) ACEPHALI
MONOPLANE TAUBE PARASOL
MONOPODE SKIAPOD
MONOPOLIZE LURCH ABSORB
CONSUME ENGROSS
MONOPOLY REGIE TRUST CARTEL
APPALTO
MONOSACCHARIDE OSE DIOSE
HEXOSE MONOSE GLYCOSE
HEPTOSE
MONOTONOUS ARID DEAD DULL
FLAT WASTE DREARY SAMELY
SODDEN ADENOID HUMDRUM
INSIPID IRKSOME TEDIOUS
BORESOME DRUDGING SAMESOME
UNVARIED VEGETABLE

MONOTONY DRAB DRYNESS
DULLNESS SAMENESS
MONOXENOUS DIRECT
MONSOON VARSHA
MONSTER OGRE BILCH LARVA
MORMO RAHAB TERAS UNMAN
ELLOPS GERYON MAKARA SHRIMP
TYPHON BICORNE CHIMERA
CYCLOPS DIDYMUS DIPYGUS
ECHIDNA GRENDEL GRIFFIN
GRIFFON SLAPPER UNBEAST
WARLOCK JANICEPS LINDWORM
MOONCALF TARASQUE TYPHOEUS
UROMELUS LEVIATHAN
(— WITH 100 EYES) ARGUS
(— WITH 100 HANDS) BRIAREUS
(9-HEADED —) HYDRA
(FABULOUS —) KRAKEN TANIWHA
(FEMALE —) HARPY LAMIA SCYLLA
(HALF-BULL HALF-MAN —)
MINOTAUR
(MAN-DEVOURING —) OGRE LAMIA
(MYTHICAL —) HARPY SCYLLA
SPHINX CHIMERA WARLOCK
MINOTAUR
(SEA —) BELUE KRAKEN PISTRIX
(SUPERNATURAL —) LARVA
(TWO-BODIED —) DISOMUS
(WATER —) NICKER
MONSTRANCE SUN
MONSTROSITY FREAK DIPYGUS
MONSTER ABORTION IMMANITY
MOONCALF TERATISM
MONSTROUS VAST ENORM GIANT
FIENDLY FLAMING HIDEOUS TITANIC
BEHEMOTH COLOSSAL DEFORMED
ENORMOUS FLAGRANT GIGANTIC
PYTHONIC SLAPPING
MONTAGNARD SEKANI

MONTANA
CAPITAL: HELENA
COLLEGE: CARROLL
COUNTY: HILL TETON FERGUS
WIBAUX PONDERA MISSOULA
INDIAN: CROW ATSINA SALISH
ARAPAHO KUTENAI SIKSIKA
SHOSHONE
LAKE: HEBGEN FLATHEAD
FORTPECK MEDICINE
MOUNTAIN: AJAX BALDY COWAN
SPHINX TORREY GRANITE
HILGARD TRAPPER GALLATIN
PENTAGON SNOWSHOE
MOUNTAIN RANGE: CRAZY LEWIS
POCKY BIGBELT
NICKNAME: BIGSKY TREASURE
RIVER: MILK TONGUE KOOTENAI
MISSOURI
STATE BIRD: MEADOWLARK
STATE FLOWER: BITTERROOT
TOWN: BUTTE HAURE MALTA
HARDIN HELENA BOZEMAN
CHINOOK CHOTEAU FORSYTH
GLASGOW ROUNDUP BILLINGS
MISSOULA

MONTANIST PHRYGIAN

MONTENEGRO
COIN: PARA FLORIN PERPERA
LAKE: SCUTARI SHKODER
MOUNTAIN: DURMITOR
NAME: ZETA ILLYRIA CRNAGORA
PORT: BAR ULCINJ ANTIVARI
DULCIGNO
RIVER: ZETA MORACA
TOWN: NIKSIC CETINJE TITOGRAD
PODGORICA

MONTH AB AV BUL MAY PUS SOL
ZIF ZIW ABIB ADAR AHET APAP ASIN
ELUL IYAR JETH JULY JUNE KUAR
MAGH MOON TYBI AGHAN APRIL
ASARH CHAIT IYYAR MAIUS MARCH
NISAN PAYNI RABIA RAJAB SAFAR
SAWAN SEBAT SHVAT SIVAN SIWAN
TEBET THOTH TIZRI UINAL AUGUST
BHADON CHOIAK JUMADA JUNIUS
KARTIK KISLEV KISLEW KISLEY
MECHIR MESORE NISSAN NIVOSE
PAOPHI PHAGUN SAPHAR SHABAN
SHABAT TAMMUZ TISHRI VEADAR
ABAGHAN APRILIS BAISAKH BYSACKI
CHAITRA CHISLEV ETHANIM
FLOREAL HESHVAN JANUARY
MARTIUS OCTOBER PACHONS
PHALGUN RAMADAN SARAWAN
SHAABAN SHAWWAL THAMMUZ
VENTOSE BRUMAIRE DECEMBER
DULKAADA FEBRUARY FERVIDOR
FRIMAIRE GAMELION GERMINAL
MESSIDOR MUHARRAM NOVEMBER
PLUVIOSE POSEIDON PRAIRIAL
SEXTILIS ZULKADAH SEPTEMBER
(IN NEXT —) PROXIMO
(IN PRECEDING —) ULTIMO
(PRESENT —) INSTANT
(SIX —S) SEMESTER
MONTHLY MENSAL
MONUMENT VAT WAT LECH TOMB
CROSS STONE TABUT TITLE BILITH
DOLMEN HEARSE MEMORY RECORD
TROPHY CHAITYA CHHATRI
CHORTEN DENKMAL FUNERAL
TRILITH BILITHON CENOTAPH
MEMORIAL MONOLITH TROPAION
(— OF HEAPED STONES) CAIRN
(PILLARLIKE —) SHAFT STELA
STELE
MOO LOW
MOOCH BUM CADGE SPONGE
MOOCHER MIKER CADGER GRAFTER
MOOD CUE FIT TID MIND TIFF TIFT
TONE TUNE VEIN WHIM DEVIL
FRAME FREAK HEART HUMOR SPITE
PLIGHT SPIRIT SPLEEN SPRITE
STRAIN TALENT TEMPER CAPRICE
FANTASY FEATHER JUSSIVE
ATTITUDE
(— IN LOGIC) BARBARA
(— OF BAD TEMPER) DORTS
(— OF DEPRESSION) LETDOWN
(CROSS —) FRUMPS
(FRIVOLOUS —) JEST
(GROUCHY —) DODS
(IRRITABLE —) GRIZZLE

(SULKY —) PET
(SULLEN —) STRUNT SULLENS
MOODY SAD GLUM SULKY BROODY
GLOOMY MOROSE SULLEN MOODISH
PENSIVE
MOON BUAT LAMP LUNA MAHI DIANA
LUNET LUCINA PHOEBE CHANDRA
CYNTHIA LEWANNA LUNETTE
MOONLET FOGEATER MENISCUS
SATELLES
(FULL —) PLENILUNE
(NEW —) PRIME
(PART OF COURSE OF —) MANSION
(WANING —) WANIAND
MOONBLIND LUNATIC
MOONEYE HIODONT
MOONEYE CISCO BLOATER
MOON-EYED LUNATIC
MOONFISH SUNFISH JOROBADA
MOONFLOWER ACHETE
MOONLIGHT FLESH MOONGLOW
MOONRAT GYMNURE
MOONSET MOONDOWN MOONFALL
MOONSHINE MOON SHINE SHINNY
BOOTLEG BLOCKADE
MOONSTRUCK LUNATIC
MOONWORT LUNARY HONESTY
MOOR FEN BENT FELL POST BEACH
BERTH HOVEL TURCO COMMOTY
COMONTE MARRANO MOGRABI
MOORMAN MORESCO MORISCO
(INFERTILE —) LANDE
MOOR COCK GORCOCK MUIRCOCK
MOORING DOCK MOORAGE
MOORLAND OUTFIELD
MOOSE BELL ELAND CERVID
ORIGNAL
MOOSEWOOD DIRCA
MOOT MUTE STIR PORTMOOT
MOP BOB SOP SWAB MALKIN MERKIN
MOPPET SCOVEL
(— FOR CLEANING CANNON)
MERKIN
(— OF HAIR) TOUSLE
(BAKER'S —) MALKIN MAWKIN
MOPANE IRONWOOD
MOPCAP MOB
MOPE MUMP POUT SULK BROOD
GLOOM
MOPING FUSTY DUMPISH
MORA LOVE TIME LIMMA SEMEION
MORAL TAG PURE CIVIL ETHIC
EPIMYTH ETHICAL UPRIGHT
HONORARY
(PL.) THEW
MORALISTIC DIDACTIC
MORALITY MORALS VIRTUE
MORALIZING PI
MORASS BOG FLOW MOSS ROSS
SUMP FLUSH MARSH SLACK
SLOUGH QUAGMIRE
MORAY PUSI ELGIN HAMLET
MURAENA
MORBID SICK MORBOSE PECCANT
MORDANT HANDLE SPIRIT CAUSTIC
STRIKER SCATHING
MORE MO MAE PIU HELDER
(— OR LESS) HALFWAY
(— THAN ADEQUATE) AMPLE

(— THAN ENOUGH) TOO
(— THAN HALF) BETTER
(— THAN ONE OR TWO) SUNDRY
(— THAN ONE) SEVERAL
(— THAN SUFFICIENT) ABUNDANT
(— THAN THIS) YEA
(— THAN) BUT OVER ABOVE RISING
PLUSQUAM
(LITTLE —) ADVANTAGE
MOREEN TABBY
MOREL HELVELLA MORIGLIO
MORELLO MOREL GRIOTTE
MULBERRY
MOREOVER EKE TOO ALSO MORE
AGAIN EITHER BESIDES FARTHER
FURTHER THERETO LIKEWISE
OVERMORE
MOREPORK PEHO RURU MOPOKE
MOPEHAWK
MORGUE LIBRARY MORTUARY
MORION CABASSET
MORMON COHAB SAINT DANITE
(— STATE) UTAH
MORNING GAY MORN MATIN
MORROW UNDERN COCKCROW
MORNTIME
(IN THE —) MANE
MORNING GLORY NIL KOALI
TWINER GAYBINE IPOMOEA
MANROOT PILIKAI BINDWEED
SCAMMONY
(— GROWING AMONG GRAIN) BEAR
MORNING STAR VENUS DAYSTAR
LUCIFER MERCURY BARTONIA
MORO LUTAO SAMAL YAKAN ILLANO
DOLOANO MALANAO
MOROCCO MAROQUIN

MOROCCO

CAPE: NUN NOUN
CAPITAL: RABAT
COIN: OKIA RIAL OKIEH DIRHAM
MOUZOUNA
DISTRICT: ERRIF
MEASURE: KALA SAAH FANEGA
IZENBI TOMINI
MOUNTAIN: TOUBKAL
MOUNTAIN RANGE: RIF ATLAS
PEOPLE: MOOR BERBER KABYLE
MOSLEM MUSLIM
PORT: SAFI CEUTA RABAT SAFFI
AGADIR TETUAN LARACHE
MAZAGAN MELILLA MOGADOR
TANGIER
PROVINCE: CEUTA MELILLA
RIVER: DRA MOULOUYA
TOWN: FES FEZ SAFI RABAT
AGADIR MEKNES TANGIER
MARRAKECH
WEIGHT: ROTL ARTAL ARTEL
GERBE RATEL KINTAR QUINTAL

MORON FOOL AMENT IMBECILE
MORONITY MOROSIS
MOROSE GLUM GRUM SOUR MOODY
RUSTY SURLY CRUSTY GLOOMY
STINGY SULLEN CRABBED CROOKED
PEEVISH STROUNGE

MOROSENESS ASPERITY
MORPHEME BASE ETYMON
COGNATE
MORPHOLOGICAL FORMAL
MORRIS MILL MERELS
MORSEL BIT NIG ORT TIT BITE GNAP
SNAP SCRAN BUCKONE MORCEAU
NOISETTE PARTICLE SKERRICK
(— OF CHEESE) TRIP
(— OF CHOCOLATE) BUD
(— OF SEASONED MEAT) GOBBET
(CHOICE —) TIDBIT TITBIT
MORTAL BEING DYING FATAL HUMAN
VITAL DEADLY FINITE LETHAL
BRITTLE DEATHLY DEATHFUL
MORTALITY FLESH MURRAIN
MORTALLY DEADLY FATALLY
MORTAR DAB COMPO DAGGA
GROUT LARRY ROYAL SORKI SWISH
CANNON CEMENT HOLMOS MINNIE
POTGUN BEDDING COEHORN
DAUBING PERRIER POUNDER
PUGGING SOORKEE
(— AND PESTLE) DOLLY DOLLIE
(— EXTRUDED BETWEEN LATHS)
KEY
(— FOR ROCKETS) TROMBE
(— FOR SALUTES) CHAMBER
(— MADE WITH STRAW) BAUGE
(INFERIOR —) SLIME
(SMALL —) HOBIT ROYAL TINKER
(THIN —) LARRY
MORTARBOARD CATERCAP
TRENCHER
MORTAR BOAT PALANDER
MORTGAGE DIP LAY BOND LIEN
ENGAGE MONKEY OBLIGE WADSET
WEDDEED THIRLAGE
MORTGAGOR REVERSER
MORTIFICATION ENVY SHAME
SPITE CHAGRIN GANGRENE
NECROSIS VEXATION
MORTIFIED ASHAMED
MORTIFY ABASE ABASH SHAME
SPITE HUMBLE CHAGRIN CRUCIFY
MACERATE
MORTISE GAIN COCKET
(SIDE OF —) CHEEK
MORTUARY MORGUE FUNERARY
SAWLSHOT
MORWONG TARAKIHI
MOSAIC AUCUBA EMBLEM MUSIVE
SCREEN FRISOLEE INTARSIA
TERRAZZO
(POTATO —) CRINKLE
MOSLEM MOOR HADJI HAFIZ HANIF
ISLAM MALAY SALAR TURBAN
ISLAMIC MOORMAN SANGGIL
SARACEN ISLAMITE SANGUILE
MOSQUE JAMI MOSCH DURGAH
MASJID MESKED
MOSQUITO GNAT CULICID GAMBIAE
SKEETER ANOPHELE DIPTERAN
MOSS FOG MNIUM USNEA HYPNUM
MUSKEG FOXFEET GULAMAN
HAIRCAP PILIGAN TORTULA
CROWFOOT MOSSWORT SPHAGNUM
STAGHORN
(— HANGING FROM TREE) WEEPER

MOSSBUNKER MENHADEN
MOSSI MOLE MORE
MOSSI-GURUNSI GUR
MOSS PINK PHLOX
MOSSTROOPER RIDER
MOSSY FOGGY HOARY MUSCOSE
MOST BEST MOSTLY FARTHEST
MOSTLY MOST FECKLY CHIEFLY
MOSTDEAL
MOT JEST
MOTE ATOM ATOMY FESCUE
MOATHILL
MOTEL COURT
MOTH GEM NUN PUG HAWK MOTE
PAGE APPLE ATLAS EGGAR EGGER
FLAME GAMMA IMAGO PISKY PLUME
SAMIA SWIFT THORN USHER WITCH
ANTLER BAGONG BURNET COSSID
DAGGER DATANA HERALD HUMMER
JUGATE LACKEY LAPPET MILLER
MOODER PLUSIA QUAKER RUSTIC
SPHINX THISBE TINEID TISSUE
TUSSUR ARCTIAN ARCTIID
BAGWORM BUDWORM CRAMBID
CRININE DELTOID DRINKER
EMERALD EMPEROR EUCLEID
FESTOON FIGWORM FOOTMAN
FRENATE HOOKTIP NOCTUID
PEGASUS PSYCHID PYRALIS
SLICKER STINGER SYLINID TINEOLA
TORTRIX TUSSOCK URANIID
VAPORER ZYGENID AEGERIID
ARMYWORM BOMBYCID CATOCALA
CECROPIA CINNABAR COCHYLIS
FISHTAIL FORESTER GEOMETER
GOLDTAIL GRISETTE HAWKMOTH
HEPIALID KNOTHORN MOTHWORM
PHYCITID PLUTELLA SPHINGID
SPRAWLER WAINSCOT
(— **BREEDER**) AURELIAN
(**VERY SMALL** —) MICRO
MOTH BALL REPELLER
MOTHER INA MOM DAME MAMA
MADRE MAMMA MAMMY MATER
MINNY MODUR MITHER MULIER
VENTER GENETRIX
(— **OF THE GODS**) RHEA
(**DIVINE** —) MATRIGAN
(**GREAT** —) AGDISTIS
(**NOURISHING** — **OF MAN**) CYBELE
(**SEVEN** —**S**) MATRIS
(**SIDE OF** —) ENATE
MOTHERLAND COUNTRY
MOTHERLY MATERNAL MATRONAL
MOTHER-OF-PEARL NACRE PEARL
MOTIF SPRIG DESIGN DEVICE MOTIVE
SCALLOP APPLIQUE
MOTILE ZO ZOO
MOTION WAY FARD FEED GIRD
MOVE SIGN WHID HURRY PAVIE
APPORT MOMENT MOTIVE TRAVEL
UNREST IMPULSE ACTIVITY
MOVEMENT OVERTURE
(— **OF AIR**) AIRFLOW
(— **OF HORSE**) AIR
(— **TO**) ALLATIVE
(**ABRUPT** —) CHOP
(**CAM** —) COULIER
(**CIRCULAR** —) GYRE COMPASS

(**CONFUSED** —) GURGE
(**DANCE** —) CAPER
(**DIZZY** —) SWIMBEL
(**EXPRESSIVE** —) GESTURE
(**FORWARD** —) HEADWAY
(**GLIDING** —) SWIM SKITTER
(**HEAVING** —) ESTUS AESTUS
(**HURRIED** —) HUSTLE
(**ILLEGAL** —) BALK BAULK
(**IRREGULAR** —) SWAG
(**JERKING** —) BOB LIPE JIGGLE
(**LATERAL** —) DRIFT
(**QUIVERING** —) TREMOR
(**RAPID** —) SCOUR
(**REARING** —) PESADE
(**RECIPROCATING** —) SEESAW
(**ROTARY** —) SWAY BACKSPIN
SIDESPIN
(**SHOWY** —) FANFARE
(**SIDEWAYS** —) CRAB
(**SLOW** —) CRAWL
(**SPINNING** —) ENGLISH
(**SWIMMING** —) FLUTTER
(**UPWARD** —) HEAVE
(**VIGOROUS** —) SKELP
(**VIOLENT** —) JERK RAPT BENSEL
(**WAVERING** —) SHAKE
(**WAVING** —) WAFF
(**WHIRLING** —) SWIRL
MOTIONLESS DEAD ASLEEP
IMMOBILE STAGNANT STIRLESS
MOTION PICTURE CINE FILM FLICK
MOVIE BIOPIC CINEMA TALKIE
CHEAPIE SMELLIE FLICKERS
(**PL.**) SILENTS
MOTIVATE ANIMATE INSPIRE
MOTIVATED COVERT
MOTIVE GOAD SAKE SPUR CAUSE
MOTIF SCORE ACTUAL DESIRE
OBJECT SPRING ATTACCO IMPULSE
PATTERN RESPECT RINCEAU
SUBJECT INSTANCE STIMULUS
(**ALLEGED** —) PRETEXT
MOTLEY MIXED MEDLEY RAGTAG
MOTTLED PIEBALD
MOTMOT HOUTOU SAWBILL
PICARIAN
MOTOR AUTO TOOT MOVER ENGINE
ROTATOR TURBINE EFFERENT
MOTORBOAT LAUNCH AUTOBOAT
RUNABOUT
MOTORCAR MOTOR DOODLEBUG
MOTORCYCLE CYCLE MOTOR
STEED TRICAR AUTOETTE TRICYCLE
MOTORIST AUTOIST
MOTORMAN CARMAN WATTMAN
TROLLYMAN
MOTORTRUCK DRAY LORRY
CAMION BOBTAIL FLATBED
MOTTLE CHECK TABBY SPONGE
MOTTLED JAZZ PINTO MOTLEY
RUMINATE SPLASHED
MOTTO MOT WORD AXIOM CACHET
DEVICE EUREKA LEGEND REASON
IMPRESA EPIGRAPH
(— **IN A RING**) POSY
(— **OF CALIFORNIA**) EUREKA
(— **OF MAINE**) DIRIGO
MOUE FACE

MOUFLON MUSIMON
MOULIN CHIMNEY
MOUND AHU COP HOW LAW LOW
BALK BANK BOSS BUND BUTT GOAL
HILL HUMP KNOW MOLE POME TELL
TEPE TERP TUFT TUMP AGGER
BERRY DHERI ESKAR ESKER KNOLL
MONDE MOTTE MOUNT PINGO RAISE
STUPA TOMAN BARROW CAUSEY
MEILER RIDEAU ANTHILL BOUROCK
HILLOCK MAMELON BACKSTOP
BARBETTE SNOWBANK TEOCALLI
(— **ABOUT A PLANT**) TUMP
(— **FOR MEMORIAL**) CAIRN
(— **IN BUILDING MATERIAL**) DIMPLE
(— **OF DETRITUS**) WASH
(— **OF ICE**) DOME
(— **OF WOOD TO BE CHARRED**)
MEILER
(**BURIAL** —) LAW LOW TOR TOLA
BERRY GUACA HUACA BARROW
KURGAN TUMULUS
(**FORTIFIED** —) DUN
(**GLACIAL** —) KAME
(**MILITARY** —) BARBETTE
(**PALISADED** —) MOTTE
(**VOLCANIC** —) HORNITO
MOUNT BEN STY BACK HEAD RIDE
RISE SCAN ARISE BIPOD BOARD
CLIMB HEAVE HINGE SPEEL SPIRE
SWARM ASCEND ASPIRE MORIAH
CHARGER COLLINE HAIRPIN
HARNESS BESTRIDE MOUNTAIN
MOUNTING MOUNTURE SURMOUNT
(— **A HORSE**) FORK LIGHT WORTH
(— **BY STEPS**) SCAN
(— **ON PIN**) STICK
(— **ON WINGS**) SOAR
(**STEREOTYPE** —) CORE
MOUNTAIN BEN KOP BERG CIMA
DAGH FELL KLIP KNOB MONS MONT
NEBO PICO PIKE JEBEL MOUNT
RANGE BARROW BUNDOC GILEAD
GUNONG HEIGHT PISGAH HELICON
MONTURE NUNATAK BUNDUCKS
(— **INHABITED BY SPIRIT**) GUACA
HUACA
(— **MASS**) OROGEN
(— **PASS**) GHAT GHAUT
(— **STATE**) MONTANA
(— **TRACT**) DUAR
(**AT BASE OF** —) PIEDMONT
(**FABLED** —) KAF MERU
(**GREEK** —) OSSA PELION HELICON
OLYMPUS MAENALUS
(**HIGH** —) ALP
(**ROUND** —) REEK
(**SMALL** —) NOB KNOB BUTTE
(**SNOW** —) JOKUL
(**SUBMARINE** —) GUYOT SEAMOUNT
MOUNTAIN ASH SORB SORBUS
DOGBERRY MOZEMIZE ROUNTREE
WINETREE
MOUNTAIN BEAVER SEWELLEL
MOUNTAIN BINDWEED SOLDANEL
MOUNTAIN CAP SCALP
MOUNTAIN CLIMBER CRAGSMAN
MOUNTAIN CRANBERRY
FOXBERRY

MOUNTAINEER WASIR WAZIR
HEIDUC HAYDUCK HILLMAN
ORESTES MONTESCO TIERSMAN
(PL.) GUTI GUTIANS
MOUNTAIN GOAT IBEX MAZAME
MOUNTAIN LAUREL IVY HEATH
ERICAD KALMIS LAUREL IVYWOOD
CALFKILL
(THICKET OF —) SLICK
MOUNTAIN LINNET TWITE
MOUNTAIN LION PUMA COUGAR
MOUNTAIN MAHOE EMAJAGUA
MOUNTAIN MISERY TARWEED
MOUNTAINOUS RANGY VICIOUS
MOUNTAIN PARSLEY FLUELLEN
MOUNTAIN RANGE KAF QAF TIER
SIERRA SAWBACK DINDYMUS
MOUNTAIN SICKNESS VETA
MOUNTAINSIDE FELLSIDE
MOUNTAINTOP MAN DOME
MOUNTAIN WOOD ROCKWOOD
MOUNTEBANK IMPOSTOR
OPERATOR
MOUNTED CARDED SADDLE
EASELED EQUITANT
MOUNT ETNA MONGIBEL
MOUNTING MOUNT SCAPE ASCENT
FLIGHT MONTANT SOAKING
INCABLOC MOUNTURE
(— OF GEM) CHASE
(STYLE OF —) SETTING
MOURN DOLE KEEN SIGH WAIL
PLAIN GRIEVE LAMENT SORROW
GRIZZLE
MOURNER WAILER WEEPER
(HIRED —) SAULIE
(PROFESSIONAL —) BLACK KEENER
MOURNFUL SAD BLACK SORRY
WEEPY RUEFUL DERNFUL SIGHFUL
WAILFUL DEJECTED DIRGEFUL
ELEGIOUS FUNEREAL MAESTIVE
MESTFULL YEARNFUL PLAINTIVE
MOURNING DOLOR SHIVA DISMAL
WIDOWED
(— CLOTH) RADZIMIR
MOUSE MURINE MYGALE RODENT
VERMIN ARVICOLE CRICETID
MYOMORPH
(LIKE A —) MURIFORM
(MEADOW —) VOLE
(STRIPED —) KUSU
MOUSEBIRD COLY
MOUSE DEER PLANDOK
MOUSETRAP TIPE
MOUSING KEEPER
MOUTH OS GAB GAM GOB JIB MUG
MUN NEB ORF ROW YAP BEAK BEAL
BOCA HEAD MUSS PUSS SHOP TRAP
YAWN BAZOO BOCCA BRACE CHOPS
CODON STOMA TUTEL GEBBIE
KISSER MUZZLE RABBLE RICTUS
SUCKER THROAT CLAPPER
FLUMMER OSTIOLE STOMACH
LORRIKER PAVILLON
(— AND THROAT) COPPER WHISTLE
(— OF CANYON) ABRA
(— OF GLASS FURNACE) BOCCA
(— OF HARBOR) BOCA
(— OF PERITHECIUM) OSTIOLE

(— OF RIVER) BEAL BOCA LADE
ENTRY INFLUX ESTUARY OSTIARY
(— OF SHAFT) BRACE
(— OF TRUMPET) BELL CODON
PAVILLON
(— PARTS OF ARTHROPOD) TROPHI
(KILN —) KILNEYE KILNHOLE
(SORE — OF SHEEP) ECTHYMA
(WRY —) MURGEON
(PL.) ORA
MOUTHFUL GAG GOB SUP GNAP
GOLEE GOBBET
MOUTHPART BILL
MOUTHPIECE BAR BEAK BOCAL
MOUTH FIPPLE SYRINX PROPHET
(— OF BAGPIPE) MUSE
(— OF PIPE) STEM
MOUTHWASH GARGLE
MOUTH-WATERING SALIVANT
MOVABLE FREE LOOSE MOBILE
PORTABLE REMUABLE
(PL.) MEUBLES
MOVE GO ACT FIG GEE GET WAG
BOOM BORE BUCK BUMP CALL
DRAW FIRK FLIT GOAD HEAT KNEE
MAKE PIRL ROLL SILE SPUR STEP
STIR SWAY WORK ANKLE BLITZ
BUDGE CARRY CAUSE CROWD
DRAFT HEAVE IMPEL LIGHT MARCH
MUDGE QUECH REMUE ROUSE
SHAKE SHIFT GAMBIT HANDLE
HUSTLE INCITE INDUCE KINDLE
MOTION PROMPT QUITCH REMBLE
SASHAY STRAKE ACTUATE AGITATE
ANIMATE DISTURB DRAUGHT
FLUTTER INSPIRE MIGRATE
PROVOKE AMBULATE BULLDOZE
CATAPULT DEMARCHE DISLODGE
DISPLACE MOTIVATE
(— A RESOLUTION) FIRST
(— ABOUT) WEND DISPACE
SHUFFLE CONVERSE LOCOMOTE
(— ACROSS) THWART
(— ACTIVELY) YANK
(— AIMLESSLY) BOGUE
(— ALONG) SHOG
(— APART) SPREAD
(— AS IN STUPOR) DAVER
(— ASIDE) SKEW
(— ASUNDER) SINGLE
(— AT TOP SPEED) LICK
(— AWAY) CUT MOG DECAMP
RECEDE
(— AWKWARDLY) HODGE HIRSEL
LARRUP SHAMBLE
(— BACK) FADE ARSLE RECUR
RECEDE RETIRE RETREAT
(— BACKWARD AND FORWARD) GIG
SWAY DARTLE DIDDLE SHUFFLE
SHUTTLE
(— BOOM OR SAIL) JIB
(— BRISKLY) FAN HALE STIR FRICK
FRIKE FRISK KNOCK SQUIRT
TRANCE TRAVEL WHIPPET
(— BY FITS AND STARTS) JIFFLE
(— BY JERKS) HITCH JIGGET JIGGLE
JINKLE
(— BY SMALL SHOCKS) JOG
(— BY WHEELS) ROLL TRUNDLE

(— CHESS PIECE) DEVELOP
(— CLUMSILY) HOIT JOLL PAUT
BARGE KEVEL HIRSEL LUMBER
TOLTER GALUMPH STUMBLE
(— DIAGONALLY) CATER
(— DOWN) SILE STOOP DECLINE
DESCEND
(— FORCIBLY) SHOVE
(— FORWARD) BREAK ADVANCE
PROGREDE
(— FURTIVELY) LEER GLIDE SLINK
SLIVE SNEAK STEAL
(— GRADUALLY) EDGE
(— HAPHAZARDLY) BUCKET
(— HASTILY) SCUR SKIRR
(— HAUGHTILY) SWOOP
(— HEAVILY) LUG LUMP FLUMP
LUMBER
(— IN AGITATION) SEETHE
(— IN CIRCLES) MILL PURL
(— IN MARBLES) FULK
(— IN RIPPLES) CURL
(— IN SHUFFLING MANNER) MOSEY
(— IN SMALL DEGREES) INCH
(— IN WATER) SQUELCH
(— IN WAVES) LAP CRINKLE
(— INWARDLY) ENMOVE
(— JERKILY) JAG BUCK FLIP KICK
FLIRT BUCKET TWITCH
(— LANGUIDLY) MAUNDER
(— LAZILY) HULK
(— LEISURELY) AMBLE
(— LIGHTLY) BRUSH FLUFF
(— LOOSELY) SLOP
(— NERVOUSLY) DITHER
(— NIMBLY) KILT WHIP DANCE
(— OFF) FIRK RYNT MORRIS
(— ON) MOG VAMP SUCCEED
WHIGFARE
(— OUT OF SIGHT) SINK
(— OUT) BLOW
(— QUICKLY) BOB FIG DUCK FIRK
FLAX FLIT GIRD JINK KITE WHAP
WHEW YANK FLASH GLENT SKEET
SKITE SPANK SQUIB STAVE STOUR
THROW NIDDLE STRIKE WALLOP
SKIMMER
(— QUIETLY) SLIP
(— RAPIDLY) BANG BOLT BUZZ
HEEL HURL THUD CHASE GLINT
SCOUR CAREER GIGGIT HURTLE
AGITATE CLATTER HIGHTAIL
(— RESTLESSLY) FIG FIKE ITCH
SQUIB JIFFLE KELTER
(— SHAKILY) HOTTER
(— SIDEWISE) CRAB EDGE SIDLE
SLENT
(— SLOWLY) LAG MOG INCH PANT
PAUT SLUG BOGUE CRAWL CREEP
DRAWL FUDGE SLOOM SNAIL
HAGGLE LINGER TRINTLE
(— SMOOTHLY) SLIP DRIFT FLOAT
GLIDE SLEEK GLISSADE
(— SPIRALLY) GYRATE
(— STEADILY) FORGE
(— STEALTHILY) GLIDE SLINK
SMOOT SNAKE
(— STIFFLY) CRAMBLE CRAMMEL
(— SUDDENLY) BOLT LASH YERK

GLENT START FLOUNCE STARTLE
(— **SWIFTLY**) CUT FLY BOOM LEAP
RAKE SCUD SPIN BREEZE COURSE
SWIFTEN
(— **THROUGH AIR**) FLY
(— **TO AND FRO**) FAN FLOP DODGE
SHAKE WIGWAG AGITATE
(— **TO ANOTHER PLACE**) ADJOURN
(— **TO LEEWARD**) DRIVE
(— **UNEASILY**) FIDGET
(— **UNSTEADILY**) BICKER BUMBLE
FALTER HOBBLE WABBLE WAMBLE
WELTER WOBBLE BLUNDER
STAGGER STUMBLE
(— **UP AND DOWN**) BOB HOWD
SEESAW TEETER
(— **UPWARD**) ARISE ASCEND
GRADUATE
(— **VESSEL**) KEDGE
(— **VIGOROUSLY**) FLOG STRAY
(— **VIOLENTLY**) DASH FLOG HURL
LASH LEAP SWASH AGITATE
COMMOVE
(— **WAVERINGLY**) FLEET
(— **WEAKLY**) FLAG
(— **WITH BEATING MOTION**) FLAP
(— **WITH EFFORT**) ACHE
(— **WITH LEAPS**) SKIP SPRING
(— **WITH NOISY ACTIVITY**) BUSTLE
(— **WITH SHORT TURNS**) ZIGZAG
(**CHESS** —) KEY COOK NECK PLOY
GAMBIT KEYMOVE
(**SUCCESSFUL** —) SCORE
(**SUDDEN** —) GAMBADE
MOVED MOSSO ANIMATE FRANTIC
(— **BY LOVE**) AMOROUS
(**EASILY** —) FLESHLY SKINLESS
MOVEMENT EDDY MOTO PLAY STIR
CARRY CAUSE FLICK FLISK FLOAT
FRONT GESTE MUDGE TREND UKIYO
ACTION CURSUS ENTREE MOMENT
MOTION PIAFFE SPRAWL STROKE
CURRENT FURIANT GAMBADO
GESTURE KINESIS PIAFFER UKIYOYE
BUSINESS FEMINISM FUTURISM
HASKALAH STIRRING
(— **BY ORGANISMS**) TAXIS
(— **FOR POLITICAL UNION**) ENOSIS
(— **FROM POINT TO POINT**)
PASSAGE
(— **IN BULLFIGHT**) SUERTE
(— **OF AIR**) SPIRIT
(— **OF CHORUS**) STROPHE
(— **OF CLOUDS**) CARRY
(— **OF HORSE**) LEVADE
(— **OF LOOM**) MOUSING
(— **OF PROTOPLASM**) CYCLOSIS
(— **OF ROPE**) SURGE
(— **OF SHIP**) STERNWAY
(— **OF TIDE**) LAKIE
(— **OF TROOPS**) LIFT
(— **TOWARD GOAL**) STRIDE
(**AGITATED** —) WORKING
(**ART** —) CUBISM
(**BACKWARD** —) BACKUP BACKLASH
BACKWASH
(**BALLET** —) FRAPPE FOUETTE
FLICFLAC
(**BOBBING** —) BOBBLE

(**BODILY** —) ACTION
(**BOWEL** —) LAXATION
(**BOXING** —) SPAR
(**BRISK** —) SNAP
(**CIRCULAR** —) CYCLING
(**CLEVER** —) PAW
(**DANCE** —) BRISE CLOSE GIGUE
GLIDE SPIRAL BATTERIE
(**DARTING** —) FLIRT
(**DOWNWARD** —) DECLINE
(**DROLL** —) GAMBADE GAMBADO
(**ENLIGHTENMENT** —) HASKALAH
(**EXPANSION** —) BOOM
(**FENCING** —) VOLT
(**FLAPPING** —) FLAFF
(**FORWARD** —) SWEEP ADVANCE
PROGRESS INCESSION
(**FROLICKING** —) FRISK GAMBOL
(**GRADUAL** —) CREEPISM
(**GYMNASTIC** —) KIP SWING
DISMOUNT
(**HUMOROUS** —) BURLA
(**INDEPENDENCE** —) SWADESHI
(**INVOLUNTARY** —) REFLEX
(**JERKING** —S) BALLISM
(**JERKY** —) SNATCH
(**LATERAL** —) LEEWAY
(**MASS** —) STAMPEDE
(**MILITARY** —) BOUND MANEUVRE
(**MUSICAL** —) AIR DUET BURLA
DUMKA LARGO ENTREE FINALE
SARABAND SYMPHONY
(**OSCILLATING** —) HUNT
(**PAINTING** —) FAUVISM
(**POETRY** —) IMAGISM
(**POLITICAL** —) LEFTISM GAULLISM
(**QUICK** —) PAW DART WHIP YERK
GLENT SHAKE GLANCE
(**RATIONALISTIC** —) DEISM
(**REELING** —) STAGGER
(**RELIGIOUS** —) JOCISM STUNDISM
(**RETROGRADE** —) SLIP CREEP
(**RETURN** —) BACKHAUL
(**RHYTHMIC** —) DANCE
(**ROCKING** —) HOWD
(**ROWING** —) HOICK
(**SKILLED** —) SUERTE
(**SPASMODIC** —) JUMP HICCUP
SPRUNT HICCOUGH
(**SPRINGY** —) LILT
(**STEALTHY** —) SLINK
(**SUDDEN** —) HITCH SPANG START
FLICKER
(**SWAYING** —) SWAG
(**SWIFT** —) SWOOSH
(**THEOLOGICAL** —) ARIANISM
(**TUMULTUOUS** —) HORROR
EMOTION
(**TURNING** —) CARACOLE
(**UP AND DOWN** —) SEESAW
(**UPWARD** — **OF VESSEL**) SCEND
(**UPWARD** —) BULGE SCEND
(**WALKING** —) AMBLE
(**WATCH** —) EBAUCHE BAGUETTE
(**ZIGZAG** —) TACK
MOVER MOTIVE
MOVIE (ALSO SEE MOTION PICTURE)
FLICK FLICKS SLEEPER
MOVING WAY HIGH ASTIR GOING

QUICK AFLOAT MOVENT ANIMATE
CURRENT AMBULANT FLITTING
POIGNANT TOUCHING
(— **ABOUT**) AROUND AMBULANT
(— **AIMLESSLY**) ERRANT
(— **BACKWARDS**) CRAB
(— **DOWN LINE**) ACTIVE
(— **FORWARD**) ADVANCE
(— **HAPHAZARDLY**) AFLOAT
(— **IN MANY DIRECTIONS**) DIFFUSE
(— **RAPIDLY**) STICKLE SKELPING
(— **SLOWLY**) SOFT GLACIAL
(— **TO AND FRO**) AGITATED
(**NOT** —) STICKY STABILE
MOVINGLY PATETICO
MOW CUT BARB GOAF SKIM CRADLE
SCYTHE SICKLE DESECATE
(— **BEANS**) THROAT
(— **FOR STORING GRAIN**) TOSS
(— **OF CORN**) CANSH
(**HAY** —) TASS
MOWER MEADER
(**FOREMOST** —) LORD
MOWING MATH MOWTH SHEAR
MOZAMBIQUE (**LAKE OF** —) CHUALI
NHAVARRE
(**RIVER OF** —) SAVE MSALU
LUGENDA ZAMBEZI
(**TOWN OF** —) TETE BEIRA ZUMBO
CHEMBA PAFURI
MOZZETTA CAMAIL
MR HERR SIGNOR SIGNIOR SIGNORE
MRS FRAU MISS PANI HANOUM
SENORA SENHORA SIGNORA
GOODWIFE
MUCH FAR FELE MICH REAL WELL
GREAT HEAPS MOLTO MOULT SIZES
MICKLE MUCHLY ABUNDANT
MUCHWHAT
(— **CALLED FOR**) LEEFTAIL
(**PRETTY** —) GAILY GAYLY
(**SO** —) ALL SUCH TANTO
INSOMUCH
(**TOO** —) TROP TROPPO
(**VERY** —) ALL BADLY GREAT HEAPS
LOADS SWITHE SWYTHE APLENTY
GEYLIES GREATLY
MUCILAGE GUM MUCUS MUCAGO
MUCILAGINOUS MALACOID
MUCK CACK SOIL
MUCOID BLENNOID
MUCUS SNOT MUCOR BUBBLE
MUCAGO PHLEGM SNIVEL PITUITE
MUD DAB FEN CLAY DIRT FANC
GLAR LAIR MIRE MOIL SAUR SIND
SLAB SLEW SLOB SLOP SLUB SLUD
SLUE SLUR SUMP CLART FANGO
GLAUR GUMBO SLAKE SLIME SLOSH
SLUSH SPOSH SQUAD WAISE
PELOID SLOUGH SLUDGE CLABBER
GUTTERS MURGEON SLOBBER
SLODDER SLUDDER SLUTHER
SULLAGE
(**LACUSTRINE** —) GYTTJA
MUDAR AK AKUND ASHUR MADOR
YERCUM AKMUDDAR
MUDCAP ADOBE
MUD CAT FLATHEAD
MUDCAT STATE MISSISSIPPI

MUDDLE MIX BALL DOZE HASH MASH MESS MULL MUZZ SOSS ADDLE SNAFU BEMUSE BURBLE FOITER FUDDLE HUDDLE JUMBLE MAFFLE MIZZLE MOFFLE MUCKER POTHER PUDDLE TANGLE BECLOUD BEDEVIL BLUNDER FLUSTER POOTHER STUPEFY BEFUDDLE BEWILDER CONFOUND DISORDER FLIUNDER

MUDDLED ADDLE BEERY FOGGY FUZZY MUSED MUZZY DRUMLY GROGGY BESOTTED CONFUSED

MUDDY DEEP FOUL GLET OOZY SICK DIRTY DROVY DUBBY GUMLY SLAKY CLAGGY CLARTY CLASHY DREGGY DROUMY DRUMLY LIMOUS PUDDLY SALLOW SLABBY SLOBBY SLOPPY SLUBBY SLUDGY TURBID CLATCHY GUTTERY MUDDIFY MUDDISH SLOUGHY CLABBERY LUTULENT SLOBBERY

(— BY STIRRING) STUDDLE

MUDFISH BOWFIN KOMTOK

MUDFLOW LAHAR MUDSPATE

MUDGUARD WING CUTTOO SPLASHER

MUDHOLE PULK SLOUGH LOBLOLLY

MUD MINNOW DOGFISH MUDFISH

MUD PUPPY DOGFISH

MUERMO ULMO

MUFF BLOW BOBBLE MUFFLE SNUFFKIN

MUFFIN COB GEM SINK COBBE HAZEL SINKER MANCHET

MUFFLE MOB MOP PAD DAMP DULL MUTE NOSE WRAP BUMBLE DEADEN MUZZLE SHROUD STIFLE ENVELOP

(— A BELL) CLAM

(— THE HEAD) MOBLE

MUFFLED DEAD DEAF DULL CLOSE THICK HOLLOW INWARD WRAPPED

MUFFLER SCARF MUFFLE SILENCER

MUG TOT CANN FACE STEIN NOGGIN PEWTER SEIDEL CANETTE GODDARD BLACKPOT SCHOPPEN

(ALE —) TOBY

(LIQUOR —) CAN GUN

MUGGER GOA

MUGGING YOKING

MUGGINS SNIFF

MUGGY FOZY MUNGY PUGGY STICKY MUGGISH PUTHERY

MUGWORT BULWAND MUGWEED

MUISCA CHIBCHA

MUISHOND ZORIL ZORILLE

MULATTO PARDO GRIFFE GRIQUA GRIFFIN TERCERON

MULBERRY AL AAL ACH AUTE KOZO MORE WAUKE ALROOT MURREY MORELLO SOURBUSH SYCAMINE

MULBERRY FIG SYCAMORE

MULCT FINE CHECK AMERCE SCONCE FORFEIT PENALTY

MULE BUCKER HYBRID ACEMILA IRONMAN JARHEAD JUGHEAD RATTAIL SUMPTER CENCERRO HARDTAIL QUADROON QUATERON

(DROVE OF —S) ATAJO MULADA

MULE ARMADILLO MULITA

MULE DRIVER SKINNER

MULE SHOE PLANCHE

MULETEER ASSMAN ARRIERO

MULISH STUPID STUBBORN

MULL CHAW BOSOM FETTLE MULMUL STEATIN

MULLEIN TORCH AGLEAF ICELEAF DOVEWEED FELTWORT FOXGLOVE HAGTAPER LUNGWORT VERBASCO

MULLER DAMPENER

MULLET BOBO LISA LIZA BOURI GARAU KANAE MOLET HARDER MULLOID GOATFISH MUGILOID SPRINGER

(UNPIERCED —) STAR

MULLOWAY JEWFISH KINGFISH SCIAENID

MULTICOLORED CALICO

MULTIFARIOUS MANIFOLD

MULTIFARIOUSNESS VARIETY

MULTIFORM DIVERSE

MULTILINGUAL POLYGLOT

MULTIPLE DECUPLE SEPTUPLE

MULTIPLICAND FACIEND

MULTIPLICATION INCREASE DUPLATION

MULTIPLICITY MULTEITY

MULTIPLIER FACIENT COFACTOR

MULTIPLY VIE BREED LAYER DOUBLE INVOLVE ENGENDER INCREASE MANIFOLD

MULTITUDE ARMY CRAM HEAP HIVE HOST ROUT RUCK CLOUD CROWD FLOTE POWER SHOAL SWARM HIRSEL HOTTER LEGION MAMPUS MEINIE NATION THRONG SMOTHER

(PL.) FLOCKS

MULTITUDINOUS MYRIAD MANIFOLD NUMEROUS

MULTIVALENT POLYAD

MULTURE THIRL THIRLAGE

MUM CLUM DARK MUMMER

MUMBLE CHEW MUMP BROCK CHELE MOUTH CHAVEL FAFFLE FUMBLE HOTTER HUMMER MAFFLE MOFFLE PALTER DRUMBLE FLUMMER GRUMBLE

MUMBLER MAFFLER

MUMBLETY-PEG KNIFE

MUMMER ACTOR GUISER GUISARD

MUMMERY MORRIS HODENING PUPPETRY

MUMMICHOG MUDFISH

MUMMY CONGO MUMMIA SKELET

MUMMY BROWN BAY SNUFF TAMARACK

MUMMY CASE SLEDGE

MUMPS BRANKS

MUNCH CHEW CHUMP MANGE MUNGE

MUND GRITH

MUNDANE WORLD EARTHLY FLESHLY SECULAR TERRENE SUBSOLAR

MUNG BEAN MUG GRAM MONGOE BALATONG

MUNIA MAYA PADDA

MUNICIPAL TOWN

MUNICIPALITY CITY TOWN CABILDO

MUNIFICENCE BOUNTY ROYALTY

MUNIFICENT ROYAL LIBERAL MUNIFIC PROFUSE MAGNIFIC PRINCELY

MUNJ MOONJA MANJEET

(CULMS OF —) SIRKI SIRKY

MUNTIACUS CERVULUS

MUNTJAC KAKAR RATWA KIDANG

MURAL TOPIA FRESCO

MURCIA (RIVER OF —) SEGURA

(TOWN OF —) MULA LORCA TOTANA

MURDER BANE KILL SLAY BLOOD BURKE DEATH SCRAG FELONY MURDUM KILLING MURTHER THUGGEE HOMICIDE MASSACRE THUGGERY THUGGISM

MURDERER BANE CAIN KILLER ASSASSIN

MURDEROUS FELL GORY CRUEL FELON BLOODY SAVAGE DEATHFUL

MURKINESS GLOOM

MURKY DARK BLACK DIRTY MIRKY MUDDY CLOUDY PUDDLY

MURMUR HUM BRUM BURR CLUM HUZZ MUSE BROOL GRANK INKLE MOURN RUMOR SOUCH SOUGH BABBLE GRUDGE GRUTCH HUMMER MUTTER PIPPLE RUMBLE MURGEON WHIMPER WHISPER WHITTER COMPLAIN

(— AGREEABLY) CHIRM

(CONFUSED —) BABBLE

(DEEP —) BROOL

MURMURING BUZZ BRABBLE MURGEON RUMOROUS

MURRAH SURTI

MURRAL DALAG

MURRE TINK ARRIE LUNGIE STRANY TINKER ROCKBIRD

MURREY SANGUINE

MUSA SABA

MUSANG POWCAT POLECAT

MUSCA FLY

MUSCADINE BULLACE

MUSCAT (SEE OMAN)

MUSCLE EYE LIRE THEW FLESH MOUSE SINEW BENDER BICEPS CORACO FLEXOR LACERT PENNON RECTUS SOLEUS TENSOR AGONIST AMBIENS CANINUS DELTOID DILATOR ERECTOR EVERTOR FLECTOR GLUTEUS ILIACUS LEVATOR MUSCULE NASALIS OBLIQUE ROTATOR SCALLOP TRICEPS VAGINAL ABDUCTOR ADDUCTOR ADJUSTER ANCONEUS ARRECTOR BIVENTER DIDUCTOR EXTENSOR GEMELLUS GRACILIS INVERTOR MASSETER MENTALIS OBLIQUUS OMOHYOID OPPONENS PALMARIS PATHETIC PECTORAL PERONEUS PROCERUS PRONATOR RETENTOR SCALENUS SERRATUS SPINALIS SPLENIUS TEMPORAL TIBIALIS

(HAVING LUMPY —S) LOADED

(PL.) BRAWN THEWS

MUSCLE SUGAR INOSITE INOSITOL

MUSCOVY DUCK PATO SCOVY
MUSCULAR ROPY HUSKY THEWY
BRAWNY ROBUST STRONG TOROSE
ATHLETIC
MUSCULATURE DETRUSOR
MUSE CLIO DUMP REVE AMUSE
DREAM ERATO STUDY THINK THALIA
URANIA EUTERPE REFLECT
CALLIOPE COGITATE CONSIDER
MEDITATE POLYMNIA RUMINATE
(PL.) PIERIDES
MUSEUM MUSEE
MUSH KASHA SLUSH MUSHER
SEPAWN SOFKEE POLENTA
SAGAMITE SCRAPPLE
MUSHROOM FAT CEPE FLAT DEATH
MITRA AGARIC BEAVER BUTTON
FUNGUS BLEWITS BOLETUS
BROILER LEPIOTA MUSHRUMP
WHITECAP
MUSHY SOPPY
MUSIC RAG DRAG GLEE JAZZ NOME
CANOR CHIME GIMEL GYMEL MURKY
NOISE SWING DREHER MUSICA
DESCANT FORLANA LANCERS
LANDLER MUSICAL MUSICRY
FALSETTO FANDANGO GUARACHA
(CALYPSO —) GOOMBAY
(CONCERTED —) ENSEMBLE
(EVENING —) DREAM SERENA
(IDENTIFYING —) SIG
(LIVELY —) GALOP FURLANA
(MORNING —) AUBADE
(RESOUNDING —) HIGGAION
(SAD —) MESTO
(SENTIMENTAL —) SCHMALZ
SCHMALTZ
(STACCATO —) SECCO
MUSICAL LYRIC SWEET LIQUID
LYRICAL TUNEFUL HARMONIC
NUMEROUS
MUSICAL INSTRUMENT GLY GUE
KIN TAR UKE ZEL ALTO ASOR BELL
CRUT DRUM GLEE GLEW GORA
HARP HORN LIRA LUTE LYRE OBOE
SANG SAWM TAAR TUBA VINA VIOL
ANVIL AULOS BANJO BLOCK BUGLE
CELLO CHENG CRWTH CUICA
DOMRA FLUTE GORAH GOURA
GUDOK GUIRO GUSLA GUSLE
KAZOO NABLA ORGAN REBAB
REBEC ROCTA RUANA SAROD
SHAWM SHENG TARAU TELYN
TRUMP VIOLA ZANZE ZINKE BALAFO
BONANG CABASA CITOLE CORNET
CROUTH CYMBAL DOUCET FIDDLE
GENDER GLARIN GUITAR GUSLEE
JARANA RAPPEL REBECK RIBIBE
SABECA SANTIR SPINET TABRET
TREBLE TYMPAN URHEEN VIOLET
VIOLIN ZITHER ALTHORN ANGELOT
ANKLONG ARGHOOL BAGPIPE
BANDORE BANDURA BASSOON
BAZOOKA CELESTA CHEKKER
CITHARA CLARINA CLAVIER CLAVIOL
DICHORD DOLCIAN DOLCINO
DULCIAN FISTULA FLUTINA GAMELIN
GITTERN HELICON KANTELE
MAGADIS OCARINA PANDURA

PIBCORN RACKETT SAMISEN
SARANGI SARINDA SAXHORN
SERPENT SISTRUM THEORBO
TRUMPET UKULELE URANION
ADIAPHON AKALIMBA AUTOHARP
AUTOPHON BARBITON CALLIOPE
CASTANET CLARINET CORNPIPE
CRESCENT DULCIMER DYOPHONE
EUPHONON FIDICULA FLAUTINO
HORNPIPE HUMSTRUM KRUMHORN
LAPIDEON MELODION NEGILOTH
NEHILOTH PENORCON PHONIKON
PSALTERY SCHWEGEL SERINGHI
SOURDINE SYMPHONY TAMBOURA
TAROGATO TRICHORD TROMBONE
VIRGINAL ZAMBOMBA
(PL.) BRASS FAMILY STRINGS
MUSICALITY HARMONY
MUSIC HALL GAFF MELODEON
MUSICIAN BARD WAIT ASAPH LINOS
VIOLA BOPPER MUSICO VIOLER
VIOLIN BANDMAN BOPSTER CELLIST
GAMBIST ORPHEUS TWANGER
VIOLIST KORAHITE MARIACHI
MINSTREL MUSICKER THRUMMER
TWANGLER
(PL.) ENSEMBLE WAITSMEN
MUSING PENSIVE MUSARDRY
MUSK MOOST CATTAIL AMBRETTE
FIXATIVE
MUSK DEER CERVID KASTURA
MUSKELLUNGE LONGE MUSKIE
MUSKET FUSIL FUZIL MATCH
DRAGON JINGAL ENFIELD GINGALL
BANDHOOK BISCAYEN CULVERIN
ESCOPETA SNAPHAAN TOPHAIKE
MUSKET BALL GOLI
MUSKETEER FUSILEER STRELITZ
MUSKET FORK GAFFLE
MUSKMELON MANGO ATAMON
WUNGEE SPANSPEK
MUSKOGEE CREEK SEMINOLE
MUSK OX OVIBOS
MUSKRAT SQUASH ONDATRA
MUSQUASH
MUSK SHREW SONDELI
MUSK TURTLE STINKER STINKPOT
MUSKWOOD CAOBA
MUSKY MOSCHATE
MUSLIM LAZ ALIM SIDI SWAT TURK
ARAIN HAFIZ IBADHI KAZAKH
TURBAN ABBADID AYYUBID BAGIRMI
BASHKIR IBADITE KHAKSAR
MUDEJAR SUNNITE ALAOUITE
ISLAMIST ISLAMITE QADARITE
SIFATITE
(— BEADS) TASBIH
(— BROTHERHOOD) TARIQA
(— CHIEF) RAIS REIS
(— DOCTRINE) TAWHID
(— FOUNDATION) WAKF WAQF
(— JUDGE) CAID QAID
(— MYSTIC) SUFI
(— PLAY) TAZIA
(— PRACTICE) PURDAH
(— PRINCIPLE) TAQIYA
(— SCHOLARS) ULAMA ULEMA
(— SECT) WAHHABI MURJIITE
(— TOMB) TABUT

(— TREE) TUBA
(PL.) SHIA SHIAH SUNNI
MUSLIN BAN MULL DORIA SWISS
GURRAH MULMUL SHALEE SHILLA
TANJIB BETEELA FACTORY JAMDANI
ORGANDY STENTER SEERHAND
TARLATAN
(PL.) COSSAS
MUSS FUFFLE RUMPLE GLOMMOX
UNDRESS
MUSSEL CLAM UNIO NAIAD ANODON
JINGLE LACERT MUCKET PALOUR
BIVALVE GLOCHID MYTILID UNIONID
BULLHEAD DEERHORN
MUSSELCRACKER BISKOP
MUST BIT BUD BUT MAN MAY MUN
BOOD MAUN SAPA STUM DULCE
SHALL
(— BE TAKEN) SUM
(— NOT) MAUNNA
MUSTACHE WALRUS VALANCE
WHISKER
MUSTACHE MONKEY MOUSTOC
MUSTANG PONY BRONCO SPHINX
MUSTARD CRESS SENVY SINEWY
AWLWORT CADLOCK KEDLOCK
SINAPIS AUBRIETA CHADLOCK
CHARLOCK FLIXWEED
MUSTARD GAS YPERITE
MUSTELUS GALEUS
MUSTER LEVY RAISE SPUNK GATHER
HOSTING MARSHAL RECRUIT
MUSTINESS FUST MUST
MUSTY HOAR FUNKY FUSTY HOARY
MOLDY MUCID RAFTY VINNY FOISTY
FROWZY FOUGHTY FROWSTY
COBWEBBY
MUTABLE FICKLE MUTATORY
VARIABLE
MUTATE SPORT
MUTATION SHIFT SPORT CHANGE
MUANCE SILKIE ANAGRAM
(VOWEL —) UMLAUT
MUTE PAD DUMB ECHO LENE SURD
BLACK MEDIA WHIST DAMPER
MUFFLE SILENT STIFLE TENUIS
SORDINE SOURDINE
(— FOR TRUMPET) DERBY
MUTED DULL SORDO STILL
DISCREET SOURDINE
MUTENESS SILENCE DUMBNESS
MUTILATE MAR HACK MAIM BREAK
GARBLE INJURE MANGLE MARTYR
MITTLE CONCISE CASTRATE
EMBEZZLE
(— AN ANIMAL) LAW
MUTILATION STRIP
MUTINEER PANDY MUTINADO
MUTINOUS UNRULY
MUTINY REVOLT STRIFE
MUTISM ALALIA
MUTTER CROOL MOTRE HOTTER
HUMMER MUMBLE MURMUR PATTER
THROAT CHANNER CHUNNER
CHUNTER GRUMBLE MAUNDER
TOOTMOOT
MUTTERING GROWL
MUTTON BRAXY VIFDA VIVDA
MOUTON BRAXIES

(LEG OF —) CABOB WABBLER
 WOBBLER
MUTTONBIRD OII
MUTTONFISH SAMA ABALONE
 EELPOUT MOJARRA
MUTUAL COMMON
MUZZLE NOSE MOUTH SNOUT
 FOREFACE
 (— FOR FERRET) COPE
 (— OF CANNON) CHOPS
MUZZLE-LOADER CAPLOCK
 MUZZLER
MYALL YARRAN WARRIGAL
MYCELIUM SPAWN MYCELE
 TAPESIUM
MYCTERIA TANTALUS
MY DEAR MACHREE
MYIASIS STRIKE

MYNA MINA MYNAH GRACKLE
MYOCOMMA FLAKE
MYRIAD HOST COUNTLESS
MYRIAPOD JULID POLYPOD
 PAUROPOD MILLIPEDE
MYRRH STACTE
MYRTLE MYRT LILAC BALTIC
 JAROOL ARRAYAN JAPONICA
 RAMARAMA
MYSELF SELF MYSEN HERSELF
MYSID SHRIMP
MYSOST PRIMOST
MYSTERIOUS DIM DARK DEEP EERY
 SELI EERIE SABLE WAKON ARCANE
 EXOTIC MYSTIC OCCULT SECRET
 CRYPTIC PUCKISH UNCANNY
 UNCOUTH ABSTRUSE ESOTERIC
 NUMINOUS SIBYLLIC

MYSTERIOUSLY DARKLY EERILY
 HEIMLICH
MYSTERY MIST RUNE CABALA
 ENIGMA SECRET ARCANUM
 SECRECY
MYSTIC SUFI OCCULT ORPHIC
 SECRET EPOPTIC ESOTERIC
MYSTICAL MISTY MYSTIC ANAGOGIC
 TELESTIC
MYSTICALLY GHOSTLY
MYSTICISM SUFIISM
MYSTIFY BEAT BEFOG BOTHER
 MUDDLE PUZZLE BECLOUD
 CONFUSE BEWILDER
MYTH SAGA FABLE LEGEND MYTHOS
 ALLEGORY
MYTHICAL FABLED FABULOUS
 FICTIOUS

N EN NU NAN
NAASSENE OPHITE
NAB HAT NIB GRAB HEAD KNAB
CATCH SEIZE ARREST CLUTCH
COLLAR NIBBLE NOBBLE SNATCH
CAPTURE APPREHEND
NABAL (WIFE OF —) ABIGAIL
NABALOI IBALOI IGOROT
NABK NUBK NABAK NEBUK NABBUK
NEBACK NEBBUK NEBBUCK
NABOB DIVES NAWAB NOBOB
DEPUTY VICEROY GOVERNOR
PLUTOCRAT
(— **DEPUTY)** NAWAB
(PL.) NABOBRY
NACELLE CAR BOAT BASKET
CHASSIS COCKPIT SHELTER
NACHSCHLAG SPRINGER
AFTERNOTE
NACKET BOY CAKE LUNCH NOCKET
NACRE PEARL SHELLFISH
NADIR BATHOS BEDROCK
(OPPOSED TO —) ZENITH
NAG CUT TIT BAIT FRAB FRET FUSS
GNAW JADE PLUG PONY PROD
SNAG TWIT ANNOY COBRA HOBBY
HORSE SCOLD SKATE SNAKE STEED
TEASE BADGER BERATE BOTHER
DOBBIN GARRAN GLEYDE HAGGLE
HARASS HECKLE HECTOR KEFFEL
PADNAG PESTER PLAGUE WANTON
HACKNEY HENPECK TORMENT
DINGDONG HARANGUE IRRITATE
PARAMOUR
(AMBLING —) HOBBY
NAGA SEMA COBRA KABUI LHOTA
SNAKE
NAGKASSAR SURIGA
NAGOR TOHI ANTELOPE REEDBUCK
NAHANE KASKA
NAHOOR SHA SNA SHEEP URIAL
BHARAL OORIAL
NAHUATL AZTEC CAZCAN MEXICA
NAHUM ELKOSHITE
NAIAD NAIS NYMPH MUSSEL
HYDRIAD
NAIL CUT FIX HOB PIN TEN BOSS
BRAD BRAG BROD CLAW CLOY
DUMP HOOF PILE SLUG SPAD STUB
STUD TACK TRAP AFFIX CATCH
CLOUT DRIVE GROPE PLATE SCALE
SEIZE SPEED SPIKE SPRIG TALON
BULLEN CLENCH CLINCH COOLER
CORKER DETAIN FASTEN GARRON
HAMMER SECURE SINKER TACKET
TENTER TINGLE UNGUIS UNGULA
CAPTURE FASTENER HOLDFAST
ROSEHEAD SPARABLE SPIKELET
TENPENNY TRICOUNI
(— **BITING)** ONYCHOPHAGIA
(— **GROWTH)** ONYCHAUXIS
(HEADLESS —) SPRIG
(HOOKED —) TENTER TENTERHOOK
(INGROWN —) ONYXIS ACRONYX
(MARKING —) SPAD SPEED
(OLD HORSESHOE —) STUB
(SHOEMAKER'S —) SPARABLE
(TOED —) TOSHNAIL
NAILROD STICKWEED

NAIVE OPEN RACY FRANK GREEN
CANDID SIMPLE ARTLESS NATURAL
CHILDISH INNOCENT UNTAUGHT
CHILDLIKE GUILELESS INGENUOUS
UNTUTORED UNWORLDLY
(— **GIRL)** INGENUE
NAIVETE GREENNESS SIMPLICITY
NAKED BALD BARE MERE NUDE
OPEN CLEAR EXACT PLAIN STARK
BARREN CUERPO SCUDDY SIMPLE
EXPOSED LITERAL OBVIOUS
MANIFEST STRIPPED SMOCKLESS
UNADORNED UNCLOTHED
UNCOVERED
NAKED OAT PILLAS PILCORN
PILKINS
NAKEDWOOD MABI SNAKEWOOD
NAKHI MOSO MOSSO
NAMAYCUSH CREE FISH LAKER
LONGE LUNGE TOGUE TROUT
LONGUE SISCOWET
NAMBY-PAMBY INANE SILLY VAPID
CODDLE INSIPID KEEPSAKE
NAME DUB FIX NOM SET CALL CITE
FAME NAIL NOMB NOUN TERM
ALIAS CLAIM CLEPE COUNT ETHIC
NEVEN NOMEN POINT QUOTE STYLE
TITLE ADDUCE APPEAL GOSSIP
MONICA REPUTE SELECT ALLONYM
APPOINT BEHIGHT DECLARE
ENTITLE EPITHET MENTION MONIKER
SPECIFY VOCABLE CATEGORY
CHRISTEN COGNOMEN IDENTIFY
IDENTITY INDICATE ENUMERATE
(— **TABLET)** FACIA
(— **WRITTEN BACKWARDS)** ANANYM
(ADDED —) AGNAME AGNOMEN
(ALTERNATIVE —) BUNCH
(ANCESTOR'S —) EPONYM
(ANOTHER —) ALIAS
(ASSUMED —) PEN ALIAS
ONOMASTIC PSEUDONYM
SOBRIQUET
(BAD —) CACONYM
(DAY —) AHAU
(DERIVATION OF —) EPONYMY
(FIRST —) FORENAME PRAENOMEN
(GOOD —) HONOR CREDIT
(REGISTERED —) AFFIX
(TECHNICAL —) ONYM
(WELL-SUITED —) EUONYM
NAMED CITED HIGHT DUBBED
YCLEPT ONYMOUS YCLEPED
NAMELESS BAS
NAMELY FOR VIZ SCIL NOTED TOWIT
FAMOUS SCILICET
NAMEPLATE MASTHEAD
NAMESAKE EPONYM JUNIOR
HOMONYM
NANDI BANANDE MUNANDI KIPSIKIS
NANDU RHEA
NANISM DWARFISM
NANNAR SIN
NANNY GOAT NURSE
NANTICOKE TOAG
NAOMI MARA
(DAUGHTER-IN-LAW OF —) RUTH
NAOS CELLA SHRINE TEMPLE
NAP GIG NOD RAS CALK CAMP

DOWN DOZE FUZZ LINT PILE RUFF
SHAG WINK COVER DOVER FLUFF
GRASP SEIZE SLEEK SLEEP STEAL
CATNAP DROWSE SIESTA SNOOZE
EMERIZE SLUMBER
(TO RAISE —) TEASE
NAPE NOD CUFF NECK NUKE POLL
NUCHA NUQUE SCRAG SCURF
NODDLE SCRUFF TURMP NIDDICK
NAPERY LINEN DOILIES NAPKINS
NAPHTALITE ENAN AHIRA
NAPHTHA NEFTE PETROLEUM
NAPKIN CLOTH DOILY TOWEL
DIAPER NAPERY KERCHIEF
SUDATORY HANDCLOTH SERVIETTE
NAPLES BISCUIT LADYFINGER
NAPLESS HARD
NAPOLEON (— **III)** LOUIS
BOUSTRAPA
(BATTLE OF —) ULM ACRE JENA
WATERLOO
(BIRTHPLACE OF —) CORSICA
(BROTHER-IN-LAW OF —) MURAT
(GAME LIKE —) PAM
(ISLAND OF —) ELBA HELENA
CORSICA
(MARSHALL OF —) NEY
(MOTHER OF —) HORTENSE
(PLACE OF VICTORY FOR —) LODI
LIGNY
NAPPE DECKE
NAPPY ALE DISH DOWNY HEADY
WOOLY LIQUOR SHAGGY STRONG
WOOLLY COTTONY FOAMING
VILLOUS
NARCISSUS LILY PLANT CRINUM
EGOIST FLOWER LILIUM JONQUIL
(LOVED BY —) ECHO
(TRUMPET --) DAFFODIL
NARCOTIC KAT BANG DOPE DRUG
HEMP JUNK BHANG DAGGA ETHER
OPIUM HEROIN OPIATE ANODYNE
COCAINE CODEINE HASHISH
NARCEIN HYPNOTIC MORPHINE
TAKROURI DIACODION MARIJUANA
SOPORIFIC
(— **AGENT)** GAZER
(— **DOSE)** LOCUS
(— **PLANT)** DUTRA MANDRAKE
(SMALL AMOUNT OF —) SNIFTER
(PL.) JUNK STUFF
NARCOTINE OPIANE
NARD SPICE ANOINT RHIZOME
MUSKROOT SPIKENARD
NARDOO ARDOO NARDU CLOVER
NARGIL COCONUT
NARGILEH PIPE HOOKA HOOKAH
NARGHILE
NARK SPY VEX NOTE ANNOY TEASE
OBSERVE INFORMER IRRITATE
NARRA NAGA ASANA APALIT
NARRATE SPIN TELL BRUIT STATE
STORY DEPICT DETAIL DEVISE
RECITE RELATE REPORT DISCUSS
RECOUNT STORIFY DESCRIBE
REHEARSE
NARRATION TALE FABLE STORY
DETAIL ACCOUNT HAGGADA
SYNAXAR DELIVERY HAGGADAH

NARRATIVE EPIC JOKE MYTH SAGA TALE CONTE DRAMA FABLE PROSE STORY COMEDY JATAKA LEGEND ACCOUNT EPISODE HISTORY MEMOIRS MIDRASH NOVELLA PARABLE RECITAL ALLEGORY ANECDOTE APOLOGUE ARETALOGY HAGIOLOGY
(— **POEM**) EPIC EPOS SAGA
(**BRIEF** —) ANECDOTE
(PL.) ACTA EXEMPLA
NARRATOR TESTO TELLER RELATOR SAGAMAN TALESMAN RACONTEUR
NARROW JERK LEAN MEAN NEAR POKY SLIT TRUE BORNE CLOSE RIGID SCANT SHARP SMALL SOUND TAPER ANGUST BIASED LINEAR LITTLE MEAGER STRAIT STRICT TWITCH BIGOTED ERICOID LIMITED PRIMARY SLENDER THRIFTY CONDENSE CONTRACT PAROCHIAL
(— **DOWN STAVES**) BUCK
(— **DOWN**) CONFINE
(— **INLET**) RIA
(**NOT** —) CATHOLIC
(**VERY** —) HAIRBREADTH
NARROWED LISTED INSWEPT CONTRACT
NARROWING CAP CHOKE INTAKE STENOSIS
NARROWLY WIDE STRAITLY
NARROW-MINDED BORNE
NARROWNESS BIAS BIGOTRY
NARSINGA TRUMPET
NARTHECIUM ABAMA
NARTHEX HALL STOA ENTRY FOYER LOBBY PORCH PORTICO PRONAOS VESTIBULE
NASAB NUSUB KINSHIP
NASAL NOSY NARINE RHINAL TWANGY ADENOID STRINGY
NASCENCY BIRTH ORIGIN GENESIS BEGINNING
NASEBERRY SAPODILLA
NASHGAB OAF GOSSIP
NASI OFFICER PATRIARCH
NASICORN RHINOCEROS
NASTIKA ATHEIST
NASTURTIUM CAPUCINE NOSEWORT RADICULA STURSHUM STURTION
NASTY BAD PAH FOUL MEAN UGLY DIRTY FILTHY HORRID ODIOUS RIBALD BAGGAGE DEFILED HARMFUL OBSCENE SQUALID UNCLEAN INDECENT NAUSEOUS DANGEROUS MALICIOUS OFFENSIVE
NAT NOT DEMON SPIRIT
NATAL INBORN INNATE NATIVE GLUTEAL CONGENIAL
NATAL PLUM AMATUNGULA
NATANT AFLOAT FLOATING SWIMMING
NATATORIUM BATH POOL
NATCHEZ STINKER STINKARD
NATION BENI FOLK GEAT HOST LAND LEDE RACE VOLK AEDUI CASTE CLASS FANTE FANTI REALM STATE TRIBE FANTEE GEATAS PEOPLE WAGOGO ARVERNI

COUNTRY SOCIETY LANGUAGE COMMUNITY MULTITUDE
(— **SYMBOL**) FLAG CREST
(**HEBREW** —) JACOB
(**LARGE** —) COLOSSUS
NATIONAL CITIZEN FEDERAL GENTILE GENTILIC
(— **DEMOCRACY**) ENDEX
NATIONALISM JINGOISM PHYLETISM
NATIONALITY FLAG
NATIVE ITE RAW SON TAO BORN FREE GOOK HOME KIND LIVE NEIF WILD INNER NATAL PUNTI EPIROT GENIAL INBORN INNATE KINDLY NORMAL SIMPLE VIRGIN CITIZEN DENIZEN DZUNGAR ENDEMIC GENUINE NATURAL PAISANO POLISTA DOMESTIC GRASSCUT HABITUAL HOMEBORN HOMEMADE INHERENT LANDSMAN ORIGINAL PRIMEVAL PRISTINE RESIDENT YAMMADJI ABORIGINE CONGENIAL INGRAINED INHERITED INTRINSIC ORIGINARY TAWNYMOOR
(— **BEAR**) KOALA
(— **BEECH**) FLINDOSA
(— **MINERAL**) LIVE
(— **OF BENGAL**) KOL
(— **OF CHINA**) CELESTIAL
(— **OF FENS**) SLODGER
(— **OF FLORIDA KEYS**) CONK CONCH
(— **OF ILLINOIS**) SUCKER
(— **OF IRELAND**) BOGTROTTER
(— **OF LONDON**) COCKNEY
(— **OF LOW CLASS**) TAO
(— **OF MADAGASCAR**) HOVA
(— **OF MALAYA**) INFIEL
(— **OF MARITIME PROVINCES**) BLUENOSE
(— **OF N. CAROLINA**) TARHEEL
(— **OF NEW GUINEA**) BOONG
(— **OF NEW SOUTH WALES**) CORNSTALK
(— **OF PHILIPPINES**) GUGU
(— **OF SCOTLAND**) GEORDIE
(— **OF SOUTHERN ILLINOIS**) EGYPTIAN
(— **OF W. AUSTRALIA**) GROPER
(— **PLANT**) INDIGINE
(— **WHO TEACHES**) CATECHIST
(**BORN AND BRED AS A** —) CREOLE
(**FREE** —) TIMAWA
(**UNCIVILIZED** —) MYALL
NATIVITY BIRTH GENESIS GENITURE HOROSCOPE
NATTERJACK NEWT TOAD
NATTY CHIC NEAT POSH TIDY TRIG TRIM NIFTY SMART SPICY DAPPER JAUNTY SPRUCE FOPPISH
NATURAL RAW BORN EASY FOOL HOME KIND OPEN RACY REAL WILD NAIVE USUAL CANCEL CASUAL COMMON CONJON CRETIN DIRECT HOMELY INBORN INBRED INNATE KINDLY NATIVE NORMAL PHYSIC ARTLESS GENUINE QUADRUM REGULAR INHERENT LIFELIKE ORDINARY PHYSICAL UNCOINED

PRIMITIVE REALISTIC UNASSUMED UNFEIGNED
(— **LOGARITHM**) LN
(— **TALENT**) DOWER FLAIR
(**NOT** —) AFFECTED
NATURALIZE ADAPT ADOPT ACCUSTOM ACCLIMATE ENDENIZEN HABITUATE
NATURALLY SN KINDLY GENIALLY
NATURALNESS EASE NAIVETE
NATURE ILK BENT BIOS CAST CLAY FORM HAIR KIND MAKE MOOD RACE SORT TYPE COLOR OUSIA SHAPE STATE TENOR ANIMAL DHARMA FIGURE HEAVEN KIDNEY PHYSIS STRIPE ESSENCE FEATHER QUALITY SPECIES PRAKRITI UNIVERSE CHARACTER
(— **DIVINITY**) NYMPH
(— **GOD**) PAN
(— **GODDESS**) CYBELE ARTEMIS
(— **OF GOD**) DIVINITY
(— **PRINT**) PHYTOGRAPH
(— **SPIRIT**) NAT
(— **WORSHIP**) PHYSIOLATRY
(**APPARENT** —) STUDY
(**CONCEALED** —) LATENCY
(**DIVINE** —) DEITY
(**EMOTIONAL** —) HEART
(**ESSENTIAL** —) ESSE FORM GENIUS
(**HUMAN** —) FLESH MANHEAD MANKIND
(**INHERENT** —) GENIUS
(**INTRINSIC** —) BOTTOM
(**MORAL** —) ETHNOS
(**OF THE SAME** —) HOMOGENEOUS
(**ORGANIC** —) BIOS
(**PERT. TO** —) COSMO
(**ROUGH** —) SPINOSITY
(**SPECIAL** —) IDIOM
(**SPIRITUAL** —) INTERNAL
(**ULTIMATE** —) ESSENCE
NAUGHT NIL EVIL ZERO AUGHT NAGHT OUGHT CIPHER NOUGHT WICKED NOTHING USELESS WORTHLESS
NAUGHTY BAD PAW SAD EVIL WRONG PAWPAW SHREWD WICKED OBSCENE WAYWARD IMPROPER
NAUPATHIA SEASICKNESS
NAUSEA PALL QUALM DISGUST NAUSITY LOATHING SICKNESS ANTIPATHY DIZZINESS
NAUSEATE TURN TWIST WLATE REVOLT SICKEN DISGUST STOMACH DISTASTE
NAUSEATED ILL SICKISH QUALMISH SQUEAMISH
NAUSEATING NASTY WAUGH QUEASY BILIOUS FULSOME BRACKISH STAWSOME LOATHSOME REVOLTING SICKENING
NAUTICAL (ALSO SEE NAVIGATION) NAVAL MARINE MAUTIC MARINAL OCEANIC TARRISH MARITIME NAVIGABLE
(— **FLAG**) CORNET PENNON
NAUTILUS MOLLUSK ARGONAUT ARGONAUTA

(— **COMMANDER**) NEMO
NAVAHO DINE NAVAJO LONGHAIR
(— **GROUP**) OUTFIT
(— **RITE**) WAY
NAVAL SEA MARINE NAUTICAL
NAVIGABLE
(— **DEPOT**) BASE
(— **FORCE**) NAVY FLEET ARMADA
SQUADRON
(— **JAIL**) BRIG
NAVE HOB HUB NEF APSE BODY FIST
PACE AISLE NATHE NIEVE CENTER
NAVEL NOMBRIL OMPHALOS
UMBILICUS
NAVIGABLE BOATABLE PORTABLE
NAVIGATE KEEL SAIL DRIVE GUIDE
SKIFF STEER AVIATE COURSE
CRUISE DIRECT MANAGE TRAVEL
CONDUCT CONTROL JOURNEY
OPERATE TRAVERSE ASTROGATE
NAVIGATION HOMING VOYAGE
NAUTICS PASSAGE SAILING TRAFFIC
CABOTAGE SHIPPING
(— **MEASURE**) TON KNOT SEAM
FATHOM
(— **SYSTEM**) LORAN
NAVIGATOR FLYER NAVVY PILOT
AIRMAN AVIATOR COPILOT LABORER
AERONAUT SEAFARER SPACEMAN
NEPTUNIAN NEPTUNIST
NAVITE BASALT
NAVVY HAND WORKER LABORER
NAVIGATOR
NAVY FLEET SHIPFERD
(— **BOARD**) ADMIRALTY
(— **OFFICER**) CPO AIDE MATE
BOSUN CHIEF ENSIGN ADMIRAL
ARMORER CAPTAIN COMMANDER
COMMODORE
(— **RADIO OPERATOR**) SPARKS
(— **VESSEL**) PT SUB CARRIER
CRUISER FLATTOP DESTROYER
SUBMARINE TRANSPORT
NAWOB NABOB NUWAB RULER
VICEROY
NAY NO NAI NEI NOT DENY EVEN
NYET FLUTE NEVER DENIAL REFUSE
REFUSAL NEGATIVE
NAZARD STOP NASAT
NAZE NASE HEADLAND
NAZI BROWN HITLERITE
(— **SYMBOL**) FYLFOT SWASTIKA
NAZIM VICEROY GOVERNOR
NEANDERTHAL CAVEMAN
NEANIC IMMATURE YOUTHFUL
NEAR AD AT BY IN GIN KIN NAR AKIN
BAIN DEAR FAST GAIN HARD HEND
INBY NEXT NIGH ABOUT ANEAR
ANENT ASIDE CLOSE FORBY HANDY
HENDE JUXTA MATCH NUDGE
ROUND SHORT TOUCH ALMOST
AROUND BESIDE CLIMAX HEREBY
NARROW STINGY TOWARD WITHIN
ADVANCE AGAINST FORTHBY
SIMILAR THRIFTY VICINAL ADJACENT
APPROACH IMMINENT INTIMATE
(— **AKIN**) GERMANE
(— **POINT**) PP

(— **THE BEGINNING**) EARLY
FORMER
(— **THE EQUATOR**) LOW
(— **THE MOUTH**) ADORAL
(— **THE SURFACE**) EBB FLEET
(— **THE WIND**) HIGH AHOLD
(**CONVENIENTLY** —) HANDSOME
NEARBY AROUND GAINLY LOCALLY
ADJACENT
NEARER HITHER
(— **FRANCE**) CISALPINE
(— **ROME**) CISALPINE
(— **THE REAR**) AFTER
NEAREST NEXT EWEST CLOSEST
NEARMOST PROCHAIN IMMEDIATE
PROXIMATE
(— **THE STERN**) AFTERMOST
NEARLY GAIN JUST LIKE MOST
MUCH ABOUT ALMOST FECKLY
NEARSIGHTED MYOPIC PURBLIND
NEAT GIM NET COSH COWS DEFT
DINK FEEL FEIL GENT JIMP MACK
NICE OXEN PRIM PURE SMUG SNOD
SNUG TIDY TOSH TRIG TRIM BULLS
CLEAN CLEAR COMPT CRISP DINKY
DONCY DONSY DOUCE EXACT
FEATY FETIS JEMMY NATTY PREST
QUEME SMART SMIRK TERSE TIGHT
ADROIT BOVINE CATTLE CLEVER
DAINTY DAPPER DIMBER DONSIE
HEPPEN MINION POLITE QUAINT
SPANDY SPRUCE BANDBOX
CONCISE ORDERLY PERJINK
PRECISE REFINED SHAPELY
UNMIXED MENSEFUL SKILLFUL
STRAIGHT TASTEFUL DEXTEROUS
SHIPSHAPE UNDILUTED WHOLESOME
NEATLY SNUG DEFTLY FAIRLY
FEATLY SMARTLY SPRUCELY
NEATNESS MENSE DEFTNESS
ELEGANCE SPRUCERY
NEB EAR NIB TIP BEAK BILL NOSE
POINT SNOUT

NEBRASKA

CAPITAL: LINCOLN
COLLEGE: DANA DOANE
DUCHESNE HASTINGS
COUNTY: LOUP OTOE DEUEL
SARPY COLFAX NEMAHA
INDIAN: OTO OMAHA PONCA
PAWNEE
RIVER: LOGAN DISMAL PLATTE
ELKHORN NIOGRARA
STATE BIRD: MEADOWLARK
STATE FLOWER: GOLDENROD
STATE NICKNAME: CORNHUSKER
STATE TREE: ELM
TOWN: COZAD OMAHA GERING
UNIVERSITY: CREIGHTON

NEBRIS FAWNSKIN
NEBULA SKY CRAB SPOT VAPOR
BALAXY SPIRAL PLANETARY
NEBULIZE ATOMIZE
NEBULOUS DIM DARK HAZY FOGGY
MISTY MUDDY VAGUE CLOUDY
MYSTIC TURBID CLOUDED EVASIVE
SHADOWY UNCLEAR DREAMLIKE

NEBULA SKY CRAB SPOT VAPOR
GALAXY SPIRAL PLANETARY
NEBULIZE ATOMIZE
NEBULOUS DIM DARK HAZY FOGGY
MISTY MUDDY CLOUDY MYSTIC
TURBID CLOUDED SHADOWY
UNCLEAR
NECESSARILY NEEDS NEEDLY
PERFORCE
NECESSARY NEEDY PRIVY VITAL
FRIEND TOILET KINSMAN NEEDFUL
FORCIBLE INTEGRAL ESSENTIAL
INTRINSIC
(PL.) ALIMENT MISTERS
NECESSITATE FORCE IMPEL
COMPEL DEMAND ENTAIL OBLIGE
REQUIRE CONSTRAIN
NECESSITY USE CALL DUTY FATE
FOOD LACK MUST NEED TASK
WANT DRINK ANANKE BESOIN
MISTER MUSCLE NEEDBE URGENCY
PERFORCE
(— **OF MOVING**) ZUGZWANG
(**BY** —) PRESENTLY
(PL.) BREAD
NECK COL NUB PET CAPE CRAG
CROP HALS KISS WAKE BEARD
CHOKE CRAIG HALSE SCRAG SPOON
SWIRE TRAIL BEHEAD CARESS
CERVIX COLLET COLLUM FONDLE
STRAIT CHANNEL EMBRACE
ISTHMUS SQUEEZE TUBULUS
LALLYGAG
(— **ARTERY**) CAROTID
(— **MUSCLE**) SCALENUS
(— **OF BOTTLE**) THROTTLE
(— **OF LAMB**) TARGET
(— **OF VOLCANO**) CORE
(**BACK OF** —) NOD NAPE NUCH
NUQUE SCRUFF NIDDICK
(**PERT. TO** —) JUGULAR CERVICAL
(**RED** —) ROOINEK
NECK AND NECK TIE EVEN CLOSE
NECKBAND BAND COLLAR COLLET
SHIRTBAND
NECKCLOTH BOA TIE RUFF AMICE
CHOKE SCARF STOLE CHOKER
CRAVAT BURDASH NECKTIE
PANUELO STARCHER BARCELONA
SOLITAIRE STEINKIRK
NECKERCHIEF GIMP RAIL FOGLE
BELCHER FOULARD NECKLET
KERCHIEF NECKATEE NECKCLOTH
NECKENGER
NECKING COLLAR GORGERIN
NECKLACE BEE LEI TORC BEADS
CHAIN NOOSE CARCAN CHOKER
COLLAR GORGET SANKHA TAWDRY
TORQUE BALDRIC CHAPLET RIVIERE
SAUTOIR LAVALIER NEGLIGEE
ESCLAVAGE
NECKLINE COWL SCOOP
NECK RUFF FRAISE QUELLIO
NECKTIE BOW TIE ASCOT SCARF
CHOKER CRAVAT GRAVAT OVERLAY
(— **PARTY**) HANGING LYNCHING
NECROMANCER GOETIC MAGICIAN
NECROMANCY GOETY MAGIC

GRAMARY SORCERY WIZARDRY
EGROMANCY
NECROPOLIS CEMETERY
NECROPSY AUTOPSY
NECTAR N HONEY AMBROSIA
NECTAR BIRD EATER HONEY
SUNBIRD
NECTARINE NECTRON NECTARIN
NECTARY SPUR GLAND NECTARIUM
NEDDER ADDER
NEDDY HORSE DONKEY
NEE BORN
NEED ASK NUD LACK TAKE THAR
WANT CRAVE DRIVE THARF BEHOVE
BESOIN DEMAND DESIRE MISTER
STRAIT BEHOOVE NEEDHAM
POVERTY REQUIRE URGENCY
DISTRESS EXIGENCY MISCHIEF
EMERGENCE EXTREMITY NECESSITY
NEEDFIRE WILDFIRE
NEEDFUL VITAL INTEGRAL
ESSENTIAL NECESSARY REQUISITE
NEEDLE SEW VEX YEN ACUS DARN
GOAD TIER WIRE ANNOY BLUNT
POINT SHARP SPIKE STRAW STYLE
BODKIN DARNER STYLUS OBELISK
PRICKER PROVOKE SPICULE
TUMBLER
(— HOLE) EYE
(— SORTER) HANDER
(COMB. FORM) ACU
(PINE —) SPILL
(PINE —S) PININGS
(PL.) TWINKLES
NEEDLE BUG NEPID RANATRA
NEEDLEBUSH URY PINBUSH
NEEDLEFISH GAR SNOOK AGUJON
BELONID LONGJAW
NEEDLE GUN RIFLE DREYSE
NEEDLELIKE ACUATE ACERATE
ACEROSE ACEROUS ACIFORM
ACICULAR BELONOID SPLINTERY
NEEDLEMAN TAILOR
NEEDLESS AMOK
NEEDLEWORK SEWING SAMPLER
SEAMING TATTING KNITTING
WOOLWORK HEMSTITCH INSERTION
NEEDY BARE POOR INDIGENT
NEEDSOME HUNGARIAN PENNILESS
NEEP NEPE TURNIP
NE'ER-DO-WELL BUM PELF LOSEL
SCHLEMIEL SHIFTLESS WORTHLESS
NEFANDOUS IMPIOUS EXECRABLE
NEFARIOUS WICKED HEINOUS
IMPIOUS FLAGRANT HORRIBLE
INFAMOUS ATROCIOUS
NEGATE DENY SUBLATE
NEGATION NAY NOT EMPTY DENIAL
REFUSAL ANNULMENT NONENTITY
NEGATIVE NA NE NO CON NAE NAY
NIT NIX NON NOR NOT NUL DENY
FILM VETO NEVER NAYWARD
STAMPER APOPHATIC PRIVATIVE
(— PREFIX) IL IM IN IR UN DIS NON
(— PRINCIPLE) YIN
NEGLECT DEBT FAIL HANG OMIT
SLIP FAULT FORGO SHIRK SLOTH
WAIVE BYPASS CESSER FOREGO
FORGET IGNORE LACHES LOITER

PERMIT SLIGHT DEFAULT DISOBEY
FAILURE OVERSEE RESPECT
FORSLACK OMISSION OVERLOOK
OVERSLIP RECKLESS DISREGARD
MISLIPPEN OVERSIGHT PRETERMIT
NEGLECTED TACKY SHABBY
UNDONE DORMANT OBSOLETE
NEGLECTFUL LAX REMISS
CARELESS DERELICT HEEDLESS
RECKLESS DISSOLUTE
NEGLIGEE ROBE MANTEAU MATINEE
UNDRESS PEIGNOIR DISHABILE
NIGHTGOWN
NEGLIGENCE CULPA LACHES
DEFAULT LASCHETY DISREGARD
OVERSIGHT
NEGLIGENT LAX LASH SOFT SLACK
OVERLY REMISS CARELESS
DISCINCT SLOVENLY YEMELESS
DISSOLUTE
NEGLIGIBLE FAT
NEGOTIATE DEAL SELL BROKE
FLOAT TREAT TROKE TRUCK TRYST
ADVISE ASSIGN CONFER DICKER
DIRECT MANAGE PARLEY SETTLE
ARRANGE BARGAIN CHAFFER
CONDUCT CONSULT DISCUSS
ENTREAT CONCLUDE ENTREATY
TRANSACT TRANSFER TEMPORIZE
NEGOTIATION DEAL DICKER
PARLEY TREATY PASSAGE
ENTREATY PRACTICE
NEGRITO ATA ATI ITA AETA AKKA
BATWA BLACK KARON SEMANG
TAPIRO ABENLEN BAMBUTE
NEGRO FON JUR LUO LWO SUK
AKIM ALUR BENI BINI BONI BUCK
CROW EGBA FONG IRON MADI
MOKE NUBA NUPE SIDI BENIN
BLACK BONGO CUFFY DARKY DINKA
DJUKA FULUP FUZZY HATSA MUNGO
SAMBO SEPIA SEREC SMOKE TEMNE
GULLAH HUBSHI AKWAPIM
DAHOMAN GEECHEE QUASHIE
SANDAWE SHILLUK SWELLUH
BECHUANA ETHIOPIAN MANGBATTU
(— BLOOD) TARBRUSH
(GOLD COAST —) GA FANTI
(LIBERIAN —) KRU VAI VEI GREBO
ICROO KRUMAN KROOBOY
(MALE —) BUCK
(OLD —) UNCLE
NEIGH NIE NVE WHI HINNY NICKER
WHINNY WIGHER WHICKER
NEIGHBOR BOR ADJOIN BORDER
FELLOW NEIPER ACCOLENT
BORDERER CONFINER UCALEGON
(PL.) KITH CONFINES
NEIGHBORHOOD WAY AREA HAND
VENUE BARRIO LOCALE REGION
PURLIEU SECTION DISTRICT
ENVIRONS PROCINCT VICINAGE
VICINITY BAILIWICK COMMUNITY
PROXIMITY TERRITORY
NEIGHBORING NIGH NEARBY
CONFINE VICINAL ACCOUENT
ADJACENT
NEIGHBORLY FOLKSY FOLKSEY
AMICABLE

NEITHER NOT NATHER NITHER
NOWDER
(— RIGHT NOR WRONG)
ADIAPHOROUS
NELEUS (BROTHER OF —) PELIAS
(DAUGHTER OF —) PERO
(FATHER OF —) NEPTUNE
(MOTHER OF —) TYRO
(SON OF —) NESTOR
(WIFE OF —) CHLORIS
NELLORE ONGOLE
NEMA EELWORM FILAMENT
NEMATODE ROUNDWORM
NEMATOCYST CNIDA DESMONEME
PENETRANT
NEMESIS BANE FATE UPIS AGENT
AVENGER PENALTY
NENTSI SAMOYED SAMOYEDE
NEOPHYTE TYRO EPOPT NOVICE
AMATEUR CONVERT BEGINNER
PROSELYTE YOUNGLING
NEOPLASM TUMOR GROWTH
TUMOUR SARCOMA NEWGROWTH
NEOTERIC NEW LATE FRESH NOVEL
MODERN RECENT
NEP KNOT CATNIP CATMINT CLUSTER

NEPAL
CAPITAL: KATMANDU
COIN: MOHAR RUPEE
MOUNTAIN: EVEREST
NATIVE: AOUL LIMBU MURMI
NEWAR GURKHA GORKHALI
RIVER: KALI KOSI MUGU SETI BABAI
BHERI RAPTI SARDA GANDAK
KARNALI NARAYANI
TOWN: PATAN BIRGUNJ
BHADGAON LALITPUR
BHAKTAPUR

NEPENTHE DRUG PLANT POTION
ANODYNE
NEPHELINE LENAD MINERAL
SOMMITE ELEOLITE
NEPHEW OY OYE NEVE VASU NEFFY
NEVOY NIECE NEPOTE BENVOLIO
NEPHRITE JADE POUNAM AXSTONE
POUNAMU TREMOLITE
NEPTUNE LER PAN SEA GREEN
OCEAN PLATE SEAGOD
(BROTHER OF —) PLUTO JUPITER
(CONSORT OF —) SALACIA
(DISCOVERER OF —) GALLE
(EMBLEM OF —) TRIDENT
(FATHER OF —) SATURN
(MOTHER OF —) RHEA
(SISTER OF —) JUNO
NEREID NYMPH NEREIS THALIA
THETIS CYMODOCE
NEREIDES (FATHER OF —) NEREUS
(MOTHER OF —) DORIS
NERO TYRANT FIDDLER
(MOTHER OF —) AGRIPPINA
(SUCCESSOR TO —) GALBA
(VICTIM OF —) LUCAN SENECA
(WIFE OF —) OCTAVIA
NERVE RIB CORD GALL GRIT GUTS
LINE SAND VEIN CHEEK CHORD

'CRUST PLUCK PUDIC SINEW SPUNK STEEL TENON VAGUS VIGOR APLOMB COSTAL DARING DENTAL ENERGY FACIAL LUMBAR RADIAL SACRAL STRING AXILLAR COELIAC COURAGE SAPHENA SCIATIC SPINDLE ABDUCENS AUDACITY BOLDNESS CERVICAL COOLNESS EFFERENT EMBOLDEN STRENGTH TEMERITY AUTONOMIC ENCOURAGE EYESTRING
(— **CELL**) ANAXON NEURON DIAXONE DENDRAXON
(— **CENTER**) BRAIN CORTEX PLEXUS
(— **FIBERS**) PONS
(— **NETWORK**) RETIA PLEXUS
(— **SLEEP**) NEURO HYPNOTISM
(PL.) HORRORS JITTERS

NERVELESS DEAD WEAK BRAVE INERT UNNERVED FOOLHARDY POWERLESS

NERVOUS EDGY TOEY FUSSY GOOSY JUMPY TENSE TIMID WINDY FIDGET SINEWY SPOOKY TOUCHY UNEASY FEARFUL FRETFUL JITTERY RESTIVE SCADDLE NEUROTIC TIMOROUS EXCITABLE SENSITIVE TREMULOUS TWITTERLY
(— **MALADY**) APHASIA NEURITIS
(— **SEIZURE**) TIC ANEURIA

NERVURE RIB NERVE NEURON CUBITAL

NERVY BOLD RASH JERKY PUSHY BRAZEN SINEWY STRONG FORWARD JITTERY IMPUDENT INTREPID VIGOROUS EXCITABLE

NESS RAS CAPE SUFFIX HEADLAND

NEST BED DEN EST JUG WEB AERY BIKE BINK DRAY DREY EYRY HOME LAIR NIDE REDD SHED TRAP ABODE AERIE BROOD EYRIE HAUNT HOUSE NIDUS SWARM CLUTCH COLONY CUDDLE HOTBED RESORT WURLEY CABINET LODGING RETREAT VESPIARY WITHYPOT LARVARIUM PENDULINE RESIDENCE TERMITARY
(— **OF ANIMALS**) BED
(— **OF ANT**) FORMICARY
(— **OF BOXES**) INRO
(— **OF EGGS**) CLUTCH

NESTLE JUG LAP LIE PET NEST SNUG NICHE SPOON BURROW CUDDLE FIDGET NUZZLE PETTLE SETTLE SNUDGE CHERISH SHELTER SNUGGLE SNUZZLE

NESTLING BABY BIRD EYAS NEST POULT SQUAB CUDDLE RETREAT BIRDLING NIDULATE FLEDGLING

NESTOR SAGE SOLON LEADER ADVISER ADVISOR COUNSELOR PATRIARCH

NET BAG GIN HAY LAM POT WEB CAUL FIKE FLAN FLEW FLUE FYKE GAIN HAAF KELL LACE LAUN LAWN LEAD MESH MOKE NEAT PURE RETE SALE TOIL TRAP TRIM WEIR BRAIL CATCH CLEAN CLEAR DRIFT GAUZE LACIS PITCH POUND SCOOP SEIZE SNARE SNOOD TRAWL TRINK TULLE YIELD BAGNET BASKET BRIGHT COBWEB ENTRAP FABRIC GROUND LEADER MALINE MASILE PANTER PROFIT RAFFLE SAGENE SAPIAO TOWNET TUNNEL DRAGNET ENSNARE FLYTAIL LAMPARA MALINES NETWORK PROTECT RETICLE RINSING SCRINGE SHELTER SPILLER STALKER TRAINEL TRAMMEL MESHWORK SALAMBAO BUCKSTALL RETICULUM

NETHER DOWN BELOW LOWER UNDER NEDDER DOWNWARD INFERIOR INFERNAL

NETHERLANDS
CANAL: ORANJE JULIANA DRENTSCH
CAPITAL: AMSTERDAM
CHEESE: EDAM GOUDA LEYDEN
COIN: CENT DOIT RYDER FLORIN GULDEN STIVER DUCATON ESCALIN GUILDER STOOTER
ISLAND: TEXEL AMELAND VLIELAND
MEASURE: EL AAM AHM AUM ELL KAN MUD VAT ZAK DUIM LOOD MIJL ROOD ROPE VOET ANKER CARAT ROEDE STOOP WISSE BUNDER KOPPEN LEGGER MAATJE MUDDLE MUTSJE STREEP SCHEPEL MIMGELEN OKSHOOFD STEEKKAN
NAME: HOLLAND
NATIVE: DUTCH DUTCHMAN
PROVINCE: DRENTHE LIMBURG UTRECHT ZEELAND FRIESLAND GRONINGEN GELDERLAND OVERIJSSEL
RIVER: EEM LECK MAAS WAAL YSEL DONGE HUNSE MEUSE YSSEL DINTEL DOMMEL KROMME SCHELDT
TOWN: EDE ASTEN BREDA HAGUE AALTEN ARNHEM LEIDEN HAARLEM TILBURG UTRECHT AALSMEER ENSCHEDE NIJMEGEN AMSTERDAM EINDHOVEN GRONINGEN ROTTERDAM
WEIGHT: ONS LAST LOOD POND BAHAR GREIN KORREL WICHTJE ESTERLIN

NETHERWORLD HADES SHADES

NETLIKE MESHY NETTY RETIARY RETICULAR

NETTING BAR CAUL LING MESH SCREEN DEEPING FISHNET FOOTING BOBBINET WIREWORK

NETTLE VEX FRET LINE ANNOY CNIDA ETTLE PEEVE PIQUE STING HENBIT ORTIGA RUFFLE SPLICE URTICA AFFRONT BLUBBER BLUETOP KNITTLE PROVOKE STINGER IRRITATE CLOWNHEAL GLIDEWORT SMARTWEED
(— **RASH**) HIVES UREDO URTICARIA

(— **TREE**) LOTUS GYMPIE
(**WHITE DEAD** —) ARCHANGEL

NETWORK WEB CAUL FRET MAZE MESH MOKE RETE CHAIN LACIS BRIDGE COBWEB CRADLE PLEXUS RESEAU SAGENE SYSTEM DRAGNET DIPLEXER GRIDIRON KNITTING WATTLING RETICULUM
(— **OF CRACKS**) CRACKLE
(— **ON MAP**) GRATICULE

NEUME PES VIRGA CLIVIS PNEUMA PODATUS PUNCTUM VIRGULA CLIMACUS QUILISMA SEQUENCE TORCULUS SCANDICUS

NEURAL DORSAL NERVAL NEURIC

NEURALGIA SCIATICA COSTALGIA

NEURITE AXON AXONE

NEUROTIC DRUG NERVOUS
(— **CONDITION**) LATAH

NEUTRAL GRAY INERT SWEET AMORAL MIDDLING NEGATIVE UNBIASED COLORLESS IMPARTIAL
(— **IN COLOR**) SOBER
(**OPTICALLY** —) INACTIVE

NEUTRALIZE KILL ANNUL BLUNT ERASE CANCEL ABOLISH BALANCE CORRECT DESTROY NULLIFY VITIATE NEGATIVE SATURATE FRUSTRATE

NEUTRINO LEPTON

NEVADA
CAPITAL: CARSONCITY
COUNTY: NYE ELKO STOREY WASHOE
INDIAN: WASHO PAIUTE
LAKE: MEAD RUBY TAHOE WALKER PYRAMID
RIVER: REESE TRUCKEE HUMBOLDT
STATE BIRD: BLUEBIRD
STATE FLOWER: SAGEBRUSH
STATE NICKNAME: SILVER
STATE TREE: PINON
TOWN: ELY ENKO RENO FALLON NELLIS SPARKS LASVEGAS

NEVE ICE FIRN SNOW NEPHEW GLACIER

NEVER NAY NIE NOT NARY NARRA NIVER NOWHEN

NEVER-NEVER DREAMLAND

NEVERTHELESS BUT YET STILL ALWISE ALGATES HOWBEIT HOWEVER WHETHER

NEVUS MOLE SPOT TUMOR NAEVUS SPIDER SPILUS FRECKLE LENTIGO SPILOMA BIRTHMARK

NEW NEO NEU RAW LATE NOVA FRESH GREEN MOIST NOVEL YOUNG MODERN RECENT UNUSED VIRGIN ANOTHER FOREIGN STRANGE UNTRIED UPSTART INITIATE NEOTERIC ORIGINAL YOUTHFUL BEGINNING
(— **BUT YET OLD**) NOVANTIQUE
(**BRAND** —) SPICK
(**COMB. FORM**) NEO

NEWBORN YEANLING
NEW CALEDONIA (— BIRD) KAGU
(CAPITAL OF —) NOUMEA
(ISLAND OF —) HUON BELEP DEPINS
LOYALTY WALPOLE
(SEAPORT OF —) NOUMEA
NEWCASTLE GOTHAM
NEWCOMER SETTLER COMELING
FRESHMAN MALIHINI RINGNECK
GREENHORN IMMIGRANT KIMBERLIN
NEW DEAL (— AGENCY) CCC NRA
NYA TVA
NEWEL POST SPINDLE
NEW ENGLAND (— INHABITANT)
YANK YANKEE JONATHAN
(— SETTLER) PILGRIM PURITAN
NEWFOUNDLAND (— CAPE) RACE
(— HOUSE) TILT
(— INHABITANT) OUTPORTER

NEW GUINEA
BAY: ORO MILNE
GULF: HUON PAPUA
ISLAND: BUKA MANUS MUSSAU
ISLAND GROUP: CRETIN NINIGO
SAINSON SOLOMON
MOUNTAIN: ALBERT VICTORIA
NATIVE: KARON PAPUAN
PORT: LAE DARU WEWAK MADANG
RIVER: FLY HAMU SEPIK AMBERNO
TOWN: LAE WAU DARU SORON
AITAPE KIKORI RABAUL

NEW HAMPSHIRE
CAPITAL: CONCORD
COLLEGE: DARTMOUTH
COUNTY: COOS BELKNAP
LAKE: SQUAM OSSIPEE SUNAPEE
UMBAGOG WINNIPESAUKEE
MOUNTAIN: MORIAH PAUGUS
WAUMBEK CHOCORUA
MONADNOCK
MOUNTAIN RANGE: WHITE
NOTCH: CRAWFORD FRANCONIA
PRESIDENT: PIERCE
RIVER: SACO ISRAEL BELLAMY
SOUHEGAN MERRIMACK
STATE BIRD: FINCH
STATE FLOWER: LILAC
STATE TREE: BIRCH
TOWN: KEENE EXETER NASHUA
HANOVER LACONIA

NEW HEBRIDES (CAPITAL OF —)
VILA
(ISLAND OF —) EPI TANA EFATE
MAEWO MABRIM MALEKULA

NEW JERSEY
CAPITAL: TRENTON
COLLEGE: UPSALA
COUNTY: ESSEX UNION BERGEN
CAMDEN MORRIS PASSAIC
MONMOUTH
INDIAN: DELAWARE
PRESIDENT: CLEVELAND

RIVER: DENNIS HAYNES MANTUA
RAMAPO MULLICA PASSAIC
RARITAN COHANSEY TUCKAHOE
STATE BIRD: GOLDFINCH
STATE FLOWER: VIOLET
STATE NICKNAME: GARDEN
STATE TREE: REDOAK
TOWN: LODI CAMDEN NEWARK
NUTLEY RAHWAY TOTOWA
BAYONNE HOBOKEN HOHOKUS
MATAWAN NETCONG ORADELL
PARAMUS PASSAIC TEANECK
TENAFLY WYCKOFF CARTERET
FREEHOLD METUCHEN
SECAUCUS WATCHUNG
UNIVERSITY: RUTGERS PRINCETON

NEWLY ANEW AGAIN AFRESH
LATELY FRESHLY NEWLINS
RECENTLY
NEWMARKET MICHIGAN SARATOGA
GRABOUCHE

NEW MEXICO
CAPITAL: SANTAFE
COUNTY: LUNA MORA QUAY TAOS
OTERO CATRON CHAVES
HIDALGO
CULTURE: MIMBRES
INDIAN: TEWA TIWA ZUNI JEMEZ
PECOS APACHE NAVAHO
NAVAJO PUEBLO
RIVER: UTE GILA PECOS SANJOSE
STATE BIRD: ROADRUNNER
STATE FLOWER: YUCCA
STATE TREE: PINON PINYON
TOWN: JAL BELEN RATON CLOVIS
DEMING GALLUP GRANTS
ARTESIA SOCORRO

NEWS BUZZ DOPE UNCA UNKO
WORD CLASH FERLY ADVICE
CRACKS FERLIE GOSPEL NOTICE
REPORT EVANGEL KHUBBER
TIDINGS WITTING NOUVELLE
KNOWLEDGE SPEERINGS
(— AGENCY) AP UP DNB INS UPI
TASS ANETA DOMEI REUTERS
(— BEAT) SCOOP
NEWSBOY NEWSY CAMELOT
CARRIER
NEWSMONGER GOSSIP TATTLER
NOVELANT NOVELIST QUIDNUNC
REPORTER
NEWSPAPER RAG NEWS DAILY
ORGAN PAPER PRESS SHEET TIMES
ARRIBA HERALD SERIAL SUNDAY
COURANT DIURNAL GAZETTE
JOURNAL MERCURY TABLOID
TRIBUNE NEWSPRINT
(— USED BY PICKPOCKET) STIFF
(PL.) PRESS
NEWSPAPERMAN PRESSMAN
NEWSSTAND BOOTH KIOSK STALL
STAND BOOKSTALL
NEWT ASK EFT ESK EVET EBBET
EFFET LIZARD TRITON AXOLOTL

CRAWLER CREEPER REPTILE
MANKEEPER
NEW YEAR'S DAY NAURUZ
NOROOSE NOWROZE
NEW YEAR'S EVE HAGMENA
HOGMANAY

NEW YORK
AVENUE: PARK FIFTH MADISON
FLATBUSH
BAY: JAMAICA PECONIC MORICHES
BOROUGH: BRONX KINGS QUEENS
BROOKLYN MANHATTAN
BUILDING: RCA PANAM CHRYSLER
FLATIRON
CANAL: ERIE GOWANUS
CAPITAL: ALBANY
COLLEGE: BARD CCNY IONA PACE
FINCH UNION HUNTER VASSAR
WAGNER ADELPHI BARNARD
CANISIUS HAMILTON SKIDMORE
COUNTY: ERIE KINGS TIOGA
YATES BROOME CAYUGA
NASSAU ONEIDA OSWEGO
OTSEGO PUTNAM QUEENS
SENECA ULSTER CHEMUNG
GENESEE NIAGARA STEUBEN
SUFFOLK CHENANGO DUTCHESS
HERKIMER ONONDAGA
RICHMOND ROCKLAND
SARATOGA SCHUYLER
INDIAN: CAYUGA MOHAWK ONEIDA
SENECA MOHICAN MONTAUK
IROQUOIS ONONDAGA
ISLAND: FIRE LONG ELLIS STATEN
FISHERS LIBERTY SHELTER
GOVERNORS MANHATTAN
LAKE: ERIE CAYUGA GEORGE
ONEIDA OTISCO OTSEGO
OWASCO PLACID SENECA
CONESUS HONEOYE ONTARIO
SARANAC SCHROON SUCCESS
SARATOGA
MOUNTAIN: BEAR MARCY
MOUNTAINS: TACONIC CATSKILL
ADIRONDACK
NICKNAME: EMPIRE GOTHAM
PRESIDENT: FILLMORE VANBUREN
ROOSEVELT
PRISON: TOMBS ATTICA SINGSING
RIVER: TIOGA HARLEM HOOSIC
HUDSON MOHAWK OSWEGO
GENESEE NIAGARA
SQUARE: TIMES UNION HERALD
MADISON
STATE BIRD: BLUEBIRD
STATE FLOWER: ROSE
STATE NICKNAME: EMPIRE
STATE TREE: SUGARMAPLE
STREET: WALL BOWERY
BROADWAY
SUBWAY: BMT IND IRT LEX
TOWN: RYE ROME ILION ISLIP
NYACK OLEAN OWEGO UTICA
ATTICA AUBURN COHOES
ELMIRA GOSHEN ITHACA ONEIDA
OSWEGO TAPPAN ARDSLEY
BABYLON BATAVIA BUFFALO
CONGERS ENDWELL GENESEO

HEWLETT MAHOPAC MASSENA
MERRICK MINEOLA MONTAUK
ONEONTA PENNYAN POTSDAM
SUFFERN SYOSSET WANTAGH
YAPHANK YONKERS BETHPAGE
CATSKILL HERKIMER KINGSTON
OSSINING SYRACUSE TUCKAHOE
ROCHESTER
UNIVERSITY: LIU NYU ADELPHI
COLGATE CORNELL FORDHAM
HOFSTRA YESHIVA COLUMBIA
WATERFALL: NIAGARA

NEW ZEALAND
BAY: OHUA HAWKE LYALL
AWARUA CLOUDY GOLDEN
FITZROY PEGASUS POVERTY
RANGAUNU
CAPE: EGMONT FAREWELL
PALLISER
CAPITAL: WELLINGTON
GULF: HAURAKI
ISLAND: OTEA STEWART
PUKETUTU
LAKE: OHAU HAWEA TAUPO
PUKAKI PUPUKE TEKAPO
WANAKA BRUNNER ROTORUA
WAKATIPU
MOUNTAIN: COOK FLAT OWEN
CHOPE LYALL MITRE OTARI
STOKES AORANGI PIHANGA
TUTAMOE TYNDALL ASPIRING
EARNSLAW
NATIVE: ATI ARAWA MAORI
RINGATU
PENINSULA: MAHIA OTAGO
RIVER: MOKAU WAIPA CLUTHA
TAMAKI WAIHOU WAIROA
WAIKATO MANAWATU
STRAIT: COOK FOVEAUX
TOWN: LEUIN ORETI OTAKI TAUPO
CLUTHA FOXTON NAPIER
OAMARU PICTON TIMARU
DUNEDIN RAETIHI ROTORUA
AUCKLAND KAWAKAWA
VOLCANO: RUAPEHU NGAURUHOE
TONGARIRO

NEXT POI NEAR SYNE THEN UNTO
WISE AFTER EWEST FIRST LATER
NEIST RIGHT BESIDE COMING
SECOND TIDDER TOTHER CLOSEST
NEAREST DIRECTLY PROCHAIN
PROCHEIN ADJOINING IMMEDIATE
(— AFTER) THEN FOLLOWING
(— IN ORDER) EKA
(— MONTH) PROXIMO
(— OF KIN) GOEL
(— TO LAST) PENULT
NEXUS TIE BOND LINK CHAIN
NGAIO KIO KAIO NAIO TREE
NHANG GIAI
NIAM-NIAM ZANDE AZANDE AZANDI
ZANDEH AZANDEH BABUNGERA
NIB NEB PEN BEAK BILL KINK TEAT
POINT PRONG SCORER

NIBBLE EAT NAB NIB NIP BITE GNAW
KNAB KNAP MOOP MOUP PECK PICK
CHAMP GNARL MOUSE PIECE SHEAR
ARRODE BROWSE CHAVEL NATTLE
PICKLE PILFER CHIMBLE GNABBLE
GNATTER KNABBLE SNAGGLE

NICARAGUA
CAPITAL: MANAGUA
COIN: PESO CENTAVO CORDOBA
ISLAND: OMETEPE
LAKE: MANAGUA
MEASURE: VARA CAHIZ MILLA
SUERTE TERCIA CAJUELA
ESTADAL MANZANA
MOUNTAIN: MADERA MOGOTON
PORT: CORINTO
RIVER: COCO TUMA WANKS
GRANDE ESCONDIDO
TOWN: LEON MASAYA GRANADA
MANAGUA JINOTEGA
MATAGALPA
WEIGHT: BAG CAJA TONELADA

NICCOLITE ARITE KUPFERNICKEL
NICE APT FIT FEAT FINE GOOD JUMP
KIND NEAT NYCE PURE CANNY
EXACT FUSSY NIECE SWEET BONITA
BONITO DAINTY GENTIL MINUTE
PEACHY QUAINT QUEASY SPICED
STRICT SUBTLE TICKLE CORRECT
ELEGANT FINICAL GENTEEL MINCING
PERJINK PICKING PRECISE PRUDISH
REFINED DECOROUS DELICATE
EXACTING PLEASANT PLEASING
TICKLISH
(TOO —) SUPERFINE
NICELY JUMP
NICETY HAIR DELICACY JUSTNESS
CRITICISM CURIOSITY PRECISION
(PL.) PERJINKITIES
NICHE BAY WRO APSE CANT COVE
NOOK SLOT HERNE HOVEL NIECE
NITCH ALCOVE ANCONA COVERT
CRANNY GROOVE MIHRAB RECESS
RINCON EDICULE HOUSING RETREAT
ROUNDEL AEDICULA CREDENCE
TOKONOMA HABITACLE
NICK CUT JAG MAR NAG NOB CHIP
DENT DINT HACK NACK SLAP SLIT
CHEAT CHICK GOUGE NITCH NOTCH
PRICK SCORE SLACK SNICK TALLY
TRICK ARREST RECORD DEFRAUD
(— OF TIME) GODSPEED
NICKEL JIT COIN JITNEY NIMBUS
(ALLOY OF —) INVAR KONEL MONEL
(CONTAINING —) NICCOLIC
(SYMBOL OF —) NI
NICKELODEON JUKEBOX
NICKER NEIGHER
NICKNAME DUB DOEG NICK ALIAS
AGNAME BYWORD HANDLE MONICA
TONAME CRACKER EKENAME
MISNAME MONIKER NICKERY
COGNOMEN MONARCHO MONICKER
TARTUFFE SOBRIQUET
NICKNAMING PROSONOMASIA
NICTATE WINK BLINK CLOSE TWINK
TWINKLE NICTITATE

NIDDICK NAPE
NIDE NID NEST BROOD LITTER
NIDGE NIG SHAKE QUIVER
NIDGET HOE FOOL IDIOT
NIDOR ODOR AROMA SAVOR SCENT
SMELL
NIECE OY OYE NEPHEW
NIELLO TULA
NIEPA NIOTA KARINGHOTA
NIEVE FIST HAND NEIF SERF NATIVE
NIFTY FINE GOOD KEEN SMART
STYLISH
NIGER JOLIBA KWORRA RAMTIL
(CAPITAL OF —) NIAMEY
(MOUTH OF —) NUN
(NATIVE OF —) PEUL HAUSA
DJERMA FULANI SONGHA TOUBOU
TUAREG
(OASIS IN —) KAOUAR
(RIVER OF —) DILLIA
(TOWN OF —) MARADI TAHOUA
ZINDER

NIGERIA
CAPITAL: LAGOS
NATIVE: ARO EBO EDO IBO IJO
VAI BENI EBOE EFIK EJAM EKOI
NUPE BENIN HAUSA FULANI
YORUBA
PORT: LAGOS CALABAR
PROVINCE: ISA OYO KANO NUPE
ONDO IJEBU OGOJA WARRI
OWERRI ADAMAWA
RIVER: OLI GANA YOBE BENUE
NIGER KADANU SOKOTO
GONGOLA KOMADUGU
TOWN: ABA ADO EDE ISA IWO JOS
BIDI BUEA KANO OFFA YOLA
LAGOS ZARIA IBADAN ILESHA
ILORIN KADUNA MUSHIN
TAKOBA CALABAR ONITSHA
OSHOGBO ABEOKUTA
TREE: AFARA

NIGGARD CHURL CLOSE MISER
NIGON PIKER SCART TIGHT NIGGER
SCRIMP SCRUNT STINGY CHINCHE
DRYFIST NITHING PUCKFIST
SCRIMPER EARTHWORM PINCHBECK
PINCHFIST PUCKFOIST SKINFLINT
NIGGARDLY MEAN CLOSE STINT
NARROW NIGHLY SCANTY SCREWY
SKIMPY SORDID STINGY STRAIT
CHINCHE MISERLY
NIGGERFISH CONY HIND CONEY
GROUPER GUATIVERE
NIGH AT NEAR ANEAR ANIGH CLOSE
ALMOST NEARLY ADJACENT
NIGHT PM EVE DARK NUIT DARKY
DEATH NACHT NOCHE SLEEP
DARKMANS DARKNESS
(— AND DAY) NYCHTHEMERON
(COMB. FORM) NYCTI
(DEPTH OF —) HOLL
(GODDESS OF —) NOX NYX
(LAST —) YESTREEN
(NORSE —) NATT NOTT
(PERT. TO —) NOCTURNAL

(STAY OUT ALL —) PERNOCTATE
NIGHT APE DURUKULI
NIGHT BLINDNESS NYCTALOPIA
NIGHTCAP HOW COWL DOWD
HOUVE PIRNY BIGGIN PIRNIE
DOREMEUSE SUNDOWNER
NIGHTCLUB CAFE CLUB SPOT BOITE
BISTRO CABARET DANCERY
NIGHTERY
NIGHTDRESS SLOP WILYCOAT
WYLIECOAT
NIGHTFALL EEN EVE DUSK EVEN
SHUTTING TWILIGHT
(OCCURRING AT —) ACRONICAL
NIGHTGOWN TOOSH BEDGOWN
NIGHTIE WYLIECOAT
NIGHTHAWK PISK CUIEJO BULLBAT
NIGHTINGALE JUG BULBUL
FLORENCE PHILOMEL
(— SOUND) JUG
(SWEDISH —) LIND JENNY
(PL.) WATCH
NIGHTJAR POTOO EVEJAR
DERHAWK SPINNER WHEELER
MOREPORK
NIGHT LAMP VEILLEUSE
NIGHTMARE ALP HAG MARA MESS
DREAM FANCY FIEND VISION
INCUBUS CACODEMON CAUCHEMAR
EPHIALTES
(— CAUSER) MARE
NIGHTSHADE HERB DWALE MOREL
HENBANE MORELLE SANDBUR
SOLANUM TROMPILLO
NIHIL NIL NICHIL NOTHING
NIHILIST ANARCHIST SOCIALIST
NIL ZERO NILGAI IPOMOEA NOTHING

NILE
AS GOD: HAPI
BIRD: IBIS WRYNECK
BOAT: BARIS CANGIA NUGGAR
DAHABEAH
CAPTAIN: RAIS REIS
DAM: ASWAN
FALLS: RIPON
FISH: BAGRE SAIDE BICHIB
DOCMAC MORMYRID
MORMYROID
ISLAND: RODA PHILAE
NATIVE: MADI NILOT
NEGRO: JUR LUO LWO SUK
PLANT: SUDD LOTUS
REGION: NUBIA
SOURCE: TSANA
TOWN: QUS ABRI ARGO IDFU ISNA
QINA ASYUT CAIRO REJAF SAITE
ROSETTA
TRIBUTARY: ATBARA KAGERA
VALLEY DEPRESSION: KORE

NILGAI NIL NYLGAU ANTELOPE
NEELGHAW
NIMBLE FLY DEFT FLIP FLIT GLEG
LISH SPRY SWAK YARE AGILE BRISK
FLEET LIGHT QUICK SWACK TRICK
WIGHT ACTIVE CLEVER FEIRIE
LIMBER LISSOM LIVELY PROMPT
QUIVER SPRACK SUPPLE VOLANT
DELIVER LISSOME SWIPPER
FLIPPANT TRIPPING SENSITIVE
SPRIGHTLY
NIMBLENESS HASTE SLEIGHT
LEGERITY DEXTERITY LIGHTNESS
NIMBLE-WITTED VOLABLE
NIMBUS AURA HALO NIMB CLOUD
GLORY SHINE VAPOR GLORIA
AUREOLA AUREOLE
NIMIETY EXCESS
NINCOMPOOP ASS DOLT FOOL
POOP NINNY NINCOM WITLING
BLOCKHEAD SIMPLETON
NINE IX NIE NYE TEAM COMET
POTHOOK
(— A.M.) UNDERN MIDMORN
(— ANGLED FIGURE) NONAGON
(— DAYS DEVOTION) NOVENA
(— FOLD) NONUPLE
(— HEADED MONSTER) HYDRA
(— HUNDRED) SAN
(— INCHES) SPAN
(— OF CLUBS OR DIAMONDS)
COMET
(— OF DIAMONDS) BRAGGER
(— OF TRUMPS) DIX MENEL
SANCHO
(— YEAR CYCLE) JUGLAR
(GROUP OF —) ENNEAD
(MUSIC FOR —) NONET
NINEBARK ROSACEAN SEVENBARK
NINEHOLES BUMBLEPUPPY
NINEPIN SQUAIL SKITTLE SKITTLES
(PL.) KEELS KAYLES NINEPEGS
NINETEENTH LARIGOT
NINETIETH NONAGESIMAL
NINETY KOPPA
NINEVEH (FOUNDER OF —) NINUS
NINE WORLDS HEL ASGARD
ALFHEIM MIDGARD NIFLHEIM
VANAHEIM JOTUNNHEIM
MUSPELLSHEIM SVARTALFAHEIM
NINNI ISHTAR
NINNY DOLT FOOL LOUT DUNCE
IDIOT NONNY PATCH SAMMY SPOON
FONDLE NOODLE FONDLING
BLOCKHEAD NIDDICOCK
PEAKGOOSE SIMPLETON
NINON SHEER
NINTH (EVERY —) NONAN ENNEATIC
NIOBATE TODDITE SIPYLITE
COLUMBATE
NIOBE HERB HOSTA FUNKIA
(BROTHER OF —) PELOPS
(FATHER OF —) TANTALUS
(HUSBAND OF —) AMPHION
(SISTER-IN-LAW OF —) AEDON
NIOBIUM COLUMBIUM
NIP CUT SIP VEX BITE BUMP CLIP
DRAM GIVE KNIP NIPE PECK SNUB
TANG TAUT TUCK BLAST CHEAT
CHECK CHILL CLAMP DRAFT FROST
PINCH SEIZE SEVER SNAPE SNEAP
THIEF BENUMB BLIGHT CATNIP
TIPPLE TWITCH WITHER SARCASM
SQUEEZE WETTING COMPRESS
FROSTBITE VELLICATE
NIPA PALM ATAP ATTAP DRINK
NIPPER BOY LAD CLAW CRAB GRAB
HAND BITER CHELA MISER THIEF
CUNNER URCHIN GRIPPER INCISOR
BRAKEMAN
NIPPERS DOG NIP BITS NIPS TONGS
GRATER PLIERS TURKIS FORCEPS
PINCERS OSTEOTOME
NIPPLE BUD DUG PAP TIT BEAN
TEAT DIDDY DUMMY SPEAN NIBBLE
PILLAR MAMILLA PAPILLA THELIUM
(— POINT) THELION
NIPPLEWORT BALLOGAN
WARTWEED WARTWORT
NIPPY BOLD
NIRVANA EMPTINESS
NIS NIX NISSE GOBLIN KOBOLD
BROWNIE
NISUS POWER EFFORT IMPULSE
ENDEAVOR
(DAUGHTER OF —) SCYLLA
NITER NITRE PETER PETRE POTASH
SALTPETER
NITHER BLAST DEBASE SHIVER
TREMBLE
NITID GAY BRIGHT GLOSSY SPRUCE
SHINING LUSTROUS NITIDOUS
NITO AGSAM
NITON RADON
NITRATE SALT ESTER COTTON
AZOTATE
NITRIC AZOTIC
NITRIDE BORAZON
NITRITE AZOTITE
NITROGEN GAS AZOTE ALKALIGEN
NITROGLYCERIN TNT SOUP SIRUP
SYRUP GLONOIN GLONOINE
NITWIT DAW DOPE DIZZARD
SIMPLETON
NIX NO HARD NECK NICKER NOBODY
SPIRIT SPRITE UNDINE NOTHING
NJAVE ADJAB DIAVE
NO NA NE NAE NAH NAW NAY NIT
NIX NUL BAAL BAIL BALE NONE
NYET NAPOO NAPOOH NOGAKU
(— ONE) NIX NEMO
(— POINTS IN TENNIS) LOVE
NOAH NOE
(DOVE OF —) COLUMBA
(FATHER OF —) LAMECH
(GRANDSON OF —) ARAM
(GREAT-GRANDSON OF —) HUL
(MEXICAN —) COXCOX
(RAVEN OF —) CORVUS
(SON OF —) HAM SEM SHEM
JAPHETH
(WINE CUP OF —) CRATER
NOB NAB BLOW HEAD NAVE KNAVE
SWELL HANDLE TIPTOPPER
NOBILITY RANK ELITE GRACE
GENTRY STATUS DIGNITY KWAZOKU
PEERAGE QUALITY STATION
BARONAGE SZLACHTA ELEVATION
(MEMBER OF TATAR —) MURZA
(ROMAN —) RAMNES
NOBLE DON ALII DOGE DUKE EARL
EDEL EPIC FAME FREE GENT GOOD
GRAF HIGH JARL JUST KAMI KUGE
LORD PEER PURE RIAL ARIKI ATHEL
BARON BROAD BURLY COUNT
DUCAL ERECT ETHEL FURST GRAND

GREAT HIRAM KHASS LOFTY MANLY
MORAL MURZA PROUD ROYAL
STATE AUGUST COUSIN EPICAL
FLAITH GENTLE GESITH HAUGHT
HEROIC JUNKER KINGLY LORDLY
LUCUMO MANFUL SIRDAR SUPERB
THAKUR WORTHY YONKER
ACERBAS CACIQUE GALLANT
GLAUCUS GLORIED GRANDEE
HIDALGO LIBERAL MAGNATE
MARQUIS PATRICK STAROST
STATELY STEWARD SUBLIME
VOLPONE PANGLIMA

NOBLEMAN DUKE EARL EMIR LORD
PEER BARON COUNT ORLOV PARIS
THANE COUSIN MILORD ORLOFF
THAKUR YONKER GRANDEE
HIDALGO MAGNATE MARQUIS
STAROST VOLPONE YOUNKER
ADELIGER ALMAVIVA BELARIUS
MARCHESE MARQUESS LANDGRAVE

NOBLENESS HONOR DIGNITY
(— OF BIRTH) EUGENY

NOBLEWOMAN LADY MILADY
DUCHESS PEERESS BARONESS
COUNTESS

NOBODY NIX NEMO NONE NADIE
NOMAN SCRUB SCARAB NOTHING
JACKSTRAW

NOCENT GUILTY HARMFUL HURTFUL
NOXIOUS CRIMINAL

NOCTURNAL NIGHT NOXIAL
NIGHTLY NIGHTISH MOONSHINE
(— ANIMAL) COON POSSUM
OPOSSUM
(— BIRD) OWL
(— CARNIVORE) RATEL
(— MAMMAL) BAT LEMUR
(— SIGNS) ZODIAC

NOCTURNE LULLABY UHTSONG
PAINTING SERENADE

NOD BOB BOW ERR NAP NID NIP
BECK BEND DOZE NAPE SIGN SLIP
SWAY WINK DROOP LAPSE ASSENT
BECKON DODDLE DROWSE NODDLE
NUTATE SALUTE SIGNIFY

NODDING DROWSY NUTANT
ANNUENT CERNUOUS DROOPING
NUTATION

NODDY AUK FOOL JACK NOIO TERN
KNAVE NINNY DROWSY FULMAR
NOODLE SLEEPY HACKNEY
TOMNODDY SIMPLETON

NODE BOW BUMP KNOB KNOT LUMP
PLOT JOINT NODUS POINT TUMOR
BULBIL NODULE DILEMMA GRANULE
KNUCKLE FOLLICLE PHYTOMER
SWELLING TUBERCLE
(— OF GRASS) KNOT
(— OF POEM) PLOT
(— OF STEM) JOINT

NODULE BOB AUGE BUMP KNOT
LUMP MASS NODE YOLK FLINT
GEODE PHYMA MILIUM BLISTER
CATHEAD GRANULE LEPROMA
NABLOCK SARCOID AMYGDALE
AMYGDOLE TUBERCLE WHITEHEAD
(— OF FLINT) CORE
(PL.) BEADING

NOEL XMAS CAROL NOWEL NATALIS
CHRISTMAS

NOGGIN ALE CUP MUG NOG PEG PIN
GILL HEAD PAIL PATE DRINK
GOGGAN NAGGIN NOODLE

NOIL FIBER PINION

NOISE (ALSO SEE SOUND) ADO AIR
BUM DIN GIG HUM POP ROW BANG
BOOM BRAY BUMP BURR HOOT
KLOP MUSH PEAL RALE RASH REEL
RERD ROTE ROUT SLAM ZING
ALARM BABEL BLARE BLAST BLOOP
BRAWL BRUIT BURLE CHANG CHIRM
CLICK DREAM GRASS JERRY KNOCK
LARRY LEDEN PLASH QUONK REERE
RERDE RUMOR SLORP SNORE
SOUND STEER SWISH CACKLE
CLAMOR DUNDER GOBBLE GOSSIP
HUBBUB NORATE OUTCRY RACKET
RANTAN RATTLE REPORT SPLASH
SQUAWK STEVEN STRIFE TUMULT
UPROAR BLUSTER BRATTLE
CLITTER CRACKLE ORATION
SCANDAL SPATTER STREPOR
STRIDOR FLICFLAC QUONKING
TINTAMAR CONFUSION
(ELECTRIC —) GRASS

NOISELESS QUIET STILL SWEET
TACIT SILENT APHONIC CATLIKE

NOISEMAKER BELL HORN GRAGER
RATTLE CLAPPER SQUEAKER

NOISETTE HAZEL HAZELNUT

NOISOME FOUL RANK FETID NASTY
PUTRID RANCID HARMFUL HURTFUL
NOXIOUS NUISOME STINKING
OFFENSIVE

NOISY LOUD CLASHY CREAKY
BLATANT DINSOME FRANTIC
MOILING RACKETY RIOTOUS
ROUTOUS BRAWLING CLATTERY
SONOROUS STREPENT HILARIOUS
RATTLEBAG

NOLL HEAD NODDLE NOODLE

NOMA CANKER

NOMAD ARAB BEJA LURI MOOR
SAKA SHUA ALANI GYPSY IGDYR
JAREG ROVER SHUWA NOMADE
ROAMER ROVING SEMITE SLUBBI
TUAREG BAZIGAR BEDOUIN
SARACEN SCENITE SHORTZY
SHUKRIA SOLUBBI TOUAREG
KABABISH SCYTHIAN SHINWARI
AMALEKITE MIGRATORY
(— PEOPLE) ALANI
(PL.) AKHLAME

NOMADIC ERRATIC VAGRANT
VAGABOND FOOTLOOSE ITINERANT

NOM DE PLUME PENNAME
TELONISM PSEUDONYM

NOME ELIS NOMOS MELODY
NOMARCHY PROVINCE

NOMENCLATURE LIST NAME TERM
ONYMY NAMING GLOSSARY
REGISTER CATALOGUE

NOMINAL PAR BASIC PAPER
FORMAL SLIGHT UNREAL TITULAR
TRIVIAL PLATONIC TRIFLING
(— RECOGNIZANCE) DOE

NOMINATE CALL LEET NAME ELECT

NEVEN SLATE SELECT APPOINT
ENTITLE PRESENT PROPOSE
SPECIFY DESIGNATE POSTULATE

NOMINY SPEECH RIGMAROLE

NONAGE NEANT INFANCY MINORITY
PUPILAGE

NONAGREEMENT DISSENT

NON-ALCOHOLIC SMALL

NON-ARAB SHANGALLA

NONASPIRATE LENE

NONBELIEVER PAGAN ATHEIST
AGNOSTIC

NONCE NANES NONES NOANCE
PRESENT PURPOSE OCCASION

NONCHALANT COOL GLIB ALOOF
CASUAL JAUNTY CARELESS
DEBONAIR

NON-CHRISTIAN INFIDEL

NONCITIZEN TENSOR PEREGRINUS

NONCLERIC LAY LAIC

NONCOMBUSTIBLE APYROUS

NONCOMMITTAL NEUTRAL

NONCONFORMIST REBEL NONCON
BEATNIK FANATIC HERETIC
SECTARY BOHEMIAN RECUSANT
DISSENTER
(— IN ART) FAUVE

NONCONFORMITY HERESY
ADHARMA DISSENT NEGLECT
REFUSAL RECUSANCE RECUSANCY

NONCONTINUOUS DISCRETE

NONDISCLOSURE FRAUD

NONDO LOVAGE ANGELICO

NONDUALISM ADVAITA

NONE NO UN NAE NIN NANE NARY
NEEN NONES

NONEGO NOTSELF

NONELASTIC BROAD

NONENTITY ZERO AUGHT CIPHER
NOBODY NOUGHT NOTHING NULLITY

NONESSENTIAL CASUAL FRILLY
UNNEEDED EXTRINSIC
(— IN RELIGION) ADIAPHORON

NONESUCH APPLE MODEL PARAGON
PATTERN PARADIGM MATCHLESS
NONPAREIL UNRIVALED

NONEXISTENT NULL NAPOOH
NOUGHT NONBEING
(PRACTICALLY —) FAT

NONFEASANCE BREACH

NON GRATA UNWELCOME

NONGYPSY GAJO

NONINJURY AHIMSA

NON-JEW GOI GOY

NONJUROR USAGER

NON-LATIN SAXON

NONLEGATO DETACHE DETACHED

NON-MOSLEM GENTILE

NONPAREIL BEST POPE TYPE
PARAGON PERFECT SUPREME
UNEQUAL NONESUCH PEERLESS
UNRIVALED

NONPAYMENT DISHONOR

NONPLUS SET FAZE POSE STOP
BLANK FLOOR POSER STICK STUMP
TRUMP BAFFLE GRAVEL PUZZLE
RATTLE CONFUSE MYSTIFY
PERPLEX STAGGER QUANDARY
DULCARNON EMBARRASS

NONPLUSSED FOOLISH
NONPOISONOUS EDIBLE
NONPROFESSIONAL BUM LAY LAIC
AMATEUR
NONSENSE BAH GAS GUP PAH ROT
BILK BLAA BLAH BOSH BUFF BUNK
COCK CRAP FLAM FLUM GOOK
JUNK PISH POOH PUNK TOSH BALLS
BLASH DROOL FOLLY FUDGE HAVER
HOOEY SPOOF STITE STUFF TRASH
TRIPE WAHOO BABBLE BUNKUM
DRIVEL FADDLE FOLDER KIBOSH
LINSEY NAVERS RUBBLE SQUISH
TRIVIA BLARNEY BLATHER
BUNCOME EYEWASH FARRAGO
INANITY LOCKRAM TOSHERY
TRIFLES TWADDLE CLAPTRAP
DISHWASH FALDEROL FLIMFLAM
FLUMMERY GALBANUM MACARONI
MOROLOGY PISHTOSH SKITTLES
SPLUTTER TRUMPERY ABSURDITY
FRIVOLITY MOONSHINE POPPYCOCK
SILLINESS
(— **CREATURE**) GOOP SHOO SNARK
SHIMOO
NOODLE BEAN FOOL HEAD NIZY
NOLL PATE NINNY NIZEY NODDY
PASTA PASTE BOODLE NODDLE
NOGGIN LOKSHEN NOGHEAD
NOUILLE BLOCKHEAD SIMPLETON
(— **DISH**) PANSIT RAVIOLI
KREPLACH
(PL.) MEIN FARFEL FERFEL LASAGNA
LASAGNE LOKSHEN FETTUCINI
NOOK IN BAY OUT WRO CANT COVE
GLEN HERN HOLE NALK NUCK NUIK
ANGLE HALKE HERNE NEUCK NICHE
ALCOVE CANTLE CORNER CRANNY
RECESS CREVICE NOOKERY
RETREAT
NOON M APEX DINE NOWN SEXT
DINNER MIDDAY UNDERN MIDNOON
MERIDIAN
NOONDAY (— **REST**) NAP SIESTA
MERIDIAN
NOOSE TIE TOW BOND DULL GIRN
HEMP LACE LOOP ROPE TRAP
BIGHT CATCH GRANE HITCH HONDA
KINCH LASSO LATCH LEASH SNARE
SNARL WIDDY CAUDLE CHOKER
CLINCH ENTRAP HALTER LARIAT
SPRING TETHER TIPPET TWITCH
CHOCKER ENSNARE EXECUTE
LANIARD LANYARD SPRINGE
NECKLACE SQUEEZER TWITCHEL
(— **FOR HAULING LOG**) CHOKER
CHOCKER
(— **FOR SNARING FISH**) DULL
(— **IN A CORD**) KINCH
(**HANGMAN'S** —) SQUEEZER
NOOTKA AHT AHOUSAHT MOATCAHT
MOOACHAHT
NORATE NOISE RUMOR GOSSIP
NORDIC ARIAN ARYAN
NORI AMANORI
NORITE GABBRO OLIGOSITE
NORM PAR RULE TYPE CANON
GAUGE MODEL NORMA DHARMA
MEDIAN AVERAGE MODULUS

PATTERN STANDARD TEMPLATE
NORMA MOLD RULE GAUGE MODEL
SQUARE PATTERN TEMPLET
STANDARD TEMPLATE
NORMAL PAR FULL HOME JUST
MEAN SANE CLEAR ERECT USUAL
FORMAL NATIVE SCHOOL AVERAGE
NATURAL NEUTRAL REGULAR
, TYPICAL ORDINARY STANDARD
CUSTOMARY
NORMANDY (**BEACH IN** —) OMAHA
(**CAPITAL OF** —) ROUEN
(**RIVER IN** —) EURE ORNE SEINE
NORN FATE URTH WURD WYRD
NORNA SKULD URDHR URTHR
VERDHANDI VERTHANDI
NORSEL BAND LINE ORSEL FILLET
NOSSEL ORSELLER
NORTH SEPTENTRION

NORTH CAROLINA
CAPE: FEAR LOOKOUT HATTERAS
CAPITAL: RALEIGH
COLLEGE: ELON CATAWBA
DAVIDSON
COUNTY: ASHE DARE HOKE WAKE
BERTIE BLADEN ONSLOW
YADKIN YANCEY CATAWBA
PAMLICO
INDIAN: ENO COREE CHERAW
MORATOK PAMLICO CHOWANOC
HATTERAS
MOUNTAIN: HARRIS MITCHELL
PRESIDENT: POLK JOHNSON
RIVER: HAW TAR NEUSE CHOWAN
LUMBER PEEDEE YADKIN
ROANOKE
SOUND: BOGUE CROATAN
PAMLICO
STATE BIRD: CARDINAL
STATE FLOWER: DOGWOOD
STATE NICKNAME: TARHEEL
STATE TREE: PINE
TOWN: DURHAM LENOIR SHELBY
EDENTON HICKORY ROXBORO
TARBORO GASTONIA
CHARLOTTE
UNIVERSITY: DUKE

NORTH DAKOTA
CAPITAL: BISMARCK
COLLEGE: JAMESTOWN
COUNTY: EDDY TRAILL PEMBINA
INDIAN: MANDAN ARIKARA
HIDATSA
RIVER: RUSH CEDAR HEART
JAMES SOURIS DESLACS
SHEYENNE WILDRICE
STATE BIRD: MEADOWLARK
STATE FLOWER: PRAIRIEROSE
STATE NICKNAME: SIOUX
FLICKERTAIL
STATE TREE: ELM
TOWN: FARGO MINOT

NORTHERN PIKE ARCTIC BOREAL
NORTHEN

(— **BEAR**) POLAR RUSSIA
(— **CONSTELLATION**) URSA
ANDROMEDA

NORTH KOREA
CAPITAL: PYONGYANG
COIN: WON HWAN
RIVER: NAM YALU IMJIN TUMEN
TAEDONG
TOWN: HAEJU HEIJO KEIJO
ANDONG ANTUNG JUSHIN
POCHON WONSAN HAMHUNG
HUICHON HUNGNAM KAESONG
SINUIJU CHONGJIN

NORTH STAR STATE MINNESOTA

NORTH VIETNAM
CAPITAL: HANOI
COIN: DONG
COMMUNIST PARTY: VIETCONG
GULF: TONKIN TONKING
MOUNTAIN: FANSIPAN
NATIVE: HOA MAN MEO TAY KINH
NUNG THAI MUONG
NEWSPAPER: NHANDAN
PORT: BENTHUY HONGGAI
HAIPHONG
REGION: ANNAM TONKIN
RIVER: BO CA DA LO MA CHU
GAM KOI CHAY NHIHA
TOWN: BACNINH CAOBANG
DONGHOI NAMDINH VIETTRI
THANHHOA HAIPHOANG

NORWAY
CAPE: NORDKAPP
CAPITAL: OSLO
COIN: ORE KRONE
COUNTY: AMT OSLO FYLKE
TROMS BERGEN OPLAND
TROMSO FINMARK HEDMARK
OSTFOLD NORDLAND ROGALAND
TELEMARK VESTFOLD
DANCE: GANGAR HALLING
SPRINGAR SPRINGLEIK
INLET: IS KOB RAN ALST ANDS
BOKN NORD OFOT SALT SUNN
TYRI VEST FIORD FJORD FOLDA
LAKSE SOGNE BJORNA HADSEL
HORTENS TRONDHEIM
ISLAND: VEGA BOMLO DONNA
FROYA HITRA HOPEN SENJA
SMOLA ALSTEN AVEROY
BOUVET HINNOY KARMOY
SOLUND VANNOY GURSKOY
LOFOTEN MAGEROY SEILAND
JANMAYEN SVALBARD
LAKE: ALTE ISTER MJOSA SNASA
FEMUND ROSTAVN TUNNSJO
MEASURE: FOT MAL POT ALEN
MAAL KANDE FATHOM SKIEPPE
MOUNTAIN: SOGNE KJOLEN
NUMEDAL BLODFJEL SNOHETTA
TELEMARK USTETIND

PARLIAMENT: LAGTING STORTING
ODELSTING
PLATEAU: DOURE FJELD
HARDANGER
RIVER: OI ENA ALTA OTRA RANA
TANA BARDU BEGNA LAGEN
ORKLA OTTER RAUMA REISA
GLOMMA LOUGEN NAMSEN
PASVIK
TOWN: GOL NES BODO MOSS
ODDA OSLO VOSS BJORT
FLORO HAMAR MOLDE SKEIN
SKJAK BERGEN HORTEN LARVIK
NARVIK ALESUND ARENDAL
DRAMMEN SANDNES
STAVANGER
WEIGHT: LOD MARK PUND
SKAALPUND BISMERPUND

NOSE CAP NEB NIZ PRY PUG SPY
BEAK BOKO CONK NASE GROIN
LORUM NASUS SCENT SMELL SNIFF
SNOOP SNOUT TRUNK BEEZER
CYRANO DETECT GNOMON MUFFLE
MUZZLE NOZZLE PECKER SEARCH
SNITCH SOCKET ADVANCE PERFUME
SMELLER DISCOVER INFORMER
OLFACTOR PERCEIVE PROBOSCIS
SCHNOZZLE
(— A LOG) SNIPE
(— BAG) MORRAL
(— CARTILAGE) SEPTUM
(— DISEASE) OZENA OZOENA
(— DIVE) VRILLE
(— FLUTE) PUNGI POOGYE
(— INFLAMMATION) CORYZA
RHINITIS
(— MEDICINE) ERRHINE
(— OF ANIMAL) GROIN
(— OPENING) NARE
(— PARTITION) VOMER
(— PIECE) NASAL
(— RING) PIRN
(BLUNT —) SNUB
(FLAT —) PUG SNUB
NOSEBAND BOSAL MUSROL
CAVESSON
NOSEBLEED EPISTAXIS
RHINORRHAGIA
NOSEGAY BOB ODOR POSY POESY
SCENT TUTTY BOUQUET CORSAGE
PERFUME
NOSINESS CURIOSITY
NOSING CURB
NOSTALGIA LONGING YEARNING
NOSTALGIC ELEGIAC ELEGIACAL
NOSTOLOGY GERIATRICS
NOSTRADAMUS SEER PROPHET
PHYSICIAN
NOSTRIL ALA NARE THIRL THRILL
BLOWHOLE
(PERT. TO —) NARIAL NARINE
(PL.) NARES NARIS SNUFFERS
NOSU LOLO
NOSY BEAKY PRYING CURIOUS
FRAGRANT INTRUSIVE
NOT NA NE NAE NAY NOR PAS BAAL
BAIL BALE NICHT SHORN SORRA

NOUGHT POLLED SHAVEN NEITHER
HORNLESS NEGATIVE
(— ANY) NO NUL NANE NARY NONE
NAIRY NOKIN STEAD
(— AT ALL) NEVER LITTLE NOWAYS
NOWHIT NOWISE
(— FINAL) NISI
(— THE SAME) OTHER ANOTHER
DIFFERENT
(— TO BE REPEATED) NR
(— WANTED) DETROP
SUPERFLUOUS
(ALMOST —) SCARCELY
(COULD —) NOTE
(PREFIX MEANING —) IL IM IN IR UN
NON
NOTABLE VIP FINE FABLED FAMOUS
GIFTED NOTARY SIGNAL UNIQUE
EMINENT STORIED SUBLIME
DISTINCT ESPECIAL EVENTFUL
HISTORIC MEMORABLE NOTORIOUS
NOTARY NOTAR GRAFFER
NOTEBOOK OBSERVER OFFICIAL
SCRIVENER
NOTARY PUBLIC TABELLION
NOTATION HOLD MEMO NOTE
ENTRY SYSTEM MARKING
(— PHONETIC) ROMIC
NOTATOR NOTER RECORDER
NOTCH CUT DAG DAP GAP HAG JAG
JOG PEG COPE DENT DINT GAIN
GIMP KERF MUSH NICK NOCK SLAP
SLOT SNIP STEP WARD CRENA
GABEL GRADE HILUM SCORE SHARD
SHERD TALLY CROTCH DEFILE
DEGREE HOLLOW INDENT JOGGLE
RECORD SCOTCH CRENATE
GUDGEON SERRATE INCISION
UNDERCUT
(— BETWEEN HILLS) SLAP
(— ON VERTEBRAE) HYPANTRUM
(— TO FELL TREE) UNDERCUT
NOTCHED EROSE JAGGY RAGULE
RAGULY SERRATE CRENATED
NOTE BON DOG IOU JOT KEY SEE
TEN UNE BILL CARD CENT CHIT
ESPY FAME FLAT GOOD HEED MARK
MEMO NAME NOIT SIGN SOLE SONG
TONE TUNE VIEW CHECK FIVER
GLOZE LABEL PRICK SHORT SIXTH
SOUND STIFF TENTH TOKEN TRAIT
TWANG ATTEND BILLET DEGREE
EXCUSE FIGURA FLIMSY LETTER
MELODY MINUTE NOTICE POLICY
RECORD REGARD REMARK RENOWN
REPORT SECOND STRAIN TENNER
BETOKEN COMMENT DISCORD
MESSAGE MISSIVE NATURAL
OBSERVE PUNCTUS REDBACK
ANNOTATE BLUEBACK BRADBURY
BREVIATE DISPATCH EMINENCE
MARGINAL PERCEIVE POSTFACE
TREASURY GREENBACK
(— FROM TRAIN) BUTTERFLY
(— OF ASSAULT) WARISON
(— OF HUMOR) TRAIT
(— OF SCALE) DO FA LA MI RE SI
SO TI UT ARE SOL
(— OF SNIPE) SCAPE

(— OF WARNING) WATCHWORD
(— ON SHOPHAR) TEKIAH
(— TO RECALL DOG) FORLOIN
(—S ON HUNTING HORN) SEEK
(100-POUND —) CENTURY
(ALTERED —) ACCIDENTAL
(BANK —S) CABBAGE
(BASS —) DRONE
(BIRD'S —) JUG CHIRP
(EIGHTH —) UNCA QUAVER
(ESCAPE —) ECHAPPEE
(EXPLANATORY —) SCHOLIUM
ANNOTATION
(GRACE —) NACHSCHLAG
(HALF —) MINIM
(HARSH —) BLOB
(HIGH-PITCHED —) BEEP
(HIGHEST —) ELA
(LONG —) LARGE
(LOVE —) POULET
(LOWEST —) KEY GAMUT
(MARGINAL —) TOT QUOTE POSTIL
APOSTIL
(MUSICAL —) ALT MESE MIND
BREVE GAMUT SHARP ALAMIRE
MEDIANT PUNCTUS PARAMESE
(NONHARMONIC —) CAMBIATA
(POUND —) BRADBURY
(PROMISSORY —) DOG GOOD HUNDI
(QUARTER —) CROTCHET SEMIMINIM
(SIXTEENTH —) DEMIQUAVER
SEMIQUAVER
(SIXTY-FOURTH —)
HEMIDEMISEMIQUAVER
(THIRTY-SECOND —) SUBSEMIFUSA
DEMISEMIQUAVER
(TWO —S) DUPLET
(WHOLE —) SEMIBREVE
(PL.) ANA GAMUT STRAIN NUMBERS
TIRALEE
NOTEBOOK LOG DIARY NOTARY
RECORD STREET JOURNAL
NOTECASE WALLET POCKETBOOK
NOTED COUTH FAMED GREAT
NAMELY EMINENT INSIGNE
RENOWNED DISTINGUE
NOTEWORTHY BIG SOLEMN
EMINENT NOTABLE SPECIAL
BODACIOUS
NOTHING NIL NIX FREE LUKE NILL
WIND ZERO AUGHT BLANK NIHIL
CIPHER NAUGHT NOBODY NOUGHT
TRIFLE NULLITY SCRATCH USELESS
BAGATELLE
(— BUT) ALL
(— DOING) NAPOO NAPOOH
(— MORE THAN) MERE
(— OTHER THAN) ONLY
NOTHINGNESS NOT NADA ZERO
NOUGHT VACUITY NIHILITY
NOTICE AD BAN SEE SPY CALL ESPY
GOME HEED IDEA KEEP MARK MIND
NEWS NOTE PIPE RIDE SIGN SPOT
TWIG ALARM AWAIT COUNT EDICT
FLOAT NOTAM ORDER QUOTE
ADVICE ALLUDE BILLET ESPIAL
NOTION PERMIT READER REGARD
REMARK REWARD AFFICHE ARTICLE
DISCERN MENTION OBSERVE

PLACARD PROGRAM WARNING
BULLETIN MONITION PERCEIVE
WITTERING
(— **UNEXPECTEDLY**) CATCH
(**ADVANCE** —) HERALDRY
(**COMMENDATORY** —) BLURB
(**DEATH** —) OBIT OBITUARY
(**FAVORABLE** —) RAVE
(**LEGAL** —) CAVEAT
(**MARRIAGE** —) BANS BANNS
(**OFFICIAL** —) EDICT SUMMONS
BULLETIN CITATION
(**PUBLIC** —) BAN EDICT BULLETIN
SPOTLIGHT
NOTICEABLE CRUDE GROSS
FLASHY SIGNAL EVIDENT NOTABLE
POINTED SALIENT HANDSOME
PALPABLE STRIKING PROMINENT
(**UNDESIRABLY** —) CONSPICUOUS
NOTIFICATION DRUM NOTE NOTICE
SUMMONS
(**PUBLIC** —) SIGN
NOTIFY ALL BID CRY JOG CITE PAGE
TELL WARN INFORM NOTICE SIGNAL
APPRISE DECLARE FRUTIFY PUBLISH
ACQUAINT INTIMATE
NOTION BEE GEE BUZZ IDEA IDEE
KINK MAZE OMEN VIEW WHIM
FANCY FREIT IMAGE SENSE THING
WARES BELIEF CEMENT DESIRE
DONNEE GADGET NAGGOT NOTICE
THEORY VAGARY BROMIDE CONCEIT
CONCEPT FANTASY INKLING
MAROTTE OPINION THOUGHT
WRINKLE CATEGORY FOLKLORE
PHANTASY SUPPOSAL WHIMWHAM
INTENTION SENTIMENT WHIRLIGIG
(**FALSE** —) IDOL
(**FIXED** —) TICK
(**FOOLISH** —) VAPOR VAPOUR
(**PUERILE** —) BOYISM
(**SUPERSTITIOUS** —) FREET FREIT
(**PL.**) SMALLS SMALLWARE
NOTORIETY FAME ECLAT GLORY
HONOR RUMOR RENOWN REPUTE
PUBLICITY
NOTORIOUS BIG KNOWN ARRANT
COMMON CRYING FAMOUS NOTARY
STRONG EVIDENT NOTABLE
NOTOIRE APPARENT FLAGRANT
INFAMOUS MANIFEST EGREGIOUS
NOTORNIS TAKAHE
NOTWITHSTANDING BUT FOR THO
YET EVEN WITH ALGATE MAUGER
MAUGRE AGAINST ALGATES
DESPITE HOWBEIT HOWEVER
ALTHOUGH NATHLESS WHATRECK
NOUGAT NUT CANDY NUTSHELL
NOUGHT BAD NIL NOT NOWT ZERO
NOCHT WRONG NOTHING USELESS
WORTHLESS
NOUMENAL ONTAL ONTIC
NOUN MANE WORD THING SUPINE
NOMINAL CONSTRUCT INCREASER
(**INDEFINABLE** —) APTOTE
(**KIND OF** —) COMMON PROPER
DIPTOTE REGULAR TRIPTOTE
MONOPTOTE
(**QUOTATION** —) HYPOSTASIS

(**VERBAL** —) GERUND
NOURISH AID FEED FOOD GROW
BREED NORSH NURSE TRAIN
BATTLE BREAST FOISON FOSTER
NORICE REFETE SUCCOR SUCKLE
SUPPLY CHERISH DEVELOP
EDUCATE NURTURE NUTRIFY
PROVIDE SUPPORT SUSTAIN
MAINTAIN CULTIVATE STIMULATE
NOURISHING ALMA RICH ALIBLE
BATTLE HEARTY STRONG NUTRIENT
ALIMENTAL HEALTHFUL NUTRITIVE
WHOLESOME
NOURISHMENT DIET FETE FOOD
KEEP MEAT MANNA FOISON FOSTER
ALIMENT PABULUM PASTURE
NUTRIMENT REFECTION
NOUS MIND REASON ALERTNESS
INTELLECT
NOUVEAU RICHE PARVENU
UPSTART
NOVEL HOT NEW BOOK EPIC RARE
FRESH PROSE RECIT ROMAN STORY
DARING RECENT SERIAL THRILL
FICTION ROMANCE STRANGE
UNUSUAL NEOTERIC ORIGINAL
THRILLER UNCOMMON NARRATIVE
PAPERBACK
(**BRIEF** —) CONTE
NOVELTY FAD NEWEL RENEW
CHANGE NEWNESS PRIMEUR
WRINKLE FRESHNESS
NOVEMBER 1 SAMUIN SAMHAIN
NOVICE DUB HAM BOOT COLT PUNK
PUNY TIRO TYRO CHELA GOYIN
PUPIL ROOKY YOUTH DRONGO
RABBIT ROOKIE TYRONE AMATEUR
CONVERT LEARNER STARTER
STUDENT YOUNKER BACHELOR
BEGINNER FRESHMAN INEXPERT
NEOPHYTE ARCHARIOS GREENHORN
NOVITIATE FUCHS NOVICERY
PROBATION
NOW NOO YET ARAH HERE ARRAH
NONCE SINCE TODAY EVENOO
EXTANT ANYMORE CURRENT
INSTANT PRESENT FORTHWITH
(— **AND THEN**) SOMETIMES
STOUNDMEAL
(**BUT** —) ERSTWHILE
(**JUST** —) ENOW FRESH
NOWADAYS ANYMORE
NOWEL DRAG
NOX NYX
(**BROTHER OF** —) EREBUS
(**FATHER OF** —) CHAOS
NOXIOUS ILL EVIL FETID DEADLY
NOCENT NOYOUS PUTRID BANEFUL
DAMPISH HARMFUL HURTFUL
NOCUOUS NOISOME SCADDLE
TEDIOUS VICIOUS INFAMOUS
VIRULENT INJURIOUS MIASMATIC
OFFENSIVE PESTILENT POISONOUS
(— **AIR**) MALARIA
(**MORALLY** —) UNWHOLESOME
NOZZLE BIB JET TIP BEAK BIBB
NOSE ROSE VENT GIANT SNOUT
SPOUT TWEER GROVEL OUTLET
MONITOR NIAGARA ORIFICE

SHUTOFF ADJUTAGE ROSEHEAD
VERMOREL NOSEPIECE
(**BLAST FURNACE** —) TUYERE
(**MINING** —) GIANT
NUANCE SHADE NICETY FINESSE
GRADATION VARIATION
NUB EAR HUB JAB JAG KEY NOB
CORE CRUX GIST HANG KNOB KNOT
KNUB LUMP NECK PITH SNAG
HEART NUDGE POINT KERNEL
NUBBIN EXECUTE
NUBBIN EAR STUB STUMP
NUBIA WRAP CLOUD SCARF
NUBIAN NUBA BARABRA HADENDOA
(— **MUSICAL INST.**) SISTRUM
NUBILOUS FOGGY MISTY VAGUE
CLOUDY OBSCURE
NUCHA NAPE NECK NUKE NUCHE
NUCLEAR ELEMENTARY
NUCLEATE SEED
NUCLEOSIDE VICINE INOSINE
CYTIDINE ADENOSINE
NUCLEUS HUB CELL CORE GERM
KERN PITH ROOT SEED CADRE
FOCUS HEART MIDST SPERM UMBRA
CENTER COLONY DEUTON KARYON
KERNEL MIDDLE ISOTOPE NIDULUS
MEROCYTE HABENDULA MESOPLAST
(— **OF CELL**) KARYON
(— **OF STARCH GRAIN**) HILUM
(— **OF SUNSPOT**) UMBRA
(**ATOMIC** —) SPECIES
(**CELL** —) SYNCARYON HEMIKARYON
NUDE BARE LOOSE MODEL NAKED
SEASAN STATUE UNCLAD DENUDED
EXPOSED PICTURE PAINTING
STRIPPED UNDRESSED
(**FRENCH** —) ALESAN
(**NOT** —) DECENT
(**RUN** —) STREAK
NUDGE JOG NOG NUB WAG GOAD
JOLT KNUB LUMP POKE POTE PROD
PUSH BLOCK CHUCK DUNCH ELBOW
NUDISM NATURISM GYMNOSOPHY
NUDIST ADAMITE NUDIFIER
GYMNOSOPH
NUGATORY IDLE NULL VAIN EMPTY
PETTY FUTILE HOLLOW INVALID
TRIVIAL USELESS TRIFLING
FRUSTRATE WORTHLESS
NUGGET EYE LOB GOLD HUNK LUMP
MASS SLUG PRILL YELLOW
NUISANCE BANE BORE EVIL HARM
HURT PAIN PEST STING INJURY
PLAGUE TERROR VEXATION
ANNOYANCE
NULL NIL VOID EMPTY INEPT IRRITE
INVALID NULLIFY USELESS VACUOUS
NUGATORY FRUSTRATE
NULLAH GORGE GULLY NULLA
NALLAH RAVINE
NULLIFY BEAT FLAW LAME NULL
UNDO VETO VOID ABATE ANNUL
ELIDE ERASE LAPSE CANCEL
DEFEAT NEGATE OFFSET REPEAL
REVOKE ABOLISH COUNTER
DESTROY ABROGATE EVACUATE
STULTIFY FRUSTRATE
NUMB DEAD DRUG DULL DAZED

FUNNY STONY ASLEEP BENUMB
CLUMSY DEADEN STUPID TORPID
STUPEFY ENFEEBLE HEBETATE
HELPLESS RIGESCENT TABETLESS
NUMBER SUM BAND BODY COPY
CURN DRAW HERD HOST LOTS MAIN
MANY MESS MORT SLEW SURD
TALE TELL COUNT DATUM DIGIT
FOLIE GRIST GROUP INDEX ISSUE
SCADS SCORE STAND TOTAL
WHOLE ADDEND AMOUNT BUNDLE
CIPHER ENCORE FACTOR FIGURE
FILLER HIRSEL MYRIAD POLICY
RECKON SCALAR TICHEL CHIFFER
COMPUTE DECIMAL DIVISOR
FOLIATE SEVERAL CARDINAL
FRACTION NUMERATE QUANTITY
CALCULATE MULTITUDE
(— OF ARROWS) END
(— OF ATOMS) CHAIN
(— OF BEASTS) HERD
(— OF BOMBS) STICK
(— OF BRICKS) CLAMP
(— OF CATTLE) SOUM
(— OF FUR SKINS) TIMBER
(— OF HANKS OF YARN TO POUND)
COUNT
(— OF HAWKS) CAST
(— OF HONEYBEES) CLUSTER
(— OF NEEDLES) GAGE GAUGE
(— OF POEMS) EPOS
(— OF SHEARERS) BOARD
(— OF TEA CHESTS) BREAK
(— OF TRICKS) BOOK
(— OF WORDS) FOLIO
(—S GAME) BUG
(BALLET —) ENTREE
(CARDINAL —) ONE TWO ALEF
ALEPH THREE
(COMPLEX —) IMAGINARY
(CONSIDERABLE —) WHEEN HATFUL
FISTFUL
(DESCRIBABLE —) SCALAR
(EXCESS —) ADVANTAGE
(EXCESSIVE —) SPATE
(EXTRA —) ENCORE
(GOLDEN —) PRIME
(GREAT —) LAC HEAP HOST LAKH
MORT BREAK HIRST MEINY POWER
SHOAL SIGHT SWARM LEGION
MYRIAD INFINITE INFINITY
THOUSAND MULTITUDE
(GREAT —S) FLOCKS
(GREATER —) MO
(INDEFINITE —) LAC STEEN SUNDRY
THARVE JILLION SEVERAL THREAVE
UMPTEEN
(IRRATIONAL —) SURD
(LARGE —) ARMY FECK HERD HOST
LUMP PECK SLEW ARRAY CROWD
FORCE SCADS SHEAF SPATE STACK
STORE WORLD GALLON HIRSEL
HIRSLE LEGION MELDER BILLION
JILLION
(LARGE —S) STRENGTH
(LEAF —) FOLIO
(LEAST WHOLE —) UNIT
(ODD —S) IMPAIR
(OPPOSITE —) COUSIN

(ORDINAL —) FIRST THIRD SECOND
(PUT ON SERIAL —) FOLIO
(SMALL —) FEW CURN CURRAN
HANDFUL PAUCITY SPATTER
(TOTAL —) AMOUNT
(VAST —) HORDE
(WHOLE —) ALL DIGIT INTEGER
NUMBERED MENE
NUMBERING TALE COUNT
FOLIATION
NUMBFISH TORPEDO
NUMBING WARELESS
NUMBLES UMBLES INNARDS
NOMBLES VISCERA ENTRAILS
NUMBNESS STUPOR STUPIDITY
NUMEN DEITY GENIUS SPIRIT
VESTAL DIVINITY
NUMERAL (ALSO SEE NUMBER) SUM
WORD DIGIT CIPHER FIGURE LETTER
CHAPTER
(— STYLE) ROMAN ARABIC
(CLOCK —) CHAPTER
NUMERATIVE PEN SEGREGATIVE
NUMEROUS BIG LOTS MAIN MANY
RANK RIFE GREAT LARGE STOUR
DIVERS GALORE LEGION MYRIAD
SUNDRY UNRIDE COPIOUS
CROWDED ENDLESS FEARFUL
FERTILE PROFUSE SEVERAL
TEEMING UMPTEEN ABUNDANT
FREQUENT MANIFOLD MULTIPLE
POPULOUS THRONGED EXTENSIVE
MULTIFOLD NUMBERFUL PLENTIFUL
(— AND POWERFUL) MAIN
(MODERATELY —) FAIR
(VERY —) EXCESSIVE
NUMIDIA (BIRD OF —) DEMOISELLE
(CITY OF —) HIPPO
(KING OF —) JUGURTHA
NUMSKULL NUM DAFF DOLT FLAT
DUNCE LACKWIT BONEHEAD
BLOCKHEAD
NUN BIRD SMEW CLARE CLERK
MONIAL PIGEON SISTER TERESA
VESTAL VOWESS CONFINE DEANESS
DEVOTEE EXTERNE MINCHEN
MONKESS RECLUSE TEATINE
THEATIN CHAPLAIN CLARISSE
PRIORESS TITMOUSE URBANIST
URSULINE VISITANT VOTARESS
ANGELICAL LORETTINE PRIESTESS
RELIGEUSE
(— BIRD) MONASE TITMOUSE
(— HEADDRESS) WIMPLE
(— HOOD) FAILLE
(— MOTH) TUSSOCK
(— ORDER) MARIST TRAPPIST
LORETTINE OOMINICAN
(CHIEF —) ABBA ABBESS MOTHER
(LATIN —) VESTA
(SON OF —) JOSHUA
NUNCIATE NUNCIO ANNOUNCER
MESSENGER
NUNCIO ENVOY NUNCE LEGATE
NUNTIUS DELEGATE MESSENGER
NUNCUPATE DECLARE DEDICATE
INSCRIBE PROCLAIM DESIGNATE
PRONOUNCE

NUNCUPATIVE ORAL SPOKEN
UNWRITTEN
NUNNERY ABBEY NUNRY CONVENT
CLOISTER MINCHERY
(HEAD OF —) ABBESS
NUPSON FOOL SIMPLETON
NUPTIAL BRIDAL GENIAL THORAL
MARITAL WEDDING ESPOUSAL
HYMENEAL MARRIAGE
(PL.) SPOUSAL ESPOUSAL
HYMENEALS WIFETHING
NUQUE NAPE NECK
NURSE AMAH AYAH CARE DHAI FEED
NANA NUSS REAR SABA SUCK TEND
BONNE MAMMY NANNY NORSH
ATTEND BAYMAN CRADLE FOMENT
FOSTER GRANNY KEEPER NANNIE
NORICE NUZZLE SISTER SITTER
SUCKLE UMFAAN CHERISH FURTHER
NOURISH NURTURE PROMOTE
CULTIVATE ENCOURAGE NURSEMAID
(— A GRIEVANCE) SULK
(— OF HIAWATHA) NOKOMIS
(— OF ULYSSES) EURYCLEA
(— OF ZEUS) AMALTHEA CYNOSURA
(— SHARK) GATA
(GULLIVER'S —) GLUMDALCLITCH
(WET —) DHAI DHOLL
NURSERY RACE CRECHE BROODER
FOSTERAGE
NURSLING BABY NORRY NURRY
FOSTER FOUNDLING
NURTURE CARE DIET FEED FOOD
REAR TEND BREED NURSE TRAIN
COCKER FOSTER NUZZLE CHERISH
EDUCATE SUPPORT BREEDING
NORTELRY TRAINING EDUCATION
ESTABLISH NUTRIMENT
NUSAIRI ANSARIE
NUT ACA BEN BUR COB GUY JOU NIT
TAP ANTA BURR COLA CORE DOLT
FOOL FROG HEAD KOLA LORE MAST
NITE PILI PITH SEED TASK ACORN
BETEL BONGA BUNGA CRANK FRUIT
GLANS HAZEL HICAN JUVIA PECAN
TRYMA ALMOND BONDUC BRAZIL
CASHEW FELLOW HICCAN ILLIPE
KERNEL PEANUT PIGNON PINION
PYRENE CASTANA FILBERT HICKORY
PROBLEM APPLENUT BEECHNUT
BREADNUT CHESTNUT GOORANUT
LARRIKIN CAPOTASTO CHINKAPIN
ECCENTRIC MACADAMIA PHILOPENA
(— COAL) ANTHRACITE
(— GRASS) SEDGE
(— OF VIOLIN BOW) FROG
(— PINE) PIGNON PINOON PIGNOLIA
(CASHEW —) SEDGE
(CONSORT OF —) GEB KEB
(DAUGHTER OF —) ISIS NEPHYTHYS
(FALLEN —S) SHACK
(PALM —) BETEL LICHI COCOANUT
(PERT. TO —) NUCAL
(RIPE —) LEAMER
(RUSH —) CHUFA
(SON OF —) RA
(PL.) MASTAGE
NUT-BEARING NUCIFEROUS
NUTCRACKER XENOPS CRACKER

PILLORY MEATBIRD NUTCRACK
NUTHATCH NUTPECKER
NUTHATCH SITTA TOMTIT XENOPS
JARBIRD SITTINE TITMOUSE
NUTJOBBER
NUTHOOK BEADLE CONSTABLE
NUTLET NUCULE PYRENA PYRENE
GYROLITH
NUTMEG SEED TREE SPICE BEAVER
CALABASH NOTEMIGGE NOTEMUGGE
(— COVERING) MACE
(— STATE) CONNECTICUT
NUTRIA FUR COYPU GREGE NEUTRIA
RAGONDIN
NUTRIENT STARTER
(PL.) FOOD HEMOTROPHE
NUTRIMENT DIET FOOD KEEP
VIANDS ALIMENT PABULUM
SUPPORT
NUTRITION EUTROPHY TROPHISM
(IMPERFECT —) DYSTROPHY
DYSTROPHIA
NUTRITIOUS BATTLE BAITTLE
TROPHIC
NUT-SHAPED NUCIFORM
NUTSHELL SHELL INCLUDER
NUTTY GAGA NUTS RACY ZANY
BUGGY QUEER SPICY FRUITY

LOVING SPRUCE AMOROUS FOOLISH
PIQUANT ZESTFUL DEMENTED
PLEASANT ECCENTRIC FLAVORFUL
NUX VOMICA SNAKEWOOD
NUZZLE DIG PET ROOT NURSE
SNUFF BURROW CARESS FONDLE
FOSTER NESTLE NUDDLE NURTURE
SNOOZLE SNUGGLE SNUZZLE
NYE EYAS NEST NIDE BROOD FLOCK
NYMPH FLY GIRL MAIA MITE MUSE
PINK PIXY PUPA TICK AEGLE DRYAD
HOURI LARVA NAIAD NIXIE OREAD
SIREN SYLPH BYBLIS CYRENE
DAMSEL DAPHNE HELICE HESTIA
KELPIE MAIDEN NEREID SPRITE
SYRINX UNDINE CORYCIA ERYTHEA
HESPERA LIRIOPE OCEANID
CALLISTO CYNOSURA EURYDICE
MARPESSA PROSOPON BUTTERFLY
HAMADRYAD
(— BELOVED BY PAN) SYRINX
(— BELOVED OF NARCISSUS) ECHO
(— OF FOUNTAIN) EGERIA
SALMACIS
(— OF HILLS) OREAD
(— OF MEADOWS) LIMONIAD
(— OF MESSINA STRAIT) SCYLLA

(— OF MT. IDA) OENONE
(CITY —) POLIAD
(LAKE —) NAIAD LIMNIAD
(OCEAN —) SIREN GALATEA
OCEANID
(QUEEN OF —S) MAB
(RIVER —) NAIS NAIAD
(SEA —) MERROW NEREID CALYPSO
GALATEA MERMAID
(WATER —) NAIS EGERIA LURLEI
UNDINE APSARAS HYDRIAD
JUTURNA EPHYDRIAD
(WOOD —) DRYAD NAPEA
ARETHUSA
(PL.) HYADS THRIAI CAMENAE
NYMPHAEA CASTALY CASTALIA
NYMPHOMANIAC (BOVINE —)
BULLER
NYROCA AYTHYA
NYSSA TUPELO
NYSTAGMUS TIC WINK
NYX NOX NIGHT
(— PERSONIFIED) NIGHT
(BROTHER OF —) EREBUS
(DAUGHTER OF —) DAY ERIS LIGHT
(HUSBAND OF —) CHAOS
(SON OF —) CHARON

O HO OH OCH ZERO CIPHER OMICRON

OAF AUF BOOR DOLT FOOL LOUT CLOWN DUNCE IDIOT OUPHE YOKEL MUCKER NASHGAB PALOOKA POMPION BLOCKHEAD FOUNDLING SCHLEMIEL SIMPLETON

OAHU (— BIRD) JIBI

OAK CLUB CORK HOLM ILEX BRAVE BRIAR EMORY HOLLY ROBLE ROBUR ACAJOU BAREEN CERRIS ENCINA KERMES STRONG TOUMEY VALOMA AMBROSE BELLOTA BELLOTE DURMAST EGILOPS KELLOGG PALAYAN TURTOSA BEEFWOOD BLUEJACK CHAMPION CHAPARRO FLITTERN WAINSCOT BLACKJACK CHINKAPIN
(— **BARK**) CRUT
(— **FRUIT**) MAST ACORN CAMATA BELLOTE
(**JERUSALEM** —) AMBROSE
(**WHITE** —) ROBLE
(**YOUNG** —) FLITTERN

OAKUM OCCAM

OAKWOOD MESA

OAR AIR BOW PLY ROW PALM PEEL POLE ALOOF BLADE ROWER SCULL SPOON SWAPE SWEEP YULOH PADDLE PALLET PROPEL OARSMAN PROPELLER
(— **BLADE**) PALM PEEL WASH
(— **FULCRUM**) LOCK THOLE OARLOCK ROWLOCK
(**BOW** —) GOUGER
(**HANDLE OF** —) GRASP
(**INBOARD PORTION OF** —) LOOM
(**STERN** —) SCULL SKULL

OARLOCK LOCK THOLE ROWLOCK

OARSMAN OAR REMEX ROWER BOWMAN STROKE BENCHER SCULLER WATERMAN

OASIS BAR OJO SPA MERV SIWA WADI WADY SPRING

OAST HOST KILN OVEN COCKLE OASTHOUSE

OAT AIT WOT FEED FOOD PIPE POEM SKEG SONG AUCHT CHEAT GRAIN HAVER PEARL ANGORA EGILOPS
(— **HUSK**) SHOOD FLIGHT
(— **RENT**) AVENAGE
(**EDIBLE PORTION OF** —) GROATS
(**FALSE WILD** —**S**) FATUOID
(**HUSKED** —) SHEALING
(**NAKED** —) PILLAS PILCORN
(**UNTHRASHED** —) OATHAY
(**WILD** —**S**) HAVERGRASS
(PL.) CORN GRAIN HAVER GROUTS PROVENDER WHITECORN

OATCAKE CAPER HAVERCAKE SOURBREAD

OATEN AITEN

OATH OD ADS BAN DAD DOD GAD GAR GOL GOR GUM ODD SAM VOW BOND CRUM CUSS DARN DRAT ECOD EGAD EGOD GEEZ GOSH HECK JEEZ JING NIGS SANG SLID SLUD WORD BEDAD BEGAD BEGOB BLIMY CURSE DAMME DEUCE GOLLY

HOKEY MORDU PARDY SACRE SFOOT SLIFE SNIGS SWEAR YERRA ADSBUD APPEAL CRACKY CRIKEY CRIPES CRUMBS FEALTY JABERS JERNIE NEAKES PARDIE PLEDGE RAPPER SBLOOD SLIGHT STRUTH ZOUNDS BEGORRA BEGORRY BEJESUS BYRLADY CORBLEU GADSLID GEEWHIZ GEEWIZZ JEEPERS JIMMINY MORBLEU ODSFISH ODZOOKS PROMISE THUNDER ANATHEMA BEJABERS BODYKINS CRICKETY GADZOOKS JURAMENT PITIKINS SANCTION SEREMENT SNIGGERS SPLUTTER AFFIDAVIT BEJABBERS BLASPHEMY DODGASTED EXPLETIVE PROFANITY SACRAMENT SLIDIKINS SWEARWORD

OATMEAL OATS STODGE YELLOW POTTAGE DRAMMOCK PORRIDGE
(— **BREAD**) ANACK JANNACK
(— **CAKE**) PONE SCONE

OBCLUDE HIDE OCCLUDE

OBDURATE FIRM HARD BALKY HARSH INERT ROCKY ROUGH STARK STONY DOGGED INURED MULISH RUGGED SEVERE STURDY SULLEN ADAMANT CALLOUS HARDENED PERVERSE STUBBORN IMPASSIVE UNBENDING

OBEAH OBI OBIA CHARM FETISH VOODOO

OBECHE ARERE AYOUS SAMBA

OBEDIENCE ORDER FEALTY CONTROL SERVICE DOCILITY OBEISANCE

OBEDIENT RULY TALL TAME BUXOM DOCILE PLIANT DEVOTED DUTEOUS DUTIFUL HEEDFUL MINDFUL ORDERLY SUBJECT AMENABLE BIDDABLE YIELDING ATTENTIVE OBSERVING SERVIABLE TRACTABLE
(— **TO THE HELM**) HANDY

OBEDIENTARY PRIOR

OBEDIENT PLANT DRAGONHEAD

OBEISANCE BOW LEG JOUK BINGE CONGE HONOR SALAM CONGEE CURTSY FEALTY HOMAGE SALAAM CURTSEY DEFERENCE HUMBLESSO REFERENCE

OBELISK MARK PYLON SHAFT DAGGER GUGLIA GUGLIO NEEDLE OBELUS PILLAR AGUGLIA MONUMENT HAGIOLITH

OBERON KING POEM FAIRY OPERA SATELLITE
(**WIFE OF** —) TITANIA

OBESE FAT FOZY PLUMP PUDGY PUFFY PURSY STOUT FLESHY PORTLY PYKNIC ROTUND TURGID ADIPOSE PURSIVE BLUBBERY LIPAROUS CORPULENT

OBESITY FAT FATNESS LIPOSIS ADIPOSIS FOZINESS ADIPOSITY

OBEY EAR HEAR HEED MIND DEFER YIELD COMPLY FOLLOW OBEISH SUBMIT EXECUTE OBSERVE OBTEMPER
(— **HELM**) STEER

OBFUSCATE DIM CLOUD DARKEN MUDDLE OBFUSK CONFUSE MYSTI[F] OBSCURE PERPLEX STUPEFY BEWILDER

OBI OBE SASH CHARM OBEAH FETICH FETISH GIRDLE

OBIT MASS REST DEATH NOTICE OBITAL DECEASE RELEASE SERVIC[E] OBITUARY NECROLOGY OBSEQUIE[S]

OBJECT AIM END TAP BALK BEEF CARE CARP FINE GOAL IDEA ITEM KICK MAIN MIND PASS WHAT ARGU[E] CAVIL DEMUR GRIPE PINCH POINT SCOPE SIGHT TELOS THING AFFAIR DESIGN EMBLEM ENTITY FIGURE GADGET INTENT MATTER MOTIVE OPPOSE TARGET ARTICLE DINGBA[T] DISLIKE DISSENT MEANING PROTES[T] PURPOSE QUARREL REALITY RECLAIM NOUMENON TENDENCY CHALLENGE INTENTION SPECTACL[E]
(— **HAVING FLAWS**) SPOIL
(— **OF AMBITION**) MAIN
(— **OF ART**) VASE CURIO VIRTU ANTIQUE BIBELOT FIGURINE
(— **OF CRITICISM**) BUTT
(— **OF DEVOTION**) IDOL TOTEM FETISH
(— **OF DISGUST**) UG
(— **OF DREAD**) BOGY BOGEY BOGI[E] BOGGIE BUGBEAR
(— **OF KNOWLEDGE**) SCIBILE
(— **OF PILGRIMAGE**) CAABA KAABA[H]
(— **OF PURSUIT**) SHADOW
(— **OF RELIANCE**) STAY
(— **OF RIDICULE**) FUN GAME
(— **OF SCORN**) GECK SCOFF BYWORD HISSING DERISION
(— **OF THOUGHT**) CONSTRUCT
(— **OF WONDER**) ADMIRATION
(— **TO BE TILTED AT**) QUINTAIN
(**BELOVED** —) MINION DARLING MISTRESS
(**BULKY** —) WODGE
(**CONICAL** —) ACORN
(**CONSPICUOUS** —) LANDMARK
(**CONTAMINATED** —**S**) FOMITES
(**CURVED** —) BELLY
(**CYLINDRICAL** —) BOLE
(**DECORATIVE** —) BIBELOT
(**DESIRABLE** —) GRAIL
(**FACTORY-MADE** —**S**) ARTWORK
(**MINUTE** —) ATOM MITE
(**ROUND** —) RONDEL TRINDLE TRUNDLE
(**SACRED** —) URIM ZOGO GUACA HUACA SHRINE CHURINGA
(**SILLY** —) INANITY
(**SMALL** —) PIRLIE
(**TRANSCENDENTAL** —) ENTITY
(**ULTIMATE** —) TELOS
(**VILE** —**S**) SCUM
(**WORTHLESS** —) SPLINTER

OBJECTION OB BAR BUT BEEF CRAB FUSS KICK CAVIL DEMUR DOUBT CHESON QUARREL QUIBBL[E] SCRUPLE QUESTION CHALLENGE CRITICISM EXCEPTION

OBJECTIONABLE VILE AWFUL

HORRID GHASTLY UNLUSTY
UNLIKELY FRIGHTFUL OBNOXIOUS
OFFENSIVE
OBJECTIVE AIM END FAIR GAME
GOAL HOME REAL SAKE OUTER
ACTUAL AMORAL ANIMUS DESIGN
MOTIVE TARGET PURPOSE
DETACHED TANGIBLE UNBIASED
DIRECTION INTENTION POSITIVAL
QUAESITUM ULTIMATUM
OBJURGATE BAN JAW DAMN ABUSE
CHIDE CURSE DECRY BERATE
REBUKE REPROVE UPBRAID
VITUPER EXECRATE CASTIGATE
OBLATE MONK OFFER DEDICATE
MONASTIC
OBLATION CORBAN OFLETE SACRED
CHARITY ANAPHORA DEVOTION
OFFERING SACRIFICE
OBLIGATE COMMIT STRICT
OBLIGATED LIABLE
OBLIGATION DUE IOU TIE VOW BAIL
BAND BOND CALL DEBT DUTY KNOT
LOAD LOAN MUST NOTE OATH
ONUS SEAL CHECK OUGHT SCORE
ARREAR BURDEN CHARGE CONSOL
CUSTOM FEALTY PLEDGE ANNUITY
BONDAGE PROMISE TRIBUTE
CONTRACT HYPOTHEC SECURITY
WARRANTY AGREEMENT LIABILITY
(— NOT TO MARRY) CELIBACY
(— TO RENDER RENT) CUSTOM
(MORAL —) BOND DUTY
(PL.) STRINGS
OBLIGATORY BINDING BOUNDEN
FORCIBLE IMPOSING LIGATORY
INCUMBENT MANDATORY
OBLIGE PUT HOLD PAWN DRIVE
FAVOR FORCE COMPEL ENGAGE
PLEASE GRATIFY REQUIRE
CONCLUDE MORTGAGE CONSTRAIN
OBLIGED FAIN BOUND DEBTED
BOUNDEN DEBTFUL FAVORED
PLEASED PLEDGED BEHOLDEN
GRATEFUL OBSTRICT BEHOLDING
OBLIGATED
OBLIGING KIND BUXOM CIVIL
CLEVER TOWARD AMIABLE
FAVOROUS AGREEABLE COURTEOUS
FAVORABLE OFFICIOUS
OBLIQUE AWRY BIAS SIDE SKEW
ASKEW BEVEL CROSS SLANT
ASLANT ASWASH LOUCHE SQUINT
THWART ASKANCE CROOKED
EMBELIF EVASIVE SCALENE SIDLING
SLOPING DIAGONAL INCLINED
INDIRECT SIDELONG SIDEWAYS
SIDEWISE SLANTING TORTUOUS
INDICULAR UNDERHAND
(— IN MINING) CLINIC
(— STROKE) SLASH SOLIDUS
(— WORK) SWASHWORK
OBLIQUELY AGEE AWRY BIAS
AGLEE ASIDE ASKEW AWASH SLANT
SLOPE ASLANT ASWASH ASKANCE
EMBELIF BIASWISE SIDELONG
SIDEWAYS SIDEWISE
OBLIQUITY DIRT SWEEP DIRTINESS
OBLITERATE INK BLOT DELE RASE

RAZE WIPE ANNUL BLACK COVER
ERASE SMEAR CANCEL DELETE
EFFACE SPONGE ABOLISH DESTROY
EXPUNGE OUTRAZE SCRATCH
OVERSCORE
OBLITERATION BLOT RASURE
ERASURE NEGATION SYNIZESIS
OBLIVION LETHE LIMBO PARDON
AMNESTY NIRVANA SILENCE
OUBLIANCE
OBLIVIOUS AMORT BLISSFUL
HEEDLESS OBLIVIAL FORGETFUL
OBLONG CHITON EVELONG
AVELONGE EVENLONG ELONGATED
(ROUNDED —) ELLIPSE
OBLOQUY ABUSE BLAME ODIUM
INFAMY CALUMNY CENSURE
REPROOF CONTEMPT DISGRACE
DISHONOR OBLICQUE
OBNOXIOUS FOUL PERT VILE CURST
CURSED FAULTY HORRID LIABLE
ODIOUS RANCID SEPTIC HATEFUL
INVIDIOUS OFFENSIVE REPUGNANT
VERMINOUS
OBOE PIPE REED WAIT AULOS
SHAWM SURNAI SURNAY HAUTBOY
MUSETTE PIFFERO CHIRIMIA
HAUTBOIS SCHALMEY SZOPELKA
CHALUMEAU
(— DI CACCIA) TENOROON
FAGOTTINO
(BASS —) RACKETT
OBOLE MAIL MAILLE
OBSCENE PAW FOUL LEWD NAST
BAWDY GROSS NASTY ROCKY
COARSE FILTHY IMPURE RIBALD
SMUTTY VULGAR KNAVISH PROFANE
IMMODEST INDECENT LOATHSOME
OFFENSIVE REPULSIVE SALACIOUS
(— CULT) AISCHROLATREIA
OBSCURATION COVER ECLIPSE
OBSCURE DIM FOG BLOT BLUR
DARK DEEP HARD HART HAZY HIDE
PALE SLUR BEDIM BEFOG BLANK
BLIND CLOUD COVER DUSKY FAINT
FOGGY GLOOM INNER LOWLY
MIRKY MISTY MUDDY MURKY SHADE
SMEAR STAIN VAGUE BEMIST
CLOUDY DARKEN DARKLE DEADEN
DELUDE GLOOMY HUMBLE MYSTIC
OCCULT OPAQUE REMOTE SHADOW
SOMBER SUBTLE BECLOUD BENIGHT
CLOUDED CONCEAL CONFUSE
CRABBED CRYPTIC ECLIPSE
ENCRUST ENVELOP OBLIQUE
OVERLAY OVERTOP SHADOWY
SLUBBER TARNISH UNCLEAR
UNKNOWN UNNOTED ABSTRUSE
DARKLING DISGUISE DOUBTFUL
FAMELESS MYSTICAL NAMELESS
OBSTRUSE OVERSILE
(MAKE —) BECLOUD
OBSCURED HAZY HIDDEN BLINDED
CLOUDED DUSKISH DARKSOME
DISGUISED INFUSCATE
OBSCURITY FOG MIST CLOUD
GLOOM SHADE CALIGO SHADOW
DIMNESS OPACITY PRIVACY SILENCE

DARKNESS TENEBRES BLINDNESS
SECLUSION
(PL.) MURLEMEWES
OBSECRATE BEG PRAY BESEECH
ENTREAT PETITION
OBSEQUIES MASS OBIT PYRE WAKE
RITES SERVICE FUNERALS
OBSEQUIOUS SLICK MENIAL SUPPLE
COURTLY DEVOTED DUTEOUS
DUTIFUL FAWNING SERVILE SLAVISH
VERNILE CRINGING OBEDIENT
OBEISANT TOADYING ASSIDUOUS
ATTENTIVE COMPLIANT
(— PERSON) LIMBERHAM
OBSEQUY RITE EXEQUY RITUAL
FUNERAL CEREMONY
OBSERVANCE ACT FORM RITE RULE
FREET HONOR CUSTOM REGARD
KEEPING CEREMONY PRACTICE
ADHERENCE ATTENTION DEFERENCE
INDICTION SOLEMNITY
(— OF PROPRIETIES) DECORUM
BREEDING ETIQUETTE
(RELIGIOUS —) NOVENA
SACRAMENT
(SUPERSTITIOUS —) FREET FREIT
(PL.) FUNERAL CEREMONY
OBSERVANT ALERT EYEFUL
CAREFUL HEEDFUL MINDFUL
DILIGENT VIGILANT WATCHFUL
OBSERVATION EYE SPY HEED IDEA
NOTE RAOB VIEW SIGHT ESPIAL
LOGION NOTICE REGARD REMARK
AUSPICE AUTOPSY COMMENT
CONTACT DESCANT OPINION
EYESIGHT GAZEMENT SCHOLION
SCHOLIUM ASSERTION ATTENTION
ESPIONAGE
(ECOLOGICAL —S) ANNUATION
(PRELIMINARY —) PROEM
OBSERVATIONISM SCHAULUST
OBSERVATORY LICK TOWER
LOOKOUT PALOMAR
OBSERVE LO EYE SEE SPY ESPY
HEED HOLD KEEP LOOK MAKE
MARK MIND NARK NOTA NOTE OBEY
SPOT TENT TOUT TWIG WAIT YEME
ABIDE QUOTE SMOKE STUDY UTTER
WATCH ADHERE ADVERT ATHOLD
BEHOLD DETECT DEVISE FOLLOW
NOTICE NOTIFY REGARD REMARK
SURVEY COMMENT DISCERN
EXPRESS MENTION PROFESS
RESPECT WITNESS PERCEIVE
PRESERVE SPECTATE ADVERTISE
CELEBRATE SOLEMNIZE
(— CLOSELY) SMOKE
(— DULLY) BLEAR
OBSERVER O BIRDER CORNER
WATCHER AUDIENCE INFORMER
ONLOOKER BYSTANDER SCRUTATOR
SPECTATOR
OBSESS RIDE BESET HAUNT HARASS
INVEST OBSEDE BESIEGE HAGRIDE
POSSESS PREOCCUPY
OBSESSED CRAZY DOTTY HAPPY
HIPPED BESOTTED
OBSESSION TIC CRAZE MANIA
SIEGE MAGGOT ECSTASY FIXATION

OBSIDIAN CORE LAVA IZTLE IZTLI LAPIS

OBSOLETE OLD DEAD PAST DATED PASSE BYGONE EFFETE ABOLETE ANCIENT ARCHAIC CLASSIC DISUSED EFFACED EXTINCT OUTWORN OUTDATED OUTMODED OVERWORN DISCARDED

OBSTACLE BAR DAM LET BOYG BUMP DRAG JUMP OBEX SNAG STAY STOP BLOCK CHECK CLAMP CRIMP FENCE HITCH HYDRA SPOKE STICK STILE ABATIS BUNKER FRAISE HOCKET HURDLE OBJECT RETARD ANSTOSS BARRIER CHICANE FIVEBAR STOPPER BLOCKADE MOLEHILL BARRICADE CONDITION HINDRANCE ROADBLOCK TURNAGAIN
(— TO VIRTUE) SLANDER
(GOLF —) HAZARD
(INSURMOUNTABLE —) IMPASSE

OBSTETRICIAN ACCOUCHEUR

OBSTETRICS MAIEUTICS MIDWIFERY

OBSTINATE SET SOT DOUR FIRM SULY BALKY FIXED ROWDY RUSTY STIFF STOUT TOUGH ASSISH CUSSED DOGGED KNOBBY MULISH STEEVE STUFFY STUPID STURDY SULLEN UNRULY ASININE BULLISH CRABBED FROWARD PEEVISH RESTIVE WILLFUL CROTCHED OBDURATE PERVERSE PREFRACT RENITENT STOMACHY STUBBORN FORERIGHT PIGHEADED STONEWALL TENACIOUS
(NOT —) SUPPLE

OBSTREPEROUS LOUD WILD NOISY UNRULY CLAMOROUS

OBSTRUCT BAR DAM DIT GAG JAM CLOG COOP DITT FILL FOUL JAMB STOP TRIP BESET BLANK BLOCK CHAIN CHECK CHOKE CROSS DELAY HEDGE THROW ARREST CUMBER FORBAR HAMPER HOBBLE IMPEDE OPPOSE PESTER RETARD STIFLE THWART WAYLAY WINDER BARRIER FORELAY OCCLUDE BLOCKADE EMBOLIZE ENCUMBER FLOUNDER OPPILATE BARRICADE EMBARRASS INCOMMODE

OBSTRUCTION BAR DAM GAG LET RUB BOOM BUMP SLUG SNAG STAY STOP BLOCK CHOKE GORCE HITCH SPOKE HAMPER TAPPEN THWART BARRACE BARRAGE BARRIER BLINDER CHOKAGE EMBOLISM OBSTACLE STOPPAGE EMPHRAXIS
(— IN OILWELL) BRIDGE
(— IN RIVER) GORGE
(— IN TEAT) SPIDER
(— IN VALVE) GAG
(— OF BLOOD VESSEL) EMBOLISM
(— OF PINE LEAVES) TAPPEN
(INNER —) LOAD

OBTAIN BEG BUM BUY EKE GET WIN EARN FANG FIND GAIN HENT REAP ANNEX CADGE CATCH ETTLE REACH AREACH ARECHE ARRIVE ATTAIN BORROW DERIVE EXPEDE SECURE SPONGE ACHIEVE ACQUIRE CAPTURE CHEVISE COMPASS DEMERIT EXTRACT POSSESS PREVAIL PROCURE RECEIVE SUCCEED PURCHASE SCROUNGE
(— BY CHANCE) DRAW
(— BY HEAT) EXCOCT
(— BY REQUEST) IMPETRATE
(— BY THREAT) EXTORT
(— CONTROL) ENGROSS
(— DISHONESTLY) CROOK SHARP FLEECE NOBBLE SKELDER
(— MONEY FROM) BLEED
(— PERMISSION) CLEAR

OBTAINABLE GOING GETTABLE AVAILABLE DERIVABLE SECURABLE

OBTAINED (— AT SCENE OF CRIME) LATENT

OBTRUDE JET SORN EJECT EXPEL GLARE FLAUNT IMPOSE MEDDLE THRUST INTRUDE INTERFERE

OBTRUSIVE FRESH PUSHY GARISH BLATANT FORWARD PUSHING BUMPTIOUS INTRUSIVE

OBTUND DULL BLUNT QUELL DEADEN

OBTURATOR MUSHROOM

OBTUSE DIM DULL BLINK BLUNT CRASS DENSE THICK OPAQUE STUPID BOEOTIAN HEBETATE PURBLIND
(NOT —) ACUTE

OBVERSE FACE FRONT CONVERSE
(— OF COIN) MAN HEAD

OBVIATE PREVENT PRECLUDE FORESTALL

OBVIOUS LOUD OPEN BROAD CLEAR CRUDE FRANK GROSS NAKED OVERT PLAIN SLICK STARK LIABLE PATENT BLATANT EVIDENT EXPOSED GLARING SHALLOW SUBJECT VISIBLE APPARENT DISTINCT MANIFEST PALPABLE BAREFACED PROMINENT
(NOT —) DEEP INNER ARCANE HIDDEN MASKED OCCULT SECRET SUBTLE DELICATE DOUBTFUL PROFOUND INEVIDENT

OBVOLUTE CONTORTED OVERLAPPING

OCA OKA TUBER OXALIS SORREL SOURSOP

OCARINA CAMOTE

OCCASION SEL BOUT CALL GIVE HINT NEED SELE SITH TIDE TIME TURN BREAK CASUS CAUSE CHARE EVENT INFER NONCE RAISE SITHE SLANT STOUR WHILE YIELD AFFAIR AUTHOR CHANCE COURSE EXCUSE PERIOD REASON STOUND CHASOUN INSPIRE PRETEXT QUARREL CEREMONY ENGENDER EXIGENCY FUNCTION INCIDENT INSTANCE CONDITION ENCHEASON HAPPENING
(— GRIEF) GRIEVE
(— OF EXCITEMENT) ALARM ALARUM
(DEFINITE —) TIDE

(FAVORABLE —) ADVANTAGE
(FESTIVE —) UTAS BEANO HOLIDAY SHINDIG BEANFEST
(HAPPY —) SIMHAH SIMCHAH
(SOCIAL —) COFFEE
(SPECIAL —) CEREMONY

OCCASIONAL ODD ORRA STRAY ANTRIN CASUAL DAIMEN SCARCE POPPING EPISODIC FUGITIVE SPORADIC IRREGULAR

OCCASIONALLY EVERY BETIMES SOMETIME SOMETIMES

OCCASIVE SETTING WESTWARD

OCCIDENTAL WEST PONENT WESTERN HESPERIAN WESTERNER

OCCLUDE SORB CLOSE ABSORB OBSTRUCT

OCCLUSAL MORSAL

OCCLUSION CORONARY ARTICULATION

OCCULT MAGIC ARCANE HIDDEN LATENT MYSTIC SECRET VOODOO ALCHEMY CRYPTIC ECLIPSE UNKNOWN ESOTERIC MYSTICAL SIBYLLIC CONCEALED RECONDITE SIBYLLINE
(— SCIENCE) ESOTERICS

OCCULTATION ECLIPSE

OCCULTISM MAGIC CABALA MYSTERY

OCCUPANT HOLDER INMATE RENTER TENANT CITIZEN DWELLER RESIDENT INCUMBENT
(— OF THEATER GALLERY) GOD

OCCUPATION ART JOB LAY USE CALL GAME LINE NOTE TOIL WORK BERTH CRAFT GRAFT TRADE CAREER EMPLOY METIER RACKET SPHERE TENURE THRIFT CALLING CONCERN CONTROL MYSTERY PURSUIT QUALITY SERVICE ACTIVITY BUSINESS FUNCTION INDUSTRY INVASION VOCATION
(— OF MIND) ABSORPTION
(SUBORDINATE —) HOBBY AVOCATION

OCCUPIED BUSY FULL HELD KEPT RAPT TOOK ACTIVE INTENT ENGAGED ABSORBED CAPTURED
(FULLY —) ENGROSSED

OCCUPY LIE SIT USE BUSY FILL HAVE HOLD KEEP TAKE WARM AMUSE BELAY BESET DWELL ABSORB BETAKE EMPLOY ENGAGE EXPEND FULFIL OBTAIN TENANT COHABIT CONCERN CONTAIN ENGROSS ENTREAT IMPROVE INHABIT INVOLVE OVERSIT PERVADE POSSESS SWALLOW DISSOLVE GARRISON INTEREST POURPRISE
(— ILLEGALLY) JUMP
(— QUARTERS) CAMP

OCCUR BE GO COME COOK FALL GIVE MAKE MEET PASS RISE SORT ARISE BREAK CLASH EXIST INCUR LIGHT APPEAR ARRIVE BEFALL BETIDE CHANCE HAPPEN PROCEED TRANSPIRE
(— AGAIN) RECUR REPEAT

(— BY CHANCE) LIGHT
(— TO) CROSS ENTER STRIKE
OCCURRENCE GO HAP CASE FACT
ITEM NOTE REDE EVENT WEIRD
EPISODE PASSAGE INCIDENT
JUNCTURE OCCASION ENCOUNTER
FREQUENCE HAPPENING
(CHANCE —) ADVENTURE
CONTINGENT
(COMMON —) USE FREQUENCY
(FREQUENT —) COMMUNITY
(SIMULTANEOUS —) COINCIDENCE
(SUPERNATURAL —) MIRACLE
(UNEXPECTED —) SUDDEN
BLIZZARD BOMBSHELL
(UNFORTUNATE —) CASUALTY
(UNUSUAL —) ODDITY
OCCURRING (— AT NIGHTFALL)
ACRONICAL
(— AT REGULAR INTERVALS) HORAL
(— AT TWILIGHT) CREPUSCULAR
(— BY TURN) ALTERNATE
(— EVERY EIGHT DAYS) OCTAN
(— EVERY FOURTH YEAR)
PENTETERIC
(— FREQUENTLY) COMMON
(— IN USUAL PLACE) ENTOPIC
OCEAN SEA BLUE BRIM DEEP MAIN
POND BRINE DRINK ARCTIC INDIAN
EXPANSE NEPTUNE PACIFIC
ATLANTIC ANTARCTIC
(— FLOATING MATTER) ALGAE
LAGAN FLOTSAM
(— ROUTE) LANE
(— SPRAY) IRONWOOD CREAMCUPS
(— SWELL) SEA
(ON THE —) ASEA
OCEANIA MALAYA AUSTRALIA
MELANESIA POLYNESIA
(SACRED OBJECT OF —) ZOGO
OCEANIC NAVAL MARINE PELAGIC
NAUTICAL AEQUOREAL
OCEANUS TITAN
(DAUGHTER OF —) DORIS OCEANID
EURYNOME
(FATHER OF —) URANUS OURANOS
(MOTHER OF —) GAEA GAIA
(SISTER OF —) TETHYS
(SON OF —) NEREUS
(WIFE OF —) TETHYS
OCELLUS EYE EYELET STEMMA
EYESPOT
OCELOT CAT TOGER LEOPARD
WILDCAT
OCHER RUD SIL KEEL OAKER OCHRE
TIVER ABRAUM RADDLE ALMAGRA
TANGIER
(BLACK —) WAD WADD
(RED —) RUD KEEL TIVER ABRAUM
REDDLE RUBRIC RUDDLE KOKOWAI
(YELLOW —) SIL SPRUCE
OCOTILLO COACHWHIP
CANDLEWOOD
OCREA OCHREA SHEATH
OCTAHEDROID HYPERCUBE
TESSERACT
OCTAVE UTAS UTIS EIGHT EIGHTH
OTTAVA HUITAIN DIAPASON
SHEMINITH

(— FLUTE) FLAUTINO
(— OF THE SEVENTH) FOURTEENTH
(— SINGING) MAGADIZE
(DIMINISHED —) SEMIDIAPASON
(TRIPLE —) TRIDIAPASON
OCTAVO EIGHTS
OCTET OCTAVE OCTUOR HUITAIN
OTTETTO
OCTAVIA (BROTHER OF —)
AUGUSTUS
(HUSBAND OF —) ANTONY
OCTOPUS HEE POLYP POULP PREKE
SQUID CUTTLE CATFISH POLYPOD
POLYPUS SCUTTLE DIBRANCH
OCTOPEAN DEVILFISH
(— ARM) TENTACLE
(SECRETION OF —) INK
OCTOROON METIS MESTEE MUSTEE
MESTIZO METISSE OCTAROON
OCTROI TAX GRANT PRIVILEGE
OCTUPLE EIGHTFOLD
OCUBY RUM
OCULAR OPTIC VISUAL OCULARY
OPTICAL ORBITAL EYEPIECE
ODD AUK AWK OUT RUM FELL LEFT
LONE ORRA RARE CRAZY DIPPY
DROLL EXTRA FUNNY IMPAR OUTRE
QUEER UNKET UNKID WEIRD IMPAIR
QUAINT SINGLE UNEVEN UNIQUE
AZYGOUS BIZARRE COMICAL
CURIOUS ERRATIC STRANGE
UNEQUAL UNUSUAL FANCIFUL
FREAKISH PECULIAR SINGULAR
UNPAIRED BURLESQUE ECCENTRIC
FANTASTIC GROTESQUE LAUGHABLE
SQUIRRELY UNMATCHED WHIMSICAL
(— JOBMAN) JOEY
ODDBALL SPOOK
ODDITY GIG QUIP RUMNESS
QUIZZITY
(PL.) PURLICUES
ODDMAN UMPIRE ARBITER FLOATER
REFEREE
ODDS BISK EDGE CHALK PRICE
BISQUE DISCORD DISPUTE QUARREL
HANDICAP VARIANCE ADVANTAGE
DISPARITY
(— AND ENDS) ORTS BROTT
REFUSE SCRAPS GIBLETS SECONDS
FEWTRILS REMNANTS SHAKINGS
ETCETERAS FRAGMENTS
(AT —) ACROSS
(EXTRAVAGANT —) POUNDAGE
ODE HYMN POEM SONG LYRIC
PAEAN PSALM MONODY ODELET
CANZONA CANZONE EPICEDE
CANTICLE PALINODE PINDARIC
SERENATA STASIMON EPICEDIUM
EPINICION PARABASIS
ODEON HALL ODEUM GALLERY
THEATER
ODIN OTHIN WODAN WODEN WOTAN
(BROTHER OF —) VE VILI
(CREATED BY —) ASK EMBLA
(DAUGHTER-IN-LAW OF —) NANNA
(DESCENDANT OF —) SCYLD
(FATHER OF —) BOR BORR
(HALL OF —) VALHALLA
(HORSE OF —) SLEIPNER

(MOTHER OF —) BESTLA
(PALACE OF —) SYN
(SON OF —) TYR THOR VALI BALDR
BALDER
(SWORD OF —) GRAM
(WIFE OF —) FRIA RIND FRIGG
RINDR FRIGGA
ODIOUS FOUL LOTH UGLY VILE
LOATH INFAND ODIBLE HATABLE
HATEFUL HEINOUS HIDEOUS
DAMNABLE FLAGRANT INFAMOUS
ABHORRENT INVIDIOUS OBNOXIOUS
OFFENSIVE REPUGNANT
ODIUM HATRED STIGMA DISLIKE
AVERSION DISFAVOR DISGRACE
DISHONOR ANTIPATHY
(PUBLIC —) ENVY
ODOMETER ODOGRAPH VIAMETER
WAYWISER HODOMETER
PEDOMETER
ODONTALGIA TOOTHACHE
ODOR AIR FUME FUNK NOSE OLID
TANG WAFF WAFT AROMA EWDER
FETOR FLAIR FUMET NIDOR SCENT
SMACK SMELL SNUFF SPICE STINK
BREATH FLAVOR FOETOR HODURE
REPUTE STENCH BOUQUET
ESSENCE FUMETTE NOSEGAY
PERFUME VERDURE PUNGENCE
EFFLUVIUM EMPYREUMA
FRAGRANCE REDOLENCE
(— FROM FLOWERS) FUME
(— OF GAME) FUMET
(— OF HAY) NOSE
(BAD —) EWDER FROWST STENCH
(DISGUSTING —) STINK
(FOUL —) FIST
(FRESH —) YMUR
(PUNGENT —) SPICE
(SPICY —) BALM
(STUDY OF —S) OSMICS
ODORIFEROUS BALMY OLENT
ODOROUS FRAGRANT
ODOROUS FOUL BALMY OLENT
SMELLY ODORANT AROMATIC
FRAGRANT NIDOROSE NIDOROUS
PERFUMED REDOLENT SCENTFUL
SMELLFUL
ODYSSEUS ULYSSES
(DOG OF —) ARGOS
(FATHER OF —) LAERTES SISYPHUS
(FRIEND OF —) MENTOR
(ISLAND OF —) ITHACA
(SON OF —) TELEGONUS
TELEMACHUS
(WIFE OF —) PENELOPE
OECIST OEKIST COLONIZER
OEDIPUS OEDIPAL
(BROTHER-IN-LAW OF —) CREON
(DAUGHTER OF —) ISMENE ATIGONE
(FATHER OF —) LAIUS
(FOSTER MOTHER OF —) PERIBOEA
(MOTHER OF —) JOCASTA
(SON OF —) ETEOCLES POLYNICES
(WIFE OF —) JOCASTA
OEIL-DE-BOEUF OCULUS
OEILLADE OGLE ELIAD EYLIAD
GLANCE ILLIAD
OENOCHOE OLPE PROCHOOS

OENOMETER VINOMETER
OESTRID FLY
(— **LARVA**) BOT
OESTRUS RUT FURY HEAT STING
DESIRE ESTRUS FRENZY IMPULSE
STIMULUS
OEUVRE OPUS WORK
OF A O BY DE OFF VAN VON FROM
HAVE TILL WITH ABOUT
(— **AGE**) AE
(— **ALL**) AVA ALDER ALLER
(— **DEATH**) M
(— **EACH**) ANA PER SING
(— **THIS DAY**) HODIERNAL
(— **THIS MONTH**) HM
OFF BY AFF FAR ODD WET AFAR
AGEE AWAY DOFF DOWN GONE
ALONG ASIDE RIGHT WONKY
WRONG ABSENT CUCKOO DEPART
REMOTE DISTANT FURTHER
REMOVED SEAWARD TAINTED
ABNORMAL OPPOSITE
(— **GUARD**) TARDY
(— **THE PATH**) ASTRAY
(— **THE SUBJECT**) AFIELD
(— **THE WIND**) ROOM ROOMWARD
(**FAR** —) DISTANT
OFFAL GURRY WASTE REFUSE
CARRION DOGMEAT GARBAGE
LEAVING RUBBISH GRALLOCH
(— **OF FISH**) GURRY STOSH
(**MILLING** —**S**) GRIT
OFFBREAK GOOGLY
OFF-CENTER ECCENTRIC
EXCENTRIC
OFF-COLOR BLUE SUGGESTIVE
OFFEND CAG ERR PET SIN VEX GALL
HARM HUFF HURT MIFF RASP RASS
ABUSE ANGER ANNOY GRATE GRILL
PIQUE SHOCK SPITE TOUCH WRONG
AGUILT ATTACK GRIEVE INJURE
INSULT NETTLE REVOLT AFFRONT
DEFAULT DISDAIN MORTIFY
OUTRAGE PROVOKE REGRATE
STOMACH UMBRAGE VIOLATE
CONFRONT DISTASTE IRRITATE
TRESPASS DISOBLIGE DISPLEASE
OFFENDED HUFF MIFF SORE
AVERTED FROISSE INJURED
INSULTED
OFFENDER SINNER CULPRIT
MISDOER PECCANT HABITUAL
OFFENDANT
(**FIRST** —) STAR
OFFENSE PET SIN HUFF LACK SLIP
WITE ABUSE CRIME ERROR FAULT
GRIEF GUILT MALUM PIQUE SNUFF
ATTACK BIGAMY DELICT FELONY
PIACLE PRITCH REATUS STRUNT
AFFRONT DEFAULT DEMERIT
DUDGEON LARCENY MISDEED
OUTRAGE SCANDAL UMBRAGE
PECCANCY TRESPASS EXTORTION
INDECORUM INDIGNITY THEFTBOTE
(— **AGAINST LAW**) MALUM DELICT
DELICTUM
(— **AGAINST MORALITY**) EVIL CRIME
OFFENSIVE BAD ACID EVIL FOUL
HARD UGLY BILGY CRUDE DIRTY

FETID GROSS NASTY SLIMY COARSE
FROWZY GARISH HORRID RANCID
RIBALD ROTTEN ABUSIVE BEASTLY
FULSOME HATEFUL HIDEOUS
NOISOME RASPING SCARLET
DREADFUL INVADING MEPHITIC
SHOCKING STINKING UNSAVORY
LOATHSOME OBNOXIOUS
REPUGNANT REVOLTING
OFFER GO BID PUT BODE GIVE HAND
LEND PLEA SHOW TAKE TEND
DEFER HEAVE PARTY SHORE START
ADDUCE AFFORD ALLEGE DELATE
INJECT OBLATE OPPOSE PREFER
SUBMIT SUPPLY TENDER ADVANCE
BIDDING COMMEND EXHIBIT
PRESENT PROFFER PROPINE
PROPOSE SUGGEST OVERTURE
VOLUNTEER
(— **EXCUSE**) ALIBI
(— **FOR SALE**) HAWK EXPOSE
(— **IN SACRIFICE**) IMMOLATE
(— **PROOF**) APPROVE
(— **PUBLICLY**) JACTITATE
(— **TO VERIFY**) AVER
(**LAST** —) ULTIMATUM
(**SOLEMN** —) PLEDGE
(**UNACCEPTED** —) POLLICITATION
OFFERING BID ALMS BALI DALI DEAL
GIFT HOST SOMA DOLLY ENTRY
CORBAN NUZZER OFLETE PIACLE
PRESENT RETABLO TRIBUTE
ANATHEMA DEVOTION DONATION
LIBATION OBLATION PESHKASH
PIACULUM SACRIFICE
(— **TO GOD**) CORBAN DEODATE
(— **TO HOUSEHOLD DEITIES**) BALI
(**PEACE** —**S**) PACIFICS
(**RELIGIOUS** —) OBLATION
(**SACRIFICIAL** —) HOLOCAUST
(**THEATRICAL** —) FLUFF
(**PL.**) HIERA ALTARAGE INFERIAE
OFF-GLIDE EXIT VOCULE DETENTE
OFFHAND CURT GLIB SOON ADLIB
BLUSH HASTY ABRUPT BREEZY
CASUAL BRUSQUE READILY
CARELESS CAVALIER GLANCING
INFORMAL EXTEMPORE IMPROMPTU
UNSTUDIED
OFFICE HAT JOB SEE BOMA DUTY
NONE PART POST ROLE ROOM
SHOP TASK TOGA WIKE WORK
PLACE STINT TRUST WIKEN YAMEN
ABBACY AGENCY BUREAU CHARGE
DAFTAR DIWANI DUFTER METIER
MISTER BULLPEN CAMARIN
CENTRAL DEWANEE DROSTDY
EDILITY PYSTERY SERVICE STATION
SURGERY AEDILITY CAPACITY
CUTCHERY ENSIGNCY FUNCTION
KINGSHIP MINISTRY POSITION
PROVINCE WOOLPACK BAILIWICK
BANKSHALL SITUATION
(— **BOY**) CHOKRA
(— **CHIEF**) BOSS MANAGER
(— **OF BISHOP**) LAWN
(— **OF JUDGE**) BENCH ERMINE
(— **OF PROFESSOR**) CHAIR

(— **OF ROMAN CURIA**) DATARY
DATARIA
(— **OF RULER**) REGENCY
(— **OF THE DEAD**) DIRGE
(— **WORKER**) CLERK STENO TYPIST
SECRETARY
(**BRANCH** —) WING
(**CASHIER'S** —) CAISSE
(**CLERICAL** —) CASSOCK
(**DIVINE** —) AKOLUTHIA
(**ECCLESIASTICAL** —) FROCK
BENEFICE EXORCIST
(**HIGH** —) DIGNITY
(**LITURGICAL** —) SEXT SERVICE
(**MORNING** —) ORTHRON ORTHROS
(**NAVAL** —**S**) BEACH
(**PRIESTLY** —) SACERDOCY
(**PRINTING** —) CHAPEL IMPRIMERY
(**RECORD** —) CHANCERY
(**RESIGN AN** —) DEMIT
(**TIMEKEEPER'S** —) PENNYHOLE
OFFICEHOLDER IN WINNER
OFFICIAL PLACEMAN
OFFICER (ALSO SEE OFFICIAL) COP
TAB AIDE EXEC EXON FLAG HOLD
NASI SWAB VOGT AGENT CHIEF
CRIER DEWAN DIWAN GRAND
GRAVE GROOM JURAT SEWER
TAXOR USHER ALCADE BEADLE
BEAGLE BUTLER CENSOR DEPUTY
DIRECT ENSIGN GAILLI GEREFA
HERALD KOTWAL LAWMAN LICTOR
MANAGE ORATOR PARNAS REDTAB
SYNDIC TINDAL ALNAGER ASSIZER
BAILIFF COMMAND CONDUCT
CORONER DUUMVIR EPAULET
FEDERAL FEODARY GAVELER
GENERAL JEMADAR KLEAGLE
LOBSTER MUSTANG NAPERER
PANTLER PATROON REGIDOR
SANCTUM SCHEPEN SHERIFF
SPEAKER STEWARD WHIPPER
WOODMAN ADJUTANT ALDERMAN
ALGUACIL ANDREEVE BANNERET
CHAFFWAX COFFERER CURSITOR
DOORWARD FORESTER GOVERNOR
GRASSMAN MERESMAN MINISTER
QUESTEUR REPORTER TIPSTAFF
VISCOUNT WOODWARD CONSTABLE
DIKEGRAVE FINANCIER INTENDANT
SCHOOLMAN TAHSILDAR
(— **OF CHURCH**) ABBOT ELDER
DEACON SEXTON ANTISTES
DEFENSOR LAMPADARY SACRISTAN
(— **OF COURT**) MACER BAILIFF
FEODARY FILACER CURSITOR
DEMPSTER EXAMINER SERGEANT
ASSOCIATE BYRLAWMAN
SURROGATE
(— **OF FORESTS**) AGISTER AGISTOR
(— **OF KING'S STABLES**) AVENER
(**BARDIC** —) DRUID
(**CHIEF** —) NASI DEWAN DAROGA
PARNAS
(**CUSTOMS** —) GAGER SHARK
GAUGER JERQUER DOUANIER
SEARCHER SURVEYOR TIDESMAN
(**GREEK** —) STRATEGOS STRATEGUS
(**JAPANESE** —) SHIKKEN

(MASONIC —) EAST KING DEACON STEWARD

(MILITARY —) NAIG NAIK COMES MAJOR SUBAH ENSIGN NAIQUE RANKER SARDAR SIRDAR CAPTAIN COLONEL GENERAL JEMADAR MARSHAL SUBADAR WARRANT COMMANDER RABSHAKEH SHAVETAIL

(MINOR —) CHINOVNIK

(NAVAL —) CPO EXON MATE SWAB BOSUN ENSIGN PURSER YEOMAN ADMIRAL CAPTAIN MUSTANG SPOTTER YOUNKER SUNDOWNER

(POLICE —) PIG RURAL EXEMPT JAVERT KOTWAL RUNNER SBIRRO ALYTARCH SEARCHER THANADAR DETECTIVE

(PUBLIC —) JUDGE FISCAL NOTARY PODESTA

(ROMAN —) LICTOR

(SHERIFF'S —) FANG BEAGLE BAILIFF BULLDOG HUISSIER

(STAFF —) TAB AIDE REDTAB ADJUTANT

(TURKISH —) AGA AGHA MUTE VIZIR VIZIER BINBASHI

(PL.) BRAID BRASS STAFF

OFFICIAL (ALSO SEE OFFICER) AGA BEG DEY VIP AMIN BOSS KUAN KWAN TRUE AGENT AHONG AMALA AMBAN AMEEN AMLAH CLERK EDILE EPHOR GYANI HAJIB HOMER JURAT LIMMU LINER MAYOR NAZIR REEVE SAHIB AEDILE ARCHON ATABEG BASHAW CENSOR CONSUL EPARCH EPONYM FISCAL FORMAL GABBAI GRIEVE HAZZAN HERALD LAWMAN MASTER NOTARY PANDIT PREVOT RABMAG SATRAP SCRIBE SEALER SINGER TAOTAI TAOYIN TRONER VERGER WARDEN WEDANA ALMONER APOSTLE ASIARCH BURGESS CERTAIN JEMADAR LANDRAT MARSHAL MOORMAN PRISTAW REFEREE STALLAR STARTER SUBASHI APPROVED CARDINAL CELLARER CUSTOMER DOGBERRY GOVERNOR LINESMAN MANDARIN PRYTANIS VESTIARY EXECUTIVE MAJORDOMO

(— APPROVAL) VISA VISE

(— DECREE) WRIT UKASE

(BLUNDERING —) DOGBERRY

(POMPOUS —) BUMBLE

(PL.) KEYS PHAR OMLAH

OFFICIATE ACT FILL SERVE SUPPLY PERFORM CELEBRATE

OFFICIATOR DEICIDE

OFFICIOUS BUSY COOL PERT SAUCY FORMAL FORTHY PUSHING ARROGANT IMPUDENT INFORMAL MEDDLING OFFICIAL INBEARING

OFFING OFF FUTURE PICTURE

OFFISH CLAMMY UPSTAGE

OFFSCOURINGS MUD SCURF

OFF-SEASON LAYOFF

OFFSET SLAB STEP ALTAR CRIMP ERASE POISE CANCEL CONTRA

JOGGLE REDEEM SETOFF BALANCE COUNTER LATERAL RETREAT SETBACK PROPAGULE

(— ON BULB) SPLIT

OFFSHOOT GET PUP ROD SON LIMB SPUR BOUGH ISSUE SCION SHOOT SPRIG BRANCH FILIAL GROWTH MEMBER SPROUT ADJUNCT APOPHYSIS FILIATION OUTGROWTH

(— OF LAKE) BAYOU

OFFSHORE DEEPWATER

OFFSPRING BOY FRY IMP KID KIN SON BRAT CHIT HEIR SEED SLIP BIRTH BREED BROOD CHILD FRUIT ISSUE SCION SPAWN BEGATS DUSTEE EMBRYO FOSTER GRIQUA JUMART PROLES RESULT STRAIN STRIND MORISCO NISHADA OUTCOME PRODUCE PRODUCT PROGENY YOUNGER CHILDREN DAUGHTER DEMISANG GENITURE INCREASE KINDLING BAIRNTEAM MUSTAFINA

(— OF FAIRIES) CHANGELING

(— OF NEGRO AND MULATTO) GRIFFE

(— OF WITCH) HAGSEED HOLDIKEN

(MYTHICAL —) JUMART

(PREMATURE —) CASTLING

OFICINA WORKS OFFICE FACTORY

OFLETE WAFER OBLATION OFFERING

OFTEN OFT AFTEN OFTLY COMMON EFTSOONS FREQUENT REPEATED

(VERY —) CONTINUALLY

OGDOAD EIGHT OCTOAD OGDOAS OCTONARY

OGEE (ALSO SEE MOLDING) CYMA GULA TALON MOLDING

OGIVAL HEATER

OGLE EYE GAZE LEER LOOK MASH STARE GLANCE EXAMINE MARLOCK SMICKER OEILLADE

OGRE ORC BRUTE DEMON GHOUL GIANT HUGON TYRANT YAKSHA BUGABOO BUGBEAR MONSTER WINDIGO

OGRESS PELLET GUNSTONE

OGTIERN LORD MASTER

OGYGIAN ANCIENT PRIMEVAL

OH OU OW ACH OUCH

OIL BEN FAT ILE ULE BALM CHIA DIKA FUEL ZEST BRIBE CRUDE JUICE OLEUM SMEAR STOCK TRAIN ULYIE ULZIE ACEITE ANOINT BINDER BUTTER CARDOL CHRISM EUPION GREASE LIQUOR SAFROL SMOOTH ZACHUN CEDRIUM ESSENCE LANOLIN MYRRHOL PHLOROL RETINOL VETIVER BERGAMOT COUMARAN ERIGERON GINGEROL PHTHALAN SDRAVETS TETRALIN CARVACROL LUBRICATE PETROLEUM

(— BEETLE) MELOE MELOID

(— CAKE) SEEDCAKE

(— CAN) OILER

(— CASK) RIER

(— LAMP) LUCIGEN

(— OF TURPENTINE) CAMPHENE CAMPHINE

(— PALM) OILBERRY

(— PAN) SUMP

(— PLANT) SESAME

(— ROCK) SHALE LIMESTONE

(— TREE) EBOE POON TUNG MAHWA

(— VESSEL) DRUM OLPE CRUET CRUSE TANKER CRESSET

(— WELL) DUSTER GASSER GUSHER WILDCAT

(BUTTER —) GHEE

(COAL —) PHOTOGEN

(CONSECRATED —) CHRISM

(FISH —) GURRY

(FIXED —) COCUM KOKAM KOKUM

(FLOWER —) ABSOLUTE

(FRAGRANT —) ATAR OTTO ATTAR OTTAR CAFFEOL CAFFEONE GERANIOL

(INFERIOR —) MIDDLING

(LINSEED —) CARRON LINOLEUM

(MINERAL —) NAPHTHA KEROSENE

(PINE —) FROTHER

(SOLID —) KIKUEL

(VEGETABLE —) MACASSAR

(VULCANIZED —) FACTICE

(WHALE —) SPERM

OILBIRD FATBIRD GUACHARO

OILFISH ESCOLAR

OILSEED TIL TEEL SESAME LINSEED RAPESEED

OILSKIN OIL OILER SQUAM OILCASE OILCOAT SLICKER

OILSTONE HONE SHALE WHETSTONE

OILY FAT GLIB BLAND FATTY LOEIC SOAPY SUAVE GREASY OILISH OLEOSE OLEOUS SMARMY SMOOTH SUPPLE PINGUID SERVILE SLIPPERY UNCTUOUS COMPLIANT PLAUSIBLE

OINTMENT BALM MULL NARD SALVE BALSAM CERATE CEROMA UNGUENT SPIKENARD

OILBIRD FATBIRD GUACHARO

OILFISH ESCOLAR
OILSEED TIL TEEL SESAME LINSEED RAPESEED
OILSKIN OIL OILER SQUAM OILCASE OILCOAT SLICKER
OILSTONE HONE SHALE WHETSTONE
OILY FAT GLIB BLAND FATTY OLEIC SOAPY SUAVE GREASY OILISH OLEOSE OLEOUS SMARMY SMOOTH SUPPLE PINGUID SERVILE SLIPPERY UNCTUOUS COMPLIANT PLAUSIBLE
OINTMENT UNG BALM MULL NARD PASTE SALVE SMEAR BALSAM CERATE CEROMA CHARGE CHRISM GREASE POMADE REMEDY UNGUENT EYESALVE POPULEON REMOLADE SPIKENARD WHITFIELD
(— OF GODS) AMBROSIA
OJIBWAY CHIPPEWA SAULTEUR CHIPPEWAY
OKA OCHA OQUE OQUI OCQUE
OKAPI GIRAFFINE
OKAY OK YES HUNK OKEH HUNKY APPROVE CORRECT SANCTION AUTHORIZE
OKIA OKET OUNCE
OKINAWA (CAPITAL OF —) NAHA

OKLAHOMA

CAPITAL: OKLAHOMA CITY
COLLEGE: CAMERON LANGSTON PHILLIPS
COUNTY: KAY ATOKA CADDO ALFALFA OKFUSKEE OKMULGEE
INDIAN TRIBE: WACO WICHITA TAWAKONI
LAKE: EUFAULA OOLOGAH
MOUNTAINS: OZARK OUACHITA
NATIVE: OKIE SOONER
RIVER: RED GRAND WASHITA ARKANSAS CANADIAN CIMARRON
STATE BIRD: FLYCATCHER
STATE FLOWER: MISTLETOE
STATE TREE: REDBUD
TOWN: ADA ALVA ENID HUGO ALTUS MIAMI PONCA TULSA ELRENO GUYMON IDABEL LAWTON SAPULPA SHAWNEE ANADARKO FORTSILL MUSKOGEE

OKRA GOBO OKRO BAMIA BENDY GOBBO GOMBO GUBBO GUMBO OCHRA BENDEE MALLOW BANDAKA BANDICOY BANDIKAI
OLD AGY ELD AGED AULD COLD WOLD YALD ANILE HOARY STALE WOULD FORMER FOROLD INFIRM MATURE SENILE SHABBY VETUST AGEABLE ANCIENT ANTIQUE ARCHAIC ELDERLY FORWORN UMWHILE DECREPIT MEDIEVAL OBSOLETE DODDERING HACKNEYED SENESCENT VENERABLE
(— AND MELLOW) CRUSTY
(— BAILEY) GAOL JAIL PRISON
(— CLOTHESMAN) POCO

(— FAITHFUL) GEYSER
(— HAND) LONGTIMER
(— MAID) SPINSTER THORNBACK
(— MAN) ANTIQUITY WHITEBEARD
(— SOD) EIRE ERIN IRELAND
(— SQUAW) DIVER HOUND MOMMY CALLOO CALLOW COWEEN DUCKER QUANDY OLDWIFE SCOLDER COCKAWEE LONGTAIL SHARPTAIL SOUTHERLY
(— WOMAN) HAG CRONE GAMMER
(GROWING —) SENESCENT
(OF —) WHILOM ERSTWHILE
OLD BAY STATE MASSACHUSETTS
OLD DOMINION STATE VIRGINIA
OLDER MORE ALDER ELDER SENIOR ANCESTOR
OLD-FASHIONED CORNY DOWDY FUSTY PASSE FOGRAM FOGRUM QUAINT STODGY ANCIENT ANTIQUE ARCHAIC ELDERLY VINTAGE FRUMPISH OBSOLETE CRINOLINE PRIMITIVE
OLD FRANKLIN STATE TENNESSEE
OLD LINE STATE MARYLAND
OLD-WOMANISH ANILE
OLEANDER LAUREL DOGBANE ROSEBAY
OLEFIN ALKENE
OLEIC RAPIC RAPINIC
OLEORESIN GUM ANIME APIOL ELEMI TOLUS BALSAM GURJUN IRIDIN COPAIBA GALIPOT LABDANUM TACAMAHAC
OLFACTION SMELL OSMESIS SMELLING ESPHRESIS
OLIGARCHY KREMLIN
OLIGARCHIC FEUDAL
OLIGOCLASE SUNSTONE
OLIO STEW MEDLEY MELANGE MIXTURE MISHMASH PASTICCIO POTPOURRI
OLIPHANT HORN ELEPHANT
OLIPRANCE ROMP SHOW FROLIC JOLLITY
OLIVE OLEA MORON BRUNET LIERRE OLIVER OXHORN PIMOLA RESEDA BAROUNI CITRINE MISSION MORILLON OLEASTER
(— FLY) DACUS
(AMERICAN —) DEVILWOOD
(OVERRIPE —) DRUPE
OLIVER NOLL HAMMER HOLLIPER
OLIVET PEARL
OLLA JAR JUG OLE POT OLAY PUCHERA PUCHERO
OLLA PODRIDA HASH OLIO MEDLEY POTPOURRI
OLM PROTEUS SALAMANDER
OLOGY ISM SCIENCE
OLYMPIAN CELESTIAL
OLYNTHUS ASCULA
OMAGUA CAMBEVA
OMAN (CAPITAL OF —) MASQAT MUSCAT
(LANGUAGE OF —) ARABIC BALUCHI
(MOUNTAIN OF —) SHAM HAFIT HARIM NAKHL TAYIN AKHDAR

(NATIVE OF —) ADNAN QAHTAN BALUCHI
(TOWN IN —) SUR NIGWA MASQAT MATRAH SALALAH
OMASUM BOOK BOUK BIBLE FARDEL MANYPLIES
OMBER SOLO UMBRE HOMBRE MEDIATOR QUADRILLE
OMEGA END LAST
OMELET AMLET AMELET FOOYUNG FOOYOUNG FRITTATA
OMEN BODE LUCK SIGN ABODE AUGUR BODER FREET FREIT GUEST TOKEN WEIRD WHATE AUGURY HANDEL HANSEL AUSPICE PORTENT PRESAGE PRODIGY WARNING CEREMONY FOREBODE SOOTHSAY HARBINGER
OMENTUM WEB CAUL ZIRBUS EPIPLOON
OMINOUS DIRE DOUR GRIM FATAL BODING DISMAL SHREWD AUGURAL BALEFUL BANEFUL BODEFUL DIREFUL DOOMFUL FATEFUL MENACING SINISTER THUNDERY PROPHETIC
OMISSION OUT CHASM SALTUS DEFAULT FAILURE MISPICK NEGLECT SILENCE PASSOVER OVERSIGHT
(— OF A LETTER) APOCOPE
(— OF SYLLABLES) SYNCOPE
(TACIT —) SILENCE
OMIT CUT LET BALK BATE DROP EDIT KILL MISS PASS SKIP SLIP ABATE ELIDE OBMIT SPARE BELEVE CANCEL DELETE EXCEPT FORGET IGNORE DISCARD EXPUNGE NEGLECT DISCOUNT OVERLOOK OVERSKIP OVERSLIP DISREGARD
OMITTED VIDE
OMMATIDIUM FACET FACETTE
OMNIBUS BUS BUSS BARGE HERDIC JOGGER PIRATE AUTOBUS MOTORBUS KITTEREEN
OMNIPOTENT GOD ABLE DEITY GREAT ARRANT MIGHTY ALMIGHTY POWERFUL UNEQUALED UNLIMITED
OMNISCIENT WISE LEARNED POWERFUL PANSOPHIC
OMOPLATE SCAPULA
OMPHALOS HUB BOSS KNOB NAVEL CENTER UMBILICUS
ON O AN IN TO ONE SUR ATOP AWAY OVER UPON ABOUT ABOVE AHEAD ALONG ANENT WITHIN FORWARD
(— A HATCH) ABROOD
(— ACCOUNT OF) IN FOR
(— ALL SIDES) ABOUT AROUND
(— AND ON) EVER FOREVER TEDIOUS
(— EARTH) BELOW
(— END) TOGETHER
(— FOOT) UP AFOOT TOWARD FOOTBACK
(— HAND) ALONG
(— HIGH) ALOFT
(— THE CONTRARY) BUT RATHER

(— THE MOVE) AFOOT

(— THE OTHER HAND) BUT AGAIN
HOWEVER ALTHOUGH

(— THE OTHER SIDE) OVER ACROSS

(— THE WAY) AWAY AGATE

(— TIME) PROMPT

(— TOP OF) ATOP ABOVE ALOFT

(— WHAT ACCOUNT) WHY

ONAGER ASS GOUR KULAN KOULAN
ONAGRA ALACRAN CATAPULT
SCORPION

ONCE ANE EEN ERST AINCE ONCET
WHILE YANCE FORMER WHILOM
QUONDAM UMWHILE FORMERLY
SOMETIME UMQUHILE WHENEVER
ERSTWHILE

(— MORE) YET AGAIN ENCORE
ITERUM

ONDRATA FIBER

ONE J AE AN HE UN AIN ANE ANY
EIN MAN OON TAE UNA UNE WON
YAE YAN YEN YIN YOU SAME SOLE
SOME TANE TEAN THIS TONE TOON
UNAL UNIT WHON WONE ALONE
ALPHA UNITY WOONE FELLOW
PERSON SINGLE UNIQUE UNITED
NUMERAL PRONOUN SIMPLUM
UNBROKEN SINGLETON UNDIVIDED
UNMARRIED

(— AFTER ANOTHER) ABOUT
TANDEM SERIALLY SERIATIM

(— BORN A SERF) NEIF NEIFE

(— BY ONE) APIECE SINGLY
OVERHEAD

(— CONDEMNED WRONGFULLY)
CALAS

(— CURIOUS TO KNOW ALL)
QUIDNUNC

(— DETESTED) WARLING

(— DEVOTED TO PARTICULAR ART)
IST

(— EASILY TRICKED) CULLY

(— ENGAGED IN MARAUDING)
LOOTIE

(— ENROLLED IN ARMY) DRAFTEE

(— GIVEN TO DEVILTRY) HELLION

(— INSTRUCTED IN SECRET
SYSTEM) EPOPT

(— LATE) SERO

(— NOT A REGULAR MASON)
COWAN

(— OF PAIR) FELLOW DOUBLET

(— OVERZEALOUS) HYPER

(— SENT FORTH) APOSTLE

(— TENTH) TITHE

(— THAT UNDERGOES CHANGE)
MUTANT

(— THOUSAND) MIL

(— TWENTY-FOURTH) CARAT

(— UNKNOWN) QUIDAM

(— VERSED IN LITERATURE) SAVANT

(— WHO BRINGS MEAT TO TABLE)
DAPIFER

(— WHO DISPLAYS
FASTIDIOUSNESS) EPICURE

(— WHO DOCTORS SOMETHING)
COOK

(— WHO EXCELS) ACE

(— WHO FABRICATES) SMITH

(— WHO FOLLOWS ARMY) SUTLER

(— WHO FORSAKES FAITH)
APOSTATE

(— WHO FRUSTRATES PLAN)
MARPLOT

(— WHO HAS ATTAINED
PERFECTION) SIDDHA

(— WHO IS AWAY) ABSENTEE

(— WHO LOADS SHIP) BUNKER

(— WHO MAKES LIVING BY
TRICKERY) CADGER

(— WHO MANAGES) GERENT

(— WHO REGULATES GUN) TRAINER

(— WHO REMOVES NUISANCE)
ABATOR

(— WHO REPRESENTS NEWEST)
NEO

(— WHO TESTS) CONNER

(— WHOSE MIND IS IMPAIRED BY
AGE) DOTARD

(— WITH FIRST-HAND INFORMATION)
INSIDER

(BLESSED —) BHAGAVAT

(EVIL —) WOND SHAITAN SHEITAN

(EXTRAORDINARY —) BUTCHA
TICKANINNY

(LOVED —) MINION

(SWEET —) HONEYCOMB

(TIMELESS —) AKAL

ONEGITE AMETHYST GEMSTONE

ONENESS UNION UNITY CONCORD
ONEHOOD UNICITY UNITUDE
IDENTITY SAMENESS AGREEMENT

ONE-NIGHT STAND GIG

ONEROUS HARD HEAVY ARDUOUS
ONEROSE WEIGHTY EXACTING
GRIEVOUS LABORIOUS

ONE-SIDED ECCENTRIC UNILATERAL

ONETIME FORMER FORMERLY
ERSTWHILE

ONFALL ONSET ATTACK ASSAULT

ON-GLIDE TENSION ENTRANCE

ONION BOLL CEPA LEEK LILY CIBOL
PEARL ALLIUM LILIUM PORRET
BERMUDA HOLLEKE PICKLER
SHALLOT AYEGREEN RARERIPE
SCALLION VALENCIA

(ROPE OF —S) REEVE

(SEASONED WITH —S) LYONNAISE

(STRING OF —S) TRACE

ONKOS TOPKNOT

ONLOOKER BOOK GAZER WITNESS
AUDIENCE BEHOLDER OVERSEER
BYSTANDER SPECTATOR

ONLY ALL BUT JUST LONE MERE
ONCE SAVE SOLE AFALD ALONE
ARRAH FIRST MERED NOBUT OLEPY
ANERLY BARELY MERELY NOBBUT
SIMPLE SINGLE SINGLY SOLELY
ALLENARLY EXCEPTING

(— THIS) MERE

(BEING —) SIMPLE

ONMUN HANGUL HANKUL

ONOMATOPOEIC ECHOIC IMSONIC
MIMETIC IMITATIVE

ONRUSH BIRR SHAKE ATTACK
TIDEWAY

ONSET DASH DINT FALL FARD RESE
RUSH BRAID BRUNT FAIRD FRUSH

START STORM STOUR VENUE
ACCESS AFFRET ATTACK CHARGE
COURGE IMPACT INSULT ONFALL
POWDER THRUST ASSAULT
BRATTLE BEGINNING ENCOUNTER
ONSLAUGHT

ONSETTER CAGER HITCHER

ONSLAUGHT LASH BLAST ONSET
ATTACK ASSAULT DESCENT
SISERARA SALIAUNCE

ONSTEAD ONSET FARMHOUSE
HOMESTEAD

ONTARIO (CANAL IN —) TRENT
RIDEAU

(CAPITAL OF —) TORONTO

(LAKE IN —) SIMCOE

(TOWN IN —) GALT LONDON
OTTAWA WINDSOR HAMILTON
KINGSTON KITCHENER

ONTO ATOP ABOARD

ONTOGENY DEVELOPMENT

ONUS DUTY LOAD BLAME BURDEN
CHARGE WEIGHT INCUBUS

ONWARD AWAY AHEAD ALONG
FORTH UPWARD FORTHON
FORWARD TOWARDS FORERIGHT

ONYX ONIX NICOLO TECALI ONYCHIN
JASPONYX SARDONYX

(MEXICAN —) ALABASTER

OOCYTE PROGAMETE GAMETOCYTE

OODLES HEAP LOTS MANY SCADS
LASHINGS SLITHERS ABUNDANCE

OOGONIUM NUCULE OOCYST
OOGONE

OOLAK WOLLOCK

OOLONG TEA

OOMPH PEP VIGOR ENERGY

OOPAK TEA

OORALI CURARE

OORIAL SHA SHEEP URIAL

OOTHECA OVISAC

OOZE OZ BOG MUD SOP DRIP EMIT
LEAK MIRE SEEP SLEW SLOB SLUE
WEEP EXUDE GLEET MARSH SLIME
SWEAT WEEZE EXHALE SICKER
SLEECH SLOUGH SLUDGE SQUASH
SQUDGE STRAIN SCREEVE TEICHER
PERCOLATE

(— OUT) SEW SPEW SPUE

OOZING WEEPY SQUDGY SEEPAGE
SPEWING WEEPING

OOZY OASY SEEPY WASHY SLEECHY
ULIGINOUS

OPAH CRAVO SUNFISH KINGFISH
MARIPOSA MOONFISH

OPAL GEM NOBLE RESIN FIORITE
GIRASOL HYALITE ISOPYRE
JASPOPAL MENILITE SEMIOPAL
CACHOLONG GEYSERITE

OPALESCENT OPALED OPALINE
IRISATED

OPALEYE GREENFISH

OPAQUE DIM DARK DULL DENSE
MUDDY SHADY THICK VAGUE
OBTUSE STUPID CLOUDED OBSCURE
ABSTRUSE EYESHADE

OPEN GO DUP LAX OPE AIRY AJAR
BARE FAIR FLUE FREE GIVE PERT
UNDO VIDE AGAPE APERT BEGIN

BLOWN BREAK BROAD BURST
CHINK CLEAR CRACK FLARE FRANK
FRESH LANCE LOOSE MUSHY
NAKED OVERT PLAIN RELAX SPALD
SPLAT SPLAY START UNBAR UNPEG
UNTIE APPERT CANDID DIRECT
ENTAME EXPAND EXPOSE FACIAL
FORTHY GAPING HONEST LIABLE
OUVERT PATENT PUBLIC SINGLE
SPREAD UNBOLT UNFOLD UNFURL
UNGLUE UNLOCK UNROLL UNSEAL
UNSHUT UNSPAR UNSTOP UNTINE
UNWINK VACANT ARTLESS
BLOSSOM DISPART FIELDEN
OBVIOUS OUTLINE SINCERE
UNCLOSE UNHINGE APPARENT
COMMENCE DISCLOSE EXPLICIT
EXTENDED INITIATE MANIFEST
PERVIOUS RESERATE UNFASTEN
(— A VEIN) BROACH
(— AIR) ALFRESCO
(— AND CLEANSE) WILLOW
(— CLOTH) SCUTCH
(— COUNTRY) VELDT WEALD
(— EYES OR LIPS) SEVER
(— THE WAY) INVITE PIONEER
(— TO PURSUIT) FAIR
(— UP) START DEVELOP DISPART
DISCLOSE
(— VIOLENTLY) SPORT
(— WIDE) YAWN EXPAND STRETCH
(— WIDELY) GAPE
(FULLY —) WIDE AGAPE YAWNING
(HALF —) MID AJAR
(TOO —) OVERBARISH
OPENBILL OPENBEAK
OPENED APPAUME ECHAPPE
OPENER KEY KNOB LATCH SESAME
APERIENT
(— IN POKER) PAIR JACKS
(FURROW —) SHOE STUBRUNNER
(OYSTER —) HUSKER
OPENHANDED FREE LIBERAL
GENEROUS RECEPTIVE
OPENING OS CUT EYE GAP YAT
ANUS BORE DAWN DOOR DROP
FENT FLUE GATE HOLE LOOP PASS
PORE PORT PYLA RIFT RIMA SLAP
SLIT SLOT SPAN VENT VOID YAWN
YEAT BLEED BRACK BREAK CHASM
CHINK CLEFT CROSS DEBUT GRILL
HILUM INLET LIGHT MOUTH SCOOT
SINUS START THIRL WIDTH ADITUS
AVENUE BREACH CASING CHANCE
GRILLE HIATUS INTAKE LACUNA
MEATUS OILLET OUTLET PORTAL
SLUICE SPREAD CREVASS CREVICE
DISPLAY FISSURE ORIFICE OUTCAST
SWALLET APERTURE BUNGHOLE
CREVASSE ENTRANCE OVERTURE
PLUGHOLE SCISSURE TEASEHOLE
(— IN EARTH) GROTTO CHIMNEY
SWALLOW
(— BELOW PENTHOUSE) GALLERY
(— FOR ESCAPE) MUSE MEUSE
(— FROM SEA) INDRAFT
(— IN ANTHER) STOMIUM
(— IN DECK) SCUTTLE

(— IN FLOOR OR ROOF) HATCH
SKYLIGHT
(— IN GARMENT) FENT ARMHOLE
(— IN LOCK TUMBLER) GATING
(— IN MINE) EYE ADIT RAISE SHAFT
WINZE WINNING
(— IN MOLD) POUR
(— IN PICTURE FRAME) SIGHT
(— IN PILLAR OF COAL) JENKIN
JUNKING
(— IN ROCK) GRIKE
(— IN SALMON TRAP) SLAP
(— IN SEA CAVE) GLOUP
(— IN SKIRT) PLACKET
(— IN SPONGE) APOPYLE
(— IN STAGE) DIP
(— IN TENNIS COURTS) GRILLE
HAZARD GALLERY
(— IN TROUSERS) SPARE
(— IN VAULT) LUNET LUNETTE
(— IN WALL) BOLE DREAMHOLE
(— OF EAR) BUR BURR
(— OF ESOPHAGUS) CARDIA
(— OF GEYSER) CRATER
(— OF PRAIRIE) BAY
(— OF SHELL) GAPE
(— THROUGH BULWARKS)
GANGWAY GUNPORT SCUPPER
(— TO ASH PIT) GLUT
(— WIDE) DEHISCENT
(— WITH LID) SCUTTLE
(— WITHOUT TREES) BLANK
(ARCHED —) ALCOVE ARCADE
(CHECKERS —) ALMA DYKE FIFE
CROSS CENTER SOUTER BRISTOL
GLASGOW PAISLEY WHILTER
DEFIANCE SWITCHER
(CHESS —) DEBUT GAMBIT
DEFENCE DEFENSE
(EROSIONAL —) FENSTER
(FUNNELLIKE —) CHOANA
(GRILL —) GUICHET
(JAR —) PITHOIGIA
(MOUTHLIKE —) STOMA OSTIUM
(SMALL —) PORE SLOT CHINK
STOMA CRANNY EYELET LACUNA
CATHOLE CREVICE DOGHOLE
FORAMEN PINHOLE QUARREL
FENESTRA
(WINDOWLIKE —) SPLITE FENESTRA
OPENLY FREELY BROADLY FRANKLY
PUBLICE ROUNDLY STRAIGHT
OPEN-MINDED LIBERAL
OPENMOUTHED GAPING GREEDY
RAVENOUS CLAMOROUS
OPENNESS FREEDOM PATENCY
DAYLIGHT FRANKNESS ROUNDNESS
OPENWORK LATTICE TRACERY
CAGEWORK FILIGREE FRETTING
FRETWORK
OPEN-WORKED AJOURISE
OPERA AIDA FAUST LAKME MANON
NORMA THAIS TOSCA BOHEME
CARMEN DAPHNE ERNANI LOUISE
MIGNON OTELLO RIENZI SALOME
ELEKTRA FIDELIO BURLETTA
FALSTAFF IOLANTHE LOKACOLO
PARSIFAL TRAVIATA WALKYRIE
LOHENGRIN PAGLIACCI RHEINGOLD

RIGOLETTO SIEGFRIED TROVATORE
(— DIVISION) SCENA
(— GLASS) GLASS JUMELLE
LORGNET LORGNETTE
(— HAT) GIBUS CLAQUE
(— SONG) ARIA
(— STAR) DIVA
(16TH CENTURY —) PASTORALE
(COMIC —) BUFFA
(HORSE —) WESTERN
(SPANISH —) ZARZUELA
(TV OR RADIO —) SOAP
OPERANT EFFICIENT OPERATIVE
OPERATE GO ACT CUT MAN RUN
PUSH TAKE WORK DRIVE MULES
AFFECT EFFECT MANAGE CONDUCT
PROCEED FUNCTION
(— BY HAND) MANIPULATE
(— GUNS) SERVE
(— MINE) FLUSH
(— RADIO) BLOOP
OPERATIC LYRIC
OPERATING GOING
(FULLY —) AFLOAT
OPERATION DEED PLAY BLAST
AGENCY EFFECT VIRTUE PROCESS
CREATION EXERCISE FUNCTION
PRACTICE EXECUTION INFLUENCE
PROCESSUS
OPERATIVE EYE HAND ARTIST
LIVING ARTISAN MECHANIC
DETECTIVE EFFECTIVE
OPERATOR DEL DOER AGENT
BAKER DEWER NABLA PILOT QUACK
BEAMER BILLER BOLTER BUMPER
BUSMAN CAPPER DEALER DEGGER
DRIVER DUNGER DYADIC GAGGER
JOCKEY KICKER RAGGER TRADER
AVIATOR BREAKER CENTRAL
CHEESER DENTIST FACIENT
GLASSER JOGGLER MANAGER
OPERANT SURGEON IDENTITY
CONDUCTOR
(INFERIOR —) PLUG
(RADIO —) HAM SPARKS SPARKER
(TRUCK —) GIPSY GYPSY
OPERCULUM LID FLAP ONYCHA
OPERCLE APTYCHUS COVERING
EYESTONE MANDIBLE
OPERETTA ZARZUELA
OPEROSE BUSY IRKSOME DILIGENT
LABORIOUS
OPHIDIAN ASP EEL SNAKE CONGER
REPTILE SERPENT
OPHITE CAINIAN CAINITE
OPIATE DOPE DRUG HEMP DWALE
OPIUM DEADEN ANODINE HYPNOTIC
NARCOTIC SEDATIVE DORMITARY
PAREGORIC SOPORIFIC
OPIFICER OPIFEX WORKMAN
ARTIFICER
OPINE DEEM JUDGE THINK PONDER
BELIEVE SUPPOSE OPINIATE
OPINION CRY EYE MOT BOOK DOXY
FAME IDEA MIND VIEW WEEN
DOGMA FANCY FUTWA GUESS
HEART SENSE SIGHT TENET THINK
VARDI VARDY VOICE ADVICE
ASSENT BELIEF DEVICE DICTUM

ESTEEM GROUND NOTION REPUTE
SCHISM CENSURE CONCEIT
CONCEPT CONSENT COUNSEL
DIANOIA FEELING HOLDING
MEASURE SEEMING THINKSO
THOUGHT TROWING VERDICT
DECISION DOCTRINE JUDGMENT
SUFFRAGE SENTIMENT
(COLLECTION OF —S) SYMPOSIUM
(EXAGGERATED —) BIGHEAD
(EXPRESSION OF —) VOTE
(FAVORABLE —) BROO ESTEEM
(MOHAMMEDAN —) FUTWA
(SET OF PROFESSED —S) CREDO
(UNORTHODOX —) HERESY
OPINIONATED DOGMATIC
CONCEITED OBSTINATE PRAGMATIC
OPIUM HOP MUD DRUG OPIE POST
CHANDU CHANDOO MECONIUM
TOXICANT
(— ALKALOID) CODEIN CODEINE
MORPHINE NARCOTIN NARCOTINE
PAPAVERIN
(— POPPY) NEPENTHE
OPIUMISM THEBAISM
OPOSSUM QUICA YAPOK POSSUM
YAPOCK OYAPOCK SARIGUE
VULPINE MARSUPIAL PHILANDER
TACUACINE
(— SHRIMP) MYSID MYSOID
OPPONENT FOE ANTI ENEMY PARTY
RIVAL ALOGIAN OPPOSER ASSILANT
ADVERSARY
(— OF GOV CLINTON) BUCKTAIL
(BOORISH —) BOEOTIAN
(IMAGINARY —) WINDMILL
OPPORTUNE FIT PAT HAPPY LUCKY
READY TIMELY APROPOS FITTING
TIMEFUL SUITABLE FAVORABLE
OPPORTUNELY TIMELY APROPOS
HAPPILY
OPPORTUNIST CREEPER
OPPORTUNISTIC SHUFFLING
OPPORTUNITY GO MAY OPE SEL
EASE HENT MEAN MINT ROOM SELE
SHOT TIDE TIME SIGHT SLANT
SPACE CHANCE SEASON SQUEAK
LEISURE OPENING RESPITE
VANTAGE APPROACH FACILITY
OCCASION ADVANTAGE
(— TO PROCEED) WAY
(FAVORABLE —) SHOW TIME
OPPOSE PIT VIE WAR BUCK COPE
DEFY FACE HEAD MEET NOSE STEM
WARN WEAR ARGUE BLOCK CHECK
CLASH CROSS FIGHT FRONT OCCUR
REBEL REBUT REPEL BATTLE
BREAST COMBAT DEFEND NAYSAY
OBJECT OBTEND OPPUGN REPUGN
RESIST THWART WITHER CONTEST
COUNTER GAINSAY OBVIATE
REVERSE WITHSET CONFLICT
CONFRONT CONTRAST FRONTIER
OBSTRUCT ENCOUNTER WITHSTAND
(— BY ARGUMENT) REBUT
(— ONE IN AUTHORITY) REBEL
DEFORCE
OPPOSED ANTI ALIEN AVERSE
ADVERSE AGAINST COUNTER

HOSTILE CONTRARY ANTARCTIC
REPUGNANT
(PERSISTENTLY —) RENITENT
OPPOSITE TO ANENT POLAR
ACROSS ANENST AVERSE FACING
WITHER ADVERSE COUNTER
FORNENT INVERSE OBVIOUS
REVERSE ANTIPODE CONTRARY
CONTRAST CONVERSE ANTIPODAL
REPUGNANT
(— MIDDLE OF SHIP'S SIDE) ABEAM
(— OF TRUTH) DEVIL
(— THE ALTAR) WEST
(— THE SUN) ANTISOLAR
OPPOSITION CON ATILT STOUR
THWART DISCORD CONTRAST
OBSTACLE ANIMOSITY COLLISION
HOSTILITY RENITENCY
(ELECTRICAL —) IMPEDANCE
OPPRESS SIT HOLD LADE LOAD PEIS
RACK RAPE RIDE SWAY THEW
CROWD CRUSH GRIND GRIPE HEAVY
PEISE POISE PRESS WEIGH WRONG
BETOIL BURDEN DEFOIL DEFOUL
EXTORT HARASS HARROW NIDDER
NITHER RAVISH SUBDUE THREAT
AFFLICT DEPRESS INGRATE
OVERLAY REPRESS SQUEEZE
TRAMPLE CONFRONT DISTRESS
ENCUMBER PRESSURE SUPPRESS
OVERPOWER OVERTHROW
OVERWHELM
(— WITH DREAD) HAGRIDE
(— WITH HEAT) SWELTER
OPPRESSED SERVILE
OPPRESSION GRIPE PRESS THRALL
MIZRAIM DULLNESS PRESSURE
EXTORTION GRIEVANCE LASSITUDE
OPPRESSIVE HOT DIRE DOWY HARD
CLOSE DOWIE FAINT HARSH HEAVY
BITTER LEADEN SCREWY SEVERE
SMUDGY SULTRY TORRID URGENT
WEIGHT ONEROUS SLAVISH
GRIEVOUS GRINDING RIGOROUS
OPPRESSIVELY STRAIT
OPPRESSOR CSAR CZAR NERO
TSAR TZAR EGLON TYRANT
INCUBUS
OPPROBRIUM ENVY ABUSE ODIUM
SCORN SHAME INFAMY INSULT
CALUMNY DISDAIN OFFENSE
SCANDAL DISGRACE DISHONOR
REPROACH CONTUMELY
OPS (ASSOCIATE OF —) CONSUS
(CONSORT OF —) SATURN
(DAUGHTER OF —) CERES
(FESTIVAL OF —) OPALIA
(PERSONIFICATION OF —) FAUNA
TERRA TELLUS
OPT CULL PICK WISH ELECT CHOOSE
DECIDE OPTATE SELECT
OPTIC EYE OCULAR VISUAL
OPTICAL (— APPARATUS) LENS
GLASS ALIDAD ALIDADE
OPTOMETER PERISCOPE TELESCOPE
OPTIMIST UTOPIANIST
OPTIMISTIC GLAD ROSY SUNNY
JOYOUS BULLISH HOPEFUL

ROSEATE EUPEPTIC SANGUINE
EXPECTANT
OPTION UP CALL DOWN CHOICE
SPREAD REFUSAL STRADDLE
PRIVILEGE
OPTIONAL ELECTIVE VOLUNTARY
OPULENT FAT LUSH RICH WELI
AMPLE FLUSH PLUSH SHOWY
LAVISH MONEYED PROFUSE
WEALTHY ABUNDANT AFFLUENT
LUXURIANT PLENTIFUL SUMPTUOUS
OPUS WORK ETUDE STUDY
(OVERLABORED —) LUCUBRATION
OQUASSA QUASKY
OR NE ARE AUT ERE ORE GOLD
OTHER TOPAZ EITHER YELLOW
ORACHE SALTBUSH GREASEWOOD
ORACLE SEER TRIP SIBYL TRIPOD
TRIPOS DIVINER AUTOPHONE
ORACULAR OTIC VATIC ORPHIC
DELPHIC VATICAL DELPHIAN
PYTHONIC PROPHETIC
ORAL ALOUD PAROL VOCAL BUCCAL
PAROLE SONANT SPOKEN VERBAL
UTTERED UNWRITTEN
ORALE FANON
ORANGE KING MOCK CERES CHILE
CHILI CHINO FLAME GENIP HEDGE
NAVEL OSAGE TENNE AURORA
BODOCK BRAZIL COPPER MIKADO
NAVAHO SUNTAN TEMPLE TITIAN
UVALHA COWSLIP FLORIDA
LEATHER MACLURA PAPRIKA
PONCEAU PUMPKIN RANGPUR
SEVILLE TANGELO TANGIER
BERGAMOT BIGARADE CHINOTTI
CLAYBANK FLAMINGO HONEYDEW
JACINTHE MANDARIN MARATHON
MOROCCAN POMANDER SUNBURST
VALENCIA BUCCANEER CARNELIAN
PERSIMMON TANGERINE
(— GRASS) KNITWEED PINEWEED
(— HAWKWEED) FIREWEED
HIERACIUM
(— MEMBRANE) ZEST
(— MILKWORT) CANDYWEED
(— PIECE) LITH SEGMENT
(— ROCKFISH) FLIOMA
(— SEED) PIP
(BROWNISH —) SPICE
(LARGE —) KING
(MOCK —) SERINGA
(OSAGE —) HEDGE BODOCK
(SOUR —) CURACAO BIGARADE
CHINOTTO
(SWEET —) CHINA CHINO
ORANGEBIRD TANAGER
ORANGELEAF KARAMU
ORANGEMAN MARKSMAN
ORANGEWOOD OSAGE
ORANG LAUT BAJAU
ORANGUTAN APE MIAS ORANG
PONGO SATYR SATIRE SATURY
PRIMATE SALTIER WOODMAN
WOODSMAN
ORAON KURUKH
ORATE PLEAD SPEAK SPIEL SPOUT
ADDRESS DECLAIM LECTURE
BLOVIATE HARANGUE DISCOURSE
SPEECHIFY

ORATION EULOGY HESPED SERMON ADDRESS CONCION HARANGUE SUASORIA OLYNTHIAC PANEGYRIC PHILIPPIC
(— OF CICERO) PHILIPPIC
(FUNERAL —) ELOGE ELOGY MONODY ELOGIUM ENCOMIUM
ORATOR RHETOR DEMAGOG SPEAKER STUMPER CICERONE BOANERGES DEMAGOGUE PLAINTIFF SPOKESMAN
ORATORIO ELIJAH RORATORIO
ORATORICAL ELOQUENT RHETORICAL
ORATORY CHAPEL SACRARY ORACULUM SPEAKING ELOCUTION ELOQUENCE PROSEUCHE
ORB EYE SUN BALL MOON STAR EARTH GLOBE MOUND ORBIT CIRCLE PLANET SPHERE CIRCUIT ENCLOSE ENCIRCLE SURROUND FIRMAMENT
ORBED LUNAR ROUND GLOBATE
ORBIT AUGE PATH APSIS CYCLE TRACK CIRCLE SOCKET SPHERE CIRCUIT ELLIPSE EYEHOLE ECCENTRIC
(POINT IN —) APSIS APOGEE EPIGEE SYZYGY PERIGEE
ORC OGRE ORCA GIANT WHALE GRAMPUS
ORCHARD TOPE ARBOR GROVE ARBOUR GARDEN HUERTA OLIVET VERGER ARBUSTUM FRUITERY PEACHERY POMARIUM SUGARBUSH
(— GRASS) DOGFOOT COCKSFOOT
ORCHESTRA BAND GROUP CHAPEL CAPELLE GAMELAN KAPELLE ENSEMBLE GAMELANG SYMPHONY
(— BELLS) GLOCKENSPIEL
(— CIRCLE) PARQUET PARTERRE
(SECTION OF —) BRASS WINDS WOODS STRINGS WOODWINDS PERCUSSION
ORCHESTRATE SCORE ARRANGE COMPOSE
ORCHESTRION HARMONICON APOLLONICON
ORCHID FAAM FAHAM PETAL VANDA CYMBID DUFOIL LAELIA PURPLE AERIDES ANGULOA BOATLIP CALYPSO CULLION FLYWORT LYCASTE POGONIA VANILLA ARETHUSA CALANTHE DENDROBE GYNANDER LABELLUM RAMSHEAD SATYRION CORALROOT HABENARIA TWAYBLADE
ORCHIS CROWTOE CROWFOOT CRAKEFEET
ORDAIN LAW PUT DEEM DOOM LOOK MAKE SEND WILL WITE ALLOT ENACT JAPAN ORDER SHAPE WIELD WRITE DECREE PRIEST ADJUDGE APPOINT ARRANGE BEHIGHT COMMAND DESTINE DICTATE FORTUNE INSTALL PREPARE
ORDEAL FIRE GAFF TEST TRIAL CALVARY GAUNTLET
(— TREE) AKAZGA TANGHIN TANGUIN

ORDER BAN BID RAY SAY TAX BOON CALL CASE CHIT FIAT FORM ORDO RANK RULE SAND SECT STOP SUIT TELL TIFF TRIM WILL WORD ALIGN ARRAY CHIME CLASS DIGHT EDICT GENUS GRADE GUIDE HAVOC PRESS QUIET RANGE SHIFT STATE TAXIS WHACK ASSIGN AVAUNT BILLET CEDULA CHARGE COSMOS CURFEW DECREE DEGREE DEMAND DIRECT ENJOIN FIRMAN FOLLOW GRAITH HOOKUM INDENT KILTER MANAGE METHOD NATURE ORDAIN POLICE POTENT SERIES SETTLE SYNTAX SYSTEM ADJUDGE ARRANGE BESPEAK BIDDING BOOKING COMMAND COMPOSE DISPOSE EMBARGO FLOATER MANDATE PRECEPT PROCESS SOCIETY KODASHIM
(— OF ANGELS) CHOIR QUIRE MIGHTS THRONES DOMINIONS
(— OF BELLS) CHANGE
(— OF COURT) SIST VACATUR
(— OF HOLY BEINGS) HIERARCHY
(— OF WORSHIP) AGODUM
(— OFF) TURN
(— TOBACCO LEAF) CASE
(CIVIL —) EUNOMY
(COSMIC —) TAO RITA
(GOOD —) EUTAXY
(KNIGHTHOOD —) DANNEBROG
(LACKING —) AMISS MESSY MUSSY ROUGH CHAOTIC UNKEMPT CONFUSED
(LEGAL —) SIST STET WRIT DAYWRIT SUMMONS SENTENCE SUBPOENA
(LOWER — OF MAN) ALALUS
(MINOR CHURCH —) BENET
(MONASTIC —) SAMGHA SANGHA
(TRAIN —) FLIMSY
(UNIVERSAL —) KIND
(WRITTEN —) CHECK DRAFT BILLET DRAUGHT
ORDERED BANDBOX BESPOKE REGULAR SCRAPED COHERENT
(WELL —) TRIM
ORDERLINESS METHOD SYSTEM CLARITY DECORUM
ORDERLY AIDE DULY NEAT RULY SNOD TIDY TRIM CRISP SOWAR SUWAR BATMAN BURSCH COSMIC FORMAL MODEST ORDENE GRADELY REGULAR SHAPELY DECOROUS GALLOPER GRAITHLY OBEDIENT PEACEABLE SHIPSHAPE
ORDINANCE LAW DOOM FIAT RITE BYLAW EDICT ASSIZE DECREE RECESS CONTROL MANDATE SETNESS STATUTE WORKING DECRETUM JUDICIAL REGIMENT TAKKANAH DIRECTION
ORDINANT DIHELY DIHELIOS DIHELIUM
ORDINARY LAY LOW SOS FESS LALA MEAN PALL RUCK BANAL CROSS NOMIC PLAIN PROSE USUAL COMMON FILLET MODERN NORMAL

PAIRLE SIMPLE VULGAR AVERAGE NATURAL PROSAIC SALTIRE SAUTIER TRIVIAL VULGATE EVERYDAY FAMILIAR HABITUAL MEDIOCRE MIDDLING PLEBEIAN RUMTYTOO WORKADAY QUOTIDIAN SHAKEFORK
ORDINATE ORDER ORDAIN APPOINT ORDERLY REGULAR MODERATE TEMPERATE
ORDNANCE LAW GUNS ARMOR ORGUE FALCON MINION PETARD PEDRERO RABINET SERPENT WEAPONS BASILISK PETERERO ARTILLERY
ORDO ORDER ALMANAC DIRECTORY
ORE (ALSO SEE MINERAL) TIN CHAT DISH DRAG FELL GOLD IRON LEAD MINE POST PULP ROCK CRAZE CRUDE FAVOR GLORY GRACE HONOR MANTO MERCY METAL PRILL COPPER CUPRITE FLOATER RESPECT SEAWEED SMEDDUM CLEMENCY KNOCKING CARBONATE REVERENCE
(— CRUSHER) DOLLY
(— DEPOSIT) LODE SCRIN BONANZA
(— LAYER) SEAM STOPE
(— LOADING PLATFORM) PLAT
(— MASS) SQUAT
(— NOT DRESSED) WORK
(— WITH STONE ADHERING) CHAT CHATS
(BROKEN —) DIRT
(CRUDE —) HEADS
(CUBE —) SIDERITE
(EARTHY-LOOKING —) PACO
(HORSEFLESH —) BORNITE
(IMPURE —) SPEISS HALVANS
(IRON —) OCHER OCHRE MINION IRONMAN LIMNITE MINETTE OLIGIST TURGITE HEMATITE JACUTINGA
(LEAD —) BOOZE GALENA
(LUMP OF —) HARDHEAD
(MERCURY —) GRANZA CINNABAR
(SOLID —) RIB
(TIN —) ROWS CRAZE SCOVE WHITS FLORAN TINSTUFF
(WORTHLESS —) SLAG DROSS MATTE
OREAD PERI NYMPH

MOUNTAIN RANGE: BLUE COAST
CASCADE
RIVER: ROGUE IMNAHA OWYHEE
POWDER UMPQUA BLITZEN
KLAMATH SILVIES COLUMBIA
DESCHUTES
STATE BIRD: MEADOWLARK
STATE FLOWER: GRAPE
STATE NICKNAME: BEAVER
STATE TREE: FIR
TOWN: NYSSA EUGENE ASTORIA
PORTLAND CORVALLIS

ORE-PRODUCING QUICK
ORESTES (FATHER OF —)
AGAMEMNON
(FRIEND OF —) PYLADES
(MOTHER OF —) CLYTEMNESTRA
(SISTER OF —) ELECTRA IPHIGENIA
(WIFE OF —) HERMIONE
ORGAN CUP GILL LIMB PART CHELA
FLOAT GREAT HEART MEANS PAPER
REGAL SERRA ELATER FEEDER
FEELER HAPTOR MEDIUM SPLEEN
SUCKER CONSOLE JOURNAL
ARMATURE EFFECTOR ISOGRAFT
MAGAZINE MELODICA MYCETOME
EQUIPMENT HARMONIUM
NEWSPAPER PORTATIVE
(— GALLERY) LOFT
(— OF HEARING) EAR
(— OF SENSE) SENSE SENSORY
(— OF SILKWORM) FILATOR
(— OF TOUCH) TACTOR TACTUS
(— PIPE) REED FLUTE SCHWEGEL
(— STOP) ECHO HARP OBOE SEXT
TUBA VIOL ACUTA DOLCE FLUTE
ORAGE QUINT TENTH VIOLA BIDARA
CURTAL CYMBAL DECIMA DULCET
FUGARA GEDACT NASARD OCTAVE
SCHARF TIERCE TROMBA BASSOON
BOMBARD BOURDON CELESTE
CLARION CREMONA DOLCIAN
DOUBLET DULCIAN FAGOTTO
GEDECKT PICCOLO POSAUNE
SERPENT TERTIAN TRUMPET
TWELFTH VIOLINA BOMBARDE
CARILLON CLARINET DIAPASON
DULCIANA GEMSHORN REGISTER
TENOROON TROMBONE WALDHORN
DOUBLETTE HARMONICA PRINCIPAL
SAXOPHONE
(— VIBRATO) TREMOLO
(BRISTLELIKE —) SETA
(CHINESE —) CHENG
(HAND —) SERINETTE
(OLFACTORY —) NOSE
(RESPIRATORY —) LUNG
(SMALL —) REGAL
(VOCAL — OF BIRDS) SYRINX
(WASTE —) KIDNEY
ORGANIC VITAL INBORN NATURAL
INHERENT
ORGANISM WOG BODY ECAD GERM
GUEST PLANT AEROBE ANIMAL
EMBRYO SYSTEM DIPLONT DISEASE
MACHINE PLANONT SUSCEPT

HEMAMEBA PATHOGEN PLANKTER
MESOPHILE
(— CHARACTERISTIC) MIXIS
(COMPOUND —) STOCK
(MINUTE —) AMEBA MONAD SPORE
(MODIFIED —) ECAD
(PELAGIC —S) NEKTON
(POLITICAL —) LEVIATHAN
(SIMPLE —) MONAD
(PL.) BENTHON BENTHOS HAYSEED
NEUSTON
ORGANIZATION ART BIG ITO CLUB
FIRM KLAN CADRE FIDAC FORUM
HOUSE MAFIA SETUP AUMAGA
CHURCH OUTFIT SURVEY SYSTEM
CHARITY COMPANY CONCERN
DEMOLAY ECONOMY GIDEONS
MENORAH SOCIETY CONGRESS
PATRONAGE STRUCTURE
(— OF ACTORS) COMPANY
(— OF DEALERS) AUCTION
(— OF EXPERIENCE) SCHEMA
(— WITH MANY BRANCHES)
OCTOPUS
(ARMY —) LANDSTORM
(AUXILIARY —) AID SYNODICAL
(COLLEGE —) FRAT ALUMNA
ALUMNI ALUMNUS SORORITY
(JEWISH —) ITO MENORAH
(MUSICAL —) BAND COMBO
CAPELLE KAPELLE ENSEMBLE
ORCHESTRA
(POLICE —) GESTAPO
(POLITICAL —) PARTY VEREIN
HETAERIA HETAIRIA APPARATUS
(SAMOAN —) AUMAGA
(SECRET —) WOW BPOE ELKS
MOOSE MASONS MIDEWIN
(SOCIAL —) POLICE
(WAR VETERANS —) AVC DAV GAR
SAR VFW FIDAC AMVETS
(WOMEN'S —) DAR WAF WRC WCTU
SORORITY
ORGANIZE FORM EDIFY FOUND
MODEL RALLY DESIGN EMBODY
ARRANGE MODULIZE REGIMENT
UNIONIZE BLUEPRINT INSTITUTE
INTEGRATE STRUCTURE
ORGANIZED FORMED ORGANIC
(BADLY —) INCONDITE
ORGIASTIC SATURNALIAN
ORGY LARK RITE ROMP BINGE
REVEL SPREE FROLIC SHINDY
REVELRY WASSAIL CAROUSAL
CEREMONY
(PL.) ORGIACS DEBAUCHERIES
ORIANA (FATHER OF —) LISUARTE
(LOVER OF —) AMADIS
ORIBI OUREBI ANTELOPE BLEEKBOK
PALEBUCK
ORIEL BAY CHAPEL DORMER RECESS
WINDOW BALCONY GALLERY
MIRADOR PORTICO CORRIDOR
ORIENT DAWN EAST ADAPT BUILD
PEARL PLACE SHEEN ADJUST
LEVANT LOCATE LUSTER RISING
GLOWING INCLINE RADIANT SUNRISE
LUSTROUS SPARKLING
ORIENTAL ASIAN PEARL BRIGHT

INDIAN ORTIVE RISING EASTERN
SHINING INDOGEAN LUSTROUS
PELLUCID PRECIOUS BRILLIANT
LEVANTINE
ORIENTATION ASPECT PHORIA
STRIKE COLORING LOCALITY
ORIFICE BUNG HOLE PORE VENT
INLET MOUTH STOMA BLOWER
CAVITY OUTLET RICTUS SIPHON
THROAT CHIMNEY EARHOLE
FORAMEN OPENING OSCULUM
OSTIOLE APERTURE FUMAROLE
INTROITUS
(— IN VOLCANIC REGION)
FUMAROLE
(— OF INFUNDIBULUM) LURA
(BREATHING —) SPIRACLE
(VOLCANIC —) BLOWER
ORIGANUM ORGANY MARJORAM
ORGAMENT
ORIGIN NEE GERM KIND RISE ROOT
SEED BIRTH CAUSE START STOCK
FATHER GROWTH NATURE PARENT
SOURCE SPRING EDITION GENESIS
LINEAGE UPSTART NASCENCE
UPSPRING BEGINNING INCEPTION
OFFSPRING PARENTAGE
(— ON EARTH) EPIGENE
(FOREIGN —) ECDEMIC
ORIGINAL NEW HOME SEED FIRST
FRESH NOVEL PRIME STOCK
FONTAL NATIVE PRIMAL PRIMER
SAMPLE PRIMARY RADICAL SEMINAL
NASCENCY PRISTINE AUTHENTIC
AUTOGRAPH BEGINNING INVENTIVE
OFFSPRING PRIMITIVE
(NOT —) DERIVED
ORIGINALITY INGENUITY
ORIGINATE COIN COME DATE GROW
HEAD MAKE MOVE OPEN REAR RISE
SIRE ARISE BEGIN BIRTH BREED
CAUSE ENDOW FOUND HATCH
RAISE START AUTHOR CREATE
DERIVE DESIGN DEVISE FATHER
INVENT SPRING CAUSATE DESCEND
EMANATE PROCEED PRODUCE
COMMENCE CONCEIVE CONTRIVE
DISCOVER GENERATE INITIATE
INSTITUTE
ORIGINATION DESCENT GENESIS
BREEDING ORIGINAL COSMOGONY
ETYMOLOGY
ORIGINATOR AUTHOR FATHER
CREATOR INVENTOR GENERATOR
ORIOLE PIROL BUNYAH LARIOT
LORIOT CACIQUE FIGBIRD PEABIRD
FIREBIRD GOLDBIRD HANGBIRD
HANGNEST TROUPIAL
ORION RIGEL ALGEBAR
(BELT OF —) ELLWAND
(HOUND OF —) ARATUS
(SLAYER OF —) ARTEMIS
ORKNEY ISLANDS (CAPITAL OF —)
KIRKWALL
(ISLAND OF —) HOY POMONA
ROUSAY SANDAY STRONSAY
ORLE ORLET BORDER FILLET
WREATH BEARING CHAPLET
TRESSURE

ORLOP DECK ARLOUP
ORMER ABALONE
ORMOLU GILT GOLD ALLOY BRASS VARNISH
ORNAMENT BOB DUB FLY FOB GAY JOY PIN POT TAG TEE TOY URN BALL BOSS CURL DICE ETCH FALL FRET FROG GAUD GEAR HUSK KNOP LEAF NULL OUCH RULE STAR TOOL TRIM WALY WING ADORN BRAID BULLA CHASE CROSS CROWN DECOR EXORN FUSEE GRACE GUTTA HELIX HONOR INLAY LUNET MENSK MENSO OVOID PATCH POPPY PRUNT SPANG SPRAY SPRIG STALK TRAIL TRICK WALLY AMULET ANKLET ATTIRE BEDAUB BEDECK BILLET BRANCH BROOCH BUTTON CIMIER COLLAR DIAPER DOODAD EDGING EMBOSS ENRICH FINERY FLORET FLOWER GORGET INSERT LABRET LUNULA NIELLO OFFSET PAMPRE PARURE PATERA ROCOCO ROSACE RUNTEE SETOFF TABLET TAHALI TEMPLE TIRADE AGREMEN AKROTER AMALAKA BIBELOT BUCRANE CIRCLET COCARDE CORBEIL CROCKET EARPLUG ECHINUS ENGRAVE ENHANCE FURNISH GADROON GARNISH NETSUKE RINCEAU SEXFOIL STRIGIL TREFOIL TRINKET APPLIQUE DECORATE FLOURISH GIMCRACK LAVALIER SWASTIKA
(— FOR HEAD) MIND TARGET
(— ON SHIP) BADGE
(CHILD'S —) GAY
(CLAW-LIKE —) GRIFFE
(DRESS —) FROG LACE JABOT SEQUIN SPANGLE
(HEAD —) TIARA TEMPLE
(HORSE COLLAR —) HOUNCE
(MUSICAL —) TURN
(PENDANT —) BOB BULLA ANADEM BANGLE TASSEL EARRING LAVALIER
(SHOULDER —) EPAULET
(TAWDRY —) GINGERBREAD
(PL.) FIGGERY KNAVERY AGREMENS
ORNAMENTAL FANCY CHICHI FRILLY LILYTURN BLUEBEARD
ORNAMENTATION BOSS FOIL ACORN DECOR ADORNO BABERY CHICHI CILERY DICING CUSPING ECHELLE LACWORK STYLING FROUFROU HEADWORK PURFLING ROCAILLE STAFFAGE TRESSURE
(CHEAP —) TINSEL
(EXTRAVAGANT —) ROCOCO
(MUSICAL —) GRUPPO GRUPPETTO
ORNAMENTED FIGURY FOILED ORNATE TAWDRY ADORNED FLOUNCY FROSTED TREFLEE WROUGHT GOFFERED SINNOWED ELABORATE STELLATED
ORNATE GAY FINE FANCY FUSSY GIDDY SHOWY DRESSY FLORID FLOSSY PURPLE SUPERB AUREATE BAROQUE FLOWERY TAFFETA MANDARIN OVERRIPE SPLENDID

ELABORATE UNNATURAL
(EXTREMELY —) GIDDY
ORNERY CONTRARY
ORNITHOLOGIST AUDUBON BIRDMAN
OROTUND FULL CLEAR SHOWY MELLOW STRONG POMPOUS RESONANT SONOROUS BOMBASTIC
ORP FRET WEEP
ORPHAN PIP WARD FOUNDLING STEPCHILD
ORPHANED ORBATE
ORPHEUS (BIRTHPLACE OF —) PIERIA
(FATHER OF —) APOLLO OEAGRUS
(MOTHER OF —) CALLIOPE
(WIFE OF —) EURYDICE
ORPHREY BAND BORDER
ORPIMENT ORPIN HARTAL SPIRIT ARSENIC HARTAIL
ORPINE SEDUM LIVELONG BAGLEAVES EVERGREEN
ORRA ODD IDLE ORROW WORTHLESS
ORRIS GIMP IRIS LACE BRAID ORRICE GALLOON
ORT BIT END CRUMB SCRAP MORSEL REFUSE TRIFLE LEAVING REMNANT FRAGMENT LEFTOVER
ORTHODOX GOOD GREEK SOUND USUAL PROPER CANONIC CORRECT ACCEPTED STANDARD CUSTOMARY
ORTHODOXY TRUTH SOUNDNESS
ORTHOGRAPHY WRITING
ORTHOPTERON WALKER
ORTOLAN BIRD RAIL SORA BUNTING BOBOLINK WHEATEAR
ORTSTEIN HARDPAN
ORYX BEISA PASANG PASENG GAZELLE GEMSBOK ANTELOPE LEUCORYX
OS BONE ESKAR ESKER MOUTH OPENING ORIFICE
OSAGE ORANGE HEDGE OSAGE BODOCK BOWWOOD
OSCILLATE LOG WAG HUNT ROCK SWAY VARY SQUEG SWING WAVER WEAVE SHIMMY FEATHER VIBRATE FLUCTUATE
OSCILLATION HOWL WAVE SHOCK SEICHE SHIMMY SQUEAL FLUTTER LIBRATION VIBRATION
OSCULATE BUSS KISS
OSCULATORY PAX
OSIER ROD WAND EDDER SALIX SKEIN SPLIT WITHY BASKET SALLOW WICKER WILLOW DOGWOOD WILGERS REDBRUSH
(— CAGE) TUMBREL
(— WILLOW) TWIGWITHY
OSIRIS HERSHEF UNNEFER
(BROTHER OF —) SET SETH
(CROWN OF —) ATEF
(FATHER OF —) GEB KEB SEB
(MOTHER OF —) NUT
(SISTER OF —) ISIS
(SON OF —) HORUS ANUBIS
(WIFE OF —) ISIS
OSMANLI TURK TURKISH
OSPREY GLED HAWK OSSI GLEDE

BALBUSARD OSSIFRAGE
OSSATURE SKELETON OSSEMENTS
OSSE DARE ATTEMPT PRESAGE PROMISE VENTURE PROPHESY RECOMMEND UTTERANCE
OSSEOUS BONE BONY SPINY LITHIC OSTEAL
OSSICLE BONE INCUS ADORAL STAPES ALVEOLE BONELET MALLEUS SCUTELLA
OSSIFICATION OSTOSIS UROSTEON METOSTEON SIDEBONES
OSSUARY URN TOMB GRAVE VAULT OSSARIUM
OSTEND SHOW REVEAL EXHIBIT MANIFEST
OSTENSIBLE SEEMING APPARENT SPECIOUS
OSTENT AIR MIEN SIGN TOKEN DISPLAY PORTENT
OSTENTATION POMP SHOW CLASS ECLAT FLARE PRIDE STRUT SWANK VAUNT PARADE DISPLAY FLUTTER PAGEANT PORTENT PRESAGE FLOURISH FRIPPERY PRETENSE SHOWINESS SPECTACLE
OSTENTATIOUS ARTY LOUD GAUDY SHOWY SWANK FLASHY SPORTY SWANKY TURGID FLAUNTY GLARING OBVIOUS POMPOUS SPLASHY FASTUOUS ELABORATE
OSTERIA INN TAVERN
OSTIOLE PORE MOUTH STOMA OPENING ORIFICE APERTURE
OSTRACIZE BAN BAR CUT SNUB EXILE BANISH PUNISH REJECT ABOLISH CENSURE EXCLUDE BLACKBALL PROSCRIBE
OSTRACON SHELL FRAGMENT POTSHERD
OSTRICH EMU RHEA NANDU BREVIPEN STRUCION
(— FEATHER) BOO
(JERKED —) BILTONG
OSTYAK KHANTY
OSWEGO TEA BALM
OTAHEITE TAHITI
(— APPLE) HEVI MACUPI
OTALGIA EARACHE
OTHELLO MOOR
(FRIEND OF —) IAGO
(WIFE OF —) DESDEMONA
OTHER HE MO ELSE MORE ALTER FORMER NOTHER SECOND TIDDER TOTHER ALTERUM FURTHER DISTINCT DIFFERENT
() HETERO
(PL.) LAVE REST LUTRA
OTHERNESS ALTERITY
OTHERWISE OR NOT ELSE ENSE ALIAS SECUS ALITER EXCEPT BESIDES ELSEHOW ELSEWAY
OTIC AURAL AUDITORY ORACULAR AURICULAR
OTIOSE IDLE LAZY VAIN ALOOF FUTILE OTIANT REMOTE STERILE USELESS INACTIVE INDOLENT REPOSING

TOLITH SAGITTA LAPILLUS
OTOSTEON
TOLOGIST AURIST
TTAVINO PICCOLO
TTER DOG FUR PUP FISH NAIR
PELT BITCH HURON LOUTRE
SIMUNG TACKLE ANNATTO PERIQUE
MAMPALON MUSTELIN PARAVANE
(— TAIL) POLE
(DEN OF — S) HOLT
(SEA —) KALAN
TTOMAN (ALSO SEE TURKEY)
POUF SEAT TURK COUCH DIVAN
SQUAB STOOL FABRIC OTHMAN
POUFFE SULTANE FOOTSTOOL
(— COURT) PORTE
(— GOVERNOR) PASHA
(— LEADER) OSMAN
(— PROVINCE) VILAYET
(— STANDARD) ALEM
(— SUBJECT) RAIA RAYAH
UABE HOGNUT
UAKARI ACARI UKARI MONKEY
UAKARI
UCH OH OW ADORN BEZEL CLASP
JEWEL NOUCH BROOCH FIBULA
NOUCHE BRACELET NECKLACE
ORNAMENT
UGHT BIT BUD BUT MOW BOOD
BOOT MOTE MUST ZERO SHALL
BELONG CIPHER NAUGHT NOUGHT
SHOULD BEHOOVE
UNCE URE OKET OKIA ONCA ONCE
ONZA OKIEH UNCIA CHEETAH
LEOPARD WILDCAT
(EIGHT —S) CUPFUL
(ONE-16TH OF —) DRAM
(ONE-20TH OF —) EASTERLING
(ONE-8TH OF —) DRAM
UPHE ELF OOF OUF GOBLIN
UR UR ORE URE WER WIR HORE
NOTRE UNSER
(— LORD) NS
(— SAVIOR) NSIC
URICURY LICURI LICURY
CABECUDO
URSELVES USSELF USSELS
USSELVEN
USIA NATURE ESSENCE
SUBSTANCE
UST BAR BUMP FIRE SACK CHUCK
EJECT EVICT EXPEL BANISH
DEBOUT REMOVE CASHIER DISCARD
DISMISS SUSPEND DISSEIZE
FORJUDGE ELIMINATE
USTING AMOTION
UT EX AWAY DOWN HORS FORTH
ABSENT BEGONE ISSUED OOTWITH
OUTWARD EXTERNAL PUBLISHED
(— LOUD) BOST
(— OF BREATH) BLOWN
(— OF COMMISSION) BUNG
(— OF DATE) OLD DOWDY PASSE
OUTWORN TIMEWORN OVERDATED
(— OF DOORS) FOREIGN THEREOUT
(— OF EXISTENCE) AWAY
(— OF KILTER) ALOP AWRY CRANK
BROKEN

(— OF ONE'S MIND) FEY DAFT
DELEERIT
(— OF ORDER) AMISS KAPUT
FAULTY DEFICIENT
(— OF PLACE) AMISS INEPT
(— OF PLAY) DEAD FOUL
(— OF SIGHT) DOGGO INVISIBLE
(— OF SORTS) CROOK CROSS
HUMPY NOHOW COMICAL PEEVISH
(— OF THE WAY) BY BYE ASIDE
BLIND CLEAR CLOSE AFIELD
REMOTE
(— OF THIS LIFE) HYNE
(— OF TUNE) FALSE SCORDATO
(— OF) EX FROM DEHORS OUTWITH
(FARTHER —) UTTER
OUTAGE VENT ULLAGE HEADSPACE
OUT-AND-OUT GROSS SHEER
SWORN UTTER ARRANT DIRECT
WHOLLY ABSOLUTE COMPLETE
CRASHING
OUTBREAK FIT ROW RASH RIOT
BURST SALLY EMEUTE PLAGUE
REVOLT RUCKUS TUMULT UPROAR
BOUTADE OUTCROP RUCTION
BLIZZARD ERUPTION OUTBURST
EXPLOSION
(— OF EMOTIONALISM) HYSTERIA
(— OF TEMPER) MOORBURN
(SUDDEN —) SPURT
OUTBUILDING BARN SHED LODGE
PRIVY BARTON GARAGE HEMMEL
OUTHOUSE SKEELING SKILLING
BACKHOUSE
OUTBURST BOUT CROW FLAW FUME
GALE GUST RAGE TIFF AGONY
BLAST BLAZE BREAK BRUNT BURST
FLARE FLASH GEARE SALLY SPATE
START STORM ACCESS BLOWER
BLOWUP ESCAPE FANTAD FANTOD
GOLLER TIRADE TUMULT BLOWOUT
OUTCROP PASSION TANTRUM
TORRENT ERUPTION EXPLOSION
(— OF ANGER) FIT GERE GEARE
TATTER
(— OF ORATORY) SQUIRT
(— OF SPEECH) STRAIN
(— OF TEMPER) FUFF TIFF
BLOWOUT
(SPACE —) SUPERNOVA
OUTCAST EXILE LEPER RONIN
SHREW ABJECT PARIAH AOUTLET
ISHMAEL MISSILE OUTWALE
CASTAWAY CHANDALA REJECTED
VAGABOND DIALONIAN
(HOMELESS —) ARAB
(JAPANESE —) ETA RONIN
OUTCOME END OUT FATE TERM
CLOSE EDUCT EVENT HATCH ISSUE
LOOSE PROOF UPSET BROWST
EFFECT EXITUS OUTLET PERIOD
RESULT SEQUEL UPSHOT EMANATE
PROGENY SUCCESS FATALITY
AFTERMATH
OUTCROP CROP LEDGE BASSET
BLOSSOM BLOWOUT OUTBREAK
OUTBURST
OUTCROPPING BULT SCABROCK
OUTCRY CAW CRY HUE YIP BAWL

BRAY DITE GAFF HOWL REAM ROAR
SCRY UTAS YARM YELL ALARM
BOAST DITTY NOISE OUTAS SHOUT
STINK WHAUP BELLOW CLAMOR
HOLLER RACKET SCREAM SHRIEK
STEVEN TUMULT CALLING EXCLAIM
PROTEST SCREECH SHILLOO
COMPLAINT PHILLILEW
(PUBLIC —) STINK
OUTDATED CRINOLINE
OUTDISTANCE DROP SKIN OUTGO
SURPASS OUTSTRIP
OUTDO CAP COB COP COW POT TOP
BANG BEAT BEST FLOG EXCEL
OUTGO TRUMP WORSE DEFEAT
EXCEED OUTACT NONPLUS
SURPASS OVERCOME
OUTDOORS FORTH OUTBY OUTBYE
OUTSIDE
OUTER BUT ALIEN ECTAD ECTAL
UPPER UTTER FOREIGN OUTSIDE
OUTWARD EXTERIOR EXTERNAL
FORINSEC
OUTERMOST FINAL UTTER UTMOST
EVEREST EXTREME OUTWARD
FARTHEST REMOTEST
OUTFACE DEFY RESIST SUBDUE
CONFRONT OVERCOME
OUTFIELDER GARDENER OUTSCOUT
OUTFIT KIT RIG GANG GARB REAR
REEK SUIT TEAM UNIT DRESS EQUIP
GETUP HABIT TROUP ATTIRE
CONREY DUFFEL FITOUT LAYOUT
CLOTHES FURNISH SHEBANG
EQUIPAGE FURNITURE GRUBSTAKE
(INFANT'S —) LAYETTE
(SPARE —) CHANGE
OUTFLANK OUTWING OVERWING
OUTFLOW FLUX DRAIN ISSUE
OUTGO EFFLUX ESCAPE OUTPOUR
OUTGO EXIT EXCEL ISSUE OUTDO
EFFLUX EGRESS EXCEED OUTLAY
OUTLET OUTRUN OUTCOME
PRODUCT SURPASS OUTSTRIP
OUTGROWTH BUD JAG FOOT HAIR
LEAF MOSS SPUR CLAMP FRUIT
HILUM HYPHA SCALE SPINE ACULEA
COCKLE CUPULE FIBRIL ENATION
FEATHER ISIDIUM APPENDIX
EPIDERMA HAPTERON INDUSIUM
OFFSHOOT CARBUNCLE
EMERGENCE
OUTHOUSE SHED SKEO BIFFY
LODGE PRIVY BIGGIN LINHAY
OUTHUT LATRINE SKEELING
SKILLION
OUTING OUT SKIP STAY TRIP
JUNKET PICNIC COOKOUT HOLIDAY
CLAMBAKE VACATION WAYGOOSE
EXCURSION WAYZGOOSE
OUTLANDER PARDESI
OUTLANDISH ALIEN EXOTIC REMOTE
BIZARRE FOREIGN STRANGE
UNCOUTH PECULIAR BARBAROUS
FANTASTIC GROTESQUE UNEARTHLY
OUTLAST ELAPSE SURVIVE
OVERBIDE
OUTLAW BAN BAR CACO HORN
TORY EXILE EXLEX FLEME RONIN

ARRANT BADMAN BANDIT BANISH BRUMBY COWBOY DACOIT UNLEDE BANDIDO ISHMAEL FUGITATE FUGITIVE PROHIBIT PROSCRIBE PROSCRIPT
(IRISH —) WOODKERN
(JAPANESE —) RONIN
(PL.) MANZAS

OUTLAWED ILLEGAL ILLICIT LAWLESS

OUTLAWRY EXILE UTLAGARY

OUTLAY COST OUTGO EXPENSE PENSION

OUTLET BORE DRIP EXIT VENT ISSUE EGRESS ESCAPE EXITUS FUNNEL OUTAGE OPENING FUMEDUCT OVERFLOW SINKHOLE AVOIDANCE
(— FOR COASTAL SWAMP) BAYOU
(— OF CARBURETOR) BARREL
(— OF SPRING) EYE
(AIR —) GRILL GRILLE

OUTLIER KLIP KLIPPE

OUTLINE MAP BOSH ETCH FLOW FORM LINE PLAN PLAT BRIEF CHALK CHART DRAFT FRAME MODEL SHAPE TRACE AGENDA APERCU DESIGN DOODLE FIGURE FILLET LAYOUT SCHEMA SCHEME SCROLL SKETCH SURVEY CAPSULE CONTOUR DRAUGHT ELEMENT EXTRACT FEATURE GABARIT ISOTYPE PROFILE SUMMARY DESCRIBE SKELETON SYLLABUS SYNOPSIS GUIDELINE TREATMENT
(— HASTILY) SPLASH
(— OF A SCIENCE) GRUNDRISS
(— OF ANIMAL'S BODY) UNDERLINE
(— OF PLAY) SCENARIO
(— SHARPLY) ITALICIZE
(CURVING —) SWING
(DOUBLE —) FRINGE
(SHADOWY —) GHOST

OUTLIVE OUTLAST OUTWEAR SURVIVE OVERBIDE

OUTLOOK MIND VIEW FRONK FRONT VISTA ASPECT CLIMATE LOOKOUT PURVIEW FRONTAGE OUTSIGHT PROSPECT
(BRASH —) FACE
(MEDICAL —) PROGNOSIS
(SELF-CONFIDENT —) SWAGGER

OUTMANEUVER HAVE OUTPLAY

OUTMODED COLD DATED KARUT PASSE RUSTY BYGONE EFFETE ANTIQUE ELDERLY OBSOLETE

OUTPLAY HAVE

OUTPOST STATION FOREPOST OUTGUARD

OUTPOURING FLOW GALE GUSH FLOOD RIVER EARFUL LAVISH STREAM OUTFLOW FUSILLADE

OUTPUT CUT GET CROP MAKE EXPEL GRIST POWER YIELD ENERGY UPCOME TURNOUT

OUTRAGE RAPE ABUSE INSULT OFFEND RAVISH ABUSION AFFRONT OFFENSE VIOLATE VIOLENCE INDIGNITY

OUTRAGEOUS ENORM DAMNED HEINOUS OBSCENE UNGODLY FLAGRANT INFERNAL SHAMEFUL SHOCKING ATROCIOUS DESPERATE MONSTROUS

OUTRANK CAMP PREFER SURPASS

OUTRE ODD BIZARRE STRANGE ECCENTRIC

OUTREACH CHEAT EXCEED EXTEND OUTWIT SEARCH DECEIVE SURPASS OVERREACH

OUTRIDER HAYDUK HEIDUK HEYDUCK
(PL.) SWING

OUTRIGGER BOOM PROA BUMKIN RIGGER SPIDER

OUTRIGHT RUN BALD CLEAN TOTAL WHOLE DIRECT ENTIRE OPENLY WHOLLY ABSOLUTE COMPLETE DIRECTLY ENTIRELY

OUTRIVAL WIN EXCEL OUTDO DEFEAT ECLIPSE SURPASS

OUTRUN BEAT COTE NICK PASS OUTGO EXCEED ATRENNE FORERUN OUTFOOT PREVENT

OUTRUSH GUST

OUTSET START SETOUT BEGINNING THRESHOLD

OUTSHINE BLIND EXCEL OUTDO STAIN DAZZLE DEFACE DISTAIN SURPASS OVERSHINE

OUTSIDE BUT OUT BOUT FREE OUTBY UTTER AFIELD OUTFACE SURFACE EXTERIOR EXTERNAL
(— BOUNDS) ALOGICAL
(— OF) BESIDE
(COMB. FORM) ECTO

OUTSIDER ALIEN OUTMAN BOUNDER ISHMAEL EXOTERIC STRANGER EXTRANEAN FOREIGNER PHILISTER

OUTSKIRTS SIDE SKIRTS OUTSHIFTS

OUTSMART SLICK

OUTSPOKEN BOLD FREE LOUD APERT BLUFF BLUNT BROAD FRANK NAKED PLAIN ROUND CANDID DIRECT ARTLESS EXPRESS EXPLICIT

OUTSTANDING ACE BIG ARCH RARE AMONG FAMED NOTED SMASH BANNER FAMOUS GIFTED HEROIC MARKED SIGNAL SNAZZY UNPAID EMINENT PALMARY STELLAR SUBLIME SUPREME FABULOUS INSPIRED SEASONED SKELPING SLAMBANG SMACKING STANDOUT BEAUTIFUL PRINCIPAL PROMINENT UNSETTLED

OUTSTAY TARRY

OUTSTRETCHED STENT EXPANDED EXTENDED

OUTSTRIP CAP TOP WIN BEST COTE LEAD LOSE PASS EXCEL OUTDO STRIP EXCEED OUTRUN DEVANCE SURPASS DISTANCE OVERCOME TRANSCEND

OUTVIE SURPASS OUTSTRIP

OUTWARD ECTAD OUTER OVERT DERMAD EXODIC EXTERN FORMAL EXTREME VISIBLE APPARENT EXTERIOR EXTERNAL OBSOLETE

OUTFORTH EXTRINSIC

OUTWEIGH WEIGH OUTPOISE OVERBEAR

OUTWIT FOX POT BALK BEST FOIL HAVE BLOCK CHECK CROSS BAFFLE EUCHRE FICKLE JOCKEY OVERGO THWART STONKER OUTSHARP CROSSBITE OVERREACH

OUTWORK BRAY JETTY FLECHE TENAIL HORNWORK HORSEHOE TENAILLE

OUTWORN WAPPENED

OUZEL PIET AMSEL COLLY OUSEL OWZEL DIPPER THRUSH WHISTLER

OVAL O ELLIPSE STADIUM VESICAL VULVATE AVELONGE NUMMULAR VULVIFORM

OVARY CORAL GONAD GERMEN OARIUM OOPHORON

OVATION HAND APPLAUSE

OVEN OON UMU KILN LEAR LEER LEHR OAST BAKER BENCH GLAZE GLOOM HANGI KOHUA TANUR TILER CALCAR MUFFLE CABOOSE FURNACE KITCHEN
(— FORK) FRUGGAN FRUGGIN
(— MOP) SCOVEL

OVENBIRD BAKER FURNER HORNERO TEACHER ACCENTOR

OVER BY BYE OER TOO ALSO ANEW ATOP BACK DEAD DONE GONE UPON ABOVE AGAIN ALOFT ATOUR ATURN CLEAR ENDED EXTRA VAULT ABROAD ACROSS AROUND BEYOND DESSUS EXCESS UPWARD SURPLUS THROUGH FINISHED
(— AGAINST) FORNENT
(— AND ABOVE) ATOP ATOUR BESIDES
(ALL —) NAPOO NAPOOH SURTOUT
(PREFIX) SUR SUPER SUPRA

OVERABUNDANCE WASTE EXCESS SURPLUS PLETHORA

OVERACT HAM EMOTE OUTDO BURLESQUE

OVERALLS SLIP CHAPS JEANS TONGS DENIMS

OVERAWE COW ABASH DAUNT BUFFALO BROWBEAT

OVERBEARING HIGH PROUD LORDLY OVERLY HAUGHTY ARROGANT BULLYING INSOLENT SNOBBISH IMPERIOUS MASTERFUL

OVERBURDEN COVER HOIST PESTER CONGEST OVERLAY ENCUMBER STRIPPING SURCHARGE

OVERBUSY FUSSY PRAGMATIC

OVERCAST DIM SEW BIND DARK DULL GLUM CLOUD HEAVY SERGE CLOUDY DARKEN GLOOMY LOWERY CLOUDED

OVERCHARGE GYP SOAK CROWD GOUGE STICK STING BURDEN EXCISE OPPRESS EXTORTION

OVERCOAT MINO BENNY GREGO SHUBA BANGUP CAPOTE RAGLAN SLIPON TOPPER ULSTER PALETOT SPENCER SURTOUT TOPCOAT BENJAMIN COONSKIN TAGLIONI

COTHAMORE GREATCOAT
INVERNESS
OVERCOATING DUFFEL DUFFLE
OVERCOME DO AWE GET WAR WIN
BEAT BEST DING LICK LOCK MATE
POOP SACK SUNK TAME WAUR
CHARM CRUCH DAUNT DROUK
DROWN FORDO STILL STOOP
THROW APPALL BEATEN BUSHED
CRAVEN DEFEAT EXCEED FOREDO
HURDLE MASTER OUTRAY PLUNGE
SUBDUE VICTOR CONFUTE
CONQUER DEPRESS ENFORCE
RECOVER SMOTHER CONVINCE
OUTSTRIP SUPERATE SURMOUNT
SURPRISE
(— DIFFICULTIES) SWIM
(— WITH FATIGUE) FORDO FOREDO
(— WITH WEARINESS) HEAVY
(BE — BY HEAT) SWELTER
OVERCONFIDENT SECURE POSITIVE
OVERCROWD CONGEST
SURCHARGE
OVERDECORATED GARISH
OVERDEVELOPED GAUDY
OVERDO EXCEED EXHAUST FATIGUE
PERCOCT OVERCOOK OVERWORK
BURLESQUE
OVERDONE FUSTIAN EXUBERANT
OVERDOSE SICKENER
OVERDRESS SAC SACK DIZEN
SAQUE POLONAISE
OVERDRIED SLEEPY
OVERDUE BACK LATE TARDY
UNPAID ARREARS BELATED
DELAYED EXCESSIVE
OVEREAGER FEVERISH FEVEROUS
OVEREAT GORGE SLOFF SATIATE
GOURMAND
OVERELABORATE NIGGLE
OVEREXERT TORLE TORFEL
OVERPLY
OVERFED RANK FULSOME
OVERFLOW REE COME FLUX SLOP
SWIM TEEM VENT BRIME FLOAT
FLOOD SPATE SPILL ABOUND
DEBORD OUTLET OVERRUN
REDOUND BOILOVER EXUNDATE
INUNDATE OUTSWELL SUBMERGE
(— FROM MOLD) SPEW SPUE
OVERFLOWING FLOW AWASH
FLOAT DELAVY DELUGE ALLUVIO
COPIOUS FRESHET PROFUSE
INUNDANT EXUBERANT LANDFLOOD
SUPERFLUX
OVERGARMENT SMOCK BLOUSE
DUSTER
OVERGROWN FOZY RANK GAWKY
BRANCHY FULSOME SPRATTY
SPRITTY
OVERHAND WHIP
OVERHANG JUT BEND EAVE RAKE
BULGE JETTY BEETLE SHELVE
TOPPLE FANTAIL OVERLAP PROJECT
SUSPEND
OVERHANGING BEETLE SHELVY
HANGING PENDENT IMMINENT
OBUMBRANT PENTHOUSE
OVERHAUL EXAMINE OVERHAIL

RENOVATE FOREREACH
OVERHEAD COST ABOVE ALOFT
BURDEN ONCOST UPKEEP EXPENSE
OVERTOP
OVERHEAT PARBOIL
OVERLAP LAP RIDE SYPHER
SHINGLE IMBRICATE INTERSECT
OVERLAPPING JUGATE RIDING
EQUITANT OBVOLUTE IMBRICATE
(— IN FUGUE) STRETTA STRETTO
OVERLAY CAP LAP CEIL COAT
APPLY COUCH COVER GLAZE
PATCH PLATE CEMENT CRAVAT
SPREAD STUCCO VENEER ENCRUST
OPPRESS OVERLIE SMOTHER
APPLIQUE TEMPLATE
(— WITH GOLD) BEAT GILD
OVERLOAD GLUT CHARGE
ENCUMBER SURCHARGE
OVERLOADED PLETHORIC
PLETHOROUS
OVERLOOK BALK MISS OMIT PASS
SKIP SLIP WINK FORGO ACQUIT
EXCUSE FOREGO FORGET IGNORE
MANAGE OVERGO ABSOLVE
COMMAND CONDONE FORGIVE
INSPECT MISKNOW NEGLECT
CONFOUND DOMINATE DISREGARD
DISSEMBLE
OVERLOOKER GAITER
OVERLORD LIEGE DESPOT ISWARA
SATRAP TYRANT ISHVARA SUZERAIN
TYRANNIZE
OVERLY CAP TOO
OVERLYING BROCHANT INCUMBENT
OVERMAN CHIEF LEADER ARBITER
FOREMAN REFEREE OVERSEER
SUPERMAN
OVERMANTLE (— TREATMENT)
TRUMEAU
OVERMASTER GET
OVERMATCH BEST DEFEAT EXCEED
SURPASS VANQUISH
OVERMODEST PRIM PRUDISH
OVERMUCH TOO EXCESS SURPLUS
EXCESSIVE
OVERNICE FEAT FUSS SAUCY
DAINTY QUAINT SPRUCE FINICKY
PRECISE DENTICAL PRECIOUS
SQUEAMISH
OVERPLAY HAM
OVERPOWER AWE BEAT ROUT
RUSH CRUSH DROWN QUELL
SWAMP WHELM COMPEL DEFEAT
DELUGE ENGULF MASTER OVERGO
SUBDUE WRIXLE CONQUER
CONTROL OPPRESS REPRESS
CONVINCE OUTSCOUT SCUMFISH
SURPRISE
(— WITH HEAT) SWELT
(— WITH LIGHT) DAZZLE
OVERPOWERING DIRE FIERCE
KILLING DAZZLING STUNNING
DESPERATE MONSTROUS
OVERPRECISE FINICKY CLERKISH
PRECIEUSE
OVERREACH DO POT DUPE GRAB
CHEAT COZEN CHOILE GREASE
NOBBLE OUTWIT OVERGO DECEIVE

OVERREADY FORWARD
OVERREFINED QUAINT PRECIOUS
OVERRIPE FRACID SQUSHY
SQUUSHY
OVERRIPENESS SEED
OVERRULE VETO GOVERN
ABROGATE OVERCOME
OVERRULING GREAT PREDOMINANT
OVERRUN TEEM BESET CRUSH
SWARM DELUGE EXCEED INFEST
INVADE OVERGO RAVAGE SPREAD
DESTROY
OVERSEE TEND WATCH DIRECT
HANDLE MANAGE SURVEY EXAMINE
INSPECT NEGLECT DISREGARD
SUPERVISE
OVERSEER BOSS CORK JOSS
EPHOR GRAVE REEVE BISHOP
CENSOR DRIVER GAFFER GRIEVE
KEEKER MIRDHA TINDAL WARDEN
BAILIFF CAPATAZ CAPORAL
CURATOR FOREMAN HEADMAN
KANGANI MANAGER MANDOER
MAYORAL OVERMAN PRISTAW
TAPSMAN BANKSMAN CHAPRASI
DECURION MARTINET SURVEYOR
VILLICUS
(— OF MACHINERY) TENTOR
(SPIRITUAL —) PASTOR PRIEST
OVERSENSITIVE TICKLISH
OVERSENTIMENTAL SLOPPY
OVERSHADOW DIM CLOUD COVER
DWARF SHADE TOWER DARKEN
EFFACE ECLIPSE OBSCURE
UMBRAGE DOMINATE OVERCAST
OVERSHOE GUM BOOT GUME
ARCTIC GAITER GALOSH GOLOSH
PATTEN RUBBER SANDAL FLAPPER
EXCLUDER FOOTHOLD PANTOFLE
OVERSIGHT EYE CARE HOLE SLIP
ERROR FAULT GAFFE LAPSE WATCH
CHARGE BLUNDER CONTROL
JEOFAIL MISTAKE OMISSION
TUTELAGE DIRECTION
(LEGAL —) JEOFAIL
OVERSKIRT PEPLUM PANNIER
OVERSOFT QUASHY
OVERSPREAD FOG CAST CLOT
DECK PALL BATHE BREDE CLOUD
COVER SMEAR STREW CLOTHE
DELUGE DOODLE INDUCE SCATTER
SUFFUSE BESPREAD
OVERSTATE MAGNIFY EXAGGERATE
OVERSTEP PASS EXCEED SURPASS
OVERSUPPLIED RANK
OVERT OPEN PATENT PUBLIC
OBVIOUS APPARENT MANIFEST
OVERTAKE PASS ATAKE CATCH
ATTAIN DETECT ENSNARE OVERHIE
FOREHENT OVERHAUL
(— BY DARKNESS) BENIGHT
OVERTASK DRIVE
OVERTAX HOIST EXCEED STRAIN
STRESS
OVERTHROW TIP CAST DASH DOWN
FALL FELL FOIL FOLD HURL RAZE
ROUT RUIN RUSH WALT WEND
ALLAY EVERT FLING LEVEL QUASH
UPSET WORST WRACK WRECK

DEFEAT DEJECT REPUTE SLIGHT
TOPPLE TUMBLE UNSEAT WRITHE
AFFLICT CONQUER CONVELL
DESTROY DISMISS RUINATE
SUBVERT UNDOING UNHORSE
CONFOUND DEMOLISH OVERCOME
REVERSAL SUPPLANT VANQUISH
CHECKMATE CONFUSION
(— **BY TRIPPING**) CHIP
OVERTONE PARTIAL HARMONIC
OVERTOP COW OVERREACH
OVERTURE OFFER PROEM ADVANCE
OPENING PRELUDE APERTURE
PROPOSAL SINFONIA VORSPIEL
(**INDECENT** —) ASSAULT
OVERTURN TIP CAVE COUP KEEL
TILT WALT WELT TERVE THROW
UPSET WELME WHALM WHELM
SLIGHT TIPPLE TOPPLE WELTER
CAPSIZE DESTROY PERVERT
REVERSE SUBVERT
OVERWEIGHT OUTGANG
OVERWHELM BOWL BURY SINK
SLAY AMAZE COVER CRUSH DROOK
DROUK DROWN FLOOD SEIZE SPATE
SWAMP CUMBER DEFEAT DELUGE
ENGULF OBRUTE PLUNGE QUELME
QUENCH ASTOUND CONFUTE
CONQUER ENGROSS FLATTEN
IMMERSE INFLOOD OPPRESS
ASTONISH DISTRESS INUNDATE
SUBMERGE AVALANCHE
OVERWORK HOIN TIRE TOIL SWEAT
SURMENAGE
OVINE OVIN OVILE SHEEP SHEEPLIKE
OVOID OVATE OBOVOID
OVOLO OVAL THUMB BOLTEL
OVULE EGG NIT GERM SEED
EMBRYO OVULUM GEMMULE
SEEDLET
OVUM EGG OVAL SEED SPORE
OOSPHERE
OWAIA TREE BOBO
OWE DUE OWN REST AUGHT OUGHT
SHALL POSSESS ATTRIBUTE
OWER DEBTOR
OWL ULE BUBO LULU MOMO RURU

SURN TYTO UTUM JENNY MADGE
NINOX PADGE SCOPS STRIX TAWNY
WEKAU AZIOLA HOOTER HOWLET
KETUPA MUCARO RAPTOR STRICH
VERMIN WHEKAU BOOBOOK
HARFANG KATOGLE WAPACUT
WOOLERT BILLYWIX POREPORK
(— **CALL**) HOOT
(**LIKE AN** —) STRIGINE
(**YOUNG** —) UTUM OWLET
OWN AiN OWE AVOW FESS HAVE
HOLD HOWE MEET NAIN SELF ADMIT
AUGHT OUGHT MASTER CONCEDE
CONFESS POSSESS
OWNER BEL MALIK WALLA HOLDER
DOMINUS HERITOR ODALLER
(— **OF ESTATE**) ALIRD
(— **OF FISHING PLANT**) PLANTER
(— **OF YACHT**) AFTERGUARD
(**PLANTATION** —) COLON
(**SHEEP** —) NABAL
OWNERSHIP ODAL UDAL AUGHT
TITLE CORNER SEIZIN SEIZURE
SEVERAL TENANCY DOMINIUM
PROPERTY COMMUNITY
OX YAK ANOA AVER BEEF BUFF BULL
GAUR MUSK NAWT NEAT NEWT
NOWT OWSE REEM RUNT STOT
URUS ZEBU AIVER BISON BUGLE
GAYAL SANGA STEER TOLLY TSINE
BOVINE MITHAN BANTENG BUFFALO
KOUPREY TWINTER SELADANG
TALLOWER
(**CAMBODIAN** —) KOUPREY
KOUPROH
(**HORNLESS** —) MOIL
(**SMALL** —) RUNT
(**TAME** —) COACH
(**WILD** —) URE ANOA BUFF GAUR
REEM URUS BISON BUGLE BANTIN
BANTENG BUFFALO SELADANG
(**YEARLING** —) STIRK
(**YOUNG** —) STOT
OXBLOOD KAZAK COPTIC KAZAKH
OXEN NOWT OWSEN CATTLE
OXEYE BOCE GOLD ASTER CLOUD

DAISY GOLDE DUNLIN PLOVER
TARPON
OXFORD DOWN SHOE CLOTH
OXONIAN SLIPPER
OXGANG OSKEN BOVATE OXGATE
OXLAND PLOWGANG
OXIDATION RUST
OXIDE EARTH FLOSS CADMIA MOILES
ZAFFER CALCINE LIMONITE
DJALMAITE
(— **OF CALCIUM**) LIME
(— **OF IRON**) RUST COLCOTHAR
MAGNETITE
OXLIP PAGLE PAIGLE PRIMULA
MILKMAID PRIMROSE PRIMWORT
OXSHOE CUE
OXYGEN GAS OZONE OXYGENIUM
OXYGENATE AERATE VENTILATE
OYSTER COPIS COUNT PINNA PLANT
SHELL COTUIT HUITRE NATIVE
REEFER BIVALVE MOLLUSK
RATTLER SHARPER BLUEPOINT
GREENGILL LYNNHAVEN
(— **BED**) PARK STEW LAYER SCALP
CLAIRE SCALFE OYSTERAGE
(— **CATCHER**) OLIVE PYNOT TIRMA
KROCKET PIANNET REDBILL
SCOLDER SHELDER PILWILLET
SKELDRAKE
(— **CRAB**) PINNOTERE
(— **FOSSIL**) OSTRACITE
(— **MEASURE**) WASH
(— **PLANT**) SALSIFY
(— **SHELL**) HUSK TEST SHUCK
(— **SMALLER THAN QUARTER**)
BLISTER
(— **SOLD BY POUND**) COUNT
(**2,3, OR 4 —S**) WARP
(**IRISH** —) POWLDOODY
(**ROCK** —) CHAMA
(**VEGETABLE** —) SALSIFY
(**YOUNG** —) SET SPAT
OYSTERFISH TAUTOG TOADFISH
OZARK STATE MISSOURI
OZOCERITE MALTHA NEFTGIL
OZONE AIR

P PAPA PETER

PA DAD PAW FORT PAPA DADDY
FATHER VILLAGE STOCKADE

PABULUM FOOD FUEL PROG CEREAL
ALIMENT SUPPORT NUTRIMENT

PAC BOOT SHOE MOCCASIN

PACA CAPA CAVY LAVA LABBA
AGOUTI RODENT

PACE FIG PAD RIP WAY BEMA CLIP
GAIT LOPE PASS PELT RACK RATE
STEP TEAR TROT WALK AMBLE
BRAWL CANTO SLINK SPACE SPEED
STEEK SWING TEMPO TRACE TREAD
CANTER GALLOP STRAIT STRIDE
CHANNEL CHAPTER DOGTROT
MEASURE PASSAGE SCUTTLE
(FAST —) ROMP
(RAPID —) CRACKER
(SLOW —) JOG CREEP
(PL.) MANAGE

PACER HORSE AMBLER SPANKER
TRIPPLER

PACHISI LUDO UCKERS PARCHESI

PACHYDERM HIPPO RHINO
ELEPHANT

PACIFIC CALM MEEK MILD IRENE
IRENIC PLACID SERENE PEACEFUL
TRANQUIL PEACEABLE
(— ISLAND PINE) IE KOU IEIE LEHUA

PACIFIER DUMMY COMFORTER

PACIFIST BOLO

PACIFY PAY CALM EASE LULL STAY
ABATE ALLAY AMESE MEASE PEASE
QUELL QUIET STILL PECIFY SERENE
SETTLE SOFTEN SOOTHE APPEASE
ASSUAGE MOLLIFY PLACATE
QUALIFY STIEKLE MITIGATE
ALLEVIATE RECONCILE

PACK JAM PUN WAD BALE CADE
CRAM DECK FILL GANG JAMB LADE
LOAD PAIR STOW SWAG TAMP TUCK
COUCH CRAME CROWD DRESS
FLOCK HORDE SKULK SOMER STEVE
STORE STUFF TRUSS BARREL
BODDLE BUDGET BUNDLE CARTON
DUFFLE EMBALE ENCASE FARDEL
HAMPER IMPACT THWACK TURKEY
WALLET PANNIER PORTAGE
RUMMAGE SUMPTER KNAPSACK
(— ANIMAL) ASS MULE BURRO
CAMEL HORSE LLAMA DONKEY
PACKER
(— BUILDER) GOBBER
(— JURY) WATER
(— LOOSELY) HOVER
(— OF BEARS) SLOTH
(— OF CARDS) STOCK
(— OF DOGS) CRY KENNEL
(— OF FOXES) GROUP SKULK
(— OF HOUNDS) CRY HUNT MUTE
(— OFF) WAG SHANK TURSE
(— ROAD) PACKWAY
(— TIGHTLY) STIVE

PACKAGE PAD BALE BOLT PAIR
DUMMY TRUSS BINDLE BUNDLE
PACKET PARCEL SAMPLE SEROON
DORLACH
(— OF CIGARETTES) DECK
(— OF GOLDBEATER'S SKINS)
SHODER

(— OF LEAF) BOOK
(— OF PEPPERS) ROBBIN
(— OF STAMPS) KILOWARE
(— OF VELLUM) KUTCH
(— OF VENEER) FLITCH
(— OF WOOL) BAG PAD BUTT
FADGE
(YARN —) CONE CHEESE

PACKER BALER LINER ROPER
CANNER

PACKET BOAT BOOK DECK ROLL
SCREW BUNDLE PARCEL SACHET
(— OF VELLUM) CUTCH KUTCH

PACKHORSE SOMER JAGGER
PACKER SUMPTER

PACKING CUP RAGS GAUZE PAPER
STRAW WASTE GASKET GROMMET
STOWAGE STOPPING
(— MATERIAL) BALINE GASKET
(CLAY —) LUTE

PACKINGHOUSE MEATWORKS

PACKMAN HAWKER

PACKSACK KYACK

PACKSADDLE BAT BARDEL
APAREJO

PACT CARTEL PACTUM TREATY
BARGAIN COMPACT LOCARNO
ALLIANCE CONTRACT COVENANT
AGREEMENT

PAD MAT WAD WAY BLAD BOSS
FROG LURE MUTE PATH PUFF ROAD
ROLL SHOE WALK WASE BLOCK
INKER PERCH PILCH QUILT STENT
STINT STUFF TABBY TRAMP BASKET
BUFFER BUSTLE DAUBER HOLDER
JOCKEY NUMNAH PADDLE PADNAG
PANNEL PILLOW SPONGE TABLET
TRUDGE VELURE WREATH BOLSTER
BOMBAST CUSHION FOOTPAD
PILLION SASHOON
(— IN CRIB) BUMPER
(— OF STRAW) SUNK WASE
(— ON HORSE'S FOOT) FROG
(ETCHER'S —) DABBER
(HAIR —) RAT MOUSE TOQUE
(INKING —) INKER TOMPION
(PERFUMED —) SACHET
(SADDLE —) PANEL PILLOW PILLION

PADAUK CORAIL

PADDER MANGLE

PADDING TABBY CADDIS BOLSTER
BOMBAST BUSHING CADDICE
FILLING PACKING ROBBERY
WADDING MAHOITRE STUFFING

PADDLE OAR ROW SPUD WADE
ALOOF CANOE SLICE SPANK
BUCKET DABBLE PETTLE PUNISH
STRIKE TODDLE SPANKER SPURTLE
LUMPFISH
(— BOX) WHEELHOUSE
(— FOR FLOUR) SLICK
(TAILOR'S —) BEATER

PADDLEFISH GANOID DUCKBILL
STURGEON POLYODONT SPADEFISH
SPOONBILL

PADDOCK LOT FROG PARK CLOSE
FIELD SLEDGE GARSTON LOANING
BIRDCAGE

PADDYMELON QUOKKA PADMELON

PADISHAH SULTAN PADASHA
POTSHAW

PADLOCK LOCK FASTEN SECURE
CLOSING FASTENER HORSELOCK
(— LINK) SHACKLE

PADRE MONK CLERIC FATHER
PRIEST CHAPLAIN

PADRONA LANDLADY MISTRESS

PADRONE BOSS CHIEF MASTER
PATRON LANDLORD INNKEEPER

PAEAN ODE HYMN SONG PRAISE
OUTBURST TRIUMPHAL

PAGAN ATA BUID BATAK BUKID
APAYAO BAGOBO BANGON BILAAN
BONTOC ETHNIC PAYNIM SABIAN
ALANGAN DUMAGAT GENTILE
HEATHEN INFIDEL SARACEN
SUBANUN UNGODLY IDOLATOR

PAGANDOM PAYNIM

PAGE BOY CALL LEAF MOTH SIDE
CHILD FACER FOLIO GROOM SHEET
DONZEL ERRATA SUMMON VARLET
BUTTONS CALLBOY FUNNIES
PAVISER SERVANT HENCHMAN
ICHOGLAN
(— BOTTOM) TAIL
(BLANK —S) CANCEL
(FACING —S) SPREAD
(LADY'S —) ESCUDERO
(LAST FEW —S) BACK
(LEFTHAND —) VERSO
(RIGHTHAND —) RECTO OUTPAGE
(TITLE —) TITLE UNWAN RUBRIC
(PL.) ODDMENTS

PAGEANT JEST POMP SHOW ANTIC
PARADE RIDING TABLEAU TAMASHA
TRIUMPH AQUACADE CAVALCADE
SPECTACLE WATERWORK

PAGEANTRY POMP PARADE
HERALDRY SPLENDOR

PAGODA PON TAA HOON WATT
TEMPLE VARELLA

PAHOUIN FAN FANG

PAHUTAN PAHO

PAID EVEN RESOLUTE
(— IN COIN) DRY
(— IN FULL) SATISFIED

PAIL CAN COG PAN SOA SOE BEAT
BOWK GAWN MEAL STOP TRUG
BOWIE COGUE CRUCK DANDY ESHIN
SKEEL STOOP BLICKY BUCKET
COGGIE HARASS KETTLE LEGLEN
NOGGIN PIGGIN SITULA THRASH
COLLOCK
(MILK —) KIT SOE TRUG ESHIN
LEGLEN
(ON WHEELS) DANDY
(POTTERY —) SEAL
(SMALL —) KIT BLICKY BLICKIE
(WOODEN —) COG COGUE LUGGIE
PIGGIN

PAIN ACHE AGRA BALE CARE CARK
FRET GRUE HARM HURT PANG SITE
SORE TEEN TINE WARK AGONY
BEANS CRAMP DOLOR GRIEF GRIPE
PINCH PINSE SCALD SMART STING
STOUN THRAW THROE WOUND
BARRAT GRIEVE MISERY SHOWER
STITCH TWINGE AFFLICH ALGESIS

ANGUISH EARACHE HURTING
MYALGIA OFFENCE PENALTY
TORTURE TRAVAIL TROUBLE
DISTRESS FLEABITE
(— IN BACK) NOTALGIA SCIATICA
(— IN HAND) CHIRAGRA
(— IN SIDE) STEEK
(— OF MIND) AGONY
(— RELIEVER) OPIATE ANODYNE
ASPIRIN
(FILL WITH —) YEARN
(SHARP —) WRING
(STOMACH —) GRIPES GNAWING
(WRENCHING —) TORSION
(PL.) LABOR WHILE EFFORT
TROUBLE
PAINFUL BAD ILL DIRE EVIL FELL
SORE SOUR TART ANGRY CRUEL
SHARP SORRY BITTER STICKY
GRIPING HURTFUL IRKSOME
PENIBLE PUNGENT EXACTING
TERRIBLE TORTUOUS DIFFICULT
HARROWING
PAINSTAKING BUSY LOVING
CAREFUL PENIBLE DILIGENT
EXACTING ASSIDUOUS ELABORATE
PAINT BLOT COAT DAUB DRAW FARD
GAUD LIMN PENT PICT SOIL COLOR
FEIGN FUCUS GRAIN ROUGE STAIN
BEDAUB DAZZLE DEPICT ENAMEL
FRESCO OPAQUE SHADOW SKETCH
BESMEAR PORTRAY PRETEND
SCUMBLE AIRBRUSH DECORATE
DESCRIBE DISGUISE URFIRNIS
CALCIMINE
(— A PIPE) SOIL
(— FACE OR BODY) FUCUS PARGET
(— HASTILY) SQUIGGLE
(— SKETCHILY) SPLASH
(— THROUGH PATTERN) STENCIL
(— WITH COSMETICS) POP POT
FARD
PAINTBRUSH WICKAWEE
NOSEBLEED
PAINTED PINTO FUCATE PASTOSE
GOFFERED
(— BEAUTY) VANESSA
(— BUNTING) POP NONPAREIL
(— CUP) WICKAWEE PAINTBRUSH
(— WAKE-ROBIN) SARA
PAINTER FAUVE ARTIST DAUBER
PICTOR PANTHER SIGNIST SIGNMAN
WORKMAN BRUSHMAN LUMINIST
MURALIST NAZARENE STIPPLER
DECORATOR TACTILIST
(PL.) ECLECTICS
PAINTING ART OIL PAT PATA DRAFT
MURAL PIECE TABLE WATER
CANVAS CROUTE FRESCO MINERY
TITIAN BODEGON CAMAIEU
CARTOON DAUBING GRADINO
GRAPHIC HISTORY FROTTAGE
PREDELLA SEAPIECE SYMPHONY
(— EQUIPMENT) OIL BRUSH EASEL
PAINT CANVAS PALLET
(— IN COLLOIDAL MEDIUM)
TEMPERA
(— OF EVERYDAY LIFE) GENRE
(— OF FOLIAGE) BOSCAGE

(— ON PLASTER) SECCO FRESCO
(— WITH OPAQUE COLORS)
GOUACHE
(CIRCULAR —) TONDO
(RELIGIOUS —) PIETA TANKA
(SCENIC —) SCAPE
(SMALL —) TABLET
(THREE PANEL —) TRIPTYCH
(PL.) GENRE
PAIR DUO TWO ZYG CASE DIAD
DUAD DUAL MATE SIDE SPAN TEAM
TWIN YOKE BRACE MARRY MATCH
TWAIN UNITE COUPLE GEMINI
COUPLET DOUBLET JUMELLE
TWOSOME
(— OF FILMS) BIPACK
(— OF MILLSTONES) RUN
(— OF SHOTS) BRACKET
(— OF TONGS) GRAMPUS GRAPPLE
(— OF WINGS) SHEARS
(— ROYAL) PARIAL
(ONE OF —) IMPAIR NEIGHBOR
(PL.) GEMELS
PAIRED GEMEL JUGATE ZYGOUS
JUMELLE
PAISLEY PRINT SHAWL DESIGN
FABRIC
PAIUTE DIGGER
PAJAMAS SHALWAR SLEEPER

PAKISTAN
BAY: SOYMIANI
CANAL: NARA ROHRI
CAPE: FASTA JADDI JIWANI
CAPITAL: ISLAMABAD
COIN: ANNA RUPEE
DAM: TARBELA
LANGUAGE: URDU PUSHTU SINDHI
  BALUCHI BENGALI PUNJABI
MOUNTAIN: TIRICHMIR
MOUNTAIN RANGE: MAKRAN
  KIRTHAR HIMALAYA SULAIMAN
NATIVE: BENGAL PATHAN SINDHI
  BALUCHI PUNJABI
PORT: CHALNA KARACHI
RIVER: NAL BADO RAVI ZHOB
  DASHT INDUS CHENAB GANGES
  JHELUM KUNDAR PORALI
  JAMUNNA
STATE: DIR SWAT KALAT KHARAN
  CHITRAL KHAIRPUR
TOWN: DACCA CHALNA KHULNA
  LAHORE MULTAN QUETTA
  KARACHI SIALKOT LYALLPUR
  PESHAWAR SARGODHA
WEIGHT: SEER TOLA MAUND

PAKTONG TUTENAG
PAL ALLY CHUM JACK PARD BILLY
BUDDY CHINA CRONY LOUKE
COBBER COPAIN DIGGER FRIEND
COMRADE PARTNER COMPANION
PALACE SALE CHIGI COURT SERAI
STEAD CASTLE ELYSEE LOUVRE
PALAIS ALCAZAR EDIFICE LATERAN
MANSION PALAZZO TRIANON
VATICAN ZWINGER SERAGLIO
WHITEHALL

(— OF SATAN) PANDEMONIUM
(FAIRY —) SHEE SIDHE
PALADIN HERO PEER ANSEIS
ASTOLF KNIGHT CHAMPION
DOUZEPER
PALAMON (RIVAL OF —) ARCITE
(WIFE OF —) EMELYE
PALANQUIN JAUN JUAN KAGE KAGO
DANDI DOOLI DOOLY PALKI SEDAN
DOOLIE LITTER PALKEE TONJON
PALATABLE SAPID SPICY TASTY
DAINTY SAVORY MOREISH DELICATE
LUSCIOUS PLEASING SAPOROUS
AGREEABLE DELICIOUS TOOTHSOME
PALATAL SOFT FRONT VELAR
GUTTURAL
PALATE TASTE VELUM RELISH
GOURMET URANISCUS
PALATIAL LARGE ORNATE STATELY
SPLENDID
PALATINE CAPE OFFICER PALADIN
PALATIAL
PALAVER GASH SLUM TALK CAJOLE
DEBATE GLAVER JARGON PARLEY
CHATTER FLATTER WHEEDLE
CAJOLERY FLATTERY
PALE DIM WAN ASHY BLOC FADE
GREY GULL LILY PALL SICK WHEY
ASHEN BLAKE BLATE BLEAK CLOSE
FAINT FENCE GREEN LIGHT LINEN
LIVID LURID MEALY STAKE STICK
WHITE ANEMIC BLANCH CHALKY
CHANGE DOUGHY FALLOW FEEBLE
PALLID PASTEL PICKET REGION
REMISS SICKLY SILVER WATERY
WHITEN DEFENSE GHASTLY
HAGGARD INSIPID OBSCURE
WATERISH
(IN —) HAURIENT
PALEA PALET SQUAMELLA
PALENESS WAN PALLOR ACHROMA
PALESTINE (SEE ISRAEL)
PALETOT COAT JACKET OVERCOAT
GREATCOAT
PALFREY HORSE PALFRY
PALIMPSET TABLET PARCHMENT
PALING PALE FENCE FLAKE LIMIT
PALIS STAKE PICKET FENCING
BLENCHING
PALISADE HAY BOMA PALE PEEL
CLIFF FENCE RIMER STAKE HURDIS
PICKET BARRIER ENCLOSE FORTIFY
HURDIES STACKET TAMBOUR
ESPALIER
(MILITARY —) CIPPUS
(PL.) BAIL BARRIER
PALL FOG BORE CLOY PALE SATE
CLOAK CLOTH FAINT QUALM STALE
WEARY MANTLE NAUSEA SHROUD
DISGUST SATIATE ANIMETTA
MORTCLOTH
PALLET BED COT PAD COUCH QUILT
BLANKET MATTRESS PLANCHER
PALLIARD BEGGAR LECHER RASCAL
VAGABOND
PALLIATE EASE HIDE MASK VEIL
ABATE CLOAK COLOR COVER
GLOSS GLOZE LITHE BLANCH
LESSEN REDUCE SMOOTH SOFTEN

SOOTHE CONCEAL CUSHION SHELTER DISGUISE MITIGATE
PALLID WAN ASHY PALE PALY BLEAK WASHY WAXEN WHITE SALLOW GHASTLY BLOODLESS COLORLESS INNOCUOUS
PALL-MALL MAIL
PALLOR ASH WAN PALE ASHES PALENESS
PALM DOM ATAP BRAB BURI BUSU COCO DATE DOUM FLAT HIDE JARA KOKO LOOF NIOG NIPA PAWN SAGO SLIP TARA ARCHA ARECA ARENG ASSAI BONGA BUNGA CARRY COCOA COYOL CURUA DATIL FOIST HOWEA INAJA JAGUA LOULU MERUS NIKAU RATAN SABAL SALAK TECUM TUCUM UNAMO YAGUA YARAY ANAHAO ASSAHY BACABA BURITI CHONTA COHUNE CONTAR COROJO GEBANG GOMUTI GRUGRU JAMBEE JUPATI KENTIA KITTUL LAWYER NIBONG PACAYA RAFFIA ROTANG THENAR TOOROO TROPHY APRICOT BABASSU CARANDA CONCEAL COQUITO ERYTHEA GEONOMA MORICHE PUPUNHA SAGWIRE TALIPOT URUCURI JACITARA LATANIER
(— **FERN**) PONJA
(— **FOOD**) NUT COCO DATE NIPA SAGO SURA ASSAI TAREE TODDY COCONUT
(— **JUICE**) SURA
(— **LEAF**) OLA OLLA CAJAN FROND
(— **LILY**) TI
(— **OF HAND**) FLAT LOOF VOLA TABLE THENAR
(— **OFF**) COG FOB TOP SHAB FOIST TRUMP
(— **OUT**) APPAUME
(**BETEL** —) ARECA BONGA PUGUA PINANG
(**CLIMBING** —) RATTAN
(**FEATHER** —) HOWEA GOMUTI URUCURI
(**SPINY** —) PEACH GRIGRI GRUGRU
PALMARY CHIEF PALMAR SUPERIOR
PALMATE FLAT BROAD LOBED WEBBED
PALMER LOUSE FERULE STROLL TRAVEL VOTARY WANDER FOISTER PILGRIM
PALMETTO CABBAGE PALMITO BIGTHATCH
(— **STATE**) SOUTHCAROLINA
PALMODIC JERKY
PALMYRA BRAB TALA LONTAR RONIER TADMOR BASSINE
(**QUEEN OF** —) ZENOBIA
PALP FEEL TOUCH CAJOLE FEELER HANDLE PALPUS FLATTER TENTACLE
PALPABLE BALD RANK PLAIN PATENT AUDIBLE EVIDENT OBVIOUS TACTILE APPARENT DISTINCT MANIFEST TANGIBLE CORPOREAL
PALPATION THROB WALLOP DIPPING PITAPAT

PALPEBRA EYELID
PALPITATE PANT QUAP THROB FLACKER FLICKER FLUTTER PULSATE
PALPITATION BEAT DUNT PANT FLICKER FLUTTER PULSATION THROBBING
(— **OF HEART**) THUMB
PALSIED SHAKY SHAKING PARALYZED TOTTERING TREMBLING TREMULOUS
PALSY PARLESIE PARALYSIS
PALTER FIB LIE BABBLE HAGGLE MUMBLE PARLEY TRIFLE BARGAIN CHAFFER CHATTER QUIBBLE SHAFFLE
PALTRY BALD BARE BASE MEAN ORRA PUNY SCAB VILE WAFF FOOTY MINOR PETTY SCALL SCRUB SILLY TRASH CHETIF FLIMSY SHABBY SLIGHT TRASHY WOEFUL HILDING PELTING PIMPING PITIFUL RUBBISH SCABBED SCRUBBY TRIVIAL PICAYUNE PICKLING PIDDLING TRIFLING
PALUDAL MARSHY
PAMPA PLAIN PRAIRIE
PAMPAS (— **CAT**) KODKOD PAJERO
(— **DEER**) MAZAME
PAMPER PET BABY CRAM DELT GLUT POMP HUMOR SPOIL TUTOR WALLY CARESS COCKER CODDLE COSHER COSSET CUDDLE DANDLE FONDLE MAUNGE POSSET TIDDLE CHERISH COCKNEY FORWEAN GRATIFY INDULGE SATIATE SMOODGE SAGINATE
PAMPHLET JACK LEAD QUIRE SHEET TRACT FOLDER BOOKLET CATALOG LEAFLET NOVELET BROCHURE CHAPBOOK WORKBOOK CATALOGUE
PAN FIT TAB VLY MELL PART PRIG VLEI WASH AGREE BASIN BATEA COVER GRAND SHEET UNITE FRACHE LAPPET PANKIN PATINA SPIDER VESSEL CRANIUM CREAMER HARDPAN PORTION ROASTER SKILLET SUBSOIL RIDICULE
(— **FOR COALS**) BRAZIER
(— **OF BALANCE**) BOWL BASIN SCALEPAN
(— **WITH 3 FEET**) POSNET
(**EVAPORATING** —) ROOM COVER TACHE SALTPAN
(**GOD** —) FAUNUS
(**IRON** —) YET FRACHE
(**LONG-HANDLED** —) PINGLE
(**MILK** —) LEAD
(**OIL** —) SUMP
PANACEA CURE ELIXIR REMEDY SOLACE CUREALL HEALALL NEPENTHE

PANAMA

CAPITAL: PANAMA
COIN: BALBOA
CROP: ABACA CACAO
GULF: DARIEN CHIRIQUI

LAKE: GATUN
MEASURE: CELEMIN
MOUNTAIN: CHICO GANDI COLUMAN SANTIAGO
MOUNTAIN RANGE: VERAGUA
PORT: CRISTOBAL
PROVINCE: COCLE COLON CHIRIQUI VERAGUAS
RIVER: CHEPO SAMBU TUIRA BAYANO PANUGO CHAGRES
TOWN: COLON DAVID AZUERO BALBOA PANAMA PENONOME SANTIAGO
TREE: YAYA MARIA QUIRA ALFAJE CATIVO

PANAMA HAT JIPIJAPA
PANAMINT KOSO
PANCAKE FLAM AREPA CREPE FADGE FLAWN KISRA LEFSE TOURT BLINTZ FRAISE FROISE CRUMPET FLAPPER FLIPPER FRITTER HOTCAKE PIKELET CORNCAKE FLAPJACK FLIPJACK
(**PL.**) LEFSEN
PANCREAS BUR NUT
PAND PAWN DRAPERY
PANDA WA WAH BEARCAT
PANDAVA BHIMA
PANDECT COMPENDIUM
PANDEMONIUM DIN HELL CHAOS NOISE TUMULT UPROAR DISORDER CONFUSION
PANDER BAWD PIMP BULLY CATER MICHER PURVEY RUFFIAN WHISKIN PROCURER BAWDSTROT
PANDORA BANDORE
(**BROTHER OF** —) PROMETHEUS
(**HUSBAND OF** —) EPIMETHEUS
PANE GLASS GLAZE LOZEN PANEL QUIRK SHEET SHOCK SLASH QUARRY SECTION PORTLIGHT
PANEGYRIC ELOGE ELOGY EULOGY PRAISE ORATION TRIBUTE ENCOMIUM LAUDATION
PANEL FIN PAN JURY SKIN BOARD GROUP LABEL TABLE ABACUS ASSIZE COFFER HURDLE MIRROR PADDLE PILLOW ROSACE TABLET TYMPAN CAISSON CONSOLE FLIPPER LACUNAR DECORATE MANDORLA
(— **IN FENCE**) LOOP
(— **IN GARMENT**) LAP STEAK
(**3-PART** —) TRIPTYCH
(**CIRCULAR** —) ROUNDEL
(**GAUZE** —) SCRIM
(**GLAZED** —) LAYLIGHT
(**LEGAL** —) ARRAY
(**RECESSED** —) ORB COFFER LACUNAR
(**SUNKEN** —) CAISSON CASSOON
PANFISH SCUP
PANG ACHE CRAM FILL GIRD PAIN STAB TANG AGONY PINCH PRONG SPASM STANG STOUN STUFF THROE SHOWER STOUND TWINGE ANGUISH TRAVAIL

(PL.) GNAWINGS
PANGOLIN MANID MANIS ANTEATER
EDENTATE TANGILIN
PANGWE FAN FANG
PANHANDLE BEG CADGE SKELB
SKILDER
(— STATE) WV WVA
PANIC FEAR FRAY FUNK WILD
ALARM AMAZE CHAOS SCARE
FRIGHT SCHRIK TERROR SWITHER
PANICKY FUNKY
PANICLE JUBA WHISK ANTHELA
PANNIER BAG PED SERON BASKET
CAJAVA CURAGH DORSEL DORSER
DOSSAL DOSSER PANTRY CORBEIL
CURRACK KAJAWAH KEDJAVE
PANOPLY POMP ARMOR UNIFORM
PANORAMA VIEW RANGE SCENE
SWEEP VISTA NEORAMA PICTURE
SCENERY CYCLORAMA POLYORAMA
PANPIPE SICU SIKU QUILL ANTARA
SYRINX ZAMPOGNA
PANSY FANCY PENSE VIOLA KISSES
PENSEE VIOLET TRINITY FANTASQUE
HEARTEASE
PANT FAB ACHE BEAT BLOW FUFF
GAPE GASP HECH LONG PANK PECH
PEGH PINE PIPE PUFF TIFT HEAVE
QUIRK STECH SUGGE THROB YEARN
ANHELE ASPIRE FRIESE PANTLE
PULSATE
PANTAGRUEL (COMPANION OF —)
PANURGE
(FATHER OF —) GARGANTUA
(MOTHER OF —) BADEBEC
PANTALOONS PANTS TROUSERS
PANTHEIST AMALRICIAN
PANTHEON TEMPLE ROTUNDA
VALHALL VALHALLA
PANTHER CAT PARD PUMA COUGAR
JAGUAR LEOPARD PAINTER PANTILE
PANTIES SCANTIES
PANTILE TILE IMBREX BISCUIT
HARDTACK
PANTING ANHELOSE ANHELOUS
PANTOGRAPH EIDOGRAPH
POLYGRAPH
PANTOMIME PLAY PANTO
PANTRY CAVE STUE AMBRY COVEY
CUDDY CLOSET LARDER SPENCE
BUTLERY BUTTERY PANNIER
PANTLER SERVERY SPICERY
CUPBOARD
PANTS JEANS LEVIS BRIEFS SLACKS
DRAWERS JODHPUR BREECHES
BRITCHES KICKSIES KNICKERS
SNUGGIES TROUSERS
(LEATHER —) CHAPS LEDERHOSEN
PANUELO COLLAR RUFFLE
KERCHIEF NECKCLOTH
PANZER TANK
PAP DUG TIT POBS TEAT NIPPLE
EMULSION FLUMMERY
PAPA PA DAD PAP PAW POP SIN
BABA EVIL DADDY LOVER PAPPY
BABOON FATHER POTATO PRIEST
HUSBAND VULTURE
PAPAL (ALSO SEE POPE) POPAL
PAPANE POPELY APOSTOLIC

PAPAW PAPA ASIMEN PAPAIO
ASIMINA CORAZON JASMINE
PAPAYA PAWPAW LECHOSA
PAPER LIL WEB BILL BOND BLANK
BROKE ESSAY STUDY THEME
ASTHMA BINDLE CARTEL PAPIER
REPORT RETREE VESSEL CHEVIOT
EXHIBIT JOURNAL WRITING YOSHINO
DOCUMENT MONOGRAPH VALENTINE
(— FOLDER) STROKER
(— MAKER) WASHERMAN
(— NAUTILUS) ARGONAUT
(— PULP) WATERLEAF
(— QUANTITY) PAGE REAM QUIRE
SHEET BUNDLE
(ABSORBENT —) BLOTTER
TOWELLING
(BUILDING —) FELT
(BUNDLE OF —S) DUFTER DOSSIER
(CHINESE —) INDIA
(DAMAGED —) BROKE CASSE SALLE
RETREE
(FOLDED —) SADDLE AIRPLANE
(GLOSS —) GILL
(HARD —) PELURE
(HEAVY —) FELT
(LINING —S) SKIPS
(NEGOTIABLE —) STIFF
(OFFICIAL —) TARGE HOOKUM
DOCUMENT
(PARCHMENT —) VELLUM
PERGAMYN
(PHOTOGRAPHIC —) SEPIA
(SIZE OF —) CAP COPY DEMI NOTE
POST POTT TOWN ATLAS CROWN
FOLIO LARGE LEGAL ROYAL SIXMO
ALBERT BILLET CASING LETTER
MEDIUM THIRDS BASTARD CABINET
EMPEROR THEOREM ELEPHANT
FOOLSCAP IMPERIAL
(STRIP OF —) TAPE
(THIN —) FLIMSY PELURE TISSUE
ONIONSKIN
(TOILET —) BUMF
(UNCUT —) BOLT
(WALL —) TENTURE
(WATERMARKED —) BATONNE
(WRAPPING —) SKIP KRAFT
SEALING SCREENING
(WRITING —) FLAT LINEN WEDDING
PAPERBARK CAJEPUT MILKWOOD
PAPERBOARD BENDER VENEER
CARDBOARD CHIPBOARD
PULPBOARD
PAPILLA CERAS DEIRID NIPPLE
PAPULA MAMMULA THELIUM
(PL.) CERATA
PAPILLOMA ANGLEBERRY
PAPIO MORMON
PAPIST TORY PAPANE CATHOLIC
POPELING
PAPPUS DOWN THISTLEDOWN
PAPPY PA DAD PAW PAPA SOFT
MUSHY PULPY FATHER SUCCULENT
PAPRIKA PIMENTO PIMIENTO
PAPUA (BAY OF —) DYKE MILNE
ACLAND HOLNICOTE
(RIVER OF —) FLY KIKORI PURARI

(TOWN OF —) BUNA DARU KIKORI
SAMARAI
PAPUAN ARAU BIAK HULA KATE
BUANG EKARI KIWAI KWOMA SIVAI
SULKA BAITSI BANARO IATMUL
KEREWA KOIARI ARAPESH BAINING
PAPULE WHELK PIMPLE
PAPYRUS REED PAPER SEDGE
BIBLOS GLUMAL SCROLL BULRUSH
(— STRIP) ORIHON
PAR BY NORM EQUAL NORMAL
AVERAGE EQUALITY
(ONE OVER —) BOGIE
(ONE UNDER —) BIRDIE
(TWO UNDER —) EAGLE
PARA FODDA PERAU PARRAH
PARABLE MYTH TALE FABLE STORY
APOLOG BYWORD MASHAL SAMPLE
BYSPELL PROVERB ALLEGORY
FORBYSEN LIKENESS
PARABOLA ARC CURVE ANTENNA
PARACHUTE SILK CHUTE BROLLY
DROGUE STREAMER
PARACHUTIST PATHFINDER
(PL.) STICK
PARACLETE AIDER HELPER
PLEADER ADVOCATE CONSOLER
COMFORTER
PARADE JET TOP POMP SHOW WALK
MARCH STRUT FLAUNT MUSTER
REVIEW STROLL CORTEGE DISPLAY
EXHIBIT MARSHAL CEREMONY
EXERCISE FLOURISH GRANDEUR
SPLENDOR PAGEANTRY
(— GROUND) MAIDAN
(UNSUBSTANTIAL —) PAGEANT
PARADED AFFICHE
PARADISE EDEN JODO BLISS JENNA
AIDENN GOLOKA HEAVEN ELYSIUM
NIRVANA
(— OF INDRA) SVARGA SWARGA
(— TREE) ACEITUNA STAVEWOOD
PARADOX KOAN ANTINOMY
PARADOXURE MUSANG
PARAFFIN ALKANE
PARAGON GEM PINK TYPE IDEAL
MODEL APERSEE PATTERN
PEROPUS PHOENIX NONESUCH
NONPARIEL
PARAGRAPH ITEM SIGN CAPUT
PAUSE CLAUSE NOTICE RUBRIC
ARTICLE INITIAL PILCROW SECTION
MATERIAL PEELCROW PERSONAL
SUBLEADER
(— MARK) PILCROW

PARAGUAY

CAPITAL: ASUNCION
COIN: GUARANI
DEPARTMENT: GUAIRA ITAPUA
OLIMPO CAAZAPA BOQUERON
LAKE: VERA YPOA YPACARAI
LANGUAGE: GUARANI
MEASURE: PIE LINE LINO VARA
LEGUA LINEA CORDEL CUADRA
CUARTA FANEGA
PLAIN: CHACO

RIVER: YPANE ACARAY PARANA
CONFUSO
TOWN: LUQUE PILAR CAACUPE
CAAZAPA TRINIDAD
CONCEPCION VILLARRICA
WEIGHT: QUINTAL

PARAKEET CONURE PARROT
WELLAT ARATINGA KAKARIKI
POPINJAY ROSEHILL GREENLEEK
PARALLEL EVEN LIKE ALONG EQUAL
MATCH SECOND EXAMPLE FRONTAL
PARAGON ANALOGUE LIKENESS
MULTIPLE QUANTITY
PARALLELOGRAM RHOMB OBLONG
SQUARE RHOMBUS RHOMBOID
RECTANGLE
PARALYSIS CRAMP PALSY SHOCK
PARESIS DIPLEGIA
PARALYZE DARE DAZE STUN PALSY
SCRAM ASTONY CONGEAL IMPALSY
TORPEDO
PARALYZED NUMB PALSIED
CRIPPLED
PARAMOUNT ABOVE CHIEF RULER
SOVRAN CAPITAL SUPREME
DOMINANT SUPERIOR SUZERAIN
SOVEREIGN
PARAMOUR DOLL PRIM PURE
LEMAN LOVER WOMAN WOOER
AMORET FRIEND MASTER MINION
FRANION GALLANT HETAERA
RUFFIAN SERVANT SPECIAL
SULTANA STALLION BOYFRIEND
PARAPET BUTT WALL BAHUT REDAN
BARBET BONNET TRENCH BULWARK
PLUTEUS RAILING RAMPART
ENVELOPE TRAVERSE
PARAPH RUBRIC
PARAPHERNALIA GEAR EQUIPAGE
APPARATUS EQUIPMENT TRAPPINGS
PARAPHRASE FARSE REWORD
TARGET TARGUM PREFACE
THARGUM VERSION TRANSLATE
PARASITE BUG BUR FLY BURR
MOSS SPIV TRYP CHARK DRONE
LEECH SHARK TOADY VIRUS
FEEDER FUNGUS GNATHO SHADOW
SPONGE SUCKER BLEEDER
SPONGER TAGTAIL DICYEMID
ENTOZOON HANGERON SLAVERER
INFESTANT POTHUNTER SACCULINA
SPARGANUM TOADEATER
TUBHUNTER
(— ON TROUT) SUG
(PL.) ECTOZOA ENTOZOA
DRIFTWOOD
PARASITIC CYTOZOIC TRENCHER
BIOPHILOUS
(— JAEGER) SHOOI DIRTBIRD
PARASOL SHADE AOGIRI SHADOW
ROUNDEL TIRESOL KITTYSOL
SUNSHADE UMBRELLA
(— MUSHROOM) LEPIOTA
PARAVANE OTTER
PARBOILED LEEPIT
PARCEL LOT DEAD DEAL DOLE METE
PACK PART WISP BULSE BUNCH

GROUP PIECE BUNDLE DIVIDE
FARDEL PACKET PASSEL CONACRE
PACKAGE PORTION COMMODITY
(— OF DIAMONDS) SERIES
(— OF GROUND) LOT PICK CLOSE
SOLUM SUERTE CONACRE PENDICLE
(— OF HEMP FIBER) PIG
(— OF JEWELS) BULSE
(— OUT) ALLOT
PARCH DRY FRY BURN COOK SEAR
ROAST TOAST PEARCH RIZZER
SCORCH BRISTLE BRUSTLE
GRADDAN SHRIVEL TORREFY
TORRIFY
PARCHED ARID HUSK SERE ADUST
FIERY GIZZEN TORRID THIRSTY
SCORCHED
PARCHING URENT
PARCHMENT LARK FOREL CHARTA
MEZUZAH PAPYRIN SCYTALE
DRUMHEAD PALIMPSEST
(— PAPER) DOCKET PERGAMYN
(FINE —) VEL VELLUM
(PIECE OF —) MEMBRANE
(ROLL OF —) PELL SCROLL
PARD PAL CHUM TIGER FRIEND
LEOPARD PANTHER PARTNER
COMPANION
PARDON FREE CLEAR COVER GRACE
MERCY REMIT SPARE ACQUIT
ASSOIL EXCUSE SHRIVE ABSOLVE
AMNESTY CONDONE FORGIVE
REPRIEVE TOLERATE EXCULPATE
PARDONABLE VENIAL VENIABLE
EXCUSABLE
PARDONER QUESTOR QUAESTOR
PARE CUP CHIP COPE FLAY PEEL
SKIN FRIZZ SHAVE SKELP SLIPE
SPADE CHISEL REDUCE REMOVE
RESECT CURTAIL WHITTLE
(— LEATHER) SKIVE
(— SOD) BURNBEAT
(— STAVES) BUCK
(— STONE) BOAST
PAREGORIC ANODYNE MITIGATING
PAREL PARELL APPAREL CLOTHING
ORNAMENT
PARENCHYMA AMYLOM MESOPHYL
PARENT DAD DAM MAMA PAPA SIRE
DADDY ELDER MATER PATER
AUTHOR FATHER MOTHER ORIGIN
FORBEAR GENITOR ANCESTOR
BEGETTER FILICIDE GUARDIAN
PARENTAGE KIND BIRTH BROOD
FAMILY ORIGIN PROGENY
ENGENDURE
PARENTHESIS HOOK ASIDE PAREN
BRACKET TOENAIL INNUENDO
INTERVAL INTERLUDE
(PL.) HOOKS CURVES
PAREVE NEUTRAL
PARGET COAT GYPSUM PARIET
PLASTER DECORATE WHITEWASH
PARGO MUTTONFISH
PARHELION DOG SUN SUNDOG
PARIAH PAREA ISHMAEL OUTCAST
PARIAN CHINA MARBLE PORCELAIN
PARIETAL SOMAL SOMATIC
PARI-MUTUEL TOTE TOTALIZER

PARING CHIP FOIL SHRED SPECK
GUBBIN PARURE PEELING
(FISH —S) GUBBINS
(PL.) BOXING
PARIS ALEXANDER
(— AIRPORT) ORLY
(FATHER OF —) PRIAM
(MOTHER OF —) HECUBA
(PALACE IN —) ELYSEE LOUVRE
TUILERIES
(RIVER OF —) SEINE
(STOCK EXCHANGE IN —) BOURSE
(SUBWAY IN —) METRO
(WIFE OF —) OENONE
PARISH CURE HOUSE TITLE CHARGE
SOCIETY PECULIAR OUTPARISH
(— HEAD) PASTOR PRIEST MINISTER
(— MEETING) VESTRY
PARISON BLOW GATHERING
PARITY ANALOGY EQUALITY
LIKENESS GRAVIDITY
PARK HAY PEN HOLE STOP WAIT
GREEN LEAVE CIRCLE DAPHNE
GARDEN PRATER COMMONS
DIAMOND PADDOCK TERRACE
PARADISE TETRAGON
PARKA PARCA ANORAK
PARLANCE TALK IDIOM SPEECH
DICTION DISCOURSE
PARLAY DOUBLE
PARLEY DODGE PARLE SPEAK
TREAT UTTER CONFER INDABA
PALTER PAROLI DISCUSS PALAVER
PARLING DISCOURSE TEMPORIZE
PARLIAMENT DIET RUMP TING
COURT SENAT CORTES FANTAN
MAJLIS SAEIMA COUNCIL ESTATES
LAGTING RIKSDAG CONGRESS
CONVERSE STORTING VOLKSRAAD
(SCAND. —) THING
PARLIAMENTARIAN APRONEER
PARLOR BEN BOOR HALL
FOREROOM LOCUTORY SNUGGERY
SOLARIUM
(COUNTRY —) SPENCE
(MILKING —) BAIL
PARLORMAID MATRON
PARLOUS KEEN RISKY CLEVER
SHREWD CUNNING CRITICAL
PERILOUS DANGEROUS HAZARDOUS
PARMESAN GRANA
PAROCHIAL PETTY NARROW
PAROCHIAN SECTARIAN
PARODIST SPOOFER
PARODY RIB SKIT SPOOF SATIRE
TRAVESTY BURLESQUE IMITATION
PAROLE FAITH PLEDGE LICENSE
PROMISE
PARONOMASIA PUN AGNOMINATION
PARONYCHIA FELON PANARIS
NAILWORT
PAROTITIS MUMPS
PAROXYSM FIT KINK PANG AGONY
COLIC QUIRK SPASM STORM STOUR
THROE ACCESS ATTACK FRENZY
ORGASM RAPTUS SHOWER
RAPTURE EPITASIS AGITATION
PARR PAR SAMLET SCEGGER
SKEGGER BRANDLIN BRANDLING

PARROT ARA HIA KEA COPY ECHO JAKO KAKA LORO LORY POLL VAZA ARARA CAGIT MACAW MIMIC POLLY AMAZON CAIQUE CONURE KAKAPO REPEAT TIRIBA CORELLA GRASSIE LORILET COCKATOO LORIKEET LOVEBIRD PARAKEET PICARIAN POPINJAY BROADTAIL COCKATEEL

PARROT FISH LORO SCAR LANIA LAUIA SCAUR VIEJA COTORO SCARUS LABROID MUDFISH OLDWIFE BLUEFISH

PARRY FEND STOP WARD AVOID BLOCK DODGE EVADE FENCE PRIME QUART SIXTE OCTAVE PARADE QUINTE SECOND THWART TIERCE COUNTER DEFLECT EVASION

PARSE PACE PEARCE ANALYZE DIAGRAM DISSECT CONSTRUE ANATOMIZE

PARSI ZOROASTRIAN
(— **HOLY BOOK**) AVESTA
(— **PRIEST**) MOBED DASTUR

PARSIMONIOUS GARE MEAN NEAR NIGH CLOSE SCANT SPARE TIGHT FRUGAL NARROW SCARCE SCOTCH SKIMPY SORDID STINGY STRAIT MISERLY SCRIMPY SPARING COVETOUS GRASPING GRUDGING SCREWING WRETCHED MERCENARY NIGGARDLY PENURIOUS RETENTIVE

PARSLEY ACHE CUMIN UMBEL CICELY CONIUM ELTROT KARPAS CHERVIL HOGWEED FLUELLIN

PARSLEY CAMPHOR APIOL APIOLE

PARSNIP TANK WYPE UMBEL CONIUM MADNEP CADWEED HOGWEED BUNDWEED QUEENWEED

PARSON RECTOR CROAKER PATRICO PERSONA MINISTER PREACHER GUIDEPOST
(**COUNTRY** —) RUM
(PL.) PARSONRY

PARSONAGE GLEBE MANSE RECTORY PASTORATE PASTORIUM

PARSON BIRD POE TUI KOKO TUWI POEBIRD POYBIRD

PART DEL END LOT PAN DEAL DOLE FECK GRIN HAET HALF HAND PANE ROLE ROVE SECT SHED SIDE SOME TWIN PARTY PIECE QUOTA SEVER SHARE SHODE SNACK SPLIT TWAIN BEHALF CANTON CLEAVE DEPART DETAIL DIVIDE FEEDER FINGER MEMBER MINUTE MOIETY PARCEL PORTIO QUORUM SECTOR SINGLE SUNDER UNYOKE DISJOIN ELEMENT FEATURE FRUSTUM PORTION SECTION SEGMENT SEVERAL ALIENATE DISSEVER DIVISION ELIQUATE FRACTION LIRIPIPE
(— **HAIR**) SHADE
(— **OF ANIMAL'S TAIL**) DOCK
(— **OF BEEF**) CHUCK SKINK
(— **OF BLAST FURNACE**) BOSH BELLY
(— **OF BOW**) PEAK
(— **OF CAM WHEEL**) LOBE
(— **OF CANNON**) CHASE

(— **OF CHAIR**) SPLAT
(— **OF COMPASS**) FLY
(— **OF CONCERTO**) CEMBALO
(— **OF CROSSBOW**) LATH
(— **OF DIAMOND**) BEZEL
(— **OF FLEECE**) LEECH
(— **OF FOWL'S COMB**) BLADE
(— **OF GUN SHIELD**) APRON
(— **OF HARBOR**) FAIRWAY
(— **OF HAWK'S BEAK**) CLAP
(— **OF HIDE**) RANGE
(— **OF HOOKAH**) CHILLUM
(— **OF POETIC FOOT**) ARSIS
(— **OF PORK LOIN**) GRISKIN
(— **OF RIVER**) FRESH
(— **OF SADDLE TREE**) FORK
(— **OF STAIR TREAD**) NOSING
(— **OF STAMEN**) ANTHER
(— **OF SWORD BLADE**) FOIBLE
(— **OF SWORD**) FORTE
(— **OF TEMPLE**) CELLA
(— **OF TONGUE**) DORSUM
(— **OF TURTLE**) CALIPEE
(— **OF VIOLIN BOW**) BAGUET
(— **OF WHEEL**) SPEECH
(— **THAT REVOLVES**) ROTOR
(— **WITH**) GIVE LOSE SELL LEAVE DONATE ABANDON
(**24TH** —) CARAT
(**360TH** —) DEGREE
(**ACCOMPANYING** —) BURDEN OBBLIGATO
(**ASSUMED** —) FIGURE
(**BAGLIKE** —) SAC
(**BEST** —) FAT YOLK CREAM FLOWER MARROW
(**BRISTLELIKE** —) SETA
(**BROADEST** — **OF PLANK**) TOUCH
(**CENTRAL** —) HUB BODY CORE HEART KERNEL
(**CHOICE** —) ELITE
(**CLEAR** — **OF LIQUID**) SWIM
(**CLOSING** —) HEEL
(**COARSE** — **OF FLAX**) HURDS
(**CONICAL** —) BULLET
(**CURVED** —) START
(**DEPRESSED** —) HOLLOW
(**DISTANT** —S) FARNESS
(**DUPLICATE** —) SPARE
(**EDIBLE** — **OF CLAM**) CHEEK
(**ESSENTIAL** —) PITH
(**ESSENTIAL** —S) STAMINA
(**FIFTH** —) QUINTUS
(**FINAL** —) LAST SHANK EPILOG
(**FIRST** —) FRONT PRIME INITIAL BEGINNING
(**FOURTH** —) FARDEL FERLING
(**FRONT** —) VAUNT BREAST FORESIDE
(**GREATER** —) HEFT SUBSTANCE
(**HARDEST** —) BRUNT
(**HIGHEST** —) CROP CROWN HEIGHT
(**HUNDREDTH** —) CENTESM
(**IMPAIRING** —) ALLOY
(**IN** —) HALVES
(**INNERMOST** —) FUND
(**INSTRUMENTAL** —) HAND CONTINUO
(**INTERLACED** —) TWINE

(**LARGE** —) FORCE
(**LATERAL** — **OF HEAD**) CHEEK
(**LATTER** —) HEEL
(**LEAST** —) STITCH
(**LOWER** — **OF ROBE**) BASES
(**LOWER** —) SECONDO
(**LOWEST** —) FOOT BOTTOM GROUND DESCENT
(**MAIN** —) BODY BULK SUBSTANCE
(**MATERIAL** —) GIST
(**MIDDLE** — **OF NIGHT**) HOWE
(**MIDDLE** —) DEEP CENTER
(**MINOR** —) BIT COG
(**MINUTE** —) PRICK TITTLE
(**MISSING** —) LACUNA
(**MOST IMPORTANT** —) EYE FOREHAND
(**MOST SERIOUS** —) DICKENS
(**OF HORSE'S THIGH**) GASKIN
(**OVERDUE** —) ARREAR
(**PRINCIPAL** —) BODY MAIN GROSS
(**PRIVATE** —) THING MEMBER
(**PROJECTING** —) ARM JAG JET JOG APSE LOBE SPURN
(**PROTUBERANT** —) BOSS BULGE
(**REJECTED** —S) CHANKINGS
(**REMAINING** —) BUTT DREG HEEL
(**REMOTEST** —) EXTREMITY
(**RINGLIKE** —) ANNULUS
(**ROOTLIKE** —) RADICLE
(**ROUNDED** —) BULB
(**SAWLIKE** —) SERRA
(**SECRET** —) RECESS
(**SLENDER** —) NECK
(**SMALL** —) BIT ATOM FLOW TITHE DETAIL MINUTE SNIPPET
(**SMALLEST** —) ATOM WHIT MINIM
(**SOFT** — **OF BREAD**) CRUMB
(**SOFT** — **OF VEIN**) LEATH
(**SOLO** —) CALL
(**STILL** — **OF WATER**) KELD
(**SWINGING** —) FLAIL
(**TELLING** —) POINT
(**TENTH** —) TITHE
(**THIN** — **OF WALL**) ALLEGE
(**THIRD** —) THIRDENDEAL
(**TOP** —) HEADPIECE
(**TWELFTH** —) INCIA POINT UNCIAL
(**UPPER** —) CHIEF RIDGE OVERPARTY
(**UPPERMOST** —) TOP PEAK CHIEF UPSIDE TOPSIDE
(**VAUDEVILLE** —) OLIO
(**VITAL** —) HEART
(**WINGLIKE** —) ALA
(**WORST** —) DEPTH
(**WORTHLESS** —) DREGS

PARTAKE BITE PART SHARE DIVIDE PARTEN
(— **OF**) USE HAVE SHARE TASTE TOUCH IMPART

PARTAN CRAB

PARTED PARTITE

PARTHAON (**FATHER OF** —) AGENOR
(**MOTHER OF** —) EPICASTE
(**SON OF** —) OENEUS
(**WIFE OF** —) EURYTE

PARTIAL HALF PART SEMI BIASED UNFAIR COLORED HALFWAY

UNEQUAL HARMONIC INCLINED
PARTISAN PROPENSE SKELETON
FAVORABLE

PARTIALITY FAVOR RESPECT
AFFECTION SPECIALTY

PARTIALLY HALF HALFWAY
HALFWISE

PARTICIPANT BOOK ACTOR PARTY
MEMBER PARTNER DUETTIST
PARTABLE PARTISAN
(SUBORDINATE —) STOOGE
(PL.) FIELD

PARTICIPATE JOIN SIDE ENTER
SHARE ENGAGE ENLIST IMPART
COMPETE PARTAKE
(— IN) GO HAVE JOIN STAY STAND
TASTE COMMON STICKLE

PARTICIPATION HAND PLOT
SOCIETY INTEREST
(COMMON —) COMMUNITY

PARTICIPLE VERBID

PARTICLE ACE BIT DOT FIG GRU
JOT RAY ATOM BETA CORN CROT
DUST GRUE HAET IOTA KNIT MITE
MOTE SNIP SPOT STIM WHIT ALPHA
BOSON FLAKE FLECK GHOST GRAIN
MESON POINT SHRED SPECK STARN
STIME THRUM TWINT FILING GEIGER
LEPTON MOMENT PANGEN RIZZOM
SMIDGE SMITCH TITTLE AMICRON
FERMION GEMMULE GRANULE
NUCLEUS PSYCHON SMIDGIN
ACCEPTER SMIDGEON POSITRINO
SCINTILLA
(— IN BLOOD) EMBOLUS
(— IN INTERNAL EAR) OTOCONIUM
(— OF FIRE) SPARK
(— OF GOLD) COLOR
(— OF SOOT) ISEL IZLE SMUT AIZLE
(—S IN BEER) FLOATERS
(—S OF GRAIN) CHOP
(ATOMIC —) ION ELECTRON
(ELECTRIFIED —) ION ANION
PROTON THERMION
(FINE ICY —S) SLEET
(JAGGED —) SPLINTER
(LEAST POSSIBLE —) MINIM
(LINGUISTIC —) SERVILE
(MINUTE —) JOT ORT RAY ATOM
GRAIN SPECK RAMENT GRANULE
MOLECULE RAMENTUM
(NEGATIVE —) NOR NOT
(NUCLEAR —S) FALLOUT
(POSITIVELY-CHARGED —) CATION
KATION
(SMALL —) NIP BLEB CORN MOTE
GRAIN SPECK AMICRON GRANULE
SPRINKLE SUBMICRON
(TINY —) ATOMY
(ULTIMATE —) PSYCHON
(PL.) DUST FINES SWARF SIZINGS
CUTTINGS FURFURES

PARTI-COLORED PIED FANCY
MOTLEY PARTED PIEBALD
BUTTERFLY HARLEQUIN

PARTICULAR AND ATOM FIXY ITEM
NICE SELF FUSSY PARTY POINT
THING CHOOSY DAINTY DETAIL
MINUTE MOROSE REGARD SINGLE

STICKY ARTICLE CAREFUL CERTAIN
CORRECT FINICKY PRECISE PRIVATE
RESPECT SEVERAL SPECIAL
UNUSUAL CLERKISH CONCRETE
ESPECIAL PECULIAR PICKSOME
PRECIOUS SINGULAR SUBALTERN
(NOT —) INCURIOUS

PARTICULARLY ONLY EXTRA
SINGLY SPECIAL EXPRESSLY
SPECIALLY

PARTING DEATH GOODBYE
FAREWELL
(— AS OF HAIR) SHED

PARTISAN PIKE SIDER STAFF BIASED
FACTOR FAUTOR MARIAN ZEALOT
CALOTIN DEVOTEE GUISARD
PARTNER ADHERENT CRISTINO
ESPOUSER FAVORITE FENNOMAN
FOLLOWER JACOBITE MOSSBACK
SIDESMAN STALWART URBANIST
HIGHFLIER MAZZINIST OCHLOCRAT
OLIVERIAN SECTARIAN TERRORIST
(NOT —) CATHOLIC
(PL.) FOLLOWING

PARTITION BAR CUT DAM FIN FLAG
SEPT WALL SHOJI SPEER STAGE
WITHE BAFFLE DIVIDE PARPAL
SCONCE SCREEN SEPTUM BARRIER
ENCLOSE GRATING PINFOLD
PORTION SCANTLE BRATTICE
BULKHEAD CLEAVAGE DIVISION
STOPPING TRAVERSE DASHBOARD
DAYABHAGA ICONOSTAS
STOOTHING
(— BETWEEN STALLS) TRAVIS
TREVIS TRAVISS
(— IN CHIMNEY) WITH WITHE
(— IN COTTAGE) SPEER HALLAN
(— IN LOUDSPEAKER) BAFFLE
(— IN WATERWHEEL) WREST
(— OF ESTATE) BOEDELSCHEIDING
(— OF LATH AND PLASTER)
STOOTHING
(HORIZONTAL —) STAGE
(MINING —) SOLLAR STOPPING
(PL.) CANCELLI

PARTLET HEN WOMAN PERTELOT

PARTLY WHAT PARCEL PARTIM
HALFLINGS

PARTNER BOY PAL ALLY HALF MATE
PARD WIFE BUDDY BUTTY PARTY
FELLOW MARROW SHARER
COMRADE CONSORT HUSBAND
CAMARADA COPEMATE SIDEKICK
YOKEMATE
(— OF DUMMY) VIVANT
(DANCING —) GIGOLO CAVALIER

PARTNERSHIP HUI AXIS FIRM
HOUSE FUSION CAHOOTS COMPANY
SOCIETY SOCIETEIT

PARTRIDGE HUN BIRD KYAH YUTU
LERWA RUDGE TITAR CHUKAR
REDLEG SEESEE CHEEPER PATRICK
SHRIMPI TINAMOU BOBWHITE
FRANCOLIN FRENCHMAN TETRAONID
(— NOISE) JUCK
(SAND —) TEHOO
(YOUNG —) CHEEPER SQUEALER

PARTRIDGEBERRY BOXBERRY

COWBERRY EYEBERRY ONEBERRY
SNOWBERRY TWINBERRY

PART-TIME PARCEL

PARTURITION EUTOCIA TRAVAIL
CHILDBED DELIVERY DYSTOCIA

PARTY DO BAL BEE CRY TEA CLAN
DRUM GALA SECT SIDE BINGE
BRAWL CABAL CRUSH GROUP
LEVEE COMITE FIESTA FROLIC
FRONDE GERMAN INFARE JUNKET
PERSON SETOUT SHINDY SHOWER
BLOWOUT CANTICO COMPANY
FACTION GREGORY PATARIA
SHINDIG DRINKING FENNOMAN
POTLATCH POUNDING SOCIABLE
SQUANTUM TERTULIA CONCISION
INCLINING
(— GIVEN AT HOME) HUDDLE
(AFTERNOON —) TEA RECEPTION
(BEACH —) CLAMBAKE
(BRIDAL —) SEND SHOWER
(DANCING —) HOP GERMAN
CANTICO HOEDOWN FANDANGO
(DRINKING —) KNEIPE POTATION
SYMPOSIUM
(DRUNKEN —) BLIND
(EVENING —) BALL SOIREE
GREGORY TERTULIA
(FISHING —) HUKILAU
(HUNTING —) FAID
(INFORMAL —) SOCIABLE TERTULIA
(IRISH —) HOOLEY
(MASQUERADE —) GUISE
(MEN'S —) STAG SMOKER
(POLITICAL —) SAM SIDE WAFD
HOOKS LABOR CAUCUS FRONDE
SWARAJ ZENTRUM MINSEITO
KENSEIKAI SQUADRONE
(POPULAR —) HOOKS
(SCOUTING —) ESPIAL
(SUPPLY —) BRIGADE
(TEA —) DRUM TEMPEST
(THIRD —) STRANGER

PARULIS GUMBOIL

PARVENU SNOB ARRIVE UPSTART
ARRIVIST MUSHROOM ARRIVISTE

PASCH PACE PAQUE EASTER
PASSOVER

PASCHAL LAMB CANDLE SUPPER
PASSOVER

PAS DE DEUX DUET

PASE FAROL NATURAL VERONICA

PASEAR WALK AIRING EXCURSION
PROMENADE

PASHA DEY EMIR PASAHAW

PASHTO AFGHAN

PASIPHAE (CHILD OF —) ARIADNE
PHAEDRA
(HUSBAND OF —) MINOS

PASQUEFLOWER BADGER GOSLING
APRILFOOL

PASQUINADE PIPE SQUIB SATIRE
LAMPOON PASQUIL

PASS BY GO COL DIE END FIG GAP
SAG USE ABRA BEAL CEDE CHIT
COMP COVE DREE DROP FALL FARE
FLIT FOIN GATE GHAT GULF HAND
HAVE LANE LEAD PACE RIDE ROLL
SEEK SILE SLAP SLIP STEP WADE

WALK WEAR WEND WIND CANTO
DREIE ENACT FLEET GHAUT GORGE
HALSE HURRY KOTAL LAPSE LITHE
LUNGE NOTCH OCCUR ORDER
PAPER PUNTA REACH RELAY SHAKE
SHOOT SMITE SPEND STRIP TRADE
UTTER WASTE WHELM YODEL
BILLET CONVEY DEFILE DEMISE
ELAPSE EXCEED HAPPEN PASSUS
PERMIT SPIRAL TICKET TRAVEL
TWOFER ABSOLVE ALLONGE
APPROVE BREATHE DESCEND
DEVOLVE DIFFUSE LATERAL
OVERGET PASSAGE UNDERGO
JUNCTURE REBOLERA PURWANNAH
(— A BALL) FEED HEEL
(— ABRUPTLY) LEAP
(— ALONG) DERIVE
(— AWAY) DIE SET FLEE WING
DEPART EXPIRE PERISH FORFARE
FORTHGO OVERDRIVE
(— BACK AND FORTH) FIG
CRISSCROSS
(— BAD COIN) SMASH
(— BETWEEN HILLS) BEAL SLAP
SLACK
(— BY) COTE OMIT SKIP VADE
WEND APASS CLEAR FORGO
FOREGO IGNORE OVERGO INTERMIT
OVERHEAVE
(— GRADUALLY) FADE
(— IN BULLFIGHT) SUERTE
(— IN POKER) BREATHE
(— INTO USE) ENURE INURE
(— JUDGMENT ON) DEEM
SENTENCE
(— LIGHTLY) BRUSH SKATE SKITTER
(— OFF) SHAM FOIST
(— ON) LEAK PACE
(— ONE'S LIFE) TRADE
(— OUT) CONK DEBOUCH EXHAUST
(— OVER LIGHTLY) SKIM SWEEP
OVERSKIP
(— OVER QUICKLY) SCUD FLEET
(— OVER) DO HIP BALK FREE SKIM
SKIP SLIP COVER CROSS ELIDE
FLEET SCOUR SWEEP TRANCE
OVERHIP INTERMIT OVERLOOK
OVERPOST PROGRESS TRAVERSE
(— QUICKLY) FLIT SPIN SPEED
STRIKE
(— THROUGH A BLOCK) REEVE
(— THROUGH NARROW WAY) THRID
THREAD
(— THROUGH) CROSS REEVE TRACE
DIVIDE OVERGO PIERCE SUFFER
EXCURSE PERVADE OVERPASS
OVERRIDE PERMEATE PROGRESS
PENETRATE
(— TIME) DRIVE SPEND TRADE
(— UNHAPPILY) DREE
(— UP) REJECT DECLINE
DISREGARD
(— WITH DIFFICULTY) WADE
(— WITH VIOLENCE) RAKE
(CUSTOMS —) CARNET
(FENCING —) FOIN LUNGE PUNTA
(FORWARD —) AERIAL
(HOCKEY —) CENTER

(MOUNTAIN —) COL GAP SAG GATE
GHAT SLIP CLOVE GHAUT KLOOT
KOTAL POORT SWIRE SWIRL
BEALACH
(NARROW —) ABRA GULF SLYPE
DEFILE
(SUDDEN —) LUNGE
PASSABLE FIT FAIR SOSO TOLLOL
GENUINE ADEQUATE MEDIOCRE
MODERATE POSSIBLE TRAVELED
PERMEABLE TOLERABLE
PASSABLENESS INDIFFERENCE
PASSABLY SEEMLY
PASSAGE CUT GAT GUT ROW VIA
WAY WRO ADIT BELT BORD DOOR
EXIT FARE FLUE FORD GANG GATE
HALL ITER LANE PACE PASS PAWN
RACE RAMP SLIP SLUM VENT WELL
AISLE ALLEY ALURE BAYOU BEARD
BOGUE CANAL CHOPS CHUTE
CLOSE CREEK CRUSH DRAFT DRIFT
DRIVE ENTRY FLYBY FORTE GLADE
GOING GORGE INLET JETTY MEUSE
PATCH PORCH SHUNT SLYPE
SOUND ACCESS ADITUS APORIA
ARCADE ATRIUM AVENUE BRIDGE
BURROW BYPASS CAREER COURSE
DEFILE DROMOS EGRESS ELAPSE
FAUCES HIATUS MEATUS PARODE
RELIEF SCREEN SLUICE STRAIT
TRAJET TRANCE TRAVEL TUNNEL
VOYAGE ARCHWAY BALTEUS
CHANNEL CHAPTER CONDUIT
COULOIR DIAZOMA DOGTROT
DRAUGHT ESTUARY EXCERPT
FISTULA FRAUGHT GALLERY
GANGWAY GATEWAY ISTHMUS
JOURNEY MANHOLE OFFTAKE
OUTTAKE PARADOS PROCESS
TRANSIT APPROACH AQUEDUCT
CLOISTER COMMERCE DEBOUCHE
DELETION PARADIGM SENTENCE
SHIPPING SINUSOID SPILLWAY
(— IN BOOK) WHERE EXCERPT
(— OF THREAD) FLOAT
(— TO STOMACH) SWALLOW
(— TO TOMB) DROMOS SYRINX
(—S OF LITERATURE) BEAUTIES
(AIR —) FLUE THIRL WINDWAY
THIRLING VENTIDUCT
(CENSORED —) CAVIAR
(CONTINUOUS —) LAPSE
(COVERED —) OPE PAWN PEND
(DIFFICULT —) APORIA
(LITERARY —) TEXT QUOTE
EXCERPT SNIPPET QUOTATION
(MINE —) RUN ADIT HEAD ROOF
SLUM DRIVE LEVEL SHAFT THIRL
AIRWAY STENTON UNDERCAST
(MUSICAL —) CUE CODA LINK
BREAK FORTE STAVE ARIOSO
FUGATO LEGATO REPEAT CADENZA
CODETTA FANFARE STRETTO
FLOURISH SPICCATO STACCATO
SYMPHONY VOCALISE
(NARROW —) GUT HASS ALLEY
GORGE JETTY NOTCH SLYPE
SMOOT DEFILE NARROW STRAIT
(SECURE — OF) CARRY

(SUBTERRANEAN —) POSTERN
(SWIFT —) FLIGHT
(WATER —) TICKLE TICKLER
PASSAGE HAWK TARTARET
PASSENGER
PASSAGEWAY (ALSO SEE PASSAGE)
BORD FLUE GANG HALL LANE PACE
PASS PEND PORT RACE SHED SLIP
WENT YAWN AISLE ALLEY ALURE
CHUTE DRIFT DRONG ENTRY GOING
LUMEN RAISE SHOOT SMOOT
STULM ACCESS AIRWAY AVENUE
COURSE DINGLE FUNNEL GUTTER
INTAKE MANWAY RUNWAY TRANCE
ZAGUAN DOORWAY GALLERY
SLIPWAY TWITTEN WALKWAY
WAYGATE CALLEJON CORRIDOR
HATCHWAY
(CLEARED — IN CROWD) HALL
(COVERED —) ARCADE CLOISTER
(MINE —) BORD BOARD DRIFT
SLANT STULM WINZE
(NARROW —) SLIP AISLE SMOOT
(SLOPING —) RAMP
PASSANT PAST CURRENT CURSORY
PASSING EPHEMERAL
PASSE AGED PAST WORN FADED
BELATED OBSOLETE OUTMODED
PASSENGER FARE INSIDE
FERRYMAN TRAVELER WAYFARER
(— WHO AVOIDS PAYING FARE) NIP
STOWAWAY
(— WITHOUT TICKET) HARE
(AIRPLANE —) BIRDMAN
(UNBOOKED —) CAD
(PL.) WAYBILL
PASSEPARTOUT SPANDREL
PASSERBY PASSER PASSANT
BYPASSER SAUNTERER
PASSERINE PERCHER
PASSIFLORA TACSO
PASSING DEATH DYING ELAPSE
CURSORY PASSADO RUNNING
SLIDING ELAPSING FLEETING
ENACTMENT EPHEMERAL
WAYFARING
(— BETWEEN) INTERCURRENT
(— BY) COTE
(— INTO EACH OTHER) FONDU
(— OF HOURS) TIME
(— OF TIME) EFFLUX
(SLOWLY —) LAG
PASSAGEWAY (NARROW —) SLIP
AISLE SMOOT
PASSANT PAST CURRENT CURSORY
PASSING EPHEMERAL
PASSE AGED PAST WORN FADED
BELATED OBSOLETE OUTMODED
PASSENGER FARE INSIDE
FERRYMAN TRAVELER WAYFARER
(— WHO AVOIDS PAYING FARE) NIP
STOWAWAY
(— WITHOUT TICKET) HARE
(AIRPLANE —) BIRDMAN
(UNBOOKED —) CAD
(PL.) WAYBILL
PASSEPARTOUT SPANDREL
PASSERBY PASSER PASSANT
BYPASSER SAUNTERER

PASSERINE PERCHER
PASSIFLORA TACSO
PASSING DEATH DYING ELAPSE
CURSORY PASSADO RUNNING
SLIDING ELAPSING FLEETING
ENACTMENT EPHEMERAL
WAYFARING
(— **BETWEEN**) INTERCURRENT
(— **BY**) COTE
(— **INTO EACH OTHER**) FONDU
(— **OF HOURS**) TIME
(— **OF TIME**) EFFLUX
(**SLOWLY** —) LAG
PASSION IRE FIRE FURY HEAT LOVE
LUST RAGA RAGE TEAR TIDE WILL
ZEAL ANGER ARDOR BLOOD BRAME
CHAFE DEVIL ERROR FLAME LETCH
MANIA RAJAS SPUNK WRATH
AFFECT CHOLER DESIRE FERVOR
MOTHER PELTER SATTVA SPLEEN
TALENT WARMTH EARNEST
EMOTION EROTISM FEELING
OUTRAGE VULTURE APPETITE
DISTRESS VIOLENCE PADDYWACK
(— **FOR DOING GREAT THINGS**)
MEGALOMANIA
(— **FOR MUSIC**) MELOMANIA
(**ANGRY** —) FUNK
(**ANIMAL** —) KAMA
PASSIONATE HOT FOND WARM
FIERY GUTSY QUICK WHITE ARDENT
FERVID FIERCE FUMOUS IREFUL
STORMY SULTRY TORRID AMOROUS
FLAMING PEPPERY THERMAL
CHOLERIC FRENETIC VASCULAR
VEHEMENT WRATHFUL DIONYSIAN
IRASCIBLE
PASSIONATELY HASTILY FERVIDLY
PASSIONFLOWER MAYPOP
BULLHOOF
PASSIONLESS COLD FREDDO
PASSIVE INERT STOIC PATHIC
STOLID PATIENT FEMININE INACTIVE
SIGNLESS YIELDING APATHETIC
PASSIVENESS QUIETISM
PASSOVER PESAH PHASE PASQUE
PESACH
(— **FESTIVAL**) SEDER
(**JEWISH** —) EASTER
PASSPORT CHOP PASS CONGE
CONGEE DUSTUK DUSTUCK
FURLOUGH TESCARIA TEZKIRAH
SAFEGUARD
PASSUS PACE PART PASS STEP
CANTO DIVISION
PASSWORD WORD TOKEN DUSTUK
TESSERA WATCHWORD
PAST BY AGO WAS GONE YOND
YORE AFTER AGONE APAST ASIDE
ENDED SINCE BEHIND BYGONE
FOREBY PRETER ANOTHER
FOREGONE PRETERIT COMPLETED
(**LONG** —) HIGH
(**TIME NOT LONG** —) YESTERDAY
PASTE HIT PAP BEAT BLOW DIKA
DUFF GLUE MISO PACK PATE
CREAM DOUGH FALSE GESSO
HENNA PUNCH STICK ATTACH
BATTER FASTEN GROUND PANADA

RASTIK STRASS BUCKETY CLOBBER
COLOGNE DRAWOUT FILLING
GORACCO GUARANA STICKUM
BADIGEON BARBOTINE
(— **FOR CAULKING**) BLARE
(— **FOR LINING HEARTHS**) BRASQUE
(— **FOR SHOES** BOOTS) CLOBBER
BLACKING
(— **OF CLAY**) BATTER
(— **TO FILL HOLES IN WOOD AND**
STONE) BADIGEON
(**ALIMENTARY** —) FEDELINI
SCUNGILLI SPAGHETTI
(**AROMATIC** —) PASTILE
(**COLORING** —) HENNA
(**DRIED** —) GUARANA
(**EARTHY** —) ENGOBE
(**FISH** —) BAGOONG
(**MEDICATED** —) ELECTUARY
(**PORCELAIN** —) PATE
(**POTTER'S** —) BARBOTINE
(**TOBACCO** —) GORACCO
(**WEAVER'S** —) SOWENS BUCKETY
PASTEBOARD CARD SHAM FLIMSY
TICKET MATBOARD
PASTEDOWN LINING
PASTEL WOAD LIGHT CRAYON
PICTURE DELICATE
PASTEN HOBBLE TETHER PASTOUR
SHACKLE
PASTILLE CACHOU CANDLE
LOZENGE
PASTIME GAY TOY GAME PLOY
HOBBY SPORT GOSSIP OLEARY
SAILING AMUSEMENT DIVERSION
PASTOR HERD ANGEL RABBI
CURATE KEEPER PRIEST RECTOR
DOMINIE VICAIRE GUARDIAN
MINISTER SHEPHERD
PASTORAL POEM DRAMA RURAL
RUSTIC BUCOLIC CROSIER IDYLLIC
ROMANCE ARCADIAN
PASTORALIST SQUATTER
PASTRY PIE FLAN HUFF PUFF SOCK
TART TUCK CORNET DANISH ECLAIR
ABAISSE CARCAKE STRUDEL
NAPOLEON TALMOUSE TURNOVER
APPLEJACK
(— **COOK**) PASTLER
(— **SHELL**) BOUCHEE DARIOLE
TIMBALE TALMOUSE
(— **STRIPS**) LATTICE
(— **WHEEL**) JAGGER
(**SWEET** —) DOUCET
PASTURAGE FEED GANG GATE
STRAY COLLOP EATAGE FORAGE
HERBAGE SHEEPGATE
PASTURE ALP FOG HAG HAM ING
LEA PEN TYE BENT FEED GAET
GANG GATE GISE GIST HAFT HALF
HEAF HOGA INGE KEEP PARK AGIST
DRIFT EJIDO GRASS GRAZE LAYER
LEASE RANGE VELDT INTAKE
MEADOW OUTRUN SAETER
COWGATE FOGGAGE GRAZING
HERBAGE LEALAND POTRERO
VACCARY VICTUAL HERDWICK
OUTFIELD SHEEPWALK
(— **GRASS**) TORE GRAMA

(— **IN STUBBLE**) SHACK
(— **LAND**) RAKE TACK LEASOW
(**HILL** —) HOGA
(**MOUNTAIN** —) SETER SAETER
SHIELING
(**SHEEP** —) HEAF EWELEASE
(**SHETLAND I.** —) SETER
(**SUMMER** —) AGOSTADERO
(**WET** —) SLINK
PASTURELAND BENT SOUM
PASTURING RELIEF PANNAGE
PASTY PIE PATE PATTY DOUGHY
FRACID SAMBOUGE
PAT APT DAB DIB TAP TIG BLOW
CLAP GLIB JUMP PALP TICK CHUCK
FITLY FIXED IMPEL THROW CARESS
DABBLE SMOOGE SOOTHE STRIKE
STROKE TIMELY APROPOS CHERISH
FITTING PATAPAT READILY
SUITABLE PERTINENT
PATAGIUM TEGULA TIPPET SCAPULA
PARACHUTE PTERYGODE
PATAGONIA (**DEITY OF** —) SETEBOS
(**RODENT OF** —) CAVY MARA
(**TREE OF** —) MANIU ALERCE
ALERSE
PATAMAR COURIER PATTAMAR
MESSENGER
PATAYAN YUMAN
PATCH BIT EKE FLY BOUT LAND
MEND SKIP SPOT SWAB SWOB
VAMP BLAZE BODGE CLOUT CLUMP
COVER FRIAR FUDGE PIECE SAVER
SCRAP SPECK SPLAT BLOTCH
COBBLE DOLLOP GORGET MOUCHE
PARCEL REVAMP SOLDER SPETCH
SWATCH TINKLE CLAMPER CLOBBER
INWEAVE PELIOMA REMNANT
(— **AS ORNAMENT**) MOUCHE
(— **CLUMSILY**) BOTCH CLOUT
CLAMPER
(— **OF COLOR**) CLOUP DAPPLE
SPLASH SPECULUM
(— **OF DARK HAIR**) SMUT
(— **OF DIRT**) MIRE
(— **OF FEATHERS**) BIB CAP
(— **OF ICE**) RONE
(— **OF LAND**) RODHAM
(— **OF LEATHER**) SPECK
(— **OF LIGHT**) GLADE
(— **OF PRINT**) FUDGE
(— **OF RUFFLED WATER**) ACKER
(— **OF SALIVA**) SIXPENCE
(— **OF TIRE**) BOOT
(— **ON BOAT**) TINGLE
(— **ON PRINTED PAGE**) FRIAR
(— **ON THROAT**) GORGET
(— **TOGETHER**) CONSARCINATE
(— **UP**) HEAL MEND
(**BALD** —) AREA
(**LIVID** —) PELIOMA
(**OOZY** —) SPEW SPUE
(**OPEN — IN FOREST**) CAMPO
(**SHOULDER** —) FLASH
PATCHOULI PACCIOLI PATCHLEAF
PATCHWORD WASTEWORD
PATCHWORK BOTCH CENTO
CENTON JUMBLE SCRAPS
PATCHERY FRAGMENTS PASTICCIO

PATE PIE TOP HEAD BROWN PASTE
PASTY PATTY BADGER NOGGIN
NOODLE COSTARD COXCOMB

PATELLA CAP PAN DISH VASE
ROTULA KNEECAP KNEEPAN
WHIRLBONE

PATEN ARCA DISC DISH DISK PLATE
PATINA PLATEN VESSEL

PATENT ARCA BALD OPEN BERAT
BROAD OVERT PLAIN SUNNUD
EVIDENT LICENSE OBVIOUS
APPARENT ARCHIVES MANIFEST
PALPABLE PRIVILEGE

PATER FATHER PRIEST

PATERFAMILIAS MASTER

PATERNAL FATHERLY

PATERNITY FATHER ORIGIN

PATESI ISHSHAKKU

PATH ARC PAD RUN RUT TAN WAY
BERM FARE GATE LANE LEAD LINE
LODE RACE RACK ROAD TRIG TROD
WALK ALLEY BYWAY GOING JETTY
PISTE ROUTE SPACE TRACK TRACT
TRADE TRAIL BOSTAL BYPASS
CAMINO CASAUN CIRCLE COMINO
COURSE GROOVE SLEUTH SPHERE
SWATHE TRENCH CHANNEL
ERGODIC FAIRWAY FOOTWAY
HIGHWAY LANDWAY MEANDER
PASSAGE RODDING SIDEWAY
TARIQAT TOWPATH TRAFFIC
TRUNDLE WAYGATE BORSTALL
CENTRODE CROSSCUT DRIFTWAY
TRAILWAY TWITCHEL CROSSWALK
(— **BETWEEN HEDGES**) TWITCHEL
(— **CUT IN MOWING**) SWATH
SWATHE
(— **FOLLOWED BY ENERGY**)
ERGODIC
(— **MADE BY ANIMAL**) PIST PISTE
(— **OF CELESTIAL BODY**) ORBIT
(— **OF CLOUDS**) RACK
(— **OF MOVING POINT**) CURVE
LOCUS
(— **OF RACE**) STRIP
(— **UP STEEP HILL**) BOSTAL
BORSTAL BORSTALL
(**BRIDLE** —) SPURWAY
(**CLOSED** —) CIRCUIT
(**NARROW** —) BERM RACK TRIG
RODDIN TROCHA RODDING
(**P. I. FOOT** —) SENDA
(**STONE-PAVED** —) STEEN
(**SUFI** —) TARIQAT
(**WINDING** —S) AMBAGES

PATHAN TURI AFRIDI SIVATI BAJOURI
BANGASH PAYTHAN DANGARIK

PATHETIC SAD SILLY TEARY
TENDER FORLORN PITIFUL
DOLOROSO PATETICO STIRRING
TOUCHING AFFECTING

PATHIC MORBID VICTIM PASSIVE
CATAMITE DISEASED SUFFERER
SUFFERING

PATHOGEN VIRUS

PATHOS BATHOS SNIVEL

PATHWAY (ALSO SEE PATH) RUN
LANE PATH RACK COURSE RAMBLA
RAMBLE RODDIN BORSTAL RODDING

PATIENCE CALM THILD BEARANCE
STOICISM COMPOSURE ENDURANCE
FORTITUDE

PATIENT CASE CURE MEEK SOBER
BOVINE PASSIVE ENDURING
THOLEMOD SUFFERANT
(— **OF ASYLUM**) BEDLAM
(**BE** —) BEAR
(**HYDROPATHIC** —) WATERER
(**MEDICAL** —) CURE

PATIO COURT COURTYARD

PATOIS CANT GOMBO GUMBO
CREOLE JARGON DIALECT

PATRIARCH JOB ABBA ENOS LEVI
NASI NOAH PAPA POPE ALDER
ELDER JACOB PITRI DESPOT
JOSEPH NESTOR ABRAHAM ANCIENT
VETERAN VENERABLE

PATRICIAN NOBLE EMPEROR
PATRICK NOBLEMAN GENTLEMAN

PATRIMONY PORTION ANCESTRY
HERITAGE LONGACRE

PATRIOT LOVER AMATEUR

PATRIOTIC PUBLIC ENVELOPE
NATIONAL

PATROL GUARD SCOUT WATCH
STOOGE PATROLE PROTECT

PATROLMAN COP GUARD FLATFOOT
INSPECTOR

PATRON BUYER GUEST STOOP
AVOWRY CLIENT FATHER FAUTOR
JAJMAN ACCOUNT PADRONE
PATROON PROCTOR SPONSOR
ADVOCATE CHAMPION CUSTOMER
DEFENDER GUARDIAN MAECENAS
(**PL.**) FOLLOWING

PATRONAGE AEGIS FAVOR AVOWRY
CUSTOM FAVOUR ACCOUNT
AUSPICE FOMENTO HEARING
BUSINESS PADROADO
(— **AND CARE**) AUSPICE

PATRONAL TITULAR

PATRONIZE USE DEIGN FAVOR
DEFEND FATHER PROMOTE
PROTECT EMPATRON FREQUENT

PATROON TRACT CAPTAIN
SUPPORTER

PATTEE FORMY FORMEE

PATTEN BASE CLOG FOOT SHOE
SKATE STAND STILT CHOPIN
GALOSH RACKET SANDAL CREEPER
RACQUET SUPPORT CIOPPINO
SNOWSHOE

PATTER CANT TALK TIRL LINGO
HAPPER JARGON BLATHER BLATTER
CHATTER DIALECT

PATTERING PITAPAT

PATTERN CUT FUR SET BASE CAST
COMB COPY FORM GIMP IDEA LAUE
MOLD NORM PLAN SEME STAR
WAVE BISON BYSEN CHECK DECOR
DISME DRAFT EPURE GUIDE IDEAL
INLAY MODEL MOIRE MOULD NOTAN
PLAID SEMEE WATER BASKET
BURELE CANVAS CHECKS DESIGN
DIAPER ENTAIL ETOILE FABRIC
FIGURE FLORAL FORMAT FORMER
LACERY MAGPIE MATRIX MIRROR
MODULE MUSTER ONDULE PATRON

POUNCE RANDOM RECIPE SAMPLE
SQUARE STRIPE SYSTEM ALLOVER
CHEVRON EXAMPLE FACONNE
FILLING FOLKWAY GESTALT
GRIZZLE HOBNAIL MEANDER
MEANING MULLION PARAGON
PROJECT SAMPLER SLEIGHT
STENCIL TEMPLET CALENDAR
DYNAMICS FILIGREE HATCHING
ILLUSION PARADIGM PLATFORM
STRICKLE PROTOTYPE
(— **IN BRAIN**) GYRATION
(— **OF BEHAVIOR**) HABIT DISPLAY
(— **OF CADENCE**) CURSUS
(— **OF LARGE SQUARES**) DAMIER
(— **OF SCARS**) KELOID
(— **OF SEPARATE OBJECTS**) SEME
(— **OF STRESS**) SUPERFIX
(— **OF TARTAN**) SET SEET SETT
SETTE
(— **ON PAPER**) BURELAGE
(— **ON STAMP**) GRILL GRILLE
(— **USED BY SILVERSMITHS**) WORK
BOROON
(**CROSS-BARRED** —) PLAID
(**FACIAL** —) BLAZE
(**GARMENT** —) SLOPER
(**HAT** —) BLOCK
(**KNITTING** —) ARGYLE
(**PORCELAIN** —) FITZHUGH
(**RUG** —) AINALEH
(**SHOE** —) FORME
(**SKATING** —) EDGE
(**SOCIAL** —) FAMILISM
(**SPEECH** —) IDIOLECT
(**STRIPED** —) BARRE
(**TAILOR'S** —) PROTRACTOR
(**TATTOO** —) MOKO
(**TREE** —) HOM HOMA
(**WEAVING** —) DRAW

PATTERNED GOFFERED

PATTY TABLET BOUCHEE PRALINE
PATTYPAN VOLAUVENT
(— **SHELL**) DARIOLE TALMOUSE
CROUSTADE

PATULOUS OPEN SPREAD
DISTENDED

PAUCITY LACK DEARTH FEWNESS
EXIGUITY SCARCITY

PAUL PAOLO
(**ASSOCIATE OF** —) DEMAS SILAS
TITUS ARTEMAS BARNABAS

PAULDRON POLLET EPAULET
PALERON POLDRON POLLETTE

PAULOPOST DEUTERIC

PAULOWNIA KIRI

PAUNCH TUN BELLY PENCH RUMEN
ABDOMEN STOMACH GUNDYGUT
POTBELLY

PAUNCHY BLOATED

PAUPER BEGGAR INDIGENT
ROUNDSMAN

PAUPERISM BEGGARY

PAUSE HO HEM HALT HANG HOLD
LULL REST RUFE STAY STOP WAIT
ABIDE BREAK CEASE CHECK COMMA
DELAY DEMUR DEVAL DWELL
HOVER LIMMA POISE SELAH TARRY
TENOR BREACH BREATH CORONA

CUTOFF FALTER HANKER HIATUS
PERIOD STANCE CAESURA FERMATA
RESPITE VIRGULE BREATHER
INTERVAL
(— BEFORE HURDLE) DWELL
(SUDDEN —) CHECK
(PL.) LIMMATA CAESURAE
PAUT PAW POKE POWT STAMP
FINGER
PAVANE DANCE PADUAN
PAVE LAY PATH STUD TILE COVER
FLOOR CAUSEY COBBLE QUARRY
SMOOTH OVERLAY PREPARE
RUDERATE
(— WITH STONES) STEEN CAUSEY
PAVED COBBLED
PAVEMENT SLAB HEARTH PAEPAE
TELFORD ASAROTUM FLAGGING
FLOORING PATHMENT PEDIMENT
PITCHING SIDEWALK TROTTOIR
WASHBOARD
PAVER CUBER PAVIOR
PAVID TIMID AFRAID FEARFUL
PAVILION BASE FLAG TELD TENT
FOLLY KIOSK PINNA ROYAL CANOPY
ENSIGN HOWDAH LITTER PANDAL
PALLION COVERING GLORIETTE
PAVILLON CHINOIS CRESCENT
PAVING FLAG SETT BLOCK BRICK
DALLE PAVER STEAN STEEN STONE
COBBLE TARMAC ASPHALT
TELFORD PITCHING FLAGSTONE
(SQUARE —) MITCHEL
PAVIS COVER PAVADE PAVOIS
SHIELD PROTECT
PAW PAT PUD TOE CLAW FOOT
GAUM GRAB HAND MAUL PATY
PAUT PORT FLAIL PATTE TRICK
CLUTCH FUMBLE HANDLE PATTEE
CRUBEEN FLIPPER FORELEG
FOREFOOT
PAWKY SLY ARCH BOLD CANNY
SAUCY CRAFTY LIVELY SHREWD
CUNNING FORWARD SQUEAMISH
PAWL COG DOG BOLT HAND SEAR
STOP TENT TRIP CATCH CLICK ·
DETENT FINGER PALLET TONGUE
CLAWKER RATCHET
PAWN DIP POP WED FINE GAGE
HOCK SOAK VAMP WAGE SPOUT
SWEAT ENGAGE LUMBER OBLIGE
PIGNUS PLEDGE WADSET COUNTER
HOSTAGE PEACOCK CHESSMAN
MOSKENEER .
(PL.) PHALANX
PAWNBROKER MOUNT UNCLE
BROKER LUMBERER
PAWNEE PANEE SKIDI WATER
ALMOND BISCUIT PLEDGEE
PAWNIE PAWN PEACOCK
PAWNSHOP PAWN SPOUT LOMBARD
POPSHOP
PAX BOARD PEACE TRUCE FRIEND
TABLET
PAY DO BUY FEE TIP ANTE FOOT
FORK GIVE MEET RENT SOLD WAGE
BATTA CLEAR COUGH DOUSE
PLANK SCREW SHEPE SOUND
WAGES YIELD ANSWER BETALL

DEFRAY IMPEND REWARD SALARY
SETTLE COMMUTE DEADRAY
HALVANS IMBURSE REQUITE
SATISFY SOULDIE STIPEND TRIBUTE
(— ATTENTION) DIG SEE COME
GAUM HARK HEED TENT ADVERT
REGARD
(— COURT TO) NUT SUE GALLANT
(— DOWN) DOUSE
(— FLIRTATIOUS ADVANCES) QUEEN
(— FOR LIQUOR) BIRL
(— FOR) ABY BUY BYE COUP ABIDE
COVER STAND ABEGGE
(— HEAVY PENALTY) SMART
EXPIATE
(— HOMAGE) CHEFE CHEVE CHIVE
SALAAM ADULATE
(— IN ADVANCE) IMPRESS
(— MONEY) PINGLE
(— OF SOLDIER) SAWDEE
(— OFF) LIFT SINK ACQUIT
(— OUT) BLEED SPEND STUMP
EXPEND DISBURSE
(— TAXES) GILD
(— UP) ANTE QUIT SETTLE
LIQUIDATE
(— WITH IOU) VOWEL
(ADVANCE —) IMPREST
(DAILY —) DIET
(EXTRA —) BATTA BONUS KICKBACK
(SMALL —) SCREW
PAYABLE DUE C4RTAL
PAYEE HOLDER ENDORSER
PAYMASTER BAKSHI BUKSHI
PURSER BUKSHEE PAGADOR
PAYMENT CRO DUE FEE TAX BILL
CENS DOES DOLE DUTY ERIC FEAL
FINE GALE GILD HIRE LEVY MAIL
TACK TOLL BONUS CANON CLAIM
GAVEL MAILL MENSE PREST PRICE
YIELD ANGILD BOUNTY CHARGE
LINAGE PAYOLA PLEDGE REBATE
RETURN REWARD TARIFF ADVANCE
ALIMONY ANNUITY BENEFIT
CUSTOMS DEPOSIT FOOTAGE
GARNISH PANNAGE PENSION
PRIMAGE SOLUTIO STIPEND
SUBSIDY SUBSIST TREWAGE
TUITION CASUALTY FOREGIFT
GRATUITY KICKBACK MALIKANA
MARITAGE MONEYAGE TREASURY
WOODGELD HEADPENNY
MALGUZARI
(— FOR INJURY) UTU
(— FOR LABOR) MEED
(— FOR OFFENSE) ENACH
(— FOR RELEASE) LOOSING
(— OF FEE) FEAL
(— OF MINERS) FOOTAGE YARDAGE
(— ON DELIVERY) COD
(DEMAND —) DUN BILL
(EVADE —) BILK DEFAULT
(HOMICIDE'S —) KELCHIN
(PERIODICAL —) GALE GAVEL
PAYNIM PAGAN PANIME HEATHEN
INFIDEL PAGANDOM
PAYOFF FIX BRIBE CLIMAX PROFIT
REWARD DECISIVE RECKONING
PEA DAL TUR DHAL GRAM LANG

SEED ARHAR CHICK CICER GANDUL
LEGUME PIGEON PODDER CARMELE
CATJANG KHESARI POWDARE
TANGIER GARVANRO
(— DOVE) ZENAIDA
(— HARVESTER) VINER
(— PETAL) KEEL
(EARLY —S) HASTINGS
(PARCHED —S) CARLS CARLINS
(PL.) POIS GRAIN
PEABIRD ORIOLE WRYNECK
PEACE PAX CALM EASE FINE LIOS
LISS REST AMITY FRITH GRITH
LISSE QUIET TRUCE REPOSE
SAUGHT SHALOM CONCORD
HARMONY REQUIEM
(GODDESS OF —) IRENE
(SYMBOL OF —) DOVE TOGA OLIVE
PEACEABLE FAIR SOME CIVIL QUIET
STILL GENTLE SILVER ORDERLY
PACIFIC SOLOMON AMICABLE
SACKLESS
PEACEFUL CALM SOME SOBER
STILL IRENIC PLACID SILVER
HALCYON PACIFIC
PEACE PIPE CALUMET
PEACH BLAB PAVY CLING PAVIE
SNEAK SPLIT TRUMP ACCUSE
BETRAY CARMAN CROSBY FOSTER
INDICT INFORM OREJON PEENTO
SALWEY ELBERTA PERSIAN PIENTAO
WHITTLE CRAWFORD ISABELLA
ROSEWORT
(— STATE) GEORGIA
(— STONE) PUTAMEN
PEACHBLOW FAKIR
PEACOCK MAO PAON PAVO PAWN
POSE PEKOK STRUT PAJOCK
PAVONE POWNIE PEAFOWL
PHASIANID
(— TAIL) TRAIN
(CONGO —) AFROPAVO
PEACOCK BITTERN SUN
PEACOCK BUTTERFLY IO
PEACOCK FISH WRASSE
PEACOCK FLOWER FLAMBEAU
POINCIANA
PEA CRAB PINNOTERE
PEAG TAX TOLL BEADS PAAGE
PEACK PEAGE PEDAGE WAMPUM
PEAI PIAY PIACHE
PEA JACKET PEACOAT
PEAK BEN NAB NOB PAP PIC TOP
TOR ACME APEX BEAK CIMA CUSP
DENT DOLT DOME KNOB KNOT PICO
PIKE TOLT BLOOM CREST CROWN
PIQUE PITCH PITON POINT SLINK
SNEAK STEAL STUMP CLIMAX
CUPULA SHASTA SHRINK SUMMIT
ZENITH EPITOME MAXIMUM
CENTROID
(— OF ANCHOR) PEE
(— OF CAP) SCOOP
(ICE —) SERAC
(ISOLATED —) TOLT
(SHARP —) HORN
(SNOW-CAPPED —) DOME CALOTTE
PEAKED WAN PALE THIN DRAWN
PIKED SHARP COPPED SICKLY

SLIMSY POINTED SLIMPSY
PEAKEDNESS KURTOSIS
PEAL CLAP RING TOLL CHIME CRACK
GRILSE SHOVEL MINNING RESOUND
SUMMONS THUNDER CARILLON
(— **OF THUNDER**) CLAP REEL
PEANUT BUR FLAX MANI MEAN
PETTY PINDA GOOBER PINDAL
ARACHIS BEENNUT ARACHIDE
EARTHPEA GRASSNUT KATCHUNG
VALENCIA MONKEYNUT
(— **DISEASE**) TIKKA
PEA POD COB PYSE QUASH PESCOD
(**POORLY FILLED** —) POP
(**UNRIPE** —) SQUASH
PEAR BOSC DIEGO MELON SABRA
BEURRE BURREL PANINI SECKEL
WARDEN WINTER KIEFFER PRICKLY
AMBRETTE BERGAMOT TASAJILLO
(**PRICKLY** —) TUNA NOPAL OPUNTIA
PEAR HAW THORN
PEARL GEM MABE TERN GRAIN
NACRE ONION PICOT UNION
BOUTON OLIVET ORIENT BAROQUE
BDELIUM BLISTER CATARACT
MOONBEAM MARGARITE
(— **WEIGHT**) TANK
(**IMITATION** —) OLIVET
(**IRREGULAR** —) SLUG
(**PIERCED** —) WIDOW
(**SEED** —) ALIOFAR
(**SMOKED** —) MITRAILLE
PEARL BLUSH ROSETAN
PEARL MILLET KOUS CUMBU
DUCHN DUKHN KOUSE JONDLA
DAGASSA
PEARLSIDES ARGENTIN
PEARLWEED SAGINA POVERTY
SEALWORT
PEARLY NACRY NACROUS PRECIOUS
PEARLY EVERLASTING LIVELONG
MOONSHINE
PEAR-SHAPED FULL MELLOW
ROUNDED PYRIFORM
PEASANT TAO BOND BOOR HERA
HIND KERN KONO KOPI PEON RAYA
RYOT SERF BAIRU BOWER CHURL
KNAVE KULAK RAYAH SWAIN
COTMAN COTTAR FARMER FELLAH
RASCAL RUSTIC BONDMAN
LABORER PAISANO VILLAIN
CHOPSTICK
(— **CLASS**) JACQUERIE
(— **OF INDIA**) RYOT KISAN RAIYAT
(**ARABIC** —) FELLAH
(**IRISH** —) KERN KERNE
(**RUSSIAN** —) KULAK MUZHIK
MUZJIK
PEASE CROW TERN
PEASHOOTER TRUNK BLOWER
PISTOL BLOWGUN
PEAT GOR PET SOD VAG COOM FUEL
MOOR MUCK MULL TURF COOMB
LAWYER MINION YARPHA DARLING
FAVORITE
(— **BOG**) CESS YARPHA
(— **CUTTER**) PINER
(— **SPADE**) SLADE TUSKAR TWISCAR
(**DRIED — FOR FUEL**) VAG
(**LAYER OF** —) FLAW

PEA TREE KATURAI
PEATY KETTY
PEBA PEVA ARMADILLO
PEBBLE DIB FLAX JACK PLUM
CHUCK SCREE STONE BANTAM
GIBBER GRAVEL QUARTZ SHILLA
SYCITE CHUCKIE CRYSTAL STANNER
JACKSTONE
(**PL.**) BEACH DREIKANTER
PECAN NOGAL PACANE
PECCADILLO FAULT OFFENSE
MISCHIEF
PECCANT FAULTY MORBID CORRUPT
SINNING DISEASED
PECCARY JAVALI WARREE TAGASSU
TAYASSU JAVELINA TAYASSUID
PECK DAB DOT JOB NIP BEAK BILL
CARP FOOD GRUB HOLE JERK KISS
PYKE PITCH PRICK STOCK THROW
HATFUL NIBBLE PEGGLE PICKLE
PIERCE STROKE CHIMBLE
(**1-4TH OF** —) LIPPY FORPET FORPIT
LIPPIE
PECKER BILL NOSE COURAGE
SPIRITS
PECTEN COMB MARSUPIUM
PECTORAL SANDPIPER JACK PERT
PEERT BROWNY BROWNIE
CHOROOK CREAKER FATBIRD
HAYBIRD KRIEKER SQUATTER
TRIDDLER JACKSNIPE
PECULATE STEAL MISUSE
EMBEZZLE
PECULIAR ODD VERY QUEER
PROPER QUAINT UNIQUE CURIOUS
PRIVATE SEVERAL SPECIAL
STRANGE UNUSUAL SEPARATE
SINGULAR SPECIFIC
PECULIARITY KINK IDIOM QUIRK
TRAIT TRICK TWIST IDIASM ODDITY
AEOLISM FEATURE IRISHRY
CROTCHET HEADMARK
(— **IN BOWL**) BIAS
(— **OF SPEECH**) IDIOLOGISM
(**CROTCHETY** —) FIKE
PECUNIARY POCKET MONETARY
FINANCIAL
PED BASKET HAMPER PANIER
PEDAGOGUE TUTOR PEDANT
DOMINIE SQUEERS TEACHER
THWACKUM
PEDAGOGY SCHOOL DIDACTICS
EDUCATION
PEDAL LEVER SWELL TREADLE
FOOTFEED PEDALIAN THROTTLE
(— **COUPLER**) TIRASSE
(**PIANO** —) CELESTE
PEDANT PRIG DUNCE TUTOR
DORBEL PURIST TASSEL ACADEME
PEDAGOG GAMALIEL DRYASDUST
OLOFERNES
PEDANTIC STODGY BOOKISH
DONNISH ERUDITE INKHORN
TEACHING
PEDDLE HAWK SELL CADGE SHOVE
TRANT TRUCK HIGGLE MEDDLE
PIDDLE RETAIL COLPORT
PEDDLER ARAB SMOUS BADGER
CRAMER JAGGER JOWTER MUGGER

STROLL WALKER NIGGLER
ROADMAN SANDBOY SWADDER
TROGGER TRUCKER HUCKSTER
BOXWALLAH DUSTYFOOT
(— **OF DOPE**) FIXER
(— **OF DRESS PIECES**) DUDDER
(— **OF FISH**) RIPIER RIPPER
(**ITINERANT** —) SMOUS SMOUSE
SMOUSER STROLLER
(**MOHAM.** —) BORA
(**STREET** —) CAMELOT
(**WARES OF** —) TROGGAN
PEDESTAL ANTA BASE BASIS BLOCK
STAND PILLAR PODIUM ROCKER
AKROTER SUPPORT PADMASANA
PEDESTRIAN PED DULL FOOT SLOW
HIKER FOOTER HOOFER WALKER
FOOTMAN PROSAIC PLODDING
WINGLESS
PEDICEL RAY STEM SCAPE STALK
PEDUNCLE FOOTSTALK
PEDIGREE STEMMA DESCENT
LINEAGE ANCESTRY PETEGREU
PUREBRED
PEDIMENT FRONTAL FRONTON
FASTIGIUM
PEDIPALP(**PL.**) LABIUM
PEDOMETER ODOGRAPH WAYWISER
PEDRERO PERRIER PETRARY
PEDUNCLE STEM SCAPE STALK
STIPES PEDICEL EYESTALK
HYPOCARP
(**PL.**) CRURA
PEEK PEEP PIKE GLANCE GLIMPSE
PEEKABOO PEEP BOPEEP PEEPEYE
PEEL BARK HARL HULL HUSK PARE
RIND SKIN FLAKE FLIPE SCALE
SLIPE STAKE STRIP CORTEX
SHOVEL SPITTLE UNDRESS
BARKPEEL ORANGEADO
(— **OFF**) HARL CRAZE FLAKE SHUCK
(**BAKER'S** —) PALE SPITTLE
(**ORANGE OR LEMON** —) ZEST
ORANGEAT
PEELER CRAB BOBBY CORER
HUSTLER SHEDDER SPUDDER
PILLAGER
PEELING RIND SKIN PARING PARURE
PEEN PIN PYNE RIVET
PEEP PRY SPY JEEP PEEK PEER
PULE SKEG STEP TOOT TOTE TOUT
CHEEP CHIRP DEKKO GLINT PIPIT
SNOOP TWEET DEGREE GLANCE
SQUEAK SQUINNY PEEKABOO
(— **SHOW**) RAREE
PEEPER EYE TOM FROG KEEK
VOYEUR
PEEPHOLE PEEP JUDAS EYELET
CREVICE
PEEPING NOSY PRYING
PEER PRY DUKE EARL FEAR GAZE
LOOK LORD MATE PEEP TOUT
BARON EQUAL GLINT GLOZE MATCH
NOBLE RIVAL STARE STIME THANE
TWIRE APPEAR FELLOW OLIVER
PINKER COMPERE
PEERAGE RANK DIGNITY BARONAGE
NOBILITY TENEMENT
PEERING SQUINNY

PEERLESS SUPREME MATCHLESS NONPAREIL UNRIVALED

PEESWEEP FINCH PEWIT LAPWING PEEWEEP

PEEVE IRK ANNOY GRUDGE NETTLE IRRITATE

PEEVISH SOUR CROSS DORTY PENSY SNACK TECHY TEENY TESTY TETTY THRAW TIFFY WEMOD CRUSTY GIRNIE HIPPED SNARLY SNUFFY SULLEN TATTER TOUCHY TWARLY TWAZZY TWITTY UPPISH UPPITY VAPORY CRABBED FRATCHY FRECKET FRETFUL FROWARD GROUCHY PETTISH SPLEENY TEDIOUS TIFFISH WASPISH PHRAMPEL PINDLING SANSHACH TWANKING

PEEWEE BOOT RUNT TINY PEWEE MARBLE LAPWING

PEG FIX HOB HUB NOB NOG PIN HOBB KING KNAG PLUG SCOB SHAG STEP CLEAT DOWEL DRINK NOTCH PERCH PITON PRONG SPELL SPILE SPILL STAKE THOLE THROW TOOTH WADDY DEGREE DOWELL FAUCET MARKER NORMAN PICKET REASON SPIGOT TAPOUN TIPCAT PINNING PRETEXT SCOLLOP SPERKET SUPPORT TRENAIL
(— FOR PLAYING GAME) CAT SPILIKIN
(— FOR SADDLES) SPERKET
(— OF STRINGED INSTRUMENT) CHEVILLE
(— OUT) DIE FAIL
(IRON —) PITON
(THATCH —) SCOB

PEGA REMORA

PEGALL BASKET PACKALL

PEGASUS QUAVIVER HYPOSTOME

PEG TOP PIRY PEERY PEERIE

PEIGNOIR GOWN DRESS KIMONO NEGLIGEE

PEISE BLOW FORCE PASSE POISE POIZE IMPACT WEIGHT BALANCE POISURE

PEKAN WEJACK

PELAGE FUR HAIR PILAGE

PELAGIC MARINE AQUATIC OCEANIC PELAGIAN

PELEUS (BROTHER OF —) TELAMON
(FATHER OF —) AEACUS
(HALF-BROTHER OF —) PHOCUS
(SON OF —) PELIDES ACHILLES
(WIFE OF —) THETIS ANTIGONE

PELF GAIN BOOTY LUCRE MONEY SPOIL TRASH PILFER PILFRE REFUSE RICHES WEALTH COMPOST

PELICAN DOVE ALCATRAS ONOCROTAL
(— STATE) LOUISIANA

PELISSE POSTIN POSTEEN

PELL BEAT PELE PELT HURRY PEELE HASTEN

PELLAGRA MAIDISM PELAGRA

PELLET BB WAD BALL CAST PILL SHOT BOLUS PRILL STONE BEEBEE BULLET FECULA OGRESS PILULE

CASTING GRANULE PALLION TRATTLE BUCKSHOT GUNSTONE HAILSTONE
(SNOW —S) GRAUPEL
(PL.) SHOT

PELLICLE FILM SCUM SKIN CRUST CUTICLE EPISTASIS

PELLITORY BERTRAM BERTRUM WALLWORT

PELL-MELL RUSH MELPELL DISORDER HEADLONG

PELLOCK PALACH PORPOISE

PELLUCID CLEAR BRIGHT LIMPID ORIENT CRYSTAL

PELMA TRACK

PELMET CORNICE VALANCE PALMETTE

PELOPONNESUS (CITY OF —) SPARTA
(PEOPLE OF —) MOREOTE
(RIVER GOD OF —) ALPHEUS

PELOPS (FATHER OF —) TANTALUS
(SON OF —) ATREUS TROEZEN PITTHEUS THYESTES
(WIFE OF —) HIPPODAMIA

PELORIA EPANODY

PELT FUR KIT BEAR BEAT BLOW CAPE CAST COON DASH FELL HIDE HURL KITT PELL PUSH RACK SKIN BESET CHUNK FITCH HURRY SABLE SLASH SPEED STONE WHACK BADGER BEAVER FISHER PELTER SERVAL SPRING BETHUMP COONSKIN
(— OF SEAL, WITH BLUBBER) SCULP
(— WITH MISSILES) BUM SQUAIL
(— WITH STONES) LAPIDATE
(BEAVER —) BLANKET

PELTAST SOLDIER

PELTATE SCUTATE

PELTER SKEET

PELTING SLASHING

PELTRY FURS SKINS

PELUDO POYOU ARMADILLO

PEN COT CUB GET HOK MEW PAR PIN STY BOLT CAGE COOP CROO CROW FAUD FOLD JAIL STUB WALK YARD BUGHT CRAWL CREEP CUBBY HUTCH KRAAL POINT QUILL STYLE WRITE BOUGHT CORRAL CRUIVE FASTEN FLIGHT HURDLE INDITE RECORD STYLUS ZAREBA CONFINE WARKLOOM
(— CATTLE) STANCE
(— FOR CATTLE) CUB LOT CREW CRUE LAIR REEVE
(— FOR ELEPHANTS) KRAAL
(— FOR HOGS OR SLAVES) CRAWL
(— OF CUTTLEFISH) GLADIUS
(— POINT) NEB NIB STUB
(— UP) FRANK STIVE
(AUTHOR'S —) STYLE STYLUS
(FOUNTAIN —) STICK
(REED —) CALAMUS

PENALIZE CHECK

PENALTY BETE CAIN DOOM FINE LOSS PAIN BEAST JUISE MULCT AMENDE AMERCE SOLACE FORFEIT NEMESIS SURSIZE BLOODWIT

HARDSHIP SCAFFOLD

PENANCE TAP SORE SHRIFT SORROW REMORSE SUFFERING

PEN CASE PENNER POPPET

PENCEL FLAG PENNON STREAMER PENNONCEL

PENCHANT BENT TASTE GENIUS LIKING LEANING FONDNESS

PENCIL PEN RED WAD BLUE LEAD WADD LINER SHEAF SKETCH STYLUS POINTEL CHARCOAL KEELIVINE
(SLATE —) SKAILLIE
(PL.) STATIONERY

PENCILWOOD MORDORE

PENDANT BOB JAG DROP FLAG JAGG PEND TAIL AGLET BULLA GUTTA POINT AIGLET LUSTER PALAOA PLAYER TABARD TARGET TASSEL EARDROP LANGUET SUPPORT LAVALIER

PENDENT LOP BAGGED ICICLE HANGING PROMISS

PENDULOUS LOP SLOUCH HANGING CERNUOUS DROOPING

PENDULUM SWING PENDLE SWINGEL SWINGLE VIBRATILE
(INVERTED —) NODDY

PENELOPE (FATHER OF —) ICARIUS
(FATHER-IN-LAW OF —) LAERTES
(HUSBAND OF —) ULYSSES ODYSSEUS
(SUITOR OF —) AGELAUS

PENEPLAIN STRATH ENDRUMPF

PENETRATE CUT DIG DIP SEE BITE BORE DIVE GORE PASS PINK SINK STAB WADE BREAK DRILL DRIVE ENTER IMBUE PROBE SEIZE THIRL CLEAVE FATHOM FICCHE GIMLET INVADE PIERCE RIDDLE SEARCH STRIKE THRILL WIMBLE DISCERN PERVADE
(— MENTALLY) ENTER
(— ONE'S MIND) SOAK

PENETRATED (EASILY —) MELLOW

PENETRATING ACID KEEN ACUTE LEVEL SHARP ASTUTE DEADLY SHREWD SHRILL SUBTLE GIMLETY INGOING INTRANT KNOWING PUNGENT PERCEANT REACHING TRENCHANT

PENETRATION DEPTH ACUMEN FATHOM INROAD INGOING INSIGHT SEEPAGE INCISION INVASION SAGACITY

PENGUIN AUK DIVER GENTU ARCTIC DIPPER GENTOO JOHNNY PINWING BREVIPED MACARONI
(PL.) IMPENNES

PENINSULA CAPE MULL NECK INDIA BILAND BYLAND ISLAND PENILE

PENITENCE RUE REGRET SORROW PENANCE PENANCY REMORSE

PENITENT RUER SORRY HUMBLE WEEPER STANDER CONTRITE
(— OF 3RD STAGE) KNEELER

PENITENTIARY JUG PEN JAIL STIR TENCH PRISON PENITENT

PENMAN CLERK AUTHOR SCRIBE WRITER

PENMANSHIP HAND SCRIPT PENSHIP WRITING

PENNANT FANE FLAG WHIP COLOR ROGER BANNER CORNET PENCIL PENNON PENSIL PINION PINNET MEATBALL REPEATER STREAMER

PENNILESS POOR BROKE NEEDY BANKRUPT INDIGENT STRAPPED PLACKLESS

PENNON FLAG VANE WING ANVIL BANNER PENCIL PENOUN PINION FEATHER

PENNON SPAR PEGGYMAST

PENNSYLVANIA

CAPITAL: HARRISBURG

COLLEGE: JUNIATA URSINUS LYCOMING

COUNTY: BERKS BUCKS TIOGA CAMBRIA JUNIATA VENANGO WYOMING LYCOMING

MOUNTAIN RANGE: POCONO ALLEGHENY

NATIVE: AMISH DUTCH

PRESIDENT: BUCHANAN

RIVER: LEHIGH CLARION JUNIATA LICKING TOWANDA CALDWELL DELAWARE SCHRADER ALLEGHENY SCHUYLKILL MONONGAHELA SUSQUEHANNA

STATE BIRD: GROUSE

STATE FLOWER: LAUREL

STATE NICKNAME: KEYSTONE

STATE TREE: HEMLOCK

TOWN: ERIE ETNA PLUM YORK AVOCA EASTON EMMAUS SHARON ALTOONA EPHRATA HERSHEY READING BRYNMAWR SCRANTON SHAMOKIN BETHLEHEM CHARLEROI GETTYSBURG PITTSBURGH

UNIVERSITY: PITT DREXEL LEHIGH TEMPLE BUCKNELL DUQUESNE VILLANOVA

PENNY DY AES MEG RED SOU GILL BROON BROWN OULAP PENCE COPPER FOLLIS SALTEE STIVER BROWNIE STERLING
(— **DREADFUL**) HORRIBLE
(**DUTCH** —) STIVER
(**HALF** —) HALFLIN
(**OLD SCOTCH** —) TURNER
(PL.) PENCE FOLLES

PENNYCRESS FANWEED STINKWEED

PENNY-PINCHING STINGY

PENNYROYAL PULIOL HEDEOMA HILLWORT TICKWEED SQUAWWEED

PENNYWEIGHT DWT PENNY WEIGHT STERLING

PENSION WAGE PAYMENT STIPEND SUBSIDY TRIBUTE GRATUITY MALIKANA

PENSIVE MESTO MOODY PENSY SOBER DREAMY MUSING PENCEY WISTFUL THOUGHTY

PENT CAGED PENNED CONFINED ENCLOSED RESERVOIR

PENTACLE STAR HEXAGRAM PENTAGRAM

PENTAD QUINTAD

PENTASTICH POEM UNIT STANZA STROPHE

PENTECOST SHABUOTH WHITSUNDAY

PENTHEUS (GRANDFATHER OF —) CADMUS
(**MOTHER OF** —) AGAVE

PENTHOUSE PENT ROOF SHED AERIE ANNEX HANGAR LOOKUM SHADOW PLUTEUS BULKHEAD SKEELING SKILLION

PENTOSAN ARABAN

PENTOSE APIOSE RIBOSE

PENTYL AMYL

PENURIOUS MEAN POOR BARREN SCANTY STINGY MISERLY WANTING INDIGENT HIDEBOUND NIGGARDLY

PENURY WANT BEGGARY BORASCO POVERTY SCARCITY INDIGENCE PRIVATION

PEON HAND PAWN SERF SLAVE PELADO THRALL FOOTMAN LABORER PEASANT SOLDIER CONSTABLE

PEONY PINY MOUTAN

PEOPLE ARO LOG MEN PUL TAT VAI YAO AKRA ASHA BENI BUGI CHIN CHUD EMIM FOLK GENS HERD HIMA HUMA IRON LAND LEDE LUBA LURI PHUD PHUL PHUT RACE RAIS REMI SAFI SARA SEBA SERE TEMA THEY TOMA TULU USUN VITI VOLK WARE AFIFI AVARS BENIN BONGO CATTI CHAGA COURS DEMOS DUALA EDONI ELYMI FOLKS GENTE GOMER HAUSA JACKS LAITY LANAO LENDU LUREM MARSI MASAI NOGAI ORANG PUNAN QUADI RAMBO ROTSE SACAE SALAR SAURA SHAKA STOCK TAURI VOLTA WARUA WORLD ABABUA ACHUAS AFSHAR AISSOR ANGAMI ANGLES ARUNTA AVIKOM BAHIMA BAKELE BAKUBA BALUBA BELTIR BOSHAS BULLOM CIMBRI COMMON DAIONE GENTRY GILAKI GILEKI HAUSSA HERERO HERULI KANWAR KPUESI KRUMAN MANTZU MINYAE MOSCHI NATION OVAMPO PAMIRI PUBLIC RAMUSI RUTULI SAFINI SAMBAL SATRAE SEMANG SHARRA TADJIK TAGAUR TELUGU TUNGUZ TURSHA VENETI VOLCAE WACAGO WAHIMA YNDOYS YUECHI ZAMBAL ACHANGO ASTOMOI BAGANDA BAGARRA BAKALAI BANGALA BANGASH BAROTSE BUNYORO DARDANI DENIZEN DURZADA FALISCI GAETULI GENERAL GEPIDAE GUHAYNA INHABIT IRISHRY ISSEDOI ITALICI KINDRED KURANKO MAKONDE MESHECH MITANNI NABALOI PICENES PICTAVI PUKHTUN ROHILLA SAMBURU SENONES SILURES

SUKKIIM TIRURAI VESTINI WABUNGA WACHAGA WAKAMBA WANGONI
(— **HAVING DISTINCT LANGUAGE**) TONGUE
(— **OF FASHION**) FLOSS
(— **OF GOOD BREEDING**) GENTRY GENTILITY
(**ABORIGINAL** —) JAKUN KHMER KODAGU SEKHWAN
(**ANCIENT** —) CARA CHAM JUNG ELYMI GETAE HURRI ICENI SACAE SERES SICULI DARDANI FALISCI FIRBOLG KIPCHAK SEQUANI SILURES
(**CAVE-DWELLING** —) HORITE
(**COMMON** —) DEMOS PLEBE VULGAR VULGUS TILIKUM SNOBBERY
(**EXTINCT** —) KOT CHONO COFAN COREE CHANGO CHATOT GUINAU HIBITO SAPONI SHIRINO
(**FOREST** —) SAKAI SAORA SAURA
(**HONORABLE** —) HONESTY
(**LOWEST CLASS OF** —) CANAILLE
(**MARITIME** —) LAMUT
(**MOUNTAIN** —) HUZUL HUTZUL
(**NOMADIC** —) SHUA HORDE IGDYR IHLAT SHUWA HABIRU SHAGIA SARACEN SHAMMAR SHORTZY SHUKRIA
(**OLD** —) ANCIENTRY
(**ORDINARY** —) LAYFOLK
(**PAGAN** —) IRAYA HANUNOO SUBANUN
(**PRIMITIVE** —) DAFLA IRULA KADIR KURUKH CHENCHU
(**WHITE** —) ALBICULI
(PL.) MAKHZAN

PEOPLED ABAD SETTLED POPULATE

PEORIA MASCOUTEN

PEP GO VIM DASH VERVE VIGOR ENERGY GINGER ANIMATE QUICKEN ACTIVITY

PEPLUM GOWN SKIRT TUNIC PEPLOS OVERSKIRT

PEPO GOURD MELON SQUASH PUMPKIN PEPONIDA PEPONIUM

PEPPER CAVA IKMO ITMO KAVA SIRI BETEL CHILI MANGO PIPER SIRIH MATICO TOPEPO CAYENNE PAPRIKA PIMENTA RELIENO JALAPENO KAVAKAVA
(**JAVA** —) CUBEB
(**RED** —) LADYFINGER

PEPPER-AND-SALT JASPER

PEPPERGRASS CRESS CANARY ANOUNOU COCKWEED

PEPPERMINT MENTHE LABIATE

PEPPER TREE MOLLE HOROPITO PIMIENTO

PEPPERWORT DITTANDER

PEPPERY HOT FIERY SAUCY SPICY TOUCHY PIQUANT PUNGENT SPIRITED STINGING

PEPPY GINGERY

PEPTONE ASCARON

PER BY THE EACH THROUGH

PERADVENTURE HAP DOUBT MAYBE CHANCE MAPPEN MAYHAP HAPPILY PERHAPS POSSIBLY

PERAMBULATE WALK RAMBLE STROLL PERAMBLE TRAVERSE
PERAMBULATION WEND
PERAMBULATOR BUGGY WAGON BASSINET VIAMETER WAYWISER PEDOMETER
PERATE OPHITE
PERCEIVE SEE ESPY FEEL FIND GAUM HEAR KNOW LOOK MIND NOTE SCAN TWIG SCENT SENSE SMELL TASTE TOUCH BEHOLD COTTON DESCRY DIVINE FIGURE NOTICE REMARK SURVEY COGNIZE DISCERN OBSERVE REALIZE SENSATE COMPRISE DESCRIBE UNDERNIM
PERCENTAGE CUT AGIO PART SHARE PROFIT PORTION SCALAGE DEFLATOR
(MINING —) LEY
PERCEPT IDEA
PERCEPTIBLE NOTABLE TACTILE VISIBLE APPARENT PALPABLE SENSIBLE TANGIBLE TRACTABLE
(FAINTLY —) SHADOWY
(HARDLY —) FAINT
PERCEPTION RAY BUMP GAUM TACT SAVOR SCENT SENSE SIGHT ACUMEN VISION CLOSURE FEELING GLIMMER NOSTRIL BEARINGS DELICACY OUTSIGHT COGNITION SENSATION SENTIMENT
(DIM —) GLIMMER
(MENTAL —) TACT TOUCH SENSATION
PERCEPTIVE QUICK SHARP SUBTLE KNOWING SENSITIVE
PERCH BAR BAS LUG PEG ROD SIT BASS JOUK MADO OKOW PERK PIKE POLE POPE SEAT BARSE BEGTI BEKTI BLOCK LIGHT REACH ROOST RUFFE STAFF ALIGHT BUGARA CALLOP PERCID SAUGER SETTLE ZANDER ZINGEL ALFIONE HOGFISH STATION ROCKFISH MARTENIKO TRUMPETER
(2-YEAR OLD —) EGLING
PERCHANCE HAPLY MAYBE AUNTERS FORTUNE PERHAPS POSSIBLY
PERCHER STAKER
PERCHTA BERTHA
PERCOLATE MELT OOZE PERK SEEP SIFT SILT SIPE SOAK WEEP DRILL EXUDE LEACH EXHALE FILTER STRAIN
PERCOLATION SIPING SEEPAGE LEACHING
PERCOLATOR SIPER BIGGIN CAFETIERE DISPLACER
PERCUSSION BLOW IMPACT STROKE PNEUMATIC
PERDITION HELL LOSS RUIN BOWWOWS BALLYWACK DAMNATION
PEREGRINATE TOUR WALK TRAVEL WANDER JOURNEY SOJOURN TRAVERSE
PEREGRINE ALIEN EXOTIC ROVING PILGRIM STRANGE IMPORTED

PEREGRINE FALCON SAKER GENTLE TASSEL TERCEL
PEREMPT QUASH DEFEAT DESTROY
PEREMPTORY FLAT FINAL UTTER EXPRESS HAUGHTY ABSOLUTE DECISIVE DOGMATIC POSITIVE ESSENTIAL
PERENNIAL HERB CAREX LIANA PEONY SEDUM BANANA CENTRO BLUEWEED CONSTANT ENDURING KNAPWEED TOADFLAX CONTINUAL EVERGREEN PERPETUAL RECURRENT
PERFECT ALL BACK CURE FILL FINE FULL HOLY PURE SURE EXACT FINAL FULLY IDEAL PLAIN RIGHT RIPEN SHEER SOUND TOTAL UTTER WHOLE ENTIRE EXPERT FINISH REFINE SPHERE CERTAIN CONCOCT CONTENT CORRECT CROWNED DEVELOP GEMLIKE IMPROVE PLENARY PRECISE SINLESS SPHERAL TYPICAL COMPLETE FLAWLESS INFINITE INTEGRAL
(— IN RIGHTEOUSNESS) HOLY
(— SCORE) MAX
PERFECTED EXACT SUMMED FINISHED PERQUEIR
PERFECTION ACME PINK BLOOM IDEAL BEAUTY FINISH PLENTY FULNESS PARAGON FINALITY FINENESS MATURITY RIPENESS ERUDITION
(TYPE OF —) PARAGON
PERFECTIVE TELIC
PERFECTLY SPAN QUITE IDEALLY PERQUEIR
PERFIDIOUS FALSE SNAKY DISLEAL SNAKISH DISLOYAL SPITEFUL FAITHLESS
PERFIDY DECEIT TREASON FALSEHOOD FALSENESS TREACHERY
PERFORATE EAT DOCK HOLE DRILL PRICK PUNCH SIEVE THIRL PIERCE POUNCE RIDDLE THRILL PINHOLE PUNCTURE PENETRATE TEREBRATE
(— A STAMP) CENTER
PERFORATED OPEN CRIBROSE
PERFORATION BORE HOLE THIRL TORET BROACH EYELET STIGMA TRESIS FORAMEN PINHOLE SEPTULA STENCIL DIABROSIS
PERFORM DO ACT CUT KIP CHAR FILL FULL HAVE KEEP LAST MAKE PLAY SHOW STEP CHARE DIGHT ENACT EXERT FETCH ACQUIT COMMIT EFFECT FULFIL RENDER ACHIEVE EXECUTE EXHIBIT EXPLOIT FUNGIFY FURNISH IWURCHE PRESENT PRESTATE
(— AWKWARDLY) BOGGLE
(— BADLY) BOLLIX
(— BRILLIANTLY) STAR SPARKLE
(— CLUMSILY) THUMB BUNGLE
(— FULLY) END
(— HASTILY) SKIMP SCAMP,
(— HURRIEDLY) SLUR
(— IN DANCING) FIGURE

PERFORMANCE ACT JOB DEED FEAT HAND SHOW TEST WORK CAPER SLANG SPORT STUNT ACTING ACTION BALLET EFFECT HORARY MASQUE ACCOUNT ACROAMA BENEFIT BOOKING CONCERT EXPLOIT MATINEE MUMMERY SHOWING FAREWELL FUNCTION PRACTICE STERACLE
(— FOR ONE) SOLO
(— OF DUTY) FEASANCE
(— OF OBLIGATION) SOLUTIO
(— VARIATIONS) COUNTER
(— WITH SENTIMENTALITY) DROOL
(ARAB —) FANTASIA
(CHRISTMAS EVE —) GOMBAY
(CLUMSY —) BUNGLE
(DRAMATIC —) TOPENG
(FIRST —) PREMIERE
(NO —) RELACHE
(PAST —) FORM
(TRIAL —) AUDITION
(VULGAR —) BLOWOFF
PERFORMER ACT DOER GEEK MOKE STAR ACTOR SHINE ARTIST DANCER KINKER LEADER PLAYER WORKER ACROAMA ARTISTE GAMBIST HORNIST HOTSHOT SOLOIST EXECUTOR SPARKLER HAMFATTER HEADLINER
(— ON SEVERAL INSTRUMENTS) MOKE
(— WITH NEGRO DIALECT) HAMBONE
(BURLESQUE —) GRINDER
(CIRCUS —) LEAPER
(INFERIOR —) HAM SHINE
PERFUME ATAR BALM FUME MUSK NOSE OTTO AROMA ATTAR CENSE CIVET MYRRH SCENT SMELL SPICE CARVOL CHYPRE EMBALM FLAVOR IONONE CARVONE DIAPASM ESSENCE INCENSE JASMINE NOSEGAY ODORIZE SWEETEN BERGAMOT MARECHAL ORANGERY PATCHOULI
(— BASE) MUSK CIVET NEROL NEROLI
(POWDERY —) PULVIL
PERFUNCTORY CURSORY CARELESS APATHETIC
PERGOLA ARBOR BOWER RAMADA BALCONY TRELLIS
PERHAPS HAPS MAYBE ABLINS BELIKE HAPPEN MAPPEN MAYHAP ABLINGS LIGHTLY PERCASE POSSIBLY
PERI ELF FAIRY SPRITE
PERIAPT CHARM AMULET
PERICARP BUR BOLL BURR BLADDER
PERICRANIUM HEAD BRAIN
PERIDOTITE PICRITE EULYSITE JOSEFITE SAXONITE WEHRLITE
PERIGEE EPIGEUM
PERIGYNIUM UTRICLE
PERIL RISK WERE WATHE CRISIS DANGER HAZARD MENACE SCYLLA THREAT THRONG TRANCE

JEOPARDY CHARYBDIS
PERILOUS KITTLE DOUBTFUL
DREADFUL INFAMOUS DANGEROUS
HAZARDOUS
PERIMETER RIM OUTLINE
BOUNDARY PERIPHERY
PERIOD GO AGE DOT END EON ERA
AEON DATE LIFE RACE SPAN STOP
TERM TIDE TIME YEAR AVAIL CLOSE
CYCLE EPACT EPOCH LABOR LAPSE
PATCH POINT SPACE SPELL STAGE
CUTOFF GHURRY HEMERA MOMENT
PARODY PICTUN SEASON STOUND
ACCOUNT DICOLON FLORUIT
PASTIME SESSION STADIUM
STRETCH DURATION INDUCIAE
INSTANCE LIFETIME SENTENCE
(— ENDING FROST) FRESH
(— FOR WHICH ENJOYED) TENURE
(— IN DEVELOPMENT) STAGE
(— OF 10 YEARS) DECADE
(— OF 100 YEARS) AGE CENTURY
(— OF 1000 YEARS) CHILIAD
MILLIAD
(— OF 14 MINUTES, 24 SECONDS)
CENTIDAY
(— OF 2 MONTHS) DIMESTER
(— OF 2 YEARS) BIENNIUM
(— OF 20 TUNS) KATUN
(— OF 20 YEARS) KATUN
(— OF 260 DAYS) TONALMATL
(— OF 5 DAYS) PENTAD LUSTRUM
(— OF 50 YEARS) JUBILE JUBILEE
(— OF 7 DAYS) HEBDOMAD
(— OF 7 YEARS) SEPTENARY
(— OF ACTION) GO BOUT
(— OF DECLINE) SUNSET EVENING
(— OF DRYNESS) DROUTH
DROUGHT
(— OF FESTIVITY) WAKES
(— OF GLOOM) DEAD
(— OF GRACE) DAY
(— OF HEAT) CALLING
(— OF HUMID WEATHER) SIZZARD
(— OF IMMATURITY) SWADDLE
(— OF INSTRUCTION) LESSON
(— OF LIFE) AGE ELD SPAN
(— OF MILITARY SERVICE) HITCH
(— OF MOTILITY) SWARMING
(— OF MOURNING) SHIVA SHIBAH
(— OF PERFORMING) STANZA
(— OF PLAY) HALF CHUKKER
QUARTER
(— OF RECREATION) HOLIDAY
VACATION
(— OF REMISSION) JUBILEE
(— OF REST) SMOKO BREATHER
(— OF REVOLUTION OF HEAVENLY
BODY) ORB
(— OF TIME) DAY HOUR WEEK
YEAR MONTH DECADE MINUTE
SECOND
(— OF WORK) SHIFT SPELL STINT
(— PRECEDING IMPORTANT EVENT)
EVE
(CLASS —) HOUR
(CULTURAL —) HORIZON
(DEFINITE —) MOMENT
(DISTINCTIVE —) EPOCH

(DULL —) SLACK
(EVOLUTIONAL —) HEMERA
(GEOLOGICAL —) JURA KAROO
EOCENE ALGOMAN HORIZON
CAMBRIAN DEVONIAN JURASSIC
SILURIAN TERTIARY TRANSVAAL
(HAPPY —) MILLENIUM
(HYPOTHETICAL —) ACME
(LONG —) EON AEON CYCLE
(MEETING —) SESSION
(MENSTRUAL —) TERMS
(OCCASIONAL —) SNATCH
(PENITENTIAL —) LENT
(RECURRING —) EMBER
(SHORT —) BIT FIT BLINK SHAKE
SPELL SPURT SNATCH
PERIODIC ERAL ANNUAL CYCLIC
ETESIAN REGULAR FREQUENT
SEASONAL
(NOT —) LOOSE
PERIODICAL DAILY PAPER SHEET
ANNUAL DIGEST REVIEW ETESIAN
FANZINE JOURNAL TABLOID
DREADFUL EXCHANGE MAGAZINE
EPHEMERIS
PERIODICALLY TERMLY
PERIPATETIC ROVING RAMBLING
ITINERANT
PERIPHERAL DEEP OUTER DISTAL
DISTANT EXTERNAL MARGINAL
PERIPHERY LIP RIM BRIM DOME
EDGE AMBIT LIMIT SKIRT AREOLA
BORDER BOUNDS FRINGE AMBITUS
CONTOUR SUBURBS SURFACE
CONFINES PERIMETER
PERISCOPE ALTISCOPE HYPOSCOPE
OMNISCOPE
PERISH DIE FADE FALL RUIN TINE
TYNE QUAIL SPILL SWELT WASTE
DEPART EXPIRE STARVE DESTROY
FORFARE MISCARRY
(— GRADUALLY) FADE
PERISHABLE SOFT DYING CADUKE
BRITTLE FUGITIVE
PERISHED MUSHY
PERISTOME FRINGE
PERITE SKILLED
PERITHECIUM ALVEOLA
PERITONEUM RIM SIPHAC
PERIWIG FLASH GALERA PERUKE
TOUPEE GALERUM PERWICK
PERIWINKLE PERY PIRE WINK
PERRY SNAIL MYRTLE WINKLE
DOGBANE PINPATCH SENGREEN
BLUEBUTTON
PERJINK NEAT TRIM PRECISE
PERJURE FORSWEAR
PERJURED MANSWORN
PERK BRISK PERCH PREEN PRINK
FRESHEN SMARTEN
PERKY AIRY PERT COCKY JAUNTY
CHIPPER
PERMANENCE STAY STABILITY
PERMANENT FIXED STABLE ABIDING
DURABLE LASTING STATIVE
CONSTANT ENDURING REMANENT
STANDING INDELIBLE
PERMANENTLY KEEPS
PERMEABLE POROUS

PERMEATE FILL SEEP SOAK BATHE
IMBUE DRENCH INFORM INVADE
ANIMATE PERVADE DOMINATE
SATURATE PENETRATE
PERMEATED SHOT
PERMIAN DYAS DYASSIC
PERMISSIBLE FREE POSSIBLE
CONGEABLE
(NOT —) NEFAS
PERMISSION MAY FIAT LIEF CONGE
DARST FAVOR GRACE GRANT LEAVE
ACCESS ACCORD CONSENT LIBERTY
LICENSE SANCTION
PERMISSIVE TOLERANT
CONCESSORY
PERMIT LET CHOP GIVE LEVE PASS
ADMIT ALLOW CONGE EXEAT FAVOR
GRACE GRANT LEAVE SERVE
ACCORD BETEEM CEDULA DUSTUK
ENDURE ENTREE SUFFER CONCEDE
CONSENT DUSTUCK FACULTY
LICENSE PLACARD POMPANO
WARRANT DISPENSE
(— NEGATIVELY) TOLERATE
(— TO TAKE) SOAK
PERMITTED FREE LOOT LICIT
ALLOWED INNOCENT SUPPOSED
(— BY LAW) LEGAL
PERMUTATION BARTER CHANGE
EXCHANGE
PERNICIOUS BAD ILL EVIL FATAL
QUICK SWIFT DEADLY MALIGN
WICKED BALEFUL BANEFUL
HARMFUL HURTFUL NOISOME
NOXIOUS RUINOUS
PERNIO CHILBLAIN
PEROPUS PARAGON
PERORATION EPILOG PERIOD
CLOSING PURLICUE
PERPEND JUMPER PARPEN PONDER
REFLECT THROUGH
PERPENDICULAR SINE ERECT
PLUMB SHEER ABRUPT NORMAL
APOTHEM UPRIGHT BINORMAL
CATHETUS EVENDOWN VERTICAL
PERPENDICULARLY BOLT SHEER
SHEERLY
PERPENDICULARITY APLOMB
PERPETRATE DO COMMIT EFFECT
PERFORM
PERPETUAL ETERN ENDLESS
ETERNAL CONSTANT INFINITO
UNENDING CONTINUAL PERENNIAL
PERPETUALLY EVER ALWAYS
FOREVER
PERPETUATE CONTINUE ETERNIZE
MAINTAIN
PERPLEX CAP MAR SET VEX BEAT
CLOG DOIT DOZE FIKE MAZE STUN
AMAZE BESET BLAIK STUMP TWIST
BAFFLE BOGGLE BOTHER CUMBER
DARKEN FICKLE GRAVEL HAMPER
HARASS HOBBLE KITTLE MAMMER
MITHER MOIDER MUDDLE PLAGUE
POTHER POTTER PUTTER PUZZLE
RAFFLE RIDDLE TWITCH WILDER
WRIXLE BEDEVIL BUMBAZE
CONFUSE DIFFUSE EMBROIL
MYSTIFY NONPLUS PLUNDER

STAGGER STUMBLE TORMENT
BEWILDER SURPRISE WINDLASS

PERPLEXED MAZY ANXIOUS
NONPLUS PUZZLED CONFUSED
TROUBLED INTRICATE

PERPLEXING HARD MAZY CRABBY
KNOBBY KNOTTY CARKING
COMPLEX CRABBED QUISCOS
BAFFLING

PERPLEXITY FOG KNOT WERE
BRAKE FOITER HOBBLE PUCKER
TANGLE ANXIETY STICKLE TROUBLE
POSEMENT SURPRISE CONFUSION
LABYRINTH
(MENTAL —) STUDY
(RELIEVE OF —) CLEAR

PERQUISITE FEE TIP PERK VAIL
GOUPIN GOWPEN INCOME ADJUNCT
APANAGE VANTAGE CONQUEST
GRATUITY
(PL.) PICKING

PERRINIST LIBERTINE

PERRIER PEDRERO

PERSE BLUE

PERSECUTE VEX BAIT ANNOY
CHASE HARRY HOUND WRACK
WRONG HARASS PESTER PURSUE
AFFLICT CRUCIFY DRAGOON
OPPRESS TORMENT TORTURE

PERSECUTED JOB REFUGEE

PERSECUTOR TORQUEMADA

PERSEPHONE KORE DESPOINA
PRAXIDIKE
(DAUGHTER OF —) CORA KORE
(FATHER OF —) ZEUS JUPITER
(HUSBAND OF —) HADES PLUTO
(MOTHER OF —) CERES DEMETER

PERSEUS RESCUER CHAMPION
(FATHER OF —) ZEUS JUPITER
(GRANDFATHER OF —) ACRISIUS
(MOTHER OF —) DANAE
(STAR OF —) ATIK ALGOL
(VICTIM OF —) MEDUSA
(WIFE OF —) ANDROMEDA

PERSEVERANCE GRIT STAMINA
INDUSTRY PATIENCE TENACITY
CONSTANCY

PERSEVERE CANK KEEP TORE
ABIDE STICK INSIST REMAIN
PERSIST CONTINUE

PERSEVERING BUSY HARD STILL
RESOLUTE ASSIDUOUS INSISTENT

PERSIA (SEE IRAN)

PERSIAN PERSE GILAKI HAJEMI
IRANIC DURZADA HADJEMI IRANIAN
MEMNONIAN
(— RED DEER) MARAL

PERSICARY REDLEG REDLEGS
REDSHANK HEARTEASE HEARTWEED
PEACHWORT

PERSIFLAGE BANTER RAILLERY

PERSIMMON KAKI SIMON SIMMON
ZAPOTE CHAPOTE HYAKUME
TRIUMPH
(— TREE) GAB GAUB LOTUS

PERSIST HOLD KEEP LAST URGE
ADHERE ENDURE INSIST REMAIN
SUBSIST CONTINUE PERSEVERE

PERSISTENCE GUTS

PERSISTENCY TENACITY

PERSISTENT SET DREE FIRM HARD
GREAT STOUT DOGGED DREECH
GRITTY HECTIC SLEUTH DURABLE
RESTANT RESTIVE CONSTANT
ENDURING HOLDFAST OBDURATE
RESOLUTE SEDULOUS STUBBORN
ASSIDUOUS OBSTINATE PRIMITIVE

PERSON CAT EGG EGO GUY MAN
ONE BABY BODY CHAL CHAP DUCK
FISH FOOD FORM GINK HOOK LEDE
LIFE NABS SELF SOUL BEING
BOSOM CHILD COOKY GHOST
HEART HUMAN PARTI PARTY PIECE
STICK THING WATCH WIGHT ANIMAL
BUGGER ENTITY FELLOW GALOOT
GAZABO JOHNNY KIPPER NUMBER
SINNER SISTER SPIRIT SPRITE
ARTICLE BLISTER WAGTAIL
SPECIMEN TILLICUM
(— ACTING FOR ANOTHER) PROXY
(— ASSOCIATED WITH WORK)
WALLAH
(— BEARING HEAVY BURDEN)
CAMEL
(— BEHIND THE TIMES) FOGY
FOGEY
(— BRINGING GOOD LUCK) MASCOT
**(— FROM WHOM FAMILY IS
DESCENDED)** STIRPS
(— NAMED) NOMINEE
(— NOT OF NOBLE BIRTH)
ROTURIER
(— OF AGE) COOT FALDWORTH
(— OF CONSEQUENCE) BIGGIE
BIGWIG TALLBOY
(— OF COURAGE) SPARTAN
(— OF INFLUENCE) CAPTAIN
HEAVYWEIGHT
(— OF MEAN BIRTH) GUTTERBLOOD
(— OF RANK) STATE MAGNATE
EMINENCE
(— RESEMBLING ANOTHER) SOSIA
(— TO SERVE WRIT) ELISOR
(— TOO STRONG FOR ASSAILANT)
TARTAR
(— WITH MENTAL TWIST) CRANK
(— WITH NERVOUS DISORDERS)
NEUROTIC
(— WITH QUEER IDEAS) ROZUM
(— WITHOUT STAMINA) JELLYFISH
(—S IN AMBASSADOR'S SUITE)
COMES
(ABJECT —) SLAVE
(ABSENT-MINDED —) MUSARD
(AFFECTED —) GIMCRACK
(AGGRESSIVE —) SHOVER HOTSHOT
(ANNOYING —) FIEND
(ARABIZED —) MOZARAB
(ARROGANT —) HUFF TENGU
(ATTRACTIVE —) CUTEY CUTIE
KNOCKOUT
(AVARICIOUS —) YISSER
(AWKWARD —) PUT GAWP HICK
RUBE SLAM STAG STEG STIFF
GUFFIN TUMFIE HOOSIER KITHOGE
LOBSTER SLOMMACK SPELDRIN
(BAD —) UNSEL

(BALD —) BALLARD BALDHEAD
SKINHEAD
(BANISHED —) WRETCH
(BAPTIZED —) MEMBER ILLUMINATO
(BASE —) CUT RASCAL CAITIFF
HILDING PUTTOCK
(BELOVED —) FLAME HEARTROOT
(BIG-BELLIED —) GORBELLY
(BLACK —) BLECK
(BOASTFUL —) BLOWER GASCON
(BOORISH —) GOOP
(CALLOW —) GORLIN SMARTY
GOSLING
(CANONIZED —) SAINT
(CARELESS —) HASH TASSEL
(CHICKENHEARTED —) HEN
(CHILDISH —) BAUBLE WHIMLING
(CHUNKY —) JUNT
(CHURLISH —) TIKE TYKE
(CIRCLE OF —S) COTERIE
(CLEVER —) BIRD WHIZ WHIZZ
MERCURY
(CLOWNISH —) BUFFOON HOBNAIL
VILLAIN
(CLUMSY —) DUB BOOB GAWK
SLOB TIKE TYKE JUMBO STAUP
STIFF DUFFER KEFFEL LUMMOX
HODMADOD
(COARSE —) COW STIRK BABOON
MUCKER
(COMBATIVE —) DRAGON
GAMECOCK
(COMMONPLACE —) MUT MUTT
BROMIDE
(CONCEITED —) IT HUFF COXCOMB
PRAGMATIC
(CONFUSED —) FOOSTERER
(CONTEMPTIBLE —) YAP HEEL PUKE
SCAB SKIN SWAB CATSO SHRUB
SKITE SKUNK SNIPE INSECT SHICER
STINKER BLIGHTER PETTITOES
(COWARDLY —) FUGIE SISSY SLINK
SQUIB
(CRAFTY —) TOD FILE SHARK
JESUIT
(CRAZED —) PSYCOPATH
(CRINGING —) SNAKE SNOOL
FLUNKY SPANIEL
(CRUEL —) LAMB FIEND MALISON
(CUNNING —) PIE
(DAINTY —) MIMMOCK
(DEAD —) DEFUNCT DECEASED
DECEDENT
(DECREPIT —) WITHERLING
(DEFORMED —) CRILE CALIBAN
HODMADOD
(DENSE —) DUFFER
(DEPRAVED —) SKATE
(DESPICABLE —) HOUND SLAVE
CAITIFF
(DESTITUTE —) PAUPER
(DIMINUTIVE —) BANTY MIDGE
BANTAM MIDGET
(DIRTY —) DRIVEL HOWLET
(DISABLED —) DUCK CRIPPLE
INVALID
(DISAGREEABLE —) GOOP PILL
QUAT SKITE RATBAG
(DISGRUNTLED —) SOREHEAD

(DISHONEST —) ROGUE ROTTER BEZONIAN
(DISLIKED —) WARLING
(DISSOLUTE —) RIBALD STRIKER
(DOLTISH —) BLOCK SWINE
(DRUNKEN —) LUSH TUMBREL TUMBRIL
(DULL —) LOB BORE DODO GOON GOOP GRUB LUMP MOME MOPE SLOB CLUNK DROUD STICK STOCK LACKWIT LOBCOCK OPACITY
(DULL-WITTED —) DOPE GUMP DUNCE
(DWARFISH —) CROWL SHURF
(DYING —) MORIBUND
(ECCENTRIC —) COON GINK TIKE TYKE GAZABO GAZEBO FANTAST
(EFFEMINATE —) SOFTY SQUAW SOFTIE BADLING SOFTLING SMOCKFACE
(ELDERLY —) SENIOR SOAKER GRAYHEAD
(EMACIATED —) FRAME WASTREL SKELETON
(EMPTY-HEADED —) NITWIT
(ENROLLED —) MEMBER
(ENTERTAINING —) COMÉDIAN
(EVIL —) QUED SCUM QUEDE SHREW
(EXPERIENCED —) EXPERT SOAKER STAGER
(EXTORTIONATE —) SCREW
(EXTRAORDINARY —) ONER BUSTER
(FADED —) SHARGAR SHARGER
(FAMOUS —) DON NOTORIETY
(FANTASTIC —) KICKSHAW
(FASHIONABLE —) GIMCRACK
(FASTIDIOUS —) MIMMOCK DELICATE
(FAT —) GURK BLIMP FATSO QUILT SQUAB STOUT
(FAWNING —) COGGER SPANIEL
(FEEBLEMINDED —) FEEB IDIOT MORON IMBECILE
(FEROCIOUS —) LAMB
(FICKLE —) ROVER MOONCALF
(FINE —) WHIPPA
(FLABBY —) HUDDERON
(FLASHY —) KID FLASHER
(FOOLISH —) FOP GUMP HOIT JERK BOOBY SOFTY BAUBLE DOODLE DOTARD DRIVEL HOWLET GOSLING GUBBINS
(FRANK —) TELLTRUTH
(FUSSY —) FAD FADDLE GRANNY SPOFFY GRANNIE
(GAY —) GRIG HUZZA
(GOOD-FOR-NOTHING —) KET PELF TASSEL WASTER WANHOPE WASTREL
(GOSSIPING —) SHULER SHUILER
(GOSSIPY —) BIGMOUTH NEWSMONGER
(GRAVE —) SOBERSIDES
(GREEDY —) GORB GRASPER PUTTOCK
(GROTESQUE —) GUY GOLLIWOGG
(GRUMPY —) SOURBELLY
(GULLIBLE —) JAY BOOB GULPIN

LOBSTER FLATHEAD SHLEMIEL WOODCOCK
(GYPSY —) CHI CHAI
(HARD —) MALISON
(HATEFUL —) TOAD
(HEAVY —) STODGER
(HEAVY-SET —) LUMP
(HOT-TEMPERED —) SPARK
(HUMPBACKED —) LORD
(HUNGRY —) HUNGARIAN
(IDLE —) RAGABASH SLUGGARD
(IGNORANT —) BABE BOOB PORK IDIOT
(ILL-BRED —) BOOR CHURL CLOWN
(ILL-MANNERED —) GRUB SKUNK
(ILL-NATURED —) CRAB HUNKS
(ILL-TEMPERED —) CRAB ETTERCAP TAISTREL
(IMMATURE —) BUD SQUAB GORLIN
(IMMORAL —) PERDU IMPURITAN
(IMPERTINENT —) PAUK PAWK SNIP
(IMPORTANT —) HONOR MUGWUMP
(IMPOTENT —) SPADO
(IMPUDENT —) SAUCE SQUIRT SAUCEBOX
(INANE —) SHAUP
(INEXPERIENCED —) BABE INGENUE BEGINNER
(INFERIOR —) BATA SHRUB SHABBLE
(INSIGNIFICANT —) DAB MUT MUTT BILSH CREEP JOKER SHURF SPRAT SQUIB ABLACH PEANUT PINKEEN WHIFFET GNATLING GRILDRIG PIGWIGEON
(INTRACTABLE —) BUCKIE TARTAR HAGGARD HARDCASE
(IRASCIBLE —) TOUCHWOOD
(LAME —) VULCAN
(LANK —) TANGLE GANGEREL
(LARGE —) CHUNK WHIPPA SKELPER STODGER STRAPPER
(LASCIVIOUS —) SUCCUBUS
(LAST — IN CONTEST) MELL
(LAZY —) BUM DAW HOIT POKE IDLER TRAIL LORDAN LURDAN BLELLUM LAZYLEGS SLUGGARD
(LEAN —) RIBE SHARGER THINGUT
(LEARNED —) CLERK ERUDIT ACHARYA SCHOLAR LITERATO WISEACRE LITERATUS
(LIGHTHEADED —) BEEHEAD
(LITERATE —) SCHOLAR
(LITTLE —) SMOLT SMOUT
(LIVELY —) GRIG BIRKIE HEMPIE WHISKER
(LOUD-VOICED —) STENTOR
(LOW —) PACK SCUM RASCAL BEASTMAN
(LOW SOCIETY —) MUDSILL
(LUBBERLY —) OAF
(LUMBERING —) PUMPKIN TUMBREL TUMBRIL
(LUMPISH —) DROUD
(LUSTY —) BILCH BILSH
(MAD —) MADLING
(MARRIED —) WIFE SPOUSE HUSBAND MATRIMONY
(MEAN —) RIP SCAB CHURL HOUND

MISER SKATE SNEAK SHICER BASTARD DOGBOLT BEZONIAN HUCKSTER STINKARD EARTHWORM
(MEDDLESOME —) BREVIT HESSIAN
(MISCHIEVOUS —) IMP LIMB PEST TOOL HEMPIE HELLION WHIPSTER
(MISERABLE —) SNAKE SWELP WRETCH
(MISERLY —) SKATE SCROOGE PINCHGUT PINCHBACK
(MONSTROUS —) WAMPUS
(NAIVE —) JERK CLUCK GUNSEL INGENUE INNOCENT
(NEGLECTED —) TACKY TACKEY
(NIMBLE —) MERCURY
(NOISY —) YAP HOWLET
(OBJECTIONABLE —) CUR COYOTE FOUTER
(OBSTINATE —) DONKEY STIFFNECK
(ODD —) GIG CURE QUIZZY RATBAG
(OFFENSIVE —) TICK SKITE STINKER
(OLD-FASHIONED —) FRUMP
(PALTRY —) PELTER
(PECULIAR —) BIRD CASE
(PEEVISH —) GRIZZLER SPLENETIC
(PERT —) PIE FLIRT
(POMPOUS —) PUFFIN POMPIST
(POT-BELLIED —) GORREL
(PRIVATE —) JUDEX
(PROSAIC —) PHILISTINE
(PRYING —) POKER PEEPER SMELLER
(PUGNOSED —) CAMUS CAMUSE
(PUNY —) SCART SHILP SHRIMP TITMAN
(PURITANICAL —) WOWSER
(QUEER-LOOKING —) JIGGER
(QUERULOUS —) GRUMP JACKDAW
(QUICK-TEMPERED —) SPUNKIE WILDCAT SPITFIRE
(RAGGED —) ROTO SHAGRAG TATTERWAG
(RAPACIOUS —) SHARK CATERER
(RECKLESS —) MADCAP RAMSTAM
(RED-HAIRED —) BRIQUE
(RESTLESS —) RAMPLER RAMPLOR RANTIPOLE
(RETICENT —) CLAM
(RICH —) MONEYBAGS
(RIDICULOUS —) GOOF HARE MONIMENT MONUMENT
(RIOTOUS —) ROARER
(ROUGH —) TOWSER
(ROUGH-LOOKING —) RULLION
(RUDE —) HICK PORK RULE CHURL CLOWN GROBIAN
(RUSTIC —) COON KERN KERNE HAYSEED HOMESPUN
(SAINTLY —) SADDIK
(SAUCY —) PIET
(SCRAWNY —) SCART SCRAG
(SELF-CENTERED —) HEEL DEVIL FLANEUR
(SELF-RIGHTEOUS —) PHARISEE
(SENSUAL —) SWING CARNALIST
(SHAMEFUL —) BISMER
(SHORT —) CRILE FADGE KNURL STUMP

(SHOWY —) FLASH FLASHER
HOTSHOT
(SHREWD —) FILE YEPE HARDHEAD
(SICK —) SICK MALADE PATIENT
AEGROTANT
(SILENT —) MUM MUMCHANCE
(SILLY —) FOP CAKE GUMP SOFT
DOBBY GOOSE SOFTY SPOON
CUCKOO NIMSHI SOFTIE GOOSECAP
LIRIPIPE LIRIPOOP SOFTHEAD
(SIMPLE —) DRIP LAMB IDIOT
PIGWIGEON
(SKINNY —) SCRAE SCARECROW
(SLATTERNLY —) SLATE
(SLIM —) SWABBLE
(SLOTHFUL —) SLOWBELLY
(SLOVENLY —) HASH SLOB SLORP
TRAIL STREEL SLOMMACK
STREELER
(SLUGGISH —) LUMP DOLDRUM
DRUMBLE LOBCOCK
(SLY —) COON SLYBOOTS
SNECKDRAW SNICKDRAW
(SMALL —) GRIG AGATE DWARF
SPRAT INSECT MORSEL POPPET
SACKET GNATLING
(SOPHISTICATED —) WELTKIND
(SPIRITLESS —) MOPE STICK
(SPITEFUL —) HELLCAT ETTERCAP
(SPRUCE —) SPRUSADO
(STINGY —) CHURL HAYNE STINGY
(STOCKY —) STUMP
(STOLID —) CLAM THICKSKIN
(STRANGE —) WAMPUS
(STRAY —) WAIF
(STUBBORN —) STOUT
(STUNTED —) URF SCRUNT
SHARGAR
(STUPID —) ASS DUB JAY MUT
BETE BOOB DODO DOLT DOPE DRIP
GAUM GAWP GOOF GUMP HASH
HOIT JERK MOKE MUTT BLOCK
BUCCA CLUCK CLUNK DUNCE
HOBBY JUKES LOACH MORON
SHEEP STIRK STOCK STUPE SUMPH
SWINE THICK WAMUS BOODLE
DAWKIN DIMWIT DODUNK DONKEY
DUFFER GANDER GILLIE GRANNY
GUNSEL LUMMOX LURDAN NITWIT
NOODLE SACKET STUPEX TUMFIE
TUMPHY BLUNTIE DULLARD
FATHEAD FUSSOCK HOWFING
JACKASS JUGHEAD MUDHEAD
SAPHEAD SCHNOOK BONEHEAD
BULLHEAD DOTTEREL DUMBBELL
FLATHEAD GAMPHREL IRONHEAD
MOLDWARP MUMPHEAD STUNPOLL
THICKWIT HODMANDOD
MUMCHANCE THICKHEAD
(STURDY —) LUMP CHUNK
STALWART
(SULKY —) GLUMP GRUMP SUMPH
GROUCH
(SURLY —) CRUST HUNKS
(TACITURN —) OYSTER
(TALKATIVE —) GASSER BLELLUM
BIGMOUTH
(TALL, AWKWARD —)
GAMMERSTANG

(TENDER —) LAMBKIN
(THICKSET —) NUGGET
(THIRD —) GOOSEBERRY
(THOUGHTLESS —) AIRLING
SKIPPER BIRDBRAIN
(TINY —) KEEROGUE
(TIRESOME —) BROMIDE PILLBORE
(TREACHEROUS —) JUDAS SNAKE
VIPER GUNSEL SERPENT
(TROUBLESOME —) COW PEST
HELLION HESSIAN
(TRUSTWORTHY —) TRAIST
STANDBY
(UNATTRACTIVE —) GOON GRUB
SCUG CREEP
(UNBENDING —) STIFF
(UNCHASTE —) SHORTHEELS
(UNCIVILIZED —) VISIGOTH
(UNCOUTH —) APE PUT STIFF
BABOON SLOMMACK
(UNDERSIZED —) DURGAN
SPARROW
(UNFAITHFUL —) INFIDEL
(UNHANDY —) FOUTER
(UNHAPPY —) UNSEL
(UNIQUE —) ONER
(UNKNOWN —) INCONNU STRANGER
(UNMARRIED —) MAIDEN AGAMIST
BACHELOR CELIBATE SPINSTER
(UNREASONABLE —) DUFFER
(UNSCRUPULOUS —) CATSO KNAVE
(UNSOPHISTICATED —) JAY HICK
NYAS HAYSEED CORNBALL
INNOCENT
(UNTHANKFUL —) INGRATE
(UNTIDY —) STREEL
(UNWIELDY —) FUSTILUGS
(USELESS —) POOP SWAB UNSEL
(VALOROUS —) HERO
(VENOMOUS —) SPITPOISON
(VIGOROUS —) SNEEZER
(VIOLENT —) DRAGON SPITFIRE
(VORACIOUS —) HUNGARIAN
(VULGAR —) MUCKER
(WANTON —) FLIRT WHIPSTER
(WEAK —) SHILP SOFTY WHIMLING
(WEAK-MINDED —) SAPHEAD
TOTTYHEAD
(WELL-BORN —) FREE
(WHITE —) FAY OFAY GRIFFIN
EUROPEAN PALEFACE
(WICKED —) DEVIL SATAN SHREW
UNLEAD UNLEDE SATANIST
(WILD —) HELLCAT RANTIPOLE
(WILY —) PIE
(WITHERED —) RUNT
(WITLESS —) WITHAM WITTOME
SLABBERER
(WITTY —) WITSHIP SPARKLER
(WORNOUT —) HUSHEL
(WORTHLESS —) YAP FILE GEAR
HOIT JADE LOON SCUM TOOT
CRUMB LOREL LOSEL SCOUT
SHAND BAUBLE BUGGER FELLOW
FOUTRA SHICER BUDMASH GULLION
BLIGHTER VAGABOND PHARMAKOS
(WRETCHED —) MISER MISERY
(YOUNG —) CUB KID COLT LAMB
CHILD HEMPY SMOLT SMOUT SPRIG

YONKE GUNSEL HEMPIE JUNIOR
CHICKEN CHOOKIE GRISTLE
LAMBKIN JUVENILE STRIPLING
(PL.) FRY
PERSONABLE COMELY SHAPELY
HANDSOME
PERSONAGE DON DUSE NIBS BLOKE
FIGURE SHOGUN TYCOON
(GREAT —) SOPHI SOPHY SUFFEE
PERSONAL SELF PRIVY DIRECT
PRIVATE CHATTELS CORPORAL
INTIMATE
(— EFFECTS) DUNNAGE
PERSONALITY EGO DRAW SELF
SOUL BEING ETHOS HEART EGOITY
FIGURE CONTROL FACULTY
DEMIURGE PRESENCE SELFHOOD
SELFNESS
PERSONATE ACT FEIGN MIMIC
MASKED PERSON TYPIFY PRESENT
PERSONATION (SHAM —) IDOL
PERSONIFICATION SOUL GENIUS
(— OF DIVINE VIRTUE) EON
(— OF JUSTICE) THEMIS
PERSONIFY EMBODY INCARNATE
PERSONIZE
PERSONNEL BLOOD STAFF KITCHEN
PHYSIQUE
PERSPECTIVE OPTICS DISTANCE
TELESCOPE
PERSPICACIOUS KEEN ACUTE
SHREWD
(MAKE —) CLEAR
PERSPICACITY WIT ACUMEN
PERSPICUOUS CLEAR LUCID PLAIN
PRECISE VISIBLE MANIFEST
LIGHTSOME
PERSPIRATION DEW SUDOR SUINT
SWEAT HIDROSIS OLIGIDRIA
SUDORESIS
PERSPIRE PUG MELT BREAN SWEAT
SWELTER TRANSPIRE
PERSUADE CON GET WIN COAX
GAIN RULE SNOW TICE URGE WISE
ARGUE BRING EDUCE SUADE
SWADE WEISE ADVISE ARGUFY
ASSURE CAJOLE ENGAGE ENTICE
INDUCE REMOVE SUBORN CONVERT
DISPUTE ENTREAT IMPRESS
PREVAIL SATISFY CANOODLE
INFLUENCE
PERSUADED PLIABLE GULLIBLE
RESOLVED SENSIBLE
PERSUASION KIND SORT BELIEF
SUASION JUDGMENT
PERSUASIVE COGENT INDUCTIVE
PROTEPTIC
PERT BOLD CHIC FESS FLIP KECK
SPRY TRIM ALERT ALIVE BARDY
BRISK COCKY DONSY KISKY PEART
PIERT QUICK SASSY SAUCY SMART
TAUNT CLEVER COCKET COMELY
DAPPER FRISKY SWASHY THWART
PAUGHTY INSOLENT PETULANT
(— TALK) CHELP
PERTAIN BE LIE BEAR COME LONG
BELIE TOUCH AFFEIR BEFALL
BELIMP BELONG RELATE RETAIN

CONCERN
(— TO) RINE
PERTAINING (— TO A BISHOP)
LAWN
(— TO AIR) AURAL PNEUMATIC
(— TO ALL NATURE) PAMPHYSIC
(— TO ANIMALS) ZOIC
(— TO ANKLE) TARSAL
(— TO APOLLO) PYTHIAN PAEONIAN
(— TO APOSTLE) PETRINE
(— TO ARMPIT) AXILLAR
(— TO ARMY) MARTIAL STRATONIC
(— TO ARROW) SAGITTAL
(— TO ATHENA) PALLADIAN
(— TO BACK) DORSAL TERGAL
(— TO BATH) BALNEAL
(— TO BEAM) TRAGAL
(— TO BEARD) BARBAL
(— TO BED) THORAL
(— TO BEES) APIAN APIARIAN
(— TO BELLY) ALVIN ALVINE
VENTRAL VENTRIC
(— TO BIBLICAL LAW) LEVITIC
(— TO BIRDS) AVIAN AVINE
ORNITHIC VOLUCRINE
(— TO BIRTH) NATAL
(— TO BODIES AT REST) STATIC
(— TO BODY) SOMAL SOMATIC
(— TO BONE) OSSAL OSTEAL
(— TO BOSOM) GREMIAL
(— TO BRACELET) ARMILLARY
(— TO BRANCHES) RAMOUS
(— TO BREADMAKING) PANARY
(— TO BREAKFAST) ENTACULAR
(— TO BREAST) PECTORAL
(— TO BREASTBONE) STERNAL
(— TO BRISTLES) SETAL
(— TO BROTHEL) STEWISH
(— TO BUNCH) COMAL
(— TO CALF OF LEG) SURAL
(— TO CALF) VITULINE
(— TO CART) PLAUSTRAL
(— TO CARTHAGINIANS) PUNIC
(— TO CARVING) GLYPHIC
(— TO CAVE) SPELEAN SPELUNCAR
(— TO CHAIN) CATENARY
(— TO CHAMBER) CAMERAL
(— TO CHARIOTEER) AURIGAL
(— TO CHEEK) MALAR
(— TO CHESS) SCACCHIC
(— TO CHINA) SINIAN SINISIAN
(— TO CITY) CIVIC URBAN
(— TO CLAN) SEPTAL
(— TO CLAY) BOLAR
(— TO CLOTHES) VESTIARY
VESTURAL
(— TO COINS) NUMMARY
NUMISMATIC
(— TO COLOR) CHROMATIC
(— TO COMB) PECTINAL
(— TO CONSTRUCTION) TECTONIC
(— TO CORK) SUBERIC SUBEROUS
(— TO COUGH) TUSSAL TUSSIVE
(— TO COURT) AULIC JUDICIAL
JUDICIARY
(— TO CROCKERY) PIG
(— TO CROWN) CORONAL
(— TO DANCING) SALTATORY
TRIPUDIAL

(— TO DAUGHTER OR SON) FILIAL
(— TO DAWN) EOAN
(— TO DEFENSE) PHYLACTIC
(— TO DESERTS) EREMIC
(— TO DIAPHRAGM) PHRENIC
(— TO DINNER) CENATORY
(— TO DOVE) COLUMBINE
(— TO DREAMS) ONEIRIC ONIROTIC
(— TO DRINKING) BIBITORY
(— TO EARTH) GEAL TELLURIC
TERRANEAN
(— TO EARTHQUAKE) SEISMAL
SEISMIC
(— TO EAST) EOAN
(— TO ESSENCE) BASIC
(— TO EUNUCH) SPADONIC
(— TO EVENING) VESPER
(— TO EYELIDS) BLEPHARAL
(— TO FACE) PROSOPIC
(— TO FAIR) NUNDINAL
(— TO FAITH) PISTIC
(— TO FEET) PEDAL PEDARY
(— TO FERMENTATION) ZYMIC
ZYMOTIC
(— TO FIELDS) AGRARIAN
(— TO FINGERS) DIGITAL
(— TO FISHING) HALIEUTIC
(— TO FLEAS) PULICENE PULICOSE
(— TO FLESH) SARCOUS
(— TO FLOCK) GREGAL
(— TO FLOOD) DILUVIAL DILUVIAN
(— TO FLOWERS) FLORAL ANTHINE
(— TO FOREARM) CUBITAL
(— TO FOREHEAD) METOPIC
(— TO FORM) MORPHIC
(— TO FOX) VULPINE
(— TO FRESH WATER) LIMNETIC
(— TO FROGS) ANURAN RANINE
(— TO FRUIT) POMONAL POMONIC
(— TO FUNERALS) EXEQUIAL
(— TO FUNGUS) MYCETOID
(— TO FURNACE) FORNACIC
(— TO GARDEN) HORTULAN
(— TO GARRISON) PRESIDIAL
(— TO GENTILES) ETHNIC
(— TO GLASS) VITREOUS
(— TO GOVERNMENT) ARCHICAL
POLITICAL
(— TO GRANDPARENTS) AVAL
(— TO GRINDING) MOLINARY
(— TO GROUND) SOLARY
(— TO GROVE) NEMORAL
(— TO GUMS) ULETIC GINGIVAL
(— TO HAIR) PILAR CRINAL PILARY
(— TO HAND) CHIRAL MANUAL
(— TO HEAD) CEPHALIC
(— TO HEAP) ACERVAL
(— TO HEART) CARDIAC
(— TO HEAT) CALORIC THERMAL
THERMIC
(— TO HIPS) SCIATIC
(— TO HOLIDAY) FERIAL
(— TO HORIZON) MUNDANE
(— TO HORSE) EQUINE HIPPIC
CABALLINE
(— TO HOSPITALITY) XENIAL XENIAN
(— TO HOUSE) DOMAL
(— TO HUNGER) FAMELIC
(— TO HUNTING) VENATIC VENERIAL

(— TO INTELLECT) NOETIC
(— TO INTESTINES) ALVIN ALVINE
(— TO JAW) MALAR GNATHAL
GNATHIC
(— TO JOURNEY) VIATIC
(— TO KIDNEY) RENAL NEPHRIC
(— TO KNOWLEDGE) GNOSTIC
(— TO LAP) GREMIAL
(— TO LAUGHING) GELASTIC
(— TO LAUGHTER) RISORIAL
(— TO LEARNING) PALLADIAN
(— TO LEG) CRURAL
(— TO LIFE) VITAL ZOETIC
(— TO LINE) FILAR
(— TO LIPS) LABIAL
(— TO LIVER) HEPATIC JECORAL
(— TO LOINS) LUMBAR
(— TO LOVE) EROTIC AMATORY
(— TO LUCK) ALEATORY
(— TO LUNGS) PULMONIC
PNEUMONIC PULMONARY
(— TO MANKIND) COMMON
ANTHROPIC
(— TO MARBLE) MARMORIC
(— TO MARKET) NUNDINAL
(— TO MARRIAGE) MARITAL
HYMENEAL
(— TO MARS) AREAN MAMERTINE
MAVORTIAL
(— TO MASS) MOLAR
(— TO MASTER) HERILE
(— TO MEADOWS) PRATAL
(— TO MECCA) MECCAWEE
(— TO MEMORY) MNESTIC
MNEMONIC
(— TO MIDDAY) MERIDIAN
(— TO MILK) LACTARY LACTEAL
(— TO MILL) MOLINARY
(— TO MIRROR) SPECULAR
(— TO MOISTURE) HYGRIC
(— TO MOON) LUNAR SELENIC
SELENIAN
(— TO MORNING) MATIN MATINAL
(— TO MOTION) GESTIC KINETIC
(— TO MOUNTAINS) MONTANE
(— TO MOUTH) ORAL OSCULAR
STOMATIC
(— TO MUSCLE) SARCOUS
(— TO MUSIC) HARMONIC
(— TO NAVEL) OMPHALIC
(— TO NECK) JUGULAR
(— TO NEPHEW) NEPOTAL
(— TO NIGHT) NOCTURNAL
(— TO NOSE) NASAL RHINAL
(— TO NUT) NUCAL
(— TO NUTRITION) TROPHIC
(— TO OAK) QUERCINE ROBOREOUS
(— TO OCEAN) PELAGIC OCEANOUS
THALASSIC
(— TO OLD AGE) SENILE GERATIC
GERONTIC
(— TO OPEN SKY) SUBDIAL
(— TO PARLOR) BEN BOOR
(— TO PASTURES) PASCUAL
(— TO PAWNBROKER) AVUNCULAR
(— TO PEACOCK) PAVONINE
(— TO PERSPIRATION) SUDORIC
(— TO PICTURE) ICONIC
(— TO PIGS) PORCINE

(— TO PINE) WARRYN
(— TO PLAGUE) LOIMIC
(— TO PLEASURE) HEDONIC
(— TO POETRY) MUSAL IAMBIC
(— TO POISON) TOXIC
(— TO POTTERY) CERAMIC
(— TO PRIESTS) SACERDOTAL
(— TO PRISON) CARCERAL
(— TO PULSE) SPHYGMIC
(— TO PUNISHMENT) PENAL
PUNITIVE
(— TO QUEEN) REGINAL
(— TO RAIN) HYETAL PLUVIAL
(— TO RAINBOW) IRIDAL
(— TO REMOTE PLACE) FORANE
(— TO RESONANCE) SYNTONIC
(— TO RING) ARMILLARY
(— TO RISING) ORTIVE
(— TO RIVER BANK) RIPARIAN
(— TO RIVER) AMNIC POTAMIC
RIVERINE FLUMINOSE
(— TO ROAD) VIATIC
(— TO ROCK) PETREAN SAXATILE
(— TO ROD) BACULINE
(— TO SABLES) ZIBELINE
(— TO SAIL) VELIC
(— TO SALVATION) SOTERIAL
(— TO SANDARAC) THYINE
(— TO SATURDAY) SABBATINE
(— TO SEAL) SIGILLARY
SPHRAGISTIC
(— TO SEAM) SUTURAL
(— TO SEASHORE) LITTORAL
(— TO SEAWEED) ALGOUS
(— TO SENSE OF TASTE)
GUSTATIVE
(— TO SHEEP) VERVECINE
(— TO SHEPHERDS) PASTORAL
(— TO SHERIFF) VICONTIEL
(— TO SHIN) CNEMIAL
(— TO SHIP) NAVICULAR
(— TO SHOPMAN) APOTHECAL
(— TO SHOULDER) ALAR SCAPULAR
(— TO SIGNS) SEMIC SEMANTIC
(— TO SILVER) ARGENTAL
(— TO SISTER) SORORAL
(— TO SKIN) DERIC DERMAL
CUTICULAR
(— TO SLEEP) SOMNIAL MORPHETIC
(— TO SNAKE) ANGUINE
(— TO SOFT PALATE) VELAR
(— TO SONG) MELIC
(— TO SPECTACLE) THEORIC
(— TO SPEECH) PHEMIC
(— TO SPINAL CORD) MYELIC
(— TO SPRING) VERNAL
(— TO STARS) ASTRAL STELLAR
SIDEREAL
(— TO STATE AFFAIRS) PRAGMATIC
(— TO STEPMOTHER) NOVERCAL
(— TO STOMACH) GASTRIC
(— TO STORKS) PELARGIC
(— TO SULPHUR) THIONIC
(— TO SUMMER) ESTIVAL AESTIVAL
(— TO SUN) SOLAR HELIAC
(— TO SUNDAY) DOMINICAL
(— TO SUNDIAL) SCIATHERIC
(— TO SUPPER) CENATORY
(— TO SURFACE OF ANYTHING)
FACIAL

(— TO SWALLOWS) HIRUNDINE
(— TO SWEAT) SUDORIC
(— TO SWIMMING) NATATORY
(— TO SWINEHERD) SYBOTIC
(— TO TAIL) CAUDAL
(— TO TAILOR) SARTORIAL
(— TO TEARS) LACRIMAL
LACHRYMAL
(— TO TEMPO) AGOGIC
(— TO THE BEAUTIFUL) ESTHETIC
AESTHETIC
(— TO THIEVING) KLEPTISTIC
(— TO THIGH) CRURAL
(— TO THREAD) FILAR
(— TO THROAT) GULAR JUGULAR
(— TO TILE) TEGULAR
(— TO TIN) STANNIC
(— TO TITHES) DECIMAL
(— TO TITMICE) PARINE
(— TO TOMB) TOMBAL
(— TO TONGUE) GLOSSAL LINGUAL
(— TO TORTOISES) CHELONIAN
(— TO TOUCH) TACTILE
(— TO TOWER) TURRICAL
(— TO TREES) DENDRAL ARBOREAL
(— TO TWENTY) VICENARY
(— TO UNCLE) AVUNCULAR
(— TO VESSEL) VASAL
(— TO VIRGIN) PARTHENIAN
(— TO VOW) VOTAL
(— TO WAGON) PLAUSTRAL
(— TO WALLS) MURAL PARIETAL
(— TO WAR) POLEMICAL
(— TO WASPS) VESPAL VESPINE
(— TO WAX) CERAL
(— TO WEAVING) TEXTORIAL
(— TO WEIGHT) BARIC PONDERAL
PONDERARY
(— TO WELL) PHREATIC
(— TO WHALES) CETIC
(— TO WHEAT) VULGARE
(— TO WHEELS) ROTAL
(— TO WIFE) UXORIAL
(— TO WIND) EOLIAN ONEUMATIC
(— TO WINE) VINIC VINOUS
(— TO WINE-MAKING) OENOPOETIC
(— TO WINGS) ALAR PTERIC
EXRUPEAL PTEROTIC
(— TO WINTER) HIEMAL
(— TO WISDOM) PALLADIAN
(— TO WOMANKIND) MULIEBRAL
(— TO WOODPECKERS) PICINE
(— TO WOODS) SYLVAN NEMORAL
(— TO WORMS) VERMICULAR
(— TO WOUNDS) VULNERAL
(— TO WRIST) CARPAL
(— TO YESTERDAY) PRIDIAN
(— TO YEW) TAXINE
PERTINACIOUS FIRM STIFF DOGGED
ADHERING STUBBORN OBSTINATE
PERTINENCY FORCE
PERTINENT APT FIT PAT HAPPY
COGENT PROPER TIMELY ADAPTED
APROPOS GERMANE POINTED
TELLING INCIDENT MATERIAL
RELATIVE RELEVANT
PERTURB BITE GRATE UPSET
WORRY DISMAY AGITATE CONFUSE

CONTURB DERANGE DISTURB
TROUBLE
PERTURBATION DISMAY FLIGHT
POTHER POOTHER STICKLE
TROUBLE TURMOIL EVECTION
AGITATION
PERTURBED UNEASY
PERTUSSIS COUGH CHINCOF
CHINCOUGH

PERU
CAPITAL: LIMA
COIN: SOL LIBRA DINERO
CENTAVO
DEPARTMENT: ICA LIMA PUNO
CUSCO CUZCO JUNIN PIURA
TACNA ANCASH LORETO
TUMBES
ISLAND: CHINCHA
LAKE: TITICACA
LANGUAGE: AYMARA QUECHUA
MEASURE: TOPO VARA GALON
CELEMIN FANEGADA
MOUNTAIN: HUAMINA COROPUNA
HUASCARAN
PERIOD: RECUAY
RIVER: NAPU RIMAC SANTA TIGRE
YAGUAS YAVARI CURARAY
MARANON PASTAZA UCAYALI
AMAZONAS APURIMAC
HUALLAGA URUBAMBA
TOWN: ICA LIMA PUNO CUZCO
PAITA PISCO CALLAO IQUITOS
AREQUIPA TRUJILLO
VOLCANO: MISTI YUCAMANI
WEIGHT: LIBRA QUINTAL

PERUKE WIG FLASH GALERA
TOUPEE GALERUM PERIWIG
WIGGERY
PERUSAL SIGHT LECTURE SCRUTINY
PERUSE CON READ SCAN STUDY
HANDLE SEARCH SURVEY EXAMINE
INSPECT
PERVADE FILL BATHE IMBUE
DRENCH INSTIL OCCUPY INSTILL
PERMEATE TRAVERSE
PERVADED STIFF
PERVERSE AUK AWK CAM CAR
AWRY WOGH WRAW CROSS DONSY
GAMMY THRAW WROTH CUSSED
DIVERS LOUCHE THRAWN THWART
WICKED WILFUL WRAIST AWKWARD
DIVERSE FORWARD FROWARD
OBLIQUE WAYWARD CAMSHACH
CRANKISH STUBBORN
PERVERSELY AUK AWK ATHWART
OVERWART
PERVERSION WREST ABUSION
(— OF TASTE) MALACIA
PERVERT WRY DRAW RACK RUIN
SKEW TURN WARP ABUSE CROOK
GLOSS TWIST UPSET DEBASE
DETORT DIVERT GARBLE INVERT
MISUSE POISON WRENCH WRITHE
CONTORT CORRUPT DEGRADE
DEPRAVE DEVIATE DISTORT
MISTURN SUBVERT TRADUCE

VITIATE MISWREST

PERVERTED BAD WICKED ABUSIVE
CORRUPT TWISTED VICIOUS

PERVERTER WRESTER

PERVIOUS LEACHY PERVIAL
PERVADING

PES NEUME TENOR PODATUS

PESKY VERY PLAGUY ANNOYING
DEVILING EXTREMELY

PESO DURO CONANT DOLLAR
CAROLUS PATACAO

PESSIMISM WELTSCHMERZ
MISERABILISM

PESSIMIST ALARMIST JEREMIAH
WORRYWART

PESSIMISTIC GLOOMY ALARMED
BEARISH CYNICAL DOWNBEAT

PEST BANE TICK WEED MOUSE
MYZUS TRAIK INSECT PLAGUE
SCHELM SORROW VERMIN NUDNICK
SANDMITE BUTTINSKY

PESTER DUN HOX NAG RIB TIG HAKE
ANNOY DEVIL TEASE WORRY
BADGER BOTHER HARASS INFEST
MOLEST BEDEVIL TORMENT
TROUBLE OBSTRUCT

PESTHOUSE LAZARET LAZARETTO

PESTICIDE BIOCIDE FUMIGANT

PESTILENCE PEST DEATH QUALM
PLAGUE MURRAIN EPIDEMIC
MORTALITY

PESTILENT FATAL DEADLY VEXING
NOXIOUS

PESTLE MIX BRAY GRIND PESTL
PILUM STAMP BEETLE BRAYER
MULLER PISTIL CHAPPER POUNDER
STAMPER

PET TOY CADE COAX DAUT DEAR
DUCK HUFF LAMB NECK PEAT SOCK
SULK TIFF DRUNT DUCKY HUMOR
QUIET SPOIL SPOON TETCH CARESS
CODDLE COSHER COSSET CUDDLE
DANDLE DAUTIE DAWTIE FADDLE
FANTAD FANTOD FONDLE GENTLE
PAMPER PETKIN SMOOCH SQUALL
STROKE WANTON CHERISH DARLING
INDULGE PINKENY TANTRUM
TIDLING UMBRAGE WHITHER
CANOODLE FAVORITE TIDDLING
PADDYWACK

PETAL ALA HELM HOOD LEAF WING
BANNER
(— **IN PEA FLOWER**) VEXILLUM
(— **OF IRIS**) STANDARD
(**UPPER** —) HOOD BANNER
(PL.) COROLLA

PETALIA NYCTERIS

PETARD PITTARD FIREWORK

PETATE BANIG

PETECHIA STIGMA

PETER P FADE FAIL PEAK SAFE
WANE CEASE PEDRO PIERS PIERRE
SIGNAL DWINDLE
(— **OUT**) FIZZLE

PETIOLE STEM SPINE STALK STIPE
PODEON PEDUNCLE PHYLLODE

PETITE SMALL LITTLE MIGNON
MIGNONNE

PETITION ASK BEG SUE BILL BOON

PLEA PRAY SUIT VOTE WISH APPLY
ORATE PLEAD APPEAL DESIRE
INVOKE MOTION PLACIT PRAYER
STEVEN ADDRESS BESEECH
ENTREAT IMPLORE ORATION
SOLICIT ROGATION SUFFRAGE
(**MAKE** —) SUE
(PL.) PRECES

PETITIONER BEGGAR ORATOR
SUITOR BEADSMAN ENTREATER
PLAINTIFF

PETO WAHOO

PETREL BILL TITI CAHOW MITTY
NELLY PRION WITCH SPENCY
TEETEE ASSILAG GLUTTON KAEDING
SEABIRD SEAFOWL STINKER
ALLAMOTH FORKTAIL STINKPOT
ALLAMOTTI NIGHTHAWK

PETRIFY DAZE DEADEN STONIFY
STUPEFY LAPIDIFY FOSSILIZE
GORGONIZE

PETRIFYING STONY GORGON

PETROL GAS GASOLINE

PETROLATUM VASELINE

PETROLEUM OIL CRUDE PETROL
NAPHTHA
(— **INDUSTRY**) OILDOM

PE-TSAI PECHAY

PETTED CADE DANDILY

PETTICOAT BAJO GORE KILT SLIP
SOUS DICKY GREEN JUPON PAGNE
SOUSE KIRTLE LUHINGA PLACKET
WHITTLE BALMORAL BASQUINE
WILYCOAT
(— **OF TARGET**) GREEN

PETTIFOG FOG CAVIL BICKER

PETTIFOGGER FOGGER SHYSTER
LEGULEIAN

PETTINESS NAGGLE PARVINIMITY

PETTING COLLING

PETTISH HUFFY FRETFUL PEEVISH
PLAINTIVE

PETTY TIN BASE JERK MEAN ORRA
PUNY VAIN GRIMY MINOR PETIT
PUNEE SMALL MEASLY MINUTE
PALTRY PEANUT POKING PUISNE
PUSILL SNIFTY KITLING PIMPING
TRIVIAL TWATTLE CHILDISH
FIDDLING INFERIOR NIGGLING
NUGATORY PICAYUNE SNIPPETY
TRIFLING PAROCHIAL

PETULANT PERT CROSS SAUCY
SHORT TESTY TIFFY FEISTY SULLEN
WANTON WILFUL CRABBED FRETFUL
FROWARD HUFFISH PEEVISH
WASPISH PERVERSE SNAPPISH

PEUMUS BOLDU

PEW PUE BOUT DESK PFUI PUGH
SEAT SLIP BENCH BUGHT STALL
BOUGHT

PEWEE PEWIT PEEWEE

PEWTER CUP BIDRI BIDRY MONEY
PUDER BIDERY TRIFLE PEAUDER
SADWARE TUTENAG
(— **MARK**) TOUCHMARK

PEYOTE HIKULI

PFENNIG PENNING

PHAEDRA (**FATHER OF** —) MINOS
(**HUSBAND OF** —) THESEUS

PHAETON DUKE FAETON SPIDER
STANHOPE

PHAETON BUTTERFLY BALTIMORE

PHALANGER ARIEL TAPOA CUSCUS
OPOSSUM PENTAIL SQUIRREL

PHALAROPE LOBIPED COOTFOOT
LOBEFOOT WHALEBIRD

PHALERA BEAD BOSS DISK STUD
CAMEO

PHANTASM DREAM FANCY GHOST
VAPOR FIGURE SHADOW SPIRIT
FANTASY PHANTOM SPECIES
SPECTER SPECTRE

PHANTASMAL UNREAL SPECTRAL

PHANTASY FANCY FANTASY
PHANTASIA

PHANTOM IDOL BOGEY BOGLE
DUMMY GHOST IMAGE PHASM
SHADE SHAPE UMBRA BOGGLE
DOUBLE FANTOM IDOLON IDOLUM
SHADOW SPIRIT BUGBEAR EIDOLON
ELUSIVE FANTASY SPECIES
SPECTER ILLUSORY ADAMASTOR

PHARAOH ALE FARO PHARO TYRANT
BUSIRIS

PHARAOH'S HEN VULTURE

PHARISEE MUGWUMP NICODEMUS

PHARMACIST DRUGGIST DISPENSER

PHARMACY FERMACY DRUGSTORE

PHAROS CLOAK LIGHT TORCH
BEACON LANTERN

PHARYNGEAL FAUCAL

PHARYNX MASTAX PROBOSCIS

PHASE EFT END LEG FAZE SIDE
ANGLE FACET GRADE STAGE
ASPECT AVATAR BACKLASH
PASSOVER DICHOTOMY
(**INITIAL** —) BUD
(**LOWEST** —) BATHOS
(**TRANSITORY** —) STREAK

PHASM FANTOM METEOR PHASMA
PHANTOM

PHEASANT CHIR GUAN ARGUS
CHEER KALIJ MINAL MONAL
GROUSE LEIPOA MAGPIE MONAUL
MOONAL PUKRAS KALLEGE
FIREBACK ITHAGINE RINGNECK
TRAGOPAN MACARTNEY
(**BREEDING PLACE FOR** —**S**) STEW
(**BROOD OF** —**S**) NID NYE NIDE
(**YOUNG** —) POULT

PHEASANT CUCKOO COUCAL

PHEASANT DUCK PINTAIL
MERGANSER

PHEASANT FINCH WAXBILL

PHEASANT'S-EYE ROSARUBY

PHELLEM CORK SUBER

PHENOBARBITOL LUMINAL

PHENOCRYST INSET

PHENOL LACCOL THYMOL ALOESOL
CREOSOL DURENOL EUGENOL
ORCINOL CHAVICOL RESORCIN

PHENOMENON FIRE ANOMY COLOR
EVENT IMAGE ARTHUS EFFECT
METEOR MIRAGE SHADOW ISOTOPY
MIRACLE PARADOX PROCESS
SYMPTOM ASTERISM PRAKRITI
SIDERISM SUNQUAKE LANDSPOUT

PHENYLSALICYLATE SALOL

PHIAL CUP FIAL VIAL BOTTLE
VESSEL
PHILABEG KILT FILIBEG
PHILANDER FOOL WOLF DALLY
FLIRT SMOCK
PHILANTHROPIC HUMANE
PHILANTHROPIST ALTRUIST
HUMANITARIAN
PHILANTHROPY CHARITY
ALMSGIVING
PHILIP PIP PHILP SPARROW
PHILIPPIC SCREED TIRADE ABUSIVE
DIATRIBE

PHILIPPINES
ARCHIPELAGO: SULU
CAPITAL: BAGUIO MANILA
QUEZONCITY
COIN: PESO PESETA CENTAVO
FIBER: ERUC ABACA BUNTAL
ISLAND: CEBU BOHOL LEYTE
LUZON PANAY SAMAR NEGROS
MASBATE MINDORO PALAWAN
MINDANAO
LAKE: TAAL LANAO
LANGUAGE: MORO BICOL IBANAG
ILOCANO TAGALOG VISAYAN
MEASURE: LOAN BRAZA CABAN
CAUAN CHUPA GANTA APATAN
BALITA QUINON
MOUNTAIN: APO IBA MAYON
PULOG BANAHAO
NATIVE: ATA ATI ITA TAO AETA
ATTA ETAS MORO SULU BICOL
TAGAL VICOL IGOROT TIMAUA
BISAYAN TAGALOG FILIPINO
PROVINCE: ABRA ALBAY CAPIZ
DAVAO LANAO RIZAL CAVITE
ILOILO TARLAC SURIGAO
RIVER: ABRA AGNO MAGAT PASIG
AGUSAN LAOANG CAGAYAN
MINDANAO PAMPANGA
TOWN: AGOA CEBU ALBAY DAVAO
LAOAG PASAY VIGAN APARRI
BAGUIO CAVITE ILAGAN ILOILO
MANILA BACALOD BASILAN
DAGUPAN CALOOCAN
TREE: DAO IBA TUA TUI ACLE
ANAM ATES BOGO DITA IPIL
GUIJO LAUAN LIGAS ALUPAG
ANAHAU ARANGA ANONANG
APITONG TINDALO ALMACIGA
AMPALAYA
VOLCANO: APO MAYO CANLAON
WEIGHT: CATTY FARDO PICUL
PUNTO LACHSA QUILATE
CHINANTA

PHILISTINE BOOB GIGMAN MUCKER
BABBITT GITTITE BOEOTIAN
BARBARIAN BOURGEOIS HYPOCRITE
(PL.) PULESATI PURASATI
CAPHTORIM
PHILOLOGIST LAVENGRO LINGUIST
PHILOLOGY SEMITICS
PHILOMACHUS MACHETES
PHILOMELA STOP FILOMEL
(FATHER OF —) PANDION
(RAVISHER OF —) TEREUS

(SISTER OF —) PROCNE
(SLAIN BY —) ITYS
PHILOSOPHER WIT SAGE CYNIC
STOIC ARTIST IONIAN LEGIST
DOTTORE ELEATIC ERISTIC
SCHOLAR SOPHIST SUMMIST
THINKER ZETETIC ACADEMIC
EPOCHIST MAGICIAN VIRTUOSO
ACADEMIST ALCHEMIST DIALECTIC
PHYSICIAN SCHOOLMAN
PHILOSOPHER'S STONE ADROP
MICROCOSM
PHILOSOPHIC SAGE
PHILOSOPHY ETHICS GOSPEL
SYSTEM TAOISM APRISMO COSMISM
DUALISM INQUIRY MIMAMSA
SCEPSIS HINDUISM HUMANISM
IDENTISM IDEOLOGY LEGALISM
OCCAMISM STOICISM NOUMENISM
SOCRATISM VEDANTISM
(— OF LIFE) LIGHTS
PHILTER DRUG CHARM WANGA
FILTER POTION AMATORY
PHLEBOTOMIZE BLEED VENESECT
PHLEBOTOMUS TATUKIRA
PHLEGM FLEM GLEET MUCUS
WATER FLEUME PITUITE MOUSEWEB
PHLEGMATIC CALM COOL DULL
SLOW INERT MUCOID SLEEPY
WATERY VISCOUS COMPOSED
SLUGGISH APATHETIC IMPASSIVE
PHLOEM BAST LEPTOME
PHLOGISTIC FIERY HEATED
BURNING FLAMING
PHLOMIS SAGELEAF
PHLOX CYME FLOX ALBION BEACON
COBAEA
PHOEBE FEBE FIVE MOON DIANA
PEWEE ARTEMIS
(DAUGHTER OF —) LETO
(MOTHER OF —) GAEA
PHOEBUS SUN APOLLO PHOIBUS
PHOENICIA (COLONY OF —)
CARTHAGE
(GODDESS OF —) TANIT BALTIS
TANITH ASTARTE
(KING OF —) AGENOR
(TOWN OF —) ACRE TYRE SIDON
SAREPTA
PHONEME MORPH TONEME
LARYNGAL
PHONEMIC BROAD
PHONOGRAM LOGOGRAM
SINOGRAM
PHONOGRAPH VIC PHONO
VICTROLA
(— RECORD) DISK PLATTER
PHONY FAKE SHAM BOGUS FAKER
FALSE BRUMMY BUNYIP PHONEY
IMPOSTOR SPURIOUS
PHOSPHATE EHLITE FLOATS
APATITE CABOCLE CACOXENE
GRIPHITE
PHOSPHORESCENCE BRIMING
MARFIRE
PHOSPHORESCENT PHOSPHOR
NOCTILUCOUS
PHOTISM SYNOPSY
PHOTOENGRAVER ZINCOGRAPHER

PHOTOENGRAVING HALFTONE
HELIOGRAPH
PHOTOGRAPH MUG FILM LENS
SNAP CARTE IMAGE PHOTO SHOOT
STILL CANDID GLOSSY MOSAIC
RETAKE SCENIC STEREO AIRVIEW
PICTURE TINTYPE LIKENESS
PORTRAIT SNAPSHOT TABLETOP
CYCLOGRAM
(— SIZE) PANEL
(X-RAY —) SKIAGRAM
PHOTOGRAPHER LENSMAN
CAMERIST CAMERAMAN
PHOTOGRAPHY STEREO
PHOTOGENY
PHOTOMETER LUCIMETER
PHOTOMONTAGE COLLAGE
PHOTON BOSON TROLAND
PHRASE CRY HIT MOT SET CRIB
FUSS HAVE IDEA TERM WORD
COMMA COUCH IDIOM LABEL
LEMMA POINT STATE STYLE TOPIC
TROPE BYWORD CLAUSE CLICHE
DITTON DORISM GRUPPO HOBNOB
NOTION PNEUMA PRAISE SAVING
SLOGAN ATTACCO DICTION EPITHET
PASSAGE CONCEIVE DIVISION
DORICISM FLATTERY IDEOGRAM
IRISHISM LATINISM LEITMOTIV
(— DIFFERENTLY) TURN
(— UNCTUOUSLY) DROOL
(MUSICAL —) ATTACCO SUBJECT
(PET —) SHIBBOLETH
(REDUNDANT —) CHEVILLE
(STOCK —) CANT
(TRITE —) CLICHE
(WELL-TURNED —) STROKE
PHRASEOLOGY CANT STYLE
DIALECT DICTION WORDING
LOCUTION PARLANCE
PHRATRY CLAN
PHRENETIC PYTHIAN FRENETIC
PHRENIC MENTAL
(PL.) PSYCHOLOGY
PHRIXOS (FATHER OF —) ATHAMUS
(MOTHER OF —) NEPHELE
(SISTER OF —) HELLE
PHRYGIA (GOD OF —) ATYS ATTIS
SABAZIOS
(KING OF —) MIDAS
PHRYNIN BUFIDIN
PHTHISIS DECAY
PHYLACTERY FILACTERY
(PL.) TEFILLIN TEPHILLIN
PHYLE TRIBE
PHYLUM HOKA CLASS HOKAN
NADENE BRYOZOA ANNELATA
ANNELIDA CHORDATA DIVISION
LIGNOSAE
PHYMA TUMOR
PHYSALIS POP POPPER TOMATILLO
PHYSETER CATODON
PHYSIC CURE HEAL FISIC PURGE
TRADE REMEDY MEDICAL NATURAL
RELIEVE DRUGGERY
PHYSICAL ILL LUSTY SOMAL BODILY
CARNAL DISTAL NATURAL SOMATIC
CORPORAL CURATIVE EXTERNAL
MATERIAL CORPOREAL

(PURELY —) BRUTE
PHYSICIAN ASA DOC PILL CURER
GALEN HAKIM LEECH MEDIC QUACK
ARTIST BAIDYA DOCTOR FELLOW
HEALER INTERN MEDICO DOTTORE
EMPIRIC SURGEON ALIENIST
RESIDENT SAWBONES SUNDOWNER
PHYSICIST HYLOZOIST
PHYSIC NUT TUBA CURCAS PIGNON
TARTAGO
PHYSIOCRAT ECONOMIST
PHYSIOGNOMY MUG FACE PHIZ
PHIZZ VIZNOMY PORTRAIT
VISENOMY
PHYSIOLOGY BIONOMY ZOONOMY
PHYSIQUE BODY BUILD COOST
HABIT FIGURE STRENGTH
PHYSOCARPUS NEILLIA OPULASTER
PHYSOSTIGMINE ESERE ESERINE
PHYTOMER PHYTON PODIUM
PI JUMBLE CONFUSE PREACHY
CONFUSION
PIA PI GABI GABGAB MARMOT
PIACLE SIN CRIME GUILT OFFENSE
PIAN YAWS FRAMBESIA
PIANETTE PYNOT PIANINO
PIANIST CEMBALIST CLAVIERIST
PIANO SOFT FLOOR GRAND GRANT
STORY FLUGEL GENTLY SOFTLY
SPINET SQUARE CLAVIAL CLAVIER
GIRAFFE PIANOLA QUIETLY UPRIGHT
MELOTROPE
PIASSAVA IYO JARA BAHIA PIACABA
PIASTER KURUS
PIATTI CYMBALS
PIAZZA PORCH SQUARE BALCONY
GALLERY PORTICO VERANDA
PIAZZETTA
PIC PEAK LANCE PIQUE PICADOR
PICA M EM LINE
PICARD PYKAR
PICARO KNAVE ROGUE TRAMP
BOHEMIAN VAGABOND
PICAROON ROGUE PICARO PIRATE
CORSAIR WRECKER
PICAYUNE PIC PETTY MEASLY
PALTRY PISTAREEN
PICCADILL RABATA REBATE REBATO
PICCOLO BUSBOY JUKEBOX
FLAUTINO OTTAVINO
PICHICIAGO ARMADILLO
CHLAMYPHORE
PICK NIB BILL CULL GAFF HACK LIFT
PIKE PILK SHOT WALE ADORN
BEELE BREAK CAVIL ELECT FLANG
LEASE PILCH PLUCK PRIDE CHOICE
CHOOSE GATHER PICKAX PUDDLE
TWITCH BARGAIN CASCROM
DIAMOND DRESSER MANDREL
(— APART) TOW
(— OUT) CULL SPOT TAKE WELE
CRONE GLEAN GARBLE SELECT
(— POCKETS) FIG FILE FOIST
TOUCH
(— TOBACCO) STRIP
(FILLING —) ABB
PICKAX PIX BEDE BILL PIKE GURLET
TUBBER TWIBIL TWIBILL
PICKED PICK TRIM PIKED CHOSEN

DAINTY PEAKED SELECT ADORNED
POINTED
PICKER COD HOPPER
(BERRY —) HURTER
(PEA —) VINER
PICKEREL JACK SNAKE DUNLIN
SAUGER SLINKER WALLEYE
PICKERELWEED TULE WAMPEE
PICKER-UP FINDER
PICKET PEG PALE POST TERN
FENCE STAKE FASTEN PALING
TETHER ENCLOSE FORTIFY PICQUET
PALISADE OUTPICKET
PICKLE BOX ALEC DILL MESS PECK
ACHAR BRINE GRAIN MANGO SAUCE
SOUSE ATSARA CAPERS DAWDLE
HIGDON KERNEL KIMCHI MUDDLE
NIBBLE PIDDLE PILFER PLIGHT
TRIFLE CONDITE CONFECT TROUBLE
VITRIOL MARINADE
(FISH —) ALEC
PICKLED DRUNK MURIATED
POWDERED MARINATED
PICKLOCK LOCK PICKER
PICK-ME-UP SCREW PICKUP
PICKPOCKET DIP FIG GUN NIP
BUNG FILE WIRE DIVER FILER FOIST
BUZZER CANNON DIPPER FIGBOY
HOOKER RATERO FOISTER
MOBSMAN CLYFAKER CUTPURSE
KNUCKLER BUZZGLOAK
(HELPER OF —) STALL BULKER
PICKUP BRUSH TRUCK ARREST
BRACER ANACRUSIS
PICNIC FRY BALL GIPSY GYPSY
BURGOO FROLIC MAROON OUTING
SHOULDER SQUANTUM SUMMERING
PICOT LOOP PEARL PERLE
PICOTAH SWEEP PACOTA
PICTOGRAPH GLYPH PICTOGRAM
PICTORIAL GRAPHIC
PICTURE GAY MAP OIL COPY DAUB
ICON IKON LIMN SIGN VIEW DECAL
FRAME IMAGE LINER PAINT PHOTO
PIECE PINAX PRINT SCENE SHAPE
STAMP STORY TABLE CACHET
CANVAS CHROMO CUTOUT DEPICT
EMBLEM MARINE PASTEL SEMBLE
SHADOW STEREO TABLET CUTAWAY
DIORAMA DIPTYCH EMBLEMA
ETCHING EXHIBIT FASHION FEATURE
GOUACHE GRAPHIC HISTORY
MIZRACH PAYSAGE PORTRAY
PORTURE RETRAIT SCENERY
TABLEAU VANDYKE AIRSCAPE
AUTOTYPE DESCRIBE DROLLERY
ENVISION IDEOGRAM KAKEMONO
LANDSKIP LIKENESS MAKIMONO
MONOTINT OVERDOOR PAINTING
PORTRAIT PROSPECT RITRATTO
SEASCAPE SINGERIE SKYSCAPE
TRIPTYCH VIGNETTE ENCAUSTIC
(— IN 3 COMPARTMENTS) TRIPTYCH
(— IN BOOK) GAY
(— MAT) SPANDREL
(— OF MONKEYS) SINGERIE
(— ON ROLLER) KAKEMONO
MAKIMONO
(— PUZZLE) REBUS JIGSAW

(—S IN BOOKS) BABY
(COMIC —) DROLLERY
(RELIGIOUS —) TANKA
(STEREOSCOPIC —) ANAGLYPH
PICTURESQUE VIVID EXOTIC QUAINT
SCENIC GRAPHIC IDYLLIC ROMANTIC
PICTORIAL
PICUL TAN PICO PIKOL
PIDDLE PICK PLAY DAWDLE PICKLE
PUTTER TRIFLE
PIDDLING JERK PALTRY TRIVIAL
USELESS FOOTLING TRIFLING
JERKWATER
PIDDOCK DACTYL PHOLAD PHOLAS
PIDGIN LANGUAGE SABIR
PIE PAI FLAM FLAN HEAP MESS PATE
PILE TART DOWDY FLAWN PASTY
PATTY TORTA TOURT AFFAIR
BRIDLE CHEWET MAGPIE PASTRY
TOURTE COBBLER SMASHER
STRUDEL BAKEMEAT CRUSTADE
FLAPJACK PANDOWDY SURPRISE
TURNOVER SMASHOVER
PIEBALD PIE PIED PIET MIXED PIETY
PINTO CALICO MOTLEY SKEWBALD
PIECE BAT BIT COB CUT DAM FIG
JOB LAB LOG MAN TUT GIRL MIND
PART PISE PLAY DAGON DRAMA
DWANG FLOOR PEZZO SCRAP
SHARD SHERD SHRED SLICE SNODE
STEEK STUCK THROW COLLOP
FARDEL FUGATO GOBBET PARCEL
STITCH CANTLET EXAMPLE FLINDER
FLITTER MORCEAU OPINION
PICTURE PORTION SEGMENT
DUOLOGUE EMBOLIUM FANDANGO
PAINTING
(— AT END) HEELPIECE
(— FOR TWO) DUET DUOLOGUE
(— IN CHECKERS) DAM
(— IN ORGAN) THUMPER
(— OF ARMOR) JAMB JAMBE
(— OF BAD LUCK) DIRDUM
(— OF BLANKET) DAGON
(— OF BLUBBER) BIBLE
(— OF DECEPTION) BEGUNK
(— OF DECORATED METAL) NIELLO
(— OF FALSE HAIR) JANE
(— OF FIBER) NOIL
(— OF FIRED CLAY) TILE
**(— OF GROUND SURROUNDED BY
WASTE)** HOPE
(— OF HARD WOOD) MOOT
(— OF LAND) HAM LOT BUTT GORE
LEASE SPONG SQUAT HUERTA
RINCON SECTION SOLIDATE
(— OF LIGHT ORDNANCE) ASPIC
(— OF LINEN) AMIT AMICE
(— OF LOG) SLAB
(— OF MAST) TONGUE
(— OF MATZOTH) AFIKOMEN
(— OF MEAT) EYE HEEL RAND
COLLOP EPIGRAM
(— OF METAL) JAG COIN JAGG
SPRAG
(— OF MONEY) COG SOU SHINER
(— OF NEEDLEWORK) SAMPLER
(— OF NONSENSE) FUDGE
TRIMTRAM

(— **OF ORE**) CHAT
(— **OF SAIL**) HULLOCK
(— **OF SEPARATED LAND**) BUTT
(— **OF SKIN FOR GLOVE**) TRANK
(— **OF SKIN**) BLYPE
(— **OF SLATE**) SLAT
(— **OF SOAP**) BALL
(— **OF SOMETHING EDIBLE**) STULL
(— **OF TIMBER**) FISH COULISSE FOREHOOK
(— **OF TOAST**) SLINGER
(— **OF TOBACCO**) FIG
(— **OF TRACK**) LEAD RUNBY
(— **OF TRICKERY**) CROOK
(— **OF TURF**) FLAG DIVOT SCRAW SHIRREL
(— **OF WOOD**) KIP LATH APRON BOARD CHUMP CHUNK PLANK SPOON WADDY BILLET COMMON STOWER TIMBER LIPPING
(— **OF WORK**) JOB CHAR TURN
(— **OF WRITING**) SCREED SCREEVE
(— **OUT**) EKE
(— **SPLIT OFF**) SPLINT
(— **TO PREVENT SLIPPING**) CLEAT
(—**S OF MACARONI**) DITALI DITALINI
(**100-REAL GOLD** —) ISABELLA
(**25-CENT** —) CUTER
(**4-DOLLAR GOLD** —) STELLA
(**ARTILLERY** —) DRAKE SAKER LANTACA
(**BACKGAMMON** —) STONE
(**BROAD** —) SHEET
(**BROKEN** —) BRACK FRACTION
(**BUTTING** —) HURTER
(**CHESS** —) PIN KING PAWN ROOK QUEEN BISHOP CASTLE KNIGHT OFFICER
(**END** — **OF BUCKET**) CANT
(**FLAT** —) FLAP FLAKE
(**FUR** —) PALATINE
(**GOLD** —) SLUG TALI
(**IN** —**S**) LIMBMEAL
(**IRREGULAR** —) SNAG
(**LARDED** — **OF MEAT**) DAUB
(**LARGE** —) HUNK MOLE STULL DOLLOP
(**LITERARY** —) CAMEO
(**LITTLE** —) STNEKI
(**LONG** —) STRIP
(**MOVABLE** — **IN VIOLIN BOW**) NUT
(**MUSICAL** —) ITEM CHORO DANCE ETUDE CHASER LESSON ALLEGRO ANDANTE CONCERTO DUOLOGUE ENTRACTE INVENTION
(**NARROW** —) LABEL STAVE STRIP
(**ODD** — **OF CARPENTRY**) DUTCHMAN
(**ROTATING** —) CAM ROTOR SPINDLE
(**SAMPLE** —) SWATCH
(**SHAPELESS** —) DUMP MAMMOCK
(**SIDE** —) RIB JAMB JAMBE
(**SINGLE** —) LENGTH
(**SLENDER** —) SPILL SLIVER
(**SMALL** — **OF FLESH**) GIGOT
(**SMALL** — **OF WOOD**) KIP
(**SMALL** —) BIT BOB NOB PEA CHIP SNIP TATE CRUMB PATCH PRILL

SCRAP SPECK MORSEL SIPPET DRIBLET FLITTER PALLION SPLINTER
(**SMALL** —**S**) MATCHWOOD
(**STRENGTHENING** —) DWANG HURTER
(**TAPERING** —) GORE GUSSET
(**THICK** —) JUNK HUNCH
(**THIN** —) SHIM FLAKE SHIVE SLICE
(**WEDGESHAPED** — **OF WOOD**) GLUT SHIM
(**PL.**) MATERIAL NOBLEMEN
PIECEWORK SETWORK TUTWORK TASKWORK
PIECEWORKER JOBBER
PIECRUST BREAD COFFIN ABAISSE
PIED PINTO SHELD MAGPIED PIEBALD
PIED ANTELOPE BONTEBOK
PIEDFORT PATAGON
PIED WAGTAIL COB COBB PEER PILE PILLAR WAGGIE WASHER WATERIE SEEDBIRD WASHDISH WASHTAIL
PIEPLANT RHUBARB RHAPONTIC
PIER COB ANTA BELT COBB DOCK MOLE PILE QUAY TILT GROIN JETTY JOWEL JUTTY LEVEE STILT WHARF BRIDGE BUNDER MULLION STAGION PIEDROIT STELLING
(— **CAP**) SUMMER
(**HALF** —) RESPONSE
PIERCE CUT DAB DAG DEG DIG JAB RIT BARB BEAR BITE BORE BROB BROD CLOY DART DIRL GORE HOLE HOOK LACE LACK PASS PINK PROB RIVE ROVE STAB STOB TAME TANG WHIP BREAK DRILL ENTER GOUGE GRIDE LANCE PERCH PITCH POACH PREEN PROBE PRONG SHEAR SNICK SPEAR SPIKE STEEK STICK STING THIRL ATTAME BROACH CLEAVE DAGGER EMPALE FICCHE GIMLET IMPALE LAUNCH PRITCH RIDDLE SEARCH SKEWER STITCH STRIKE THRILL THRING THRUST WIMBLE ASSAGAI JAVELIN ENTHRILL LACERATE PUNCTURE
PIERCED AJOURE CRIBRAL PERTUSE CRIBROSE PERFORATE
PIERCING SHY FELL HIGH KEEN LOUD TART CLEAR EAGLE SHARP SNELL ARROWY BITTER BORING SHREWD SHRILL SNITHE SNITHY CUTTING GIMLETY POINTED PUNGENT DRILLING INCISIVE PERCEANT POIGNANT POUNCING STABBING STICKING
PIERHEAD MOLEHEAD
PIET PYOT DIPPER MAGPIE
PIETIST LABADIST
PIETISTIC DEVOUT
PIETY HONOR LOYALTY PIETISM DEVOTION SANCTION GODLINESS
PIFFLE FOLDEROL
PIG (ALSO SEE HOG, SWINE) COW FAR HAM HOG SLIP BACON BONAV BROCK CHEAT CHUCK GRICE INGOT PIGGY SHOAT APEREA BONHAM COCHON FARROW GUSSIE HOGGIE PORKET PORKIN SUCKER TITMAN

WEANER BONNIVE GLUTTON GRUMPHY HOGLING PIGLING ROOKLER GRUNTLING
(**BROOD OF** —**S**) TEAM
(**EIGHT** —**S**) FODDER
(**SMALLEST** — **OF LITTER**) TITMAN ANTHONY DILLING TANTANY TANTONY
(**SUCKLING** —) ROASTER
(**UNDERSIZED** —) RUNT TITMAN TEATMAN
(**YOUNG** —) ELT FAR SLIP GRICE GURRY BONEEN BONHAM SQUEAKER
PIG DEER BABIRUSA
PIGEON DOO NUN OWL TOY BARB CLAY DOVE JACK KING KITE LUPE RUFF RUNT SPOT BALDY DOWVE FRILL HOMER KOKLA PIPER SQUAB WONGA CULTER CULVER CUSHAT DODLET DRAGON FEEDER HELMET JEWING MAGPIE MANUMA MAUMET MODENA POUTER PRIEST ROCKER SHAKER THROON TURBIT TURNER WATTLE ANTWERP CARNEAU CARRIER CROPPER FANTAIL FINIKIN JACOBIN MALTESE PINTADO SWALLOW TIPPLER TUMBLER BALDHEAD CAPUCHIN FINIKING HORSEMAN MANUTAGI RINGDOVE SQUABBER SQUEAKER SQUEALER FRILLBACK TOOTHBILL
(**CLAY** —) BIRD GYROPIGEON
(**STOOL** —) PIG NARK
PIGEON BLOOD GARNET
PIGEON HAWK MERLIN
PIGEONHOLE BOX SLOT LABEL SHELVE ANALYZE CELLULE CLASSIFY CUBBYHOLE
(**PL.**) STOCK
PIGEON HOUSE COT DOOKET DOVECOT COLUMBARY
PIGEON PEA DAL TUR TARE ARHAR DAHIL GANDUL TURNER TURNOR CATJANG
PIGEON WOODPECKER FLICKER
PIGGERY PIGS PIGSTY HOGGERY POTTERY SWINERY CROCKERY
PIGGIN HANDY PIPKIN
PIGHEADED WILLFUL PERVERSE STUBBORN OBSTINATE
PIGHTLE PIKLE PICKLE PIDDLE PIGTAIL
PIG IRON GRUNDY
PIGLET PORKLING
PIGLIKE SUIFORM SUILINE
PIGMENT (ALSO SEE DYE, COLOR) BLUE HEME BROWN COLOR EARTH GREEN HUMIN MORIN PAINT STAIN TONER BRONZE CEROID CERUSE IDAEIN LITHOL MALVIN ORANGE PURPLE SIENNA VIOLET GOUACHE PAINTRY PUCCOON STAINER TURACIN ALTHAEIN COLORANT EXTENDER GOSSYPOL PAINTURE TINCTURE UROPHEIN
(— **FOR WOODWORK**) KOKOWAI
(**BLACK** —) ABAISER MELANIN
(**BLUE** —) BICE SMALT CYANIN

ALTHEIN CERULEUM MARENNIN
(BLUE-GREEN —) LEUCOCYAN
(BROWN —) MUMMY SEPIA UMBER
BISTER FUSCIN ASTERIN
(BROWNISH-YELLOW —) SIENNA
(GREEN —) VERDITER
(MADDER-ROOT —) RUBIATE
(ORANGE-RED —) REALGAR
(RED —) HAEM LAKE ARUMIN
PATISE SANDYX AMATITO KOKOWAI
PUCCOON SCARLET SINOPIA
CAPSUMIN URORUBIN URRHODIN
VERMILION
(RED-VIOLET —) TURACIN
(WHITE —) CERUSE ANATASE
LITHOPONE
(YELLOW —) FLAVIN ETIOLIN
FISETIN GAMBOGE PUCCOON
DIATOMIN GALANGIN GENTISIN
ORPIMENT UROBILIN
PIGMENTATION COLOR LENTIL
LENTIGO JAUNDICE NIGRITIES
PIGNUS PAWN PLEDGE
PIGNUT HOGNUT
PIGS' FEET CRUBEEN PETTITOES
PIGSKIN SADDLE FOOTBALL
PIGSNEY EYE DARLING
PIGSTY FRANK HOGCOTE HOGGERY
PIGGERY SWINESTY
PIGTAIL PLAIT QUEUE COLETA
PIGWASH SWILL
PIGWEED QUINOA BEETROOT
CARELESS GOOSEFOOT
PIK DRA PICKI PICKL ENDAZE
ENDASEH
PIKA CONY HAIR HARE LEPORID
LAGOMORPH
PIKE GED DORE DORY GADE GEDD
JACK LUCE TANG TOUG TUCK
HAKED LUCET SNAKE SNOOK STING
VOUGE SALMON SAUGER JAVELIN
WALLEYE BLOWFISH GLASSEYE
JACKFISH NORTHERN PARTISAN
PICKEREL POULAINE TURNPIKE
PIKELET CRUMPET
PIKEMAN PIKE WATTLEBOY
PIKE PERCH PERCID SANDER
SAUGER ZANDER
PIKER TRAMP VAGRANT TELLTALE
TIGHTWAD VAGABOND
PILASTER ANTA PIER RIDGE ALETTE
RESPOND TELAMON
PILCHARD FUMADO ALEWIFE
SARDINE MENHADEN
PILE COP FUR LOT NAP PIE TIP BALE
BANK BING BULK BUNG BURR COCK
DASS DECK DESS DOWN HACK HAIR
HEAP LEET LOAD PEEL PIER POLE
POOK PYRE REEK RUCK SESS SHAG
SPUD AMASS CANCH CLAMP
CROWD FAGOT POINT SPILE SPIRE
STACK STILT TOWER CASTLE
FAGGOT FENDER FILLER GALGAL
PILLAR RICKLE RUCKLE FORTUNE
JAVELIN PYRAMID REACTOR
SPINDLE CROWBILL INCREASE
SANDPILE
(— CROSSWISE) COB
(— CURD) CHEDDAR

(— OF BRICKS) HACK
(— OF CLOTH) LAY
(— OF HAY) RICK SHOCK DOODLE
HAYCOCK HAYRICK
(— OF ICE) HUMMOCK
(— OF LOGS) DECK
(— OF PLATES) BUNG
(— OF REFUSE) DUSTHEAP
(— OF SALT FISH) BULK
(— OF SEALSKINS) PAN
(— OF SHEAVES) SESS
(— OF SHEETS) LIFT
(— OF STONES) ISLAND STONAGE
WARLOCK
(— OF TOBACCO) BULK
(— OF WOOD) STRAND
(— TO BE BURNT) PYRE
(— UP) CORD RICK COMPILE
(— WHEAT SHOCKS) STITCH
(IRON —) SPINDLE
(LITTLE —) HOT HOTT
(LOOSE —) RICKLE
(ROCK —) HOODOO
(SMALL —) COCK CANCH
(PL.) FIG DRIFT
PILEA ADICEA
PILEATED WOODPECKER
LOGCOCK WOODCOCK
PILE DRIVER TUP FISTUCA
HERCULES IMPACTER
(— DOLLY) FOLLOWER
(— WEIGHT) RAM TUP MONKEY
PILEUS CAP MITRA PILEOLUS
PILEWORT CRAIN CRANE FICARY
FIGWORT CELANDINE
PILFER ROB CRIB HOOK PELF PICK
PILK PRIG SMUG SNIG FILCH
MOOCH PILCH PROWL SHARP
SLOCK STEAL SWIPE FINGER
MAGPIE MOOTCH NIBBLE PICKLE
SMOUCH SNITCH CABBAGE
MANAVEL PLUNDER PURLOIN
SNAFFLE UNHITCH PETTIFOG
SCROUNGE
PILFERER PRIG TAKER SLOCKER
FINGERER SLOCKSTER
PILFERING MICHING PICKING
THIEVISH
PILGRIM HAJI HADJI HAJJI PALMER
PELERIN PEREGRIN WAYFARER
PILGRIMAGE TRIP TURUS VOYAGE
JOURNEY
(— TO MECCA) HADJ
PILING SPILING STOCKADE
(PL.) STARLING
PILL PIL ROB BALL BARK GOLI PEEL
POOL CREEK CACHOU EXTORT
UNHAIR DESPOIL DIURNAL GLOBULE
GRANULE PARVULE PILLULE
PREFORM BASEBALL GOOFBALL
BLACKBALL CIGARETTE
(AROMATIC —) CACHOU
(LARGE —) BALL BOLUS
(LITTLE —) PILULA PILULE
PILLAGE LOOT PEEL PILL PREY
SACK BOOTY FORAY HARRY REAVE
RIFLE SPOIL HARROW MARAUD
PICORY RAPINE RAVAGE DESPOIL
PICKEER PLUNDER RANSACK

ROBBERY BOOTHALE EXPILATE
PURCHASE SPOLIATE DEVASTATE
PILLAGER PEELER PILLER ROBBER
SACKER SPOILER SNAPHANCE
PILLAGING EXECUTION PREDATORY
PILLAR COG HERM JAMB PACK PIER
PILE POST PROP STUD TERM JAMBE
NEWEL SHAFT STELA STELE STOCK
STONE STOOP STUMP CIPPUS
COLUMN HERMES PILLER STAPLE
BEDPOST DEADMAN TRESTLE
TRUMEAU BOUNDARY MASSEBAH
PEDESTAL RESPONSE STANCHION
(— CAPPED WITH SLAB) BILITH
(— IN LARGE DOORWAY) TRUMEAU
(— IN MINE) STOOK STUMP
(— OF COAL) SPURN STOOK STOOP
(— SUPPORTING ARCH) RESPONSE
(— SURMOUNTED BY HEAD)
HERMES
(—S OF HERCULES) ABILA CALPE
(4-SIDED —) OBELISK
(BUDDHIST —) LAT
(CHANGED TO —) OLENUS
(EARTH —) HOODOO
(SACRED —) ASHERAH
(SEMITE —) MASSEBAH
(STONE —) CIPPUS
(TEMPORARY —) DEADMAN
(PL.) CRURA
PILLARIST STYLITE
PILLAS PILCORN PILKINS
PILLBOX SCATULA
PILLBUG ISOPOD KEESLIP MILLEPED
PILLWORM CHEESELIP
PILLED BALD SHAVEN TONSURED
PILLION PAD PILLOW SADDLE
CUSHION
PILLORY THEW JOUGS TRONE
CRUCIFY HALSFANG
PILLOW COD BOTT DAWN PEEL PILE
REST FLOAT WANGER BOLSTER
CUSHION FUSTIAN HEADING
OREILLER
PILLOWCASE BEAR PILL SHAM
PILLIVER
PILM DUST
PILON BONUS LAGNIAPPE
PILOSE HAIRY PILEOUS
PILOT ACE SPY KIWI COACH GUARD
GUIDE STEER AIRMAN ESCORT
MANAGE THAMUS AVIATOR CAPTAIN
CONDUCT HOBBLER LODEMAN
SHIPMAN WINGMAN AIREDALE
GOVERNOR HELMSMAN PALINURUS
WHEELSMAN
PILOT BIRD PLOVER
PILOT FISH ROMERO JACKFISH
AMBERFISH
PILOTHOUSE TEXAS CHARTHOUSE
PILUM PESTLE JAVELIN
PIMENTA MYRTAL
PIMENTO PIMINTA ALLSPICE
PIMIENTO
PIMP MACK BULLY CADET FAGOT
PONCE SNEAK MACRIO PANDER
RUFFIAN INFORMER PROCUROR
PURVEYOR SCOUNDREL
PIMPERNEL BURNET WAYWORT

EYEBRIGHT MARGELINE WINCOPIPE

PIMPLE GUM NOB PAP BURL KNOB
PUSH QUAT SPOT HICKY PLOOK
PLOUK PLUKE PAPULA PAPULE
TETTER BUBUKLE PUSTULE
PIMGENET WHEYWORM

PIN FID FIX HOB HUB LAG LEG NOG
PEG PEN ACUS APEX AXLE BANK
BOLT MOOD PEEN POST PRIN PROP
PYNE RUNG STUD DRIFT HUMOR
KAYLE POINT PREEN SPILL THOLE
BOBBIN BROACH BROOCH CALIGO
COTTER CURLER FASTEN HATPIN
NORMAN PINNET SKEWER SPIGOT
TEMPER TENPIN TOGGEL TONGUE
TRIFLE BAYONET CONFINE ENCLOSE
GUDGEON IMPOUND LOCKPIN
PAIRPIN PUSHPIN SPINDLE TAMPION
TANGENT TUMBLER FORELOCK
PINNACLE

(— FOR FITTING PLANKS) SETBOLT
(— IN AXLETREE) LINCHPIN
(— IN RIFLE) TIGE
(— OF DIAL) STYLE GNOMON
(— OF LANTERN PINION) RUNDLE
(— OF WATCH) DART
(— ON CLAVICHORD KEY) TANGENT
(— TO HOLD BEDCLOTHES)
BEDSTAFF
(— USED AS TARGET) HOB
(BELAYING —) CAVIL
(BOWLING —) DUCKPIN HEADPIN
KINGPIN SLEEPER
(BOWLING —S) DEADWOOD
(CARPENTRY —) DOWEL
(COUPLING —) DRAWBOLT
(ENGAGING —) BAYONET
(HAIR —) BARRETTE
(HEADED —) RIVET
(JEWELED —) PROP
(OAR —) THOLE
(ORNAMENTAL —) AGLET AIGLET
(PIVOT —) PINTLE
(SMALL —) LILL MINIKIN MICROPIN
(SPLIT —) COTTER FORELOCK
(SURVEYOR'S —) ARROW
(TAPERED —) DRIFT
(TIRLING —) RISP
(WOODEN —) SPILE TRENAIL
(PL.) LEGS KAILS DEADWOOD

PINACOID BASE HEMIDOME
PINAFORE SLIP TIDE TIDY TIER
TYER DAIDLY SAVEALL SLIPPER
GABERDINE
PINBALL MACHINE PACHINKO
PINCASE POPPET
PINCE-NEZ NIPPER LORGNON
NOSEPINCH
PINCERS TEU TEW CLAM CHELA
TUARN PLIERS TURKIS WYNRIS
FORCEPS MULLETS NIPPERS
PINCHER PINSONS TWEEZERS
PINCH NIP TOP VEX WRY BITE CLAM
HURT PUSH STOP TUCK CRIMP
GRIPE HINCH PUGIL SNUFF SQUAT
STEAL STINT TAPER THEFT TWEAK
WRING ARREST CLUTCH EXTORT
HARASS NARROW SNITCH STRAIT
STRESS TWINCH TWITCH SCRINCH

SQUEEZE JUNCTURE PRESSURE
SHORTAGE STRAITEN VELLICATE
(— OF SNUFF) SNEESH SNEESHIN
(— WITH HUNGER) CLAM CLEM
PINCHBECK SHAM CHEAP SPURIOUS
PRETENDED
PINCHED CHITTY WASTED HAGGARD
PUNGLED SQUINCH
PINCHPENNY CARL MISER NIGGARD
NIGGARDLY
PINDARIC ODE WILD
PINE IE ARA LIM CHIL CHIR FADE
FLAG HALA HONE IEIE KAIL WANT
AGGAG DROOP DWAIN GRIEF KAURI
MATAI MATSU MOURN OCOTE PINON
WANZE WEARY WRIST YEARN
APACHE AROLLA DUSTER FAMINE
GRIEVE HUNGER LAMENT PANDAN
SHRINK SORROW STARVE TOATOA
TORFEL WITHER CYPRESS DAISING
DWINDLE FORPINE FOXTAIL
JEFFREY LAUHALA TARWOOD
TORMENT TORTURE AKAMATSU
AUSTRIAN GALAGALA LANGUISH
LOBLOLLY LONGLEAF PINASTER
STAGHORN TANEKAHA VANQUISH
(— AWAY) DROOP DWINE SNURP
WANZE WINDER FORPINE
MACERATE
(AUSTRALIAN —) BEEFWOOD
(GROUND —) FOXTAIL
(PITCH —) THYME
PINEAPPLE BOMB NANA PINA PINO
PITA ANANA ANANAS ABACAXI
GRENADE
PINE FINCH SISKIN
PINE MARTEN SABLE
PINE NEEDLE SHAT SPILL PINING
ALFILARIA
(PL.) TWINKLES
PINE TREE STATE MAINE
PINFEATHER PEN STUMP STIPULE
PINFISH CHUB SPOT JIMMY PORGY
SARGO
PINFOLD POUND
PING KNOCK
PINGUIN MAYA ANANAS AGUAMAS
PINUELA HUIPILLA
PINGUITUDE FATNESS OBESITY
OILINESS
PINION NOIL WING PINON QUILL
PENNON SECURE LANTERN PINACLE
SHACKLE TRUNDLE FLIGHTER
WALLOWER
PINION WHEEL MOBILE
PINITOL SENNITE MATEZITE
PINK JAG PIP CYME DAWN DECK
FADE MICE PING STAB WINK ADORN
BLINK CORAL ELITE MOVED SWELL
WOUND AURORE BISQUE CHERUB
FIESTA HEIGHT MINNOW POUNCE
SHRIMP SILENE TATTOO ZEPHYR
ANNATTO ARBUTUS BEGONIA
BERMUDA BLOSSOM EXTREME
PARAGON REVEREE SANDUST
TUSSORE CONFETTI COQUETTE
DECORATE DIANTHUS GILLIVER
LIMEWORT RADIANCE RECAMIER
PINKED JAGGED

PINKIE PIRLIE
PINKROOT REDROOT WORMWEED
STARBLOOM
PINNA EARFLAP PINNULE APHLEBIA
AURICULA PAVILION
PINNACE BARK CROWN WOMAN
BARQUE PINNAGE MISTRESS
PINNACLE IT PIN TOP ACME APEX
CREST CROWN SERAC SPIRE
THUMB FINIAL HEIGHT SUMMIT
GENDARME
(ICE —) SERAC
(ROCKY —) TOR HOODOO AIGUILLE
GENDARME
PINNATE WINGED
PINNER PINDER FLANDAN STICKER
PINOCHLE BINOCLE GOULASH
AIRPLANE
(— SCORE) MELD
PINPILLOW PIMPLO
PINPOINT ISOLATE
(— OF LIGHT) GLEAM
PINT O GULL PINNET SWIGGER
OCTARIUS
(9-10THS —) MUTCHKIN
(FOURTH —) GILL JACK
(HALF —) CUP NIP GILL JACK
CUPFUL NIPPERKIN
PINTADO CERO PIED SIER SEARER
SIERRA SPOTTED KINGFISH
PINTAIL DUCK SMEE SPIKE SPRIG
GROUSE SMETHE CRACKER
LADYBIRD LONGNECK PIKETAIL
PINTANO PILOT COCKEYE CHIRIVITA
PINTID EMPEINE
PINTO BEAN ROSILLO
PINWEED(PL.) LECHEA
PINWHEEL WINDMILL
PINWORM NEMA OXYURID
PIN WRENCH SPANULE
PIONEER BLAZE GUIDE MINER
GROPER HALUTZ SETTLE CHALUTZ
EXPLORE EARLIEST EMIGRANT
ORIGINAL RAWHIDER
PIOUS PI HOLY FROOM GODLY
MORAL SEELY DEVOUT DIVINE
INWARD PIETIC CANTING DUTIFUL
GODDARD PITEOUS SAINTED
SAINTLY FAITHFUL RELIGIOUS
PIP DIE CHIP ECHO KILL PAIP PEEP
SPOT SPECK DEFEAT PIPPIN
BLACKBALL
PIPAL BO FIG
PIPE TD BIN GUN HUB TAP TEE CALL
CANE DALE DRIP DUCT FLUE HOSE
LINE MAIN MUTE PULE REED TILE
TUBE WEEP WORM BLAST BRAIL
BRIAR CANAL CANEL CINCH CRANE
CROSS CUTTY HOOKA PROBE PUNGI
QUILL RIDER RISER SPOUT STAND
STRAW TEWEL TRUMP TRUNK VOICE
BRANCH BURROW CALEAN CASING
DUCTUS FAUCET FILLER GEWGAW
HEWGAG HOGGER KINURA NIPPLE
NOTICE NOZZLE OFFLET OFFSET
POOGYE RANKET SLEEVE SLOUCH
SLUICE SUCKER TROWEL TUBULE
TUNNEL UPTAKE WEEPER CHANNEL
CHANTER CHIBOUK CONDUIT

DUCTURE FISTULA HYDRANT
SERVICE SPARGER SPINDLE
SUCTION TALLBOY TWEEDLE
WHISTLE CALIDUCT DOWNTAKE
GALOUBET LAMPHOLE MIRLITON
NARGHILE NARGILEH PENSTOCK
SEMIDOLE SUSPIRAL TELLTALE
THRIBBLE
(— AS NAVIGATION AID) SPINDLE
(— BENDER) HICKEY
(— BOWL) STUMMEL
(— FOR CONDUCTING WATER)
LEADER
(— JOINT) TURNOUT
(— OF ORE) BUNNY
(— OF PAN) SYRINX
(— OF QUEEN BEE) TEET
(— ON BAGPIPE) DRONE CHANTER
(— SUPPORT) CRADLE
(— TAB) TACK
(— TO MUFFLE TRUMPET) SORDINE
(— USED IN WELL) STRING
(— WITH SOCKET ENDS) HUB
(4 LENGTHS OF —) FOURBLE
(CEREMONIAL —) CALUMET
(CLAMMING —) BRAIL
(CONNECTING —) HOGGER
(FLUE —) LABIAL
(HEATING —) CALIDUCT
(MUSICAL —) BODY GEWGAW
FISTULA SORDINE HORNPIPE
SCHWEGEL
(OATEN —) OAT
(ORGAN —) FLUE KINURA LABIAL
ERZAHLER SCHWEGEL TREMOLANT
(PEACE —) CALUMET
(SEWER —) SLANT
(SHEPHERD'S —) REED LARIGOT
(SNAKE-CHARMER'S —) PUNGI
(TOBACCO —) GUN CLAY BRIAR
BRIER CUTTY HOOKA STRAW
CALEAN DUDEEN HOOKAH BULLDOG
CHIBOUK CHILLUM CORNCOB
BILLIARD CALABASH
(TOY —) HEWGAG
(VERTICAL —) STACK LAMPHOLE
(WATER — FOR ENGINE) SLOUCH
PIPED DRUNK JETTED
PIPEFISH EARL LONGJAW
PIPELAYER YARNER
PIPESTEM STOPPEL STOPPLE
PIPETTE PIPET TASTER
PIPEWORT HATPIN WOOLWEED
PIPING HOSE SOFT VERY CRYING
ROULEAU WAILING WEEPING
TRANQUIL
PIPING CROW CASSICAN FLUTEBIRD
PIPIRI PITIRRI
PIPISTRELLE BAT NOCTULE
PIPIT PEEP TEETAN WEKEEN
CHEEPER SKYLARK TIETICK TITLARK
TITLING WAGTAIL LINGBIRD
TWITLARK
PIPPIN PIP APPLE PEPPIN RIBSTON
PIPSISSEWA EVERGREEN
WINTERGREEN
PIQUANCY SALT ZEST FLAVOR
GINGER TARTNESS
PIQUANT BOLD RACY JUICY NUTTY

SALTY SHARP SPICY TASTY ZESTY
LIVELY SEVERE CUTTING PEPPERY
PUNGENT STINGING
PIQUE FRET GOAD PEAK PICK PIKE
PYKE TICK ANNOY PRISE SNUFF
SPITE STING HARASS MALICE
NETTLE PRITCH STRUNT CHIGGER
OFFENSE PROVOKE UMBRAGE
IRRITATE MARCELLA
PIRACY CAPTURE PIRATISM
PIRAGUA CANOE DUGOUT PIROGUE
PETTIAGUA
PIRANHA PIRAI CARIBE PIRAYA
PIRARUCU PAICHE ARAPAIMA
PIRATE CAPER ROVER ROBBER
VIKING CATERAN CORSAIR PICKEER
SCUMMER ALGERINE MAROONER
PICAROON BUCCANEER SALLEEMAN
(— FLAG) ROGER BLACKJACK
PIRIPIRI BIRK BIRCH MAPAN
PIRL SPIN TWINE TWIST REVOLVE
PIRN QUILL BOBBIN PIRNIE SPINDLE
PIROGUE CANOE PERIOQUE
PIROPLASM BABESIA
PIROSHKI PIROGEN
PISCINA POOL TANK BASIN
SACRARY LAVATORY SACRARIUM
PISE CAJON PISAY
PISHOGUE CHARM SPELL SORCERY
WITCHERY
PISMIRE ANT EMMET
PISOLITE PEASTONE
PISTACHIO FISTIC PISTICK
PISTIL CHIVE CARPEL UMBONE
POINTEL
(PL.) GYNECIUM
PISTILLATE FEMALE
PISTOL DAG GAT GUN POP ROD
BULL DAGG IRON TACK FLUTE
RIFLE STICK BARKER BUFFER
BULDER BULLER CANNON DRAGON
HEATER POTGUN RIFFLE BULLDOG
DUNGEON SHOOTER TICKLER
DERINGER REPORTER REVOLVER
(TOY —) SPARKLER
PISTON BUCKET FORCER PALLET
SUCKER EMBOLUS PLUNGER
(— HUB) SPIDER
PIT PET POT PUT BURY CIST DELF
DELL DISC DISK FOSS HELL HOLE
KIST LAKE MINE PLAY PUTT SILO
SINK SUMP SWAG TURN WEEM
WELL ABYSM ABYSS CRYPT DELFT
DITCH FOSSA FOVEA FROST GRAVE
LEACH MATCH PITCH PORUS SLACK
SLUIG TREAD AREOLE BORROW
BUNKER KERNEL OPPOSE RADDLE
WALLOW ABADDON ALVEOLA
AMPULLA BOTHROS CHARPIT
FOSSULA FOXHOLE HANDLER
LATRINE MEGARON PINHOLE
VARIOLE WINNING CYPHELLA
DOWNFALL FAVEOLUS FENESTRA
POCKMARK PUNCTULE WELLHOLE
(— FOR BAKING) IMU UMU
(— FOR OFFERINGS) BOTHROS
(— OF STOMACH) MARK WIND
(— OF THEATER) GROUND

(— ON COCKROACH HEAD)
FENESTRA
(— ON LICHENS) LACUNA CYPHELLA
(— SACRED TO DEMETER)
MEGARON
(BITTER —) STIPPEN
(BOTTOMLESS —) ABYSS ABADDON
BARATHRUM
(COAL —) HEUCH HEUGH
(FODDER —) SILO
(MAORI —) RUA
(MIRY —) SLUIG
(RIFLE —) SANGAR
(ROOFED —) CIST KIST
(SALT —) VAT PEZOGRAPH
(SAND —) BUNKER
(SMALL —) AREOLE LACUNA
STAPLE
(TANNING —) LIME LAYER LEACH
HANDLER LAYAWAY SUSPENDER
PITA PITO YUCCA ARGHAN
PITCH DIP FIT KEY LAB MEL PIC
BUCK CANT CHAT CODE COOK DING
FALL FORK HURL PECK PICK PLUG
RAKE TELL TONE TOSS ABODE
BOOST BUNCH FLING LABOR LURCH
PLANT SLENT SLOPE SPIEL THROW
TWIRL BINDER DIRECT ENCAMP
FILLER LENGTH MALTHA MANJAK
PLUNGE SQUARE TOTTER TUMBLE
VOLLEY WICKET CURRENT NARRATE
ALKITRAN OVERHANG
(— AT A MARK) LAG
(— FROM FIR TREES) ALKITRAN
(— OF HELIX) JAW
(— TENT) TELD
(ABOVE —) SHARP
(AUCTION —) SETBACK
(BASEBALL —) CURVE STRIKE
CRIPPLE SPITTER FADEAWAY
KNUCKLER SPITBALL
(BELOW —) FLAT
(COBBLER'S —) CODE
(FULL —) VOLLEY
(GLANCE —) MANJAK MANJACK
(HIGH —) BLOOPER
(HIGHEST —) PRIDE
(IDENTITY IN —) UNISON
(MINERAL —) BITUMEN
PITCH APPLE COPEI CUPAY
PITCHED SET
PITCHER JUG JACK OLLA PILL PRIG
BUIRE CRUET GALON GORGE
GOTCH AFTABA CROUKE GALLON
HURLER POURIE STRAIN URCEUS
CANETTE CHUCKER FLINGER
GROWLER STARTER STOPPER
TWIRLER URCEOLE AIGUIERE
ASCIDIUM OENOCHOE SOUTHPAW
MOUNDSMAN
(— AND CATCHER) BATTERY
(— FOR BEER) GROWLER
(— SHAPED LIKE MAN) TOBY
(— WITH ONE HANDLE) URCEUS
(BULGING —) GOTCH
(EARTHEN —) GEORG GORGE
(RELIEF —) FIREMAN
(RELIEF —S) BULLPEN
(WIDEMOUTHED —) EWER

PITCHER PLANT BISCUIT FLYTRAP
FEVERCUP FOXGLOVE WATERCUP
NEPENTHES SKUNKWEED
PITCHFORK EVIL PICK PIKE PICKEL
SHEPPECK PITCHPIKE
(THATCHER'S —) GROOM
(PL.) HARD
PITCHHOLE CAHOT
PITCHMAN VENDER SALESMAN
PITCH PIPE TUNER EPITONION
PITEOUS MEAN PALTRY PITIFUL
MERCIFUL MOURNFUL PIERCING
PITFALL PIT FALL TRAP SNARE
DANGER TRAPFALL
PITH JET PUT SAP CORE GIST MEAT
PULP PUTT HEART VIGOR ENERGY
KERNEL MARROW ESSENCE
EXTRACT MEDULLA NUCLEUS
PAPYRUS STRENGTH
PITH HELMET TOPI TOPEE
PITH TREE AMBATCH
PITHY CRISP MEATY SAPPY TERSE
STRONG CONCISE LACONIC
MARROWY
PITIABLE SAD SEELY WOFUL
RUEFUL WOEFUL FORLORN PITIFUL
PITIFUL MEAN MEEK RUTH SILLY
SORRY PALTRY RUEFUL TENDER
HANGDOG RUESOME RUTHFUL
MERCIFUL PATHETIC
PITILESS GRIM CRUEL STERN STONY
SAVAGE RUTHLESS UNPITIED
MERCILESS
PITTANCE BIT ALMS DOLE GIFT MITE
SONG TRIFLE BEQUEST
PITTED FOVEATE OPPOSED
ALVEOLATE
PITTER STONER
PITURI BEDGERY PITCHERY
PITY RUE MEAN MOAN PETE PITE
RUTH MERCY PIETY REIVE SCATH
PATHOS MERCIFY REMORSE
WAESUCK CLEMENCY SYMPATHY
PIVOT TOE CRUX SLEW TURN HEART
CENTER SLOUGH WORDLE
GUDGEON TRAVERSE TRUNNION
PIVOTAL POLAR CENTRAL
(— POINT) KNUCKLE
PIVOTING DISHRAG
PIVOT STAND PEDESTAL
PIXY ELF FAIRY PYGMY ROGUE
IMPISH RASCAL SPRITE PUCKISH
ROGUISH
PIXILATED DAFFY DOTTY DRUNK
PIXIE BEMUSED PUCKISH TOUCHED
CONFUSED
PIZE OATH PISE CURSE
PLACABLE WEAK QUIET PACABLE
PEACEFUL YIELDING FORGIVING
PLACARD BILL POST TITLE POSTER
TICKET AFFICHE REDLINE
STOMACHER
PLACATE CALM GENTLE PACIFY
PLEASE SOOTHE APPEASE FORGIVE
PLACE L DO BIT FIX PUT SET AREA
HOLE LIEU PLAT PLOT POSE POST
RANK ROOM SEAT SITE SITU SPOT
STEP STOW TEXT VICE YARK BEING
ESTER ESTRE HOUSE JOINT LOCUS

PLAZA POSIT SCENE SITUS STALL
STATE STEAD STELL STOUR WHERE
BESTOW CHARGE GROUND IMPOSE
INVEST LAYOUT LOCALE LOCATE
OFFICE POSSIE ROOMTH ALLODGE
ARRANGE DEPOSIT KITCHEN
STATION ABDITORY DIGGINGS
EMPORIUM LOCATION POSITION
(— ALONE) ISOLATE
(— ALTERNATELY) STAGGER
(— APART) ENISLE
(— BEFORE) APPOSE PREFIX
(— BY FORCE) PILT
(— CROSSWISE) THWART
(— FISH IN SALTING BIN) KENCH
(— FOR CATTLE) CAMP
(— FOR DUMPING RUBBISH) SHOOT
(— FOR MORTAR AND BRICK) FROG
(— FOR PHEASANTS) STEW
(— FOR PRAYERS) IDGAH
(— FOR RABBITS) WARREN
(— FOR RECEPTION) RECEIPT
(— FOR RUBBISH DEPOSITS)
LAYSTALL
(— FOR SEETHING) STEW
(— FOR SLEEPING) BED BUNK DOSS
FLOP LAIR LIBKIN
(— FOR TRAINING HORSES) LONGE
(— FROM WHICH JURY IS TAKEN)
VENUE
(— IN COMPACT MASS) STOW
(— IN ORDER) ARRAY ENRANK
(— IN WATERFALL) LEAP
(— IN) INNEST
(— OF AMUSEMENT) GAFF
(— OF ASSEMBLY) AGORA CURIA
SYNAGOG
(— OF BURIAL) AHU KIL KILL LAIR
GRAVE LAYSTOW CATACOMB
CEMETERY GOLGOTHA LAYSTALL
(— OF BUSINESS) BANK AGENCY
KNACKERY
(— OF CONCEALMENT) DEN BOMA
BLIND STALE HIDING HIDEOUT
HIDEAWAY
(— OF CONFINEMENT) BRIG CAGE
COOP LIMBO PRISON BULLPEN
(— OF CONFUSION) BABEL
TROYTOWN
(— OF DESTRUCTION) ABADDON
(— OF DWELLING) WANE
(— OF ENTERTAINMENT) INN JOINT
DANCERY HANGOUT HOSTELRY
(— OF EXERTION) ARENA
(— OF EXILE) PATMOS
(— OF MISERY) HELL
(— OF NETHER DARKNESS) EREBUS
(— OF NOISE) BABEL
(— OF PROTECTION) PORT SCUG
(— OF REFUGE) ARK BAST HOLD
ASYLUM ADULLAM HIDEOUT
(— OF RESIDENCE) SOIL DOMICILE
(— OF RESORT) PURLIEU
(— OF RESTRAINT) LIMBO
(— OF SACRIFICE) ALTAR
(— OF SAFETY) GRITH HAVEN
WARRANT
(— OF SECURITY) GRITH ASYLUM
CORRAL HARBOR GARRISON

(— OF SHELTER) LEW HOLD JOUK
COVER
(— OF SUBMISSION) CANOSSA
(— OF TORMENT) GOLGOTHA
(— OF WORSHIP) HEIAU BETHEL
CHAPEL CHURCH DESERT SHRINE
TEMPLE GURDWARA SYNAGOGUE
(— WHERE 4 OR MORE WAYS MEET)
CARFAX
(— WHERE FOOD IS KEPT) LARDER
(— WHERE MEAT IS SMOKED)
BUCAN BUCCAN
(— WHERE OUTCASTS GATHER)
HELL
(— WHERE ROADS CROSS) LEET
(— WHERE STREAM IS RAPID)
SHARP
**(— WHERE TROOPS HALT
OVERNIGHT)** ETAPE
(BOGGY —) SLUMP
(BREEDING —) NIDUS LOOMERY
PELICANRY
(CHIEF —) HEADSHIP
(CIRCULAR —) ORBELL
(CONSECRATED —) HIERON
(DRINKING —) BOOZER MUMHOUSE
(DRY —) SEARING
(DWELLING —) BY BYE DEN SEE
HAFT HIVE HOME BEING HOUSE
HOWFF SOJOURN HABITACLE
(EATING —) CAFE GRUBBERY
(EMPTY —) BLANK SPACE
(ENCLOSED —) BIN HAY WORTH
SEVERAL
(ESSENTIAL —) EYE
(FAMILIAR —) KITH
(FAULTY — IN THREAD) TRAP
(FILTHY —) STY
(FIRST —) BLUE LEAD STRAIGHT
(FORTIFIED —) LIS LISS CASTLE
FASTNESS
(GATHERING —) SHOP AGORA
FOYER JOINT LESCHE
(HALTING —) MARAH
(HIDING —) MEW CACHE HIDEL
HOARD STASH COVERT HIDDELS
RETREAT STOWAWAY
(HIGH —) EMINENCE
(HOLLOW —) GULF HOLE HOLL
SCOOP CAVITY ALBERCA SINKHOLE
(INHABITED —) ABADI
(LANDING —) GHAT HARD LEVEE
SCALE PALACE HELIPORT
(LEVEL —) PLANILLA
(LODGING —) CAMP LOGIS BIDING
BILLET LIBKEN
(LURKING —) HOLD HOLE HOARD
HULSTER
(MARKET —) AGORA TRONE
MARKET RIALTO
(MARSHY —) SLEW SLOO SLUE
SLUMP SLOUGH
(MEETING —) CLUB COURT FORUM
GUILD TRYST TOLSEL TOLZEY
AMBALAM KLAVERN TINWALD
(MUDDY —) SOIL
(NESTING —) JUG NIDARY
(OPEN —) ENAJIM
(OTHERWORLDLY —) EMPYREAN

(RAVELED —) FRAY
(REMOTE —) JERICHO
(RESTING —) LAY CAMP FORM GIST
LAIR PARAO CRADLE
(ROCKY —) ROCHER
(SACRED —) HAREM HIERON
CHAITYA SANCTUM
(SALTING —) SALADERO
(SECRET —) LAIR CORNER CRANNY
(SHADY —) GLOOM SWALE
FRESCADE UMBRACLE
(SHELTERED —) NOOK SCUG
SUCCOR
(STOPPING —) HALT MANZIL
(STORAGE —) DEPOT HOARD
LODGE SPICERY STORAGE
STOWAGE DOCKYARD
(SWAMPY —) FLUSH SOUGH
(THIRD —) SHOW
(TIGHT —) JAM JAMB
(WATCH —) TOOTHILL
(WRETCHED —) DEN MISERY
(PL.) LOCI
PLACEBO TOADY VESPERS
PARASITE
PLACED FIXED BESTEAD
(— ON ITS SIDE) LAZY
PLACEHOLDER VARIABLE
PLACE-NAME TOPONYM
PLACENTA MAZA
PLACENTAL MAZIC
PLACID CALM COOL EVEN MEEK
MILD SOFT DOWNY QUIET SUANT
SUENT GENTLE SEDATE SERENE
SMOOTH PACIFIC TRANQUIL
THROBLESS
PLACKET FENT SPARE WOMAN
CLOSING PETTICOAT
PLAGIARISM CRIB PLAGIUM
PLAGIARIST TAKER COPYIST
PLAGIARIZE CRIB LIFT STEAL
PLAGUE DUN IMP VEX FRAB FRET
GNAW PEST TWIT BESET CURSE
DEATH DEUCE HARRY QUALM
TEASE TRAIK WEARY WORRY
WOUND BURDEN HAMPER HARASS
INFEST PESTER PESTIS SORROW
WANION DESTROY MURRAIN
PERPLEX SCOURGE TORMENT
TORTURE TROUBLE HANDICAP
OUTBREAK
PLAGUY VERY PESKY VEXING
MURRAIN PESTFUL INFERNAL
PLAICE FLUKE FLATFISH FLOUNDER
PLAID CALM FAKE MAUD PLOD
TARTAN BRACKEN BRECHAN
PLAIN DRY LOW BALD BARE CHOL
EASY EVEN FLAT OPEN PLAT RIFE
VEGA WALD WOLD BLAIR BLUNT
BROAD CAMPO CORAH FIELD FRANK
GREEN GROSS LAUND LEVEL LLANO
MOURN NAKED PAMPA PROSE
ROUND SEBKA SILLY SMALL TALAO
UNORN BEMOAN BEWAIL CHASTE
CUESTA GRAITH HOMELY HONEST
HUMBLE LENTEN MACHAR PUSZTA
RUSTIC SABANA SEVERE SIMPLE
SINGLE SMOOTH ARTLESS EVIDENT
GENUINE IDAVOLL INARTED LEGIBLE

OBVIOUS POPULAR TERRACE
APPARENT CAMPAIGN DISTINCT
EVERYDAY EXPLICIT FAMILIAR
HOMEMADE HOMESPUN ITHAVOLL
PALPABLE PIEDMONT SEMPLICE
STRAIGHT
(— AMONG TREES) LAUND
(— OF ARGENTINA) PAMPA
(— OF RUSSIA) STEPPE
(ALKALI —S) USAR
(ALLUVIAL —) APRON HAUGH
(ARCTIC —) TUNDRA
(DESOLATE —) CHOL
(LOW-LYING —) MACHAR MACHAIR
(MARSHY —) BLAIR
(SALINE —) SEBKA SEBKHA
(SALT —) SALADA
(SLOPING —) HOPE CUESTA
CONOPLAIN
(SMALL GRASSY —) CAMAS CAMASS
QUAMASH
(TREELESS —) BLED TUNDRA
SAVANNA SAVANNAH
(UNOCCUPIED —) DESERT
(PL.) VIZCACHA
PLAIN CHANT CF
PLAINCLOTHESMAN SPLIT
PLAINLY FAIR BARELY FAIRLY
FLATLY SIMPLY BROADLY FRANKLY
DIRECTLY
PLAINNESS PROSE INNOCENCE
PLAINSMAN LLANERO
PLAINSONG GROUND
PLAINT WAIL PLANT LAMENT
COMPLAINT
PLAINTEXT CLEAR
PLAINTIFF SUER ACTOR ORATOR
PURSUER QUERENT
PLAINTIVE SAD CROSS PINING
DOLENTE ELEGIAC FRETFUL
MOANFUL PEEVISH PETTISH
DOLOROSO MANGENDO PETULANT
WAILSOME SORROWFUL
PLAIT CUE PLY KNIT PAIR PLAT RUFF
TURN WALE WAND BRAID BREAD
CRIMP FETCH FITCH PEDAL PINCH
QUEUE QUILL QUIRK TRACE TRESS
WEAVE BOHDER DOUBLE GATHER
GOFFER PLEACH PLIGHT RUMPLE
TUSCAN WIMPLE WRITHE FROUNCE
PIGTAIL SCALLOM COMPLECT
(— FOR HAT) DUNSTABLE
(— OF STRAW) MILAN TRACE
(SERIES OF —S) KILTING
PLAITED PLISSE DEVIOUS PLICATE
PLAITING PLISSE LEGHORN
PLAN AIM ART LAY WAY CARD CAST
COUP DART FOOT GAME HANG IDEA
MIND MOOD PLAT PLOT REDE WENT
ALLOW BRIEF CHART DARTY DRAFT
DRIFT ETTLE FRAME HOBBY MODEL
REACH SHAPE TRACE ADVICE
AGENDA BEREDE BUDGET CIPHER
DECOCT DESIGN DEVISE ENGINE
FIGURE INTEND LAYOUT METHOD
MODULE ORDAIN PROJET SCHEMA
SCHEME SURVEY THEORY ARRANGE
CONCERT COUNSEL DRAWING
FORELAY NOSTRUM PATTERN

PROJECT PURPOSE COGITATE
CONSPIRE CONTRIVE ENGINEER
FORECAST FOREGAME LANDSKIP
MEDITATE PLATFORM PRACTICE
SCHEDULE SKELETON STRATEGY
(— AHEAD) FORECAST
(— OF FUTURE PROCEDURE)
PROGRAM
(— ON A FLOOR) EPURE
(— TOGETHER) CONCERT
(5-YEAR —) PIATILETKA
(GROUND —) TRACE GRUNDRISS
PLANARIAN PLATODE TRICLAD
FLATWORM
PLANE AXCI BEAD DADO FACE FLAT
HOLL MILL AXIAL CHUTE CROZE
FACET GLIDE HOULE HOWEL LEVEL
MESON SHOOT STICK TABLE WHISK
AEQUOR BEADER HOLLOW REEDER
ROUTER SMOKER SNIBEL COURIER
INSHAVE JOINTER SURFACE
WITCHET BULLNOSE DECLINER
LEEBOARD MERIDIAN RECLINER
SYCAMORE TRAVERSE
(— HANDLE) TOAT TOTE
(— OF CLEAVAGE) BACK
(— OF EARTH'S ORBIT) ECLIPTIC
(— OF ROCK) BED
(—S OF GUNNERY FIRE) SHEAF
(ENEMY —) BANDIT
(INCLINED —) RAMP SLIP
(MOLDING —) HOLL HOULE HOLLOW
(PERSPECTIVE —) TABLE
(RABBET —) PLOW RABAT PLOUGH
REBATE FILLETER
(SLOPING —) CUESTA
PLANER JOINTER SURFACER
PLANER TREE HORNBEAM
SYCAMORE
PLANET SUN BODY IRIS JOVE MARS
MOON STAR EARTH GLOBE HYLEG
PLUTO SHREW VENUS WORLD
SATURN SPHERE URANUS VULCAN
ALMUTEN ANARETA BENEFIC
FORTUNE JUPITER MERCURY
NEPTUNE PRIMARY CHASUBLE
LUMINARY RECEPTOR TERRELLA
WANDERER
(— IN A NATIVITY) ALMUTEN
(BENEVOLENT —) FORTUNE
(CONTROLLING —) LORD
(HYPOTHETICAL —) VULCAN
(MALEFICENT —) SHREW
(RULING —) DOMINATOR
(SMALL —) IRIS ASTEROID
TERRELLA
PLANETARIUM ORRERY
PLANETOID UNDINE ASTEROID
PLANE TREE CHINAR PLATAN
COTONIER PLANTAIN SYCAMORE
PLANET-STRICKEN SIDERATED
PLANISPHERE ASTROLABE
METEORSCOPE
PLANK CLAM HOOD PATA PLAT RAIL
SOLE WAIR BOARD CLAMP PATTA
SHIDE SWALE THEAL DAGGER
FLITCH ROOFER CLAPPER CROSSER
DEPOSIT MADRIER RIBBAND

STEALER FOREPOLE GARBOARD
STRINGER
(— 6 FT. X 1 FT.) WARE
(— AS PROTECTION) SHOLE
(— OVER BROOK) CLAM
(—S IN BRIDGE) CHESS
(—S LESS THAN 6 FT.) DEAL
(CURVED —) SNYING
(ROUGHHEWN —) SLAB
PLANK DRAG RUBBER
PLANK END STUB
PLANKING GORE RACK HATCH
SWALE CEILING LAGGING BERTHING
BRATTICE GARBOARD WATERWAY
PLANKSHEER WATERWAY
PLANKTON KRILL
PLANOMILLER SLABBER
PLANT AJI BED SET SOW ACHE ALGA
ARUM BURY CROP FAST HERB HIDE
MORE RAPE SALT SEED SLIP TREE
WORT ABACA AGAVE ARGEL CAROA
CHIVE CLOTE CLOVE EARLY FANCY
GRAFT HEATH INTER INULA JALAP
KEIKI PITCH SHRUB YERBA ACACIA
AKELEY ALASAS ANNUAL BEDDER
CACOON CALALU CARROT COKERY
COTTON ESCAPE FICOID FORCER
GALAXY GROWTH KARREE LENTIL
LIGGER MANUKA MEDICK MESCAL
PEPINO SETTLE SPRING ULLUCU
YARROW ABANDON ALKANET
ALYSSUM BREWERY CONCEAL
CUTTING DAGGERS ENCELIA
HAEMONY IMPLANT JIKUNGU
LETTUCE PICKERY RAMBONG
SAWMILL ABUTILON AGERATUM
AGRIMONY ANGLEPOD BIENNIAL
BLUEBELL CONSOUND DRAWLING
DYEHOUSE EMERGENT ENGINERY
FUMEROOT GASWORKS GROMWELL
HAWKWEED HONEWORT KNAPWEED
LARKSPUR
(— 2ND CROP) ETCH
(— BY SPADING) SPIT
(— DEEPLY) HEEL
(— FIRMLY) BRACE
(— GROWING IN WATER) BILDERS
HYDROPHYTE
(— IN ROWS) DRILL
(— OF MEADOWS) POOPHYTE
(— ROOTED IN GROUND) LIANA
LIANE
(— SUPPORTING PARASITES)
SUSCEPT
(— TREE) MOTCH
(— WITH NO DISTINCT MEMBERS)
THALLUS
(— WITH THREE PISTILS) TRIGYN
(— WITH THREE STAMENS)
TRIANDER
(AIR —) FLOPPERS
(ANCIENT —) CYCAD
(AQUATIC —) ALISMA NUPHAR
SUGAMO TAWKEE AMBULIA
AWLWORT FROGBIT DUCKWEED
(AROMATIC —) MINT NARD BASIL
CUMIN TANSY THYME AMOMUM
CUMMIN DITTANY ALBAHACA
LAVENDER SPIKENARD

(AUSTRALIAN —) LILAC STYLO
LIGNUM LANCEPOD
(BULBOUS —) GALTONIA
(CLIMBING —) VETCH LAWYER
ULLUCE CORALITA
(COMPOSITE —) SUCCORY
HAWKWEED
(CONSECRATED —) HAOMA
(CREATED —) BARAMIN
(CREEPING —) IPECAC KAREAO
KAREAU
(CROSSBRED —) HYBRID
(CRUSHING —) BREAKER
(DWARF —) CUMIN STUNT
(DYE —) WAD ANIL WOAD WOLD
WOALD MADDER
(E. INDIAN —) JATI
(ETIOLATED —) ALBINO
(FIBER —) ALOE FLAX HEMP PITA
CAJUN RAMIE SISAL
(FLOWERING —) HOP ROSE DAISY
HOLLY POPPY ORCHID VIOLET
HAWTHORN LARKSPUR POLYGALA
PRIMROSE SNOWDROP
(FORAGE —) RAPE ALFALFA
DAINCHA
(GERMINATING —) SPIRE
(GRAIN —) TEFF
(HEDGE —) ESPINO
(HEMP —) FIMBLE
(IMMATURE —) KEIKI
(LEAFLESS —) ULEX DODDER
RESTIAD TRIURID
(MALE —) MAS MACRANDER
(MARSH —) FERN JUNCUS CATTAIL
(MEDICINAL —) ALOE HERB ERICA
ARNICA CATNEP CATNIP IPECAC
SIMPLE ACONITE BONESET GENTIAN
LOBELIA CAMOMILE
(NON-FLOWERING —) FERN
(NURSERY —) SEEDLING
(PEPPER —) ARA
(PISTILLATE —) FEMALE
(POISONOUS —) COWBANE DEATHIN
(POTTED —) BONSAI
(POWER —) HYDRO
(PRICKLY —) BRIAR BRIER CACTUS
CARDON NETTLE TEASEL TEAZEL
PRICKFOOT
(PUNGENT —) PEPPER
(RAPIDLY-GROWING —) FILLER
(REEDY —) SPRIT
(RENDERING —) KNACKERY
(SENSITIVE —) MIMOSA
(SIBERIAN —) BADAN
(SPINOUS —) KANTIARA
(STAMINATE —) HUSBAND
(SUBMERGED —) ENALID
(SUCCULENT —) ALOE HERB
GASTERIA HAWORTHIA LOUSELEEK
(SWORD-LEAVED —) LEVERS
(THALLOPHYTIC —) LICHEN
(TRAILING —) ARBUTUS
(TUFTED —) DRYAS
(TWINING —) SMILAX CLIMBER
BINDWEED SCAMMONY
(UNIDENTIFIED —) HORDOCK
(WATER —) LIMU LOTUS AQUATILE
STARFRUIT

(WEEDY —) DOCK KNAWEL
(YOUNG —) SET SPRINGER
(PL.) FLORA
PLANTAGENET ANGEVIN
PLANTAIN COCK PALA ALISMA
FINGER PISANG WABRON BENTING
NETLEAF PANTANO RIBWORT
SITFAST BALISIER BUCKHORN
FIREWEED FLEAWORT ISPAGHUL
RATSBANE ROADWEED WAYBREAD
PLANTAIN EATER TOURACO
SPLITBEAK
PLANTAIN LILY FUNKIA
PLANTATION PEN HOLT WALK
FINCA GROVE BOSKET BOWERY
COLONY ESTATE SHAMBA SPRING
YERBAL CAFETAL FAZENDA
NOPALRY PINETUM THICKET
ARBUSTUM HACIENDA TRAPICHE
VINEYARD
(HEMP —) LATE
PLANTED LISTED
PLANTER SNAG COLON SOWER
FARMER SETTLER PLANTATOR
PLANTING GROVE SATION
PLANTING STICK DIBBLE
PLANT LOUSE APHID PSYLLID
PUCERON HOMOPTER
PLAQUE CHIP PINAX PLATE PLATEAU
SARCOID NAMEPLATE STOMACHER
PLASH LIP DASH BLASH PLOSH
PLOUT PLEACH PUDDLE SPLASH
SPATTER SPECKLE
PLASMA LATEX PLASM
PLASTER CAST DAUB HARL LEEP
LOCK TEER CLEAM GATCH PARGE
SLICK SMALM STAFF TOPIC TREAT
CHARGE CHUNAM GAGING MORTAR
PARGET SPARGE STOOTH STUCCO
BLISTER MALAGMA DIACULUM
DIAPALMA SINAPISM VESICANT
(- WITH COW DUNG) LEEP
(— BETWEEN LATHS) CAT
(— OF PARIS) GESSO GYPSUM
(2 COATS OF —) RENDERSET
(COARSE —) GROUT
(MEDICAL —) TOPIC TREAT CHARGE
SPARADRAP
(MUSTARD —) SINAPISM
PLASTERBOARD GYPSUM
PLASTERED DRUNK SOUSED
SWACKED
PLASTERER DAUBER DAUBSTER
PARGETER SPREADER
PLASTERING KEY SETWORK
ROUGHCAST
PLASTIC FOAM RICH SIRUP LABILE
PLIANT ACETATE CATALIN CRYSTAL
DUCTILE ORGANIC CREATIVE
FLEXIBLE LAMINATE MELAMINE
TECTONIC UNCTUOUS FORMATIVE
PLASTICIZER CAMPHOR
PLASTRON DICKEY CALIPEE
PLAT BED FLAT FOOD PLAN PLOT
SLAP BRAID LEVEL PLACE PLAIN
PLAIT BUFFET WATTLE ARRANGE
FLATTEN PLATEAU QUADRAT
PLATANIST SUSU

PLATANUS PLANE COTONIER
SYCAMORE
PLATBAND IMPOST LINTEL EPISTYLE
PLATE BAT CAP CUT DIP DOD EAR
FIN GIB WEB ANAL BACK BRIN CASE
CAST CURB DIAL DISK DROP FISH
GILL GONG GULA HOME HOOF LAME
LEAF MOLD NAIL ORAL RETE ROSE
SHOE SHUT SLAB SOLE STUD TACE
TRAY AMPYX ANODE BASAL BELLY
BLADE CHAIR CLAMP CLEAT CLOUT
FACIA FENCE FLOOR FLUKE FORCE
GLAND GUARD GULAR LAMEL
PATEN PYGAL SCALE SCUTE SHEET
SHOLE SLICE STAMP STAVE STRAP
TABLE TASSE TERNE TRAMP UNCUS
WATER ADORAL BAFFLE BRIDGE
BUCKLE CASTER CIRCLE CLICHE
COLLAR COPPER COSTAL CRUSTA
DAMPER DASHER EPIGNE FASCIA
FILLER FOLIUM FRIZEL GENIAL
GNOMON GORGET GUSSET LABIAL
LAMINA LOREAL MASCLE MATRIX
MENTAL MENTUM MOTHER PALLET
PATTEN PLATEN RADIAL SCREEN
SCUTUM SEPTUM SERVER SHEATH
SHROUD SPLINT STAPLE TARSUS
TEGMEN TURTLE TYMPAN VESSEL
BESAGNE BOLSTER BRACKET
BRACTEA BUCCULA BUCKLER
CHARGER CLYPEUS COASTER
CORNULE CORONET CRYSTAL
DOUBLER ETCHING FRIZZLE
FRONTAL GRAVURE HUMERAL
INKBLOT MORDANT MYOTOME
NEPTUNE PETALON PRIMARY
ROSTRAL ROUNDEL SPANGLE
STEALER STEELER TERGITE
TESSERA VENTRAL ASSIETTE
BEDPLATE BIQUARTZ BRACHIAL
CELLOCUT DIASCOPE DRAWBACK
ELECTRUM EPIGYNUM EPIPROCT
EPISTOME FIREBACK FLOUNDER
SKEWBACK STAPLING STRINGER
SUBPLATE SURPRINT
(— **COVERING KEYHOLE**) DROP
(— **COVERING MIDDLE EAR**)
TEGMEN
(— **IN AIRPLANE WING**) SPOILER
(— **IN BATTERY**) GRID
(— **IN ORGAN PIPE**) LANGUET
(— **IN STEAM BOILER**) SPUT
DASHER
(— **OF BALEEN**) BLADE
(— **OF CTENOPHORE**) COMB
(— **OF GELATIN**) BAT
(— **OF GLASS**) SLIDE
(— **OF JAW**) AURICLE
(— **OF PRECIOUS METAL**) BRACTEA
(— **OF SOAP FRAME**) SESS
(— **OF SUNDIAL**) GNOMON
(— **ON LANCE SHAFT**) VAMPLATE
(— **ON SADDLE**) SIDEBAR
(— **ON SATCHEL STRAP**) OLIVE
(— **ON THROAT OF FISH**) GULAR
(— **ON WATERWHEEL**) SHROUD
(—**S OF CARDING MACHINE**) ARCH
(—**S OF GUN CARRIAGE**) FLASK
(**ARMOR** —) SPLINT AILETTE

(**COMMUNION** —) PATEN
(**DEEP** —) MAZARINE
(**DORSAL** —) ALINOTUM
(**EARTHEN** —) MUFFIN
(**FASHION** —) SWELL
(**FIREPLACE** —) IRONBACK
(**FLAT** —) APRON
(**GOLD** — **ON FOREHEAD**) PATA
PATTA
(**GROOVED TRAM** —) GULLY GULLEY
(**GUARD** —) SHELL
(**HINGED** —) SHUT
(**HOME** —) DISH
(**HOT** —) GRILL GRILLE
(**IRON** —) STAVE LATTEN MARVER
LAPSTONE SKEWBACK MOLDBOARD
TURNPLATE TURNSHEET
(**LARGE** —) DOUBLER
(**LOCK** —) SELVEDGE
(**NAME** —) FACIA
(**PERFORATED** —) DOD GRID
PINNULE
(**PITCHER'S** —) SLAB MOUND
(**RIMLESS** —) COUPE
(**SIEVE** —) LATTICE
(**THIN** —) LAME LAMP LAMINA
LAMELLA
(**THIN TIN** —) TAIN TAGGERS
(**WALL** —) PAN RASEN
(**WOODEN** —) TRENCHER
PLATEAU PLAT FJELD KAROO KARST
TABLE CAUSSE HAMADA MESETA
NIVEAU PARAMO SABANA UPLAND
ANASAZI PLATFORM
PLATEHOLDER CASSETTE
PLATER VATMAN CLAIMER
COLLARMAN
PLATFORM TOP BANK BEMA DAIS
DECK DRIP DROP DUCK FLAT GHAT
KITE PACE PLAT STEP WING APRON
BENCH BLIND BLOCK CHAIN DUKAN
FLAKE FLOAT HEIAU SOLEA STAGE
STAND STOEP STOOL STOOP STULL
STUMP TOLDO ARBOUR AZOTEA
BRIDGE DESIGN GANTRY HURDLE
ISLAND MACHAN PAEPAE PALLET
PERRON PILLAR PODIUM PULPIT
RUNWAY SETTLE SLEDGE ALMEMAR
BALCONY BATTERY CATWALK
ESTRADE FORETOP GALLERY
LANDING LOGEION PADDOCK
PATTERN ROLLWAY ROSTRUM
SKIDWAY SOAPBOX TRIBUNE
FOOTPACE HUSTINGS SCAFFOLD
STALLAGE
(— **FOR ACTORS**) LOGEION
THEOLOGIUM
(— **FOR ALTAR**) PREDELLA
(— **FOR DRYING FISH**) FLAKE
(— **FOR PUBLIC SPEAKING**) BEMA
PODIUM TRIBUNE
(— **FOR STORING FOOD**) WHATA
(— **IN CHURCH**) SOLEA
(— **IN SYNAGOGUE**) ALMEMAR
(— **IN TEMPLE**) DUKAN
(— **IN TREE**) MACHAN
(— **OF GALLOWS**) DROP
(— **ON RUNNERS**) SLEDGE
(— **ON TOP OF HOUSE**) AZOTEA

(— **ON WHEELS**) SKID DOLLY FLOAT
(— **TO SUPPORT MINERS**) STULL
(**GUN** —) BARBET SPONSON
BARBETTE
(**LEADSMAN'S** —) CHAIN
(**MINE** —) STULL SOLLAR SOLLER
(**MOHAMMEDAN STONE** —)
MASTABA
(**MOUNTED** —) SKID
(**NAUTICAL** —) FORETOP MAINTOP
ROUNDTOP
(**ORE** —) BUDDLE
(**RAILROAD** —) DOCK DOCKEN
TRAINWAY
(**RAISED** —) DAIS PYAL STAND
STOEP STOOL STOOP LISSOM
PANTALAN
(**ROCK** —) STANCE
(**SLEEPING** —) KANG
(**STAIRCASE** —) HALFPACE
HATHPACE
(**WOOD** —) PLANCHER
PLATING ARMOR SKIRT
PLATINUM COSTLY PLATINA
PLATITUDE TRUISM BROMIDE
DULLNESS STALENESS TRITENESS
PLATONIST IDEIST
PLATOON SQUAD VOLLEY PELOTON
PLOTTON
PLATTER DISH DISK LANX ASHET
GRAIL PLATE RECORD CHARGER
TRENCHER
PLATY MOON MOONFISH
PLATYPUS DUCKBILL DUCKMOLE
MALLAGONG
PLAUDIT APPLAUD APPROVAL
ENCOMIUM
(**PL.**) PRAISE APPLAUSE
PLAUSIBILITY COLOR
PLAUSIBLE FAIR OILY SNOD GLOSSY
AFFABLE POPULAR CREDIBLE
PROBABLE PROVABLE SPECIOUS
SUITABLE
PLAY FUN JEU JIG RUN RUX TOY
AUTO BEAR COME DAFF DEAL DICE
DRAW FAIR GAME JEST LAKE MOVE
MUCK PLEE PUNT ROMP SPIN TUNE
WAKE CARRY CHARM DALLY DRAMA
ENACT FLIRT FROST HORSE SHOOT
SOTIE SOUND SPIEL SPORT STUCK
WREAK YEDDE ACTION COMEDY
COQUET DANDLE DIVIDE FILLER
FROLIC GAMBLE GAMBOL GAMING
GHOSTS MUSERY NUMBER PIDDLE
ROLLIX TRIFLE CONSORT CUTBACK
DISPORT EXECUTE EXPLOIT
GUIGNOL HISTORY HOLIDAY
MIRACLE PAGEANT PASSION
PRELUDE STAGERY VENTURE
BURLETTA MORALITY SKITTLES
(— **A DOMINO**) SET POSE
(— **A PART**) DO ACT ENTER
GAMMON GUIZARD
(— **A PIPE**) CHARM
(— **ABOUT**) SPANIEL
(— **AGAINST**) BUCK
(— **AN INSTRUMENT**) BOW BLOW
SWAY FINGER TWEEDLE
(— **AT COURTSHIP**) FLIRT

(— **BAGPIPE**) SKIRL DOODLE DOUDLE
(— **BY STROKES**) STRIKE
(— **FANFARE**) FLOURISH
(— **FAST AND LOOSE**) PALTER
(— **FIRST CARD**) LEAD
(— **FLORIDLY**) DIVIDE
(— **FOR TIME**) STALL
(— **GOLF BALL**) DRIVE
(— **IMPOSTER**) MUMP
(— **IN MUD**) MUDLARK
(— **IN POOL**) BURST
(— **IN STREAKS**) FORK
(— **IN TRIGGER**) CREEP
(— **JAZZ**) BLOW
(— **LEGATO**) SUSTAIN
(— **LOOSELY**) WAVE
(— **LOUT**) SWAB SLUBBER
(— **MEAN TRICKS**) SHAB
(— **NERVOUSLY**) FIDGET
(— **OF COLORS**) IRIS
(— **OF FOAM**) HOOD
(— **OF LIGHT**) GLORY
(— **ON WORDS**) PUN CLENCH CLINCH
(— **THE BUFFOON**) DROLL
(— **THE BULLY**) BLUSTER
(— **THE FOOL**) HOIT
(— **THE HYPOCRITE**) FACE
(— **THE TOADY**) SUPE
(— **TRICKS**) JAPE JINK
(— **TRUANT**) WAG JOUK MICHE MOOCH MOUCH PLUNK TRONE MOOTCH
(— **UNSKILLFULLY**) STRUM FOOZLE
(— **WITH**) DANDLE
(**AMOROUS** —) GAME
(**BOISTEROUS** —) ROMP
(**BRIDGE** —) COUP ECHO SIGNAL SQUEEZE
(**END** —) SHAKE
(**FARCICAL** —) SOTIE
(**FOOTBALL** —) DOWN KEEP SAFETY CUTBACK SPINNER
(**IN** —) ALIVE
(**MASKED** —) GUISE
(**MIRACLE** —) AUTO GUARY MIRACLE
(**RAPID CHESS** —) SKITTLES
(**USED IN** —) LUSORY
(PL.) THEATER VANGELI
PLAYA BEACH SEBKA SALINA SEBKHA
PLAY-BY-PLAY DETAILED
PLAYER IT CAP END BACK DUCK SIDE ACTOR BLACK COLOR GUARD BANKER BUSKER FEEDER STAGER STROLL TENTER ALTOIST FIELDER FORWARD GAMBLER STRIKER TRIFLER TURQUET BUDGETER GAMESTER HORNSMAN STROLLER
(— **IN CHESS**) BLACK WHITE
(— **IN CHOUETTE**) CAPTAIN
(— **OF JAZZ**) CAT
(— **WHO CUTS CARDS**) PONE
(— **WHO IS IT**) HE
(— **WHO SCORES ZERO**) DUCK
(— **WITH LOWEST SCORE**) BOOBY
(**BACKGAMMON** —) TABLER

(**BASEBALL** —) SHORT SACKER CATCHER FIELDER LEADOFF PITCHER BACKSTOP
(**BASKETBALL** —) CAGEMAN HOOPMAN HOOPSTER
(**BOWLING** —) LEAD
(**CARD** —) EAST HAND PONE WEST BLIND DUMMY NORTH SOUTH JUNIOR SENIOR BRAGGER DECLARER
(**CRICKET** —) LEG BOWLER INNING
(**CROQUET** —) MALLET
(**DICE** —) SHOOTER
(**FLUTE** —) AULETE
(**FOOTBALL** —) END GUARD SLANT BUCKER CENTER TACKLE BLOCKER FLANKER GRIDDER SNAPPER FULLBACK HALFBACK SCATBACK
(**LACROSSE** —) HOME COVER ATTACK STICKMAN
(**LEAPFROG** —) BACK
(**POKER** —) AGE
(**RUGBY** —) SCRUM HOOKER
(**SOCCER** —) CAP INNER BOOTER
(**STUPID** —) HAM
(**TENNIS** —) SMASHER
(**UNSKILLFUL** —) DUB
(**VOLLEYBALL** —) SPIKER
(**WEAK** —) RABBIT
PLAYFUL ELFIN MERRY FRISKY GAMBOL JOCOSE LUSORY TOYISH WANTON COLTISH GIOCOSO JIGGISH JOCULAR TOYSOME GAMESOME HUMOROUS LARKSOME SPORTFUL SPORTIVE KITTENISH
PLAYFULNESS FUN BANTER GAMMICK GAMMOCK
PLAYGROUND OVAL CLOSE PLAYSTOW PLAYSTEAD
PLAYHOUSE HOUSE MOVIE CINEMA THEATER
PLAYING FROLIC LAKING
(— **CARD**) ACE JACK KING TREY DEUCE QUEEN TAROT
(— **CARDS**) DECK
(— **LIGHTLY**) LAMBENT
PLAYTHING DIE TOY HOOP KNACK PLAIK SPORT BAUBLE LAKING SUCKER TRIFLE PLAYOCK
PLAYWRIGHT AUTHOR DRAMATIST PLAYMAKER
PLAZA PLEIN SQUARE ZOCALO
(— **DE TOROS**) BULLRING
PLEA BAR BID PLY MOOT NOLO SUIT ALIBI CLAIM PLEAD ABATER APPEAL EXCUSE REFUGE APOLOGY CONTEND DEFENCE LAWSUIT PRETEXT QUARREL DILATORY ENTREATY PRETENSE
PLEACH PLAIT PLASH INTERLACE
PLEAD BEG SUE MOOT PLEA PRAY PRIG SHOW URGE COUNT ORATE ALLEGE APPEAL ASSERT PLAYTE PURSUE ENTREAT IMPLORE SOLICIT WRANGLE ADVOCATE LITIGATE
(— **FOR**) SOLICIT PETITION
PLEADER ACTOR VAKIL PATRON SUITOR VAKEEL COUNTOR ADVOCATE

PLEADING PLEA PAROL ANSWER PAROLE ADVOCACY COGNOVIT DEMURRER INTENDIT MEMORIAL
PLEASANT FUN GAY BEEN BIEN BRAW FAIR FINE GLAD GOOD HEND JOLI NEAT TRIM WEME BIGLY BONNY CANNY COUTH CUSHY DOUCE DRUNK DUCKY GREEN HAPPY HENDE HODDY JOLLY LEPID LISTY MERRY NUTTY QUEME SMIRK SUAVE SWEET TIPSY WALLY WETHE COMELY DAINTY DULCET GENIAL KINDLY SAVORY SMOOTH AFFABLE ELEGANT FARRAND JANNOCK LEESOME WINSOME DELICATE GLORIOUS GRATEFUL HEAVENLY LIEFSOME LIKESOME LOVESOME THANKFUL TOWARDLY
PLEASANTLY FAIR WINLY FAIRLY AFFABLY SWEETLY GENIALLY LIKINGLY
PLEASANTNESS GAIETY NAAMAN AMENITY SUAVITY JOCUNDITY
PLEASANTRY WIT JEST JOKE SPORT BANTER JESTING JOLLITY WAGGERY
PLEASE PAY GAME LIKE LIST LUST SUIT WANT WISH AGREE AMUSE BITTE CHARM ELATE FANCY HUMOR QUEME SAVOR TASTE ARRIDE KITTLE OBLIGE REGALE SOOTHE TICKLE CONTENT DELIGHT GLADDEN GRATIFY PLACATE REJOICE SATISFY APPLEASE
(— **FORWARD**) FS
PLEASED FAIN FOND GLAD APAID HAPPY PROUD BUCKED CONTENT GLADSOME
(**BE** —) GAME
PLEASING AMEN GLAD GOOD LIEF NICE SOFT AMENE DICTY SOOTH SWEET CLEVER DREAMY FACILE FLASHY GAINLY LIKING LUSTLY AMIABLE BLESSED CORKING DARLING LIKEFUL TUNABLE WELCOME CHARMING DELICATE FAVOROUS FETCHING GRACEFUL GRACIOUS GRATEFUL HEAVENLY INVITING LIKESOME PLACABLE PLAUSIVE SPECIOUS
(— **TO EAR**) HARMONIC
(— **TO EYE**) EESOME
(— **TO HEAR**) FAIR
(**VERY** —) SNAZZY
PLEASURABLE GOOD JOLLY ANIMAL MIRTHFUL
PLEASURE JO EST FUN JOY BANG BOOT EASE ESTE GREE KAMA LIST LUST PLAY WILL KICKS MIRTH SAVOR SOOTH TASTE DAINTY DEDUIT GAIETY GAYETY LIKING LUXURY NICETY VOLUPT COMFORT DELIGHT GRATIFY JOLLITY JOYANCE VOLUPTY DELICACY FRUITION GLADNESS HILARITY VOLUPTAS
(**SELFISH** —) LECHERY
(**STOLEN** —) STOUTH STOWTH
(PL.) DELICIAE
PLEASURE SEEKER FRANION

PLEAT SET FOLD POKE FLUTE FRILL PINCH PLAIT PRANK GUSSET SUNRAY

PLEATED SUNBURST

PLEBE PLEBS FRESHMAN

PLEBEIAN LOW BASE PLEB SNOB COMMON HOMELY VULGAR IGNOBLE LOWBORN POPULAR BASEBORN EVERYDAY HOMESPUN INFERIOR MECHANIC ORDINARY RUPTUARY

PLEBISCITE VOTE DECREE

PLECTRUM PICK SPUR QUILL UVULA MALLEUS POINTEL PLECTRON (— OF HARP) FESCUE

PLEDGE LAY VAS VOW WAD WED BAND CLAP EARL GAGE HAND HEST HOCK PASS PAWN WAGE WOID WORD FAITH SIKER SPOUT STAKE SWEAR SWEAT TOKEN TROTH TRUTH WAGER ARREST BORROW COMMIT ENGAGE IMPAWN IMPONE LUMBER PIGNUS PLEVIN PLIGHT SICCAR SICKER VADIUM WADSET BARGAIN BETROTH CAUTION EARNEST HOSTAGE PROMISE BOTTOMRY MORTGAGE SECURITY SPONSION VADIMONY (— IN DRINKING) PROPINE

PLEDGED HIGHT SWORN ASSURED ENGAGED PIGNORATE (— TO MARRY) SURE

PLEDGET DOSSIL

PLEIADES MAIA MEROPE ALCYONE CELAENO ELECTRA STEROPE TAYGETA

PLEIN-AIRIST LUMINIST

PLEISTHENES (FATHER OF —) ATREUS (MOTHER OF —) AEROPE (SON OF —) MENELAUS AGAMEMNON

PLENARY FULL ENTIRE PLENAL PERFECT ABSOLUTE COMPLETE

PLENITUDE PLENITY PLEROMA FULLNESS PLETHORA ABUNDANCE

PLENTEOUS RICH COPIOUS FERTILE AFFLUENT FRUITFUL GENEROUS ABOUNDING EXUBERANT

PLENTIFUL OLD FULL RANK RICH RIFE AMPLE HEFTY LARGE ROUTH SONSY STORE ENOUGH GALORE LAVISH SONSIE COPIOUS FERTILE LIBERAL OPULENT PROFUSE UBEROUS ABUNDANT FRUITFUL NUMEROUS EXUBERANT

PLENTIFULLY RIFE FREELY GALORE APLENTY

PLENTY WON BAIT COPY MANY RAFF SONS AMPLE CHEAP COPIA FOUTH PRICE ROUTH SONSE TEEMS FOISON SCOUTH UBERTY LASHINGS (GREAT —) LASHINGS

PLEON TELSON ABDOMEN

PLEONASM ITERATION MACROLOGY TAUTOLOGY

PLETHORA EXCESS PLURISY FULLNESS PLEURISY POLYEMIA PROFUSION REPLETION

PLETHORIC TUMID TURGID

SWOLLEN INFLATED

PLEURISY EMPYEMA

PLEURON SCAPULA

PLEXUS RETE GLOMUS NETWORK PROPLEX GENIPLEX

PLIABLE WAXY WEAK LITHY WAXEN DOCILE LIMBER PLIANT SEMMIT SUPPLE BOWABLE FICTILE FINGENT FLEXILE PLASTIC WINDING CUSHIONY FLEXIBLE COMPLIANT

PLIANCY FLEXURE FACILITY

PLIANT APT FLIP SWAK BUXOM LITHE SWACK YOUNG DOCILE LIMBER SUPPLE DUCTILE FLEXILE PLIABLE SLIPPER WILLOWY APPLIANT FLEXIBLE SUITABLE WORKABLE

PLICA FOLD TRICHOMA

PLICATE FOLD PLEAT FOLDED FANLIKE PLAITED

PLIERS BENDER FLEXOR GRATER FLECTOR PINCERS

PLIGHT PLY FOLD ARRAY BRAID DRESS PLAIT POINT STATE WOVEN ATTIRE ENGAGE PICKLE PLEDGE PLISKY TAKING BETROTH MISCHIEF

PLIGHTED ASSURATE

PLIM PLUM STOUT SWELL INFLATE PLIABLE

PLINTH ORLE ORLO BLOCK ABACUS PATAND QUADRA SUBBASE FOOTSTALL SCAMILLUS

PLOD JOG GRUB PLOT SLOG STOG TORE TROG VAMP POACH TRAMP TRASH DRUDGE SLOUCH TRUDGE PLUNTHER (— ALONG) PEG TORE (— THROUGH MUD) SLOUGH

PLODDER GRUB DIGGER SLOGGER

PLOIARIA EMESA

PLOP FLUMP PLUMP HEAVILY

PLOT BREW CAST PACK PLAN PLAT CABAL DRIFT FRAUD GLEBE GRAPH GREEN HATCH MODEL PLECK SCALD STORY STUDY WATCH ACTION BRIGUE CLIQUE DESIGN DEVISE GARDEN MALIGN MYTHOS SCHEME SHAMBA TAMPER AGITATE COLLUDE COMPACT COMPASS CONJECT CONNIVE CONTOUR DRAUGHT FEEDLOT LAZYBED MACHINE PRETEND QUADRAT QUARTER SWIDDEN ARGUMENT COGITATE CONSPIRE CONTRIVE INTRIGUE PRACTICE PROTRACT SEMINARY (— OF 1-2 ACRE) ERF (— OF GRASS) SONK (— OF LAND) ERF LOT PLAT SHOT FORTY MILPA PATCH PLECK SPLAT COMMON SCHERM SHAMBA HAGGARD LAZYBED SEVERAL (GARDEN —) BED ERF QUINTA QUARTER (UNPRODUCTIVE —) HIRST

PLOTTER PACKER HATCHER JACOBIN SCHEMER DESIGNER ENGINEER

PLOUK KNOB PIMPLE

PLOVER DROME KOLEA OXEYE PILOT SANDY STILT KILDEE QUAILY TURNIX COLLIER COURSER DOTTREL LAPWING MAYCOCK OWLHEAD PAPABOT WRYBILL BULLHEAD DULWILLY HILLBIRD KILLDEER RINGNECK SPURWING SQUEALER TOADHEAD WHISTLER WIREBIRD

PLOW EAR ERE BOUT DISK FOIL HINT MOLE PLOD RIVE ROVE SLUG STIR SULK SULL TILL BREAK FLUNK SPLIT SULKY THROW ARAIRE BUSTER DIGGER FALLOW FURROW GOPHER JUMPER LISTER PLOUGH RAFTER ROOTER RUTTER SULLOW BACKSET BREAKER HUSBAND SCOOTER SULCATE TWISTER FIREPLOW FURROWER GANGPLOW SNOWPLOW TURNPLOW (— CROSSWISE) THORTER (— HANDLE) STILT (— LIGHTLY) SKIM RIFFLE (— PART) PINHEAD (PL.) OUTSIGHT

PLOWBOY YOKEL

PLOWING ARDER EARTH ARDURE ARATION CARUAGE STIRRING

PLOWLAND CARUE CARVE TILTH CARUCATE TEAMLAND

PLOWMAN PLOWER TILLER ACREMAN

PLOWSHARE LAY SLIP SOCK LAVER REEST SHARE JUMPER (— BONE) VOMER PYGOSTYLE

PLOY BENT BOWED SPORT RAMBLE TACTIC PURSUIT ACTIVITY ESCAPADE

PLUCK GO PUG ROB TUG BOUT CROP CULL DRAG GAME GRAB PELT PICK PILL POOK PULL RACE RASE RASH SAND TUCK ARBER ARBOR BREAK DRAFT HANGE NERVE PILCH PLOAT PLUME RANCH SMITE SPUNK STEAL STRIP AVULSE DECERP EVULSE FLEECE GATHER PIGEON PLITCH PLOUGH QUARRY SNATCH SPIRIT TWINGE TWITCH COURAGE DEPLUME PLUNDER BOLDNESS DECISION DEMOLISH GAMENESS (— AS A STRING) TIRL PINCH (— FEATHERS) STUB (— LEAVES) BLADE (— OF SHEEP OR CALF) RACE GATHER (— UP COURAGE) CHEER (— WOOL BY HAND) ROO

PLUCKED PLUMED PIZZICATO

PLUCKY GAMY SANDY GRITTY SPUNKY FIGHTING

PLUG BUG FID PEG PIN TAP TOP WAD BLOW BONE BOTT BUNG FILL JADE ROOT SHOT SLOG STOP SWAT SWOT BOOST DOWEL DUMMY PILOT PUNCH SHACK SKATE SPILE STUFF SWEAT BOXING BULLET COMEDO DOSSIL DOTTLE FIDDLE SPIGOT BOUCHON BUSHING CHAMBER CHUGGER FERRULE STOPPER

STOPPLE DRIVECAP FUSEPLUG
PELELITH STOPCOCK
(— FOR CANNON) TAMPION
(— IN GRENADE) BOUCHON
(— IN ORGAN PIPE) STOPPLE
TAMPION
(— OF CLAY) BOTT
(— OF OAKUM) FID
(— OF VOLCANO) CORE
(— UP) CLAM STOP ESTOP
RAMFORCE
(FISHING —) BUG
(NOSE —) TEMBETA TEMBETARA
(WASTE —) WASHER
(WATER —) HYDRANT
PLUG-IN JACK
PLUG-UGLY THUG ROWDY TOUGH
RUFFIAN ROUGHNECK
PLUM GAGE JOBO RISE ISLAY JAMAN
PRUNE SWELL BEAUTY CHENEY
DAMSEL DAMSON KELSEY SAPOTE
APRICOT BULLACE BURBANK
FORTUNE ORLEANS PRUNELLO
ROSACEAN ROSEWORT VICTORIA
WINDFALL
(COCO —) ICACO
(JAVA —) DUHAT JAMBUL JAMBOOL
JAMBOLAN
(WILD —) SKEG SLOE ISLAY
PLUMAGE ROBE FLUFF HACKLE
SHROUD FEATHER FLOCCUS
JUVENAL PENNAGE FEATHERS
PARADISE PTILOSIS
PLUMB BUNG BOTTOM SINKER
EXACTLY PLUMMET UTTERLY
ABSOLUTE COMPLETE DIRECTLY
ENTIRELY VERTICAL
PLUMBAGO LUSTER LUSTRE
GRAPHITE LEADWORT
PLUMB BOB PLUMMET
PLUMB LINE MERKHET
PLUM CURCULIO TURK WEEVIL
PLUME PEN TIP TUFT CREST EGRET
PRIDE PRUNE DEPRIVE DESPOIL
FEATHER PANACHE AIGRETTE
(— ON HELMET) CREST PANACHE
(— ON HORSE) PLUMADE
(— ON TURBAN) CULGEE
(EGRET —) OSPREY
(MILITARY —) PANACHE
PLUME NUTMEG SASSAFRAS
PLUMMET LEAD FLOAT PLUMB
WEIGHT
PLUMMING BRONZING
PLUMP FAT BOLD FAIR FLOP FULL
PLOP SLAP SOSS TIDY BLUNT
BONNY CLUMP FLUMP FUBBY
FUBSY GROUP JOLLY PLUNK SAPPY
SLEEK SMACK SQUAB STOUT THICK
BONNIE CHUBBY CRUMBY CRUMMY
DIRECT FATTEN FLATLY FLESHY
FODGEL GAWSIE PLUNGE PUBBLE
ROTUND BLUNTLY BUNTING
CLUSTER DISTEND FULSOME
RIBLESS THRODDY FLESHFUL
(— AND ROSY) BUXOM
(— AND ROUND) CHUBBY
PLUM POCKET FOOL
PLUMULE FEATHER GEMMULA
GEMMULE GEOBLAST ACROSPIRE

PLUNDER GUT ROB BOOT FANG
JUNK LOOT PILL POLL PREY RAPE
REIF RIPE RUMP SACK SWAG
BOOTY CHEAT GAINS HARRY PLUCK
PREDE RAVEN RENNE RIFLE SCOFF
SHAVE SPOIL STRIP BEZZLE
BOODLE CREACH DACOIT FLEECE
FORAGE HARROW MARAUD PANYAR
PROFIT RAPINE RAVAGE DESPOIL
ESCHEAT FREIGHT PILFERY PILLAGE
SACKAGE SPULZIE BOOTHALE
FREEBOOT
PLUNDERER THIEF BANDIT BUMMER
POLLER RAPTOR ROBBER VANDAL
ROUTIER SPOILER MARAUDER
RAPPAREE
PLUNDERING PREY SACK MARAUD
RAPINE ESCHEAT PURCHASE
SPECHERY SPOILFUL SPOILING
PREDATORY
PLUNGE BET DIG DIP CAVE DIVE
DOOK DUCK DUMP JUMP PURL
PUSH RAKE RISK SINK SOSS BURST
DOUSE FLING PITCH PLUMP SOUSE
SWOOP FOOTER GAMBLE HEADER
LAUNCH SPLASH THRUST WALLOP
BRAINGE IMMERSE PLOUNCE
SUBMERGE
(— INTO WATER) ENEW
(— INTO) CLAP ENGULF IMMERGE
PLUNGER RAM SWAB FORCE
DUCKER POMMEL BLUNGER
STRIKER
PLUNGING FLING
PLUNK DIVE PLONK PLUCK PLUMP
DOLLAR SUPPORT SUDDENLY
PLUNTHER PLOD FLOUNDER
PLURALIST TOTQUOT
PLURALITY MAJORITY MORENESS
TRIALITY
PLUS GAIN WITH EXTRA SURPLUS
ADDITION INCREASE POSITIVE
PLUSH EASY BEAVER VELOUR
SUPERIOR
PLUSHY SWANK SWANKY
PLUTEUS WAGON PARAPET
PLUTO DIS HADES ORCUS
(BROTHER OF —) JUPITER NEPTUNE
(FATHER OF —) SATURN
(WIFE OF —) PROSERPINE
PLUTOCRAT NABOB RICHARD
PLUTONIC HYPOGENE INTRUSIVE
VULCANIAN
PLUTUS (ASSOCIATE OF —) TYCHE
EIRENE
(FATHER OF —) IASION
(MOTHER OF —) DEMETER
PLY RUN BEAT BEND BIAS CORD
CORE DRAM FOLD MOLD SAIL URGE
ADAPT APPLY EXERT LAYER STEER
TWIST WIELD YIELD COMPLY
DOUBLE HANDLE TRAVEL EXERCISE
(— WITH DRINK) BIRL ROSIN
(— WITH DRUGS) HOCUS
(OF ONE —) SINGLE
PNEUMA NEUM SOUL NEUME
BREATH SPIRIT
PNEUMATIC HAMMER GUN
PNEUMATOCYST FLOAT

PNEUMONIA PULMONITIS
POACH PUG ROB COOK DROP POKE
PUSH SINK BLACK DRIVE FORCE
POTCH STEAL BLEACH PLUNGE
INTRUDE
POACHED EGGS MOONSHINE
POACHER BLACK POGGE SPOACH
LURCHER STALKER WIDGEON
BALDPATE BULLHEAD
(SALMON —) REBECCA REBEKAH
(PL.) BLACKS
POALES GLUMALES
POCHARD DUCK SMEE DIVER POKER
SCAUP DUNAIR DUNKER DUNBIRD
REDHEAD WHINGER GOLDHEAD
WHINYARD
POCHETTE KIT VIOLIN HANDBAG
POCKET BOX CLY FOB PIT CLAY
KICK POKE PRAT BASIN BURSE
MEANS POUCH PURSE STEAL
ACCEPT BECKET CASING CANTINA
PLACKET SWALLOW TROUSER
ENVELOPE ISOLATED MONETARY
PROFONDE SUPPRESS CONDENSED
MINIATURE
(— A WRONG) PURSE
(BILLIARD —) POT HOLE HAZARD
(MAGICIAN'S —) PROFONDE
(NOODLE —S) KREPLACH
(ORE —) CHURN BONANZA
(SMALL —) FOB
(TROUSER —) FOB PRAT BECKET
(WATER —) TINAJA ALBERCA
(PL.) KREPLACH
POCKETBOOK BAG KICK SKIN
PURSE INCOME READER WALLET
HANDBAG LEATHER BILLFOLD
NOTECASE
POCKET GOPHER TUZA QUACHIL
POCKETING COUP
POCKETKNIFE PIGSTICKER
POCKMARK PITHOLE
POD BAG COD GAM KID POP SAC
BALL BEAN BOLL HUSK POKE SWAD
BURSE CAROB FLOCK POUCH
QUASH SHAUP SHELL SHUCK SNAIL
WHAUP LEGUME PESCOD SCHOOL
HARICOT PEASCOD PEASECOD
PODOCARP POTBELLY SEEDCASE
TAMARIND
(— FORMING) KID
(— OF LEGUME) KID
(— OF MESQUITE) HONEYPOD
(EXPLOSIVE —) SANDBOX
(SUBTERRANEAN —) EARTHNUT
(UNRIPE —) SQUASH
(PL.) SUNT GARAD BABLAH GARRAT
GONAKIE ALGAROBA
PODIUM DAIS FOOT WALL LECTERN
PODOCARP YACCA
PODWARE PODDER
POEM GEM LAI LAY ODE DUAN EPIC
JOSE MELE POSY RUNE SONG
DIRGE DITTY HAIKU IWEIN METER
STAFF VERSE AMHRAN AUBADE
BALLAD CACCIA CARMEN CYCLIC
DIXAIN EPOPEE EROTIC ESTRIF
HEROID MELODY MONODY PIYYUT
SESTET SONNET TENSON TERCET

BUCOLIC CANTARE CANTATA
CANZONE DESCORT DIZAINE
ECLOGUE ELEGIAC FLITING
GEORGIC SOTADIC TRIOLET VIRELAI
VIRELAY VOLUSPA ACROSTIC
AMOEBEUM BRINDISI CANTICLE
DINGDONG DOGGEREL INVICTUS
LIMERICK MADRIGAL TELESTIC
THEOGONY TRISTICH TROCHAIC
VERSICLE
(— **ABOUT DEBATE**) ESTRIF
(— **ABOUT SHEPHERDS**) ECLOGUE
(— **GREETING DAWN**) AUBADE
(— **OF 10 LINES**) DIZAINE
(— **OF 14 LINES**) SONNET
(— **OF LAMENTATION**) ELEGY
(**AMATORY** —) EROTIC SONNET
(**EPIC** —) EPOS EPOPEE LUSIAD
THEBAID
(**HOMELY** —) DIT
(**IRISH** —) AMHRAN
(**JAPANESE** —) HAIKU
(**LITURGICAL** —) VIDDUI VIDDUY
SELIHOTH
(**LOVE** —) AMORETTO
(**LYRIC** —) LAI LAY ODE ALBA
EPODE GHAZEL RONDEL CANZONA
PARTIMEN
(**PART OF** —) PASSUS
(**PASTORAL** —) IDYL IDYLL BUCOLIC
(**PERSIAN** —) GHAZAL
(**RELIGIOUS** —) HYMN
(**RURAL** —) GEORGIC
(**SACRED** —) PSALM YIGDAL
(**SATIRICAL** —) IAMBIC KASIDA
(**SHORT** —) DIT DITTY EPILOG
SONNET EPIGRAM EPILOGUE
EPYLLION
(**TONE** —) BALLADE
(**WELSH** —) CYWYDD
(**PL.**) AZAHROT MAKINGS
POET OG RSI BARD FILE FILI FIRI
LARK MUSE SCOP SWAN ARION
LAKER LINOS LINUS LYRIC MAKAR
MAKER ODIST RISHI SAYER SCALD
SKALD FINDER GNOMIC IBYCUS
LAKIST LYRIST SHAPER SINGER
DICHTER ELEGIAC EPICIST IDYLIST
IMAGIST MUSAEUS ORPHEUS
PROPHET FERAMORZ GEORGIAN
LAUREATE LUTANIST MINSTREL
SONGSTER TROUVERE
(**IRISH** —) FILI
(**MEDIOCRE** —) RIMER RHYMER
(**MINOR** —) BARDIE
POETASTER BARDET BAVIAN BAVIUS
POETITO BARDLING VERSEMAN
POETIC ODIC LYRIC STILTED
PEGASEAN POEMATIC
POETRY SONG BLANK MELIC POEMS
VERSE EPOPEE POESIS SONIOU
DOGGREL KALEVALA
(**FINNISH** —) RUNES
(**GOD OF** —) BRAGI
(**MUSE OF** —) ERATO THALIA
EUTERPE CALLIOPE
POGROM RIOT PILLAGE MASSACRE
POGY POGIE MENHADEN
POIGNANT APT HOME KEEN ACUTE

SHARP SMART BITING BITTER
MOVING SEVERE URGENT CUTTING
POINTED PUNGENT SATIRIC INCISIVE
PIERCING PRESSING STINGING
STRIKING TOUCHING AMAREVOLE
POINCIANA DELONIX FLAMBEAU
GULMOHAR FLAMBOYER
POINSETTIA BANNER FIREFLOWER
POINT AIM DOT JOT NAK NEB NIB
NUB PEG PIN RES WAY APEX BACK
BOKE CHAT CUSP FORK GAFF GAME
GOOD HEAD HOLD ITEM KNOT LACE
LOOK NAIL PEAK PICK PILE PINT
SPOT STOP WHET BEARD CHALK
DIGIT FOCUS INDEX LEVEL MUCRO
PITCH PRICK PUNCH PUNCT PUNTA
PUNTO REFER STAND TEACH THING
TOOTH ALLUDE BROACH CRAYON
CUSPIS CUTOFF DEGREE DIRECT
FLECHE JUGALE MATTER NOSING
PERIOD THESIS TITTLE VERTEX
ZYGION APICULA ARTICLE BENEFIT
CRUNODE ESSENCE GATEWAY
PUSHPIN SHARPEN TANJONG
TRAGION ANNOUNCE PUNCTULE
STRIPPER
(— **AT ISSUE**) BEEF CRUX
(— **AT WHICH LEAF SPRINGS**) AXIL
(— **BEHIND EAR**) ASTERION
(— **FOR PHONOGRAPH RECORD**)
STYLE
(— **IN CAPSTAN**) STRIPPER
(— **IN CONSONANT**) DAGHESH
(— **IN DEBATE**) ISSUE
(— **IN ORBIT OF PLANET**) AUGE
APSIS APOGEE SYZYGY APOJOVE
PERIGEE APASTRON APHELION
(— **IN QUESTION**) ISSUE
(— **IN SEVEN-UP**) GIFT
(— **IN SOME GAMES**) PUNT
(— **NEAREST EARTH**) PERIGEE
(— **OF A BORDER**) VANDYKE
(— **OF ANCHOR**) BILL
(— **OF ANTLER**) PRONG
(— **OF ANVIL**) HORN
(— **OF CELESTIAL SPHERE**)
ANTAPEX
(— **OF CHIN**) BUTTON
(— **OF CONTACT**) EPHAPSE
(— **OF CRESCENT MOON**) CUSP
(— **OF DECLINE**) EBB
(— **OF DIVERGENCE**) AXIL
(— **OF ECLIPTIC**) LAGNA SOLSTICE
(— **OF EPIGRAM**) STING
(— **OF HONOR**) PUNDONOR
(— **OF INTEREST**) CLOU
(— **OF INTERSECTION**) FOOT
STAURION
(— **OF JAVELIN**) SAGAIE
(— **OF JUNCTION**) MEET BREGMA
LAMBDA
(— **OF LABEL**) LAMBEAU
(— **OF LAND**) ODD CAPE SPIT
MORRO HEADLAND
(— **OF LEAF**) MUCRO
(— **OF LIFE**) HYLEG
(— **OF LIGHT**) GLINT SPANGLE
(— **OF LIGHTNING ROD**) AIGRETTE
(— **OF LIPS**) CHEILION

(— **OF MANGO**) NAK
(— **OF ONSET**) BRINK
(— **OF ORIGIN**) HIVE SOURCE
FOUNTAIN
(— **OF PEN**) NEB NIB
(— **OF PETAL**) LACINULA
(— **OF REFERENCE**) STYLION
(— **OF STAG'S HORN**) START
(— **OF STORY**) KNOT
(— **OF STYLUS**) CUTTER
(— **OF SUPPORT**) BEARING
(— **OF TEMPERATURE**) SOLIDUS
(— **OF TIME**) DATE INSTANT
JUNCTURE
(— **OF TOOTH**) CUSP
(— **OF UMBRELLA**) FERRULE
(— **OF VIEW**) EYE ANGLE FRONT
SLANT COLORS CORNER GROUND
RESPECT FUTURISM
(— **OF VIOLIN BOW**) HEAD
(— **OF WEAPON**) BARB
(— **ON AUGER OR BIT**) SPUR
(— **ON BACKGAMMON BOARD**)
FLECHE
(— **ON CURVE**) TACNODE
(— **ON JAW**) GONION
(— **ON STAG'S HORN**) BROACH
(— **ON SUNDIAL**) NODE
(— **OUT**) SHOW DIGIT INFER ASSIGN
DIRECT ENSIGN FINGER MUSTER
NOTIFY REMARK PRESAGE INDICATE
(**ASTROLOGICAL** —) INGRESS
(**BARBED** —) FORK
(**BLUNT** —) MORNETTE
(**CARBON** —) CRAYON
(**CARDINAL** —) EAST WEST HINGE
NORTH SOUTH
(**CARDINAL** —S) CARDINES
(**CHRONOLOGICAL** —) ERA EPOCH
(**COMPASS** —) E N S W NE NW SE
SW ENE ESE NNE NNW SSE SSW
WNW WSW AIRT AIRTH RHUMB
COURSE
(**CRITICAL** —) JUMP
(**CROWNING** —) CAPSHEAF
CAPSTONE
(**CRUCIAL** —) CRUX
(**CULMINATING** —) HEAD COMBLE
(**DOUBLE — OF CURVE**) ACNODE
CRUNODE
(**ESSENTIAL** —) MAIN
(**EXACT** —) TEE
(**EXCESS** —S) LAP
(**EXCLAMATION** —) BANG
SCREAMER
(**EXTREME** —) END
(**FARTHEST** —) APOGEE SOLSTICE
(**FINAL** —) UPCOME
(**FIXED** —) ABUTMENT
(**GLAZIER'S** —) SPRIG
(**HALFWAY — IN CRIBBAGE**)
CORNER
(**HIGHEST** —) TIP ACME APEX AUGE
NOON PEAK CREST FLOOD APOGEE
CLIMAX HEIGHT PERIOD SUMMIT
VERTEX ZENITH EVEREST MAXIMUM
MERIDIAN SOLSTICE
(**LAST** —) END
(**LATERAL** —) ALARE

(LOWEST — OF HULL) BILGE
(LOWEST —) NADIR BOTTOM
BEDROCK
(MAIN —) JET SUM GIST
(MEDIAN —) HORMION
(NO —S) LOVE
(ONE'S STRONG —) FORTE
(PEDAL —) DRONE
(PIVOTAL —) KNUCKLE
(PRECISE —) NICK
(PROJECTING —) CRAG PEAK
BEARD
(SHARP —) PRICK PRICKLE
(SINGLE —) ACE
(SKULL —) TYLION
(STATIONARY —) SPINODE
(STRIKING —) SALIENCE
(STRONG —) FORTE
(TAPERING —) ACUMEN
(TENNIS —) LET CHASE BISQUE
(TENTH OF —) MOMENT
(TERMINAL —) GOAL BOURN BREAK
AIRPORT
(TO THE —) COGENT
(TOP —) TUFT
(TURNING —) CARDO EPOCH CRISIS
(UNIPLANAR —) UNODE
(UTMOST —) EXTREME SUBLIME
(VANTAGE —) TOWER
(VOWEL —) SERE
(WEAK —) BLOT
POINT-BLANK BLUNT PLAIN POINT
DIRECT WHOLLY EXPRESS DIRECTLY
POINTED SET HOME ACUTE EXACT
FIXED PEAKY PIKED TANGY TERSE
FITCHE LIVELY OXEOTE PEAKED
PECKED PICKED SPIRED ANGULAR
FITCHEE LACONIC PRECISE SPICATE
ZESTFUL ACICULAR ACULEATE
CULTRATE DIACTINE PUNCTUAL
STELLATE
POINTER TIP YAD COCK HAND
WAND DUBHE INDEX POINT FESCUE
FINGER GUNDOG INDICE SILKER
STYLUS FLUSHER INDICANT
SIGNITOR
(— IN GREAT BEAR) DUBHE DUBBHE
(— ON ASTROLABE) ALMURY
(— ON GAUGE) ARM
(TEACHER'S —) FESCUE
(PL.) MEN GUARDS YADAYIM
POINTLESS DRY ILL DULL FLAT
INANE SILLY VAPID FRIGID STUPID
INSIPID WITLESS
POINTSMAN TRAPPER LATCHMAN
SWITCHMAN
POISE PEE CALM HEAD REST SWAY
TACT BRACE PEIZE APLOMB OFFSET
PONDER BALANCE BEARING DIGNITY
OPPRESS POISURE DELIVERY
EASINESS SERENITY
(— RECIPROCAL) RHE
POISED SET FACILE HOVERING
(BE —) LIBRATE
POISER HALTER
POISON FIG GAS BANE BIKH DRAB
DRUG GALL TUBA VERY ATTER
TAINT TOXIN VENOM VIRUS ANTIAR
DERRIS INFECT RANKLE TOXIFY

TOXOID BABASCO CORRUPT
ENVENOM FLYBANE PERVERT
PHALLIN TANGHIN VITIATE
ACQUETTA DELETERY RATSBANE
VENENATE
(— IN DEATH CUP) PHALLIN
(ARROW —) HAYA INEE URALI
ANTIAR ANTJAR CURARE CURARI
DERRIS
(FISH —) AKIA CUBE DERRIS HAIARI
BABASCO BARBASCO
(RAT —) ANTU
(VIRULENT —) BIKH TANGHIN
POISONED BUCKEYED TOXICATE
VENENATE VENOMOUS
POISONER SEPSIN CANIDIA VENEFIC
VENOMER
POISON HEMLOCK BUNK CICUTA
POISONING PYEMIA GASSING
JIMMIES BOTULISM MYCETISM
PLUMBISM ICHTHYISM LATHYRISM
POISON IVY CLIMATH MARKERY
MERCURY MARKWEED
POISON OAK YEARA
POISONOUS ATTRY TOXIC ATTERY
VENENE VIROSE VIROUS NOISOME
NOXIOUS DELETERY MEPHITIC
TOXICANT VENENATE VENOMOUS
VIRULENT MALIGNANT
POISON SUMAC BURTREE
DOGWOOD
POISON TOBACCO HENBANE
POISONWOOD BUMWOOD
POITREL ARMOR PECTRON
POKE BAG DAB DIG DUB HIT JAB
JOG PUG PUR TIG WAD BROD PAUT
PORR PROD PROG RAUK RUCK
SACK SOCK STAB STIR NIDGE
POACH PROKE PROTE PUNCH
ROUSE STEER STOKE COWBOY
DAWDLE INCITE PIERCE POCKET
POUNCE POUTER PUGGLE PUTTER
WALLET PRODDLE
(— ABOUT) ROKE
(— AROUND) ROOT SCROUNGE
(— LIGHTLY) POTTER PUTTER
(— WITH FOOT) SCUFF
(— WITH NOSE) SNUZZLE
POKE-IN STRANDER
POKELOKEN BOGAN LOGAN
POKER DART DRAW FLIP POIT PORR
POTE STUD BLUFF BOGIE CURATE
GOBLIN STOKER ACEPOTS
FRUGGAN LOWBALL PASSOUT
POCHARD SHOTGUN BASEBALL
COALRAKE JACKPOTS MISTIGRI
SHOWDOWN
(— CHIP) JETON JETTON
(— HAND) RUNT FLUSH SKEET
KILTER PELTER STRAIGHT
(FORM OF —) DRAW STUD
POKEWEED POKE POCAN SCOKE
COAKUM GARGET FOXGLOVE
INKBERRY REDBERRY
POKY DEAD DULL JAIL SLOW DOWDY
POKEY POKING SHABBY STODGY
STUFFY STUPID CRAMPED TEDIOUS

POLAND
CAPITAL: WARSAW
COIN: DUCAT GROSZ MARKA
ZLOTY FENNIG HALERZ KORONA
DANCE: POLKA MAZURKA
KRAKOWIAK POLONAISE
GENTRY: SZLACHTA
LAKE: GOPLO MAMRY SNIARDWY
MEASURE: CAL MILA MORG PRET
LINJA MORGA SAZEN STOPA
VLOKA WLOKA CWIERK KORZEC
KWARTA LOKIEC GARNIEC
MOUNTAIN: TATRA SUDETEN
NAME: POLONIA SARMATIA
NATIVE: SLAV MARUR SILESIAN
PARLIAMENT: SEJM SEYM SENAT
RIVER: BUG SAN BRDA GWDA
LYNA NYSA ODER STYR BIALA
BZURA DRANA DWINA NOTEC
SERET WARTA WISTA NEISSE
NIEMEN PILICA PRIPET PROSNA
STRYPA WIEPRZ VISTULA
WISTOKA DNIESTER
TITLE OF ADDRESS: PAN PANI
PANIE
TOWN: LWO KOLO LIDA LODZ
LVOV OELS BREST BYTOM
CHELM POSEN RADOM SRODA
TORUN VILNA GDANSK GDYNIA
GRODNO KRACOW KRAKOW
LUBLIN POZNAN TARNOW
WARSAW ZABRZE BEUTHEN
BRESLAU CHORZOW GAROCIN
GLIWICE LEMBERG LITOUSK
WROCLAW GLEIWITZ KATOWICE
SZCZECIN TARNOPOL
WEIGHT: LUT FUNT UNCYA
KAMIAN CENTNER SKRUPUL

POLAK BALSA POLLACK
POLAR ARCTIC EMANANT PIVOTAL
DIRECTRIX
POLARIS ALRUCABA
POLE BAR LAT LEG LUG POL POY
ROD SKY XAT BEAM BIND BROG
COPE FALL HOOK KENT MAST NEAP
PALO PERK PIKE PROP SKID SPAR
TREE UFER CABER FOCUS MASUR
MAZUR PERCH QUANT REACH
SHAFT SPEAR SPOKE STAFF STANG
STILT STING STODE SWAPE SWIPE
BEACON BORITY CROTCH FLOWER
IMPOSE JUFFER KILHIG RICKER
RISSLE RYPECK SPONGE STOWER
TONGUE BARLING HEAVENS
TOWMAST ALESTAKE FLAGPOLE
FOOTPICK POLANDER STANDARD
(— AS EMBLEM OF SOVEREIGNTY)
KAHILI
(— AS HOLDFAST FOR BOATS)
RYPECK
(— FOR BEARING COFFIN) SPOKE
(— FOR PROPELLING BOAT) POY
(— FOR TOSSING) CABER KEBAR
(— HOLDING SAIL) BOOM MAST
SPRIT
(— OF TIMBER WAGON) NIB JANKER

(— OF VEHICLE) NEAP
(— ON TWO WHEELS) JANKER
(— USED AS SIGN) ALEPOLE
ALESTAKE
(— WITH BIRD DECOY) STOOL
(BOAT —) SPRIT
(CARRIAGE —) BEAM
(COUPLING —) REACH
(FIR —) UFER UPHER JUFFER
(FISHING —) WAND
(FORKED —) CROTCH
(LOGGING —) JANKER KILHIG KILLIG
(LONG —) PEW
(MANGROVE —) BORITY
(MINE —S) LAGGING
(NEGATIVE —) CATHODE
(PUNT —) QUANT STOWER
(RANGE —) FLAG
(SACRED —) ASHERAH
(SHEPHERD'S —) KENT
(SPRINGY —) BINDER
(STABLE —) BAIL
(STOUT —) KILHIG RICKER
(WATER-RAISING —) SWEEP
POLEAX STAFF POLEARM
POLECAT FITCH SKUNK ZORIL
FERRET FICHAT WEASEL FOUMART
FOULMART PERWITSKY SARMATIER
(— PELT) FITCH
POLE FLOUNDER SOLE
POLEHEAD TADPOLE
POLESTAR STAR GUIDE POLARIS
LODESTAR
POLICE GUARD WATCH GOVERN
CONTROL JEMADAR OCHRANA
POLIZEI PROTECT TOXOTAE
OPRICHNIC
(SECRET —) CHEKA
POLICEMAN COP JOE KID NAB PIG
BULL FLIC FUZZ GRAB JACK JOHN
PEON SLOP TRAP ZARP BOBBY
BULKY BURLY GAZER PEACE RURAL
SCREW SEPOY ASKARI BADGER
BOBBIE COPPER FISCAL FLATTY
HARMAN JOHNNY PEELER REDCAP
RUNNER SHAMUS CRUSHER
FOOTMAN GHAFFIR GUMSHOE
JEMADAR OFFICER SHOOFLY
TROOPER ZAPTIAH BARGELLO
BLUECOAT DOGBERRY FLATFOOT
GENDARME MINISTER
(CLUB OF —) BILLY STAFF
SPONTOON TRUNCHEON
(PL.) FINEST
POLICE STATION THANA BARGELLO
KOTWALEE
POLICY WIT DEAL FRONT ORDER
GOVERN NUMBER TICKET WISDOM
AUTARKY COUNSEL CUNNING
FLOATER LEFTISM LOTTERY
TONTINE VOUCHER ARTIFICE
SAGACITY STATEWAY
(CHOSEN —) COURSE
(PL.) APRISMO
POLISH BOB LAP MOP RUB RUD
BUFF DUCO FILE POLE CLEAN
FRUSH GLAZE GLOSS GRACE RABAT
ROUND SHINE SLICK STONE AFFILE
BARREL LUSTER PUNISH REFINE

RUMBLE SHAMMY SLIGHT SMOOTH
STREAK BEESWAX BURNISH
CHAMOIS FURBISH LACQUER
PERFECT VARNISH ELEGANCE
LEVIGATE SIMONIZE URBANIZE
POLISHED FINE COMPT ROUND
SHINY SLICK TERSE BUFFED FACETE
GLOSSY ELEGANT GALLANT
GENTEEL POLITIC REFINED
CULTURED
(NOT —) BLIND
POLISHER BUFFER GLAZER
WAGWAG WIGWAG DOLLIER
GLOSSER LAPIDARY SMOOTHER
POLISHING SANDING FROTTAGE
LIMATION
(— MATERIAL) RABAT
POLITE NEAT TIDY TRIM CIVIL SUAVE
GENTLE SMOOTH URBANE COURTLY
GALLANT GENTEEL DISCREET
LUSTROUS COURTEOUS
POLITENESS FINISH TASHRIF
COURTESY ELEGANCE URBANITY
POLITES (FATHER OF —) PRIAM
(MOTHER OF —) HECUBA
POLITIC WARY WISE SUAVE AROFUL
CRAFTY CUNNING TACTFUL
DISCREET PROVIDENT
POLITICAL (— ASSN.) VEREIN
(— PARTY) GOP TORY WHIG LABOR
POLITICIAN BOSS STATIST
WARWICK PIPELAYER STATESMAN
POLITY SERFISM
POLL COW DOD NOT POW ROB CHUB
COLL DODD HEAD NAPE NOTT PASH
CROWN SKULL STRIP CENSUS
FLEECE PARROT CANVASS DESPOIL
PILLAGE PLUNDER POLLARD
POLLACK LOB GADE LAIT GADID
LYTHE BILLET LAITHE BADDOCK
SILLOCK WALLEYE BLUEFISH
COALFISH GRAYFISH LORICATE
MOULRUSH
POLLARD CHU COW BRAN POLL
STAG SHEEP CHEVAN DODDLE
DOTARD BOLLING LOPPARD
WOOSERE
POLLARD TREE DOTARD RUNNEL
POLLED NOT NOTT POLEY
HORNLESS
POLLEN DUST MEAL FLOUR FARINA
POWDER BEEBREAD
(— BRUSH) SCOPA
(— TUBE) SPERMARY
POLLER VOTER BARBER POLLSTER
POLLEX THUMB
POLLINATE SELF FECUNDATE
FECUNDIZE FERTILIZE
POLLINATING SIBBING
POLLIWOG TADPOLE
POLLOCK PODLER
POLLUTE FOIL FOUL SOIL BLEND
DIRTY SMEAR TAINT BEFOUL DEFILE
INFECT MUDDLE RAVISH ADULTER
DEBAUCH PROFANE VIOLATE
POLLUTED FOUL DRUNK TURBID
CORRUPT
POLLUTING FILTHY
POLLUTION STAIN SULLAGE

FOULNESS IMPURITY
POLLUX POL HERCULES
(BROTHER OF —) CASTOR
(MOTHER OF —) LEDA
POLO (PERIOD IN —) CHUKKER
POLONAISE POLACCA FACKELTANZ
POLONIUS CORAMBIS
(DAUGHTER OF —) OPHELIA
(SON OF —) LAERTES
POLT BLOW THUMP STROKE
POLTERGEIST GHOST SPIRIT
POLTROON IDLER COWARD CRAVEN
WRETCH DASTARD COWARDLY
SLUGGARD
POLYANDRIUM CEMETERY
POLYGALA GAYWINGS
POLYGON DECAGON HEXAGON
NONAGON HEPTAGON PENTAGON
CHILIAGON MULTANGLE
POLYGRAPH KEELER
POLYHEDRON BEAD
POLYMER DIMER HYDROL HEXAMER
(— UNIT) MER

POLYNESIAN MAORI KANAKA
TONGAN FUTUNAN
POLYNICES (BROTHER OF —)
ETEOCLES
(FATHER OF —) OEDIPUS
(MOTHER OF —) JOCASTA
(WIFE OF —) ARGIA
POLYNOMIAL CUBIC
POLYP CORAL HYDRA TUMOR ZOOID
ISOPOD HYDRULA OCTOPOD
POLYPARY ZOARIUM
POLYPHONY FABURDEN
COUNTERPOINT
POLYPIDOM CORMUS
POLYSACCHARIDE LEVAN GELOSE
GLYCAN INULIN IRISIN MANNAN
AMYLOSE DEXTRAN FUCOSAN
HEXOSAN POLYOSE GALACTAN
GLYCOGEN LICHENIN SECALOSE
SINISTRIN
POLYZOAN POLYP CESTODE
RADIATE
POMACE MUST RAPE POMMY STOCK
STOSH CHEESE
POMADE CIDER POMATUM LIPSTICK
OINTMENT
POMANDER POUNCET
POMATO TOPATO
POME BALL APPLE GLOBE
JUNEBERRY

POMEGRANATE GRENAT GRENADE BALAUSTA
POMELO SHADDOCK GRAPEFRUIT
POMERANIA (CAPITAL OF —) STETTIN
(CITY IN —) THORN TORUN ANKLAM
(ISLAND IN —) RUGEN USEDOM
(PROVINCE IN —) POMORZE
POMFRET BULLY HENFISH
POMME DE TERRE POTATO
POMMEL BOB FIB NOB BEAT HORN KNOB PAIK PAKE TORE NEVEL BRUISE BUFFET CRUTCH FINIAL PLUMMET
POMP BRAG FARE WEAL BOAST PRIDE STATE ESTATE PAMPER PARADE RIALTY SCHEME SPRUNK BOBANCE DISPLAY PAGEANT PANOPLY SPLURGE CEREMONY EQUIPAGE GRANDEUR SEMBLANT SPLENDOR
POMPANO DART JUREL ALLICE CARANX PERMIT ALEWIFE COBBLER OLDWIFE CARANGID MACKEREL
(— CLAM) COQUINA
POMPOSITY TUMOR TUMOUR BIGHEAD BIGNESS
POMPOUS BIG BUG BUDGE JELLY LARGE SHOWY TUMID WIGGY AUGUST TURGID BLOATED BOMBAST FUSTIAN OROTUND STILTED SWOLLEN TURGENT BEWIGGED INFLATED SWELLING IMPORTANT
PONCEAU GRANAT
PONCHO MANGA RUANA
POND (ALSO SEE POOL) LAY LUM DELF DIKE MOAT PULK SLEW STEW TANK VLEI VLEY CANAL DECOY DELFT LACHE LETCH STANK WAYER CLAIRE LAGOON LOCHAN PUDDLE SALINA SLOUGH SPLASH STAGNE MULLETRY
(— FOR OYSTERS) CLAIRE
(— MAN) JACKER
(ARTIFICIAL —) AQUARIUM
(DIRTY —) SOAL
(FISH —) GURGES
(FISH STORING —) STEW
(SMALL —) KHAL
(STAGNANT —) DUB
PONDER CON CAST CHAW MUSE PORE ROLL TURN BROOD STUDY WEIGH ADVISE EXPEND REASON RECORD REMORD BALANCE COMPASS EXAMINE IMAGINE PERPEND REFLECT REVERIE REVOLVE APPRAISE COGITATE CONSIDER MEDITATE
PONDERABILITY WEIGHT GRAVITY
PONDEROUS DULL SLOW BULKY GRAVE HEAVY SOGGY AWKWARD WEIGHTY UNWIELDY IMPORTANT
PONDEROUSNESS HEFT
POND HEN COOT
PONDMAN JACKER
PONDOKKIE HUT HOVEL
PONE CAKE LUMP WRIT PAUNE PUDDING SWELLING

PONGEE PAUNCHE SHANTUNG
PONIARD STAB BODKIN DAGGER STYLET POINADO
PONT FERRY FLOAT BRIDGE FERRYBOAT
PONTIC DUMMY
PONTICELLO BREAK MAGAS
PONTIFF POPE BISHOP PRIEST PONTIFEX
PONTOON FLOAT RHINO BRIDGE
PONY CAB RAW TAT CAVY YABU DALES GRIFF PAINT PINTO POWNY TACKY TRICK WELCH WELSH BASUTO BHUTIA BRONCO CAYUSE EXMOOR GARRAN SHELTY TANGUN TATTOO ENGLISH HACKNEY MANIPUR MUSTANG SHELTIE FORESTER GALLOWAY SHETLAND
(STUDENT'S —) CRIB TROT BICYCLE
(PL.) DALES
POODLE SHOCK BARBET
POOK HEAP PICK PULL PLUCK STACK
POOKA PUCK GOBLIN SPECTER
POOL (ALSO SEE POND) CAR DIB DUB LAY LUM PIT POL POT POW BOOK CARR DIKE FARM JHIL LAKE LIDO LINN LLYN LUMB MERE PANT PEEL PLUD POLK POND PULE PULK RING SINK SLEW SOIL SWAG TANK TARN WEEL BAYOU BOWLY DECOY FLASH FLUSH FRESH JHEEL KITTY LETCH LOUGH MEARE PLASH PLUMB SLACK STANK STELL STILL THERM TRUNK CARTEL CHARCO FLODGE LAGOON LASHER PLUNGE PUDDLE SILOAM SPLASH STABLE CARLINE CATHOLE CUSHION JACKPOT PLASHET SNOOKER STAGNUM INTERLOT QUINIELA
(— AT JERUSALEM) BETHESDA
(— BELOW WATERFALL) LIN LINN LLYN
(— WITH SALMON NETS) STELL
(— WITHOUT OUTLET) STAGNUM
(ARTIFICIAL —) CUSHION
(AUCTION —) CALCUTTA
(DIRTY —) SUMP
(FISH —) TRUNK STEWPOND
(MOUNTAIN —) TARN
(MUDDY —) LETCH
(SWIMMING —) BATH LIDO NATATORY
POON DILO PEON PUNA DOMBA KEENA TAMANU SIRPOON MASTWOOD
POONGHIE RAHAN PRIEST PUNGYI PHONGHI TALAPOIN
POOP DOCK FIRE GULP TOOT CHEAT COZEN STERN BEFOOL ISLAND DECEIVE EXHAUST HINDDECK OVERCOME
POOR BAD SAD BASE EVIL FOUL LEAN LEWD PUNK SICK SOUR THIN DINKY EXILE FOOTY GROSS JERRY KETTY SCALY SEELY SILLY SOBER SORRY UNORN FEEBLE HUMBLE HUNGRY LEADEN MEAGER MEAGRE MEASLY PILLED PORAIL PRETTY

SCANTY SHABBY STREET CODFISH HAPLESS NAUGHTY SCRAWNY SCRUBBY SQUALID TRIVIAL UNLUCKY INDIGENT PRECIOUS SCRANNEL SNEAKING UNTHENDE
(— BOY) HERO
POORHOUSE MEASONDUE
POORLY ILL BADLY SADLY BARELY FEEBLY SIMPLY SLIGHT SHABBILY
POOR SOLDIER FRIARBIRD
POORTITH POVERTY
POP GO DOT GUN HIT TRY BLOW DART HOCK JUMP PAWN SODA BREAK CRACK KNOCK SHOOT ATTACK EFFORT FATHER POPPER STROKE THRUSH ASSAULT ATTEMPT CONCERT EXPLODE INSTANT REDWING BACKFIRE SUDDENLY
POPDOCK FOXGLOVE
POPE PAPA PAPE RUFF BISHOP PUFFIN SHRIKE PONTIFEX FISHERMAN
POPERY POPEISM PAPISTRY
POPE'S-EYE NUT NOIX
POPGUN SCOOT PENGUN POTGUN PLUFFER
POPINJAY PARROT PAPINGO
POPLAR ABBEY ABELE ALAMO ASPEN BAHAN LIARD BALSAM POPPLE BAUMIER ABELTREE WHITEBARK
POPLIN TABINET
POPOLOCA CHOCHO
POPPY HEAD BLAVER CANKER COPROSE EARACHE PONCEAU REDWEED ARGEMONE BALEWORT BOCCONIA HEADACHE DANNEBROG SQUATMORE
(CORN —S) SOLDIERS
POPPYCOCK BOSH FOLLY STUFF HAVERS
POPPYFISH POMPANO
POPPY SEED MAW MOHNSEED
POPULACE MOB MASS CROWD DEMOS PLEBS MASSES MOBILE PEOPLE COUNTRY
POPULAR LAY POP COMMON GOLDEN SIMPLE VULGAR CROWDED DEMOTIC VULGATE APPROVED FAVORITE PEOPLISH PLEBEIAN
POPULARITY VOGUE CLAPTRAP
POPULATE MAN BREED PLANT WORLD PEOPLE INHABIT
POPULATION DEME COLONY FLOTSAM KINDRED TOPODEME UNIVERSE
POPULUS SALIX
PORBEAGLE LAMNA SHARK LAMNID LAMNOID
PORCELAIN JU KO CHINA MURRA SPODE MURRHA NANKIN BISCUIT CELADON DRESDEN NANKEEN MANDARIN STEATITE
(VARIETY OF —) CAEN KUAN ARITA HIZEN IMARI KYOTO AMSTEL SEVRES BUDWEIS DRESDEN LIMOGES MEISSEN SWANSEA HAVILAND KAKIEMON CHANTILLY
PORCH HOOD STOA LANAI STOEP

STOOP INGANG PARVIS PIAZZA
PORTAL RAMADA BALCONY GALILEE
NARTHEX PASSAGE POIKILE
PORTICO PRONAOS VERANDA
ANTENAVE GALLERIE SOLARIUM
TRANSEPT VESTIBLE
(FRONT —) ANTICUM

PORCUPINE QUILL URSON
CAWQUAW COENDOU ERECTER
ERICIUS PORKPEN HEDGEHOG
HEDGEPIG

PORCUPINE ANTEATER ECHIDNA

PORCUPINE FISH ERIZO ATINGA
BURFISH DIODONT

PORCUPINE GRASS SPINIFEX

PORE GAZE GLOSE GLOZE STARE
STUDY TRYPA PONDER ALVEOLA
CINCLIS OSTIOLE TUBULUS
BAJONADO JOLTHEAD LENTICEL

PORGY TAI SCUP PARGO PLUMA
POGGY BESUGO MAMAMU PAGRUS
SPARID MARGATE MENHADEN
SPADEFISH

PORK HAM HOG PIG LARD BACON
BRAWN MONEY SWINE BALDRIB
LARDOON MIDDLING
(CHOP) BALDRIB GRISKIN
(— AND SALMON) LAULAU
(— SHOULDER) HAND
(SALT —) BACON SPECK SOWBELLY

PORKFISH SISI CATALINETA

PORKY FAT GREASY

PORNOGRAPHIC LEWD CURIOUS
OBSCENE

PORNOGRAPHY CURIOSA
ESOTERICA

POROUS OPEN LIGHT LEACHY
CELLULAR

PORPHYRY ELVAN EURITE ELVANITE
GRORUDITE

PORPOISE WHALE PALACH PUFFER
COWFISH DOLPHIN HOGFISH
PELLOCK PULLOCK SNUFFER
CETACEAN GAIRFISH

PORRECT EXTEND TENDER PRESENT

PORRET LEEK ONION PORETT
SCALLION

PORRIDGE KHIR POBS ATOLE
BROSE GROUT GRUEL BURGOO
CROWDY SKILLY SOWENS TARTAN
BROCHAN BURGOUT OATMEAL
POBBIES POLENTA POTTAGE
FLUMMERY SAGAMITE

PORRINGER TASTER TRINKET

PORT GATE GOAL LEFT MIEN WICK
WINE CARRY CREEK HAVEN HITHE
SALLY SCALE STATE APPORT
HARBOR INPORT REFUGE AIRPORT
BEARING DIGNITY LIBERTY
OUTPORT ANTEPORT DEMEANOR
LARBOARD MALTOLTE PORTHOLE
PRESENCE

PORTABLE MOBILE MOVABLE
BEARABLE

PORTAGE PACK CARGO CARRY
TARBET FREIGHT TONNAGE
HAULOVER

PORTAL DOOR GATE PORCH
DOORWAY ENTRANCE

PORTAMENTO DRAG GLIDE SCOOP

SLIDE PORTATO GLISSADE

PORTCULLIS BAR SHUT HERSE
ORGUE CATARACT

PORTE-MONNAIE PURSE

PORTE GATE

PORTEND BODE AUGUR DIVINE
EXTEND BESPEAK BETOKEN
PREDICT PRESAGE DENOUNCE
FOREBODE FORECAST FORETELL

PORTENT AYAH LUCK SIGN SOUND
TOKEN AUGURY MARVEL OSTENT
WONDER AUSPICE PREDICT
PRESAGE PRODIGY CEREMONY
DISASTER SOOTHSAY

PORTENTOUS AWFUL GRAVID
BODEFUL DOOMFUL FATEFUL
OMINOUS POMPOUS DOOMLIKE
DREADFUL INFLATED SINISTER

PORTER BEER MOZO HAMAL STOUT
TAMEN BADGER BEARER COOLIE
DARWAN DURWAN ENTIRE KHAMAL
REDCAP SUISSE DROGHER
HUMMAUL JANITOR PITCHER
REMOVER BADGEMAN CARGADOR
CHAPRASI LODGEMAN PORTITOR
RECEIVER
(— AND STOUT) COOPER
(JAPANESE —) AKABO
(MEAT —) PITCHER
(MEXICAN —) TAMEN

PORTFOLIO BLAD

PORTIA (HUSBAND OF —) BRUTUS
(LOVER OF —) BASSANIO
(MAID OF —) NERISSA

PORTIA TREE MAHO BENDY MAHOE

PORTICO STOA WALK XYST ORIEL
PORCH XYSTA ZAYAT PARVIS
PIAZZA SCHOOL XYSTUS BALCONY
GALLERY NARTHEX PRONAOS
TERRACE VERANDA PORTICUS
POSTICUM VERANDAH

PORTION BIT CUP CUT DAB JAG LAB
LOT PAN BLAD DALE DEAL DOLE
DOSE FATE FECK JAGG PART SIZE
WHAT DOWER PIECE RATIO SHARE
SLICE SNACK WHACK CANTLE
CANTON COLLOP DETAIL GOBBET
MATTER PARCEL RASHER EXCERPT
PARTAGE SECTION SEGMENT
TODDICK TRANCHE FRACTION
FRAGMENT PITTANCE QUANTITY
SCANTLET FODDERING
(— DRUNK) DRAFT DRAUGHT
(— OF ACTOR'S PART) LENGTH
(— OF ARROW) BREAST
(— OF BIRD SONG) TOUR
(— OF BREAD OR BEER) CUE
(— OF CITRUS RIND) ALBEDA
(— OF ESTATE) LEGITIM
(— OF FARMLAND) BEREWICK
(— OF FLOODPLAIN) BANCO
(— OF FODDER) JAG
(— OF FOOD) HELP GOBBET
HELPING
(— OF HIDE) HEAD
(— OF LAND) BLOCK PATTI INTAKE
DIVISION DONATION
(— OF LIQUOR) STICK DIVIDEND
(— OF LITURGY) ANAPHORA

(— OF MAST) HOUSING HOUNDING
(— OF PASTURE) BREAK
(— OF POEM) STRAIN
(— OF RUG) GRIN
(— OF SERPENT'S BODY) TRAIN
(— OF STEM) BOON
(— OF STORY) SNATCH
(— OF STREAM) LAVADERO
(— OF TEA) DRAWING
(— OF TIME) SPAN DISTANCE
(— OF TOBACCO) CUD
(— OF TONGUE) BLADE
(ADDITIONAL —) RASHER
(ALLOTTED —) MOIRA SCANTLING
(BRIDE'S —) DOWRY
(CLOTTED — OF BLOOD) CRUOR
(COARSER —) BOLTINGS
(EARLY —) SPRING
(INHABITED — OF EARTH) ECUMENE
(LATTER —) AUTUMN EVENING
(MAIN —) CORPSE
(MARRIAGE —) DOT DOTE TOCHER
(MINUTE —) GRAIN
(MOST VALUABLE —) CHIEF
(PERCEPTIBLE —) KENNING
(REPRESENTATIVE —) SAMPLE
(SIGNIFICANT —) CHAPTER
(SIZABLE —) DUNT
(SMALL — OF LIQUOR) DOLLOP
HEELTAP
(SMALL —) BIT DAB DOT DRAM
DROP SOSH CHACK SPICE SPUNK
SHADOW MODICUM REMNANT
SCANTLE SMIDGEN SOUPCON
SCANTLET
(TRIFLING —) SMACK

PORTLY FAT FULL AMPLE STOUT
GOODLY STATELY SWELLING

PORTMANTEAU BAG HOOK VALISE
POCKMANKY

PORTRAIT BUST ICON IKON IMAGE
IMAGO MODEL PIECE STATUE
VISAGE PORTRAY RETRAIT
LIKENESS RITRATTO VERONICA
(— ON COIN) EFFIGY

PORTRAY GIVE LIMN LINE BLAZE
ENACT IMAGE PAINT CIPHER
CLOTHE DEPICT FIGURE SHADOW
FEATURE IMITATE PICTURE
DECIPHER DESCRIBE RESEMBLE

PORTUGAL

BAY: SETUBAL
CAPITAL: LISBON
CAPE: MONDEGO ESPICHEL
COIN: JOE REI PECA REAL CONTO
COROA DOBRA INDIO ESCUDO
MACUTA PATACA TESTAO
VINTEM CENTAVO CRUSADO
MOIDORE EQUIPAGA
COLONY: MACAO TIMOR ANGOLA
GUINEA PRINCIPE
ISLAND: TIMOR
ISLANDS: MADEIRA
MEASURE: PE ALMA BOTA MEIO
MOIO PIPA VARA ALMUD BRACA
FANGA GEIRA LEGOA LINHA
MILHA PALMO ALMUDE CANADA

COVADO QUARTO ALQUIER ESTADIO FERRADO SELAMIN ALQUEIRE TONELADA
MOUNTAIN: ACOR GEREZ MARAO MOUSA PENEDA ESTRELA MONCHIQUE
RIVER: SOR TUA LIMA MINO MIRA SADO SEDA TAGO TEJO DOURO MINHO SABAR TAGUS VOUGA ZATAS CAVADO CHANCA TAMEGA ZEZERE MONDEGO GUADIANA
TOWN: FARO OVAR BRAGA EVORA PORTO GUARDA OPORTO COIMBRA FUNCHAL SETUBAL BRAGANCA
UNIVERSITY: COIMBRA
WEIGHT: GRAO ONCA LIBRA MARCO ARROBA OITAVA ARRATEL QUINTAL
WINE: PORT

PORTULACA MOSS PURSLANE
PORWIGLE TADPOLE
POSAUNE TROMBONE
POSE SET SIT HOARD MODEL OFFER PLANT STICK BAFFLE NONPLUS PEACOCK POSTURE PRESENT POSITION PRETENSE PROPOUND QUESTION
POSEIDON NEPTUNE EARTHSHAKER
(**BROTHER OF** —) ZEUS
(**FATHER OF** —) KRONOS
(**MOTHER OF** —) RHEA
(**WIFE OF** —) AMPHITRITE
POSER FACER POSEUR PUZZLE STAYER STICKER STUMPER TWISTER EXAMINER STICKLER BANDARLOG
POSH SWAGGER
POSING OPPOSAL
(**— TECHNIQUE**) PLASTIQUE
POSIT FIX PUT SET PLACE AFFIRM ASSUME
POSITING PONENT
POSITION LAY LIE HANG LINE POSE RANK SITE CENSE COIGN PLANT POSTE SITUS STAND STATE STEAD ASSIZE FIGURE HEIGHT OCTAVE OFFICE STANCE UBIETY VALGUS POSTURE STATION ATTITUDE CAPACITY DOCTRINE VOCATION
(**— OF AFFAIRS**) STATUS
(**— OF FEAR**) GAZE
(**— OF HEAVENLY BODY**) HARBOR
(**— OF VESSEL**) GAUGE HEIGHT
(**— WITH NO ESCAPE**) IMPASSE
(**— WITH NO RESPONSIBILITY**) SINECURE
(**DISTINGUISHED** —) HONOR
(**EMBARRASSING** —) FIX HOLE
(**FENCING** —) CARTE SIXTE SIXTH QUARTE TIERCE SACCOON SECONDE SEPTIME
(**FOREMOST** —) HEAD LEAD STEM
(**INITIAL** —) ANLAUT
(**MEDIAL** —) INLAUT
(**RELATIVE** —) RANK TERMS

BEARING FOOTING STANDING
(**SOCIAL** —) CASTE STATE VALOUR
(**SYMBOLIC** —) HASTA
POSITIONAL SITUAL
POSITIVE POS POZ COOL DOWN FLAT PLUS SURE BASIC SHEER UTTER ACTIVE DIRECT THETIC GENUINE HEALTHY ABSOLUTE CONCRETE DEFINITE DOGMATIC EXPLICIT INHERENT RESOLUTE SIGNLESS THETICAL
(**THREE —S**) KROMOGRAM
POSITIVELY BUT POS FLAT PLUS QUITE FAIRLY INDEED STRICTLY
POSITIVISM COMTISM CERTAINTY DOGMATISM
POSITRON LEPTON
POSSESS GET OWE OWN HAVE HOLD WALD BOAST BROOK OUGHT REACH WIELD MASTER OBTAIN OCCUPY BEDEVIL ENVELOP FURNISH INHABIT INHERIT INSTALL INSTATE SMITTLE ACQUAINT DOMINATE INSTRUCT
POSSESSED MAD CALM COOL OUGHT CRAZED JERUSHA ENTHEATE
(**— BY EVIL SPIRIT**) DEMONIAC
POSSESSION AVER HAND HOLD YHTE AUGHT GRASP STATE CLUTCH CORNER HAVIOR SASINE SEISIN SEIZIN WEALTH CONTROL COUNTER DEMESNE DEWANEE FINGERS KEEPING MASTERY SEIZURE CONQUEST DEFIANCE PROPERTY
(**— OF COMMON FEATURES**) AFFINITY
(**— OF KNOWLEDGE**) SCIENCE
(**— WITH QUIET ENJOYMENT**) SEISIN SEIZIN
(**BURDENSOME** —) ELEPHANT
(**RELIGIOUS** —) POWER
(**TEMPORAL —S**) WORLD
(**TEMPORARY** —) LEND
(PL.) ALLS STORE STUFF WRACK DOMAIN ESTATE GRAITH PROPER CAPITAL FORTUNE HAVINGS LIVINGS
POSSET CURDLE PAMPER POWSOWDY BALDUCTUM MERRYBUSH
POSSIBILITY MAY MAYBE POSSE CHANCE
POSSIBLE ABLE RIFE MAYBE LIKELY EARTHLY ELIGIBLE FEASIBLE PROBABLY POTENTIAL
POSSIBLY MAPPEN LIGHTLY PERHAPS PERCHANCE
POSSUM TAIT FEIGN PRETEND
POST DAK SET TIE BITT BOMA CAMP DAWK DOLE FAST FORT MAIL META POLE ROOM SPOT SPUD STOB STUD TREE BERTH CHEEK CLOSH CRANE NEWEL PLACE SPILE SPRAG STAKE STAND STILT STING STOCK STODE STOOP STULP STUMP BILLET CIPPUS COLUMN CROTCH FENDER GIBBET INFORM OFFICE PICKET PILLAR SAMSON SCREEN STAPLE STOOTH STOWER TRUNCH ASHERAH

BOLLARD COURIER GARETTA PLACARD POSTAGE POSTBOX QUARTER STATION STUDDLE UPRIGHT BANISTER DEADHEAD LEGPIECE MAKEFAST PRESIDIO PUNCHEON QUINTAIN STRADDLE
(**— AS RACE MARKER**) META
(**— ON PIER**) FAST BOLLARD DEADHEAD
(**BOUNDARY** —) TERM STOOP TERMINUS
(**CHIMNEY** —) SPEER
(**CUSTOMS** —) CHOKEY
(**DOOR OR GATE** —) DURN
(**ECCLESIASTIC** —) BENEFICE
(**FENCE** —) DROPPER
(**HANGING** —) GIBBET
(**INDIAN MILITARY** —) TANA TANNA THANA
(**MILITARY** —) FORT GARRISON
(**MOORING** —) DOLPHIN
(**OBSERVATORY** —) CUPOLA
(**SACRED** —) ASHERAH
(**SIGN** —) PARSON
POSTAGE POST STAMPAGE
POSTAGE-FREE FRANCO
POSTAGE STAMP DUE HEAD STICKER
POSTBOY YAMSHIK YEMSCHIK POSTILION
POST CHAISE JACK POCHAY POSCHAY
POSTER BILL CLAP SNIPE CLAPPE AFFICHE PLACARD SHOWING STICKER STREAMER
POSTERIOR BACK REAR CAUDAL DORSAL POSTIC RETRAL ADAXIAL BUTTOCKS
(PL.) WHEERIKINS
POSTERIORLY RETRAD
POSTERITY SEQUEL KINDRED FUTURITY
POSTERN SIDE CLOCKET KLICKET PRIVATE POSTICUM
POSTHOUSE YAM MUTATION
POSTICHE WIG SHAM SWITCH TOUPEE PRETENSE SPURIOUS
POSTIL HOMILY COMMENT
POSTILION COURIER POSTBOY YAMSHIK
POSTLUDE SORTIE SORTITA EPILOGUE
POSTMAN MAIL CORREO MAILBAG MAILMAN
POST OFFICE BOMA CORREO POSTHOUSE
POSTPONE OFF STAY WAIT DEFER DELAY FRIST REFER REMIT WAIVE FUTURE LINGER RELONG RETARD ADJOURN DEGRADE OVERSET PROLONG RESPECT SUSPEND CONTINUE PROROGUE REPRIEVE WITHHOLD
POSTPONED DEFERRED
POSTPONEMENT MORA STAY DELAY RESPECT RESPITE
POSTRIDE COURIER POSTILION
POSTSCRIPT EKE ENVOY
POST SUPPORT CROWFOOT

POSTULANT NOVICE
POSTULATE AXIOM CLAIM ASSERT
ASSUME DEMAND THESIS PERHAPS
PETITION PRINCIPLE
POSTURE SET POSE SEAT SITE
ASANA FRONT HEART PLACE SHAPE
SQUAT STATE LOUNGE SLOUCH
STANCE BEARING CROWHOP
STATION STATURE ATTITUDE
CARRIAGE POSITION
(— OF DEFENSE) GUARD
(DANCE —) HOLD
(KNEELING —) SHIKO
POSY POESY TUTTY FLOWER
BOUQUET NOSEGAY ANTHOLOGY
POT BAG CAN COOP FOOL JUST
LEAD OLLA PINT POOL RUIN CREWE
CROCK CRUSE DIXIE KITTY SHANT
SHOOT ALUDEL CHATTY CHYTRA
JORDAN JORDEN KETTLE MARMIT
MASLIN MONKEY OUTWIT PINGLE
PIPKIN POCKET POSNET CHAMBER
CUVETTE DECEIVE POTSHOT
SEETHER SKILLET YETLING
FAVORITE JACKSHEA PRESERVE
MARIJUANA
(— FOR CATCHING FISH) COOP
(— OF BRASS) MASLIN
(— OF DRINK) SHANT
(— WITH 3 FEET) POSNET
(12-GALLON —) DIXY DIXIE
(BULGING —) OLLA
(BUSHMAN'S —) JACKSHAY
JACKSHEA
(CHAMBER —) JERRY JORDAN
JORDEN COMMODE JEROBOAM
(CHIMNEY —) CAN TUN
(EARTHEN —) OLLA CROCK CHATTY
PIPKIN
(LEATHER —) GISPIN
(LOBSTER —) COY TRUNK
(LONG-HANDLED —) PINGLE
(MELTING —) CRUCIBLE
(PEAR-SHAPED —) ALUDEL
(SMALL ROUND —) LOTAH
(TEA —) TRACK
POTABLE DRINK BEVERAGE
POTATORY
POTAGE SOUP BROTH
POTAMOGETON PONDWEED
PONDGRASS
POTASH KALI SALINE PEARLASH
POLVERINE
(— FACTORY) ASHERY
POTASSIUM K KALIUM POTASS
(— DICHROMATE) CHROME
POTASSIUM NITRATE GROUGH
POTATION POT DRAM DRAFT DRINK
LIBATION
POTATO PAP YAM CHAT PAPA SPUD
YAMP IDAHO RURAL TATER TUBER
BATATA CAMOTE KUMARA LUMPER
MURPHY PRATEY SKERRY BURBANK
EPICURE SOLANUM BLUENOSE
(— BALL) NOISETTE
(— MASHER) RICER CHAPPER
(— SLICES) LATTICE
(— STATE) IDAHO MAINE
(—S AND CABBAGE) COLCANNON

(FRENCH FRIED —) CHIP
(FRENCH FRIED —S) GAUFRETTES
(JAPANESE —) IMO
(STEWED —S) STOVIES
(WITH —S) PARMENTIER
(PL.) WARE CHUNO
POT BEARER POTIFER
POTBELLIED PODDY STOMACHY
POTBELLY PAUNCH TUNBELLY
POTBOY GANYMEDE
POTE KICK MOPE POIT POKE PUSH
NUDGE PLATE POKER SHOVE
THRUST
POTEEN POTHEEN WHISKEY
POTWHISKY
POTENCE STUD CROSS GIBBET
POTENCY FORCE POWER VIGOR
ORENDA VIRTUE EFFICACY
STRENGTH VITALITY
POTENT ABLE MAIN RICH STAY
STIFF CAUSAL COGENT CRUTCH
MIGHTY STRONG DYNAMIC SUPPORT
WARRANT FORCIBLE POWERFUL
PUISSANT VIGOROUS VIRTUOUS
VIRULENT
POTENTATE KING RULER POTENT
PRINCE DICTATOR DOMINION
SOVEREIGN
POTENTIAL EH LATENT VIRTUAL
IMPLICIT INCHOATE POSSIBLE
PREGNANT
(— ENERGY) ERGAL
POTENTIALITY POSSE POWER
DUNAMIS DYNAMIS CAPACITY
PREGNANCY
POTGUN PISTOL POPGUN BRAGGART
POTHER ADO VEX FUSS STEW STIR
WORRY BOTHER BUSTLE HARASS
POTTER PUTTER PUZZLE PERPLEX
TURMOIL
POTHERB WORT WERTE GREENS
OLITORY POTWORT QUELITE
SPINACH TAMPALA
POTHOLE POT KETTLE TINAJA
POTHOOK HAIK HAKE CROOK
HANGLE RACKAN SLOWRIE
TRAMMEL COTTEREL
POTHOUSE TAVERN ALEHOUSE
MUGHOUSE
POTION DOSE DRUG DRAFT DRINK
DWALE STUFF DRENCH POISON
AMATORY MIXTURE PHILTER
PHILTRE NEPENTHE
POTLATCH GIFT FEAST PARTY
POTLACH FESTIVAL
POT MARIGOLD GOLD GOLDE
SUNFLOWER
POTPOURRI OLIO STEW MASLIN
MEDLEY POTPIE RAGOUT FANTASIA
PASTICHE JAMBALAYA
POTRO COLT
POTSHERD BIT TEST CROCK SHARD
SHERD FRAGMENT OSTRACON
PANSHARD
POTTAGE SEW SOUP SOWL STEW
BROTH BRUET BREWIS BROWET
POTAGE OATMEAL PULMENT
POTTED DRUNK CANNED
(— MEAT) RILLETT

POTTER FAD FUSS MUCK POKE
ANNOY DAKER TRUCK BOTHER
DABBLE DACKER DIDDLE DISHER
DODDER FIDDLE FOOTLE FOTTER
JOTTER KUMHAR MUDDLE NANTLE
NIGGLE PETTLE POUTER TIDDLE
TIFFIE TIFFLE TRIFLE CLOAMER
CROCKER DISTURB FIGURER
FOSSICK HANDLER NAUNTLE
PERPLEX PLOWTER PRODDLE
THROWER TROUBLE CERAMIST
TERRAPIN
(— OFFICIOUSLY) TEW
(MACHINE OF —) JOLLY
POTTERER TWIRLER
POTTERY POT BANK CHUN DELF
GROG WARE BIZEN CROCK DELFT
GLOST ROUEN SPODE BASALT
FICTIL KASHAN MIMPEI ASTBURY
BELLEEK BOCCARO BRISTOL
DIPWARE FIGMENT JETWARE
KAMARES POTBANK POTWARE
POTWORK REDWARE SATSUMA
TICKNEY TZUCHOU BUCCHERO
CERAMICS FIGULINE GRAYWARE
SLIPWARE
(— CIVILIZATION) MINYAN
(— CULTURE) PUCARA
(— DECOR) MISHIMA
(— DECORATED WITH SCRATCHING)
GRAFFITO
(ANCIENT —) KAMARES GRAYWARE
(BLACK —) BASALT
(CHINESE —) KUAN
(CRUSHED —) GROG
(HINDU —) UDA
(RICHLY COLORED —) MAJOLICA
POTTERY TREE CARAIPE
POTTINGER COOK POTYCARY
POTTO LEMUR APOSORO KINKAJOU
POTTY CRAZY FOOLISH TRIVIAL
SNOBBISH
POUCH BAG COD JAG POD SAC
BELL CYST POKE BULGE BURSA
POKKE PURSE BUDGET CAECUM
CRUMEN GIPSER PACKET POCKET
PURSET SACHET ALFARGA ALFORJA
CANTINA CRUMENA GIPSIRE MICHILA
OVICYST SCROTUM SPORRAN
SWALLOW BURSICLE PROTRUDE
SPEUCHAN
(— OF FLY) AEROSTAT
(— ON DEER'S NECK) BELL
(TOBACCO —) DOSS
POUF PUFF OTTOMAN
POULAINE PIKE CRAKOW
POULPE POULP CUTTLE OCTOPUS
POULTICE QUILT STUPA STUPE
MALAGMA EPITHEME SINAPISM
POULTRY FOWL HENS DUCKS GEESE
PULLEN PEAFOWL PIGEONS
PULLERY TURKEYS CHICKENS
PULLAILE VOLAILLE
POUNAMU JADE PUNAMU NEPHRITE
POUNCE NAB CHOP CLAP JUMP
POKE SWAP SWOP FLECK PRICK
PUNCH SOUSE SWOOP TALON
EMBOSS PIERCE TATTOO BOBCAT
DESCEND SPRINKLE

(— **UPON**) TIRE STOOP

POUND L LB BUM DAD LIB PIN PUN
SOV BEAT CHAP DRUB FRAM PELT
PIND POON POSS PUND QUID SKIT
THUD TRAP TUND CRUSH FRAME
KNOCK LABOR LIVRE STAMP THUMP
TRAMP WEIGH BATTER HAMMER
LUMBER NICKER POUNCE PRISON
THRASH CONTUND CONTUSE
PINFOLD THUNDER LAMBASTE
RESTRAIN
(— **FINE**) BRAY
(**1-8TH OF** —) HANDFUL
(**100** —**S**) CENTAL CENTURY
(**12** —**S OF BUTTER**) GAUN
(**25** —**S**) PONY PONEY
(**32, 56, OR 75** —**S OF RAISINS**)
FRAIL
(**500** —**S**) MONKEY
(**FISH** —) KEEP MADRAGUE
(**ISRAELI** —**S**) LIROTH

POUNDMASTER PINDER PINNER
PONDER

POUR JAW RUN TUN YET BIRL BREW
DROP EMIT FILL FLOW GOSH GUSH
HELD LASH LAVE RAIN TEEM TOOM
VENT FLOOD FLUSH HEELD HIELD
POWER SLIDE SOUSE SPILL SPOUT
SWARM AFFUSE DECANT SLUICE
STREAM CASCADE CHANNEL
DIFFUSE SUFFUSE
(— **AWAY**) STAVE
(— **BACK**) REFUND
(— **BEER OR WINE**) BIRL
(— **CLUMSILY**) SLOSH
(— **COPIOUSLY**) HALE
(— **DOWN**) RASH SILE SHOWER
DESCEND DISPUNGE
(— **FORTH**) SHED TIDE VENT WELL
DISTILL OVERFLOW
(— **FREELY**) SWILL
(— **FROM ONE VESSEL TO**
ANOTHER) DECANT JIRBLE
TRANSFUSE
(— **IN DROP BY DROP**) INSTIL
INSTILL
(— **IN**) INFUSE INFOUND INHELDE
(— **LIKE RAIN OR TEARS**) LASH
(— **MELTED WAX**) BASTE
(— **MOLTEN LEAD**) YOTE
(— **OFF**) SLUICE
(— **OIL UPON**) ANOINT
(— **OUT**) FILL SEND SHED SKINK
STOUR UTTER EFFUSE LIBATE
DIFFUND DIFFUSE
(— **UPON**) AFFUSE

POURBOIRE TIP GRATUITY
TRINKGELD

POURER TEEMER INFUSER

POURPOINT GIPON JUPON QUILT
DOUBLET

POUT BIB MOP MAID MOUE PUSS
SULK BOODY GROIN CATFISH
EELPOUT BULLHEAD PROTRUDE

POUTERIA LUCUMA

POUTING BOUDERIE

POVERTY LACK NEED WANE WANT
DEARTH PENURY BEGGARY
DEFAULT TENUITY DISTRESS
PUIRTITH SCARCITY WANDRETH

POVERTY PLANT HEATH HEATHER
LINGWORT

POVERTY-STRICKEN POOR NAKED
NEEDY SQUALID SHIRTLESS

POWDER DUST KISH MILL MULL
SAND CHALK CURRY ERBIA FLOUR
GRIND HEMOL KOSIN PICRA STOUR
CEMENT CHARGE CHINOL DECAMP
DERMOL EMPASM ESCAPE FARINA
FILITE GERATE KAMALA KERMES
KUMKUM MELLON PEYTON PINOLE
POUNCE RACHEL SMEETH YTTRIA
ALCOHOL BESTREW BROCADE
LUPULIN SCATTER SMEDDUM
SPACKLE SPODIUM ALGAROTH
CATAPASM DYNAMITE FLUMERIN
PALEGOLD
(— **A SHIELD**) GERATE
(— **FOR BRONZING**) BROCADE
(— **OBTAINED BY SUBLIMATION**)
FLOWERS
(— **TO MASK SWEAT ODOR**)
EMPASM EMPASMA
(— **USED IN CHOCOLATE**) PINOLE
(**ABRASIVE** —) EMERY
(**ANTHELMINTIC** —) KOSIN
(**ANTIMONY** —) KOHL
(**ASTRINGENT** —) BORAL
(**BLEACHING** —) CHEMIC
(**BROWNISH** —) LIGNIN
(**CATHARTIC** —) KAMALA
(**COLORING** —) HENNA
(**FINE** —) DUST POUNCE ALCOHOL
(**FLUORESCENT** —) FLUMERIN
(**GOA** —) ARAROBA
(**GOLD** —) VENTURINE
(**GRAPHITIC** —) KISH
(**GRAY** —) ANTU
(**HAIR** —) MUST
(**MALT** —) SMEDDUM
(**PERFUMED** —) ABIR SACHET
(**PINK** —) CALAMINE
(**POISONOUS** —) ROBIN
(**REDDISH** —) ABIR KUMKUM
SIMMON
(**ROSE-COLORED** —) ERBIA
(**SACHET** —) PULVIL
(**SILICEOUS** —**S**) SILEX
(**SMOKELESS** —) FILITE PEYTON
CORDITE AMBERITE INDURITE
SOLENITE
(**WHITE** —) CHINOL YTTRIA HYPORIT
SCANDIA HALAZONE LANTHANA
PARAFORM
(**YELLOW** —) KOSIN DERMOL
MELLON LUPULIN MALARIN SAMARIA
TANNIGEN

POWDERED SEME SPICED PICKLED
SEASONED

POWDER PUFF PLUFF

POWER ARM ART JUS ROD SAY SUN
VIS BEEF BULK DINT GIFT GRIP
HAND HANK HEAP HORN IRON KAMI
MAIN MANA MAYA SOUP SWAY
WALD WILL AGENT CROWN DEMON
DEVIL FORCE GRACE HUACA HYDRO
INPUT LURCH MIGHT SINEW SKILL
STEAM VALUE VIGOR WAKON WIELD
YARAK APPEAL BREATH CLUTCH
CREDIT DANGER DEGREE DOUGHT
EFFORT ENERGY FOISON IMPACT
MOLOCH SHAKTI STROIL STROKE
SWINGE TALENT VIRTUE WEIGHT
BALANCE BOSSDOM COMMAND
CONTROL DEMESNE DESTINY
DUNAMIS DYNAMIS ENTHEOS
FACULTY POTENCY VALENCY
VOLTAGE WAKONDA ACTIVITY
AUTONOMY CAPACITY COERCION
DELEGACY DEMIURGE DISPOSAL
DOMINION INTEREST LEVERAGE
LORDSHIP SEIGNORY STRENGTH
(— **OF ACID**) BASICITY
(— **OF ATTRACTION**) ALLURE
(— **OF CHOICE**) LIBERTY
(— **OF DIVORCE**) TAFWIZ
(— **OF ENTRY**) INGRESS
(— **OF GIVING**) PROPINE
(— **OF HEARING**) AUDITION
(— **OF KNOWING**) JNANASHAKTI
(— **OF MANIFESTATION**) MAYA
(— **OF MOVING AT SEA**) YARAGE
(— **OF PERFORMING**) ART
(— **OF RESISTANCE**) STAMINA
(— **OF TRANSMUTATION**) ALCHEMY
(— **OF VISION**) KEN
(— **OF WINE**) SEVE
(— **TO CONVINCE**) FORCE
(—**S OF EVIL**) HELL
(**CIVIL** —) CAESAR
(**COERCIVE** —) SWORD
(**DIVINE** —) MOIRA
(**ELEVATING** —) LIFT
(**EMOTIONAL** —) STOMACH
(**EXTRAPHYSICAL** —) MANA
(**FIFTH** —) SURSOLID
(**FOCAL** —) DIOPTRY
(**GROWTH** —) BATHMISM
(**HYPOTHETICAL** —) FORTUNE
(**IMPERSONAL** —) WAKAN WAKON
WAKANDA
(**INTELLECTUAL** —) WIT
(**LEGAL** —) JUS
(**MAGIC** —) ORENDA
(**MAGNETIC** —) MAGNES
(**MENTAL** —) HABITUS
(**MORMON** —) KEYS
(**NATURAL** —) OD
(**OCCULT** —) MAGIC
(**PERSUASIVE** —) RHETORIC
(**PERUVIAN** —) HUACA
(**POLITICAL** —) DOMINIUM
(**RATIONAL** —) EYE
(**REFLECTIVE** —) ALBEDO
(**ROYAL** —) RIAL
(**SACRED** —) KAMI
(**SECOND** —) SQUARE
(**SOVEREIGN** —) SWAY THRONE
(**SPIRITUAL** —) NGAI
(**STAYING** —) STAMINA
(**SUPERNATURAL** —) CHARISMA
(**SUPREME** —) EMPIRE HEAVEN
IMPERIUM
(**THIRD** —) CUBE
(**VITAL** —) SPIRITS

POWERBOAT SEDAN SKIFF GLIDER
CRUISER STINKPOT GASOLINER

POWERFUL BIG FAT ABLE DEEP HIGH MAIN RANK RICH VERY FORTE HEFTY HUSKY LUSTY STARK STOUT VALID VIVID WIGHT WILDE COGENT HEROIC MIGHTY POTENT SEVERE STRONG CAPABLE FECKFUL INTENSE POLLENT RICHARD SKOOKUM STAVING VALIANT FORCIBLE PUISSANT VIGOROUS

POWERLESS WEAK FEEBLE UNABLE HELPLESS IMPOTENT

POWWOW PAWAW CONFAB FROLIC COUNCIL MEETING SESSION CONJURER

POX ROUP CANKER PLAGUE VARIOLA
(FOWL —) SOREHEAD
(SHEEP —) OVINIA

POYOU PELUDO ARMADILLO

PRABHU LORD CHIEF WRITER

PRACTICABLE AGIBLE DOABLE USABLE FEASIBLE POSSIBLE

PRACTICAL HARD UTILE ACTUAL THINGY USEFUL OPERARY VIRTUAL WORKING BANAUSIC HOMESPUN PRACTIVE THINGISH
(— JOKE) WAGGERY
(NOT —) PROFESSORY

PRACTICALLY ALMOST NEARLY REALLY VIRTUALLY

PRACTICE ACT ISM LAW SUE TRY URE USE KEEP LIVE PLAN PLOT ADOPT APPLY ASSAY DRILL FOUND GUISE HABIT HAUNT TRADE TRAIN TREAD USAGE CUSTOM EMPLOY FOLLOW GROOVE OCCUPY PRAXIS RECORD BRUSHUP ENHAUNT KNOCKUP OPERATE PROCEED PROFESS RANDORI USAUNCE ACTIVISM ALARMISM EXERCISE FREQUENT GALENISM
(— CHEATING) FOIST
(— DECEPTION) DEACON
(— DILIGENTLY) PLY
(— FRAUD) SHARK
(— HYPOCRISY) CANT
(— OF AN ART) PRAXIS
(— OF MEDICINE) GALENISM
(— ROWING) TUB
(— WITCHCRAFT) HEX
(BINDING —) LAW
(CEREMONIAL —) RITE
(COMMUNAL —) SUNNA SCHEME SUNNAH INTRIGUE
(CORRUPT —) ABUSE WHORE
(DIPLOMATIC —) ALTERNAT
(DISHONEST —S) CROSS
(HORTICULTURAL —) CUTTAGE
(MEDICAL —) ALLERGY
(RELIGIOUS —) CULT CULTUS
(SUPERSTITIOUS —) FREET
(UNDERHAND —) JUGGLING
(VICIOUS —) MOLOCH

PRACTICED EXPERT VERSED PRACTIC SKILLED VETERAN HACKNEYED

PRACTICING EXERCENT

PRACTITIONER DOCTOR HEALER LAWYER NOVICE LEARNER EXERCENT FELDSHER HUMANIST HERBALIST HOMEOPATH

PRAD HORSE

PRAENOMEN AULUS CAIUS GAIUS TITUS GNAEUS LUCIUS MANIUS MARCUS SEXTUS SERVIUS SPURIUS MAMERCUS NUMERIUS TIBERIUS

PRAESEPE CRIB CRATCH MANGER BEEHIVE

PRAGMATIC BUSY BUSYBODY DOGMATIC MEDDLING OFFICIOUS PRACTICAL

PRAIRIE BAY BLED CAMAS CAMASS MEADOW PLATEAU QUAMASH
(— STATE) ILLINOIS

PRAIRIE BERRY TROMPILLO

PRAIRIE CHICKEN GROUSE

PRAIRIE DOG GOPHER MARMOT

PRAIRIE WOLF COYOTE

PRAISE CRY LOF FUME HERY LAUD LOSE LOVE PRES ADORE ALLOW ALOSE BLESS CAROL CHANT CRACK DEIFY EXTOL GLORY HERSE HONOR KUDOS PLAUD PRIZE ROOSE SALVE VALUE WURTH ANTHEM BELAUD EULOGY FRAISE HILLEL KUDIZE LOANGE LOVING ORCHID SALUTE TONGUE ACCLAIM ADULATE APPLAUD COMMEND FLATTER GLORIFY MAGNIFY NOSEGAY PLAUDIT PUFFING TRIBUTE WORSHIP APPLAUSE BLESSING DOXOLOGY ENCOMIUM EULOGIZE
(— BE TO GOD) LD
(— IN THANKSGIVING) JOY
(— INORDINATELY) FUME
(— OF ANOTHER'S FELICITY) MACARISM
(— TO GOD ALWAYS) LDS
(EFFUSIVE —) FUSS
(EXCESSIVE —) FLATTERY ADULATION
(INSINCERE —) CLART DAUBING
(PUBLIC —) PRECONY
(SING FALSE —S) CHANT

PRAISED JUDAH JUDITH LAURELED
(UNDULY —) BEPUFFED

PRAISEWORTHY WORTHY AMIABLE GLORIOUS LAUDABLE SPLENDID EXEMPLARY

PRAJAPATI KA PITRI

PRAKRIT PALI MAGADHI

PRAM CARRIAGE HANDCART PUSHCART STROLLER

PRANCE STIR BRANK CAPER DANCE JAUNT PRANK CAREER CAVORT CURVET GAMBOL JAUNCE TITTUP TRANCE PRANKLE SWAGGER CAKEWALK

PRANCER HORSE DANCER CAPERER

PRANK JIG RAG RIG DECK DIDO FOLD GAME JEST LARK PRAT REAK ADORN CAPER FREAK SHINE SKITE TRICK VAGUE BROGUE CURVET FEGARY FIGARY FROLIC GAMBOL SHAVIE VAGARY MARLOCK SPANGLE ESCAPADE PRANCOME RIGWIDDIE
(PL.) REX GAMES JINKS

PRANKISH TRICKSY

PRASINE LEEK

PRAT PUSH NUDGE TRICK

PRATE GAB BUCK BUKH BUKK CARO CHAT CLAP CLAT TALK BLATE BOAST CLASH SCOLD BABBLE CACKLE CLAVER JANGLE SQUIRT TONGUE BLATHER BLATTER CHATTER CLATTER PRATTLE TWATTLE

PRATING GAFF CHATTER

PRATIQUE CUSTOM PRODUCT

PRATTLE CHAT CLACK BABBLE BURBLE JANNER JAUNER YATTER BLATTER CHATTER CLATTER JAUNDER PRITTLE TRATTLE TWADDLE BAVARDAGE

PRATTLING CHAVISH

PRAWN CARID NIPPER PENEID SHRIMP SQUILLA CARIDEAN CARIDOID CREVETTE MACRURAN

PRAWN KILLER SQUILLA

PRAXIS HABIT ACTION CUSTOM PRACTICE

PRAY ASK BEG BID BLESS CRAVE DAVEN SOUGH VOUCH INVITE ENTREAT IMPLORE REQUEST WRESTLE INVOCATE
(— FOR) BOON

PRAYA BUND BEACH STRAND

PRAYER ACT AHA AVE VOW BEAD BENE BOON PLEA SUIT VOTE AGNUS ALENU NAMAZ SALAT ABODAH APPEAL ECTENE ERRAND LITANY MANTRA MATINS ORISON STEVEN VESPER YIZKOR BIDDING COMPLIN FATIHAH GAYATRI GEULLAH KADDISH MEMENTO ORATION PRECULE PREFACE TAHANUN ANAPHORA APOLYSIS CATHISMA DEVOTION KEDUSHAH MISERERE PETITION SUFFRAGE TEHINNAH
(— BEADS) ROSARY
(— BOOK) MAHZOR MISSAL SERVICE
(— LEADER) IMAM
(— OF DISMISSAL) APOLYSIS
(— RUG) NAMAZLIK
(— SHAWL) TALLITH
(— STICK) BAHO PAHO
(— TOWER) MINARET
(CANONICAL —S) BREVIARY
(CHIEF MOHAMMEDAN —) NAMAZ
(HINDU —) GAYATRI
(INWARD —) ACT
(JEWISH —) ALENU ABODAH GEULLAH HOSHANA KADDISH
(LAST — OF DAY) COMPLIN
(LONG —) CATHISMA
(MUSLIM —) SALAH SALAT
(OPENING —) COLLECT
(SHORT —) GRACE COLLECT
(SILENT —) SECRET
(PL.) HOURS NORITO TIKKUN CHAPLET

PRAYING ORISON IMPRECANT

PREACH EDIFY SOUGH TEACH EXHORT GOSPEL SERMON DELIVER HOMILIZE

PREACHER KHATIB MAGGID PARSON

TUBMAN DARSHAN LOLLARD
MARTEXT PROPHET ROUNDER
TEACHER TUBBIST TUBSTER
EXHORTER KOHELETH MINISTER
PARDONER PULPITER QOHELETH
SERMONER SPINTEXT SWADDLER
VARTABED
(PL.) PULPIT
PREACHING SPELL PULPIT SERMON
HEARING KERUGMA KERYGMA
PROPHECY PULPITRY SPELLING
PREACHY DIDACTIC
PREAMBLE PREFACE WHEREAS
PREARRANGED SET
PREBEND CANONRY
PREBENDARY PROVEND
PRE-CAMBRIAN MOINE EOZOIC
ARCHEAN
PRECARIOUS DICKY RISKY SHAKY
CASUAL INFIRM UNSURE DUBIOUS
CATCHING DELICATE INSECURE
PERILOUS UNSTABLE DANGEROUS
UNCERTAIN
PRECAUTION CARE GUARD CAUTEL
PRECEDE LEAD FOREGO HERALD
FORERUN PREFACE PREVENT
ANTECEDE PREAMBLE
PRECEDENCE LEAD PRIMACY
HERALDRY PRIORITY
(RIGHT OF —) PAS
(SOCIAL —) LEVEL
PRECEDENT LEAD SIGN MODEL
TOKEN USAGE INSTANCE ORIGINAL
SPECIMEN STANDARD AUTHORITY
PRECEDING OLD FORE WEST
BEFORE FORMER LEADING
ADJACENT PREVIOUS
(— ALL OTHERS) FIRST
PRECENTOR CANTOR PSALMIST
LETTERGAE
PRECEPT LAW HEST LINE RULE
TORA WRIT ADAGE AXIOM BREVE
MAXIM ORDER SUTRA SUTTA TORAH
BEHEST DICTATE MANDATE
WARRANT DOCTRINE DOCUMENT
LANDMARK
PRECEPTIVE DIDACTIC MANDATORY
PRECEPTOR TUTOR MASTER
PRECINCT BEAT AMBIT BOUND
CLOSE DOMAIN HIERON COLLEGE
LENAEUM SOCIETY TEMENOS
DISTRICT ENVIRONS
(PL.) AMBIT
PRECIOUS DEAR FINE LIEF RARE
VERY CHARY CHERE GREAT HONEY
CHOICE COSTLY DAINTY GOLDEN
POSING SILVER TENDER PRECISE
AFFECTED ORIENTAL OVERNICE
VALUABLE WORTHFUL
PRECIOUSNESS PRICE
PRECIPICE LIN KHUD LINN LLYN
PALI CLIFF KRANS SCREE SHEER
STEEP KRANTZ CLOGWYN
DOWNFALL HEADWALL
PRECIPITATE GEL CURD HURL
RASH HASTY HURRY SHOOT SPEED
STEEP ABRUPT COAGEL HASTEN
SLUDGE SUDDEN TUMBLE UNWARY
DISTILL LYCOPIN SUBSIDE

CATALYZE HEADLONG PROCLIVE
SETTLING
(— DYE) STRIKE
PRECIPITATELY HEADLING
HEADLONG SLAPDASH
PRECIPITATION HAIL MIST RAIN
SNOW HASTE SLEET VIRGA
PRECIPITOUS FULL RASH BRANT
BRENT HASTY STEEP ABRUPT
CHICHI STEEPY SUDDEN PRERUPT
HEADLONG
PRECIS JUNONIA SUMMARY
ABSTRACT
PRECISE SET FLAT HARD JUMP JUST
TIDY TRIG TRUE VERY CLEAN
CLOSE EXACT PRESS RIGID SOUND
FORMAL STARCH STRICT BUCKRAM
CAREFUL CERTAIN CLERKLY
CORRECT EXPRESS PERFECT
PERJINK STARCHY ABSOLUTE
ACCURATE DEFINITE EXPLICIT
HAIRLINE PUNCTUAL
PRECISELY BUT EVEN JUST CLEAN
SHARP FINELY JUSTLY STRAIT
EXACTLY
PRECISENESS RIGOR RIGOUR
PRIMNESS
PRECISIAN PRIG PURITAN
PRECISION NICETY CLARITY
ACCURACY DELICACY ELEGANCE
JUSTNESS
PRECISIONIST PEDANT
PRECLUDE BAR DENY STOP CLOSE
CROSS DEBAR ESTOP FORBID
HINDER IMPEDE OBVIATE PREVENT
SILENCE CONCLUDE INTERPEL
PRECOCIOUS PRECOX UNRIPE
FORWARD PREMATURE RATHERIPE
PRECONCEIVE IDEATE
PRECONDITION PRIUS
PRECURSOR USHER HERALD INITIAL
ANCESTOR PRODROME WAYMAKER
HARBINGER HEMIAUXIN
PREDACITY RAVEN RAVIN
PREDATOR COACTOR
PREDATORY HUNGRY HARMFUL
RAVENOUS
PREDECESSOR ANCESTOR
FOREGOER
(PL.) OLDERS
PREDELLA FOOTPACE
PREDESTINATION FATE DESTINY
ELECTION
PREDESTINE DOOM SLATE
FOREDOOM FOREPOINT
PREDETERMINE DESTINE FORECAST
PREDICAMENT FIX JAM SOUP SPOT
CLASS STATE STEAD PICKLE PLIGHT
SCRAPE DILEMMA IMPASSE
CATEGORY JUNCTURE QUANDARY
PREDICANT FRIAR PREACHER
DOMINICAN
PREDICATE BASE FOUND AFFIRM
ASSERT PRAISE PREACH COMMEND
DECLARE EXTREME PREDICT
PROCLAIM
PREDICT LAY BODE CALL DOPE
READ REDE AUGUR WEIRD HALSEN
FORESAY PRESAGE FOREBODE

FORECAST FORETELL PROPHESY
SOOTHSAY
(— EVIL) CROAK
PREDICTION DOPE WEIRD AUGURY
BODING BODWORD PORTENT
PRESAGE BODEWORD FORECAST
PROPHECY VATICINE
PREDILECTION BIAS HANG FANCY
FAVOR LIKING RELISH FONDNESS
PREDISPOSE BEND INCLINE
SUBJECT
PREDISPOSED PRONE PARTIAL
TENDING INCLINED
PREDISPOSITION ITCH DIATHESIS
PREDOMINANT GREAT RULING
CAPITAL REIGNING SUPERIOR
CULMINANT HEGEMONIC
PREDOMINATE RULE DOMINE
EXCEED GOVERN PREVAIL
PREE KISS PRIE TEST TASTE TRIAL
PRYING SAMPLE PROVING TASTING
PREEMINENT BIG TOP HIGH STAR
FIRST GRAND GREAT PALMARY
PASSING STELLAR SUPREME
FOREMOST PRECLARE SPLENDID
SUPERIOR PARAMOUNT
PREEMPT COLLAR
PREEN PIN PERK PICK TRIM DRESS
GLOAT PLUME PRINK PRUNE SWELL
TRICK BROOCH GODWIT SMOOTH
REPLUME
(— WINGS) WHET
PREFACE FRONT PROEM USHER
HERALD PRESAY PRECEDE
PREPOSE EXORDIUM FORETALK
FOREWORD PREAMBLE PROLOGUE
PREFATORY PROEMIAL
PREFECT WALI EPARC EPARCH
MONITOR PROVOST GOVERNOR
PRESIDENT
PREFECTURE EPARCHY
(CHINESE —) FU
(JAPANESE —) KEN
(TIBETAN —) JONG
PREFER LAY LIKE LOVE BRING
ELECT EXALT FAVOR OFFER
CHOOSE PROFER SELECT OUTRANK
PREFECT PRESENT PROMOTE
PROPOSE SURPASS
PREFERABLE LIEF RIGHT RATHER
ELIGIBLE
PREFERENCE GOO LIKE FAVOR
DESIRE LIKING RATHER DRUTHERS
FAVORITE PRIVILEGE PROMOTION
PREFIGURE TYPE IDEATE SHADOW
TYPIFY FORERUN FORESEE PREDICT
FORESHOW
PREFIX DUN DOON PREPOSE
PREGNANCY CYESIS TROUBLE
ACCYESIS FETATION OOCYESIS
GESTATION
PREGNANT BIG GONE OPEN GREAT
HEAVY QUICK READY BAGGED
CAUGHT COGENT GRAVID PAROUS
ENCEINT FERTILE GESTANT
TEEMING WEIGHTY CHILDING
FORCIBLE GERMINAL PRESSING
PREHALLUX CALCAR
PREHEND SEIZE

PREHISTORIC IMMEMORIAL
PREINDICATE PRESAGE FORESHOW
PREJUDICE BIAS DOWN HARM HURT
KINK TURN DERRY DAMAGE IMPAIR
INJURY SCUNDER SCUNNER
JAUNDICE PREJUDGE
PREJUDICED BIGOTED INSULAR
PARTIAL
PREJUDICIAL BIASED HURTFUL
CONTRARY DAMAGING INIMICAL
SINISTER
PRELATE CHIEF LEADER PRIEST
HIERARCH ORDINARY SUPERIOR
PRELIMINARY PRIOR PRELIM
PREFACE PRELUDE LIMINARY
PREAMBLE PREVIOUS
PRELUDE PROEM VERSET DESCANT
FORERUN INTRADA PREFACE
ANTELUDE BORSPIEL OVERTURE
RITORNEL VERSETTE VORSPIEL
PREMATURE UNRIPE IMMATURE
PREVIOUS TIMELESS UNTIMELY
PREMEDITATE FORNCAST
PURPENSE
PREMEDITATED SET STUDIED
PREPENSE
PREMIER CHIEF FIRST OLDEST
LEADING EARLIEST
PREMISE LEMMA MAJOR ASSUME
GROUND REASON SUMPTION
PREMIXED INSTANT
PREMIUM USE AGIO BACK AWARD
BONUS FANCY PRIZE SHAVE USURY
BOUNTY DEPORT REWARD
CONTANGO DONATIVE FOREGIFT
GIVEAWAY
PREMONITION OMEN HUNCH
NOTICE BODWORD PRESAGE
WARNING BODEWORD FORESCENT
PREMUNE SALTED
PREOCCUPATION HEART INSIGHT
FIXATION
PREOCCUPIED DEEP LOST RAPT
CRAZY ABSENT FILLED INTENT
CRACKED ABSORBED ENGROSSED
PREPARATION DIA FIG BALM DIBS
DOPE PREP CREAM FLASH GLAZE
JELLY READY ACETUM BLEACH
BLUING DERRIS FACIAL LOTION
MEGILP NEBULA PEPSIN SIMPLE
APPREST CLEANER DIPPING
EMANIUM ESSENCE ETHIOPS
EXTRACT FITNESS FONDANT
LINCTUS MELLITE PLACEBO
TRYPSIN VARNISH ABSTRACT
CONSERVE COSMETIC FIXATURE
GELOSINE INHALANT LAUDANUM
MEDICINE RACAHOUT TRAINING
MAKEREADY
(— CONTAINING HONEY) MELLITE
(— FOR COLORING LIQUORS) FLASH
(— OF GRAPEJUICE) DIBS
(AROMATIC —) ELIXIR
(CHEESE —) FONDU
(CHEESELIKE —) YOGURT YOGHURT
(COSMETIC —) HENNA
(ENZYME —) KOJI
(EYELID —) KOHL
(IMPURE RADIOACTIVE —) EMANIUM

(INTOXICATING —) BOZA
(MEDICAL —) STUFF
(OPIUM —) LAUDANUM
(SALINE —) LICK
(SLOPPY —) SLIBBERSAUCE
(SWEET —) DULCE
(UNCTUOUS —) CERATE
PREPARATORY PIONEER
PREPARE DO FIT FIX GET LAY ABLE
BUSK COOK GIRD MAKE PARE PLOT
PREP TILL YARK ATTLE BLEND
BRACE DIGHT DRAFT DRESS EQUIP
FRAME ORDER PREDY READY TRAIN
ADJUST DESIGN GRAITH ORDAIN
ADDRESS AFFAITE APPAREL
APPOINT CONCOCT CONFECT
DISPOSE EDUCATE PRODUCE
PROVIDE QUALIFY INSTRUCT
(— BANQUET) COVER
(— BY BOILING) BREW DECOCT
(— BY HEAT) FRIT
(— CAPON) SAUCE
(— FISH) CALVER
(— FOOD) DO COOK
(— FOR BUILDING) FRAME
(— FOR BURIAL) EMBALM
(— FOR DISPLAY) DRESS
(— FOR PUBLICATION) EDIT
(— HASTILY) RASH
(— HEMP) TAW
(— LAND) CURE
(— ONESELF) ADDRESS
(— TEASEL HEADS) CARP
PREPARED UP APT BUN FIT SET
BAAN BOON BOUN BOWN GIRT RIPE
YARE ALERT BOUND PREST READY
GRAITH CURRIED EQUIPPED
(QUICKLY —) RUNNING
PREPENSE DESIGN FORETHOUGHT
PREPONDERANCE MAJORITY
DOMINANCE
PREPONDERATE EXCEED INCLINE
SURPASS DOMINATE OUTWEIGH
PERSUADE
PREPOSSESS BIAS PREVENT
PREPOSSESSION BENT BIAS FETICH
FANTASY PREJUDICE
PREPOSTEROUS RICH INEPT
ABSURD FOOLISH LAPUTAN
GROTESQUE
PREROGATIVE GRACE HONOR
RIGHT ESNECY REGALE FACULTY
PECULIAR PRIVILEGE
PRESA LEAD
PRESAGE BODE HINT OMEN OSSE
SIGN ABODE AUGUR TOKEN
AUGURY BETIDE BETOKEN FORESEE
OMINATE PORTEND PREDICT
FOREBODE FORECAST FOREDOOM
FORETELL INDICATE PREAMBLE
PROPHESY
PRESBYTER ELDER PRIEST PRESTER
ANTISTES MINISTER
PRESBYTERIAN WHIG
PRESBYTERY SENIORY EXERCISE
PARSONAGE
PRESCIENCE PRESAGE FORESIGHT
PREVISION
PRESCIND SEVER DETACH

PRESCRIBE SET TAX ALLOT GUIDE
LIMIT ORDER ASSIGN DEFINE
DIRECT ENJOIN INDITE ORDAIN
APPOINT CONFINE CONTROL
DICTATE RESTRAIN
PRESCRIBED SET BASIC THETIC
THETICAL FORMULARY
PRESCRIPT LAW COMMAND
MANDATE PRECEPT
PRESCRIPTION RX BILL FORM
CIPHER RECIPE DICTATE FORMULA
PRESENCE EYE FACE SELF BEING
ASPECT BEARING COMPANY
ASSEMBLY INSTANCE
(DIRECT —) IMMEDIACY
PRESENT AIM BOX NOW BILL BOON
GIFT GIVE HAND HERE NEAR NIGH
SAND SHOW BEING CUDDY DOLLY
ENTER FEOFF GRANT NONCE OFFER
PLACE RAISE READY STAGE THERE
ACCUSE ACTUAL ADDUCE ALLEGE
AROUND BESTOW BOUNTY BROACH
CLOTHE CUMSHA DONATE DURANT
HANSEL KHILAT LATTER MODERN
NEARBY PREFER REGALE REGALO
XENIUM COMMEND CUMSHAW
DISPLAY DOUCEUR ETRENNE
EXHIBIT EXPOUND FAIRING FURNISH
HANDSEL INSTANT LARGESS
PERFORM PORRECT PRETEND
PROPINE RESIANT TASHRIF
BLESSING CONGIARY DONATION
GRATUITY INSTANCE LAGNAPPE
OFFERING PESHKASH RESIDENT
SOULCAKE SPORTULA
(— AS GIFT) DASH
(— FOR ACCEPTANCE) TENDER
(— FROM PUPIL TO TEACHER)
MINERVAL
(— IN DETAIL) DISCUSS
(— IN MIND) DEAR
(— ONESELF) APPEAR
(— TO SOLDIERS) CONGIARY
(— TO STRANGER) XENIUM
(— TO VIEW) YIELD
(— WITHOUT WARRANT) OBTRUDE
(ALWAYS —) CHRONIC
(BRIDEGROOM'S —) HANDSEL
(CEREMONIAL —) KHILAT
PRESENTATION BILL GALA GIFT
SHOW DROLL IMAGE DHARMA
MUSTER SCHEMA BILLING DISPLAY
EPITOME HOOKUPU PRESENT
SPECIES ANALYSIS BESTOWAL
DELIVERY DONATION EXPOSURE
CANDLEMAS
PRESENTIMENT FEELING PRESAGE
BODEMENT FOREFEEL PRENOTION
PRESENTLY NOW ANON ENOW
SOON SHORTLY DIRECTLY
PRESERVATION FILING SAVING
KEEPING SERVATION
PRESERVATIVE SALT BORAX SPICE
SUGAR CONSERVE TREATMENT
PRESERVE CAN JAR CORN HAIN
HOLD KEEP SAVE BLESS GUARD
SERVE SPARE SWEET WITIE ATHOLD
BOTTLE COMFIT DEFEND EMBALM
FREEZE GOGGLE POWDER RETAIN

SECURE SHIELD UPHOLD CONDITE
FORFEND KYANIZE PROTECT
RAISINE RESERVE SUCCADE
SUSTAIN CHOWCHOW CONSERVE
ENSHRINE MAINTAIN MOTHBALL
PARADISE WITHSAVE
(— BY BOILING WITH SUGAR)
CANDY
(— BY SALTING) CORN CURE SALT
(— OF GRAPES) RAISINE
(— WOOD) KYANIZE
(GAME —) MOOR SHIKARGAH
(HUNTING —) WALK
(PL.) KONFYT
PRESERVED WET CONFECT
BRANDIED POWDERED
PRESIDE RULE GUIDE DIRECT
MODERATE
(— OVER) KEEP
PRESIDENCY MADRAS PRYTANY
PRESIDENT MIR FOUD PREX PROXY
REEVE DEACON RECTOR PRAESES
PREFECT
(— OF SUPREME COURT) LAWMAN
(— OF TRADE) DEACON
PRESIGNIFY PRESAGE FORETOKEN
PRESS FLY HUG JAM SIT BEAR BEND
CRAM DOME DROP DRUK HORN
HUSH IRON JAMB KISS PLOT SERR
THEW TUCK URGE VICE YERK
ARGUE BESET BRIZZ CHAFE CHIRT
CROWD CRUSH DRIVE EXACT
FORCE KNEAD MIDST PRIZE SCREW
SHREW SMASH STAMP STUFF TWIST
WEIGH WRING ASSAIL CHISEL
CLOSET COARCT CRUNCH GOFFER
HARASS JOBBER MANGLE NUDDLE
PREACE SQUASH STRAIN STRESS
THRAST THREAP THREAT THREEP
THRIMP THRING THRONG THRUST
AFFLICT ATTEMPT BESEECH
BESIEGE CONCISE CRUMPLE
EMBRACE ENVIRON FLATBED
IMPRESS MACHINE OPPRESS
SCROOGE SCRUNGE SQUEEZE
THRUTCH CALENDER COMPRESS
PRESSURE SCROUNGE SQUEEGEE
SURROUND
(— AGAINST) CONTACT
(— CLOSE) NUDDLE
(— CLOSELY AND PAINFULLY) MASH
(— DOWN) QUAT
(— FOR WINE) TORCULAR
(— FORWARD) DRIVE BREAST
(— HARSHLY) GRIND
(— IN CHEESE VAT) CHISEL
CHIZZEL
(— INTO) THRIMBLE THRUMBLE
(— ON ANVIL) HORN
(— ONWARD) STRETCH
(— OUT) EXTRUDE
(— PAPER) COUCH
(— TOGETHER) SERRY
(— UPON) ELBOW DOWNBEAR
(— WITH HEAD OR HORNS) BOX
(— WITH VIOLENCE) DRIVE
PRESS AGENT FLACK
PRESSED SERRIED
(— WITH BUSINESS) THRONG

(— WITH LEFTHAND FOREFINGER)
BARRED
PRESSING RASH CRYING URGENT
CLAMANT EARNEST EXIGENT
INSTANT SQUEEZE CRITICAL
PREGNANT
PRESSMAN PIG MINDER PROVER
PRINTER
PRESSURE JAM HEAD HEAT PEND
PUSH SWAY DRIVE FORCE IMAGE
PINCH STAMP DURESS STRESS
THRONG WEIGHT BEARING
MERCURY PUSHING SQUEEZE
TENSION URGENCY EXACTION
EXIGENCY FUGACITY PRESSION
(— GROUP) LOBBY
(— OF 1 DYNE) BARAD
(— ON INSTRUMENT STRING) STOP
(— UNIT) TORR MICRON
(LIQUID —) HEAD
(MANUAL —) TAXIS
(VAPOR —) FUGACITY
PRESSURE COOKER STEAMER
AUTOCLAVE
PRESSWORK BACKUP
PRESTIDIGITATOR PALMER
JUGGLER PYTHONIC
PRESTIGE FACE MANA CASTE IKBAL
IZZAT KUDOS CACHET STATUS
STATURE ILLUSION INFLUENCE
PRESTO QUICKLY SPEEDILY
PRESUME BEAR DARE GROW IMPLY
INFER ASSUME EXPECT DARESAY
SUPPOSE
PRESUMING ARROGANT FAMILIAR
PRESUMPTION JOLLITY OUTRAGE
PRESUME AUDACITY SUCCUDRY
SURQUIDY
PRESUMPTUOUS BOLD PERT FRESH
PROUD WICKED WILFUL FORWARD
HAUGHTY ARROGANT ASSUMING
FAMILIAR INSOLENT FOOLHARDY
PRESUPPOSE IMPLY POSIT ASSUME
EXPECT PREMISE FORETAKE
PRETA PETA
PRETEND ACT LET FAKE MAKE
MOCK SHAM CLAIM FEIGN AFFECT
ASPIRE ASSERT ASSUME GAMMON
INTEND OBTEND POSSUM RECKON
SEMBLE ATTEMPT PORTEND
PRESUME PROFESS SUPPOSE
VENTURE SIMULATE
(— IGNORANCE) CONNIVE
(— TO) FA
PRETENDED FAKE SHAM BOGUS
FALSE IRONIC UNREAL ALLEGED
ASSUMED COLORED FEIGNED
SEEMING AFFECTED IRONICAL
SIMULATE
PRETENDER FOP FAKE IDOL CHEAT
COWAN FAKER FRAUD QUACK
PSEUDO SEEMER AEOLIST
CLAIMANT IMPOSTOR INTENDER
TARTUFFE
(— TO LEARNING) SCIOLIST
PRETENDING FICTION
PRETENSE ACT AIR FACE GRIM
MIEN PLEA RUSE SCUG SHAM SHOW
SIGN WILE CLOAK COLOR COVER

FEINT GLOSS GLOZE STUDY
EXCUSE HUMBUG CHARADE FAITERY
FASHION FICTION GRIMACE
PRETEXT PURPOSE UMBRAGE
ARTIFICE DISGUISE POSTICHE
POSTIQUE SEMBLANT
PRETENSION PARADE VANITY
PRETEXT
PRETENTIOUS BIG BRAG HIGH SIDY
FLASH GAUDY PUFFY SHOWY
BRAGGY GEWGAW GLOSSY PUFFED
ROCOCO SHODDY TINSEL BOMBAST
POMPOUS TOPPING BRAGGART
PRETENTIOUSNESS SIDE SWANK
PRETERMIT OMIT NEGLACT
SUSPEND INTERRUPT
PRETERNATURAL GOUSTY GOUSTIE
STRANGE ABNORMAL UNCOMMON
UNEARTHLY
(— BEING) MARE
PRETEXT PEG FLAM MASK PLEA
CLOAK COLOR COVER GLOSS
SALVO STALL EXCUSE REFUGE
SCONCE APOLOGY UMBRAGE
OCCASION PRETENCE
PRETTIFY EYEWASH
PRETTY APT GEY PAT ABLE BRAW
CUTE DEFT FAIR FEAT FINE GAIN
GENT GOOD JOLI MILD POOR TRIM
BONNY DINKY JOLIE POOTY PURTY
QUITE SWEET BONITA DIMBER
FINELY INCONY MINION PRATTY
RATHER TRETIS CLEMENT CUNNING
DOLLISH GENTEEL BUDGEREE
PRECIOUS
(— WELL) GAILY GAYLY
PRETTY-PRETTY KEEPSAKE
PREVAIL WIN BEAR BEAT REIGN
WIELD INDUCE OBTAIN CONQUER
PERSIST SUCCEED TRIUMPH
DOMINATE
(— BECAUSE BEYOND CONTROL)
RAGE
(— OVER) SURMOUNT
(— UPON) GET FOLD LEAD ARGUFY
ENTICE INDUCE OBTAIN ENTREAT
OVERSWAY
PREVAILING RIFE GOING USUAL
CURRENT DOMINANT
PREVALENCE RUN
PREVALENT UP RIFE BRIEF
COMMON POTENT CURRENT
GENERAL POPULAR REGNANT
CATHOLIC EPIDEMIC POWERFUL
PREVARICATE LIE EVADE STRAY
WANDER QUIBBLE SHUFFLE
PREVENT BAR LET HELP KEEP NILL
SHUN STAY STOP TENT WARN
AVERT CHECK DEBAR DETER ESTOP
ARREST DEFEND FORBID FORLET
HINDER OUTRUN RETAIN REVOKE
SECURE FORFEND FORLEIT
IMPEACH INHIBIT PRECEDE RETRACT
ANTEVERT INTERPEL PRECLUDE
WITHHOLD
(— OPPONENT FROM SCORING)
CHICAGO
PREVENTION PREFACE ESTOPPEL
OBSTACLE PREJUDICE

PREVIEW SNEAK FUTURAMA
PREVIOUS HASTY PRIOR BEFORE FORMER RATHER EARLIER LEADING FOREGONE
PREVIOUSLY ERE YET ERST FORE SUPRA BEFORE ALREADY HASTILY PRIORLY FORMERLY HITHERTO
PREVISION FORESEE FORECAST FORESIGHT
PREY ROB FEED GAME SOYL TIRE BOOTY PREDE RAVEN RAVIN SPOIL QUARRY RAVAGE RAVINE VICTIM CAPTURE PILLAGE PLUNDER ROBBERY SPREATH VULTURE
(— UPON) DEVOUR PICAROON DEPREDATE
PREYER KITE
PRIAM (DAUGHTER OF —) CREUSA POLYXENA CASSANDRA
(SLAYER OF —) PYRRHUS
(SON OF —) PARIS HECTOR TROILUS
(WIFE OF —) HECUBA
PRIAPISM TENTIGO
PRICE LAY ANTE COST FARE FEER FIAR FIER FOOT ODDS PRYS RATE BRIBE CHEAP CLOSE VALUE WORTH CHARGE FIGURE HANSEL TARIFF AVERAGE CATALOG CRANAGE EXPENSE FURNACE HANDSEL PRETIUM STORAGE CARRIAGE FERRIAGE INTEREST
(— FOR KEEPING GOODS) STORAGE
(LOW —) WANWORTH
(PROPER —) VALUE
(REDUCED —) SALE BARGAIN
(RISING —S) BOOM INFLATION
PRICELESS RARE COSTLY UNIQUE UNSALABLE
PRICK DOT JAG BROD DROB FOIN GOAD JAGG PECK PING PROG SPUR STAB TANG URGE DRESS ERECT POINT PREEN PUNCH STEEK BROACH GALLOP INTENT LAUNCH POUNCE PRITCH SKEWER STITCH TARGET THRUST TWINGE POINTED BULLSEYE
(— OUT) SPOT
(— PAINFULLY) STING
(— WITH NAIL) CLY CLOY
PRICKED PIQUE
PRICKER PROD NEEDLE STABBER
PRICKET DAG SNUFFER SPITTER
PRICKING SMART PUNGENT RETRACT POIGNANT POINTURE PUNCTION
PRICKLE PIKE SETA SPEAR THORN BASKET ACANTHA ACULEUS PRINKLE SPICULA
PRICKLY BURRY JAGGY SHARP SPINY URCHIN SPINOSE SPINOUS STICKLY THISTLY ECHINATE MURICATE SCABROUS SCRATCHY SPICULAR STICKERY STINGING VEXATIOUS
PRICKLY ASH RUEWORT
PRICKLY PEAR TUN TUNA NOPAL SABRA OPUNTIA PINPILLOW
PRICKLY-POINTED PUNGENT

PRICKLY POPPY COCKSCOMB
PRIDE HEAT HORN LUST POMP RUFF ADORN CREST GLORY ORGUL PLUME PRIME WLANK EXCESS HUBRIS METTLE NOSISM VANITY COMPANY CONCEIT DISDAIN EGOTISM GLORIFY HAUTEUR STOMACH SURQUIDY WLONKHEDE
(— ONESELF) PIQUE
(EXCESSIVE —) SWELLING
PRIDEFUL FASTUOUS
PRIEST EN CURA CURE DEAN EZRA IMAM MAGA COHEN EPULO IMAUM ISIAC MOBED PADRE PATER SABIO SARIP VICAR ZADOK ABACES AMAUTA BHIKKU BISHOP DASTUR DIVINE FALMEN FATHER FLAMEN GALLAH GALLUS GELONG GETSUL GOSAIN JETHRO KAHUNA LEVITE POWWOW SHAMAN ANANIAS ARBACES CALCHAS CASSOCK CHANTER DESTOUR DUSTOOR GALLACH LAOCOON PANDITA PAPALOI PATENER PATRICO PHINEAS POONGEE PRESTER STOLIST TEACHER TOHUNGA BABAYLAN BEROSSOS CASERDOS CHRYSEIS HANANIAH KASHYAPA MINISTER PANDARAM PENANCER PONTIFEX POONGHIE SEMINARY SOGGARTH SYRIARCH TALISMAN VARDAPET ZADOKITE
(— OF APOLLO) CALCHAS CHRYSEIS
(— OF CYBELE) CORYBANT
(— OF RAMA) KASHYAPA
(— OF RHEA) CURETE
(BABYLONIAN —) BEROSSOS
(BUDDHIST —) LAMA BHIKKU GELONG POONGEE POONGHIE
(CHIEF — OF SHRINE) EN
(CHIEF —) SYRIARCH
(EGYPTIAN —) ARBACES CHOACHYTE
(EUNUCH —) GALLUS
(FRENCH —) PERE SULPICIAN
(GYPSY —) PATRICO
(HIGH —) ELI SARIP DASTUR KAHUNA DESTOUR PHINEAS PONTIFF PRELATE CAIAPHAS HIERARCH JEHOIADA PONTIFEX
(HINDU —) PANDARAM
(INCA —) AMAUTA
(LAMAIST —) GETSUL
(MAORI —) TOHUNGA
(MORO —) SARIP PANDITA
(MOSLEM —) TALISMAN
(PAGAN —) BABAYLAN
(PARISH —) CURA CURE PAPA POPE PARSON PERSON SECULAR
(ROMAN —) EPULO FLAMEN
(TIBETAN —) LAMA
(VAISHNAVA —) GOSAIN
(PL.) LUPERCI
PRIEST-DOCTOR SHAMAN WABENO
PRIESTESS NUN ENTUM HORSE MAMBO MAMBU BACBUC PYTHIA DIOTIMA MAMALOI PHOIBAD PHITONES
(— OF APOLLO) PYTHIA PHOEBAD

(— OF THE BOTTLE) BACBUC
(BABYLONIAN —) ENTUM
(VOODOO —) HORSE
PRIESTFISH CHERNA ROCKFISH
PRIESTHOOD SALII SACERDOCY
PRIEST-KING PATESI
PRIESTLY LEVITIC SACERDOTAL
PRIG BEG FOP BRAD BUCK NAIL SMUG DANDY FILCH PLEAD STEAL THIEF FELLOW HAGGLE PERSON PILFER TINKER ENTREAT PURITAN QUIBBLE
PRIGGER THIEF
PRIM MIM NEAT TRIG TRIM MIMZY DEMURE FORMAL MIMSEY PRIVET PROPER STUFFY MISSISH PRECISE PRIMSIE
PRIMACY CHIEFTY PRIMITY HEADSHIP
PRIMA DONNA DIVA STAR
PRIMARY CYAN BASIC CHIEF FIRST PRIME CAUCUS DIRECT FONTAL MANUAL MAGENTA RADICAL ARCHICAL CARDINAL HYPOGENE ORIGINAL PRIMEVAL
PRIMATE BISHOP GALAGO LEADER PREMAN PRINCIPAL
PRIME MAY FANG FILL LOAD MAIN CHIEF COACH FIRST PRIDE TONIC YOUTH CHOICE FLOWER SPRING CENTRAL LEADING LUSTFUL PREPARE DOMINEER ORIGINAL YOUTHFUL PRINCIPAL
PRIME MINISTER ATABEG PREMIER
PRIMER ABC CAP WAFER CORDERY HORNBOOK
PRIMEVAL OLD NATIVE ANCIENT OGYGIAN PRIMARY PRISTINE PRIMITIVE
PRIMING MORSING TWOPENNY CLEARCOLE
PRIMING IRON DRIFT
PRIMING WIRE PICKER
PRIMITIVE DARK CRUDE EARLY FIRST GROSS NAIVE PLAIN PRIME FANTEE GOTHIC PRIMAL SAVAGE SIMPLE ANCIENT ARCHAIC PRIMARY PRISCAN BARBARIC EARLIEST IGNORANT ORIGINAL PRISTINE
PRIMNESS PRUDERY
PRIMORDIAL CRUDE FIRST PRIMARY ARCHICAL EARLIEST PRIMEVAL
PRIMORDIUM BUD
PRIMP PRIM ADORN PREEN PRINK
PRIMROSE GAY OXLIP SPINK FLOWER SUNCUP COWSLIP FLOWERY SCABISH AURICULA PLUMROCK SCURVISH AFTERGLOW PIMPERNEL
PRIMULA OXLIP COWSLIP PRIMWORT
PRINCE MIN RAS DUKE EARL EMIR IMAM KHAN KING KNEZ LORD NASI RAJA RANA RIAL SAID WANG ALDER EBLIS EMEER FURST GEBIR PWYLL RAJAH SAYID ARJUNA DESPOT DYNAST SHERIF SOLDAN BHARATA ELECTOR GLAUCUS HELENUS MONARCH TANCRED TOPARCH ZERBINO ARCHDUKE CARDINAL

MAMILIUS OROONOKO PLORIZEL RASSELAS SARPEDON
(— **OF ABYSSINIA**) RAS RASSELAS
(— **OF APOSTATE ANGELS**) DEVIL EBLIS
(— **OF ARGO**) DIOMED DIOMEDES
(— **OF BOHEMIA**) FLORIZEL
(— **OF DARKNESS**) DEVIL SATAN
(— **OF DEMONS**) BEELZEBUB
(— **OF DYFED**) PWYLL
(— **OF SALERNO**) TANCRED
(— **OF SCOTLAND**) ZERBINO
(— **SOLD INTO SLAVERY**) OROONOKO
(— **WITH CHARLEMAGNE**) ASTOLF ASTOLFO
(**ANGLO-SAXON** —) ADELING ATHELING
(**ARAB** —) SHERIF
(**CHINESE** —) WANG
(**GERMAN** —) FURST ELECTOR
(**INDIAN** —) RAJA RANA RAJAH BHARATA AHLUWALIA
(**LYCIAN** —) GLAUCUS SARPEDON
(**MOHAMMEDAN** —) SOLDAN
(**MOSLEM** —) IMAM SAID SAYID SAYYID SHEIKH SOLDAN
(**PETTY** —) SATRAP VERGOBRET
(**SERVIAN** —) CRAL
(**SLAVIC** —) KNEZ
(**TROJAN** —) HELENUS
PRINCELY NOBLE ROYAL KINGLY STATELY SOVEREIGN
PRINCE'S FEATHER LILAC PILEWORT
PRINCESS AIDA ELSA RANI DANAE PALLA RANEE SARAH CREUSA GLAUKE ILDICO MADAME PSYCHE ANTIOPE CORONIS PHYLLIS DRAUPADI MAHARANI
(— **CHANGED INTO CROW**) CORONIS
(— **MOTHER OF ZEUS**) ANTIOPA ANTIOPE
(— **OF ARGOS**) DANAE
(— **OF CORINTH**) CREUSA GLAUKE
(— **WHO SLEW ATTILA**) ILDICO
(**MOHAMMEDAN** —) BEGUM
(**THRACIAN** —) PHYLLIS
(**TYRIAN** —) DIDO
PRINCEWOOD CYP BARIA CYPRE CERILLO CANALETE SALMWOOD
PRINCIPAL ARCH BOSS HEAD HIGH MAIN STAR CHIEF FIRST GRAND GREAT PRIME STOCK AUCTOR CORPUS MASTER STAPLE CAPITAL CAPTAIN CENTRAL CHATTEL DOMINUS PREMIER PRIMARY SALIENT STELLAR FOREMOST OFFICIAL PRESTANT PRINCELY
(— **OF SCHOOL**) PRECEPTOR HEADMASTER
PRINCIPALITY ZUPA ARZAVA ARZAWA ORANGE SATRAPY APPANAGE DESPUTAT
PRINCIPLE JUS LAW RTA TAO BASE FATE RITA RULE SEED YANG AGENT AXIOM BASIS CANON CAUSE DATUM PRANA SPARK STUFF TENET

ANIMUS CNICIN COGITO CORTIN ELIXIR EMBRYO FAGINE GOSPEL ARCHEUS BROCARD BUFAGIN CLYSSUS ELEMENT FORMULA GENERAL PRECEPT QUASSIN RADICAL THEOREM URGRUND DOCTRINE GOSSYPOL INTIMISM LANDMARK NICOTINE SANCTION SPECIFIC TINCTURE
(— **ACCEPTED AS TRUE**) CANON
(— **FROM TOAD**) BUFAGIN
(— **IN BEECHNUTS**) FAGINE
(— **OF BLESSED THISTLE**) CNICIN
(— **OF COTTONSEED**) GOSSYPOL
(— **OF EXISTENCE**) TATTVA
(— **OF INDIVIDUATION**) AHANKARA
(— **OF KEY IN MUSIC**) TONALITY
(— **OF REST**) ADHARMA
(**COSMIC** —) HEAVEN URGRUND PRAJAPATI
(**DOGMATIC** —) DICTUM
(**ELEMENTARY** —) BROCARD
(**FEMALE** —) YIN
(**FIRST** —) ABC SEED ARCHE
(**FUNDAMENTAL** —) GROUNDSEL
(**GERMINAL** —) STAMEN
(**GOVERNING** —) HINGE
(**GUIDING** —) SQUARE
(**LIFE** —) SOUL GHOST PRANA
(**MALE** —) YANG PURUSHA
(**MOHAMMEDAN THEOLOGICAL** —) IJMA
(**MORAL** —) SCRUPLE
(**NARCOTIC** —) FAGINE
(**ONTOLOGICAL** —) DHARMA
(**PRIMAL** —) APEIRON
(**PROMINENT** —) KEY
(**RHYTHMICAL** —) ACCENT
(**SPIRITUAL** —) SOUL
(**SUMMARY OF** —**S**) CREED
(**VITAL** —) JIVA SPIRIT STAMEN ARCHAEUS
PRINK PERK PRIG WINK ADORN PRICK PRIMP PRUNE BEDECK SMUDGE
PRINT CUT GAY GUM DRUK MARK TYPE FUDGE PORTY PRESS SEPIA STAMP BANNER BORDER CARBON CARBRO ENFACE LETTER STRIKE BROMOIL DROPOUT DUOTYPE ENGRAVE GRAPHIC GRAVURE IMPRESS PUBLISH TRACING VANDYKE VESTIGE WOODCUT AQUATONE CALOTYPE CHLORIDE DRYPOINT HALFTONE INSCRIBE LEIMTYPE MONOTYPE POSITIVE URUSHIYE
(— **OTHER SIDE**) BACK
(— **TO RIGHT**) ADSCRIPT
PRINTED FONTED
PRINTER TYPO TWICER PRESSMAN IMPRIMENT
(**AID TO** —) DEVIL
(**PL.**) TYPOTHETAE
PRINTER'S DEVIL FLY
PRINTING TIRAGE EDITION VIGOREUX CHARACTER IMPRIMERY
(**LAST** —) THIRTY
PRION PETREL

PRIONID BEETLE
PRIONODON LINSANG
PRIOR ERE OLD FORE PAST EIGNE ELDER FORMER RATHER ALREADY EARLIER FARTHER ANTERIOR FOREHAND HITHERTO PREVIOUS
PRIORITY PRIVILEGE PRECEDENCE
PRIORY ABBEY NUNNERY CLOISTER PRIORATE
PRISM BLOCK NICOL CYLINDER SPECTRUM WERNICKE
PRISMATIC SHOWY BRILLIANT
PRISON GIB JUG BRIG COOP GAOL HELL HOCK HOLD HOLE JAIL KEEP LAKE QUAD QUOD SHOP STIR WARD BAGNE CLINK FLEET GRATE KITTY LODGE POUND RATEL TENCH TRONK VAULT BAGNIO BAILEY BUCKET CARCEL CARCER COOLER JIGGER RATTLE BASTILE BOCARDO BULLPEN COLLEGE COMPTER CONFINE COUNTER DUNGEON FREEZER GEHENNA KIDCOTE LUDGATE NEWGATE DARTMOOR HOOSEGOW TOLBOOTH TRIBUNAL
(— **CAMP**) OFLAG
(— **IN ROME**) TULLIANUM
(**AUSTRALIAN** —) TENCH
(**UNIVERSITY** —) CARCER
PRISONER CON POW MUTE LIFER DETENU INMATE REMAND CAITIFF CAPTIVE CONVICT GAOLBIRD JAILBIRD LONGTIMER
PRISONER'S BASE CHEVY CHIVY
PRISSY PRIM FUSSY DAINTY FINICKY PRUDISH PRIGGISH SISSIFIED
PRISTINE NEW PURE FIRST FRESH ANCIENT PRIMARY ORIGINAL PRIMEVAL PRIMITIVE UNSPOILED
PRIVACY RECESS SECRET PRIVITY RETREAT SECRECY DARKNESS INTIMACY INTIMITY SOLITUDE SECLUSION
(**IN** —) ASIDE
(**PL.**) VERENDA
PRIVATE SNUG ALONE GUIDE KHASS PRIVY SHARE CLOSET COVERT INWARD POCKET SECRET STANCH POSTERN SECRECY SEVERAL SOLDIER CIVILIAN ESOTERIC HOMEFELT INTERNAL INTIMATE PERSONAL SINGULAR UMBRATILE
PRIVATEER CAPER PIRATE ALABAMA CORSAIR DUNKIRK PICKEER
PRIVATELY ASIDE INWARDLY SECRETLY
PRIVATION LOSS WANT PENURY PERISH ABSENCE POVERTY HARDSHIP
PRIVET PRIM HEDGE SKEDGE IBOLIUM PRIMWORT PRIMPRINT
PRIVILEGE UP PUT SOC DOWN HAND STAR TEAM CLAIM ENTRY FAVOR FRANK GRACE HONOR REGAL RIGHT THEAM EXCUSE INDULT MUNITY OCTROI OPTION PATENT WARREN CHARTER FALDAGE FREEDOM LIBERTY MITZVAH PASSAGE GRANDEZA STANDAGE

(— TO USE THINGS) BOTE
(ACQUIRED —) EASEMENT
(POKER —) EDGE
(POOL —) STAR
PRIVILEGED CURULE EXEMPT
LICENSED
(— PLACE) WARREN
PRIVY WC GONG BIFFY DRAFT ISSUE
JAKES PETTY QUIET SIEGE CLOSET
OFFICE SECRET DRAUGHT FOREIGN
LATRINE PRIVATE DONICKER
FAMILIAR INTIMATE OUTHOUSE
PERSONAL STEALTHY WARDROBE
PRIZE CUP FEE GEM PRY BELL BEND
GAME GREE PALM PREY PRIX RATE
RISK AWARD BACON BOOTY LEVER
PLATE PLUME PRICE PURSE STAKE
VALUE WAGER ESTEEM GLAIVE
PRAISE PREMIO TROPHY BENEFIT
CAPTURE GARLAND PREMIUM
ESTIMATE LEVERAGE PURCHASE
REPRISAL TREASURE
(— FOR LAST) MELL
(FIRST —) BLUE
(LOTTERY —) LOT TERN
PRIZE CUP PEWTER
PRIZED DEAR CHARY
PRIZEFIGHT GO BOUT MILL MATCH
SCRAP
PRIZEFIGHTER BOXER BLEEDER
FIGHTER SLUGGER PUGILIST
PRIZE MONEY GUNNAGE
PRO TO FOR FAVORING
PROA PARO PRAU PROW PAROO
PRAHU CARACOA
PROBABILITY ODDS SHOW CHANCE
PROBABLE MAYBE LIKELY PROBAL
TOPICAL APPARENT FEASIBLE
POSSIBLE
PROBABLY BELIKE LIKELY
PROBATION TEST PROOF TRIAL
PAROLE EVIDENCE
PROBATIONER STIBBLER
PROBE SEEK SIFT STOG TENT ENTER
GROPE SOUND FATHOM SEARCH
SEEKER STYLET THRUST ACCOUNT
EXAMINE INQUIRY SOUNDER
GYROMELE
PROBITY HONESTY INTEGRITY
RECTITUDE
PROBLEM NUT SUM WHY BOYG
CRUX DUAL ISSE KNOT BLAIK
HYDRA POSER APORIA ENIGMA
BUGBEAR DILEMMA FUNERAL
GORDIAN GRUELER TICHLER
EXERCISE HEADACHE JEOPARDY
QUESTION STICKLER
(CHESS —) DUAL MOVER SUIMATE
MINIATURE
PROBLEMATICAL DUBIOUS
DOUBTFUL PUZZLING UNCERTAIN
UNDECIDED
PROBOSCIS NOSE SNOUT TRUMP
TRUNK ANTLIA LINGUA SIPHON
SYPHON TONGUE ROSTRUM
PROBOSCIS MONKEY KAHA KAHUA
PROCAVIA HYRAX
PROCEDURE BIAS FORM HAVE VEIN
DRAFT ORDER TENOR TRACK

AFFAIR COURSE METHOD POLITY
SYSTEM DRAUGHT PROCESS
PRODUCT ACTIVITY PROTOCOL
(PRESCRIBED —S) CEREMONY
(ROUNDABOUT —) CIRCUITY
(SECRET —) STEALTH
(UNWISE —) FOLLY
PROCEED DO GO BANG BEAR FAND
FARE FLOW FOND HAVE MAKE
MARK MOVE PASS ROAM ROLL
SEEK STEP TAKE TOOL TOUR WEAR
WEND WIND YEDE AMBLE ARISE
DRESS FOUND FRAME ISSUE MARCH
REACH BREEZE INTEND PURSUE
RESULT SPRING STRAKE STRIKE
ADVANCE AGGRESS DEVOLVE
EMANATE FORTHGO PRETEND
STRETCH CONTINUE PROGRESS
(— AIMLESSLY) CIRCLE
(— ALONE) SINGLE
(— CLUMSILY) FLOUNDER
(— OBLIQUELY) CUT
(— RAGGEDLY) HALT
(— RAPIDLY) STRETCH
(— UNSTEADILY) DRIDDLE
(— WITH DIFFICULTY) STRUGGLE
(PL.) TAKE VAIL AVAILS INCOME
PROFITS PROVENT RETURNS
PREVENUE
PROCEEDING ACT DEED FARE PLOY
STEP AFFAIR AMPARO COURSE
DOMENT ISSUANT MEASURE
ONGOING PASSANT QUIETUS
TEMANET WARRANT CONCURSO
INSTANCE PLACITUM PRACTICE
(— BY THREES) TERNARY
(— FROM GOD) DIVINE
(— FROM THE EARTH) TELLURIC
(COURT —S) TRIAL
(INDIRECT —S) AMBAGES
(PARLIAMENTARY —S) HUSTINGS
(RECORDED —S) ACTA
PROCERITY HEIGHT TALLNESS
PROCESS RUN FANG FOOT TINA
WRIT CREST FURCA HAMUS MUCRO
SPINA CALCAR CAPIAS CILIUM
COURSE FEELER HABEAS INTEND
METHOD REPORT ACCOUNT
FURCULA GOBBING HAMULUS
ISOLATE LAMELLA MANDATE
SPATULA SUMMONS ACTIVITY
APPENDIX FILAMENT FRENULUM
GRAINING INSTANCE
(— OF BONE) HORN
(— OF CHANGE) ACTION
(— OF CREATING VACUUM)
EXHAUST
(— OF DYEING) BATIK HANKING
(— OF METALPLATING) ACIERAGE
(— OF PACKING) GOBBING
(— OF REASONING) ALGEBRA
(— OF SUPPLYING WANTAGE)
ULLING
(— ON FISH'S HEAD) LACINIA
(— PAPER) CONVERT
(— TO RECOVER LAND) DADENHUDD
(ABRUPT —) MUCRO
(ALCHEMICAL —) DIPLOSIS
(ARTISTIC —) FROTTAGE

(CALENDERING —) SWISSING
(CARBON —) AUTOTYPE
(CERAMIC —) FIRING
(COATING —) BLOOMING
(CURVED —) HAMUS
(DEVELOPMENTAL —) ANCESTRY
(EARLIKE —) AURICLE
(FALCONRY —) IMPING
(FINISHING —) BRUSHING CRABBING
(FORKED —) FURCA FURCULA
(HELMETLIKE —) CASQUE
(HOOKLIKE —) HAMULUS
(HORNSHAPED —) CORNICLE
(INTELLECTUAL —S) COGITO
(KNOBLIKE —) BOSS
(LEGAL —) BAIL SUIT CAUSE
ATTAINT INSTANCE
(MATHEMATICAL —) ADDITION
DIVISION
(MENTAL —) COMPOUND
(MINING —) STOPING
(MOVIE-MAKING —) SLATING
(NERVELIKE —) AXON AXONE
(PHOTOGRAPHIC —) CARBRO
(POINTED —) AWN SPINE STYLUS
LANGUET
(PRINTING —) GRAVURE STENCIL
INTAGLIO
(REORGANIZATION —) HEMIXIS
(SMALL POINTED —) AWN
(SPINNING —) JACKING
(TEXTILE —) DECATING
(WEAVING —) HATCHING
(WINGLIKE —) ALA FIN
PROCESSED DOWN FINISHED
PROCESSION POMP WALK CORSO
DRIVE TRACE TRAIN BRIDAL
EXEQUY LITANY PARADE STREAM
CORTEGE FUNERAL THIASOS
TRIONFO TRIUMPH ENTRANCE
PROGRESS
(BOISTEROUS —) SKIMMITY
(IRISH CIVIC —) FRINGES
PROCLAIM BID CRY BAWL DEEM
HORN OYES OYEZ SCRY SING TOOT
TOUT BLARE BOAST CLAIM GREDE
KNELL SOUND SPEAK BLAZON
BOUNCE DEFAME HERALD INDICT
OUTCRY CLARION DECLARE
DIVULGE PROTEST PUBLISH
TRUMPET ANNOUNCE DENOUNCE
RENOUNCE
(— ALOUD) ROAR
(— PUBLICLY) PRECONIZE
(— WITH BIG TALK) BOUNCE
PROCLAMATION CRY HUE BANS
FIAT RERD BANDO BANNS BLAZE
EDICT UKASE PLACARD PROGRAM
PROCLIVITY BENT ANLAGE APETITE
APTNESS LEANING TENDENCY
PROCNE (FATHER OF —) PANDION
(HUSBAND OF —) TEREUS
(SISTER OF —) PHILOMENA
(SON OF —) ITYS
PROCONSUL GALLIO PROVOST
PROCRASTINATE LAG TIME DEFER
DELAY LINGER ADJOURN POSTPONE
PROROGUE TEMPORIZE
PROCRASTINATION DELAY
CUNCTATION

PROCREANT FRUITFUL
PROCREATE WIN SIRE BEGET ENGENDER GENERATE OCCASION
PROCREATION INCREASE
PROCREATOR AUTHOR
PROCTOR LIAR PROG ACTOR AGENT PROXY BEGGAR RECTOR MONITOR PROCUTOR
PROCUMBENT HUMIFUSE PROSTRATE
PROCURABLE PARABLE
PROCURATOR PROXY PILATE PROCTOR
PROCURE GET WIN FANG FIND GAIN GIVE HALE BRING INFER TOUCH EFFECT INDUCE OBTAIN ACHIEVE ACQUIRE COMPARE CONQUER CONTRIVE PURCHASE
PROCURER PIMP PROXENET PURVEYOR
PROCURESS HACK LENA PANDER COMMODE PINNACE
PROD DAB EGG GIG JAB JOG BROD BROG GOAD HEEL POKE PROG HURRY NUDGE PROBE INCITE JOSTLE THRUST IRRITATE
PRODIGAL PROD FLUSH LARGE COSTLY LAVISH WANTON WASTER PROFUSE SPENDER WASTRIE WASTRIFE
PRODIGALITY WASTE WASTRY WASTRIFE PROFUSION
PRODIGIOUS HUGE VAST GIANT AMAZING IMMENSE STRANGE ABNORMAL ENORMOUS GIGANTIC MONSTROUS
PRODIGY OMEN SIGN MARVEL OSTENT WIZARD WONDER MONSTER PORTENT CEREMONY
PRODITION TREASON BETRAYAL
PRODUCE DO GO ANTE BEAR FORM GIVE GROW MAKE REAR SHOW TEEM WAGE BEGET BIRTH BREED BRING BROOD BUILD CARRY CAUSE DRIVE FORGE FRAME HATCH ISSUE RAISE SPAWN THROW TRADE YIELD APPORT CREATE EFFECT GROWTH INCOME INVENT INWORK SECURE ADVANCE ANIMATE COMPOSE DEPROME GIGNATE INSPIRE OUTWORK PRODUCT PROLONG PROVENT CONCEIVE CONFLATE ENGENDER GENERATE INCREASE LENGTHEN OFFSPRING
(— A COPY OF) TYPE
(— AN EFFECT) ACT AFFECT
(— AUDIBLE EFFECT) SOUND
(— CROPS) CARRY
(— DULL APPEARANCE) CHILL
(— FRUIT) TEEM
(— HEAT) ENRAGE
(— PAID FOR RENT) CAIN
(— SHARP NOISE) CRINK
(AGRICULTURAL —) PODWARE
(FARM —) HUSBANDRY
(MINING —) LEY
PRODUCER GASMAN BEARING SHOWMAN DIRECTOR GAZOGENE OUTPUTTER

PRODUCING IN PROCREANT
PRODUCT HEIR ITEM BRAND CHILD FRUIT GROSS OUTGO SPAWN ALCLAD EFFORT FABRIC GROWTH RESULT UPCOME OUTTURN PRODUCE PROGENY TURNOUT OUTBIRTH
(— OF ROCK DECAY) LATERITE
(—S OF LAND) ESPLEES
(—S OF ORCHARD) BIKKURIM
(ADDITION —) ADDUCT
(CHEESE AND MILK —S) GERVAIS
(CHOICE —) CAVIAR
(COMPLETED —) TURNOFF
(LEGISLATIVE —) ACT
(MATHEMATICAL —) SQUARE
(MINERAL —) HUTCH
(OXIDATION —) SUBSCALE
(RESIDUAL —) LATERITE
(SECONDARY —) CONGENER
(SURPLUS —S) ARISINGS
(TRANSFORMATION —) BAINITE
(WASTE —) RESIDUENT
(WORTHLESS —) CHAFF
PRODUCTION WORK FORGE FRUIT GROSS PIECE YIELD GROWTH EDITION GUIGNOL PRODUCE ARTIFICE INDUCTION OPERATION
(— OF MEDIUM) APPORT
(— OF YOUNG) INCREASE
(BEST —S) FAT
(SUCCESSFUL —) HIT
PRODUCTIVE FAT RICH LOOSE QUICK ACTIVE BATTLE PAROUD STRONG CAUSING FERTILE GAINFUL HEALTHY TEEMFUL TEEMING CHILDING CREATIVE FRUITFUL GERMINAL
PROEM PREFACE PRELUDE PROHEIM FOREWORD OVERTURE PREAMBLE
PROETUS (BROTHER OF —) ACRISIUS
(FATHER OF —) ABAS
(MOTHER OF —) OCALEA
(WIFE OF —) ANTEA
PROFANATION VIOLENCE SACRILEGE
PROFANE LAY NOA BLUE FOUL ABUSE COARSE DEBASE DEFILE DEFOIL DEFOUL UNHOLY VULGAR WICKED GODLESS IMPIOUS POLLUTE SECULAR UNGODLY VIOLATE WORLDLY TEMPORAL UNHALLOW
PROFANITY OATH CURSE LANGUAGE BLASPHEMY
PROFESS OWN AVOW ADMIT CLAIM AFFECT AFFIRM ALLEGE ASSERT ASSUME FOLLOW PRESUME PRETEND PURPORT PRACTICE
PROFESSION ART BAR LAW COAT FEAT GAME WALK CRAFT FAITH FORTE TRADE CAREER CHURCH EMPLOY METIER CALLING FACULTY QUALITY SERVICE ADVOCACY BUSINESS COACHING FUNCTION SOLDIERY VOCATION
PROFESSIONAL PRO COLT PAID HIRED EXPERT SKILLED TRAINED FINISHED

PROFESSOR DON PROF HANIF LAWYER REGENT ADJOINT ACADEMIC EMERITUS
PROFESSORSHIP CHAIR FAUTEUIL
PROFFER BID CAP GIVE TEND TENT DEFER DODGE ESSAY OFFER EXTEND OPPOSE PREFER PROFRE TENDER ATTEMPT PRESENT HESITATE
PROFICIENCY SIGHT SKILL ABILITY APTNESS MAITRISE
PROFICIENT ADEPT EXPERT SALTED VERSED SKILLED SKILLFUL
PROFILE FORM FLANK SKETCH CONTOUR OUTLINE SECTION
PROFIT AID GET NET WIN BOOT GAIN MEND NOTE SKIN VAIL AVAIL EDIFY FRAME LUCRE SCALP SPEED BEHOOF INCOME MAKING RETURN ACCOUNT ADVANCE BENEFIT CLEANUP FURTHER GETTING IMPROVE MILEAGE PLUNDER REVENUE VANTAGE WINNING CLEANING INCREASE INTEREST
(— BY) BROOK
(UNDERCOVER —) SQUEEZE
(PL.) GRAVY ISSUE AVAILS JALKAR ESPLEES
PROFITABLE FAT GOOD UTILE GOLDEN GAINFUL HELPFUL PAYABLE BEHOVELY ECONOMIC PROVABLE REPAYING VAILABLE REWARDING
PROFLIGATE DEFEAT CORRUPT IMMORAL RIOTOUS SPENDER VICIOUS WASTREL DEPRAVED FLAGRANT OVERCOME RAKEHELL WASTEFUL
PROFOUND DEEP HARD WISE ABYSS DEPTH HEAVY OCEAN SOUND THICK PITCHY STRONG ABYSMAL INTENSE ABSTRUSE COMPLETE REACHING THOROUGH
PROFUNDITY ABYSS DEPTH FATHOM DEEPNESS
PROFUSE FREE LUSH SLAB FRANK GALORE LAVISH COPIOUS LIBERAL ABUNDANT GENEROUS PRODIGAL SQUANDER WASTEFUL
PROFUSELY HEARTILY
PROFUSION WASTE EXCESS LAVISH FLUENCY OPULENCE
PROG FOOD GOAD POKE PROD PROWL TRAMP BEGGAR FORAGE PROCTOR
PROGENITOR BURI MANU ROOT SIRE PITRI STOCK PARENT ANCESTOR
PROGENY BED GET IMP KIN CLAN KIND SEED TEAM BROOD CHILD FRUIT ISSUE STRAIN STRIND INCROSS KINDRED LINEAGE OUTCOME PRODUCT CHILDREN FRUITAGE INCREASE OUTBIRTH OUTCROSS OFFSPRING
(— OF WATER-BUFFALO AND YAK) DZO
(— OF WITCH AND DEMON) HOLD
(INSECT —) SOCIETY

PROGNOSIS FORECAST PROPHASIS

PROGNOSTIC OMEN SIGN TOKEN
PRESAGE PROPHECY

PROGNOSTICATE BODE AUGUR
SPELL BETOKEN CONJECT PREDICT
PRENOTE FOREBODE FORESHOW
FORETELL PROPHESY

PROGNOSTICATION RACE
PRESAGE FOREBODE FORECAST
PROGRESS PROPHECY

PROGNOSTICATOR SEER DOOMER
PROPHET HARUSPEX

PROGRAM CARD SHOW FORUM
AGENDA DESIGN SCHEME AGENDUM
PREFACE CLAMBAKE FESTIVAL
GIVEAWAY GUIDANCE JAMBOREE
PLAYBILL SCHEDULE SEQUENCE
SYLLABUS

PROGRAMMA EDICT DECREE
PREFACE PROGRAM

PROGRESS WAY BIRL DENT FARE
GAIN GROW MOVE RACE RISE STEM
STEP TOUR WEAR WEND WENT
BUILD DRIFT FORGE GOING MARCH
SWING WEENT ASCENT BUFFET
COURSE GROWTH STREEK ADVANCE
DEVELOP FOOTING HEADWAY
IMPROVE JOURNEY ONGOING
PASSAGE PROCESS
(— **CLUMSILY**) SCRAMBLE
(— **ERRATICALLY**) FLAIL
(— **FEEBLY**) DODDER
(— **INTELLIGENTLY PLANNED**)
TELESIA TELESIS
(— **NOISILY**) CHORTLE
(— **SLOWLY**) CRAWL
(**SINGLE** —) THROUGH

PROGRESSED FAR

PROGRESSION WAY SWING COURSE
GALLOP ADVANCE PASSAGE
PROGRESS SEQUENCE
(— **OF CHORDS**) SWIPE
(**MUSICAL** —) SKIP
(**SMOOTH** —) SLIDE

PROGRESSIVE ACTIVE ONWARD
FORWARD GRADUAL LIBERAL

PROGRESSIVELY STILL

PROHIBIT BAN BAR STOP VETO
BLOCK DEBAR ESTOP DEFEND
ENJOIN FORBID HINDER OUTLAW
FORFEND FORWARN INHIBIT
PREVENT DISALLOW PRECLUDE
SUPPRESS

PROHIBITED HOT TABU TABOO
ILLEGAL ILLICIT UNLAWFUL
VERBOTEN

PROHIBITION BAN NAY NON VETO
ORDER BARRIER DEFENCE DEFENSE
EMBARGO FORBODE ESTOPPEL

PROHIBITING VETITIVE

PROHIBITIONIST DRY PUSSYFOOT

PROJECT GAB GAG JET JUT LAP
TUT BEAM CAST GAME IDEA PLAN
POKE SWIM BULGE CHART DRAFT
DRIVE IMAGE JETTY JUTTY SETUP
SHOOT STICK THROW BEETLE
DESIGN DEVICE ESTATE EXTEND
FILLIP OUTJUT PROPEL SCHEME
SCREEN SHELVE EXTRUDE GOSPLAN

IMAGINE KNUCKLE PATTERN
BUSINESS CONTRIVE OUTREACH
OUTSHOOT PROPOSAL PROTRUDE
SPANGHEW
(**UNETHICAL** —) SCHEME
(**VISIONARY** —) BABEL

PROJECTILE BALL BOLT CASE SHOT
SHAFT TRACER OUTCAST POUNDER
SHRAPNEL
(— **DESIGNED TO SET FIRE TO
HOUSES**) CARCASS
(**EXPLOSIVE** —) BOMB SHELL
(**SUBMARINE** —) TORPEDO
(PL.) LEAD SHOT SALVO STUFF

PROJECTING BEETLE SHELVY
EMINENT JUTTING OUTSHOT
SALIENT SNAGGLED

PROJECTION ARM CAM COG DOG
EAR FIN GIB JET JOG JUT NAG NUT
TOE BEAK BOSS BROW BUHR COAK
COCK CROC CUSP HEEL HORN KEEL
KICK KINK KNAG KNOB KNOP LOBE
RIDE SNUG SPUD SPUR TEAT WING
BULGE CLEAT EJECT ELBOW FENCE
FURCA JUTTY SHANK SHOOT SPIKE
TOOTH BRANCH CORBEL CROSET
FUSULA HEARTH ICICLE MENTUM
PALATE RELISH TAPPET BREAKER
DRAWING EPAULET EYEBROW
FETLOCK KNUCKLE LANGUET
ORILLON PRICKER PRICKLE
RESSAUT AJUTMENT CASCABEL
DENTICLE EMINENCE FOOTLOCK
OVERHANG SALIENCE SHOULDER
SPROCKET STERIOMA OUTTHRUST
(— **CONNECTING TIMBER**) COAK
(— **EXTENDING BACKWARD**) BARB
(— **FROM CASTING**) SPRUE
(— **FROM SHIP'S KEEL**) SPONSON
(— **IN CLOCK**) SQUARE
(— **IN ORCHIDS**) MENTUM
(— **OF FOREHEAD**) ANTINION
(— **OF JAW**) GNATHISM
(— **OF PEAT**) HAG
(— **OF RAFTER**) SALLY
(— **ON CANNON**) CASCABEL
(— **ON GUN**) CROC LUMP
(— **ON HARNESS**) HAME
(— **ON HORSE'S LEG**) FETLOCK
(— **ON HORSESHOE**) STICKER
(— **ON LOCK**) FENCE STUMP
(— **ON MAST**) STOP
(— **ON OVARY**) STIGMA
(— **ON POCKETKNIFE**) KICK
(— **ON SALMON JAW**) GIB
(— **ON WHEEL**) GUB GROUSER
GROUTER
(— **OVER AIR PORT**) EYEBROW
(**FIREPLACE** —) HOB
(**JAGGED** —) SNUG
(**SHARP** —) BARB FANG
(**SUBMERGED** —) KNOLL
(PL.) GRAIN BARLEY

PROJECTOR KINO LANTERN
PLANNER SCHEMER BIOSCOPE
EPISCOPE VITASCOPE

PROLAMIN ZEIN SEINE GLIADIN
HORDEIN KAFIRIN SECALIN

PROLAPSE PTOSIS BLOWOUT
FALLING

PROLETARIAN POPULAR

PROLETARIAT MASSES

PROLIFIC BIRTHY BREEDY BROODY
FECUND FERTILE PROFUSE TEEMING
ABUNDANT FRUITFUL SPAWNING
(**BE** —) INCREASE

PROLIX LARGE WORDY DIFFUSE
LENGTHY PROSAIC TEDIOUS
VERBOSE TIRESOME WEARISOME

PROLOGUE BANS BANNS INDEX
PREFACE

PROLONG DREE LENG LONG SPIN
DEFER DELAY DRIVE ELONG TWINE
DILATE EXTEND LINGER SPREAD
DISPACE PRODUCE RESPITE
SUSTAIN CONTINUE ETERNIZE
LENGTHEN POSTPONE PROROGUE
PROTRACT

PROLONGATION BEAK AORTA
CONUS STIPE STYLE FERMATA
ACROSOME GYNOBASE LABELLUM

PROLONGED GREAT PROLIX
DELAYED EXTENDED SOSTENUTO

PROMENADE MAIL MALL PIER PROM
WALK CORSO FRONT PASEO PRADO
MARINA PARADE PASEAR ALAMEDA
GALLERY FRESCADE
(**CARRIAGE** —) TOUR

PROMETHEUS (**FATHER OF** —)
IAPETUS
(**MOTHER OF** —) CLYMENE

PROMINENCE BUR NOB BURR KNOB
NOOP UMBO AGGER BULLA CREST
GRAIN OLIVA SWELL TYLUS ACCENT
CALCAR NODULE TRAGUS BILLING
BUTTOCK CONDYLE FASHION
HAMULUS KNUCKLE LINGULA
AMYGDALA EMINENCY EMPHASIS
GLABELLA PULVINAR SALIENCE
TUBERCLE

PROMINENT BIG BOLD BEADY
BRENT GREAT STEEP BEETLE
MARKED SIGNAL BLATANT BOLTING
CAPITAL EMINENT JUTTING LEADING
NOTABLE OBVIOUS SALIENT
AQUILINE MANIFEST STRIKING
(**SOCIALLY** —) SWELL

PROMISCUOUS LIGHT CASUAL
RANDOM CARELESS

PROMISCUOUSLY TAGRAG

PROMISE VOW AVOW BAND HEST
HETE HOPE HOTE OSSE PASS PLEA
SURE WORD FAITH GRANT HIGHT
TRUTH ASSURE BEHEST ENGAGE
FIANCE HALSEN INSURE PAROLE
PLEDGE PLIGHT PROMIT BEHIGHT
BETROTH WARRANT CONTRACT
COVENANT GUARANTY BETROTHAL
(— **IN MARRIAGE**) BETROTH
ESPOUSE AFFIANCE
(— **TO PAY**) NOTE
(— **TO TAKE IN MARRIAGE**) AFFY

PROMISED VOTARY
(— **IN MARRIAGE**) SURE HIGHT
ENGAGED

PROMISING APT FAIR BRIGHT
LIKELY PROOFY TOWARD GRADELY
TOWARDLY

PROMISSORY NOTE IOU HUNDI
HOONDI TICKET

PROMONTORY HOE NAB BEAK BILL
HEAD MULL NAZE NESS NOOK
NOUP PEAK SCAW SKAW TOOT
ELBOW POINT REACH SNOUT
SALIENT FORELAND HEADLAND

PROMOTE AID HELP LOFT AVAIL
BOOST EXALT NURSE RAISE SERVE
SPEED ASSIST EXCITE FOMENT
FOSTER LAUNCH PREFER ADVANCE
DIGNIFY ELEVATE FORWARD
FURTHER IMPROVE PREFECT
PRODUCE PROMOVE SUCCEED
SUPPORT INCREASE SUBSERVE

PROMOTER AGENT FRIEND
ABETTOR BOOSTER BUBBLER
BROACHER HUMANIST

PROMOTION LIFT REMOVE ADVANCE
PROMOVAL

PROMPT APT CUE MOVE URGE YARE
ALERT PREST QUICK READY SERVE
SWIFT WILLY YEDER EXCITE INDITE
MATURE NIMBLE SPEEDY SUDDEN
ANIMATE FORWARD PROVOKE
SUGGEST PUNCTUAL REMINDER
(— TO EVIL) SUGGEST

PROMPTER CUER CALLER
MEMORIST ORDINARY SOUFFLEUR

PROMPTING CALL BEHEST BEHIND
MOTIVE
(SPIRITUAL —) LEADING

PROMPTLY UP PAT TID TIT SOON
TITE PRONTO YARELY PRESTLY
QUICKLY DIRECTLY SPEEDILY

PROMPTNESS ALACRITY CELERITY
DISPATCH

PROMULGATE SPREAD DECLARE
PUBLISH PROCLAIM

PRONAOS ANTICUM

PRONE APT BENT EASY FLAT FREE
GRUF BUXOM GIVEN GROOF JACENT
LIABLE SUPINE BEASTLY BESTIAL
DORMANT SUBJECT ADDICTED
COUCHANT DISPOSED DOWNWARD
PROPENSE
(— TO TAKE UP FADS) ISMY
(NATURALLY —) PROLIVE

PRONG NEB NIB PEG PEW BILL
FANG FORK HOOK PUGH SPUR
TANG TENG TINE TING GRAIN
SPADE SPEAN SPRONG FOURCHE
TICKLER GRAINING
(— FOR EXTRACTING BUNG)
TICKLER
(— FOR FISH) PEW PUGH
(— OF ANTLER) KNAG TIND TINE
(— OF FORK) SPEAN

PRONGHORN CABREE CABRIT
MAZAME BERENDO BERRENDO

PRONOUN HE IT ME MY WE YE ANY
HER HIM HIS ONE OUR SHE THY
WHO YOU OURS THAT THEM THEY
THOU WHAT WHOM YOUR THINE
WHICH WHOSE ITSELF MYSELF
HERSELF HIMSELF OURSELF
WHOEVER YOURSELF OURSELVES
(GENDERLESS —) THON

PRONOUNCE SAY PASS ACUTE

SPEAK UTTER PREACH RECITE
TONGUE ADJUDGE BEHIGHT
CENSURE MOUILLE
(— FREE) ABSOLVE
(— GUILTY) CONDEMN
(— HOLY) BLESS

PRONOUNCED HIGH MARKED
DECIDED HOWLING INTENSE
MOVABLE
(— AS FRICATIVE) GRASSEYE
(NOT —) SOFT

PRONOUNCEMENT FIAT CURSE
DICTUM DICTAMEN

PRONTO QUICK QUICKLY PROMPTLY

PRONUNCIATION BROGUE DICTION
ETACISM LIAISON DELIVERY
ENCLISIS ORTHOEPY
(BAD —) CACOEPY LABDACISM
(BROAD —) PLATEASM
(CORRECT —) ORTHOEPY
(ROUGH —) BUR BURR

PROOF MARK SLIP TEST ESSAY
PREWE TOKEN TOUCH TRIAL
GALLEY ORDEAL REASON RESULT
REVISE ATTEMPT OUTCOME
PROBATE SHOWING UTTERLY
VOUCHER WARRANT ANALYSIS
CACOLOGY DOCUMENT EVICTION
EVIDENCE GOODNESS MONUMENT
(— SPIRIT OF WINE) SVT
(— OF WRONGDOING) GOODS
(PL.) STRING WARRANTY

PROOFREADER MARK CAP DELE
STET CARET

PROP LEG BROB POST REST SPUR
STAY STUD TRIG APPUI BRACE
PERCH PUNCH RANCE SCOTE
SHORE SHOVE SOUSE SPRAG
SPURN STAFF STELL STOOP STULL
COLUMN CROTCH CRUTCH SCOTCH
SHORER STAYER UPHOLD FULCRUM
PINNING STUDDLE SUPPORT
SUSTAIN BUTTRESS CROTCHET
DUTCHMAN UNDERLAY UNDERSET
(— AS TRAP) TEEL
(— FOR ROOF OF MINE) GIB
(— UP) CUSHION

PROPAGANDA BOLOISM AGITPROP

PROPAGATE BREED HATCH LAYER
EXTEND SPREAD STRIKE DIFFUSE
GEMMATE PRODUCE PUBLISH
ENGENDER GENERATE INCREASE
POPULATE TRANSMIT

PROPAGATION BREED BREEDING
DIVISION INCREASE LAYERAGE
OFFSPRING

PROPEL ROW CALL CAST FIRE FLIP
KENT POLE PUSH SEND URGE DRIVE
FLICK IMPEL KNOCK PRICK RANGE
SPANK THROW HURTLE LAUNCH
PROJECT
(— BALL) STROKE
(— BOAT WITH FEET) LEG
(— BOAT) OAR ROW SET KENT
POLE SCULL BUSHWACK
(— ONESELF) HAUL
(— PUCK) CARRY

PROPELLER FAN SCREW AIRSCREW
WINDMILL

PROPENSITY YEN BENT ITCH LURCH
APTNESS IMPULSE LEANING
PRONITY APPETITE FONDNESS
INTEREST TENDENCY

PROPER FIT OWN GOOD JUST MEET
TRUE WELL PREST RIGHT UTTER
COMELY DECENT HONEST LAWFUL
MODEST SEEMLY CAPITAL CORRECT
FITTING GRADELY SEEMING SKILFUL
THRIFTY ABSOLUTE BECOMING
CONGREVE DECOROUS FORMULAR
IDONEOUS PECULIAR RIGHTFUL
SORTABLE SUITABLE VIRTUOUS
(APPARENTLY —) SPECIOUS
(BE — TO) BESEEM

PROPERLY DULY WELL FITLY TRULY
FAIRLY FEATLY GLADLY MEETLY
RIGHTLY

PROPERTY AVER BONA DHAN TOOL
WAIF ASSET AUGHT GOODS GRANT
MOYEN STATE STOCK THING
WORTH APPEAL DEVISE ESTATE
HAVIOR KELTER LIVING MUSHAA
REALTY TALENT USINGS WEALTH
ACQUEST APANAGE CHATTEL
DEMESNE ESCHEAT ESSENCE
FACULTY FITNESS HARNESS
HAVINGS QUALITY WARISON
ALLODIAL CATALLUM HOLDINGS
PECULIUM
(— BELONGING TO WOMAN)
STRIDHAN
(— FROM WIFE TO HUSBAND) DOS
(— GIVEN BY WILL) DEVISE
(— OF MATTER AT REST) INERTIA
(— SECURED DISHONESTLY) HARL
(— SEIZED BY FORCE) SPOIL
(ABSOLUTE —) ALODIUM
(ENEMY —) HEREM
(LANDED —) DOMAIN ESTATE
DEMESNE PRAEDIUM
(MOVABLE —) GEAR CHATTEL
EFFECTS CATALLUM
(PERSONAL —) FEE BONA GOODS
STUFF INSIGHT PLUNDER
(PRIVATE —) SEVERAL
(RURAL —) FINCA
(STOLEN —) PELF STEALTH
(THEATRICAL —S) PROPS
(WITHOUT —) LACKLAND

PROPHECY SPAE WEIRD EXHORT
PREACH PREDICT BODEMENT
FORECAST FORESHOW SOOTHSAY
VATICINE SIBYLLISM

PROPHESY OSSE SPAE AREAD
AUGUR DIVINE EXHORT PREACH
OMINATE PORTEND PREDICT
ARIOLATE FORETELL

PROPHET GAD AMOS JOEL SEER
ANGEL AUGUR DRUID ELIAS HOSEA
JONAH MICAH MOSES NAHUM SILAS
SYRUS ARIOLE BALAAM DANIEL
ELIJAH HAGGAI ISAIAH MERLIN
MORONI NATHAN PYTHON SAMUEL
EZEKIEL MALACHI SPAEMAN
HABAKKUK JEREMIAH
(PL.) VATES NEBIIM

PROPHETESS ANNA ANNE HULDA
SIBYL PYTHIA DEBORAH PHOIBAD

SEERESS VOLUSPA DRUIDESS
SPAEWIFE CASSANDRA PYTHONESS
PROPHETIC FATAL MANTIC FATEFUL
FATIDIC DELPHIAN SIBYLLIC
VATICINAL
PROPINE TIP GIFT EXPOSE PLEDGE
PROFFER
PROPINQUITY KINSHIP AFFINITY
NEARNESS VICINITY PROXIMITY
PROPITIATE MILD ATONE PACIFY
APPEASE RECONCILE
PROPITIATORY HILASMIC
PROPITIOUS FAIR KIND HAPPY
LUCKY BENIGN DEXTER KINDLY
HELPFUL PRESENT FRIENDLY
GRACIOUS MERCIFUL FAVORABLE
PROMISING
PROPONENT BACKER ADVOCATE
SUPPORTER
PROPORTION END LOT DOSE SIZE
CHIME FRAME QUOTA RATIO SCALE
SHARE ACCORD DEGREE EXTENT
FORMAT QUOTUM ANALOGY
BALANCE COMPASS CONTENT
MEASURE EURYTHMY QUANTITY
SYMMETRY
(— OF CATTLE TO GIVEN AREA)
SOUM
(— OF MALT IN BREWING) STRAIK
(ALLOTTED —) STENT STINT
(EXACT —) SQUARE
(SMALL —) TITHE
PROPORTIONATENESS CONTOUR
PROPOSAL BID KITE MOVE PLAN
PLEA VOEU GRACE OFFER PARTY
DEMAND FEELER MOTION MOTIVE
PROJECT PROPOSE PURPOSE
OVERTURE SCHEDULE SENTENCE
(TENTATIVE —) SNIFF
PROPOSE FACE MOVE PLAN POSE
SHOW WISH OFFER ALLEGE DESIGN
INJECT INTEND MOTION ADVANCE
EXHIBIT IMAGINE PROPINE PURPOSE
SUPPOSE CONFRONT CONVERSE
PROPOUND
(— FOR DISCUSSION) MOOT
(— RESOLUTION) FIRST
(— TENTATIVELY) SUGGEST
PROPOSITION R FACT AXIOM
MODAL OFFER THEME AFFAIR
CONNEX MEMBER PORISM GENERAL
INVERSE PREMISS PROBLEM
THEOREM TYCHISM BUSINESS
CONTRARY EMPIREMA IDENTITY
IRENICON JUDGMENT NEGATION
OVERTURE PROPOSAL PROTASIS
SENTENCE SINGULAR SUPPOSAL
(— IN LOGIC) TERMAL
(— LEADING TO CONCLUSION)
PREMISE
(PARTICULAR NEGATIVE —) O
(PRELIMINARY —) LEMMA
(UNIVERSAL NEGATIVE —) E
PROPOUND POSE OFFER POSIT
START STATE INVOKE PROPOSE
PURPOSE
PROPOUNDER HYLICIST
PROPRIETOR LORD LAIRD MALIK
OWNER MASTER PATRON TANIST

YEOMAN ESQUIRE PATROON
ABSENTEE BONIFACE SQUARSON
TALUKDAR YEOWOMAN
PROPRIETY GRACE IDIOM MENSE
ESTATE NATURE REASON DECENCY
DECORUM ESSENCE FITNESS
HOLDING CIVILITY PROPERTY
ETIQUETTE
PROPROCTOR RECTOR
PROPULSION DRIFT EJECTION
PROPULSIVE ELASTIC
PRORATE ALLOT ASSESS DIVIDE
APPORTION
PROROGUE DEFER ADJOURN
PROLONG POSTPONE PROTRACT
PROSAIC DRAB DULL FLAT FOOT
PROSE PROSY PROLIX STODGY
STOLID STUPID FACTUAL HUMDRUM
INSIPID LITERAL TEDIOUS TIRESOME
WORKADAY
PROSCENIUM FRAME STAGE
PROSCRIBE BAN TABU EXILE TABOO
FORBID OUTLAW REJECT PROHIBIT
PROSCRIPTION EXILE OUTLAWRY
PROSE CHAT PROSY GOSSIP
PROSAIC TEDIOUS SEQUENCE
ELOQUENCE
PROSECUTE LAW SUE HOLD URGE
CARRY ENSUE ACCUSE CHARGE
DEDUCE FOLLOW INDICT INTEND
PURSUE IMPLEAD
PROSECUTOR DA FISCAL PURSUER
SAKEBER PROMOTER QUAESTOR
(PUBLIC —) ACTOR
PROSELYTE CONVERT NICOLAS
NEOPHYTE PURSUANT
(JEWISH —) GER
PROSER HAVERER GRATIANO
PROSODY METER METRICS
PROSPECT HOPE VIEW SCENE
SPECK VISTA CHANCE CHIEVE
FUTURE REGARD SEARCH SURVEY
COMMAND EXPLORE FOSSICK
HORIZON LOOKOUT OUTLOOK
PROJECT RESPECT LANDSKIP
OFFSCAPE
(— FOR GOLD) SPECK
(— WITHOUT SYSTEM) GOPHER
(FORBIDDING —) DESERT
PROSPECTING LOAMING
PROSPECTIVE VIEW WATCH
LOOKOUT EXPECTED
PROSPECTOR SNIPER FOSSICKER
SOURDOUGH
(LONE —) HATTER
PROSPECTUS PROGRAM
PROSPER DO DOW FAY HIE LIKE
RISE THEE CHEVE CHIVE EDIFY
FRAME LIGHT SPEED BATTEN
THRIVE BLOSSOM SUCCEED
WELFARE FLOURISH
PROSPERITY HAP GLEE GOOD SEEL
SONS WEAL IKBAL SONSE HEALTH
THRIFT FORTUNE SUCCESS
THEEDOM WELFARE FLOURISH
(GOD OF —) FREY
PROSPERO (DAUGHTER OF —)
MIRANDA
(SERVANT OF —) ARIEL

PROSPEROUS UP FAT BEEN BEIN
BIEN BOON GOOD FELIX FLUSH
HAPPY LUCKY PALMY SONSY
EUROUS GILDED SONSIE WELSOM
HALCYON HEALTHY THRIVEN
WEIRDLY SUNSHINE THRIVING
WEALSOME
PROSTITUTE BAG BAT CAT COW
DOG MOB AUNT BAWD DOXY DRAB
HACK MAUX MISS MUFF PUNK SLUT
STEW TRUG BROAD CRACK MAWKS
PAGAN STALE WHORE BULKER
CALLET CHIPPY DEBASE GIRLIE
HARLOT HOOKER LIMMER MUTTON
RANNEL TOMATO TRADER VIZARD
BAGGAGE BROTHEL CRUISER
CYPRIAN HACKNEY HETAERA
HUSTLER PAPHIAN PINNACE
POLECAT PUCELLE SELLARY
BERDACHE COMMONER CUSTOMER
HACKSTER MAGDALEN MERETRIX
OCCUPANT RUMBELOW SLATTERN
STRUMPET VENTURER
PROSTITUTION BORDEL SACKING
BORDELLO HARLOTRY PUTANISM
PROSTRATE LOW FELL FLAT GRUF
RASE RAZE FLING GROOF PRONE
STOOP THROW ATTERR CUMBER
FALLEN REPENT WEAKEN FLATTEN
DEJECTED HELPLESS OVERCOME
PROSTERN DEPRESSED
(— ONESELF) HURKLE
(BECOME —) FALL
PROSTRATION SHOCK KOWTOW
COLLAPSE
PROSY DRY DULL JEJUNE HUMDRUM
INSIPID PROSAIC PROSISH TEDIOUS
TIRESOME
PROTAGONIST HERO ACTOR
LEADER PALADIN ADVOCATE
CHAMPION
PROTAMINE SALMINE STURINE
CLUPEINE
PROTEAN EDESTAN VARIABLE
PROTECT CAP BANK BIEL BIND DIKE
FEND FORT HILL KEEP REDE SAVE
WARD WEAR BLESS CHAIN CLOUT
COURE COVER FENCE GANGE
GRATE GUARD HEDGE PAVIS SHADE
SHEND UMBER ASSERT BORROW
CHIELD DEFEND SCREEN SHADOW
WARISH BULWARK CHERISH
CUSHION FASCINE FORFEND
SECLUDE SHELTER SUPPORT
WARRANT BESTRIDE CHAMPION
DEFILADE PRESERVE
(— AGAINST RAIN) FLASH
(— BY COVERING) HILL
(— BY WINDING WITH WIRE) GANGE
(— FROM INTRUSION) TILE TYLE
(— IRON OR STEEL) BARFF
PROTECTED SHADY IMMUNE
CLOUTED GUARDED SHEATHED
SHIELDED
PROTECTING TUTELAR TUTELARY
SECUREFUL
PROTECTION LEE EGIS HOLD WARD
AEGIS ARMOR BIELD COVER GRITH
GUARD SHADE TARGE TOWER

AMULET ASYLUM AVOWRY ESCORT
FENDER REFUGE SAFETY SCONCE
SCREEN SHADOW SHROUD AUSPICE
CUSTODY DEFENCE HOUSING
MANTLET SHELTER TUITION
UMBRAGE WARRANT BLINDAGE
COVERAGE DEFILADE PASSPORT
SECURITY TUTAMENT TUTELAGE
(— FOR SAILOR) HORSE
(— FROM LOSS) INDEMNITY
(— FROM RAIN) OMBRIFUGE
(— FROM SUN) HAVELOCK
(— FROM WEATHER) LEWTH
(— RIGHT) MUND
(VALUABLE —) EDMUND
(WISE —) RAYMOND
PROTECTIVE (— **SURFACE**) LAGGING
PROTECTOR BIB GUARD BRACER
FAUTOR KEEPER PATRON REGENT
WARRANT DEFENDER GUARDIAN
PECTORAL PRESIDENT
(— OF PROSTITUTE) BULLY
(— OF VINEYARDS) PRIAPUS
PROTEGE WARD PUPIL SMIKE
PROTEIN ABRIN ACTIN RICIN SOZIN
AVIDIN CASEIN FIBRIN GLOBIN
MYOGEN ALBUMIN AMANDIN
ELASTIN GELATIN GLIADIN HISTONE
HORDEIN KERATIN LIVETIN MUCEDIN
SERICIN ALEURONE COLLOGEN
FERRITIN GLOBULIN GLUTELIN
GORGONIN IPOMOEIN PROLAMIN
(RICH IN —S) NARROW
PROTEOSE ALBUMOSE ELASTOSE
GELATOSE
PROTEST AVER BEEF FUSS HOWL
KICK BROCK CROAK DEMUR AFFIRM
ASSERT BOWWOW EXCEPT HOLLER
OBJECT OBTEST PLAINT SQUAWK
SQUEAL CONTEST INVEIGH PUBLISH
RECLAIM RHUBARB SCRUPLE
TESTIFY HARRUMPH PROCLAIM
(— AGAINST INJUSTICE) HARO
PROTESTANT ALASCAN GENEVAN
GOSPELER HELVETIC HUGUENOT
SWADDLER
PROTEUS OLM AMOEBA
PROTHESIS CREDENCE PARABEMA
PROTHORAX COLLAR CORSELET
MANITRUNK
PROTOPINE FUMARINE
PROTOPLASM PLASMA PLASSON
SARCODE OVOPLASM PERIPLAST
SOLEPLATE
PROTOPLAST CELL ENERGID
PROTOTYPE IDEAL MODEL FATHER
EXAMPLE PATTERN ANTITYPE
EXEMPLAR
PROTOZOAN AMEBA FORAM MONAD
MONER AGAMETE ARCELLA BABESIA
BODONID CILIATE PROTIST RADIATE
STENTOR DIDINIUM HYPOZOAN
(PL.) MICROZOA
PROTRACT DRAG DRAW DREE PLOT
SPIN DEFER DELAY DRIVE TRACT
TRAIL TRAIN DILATE EXTEND
LINGER SPREAD DETRACT PROLONG
CONTINUE LENGTHEN
PROTRACTED DREE LONG DREICH

PROLIX LENGTHY DRAGGING
EXTENDED
PROTRUDE BUG JUT LILL LOLL
POUT BLEAR BULGE BUNCH POUCH
SHOOT START STICK STRUT SWELL
EXSERT EXTEND EXTRUDE KNUCKLE
PROJECT HERNIATE OUTPOINT
OUTREACH OUTSHOOT
PROTRUDING STEEP BUNCHY
GOGGLE BLABBER EMINENT
JUTTING
PROTRUSION LAP NOB BURR KNOB
POUT HERNIA SALIENCE SHOULDER
TYLOSOID
PROTUBERANCE BUD HUB JAG
NOB NUB WEN BEAN BOLL BOSS
BULB BUMP HEEL HUMP JAGG KNOB
KNOP KNOT LUMP NODE PUFF SCAB
SNAG STUB UMBO WART BULGE
BUNCH CAPUT GLAND GNARL
HUNCH KNURL SWELL TORUS
TUBER TUMOR CALLUS HUBBLE
PIMPLE POMMEL EXTANCY PAPILLA
EMINENCE FLANKARD NODOSITY
SWELLING
(— AT BASE OF BIRD'S BILL) CERE
SNOOD
(— BEARING SPINE) UMBO
(— FROM SWELLING) PUFF
(— IN SIDE OF DEER) FLANKARD
(— ON A CASTING) SCAB
(— ON BONE) EMINENCE
(— ON HORSE'S HOOF) BUTTRESS
(— ON MANDIBLE OF GEESE) BEAN
(— ON SADDLEBOW) POMMEL
(— ON SALAMANDER) BALANCER
(— ON TONGUE) PAPILLA
(KNOBLIKE —) CAPUT
(OCCIPITAL —) INION
(RAGGED —) JAG JAGG
(ROUGH —) HUB
(SKIN —) WEN MOLE WART PIMPLE
PROTUBERANT BULGY BUMPY
PROUD STRUT TUMID BUCKED
EXTANT GOGGLE BOTTLED BULGING
EMINENT GIBBOUS SALIENT
SWOLLEN
(REGULARLY —) CONVEX
PROUD FESS GLAD HIGH IKEY LOFT
PERK RANK SIDE VAIN BRANT
CHUFF GELLY GREAT JELLY LOFTY
NOBLE ORGUL PRIDY SAUCY STEEP
STIFF STOUT VOGIE WINDY WLONK
COPPED ELATED FIERCE LORDLY
ORGUIL PENCEY QUAINT SKEICH
SKEIGH UPPISH UPPITY VAUNTY
HAUGHTY SUBLIME SWOLLEN
TOPPING ARROGANT EXULTANT
GLORIOUS IMPOSING INSOLENT
ORGULOUS SPLENDID STOMACHY
PROUDLY HIGH
PROVE TRY FAND FOND PREE SHOW
TEST ARGUE ASSAY EVICT TAINT
TASTE TEMPT ARGUFY EVINCE
SUFFER VERIFY BALANCE CONFESS
CONFIRM CONVICT DERAIGN
IMPROVE JUSTIFY CONCLUDE
CONVINCE EVIDENCE INDICATE
INSTRUCT MANIFEST

(— FALSE) BELIE BETRAY FALSIFY
(— GUILTY) ATTAINT
(— OUT) SERVE
(— TITLE) DEDUCE
(— VALID) DEFEND
PROVED TRIED EXPERT PROBATE
PROVENCAL LANGUEDOC
ROMANESQUE
PROVENDER HAY CORN FEED FOOD
OATS STRAW PROVAND PROVIANT
PROVERB SAW SAY REDE WORD
ADAGE AXIOM CREED GNOME
SOOTH BALLAD BYWORD DITTON
DIVERB MASHAL SAYING SPEECH
SYMBOL WHEEZE BYSPELL IMPRESA
NAYWORD PARABLE APHORISM
FORBYSEN PAROEMIA SCHOLION
SCHOLIUM SENTENCE SOOTHSAY
PROVIDE DO FIT SEE FEND FILL
FIND GIRD LEND LOOK BLOCK
CATER ENDOW ENDUE EQUIP SPEED
STOCK STORE AFFORD FOISON
PURVEY SUBORN SUPPLY EXHIBIT
FORESEE FURNISH INSTORE
PREPARE ACCOUTER APPANAGE
DISPENSE PURCHASE
(— AHEAD OF TIME) ADVANCE
(— AMUSEMENT) DISTRACT
(— FOOD) GRUB CATER SCAFF
(— FOR) FEND SERVE CHEVEYS
CHEVISE PROVANT
(— STINGILY) SKINCH
(— SUPPORT) ESCOT
(— WITH DOWRY) DOT
(— WITH HIP-ROOF) COOT
(— WITH) BESEE
PROVIDED IF BODEN FIXED READY
SOBEIT PROVISO INSTRUCT
PREPARED
PROVIDENCE THRIFT ECONOMY
PRUDENCE
PROVIDENT WARY WISE FRUGAL
SAVING CAREFUL PRUDENT THRIFTY
PROVINCE LAN AREA NOME WALK
AIMAK BANAT FIELD MOUTH NATAL
NOMOS REALM SHENG SHIRE
SUBAH BANNAT EMPIRE EYALET
MALAGA MONTON REGION SIRCAR
SPHERE SYSSEL YAMATO DEMESNE
DONGOLA EPARCHY MUDIRIA
PURVIEW RECTORY VILAYET
APPANAGE DISTRICT FUNCTION
MUDIRIEH NOMARCHY
(SUBDIVISION OF EGYPTIAN —)
KISM
(PL.) OUTLAND
PROVINCIAL HICK BORNE CRUDE
NARROW RUSTIC STUFFY INSULAR
SUBURBAN
PROVISION BOARD CHECK GRIST
FODDER MATTER PURVEY STOVER
UNLESS WRAITH APPREST CAUTION
CODICIL DOWNSET KEEPING
SLEEPER VICTUAL WARNISH
WARNISON
(BOUGHT —S) ACATERY
(SUBORDINATE —) ITEM
(PL.) CHOW FOOD JOCK KEEP LOAN
BOUGE CATES SCRAN STORE

TERMS TOMMY ANNONA VIANDS
VIVRES COMMONS WARNAGE
WAYFARE VICTUALS

PROVISO SALVO CAVEAT CLAUSE
CAUTION CONDITION

PROVOCATION APPEAL INCENTIVE

PROVOCATIVE GUTTY SALTY
AGACANT PIQUANT IRRITANT
APPEALING

PROVOKE BOG EGG GIG IRE TAR
VEX BEAR DARE HUFF MOVE PICK
STIR TARR TEEN URGE WORK
ANGER ANGRY ANNOY EAGER
EVOKE FRUMP PIQUE TAUNT TEMPT
APPEAL ELICIT EVINCE EXCITE
GRIEVE HARASS INCITE KINDLE
NETTLE PROMPT SUMMON TICKLE
AFFRONT ILLICIT INCENSE INFLAME
INSPIRE VROTHER CATALYZE
IRRITATE

PROVOST JUDGE PRIOR REEVE
KEEPER WARDEN STEWARD

PROW BOW BEAK SPUR STEM
PRORE SNOUT SPERON STEVEN
DIVIDER GALLANT VALIANT
(**— OF GONDOLA**) FERRO

PROWESS FEAT PROW VALOR
NOBLEY BRAVERY COURAGE

PROWL OWL PROG ROAM LURCH
MOOCH MOUSE RAVEN BREVIT
RAMBLE

PROWLER WALKER SLASHER
TENEBRION

PROWLIKE PROREAN

PROWLING GRASSANT

PROXIMATE NEXT CLOSE DIRECT
CLOSEST NEAREST PROXIME
IMMINENT PROXIMAL

PROXIMITY SHADOW NEARNESS
PRESENCE VICINITY

PROXY VICE AGENT VICAR BALLOT
MANDAT PROCTOR
(**PL.**) ELECTION

PRUDE COMSTOCK

PRUDENCE CARE ADVICE CAUTEL
WISDOM CAUTION COUNSEL
SLEIGHT FORECAST FORELOOK

PRUDENT FIT SAGE WARE WARY
WISE CANNY DOOSE DOUCE SOLID
SYKER VERTY FRUGAL QUAINT
SEKERE SICCAR POLITIC THRIVEN
CAUTIOUS DISCREET

PRUDISH NICE PRIM MIMZY MIMSEY
PRIGGISH RUDIBUND VICTORIA

PRUDISHNESS NICETY PUDENCY

PRUNE COW LOP TOP CLIP COLL
COUL GELD PLUM SNED SPUR TAME
TRIM CLEAN DRESS KNIFE PLUMB
PREEN PRIME PURGE SHEAR SHRED
SHRUB TWIST DEHORN REFORM
SHRIDE SNATHE SWITCH AMPUTATE
CASTRATE RETRENCH
(**— SEVERELY**) DEHORN
(**IMPERFECTLY RIPENED —**) FROG

PRUNING HOOK SARPE CALABOZO

PRUNING KNIFE CALABOZO
SERPETTE

PRUNING SHEARS SECATEUR

PRURIENT ITCHY

PRURITIS ITCH

PRUSSIAN PRUTENIC

PRY GAG NOSE NOTE PEEK PEEP
PEER TEET JIMMY LEVER PRIZE
SNOOP BREVIT FERRET PIGGLE
POTTER PUTTER CROWBAR
GUMSHOE LEVERAGE
(**— ABOUT**) OWL MOUSE SNOOK
SCROUNGE
(**— INTO AND REPEAT**) RAVE
(**— INTO**) BREVIT

PRYING NOSY NOSEY CURIOUS
PEEPING

PSALM ODE HYMN SONG DIRGE
GATHA ANTHEM CANTATE CHORALE
INTROIT MISERERE
(**100TH —**) JUBILATE
(**95TH —**) VENITE
(**98TH —**) CANTATE

PSALMS HALLEL
(**BOOK OF —**) PSALTER

PSALTERIUM BOOK LYRA OMASUM
PSALTER PSALTERY

PSALTERY GUSLA SAUTREE

PSEUDO FAKE MOCK SHAM BOGUS
FALSE FEIGNED SPURIOUS

PSEUDOCARP HIP

PSEUDONYM ALIAS ANONYM JUNIUS

PSHAW SHA POOH SUGAR SHUCKS

PSORIASIS ALPHOS

PSYCHE MIND SELF SOUL

PSYCHIATRIST ALIENIST

PSYCHOANALYST FREUDIAN

PSYCHOLOGY HORMISM HEDONICS
ANIMASTIC FORMALISM

PSYCHOPATH MATTOID

PSYCHOSIS INSANITY SENILITY

PSYCHOTIC MAD CRAZY INSANE

PSYLLA DIMERAN

PSYLLIUM FLEAWORT

PTAH (**— EMBODIED**) APIS
(**ASSOCIATED WITH —**) SEKHET

PTARMIGAN RYPE GROUSE
LAGOPODE

PTEROCARPUS LINGOUM

PTEROSAUR DIAPSID

PTERYGIUM WEBEYE

PTERYGOID EXTERNUM

PTERYLA TRACT

PTISAN TEA TISANE

PTOLEMY SOTER
(**WIFE OF —**) CLEOPATRA

PTOMAINE NEURIN SEPSIN SAPRINE
GADININE

PUB BAR INN BOOZER LOUNGE
SHANTY TAVERN

PUBBLE FAT FULL PLUMP

PUB-CRAWL BARHOP

PUBESCENCE DOWN SCURF YOUTH
TOMENT

PUBESCENT HIRSUTE VILLOUS

PUBLIC KUNG OPEN TOWN CIVIC
OVERT WORLD COMMON SOCIAL
VULGAR GENERAL OMNIBUS
POPULAR EXTERNAL MATERIAL
NATIONAL
(**GENERAL —**) GALLERY

PUBLICAN FARMER KEEPER
ZACCHEUS CATCHPOLL

PUBLICATION BOOK ORDO BIBLE
FOLIO ISSUE SHEET ANNUAL
BLAZON DIGLOT SERIAL WEEKLY
ALMANAC BOOKLET ELZEVIR
JOURNAL MONTHLY WRITING
BIWEEKLY BULLETIN DOCUMENT
EMISSION EXCHANGE PRODROME
EPHEMERIS

PUBLIC HOUSE BAR INN PUB
BOOZER PUBLIC SALOON HOSTELRY
POTHOUSE

PUBLICIST AGENT SOLON WRITER

PUBLICITY AIR ECLAT BUILDUP
PUFFERY RECLAME BALLYHOO
BROUHAHA DAYLIGHT HERALDRY
PROMOTION

PUBLICIZE CRY BLURB BREAK
BRUIT HERALD BALLYHOO HEADLINE

PUBLIC SQUARE PLAZA PLEIN
ZOCALO

PUBLISH ASH BLOW CALL EDIT EMIT
VEND VENT CARRY ISSUE PRINT
SPEAK UTTER BLAZON BROACH
DEFAME EVULGE EXPOSE SPREAD
CENSURE DECLARE DIFFUSE
DIVULGE GAZETTE PROTEST
DENOUNCE DISCLOSE EVULGATE
PROCLAIM PROMULGE
(**— BANNS OF MARRIAGE**) CRY
SPUR OUTASK
(**— IN CHURCH**) ASK
(**— WITHOUT AUTHORIZATION**)
PIRATE

PUBLISHER CRIER EDITOR PRINTER
STATIONER

PUCCOON GROMYL ALKANET
GROMWELL BLOODROOT

PUCE FLEA

PUCK ELF LOB PUG BLOW BUTT
DISK POKE POOK DEMON DEVIL
FAIRY PEWKE SPORT RUBBER
SPRITE STRIKE PUCKREL
HOBGOBLIN

PUCKER DRAW FULL RUCK PURSE
REEVE TIZZY COCKLE COTTER
FURROW LUCKEN WRINKLE
CONTRACT AGITATION CONSTRICT

PUCKERED BULLATE COCKLED
WRINKLED BULLIFORM

PUCKFIST BRAGGART PUFFBALL

PUCKISH PUXY ELFIN IMPISH
WHIMSICAL

PUDDING DICK DUFF LINK SAGO
DOWDY KUGEL MERIT BURGOO
FENDER HACKIN HAGGIS HAUPIA
JAUDIE SPONGE TANSEY TARTAN
DESSERT ADEQUACY BLOODING
HEDGEHOG LIVERING PANDOWDY
WHITEPOT CHARLOTTE
(**— CONTAINING KALE**) TARTAN
(**— OF FLOUR**) DUFF
(**BOILED —**) HOY
(**FRUIT —**) HEDGEHOG
(**HASTY —**) MUSH SEPON SUPAWN
(**HAWAIIAN —**) HAUPIA
(**MEAT —**) ISING HACKIN HACKING
(**SUET —**) KUGEL

PUDDINGWIFE PUDIANO DONCELLA
GLUEFISH

PUDDLE DUB PANT PLUD POOL PULK ROIL SLAB SLOP SOSS SUMP PLANT PLASH PUDGE CHARCO FLODGE MUDDLE PUDDER SPLASH TAMPER CONFUSE PLASHET SLODDER SPUDDLE BEFUDDLE **(MUD —)** DUB SLOP LOBLOLLY

PUDDLER'S RABBLE STRIKE

PUDENCY MODESTY DELICACY

PUDGY MIRY BULKY MUDDY SQUAT CHUBBY SPUDDY

PUDU VENADA

PUEBLO ANASAZI

PUELCHE PAMPA TEHUELET

PUERILE WEAK SILLY BOYISH JEJUNE TRIVIAL CHILDISH IMMATURE YOUTHFUL

PUERTO RICO

BAY: SUCIA RINCON BOQUERON AQUADILLA
CAPITAL: SANJUAN
ISLAND: MONA CULEBRA VIEQUES
LAKE: LOIZA CARITE CAONILLAS
MEASURE: CUERDA CABALLERIA
RIVER: CAMUY CANAS YAUCO ANASCO TANAMA FAJARDO
TOWN: CAYEY COAMO PONCE DORADO MANATI ARECIBO FAJARDO GUAYAMA HUMACAO MAYAGUEZ

PUFF GUF POP BLOW BRAG DRAG FLAM FLAN GUFF GUST HUFF PANT SHOW WAFF WAFT ELATE ERUPT EXTOL FLUFF GLURB QUIFF STECH SWELL WHIFF CAPFUL EXPAND FLATUS BLUSTER EXPLODE GRATIFY INFLATE WHIFFET BRAGGART OVERRATE WINDGALL BOUILLONE **(— FROM SHELL BLAST)** BURST **(— OF WIND)** FLAM TIFT SCART FLATUS HUFFLE **(— OUT SMOKE)** EFFUME **(— OUT)** BELL BLUB VENT BLUBBER EFFLATE INFLATE **(— UP)** BLOW HUFF RISE BLOAT HEAVE BLADDER **(— VIOLENTLY)** BLAST **(CREAM —)** DUCHESSE **(SUDDEN —)** FLAN FLAW GUST

PUFFBALL FIST FUZZ PUFF SMOKE FUNGUS PUFFIN BULLFICE BULLFIST PUCKFIST SNUFFBOX

PUFFBIRD BARBET MONASE NUNLET DREAMER NUNBIRD BARBACOU

PUFFED BLUB BOLLEN BLOATED SOUFFLE SWOLLEN ARROGANT INFLATED **(— OUT)** BAGGY BOUFFANT **(— UP)** RANK POBBY ASTRUT BLOATED SWOLLEN TURGENT **(BE — UP)** BELL

PUFFER ATINGA BALLER BLOWER SLIMER TAMBOR BURFISH EGGFISH BLOWFISH TOADFISH

PUFFIN LOOM PAPE POPE MARROT MULLET MARROCK WILLOCK

COCKANDY PARAKEET TOMNODDY TOMNORRY **(HAWAIIAN —)** AO

PUFFY SOFT BLOAT FAFFY GUMMY GUSTY PURSY CHUBBY FLUFFY PURFLY PERSIVE SWOLLEN BLADDERY BOUFFANT DROPSICAL

PUG FOX IMP PET BOXER CHAFF GOUGE SPOOR TRACK TRAIL CAMOIS CAMUSE GOBLIN MONKEY MISTRESS PUGILIST FOOTPRINT

PUGILIST PUG MILLER BRUISER SLOGGER

PUG-NOSED CAMUS CAMUSE

PUISNE PUNY LATER PETTY JUNIOR YOUNGER INFERIOR

PUISSANCE ARMY FORCE POWER CONTROL POTENCY PROWESS DOMINION STRENGTH

PUJUNAN MAIDU

PUKKA GOOD REAL GENUINE LASTING COMPLETE SUPERIOR AUTHENTIC

PUKRAS PHEASANT KOKLAS

PULCHRITUDE GRACE BEAUTY

PULE CRY PEEP CHIRP COWRY WHINE SNIVEL WHIMPER

PULING PULY SPINDLY WHINING

PULL IN PU EAR LUG POO POU ROG RUG TIT TOW CHUG CLAW DRAG DRAW DUCT HALE HARL HAUL HOOK RUGG SWIG TIRE TREK TUSH TWIG YANK BOUSE BREAK BUNCH DRAFT HEAVE HITCH IMPEL PLUCK POLLE PROOF TRICE TWEAK ASSUME COMMIT GATHER OBTAIN PLITCH RUGGLE SECURE TWITCH UPROOT WRENCH ATTRACT EXTRACT **(— A BELL)** SET **(— ABOUT)** TEW SOOL TOSE TOZE MOUSLE **(— APART)** RAVE REND TEAR DIVULSE **(— AWAY)** AVEL AVELL WREST REVULSE **(— BY EARS)** SOLE SOWL **(— DOWN)** UNPILE DESTROY DEMOLISH **(— HERE AND THERE)** TOOZLE TOUSLE **(— NOSE)** SNITE **(— OF DRUM)** EAR **(— OFF)** CROP DRAW STRIP AVULSE **(— ON FISHING ROD)** STRIKE **(— OUT)** RAX EXTRACT OUTBRAID **(— QUICKLY)** YANK **(— ROUGHLY)** WAP TOWSE WOUSE **(— SUDDENLY)** TRICE **(— THE LEG)** STRING **(— TOGETHER)** KNOT ATTRACT **(— TRIGGER)** SQUEEZE **(— UP BY THE ROOTS)** ARACE **(— UP)** LOUK **(— WITH JERK)** HOICK SWITCH **(ZIPPER —)** SLIDER

PULLDEVIL SCROUGER SCRODGILL

PULLER KNOCKER

PULLER-IN CLICKER

PULLET HEN EAROCK EEROCK EIRACK MABYER POULARD POULAINE

PULLEY RIM CONE DRUM BLOCK FUSEE FUZEE IDLER WHEEL DRIVEN IDLEBY JOCKEY POLYVE RIGGER SHEAVE SHIVER WHARVE CAPSTAN FERRULE TIGHTER TRUCKLE WHARROW PULLISEE PURCHASE TROCHLEA **(PL.)** TRISPAST JACKANAPES

PULLOVER JERSEY SWEATER

PULLULATE BUD TEEM SWARM MULTIPLY

PULMONATE LUNGED

PULP PAP PUG CHUM BROKE JELLY NERVE SLUSH STOCK STUFF MARROW SQUEEZE SQUELCH

PULPIT PEW TUB AMBO BEMA DESK WOOD CHAIR PREACH ROSTRUM TRIBUNE **(— BOARD)** TYPE **(— FOR CHOIR BOOKS)** ANALOGION **(MOSLEM —)** MIMBAR MINBAR **(OPEN-AIR —)** TENT

PULPY SOFT SPEWY FLABBY FLESHY SIDDER SIDDOW BACCATE SQUELCHY

PULSATE BEAT BRIM FLAP PANT PUMP THROB COURSE STRIKE PALPITATE

PULSATION BEAT HEARTBEAT LIFEBLOOD VIBRATION **(— OF ARTERY)** ICTUS

PULSE DAL BEAT DOHL TAKT URAD WAVE POUCE STUFF THROB BATTUTA IMPULSE PULSIDGE SPHYGMUS VITALITY

PULVERIZE BUCK DRAG FINE MEAL MULL STUB CRUSH FLOUR GRIND POUND POWDER ATOMIZE DEMOLISH VANQUISH COMMINUTE

PULVERIZED FINE POWDERED

PULVERIZER MULLER

PULVERULENT DUSTY CRUMBLY POWDERY

PUMA COUGAR PAINTER PANTHER

PUME YARURA

PUMICE PUMEX PUMIE

PUMMEL FIB BEAT DRUB PAIK SLAT POUND SLATE THUMP POUNCE

PUMP GIN GUN FORK JACK COURT FORCE HEART PLUMB SLUSH DOCTOR DORSAY FORCER SINKER VOLUTE BOOSTER DOWNTON EJECTOR EVACTOR PITWORK SLUDGER SYRINGE TOEPLER BEERPULL ELEVATOR INFLATER INJECTOR PULSATOR **(— ON SHIPS)** DOWNTON **(GAS —)** BOWSER **(HAND —)** GUN **(MINE —S)** SET **(SET OF —S)** LIFT

PUMP DOCTOR GRATHER

PUMPER RACKER

PUMPERNICKEL BOMBERNICKEL

PUMPKIN PEPO CHUMP GOURD PEPON QUASH CITRUL CUCURB

CUSHAW SQUASH QUASHEY
CUCURBIT PEPONIDA

PUMPKINSEED RUFF SUNNY
FLATFISH FLOUNDER REDBELLY

PUN NICK WHIM ALLUDE CLINCH
QUIBBLE EQUIVOKE PARAGRAM
CALEMBOUR

PUNCH DAB DIG HUB JAB SET BASH
BLOW BOFF BUST DING PLUG POKE
SETT SOAK SOCK TIFF DOUSE
DRIFT FORCE GLOGG PASTE PENCH
SHORT SLOSH CANCEL INCUSE
PATRIX PAUNCH SHAPER STRIKE
TRACER MATTOIR PERLOIR
STARTER EMBOSSER GROUNDER
PRITCHEL PUNCTURE SWATCHEL
THICKSET

(CHASING —) TRACER
(ETCHER'S —) MATTOIR
(HORSESHOE —) PRITCHEL
(OVAL —) PLAISHER

PUNCHBOARD PUSHCARD
PUNCH BOWL SNEAKER
PUNCHED PERTUSE
PUNCHEON CASK PULE SNAP
PUNCH

PUNCHER COWBOY SOCKER
PUNCHINELLO CLOWN BUFFOON
PUGENELLO

PUNCH PRESS BEAR DROP
PUNCHY POUNCY FORCEFUL
PUNCTILIOUS NICE EXACT STIFF
FORMAL CAREFUL POINTED
PRECISE PUNCTUAL

PUNCTUAL DUE EXACT PROMPT
CAREFUL PRECISE ACCURATE
DEFINITE DETAILED EXPLICIT

PUNCTUATE MARK STOP
EMPHASIZE

PUNCTUATION MARK DOT DASH
STOP BRACE COLON COMMA PRICK
SLASH HYPHEN PERIOD STIGME
BRACKET VIRGULE ELLIPSIS
SEMICOLON

PUNCTURE HOLE PICK PINK PROD
STAB DRILL POINT PRICK PUNCH
STICK NEEDLE PIERCE PIQURE
DEFLATE DESTROY PUNCTUM
CENTESIS

PUNDIT SVAMI SWAMI CRITIC PANDIT
TEACHER

PUNGENCY HEAT SALT SNAP
ACRIMONY KEENNESS PIQUANCY
SALTNESS

PUNGENT HOT TEZ BOLD FELL
KEEN RACY SALT TART ACRID
ACUTE BRISK QUICK SHARP SMART
SNELL SPICY BITING BITTER SHRILL
SNAPPY CAUSTIC MORDANT
PEPPERY PIQUANT POINTED
TELLING CAYENNED PIERCING
POIGNANT STABBING STINGING

PUNGI BIN
PUNIC PUNICAL FAITHLESS
PUNISH FIT FIX PAY BUCK CANE
COLT COOK CUCK FINE FLOG GATE
SORT WIPE ABUSE BIRCH CURSE
ORDER SCOUR SHEND SLATE SPILL
STOCK STRAP TWINK WREAK

AMERCE AVENGE CAMPUS FERULE
FOLLOW IMMURE LESSON REFORM
SCHOOL STRIKE CHASTEN
CONSUME CORRECT CORRIGE
DEPLETE PENANCE REQUITE
SCOURGE CARTWHIP CHASTISE
DISTRAIN

(— BY COMPENSATION) FINE
AMERCE

(— BY CONFINEMENT) GATE
(— BY FINE) MULCT
(— BY LASHING WRISTS) BUCK

PUNISHING HARD GRUELING
PUNISHMENT GIG FINE LASH PAIN
PINE RACK SACK WITE YARD BEANS
GRUEL LIBEL PANDY PEINE SMART
WRACK WREAK DESERT DIRDUM
FERULE LESSON PICKET EXAMPLE
GALLOWS GANTLET JANKERS
PAYMENT PENALTY PENANCE
PENANCY REVENGE SCOURGE
HERISSON JUDGMENT PUNITION
STOCKING SUPPLICE EXECUTION

(CAPITAL —) SCAFFOLD
(MILITARY —) JANKERS

PUNITIVE PENAL PUNITORY
PUNK BAD BOY FUNK JERK MONK
POOR PUNG CONCH SPONK SPUNK
AMADOU BUNKUM NOVICE
HOODLUM RUFFIAN BEGINNER
GANGSTER INFERIOR NONSENSE
STRUMPET TERRIBLE TOUCHWOOD

PUNKIE MIDGE MIDGET
PUNNING ALLUSIVE BIVERBAL
PUNSCH ARRACK
PUNSTER SPEED
PUNT BET HIT POY KENT KICK
QUANT GAMBLE GARVEY SKERRY

PUNTER BIDDER GAMBLER SCALPER
SERVITOR

PUNY WEAK DAWNY DEENY DWARF
FRAIL PETTY SCRAM WEARY JUNIOR
MAUGER NOVICE PUISNE RECENT
SICKLY SPROTY MANIKIN PIMPING
QUEECHY SHILPIT YOUNGER
DROGHLIN INFERIOR PINDLING

(— PERSON) TITMAN

PUP PUPPY WHELP
PUPA EGG NYMPH PUPPET TUMBLER
WIGGLER FLAXSEED WRIGGLER
CHRYSALIS

PUPIL BOY GYTE TYRO WARD BLACK
CADET CHILD ELEVE NORRY NURRY
RAPIN TUTEE ALUMNA GRADER
INFANT JUNIOR SENIOR LEARNER
PAULINE SCHOLAR SOJOURN
STUDENT ABSENTEE DISCIPLE
RUGBEIAN SCHOOLER

(— AT HEAD OF CLASS) DUX
(— IN STUDIO) RAPIN
(— OF EYE) BLACK PEARL SIGHT
(ANGLO-INDIAN —) CHELA
(BOARDED —) SOJOURN

PUPILAGE (WARDSHIP PEDANTISM
PUPPET BABY DOLL DUPE IDOL
MOTE BABBY DROLL DUMMY
MAUMET MOTION POPPIN STOOGE
WAJANG WAYANG GUIGNOL
DROLLERY MARIONET

(— PLAY) WAJANG
(— SHOW) VERTEP

PUPPIS STERN
PUPPY FOP PUP DOLL DOUGH
WHELP PUPPET

(FEMALE —) GYP
(GREYHOUND —) SAPLING

PURBLIND BISME BISSON
PURCHASABLE VENAL CORRUPT
PURCHASE BUY WIN EARN FISH
GAIN KOOP WHIP BOOTY HEDGE
PRIZE DUPLEX EFFECT EMPTIO
TACKLE ACQUIRE BARGAIN EMPTION
PILLAGE PROCURE BARRATRY

(— AND FATTEN CATTLE) HIGGLE

PURCHASER BUYER EMPTOR
VENDEE CHAPMAN POULTER
SHOPPER CUSTOMER

PURE NET CAST EVEN FAIR FINE
FREE FULL GOOD HOLY MERE NEAT
PUTE TRUE CLEAN CLEAR FRESH
MORAL NAKED SHEER STARK
SYCEE UTTER WHITE WHOLE
CANDID CHASTE ENTIRE IMMIXT
LIMPID PISTIC SIMPLE VESTAL
VIRGIN CATHARI GENUINE PERFECT
SINCERE ABSOLUTE ABSTRACT
COMPLETE DOVELIKE INNOCENT
SERAPHIC SPOTLESS VIRGINAL
VIRTUOUS

PUREE SOUP CREAM
PURGATIVE PURGE SENNA DIASENE
DRASTIC TURPETH ALOEDARY
CLEANSER EVACUANT CATHARTIC

PURGATORY PAIN SWAMP
PURGE LAX RID FIRE FLUX SOIL
CLEAR SCOUR DRENCH PHYSIC
REMOVE SEETHE SHRIVE SPURGE
CHISTKA CLEANSE DETERGE
ABSTERGE

PURIFICATION BAPTISM ELUTION
LUSTRUM VASTATION

PURIFY TRY BOLT FINE PURE WASH
CLEAN PURGE SNUFF BLEACH
DISTIL FILTER REFINE SETTLE
SPURGE WINNOW BAPTIZE CHASTEN
CLEANSE EPURATE EXPIATE
LAUNDER SUBLIME SWEETEN
DEPURATE EXORCISE FILTRATE
LUSTRATE SANCTIFY SCAVENGE
SPRINKLE

(— ORE) DILVE

PURIFYING SMECTIC DEPURANT
PURIRI TEAK BULREEDY IRONWOOD
PURITAN PRIG SAINT CANTER
CROPPY BLUENOSE CATHARAN
GOSPELER ROUNDHEAD

PURITANICAL BLUE STRICT
GENTEEL PRECISE

PURITY PURE ASSAY HONOR WHITE
CANDOR SATTVA VIRTUE FINESSE
CHASTITY FINENESS PURENESS

PURL RIB EDDY KNIT PEARL UPSET
RIPPLE TOTTLE CAPSIZE OVERTURN

PURLIEU HAUNT
(PL.) BOUNDS CONFINES ENVIRONS

PURLOIN CAB CRIB WEED BRIBE
FILCH STEAL SWIPE FINGER PILFER
PIRATE CABBAGE SURREPT
ABSTRACT

PURPLE GAY VIOL REGAL SHOWY BLATTA BLOODY CROCUS EVEQUE MIGNON ARDOISE FUCHSIA FUCHSIN HEATHEN LOGWOOD PETUNIA PONTIFF AMARANTH BURGUNDY CAMERIER CYCLAMEN EGGPLANT EMINENCE IMPERIAL MAUVETTE WISTARIA
(DELICATE —) MAUVE
(VISIBLE —) RHODOPSIN
PURPLE FISH MUREX
PURPLE GALLINULE SULTAN SULTANA HYACINTH
PURPLE LOOSESTRIFE KILLWEED
PURPLE RAGWORT JACOBY
PURPLE SANDPIPER REDLEG REDLEGS ROCKBIRD
PURPORT FECK GIST PORT DRIFT SENSE TENOR DESIGN EFFECT IMPART IMPORT INTEND INTENT BEARING MEANING PROFESS PURPOSE COVERING DISGUISE STRENGTH
PURPOSE GO AIM END GOAL IDEA MAIN MEAN MIND MINT PLAN SAKE TALK TEND WEEN WILL ARTHA CAUSE ETTLE HEART LEVEL SCOPE STUDY THINK DESIGN DEVICE EFFECT INTEND INTENT OBTENT PREFIX SCHEME COMPASS COUNSEL DESTINE EARNEST IMAGINE MEANING PROPOSE DEVOTION FUNCTION PLEASURE PROPOUND DISCOURSE
(FIXED —) HEART
(MORAL —) ETHOS
PURPOSEFUL AIMFUL POINTED
PURPOSIVE TELIC HORMIC
PURPOSELESS WASTE AIMLESS FECKLESS
PURPURA MUREX PURPLES PELIOSIS
PURPURE GOLP GOLPE PURPLE MERCURY
PURR MURR THRUM WHURL DUNLIN
PURSE BAG CLY JAN BUNG CLAY CLOY KNIT POKE PUSS SKIN BULSE BURSE DUMMY FUNDS MEANS POUCH SPUNG COMMON FOLLIS GIPSER POCKET PUCKER READER SHAMMY ALMONER GIPSIRE LEATHER SPORRAN BUCKSKIN BURSICLE CRUMENAL
PURSE CRAB PAGURID
PURSER CLERK BURSAR BOUCHER PINCHGUT NIPCHEESE
PURSING MIMP
(— OF MOUTH) PRIM
PURSLANE PUSSLY PIGWEED
PURSLANE TREE SPEKBOOM
PURSUANCE SUING SEQUENCE
PURSUE BAY RUN SUE HUNT SEEK CHASE CHEVY CHIVY ENSUE HOUND QUEST SLATE STALK TRADE COURSE FOLLOW GALLOP TRAVEL BEDEVIL HOTFOOT CONTINUE PRACTICE
(— ZIGZAG COURSE) TACK
PURSUER FOLLOWER PLAINTIFF QUESTRIST

PURSUIT FAD HUNT SUIT CAPER CAUSE CHASE CRAFT HOBBY COURSE SEARCH ASSAULT ACTIVITY ENTREATY
PURSUIVANT BUTE MARCH FALCON ORMOND ATHLONE CARRICK ANTELOPE DINGWALL FOLLOWER
PURSY FAT OBESE PUFFY ASTHMATIC
PURULENT PYIC ATTRY ATTERY
PURVEY PANDER SUPPLY FORESEE PROVIDE
PURVEYOR CATER TAKER ACHUAS PROWER CATERER ACHATOUR MANCIPLE
PUS WARE AMPER FESTER MATTER WORSUM QUITTER
PUSH CA DUB JAM JOG JUR PUT BANG BIRR BOIL BOOM BORE BUNT DING DUSH FLOG KENT PICK PILT PING PORR POSS POTE STOP BLITZ BOOST BRUSH BUNCH CROWD CRUSH DRIVE DUNCH ELBOW HUNCH NUDGE PINCH POACH POUSE SCAUT SHOVE SKELP STICK STOVE EXTEND HURTLE HUSTLE JOGGLE JOSTLE POTTER PROPEL THRING THRONG THRUST ASSAULT IMPETUS IMPULSE OPERATE PERPLEX SHUFFLE THRUTCH CONTRUDE INCREASE SHOULDER STRAITEN DISMISSAL
(— ALONG) TUSH
(— APART) SPREAD
(— ASIDE) SHOG
(— BY STICK) KENT POLE
(— FORWARD) ADVANCE
(— GENTLY) NUDGE
(— INTO) INVADE
(— MONEY) SPIFF
(— ON) BEAR YERK
(— OUT) DEBOUT LAUNCH
(— RUDELY) HORSE HUSTLE
(— TO FULL STRIDE) EXTEND
(— TOGETHER) CONTRUDE
(— UP) BOOST
(— WITH ELBOW) ELBOW HUNCH
(— WITH FEET) DIG SCAUT
(— WITH HEAD) BUNT BUTT
(STRONG —) BEVEL
PUSH BUTTON PUSH PRESSEL
PUSHCART BARROW TROLLEY
PUSHER PLUNGER TRAILER TRAMMER WHEELER
PUSHY FORWARD AGGRESSIVE
PUSILLANIMOUS WEAK TIMID FEEBLE COWARDLY TIMOROUS
PUSS CAT FACE HARE CHEET CHILD MOUTH RABBIT BAUDRONS
PUSTULE NOB BEAL BURL KNOB POCK PUSH QUAT WART ACHOR AMPER BLAIN WHEAL WHELK BLOTCH FESTER PIMPLE TETTER ANTHRAX BLISTER ERUPTION WHEYWORM
PUT DO BET LAY PIT SET BANG BUTT FILL GIVE GROW PILT REST URGE ADAPT APPLY DIGHT DRIVE FOCUS PLACE STALL STATE STEAD STEEK

STELL WAGER ASSIGN BESTOW DECAMP IMPOSE INVEST PHRASE REPOSE SPROUT THRUST DEPOSIT EMPLACE EXPRESS INFLICT SUBJECT
(— AN END TO) DATE SNIB ABATE NAPOO SNUFF SPIKE STASH STILL STINT SOPITE STANCH ASSUAGE EXPIATE SATISFY ABROGATE DEMOLISH SURCEASE
(— ANOTHER IN PLACE OF) RELIEVE
(— APART) DISPART
(— ASIDE) BLOW HAIN SAVE SHUNT SHUFFLE
(— AT REST) HUSH
(— AWAY) STOW COVER ELONG HUTCH SHIFT RECOND DIVORCE
(— BACK INTO USE) RESTORE
(— BACK) REMIT REMISE
(— BEFORE) PROFER ANTEPONE
(— DOWN) LAY DEMIT QUELL DEPOSE SQUASH DEPRESS OPPRESS REPRESS SILENCE DIMINISH SUPPRESS
(— EDGE ON) TED
(— FLAX UPON A DISTAFF) DIZEN
(— FORTH BLOSSOMS) GEM
(— FORTH) GEM CAST GIVE PUSH EXERT LANCE PROFER STRETCH
(— GRAIN IN BARN) END
(— IN AGONY) THROE
(— IN CHARGE) COMMIT
(— IN COMPETITION) PIT
(— IN DANGER) SCUPPER
(— IN DREAD) ADRAD
(— IN MOTION) AROUSE
(— IN OPERATION) LAUNCH
(— IN ORDER) DO SET REDD SIDE SORT TRIM DIGHT MENSE SHIFT TRICK ADJUST DAIKER GRAITH ORDAIN SETTLE ARRANGE CLARIFY DISPOSE REDRESS INSTRUCT
(— IN PLACE) POSE
(— IN POSSESSION) SEISE
(— IN PRISON) WARD
(— IN) ENTER INSERT INTROMIT
(— INFORMATION INTO) ADDRESS
(— INTO BARN) END
(— INTO CASE) SHEATHE
(— INTO CIRCULATION) EMIT SPRING
(— INTO ECSTASY) ENTRANCE
(— INTO EFFECT) EXECUTE SANCTION
(— INTO IRONS) BOLT
(— INTO RHYTHM) METER METRE
(— LIQUOR INTO CASK) TUN
(— OFF) DOFF HAFT DEFER DELAY DEMUR FOIST PARRY REMIT REPRY SHIFT TARRY THROW LINGER RETARD SHELVE ADJOURN FORSLOW PROLONG RESPITE POSTPONE
(— ON AIRS) PROSS FINICK REVEST
(— ON ALERT) ALARM
(— ON COVER) HACKLE
(— ON GUARD) ALERT CAUTION
(— ON HAT) COVER
(— ON PRETENSE) AFFECT

(— **ON SALE**) SHOP
(— **ON SHORT ALLOWANCE**) SCRIMP
(— **ON STRING**) ENFILE
(— **ON**) DON APPLY CRACK DRAPE
ENDUE MOUNT STAGE ASSUME
INVEST ADDRESS
(— **OUT BATSMAN**) SKITTLE
(— **OUT OF ACTION**) HAMPER
(— **OUT**) GET OUT DOUT OUST
DOWSE EVICT EXERT OUTED SLAKE
SLOCK RETIRE DISMISS EXCLUDE
EXTINCT FORJUDGE
(— **RIGHT**) AMEND
(— **ROAD METAL ON**) STEEN
(— **THROUGH A STRAINER**) TAMMY
(— **TO FLIGHT**) AFLEY FEAZE GALLY
(— **TO RIGHTS**) SORT DIGHT
(— **TO SHAME**) DASH ABASH SHEND
UPBRAID
(— **TO SLEEP**) OPIATE SOPITE
SOPORATE
(— **TO USE**) STOW APPLY BESTOW
(— **TO WORK**) HARNESS
(— **TOGETHER**) ADD JOIN BUILD
COMPILE COMPOSE CONCOCT
CONFECT ASSEMBLE COMPOUND
(— **UP HAY**) BOTTLE
(— **UP WITH**) GO BEAR BIDE HACK
BROOK ENDURE SUFFER COMPORT
STOMACH SWALLOW TOLERATE
(— **UP**) ANTE ERECT FLUSH
DISPENSE
(— **UPON**) GAMMON
(— **WITH ANOTHER**) APPOSE
PUTCHER PUTLOG PUTCHEN
PUTLOCK
PUTREFACTION ROT DECAY
PUTREFACTIVE SEPTIC
PUTREFY ROT DECAY SWEAT
FESTER POLLUTE PUTRESCE
PUTRESCENT PUTRID ROTTEN
PUTRID FOUL SOUR VILE LOUSY

ROTTEN CORRUPT DECAYED
FRIABLE VICIOUS DEPRAVED
PUTT CLOWN BORROW GOBBLE
PUTTEE PAT PATA GAITER BANDAGE
LEGGING
PUTTER FUSS MESS MUCK TRUCK
CADDLE DAWDLE MUCKER MUCKLE
PIDDLE TINKER FRIGGLE
PUTTY BEDDING
PUTTYROOT CRAWFOOT
PUTZ CRECHE
PUXY SWAMPY QUAGMIRE
PUZZLE CAP GET SET BEAT CRUX
DEAD LICK POSE BEFOG GRIPH
POSER QUEER REBUS STICK BAFFLE
BOTHER ENIGMA FICKLE FOITER
GLAIKS JIGSAW KITTLE RIDDLE
CONFUSE MYSTERY MYSTIFY
NONPLUS PERPLEX STICKER
TAISSLE TANGRAM TRANGAM
ACROSTIC BEFUDDLE BEWILDER
CONFOUND DISTRACT DUMFOUND
ENTANGLE INTRIGUE REMBLERE
CROSSWORD
PUZZLED ASEA
PUZZLING KNOTTY KNOTTED
RIDDLING DIFFICULT
PYCNANTHEMUM KOELLIA
PYCNOGONID SPIDER
PYGARG ADDAX OSPREY
PYGIDIUM PODEX
PYGMALION (FATHER OF —) BELUS
MUTGO AGENOR
(**MURDERED BY** —) SICHAEUS
(**SISTER OF** —) DIDO
(**STATUE FASHIONED BY** —)
GALATEA
PYGMY ELF AKKA AMBA DOKO
ACHUA AFIFI ATOMY BATWA DWARF
GNOME PIXIE PIGMEW WOCHUA
ACHANGO ASHANGO MANIKIN
DWARFISH NEGRILLO VAALPENS
DANDIPRAT

PYGMY GOOSE GOSLET
PYGMY RATTLESNAKE
MASSASAUGA
PYGOSTYLE VOMER
PYKNIC SQUAT STOCKY STHENIC
MUSCULAR
PYRAMID BENBEN HOPPER
TEOCALLI
(— **OF CRAYFISH**) BUISSON
(**DOUBLE** —) TWIN ZIRCONOID
(**INVERTED** —) HOPPER
PYRAMIDAL HUGE ENORMOUS
IMPOSING
PYRAMIDICAL TAPER
PYRAZINE ALDINE PIAZIN DIAZINE
PYRE BALE TOPHET BONFIRE
BALEFIRE
PYRITE BALE MUNDIC
(**PL.**) BRAZIL STANNITE FIRESTONE
MAGISTRAL MARCASITE
PYROLA LIMONIUM SHINLEAF
PYROMANIAC FIREBUG ARSONIST
PYRONE CUMALIN
PYROPHYLLITE PENCIL
PYROTECHNICS FIREWORKS
PYROXENE AUGITE SALITE SAHLITE
DIALLAGE DIOPSIDE
PYROXENITE ARIEGITE MARCHITE
OSTRAITE NIKLESITE
PYRRHIC DIBRACH
PYRRHULOXIA GROSBEAK
BULLFINCH
PYRROLE AZOLE
PYTHON ADJIGER PEROPOD
ANACONDA
PYTHONESS WITCH PHITONES
PYTHONIC HUGE INSPIRED
ORACULAR MONSTROUS PROPHETIC
PYX BOX CAPSA CASKET VESSEL
BINNACLE CIBORIUM
PYXIDIUM CAPSULE

Q KU CUE KUE QUEEN QUEUE
QUEBEC
QUA HERON QUABIRD
QUACK PUFF WHACK SALVER
SUBTLE EMPIRIC IMPOSTOR
OPERATOR SANGRADO CHARLATAN
QUACKERY HUMBUG
QUADRAGESIMA LENT
QUADRANGLE QUAD CLOSE COURT
TETRAGON
QUADRANT BOW RADIAL SQUARE
QUARTER TETRANT ALTIMETER
QUADRATE SUIT AGREE IDEAL
QUADER SQUARE PERFECT
BALANCED
QUADRIC CONICOID
QUADRILATERAL TRAPEZIA
TETRAGRAM
(PL.) TESSARA
QUADRILLE CONTREDANSE
(PL.) LANCERS
QUADROON QUATERON TERCERON
QUADRUPED BABIRUSA
QUADRUPLE FOURBLE FOURFOLD
QUADRUPLET FOURLING QUARTOLE
QUAFF QUAX TOOT DRINK QUASS
WAUCHT CAROUSE TRILLIL
QUAG BOG MARSH SHAKE QUIVER
QUAGMIRE BOG FEN GOG HAG QUA
SOG LAIR PUXY QUAW MARSH
MIZZY SWAMP MORASS PUDDLE
BOGMIRE PUCKSEY
QUAHOG CLAM COHOG VENUS
BULLNOSE
QUAIL COW LOWA WEET COLIN
DAUNT QUAKE SPOIL WASTE
BLENCH CURDLE FLINCH SHRINK
TURNIX WITHER DECLINE HEMIPOD
TREMBLE BOBWHITE
(YOUNG —) SQUEALER
QUAINT DRY ODD NAIVE STRANGE
FANCIFUL HANDSOME
QUAKE JAR QUOG RESE CHILL
QUAIL SHAKE QUIVER SHIVER
FLUTTER SHUDDER TREMBLE
QUAKER ASPEN HERON FRIEND
OBADIAH WHACKER HICKSITE
TREMBLER BEACONITE BROADBRIM
SHADBELLY
(— STATE) PENNA PENNSYLVANIA
QUAKER GRAY ACIER
QUAKING ASPEN QUAKY TREPID
SHAKING TREMBLING
QUAKING GRASS COWQUAKE
WAGWANTS
QUALIFICATION NATURE RESERVE
SHADING CAPACITY
QUALIFIED FIT ABLE MEET FITTED
FITTEN LIKELY CAPABLE ELIGIBLE
SUITABLE AUTHENTIC
(NOT —) INAPT INHABILE
QUALIFIER MODIFIER
QUALIFY FIT DASH ADAPT ALLAY
EQUIP HEDGE ENABLE MODIFY
SOFTEN TEMPER ABSOLVE CERTIFY
ENTITLE LICENSE PREPARE
GRADUATE MODERATE RESTRAIN
RESTRICT
QUALITY Y BRAN BUMP CHOP COST

FEEL GUNA LEAD SORT COLOR
GRACE STATE TRAIT ASSIZE
BARREL FABRIC STRAIN THREAD
TIMBER ADJUNCT CALIBER KINSHIP
STATURE ACCIDENT MOVEMENT
PROPERTY
(— OF PERSONAL EMOTIONS)
PATHOS
(— OF PHOTOGRAPH) CONTRAST
(— OF TONE) TIMBRE
(— OF VOWELS) LENGTH
(— PECULIAR TO ONESELF) SEITY
(AESTHETIC —) TASTE
(ARTISTIC —) VIRTU
(ATTRACTIVE —) TAKE
(BASIC —) GRAIN
(BASIC —S) STUFF
(COLOR —) TONE
(ESSENTIAL —) ALLOY SPECIES
SUCHNESS
(GOOD —) THEW
(HEREDITARY —) STRAIN
(IMPECCABLE —) FINISH
(INCISIVE —) BITE
(INNATE —) LARGESS
(INTELLECTUAL —) BROW
(NATURAL —) TARAGE
(OBJECTIONABLE —) ANILITY
(OF HIGH —) FRANK
(PERVASIVE —) AROMA
(PHYSICAL —S) BOTTOM
(PRIMAL —) GUNA
(PUNGENT —) SNAP
(RELATIVE —) RATE
(SPRINGY —) SPINE
(STRUCTURAL —) TEXTURE
(SUBDUED —) SHADE
(SUBTLE —) BOUQUET
(SUPERIOR —) SUPER FINENESS
(TRIED —) TOUCH
(UNUSUAL —) SURD
(WAVY — OF HAIR) FLIX
QUALM CALM DROW PALL NAUSEA
SQUEAM SCRUPLE
QUALMISH TEWLY SICKISH
SQUEAMISH
QUAMOCLIT MOONFLOWER
QUANDARY FIX PUXY TANGLE
DILEMMA NONPLUS SWITHER
DOLDRUMS JUNCTURE
QUANDONG PEACH
QUANTIC NONIC OCTIC SEPTIC
SEXTIC QUADRIC QUINTIC
QUANTIFIER PREFIX
QUANTITY JAG SUM SUP BODY
DEAL DISH DOSE FECK JAGG LIFT
MASK SOME SOUD WARE BATCH
BREAK CLASH GRIST KITTY SIEGE
TROOP WHEEN ACTION ADDEND
AMOUNT BAGFUL BOTTLE BUDGET
DICKER EFFECT HANTLE NUMBER
SPINOR THRAVE CONTENT FOOTAGE
PORTION QUANTUM GLASSFUL
KNIFEFUL LADLEFUL
(— OF ARROWS) SHEAF
(— OF BUTTER) CHURNING
(— OF CLOTHES) BUCKING
(— OF COTTONSEED) CRUSH
(— OF CUT TREES) FALL

(— OF DRINK) HOOP DRAFT
DRAUGHT
(— OF ELECTRICITY) FARADAY
(— OF EXPLOSIVE) CHARGE
(— OF FISH OR GAME) TAKE CATCH
DRAFT DRAUGHT
(— OF GRAIN) GAVEL
(— OF HAY) TRUSS
(— OF IRRIGATION WATER) DUTY
(— OF LIQUID) DROP JAUP SLASH
GOBBET
(— OF LIQUOR) HEELTAP
(— OF LUMBER) RUN
(— OF METAL) BLOW
(— OF MUD) CLASH
(— OF NARCOTICS) BINDLE
(— OF PAPER) TOKEN
(— OF PRODUCE) BURY
(— OF RAISINS) FRAIL
(— OF THREAD) LEASE
(— OF WOOD) HAG FATHOM
(ESTIMATED —) WEY
(EXCESSIVE —) GLUT SPATE
(FIXED —) CONSTANT
(GREAT —) HOST MORT MUCH
HIRST SIGHT STORE BARREL
FOREST SLATHER TUMMELS
(LARGE —) ACRE BOLT DEAL FECK
HEAP MASS PECK SCAD SLEW
FLOOD FORCE GRIST JORUM
POWER SCADS SHEAF STACK
STORE BUCKET BUSHEL DICKER
DOLLOP GALLON MATTER MELDER
CLUTHER SKINFUL HECATOMB
MOUNTAIN
(LEAST —) BEDROCK
(MINUTE —) DRAM DROP SHADE
SCRUPLE
(NOTEWORTHY —) CHUNK
(RELATIVE —) DEGREE
(SETTLED —) SIZE
(SIZABLE —) SCUMP
(SMALL —) ACE BIT SUP DASH
DUST HAET HAIR HARL IOTA PEAK
SOSH SPOT CANCH PRILL SMACK
SPICE SQUIB TOUCH JOBBLE
MORSEL PICKLE SAMPLE SONGLE
STIVER CAPSULE CURTSEY DRIBBLE
DRIBLET EPSILON HANDFUL
MODICUM SMICKET SPATTER
TODDICK FARTHING MOUTHFUL
PENNORTH SCANTLET
(UNDIRECTED —) SCALAR
(VARYING —) SKID
QUANTUM PHONON PHOTON
QUAPAW KWAPA ARKANSAS
QUARANTINE DETAIN ISOLATE
SANCTION
QUARENTENE ROOD FURLONG
QUARREL JAR YED BEEF CHIP DEAL
FEUD FRAY FUSS JARL JOWL MIFF
NIFF ODDS PICK PLEA SPAT BRACK
BRAWL BRIGE BROIL FLITE FLUSK
GRUFF HURRY JOWER NOISE PIQUE
SCOLD SCRAP SHINE STOUR UPSET
WRALL AFFRAY BARNEY BREACH
BREEZE BRIGUE DEBATE DIFFER
DUSTUP FRACAS FRATCH GARROT
JANGLE MATTER QUARRY RIPPET

SQUARE SQUEAL STRIFE THREAP
THREEP THWART BRABBLE DISGUST
DISPUTE FACTION OUTCAST
PRABBLE RUCTION SIMULTY
STASHIE SWAGGER TUILZIE
WRANGLE DISAGREE MOORBURN
SPLUTTER SQUABBLE TRAVERSE
(— IN WORDS) JANGLE
(NOISY —) ROW FRACAS KICKUP
(PETTY —) MIFF SPAT TIFF
QUARRELING BICKER CONTEK
CHIDING CONTECK
QUARRELSOME RIXY UGLY ROWTY
FEISTY SCRAPPY DRAWLING
FRAMPOLD FRATCHED PETULANT
PHRAMPEL FRACTIOUS
(NOT —) AMICABLE
QUARRELSOMENESS SQUARING
WARIANCE
QUARRIED (NOT —) LIVE
QUARRIER FACEMAN QUARION
QUARRY DELF GAME LODE MEAT
CHASE DELFT DELPH PLUCK
LATOMY REWARD LATOMIA
LOZENGE
(HAWK'S —) MARK
QUARRYMAN SCABBLER SCAPPLER
QUART SHANT WHART
(1-8TH —) GILL
(2 —S) FLAGON
(4 —S) GALLON
(METRIC —) LITER
(ONE-HALF —) PINT
QUARTE FOURTH
QUARTER PART STUD EAVER GRITH
TRACT BARRIO BEHALF BESTOW
CANTON COLONY FARDEL HARBOR
SECTOR CONTRADA FAUBOURG
FIERDING STANDARD POBLACION
(— IN BATTLE) GRITH
(— OF A POUND) TRIPPET
(— OF BEEF OR MUTTON) BOUT
(— OF CITY) BLOCK GHETTO
(— OF COMPASS) PLAGE
(— OF FLAG) CANTON
(— OF HOUR) POINT
(— OF HUNDRED) FIERDING
(— OF YEAR) RAITH
(— ONESELF) SORN
(— UPON) LAY
(JEWISH —) ALJAME
QUARTERING LASKING CHUMMAGE
QUARTER NOTE CROTCHET
QUARTER REST SOSPIRO
QUARTERS BOTHY BILLET BOTHIE
LIVERY MENAGE FARDELS
CHUMMERY DIGGINGS LODGMENT
(— FOR IMMIGRANTS) HOSTEL
(— OF SALVATION ARMY)
BARRACKS
(HIGH —) AERY EYRY AERIE EYRIE
(JUNIOR OFFICERS' —) GUNROOM
(MEN'S —) SELAMLIK
(MONASTERY —) FRATRY
QUARTET FOURSOME
QUARTILE SQUARE TETRAGON
QUARTO FOURS
QUARTZ IRIS ONYX SARD AGATE
FLINT PRASE TARSO TOPAZ JASPER

MORION PEBBLE PLASMA SILICA
ALENCON CITRINE CRYSTAL
RUBASSE SINOPLE AMETHYST
BASANITE SARDONYX SIDERITE
YENTNITE
QUARTZITE GANISTER SILCRETE
QUASH CASS CRUSH QUELL SPIKE
SQUAT SOPITE CASSARE PEREMPT
SUPPRESS
QUAT FOUR GLUT SQUASH SATIATE
UPSTART
QUATERNION TETRAD QUADRATE
QUATREFOIL TRESSURE
(DOUBLE —) EIGHTFOIL
QUAVER QUAP CROMA SHAKE TRILL
WAVER CHROMA FALTER QUIVER
WABBLE WOBBLE WRIBLE FREDDON
VIBRATE
QUAVERY WARBLY UNSTEADY
QUAY KEY POW QUAI LEVEE BUNDER
STRAND
QUEACH BOG FEN MARSH THICKET
QUEASINESS KECK SICKNESS
QUEASY NICE SICK SQUEEZY
DELICATE NAUSEATED SQUEAMISH
QUEBRACHO BREAKAX AXMASTER
IRONWOOD AXBREAKER
QUEBRADA BROOK GULLY RAVINE
FISSURE
QUECHUA INCAN KICHUA
QUEEN REG DAME FERS LADY MEDB
RANI AEDON BEGUM FIERS RANEE
ATOSSA REGINA ROXANA TAILTE
TAMARA ARGANTE ATHALIA
CANDACE JOCASTE OMPHALE
PHEARSE STATIRA TITANIA
BRUNHILD GERTRUDE GLORIANA
GUINEVER MAHARANI
(— AND KING OF TRUMPS) BELLA
(— CITY) CINCINNATI
(— IN CHESS) FERS LADY FIERS
(— OF CLUBS) SPADILLA
(— OF DENMARK) GERTRUDE
(— OF ETHIOPIA) CANDACE
(— OF FAIRY LAND) MEDB
GLORIANA
(— OF GEORGIA) TAMARA
(— OF GOTHS) TAMORA
(— OF HEARTS) ELIZABETH
(— OF HEAVEN) HERA
(— OF JUDAH) ATHALIA
(— OF LYDIA) OMPHALE
(— OF SHEBA) BALKIS BILKIS
(— OF SPADES) BASTA LIZZY
(— OF THE ADRIATIC) VENICE
(— OF THE ANTILLES) CUBA
(— OF THE EAST) ZENOBIA
(— OF THEBES) JOCASTA
(— OF TRUMPS) HONOR
(FAIRY —) MAB ARGANTE TITANIA
(INDIAN —) RANI SUNK MAHARANI
(MOHAMMEDAN —) BEGUM
QUEEN ANNE'S LACE UMBEL
QUEEN BEE KING
QUEEN ELIZABETH DIANA ORIANA
CYNTHIA
QUEENFISH WAHOO CROAKER
DRUMFISH
QUEENLY HAUGHTY REGINAL
MAJESTIC

QUEENROOT YAWSHRUB
QUEEN'S-DELIGHT YAWSHRUB
QUEENSLAND HEMP SIDA
JELLYLEAF
QUEER HEX ODD RUM HARM DICKY
DIPPY DROLL FAINT FUNNY GIDDY
NUTTY RUMMY COCKLE HIPPED
QUEASY QUISBY UNIQUE AMUSING
COMICAL CURIOUS DISRUPT
ERRATIC STRANGE TOUCHED
WHIMSIC FANCIFUL OBSESSED
PECULIAR
(— THING) QUOZ
QUEERNESS ODDITY
QUEEST RINGDOVE
QUELL DIE CALM FLOW HUSH KILL
QUAY SLAY ABATE ALLAY CRUSH
QUASH QUIET YIELD PACIFY PERISH
REDUCE SOOTHE SPRING STANCH
STIFLE KILLING REPRESS SQUELCH
SUPPRESS
QUEME QUIM HANDY WHEAM
COMELY PLEASE GRATIFY
PLEASANT
QUENCH COOL DAMP SIND ALLAY
CHECK CRUSH SLAKE SLOCK STILL
STANCH STIFLE ASSUAGE SLOCKEN
AUSTEMPER
QUENCHED EXTINCT
QUENCHER STANCH
QUENCHING FRITTING
QUERECHO VAQUERO
QUERELA AUDITA
QUERENT INQUIRER PLAINTIFF
QUERN KERN MILL METATE
MILLSTONE
QUERULOUS WHINY FRETFUL
PEEVISH NATTERED PETULANT
IRRITABLE
QUERY ASK DOUBT DEMAND
INQUIRE INQUIRY QUESTION
QUEST ASK BAY GAPE SEEK
DEMAND EXAMINE PURSUIT SEEKING
VENTURE
QUESTING OUTREACH
QUESTION ASK HOW SPY POSE
QUIZ TALK ARGUE DOUBT DREAD
QUERY ACCUSE CHANCE CHARGE
DEMAND LEADER MATTER PONDER
REASON SHRIVE EXAMINE INQUIRE
INQUIRY PROBLEM SCRUPLE
OVERTURE RELEVANT RESEARCH
STICKLER
(— AMBIGUOUSLY WORDED) RIDDLE
(— FRETFULLY) RAME
(BAFFLING —) POSER
(PERPLEXING —) STUMPER
(UNSOLVED —) CRUX
QUESTIONABLE (NOT —) DECENT
QUESTIONER APPOSER INQUIRER
QUESTIONING DUBIOUS
QUESTIONABLE FISHY QUEER
SHAKY UNSAFE CLOUDED DUBIOUS
DOUBTFUL
QUESTION MARK QUERY QUAERE
EROTEME
QUESTIONNAIRE POLL INVENTORY
QUETCH STIR TWITCH
QUETZAL QUESAL TROGON

QUEUE CUE COLA LINE BRAID PIGTAIL CROCODILE

QUEY KOY WHY WHEY HEIFER

QUIBBLE COG PUN BALK CARP QUIB QUIP CAVIL DODGE EVADE QUIRK SALVO AMBAGE BAFFLE BICKER HAFFLE BRABBLE CAPTION CHICANE QUIBLET QUIDDIT QUILLET SHUFFLE QUILLILITY CONUNDRUM

QUICA OPOSSUM SARIGUE

QUICK APT RAD YAP FAST FLIT GLEG KECK KEEN LISH LIST PERT RATH RIFE SNAP SOON WHAT WHIT WICK AGILE ALIVE APACE BRISK CHEAP FLEET HASTY MERRY PREST RAPID READY SHARP SHORT SNACK SNELL SWIFT SWITH TOSTO TRICK VISTO YARRY ACTIVE CLEVER FACILE KITTLE NIMBLE PROMPT PRONTO SNAPPY SPEEDY SUDDEN DARTING SCHNELL SHUTTLE DEXTROUS TRIPPING

(— AND NEAT) DEFT

(— AS A FLASH) WHIP

(— IN PERCEPTION) ACID

(— IN RESPONSE) GNIB

(— TO DETECT) SMOKY

(— TO FLARE UP) GASSY

(— TO LEARN) APT

(— TO MOVE) YARE

(LIGHT AND —) VOLANT

QUICKEN PEP MEND STIR WHET HURRY SPEED ACUATE AROUSE HASTEN INCITE KINDLE REVIVE VIVIFY ANIMATE ENLIVEN REFRESH SHARPEN EXPEDITE INSPIRIT

QUICKENING FLICKER REVIVAL STIRRING

QUICKLY TID TIT CITO FAST RIFE SOON TIVY WHIP YARE NEWLY RADLY RATHE SHARP SKELP SNACK SNELL SWITH TIGHT WIGHT YEPLY ASTITE BELIVE HOURLY PRESTO PRONTO RASHLY EFTSOON PRESTLY READILY SPEEDILY WIKIWIKI

(— AND WITH FORCE) SWAP

(MORE —) TIDDER TITTER STRETTO

QUICKNESS HASTE SPEED AGILITY ACTIVITY CELERITY DISPATCH KEENNESS SAGACITY

(MENTAL —) NOUS SLEIGHT LEGERITY

QUICKSAND FLOW SYRT SYRTIS SWALLOW

QUICK-SELLING LEEFTAIL

QUICKSILVER OREMIX MERCURY TIERRAS HEAUTARIT

QUICK-SPEAKING PROMPT

QUICK-TEMPERED DONCY DONSY IRASCIBLE

QUICK-WITTED APT SHARP SMART NIMBLE KNOWING

QUID FID CHEW SOVEREIGN

(— OF TOBACCO) CUD FID

QUIDDANY JELLY SYRUP CODINIAC

QUIDDITY QUIBBLE WHATNESS

QUIDNUNC GOSSIP BUSYBODY

QUIESCENCE STASIS DORMANCY

QUIESCENT QUIET LATENT STATIC RESTING INACTIVE

QUIET QT ST COY LAY CALM COSH DEAD DUMB EASE EASY HUSH LOUN LOWN LULL REST ROCK SNUG SOFT WEME ACCOY CANNY CIVIL DOWNY LEVEL PEACE PEASE QUATE QUELL QUEME RESTY SALVE SHADY SILKY SLEEP SOBER SQUAT STILL SUANT WHIST DREAMY GENTLE PACIFY PLACID RETIRE SAUGHT SEDATE SERENE SETTLE SILENT SMOOTH SOFTLY SOOTHE SOPITE STEADY STILLY HUSHFUL ORDERLY REQUIEM RESTFUL SILENCE DECOROUS PEACEFUL TRANQUIL UNRUFFLE

(— DOWN) DILL

(MAKE —) ALLAY

(STEALTHILY —) SLINKY

QUIETISM MOLINISM

QUIETLY FAIR CANNY STILL WINLY EVENLY GENTLY SOFTLY TIPTOE

QUIETNESS REST REPOSE SERENITY

QUIETUDE CALM INERTION

QUIETUS REST DEATH RELEASE

QUILL COP PEN RIB PIRN FLOAT STALK BOBBIN FESCUE PINION SLEEVE CALAMOS PRIMARY TRUNDLE

(— FOR WINDING THREAD) COP

(PORCUPINE —) PEN

QUILLBACK SAILFISH SKIMBACK

QUILLWORT ISOETES FERNWORT

QUILT BEAT GULP WALT WELT WHIP DUVET REZAI CADDOW CHALON PALLET THRASH SWALLOW MATTRESS POULTICE COMFORTER

QUILTING MARCELLA

QUIMPER NICE

QUINCE COYNE ANGERS SQUINCH JAPONICA

(BENGAL —) BEL BAEL

QUINCE SEED CYDONIUM

QUININE KINA SPECIFIC

QUINK BRANT

QUINONE EMBELIN

QUINTAIN FAN

QUINTE FIFTH

QUINTESSENCE CREAM ELIXIR CLYSSUS OSMAZOME

QUINTUPLE QUINARY FIVEFOLD QUINIBLE

QUIP GIBE JEST JOKE CRACK QUIRK SALLY SCOFF TAUNT CONCEIT QUIBBLE

QUIRA CAOBA ROBLE HORMIGO VENCOLA MACAWOOD

QUIRE CHOR SEXTERN

(20 —S) REAM

(PL.) INSIDES

QUIRK BEND KINK QUIP TURN CLOCK CROOK TWIST CONCEIT QUIBBLE FLOURISH PAROXYSM MANNERISM

QUIRQUINCHO PICHI PELUDO

QUIRT WHIP ROMAL

QUIS WOODCOCK

QUIT GO DROP NASH PART QUAT AVOID BELAY CEASE DOUSE LEAVE SHIFT SHOOT STASH WHITE BEHAVE CIVITE DESERT DESIST FOREGO RESIGN SECEDE VACATE ABANDON FORSAKE RELEASE UNTENANT

QUITCH COUCH QUICK SCUTCH TWITCH

QUITCLAIM ACQUIT RELEASE DISCHARGE

QUITE SO ALL BUT GEY BRAW EVEN FAIR FREE FULL JUST PLAT WELL CLEAR CLOSE FULLY SHEER STARK CLEVER DAMNED ENOUGH JUSTLY MERELY TOTALLY

(NOT —) HARDLY

QUITRENT CANON

QUITS EVEN EVENS UPSIDES

QUITTER PUS SLAG PIKER COWARD JUMPER SHIRKER TURNBACK

QUIVER DIRL QUAG QUOG BEVER NIDGE QUAKE SHAKE TRILL WAVER WIVER BICKER COCKER DIDDER DINDLE SHEATH SHIMMY SHIVER TREMOR WAMBLE DORLACH FLUTTER FRISSON SHUDDER TREMBLE TWIDDLE TWITTER VIBRATE FLICHTER WERSLETE

QUIVERING ASPEN AGUISH DIDDER DITHER QUAGGLE QUAKING AGITATED ATREMBLE

QUIVER TREE KOKERBOOM

QUIXOTIC IMAGINARY VISIONARY

QUIZ ASK GUY HOAX MOCK CHAFF EXAMINE QUESTION RIDICULE

QUIZZICAL ODD QUEER QUIZZY CURIOUS WHIMSICAL

QUO KA

QUOD JAIL QUAD PRISON

QUOIN COIN ANGLE GOIGN CORNER LOZENGE KEYSTONE VOUSSOIR

QUOIT CIST DISC DISH DISK LINER DISCUS HOBBER CROMLECH

QUOMODO HOW WAY MEANS MANNER

QUONDAM OLD ONCE WHILE FORMER ONETIME SOMETIME

QUORATEAN KAROK

QUORUM CORAM HOUSE MINYAN MAJORITY

QUOTA PART BOGEY SHARE QUOTIENT

QUOTATION PRICE QUOTE EXTRACT SNIPPET EPIGRAPH

(— DEVELOPED INTO ESSAY) CHRIA

QUOTATION MARK GUILLEMET

QUOTE CITE COAT COTE MARK NAME NOTE ADDUCE ALLEGE RECITE REPEAT EXCERPT EXTRACT OBSERVE REHEARSE

(— SARCASTICALLY) FLOUT

QUOTH CO KO CUTH QUAD QUOD SAID SPOKE UTTERED

QUOTIDIAN DAILY TRIVIAL ORDINARY

QUOTIENT QUOTE FRACTION

QUTB POLE

Quisling — Traitor

R AR ROGER ROMEO
(**UVULAR —**) BURR
RA RE RAE SHU TEM ATMU BACIS
HORUS MENTU KHEPERA SOKARIS
RABBAN MASTER TEACHER
RABBET CHECK GROOVE BACKJOINT
FILLISTER
RABBI TANA AMORA CACAM HAKAM
TANNA MASTER SABORA KHAKHAM
TEACHER GAMALIEL SABORAIM
(**PL.**) AMORAIM TANNAIM
RABBIT BUN REX TAN BUNT CONY
JACK POLE RACK BUNNY CAPON
CREAM CUNNY DUTCH FRIER LAPIN
ANGORA ASTREX CONEEN HAVANA
OARLOP PARKER POLISH SILVER
TAPETI WOOLER BEVEREN
CONYNGE FLEMISH LEPORID
SNOWSHOE WARRENER
(**— BURROW**) CLAPPER
(**— FUR**) CONY SCUT CONEY FLICK
LAPIN FLITCH
(**— MEAT**) LAPAN
(**— SKIN**) RACK
(**— TAIL**) SCUT
(**— WARREN**) CONYGER
(**CASTRATED —**) CAPON
(**FEMALE —**) DOE
(**MALE —**) BUCK
(**YOUNG —**) KITTEN
(**PL.**) FLICK WARREN
RABBITFISH SPINY
RABBLE MOB TAG GING HERD ROUT
SCUM FRAPE SCAFF SCUFF TRASH
MEINIE RADDLE RAFFLE RAGTAG
RASCAL TAGRAG DOGGERY
PUDDLER RABBLER RANGALE
TRAFFIC BRAGGERY CANAILLE
RAGABASH RIFFRAFF VARLETRY
(**DISORDERLY —**) HERD
RABBLE-ROUSER DEMAGOG
RABID MAD RAGING FRANTIC
FURIOUS RABIOUS RABITIC
FRENZIED RAVENING VIRULENT
RABIES LYSSA MADNESS PIBLOKTO
RAVENING
RACCOON COON COATI GUARA
TEJON AGUARA MAPACH WASHER
AGOUARA ARCTOID RATTOON
CRABEATER
RACE CAP CUP LOG ROD RUN BENT
CONE DASH DRAG GEST HUMP KIND
LINE NAME RAIS RAZE RINK TEAM
TRAM BLOB BREED CASTE FLESH
CHEVY CORSO DERBY FLESH
HOUSE ISSUE PLATE PURSE RATCH
REACH ROUTE SPEED STAKE
STAMM STIRP STOCK BROOSE
CHEVVY COURSE FAMILY NATION
PEOPLE PHYLON RUNOFF SPRING
STIRPS STRAIN STRIND BIOTYPE
CENTURY CLAIMER CLASSIC
HACKNEY HUNDRED KINDRED
LINEAGE MATINEE NURSERY
PROGENY PROSAPY RACEWAY
REGATTA STADIUM FUTURITY
HANDICAP MARATHON WALKOVER
OFFSPRING
(**— A HORSE**) CAMPAIGN

(**— AT WEDDING**) BROOSE BROUZE
(**— FOR BALL-BEARINGS**) CONE
(**— OF BARLEY**) BENT
(**— OF GODS**) VANIR
(**— OF PEOPLE**) VANS AMALS VANIR
HAZARA YADAVA BAMBUTE FIRBOLG
GIANTRY NISHADA RASENNA
REPHAIM AMALINGS
(**— OF UNDERGROUND ELVES**)
DROW
(**— OF WINDMILL**) CURB
(**HORSE —**) DERBY PLATE SPRINT
MATINEE FUTURITY WALKOVER
(**HUMAN —**) MAN MANKIND SPECIES
(**IMPROMPTU —**) BRUSH
(**JUMPING —**) SCURRY
(**LENTEN —S**) TORPIDS
(**MILL —**) LADE
(**PRELIMINARY —**) HEAT
(**ROWING —**) SCULLS REGATTA
(**RUNNING —**) MILE RELAY SPRINT
HUNDRED HURDLES
(**SHORT —**) BICKER
(**SHORT-DISTANCE —**) DASH
SCURRY SPRINT
(**SKI —**) SLALOM DAUERLAUF
(**PL.**) FOURS
RACECOURSE LIST OVAL PIST RING
TURF EPSOM CAREER CIRCUS
STADIE STRETCH GYMKHANA
SPEEDWAY
RACEHORSE DOG PACER RACER
SLEEPER TROTTER BANGTAIL
(**— THAT HAS NEVER WON**) MAIDEN
(**2-YEAR OLD —**) JUVENILE
(**INFERIOR —**) PLATER HAYBURNER
(**PL.**) RUCK
RACEME STRIG
RACER CRACK SNAKE RUNNER
BICYCLIST CINDERMAN
RACETRACK DROMOS FURLONG
RACEWAY CANAL TRACK GROOVE
CHANNEL FISHWAY
RACHEL POWDER
(**HUSBAND OF —**) JACOB
(**SON OF —**) JOSEPH BENJAMIN
RACHIS SPINE SPINDLE
(**— OF HOP STROBILE**) STRIG
RACHITIS RICKETS
RACIAL GENTILE GENTILIC PHYLETIC
RACIST COLOR
RACK GIN RAK RAT TUB BINK BUCK
CASE HACK HECK SHOG TACK
AMBLE BRAKE DRIER DRYER FLAKE
FRAME POKER THROW TOUSE
TRAIN WRACK WRECK WRING
CIRCLE CRATCH CUDGEL ENGINE
NIPPER PULLEY TREBLE WRENCH
AFFLICT AGONIZE PENRACK
POTTARO TORMENT TORTURE
BARBECUE EQUULEUS PINEBANK
SAWHORSE
(**— ATTACHED TO WAGON**)
SHELVING OUTRIGGER
(**— FOR BARRELS**) JIB
(**— FOR CHINAWARE**) FIDDLE
(**— FOR DISHES**) BINK
(**— FOR FEEDING**) HACK HAYRACK
(**— FOR FODDER**) HECK CRATCH

(**— FOR PLATES**) CREEL
(**— FOR STORAGE**) FLAKE
(**— IN THRESHER**) SHAKER
(**DRYING —**) CRIB TREBLE
(**WOODEN —**) BUCAN
RACKED WRUNG TORTURED
RACKET BAT DIN GAME BANDY
MUSIC RAZOO CLAMOR CROSSE
DRIVER HUBBUB HUSTLE RAQUET
RATTLE BUSINESS REVELING
STRAMASH
(**TENNIS —**) SCUFE
RACKETEER HOOD HUSTLER
GANGSTER
RACKETT CERVALET CERVELAT
RACKING FIERCE
RACKMAN TOPMAN
RACON BEACON
RACONTEUR STORYTELLER
RACQUET GAZELLE
RACY GAMY LEAN SEXY JUICY
SALTY SMART SPICY LIVELY RISQUE
PIQUANT PUNGENT ZESTFUL
SPIRITED
RAD EAGER QUICK READY AFRAID
ELATED
RADAR (**— NAVIGATION SYSTEM**)
LANAC
(**— SYSTEM**) OBOE
RADARSCOPE PPI HSCOPE
RADDLE PIT BEAT SCAR RAVEL
RUDDLE THRASH SEPARATOR
RADIAL RAY QUADRANT
RADIANCE RAY GLOW LEAM GLARE
GLEAM GLINT GLORY LIGHT SHINE
LUSTER AUREOLA GLITTER
SPLENDOR
RADIANT BEAMY SHEEN SHINY
ABLAZE BRIGHT GOLDEN LUCENT
SHEENY AURORAL BEAMFUL
BEAMING FULGENT LAMBENT
GLORIOUS LUSTROUS RELUCENT
SPLENDID
(**— INTENSITY**) J
RADIATE RAY BEAM POUR SHED
SHINE EFFUSE SPREAD EFFULGE
EMANATE
RADIATED PENCILED STELLATE
RADIATION AURA LIGHT INFRARED
(**— DOSAGE**) REM REP
(**— UNIT**) LANGLEY
RADIATOR HEATER EMANATOR
(**SET OF —S**) STACK
RADICAL KEY SURD BASAL GROUP
RADIX ROUGE ULTRA CAPRYL
HEROIC CAPITAL CAPROYL DRASTIC
EXTREME FORWARD HERETIC
JACOBIN LEFTIST LEVELER LIBERAL
PRIMARY CARDINAL LOCOFOCO
(**CHEMICAL —**) AMYL CARYL CETYL
GROUP ACETYL CAPRYL PHENYL
PHYTYL HALOGEN LINALYL
CARBAMYL QINNAMAL
RADICALISM EXTREMISM
JACOBINISM
RADICEL ROOTLET
RADICLE (**— THAT DEVELOPS IN
GRAIN**) COME
RADIENT ORIENT

RADIO AIR SET WIRELESS
(— **OPERATOR**) HAM SPARKS
(— **SYSTEM**) TBS
RADIOGRAM FLIMSY
RADIOGRAPH EXOGRAPH SKIAGRAM
RADISH RUNCH DAEKON DAIKON
RIFART CADLOCK CRADLOCK
CRUCIFER CROSSWEED
RADIUS RAYON SPOKE SWEEP
THROW ADRADIUS
RADIX BASE ROOT ETYMON RADICLE
RADON NITON THORON ACTINON
EXRADIO
RADULA RIBBON TONGUE
RAFF LOW IDLE SCUM SWEEP TRASH
COMMON JUMBLE LUMBER RABBLE
RAFFLE RAGTAG SNATCH RUBBISH
RAFFISH RAKISH TAWDRY UNKEMPT
RAFFLE MOVE RAFF JUMBLE RABBLE
REFUSE RUBBISH
RAFT COW CRIB MOKI BALSA BATCH
FLOAT TABLE DINGEY DINGHY
JANGAR MOKIHI PIPERY RADEAU
JANGADA ZATTARE CATAMARAN
(— **OF INVERTED POTS**) GHARNAO
(— **OF LOGS**) BOOM CRIB
(— **WITH CABIN**) COW
(**BAMBOO** —) RAKIT
(**FIRE** —) CATAMARAN
(**LUMBER** —) BATCH
RAFT DOG RAKER
RAFTER HIP BALK BLAD FIRM SILE
SOIL SPAR SPUR VIGA BLADE
CABER RIDGE BOUGAR CARLINE
RAFFMAN SLEEPER
(— **OF TURKEYS**) FLOCK
RAFTY RAW DAMP FUSTY MUSTY
RANCID
RAG JAG TAT HOAX JAGG SAIL
ANNOY CLOUT PRANK SCOLD
SCRAP SHRED WIPER GIBBOL
LIBBET RAGGLE TAGRAG TATTER
FLITTER REMNANT TORMENT
RAGSTONE STRAGGLE NEWSPAPER
(— **GATHERER**) TATTER
(PL.) DUDS CADDIS FITTERS
RAGGERY FLITTERS
RAGAMUFFIN MUFFLIN BEGGARLY
SHABROON TITMOUSE
RAGE GO AWE FAD RAG WAX BAIT
BEEF FARE FOAM FRET FUFF FUME
FUNK FUNX FURY GLOW GRIM HEAT
PELT RAMP RASE RESE TAVE TEAR
WOOD ANGER BRETH CHAFE CRAZE
FUROR PADDY STORM TEAVE TEVEL
VOGUE WRATH FRENZY FURORE
PELTER TYAUVE BLUSTER FASHION
FUFFIAN MADNESS PASSION
TEMPEST INSANITY WOODNESS
PADDYWACK
(**BE IN A** —) RANT
RAGFISH ICOSTEID
RAGGED DUDDY HARSH FRAYED
JAGGED SCOURY UNEVEN SHAGRAG
SHREDDY TATTERY SCRAGGLY
SCRATCHY TATTERED
RAGGED ROBIN ROBIN CUCKOO
RAGGEE MAND RAGI MARUA
MANDUA KORAKAN ELEUSINE

RAGGLE-TAGGLE MOTLEY
RAGING HOT GRIM WILD YOND
RABID FIERCE FURIAL FERVENT
PELTING VIOLENT FLAGRANT
FURIBUND WRATHFUL
RAGOUT GOULASH HARICOT
TERRINE SALPICON CHIPOLATA
PULPATONE
(— **OF GAME**) SALMI SALMIS
RAGPICKER BUNTER RAGMAN
TATTER
RAGWEED HAYWEED HOGWEED
AMBROSIA IRONWEED KINGHEAD
KINGWEED RICHWEED FRANSERIA
RAGWORT CUSHAG JACOBY
BENWEED CAMMOCK SEGGROM
LIFEROOT
RAID RADE ROAD TALA FORAY
HARRY PINCH REISE REIVE CREACH
FORAGE HARASS INROAD MOLEST
PANYAR RAZZIA BODRAGE
BORDRAG CHAPPOW DESCENT
JAYHAWK OUTFALL OUTRAKE
OUTRIDE OUTROAD SPREATH
COMMANDO SPOILING
(**AIR** —) BLITZ
(**CATTLE** —) SPREAGH SPREATH
(**WARLIKE** —) HERSHIP
RAIDER REDLEG BUSHWACK
RAIL BAR BULL COOT GIRD JEST
KOKO LIST MOHO RANT RAVE SKID
SORA TRAM WEKA WING CRAKE
EASER FENCE GUARD PLATE RAVEL
REILE SCOFF SCOLD SLENT STANG
STANK STEEL SWEAR BANTER
BEDWAY CALLET FENDER RUNNER
SKITTY TIKLIN BIDCOCK BILCOCK
COURLAN INVEIGH OARCOCK
RACKWAY TOPRAIL BULLHEAD
CANCELLI CORNBIRD PORTLAST
TOADBACK VIGNOLES
(— **AT**) JEST CURSE SCOFF RATTLE
REVILE
(— **OF BED**) STOCK
(— **OF RAILWAY SWITCH**) TONGUE
(— **ON GUN PLATFORM**) TRINGLE
(— **ON HAY VEHICLE**) THRIPPLE
(— **ON SHIP**) FIFE
(**ALTAR** —) SEPTUM
(**ARCHED** —) HOOPSTICK
(**CHAIR** —) LEDGE
(**FENCE** —) RIDER
(PL.) RAILING CANCELLI RAILROAD
RAIL CHAIR CARRIAGE
RAILING BAR SEPT GRATE RAVEL
FENDER FIDDLE GITTER VEDIKA
BARRIER GALLERY PARAPET
CANCELLI ESPALIER HANDRAIL
PARCLOSE TRAVERSE
RAILLERY GAFF HASH JEST JOKE
RAGE CHAFF RALLY SPORT BANTER
BLAGUE HOORAY HURRAH SATIRE
TRIFLE MOCKERY BADINAGE
DICACITY RABULOUS RIDICULE
RAILROAD EL ROAD YARD STEEL
COALER FEEDER GRANGER
TRAMWAY CEINTURE ELEVATED
(— **CAR**) IDLER
RAILROAD CHAIR SADDLE

RAILSPLITTER MAULER
RAILWAY ROAD TUBE COGWAY
SUBWAY COGROAD INCLINE
TRANVIA WIREWAY ASCENSOR
PLATEWAY TRAMROAD FUNICULAR
RAIMENT RAY GARB CLOTH
APPAREL CLOTHES VESTURE
CLOTHING DRESSING
(**SPLENDID** —) SHEEN
RAIN WET ISLE MIST SMUR ULAN
WEET STORM DELUGE MIZZLE
SERENE SHOWER SOAKER DRIZZLE
DOWNPOUR SPRINKLE
(— **AND SNOW**) SLEET
(— **HEAVILY**) TEEM
(— **LIGHTLY**) SMUR SPIT SPRINKLE
(— **OF SPARKS**) SHOWER
(**DRIZZLING** —) DAG
(**FINE** —) MIST SEREIN SERENE
(**GOD OF** —) PARJANYA
(**HEAVY** —) PASH SPOUT
(**LIGHT** —) WEATHER HEATDROPS
(**SHORT** —) SHOWER
(**SUDDEN** —) SKEW
(**WHIRLING** —) SKIRL
(**WIND-DRIVEN** —) SCAT
(PL.) VARSHA
RAINBIRD KOEL TOMFOOL
STORMBIRD
(— **OF JAMAICA**) HUNTER
RAINBOW ARC BOW ARCH IRIS
GAMUT METEOR SUNBOW ILLUSION
(**BROKEN** —) WINDDOG WINDGALL
RAINBOW FISH GUPPY MAORI
RAINBOW RUNNER SKIPJACK
SHOEMAKER
RAINBRINGER KACHINA
RAINCOAT MAC MACK PONCHO
BURSATI OILSKIN SLICKER
GOSSAMER
RAINFALL PLOUT SKIFF SKIFT
ONDING STEMPLOW
RAIN GAGE UDOMETER
RAINSPOUT RONE
RAINSTORM WET SPATE
RAIN TREE SAMAN ZAMAN GUANGO
ZAMANG ALGAROBA GENISARO
MONKEYPOD
RAINY WET KICK FRESH JUICY
RAYNE SAPPY WEETY BLASHY
DRIPPY PLUNGY SPONGY PLUVIAL
PLUVINE SHOWERY WEEPING
CLUTTERY PLUVIOUS SLATTERY
(— **SEASON**) VARSHA
RAISE END SET WIN BUMP BUOY
GROW HAIN HEFT HIGH HIKE HOVE
JACK KICK LEVY LIFT MAKE OVER
REAR ROOF STIR TELD TOSS AREAR
BLOCK BOOST BREED BUILD CAIRN
CHOCK CRANE DIGHT ELATE ENSKY
ERECT EXALT FORCE GREET HANCE
HEAVE HEEZE HEVEN HOISE HOIST
HORSE LEAVE MOUND MOUNT
PRICK RISER ROUSE VOICE ASSIST
BETTER CREATE DOUBLE EMBOSS
EXHALE GATHER LEAVEN MUSTER
NANTLE PREFER REMOVE RISING
UPHOLD UPLIFT ADDRESS ADVANCE
COLLECT ELEVATE ENHANCE

LIGHTEN NOURISH PRESENT PROMOTE RECRUIT UPSHOOT ANGELIZE HEIGHTEN INSPIRIT RELEVATE
(— **A BUMP**) CLOUR
(— **A NAP**) TEASE TEASEL TEAZLE
(— **ALOFT**) SPHERE
(— **BY ASSESSMENT**) LEVY
(— **BY HAND**) NOB
(— **CLAMOR**) BRAWL
(— **IN PITCH**) SHARP
(— **OBJECTIONS**) CAVIL BOGGLE
(— **ONESELF**) CHIN
(— **TO 3RD POWER**) CUBE
(— **TO HIGH DEGREE**) STRAIN
(— **UP**) BUOY AREAR ELATE EXALT EXTOL ELEVATE CIVILIZE

RAISED HIGH UPSET ARRECT HOGGED EXALTED ELEVATED MOUNTANT UPLIFTED UPRAUGHT

RAISIN FIG PASA PLUM LEXIA ZIBEB REYSON CURRANT SULTANA MUSCATEL
(PL.) SPICE

RAJ RULE REIGN

RAJA KING CHIEF RULER PRINCE PANGLIMA

RAJMAHAL CREEPER JITI CHITI JETEE JEETEE

RAJPUT SAMMA SUMRA GAHRWAL RAZBOOCH

RAKE GO HOE RIP WAY COMB PATH RACK RAFF RAVE REAP ROAM ROUE ROVE RUCK BLOOD CLAUT PITCH SCOOP SCOUR SULKY TIGER PLUNGE RABBLE ROLLER SEARCH RANSACK SCRATCH LOTHARIO SCRAPPLE
(— **GRAIN**) GAVEL
(— **UP IN ROWS**) HACK
(— **WITH GUNFIRE**) SCOUR STRAFE ENFILADE
(— **WITHOUT TEETH**) LUTE
(**BUCK** —) SWEEP
(**CRANBERRY** —) SCOOP
(**HORSE-DRAWN** —) GLEANER
(**OYSTER** —) GLEANER

RAKEHELL RASCAL IMMORAL LIBERTINE

RAKER GUMMER ROOKER

RAKISH SLANG JAUNTY SPORTY WANTON DASHING CARELESS DEVILISH RANTEPOLE

RALE RATTLE SIFFLE SIBILUS

RALLENTANDO DRAG RITARD

RALLY KID DRAG JOKE MOCK RELY STIR BULLY JOLLY QUEER BANTER DERIDE REVIVE COLLECT CLAMBAKE RIDICULE SPEAKING

RAM PUN TIP TUP BUCK CRAM PACK RAME STEM TEAP TOOP ARIES CHOKE CRASH POACH ROGER SLIDE BEETLE CHASER RANCID ROSTRUM BULLDOZER WETHERHOG WETHERTEG
(— **OF WAR VESSEL**) SPUR
(**CASTRATED** —) WETHER

RAMA MELCHORA
(**WIFE OF** —) SITA

RAMADA ARBOR PORCH

RAMAGE WILD RAMMISH UNTAMED

RAMAGE HAWK BRANCHER

RAMBLE RAKE ROAM ROVE WALK JAUNT PROWL RANGE TRACE TROLL RUMBLE STROLL VAGARY WAMBLE WANDER ENRANGE EXCURSE SPROGUE TROUNCE FLAGARIE SCRAMBLE SPATIATE
(— **AIMLESSLY**) HAZE

RAMBLING GAD CURSORY DEVIOUS WINDING DESULTORY SCATTERED

RAMBUNCTIOUS RUDE WILD ROUGH UNRULY UNTAMED VIOLENT

RAMBUTAN SOAPWORT

RAMENTUM PALEA PALET SCALE SHAVING

RAMIE ORTIGA

RAMIFICATION ARM RAMUS BRANCH OFFSHOOT OUTGROWTH

RAMIFY BRANCH SPRANGLE

RAMMAN ADAD ADDA ADDU

RAMMED EARTH PISE

RAMMEL TRASH RUMMLE RUBBISH

RAMMER HEAD BOSER PUNNER WORMER

RAMOSE CLADOSE BRANCHED

RAMP RUN BANK EXIT RAGE RANK SLIP STORM EASING FROLIC FOOTPAD SLIPWAY GRADIENT

RAMPAGE RAGE ROMP BINGE SPRAY SPREE STORM RANDAN

RAMPAGEOUS UNRULY GLARING RAMPANT VIOLENT

RAMPANT RANK PROFUSE SALIANT SALIENT SEGREANT

RAMPART BRAY LINE WALL AGGER ARGIN VALLUM BULWARK DEFENSE PARAPET RAMPIER BARBICAN MUNITION BARRICADE

RAMPER LAMPREY

RAMPIKE SNAG RAUNPICK ROUNSPIK

RAMROD FORMAL GUNSTICK

RAMSHACKLE RUDE UNRULY RICKETY SHACKLY UNSTEADY

RAMSON RAMP GARLIC BUCKRAM
(PL.) RAMS

RAMSTAM RASH HEADLONG RECKLESS

RAN ARN

RANCEL SEARCH RANSACK

RANCH RUN FARM TEAR FINCA CHACRA OUTFIT SPREAD WRENCH STATION ESTANCIA HACIENDA

RANCHE NATURAL

RANCHER COWMAN GRAZIER SHEEPMAN CATTLEMAN

RANCID RAM RANK SOUR FROWY RAFTY RASTY REEST RESTY FROWZY ODIOUS ROTTEN

RANCOR GALL HATE SPITE ENMITY GRUDGE HATRED MALICE ACRIMONY

RANCOROUS ACRID VENOMOUS MALIGNANT
(**NOT** —) GOOD

RAND EDGE ROON RUND BORDER HIGHLAND

RANDAN SPREE RANTAN UPROAR RAMPAGE

RANDOM BANK FORCE LOOSE STRAY CASUAL CHANCE CHANCY AIMLESS RANDALL RENDOUN SHOTGUN UNAIMED VAGRANT
(**AT** —) HOBNOB
(**SOMEWHAT** —) LONG

RANDY LEWD RUDE SPREE BEGGAR VIRAGO LUSTFUL RIOTOUS CAROUSAL

RANGE KEN ROW ALLY AREA BEAT GATE GAUT GHAT LINE RANK ROAM ROVE SCUM SHOT TOUR WALK ALIGN BLANK CARRY FIELD GAMUT HILLS ORBIT REACH SCOPE SHOOT SPACE STAND START SWEEP SWING VERGE COURSE DANGER EXTEND EXTENT LENGTH RADIUS RAMBLE SCOUTH SPHERE STROLL WANDER BOWSHOT COMPASS DEMESNE EARSHOT GUNSHOT HABITAT HORIZON PURVIEW CLASSIFY DIAPASON EARREACH EYEREACH LATITUDE PANORAMA
(— **OF ARROW**) FLIGHT
(— **OF BRICK**) COURSE
(— **OF FOOD**) FARE
(— **OF FREQUENCIES**) SPECTRUM
(— **OF GOVERNANCE**) DOMAIN
(— **OF GUN**) CARRY RANDOM GUNSHOT
(— **OF HILLS**) GAUT GHAT HUMP TIER CHAIN GHAUT RIDGE SIERRA SAWBACK BACKBONE
(— **OF ORGANISM**) BIOZONE
(— **OF PASTURE**) GANG
(— **OF PLANKS**) STRING
(— **OF PRINTING TYPES**) SERIES
(— **OF SIGHT**) KEN SCAN EYESHOT KENNING
(— **OF TONES**) KEY SCALE GRADATION
(— **OF VISION**) EYE SIGHT KENNING
(— **OF WAVELENGTH**) BAND
(— **OVER**) SWEEP
(**ARCHERY** —) BUTTS GREEN
(**COOKING** —) KITCHENER
(**SHOOTING** —) MES GALLERY
(**TEMPERATURE** —) CONE

RANGE FINDER STADIA MEKOMETER

RANGE POLE PICKET

RANGER ROVER ROBBER MONTERO FIREWARD

RANGOON SHERRY

RANGY OPEN ROOMY SPACIOUS

RANK RAY ROW SEE DANK FOOT FORM FOXY GOLE GREE LINE RAMP RATE ROOM SEED SOUR STEP TIER CENSE CHOIR CLASS FETID FRANK FUSTY GRADE GROSS HONOR LEVEL MARCH ORDER QUIRE RANGE ROWTY SIEGE SPACE STALL STAND STATE TCHIN TRAIN AFFAIR AGREGE DEGREE ERMINE ESTEEM FIGURE LAVISH PARAGE RATING SPHERE STATUS STRONG CALIBER CALLING DIGNITY DUKEDOM EARLDOM

FOOTING GLARING RAMMISH
RAMPANT STATION WORSHIP
ABSOLUTE EARLSHIP ENSIGNCY
EQUIPAGE FLAGRANT GENTRICE
LADYSHIP PALPABLE STINKING
(— AND FILE) RANGALE
(— OF GENTLEMEN) GENTRY
GENTILITY
(— OF SERGEANT-AT-LAW) COIF
COIFFE
(ACADEMIC —) AGREGE
(BOTTOMMOST —) CELLAR
(HIGH —) DIGNITY EMINENCE
(LOWEST —) SCOURING
(MILITARY —) GRADE AIRMAN
CORNET CHAOUSH
(NOBLE —) ADELAIDE
(SAME —) KIND
(SOCIAL —) CLASS ESTATE
HERALDRY POSITION
RANKLE FRET CHAFE FESTER
INJURE RANCOR DESTROY INFLAME
RANSACK RIG DRAG RAKE RIPE
SACK SEEK RIFLE DACKER RANCEL
SEARCH PLUNDER RUMMAGE
RANSOM FINE RAME REDEEM
RESCUE RESGAT EXPIATE
RANSTEAD TOADFLAX
RANT CAVE HUFF RAIL RAND MOUTH
REVEL ROUSE SCOLD SPOUT
STEVEN BOMBAST CAROUSE
DECLAIM FROTHING
(— AND RAVE) FAUNCH
RANTING RANTISM TEARCAT
RANTIPOLE WILD CARROT RAKISH
SEESAW ROMPING
RANULA CYST FROGTONGUE
RANUNCULUS MOSS GOLLAND
CROWFOOT HEDGEHOG BUTTERCUP
RAOULIA HAASTIA
RAP BOB CON CHAP GRAB KNAP
TIRL TUNK WRAP CLICK CLINK
KNOCK STEAL TOUCH BARTER
HANDLE
RAPACIOUS CRUEL GREEDY TAKING
RAVENING RAVENOUS
RAPACITY RAVEN RAVIN CUPIDITY
EXTORTION
RAPE COLE ABUSE COLZA FORCE
NAVET NAVEW TOUCH ATTACK
FELONY RAPEYE TURNIP ASSAULT
DESPOIL NAVETTE OPPRESS
PLUNDER RAPTURE STUPRUM
COLESEED COLEWORT DISHONOR
STUPRATE SUPPRESS
RAPESEED COLZA RAVISON
RAPHUS DIDUS
RAPID GAY FAST CHUTE HASTY
MOSSO QUICK ROUND SAULT
SHARP SHUTE TOSTO WINGY RIFFLE
SPEEDY WINGED SCHNELL SKELPIN
STICKLE TANTIVY SLAPPING
SPEEDFUL
(—S IN RIVER) SAULT DALLES
RIFFLE STICKLE CATARACT
(MORE —) STRETTO
RAPIDITY HASTE SPEED RADEUR
CELERITY VELOCITY
RAPIDLY APACE CHEAP FLEETLY

HASTILY SPEEDILY QUICKFOOT
RAPIER TUCK TUKE BILBO ESTOC
SHARP STOCK VERDUN TOASTER
RAPINE FORCE RAVIN PILLAGE
PLUNDER VIOLENCE
RAPPAREE ROBBER CREAGHT
VAGABOND
RAPPORT ACCORD HARMONY
RELATION AGREEMENT
RAPSCALLION ROGUE RASCAL
VILLAIN HOSEBIRD VAGABOND
RAPT LOST WRAP TENSE INTENT
RAVISH TRANCE CARRIED ENGAGED
RAPTURE ABDUCTED ABSORBED
ECSTATIC
RAPTORES RAPACES
RAPTURE JOY BLISS DELIGHT
ECSTASY PAROXYSM RHAPSODY
RARA AVIS PHENIX RARITY WONDER
PHOENIX
RARE FINE REAL SELD THIN ALONE
EARLY GREAT ANTRIN CHOICE
GEASON INCONY SCARCE SEENIL
SELDOM SINDLE SUBTLE SULLEN
UNIQUE ANTERIN CURIOUS
TENUOUS UNUSUAL CRITICAL
SELDSEEN SINGULAR UNCOMMON
RAREFACTION POROSIS
RAREFIED HIGH THIN SUBTILE
ABSTRUSE AETHERED ESOTERIC
RAREFY THIN DILUTE EXTENUATE
RARELY SELDEN SELDOM
RARENESS RARITY TENUITY
SCARCITY
RARITY SWAN CURIO RELIC RARIETY
TENUITY RARENESS
(PL.) CURIOSA
RASCAL BOY CAD DOG IMP LOW
RAP BASE DUCK FILE KITE LOON
MEAN SHAG SMAK CATSO FILTH
GANEF GIPSY KNAVE ROGUE SCAMP
SHELM SLAVE SMAIK THIEF ABLACH
BRIBER BUDZAT BUGGER COQUIN
HARLOT LIMMER RABBLE RAGGIL
RIBALD SCHELM SORROW TINKER
BLEEDER CAMOOCH GLUTTON
HESSIAN NEBULON PEASANT
RAPTRIL SHELLUM SKEEZIX
SKELLUM VILLAIN HOSEBIRD
LIDDERON PALLIARD PICAROON
RAKEWELL RUBIATOR SKALAWAG
SPALPEEN TAISTREL VAGABOND
WIDDIFOW
RASCALITY FOIST RABBLE KNAVERY
ROGUING RASCALRY
RASCALLY BASE MEAN ROOKY
GALLUS LIMMER GALLOWS KNAVISH
RAGGILY SHAGRAG WIDDIFOW
RASE PULL RAIS RAZE ERASE PLUCK
INCISE SNATCH
RASH ID CUT BRASH HARDY HASTY
HEADY SLASH SLICE DARING
SUDDEN UNWARY URGENT BULRUSH
HOTSPUR RABBISH BLIZZARD
CARELESS ERUPTION EXANTHEM
HEADLONG HEEDLESS MADBRAIN
OVERSEEN PRESSING RECKLESS
TEMEROUS

RASHER SLICE COLLOP TRIFLE
COLOPPE
RASHLY HEADILY HEADLONG
RASHNESS RAGE RESE ACRISY
TEMERITY HEADINESS
RASKOLNIK POPOVETS
RASP RUB FILE RAPE ERUCT GRATE
TOOTH RAPEYE RUBBER RIFFLER
DENTICLE
(SHOEMAKER'S —) FLOAT
RASPBERRY AKPEK BAZOO MOLKA
AVARIN RASPIS PLUMBOG
ARNBERRY BLACKCAP BOGBERRY
CUTHBERT MULBERRY RESPASSE
ROSACEAN
RASPING HARSH ROUGH STOOR
STOUR HOARSE RASION RAZZLY
GRATING RAUCOUS GUTTERAL
(PL.) SCOBS
RASPY HARSH GRATING SCREAKY
SCRABBLY
RASSE CIVET WEASEL
RAT BUCK DAMN DRAT HEEL NOKI
ROTN SCAB VOLE KIORE LOUSE
METAD RATON SELVA ZEMMI ZEMNI
CRABER MURINE RODENT ROTTAN
SLEPEZ VERMIN YUNGAS CUSHION
CONFOUND INFORMER MYOMORPH
(INDIAN —) KOK
RATAPLAN RATTAN RATTLE
RATCH RASH REND ROCH SPOT
NOTCH STREAK RATCHET STRETCH
RATCHET DOG PAWL CLICK DETENT
ROCHET
RAT CHINCHILLA ABROCOME
RATE LAY RAG SET CESS CHOP GAIT
GIVE HAND KIND RANK RATA ABUSE
CULET CURVE PRIZE RATIO REBUT
SCOLD STENT STYLE VALUE ZAKAT
ASSIZE GALLOP ACCOUNT CARTAGE
DESERVE FASHION MILLAGE
REPROVE CLASSIFY ESTIMATE
QUANTIFY
(— HIGHLY) PRICE
(— OF ASCENT) GRADE
(— OF DRAINAGE) FREENESS
(— OF EXCHANGE) BATTA
(— OF INTEREST) DISCOUNT
(— OF MOTION) BAT SPEED
(— OF MOVEMENT) PACE TEMPO
(— OF RECKONING) FOOT
(— OF SPEED) BAT AGOGE
(— OF TRANSFER) FLUX
(— OF TUITION) CULET
(— SCHEDULE) TARIFF
(AT ANY —) HURE
(BIRTH —) NATALITY
RATE BOOK STREET
RATEL BADGER BURIER
RATH CAR HILL REUT RUTH EARLY
MOUND QUICK REUTE SWIFT
BETIMES CHARIOT YOUTHFUL
RATHER Y BUT GEY LIKE SOON
LOURD QUITE ASTITE BEFORE
FAIRLY HELDER KINDLY PRETTY
RUTHER SEEMLY TIDDER TITTER
EARLIER INSTEAD MIDDLING
SOMEWHAT
(— THAN) ERE BEFORE

RATIFICATION AMEN RATE
SANCTION
RATIFY AMEN PASS SEAL SIGN VISA
ENSEAL FASTEN OBSIGN APPROVE
CONFIRM SCEPTER CANONIZE
ROBORATE SANCTION
RATING E RANK CENSE CLASS
GRADE WRITER STANDING
RATIO Q PI GAIN RATE SINE SLIP
INDEX RESON SETUP SHEAR
ASPECT CAMBER DECADE QUOTUM
REASON REYSON SECANT AVERAGE
PORTION CONTRAST SOLIDITY
RATIOCINATION LOGIC THOUGHT
REASONING
RATION DOLE RATIO ALLOCATE
(**— OF BREAD**) TOMMY
(**ANIMAL —**) CHOW
(**EXTRA —S**) BUCKSHEE
(**HOG —**) SWILL
(**PL.**) FOOD BOUCH COMMON
RATIONAL SANE SOBER LOGICAL
REASONAL SENSIBLE THINKING
RATIONALIZE THOB EXPLAIN
RATITE EMU MOA KIWI RHEA
OSTRICH STRUTHIAN
RAT KANGAROO TUNGO POTOROO
SQUEAKER
RATOON SHOOT SPROUT SUCKER
RATTAIL MULE ARREST GRENADIER
RATTAN CANE SEGA ROTAN BEJUCO
ROTANG SWITCH RATTOON
RATTLE DIN BIRL BURL RICK TIRL
CLACK CROTAL GRAGER HENPEN
MARACA RACKLE RICKLE RIFFLE
ROTTLE RUCKLE RUTTLE CHACKLE
CLACKER CLAPPER CLATTER
CLICKET CREAKER GNATTER
GROGGER SHATTER SISTRUM
SKELLAT CAIXINHA CHOCALHO
COWWHEAT
(**CRIER'S —**) CLAPPER
(**IRON —**) SKELLAT SKILLET
RATTLER LIE ROMBLE RUMBLER
RATTLESNAKE BELLTAIL CASCABEL
CASCAVEL
(**— PLANTAIN**) NETLEAF RATSBANE
RATTLESNAKE ROOT BUGBANE
JOYLEAF
RATTLETRAP GEWGAW TRIFLE
RICKETY
RATTLING BRISK HUSKY SLAPPING
SPLENDID CREPITANT
RATTY NASTY SHABBY UNKEMPT
WORTHLESS
RATWA MUNTJAC
RAUCOUS LOUD HARSH COARSE
HOARSE SQUAWKY STRIDENT
RAUN ROE ROWN SPAWN
RAUPO CATTAIL
RAVAGE EAT PREY RIOT RUIN SACK
FORAY HARRY HAVOC SPOIL WASTE
FORAGE DESPOIL DESTROY
OVERRUN PILLAGE PLUNDER
DEFLOWER DESOLATE POPULATE
SPOLIATE
RAVE MAD RAGE RAND WOOD
AWEDE BLURB CRUSH RATHE
ROUSE STORM DELIRE WANDER

RAVEL FAG RUN FRAY FRET REYLE
SNARL EVENER LADDER RADDLE
RUNNER SLOUGH TANGLE CONFUSE
INVOLVE PERPLEX RAILING
UNWEAVE
RAVELIN RABLIN OUTWORK
DEMILUNE
RAVEN RALPH CORBEL CORBIE
CORBIN FORAGE RAVINE WAYBIRD
(**BRIGHT —**) BERTRAM
RAVENING CRUEL RABIES
RAVENOUS GREEDY LUPINE TOOTHY
WOLFISH RAPACIOUS VORACIOUS
RAVINE DEN GAP GUT LIN DELL
DRAW GILL GULL KHOR KHUD LINN
LLYN SIKE WADI BREAK BUNNY
CHASM CHINE CLOVE DONGA FLUME
GHYLL GLACK GORGE GOYAL
GOYLE GRIFF GRIKE GULCH GULLY
HEUCH KLOOF SLADE SLAKE STRID
ARROYO CLEUCH CLOUGH COULEE
DIMBLE DINGLE DUMBLE GULLEY
HOLLOW NULLAH RAMBLA SHEUGH
STRAIT BARRANCA QUEBRADA
RAVING RAVERY DELIRANT
FRENZIED DELIRIOUS
RAVISH ROB RAPE ABUSE CHARM
FORCE HARRY SPOIL ABDUCT
ATTACK DEFILE AFFORCE CORRUPT
DELIGHT ENFORCE OPPRESS
OUTRAGE OVERJOY PLUNDER
POLLUTE VIOLATE DEFLOWER
ENTRANCE STUPRATE SUPPRESS
UNMAIDEN
RAVISHER RAPTER RAVENER
RAVISHMENT ECSTASY RAPTURE
TRANSPORT
RAW RA ROW BRUT LASH RUDE
BLEAK CHILL CRUDE FRESH GREEN
HARSH NAKED RAFTY SHARP
BITTER COARSE CUTCHA KUTCHA
UNRIPE VULGAR WAIRSH NATURAL
NOUVEAU UNBOUND VERDANT
WEARISH WEERISH IMMATURE
RAWBONED UNCOOKED UNEDITED
VISCERAL
(**— AND COLD**) CRIMPY
RAWBONED RAW BONY LEAN
GAUNT LANKY SCRAG SCRAWNY
RAWHIDE WHIP WHANG COWHIDE
COWSKIN GREENHIDE PARFLECHE
RAWNESS CRUDITY
RAY BEAM BETA DORN SOIL WIRE
ALPHA BRAND DRESS EQUIP FLAIR
FLAKE FLATH GLEAM GLEED ORDER
RAYON ROKER SKATE BATOID
CHUCHO OBISPO RADIAL RADIUS
RAIOID SEPHEN STREAM TRYGON
VISUAL BATFISH COWFISH
DEWBEAM DRILVIS FIDDLER
HOMELYN PLACOID RAIMENT
TORPEDO WAIREPO BRACHIUM
MOONBEAM NUMBFISH PLOWFISH
PYLSTERT STINGRAY
(**— OF LIGHT**) GLINT SPEAR GLANCE
SUNRAY SUNBEAM
(**— OF STARFISH**) ARM
(**FEMALE —**) MAID
(**FIN —**) SPINE

RAYON BEAM RADIUS DUCHESS
RAZE CUT FLAT RUIN ARASE ERASE
LEVEL STREW ARRACE EFFACE
SCRAPE SLIGHT UNPILE DESTROY
SCRATCH SUBVERT UNBUILD
DEMOLISH
RAZOR SHIV TUSK MUSSEL RASOIR
SHAVER RATTLER SLASHER
CUTTHROAT
RAZORBACK STATE ARKANSAS
RAZOR-BILLED AUK FALK TINK
MURRE NODDY SCOOT SCOUT
SKOOT TINKER SKIMMER WILLOCK
ROCKBIRD
RAZOR CLAM PIROT RASOR SOLEN
SPOUT RASOIR
RAZZ CHIACK RIDICULE RASPBERRY
RAZZIA RAID FORAY INCURSION
RAZZING RAZOO
RE RAY ANENT ACTION MATTER
REGARDING
REACH GO GET HIT RAX RUN WIN
BEAT COME FIND GAIN HAWK HENT
MAKE REEK REIK RYKE SHOT SORT
SPAN SPIT TEND BRACE CROSS
FETCH GRASP PERCH RANGE
RETCH TOUCH ADVENE ARRIVE
ATTAIN DANGER EXTEND FATHOM
LENGTH OBTAIN SNATCH STREEK
STRIKE ACHIEVE COMPASS
CONTACT GUNSHOT OVERGET
POSSESS RECOVER STRETCH
(**— ACROSS**) SPAN OVERSTRIDE
(**— AN END**) STAY
(**— BY EFFORT**) ATTAIN
(**— BY FIGURING**) STRIKE
(**— FORTH**) EXTEND
(**— GOAL**) HAIL
(**— OUT**) UTTER SPREAD STRETCH
(**— TO**) LINE
(**— TOTAL**) AMOUNT
(**— UNDERSTANDING**) AGREE
(**— WITH END**) ABUT
(**EXTREME —**) PITCH STRETCH
(**TRY TO —**) ASPIRE
REACHER INGIVER
REACT ACT BUCK BEHAVE
RETROACT
REACTION BELT BUZZ KAHN WOHL
START WIDAL FAVISM RECOIL
BLOWOFF EMOTION FEELING
SETBACK BACKLASH EXCHANGE
GUARDING KICKBACK
(**— TIME**) LATENCY
(**VIOLENT —**) SONG
REACTIONARY WHITE BOURBON
BACKWARD
REACTIVATED AWAKE ACTIVE
REACTIVATOR ACTIFIER
REACTOR CHOKER FURNACE
INDUCTOR
READ GO CON KRI QRI SEE CALL
KERE QERI TURN CHOKE JUDGE
SOLVE WRITE PERUSE RELATE
FORESEE LEARNED LECTION
PREDICT ABOMASUM DECIPHER
FORETELL INDICATE OVERLOOK
(**— ALOUD**) LINE DEACON
(**— HERE AND THERE**) BROWSE

(— **MECHANICALLY**) RETINIZE
(— **OF**) SEE
(— **OFF**) DICTATE
(— **PROOF**) HORSE
(— **RAPIDLY**) DIP SKIM GOBBLE
(— **SLOWLY**) SPELL
(— **SYSTEMATICALLY**) FREQUENT
(— **WITH PROFOUND ATTENTION**)
PORE STUDY

READER PURSE DIPPER LECTOR
LISTER MAFTIR GRANTHI PISTLER
DEVOURER
(**CHILD'S** —) TENPENNY
(**CHURCH** —) LECTOR ANAGNOST
(PL.) FOLLOWING

READILY PAT YERN APTLY PREST
YERNE EASILY GAINLY PROBABLY
SPEEDILY

READINESS ART EASE GIFT PRESS
SKILL BELIEF GRAITH ADDRESS
FLUENCY FREEDOM ALACRITY
FACILITY GOODWILL
(**IN** —) APOISE AGAINST

READING KRI QRE QRI KERE KERI
QERI KTHIB KETHIB LESSON
LECTION LECTURE PERUSAL
SETTING
(PL.) PROCINCT

READING DESK AMBO LECTERN
READJUST MEND ADVANCE
READY UP APT BUN FIT RAD YAP
BAAN BAIN BOON BOWN FREE
GIRT GLIB GNIB RIFE RIPE TALL
YARE APERT EAGER FRACK HANDY
HAPPY PREDY PREST PRIME QUICK
SWIFT THERE TIGHT ADROIT
APPERT FACILE GRAITH HEARTY
PROMPT PRESENT RENABLE
WILLING CHEERFUL DEXTROUS
HANDSOME PREGNANT PREPARED
PROVIDED SKILLFUL
(— **FOR ACTION**) ARM EXPEDITE
(— **WITH WORDS**) FLUENT
(**NOT** —) SET BOUND GROOM
FORWARD DISPOSED IMPROMPT
INCLINED

READY-MADE SALE STORE BOUGHT
REAGENT ETCHANT REACTOR
ALTERANT REACTIVE

REAL BODY FAIR GOOD LEAL LEVY
PURE RIAL TRUE VERY VRAI PAKKA
PUCKA PUKKA RIGHT ROYAL SOLID
SOOTH ACTUAL ENTIRE HONEST
THINGY CORDIAL GENUINE GRADELY
SINCERE THINGAL CONCRETE
DEFINITE EXISTENT GRAITHLY
POSITIVE THINGISH
(**1-8TH** —) TLAC TLACO
(**EXTERNALLY** —) TANGIBLE

REALGAR ARSENIC ROSAKER
SANDARAC

REALISM REALITY LITERALISM
REALISTIC HARD SOBER VIVID
EARTHLY LIFELIKE PROBABLE

REALITY FEAT TRUE BEING SOOTH
THING TRUTH ACTUAL DASEIN
EFFECT VERITY SUBJECT IDENTITY
OVERSOUL REALNESS TRUENESS
(**LIMITED** —) SOMEWHAT

(**ULTIMATE** —) GOD SOURCE
DIVINITY SUBSTANCE
(PL.) REALIA

REALIZATION SENSE CRUSHER
FRUITION AWAKENING

REALIZE GAIN KNOW FETCH LEARN
SENSE EFFECT FULFIL ACQUIRE
CONCEIVE

REALIZED BODILY
(**FULLY** —) COMPLETE

REALLY ARU WIS ARAH HALF JUST
ARRAH TRULY WISHA FINELY
INDEED SIMPLY SURELY ACTUALLY
(**NOT** —) ILL ALMOST

REALM LAND SOIL BOURN CLIME
RANGE REIGN REWME RICHE
CIRCLE DEMAIN EMPIRE HEAVEN
REALTY REGION SPHERE DEMESNE
GAELDOM KINGDOM NOTALIA
ROYALME TERRENE CLUBLAND
DEVILDOM DOMINION ELDORADO
GHOSTDOM GIPSYDOM NOTOGAEA
(— **OF DARKNESS**) PO
(— **OF FABULOUS RICHNESS**)
ELDORADO
(— **OF THOR**) THRUTHHEIM
THRUTHVANG
(**MARINE** —) NOTALIA TROPICALIA
(**VISIONARY** —) CLOUDLAND

REALTY FEALTY REAUTE ROYALTY
REAM FOAM RIME SEED SKIM CHEAT
CREAM FROTH FRAISE RHYMER
STRETCH
(PL.) INSIDES OUTSIDES

REAMER BUR BURR SPUD DRIFT
RIMER BROACH CHERRY FRAISE
RANCER RHYMER RIMMER WIDENER

REANIMATE WAKE RENEW REVIVE
RECREATE

REANIMATED AWAKE
REAP BAG CUT REP CROP RIPE
GLEAN SHEAR GARNER GATHER
SICKLE HARVEST

REAPER LORD COCKER TASKER
WINNER CRADLER SICKLER
(**GRIM** —) DEATH

REAPING HOOK SICKLE TWIBIL
CROTCHET

REAPPEARANCE RENTREE
EMERSION

REAR AFT BACK HIND HINT JUMP
LIFT STEN TOSS BREED BUILD
CARVE ERECT JUNCH STEND
ACHTER AROUSE CRADLE FOSTER
NURSLE SUCKLE APPREAR ARRIERE
EDUCATE ELEVATE NOURISH
NURTURE UPBRING BUTTOCKS
HINDMOST REARWARD
(— **CAREFULLY**) TIDDLE
(**NEARER THE** —) AFTER
(**TO THE** — **OF**) ABAFT
(**TO THE** —) BACK BEHIND

REARED (— **BY HAND**) CADE
(**DELICATELY** —) SOYLED

REARHORSE MANTIS
REARING FRESNE PESADE FORCENE
RAMPANT
(— **UP**) STEND

REARRANGE DO ADJUST JIGGER

REORDER READJUST
REARRANGEMENT WAGNER
DIAGENESIS
REARWARD AFT BACKWARD
REASON PEG WAY HOTI NOUS REDE
SAKE TALK ARGUE CAUSE COUNT
LOGOS PROOF RATIO SCORE SENSE
SKILL THING THINK TOPIC EXCUSE
GROUND MANNER MATTER MOTION
NOESIS ACCOUNT PREMISE
QUARREL SUBJECT TUITION
ARGUMENT ENCHESON LOGICIZE
VERNUNFT
(— **FOR PRIDE**) BOAST
(**LACKING** —) INEPT

REASONABLE FAIR JUST SOBER
SKILFUL FEASIBLE MODERATE
RATIONAL SENSIBLE

REASONABLENESS EPIKY EPIKIKA
FITNESS FAIRNESS SOBRIETY

REASONABLY SOON
REASONER (**FALLACIOUS** —)
SOPHIST

REASONING LOGIC ERGOTISM
RATIONAL
(**CLUMSY** —) ARGAL
(**FALLACIOUS** —) CIRCLE SOPHISTRY

REASSEMBLE RELY
REASSUME REVOKE REPRISE
REAVE ROB REFE SEIZE SPLIT
REMOVE DESPOIL PILLAGE PLUNDER
UNRAVEL

REB RABBI REBEL MISTER
REBAB GUSLE
REBATE BLUNT CHECK LESSEN
RIBBET DIMINISH DISCOUNT
DRAWBACK KICKBACK

REBEC LYRE SAROD RIBIBE RUBIBLE
REBEKAH (**HUSBAND OF** —) ISAAC
(**SON OF** —) ESAU JACOB

REBEL REB KICK RISE TURN BRAND
FAUVE ANARCH CROPPY MUTINE
REVOLT FRONDEUR
(— **IN ART**) FAUVE
(PL.) REBELDOM

REBELLION MUTINY PUTSCH
REVOLT MISRULE UPRISING

REBELLIOUS RUSTY ANARCHIC
MUTINOUS AUDACIOUS INSURGENT

REBIRTH REVIVAL
REBOUND DAP HOP HANG KISS
STOT CANON CAROM STITE BOUNCE
CARROM RECOIL RESULT BRICOLE
REDOUND RICOCHET SNAPBACK
(— **ERRATICALLY**) KICK

REBOUND CLIP RETAINER
REBUFF SLAP SNIB SNUB CHECK
FLING REPEL DEFEAT DENIAL
REBUKE REBUTE REPULSE

REBUKE NIP WIG BAWL RATE REDD
SNEB SNIB SNUB TRIM BARGE
BLAME CHECK CHIDE DRESS SAUCE
SCOLD SNAPE SNEAP TOUCH
DIRDUM GANSEL LESSON RATING
RATTLE REHETE REMORD CHIDING
CORRECT HOTFOOT LECTURE
REPROOF REPROVE SARCASM
BLESSING BUSINESS CHASTISE
KEELHAUL REPROACH SCORCHER

THREAPEN UNDERNIM

REBUS BADGE ENIGMA PUZZLE
RIDDLE

REBUT REPEL RECOIL REFUTE
REPULSE RETREAT DISPROVE

RECALCITRANT UNRULY RENITENT
OBSTINATE RESISTANT

RECALL CITE BRING UNSAY REMAND
REMIND RETURN REVOKE UNLOOK
RECLAIM RETRACE RETRACT
REVIVAL UNSHOUT REMEMBER
WITHCALL WITHDRAW
(— **FONDLY**) CHERISH

RECANT UNSAY ABJURE REVOKE
UNSING DISAVOW RETRACT
SWALLOW PALINODE RENOUNCE

RECAPITULATE SUM UNITE RECITE
REPEAT RECOUNT REHEARSE
REITERATE SUMMARIZE

RECAPTURE RETAKE RECOVER

RECEDE DIE EBB BACK FADE STEP
VARY RECUR DEPART DIFFER
RETIRE SHRINK DECLINE DIGRESS
RETREAT CONTRACT DIMINISH
ELONGATE WITHDRAW

RECEIPT CHIT RECU RESET APOCHA
BINDER RECIPE WARRANT
(PL.) GATE TAKE SALES INCOME
ENTRADA

RECEIVE GET BEAR FALL GAIN HAVE
HOLD TAKE ADMIT AFONG CATCH
GREET GUEST LATCH RESET
ACCEPT ASSUME BORROW DERIVE
GATHER HARBOR RECULE BELIEVE
CONTAIN EMBRACE INHERIT
SUSTAIN UNDERFO PERCEIVE
(— **A CRIMINAL**) RESET
(— **AS GUEST**) FANG HOST VANG
GREET
(— **AS MEMBER**) INCEPT
(— **AS REWARD**) REAP
(— **FROM LOTTERY**) DRAW
(— **SHEETS**) FLY
(— **WITH PLEASURE**) GRATIFY

RECEIVER FENCE PHONE PERNOR
SINDICO CYMAPHEN DONATARY
REHEATER
(— **IN BANKRUPTCY**) SINDICO
(— **OF INCOME**) PERNOR
(— **OF STOLEN GOODS**) LOCK
FENCE
(**TELEGRAPH** —) INKER INKWRITER
(**TELEPHONE** —) PHONE CYMAPHEN

RECENSION REVIEW SURVEY
CENSURE CRITIQUE

RECENT HOT NEW LATE PUNY
ENDER FRESH GREEN HOURLY
LATELY LATTER MODERN CURRENT
HOLOCENE NEOTERIC
(**MOST** —) LAST

RECENTLY ANEW JUST LATE NEWLY
LASTLY LATELY FRESHLY LATTERLY

RECENTNESS YOUTH

RECEPTACLE ARK BIN BOX CAN
CUP DIP FAT PAN TIN TUB URN VAT
BATH BOAT BOWL CASE CELL CIST
DOVE DROP FACK FONT HELL HOLD
LOOM RACK RECU SAFE SINK TIDY
TOUR ARBOR CARRY CREEL KIOSK

KITTY RESET SCOOP STEAN STEEN
TABLE TORUS BASKET BUCKET
BUTLER CARTON CUPULE DIPPER
DRAWER HAMPER HOPPER MORTAR
PITCHI POCKET RECEIT SHRINE
TABLET TROUGH ASHTRAY CAPSULE
CARRIER CORBULA DUSTBIN
ENVELOP HEADBOX LATRINE
OMNIBUS OSSUARY PARISON
SANDBOX SETTLER SOAPBOX
STOWAGE TRAVOIS BURSICLE
CANISTER CESSPOOL FOREBOOT
GYNOBASE HONEYPOT LOCKFAST
OSSARIUM OVERFLOW PERFUMER
SPITTOON STOCKPOT SEPULCHER
(— **FOR ABANDONED INFANTS**)
TOUR
(— **FOR BONES**) OSSUARY
OSSARIUM
(— **FOR BROKEN TYPE**) HELL
(— **FOR BUTTER**) RUSKIN
(— **FOR COAL**) BUNKER
(— **FOR CONVEYING**) APRON
(— **FOR DRY ARTICLES**) FAT
(— **FOR FOUL THINGS**) SINK
(— **FOR GLASS BATCH**) ARBOR
(— **FOR HOLY WATER**) FONT
(— **FOR ORE-CRUSHING**) MORTAR
(— **FOR POKER CHIPS**) KITTY
(— **FOR SACRED RELICS**) TABLE
SHRINE TABLET SEPULCHRE
(— **FOR SAVINGS**) SOCK
(— **FOR SEWING MATERIALS**) TIDY
(— **FOR TREASURE**) HANAPER
(— **FOR TYPE CASES**) RACK
(— **FOR VOTES**) SITULA
(— **IN BOTTLE-MAKING MACHINE**)
PARISON
(— **OF CLAY OR STONE**) STEAN
STEEN
(— **ON WEIGHING SCALES**) PAN
(— **OVER ALTAR**) DOVE
(**CLAY** —) BOOT
(**DILATED** —) GYNOBASE
(**ELECTRICAL** —) BASEPLUG
(**INCENSE** —) ACERRA
(**OPEN** —) TRAY
(**PURSELIKE** —) BURSICLE
(**TAILOR'S** —) HELL
(**WOODEN** —) SEBILLA

RECEPTION TEA ROUT COURT
CRUSH DIFFA LEVEE SALON TREAT
ACCOIL DURBAR RUELLE SOIREE
SQUASH ACCUEIL COUCHEE
MATINEE OVATION PASSAGE
RECEIPT RECUEIL TEMPEST
FUNCTION GREETING PERNANCY
REACTION SOCIABLE
(— **AT BEDTIME**) COUCHEE
(— **OF NATIVE PRINCES**) DURBAR
(— **OF SOUND**) AUDIO
(**ARABIC** —) DIFFA
(**CORDIAL** —) WELCOME
(**CROWDED** —) SQUASH
(**FASHIONABLE** —) LEVEE SALON
(**WEDDING** —) INFARE

RECEPTIVE SENSORY OPENHANDED

RECEPTOR STOCK RECEIVER
DOMINATOR

RECERCELEE SARCELLY

RECESS ALA ARK BAY BOX COD
CUP PAN BOLE COVE DEEP HOLE
NOOK TRAP AMBRY BOSOM CANAL
CAVUM CLEFT CREEK HAVEN HITCH
INLET NICHE ORIEL PRESS SINUS
ALCOVE ANCONA CAVERN CENTER
CHAPEL CIRQUE CLOSET COFFER
CRANNY GROTTO INDENT LOCULE
RABBET REBATE BEDSITE CONCAVE
CREVICE LOCULUS MANHOLE
RETREAT SINKING INTERVAL
LOCKHOLE OVERTURE TABLINUM
TOKONOMA TRAVERSE VACATION
(— **BETWEEN CAPES**) BAY
(— **FOR FAMILY RECORDS**)
TABLINUM
(— **FOR HINGE LEAF**) PAN
(— **FOR PIECE OF SCULPTURE**)
ANCONA
(— **IN CHURCH WALL**) AMBRY
(— **IN COLON**) HAUSTRUM
(— **IN JAPANESE HOUSE**)
TOKONOMA
(— **IN MOUNTAIN**) CIRQUE
(— **IN ROCK**) HITCH
(— **IN SIDE OF HILL**) CORRIE
(— **IN SIDE OF ROOM**) ALA
(— **IN WALL**) BOLE NICHE ALCOVE
(— **ON STAGE**) CANOPY
(**INMOST** —) BOSOM
(PL.) FLASH

RECESSED SUNK SUNKEN

RECESSION BUST RETREAT

RECESSIVE BACKWARD RECEDING
RETIRING WITHDRAWN

RECHERCHE RARE CHOICE EXOTIC
CURIOUS PRECIOUS UNCOMMON
EXQUISITE

RECIDIVIST REPEATER

RECIPE RX FORM RULE FORMULA
RECEIPT

RECIPIENT HEIR DONEE ALMSMAN
DONATEE LAUREATE

RECIPROCAL CROSS COMMON
MUTUAL SECANT SEESAW
(— **OF A POISE**) RHE
(— **OF VISCOSITY**) FLUIDITY

RECIPROCATE REPAY RETURN
REQUITE RETROACT

RECIPROCITY SHU ISOPOLITY
MUTUALITY

RECITAL TALE ASHRE CITAL RECIT
STORY EXPOSE LITANY PARADE
REPEAT TIKKUN READING RELATION
(— **OF PRAYER**) GEULAH HAMOTZI
KEDUSHAH
(**UNTRUE** —) TALE

RECITATION DHIKR READING
RECITAL RHAPSODY

RECITATIVE SCENA CHANSON

RECITE SAY CARP TELL STATE
INTONE RECKON RELATE RENDER
REPEAT DECLAIM DECLINE DICTATE
NARRATE RECOUNT REHEARSE
(— **AS ELOCUTION EXERCISE**)
DECLAIM
(— **IN MONOTONE**) INTONE
(— **METRICALLY**) SCAN

(— **MONOTONOUSLY**) CHANT
CHAUNT
(— **NUMBERS**) COUNT
(— **PRAYERS**) BENSH DAVEN
(— **TIRESOMELY**) THRUM
(— **WITH GREAT EASE**) RUSH
RECITER SCALD SKALD ANTERI
DISEUR CONTEUR DISEUSE
HOMERIST ILIADIST RHAPSODE
RECITING CHARM
RECK RAK CARE DEEM PASS
MATTER REGARD CONCERN
CONSIDER ESTIMATE
RECKLESS RASH WILD FOLLE
PERDU MADCAP RACKLE SAVAGE
GALLOWS RAMSTAM CARELESS
HEADLONG HEEDLESS BLINDFOLD
RECKLESSLY FAST BLIND RAMSTAM
HEADLONG HEADFIRST
RECKON RET ARET CAST DATE ITEM
RATE RECK RELY TALE TELL TOTE
ALLOT AUDIT CLAIM CLASS COUNT
JUDGE PLACE RETTE SCORE TALLY
THINK ASSIGN FIGURE IMPUTE
NUMBER REPUTE TOTTLE ACCOUNT
ASCRIBE COMPUTE INCLUDE
PRETEND RECOUNT SUPPOSE
SUPPUTE CONSIDER ESTIMATE
(— **IN**) INCLUDE
RECKONING TAB BILL NICK POST
SHOT TAIL TALE COUNT SCORE
TALLY COMPOT LAWING REASON
TAILYE TOTTLE ACCOUNT DAYTALE
TAILZEE COMPUTUS
RECLAIM IN TAME OBJECT RECALL
REDEEM REFORM RESCUE SUBDUE
PROTEST RECOVER RESTORE
(— **FROM SAVAGE STATE**) CIVILIZE
RECLAIMANT GOEL
RECLINE LIE LIG LEAN LOLL REST
COUCH ACCUMB RECUMB UPLEAN
DISCUMB
(— **LANGUIDLY**) GAULSH
RECLUSE NUN MONK CULDEE
HERMIT REMOTE ASCETIC EREMITE
INCLUSA INCLUSE ANCHORET
INCLUSIS SECLUDED SOLITARY
(PL.) SECLUSE
RECOGNITION FAME SPUR HONOR
SENSE CREDIT STATUS FEELING
KENNING KNOWING AGNITION
SANCTION
(— **OF ACHIEVEMENT**) LAUREL
RECOGNIZE KEN SEE ESPY FACE
KNOW SPOT TELL ADMIT ALLOW
BLINK CROWN HONOR KEETH KITHE
KYTHE ACCEPT ACKNOW AGNIZE
BEKNOW COUTHE REVISE CORRECT
DISCERN REALIZE ACCREDIT
(— **IN ANY CAPACITY**) AGNIZE
RECOGNIZED GOOD CLEAR KNOWN
CLASSIC FAMILIAR
RECOIL SHY BALK KICK TURN REBUT
SHRUG SHUCK START STRAM
BLENCH BOUNCE FLINCH RECULE
RESILE RESULT RETORT SHRINK
REBOUND REDOUND REVERSE
BACKLASH REJOUNCE
(**WITHOUT** —) DEADBEAT

RECOLLECT RECALL RECORD
RETAIN COMPOSE RECOVER
RECOLETO REMEMBER
RECOLLECTION MIND MEMORY
RECALL RECORD MINDING THOUGHT
MEMORIAL SOUVENIR
RECOMMENCE RENEW REOPEN
RESUME REPRISE
RECOMMEND MOVE OSSE PLUG
TOUT WISH ADVISE COMMIT PRAISE
PREFER COMMEND CONSIGN
COUNSEL ENTRUST ADVOCATE
RECOMMIT
RECOMMENDATION CHIT VOEU
ADVISE COUNSEL TESTIMONY
(**PARTY** —) COUPON
(**SERVANT'S** —) CHIT
RECOMPENSE PAY MEED MEND
MENSE QUITS REPAY YIELD AMENDS
BOUNTY HADBOT REWARD SALARY
GUERDON IMBURSE PAYMENT
PREMIUM REQUITE RESTORE
SATISFY SERVICE
RECONCILE GREE WEAN ADAPT
AGREE ATONE ACCORD ADJUST
SETTLE SHRIVE REUNITE
HARMONIZE
RECONCILED FAIN VAIN SAUGHT
RECONCILIATION ATONE ACCORD
SAUGHT REUNION IRENICON
RECONDITE DARK DEEP HIGH
HIDDEN MYSTIC OCCULT SECRET
CRYPTIC CURIOUS OBSCURE
RETIRED ABSTRACT ABSTRUSE
ESOTERIC
RECONNAISSANCE RECCE RECCO
RECCY SURVEY
RECONNOITER SCOUT RECALL
SURVEY EXAMINE PICKEER
DISCOVER REMEMBER
RECONSIDER REVIEW FORTHINK
RECONSTRUCT REPAIR REEVOKE
REMODEL RESTORE
RECORD CAN CUT BOOK CARD DATE
DISC ITER NICK PAGE ROLL SING
SLIP WICK ALBUM CHART DIARY
ENACT ENTER ENTRY FASTI GRAPH
JUMBO PRICK QUIPO QUIPU SIJIL
SLATE STYLE TITLE ANNALS
CHARGE DOCKET LEGEND MEMOIR
SCROLL SPREAD WARBLE ACCOUNT
CALENDS CITATOR DUBBING
KALENDS LEXICON MENTION
MYOGRAM SHOWING TICKLER
TRACING ANAGRAPH ARCHIVES
CYLINDER ENTRANCE ERGOGRAM
HERDBOOK INSCROLL JUDGMENT
KYMOGRAM LAUEGRAM MARIGRAM
MELOGRAM MEMORIAL MONUMENT
ONDOGRAM PANCHART PRESSING
REGISTER REMEMBER SCHEDULE
STUDBOOK
(— **BY NOTCHES**) SCORE
(— **OF CAR MOVEMENTS**) JUMBO
(— **OF DOCUMENT**) PROTOCOL
(— **OF EVENTS**) FASTI
(— **OF HUMANITY'S FATE**) SIJIL
SIJILL

(— **OF JOURNEY**) JOURNAL
ITINERARY
(— **OF LOAN**) CHARGE
(— **OF MUHAMMAD'S SAYINGS**)
HADIT
(— **OF MUSCULAR WORK**)
ERGOGRAM
(— **OF PROCEEDINGS**) ACTA ITER
JOURNAL MINUTES
(**COURT** —) EYRE
(**DAILY** —) DIARY
(**FORMAL** —) ACT
(**HISTORICAL** —) STORY
(**PHONOGRAPH** —) DISC DISK
SINGLE BISCUIT SHELLAC
(**SHIP'S** —) LOG
(PL.) LIBER ANNALS ARCHIVE
RECORDER FLUTE BOOKER FLAUTO
NOTATOR GREFFIER REGISTER
RECORDING ALBUM ALIVE LABEL
CUTTING
RECOUNT MING TELL COUNT DEVISE
RECITE REGARD RELATE REPEAT
SPREAD EXPRESS HISTORY
NARRATE CONSIDER DESCRIBE
REHEARSE
RECOUP DEDUCT REGAIN RECOVER
INDEMNIFY
RECOUPLING HOOKUP
RECOURSE SUIT ACCESS REFUGE
RESORT STRING REGRESS RESTAUR
RISORSE
(**HAVE** —) RECUR
RECOVER DOW COUR COWR CURE
FIRM HEAL KERE COVER REACH
UPSET BOUNCE RECURE REGAIN
RESCUE RESUME RETAKE RETIRE
REVERT REVOKE WARISH DELIVER
OVERGET OVERPUT OVERSET
READEPT RECLAIM RECRUIT
REPAREL REPRISE RESTORE
RETRIEVE
RECOVERER DIGESTER
RECOVERY CURE RECOUR RECURE
REMEDY RETURN SALVAGE
COMEBACK SNAPBACK
RECREANT FALSE CRAVEN YELLOW
APOSTATE COWARDLY DESERTER
RECRAYED
RECREATE AMUSE EVOKE REVIVE
RECREATION PLAY SPORT SOLACE
RENEWAL ACTIVITY DIVERSION
PALINGENY
(**PERIOD OF** —) HOLIDAY VACATION
RECREATIVE PLAYING
RECREMENT SLAG DROSS SCORIA
RECRUIT BLEU BOOT FRESH RAISE
GATHER INTAKE MUSTER RECREW
REPAIR REVIVE RECOVER REFRESH
RESTORE ASSEMBLE BEZONIAN
CONSCRIPT
(**RAW** —) ROOKY ROOKIE
RECTANGLE BOX SQUARE CHECKER
(**COTTON** —) HUIPIL
(**CURVILINEAR** —) TESSERA
(**WOVEN** —) SINKER
RECTANGULAR SQUARE BOXLIKE
EMERALD
RECTIFICATION LIMATION

RECTIFIER DIODE COLUMN DETECTOR EXCITRON

RECTIFY AMEND EMEND RIGHT ADJUST BETTER DETECT REFORM REMEDY CORRECT IMPROVE REDRESS EMENDATE REGULATE

RECTITUDE DOOM EQUITY JUSTICE PROBITY

RECTOR RULER LEADER PARSON PERSONA INCUMBENT

RECTUM SIEGE TEWEL

RECUMBENT IDLE JACENT CUMBENT LEANING RESTING INACTIVE REPOSING

RECUPERATE RALLY REFETE REGAIN RECOVER RECRUIT RETRIEVE

RECUR CYCLE REFER REPEAT RESORT RETURN REOCCUR REVOLVE REAPPEAR
(— **CONSTANTLY**) HAUNT

RECURRENCE RESORT RETURN ATAVISM REPRISE ITERANCE ITERANCY RECOURSE
(— **OF SOUND**) CADENCE

RECURRENT CYCLIC FREQUENT

RECURRING ROLLING CONTINUAL
(— **ANNUALLY**) ETESIAN
(— **EVERY THIRD DAY**) TERTIAN
(— **ON NINTH DAY**) NONAN NONANE
(— **ON SEVENTH DAY**) SEPTAN
(**CONSTANTLY** —) ETERNAL
(**CONTINUALLY** —) CONSTANT

RECURVED ERICOID

RECUTTING FRESHING

RED (ALSO SEE COLOR) GOYA GULY PINK PUCE ROJO ROSY RUBY ANGRY CANNA CORAL FIERY JUDAS ROUGE RUDDY RUFUS ARCHIL AZALEA BLOODY CERISE FLORID FULGID GARNET HECTIC NECTAR ORCHIL ORIENT RAISIN RUBRIC TITIAN TRYPAN VERMIL WANTON CARMINE GLOWING NACARAT PIMENTO RADICAL RUBELLE RUBIOUS STAMMEL VERMILY ARMENIAN AUBUSSON BORDEAUX CARDINAL CHOLERIC COLORADO FLAGRANT MANDARIN MOROCAIN RUBICUND SANGUINE ARTILLERY
(— **AND INFLAMED**) BLOODSHOT
(— **PLANET**) MARS
(**ANTIQUE** —) CANNA
(**BRIGHT** —) TULY CHERRY PUNICIAL VERMILION
(**DARK** —) CLARET
(**EUREKA** —) PUCE
(**FIERY** —) MINIUM
(**GRAYISH** —) AZALEA
(**HERALDIC** —) GULES
(**IRON OXIDE** —) AGATE TARRAGONA
(**PURPLISH** —) LAKE MAGENTA
(**WAX** —) COPPER
(**YELLOWISH** —) MAROON

RED ADMIRAL VANESSA

RED-BACKED SHRIKE POPE

RED BANEBERRY REDBERRY TOADROOT

RED BAY PERSEA

RED-BELLIED (— **TERRAPIN**) SLIDER SKILPOT
(— **WOODPECKER**) CHAB

RED-BREASTED BREAM FLATFISH FLOUNDER

RED-BREASTED KNOT GRAYBACK GREYBACK

REDBUD CERCIS JUNEBUD

RED CAMPION ROBIN SOLDIER

RED CEDAR SAVIN SABINA JUNIPER

RED CLOVER SAPLING TREFOIL TRIFOLY

RED CURRANT GOYA RIZZLE TIZZAR

REDD RID COMB OPEN LITTER NEATEN REFUSE RESCUE SETTLE ARRANGE DELIVER SMARTEN UNBLOCK UNRAVEL

RED DEER OLEN STAG
(**FEMALE** —) HIND
(**MALE** —) HART STAG

REDDEN RUD FIRE RUBY BLUSH FLUSH LIGHT ROUGE RUDDY BLOODY RUBIFY RUBRIC RUDDLE EMPURPLE

REDDISH REDDY RUDDY RUFUS FLUSHY RUFOUS COLORADO PYRRHOUS

RED DRUM SPOT REDFISH

REDEEM BUY WIN SAVE ALESE CLEAR REPRY BORROW OFFSET RANSOM DELIVER FULFILL JUSTIFY RECLAIM WITHBEG AGAINBUY LIBERATE

REDEEMER GOEL SAVIOR

REDEMPTION RANSOM REFORM SAFETY SALVATION

REDEYE BASS RUDD VIREO WHISKY SUNFISH

RED-EYE CATSUP CICADA WHISKY

RED-EYED VIREO REDEYE GRASSET PREACHER

RED-FACED FLUSHED SCARLET

REDFIN DACE SHINER REDHORSE YELLOWFIN

REDFISH SALMON FATHEAD ROSEFISH

RED GOOSEFOOT PIGWEED SOWBANE

RED GROUPER MERO NEGRE REDBELLY

RED GROUSE GORHEN GORCOCK LAGOPODE MOORBIRD MUIRFOWL

RED GUM JARRAH EUCALYPT

RED GURNARD CUR ELLECK ROCHET SOLDIER

REDHAIRED RUFUS

REDHEAD DIVER FINCH POCHARD KIZILBASH

RED HIND GRAYSBY GROUPER CABRILLA

REDHORSE REDFIN SUCKER

REDIA SPOROSAC

REDIRECT DISPLACE READDRESS

REDISTILL COHOBATE

REDISTRIBUTE FRESHEN REASSIGN

RED LAVER SLOKE

REDNESS RED RUD GLOW HEAT

RUDD RUBOR ERYTHEMA RUBEDITY
(— **OF SKY**) AURORA

REDO REDACT RESTYLE
(— **UNSKILLFULLY**) BOTCH

RED OCHER TIVER ABRAUM RUDDLE

REDOLENCE BALM AROMA SCENT

REDOLENT RICH ODOROUS SCENTED AROMATIC FRAGRANT SMELLING

RED OSIER WILLOW REDBRUSH

REDOUBT FEAR MASK DREAD SCHANZ SCONCE

REDOUBLE REECHO INTENSIFY

REDOUND TURN ACCRUE BILLOW CONDUCE REFLECT OVERFLOW

RED RASPBERRY CUTHBERT

REDRESS HEAL DRESS REDUB AVENGE OFFSET REFORM RELIEF REMEDE REMEDY REPAIR ADDRESS CORRECT RECTIFY REFOUND RELIEVE

RED ROCKFISH TAMBOR

RED SAGE LANTANA

RED SANDALWOOD CHANDAM

REDSHANK CLEE TEUK SHAKE GAMBET REDLEG YELPER PELLILE TATTLER

REDSKIN RED ROJO TAWNY INDIAN

REDSTART YELPER BRANTAIL FIRETAIL WHITECAP FIREFLIRT

RED STOPPER EUGENIA IRONWOOD

RED-TAILED (— **HAWK**) REDTAIL
(— **TROPIC BIRD**) KOAE

RED-TAPISM BEADLEDOM

RED-THROATED LOON WABBY

REDTOP COUCH FIORIN FINETOP FINEBENT FURZETOP BLUEJOINT

REDUCE CUT BATE DOCK DROP EASE PARE PULL THIN ABASE ABATE ALLAY APPAL BREAK DRAFT ELIDE LOWER QUELL SCANT SHAVE SLAKE SLASH SMELT DEDUCE DEFALK DEJECT DELETE DEPOSE DILUTE HUMBLE LESSEN REBATE REDUCT SHRINK SUBACT SUBDUE WEAKEN ABANDON ABRIDGE ASSUAGE ATOMIZE CHANCER CONQUER CURTAIL DEFLATE DEGRADE DEPLETE DWINDLE ECLIPSE FRITTER INHIBIT RESOLVE RETREAT SCISSOR SHORTEN SUBJECT ATTEMPER CONDENSE DECREASE DIMINISH MINIMIZE
(— **ACCORDING TO FIXED RATIO**) SCALE
(— **ANGLE**) CHAMFER
(— **BULK**) BLEND
(— **LUMBER**) SIZE
(— **PROFITS**) SQUEEZE
(— **PURITY**) ALLOY
(— **STONE BLOCKS**) SPALL SPAWL
(— **THE VALUE**) DECRY BEGGAR DEPRAVE
(— **TO A MEAN**) AVERAGE
(— **TO ASHES**) CREMATE
(— **TO CARBON**) CHAR
(— **TO FINE PARTICLES**) ATOMIZE
(— **TO FLAT SURFACE**) LEVEL
(— **TO INSIGNIFICANCE**) DROWN

(— **TO LOWER GRADE**) BREAK DEMOTE DEGRADE
(— **TO NIL**) CLOSE
(— **TO NOTHING**) ANNUL
(— **TO PASSIVITY**) CHINAFY
(— **TO POWDER**) GRIND PULVERIZE
REDUCED SUNK TAIL BROKEN DWARFED DEGRADED WEAKENED VESTIGIAL
REDUCTION BUST LETUP SLASH CUTBACK CUTDOWN DOCKAGE SHAVING ANALYSIS DILUTION DISCOUNT SHRINKAGE
(— **IN FORCE**) RIF
(— **IN PITCH**) DROP
(— **IN PRICE**) SAVING CONCESSION
REDUNDANCY EXCESS NIMIETY SURPLUS PLEONASM PLETHORA VERBIAGE TAUTOLOGY
REDUNDANT WORDY LAVISH PROFUSE SURPLUS VERBOSE SWELLING EXCESSIVE
REDWING POP THRUSH WINDLE GADWALL WINNARD
REDWOOD MAD AMBOYNA BARWOOD FURIOUS SEQUOIA MAHOGANY
RE-ECHO REWORD REBOUND RESOUND REDOUBLE
REED NAL RIE RIX SAG BENT JUNK PIPE PIRN RODE SLEY TULE ARROW DONAX SPEAR TWILL BENNEL RADDLE SAGGON CALAMUS FISTULA WHISTLE WINDING
(— **FOR WARPING**) WRAITHE
(— **FOR WINDING THREAD**) PIRN SPOOL
(— **IN ORGAN**) VIBRATOR
(— **OF LOOM**) COMB
(**FOXTAIL** —) DOD
(**GIANT** —) DONAX
(**MUSICAL** —) OAT
(**WEAVER'S** —) SLAY SLEY RADDLE SLEIGH
(**PL.**) SPEAR
REED BENT CARRIZO
REEDBIRD BOBOLINK
REEDBUCK BOHOR NAGOR REITBOK
REED BUNTING RINGBIRD
REED CANARY GRASS SPIRE DAGGERS
REED END TONGUE
REEDING GADROON MILLING STRIGIL GRAINING
REED MACE RAUPO CATTAIL MATREED
REED ORGAN MELODEON HARMONIUM
REED PIPE MIRLITON
REED WARBLER PITBIRD
REEDY THIN WEAK FRAIL TWILLED
REEF CAY KAY KEY CAYO LODE RYFT VEIN ATOLL LEDGE SHELF STICK BOILER REEFER SADDLE SKERRY BAGREEF BALANCE BIOHERM MAKATEA TOMBOLO
REEFER CAR COAT STICK JACKET MUGGLES
REEK FOG FUG EMIT FUME HEAP

MIST PILE RICK RISE VENT EQUIP EXUDE ISSUE NIDOR SMEEK SMOKE STEAM VAPOR EXHALE OUTFIT EMANATE
(— **WITH CORRUPTION**) FESTER
REEL PIRN ROCK SPIN SWAB SWIM TURN GIDDY SPOOL SWIFT TRULL WAVER WHEEL WHIRL WINCE BOBBIN RECOIL SWERVE TUMULT WAGGLE WALTER WELTER WINDER WINDLE WINNLE WINTLE BALLOON STAGGER SWABBLE TITUBATE
(— **FOR DRAWING SILK**) FILATURE
(— **FOR WARP DRYING**) BALLOON
(— **FOR WINDING YARN**) PIRN SWIFT
(— **OFF A STORY**) SCRIEVE
(— **USED FOR YARN**) CRIB
(**DYEING** —) WINCE
(**FISHING** —) TROW TROLL TRULL WINCH
(**PL.**) REVELS
REELER TWINER
REELING TURN AREEL STAGGERY WAMBLING
REEM MOAN URUS UNICORN
REEVE REE REFE THREAD BAILIFF PROVOST STEWARD OVERSEER
REFECTION MEAL RELIEF REPAST
REFECTORY FRATER FRATRY
REFER DEFER LEAVE POINT ADVERT ALLUDE APPEAL ASSIGN CHARGE COMMIT DELATE DIRECT IMPUTE PREFER RELATE SUBMIT ASCRIBE REJOURN RELEGATE
(— **TO SOMETHING REPEATEDLY**) HARP
(— **TO**) SEE CITE INTEND CONCERN CONSULT MENTION INTIMATE
REFEREE BREHON UMPIRE ARBITER AUDITOR
REFERENCE TAB FOLIO REMIT SIGIL APPEAL REGARD RENVOI MEANING RESPECT ALLUSION HANDBOOK INNUENDO RELATION
(**SATIRICAL** —) GLANCE
REFERENDUM POLL MANDATE
REFINE RUN TRY BOLT EDIT FILE FINE PURE CUPEL EXALT PLAIN SLICK SMELT AFFINE DECOCT EXCOCT FILTER GARBLE SMOOTH CONCOCT ELEVATE SUBLIME SWEETEN HUMANIZE URBANIZE
(— **AS GOLD**) TEST CARAT
(— **PULP**) JORDAN
(— **SUGAR**) CLAY
(— **WINE**) FORCE
REFINED FINE GENT NEAT NICE TRIE EXACT PURED TERSE CHASTE EXCOCT INLAND NIMINY POLITE QUAINT SUBTLE CLEANLY COURTLY ELEGANT GENTEEL PRECISE SCRAPED DELICATE ELEVATED HIGHBRED PRECIEUX SERAPHIC
(**NOT** —) CRUDE
(**TOO** —) FINESPUN
REFINEMENT GRACE POLISH CULTURE FINESSE DELICACY ELEGANCE POLITURE SUBTLETY URBANITY

REFINER TRIER JORDAN PURIFIER
REFINING HUMAN FINING CULTURE AFFINAGE
REFINISH ANTIQUE
REFLECT COW MUSE PORE SHOW BLAZE FLASH GLASS GLINT IMAGE SHINE STUDY THINK DAZZLE DEBATE MIRROR PONDER RECORD REFLEX RELUCE RETORT RETURN REVISE STEVEN EXPRESS REDOUND REFRACT SHIMMER COGITATE CONSIDER MEDITATE REDOUBLE RUMINATE
(— **IRREGULARLY**) SCATTER
(— **UPON**) SPECULATE
REFLECTED DERIVED MIRRORED SPECULAR
REFLECTION ECHO FOLD IDEA SKIT BLAME GHOST GLARE GNOME DEBATE MUSING PONDER REFLEX RETURN SHADOW CENSURE COUNSEL SPECIES THOUGHT EYESHINE MOONPATH THINKING
(— **OF SELF IN ANOTHER'S EYES**) BABY
REFLECTIVE PENSIVE THOUGHTFUL
(— **POWER**) ALBEDO
REFLECTOR FLAT CRITIC HASTER SHINER HORIZON DIFFUSER HASTENER SPECULUM
REFLEX COPY IMAGE TROPISM ALLUSION
(**NOT** —) IDEOMOTOR
REFLUX EBB EBBING REFLOW
REFOREST REBOISE
REFORM MEND AMEND EMEND PRUNE BETTER REBUKE REPAIR CENSURE CORRECT DISBAND RECLAIM RECTIFY REDRESS
REFORMATORY COLLEGE MAGDALEN
REFORMER APOSTLE UTOPIAN UTOPIAST JANSENIST
REFRACT DIVIDE REFLECT REFRINGE
REFRACTION REBATE REBOUND DIACLASIS
REFRACTORY SULLEN UNRULY WANTON ALUNDUM FROWARD RESTIVE VICIOUS WAYWARD MUTINOUS PERVERSE STUBBORN CAMSTEERY
REFRAIN BOB TAG CURB DOWN KEEP SHUN AVOID FORGO SPARE WONDE BURDEN CHORUS DESIST FOREGO LUDDEN RETAIN THRAIN ABSTAIN FORBEAR LULLABY REFREIT TORNADA FALDERAL OVERCOME OVERWORD REPETEND RESTRAIN WITHDRAW
(— **FROM INDULGENCE**) ABSTAIN
(— **FROM TELLING**) LAYNE
(— **FROM USING**) BOYCOTT
(— **FROM**) CAN HELP AVOID SPARE WAIVE FOREGO RESIGN
(— **OF SONG**) BOB TAG DOWN FOOT WHEEL BURDEN CHORUS FALDEROL
(**MEANINGLESS** —) DERRY
REFRESH FAN COOL REST CHEER

FRESH SLAKE CAUDLE REFECT REFETE REHETE REPOSE REVIVE UNTIRE COMFORT FORTIFY FRESHEN QUICKEN RECRUIT IRRIGATE RECREATE

REFRESHING DEWY BALMY FRESH TONIC CALLER LIVING COOLING

REFRESHMENT BAIT LUNCH CHARITY NUNCHEON REFRESCO COLLATION
(PL.) FOURS

REFRIGERANT ICE COOLER AMMONIA COOLING CRYOGEN

REFRIGERATE CHILL

REFRIGERATOR FRIG FRIDGE ICEBOX FREEZER CONDENSER
(— CAR) REEFER

REFUGE ARK HOME PORT ROCK SOIL BIELD GRITH HAVEN RESET ASYLUM BILBIE COVERT HARBOR REFUTE RESORT SPITAL SUCCOR ALSATIA CRANNOG RESERVE RETREAT SHELTER UMBRAGE WARRANT CRANNOGE FORTRESS HIDEAWAY MAGDALEN RESOURCE SAFEHOLD

REFUGEE REFFO COWBOY FUIDHIR FUGITIVE

REFULGENT BRIGHT SHINING RELUCENT BRILLIANT

REFUND REPAY UPSET REFOUND RESTORE DRAWBACK KICKBACK

REFURBISH DUST RENEW REVAMP FRESHEN BRIGHTEN RENOVATE

REFUSAL NAY VEE WARN WONT DENIAL MITTEN NAYSAY REPULSE ACCISMUS DECLINAL NEGATION
(— TO SPEAK) APHRASIA

REFUSE NAY NIL SUD BALK COOM DENY DUST JUNK KEMP NAIT NILL NITE PELF PELT REDD SCUM SKIM SOIL SUDS WARN BAVIN COOMB CRAWN DEADS DRAST DROSS EXPEL FLOCK NITTE OFFAL RENAY REPEL SCRAN STENT STUFF SWASH SWILL TRADE TRASH WAIVE WASTE COLDER DANDER DEBRIS FORBID LITTER LUMBER MIDDEN NAYSAY PALTRY PELTRY RAFFLE RECUSE REFUGE REJECT SCRUFF SCULCH SHORTS SORDES SORDOR SPILTH BACKING BAGGAGE BROCKLE DECLINE DETRACT DETRECT DISAVOW DISOBEY FORSAKE GARBAGE GUBBINS MULLOCK OFFSCUM OUTCAST PRUNING SOILAGE SULLAGE WITHNAY WITHSAY CRASSIER DENEGATE DISALLOW DISCLAIM GARBLING LEAVINGS RIFFRAFF SWEEPAGE WITHHOLD
(— ADMISSION) CLOSE
(— FROM CHARCOAL OR COKE) BREEZE
(— FROM COFFEE BERRIES) TAILINGS
(— FROM CUTTING UP WHALE) GURRY
(— FROM MELTING METALS) SLAG DROSS SCORIA

(— FROM SIFTING COFFEE-BEANS) TRIAGE
(— FROM THRESHING) HUSK COLDER
(— GREASE) COOM COOMB
(— OF MINE) DEAD
(— OF CROP) STOVER
(— OF FLAX) PAB POB HARDS HURDS
(— OF FRUITS) MUST
(— OF GRAIN) PUG
(— OF GRAPES) MARC
(— OF INSECT) FRASS
(— OF OIL MILLS) SHODE
(— OF SILK) STRASS
(— OF SPICES) GARBLE
(— OF WHALE) GURRY TWITTER
(— OF WOOL) BACKINGS
(— TO APPROVE) VETO
(— TO GO) JIB BALK
(— TO RECOGNIZE) CUT
(— TO SUPPORT) BOLT
(— TO TALK) DUMMY
(BREWERY —) DRAFF
(FISH —) CHUM GUBBINS
(FOOD —) SWILL
(LEATHER —) SPETCHES
(PLANT —) SCROFF
(STREET —) FULLAGE

REFUTATION DISPROOF ELENCHUS HYPOBOLE

REFUTE DENY AVOID REBUT REFEL ASSOIL CONFUTE CONVELL CONVICT REPROVE REVINCE CONFOUND DISPROVE INFRINGE REDARGUE

REGAIN READEPT RECOVER RETRIEVE
(— SOMETHING LOST) RECOUP

REGAL REAL ROYAL KINGLY PURPLE RIGGAL RIGOLE STATELY IMPERIAL MAJESTIC PRINCELY REGALIAN SPLENDID

REGALE FETE FEAST TREAT PLEASE DELIGHT REFRESH

REGALIA KIT ROYALTY

REGALO GIFT BONUS TREAT

REGARD CON CARE DEEM FIND GAZE GIVE HEED HOLD LIKE LOOK MARK MIND RATE RECK TELL YEME ADORE COUNT FAVOR HONOR TREAT WEIGH ADMIRE ASPECT BEHOLD ESTEEM FIGURE GLANCE HOMAGE IMPUTE INTEND LIKING MOTIVE NOTICE RECKON REMARK REWARD SURVEY ACCOUNT ADJUDGE OBSERVE RESPECT RESPITE CONSIDER ENVISAGE ESTIMATE
(— AS HOPELESS) DEPLORE
(— AS OBJECT OF GREAT INTEREST) LIONIZE
(— AS PROPER) ACCEPT
(— AS) SEE
(— HIGHLY) ADMIRE CONSIDER
(— WITH PROFOUND RESPECT) REVERE VENERATE
(— WITH REPUGNANCE) ABHOR
(ATTENTIVE —) EYE

(MENTAL —) EYE
(PL.) COMPLIMENTS

REGARDED (— WITH AFFECTION) DEAR AFFECTED

REGARDING ABOUT ANENT APROPOS

REGARDLESS DEAF CARELESS HEEDLESS RECKLESS
(— OF THAT) BUT

REGATTA HENLEY LIBERTY

REGENCY RULE DOMINION

REGENERATE RENEW REFORM REVIVE RECLAIM GRACIOUS RENOVATE
(NOT —) CIVIL

REGENT RULER RULING WARDEN SHIKKEN GOVERNOR PANGERANG
(— DIAMOND) PITT
(— OF NORTH) KUBERA KUVERA

REGIME FASCISM CAFETERIA

REGIMEN CURE DIET KEEP RULE REGIMENT

REGIMENT BUFF RULE COLOR TERCIO GUIDANCE INFANTRY SLASHERS
(28TH —) SLASHERS
(BRITISH —) GRAYS GREYS
(COSSACK —) PULK
(FRAMEWORK OF —) CADRE
(INDIA —) PULTON PULTUN
(SPANISH —) TERCIO
(TURKISH —) ALAI

REGION DO ERD EYE GAU WON AREA BELT KITH KNOT PART SOIL WONE WOON ZONE CLIME COAST EARTH EXURB INDIA MARCH PAGUS PLACE PLAGE REALM SHIRE TRACT TROAD ALKALI BORDER CENTER DESERT DOMAIN EXTENT GILEAD GROUND GUIANA TATARY CLIMATE CONFINE COUNTRY DEMESNE ENCLAVE IMAMATE KINGDOM MALABAR STATION TARTARY CHIEFDOM CLUBLAND DEMERARA DISTRICT ENVIRONS EPISTOME FLATLAND FORTRESS FRONTIER KRATOGEN LAKELAND LATITUDE NAPHTALI PROVINCE REGIMENT SERICANA STANNARY
(— ABOVE MOUTH) EPISTOMA EPISTOME
(— ADJACENT TO BOUNDARY) MARCH
(— BEYOND ATMOSPHERE) SPACE
(— BEYOND DEATH) CANAAN
(— BORDERING ON HELL) LIMBO
(— FAR AWAY) STRAND
(— NEAR EQUATOR) DOLDRUMS
(— NOTED FOR MANY CONFLICTS) COCKPIT
(— OF AMPLITUDE) ANTINODE
(— OF COLD AND DARKNESS) NIFLHEL NIFLHEIM
(— OF DEAD) AMENTI UTGARTHAR
(— OF JAPAN) DO
(— OF MARS) LIBYA
(— OF OCEAN) COUNTRY
(— OF ORIGIN) CRADLE
(— OF PHOTOSPHERE) FACULA

(— **OF SHIFTING SAND**) ERG
(— **OF SIMPLE PLEASURE**) ARCADY
ARCADIA
(— **OF SOURCE OF GOLD**) OPHIR
(— **OF TISSUE**) FIELD
(— **WITHOUT LAW**) ALSATIA
(— **WITHOUT WOODS**) WOLD WEALD
(**CELESTIAL —S**) LANGI
(**COASTAL —**) LITTORAL
(**CULTIVATED —**) GARDEN
(**DARKISH —S ON MARS**) MARE
(**DESERT —**) ERG HAMADA
(**DESERTED —**) WASTE
(**DESOLATE —**) PUNA
(**DISTANT —-**) THULE
(**E. INDIAN —**) DESH
(**ELEVATED —**) ALTITUDE
(**FOREST —**) TAIGA
(**FORESTED —**) MONTANA
(**GEOGRAPHICAL —**) BOWL SIDE
(**HEAVENLY —**) SPHERE
(**IDEAL —**) JINNESTAN
(**INFERNAL —S**) ABYSS TARTAR
TARTARUS
(**LARGE —**) COMPAGE
(**LIMESTONE —**) KARST
(**MOUNTAINOUS —**) SIERRA
(**OPEN —**) SAVANNAH
(**ORIENTAL —**) INDOGAEA
(**STAGNANT —**) EDDY
(**SUPERIOR —**) HIGH
(**TREELESS —**) HIGHMOOR
(**UPPER —**) HIGH LOFT
(**UPPER —S**) ETHER
(**WOODED —**) FOREST
(PL.) DIGGINGS
REGIONAL LOCAL SECTIONAL
REGISTER PIE BEAR BOOK FREE
LIST PILE POLL READ ROLL STOP
ALBUM DIARY ENROL ENTER FASTI
GRILL SIJIL SLATE ANNALS BEHAVE
LEDGER MUSTER RECORD REGEST
ASCRIBE CALENDS CATALOG
COUCHER INDORSE KALENDS
NOTITIA ROTULET ARCHIVES
CADASTER CALENDAR GREFFIER
INDICATE INSCRIBE MENOLOGY
PEDIGREE POLLBOOK TOLLBOOK
STROHBASS
(— **OF JUDGMENTS**) DOCKET
(**LOWEST —**) CHALUMEAU
(**MIDDLE —**) CLARINO
(**OFFICIAL —**) TABLEAU CADASTER
REGISTRAR GUARD ACTUARY
PATWARI PUTWARI GREFFIER
RESIDENT
REGISTRY FLAG STUDBOOK
REGLET FILET BATTEN FILLET
RIGLET
REGRATER HUCKSTER
REGRESS EGRESS RETURN
ANALYSIS RECOURSE
REGRET REW RUE RUTH GRIEF
DESIRE RELENT REPENT SORROW
DEPLORE REGRATE REMORSE
FORTHINK REPINING
REGRETFUL BAD SORRY REPINING
REGRETTABLE DIRTY DOLOROUS
REGULAR DUE SET EVEN FULL JUST

WEAK SOBER SUANT SUENT USUAL
FORMAL NORMAL SQUARE STATED
STEADY CORRECT NATURAL
ORDERED ORDERLY ORDINAL
PERFECT TYPICAL UNIFORM
COMPLETE CONSTANT DECOROUS
FORMULAR HABITUAL ORDINARY
ORDINATE TESSERAL
REGULARITY METHOD SQUARE
SYSTEM EVENNESS SYNAPHEA
(— **OF NATURE**) LAW
REGULARLY DULY EVEN ORDERLY
PROPERLY STATEDLY
REGULATE SET RULE WIND BOOST
FRAME GUIDE ORDER RIGHT SHAPE
ADJUST ASSIZE BEHAVE DIRECT
GOVERN MASTER RADDLE SETTLE
SQUARE TEMPER ARRANGE
CONTROL DISPOSE MEASURE
QUALIFY RECTIFY ATTEMPER
MODERATE MODULIZE
(— **FOOD**) DIET
(— **PITCH**) KEY STOP
REGULATED ORDENE ORDERED
REGULATING BEHIND
REGULATION LAW RULE BYLAW
ORDER REGLE USUAL CURFEW
ZABETA CONTROL PRECEPT
STATUTE VOICING DISPOSAL
STEERAGE
(— **OF PRICE**) ASSIZE
REGULATOR GUIDE DISPOSER
GOVERNOR
REGULUS MATTE SLURRY KINGLET
REHABILITATE REABLE RESTORE
REINSTATE
REHASH RECHAUFFE
REHEARSAL CALL HEARSAL
HERSALL PREVIEW CLAMBAKE
NARRATION
REHEARSE TELL TRAIN DETAIL
RECITE RELATE DECLINE NARRATE
RECOUNT DESCRIBE PRACTICE
REHEAT FLASH
REHOBOAM ROBOAM
(**FATHER OF —**) SOLOMON
REICHSTAG DIET
REIF PLUNDER ROBBERY
REIGN RING RULE REALM RICHE
EMPIRE GOVERN KINGDOM PREVAIL
REGIMENT
(— **IN INDIA**) RAJ
REIMBURSE PAY REPAY DEFRAY
RECOUP REFUND REBURSE
INDEMNIFY
REIN CURB STOP CHECK SWING
THONG GOVERN BABICHE LEATHER
PLOWLINE RESTRAIN
(PL.) LINES RIBBONS
REINDEER REIN CERVID TARAND
CARIBOU CERVINE CERVOID
REINDEER MOSS SWARD
REINFORCE BAR GUY BACK FACE
STAY BRACE FORCE INLAY STUFF
SUPER CRADLE DOUBLE GUSSET
HARDEN MUSCLE SUPPLY AFFORCE
BOLSTER BULWARK ENFORCE
GROMMET NERVATE STIFFEN
SUPPORT

(— **ROAD**) SKID
REINFORCED KEYED SPLICED
REINFORCEMENT CREW FUEL STAY
BRACE HURTER CUNETTE SPLICING
STRAINER
(PL.) SUCCOR SUPPLY
REINVIGORATE QUICK REVIVE
RECRUIT RENERVE
REITERATE BACK REITER REPEAT
RESUME ITERATE REHEARSE
REJECT BEG ORT CAST DICE JILT
NILL SPIN ABHOR BANDY BELIE
BRUSH EJECT SCOUT ABJECT
ABJURE DELETE DESERT IGNORE
RECUSE RESPUE CASHIER DISCARD
FORSAKE REPULSE ATHETIZE
DISCLAIM DEFY FAIL KICK CHECK
REFEL REPEL SPURN WAIVE REFUSE
RETORT ABANDON CONTEMN
DECLINE DISCARD DISMISS
FORSAKE PROJECT REPROVE
REPULSE ABNEGATE DISALLOW
FORSWEAR RENOUNCE THROWOUT
(— **A STUDENT**) PLUCK PLOUGH
(— **COPY**) SPIKE
REJECTED OFFCAST OUTCAST
CASTAWAY
REJECTION SACK BRUSH SPURN
DENIAL MITTEN REBUFF REFUSAL
REPULSE DEFIANCE TURNDOWN
(— **OF DOCTRINE**) HERESY
REJOICE JOY FAIN GAME CHEER
ENJOY EXULT GLORY BLITHE
PLEASE DELIGHT GLADDEN
JUBILATE
REJOICING GLEE MIRTH FESTIVITY
REJOIN TAUNT ANSWER REUNITE
REJOINDER REPLY ANSWER
COUNTER RESPONSE
REJUVENATE UNOLD
REKINDLE RELUME REVIVE
RELAPSE SINK WEED LAPSE RECIDE
RETURN BACKSET SUBSIDE
BACKCAST WITHDRAW
RELATE SAY ALLY BEAR JOIN READ
TELL PITCH REFER SPELL STATE
TOUCH ALLUDE ASSERT DELATE
DETAIL DEVISE RECITE REPORT
REPUTE COGNATE CONCERN
DECLARE INVOLVE NARRATE
PERTAIN RECOUNT CALABASH
DESCRIBE REHEARSE
(— **TO**) TOUCH
RELATED KIN SIB AKIN ALLIED
(— **BY FATHER'S SIDE**) AGNATE
(— **ON MOTHER'S SIDE**) ENATE
ENATIC COGNATE
RELATING (ALSO SEE PERTAINING)
(— **TO A RECENT PAST**) ERST
(— **TO**) AGAINST
RELATION KIN SIB TALE BLOOD
FETII AFFINE DATIVE REGARD
ACCOUNT BEARING HISTORY
KINSHIP KINSMAN RAPPORT
RESPECT SCHESIS TELLING
AFFINITY HABITUDE RELATIVE
TENDENCY REHEARSAL RISHTADAR
(— **BETWEEN SPECIES**) AFFINITY
(— **OF LIKENESS**) ANALOGY

(BLOOD —) KIN SIB
(FIXED —) RATIO
(FRIENDLY —S) AMITY
(SYNTACTIC —) FUNCTION
(WORKING —) GEAR
RELATIONSHIP KIN BLOOD ACTION
AGENCY AMENITY AMITATE
ANGULUS BEARING CONTACT
KINDRED KINSHIP LIAISON RESPECT
SIBNESS SIBREDE SOCIETY AFFINITY
AGNATION CONTRAST GOSSIPRY
RELATIVE SYMPATHY COGNATION
FILIATION
(BUSINESS —) ACCOUNT
(CLOSE —) BOSOM AFFIANCE
INTIMACY BELONGING
(INHARMONIOUS —) OUTS
(MARITAL —) BED
(MUTUAL —) TERMS SYMMETRY
(SEXUAL —) AFFAIR
(SOCIAL —) FOOTING
RELATIVE KIN ALLY BLOOD AFFINE
AGNATE ALLIED COUSIN GERMAN
KINDRED KINSMAN APPOSITE
COGNATUS RELATION RELEVANT
PERTINENT
(PL.) KIN SIB FOLK KINDRED
KINFOLK KINNERY KINSFOLK
RELAX LAX GIVE REST ABATE BREAK
LOOSE REMIT SLACK DIVERT
LAXATE SOFTEN UNBEND UNGIVE
UNKNIT DEBLOCK RELEASE
RESOLVE SLACKEN UNPURSE
MITIGATE UNBUCKLE UNCLENCH
RELAXATION EASE LAZE REST
CREEP LETUP RELAX SOLACE
DETENTE LETDOWN BREATHER
DIVERSION
RELAXED LAX LASH LOOSE SLACK
SONSY REMISS SONSIE INFORMAL
RESOLVED UNBENDED UNBRACED
RELAXING ANIMAL ANODYNE
DETENTE
(— POINT) SEAR
RELAY SPELL RELIEF REMUDA
AVANTLAY REPEATER
(— OF DOGS) VAUNTLAY
(— OF PALANQUIN BEARERS) DAK
RELEASE LES LET BAIL DROP EMIT
FREE LESE LIOS LISS SHED SLIP
TRIP UNDO ERUPT LEISS LOOSE
MUKTI REMIT SLAKE ASSOIL DEMISE
EXCUSE EXEMPT LAUNCH MOKSHA
REMISE SPRING UNBEND UNTACK
UNWORK ABSOLVE APATHIA
DELIVER DETENTE DISBAND
FREEDOM QUIETUS SOLUTIO
UNSTICK DELIVERY DISPENSE
DISSOLVE LIBERATE DISCHARGE
(— AS DOGS) UNLEASH
(— DANCING PARTNER) BREAK
(— EMOTION) ABREAST
(— FROM CONFINEMENT) UNMEW
UNPEN SPRING STREET
(— FROM DEBT) FREITH
(— FROM MILITARY) INVALID
(— FROM SLAVERY) MANUMIT
(— ON ONE'S WORD) PAROLE
(PRESS —) HANDOUT

RELEASED OFF FREE EXEMPT
RELEGATE DOOM EXILE BANISH
COMMIT DEMOTE REJECT DEGRADE
(— TO OBSCURITY) DOWN
RELENT COME MELT ABATE YIELD
REGRET REPENT LIQUEFY MOLLIFY
SLACKEN
RELENTLESS GRIM HARD HARSH
STERN STONY BITTER SAVAGE
STRICT AUSTERE PITILESS
RIGOROUS
RELEVANT APT VALID GERMAN
APROPOS GERMANE APPOSITE
MATERIAL PERTINENT
RELIABILITY STEEL CREDENCE
RELIABLE GOOD HARD SURE TRUE
SOLID SOUND THERE TRIED TRUST
DINKUM STEADY TRUSTY CERTAIN
FAITHFUL SOOTHFUL STRAIGHT
RELIANCE HOPE TRUST CREDIT
AFFIANCE MAINSTAY
(— ON FAITH) FIDEISM
RELIC HUACO REMAIN ANTIQUE
HALIDOM LEAVING MEMENTO
RELIQUE VESTIGE SOUVENIR
SURVIVAL
(PL.) CORPSE HALIDOM REMAINS
RELICT WIDOW REMANIE RESIDUAL
SURVIVOR EPIBIOTIC
RELIEF AID LAX SOB BOOT BOTE
EASE HELP RELAY SCRUB SPELL
SWING ESCAPE REMEDY SUCCOR
COMFORT FEEDING REDRESS
RILIEVO EASEMENT REPOUSSE
(TEMPORARY —) HITCH
RELIEVE ROB BEET EASE FREE HELP
LIOS LISS ALLAY LIGHT LISSE LITHE
RIGHT SLAKE SPARE SPELL ASSIST
LESSEN PHYSIC REMEDY REMOVE
RESCUE SOOTHE SUCCOR UNMAZE
ASSUAGE COMFORT DELIVER
DEPRIVE FRESHEN LIGHTEN
REDRESS REFRESH SUCCEED
SUPPORT SUSTAIN SWEETEN
ALIGHTEN DIMINISH MITIGATE
RELEVATE
(— A SAIL) SPILL
(— OF OFFICE) AX AXE
(— OF SIN) CONFESS
RELIGIEUSE NUN CLERGESS
RELIGION BON DIN LAW SECT
BONBO CREED DAENA FAITH OBEAH
PIETY SOPHY DHARMA SHINTO
SYSTEM TAOISM ELOHISM JAINISM
JUDAISM ORPHISM PERSISM RELIGIO
SIKHISM SYNAGOG BUDDHISM
CAODAISM HINDUISM MAZDAISM
PEYOTISM
(— OF ABRAHAM) HANIFIYA
(— OF TIBET) BON
(CHRISTIAN —) WAY
(UNORTHODOX —) CULT
RELIGIOUS HOLY EXACT GODLY
PIOUS RIGID DEVOUT DIVINE
SACRED FERVENT GHOSTLY
ZEALOUS
(— HOUSE) KELLION
RELINQUISH LAY LET CEDE DROP
QUIT DEMIT FORGO GRANT LEAVE

WAIVE YIELD CANCEL DESERT
RESIGN ABANDON FORSAKE
RELEASE ABDICATE ABNEGATE
LINQUISH RENOUNCE
RELIQUARY ARCA CASKET CHASSE
COFFER MEMORY SHRINE STEEPA
TABLET CHORTEN HALIDOM
MEMORIA FERETORY
RELISH CHOW DASH EDGE GOUT
GUST LIKE SOUL SOWL TANG ZEST
ACHAR ENJOY GUSTO RELES
SAVOR SOWLE SPICE TASTE TRACE
ATSARA DEGUST FLAVOR LIKING
SAVOUR BOTARGO OUTWORK
STOMACH APPETITE FONDNESS
(— FOR FOOD) CHAW
(INTELLECTUAL —) TASTE
(MENTAL —) PALATE
(ROMAN —) GARUM
(SALT OR ACID —) ACHAR
RELUCENT RADIANT SHINING
GLEAMING
RELUCTANCE GRUDGE AVERSION
ANTIPATHY RENITENCE
(— UNIT) REL
RELUCTANT SET SHY CAGY LOTH
NICE CHARY LOATH SWEER THRAW
AFRAID AVERSE DAINTY FORCED
SWEERT UNFAIN ASHAMED HALTING
BACKWARD GRUDGING LOATHFUL
THRAWART
RELY AFFY BANK BASE LEAN LITE
REST STAY COUNT RALLY TRUST
DEPEND GROUND RECKON REPOSE
CONFIDE
(— ON) LIPPEN VENTURE
REMAIN LIE SIT BIDE REST STAY
STOP ABIDE CLING DWELL LEAVE
STAND TARRY THOLE BELIVE
ENDURE MANENT RESIDE SUBSIST
SURVIVE CONTINUE
(— AWAKE) VIGILATE
(— IN DEADLOCK) HANG
(— MOTIONLESS) STAGNATE
(— UNDER HEAT TREATMENT) SOAK
**(— UNDISTURBED AFTER HEAT
TREATMENT)** AGE
(— UNUSED) LIE
(— UPRIGHT) STAND
(—S IN MASH TUN) GRAINS
(—S IN PIPEBOWL) TOPPER
(—S OF CANE) BEGASS BAGASSE
(—S OF FIRE) EMBER EMBERS
(—S ON STAGE) MANET
(ANIMAL —S) SPOILS
(FOUL —S) SCURF
(PL.) CHAR DUST ASHES DECAY
DRAFF GHOST SHARD SHERD
BURIAL DEBRIS FOSSIL RELIEF
CARCASS REMNANT RESIDUE
REMAINDER HEEL LAVE REST
PLUGS ARREAR EXCESS RELIEF
BALANCE REMNANT RESIDUE
SURPLUS LEAVINGS LEFTOVER
RESIDUAL RESIDUUM
(— OF ATOM) CORE
(PL.) GARBLINGS LEFTMENTS
REMAINING BIDING REMNANT
LEFTOVER REMANENT RESIDUAL

REMARK DIG SAY SEE GIRD HEED
NOTE WORD GLOSS STATE TOKEN
EARFUL GAMBIT NOTICE REGARD
COMMENT DESCANT DISCANT
OBSERVE PERCEIVE
(— BRIEFLY) GLANCE
(AMIABLE —) DOUCEUR
(AMUSING —) GAG
(BITING —) BARB
(CONCLUDING —S) ENVOI
(CUTTING —) DIG SPINOSITY
(EMBARRASSING —) BREAK
(EXPLANATORY —) SCHOLION
SCHOLIUM
(FOOLISH —) INANITY
(INSULTING —) SLUR
(JEERING —) JEST SKIT
(LAUGH-PROVOKING —) GAG
(SARCASTIC —) HIT GIRD SLANT
(SATIRICAL —) JEST SKIT SGAFT
(SHARP —) GANSEL STINGER
(SILLY —) FADAISE
(STALE —S) BILGE
(UNCOMPLIMENTARY —) BRICKBAT
(WITTY —) JEST CRACK
REMARKABLE FORBY GREAT
SIGNAL STRONG NOTABLE STRANGE
UNUSUAL FABULOUS MARKABLE
SINGULAR SPANKING STRIKING
UNCOMMON BODACIOUS
(NOT —) INCURIOUS
REMARKABLY UNCO UNKO JOLLY
UNCOW DEUCED UNCOLY SIGNALLY
REMEDIAL RELEVANT SALUTARY
REMEDILESS BOOTLESS
REMEDY AID BOT BOOT BOTE CURE
GAIN HALE HEAL HELP REDE AZOTH
MANDS REDUB SHERE TOPIC
PHYSIC RECOUR RECURE RELIEF
REPAIR RESIDY URETIC ANTACID
CORRECT DRASTIC ICTERIC
OTALGIC PLASTER RECTIFY
REDRESS RELIEVE ANTIDOTE
MEDICINE PHARMACY RECOVERY
REMEDIAL SPECIFIC
(— COUNTERACTING POISON)
TREACLE ANTIDOTE
(— FOR ALL DISEASES) PANACEA
CATHOLICON
(— FOR JAUNDICE) ICTERIC
(— TO REDUCE FEVER) FEBRIFUGE
(CHINESE —) SENSO
(EXTERNAL —) TOPIC
(FAVORITE —) NOSTRUM
(SECRET —) ARCANUM
(TAPEWORM —) EMBELIA
(UNIVERSAL —) AZOTH
(WITHOUT —) BOOTLESS
REMEMBER MEM MIN MEAN MIND
MINE MING IDEATE MEMBER RECALL
RECORD REMIND RETAIN REWARD
BETHINK MENTION
(— REMORSEFULLY) REMORD
REMEMBRANCE MiN MIND MEMORY
RECORD MEANING MINDING MINNING
MEMORIAL REMINDER SOUVENIR
REMIND JOG MIN MIND MINE MING
IMMIND PROMPT REMEMBER
REMINDER MEMO PROD TWIT

TOUCH PROMPT MINDING MONITOR
SOUVENIR
REMINISCENCE MEMORY RECALL
ANAMNESIS
REMISE RETURN RELEASE REPLACE
CARRIAGE
REMISS LAX LAZY MILD PALE FAINT
SLACK TARDY BEHIND DILUTED
LANGUID CARELESS DERELICT
DILATORY HEEDLESS
REMISSION CURE LIOS LISS
PARDON REMISE LOOSING
REMITTAL
REMISSNESS LACHES LASHNESS
REMIT SEND COVER LOOSE RELAX
CANCEL EXCUSE PARDON REMAND
REMISS RESIGN ABSOLVE FORGIVE
RELEASE SUSPEND ABROGATE
MITIGATE MODERATE
REMNANT END TAG DREG FENT
REST RUMP RUND RELIC STUMP
TRACE REMAIN LEAVING REMAINS
SURVIVOR
(— OF CLOTH) FENT
(— OF FOOD) CRUST
(— OF ROCK MASS) KLIP KLIPPE
(— OF VEIL) ANNULUS
(—S OF FILLETS) SCISSEL
(—S OF VEIL) CORTINA
(VESTIGIAL —) SHADOW
(PL.) EPIPLASM
REMODEL MEND RECAST CONVERT
REMONSTRANCE PROOF ADVICE
COUNSEL PROTEST REPROOF
EVIDENCE
REMONSTRANT ARMINIAN
REMONSTRATE ARGUE PROTEST
REPROVE COMPLAIN
REMORA CLOG DRAG PEGA SUCKER
GUAICAN PEGADOR ECHENEID
LOOTSMAN STAYSHIP STOPSHIP
SUCKFISH
REMORSE HELL PITY RUTH PRICK
REGRET REMORD
(— OF CONSCIENCE) GRUDGE
REMORSEFUL BAD PITIFUL
CONTRITE GUILTSICK
REMOTE FAR OFF DEEP FERN HIGH
LONG ALOOF HOARY UTTER
ALENGE DISTAL ELENGE EXEMPT
OTIOSE SECRET DEVIOUS DISSITE
DISTANT EXTREME FAILING
FARAWAY FOREIGN OBSCURE
OUTSIDE ADDITIVE ARMCHAIR
INTERIOR OUTLYING OUTWORLD
SECLUDED
(— FROM LIFE) SCHOOLISH
(MOST —) ULTIMA EXTREME
HINDMOST ULTIMATE
REMOTELY CLEAN DISTANTLY
REMOTENESS AWAYNESS DISTANCE
REMOTER FARTHER ULTERIOR
REMOVABLE DATIVE REMOTIVE
REMOVAL AX AXE EXILE AMOTION
CLEANUP ERASION ABLATION
EXCISION EXERESIS OFFGOING
REMOTION
(— OF COAL) GETTING

(— OF ICE FROM GLACIER)
ATTRITION
REMOVE GET PUT RID BATE COMB
DELE DRAW FILE FLIT FREE LIFT
MOVE PARE QUIT RAZE VOID WEED
APART AUFER AVOID BLAST BRUSH
CLEAR EMITY ERASE EVOID HEAVE
HOIST LIGHT PLANE RAISE REPEL
SHIFT SHUCK SLASH SLIPE STRIP
SWEEP WAIVE BANISH CANCEL
CHANGE CONVEY DEDUCT DEGREE
DEPART DEPOSE EFFACE ELOIGN
EXEMPT EXPORT MINISH RELEVE
SPIRIT AMOLISH DEPRIVE DESCENT
DISMISS DISPOST DIVORCE
EXCERPT RESCIND RETRACT
REVERSE STRANGE SUBDUCT
SUBLATE ABSTRACT ASPIRATE
DISPLACE DISPLANT ESTRANGE
EVACUATE RETRENCH SUPPLANT
TRANSFER WITHDRAW
(— A STITCH) DECREASE
(— BARK FROM LOG) ROSS
(— BIT BY BIT) SCAMBLE
(— BY CUTTING) ABLATE
(— BY DEATH) SNATCH
(— CLOTHING) DOFF STRIP
(— COLOR) BLEACH
(— COVER) UNCAP
(— DEFECTS) SCARF
(— DIRT) BLADE GARBLE
(— EXCESS METAL) CUT
(— FROM CHECKER BOARD) HUFF
(— FROM OFFICE) DEPOSE RECALL
DISMISS
(— FROM REMEMBRANCE) COVER
(— GILLS) BEARD
(— HAIR) DEPILATE
(— HUSKS AND CHAFF) GELD
(— INSIDES OF FISH) GIB GIP
(— JUDGE) ADDRESS
(— LOWER BRANCHES) BRASH
(— MAST) UNSTEP
(— ORE) EXTRACT
(— PARTICLES OF GOLD LEAF)
SKEW
(— POTATOES) GRABBLE
(— QUEEN BEE) DEMAREE
(— ROOTS) GRUB
(— SEED FROM FLAX) RIBBLE
(— SEEDS) STONE
(— SKIN) HULL HUSK
(— SPROUTS FROM) CHIT
(— STALK FROM) STRIG
(— STAMENS) CASTRATE
(— TABLECLOTH) DRAW
(— THE TOP OF) COP
(— TROUSERS) DEBAG
(— WASTE TO FIBER) GARNETT
(— WOOL) BELLY
(— WORKS OF STOLEN WATCH)
CHURCH
REMOVED UP OFF AWAY ALIEN
ALOOF APART REMOTE DISTANT
SEMOTED ABSTRACT
REMOVER MOVER CROPMAN
KNOTTER
REMUDA CAVY CAVAYARD
CAVYYARD

REMUNERATE PAY REPAY REWARD
GRATIFY SATISFY CONSIDER
REIMBURSE
REMUNERATION PAY REWARD
SALARY PAYMENT
REMUNERATIVE GAINFUL
REWARDING
REMUS (BROTHER OF —) ROMULUS
RENAISSANCE NARA REBIRTH
REVIVAL
RENAL NEPHRIC
RENCOUNTER CLASH FIGHT
DEBATE CONTEST CONFLICT
REND PULL RENT RIVE TEAR TOIL
BREAK BURST DIVEL RATCH ROWEL
SEVER SPLIT WREST CLEAVE
SCREED WRENCH DIVULSE
RUPTURE WREATHE DISPIECE
DISTRAIN FRACTURE LACERATE
SPLINTER
(— AND DEVOUR) TIRE
RENDER DO PAY PUT TRY BEAR
DRAW ECHO EMIT MAKE RENT RIND
DEFER PRICK REPAY YIELD RECITE
REPEAT RETURN DELIVER PRECARY
REFLECT REQUITE RESTORE
SERVICE TALLAGE TRANSMIT
(— ACID) PRICK
(— AGREEABLE) DULCIFY
(— AS LARD) TRY
(— ASSISTANCE TO SHIP) FOY
(— CAPABLE) ACTIVATE
(— CLEAR) OPEN
(— FIT) ADAPT
(— GODLIKE) DEIFY
(— HEAVY WITH FOOD) STODGE
(— HOMAGE) ATTORN
(— IMMUNE) FRANK VASTATE
(— INEFFECTIVE) VITIATE
(— KNOTTY) GNARL
(— OBLIQUE) SPLAY
(— OBSCURE) DARKLE
(— OF BOON WORK) PRECARY
(— QUIET) ACCOY
(— SENSELESS) STUN ASTONISH
(— TURBID) ROIL
(— UNFIT) DENATURE
(— UNSTABLE) UNHINGE
(— VERDICT) PASS
(— VOID) CASS DEFEAT
RENDERED RENDU TRIED
RENDERING RENDU ENGLISH
VERSION RENDITION
(— OF SCENE) STUDY
RENDEZVOUS DATE HAUNT TRYST
REFUGE HANGOUT MEETING
RETREAT
(— FOR SHIPS) DOWN
RENDITION ACCOUNT CONDUCT
DELIVERY
RENEGADE DORAX PERVERT
TRAITOR APOSTATE RENEGADO
RUNAGADO RUNAGATE TURNCOAT
RENEGE BEG NIG DENY RENIG
DESERT REVOKE RETRACT
FAINAIGUE
RENEW NEW REST FRESH RECALL
REFORM RENOVE REPEAT RESUME
REVIVE INSTORE REBUILD REFRESH

REPLACE RESTORE
(— WINE) STUM
RENEWAL RENEW REVIVAL
NOVATION
RENNET LAB RUEN VELL STEEP
RENNIN RUNNET EARNING
ABOMASUM YEARNING CHEESELIP
RENOUNCE PUT CEDE DEFY DENY
QUIT DEVOW FORGO RENAY WAIVE
ABJURE DISOWN FORLET FORSAY
RECANT REFUSE REJECT RENEGE
RESIGN REVOKE ABANDON
DECLARE FORLEIT FORSAKE
RETRACT WITHSAY ABDICATE
ABNEGATE DISCLAIM FORSPEAK
FORSWEAR MANSWEAR PROCLAIM
RENOVATE DUST RENEW REVIVE
FURBISH REFRESH RESTORE
RENOVIZE
(— HAT) MOLOKER MOLOCKER
RENOWN BAY BRAG FAME ECLAT
GLORY KUDOS PRICE RUMOR
ESTEEM LUSTER RENONE REPORT
EMPRISE SWAGGER WORSHIP
PRESTIGE NOTORIETY
RENOWNED FAMED NOBLE NOTED
FAMOUS EMINENT RENOMME
GLORIOUS MAGNIFIC RENOMMEE
RENT LET SET TAX FARM GALE
GAPE HIRE MAIL RACK RIME RIVE
SLIT TEAR TOLL WAGE BREAK
CANON CENSO CUDDY ENDOW
GANCH GAVEL SPLIT BLANCH
BREACH BROKEN CENSUS CHASMA
CUSTOM GAUNCH INCOME SCHISM
SCREED STRENT CHARTER CHIEFRY
FISSURE MAILING MOLLAND
ONSTAND RENTAGE REVENUE
RUPTURE TRIBUTE CHAMPART
CHIEFERY HEADRENT STALLAGE
VECTIGAL WAYLEAVE LANDGAFOL
(— BY BOAR'S TUSK) GANCH
GAUNCH
(— IN LIEU OF SUPPER) CUDDY
(— OF LAND PAID IN KIND) CAIN
(ANNUAL —) CANON
(EARTHQUAKE —) SCARPLET
(GROUND —) CENSO CENSUS
(OATS IN LIEU OF —) AVENAGE
RENTAL PORT TONNAGE TRIBUTE
TUNNAGE
RENTED LETTEN
RENTER FARMER RANTER CHIPPER
BOXHOLDER
RENUNCIATION DENIAL APOSTASY
DEFIANCE DISAVOWAL REJECTION
SACRIFICE
REP CANNELE DROGUET POPELINE
REPAIR DO EIK EKE FIX IMP HEAL
HELP MEND TINE AMEND BOTCH
DIGHT EMEND HAUNT RALLY REDUB
RENEW STORE TRADE UPSET
ASTORE BUSHEL COBBLE COGGLE
DOCTOR FETTLE RECURE REFORM
REMEDY REPASS RESORT RETURN
UPKEEP CORRECT INFAINT REDRESS
REPAREL RESTORE SERVICE
FLOCKING RETRIEVE REVIVIFY
(— BOAT) CAREEN

(— CLUMSILY) BOTCH
(— FENCE) MOUND
(— ROAD) SKID
(— SHOE) FOX TAP
REPAIRED VAMPED
REPAIRER DOCTOR COBBLER
WOFFLER CEMENTER
(SHOE —) JACKMAN BENCHMAN
(TEXTILE —) SMASHER
REPAIRMAN FETTLER
REPARATION BOTE AMENDS
REMEDY REWARD DAMAGES
REDRESS REPAIRS REQUITAL
REPARTEE WIT KNACK REPLY
RETORT RIPOST RIPOSTE
BACKCHAT BADINAGE COMEBACK
GIFFGAFF
REPAST BAIT FEED FOOD MEAL
BEVER FEAST TREAT DRINKING
(— BETWEEN MEALS) BEVER
BRUNCH BANQUET
(HASTY —) SNACK
(LIGHT —) BAIT VOID VOIDEE
COLLATION
REPAY MEED QUIT APPAY TALLY
YIELD ACQUIT ANSWER REFUND
RETORT RETURN REWARD REQUITE
RESTORE
REPEAL ANNUL CANCEL RECALL
REVOKE ABANDON ABOLISH
RESCIND REVERSE ABROGATE
DEROGATE DISENACT RENOUNCE
REPEAT SAY ECHO GAIT RAME RANE
SHOW TELL DITTO QUOTE RECUR
RENEW RESAY REVIE THRUM
ANSWER RENDER RESUME RETAIL
SECOND DECLINE DIVULGE ITERATE
PRESENT REPLICA DINGDONG
REDOUBLE REHEARSE
(— BY ROTE) PARROT
(— MONOTONOUSLY) CUCKOO
DINGDONG
(— OF PATTERN) GAIT
(— TIRESOMELY) DIN
REPEATED OFTEN CONSTANT
FREQUENT
REPEATEDLY OFT EVERY THRICE
REPEATER GUN RIFLE WATCH
PISTOL FLOATER HOLDOVER
REPEL FEND TURN WARD FENCE
REBUT DEFEND REBEAT REBUFF
REFUSE REJECT REPUGN RESIST
REVOLT DISGUST PELLATE REPULSE
PROPULSE
REPELLENT DOPE GRIM HARSH
CAMPHOR HATEFUL SQUALID
REPELLING HARD SICKLY
REPENT REW RUE MOURN GRIEVE
REGRET REPTANT CREEPING
FORTHINK
REPENTANCE REW RUE PITY RUTH
RUING REGRET SORROW PENANCE
REMORSE
REPERCUSSION ECHO TENOR
RECOIL REPULSE BACKWASH
REPERTORY REP BOOK LIST INDEX
ARSENAL CATALOG
REPETITION BIS REP COPY ECHO
PLOCE REVIE TROLL DILOGY

REPEAT MENTION RECITAL REPRISE
IDENTITY ITERANCE ITERANCY
NEMBUTSU PALILOGY PARROTRY
RECOVERY REDOUBLE REHEARSAL
(— **IN REVERSE ORDER**) EPANODOS
(— **OF HOMOLOGOUS PARTS**)
MERISM
(— **OF SPEECH FORMS**) ROTE
(— **OF WORD**) ANAPHORA
(**UNINSPIRED** —) STENCIL
REPHAIM EMIM
REPINE FRET PINE WEAKEN
COMPLAIN
REPINING MURMUR REGRET
PLAINTIVE
REPLACE SWAP SWOP RENEW
REPAY SHIFT STEAD CHANGE
FOLLOW REFUND REMISE REPONE
SUPPLY FRESHEN RESTORE
SUCCEED DISPLACE SUPPLANT
REPLACEMENT CUT ERSATZ
(— **FOR HAND**) HOOK
(— **OF CONSONANT**) LENITION
REPLENISH CHUNK REFIT RENEW
SUPPLY NOURISH PERFECT PLENISH
REPLETE RESTORE SUFFICE
REPLETE FAT FULL RIFE SATED
STOUT STUFF FILLED GORGED
IMPLETE COMPLETE HONEYPOT
REPLETION FULTH FULNESS
SURFEIT FULLNESS PLETHORA
SATURITY
REPLICA BIS PUP COPY IDEA CHARM
IMAGE REVIE FACSIMILE
REPLICATION ECHO REPLY ANSWER
REJOINDER
REPLY CAP JAWAB KNACK RESAY
ANSWER REJOIN RETORT RETURN
REPLIAL RESOUND RESPOND
REPARTEE REPLIQUE RESPONSE
SIMILITER
REPORT CRY POP FAME ITEM NOTE
TELL VENT VOTE WORD AUDIT
BRUIT COVER CRACK NOISE REFER
ROUND RUMOR SCALE STATE
STORY VOICE BREEZE CAHIER
CREDIT DELATE DETAIL FINGER
GOSSIP RAPORT RECITE RELATE
RENOWN REPUTE RUMOR RUMBLE
SPEECH STEVEN SURVEY THREAP
ACCOUNT HANSARD HEARING
HEARSAY INKLING KHUBBER
NARRATE OPINION PROCESS
RECITAL ADVISORY DECISION
DESCRIBE HEMOGRAM VERBATIM
GRAPEVINE
(— **NEWS**) COVER
(— **OF GUN**) CLAP
(— **OF INFRACTION**) GIG
(— **OF PROCEEDINGS**) CAHIER
(— **OF TIMBER SURVEYOR**) CRUISE
(**ABSURD** —) CANARD
(**BELIEVED** —) CREDIT
(**CASUAL** —) FABLE
(**COMMON** —) CRY FAME SPEECH
(**FALSE** —) SHAVE CANARD FURPHY
SLANDER
(**FLYING** —) SOUGH
(**HONORABLE** —) TONGUE

(**LAW** —) CASE
(**MILITARY** —) STATE SITREP
(**NEWS** —) FLASH SCOOP
(**NOISY** —) RUMBLE
(**OFFICIAL** —) HANSARD
(**POPULAR** —) RUMOR RUMOUR
(**PUBLIC** —) FAME
(**UNFAVORABLE** —) SKIN
(**UNVERIFIED** —) VOICE GRAPEVINE
(**VAGUE** —) BREEZE
REPORTER LEGMAN PISTOL
CREEPER PRESSMAN STRINGER
(**YOUNG** —) CUB
REPORTING BEAT COVERAGE
REPOSE RO BED LIE CALM EASE
RELY REST PEACE PLACE POISE
QUIET SLEEP REPAST RECLINE
EASINESS QUIETUDE SERENITY
(— **LAZILY**) FROWST
REPOSITORY ARK AMBRY CAPSA
DEPOT HOARD VAULT ARMORY
CASKET MUSEUM VESTRY ARCHIVE
CABINET CAPSULE GENIZAH
GRANARY HANAPER SPICERY
MAGAZINE TREASURY SEPULCHER
REPOSOIR REPOSE
REPOSSESS PULL RECOVER
REPREHEND WARN BLAME CHIDE
REBUKE CENSURE REPRISE
REPROVE CRITICIZE
REPREHENSIBLE ILL AMISS
BLAMABLE CRIMINAL CULPABLE
SCABROUS
REPREHENSION BLAME REBUKE
CENSURE OBLOQUY REPROOF
REPRESENT GIVE LIKE LIMN SHOW
TYPE SHADE DEPICT SEMBLE
TYPIFY DISPLAY EXHIBIT FASHION
PICTURE PORTRAY PROTEST
TRADUCE DEFIGURE DESCRIBE
RESEMBLE
(— **CONCRETELY**) THING
(— **IN LANGUAGE**) ACT BODY DRAW
ENACT IMAGE SPEAK BLAZON
CLOTHE EMBODY FIGURE SAMPLE
BETOKEN EXPRESS DECIPHER
(— **ON STAGE**) ACT
REPRESENTATION SUN BUST FORM
ICON IDEA IDOL IKON SHOW SWAG
ANGLE DRAFT FANCY IMAGE INSET
LABEL MEDAL TABUT AVOWAL
BUDDHA EFFIGY FIGURE FLEECE
MODULE OBJECT SCHEMA SCHEME
SKETCH SUNRAY WAYANG
ANATOMY DIORAMA DRAUGHT
DRAWING EPITOME EXPRESS
EXTRACT FOLIAGE MAJESTY
SCENERY TABLEAU BESTIARY
BLAZONRY CREATION EPIPHANY
EXTERIOR IDIOGRAM LIKENESS
TYPORAMA
(— **OF SERPENT**) BASIL DRAGON
BASILISK
(— **OF SHRINE OF HUSAIN**) TABUT
(— **OF VISION**) AISLING
(**DIPLOMATIC** —) DEMARCHE
(**FACSIMILE** —) TYPORAMA
(**FAINT** —) SHADOW
(**FUNERAL** —) CADAVER

(**GRAPHIC** —) CHART BISECT
(**HERALDIC** —) LEOPARD LIONCEL
(**MENTAL** —) FANCY IMAGE
(**MINIATURE** —) MODEL
(**SYMBOLIC** —) ALLEGORY
REPRESENTATIVE REP FAIR TYPE
AGENT ENVOY VAKIL ASSIGN
COMMON DEPUTY EMBLEM LEDGER
SAMPLE VAKEEL BURGESS GRIEVER
TRIBUNE TYPICAL DECURION
DELEGATE EMISSARY EXPONENT
FIELDMAN GASTALDO INTIMATE
OBSERVER SALESMAN SPECIMEN
(— **OF ATMOSPHERE**) AERIAL
(**MANUFACTURER'S** —) BLOCKMAN
(**PL.**) COMMONS
REPRESS CURB HUSH BLUNT BRIDE
CHAIN CHECK CHOKE CRUSH DAUNT
DROWN QUELL SQUAT COERCE
DEADEN REBUKE STIFLE CONTROL
DEPRESS INHIBIT REPRIME SILENCE
SWALLOW COMPRESS RESTRAIN
RESTRICT RETRENCH REVOCATE
STRANGLE SUPPRESS WITHHOLD
REPRESSED SULLEN STIFLED
REPRIEVE DELAY GRACE ESCAPE
REPRISE RESPITE SUSPEND
POSTPONE
REPRIMAND WIG BAWL CALL CHEW
JACK SKIN SLAP SLON SNEB SNIB
TASK CHECK CREED SLATE SLOAN
SPANK TARGE CARPET EARFUL
REBUKE CENSURE CHAPTER
LECTURE REPROOF REPROVE
DRESSING
REPRINT COPY DEPRINT OFFPRINT
REIMPOSE TAUCHNITZ
REPRISAL PRIZE REPRISE REQUITAL
RECAPTION
REPROACH ILL TAX BLOT GIBE JIBE
LACK NOSE NOTE SLUR SPOT TEEN
TWIT WITE ABUSE BLAME BRAID
CHIDE SCOLD SHEND TAUNT WHITE
BISMER INFAMY REBUKE REVILE
UPCAST VILIFY CENSURE CONDEMN
REPROOF REPROVE SLANDER
UMBRAID UPBRAID WITHNIM
DISHONOR REDARGUE REVILING
REPROACHFUL BITTER ABUSIVE
SHAMEFUL
REPROBATE HARD LOST SCAMP
DISOWN RASCAL REJECT SINNER
ABANDON CENSURE CORRUPT
EXCLUDE REPROVE DEPRAVED
DISALLOW HARDENED SCALAWAG
SKALAWAG
REPRODUCE BUD HIT COPY BREED
SPORE RECITE REPEAT PORTRAY
MULTIPLY REFIGURE REMEMBER
REPRODUCTION CAST COPY REVI
IMAGE ECTYPE RECALL STEREO
EDITION ELECTRO EXOGAMY
FISSION REPLICA REVIVAL APOMIXIS
BLOCKOUT GAMOGAMY HOMOGAMY
LIKENESS
(— **OF SOUND**) AUDIO
REPROOF PROD RATE BLAME
CHECK LESSON REBUKE CHIDING
LECTURE SETDOWN JOBATION

REPROACH REPROVAL SCOLDING
TAXATION JAWBATION
REPROVE TAP BAWL FLAY FRIE
JOBE RATE SNIB TRIM BLAME
CHECK CHIDE CRAWL SCOLD SHEND
SHENT SNEAP BERATE CHASTE
REBUKE REFORM SCHOOL THREAT
CENSURE CONDEMN CORRECT
IMPROVE LECTURE UPBRAID
WITHNIM ADMONISH CHASTISE
REDARGUE REPROACH UNDERNIM
WITHTAKE
REPTILE LOW MEAN WORM GUANA
SNAKE GAVIAL LIZARD MOLOCH
TURTLE CRAWLER CREEPER
DIAPSID GHARIAL PROTEUS
SAURIAN SERPENT TUATARA
BASILISK CREEPING CYNODONT
DINOSAUR GALESAUR MESOSAUR
MOSASAUR PLIOSAUR STEGOMUS
SYNAPSID TORTOISE ALLIGATOR
CROCODILE
REPTILIAN HERPETIC
REPUBLIC STATE SOVIET POBLACHT
(FRENCH —) MARIANNE
(IDEAL —) ICARIA
(IMAGINARY —) OCEANA
REPUBLICAN RED QUID STALWART
SANSCULOT
REPUDIATE DEFY ABJURE DISOWN
RECANT REJECT DECLINE DISAVOW
DISCARD DIVORCE RETRACT
DISCLAIM DISVOUCH RENOUNCE
REPUDIATING NAKIR
REPUGNANCE ENMITY HATRED
HORROR DISGUST DISLIKE DISTASTE
LOATHING
REPUGNANT ALIEN DIRTY ADVERSE
HATEFUL OPPOSED INIMICAL
OPPOSITE REPULSIVE
REPULSE FOIL ROUT RUSH CHECK
FLING REBUT REFEL REPEL SMEAR
DEFEAT DENIAL REBUFF REBUTE
REFUSE REJECT
REPULSIVE COLD DAIN EVIL LOTH
UGLY VILE LOATH GREASY LAIDLY
FULSOME HATEFUL LOATHLY
SQUALID SCABROUS UNHONEST
REPULSION UG DISLIKE AVERSION
REPUTABLE GOOD HONEST
WORTHY CREDIBLE ESTIMABLE
REPUTATION REP FAME LOSE NAME
NOTE PASS GLORY HONOR IZZAT
NOISE RUMOR SAVOR VOICE CREDIT
ESTEEM RECORD RENOWN SHADOW
LAURELS OPINION RESPECT
WORSHIP STANDING
(EVIL —) INFAMY
(GOOD —) STANDING
REPUTE FAME ODOR RANK WORD
NOISE SAVOR THINK RECKON
REGARD STATUS OPINION RESPECT
WORSHIP ESTIMATE JUDGMENT
POSITION
(ILL —) SLANDER
REPUTED DIT PUTATIVE
REQUEST ASK BEG CALL PLEA PRAY
SEEK SUIT TELL WISH CLAIM LIBEL
QUEST YEARN APPEAL BEHEST

DEMAND DESIRE DIRECT ENCORE
INVITE MOTION BESPEAK COMMAND
ENTREAT INQUIRY REQUIRE SOLICIT
ENTREATY INSTANCE PETITION
ROGATION
(— FOR HELP) SOS
(STRONG —) DUN DEMAND
REQUIEM HYMN MASS REST DIRGE
PEACE QUIET REPOSE REQUIN
REQUIN SHARK TOMMY
REQUIRE ASK HAVE LACK NEED
TAKE WANT CLAIM CRAVE EXACT
FORCE GAVEL COMPEL DEMAND
DEPEND DESIRE ENJOIN ENTAIL
EXPECT GOVERN MISTER OBLIGE
BEHOOVE DICTATE INVOLVE SOLICIT
REQUIRED DUE SET SUPPOSED
REQUIREMENT CALL NEED LEGAL
ORDER BEHEST DEMAND NECESSITY
(PL.) EXIGENCE EXIGENCY
REQUISITE DUE NEED NEEDY VITAL
NEEDFUL ESSENTIAL NECESSARY
REQUISITION ORDER DEMAND
INDENT EMBARGO REQUEST
REQUITAL WAR APPAY MERIT
REPAY SERVE TALLY YIELD ACQUIT
DEFRAY REWARD GRATIFY
PAYMENT REVENGE CONSIDER
FORYIELD REPRISAL
RERAILER DIAMOND
REREAD DOUBLE
RERECORD DUB
REREDOS SCREEN BRAZIER
DRAPERY RETABLO FIREBACK
REARDOSS
REREMOUSE BAT
RES POINT THING MATTER SUBJECT
RESCIND LIFT ANNUL CANCEL
REMOVE REPEAL REVOKE ABOLISH
RETRACT RETREAT ABROGATE
RESCRIPT EDICT ORDER DECREE
LETTER EPISTLE
RESCUE RID FREE HELP REDD SAVE
BORROW RANSOM REDEEM RESKEW
SUCCOR WARISH DELIVER RECLAIM
RECOVER RELEASE SALVAGE
DELIVERY LIBERATE RECOURSE
RESEARCH ARBEIT SEARCH
ENQUIRY INQUIRY
RESECT EXCISE
RESEDA LEEK MENNUET
RESEMBLANCE SWAP SIMILE
ANALOGY AFFINITY LIKENESS
PARALLEL VICINITY
(DIM HAZY —) BLY
(SLIGHT —) BLUSH
RESEMBLE AGREE BRAID FAVOR
IMAGE LIKEN APPEAR DEPICT
FIGURE SEMBLE COMPARE IMITATE
PORTRAY ASSEMBLE SIMULATE
RESEMBLING LIKE SAME SEMBLE
SIMILAR SEMBLANT
(— AN EGG) OVULARIAN
(— COMB) PECTINAL
(— GOOSE) ANSERINE
(— HORSE) EQUOID
(— IVORY) EBURNEAN EBURNOUS
EBURNEOID
(— SALT) HALOID

(— STAR) STELLATE
(— WALL) MURAL
RESENT HATE MEAN INDIGN MALIGN
STOMACH SUGGEST
RESENTFUL HARD HURT BITTER
ENVIOUS JEALOUS STOMACHY
RESENTMENT HURT DEPIT PIQUE
SNUFF SPITE CHOLER ENMITY
GRUDGE HATRED MALICE RANCOR
DISDAIN DUDGEON OFFENCE
OFFENSE STOMACH UMBRAGE
JEALOUSY HEARTBURN
RESERVATION DIBS SALVO SPACE
SAVING UNLESS BOOKING CAUTION
KEEPING PROVISO RESERVE
FORPRISE RESERVAL
(MENTAL —) SALVO SCRUPLE
RESERVE BOOK CAVE FUND HOJU
HOLD KEEP SALT SAVE SPARE
BACKUP NICETY SEPONE SEPOSE
TRIARY BACKLOG CAUTION
CONTROL DIGNITY SEPOSIT
SHYNESS TENENUE COLDNESS
DISTANCE FALLBACK FORPRISE
IMMODEST WITHHOLD STOCKPILE
(HOME —S) LANDSTURM
(MILITARY —) HOJU YOBI TRIARY
TRIARII
(MONETARY —) CUSHION
(PL.) FAT KOKUMIN STRENGTH
RESERVED COY DRY SHY COLD
UNCO ALOOF CHARY SAVED
BOOKED DEMURE MODEST SILENT
STANCH COSTIVE DISTANT RETIRED
STRANGE RETICENT RETIRING
STANDOFF WITHHELD
(— FOR ROYAL USE) KHASS
(NOT —) COMMON
RESERVOIR DAM BOSS FONT KEEP
LAKE PENT SUMP TANK BASIN
FOUNT STANK STORE CENOTE
SIPHON SOURCE SYPHON CISTERN
CLEARER FAVISSA FOREBAY
IMPOUND PISCINA RECEIPT
AFTERBAY DEPOSITO FOUNTAIN
MAGAZINE STANDAGE
(— OF WEATHERGLASS) STAGNUM
RESET HELP ABODE ALTER RECEPT
RESORT SUCCOR RECEIPT REPLANT
SHARPEN WELCOME
RESIDE BIG WIN BIGG HOME LIVE
STAY TELD WONT ABIDE DWELL
LODGE REMAIN CONSIST SOJOURN
HABITATE
(— TEMPORARILY) LIE STOP
RESIDENCE DUN WON DOON HALL
HOME SEAT SEMI STAY WENE WONE
ABODE COURT DAIRI DEMUR HOUSE
MAHAL MANSE YAMUN BIDING
DUKERY ELYSEE HOSTEL MANOIR
TENSER DEANERY DROSTDY
EMBASSY SOJOURN CURATAGE
DOMICILE DWELLING LEGATION
RESIANCE RESIANCY RESIDUUM
SEDIMENT SETTLING
(— FOR STUDENTS) INN
(— OF ARCHBISHOP) PALACE
(— OF CHIEF OF VILLAGE) TATA
(— OF ECCLESIASTIC) MANSE
DEANERY CURATAGE

(— OF FRENCH PRESIDENTS)
ELYSEE
(— OF MANDARIN) YAMEN YAMUN
(— OF MIKADO) DAIRI
(— OF PRIEST) CONVENTO
(— OF SOVEREIGN) PALACE
(— OF SULTAN) SERAGLIO
(FORTIFIED —) DUN
(HILL —) RATH
(OFFICIAL TURKISH —) KONAK
(RURAL —) SEAT FARMSTEAD
(SUMMER —) MAHAL
(TEMPORARY —) STAY

RESIDENT GER FIXED LEGER LIVER
INMATE LEDGER STABLE CITIZEN
DENIZEN DWELLER PRESENT
RESIANT RESIDER RESTING
HABITANT INHERENT KAMAAINA
MINISTER
(— AT A UNIVERSITY) GREMIALE
(— OF HAWAII) KAMAAINA
(— OF WEST. AUSTRALIA) GROPER
(ALIEN —) GER METIC
(CHINESE — OF TIBET) AMBAN
(FOREIGN-BORN —) ALIEN
(OLD —) STANDARD

RESIDUAL RELICT REMANIE
REMANENT

RESIDUE ASH DREG FOOT GUNK
HEEL LAFE LAVE LEES REST SILT
SLAG UNIT MAZUT SHARD SHERD
BEGASS BORING BOTTOM GRUFFS
RELICS BAGASSE CINDERS REMAINS
HARDHEAD LEAVINGS LEFTOVER
REMANENT RESIDUUM SEMICOKE
TAILINGS
(— FROM FAT) CRAP
(— FROM OLIVES) SANZA
(— FROM REFINING TIN) HARDHEAD
(— IN STILL) BOTTOM BOTTOMS
(— OF COAL) COKE SEMICOKE
(— OF COKE) BREEZE
(— OF COMBUSTION) ASH
(— OF HONEYCOMB) SLUMGUM
(— OF PETROLEUM) MAZUT
(— OF SHINGLES) SPALT
(FRIABLE —) CALX
(INSOLUBLE —) MARC
(PL.) TANKAGE

RESIDUUM TAIL BOTTOM DEPOSIT
RESIDUE SEDIMENT

RESIGN QUIT DEMIT FORGO REMIT
YIELD PERMIT SUBMIT ABANDON
COMMEND DELIVER FORGIVE
ABDICATE RENOUNCE

RESIGNATION PATIENCE DEMISSION
SURRENDER

RESILIENCE GIVE LIFE BOUNCE
RECOIL SPRING REBOUND
BUOYANCY

RESILIENT BOUNCY SUPPLE WHIPPY
ELASTIC SPRINGY FLEXIBLE

RESIN ALK LAC BALM BATU BREA
ALKYD AMBER ANIME COPAL
CUMAR ELEMI EPOXY GUGAL
GUGUL KAURI PITCH ROSEL ROSET
SIRUP SYRUP ANTIAR BINDER
CHARAS DAMMAR GOOGUL GUACIN
HARTIN MASTIC STORAX TAMANU

ACOUCHI ACRYLIC AMBRITE
BENZOIN BISABOL DERRIDE FLUAVIL
GAMBOGE SAGAPEN SHELLAC
ALKITRAN ALMACIGA BAKELITE
BDELLIUM CACHIBOU CANNABIN
COLOPHAN EUOSMITE FORMVAIL
GALAGALA GALLIPOT GEDANITE
GUAIACUM MALAPAHO MELAMINE
OPOPANAX SANDARAC SCAMMONY
(— DRAWN FROM TREES) CHIP
(— FROM HEMP) CHARAS
(— FROM NORWAY SPRUCE) THUS
(— OF FIR TREE) BLOB
(FOSSIL —) AMBER AMBRITE
HARTITE GEDANITE GLESSITE
RETINITE
(GRADE OF —) SORTS
(GUM —) GUGUL LASER MYRRH
ANTIAR BISABOL GAMBOGE
BDELLIUM
(NARCOTIC —) CHARAS CHURUS
(TURPENTINE —) ALK GALIPOT

RESINOID ALNUIN HELONIN LOBELIN
ASCLEPIN CERASEIN CHELONIN
TRILLIIN

RESINOUS ROSETY ROSETTY

RESIST BUCK FACE STAY REPEL
STAND DEFEND IMPUGN OPPOSE
REPUGN WITHER CONTEST DISPUTE
GAINSAY KNUCKLE RESERVE
WITHSET OUTSTAND
(— AUTHORITY) REBEL DEFORCE
(— SEPARATION) ATTRACT

RESISTANCE DRAG LOAD OHMAGE
REBUFF WITHER BALLAST ANTITYPY
BLOCKAGE FASTNESS FRICTION
HARDNESS OBSTACLE SEDITION
(— OF COTTON FIBERS) DRAG
(— OF KEYS) ACTION
(— THAT EXPLOSIVE MUST
OVERCOME) BURDEN BURTHEN
(— TO ATTACK) DEFENCE DEFENSE
(— TO CHANGE) INERTIA
(— TO COLOR CHANGE) FASTNESS
(— TO SLIPPING) BOND

RESISTANT HARD STOUT STABILE
STUBBORN
(— TO CHANGE) FAST STICKY

RESISTING OBSTANT RELUCTANT

RESISTOR BLEEDER REOSTAT
DIVERTOR RHEOSTAT

RESOLUTE BOLD FIRM GRIM BRAVE
FIXED HARDY MANLY STERN STIFF
STOUT GRITTY MANFUL PLUCKY
STANCH STEADY STUFFY STURDY
ANIMOSE ANIMOUS DECIDED
CONSTANT FAITHFUL INTREPID
POSITIVE STALWART STUBBORN
UNSHAKEN

RESOLUTELY TALLY FIRMLY
STOUTLY

RESOLUTION VOW SAND THEW
NERVE PARTY PLUCK POINT
STARCH ACUERDO BESLUIT
CENSURE COURAGE MANHEAD
MANHOOD PURPOSE RESOLVE
ANALYSIS DECISION DIERESIS
ENACTURE STRENGTH

RESOLVE ACT BEND MELT SOIL
UNDO LAPSE RELAX SALVE SOLVE
SOYLE UNTIE VOUCH ADJUST
ADVICE ASSOIL DECIDE DECREE
FACTOR INCIDE REDUCE SETTLE
STEVEN ABSOLVE ANALYZE
APPOINT BETHINK CONSULT
PURPOSE CONCLUDE DISSOLVE
UNRIDDLE UNTANGLE
(— GRAMMATICALLY) PARSE
(— INTO ELEMENTS) ANALYSE
ANALYZE

RESOLVED BENT BOUND INTENT
INTENSE RESOLUTE
(HALF —) GOOD

RESONANCE BODY EMPATHY
RAPPORT RESOUND SYNTONY
TYMPANY SONORITY VIBRANCY

RESONANT BIG BRASS RINGY
OROTUND RINGING SILVERY
VIBRANT PLANGENT SONORANT
SONOROUS SOUNDFUL SOUNDING

RESORT GO RUN SPA BEAT DOME
HOWF LIDO SEEK TEEM TOUR TURN
CAUSE FRAME HAUNT HOWFF JOINT
RECUR RESET VISIT ESCORT FINISH
REPAIR RETURN REVERT THRONG
COMPANY PIMLICO RECOURSE
RESOURCE TEETOTUM
(— TO DEVIOUS METHODS) FINAGLE
(— TO) SEEK
(DISREPUTABLE —) KEN DIVE
(LOW —) KEN DIVE STEW SPITAL
(MEANS OF —) REFUGE
(WORKINGMEN'S —) TEETOTUM

RESOUND DIN DUN ECHO PEAL RING
SOUND REECHO EXPLODE REBOUND
RESPEAK

RESOUNDING BRASS REVERB
EMPHATIC FORCEFUL RESONANT
RUMOROUS
(— WITH TALK) ABUZZ

RESOURCE WON BOOT FUND WONE
MEANS SHIFT REFUGE RESORT
STOPGAP PURCHASE
(PL.) EASE FOND GAIN FUNDS
MEANS SINEW FACULTY FOISONS
PURCHASE STRENGTH

RESOURCEFUL APT FENDY SHARP
SMART CLEVER FACILE SHIFTY
PLANFUL

RESOURCEFULNESS SENSE SHIFT
AGILITY

RESPECT ORE WAY DUTY FACE
HEED HORE LOOK MARK DEFER
DULIA FRONT HONOR IZZAT PARTY
VALUE ASPECT BEHALF DETAIL
ESTEEM HALLOW HOMAGE NOTICE
REGARD CONCERN OBSERVE
RESPITE SUSPECT TASHRIF
WORSHIP CONSIDER HABITUDE
RELATION VENERATE
(PL.) DEVOIR

RESPECTABLE GOOD SMUG DOUCE
DECENT PROPER FRUSANT
CULOTTIC

RESPECTFUL AWFUL CIVIL CAREFUL
DUTEOUS DUTIFUL HEEDFUL
REVERENT

RESPIRATION SIGH EUPNEA
ANAPNEA DYSPNEA EUPNOEA
ROARING GRUNTING
RESPIRATOR MUZZLE CUIRASS
RESPIRE BLOW LIVE REST EXHALE
REVIVE BREATHE SNUFFLE SUSPIRE
RESPITE SOB REST STAY TRUE
DELAY PAUSE BARLEY BREATH
LAYOFF REGARD REMISE LEISURE
RESPECT INTERVAL REPRIEVE
SURCEASE
RESPLENDENCE GLORY FULGENCE
FULGENCY SPLENDOR
RESPLENDENT LUCID SHEEN
BRIGHT GILDED ORIENT SILVER
AUREATE SHINING GLORIOUS
GORGEOUS LUSTROUS SPLENDID
SUNSHINY
RESPOND REACT REPLY ANSWER
RETURN TRISAGION
(— **TO LURE**) STOOL
RESPONDENT ANSWERER APPELLEE
RESPONSE AMEN ECHO CHORD
REPLY SNAFF ANSWER EARFUL
VOLLEY INTROIT RESPOND
ANTIPHON BEHAVIOR INSTINCT
REACTION REANSWER
(— **OF KEYS**) ACTION
(— **OF SHIP**) STEERING
RESPONSIBILITY BALL CARE DUTY
ONUS WITE BLAME GUILT CHARGE
RESPONSIBLE GOOD SOLID DIRECT
LIABLE AMENABLE
RESPONSION REPLY ANSWER
(PL.) SMALLS
RESPONSIVE OPEN SOFT WARM
GUILTY MUTUAL SUPPLE TENDER
MEETING AMENABLE SENSIBLE
(— **TO BEAUTY**) ESTHETIC
(**NOT** —) IMMUNE
RESPONSIVENESS TOUCH FEELING
RESPONSORY ANTHEM LIBERA
GRADUAL RESPOND
REST BED LAY LIE SET SIT SOB
BASE BLOW CALM CAMP EASE
HANG HEEL LAIR LAVE LEAN LIOS
LISS PROP RELY RIDE RUST STAY
STOP COUCH FOUND LEATH PAUSE
PEACE POISE QUIET RENEW ROOST
SLEEP SPELL STAND TRUST WREST
ANCHOR BOTTOM FAUCRE FEWTER
GROUND INSIST REMAIN REPOSE
SETTLE SIESTA STEADY UNTIRE
ADHARMA BALANCE BREATHE
CAESURA CLARION COMFORT
GALLOWS NOONING RECLINE
REFRESH REMNANT REQUIEM
RESIDUE RESPITE SILENCE
SLUMBER SOJOURN SUFFLUE
SUPPORT SURPLUS AKINESIS
INTERVAL QUIETUDE STANDOFF
VACATION
(— **FOR SPEAR OR LANCE**) QUEUE
FAUCRE FEWTER
(— **FOR SUPPORT**) ABUT
(— **FOR TYMPAN**) GALLOWS
(— **HORSE**) WIND
(— **IDLY**) SLUG
(— **LAZILY**) FROWST

(— **ON PLANER**) SIDEHEAD
(— **ON SUPPORT**) BOTTOM
(— **UPRIGHT**) STAND
(**HALF** —) MINIM SOSPIRO
(**LATHE** —) STEADY
(**LEG** — **ON SADDLE**) CRUTCH
(**MUSKET** —) GAFFLE
(**NOONDAY** —) NAP SIESTA
(**QUARTER** —) SOSPIRO
RESTATE REHASH
RESTATEMENT HASH SUMMARY
RESTAURANT CAFE DINER GRILL
HOUSE PLACE BISTRO BUFFET
EATERY AUTOMAT BEANERY
CABARET CANTEEN OSTERIA
TEAROOM HIDEAWAY BRASSERIE
CHOPHOUSE TRATTORIA
(— **KEEPER**) BISTRO TRAITEUR
RESTFUL COOL SOFT QUIET PLACID
EASEFUL RELAXED SOOTHFUL
TRANQUIL
RESTHARROW WHIN CAMMOCK
SITFAST LANDWHIN
RESTHOUSE KHAN SERAI AMBALAM
CHHATRI KHANKAH
RESTING DORMANT
RESTING PLACE (ALSO SEE
RESTHOUSE) FORM GIST GITE
STAGE CHHATRI DHARMSALA
RESTITUTION AMENDS RETURN
RECOVERY
RESTIVE BALKY FUDGY ITCHY
RESTY RUSTY FIDGETY UNRESTY
UNWAYED CONTRARY INACTIVE
RESTLESS SKITTISH SLUGGISH
STUBBORN UNWIELDY
RESTLESS ANTSY FIKIE FUDGY
ITCHY FITFUL HAUNTY HECTIC
ROVING UNEASY AGITATO ERETHIC
FIDGETY FLIGHTY FRETFUL INQUIET
RAMPLER RAMPLOR RESTIVE
TEWSOME TOSSING UNQUIET
UNRESTY VARIANT WAKEFUL
FEVERISH FEVEROUS STEERING
(— **FLYCATCHER**) GRINDER
RESTLESSNESS STIR FIDGET
UNREST DISQUIET JACTATION
RESTORATION REPAIR RETURN
RENEWAL RESTORE REVIVAL
EXCHANGE RECOVERY REMITTER
RESTORAL
RESTORATIVE ACOPON BALSAMIC
SALUTARY SANATIVE ANALEPTIC
RESTORE FIX CURE HEAL AMEND
BLOCK COVER REDUB REFER
RENEW REPAY STORE YIELD
ASTORE DOCTOR RECALL REDEEM
REFORM REFUND RELATE RENDER
REVERT REVIVE CONVERT ENSTORE
INPAINT REBUILD RECLAIM
RECOVER RECRUIT REFOUND
REFRESH REPLACE REVOLVE
DECOHERE REANSWER RESTITUE
RETRIEVE
(— **CONFIDENCE**) REASSURE
(— **TO CIVIL RIGHTS**) INLAW
(— **TO HEALTH**) CURE HEAL MEND
(— **TO ORDER**) STILL
RESTRAIN DAM BATE BIND BOLT

BUCK COOP CRIB CURB DAMP GRAB
GYVE HEAD HEFT KEEP REIN SHUT
SINK SNEB SNIB SNUB STAY STEM
STOP STOW CHAIN CHECK COART
CRAMP DETER GUARD LEASH MINCE
REPEL SHUNT SOBER STILL STINT
TRASH ARREST BOTTLE BRIDLE
CHASTE COERCE DETAIN ENJOIN
FETTER FORBID GOVERN HALTER
HAMPER HINDER KENNEL OBLIGE
REBUKE RETAIN RETIRE REVOKE
STIFLE STRAIN TEMPER ABRIDGE
CHASTEN COHIBIT CONFINE
CONTAIN CONTROL ENCHAIN
EXCLUDE INHIBIT INJUNCT QUALIFY
RECLAIM REFRAIN REPRESS
RETRACT SHACKLE SNAFFLE
SWADDLE BULLDOZE COMPESCE
COMPRESS HANDCUFF IMPRISON
RESTRICT SIDELINE WITHDRAW
WITHHOLD
(— **BY FEAR**) OVERAWE
(— **HAWK'S WING**) BRAIL
(— **MOTION**) SNUB
RESTRAINED SOBER CHASTE
SEVERE ASHAMED DISCREET
RESERVED
RESTRAINT BIT BEND CLOG CURB
HEFT STAY STOP CHECK CRAMP
FORCE LEASH SPARE STENT STINT
ARREST BRIDLE DURESS FETTER
STAYER AWEBAND BONDAGE
CONTROL DURANCE EMBARGO
MANACLE RESERVE SNAFFLE
TRAMMEL SOBRIETY
(— **OF GOODS**) HOCK
RESTRICT TIE CURB HOLD BOUND
CHAIN COART FENCE HEDGE STINT
THIRL COARCT COERCE CORRAL
CORSET ENTAIL HAMPER NARROW
ASTRICT COHIBIT QUALIFY REPRESS
SCANTLE SWADDLE CONTRACT
DEROGATE DIMINISH RESTRAIN
STRAITEN
(— **MEANING**) MODIFY
RESTRICTED CLOSE LOCAL CLOSED
FINITE NARROW STRAIT STRICT
OBLIGATE
RESTRICTION STENT STINT BURDEN
DENIAL BARRIER CONFINE RESERVE
BLACKOUT CABOTAGE
(PL.) BARS SWADDLE
RESTRICTIVE SEVERE BINDING
STYPTIC COACTIVE LIMITARY
LIMITING CONFINING
RESTY LAZY RESTIVE INACTIVE
INDOLENT SLUGGISH
RESULT GO END OUT ECHO FALL
FAVE GROW RISE TAKE BACON
BRING CHILD ENSUE EVENT FRUIT
FUDGE ISSUE PROOF EFFECT
EFFORT ENDING FINISH FOLLOW
GROWTH RECOIL REVERT SEQUEL
SPRING UPCOME UPSHOT ENTRAIN
FINDING OUTCOME PROCEED
REBOUND REDOUND SUCCEED
SUCCESS FRUITAGE SEQUENCE
(— **FAVORABLY**) SUCCEED
(— **FROM**) SUE

(ALGEBRAIC —) DUAL EXPANSION
(AS A —) AGAIN
(INCONCLUSIVE —) DOGFALL
(INEVITABLE —) NEMESIS
(PATHOLOGICAL —S) ALCOHOLISM
(REWARDING —) HAY
(SECONDARY —) SEQUELA
(PL.) AFTERINGS
RESULTANT CONCEPT OUTCOME
  PROGENY
RESUME RENEW REOPEN RECOVER
  SUMMARY CONTINUE PURLICUE
  REASSUME RENOVATE REOCCUPY
  (PL.) EXCERPTA
RESURRECTION RISE RIST UPRIST
  REBIRTH REVIVAL
RESURRECTION PLANT FERNWORT
RESUSCITATE REVIVE QUICKEN
  SUSCITE REVIVIFY
RESUSCITATION KATSU RENEWAL
  REVIVAL
RET RAIT RATE SOAK DEWROT
RETAIL REGRATE HUCKSTER
  (— STORE) WAREHOUSE
RETAILER DEALER CLOTHIER
  HUCKSTER
RETAIN HAVE HOLD KEEP SAVE
  CATCH ATHOLD CONTAIN RESERVE
  CONTINUE MAINTAIN PRESERVE
  (— MOMENTUM) DRIFT
RETAINER FOOL HEWE LACKEY
  MENIAL RIBALD SEQUEL YEOMAN
  HOBBLER HUSCARL JACKMAN
  LACQUEY PANDOUR SERVANT
  TRAVERS EMPLOYEE FOLLOWER
  HENCHMAN MYRMIDON BURKUNDAZ
  (JAPANESE —) SAMURAI
  (PL.) FOLK
RETALIATE REPAY AVENGE RETORT
  REQUITE
RETALIATION QUITS MARQUE
  TALION REPRISAL REQUITAL
  (MAKE —) TURN
  (VINDICTIVE —) REVENGE
RETALIATORY COUNTER
RETARD LAG CHOP DAMP DRAG
  SLOW STEM BRAKE DEFER DELAY
  ELONG TARDY TARRY THROW
  TRASH BACKEN BELATE DEADEN
  DETAIN HINDER INHIBIT SLACKEN
  ENCUMBER OBSTRUCT PROTRACT
  RESTRAIN
RETARDANT (FIRE —) BORAX
RETARDATION LAG DRAG DELAY
RETARDED DARK BEHIND LAGGED
  SIMPLE OVERAGE
RETARDING LENTANDO
RETCH GAG BOKE KECK HEAVE
  REACH VOMIT KECKLE RECCHE
  STRAIN
RETEM JUNIPER
RETENTION MEMORY RETAIN
  HOLDING KEEPING RETINUE
RETIARIUS RETIARY GLADIATOR
RETICENCE RESERVE SECRECY
  RESTRAINT
RETICENT DARK SNUG SECRET
  SILENT MIMMOUD SPARING
RETICENTLY HEIMLICH

RETICULATE MESHED NETTED
RETICULE BAG CABAS SACHET
  WORKBAG CARRYALL RIDICULE
RETICULUM NET MITOME NETWORK
  MATTULLA
RETINOL CODOL
RETINOPHORE VITRELLA
RETINUE CREW GING PORT ROUT
  SUIT TAIL MEINY SUITE TIRED TRAIN
  FAMILY REPAIR RETAIN COMPANY
  CORTEGE SOWARRY EQUIPAGE
  TENDANCE BODYGUARD
  (— OF CAVALRY) SOWARRY
  (VILLAINOUS —) BLACKGUARD
RETIRE GO GET DRAW GIVE AVOID
  LEAVE MICHE REBUT DEPART
  LOCATE RECALL RECEDE RECESS
  RECOIL SHRINK SURVEY PENSION
  REGRADE RETRACT RETREAT
  WITHDRAW
  (— IGNOMINIOUSLY) SLINK
RETIRED QUIET SECRET DEVIOUS
  OBSCURE OUTGONE PRIVATE
  SECLUSE SHADOWY ABSTRUSE
  EMERITUS
  (— FROM PLAY) DOWN
RETIREMENT SHADE RECESS
  SECESS PRIVACY PRIVATE RETREAT
  FIRESIDE SOLITUDE
RETIRING SHY NESH TIMID DEMURE
  MODEST FUGIENT RESERVED
  UMBRATIC
  (— ROOM) RECAMERA
RETORT MOT QUIP RISE SNAP VENY
  QUIRK REPAY REPLY ANSWER
  REGEST RETURN RIPOST BOMBOLA
  CORNUTE CRUSHER PELICAN
  REFLECT SQUELCH BACKWORD
  BLIZZARD COMEBACK MAGAZINE
  RECEIVER REPARTEE
  (CURT —) SNAPHANCE
  (GROUP OF —S) SETTING
  (WITTY —) KNACK
RETRACE RECALL FLYBACK
  RETREAT UNTREAD BACKTRACK
RETRACT BACK UNSAY ABJURE
  DISOWN RECALL RECANT RECEDE
  REVOKE SHRINK UNLOOK RESCIND
  RETREAT SWALLOW PALINODE
  RENOUNCE WITHDRAW
RETRACTED INNER
RETRACTION PALINODE PALINODY
RETREAT DEN DOME DROP FADE
  GIVE NEST ROUT ARBOR AVOID
  BOWER NICHE QUAIL QUIET SHADE
  START ASHRAM ASYLUM BACKUP
  CASTLE RECEDE RECESS REFUGE
  RETIRE REVOLT CABINET DESCEND
  PRIVACY RETIRAL RETRACT
  SHELTER ANABASIS CRAWFISH
  DISMARCH FALLBACK FASTNESS
  NESTLING RECOURSE RECULADE
  SOLITUDE STAMPEDE WITHDRAW
  CREEPHOLE KATABASIS
  (— FOR FISH) HOD
  (RELIGIOUS —) ASRAM ASHRAM
  (SECURE —) STRENGTH
RETRENCH OMIT EXCISE LESSEN

REDUCE ABRIDGE CURTAIL
  SHORTEN
RETRENCHMENT CUT RAMPART
  EXCISION RETIRADE LESSENING
RETRIBUTION PAY RETURN
  REWARD WISSEL MANNAIA PENALTY
  REVENGE REQUITAL
RETRIEVE SHACK RECALL RECURE
  REGAIN REPAIR RESCUE REVIVE
  CORRECT RECOVER RESTORE
  SALVAGE
RETRIEVER FINDER GUNDOG
  LABRADOR WATERRUG
RETROFLEX DEMAL CORONAL
  CEREBRAL INVERTED REFLEXED
RETROGRADE RECEDE RETRAL
  DECLINE INVERSE OPPOSED
  REGREDE RETREAT BACKWARD
  DECADENT REARWARD WITHDRAW
RETROGRESS SINK REGRESS
  BACKSLIDE
RETROGRESSION SINK REGRESS
  RETREAT FALLBACK
RETUND DULL TURN BLUNT REFUTE
RETURN EBB GET COME TURN VAIL
  RECUR REFER REPAY REPLY VISIT
  YIELD AIRWAY ANSWER HOMING
  REMISE RENDER REPAIR REPASS
  REPORT RESORT RETIRE RETORT
  RETOUR REVERT CLEANUP
  PAYMENT REBOUND REDOUND
  REFLECT REPRISE REQUITE
  RESTORE REVENUE ATTOURNE
  DIVIDEND ELECTION EPANODOS
  FEEDBACK REACCESS REANSWER
  RECOURSE RECOVERY REDITION
  (— FROM DEATH) ARISE
  (— OF MERCHANDISE) COMEBACK
  (— TO ZERO) FLYBACK
  (GROUNDED —) BOND
  (TENNIS —) GET BOAST
RETURNING REDIENT REMEANT
  REDITION
REUNION COLLEGE HERENIGING
  (— WITH BRAHMA) NIRVANA
REUNITE RALLY REUNE REJOIN
  RECONCILE
REVEAL BID BARE BLAB HINT JAMB
  KNOW OPEN SHOW TELL WRAY
  BREAK EXERT SPEAK SPLIT UNRIP
  UNTOP UTTER YIELD ACCUSE
  APPEAR BETRAY BEWRAY DESCRY
  DETECT EVINCE IMPART OSTEND
  PATEFY SPRING UNHELE UNLOCK
  UNMASK UNVEIL UNWRAP BESPEAK
  CLARIFY CONFESS DEVELOP
  DISPLAY DIVULGE UNCLOAK
  UNCOVER UNSHALE UNTRUSS
  DECIPHER DISCLOSE DISCOVER
  INDICATE MANIFEST UNBURDEN
  UNSHADOW UNSHROUD
  (— BY SIGNS) EXHIBIT
  (— SECRETS) BABBLE
  (— UNINTENTIONALLY) BETRAY
REVEILLE LEVET ROUSE SIGNAL
  TRAVALLY
REVEL JOY MASK RANT RIOT BIZLE
  FEAST GLOAT GLORY WATCH
  BEZZLE FROLIC GAVALL SPLORE

TRESCA WALLOW WANTON
CAROUSE DELIGHT ROISTER
TRESCHE CAROUSAL DOMINEER
FESTIVAL WITHDRAW
(PL.) REVELRY
REVELATION TORA TORAH EXPOSE
ORACLE REVEAL BATHKOL
BATHQOL SHOWING GIVEAWAY
OVERTURE
(— OF GOD'S WILL) LAW
(SUDDEN —) KICK
REVELER GREEK RANTER RIOTER
FRANION PIERROT ROISTER
BACCHANT CAROUSER
REVELRY JOY ORGY RIOT RIOTISE
WASSAIL CARNIVAL CAROUSAL
FESTIVAL
REVENANT GHOST WRAITH SPECTER
REVENGE HELL WREAK WROIK
AVENGE ULTION REQUITE REQUITAL
REVANCHE
REVENGED EVEN
REVENUE RENT JAGIR MANSE YIELD
INCOME ENTRADA FINANCE PROFITS
HACIENDA INCOMING
(— FROM WATER RIGHTS) JALKAR
(— REVENUE PAID TO POPE) ANNAT
(STATE —) HACIENDA
REVERBERATE DIRL ECHO RING
REPEL RETORT REVERB REBOUND
REDOUND REFLECT RESOUND
REVERBERATING REBOANT
RESONANT SOUNDING
REVERBERATION ECHO REDOUND
REBOATION
REVERE ADORE HONOR ADMIRE
ESTEEM HALLOW RESPECT
WORSHIP VENERATE
REVERENCE AWE ORE CULT FEAR
DREAD HONOR MENSK PIETY
WURTH HOMAGE REGARD WORSHIP
DEVOTION VENERANT VENERATE
WORTHING
(— FOR ANIMALS) ZOISM
(IRRATIONAL —) FETICH FETISH
REVEREND SRI SHRI SHREE SVAMI
SWAMI POTENT STRONG
REVERENT DEVOUT STRONG
AWESOME DUTIFUL
REVERENTIAL PIOUS SOLEMN
REVERIE DUMP DWAM DREAM
DWALM STUDY PONDER MEMENTO
MOONING DAYDREAM TRAUMEREI
REVERSAL KNOCK CHANGE DOUBLE
SWITCH BACKCAST BACKFLIP
OVERTURN THROWBACK
TURNABOUT
REVERSE BACK DOWN FACE FLOP
JOLT ANNUL CHECK UPSET VERSO
CHANGE DEFEAT INVERT REPEAL
RETURN REVERT REVOKE BACKSET
COUNTER INVERSE PUTBACK
RETREAT REVERSO SETBACK
SNIFTER SUBVERT BACKCAST
CONTRARY CONVERSE OPPOSITE
OVERTURN RAMVERSE TRAVERSE
WATERLOO
(— OARS) SHEAVE
(— OF COIN) PILE TAIL WOMAN

(— OF NOTE) BACK
(— PAGE OF BOOK) VERSO
REVERSO
REVERSED INVERSE REVERTED
ROVESCIO
(NOT —) DIRECT
REVERSI QUINOLAS
REVERSION SCRAPS ATAVISM
ESCHEAT REMNANT FEEDBACK
REVERTAL REVERTER THROWBACK
REVERT ANNUL ADVERT RESORT
RESULT RETOUR RETURN REVOKE
ESCHEAT RESTORE RECOURSE
BACKSLIDE
(— TO A SUPERIOR) FALL
REVETMENT SODWORK
REVIEW HASH VIEW REVIE NOTICE
REVISE SURVEY BRUSHUP RECENSE
REJUDGE CRITIQUE REVIEWAL
REVISION
REVILE CALL RAIL ABUSE BLEIR
BRAWL REBUT SCOLD SHEND
SHENT MISUSE VILIFY MISCALL
MISNAME BACKBITE DISGRACE
EXECRATE REPROACH
REVILING ABUSION BLASPHEMY
REVISE EDIT ALTER REDACT
REFORM REVIEW CORRECT
RECENSE REFLECT REVISIT
REVISER REDACTOR REFORMER
REVIEWER
REVISION REVIEW SURVEY REVISAL
REVIEWAL EPANAGOGE
REVITALIZER BRACER
REVIVAL IMAGE REBIRTH WAKENING
REVIVE DAW EBB WAKE FETCH
QUICK RALLY RENEW ROUSE
EXHUME GINGER RECALL RELIVE
REVERT REVOKE EKPHORE ENLIVEN
FRESHEN FURBISH QUICKEN
REFRESH RESPIRE RESTORE
REDIVIVE REKINDLE RENOVATE
RETRIEVE
(— FIRE) CHUNK
REVOCATION REPEAL REVERSAL
ADEMPTION
REVOICE ECHO
REVOKE LIFT ADEEM ANNUL RENIG
CANCEL RECALL RECANT RENEGE
REPEAL REVERT ABOLISH COMMUTE
FINAGLE RECLAIM RESCIND
RETREAT REVERSE ABROGATE
REVOCATE
(— A LEGACY) ADEEM
REVOLT REBEL REPEL START
MUTINY OFFEND RELUCT UPROAR
MUTATION SEDITION UPRISING
JACQUERIE
REVOLTING GARISH HORRID
BILIOUS FEARFUL HATEFUL
HIDEOUS DREADFUL
REVOLUTION GYRE RIOT TOUR
TURN CYCLE WHEEL CHANGE
ANARCHY CIRCUIT REVOLVE
GYRATION MUTATION NOVATION
ROTATION SEDITION
REVOLUTIONARY RED RADICAL
ROTATING BOLSHEVIK
REVOLUTIONIST REDSHIRT

REVOLVE BIRL GYRE PIRL ROLL
SPIN TIRL TURN WELT PIVOT
THROW TREND TROLL TWINE VERSE
WHEEL WHIRL CENTER CIRCLE
GYRATE PONDER ROTATE SPHERE
SWINGE WAMBLE AGITATE VERSATE
CONSIDER OVERTURN REVOLUTE
(CAUSE TO —) TRUNDLE
REVOLVER GAT GUN ROD RIFLE
STICK CANNON CUTTER HOGLEG
PISTOL RIFFLE BULLDOG DUNGEON
REVOLVING ORBY VOLUBLE
GYRATORY VOLUTION
REVUE SHOW REVIEW FOLLIES
REVULSION FEAR REACTION
REWARD FEE PAY UTU GREE MEED
RENT SPUR WAGE AMEED BOOTY
BRIBE CROWN LOWER MERIT PLUME
SHEPE YIELD BOUNTY DESERT
GERSUM SALARY TROPHY WEDFEE
AUREOLE GUERDON PREMIUM
RENTAGE STIPEND WARISON
DIVIDEND EXACTION REMEMBER
REQUITAL
(— FOR INFORMATION ON CATTLE
THIEVES) TASCAL
(— OF VICTORY) CROWN
(— TO HOUNDS) HALLOW
(ILLUSORY —) CARROT
(UNEXPECTED —) JACKPOT
REWARDED APAID BOUNTIED
REWARDING FAT PREMIANT
(FINANCIALLY —) JUICY
REWRITTEN PALIMPSEST
REZAI ROSEI COVERLET MATTRESS
RHABDUS SCOPULA
RHADAMANTHUS (FATHER OF —)
JUPITER
(MOTHER OF —) EUROPA
RHAPSODIC CONFUSED EFFUSIVE
RAPTUROUS
RHAPSODY JUMBLE MEDLEY
BOMBAST ECSTASY RAPTURE
(— SECTION) LASSU
RHATANY LEGUME
RHEA EMU EMEU NANDU NANDOW
RATITE OSTRICH AGDISTIS
AVESTRUZ
(DAUGHTER OF —) JUNO CERES
VESTA
(FATHER OF —) URANUS
(HUSBAND OF —) SATURN
(MOTHER OF —) GAEA
(SON OF —) PLUTO NEPTUNE
RHEBOK PEELE REHBOC
RHENIUM BOHEMIUM
RHEOMETER STROMUHR
RHEOSTAT DIMMER
RHESUS BANDAR BUNDAR MONKEY
BHUNDER MACAQUE
RHETORIC SPEECH BOMBAST
PROSAIC ELOQUENCE
RHETORICAL FLORID FORENSIC
SWELLING
RHETORICIAN ORATOR RHETOR
RHEUM GORE TEARS CHOLER
SPLEEN
RHINARIUM MUFFLE
RHINE DITCH RUNNEL

RHINESTONE DEWDROP
(PL.) GLITTER
RHINO CASH MONEY PONTOON
RHINOCEROS FOW ABADA BADAK
RHINO BORELE KEITLOA UNICORN
UPEYGAN NASICORN
RHINOCEROS BEETLE UANG
SCARABAEID
RHINOCEROS HORNBILL TOPAU
RHIPIDION FLABELLUM
RHIZOID RHIZINA ROOTLET
RHIZOME KAVA NARD ARUKE CAAPI
STOCK ARALIA ARNICA ASARUM
GINGER IPECAC STOLON BERBERY
CALAMUS CULVERS GENTIAN
SCOPOLA ZEDOARY ASPIDIUM
BARBERRY BERBERIS HELONIAS
KAVAKAVA TRILLIUM TRITICUM
VERATRUM
(PL.) INULA GERANIUM

RHODE ISLAND

CAPITAL: PROVIDENCE
COLLEGE: BROWN BRYANT
INDIAN: NIANTIC
MOTTO: HOPE
NATIVE: GUNFLINT
RIVER: PAWTUXET
STATE FLOWER: VIOLET
STATE TREE: MAPLE
TOWN: BRISTOL NEWPORT
CRANSTON KINGSTON

RHODE ISLAND BENT FURZETOP
RHODE ISLANDER GUNFLINT

RHODESIA

CAPITAL: SALISBURY
LANGUAGE: ILA BANTU
PEOPLE: BANTU MASHOMA
MATABELE BALOKWAKWA
RIVER: SABI LIMPOPO ZAMBEZI
RUINS: ZIMBABWE
TOWN: GWELO UMTALI BULAWAYO

RHODODENDRON ROSEBAY
SPOONHUTCH
(THICKET OF —) SLICK
RHOMB LOZEN WHEEL CIRCLE
LOZENGE
RHOMBUS DIAMOND LOZENGE
RHUBARB ROW HASSEL CITRINE
DISPUTE YAWWEED PIEPLANT
RHYME CHIME CLINK VERSE
CRAMBO POETRY RHYTHM TINKLE
MEASURE
(— ROYAL) TROILUS
(PL.) RIMUR
RHYTHM BEAT STOT TIME CHIME
METER PULSE SWING CADENCE
RAGTIME MOVEMENT SEQUENCE
RHYTHMICAL CADENCED MEASURED
NUMEROUS
RIA CREEK INLET
RIAL COIN RYEL ROYAL KINGLY
SPLENDID
RIALTO MART BRIDGE EXCHANGE

RIANT GAY RIDENT LAUGHING
MIRTHFUL
RIATA LASSO LARIAT
RIB FIN KID BULB CORD DIKE JOKE
PURL SLAT WALE WIFE CORSE
COSTA GROIN NERVE OGIVE PEARL
RIDGE VARIX VITTA WHELP BRANCH
LIERNE PARODY RIPPLE SCROLL
TIMBER TONGUE BRISTLE FEATHER
NERVURE PLEURAL STRATUM
FORMERET SIDEBONE
(— IN GROINED ROOF) SPRINGER
(— OF INSECT WING) VEIN
(— OF SHIP) WRONG
(— OF VIOLIN) BOUT
(—S OF UMBRELLA) FRAME
(SHORT —S) CROP
(STRENGTHENING —) FEATHER
(PL.) SLATS
RIBALD ROGUE COARSE RASCAL
VULGAR
RIBALDRY HASH HARLOTRY
RIBAND RIBBON SCROLL
RIBBED RIBBY CORDED
RIBBING SPOOFERY
RIBBON BAR BOW FOB PAN BEND
COST PADS BRAID CORSE FILET
LABEL PADOU PIECE RUBAN SHRED
TASTE BENDEL CADDIS CORDON
FERRET FILLET LISERE RADULA
RECORD RIBAND SHOWER STRING
TAWDRY TISSUE TONGUE BANDING
SAUTOIR TORSADE BANDEROL
BOOKMARK FRAGMENT TRESSURE
(— AS BADGE OF HONOR) CORDON
(— AS HEADDRESS) TRESSOUR
TRESSURE
(— FOR BORDER) LISERE
(— HANGING FROM CROWN) JESS
(— USED FOR GARTERS) CADDIS
CADDICE
(COLORED —S) DIVISA
(END OF —S) FATTRELS
(FLOATING —) PAN
(KNOT OF —S) SORTIE
(LINGUAL —) TONGUE
(SILK —) CORSE PADOU TASTE
(WATERED —) PADS
(PL.) REINS
RIBBON FERN PTERIS
RIBBONFISH GARFISH GUAPENA
AGUAVINA BANDFISH DEALFISH
RIBBONLIKE TAENFORM TAENIATE
TAENIOID
RIBBON TREE AKAROA HOIHERE
HOUHERE LACEBARK
RIBGRASS WINDLES BUCKHORN
HARDHEAD PLANTAIN
RIBWORT KLOPS HEADMAN RATTAIL
SOLDIER WINDLES HARDHEAD
HEADSMAN PLANTAGO
RICE AUS AMAN BORO PADI PAGA
RISE SELA TWIG ARROZ BATTY
BIGAS CANIN CHITS GRAIN MACAN
PADDY PALAY PATNA BRANCH
CEREAL CONGEE SIDDHA ANGKHAK
MANOMIN RISOTTO
(— BOILED WITH MEAT) PILAF PILAU
PILAW

(— COOKED WITH MEAT) RISOTTO
JAMBALAYA
(— FIELD) SAWAH
(— IN HUSK) PALAY
(— OF 2ND OR 3RD GRADE) CHITS
(— POLISHINGS) DARAC
(BOILED —) CANIN KANIN
(HUSKED —) CHAL
(INFERIOR —) PAGA
(LONG-STEMMED —) AMAN
(MOUNTAIN —) SMILO
(SHORT-STEMMED —) AUS
(SPRING —) BORO
(UNCOOKED —) BIGAS
(UNMILLED —) PADI PADDY
(WILD —) MANOMIN
RICEBIRD BUNTING CACIQUE
SPARROW BOBOLINK
RICE FLOWER PIMELEA
RICEGRASS BARIT SACATE ZACATE
RICH FAT ABLE DEEP FAIR HIGH
LUSH OOFY WARM GLEBY OPIME
PLUMP ROUND TINNY VIVID BATFUL
COSTLY DAEDAL FRUITY HEARTY
PLUMMY PLUSHY PODDED SUPERB
ULRICA AMUSING BAITTLE COPIOUS
FERTILE MONEYED OPULENT
PINGUID PLASTIC WEALTHY
ABUNDANT AFFLUENT GENEROUS
HUMOROUS
(— IN FAME) RODERICK
(— IN GIFTS) PREMIOUS
(— IN INTEREST) JUICY
(— IN MALT) HEAVY
(— IN SILICA) ACID
(— IN TIMBRE) GOLDEN
(— MAN) DIVES
(— OF SOIL) PINGUID
RICHARD DICCON
RICHES GOLD PELF WEAL LUCRE
WORTH MAMMON TALENT WEALTH
FORTUNE OPULENCE RICHESSE
TREASURE
RICHLY HIGH AMPLY FATLY FULLY
DEARLY
RICHNESS BODY SUMEN LUXURY
ELEGANCE FECUNDITY
RICHWEED RAGWEED COOLWEED
RICK GOAF GOFE REKE CANCH
RICKLE SPRAIN WRENCH CORNRICK
RICKETY SHAKY SHACKY SHACKLY
UNSOUND RACHITIC SHATTERY
UNSTABLE TOTTERING
RICKMATIC CONCERN BUSINESS
RICOCHET SKIP SKITE GLANCE
REBOUND
RICTUS GRIN GRIMACE
RID FREE QUIT SHED SHUT CLEAR
EGEST REDDE SCOUR SHIFT ACQUIT
REMOVE DELIVER
(— OF INSECTS) BUG
(— OF WEEDS) CLEAN
(— ONESELF OF) DOFF DEPOSIT
DISPATCH
RIDDANCE SHUT RELIEF DISPATCH
RIDDER SIFT SIEVE RIDDLE
RIDDLE SIFT BLAIK GRIPH REBUS
DEBASE ENIGMA FOITER PUZZLE
RUDDLE SCREEN CORRUPT EXPLAIN

GRIDDLE GRIPHUS MYSTIFY
PERPLEX PROBLEM CRATEMAN
PERMEATE
(— AS GRAIN) REE
(PL.) MURLEMEWES
RIDDLER CRATEMAN
RIDE GO RIB BAIT DOSA HACK HURL
LAST LIFT PRIG SAIL TOOL CROSS
DRIVE TEASE BANTER CANTER
DEPEND DODGEM GALLOP JUMBLE
NOTICE SADDLE HAYRIDE JOYRIDE
OVERLAP SURVIVE TANTIVY
BESTRIDE
(— FAST) PRICK POWDER
(— HARD) POUND BUCKET
(— IN HIRED VEHICLE) JOB
(— ON HORSE) BOOT LARK BURST
JOCKEY SCHOOL
(— TO HOUNDS) GO
(AMUSEMENT PARK —) SWING
RIDER TACK ANNEX CROSS HAZER
LABEL COWBOY JOCKEY SITTER
ALLONGE CODICIL NAGSMAN
PRICKER CAVALIER DESULTOR
HORSEMAN
(DUKEY —) BRAKEMAN
(DUMMY —) CROSS
RIDGE AAS ARM FIN RIB RIG RYG
BALK BAND BANK BARB BROW BULT
BURR BUTT COMB DRUM FRET FULL
HACK HILL KEEL LINK LIST PAHA
PUFF RAIN REAN ROLL SHIN SPUR
WAVE WELT BARGH CHINE COSTA
CREST EARTH EAVES GONYS
GYRUS JUGUM KNURL LEDGE RINGE
RUDGE SCOUT SHANK SPINE TORUS
VARIX WHELP BRIDGE CARINA
COLLOP CREASE CRISTA CUESTA
CULMEN DIVIDE DORSUM FRENUM
RAFTER RIDEAU SADDLE SELION
SUMMIT ANNULET APODEMA
BREAKER BUCCULA COLLINE
COSTULA EYEBROW EYELINE
HOGBACK HUMMOCK INTHROW
PROPONS RIGGING SOWBACK
WINDROW WITHERS WRINKLE
YARDANG CATOCTIN CINGULUM
FOREDUNE HEADLAND RESTBALK
SHOULDER
(— BETWEEN FURROWS) STITCH
RESTBALK
(— IN BREASTPLATE) TAPUL
(— IN COAL SEAM) HORSEBACK
(— IN HORSE'S MOUTH) EAR
(— MADE BY PLOWING) HACK
SELION
(— MADE BY TOOL) BUR BARB
BURR
(— OF BIRD'S BILL) CULM CULMEN
(— OF BRAIN CORAL) COLLINE
(— OF BREASTBONE) KEEL
(— OF CLAY) DOWLE
(— OF EARTH) BALK
(— OF FLESH) COLLOP
(— OF HORSE'S NECK) CREST
(— OF LAND) BULT RAIN SELION
STITCH HOGBACK
(— OF SAND IN WATER) REEF
SANDBAR

(— OF SCAPULA) SPINE
(— OF SNOW) SASTRUGA
ZASTRUGA
(— OF UNPLOWED LAND) LINCH
LINCHET
(— OF WAVE) CREST
(— ON BOOK) HUB
(— ON CLOTH) WALE
(— ON CROWN OF TOOTH)
CINGULUM
(— ON FINGERBOARD OF GUITAR)
FRET
(— ON FISH SCALE) CIRCULUS
(— ON FRUITS OF CARROT FAMILY)
JUGUM
(— ON GLUMES) CARINA
(— ON MOLLUSK SHELL) COSTULA
(— ON SEA FLOOR) SWELL
(— ON SEASHORE) STANNER
(— ON SHEET METAL) BEAD
(— ON SIDE OF SADDLE) PUFF
(— ON SKIN) WALE
(— ON VIOLIN) NUT
(— PROTECTING CAMP) RIDEAU
(— WITH SHARP SUMMIT) HOGBACK
(—S ON ROCK) LAPIES
(ANATOMICAL —) CARINA
(BEACH —) FULL
(CHEWING —) ENDITE
(CONNECTING —) HAUSE
(CONVOLUTED —) GYRUS
(DRAINAGE —) BREAKER
(GLACIAL —) OS KAME PAHA ESKAR
ESKER ESCHAR
(HAIRLIKE —) LIRA
(ICE —) SERAC
(ISOLATED —) BARGH
(LONG STONY —) RAND
(MOUNTAIN —) COMB SIERRA
BACKBONE
(NARROW —) DRUM RAZORBACK
(PROJECTING —) SCOUT
(RESIDUAL —) CATOCTIN
(SAND —) DUNE WAVEMARK
(SHARP-CRESTED —) ARETE
(SLIGHT —) PROPONS
(UNPLOWED —) BALK BAULK
(WOODED —) CHENIER
(PL.) KNURLING
RIDGED RIDGY SHARP CARINATE
RIDGELING RIG REGALD RIDGIL
RIGGOT RIGINAL
RIDGEPOLE ROOFTREE
RIDICULE FUN GUY MOB PAN RIG
TAX GAME GIBE JEER JEST JIBE
JOEY MOCK PLAY QUIZ RAZZ SKIT
TROT TWIT BORAK CHAFF CLOWN
HORSE IRONY MIMIC MOMUS QUEER
RALLY SCOFF SMOKE SNEER TAUNT
BANTER DERIDE EXPOSE RAILLY
SATIRE BUFFOON LAMPOON
MOCKERY SARCASM DERISION
RAILLERY SATIRIZE SPOOFERY
RIDICULOUS DOTTY DROLL FUNNY
SILLY ABSURD INSANE COMICAL
FOOLISH MOCKING DERISIVE
DERISORY FARCICAL INDECENT
RIDING AWHEEL LIVELY OVERLAP
PRICKANT SHIVAREE TRITHING
CHEVACHIE

(— ACADEMY) MANAGE MANEGE
(— CROP) ROD
(— WHIP) CROP QUIRT
RIDOTTO BALL REDOUTE
RIEM RHEIM RIMPI STRAP THONG
RIFE EASY FULL RANK QUICK READY
ACTIVE FILLED NIMBLE STRONG
CURRENT REPLETE ABUNDANT
INCLINED MANIFEST NUMEROUS
RIFFLE RIFF WAVE RAPID RIPPLE
SHUFFLE WATERFALL
RIFFRAFF MOB RAFF SCAFF TRASH
RABBLE REFUSE RUBBISH CANAILLE
POPULACE RAGABASH
RIFLE RIG ROB KRAG RIPE PIECE
YAGER CARBIN JEZAIL JUZAIL
RIFFLE SNIDER ARISAKA BULLPUP
BUNDOCK BUNDOOK CARABIN
CARBINE DESPOIL ENFIELD
ESCOPET MARTINI PILLAGE
PLUNDER RANSACK SPORTER
BANDHOOK BUNDHOOK REPEATER
SPLITTER STRICKLE TAKEDOWN
CHASSEPOT
(— BALL CASING) THIMBLE
(— PIN) TIGE
RIFLEMAN JAGER JAEGER
(PL.) RIFLERY
RIFT RIVE BELCH CHASM CRACK
SPLIT CLEAVE DIVIDE BLEMISH
FISSURE CREVASSE
(— IN TIMBER) LAG
RIG RI FIG REG HOAX JEST JOKE
REEK WIND DRESS EQUIP GETUP
PRANK RIDGE SPORT STORM TRICK
BANTER CLOTHE GUNTER ROTARY
SADDLE SCHEME MARCONI
SPUDDER SWINDLE BACKSTAY
RIDICULE
(TRUCKING —) SEMI
RIGADOON DANCE RIGODON
RIGEL REGEL ALGEBAR
RIGGED (FULLY —) ATAUNT
RIGGER CLIMBER SLINGER
SCAFFOLD
RIGGING NET GEAR ROOF RIDGE
TACKLE CLOTHING JACKSTAY
TACKLING
RIGHT DUE FEE FIT IUS OFF REE
SAY SOC BANG DUTY FAIR FLOP
GALE GOOD HAND ITER JUST LIEN
REAL RECT REET SANE SLAP SOKE
TEAM TRUE WELL CLAIM DRESS
DROIT ENTRY EXACT FAVOR FERRY
LEGAL RICHT SOUND STRAY TECHT
TITLE ACTION ACTUAL BALLOT
DEMAND DEXTER EATAGE EQUITY
PROPER PUTURE ANNUITY APANAGE
AUBAINE CORRECT DERECHO
DESIRED FACULTY FALDAGE FITTING
FOLDAGE FREEDOM GENUINE
HAYBOTE LIBERTY LICENSE
PRENDER RECTIFY RELIEVE
SLAPDAB UPRIGHT WARRANT
BANALITY BLOODWIT FIREBOOT
FORESTRY HEIRSHIP INTEREST
LIFERENT SEIGNORY SLAPDASH
STALLAGE STRAIGHT SUFFRAGE
SUITABLE THIRLAGE

(— AND LEFT) HAY HEY
(— AS COMMAND TO HORSES) REE
(— EYE) OD
(— HAND) MD OPENBAND
(— IN A THING) INTEREST
(— IN WIFE'S INHERITED PROPERTY)
CURTESY
(— OF CHOICE) OPTION
(— OF EXIT) ISH
(— OF FREE QUARTERS) CORODY
(— OF HOLDING COURT) TEAM
(— OF INQUIRY) SOKEN
(— OF OWNERSHIP) TITLE
COMMONTY
(— OF PASTURAGE) FEED STINT
EATAGE COWGATE COMMONAGE
HORSEGATE
(— OF PRECEDENCE) PAS
(— OF PROTECTION) MUND
(— OF USING ANOTHER'S
PROPERTY) EASEMENT
(— OF USING GRASSLAND) EATAGE
(— SIDE) OFFSIDE
(— TIME) TID
(— TO COLLECT REVENUE) DIWANI
DEWANEE DEWANNY
(— TO COMMAND) IMPERIUM
(— TO CUT WOOD) VERT
GREENHEW
(— TO DRAW WATER) HAUSTUS
(— TO DRIVE BEAST) ACTUS
(— TO PASS OVER LAND) ITER
(— TO SEIZE PROPERTY) ANGARY
(— TO SHOOT FIRST) CAST
(— TO WORK IN MINE) BEN
(ALL —) HUNK JAKE HUNKY
(FEUDAL —) THIRL THIRLAGE
(INDIAN LEGAL —) HAK HAKH
(LEGAL —) IUS JUS JURE DROIT
ACCESS APPEAL COMMON FISHERY
HYPOTHEC
(LEGAL —S) JURA
(MINING —) GALE
(NOT —) ACUTE
(PROPERTY —) DOMINIUM
(WIDOW'S —) TERCE TIERCE
(PL.) DIBS JURA
RIGHT ANGLE RECTANGLE
(HUNDREDTH OF —) GRAD GRADE
RIGHTEOUS GOOD JUST GODLY
MORAL ZADOC ZADOK DEVOUT
FITTING PERFECT SKILFUL UPRIGHT
INNOCENT VIRTUOUS
RIGHTEOUSNESS DOOM DHARMA
EQUITY JUSTICE HOLINESS
JUDGMENT JUSTNESS MORALITY
RECTITUDE
RIGHTFUL DUE JUST TRUE LEGAL
KINDLY LAWFUL PROPER FITTING
RIGHTFULNESS JUSTICE
RIGHT-HANDED DEXTRAL SKILLED
DEXTROUS CLOCKWISE
RIGHT-HANDWISE DEASIL DESSIL
DEISEAL CLOCKWISE
RIGHTLY RITE FITLY ARIGHT FAIRLY
JUSTLY HANDILY PERQUEER
SUITABLY
RIGHT WHALE BOWHEAD BALAENID
MYSTICETE NORDCAPER

RIGID SET ACID CARK FIRM HARD
HIGH FIXED SOLID STARK STERN
STIFF STONY STOUT TENSE TOUGH
FORMAL FROZEN MARBLY SEVERE
STARCH STICKY STRICT AUSTERE
IRONCLAD RIGOROUS STRAIGHT
INELASTIC STRINGENT
(— IN SELF-DENIAL) ASCETIC
RIGIDITY FROST RIGOR RIGOUR
BUCKRAM SETNESS HARDNESS
STIFFNESS
RIGMAREE COIN TRIFLE
RIGMAROLE RANE NOMINY RABBLE
SLAMPAMP SLAMPANT AMPHIGORY
RIGOR TYRANNY ASPERITY
HARDNESS SEVERITY
RIGOROUS FIRM HARD CLOSE
CRUEL EXACT HARSH HEFTY RIGID
STERN STIFF BITTER FLINTY SEVERE
STRICT STRONG AUSTERE DRASTIC
PRECISE DISTRICT DRACONIC
EXACTING IRONCLAD STRAIGHT
(MORALLY —) PURITANIC
(NOT —) INEXACT
(UNDULY —) HARSH
RILE VEX ROIL ANGER IRRITATE
RILL PURL SIKE CLEFT DRILL PRILL
GROOVE RILLOCK RIVULET
BROOKLET RIVELING TRICKLET
ARROYUELO WATERSHUT
RILLSTONE VENTIFACT
RIM HEM LIP BEAD BRIM CURB EDGE
SHOE BEZEL BRINK CHIME EAVES
FELLY FRAME HELIX SKIRT BORDER
CALKER CHOANA FILLET FLANGE
MARGIN EXCIPLE
(— HOLDING WATCH CRYSTAL)
BEZEL BEZIL
(— OF BASKET) HOOP
(— OF COROLLA) ANNULUS
(— OF CRATER) SOMMA
(— OF EAR) HELIX
(— OF HORSESHOE) WEB
(— OF INSECT'S WING) TERMEN
(— OF SANIO) CRASSULA
(— OF TIN) LIST
(— OF WHEEL) FELLY FELLOE
(— ON CASK) CHIMB CHIME CHINE
(— ON CLOG) CALKER
(— SURROUNDING FLAGELLUM)
CHOANA
(EXTERNAL —) FLANGE
(PROTECTIVE —) BANK
(RAISED —) BOSS
RIMA CHINK CLEFT RIMULA FISSURE
RIME RIM HOAR RIND RUNG CRACK
CRUST FROST ROUND CRANREUCH
RIMPLE FOLD RIPPLE WRINKLE
RIND BARK PEEL PILL RYND SKIN
CRUST FROST SWARD CITRON
SWARTH
(— OF HAM) SKIN
(— OF MEAT) SPINE
(— OF POMEGRANATE) GRANATUM
(— OF ROASTED PORK) CRACKLING
RING GO BEE BOW BUR CUP DEE DIE
EKE FAM JOW ORB PIT RIM AMBO
BAIL BAND BELL BONG BURR CRIC
CURB DING DIRL ECHO GYRE HOOP

JING LOOP MAIL PASS PEAL RACE
RINK RUSH SHUT SING TANG TOLL
VIRL WISP AMBON ANLET ARENA
BAGUE CAROL CHIME CLANG CYCLE
GRAIN GROUP GUARD GUIDE JEWEL
KNELL LUNET PISTE RIGOL ROUND
ROWEL TORUS VERGE WAFER
WITHE BECKET BROUGH BUTTON
CIRCLE CIRCUS CLIQUE COLLAR
COLLET DINDLE EYELET FAMBLE
GIMMER GIRDLE HARROW KEEPER
LARIGO LEGLET RINGLE RUNDLE
RUNNER SIGNET TORQUE TURRET
VIROLE WASHER ANNULUS ARMILLA
CIRCUIT CLAPPER COMPASS
COUPLER CRINGLE DIAMOND
FAMELEN FERRULE GALLERY
GARLAND GROMMET GUDGEON
MANILLA NUCLEUS PACKING
RESOUND ROWLOCK SHACKLE
STIRRUP THIMBLE BRACELET
BULLRING CINCTURE CORONULE
DINGDONG DRAUPNIR DUSTBAND
ENCIRCLE FAIRLEAD PACIFIER
SONORITY SURROUND TRAVELER
(— A TREE) FRILL
(— AROUND ARTICULAR CAVITY)
AMBON
(— AROUND MOON) BROCH
(— AROUND NIPPLE) AREOLA
(— AT EACH END OF CINCH)
LARIGO
(— ATTACHED TO JIB) HANK
(— BELLS) FIRE
(— FOR CARRYING SHOT) LADLE
(— FOR SECURING BIRD) VERVEL
(— FOR TRAINING HORSES) LONGE
(— FORMING HANDLE OF KEY) BOW
(— OF ANNULATED COLUMN)
BAGUE
(— OF BOILER) STRAKE
(— OF COLOR) STOCKING
(— OF DOTS AROUND EDGE OF
COIN) GRAINING
(— OF LIGHT) GLORY
(— OF ODIN) DRAUPNIR
(— OF RIDING SCHOOL) PISTE
(— OF ROPE) HANK BECKET
GARLAND GROMMET SNORTER
SNOTTER
(— OF SPINES) CORONULE
(— OF STANDING STONES) CAROL
(— OF TWO HOOPS) GEMEL
GEMMEL
(— ON BATTLEAX) BUR BURR
(— ON BIRD'S TIBIA) ARMILLA
(— ON DECK) CRANCE
(— ON GUN CARRIAGE) LUNET
LUNETTE
(— ON HINGE) GUDGEON
(— ON LAMP) CRIC
(— ON LANCE) BURR
(— ON UMBRELLA ROD) RUNNER
(— SUPPORTING LAMPSHADE)
GALLERY
(— SURROUNDING BUGLE) VIROLE
(— SUSPENDING COMPASS) GIMBAL
(— TO ENCLOSE DEER) TINCHEL
TINCHILL

(— **UNDER BEEHIVE**) EKE
(— **USED AS MONEY**) MANILLA
(— **USED AS VALVE**) WAFER
(— **WITH GROOVED OUTER EDGE**) THIMBLE
(— **WITH VIBRATION**) DIRL
(**BRIGHT** —) HALATION
(**CERVICAL** —) TORQUE
(**CURTAIN** —) EYE
(**FINGER** —) HOOP
(**FLESHY** —) ANNULUS
(**HARNESS** —) DEE BUTTON LARIGO TERRET TORRET TURRET
(**INTERLINKED METAL —S**) MAIL
(**JOINED** —) GIMMER GIMMOR
(**LITTLE** —) ANNULET
(**LUMINOUS** —) BROUGH
(**NOSE** —) PIRN
(**OIL** —) WIPER
(**PACKING** —) LUTE
(**PLAITED** —) RUSH WISP
(**SURGICAL** —) CURETTE
(**TAPERING SHANK** —) BELCHER
(**TARGET** —) SOUS SOUSE
(**TOOTHED IRON** —) HARROW
(**TOP OF** —) BEZEL BEZIL

RINGDOVE QUIST CUSHAT CUSHIE QUEEST TOOZOO ZOOZOO COWSHOT COWSHUT
RINGED GYRATE ZONATE ANNULAR
RINGED SNAKE COLUBRID
RINGER CHEER YOUTH COWBOY CROWBAR STOCKMAN
RINGHALS COBRA
RINGING BELL BRIGHT FERVID JANGLE CLANGOR OROTUND SINGING DECISIVE RESONANT SONORANT SONOROUS TINNIENT
(**CHANGE** —) CINQUES SINGLES
RINGLET CURL LOCK TENDRIL
(— **ON FOREHEAD**) FAVORITE
RING-NECKED TORQUATE
RING-NECKED DUCK DOGY SCAUP MOONBILL RINGBILL BLACKJACK
RING OUZEL AMSEL THRUSH WHISTLER
RING PLOVER SANDY COLLIER DULWILLY RINGNECK
RING-SHAPED ANNULAR ANNULARY ANNULATE CIRCULAR
RINGWORM TINEA KERION TETTER SERPIGO
RINGWORM BUSH SENNA
RINK GLACIARIUM
RINSE NET SIND WASH RANGE RENCH RENSH RINGE SCIND SWILL BLUING DOUCHE CLEANSE
RINSING NET SIND FLUSH RESIDUE
RIOT DIN HURL BRAWL REVEL WORRY ATTACK CLAMOR EXCESS JUMBLE MEDLEY RANTAN SPLORE TUMULT ANARCHY CONFUSE DESPOIL REVELRY BLOODWIT CAROUSAL
RIOTOUS ROID ROYD WILD NOISY RANDY RANTY HEMPIE RANDIE STORMY WANTON BACCHIC PROFUSE ROARING ABUNDANT BACCHIAN

RIP RIT COOP REAT TEAR BREAK SHARK SHRED SLITE UNSEW BASKET RIPPLE UNSEAM
RIPE FIT BOLD LATE DRUNK READY MATURE MELLOW SIDDER SIDDOW DIGESTED FINISHED SEASHORE SUITABLE
(**EARLY** —) HASTY RARERIPE
RIPEN AGE ADDLE AUGUST DIGEST MELLOW CONCOCT CRIMSON DEVELOP PERFECT COMPLETE MATURATE
RIPENESS MATURITY
RIPOSTE REPLY RETORT THRUST REPARTEE
RIPPER RIPSAW BOBSLED HUMDINGER
RIPPET FUSS TUMULT UPROAR DISPUTE QUARREL
RIPPING FINE GRAND SWELL CAPITAL TIPPING SPLENDID
RIPPLE FRET RIFF SEED WAVE ACKER CRISP TWINE COCKLE DIMPLE JABBLE LIPPER RIMPLE RUFFLE RUMBLE WIMPLE CRINKLE WAVELET WRINKLE
(— **ALONG**) DADE
RIPPLING BREAK BULGE JABBLE ARIPPLE
(— **ON SURFACE**) HORROR
RIPSAW RIPPER SPLITSAW
RIPSNORTER SNIFTER HUMDINGER
RISE COME DRAW FLOW GROW HEAD HIGH HIKE HOLT HOVE LIFT PLUM SOAR ARISE BEGIN CANCH CHEER CLIMB ERECT HEAVE HOIST MOUNT OCCUR PITCH PLUFF RAISE ROUSE SCEND SOURD STAND START SURGE SWELL TOWER YEAST ASCEND ASCENT ASPIRE AURORA BILLOW EMERGE GROWTH HAPPEN HEIGHT ORIGIN RESULT RETORT SOURCE SPRING THRIVE UPDIVE UPREAR ADVANCE APPLAUD HUMMOCK REDOUND UPHEAVE UPSHOOT EMINENCE FLOURISH HEIGHTEN INCREASE LEVITATE SCENSION UPSPRING
(— **ABOVE**) SURMOUNT
(— **ABRUPTLY**) SKYROCKET
(— **AGAIN**) RESURGE
(— **AND FALL**) LOOM HEAVE WELTER
(— **AS PRICE**) MEND
(— **GRADUALLY**) LOOM
(— **IN BLISTERS**) YAW
(— **IN CLOUDS**) STOOR
(— **IN MINE FLOOR**) HOGBACK
(— **IN PRICES**) BULGE
(— **IN VALUE**) IMPROVE
(— **OF CURVE**) CAMBER
(— **OF HAWK AFTER PREY**) MOUNTY
(— **OF SHIP'S LINES**) FLIGHT
(— **OF WATER**) FLOOD
(— **PRECIPITOUSLY**) SKY
(— **RAPIDLY**) KITE
(— **SHARPLY**) BREAK
(— **SUDDENLY**) BOOM SPRING
(— **SWIFTLY**) BOIL

(— **TO BAIT**) TAKE
(— **TO GREAT HEIGHT**) TOWER
(— **TO PEAK**) SWELL
(— **UP**) FUME REAR ASCEND INSURRECT
(**SHARP** —) HOGBACK
RISER HEAD RAISE FEEDHEAD INSURGENT
RISHI RSI POET SAGE SAINT DEVARSHI KASHYAPA MAHARSHI
RISIBLE FUNNY GELASTIC LAUGHABLE
RISING BOIL BULL RIST ARISE ARIST ORIENT SOURCE STRAKE UPREST UPWITH MONTANT PUSTULE SURGENT EMERGENT INCREASE MOUNTANT EXCEEDING
(— **ABRUPTLY**) BOLD
(— **AND FALLING**) TIDAL
(— **AS OF HAWK**) SOURCE
(— **BY DEGREES**) GRADIENT
(— **GRADUALLY**) SOFT
(— **HIGH**) AERIAL
(— **SHARPLY**) ABRUPT
(— **STEEPLY**) BLUFF
RISK GO RUN SET GAGE JUMP LUCK PAWN PERIL RISCO STAKE STAND THROW WAGER WATHE CHANCE DANGER GAMBLE HAZARD PLIGHT THREAT BALANCE IMPERIL VENTURE ENDANGER EXPOSURE
RISKY BOLD CHANCY DARING KITTLE RISQUE PARLISH PARLOUS TECHOUS TICKLISH
RISP BUSH RASP STEM TWIG STALK BRANCH SCRATCH
RISQUE BLUE RACY BROAD DARING SCABROUS
RISS-WURM NEUDECKIAN
RIT CUT RIP RUT REND SLIT TEAR SCRATCH
RITE KEX ASAL BORA BRIS FORM HAKO SOMA BRITH HONOR RIGHT SRADH ABDEST AUGURY EXEQUY FETISH OFFICE PANSIL PIACLE POOJAH RITUAL BAPTISM FUNERAL KATCINA LITURGY MYSTERY OBSEQUY SRADDHA TASHLIK CEREMONY HIERURGY HUSKANAW MORTUARY PIACULUM
(**PL.**) CULT SACRA SERVICE
RITUAL FORM RITE SOLEMN AGENDUM HAGGADA LITURGY OBSEQUY SERVICE CEREMONY VISPARAD VISPERED
RITZY HAUGHTY SNOBBISH
RIVAGE BANK RIVE COAST SHORE
RIVAL VIE EVEN PEER SIDE MATCH COMPETE CORRIVE EMULATE CORRIVAL EMULATOR OPPONENT
RIVALRY VIE GAME PARAGON JEALOUSY STRIVING EMULATION
RIVE RIP PLOW REND STAB TEAR CRACK REAVE SEVER SPLIT WEDGE CLEAVE SUNDER THRUST SHATTER FRACTURE
RIVER EA LE LEE REE RIO TJI ALPH BAHR GEON ILOG KILL WADI WADY BAYOU FLOOD GANGA GIHON GJOLL

GLIDE HABOR INLET KIANG TCHAI
BARCOO GUTTER KHUBUR NYANZA
STRAIT STREAM CHANNEL COCYTUS
ESTUARY FROEMAN ILISSUS
PHARPAR RUBICON SENEGAL
AFFLUENT ERIDANUS PACTOLUS
STAIRCASE
(— CHANNEL) ALVEUS
(— NEAR GATE OF HEL'S ABODE)
GJOLL
(— OF ATTICA) ILISSUS
(— OF DAMASCUS) PHARPAR
(— OF LYDIA) PACTOLUS
(— OF PARADISE) GEON GIHON
(— OF QUEENSLAND) BARCOO
(— OF UNDERWORLD) STYX LETHE
ACHERON COCYTUS FLEGETON
(AFRICAN —) NYANZA SENEGAL
(CHINESE —) HO KIANG
(EGYPTIAN —) BAHR NILE
(FULL —) BANKER
(JAVANESE —) TJI
(MINOR —) BAYOU
(SACRED —) ALPH GANGA
(SMALL —) BACHE TCHAI
RIVERBANK RIPA RIPE
RIVERBED LAAGTE BATTURE
(DRY —) WADI WADY
RIVERBOAT COG BARGE FOIST
PULWAR
RIVER DUCK TEAL MALLARD
WIDGEON GREENWING
RIVERINE (— FISH) HUCHO
RIVERWEED WATERWEED
RIVET STUD ROOVE PANHEAD
FLATHEAD
(— ATTENTION) GRIP
(— HEAD) CUPHEAD
RIVULET RUN BURN GILL LAKE
MOTH RILL BACHE BATCH BAYOU
BOURN BROOK GHYLL RITHE
RINDLE RUNLET RUNNEL STREAM
STRIPE STRYPE CHANNEL RIVERET
BROOKLET
RIXY TERN
RIZZAR DRY PARCH RASOUR
RAZOUR CURRANT HADDOCK
RIZZOM BIT EAR RISOM STALK
STRAW RISSOM
ROACH HOG BUTT ROCK SPOT
BRAISE BLATTID SUNFISH
ROAD LEG PAD TAO WAY BELT
BORD CASH DRAG DRUN FARE
GAET GANG GATE LINE LODE LOKE
PASS PATH PAVE PIKE RADE RAID
RIDE RODE ROTE ROUT SLAB SPUR
WENT BARGH BLAZE BYWAY CLOSE
DRIFT DRIVE DROVE FORAY GAITE
GOING METAL PRAYA ROUTE TRACE
TRACK BYROAD CAMINO CAREER
CAUSEY CHEMIN COURSE DUGWAY
FEEDER RIDING ROUGHT RUNWAY
SLOUGH STREET TARMAC TRAJET
CALZADA CARTWAY ESTRADA
GANGWAY HIGHWAY LANDWAY
OUTGANG PACKWAY PASSAGE
RAILWAY RAMPIRE ROADWAY
ROLLWAY SKIDWAY TELFORD
AUTOBAHN BEALLACH BLACKTOP

BROADWAY CHAUSSEE CORDUROY
FOOTRILL HORSEWAY OVERPASS
RIDGEWAY SPEEDWAY TRACKWAY
TRAMROAD TRAVERSE TURNPIKE
WAGONWAY
(— BORDERING SHORE) PRAYA
(— FOR LOGGING) SKIDWAY
CROSSHAUL
(— IN COAL MINE) BORD BOARD
FOOTRILL
(— ON CLIFF) CORNICHE
(— SCRAPER) HARL HARLE
(— SURFACE) TELFORD
(CEMENT OR CONCRETE —) SLAB
(COUNTRY —) BOREEN DRIFTWAY
(DESCENDING —) BAHADA BAJADA
(IMPASSABLE —) SLOUGH IMPASSE
(IMPROVISED —) CASH
(MILITARY OR PUBLIC —) AGGER
(NARROW —) DRANG DRUNG
RODDIN
(PAVED —) CALZADA CHAUSSEE
(PRINCIPAL —) ARTERY
(PRIVATE —) LOKE DRIVE DRIVEWAY
(RAISED —) AGGER RAMPIRE
CAUSEWAY
(ROMAN —) ITER CAUSEY
(SIDE —) BRANCH SHUNPIKE
(STEEP —) BRAE PATH BARGH
SPRUNT
(TEMPORARY —) SHOOFLY
(UNIMPROVED —) DROVE
(ZIGZAG —) SWITCHBACK
ROADBED BALLAST BITUMEN
ROADBOOK MAP ITINERARY
ROAD DONKEY ROADER
ROADMAN PEDDLER SALESMAN
CANVASSER
ROADMASTER OVERSEER
ROAD RUNNER CUCKOO PAISANO
ROADSIDE HEDGE
ROADSTEAD RAID DOWNS
ROADSTER BUGGY TRAMP DRIVER
BICYCLE RUNABOUT RACEABOUT
SPEEDSTER
ROADWAY DECK EXIT STREET
MACADAM SLIPWAY TRUCKWAY
ROAM GO ERR RUN WAG RAKE
RAME RAVE ROIL ROLL ROVE WALK
GIPSY GYPSY KNOCK RANGE SCAMP
SPACE STRAY TAVER VAGUE
WAVER BANGLE RAMBLE STROLL
SWERVE TAIVER VAGARY WANDER
GALLANT PROCEED SQUANDER
VAGABOND
(— FURTIVELY) PROWL
ROAMING ERROR ROAMAGE
FUGITIVE
ROAN HORSE GRIZZLE
ROANOKE WAMPUM
ROAR CRY BAWL BEAL BELL BERE
BOOM BRAY HOWL HURL RAIR
RARE RERD ROIN ROME ROUT YELL
BROOL CRACK RERDE ROUST
SHOUT SNORE BELLOW BULDER
BULLER CLAMOR GOLLAR GOLLER
RUMMES SCREAM SHRIEK STEVEN
BLUSTER RUMMISH ULULATE

(— AS BOAR) FREAM
(— LIKE WIND) HURL
(— OF SURF) ROTE
(LOW —) BROOL
ROARING RUT LOUD AROAR BRISK
ROUST BELLOW BOOMING RIOTOUS
THRIVING
ROARING BOY TWIBIL TWIBILL
ROARING GAME CURLING
ROARING MEG CANNON
ROAST RAZZ ROTI SOAK BREDE
PARCH ASSATE CODDLE REMOVE
TORREFY TORRIFY BARBECUE
RIDICULE
(STUFFED —) FARCI
ROASTED ASADO
(NOT —) GREEN
ROASTER BURNER SCORCHER
ROASTING ASSATION
ROASTING JACK TURNSPIT
ROB COP EASE FAKE FLAP NICK
PEEL PELF PICK PILL POLL PREY
PULL RAMP RIPE ROLL TOBY BENIM
BRIBE FLIMP HARRY HEAVE HEIST
LURCH PINCH PLUCK PLUME PROWL
REAVE RIFLE ROIST SHAKE SPOIL
SPUNG STEAL STRUB TOUCH
HARROW HIJACK HUSTLE PILFER
RAVISH STRIKE THIEVE DEPRIVE
DESPOIL PLUNDER RUMPADE
SNAFFLE UNPURSE DEFLOWER
SPOLIATE
(— HOUSE) MILL
(— OF CHASTITY) DEFILE
(— OF FORCE) COOL
(— OF JOY) DESOLATE
(— OF VIGOR) ETIOLATE
(— WITH VIOLENCE) RAMP
ROBALO SNOOK SNOWK SERGEANT
ROBBED RUBATO
(NOT —) UNPILLED
ROBBER PAD FOMOR LARON THIEF
BANDIT BRIBER DACOIT FORMOR
HOLDUP LATRON RIFLER BRIGAND
FOOTPAD HEISTER LADRONE
MOONMAN PRANCER RAVENER
ROUTIER SPOILER TOBYMAN
BARRABAS FOMORIAN PILLAGER
RABIATOR
(— ON HIGH SEAS) PIRATE
(— WHO USES VIOLENCE)
RABIATOR
(GRAVE —) GOUL GHOUL
(HIGHWAY —) PAD FOOTPAD
TOBYMAN
(INDIAN MURDEROUS —) DACOIT
(IRISH —) WOODKERN
(MOUNTAIN —) CHOAR
(NIGHT —) MOONMAN
(SEA —) FOMOR FORMOR
FOMORIAN
(WANDERING —) ROUTIER
ROBBERY JOB JUMP REIF RIFE
HEIST SCREW STALE FELONY
HOLDUP STOWTH BRIBERY DACOITY
LARCENY PILLAGE PLUNDER
REAVERY STICKUP THUGGEE
PURCHASE
(— ON HIGH SEAS) PIRACY

(HIGHWAY —) TOBY
ROBE GOWN VEST KANZU STOLA
CHIMER KIMONO KITTEL MANTLE
REVEST ARISAID BUFFALO GALABIA
SURCOAT VESTURE WOLFSKIN
(— FOR THE DEAD) HABIT
(— OF MONARCH) PLUVIAL
(— PRESENTED BY DIGNITARY)
KHALAT KHILAT
(— REACHING TO ANKLES) TALAR
(ACTOR'S —) SYRMA
(BAPTISMAL —) CHRISOM
(BISHOP'S —) CHIMER CHIMERE
(CIRCULAR —) CYCLAS
(CORONATION —) COLOBIUM
DALMATIC
(DERVISH'S —) KHIRKA KHIRKAH
(EMPEROR'S —) PURPLE
(FUNERAL —) SABLE
(JEWISH —) KITTEL
(KING'S —) DALMATIC
(LOOSE —) MANT CAMIS CAMUS
CYMAR SIMAR SYMAR MANTUA
MANTEAU
(MASQUERADE —) VENETIAN
(MEXICAN —) MANGA
(MONK'S —) HAPLOMA
(OUTER —) JAMA
(TARTAN —) ARISAID
(TURKISH —) DOLMAN
(WHITE —) CHRISOM
ROBERT DOB POP RAB DOBBIN
POPKIN
ROBERT OF LINCOLN BOBOLINK
ROBIN PINFISH REDDOCK RUDDOCK
TOOTLER WINGFISH REDBREAST
ROBIN GOODFELLOW ELF PUCK
FAIRY SPRITE HOBGOBLIN
ROBINIA LOCUST
ROBIN SANDPIPER KNOT
DOWITCHER
ROBORANT TONIC
ROBOT GELEM GOLEM AUTOMAT
TELEVOX
ROBUST ABLE FIRM HAIL HALE HARD
IRON RUDE HARDY HUSKY LUSTY
RENKY SOUND STARK STIFF STOUR
STOUT TOUGH VALID WALLY
HEARTY RUGGED SINEWY STRONG
STURDY HEALTHY VALIANT
MUSCULAR PITHSOME SWACKING
VIGOROUS STRAPPING
(NOT —) SLENDER
ROBUSTNESS VALIDITY
ROC BIRD BOMB RUKH ROQUE
SIMURG SIMURGH
ROCHET CLOAK SMOCK CAMISIA
ROCK CAP JOW LOG PAY RAG DAZE
HOST KLIP REEL RUKH SIAL SIMA
SWAY SWIG TOSS BRACK CLIFF
FLOOR GREET GRUSS HORSE
LEDGE ROACH ROQUE SHAKE
SHOWD SKARN STONE TRILL FACIES
GROUND TOTTER COUNTRY FOLIATE
(— AROUND DRILL HOLE) COLLAR
(— CHUNK) KNUCKLE
(— IN ANOTHER ROCK) XENOLITH
(— IN MINE) CAPPING
(— IN SEA) STACK

(— SURFACE) KARREN
(— VIOLENTLY) STAGGER
(ARTIFICIAL —) GRANOLITH
(BANDED —) BAR
(BARE —) SCARTH
(CAP —) COVER
(COMPACT —) BASEMENT
(COUNTRY —) RIDER
(CRUSHED —) GREET
(CRYSTALLINE —) SCHIST DIORITE
GREISEN
(DECAY OF —S) GEEST LATERITE
(DECOMPOSED —) GOSSAN GOZZAN
(DENSE —) ADINOLE
(EXTRUSIVE —) DACITE SPILITE
ANDESITE CIMINITE
(FISSILE —) SHALE SHAUL
(FLUID —) LAVA
(FRAGMENTAL —) PSEPHITE
(GRANULAR —) GABBRO OOLITE
DIORITE IJOLITE KOSWITE
(GRANULATED —) GRUSS
(HARD —) WHIN
(HIGH —) SCOUT
(IGNEOUS —) BOSS SIAL SIMA TRAP
BASALT DUNITE GABBRO URTITE
FELSITE GRANITE MINETTE SYENITE
ESSEXITE TONALITE
(IMPURE —) CHERT
(INSULAR —) SKERRY
(INSULATED —) SKERRY
(INTRUSIVE —) HORTITE MAENAITE
(IRON-BEARING —) GAL
(ISOLATED —) SCAR SCARR SCAUR
(JUTTING POINT OF —) KIP
(METAMORPHIC —) SKARN GNEISS
SCHIST BUCHITE GONDITE LEPTITE
ECLOGITE HORNFELS LIMURITE
(MICA-BEARING —) DOMITE
(MOLTEN —) MAGMA
(PLUTONIC —) TAWITE HOLLAITE
TURJAITE
(POROUS —) TUFA TUFF ARSOITE
(PROJECTING —) CLINT
(PULVERIZED —) FLOUR
(RARE —) ALNOITE
(ROUGH —) CRAG KNAR SCARTH
(ROUNDED —) ROGNON SHEEPBACK
(SEDIMENTARY —) CRAG
IRONSTONE SANDSTONE
(SLATY —) PLATE SCHALSTEIN
(SOLID —) GIBBER
(STUDY OF —S) LITHOLOGY
(SUBMERGED —) SHELF
(UNDERLYING —) FLOOR
(VOLCANIC —) TUFA TUFF BASALT
DOMITE LATITE TAXITE ASHSTONE
RHYOLITE TEPHRITE TRACHYTE
(WORTHLESS —) GANG GANGUE
(PL.) ROCHER
ROCKAWAY CARRIAGE
ROCK BADGER CONY HYRAX
ROCK BASS REDEYE CABRILLA
ROCKBRUSH ROSILLA
ROCK CEDAR SABINO
ROCK CRESS SICKLEPOD
ROCK DEBRIS TALUS
ROCK DOVE SOD
ROCKER CRADLE SHOOFLY

ROCKET DRAKE REBUKE STREAK
YELLOW CONGREVE SKYLIGHT
STARSHIP FIREDRAKE
(DYER'S —) WELD WOLD WOALD
WOULD
ROCKET SALAD ROQUETTE
ROCKFISH JACK RENA REINA VIUVA
FLIOMA GOPHER RASHER TAMBOR
CORSAIR GARRUPA GROUPER
BOCACCIO CHINAFISH GREENLING
ROCK HARE KLIPHAAS
ROCK HIND MERO AGAUJI
ROCK HOPPER MACARONI
ROCKLING BAUD GADE ROKER
SORGHE WHISTLER
ROCK NATIVE SNAPPER
ROCK PIPIT TIETICK
ROCK RABBIT PIKA HYRAX
HYRACOID
ROCKROSE CISTUS HUDSONIA
ROCKCIST SAGEROSE DAYFLOWER
SUNFLOWER
ROCK SALT EMOL AMOLE HALITE
(BLOCK OF —) PIG
ROCK SANDWORT CYME
ROCKSHAFT SHAFT ROCKER
WEIGHBAR
ROCK TROUT BOREGAT GREENLING
ROCKWEED TANG FUCUS FUCOID
SEATANG SEAWEED
ROCK WHITING KELPFISH
STRANGER
ROCKY DAFT HARD STONY CLINTY
OBSCENE PETREAN PETROUS
UNCOUTH OBDURATE UNSTABLE
DIFFICULT RUPELLARY
ROCKY MOUNTAIN (— GOAT)
MAZAME
ROCOCO ORNATE QUAINT BAROCCO
BAROQUE OUTMODED
ROD BAR BOW CUE GAD GUY LUG
PIN TIE BOLT CALM CAME CANE
CORE FALL FORK GOAD GONG LINK
MACE POLE RAVE SCOB SNAP STEM
STUD WAND WHIP YARD ARBOR
BIRCH CATCH DOWEL LYTTA OSIER
PERCH POWER PUNCH REACH
ROUND SETUP SHOOT SPELK SPILL
SPOKE SPRAG STAFF STEEL STICK
STING TEYNE TOMMY TRACE VERGE
WIPER BALEYS BROACH CANARY
CARBON CENTER CRUTCH ETALON
FERULA FINGER GLOWER HANGER
PISTOL PITMAN PODGER RADDLE
RAMMER SKEWER SPRING STADIA
SWITCH TOGGLE WATTLE WICKER
BACULUS CROPPIE DRAWROD
ELLWAND FEATHER FESTUCA
PLUNGER POINTER POTHOOK
PRICKER PROBANG PROLONG
SCALLOM SCEPTER SPINDLE
STADIUM STICKER TYRANNY
VIRGULA WHISKER WINDING
AXOSTYLE BACKSTAY BILBERRY
BODSTICK BOWSTAVE DIPSTICK
JACKSTAY KINGBOLT REVOLVER
STRAINER TRAVELER WEEDHOOK
(— AS SYMBOL OF OFFICE) VERGE
(— BEARING TRAFFIC SIGNAL)
STANCHION

(— **FOR ALIGNING HOLES**) PODGER
(— **FOR CARRYING GLASS**) FORK
(— **FOR DISCIPLINE**) YARD FERULA
FERULE
(— **FOR FASTENING THATCH**) SPELK
SPRINGLE
(— **FOR FIREARM BORE**) WIPER
(— **FOR GLASS-MAKING**) PUNTY
FASCET PONTEE PONTIL CROPPIE
(— **FOR HOLDING MEAT**) SPIT
(— **FOR TRANSMITTING MOTION**)
TRACE
(— **IN ARC LAMP**) CARBON
(— **IN CRICKET**) STUMP
(— **IN INTERFEROMETER**) ETALON
(— **IN MINE PUMP**) SPEAR
(— **IN NERNST LAMP**) GLOWER
(— **IN SPINNING WHEEL**) SPINDLE
(— **OF FOUNDRY MOLD**) LANCE
(— **OF LOOM**) SHAFT
(— **OF WOOD**) SCOB
(— **ON LOGGING TRUCK**) RAVE
(— **POINTED AT BOTH ENDS**)
SKEWER
(— **SYMBOLIZING AUTHORITY**)
BACULUS
(— **TO BIND A CONTRACT**) FESTUCA
(— **TO FASTEN SAILS**) JACKSTAY
(— **TO IMMERSE SHEEP**) CRUTCH
(— **TO URGE BEAST**) GOAD PROD
(— **UPSET AT ONE END**) SETUP
(— **USED AS KEY**) TOMMY
(— **WITH ENDS AT RIGHT ANGLES**)
STRAINER
(— **WITH SPONGE ON END**)
PROBANG
(— **WITH T-HEAD**) TOGGLE
(**AXIAL** —) VIRGULA AXOSTYLE
(**BASKETRY** —) OSIER
(**BUNDLE OF** —S) DRIVER
(**CARTILAGINOUS** —) LYTTA
COLUMELLA
(**CLAMMING** —) BRAIL
(**CONNECTING** —) PITMAN
(**CURTAIN** —) TRINGLE
(**DANCER'S** —) CROTALUM
(**DIVINING** —) TWIG DOWSER
(**FISHING** —) GAD CALCUTTA
(**FLEXIBLE** —) RADDLE WATTLE
(**FORKED** —) CRUTCH
(**GEM-CUTTING** —) SETTER
(**GRADUATED** —) STADIA STADIUM
(**IRON** —) SNAP
(**KNITTING** —) NEEDLE
(**LEAD** —) CAME
(**LOGGING** —) CANARY
(**MEASURING** —) JUDGE SPILE
STADIA ELLWAND METEWAND
METEYARD
(**PLIABLE** —) WINDING
(**SMALL** —) LANCE
(**STRENGTHENING** —) RIB
(**SUPPLE** —) SWABBLE
(**TETHERING** —) STAKE
(**THIN** —) TEYNE SCALLOM
(**TIE** —) ANCHOR
(**UMBRELLA** —) STRETCHER
(**WITHE** —) BILBERRY
RODENT RAT CONY DEGU HARE

MARA MOCO MOLE PACA PIKA UTIA
VOLE CONEY COYPU GUNDI HUTIA
JUTIA LEROT MOUSE TUCAN ZOKOR
AGOUTI BEAVER BITING CURURO
GERBIL GLIRID GNAWER GOPHER
JERBOA MARMOT MURINE MUROID
RABBIT SOKHER BLESMOL CHINCHA
DIPODID GEOMYID GNAWING
HAMSTER LEMMING LEVERET
MUSKRAT ABROCOME CAPIBARA
DORMOUSE LEPORIDE OCTODONT
SEWELLEL SPALACID SQUIRREL
TUCOTUCO VISCACHA VIZCACHA
RODEO ROUNDUP
RODLIKE VIRGATE
RODMAN CLASHY CLASHEE
CHAINMAN
RODOMONTADE BRAG RANT BOAST
BLUSTER BOMBAST BRAGGART
ROD-SHAPED RHABDOID VIRGULATE
ROE RA DOE FRY PEA RAA RAE HIND
KELK RAUN ROUN ROWN CORAL
TRUBU CAVIAR
ROEBUCK GIRL CHEVREUIL
ROGER RAM HODGE ROGUE
ROGUE BOY GUE IMP NYM KEMP
KITE ROAG CATSO CRACK CRANK
GIPSY GREEK GYPSY HEMPY KNAVE
SCAMP SHELM BEGGAR BORGER
BUGGER CANTER COQUIN CURTAL
HARLOT LIMMER PICARA PICARO
RASCAL SORROW TINKER BLEEDER
ERRATIC FOISTER HALLION
LADRONE PANURGE SHARPER
SKELLUM SWINGER VILLAIN
COMROGUE HEMPSEED PICAROON
SWINDLER WHIPJACK
ROGUERY ROPERY KNAVERY
LOONERY WAGGERY PATCHERY
PRIGGISM TRICKERY TRUANTRY
ROGUISH SLY ARCH ROGUY WICKED
KNAVISH TRICKSY VAGRANT
WAGGISH ESPIEGLE SCAMPISH
DISHONEST
ROGUISHNESS KNAVERY ARCHNESS
ROIL VEX FOUL RILE ANNOY
BLUNDER DISTURB STUDDLE
BEWILDER DISORDER IRRITATE
ROILED TURBID
ROISTER REVEL ROIST SCOUR
CAROUSE GALRAVAGE
ROISTERER MUN GREEK HUZZA
HECTOR RIOTER SCOURER TWIBILL
EPHESIAN
ROISTERING HOYDEN
ROKE FOG DAMP MIST REEK ROWK
STIR FOGGY SMOKE STEAM VAPOR
ROKELAY ROCOLO
ROLE BIT JOB LEAD PART ROTE
HEAVY FIGURE CLOTHES BUSINESS
FUNCTION LIRIPIPE
ROLL BAP BUN ROW WEB BOLT COIL
CURL FILE FLOW FURL LIST MILL
PASS REEL ROAM ROTA SWAG
WELT WIND WRAP BAGEL BREAD
BUILD DANDY DICKY ENROL FLUTE
ROYLE SPLIT TRILL TROLL WHELM
BILLOW BUNDLE CIRCLE ELAPSE
ENFOLD GOGGLE GROVEL KIPFEL

LEGEND MUSTER PONDER ROSTER
ROTATE SCROLL UPWIND VOLUME
WAMBLE WANDER WHELVE WINTLE
WREATH BISCUIT BRIOCHE
CROCKET ENVELOP MANCHET
REVOLVE ROTULET ROTULUS
STRETCH TERRIER TRUNDLE
TWISTER BROTCHEN CANNELON
CONSIDER CRESCENT JACKROLL
LAMINATE PORTEOUS REGISTER
SEDERUNT SPREADER VOLUTATE
(— **A BALL**) BOWL
(— **ABOUT**) WALTER SCAMBLE
(— **AS A SHIP**) SEEL LURCH
(— **AS STONE**) REEL
(— **BY**) WALK
(— **CLOSELY**) FURL
(— **EYES**) WALL WAUL WHAWL
GOGGLE
(— **GLASS**) MARVER
(— **INTO A BALL**) CLEW CLUE
(— **OF BREAD**) BAP SEMMEL
TAMMIE
(— **OF CLOTH**) BOLT WREATH
(— **OF COINS**) ROULEAU
(— **OF DOUGH**) TWIST
(— **OF DRIED BARK**) QUILL
(— **OF DRUM**) HURRY
(— **OF DUST**) KITTEN
(— **OF HAIR**) ROACH ROWEL
CROCKET
(— **OF HAY**) WAKE
(— **OF LINT OR LINEN**) TENT DOSSIL
(— **OF LUGGAGE**) SWAG
(— **OF MINCED MEAT**) RISSOLE
(— **OF OFFENDERS**) PORTEOUS
(— **OF PAPER**) SPILL STOMP STUMP
(— **OF PARCHMENT**) BOOK PELL
(— **OF ROULETTE WHEEL**) COUP
(— **OF SPUN YARN**) PRICK
(— **OF TOBACCO**) CAROT CIGAR
PRICK SEGAR CAROTTE
(— **OF WALLPAPER**) BOLT
(— **OF WHEAT BREAD**) MANCHET
(— **OF WOOL**) ROVE ROVING
CARDING
(— **ON LITTLE WHEELS**) TRUNDLE
(— **ONWARD**) DEVOLVE
(— **OVER**) COMB JOLL WELTER
(— **TO RUB DOWN DRAWING**)
STUMP
(— **TOGETHER**) CONVOLVE
(— **UP SLEEVES**) REEVE
(— **UP**) FURL STOW COLLAR
(**BLANKET** —) BINDLE SHIRALEE
(**DANDY** —) DANCER
(**HOLLOW** —) CANNELON
(**LONG** —) FLUTE
(**PADDED** —) BURLET
(**PENNY** —) TOMMY
(**TWISTED** — **OF WOOL**) SLUB
(**WHIP** —) BACKREST
ROLLED (— **IN SUGAR**) SANDED
ROLLER FLY BOWL BRAY DRUM
JACK LEAD MILL PUCK RUBY BREAK
DANDY FINER GODET INKER RIDER
SHELL WAVER WINCH BRAYER
BREAST DOFFER DUCTOR FASCIA
MANGLE ROWLET RUNNER CARRIER

CLEARER MOIETER TRUCKLE
HEDGEHOG SQUEEGEE STRIPPER
TROUPAND
(— **FOR MASSAGER**) ROULETTE
(— **IN HORSE'S BIT**) CRICKET
(— **IN ORGAN**) TRUNDLE
(— **IN STEELWORKS**) COGGER
(— **TO CLEAR FABRIC**) MOIETER
(**CARDING** —) BREAST WORKER
SQUIRREL STRIPPER
(**CHINESE** —) SIRGANG
(**DREDGING** —) HEDGEHOG
(**DROP** —) DUCTOR
(**GRINDING** —) BREAK
(**INKING** —) BRAYER
(**PRINTING** —) DANDY SHELL
BRAYER DAMPENER
(**STONE** —) MAMMY TOTER
(**SURGICAL** —) FASCIA
(**TOOTHED** —) PRICK PRICKER
ROLLER COASTER SWITCHBACK
ROLLERMAN BRAKER JACKMAN
LEVERMAN
ROLLER SKATE PEDOMOTOR
ROLLICK PLAY ROMP FROLIC ROLLIX
ROLLICKING GAY WILD MERRY
JOVIAL LIVELY
ROLLING CURL GOGGLE WHEELY
SWAYING TRILLED LURCHING
VOLUTION
(— **OF SCROLL**) GELILAH
(— **OF SHIP**) LABOR
ROLLTOP TAMBOUR
ROLY-POLY ROTUND PUDDING
TUMBLER SALTWORT
ROM RO GYPSY ROMANY
ROMAN BRAVE LATIN NOBLE PAPAL
ANTIQUA UPRIGHT GOWNSMAN
(— **COLLAR**) RABAT
ROMAN CATHOLIC ROME ROMAN
PAPIST ROMIST BABYLONIC
ROMANCE WOO GEST ANTAR FANCY
FEIGN GESTE KATHA NOVEL STORY
ANTARA UTOPIA FANTASY FICTION
ROMANZA
(— **LANGUAGE**) FRENCH ITALIAN
SPANISH
ROMAN-FLEUVE SAGA

ROMANIA
CANAL: BEGA
CAPITAL: BUCHAREST
COIN: BAN LEI LEU LEY
DISTRICT: ALBA BANAT BIHOR
DOBRUJA DOBROGEA
MARAMURES
LAKE: SINOE
MOUNTAIN: BIHOR NEGOI CODRUL
RODNEI CALIMAN PIETROSU
OLD NAME: DACIA
PASS: ROSUL
PROVINCE: ARDEAL MOLDAVIA
WALACHIA
RIVER: ALT JIU OLT PRUT ALUTA
ARGES BUZDU MOROS MURES
OLTUL SCHYL SIRET VEDEA
CRASNA DANUBE ARGESUL
BISTRITA IALOMITA

RIVER PORT: BRAILA GALATI
GALATZ
TOWN: ARAD CLUJ IASI BACAV
CERNA JASSY NEAMT SIBIU
TURNU BRAILA BRASOV GALATI
GALATZ LVPENI CRAIOVA
FOCSANI PLOESTI SEVERIN
CERNAVTI KISHENEF KOLSOVAR
TEMESVAR

ROMANIST MISSARY
ROMANIZATION LATINXUA
ROMANSH LADIN
ROMANTIC AIRY WILD IDEAL
ADRENT DREAMY GOTHIC POETIC
UNREAL FERVENT FABULOUS
FANCIFUL
ROMANY RO ROM GIPSY GYPSY
ROMAN
ROME (CHAPEL IN —) SISTINE
(**FOUNDER OF** —) ROMULUS
(**HILL IN** —) CAELIAN VIMINAL
AVENTINE PALATINE QUIRINAL
(**RIVER IN** —) TIBER
ROMP REG RIG LARK PLAY ROIL
FRISK SHIRL SPORT TRAIN FROLIC
GAMBOL HOORAY HOYDEN HURRAH
RIPPET COURANT GAMMOCK
RAMMACK RUNAWAY
ROMPERS JUMPER JUMPERS
ROMPING ROYT ROYET
RONCADOR GRUNT CROAKER
SCIAENID
RONE BUSH BRAKE GUTTER THICKET
RONG LEPCHA
RONGA THONGA
RONSDORFER ZIONITE ELLERIAN
ROOD RUD REED ROPE CROSS
SPAWN STANG CRUCIFIX
ROODLES RANGDOODLES
ROOF TOP ATAP BACK DECK DOME
FLAT ATTAP COVER HOUSE RAISE
RISER SHELL THACK AZOTEA
BONNET CUPOLA SUMMIT TECTUM
CHOPPER CRICKET GAMBREL
MANSARD RIGGING TECTURE
BULKHEAD HOUSETOP SAWTOOTH
SEMIDOME
(— **MEMBER**) PURLIN
(— **OF CARRIAGE**) IMPERIAL
(— **OF CAVERN**) DOME
(— **OF MINING CAGE**) BONNET
(— **OF MOUTH**) PALATE
(— **OF NASOPHARYNX**) VAULT
(— **OF RAILWAY CAR**) DECK
(— **OVER STAGE**) SHADOW
(— **PORTION**) MONITOR
(**CLOTH** —) CHUTT
(**FALSE** —) CRICKET
(**FLAT** —) LEADS AZOTEA TERRACE
(**STEEPLY TAPERING** —) SPIRE
(**THATCHED** —) ATAP ATTAP
CHOPPER
(**VAULTED** —) DOME
ROOFING HEALING SHINDLE
PANTILING
ROOK ROC CROW DUPE RUKH
CHEAT CRAKE JUDGE TOWER

BLACKY CASTLE DEFRAUD
CASTILLO SWINDLER
ROOKERY ROOST RUMPUS BUILDING
ROOKIE COLT DRONGO NOVICE
RECRUIT BEGINNER
ROOM WON AULA CAFE CRIB FARM
HALL KILN LIEU PLAY SALA SEAT
SLUM WAME WENE WONE ATTIC
BERTH CUDDY DIVAN EWERY HOUSE
LODGE OECUS PLACE SALLE SCOPE
SHACK SOLAR SPACE STALL STOVE
STUDY BELFRY BREAST CAMERA
CASINO CHAPEL ESTUFA EXEDRA
HAMMAM LEEWAY MARGIN PARVIS
SCOUTH SINGLE SMOKER SOLLAR
STANCE STANZA STUDIO CABINET
CAMARIN CHALMER CHAMBER
EPINAOS FREEZER GALLERY
HOLDING HYPOGEE KITCHEN
LAUNDRY LIBRARY SEMINAR
SERVERY SMOKERY SURGERY
AEDICULA ASSEMBLY BASEMENT
DRYHOUSE HOTHOUSE HYPOGEUM
LAVATORY NYMPHEUM SCULLERY
SWEATBOX TABLINUM THALAMUS
(— **BEHIND FACADE**) ATTIC
(— **BETWEEN KITCHEN AND DINING
ROOM**) SERVERY
(— **CONTAINING FOUNTAIN**)
NYMPHEUM
(— **DUG IN CLIFF**) HYPOGEE
HYPOGEUM
(— **FOR ACTION**) LEEWAY
(— **FOR BATHING**) HAMMAM
(— **FOR CONVERSATION**) EXEDRA
(— **FOR FAMILY RECORDS**)
TABLINUM
(— **FOR KEEPING FOOD**) LARDER
PANTRY
(— **FOR PAINTINGS**) GALLERY
(— **FOR PRIVATE DEVOTIONS**)
ORATORY
(— **FOR PUBLIC AMUSEMENTS**)
CASINO THEATER
(— **FOR STOWAGE**) LASTAGE
(— **FOR TABLE LINEN**) EWERY
(— **IN COAL MINE**) BREAST
(— **IN HAREM**) ODA
(— **IN KEEP**) DUNGEON
(— **IN PREHISTORIC BUILDING**) CELL
(— **IN REAR OF TEMPLE**) EPINAOS
(— **IN SIDE OF LARGER ROOM**) ALA
(— **IN TOWER**) BELFRY
(— **OF STUDENTS' SOCIETY**) HALL
(— **ON SHIP**) CABIN STOKEHOLD
(— **OVER CHURCH PORCH**) PARVIS
(— **OVER STAGE**) SHADOW
(— **TOGETHER**) CHUM
(— **UNDER BUILDING**) CELLAR
(**CHILDREN'S** —) NURSERY
(**DINING** —) CENACLE DINETTE
REFECTORY
(**DRAWING** —) SALON SALOON
(**DRESSING** —) SHIFT BOUDOIR
CAMARIN VESTUARY WARDROBE
TIREHOUSE
(**ESKIMO ASSEMBLY** —) KASHGA
(**EXHIBITION** —) THEATER
(**GRINDING** —) HULL

(HEATED —) STEW
(HIGH —) AERY EYRY AERIE EYRIE
(INNER —) BEN INBY INBYE SPENCE
(INSULATED —) FREEZER
(LIVING —) HOUSE LANAI SALON
SERDAB SOLARIUM VOORHUIS
(MONASTERY —) CELL LAVABO
(NARROW —) CRIB
(OCTAGONAL —) TRIBUNA
(PRIVATE —) SNUG SCHOLA
(PUEBLO ASSEMBLY —) ESTUFA
(READING —) ATHENEUM
(RECEPTION —) DIVAN PARLOR
MANDARAH
(REFRIGERATED —) COOLER
(RETIRING —) RECAMERA
(ROMAN —) ATRIUM AEDICULA
FUMARIUM
(ROUND —) ROTUNDA
(SEA —) BERTH
(SECLUDED —) DEN
(SERIES OF —S) SWEEP
(SITTING —) SITTER BOUDOIR
(SLEEPING —) DORMER BEDROOM
DORMITORY
(SMALL —) ALA CELL SNUG STEW
CUBBY CUDDY LOBBY CLOSET
CUBICLE SNUGGERY
(SMOKING —) DIVAN DIWAN
TABAGIE
(SORTING —) SALLE
(STEAM —) STOVE
(STORAGE —) CAMARIN MAGAZINE
THALAMUS
(SWEATING —) SUDARIUM
SUDATORY LACONICUM
(THRONE —) AIWAN
(TOP —) GARRET IMPERIAL
(UPPER —) SOLAR
ROOMMATE CHUM ROOMY ROOMIE
ROOMY WIDE LARGE RANGY SPACY
ROOMSOME SPACIOUS
ROOSE RUSE EXTOL PRAISE
FLATTER BOASTING BRAGGING
ROOST EVE SIT BAUK JOUK TIDE
PERCH GARRET HARBOR LODGING
ROOKERY SHELTER
ROOSTER COCK GAME GALLO
MANOC GAMECOCK
ROOT DIG PRY ROI TAP BASE BULB
CHAY CHOY GRUB MOOR MOOT
MORE RACE SPUR TAIL CHEER
FIBER FRUIT GROOT GROUT HEART
IREOS LAPPA RADIX STOCK ALRAUN
BOTTOM CARROT CATGUT GROUND
MUZZLE ORIGIN SENEGA SETTLE
SUMBAL SUMBUL ACONITE ALKANET
AZAFRAN BIACURU BONIATA
CALUMBA CHICORY COLUMBO
CRAMPON GINSENG IMPLANT
IPOMOEA NUNNARI PARIERA
RADICAL RUMMAGE TURPETH
DEDENDUM EARTHNUT
(— BRANCH) TAPOUN
(— CONTAINING STARCH) KOONTI
(— DEEPLY) SCREW
(— OF GINGER) RACE
(— OF ORCHID) CULLIONS
(— OF TOOTH) FANG

(— OF TREE) TANG SPURN
(— OF WORD) THEME
(— OUT) GRUB STUB STOCK
EVULSE DISPLANT SUPPLANT
(— TUBERCLE) CLOG
(— WORD) ETYMON
(— YIELDING RED DYE) CHAY CHOY
CHAYA
(—S FOR SEWING CANOES) WATAP
WATAPEH
(—S OF ACONITE) BIKH NABEE
(CANDIED —) ERYNGO
(DRIED —) JALAP ALTHEA SENECA
BRYONIA KRAMERIA LICORICE
SCAMMONY
(DRIED —S) INULA IPECAC
KRAMERIA VERATRUM
(EDIBLE —) YAM BEET EDDO
RADISH TURNIP WASABI PARSNIP
RUTABAGA TUBERCLE
(FERN —) ROI
(FINE —) STRING
(FRAGRANT —S) VETIVER
(MASS OF FIBROUS —S) SPONGE
(MEDICINAL —) JALAP LAPPA
GINSENG
(PROJECTING —) SPUR
(ROASTED BEET —) BONKA
(STUMP AND —) MOCK
(PL.) CULVERS
ROOTCAP CALYPTRA SPONGIOLE
ROOTED FIXED CHRONIC
(DEEPLY —) BESETTING
ROOTER FAN PLUGGER
ROOTLET CRAMPON RADICEL
RADICLE
(PL.) COME CULMS
ROOTSTOCK PIP ROI TARO ORRIS
CASAVA DANNUM GINGER ORIGIN
PANNUM STOLON BISCUIT
TURMERIC
ROPE GAD GUY TIE TOW TUG CEEL
COLT CORD FALL FAST GUSS HEMP
JEFF JUNK LIFT LINE ROOD SEAL
SOAM SPAN STAY TACK TAIL TAUM
TOME VANG WARP BRACE BRAIL
CABLE CABUL CHECK CHORD
LASSO LONGE SHANK STRAP STROP
SWEEP TRACE TWIST WANTY WIDDY
WITHE CABLET HALTER INHAUL
LARIAT LISSOM LIZARD MECATE
PINION RAPEYE RUNNER SHROUD
SLATCH STRAND STRING TETHER
WARROK AWEBAND BEDCORD
BOBSTAY CATFALL CRINGLE
ENTRAIL HALYARD LASHING
LEEFANG OUTHAUL PAINTER
PAZAREE PENDANT PIGTAIL
SEAMING SERPENT SERVICE
STIRRUP SWIFTER BACKBONE
BACKSTAY BUNTLINE CABESTRO
CORDELLE DOWNHAUL DRAGLINE
FOREFOOT FORETACK HALLIARD
HAULYARD INHAULER JACKSTAY
LIFELINE NECKLACE PASSAREE
PROLONGE ROUNDING SEQUENCE
THRAMMLE BREECHING
(— A STEER) HEEL
(— COLLAR) PARRAL PARREL

(— COVERING) QUILTING
(— FOR FASTENING GATE) CRINGLE
(— FOR FISH) STRINGER
(— FOR TRAINING HORSE) LONGE
(— FOR TYING CATTLE) CEEL SEAL
AWEBAND
(— HANDLE) FETTLE SHACKLE
(— HOLDING RAFT TOGETHER)
BRAIL
(— JOINT) TUCK
(— OF 10 OR MORE INCHES) CABLE
(— OF HAIR) CABESTRO
(— OF ONIONS) REEVE
(— OF STRAW) GAD SIME VINE
SIMON SUGAN FETTLE SIMMON
SOOGAN
(— ON DERRICK) TELEGRAF
(— ON FISHING NET) PINION
SEAMING
(— ORNAMENTATION) TORSADE
(— PASSING AROUND DEADEYE)
STRAP STROP
(— STOLEN FROM DOCKYARD)
RUMBO
(— WITH HOOK AND TOGGLE)
PROLONGE
(— WITH SWIVEL AND LOOP)
TOGGEL TOGGLE
(— WOUND AROUND CABLE)
KECKLING
(—S IN RIGGING) CORDAGE
(ANCHOR —) RODE VIOL VOYAL
(BELL —) TYALL HANGER
(CIRCUS —) JEFF
(DRAFT —) SOAM
(DRAG —) GUSS
(FLAG-RAISING —) HALYARD
(FOOT —) HORSE
(GRASS —) SOGA
(GUIDE —) DRAGLINE
(HANDLE —) FETTLE
(HANGMAN'S —) HEMP TIPPET
(HARNESS —) TRACE HALTER
(HARPOON —) FOREGOER
(NAUTICAL —) TIE TYE COLT FANG
LIFT STAY VANG BRACE BRAIL
SHEET SLING STRAP STROP GILGUY
HAWSER INHAUL LACING RATLIN
SHROUD BOBSTAY BOWLINE
CATFALL GESWARP LANYARD
LEEFANG OUTHAUL PAINTER
PAZAREE PENDANT PENNANT
PIGTAIL RATLINE SNORTER
SNOTTER STIRRUP STOPPER
SWIFTER BACKBONE BACKSTAY
BUNTLINE DOWNHAUL FORETACK
JACKSTAY PASSAREE ROUNDING
SELVAGEE WOOLDING
(PART OF —) SLATCH
(SHORT —) SHANK
(SHORT CART —) WANTY
(SMALL HANDMADE —) FOX
(SMUGGLER'S —) LINGTOW
(TALLOWED —) GASKET
(TOW —) CORDELLE
(WIRE —) HAULBACK JACKSTAY
(WORN OR POOR —) JUNK
(PL.) CORDAGE
ROPEBAND RABAND

ROPEMAKER FOLLOWER RATLINER
ROPEWALKER FUNAMBULO
ROPEWAY TRAMWAY WIREWAY
CABLEWAY
ROPY SINEWY STRINGY VISCOUS
MUSCULAR GLUTINOUS
ROQUE CROQUET
ROQUELAURE CLOAK ROCOLO
ROCKLAY
RORIPA RADICULA
RORQUAL SEI FINBACK
ROSARY BEADS CORONA TASBIH
BEADING BEADROLL
(— BEAD) GAUD GAUDY
(MOHAMMEDAN —) COMBOLOIO
ROSE ASH GUL KNOT MOSS ROIS
BRIAR BRIDE BUCKY FLUSH RHODA
CANKER POMPON BOURBON
BURBANK GLAIEUL HUGONIS
LOZENGE MANETTI MONTHLY
OPHELIA RAMBLER AGRIMONY
COLUMBIA DOGBERRY LOKELANI
PEDELION
(COTTON —) CUDWEED
ROSE ACACIA ROBINIA
ROSE APPLE JAMBO JAMBOS
JAMBOSA
ROSEATE SPOONBILL AJAJA
ROSE-BREASTED (— COCKATOO)
GALAH
ROSEBUSH ROSER BALWARRA
ROSE CAMPION LYCHNIS
ROSE-COLORED OPTIMISTIC
(— STARLING) PASTOR TILYER
ROSEFISH BRIM BREAM BERGYLT
REDFISH
(YOUNG —) SNAPPER
ROSE HIP CHOOP CHOUP
ROSELLE SORREL SABDARIFFA
ROSEMARY COSTMARY MOORWORT
ROSMARINE
ROSE MOSS PURSLANE PORTULACA
ROSET BRAZIL
ROSETTE CHOU KNOT COCKADE
ROSEWOOD BUBINGA MOLOMPI
JACARANDA
ROSIN FLUX COLOPHONY
(— SPIRIT) PINOLIN
ROSS SCALP
ROSSER BARKER PEELER SCALPER
SLIPPER
ROSTER LIST ROTA SCROLL
REGISTER
ROSTRATE BEAKED
ROSTRUM PEW AMBE BEAK GUARD
SNOUT PULPIT ACROTER TRIBUNE
ROSY ROSEN BLUSHY AURORAL
HEALTHY AUROREAN BLOOMING
BLUSHFUL
ROT COE RET DOTE DOZE DROP
FOUL JOKE LEAK POKE SOUR WROX
DECAY SPOIL TEASE BLUING
FESTER ROTTEN CORRUPT
HOOFRUT PUTREFY NONSENSE
STAGNATE
(— BY EXPOSURE) RET
(— OF GRAPES) SLIPSKIN
(APPLE —) FROGEYE
(FOOT —) FOUL

(FRUIT —) LEAK
(LIVER —) COE
ROTA LIST ROLL ROSTER ROTULA
ROTARY CIRCLE GYRATORY
ROTATE RUN BIRL GYRE ROLL SPIN
TURN PIVOT SCREW WHEEL GYRATE
REVOLVE TRUNDLE ROTIFORM
ALTERNATE
(— HIPS) GRIND
ROTATING VOLUBLE
ROTATION SPIN TURN ROUND TWIRL
GYRATION SPINNING WHIRLING
(— ON BALL) STUFF
ROTCHE BULL RATCH ROTGE
DOVEKEY DOVEKIE BULLBIRD
ROTE CRWTH HEART ROTTA REPEAT
ROTIFER POLYP LIPOPOD LORICATE
PLOIMATE
ROTL RATTEL WEIGHT ROTTOLO
(PL.) ARTAL ARTEL
ROTOGRAVURE ROTO COLOROTO
ROTOR IMPELLER
ROTTED PECKY
ROTTEN BAD FOUL ROXY SOUR
ADDLE DAZED MOSEY PUTID
AMPERY FRACID MOOSEY PUTRID
DECAYED SPOILED DEPRAVED
UNSTABLE
(HALF —) DOTED DOATED
(PARTIALLY —) DRUXY
ROTTING SLEEPY CARIOUS
ROTTLERA KAMALA
ROTULA ROUND TROCHE KNEEPAN
PATELLA
ROTUND FAT PLUMP ROUND STOUT
CHUBBY SUBROUND
ROTURIER PEASANT PLEBEIAN
RUPTUARY
ROUE RAKE DEBAUCHEE
ROUGE RED FARD BLUSH PAINT
FUCATE REDDEN RUDDLE CLINKER
SCRIMMAGE
(ANIMAL —) CARMINE
ROUGH RU ROW RUF BEAT FOUL
GURL HARD HASK LAMB ROID ROYD
RUDE THUG WILD ACRID BLUFF
BLUNT BRUTE CHURL CRUDE DIRTY
GOBBY GROFF GURLY HAIRY HARSH
HEFTY JAGGY LUMPY REWCH
ROUCH ROWDY RUGGY RUVID
STARK STEER STERN STOUR TOUGH
TOUSY WIGHT BORREL BROKEN
BRUSHY BURRED CHOPPY COARSE
COBBLY CRABBY CRAGGY ELBOIC
ENEVEN HACKLY HISPID HOARSE
HOBBLY HORRID HUBBLY INCULT
JAGGED KNAGGY KNOTTY NOGGEN
RAGGED RAMAGE RASPED ROBUST
RUFFLE RUGGED RUMBLY RUSTIS
SEVERE SHAGGY SKETCH TOOSIE
TRYING UNFEEL UNFELE UNFINE
UNKIND UNMILD UNRIDE ABUSIVE
AUSTERE BOORISH CRABBED
HIRSUTE INEQUAL INEXACT JARRING
RABBISH RAMMAGE RAPLOCH
RUFFLED SCABRID STICKLE STICKLY
UNCOUTH UNKEMPT VICIOUS
ASPERATE CHURLISH DEPOLISH
IMPOLITE LARRIKIN OBDURATE

SCABROUS SCRAGGED STUBBORN
UNGENTLE UNTENDER MANHANDLE
(— EDGES) FASH
(— IT) SIWASH
(— UP ARROW FEATHERS)
SPRANGLE
(MAKE —) SHAG
ROUGHAGE FODDER AVERAGE
BALLAST CELLULOSE
ROUGH-AND-READY BURLY TOWSY
TOWZIE MAKESHIFT
ROUGHCAST PARGET SPARGE
ROUGHHEW SLAPDASH
ROUGHEN FRET GAIG HACK EMERY
FEAZE FLOCK FROST TOOTH
ABRADE CRISLE STIVER CRIZZLE
ENGRAIL SCRATCH UNSMOOTH
(— BRICK WALL) STAB
ROUGHER BULLDOGGER
(PONY —) STRANDER
ROUGH-HOB GASH
ROUGH-MILL GASH
ROUGHNECK ROWDY TOUGH
MUCKER UNCOUTH BANGSTER
ROUGHNESS GAFF GRAIN SCUFF
TOOTH RUFFLE CRIZZLE CRUDITY
ACRIMONY ASPERITY
(— OF SEA) LIPPER
(— OF SKIN) GOOSESKIN
GOOSEFLESH
(— OF WALL) KEY
ROUGHOMETER VIAGRAPH
ROULADE VOLATA ARPEGGIO
ROULETTE FILET FILLET TROCHOID
(1-18 IN —) MANQUE
(13-24 IN —) MILIEU
(HIGH — NUMBERS) PASSE
ROUNCEVAL GIANT LARGE
MONSTER GIGANTIC
ROUND BALL BEAT BEND BOLD
BOUT FAST FULL GIRO HEAD RICH
ROON ROTA TOUR TRIM WALK
ABOUT AMPLE BEADY BRISK CATCH
DANCE GLOBE HAMBO HARSH
LARGE MOONY ORBED PLAIN
ROMAN RONDO SPOKE TROLL
TUBBY CIRCLE COURSE ENTIRE
MELLOW NEARLY ROTUND ROUNDY
RUBBER RUNDLE SPHERY SPIRAL
STOWER STREAK ZODIAC ANNULAR
CIRCUIT SHAPELY CIRCULAR
COMPLETE CROSSBAR ENCIRCLE
GLOBULAR SONOROUS LABIALIZE
(— EDGES OF TIMBER) BEARD
(— END OF LOG) SNIPE
(— FREQUENTLY GONE OVER) BEAT
(— IN BOWLING) FRAME
(— IN CARDS) GRAND
(— OF ACTIVITIES) SWING
(— OF APPLAUSE) HAND JOLLY
PLAUDIT
(— OF CHAIR) BALUSTER
(— OF KNITTING) BOUT
(— OF LADDER) STAVE
(— OF PLAY) LAP
(— OFF) TOP CROWN FILLET
(— OUT) ORB BELLY INTEGRATE
(— UP) CORRAL WRANGLE
SCROUNGE

(PLUMP AND —) CHUBBY
(SWEDISH —) HAMBO
ROUNDABOUT PLUMP DETOUR
  ROTARY CURVING DEVIOUS
  CIRCULAR INDIRECT TORTUOUS
  (— MOVEMENT) WINDLASS
ROUNDED FULL BOMBE BOWLY
  CONVEX MELLOW ROTUND TERETE
  ARRONDI BUNTING CONCAVE
  GIBBOUS SHAPELY COMPLETE
  FINISHED HOOPLIKE SONOROUS
  (— OUT) PLUM
ROUNDEL HEURT PLATE POMME
  PELLET FOUNTAIN
  (— AZURE) HURT
  (— GULES) TORTEAU TORTEAUX
  (— OR) BEZANT BYZANT
  (— PURPURE) GOLP GOLPE
  (— SABLE) GUNSTONE
  (— SANGUINE) GUZE
  (— VERT) POMEY
ROUNDER SOAKER WASTREL
  INFORMER
ROUNDERS TUT PATBALL TUTBALL
ROUNDHEAD SWEDE CROPPY
  WEAKFISH
ROUND HERRING SHADINE
  STRADINE
ROUNDHOUSE BARN POOP LOCKUP
ROUNDNESS ROTUND SPHERICITY
  (— OF RIBS) SPRING
ROUND POMPANO PERMIT
  PALOMETA
ROUND ROBIN ANGLER SERIES
  PANCAKE SEQUENCE
ROUNDSMAN VANMAN SWINGMAN
  WATCHMAN
ROUNDUP RODEO CAMBER GATHER
ROUNDWORM NEMA ASCARID
  EELWORM GORDIAN HELMINTH
  NEMATODE STRONGYL
ROUP ROLP ROOP CROAK CLAMOR
  AUCTION SHOUTING
ROUSE DAW GIG HOP JOG BAIT
  CALL DRAW FIRK GOAD MOVE RANT
  RAVE STIR WAKE WHET AMOVE
  ERECT MOUNT RAISE START STEER
  UPSET WAKEN AROUSE BESTIR
  EXCITE FOMENT KINDLE NETTLE
  RATTLE REVIVE RUFFLE WECCHE
  AGITATE ANIMATE DISTURB
  EKPHORE ENLIVEN HEARTEN
  INFLAME STARTLE INSPIRIT
  IRRITATE
  (— TO ACTION) HIE ALARM ALARUM
  BESTIR ALACRIFY
ROUSTABOUT FLOORMAN
  RAZORBACK
ROUT MOB DRUM FUSS HERD BRANT
  CHASE COHUE CROWD EJECT
  FLOCK LURCH SMEAR SNORE
  CLAMOR DEFEAT FLIGHT NUMBER
  RABBLE SOIREE THRONG UPROAR
  CONFUSE CONQUER DEBACLE
  SCATTER SPARPLE TEMPEST
  ASSEMBLY CONFOUND DISTRESS
  VANQUISH
ROUTE WAY BELT GATE GEST LINE
  PASS PATH SEND TRACE TRACK

AIRWAY CAREER COURSE CUTOFF
SKYWAY TRAJET CHANNEL CIRCUIT
LANDWAY SHUTTLE CORRIDOR
DISTANCE LIFELINE SHORTCUT
TRAVERSE
(— MARKED OUT) ITER
(— TO DEFEAT) SKIDS
(CIRCUITOUS —) DETOUR
(MIGRATION —) FLYWAY
(OCEAN —) LANE
ROUTH PLENTY ABUNDANT
ROUTINE RUT GRIND ROUTE TROLL
  GROOVE HARNESS EVERYDAY
  (DOMESTIC —) HOMELIFE
  (WEARISOME —) TREADMILL
ROVE RUN RAKE RAVE ROAM GUESS
  KNOCK RANGE ROWAN SPACE
  STRAY FORAGE MARAUD RAMBLE
  STROLL WANDER SPATIATE
  STRAGGLE TRANSCUR
  (— ON THE WING) FLIT
ROVER FLIRT HOYLE STAKE STRAY
  MASHER RANGER VIKING GANGREL
  SCUMMER MARAUDER SLIVERER
  TRAVELER WANDERER COLORADAN
ROVING END SLUB NOMAD ARRANT
  ERRANT DEVIOUS NOMADIC
  RAMPLER VAGRANT GADABOUT
  RAMBLING RESTLESS SLUBBING
  (— IN SEARCH OF KNIGHTLY
  ADVENTURE) ERRANTRY
ROW LAY OAR RIG SET DUST FILE
  LINE MUSS PULL RULE TIER ALLEY
  BRAWL CHESS FIGHT MOUTH NOISE
  ORDER RANGE RINGE SCOLD
  SWATH TRAIN BARNEY BERATE
  COURSE DUSTUP GARRAY KICKUP
  LISSOM PADDLE POTHER RACKET
  RUCKUS SHINDY STREET STROKE
  BOBBERY BRULYIE QUARREL
  SHINDIG CATEGORY OUTBURST
  REMIGATE SQUABBLE
  (— BACKWARD) STERN
  (— OF BENCHES) STACK
  (— OF CASKS) LONGER
  (— OF CORN, BARLEY, ETC.) RIG
  (— OF DRY HAY) STADDLE
  (— OF GRAIN) SWATH SWATHE
  (— OF GRASS) HACK SWATH
  (— OF GUNS) TIRE
  (— OF HOUSES) CRESCENT
  (— OF SEATS) BARRERA
  (— OF SEED) DRILL
  (— OF VEGETABLES) RINGE
  (PL.) EPEIRA
ROWAN RAN RODDIN
ROWAN TREE CARE SORB WICKY
  WITCH RODDEN RODDIN WICKEN
  WIGGEN QUICKEN RANTREE
  WHITTEN WITCHEN ROUNTREE
ROWBOAT GIG OAR BARK OARS
  PLAT BARIS COBLE DINGY FUNNY
  KOBIL SCULL SKIFF BARQUE CAIQUE
  DINGHY LURKER WHERRY SCULLER
  (— SEAT) TAFT
  (CLINKER-BUILT —) FUNNY
  (FLAT-BOTTOMED —) DORY
  (SMALL —) COG
ROWDY TOU BHOY CASH MONEY

ROUGH TOUGH TOMBOY UNRULY
VULGAR HOODLUM RAFFISH
BARRATER LARRIKIN STUBBORN
ROWDYISM YAHOOISM
ROWEN EDGROW RAWING
  AFTERMATH ROUGHINGS
ROWER URGER GALIOT STROKE
  OARSMAN STERNMAN CAIQUEJEE
  (— ON UPPER SEATS) THRANITE
  (OUTERMOST —) THALAMITE
  (SECOND LEVEL —) ZYGITE
ROWING CREW
ROWLOCK LOCK CRUTCH OARLOCK
  RULLOCK
ROYAL EASY REAL RIAL ELITE
  REGAL SMALT AUGUST KINGLY
  REGIUS SOVRAN SUPERB BASILIC
  GLORIOUS IMPERIAL IMPOSING
  MAJESTIC PAVILION
  (— MACE) SCEPTER SCEPTRE
ROYAL ANTELOPE MADOQUA
  KLEENEBOC
ROYAL FERN OSMOND OSMUND
ROYALIST TORY ULTRA REGIAN
  TANTIVY CAVALIER MUSCADIN
ROYALLY PURPLEY
ROYAL PALM COYAL
ROYALTY LOT ALII GALE BONUS
  REGAL REALTY MAJESTY PENALTY
  LORDSHIP NOBILITY REGALITY
ROYET WILD HARSH UNRULY
  ROMPING
RUB DUB BARK BILL FILE FRAY FRET
  FRIG FROT RISP WIPE CHAFE DIGHT
  FEEZE FRUSH GRATE GRAZE GRIDE
  LABOR SCOUR SCRUB SMEAR
  STONE FRIDGE RUBBER STREAK
  BEESWAX FRICACE FURBISH
  MASSAGE
  (— AS A ROPE) SNUG
  (— AS ANIMALS) SHAB
  (— AWAY) ERODE ABRADE
  (— BOOT) BONE
  (— DOWN) WIPE STRAP
  (— ELBOWS) JOSTLE JUSTLE
  (— GENTLY) STRIKE STROKE
  (— HARD) SCOUR SCRUB
  (— HARSHLY) GRIND
  (— LIGHTLY) GRAZE
  (— OFF) CROCK ABRADE ABRASE
  (— OUT) ERASE EFFACE EXPUNGE
  (— ROUGHLY) GRATE
  (— SNUFF) DIP
  (— THE SKIN OFF) SHAW
  (— TOGETHER) FIDDLE
  (— VELVET FROM ANTLERS)
  BURNISH
  (— WITH GREASE) DUB
  (— WITH OIL) ANOINT
RUBBED TERSE
RUBBER BUNA FOAM PARA BUTYL
  CREPE RASER ALASKA BISUIT
  CAUCHO DAPICO ERASER NIGGER
  RUNNER BURUCHA EBONITE
  ELASTIC GUAYULE RAMBONG
  BORRACHA FRICTION NEOPRENE
  SERNAMBY SERWAMBY SOVPRENE
  (— CITY) AKRON
  (HARD —) EBONITE

(RECLAIMED —) SHODDY
(PL.) SHAB
RUBBERIZE FRICTION
RUBBER TREE ULE MILKER
RAMBONG
RUBBING CHAFE CARESS ABRASION
FRICTION FROTTAGE FRICATION
RUBBISH KET CRAB FLAM FLUM
GEAR GWAG MULL PELF PELT RAFF
ROSS TRAG BRASH CRAWM CULCH
OFFAL SCOWL SLUSH STENT STUFF
TRADE TRASH TRUCK WASTE
COLDER DEBRIS GARBLE KELTER
LITTER PALTRY RAFFLE REFUSE
RUBBLE SCULCH SHRUFF SPILTH
BAGGAGE BEGGARY MULLOCK
RUMMAGE SLITHER TAFFIKE
TRAFFIC FIRETRAP NONSENSE
RIFFRAFF TRASHERY TRUMPERY
(VEGETABLE —) WRACK
RUBBISHY POUCY PALTRY TRASHY
BAGGAGE RUMMAGY
RUBBLE BRASH STENT TALUS
BACKING SLITHER
RUBE JAY BOOR HICK JAKE JASPER
BUMPKIN BUSHMAN HAYSEED
CORNBALL
RUBELLA ROTELN
RUBICUND RED ROSY RUDDY
FLORID FLUSHED
RUBIGINOUS RUSTY
RUBLE RO RUBLIS
(ONE-HALF —) POLTINIK
RUBRIC RED NAME CANON CLASS
TITLE CONCEPT CATEGORY
RUBRICATE MINIATE
RUBY AGATE RUBIN PYROPE
ANTHRAX SPARKLE VERMEIL
RUBY SPINEL BALAS ALMANDINE
RUCHING COQUILLE
RUCK RUT HEAP PILE RICK CROWD
SQUAT STACK TRASH CREASE
FURROW HUDDLE PUCKER RUBBISH
WRINKLE
RUCKUS ADO ROW FIGHT FRACAS
ROOKUS
RUCTION HURRY RUCKUS QUARREL
RUPTION FRACTION
RUDD REDEYE
RUDDER HELM STEER STERN TIMON
HELLIM RUTHER STEERER
STEERAGE GOVERNAIL
(— BACK) TALON
(— EDGE) BEARDING
(— OF WINDMILL) TAIL
(DIVING —) HYDROVANE
(PART OF —) STOCK
RUDDERFISH CHOPA OPALEYE
RUDDINESS RUBEDITY
RUDDLE RED BOLE KEEL SMIT
ROUGE
RUDDY RED RODE RUDE FRESH
VIVID BLOWSY BLOWZY FLORID
LIVELY GLOWING RUDDISH
BLUSHFUL RUBICUND SANGUINE
RUDDY DUCK ROOK BOOBY NODDY
PADDY SPRIG BOBBER DUNBIRD
GREASER PINTAIL SLEEPER
SPATTER BLUEBILL BULLNECK

HARDHEAD WIRETAIL
RUDE ILL RAW BOLD IRON LEWD
WILD BLUFF BLUNT GREEN GROSS
PLUMP ROUGH STOUR SURLY
UNORN ABRUPT BITTER BORREL
CALLOW CLUMSY COARSE DUDGEN
GOTHIC HOMELY HOYDEN INCULT
RIBALD ROBUST RUGGED RUSTIC
SAVAGE SHAGGY SIMPLE STORMY
UNFEEL UPLAND VULGAR ARTLESS
BOORISH CARLAGE CARLISH INCIVIL
LOUTISH LOWBRED NATURAL
UNCOUTH UNHENDE CHURLISH
CLUBBISH HOMESPUN IMPOLITE
INSOLENT MECHANIC PORTERLY
STUBBORN SYLVATIC UNGENTLE
UNPOLITE YOKELISH
(— AND BOLD) HOIDEN HOYDEN
RUDENESS GAFF
RUDIMENT GERM ANLAGE VESTIGE
BEGINNING
(PL.) ABC ALPHABET ELEMENTS
GRAMMATES
RUDIMENTARY BASIC GERMING
ABORTIVE ABECEDARY ELEMENTAL
EMBRYONIC
(MOST —) FIRST
RUE RU REWE MOURN CATGUT
REGRET REPENT SORROW BORONIA
TENTWORT
RUEFUL SAD RUELY WOEFUL
DOLEFUL PITIABLE
RUFF SET APEX FURY PAPE POPE
CREST PRIDE REEVE TEASE TEAZE
TRUMP COLLAR RABATO RUFFLE
TIPPET ZENITH ELATION PASSION
QUELLIO REBATER ROTONDE
PICKADILL
RUFFED BUSTARD HOUBARA
RUFFED LEMUR VARI
RUFFIAN MUN LAMB PIMP THUG
TORY BULLY DEVIL ROUGH ROWDY
TIGER APACHE BRUTAL COARSE
CUTTER CUTTLE MOHAWK MOHOCK
PANDER TOWSER HOODLUM
SWEATER TUMBLER HACKSTER
HOOLIGAN
RUFFLE VEX BAIT FRET HOOP ROOL
RUFF BULLY FRILL GRAZE JABOT
PLEAT ROUSE SHIRR ABRADE
ATTACK GATHER NETTLE RIPPLE
BLUSTER BRISTLE DERANGE
FLOUNCE FLUTTER PANUELO
STIFFEN SWAGGER TROUBLE
DISHEVEL DISORDER DISTRACT
FURBELOW IRRITATE QUILLING
SKIRMISH
(— THE TEMPER) ROIL
RUFFLED ROUGH UNKEMPT
**RUFFLING (— ON THE SURFACE OF
WATER)** HORROR
RUG TUG BAKU COZY HAUL MAUD
PULL SNUG TEAR WRAP BIJAR
HERAT HEREZ JURUK KAZAK KHILA
KONIA KULAH KUMEH LADIK MECCA
MELAS MOSUL NAMDA SENNA
TEKKE TUZLA USHAK YURUK ZOFRA
AFSHAR BALUCH KANARA KAROSS
KASHAN KIRMAN MOGHAN NAMMAD

PERGAM RUNNER SHIRAZ SMYRNA
TABRIZ TILPAH TOUPEE WILTON
BALUCHI BERGAMA BOKHARA
BUFFALO DERBEND DRUGGET
FERAHAN GIORDES GOREVAN
HAMADAN ISPAHAN SHEERAZ
SHIRVAN YARKAND AUBUSSON
DOMESTIC FOOTPACE PANDERMA
SARABAND SEDJADEH SERABEND
WOLFSKIN
(— OF SKINS) KAROSS WOLFSKIN
(PLAID —) MAUD
(PRAYER —) GHIORDES NAMAZLIK
(REVERSIBLE —) KILIM
RUGA FOLD CREASE WRINKLE
RUGBY FOOTER RUGGER FOOTBALL
(— PLAY) SCRUM
RUGGED RUDE WILD HAIRY HARDY
ROUGH STIFF COARSE CRAGGY
HORRID JAGGED KNAGGY KNOTTY
ROBUST SAVAGE STRONG STURDY
UNEVEN CRABBED GNARLED
OBDURATE SCRAGGED VIGOROUS
RUIN DO MAR POT BANE BANG
COOK CRAB DAMN DASH DOOM
FALL FATE FELL HELL JACK KILL
LOSS RASE RAZE SINK TALA BLAST
BOTCH BREAK CRUSH DECAY EXILE
GUBAT HUACA LEESE LEISS SHEND
SHOOT SMASH SPEED SPILL SPLIT
SPOIL SWAMP WRACK WRAKE
WRECK BEDASH BLIGHT CANCEL
COOPER DAMAGE DEFACE DEFEAT
DIDDLE DISMAY FOREDO INJURY
RAVAGE UNMAKE BOWWOWS
CORRUPT DESTROY FLATTEN
FORLESE FORWORK LEESING
PERVERT SHATTER SUBVERT
TORPEDO UNDOING BANKRUPT
COLLAPSE DEMOLISH DESOLATE
DISASTER DOWNFALL
(— AT GAMBLING) SHRUB
(SPIRITUAL —) FALL
(PL.) ASHES DEBRIS RELICS RUDERA
ZIMBABWE
RUINATION DOGS
RUINED FLAT GONE LORN KAPUT
BROKEN FALLEN NAUGHT NOUGHT
FORLORN BANKRUPT DESOLATE
RUINER MARPLOT
RUINOUS DEADLY BANEFUL
DECAYED SHENDFUL WASTEFUL
CUTTHROAT
RULE LAW MAN RAJ WIN DASH KING
NORM SWAY WALD WARD YARD
AXIOM CANON GUIDE JUDGE MAXIM
NORMA ORDER REGLE REIGN RICHE
RIGHT RULER SPILE STAFF SUTRA
SUTTA WIELD ALIDAD CUTOFF
DECIDE DECREE DITION DOMINE
EMPIRE ENTAIL GNOMON GOVERN
MANAGE MASTER METHOD REGNUM
SQUARE VASSAL BROCARD
COMMAND CONTROL COUNSEL
DICTATE DIETARY FORMULA
PLUMMET PRECEPT PRESIDE
REGENCY REGIMEN THEOREM
DICTAMEN DOCTRINE DOMINATE
FUNCTION LEGALISM MODERATE

ORDINARY OVERLEAD PERSUADE
REGIMENT REGNANCY STANDARD
TYRANNIS
(— **OUT**) EXCLUDE
(— **TYRANNICALLY**) HORSE
(—**S OF CONDUCT**) ETIQUETTE
(—**S OF DUELING**) DUELLO
(**ABSOLUTE** —) AUTARCHY
(**OPPOSING** —) ANTINOMY
RULER DEY GOG JAM MIN OBA AMIR
CZAR DAME DUKE EMIR INCA KING
LORD OBBA RULE TSAR TZAR
ALDER AMEER DECAN EMEER HAKIM
MPRET MWAMI NAGID NAWAB
SCALE SOPHI STEER SUBAH ZUPAN
APHETA ARCHON AUTHOR CAESAR
DESPOT DUARCH DYNAST EPARCH
FERULE HERSIR ISWARA KABAKA
KAISER MASTER NIMROD PATESI
PENLOP RECTOR REGENT SAWBWA
SHERIF SOLDAN SUFFEE SULTAN
TYRANT ADMIRAL ALIDADE
BOURBON DEMARCH FAIPULE
ISHVARA KHEDIVE MONARCH
MORMAER PTOLEMY RECTRIX
REGULUS REIGNER TOPARCH
TRIARCH WIELDER AUGUSTUS
BASILEUS DRIGHTEN EXILARCH
GOVERNOR HEPTARCH INTERREX
OLIGARCH PADISHAH PENTARCH
PHYLARCH REGINALD TARAFDAR
WHIPKING
(— **IN A NATIVITY**) APHETA
(— **OF ENCLOSURE**) HENRY
(**CURVED** —) SWEEP
(**ELF** —) AUBREY
(**INCA** —) CURACA
(**JEWISH** —) EXILARCH
(**MONGOLIAN** —) HUTUKTU
(**MOSLEM** —) SOLDAN
(**STRONG** —) REGINALD
(**TATAR OR MOGUL** —) CHAM
RULING CALL CHIEF REGENT
SOVRAN CURRENT HOLDING
REGITIVE HEGEMONIC
RUM ODD ROME OCUBY QUEER
RUMBO TAFIA TAFFIA BACARDI
CACHACA JAMAICA PECULIAR
SWITCHEL EXCELLENT
RUMBLE CROWL DICKY GROWL
RUMOR SNORE BUMBLE HOTTER
HUMBLE LUMBER WAMBLE
GRUMBLE QUARREL
RUMBO RUM GROG LIQUOR
RUMEN CUD PAUNCH STOMACH
RUMINANT OX COW YAK BULL DEER
GOAT CAMEL LLAMA MOOSE SHEEP
STEER TAKIN ALPACA MAZAME
VICUNA GIRAFFE QUIDDER
ANTELOPE TUBICORN
RUMINATE CHAW CHEW MULL MUSE
CONCOCT REFLECT SAUNTER
CONSIDER
RUMINATION MERYCISM
RUMKIN RUMMER
RUMMAGE GRUB ROUT SEEK
BUSTLE FORAGE TOUSLE UPROAR
FOSSICK RANSACK ROMMACK
DISORDER SKIRMISH UPHEAVAL

(— **ABOUT FOR A PROFIT**) FOSSICK
(— **SALE**) JUMBLE
RUMMY GIN RUM TUNK QUEER
CANASTA COONCAN DRUNKARD
OKLAHOMA
RUMOR CRY SAW BUZZ FAMA FAME
TALK WORD BRUIT MUDGE NOISE
SOUGH SOUND STORY VOGUE
VOICE BREEZE FURPHY GOSSIP
MURMUR POTGUN RENOWN REPORT
RUMBLE CLATTER HEARING
HEARSAY INKLING OPINION
WHISPER NORATION GRAPEVINE
RUMORED AFLOAT
RUMP ASS FUD ARSE BEAM CULE
DOCK DOUP CROUP NATCH PODEX
STERN BOTTOM CURPIN CROUPON
CRUPPER HURDIES PLUNDER
BANKRUPT BUTTOCKS DERRIERE
RUMPF CORE
RUMPLE FOLD MUSS WISP TOUSE
TOWSE MOUSLE ROMBLE CRUMPLE
SCRUNCH WRINKLE
RUMPUS RAG ROW BRAWL SHINE
CLAMOR FRACAS HUBBUB RUCKUS
TOWROW UPROAR ROOKERY
ROWDYDOW
RUMSHOP BAR SALOON TAVERN
BARROOM TAPROOM DRUNKERY
RUN GO BYE ERN FLY FOG GAD HOP
JOG LAM LEG PLY RIN RUB URN
BUNK CALL FLEE FLOW FUSE HARE
HEAT HEEL HUNT IRNE KITE LEAD
LEAP MELT PASS PLAY RACE RAKE
RINN ROAM ROVE TEND TRIG TRIP
TROT TURN WALK WEEP WORK
ASSAY BLEND BREAK CHASE COAST
EXTRA GOING HURRY NOTCH POINT
SCOUP SPEED SPEND STAND TABLE
TRACE BICKER CAREER COURSE
ELAPSE ESCAPE EXTEND GALLOP
HASTEN LADDER MANAGE RESORT
ROTATE SPRENT SPRINT STREAM
TUMBLE VOLATA ACCURRE
CONDUCT CONTAIN FLUTTER
LIQUEFY OPERATE PASSAGE
RETREAT SKELTER STRETCH
FUNCTION TRANSCUR
(— **ABOUT**) TIG FISK DISCURRE
(— **ACROSS**) STRIKE
(— **AGAINST**) JOSTLE
(— **AGROUND**) BEACH GRAVEL
HURTLE STRAND STRIKE
(— **ALONG EDGE OF**) SKIRT
(— **AS STOCKING**) LADDER
(— **AT HIGH SPEED**) SCORCH
(— **AT THE NOSE**) SNIVEL
(— **AT TOP SPEED**) SPRINT
(— **AWAY FROM DEBTS**) LEVANT
(— **AWAY IN PANIC**) STAMPEDE
(— **AWAY**) FLY GUY FLEE HIKE JINK
JUMP SMUG ELOPE SCRAM SMOKE
DECAMP SCAMPER SCARPER
FUGITATE SKEDADDLE
(— **BEFORE A GALE**) SCUD
(— **BEFORE A JUMP**) FEAZE FEEZE
(— **BETWEEN**) INTERCUR
(— **BLINDLY**) SKITTLE
(— **CLUMSILY**) LOPPET TUMBLE

(— **COUNTER**) BELY BELIE CROSS
(— **DOWN**) SLUR OVERRUN
(— **HARD**) DIG
(— **HIGH**) FLOOD
(— **IN CRICKET**) BYE WIDE EXTRA
NOTCH
(— **IN DROPS**) WEEP
(— **INTO**) INCUR
(— **ITS COURSE**) LAPSE
(— **OBLIQUELY**) SQUINT
(— **OF CLAPBOARDING**) STRAKE
(— **OF MULE CARRIAGE**) DRAW
(— **OF SHAD**) SPURT
(— **OF STAIRS**) GOING
(— **OFF**) BOLT SCADDLE
(— **ON SKIS**) SCHUSS
(— **OUT**) EXCUR ISSUE PETER
(— **OVER**) HEAT TRAMP OVERFLOW
(— **RAPIDLY**) KITE RAKE SCUR
SCOUR SKIRR SPLIT CAREER
(— **SOAP**) FRAME
(— **SPEEDILY**) CHASE CAREER
(— **SWIFTLY**) HARE LEAP SCUD
CHEVY CHIVY
(— **THROUGH**) PIERCE DISCURRE
(— **TO EXERCISE HORSE**) HEAT
(— **TO**) ACCURRE
(— **TOGETHER**) HERD MUDDY
CLUTTER
(— **TRAINS**) BLOCK
(— **WILD**) GAD ESCAPE STARTLE
(— **WILDLY**) STARTLE
(— **WITH AFFECTED PRECIPITATION**)
SCUTTLE
(— **WITH SKIPS**) SCOUP
(— **WITH VELOCITY**) DART
(**BRIEF** —) STREAK FLUTTER
(**END** —) SWEEP
(**GLASS FURNACE** —) BLAST
(**OBSTACLE** —) GYMKHANA
(**RAPID MUSICAL** —) TIRADE VOLATA
(**SAILING** —) STRETCH
(**SHEEP** —) SLAIT STATION
(**SHORT** —) FAIL BICKER SCURRY
FLUTTER RAMRACE SCUTTLE
RUNAGATE APOSTATE FUGITIVE
RENEGADE RUNABOUT VAGABOND
WANDERER
RUNAWAY ROMP RUNNER DECISIVE
DESERTER FUGITIVE RUNAGATE
RUNDI HUTU
RUNDLE DRUM RUNG ORBIT CIRCLE
SPHERE WINDLASS
RUNDLET KEG BARREL
RUN-DOWN BAD SHODDY SQUALID
DERELICT
RUNE WEN WYN WYNN CHARM
OGHAM SPELL SECRET MYSTERY
RUNG RIM GREE RIME STEP ROUND
SCALE SPELL SPOKE STAFF STAIR
STALE STAVE STEAL TREAD WRUNG
DEGREE RUNDLE STOWER STREAK
CROSSBAR TRAVERSE
(— **OF CHAIR**) SPELL
(— **OF LADDER**) RIME STEP RANGE
SPOKE STALE RONDLE STREAK
(— **OF ROPE WALK**) STAKE
(**PL.**) STILE

RUNIC ALPHABET FUTHARK
FUTHORC
RUNIC LETTER THORN
RUNLET RUSH RINDLE RUNNEL
STREAM RIVELING
RUNNEL RILL BROOK RHINE RINDLE
RUNLET POLLARD RIVULET
STREAMLET
RUNNER SOW GOER POST SCUD
SHOE SKID BLADE COBIA FLOAT
RACER SCARF SKATE SLIDE SPRAY
TEDGE CURSOR HEELER KANARA
RENNER STOLON TOUTER CHANNEL
COURIER HARRIER SARMENT
CURSITOR SKIPJACK TRAILING
(— **FOR GRINDING STONE**) MARTIN
(**BLUE** —) HARDTAIL
(**FLUME** —) HERDER
(**PAIR OF** —S) SLOOP
(**RACE** —) SCUTTLER
(**SLED** —S) BOB
(**SLEDGE** —S) SLIPES
RUNNING RUN CARE EASY RACE
FLUID QUICK COURSE LIVING
COURANT CURRENT CURSIVE
FLOWING HOTFOOT SCUTTER
SLIDING FUGITIVE
(— **ABOUT**) COURANT CURSORY
(— **ACROSS**) DIAGONAL
(— **OF SHIPS TOGETHER**) ALLISION
(— **TOWARD**) APPULSE
(— **VERTICALLY**) DOWN
(**FIRST** —S) HEAD
(**NOT** —) DEAD
RUNNING GEAR MOBILE
RUNT BOOR SCRUB SLINK STEER
STUMP STUNT HEIFER PEEWEE
SCRUMP TITMAN URLING BULLOCK
SHARGAR SHARGER SLINKER
RECKLING
RUNTY MEAN SURLY SCRUBBY
SCRUNTY STUNTED DWARFISH
RUNWAY RUN TIP DUCT TRAIL
TARMAC SLIPWAY AIRSTRIP
DOLLYWAY
(— **OF HARE**) FILE
RUPEE DIB CHIP SICCA ROUPIE
(**100,000** —S) LAC LAKH
(**ONE-SIXTEENTH** —) ANNA
(**TENS OF** —S) RX
RUPERT'S DROP TEAR
RUPIA RUPEE ERUPTION
(**HALF** —) PARDO PARDAO
RUPTURE BLOW REND RENT BREAK
BURST CRACK SPLIT BREACH
HERNIA RHEXIS DISRUPT RUPTION
FRACTION FRACTURE HERNIATE
RUPTURED BROKEN
RURAL RUSTIC BUCOLIC COUNTRY
AGRESTIC ARCADIAN LANDWARD
PASTORAL VILLATIC
RUSE HOAX ROSE SHIFT STALL
TRICK WREST ARTIFICE TRICKERY
RUSH FLY FOG RIP RIX RUB SAG
BANG BENT CLAP DASH DUSH FALL
GIRD HURL HUSH JUNK LASH LEAP
LUSH PASH RACE RACK RASH RESE
RISH ROUT SCUD SHOT SLUR SPUR
SWIP TEAR TILT WHIP WIND ADRUE

CARRY CHASE CHUTE DRASH DRIVE
FEEZE FLASH FLUSH FRAIL FRUSH
HURRY ONSET PIPES PREEL SCOUR
SEAVE SHOOT SPART SPATE SPRAT
SPRIT SPROT START STAVE STORM
WHIRL CHARGE DELUGE FESCUE
HURTLE JUNCUS POWDER RAMACK
RANDOM RAVINE STREAK THRESH
ASSAULT BRATTLE BULRUSH
DAILIES DEBACLE JUNCITE RAMMISH
RAMRACE SKELTER SMOTHER
SWITHER TANTIVY TORNADO
WHITHER CATARACT DEERHAIR
SALTWEED SPLATTER VANQUISH
(— **ABROAD**) FLUSH
(— **AGAINST**) CHARGE
(— **AWAY**) BOLT FLEE
(— **DOWN**) TRACE
(— **FOR WEAVING**) FRAIL
(— **HEADLONG**) BOIL RUIN SPURN
STAMPEDE
(— **OF LIQUID**) HEAD FLUSH
(— **OF WATER**) FRESH SHOOT
SPOUT SWASH
(— **OF WORDS**) SPATE
(— **OUT**) SALLY
(**CLUMP OF** —S) RASHBUSS
(**COMMON** —) FLOSS
(**DOWNWARD** —) HURL
(**FLAT** —) SHALDER
(**FORCEFUL** —) JET
(**NOISY** —) SCUTTER
(**ONWARD** —) BIRR SURGE
(**PL.**) REXEN
RUSHING HURL SCUD FURIOUS
HUDDLING IMPETUOUS
(— **OF WIND**) GUST
RUSHLIGHT SEAVE
RUSH NUT CHUFA
RUSK ZWIEBACK
RUSSELL'S VIPER DABOIA DABOYA
JESSUR KATUKA

RUSSIA
CAPITAL: MOSCOW
COIN: KOPEK RUBLE GRIVNA
KOPECK
COLLECTIVE FARM: KOLHOZ
KOLKHOZ
DISTRICT: KARELIA
FORTRESS: KREMLIN
LAKE: ARAL NEVA SEGO CHANY
ELTON ILMEN ONEGA BAYKAL
SELETY TAYMYR TENGIZ
ZAYSAN BALKHASH
MEASURE: FUT LOF DUIM FASS
LOOF STOF FOUTE KOREC
LIGNE OSMIN PAJAK STOFF
VEDRO VERST ARSHIN CHARKA
LINIYA PALETZ SAGENE TCHAST
BOTCHKA CHKALIK GARNETZ
VERCHOC BOUTYLKA CHETVERT
KROUSHKA
MOUNTAIN: POBEDY BELUKHA
MOUNTAIN RANGE: ALAI URAL
CAUCASUS
NAME: USSR SOVIET MUSCOVY

PENINSULA: KOLA CRIMEA
KARELIA KAMCHATKA
PORT: EISK ANAPA ODESSA
RIVER: IK OB DON ILI KET NER
OKA ROS TAZ TYM USA AMGA
AMUR KARA LENA NEVA OREL
SURA SVIR URAL LOVAT MEZEN
NADYM ONEGA TEREK TOBOL
VOLGA ABAKAN DONETS IRTYSH
DNIEPER PECHORA
SEA: ARAL AZOV KARA BLACK
BAIKAL OKHOTSK
TOWN: KIEV OMSK OREL PERM
GOMEL KASAN KAZAN KYZYL
MINSK PENSA PSKOV TOMSK
IGARKA KERTCH KURGAN NIZHNI
ODESSA ROSTOV SARTOV
URALSK ALMAATA BATAISK
DONETSK IRKUTSK IVANOVO
KALININ RYBINSK KOSTROMA
ORENBURG SMOLENSK
TAGANROG TASHKENT VLADIMIR
VORONEZH YAROSLAV

RUSSIAN IVAN RUSS SLAV VELIKA
(— **BRAID**) SOUTACHE
(— **HEMP**) RINE
(— **POOL**) CARLINE
(**LITTLE** —) RUSSENE RUTHENE
UKRAINIAN
RUSSIAN BANK CRAPETTE
RUSSIAN CALF FUDGE
RUSSIAN THISTLE SALTWORT
TUMBLEWEED
RUSSIAN TURNIP RUTABAGA
RUSSIAN WOLFHOUND BORZOI
RUST CLOWN DROSS ROOST ROUST
UREDO AERUGO CANKER CORRODE
FERRUGO OXIDIZE
(— **OF PLANTS**) HEMIFORM
LEPTOFORM
(**KNOT OF** —) TUBERCULE
RUSTIC HOB JAY PUT BOOR CARL
CHAW HICK HIND JAKE JOCK RUDE
BACON BUSHY CARLE CHUFF
CHURL COLIN DAMON DORIC HODGE
ROUGH RURAL RURIC SILLY YOKEL
AGREST BUMKIN COARSE FARMER
GAFFER HONEST JOBSON RUSSET
SAVAGE SCOLOC SCOLOG STURDY
SYLVAN UPLAND ARTLESS BOORISH
BUCOLIC BUMPKIN BUSHMAN
COUNTRY DAPHNIS FIELDEN
GEORGIC HAYSEED HOBNAIL
HOOSIER LANDMAN PAISANO
PEASANT PLOWMAN THYRSIS
WAYBACK AGRESTIC DAMOETAS
GEOPONIC LANDWARD MOSSBACK
CHAWBACON
(**NOT** —) CIVIL
(**UNCOUTH** —) JAKE
(**YOUTHFUL** —) SWAIN
(**PL.**) COUNTRYFOLK
RUSTLE FISLE STEAL FISSLE FISTLE
HIRSEL REESLE BRUSSEL BRUSTLE
CRINKLE REESTLE SKITTER WHISTLE
(— **OF SILK**) SCROOP
(— **UP**) SNAVVLE

RUSTLER THIEF WADDY DUFFER
   WADDIE HUSTLER
RUSTLING ARUSTLE CRINKLY
   FROUFROU SOUGHING FRICATION
   SUSURROUS
RUSTY HOARY MOROSE ROOSTY
   SULLEN CANKERY OUTMODED
RUT RAT BRIM RACK RAIK RUCK
   TRACK TREAD CREASE FURROW
   GROOVE STRAKE UPROAR CHANNEL
   OESTRUS WRINKLE
   (— IN PATH) GAY
RUTABAGA BAGA SWEDE TURNIP
RUTH PITY MERCY MISERY REGRET
   SORROW CRUELTY REMORSE
   SADNESS SYMPATHY
   (HUSBAND OF —) BOAZ

(MOTHER-IN-LAW OF —) NAOMI
(SON OF —) OBED JESSE
RUTHENIAN RUSSENE RUSSNIAK
   UKRAINIAN
RUTHLESS GRIM CRUEL BRUTAL
   PITILESS CUTTHROAT
RUTILE NIGRINE SAGENITE
RUTTER PLOW DRAGOON GALLANT
   TROOPER
RUTTISH RANK LUSTFUL

RWANDA
CAPITAL: KIGALI
LAKE: KIVU
LANGUAGE: KIRUNDI SWAHILI
MOUNTAIN: KARISIMBI

MOUNTAIN RANGE: MITUMBA
PEOPLE: TWA HUTU TUTSI
RIVER: KAGERA AKANYARU
   LUVIRONZA
TRIBE: BATWA BAHUTU WATUSI
   BATUTSI

RYE RAY RIE ERAY REYE SPELT
   WHISKY GENTLEMAN
RYEGRASS RAY EAVER DARNEL
RYMANDRA KNIGHTIA
RYND BAIL RHIND MILRIND
RYOT RAYAT FARMER RAIYAT
   TENANT TILLER PEASANT

S ESS SUGAR SIERRA
SABBATH SUNDAY SABAOTH
SHABBAT SHABBOS
SABER KUKRI SABRE BANCAL
BASKET TULWAR TUWAUR ATAGHAN
CIMETER YATAGAN ACINACES
SCIMITAR
SABICU JIQUE JIQUI
SABLE DWALE SAPLE OGRESS
SATURN DIAMOND ZIBELINE
(ROUNDEL —) PELLET
SABLEFISH SKIL BESHOW COALFISH
SKILFISH
SABOTAGE MASTIC DESTROY
SAC BAG GUT POD CYST SACK
ASCUS BURSA FLOAT POUCH THECA
VOLVA ACINUS AMNION SACCUS
AMPULLA BLADDER CAPSULE
CISTERN HYGROMA UTRICLE
VESICLE BROODSAC FOLLICLE
SACCULUS SPERMARY
SACCHARIN SWEET STICKY SUGARY
GLUCOSE GLUSIDE
SACCHAROSE SUCROSE
SACERDOTAL HIERATIC PRIESTLY
SACHEM SAGAMORE
SACK BAG BED MAT SAC LOOT
POCK POKE BAYON GOOSE HARRY
POUCH SPOIL BUDGET POCKET
RAVAGE SACKET SACQUE DISMISS
PILLAGE PLUNDER RANSACK
SACKAGE SACKBAG DESOLATE
PACKSACK PEIGNOIR
(— OF PALM LEAVES) BAYONG
(MAIL —) BUM
(PACK —) KYACK
(SAD —) BOLO
SACKBUT SAMBUKE TROMBONE
SACKING SACK GUNNY CROCUS
SACKEN HESSIAN POLDAVY
SOUTAGE
SACRAMENT BAPTISM MYSTERY
PENANCE
SACRED HOLY TABU HUACA SACRE
SAINT SANCT SANTO TABOO DIVINE
SACRAL HALLOWED HEAVENLY
NUMINOUS REVEREND
SACRED FIG PIPAL
SACRED FISH KANNUME
SACREDNESS CHURINGA SANCTITY
TJURUNGA
SACRIFICE GIVE HOST LOSS OFFER
SPEND YAJNA CORBAN FOREGO
VICTIM EXPENSE CHILIOMB
IMMOLATE KAPPARAH LITATION
OBLATION OFFERING PASSOVER
SPHAGION
(— OF 100 OXEN) HECATOMB
(— OF 1000 OXEN) CHILIOMB
(— OF CARGO) JETTISON
(PL.) HAGIGAH CHAGIGAH
SACRIFICIAL PIACULAR
SACRILEGIOUS IMPIOUS
SACRISTAN SEXTON SACRIST
SACRISTY SEXTRY SACRARY
VERGERY PARATORY
SACROSANCT SACRED
SAD WAN DARK DOWY DRAM BLACK
DREAR DUSKY MESTO MOODY

SABLE SOBER SORRY WEARY
YEMER DREARY SOLEMN SULLEN
TRISTE WOEFUL DOLEFUL DUMPISH
FORLORN FUNEBRE LUCTUAL
MOANFUL SOBERLY UNHAPPY
DEJECTED GROANFUL MOURNFUL
MOURNING PITIABLE SUBTRIST
TRISTIVE UNBLITHE
SADDEN SAD DUMP GLOOM GRIEVE
ATTRIST CONTRIST DISTRESS
SADDENED BROKEN
SADDENING LUCTUAL
SADDLE PAD RIG SAG TAG LOAD
SUNK CHINE PANEL PILCH SELLE
STICK BURDEN HEADER RECADO
PIGSKIN PILLION
(— COVER) MOCHILA
(— FOR ONE-LEGGED RIDER)
SOMERSET
(— STUFFED WITH STRAW) SODS
(— WITH) STICK
(— WORKER) LORIMER
(LIGHT —) PILCH PILLION
(MOTORCYCLE —) PILLION
(PACK —) BAT
(STRAW —) SUNK SUGGAN
(WITHOUT A —) ASELLATE
SADDLEBACK JACK JACKBIRD
SADDLEBAG ALFORJA CANTINA
SUMPTER TEETSOOK
(PL.) JAGS JAGGS
SADDLE BLANKET CORONA
SADDLEBOW BOW ARSON
SADDLECLOTH HOUSE NAMDA
HOUSING PADCLOTH SHABRACK
SADDLEMAKER FUSTER KNACKER
SADDLE MAT FLET
SADDLEPAD PANEL PILLOW
SADDLER CODDER KNACKER
LORIMER WHITTAW
SADISTIC SICK CRUEL SADIC
SADLY SAD UNWINLY
SADNESS DUMP RUTH DREAR
DUMPS GLOOM GRIEF UNWIN
SORROW
SAD SACK BOLO
SAFAWID SUFI
SAFE RUG CRIB PETE SURE WELL
SALVA SIKER SOUND SECURE
SICCAR HEALTHY SYKERLY
COCKSURE SILVENDY
(— FOR MEAT) KEEP
(— TO DEAL WITH) CANNY
SAFEBLOWER PETEMAN
SAFEBREAKER YEGG YEGGMAN
SAFE-CONDUCT COWLE GRITH
CONDUCT PASSPORT
SAFECRACKER BOXMAN PETEMAN
PETERMAN TORCHMAN
SAFEGUARD SAVE WARD GUARD
HEDGE SALVE DEFEND SAFETY
SECURE BASTION BULWARK
WARRANT FREEWARD
SAFEKEEPING CUSTODY STORAGE
SAFELY SAFE SICCAR SICKER
SURELY SECURELY
SAFETY SALUTE SURETY WARRANT
SECURITY

SAFETY ZONE ISLET ISLAND
REFUGE
SAFFLOWER KUSUM ALAZOR
SAFFRON
SAFFRON CROCUS AZAFRAN
CROCEUS
SAFROLE SHIKIMOL
SAG BAG DIP TIE SWAG CREEP
DROOP PLANK SLUMP SAGGON
CURTAIN DEFLATE
SAGA EDDA EPIC MYTH TALE RIMUR
LEGEND NJALSAGA
SAGACIOUS DEEP CANNY SHARP
ARGUTE SHREWD CORDATE
SAPIENT
SAGACITY POLICY WISDOM
YEPHEDE SAPIENCE
SAGE RSI WARE WISE WITE CLARY
IMLAC KATHA RISHI SABIO SOLON
SOPHY ABARIS DHARMA SALVIA
SAULGE SHREWD WIZARD EYESEED
MAHATMA SAPIENT SOPHIST
TOHUNGA WISEMAN DEVARSHI
MAHARSHI WISEACRE
SAGEBRUSH SAGE HYSSOP
SAGEWOOD
SAGENESS SAPIENCE
SAGGER COFFIN SETTER CASSETTE
SAGGING DRAG SWAG PTOSIS
SAGITTA ARROW
SAGITTARIUS ARCHER
SAGO PALM CYCAD
SAGRADA CASCARA
SAGUARO SUAHARO SUWARRO
PITAHAYA
SAHIDIC THEBAIC
SAIBLING TORGOCH
SAID DIT QUOTH STATED RELATED
SAIL JIB LUG RAG BEAT GALE HAUL
MAIN SCUN SLAT SWAN SWIM WING
DANDY FLEET FLIER FLOAT FLYER
JUMBO RAFFE SCALE SHEET
ACCOST CANVAS COURSE CRUISE
DRIVER JIGGER LATEEN MIZZEN
MUSLIN SINGLE ARTEMON LUGSAIL
SKYSAIL SPANKER SPENCER
TRYSAIL BACKWIND FORESAIL
GAFFSAIL HEADSAIL MAINSAIL
MOONSAIL NAVIGATE RINGSAIL
STAYSAIL STUNSAIL
(— ALONG COAST) COAST ACCOST
(— AROUND) TURN DOUBLE
(— BRISKLY) SPANK
(— BY THE WIND) STRETCH
(— CLOSE TO WIND) PINCH
(— DOWN) AVALE AWALE
(— FASTER) FOOT
(— IN SPECIFIED DIRECTION) STAND
(— OF WINDMILL) ARM AWE EIE
FAN VAN EIGHE FLIER FLYER
SWEEP SWIFT
(— ON COURSE) HAUL WORK
(— QUIETLY) GHOST
(— RAPIDLY) SCUR SKIRR
(— SWIFTLY) RAMP
(— TO WINDWARD) THRASH
(— WITH WIND ABEAM) LASK
(3-CORNERED —) JIB TRINKET
(FRAGMENT OF —) HULLOCK

(LIGHT —) SHADOW
(LOWEST —) COURSE
(PART OF —) SLAB
(SMALL —) ROYAL
(TRIANGULAR —) RAFFE LATEEN
BENTINCK
(WIND —) BADGIR
(PL.) VELA KITES LINENS SAILAGE
CLOTHING
SAILBOAT SAIL SCOW BULLY DANDY
NABBY SAPIT SCOUT SHARP SKIFF
SLOOP SNIPE CANGIA DINGHY
QUODDY SAILER SATTIE CATBOAT
SCOOTER SHALLOP SHARPIE
KEELBOAT SAILSHIP SKIPJACK
(WITCH'S —) SIEVE
SAILFISH BOHO WOOHOO GUEBUCU
LONGJAW VOILIER VOLADOR
BILLFISH
SAILOR GOB TAR JACK TOTY GUARD
KLOSH LAKER LIMEY CALASH
CLASHY DAYMAN DECKIE HEARTY
MARINE MATLOW SEAMAN TARPOT
TIERER TOPMAN MARINAL MARINER
MATELOT SHIPMAN SWABBER
WARRIOR YARDMAN CANOTIER
COXSWAIN DECKHAND FLATFOOT
GALIONJI GUNLAYER LANDSMAN
LITHSMAN MASTHEAD SHIPMATE
WATERDOG WATERMAN WATERRUG
YARDSMAN
(EAST INDIAN —) LASCAR
(OLD —) SALT
(SCANDINAVIAN —) KLOSH
SAILORLIKE TARRISH
SAILOR'S-CHOICE BREAM PIGFISH
PINFISH WHITING
SAIL YARD RAE
SAINFOIN ESPARCET
SAINT PIR RSI DADU HOLY QUTB
WALI ALVAR ARHAT RISHI SANTO
BHAGAT HALLOW PATRON SANTON
CANONIZE MARABOUT
(CHINESE —) IMMORTAL
(PATRON —) AVOWRY
(PILLAR —) STYLITE
(PL.) SS
SAINT ELMO'S FIRE HERMO
CASTOR FUROLE HELENA
ST-JOHN'S-BREAD CAROB
ST-JOHN'S-WORT AMBER TUTSAN
CAMMOCK
SAINTLINESS HOLINESS SANCTITY
SAINTLY DEVOUT ANGELIC SAINTED
BEATIFIC SAINTISH
(— PERSON) ZADDIK
ST REGIS RANERE
SAJ SAIN
SAKE SAKI SCORE
SAKI BISA MONK COUXIA MONKEY
YARKEE
SALABLE VENAL SELLING SELLABLE
VENDIBLE
SALACIOUS LEWD SALT RUTTISH
SCARLET SCABROUS
SALAD SALLET COLESLAW
(CORN —) FETTICUS
SALADA SALINA
SALAL SHALLON

SALAMANDER OLM SOW BEAR
NEWT TWEEG GOPHER LIZARD
TRITON AXOLOTL CRAWLER
CREEPER DOGFISH MECODONT
SALAMICH SHADRACH
SAL AMMONIAC SPIRIT SALMIAC
SALARY PAY HIRE SCREW WAGES
INCOME PACKET PENSION STIPEND
SALE FAIR VENT BREAK HEDGE
TOUCH BOURSE VENDUE AUCTION
MOHATRA SELLING HANDSALE
KNOCKOUT PORTSALE
(— BY AUCTION) CANT BLOCK
(— BY OUTCRY) ROUP ROWP
HAMMER
(— OF OFFICE) BARRATRY
(— OF TOBACCO) BREAK
(PUBLIC —) AUCTION
(RUMMAGE —) JUMBLE
SALESMAN CLERK BAGMAN RUNNER
SELLER BOOKMAN DRUMMER
OUTRIDER
SALESMANSHIP SELLING
SALESPERSON CLERK
SALESWOMAN WINSTER SHOPGIRL
VENDEUSE
SALIENT SPUR BULGE CHIEF ARGINE
BASTION SALTANT
SALIENTIA ANURA ANOURA
ECAUDATA
SALINA SHOR SALINE
SALINE SALT SALAR SALTY MARINAL
SALIVA SPIT DROOL WATER DRIVEL
SLAVER SPUTUM SPITTLE
(— FLOW) PTYALISM
SALIVARY SIALIC
SALIVATION PTYALISM SLOBBERS
SALLET SALADE
SALLOW WAN SICK ADUST LURID
MUDDY SALIX SAUCH SAUGH PALLID
YELLOW
SALLY GRIP JERK PASS QUIP SAIL
QUICK START ESCAPE GAMBIT
SORTIE GAMBADE OUTFALL
OUTLEAP DEMARCHE
SALMON DOG LAX LOX SAM KETA
MASU PINK AMOUT COHOE COUNT
HADDO HOLIA SMOLT SMOOT
SPROD TECON ALEVIN BAGGIT
KIPPER LAUREL MYKISS SAMLET
SAUQUI SILVER TAIMEN ANADROM
ANNATTO BLUECAP BOTCHER
CHINOOK DOGFISH GILLING
KAHAWAI KOKANEE NEWFISH
REDFISH RUNFISH SAWMONT
SHEDDER SOCKEYE BLUEBACK
BRANDLIN GOLDFISH HUMPBACK
LASPRING SALMONID SPRINGER
(— AFTER SPAWNING) KELT
SHEDDER
(— BEFORE SPAWNING) GILLING
GIRLING
(— ENCLOSURE) YAIR
(— IN 2ND OR 3D YEAR) SMOLT
(— IN 2ND YEAR) SPROD HEPPER
GILLING
(— IN 3D YEAR) PUG MORT
(— ON FIRST RETURN FROM SEA)
GRILSE

(BLUEBACK —) NERKA SAUQUI
SOCKEYE
(CURED —) KIPPER
(DOG —) CHUM KETA
(FEMALE —) RAUN BAGGIT
(HUMPBACK —) HADDO HOLIA
(MALE —) GIB BUCK COCK
(MILTER —) EKE
(NEWLY HATCHED —) PINK ALEVIN
(SMALL —) PEAL SKIRLING
(SPENT —) JUDY SLAT RUNFISH
(YOUNG —) FOG PARR PEAL GRILSE
HEPPER JERKIN SAMLET BOTCHER
ESSLING SKEGGER LASPRING
SALMONELLOSIS KEEL
SALON HALL SALOON GALLERY
SALOON CAFE CUDDY DIVAN SALON
SHADE BARROOM CANTINA
RUMSHOP SCATTER DEADFALL
DRINKERY DRUNKERY EXCHANGE
SALPA SALP THALIA
SALSIFY GOATBEARD
SALT SAL CORN KERN SAWT BRINY
ZIRAM AMIDOL AURATE GAMMON
HALITE MALATE OLEATE OSMATE
POWDER SALINE URANIN KAINITE
LACTATE MALEATE NIOBATE
PHYTATE TROPATE ABIETATE
BRACKISH HALINOUS PIMELATE
PLUMBITE
(— OUT) CUT GRAIN
(DOUBLE —) ALUM
(HAIR —) ALUNOGEN
(LUMP OF —) SALTCAT
(METAL —) SILICATE
(MIXTURE OF —S) REH
(ROCK —) PIG HALITE
SALTATE JUMP
SALT BOILER WELLER
SALTBUSH BLUEBUSH
SALTCELLAR SALT CELLAR SELLER
SHAKER SALTFAT SALTFOOT
SALTED SALEE
SALTICID ATTID
SALT PAN PLAYA
SALTPETER NITER NITRE PETER
ANATRON PRUNELLA
SALT PIT VAT WICH WYCH
SALT PORK SOWBELLY
SALTWORKS SALINA SALTERN
SALTERY SALTPANS
SALTWORT KALI BARILLA SALSOLA
KELPWORT
SALTY SALT BRINY SALINE HALINOUS
SALUBRIOUS HEALTHY SALUTARY
SALUTARY GOOD BENIGN HEALTHY
HELPFUL BENEDICT
SALUTATION AVE HAIL ALOHA
SALUS MIZPAH SALAAM SALUTE
REGREET SLAINTE WELCOME
DIEUGARD GREETING HAEREMAI
(DRINKING —) SKOAL PROSIT
PROFACE
SALUTE CAP HAIL HEIL KISS MOVE
YULE CHEER DRINK GREET HALCH
HONOR SALUE SALVO COLORS
EMBRACE CONGREET
SALVADOR BAHIA

SALVAGE SAVE SALVE RECOVERY SCROUNGE
SALVAGER SALVOR
SALVATION BODAI MOKSHA SAFETY NIRVANA KAIVALYA SAVEMENT SOULHEAL
(— APPROACH) MARGA
SALVE SAW TAR SALVO SAUVE NERVAL SUPPLE PLASTER UNGUENT OINTMENT
SALVER TRAY SERVER WAITER PLATEAU
SALVIA CHIA SAGE CLARY MEJORANA MINTWEED
SALVO SALUTE SPREAD PROVISO TRIBUTE STRADDLE
(PL.) LADDER
SAMARA KEY CHAT
SAMARIA AHOLAH
SAMARITAN CUTHEAN CUTHITE
SAMBA CARIOCA
SAMBAR ELK MAHA RUSA
SAME A ID EAD ILK ONE IDEM LIKE SELF VERY DITTO EQUAL SAMEN IDENTIC SELFSAME
(— AS) IQ
(— PLACE) IB
(THAT —) THILK THICKE
SAMENESS ONENESS EQUALITY IDENTITY MONOTONY
SAMNITES SABELLI
SAMOA (CAPITAL OF —) APIA PAGOPAGO
(COIN OF —) TALA
(ISLAND OF —) OFU TAU ROSE MANUA UPOLU SAVAII OLOSEGA TUTUILA
(MOUNTAIN OF —) FITO SAVAII MATAFAO
SAMOGITIAN ZHMUD
SAMOYED TUBA KOIBA YURAK BELTIR KAIBAL NENTSI KAMASSIN
SAMPHIRE SALTWEED
SAMPLE DIP CAST PREE CHECK ESSAY TASTE TRIAL CHANCE COUPON FLOWER MUSTER SWATCH TASTER EXAMPLE EXCERPT PATTERN SAMPLER TASTING INSTANCE PULLDOWN SPECIMEN
(— OF METAL) DIET
SAMPLING SOUNDING
SAMURAI BUSHI RONIN
SAN SAMPI
SANAD SUNNUD
SANBENITO SAMARRA
SAN BLAS TULE
SAN CARLOS ARIVAIPA
SANCTIFICATION HOLINESS
SANCTIFY SACRE SACRI DEDICATE
SANCTIMONIOUS DEVOUT
SANCTION AMEN FIAT ALLOW PIETY ASSENT BISHOP RATIFY APPROVE ENDORSE JUSTIFY PASSAGE SUPPORT ACCREDIT APPROVAL CANONIZE COURTESY SUFFRAGE
SANCTIONED CANONICAL
SANCTITY SANTY HALIDOME HOLINESS
SANCTUARY ADYT BAST BEMA FANE

HOLY SOIL ABBEY ALTAR BAMAH GIRTH GRITH SECOS SEKOS TOWER ADYTON ADYTUM ASYLUM CHAPEL HAIKAL REFUGE SENTRY SHRINE SACRARY SHELTER CABIRION DELUBRUM HALIDOME HOLINESS
(— FOR LAWBREAKERS) ALSATIA
SANCTUM ADYT ADYTON ADYTUM
SAND DIRT GRIT ARENA GRAIL SONDE GRAVEL ISERINE ISERITE PARTING ASBESTIC BLINDING
(— FOR STREWING ON FLOORS) BREEZE
(— HILL) DENE DUNE
(— IN KIDNEYS) ARENA
(— MIXED WITH GRAVEL) GARD DOBBIN
(— ON SEA BOTTOM) PAAR
(BRAIN —) SABULUM ACERVULUS
(COLORED —) SMALT
(DEAUVILLE —) STUCCO
SANDAL TIP BAXA FLAT SOCK TEGUA CALIGA CHARUK PATTEN TATBEB RULLION SCUFFER FOOTHOLD GUARACHE HUARACHO
SANDAL TREE SANTOL
SANDALWOOD NAIO ALGUM ALMUG MAIRE CHANDAM SAUNDERS
SANDALWOOD TREE ILIAHI
SANDARAC TREE ARAR LIGNUM
SANDBAG SANDCLUB
SAND BANK AIR CHAR MEAL SAND BATCH HURST HYRST KNOCK SHELF SHOAL
SANDBAR BALK LOOP SAND BARRA SHOAL TOWHEAD
SANDBLASTER FROSTER BLASTMAN
SAND BORER SMELT
SANDBOX TREE ASSACU
SAND COLIC SABURRA
SAND DARTER SPECK
SAND DUNE TOWAN BARCHAN
SAND EEL GRIG SANDFISH
SANDEMANIAN GLASSITE
SANDERLING OXBIRD
SAND FLEA SCREW SCROW SANDBOY
SAND-FLY BUSH TURMERIC
SAND GROUSE GANGA ROCKER ATTAGEN PINTAIL
SAND HOLE BUNKER
SANDIVER NATRON
SAND LAUNCE LANT SMELT WRIGGLE AMMODYTE SANDLING SCRIGGLE
SAND LILY SOAPROOT
SANDMAN DUSTMAN
SANDPAPER TREE CHAPARRO
SANDPIPER JACK KNOT PEEP RUFF STIB WEET OXEYE SNIPE STINT TEREK TIPUP WADER DUNLIN GAMBET OXBIRD PLOVER REDLEG TEETER TILTER TILTUP TRINGA BROWNIE CHOROOK CREEKER FATBIRD FIDDLER HAYBIRD KRIEKER MONGLER MONGREL REDBACK TATTLER TIPTAIL GRAYBACK LEADBACK PEETWEET ROCKBIRD SANDPEEP SHADBIRD SQUATTER

SWEESWEE TELLTALE TRIDDLER
(FEMALE —) REEVE
(FLOCK OF —S) FLING
SAND PIT BUNKER
SAND ROCKET FLIXWEED
SAND SHARK BONEDOG
SANDSTONE FAKE FLAG GRES GRIT SAND GAIZE HAZEL ARCOSE ARKOSE ARENITE CARSTONE COCONINO GANISTER PSAMMITE RUBSTONE SANDROCK
(BLOCK OF —) SARSEN
SANDSTORM BURAN HABOOB TEBBAD
SANDUST VANITY
SANDWICH BURGER GRINDER WESTERN
SANDWORT LONGROOT SANDWEED
SANDY DEEP GRISTY SANDED ARENOSE PSAMMOUS SABULINE SABULOUS
SANE SAFE WISE LUCID RIGHT FORMAL HEALTHY RATIONAL SENSIBLE
SANGA-SANGA ESSANG
SANGUINARY GORY CRUEL BLOODY CRIMSON SANGUINE
SANGUINE FOND GUZE MURREY HEMATIC HOPEFUL SARDONYX
SANHEDRIN GEROUSIA
SANICLE ALLHEAL SELFHEAL
SANIOUS ICHOROUS
SANITARY HYGIENIC
SANITY SENSE REASON BALANCE LUCIDITY SANENESS
SAN MARINO (CHURCH OF —) PIEVE
(DISTRICTS OF —) CASTELLI
(MOUNTAIN OF —) TITANO
(SUBURB IN —) BORGO
SANNUP SQUAW
SANSKRIT HINDU
(— SOUND OR SIGN) VISARGA
(— WORK) VEDANGA
SANS SERIF DORIC GOTHIC
SANTA MARIA TREE BIRMA GALBA CALABA
SANTONICA WORMSEED
SAP GOON MINE OOZE RASA SEVE HUMBO KEEST LYMPH SAPPER WEAKEN ALVELOZ FLUXURE SAPHEAD
(— COURAGE) DAUNT
(PALM —) TODY TODDY
(POISONOUS —) UPAS
(SUGAR MAPLE —) HUMBO
SAPAJOU SAJOU WARINE
SAPANWOOD BOKOM SIBUCAO
SAPEK DONG
SAPID SIPID FLAVORY
SAPIENT WISE SHREWD KNOWING
SAPLING SCOB PLANT SAPLE SPIRE RUNNEL SPRING TILLER STADDLE ASHPLANT SEEDLING SHILLALA SPRINGER
(— AMONG FELLED TREES) WAVER
SAPODILLA GUM CHICA CHICO DILLY ACHRAS MAMMEE SAPOTA SAPOTE ZAPOTE NISPERO NISBERRY

SAPONIFYING KILLING
SAPONIN GITONIN SENEGIN
CYCLAMIN STRUTHIN
SAPONITE PIOTINE
SAPOTA MATASANO
SAPPHIRE SAFIR TOPAZ ADAMAS
ASTRION HYACINTH
SAPPHIRINE GURNARD TUB
SAPPY FRIM FRUM SAPFUL
SAPSAP PEPEREK
SAPUCAIA COCO COCOA KAKARAL
SAPWOOD SAP BLEA SPLENT SPLINT
GUAYABI LISTING ALBURNUM
SARA (— WOMAN) UBANGI
SARABAITES REMOBOTH
SARACEN CORSAIR
SARAH ATOSSA
SARAKOLLE WAKORE
SARASVATI VAC VACH BENTEN
SARCASM RUB GIBE WIPE FLING
IRONY TAUNT RUBBER SATIRE
BROCARD RIDICULE SCORCHER
SARCASTIC ACID WITTY BITING
IRONIC ACERBIC CUTTING MORDANT
INCISIVE SARDONIC SATIRICAL
SARCASTICALLY DRILY DRYLY
ACIDLY
SARCOCARP FLESH
SARCOPHAGUS TOMB COFFIN
SARCOPSYLLA TUNGA
SARDINE BANG LOUR SARD SILD
CLUPEID PILCHARD SARDELLE

SARDINIA

CHEESE: ROMANO PECORINO
COIN: CARLINE
GREEK COLONY: OLBIA
GULF: OROSEI ASINARA CAGLIARI
ORISTANO
MOUNTAIN: RASU FERRY LINAS
GALLURA LIMBARA SERPEDDI
VITTORIA
NAME: SARDEGNA
PROVINCE: NUORO SASSARI
CAGLIARI
RIVER: MANNU TIRSO LASCIA
COGHINAS
TOWN: NUORO SASSARI THATARI
CAGLIARI IGLESIAS

SARGASSUM GULFWEED
SARGO ZEBRA
SARI PATOLA TAMEIN
SARONG PAU KAIN COMBOY KIKEPA
SARSAPARILLA NUNNARI SHOTBUSH
SASH BAR BELT BENN FAJA GATE
TOBE SCARF TAPIS TOWEL FASCIA
GIRDLE BURDASH CHASSIS
TUBBECK CASEMENT CORSELET
(JAPANESE —) OBI
(WINDOW —) CHESS
SASHAY CHASSE
SASH BAR MUNTIN ASTRAGAL
SASSABY TSESSEBE
SASSAFRAS FILE SALOP SALOOP
SAXIFRAX
SASSY KICKY
SATAN ANGEL DEVIL EBLIS FIEND

SHREW BELIAL LUCIFER SATANAS
DIABOLUS SATANAEL
SATANIC SABLE INFERNAL
SATCHEL HANDBAG KEESTER
SATE GLUT SATIATE SATISFY
SATURATE
SATED SAD BLASE
SATEEN VENETIAN
SATELLITE MOON ARIEL LUNET
DEIMOS MOONET OBERON PHOBOS
ACOLYTE ACOLYTH LUNETTE
ORBITER SPUTNIK TRABANT
UMBRIEL COURTIER FOLLOWER
(— OF JUPITER) IO EUROPA
CALLISTO GANYMEDE
(— OF SATURN) RHEA DIONE MIMAS
TITAN PHOEBE TETHYS IAPETUS
JAPETUS HYPERION
SATIATE CLOY FILL GLUT PALL
QUAT SADE SATE FLESH GORGE
SERVE STALL ENGLUT STODGE
RASSASY SATISFY SURFEIT
SATURATE
SATIATED SICK JADED SATED
SATIATING STODGY FULSOME
SATIETY FULNESS SURFEIT
CLOYMENT
SATIN SAY ATLAS CYPRUS MUSHRU
COOTHAY CYPRESS SATINET
(SILK —) DUCHESS
SATINFLOWER SAFFRON
SATINPOD HONESTY LUNARIA
SATINWOOD HAREWOOD
SATIRE WIT GRIND IRONY IAMBIC
LAMPOON SARCASM SOTADIC
RIDICULE
SATIRIC BITTER IRONIC ABUSIVE
CAUSTIC CUTTING POIGNANT
SLASHING
SATIRIST GRIND SATIRE JUVENAL
PASQUIN
SATIRIZE SKIN SKIT GRIND EXPOSE
IAMBIZE LAMPOON PASQUIN
SATISFACTION CRO FIN PAY UTU
EASE GREE BELLY ENACH TREAT
AMENDS ASSETH REASON COMFORT
CONTENT DELIGHT GLADNESS
PLEASURE
SATISFACTORILY SPROWSY
CLEVERLY
SATISFACTORY FAIR GOOD WELL
DUCKY HUNKY CLEVER DECENT
ADEQUATE LAUDABLE
SATISFIED SAD FAIN FULL GLAD
PAID VAIN APAID CHUFF PROUD
ASSURED CONTENT GRUNTLED
SENSIBLE WILCWEME
SATISFY PAY EVEN FEED FILL MEET
SAIR SATE SUIT ADEEM APPAY
QUEME SERVE SLAKE SPEED
ANSWER DEFRAY PLEASE STODGE
SUPPLY ASSUAGE CONTENT
EXPLETE FULFILL GRATIFY GRUNTLE
RESPOND SATIATE STAUNCH
SUFFICE SATURATE
(— APPETITE) STAY
(— BY PROOF) CONVINCE
(— NEEDS) DO ADJUST
SATISFYING DUE AMPLE SQUARE
PERFECT

SATURATE SOG GLUT SATE SOAK
DRAWK IMBUE SOUSE STEEP
DRENCH IMBIBE SEETHE SODDEN
DRUNKEN INGRAIN SATIATE
SLOCKEN
(— WITH SYRUP) CANDY
SATURATED SOBBY SOGGY SOPPY
SODDEN SPONGY DRUNKEN
SATURATION CHROMA PURITY
SATURITY
SATURN: (FATHER OF —) URANUS
(MOTHER OF —) GAEA
(SATELLITE OF —) RHEA DIONE
MIMAS TITAN TETHYS JAPETUS
HYPERION ENCELADUS
(SON OF —) JUPITER
SATURNINE SULLEN SATANIC
SATYAGRAHA GANDHISM
SATYR FAUN SAUMON SALTIER
WOODMAN WOODWOSE
SATYRIASIS TENTIGO
SAUCE MOLE SASS SOWL BERCY
CHILE CHILI CREAM CREME CURRY
GRAVY PESTO CATSUP GANSEL
MORNAY ROBERT KETCHUP
MARENGO SOUBISE SUPREME
TABASCO VELOUTE BECHAMEL
CHAWDRON DRESSING DUXELLES
MATELOTE POIVRADE RAVIGOTE
REMOLADE
(CURRY —) SAMBAL
(FISH —) ALEC BAGOONG
(SALAD —) DRESSING
(SAVORY —) DIP
(THICK —) LEAR
SAUCEDISH SAUCER BIRDBATH
SAUCEPAN GOBLET POSNET
SKILLET STEWPAN
SAUCER BIRD PATERA PHIALE
CAPSULE
SAUCINESS SAUCE DICACITY
SAUCY BOG ARCH BOLD COXY
BRASH DONSY DORTY FRESH LIPPY
PAWKY POKEY SASSY SMART
BANTAM COCKET COPPED CROUSE
THWART FORWARD PAUGHTY
MALAPERT PETULANT SANSHACH
SAUDI ARABIA: (CAPITAL OF —)
JIDDAH RIYADH
(COIN OF —) RIYAL
(DESERT REGION OF —) NEFUD
DAHANA ALNAFUD
(PLATEAU OF —) NEJD
(TOWN OF —) HAIL MECCA MEDINA
ALHOFUF
(WEIGHT OF —) OKE
SAUNTER IDLE ROAM ROVE TOIT
AMBLE RANGE SHOOL SIDLE STRAY
TRAIK BUMMEL DACKER DANDER
FAFFLE LINGER LOITER LOUNGE
POTTER PUTTER RAMBLE SOODLE
STREEL STROLL TODDLE WANDER
SNAFFLE STAIVER STRAVAGE
SAURA MAGA
SAUREL SCAD XUREL GASCON
BLUEFISH SKIPJACK
SAURY LONGJAW SKIPPER BILLFISH
GOWDNOOK SKIPJACK
SAUSAGE POT LINK COPPA GIGOT

BOUDIN POLONY SALAMI BOLOGNA
BOLONEY CHORIZO PUDDING
SAVELOY BLACKPOT CERVELAT
DRISHEEN KIELBASA LIVERING
ROLLICHE
(KIND OF —) METT
SAUTE PANFRY
SAUTERNE YQUEM
SAVAGE ILL FELL GRIM RUDE WILD
BRUTE CRUEL EAGER FELON FERAL
STERN FIERCE GOTHIC BRUTISH
FERVENT HOWLING INHUMAN
MANKEEN MANKIND ROPABLE
UNCIVIL VIOLENT WILROUN
CANNIBAL PITILESS THEREOID
WARRAGAL
SAVAGELY FELLY UNMANLY
SAVAGERY FURY FEROCITY
SAVANNA CAMPO SABANA
(— LANDS) LALANG
SAVANT ARTIST VIRTUOSO
SAVE BAR WIN HAIN HELP KEEP
SAFE STOP SALVE SPARE SPELL
DEFEND EXCEPT RESCUE SAVING
SCRIMP DELIVER HUSBAND
SALVAGE WARRANT CONSERVE
PRESERVE
SAVIN HEATH SABINE JUNIPER
SAVING FRUGAL THRIFT ECONOMY
SPARING THRIFTY
SAVINGS FAT ADDLINGS
(— CLUB) MENAGE
SAVIOR LORD SAVER SOTER
REDEEMER
SAVOR EDGE SALT SAPOR SMACK
TASTE DEGUST FLAVOR RELISH
RESENT SAVOUR SEASON TASTEN
SAPIDITY
SAVORLESS FOND INSIPID
SAVORY GUSTY MERRY SAPID
TASTY DAINTY SMERVY GUSTFUL
GUSTABLE TASTEFUL
SAVVY SABE
SAW SAG SEY WEB BUCK REDE
ADAGE FREIT GNOME SCEAR SPOKE
JIGSAW PITSAW RIPSAW SAYING
SCRIBE BACKSAW BUCKSAW
CONVERT DRAGSAW FRETSAW
HACKSAW HANDSAW HEADRIG
HEADSAW PROVERB SLABBER
WHIPSAW CROSSCUT SENTENCE
(— INTO LOGS) BUCK
(— LENGTHWISE OF GRAIN) RIP
(— OF SAWFISH) SERRA
(— WITH TWO BLADES) STADDA
(CIRCULAR —) BUR BURR EDGER
DAPPER TRIMMER
(CROSSCUT —) BRIAR
(CYLINDER —) CROWN TREPAN
TREPHINE
SAWAN SRABAN SHRAVAN
SAWDUST COOM COOMB SAWINGS
SAW FERN DYGAL BUNGWALL
HARDFERN
SAWFISH RAY BATOID COMBFISH
SAWFLY CEPHID
SAW GATE FRAME
SAWHORSE BUCK JACK SETTER
SAWBUCK TRESTLE

SAW KERF SKAFF
SAWMILL RASPER
(— DEVICE) KICKER
(— WORKER) PONDMAN LEVERMAN
SAWYER WETA SAWER PITMAN
TOPMAN KNOTTER
SAXHORN ALTO TUBA ALTHORN
SAXTUBA BARITONE BARYTONE
SAXIFRAGE BAUERA BENNET SESELI
ASTILBE ROCKFOIL SELFHEAL
SENGREEN
SAXONIAN MINDEL
SAXOPHONE SAX ALTO TENOR
SOPRANINO
SAY DEED MEAN MOVE TAKE TELL
SPEAK SPELL AUTHOR QUETHE
RELATE REMARK SAYING REHEARSE
(— A BLESSING) BENSH
(— FOOLISHLY) BLABBER
(— FURTHER) ADD
(— GLIBLY) SCREED
(— NO TO) NAIT NICK
(— OVER AGAIN) REPEAT
(— SPITEFUL THINGS) BACKBITE
(— TOO MUCH) OVERSAY
(— UNDER OATH) DEPOSE
SAYING DIT SAW SAY DICT ITEM
REDE TEXT WORD ADAGE AXIOM
CHRIA DITTY FREIT MAXIM SPEAK
BALLAD BYWORD DICTUM DIVERB
LOGION DICTION PROVERB
APOTHEGM SENTENCE SPEAKING
(— LITTLE) DUMB
(—S OF JESUS) AGRAPHA
(—S OF RELIGIOUS TEACHER)
LOGIA
(CLEVER —) QUIP
(CURRENT —) DICTUM
(OBSCURE —) ENIGMA
(QUICK —) JERK
(TERSE —) EPIGRAM
(TRUE —) SOOTHSAW
(WISE —) SCHOLIUM
(WITTY —) MOT SALLY DICTERY
WITNESS
(WITTY —S) FACETIAE
SCAB RAT ROIN SHAB SNOB CRUST
CANKER ESCHAR RATTER GREENER
RUBBERS BLACKLEG BLACKNEB
SCABBARD CHAPE SHEATH PILCHER
SCABBARD FISH HIKU
SCABBLE SCAB SCALP
SCABBY MANGY SCALD ROINISH
SCABIOUS
SCABIES ITCH SCAB PSORA
SCABIOSA KNAUTIA
SCABIOUS SCABIA BLUECAP
BUNDWEED PREMORSE
SCABROUS SULTRY ASPEROUS
SCAD AKULE XUREL GOGGLER
QUIAQUIA
SCAFFOLD CAGE PEGMA STAGE
BRIDGE CATASTA HAYLOFT
STAGING HOARDING
SCAFFOLDING DOCK STAGING
SCALD BURN LEEP PLOT SCAD
BLAST PLOUT SCAUD BLANCH
SCALDER
SCALE LEAF PELA STEP TAPE CLIMB

FLAKE GAMUT GENUS GULAR PALEA
PELOG PELOK PELTA POISE SCUTE
SHALE SHARD SHELL SHERD SHIVE
TRUNK ASCEND CAUDAL CINDER
COCCID FORNIX GUNTER IMBREX
KELVIN LABIAL LADDER LAMINA
LIGULE LOREAL MENTAL OCULAR
PERULE RAMENT RONDLE RUSTRE
SHIELD SQUAMA STRIGA BALANCE
CLINKER ELYTRON FRONTAL
FULCRUM HUMERAL LATERAL
NUCHALE REAUMUR ROSTRUM
VENTRAL VERNIER ANALEMMA
BRACHIAL LECANIUM LODICULE
MEALYBUG ODOPHONE RAMENTUM
SCRAMBLE SQUAMULE TEMPORAL
UROSTEGE
(— DOWN) DEGRADE
(— OF 7 TONES) SEPTAVE
(— OF CORNSTALK) SHIVE
(— USED BY TAILORS) LOG
(GRADUATED —) RETE
(GREAT —) GAMUT
(SHAD —) CENIZO
(PL.) CHAFF DANDER
SCALEBOARD SCABBARD
SCALEPAN BASIN
SCALER CULLER SOOTER
SCALES TRON TRONE BALANCE
SCALETAIL SQUIRREL
SCALLION PORRET
SCALLOP CRENA QUEEN SQUIN
PECTEN COQUILLE DOUGHBOY
ESCALLOP PECTINID
SCALLOPED INVECTED
SCALP SCAUP SKELP ATTIRE
SCALPER PUNTER
SCALY SCABBY SQUAMY LEPROSE
PALEATE LEPIDOTE SCABROUS
SQUAMOSE
SCAMP LAD RIP LIMB SLIM ROGUE
SKEMP SKIMP THIEF BOOGER
BUGGER NICKUM SINNER SORREL
SORROW HALLION HESSIAN
PEASANT RAMMACK SCUBBER
SKELLUM SNOOZER SCALAWAG
SLYBOOTS SPALPEEN VAGABOND
WIDDIFOW
SCAMPER CHEVY SCOUP CHIVVY
BRATTLE SKITHER SKITTER
SCAN PIPE GLASS METER DEVISE
SURVEY EXAMINE
SCANDAL GUP CLASH CRACK ECLAT
SHAME CALUMNY SCANMAG
SLANDER
SCANDALIZE SHOCK
SCANDALMONGER CLAT
SCANDALOUS UNHOLY SHAMEFUL
SCANDINAVIAN DANE LAPP NORSE
SWEDE VIKING LOCHLIN NORSEMAN
NORTHMAN SCANDIAN VARANGIAN
(PL.) OSTMEN
SCANT SHY JIMP LEAN MEET POOR
SCAMP SHORT SKIMP SPLAY
BARISH GEASON LITTLE SCANTY
SKINNY STINGY STINTY SLENDER
SCRATCHY
SCANTILY BARELY FEEBLY SMALLY
SCANTLY SPARSELY

SCANTINESS PENURY PARCITY
EXIGUITY SPARSITY
SCANTLING STUD FILET JOIST
FILLET BOLSTER RIBBAND
STUDDING
SCANTY BARE JIMP LANK LEAN
POOR SLIM EXILE GNEDE SCANT
SHORT SILLY SKIMP SPARE FRUGAL
MEAGER SCRIMP SKIMPY SLIGHT
SPARSE SCRANNY SCRIMPY
SLENDER SPARING EXIGUOUS
SCAPOLITE DIPYRE
SCAPULA BLADE OMOPLATE
SCAPULAR CUCULLA
SCAR ARR EYE WEM SEAM SEAR
CHALK FESTER KELOID RADDLE
STIGMA TRENCH CHELOID SCARIFY
CICATRIX SMALLPOX CICATRICE
(— **ON SAWED STONE**) STUN
(— **ON SEED**) HILUM
(— **ON TREE**) CATFACE
SCARAB ATEUCHES
SCARCE DEAR RARE THIN SLACK
DAINTY GEASON CLASSIC
UNCOMMON
SCARCELY ILL VIX JIMP SCANT
BARELY HARDLY MERELY ONETHE
SCARCE SCRIMP WENETH SCANTLY
UNEATHS UNNETHE
SCARCITY LACK WANT FAULT
SCANT DEARTH FAMINE RARITY
PAUCITY
SCARE COW BOOF BREE FAZE FEAR
FLEG FLIG FRAY GAST HUSH SHOO
ALARM GLIFF GLOFF SPOOK
AFFRAY FRIGHT GASTER SCARIFY
STARTLE TERRIFY AFFRIGHT
FRIGHTEN
(— **BIRDS**) KEEP
SCARECROW BOGLE BUCCA MOGGY
BOGGLE DUDMAN MALKIN MAUMET
MAWKIN SCARER SHEWEL BOGGART
BUGABOO DEADMAN HODMADOD
SHAWFOWL
SCARED SCART SCARY AFRAID
GOOSEY STREAKED
SCAREMONGER ALARMIST
SCARF BARB HOOD SASH ABNET
ASCOT BARBE CLOUD CYMAR FICHU
LUNGI NUBIA SHADE STOCK STOLE
TABLE THROW CRAVAT REBOZO
SCREEN SQUARE TAPALO TIPPET
UPARNA BURDASH DOPATTA
FOULARD MUFFLER NECKTIE
OVERLAY PUGGREE SAUTOIR
TALLITH CLAUDENT COINTISE
LIRIPIPE LIRIPOOP MANTILLA
MUFFETEE SLENDANG
(— **ON KNIGHT'S HELMET**) COINTISE
(**ARABIAN** —) CABAAN
(**FEATHER** —) BOA
(**PRAYER** —) TALLIS TALLITH
SCARFING GRAFTING
SCARIFY LIFT
SCARLET LAC RED PINK TULY GRAIN
KERMES
SCARLET HAW HAWTHORN
SCARLET IBIS GUARA
SCARLET LYCHNIS FIREBALL
NONESUCH

SCARLET TANAGER REDBIRD
FIREBIRD
SCARLIKE ULOID
SCARP CLIFF SCARF ESCARP
SCARPLET
SCATHING MORDANT SCALDING
SCATHINGLY ROUNDLY
SCATOLOGICAL BARNYARD
SCATTER DAD SOW TED FLEE SALT
SCAT SEED SHED SPEW VOID FLING
SCALE SCHAL SEVER SHAKE SPRAY
STREW STROW DISPEL SHOWER
SKIVER SPARSE SPREAD SPRENG
WINNOW DIFFUSE DISBAND DISJECT
FRITTER RESOLVE SCAMBLE
SHATTER SKINKLE SKITTER
SLATTER SPARKLE SPARPLE
SPATTER SWATTER DISPERSE
INTERSOW SEPARATE SPLUTTER
SPRINKLE SQUANDER SQUATTER
(— **BAIT FOR FISH**) TOLE TOLL
(— **OVER**) BESTREW
(— **WATER**) SPLASH
SCATTERED LAX OPEN STRAY
DAIMEN SPARSE DIFFUSE SPOTTED
FUGITIVE SPARSILE
SCATTERING SOWING DIASPORA
SCATTERY
SCAUP DUCK DOGS DIVER DUCKER
DUNBIRD POCHARD BLUEBILL
GRAYBACK SHUFFLER
SCAVAGE SCEWING
SCAVENGE CLEANSE GARBAGE
SCAVENGER BUNGY BHANGI
BHUNGI MEHTAR REMOVER SCAFFIE
CORYDORA HALALCOR
SCAZON CHOLIAMB
SCEAT SKEAT STYCA
SCENE JOG SET CODA CYKE FLAT
SITE VIEW ARENA STAGE BRIDGE
VISION EPISODE PAGEANT COULISSE
EXTERIOR INTERIOR PROSPECT
TABLETOP
(— **IN OPERA**) SCENA
(— **OF ACTION**) STAGE
(— **OF ACTIVITY**) BEEHIVE
(— **OF CONFUSION**) BABEL BEDLAM
(**CLOSING** —) FINALE
(**FINAL** —) CURTAIN EPILOGUE
SCENERY DROP FLAT DECOR
CUTOUT IMAGERY PROFILE
(**PIECE OF** —) MASKING
SCENESHIFTER GRIP
SCENT AIR DRAG NOSE ODOR VENT
WIND CIVET FAULT FLAIR RELES
SAVOR SMACK SMELL SNIFF SNUFF
SPOOR TASTE ESSENCE INCENSE
NOSEGAY ODORIZE VERDURE
FUMIGATE MARECHAL PASTILLE
(— **OF ANIMAL FOLLOWED BY**
HOUNDS) FEUTE
(— **OF COOKING**) NIDOR
(— **OF FOX**) DRAG
(**FALSE** —) RIOT
(**LOST** —) FAULT
SCENTED OLENT ODORATE
PERFUMY ESSENCED
SCAPTER ROD WAND VERGE
BAUBLE CEPTER FERULA WARDER

SCHEDULE BOOK CARD HOLD LIST
SKED TIME PANEL SCRIP SCROW
SETUP SLATE TABLE SCROLL
CATALOG TABLEAU CALENDAR
REGISTER
(— **OF DUTIES**) TARIFF
(— **OF GAMES**) SEASON
SCHEDULED DUE
SCHEELITE TUNGSTEN
SCHEMA FORM
SCHEME AIM GIN LAY WAY WEB
CAST DART GAME PLAN PLAT PLOT
REDE SWIM ANGLE BABEL CADRE
DODGE DRAFT DRIFT KNACK PINAX
REACH SCALE SETUP SHIFT TABLE
THINK TRAIN BRIGUE BUBBLE
CIPHER DESIGN DEVICE DEVISE
FIGURE HOOKUP POLICY SCHEMA
SYSTEM TAMPER THEORY UTOPIA
COUNSEL DRAUGHT GIMMICK
IMAGINE KNAVERY NOSTRUM
PROJECT PURPOSE CONTRIVE
FORECAST GIMCRACK IDEOLOGY
INTRIGUE MANEUVER PLATFORM
PRACTICE TRIPOTER WINDMILL
(— **OF RANK**) LADDER
(**BETTING** —) SYSTEM
(**DECEITFUL** —) SHIFT
(**DELUSIVE** —) BUBBLE
(**DIAGRAMMATIC** —) PINAX
(**FANCIFUL** —) WINDMILL
(**FAVORITE** —) NOSTRUM
(**VISIONARY** —) BABEL
SCHEMER ARTIST DESIGNER
ENGINEER SCHEMIST SLEEVEEN
SCHEMING SCHEMY PLANFUL
SPIDERY FETCHING PRACTICE
SCHISM RENT SCISSION SCISSURE
SCHISMATIC HERETIC
SCHIST RAG AMPELITE MICACITE
MYLONITE OLLENITE PHYLLITE
SCHIZONT MONONT AGAMONT
SCHIZOPHRENIA CATATONY
SCHNAPPER WOLLOMAI
SCHOLAR TUG DEMY GAON IMAM
CLERK PUPIL DIVINE DOCTOR
FELLOW JURIST LAMDEN MASTER
PANDIT SABORA SAVANT SCOLOG
SHEIKH BIBLIST BOOKMAN DANTIST
LATINER LEARNER MAULANA
STUDENT DISCIPLE HEBRAEAN
HUMANIST ISLAMIST MASORITE
TABERDAR THAUMASTE
SCHOLARLY CLERKLY ACADEMIC
SCHOLARSHIP ART BOOK BURSE
BURSARY DEMYSHIP LEARNING
SCHOOL GAM TOL EDDY PREP
AGGIE BOOKS ECOLE HEDER MYAYA
SAKHA TEACH TRADE TRAIN TUTOR
ALJAMA CAMPUS CHEDER CHURCH
KUTTAB KYAUNG MADHAB MALIKI
RABFAK SCHOLA SCHULE SQUEEL
TRIPOS ACADEME ACADEMY
CRAMMER MADRASA PENSION
STUDIUM YESHIVA AUDITORY
DOCUMENT EXERCISE EXTERNAT
PEDAGOGY SEMINARY
(— **FOR SINGERS**) MAITRISE
(— **OF BLACKFISH**) GRIND

(— OF BUDDHISM) CHAN DHYANA SANRON
(— OF FISH) HERD SCALE
(— OF HINDU PHILOSOPHY) NYAYA
(— OF PAINTING) GENRE
(— OF PHILOSOPHY) SECT ACADEMY AUDITORY
(— OF VEDA) SAKHA SHAKHA
(— OF WHALES) GAM POD
(ART —) LUMINISM
(AZTEC —) CALMECAC
(COMPARATIVE —) FOLKLORE
(DAY —) EXTERNAT
(ELEMENTARY —) GRADES
(HIGH —) HIGH ACADEMY COLLEGE
(MOSLEM —) HANAFI KUTTAB SHAFII HANBALI
(REFORM —) BORSTAL
(RELIGIOUS —) ALJAMA YESHIVA
(RIDING —) MANEGE
(SANSKRIT —) TOL
(SCOTCH —) SQUEEL
(SECONDARY —) LYCEE LYCEUM COLEGIO
(WRESTLING —) PALESTRA
SCHOOLBOOK COCKER
SCHOOLBOY SCUG PETTY CLERGION
SCHOOLHOUSE PORTABLE
SCHOOLING LEARNING
SCHOOLMASTER CAJI CAXI AKHUN KHOJA KHODJA MASTER PEDANT AKHOOND DOMINIE PEDAGOG ORBILIUS
SCHOOLROOM HOMEROOM
SCHOOL SHARK TOPE TOPER
SCHOOLWORK BOOKWORK
SCHOONER JACK TERN QUART QUINT WUINT PUNGEY BALLAHOO
SCHORL COCKLE
SCHRADAN OMPA
SCHROTHER SHREDDER
SCHUYT SHOE SCOUT EELBOAT
SCIATICA BONESHAW
SCIENCE ART OLOGY SOPHY MATHESIS SCIENTIA
(— OF ALGAE) ALGOLOGY
(— OF ANIMALS) ZOOLOGY
(— OF AQUEOUS VAPOR) ATMOLOGY
(— OF ATOMS) ATOMICS
(— OF BEING OR REALITY) ONTOLOGY
(— OF BIOLOGICAL STATISTICS) BIOMETRY
(— OF BREEDING) GENETICS
(— OF CAUSES) ETIOLOGY
(— OF CHARACTER) ETHOLOGY
(— OF CLASSIFICATION OF DISEASES) NOSOLOGY
(— OF DOSES) DOSOLOGY POSOLOGY
(— OF EARTH'S FORMATION) GEOGONY
(— OF EXCHANGE) CAMBISTRY
(— OF FERMENTATION) ZYMOLOGY
(— OF FORMS OF SPEECH) GRAMMAR
(— OF FRUIT GROWING) POMOLOGY

(— OF FUNDS MANAGEMENT) FINANCE
(— OF GEMS) GEMMARY GEMOLOGY
(— OF GOD) DIVINITY
(— OF GOVERNMENT) POLITICS
(— OF HEALTH MAINTENANCE) HYGIENE
(— OF HEAT) PYROLOGY
(— OF HISTORY OF EARTH) GEOLOGY
(— OF IDEAS) IDEOLOGY
(— OF LAW) NOMOLOGY
(— OF LIFE INFLUENCES) EUGENICS
(— OF LIFE OF TREES) SILVICS
(— OF LIFE) BIOLOGY
(— OF LIGHT) OPTICS
(— OF MEASURING TIME) HOROLOGY
(— OF MEDIEVAL CHEMISTRY) ALCHEMY
(— OF MIDWIFERY) TOKOLOGY
(— OF MORAL DUTY) ETHICS
(— OF MOSSES) BRYOLOGY
(— OF MOUNTAINS) OROLOGY
(— OF MUSCLES) MYOLOGY
(— OF NUMBERS COMBINATIONS) ALGEBRA
(— OF PERSUADING A GOD) THEURGY
(— OF PLANTS) BOTANY
(— OF RACIAL IMPROVEMENT) EUGENICS
(— OF REASONING) LOGIC
(— OF RECORDING GENEALOGIES) HERALDRY
(— OF REFRIGERATION) CRYOLOGY
(— OF REMEDIES) ACOLOGY
(— OF SERUMS) SEROLOGY
(— OF SOUND) PHONICS ACOUSTICS
(— OF SPATIAL MAGNITUDES) GEOMETRY
(— OF STRUCTURE OF ANIMALS) ANATOMY
(— OF THE EAR) OTOLOGY
(— OF TIDES) TIDOLOGY
(— OF VERSIFICATION) PROSODY
(— OF VIRTUE) ARETAICS
(— OF WEIGHT OR GRAVITY) BAROLOGY
(— OF WINES) ENOLOGY OENOLOGY
(LEGAL —) LAW .
(MILITARY —) STRATEGY
(NATURAL —) STINKS PHYSICS
(RELIGIOUS —) THEOLOGY
SCIMITAR SAX SEAX TURK KHEPESH TULWAUR
SCINDAPSUS POTHOS
SCINTILLATE SNAP FLASH GLEAM GLANCE GLITTER SPARKLE TWINKLE
SCINTILLATION SPARKLE SPARKLET
SCION IMP ROD CION CYON ROOT SLIP GRAFT SPRIG BRANCH SPROUT SARMENT SETLING
SCISSORS SHEARS CLIPPER SECATEUR
SCLERITE TORMA LABIUM PLANTA PLAGULA AXILLARY EPIMERON

SCLERODERMA MORPHEA
SCLEROPROTEIN SPONGIN
SCLEROTIUM ERGOT SCLEROTE TUCKAHOE
SCOFF DOR GAB GALL GIBE GIRD JEER JIBE MOCK RAIL CURSE FLEER FLOUT GLEEK SCORN SCOUT SNEER TAUNT DERIDE REPROVE RIDICULE
SCOFFER MOCKER ABDERITE
SCOLD JAW MAG MOB NAG RAG ROW WIG YAP BAWL CALL CAMP CANT DING FRAB FUSS HAZE JACK JOBE JOWL JUMP RAIL RANT RATE REDD RICK SHAW SNAG SNUB TUCK YAFF ABUSE BARGE BASTE BOAST CHIDE DRESS FLIRT FLITE PRATE SCALD SCORE SHORE SHREW SLANG TARGE VIXEN BERATE BOUNCE CALLET CAMPLE CARPET HAMMER HOORAY HURRAH MAGPIE RATTLE REHETE REVILE TATTER THREAP TONGUE YAFFLE CHANNER REPROVE TRIMMER TROUNCE BALLYRAG BERATTLE CHASTISE CIDESTER DINGDONG LIPBRAID RIXATRIX
SCOLDING JAW HURL JESSE SCOLD DIRDUM JAWING RAKING RATTLE SISERA FLITING HEARING LECTURE RAGGING WIGGING BLESSING CARRITCH JOBATION
SCOLEX HEAD
SCOLYTUS IPS
SCONCE SWAPE APPLIQUE
SCONE FARL FARLE
SCOOP BAIL DRAG ROUT DIDLE GOUGE KEACH SHAUL SKEET BUCKET DIPPER DISHER SHOVEL WIMBLE SCRAPER SKIMMER SKIPPET SCOOPFUL
(— FOR CANNON) LADLE
(— FOR DAMPENING CANVAS) SKEET
(— FOR GRAIN) WECHT
(— UP) LAP LAVE GATHER
(CHEESE —) PALE
(JAI ALAI —) CHISTERA
(LONG-HANDLED —) DIDLE
(SURGICAL —) CURET CURETTE
SCOOT SCOUT SKEET SKYHOOT
SCOPE AREA AMBIT RANGE REACH SCOOP SWEEP VERGE SCOUTH SPHERE TETHER BREADTH CIRCUIT OPERAND PURVIEW CONFINES DIAPASON LATITUDE
(— OF VISION) COMMAND
(FREE —) SWING
SCOPOLINE OSCIN OSCINE
SCORCH BURN CHAR PLOT SCAM SEAR ADURE ADUST PARCH PLAUT REESE SCALD SCAUM SINGE SWEAL SWELT BIRSLE BISHOP DEGREE SMITCH SOTTER SPARCH SWINGE SWITHE BLISTER BRISTLE FRIZZLE SCORKLE SCOWDER SWITHEN SWITHER TORRIFY FIREFANG SCOWTHER
SCORCHED ADUST LEEPIT
SCORCHER SIZZLER

SCORCHING BAKING FIRING ADURENT SCALDING

SCORE ACE CUT RUN CARD DROP GAME GOAL HOLE MAKE MARK NICK POST RIDE SLOG CHASE CORGE COUNT EXTRA NOTCH OPERA TALLY COOREE FURROW SAFETY SCOTCH SCRIVE SPADES STRING TARGET TICKET TWENTY CONVERT SCORING SCRATCH SQUEEZE GAMEBALL PARTITUR

(— FOR ALE) ALESHOT

(— IN BRIDGE) BOARD BONUS SWING

(— IN CRIBBAGE) GO PEG FIFTEEN

(— IN CRICKET) BLOB CENTURY

(— OF NOTHING) DUCK

(APTITUDE —) STANINE

(BASKETBALL —) HOOP

(BOWLING —) PINFALL

(GOLF —) DEUCE EAGLE BIRDIE BUZZARD

(PINOCHLE —) LAST

(TENNIS —) CALL FIVE LOVE DEUCE FORTY FIFTEEN

(TIE —) HALVE DEADLOCK

(PL.) MUSIC

SCORED SULCATE SULCATED

SCOREKEEPER SCORER TALLIER TALLYMAN

SCORER NIB MARKER NOTCHER

SCORIA SCUM SLAG CINDER SULLAGE

SCORIFIER CAPSULE

SCORIFY SMELT

SCORN GECK LOUT HOKER SCARN SPURN BISMER SLIGHT CONTEMN DESPISE DESPITE DISDAIN CONTEMPT DERISION MISPRIZE

SCORNFUL SAUCY SCORNY SNIFFY SNIFTY HAUGHTY FRUMPISH INSOLENT

SCORNFULLY ASKEW ASWASH

SCORPION NEPA ALACRAN STINGER UROPYGI ARACHNID PEDIPALP WHIPTAIL

SCORPION FISH LAPON SERRAN HOGFISH SCULPIN LORICATE RASCACIO

SCORPION FLY PANORPID

SCOT (ALSO SEE SCOTSMAN) CELT JOCK KELT SAXON SCOTTY BLUECAP SCOTSMAN

(PL.) SAWNY SAWNEY LALLANS

SCOTCH TRIG SCOTS SCOTTISH

SCOTCHMAN MAC GAUL SANDY TARTAN SCOTCHY SCOTTIE SCOTSMAN

SCOTER COOT FILK DIVER SCOUT WHILK BASQUE DUCKER SURFER PISHAUG SCOOTER SKUNKTOP

SCOTIA MOUTH

SCOTIST DUNCE

SCOTLAND

BAY: SCAPA
CAPITAL: EDINBURGH

COIN: DEMY BODLE GROAT PLACK RIDER BAWBEE

COUNTY: AYR BUTE FIFE ROSS ANGUS BANFF MORAY NAIRN PERTH ARGYLL LANARK ORKNEY BERWICK KINROSS PEEBLES RENFREW SELKIRK WIGTOWN ABERDEEN AYRSHIRE CROMARTY DUMFRIES ROXBURGH SHETLAND STERLING

FIRTH: LORN CLYDE FORTH MORAY SOLWAY PENTLAND

ISLAND: JURA LONA MULL RHUM SKYE ARRAN BARRA ISLAY LEWIS HARRIS ORKNEY SHETLAND

ISLANDS: ORKNEY HEBRIDES SHETLAND

LAKE: TAY NESS MORAR LAGGAN LINNHE LOMOND KATRINE RANNOCH

LANGUAGE: ERSE LALLAN LALLAND

MEASURE: COP BOLL CRAN FALL MILE PECK PINT ROOD ROPE SPAN CRANE LIPPY FIRLOT AUCHLET CHALDER CHOPPIN MUTCHKIN STIMPART

MOUNTAIN: HOPE ATTOW DEARG NEVIS TINTO WYVIS CHEVIOT MACDHUI

NATIVE: GAEL PICT SCOT

ORDER: THISTLE

RESORT: OBAN

RIVER: AYR DEE DON ESK TAY DOON GLEN NITH NORN SPEY AFTON ANNAN FORTH GARRY TWEED YTHAN AFFRIC TEVIOT TUMMEL DEVERON FINDHORN

SEAPORT: ALLOA LEITH DUNDEE ABERDEEN

TOWN: AYR DUNS OBAN ALLOA BRORA CUPAR ELLON LEITH PERTH SALEN TROON DUNDEE GIRVAN HAWICK DUNKELD GLASGOW PAISLEY ABERDEEN DUMFRIES GREENOCK KIRKWALL STIRLING

WEIGHT: BOLL DROP TRONE BUSHEL

SCOTLAND ALBANY ALBION SCOTIA ALBAINN ALBANIA

(NORTHERN —) PICTLAND

SCOTSMAN SANDY SAWNY

SCOTTISH SCOTCH SCOTLAND

SCOTTISH TERRIER DIEHARD SCOTTIE VERMINER

SCOUNDREL RAP PIMP SCAB VILE WARY BLECK FILTH KNAVE SHREW SMAIK SWEEP THIEF WHAUP BRIBER LIMMER SLOVEN VARLET CATAIAN GLUTTON HALLION NITHING SCROYLE SKELLUM VILIACO VILLAIN WARLOCK BEZONIAN LIDDERON MASCHANT

SCOUNDRELLY VILLAIN

SCOUR ASH BEAT RAKE SCUM SEEK SCOOR SCRUB SKIRR SWEEP DRENCH SCURRY SLUICE DEGRADE FURBISH BACKWASH STONEFILE

(PL.) SKIT

SCOURER BLOOMER DOLLIER PICKLER

SCOURGE EEL TAW LASH CURSE FLAIL KNOUT SLASH SWING BALEYS PLAGUE SWINGE SCORPION

SCOURGER WHIPSTER

SCOURING BEAT SCOUR HUSHING SCRUBBING

SCOUT SPY BEAR LION SKIP ROVER SPIAL VISOR ESPIAL GAYCAT DESPISE MARINER PICKEER PIONEER SCOURER WATCHER EMISSARY OUTRIDER OUTSCOUT SCURRIER SKIRMISH

(BOY —) CUB BOBCAT SCOUTER WEBELOS EXPLORER

SCOW ACCON FLOAT GARVEY

SCOWL LOUR FROWN GLARE GLOOM GLOUT LOWER SKIME GLOWER VENNER GLOOMING

SCOWLING FROWNY GLARING

SCRAGGY WEEDY

SCRAM HOP LAM BUNK BUGGER

SCRAMBLE MUSS SPURL SCRAWM SPRAWL CLAMBER LOUSTER SCRABBLE SCRAFFLE SCRATTLE SPRACHLE

SCRAP BIT END JAG PIP CRAP ITEM JAGG JUNK PICK SNAP BRAWL GRAIN PATCH SCRAN SHRED THRUM WASTE DISCARD MAMMOCK REMNANT FRACTION SCRAPPET SKERRICK SNATTOCK

(— FOR PATCHING) SPETCH

(— OF PAPER) SCRIP

(— OF SONG) CATCH

(— OF WRITING) SCRAPE

(LITERARY —S) ANA

(RAGGED —) SCART

(PL.) ORTS SCRAN RELICS SCROFF GARBAGE GUBBINGS

SCRAPE LEG RUB CLAW COMB RAZE CLAUT CURET ERADE ERODE GRATE GRAZE GRIDE SCALP SCART SCUFF SHAVE ABRADE RUGINE SCREED SCROOP CORRADE CURETTE JACKPOT SCRATCH SCRABBLE

(— ALONG) HARL HARLE SHOOL

(— GOLF CLUB ON GROUND) SCLAFF

(— OFF) SPUD

(— OUT) ERASE HOLLOW

(— SKINS) MOON SCUD FLESH HARASS

(— TOGETHER) RAKE GLEAN MUCKER SCAMBLE

(— WITH FEET) SCAUT

SCRAPED BRIGHT

SCRAPER PAN HARL SLIP CURET GLOVE HARLE QUIRL RASER SPOON DOCTOR FRESNO GRADER GRATER CURETTE FLANGER LEVELER SLUSHER STRIGIL GRATTOIR SCRAPPLE TERRACER UNHAIRER

SCRAPING GRIDE RASURE
(CRACKER —S) CUSH
(METAL —S) DIET
(PL.) RAMENTA
SCRAPMAN CHIPMAN
SCRAPPER BREAKER FIGHTER
SCRAPPLE PANHAS PONHAWS
SCRAPPY BITTY
SCRATCH RAT RIT CLAW CRAB
RACE RAIN RAKE RAPE RASE RAUK
RAZE RISP RIST SLUG STUN CHALK
CLAUT CLAWK FRUSH GRAZE
RANCH SCART SCLUM SCORE
SCRAB SCRAT SCROB SCRUB
SHRUB SKELP TEASE TOUCH
BRUISE CANCEL CRATCH RASURE
RIPPLE SCORCH SCOTCH SCRAPE
SCRAWK SCRAWL SCRAWM SCRAZE
SCRIVE TORACE DECLARE EMERIZE
EXPUNGE SCARIFY SCRABBLE
SCRATTLE SCRIBBLE
SCRATCHER RASER
SCRAWL SCRAWM SPRAWL
SCRATCH SCRABBLE SCRIBBLE
SQUIGGLE
SCRAWNY BONY LEAN SLINK
SCRANK SCRAGGY SCRANKY
SCRANNY SCRAGGED
(— PERSON OR ANIMAL) RIBE
SCREAM CRY YAW REME WEAK
YARM YAUP YAWL YAWP YOWT
SKIRL SHRAME SHRIEK SHRILL
SQUALL SQUAWL YAMMER
SCREECH YELLOCH SKELLOCH
SCREAMER CHAJA ANHIMA
SCREECH QUAWK QUOCK SCREAM
SCREEK SCRITCH SKREIGH
SKELLOCH
SCREECH OWL STRICH
SCREED TIRADE
SCREEN TRY CAGE GOBO HARP
HIDE LAWN MASK PICK REJA SCUG
SEPT SIFT TENT ARRAS BLIND
CHEEK CHICK CLOAK CLOSE COVER
FIGHT GAUZE GRATE HOARD SHADE
SHOJI SIEVE SPEER SPIER TATTY
BAFFLE BASKET CANVAS DEFEND
ESCORT MEDIUM PURDAH RESEAU
SCHERM SCONCE SHAKER SHIELD
SHROUD THREAD VOIDER CEILING
CONCEAL CURTAIN FLYWIRE
GOGGLES GRIZZLY REREDOS
SECLUDE SHELTER SHUTTER
TESTUDO TROMMEL BACKSTOP
BESCREEN BLINDAGE COVERING
DIFFUSER ECLIPSER EXCLUDER
HOARDING OCCULTER PARAVENT
PARCLOSE PAVISADE SCREENER
SPLASHER STRAINER TRAVERSE
UMBRELLA
(— ALONGSIDE SHIP) PAVISADE
(— BEHIND ALTAR) REREDOS
(— FOR BATTING PRACTICE) CAGE
(— FOR SHIP'S COMBATANTS)
FIGHT
(— FOR SIZING ORE) GRATE
TROMMEL
(— FOR THEATER LIGHT) JELLY
MEDIUM

(— OF BAMBOO SLIPS) CHEEK
CHICK
(— OF BRUSHWOOD) SCHERM
(— OF FIRE) BARRAGE
(— OF SHIELDS FOR TROOPS)
TESTUDO
(— OF TAPESTRY) ARRAS CEILING
(— ON AUTOMOBILE) GRILL GRILLE
(— TO PROTECT LOOKOUTS)
DODGER
(— USED BY ARCHERS) PANNIER
(BULLETPROOF —) MANTA MANTEL
MANTELET
(CHANCEL —) JUBE
(FIRE —) FENDER
(MECHANICALLY ACTUATED —)
GRIZZLY
(PAPER —) SHOJI
(PL.) CANCELLI
SCREENED BLIND SECLUDED
SCREENINGS CULM SLACK SLECK
SCREENPLAY SCENARIO
SCREW HOB VISE WORM CRICK
FEEZE SCROW TEMPER TOGGLE
COCHLEA AIRSCREW FLATHEAD
SETSCREW THUMBKIN WINDMILL
(KIND OF —) ALLEN MEANTIME
SCREW BEAN MESQUITE
SCREWPOD TORNILLA
SCREWED SQUINCH
SCREWER WORMER
SCREWMAN JACKMAN
SCREW PINE IE ARA HALA IEIE
AGGAG PALMA VACOA VACONA
LAUHALA PANDANUS
SCREW TREE TWISTY
SCRIBBLE SQUIB DOODLE SCRAWL
SCRATCH SCRABBLE SQUIGGLE
SCRIBE EZRA CLERK THOTH
BOOKER SCRIVE SOPHER WRITER
GRAFFER MASORET SCRIVAN
NOVERINT PENCLERK SCRIPTOR
SCRIVANO
(PL.) SOPHERIM
SCRIMMAGE BULLY ROUGE BICKER
SPLORE SKIRMISH
SCRIMP HINCH SCREW SKIMP
SCRIPT BOOK NEUM RONDE SERTA
SERTO NASKHI NESKHI SCRITE
SOOLOOS THULUTH BASTARDA
GURMUKHI HIRAGANA KANARESE
MAGHRIBI MAITHILI MEROITIC
NASTALIQ SCENARIO
SCRIPTURE WRIT AGAMA CHING
SUTRA SUTTA
(PL.) BIBLE GRANTH GRUNTH
TANACH TENACH SHASTRA
SCRIVENER PENMAN WRITER
GRAFFER SCRIVER NOVERINT
SCROFULA EVIL CRUELS
SCROLL BEND ROLL LABEL SCRIT
AMULET ESCROL LEGEND SCRAWL
STEMMA VOLUME VOLUTE EVOLUTE
PAPYRUS RINCEAU BANDEROL
CARTOUCH
SCROLL-LIKE TURBINAL
SCROPHULARIA FIGWORT
SCROTUM BAG COD PURSE

SCRUB FILE SCROG COPPET
SCODGY CLEANSE SCRUBBER
YANNIGAN
SCRUBBY SHRUBBY
SCRUBLAND GARIGUE GARRIGUE
SCRUFF CUFF SCUFF SCROFF
SCRUPLE PASS DEMUR DOUBT
FORCE POINT QUALM STAND STICK
BOGGLE SCOTCH STRAIN STICKLE
STUMBLE
SCRUPULOUS NICE SPICED TENDER
CAREFUL FINICKY PRECISE
DELICATE
SCRUTINIZE PRY SEE SPY SCAN
AUDIT PROBE SIGHT SOUND VISIT
SURVEY EXAMINE INSPECT
ENSEARCH
SCRUTINIZING NARROW SCANNING
SCRUTINY EYE SEARCH CANVASS
EXAMINE HAWKEYE PERUSAL
SCRYER SEER
SCUD RACK RAMP SKID SKIM SCOOT
SCUDO FILIPPO
SCUFF SLARE SLIDE SCLAFF
SCUFFER SCUFFLE SHUFFLE
SCUFFLE CUFF BUSTLE CLINCH
TUSSLE WISTER BRULYIE SHAMBLE
SHUFFLE SCRUFFLE
SCULL FUNNY SKULL
SCULLERY SINKROOM
SCULLION GIPPO SCULL SLUSH
GALOPIN SWILLER CUSTRON
QUISTRON
SCULPIN COTTID GRUBBY JOHNNY
BIGHEAD DRUMMER BULLHEAD
BULLPOUT CABEZONE HARDHEAD
LORICATE SCALAWAG
SCULPTOR GRAVER IMAGER
MARBLER PLASTIC
SCULPTURE CAMEO DRAFT GRAVE
SCULP BRONZE ENTAIL GISANT
SCULPT CARVING DRAUGHT
ENGRAVE GRADINO IMAGERY
INSCULP STABILE MORTORIO
NATIVITY PORTRAIT PREDELLA
SCULLION
SCULPTURED GRAVEN GLYPHIC
SCUM BRAT FOAM GALL HEAD REAM
SCUD SILT SKIM SKIN DROSS FROTH
SCURF SLOAK SLOKE SPUME
FLURRY REFUSE RIDDAM SCRUFF
BLANKET CACHAZA OFFSCUM
LAITANCE SANDIVER SCOURING
SCUMMING
SCUP BREAM PORGY SPARID
SCUPPAUG
SCURF SCALD DANDER FURFUR
SCRUFF DANDRUFF
SCURFY SCALD SCURVY LEPROSE
SCRUFFY SCABROUS
SCURRILITY ABUSE REPROACH
SCURRILOUS LOW FOUL VILE DIRTY
GROSS RIBALD VULGAR ABUSIVE
SCURRIL INDECENT
SCURRY BELT CRAB SKIN CURRY
HURRY SKICE SKURRY SCUFFLE
SCUTTER SCUTTLE SKELTER
SKITTER
SCURRYING SKITTER

SCURVY SCALD SCUMMY SHABBY ROYNOUS SCORBUCH SCORBUTE UNLIKING
SCUTAGE ESCUAGE
SCUTATE CLYPEATE
SCUTCH SCOTCH SWINGLE
SCUTE PLATE SCUTUM SCUTELLA
SCUTELLATION SCALING
SCUTIFORM PELTATE
SCUTTLE HOD CRAB SKEP BEETLE MANHOLE SCUDDLE SCUTTER
SCYLLA (FATHER OF —) NISUS TYPHON
SCYLLITOL INOSITOL
SCYPHUS PYXIS
SCYTHE SY LEA HOOK MEAK CRADLE
SCYTHIAN LAMB BAROMETZ
SEA ZEE BAHR BLUE BRIM FOAM FRET GULF HOLM LAVE MAIN RACE TIDE WAVE BRINE BRINY FLOAT FLOOD LOUGH OCEAN AEQUOR PONTUS SEALET STRAND TETHYS CHANNEL HYALINE NEPTUNE BOSPORUS DEEPNESS SEAFLOOD THALASSA
(— DIVINITY) TRITON
(— GOD) PROTEUS
(— LETTER) PASSPORT
(HEAVY —) POPPLE
(MODERATE —) SEAWAY
SEA ANEMONE POLYP DAHLIA OPELET ACTINIA VESTLET ACTINIAN ZOANTHID
SEA BASS HANAHILL HUMPBACK SERRANID TALLYWAG
SEA BEAR OTARIOID
SEABIRD HAGDON
SEA BISCUIT BREAD GALETTE PANTILE
SEABOARD COAST
SEA BREAD HARDTACK
SEA BREAM CARP CHAD PORGY ROMAN BRAISE SARGUS SPARID TARWHINE
SEACOAST BANK SEABOARD SEASHORE
SEA COW SIREN DUGONG RHYTINA SIRENIAN
SEA CUCUMBER BALATE TREPANG CUCUMBER SYNAPTID TEATFISH
SEADOG FOGBOW
SEA DRAGON PEGASID QUAVIVER
SEA DUCK DIVER EIDER DIPPER DUCKER SCOTER
SEA EAGLE ERN ERNE PYGARG PYGARGUS
SEAFARER SEAGOER
SEA FOX THRASHER
SEA GIRDLE CUVY CUTWEED
SEA GULL COB GOR MEW COBB ANNET COBBE POPELER
SEA-GYPSY SELUNG
SEA HOLLY ERYNGO ERYNGIUM
SEA KALE COLE
SEAL CAN FIX FOB GUM BULL CHOP CORK HARP HOOD JARK LUTE BLANK BULLA CLOSE EAGLE PHOCA SIGIL STAMP SWILE THONG UGRUG

URSUK WAFER ASSEAL BEATER CACHET COCKET DOTARD ENSEAL ENSIGN FASTEN GASKET MAKLUK MATKAH OBSIGN PHOCID RANGER SEALCH SECURE SIGNET CONFIRM CONSIGN COWROID ENGLUTE HOODCAP IMPRESS QUITTER SADDLER SEALING SEALKIE SIGNARY WEDDELL ADHESIVE BACHELOR BEDLAMER BRELOQUE CYLINDER MANDORLA PINNIPED SECRETUM SEECATCH SIGILLUM SIGNACLE TANGFISH VALIDATE
(— FOR WATCH CHAIN) ONION BRELOQUE
(— OFF) CAP
(— OVER CORK) CAPSULE
(3-YEAR OLD —) TURNER
(BEARDED —) URSUK MAKLUK
(EARED —) OTARY
(FEMALE —) MATKA
(GOLD —) BEZEL
(HARBOR —) DOTARD RANGER TANGFISH
(HERD OF —S) PATCH
(IMMATURE —) BEDLAMER
(MALE —) WIG SADDLER BACHELOR SEECATCH
(NEWFOUNDLAND —) SWILE RANGER
(PAPAL —) BULL BULLA
(SHETLAND —) SILKIE
(YEARLING —) HOPPER
(YOUNG —) PUP BEATER JACKET BLUEBACK
SEA LACE WHIPLASH
SEA LAVENDER INKROOT STATICE
SEALED CLOSE
SEALER CAPPER GASKET
SEA LETTUCE LAVER SLAKE SLOKE SEAWEED
SEALSKIN SKIN SCULP MATARA
SEALSKIN COAT NETCHA
SEALYHAM TERRIER
SEAM DRY BAND DART FASH FELL PURL REND DEVIL PEARL SPILL FAGGOT INSEAM STREAK SUTURE SEAMLET JUNCTURE OVERSEAM
(— IN INGOT) SPILL
(— IN SHIP'S HULL) DEVIL
(— OF COAL) RIDER SPLIT STREAK
(IRREGULAR —) FASH
SEAMAN SALT JACKY ARTIST CALASH LUBBER SAILOR MARINER MASTMAN SHIPMAN SHIPPER SMASHER WAISTER YOUNKER DESERTER SEASONER
SEAMARK MEITH
SEAMED SEAMY RUGGED
SEA MILE NAUT
SEAMOUNT GUYOT
SEAMSTER TAILOR SEMPSTER
SEAMSTRESS SEAMER SEWSTER
SEANCE SITTING
SEA NETTLE BLUBBER
SEA ONION SCILLA
SEA OTTER KID KALAN
SEA OXEYE SALTWEED SAMPHIRE
SEA PINK THRIFT SABBATIA

SEAPLANE HYDRO AIRBOAT AEROBOAT
SEA PLANTAIN GIBBALS
SEA POACHER BULLHEAD
SEAPORT PARA PORT GROIN NATAL HARBOR MACASSAR
SEA PUSS OFFSET
SEAR BURN FIRE SERE FLAME FRIZZ ENSEAR SCORCH SIZZLE FRIZZLE
SEA RAVEN SCULPIN
SEARCH FAN SPY BEAT COMB DRAG DRAW FAND FOND GAPE HUNT LAIT RAKE RIPE ROUT SEEK SIFT WAIT FRISK PROBE QUEST SNOOP VISIT DACKER DREDGE FERRET FUMBLE RANCEL SLEUTH ENQUIRE EXPLORE FOSSICK INQUEST INQUIRE INSPECT RANSACK SCRINGE ZETETIC FINECOMB OUTREACH SCRABBLE SCROUNGE
(— ABOUT) GRUB PROG GROPE
(— BY FEELING) GROPE
(— DEEPLY) TENT
(— EVERYWHERE) BUSK
(— FOR FOX'S TRAIL) CIPHER
(— FOR GAME) DRAW GHOOM QUEST
(— FOR GOLD) FOSSICK
(— FOR KNOWLEDGE) OUTREACH
(— FOR PROVISIONS) FORAGE
(— FOR SMUGGLED GOODS) DACKER JERQUE
(— FOR WEAPONS) FRISK
(— FOR) FORK HUNT LAIT REQUIRE
(— GROPINGLY) GLAMP
(— INTO) EXQUIRE INDAGATE
(— OUT) FERRET INVENT EXQUIRE
(— SHIP) RUMMAGE
(— SYSTEMATICALLY) COMB
(— THROUGH) TURN
(— UNDERWATER) FISH
(SYSTEMATIC —) SWEEP
SEARCHER FINDER
SEARCHING HARD SHREWD CURIOUS GROPING
SEARED ADUST
SEARING CAUTERY
SEA ROBIN GURNARD WINGFISH
SEA ROVER VIKING SCUMMER
SEASAN NUDE
SEASCAPE SEAPIECE
SEA SCORPION COBBLER
SEA SERPENT ELOPS
SEASHELL PROP
SEASHORE SEA RIPE CLEVE COAST MARINE SEASIDE SEABEACH SEABOARD SEACOAST
SEASICKNESS HILO NAUPATHIA
SEA SNAIL LIPARIAN
SEA SNAKE CHITAL KERRIL
SEASON BEEK CORN DASH FALL PERT SALT SEEL TIDE TIME GRASS SAUCE SAVOR SHEMU SPICE AUTUMN EASTER FLOWER HARDEN HAYING MASTER SPRING STEVEN STOUND SUMMER WINTER BUDTIME FLYTIME HARVEST KITCHEN OATSEED SEEDTIME
(— FOR HERRING FISHING) DRAVE

(— **HIGHLY**) DEVIL
(— **IN THE SUN**) HAZE
(— **OF JOY**) JUBILEE
(— **OF MERRYMAKING**) CARNIVAL
(**CLOSED** —) SHUTOFF
(**DULL** —) SLACK
(**EGYPTIAN** —) AHET PERT SHEMU
(**HAYING** —) HAYING HAYSEL
(**LENTEN** —) CAREME
(**RAINLESS** —) DRY
(**RAINY** —) KHARIF VARSHA
(**REGULARLY RECURRING** —) EMBER
(**SPRING** —) WARE APRIL GRASS
(**THE RIGHT** —) TID
SEASONABLE PAT TIDY TIMELY
TIDEFUL TIMEFUL VETERAN
TOWARDLY
SEASONABLY TIMELY APROPOS
BETIMES
SEASONED SAGY SALT SALTED
INDIENNE POWDERED
(**MILDLY** —) SWEET
SEASONER SURFACER
SEASONING SALT SPICE SEASON
SPICING
SEA SQUIRT ASCIDIAN
SEA SWALLOW TERN
SEAT BOX CAN SEE SET BANK BOSS
COSY DAIS FLOP FORM FROG ROOM
SILL SLIP SUNK TOIT ASANA BENCH
CELLE CHAIR DICKY SELLA SELLE
SETTE SIEGE SLIDE STALL STOOL
BOUGHT DODONA EXEDRA HUMPTY
INSIDE RUMBLE SADDLE SEATER
SEGGIO SETTEE SETTLE THWART
BUTTOCK CUSHION GRADINE
GRADINO INSTALL OTTOMAN
SEATING TABORET TRANSOM
BLEACHER ENTHRONE PULVINAR
SEGGIOLA SUBSELLA WOOLPACK
(— **AT PUBLIC SPECTACLE**)
PULVINAR
(— **FOR CLERGY**) SEDILE
(— **FOR GRINDER**) HORSING
(— **FOR PLANE IRON**) FROG
(— **OF BIRTH**) SIDE
(— **OF EMOTIONS**) CHEST SPLEEN
(— **OF FEELINGS**) STOMACH
(— **OF HARE**) FORM
(— **OF INTELLECT**) HEAD
(— **OF KNOWLEDGE**) RUACH
(— **OF ORACLE**) DODONA
(— **OF PITY**) BOWEL
(— **OF POWER**) SEE
(— **OF REAL LIFE**) SOUL
(— **OF RESPONSIBILITY**) SHOULDER
(— **OF RULE**) OGDOAD
(— **OF TURF**) SUNK
(— **OF UNDERSTANDING**) SKULL
(— **ON ELEPHANT'S BACK**) TOWER
CASTLE HOWDAH
(— **ONESELF**) LEAN PITCH
(— **SLUNG ON POLES**) HORSE
(— **WITH BRAZIER BELOW**)
TENDOUR
(— **WITHIN WINDOW OPENING**)
CAROL
(**AIRPLANE** —) DORMETTE
(**BACKLESS** —) STOOL HASSOCK

(**BISHOP'S** —) APSE BISHOPRIC
(**CANOPIED** —) COSY COZY
(**CARRIAGE** —) DICKY
(**CHIMNEY** —) SCONCE
(**CHURCH** —) PEW DESK STALL
SEDILE
(**COACH** —) BOOT POOP
(**COUNTRY** —) TOWER GRANGE
QUINTA
(**DRAPED** —) MUSNUD
(**DRIVER'S** —) BOX DICKY FORETOP
(**ELEVATED** —) PERCH
(**FIXED** —) DAIS
(**KEY** —) KEYWAY
(**LONG** —) BANK FORM BENCH
(**NIPPLE** —) LUMP
(**OARSMAN'S** —) TAFT
(**PORCH** —) GLIDER
(**RECLINING** —) DORMEUSE
(**ROWER'S** —) THWART
(**ROYAL** —) SIEGE STEAD THRONE
(**STAGECOACH** —**S**) BASKET
(**STRAW** —) BOSS
(**TIER OF** —**S**) TENDIDO
(**UNRESERVED** —**S**) BLUES
SEA TANGLE FURBELOW
SEA TROUT SEWEN SMELT KIPPER
HERLING HIRLING BODIERON
(— **AFTER SPAWNING**) KELT
(**YOUNG** —) PEAL
SEA TURTLE CHELONID
SEA URCHIN WANA REPKIE ARBACIA
CIDARID ECHINID ECHINUS RADIATE
(**FOSSIL** —) ECHINITE
SEAWALL BULWARK
SEAWARD OFF MAKAI
SEAWEED ORE AGAR ALGA KELP
LIMU MOSS NORI OOZE REEK REIT
TANG WARE DRIFT DULSE KOMBU
LAVER SLAKE SLOKE VAREC VRAIC
WRACK DELISK FUCOID FUNORI
TANGLE HAITSAI OARWEED
OREWEED OREWOOD REDWARE
SEATANG SEAWARE CARAGEEN
CORALINE GULFWEED HEMPWEED
ROCKWEED SARGASSO SEABEARD
WHIPCORD WHIPLASH
(**PL.**) LUMUT
SEBESTEN MYXA
SECANT SEC CHORD
SECCO FRESCO
SECEDE SPLINTER
SECESSIONIST SECESH SEPARATE
SECLUDE TACKLE ENCLOSE ISOLATE
RECLUSE CLOISTER
SECLUDED COY SHY DEEP CLOSE
QUIET HIDDEN REMOTE SECRET
PRIVATE RETIRED SECLUSE
HIDEAWAY MONASTIC SEPARATE
UMBRATIC
SECLUSION RECESS SHADOW
PRIVACY PRIVITY RETREAT
SECRECY SEQUEST SOLITUDE
SECOND AID SEC ABET BACK BETA
TICK OTHER VOUCH ASSIST LATTER
MOMENT TARTAN TIDDER TOTHER
ANOTHER INSTANT SUPPORT
SUSTAIN STICKLER
(— **BASE**) KEYSTONE

(— **IN COMMAND**) DEPUTY
(— **PERSON USE**) TUISM
(**1000TH OF A** —) SIGMA
(**60TH OF A** —) THIRD
SECONDARY BY BYE SUB SLACK
DONKEY SECOND CUBITAL DERIVED
INFERIOR
(**PL.**) FLAGS
SECONDHAND USED
SECOND-RATE COMMON INFERIOR
SECOND-RATER PIKER
SECRECY DERN HUSH HIDING
SECRET PRIVACY PRIVITY SILENCE
DARKNESS SCUGGERY VELATION
SECRET SLY DARK DERN BLIND
CABAL CLOSE PRIVY QUIET ARCANE
CLOSET COVERT HIDDEN INWARD
POCKET STOLEN ARCANUM
COUNSEL CRYPTIC EPOPTIC
FURTIVE MYSTERY PRIVACY
PRIVATE PRIVITY RECLUSE RESERVE
RETIRED SECRETA UNKNOWN
ESOTERIC HIDLINGS MYSTICAL
SNEAKING STEALTHY
SECRETARY CLERK COPPY BARUCH
MUNSHI RAPTOR SCRIBE FAMULUS
MUNSHEE MOONSHEE
SECRETE HIDE NICHE RESET
SECERN SECRET CONCEAL
SECLUDE SALIVATE SEPARATE
(— **MILK**) LACTATE
(— **ONESELF**) HIVE
(— **SALIVA**) DROOL
SECRETION INK LAC GOWL LAAP
LERP MILT SPIT WOOL HUMOR
LAARP MUCUS SEPIA SLIME SPADE
CEMENT SALIVA SMEGMA CERUMEN
CHALONE FLOCOON HORMONE
SPITTLE ENDOCRIN
(**THICKENED** —) GUM
(**WAXY** —) LERP LAARP
SECRETIVE SLY DARK SNUG
COVERT SECRET SILENT INVOLVED
SECRETIVENESS SECRECY
SLYNESS
SECRETLY CLOSE DARKLY DERNLY
SECRET CLOSELY HIDLINGS
INWARDLY
SECT SET ZEN BABI CULT JODO
KIND SHIN ALOGI BHORA ISAWA
PANTH BOHORA DONMEH HERESY
SCHISM SCHOOL DHUNDIA DOCETAE
HASIDIM ISAWIYA KHALSAH
RINGATU SECTARY SEQUELA
SHAIKHI SHINGON SIVAISM SUBSECT
AGNOETAE AHMADIYA AISSAOUA
MURJIITE NAASSENE SECTUARY
SHAKTISM
(**MEMBER OF** —) KHLYST OPHITE
YEZIDI MOLOKAN NUSAIRI LINGAYAT
SECTARIAN CULTIST HERETIC
MAZHABI SECTARY SECTIST
SECTARY JESUIT HERETIC SECTIST
SECTUARY SEPARATE
SECTION CUT END AREA PACE PART
SECT UNIT CAPUT FRUST SHARE
TMEMA BILLET BRANCH BRIDGE
CANTON LENGTH MEMBER SECTOR
ARTICLE CUTTING HEADING

SEGMENT TRANCHE ADDENDUM
DIVISION FRACTION
(— **AROUND HOP KILN**) CURB
(— **OF A BODY**) LAMINA
(— **OF AVICENNA'S WORK**) FEN
(— **OF BLOOM**) STAMP
(— **OF BUILDING**) ENTRY
(— **OF FENCE**) FLAKE
(— **OF FILM**) EXPOSURE
(— **OF FILTER**) LEAF
(— **OF FISHING TACKLE**) TRACE
(— **OF GARMENT**) GORE
(— **OF GLASS**) SHAWL
(— **OF HIGH GROUND**) DIVIDE
(— **OF KORAN**) SURA
(— **OF LADDER**) FLY
(— **OF LOG**) BOLT FLITCH
(— **OF LOOM**) LAY
(— **OF NET**) DEEPING
(— **OF NEWSPAPER**) LEAD
(— **OF PARLIAMENT**) LAGTHING
(— **OF PSALTER**) CATHISMA
(— **OF RHAPSODY**) LASSU
(— **OF ROOF**) SEVERY
(— **OF ROOTSTOCK**) BIT
(— **OF SHIP**) STEERAGE
(— **OF SONG**) STOLLEN
(— **OF THREE SHEETS**) TERNION
(— **OF TRENCH**) BAY
(— **OF VIOLIN**) BOUT
(— **OF WOOD**) HAG
(— **OF YARN**) SLUB
(—**S OF SCENERY**) BOOK
(**4-PAGE** —) OUTSERT
(**CONCLUDING** —) ABGESANG
(**CONIC** —) PARABOLA
(**DULL** —) LONGUEUR
(**LOWEST** —) BOTTOM
(**MINE** —) BORASQUE BORRASCA
(**MUSICAL** —) CODA EPILOG FINALE
(**NARROW** —) STRIPE
(**NATIVE** —) KASBA CASBAH
(**ONE-SIXTEENTH OF** —) FORTY
(**PERCUSSION** —) BATTERY
SECTIONALISM LOCALISM
SECTOR AREA HOUSE
SECULAR LAIC COMMON EARTHLY
PROFANE WORLDLY TEMPORAL
SECURE FID GET GIB KEY POT SEW
WIN BAIL BOLT BOND CAUK COCK
COLD EASY FAST FIND FIRM FRAP
GAIN GIRD HOOK LAND MOOR NAIL
SAFE SEAL SHOT SNUG STAY SURE
WARM BELAY BLOCK CINCH CLEAT
SLOUR SOUND STRAP TRUST
ANCHOR ASSURE BECKET BUTTON
CLINCH DEFEND ENSURE FASTEN
OBTAIN PLEDGE SETTLE SICCAR
SICKER STABLE STAPLE TRAIST
BULWARK CONFINE DUNNAGE
FORFEND FORTIFY RAMPIRE
WARRANT GARRISON PRESERVE
(— **A SAIL**) TRICE
(— **AGAINST INTRUSION**) TILE
(— **AID OF**) ENLIST
(— **BAIT**) EBB
(— **FROM LEAKING**) COFFER
(— **WITH BARS**) GRATE
SECURED BOUND SETTLED

SECURELY FAST SAFE SICCAR
SICKER STRAIT SURELY SOLIDLY
SOUNDLY
SECURITY PUP BAIL BAND EASE
GAGE SEAL WAGE FRITH GRITH
GUARD QUIET STOCK BORROW
CEDULA EQUITY PLEDGE SAFETY
SCREEN SEVERE SURETY VADIUM
CAUTION DEFENSE DEPOSIT
FLOATER HOSTAGE SHELTER
SLEEPER WARRANT COLONIAL
COVENANT FASTNESS GUARANTY
HYPOTHEC STRENGTH VADIMONY
(**PL.**) PERCENTS
SEDAN SEDIA JAMPAN SALOON
TONJON TOMJOHN BROUGHAM
SEDATE CALM COOL DOUCE QUIET
SOBER STAID SERENE EARNEST
SERIOUS SETTLED DECOROUS
SEDATENESS SOBRIETY
SEDATIVE AMYTAL CALMANT
LENITIVE QUIETIVE SOOTHING
SEDENTARY STILL SESSILE
INACTIVE
SEDGE SAG LING RAIT REIT STAR
CAREX CHUFA TIKUG BHABAR
EHUAWA GLUMAL THATCH TOETOE
TOITOI BULRUSH MONOCOT
PAPYRUS SNIDDLE TUSSOCK
GALANGAL JIMSEDGE
SEDGE FLY GRANAM GRANNOM
SEDGE WARBLER WREN MOCKBIRD
REEDBIRD
SEDGY SAGGY SEGGY TWILLED
SEDIMENT CARR DREG FAEX FOOT
GOBI LEES MULM SILT WARP DRAST
DREGS FECES FOOTS MAGMA
BOTTOM SIMMON SLUDGE DREWITE
GROUNDS GRUMMEL SAPROPEL
SETTLING
(— **OF BEER OR ALE**) CRAP
(**IRON** —) CAR CARR
(**REDDISH** —) SIMMON
SEDITION REVOLT TREASON
SEDITIOUS RIOTOUS FACTIOUS
MUTINOUS
SEDUCE DRAW JAPE LOCK DECOY
TEMPT WRONG ALLURE BETRAY
ENTICE DEBAUCH ENSNARE
MISLEAD SUGGEST TRADUCE
INVEIGLE
(— **WITH THE EYE**) LEER
SEDUCER UNDOER LOTHARIO
SEDUCTION LURE BRIBE CHARM
SEDULOUS BUSY INTENT STUDIED
DILIGENT UNTIRING
SEDULOUSNESS INDUSTRY
SEDUM MOSS ORPINE SENGREEN
SEE LO EYE KEN SPY VID ESPY
LOOK MIND NOTE PIPE SEAT SEGE
SPOT VIDE VIEW BESEE CATCH
CHAIR SIEGE SIGHT STOOL TENEZ
WATCH ATTEND BEHOLD DESCRY
NOTICE QUAERE REMARK SURVEY
ARCHSEE DISCERN GLIMPSE
OBSERVE WITNESS CATHEDRA
CONCEIVE PERCEIVE
(— **ABOVE**) VS
(— **BELOW**) VI

(— **FIT**) CHOOSE
(— **INTO**) INSEE
(— **TO**) FIX
(— **VISIONS**) SCRY
SEED BEN MAW NIB PIP BEAN BOIL
CHAT CORN DIKA GERM KOLA LIMA
MOTE SETH TARE BEHEN BERRY
CACAO CARAT GRAIN SEMEN
SPAWN SPERM STONE ABILLA
ACHENE ACINUS CARNEL FENNEL
KERNEL LEGUME LENTIL NICKER
NUTLET PIGNON PIPPIN TILLEY
ACHIOTE ACHUETE ALPISTE
ANISEED BUCKEYE CALINUT FRIJOLE
HARICOT HAYSEED SEEDKIN
SEEDLET SEMINAL AMBRETTE
COKERNUT CYDONIUM DILLSEED
FLAXSEED FLEASEED HEMPSEED
PIGNOLIA PRINCIPE SEEDLING
SEEDNESS
(**AROMATIC** —**S**) ANISE
(**EDIBLE** —) PEA BEAN
(**FENUGREEK** —) HELBEH
(**GRAPE** —) ACINUS
(**IMMATURE** —) OVULE
(**MUSTARD** —) SENVY SINEWY
(**NUTLIKE** —) PEANUT
(**OILY** —) ABILLA
(**PALM** —) COROZO
(**POPPY** —) MAW MOHNSEED
(**SESAME** —) JINJILI GINGELLY
(**PL.**) ANISE COFFEE SESAME ZERAIM
IGNATIA LARKSPUR
SEEDCAKE WIG WIGG
SEEDCASE TEST TESTA THECA
SEED COAT TESTA SPIRICLE
SEEDED ARABLE
SEEDER SEEDMAN
SEEDLING FREE LINER
SEEDY MANGY SCUFFY
SEEING SIGHT SIGHTED
(— **THAT**) SITH SINCE
SEEK ASK BEG SIC WOO FAND FEEL
FISH FOND FORK HUNT LAIT LOOK
SICK SIFT COURT DELVE ESSAY
FETCH SCOUR APPETE BOTTOM
FERRET FOLLOW FRAIST PURSUE
SEARCH FORSEEK INQUIRE
RANSACK REQUIRE RUMMAGE
SOLICIT ENDEAVOR
(— **AFTER**) SUE SUIT ENSUE
EXPLORE
(— **AIMLESSLY**) PROG
(— **FAVOR**) WISH
(— **FOR**) APPETE EXPLORE
(— **IN MARRIAGE**) WOO PRETEND
(— **OUT**) COMB ENSEARCH
(— **TO ATTAIN**) ASPIRE
SEEKER TRACER PETITOR ZETETIC
SEARCHER
(— **AFTER FACTS**) GRADGRIND
(— **OF KNOWLEDGE**) PHILONIST
(**JOB** —) CHANCER
(**PLEASURE** —) FRANION
SEEKING SOKE SOKEN ZETETIC
SEEM BID EYE SEE FARE LOOK PEER
SOUND APPEAR BESEEM REGARD
(— **TO BE**) LIKE
(**IT** —**S**) SEMBLE

SEEMING GUISE QUASI LIKELY
SEEMLY APPARENT SEMBLANT
SEEMINGLY QUASI SEEMLY
SEEMING
SEEMLINESS GRACE DECENCY
DECORUM
SEEMLY FIT TALL CIVIL COMELY
DECENT LIKELY MODEST BECOMING
DECOROUS GRACEFUL
SEEP LEAK OOZE SIPE EXUDE
SEEPAGE SEEP SIPAGE SPRING
SEEPY WEEPY
SEER SIR SWAMI MOPSUS SCRYER
PROPHET CHALDEAN MELAMPUS
SEERBAND TURBAN
SEERESS SAGA SIBYL VOLVA
ALRUNE ALBRUNA PHOIBAD
SEESAW PUMP TILT DANDLE TEETER
TIDDLE TILTER TITTER TOTTER
SEETHE FRY JUG BOIL CREE ITCH
STEW WALL WALM BULLER HOTTER
SIMMER BLUBBER ELIXATE
FERMENT
SEETHING ASEETHE BOILING
HUMMING ITCHING SCALDING
SEGMENT CUT LAP FALL HAND LITH
MERE PART BLANK CHORD ELITE
FEMUR FURCA SHARE SLICE TMEMA
CANTLE GLOSSA LENGTH SAMPLE
SYZYGY ARTICLE DIGITUS EXERGUE
FESTOON ISOMERE MYOMERE
MYOTOME SECTION SETIGER
ANTIMERE BRACHIUM COLUMNAL
DACTYLUS DIVISION GONOTOME
HYPOMERE INTERVAL MESOMERE
METAMERE MYOCOMMA NARICORN
(— OF CASK) CANT
(— OF CAULIFLOWER) FLOWERET
(— OF CIRCLE) SECTION
(— OF COMMUNITY) FACIES
(— OF EARTH'S CRUST) GRABEN
(— OF FIBER) BAND
(— OF IRIS) FALL
(— OF LEAF) LACINIA
(— OF MAXILLA) STIPES SUBGALEA
(— OF RATTLESNAKE'S RATTLE)
BUTTON
(— OF SPEECH) DOMAIN
(HERALDIC —) FLANCH FLANCHE
(INSTRUCTIONAL —) LESSON
(MERE —) SNAPSHOT
(PEASANT —) HERA
SEGMENTATION CLEAVAGE
SEGMENTED INSECTED
SEGNO SIGN
SEGREGATE SHED SEVER INTERN
ISOLATE CLASSIFY INSULATE
SEPARATE
SEIGNORAGE ROYALTY
SEIGNORY LORDSHIP
SEINE NET FARE TUCK TRAIN
POCKET SAGENE SPILLER
MADRAGUE
SEISIN VESTURE
SEIZE BAG CAP CLY GET HAP NAB
NAP BEAK BONE CLAW CLUM FANG
GALL GLOM GRAB GRIP GRUP HAND
HENT HOOK JUMP KEEP LEVY NAIL
RAMP SMUG SNAP SPAN TAKE TIRE

YOKE CATCH CESSE CLASP CLEEK
CLICK DRIVE GRASP GRIPE LATCH
PINCH RAVEN RAVIN REACH REAVE
SNACK ARREST ASSUME ATTACH
CLUTCH COLLAR EXTEND FASTEN
FREEZE GOBBLE NOBBLE QUARRY
SECURE SNATCH ASSEIZE CAPTURE
ENCLASP ENCLOSE GRABBLE
GRAPPLE IMPOUND POSSESS
PREHEND SCAMBLE SWALLOW
ARROGATE COMPRISE DISTRAIN
SPUILZIE SURPRISE UNDERNIM
(— AND HOLD FIRMLY) TRUSS
(— BAIT) STRIKE
(— BY NECK) SCRAG COLLAR
SCRUFF
(— PREY) CHOP
(— SUDDENLY) NAB NIP SWOOP
SNATCH
(— UPON) ATTACK INFECT
(— WITH CLAWS) STRAIN
(— WITH TEETH) BITE
(— WITH WHOLE HAND) GLAUM
(— WITHOUT RIGHT) USURP
SEIZIN SASINE VESTURE
SEIZING FANG GRIP MARQUE
CAPTION SEIZURE
SEIZURE PIT BITE HOLD GRIPE
ICTUS SPELL ARREST EXTENT
PRISAL RAPTUS TAKING ANGARIA
CAPTION CONCEIT TELLACH
DISTRESS STOPPAGE
SELDOM RARE SELD RARELY
UNOFTEN
SELDOM-SEEN ANTRIN ANTERIN
SELECT ORT TAP TRY CULL PICK
SIFT SORT TAKE WALE DRAFT
ELECT ELITE PITCH TRIED ASSIGN
BALLOT CHOICE CHOOSE CLUBBY
DECIDE DESUME EXEMPT PREFER
SINGLE WINNOW DRAUGHT
EXCERPT EXTRACT OUTLOOK
EXIMIOUS HANDPICK SELECTED
(— BY LOT) DRAW
(— BY PATTERN) SWATCH
(— JURY) STRIKE
SELECTED DRAFT ELECT FANCY
DRAUGHT
SELECTING DRAFT GARBLING
SELECTION BLAD CHAP CULL ITEM
PICK CHOICE CHOOSE EXCERPT
EXTRACT ELECTION HAFTARAH
PERICOPE
(— OF PSALMS) HALLEL
(VERSE —) SINGSONG
SELECTIVE CHOOSY ECLECTIC
SELF EGO SEL SEN JIVA SELL SOUL
DAENA NATURE PERSON PSYCHE
(INNER —) ANIMA
(OWN —) AINSELL NAINSEL
(SUPREME UNIVERSAL —) ATMAN
SELF-ACCUSATION GUILT
SELF-AGGRANDIZING IMPERIAL
SELF-ASSERTIVE BRASH PERKY
CHESTY BLUSTERY
SELF-ASSURANCE CHEEK APLOMB
COOLNESS
SELF-ASSURED CALM CONFIDENT
SELF-CENTERED SELFISH

SELF-CENTEREDNESS EGOTISM
SELFHOOD
SELF-COMMAND NERVE
SELF-CONCEIT NOSISM
SELF-CONCEITED COXY PENSY
COCKSY PENCEY
SELF-CONFIDENCE CREST HUBRIS
JOLLITY OPINION
SELF-CONFIDENT FLUSH CHESTY
SELF-CONSCIOUS GAWKY BASHFUL
SELF-CONTAINED ABSOLUTE
SELF-CONTAINMENT CLOSURE
SELF-CONTRADICTORY ABSURD
SELF-CONTROL STAY WILL
ENCRATY MODESTY RETENUE
PATIENCE
SELF-DECEPTION FLATTERY
SELF-DENIAL DENIAL
SELF-DENYING ASCETIC
SELF-DESTRUCTION SUICIDE
SELF-DESTRUCTIVE SUICIDAL
SELF-DETERMINATION FREEDOM
AUTONOMY
SELF-DISCIPLINE ASCESIS
SELF-ENRICHMENT GROWTH
SELF-ESTEEM EGO PRIDE CONCEIT
SELFNESS
SELF-EVIDENT MANIFEST
SELF-EXALTATION NOSISM ELATION
SELF-EXISTENT BEER INCREATE
UNCAUSED
SELF-FERTILIZATION AUTOGAMY
SELF-FULFILLMENT FREEDOM
SAMADHI
SELF-GENERATION AUTOGENY
SELF-GLORIFICATION VANITY
SELF-GOVERNMENT SWARAJ
SELF-HEAL ALLHEAL HOOKHEAL
HOOKWEED
SELFHOOD SEITY EGOITY IPSEITY
OWNHOOD PROPRIUM SELFNESS
SELF-IDENTITY IPSEITY
SELF-IMPORTANT PURDY CHESTY
BIGGETY POMPOUS
SELF-INDULGENCE NICETY
PLEASURE
SELFISH PIGGISH SELFFUL
DISSOCIAL
SELFISHNESS EGO SELF EGOTISM
SUICISM PHILAUTY SELFHOOD
SELFNESS
SELF-LOVE CONCEIT PHILAUTY
SELF-POLLUTION ONANISM
SELF-POSSESSED COOL ASSURED
COMPOSED
SELF-POSSESSION APLOMB
COOLNESS
SELF-REALIZATION FREEDOM
ENERGISM
SELF-RELIANT BOLD FREE
SELF-REPROACH GUILT REGRET
SELF-RESTRAINT HO HOO ASCESIS
CONTROL RESERVE RETENUE
HAVLAGAH
SELF-RIGHTEOUS STUFFY
SELF-SACRIFICING HEROIC
GALLANT
SELFSAME SAME SELFSAID
IDENTICAL

SELFSAMENESS IDENTITY
SELF-SATISFIED SMUG STODGY
ASSURED
SELF-SUFFICIENCY ASEITY ASEITAS
AUTARCHY
SELF-SUFFICIENT ABSOLUTE
SELF-WILLED SET SENSUAL
WAYWARD CONTRARY
SELION BUTT
SELL DO GIVE VEND CHEAP PITCH
SHAVE TRADE UTTER AFFORD
BARTER MARKET AUCTION BARGAIN
(**— AT LOW PRICE**) DUMP
(**— BELOW COST**) FOOTBALL
(**— BY AUCTION**) CANT ROUP
(**— FOR**) BRING FETCH
(**— IN SMALL QUANTITIES**) RETAIL
(**BUY AND —**) CHOP
SELLER BOOMER BUSKER CADGER
VENDOR CHANTER FLESHER
CHANDLER
(**WINE —**) ABKAR
SELLING (SPECULATIVE —)
AGIOTAGE
SELSYN SYNCHRO
SELVAGE LIST GOUGE FORREL
LISTING STICKING
SEMANTEME RHEME
SEMANTICS SEMOLOGY
SEMAPHORE FISHTAIL
SEMBLANCE FACE SHOW SIGN
COLOR GHOST GLOSS GUISE IMAGE
SCHEME VISAGE PRETEXT SEEMING
UMBRAGE LIKENESS SEMBLANT
SKERRICK
(**— OF DIGNITY**) FACE
(**— OF REALITY**) DREAM
(**FALSE —**) COLORING
SEME SEMY GUTTY HURTY FLEURY
GOUTTE GUTTEE BEZANTE
SEME-DE-LIS FLORETTY
SEMELE (BROTHER OF —)
POLYDORUS
(**FATHER OF —**) CADMUS
(**MOTHER OF —**) HARMONIA
(**SISTER OF —**) INO AGAVE
AUTONOE
(**SON OF —**) BACCHUS
SEMEN SEED SPERM
SEMESTER HALF
SEMIDARKNESS DUSK
SEMIDIAMETER RADIUS
SEMIDOME CONCHA
SEMIFLUID SOFT HUMOR
SEMIGLOSS EGGSHELL
SEMINARY YESHIVA JUVENATE
SEMIOPAQUE HORNY
SEMIPORCELAIN GOMBROON
SEMIRAMIS (HUSBAND OF —) NINUS
(**MOTHER OF —**) DERCETO
SEMITE JEW ARAB HARARI SYRIAN
SEMITIC SHEMITE ARAMAEAN
ASSYRIAN CHALDEAN
SEMITIC JEWISH
(**— LANGUAGE**) GAFAT
SEMITONE FEINT LIMMA DEMITONE
HEMITONE
SEMOLINA SUJI SEMOLA
SENATE BOULE SENATO COUNCIL

SENATUS GEROUSIA SENATORY
(**— AND PEOPLE OF ROME**) SPQR
(**— DIVISION**) PRYTANY
SENATOR SOLON CONSUL FATHER
LAWMAKER
SENATORSHIP TOGA
SEND MIT FAST PACK SHIP ENVOY
SCEND THROW ADDRESS CHANNEL
COMMAND CONSIGN DELIVER
FORWARD DISPATCH TRANSMIT
(**— ABOUT**) TROLL
(**— ALOFT**) CROSS
(**— AWAY**) MAND SHIP AMAND
BANISH DISBAND DISMISS RELEGATE
(**— BACK**) ECHO TURN WISE REMIT
REMAND REMISE RENVOY RESEND
RETURN REFRACT
(**— BY MAIL**) DROP
(**— DOWN**) DEMIT DIMIT STRIKE
(**— FOR**) SUMMON
(**— FORTH IN RAYS**) RADIATE
(**— FORTH**) BEAR CAST EMIT MAND
DIMIT FLING EFFUSE OUTSEND
(**— IN**) IMMIT IMMISS INTROMIT
(**— MESSAGE**) BLINKER
(**— OFF UNCEREMONIOUSLY**) SHANK
(**— OFF**) WING
(**— OFFICIALLY**) ISSUE
(**— OUT**) BEAM EMIT AMAND SHOOT
SPEED DEDUCE DEPORT LAUNCH
DIFFUSE EXPEDITE
(**— TO JAIL**) LAG MITTIMUS
(**— TO PERDITION**) CONFOUND
SENDING SAND
(**— OUT**) EMISSIVE

SENEGAL

CAPITAL: DAKAR
MOUNTAIN: GOUNOU
NATIVE: PEUL SOCE DIOLA FOULA
LAOBE SERER WOLOF FULANI
SERERE BAMBARA MALINKE
TUKULER MANDINGO
RIVER: FALEME GAMBIA SALOUM
SENEGAL
TOWN: THIES KAOLACK RUFISQUE

SENILE DOLD DOTARD
SENILITY DOTAGE CADUCITY
PROGERIA
SENIOR AINE DEAN SIRE DOYEN
ELDER ANCIENT SUPERIOR
SENIORITY AGE ANCIENTY
SIGNEURY
SENNET SPET SIGNET
SENOR DON
SENORITA MISS SRTA SRITA
SENSATION FEEL ITCH SOUR SENSE
TABET TASTE TIBBIT VEDANA
FEELING ESTHESIS
(**— OF COLD**) RHIGOSIS
(**— OF FRIGHT**) FRISSON
(**— OF HEAT**) HOTNESS
(**ANTICIPATORY —**) FOREFEEL
(**BURNING —**) ARDOR
(**DARTING —**) SHOOT
(**STRONG —**) CREEP
(**SUBJECTIVE —**) AURA

(**TASTE —**) GUST BITTER
(**TINGLING —**) DIRL
(**VIBRATING —**) FREMITUS
(**VISUAL —**) PHOSE PHOTOMA
SENSATIONAL GORY YELLOW
SAFFRON SPLASHY THRILLY
STUNNING
SENSATIONALISM BLARE SENSISM
SENSE WIT FEEL SALT SMELL
LETTER MATTER REASON SCONCE
WISDOM FEELING HEARING
MARBLES MEANING SMEDDUM
CARRIAGE GUMPTION JUDGMENT
(**— OF APPREHENSION**) ANXIETY
(**— OF HEARING**) EAR
(**— OF HUMOR**) MUSIC
(**— OF ONENESS**) KINSHIP
(**— OF OUTRAGE**) SHOCK
(**— OF PANIC**) JITTERS
(**— OF RIGHT**) GRACE
(**— OF SIGHT**) VISION
(**— OF SMELL**) SCENT
(**— OF SUPERIORITY**) EGOTISM
(**— OF TOUCH**) FEEL TASTE
(**— ON ONE'S WORTH**) PRIDE
(**COMMON —**) SALT BALANCE
GUMPTION
(**DISCRIMINATING —**) FLAIR
(**LACKING —**) INEPT
(**PLAIN —**) ENGLISH
(**SOUND —**) MATTER
SENSE-DATUM SENSUM
SENSELESS MAD COLD DUMB
FRIGID STUPID UNWISE FOOLISH
IDIOTIC PEEVISH SOTTISH UNIDEAED
SENSIBILITY HEART SENSE FEELING
DELICACY ESTHESIA JUDGMENT
(**PL.**) FEELINGS
SENSIBLE SANE WISE AWARE PRIVY
ACTUAL FEELABLE MATERIAL
PASSIBLE RATIONAL SENSICAL
SENTIENT WISELIKE
SENSITIVE FINE KEEN SORE ALIVE
QUICK LIABLE NIMBLE TENDER
TETCHY FEELING NERVOUS PRICKLY
ALLERGIC DELICATE EROGENIC
SENSIBLE SENTIENT SKINLESS
TOUCHOUS
(**— TO PAIN**) TART
(**NERVOUSLY —**) TOUCHY
SENSITIVENESS SENSE TOUCH
ALGESIA DELICACY
SENSITIVE PEA HONEYCUP
SENSITIVE PLANT MIMOSA
SENSITIVITY FLESH DELICACY
FINENESS
SENSORY SENSUAL AFFERENT
SENSUAL LEWD BRUTE MUDDY
CARNAL FLESHY SULTRY WANTON
BESTIAL BRUTISH FLESHLY LESBIAN
SWINISH PANDEMIC SENSUOUS
SENSUALITY FLESH LIKING LUXURY
SENSUOUS SOFT SATINY SENSAL
FLESHLY SENSUAL LUSCIOUS
SENSIBLE
SENTENCE DIT RAP SAW DAMN
DOOM TIME AWARD FUTWA JUISE
TENER TROPE ARREST COMMIT
DECREE DEPORT JUWISE REASON

ADJUDGE CENSURE CONDEMN
FLOATER IMPRESA LAGGING
FOREDOOM JUDGMENT VERSICLE
(— **INDICATING CHARACTER**)
MOTTO
(**CONCISE —S**) LACONICS
(**IMPRISONMENT** —) LAG RAP LIFE
LAGGING STRETCH
(**MUSICAL** —) PERIOD
(**SHORT** —) CLAUSE
(**WITTY** —) ATTICISM
SENTENTIOUS CONCISE LACONIC
SENTIENCE SENSE
SENTIENT FEELING SENSILE
SENSIVE SENSEFUL SENSIBLE
SENTIMENT MIND POSY ETHNOS
GENIUS HOBNOB PLEDGE FEELING
(**SLOPPY** —) DRIP
SENTIMENTAL SLAB SOFT CORNY
GOOEY GUSHY MUSHY SAPPY
SOBBY SOPPY SOUPY FRUITY
SLUSHY SPOONY SUGARY SYRUPY
INSIPID MAUDLIN MAWKISH
ROMANTIC SCHMALZY SNIVELLY
SENTIMENTALISM BATHOS
SCHMALZ SCHMALTZ
SENTIMENTALIST SOFTHEAD
SENTIMENTALITY GOO HAM MUSH
SIRUP SYRUP BATHOS
SENTINEL WAIT DEINO GUARD
WATCH BANTAY PICKET SENTRY
PICQUET COCKATOO PEPHEDRO
WATCHMAN
(**MOUNTED** —) VEDET VEDETTE
(**PL.**) GRAEAE GRAIAE
SENTINEL BOX STATION
SENTRY KITE WATCH SENTINEL
SEPAL LEAF HELMET LEAFLET
SEPARATE CUT TOM COMB CULL
CURD DEAL FALL FRAY FREE HAZE
PART REDD SERE SIFT SORT TWIN
BLEED BREAK CALVE ELONG FENCE
FLAKE HEDGE PARTY SCALE SEVER
SIEVE SKILL SPLIT TWAIN TWIST
ABDUCT ABRUPT ASSORT AVULSE
BISECT CLEAVE DECIDE DEPART
DETACH DIGEST DIVIDE DIVISI
PROPER REMOTE SCREEN SECERN
SECRET SEJOIN SETTLE SINGLE
SOLUTE SPREAD SUNDER SUNDRY
SWATCH UNLUTE WINNOW ABSCISE
ABSCISS BRACKET CONCERN
DIALYZE DISJOIN DISLINK DISPAIR
DISPART DIVERSE EXPANSE FISSION
ISOLATE SCATTER SECTION
SEJUNCT SEVERAL SWINGLE
ABSTRACT BULKHEAD DETACHED
DIFFRACT DISCRETE DISJOINT
DISSEVER DISSOLVE DISTINCT
DISTRACT DISUNITE DIVIDANT
DIVIDUAL FRACTION LAMINATE
LEVIGATE LIBERATE PECULIAR
SEVERATE SPORADIC UNMINGLE
UNSOLDER UNSTRING
(— **BY BEATING**) SCUTCH
(— **BY CROSSWALL**) ABJOINT
(— **BY PICKING**) LEASE LEAZE
(— **COINS**) JOURNEY
(— **COMBATANTS**) STICKLE

(— **FIBERS**) HACKLE
(— **FROM HERD**) IMPRIME
(— **GRAIN FROM CHAFF**) FAN CAVE
WINNOW
(— **HAIR**) BLOCK
(— **INTO COMPONENTS**) STRIP
(— **INTO FLOCKS**) DRAFT DRAUGHT
(— **INTO SHREDS**) TEASE
(— **ONESELF**) ABDICATE
(— **ORE**) JIG SMELT DILLUE
(— **SHEEP**) DRAW
(— **THREADS**) SLEY SLEAVE
SEPARATED FREE ALONE BROKEN
DISTANT DIVIDED ABSTRACT
ISOLATED RESOLVED
(— **BY INTERVAL**) OPEN
SEPARATELY APART SINGLY
SUNDRY SEVERAL SUNDERLY
SEPARATING BETWEEN
SEPARATION GAP GULF PART SHED
CHASM SPLIT SCHISM BARRIER
DIVORCE ELUTION PARTING
ANALYSIS AUTOTOMY AVULSION
CREAMING DECISION DIALYSIS
DISTANCE DISUNION DIVISION
INCISION SHEDDING TWINNING
(— **OF LEAF**) CHORISIS
(— **OF MAN AND WIFE**) ZIHAR
DIVORCE
(— **OF METALS**) DEPART
(— **OF PIGMENT**) FLOATING
(— **OF WORD PARTS**) TMESIS
(— **OF YEAST IN BEER**) BREAK
SEPARATIST ZOARITE BIMMELER
SEPARATOR RAVEL PARTER
CREAMER SETTLER SEVERER
SUBSIDER
SEPARATRIX SLASH DIAGONAL
SEPIA COCONUT SEPIARY
SEPOY TELINGA
SEPT KIN
SEPTET SEPTUOR
SEPTIVALENT HEPTAD
SEPTUAGINT LXX
SEPTUM VITTA TABULA MYOTOME
PHRAGMA MYOCOMMA
SEPULCHER BIER GRAVE TITLE
MONUMENT MORTUARY
SEPULCHRAL HOLLOW CHARNEL
TUMULARY
SEQUEL SUITE EFFECT SEQUENT
BACKWASH SEQUENCE
SEQUENCE ROPE SUIT TRACT TRAIN
DOCKET ENTAIL SEQUEL SERIES
STRING CADENCE CORONET
SEQUENT SUCCESS SPECTRUM
STRAIGHT
(— **OF BEHAVIOR**) ACT
(— **OF BILLIARD SHOTS**) BREAK
(— **OF CARDS**) STRINGER
(— **OF CHESS MOVES**) DEFENCE
DEFENSE
(— **OF EVENTS**) CYCLE
(— **OF MELODRAMA**) CHASE
(— **OF ROCK UNITS**) SECTION
(— **OF SOUNDS**) AFFIX
(**ACTING** —) EXTERIOR
(**CUSTOMARY** —) COURSE
(**FILM** —) INTERCUT

(**LITURGICAL** —) CANON
SEQUENT ENSUANT SEQUITUR
SEQUESTER SINGLE ISOLATE
RECLUDE
SEQUESTERED LONELY PRIVATE
RECLUSE RETIRED SECLUDED
SOLITARY
SEQUIN CHICK SPANG VENTIN
ZEQUIN CHEQUIN CHEQUEEN
VENETIAN ZECCHINO
(**PL.**) GLITTER
SERAGLIO HAREM SERAI ZENANA
SERAPHIC BEATIFIC
SERBOCROATIAN ILLYRIAN
SERE SEAR SERULE UNGREEN
HALOSERE
SERENADE AUBADE HORNING
ALBORADA NOCTURNE SERENATA
(**MOCK** —) SHIVAREE
SERENADER WAIT
SERENE CALM EVEN CLEAR LITHE
SEDATE SMOOTH HALCYON
DECOROUS
SERENITY CALM PEACE REPOSE
SERF BOND THEW CHURL HELOT
SLAVE THEOW PENEST SERVUS
THRALL BONDMAN COLONUS
PEASANT ADSCRIPT PRAEDIAL
YANACONA
SERFDOM BONDAGE HELOTRY
SERFAGE SERVAGE HELOTISM
SERFHOOD SERFSHIP
SERGE SAGATHY
SERGEANT TOP SARGE CHIAUS
DESKMAN SERVANT TOPKICK
SERIAUNT
SERGEANT-AT-LAW COUNTOR
COUNTOUR
SERGEANT FISH LING CABIO COBIA
SNOOK BONITO CUBBYYEW
SERGEANT MAJOR PINTANO
SERIALLY SERIATIM
SERIEMA CARIAMA GRUIFORM
SCREAMER
SERIES RUN SET ECCA RANK SUIT
TIRE CHAIN DRIFT DWYKA ORDER
SUITE TALLY TRACE COURSE
EOCENE SEQUEL STRING SYSTEM
BATTERY CASCADE CATALOG
BEADROLL SEQUENCE
(— **GATHERED TOGETHER**) SORITES
(— **OF ABSTRACTS**) SYLLABUS
(— **OF ARCHES**) ARCADE
(— **OF BALLET TURNS**) CHAINE
(— **OF BOAT RACES**) REGATTA
(— **OF CELLS**) FILAMENT
(— **OF CHARACTERS**) CLINE
(— **OF CHESS MOVES**) COOK
(— **OF CLASHES**) CLATTER
(— **OF COMMUNITIES**) SERE
(— **OF DANCE MOVEMENTS**) ADAGIO
(— **OF DRAIN TILES**) FIELD
(— **OF EVENTS**) EPOS ACTION
(— **OF EXTRACTS**) CATENA
(— **OF FORTIFICATIONS**) CEINTURE
(— **OF IMAGES**) DREAM
(— **OF LEGENDS**) SAGA
(— **OF LIPS**) GILL
(— **OF MEETINGS**) SESSION

(— **OF METAL DISKS**) PILE
(— **OF MILITARY OPERATIONS**)
CAMPAIGN
(— **OF MOVEMENTS**) DANCE
(— **OF NEIGHBORING LOTS**) COTE
(— **OF NOTES**) GAMUT GLISSADE
(— **OF PASSES**) FAENA
(— **OF PILES**) DRIFT
(— **OF POEMS**) DIVAN DIWAN
(— **OF PRAYERS**) COURSE SYNAPTE
(— **OF RACES**) CIRCUIT
(— **OF REASONS**) ARGUMENT
(— **OF RINGS**) COIL GIMMAL
(— **OF ROOMS**) SWEEP
(— **OF SHOTS**) BURST
(— **OF SIMILAR STRUCTURES**)
STROBILA
(— **OF SLALOM GATES**) FLUSH
(— **OF SLIPS**) DOCK
(— **OF SOILS**) CECIL
(— **OF STAIRS**) FLIGHT
(— **OF STAMPS**) SET
(— **OF STITCHES**) STAY
(— **OF STRAPS**) LADDER
(— **OF TANKS**) SOAPER
(— **OF THREADS**) BINDER STUFFER
(— **OF TONES**) SCALE
(— **OF TRAVELS**) ODYSSEY
(— **OF VERSES**) ANTIPHON
(— **OF WORDS**) ACROSTIC
ALPHABET
(**CARD** —) CORONET
(**CONNECTED** —) CATENA
(**CONSECUTIVE** —) STREAK
(**DANCE** —) DOUBLE
(**GEOLOGICAL** —) ECCA DWYKA
KENAI EOCENE KEEWATIN
(**IMPRESSIVE** —) ARRAY
(**RADIOACTIVE** —) FAMILY
SERIOUS RUM SAD DEEP HIGH
ACUTE GRAVE HEAVY SOBER SOLID
STAID DEMURE SEDATE SEVERE
SOLEMN SOMBER SOMBRE SULLEN
AUSTERE CAPITAL EARNEST
SERIOSO WEIGHTY GRIEVOUS
SERIOUSLY BAD ILL DOWN SADLY
DEEPLY GRAVELY SOLIDLY
SERIOUSNESS EARNEST GRAVITY
SADNESS
SERMON SPELL HOMILY ADDRESS
FUNERAL SEREMENT SERMONET
SERMONIZING MORALITY
SEROPURULENT SANIOUS
SEROUS ICHOROUS
SEROW JAGLA SERAU
SERPENT (ALSO SEE SNAKE) AHI
SEPS WORM ABOMA ADDER APEPI
ATHER OPHIS SIREN SNAKE TRAIN
CHITAL DIPSAS DRAGON GERARD
HYDRUS PYTHON APOPHIS PRESTER
SCYTALE JARARACA
(— **WORSHIPER**) NAASSENE
(**FEATHERED** —) GUCUMATZ
KUKULKAN
(**NORSE** —) GOIN
(**SACRED** —) AVANYU AWANYU
(**SKY** —) AHI
SERPENTINE SNAKY SPIRY OPHITE
SNAKISH BOWENITE METAXITE
SCROLLED

SERPENT STAR OPHIURAN
SERRANO PERCOID GITANEMUK
SERRATE SAWED ARGUTE RAFFLE
NOTCHED SERRIED
SERRATION SERRA DENTILE
SERUM WHEY FLUID BIOLOGIC
SERVANT BOY FAG KID MAN PUG
TAG AMAH BATA COOK DASI DAVY
HELP HIND JACK LUCE MATY MOZO
ALILA BAGOT BOOTS BOULT DAVUS
GILLY GROOM HAMAL MAMMY
SEWER SLAVE SOSIA SPEED USHER
ABDIEL ANDREW BATMAN BEARER
BILDAR BUTLER CHAKAR CLASHY
DORINE EWERER FEEDER FERASH
FLUNKY GILLIE GRUMIO HAIDUK
HARLOT KHAMAL MENIAL PAMELA
SIRCAR SLAVEY TEABOY TEAGUE
TRANIO VARLET VASSAL VOIDER
ANCILLA BOOTBOY BOUCHAL
COURIER DUFTERY FAMULUS
FEODARY FERRASH FLUNKEY
FOOTMAN GENERAL GHILLIE
MALCHUS PANDOUR PANTLER
PAPELON PIQUEUR PISANIO
WASHPOT ASSIGNEE CHAPRASI
CROMWELL DOMESTIC FOLLOWER
GRASSCUT HENCHMAN HOUSEBOY
MANCIPLE MINISTER OUTRIDER
PANTHINO PHILOTUS PINDARUS
SERGEANT SERVITOR STANDARD
TRENCHER VADELECT WARDMAID
KITCHENER
(— **IN CHARGE OF BREAD**) PANTLER
(— **IN CHARGE OF DAIRY**) DEY
(— **IN OFFICE**) DUFTERY
(— **OF SCHOLAR OR MAGICIAN**)
FAMULUS
(— **WHO CARVES**) TRENCHER
(— **WHO CLEARS TABLE**) VOIDER
(— **WHO RUNS BEFORE CARRIAGE**)
PIQUEUR
(— **WHO SERVES TABLE**) SEWER
(**ARMED** —) PANDOUR
(**ARMY** —) BATMAN LASCAR
(**BENGAL** —) MEHTAR SIRCAR
(**BODY** —) VALET SIRDAR
(**BOY** —) BOY KNAVE CHOKRA
BOUCHAL
(**CAMP** —) BILDAR
(**CLOWNISH** —) SPEED LAUNCE
(**COLLEGE** —) GYP SKIP SCOUT
(**FEMALE** —) AMA NAN AMAH DASI
GIRL LASS MAID MAMMY NURSE
WENCH PAMELA SKIVVY ANCILLA
HANDMAID MUCHACHA WARDMAID
(**GENERAL** —) FACTOTUM
(**HEAD** —) BUTLER TINDAL
(**HIGH PRIEST'S** —) MALCHUS
(**HINDU** —) DAS DASI
(**HOUSE** —) COOK HEWE SEWER
DOMESTIC MATRANEE SCULLION
(**KITCHEN** —) COOK WASHPOT
(**LORD OR KING'S** —) THANE
(**LYING** —) FAG
(**MAID** —) NAN BONNE
(**MAN** —) BOY JACK MOZO SWAIN
VALET ANDREW GILLIE KNIGHT

GHILLIE KHANSAMA MUCHACHO
SERVITOR
(**MISCHIEVOUS** —) TEAGUE
(**PETULANT** —) DORINE
(**PHILIPPINE** —) BATA ALILA
(**SCOTTISH** —) JURR
(**SOLDIER'S** —) PAGE
(**TRUSTY** —) TROUT
(PL.) FOLK VOLK STAFF FAMILIA
NETHINIM
SERVE DO KA ACT AID HOP GIVE
HELP LEAP SHEW SLAP STAY TEND
TOSS WAIT COVER FRAME HORSE
SARRA STAND ANSWER ASSIST
FRIEND INTEND SAIRVE SARROW
SETTLE SPREAD SUCCOR ADVANCE
ASSERVE BESTEAD CONVENT
FORWARD FURTHER SERVICE
FUNCTION
(— **A DISH**) MESS
(— **AS ESCORT**) SQUIRE
(— **AS HOST**) GIVE
(— **AS SUBSTITUTE**) PASS
(— **AS WELL AS**) AVAIL
(— **DRINK**) SKINK
(— **FOOD**) HASH KITCHEN
(— **FOR PASTURE**) GRAZE
(— **OBSEQUIOUSLY**) LACKEY
LACQUEY
SERVER SALVER ACOLYTE MINISTER
SERVICE AID FEE CENS DUTY HELP
RITE TIDE YOKE FAVOR MUSAF
STEAD DEVOIR EMPLOY ERRAND
FACTOR OFFICE YIZKOR BENEFIT
BONDAGE CHAKARI CORNAGE
FUNERAL LITURGY OBSEQUY
RETINUE SERVAGE SERVING
BREEDING EQUIPAGE FUNCTION
HEADWARD KINDNESS MINISTRY
ROUNDING SERVITUM TENDANCE
(**ASSIGNED** —) MYSTERY
(**BODYGUARD** —) INWARD
(**BREAKFAST** —) DEJEUNER
(**CHORAL** —) MATIN
(**CHURCH** —) LAUDS CHAPEL
CHURCH HEARING STATION SYNAXIS
EVENSONG
(**COFFEE** —) CABARET
(**COMPULSORY** —) ANGARIA
(**DOMESTIC** —) CHAKARI
(**FEUDAL** —) BOON AVERA SEAWARD
HEADWARD
(**MILITARY** —) ARMS CAMP DUTY
ESCUAGE
(**MILITIA** —) COMMANDO
(**RELIGIOUS** —) AHA SEDER
COMMON
(**SECRET** —) OGPU
(**TENNIS** —) ACE LET
SERVICEABLE USEFUL DURABLE
THRIFTY FRIENDLY VAILABLE
SERVICE TREE SORB SORBUS
CHECKER
SERVILE BASE BOND ABJECT
MENIAL SUPINE VASSAL CAITIFF
SLAVISH VERNILE COISTREL
CRAWLING CRINGING SERVIENT
THEWLIKE
SERVILITY CRINGE

SERVING OBED SMACK DISHFUL
HELPING SERVIENT WHIPPING
SERVITOR FAG GROOM PUNTER
SERVANT PUNTSMAN
SERVITUDE USE VIA YOKE BONDAGE
SERVICE SLAVERY SERVITUS
THEOWDOM THIRLAGE
SERVOMECHANISM SERVO
BOOSTER
SERVOMOTOR RELAY SERVO
SESAME TIL TEEL BENNE BENNI
SEMSEM VANGLO OILSEED
WANGALA AJONJOLI BENISEED
SERGELIM
SESBANIA AGATI
SESQUITERPENE CEDROL CLOVENE
COPAENE HUMULENE
SESSION DAY BOUT DIET HOUR
SEAT COURT CLINIC SCHOOL
SEANCE ACUERDO HEARING
SEMINAR SITTING CONGRESS
SEDERUNT SEMESTER
(JAM —) CLAMBAKE
(PL.) ASSIZES
SESTERTIUS BRONZE
SESTINA SEXTAIN
SET DO DIP FIX GEL KIT LAY MOB
PUT SIC SIT SOT CASE CREW CUBE
GAGE GANG GIVE JELL KNIT KNOT
NEST PAIR PICK PILT POSE REST
SETT SORT STEP STOW BATCH
CLASS CLOCK CROWD FIXED GAUGE
GLADE GROUP INFIX PAVER PLACE
POSIT STACK STAID STAND STEAD
STEEK STICK SUITE ADJUST CIRCLE
DEFINE FASTEN FINALE FORMAL
GLAZED GROUND HARDEN IMPOSE
SERIES SETTLE SPREAD SQUARE
STATED BATTERY COMPANY
COMPOSE CONFIRM COTERIE
DEPOSIT DISPOSE ENCHASE
FACTION IMPLANT INSTATE
PLATOON SERVICE STATION
STIFFEN STRATUM EQUIPAGE
PANTALON SEQUENCE SOLIDIFY
STANDARD
(— A PERIOD) DATE
(— A PRICE) ASK
(— ABOUT) FALL FANG GANG BEGIN
ADDRESS
(— AFLOAT) LAUNCH
(— APART) SHED DESIGN DEVOTE
EXEMPT SACRED SEPONE SEPOSE
APPOINT ISOLATE RESERVE
ALLOCATE DEDICATE INSULATE
SEPARATE
(— ARROWS IN ORDER) FRUSH
(— AS ONE'S SHARE) ALLOT
(— ASIDE) BAR DISH DROP HAIN
SIDE SINK SLIP BURKE KAPUT
SEPOSE BRACKET EARMARK
PURLOIN RESERVE SUSPEND
ABROGATE DISPENSE OVERRIDE
OVERRULE REVERSED
(— AT DEFIANCE) BEARD
(— AT LIBERTY) FREE RELEASE
LIBERATE
(— BACK TO BACK) ADDORSED
ADDOSSED

(— CLOSE TOGETHER) PAVEED
(— DOG ON) SIC SLATE
(— DOWN UNDER NAME) TITLE
(— DOWN) JOT LAY GIVE LAND
SCORE EXPONE DEPOSIT
(— EDGEWISE) SURBED
(— ERECT) COCK
(— FIRMLY) FIRM STEM PLANT
POSIT
(— FORTH) DRAW ETCH SHOW
GIVEN STATE DEPART EXPOSE
SPREAD ARTICLE DISPLAY ENOUNCE
EXHIBIT EXPOUND PRESENT
PROPONE PROPOSE PURPOSE
PROPOUND
(— FORWARD) PREFER ADVANCE
(— FREE) BAIL EASE REMIT SKILL
SOLVE ACQUIT ASSOIL ABSOLVE
DELIVER ENLARGE UNLOOSE
WINFREE DISPLACE DISSOLVE
EXPEDITE UNVASSAL
(— GOING) INITIATE
(— IN EARTH) STRIKE
(— IN FROM MARGINS) INDENT
(— IN MOTION) SOW
(— IN OPERATION) DRIVE
(— IN OPPOSITION) PIT
(— IN ORDER) ARRAY FRUSH
ADIGHT DAIKER FETTLE INFORM
ADDRESS
(— INTO A GROOVE) DADO
(— INTO) INLAY
(— LIMITS TO) SPAN BOUND
(— OF 3 ANIMALS) LEASH
(— OF ACTORS) CAST
(— OF ARMS) CONVEYER
(— OF BARS) CONCAVE
(— OF BELLS) RING CHIME
CARILLON
(— OF BOOKS) PLENARY
(— OF CARS) DRAG
(— OF CHIMES) DOORBELL
(— OF CIRCUMSTANCES) CASE EGIS
FRAME
(— OF CORDS) SIMPLE
(— OF DISHES) GARNISH SERVICE
CUPBOARD
(— OF EIGHT) OGDOAD
(— OF EXERCISES) KATA
(— OF FACTS) BOOK
(— OF FISH NETS) DRIFT
(— OF FOLDED SHEETS) QUIRE
(— OF FOUR) WARP
(— OF FURNITURE) SUITE DINETTE
(— OF GARMENTS) SUIT
(— OF GEARS) GEARSET
(— OF HIDES) KIP
(— OF HOUNDS) VANLAY VAUNTLAY
(— OF IDEAS) SYSTEM
(— OF JEWELLED ORNAMENTS)
PARURE
(— OF LEAVES) COROLLA
(— OF LETTERS) ALPHABET
(— OF MUSICAL INSTRUMENTS)
CONSORT
(— OF OPINIONS) CREDO
(— OF ORGAN PIPES) STOP
(— OF PINS) KAILS KNOCKOUT
(— OF POINTS) INTERVAL

(— OF PUMPS) LIFT
(— OF QUADRILLES) LANCERS
(— OF RADIATORS) STACK
(— OF ROOMS) STORY
(— OF RULES) CODE EQUITY
DECALOG
(— OF SAILS) CANVAS
(— OF SHELVES) STAGE BUFFET
DRESSER WHATNOT
(— OF SKI FASTENINGS) BINDING
(— OF STAVES) SHOOK
(— OF STEPS) LADDER
(— OF SYMBOLS) KATAKANA
(— OF TABLES) COMPUTUS
(— OF TEETH) DENTURE
(— OF TEN) DECADE
(— OF THREE) BALE
(— OF TOOLS) STRING
(— OF TRAMS) JOURNEY
(— OF TYPEFACES) FAMILY
(— OF VALUES) CURRENCY
(— OF VATS) SOLERA
(— OF VERSES) STAVE
(— OF VOWELS) SERIES
(— OF WARP THREADS) LEA
(— OFF TO ADVANTAGE) ADORN
COMMEND
(— OFF) FOIL SEVER SHOOT
ACCENT BUNDLE BALANCE
EMBLAZE CONTRAST DECORATE
EMBLAZON
(— ON END) UPEND
(— ON FIRE) SPIT TIND LIGHT
ACCEND IGNIFY IGNITE KINDLE
ENFLAME INFLAME ENKINDLE
(— ONESELF) GO
(— OUT) FOUND SALLY START
INTEND STARTLE
(— OVER) COUCH
(— RIGHT) REDD ADJUST SCHOOL
SQUARE CORRECT REDRESS
(— SNARE) TAIL TILL
(— SOLIDLY) EMBED
(— STRAIGHT) DRESS
(— THICKLY) STUD
(— TO MUSIC) AIR DITTY
(— TRAP) TELD
(— TYPE) KEYBOARD
(— UP IN COLUMNS) TABULAR
(— UP) AREAR ERECT RAISE
INSTALL UPDRESS ACTIVATE
(— UPON) BESET ATTACK AGGRESS
BROWDEN
(— UPRIGHT) ERECT STAND
(— VALUE) APPRAISE
(— WITH BRISTLES) STRIGOSE
(— WITH GEMS) CHASE
(ANTIGEN —) SEROTYPE
(BECOME —) STRIKE
(CHESS —) MEINY MEINIE
(CHROMOSOME —) GENOME
COMPLEX
(COMPLETE —) STAND
(INFINITE —) FAMILY
(MINIATURE —) DIORAMA
(RADIO —) BLOOPER
(SMART —) TON
(STAGE —) SCENE

(UNALTERABLY —) STOUT
(PL.) DECOR
SETA STALK WHISK CHAETA SETULA
SETULE CROTCHET PODETIUM
SETBACK DASH JOLT KNOCK LURCH
BACKSET LICKING PUTBACK
BUSINESS COMEDOWN HAYMAKER
SETLINE GEAR TRAWL BULTOW
OUTLINE TROTLINE
SETTEE SETTLE WINDSOR
SETTER SOFA GUNDOG DROPPER
FLUSHER SETTLER
SETTERWORT PIGROOTS
SETTING SET FALL PAVE CHASE
MIDST SETUP CHATON MILIEU
FERMAIL MONTURE SITTING
INTERIOR MARQUISE MOUNTING
SHOWCASE
(— APART) BETWEEN
(— FREE) SOLUTION
(— OF GEM) FOIL OUCH CHASE
GALLERY
(— OF REED) CAAMING
(— OF WHEELS) CAMBER
(CAMERA —) BULB
(FAMILIAR —) HOME
(MUSICAL —) CREDO BALLAD
BALLADE
(SHUTTER —) TIME
(STAGE —) SCENE
SETTLE BED FIT FIX PAY SAG SET
SIT TAX BANK BIND CALM DAIS
DEAS FAST FIRM HAFT LEND NEST
REST ROOT SEAT SINK SNUG TOIT
AGREE CLEAR COUCH ISSUE LIGHT
LODGE ORDER PITCH PLACE PLANT
QUIET SQUAT STATE STILL ADJUST
ASSIGN CLINCH DECIDE DECREE
ENCAMP LOCATE NESTLE PURIFY
RESIDE SCREEN SECURE SOOTHE
SOPITE SQUARE ACCOUNT APPEASE
APPOINT ARRANGE BALANCE
CLARIFY COMPONE COMPOSE
CONCERT CONFIRM DEPOSIT
DERAIGN INHABIT RESOLVE SUBSIDE
COLONIZE REGULATE SQUATTLE
(— AMICABLY) COMPOUND
(— DOWN) CAMP SLUMP STEADY
DESCEND
(— ITSELF) INVEST
(— LANDS ON A PERSON) ENTAIL
(— ON) POINT
(— UPON) AFFIX AGREE TIGHT
(— VERTICALLY) SQUASH
SETTLED SAD SET FIRM FIXED QUIET
STAID FORMED RANGED SEATED
SEDATE SQUARE STAPLE STATED
CERTAIN DECIDED EMPIGHT
STATARY DECOROUS RESOLVED
STANDING
(NOT —) FARROW
SETTLEMENT AUL DEAL FINE FORK
POST BARRIO COLONY DIKTAT
MOSHAV WINDUP ACCOUNT
BIVOUAC FINANCE MAABARA
OUTPOST STATION CLERUCHY
DECISION DISPATCH JOINTURE
KEVUTZAH PRESIDIO SETTLING
SHOWDOWN TOWNSHIP

(— OF MONKS) SCETE SKETE
(COLLECTIVE —) KVUTZA KIBBUTZ
(MARRIAGE —) MAHR ARRAS
DOWNSET
(NEW ZEALAND —) PA PAH
(RAPID —) BOOM
SETTLER METIC SAHIB LIVYER
NESTER GRUELER PEOPLER
PILGRIM PIONEER TRIMMER
FINISHER GACHUPIN HABITANT
SHAGROON SIBERSKI SIBERYAK
(— IN AUSTRALIA) GROPER
SETTLING SIT
(— OF ESTATE) ENTAIL
(PL.) LEES SEDIMENT
SET-TO BOUT TURN PLUCK FETTLE
TURNUP BRANGLE
SETUP SET SITTER
SEVEN SEPT ZETA ZAYIN HEPTAD
SEPTET HEBDOMAD SEPTETTE
(— OF DIAMONDS) POPE
(— OF TRUMPS) MANILLA
(GROUP OF —) PLEIAD
SEVENFOLD SEPTUPLE
SEVEN-UP SLEDGE
SEVER AX AXE CUT BITE DEAL HACK
REND SLIT TWIN SHEAR SHRED
CLEAVE DEPART DETACH DIVIDE
SUNDER DISALLY DISCERP DISCIDE
DISJOIN OUTRIVE DISSEVER
PRESCIND SEPARATE SEVERIZE
SEVERAL ODD TEN SERE WHEEN
DIVERS SUNDRY DIVERSE VARIOUS
DISTINCT MULTIPLE
SEVERALLY APIECE SEVERAL
SEVERANCE SUNDER SOLUTION
(— OF RELATIONSHIPS) AIR
SEVERE BAD DRY ACID BLUE DEAR
DOUR DURE FIRM HARD IRON KEEN
ROID RUDE SALT SIDE SORE TART
TAUT ACUTE BREME CRUEL EAGER
GRUFF HARSH RETHE RIGID ROUGH
SHARP SMART SNELL SOBER
SOUND STARK STEER STERN STIFF
STOUR BITING BITTER BRUTAL
CHASTE COARSE FROSTY HETTER
SIMPLE SOLEMN STRICT TORVID
UNKIND UNMILD ACERBIC ASCETIC
AUSTERE CHRONIC CONDIGN
CRUCIAL CUTTING DRASTIC
SERIOUS SPARTAN TORVOUS
UNCANNY VIOLENT WEIGHTY
ACULEATE EXACTING GRIEVOUS
GRINDING HORRIBLE IRONCLAD
IRONHARD RIGOROUS SCATHING
STALWART STRAIGHT
(MOST —) EXTREME
SEVERELY BAD HARD BADLY STARK
STIFF HARDLY SORELY STRONG
HEAVILY ROUGHLY SMARTLY
SOUNDLY STITHLY SHREWDLY
SEVERIAN AGNOETE AGNOITE
SEVERITY FROST RIGOR CRUELTY
TORVITY TYRANNY ACRIMONY
ASPERITY FERVENCY HARDNESS
RIGIDITY SORENESS VIOLENCE
SEW SUE FELL SEAM SLIP PREEN
STEEK NEEDLE STITCH OVERSEW
THIMBLE OVERHAND

(— A CORPSE) SOCK
(— LOOSELY) BASTE
(— TO REINFORCE) BAR
(— WAVED PATTERN) DICE
SEWAGE SOIL WASTE SOILAGE
SULLAGE AFFLUENT DRAINAGE
SEWERAGE
SEWELLEL BEAVER BOOMER
SEWER SINK SIRE DRAFT DRAIN
FLEET ISSUE MAKER SHORE
CLOACA KILTER TACKER VENNEL
BELTMAN COPYIST CULVERT
DRAUGHT GULLION JAWHOLE
SHIRRER PIQUIERE
SEWING TACK SUTURE SEMPSTRY
SEX KIND SECT GENDER
(FEMALE —) SMOCK
(MALE —) WEPMANKIN
SEXLESS NEUTER EPICENE
SEXT MIDDAY
SEXTET SESTET SEXTUOR SESTETTO
SEXTON SAXON SHAMUS WARDEN
SACRIST SHAMASH VESTURER
SEXTUPLE SENARY
SEXTUPLET SESTOLE SEXTOLE
SESTOLET SEXTOLET
SEXUAL GAMIC INTIMATE
SEXY FREUDIAN
SHA YASHIRO
SHAB RUBBERS
SHABBINESS WAFFNESS
SHABBY BASE MEAN POKY WORN
DINGY DOWDY MANGY RATTY
SCALD SEEDY TACKY CHEESY
FROWZY GRUBBY SCABBY SCOFFY
SCOURY SCURVY SHODDY SHROVY
SLEAZY TAGRAG BUNTING MESQUIN
SCALLED SCRUBBY SCRUFFY
SCUFFED SHABBED SQUALID
PALTERLY SLIPSHOD WAFFLIKE
SHACK COE HUT CRIB SHAG HUMPY
HUTCH SHANTY
SHACKLE COP TIE BAND BIND BOLT
BOND GYVE LOCK STAY BASIL
BILBO CLAMP COPSE CRAMP CRANK
HUMPY TRASH TRAVE FETTER
GARTER HAMPER PINION SHANGY
STAYER SWATHE COTTAGE
COUPLER FETLOCK MANACLE
PASTERN SNACKLE TRAMMEL
RESTRAIN
(PL.) IRONS
SHACKLER SLOTTER
SHAD BUCK CHAD ALLIS ALOSE
TRABU ALLICE TWAITE ALEWIFE
ANADROM CLUPEID FLATFISH
SAWBELLY
SHADBUSH DOGWOOD SERVICE
SHADDOCK LUCBAN POMELO
POMPION
SHADE EYE CAST DULL SCUG SHED
TONE VEIL BLEND COLOR ENNUE
GHOST GLIDE GLOOM GRAIN SCAUM
SWALE SWILL TASTE TINCT TINGE
TRACE UMBER UMBRA DEGREE
FRESCO SHADOW SHIELD SHROUD
SPRITE STRAIN STRIPE TONING
CURTAIN ECLIPSE GRADATE
HACHURE PROTECT SECTION

SHADING UMBRAGE HALFTONE
UMBRELLA
(— OF COLOR) EYE TONE
(— OF DIFFERENCE) NUANCE
(— OFF) GRADUATE
(EYE —) UGLY
(OVERHANGING —) CANOPY
(WINDOW —) STORE
SHADED OMBRE SHADY DRUMLY
SOMBER SOMBRE DARKLING
SHADINESS GLOOM
SHADING FLUTING LAYERING
SHADOW FOX BLOT SCUG TAIL
CLOUD SHADE UMBER UMBRA
CLEEKS DARKEN FINGER SHROUD
TAILER ISOGYRE PHANTOM
SCARROW SUGGEST UMBRAGE
UMBRATE PENUMBRA PHANTASM
SHEPHERD
SHADOWED DARKLING
SHADOWINESS GLOOM
SHADOWLESS ASCIAN WHITEOUT
SHADOWY MISTY VAGUE GLOOMY
GHOSTLY OBSCURE
SHADRACH ANANIAS HANANIAH
SHADY DARK CLOUDY SHADOW
SHADOWY UMBROSE ADUMBRAL
SHAFT BAR NIB ROD BALK BOLT
DART FUST HOLE PILE POLE TRAM
WELL ARBOR HEUGH QUILL REACH
SCAPE SHANK SHOOT SNEAD
SPRAG STAFF STALE STAVE STEAL
STILT STING THILL TRUNK BOLTEL
CANNON COLUMN GNOMON SCAPUS
STAPLE TILLER UPRISE VAGINA
BOWTELL CHIMNEY INCLINE
MANDREL SPINDLE CAMSHAFT
DOWNCAST ESCONSON HOISTWAY
LAMPHOLE SHAFTWAY STANDARD
WEIGHBAR WELLHOLE
(— CONNECTING WHEELS) AXLE
(— IN GLACIER) MOULIN
(— IN WATCH) STEM
(— OF CANDLESTICK) BALUSTER
(— OF CARRIAGE) FILL SILL THILL
(— OF CART) ROD TRAM SHARP
STANG
(— OF CAVERN) DOME
(— OF CHARIOT) BEAM
(— OF CLUSTERED PIER) BOLTEL
(— OF COLUMN) FUST TIGE SCAPE
(— OF FEATHER) SCAPE SCAPUS
(— OF MINE) PIT WORK GRUFF
HEUCH HEUGH SLOPE GROOVE
STAPLE INCLINE WINNING
(— OF PADDLE) ROUND
(— OF SPEAR OR LANCE) TREE
STALE
(— OF WAGON) STAVE THILL
LIMBER
(HARNESS —) HEALD
(HOLLOW —) CANNON
(MAIN —) ARBOR
(ORNAMENTAL —) VERGE
(SCYTHE —) SNEAD
(STAIRWAY —) VICE
(TWISTED —) TORSO
(VENTILATION —) UPCAST UPTAKE
WINDHOLE

SHAG PILE
SHAGGY SHAG SWAG HARSH NAPPY
ROUGH SHOCK TATTY TOUSY
BRUSHY COMATE RAGGED TOOSIE
HIRSUTE SHAGRAG SQUALID
SWAGGED THRUMMY VILLOUS
TATTERED
SHAGREEN GALUCHAT
SHAGROON PILGRIM
SHAKE BOB DAD JAR JOG ROG WAG
JOLT JOWL PLUM QUAG RESE ROCK
SHOG STIR SWAY TOZE WEVE
WHAP WHOP HOTCH JAUNT KNOCK
NIDGE QUASH SHOCK SWING TRILL
DIDDER DITHER DODDER DODDLE
EXCUSS GOGGLE HOTTER HUSTLE
JOGGLE JOUNCE JUMBLE QUATCH
QUAVER QUITCH QUIVER ROGGLE
RUFFLE SHIMMY SHIVER TOTTER
WAMBLE WANGLE WARBLE WEAKEN
WOBBLE AGITATE BRANDLE
CHOUNCE CONCUSS SHUDDER
STAGGER SUCCUSS TREMBLE
TWITTER WHIFFLE WHITHER
BRANDISH CONVULSE ENFEEBLE
(— HERRING) SCUD
(— LIGHTLY) LIFT
(— OFF) ARISE EXCUSS
(— TO SEPARATE) HOTCH
(— UP) JABBLE JUMBLE RATTLE
(WIND —) ANEMOSIS
SHAKER DUSTER SIFTER DREDGER
JUMBLER POUNCET SANDBOX
SHAKING ASHAKE TREMOR JARRING
AGITATED
(— OF AIRPLANE) BUFFET
SHAKTI TARA PRAKRINI
SHAKTIS MATRIS
SHAKY CRANK DICKY QUAKY ROCKY
TOTTY WONKY WOOZY AGUISH
CRANKY GROGGY INFIRM WAMBLY
CASALTY DWAIBLE DWEEBLE
PALSIED RICKETY SHOGGLY
TITTUPY TOTTERY COGGLEDY
INSECURE
SHALE BAT BASS BONE CLOD FLAG
KOLM METAL PLATE XALLE KILLAS
SHILLET MUDSTONE SLIGGEEN
SHALL SE MAY MUN MUST SALL
(— NOT) SANNA SHANT SHANNA
SHALLOON CUBICA
SHALLOT CIBOL ALLIUM ESCHALOT
SCALLION
SHALLOW EBB BANK FLAN FLAT
FLUE GLIB FLEET INANE SHOAL
SILLY SMALL FLIMSY FROTHY
LITTLE RIFFLE SLIGHT UNDEEP
CRIPPLE CURSORY TRIVIAL
MAGAZINY
(PL.) FORD
SHALLOWNESS INANITY
SHAM BAM FOB FOX GIG FAKE HOAX
MOCK PUFF BLUFF BOGUS CHEAT
DUMMY FALSE FEIGN FRAUD LETON
QUEER ASSUME BRUMMY BUNYIP
CHOUSE DECEIT DUFFER HUMBUG
PSEUDO STUMER FALSITY FORGERY
GRIMACE MOCKISH PLASTER

PRETEND STUMOUR PRETENSE
SPURIOUS
SHAMAN PEAI CURER MACHI
KAHUNA WABENO ANGEKOK
TOHUNGA CONTRARY WITCHMAN
SHAMBLE SHALE SHOOL SCAMBLE
SHACHLE SHACKLE SKEMMEL
ABATTOIR SHAMMOCK
(PL.) BUTCHERY
SHAMBLING SHACKLY
SHAME SISS ABASH AIDOS SPITE
ASHAME BISMER REBUKE MORTIFY
SCANDAL SLANDER CONTEMPT
DISGRACE DISHONOR REPROACH
SHENDING VERGOYNE VITUPERY
(— BY CENSURE) TOUCH
SHAMEFACED SHY
SHAMEFACEDNESS PUDENCY
SHAMEFUL BASE FOUL MEAN
GROSS HONTOUS IGNOBLE
FLAGRANT IMPROPER INFAMOUS
SHAMELESS HARD BRASH ARRANT
BRAZEN BASHLESS BROWLESS
IMMODEST IMPUDENT
SHAMELESSNESS BRASS
SHAMPOO TRIPSIS
SHAMROCK SEAMROG SHAMROOT
SHANK BODY CRUS GAMB JAMB
TANG FENUR GAMBE CANNON
NIBBLE TARSUS KNUCKLE
(THREAD —) STEM
SHANNY BULLY
SHANTY BOIST HUMPY HUTCH
SHACK CHANTIER DOGHOUSE
SHAPE AX ADZ AXE CUT DIE HUE
ADZE BEAT BEND CAST COLE COPE
DRAW FACE FAIR FORM HACK MOLD
NICK BEVEL BLOCK BOAST BUILT
COLOR DRAPE DRESS FEIGN FORGE
FRAME GUISE HORSE JOLLY LATHE
MODEL MOULD SWAGE BROACH
CHISEL CUTOUT EFFORM FIGURE
FORMER FRAISE HAMMER JIGGER
SQUARE CHANNEL CONFORM
CONTOUR FASHION GESTALT
INCLINE PATTERN TONNEAU
CONTRIVE LIKENESS
(— BY HAMMERING) SMITH
(— DIAMOND) BRUTE
(— GARMENTS) BOARD
(— METAL) SWAGE EXTRUDE
(— OF BUST) TAILLE
(— OF ENVELOPE FLAP) KNIFE
(— ON POTTER'S WHEEL) THROW
(— ONE'S COURSE) ETTLE
(— RIGHTLY) FIT
(— ROUGHLY WITH CHISEL) BOAST
(— ROUGHLY) BOAST SCABBLE
SCAPPLE
(— STONE) BROACH SCABBLE
(CLAY —) FLOATER
(CONICAL —) BEEHIVE
(GEM —) BAGUET BAGUETTE
(GLOVE —) TRANK
(SPIRALLING —) SWIRL
(SURFACE —) GEOMETRY
(UNBLOCKED —) HOOD
SHAPED BUILT FITTED BLOCKED
FEATURED

(— **LIKE BEAN**) FABIFORM
(— **LIKE BOAT**) SCAPHOID
(— **LIKE BUCKLER**) SCUTATE
(— **LIKE CLUB**) CLAVATE CLUBBED
(— **LIKE CONE**) CONIFORM
(— **LIKE CUP**) SCYPHATE
(— **LIKE DOME**) DOMAL
(— **LIKE EAR**) AURIFORM
(— **LIKE HALBERD**) HASTATE
(— **LIKE HEART**) CORDATE
(— **LIKE HOOK**) ANKYROID
(— **LIKE KEEL**) CARINATE
(— **LIKE LEAF**) FOLIATE
(— **LIKE LENS**) LENTOID
(— **LIKE NEEDLE**) ACUATE
(— **LIKE RING**) ANNULAR
(— **LIKE ROD**) BACILLAR
(— **LIKE S**) SIGMATE
(— **LIKE SHIELD**) ASPIDATE
CLYPEATE
(— **LIKE SICKLE**) FALCULAR
(— **LIKE SPINDLE**) FUSOID
FUSIFORM
(— **LIKE SPUR**) CALCARINE
(— **LIKE STAR**) ASTROID
(— **LIKE STRAP**) LIGULATE
(— **LIKE SWORD**) GLADIATE
(— **LIKE THREAD**) FILIFORM
(— **LIKE WEDGE**) CUNEAL CUNEATE
(— **LIKE X**) SALTIRE
(— **WITH AX**) HEWN
SHAPELESS DUMPY DEFORM
DUMPTY INFORM FORMLESS
UNSHAPED
SHAPELINESS DELICACY
SHAPELY GENT TRIM CLEAN TIGHT
DECENT FORMAL GAINLY FORMFUL
SHAPABLE
SHAPING DESCENT
SHARD SCAUR SHERD SHRED
(PL.) PITCHER
SHARE CUT END LOT CANT DALE
DEAL DOLE HAND PART PLOT RENT
SCOT SNIP DIVVY ENTER PARTY
QUOTA RATIO SHEAR SHIFT SLICE
SNACK SNICK SNUCK SPLIT WHACK
COMMON COPART DEPART DIVIDE
FINGER IMPART RATION SHOVEL
PARTAGE PARTAKE PORTION
DIVIDEND DIVISION INTEREST
PURPARTY
(— **A BED**) BUNK
(— **EQUALLY**) HALVE
(— **OF EXPENSES**) LAW CLUB
(— **OF LAND**) DAIL DALE FREEDOM
(— **OF PROFIT**) LAY
(— **OF STOCK**) STOCK ACTION
(— **QUARTERS**) CHUM
(— **SECRETS**) CONFIDE
(**ALLOTED** —) DOLE
(**ANCESTRAL** —) PATTI
(**FULL** —) SKINFUL
(**GREATER** —) FECK
(**LEGAL** —) HAK
(**ONE'S** —) AFFERE
(**PROPORTIONAL** —) QUOTA
SHARECROPPER BYWONER
CROPPER
SHARED JOINT BETWEEN

SHARING (— **OF EXPENSE**) CLUB
(— **VICARIOUSLY**) ARMCHAIR
SHARK FOX GATA HAYE KULP MAKO
MANO TOPE GUMMY HOMER HOUND
LAMIA TIGER TOPER DAGGAR
GALEID PALOMA REQUIN WHALER
ACRODUS BONEDOG DOGFISH
FOXFISH HUNFYSH PLACOID
REQUIEM SLEEPER SOUPFIN
SQUALID SUNFISH TIBERON
TIGRONE TUBARON BULLHEAD
HYBODONT ROUSETTE SAILFISH
SEAHOUND SKAAMOOG SPEAREYE
SQUATINA THRASHER
(**YOUNG** —) CUB SHARKLET
SHARP DRY SHY ACID ACRE CUTE
EDGY FELL FINE GAIR GASH GLEG
GNIB HARD HIGH KEEN PERT SALT
TART ACERB ACRID ACUTE ALERT
BRASH BREME BRISK CRISP DOWNY
EAGER EDGED FALSE HARSH NEBBY
PEERY QUICK SMART SNELL SQUAB
STEEP STIFF VIVID YAULD ARGUTE
ASTUTE BITING BITTER BRIGHT
CRISPY DIESIS GLASSY JAGGED
PLUCKY SEVERE SHREWD SHRILL
SNELLY SNITHE STINGY TOOTHY
TWEAKY UNRIDE ANGULAR
AUSTERE BRITTLE CAUSTIC
CUTTING GINGERY PIQUANT
POINTED PUNGENT SHARPEN
SLICING SPINOUS VARMINT VIOLENT
HATCHETY INCISIVE POIGNANT
SHARP-EDGED CULTRATE
SHARPEN EDGE FILE FINE HONE
KEEN WHET BRISK FROST GRIND
POINT RAISE SHARP SLYPE STONE
STROP ACCENT AFFILE STROKE
ENHANCE QUICKEN SMARTEN
EXACUATE HEIGHTEN
SHARPENED ACUATE
SHARPENER SHARPER STROPPER
(**SCYTHE** —) RIP RIFLE
SHARPER GUE GYP BITE KITE ROOK
SKIN SNAP BITER CHEAT CROOK
GREEK ROGUE SHARK SHARP
BESTER COGGER NICKUM PICARO
ROOKER SHARPY BARNARD
CATATAN GAMBLER SHARKER
SPIELER BLACKLEG DECEIVER
PIGEONER SWINDLER
SHARPLY DAB SHARP SNACK ACIDLY
ROUNDLY SHEERLY SMARTLY
STEEPLY
SHARPNESS WIT EDGE SALT WHET
PLUCK ACRITY ACUITY ACIDITY
ACERBITY ACRIDITY ACRIMONY
EDGINESS PUNGENCY
SHARP-POINTED ACUATE
ACULEATE
SHARPSHOOTER VOLTIGEUR
SHARP-SIGHTED SIGHTY LYNCEAN
SHARP-TAILED GROUSE PINTAIL
SHARP-WITTED CANNY SNELL
SHREWD
SHASTRA PURANA SASTRA
(— **CLASS**) SRUTI
SHATTER BLOW DASH DICE BLAST
BREAK BURST CRASH CRAZE

CREEM FRUSH SMASH SMOKE SPLIT
WRECK SHIVER SPIDER BEGUILE
CHATTER CONVEIL EXPLODE
SMATTER TORPEDO DEMOLISH
DYNAMITE SPLINTER
(— **CLAY TARGET**) KILL
SHATTERED BROKEN BROOZLED
DODDERED
SHAVE BARB BITE DRAW PARE RAZE
GLACE GRAZE SKIVE SCHAWE
SCRAPE FLATTEN UPRIGHT
SHAVED POLLED SHAVEN
SHAVEN NOT NOTT PILLED
TONSURED
SHAVING SHAVE SHRED SPALE
SPELL RAMENT RAMENTUM
(PL.) COOM COOMB SCOBS
MOSLINGS
SHAWL MAUD LAMBA MANTA MANTO
NUBIA PATTU TOZIE AFGHAN
ANGORA KAMBAL PEPLOS PEPLUM
PEPLUS PUTTOO SERAPE TAPALO
TOILET ZEPHYR AMLIKAR PAISLEY
WHITTLE WRAPPER CASHMERE
EPIBLEMA SLENDANG TURNOVER
(**COARSE** —) KAMBAL
(**COTTON** —) FARDA
(**PLAID** —) MAUD
(**TASSELED** —) TALLITH
SHAWM WAIT SHALM BOMBARD
SCHALMEI
SHE A HE HEO HER SHU HAEC SCHO
SHEAF TIE BEAT BUNG GAIT GERB
OMER FLASH GAVEL GERBE GLEAN
BATTEN THRAVE HATTOCK
CAPSHEAF CORNBOLE
(— **LEVIED AS TAX**) CORNBOLE
(— **OF ARROWS**) FLASH
(— **OF FLAX OR HEMP**) BEAT BEET
GLEAN
(— **OF GRAIN**) GAIT GARB HOSE
GARBACE
(**LAST** — **OF CORN**) NECK
(**LAST** — **OF HARVEST**) KIRN
(**PROTECTING** —) HATTOCK
(**UNBOUND** —) REAP GAVEL
SHEAR COW CUT DOD LIP NOT CLIP
CROP NOTT TRIM BREAK FORCE
SHARE SHEER SHIRL SLIDE STRIP
FLEECE STRESS
SHEARABLE TONSILE
SHEARER SNAGGER
SHEARLING SHEARHOG
(PL.) ALPACA
SHEARS LEWIS SNIPS FORFEX
SHEARER SNOUTER SECATEUR
SHEARWATER HAG CREW COHOW
HAGDON HAGLET PETREL PUFFIN
SCRABE PIMLICO SCRABER SEABIRD
HACKBOLT
SHEATFISH WELS DORAD WALLER
CATFISH SILURID
SHEATH COT HOT BOOT CASE CYST
HOSE HOTT ARMOR CHAPE FOREL
GAINE SHADE SHEAF SPILL THECA
CONDOM FORREL MYELIN OCHREA
QUIVER SLOUGH VAGINA AXILEMMA
EPILEMMA SCABBARD STANDARD
VAGINULA

(— **FOR BOOK**) FOREL FORRIL
(— **FOR FINGER**) STALL
(— **FOR GAMECOCK'S SPUR**) HOT HOTT
(— **OF CIGARETTE**) SPILL
(— **OF PLOW**) STANDARD
(**MEDULLARY** —) CORONA
SHEATHBILL PADDY
SHEATHE CLAD COPPER MUZZLE IMPLATE
SHEATHING SKIN ARMOR COPPER FACING SHEATH INLAYER SHIPLAP SLITWORK
SHEA TREE KARITE KARITI
SHEAVE SHEAF SHIVER HATTOCK TRUCKLE
(**24** —**S OF GRAIN**) THRAVE THREAVE
SHED BOX CUB SOW ABRI CAST COTE DROP HELM HULL KILN MOLT POUR SHUD SKEO SLIP HIELD HOVEL MOULT SCALE SHADE SPILL THROW VINEA ZAYAT BELFRY BROACH DINGLE EFFUSE GARAGE HANGAR HEMMEL INFUSE LINHAY MISTAL PANDAL SLOUGH COTTAGE DIFFUSE DISCARD MUSCULE RADIATE SKIPPER EXUVIATE SKEELING SKILLION WOODSHED
(— **BLOOD**) BROACH
(— **DROPS**) DRIZZLE
(— **FEATHERS OR HORNS**) MEW
(— **FOR LIVESTOCK**) SHIPPEN
(— **FOR SHEEP**) SHEALING
(— **OVER MINE SHAFT**) COE
(— **TEARS**) GIVE
(— **TO PROTECT SOLDIERS**) TESTUDO
(**CATTLE** —) CUB HELM LAIR BELFRY
(**MOVABLE** —) SOW BAIL MUSCULE
(**TEMPORARY** —) PANDAL
(**WEATHER** —) DINGLE
SHEDDING FALL SPILTH ECDYSIS APOLYSIS
SHE-DEMON LAMIA
SHEEN GLAZE SHINE LUSTER LUSTRE SHIMMER
SHEEP SNA TEG DOWN LAMB LONK MUGS SHIP SOAY URIN ZENU ANCON BOVID DUMBA HEDER HUNIA MUGGS OVINE SAIGA SHORN TAGGE AOUDAD ARGALI BARHAL BHARAL BIDENT CHURRO DECCAN DORPER DORSET EXMOOR HIRSEL MARKER MASHAM MERINO MUTTON NAYAUR OXFORD PANAMA PAULER ROMNEY WETHER WOOLIE WOOLLY BIGHORN BLEATER BRAXIES CHEVIOT CRIOLLA DELAINE DISHLEY FREEZER FRONTER JUMBUCK KARAKUL LINCOLN POLLARD SUFFOLK TARGHEE TWINTER VERMONT BIKANERI COMEBACK COTSWOLD DARTMOOR HERDWICK LONGWOOL LUGHDOAN RUMINANT SHEARHOG SHEARING TALLOWER THRINTER
(— **DIFFICULT TO HANDLE**) COBBLER

(— **IN 2ND YEAR**) HOB TAG TEG TAGGE TWINTER
(— **THAT HAS SHED PORTION OF WOOL**) ROSELLA
(— **TO BE SHEARED**) BOARD
(**3-YEAR-OLD** —) THRINTER
(**DEAD** —) BRAXY
(**FEMALE** —) EWE GIMMER SHEDER
(**HORNLESS** —) NOT NOTT
(**LOST** —) WAIF
(**MALE** —) RAM TUP BUCK HEDER
(**MOUNTAIN** —) IBEX
(**OLD** —) GUMMER
(**THICK-WOOLED** —) MUG
(**UNSHORN** —) HOG TEG
(**WILD** —) SHA ARGAL RASSE URIAL AOUDAD ARGALI BHARAL SHAPOO BURRHEL MOUFLON
(**YOUNG** —) HOG HOGG HOGGEREL
SHEEPBERRY ALISIER VIBURNUM
SHEEPCOTE SHEPPEY
SHEEPDOG KELPIE SHELTY BOBTAIL MALINOIS SHETLAND
SHEEP FLY FAG
SHEEPFOLD REE FANK KRAAL REEVE STELL BOUGHT BARKARY SHEPPEY SHEEPCOT
SHEEPHERDER SNOOZER STOCKMAN
SHEEPISH SHY
SHEEP LAUREL IVY HEATH WICKY KALMIA LAUREL CALFKILL LAMBKILL
SHEEPLIKE OVINE
SHEEPMAN HOBBER
SHEEP PLANT RAOULIA
SHEEP ROT CAW
SHEEP RUN STATION
SHEEPSHEAD JAMES JEMMY JIMMY PARGO PORGY TAUTOG FATHEAD PERCOID SPAROID
SHEEPSHEARER GUN
SHEEPSKIN ROAN SLAT MOUTON SOLDIER CAPESKIN LAMBSKIN WOOLFELL WOOLSKIN
(— **TANNED WITH BARK**) BASAN BASIL
(— **THAT SWEATS UNEVENLY**) SOLDIER
(— **WITHOUT WOOL**) SLAT
(**ROUGH-TANNED** —) CRUST
SHEEP SORREL SOURWEED
SHEEP TICK FAG KEB KED KADE
SHEEPWALK SLAIT
SHEER BOLD FINE MAIN MERE PURE BLANK BRANT CRUDE FRANK STARK STEEP SIMPLE CLOTTED GAZETTE EVENDOWN
(**MADE OF** — **FABRIC**) PEEKABOO
SHEET FIN CARD FILM FINE FLAT FOIL LEAF SILL BLANK FLONG FOLIO NAPPE CANVAS CIRCLE DOUBLE FASCIA FENDER FLIMSY SHROUD SINDON BLANKET CHUDDER FLOGGER FRISKET LEAFLET PALLIUM PAPYRUS WRAPPER AIRSHEET EIGHTEEN FOLLOWER HANDBILL INTERLAY SHEETLET
(— **ADDED TO DEED**) FOLLOWER

(— **ATTACHED TO INVOICE**) APRON
(— **FOR BRIDGE SCORES**) FLOGGER
(— **OF CELLULOID**) CEL CELL
(— **OF CLOUDS**) PALLIUM
(— **OF DOUGH**) STRUDEL
(— **OF FIBER**) BAT LAP BATT
(— **OF ICE**) GLARE GLAZE
(— **OF IRON**) CRAMPET CRAMPIT
(— **OF LAVA**) COULEE
(— **OF LEAD**) SOAKER
(— **OF LEATHER**) BUFFING
(— **OF MICA**) FILM
(— **OF PAPER**) FLAT FOLIO FRISKET LEAFLET HANDBILL
(— **OF PARCHMENT**) SKIN FOLLOWER
(— **OF RUBBER**) DAM
(— **OF STRAW**) YELM
(— **OF SUGAR**) SLAB
(— **OF TISSUE**) FASCIA
(— **OF TOBACCO**) BINDER
(— **OF WATER**) NAPPE
(— **USED FOR MATRIX**) FLONG
(**HEATED** —) CAUL
(**METAL** —**S**) LATTENS
(**NEWS** —) GAZETTE
(**ORGANIZATION** —) BILL
(**PERFORATED** —) SIEVE
(**PROTECTIVE** —) CURTAIN
(**THEATRICAL** —) SIDE
(**THIN** —**S OF IRON**) DOUBLES
(**TRANSPARENT** —) GELATINE
(**WINDING** —) SINDON SUDARY
SHEETING DOMESTIC AMERIKANI
SHEKINAH GLORY
SHELDRAKE SHELDER BARGOOSE
SHELF BANK BERM BINK DECK DESS STEP TACK BENCH LEDGE SKELF STAGE STOOL MANTEL SCONCE SETTLE SHELVE BACKBAR BRACKET COUNTER PLATEAU CREDENCE CUPBOARD
(— **BEFORE STOVE**) HEARTH
(— **BEHIND ALTAR**) GRADINE GRADINO RETABLE
(— **IN MINE**) BUNNING
(— **OF ROCK**) CAR LENCH LENCHEON
(**ALTAR** —) BUTSUDAN
(**CONTINENTAL** —) PLATFORM
(**FIREWORKS** —) BALLOON
(**RAISED** —) SETTLE
SHELL ARD HUD PEN POD BAND CASK CHOU CONE HARD HOOF HULL HUSK MAIL OBUS PELL PILL PIPI PUPA SKIN SWAD UMBO UNIO BALAT CHANK CHINK CONCH COPIS CRUMP CRUST DRILL FRITZ GOURD MITER MITRA MUREX ORMER SCAUP SHALE SHARD SHEAL SHERD SHOCK SHUCK TESTA TIARA TROCA TURBO VALVE VENUS ANOMIA BUCKIE BULLET BURGAU CERION COCKLE CONKER COWRIE CRUSTA DENTAL DOLIUM ECLAIR JINGLE LORICA MAROON NOUGAT NUCULA PULLET PURPLE SANKHA SINGLE SLOUGH STROMB TERBRA TRITON TURBAN VANNET VENTER VOLUTE WINKLE

BALLOON CARACOL CARCASS
COCONUT DARIOLE DISCINA
GLADIUS LIMACEL MARINER
PAPBOAT PHILINE PROJECT
SCALLOP SPICULE SPINDLE
SPONDYL THIMBLE TOHEROA
TORPEDO TOXIFER TROCHID
TRUMPET UNICORN BACULITE
BACULOID CARAPACE CONCHITE
COQUILLE CYLINDER DUCKFOOT
EGGSHELL ENVELOPE ESCALLOP
FIGSHELL FOCALOID FRUSTULE
HELICINA MERINGUE OLIVELLA
PUPARIUM SEASHELL SOLARIUM
STROMBUS UNIVALVE VELUTINA
VERMETID VERMETUS WARRENER
WHIZBANG WOODCOCK
(— CONTAINING MEDICINE)
CAPSULE
(— OF DIATOM) FRUSTULE
(— OF OYSTER) HUSK SHUCK
(— OF SHIP) HULK SKIN
(— OF SLUG) LIMACEL
(— SYSTEMATICALLY) COMB
(—S FROM GUN) STUFF
(ANTIAIRCRAFT —) FLAK
(CARTRIDGE —S) BRASS
(CAST —S) EXUVIAE
(CUSTARD-FILLED —) ECLAIR
DARIOLE
(FOSSIL —) DOLITE AMMONITE
BACULITE BALANITE CONCHITE
(HOWITZER —) OBUS
(MATHEMATICAL —) HOMEOID
(OYSTER —S) CULCH CULTCH
(PASTRY —) CORNET DARIOLE
TIMBALE TALMOUSE
(SNAIL —) CONKER HODMADOD
(SPIRAL —) CHANK
(TORTOISE —) HOOF
(VEGETABLE —) DOLMA
SHELLED VINED
SHELLFISH COCK NACRE PIROT
LIMPET WIGGLE MOLLUSK PERIWIG
SHELLING RATTLES
SHELL-LESS OON
SHELL MONEY UHLLO WAKIKI
SHELTER CAB HUT LEE LOO ABRI
BURY EAVE GIDE GITE HERD HIDE
HIVE JOKE JOUK ROOF SCOG SCUG
BARTH BENAB BERRY BIELD BOIST
BOTHY BOWER CABIN CLEAD CLOAK
COVER EMBAY HAVEN HOARD
HOUSE HOVEL HOVER HOWFF
HUTCH LEWTH LITHE RESET SHADE
SHEAL ASYLUM AWNING BELFRY
BILBIE BOOLEY BOUGHT BURROW
COVERT CRADLE DEFEND DUGOUT
GABION GUNYAH HANGAR HARBOR
HOSTEL PANDAL REFUGE SCONCE
SCREEN SHADOW SHIELD SHROUD
SUKKAH BOROUGH CABINET
CARPORT CHAMBER DEFENSE
EMBOSOM EMBOWER HOUSING
NACELLE QUARTER RETREAT
ROOFING TABERNA UMBRAGE
WANIGAN WICKIUP BESCREEN
DOGHOUSE ENSCONCE LODGMENT
PALLIATE SECURITY SNOWSHED
WAYHOUSE

(— FOR CATTLE) HELM BOOLY
STELL HEMMEL
(— FOR CROP WATCHERS) KISI
(— FOR DANCES) ENRAMADA
(— FOR SENTRY) GUERITE
(— FROM WEATHER) LEWTH
(— OVER BEEHIVE) HOOD
(BULLETPROOF —) MANTLET
MANTELET
(CONCRETE-AND-STEEL —) PILLBOX
(CRAMPED —) HUTCH
(FISH —) CROY
(LEAFY —) LEVESEL
(MINING —) TALPA
(PORTABLE —) MANTA CABANA
(ROCK —) KRAPINA
(ROUGH —) JACAL
(TEEPEELIKE —) CHUM
(TEMPORARY —) HALE HOLD CABIN
BIVOUAC
SHELTERED LEE LEW LOWN BIELD
LITHE SHADY COVERT
(— SPACE) KILLOGIE
SHELTERING BIELDY SHADING
SHELTERLESS HOMELESS
ROOFLESS
SHELVE DISH BURKE SHELF
SHELVES STAGE ETAGERE
SHENG SANG CHENG SHING
(ONE-HUNDREDTH —) CHAO
SHEOL HELL
SHEPHERD HERD SHEP COLIN
CORIN GADDI GYGES SWAIN FEEDER
PASTOR TARBOX CORYDON
DAPHNIS DRAFTER GADARIA
KURUMBA THYRSIS TITYRIS
MELIBEUS MENALCAS PASTORAL
SHEEPMAN STREPHON
(GERMAN —) ALSATIAN
SHEPHERDESS DELIA MOPSA PHEBE
DORCAS BERGERE GALATEA
PASTORA PERDITA
SHEPHERD'S-PURSE TOYWORT
CASEWEED COCOWORT
SHERBET ICE GLACE SORBET
GRANITA SOUFFLE
SHERD SCARTH
SHERIFF FOUD FOWD SCULT XERIF
DEPUTY GRIEVE SCHOUT SHIRRA
BAILIFF SHREEVE SHRIEVE
ALGUACIL HUISSIER SHIREMAN
VISCOUNT
SHERRY FINO CLOVE JEREZ XERES
DOCTOR MANCHU SOLERA
OLOROSO RANGOON SHERRIS
MONTILLA
SHEVRI SESBAN
SHICER DUFFER
SHIELD ECU EGIS HIDE PELT AEGIS
APRON BIELD BOARD CLOAK COVER
FENCE GUARD GULAR MULGA
PATCH PAVIS PELTA PYGAL SCUTE
SHEND TARGE YELDE ANCILE
ANGARA BLAZON CASQUE DEFEND
FENDER GUNTUB GYROMA LINDEN
MENTAL OCULAR PAUNCH RONDEL
SCREEN SCUTUM SECURE TARGET
BUCKLER CLIPEUS CONCEAL
PANNIER PAVISSE PRIDWIN

PROTECT ROSTRAL ROTELLA
ROUNDEL SHELTER SUPPORT
TESTUDO CARTOUCH CUCULLUS
HIELAMEN INSULATE MARGINAL
PRESERVE RONDACHE STERNITE
SUNSHADE BREASTING
(— BELOW A DAM) APRON
(— FOR ARCHERS) PANNIER
(— FOR HORSE) BIB
(— FOR LAMP) BONNET CHIMNEY
(— OF A STIRRUP) HOOD
(— OF ABORIGINES) MULGA
HIELAMEN
(— OF CONTINENT) CORE
(— OF HIDE) SKILDFEL
(— OF SOMITE) STERNITE
(— OF TRILOBITE) CEPHALON
(— ON MAST) PAUNCH
(— ON THROAT OF FISH) GULAR
(— OVER BASE OF FAN) CANOPY
(BONY —) CARAPACE
(BULLETPROOF —) MANTA MANTLET
MANTELET
(HERALDIC —) BLAZON
(KING ARTHUR'S —) PRIWEN
PRIDWIN
(LEATHER —) CHAFE
(SACRED —) ANCILE
(SIBERIAN —) ANGARA
(WICKERWORK —) SCIATH
SHIELDBEARER SQUIRE ESQUIRE
PELTAST ESCUDERO SCUTIFER
SHIELD BUG STINKBUG
SHIELD FERN FERNGALE
SHIELDMAKER TYCHIOS
SHIELD-SHAPED PELTATE SCUTATE
THYROID
SHIFT JIB BACK CHOP FEND FLIT
HAUL MOVE RUSE SHIP TACK TOUR
TURN VARY VEER WEND BREAK
BUDGE CREEP CYMAR DRIFT HOTCH
QUIRK SHIRK SHUNT SIMAR SKIFT
SLIDE SMOCK SPELL TRICK BAFFLE
CHANGE DENIAL DEVICE DOUBLE
PALTER SKYFTE SWERVE SWITCH
CUTBACK EVASION FRESHEN
SHUFFLE SLEIGHT WHIFFLE
ARTIFICE DISLODGE DISPLACE
DOGWATCH DOUBLING MUTATION
REVIRADO TRANSFER TRAVERSE
TURNOVER WINDLASS
(— ABOUT AS THE WIND) LARGE
(— ABRUPTLY) JUMP
(— IN DANCING) BALANCE
(— IN TACKING) JIB
(— ORDER OF BELLS) HUNT
(— RAILROAD EQUIPMENT) DRILL
(— SUDDENLY) FLY CHOP GYBE
JIBE
(— WEIGHT) WING
(MINING —) CORE
SHIFTING FLUID QUICK CHOPPING
DRIFTING FLOATING SLIPPAGE
VARIABLE VEERABLE
SHIFTLESS DRIFTY SOZZLY
DRIFTING FECKLESS HAVELESS
SHIFTLESSNESS SLOUCH
SHIFTY GREASY DEVIOUS EVASIVE
HANGDOG SLIDING SLIPPERY

SHIITE SHIAH SECTARY SHAIKHI
TWELVER
SHILHA SHLU CHLEUH
SHILL STICK BONNET CAPPER
BOOSTER
SHILLING BOB HOG CHIP HOGG
LEVY DEENER HARPER TESTON
TEVISS THIRTEEN
(20 —S) POUND
(21 —S) GUINEA
(5 —S) CROWN DECUS
SHILLY-SHALLY BACK BOGGLE
SHIM GLUT LINER SHIMMER
SHIMMER FLASH GLIMMER SHIMPER
SKIMMER
SHIN SHANK SKINK SWARM CNEMIS
SHINNY
SHINDIG SHINDY SHIVOO
SHINE RAY SUN BEAM BUFF GLOW
LAMP LEAM LINK STAR BLARE
BLICK BLINK BLOOM EXCEL GLAIK
GLARE GLEAM GLEIT GLENT GLINT
GLISS GLORE GLORY GLOSS GLOZE
SHEEN SKYRE STARE BEACON
DAZZLE GLANCE LUSTER LUSTRE
SCANCE EFFULGE GLIMMER
GLISTEN GLITTER RADIATE REFLECT
SHIMMER SPARKLE RUTILATE
(— BRIGHTLY) BEEK FLAME LIGHT
(— FAINTLY) SCARROW
(— UPON) SUN SMITE
SHINER CHUB DACE BREAM REDFIN
CYPRINID WINDFISH
SHINER-UP PATCHER
SHINGLE SHIM BEACH SHAKE SLATE
CHESIL KNOBBLE STARTER
SHINGLER NOBBLER
SHINGLES ZONA ZOSTER
SHININESS GLARE GLAZE GLOSS
SHINING GLAD NEAT CLEAR GLARY
LIGHT LUCID SHEER WHITE ARDENT
ARGENT ASHINE BRIGHT FULGID
GLOSSY GOLDEN LUCENT NITENT
ORIENT SERENE SHEENY SPUNKY
STARRY ADAZZLE BURNING
FULGENT GLARING GLIMMER
LAMPING FLASHING GLEAMING
LUCULENT LUSTRANT LUSTROUS
NITIDOUS RELUCENT RUTILANT
SPLENDID STARLIKE SUNBEAMY
SUNSHINY
SHINLEAF PYROLA
SHINNY PEG SHINTY
SHINTO (— SECT) RYOBU
SHIP (ALSO SEE BOAT AND VESSEL)
ARK CAT COG HOY NAO BARK
BOAT BOOM GRAB HAND HULK
KEEL LADE NAVY PAHI PINE PINK
SAIL SEND SNOW TREE WOOD ZULU
CHECK LAKER OILER PINTA PRORE
RAZEE SCOUT SCREW SKIFF WHELP
ANDREW ARGOSY BARKEY BARQUE
BOTTOM CARTEL CASTLE CHASER
COALER CODMAN DECKER DIESEL
GALIOT GALLEY HOLCAD HOPPER
LANCHA LATEEN LORCHA MASTER
MISTIC MOTHER PACKET PUFFER
RUNNER SAILER SALVOR SEALER
SMOKER TONNER TRAVEL VESSEL

ADMIRAL CARRACK CLIPPER
COLLIER FACTORY FELUCCA
FOREIGN FRIGATE FRUITER
GABBARD GALLEON GUNBOAT
INVOICE MACHINE MULETTA
ONERARY PATAMAR PINNACE
POLACRE SHALLOP SHIPLET SPITKIT
STEAMER BALANDRA BALINGER
BILANDER CAPITANA DRUMBLER
FLAGSHIP GALLEASS GAYDIANG
INDIAMAN JAPANNER LANCHARA
MAGAZINE PESSONER PIPPINER
REPEATER SAILSHIP SCHOONER
SMUGGLER SPANIARD
(— BUILT FROM NAILS OF DEAD)
NAGLFAR
(— OF ARGONAUTS) ARGO
(— OF NORSEMEN) KEEL
(CLUMSY —) HULK
(DEPOT —) TENDER
(ESCORT —) CORVETTE
(FLEET OF —S) ARMADA
(JAPANESE —) MARU
(MALAY —) COUGNAR
(NOVA SCOTIAN —) BLUENOSE
(OBJECT SHAPED LIKE A —) NEF
(PIRATE —) GALLIVAT
(PRIZE —) CAPTURE
(QUARANTINE —) LAZARET
(RECEIVING —) GUARDO
(REMOTE-CONTROLLED —) DRONE
(SLOW —) BUCKET
(STORE —) FLUTER
(SUPPLY —) COPER COOPER
(UNTRIM —) BALLAHOO
(VIKING —) DRAKE
(PL.) NAVY MARINE SEACRAFT
SHIPPING
SHIPFITTER FITTER ERECTOR
SHIPMENT CARLOT RAILING
DISPATCH SHIPPAGE
SHIPSHAPE NEAT TIDY TRIM CIVIL
ATAUNT ORDERLY
SHIP SWEEPER TOPASS TOPIWALA
SHIPWAY BERTH
SHIPWORM ARTER BORER COBRA
TEREDO PILEWORM WOODWORM
SHIPWRECK WRACK NAUFRAGE
SHIPWRIGHT WAYMAN BUILDER
SHIRE DERBY SHEER COUNTY
SHIRK FUNK GOOF MIKE BLINK
BUDGE DODGE FEIGN FUDGE SKULK
SLACK RODNEY FINAGLE SHACKLE
SHAFFLE SOLDIER SHAMMOCK
SHIRKER FUNK PIKER FUNKER
ROTTER BLUDGER SLACKER
SLINKER SUGARER COBERGER
EMBUSQUE SCOWBANK
SHIRR SMOCK
SHIRT TOB JUPE SARK TOBE BLUEY
HAIRE JUPON KAMIS SHIFT BANIAN
BANIYA CAMISA CAMISE PALAKA
UNDERGO VAREUSE KAMLEIKA
(HAIR —) HAIRE CILICE
(SLEEVELESS —) FECKET
(WORKMAN'S —) FROCK
(WORNOUT —) DICKY
SHIRTING CHEVIOT HARVARD
HOLLAND SARKING

SHIRTWAIST BLOUSE GARIBALDI
SHITTIMWOOD BOXWOOD
SHIVAREE BELLING CHIVARI
HORNING SERENADE
SHIVER JAR GIRL GRUE BEVER
BREAK CHILL CREEM CREEP FRILL
GROWS QUAKE SHRUG SLICE
CHIVER DITHER DUDDER GROOSE
HOTTER NIDDER NITHER QUIVER
SHRIMP SPLINT CHITTER FLICKER
FRISSON SHATTER SHITHER
SHUDDER TREMBLE KAMLEIKA
SPLINTER
SHIVERING CHILL OURIE TREMOR
ASHIVER
SHOAL BAJO BANK FLAT REEF SPIT
BARRA DRAVE FLOTE SCULL SHELF
SCHOOL SHALLOW TOWHEAD
SHOAT GURRY SHOOT SHOTT
SHOCK COP JAR BLOW BUMP DINT
JOLT RACK SHOG STUN TURN
APPAL BRUNT GAVEL GLIFF GLOFF
SHAKE STOOK STOUR DISMAY
FRIGHT IMPACT JOSTLE JUMBLE
REJOLT RICKLE ROLLER STRIKE
ASTOUND CANVASS DISGUST
HATTOCK HORRIFY STAGGER
STARTLE STUPEFY TERRIFY
DISEDIFY GLIFFING SURPRISE
(— OF CORN) STOOK STOUT STITCH
(MENTAL —) TRAUMA
SHOCK ABSORBER SHOCK BUFFER
DASHPOT SNUBBER
SHOCKED AGHAST
SHOCKER RICKER STOOKER
SHOCKING GRIM AWFUL HORRID
UNHOLY BURNING FEARFUL
FEARING GHASTLY HIDEOUS
DREADFUL ENORMOUS HORRIBLE
SHOD CALCED
SHODDY SOFT CHEAP FOOTY SOFTS
SLEAZY
SHOE BAL CUE PAN BOOT BROG
CLOG DRAG FLAT HALF SKID SOCK
TURN BLAKE DERBY KLOMP MOYLE
ROMEO SABOT SCRAE SLING SPIKE
STOGA STOGY STRAP ANKLET
BEAKER BROGAN BROGUE BUSKIN
CALIGA CALIGO CHOPIN COBCAB
COCKER CRAKOW CREOLE DORSAY
GAITER GALOSH KILTIE MULLER
PATTEN PINSON POLISH SADDLE
SANDAL SECQUE BAUCHLE
BLUCHER CALCEUS CHOPINE
COWHIDE FLIPPER RULLION
SHOEPAC SLIPPER SNEAKER
BALMORAL BRODEKIN COLONIAL
PLIMSOLL SABOTINE SANDSHOE
SKEWBACK SLIPSLOP SOLLERET
(— FOR GRINDING) MULLER
(— FOR MULE) PLANCHE
(— IN TRUSS OR FRAME)
SKEWBACK
(— NOT FASTENED ON) PUMP
(— OF A SLEDGE) HOB
(— OF AN OX) CUE
(— OF COMIC ACTOR) BAXA
(— OF SUBWAY CAR) PAN
(— REPAIRER) JACKMAN

(— TO CHECK WHEEL) DRAG SKID
(— USED AS BRAKE) SKATE
(— WORN ON EITHER FOOT)
STRAIGHT
(—S AND STOCKINGS) FEET
(BABY'S —) CACK
(HOBNAILED —) TACKET
(LARGE —S) GUNBOATS
(LOW-CUT —) SOCK GILLY ANKLET
BUSKIN SLIPPER COLONIAL
(MILITARY —) CALIGA
(OLD —) BAUCHLE
(PIKED —) BEAKER
(RAWHIDE —) HIMMING
(SPORTS —S) GILLIES
(STEEL —) SOLLERET
(THIN —) PINSON SCLAFF
(WINGED —S) TALARIA
(WOODEN —) KLOMP SABOT
PATTEN RACKET RACQUET
(WORN —) SCRAE
(PL.) SHEEN SHOON SHUNE SCHONE
FOOTGEAR
SHOEMAKER SNOB FOXER SOLER
ARCHER CHAMAR CODGER COZIER
FUDGER GOUGER SOOTER SOUTER
VAMPER COBBLER CRISPIN
CROWNER SHOEMAN SNOBBER
UPPERER CORVISER SNOBSCAT
SHOEMAKING SNOBBING
SHOGUN TYCOON
SHOO HOOSH DISPEL
SHOOK PACK BLANK SHAKE
SHOOT DAG GUN IMP PAY POT PUT
ROD BANG BOLT BROD CANE CHIT
CION DRAW LEAF PLUG SLIP WEFT
BLAST BLAZE BROWN DRILL DRIVE
EXPEL FLUSH FROND GEMMA
GLEAM LANCE LAYER PLUFF SCION
SHEET SOBOL SPEAR SPRAY SPRIG
SPRIT SPURT SQUIB STICK STOOL
TUBER TURIO VIMEN BRANCH
FLIGHT FLOWER GERMEN GROWTH
HEADER HURTLE LAUNCH LEADER
OFFSET RATOON SALLOW SOBOLE
SPRING SPROUT STOLON STOVEN
STRIKE SUCKER TILLER TURION
BUDLING CHIMNEY DROPPER
SCOURGE SPIRING TENDRIL
TENDRON THALLUS ANAPHYTE
APOBLAST CATAPULT TRAILING
(— A MARBLE) LAG TAW KNUCKLE
(— A WHALE) STRIKE
(— ASIDE FROM MARK) DRIB
(— AT LONG RANGE) SNIPE
(— DOWN) SPLASH
(— DUCKS) SKAG
(— FORTH) JET GLEAM SPIRE
(— FROM DEER'S ANTLER) SPELLER
(— INDISCRIMINATELY) BROWN
(— MOOSE OR DEER) YARD
(— OF A TREE) STOW WHIP LANCE
BRANCH
(— OUT) JUT CHIT DART
(— SEAL) SWATCH
(— UP) SPIRE SPURT
(—S USED AS FODDER) BROWSE
(FIRST —S) BRAIRD
(FLEXIBLE —) BINE

(LATERAL —) ARM
(ORE —) BONANZA
(PAWNBROKER'S —) SPOUT
(SUGARCANE —) LALO
(TENDER —) FLUSH
(WILLOW —) SALLOW
SHOOTER SCOOT BLASTER
GUNSTER PLUFFER SHOTMAN
SKEETER
SHOOTING COCKING GUNNING
GUNPLAY HUNTING POTTING
SHOOTING STAR METEOR COWSLIP
SHOOTER PRIMWORT
SHOP CRIB TOKO BURSE STORE
KOSHER SHOPPE TIENDA WINKEL
ALMACEN APOTHEC BOTTEGA
CABARET MERCERY SPICERY
TABERNA TURNERY BOUTIQUE
COOKSHOP CREMERIE EMPORIUM
ESPRESSO EXCHANGE MAGAZINE
SHOWSHOP SLOPSHOP TENDEJON
WAREROOM
(BARBER —) BARBERY
(BLACKSMITH —) SMITHY
(LIQUOR —) SALOON
(OLD CLOTHES —) FLIPPERY
(PAWNBROKER'S —) LUMBER
SPROUT
(REPAIR —) GARAGE
(SUTLER'S —) CANTEEN
SHOPKEEPER CIT ARAB BAKAL
CHETTY SOUDAGUR
SHOPLIFT BOOST
SHOPLIFTER BOOSTER
SHORE GIB TOM BANK RIPE RIVE
SAND SIDE BEACH BENCH CLIFF
COAST RAKER RANCE SHOAR
WARTH RIVAGE STRAND BUTTRESS
DOCKSIDE LANDFALL LANDSIDE
SEACOAST
SHOREBIRD TATTLER WRYBILL
SURFBIRD
SHORE CRAB OCHIDORE
SHOREFISH OPALEYE
SHORER BRACER CRIBBER
SHORN NOT NOTT POLLED
TONSURED
SHORT AIM LAG LOW SHY BAIN
CURT NEAR NIGH SOON BLUFF
BRIEF BUNTY CLOSE CRISP CUTTY
FUBBY FUBSY PUNCH SQUAB
UNDER CRISPY SCARCE STUGGY
STUNTY SUDDEN ULLAGE BOBTAIL
BRUSQUE CURTATE LACONIC
SQUIDGY STUBBED SUMMARY
SNAPPISH SUCCINCT
(— AND FLAT) CAMUS
(— AND THICK) CHUNKY STOCKY
STUBBY STUMPY TRUNCH
TRUNCHED
(— AND THICKSET) NUGGETY
(— AS OF WOOL) FRIBBY
(— PERSON OR ANIMAL) PUNCH
(STOUT AND —) BUNTY CHUFFY
PLUGGY THICKSET
(PL.) BERMUDAS
SHORTAGE FAMINE DROUGHT
WANTAGE UNDERAGE
SHORTCHANGE FLUFF SHORT

SHORTCOMING SIN DEFECT FOIBLE
SHORT-COUPLED CHUFFY
SHORTCUT CUTOFF
SHORT-EARED OWL MOMO
SHORTEN CUT CLIP STAG ELIDE
SLASH REDUCE ABRIDGE CURTAIL
EXCERPT CONTRACT DIMINISH
RETRENCH
(— AND THICKEN IRON) JUMP
(— GRIP) CHOKE
SHORTENED CURTED BOBTAIL
CURTATE ABRIDGED
SHORTENING (— OF SYLLABLE)
SYSTOLE
SHORTEST LEAST
SHORTHORN DURHAM
SHORT-LIVED FRAGILE
SHORTLY DUMPILY DIRECTLY
SHORT-NAPPED RAS
SHORTNESS BREVITY CURTNESS
UNLENGTH
SHORT-RANGE TACTICAL
SHORT-SIGHTED SANDED PURBLIND
SHORTSIGHTEDNESS MYOPIA
SHORT-TEMPERED SNIPPY SNUFFY
SHORT-TERM FLOATING
SHORT-WINDED PURSY PURFLY
PURFLED PURSIVE
SHOT POP SET BLUE CASE JOLT
OVER SETT SLUG BLANK FLIER
FLING FLUFF FLYER OUTER PLUFF
SHOOT TOWEL WHITE CARTON
CENTER CENTRE FOLLOW MUDCAP
REBOTE ALIIPOE BOMBARD
CUTAWAY DEADEYE GUNSHOT
LANGREL PELICAN SIGHTER
BLIZZARD BUCKSHOT HAILSHOT
LANGRAGE MARKSHOT SCORCHER
(— BEYOND TARGET) OVER
(— FOR CULVERIN) PELICAN
(— IN FIFTH CIRCLE) WHITE
(— IN FOURTH CIRCLE) BLACK
(— IN THIRD CIRCLE) BLUE
(— OF NARCOTIC) FIX
(— STRIKING BULL'S-EYE) CARTON
(ARCHERY —) GREEN
(BADMINTON —) CLEAR
(BILLIARD —) DRAG STAB CAROM
MASSE SCREW FOLLOW SAFETY
SPREAD BRICOLE SCRATCH
(BOW —) DRAFT
(CAMERA —) INTERCUT
(CROQUET —) SPLIT FOLLOW
(CURLING —) INWICK OUTWICK
(FINAL —) UPSHOT
(GOOD —) SCREAMER
(PISTOL —) BARK
(POOL —) BREAK
(SIZE OF —) F T BB FF TT BBB
DUST BUCKSHOT
(TENNIS —) ACE LOB DINK SERVE
SMASH
(VOLLEY OF —S) BLIZZARD
SHOTGUN DOUBLE TUPARA
PEPPERER
SHOULD MOW SUD WANT OUGHT
(— NOT) SHUDNA SHOULDNA
SHOULDNT
SHOULDER DOD AXLE CLOD DODD

GAIN HUMP SHIP STEP SULD BOUGH
PITCH SPALL SPULE VERGE AXILLA
EPAULE RELISH SPAULD KNUCKLE
RIMBASE SHOUTHER
(— **AROUND TENON**) RELISH
(— **OF BOLT**) NAB
(— **OF FIREARM STOCK**) RIMBASE
(— **OF FLY**) CHEEK
(— **OF PORK**) HAND PICNIC
CUSHION
(— **OF RABBIT OR HARE**) WING
(— **OF ROAD**) BERM BERME
HAUNCH QUARTER
(— **PAIN**) OMODYNIA
(**BEVELED** —) GAIN
(PL.) FOREBOWS
SHOULDER BLADE SPALD SPEAL
SCAPULA
SHOUT BAY BOO CRY HOY HUE
BAWL CALL CROW GAPE HAIL HOCH
HOOP HOOT REME ROOT ROUP
ROUT SCRY TOOT YELL BRAWL
CHEER CLAIM CLEPE CRACK GREDE
HAVOC HOLLO HUZZA REERE
WHEWT WHOOP ABRAID BOOHOO
CLAMOR GOLLAR GOLLER HALLOO
HOLLER HURRAH STEVEN YAMMER
ACCLAIM SHILLOO GARDYLOO
LULLILOO SCRONACH
(— **AS CHILDREN**) BELDER
(— **DERISIVELY**) BARRACK
(— **OF APPROVAL**) BRAVO
(— **OF ENCOURAGEMENT**) HARK
(— **OF JOY**) IO
(**HUNTING** —) CHEVY
SHOUTING HUE GLAM ROUP ROUT
HOLLO CLAMOR HOLLOA JUBILEE
SHOVE JUT PUT BUNT DUSH FEND
MUCK PICK POTE PUSH SHOG SHUN
BOOST CROWD DUNCH ELBOW
HUNCH SHIVE SHUNT HUSTLE
JOSTLE JUSTLE MUSCLE THRUST
SCAMBLE
(— **IN MARBLES**) FULK
SHOVEL FAN VAN CAST PEEL SPUD
SCOOP SHOOL SPADE SPOON
SCOPPIT SCUPPIT SLUDGER
DUCKBILL DUCKFOOT STROCKLE
(— **FOR COIN**) MAIN
(— **FOR DRESSING ORE**) VAN
(**BRICKMAKING** —) CUCKHOLD
(**CASTING** —) SCUTTLE
(**CHARCOAL BURNER'S** —) RABBLE
(**FIRE** —) PEEL SLICE
(**GRATED** —) HARP
(**MINER'S** —) BANJO
(**PERFORATED** —) SKIMMER
SHOVELER SCOOPER WHINGER
BLUEWING SHOULERD WHINYARD
SHOW DO SAY SEE WIS BOSH CALL
DASH HAVE ITEM LEAD MARK MIEN
SCAW SEEM SHEW TENT VIEW
WEAR WISE ARGUE ASSAY EXERT
FLASH GLOSS GLOZE KITHE PRIDE
PROVE SHINE SIGHT SLANG SPORT
TEACH ACCUSE ASSIGN BETRAY
BLAZON CHICHI COUTHE DENOTE
DETECT DEVICE DIRECT ENSIGN
ESCORT EVINCE EXPOSE FIGURE

FLAUNT GAIETY GAYETY LAYOUT
MUSTER OBJECT PARADE REVEAL
SCHEME SPREAD SPRUNK ADVANCE
ANALYZE BALLOON BESPEAK
BETOKEN BRAVURA BREATHE
DECLARE DISPLAY DIVULGE EXHIBIT
EXPRESS FASHION MONSTER
PRESAGE PRODUCE PROPOSE
SELLOUT SHOWING SIGNIFY
TRIUMPH COLORING CONCLUDE
EVIDENCE FLOURISH FORESHOW
INDICATE MANIFEST PRETENCE
SEMBLANT SIDESHOW
(— **APPROVAL**) CLAP APPLAUD
(— **CONTEMPT**) SCOFF
(— **DISCONTENT**) GROUCH
(— **DISPLEASURE**) POUT
(— **ENTHUSIASM**) DROOL
(— **FORTH**) BLAZE CIPHER
(— **IN PUBLIC CELEBRATION**)
PAGEANT
(— **ITSELF**) APPEAR
(— **MERCY**) SPARE
(— **OF LEARNING**) SCIOLISM
(— **OF LIGHT**) BLINK
(— **OF REASON**) COLOR
(— **OF VANITY**) AIR
(— **OFF**) FLASH SPORT SWANK
PARADE
(— **ONESELF**) BE
(— **POSITION OF**) MEITH
(— **PROMISE**) FRAME SHAPE
(— **RESPECT FOR**) REGARD
(— **REVERSE TREND**) REACT
(— **SIGNS OF GIVING WAY**) WAVER
(— **SIGNS OF ILLNESS**) GRUDGE
(— **THE BOTTOM**) KEEL
(— **THE SIGHTS**) LIONIZE
(— **THE TEETH**) GIRN GRIN
(— **THE WAY**) LEAD CONDUCT
(— **TO BE FALSE**) BELIE DISPROVE
(— **UNKINDNESS**) WAIT
(— **WITHOUT SUBSTANCE**) FORM
(**ARTFUL** —) GRIMACE
(**FALSE** —) FUCUS BUBBLE TINSEL
ILLUSION
(**FLOOR** —) CABARET
(**GAUDY** —) HOOPLA BRAVERY
(**MERE** —) PHANTOM
(**MOMENTARY** —) FLASH
(**ORNATE** —) FLUBDUB
(**OSTENTATIOUS** —) SPRUNK
DISPLAY
(**OUTSIDE** —) VARNISH
(**OUTWARD** —) FUCUS VISAGE
(**PUPPET** —) DROLL MOTION
WAJANG WAYANG GUIGNOL
(**RIDICULOUS** —) FARCE
(**RUDIMENTARY** —) SATURA
(**SPECIOUS** —) GLOZE
(**SUPERFICIAL** —) GLOSS VENEER
(**TRAVELLING** —) SLANG
SHOWCASE ISLAND VITRINE
SHOWER WET HAIL RAIN SCAT SUMP
AUGER BLASH SKITE SOUSE
FLURRY PELTER SHEWER DRIBBLE
SHATTER WEATHER COMMORTH
SCOUTHER
(**CONCENTRATED** —) BARRAGE

(**HEAVY** —) SUMP
(**RAIN** —) RASH
(**SUDDEN** —) SCUD SKIT BRASH
PLUMP
SHOWERY BRASHY CLASHY SCATTY
SHOWILY GAILY BRAVELY GAUDILY
SHOWINESS DASH GLARE GLITTER
FLOURISH GEWGAWRY SPLENDOR
SHOWING SPRANK SPARKLE
(— **SAME NATURE**) AKIN
(**SUPERFICIAL** —) FACE
SHOW-ME STATE MISSOURI
SHOW-OFF CUTUP
SHOWY GAY FINE LOUD NICE RORY
DASHY FLARY FLASH FRESH GAUDY
GIDDY GRAND SPICY TOPPY VAUDY
VIEWY BRANKY BRAZEN BRUMMY
CHICHI DRESSY FLASHY FLOSSY
GARISH GEWGAW GLOSSY JAUNTY
PURPLE SHANTY SPANKY SPORTY
TAWDRY DASHING FLAUNTY
GALLANT GAUDFUL HOTSHOT
POMPOUS SHOWFUL SHOWISH
SPLASHY CLAPTRAP FASTUOUS
GIMCRACK GORGEOUS ORGULOUS
SPARKISH SPECIOUS SPLENDID
TRUMPERY
(**NOT** —) CIVIL LENTEN DISCREET
SHRED DAG HOG JAG RAG ROND
ROON SNIP WISP BLYPE CLOUT
SHRAG SHRIP CULPON SCREED
SLIVER TARGET FRITTER SHATTER
FILAMENT
(— **FISH**) SCROD
(— **OF CLOTHES**) TACK
(— **OF FLESH**) TAG
(— **OF HAIR**) TAIT
(PL.) TAVERS CADDICE TAIVERS
SHREDDED CUT
SHREDDER DEVIL
SHREW JES TANA PRESS RANNY
SOREX VIXEN CALLET JUMPER
MIGALE TARGER TARTAR TUPAIA
VIRAGO BLARINA HELLCAT
MUSKRAT PENTAIL SCYTALE
TUPAIID SINSRING SORICINE
SORICOID UROPSILE
(**TREE** —) BANXRING
SHREWD DRY SLY ACID CUTE FELL
GASH SAGE TIDY WARE WISE
ACUTE CAGEY CANNY HEADY
PAWKY POKEY SHARP SMART
SWACK ARGUTE ARTFUL ASTUTE
CLEVER CRAFTY SPRACK SUBTLE
CUNNING GNOSTIC KNOWING
PARLISH PARLOUS PRACTIC
SAPIENT
(— **PERSON**) FILE
SHREWDLY SLILY CANNILY
ASTUTELY
SHREWDNESS SAVVY ACUMEN
POLICY SLYNESS GUMPTION
SAGACITY CALLIDITY
SHREWISH CURST CURSED SHREWD
VIXENISH
SHREWMOUSE MYGALE SCYTALE
SHRIEK CRY YIP YARM YELL CHIRK
SKIRL SCREAM SCRIKE SHRIKE
SKRIKE SPRAICH

SHRIKE POPE BATARA BOUBOU BRUBRU FISCAL FLASHER FLUSHER LOGHEAD MIGRANT MINIVET TRILLER BELLBIRD FALCONET PUFFBACK WOODCHAT

SHRILL HIGH KEEN ACUTE PIPEY SHARP SHILL SHIRL ARGUTE BRASSY GLASSY PIPING SQUEAK TREBLE HAUTAIN MINIKIN SCREAKY STRIDENT

(MAKE — NOISE) POTRACK

SHRIMP GRIT APANG CARID MYSID PARVA PRAWN NIPPER PANDLE ARTEMIA BROWNIE CAMARON DECAPOD POLYPOD REDTAIL SPECTER SPECTRE CARIDEAN CRAWFISH CREVETTE MACRURAN

SHRINE ADYT NAOS GUACA HUACA ISEUM MAZAR STUPA ZIARA ADYTON ADYTUM CHASSE DAGABA DAGOBA DURGAH HALLOW HIERON MEMORY SAMADH ZIARAT CHAITYA CHORTEN EDICULE FANACLE MARTYRY MEMORIA SACRARY TEMENOS THESEUM AEDICULA DELUBRUM FERETORY FERETRUM GURDWARA LARARIUM MARABOUT PANTHEON VALHALLA

(— STUDY) NAOLOGY

SHRINK COY SHY DUCK FULL FUNK GIVE PEAK ABHOR ARGHE CLING COWER CRINE QUAIL RELAX RIVEL SHRAM SHRUG SHUCK START WINCE BLANCH BLENCH BOGGLE COTTER CRINGE FLINCH LESSEN RECOIL SCRUMP SETTLE SHRIMP WEAZEN CRIMPLE DWINDLE SCUNNER SHRIVEL COLLAPSE CONTRACT

(— FROM DRYNESS) GIZZEN

SHRINKAGE SETTLE SHRINK SINKAGE

(— OF TYPE) SQUEEZE

SHRINKING COY SHY TIMID BLETHE DASTARD FULLING LOATHFUL TIMOROUS

SHRIVE SHRIFT CONFESS SHRIEVE

SHRIVEL SEAR BLAST CLING CRINE PARCH RIVEL SHRAM SNERP WIZEN COTTER GIZZEN SCORCH SCRUMP SHRINK WEAZEN WITHER CROZZLE

SHRIVELED WEDE CLUNG CORKY THIRL GIZZEN STARKY PUNGLED SHIRPIT WIZENED WRITHEN SHRAMMED WRIZZLED

SHROPSHIRE SALOP

SHROUD HIDE SARK CLOAK CRAPE DRAPE HABIT SHEET SWIFT EMBOSK HEARSE KITTEL MUFFLE SCREEN SHADOW SINDON SUDARY BENIGHT CONCEAL CURTAIN INVOLVE SWIFTER CEREMENT

(PL.) PUTTOCK

SHROVETIDE SHROVE GUTTIDE CARNIVAL

SHROVE TUESDAY FASTENS GUTTIDE

SHRUB TI BAY HAW KAT MAY QAT TOD AKIA ALEM BUSH COCA HOYA INGA ITEA KARO KEUR KHAT MUSK ULEX AKALA AKELA ALDER ALISO ARUSA BOCCA BROOM CEIBO CUMAY ELDER GOOMA GOUMI HAZEL HENNA IXORA LEDUM LEMON LILAC MAQUI MARIA MUDAR RETEM SALAL SHROG SUMAC TOYON ZILLA ABELIA AGRITO AKONGE AMULLA ANAGUA ANILAO ARALIA ARUSHA AUCUBA AUPAKA AZALEA BLOLLY CENIZO CHEKAN CHERRY CISTUS CORREA DAPHNE DHAURI DRIMYS FEIJOA FRUTEX JACATE JOJOBA KARAMU KOWHAI LABRUM LARREA LAUREL MATICO MYRTLE NARRAS PENAEA PITURI RAETEM SAVINE STORAX STYRAX AFERNAN AGARITA AMORPHA ARBORET ARRAYAN ARRIMBY AZAROLE BANKSIA BORONIA BUCKEYE CANTUTA CHACATE CHAMISE CHANCHE DEUTZIA EHRETIA ENCELIA EPACRID EPHEDRA FUCHSIA GUMWOOD GUTWORT HOPBUSH HOPSAGE JASMINE JETBEAD JEWBUSH JOEWOOD KUMQUAT LANTANA MAHONIA NUNNARI PAVONIA PEABUSH PIMELEA RHODORA SPIRAEA TARBUSH THEEZAN ABELMOSK ALLTHORN BARBERRY CAMELLIA CARAGANA COMEBACK COPALCHE DRACAENA GOATBUSH GOWIDDIE GRAVILEA HARDHACK HARDTACK HAWTHORN HIBISCUS IRONWOOD KEURBOOM KOROMIKO MOORWORT NINEBARK OCOTILLO OLEASTER OSOBERRY PIPEWOOD PONDBUSH ROSEMARY SANDSTAY SANDWOOD SASANQUA SHRUBLET SNOWBALL SNOWBELL SNOWBUSH SOAPBARK STANDARD

(AROMATIC —) THYME CLUSIA BORONIA HOGBUSH ALLSPICE

(AUSTRALIAN —) GOOMA BUDDAH DRIMYS GEEBUNG MILKBUSH SANDSTAY

(CHINESE —) KERRIA

(CLIMBING —) CATCLAWS SOLANDRA

(DESERT —) AFERNAN

(EVERGREEN —) BOX BAGO ILEX TITI BOLDO ERICA FURZE HEATH HOLLY KOSAM PYXIE SALAL SAVIN TOYON BAUERA DAHOON KALMIA LAUREL PEPINO RUSCUS SAKAKI ARDISIA BARETTA JASMINE JUNIPER MADRONA CALFKILL CARAUNDA EVONYMUS OLEANDER SASANQUA

(FRAGRANT —) JASMINE HUISACHE MEJORANA MEZEREON ROSEMARY

(HAWAIIAN —) AKALA AKELA ILIMA KOKIO OLONA

(LOW —) AYAPANA

(MEXICAN —) BLUEBUSH

(NEW ZEALAND —) KARO KAWA TUTU KARAMU KIEKIE KAWAKAWA KOROMIKO

(PASTURE —) COWBERRY

(PHILIPPINE —) IPILIPIL

(POISONOUS —) GIF CUBE LITHI SUMAC GIFBLAAR LABURNUM

(PRICKLY —) CAPER COLIMA BRAMBLE CATCLAWS

(SPINY —) ULEX AROMA GORSE JUNCO ESPINO BUMELIA CARISSA CYTISUS GENISTA GOATBUSH GRANJENO GUAJILLO HUAJILLO

(STRONG-SMELLING —) SALTWORT

(STUNTED —) SCRAB SCROG SCRUB

(THORNY —) CHANAR HAWTHORN

(TREELIKE —) ARBUSCLE

(TROPICAL —) INGA MAJO HENNA CAMARA DERRIS MOMBIN OLACAD PERSEA HAMELIA JEWBUSH LANTANA SOAPBARK

(WEST INDIAN —) ANIL RATWOOD MILKWOOD

(XEROPHYTIC —) SAXAUL

SHRUBBERY MOGOTE ARBORET

SHRUG SHUG HURKLE SHRINK

SHRUNKEN LANK CLUNG PUNGLED SLUNKEN WIZENED CONTRACT

(— HEAD) TSANTSA

SHUCK HULL SHACK SHELL SHOCK

SHUDDER GRUE CREEP HIRCH QUAKE SHRUG AGRISE GROOSE HIRTCH HOTTER HURKLE SHIVER FRISSON TREMBLE

SHUDDERING RIGOR

SHUFFLE JANK MAKE MILK SLUR SCUFF SHALE SHIFT SHOOL JUGGLE RIFFLE RUFFLE SCLAFF SHOVEL DRAGGLE QUIBBLE SHACKLE SHAFFLE SHAMBLE SLIPPER SLUTHER

SHUN FIN SHY BALK FLEE TABU VOID WARE AVOID EVADE EVITE SHUNT TABOO ASTART DEVOID ESCAPE ESCHEW REFUSE SHRINK DECLINE FORBEAR FORSAKE

SHUNT AYRTON BRIDGE BYPASS SWITCH

SHUSH HUSH WHISH SUPPRESS

SHUSWAP ATNAH

SHUT FAST HASP MAKE SEAL SHOT SLAM SLOT SPAR TAKE TEEN TINE CLOSE LATCH STEEK STICK CLOSED CABINET OCCLUSE UPCLOSE

(— EYES) WINK

(— IN) BAR LAP CAGE COPSE EMBAR EMBAY FORBAR PENTIT TACKLE BELOUKE ENCLAVE

(— OFF) SCREEN SECLUDE

(— OUT) BAR DEBAR REPEL SKUNK HINDER DEPRIVE EXCLUDE OCCLUDE OUTSHUT PRECLUDE

(— TOGETHER) CLASP

(— UP) BAR CUB MEW PENT STOP CHOKE FRANK STIVE STOVE CLOSET EMBOSS ENJAIL IMMURE IMPARK CONDEMN CONFINE DUNGEON ENCLOSE IMPOUND INCLUDE OCCLUDE OPPRESS PARROCK RECLUSE SECLUDE CONCLUDE PRECLUDE

(HALF —) PINK

SHUTDOWN LAYOFF

SHUTOUT SKUNK

SHUTTER LID DROP SHUT BLIND SHADE CUTOFF DOUSER AUTOMAT BUCKLER SHUTTLE JALOUSIE
(— IN ORGAN) SHADE
(— OF TRIPTYCH) VOLET
SHUTTING CLAUDENT
SHUTTLE FLY FLUTE SHUNT BROCHE LOOPER SWIVEL SHITTLE
SHUTTLECOCK BIRD PETECA VOLANT
SHY COY JIB MIM SCAR SHAN SHUN SKIT UNKO WILD BLATE CAGEY CHARY DEMUR FLING SCARE SHUNT SQUAB TIMID UNCOW BOGGLE BOOGER DEMURE MODEST SHANNY SKIEGH TARTLE BASHFUL GAWKISH RABBITY STRANGE TREMBLY UPSTAGE BACKWARD DAPHNEAN FAROUCHE RETIRING SHEEPISH SKITTISH SWAIMOUS WILLYARD
SHYNESS COYNESS MODESTY RESERVE TIMIDITY
SIALAGOGUE SALIVANT
SIAM (SEE THAILAND)
SIAMANG UNGKA GIBBON
SIB SEPT AYLLU SIBLING SIBSHIP CALPULLI
SIBERIA (GULF IN —) OB
(MOUNTAIN RANGE IN —) URAL ALTAI
(NATIVE IN —) YAKU SAGAI TATAR KIRGIZ TARTAR KIRGHIZ YUKAGIR
(RIVER IN —) OB ILI KET PUR TAZ TYM AMGA AMUR LENA MAYA ONON UCUR ALDAN ISHIM NADYM SOBOL TOBOL ANGARA IRTYSH OLEKMA VILYUY
(TOWN IN —) OMSK CHITA KYZYL TOMSK IGARKA KURGAN BARNAUL IRKUTSK LENINSK YAKUTSK
SIBERIAN SQUILL SCILLA
SIBYL SYBIL SIBYLLA VOLUSPA AMALTHEA
SIC SOOL

SICILY

CAPE: BOEO FARO PASSARO
CAPITAL: PALERMO
CATHEDRAL: MONREALE
COIN: LITRA UNCIA
GULF: NOTO CATANIA
ISLAND: EGADI LIPARI USTICA
MEASURE: SALMA CAFFISO
MOUNTAIN: EREI ETNA MORO SORI IBREI NEBRODI
NATIVE: ELYMI SICEL SICANI SICULI
OLD NAME: TRINACRIA TRIQUETRA
PROVINCE: ENNA RAGUSA CATANIA MESSINA PALERMO TRAPANI SIRACUSA
RIVER: SALSO TORTO BELICE SIMETO PLATANI
SEAPORT: ACI CATANIA MARSALA MESSINA PALERMO TRAPANI
TOWN: ENNA NOTO RAGUSA CATANIA MARSALA MESSINA

TRAPANI SYRACUSE
VOLCANO: ETNA AETNA

SICK BAD ILL BADLY CRONK CROOK MORBID MAWKISH SEASICK UNWHOLE CROPSICK MALADIVE PHYSICAL STREAKED
SICKEN TIRE TURN WEARY SUNDER SUNNER WEAKEN DISGUST SURFEIT NAUSEATE
SICKENING FELL SICKLY FULSOME SICKISH NAUSEOUS
SICKISH DAUNCY
SICKLE HOOK CROOK
SICKLY WAN FLUE FOND PALE PUKY SICK DAWNY DONCY FAINT GREEN PEAKY SILLY TEWLY WEARY WISHT AMPERY CLAMMY CRANKY FEEBLE INFIRM PUKISH PULING WANKLY WEAKLY INVALID LANGUID MAWKISH PEAKING PEAKISH PIMPING QUEECHY SICKISH WEARISH WEERISH DELICATE DISEASED MALADIVE PINDLING
SICKNESS (ALSO SEE DISEASE) SICK SORE TAKING AILMENT DISEASE ILLNESS SURFEIT DISORDER
(MILK —) SLOWS TIRES
(MOTION —) KINETOSIS
(MOUNTAIN —) SOROCHE
SIDA ILIMA ESCOBA
SIDE COST EDGE FACE HALF HAND KANT LEAF PART BOARD CHEEK FLANK LATUS PARTY SITHE BEHALF PTERON ENGLISH PENDANT FORESIDE SIDELONG
(— BY SIDE) ACCOLE ACCOSTED PARALLEL
(— OF ATTIC) SKEELING SKILLING SKILLION
(— OF BOOM JAW) HORN
(— OF BOW) BELLY
(— OF CAVITY) WALL
(— OF DECK) GANGWAY
(— OF DITCH) SCARP
(— OF DIVIDERS) LEG
(— OF FACE) CHEEK
(— OF GATE) FOLD
(— OF GEM) BEZEL
(— OF HEARTH) BREAST
(— OF HILL) SCUG
(— OF HOG) FLITCH
(— OF HORSESHOE) BRANCH
(— OF LACE) FOOTING
(— OF LOG) RIDE
(— OF NAVE) AISLE
(— OF OPENING) JAW JAMB
(— OF PIG) BACON
(— OF QUADRANGLE) PANE
(— OF RABBET) LEDGE
(— OF RACECOURSE) STRETCH
(— OF RECTANGLE) SQUARE
(— OF ROOF) CATSLIDE
(— OF SHIP) BEAM WALE BOARD BULWARK LARBOARD SEABOARD
(— OF TENNIS RACKET) ROUGH SMOOTH
(— OF TRIANGLE) LEG

(— OF TYPE) BACK
(— OF VALLEY) COTEAU
(— PIECE) RAVE
(— SHELTERED FROM WIND) LEE LEW LEEWARD
(— WITH) SUFFRAGE
(—S OF GALLERY) SLIPS
(BACK —) REAR BEHIND BACKSIDE
(DRESSED —) FACE
(FOR EACH —) ALL
(MOUNTAIN —) PUNA VETA SOROCHE
(OUTER — OF SKIN) GRAIN
(RIGHT — OF SWORD) INSIDE
(RIGHT —) FACE
(UNDERNEATH —) BOTTOM
SIDEBAR HOUND
SIDEBOARD ABACUS BUFFET SERVER DRESSER CELLARET CREDENCE CREDENZA
SIDE DISH OUTWORK
SIDEPIECE BAR BOW JAMB WING CHEEK GUSSET EARPIECE LANDSIDE
SIDESLIP SKID SLIP DRIFT DRILL
SIDESMAN HOGGLER QUESTMAN
SIDESTEP BEG AVOID DODGE
SIDEWALK WALKWAY TROTTOIR
SIDEWISE ASIDE ASIDEN
SIDING CURB SPUR GARAGE
SIDLE EDGE SLIVE SAUNTER
SIDRA PARASHAH
SIEGE BOUT SEDGE ASSIEGE JOURNEY LEAGUER
(— ENGINE) WARWOLF
SIERRA CERO SERRA SAWBACK KINGFISH

SIERRA LEONE

CAPITAL: FREETOWN
COIN: LEONE
LANGUAGE: KRIO MENDE TEMNE
MEASURE: LOAD KETTLE
MOUNTAIN: LOMA
NATIVE: VAI KONO LOKO SUSU KISSI LIMBA MENDE TEMNE FULANI GALLINA SHERBRO MANDINGO
RIVER: MOA JONG SEWA ROKKEL SCARCY
SEAPORT: HEPEL BONTHE SULIMA
TOWN: BO KISSI KENEMA

SIESTA NAP MERIDIAN
SIEVE FRY TRY BOLT BUNT DRUM HARP LAWN PREE SCRY SHOE SIFT SILE SIZE TEMS GRATE RANGE SCALP TAMIS TAMMY TEMSE BOLTER RANGER RIDDER RIDDLE SEARCE SEARCH SEMMET SIFTER WEIGHT BOULTEL CHAFFER CRIBBLE DILLUER PRICKLE TIFFANY SEARCHER STRAINER
SIFT REE TRY BOLT DUST SCRY RANGE SCALP SIEVE TEMSE DREDGE GARBLE RIDDER RIDDLE SCREEN SEARCE WINNOW CANVASS CRIBBLE DRIBBLE SIFTAGE CRIBRATE

(—°FLOUR) DRESS
(— IN MINING) LUE
(— IN) INFILTER
(— MEAL) BUNT
(— SHOT) TABLE
(— WHEAT) SCALP
SIFTER SIEVE BOLTER CASTER
SIEVER
SIFTING DRIFT GARBLING
(PL.) BOLTING FANNINGS SIEVINGS
SIGH SOB PECH SIFE SOCK WIND
MOURN SIGHT SITHE SOUGH TWANK
BEMOAN BEWAIL SORROW SUTHER
DEPLORE SINGULT SUSPIRE
SIGHT EYE KEN RAY BONE ESPY
FACE GAZE PEEP SEET VIEW FERLY
RAISE SCENE SCOPE SICHT TRACK
VISIE VIZZY BEHOLD DESCRY
OBJECT TICKET VISION DISCERN
DISPLAY EYESHOT GLIMPSE
MONSTER CONSPECT DISCOVER
EYESIGHT GUNSIGHT
(— FOR GUN) LEAF PEEP SCOPE
VISIE VIZZY HAUSSE GUNSIGHT
(— OF COMPASS) VANE
(— ON SURVEYOR'S STAFF) TARGET
(— TO SEE IF LEVEL) BONE
(—S OF CITY) LIONS
(AMAZING —) STOUND
(IMAGINARY —) VISION
(PITIFUL —) RUTH
(SORRY —) BYSEN
(STRANGE —) FERLY FERLIE
SIGHTER ALINER ALIGNER
SIGHTING LANDFALL
(— DEVICE) ALIDADE
SIGHTLY VIEWLY EYEABLE
SIGLOS DARIC
SIGN INK AYAH DASH FIRM HINT
HIRE MARK NOTE OMEN TYPE
BADGE COLON FRANK GHOST
GUIDA HAMZA INDEX SIGIL SINGE
SPOOR STAMP TOKEN TRACE
ASSIGN AUGURY CARACT EFFECT
EMBLEM ENGAGE ENSIGN FUGLER
INDICE MOTION NOTICE PARAPH
REMARK SIGLUM SIGNAL SIGNET
SIGNUM SYMBOL TITTLE WITTER
ALEBUSH AUSPICE CHECKER
CHEQUER CONSIGN EARMARK
ENDORSE INDICIA INSIGNE KNOWING
PORTENT PRESAGE PRODIGY
PROFFER SHINGLE SHOWING
SIGNARY SURMISE SYMPTOM
VESTIGE WARNING CEREMONY
INDICANT INSTANCE MONUMENT
PROCLAIM SIGNACLE SYLLABIC
TELLTALE
(— DOCUMENT) FIRM
(— FOR KEYNOTE) ISON
(— OF ALEHOUSE) LATTICE
(— OF AN IDEA) EMBLEM
(— OF APPROVAL) CACHET
(— OF CONTEMPT) FIG
(— OF DANGER) SEAMARK
(— OF GLOTTAL STOP) HAMZA
HAMZAH
(— OF MULTIPLICATION) DOT
(— OF ZODIAC) LEO RAM BULL

CRAB GOAT LION ARIES HOUSE
LIBRA TWINS VIRGO ARCHER
CANCER FISHES GEMINI PISCES
TAURUS VIRGIN BALANCE SCORPIO
AQUARIUS SCORPION
(— ON MAP) ICON
(ASTROLOGICAL —) CIPHER
(MATHEMATICAL —) NAME
FUNCTOR
(MUSICAL —) GUIDA SEGNO SWELL
SIMILE FERMATA
(OUTWARD —) EVIDENCE
(SANSKRIT —) ANUSVARA
(SLIGHT —) SURMISE
(SUBSCRIPT —) SUBFIX
(SUPERSTITIOUS —) GUEST
(TAVERN —) BUSH ALEBUSH
ALEPOLE CHECKER CHEQUER
ALESTAKE
(TRAMP'S —) MONICA MONIKER
(VOWEL —) SEGOL SEGHOL
(PL.) INDICIA INSIGNIA
SIGNAL OS CUE GUN PST WAG BALK
BECK BELL BUZZ CALL COND FLAG
GATE HASH SIGN WAFT WAVE WINK
ALARM ALERT BLINK FLARE FUSEE
FUZEE LIGHT SHAPE SHORT SPEAK
TOKEN WHIFF ALARUM BANNER
BEACON BECKON BUZZER ENSIGN
HERALD MARKER OFFICE RECALL
SIGNET TARGET WAVING WIGWAG
BLINKER CHAMADE EMINENT
NOTABLE RETREAT TURNOUT
CRANTARA DIAPHONE FLAGFALL
LOGOGRAM STANDARD STRIKING
(— FISHERMEN) BALK
(— FOR A PARLEY) CHAMADE
(— FOR WHALERS) WAIF
(— IN WHIST) ECHO PETER
(— OF DISTRESS) SOS
(— ON HORN) SEEK BLAST STRAKE
(— TO ATTACK) CHARGE
(— TO BEGIN ACTION) CUE
(— WITH FLAGS) WIGWAG
(AUDIO —) HUM
(BOAT'S —) WAFF WAFT
(DEATH —; KNELL
(FOG —) FOGHORN TORPEDO
DIAPHONE
(HUNTER'S —) SEEK PRIZE GIBBET
STRAKE
(MILITARY —) FLARE TURNOUT
ASSEMBLY
(NAVAL —) SECURE
(RADIO —) BEAM
(RAILROAD —) BANJO BOARD
FUSEE FUZEE TARGET HIGHBALL
(WARNING —) ALARM KLAXON
TOCSIN
SIGNALLING TICKTACK
SIGNALMAN FLAGS BELLBOY
BELLMAN
SIGNATE SENNET
SIGNATORY SIGNEE SIGNER
SIGNATURE BOLT FIRM HAND VISA
FRANK SHEET SIGIL THEME SIGNUM
TUGHRA SECTION HANDWRIT
SIGNATOR
SIGNBOARD SIGN SHINGLE

SIGNET SIGIL
SIGNIFICANCE WIT BODY SOUND
AMOUNT IMPORT INTENT LETTER
STRESS WEIGHT BEARING CONTENT
GRAVITY MEANING SENTENCE
STRENGTH
(DEVOID OF —) JEJUNE
(HIDDEN —) HYPONOIA
(LACKING —) INANE
SIGNIFICANT REAL GREAT
AUGURAL EPOCHAL OMINOUS
POINTED SERIOUS SENSEFUL
SPEAKING
SIGNIFICANTLY SENSIBLY
SIGNIFICATION SENSE VALOR
VALUE ETYMON IMPORT MOMENT
NOTION MEANING CARRIAGE
SIGNIFIE
SIGNIFICS SENSIFICS
SIGNIFY BE SAY BEAR GIVE MAKE
MEAN NOTE SIGN WAVE AUGUR
IMPLY SKILL SOUND SPEAK SPELL
TOKEN UTTER AMOUNT ARGUFY
ASSERT BEMEAN DENOTE EMPLOY
IMPORT INTEND MATTER SIGNAL
BESPEAK BETOKEN CONNOTE
DECLARE EXPRESS PORTEND
PRETEND DESCRIBE INDICATE
INTIMATE MANIFEST
SIGNPOST GUIDE MERCURY
WAYMARK HANDPOST
SIGURD (HORSE OF —) GRANI
(SLAIN BY —) FAFNIR
(SLAYER OF —) HOGNI
(WIFE OF —) GUDRUN
SIKH AKALI SINGH UDASI MAZHABI
SIKKIM (CAPITAL OF —) GANGTOK
(NATIVE OF —) RONG BHOTIA
LEPCHA
(RIVER OF —) TISTA
SIKSIKA SIHASAPA
SILENCE GAG MUM CALK CLUM
HUSH REST CHOKE FLOOR QUIET
SHUSH SQUAT STILL CLAMOR
MUFFLE SETTLE STIFLE WHISHT
CONFUTE SQUELCH DUMBNESS
PRECLUDE SUPPRESS
SILENCED STILL
SILENCER SOURDINE
SILENT MUM CLUM HUSH HUST
MUET MUTE SNUG CLOSE STILL
TACIT WHIST MUETTE SULLEN
TIPTOE WHISHT APHONIC UNWORDY
ASPIRATE RESERVED RETICENT
TACITURN
SILHOUETTE SHADE ISOTYPE
SILICA FLINT SILEX TRIPOLI
SILICATE MICA ALVITE CERITE
EUCLASE ILVAITE LOTRITE ZEOLITE
CALAMINE ERIONITE WELLSITE
SILICEOUS SHELLY
SILICLE POUCH SILICULE
SILICOSIS CON
SILK SAY SOY CRIN ERIA LOVE
MUGA FLOSS GREGE HONAN JAPAN
TABBY BLATTA CRACKS CULGEE
DUCAPE FRISON MANTUA RADIUM
SENDAL SHALEE SHILLA SOUPLE
TUSSAH ALAMODE CHIFFON

HABUTAI PERSIAN SQUEEZE
TSATLEE TUSSORE YAMAMAI
ARMOZEEN ARMOZINE LUSTRINE
MILANESE
(— FOR LININGS) SARSNET
SARCENET
(HEAVY —) CRIN ARMOZINE
(RAW —) GREIGE MARABOU
TAYSAAM TSATLEE MARABOUT
(REFUSE —) BUR BURR
(TWILLED —) SURAH TOBINE
FOULARD LOUSINE
(UNDYED —) CORAH
(UNTWISTED —) SLEAVE
(UPHOLSTERY —) TABARET
(WASTE —) KNUB NOIL FRISON
SILK COTTON KAPOK
SILK-COTTON TREE BULAK SEMUL
SIMAL YAXCHE BENTANG MUNGUBA
POCHOTE
SILKEN SILL SERIC SILKY SUAVE
SEREAN
SILK GRASS KARATAS
SILK GUM SERICIN
SILK OAK LACEWOOD
SILKSMAN SCALPER
SILK TREE SIRIS
SILKWORM ERI ERIA SINA TUSSAH
TUSSORE YAMAMAI BOMBYCID
SILKY GLOSSY SILKEN
SILKY CORNEL REDBRUSH
SILKY TAMARIN MARIKINA
SILL GIRD SOLE PLATE PATAND
PATTEN SADDLE MUDSILL DOORSILL
SILLINESS BOSH FOLLY BETISE
GOOSERY INANITY SIMPLES
IDLENESS NONSENSE
SILLY TID BETE DAFT FOND FOOL
NICE VAIN APISH BALMY BUGGY
CAKEY DENSE DILLY DIZZY GOOFY
INANE SAPPY SEELY BLASHY
CRANKY CUCKOO DAWISH DOTARD
DOTTLE FOOTLE FRUITY GUCKED
PAULIE SAWNEY SHANNY SIMPLE
SINGLE SKIVIE SLIGHT SPOONY
VACANT ASININE FATUOUS FOOLISH
FOPPISH FRIBBLE GLAIKET PEEVISH
SCRANNY SHALLOW UNWITTY
ANSERINE FEATLESS FOOTLING
FOPPERLY
(BE —) DRIVEL
SILOXANE SILICON
SILT DREGS SLEECH DEPOSIT
RESIDUE SULLAGE BULLDUST
SILVER LUNA MOON PINA DIANA
PLATE SYCEE WEDGE WHITE
ALBATA ARGENT SILLER BULLION
VERMEIL ARGENTUM STERLING
ARGENTINE
(— STATE) NEVADA
(DEBASED —) VELLON
(GILDED —) VERMEIL
SILVER BELL HALESIA BELLWOOD
COWLICKS
SILVERFISH SHINER SLICKER
FISHTAIL WOODFISH
SILVERING BACKING
SILVERSIDES IAO BRIT TINK BRITT
FRIAR SMELT TAILOR TINKER

GRUNION ATHERINE PEIXEREY
PEJERREY SKIPJACK
SILVERSMITH SONAR
SILVER TREE IRONWOOD
SILVER TREE FERN PITAU
SILVERVINE CATVINE
SILVERWEED TANSY
SILVERWING CINDER
SILVERY WHITE ARGENT SILVER
SILVERN
SILYBUM MARIANA
SIMAR CYMAR SYMAR ZIMARRA
SIMILAR LIKE SUCH ALIKE EVENLY
LIKELY SIMILE COGNATE KINDRED
SEEMABLE SELFLIKE SUCHLIKE
SUITABLE
SIMILARITY SIMILE ANALOGY
HOMOLOGY HOMOTAXY LIKENESS
PARALLEL SAMENESS
SIMILARLY EQUALLY LIKEWISE
SIMILE ICON IKON IMAGE FIGURE
SUIVEZ COMPARE
SIMILITUDE IMAGE FIGURE
ANALOGY PARABLE PORTRAIT
SIMMER FRY CREE SILE STEW
SIMPER SOTTER TOTTLE
SIMON ZELOTES
SIMONY BARRATRY
SIMOOM SAMUM SAMIEL
SIMPER MINCE SMIRK BRIDLE
SIMPLE LOW BALD BARE EASY FOND
MERE NICE ONLY PURE RUDE SNAP
VERY WEAK AFALD BLEAK DIZZY
GREEN NAIVE NAKED PLAIN SEELY
SILLY SMALL SOBER CHASTE
GLOBAL HOMELY HONEST HUMBLE
NATIVE OAFISH RUSTIC SEMPLE
SEVERE SINGLE STUPID VIRGIN
ARTLESS ASININE AUSTERE
BABYISH FATUOUS FOOLISH
ONEFOLD POPULAR SIMPLEX
SPECIES EXPLICIT HOMEMADE
INNOCENT SACKLESS SEMPLICE
SOLITARY
SIMPLE-MINDED SEELY SILLY
INNOCENT
SIMPLETON AUF AWF COX DAW
FON NUP OAF SAP SOT BOOB CAKE
COOT CULL FLAT FOOL GABY GAUP
GAWP GOFF GOUK GOWK GOWP
GUFF PEAK SIMP SOFT TONY TOOT
ZANY COKES GALAH GOOSE IDIOT
IKONA JACOB LOACH NINNY NODDY
PRUNE SAMMY SMELT SPOON
TOMMY BADAUD DAUKIN FONDLE
GANDER GAUPUS GAWNEY GOTHAM
GREENY GULPIN JOSSER NINCUM
NOODLE NUPSON SAWNEY SIMKIN
SIMPLE DAWPATE GOMERAL
GUBBINS JUGGINS MAFFLIN
MUGGINS WIDGEON ABDERITE
FLATHEAD FONDLING INNOCENT
JEANJEAN JOCRISSE KNOTHEAD
MOONCALF MOONLING OMADHAUN
PEAGOOSE SILLYTON SOFTHEAD
WISEACRE WOODCOCK
SIMPLICITY NICETY PURITY
MODESTY NAIVETE ELEGANCE
SIMPLIFY CLARIFY EXPOUND

SIMPLY JUST ALONE FONDLY
MERELY PLATLY CRUDELY QUIETLY
NATIVELY
SIMULATE ACT FAKE MOCK FEIGN
MIMIC AFFECT ASSUME SEMBLE
SIMULE SKETCH
SIMULATED FAINT FAKED ERSATZ
FICTIOUS
SIMULATION ACTING ANALOGUE
PRETENSE
SIMULTANEOUS CONJOINT
CONJUGATE
SIMULTANEOUSLY ONCE
TOGETHER
SIN ERR CULP DEBT ENZU EVIL HELL
PAPA VICE BLAME CRIME ERROR
FAULT FOLLY GUILT SLOTH WATHE
WRONG AGUILT COMMIT FELONY
NANNAR OFFEND PIACLE PLIGHT
VENIAL FRAILTY OFFENSE
HAMARTIA INIQUITY PECCANCY
QUEDSHIP TRESPASS
(DEADLY —) ACEDIA
(ORIGINAL —) ADAM
SINCALINE CHOLINE
SINCE AS AGO FOR FRO NOW GONE
SETH SITH SYNE BEING WHERE
FORWHY BECAUSE SITHENS
WHEREAS INASMUCH SITHENCE
SINCERE GOOD REAL TRUE AFALD
FRANK DEVOUT ENTIRE HEARTY
HONEST SIMPLE SINGLE CORDIAL
EARNEST GENUINE ONEFOLD
UPRIGHT FAITHFUL
SINCERELY TRULY SIMPLY SINGLY
DEVOUTLY ENTIRELY HEARTILY
SINCERITY FAITH HEART HONESTY
REALITY
SINDON CORPORAL
SINEW THEW FIBER FIBRE NERVE
LEADER SINNER TENDON
SINEWY WIRY NERVY THEWY
ROBUST FIBROSE FIBROUS STRINGY
TENDINAL
SINFONIA SYMPHONY
SINFUL BAD EVIL VILE NEFAS
WRONG WICKED UNGODLY VICIOUS
PIACULAR
SING HUM JIG LIP CANT CARP GALE
HYMN LILT TUNE CAROL CARRY
CHANT CHIRL CROON DIRGE DITTY
DRING FEIGN LYRIC RAISE TOUCH
YEDDE CHAUNT CHORUS DIVIDE
INTONE MELODY RECORD RELISH
STRAIN WARBLE CHORTLE
COUNTER DESCANT GRIDDLE
SINGING TWEEDLE CHERUBIM
FALDERAL MODULATE SINGSONG
VOCALIZE
(— ABOUT) BESING
(— ABOVE TRUE PITCH) SHARP
(— AS A BEGGAR) GRIDDLE
(— BRISKLY) KNACK
(— CHEERFULLY) LILT
(— FLORIDLY) DIVIDE
(— HARSHLY) SCREAM
(— IN A CRACKED VOICE) CRAKE
(— IN CHORUS) CHOIR
(— IN LOW VOICE) CROON

(— IN SWISS MANNER) YODEL
(— LOUDLY) BELT TROLL TROLLOL
(— PRAISES) LAUD
(— ROMANCES) GEST GESTE
(— SECOND PART) SURCENT
(— SOFTLY) SOWF SOWTH
(— WITH FLOURISHES) ROULADE
SINGAPORE (RIVER IN —) SUNGEI
SELETAR
(STRAIT OF —) JOHORE SEMBILAN
SINGE GAS BURN SWEAL GENAPP
SCORCH SWINGE SCOWDER
SWITHEN FIREFANG
SINGER ALTO BARD LARK SWAN
BASSO BUFFA BUFFO SKALD VOICE
BULBUL BUSKER CANARY CANTOR
LYRIST SONGER BASSIST CHANTER
CROONER PRIMOMO SOLOIST
SONGMAN SOPRANO TROLLER
WARBLER BAYADERE CANTADOR
CASTRATO CHANTEUR FALSETTO
GRIDDLER MELODIST MONODIST
THAMYRIS VOCALIST
(— OF FOLK SONGS) CANTADOR
(— OF THE GODS) GANDHARVA
(FEMALE —) SONGBIRD
(MENDICANT —) BUSKER
(PRINCIPAL —) PRIMOMO
(PROVENCAL —) MUSAR
SINGING CANT SCAT CHANT LYRIC
HYMNODY JONGLERY
(— CAROLS) PLYGAIN HODENING
(CANTORIAL —) HAZANUTH
HAZZANUT
(SIMULTANEOUS —) CHORUS
SINGLE ODD ONE LAST ONLY SOLE
UNAL AFALD SIMPLE SOLEIN
SULLEN UNIQUE VERSAL ALONELY
AZYGOUS ONEFOLD SEVERAL
SIMPLEX TWOSOME PECULIAR
SEPARATE SINGULAR SOLITARY
SPORADIC
(— OUT) CUT SPOT ISOLATE
SEPARATE
SINGLE-FOOT RACK
SINGLEHANDEDLY SINGLY
SINGLENESS UNITY ONENESS
SINGLETON (— LEAD) SNEAK
SINGLY SINGLE SOLELY SLONELY
SINGPHO CHINGPAW
SINGSONG SOUGH CHANTING
SINGULAR ODD RARE QUEER SEENIL
SINGLE STRANGE PECULIAR
SINGULARISM HENISM
SINGULARITY DOUBLET ONENESS
ONLINESS
SINISTER AWK CAR KAY DARK DIRE
FELL GRIM DISMAL LOUCHE
OBLIQUE OMINOUS
SINISTRAL REVERSED
SINK DIP DOP EBB LUM SAG SET
SYE BORE DRAU DRAW DROP FADE
FAIL FALL GOWT HELD KILL LUMB
SILE SWAG AVALE DRAFT DRAIN
DROOP DROWN HIELD LAPSE
LOWER MERGE POACH SQUAT
STOOP SWAMP VERGE DOLINA
DOLINE DRENCH GUTTER PLUNGE
PUDDLE RESIDE SETTLE COMMODE

DECLINE DESCEND DRAUGHT
FOUNDER GULLION IMMERSE
RELAPSE SCUTTLE SUBSIDE
SWALLOW DECREASE SINKHOLE
SOAKAWAY
(— A WELL) DRILL
(— AND FALL) TWINE
(— AS IN MUD) LAIR
(— DOWN) BOG AVALE STOOP
DECLINE
(— FANGS INTO) STRIKE
(— INTO OOZE) WASEL
(— NAILHEAD) SET
(— SUDDENLY) SLUMP
(— UNDER TRIAL) QUAIL
SINKBOX BOX SINK BATTERY
SINKER BUR BURR SINK DIPSY
PLUMB BULLET
SINKHOLE SINK PONOR UVALA
CENOTE COLLECT
SINKING GONE SINKAGE
(— DOWN) FONDU
SINKIUSE COLUMBIA
SINLESS INNOCENT
SINLESSNESS HOLINESS
SINNER DEBTOR PECCANT
SINNING PECCANT
SINUATE GYROSE
SINUOSITY WRIGGLE
SINUOUS WAVY SNAKEY SINUATE
SNAKISH TORTILE WINDING
INDENTED SWANLIKE
SINUS BOSOM RECESS LOCULUS
TEARPIT
SINUSITIS ROUP
SIOUAN ABANIC DAKOTA SANTEE
SAPONI CATAWBA DACOTAH
SIOUX (— FORCE) WAKAN WAKON
SIP BIB NIP SUP BLEB SEEP SLUP
SUCK TIFF KEACH SNACK WHIFF
TIPPLE TICKLER DELIBATE
SIPHON CRANE THIEF VALINCH
FLINCHER
SIPPING LIBANT
SIPUNCULOIDEA ACHAETA INERMIA
SIR PO DAN DEN DON PAN AZAM
HERR MIAN STIR TUAN SAHIB
SENOR SEYID SIEUR MESSER
SAYYID SIGNOR SIRREE DOMINUS
EFFENDI MESSIRE SIGNIOR SIGNORE
GOSPODIN GOVERNOR
(PL.) LORDINGS
SIRCAR BANIAN
SIRE BEGET THROW FATHER GETTER
SIREN HOOTER LIGEIA LIGYDA
LORELEI MERMAID SIRENIAN
SIRENIAN COWFISH MUTILATE
SIRENOMELUS SYMPUS SYMMELUS
SIRICID UROCERID
SIRIS KOKO LEBBEK
SIRIUS SOTHIS TISHIVA CANICULA
SIRLOIN SEY BACKSEY
SIRMUELLERA BANKSIA
SIRUP WAX LICK GOLDY SYRUP
GOWDIE GREENS LIQUER ORGEAT
RUNOFF CLAIRCE ECLEGMA
MOLASSES QUIDDANY
SIRWASH SIDELINE
SISAL CABUYA SISALANA

SISKIN TARIN
SISSIFIED PRISSY
SISSOO TALI SHISHAM
SISSY SIS CISSIE SISTER CHICKEN
SISTER NUN SIB SIS GIRL NURSE
SISSY TITTY WOMAN EXTERN
PERSON
(YOUNGER —) CADETTE
(PL.) SISTERN SISTREN
SISTERHOOD SORORITY
SISTERLY SORORAL
SISYPHUS (FATHER OF —) AEOLUS
(WIFE OF —) MEROPE
SIT SET LEAN SEAT BENCH PRESS
ROOST SQUAT WEIGH BESTRIDE
(— ABRUPTLY) CLAP
(— ASTRIDE) CROSS HORSE
STRADDLE
(— ERECT LIKE A DOG) BEG
(— FORCIBLY) DOSS
(— IN JUDGMENT) DEEM
(— ON) BROOD COVER
(— OVER EGGS) RUCK BROOD
SITATUNGA NAKONG
SITE AREA PLOT SEAT SITU SOLE
SPOT TOFT FIELD PLACE SITUS
STAND STANCE BIVOUAC DAMSITE
HABITAT STEADING
(— OF BIRD SEXUAL DISPLAY) LEK
(— OF HUNT) DRIVE
(— OF SMELTER) BOLE
(EXCAVATION —) DIG
(THRESHING —) SETTING
SITTER DOLLY DOLLIE INSESSOR
SITTING DIET SEAT ASSIS SEANCE
SEDENT SEJANT SESSION
CONGRESS SEDERUNT
SITUATE PLACE POSITION
SITUATED SET SEATED STATURED
(— OPPOSITE) COUNTER
SITUATION JOB LIE CASE PASS
PLOT POST SEAT SITE SPOT BERTH
SIEGE SITUS STATE STEAD ASSIZE
CHANCE ESTATE OFFICE PLIGHT
STATUS EPISODE PICTURE PORTENT
POSTURE STATION INCIDENT
INSTANCE POSITURE STANDING
UBIQUITY
(— BESET BY DIFFICULTIES)
SCRAPE
(— IN CRIBBAGE) GO
(— IN FARO) CATHOP
(— OF PERPLEXITY) HOBBLE STRAIT
(AMUSING —) BAR
(AWKWARD —) SCRAPE
(CRITICAL —) CLUTCH
(DIFFICULT —) BOX PUXY BOGGLE
NINEHOLES
(DISTRESSING —) STYMIE
(EXECRABLE —) ATROCITY
(FAVORABLE —) BREAK
(FINAL — OF ACT) CURTAIN
(HOPELESSLY DOOMED —)
RATTRAP
(NECESSITOUS —) BREACH
(PAINFUL —) DISTRESS
(RELATIVE —) BEARING
(UNSATISFACTORY —) DILEMMA
(VEXATIOUS —) HEADACHE

(VILE —) DUNGHILL
(ZODIACAL —) HAYZ
SITZ BATH SITZBAD SEMICUPE
SITZMARK BATHTUB
SIVA RUDRA SHIVA ISVARA SHAMBU
BHAIRAVA MAHADEVA NATARAJA
SIX VAU WAW SICE SISE HEXAD
HEXADE SENARY SEXTET STIGMA
DIGAMMA SIXSOME
SIXFOLD SEXTUPLE
SIX-FOOTED HEXAPOD
SIXMO SEXTO
SIXPENCE HOG PIG BEND KICK
SIMON SPRAT TIZZY BENDER
FIDDLE TANNER TESTON CRIPPLE
FIDDLER TESTRIL
SIXTEENTH ANA ANNA
SIXTIETH (— PART OF DAY) GHURRY
SIXTY SAMECH SAMEKH
SIZABLE SNUG LARGE HANDSOME
SIZE WAX AREA BIND BULK MARK
MASS DRESS GIRTH MOUND PLANK
SCALE EXTENT FORMAT GROWTH
MICKLE MOISON PICNIC SIZING
BIGNESS CONTENT CORSAGE
FITTING THIRTEEN TWELVEMO
(— OF BOOK) FOLIO
(— OF CARDS) TOWN LADIES
(— OF HOLE) BORE
(— OF HOSIERY) POPE
(— OF PAPERBOARD) LARGE
(— OF PARTICLE) GRIND
(— OF ROPE) GRIST
(— OF TYPE) GEM PICA RUBY
AGATE CANON ELITE PEARL MINION
PRIMER BREVIER DIAMOND
EMERALD ENGLISH PARAGON
(— YARN) SLASH
(CLOTHING —) LONG SHORT STOUT
JUNIOR PETITE
(EXTRA LARGE —) SUPER
(RELATIVE —) SCALE
(UNUSUAL —) OUTSIZE
SIZING DRESSING SLASHING
(— LIQUID) GLAIR
SIZZLE FRIZZ
SKAT CAT NULL TOURNEE
SKATE BOB RAY TUB RAJA RINK
SKIT TINK TUBE FLAIR SCULL
BATOID DOCTOR FLATHE PATENT
PATTEN ROCKER ROLLER RUNNER
SKETCH TINKER CHOPINE FLAPPER
PLACOID SKETCHER
(— MARK) CUSP
(FEMALE —) MAID
SKATER PATTENER SKETCHER
SKEDADDLE BUNK
SKEET KELTER KILTER PELTER
SKEIN RAP HANK HASP SCAN
BOTTOM SLEAVE SELVAGE
SKEINER RANDER SLIPPER
SKELETIN SPONGIN
SKELETON CUP CAGE MORT RAME
ATOMY BONES FRAME LOOFAH
SICULA SKELET ANATOMY CARCASS
RAWBONE ARMATURE CORALLUM
MANDIBLE OSSATURE
SKELETON KEY GILT SCREW
TWIRLER

SKEPTIC DOUBTER INFIDEL ZETETIC
APIKOROS APORETIC
SKEPTICAL APORETIC DOUBTFUL
SKEPTICISM HUMISM UNBELIEF
SKETCH BIT DASH DRAW LIMN PLAN
VIEW VITA DRAFT ENTER PAINT
TRACE APERCU DESIGN DOODLE
SCHEME SPLASH CROQUIS
DRAUGHT DRAWING ETCHING
OUTLINE SCHIZZO MONOGRAM
PROSPECT VIGNETTE
(— BEFOREHAND) INDICATE
(AUTOBIOGRAPHICAL —) VITA
(BIOGRAPHICAL —) ELOGY ELOGIUM
(FIRST —) ESQUISSE
(HERALDIC —) TRICK
(OUTDOORS —) LANDSKIP
(PRELIMINARY —) DRAFT ABBOZZO
MAQUETTE
(ROUGH —) NOTE POCHADE
ESQUISSE
(SATIRICAL —) SKIT
SKEW ASKEW GAUCHE
SKEWBACK SPRINGER
SKEWER PROD PROG SPIT PRICK
TRUSS SKIVER TASTER
SKEWERER TUBER
SKI SKEE SNOWSHOE
(— DOWN SLOPE) SCHUSS
(— METHOD) PASSGANG
(— MOVEMENT) RUADE
(— POSITION) VORLAGE
(— RACING) LANGLAUF
(— TURN) TELEMARK
(PL.) BOARDS
SKID DOG DRAG SLEW SLUE TRIG
DRIFT DRILL SLOUGH SKIDPAN
SLIPPER TRIGGER SIDESLIP
(— LOGS) SNAKE TWICH TRAVOY
TWITCH
(— ON RAIL) SKATE
(FENDER —) GLANCER
SKIDDER SNAKER
SKIDI LOUP
SKIDWAY PIT
SKIER KANONE SNOWBIRD
SKIFF SKIFT CAIQUE DINGHY
SAMPAN CURRANE SKIPPET
SKIING TOURING
SKIL BESHOW SKILFISH
SKILL ART CAN WIT FEAT FEEL HAND
PATE TACT CRAFT DRAFT HAUNT
KNACK TRICK ENGINE TECHNE
ABILITY ADDRESS APTNESS
CUNNING FINESSE MASTERY
MYSTERY SCIENCE SLEIGHT
ARTIFICE CAPACITY CHIVALRY
DEFTNESS FACILITY INDUSTRY
LEARNING
(LACK OF —) INERTIA
(NAVIGATION —) SEACRAFT
SKILLED OLD WISE ADEPT ASTUTE
PERITE SCIENT SKILLY VERSED
HOTSHOT PRACTIC EDUCATED
SKILLFUL
SKILLET PRIG SPIDER
SKILLFUL APT SLY ABLE DEFT FEAT
FILE FINE GOOD PERT TIDY WISE
ADEPT CANNY FITTY HANDY HENDE

READY SLICK SWEET ADROIT
ARTFUL CLEVER CRAFTY DAEDAL
EXPERT HABILE SCIENT SKILLY
SOLERT SUBTLE CUNNING SKILLED
DEXTROUS PRACTIVE SLEIGHTY
TACTICAL
SKILLFULLY DEFTLY CRAFTILY
SKILLFULNESS CRAFT
SKIM TOP RIFF SCUD SCUM SCUN
SCUR SILE SKIP FLEET GRAZE
SCALE SKIFF SKIRR SKIVE BROWSE
RABBLE SAMPLE DESPUME SKITTER
(— ON WATER) SCHOON
SKIMMED FLAT FLET
SKIMMER FALK LARI SKEP SCOOP
LINGEL SCUMMER CUTWATER
SKIMMINGS SCRUFF
SKIMP JIMP SLUR SCAMP SKINCH
SKIMPY JIMP CHARY SPARE SCANTY
STINGY
SKIN KIP KIT BACK BARK CASE CAST
DERM FELL FLAY FLEA HIDE HILD
KITT MORT PEAU PEEL PELT RIND
BALAT BLYPE BRAWN FLOAT GENET
SLUFF STRIP SWARD PELTRY
SWARTH UNCASE CUTICLE DOESKIN
ENDERON KIDSKIN LEATHER
PELLAGE SKIMMER BUCKSKIN
DRUMHEAD LAMBSKIN PARADERM
PELLICLE SEALSKIN TEGUMENT
VITILIGO WOOLFELL
(— FOR BOOKBINDING) BASAN
(— OF BACON) SWARD
(— OF BOARDS) CARPET
(— OF FRUIT) PEEL
(— OF GOOSE) APRON
(— OF INSECT) CAST
(— OF POTATO) JACKET
(— OF POULTRY NECK) HELZEL
(— OF RABBIT) RACK CONEY
(— OF SEAL) SCULP
(— OF THE HEAD) SCALP
(— OF WALNUT) ZEST
(— OF YOUNG CALF) SLINK DEACON
(— WITH WOOL REMAINING ON IT)
WOOLFELL
(60 —S) TURN
(BARE —) BUFF
(BEAVER —) PLEW
(BOAR'S —) SHIELD
(CAST —) SPOIL SLOUGH EXUVIAE
(CHAFED OR SORE —) IRE
(CHAMOIS —) FURWA
(DEEP LAYER OF THE —) CUTIS
(FAWN —) NEBRIS
(INNER PART OF THE —) DERMA
(LAMB — PREPARED LIKE FUR)
BUDGE
(OUTER —) HUSK
(PENDULOUS FOLD OF —) DEWLAP
(ROUGHTANNED —) CRUST
(SHARK —) SHAGREEN
(SHEEP —) BASIL
(SQUIRREL —) VAIR
(THICKENED —) BRAWN
(THIN —) FILM PELLICLE STRIFFEN
SKINFLINT SKIN FLINT SCREW
HUDDLE PELTER SCRAPER SKEEZIX
SKINK ADDA SCINCID SCORPION

SKINNY BONY LEAN THIN SLINK
SKIP DAP HIP BALK BOUT FOOT
JUMP LEAP SLIP TRIP BOUND
CAPER DANCE FRISK SALTO SCOON
SCOPE SCOUP SKITE SMOKE VAULT
GAMBOL GLANCE LAUNCH SPRING
GUNBOAT SKIPPER SKITTER
TRIPPLE PORPOISE
(— **SCHOOL**) TIB
SKIPJACK SKIP BONITO SKIPPER
SKIPPER IHI SKIP LAODAH LOWDAH
SERANG SHIPPER
SKIRMISH FRAY BRUSH CLASH
MELEE SKIRM BICKER HASSLE
PICKEER RUNNING
SKIRMISHER HUSSAR
SKIRMISHING SPARRING
SKIRT CUT LAP BANK BASE COAT
ENGI JUPE SAYA TUBE COAST
JUPON LABIE PAREU PASIN STRIP
TREND TWIST BASQUE DIRNDL
HOBBLE JUMPER KIRTLE PEPLUM
SARONG TAMEIN QUARTER
BASQUINE PULLBACK SKIRTING
(**ARMOR** —) TASSES LAMBOYS
(**DIVIDED** —) CULOTTE
(**HOOPED** —) TUBTAIL
(**TARTAN** —) KILT ARISAID
(PL.) DOCK DOCKEN
SKIRTING SKIRT PLINTH
(PL.) BROKES
SKIT BLACKOUT
SKITTAGETAN HAIDA
SKITTISH SHY CORKY GOOSY WINDY
FLISKY KITTLE SKEIGH SPOOKY
FLIGHTY SCADDLE SKADDLE
STARTLY BOGGLISH SKITTERY
STARTFUL
SKITTLES KAYLES KITTLES SQUAILS
SKUA BONXIE JAEGER TEASER
TULIAC STINKPOT WHIPTAIL
SKULDUGGERY JOUKERY PAWKERY
SKULK DERN JOUK LURK LUSK
MOOCH SCOUT
SKULL BEAN POLL CRANY MOOCH
SCALP SCAUP VAULT COBBRA
PALLET SCONCE CRANIUM HARNPAN
HEADMOLD PANNICLE
(— **BONE**) VOMER
(— **POINT**) TYLION
(**BACK OF** —) OCCIPUT
(**INCOMPLETE** —) CALVARIA
(**UPPER HALF OF** —) SINCIPUT
SKULLCAP COIF PIXY PIXIE SKULL
VAULT BEANIE COIFFE CALOTTE
CAPELINE HOODWORT
(**ARABIAN** —) CHECHIA
(**JEWISH** —) YAMILKE YARMULKE
(**STEEL** —) SECRET
SKUNK ANNA PUSS HURON SKINK
SNIPE ZORIL CHINCHA POLECAT
SEECAWK SMELLER CONEPATE
CONEPATL MUSTELID PHOBYCAT
ZORRILLO
(**JAVANESE** —) TELEDU
SKUNK CABBAGE COLLARD
POCKWEED
SKY BLUE HIGH LIFT LOFT POLE TIEN
AZURE CARRY DYAUS ETHER LANGI

VAULT CAELUS CANOPY HEAVEN
REGION WELKIN ELEMENT HEAVENS
OLYMPUS TENGERE WEATHER
(**ICE** —) ICEBLINK
SKYLARK LARK YERK
SLAB BAT CANT CLAM LECH PARE
SLAT BLADE DALLE LINER PANEL
PLANK SLATE STELA STELE TABLE
WADGE ABACUS FLITCH MARVER
MIHRAB PAVIOR RUNNER FLAPPET
PLANCHE PORPHYRY PUNCHEON
SLABWOOD
(— **OF CLAY**) BAT
(— **OF COAL**) SKIP SLIP
(— **OF LIMESTONE**) BALATTE
(— **OF MARBLE**) DALLE
(— **OF PEAT**) SCAD
(— **OF SANDSTONE**) COMAL
(— **OVER BROOK**) CLAM
(**MEMORIAL** —) LEDGER
(**PAINTER'S** —) SLANT
(**STONE** —) PLANK STELA STELE
INKSTONE
SLACK DRY LAX CULM DUFF NESH
SLOW SOFT CHECK FLOWN LOOSE
SLAKE TARDY ABATED FLABBY
FLAPPY REMISS UNGIRT BACKING
MAKINGS RELAXED SLACKEN
SMEDDUM CARELESS DILATORY
INACTIVE SLOBBERY
(— **IN TRIGGER**) CREEP
(— **SHEET OF SAIL**) FLOW
(**COAL** —) COOM COOMB
(PL.) BAGS
SLACKEN LAG PAY EASE FLAG
SLOW DELAY DOWSE LOOSE RELAX
SLACK SLAKE START SURGE
EXOLVE RELENT UNBEND
(— **SPEED**) HANG
SLACKENING HANG LETUP DETENTE
LETDOWN SLACKAGE
SLACKER SPIV ROTTER COUCHER
SLINKER EMBUSQUE
SLACKNESS LACHES LASHNESS
SLADE SOLE
SLAG SCAR DROSS CINDER DANDER
SCORIA SLAKIN THOMAS QUITTER
SLACKEN
SLAIN FALLEN
SLAKE ABATE SLACK LESSEN
QUENCH REFRESH SATISFY
SLAKING FAT
SLAM CLAP DASH FLUB SLOG SLOT
VOLE CLASH GRAND PLANK SLOSH
STRAM CHELEM FLOUNCE
SLANDER CANT BELIE LIBEL NOISE
BEFOUL DEFAME INJURE MALIGN
MISSAY ASPERSE CALUMNY
OBTRECT SCANDAL TRUMPET
BACKBITE DEROGATE STRUMPET
SLANDERER JUROR
SLANDEROUS FAMOUS VILIPEND
SLANG CANT ARGOT FLASH DIALECT
SLANT TIP CANT FLUE SKEW TILT
BEVEL DRAFT SLOPE SPLAY STOOP
FLANCH SKLENT DRAUGHT
COLORING DIAGONAL
SLANTED CANTED COLORED
COCKEYED

SLANTING BIAS CANT SKEW SLOPE
ASLANT ASLOPE SKLENT SQUINT
LOXOTIC OBLIQUE SLOPING
AVELONGE COLORING OVERWART
SIDELONG
SLANTINGLY AHOO ASWASH
SLANTLY
SLANT LINE VIRGULA VIRGULE
SLAP BOX DAB BLIP BLOW CLAP
CUFF FLAP LICK PLAT SCUD SLAT
SNUB SPAT TACK BLIBE CLINK
CRACK POTCH SKEEG SKELP
SMACK SPANK TWANG TWANK
BLEEZE BUFFET SCLAFF SLIGHT
STRIKE TINGLER WHERRET
BACKSLAP
(— **HARD**) BLAD
(**RANDOM** —) FLAY
SLAPDASH BUCKEYE
SLASH CAG CUT JAG COUP GASH
HASH PANE RACE RASH SLIT TOPS
KNIFE MINCE SCORE SKICE SLISH
RAMMEL SCORCH STREAK SLITTER
DIAGONAL SLASHING
SLASHED JAGGED DECOPED
TATTERED
SLASHING ABATIS
SLAT BOW LAG FLAT PALE SLOT
WAND BLADE SCLAT STAVE SPLINE
EUPHROE BEDSTAFF
SLATE RAG SLAT FRAME KILLAS
TABLET TICKET SHALDER SHINDLE
SLATING
(— **IN SMALL IRREGULAR PIECES**)
SCANTLE
(**BLUE** —) SHIVER SKAILLIE
(**EXPOSED PART OF ROOFING** —)
BARI
(**SURFACE** —) BONE
SLATER HELER HELLIER SLATTER
SKIMMITY
(**TOOL OF** —) STAKE
SLATTERN DAB DAW MAB FROW
MAUX SLUT TRUB DOLLY FAGOT
MAWKS MOGGY MOPSY BLOUSE
CLATCH DOLLOP MALKIN STREEL
TRAPES LADRONE TROLLOP
HUCKMUCK SLUMMOCK
SLATTERNLY DOWDY BLOWSY
DAWISH FROWZY SORDID TRAPISH
SLATTERN SLOVENLY
SLAUGHTER WAL FELL KILL SLAM
SLAY BUTCH HALAL QUELL BATTUE
MURDER STRAGE BUTCHER
CARNAGE KILLING SHAMBLE
BUTCHERY MASSACRE OCCISION
SHECHITA
(— **ACCORDING TO MOSLEM LAW**)
HALAL
(— **OF LARGE NUMBER**) HECATOMB
(**WHOLESALE** —) QUELL
SLAUGHTERER KILLER SHOHET
SHOCHET
SLAUGHTERHOUSE ABBATOIR
BUTCHERY MATADERO SHAMBLES
(— **WORKER**) LIMEMAN
SLAUGHTERING SHEHITA SHECHITA
SLAV VEND WEND CZECH HUNKS

HUNKY SLAVE USKOK CROATIAN MORAVIAN

SLAVE DAS ARDU BOND DASI DUPE ESNE SERF DAVUS HELOT SWINK THEOW ALIPIN ALLTUD CUMHAL FORSAR GUINEA HIEROS MAMLUK SLAVEY THRALL VASSAL BONDMAN CAPTIVE CHATTEL FORSADO HACKNEY PEDAGOG SERVANT SLAVISH BONDMAID LORARIUS MAMELUKE MANCIPLE MORGIANA PRAEDIAL SLAVELET THEOWMAN
(— IN TEMPLE) HIEROS
(— WHO WHIPS OTHERS) LORARIUS
(DEFORMED —) CALIBAN
(FREED —) CLIENT
(FUGITIVE —) MAROON CIMMARON
(GALLEY —) FORSAR FORSADO SFORZATO
(HAREM —) ODALISK
(HINDU —) DAS DASI
(PL.) CHIURM COFFLE HELOTRY TOXOTAE
SLAVER DROOL FROTH DRIVEL DRIBBLE SLABBER SLOBBER SALIVATE
SLAVERY YOKE THRALL BONDAGE HELOTRY MIZRAIM THRALDOM
SLAVEY DRUDGE
SLAVISH MEAN MENIAL
SLAVONIC (— BEING) VILA
SLAY KILL SMITE SPILL MURDER STRIKE BUTCHER EXECUTE STRANGLE
SLAYER BANE HOGNI KILLER MURDERER
SLEAZY FLIMSY
SLED LUGE TODE JUMBO SCOOT SLIDE SLIPE SLOOP HURDLE JUMPER SLEDGE SLEIGH BOBSLED CLIPPER COASTER DOGBOAT DOGSLED MONOSKI POINTER SLIPPER TRAILER TRAVOIS HANDSLED SKELETON TOBOGGAN
SLEDGE DAN DRAG DRAY PULK SLED GURRY PULKA SLIDE SLIPE TRAIL TRAIN TROLL TRUNK SLEIGH KOMATIK PADDOCK TROLLEY TRAINEAU
(— FOR CRIMINALS) HURDLE
(— FOR STRAIGHTENING RAILS) GAG
(LOG —) SLOOP TIEBOY
(MINER'S —) MALLET
SLEDGEHAMMER SMASHER
SLEEK SNOD CLOSE JOLLY SILKY SLICK TRICK SILKEN SLEEKY SLIGHT SMARMY SMOOTH SVELTE SLEEKIT SOIGNEE SLIPPERY
SLEEKNESS GLOSS
SLEEP BED KIP LIB LIE NAP CALK CAMP DORM DOSS DOZE HALE REST WINK BALMY DORSE ROOST SWOON DROWSE SIESTA SNOOZE SOMNUS SWEVEN SLUMBER WINKING
(— BROKEN BY SNORING) GRUFF
(— ON A PERCH) JOUK
(DEEP —) SWOON

(LIGHT —) SLOOM
(PRETENDED —) DOGSLEEP
(PROFOUND —) SOPOR
(SHORT —) NAP SIESTA SNOOZE
SLEEPER TIE FENDER DORMANT DORMEUSE ELEOTRID STRINGER
SLEEPING BED ASLEEP DORMANT
SLEEPLESS LIDLESS WAKEFUL RESTLESS WATCHFUL
SLEEPLESSNESS WATCH INSOMNIA
SLEEPY DOZY HEAVY NODDY PEEPY DROWSY GROGGY MORPHIC SLEEPISH SLUMBERY SOMNIFIC
SLEET STORM
SLEEVE ARM BAND POKE ARMLET MANCHE MOGGAN BUSHING CATHEAD CUBITAL HOUSING THIMBLE
(— ON A SHAFT) CANNON
(— ON GUN) BAND
(HANGING —) TAB
(LEG-OF-MUTTON —) GIGOT
(LONG —) POKE
(TAPERED —) SKEIN
SLEIGH SLO PUNG SLED BOOBY SLIPE TRAIN BERLIN CUTTER SLEDGE CARIOLE TRAINEAU
SLEIGHT ARTIFICE
SLENDER FINE HAIR JIMP LANK LEAN PRIN SLIM THIN DELIE EXILE FAINT LATHY REEDY SLANK SLEEK SMALL SPIRY SWAMP WISPY FILATE SEMMIT SLIGHT SPINNY SPIRED STALKY SVELTE TENDER GRACILE LISSOME SLIVERY SPIRLIE SQUINNY TENUOUS THREADY WASPISH ACICULAR ETHEREAL HAIRLIKE SPINDLED
SLENDERNESS EXILITY TENUITY
SLEW LOT RAFT SLUE STROKE
SLICE CUT BITE CHOP FLAG FLAP JERK SHED STOW CANCH CAPER GIGOT LEACH SHARE SHAVE SHIVE SKELB SLIPE SLIVE CANTLE COLLOP CORNET CULPON SHIVER SLIVER TARGET THIBLE TRENCH SECTION SHAVING TRANCHE COSSETTE TURNOVER
(— CUT IN PLOWING) FLAG
(— OF BACON) BARD BARDE LARDON RASHER
(— OF BREAD) BUTTY WHANG CROUTE TRENCHER
(— OF CHEESE) KEBBOC
(— OF COAL) SKIP
(— OF FISH) COBBIN
(— OF MEAT) STEAK COLLOP CUTLET SCALLOP TAILZIE
(— OF SMOKED SALMON) CORNET
(— REMOVED FROM ROADWAY) CANCH
(— WITH MOTIONS) SAW
(—S OF APPLES) CHOPS
(LARGE —) BLAD DODGE
(THICK —) SLAB
(THIN —) CHIP SECTION
SLICED CUT
SLICK LOY GLIB SNUG SLEEK

CLASSY GLOSSY SMOOTHY SLIDDERY
SLICKER FLOAT SLICK SMOOTH SLEEKER SMOOTHER
SLIDE SCLY SKID SLEW SLIP SLUR BALOP CHUTE COAST COULE CREEP GLIDE HURRY MOUNT SCOOT SHIRL SLADE FINDER SLOUGH SLIDDER SLITHER SLUTHER FADEAWAY GLISSADE SLIDEWAY
(— A DIE) SLUR
(— CARDS) SKIN
(— DOWN) RUSE SLUMP
(— FOR LOWERING CASKS) POLEYNE
(— ON DRUMHEAD) BRACE
(— SIDEWISE) SKID
(TENT —) EUPHROE
SLIDER REGISTER
SLIDEWAY PULLEY
SLIDING COULE
SLIGHT CUT OFF EASY FINE HURT POOR SLAP SLIM SLUR SNUB THIN WEAK FILMY GAUZY LIGHT MINOR SCANT SMALL SOBER FLIMSY FORGET LACHES LITTLE MINUTE REMOTE TWIGGY FRAGILE GRACILE NEGLECT NOMINAL SHALLOW SKETCHY SLENDER SLIGHTY THREADY VILLAIN DELICATE MISPRIZE OVERLOOK SCRANNEL VILIPEND
SLIGHTER LESS
SLIGHTEST FIRST LEAST
SLIGHTINGLY LIGHTLY
SLIGHTLY FAINTLY SOMEWHAT
SLIGHTNESS DELICACY GRACILITY
SLIM THIN GAUNT WANDY SLIGHT SLENDER TENUOUS
SLIME GLIT GORE OOZE SLAB SLIP SLUM GLEET SLAKE SLOAK SLOKE SLEECH SLUDGE SCHLICH SLUBBER SLUTHER
SLIMY OOZY SLAB MUCID GLAIRY GLEETY GLETTY LIMOUS MUCOUS SNOTTY SLEECHY MUCULENT
SLINE JOINT
SLING DUST LOOP FLING HONDA SLUNG BRIDGE BRIDLE HALTER SLACKIE
(— FOR HAULING GAME) TUMPLINE
(— OF BRAIDED FIBERS) MA
SLINGER FUNDITOR
SLINGSHOT SLING SLAPPY TWEAKER CATAPULT SHANGHAI
SLINK SLY CAST HINT LEER LOOP LURK PEAK SHIRK SLING SLUNK SNEAK SLINKY
(— AWAY) SHAG SLOKE FLINCH MIZZLE SHRINK
SLIP DIP IMP NOD SLY BALK CARD CHIT DOCK FALL JINK LOOP RUSE SKEW SKID SLEW SLUR SPEW BEWET BEWIT BONER CHECK DAGGE ERROR FLIER FLYER GLIDE LABEL LAPSE SCAPE SHIFT SHIRL SKATE SKITE SLICK SLIDE SLIPE SLIVE SLUMP STALK SURGE COUPON ENGOBE LAPSUS MISCUE

SLOUGH SLURRY TICKET UNSLIP
DELAPSE FOUNDER ILLAPSE
MISSTEP MORTISE SLIDDER
SLUTHER SNAPPER STUMBLE
BOOKMARK GERTRUDE GLISSADE
HEADBAND QUICKSET SCHEDULE
SIDESLIP SLIPPAGE SLIPPING
(— **AWAY**) GO BILK SKIN WISE
EVADE ELAPSE
(— **BY**) ELAPSE
(— **FROM A PLANT**) STALLON
(— **OF FISH**) RAND
(— **OF PAPER**) ALLONGE
(— **OF WOOD**) SPILL
(— **OFF COURSE**) SLEW SLOUGH
(— **ON CARELESSLY**) SLIVE
(— **OUT**) TIB
(— **SECRETLY**) CREEM
(— **SMOOTHLY**) SWIM
(**CERAMICS** —) SLOP ENGOBE
(**INFANT'S** —) GERTRUDE
(**PILLOW** —) BIER
SLIPCASE CASE FOREL FORREL
SLIPKNOT BOW SNITTLE DRAWKNOT
SLIPMAN JACKER
SLIPOVER OVERSLIP
SLIPPER FLAT MULE NEAP PUMP
SOCK TURN GLAVE MOYLE ROMEO
SCUFF BALLET BOOTEE DORSAY
JULIET PANTON PINSON SANDAL
SCLAFF SCLIFF BAUCHLE CHINELA
CRAKOWE EVERETT SCUFFER
BABOUCHE FEWTERER PANTOFLE
SCLAFFER SLIPSHOE
SLIPPERINESS SLIDDER
SLIPPERY GLEG GLIB SLID GLARY
GLINT SLAPE SLEEK SLICK SOAPY
SWACK CRAFTY GLINSE GREASY
LUBRIC SHIFTY SLIPPY ELUSIVE
EVASIVE GLIDDER SHUTTLE SLIDDRY
SLIDING SLITHER GLIBBERY
SLABBERY SLICKERY SLIDDERY
SLITHERY
SLIPPERY DICK DONCELLA
SLIPSHOD JERRY SLOPPY UNKEMPT
SLAPDASH SLOVENLY
SLIPSTREAM RACE
SLIT CUT EYE JAG KIN NAG RIT FENT
GATE PORT RACE RENT SCAR SLOT
VENT CRACK SPARE BOUCHE
CRANNY OSTIUM STRENT FISSURE
PLACKET SLITTED SLOTTEN
WINDWAY APERTURE BOTHRIUM
(— **HIND LEG**) HARL
(— **IN EDGE OF SHIELD**) BOUCHE
(— **IN STONE**) GRIKE
(— **MADE BY CUT**) KERF
(**ORNAMENTAL** —) SLASH
SLITHER SLIDE HIRSEL SLIDDER
SLUTHER
SLIVER TOP SHAVE SKELF SLICE
SPELK SPELL SHIVER DELIVERY
SPLINTER
(— **OF WOOL**) ROLL ROVE
(**SPINNING** —) END RIBBON
DELIVERY
SLOB JOKER SLUDGE SLOBBER
SLOMMACK
SLOBBER SLOP SLUP SMALM

SMARM SLAVER SLABBER SLATHER
SLIVVER BESLAVER
SLOBBERY SLOBBY SMARMY
SLAVERY
SLOE SLA SNAG SLONE
SLOG SLOSH STRIKE
SLOGAN CRY CACHET PHRASE
CATCHCRY SLUGHORN WARDWORD
SLOOP STAR BOYER COMET SMACK
SCHUIT HOOGAARS
SLOP SLAP SOSS SQUAB SWILL
SOSSLE SOZZLE HOGWASH
SLATTER
(— **AROUND**) SLAISTER
(**PL.**) SLIVERS SLIPSLOP SLOPPAGE
SLOPE UP DIP LIE BAND BANK BENT
BRAE CANT CAST CURB DROP FALL
HANG HILL LEAN PALI RAKE RAMP
RISE SIDE SINK TILT BEVEL CLIFF
COAST GAMMA HIELD PINCH SCARP
SLANT SLENT SLOOP SPLAY STEEP
TALUS VERGE YUNGA ASCENT
BAJADA BATTER BROACH GLACIS
HADING SHELVE TUMBLE UPBROW
UPRISE CUTBANK DESCENT
DOWNSET FORESET HANDING
INCLINE LEANING PENDANT
UPGRADE VERSANT WEATHER
BANKSIDE DRIPPING GLISSADE
GRADIENT SHOULDER SIDELING
SNOWBANK
(— **BACK**) BATTER
(— **DOWN**) SHED
(— **OF CUESTA**) INFACE
(— **OF ROOF**) CURB
(— **OF STERNPOST**) RAKE
(— **UPWARD**) CLIMB ASCEND
BATTER
(**DOWNWARD** —) HANG DEVALL
DECLINE DESCENT HANGING
DOWNHILL
(**GENTLE** —) GLACIS
(**MARGINAL** —) CESS
(**MOUNTAIN** —) ADRET
(**STEEP** —) BROW HEADWALL
SLOPING CANT DEVEX SLANT SLOPE
SLOPY ASLOPE SHELVY DECLIVE
DOWNHILL SIDELING
(— **ABRUPTLY**) BOLD
(— **BACKWARD**) SUPINE
SLOPPY JUICY SOPPY SLABBY
SOZZLY SPLOSHY SLABBERY
SLAPDASH SLATTERN SLATTERY
SLIPSHOD WATERISH
SLOSH DOWSE SLASH SLUSH SOUSE
SQUDGE SPLODGE
SLOT COVE DROP SCROLL SPLINE
KEYHOLE GUIDEWAY
SLOTH AI UNAU TARDO ACEDIA
IGNAVY ACCIDIE IGNAVIA BRADYPOD
EDENTATE PIGRITIA SLUGGING
SLOTH BEAR BHALU ASWAIL
SLOTHFUL FAT ARGH IDLE LAZY
INERT LITHER THOKISH UNLUSTY
DELICATE INDOLENT SLUGGISH
SLOUCH LOUCH LARRUP LOLLOP
LOUNGE SLIDDER TROLLOP
SHAMMOCK SLOUCHER
SLOUCH HAT SMASHER

SLOUGH CORE SHED SLEW SLUE
BAYOU RAVEL SHUCK SLONK SLUFF
SPOIL SWAMP ESCHAR DISCARD
LAMMOCK
SLOVEN BESOM CLART SLUSH
TROLLY HALLION TRACHLE
HUDDROUN
SLOVENLY DOWDY GAUMY MESSY
BLOWZY CLATTY FROWZY GRUBBY
SHABBY SLOPPY SLOVEN TRAILY
UNTIDY BUNTING SLIVING SLOUCHY
UNSONCY CARELESS HUDDROUN
SLIPSHOD SLOBBERY SLUBBERY
SLUTTISH TROLLOPY
SLOW BOG LAG LAX LEK WET ARGH
DREE DULL LATE LAZY LENT SKID
SLUG SULK BLUNT DUNCH DUNNY
HEAVY HOOLY INERT POKEY SLACK
SLOTH SWEER TARDE TARDO
TARDY UNAPT ARREST BEHIND
DRIECH DUMMEL HINDER RETARD
SLOOMY SOODLY TRAILY COSTIVE
DRONISH HALTING LAGGARD
LANGUID SLACKEN SOAKING
STRANGE TARDANT TEDIOUS
UNREADY DILATORY INACTIVE
LATESOME SLUGGISH
(— **DOWN**) SEIZE
(— **IN BURNING**) SOFT
(— **IN MOVEMENT**) GRAVE INERT
SULKY
(— **OF MIND**) STUPID
(— **TO LEARN**) BACKWARD
(— **TO RESPOND**) GROSS
(— **UP**) SLACK SLACKEN
(**MODERATELY** —) ANDANTE
(**MUSICALLY** —) LENTO
(**PLEASANTLY** —) SOFT
(**VERY** —) LARGO
SLOW-BURNING PUNKY
SLOWED STIFF
SLOWER LATTER
SLOW LORIS KOKAN
SLOWLY SLOW DULLY GRAVE
HOOLY LENTO ADAGIO GENTLY
HEAVILY
SLOW-MOVING SLEEPY DORMANT
DRAWLING SLUGGISH
SLOWNESS LAG SLOTH LENTOR
TARDITY LATENESS
SLOW-WITTED FAT DENSE STUPID
SLOWWORM HAGWORM
SLUDGE GUNK SLOB
SLUE SLEW SWAMP SLOUGH
SLUG BUST LINE MILL PLOW SHOT
SNAG STEW ARION CLUMP LIMAX
SNAIL RATTLE STRIKE SNIFTER
TREPANG GEEPOUND
SLUGGARD DAW SLOW SLUG
DRONE CAYNARD LUGGARD
SWINGER SLOWBACK SLUGABED
SLUGGISH LAG DOZY DULL FOUL
LATE LAZY SLOW BROSY DOPEY
DRONY FAINT HEAVY INERT LOURD
RESTY SULKY BOVINE DRAGGY
DROWSY LEADEN SLEEPY SLOOMY
SLUGGY SUPINE TORPID COSTIVE
DORMANT DRONISH LAGGARD
LANGUID LENTOUS LUMPISH

RESTIVE DILATORY INACTIVE
INDOLENT LOURDISH SLOTHFUL
SLOTTERY SLUGGARD

SLUGGISHNESS LEAD SLOTH
APATHY LENTOR PHLEGM INERTIA
LANGUOR

SLUICE CLOW GOOL GOTE GOUT
SASSE SLUSH TRUNK CLOUGH
FENDER LAUNDER PENSTOCK
WASTWEIR

SLUICEWAY FLASH

SLUM BUSTI BUSTEE WARREN

SLUMBER DORM DOVE DOZE JOUK
REST ROUT SLEEP SLOOM DROWSE

SLUMP FALL FLOP SOSS SLOUCH
LETDOWN TROLLOP

SLUR BIND SLIM COULE GLIDE SLIME
SCRUFF SLIGHT SLUBBER LIGATURE
(— IN PRINTING) SHAKE

SLURRY SLIP

SLUSH MIRE POSH SIND SLOP FLUSH
SLOSH SPOSH STUFF SWASH
SWOSH LOPPER SLUTCH SLOBBER
SLODDER

SLUSHY SLASHY SLOPPY SLOSHY
SLUDGY STICKY SPLASHY
SLOBBERY

SLUT MAUX BITCH FILTH QUEAN
DOLLOP DRAZIL DROSSEL
SLATTERN

SLUTTISH SLUTTY SORDID

SLY ARCH FOXY SLEE SLID SLIM
CANNY COONY LOOPY PAWKY
POKEY SLOAN SNAKY ARTFUL
CRAFTY FELINE SUBTLE SUPPLE
CUNNING EVASIVE FURTIVE LEERING
SUBTILE UNFRANK GUILEFUL
SLEIGHTY SNEAKING STEALTHY
THIEVISH

SLYNESS CUNNING PAWKERY
STEALTH ARCHNESS

SMACK BANG BARK BUSS KISS SALT
SCAT SLAP TANG TROW VEIN
BAWLY GOUFF SAVOR SNACK
TASTE BARQUE FLAVOR SMATCH
SMACKEE SPANKER BRAGOZZO
SLAPDASH TINCTURE
(— OF) RELISH

SMACKING SKELPING

SMALL BIT SMA WEE BABY MEAN
PINK SEED SLIM TINY WEAK BIJOU
BITTY DAWNY DEENY DINKY ELFIN
PETIT PETTY PINKY POKEY TEENY
WEENY BANTAM FRIBBY GRUBBY
LITTLE MINUTE NARROW PEANUT
PETITE SLIGHT SMALLY CAPSULE
NAGGISH NANITIC PICCOLO
QUEECHY SCRIMPY SLENDER
THRIFTY PILULOUS SNIPPETY
(— AND NUMEROUS) MILIARY
(— AND THICK) DUMPY DUMPTY
(— BUT TANGIBLE) CERTAIN
(— PORTION) MODICUM
(DAINTILY —) MIGNON
(EXCESSIVELY —) BOXY
(NOT —) GOOD
(VERY —) WEE FINE TINY DWARF
PUSIL PYGMY TEENY MINUTE
MINIKIN TIDDLEY DWARFISH

SMALLAGE MARCH

SMALLCLOTHES SHORTS SMALLS

SMALL CRANBERRY FENBERRY

SMALLER LESS MINOR LESSER

SMALLEST FIRST LEAST MINIM
TITMAN MINIMUS

SMALLHOLDER TOFTMAN

SMALL-MINDED PETTY

SMALLNESS EXILITY FEWNESS
PAUCITY EXIGUITY SCARCITY

SMALLPOX POX VARIOLA ALASTRIM

SMALT ROYAL ESCHEL SMALTZ
ZAFFER ASMALTE

SMART YEP BRAW FESS FLIP FOXY
GNIB NICE PINK RACY SNAP SPRY
TRIG ACUTE BRISK CLEAN DINKY
FLASH HEADY JIMMY KIPPY NIFTY
NOBBY NUTTY PEERT PRANK PRIDY
SASSY SAUCY SHARP SLEEK SLICK
SMIRK SMOKE SMUSH SPICY SPRIG
STING SWANK SWISH TIGHT TIPPY
TOFFY TRICK AKAMAI BRAWLY
CHEESY CLEVER DAPPER GIGOLO
JAUNTY KITTLE PERTLY SHREWD
SPANKY SPIFFY SPRINK SPRUCE
STOUND SWANKY SWIDGE TIDDLY
KNOWING PUNGENT SWAGGER
TOFFISH VOGUISH BRUSHING
(— IN APPEARANCE) POSH
(— IN DRESS) GALLANT

SMART ALECK FLIP SMARTY

SMARTEN FINE PUSS SMUG SLICK
TITIVATE

SMARTLY SMART SNACK YEPLY
TIDELY

SMARTNESS TON SNAP SMART
SWISH

SMARTWEED CULERAGE REDKNEES

SMASH BASH BUMP CAVE DASH
PASH RUSH SCAT TRAP BREAK
CRACK CRASH CRAZE SOCKO
STAVE WRECK CRACKER SHATTER
SMASHUP DEBRUISE DEMOLISH
OVERHEAD SMARASH
(— A GAP) BREACH

SMASHED BUNG STOVEN BROOZLED

SMASHING CRACKING

SMASHUP STRAMASH

SMATTERING SMACK SMATCH
SMATTER

SMEAR RUB BLOT BLUR CLAM DAUB
DOPE GAUM GLOB GORM MOIL
CLEAM DITCH GLAIR SLAKE SLARE
SMALM SMARM SULLY BEDAUB
BESLAB DEFILE PLATCH SLAVER
SLURRY SMIRCH SMOOCH SMUDGE
SPREAD STREAK STRIKE BEPAINT
BESMEAR PLASTER POLLUTE
SPLOTCH SLAISTER
(— OVER) ENGLUTE
(— WITH BLOOD) GILD
(— WITH EGG WHITE) GLAIR
(— WITH MUD) CLART SLIME
(— WITH SOMETHING STICKY)
GAUM GORM LIME
(— WITH TAR) PAY
(— WITH WAX) CERE

SMEAR DAB FLATFISH MARYSOLE

SMEARED FOUL BROSY MUSSY

SCOVY BLOODY SMUDGY BLURRED
BEGUMMED

SMEARY DAUBY GAUMY

SMEDDUM SMITHUM

SMELL FUNK FUST GUSH NOSE
ODOR VENT AROMA FETOR FLAIR
SAVOR SCENT SMACK SNIFF SNOOK
SNUFF STIFE TASTE OLFACT
RESENT SMEECH BREATHE
PERFUME REFLAIR VERDURE
(— AFTER PREY) BREVIT
(— OFFENSIVELY) REEK
(DAMP FUSTY —) RAFT
(DISAGREEABLE —) GOO STENCH
(HAVING PLEASANT —) SNIFTY
(MUSTY —) FUST
(OFFENSIVE —) FUNK FETOR STINK
MEPHITIS
(STRONG —) HOGO
(SWEET —) SWEET

SMELLY FUGGY WHIFFY SMELLFUL

SMELT DECOCT INANGA EPERLAN
ICEFISH ELIQUATE SALMONID
SPARLING SPERLING
(FRY OF —) PRIM

SMEW NUN PIED SMEE DIVER
SMETHE

SMILAX LILY SARSA LILIUM

SMILE BEAM GRIN FLASH FLEER
SMEER ARRIDE SMUDGE SMIRKLE
(— AMOROUSLY) SMICKER
(AFFECTED —) SMIRK
(SELF-CONSCIOUS —) SIMPER

SMILING GOOD RIANT SMILY SMIRKY
TWINKLY SMILEFUL

SMIRCH SMIT SOIL SMEAR SULLY
SLURRY SOILURE TARNISH

SMIRCHED DINGY

SMIRK DRAD YIRN SIMPER SMICKER
SMIRKLE SMURTLE

SMITE DUNT FRAP GIRD SLAY FLING
SKITE STRIKE
(— WITH LIGHTNING) LEVEN

SMITH MIMIR REGIN BOSSER
FORGER SMITHY FARRIER GLUTTER
SMITHER STEELER WAYLAND
FLOORMAN FORGEMAN PANSMITH

SMITHSONITE CALAMINE

SMITHY FORGE SMIDDY STITHY
STUDDIE FARRIERY

SMITTEN EPRISE STRICKEN

SMOCK BRAT SLOP KAMIS SMOKE
JIBBAH JUMPER CHEMISE SMICKET

SMOKE PEW USE FLAN FOGO FUFF
FUME FUNK HAVE LUNT NAVE PIPE
REEK ROKE TOVE DRINK REECH
SMEEK SMORE SMUSH STIVE VAPOR
WHIFF BREATH BUCCAN POTHER
SMEECH SMUDGE INCENSE
SMOLDER SMOTHER BACONIZE
(— MARIJUANA) BLAST
(FROST —) BARBER
(OFFENSIVE —) FUNK
(TOBACCO —) BLAST

SMOKEHOUSE FUMATORY

SMOKEJACK STACKMAN

SMOKER FUNKER

SMOKESTACK STACK FUNNEL
TUNNEL CHIMNEY

SMOKE TREE ZANTE FUSTET
FUSTIC SCOTINO
SMOKING ROOM DIVAN TABAGIE
SMOKY HAZY ROKY DINGY FUMID
FUMISH FUMOSE SMUDGY SMUISTY
SMOLDER SMUSH SMOTHER
SMOLDERING PUNKY
SMOLT SMELT SMOUT SPROD
SMOOCH LALLYGAG LOLLYGAG
SMOOTH DUB FAT LAP NOT BOSS
COMB DRAG EASE EASY EVEN FACE
FAIR FILE FLAT GLAD GLEG GLIB
HONE IRON LENE NOTT REET SLID
SNOD SOFT BLAND BRENT CLEAR
COUTH DARBY DIGHT DOLCE DRESS
EMERY FLOAT FRAZE GLARE GOOSE
HOWEL LEVEL LITHE PLAIN PLANE
PRESS QUIET SCARF SILKY SLAPE
SLEEK SLICK SMOLT SNUFF SOAPY
SUANT SUAVE SUENT TERSE
ABRASE BUFFED CREAMY EQUATE
EVENLY FETTLE FLUENT GLOSSY
GREASE GREASY LEGATO LIMBER
MANGLE POLITE SCREED SILKEN
SLIGHT STREAK STRIKE STROKE
SVELTE UNFRET BOULDER ERUGATE
FLATTEN SLEEKIT EXPLICIT
GLABRATE GLABROUS GLIBBERY
GRAZIOSO LEVIGATE SARSENET
SLIDDERY SQUEEGEE STRICKLE
UNRUFFLE
(— **BY BREAKING LUMPS**) BILDER
(— **MARBLE**) GRIT
(— **ONESELF UP**) PREEN
(— **OVER**) GLOZE PLASTER
(— **TYPE**) KERN
(**HYPOCRITICALLY** —) SLEEK
(**PHONETICALLY** —) LENE LENIS
SMOOTHER GLAZER
SMOOTHLY SLICK EASILY EVENLY
GLIBLY SMOOTH SPROWSY
SWEETLY POLITELY
SMOOTHNESS EASE FLUENCY
SMOOTH-RUNNING SWEET
SMOOTH WINTERBERRY CANHOOP
SMOTHER BURKE CHOKE SMEAR
SMOKE SMORE MOIDER QUEZEN
SMUDGE STIFLE FLASKER OPPRESS
QUEASON SMOLDER SMUDDER
SMOTHERED ETOUFFE STIFLED
SMUDGE GAUM SLUR SMUT SOIL
SOOT CROCK SMEAR SMOKE
SMOOCH SMUTCH SMOLDER
SMOTHER SOILURE
SMUDGED SMUTCHY
SMUG SMUSH SUAVE SMUDGE
SMUGGLE RUN STEAL BOOTLEG
SHUFFLE
SMUGGLER OWLER RUNNER
SPOTSMAN
SMUGGLING OWLING
SMUGLY FATLY
SMUT BUNT COOM BLACK BLECK
COLLY COOMB CROCK GRIME
SMOOT SMITCH SMUTCH SMATTER
COLBRAND
SMUTCH BLOT SMIRCH SMITCH
SMOUCH SMUDGE
SMUT GRASS TUSSOCK

SMUTTY BAWDY DIRTY SOOTY
SULTRY BARNYARD FREUDIAN
SMYRNA USHAK
SNACK BIT CUT BAIT BITE SNAP
TAPA CHACK CHECK SHARE SNICK
TASTE GOUTER MUNGEY SNATCH
NUNCHEON
SNAFFLE GAG
SNAG KNAG SNUG STUB POINT
PLANTER SNAGGLE
(PL.) EMBARRAS
SNAIL HUA PILA SNAG CHINK DRILL
HELIX OLIVA PHYSA SHELL THAIS
TURBO WHELK CERION CONKER
DODMAN NATICA PHYSID PURPLE
TRITON WINKLE RISSOID UNICORN
VERTIGO ZONITID CASSIDID
ESCARGOT HODMADOD JANTHINA
LYMNAEID MELANIAN NERITOID
RAMSHORN SOLARIUM
SNAILFLOWER CARACOL
SNAKE (ALSO SEE SERPENT AND
REPTILE) ASP BOA BOM NAG BOBA
BOID BOMA JUBO NAGA NAJA SNIG
ABOMA ASPIC COBRA CONGO
CRIBO DRILL JIBOA KRAIT MAMBA
PTYAS RACER SNECK TIGER VIPER
BOIGID BONGAR CANTIL CHITAL
DABOIA ELAPID GOPHER HISSER
JESSUR KERRIL PYTHON ROLLER
RUNNER TAIPAN WENONA ADJIGER
ANILIID BOKADAM CAMOODI
CRAWLER CREEPER CULEBRA
DIAPSID HAGWORM LABARIA
LANGAHA PRESTER RATTLER
REGULUS REPTILE SERPENT
SPITTER WALPAPI ANACONDA
BONETAIL BUNGARUM CASCAVEL
CERASTES CROTALID EGGEATER
FLATHEAD HAIRWORM JARARACA
KEELBACK MOCCASIN OPHIDIAN
RINGHALS SNAKELET VIPERINE
SNAKEBARK IRONBARK
SNAKEBIRD DARTER PLOTUS
ANHINGA DUCKLAR
SNAKEHEAD MURRAL
SNAKELIKE ANGUINE
SNAKEMOUTH POGONIA
SNAKEPIECE POINTER
SNAKEROOT STEVIA BABROOT
BUGBANE SANGREL SANICLE
SAWWORT POOLWORT RICHWEED
WHITETOP
SNAKESKIN SPOIL HACKLE SLOUGH
(**CASTOFF** —S) EXUVIAE
SNAP SET ZIP BARK BITE CHOP
GNAP HUFF JERK KNAP LIRP SETT
BREAK CLACK FILIP FLICK GANCH
KNACK KNICK SMACK SNACK
BLUDGE SNAPPY SNATCH FASTENER
PUSHOVER SNAPHEAD
(— **AT**) HANCH
(— **LIGHTLY**) KNICK
(— **OFF**) SNIP
(— **TOGETHER**) CRASH
(— **UP**) SNUP SNAFFLE
(— **WITH FINGER**) LIRP FILIP THRIP
FILLIP
SNAPBACK PASSBACK

SNAPDRAGON BULL SNAPS BULLER
BULLDOG DOGMOUTH
SNAPE FLINCH
SNAPPER UKU BRIM JOCU SESI
BREAM PARGO VORAZ CUBERA
HUSSAR JENOAR LAWYER NATIVE
TAMURE ULAULA COCKNEY
CRACKER BIAJAIBA CACHUCHO
FLAMENCO GNATSNAP LUTIANID
WILLOMAI SCHNAPPER
SNAPPING DOGGISH
SNAPPING BEETLE ELATER
SKIPPER SNAPPER ELATERID
SKIPJACK
SNAPPING TURTLE LOGHEAD
SHAGTAIL
SNAPPISH CRUP EDGY PUXY CROSS
SNACK TESTY WASPY CUTTED
SNAGGY SNAPPY SNIPPY DOGGISH
PEEVISH
SNAPPY CRISP JEMMY ZIPPY
SNARE GIN HAY NET PIT SET BUKE
FANG GIRN GRIN HOOK LACE LIME
TOIL TRAP WAIT WIRE BRAKE
CATCH FRAUD GNARE LATCH LEASH
SINEW SNARL SNIRL STALE SWEEK
TRAIN COBWEB GILDER PANTER
SNATCH SPRINT TREPAN TUNNEL
ENSNARE OVERNET PITFALL
SETTING SNICKLE SPRINGE
BIRDLIME INVEIGLE LIMEBUSH
SPRINGLE TENDICLE
(— **DEER**) WITHE
(— **FOR ELEPHANTS**) KEDDAH
SNARL ARR BITE CARL GIRN GNAR
GURR HARL HURR NARR TWIT WAFF
YARR GNARL GNARR GRILL KNURL
RAVEL SNIRL TWINE BOWWOW
BUMBLE GAUNCH MUCKER TANGLE
VENNER GRIZZLE GRUMBLE
SNARLED SNAFU
SNARLER CYNIC
SNARLING LATRANT
SNATCH HAP NAB NIP GRAB HINT
RACE RASE SNAP SNIP WHIP WRAP
YERK YUCK BRAID CATCH CLAWK
CLICK EREPT GANCH GRASP GRIPE
PLUCK SNACK STRIP SWIPE SWOOP
TWEAK WREST SNITCH STRIKE
TWITCH WRENCH CLAUGHT
GRABBLE SCAMBLE VULTURE
SNEAK GRUB LEER LOOP LOUT
LURK PEAK PIMP SHUG SNIG LURCH
MEECH SCOUT SHIRK SKULK SLIDE
SLINK SLIPE SLIVE SLOKE SNEAP
SNICK SNOOK BLIFIL MICHER
WEASEL SLOUNGE SNIGGLE
SNEAKSBY
(— **AWAY**) SLIPE
(— **OFF**) MAG SHAB
(**PRYING** —) SNOOP
SNEAKER CREEPER GUMSHOE
SNEAKING HANGDOG PEAKING
SLIVING
SNEAKY FURTIVE MEECHING
SNEER SHY FLON GIBE GIRD GIRN
GULE JEER JERK JIBE MOCK FLEER
FLING FLOUT GLEEK JAUNT SCOFF
SLARE SLEER SNIRT GIZZEN

SNEEST WRINKLE RIDICULE
SNEERING FRUMPERY
SNEEZE NEESE NEEZE ARREST
(— **AT**) CONDEMN DESPISE
SNEEZEWEED ALANT ROSILLA
HELENIUM
SNEEZEWOOD NIESHOUT
SNEEZEWORT HARDHEAD
PTARMICA
SNEEZING PTARMIC
SNELL SNOOD TIPPET GANGING
SNICK TIP SNECK
SNICKER TITTER SMIRKLE SNIGGER
SNIGGLE
SNIFF NOSE TIFT VENT WIND SMELL
SNAFF SNIFT SNUFF SNIVEL
SNAFFLE SNIFFLE SNOTTER
SNIFTER SLUG BALLOON INHALER
SNIGGER WHICKER
SNIGGLE BRAGGLE
SNIP CUT CLIP CROP SHRED SNICK
SNIPE JACK NICK WISP SCAPE SNITE
WADER WILLET BLEATER BLITTER
DOWITCH HUMILITY LONGBILL
SHADBIRD
SNIPER TEASER BUSHWACK
SNIVEL BUBBLE SNIFFLE SNIFTER
SNOTTER SNUFFLE
SNOB SNAB SNOOT FLUNKY
SHONEEN SNOBBER
SNOBBISH DICKTY SNOBBY SNOOTY
UPSTAGE
SNOOK SNOOT ROBALO
SNOOP PRY PEEK PEEP SNEAK
BREVIT PIROOT GUMSHOE
SNOOPER CREEP BUSYBODY
SNOOPY CURIOUS
SNOOZE SLEEP SNOOZLE
SNORE ROUT SNARK SNORK SNORT
SNOCKER SNOTTER
SNORING STERTOR RHONCHUS
SNORT BLOW ROUT SNUR TOOT
VENT FNESE SNARK SNEER SNORE
SNORK WHOOF EXCLAIM SNIFTER
SNOCKER SNORKEL SNORTLE
SNOTTER
SNOUT NEB SAW BILL NOSE WROT
GROIN SNOOT MUFFLE MUZZLE
NOZZLE GRUNTLE ROSTRUM
SNOUT BEETLE CURCULIO
SNOUT MITE BDELLID
SNOW CORN DRIP GRUE COVER
SPOSH STORM SUGAR WHITE
POWDER COCAINE GRAUPEL
RAMPART WEATHER SCOUTHER
WINDSLAB
(— **PELLETS**) GRAUPEL
(— **SLIGHTLY**) SPIT
(**DISSOLVING** —) FLUSH
(**DRIFTED** —) WINDLE
(**GLACIER** —) FIRN NEVE BLIZZ
(**HEAVY FALL OF** —) PASH
(**MUSHY** —) SLOB
(**NEW-FALLEN** —) MANNA
(**PARTLY MELTED** —) SLUSH
(**WHIRLING** —) SKIRL
SNOWBERRY MOXA WAXBERRY
SNOWBIRD JUNCO
SNOW BUNTING OATFOWL

SNOWBIRD SNOWFOWL
SNOW COCK JERMONAL
SNOWDRIFT YOWDEN
SNOWDROP TREE BELLWOOD
COWLICKS TISSWOOD
SNOWFALL PASH SKIFF SKIFT
FLURRY ONDING
SNOWFLAKE FLAG FLAUCHT
SNOW FLEA PODURAN PODURID
SNOW GOOSE WAVY
SNOWINESS NIVOSITY
SNOW LEOPARD IRBIS
SNOWLESS GREEN
SNOWMAN YETI
SNOW MOUNTAIN JOKUL
SNOWSHOE WEB PATIN PATTEN
RACKET RACQUET
SNOWSTORM PURGA DRIFTER
BLIZZARD
SNOWY NIVAL WHITE NIVEOUS
SNUB AIR RITZ SLAP SNIB FRUMP
SNEAP SWANK REBUFF REBUTE
SIMOUS SLIGHT SNOUCH SNUBBY
SETDOWN
SNUBBING MAIL
SNUBBY PUGGISH
SNUB-NOSED SIMOUS
SNUFF TOP VENT MUSTY SNIFF
SNUSH TABAC COHOBA PULVIL
RAPPEE SNEESH STIFLE SNUFFLE
BERGAMOT MACCABOY ORANGERY
SMUTCHIN
SNUFFBOX MILL
SNUFFBOX BEAN CACOON
SNUFFER PRICK DOUTER TOPPER
PRICKER
SNUFFLE SNIVEL SNAFFLE SNIFFLE
SNIFTER
SNUG LEW RUG BIEN COSH COZY
NEAT TAUT TEAT TOSH TOSY
CANNY CLOSE COUTH POVIE QUEME
TIGHT PENTIT COUTHIE SNUGGERY
SNUGGISH
SNUGGLE SNUG BURROW CUDDLE
SNUDGE CROODLE SNUZZLE
SNUGLY SHORT COSILY
SO SAE SUCH THAT THIS THUS
THISSEN INSOMUCH SUCHWISE
THUSWISE
(— **AM I**) LIKEWISE
(— **BE IT**) AMEN
(— **FAR AS**) QUOAD
(— **TO SPEAK**) FAIRLY
(**NOT** —) SECUS
(**QUITE** —) EXACTLY
SOAK RET SOB SOD SOG SOP WET
BOWK BUCK SIPE BINGE DROUK
DROWN SOUSE STEEP TOAST
DRENCH EMBAIN IMBIBE IMBRUE
SEETHE SODDEN SPONGE INSTEEP
MICKERY SWELTER SATURATE
(— **A CASK**) GROG
(— **FLAX**) RET RATE
(— **IN**) SOP FEATHER
SOAKED SOGGY SOPPY SOBBED
SODDEN WATERY DRUNKEN
SOBBING DRAGGLED
SOAKING BATH SUING SOGGING
INFUSION

SOAP SAPO SUDS CHIPS STOCK
NIGGER CASTILE TALLATE WINDSOR
SANDSOAP
(**CAKE OF** —) TABLET TABULATE
(**LIQUID** —) FIT
SOAPBARK QUILLAI SOAPWOOD
SOAPFISH JABON
SOAP PLANT AMOLE PALMILLO
SOAPROOT SOAPWEED
SOAPSTONE ALBERENE STEATITE
SOAPSTONER TALCER
SOAPWORT BORITH COWHERB
SAPONARY SOAPROOT SOAPWEED
SOAR FLY STY KITE FLOAT MOUNT
PLANE SPIRE TOWER ASPIRE
AIRPLANE
SOARING FLIGHT ICARIAN SPIRING
ESSORANT
SOB YEX SIKE SNOB SNUB SOUGH
BLUBBER SINGULT
SOBBING GREET
SOBER SAD CALM COOL SAGE CIVIL
FRESH GRAVE QUIET STAID DOULCE
SEDATE SEVERE SOLEMN SOMBER
STEADY EARNEST PENSIVE
REGULAR SERIOUS UNFOXED
DECOROUS MODERATE
SOBRIETY DRYNESS GRAVITY
SOBRIQUET BYNAME HAWKEYE
SO-CALLED ALLEGED
SOCCER FOOTER FOOTBALL
SOCIABLE COSY CHUMMY CLUBBY
FOLKSY SOCIAL AFFABLE AMIABLE
INNERLY CLUBABLE FAMILIAR
FELLOWLY INFORMAL
SOCIAL DISTAL SUPPER SOCIABLE
SOCIETAL
(— **WORKER**) ALMONER
SOCIALISM ETATISM MARXISM
GUESDISM
SOCIALIST FABIAN NIHILIST
SOCIALIZE CIVILIZE
SOCIETY BUND HALL HERD SANG
GUILD MONDE SABHA SAMAJ SANGH
SOKOL MENAGE NANIGO PARISH
SYSTEM VEREIN ACADEMY COLLEGE
COLORUM COMPANY COUNCIL
KINGDOM SOCIETE THIASOS
EXCHANGE HETAERIA PRECINCT
SOCIETAS SODALITY SORORITY
(— **OF RELIGIOUS FANATICS**)
COLORUM
(**CHORAL** —) CHOIR
(**CLOWN** —) KOSHARE KOYEMSHI
(**CRAFT** —) ARTEL
(**DEBATING** —) POP
(**GYMNASTIC** —) SOKOL
(**HIGH** —) SWELLDOM
(**LITERARY** —) HALL
(**RELIGIOUS** —) CHURCH
(**SECRET** —) HUI EGBO HOEY PORO
TONG LODGE OGBONI PURRAH
(**UTOPIAN** —) ANARCHY
SOCINIAN RACOVIAN
SOCIOLOGY DEMOTICS
SOCK BOP ONE BIFF BUST HOSE
VAMP ANKLET ARGYLE VAMPEY
STOCKING
(— **OF GOAT'S HAIR**) UDO

(INFANT'S —) BOOTEE BOOTIE
(JAPANESE —) TABI
SOCKET BOX CUP PAD POD BUSH
CELL HOSE LEAD NOSE SHOE CHAIR
POINT SHANK BUCKET BUDGET
COLLET EYEPIT NOZZLE POCKET
SAUCER SCONCE ALVEOLE
COCKEYE FERRULE FUTCHEL
GUDGEON THIMBLE TORULUS
ALVEOLUS DRAWHEAD
(— **FOR LANCE**) PORT
(— **FOR LENS**) CELL
(— **FOR MOUTHPIECE**) BIRN
(— **IN GOLF CLUB HEAD**) HOSE
HOSEL
(— **OF BONE**) POT
(— **OF HINGE**) PAN
(— **OF MILLSTONE**) INK COCKEYE
(— **OF WATER PIPE**) BELL
(BIT —) POD
SOCLE ZOCCO
SOCRATES (— **METHOD**) MAIEUTIC
SOD HUB BEAT DELF FAIL FLAG
SCAD SONK TURF DELPH GAZON
GLEBE SCRAW SWARD CLOWER
TERRON SODDING
SODA BARILLA
SODA POP TONIC
SODDEN SAMMY SAPPY SOGGY
POACHY DRAGGLED
SODIUM NA SODA NATRIUM
SODIUM BICARBONATE SODA
BICARB
SODIUM BORATE BORAX
SODIUM CARBONATE SODA TRONA
ANATRON BARILLA SALSODA
SODIUM CHLORIDE SALT HALITE
SODIUM THIOSULFATE HYPO
SODOMITE DOG BUGGER SPINTRY
BOUGERON
SOEVER SOME
SOFA BOIST COUCH DIVAN SQUAB
CANAPE LOUNGE SETTEE
CAUSEUSE SOCIABLE
SOFFIT GATHER PLANCIER
SOFT COY TID FEIL LASH LIMP LUSH
MILD MURE NASH PLUM SART TOSY
WAXY WEAK BALMY BLAND CUSHY
DABBY DOLCE DOWNY FAINT GIVEY
HOOLY LENIS LIGHT MALMY MELCH
MUSHY PADDY PAPPY PIANO PLIFF
SILKY SLACK SMALL SOAPY SOOTH
SWASH SWEET WAXEN WETHE
YAPPY CASHIE CREAMY EFFETE
FLAGGY FLOSSY FLUFFY GENTLE
LYDIAN MELLOW PIPING PLACID
SAMMEL SIDDER SILKEN SLOPPY
SOFTLY SPONGY SPOONY TENDER
UNDURE CLEMENT COTTONY
DUCTILE FLESHLY LENIENT
SQUASHY CUSHIONY FEMININE
FLEXIBLE HOTHOUSE LADYLIKE
SARCENET SQUELCHY TRANQUIL
(— **AND FLEXIBLE**) FLOPPY
(— **AND LIFELESS**) DOUGHY
(— **IN TEXTURE**) SUPPLE
(VERY —) SQUASHY
SOFT-COVER PAPERBACK
SOFTEN CUT CREE MELT SOAK

SOFT TAME ALLAY BATCH BREAK
FRIZZ LITHE MALAX TOUCH WOKIE
DIGEST GENTLE LENIFY PACIFY
RELENT SOOTHE SUBDUE SUBMIT
TEMPER WEAKEN APPEASE
ASSUAGE CUSHION LENIATE
MOLLIFY QUALIFY SWEETEN
UNSTEEL AMOLLISH ATTEMPER
ENFEEBLE HUMANIZE MITIGATE
MODULATE PALLIATE PRETTIFY
(— **BY BOILING**) CREE
(— **BY KNEADING**) MALAX
(— **BY STEEPING**) MACERATE
(— **COLOR**) CUT SCUMBLE
(— **FIBERS**) BREAK
(— **GRADUALLY**) SQUAT
(— **JUTE**) BATCH
(— **LEATHER**) BREY FRIZ FRIZZ
(— **METAL**) ALLAY
(— **TONE**) SURD
SOFTENED ROXY ANODYNE
FLEXUOUS
SOFTENING LENIENT MALACIA
BLETTING
SOFTER MANCANDO
SOFTHEARTED TENDER
SOFTLY BAJO SOFT FAIRLY GENTLY
SWEETLY CREAMILY TENDERLY
SOFTNESS SOFT MOLLITIES
(— **IN COAL SEAM**) LUM LUMB
SOFT-SHELLED TURTLE FLAPPER
FLIPPER FLAPJACK
SOFT-SOAP CON
SOFT-SPOKEN MEALY
SOGGY SAD DUNCH SOBBY SODDEN
SPONGY WATERY
SOIL DAG DUB MUD RAY SOD BLOT
BLUR CLAY CLOD DAUB DIRT DUST
FOIL FOUL GRIT LAND MIRK MOOL
MOSS MUCK MURK MUSS SAUR SILE
SLUR SMUT SOOT TASH BULLI
CROCK EARTH GLEBE GRIME
GUMBO LAYER MUCKY ROSEL
SLUSH SMEAR SOLUM SOULE
SPARK STAIN SULLY BARING
BEDAUB BEMIRE BEMOIL GROUND
PODZOL SLURRY SMIRCH SMOOCH
SMUDGE SPLASH SUDDLE BEGRIME
BENASTY BESMEAR BESMOKE
BETHUMB FEWMAND POLLUTE
REGOSOL SEEDBED TARNISH
TRACHLE AGROTYPE ALLUVIAL
BEDABBLE BESMIRCH BUCKSHOT
FLYSPECK LATERITE RENDZINA
WOODCOCK
(— **ABOVE CLAY**) KELLY
(— **DEPOSITED BY WIND**) ELUVIUM
(— **FORMED BY DECAY**) GEEST
(— **INTERMEDIATE BETWEEN SAND
AND CLAY**) ROSEL
(— **PREPARED FOR SOWING**) TILTH
(— **REMOVED FROM ORE**) BARING
(— **WITH GREASE**) LARD
(AGGREGATE —) PED
(ALKALINE —) SOLONETZ
(ASHLIKE —) PODSOL PODZOL
(CLAYEY —) GALT MALM MAUM
ADOBE SOLOD SOLOTH
(DRY —) GROOT

(FRIABLE —) CRUMB
(GRAVELLY —) ROACH GROWAN
(HARD —) RAMMEL
(INFERTILE —) GALL
(LEACHED —S) LATOSOL
(PLUMBER'S —) SMUDGE
(POROUS —) SPONGE
(POTTING —) COMPOST
(PRAIRIE —) BRUNIZEM
(SILTY —) GUMBO
(SPRINGY —) WOODSERE
(ZONAL —) SEROZEM SIEROZEM
SOILAGE SOIL SMUDGE SOILING
SOILED FOUL BLACK DINGY DIRTY
MUSSY SOOTY TARRY SMUDGY
SMUTTY SNUFFY THUMBED
DRAGGLED SHOPWORN
SOIL-EXPOSING EROSIVE
SOIREE EVENING
SOJOURN LIE BIDE STAY STOP
ABIDE ABODE TARRY RESIDE
ALLODGE MANSION STATION
SOJOURNER PILGRIM
SOKOL FALCON
SOL SOH SOU ALCOSOL EMULSOID
HYDROSOL SOLUTION
SOLA SHOLA PAUKPAN
SOLACE CHEER CHEERER COMFORT
SWEETEN SOLATION
SOLAR SOLLER SOLARIUM
(— **SYSTEM APPARATUS**) ORRERY
SOLAR DISK ATEN ATON
(CENTER OF —) CAZIMI
SOLD SELT BOOKED
(ILLICITLY —) BOOTLEG
SOLDER PALE BRAZE FLOAT
SOWDER SPELTER
SOLDERER BROGUER
SOLDERING IRON COPPER DOCTOR
SOLDIER SON TAP BLEU BOLO
GOUM GUGU KERN LEVY SHOT
SWAD TULK WART BERNE CROAT
FRITZ GUARD GUFFY KHAKI LANCE
LIMEY LINER MINER NIZAM PERDU
PIKER PIVOT POILU SAMMY SWEAT
TOLKE TOMMY TOPAS ASKARI
BONAGH BUMMER DARTER DIGGER
EXPERT GALOOT GUNNER GURKHA
HAIDUK HEINIE HOSTER LANCER
MARKER PIETON REITER SENTRY
SKIEUR SOLDAT SWADDY THRASO
WEAPON ZOUAVE BILLJIM BLIGHTY
BRIGAND CARABIN CATERAN
CORSLET DARTMAN DOGFACE
DRAGOON FEDERAL FEEDMAN
FIGHTER GENETOR GOUMIER
HOBBLER INVALID MATROSS
ORDERLY PALIKAR PANDOUR
PAVISOR PIKEMAN POLTAST
PRIVATE REDCOAT REGULAR
REISTER SCARLET SLINGER
SOLDADO STRIKER TROOPER
VETERAN WARRIOR ARQUEBUS
BEZONIAN BLUECOAT BUCKSKIN
BUFFCOAT CAMELEER CAVALIER
DESERTER FENCIBLE FUGLEMAN
FUSILIER GALLOPER GENDARME
GRAYBACK GRAYCOAT IRONSIDE
JANIZARY KHANDAIT LANCEMAN

LINESMAN MILITANT MIQUELET
MUSTACHE PIOUPIOU RAPPAREE
SENTINEL SERVITOR SILLADAR
SPEARMAN SWORDMAN TOLPATCH
TRANSFER TRIARIAN WARFARER
WHIFFLER YARDBIRD
(— OF MUSCOVITE GUARD)
STRELITZ
(— WITH SIDE WHISKERS) BADGER
(ALBANIAN —) PALIKAR
(ALGERIAN —) ARBI
(ANT —) MAXIM
(AUSTRALIAN —) ANZAC DIGGER
BILLJIM
(BOMBAY —S) DUCKS
(BRITISH —) LIMEY TOMMY BLIGHTY
LOBSTER REDCOAT
(BRUTAL —) PANDOUR
(COWARDLY —) CAPITANO
(FILE OF 6 —S) ROT
(FILIPINO —) GUGU
(FOOT —) KERN PAGE PEON PIETON
FOOTMAN TOLPATCH
(GERMAN —) HUN FRITZ HEINE
KRAUT HEINIE
(GREEK —) EVZONE HOPLITE
(INCOMPETENT —) BOLL
(INDIAN —) SEPOY GURKHA
(INVALID —) FOGY FOGEY
(IRREGULAR —) CATERAN JAYHAWK
MIQUELET SILLADAR
(MOROCCAN —) ASKARI
(MOUNTED —) LANCER DRAGOON
GENETOR LOBSTER TROOPER
VEDETTE CAVALIER
(OLD —) GROGNARD
(PROFESSIONAL —) SAMURAI
(REVOLUTIONARY —) REDCOAT
BUCKSKIN
(ROMAN —S OF THIRD LINE) TRIARY
TRIARII
(RUSSIAN —) IVAN
(SCOTTISH —) JOCK
(TURKISH —) NIZAM REDIF
(PL.) FOOT ELITE TERZO TROOP
TERTIA CATERVA ENOMOTY MILITIA
VELITES FORAGERS INFANTRY
SOLDIERY
SOLDIERLY WARLIKE
SOLDIERY HORSE MILITIA SEBUNDY
MILITARY SIBBENDY
SOLE CORK FACE GADE MERE ONLY
SLIP SOCK SPUR AFALD ALONE
CLUMP OLEPI PELMA WHOLE
GADOID INSOLE ONLEPY PLANTA
SINGLE SOLEYN SULLEN THENAR
TONGUE UNIQUE ANACANTH
FLATFISH HOGCHOKE MARYSOLE
SINGULAR SOLITARY
(— A SHOE) SPECK
(— FOR WALKING OVER SAND)
BACKSTER
(— OF BIRD'S FOOT) PTERNA
(— OF FOOT) PLAT VOLA PELMA
PLANT
(— OF PLANE) FACE
(— OF PLOW) SLADE
(HALF —) SHOULDER
(TOWARD THE —) PLANTAD

SOLELY SOLE ALONE SIMPLY SINGLY
WHOLLY SHEERLY ENTIRELY
SOLEMN DEEP SAGE BUDGE SOBER
DEVOUT FORMAL RITUAL EARNEST
SERIOUS WEIGHTY FUNEREAL
SOLEMNITY OBIT RITE SACRE
GRAVITY SEVERITY
SOLEMNIZE KEEP SEAL
SOLEMNLY GRAVE HIGHLY
SOLENODONT AGOUTA ALMIQUE
SOLEPIECE SOLE GIRDER
SOL-FA SOLMIZATE
SOLICIT ASK BEG SUE WOO DRUM
MOVE SEEK TOUT URGE APPLY
COURT CRAVE TREAT ACCOST
HUSTLE INVITE INVOKE BESEECH
CANVASS ENTREAT IMPLORE
INSTANT PROCURE REQUEST
APPROACH PETITION
SOLICITATION SUIT QUEST
CANVASS INSTANT SOLICIT
ENTREATY INSTANCE
SOLICITOR LAWYER WRITER
ADVOCATE TRAMPLER
SOLICITOUS URGENT CAREFUL
CURIOUS JEALOUS DESIROUS
CONCERNED
SOLICITUDE CARE FEAR HEED PAIN
YEME HEART WORRY ANXIETY
CONCERN BUSINESS JEALOUSY
SOLID DRY SAD CONE CUBE FAST
FIRM FULL HARD CHAMP LEVEL
MASSY MEATY SOUND STIFF STOUT
THICK TIGHT SECURE STABLE
STRONG STURDY COMPACT
CUPRENE UNIFORM CONSTANT
GROUNDLY MATERIAL STERLING
(GEOMETRICAL —) CONE CUBE
PRISM CONOID CUPROID FRUSTUM
(PL.) POCHE
SOLIDARITY CIVILITY
SOLIDIFIED SOLID HARDENED
SOLIDIFY DRY SET JELL SHOOT
HARDEN COMPACT STIFFEN
CONCRETE
SOLIDITY SADNESS FASTNESS
FIRMNESS HARDNESS
SOLIDLY FIRMLY SQUARE STOUTLY
GROUNDLY
SOLIDUS BEZANT NOMISMA
DIAGONAL HYPERPER
(HALF —) SEMIS
SOLIPSISM EGOISM
SOLITAIRE CLARINO CANFIELD
KLONDIKE NAPOLEON PATIENCE
SOLITARY
SOLITARY ODD WAF LONE SOLE
ALONE ELYNG LONELY ONLEPY
SAVAGE SINGLE SOLEYN SULLEN
EREMITE PRIVATE RECLUSE
UNCOUTH WIDOWED DESOLATE
EREMITIC ISOLATED LONESOME
SECLUDED SEPARATE
SOLITUDE PRIVACY RETREAT
SOLITARY
SOLLERET SABBATON
SOLO ARIA CALL ARIOSO CAVATINA
SPADILLA

SOLOMON ISLANDS (CAPITAL OF
—) HONIARA
(ISLAND OF —) BUKA TULAGI
MALAITA CHOISEUL
SOLOMON'S SEAL LILY SEALWORT
SOLOMON SAM KOHELETH
SOLON SAGE GNOMIC GNOMIST
SENATOR LAWMAKER
SOLSTICE SUNSTAY SUNSTEAD
SOLUBLE FRIM FRUM FIXED SOLUTE
SOLVABLE
SOLUTION IT LYE AQUA EUSOL
STAIN TINCT ACETUM ANSWER
ASSOIL DOCTOR ERASER SALINE
EXTRACT EYEWASH LACQUER
RESOLVE SOLUTIO WORKING
ANALYSIS LEACHATE TINCTURE
(— ADDED FOR GOOD MEASURE)
INCAST
(— OF CHESS PROBLEM) COOK
(— OF FERMENTED BRAN) DRENCH
(— OF GUM TRAGACANTH) BED
(ALCOHOLIC —) ESSENCE
(PICKLING —) SOUSE
(PRESERVING —) BOLIN
(SALINE —) BRINE
(SOAP —) NIGRE
(STERILE —) JOHNIN
(VISCOUS —) GLUE
(WATERY —) EAU SAF
SOLVE DO FIX READ UNDO WORK
BREAK CRACK LOOSE SALVE
ANSWER ASSOIL CIPHER FIGURE
REDUCE RIDDLE SOLUTE RESOLVE
UNRAVEL DECIPHER DISSOLVE
SOLVENT ETHER ELUENT SPIRIT
ACETONE ALCOHOL BENZINE
COUPLER DILUENT REMOVER
SPOTTER CARBITOL SOLVABLE
STRIPPER TETRALIN
(UNIVERSAL —) ALKAHEST
SOMALI SOMAL SHUHALI
(PL.) ASHA
SOMALIA (COIN OF —) BESA
(DIVISION OF —) HAWIYA
(MEASURE OF —) TOP CABA CHELA
DARAT TABLA CUBITO
(MOUNTAIN RANGE OF —) GUBAN
(NATIVE OF —) GALLA HAWIYA
ISBAAK SOMALI DANAKIL
(RIVER OF —) JUBA NOGAL SCEBELI
(TOWN OF —) MERCA BERBERA
HARGEISA KISIMAYU
(WEIGHT OF —) PARSALAH
SOMATIC SOMAL SOMAL BODILY
SOMBER SAD DERN DULL GRAVE
SOBER GLOOMY LENTEN SOLEMN
SOMBRE SULLEN AUSTERE SERIOUS
DARKSOME SOMBROUS
SOME ANY ODD THIS CERTAIN
SOMEBODY QUIDAM SOMEONE
SOMEDAY ONCE
SOMEHOW HOW ONEHOW SOMEWAY
SOMEGATE
SOMEONE SUCH
SOMERSAULT FLIP TOPPLE FLIFFUS
SPOTTER TWISTER BACKFLIP
SOMERSET
SOMETHING WHAT ALIQUID

WHATNOT SOMEWHAT
(— **ABNORMAL)** FREAK
(— **ADDED)** IMP EXTRA DOCTOR
(— **ATTRACTIVE)** DUCK
(— **BELIEVED)** CREDIT
(— **BIG)** BOUNCER
(— **BRIGHT RED)** CORAL
(— **CHERISHED)** APPLE
(— **COMMONPLACE)** DROSS
(— **CONSECRATED)** SACRUM
(— **CONTRARY TO LOGIC)** ALOGISM
(— **CORRUPT)** CARRION
(— **COUNTERFEIT)** DUFFER
(— **DIFFICULT)** STINKER
(— **DISLIKED)** DOGMEAT
(— **DONE)** GERENDUM
(— **ELABORATE)** DEVICE
(— **ELUSIVE)** FUGITIVE
(— **EXCELLENT)** DANDY
(— **EXCESSIVE)** LUXUS
(— **EXTRAORDINARY)** SNORTER
(— **FALSE)** HOOEY
(— **FAMILIAR)** KNOWN
(— **FIRST-RATE)** CHEESE
(— **FLAWED)** CRIPPLE
(— **FOOLISH)** IDIOCY FATUITY
(— **FORGOTTEN)** CORPSE
(— **FORKED)** CORNUTE
(— **FRAUDULENT)** CROSS
(— **HORRIFYING)** SHOCKER
(— **IDENTICAL)** ISOMORPH
(— **ILL-DEFINED)** BLOB
(— **IN ADDITION TO ORDINARY)**
BONUS
(— **INCOMPLETE)** END
(— **INFERIOR)** DOG CULL LESS
CAGMAG
(— **INJURIOUS)** ENEMY
(— **INSIGNIFICANT)** STRAW
FEATHER SNICKET FRAGMENT
(— **INTRICATE)** KNOT
(— **LARGE)** GIANT SMASHER
(— **MADE UP)** FIGMENT
(— **NOT ESSENTIAL)** FRILL
(— **NOT EXPLAINED)** MYSTERY
(— **NOTABLE)** DEUCE
(— **OF GREAT VALUE)** EYETOOTH
(— **OF LITTLE VALUE)** SHUCK
FOUTER FOUTRA
(— **OF NO VALUE)** HAW DAMN
BAUBEE DOCKEN
(— **OFFERED FOR LOAN)** PREMIUM
(— **OR OTHER)** ANYTHING
(— **OUTSTANDING)** BROTH DOYEN
GASSER STANDOUT
(— **PAINFUL)** GAFF
(— **PATCHED UP)** VAMP
(— **POOR)** FLUMMERY
(— **PRECIOUS)** DUMPLING
(— **PREJUDICIAL)** FOE
(— **PROVOKING)** DEVIL
(— **REPELLENT)** SPINACH
(— **RISKED)** HAZARD
(— **SHAPELESS)** DUMP
(— **SHOWY)** FLOSS
(— **SHRIVELED)** SCRUMP
(— **SMALL)** DOT SNIP
(— **SPECTACULAR)** DILLY
(— **STICKY)** CAB

(— **STOLEN)** CRIB
(— **STRANGE)** FANTASIA
(— **SUPERLATIVE)** DARB
(— **TAUGHT)** DOCUMENT
(— **THAT IS LIGHT)** SKIFF SKIFT
(— **THAT WHIRLS)** GIG
(— **TO BIND BARGAIN)** EARNEST
(— **TRIVIAL)** CHIP FLUFF
(— **UNDECIDED)** ACRISY
(— **UNINTELLIGIBLE)** GREEK
(— **UNPLEASANT)** GUCK SOUR
(— **UNSPECIFIED)** ITEM
(— **UNSUBSTANTIAL)** FROTH
(— **UNTRUE)** HOKUM
(— **USELESS)** CRAP BLANK
(— **VILE)** DUNG
(— **WORTHLESS)** BOTH DUST
HOKUM DUFFER AMBSACE
(— **WRITTEN)** SCRIPT
SOMETIME FORMER SOMDEL
WHILOM ANCIENT QUONDAM
SOMEDEAL SOMEPART SOMEWHEN
SOMETIMES NOW TOO WHILE
WHILES UMQUHILE
SOMEWHAT BIT SOME RATHER
SLIGHT SUMMAT ALIQUID
SOMEDEAL
SOMEWHERE SOMERS SOMEGATE
SOMITE ZONITE SEGMENT TERGITE
GONOTOME MEROSOME MESOMERE
SOMATOME
SOMNIFEROUS OPIATE SOMNIFIC
SOMNUS HYPNUS
SON BEN BOY LAD ANAC FILS FITZ
ZONE CHILD KIBEI MOPSY FILIUS
JUNIOR REUBEN EPAPHUS
EPIGONUS MONSIEUR
(— **OF CHIEF)** OGTIERN
(— **OF KING OF FRANCE)** DAUPHIN
(— **OF NISEI)** SANSEI
(— **OF PEER)** MASTER
(— **OF SUDRA)** CHANDALA
(**DAVID'S FAVORITE** —) ABSALOM
(**FOURTH** —) MARTLET
(**ILLEGITIMATE** —) NEPHEW
(**YOUNG** —) MOPSY
(**YOUNGER** —) CADET
SONAR ASDIC
SONCHUS DINDLE
SONG AIR DIT JIG LAY UTA CANT
DUAN FOLK GATO GLEE LEED MELE
NOTE RANT RUNE SANG TUNE
BLUES CANSO CAROL CHANT
CROON DILDO DITTY MELOS MOLPE
VOCAL BALLAD BRANLE BUBBLE
CANTIC CANZON CARMEN CHANTY
CHORUS HIMENE JINGLE MELODY
ORPHIC SHANTY STRAIN VINATA
WAIATA WARBLE BACCHIC BALLATA
CANCION CHANSON COMIQUE
DESCANT MELISMA MELODIA
REQUIEM REVERDI ROMANCE
SCOLION SONGLET THRENOS
BIRDSONG BRINDISI CANTICLE
CANZONET COONJINE FLAMENCO
JUBILATE PALINODE RHAPSODY
SERVENTE SINGSONG ZORTZICO
(— **ACCOMPANYING TOAST)**
BRINDISI

(— **FOR TWO VOICES)** GYMEL
(— **OF BASQUES)** ZORTZICO
(— **OF BIRD)** LAY KOLLER
(— **OF JOY)** CAROL PAEAN
JUBILATE
(— **OF MINSTREL)** YEDDING
(— **OF OCEANIA)** HIMENE
(— **OF PRAISE)** HYMN CAROL
ANTHEM CHORALE
(— **UNACCOMPANIED)** GLEE
(— **WITH MONOTONOUS RHYME)**
VIRELAI VIRELAY
(—**S OF BIRDS)** RAMAGE
(**ANDALUSIAN** —) SAETA
(**ART** —) LIED
(**BOAT** —) JORRAM
(**CEREMONIAL** —**S)** AREITO
(**CRADLE** —) HUSHO
(**CUBAN** —) GUAJIRA COMPARSA
(**DANCE** —) BALLAD BAMBUCO
(**DRINKING** —) BACCHIC WASSAIL
(**EVENING** —) SERENA EVENSONG
SERENATA
(**FOLK** —) SON FADO FOLK BLUES
DOINA BYLINA CANTIGA JUBILEE
(**FUNERAL** —) DIRGE MONODY
EPICEDE THRENODY
(**FUNEREAL** —) ELEGY
(**GAY** —) LILT
(**GERMAN** —) LIED
(**HAWAIIAN** —) MELE
(**HEBREW** —) HATIKVAH
(**IMPROMPTU** —) SCOLION
(**JAPANESE** —) UTA
(**LOVE** —) CANSO CANZO FANCY
AMORET AUBADE SERENA
SERENATA
(**MELISMATIC** —) DIVISION
(**MOCKING** —) JIG
(**MORNING** —) MATIN AUBADE
(**MOURNFUL** —) DUMP PLAINT
ENDECHA
(**NEW ZEALAND** —) WAIATA
(**NIGHT** —) COMPLIN
(**NO** —**S)** UTAI
(**NUPTIAL** —) HYMEN
(**PART** —) CHACE TROLL CACCIA
CANZONET FROTTOLA MADRIGAL
(**PASTORAL** —) OAT
(**PLAIN** —) GROUND
(**PORTUGUESE** —) FADO
(**RELIGIOUS** —) HYMN CAROL
PSALM SHOUT ANTHEM POLYMNY
SIRVENT
(**SAILOR'S** —) CHANTY SHANTY
(**SANSKRIT** —) GITA
(**STUPID** —) STROWD
(**VINTAGE** —) VINATA
(**WORK** —) HOLLER
(PL.) ZEMMI AREITO
SONGBIRD CHAT IORA LARK WREN
MAVIS ROBIN SABIA SIREN VEERY
VIREO BULBUL CANARY LINNET
MOCKER ORIOLE SINGER THRUSH
CATBIRD GRASSET WARBLER
BENGALEE BLUEBIRD BOBOLINK
CARDINAL SONGSTER
SONGSTER SINGER WARBLER
SONG THRUSH MAVIE MAVIS

SON-IN-LAW GENER MAUGH
SONOROUS SHILL TONOUS
OROTUND VIBRANT RESONANT
SOUNDFUL SOUNDING
SONOROUSLY DEEPLY
SONSHIP FILIETY
SOOLOOS THULUTH
SOON ERE ANON CITO TITE EARLY
NEWLY RADLY RATHE BELIVE
SUDDEN TIMELY BETIMES ERELONG
PRESTLY SHORTLY DIRECTLY
SPEEDILY
SOONER ERE ERER ERST FIRST
BEFORE TITTER
(— **STATE**) OKLAHOMA
(— **THAN**) OR ERE
SOONEST ERST RATHEST
SOOT COOM IZLE SMUT STUP SUMI
BLECK BROOK COLLY COOMB
CROCK GRIME SOTIK FULIGO
SMOUCH SMUTCH SPODIUM
(— **ON GRATE BAR**) STRANGER
SOOTHE COY DEW BALM CALM DILL
EASE HUSH LULL ACCOY ALLAY
CHARM DULCE HUMOR QUELL
SALVE STILL BECALM PACIFY
SETTLE SMOOTH SOLACE STROKE
SUPPLE ADDULCE ASSUAGE
COMPOSE CONSOLE DEMULCE
FLATTER GRUNTLE LULLABY
PLASTER QUALIFY ATTEMPER
MITIGATE UNRUFFLE
SOOTHER ANODYNE
SOOTHING MILD BALMY BLAND
DOWNY DULCE STILL SWEET
ANIMAL DREAMY DULCET GENTLE
SMOOTH ANODYNE BALSAMIC
SEDATIVE
SOOTHSAY SORT
SOOTHSAYER SEER AUGUR WEIRD
ARIOLE DIVINE ARUSPEX DIVINER
CHALDEAN HARUSPEX TIRESIAS
SOOTY COLLY SMUTTY BROOKIE
COLLIED
SOOTY ALBATROSS NELLIE
QUAKER STINKER BLUEBIRD
STINKPOT
SOOTY SHEARWATER TITI
SOP SPONGE SUGARSOP SWEETSOP
SOPHER SCRIBE
SOPHISM FETCH ELENCH FALLACY
SOPHEME
SOPHIST SOPH DUNCE
SOPHISTICATE GARBLE MONDAINE
SOPHISTICATED WISE BLASE CIVIL
SALTY SVELTE WORLDLY
SOPHISTICATION CHIC
SOPHISTRY DECEIT FALLACY
SOPHISM
SOPORIFIC DWALE DROWSY OPIATE
SLEEPY HYPNOTIC NARCOTIC
SOMNIFIC
SOPPY JUICY SOAKY
SOPRANO CANARY TREBLE
DESCANT CASTRATO
SORB LUSATIAN
SORBIAN WENDISH
SORBOSE ACROSE
SORCERER MAGE BOYLA BRUJO

WITCH BOOLYA NAGUAL VOODOO
WIZARD KORADJI WARLOCK
WIELARE FETISHER MAGICIAN
WITCHMAN
(PL.) GOETAE
SORCERESS BRUJA CIRCE LAMIA
WITCH ARMIDA HECATE BABAJAGA
KORRIGAN WALKYRIE
SORCERY OBI MAGIC SPELL
MAKUTU PISHOGUE PRESTIGE
SORTIARY WIGELING WITCHERY
WITCHING
(**VOODOO** —) WANGA OUANGA
SORDES SABURRA
SORDID RAW BASE GAMY MEAN VILE
DIRTY DUSTY MUCKY CHETIF
GRUBBY SODDEN MESQUIN SQUALID
CHURLISH
SORE BUM FOX PET BUBA CHAP
DEAR GALL KIBE KYLE OUCH BLAIN
BOTCH GAMMY AGNAIL BITTER
BOUBAS CANKER FESTER MELLIT
MORMAL RANKLE TAKING CATHAIR
CHANCRE SORANCE SCALDING
(— **ON HORSE'S FOOT**) MELLIT
(**ARTIFICIAL** —) FOX
(**SUMMER** —**S**) CALORIS LEECHES
SORENESS FROG
SORGHUM CANE CUSH MILO BATAD
DARSO DURRA SORGO CHOLAM
HEGARI IMPHEE KAFFIR SHALLU
FETERITA KAOLIANG
SOROCHE PUNA
SORREL OCA OKA SORE CUCKOO
HEARTS OXALIS RUBICAN SOUROCK
ALLELUIA STABWORT
SORREL TREE TITI ELKWOOD
SOURWOOD
SORROW WO RUE WOE BALE CARE
DOLE HARM MOAN RUTH SORE
TEEN DOLOR GRAME GRIEF MOURN
RUING SARRA UNWIN GRIEVE
LAMENT MISERY REGRET STOUND
UNLUST ANGUISH CONDOLE
DEPLORE PENANCE REGRATE
REMORSE THOUGHT TROUBLE
WOEFARE CALAMITY DISTRESS
DOLEANCE DREARING EGRIMONY
MOURNING
SORROWFUL BAD SAD WAN CHARY
DREAR TRIST WOFUL DISMAL
DOLENT DREARY RUEFUL DOLEFUL
LUCTUAL RUESOME UNHAPPY
WAILFUL CONTRITE DESOLATE
DOLESOME DOLOROSO GRIEFFUL
MOURNFUL PITIABLE
SORROWFULLY SADLY WRATH
HEAVILY
SORRY BAD SAD WOE HURT VEXED
UNFAIN PITIFUL CONTRITE
WRETCHED
SORT KIN LOT BRAN COMB GERE
HUMP KIND RANK SUIT WING WORK
BRACK BREED GENUS GRADE
SAVOR SPICE ASSORT BARREL
DILLUE GARBLE GENDER KIDNEY
MANNER MISTER NATURE STRAIN
STRIPE FASHION SPECIES SPECKLE
VARIETY CLASSIFY SEPARATE

(— **COTTON BY STAPLE**) STAPLE
(— **MAIL**) CASE
(— **MERCHANDISE**) BRACK
(— **OF PERSON**) LIKE
SORTER SHALEMAN
SORTIE ISSUE SALLY ATTACK
OUTFALL
SORTILEGE LOT
SORTING GARBLING
(— **ROOM**) SALLE
SORVA BORRACHA
SOT LUSH SOAK DRUNK LOURD
TOPER LOURDY BLOTTER DASTARD
TOSSPOT DRUNKARD
SOTHO SUTO SESUTO
SOTIK SOOT
SOUFFLE FONDU FONDUE
SOUGHT QUESITED
SOUL BA EGO ALMA ANIMA ATMAN
GHOST HEART SHADE BUDDHI
DIBBUK NATURE PNEUMA PSYCHE
SPIRIT SPRITE NEPHESH PURUSHA
INTERNAL
(—**S OF THE DEAD**) LEMURES
(**ANIMAL** — **IN MAN**) NEPHESH
(**DISEMBODIED** —) KER
(**EGYPTIAN IMMORTAL** —) BA
(**INDIVIDUAL** —) JIVA
(**LIBERATED** —) KEVALIN
(**UNIVERSAL** —) HANSA
(**WANDERING** —) DIBBUK DYBBUK
SOULFULLY GEISTLICH
SOULLESS TURNIPY
SOU MARQUE STAMPEE
SOUND GO CRY FIT BLOW DING
DRIP FAST FERE FIRM FLOG GLUG
GOOD HAIL HALE KYLE NOTE RING
SAFE SANE TEST TONE TRIG WISE
AFFIX BLAST BUGLE CHEEP FLICK
FRESH GLIFF GLUCK GRIND GROPE
HODDY NOISE PLANG PLUMB PROBE
RIGHT SLUSH SOLID SPANG SPANK
SPEAK SWASH VALID WHOLE
BICKER BIRDIE DORSAL ENDING
ENTIRE FATHOM FAUCAL HEARTY
INTACT LAGOON ROBUST SIGNAL
SINGLE SONANT SPLASH STABLE
STURDY HEALTHY HEARING
HURLING PERFECT PHONEME
PLUMMET SCRATCH SONANCE
VOCABLE FLAWLESS FOOTFALL
GRINDING GROUNDLY LAUGHTER
RELIABLE SEARCHER SYLLABIC
WAKELESS
(— **A BAGPIPE**) DOODLE
(— **BELL**) PEAL RING KNELL KNOLL
(— **DRUM OR TRUMPET**) TUCK
(— **FORTH**) BOOM
(— **IN GREEK AND LATIN**) AGMA
(— **IN MIND**) FORMAL
(— **INDEPENDENTLY OF THE**
PLAYER) CIPHER
(— **LESS LOUD**) FALL
(— **LIKE THUNDER**) BRONTIDE
(— **LOUDLY**) TANG LARUM
(— **MELODIOUSLY**) CHARM
(— **OF BAGPIPE**) DRONE
(— **OF BEATING**) RATAPLAN
(— **OF BELL**) DING PEAL RING

KNELL STROKE DINGDONG TINGTANG
(— OF BIRD) JUG
(— OF BULLET) ZIP
(— OF CONTEMPT) HUMPH
(— OF CORK) CLOOP CLUNK
(— OF DISAPPROVAL) BOO HOOT BAZOO
(— OF DOG) BOOK
(— OF DYING PERSON'S VOICE) TAISCH
(— OF ENGINE) CHUG
(— OF EXPLOSION) BOUNCE
(— OF F) DIGAMMA
(— OF FLUTE) TOOTLE
(— OF GLOTTAL STOP) HAMZA HAMZAH
(— OF HEN) CLUCK
(— OF HOG) GRUNT
(— OF HOOF) CLOP
(— OF HORN) BEEP TOOT
(— OF HORSE) BLOWING
(— OF PLUCKED STRING) TUM
(— OF POURING LIQUID) GLUG GLUGGLUG
(— OF RAIN) SPAT
(— OF RENDING) SCAT
(— OF SHEEP) BAA BLEAT
(— OF STEAM ENGINE) CHUFF
(— OF STRAW OR LEAVES) RUSTLE
(— OF TRUMPET) CLARION
(— OF WIND IN TREES) WOOSH
(— OUT) FEEL
(—S HAVING RHYTHM) MUSIC
(ABNORMAL —) BRUIT
(ADVENTITIOUS —) RALE
(BLOWING —) SOUFFLE
(BRAWLING —) CHIDE
(BUBBLING —) BLATHER
(BUZZING —) Z WHIR WHIRR
(CLICKING —) SNECK
(CONSONANT —) ALVEOLAR
(COOING —) CHIRR TURTUR
(CRACKLING —) RISK
(CRISP —) BLIP
(CRUNCHING —) CRUMP SCRUNCH
(DELICATE —) TINK TINKLE
(DISCORDANT —) JAR BRAY JANGLE
(DISTINCTIVE —) SONG
(DULL —) CLONK FLUMP SQUELCH
(EXPLOSIVE —) POP BARK CHUG PUFF SNORT REPORT
(FAINT —) PEEP GLIFF WHISHT INKLING
(FINAL —) AUSLAUT
(GULPING —) GLUCK
(GUTTURAL —) GROWL
(HARSH —) JAR BRAY BLARE CLASH CRANK TWANG SCROOP DISCORD STRIDOR
(HEAVY —) DUMP
(HIGH-PITCHED —) TING
(HISSING —) FIZZ SIZZ SWISH SIZZLE
(HOLLOW —) CHOCK THUNGE
(HUMMING —) HUM BURR SUUM DRONE SINGING
(INDISTINCT —) BLUR SURD
(INITIAL — OF WORDS) ANLAUT

(JINGLING —) SMIT
(LAPPING —) SLOOSH
(LIGHT REPEATED —) PITAPAT
(LOUD —) PEAL BLARE CLANG CRASH CLANGOR
(LOW-PITCHED —) BASS
(MEANINGLESS —S) GABBLE
(MEDIAL —) INLAUT
(MENTALLY —) SANE WISE
(MOANING —) SUUM SOUGH
(MOURNFUL —) GROAN
(MUSICAL —) CHIME
(NASAL —) ANUSVARA
(NON-SIGNIFICANT —) GLIDE
(NONVIBRATORY —) FRICTION
(PLEASING —) EUPHONY EUPHONIA
(RASPING —) BUZZ SKIRR SCROOP
(REPEATED —) ECHO
(RESONANT —) BONG
(REVERBERATING —) PLANG
(RINGING —) CLANG CLANK CLING TWANG RINGLE DINGDONG
(ROARING —) BEAL
(RUSHING —) SWOOSH HURLING
(RUSTLING —) FISSLE FISTLE
(SCRAPING —) GRIDE
(SHARP —) POP PING SNAP CHINK CRAKE KNACK SPANG SQUIRK
(SHRILL —) CHEEP KNACK SKIRL SCREED SQUEAK STRIDOR
(SHUFFLING —) SCUFFLE
(SIBILANT —) HISS SHISH SHUSH
(SLIGHT —) SWISH
(SNORING —) SNORK
(SOBBING —) YOOP
(SPEECH —) SURD DOMAL TENUE VOWEL APICAL PHONEME CEREBRAL
(SPLASHING —) LAP CHUNK FLURR SPLAT SWASH
(SPOKEN —) BREATH
(SQUEAKY —) CREAK
(SQUELCHING —) SQUASH
(STRANGLED —) GLUB GLUG
(SWISHING —) SCHLOOP
(TELEPHONE —) SIDETONE
(TRAMPING —) STUMP
(TRILLING —) CHIRR CHIZZ HIRRIENT
(TUNEFUL —) HARMONY
(UNPLEASANT —) BLOOP
(WARNING —) ALARM SIREN ALARUM TOCSIN
(WHIRRING —) BIRR FLURR SKIRR
(WHISPERING —) SUSURRUS
(WHISTLING —) STRIDOR

SOUND-ABSORBENT ACOUSTIC
SOUNDBOARD BELLY
SOUNDER TICKER LEADMAN
SOUNDING RAWIN SONANT INKLING
SONDAGE SONATION
(— HARSH) BRAZEN
(— OF BELL) CURFEW
(— OF ORGAN PIPE) CIPHER
(— WITH REVERBERATIONS) PLANGENT
SOUNDLY FAST TIGHT FIRMLY
SOUNDNESS SANITY FITNESS SOBRIETY STRENGTH

SOUP BREE KAIL KALE BROTH GUMBO POSOL BISQUE BORSCH BURGOO JOUTES POZOLE BORSCHT GARBURE MARMITE CONSOMME GAZPACHO MINESTRA MORTREUX
(— UP) SUPE
(BARLEY —) SMIGGINS
(BEEFSKIN —) SKINK
(CABBAGE —) SHCHI STCHI
(CLEAR —) CONSOMME JULIENNE
(JELLIED —) GAZPACHO
(LARGE QUANTITY OF —) SLASH
(THICK —) BISK GUMBO HOOSH PUREE BISQUE BURGOO CHOWDER GARBURE POTTAGE HOTCHPOT MORTREWES
(THIN —) BROTH
SOUR AWA DRY YAR ACID ASIM CRAB DOUR FOXY GRIM GRUM HARD TART TURN ACERB ACRID AIGRE EAGER GOURY GRUFF MUSTY TEART BITTER CRUETY CURDLE PONTIC RUGGED SULLEN TORVID ACETOSE ACIDIFY AUSTERE SUBACID ACERBATE VINEGARY
(SLIGHTLY —) BLINK BLINKY ACESCENT
SOURCE FONS FONT HAND HEAD HIVE MINE RISE RIST ROOT SEED FOUNT SPAWN SURGE AUCTOR AUTHOR BOTTOM CENTER FATHER FONTAL ORIGIN PARENT RESORT STAPLE EDITION FOUNTAIN WELLHEAD
(— OF AID) RECOURSE
(— OF ANCESTRAL LINE) STOCK
(— OF ANNOYANCE) BOGY BOGIE HARROW BUGBEAR
(— OF ASSURANCE) FORTRESS
(— OF CONCERN) BUGABOO
(— OF CONFIDENCE) ANCHOR
(— OF DISPLEASURE) DISGUST
(— OF ENERGY) TAPAS
(— OF HAPPINESS) SUNSHINE
(— OF HARM) CURSE
(— OF HONOR) CREDIT
(— OF INCOME) TITLE REVENUE
(— OF INFORMATION) CHECK
(— OF INSPIRATION) CASTALIA CASTALIE
(— OF LAUGHTER) SPLEEN
(— OF LIGHT) LAMP
(— OF NOURISHMENT) BREAST
(— OF POWER) STRENGTH
(— OF REGRET) SCATH SCATHE
(— OF STREAM OR RIVER) FILL
(— OF STRENGTH) HORN
(— OF SUPPLY) SHOP FEEDER ARSENAL
(— OF TROUBLE) HEADACHE
(— OF WATER) BRON SPRING
(— OF WEALTH) GOLCONDA KLONDIKE
(ENCLOSED —) FLOW
(FROM ANOTHER —) ALIUNDE
(MALIGNANT —) CANCER
(PHYSICAL —) MOTHER
(PRIMARY —) RADIX
SOURDOUGH LEAVEN

SOURED FOXY QUARRED
SOURNESS ACIDITY ACERBITY
ACRIMONY ASPERITY TARTNESS
VERJUICE
SOURSOP CORRESOL GUANABANA
SOURWOOD TITI ELKWOOD
SOUSE DIP DUCK TOSH STOOP
PLUNGE SOZZLE
SOUTANE SIMAR ZIMARRA
SOUTH MIDI AUSTER MIDDAY
MERIDIAN
(**FARTHER** —) BELOW

SOUTH AFRICA
BAY: ALGOA FALSE
CAPE: AGULHAS
CAPITAL: CAPETOWN PRETORIA
COIN: CENT RAND POUND FLORIN
LANGUAGE: BANTU HINDI TAMIL
TELUGU BUJARATI
MOUNTAIN: AUX KOP KATHKIN
INJASUTI
NATIVE: YOSA BANTU NAMAS
PONDO DAMARA SWAHILI
BECHUANA HOTTENTOT
PROVINCE: TRANSVAAL
RIVER: MODDER MOLOPO ORANGE
KURUMAM LIMPOPO OLIFANTS
TOWN: AUS MARA STAD BENONI
DURBAN SEVERN UMTATA
KOKSTAD MAFEKING

SOUTH CAROLINA
CAPITAL: COLUMBIA
COLLEGE: COKER FURMAN
LANDER CITADEL CLAFFIN
CLEMSON ERSKINE WOFFORD
COUNTY: AIKEN HORRY DILLON
JASPER OCONEE SALUDA
FORT: SUMTER
INDIAN: PEDEE SEWEE CUSABO
SANTEE WAXHAW CATAWBA
SUGEREE WATEREE CONGAREE
LAKE: MARION MURRAY CATAWBA
WATEREE HARTWELL MOULTRIE
MOUNTAIN: SASSAFRAS
NATIVE: WEASEL PALMETTO
PLATEAU: PIEDMONT
PRESIDENT: JACKSON
RIVER: BROAD EDISTO PEEDEE
SALUDA SANTEE ASHEPOO
SAVANNAH
STATE BIRD: WREN
STATE FLOWER: JESSAMINE
STATE TREE: PALMETTO
TOWN: AIKEN GREER UNION
BELTON CAMDEN CHERAW
CONWAY DILLON SENECA
SUMTER BAMBERG LAURENS
MANNING BEAUFORT FLORENCE
NEWBERRY WALHALLA

SOUTH CAROLINIAN WEASEL
PALMETTO

SOUTH DAKOTA
BUTTE: MUD CROW SULLY FINGER
SADDLE THUNDER DEERSEARS

CAPITAL: PIERRE
COLLEGE: HURON YANKTON
COUNTY: DAY BRULE MOODY
SPINK CUSTER JERAULD
YANKTON MELLETTE
INDIAN: BRULE SIOUX DAKOTA
CHEYENNE
LAKE: OAHE BIGSTONE TRAVERSE
MONUMENT: RUSHMORE
MOUNTAIN: BEAR SHEEP TABLE
CROOKS HARNEY MOREAU
NICKNAME: COYOTE
RIVER: JAMES MOREAU CHEYENNE
MISSOURI
STATE BIRD: PHEASANT
STATE FLOWER: PASQUE
STATE TREE: SPRUCE
TOWN: LEAD HURON CUSTER
EUREKA LEMMON MILLER
WINNER STURGIS WEBSTER
YANKTON ABERDEEN
DEADWOOD SISSETON

SOUTHERLY AUSTRINE
SOUTHERN SUDIC AUSTRAL
MERIDIAN SOUTHRON
SOUTHERN CROSS CRUX CROSS
CROSIER
SOUTHERNER CAVALIER SOUTHRON
SOUTHERN FRANCE MIDI
SOUTHERN ILLINOIS EGYPT
SOUTHERN INDIA DRAVIDA

SOUTH KOREA
BAY: KANGHWA
CAPITAL: SEOUL
COIN: WON HWAN
MOUNTAIN: CHIRI
RIVER: HAN KUM PUKHAN SOMJIN
NAKTONG YONGSAN
TOWN: MASAN MOKPO PUSAN
SUWON TAEGU CHINJU CHONJU
INCHON KUNSAN TAEJON
KWANGJU CHUNCHON

SOUTHLAND AUSTER
SOUTH SEA ISLANDER KANAKA

SOUTH VIETNAM
CAPITAL: SAIGON
LANGUAGE: CHAM KHMER RHADE
MEASURE: GANG PHAN THON
MOUNTAIN: BADINH NINHHOA
KNONTRAN NGOKLINH
TCHEPONE
NATIVE: CHAM MALAY
PORT: DANANG SAIGON QUINHON
NHATRANG
REGION: ANNAM COCHIN
RIVER: BA MEKONG DONGNAI
TOWN: HUE HOIAN ANNHON
DANANG QUINHON SONGCAN
TAYNINH PHANRANG QUANGTRI
VINHLOI
WEIGHT: CAN YET UYEN

SOUTHWESTER SQUAM

SOUVENIR RELIC TOKEN FAIRING
NICKNACK
SOVEREIGN BEY SIR SOV BEAN
CHAM CHIP FREE KHAN QUID SHAH
SKIV JAMES NEGUS NIZAM QUEED
CHAGAN COUTER GUINEA KAISER
KINGLY MASTER PRINCE SAMORY
SHINER SOLDAN SOVRAN SULTAN
CROWNED MONARCH ZAMORIN
DOMINANT IMPERIAL SUFFRAIN
SUZERAIN
(**DIVINELY** —) THEARCHIC
(**FELLOW** —) COUSIN
(**HEAVENLY** —) TENNO HEAVEN
(**MOSLEM** —) SOLDAN
SOVEREIGNTY SWAY CROWN REIGN
DIADEM EMPERY EMPIRE THRONE
DEMESNE DYNASTY KINGDOM
MAJESTY SCEPTER SCEPTRE
AUTARCHY DOMINION IMPERIUM
MONARCHY REGALITY REGNANCY
SOVRANTY
(— **OF REASON)** AUTONOMY
(**JOINT** —) SYNARCHY
SOVIET (ALSO SEE RUSSIA) VOLOST
COUNCIL GUBERNIA
SOW HOG GILT SEED SHED YILT
DRILL PLANT PLUMP STREW
CHANNEL GRUMPHY IMPLANT
OVERSOW SCATTER ENGENDER
INTERSOW SEMINATE
SOW BUG ISOPOD SLATER
ISOPODAN
SOWENS SONS SWEENS FLUMMERY
WASHBREW
SOWER SEEDER SEEDMAN
SEEDSTER SEMINARY
SOWING SATION SEMENCE
SEEDNESS
SOWN SEME SATIVE SEEDED
SEMEED
SOW THISTLE DINDLE GUTWEED
HOGWEED MILKWEED
SOY SHOYA SHOYU
SOYBEAN SOJA SOYA
SPA BATH CURE HYDRO
SPACE AREA BLUE CORD COSO
DENT FACE LUNG PALE RANK ROOM
SIDE VOID ABYSS BLOCK CHINK
CLEFT FIELD PLACE RANGE HIATUS
INDENT MATTER ROOMTH ARRANGE
FOREIGN GUNNIES LEGROOM
ROOMAGE SPACING SPATIUM
DIASTEMA DISTANCE EXOCOELE
INTERVAL
(— **ABOVE EARTH)** AIRSPACE
(— **AMONG MUSCLES)** SINUS
(— **AROUND HOUSE)** AMBIT
(— **AT WHARF)** BERTHAGE
(— **BEHIND ALTAR)** FERETORY
(— **BETWEEN BED AND WALL)**
RUELLE
(— **BETWEEN BRIDGE PIERS)** LOCK
(— **BETWEEN CONCENTRIC**
CIRCLES) ANNULUS
(— **BETWEEN DECKS)** LAZARET
(— **BETWEEN EYE AND BILL)** LORE
(— **BETWEEN FEATHERS)** APTERYLA

(— **BETWEEN FLUTINGS**) FILET FILLET GORGERIN

(— **BETWEEN FURROWS**) RIG

(— **BETWEEN PAGES**) GUTTER

(— **BETWEEN RAILROAD TIES**) CRIB

(— **BETWEEN SAW TEETH**) GULLET

(— **BETWEEN SHIP'S BOWS AND ANCHOR**) HAWSE

(— **BETWEEN STRANDS**) CANTLINE

(— **BETWEEN TEETH**) DIASTEMA

(— **BETWEEN THUMB AND LITTLE FINGER**) SPAN

(— **BETWEEN TIMBERS**) SPIRKET

(— **BETWEEN TWO WIRES**) DENT

(— **BETWEEN VEINS OF LEAVES**) AREOLA

(— **DEVOID OF MATTER**) VACUUM VACUITY

(— **FOR SECRETION**) BAG

(— **IN CHURCH**) KNEELING

(— **IN COIL OF CABLE**) TIER

(— **IN FOREST**) GLADE

(— **IN MINE**) GOB

(— **IN THEATER**) BOX

(— **IN TYPE**) CORE

(— **OCCUPIED**) VOLUME

(— **OF TIME**) DAY PULL STEAD GHURRY STITCH INTERVAL

(— **ON BILLIARD TABLE**) BALK BAULK

(— **ON COIN**) EXERGUE

(— **OVER STAGE**) FLIES

(— **OVERHEAD**) HIGH

(— **UNDER STAGE**) DOCK

(— **USED AS LIVING-ROOM**) LANAI

(— **WITHIN LIMITS**) CONTENT

(**AIR** —) CENTRUM

(**ARCHITECTURAL** —) METOPE PEDIMENT SACELLUM

(**BARE** — **ON BIRD**) APTERIUM

(**BLANK** —) ALLEY LACUNA

(**BOUNDLESS** —) INFINITE

(**CLEAR** —) FAIRWAY HEADWAY DAYLIGHT

(**COUNTER** —) BACKBAR

(**CRAMPED** —) CUBBY

(**EMPTY** —) AIR BLANK CAPACITY

(**ENCLOSED** —) AREA BOWL HATCH VERGE CHAMBER CIRCUIT CLOSURE COMPASS PTEROMA CLOISTER CONFINES

(**EUCLIDEAN** —) FLAT

(**FLAT** —) HOMALOID

(**LEVEL** —) PLATEA PARTERRE

(**NARROW** —) SLOT STRAIT

(**OPEN** — **OF WATER**) WAKE

(**OPEN** —) OUT LAWN ALLEY COURT LAUND TAHUA MAIDAN AREAWAY FAIRWAY LOANING APERTURE DAYLIGHT KNEEHOLE

(**OVERHANGING** —) DOME

(**POPLITEAL** —) HAM HOCK

(**ROOF** —) CELL

(**SEATING** —) CAVEA

(**SHELTERED** —) KILLOGIE

(**STORAGE** —) ATTIC

(**TRIANGULAR** —) SPANDREL

(**UNFILLED** —) GAP GAPE CAVITY HOLLOW BREAKAGE

(**VAULTED** —) ALCOVE

(**VERTICAL** —) HEADROOM

(**WORKING** —) COUNTER

SPACED MEATIC

SPACIOUS ROOM SIDE WIDE AMPLE BROAD RANGY ROOMY GOLDEN BARONIAL SCOPIOUS

SPADE DIG LOY FECK LILY PEEL PICK SPIT SPUD DELVE DIDLE GRAFF SLADE SLANE TRAMP DIGGER PADDLE SERVER SHOVEL TUSKAR GRAFTER SCAFFLE SCUPPIT SPADDLE SPITTER TWISCAR

(**LONG NARROW** —) LOY

(**PEAT** —) SLADE SLANE TUSKAR

(**PLASTERER'S** —) SERVER

(**TRIANGULAR** —) DIDLE

SPADEFISH POGY PORGY MOONFISH

SPADEFUL SPIT SPITFUL

SPAGHETTI PASTA SLEEVING

SPAGNUOLO LADINO

SPAIN

CAPE: AJO NAO GATA CREUS MORAS PALOS PENAS PRIOR DARTUCH ORTEGAL SALINAS TORTOSA ESPICHEL MARROQUI SACRATIF

CAPITAL: MADRID

COIN: COB DURO PESO REAL DOBLA CUARTO DINERO DOBLON ESCUDO PESETA ALFONSO CENTIMO PISTOLE REALDOR DOUBLOON

DIALECT: BASQUE CATALAN GALICIAN

ISLAND: IBIZA PALMA GOMERA HIERRO ALBORAN MAJORCA MINORCA MALLORCA TAGOMAGO TENERIFE

ISLANDS: CANARY BALEARIC

MEASURE: PIE CODO COPA DEDO MOYO PASO VARA BRAZA CAFIZ CAHIZ CARGA LEGUA LINEA MEDIO MILLA PALMO SESMA ARROBA CORDEL CUARTA ESTADO FANEGA RACION YUGADA AZUMBRE CANTARA CELEMIN ESTADEL PULGADA ARANZADA FANEGADA

MOUNTAIN: GATA ANETO ROUCH TEIDE ESTATS NETHOU TELENO BANUELO CERREDO PERDIDO ALMANZOR MONTSENY MULHACEN PENALARA

MOUNTAIN RANGE: CUENCA GREDOS MORENA TOLEDO ALCARAZ DEMANDA MONCAYO MALADETA MONEGROS PYRENEES

NAME: ESPANA IBERIA HISPANIA

NATIVE: CATALAN IBERIAN

PORT: ADRA NOYA VIGO CADIZ GADES GADIR GIJON PALOS ABDERA CORUNA MALAGA ALMERIA ALICANTE BARCELONA

PROVINCE: JAEN LEON LUBO ALAVA AVILA CADIZ SORIA BURGOS CORUNA CUENCA GERONA HUELVA HUESCA LERIDA MADRID MALAGA MURCIA ORENSE OVIEDO TERUEL TOLEDO ZAMORA ALMERIA BADAJOZ CACERES CORDOBA GRANADA LOGRONO NAVARRA SEGOVIA SEVILLA VIZCAYA ALBACETE ALICANTE BALEARES PALENCIA VALENCIA ZARAGOZA

REGION: LEON ARAGON BASQUE MURCIA CASTILE GALICIA NAVARRE ASTURIAS CASTILLA VALENCIA

RIVER: SIL TER CEGA EBRO ESLA LIMA MINO TAJO ULLA ADAJA CINCA DOURO DUERO GENIL JALON JUCAR NAVIA ODIEL RIAZA SEGRE TAGUS TINTO TURIA ALAGON ARAGON ERESMA HUERVA JARAMA ORBIGO SEGURA TOROTE ALMERIA ALMONTE ARLANZA BARBATE CABRIEL DURATON GALLEGO HENARES MIJARES PERALES GUADIANA

TOWN: ASPE BAZA ELDA HARO IRUN JAEN LEON LUGO OLOT REUS ROTA SAMA VIGO BAENA BEJAR CADIZ CIEZA CUETA ECIJA EIBAR ELCHE GIJON IBIZA JEREZ JODAR LORCA OLIVA PALMA RONDA SIERO UBEDA XERES YECLA ZAFRA AVILES AZUAGA BILBAO BURGOS DUENCA GANDIA GERONA GETAFE GUADIX HELLIN HUELVA HUESCA JATIVA LERIDA LUCENA MADRID MALAGA MATARO MERIDA MURCIA ORENSE OVIEDO TERMEL TOLEDO UTRERA ZAMORA BADAJOS CORDOBA DAIMIEL GRANADA JUMILLA LINARES LOGRONO MANRESA SEGOVIA SEVILLA TARRASA VITORIA BADALONA FIGUERAS PAMPLONA SABADELL SANTIAGO TORRENTE VALENCIA ZARAGOZA

WEIGHT: ONZA FRAIL GRANO LIBRA MARCO TOMIN ADARME ARROBA DINERO DRACMA OCHAVA ARIENZO QUILATE QUINTAL CARACTER TONELADA

WINE: RIOJA SHERRY

SPALL SCALE SPAWL GALLET

SPAN ARCH BEAM PAIR CHORD SPANG SWING BRIDGE EXTEND SPREAD OPENING QUARTER BESTRIDE

(— **WITH FINGERS**) SPEND

(**UNSUPPORTED** —) BEARING

SPANDREL GROIN ALLEGE SPANDLE

SPANGLE AGLET PRANK SPANG SEQUIN CHEQUEEN SPANGLET ZECCHINO

SPANGLED POWDERED SPANKLED

SPANIARD DON DIEGO MULADI

SPANIEL TRASY COCKER SUSSEX
PAPILLON SPRINGER WATERRUG

SPANISH ALJAMIA

SPANISH-AMERICAN CHINO

SPANISH BAYONET IZOTE YUCCA

SPANISH HOGFISH LADYFISH

SPANISH JACINTH SCILLA

SPANISH JASMINE MALATI

SPANISH MACKEREL SIERRA

SPANISH PLUM SIRUELAS

SPANISH STOPPER IRONWOOD

SPANK PRAT SCUD SKELP SLIPPER

SPANKER DRIVER

SPANKING SMACKING

SPANNER KEY WRENCH

SPANNING ASTRIDE

SPAR BEAM BOOM CAUK CLUB GAFF
MAST RAFT SPUR YARD CABER
SPAAD SPATH SPELK SPRIT STODE
BOUGAR STEEVE BASTITE DERRICK
DOLPHIN JIBBOOM RIBBAND
BOWSPRIT LAZULITE
(BITTER —) DOLOMITE
(HEAVY —) CAUK BARITE BARYTE

SPARE BONY FAIK HAIN LEAN NICE
SAVE SLIM THIN FAVOR LANKY
SPELL LENTEN SKIMPY RESERVE
SLENDER PRESERVE

SPARGE PIPE WEEPER

SPARING CHARY GNEDE SCANT
SPARE DAINTY FRUGAL STINGY
ENVIOUS ECONOMIC SPAREFUL
(— OF WORDS) CURT
(NOT —) HANDSOME

SPARINGNESS PARCITY SCARCITY

SPARK FUNK IZLE AIZLE GRAIN
LIGHT PURSE SPERK SPUNK
FLANKER SPARKLE SPUNKIE
SPARKLET
(VITAL —) GHOST LIGHT

SPARKER IGNITER

SPARKLE FUNK SNAP WINK BLINK
FLASH GLENT GLINT SHINE SPARK
GLANCE KINDLE SIMPER CRACKLE
FLANKER GLIMMER GLISTEN
GLISTER GLITTER RADIATE SHIMMER
SKINKLE SPANGLE TWINKLE
SPRINKLE

SPARKLER TWINKLER

SPARKLING DEWY CRISP QUICK
SUNNY SPUNKY STARRY CREMANT
DIAMOND SHINING TWINKLY
MOUSSEUX SMIRKING SPERLING
(MAKE —) AERATE

SPARLING SMELT

SPARROW SPUG DICKY DONEY
FINCH HEMPY ISAAC PADDA PADDY
SPRIG SPRUG CHIPPY PHILIP
SPRONG TOWHEE CHANTER CHIPPIE
DUNNOCK FIELDIE HAYSUCK
PINNOCK SPADGER SPURDIE
TITLENE TITLING TITTLIN ACCENTOR
FIRETAIL HAIRBIRD WHITECAP

SPARROW HAWK MUSKET
SPARHAWK

SPARSE BALD THIN MEAGER SCANTY
THRIFTY

SPARTAN LACONIC

SPASM QUALM TONUS ENTASIA
FLUTTER RAPTURE SPASMUS
MYOTONIA PAROXYSM
(— OF PAIN) GRIP
(—S OF WHALE) FLURRY
(TONIC —) HOLOTONY

SPASMODIC FITFUL SNATCHY
SPASMIC SPASTIC SPURTIVE

SPAT SEED BROOD JOWER GAITER
LEGGING BOOTHOSE BOOTIKIN

SPATE SLUICE

SPATHE CYMBA SHEATH

SPATHIC SPARRY SPATHOSE

SPATIAL STERIC

SPATTER DASH JAUP BERAY SKIRP
SLART SPARK SPURT DABBLE
SPLASH SQUIRT BESPAWL BESPETE
SHATTER SMATTER SPATTLE
SPIRTLE SPLATTER SPRINKLE
(— WITH FOAM) EMBOSS
(— WITH MUD) JAP BEMUD SPARK

SPATTERDASH SPAT BONNET
GAITER CUTIKIN LEGGING
BOOTHOSE BOOTIKIN

SPATTERDOCK DUCK CLOTE TUCKY
WOKAS NUPHAR BONNETS
CANDOCK

SPATULA SPAT SLICE THIBLE THIVEL
CESTRUM SPATTLE SPLATTER

SPAVIN JACK SPAVIE VARISSE

SPAWN RUD RAUN REDD RUDD SILE
SPORE TODDER

SPAWNEATER SHINER

SPAWNING SICK MILKY SEEDING

SPAY FIX GELD ALTER DESEX SPADE
CHANGE SPEAVE CASTRATE

SPEAK ASK CUT SAY CANT CARP
MEAN MOOT MOVE TALE TALK TELL
WORD BREAK MOUTH NEVEN ORATE
PARLE SOUND SPELL SPIEL UTTER
ACCENT PARLEY PATTER QUETHE
SERMON SPEECH SQUEAK TONGUE
ADDRESS BESPEAK DECLAIM
DELIVER EXCLAIM PARRALL
CONVERSE REHEARSE
(— ABUSIVELY) JAW
(— AFFECTEDLY) MIMP KNACK
(— AGAINST) ACCUSE GAINSAY
FORSPEAK
(— ANGRILY) ROUSE CAMPLE
(— AT LENGTH) DISSERT ENLARGE
(— BROKENLY) FALTER
(— CAJOLINGLY) COLLOGUE
(— CONFUSEDLY) HATTER CLUTTER
SPLATHER
(— CONTEMPTUOUSLY) SCOFF
(— CRITICALLY) LAUNCH
(— CURTLY) BIRK SNAP
(— EVIL) BLACKEN
(— FALSELY) ABUSE
(— FAMILIARLY) HOBNOB
(— FIRST TO) ACCOST
(— FOOLISHLY) PRATE GIBBER
(— HALTINGLY) HACK HAMMER
STAMMER
(— HOARSELY) CROAK CROUP
(— ILL OF) KNOCK DEPRAVE
DETRACT

(— IMPERFECTLY) LISP

(— IMPUDENTLY) CHEEK

(— IMPULSIVELY) BLURT

(— IN DRAWL) DRANT DRAUNT

(— IN JEST) FOOL

(— IN ONE'S EAR) HARK

(— IN POINTLESS MANNER) DROOL

(— IN STUMBLING WAY) STUTTER

(— IN UNDERTONE) WHISPER

(— IN WHINING VOICE) CANT

(— INDISTINCTLY) FUMBLE JABBER
MUFFLE MAUNDER SPLUTTER

(— INEPTLY) BUMBLE

(— INSOLENTLY) SNASH

(— LOUDLY) TANG

(— MINCINGLY) NAB MIMP

(— MONOTONOUSLY) DROLL

(— OF) CALL NEVEN MENTION

(— OUT) LEVEL SHOOT

(— PLAYFULLY) BANTER

(— POMPOUSLY) CRACK

(— PROFUSELY) PALAVER

(— QUERULOUSLY) CREAK

(— RAPIDLY) TROLL GIBBER JABBER
SQUIRT CHATTER

(— RESENTFULLY) HUFF

(— RHETORICALLY) DECLAIM

(— SARCASTICALLY) GIRD

(— SHORTLY) JERK

(— SLIGHTINGLY OF) BELITTLE

(— SLOWLY) DRAWL

(— THROUGH THE NOSE) SNAFFLE

(— TRUTH) SOOTHSAY

(— WITH EMPHASIS) DWELL

(— WITH LIPS CLOSED) MUMBLE

SPEAKEASY SHEBEEN

SPEAKER VOICE BRYTHON LOCUTOR
MOUTHER STYLIST EPILOGUE
SPEECHER
(ORATORICAL —) SPOUTER
(PUBLIC —) ORATOR STUMPER

SPEAKING STEVEN LOQUENT
SPELLING
(— ARTICULATELY) MEROP
MEROPIC
(— MANY LANGUAGES) POLYGLOT
(EVIL —) PRATING

SPEAR GAD DART FRAM GAFF PIKE
GRAIN LANCE REJON SHAFT STAFF
VALET AMGARN BORDUN BROACH
FIZGIG FRAMEA GIDJEE GLAIVE
WASTER ASSEGAI BOURDON
HARPOON IMPALER JAVELIN
TRIDENT VERUTUM EELSPEAR
GAVELOCK LANCEGAY STANDARD
WALSPERE
(EEL —) ELGER PILGER
(FISH —) GIG GAFF TREN POACH
FIZGIG GRAINS FISHGIG LEISTER
SNIGGER
(SALMON —) WASTER

SPEARFISH AGUJA GOGGLE MARLIN
BILLFISH LONGJAWS

SPEAR GRASS SPANIARD

SPEARHEAD BUNT GAFF SPUD
CORONAL

SPEARMINT MENTHE LABIATE

SPEAR-SHAPED HASTATE

SPEAR THROWER ATLATL

WOMMALA WOOMERAH
SPEARWORT BANEWORT
SPECIAL VERY EXTRA KHASS
CONCRETE ESPECIAL PECULIAR
SPECIFIC
SPECIALIST SWELL EXPERT HERALD
LEGIST ALTAIST ARABIST FAUNIST
FEUDIST GRECIAN OLOGIST
SURGEON AQUINIST ARBORIST
BANTUIST BOTANIST ETHICIST
GEMARIST GEOGNOST GEOMETER
HEBRAIST HOMERIST LATINIST
URBANIST
SPECIES FOLK FORM KIND SORT
BROOD CLASS EIDOS GENRE
ESPECE MANNER MISTER APOMICT
FEATHER SPECIAL ANALOGUE
GENOTYPE INDIGENE
(ATOMIC —) DAUGHTER
SPECIFIC EXPRESS SPECIAL TRIVIAL
CONCRETE ESPECIAL
SPECIFICALLY NAMELY
SPECIFICATION MENTION
SPECIFICITY HECCEITY
SPECIFIED SET GIVEN
SPECIFY DESIGN DETAIL ARTICLE
EXPRESS MENTION INDICATE
NOMINATE
SPECIMEN CAST TEST ESSAY
FACER MODEL SPICE CHANCE
SAMPLE SWATCH EXAMPLE ICOTYPE
ISOTYPE PATTERN SAMPLER
ALLOTYPE EXEMPLAR HOLOTYPE
HYPOTYPE IDEOTYPE INSTANCE
(ADDITIONAL —) COTYPE
(EXTRAORDINARY —) BENDER
(FEMALE —) GYNETYPE
(FINEST —) PEARL
(LARGE —) ELEPHANT
(SMALL —) SPRIG
SPECIOUS GAY FAIR FALSE WHITE
FACILE GLOSSY HOLLOW TINSEL
PAGEANT PLAUSIVE PROBABLE
SPURIOUS
SPECIOUSNESS DISGUISE
SPECK DOT PIN PIP MOTE SPOT
TICK WHIT BLACK GLEBE PLECK
APHTHA SPECKLE FLYSPECK
NUBECULA
(— IN LINEN) SPRIT
(— ON FINGERNAIL) GIFT
(BLACK —) DARTROSE
SPECKLE FLECK GARLE SPECK
MIZZLE PECKLE STIPPLE
SPECKLED SHELD FIGGED MAILED
MENALD SANDED BLOBBED
BRACKET PECKLED SPECKED
SPECKLY FRECKLED IRONSHOT
IRRORATE JASPERED STIPPLED
SPECTACLE POMP SHOW SPEC
BYSEN SIGHT CIRCUS DEVICE
OBJECT EYEMARK PAGEANT
SPECIES TAMASHA MONUMENT
NAUMACHY STERACLE
(ODD —) TRACK
(SORRY —) BIZEN BYSEN
(WATER —) AQUACADE
SPECTACLES PAIR SPECS BRILLS
LUNETS PEEPER SIGHTS GLASSES

GOGGLES WINKERS CHEATERS
SPECTACULAR VIEWY PAGEANT
SPECTATOR FAN VIEWER WITNESS
BEHOLDER OBSERVER OVERSEER
RAILBIRD VIEWSTER
(PL.) DEDANS
SPECTER BUG BOGY MARE BOGIE
BOGLE GHOST LARVA POOKA
SPOOK TAIPO BOGGLE EMPUSA
PHOOKA REDCAP SHADOW SPIRIT
SPOORN WRAITH BOGGART
BUGBEAR PHANTOM RAWHEAD
REDCOWL SPECTRE GUYTRASH
PHANTASM PRESENCE REVENANT
SPECTRUM
SPECTRAL SPOOKY GHOSTLY
SHADOWY
SPECULATE JOB STAG GAMBLE
PONDER CONSIDER RUMINATE
THEORIZE
SPECULATION THEORY THEORIC
VENTURE GAMBLING IDEOLOGY
(DISHONEST —) BUBBLE
SPECULATIVE ACADEMIC
SPECULATOR PIKER GAMBLER
PLUNGER SCALPER BUMMAREE
OPERATOR
SPECULUM METAL MIRROR DILATER
DIOPTER DIOPTRIC
SPEECH GOB LIP SAW SAY TAT TOY
COAX LEED REDE RUNE TALE
DUALA FRUMP GLOZE LEDEN LINGO
SERMO SPEAK SPELL SPOKE SQUIB
VOICE BREATH DILOGY EPILOG
GAELIC GASCON GILAKI JARGON
LEMOSI ORISON REASON SALUTE
STEVEN TONGUE ADDRESS
BROCARD EASTERN MEITHEI
ORATION VULGATE EPILOGUE
GALICIAN HARANGUE LANGUAGE
LOCUTION LOQUENCE MORAVIAN
QUESTION SONORITY SPEAKING
(— FORM) LEXEME
(— IN GREEK DRAMA) RHESIS
(— IN PLAY) SIDE
(— REDUCER) VOCODER
(AFFECTED —) CANT
(BITTER —) DIATRIBE
(BOASTFUL —) BLUSTER
(BOMBASTIC —) SQUIRT HARANGUE
(COARSE —) HARLOTRY
(CONFUSED —) SPUTTER
(CONTEMPTUOUS —) FRUMP
(IRRITABLE —) SNAP
(JAVANESE —) KRAMA
(LONG —) MONOLOG
(LONG-DRAWN —) TIRADE
(MOCKING —) TRIFLE
(OBSCURE —) ENIGMA
(OFFENSIVE —) INJURY
(PRETENTIOUS —) FUSTIAN
(ROUNDABOUT —) CIRCUIT
(SANCTIMONIOUS —) SNUFFLE
(SINGSONG —) CANT
(SLANDEROUS —) EVIL
(VAPID —) WASH
SPEECHIFIER SPOUTER
SPEECHLESS DUMB MUTE SILENT
SPEECHMAKING SPOUTING

(— TO GAIN APPLAUSE) BUNKUM
BUNCOMBE
SPEED BAT HIE RIP RUN FLEE FOOT
GAIT HIGH PACE PELT PIRR POST
TILT BLAST HASTE HURRY SMOKE
WHIRL ASSIST CAREER FOURTH
HASTEN STREAK QUICKEN WHIZZLE
AIRSPEED CELERITY DISPATCH
EXPEDITE FASTNESS MOMENTUM
RAPIDITY VELOCITY
(— OF NAUTICAL MILE) KNOT
(— OF PITCH) STUFF
(— UP) HASTEN CATALYZE
EXPEDITE
(AT FULL —) AMAIN
(AUTOMOTIVE —) LOW HIGH DRIVE
FIRST THIRD FOURTH SECOND
REVERSE
(DRIVING —) SWING
(GOOD —) BONALLY
SPEEDILY CITO SOON APACE RATHE
BELIVE BETIMES HYINGLY QUICKLY
TANTIVY
SPEEDING HURTLING
SPEEDWELL CATEYE HENBIT
FLUELLEN NECKWEED NICKWELL
SPEEDY FAST SOON HASTY QUICK
RATHE SWIFT RAKING SUDDEN
POSTING TANTIVY EXPEDITE
SPEEDFUL SPINNING
SPELEOLOGIST CAVEMAN
SPELL GO FIT HEX JAG HACK JINX
MOJO PULL RUNE TACK TAKE TIFF
TIME TOUR TURN BRIEF CHARM
CRAFT CRASH MAGIC PATCH SPACE
WANGA WEIRD WHEEL ACCESS
GLAMOR GOOFER GRIGRI GUFFER
MAKUTU MANTRA PERIOD SNATCH
STREAK CANTRIP SORCERY
SPELDER CANTRAIP EXORCISM
GREEGREE MALEFICE PISHOGUE
(— OF ACTIVITY) BOUT
(— OF EXERCISE) BREATHER
(— OF LISTLESSNESS) DOLDRUMS
(— OF SHIVERING) AGUE
(— OF WEATHER) SNAP SLANT
SEASON
(BREATHING —) BLOW
(BRIEF —) SNATCH
(DRINKING —) FUDDLE
(EVIL —) JINX
(FAINTING —) DROW DWALM
(NIPPING —) SNAPE
(STORMY —) FLAW
(VOODOOISTIC —) WANGA
SPELLBIND ENCHANT
SPELLBINDING BASILISK
SPELLING GRAPH WRITING
SPELT FAR EMMER FITCH SPELTZ
SPELTZ EMMER
SPEND COST DREE DROP LEAD
PASS STOW WARE WEAR DALLY
DREIE SERVE SHOOT TRADE
BESTOW BEWARE EXPEND LAVISH
OUTRUN CONSUME DISPEND
EXHAUST UNPURSE CONFOUND
CONTRIVE DISBURSE
(— FRUITLESSLY) DAWDLE
(— IN IDLENESS) DRONE

(— LAVISHLY) BLUE SPORT DEBAUCH
(— MONEY) MELT
(— RECKLESSLY) BLOW LASH
(— SUMMER) ESTIVATE
(— TIME TEDIOUSLY) DRANT
(— TIME) DREE FOOL DREIE
(— WASTEFULLY) SPILL SQUANDER
SPENDTHRIFT WASTER PANURGE ROUNDER SPENDER WASTREL PRODIGAL
SPENSER IMMERITO
SPENT DONE WEARY EFFETE OVERWORN
SPERM SEED SEMINIUM
SPERMACETI SPERM CETACEUM
SPERMOGONIUM PYCNIUM
SPERMOPHILE MARMOT SUSLIK
SPERM WHALE CACHALOT
SPET SIGNET SINNET
SPEW PUKE SPUE VOMIT
SPHAERIUM CYCLAS
SPHAGION HIERA
SPHAGNUM MUSKEG
SPHALERITE JACK BLENDE
SPHENODON HATTERIA
SPHERE ORB AREA BALL BOWL LOKA SHOT FIELD GLOBE RANGE SCOPE CIRCLE CROTAL DOMAIN HEAVEN REGION RUNDLE COUNTRY ELEMENT GLOBOID KINGDOM ORBICLE EARTHKIN EMPYREAL EMPYREAN MOVEABLE PROVINCE
(— OF ACTION) AMBIT ARENA WORLD DOMAIN
(— OF ACTIVITY) FIELD FRONT
(— OF AUTHORITY) DIOCESE
(— OF INFLUENCE) DOMAIN SATRAPY
(— OF LIFE) EARTH WORLD STATION
(— OF OPERATION) THEATER THEATRE
(— OF WORK) TITLE
(CELESTIAL —) CYCLE ELEMENT
(ENCOMPASSING —) AMBIENT
(MAGNETIZED —) EARTHKIN TERRELLA
(METAL —) HAMMER
(SMALL —) ORBICLE SPHERULE
(TINKLING —) CROTAL
SPHERICAL ORBIC GLOBAL ROTUND GLOBATE GLOBOSE ORBICAL SPHERIC GLOBULAR
SPHERULE GLOBULE VARIOLE
SPHINX MUSTANG COLOSSUS HAWKMOTH
SPICA AZIMECH
SPICCATO PIQUE
SPICE MACE VEIN AROMA CLOVE EPICE TASTE GINGER NUTMEG PEPPER SEASON STACTE SPICERY SPICING ALLSPICE CINNAMON SEASONER
SPICEBUSH BENZOIN SNAPWOOD
SPICED SPICY POWDERED
SPICKNEL MEW SCLERE BEARWORT
SPICULE OXEA TOXA ASTER CHELA CYMBA DESMA DIACT SIGMA SPINE

STYLE ACTINE ANCHOR MONACT SCLERE STYLUS TRIACT TRIPOD TYLOTE CALTROP DIACTIN EUASTER HEXAXON MONAXON PINULUS SPERULA SPICKLE TETRACT TORNOTE TRIAENE TRIAXON TYLOTUS HEXASTER ISOCHELA OXYASTER POLYAXON SCLERITE SPHERULA SPICULUM STRONGYL TETRAXON TRICHITE TYLASTER
SPICY RACY SEXY GAMEY NUTTY SWEET SPICED GINGERY FRAGRANT SPICEFUL
SPIDER BUG COB ARAIN ATTID COBBE COPPE LOPPE NANCY TAINT ANANSI ARRAND EPEIRA HUNTER KATIPO WEAVER ARANEID CREEPER DRASSID JAYHAWK KNOPPIE POKOMOO RETIARY SERPENT SKILLET SOLDIER SPINNER ARACHNID ATTERCOP CTENIZID DICTYNID ETTERCAP KARAKURT ORBITELE PHALANGY PHOLCOID SALTICID SOLPUGID TELARIAN ULOBORID VENANTES WANDERER TARANTULA
SPIDER CRAB MAIAN MAIID
SPIDERFLOWER QUARESMA
SPIDER MONKEY SAJOU COAITA SAPAJOU
SPIDERWORT TRINITY
SPIELER BARKER
SPIGOT TAP SPILE DOSSIL DOZZLE STOPCOCK
SPIKE GAD BROB PICK PIKE PILE SPUR TINE PITON ROUGH SPEAR MOOTER PRITCH SPADIX SPIKER TENTER ALICOLE GADLING PRICKER PRICKET TRENAIL TURNPIN SPIKELET STROBILE WHEATEAR
(— OF CEREAL) EAR
(BRACTED —) AMENT
(DRIED —S) CANNABIS
SPIKED SPICATE SPINDLED
SPIKELET CHAT ALICOLE LOCUSTA SPICULE
SPIKENARD PHU NARD ARALIA SUMBUL ARALIAD IVYWORT SPIGNET SPIGNUT
SPILE TAP SPILL FOREPOLE
SPILL LET DRIP SHED SLOP FLOSH SCALE SPILE SQUAB STAVE JIRBLE PURLER SLATTER SLOBBER TURNOVER
(— FOR LIGHTING PIPES) FIDIBUS
SPIN CUT BIRL DRAW GYRE HURL PIRL PURL SCREW SPONE TWIST WEAVE WHIRL FOLLOW GYRATE VRILLE WAMBLE TWIZZLE TEETOTUM
(— AND MAKE HUM) BUM
(— AROUND) SWING
(— ON BASEBALL) STUFF
(— ON BILLIARD BALL) SIDE
(— OUT) SHOOT
(— SILK) THROW
(— SMOOTHLY) SLEEP
(— UNEVENLY) TWITTER
SPINACH SAVOY EPINARD OLITORY POTHERB

SPINAL CORD AXION NUCHA MYELON
(WHITE MATTER OF —) ALBA NUKE
SPINDLE PIN AXLE HASP SPIT STEM STUD ARBOR FLOAT QUILL SPIKE SPILL VERGE BOBBIN BROACH CANNON FUSEAU BOLSTER MANDREL SPINNEL TRENDLE WHARROW
(AXLE —) ARM
(FOURTH OF —) HASP
(ONE 24TH OF —) HEER
SPINDLE TREE GAITER DOGWOOD PEGWOOD EUONYMUS
SPINDLING SPEARY SPINDLY SPIRLIE
SPINDLY LEGGY PULING
SPINE HORN PIKE PILE SETA SPUR CHINE PRICK QUILL SPEAR SPIKE SPINA THORN ACUMEN CHAETA RACHIS ACANTHA ACICULA FULCRUM GLOCHIS PAXILLA PRICKER PRICKLE ROSTRUM SPINULE ACICULUM BACKBONE ILLICIUM PAXILLUS PELELITH SPICULUM SPINELET
(— OF SURGEON FISH) TUCK
(CURVATURE OF —) LORDOSIS
SPINEL BALAS CANDITE ESPINEL VERMEIL PICOTITE SPINELLE
SPINELESS SLAVISH
SPINET ESPINET GIRAFFE OCTAVINA SOURDINE VIRGINAL
SPINNERET GALEA MAMMULA SPINNER
SPINNING LANIFICE
(— WEB) TELARIAN
SPINNING JENNY MULE JENNY
SPINNING MULE IRONMAN
SPINNING WHEEL TURN CHARKHA CHURRUCK
SPINSTER TABBY VIRGIN
SPINULE(PL.) CTENII
SPINY PICKED THORNY
SPINY OYSTER SPONDYLE
SPINY RAT OCTODONT
SPIRACLE STOMA STIGMA BLOWHOLE
SPIRAEA MAY ROSACEAN
SPIRAL COIL CURL GYRE SPIN SCREW SNARE SPIRE BUTTON GURGES LITUUS SCREWY SCROLL SPIRED TWIRLY VOLUTE HELICAL ROLLING SPIROID STROPHE WINDING WREATHY GYROIDAL HELICINE HELICOID
SPIRANT VAU WAW HISS OPEN DURATIVE
SPIRANTHES IBIDIUM
SPIRE SHAFT SIKAR SPEAR TAPER TOLLY BROACH FLECHE PRICKET SHIKARA SIKHARA SPIRALE SPIRELET
SPIRE-BEARER SPIRIFER
SPIREME SKEAN SKEIN
SPIRIT GO FLY NAG VIM AITU AKUA ALMA ATUA BRIO DASH DOOK ELAN FIRE GALL GIMP HYLE JINN LIFE MARC MARE MIND MOOD SOUL

TONE ZEMI ZING AGIEL ARDOR
ARIEL ASURA AZOTH CHEER DEMON
DHOUL DJINN DOBBY ETHOS FLING
GEIST GHOST GORIC GUACA HAUNT
HEART HOLDA HUACA JINNI LARVA
NUMEN PLUCK POWER PRETA
RALPH SAINT SHADE SHRAB SPOOK
SPUNK VERVE ASTRAL ASUANG
BOTTOM BREATH CHULPA COURIL
DAEMON ESPRIT FAINTS FYLGJA
GENIUS GINGER INWARD KOBOLD
LESHEY METTLE MORALE ORISHA
PNEUMA PYTHON SPRAWL SPRITE
TAFFIA WRAITH ALCOHOL BRAVERY
CONTROL CORDIAL COURAGE
ENTRAIN EUDEMON KNOCKER
MANITOU PISACHI PURUSHA
RAPPIST SMEDDUM STOMACH
CALVADOS ERDGEIST FAMILIAR
FOLLETTO PHANTASM SPIRACLE
SPIRITUS
(— DWELLING IN JEWEL) AZOTH
(— DWELLING IN MINES) KNOCKER
(— HAUNTING PRINTING HOUSES)
RALPH
(— OF DEAD) CHINDI CHINDEE
(— OF DEATH) CHULPA
(— OF DECEASED) AKH
(— OF FERTILITY) YAKSA YAKSHA
YAKSHI
(— OF HOSTILITY) ANIMUS
(— OF LOYALTY) PIETAS
(— OF MAN) AKH
(— OF ONE WHO HAS MET VIOLENT
DEATH) PISACHI
(— OF PHYSICAL HEART) AB
(— OF TRAGEDY) COTHURN
(— OF UNBAPTIZED BABE) TARAN
(— WHICH ACTUATES CUSTOMS)
ETHOS
(—S OF LOWER WORLD) INFERI
(—S OF THE DEAD) MANES
(ANCESTRAL —) ANITO KATCHINA
(ARDENT —) RAK RACK ARRACK
(ASTRAL —) AGIEL ASTRAL JOPHIEL
UUCHATON
(AVENGING —) FURY ALECTO
ALASTOR MEGAERA
(COMBATIVE —) SWORD
(DISEMBODIED —) KUEI KWEI SOUL
GHOST LARVA SHADE ASUANG
SPECTER SPECTRE
(DIVINE —) ISVARA ISHVARA
(EARTH —) ERDGEIST
(EFFULGENT —S) ARDORS
(EMANCIPATED —) MUKTATMA
(EVIL —) DEV HAG IMP OKI BAKA
BENG BOKO BOLL DEVA DUSE
MARA OKEE ASURA BUGAN DAEVA
DEMON DEVIL JUMBY OTKON
DAITYA DIBBUK DYBBUK LILITH
AHRIMAN BUGGANE CASZIEL
INCUBUS KANAIMA SHAITAN
SHEITAN SKOOKUM WINDIGO
ASMODEUS BAALPEOR BEELPEOR
HOBOMOCO
(FAMILIAR —) FLY GENIUS HARPIER
(FEMALE —) DUFFY DUPPY DUSIO
HOLDA UNDINE BANSHEE ATAENSIC

BABAJAGA BELFAGOR BELFAZOR
(FIGHTING —) DEVIL
(FOREST —) MIMING
(FULL OF —) CRANK
(FULL OF —S) BRAG
(GOOD —) EUDEMON
(GOVERNING —) ANIMUS
(GUARDIAN —) ANGEL TOTEM
FYLGJA NAGUAL
(HIGH —) GINGER COURAGE
(HIGH —S) CREST GAIETY HEYDAY
ELATION
(HOSTILE —S) LEMURES
(HOUSEHOLD —S) LARES PENATES
(HUMAN —) JIVATMA
(IMPISH —) PO
(IMPURE —) FAINTS
(IN VIGOROUS —S) FIERCE
(LOW —S) DUMP BLUES DISMALS
(MALEVOLENT —) BHUT GORIC
LARVA
(MALICIOUS —) DOBBY
(MALIGNANT —) IMP KER GYRE
DEMON
(MANLY —) SPLEEN
(MISCHIEVOUS —) KOBOLD
TIKOLOSH
(MOUNTAIN —) RUBEZAHL
(MOVING —) SOUL
(MUSICAL —) BRIO
(NATURE —) NAT
(PARTY —) FACTION
(REFINED —) ELIXIR
(RESOLUTE —) SPRAWL
(SEA —) TANGIE
(SOOTHSAYING —) PYTHON
(SUPERNATURAL —) FAMILIAR
(SYLVAN —) LESHY SYLVAN
(TRICKSY —) ARIEL
(TUTELARY —S) DIS LARES
(VITAL —) TUCK
(VOLATILE —) ESSENCE
(WATER —) ARIEL KELPY UNDINE
(WICKED —) IMP THURSE
(PL.) IGIGI DAUBER
SPIRITED BRAG FELL RACY TALL
BEANY BIRKY CRANK EAGER FIERY
FLUSH KEDGE KINKY LIFEY SASSY
SEEDY SMART SPICY VIVID AUDACE
FIERCE GINGER LIVELY METTLE
PLUCKY SKEIGH SPRUCE SPUNKY
VIVACE ANIMATO DASHING
FORWARD HUMMING NERVOUS
PEPPERY SPIRITY DESIROUS
FRAMPOLD GENEROUS PHRAMPEL
SLASHING STOMACHY VASCULAR
SPIRITEDLY GAMELY
SPIRITLESS DEAD MEAN MEEK TAME
AMORT FAINT MILKY MUSTY SEEDY
SOGGY VAPID DREEPY FLASHY
LEADEN SODDEN SOFTLY WOODEN
INSIPID LANGUID FECKLESS
FLAGGING LISTLESS THEWLESS
SPIRITLESSLY DAVIELY
SPIRITLIKE ETHEREAL
SPIRITS LACE RAKI HOOCH MANES
FETTLE PECKER FEATHER LEMURES
WAIPIRO
SPIRITUAL ABOVE DEVOUT INWARD

MISTLY GHOSTLY CHURCHLY
INTERNAL NUMINOUS SUPERIOR
(— LEADER) ZADDIK
SPIRITUALISM SPOOKISM
SPIRITUALITY HEAVEN
SPIRITUALIZE REFINE
SPIRITUOUS HARD
SPIROCHETE BORRELIA
SPIT FUFF RACK FROTH REACH
SPAWL BROACH SPITTLE SANDSPIT
SPITTING
SPITE ENVY ONDE DEPIT LIVOR
PIQUE VENOM MALICE MAUGRE
RANCOR SPLEEN DESPITE AMBITION
SPITEFUL CATTY NEBBY SNAKY
ELVISH SULLEN WANTON CATTISH
ENVIOUS PEEVISH SNAKISH VICIOUS
WASPISH CANKERED KNAPPISH
VENOMOUS
SPITFIRE PEPPERBOX
SPITTING SNAKE RINGHALS
SPITTLE SPIT SPAWL SPUTUM
SLOBBER
SPITTOON GABOON PIGDAN
SPITBOX CRACHOIR CUSPIDOR
SPLANCHNIC VISCERAL
SPLASH JAW LAP DASH GLOB GOUT
JAUP LOSH LUSH SKIT SOSS SPAT
WASH BLASH FLASH FLICK FLOOD
FLOSH PLASH PLOUT QUASH SKIRP
SLART SLASH SLOSH SLUSH SQUAT
SWILK BEDASH DABBLE DOLLOP
JABBLE LABBER PLATCH SLUNGE
SOZZLE SPLOSH SPRENT SQUIRT
SPATTER SPIRTLE SPLODGE
SPLURGE SWATTER SPLAIRGE
SPLATHER SPLATTER SPLOTHER
SPLUTHER SPLUTTER
(— OF COLOR) GOUT
(SLIGHT —) GILP
SPLASHBOARD FENDER SPLASHER
SPLASHING SWASH FLASHY JABBLE
DASHING SPATTER SPLUTTER
SWASHING
SPLASHY BLASHY SLOPPY SPRAWLY
SPLATTER DASH BLASH SPLAIRGE
SPLAY FLAN
SPLAYFOOT FLATFOOT
SPLEEN BILE LIEN MELT MILT
STOMACH
SPLEENY PEEVISH
SPLENDID GAY BRAW FINE RIAL
BRAVE GRAND JOLLY NOBLE
PROUD REGAL ROYAL SHEEN
SHOWY STOUT WALLY WLONK
CANDID COSTLY SIGHTY SOLEMN
SPIFFY SUPERB ELEGANT GALLANT
SHINING SUBLIME TEARING
BARONIAL CHAMPION CLINKING
GLORIOUS GORGEOUS MAJESTIC
ORGULOUS RATTLING SLASHING
STUNNING
(CHEAPLY —) TINNY
SPLENDIDLY FINE FINELY SPROWSY
SPLENDOR SUN UMA GITE LUXE
POMP BLAZE GLARE GLEAM GLORY
SHEEN SHINE FULGOR LUSTER
LUSTRE PARADE RUFFLE CLARITY
DISPLAY JOLLITY GRANDEUR

RADIANCE SUMPTURE
SPLENETIC SULLEN VAPORY
PEEVISH
SPLENIC LIENAL
SPLICE FOOT JOIN SCAB PIECE
SCARE SKELB CROTCH PIECEN
SPLICING
SPLICER STRAPPER
SPLINE FIN FEATHER
SPLINT SCOB FANON MATCH SPELK
SPELL TASSE SPLENT THOMAS
CALIPER SPLINTER
(— **FOR FRACTURE**) JUNK
SPLINTER BROOM BURST PURSE
SHAKE SHIDE SHIVE SKELB SLICE
SPAIL SPALE SPALT SPEEL SPELK
SPELL SPILE SPILL SPLIT SPOON
SLIVER SPLEET SPLINT FLINDER
SHATTER SLITHER SPLITTER
SPLINTERY SKELVY
SPLINTWOOD ALBURNUM
SPLIT AX AXE CUT RIT BUCK CHAP
CONE DUNT GAIG MALL MAUL REND
RENT RIFT RIVE SKAG SLAT TEAR
BREAK CHECK CHINE SHAKE SHEAR
SLENT SLIVE SMASH SPALD SPLAT
CLEAVE CLOVEN CREASE DIVIDE
FLAGGY FLERRY SCHISM SPRING
SUNDER BIVALVE SHATTER SLITHER
CREVASSE SCISSION SCISSURE
SPLINTER
(— **FISH**) SCROD
(— **IN BOWLING**) BEDPOSTS
(— **OFF**) SPALL SPAWL SCREEVED
(— **TICKET**) SCRATCH
SPLITTERMAN BOLTER
SPLITTING FLAGGY FISSION
SCISSION
(PL.) FILMS
SPLOTCH DAB BLOB DASH HALO
SPOT FLICK SMUDGE SPECKLE
SPLATCH SPLURGE
SPLURGE BINGE SPRAY SPREE
SPLASH
SPLUTTER FUFF GLUTTER SPATTER
SPUTTER SPLOTHER
SPODOPTERA LAPHYGMA
SPODUMENE KUNZITE TRIPHANE
SPOIL MAR ROT BLOT BOOT COOK
DAZE FANG FOIL FRAB GAIN KILL
MANK PELF PREY ADDLE BITCH
BLEND BOOTY BOTCH CROSS
DECAY QUAIL QUEER SHEND SPILL
STAIN STRIP TOUCH WALLY
COOPER CORPSE CURDLE DEFACE
DEFORM FORAGE INJURE MANGLE
RAVAGE TIDDLE BEDEVIL BLEMISH
CONNACH CORRUMP CORRUPT
ESTREPE INDULGE MULLOCK
PILLAGE PLUNDER SPOLIUM
TARNISH VIOLATE BANKRUPT
CONFOUND DISGRACE MISGUIDE
SPOLIATE
SPOILED BAD BLOWN DAZED MUSTY
CADISH STICKIT BRATTISH
(**EASILY** —) GINGER
SPOILER HARROWER
SPOILFIVE MAW
SPOILS BAG LOOT SKIN SWAG

BOOTY FORAY SPOLIA PILLAGE
PLUNDER
SPOILSPORT NARK LETGAME
SPOILT MARDY
SPOKE RUNG QUOTH SPACK SPAKE
LOWDER SPONDIL SPONDYL
SPOKEN ORAL SAID VERBAL
SPOKESMAN MOUTH HERALD
PROPHET SPEAKER TRUMPET
SPOLIATION SPOIL RAPINE PILLAGE
PLUNDER SPOILING
SPONGE BOT FORM MUMP POLE
SILK SORN SWAB ASCON CADGE
GRASS LUFFA SCAFF SHARK SHIRK
SYCON ASCULA COSHER LEUCON
LOOFAH MALKIN MOPPET RHAGON
ROLLER YELLOW BADIAGA BLEEDER
GELFOAM RADIATE SCOURER
SCRUNGE SYCONID ZIMOCCA
DEADBEAT HARDHEAD HEDGEHOG
MANDRUKA OLYNTHUS REDBEARD
SILICEAN SPHERIDA SUBERITE
ZOOPHYTE
(**YOUNG** —) SEEDLING
SPONGER BOT TRAMP SPONGE
SCAMBLER SMOOTHER
SPONGINESS FOZINESS
SPONGING TRENCHER
SPONGY FOZY FUZZY QUAGGY
SPONSOR COACH GOSSIP SURETY
WITNESS
(— **AT BAPTISM**) HEAVE
SPONSORSHIP EGIS AEGIS
SPONTANEOUS FREE CARELESS
FREEWILL UNTAUGHT
SPONTANEOUSLY KINDLY SELFLY
SPOOK GYRE GHOST HAUNT SCARE
SPOOL COB COP REEL QUILL SPILL
SPULE TWEEL TWILL BOBBIN
BROACH CHEESE COPPIN CARRIER
(— **FOR NETS**) GURDY
SPOON HORN CUTTY LABIS SHELL
COCHLEA JUMBLER MUDDLER
SKIMMER SPINNER STIRRER
BARSPOON COCHLEAR GOBSTICK
(**EUCHARISTIC** —) LABIS
(**FISHING** —) TROLL
(**LONG-HANDLED** —) LADLE
(**SKIMMING** —) LINGEL SKIMMER
(**SNUFF** —) PEN
SPOONBILL AJAJA SPOONY
POPELER CICONIID
SPOON-SHAPED COCHLEAR
SPATULAR
SPOOR SIGN SPUR PISTE
SPORADIC POPPING ISOLATED
SPORANGIUM THECA OOTHECA
SPORE CYST SEED SPORID AGAMETE
AKINETE BISPORE ISOLATE
SPORULE SWARMER CONIDIUM
GONIDIUM
SPOROCYST ZOOCYST SPOROSAC
SPORT FUN GIG KID MUM RIE RUX
SEE TOY ALSO GAME GAUD GLEE
JEST JOKE LAKE LARK PLAY PLOY
RAGE TAIT BREAK DALLY DROLL
FREAK MIRTH FROLIC LAUGHS
POPJOY RACING SHIKAR SKIING
BOATING CAMOGIE DISPORT

DUCKING FOWLING MARLOCK
PASTIME ROLLICK ROUNDER
SAILING SPANIEL FALCONRY
PLEASURE
(— **OF HAWKING**) RIVER
(**BOISTEROUS** —) HIJINKS
(**JAPANESE** —) KENDO
(**ROUGH** —) ROMP
(**WATER** —**S**) NAUTICS AQUATICS
SPORTING VARMINT SPORTIVE
SPORTIVE GAY TAIT LARKY MERRY
FRISKY JOCUND LIVELY LUSORY
TOYFUL TOYING WANTON COLTISH
FESTIVE GAMEFUL JESTING
JOCULAR PLAYFUL TOYSOME
TRICKSY WAGGISH FROLICKY
GAMESOME PLAYSOME PLEASANT
SPORTFUL
SPORTIVENESS HELL KNAVERY
SPORTSMAN SPORT ATHLETE
SHIKARI
SPORTSMANLIKE CLEAN SPORTY
SPORTY FLASH RORTY FLASHY
RAKISH
SPORULE GRANULE
SPOT BIT DAB PIP WEM BLOT CHUB
DIRT DRAB FLAW GALL MOIL MOLE
PLOT SCAM SITE SKIP SLUR SMUT
SOIL SPAT TICK AMPER BLACK
CLOUD FLECK GARLE GOODY
GUTTA HATCH JIMMY MACLE PATCH
PLACE PLECK POINT ROACH SMEAR
SPLAT STAIN SULLY TACHE TAINT
WHERE BLANCH BLOTCH DAPPLE
FOGDOG GERATE MACULE MAZUCA
MOTTLE SMUDGE SMUTCH SPLECK
STIGMA BLEMISH CHARBON
CHECKER FLECKER FRECKLE
GUTTULA MASOOKA OCELLUS
OLDWIFE SMATTER SMITTER
SPATTER SPECKLE SPLOTCH
SPOTTLE STATION STIPPLE TERRAIN
FENESTRA LOCALITY MACULATE
PUNCTULE SPARKLET SPRINKLE
(— **A SHIELD**) GERATE
(— **IN CLOTH**) YAW
(— **IN MINERAL**) MACLE
(— **IN PAPER**) SHINER
(— **IN SAW BLADE**) BLOB
(— **IN STEEL**) STAR
(— **IN WOOD**) WEM
(— **IN YARN**) MOTE
(— **OF INK**) MONK
(— **OF PAINT**) DAUB
(— **OF QUICKSAND**) SUCKHOLE
(— **ON CAT'S FACE**) LAVALIER
(— **ON CAT**) BUTTON
(— **ON EGG**) EYE
(— **ON FINGERNAIL**) GIFT
(— **ON FOREHEAD**) TILAK TILAKA
(— **ON HAWK**) GOUT
(— **ON HORSE**) RACE SNIP STAR
RACHE
(— **ON HORSES'S TOOTH**) CHARBON
(— **ON INSECT WINGS**) BULLA
(— **ON MOTH'S WINGS**) FENESTRA
(— **ON PLAYING CARD**) PIP
(— **ON SUN**) FACULA GRANULE
SUNSPOT

(—S IN BOOKS) FOXING
(BARREN —) GALL
(BLIND —) SCOTOMA SCOTISIS
(BROWN —) SPRAIN SPRAING
(CRUSTY —) SCAB
(ESSENTIAL —) EYE
(FERTILE —) OASIS
(FIRM — IN BOG) HAG
(GREEN — IN VALLEY) HAW
(INFLAMED —) AMPER
(LEAF —) TIKKA BLACKARM
(LIVER —S) CHLOASMA
(LIVID —) TOKEN
(LOW —) DIP SWAMP HOLLOW
(RED —) FLEABITE
(RETIRED —) SHADE
(ROUGH — IN WOVEN GOODS) FAG
(SCABBY —) SCALD
(SKIN —) MOLE BLISTER FRECKLE
LENTIGO
(SMALL —) DOT PLECK STIGMA
LUNULET SPARKLET
(SOILED —) SLOP
(SORE —) BUBU BOTCH
(SWAMPY —) FLAM
(TIGHT —) JAM JACKPOT
(WEAK —) GALL HOLE CHINK NERVE
(WORN —) FRAY FRET
(PL.) MOONING
SPOTLESS FAIR PURE WEMLESS
INNOCENT
SPOTLIGHT ARC SPOT DEUCE
SPOTTED MARLY SCOVY SHELD
CALICO FIGGED HAWKED MACLED
MAILED MARLED MIRLED SPOTTY
TICKED BRACKET BROOKED
FINCHED MOTTLED PARDINE
SPARKED SPECKED SPECKLY
TIGROID FRECKLED LITURATE
MACULOSE SPECKLED STIPPLED
SPOTTED EAGLE RAY MILLER
OBISPO
SPOTTED FLYCATCHER COBWEB
RAFTER WALLBIRD
SPOTTED GUM EUCALYPT
SPOTTED JEWFISH GUASA
SPOTTED SANDPIPER TIPUP
TILTUP CREEKER TIPTAIL
SPOTTED SPURGE DOVEWEED
SPOTTED WINTERGREEN
RATSBANE
SPOTTED WOODPECKER WITWALL
SPOTTER DOTTER
SPOTTY MEALY PATCHY PLATTY
SCABBY SPOTTED
SPOUSE EX MAKE WIFE BRIDE
MATCH PARTY FELLOW MARROW
CONSORT ESPOUSE HUSBAND
SPOUT JET LIP BEAK DALE GEAT
GUSH NOSE SHOE SPILE SPUME
SPURT NOZZLE RIGGOT SPLOIT
SPROUT STRONE STROUP BUBBLER
FOUNTAIN GARGOYLE
(RAIN —) RONE
SPOUTER VAPORER
SPOUTING BLOW SALIENT
SPRAG TRAILER
SPRAGGER SCOTCHER
SPRAIN RICK CHINK STAVE THRAW

THROW WRAMP WREST WRICK
STRAIN WRENCH STREMMA
SPRAT SMY SPRET SPRIT GARVIE
ALFIONE GARVOCK
(—S CAUGHT EARLY IN SEASON)
DROVE
SPRAWL LOLL TAVE SPURL SCRAWL
GRABBLE SCAMBLE SPARTLE
SPELDER SCRAMBLE SPRADDLE
SPRANGLE STRADDLE
SPRAWLING SPRANGLY
SPRAY FOG HOSE SCUD SPRY STEW
SPREE STOUR SWISH TRAIL TWIST
SHOWER SPARGE SPLASH SPRANG
SPRITZ CURTAIN SPAIRGE SYRINGE
INHALANT SPRANGLE
(— FROM SMALL WAVES) LIPPER
(— MASH) SPARGE
(— OF GEMS) AIGRETTE
(REDUCE TO —) NEBULIZE
SPREAD BED FAN LAY RUN COAT
DRAW FLUE SPAN TELD TUCK VEIN
WALK APPLY CLEAM CREEP FLARE
KILIM PASTE SCALE SLICE SPEND
SPLAT SPLAY STALK STREW WIDEN
BUTTER EXTEND FLANGE LARDER
LAYOUT MANTLE SETOUT THRUST
UNFOLD UNFURL BROADEN
CANVASS DIFFUSE DISPLAY DISTEND
EXPANSE EXPLAIN FEATHER
OPENING SCATTER STRETCH
DIASPORA DISPENSE DISPERSE
HUMIFUSE INCREASE MULTIPLY
SPLATHER STRAGGLE
(— ABROAD) TOOT DELATE SPRING
DIVULGE EMANATE
(— APART) GAPE
(— AS GOSSIP) BUZZ
(— BY REPORT) BLOW NOISE
NORATE
(— DEFAMATION) LIBEL
(— FOR DRYING) TED
(— INTO) INVADE
(— LIKE GRAIN) FLOOR
(— NEWS) HORN
(— ON THICK) COUCH SLATHER
(— OUT) FAN FLOW OPEN SPAN
ASPAR BREDE SPLAT SPLAY SPRAY
EXPAND FLANGE FRINGE MANTLE
OUTLAY SPRAWL UNLOCK DIFFUSE
DISPAND DISTENT EXPLAIN FEATHER
DIFFUSED SPRADDLE SPRANGLE
STRAGGLY
(— OUTWARD) FLARE
(— OVER) LAP DASH COVER
SUFFUSE
(— PAINT) KNIFE
(— THINLY) BRAY DRIVE TOUCH
SCANTY
(— TO THE WIND) SET
(— TO) CATCH
(EVENLY —) SUANT
(TAPESTRY-WOVEN —) KILIM
SPREADER PLOW PLOUGH SANDER
SPREADING FLAN BUSHY FLANGE
PATENT ASPREAD DIFFUSE FLARING
SPRAYEY PATULENT PATULOUS
SPRANGLY
(— OF LIGHT) HALATION

(— RAPIDLY) RUNNING
(NOT —) ERECT
(SLOW —) CREEPAGE
SPREE BAT BUM JAG BLOW BUST
GELL RANT SOAK TEAR TIME TOOT
BEANO BINGE BOOZE BURST DRINK
DRUNK SOUSE SPRAY BENDER
BUSTER HOORAY HURRAH RANDAN
RANTAN BLOWOFF JAMBOREE
WINGDING
SPRIG POINT
(—S FOR MOURNING) CYPRESS
SPRIGGER STRIPPER
SPRIGHTLINESS GAIETY AIRINESS
ALACRITY BUOYANCY VIVACITY
SPRIGHTLY GAY TID AIRY GNIB
PERT WARM ALIVE BRISK CANTY
CRISP DESTO MERRY QUICK
ALEGER JAUNTY LIVELY SPANKY
WIMBLE CHIPPER DELIVER JOCULAR
SPARKLY LIFESOME PLEASANT
SPRING EN AIN BUG EYE FLY HOP
JET OJO URN VER WAX BATH BOLT
BOUT BUCK DART FLOW FONT
GEON HAIR HEAD JUMP KELD LEAP
PERT RISE SEEP SKIP SOAK STEM
URNA WALM WARE WELL WIND
ARISE BOUND DANCE FLIRT FOUNT
FRESH GIHON GLENT GRASS ISSUE
LYMPH PRIME QUELL SALLY SOURD
SPEND SPOUT START STEND SURGE
THROW VAULT BOUNCE CHARCO
DERIVE GAMBOL GEYSER JUMPER
LOCKET ORIGIN PIRENE RESORT
RESULT SILOAM SOURCE SPRINT
VENERO BUDTIME EMANATE
ESTUARY FLOUNCE GAMBADO
PROCEED REBOUND WRAPPER
BACKSTAY BANDUSIA CASTALIA
FOUNTAIN SPANGHEW
(— AWKWARDLY) KEVEL
(— BACK) RECOIL RESULT RETORT
REBOUND
(— DOWN) ALIGHT
(— FORWARD) LAUNCH
(— FROM) DESCEND
(— OF THE YEAR) VER VOAR
(— ON SHEARS) BACKSTAY
(— SEASON) APRIL GRASS BUDTIME
(— SUDDENLY) FLY BOUNCE
(— TO FASTEN NECKLACE) LOCKET
(— UP) ARISE SHOOT SPROUT
BURGEON UPSPRING
(BOILING —) TUBIG
(CARRIAGE —) ROBBIN
(ERUPTIVE —) WALM GEYSER
(GUSHING —) CHARCO
(HOT —) SPRUDEL
(INTERMITTENT —S) GIPSIES
GYPSIES
(LAND —) LAVANT
(MECHANICAL —) RESORT RESSORT
(MINERAL —) SPA
(SALT —) LICK SALINE
(WARM —S) THERMAE
(WATCH —) SLEEVE
SPRING BEAUTY LETTUCE
SPRINGBOARD BATULE TREMPLIN
SPRINGBOK GAZELLE SPRINGER

SPRING CHAPLET JAMMER
SPRINGILY BOUNCILY SPONGILY
SPRINGINESS GIVE LIFE
SPRINGING LAUNCH SALIENT
 (— **BACK**) RESULT ELASTIC
 (— **FROM STEPS**) GRADY
SPRINGLIKE VERNAL
SPRING ORANGE STYRAX
SPRINGTAIL PODURA FURCULA
 PODURID SKIPTAIL
SPRINGTIME VER GERMINAL
SPRINGY WHIPPY ELASTIC FLEXIBLE
SPRINKLE ASH DAG DEG BLOW
 DAMP SHED SPIT FLASH SHAKE
 SPURT WATER BEDROP DABBLE
 POUNCE SPARGE SPRENT SPRINK
 SQUIRT ARROUSE ASPERGE
 ASPERSE DRIZZLE RANTIZE
 SCATTER SKINKLE SKITTER SPAIRGE
 SPARKLE SPARPLE SPATTER
 SPATTLE SPERPLE SPURTLE
 DISPUNGE INTERSOW SPITTING
 SPRINGLE STRINKLE
 (— **IN BAPTISM**) RANTIZE
 (— **OF RAIN**) SPIT
 (— **SEED**) SPRAIN
 (— **TOBACCO**) BLOW
 (— **WITH FLOUR**) DREDGE
 (— **WITH POWDER**) DUST
 (— **WITH SALT**) CORN
 (— **WITH SAND**) SAND
SPRINKLED SEEDED SPRENT
 (— **OVER**) BESPRENT
SPRINKLER SPARGER SPRAYER
 WATERER DAMPENER STRINKLE
SPRINKLING SEME LACING SPARGE
 STRANK RANTISM STIPPLE
 STOURING
 (— **OF PEOPLE**) SALT
SPRINT BICKER SPRENT SPRUNT
SPRITE AND ELF HOB PUG SEE ALSO
 PIXY PUCK BUCCA DOBBY FAIRY
 HOLDA PIXIE GOBLIN PILWIZ SPIRIT
 SPOORN UMBRIEL COLTPIXY
 GLAISTIG WATERMAN
 (**WATER** —) NIX NECK NIXIE NICKER
SPRITELY WIMBLE
SPROCKET WHELP
SPROUT BUD PUT BROD CHIT CHUN
 CION DRAW TOOT CATCH CHICK
 SCUTE SHOOT SPEAR SPIRE SPRIT
 SPURT BRAIRD GERMEN RATOON
 SIRING STOVEN TELLER TILLER
 BURGEON COPPICE SPURTER
 TENDRON
 (— **OF BARLEY**) TAIL
 (**FIRST** —**S**) BREER BRAIRD BREIRD
 (**STUMP** —) TILLER
SPRUCE GIM DEFT JIMP NEAT POSH
 SMUG SPRY TRIG TRIM BRISK
 COMPT CRISP DINKY FRESH JEMMY
 JIMMY NATTY SLICK SMART SMIRK
 SPIFF SPRIG DAPPER PICKED
 SPONGE SPRUNT SPRUSH FINICAL
 FOPPISH SMARTEN SMICKER
 SPRUNNY EPINETTE TITIVATE
SPRUE RUNNER PSILOSIS
SPRUER GATER
SPRY AGILE BRISK QUICK NIMBLE

SPUD BARKER PADDLE SPUDDER
SPUME EST BEES FOAM FROTH
 YEAST
SPUNK GETUP SPRAWL SMEDDUM
SPUR ARM GAD GIG EDGE GAFF
 GOAD KNAG MOVE STUD TANG
 DRIVE PRICK PRONG ROWEL SPURN
 BROACH CALCAR DIGGER EXCITE
 FOMENT GAFFLE GRIFFE INCITE
 MOTIVE OFFSET RIPPON SICKLE
 SPERON WEAPON BICYCLE
 GABLOCK INCITER LORMERY
 SCRATCH COCKSPUR GAVELOCK
 (— **OF COCK**) HEEL
 (— **ON HORSESHOE**) CALK
 (—**S OF COCK**) WEAPON
SPURGE BALSAM INTISY SUNWEED
 CATEPUCE DOVEWEED FLUXWEED
 MILKBUSH MILKWEED TITHYMAL
 WARTWEED WARTWORT
SPURIOUS DOG FAKE SHAM BOGUS
 FUNNY QUEER SHICE SNIDE NOTHAL
 PSEUDO BASTARD NOTHOUS
 SYNDIETIC
SPURN FOOT TACK SCORN REJECT
 CONSPUE CONTEMN DECLINE
 DESPISE DISDAIN
SPURRY YARR FRANK COWQUAKE
 SANDWEED
SPURT JET GILP GIRD GOUT JAUP
 SPAR SPIN BURST CHIRT FLASH
 PULSE SALLY SPOUT GEYSER
 RANDOM SPLURT SPRING SPROUT
 SQUIRT SPATTER
SPUTTER SPIT FIZZLE SOTTER
 SPATTER SPLUTTER
SPUTUM SPIT
SPY FLY PRY ESPY NARK NOSE STAG
 TOOT TOUT WAIT WORM LOWER
 PERDU PLANT SCOUT SNEAP SPIAL
 SPION WATCH BEAGLE BEHOLD
 DESCRY GAYCAT MOUTON PEEPER
 PERDUE SEARCH SHADOW SPIRAL
 TOUTER WAITER EXAMINE LURCHER
 OTACUST SMELLER SPOTTER
 WATCHER DISCOVER EMISSARY
 HIRCARRA MOUCHARD
 (— **ON RACEHORSES**) TOUT
 (— **UPON**) LAY
 (**PLANTED** —) STOOGE
 (**POLICE** —) SETTER
SPYBOAT VEDET VEDETTE
SQUAB PIPER SQUABBY SQUEAKER
 SQUEALER SQUILGEE
SQUABBLE MUSS BRAWL SCRAP
 BICKER JANGLE SQUALL BOBBERY
 BRABBLE BRANGLE CONTEND
 PRABBLE QUARREL SWABBLE
SQUAD CREW DECURY TWENTY
 PLATOON
 (— **OF DETECTIVES**) HOMICIDE
SQUADRON SOTNIA SQUADER
SQUALID DINGY DIRTY MANGY
 SEEDY FILTHY FROWZY SCABROUS
SQUALL DROW FRET GUST MEWL
 WAUL BARAT FRESH PERRY SKELP
 BAYAMO FLURRY SQUAWK
 BORASCA SUMATRA TORNADO
 BORASQUE CHUBASCO

SQUALOR DIRT
SQUAMA ALULA TEGULA
SQUANDER SOT BLOW BLUE BURN
 GAME LASH WARE SPEND SPILL
 SPORT WASTE LAVISH MAFFLE
 MUDDLE PADDLE PALTER PERISH
 TIPPLE CONSUME DEBAUCH
 DEBOISE DISPEND PROFUSE
 SCATTER SKITTLE SLATHER
 SWATTER EMBEZZLE MISSPEND
 SQUATTER
SQUANDERER PRODIGAL
SQUANDERING WASTEFUL
SQUARE FIX EDGE EVEN FOUR FULL
 POST QUAD SUIT AGREE CHECK
 CROSS FRAME HUNKY PLACE PLAIN
 PLAZA SUPER BLOCKY DINKUM
 ISAGON PIAZZA QUARRY ZENZIC
 ZOCALO CARREAU CHECKER
 COMMONS EMERALD UPRIGHT
 QUADRANT QUADRATE SQUADRON
 TETRAGON
 (— **A STONE**) PITCH
 (— **FOR BOWLING SCORE**) FRAME
 (— **OF CANVAS**) SKATE
 (— **OF CLOTH**) PANE
 (— **OF DOUGH**) KNISH
 (— **OF FRAMING**) PAN
 (— **OF GLASS**) QUARREL
 (— **OF TURF**) DIVOT QUADREL
 (— **OFF**) BUTT
 (— **ON BILLIARD TABLE**) CROTCH
 (— **ON CHESSBOARD**) HOUSE POINT
 (**BUILDINGS FORMING** —) INSULA
 (**CARPENTER'S** —) NORMA
 (**LINEN** —) SUDARIUM
 (**PATTERN OF** —**S**) DAMIER
 (**WOVEN** —) SINKER
SQUARED HEWN QUARTO SQUARE
SQUARE DANCE TUCKER
SQUARE-DEALING WHITE
SQUARELY BUNG FAIR FULL FLUSH
 SPANG FAIRLY DIRECTLY
 (— **AND SHARPLY**) SMACK
SQUARISH BOXY
SQUASH PEPO QUAT GOURD SQUAB
 CASHAW CUCURB CUSHAW
 MARROW SIMNEL SQUISH SQUOSH
 TURBAN HUBBARD PUMPKIN
 CUCURBIT CYMBLING PEPONIUM
 ZUCCHINI
SQUASH BUG STINKBUG
SQUASHY SWASHY SQUUSHY
SQUAT QUAT RUCK STUB SWAT
 SWOT COWER DUMPY FUBSY
 HUNCH PUDGY SQUAB FODGEL
 HUNKER HURKLE QUATCH STOCKY
 STUBBY SQUATTY TAPPISH
 SQUATTLE THICKSET
SQUATINA RHINA
SQUATTER NESTER BYWONER
SQUAW JACK WEBB HOUND WENCH
 MAHALA SQUARK
SQUAWBUSH SHOVAL
SQUAWFISH CHUB BOXHEAD
 BIGMOUTH CHAPPAUL
SQUAWK SCRAWK SQUALL SQUARK
 SQUAWL COMPLAIN
SQUAWROOT CLAPWORT ELOTILLO

SQUEAK GIKE PEEP WEAK CHEEP
QUEAK SCRAWK SCROOP SQUEAL
SQUEAKY CREAKY
SQUEAL PIP FINK HOWL SWEEL
SCREAK WHISTLE
SQUEALER FINK CANARY
SQUEAMISH HELO NICE NAISH
PAWKY PENSY DAINTY DAUNCH
PENCEY QUAINT QUEASY SPICED
TICKLE WAIRCH WAMBLY FINICAL
MAWKISH WEARISH NAUSEOUS
OVERNICE
SQUEAMISHNESS NICETY DISGUST
DELICACY
SQUEEZE EKE HUG JAM NIP CLAM
MULL MURE VISE ZEST BUNCH
CHIRT CREEM CROWD CRUSH
PRESS SQUAB SQUAT WRING
GRUDGE QUEASE SCRUMP SCRUZE
SQUASH STRAIN THRIMP THRING
THRONG TWEEZE TWITCH SCRINGE
SCROOGE SCROUGE SCRUNCH
SCRUNGE SQUEEGE SQUINCH
COMPRESS CONTRACT PRESSURE
SHOEHORN THRIMBLE THRUMBLE
(— **FROM**) SPONGE
(— **IN**) FUDGE
(— **INTO**) THRIMBLE
(— **OUT**) PINCH STRAIN
SQUEEZED STRETTA STRETTO
SQUEEZER REAMER ALLIGATOR
SQUELCH QUELCH SQUASH SQUISH
SQUIDGE
SQUELCHER BLIZZARD
SQUETEAGUE DRUM DRUMMER
SQUETEE BLUEFISH CHICKWIT
WEAKFISH
SQUIB MOTE FILLER EXPLODER
SQUID PLUG
SQUIGGLE SCRIGGLE
SQUILL SCILLA SLANGKOP
SQUINT GLEE GLEG SKEN SKEW
BAGGE GLENT GLEDGE GOGGLE
SHEYLE SKELLY SQUINCH SQUINNY
SQUINT-EYED GLEE GLEED
SQUINTING LOUCHE
SQUIRE SWAIN DONZEL TIMIAS
ARMIGER ESQUIRE SQUIRET
YOUNKER HENCHMAN SCUTIGER
SERVITOR SQUIREEN
SQUIRM CURL WIND TWINE WRING
WRITHE WRESTLE WRIGGLE
SCRIGGLE SQUIGGLE
SQUIRREL BUN CON BUNT LEAD
SCUG BUNNY XERUS BOOMER
CHIPPY GOPHER RODENT TAGUAN
ARDILLA SCHILLU SCIURID
CHIPMUNK EGGEATER GRAYBACK
JELERANG RATATOSK
(— **SKIN**) VAIR
(**FLYING** —) ASAPAN
SQUIRRELFISH ALAIKI MARIAN
MOJARRA SERRANO SOLDIER
SANDFISH WELSHMAN
SQUIRREL SHREW TANA TUPAIA
PENTAIL
SQUIRT CHIRT SCOOT SKITE SLIRT
SPIRT SPOUT SPURT SQUIB SQUIT
SPLOIT SPRENT SPRITZ SCOOTER
SQUITTER

STAB DAB DAG JAB JAG JOB DIRK
GORE PINK PROB SHIV STOB STOG
STUG YERK CHIVE KNIFE POACH
PRICK PRONG STICK STOKE
BROACH DAGGER PIERCE POUNCE
SLIVER STITCH THRUST BAYONET
STAGGER PRICKADO STILETTO
STOCCADO STOCCATA
(— **IN MIDBREAST**) SLOT
STABBING THORNY JABBING
PUNGENT STICKING
STABILITY POISE BALANCE SADNESS
FIRMNESS SECURITY
STABILIZE FIX SET EVEN TRIM POISE
SCHOOL STEADY BALANCE BALLAST
STIFFEN
STABILIZER ACARDITE
STABLE BYRE FAST FIRM SURE
HARAS HEMEL SOLID SOUND STALL
STIFF STOUT TAMBO LINTER LIVERY
SECURE SICKER STATIC STEADY
STRONG STURDY DURABLE
EQUERRY LASTING OXHOUSE
SETTLED SHIPPEN STABILE
IMMOBILE RESIDENT STANDING
(**ROYAL** —**S**) MEWS
STABLEBOY LAD JACKBOY
STABLEMAN OSTLER HOSTLER
STACCATO TUT SECCO DETACHE
SALTATO RICOCHET SALTANDO
(**NOT** —) TENUTO
STACK COB MOW SOW BIKE DESS
LEET PACK PILE POKE RICK CANCH
CLAMP GOAVE POAKE SCROO
SHOCK STAKE STALK STOCK
COLUMN FUNNEL RICKLE CALENDER
STACKAGE
(— **BRICKS**) SCINTLE
(— **IN KILN**) BOX
(— **LUMBER**) STICK
(— **OF ARMS**) PILE
(— **OF BRICK**) LIFT
(— **OF CERAMICS**) BUNG
(— **OF CORN**) SHOCK
(— **OF FISH**) BULK
(— **OF GRAIN**) RICK
(— **OF HIDES**) BED
(— **OF PANS**) SWEATER
(— **OF SHEETS**) BOOK
(**HAY OR CORN** —) HOVEL
(**SMALL** —) COB CANCH RICKLE
(**TILE** —) WELL
STACKER CROWDER PITCHER
STACKMAN
STACKYARD MOWIE MOWHAY
HAGGARD
STADIUM BOWL STADE STAGE
FURLONG STADION COLISEUM
STAFF PIN ROD TAU TAW CANE
CLUB KENT LIMB MACE MALL MAUL
PIKE POLE RUNG TREE VARE YARD
BATON CROOK CROSS KEVEL NIBBY
PEDUM PERCH STAVE STICK SUITE
VERGE BASTON CADUCE CEPTER
CLEEKY CROCHE CRUTCH FAMILY
FERULE GROUND LITUUS MULETA
POTENT PRITCH RADIUS RISSLE
TAIAHA THYRSE WARDER BACULUS
BOURDON CAMBUCA CROSIER

CRUMMIE DISTAFF FESTUCA
PALSTER SCEPTER SCEPTRE
STADDLE THYRSUS CADUCEUS
CRUMMOCK PARTISAN PASTORAL
PLOWFOOT TIPSTAFF
(— **AT END OF NET**) BRAIL
(— **OF AUTHORITY**) VARE VERGE
(— **WITH CROSSPIECE**) POTENT
(**BISHOP'S** —) BAGLE BACULUS
CROSIER CROZIER PASTORAL
(**FIELD MARSHAL'S** —) BATON
(**FORKED** —) LINSTOCK
(**GRADUATED** —) LIMB
(**HOTTENTOT** —) KIRVI
(**MAGICIAN'S** —) RHABDOS
(**NEWSPAPER** —) DAYSIDE
(**NUBIAN** —) KUERR
(**PLASTERER'S** —) BEATER
(**SHEPHERD'S** —) KENT CROOK
(**TEACHING** —) FACULTY
(**THIEVES'** —) FILCH
STAG HART ROYAL SPADE STAIG
WAPITI BULLOCK KNOBBER POINTER
KNOBBLER
(— **OF 8 YEARS OR MORE**) ROYAL
(— **OF THE 3D YEAR**) SPIRE
(— **THAT HAS CAST HIS ANTLERS**)
POLLARD
(**3-YEAR OLD** —) SPADE
(**DEAD** —) MORT
(**HORNLESS** —) HUMMEL
(**TURNED TO** —) ACTAEON
STAG BEETLE LUCANID
STAGE LEG BANK GEST POST STEP
TREK DUMMY ETAGE FLAKE GRADE
PEGME PHASE POINT SCENE STAIR
STATE BOARDS DEGREE HEMMEL
PERIOD STRIDE CATASTA MANSION
ROSTRUM STADIUM INSTANCE
PLATFORM SCAFFOLD
(— **FOR DRYING FISH**) FLAKE
(— **FOR HAY**) HEMMEL
(— **IN DELIRIUM**) TILMUS
(— **IN FEVER**) FLUSH
(— **IN PORCELAIN FURNACE**)
HOWELL
(— **IN TRAVELING**) GEST
(— **MANAGER**) REGISSEUR
(— **OF CUPOLA**) LANTERN
(— **OF DEVELOPMENT**) ERA
BLOSSOM
(— **OF GLACIATION**) ACHEN MINDEL
(— **OF INSECT**) INSTAR
(— **OF LIFE**) AGE ASRAMA ASHRAMA
(— **OF PERSONALITY**) LATENCY
(— **OF ROCKET**) BOOSTER
(— **OF THEATER**) SCAENA
THEATRON
(— **WHERE SLAVES WERE SOLD**)
CATASTA
(**BOTTOMMOST** —) CELLAR
(**COMIC** —) SOCK
(**FINAL** —) CLOSE FINISH STRETCH
(**FIRST** —) YOUTH SPRING
(**FLOATING** —) DUMMY
(**FLOOD** —) CREST
(**GEOLOGICAL** —) GUNZ GLACIAL
(**INITIAL** —) INFANCY

(LANDING —) STAIR BRIDGE STAITH
STELLING
(MOVING —) PEGMA PEGME
(RADIO —) STEP
(THIRD —) AUTUMN
STAGECOACH DILLY STAGE
STAGEHAND DAYMAN
STAGER SOAKER
STAGGER REEL ROLL STOT DAVER
DODGE HODGE STITE STOIT
DACKER FALTER GOGGLE STIVER
SWAVER WALTER WAMBLE WELTER
WIGGLE WINTLE MEGRIMS STACHER
STACKER STAMMER STOITER
STOTTER STUMBLE SWAGGER
VANDYKE WAUCHLE TITUBATE
STAGGERBUSH LAMBKILL
STAGGERED STURTAN STURTIN
STAGGERS DUNT GOGGLES
STAVERS VERTIGO
STAGHEAD SPIKETOP
STAGING STAGE CRIPPLE DERRICK
HURRIES
STAGNANCY STASIS
STAGNANT DEAD DULL INERT STILL
STATIC COBWEBBY SLUGGISH
STAGNATE STANDING
STAGNATION STASIS TORPOR
LANGUOR
STAID SET CIVIL GRAVE SOBER
DEMURE STEADY EARNEST SERIOUS
DECOROUS
STAIN DYE LIT WEM BLOT BLUR
BUFF DIRT DRAB FILE FOIL HURT
MEAL MOLE RUST SCAM SLUR
SMAD SMIT SMUT SOIL SPOT TASH
BLACK BLEND CLOUD DIRTY HATCH
PAINT PLECK SMEAR SPECK SULLY
TACHE TAINT TINGE WEMMY
BREATH GIEMSA IMBRUE INFAMY
INFECT MACULA SMIRCH SMUDGE
SMUTCH SPLASH STIGMA SUDDLE
ATTAINT BESTAIN BLEMISH DEPAINT
DISTAIN SLUBBER SOILURE
SPATTER SPLOTCH STADDLE
TARNISH BESMIRCH CARMALUM
DISCOLOR DISGRACE DISHONOR
FLYSPECK MACULATE TAINTURE
(— BLACK) EBONIZE
(— IN LINEN) MELL
(— ON BRICK) SCUMMING
(— WITH BLOOD) ENGORE
STAINED FOXY RUSTY SMUDGY
SMUTCHY
(— BY DECAY) DOATY
(— WITH BLOOD) BLOODY IMBRUED
STAINED GLASS VITRAIL
STAINER TRACER
STAINLESS CHASTE INNOCENT
STAIR STY GREE RUNG STEP
DEGREE COCHLEA ESCALIER
(MINING —) LOB
(PL.) PAIR PITCH FLIGHT DANCERS
ESCALIER
STAIRCASE SCALE ESCALIER
(SPIRAL —) SPIRAL CARACOLE
STAIRWAY STOOP GREESE PERRON
DESCENT ESCALIER
(— ON RIVER BANK) GHAT

(CURVED —) SWEEP
(SHIP'S —) LADDER
(WINDING —) VICE TURNPIKE
STAKE BET HOB LAY SET TAW VIE
WAD WED ANTE BENT GAGE MAIN
PALE PAWN PEEL POOL RISK STAB
STOB TREE WAGE PITCH SPILE
SPOKE SPRAG STOCK STOOP
STOUR WAGER BAIKIE CAULIS
CHANCE CORNER CROTCH ENGAGE
GAMBLE HAZARD IMPONE LOGGAT
LOGGET PALING STOWER TRUNCH
WEDFEE STOATER STUCKEN
VENTURE INTEREST PALISADE
PEASTICK STUCKING
(CART —) RUNG
(COMPULSORY — IN POKER) BLIND
(POINTED —) SOULE SOWEL PICKET
(SURVEYORS' —) HUB
(TETHERING —) PUTTO
(TINSMITH'S —) TEEST
STAKE-SHAPED SUDIFORM
STALACE COLUMELLA
STALE OLD COLD HOAR PALL SICK
WORN BLOWN DUSTY FROWY
HOARY MOLDY MUSTY RAFTY
SANDY TRITE FROWZY MOULDY
STUFFY EXOLETE FROUGHY INSIPID
OVERWORN STAGNANT
(DAMP AND —) WAUGH
STALEMATE PATT STALE
STALK BUN RAY CORN MOTE POLE
RISP STAM STEG STEM TIGE QUILL
SCAPE SHANK SPEAR SPIRE STAKE
STALE STEAL STIPE STUMP WRIDE
COULIS RATOON STIPES CASTOCK
PEDICEL PETIOLE SPINDLE
FILAMENT PEDUNCLE PODETIUM
STALKLET STERIGMA
(— OF BUCKWHEAT) STRAW
(— OF CRINOID) COLUMN
(— OF GRAIN) RESSOM RIZZOM
(— OF GRASS) BENT SPEAR
(— OF HAY) RISP
(— OF PLANT) SPINDLE TENACLE
(— OF SPOROGONIUM) SETA
(— OF STAMEN) FILAMENT
(— OF SUGAR CANE) RATOON
(— OF UMBEL) RAY
(—S OF GRAIN) KARBI STRAW
(CABBAGE —) CASTOCK
(CROSSBOW —) TILLER
(DRY —) KEX KECK
(FLOWER —) SCAPE
(HOLLOW —) BUN KEX
(PL.) HAULM STRAW WRIDE IWAIWA
STALL BIN BOX CUB PEW BULK CRIB
SPAR STAW BOOSE BOOSY BOOTH
CRAME PITCH STAND STASH
CARCER CARREL TRAVIS WICKET
BALAGAN CABINET SHAMBLE
BUTCHERY STANDING TRAVERSE
(— FOR TIME) HAVER STRETCH
(— IN CLOISTER) CAROL
(— IN COAL MINE) BREAST WICKET
(— IN MUD) STOG
(— IN ROMAN CIRCUS) CARCER
(CHURCH —) PEW
(THEATER —) LOGE FAUTEUIL

STALLED STOODED
STALLION SIRE STAG STUD ENTRE
HORSE COOSER ENTIRE STALLAND
STALWART RUDE STARK STIFF
WIGHT STRONG STURDY BUIRDLY
VALIANT
STAMEN TAMIN STAMMEL
STAMINA GUTS SAND BOTTOM
STAMMER FAM HACK MANT STOT
STUT GANCH WLAFF FAFFLE
FALTER FAMBLE HACKER HAFFLE
HAMMER HOCKER HOTTER MAFFLE
MAMMER YAMMER FRIBBLE
STUMBLE STUTTER HESITATE
SPLUTTER TITUBATE
STAMMERING HACK TRAULISM
STAMP CHOP COIL DRUB FAKE
MARK NIXY PAUT POSS RUFF SEAL
SNAP TYPE APPEL BLOCK DOLLY
ERROR FRANK LABEL LOCAL NIXIE
PRINT PUNCH STOCK STOMP STUNT
TENOR TOUCH WRITE ACCENT
CACHET CLICHE DOCKER FULLER
INCUSE INCUTE INDENT LOCKUP
PASTER POUNCE SCRIBE SHAPER
SIGNET STRAMP STRIKE CARRIER
CHARACT EDITION IMPRESS IMPRINT
MINTAGE POUNDER REPRINT
SEEBECK SPECIAL SQUELCH
STICKER TAXPAID WRAPPER
HALLMARK ORIGINAL PRESSURE
PUNCHEON
(— AFTER ASSAY) TOUCH
(— BOOK COVER) BLIND
(— FOR CUTTING DOUGH) DOCKER
(— HERRING BARREL) DUNT
(— HIDES) STOCK
(— HOLES) STOACH
(— OUT) SCOTCH
(— WITH DIE) DINK
(BOOKBINDING —) BLOCK FILLET
(CANCELLING —) KILLER
(HALF OF —) BISECT
(HAND —) CANCELER
(OFFICIAL —) CHOP
(POSTAGE —) AIR DUE CAPE FAKE
HEAD ERROR LABEL LOCAL BUREAU
INVERT AIRMAIL BICOLOR CHARITY
CLASSIC REPRINT STICKER
ADHESIVE COLONIAL ORIGINAL
SPECIMEN
(REVENUE —) FISCAL TAXPAID
(SMART —) APPEL
(PL.) MIXTURE KILOWARE
STAMPEDE RUSH BLITZ CHUTE
DEBACLE STAMPEDO
STAMPER FANCIER STOMPER
STAMPING TITLING
STANCE STATION STANDING
(— OF GOLFER) ADDRESS
(— OF HORSE) GATHER
STANCH FIRM STEM STIFF STOUT
HEARTY TRUSTY STAUNCH
FAITHFUL RESOLUTE
STANCHION BAIL PITON CROTCH
CRUTCH STENCIL STANCHEL
STANCHER
STAND GO JIB SET BANK BEAR BIER
DESK HALT RACK RANK REST STAY

ZARF BLOCK ERECT FRAME FRONT
KIOSK NIPOD STALL STICK STONE
STOOL CASTER COLORS ENDURE
HASTER INSIST PATTEN PILLAR
SMOKER STANZA STOUND STRIKE
TEAPOY TRIPOD TRIVET CONSIST
DIOPTER EPERGNE FOURBLE
LECTERN STATION TABORET
TRESTLE TROLLEY ATTITUDE
BLEACHER COATRACK CROWFOOT
FRIPPERY GUERIDON HASTENER
INKSTAND POSITION SCAFFOLD
STALLAGE STANDING STANDISH
STILLAGE STILLING STILLION
(— AS SPONSOR) FANG HEAVE
CHRISTEN
(— AT AN ANGLE) CATER
(— AT ATTENTION) BACK
(— BACK) BACCARE BACKARE
(— BEFORE A FIRE) FOOTMAN
(— BEHIND) COVER
(— BY) SERVE
(— CLOSE) CROWD ENVIRON
(— FASTENED TO MESS TABLE)
CROWFOOT
(— FIRM) STAY
(— FOR AUCTIONING) BLOCK
(— FOR BARRELS) JIB THRALL
(— FOR COFFIN) BIER
(— FOR COMPASS) BINNACLE
(— FOR CONFINING HEAT) HASTER
HASTENER
(— FOR DRESSES) FRIPPERY
(— FOR DRILL PIPE) FOURBLE
(— FOR FINJAN) ZARF
(— FOR TILES) CRISS
(— FOR WRITING MATERIALS)
STANDISH
(— FOR) DENOTE
(— GUARD) COVER
(— IN AWE) FEAR
(— OF FOREST) GROWTH
(— OF PLANTS) STOOL
(— OFF) AROINT
(— ON AND OFF SHORE) BUSK
(— ON END) STARE UPEND
(— ON TWO FEET) BIPOD DUOPOD
(— OUT) CUT TOOT FLAUNT
(— READY) ABIDE
(— STILL) HO HOO HALT STAY
(— TO SHOOT) ADDRESS
(— TREAT) MUG SHOUT
(— UNSTEADILY) STAGGER
(— UP STIFF) STIVER
(— UP TO) CONFRONT
(— WITH LEGS APART) STRIDE
(CONCESSION —) JOINT
(FIRECLAY —) CRANK
(ONE-NIGHT —) GIG
(PRINTER'S —) BANK FRAME
(PULPIT-LIKE —) AMBO
(RAISED —) PERGOLA
(SCULPTOR'S —) CHASSIS
(SHOOTING —) BUTT
(THREE-LEGGED —) TRIVET
STANDARD ALEM DICK FIAR FLAG
GAGE IDEA MARK NORM SIGN TEST
TOUG ALLOY BOGEY CANON CHECK
DOLLY DRAKE EAGLE GAUGE IDEAL

JEDGE MODEL NORMA SCALE
STAND STOOL AQUILA ASSIZE
BANNER CORNET DOLLIE FILLER
SOCKET SQUARE STAPLE TIPONI
TRIPOD VIOLLE ANCIENT CLASSIC
DECORUM DRAPEAU LABARUM
MODULUS STANDER BRATTACH
GONFALON MOUNTING ORIFLAMB
ORTHODOX VEXILLUM
(— IN GATE) STRIKE
(— OF CONDUCT) LINE GNOMON
(— OF PERFECTION) IDEAL
(— OF PERFORMANCE) BOGY
BOGEY BOGIE
(— OF PITCH) DIAPASON
(— OF QUALITY) GRADE
(—S OF BEHAVIOR) ETHICS
(LIGHT —) CARCEL
(TURKISH —) ALEM TOUG
(PL.) LIGHTS HOLSTERS
STANDARD-BEARER ENSIGN
ALFEREZ ANCIENT STALLER
SIGNIFER STANDARD
STANDARDIZE FORDIZE MACHINE
CALIBRATE
STANDEL STORER
STANDING BEING ERECT STATE
CREDIT ESTEEM RESPECT
STAGNANT
(— ALONE) SEPARATE
(— BY ITSELF) ABSOLUTE
DETACHED
(— ERECT) HORRENT
(— INCOORDINATION) ASTASIA
(— ON STEPS) DEGRADED
(— OUT CLEARLY) EMINENT
(— OUT) BOLD EXTANT SALIENT
(— POSITION) OFFHAND
(MODE OF —) STANCE
(SOCIAL —) LEVEL ESTATE FASHION
STATION
STANDPATTISM TORYISM
STANDPOINT STANCE
STANDSTILL JIB SET HALT REST
STAY STAND STANCE
STANZA CALL RANN ENVOI ENVOY
STAFF STAND STAVE VERSE
BASTON DIXAIN DIZAIN OCTAVE
SEPTET SESTET SEXTET SIXAIN
STANCE STANZO HUITAIN SEXTAIN
STROPHE TRIOLET TROILUS
CINQUAIN OCTONARY QUATRAIN
QUINTAIN RISPETTO SETTAINE
TRISTICH
STAPES STIRRUP
STAPLE LOOP FLOSS STITCH
STEEPLE VERVELLE
STAR COR SUN BEID FIRE LAMP
ASTER COMES DWARF GIANT
MOLET RISHI SHINE STARN ALNATH
ASTRAL BINARY COUPLE DOUBLE
ETOILE LUCIDA MULLET NITHAM
SHINER SPHERE STELLA BENEFIC
DINGBAT ESTOILE GEMINID STARLET
STARNIE ASTERISK ASTEROID
HEXAGRAM MALEFICE PENTACLE
SUBDWARF SUBGIANT VARIABLE
(7 —S OF GREAT BEAR) CAR
(COMPANION —) COMES

(DOG —) SEPT SOPT SEPTI SIRIUS
(EVENING —) VENUS HESPER
VESPER EVESTAR HESPERUS
(FEATHER —) COMATULA
(GUIDING —) LOADSTAR LODESTAR
(MORNING —) VENUS DAYSTAR
PHOSPHOR
(NEW —) NOVA
(OFFICER'S —) PIP
(PULSATING —) CEPHEID
(SHOOTING —) METEOR SHOOTER
(SPECIFIC —) YED ADIB ALYA ATIK
CAPH ENIF ENIR IZAR KIED MAIA
NAOS PHAD SADR VEGA WEGA
ACRAB ACRUX AGENA ALCOR
ALGOL ALKES ANCHA ARNEB
CHARA DABIH DELTA DENEB DUBHE
GIEDI GUIAM GUYAM HAMAL HAMUL
JUGUM MERAK MIZAR NIBAL NIHAI
PHAET PHARD RIGEL SAIPH SPICA
TEJAT WASAT WEZEN ZOZMA
ADHARA ALHENA ALIOTH ALKAID
ALMACH ALTAIR ALUDRA APOLLO
ARIDED CASTOR CELENO CHELEB
DIPHDA ELNATH ETAMIN GIENAH
HYADES KOCHAB LESUTH MAASYM
MARKAB MARKEB MARSIC MEGREZ
MENKAB MENKAR MERACH MEROPE
MIRFAK MIRZAM NEKKAR PHECDA
POLLUX PROPUS RANICH SCHEAT
SHEDIR SIRIUS THABIT THUBAN
ACUBENS ALBIREO ALCHIBA
ALCYONE ALGENIB ALGIEBA
ALGORAH ALMAACK ALNILAM
ALNITAH ALPHARD ALPHIRK
ALSHAIN ANTARES AZIMECH
BUNGULA CANOPUS CAPELLA
ELECTRA GIANSAR GOMELZA
GRUMIUM MEBUSTA MELUCTA
MENCHIB MINTAKA MUFRIDE
POLARIS PROCYON REGULUS
ROTANIM RUCHBAR SCHEDAR
SEGINUS SHELLAK STEROPE
TARAZED TAYGETA TEGMINE
THEENIM ACHERNAR ALPHECCA
ARCTURUS ASTERION DENEBOLA
GRAFFIAS HERCULES MULIPHEN
PRAESEPE SCALOOIN SCHEMALI
SHERATAN
(THREE —S) KIDS ELLWAND
TRIANGLE
STAR APPLE CAIMITO
STARCH AMYL ARUM SAGO STIFF
TIKOR AMYDON AMYLUM FARINA
FECULA CASSAVA CURCUMA
FAECULA MARANTA TALIPOT
AMIDULIN DRESSING FIXATURE
GLUCOSAN
(ANIMAL —) GLYCOGEN
STARCHED FORMAL
STARE EYE BORE DARE GAPE GAUM
GAUP GAWK GAWP GAZE GOVE
GYPE KIKE LOOK PORE GLARE
GLORE GLOWER GOGGLE EYEBALL
(— IDLY) GOVE GOAVE
(— VACANTLY) GOWK
(COLD —) FISHEYE
STARFISH PAD STAR RADIATE
ASTEROID OPHIURAN

STARING STEEP ASTARE GOGGLE GOOGLY HAGGARD

STAR JELLY STARSHOT

STARK BUCK CARK FAIR HARD CRUDE HARSH STIFF STARCH DESOLATE METALLIC

STARLIKE ASTRAL SPHERY

STARLING SALI STARE BEAVER PASTOR TILYER SPREEUW STARNEL STAYNIL CHEPSTER CUTWATER SHEPSTER

STARRED LIZARD HARDIM

STARRING FEATURED

STARRY ASTRAL STARNY STELLED SIDEREAL

STAR SAPPHIRE ASTERIA ASTRION ASTROITE

STAR-SHAPED ASTROID

START DIG SET BOLT BOUN DART DASH HEAD JERK JUMP OPEN TURN WHIP BEGIN BIRTH BRAID BREAK BUDGE ENTER FLIRT GLENT ONSET RAISE ROUSE THROW BOGGLE BROACH FLINCH INTEND OFFSET SETOFF SETOUT STRIKE TWITCH GETAWAY OPENING STARTLE SUNRISE COMMENCE CONCEIVE INCHOATE OUTSTART
(— A HORSE) WINCE
(— ASIDE) SHY SKIT DODGE
(— BURNING) SPIT KINDLE
(— FERMENTATION) PITCH
(— OF BIRD'S FLIGHT) SOUSE
(— OUT) FRAME INTEND
(— UP) JUMP ASTART ASTERT
(SUDDEN —) SHY SQUIRT

STARTER KOJI
(BUNG —) FLOGGER

STAR THISTLE CALTROP CALTHROP

STARTING INCOMING

STARTLE SOHO ALARM SCARE SHOCK START STURT AFFRAY BOGGLE BOOGER FRIGHT FRIGHTEN SURPRISE

STARTLING ALARMING SHOCKING

STARVATION LACK FAMINE

STARVE CLEM FAST FAMINE FAMISH AFFAMISH

STARVED MEAGER MEAGRE STARVEN

STARVED-LOOKING SLINK

STARVELING SHARGAR SHARGER

STARVING CLUNG

STARWORT ASTROFEL

STATE WU LAY PUT SAY CASE MODE NAME POMP PORT TERM TIFF COVIN ESTER ESTRE POLIS SPEAK STADE TERMS TUATH WHACK AFFIRM AGENCY ASSERT ASSURE CAESAR EFFEIR EMPIRE ESTATE IMPORT NATION PLIGHT POLICY POLITY RENDER RIALTY SOVIET STATUS STEVEN CIVITAS DECLARE DESERET DUKEDOM ENOUNCE EXPOUND EXPRESS KINSHIP PROPOSE SPECIFY STATION TERMINE DEVACHAN DOMINION FRANKLIN HEGEMONY INDICATE KINGSHIP REPUBLIC STATELET

(— EXPLICITLY) DEFINE
(— FORMALLY) ENOUNCE
(— IN NORTH CAROLINA) FRANKLIN
(— OF AFFAIRS) CASE ARRAY STATUS
(— OF ALARM) GAST FEEZE SCARE
(— OF AMAZEMENT) STOUND
(— OF ANGER) FUME
(— OF APATHY) STUPOR
(— OF BEING CUT) SCISSION
(— OF BEING DRAWN) TRACTION
(— OF BEING OVERFULL) PLETHORA
(— OF BEING POISONOUS) TOXICITY
(— OF BEING WORSE) PEJORITY
(— OF CONCENTRATION) DHARANA DHAYANA SAMADHI
(— OF CONFUSION) FOG FLAP HACK MUSS CHAOS SWIRL HASSLE HUBBUB FLUMMOX TROYTOWN
(— OF CONSECRATION) IHRAM
(— OF COOPERATION) HOOKUP
(— OF DISASTER) SMASH
(— OF DISORDER) HELL MUSS FANTAD ANARCHY
(— OF DISSENSION) SCISSION
(— OF DISTURBANCE) GARBOIL
(— OF DOUBT) MIST
(— OF EAGERNESS) HURRY
(— OF ECSTASY) SWOON
(— OF ENCHANTMENT) SPELL
(— OF ENLIGHTENMENT) BODHI
(— OF EXALTATION) FURY ECSTASY
(— OF EXCITATION) FOMENT
(— OF EXCITEMENT) FRY FLAP GALE HIGH SNIT STEW FEEZE HOIGH DITHER DOODAH HUBBUB FANTEEG FLUSTER KIPPAGE SWELTER FANTIGUE
(— OF EXHAUSTION) GONENESS
(— OF FEAR) FUNK JELLY SCARE
(— OF HAPPINESS) ELYSIUM PARADISE
(— OF HEALTH) EUCRASIA
(— OF HUMILIATION) DUST
(— OF IDEAL PERFECTION) UTOPIA
(— OF IMPERFECTION) SCARCITY
(— OF INACTION) DEADLOCK
(— OF INCIPIENCE) EMBRYO
(— OF INTENSITY) BUILD
(— OF IRRITABILITY) FUME GALL FANTAD
(— OF JOY) JUBILEE
(— OF MELANCHOLY) GLOOM
(— OF MENTAL INACTIVITY) TORPOR
(— OF MENTAL READINESS) ATTITUDE
(— OF MIND) CUE HIP CASE MOOD HUMOR FETTLE CARAPACE
(— OF MISERY) HELL GEHENNA
(— OF NEGLECT) LIMBO
(— OF OPPOSITION) DEFIANCE
(— OF OSTRACISM) COVENTRY
(— OF PERTURBATION) CRISE
(— OF PREOCCUPATION) CARE
(— OF READINESS) GUARD
(— OF REALITY) ACT
(— OF REJECTION) GATE
(— OF REPOSE) CALM

(— OF RETIREMENT) GRASS
(— OF REVERIE) DUMP
(— OF SENSITIVITY) NERVES
(— OF SLUGGISHNESS) COMA
(— OF SUSPENSE) TRANCE
(— OF TENSION) FANTEEG STRETCH FANTIGUE
(— OF THE SOUL) BARDO
(— OF THINGS) FARE PASS
(— OF TRANQUILLITY) KEF KIF PEACE
(— OF UNCERTAINTY) FOG FLUX
(— OF UNREST) FERMENT
(— OF WEATHER) FREEZE
(— OF WORRY) TEW SWEAT FANTAD
(— POSITIVELY) AFFIRM
(— UNDER OATH) ALLEGE
(AGITATED —) FUSS SNIT STIR CHURN STORM LATHER SWIVET
(BUFFER —) GLACIS
(CHINESE —) WU SHU WEI
(DAZED —) DAMP
(DEPRESSED —) GLOOM WALLOW
(DISTURBED —) STIR STORM UNREST
(DOMINANT —) SUZERAIN
(DROWSY —) DOVER
(EMOTIONAL —) FEVER FEELING
(FEUDAL —) WEI
(FICTITIOUS —) FABLE
(FILTHY —) DIRT
(FREE —) SAORSTAT
(GLOOMY —) DUMP
(HIGHEST —) SUPREME
(HORIZONTAL —) LEVEL
(INDONESIAN —) NEGARA
(IRISH —) TUATH
(LIQUID —) FLUOR FLUIDITY
(MARRIED —) SPOUSAL
(MENTAL —) EARNEST DELUSION
(MORBID —) HIP IODISM
(MORMON —) DESERET
(NEUTRAL —) BUFFER
(PECUNIARY —) FACULTY
(PERTURBED —) DEVIL
(PROFOUND —) DEPTH
(SWISS —) CANTON
(ULTIMATE —) END
(UNFAVORABLE —) FOULNESS
(VERIFIED —) FACT

STATED GIVEN CERTAIN
(DIRECTLY —) EXPRESS

STATEHOUSE CAPITOL

STATELINESS STATE DIGNITY MAJESTY GRANDEUR

STATELY DATE BURLY GRAND LARGO LOFTY NOBLE REGAL STATE STOUT AUGUST COUPON PORTLY SOLEMN SUPERB TOGATE GALLANT BARONIAL IMPOSING MAESTOSO MAJESTIC STATEFUL

STATEMENT SAY BILL VOTE WORD AXIOM BRIEF COUNT DIXIT LIBEL STATE STORY BELIEF DICTUM DOCKET EXPOSE FACTUM RETURN SAYING SPEECH ACCOUNT ADDRESS ANALOGY DISSENT EPITAPH EPITOME FORMULA INVOICE MENTION SHOWING ABSTRACT

ANTINOMY ARGUMENT AVERMENT BULLETIN DELIVERY EQUATION EXPLICIT JUDGMENT PROPOSAL SCHEDULE SENTENCE SPEAKING SYNGRAPH SYNOPSIS
(— **AS PRECEDENT**) AUTHORITY
(— **OF OPINION**) CHANT
(— **OF RELATIONS**) THEOREM
(— **ON DRUG LABEL**) LEGEND
(**AUTHORITATIVE** —) DICTUM
(**CASUAL** —) REMARK
(**CONCISE** —) SCHEME APHORISM
(**CONDENSED** —) RESUME SYNOPSIS
(**DEFAMATORY** —) LIBEL
(**EXAGGERATED** —) STRETCH
(**FABRICATED** —) CANARD
(**FINAL — OF ACCOUNT**) AUDIT
(**FINANCIAL** —) BUDGET
(**FOOLISH** —) INANITY
(**FORMAL** —) CITATION
(**IRRATIONAL** —) ALOGISM
(**OBSCURE** —) ENIGMA
(**PLAINTIFF'S** —) BODY
(**POMPOUS** —) BRAG
(**SELF-CONTRADICTORY** —) PARADOX
(**SOOTHING** —) SALVE
(**UNTRUE** —) LIE
STATER COLT TURTLE PEGASUS CYZICENE
STATEROOM BIBBY CABIN
STATESMAN GENRO SOLON FATHER STATIST WARWICK JACOBEAN WEALSMAN
STATICE ARMERIA LIMONIUM
STATION BY BYE FIX ORB RUN SET GARE POST RANK ROOM STOP BEING CHOKY DEPOT PLACE POSTE SIEGE STAGE STALL STAND STATE DEGREE LOCATE STANCE CONTROL CUARTEL DIGNITY HABITAT OUTPOST GARRISON PILTDOWN POSITION STANDING TERMINAL TERMINUS TRANSFER
(— **IN BASEBALL**) BASE
(— **IN LIFE**) BEING CALLING
(— **OF HERON**) SEDGE SIEGE
(**CONCEALED** —) AMBUSH
(**CUSTOMS** —) CHOKEY
(**EXALTED** —) PURPLE
(**POLICE** —) TANA TANNA THANAH KOTWALEE
(**POST** —) DAK
(**RADIO** —S) CHAIN NETWORK
(**RAILWAY** —) GARE CABIN
(**SIGNALLING** —) BANTAY BEACON
(**SURVEYING** —) STADIA
(**TRADING** —) FACTORY
(**WAY** —) TAMBO
STATIONARY SET FAST FIXED STILL LEDGER STATIC DORMANT SITFAST STABILE STATARY IMMOBILE
STATISTICIAN ANALYST STATIST
STATOBLAST SPORE
STATUARY IMAGERY
STATUE HERM ICON IDOL IKON TERM BUSTO HERMA IMAGE MOSES AGALMA BRONZE HERMES MEMNON STATUA WEEPER XOANON ILISSUS

PASQUIN PICTURE STATURE STATUTE ACROLITH CARYATID MARFORIO MONUMENT PANTHEUM PORTRAIT VICTORIA
(— **ENDOWED WITH LIFE**) GALATEA
(— **OF GIGANTIC SIZE**) COLOSSUS
(**COLOSSAL** —) GOG MAGOG
STATUETTE WAX EMMY OSCAR WINNIE TANAGRA FIGULINE FIGURINE SIGILLUM
STATURE PITCH GROWTH HEIGHT INCHES WASTME CAPACITY
STATUS RANK SEAT PLACE STATE ASPECT FOOTING STATURE STANDING
(— **OF YOUNGER SON**) CADENCY
(**HIGH** —) CACHET
(**LEGAL** —) CAPUT
(**SECONDARY** —) BACKSEAT
STATUTE ACT LAW LEX DOOM EDICT ASSIZE DECREE SETNESS SITTING STATUTUM TANZIMAT
(— **FAIR**) MOP
STATUTORY LEGAL
STAUNCH FAST STOUT FAITHFUL
STAVE LAG SLAT STAP SHAKE STAFF STOVE VERSE BASTON STANZA WATTLE
(— **IN**) BILGE BULGE
(**SET OF** —S) SHOOK
(PL.) LAGGEN LAGGIN STICKS STAVING
STAY DAY GET LIE BASE HOLD LEND PROP REST SIST STOP WAIT ABIDE ABODE APPUI DEFER DELAY DEMUR DWELL LEAVE STINT TARRY THOLE ARREST ATTEND BIDING DETAIN EXPECT GUSSET POTENT REMAIN TIMBER UPHOLD EMBASSY JIBSTAY LAYOVER MANSION SOJOURN SUSPEND BACKSTAY CONTINUE FORESTAY HORNSTAY MAINSTAY
(— **AWAY**) SKIP
(— **BEHIND**) LAG
(— **CLEAR**) AVOID
(— **FOR**) AWAIT
(— **THE NIGHT**) BUNK HOSTLE
(— **WITH**) STICK
(**PRIEST'S** —) STATION
(**TAILORING** —) BRIDLE
(PL.) JUMPS JUPES BODICE
STAY-AT-HOME HOMEBODY HOMESTER
STAYER BONER
STAYLACE AGLET AIGLET
STAYSAIL JUMBO
STEAD LIEU ROOM VICE PLACE BEHALF
STEADFAST SAD FAST FIRM SURE TRUE ROCKY STAID STEER STABLE STANCH STEADY CERTAIN EXPRESS SETTLED STAUNCH VALIANT CONSTANT FAITHFUL RESOLUTE
STEADFASTLY FIRM FIRMLY INTENTLY
STEADILY SAD FAST STEADY
STEADINESS NERVE BALANCE
STEADING ONSET ONSTEAD
STEADY GUY SAD BEAU EVEN FIRM

SURE TRIG TRUE CANNY FRANK LEVEL SOBER STUDY SUANT TIGHT STABLE STANCH BALLAST EQUABLE STABILE STATARY STAUNCH CONSTANT DECOROUS DILIGENT FAITHFUL RESOLUTE TRANQUIL UNSHAKEN
(— **AT ANCHOR**) HOLSOM
STEAK BROIL SHELL FLITCH TUCKET GRISKIN
STEAL BAG CAB CLY COP FOX GYP LAG NAP NIM NIP RAP RIG BONE CHOR COON CRIB FAKE GLOM HOOK LIFT LURK MAGG MAKE MILL NAIL NICK PEAK PICK PRIG SLIP SMUG ANNEX BOOST BRIBE CLOUT CREEP FETCH FILCH FLIMP FRISK GLIDE HARRY HEIST HOIST LURCH MOOCH MOUCH PINCH PLUCK POACH SCOFF SHAKE SHARP SHAVE SLIDE SNAKE SNARE SNEAK STALK SWIPE TOUCH TRUFF COLLAR CONVEY FINGER HIJACK MOOTCH NOBBLE PILFER SNITCH STRIKE THIEVE BESTEAL CABBAGE PLUNDER PURLOIN SCHLEPP SKYUGLE SNABBLE SNAFFLE SURREPT ABSTRACT CRIBBAGE EMBEZZLE LIBERATE MANARVEL PECULATE SCROUNGE SHOPLIFT
(— **A GLANCE**) GLIME
(— **A WATCH**) FLIMP
(— **ALONG**) SLIME SLINK
(— **AWAY**) LOOP SLINK
(— **BY ALTERING BRANDS**) DUFF
(— **CALVES**) NUGGET
(— **CATTLE**) DUFF RUSTLE
(— **COPPER FROM VESSEL'S BOTTOM**) TOSH
(— **OFF**) RUN
(— **SLYLY**) SCROUNGE
STEALER (**CATTLE** —) DUFFER ABACTOR
STEALTHILY SIDLINS THIEFLY SIDELINS
STEALTHY CATTY PRIVY ARTFUL FELINE TIPTOE CATLIKE FURTIVE SNEAKING THIEVISH
STEAM OAM ROKE STEM BLAST SMOKE SWEAT VAPOR BREATH POTHER CUSHION
STEAMBOAT KICKUP STEAMER
STEAMER CLAM LINER TENDER STEAMER CUNARDER
STEAMER DUCK RACER LOGHEAD
STEAMSHIP SCREW STEAM STEAMER SEATRAIN SHOWBOAT
STEAM SHOVEL NAVVY NAVVIE
STEATIN MULL
STEATITE LARDITE POTSTONE SOAPROCK
STEATOPYGOUS RUMPY
STEED ROIL STEAD PEGASUS SLEIPNER
STEEL RAIL BLOOM BRACE FUSIL TERNE WEAPON WHITTLE FLEERISH
(— **FOR STRIKING FIRE**) ESLABON
(— **FOR USE WITH FLINT**) FUSIL FURISON FLEERISH

(— **INLAID WITH GOLD**) KOFT
KOFTGARI
(**DAMASCUS —**) DAMASK
(**INDIAN —**) WOOTZ
(**MOLTEN —**) HEAT
STEELER BONER
STEELING ACIERAGE
STEELWORKER HOOKER STICKMAN
STRANDER STRANNER
STEELYARD BISMER DESEMER
DOTCHIN STATERA
STEENBRAS BISKOP
STEEP SOP BATE BOLD BOWK BUCK
DRAW DUNG ELIX LIME MASH SOAK
STAY STEW STEY BRANT BRENT
HATCH HEAVY HILLY QUICK SHARP
SHEER SOUSE STIFF ABRUPT
BLUFFY CLIFFY CLIFTY DECOCT
IMBIBE INFUSE SPRUNT STEEPY
ARDUOUS BRASQUE CLIVOSE
INSTEEP PRERUPT STICKLE
HEADLONG MACETATE SATURATE
SIDELING STIFFISH STRAIGHT
STEEPED SODDEN
STEEPING SOUSE INFUSION
STEEPLE SPEAR SPIRE
STEEPLECHASE CHASE GRIND
STEER COX PLY BEEF BULL HELM
LEAD STEM STOT GUIDE SPADE
SPADO STERN TOLLY CANNER
RUDDER BULLOCK STOCKER
COWBRUTE MOSSHORN NAVIGATE
(— **VEHICLE**) DRIVE
(**FAT —**) BEAST
(**HORNLESS —**) NOT NOTT
(**VICIOUS —**) LADINO
(**WILD —**) YAW YEW COWBRUTE
(**YOUNG —**) STOT STOTT
STEERAGE STERN
STEERER CAPPER
STEERSMAN PILOT WHEEL PATRON
SLEWER CANOPUS SHIPMAN
STEERER COXSWAIN HELMSMAN
SEACUNNY STERNMAN WHEELMAN
STEIN SHANT
STELE SHAFT EUSTELE
STELLAR STARRY
STELLATE STARRY ASTROSE
STEM BUN BASE BEAM BINE BIRN
CANE CULM NOSE PIPE PROW RISP
ROOT RUNT STUD DTRAW FILUM
HAULM SCAPE SCREW SHAFT
SHANK SHOOT STALE STALK STEAL
STICK STIPE STOCK THEME TRUNK
TUBER BRANCH CAUDEX CAULIS
DERIVE SCAPUS SPRING CAULOME
CONTAIN FULCRUM HOPBINE
HOPVINE PEDICEL PETIOLE PLASHER
SPINDLE STEMLET TIGELLA
CAULICLE ENGENDER FORESTEM
PEDUNCLE PIPESTEM TIGELLUM
(— **OF ARROW**) SHAFT
(— **OF BANANAS**) COUNT
(— **OF GLASS**) BALUSTER
(— **OF GRAPES**) RAPE
(— **OF HOOKAH**) SNAKE
(— **OF MATCH**) SHAFT
(— **OF MUSHROOM**) STIPE
(— **OF MUSICAL NOTE**) TAIL FILUM
VIRGULA

(— **OF PIPE**) STAPPLE
(— **OF PLANT**) AXIS RUNT CAULIS
(— **OF SHIP**) PROW STEMPOST
(— **OF TREE**) BOLE
(—**S OF CULTIVATED PLANTS**)
HAULM
(**BULBLIKE —**) CORM
(**DRY WITHERED —**) BIRN
(**EDIBLE —**) EDDO
(**GRIEF —**) KELLY
(**MAIN — OF DEER'S ANTLERS**)
BEAM
(**ORNAMENTAL —**) STAVE
(**PITHY JOINTED —**) CANE
(**THORNY —**) LAWYER
(**TWINING —**) BINE
STEMLESS ACAULINE
STEMMA OCELLUS OCELLANA
PEDIGREE
STEMMER STRIPPER
STENCH FOGO HOGO FETOR SMELL
STINK WHIFF FOETOR MEPHITIS
STENCIL (— **PROCESS**) POCHOIR
STENCILED GOFFERED
STENOSIS SMALLING
STEP CUT FIT JOG PEG PIP BEMA
DESS FOOT GREE LINK PACE PEEP
RUNG STAP BRASS CORTE DODGE
FLIER FLYER GRECE NOTCH POINT
STAGE STAIR TOOTH TRACE TREAD
DEGREE GRADIN RUNDLE STRIDE
WINDER CURTAIL DESCENT
FOOTING GRADINE GRADING
COONJINE DEMARCHE DOORSTEP
FOOTPACE FOOTSTEP FORESTEP
PREDELLA STRATLIN
(— **ASIDE**) DIGRESS
(— **BACKWARD**) DODGE
(— **BY STEP**) GRADATIM
(— **DOWNWARD**) DESCENT
(— **FOR GEM MOUNTING**) KITE
(— **FORWARD**) ADVANCE
(— **IN A BEARING**) BRASS
(— **IN BELL RINGING**) DODGE
(— **IN DOCK**) ALTAR
(— **IN SELF-ESTEEM**) PEG
(— **IN SOCIAL SCALE**) CUT
(— **LIVELY**) SKELP
(— **OF LADDER**) RIME RUNG ROUND
RUNDLE
(— **OF TUSK**) TOOTH
(— **SUPPORTING MILLSTONE**)
TRAMPOT
(—**S OF BOWLER**) APPROACH
(**ALTAR —S**) GRADUAL
(**BALLET —**) SISSONE SISSONNE
(**BALLET —S**) ALLEGRO
(**BOUNDING —**) SKIP
(**CLUMSY —**) STAUP
(**DANCE —**) DIP PAS SET BUZZ
DRAG DRAW FLAT SHAG SKIP
BRAWL CHASS COULE GLIDE IRISH
STOMP BRANLE CANTER CHASSE
DOUBLE INTURN STRIDE BRANSLE
BUFFALO FISHTAIL GLISSADE
(**FALSE —**) HOB SLIP SPHALM
SNAPPER SPHALMA STUMBLE
(**FIRST —**) STARTER RUDIMENT
(**FLIGHT OF —S**) GRECE GRICE

PERRON GEMONIES
(**HALF —**) HALFTONE SEMITONE
(**MINING —**) LOB STEMPEL STEMPLE
(**POMPOUS —**) STRUT
(**PRIM —**) MINCE
(**SET OF —S**) STILE
(**STATELY —**) STALK
(**PL.**) STY STILE LADDER
STEPFATHER FATHER STEPSIRE
STEPLADDER TRAP STEPS
STEPMOTHER MOTHER HANGNAIL
STEPDAME
(**RELATING TO —**) NOVERCAL
STEPPE PUSZTA
STEPPED STOPEN
STEREOISOMER ANOMER EPIMER
STEREOTYPE CAST CLICHE STEREO
STEREOTYPED CHAIN STAGE TRITE
USUAL STEREO
STERILE DRY DEAD DEAF GELD
POOR AXENIC BARREN GALLED
MEAGER MULISH OTIOSE ASEPTIC
ACARPOUS BANKRUPT IMPOTENT
STERILITY ATOCIA APHORIA
STERILIZE INSULATE
STERILIZING BURNING
STERLING SOUND
(**100,000 POUNDS —**) PLUM
STERN GRIL GRIM HARD POOP
ASPER CRUEL GRUFF HARSH RIGID
ROUGH ROUND STARK STOUR
FLINTY GLOOMY GRIMLY SHREWD
STRICT SULLEN TORVID UNKIND
WICKED AUSTERE TORVOUS
STEERAGE STERNFUL STRAIGHT
(— **OF SHIP**) DOCK APLUSTRE
STERNFAST PROVISO
STERNNESS RIGOR TORVITY
SEVERITY
STERNPOST POST STEM MAINPOST
STERNUTATIVE ERRHINE PTARMIC
STERNUTATOR ERRHINE
STEROL AMYRIN STERIN AMBRAIN
STEVEDORE STOWER TRIMMER
WHARFIE CARGADOR DOCKHAND
STEVENSON, R.L. TUSITALA
STEW JUG FRET ITCH SLUM SNIT
BREDI CIVET CURRY DAUBE STIVE
STOVE SWEAT BURGOO HODDLE
MUDDLE PAELLA SEETHE SIMMER
BROTHEL CALDERA GOULASH
HARICOT NAVARIN PUCHERO
STOVIES FRIJOADA HOTCHPOT
MORTREUX MULLIGAN STEWPOND
STUFFATA
(— **A HARE**) JUG
(— **IN A SAUCE**) DAUBE
(— **MADE IN FORECASTLE**) HODDLE
(— **OF TRAMPS**) MULLIGAN
(**FISH —**) STODGE CHOWDER
(**IRISH —**) STOVIES
(**MUTTON —**) NAVARIN
STEWARD HIND VOGT DEWAN DIWAN
GRAFF GRAVE FACTOR FARMER
GRIEVE LOOKER SIRCAR SIRDAR
CURATOR DAPIFER FLUNKEY
GRANGER HUSBAND MAORMOR
MORMAOR PESHKAR PROCTOR
PROVOST SPENCER SPENDER

VILLCUS APPROVER BHANDARI
CELLARER CONSUMAH GASTALDO
HERENACH KHANSAMA LARDINER
MALVOLIO MANCIPLE PROVISOR
STEADMAN
(JOCKEY CLUB —) STIPE
STEWED SODDEN
STEWING ITCHING
STEWPAN STEW COCOTTE SKILLET
STHENELUS (FATHER OF —)
PERSEUS CAPANEUS ANDROGEOS
(MOTHER OF —) EVADNE
ANDROMEDA
(SON OF —) EURYSTHEUS
(WIFE OF —) NICIPPE
STHENOBOEA (FATHER OF —)
IOBATES
(HUSBAND OF —) PROETUS
STIBNITE SURMA STIBIUM ANTIMONY
STIBOPHEN FUADIN
STICHIC SERIAL
STICK CAT CLA DIP GAD HEW WAN
BROG BUFF CHOP CLAG CLAM CLUB
CRAB GLUE HANG HURL PALO PICK
POLE POTE RICE RUNG STAY TREE
YARD BATON BRAIL CAMAN CLAME
CLAVE CLEAM CLING CROME
DEMUR HURLY PRICK SPELK STAFF
STAKE STANG STAVE STEND STING
STOCK STOKE VALET VERGE
WADDY ADHERE ATLATL BALLOW
BATLER BATLET BATTLE BILLET
BROACH BULGER CEMENT CLEAVE
CLEEKY COHERE CUDGEL FESCUE
HOCKEY INHERE KIPPIN LIBBET
MALLET RADDLE RAMMER RISSLE
STRIKE STRING THIVEL TWITCH
BACKSET BATLING CAMMOCK
CUMMOCK GAMBREL HURLBAT
KILNRIB KIPPEEN MOLINET NOBBLER
SHANGAN SPURTLE WOOLDER
ASHPLANT BLUDGEON BRINGSEL
BRINSELL CATPIECE CATSTICK
DIPSTICK DUTCHMAN GIBSTAFF
GOBSTICK KILNTREE POTSTICK
SPREADER
(— AS ARCHERY MARK) WAND
(— FAST) JAM JAMB SEIZE FITCHER
(— FASTENED TO DOG'S TAIL)
SHANGAN
(— FOR ADMITTING TENANTS)
VERGE
(— FOR KILLING FISH) NOBBLER
(— FOR MAKING FENCE) RADDLE
(— FOR MIXING CHOCOLATE)
MOLINET
(— FOR SNUFF) DIP
(— FOR THATCHING) SPAR GROOM
SPELK SPRINGLE
(— IN MUD) STODGE
(— IN OPERATION) FREEZE
(— IT OUT) LAST
(— OF A FAN) BRIN
(— OF CANDY) GIBBY
(— OF CHALK) CRAYON
(— OF ORCHESTRA LEADER) BATON
(— OUT) BUG POKE BULGE SHOOT
EXTEND EXXERT EXTRUDE
(— REGULATING SLUICEWAY)
CATPIECE

(— SEPARATING LUMBER PILES)
STICKER
(— TO BEAT CLOTHES) BATLER
BATLET
(— TO DISTEND CARCASS) STEND
BACKSET
(— TO HOLD BOW) TILLER
(— TO HOLD LOG LOAD) DUTCHMAN
(— TO KEEP ANIMAL QUIET)
TWITCH
(— TO MARK CROSSING) BROG
(— TO POKE WITH) POTE
(— TO REMOVE HOOK FROM FISH)
GOBSTICK
(— TO STRETCH NET) BRAIL
(— TO STUFF DOLLS) RAMMER
(— TO THROW AT BIRDS) SQUAIL
(— TO TIGHTEN KNOT) WOOLDER
(— TOGETHER) CLOT BLOCK CLING
BALTER CEMENT COHERE
COAGMENT
(— UP) COCK
(— USED AS POINTER) FESCUE
(BAMBOO —) LATHI LATHEE
(BASKETRY —) LEAGUE
(BENT —) RIFLE
(FIELD HOCKEY —) BULGER
CAMMOCK
(FISHING —) GAD
(FORKED —) GROM GROOM
(HOCKEY —) CAMAN HURLY
HOCKEY HURLEY SHINNY CAMMOCK
CUMMOCK DODDART
(IRON-POINTED —) VALET
(KNOBBED —) BILLET
(LACROSSE —) CROSSE
(LARGE —) MOCK
(MARKING —) LEAD
(ODD —) JAY
(POLISHING —) BUFF
(PRAYER —) PAHO
(PRINTER'S —) SHOOTER
(RANGE-FINDING —) STADIA
(ROUND —) DOWEL SPINDLE
(STIRRING —) MUNDLE POOLER
SPURTLE POTSTICK SWIZZLER
(STOUT —) BAT LOWDER
(TALLY —) TAIL
(THROWING —) ATLATL HORNERAH
(TOBACCO —) LATH
(WALKING —) CANE KEBBY WADDY
JAMBEE JOCKEY KEBBIE WHANGEE
ASHPLANT GIBSTAFF
STICKER HINGE LABEL STRIP WAFER
HOPPER PASTER BLEEDER
CROSSER MOPSTICK STICKLER
STICK-IN STRANDER
STICKINESS TACK
STICKING ADHERENT ADHESION
COHESION COHESIVE
STICKLE DEMUR BOGGLE HAGGLE
HIGGLE
STICKLEBACK BAGGIE BANDIE
HACKLE GHOSTER PINFISH
STICKLER (— FOR FORMALITY)
TAPIST
STICKMAN DEALER
STICKY CAB CLAM CLIT ICKY DABBY
FATTY GAUMY GLUEY GOOEY

GUMMY JAMMY MALMY PUGGY
SHORT TACKY TOUGH CLAGGY
CLAMMY CLARTY CLOGGY PLUCKY
VISCID VISCOUS ADHESIVE
STIFF BUM SAD CARK HARD NASH
TRIG BUDGE CLUNG RIGID SOLID
STARK STEER STITH STOUR THARF
TOUGH BOARDY CLEDGY CLUMSY
CLUNCH FORMAL FROZEN PLUGGY
STARKY STEEVE STICKY STILTY
STOCKY STURDY UNEASY WOODEN
ANGULAR COSTIVE STARCHY
STILTED RAMRODDY RIGOROUS
STAFFISH
(SOMEWHAT —) CARKLED
STIFFEN GUM SET SIZE BRACE
STARK STIFF STRUT TRUSS HARDEN
STARCH STOVER STARKEN
(— PRICE) HARDEN
STIFFENED FUSED CARKLED
STIFFENER KNEE COUNTER
STIFFENING PUFF DRESS
STIFFNESS KINK RIGOR STARCH
BUCKRAM PRIMNESS RIGIDITY
SEVERITY
STIFLE DAMP SLAY CHOKE CRUSH
STIVE STUFF MUFFLE QUENCH
FLASKER QUERKEN SMOTHER
STRANGLE SUPPRESS THROTTLE
STIFLED DEAF ETOUFFE
STIFLING STUVY SMUDGY POTHERY
SMOTHERY
STIGMA BLOT FOIL NOTE SLUR
SPOT BRAND ODIUM STAIN TAINT
BLOTCH BLEMISH
STIGMATIZE BLOT BRAND
DENOUNCE
STILBITE DESMINE
STILE STY STICK TIMBER
STILETTO BODKIN STYLET PIERCER
POINTEL
STILL BUT COY LAY YET BODY CALM
COSH HUSH LOWN LULL WORM
CHECK QUIET WHIST HOWEER
HUSHED PACIFY QUENCH SETTLE
SILENT SOOTHE SUBDUE WITHAL
ALEMBIC CORNUTE HOWEVER
PELICAN SILENCE CUCURBIT
RECEIVER RESTRAIN STAGNANT
STILLERY SUPPRESS
(— PART) KELD
STILLAGE SLOP STILLING STILLION
STILL-HUNT STALK
STILLNESS CALM HUSH REST PEACE
SILENCE STATION
STILT KAKI POGO TILT LAWYER
PATTEN SCATCH YEGUITA
LONGLEGS STILTIFY TRIANGLE
STILTED LOFTY STIFF FORMAL
POETIC STILTY POMPOUS
STIMULANT STIM INULA BRACER
FILLIP GINGER HARMAL PHYTIN
CAMPHOR REVIVER ADONIDIN
AMMONIAC EXCITANT STIMULUS
STIMULATE FAN HOP PEP FUEL
GOAD HYPO MOVE SEED SPUR STIR
URGE WHET FILIP IMPEL ROUSE
SPARK STING AROUSE EXCITE
FILLIP INCITE SPIRIT TICKLE UPSTIR

ANIMATE ENLIVEN INNERVE INSPIRE
QUICKEN ACTIVATE FARADIZE
IRRITATE MOTIVATE
STIMULATING SEXY BRISK
PUNGENT EROGENIC EXCITING
GENEROUS INCITANT STIRRING
(— ANGER) ADRENAL
STIMULATION IMPETUS
(MENTAL —) SPRITE
STIMULUS CUE AURA BROD EDGE
GOAD HYPO SPUR STIM STING
FILLIP MOTIVE SOURCE BAHNUNG
IMPETUS OESTRUS
STING NIP BITE BURN FOIN GOAD
TANG ATTER DEVIL PIQUE PRICK
STANG TOUCH NETTLE ACULEUS
BUGBITE PIERCER IRRITATE
STIMULUS
STINGILY STRAIT SCARCELY
STINGING KEEN SMART PEPPERY
PIQUANT POINTED PRICKLY
PUNGENT ACULEATE NETTLING
SCALDING URTICANT
STINGING ANT KELEP
STINGRAY ANGLER OBISPO TRYGON
BATFISH LOPHIID STEPHEN STINGER
WAIREPO
STINGY DRY DREE GAIN GAIR HARD
MEAN NEAR NIGH CLOSE MINGY
SCALY TIGHT DRIECH GRIPPY
HUNGRY NARROW SCABBY SCARCE
SCRIMY SKIMPY SKINNY SNIPPY
STRAIT CHINCHY CHINTZY MISERLY
NIGGARD
STINK FOGO GOAD STEW SMELL
SMEECH STENCH
STINKBIRD HOACIN HOATZIN
STINKING FOUL HIGH FETID PUTID
STINKY
STINKWOOD DOGWOOD
STINT TASK GRIST PINCH SCANT
SNAPE SKINCH STINGY TANTUM
SCANTLE
(SHORT —) SNATCH
(WITHOUT —) FREELY
STIPE STEM STALK
STIPEND ANN HIRE ANNAT WAGES
SALARY PENSION PREBEND
PROVEND COMMENDA
STIPENDIARY BEAK
STIPPLE SPONGE
STIPPLED DOTTED
STIPULATE ARTICLE PROTEST
COVENANT
STIPULATION IF ANNEX CLAUSE
ARTICLE PREMISE PROVISO
COVENANT
(PL.) TERMS
STIPULE SPINE SHEATH STIPEL
STIPULA TENDRIL
STIR DO ADO FAN GOG PUG WAG
BEET BUZZ CARD FUSS MOVE PEAL
RAUK ROKE WAKE AMOVE BUDGE
CHURN CREEP ERECT FUROR
HURRY MUDGE POACH RAISE
ROUST SLICE SPARK STING STOOR
STURT TEASE TOUCH AROUSE
AWAKEN BUBBLE BUSTLE CRUTCH
EXCITE FLURRY GINGER HUBBUB

JUMBLE KIAUGH MUDDLE POUTER
QUINCH QUITCH REMBLE REMOVE
ROUNCE STODGE SUMMON TATTER
ACTUATE ANIMATE BLATHER
FLUTTER PROVOKE STARKLE
SWIZZLE TROUBLE
(— ABOUT) KNOCK
(— CALICO COLORS) TEER
(— DRINK) MUDDLE SWIZZLE
(— LIQUID) ROG
(— SOIL) CHISEL
(— UP WITH YEAST) BARM
(— UP) FAN MIX BUZZ DRUM FUSS
MOVE PROG ROIL TOSS AMOVE
AREAR AWAKE ERECT QUICK ROUSE
SNURL SPOOK STOKE TARRY
BESTIR BOTHER CHOUSE EXCITE
INCITE JOSTLE KINDLE PUDDLE
RUMBLE TICKLE UPSTIR AGITATE
ANIMATE COMMOVE DISTURB
PRODDLE PROVOKE STUDDLE
TORMENT UNQUEME DISTRACT
STIRRER HOG DOLLY ROUSER
RUMMAGER
STIRRING RACY ASTIR DEEDFUL
THRILLY EXCITING PATHETIC
STIRRUP IRON CHAPELET STEELBOW
STITCH BAR RUN SEW KNIT LOOP
PURL WHIP CABLE CLOSE POINT
PREEN PUNTO STEEK ACCRUE
FESTON SUTURE TRICOT CROCHET
POPCORN FAGOTING
(— OF CLOTHES) TACK
(PL.) JOURS FILLING
STITCHBIRD IHI
STITCHDOWN SEWROUND
STITCHER WHIPPER
STITCHING SERGING FAGOTING
STOATING WHIPPING
STITCHWORT PAIGLE ALLBONE
SNAPPER HEADACHE SNAPJACK
SNAPWORT
STITHY STUDY SMITHY STIDDY
STUDDY
STOAT VAIR ERMINE WEASEL
CLUBSTER FUTTERET WHITRACK
STOCK COP DOG KIN ROD CANT
CROP FILL FOND FUND SEED SELL
STEM TRIP BLOND BLOOD BROTH
CASTE CREAM FLESH HOARD ISSUE
STALE STIRP STORE STUFF TALON
BUDGET CHOKER COMMON FUTURE
KAFFIR SHARES STOVEN STRAIN
SUPPLY CAPITAL DESCENT PILLORY
PROSAPY PROVIDE REPLETE
RESERVE BONEYARD CROSSBAR
DIESTOCK GILLIVER GUNSTOCK
MAGAZINE MERCHANT ORDINARY
SECURITY
(— OF ANCHOR) CROSS
(— OF BREEDING MARES) STRUDE
(— OF FOOD) FARE
(— OF GRAIN) COP
(— OF MORPHEMES) LEXICON
(— OF WEAPONS) ARSENAL
(— OF WHIP) CROP
(— OF WINE) CELLAR
(— SOLD SHORT) BEAR
(FARM —) BOW

(LANGUAGE —) SALISH SIOUAN
BOROTUKE
(MEAT —) BLOND BOUILLON
(PLASTIC —) BISCUIT
(RAILROAD —) GRANGER
(PL.) FOODS CIPPUS HARMAN
TIMBER CATASTA KAFFIRS
STOCKADE BOMA PEEL ETAPE
ZAREBA BARRIER TAMBOUR
STOCKADO
STOCK EXCHANGE BOURSE
COULISSE
STOCKFISH STOCK LUTFISK TITLING
SPELDING SPELDRON
STOCKING HOSE SOCK SHANK
STOCK CALIGA MOGGAN SCOGGER
SHINNER
(FOOTLESS —) HOGGER HUSHION
(SOLELESS —) TRAHEEN
(PL.) HOSE BUSKINS BOOTHOSE
STOCKJOBBING AGIOTAGE
STOCKWORK CARBONA
STOCKY FAT COBBY DUMPY GROSS
SQUAT STOUT CHUMPY CHUNKY
DUMPTY STUBBY STUGGY STUNTY
BUNTING COMPACT HEAVYSET
STOCKISH THICKSET
STODGY STUFFY STUGGY
STOIC IMPASSIVE
STOKEHOLD FIREROOM
STOKER FIREMAN BLOCKMAN
STOLE STAW ARMIL ORARY ARMILLA
ORARION
STOLEN HOT INOME STOUN FURTIVE
(— GOODS) MAINOUR
STOLID BEEFY CLUMSE STUPID
WOODEN CLUMPST DEADPAN
PASSIVE
STOLIDITY MORGUE
STOLON WIRE SOBOL SOBOLE
SOLENIUM
STOMACH MAW CROP GUTS KYTE
MARY POKE READ TANK WAME
WOMB BINGY BROOK GORGE
GROUF HEART TUMMY BINGEE
BINGEY BONNET CROPPY GEBBIE
PECHAN CONCOCT CRAPPIN
GIZZARD ABOMASUM
(— OF ANIMAL) CRAW
(— OF CALF) VELL
(— OF RUMINANT) READ RUMEN
BONNET OMASUM PAUNCH
ABOMASUM MANIFOLD RODDIKIN
(PIG'S —) JAUDIE
STOMACHACHE FANTAD GULLION
STOMACHER GIMP TRUSS ECHELLE
PLACARD POITREL FOREPART
STOMACHIC COTO CORNUS
GENTIAN ANTHEMIS
STONE DAM GEM BOND DUCK FLAG
HERD KLIP KNAR MARK ROCK STEN
TRIG BAUTA CAPEL DRAKE GUARD
LAPIS PAVER PITCH SCRAE SCREE
SNECK STANE ASHLAR BEDDER
BENBEN CEPHAS CHATON CLOSER
COBBLE GAMAHE GIBBER HEADER
JUMPER LEDGER MARVER METATE
MULLER NUTLET PEEVER PINNER
RUNNER SUMMER TORSEL ANGRITE

CALLAIS DINGBAT DONNOCK
DORNICK GLIDDER KNEELER
KNICKER PERPEND PITCHER
PUTAMEN RATCHEL STANNER
SURFACE THROUGH BAETULUS
CABOCHON DENDRITE EBENEZER
HAGSTONE LAPIDATE LAPILLUS
LAPSTONE MACEHEAD MONOLITH
NAKHLITE SKEWBACK TOPSTONE
(— ADHERING TO LEAD ORE) KEVEL
(— AS AMULET) HAGSTONE
(— AS IT COMES FROM QUARRY)
RUBBLE
(— AS ROAD MARKER) LEAGUE
(— AT DOOR) RYBAT
(— BLOCK) ASSIZE
(— FOR GLASS-ROLLING) MARVER
(— FORMING CAP OF PIER)
SUMMER CUSHION
(— HARD TO MOVE) SITFAST
(— HEAP) MAN
(— IN BLAST FURNACE) DAM
(— IN MEMORY OF DEAD)
MONUMENT
(— IN SMALL FRAGMENTS)
RATCHEL
(— OF FRUIT) COB PIT PAIP COBBE
NUTLET PYRENE PUTAMEN
(— OF PYRAMID SHAPE) BENBEN
(— PROVIDING CHANGE OF
DIRECTION) KNEELER
(— SET IN RING) CHATON
(— SHOT FROM STONE-BOW) JALET
(— TO DEATH) LAPIDATE
(— USED AS MONUMENT) MEGALITH
(— USED IN GAME) DUCK DRAKE
(— WITH INTERNAL CAVITY) GEODE
(—S FROM CRUSHER) TAILINGS
(—S IN WATER) STANNERS
(ARTIFICIAL —) ALBOLITE
(BINDING —) PERPEND THROUGH
PIERPONT
(BOND —) GIRDER KEYSTONE
(BOUNDARY —) TERM TERMINUS
(BROKEN — USED FOR ROADS)
BALLAST MACADAM
(BUILDING —) SUMMER MITCHEL
SPERONE
(CARVED —) CAMEO CUVETTE
(CASTING —) TYMP
(CHINA —) PETUNSE
(CLAY —) LECH
(COPING —) SKEW TABLET TABLING
CAPSTONE
(CURLING —) HOG HERD GUARD
LOOFIE POTLID
(DESERT —) GIBBER
(DRUID —) SARSEN
(DRYING —) STILLAGE
(EDGING —) SETTER
(FLAT —) PLAT DRAKE LEDGER
(FOUNDATION —) BEDDER
(GLITTERING —) DAZE
(GRAVE —) BAUTA STELE
(GREEN —) CALLAIS
(GRINDING —) METATE MULLER
(HOLY —) BEAR
(HOPSCOTCH —) PEEVER PALLALL
(IMAGINARY —) ADAMANT

(KIDNEY —) NEPHRITE
(LAST — IN COURSE) CLOSER
(LOOSE —) GLIDDER
(MEMORIAL —) BAUTA EBENEZER
(METEORIC —) ANGRITE NAKHLITE
(MIDDLE —) HONEY
(MONUMENTAL —) LECH
(PAVING —) PAVER PITCHER
(PHILOSOPHER'S —) ADROP
(PRECIOUS —) GEM OPAL RUBY
EWAGE JEWEL TOPAZ ADAMAS
LIGURE SHAMIR ASTERIA ASTRION
CRAPAUD CUVETTE DIAMOND
DIONISE EMERALD GELATIA JACINTH
OLIVINE SARDIUS AMETHYST
ASTROITE HYACINTH PANTARBE
SAPPHIRE YDRIADES
(PRECIOUS —S) PERRIE
(REFUSE —) ROACH
(SACRED —) BAETYL BAETULUS
(SEMIPRECIOUS —) ONYX SARD
MURRA GARNET CITRINE TIGEREYE
(SHARPENING —) HONE WHET
(SHOEMAKER'S —) LAPSTONE
(SMALL ROUND —) JACK
(SOFTENED —) SAP
(STEPPING —) GOAT
(STRATIFIED —) FLAG SLAB
(TALISMANIC —) GAMAHE
(UNSQUARED —) BACKING
(UPRIGHT —) BAUTA MENHIR
MASSEBAH
(PL.) LAPIDES LAPILLI
STONEBASS BAFARO WHAPUKU
STONEBOAT DRAY
STONEBOW RODD
STONECHAT CHAT SMICH
WHEATEAR
STONECROP SEDUM ORPINE
PRICKET WALLWORT
STONE CURLEW BUSTARD
STONECUTTER JADDER LAPICIDE
SCABBLER SCAPPLER SQUAREMAN
STONEFLY NAIAD
STONEHAND LOCKUP
STONELIKE LITHOID
STONEMAN IMPOSER
STONE MARTEN FOIN
STONEMASON DORBIE
STONE PARSLEY HONEWORT
STONE PINE PINON
STONE ROLLER MAMMY MOMMY
TOTER
STONE TOTER CUTLIPS
STONEWALLER STICKER
STONEWARE GRES BASALT JASPER
BASALTES CANEWARE
STONINESS LAPIDITY PETREITY
STONY RIGID COBBLY PETROUS
LAPIDOSE PETROSAL
STOOL FORM MORA SEAT STAB
COPPY CROCK HORSE STOLE
TREST BUFFET CREEPY CURRIE
TRIPOD TUFFET COMMODE CREEPIE
KNEELER SHAMBLE TABORET
TRESTLE TUMBREL BARSTOOL
STILLAGE
(3-LEGGED —) THRESTLE
(CLOSE —) TOM

(CUCKING —) THEW
(LOW —) COPPY SUNKIE CREEPIE
STOOLBALL TUTBALL
STOOL PIGEON NARK SNITCH
STOOGE STOOLIE
STOOP BOW BEND LEAN LOUT SINK
COUCH DEIGN STOPE STULP
COORIE CROUCH HUCKLE BALCONY
DECLINE DESCEND RUCKSEY
SUCCUMB
(— OF HAWK) SOUSE
STOOPING DUCK ASTOOP DESCENT
STOP HO BAS COG CUT DAM DIE
DOG END HOO LIN MAR SET BALK
BODE BUNG CALK CALL COOL DROP
EASE HALT HELP HOLD HOOK KILL
QUIT REED REST SIST SNUB STAP
STAY STEM STOW TEAT TENT TOHO
TRIG VIOL WEAR WHOA ABIDE
AVAST BASTA BELAY BLOCK BRAKE
BREAK CAULK CEASE CHECK
CHOKE CLAMP CLOSE DELAY
EMBAR HITCH LEAVE MEDIA PEACE
POINT QUINT SCOTE SLAKE SPARE
SPRAG STAND STASH STEEK STICK
STINT VIOLA AEOLIN ANCHOR
ARREST ASTINT BIFARA BOGGLE
BORROW CHEESE CLAMOR COLLAR
DESIST DETAIN GRAVEL INSTOP
MONTRE NASARD PERIOD SCOTCH
SQUASH STANCE STANCH STIFLE
TENUIS TROMBA BASSOON
CAESURA MELODIA MUSETTE
OPPRESS SOJOURN STATION
TERTIAN TWELFTH ASPIRATA
BACKSTOP BOMBARDE PRECLUDE
RECORDER STOPOVER STOPPAGE
SUPPRESS SURCEASE TENOROON
WALDHORN WITHSPAR
(— AS IF FRIGHTENED) BOGGLE
(— BLAST) DAMP
(— FLOW) BAFFLE STANCH
(— FOR FOOD) BAIT
(— FOR HORSE) BLOW
(— FROM FERMENTING) STUM
(— GROWTH) BLAST
(— GUN BREECH) OBTURATE
(— IN EARLY STAGES) ABORT
(— IN SPEAKING) HAW
(— LEAK) CALK CAULK FOTHER
(— ROWING) EASY
(— SHORT) JIB
(— SWINGING) SET
(— UNDESIREDLY) STALL
(— UP) DAM CALK CLOG CLOY FILL
PLUG CHINK ESTOP STUFF STANCH
STAUNCH OPPILATE
(— USING) SINK
(— WITH CLAY) PUG
(— WORK) SECURE
(BRIEF —) CALL
(GLOTTAL —) STOD CATCH STOSS
STOSSTON
(HARPSICHORD —) LUTE
(ROUGH —) ASPIRATA
(SUCTION —) CLICK
(TEMPORARY —) PAUSE SUSPEND
(VOICELESS —) TENUIS
(PL.) REEDWORK

STOPCOCK BIB BIBB BIBCOCK
TURNCOCK
STOPLIGHT IMPEDER
STOPOVER LAYOVER
STOPPAGE JAM ALLAY CHECK
HITCH LEATH STICK STINT ARREST
DEVALL STASIS EMBARGO GASLOCK
REFUSAL SHUTOFF STOPPLE
SHUTDOWN STOPWORK
(— OF DEVELOPMENT) ATROPHY
(WORK —) LOWSIN STRIKE
STOPPED PILEATA
(— WITH HAND) BOUCHE
STOPPER WAD BUNG CORK STOP
VICE CHECK FIPPLE STANCH
BOUCHON CLOSURE SHUTOFF
STOPGAP STOPPLE TAMPION
STOPCOCK
STOPPING STAY HOLDUP STOPPAGE
STORAGE STORE STOWAGE
BESTOWAL
STORAX COPALM STACTE STYRAX
LORDWOOD
STORE CAVE CRIB DECK FOND FUND
HOLD KEEP MASS SAVE SHOP
STOW TOKO CACHE DEPOT HOUSE
HUTCH STASH STOCK UPLAY
BAZAAR GARNER GIRNEL RECOND
STEEVE SUPPLY TIENDA WINKEL
ARSENAL BHANDAR BOOTERY
GROCERY HARVEST HUSBAND
IMBURSE REPOSIT RESTORE
BOUTIQUE EMPORIUM EXCHANGE
GARRISON MAGAZINE TENDEJON
WAREROOM WARNISON
(— BEER) AGE LAGER
(— CROP) BARN
(— FODDER) ENSILE
(— IN A MOW) GOVE
(— IN LUMBER CAMP) VAN
(— KEPT BY CHINESE) TOKO
(— OF FOOD) LARDER
(— OF WEALTH) FORTUNE
(— UP) FUND POWDER IMBURSE
SQUIRREL
(ABUNDANT —) MINE
(HIDDEN —) BIKE
(LARGE —) RAFF
(LIQUOR —) GROGGERY
(RESERVE —) SLUICE
(RICH —) ARGOSY
(SMALL —S) SLOPS
(PL.) SAMAN SUPPLY
STOREHOUSE BIKE GOLA CACHE
DEPOT ETAPE STORE ARGOSY
ARMORY BODEGA GODOWN PALACE
PANARY STAPLE VINTRY ARSENAL
BHANDAR CAMALIG CAMARIN
GRANARY STORAGE MAGAZINE
SADDLERY TREASURE
(— FOR BREAD) PANARY
(RAISED —) WHATA FUTTAH PATAKA
(UNDERGROUND —) PALACE
STOREKEEPER MERCHANT
STOREMAN
STOREROOM CAVE GOLA WARD
GOLAH BODEGA CELLAR DINGLE
BOXROOM BUTTERY GENIZAH
LAZARET POULTRY THALAMUS

(PAWNBROKER'S —) LUMBER
STORESHIP FLUTE
STORK WADER ARGALA JABIRU
SIMBIL HURGILA MAGUARI MARABOU
ADJUTANT CICONIID MARABOUT
OPENBEAK OPENBILL
STORKLIKE PELARGIC
STORKSBILL ERODIUM
STORM RIG WAP BLOW HAIL HUFF
RAGE RAMP RAND RAVE WIND
BLIZZ BLOUT BRASH DEVIL DRIFT
FORCE ORAGE OSTOR ATTACK
BARBER EASTER EXPUGN WESTER
BLUSTER BRAVADO CYCLONE
DUSTING EQUINOX GAUSTER
PISACHI SHAITAN SNIFTER TEMPEST
TORMENT WEATHER BLOWDOWN
CALAMITY ERUPTION UPHEAVAL
WILLIWAW
(— OF BLOWS) STOUR
(DUST —) DEVIL DUSTER HABOOB
KHAMSIN PEESASH SHAITAN
(FURIOUS —) TEMPEST
(HAWAIIAN —) KONA
(SEVERE —) PEELER SNIFTER
(VIOLENT —) FLAW TUFAN CYCLONE
SNORTER
STORM DOOR DINGLE
STORMY FOUL GURL RUDE WILD
DIRTY DUSTY GURLY GUSTY STARK
WINDY COARSE RUGGED UNFINE
WINTRY FURIOUS NIMBOSE RIOTOUS
SQUALLY TROUBLE VIOLENT
AGITATED BLUSTERY CLUTTERY
ORAGIOUS TEMPESTY
STORMY PETREL MITTY WITCH
SPENCY
STORY GAG SAW DECK DIDO FLAT
LORE REDE TALE TEXT YARN ATTIC
CRACK ETAGE FABLE FLOOR KATHA
PITCH PROSE RECIT SOLAR SPELL
SPIEL STAGE STORE CUFFER
FABULA FLIGHT PISTLE SCREED
SOLLAR ADVANCE HAGGADA
HISTORY MANSARD MARCHEN
PROCESS RECITAL ANECDOTE
DREADFUL ENTRESOL
(— FROM THE PAST) LEGEND
(— OF BEEHIVE) SUPER
(— OF BUILDING) DECK FLAT ATTIC
CHESS ETAGE FLOOR PIANO SOLAR
STAGE FLIGHT SOLLAR MANSARD
ENTRESOL
(— OF HEROES) SAGA
(ABSURD —) CANARD
(ADVENTURE —) YARN
(AMUSING —) DROLLERY
(BIRTH —) JATAKA
(DOLEFUL —) JEREMIAD
(EERIE —) CHILLER
(FAKE —) STRING
(FALSE —) SHAVE CANARD
WHOPPER
(MADE-UP —) FUDGE
(MONSTROUS —) BANGER
(MORBIDLY SENSATIONAL —)
DREADFUL
(MYSTERY —) WHODUNIT
(NEWS —) SIDEBAR

(NEWSPAPER —) LEAD FEATURE
(OLD —) DIDO
(POMPOUS —) BRAG
(PREPOSTEROUS —) CUFFER
(RIBALD —) HARLOTRY
(SATIRICAL —) SKIT
(SHORT —) CONTE NOVELLA
(STALE —) CHESTNUT
(UPPER —) ATTIC GARRET
HYPEROON
(PL.) LEGENDA
STORY BOOK TALEBOOK
STORYTELLER CONTEUR DISCOUR
DISSOUR
STOUP STOOP BENITIER
STOUT FAT SAD FIRM STUT TRIM
BROSY BULKY BUNTY BURLY
COBBY FRACK FRECK GREAT
HARDY KEDGE OBESE PLUMP
PODDY PUNCH STARK STERN
FLESHY PORTER PORTLY PRETTY
PYKNIC ROTUND SQUARE STRONG
STUFFY STURDY BOWERLY REPLETE
FORCIBLE POWERFUL ROBOREAN
STALWART THICKSET
(— PERSON) GURK
STOUTHEARTED GOOD VALIANT
STOUTLY FAST HARDILY
STOUTNESS STRENGTH
STOVE HOD STOW BOGEY CHULA
PEACH PLATE CHULHA COCKLE
COOKER HEATER PRIMUS BRASERO
CHAUFFER FRANKLIN POTBELLY
(— FOR DRYING GUNPOWDER)
GLOOM
(— ON SHIP) GALLEY
(RUSSIAN —) PEACH
(WARMING —) KANGRI
STOVER OVENSMAN
STOW BIN BOX SET CRAM LADE
MASS CROWD DOUSE STORE
BESTOW COOPER STEEVE DUNNAGE
RUMMAGE
STOWAGE BURTON
STOWED IN
STOWER TOPPER
STOWING BINNING GOBBING
STRABISMUS CAST CROSS SQUINT
TROPIA ANOPSIA COCKEYE
WALLEYE
STRADDLE SADDLE SPREAD STRIDE
BESTRIDE SPRADDLE STRIDDLE
STRAGGLE ROVE RANGLE SPRAWL
STREEL TAGGLE WANDER DRAGGLE
MEANDER SCRAMBLE SPRANGLE
STRAGGLER STRAY
STRAGGLING RAGGED RAGGLED
SPRAYEY SCRATCHY VAGULOUS
STRAIGHT BOLT FAIR FULL GAIN
BRANT CLEAN DOGGY FLUSH RIGHT
SHORT SPANG ARIGHT DIRECT
HONEST STRAIT STRICT BOBTAIL
UPRIGHT DIRECTLY SEQUENCE
(— AHEAD) ANON PLUMP OUTRIGHT
(— UP AND DOWN) SHEER CLEVER
EVENDOWN
(NOT —) CRAZY
STRAIGHTEDGE RULER STRICKLE
STRAIGHTEN GAG ORDER STENT

EXTEND SQUARE UNKINK COMPOSE
RECTIFY STRETCH
(— BY HEATING) SET
(— NEEDLE) RUB
(— RAILS) GAG
STRAIGHT-FIBERED BROAD
STRAIGHTFORWARD EVEN PLAT
APERT FRANK LEVEL NAKED ROUND
CANDID DEXTER DIRECT HONEST
SIMPLE SQUARE JANNOCK SINCERE
EVENDOWN HOMESPUN OUTRIGHT
STRAIGHT
(NOT —) CROOKED PLAITED
STRAIGHTFORWARDLY SINGLY
SQUARE STRAIGHT
STRAIGHT-THINKING CLEAR
STRAIGHTWAY ANON AWAY RIGHT
ARIGHT BEDEEN BEDENE DIRECTLY
STRAIN FIT LAG RAX SIE TAX TRY
TUG ACHE BEND CALL DASH DRAG
HEAT HEFT LAWN NOTE PULL RANN
SILE SINE SOLO SONG VEIN WORK
BRUNT CHAFE DEMUR DRAIN FORCE
HEAVE PRESS RETCH SHADE SHEAR
STOCK SURGE TAMMY TOUCH
WREST WRICK CLENCH EFFORT
EXTEND EXTORT FILTER INTEND
SPRAIN SPRING STREAK STRESS
STRIND THRONG DESCANT DISCANT
EUPLOID FATIGUE STRAINT
STRETCH STROPHE TENSION
TORMENT DIAPASON DIATRIBE
DIHYBRID SUBBREED
(— MILK) SIE SYE
(— OF AN ARCH) THRUST
(— OF CHICKENS) ANCOBAR
(— OF RAILING LANGUAGE)
DIATRIBE
(— ON BUGLE) MOT
(— ON HORN) MOT RECHASE
RECHEAT
(— THROUGH COLANDER) COIL
(CONCLUDING —) CADENCE
(MUSICAL —) FIT SOLO POINT
(MUSICAL —S) TOUCH
(MUTANT —) SALTANT
STRAINED PENT TENSE INTENSE
LABORED INTENDED
STRAINER CAGE ROSE SILE RENGE
SIEVE STRUM TAMIS TAMMY THEAD
SEARCE SEARCH CRIBBLE
COLATORY COLATURE SEARCHER
(— OF TWIGS) HUCKMUCK
(COFFEE —) GRECQUE
(MILK —) SAY MILSEY MILSIE
(WICKER —) THEAD THEDE
STRAINING CUTE COILED ASTRAIN
INTENSE COLATURE
STRAIT CUT GUT BAND BELT FRET
KYLE NECK PACE BRAKE CANAL
PHARE PINCH SHARD ANGUST
FRETUM NARROW PLUNGE CHANNEL
EURIPUS BOSPORUS JUNCTURE
(IN —S) SET
(NEWFOUNDLAND —) TICKLER
(PL.) CHOPS PRESS EXTREMES
STRAITEN PINCH SCANT STRAIT
STRAITENED CRIMP NARROW
CRIMPED

STRAITJACKET CAMISOLE
STRAITLACED STIFF BLUENOSED
STRAKE SHEER COURSE RISING
STREAK COAMING SAXBOARD
(PL.) TIRE
STRAMONIUM DEWTRY
STRAND PLY TOP BANK CORE FLAT
TOWT BEACH BRAID CLIFF PRAYA
READY SHORE LISSOM SINGLE
SLIVER STRAIN STRIKE SUTURE
HAIRLINE
(— OF HAIR) LICK SWITCH
(— OF PROTOPLASM) BRIDGE
STRANDED ISOLATED
STRANDER EDGER
STRANGE ODD EERY FELL FREM
NICE RARE UNCO ALIEN EERIE
FREMT FUNNY NOVEL QUEER UNKET
UNKID WOOZY ALANGE FERLIE
QUAINT UNIQUE UNKENT UNKIND
CURIOUS ERRATIC HEATHEN
UNHEARD UNKNOWN UNUSUAL
FANCIFUL INSOLENT INSOLITE
PECULIAR SELCOUTH SINGULAR
UNCOLIKE UNCOMMON UNKENNED
UNKINDLY
STRANGER COME UNCO UNKO
ALIEN GUEST FRENNE GANGER
INCOME INMATE FUIDHIR INCOMER
UNCOUTH MALIHINI OUTCOMER
PEREGRIN
STRANGLE CHOKE GRAIN GRANE
SNARL WORRY STIFLE GARROTE
QUACKLE GARROTTE JUGULATE
THROTTLE
STRANGLEHOLD CHANCERY
STRANGUL
STRAP BAR TUG BAND CLIP CURB
GIRD HASP RIDE RIEM BRACE
CHEEK GIRTH GUIGE PATTE RIDER
RISER SABOT SLING STROP THONG
TRACE ANKLET BACKER RILLET
COLLAR ENARME GARTER HALTER
HANGER LAINER LATIGO SANDAL
TOGGLE WARROK BABICHE
BOWYANG CRIBBER DOLPHIN
LANYARD LATCHET LEATHER
RIEMPIE STIRRUP TICKLER WEBBING
BACKSTAY BRETELLE SQUILGEE
TURNBACK WRISTLET
(— AROUND HORSE'S THROAT)
CRIBBER
(— AROUND MAST) DOLPHIN
(— FOR SHIELD) GUIGE ENARME
BRETELLE
(— IN FLAIL) TAPLING
(— OF BRIDLE) REIN
(— OF SENNIT) BACKER
(— ON HAWK'S LEAD) JESS JESSE
SENDAL
(— WITH SLIT END) TAWS TAWSE
(ANKLE —) BRACELET
(DOOR —) HASP
(MINER'S —) BYARD
(SHOE —) BAR
(STIRRUP —S) CHAPELET
(TIE —) SHANK
(U-SHAPED —) STIRRUP
(PL.) LADDER

STRAP FERN LONGLEAF
STRAPHANGER COMMUTER
STRAPPER SPLICER
STRAPPING SWANK CHOPPING
SLAPPING SWANKING
STRAP-SHAPED LORATE LIGULAR
LIGULATE
STRATA TERRANE UNDERAIR
(— OF COAL) MEASURES
STRATAGEM JIG COUP LOCK RUSE
TRAM TURN WILE ANGLE DRAFT
FETCH FRAUD GUILE JOKER KNACK
TRAIN TRICK WREST BLENCH
DECEIT DEVICE HUMBUG POLICY
TRAPAN TREPAN WOIDRE WRENCH
FINESSE SLEIGHT ARTIFICE
CONTOISE FARFETCH INTRIGUE
LIRIPIPE LIRIPOOP PRACTICE
PRACTISE QUENTISE STRATEGY
STRATEGY GAME FINESSE
STRATIFICATION BEDDING
STRATIFIED BEDDED VARVED
STRATUM BED CAP CUT LAY RIB
FAST LAIN SEAM COUCH ELITE
FLOOR LAYER LEDGE SHELF TABLE
COUCHE GIRDLE GRAVEL LAYING
LISSOM PINNEL AQUAFER AQUIFER
ENTIRIS FISHBED SUBSOIL UPRIGHT
AQUIFUGE FAHLBAND SUBGRADE
(— OF COAL) BENCH
(— OF FIRECLAY) THILL
(— OF PALE COLOR) FAHLBAND
(— OF SANDSTONE) PINNEL
(— OF SOIL) SOD
(— OF STONE) GIRDLE
(SOCIAL —) CUT
(THIN —) SEAM LENTIL
STRAW BAKU GLOY MOTE REED
RUSH TOYO WASE HAULM PEDAL
SHILF STALK STREW YEDDA FESCUE
FETTLE PANAMA RIZZOM SIPPER
TUSCAN BANGKOK SABUTAN
STUBBLE WINDLIN STRAMMEL
(— CUT FINE) CHAFF
(— FOR MAKING HATS) SENNIT
BANGKOK LEGHORN SABUTAN
(— FOR THATCHING) YELM
(— MEASURE) KEMPLE
(— TO PROTECT PLANTS) MULCH
(BROKEN —) BHUSA BHOOSA
(COOKERY —S) PAILLES
(PLAITED —) SENNIT
(WAXED —) STRASS
STRAWBERRY BERRY DUNLAP
FRAISE RUNNER HAUTBOY FRUTILLA
HAUTBOIS KLONDIKE ROSACEAN
STRAWBERRY BUSH WAHOO
EUONYMUS EVONYMUS FISHWOOD
STRAWBERRY FINCH AMADAVAT
AVADAVAT
STRAWBERRY SHRUB BUBBY
COWBERRY
STRAWBERRY TOMATO PHYSALIS
STRAY ERR ODD FALL RAVE ROVE
WAFF WAIF WALK DRIFT RANGE
TRAIK VAGUE WAVER ESTRAY
RANGLE SWERVE VAGARY WANDER
WILDER DEVIATE FORLORN

STRAYER DIVAGATE MAVERICK STRAGGLE

STRAYING ASTRAY ERRANT ABERRANT VAGATION

STREAK PAY RAY BAND SEAM VEIN WALE FLAKE FLECK FLICK FREAK GARLE GLADE SLASH FACULA SMUDGE STRAIN STRAKE STREAM STRIPE FLECKER SPRAING STIPPLE DISCOLOR TRAVERSE
(— IN FABRIC) CRACK SHINER
(— IN GLASS) SKIM
(— IN HAIR) BLAZE
(— IN SKY) ICEBLINK
(— IN WOOD) ROE
(— OF BLUBBER) BLANKET
(— OF LIGHT) STREAM
(— ON SURFACE OF SUN) FACULA
(— WITH FINE STRIPES) LACE
(—S FROM PLANE) CONTRAIL
(BACTERIOLOGICAL —) STROKE
(LOSING —) SLUMP
(THEATRICAL —) HAM
(WHITE —) SHIM

STREAKED ROWY LACED BRINDLE BROCKED BROOKED FINCHED SPARKED STRIPED WHIPPED BRINDLED IRONSHOT PINROWED

STREAKY ROWY SCOVY STREAKED

STREAM EA PUP RIO RUN BECK BURN FLOW FLUX FORD GILL GOTE KHAL KILL LAKE PUIT PURL RILL SICK SIKE SILE SPIN TIDE BACHE BATCH BAYOU BOGUE BROOK CREEK DRILL DRINK FLARE FLASH FLEAM FLOOD FLOSS FLUOR FRESH GHYLL NYMPH PRILL RITHE RIVER SWAMP TCHAI TRAIN ARROYO BANKER BOURNE BRANCH BURNIE CANADA COULEE FILLER FLUENT GUZZLE OUTLET PIRATE RANDOM RUNDLE RUNNEL SLUICE SPRUIT STRAND STRONE CHANNEL CURRENT DRIBBLE FLUENCE FRESHET RIVULET TRICKLE AFFLUENT INFLUENT
(— ALONG) SLIDE
(— FULL TO TOP) BANKER
(— OF AIR OR SMOKE) PEW
(— OF ELECTRODES) BEAM
(— OF LAVA) COULEE
(— OF SIRUP) THREAD
(— OF SPEECH) STRAIN
(— OUT) BREAK
(FLOWING —) NYMPH
(HIGH-SPEED —) JET
(MYTHOLOGICAL —S) ELIVAGAR
(SLOW —) OOZE
(SLUGGISH —) LANE
(SMALL —) BECK LAKE SIKE DRAFT RITHE COULEE SICKET SQUIRT STRIPE DRAUGHT GRINDLE
(THIN —) TRICKLE TRICKLET
(TIDAL —) COVE SEAPOOSE
(TRANSIENT —) RILL
(TRICKLING —) DRILL
(TURBID —) DRUVE
(UNDERGROUND —) AAR SWALLET
(VIOLENT —) TORRENT

(WEAK —) DRIP

STREAMER FLAG VANE GARTER GUIDON LAPPET PENCEL PENNON SCROLL SIMPLE WIMPLE BANDEROL FILAMENT
(— OF MOSS) WEEPER
(PAPER —S) CONFETTI

STREAMING SLUICY ASTREAM CYCLOSIS DOWNPOUR

STREAMLET RILL RILLET RUNDLE RUNLET RUNNEL RIVULET

STREAMLINE SIMPLIFY
(— FLOW) LAMINAR

STREAMLINED CLEAN SLEEK

STREET ROW RUE WAY CHAR DRUM GATE PAVE STEM TOBY BLOCK BORGO CALLE CANON CHAWK CORSO DRIVE AVENUE BOWERY CANYON CAUSEY RAMBLA CHAUSEE POULTRY TERRACE THROUGH ARTERIAL BROADWAY BYSTREET CONTRADA PROSPECT
(— IN BARCELONA) RAMBLA
(— IN FLORENCE) BORGO
(MAIN —) CHAWK CHOWK TOWNGATE
(NARROW —) CHAR ALLEY CHARE
(PRINCIPAL —) ARTERY
(SIDE —) HUTUNG

STREETCAR TRAMCAR ELECTRIC

STREET CLEANER ORDERLY CLEANSER

STREET CLEANING SLOPPING

STREETWALKER CRUISER

STRENGTH EL ARM VIR BEEF DRAW GRIP GUTS HEAD HORN IRON MAIN THEW BRAWN CRAFT ETHAN FIBER FIBRE FORCE HEART JUICE MIGHT NERVE POWER SINEW VIGOR ENERGY FOISON MAUGHT STARCH VIRTUE COURAGE STAMINA STHENIA CAPACITY FIRMNESS VALIDITY
(— OF ACID OR BASE) AVIDITY
(— OF ALE) STRIKE
(— OF CARD HAND) BODY
(— OF CHARACTER) GRISTLE
(— OF CURRENT) AMPERAGE
(— OF SOLUTION) TIRE TITER
(— OF SPIRITS) PROOF
(— OF TEA) DRAW
(— OF WILL) BACKBONE
(— OF WINE) SEVE

STRENGTHEN IMP ABLE BACK BIND FIRM FRAP HELP PROP SOUD STAY BRACE CLEAT FORCE SINEW STEEL THRAP TONIC TRUSS ANNEAL ASSURE DEEPEN ENDURE ENFIRM ENFORT GABION HARDEN INTEND MUNIFY MUNITE NEEDLE SETTLE STRING STRONG AFFORCE BUCKRAM COMFORT CONFIRM ENFORCE FASCINE FORTIFY NERVATE QUICKEN RAMPIRE SUPPORT THICKEN BUTTRESS ENERGIZE ENTRENCH HEIGHTEN ROBORATE

STRENGTHENED BULLED

STRENGTHENING ROBORANT

STRENGTHLESS DOWLESS

STRENUOUS HARD EAGER ARDUOUS WILLING VIGOROUS

STREPSIPTERON STYLOPS

STRESS HIT BRUNT ICTUS PINCH SHEAR ACCENT STRAIN THRONG CENTROID DOWNBEAT EMPHASIS
(— OF SOUND) LENGTH

STRESSED TONIC STRONG

STRETCH EKE LAG LIE RAX RUN BEAT DRAW LAST MAIN PASS RACK REAM ROLL SPAN TEND BOARD BURST FETCH RATCH RETCH SIGHT SPELL SWAGE VERGE EXTEND LENGTH SMOOTH STRAIN STRAKE STREEK DISPLAY DISTEND EXPANSE SPELDER ELONGATE STRAIGHT LENGTHEN
(— CLOTH) TENTER
(— INJURIOUSLY) SPRAIN
(— IRREGULARLY) TRAIL
(— LEATHER) DRAFT STAKE DRAUGHT
(— METAL) FORM
(— OF ARMS) FATHOM
(— OF GROUND) BRECK
(— OF INTERVALE) CARSE
(— OF LAND) SWALE COMMON GALLOP COMMONS
(— OF ROAD) SIGHT
(— OF SEA) CHOP
(— OF TIME) TIFF
(— OF WALL) CURTAIN
(— OF WATER) GLIDE LEVEL LOGIN FAIRWAY
(— OUT) GROW SPIN REACH STENT STRUT TWINE INTEND OUTLIE SPRAWL SPREAD SPRING DISTEND OUTSPAN PORTEND ELONGATE
(— THE NECK) CRANE
(GRASSY —) DRINN
(LEVEL —) LAWN

STRETCHED (— OUT) PORRECT PROJECT PROLATE ELONGATE EXTENDED
(TENSELY —) TAUT TORT STIFF

STRETCHER COT GURNEY LITTER ANGAREP TROLLEY ANGAREEB STRAINER

STREW BED SOW CLOT DUST LARD SPEW BESET STRAW STRAY STROW LITTER SPREAD BESTREW SCATTER SKINKLE SPARKLE
(— WITH BULLETS) SPRAY

STREWING SEME

STREWN DOTTED BESPRENT

STRIA CORD STRIOLA DRAGLINE STRIOLET

STRIATE VEIN

STRIATION STREAK STRIGA

STRICKEN STREAKED

STRICKER TIPPLER

STRICKLE SWEEP STRIKER

STRICT HARD TAUT TRUE CLOSE EXACT HARSH RIGID STARK STERN GIUSTO SEVERE STRAIT STRONG ASCETIC AUSTERE PRECISE DISTRICT RESTRICT RIGOROUS
(NOT —) LAX SCIOLTO

STRICTLY NARROW STRAIT CLOSELY PROPERLY

STRICTNESS RIGOR RIGIDITY RIGORISM SEVERITY

STRIDE SAIL STEP FLOAT SKELP SPANG STEND STRUT LAMPER STROAM STROKE STROME BESTRIDE POINTING STRIDDLE
(— LOFTILY) STALK
(— PURPOSEFULLY) SLING

STRIDENT HARD HARSH BRASSY GLASSY SHRILL RAUCOUS YELLING GRINDING

STRIDULATE PITTER

STRIFE TUG WAR WIN BATE FEUD HOLD PLEA BRIGE CHEST FLITE JEHAD JIHAD NOISE STOUR STROW STRUT STURT BARRAT DEBATE ESTRIF MUTINY STRIVE CONTEST DISCORD DISPUTE HURLING QUARREL CONFLICT CONTRAST DISPEACE STRUGGLE
(CIVIL —) STASIS

STRIGIL COMB SCRAPER

STRIKE GO BAT BOB BOP BOX BUM COB CUE DAD DUB GET HAB HIT JOB JOW LAM LAY PUG RAP ABRE BAFF BEAK BEAT BELT BILL BLAD BLIP BUFF BUMP CHAP CLUB COIN COPE COSH CUFF DING DINT DONG DUNT FALL FANG FIRK FLAP FLOG FRAP GIRD GOWF HACK HURT JOWL KILL KNEE LASH LILT LUSH MARK NAIL PAIK PLAT PUCK ROUT SLAM SLAP SLAT SLAY SLOG SLUG SOCK SPAR SPAT SWAP SWAT SWIP TAKE WHOP WIPE ANGLE BATON CATCH CHECK CHIME CHINK CLOUT CLUNK CRACK CRUNT DEVEL DOUSE DOWSE DRIVE DUNCH FETCH FILCH FILIP FLAIL KNOCK PANDY PASTE POKER POTCH SABER SKELP SKITE SLOSH SMACK SMITE SNICK SOUND SPANK SQUAP STAMP STEEK SWACK SWEEP SWIPE SWISH THROW WHALE WHANG ACOUPE AFFECT AFFRAP ATTAIN BATTER BOUNCE BUFFET COURSE DUNDER FETTLE FILLIP HAMMER INCUSE INCUTE KEEPER SLOUGH STOUSH STRICK STRIPE SWITCH THRASH WALLOP BEARING FLYFLAP IMPINGE KNUCKLE PERCUSS STRIKER TURNOUT WHAMPLE WILDCAT STOPPAGE STOPWORK STRICKLE
(— A WICKET) BREAK
(— ABOUT) FLOP
(— AGAINST) RAM BANG STUMP ASSAULT COLLIDE
(— AND REBOUND) CAROM
(— CRICKET BALL) EDGE
(— DOWN) LAY FALL SLAY WEND FLASH FLOOR AFFLICT SIDERATE
(— DUMB) DUMFOUND
(— FEET TOGETHER) HITCH
(— FORCIBLY) GET CLOUT DEVEL SLASH
(— GENTLY) PAT
(— GOLF BALL) HOOK DRIVE SCLAFF

(— HEAVILY) BASH DUNT FLOP SLUG CLUMP SLOUGH
(— IN CURLING) WICK
(— LIGHTLY) BOB DAB SPAT FLICK
(— OF LOCK) KEEPER STRIKER
(— ON HEAD) COP NOBBLE
(— OUT) FAN TAKE CROSS ELIDE CANCEL EXPUNGE OUTLASH EXCUDATE
(— REPEATEDLY) DRUM LICK
(— SHARPLY) CUT SNICK
(— SMARTLY) NAP RAP KNAP
(— TEETH TOGETHER) GNASH
(— TOGETHER) CLASH KNACK
(— UP) LILT YERK RAISE
(— VIOLENTLY) RIP BASH DING SOUSE BENSEL
(— WITH AMAZEMENT) CONFOUND
(— WITH BAT) DRIVE
(— WITH FEAR) ALARM ASTONISH
(— WITH FIST) PLUG NODDLE
(— WITH FOOT) KICK BUNCH SPURN STAMP
(— WITH HAMMER) CHAP JOWL MELL
(— WITH HORNS) BUNT BUTT HOOK
(— WITH SPEAR) STICK
(— WITH STICK) SQUAIL
(— WITH WHIP) JERK LASH QUIRK
(— WITH WONDER) SURPRISE
(BOWLING —S) DOUBLE
(HUNGER —) ENDURA
(LABOR —) STEEK STICK TURNOUT WALKOUT
(MINING —) TREND
(THREE —S) TURKEY

STRIKEBREAKER FINK BLACKLEG

STRIKER BATMAN DRUMMER TURNOUT PULSATOR

STRIKER-OUT SETTER

STRIKING FITTY FRESH SHOWY VIVID DARING SIGNAL STRONG SALIENT SKELPIN COLORFUL CONFLICT DRAMATIC KNOCKOUT SENSIBLE SPEAKING

STRING LAG BAND CORD FILE LACE MEAN PAIR SLIP TAPE TAUM BRAID BRIDE CHORD POINT SINEW SNEAD STRAP CORDON STRAND TREBLE MINIKIN LIGATURE RHAPSODY
(— OF BEADS) ROSARY CHAPLET NECKLACE
(— OF CASH) QUAN TIAO
(— OF DRUM) SNARE
(— OF FIDDLE) THARM
(— OF FLAGS) HOIST
(— OF LOCK) KEEPER
(— OF LYRE) TRITE
(— OF MUSICAL INSTRUMENT) WIRE CHORD DRONE CATLING MINIKIN
(— OF ONIONS) REEVE TRACE
(— OF RAILWAY CARS) SET
(— OF SUGAR CRYSTALS) COB
(— OF VEGETABLES) STRAP
(— OF VIOL) MEAN
(— TOBACCO) SEW
(BONNET —) BRIDE
(E —) QUINT
(LEADING —) BAND

(ORNAMENTAL —) CORDON
(SURGICAL —) LIGATURE
(VIOLIN —) THAIRM VIBRATOR
(WEAVING —) LEASH

STRING BEAN SNAP HARICOT SNAPPER

STRINGCOURSE LEDGE TABLE CORDON STRING

STRINGENT HARD RIGID SEVERE STRICT EXTREME

STRINGER BALK BAULK

STRINGHALTED CRAMPY

STRINGY ROPY WOOLY SINEWY THONGY WOOLLY GARGETY SINEWED

STRIP BAR LAG TAG BAND BARE BEAD BELT BEND BUSK DRIP FUSE GAGE GAIR HILD HUSK LIST MALL NAKE NUDE PEEL RAND ROLL SACK SHIM SKIN TIRR WELT CLEAN DRIVE EXUTE FILET FLAKE GAUGE GLEAN GUARD HARRY LABEL LINER LYNCH PANEL PLUME REEVE SHEAR SHRED SKELP SLIPE SPEEL SPOIL STRAP STROP STRUB SWATH UNGUM UNRIG BORDER BOXING BRIDGE COLLAR CULPON DENUDE DEVEST DIVEST FEELER FILLET FLEECE LIBBET MATRIX PANUNG SCROLL SPLINE STREAK STRIPE TARGET UNBARE UNBARK UNCASE BANDAGE BEREAVE CHANNEL DEPLUME DEPRIVE DESPOIL DISROBE FEATHER FLOUNCE LAMBEAU LANGUET NAILROD PINRAIL PLUNDER UNCLOAK UNCOVER UNDRESS BOOKMARK COSSETTE DISARRAY DISENDOW DISTRUSS FOOTBAND SEPARATE
(— A PLANT) SPRIG
(— BARK) PILL
(— BINDING STALKS TO WALL) TACK
(— BLUBBER FROM WHALE) FLENSE
(— EAR OF CORN) SILK
(— FOR DRAWING CURVED LINES) SPLINE
(— FOR GUIDING PLASTER) BEAD
(— FOR MAKING TUBE) SKELP
(— HANGING AROUND SKIRT) FLOUNCE
(— IN BASKETMAKING) INSIDES
(— IN BEEHIVE) STARTER
(— IN CANING) SPLENT SPLINT
(— IN TYPEWRITER) DRAWBAND
(— OF CANVAS) FOOTBAND
(— OF CLOTH) LIST PATA RIND GUARD BANNER DUTCHMAN
(— OF CORK) SPREADER
(— OF FABRIC) FLIPPER
(— OF FAT) FATBACK LARDOON
(— OF FIELD HOCKEY AREA) ALLEY
(— OF FUR) GROTZEN
(— OF GRASS) VERGE
(— OF HIDE) SPECK DEWLAP
(— OF LAND) BUTT LAND RAIK RAIN RAKE TANG BREAK CREEK SLANG SLIPE SPONG SCREED SELION STRAKE STRIPE FURLONG ISTHMUS

CORRIDOR SIDELING
(— OF LEATHER) LAY RAND WELT
APRON RANGE THONG BACKSTAY
(— OF LEAVES) TWIST
(— OF LINEN) SETON
(— OF MASONRY) ARCHBAND
(— OF OFFICE) BREAK
(— OF OSIER) SKEIN
(— OF PALM LEAF) CADJAN CAJANG
(— OF PASTRY) STRAW
(— OF PLANKING) APRON
(— OF PRAIRIE) COVE
(— OF PROVISIONS) FORAGE
(— OF RANK) DEGRADE
(— OF ROADWAY) LANE
(— OF RUBBER) CUSHION
(— OF TURF) PARKING
(— OF UNPLOWED LAND) GAIR
HADE HEADLAND
(— OF WATER) INLET
(— OF WOOD) LAG LAT LATH LIST
SHAW SLAT WELT CHINK CLEAT
STAVE BATTEN INWALE REEPER
REGLET FOOTING FURRING STICKER
TRACKER FOOTLING
(— OFF SKIN) CASE FLAY
(— OFF) TIRL FLIPE FLYPE SLIPE
(— ON FOLDING DOORS) ASTRAGAL
(— ON PRINTER'S GALLEY) LEDGE
(— ON SQUASH COURT) TELLTALE
(— ON TIRE) CHAFER
(— SEPARATING LINES OF TYPE)
LEAD REGLET
(CAMOUFLAGING —) GARLAND
(COMIC —) FUNNY
(CONSTRUCTION —S) LAGGING
(CORSET —) BUSK
(DEPENDENT —) LAMBEAU
(DIVIDING —) CLOISON
(HORSESHOE-SHAPED —) BAIL BALE
(IRON IN —S) NAILROD
(NARROW —) SEAM SLAT SLIP TAPE
REEVE STRAKE
(PAPER —) ORIHON
(PROJECTING —) FEATHER
(RAISED —) RIDGE
(STRENGTHENING —) BEND
(THATCHING —) LEDGER
STRIPE BAR RAY BEAD BEND LIST
PALE SLAT WALE WEAL WELT ZONE
FLECK PLAGA STRIA STRIP SWATH
VITTA WHEAL BORDER CLAVUS
COTICE FRENUM LADDER RIBBON
STRAKE STREAK STREAM COTTISE
SPRAING MUSTACHE TRAVERSE
(— OF CHEVRON) ARC
(— OF COLOR ON CHEEK) FRENUM
FRAENUM
(— ON ANIMAL'S FACE) SNIP BLAZE
(— ON FABRIC) CROSSBAR
(— ON MILITARY SLEEVE) SLASH
(ENCIRCLING —) ZONE
(PURPLE —) CLAVUS
(SET OF —S) BAR
STRIPED BANDY PALED PIRNY
RAWED RAYED ROWED WALED
ZONED BARRED CORDED LISTED
PIRNED BROCKED TIGROID VITTATE
FASCIATE STRIPPED

STRIPED BASS ROCKFISH SERRANID
STRIPED MAPLE DOGWOOD
STRIPING HAIRLINE
STRIPLIGHT BORDER
STRIPLING LAD SLIP STIRRA
YONKER SPAUGHT YOUNKER
SKIPJACK SPRINGAL
STRIPPED BARE NUDE NAKED
HUSKED PICKED PLUMED UNPEELED
STRIPPER STEMMER SPRIGGER
STRIPPING STROKINGS
(PL.) JIBBINGS
STRIPTEASER STRIPPER ECDYSIAST
STRIVE AIM HIE TEW TRY TUG DEAL
FEND PAIN TOIL WORK BANDY
DRIVE EXERT FIGHT FORCE LABOR
PRESS BUCKLE BUFFET DEBATE
INTEND PINGLE STRAIN STRIKE
AGONIZE CONTEND CONTEST
DISPUTE ENFORCE SCUFFLE
CONTRAST ENDEAVOR PURCHASE
STRUGGLE
(— AFTER) SEEK FOLLOW CANVASS
(— FOR SUPERIORITY) VIE
(— IN OPPOSITION) RIVAL CONTEND
(— TO EQUAL) EMULATE
(— TO OVERTAKE) ENSUE
STRIVING NISUS HORMIC STRIFT
CONATUS CONATION
STRIX SYRNIUM
STROBILE BUR BELL BURR CHAT
CONE BRUSH
STROKE BAT COY CUT DAB FIT JOW
ODD PAT PET POP RUB BAFF BEAT
BLOW CHAP CHOP CLAP COUP
DASH DENT DING DINT DIRD DRAW
DUNT EDGE FIRK FLAP FLEG FLIP
FLOP FUNG GOWF HURT JERK JOWL
KERF LASH LICK NACK PAIK PEAL
PECK SHOT SMIT SWAP TILT TIRE
TUCK WELT WHAP WIPE BRUSH
CHASE DOUSE DOWSE DRAFT
FLACK FLICK FORCE HATCH ICTUS
MINIM PANDY PULSE SHOCK SLASH
SLING SLIVE SLOSH STRIP SWEEP
SWING SWIPE THROW TRAIT TRICE
WHACK CARESS CENTER FONDLE
FOOZLE GENTLE GLANCE PLAGUE
PLUNGE SMOOTH STRAIK STRIKE
STRIKE STRIPE DRAUGHT OUTLASH
SOLIDUS VIRGULE APOPLEXY
DRUMBEAT FOREHAND INSTROKE
SCORCHER
(— IN PAINTING) HAND
(— IN PENMANSHIP) MINIM
(— IN TENNIS) LET LOB BOAST
CHASE SMASH BRICOLE BACKHAND
FOREHAND
(— OF A LETTER) DUCT STEM SERIF
CROSSBAR
(— OF BAD FORTUNE) CLAP
(— OF BELL) JOW BELL JOWL
KNELL TELLER
(— OF FORTUNE) CAST BREAK
FELICITY
(— OF LUCK) HIT FLUKE STRIKE
TURNUP CAPTION
(— OF SCYTHE) SWATH SWATHE
(— OF SHEARS) SNIP

(— OF WIT) FLIRT
(— OF WORK) BAT CHAR
(— ON THE PALM) LOOFIE
(BILLIARDS —) SPOT STUN FLUKE
FORCE MASSE HAZARD
(CONNECTING —) LIGATURE
(CRICKET —) CUT GLANCE
(CUTTING —) GIRD
(DOUBLE SPINNING —) DRAW
(DRUM —) DRAG
(GOLF —) ODD BAFF BISK HOOK
LIKE SLICE BISQUE FOOZLE SCLAFF
APPROACH
(HOCKEY —) JOB SCOOP
(JERKY —) STAB
(LIGHTNING —) BOLT
(MEDICAL —) ICTUS APOPLEXY
(ORNAMENTAL —) FLOURISH
(QUICK —) FLIP
(SKATING —) EDGE MOHAWK
CHOCTAW
(SMART —) FIRK
(SOOTHING —) COY
(SWIMMING —) CRAWL
(SWINGING —) HEW
(SWORD —) MONTANTO
STROLL JET IDLE ROAM ROVE
ANTER JAUNT RANGE STRAY TRAIK
BUMMEL DACKER DANDER GANDER
LOUNGE PALMER RAMBLE SOODLE
STROAM STROME WANDER
SAUNTER TURNOUT SPATIATE
STRAVAGE
STROLLER SULKY TRAMP SHULER
SHUILER VAGRANT BOHEMIAN
STROLLING FLANERIE FUGITIVE
STROMA ECOID OECOID
STRONG FAT FIT HOT FELL FERE
FIRM FORT HALE HANG HARD HIGH
IRON KEEN RANK SURE TRIG TRIM
ACRID BONNY FORCY FRECK FRESH
HARDY HEAVY HOGEN HUSKY JOLLY
LUSTY NAPPY NERVY ORPED PITHY
SHARP SMART SOLID SOUND STARK
STEER STERN STIFF STOUR STOUT
SWITH THEWY VALID VIVID WIGHT
YAULD ARDENT BRAWNY BUCKRA
BUNKUM FEIRIE FIERCE MIGHTY
POTENT PRETTY ROBUST RUGGED
SECURE SEVERE SINEWY STABLE
STANCH STARCH STURDY WIELDY
BOARDLY BUIRDLY DOUGHTY
DURABLE EXALTED FECKFUL
HUFFCAP HUMMING INTENSE
LUSTFUL NERVOUS SKOOKUM
STHENIC ATHLETIC BIDDABLE
MUSCULAR REVERENT ROBOREAN
SPANKING STALWART STIFFISH
VIGOROUS
STRONGBOX PETE COFFER
DEEDBOX
STRONGEST EXTREME
STRONGHOLD HOLD KEEP PIECE
PLACE TOWER CASTLE WARDER
CITADEL KREMLIN FASTHOLD
FASTNESS FORTRESS FRONTIER
STRENGTH
STRONGLY BUT SAD BADLY SWITH
FIRMLY STRONG DURABLY FRESHLY

HEFTILY SOLIDLY STITHLY STOUTLY
HEARTILY
STRONG-SCENTED HIGH RANK
STRONG-SMELLING FOXY
STROP RIP STRAP
STROPHE ALCAIC LAISSE STANZA
SAPPHIC
STROPHIUS (FATHER OF —)
CRISSUS
(SON OF —) PYLADES
STRUCK (— SHARPLY) SMITTEN
(— WITH AMAZEMENT) AGHAST
STRUCTURAL ANATOMIC TECTONIC
(— UNIT) IDANT
STRUCTURE CAGE FALX FORM
MAKE ANNEX BOOTH CABIN FLOAT
FRAME GETUP HOUSE KIOSK PEGMA
SETUP SHAPE STOCK BRIDGE
CAGEOT FABRIC GANTRY GIRDER
ISOGEN KELSON TIMBER COTTAGE
EDIFICE FAIRING FEATURE GATEWAY
GESTALT KEELSON MANSION
NURAGHE MOUNTURE OUTCAST PAGEANT
STADIUM TURNOUT ZEUGITE
AEDICULA AIRCRAFT AIRFRAME
BUILDING BUTTRESS CRIBWORK
DOMATIUM ENDOCONE ESCORIAL
HEADWORK MOUNTURE NEOMORPH
SKELETON STANDARD
(— BUILT IN WATER) PIER
(— CONTAINING KILN) HOVEL
(— EXTENDED INTO SEA) JETTY
(— FOR PIGEONS) COTE
(— FRAMING SHIP) KEELSON
(— OF CARTRIDGE) ANVIL
(— OF PRETENSION) PERRON
(— ON ROOF) CUPOLA FEMERELL
(— ON SHIP) BLISTER
(— ON STEAMER) TEXAS
(— PRODUCING SMOOTH OUTLINE)
FAIRING
(— SHELTERING INSECTS)
DOMATIUM
**(— SUPPORTING AIRSHIP
PROPELLER)** PYLON
(— WITHIN SHELL) ENDOCONE
(ANATOMICAL —) BUD APRON
CARINA CRESCENT
(ANTICLINAL —) SWELL
(ARCHED —) FORNIX
(BODILY —) FRAME PHYSIQUE
(BRICK —) KANG HOVEL
(BRISTLELIKE —) ARISTA
(BRONZE AGE —) HENGE
(CABINLIKE —) CABANA
(CLIMBING —) LADDER
(COMPLEX —) EMBOLUS
(CONELIKE —) PYRAMID
(CONICAL —) BULLET
(CROWNLIKE —) CORONA
(CYLINDRICAL —) SILO
(DEADENING —) BAFFLE
(DEFENSIVE —) CAT
(FORTIFIED —) CAVALIER
(GENERAL —) GETUP
(GEOLOGICAL —) CAMBER
(HIGH —) TOWER
(HOLLOW —) SHELL
(KNEE-LIKE —) GENU

(LENS-SHAPED —) LENTOID
(LOFTY —) BABEL STEEPLE
(LOGICAL —) EIDOS
(ORGANIZED —) BULK
(ORIENTAL STORIED —) PAGODA
(ORNAMENTAL —) KIOSK
(PLANT —) DISC DISK
(POINTED —) BEAK
(PUEBLO —) KIVA
(RAISED —) CIMBORIO
(RAMSHACKLE —) COOP
(RINGLIKE —) ANNULUS
(RUDE STONE —S) SPECCHIE
(SACRIFICIAL —) ALTAR
(SENTENCE —) SYNTAX
(SHELTERING —) COT
(SICKLE-SHAPED —) FALX
(SLENDER —) HAIR
(STONE —) TAULA
(TEMPORARY —) HUT
(THEATER —) SKENE
(UNDERLYING —) BOTTOM
(UNSTABLE —) COBHOUSE
(WATERTIGHT —) CAMEL
(WHITE —) ALBEDO
STRUGGLE IT TEW TUG VIE WIN
AGON COPE DEAL FEND FICK FRAB
GAME PULL TAVE TOIL FIGHT FLING
HEAVE LABOR STRAY SWORD
TEAVE TWEIL WORRY WRELE
BATTLE BUCKLE BUFFET BUSTLE
COMBAT EFFORT HASSLE JOSTLE
JUSTLE PINGLE RELUCT SEESAW
SPRAWL SPRUNT STIVER STRIFE
STRIVE TERVEE TUSSLE WARSLE
WIDDLE AGONIZE CLAMBER
CONTEND CONTEST DISPUTE
FLOUNCE GRAPPLE SCUFFLE
TUILYIE WARFARE WAUCHLE
WRESTLE CONFLICT ENDEAVOR
FLOUNDER SCRAFFLE SCRAMBLE
SLUGFEST SPRANGLE SPRATTLE
(— ALONG) HOBBLE
(— CONVULSIVELY) SPRAWL
(— FOR LARGESS) SCAMBLE
(— FORTH) ELUCTATE
(— TO GAIN FOOTING) SCRABBLE
SPROTTLE
(AGONIZED —) THROE
(CONFUSED —) MUSS
(DEATH —) AGONY
(HAND-TO-HAND —) GRAPPLE
(HAPHAZARD —) SCUFFLE
(SPIRITUAL —) PENIEL
(UNCEREMONIOUS —) SCRAMBLE
STRUGGLER LAOCOON
STRUM THRUM
STRUMA GOITER GOITRE
STRUMPET BRIM PUNK TRULL
WENCH WHORE BLOWEN BULKER
STIVER TOMBOY TOMRIG COCOTTE
SUCCUBA DOLLYMOP PUNKLING
SUCCUBUS VENTURER
(WORN-OUT —) HARRIDAN
STRUT JET BRAG COCK POMP SPUR
CORSO MAJOR PRINK SWANK
SASHAY STROKE STROOT STRUNT
NAUNTLE PEACOCK STEMPLE
SWAGGER TRANSOM

STRUTTER HAM
STRUTTING COCKING
STUB BUTT SNAG SPUD STOB STUD
CHECK ERGOT GUARD HINGE
STUMP SPRUNT
STUBBLE BUN ETCH MANE SHACK
ARRISH EDDISH STOVER STUMPS
EEGRASS GRATTEN STIBBLE
STUBBORN SOT ROWDY RUSTY
STIFF STOUT STUNT THRAW TOUGH
MULISH STURDY THWART BULLDOG
PEEVISH PIGGISH RESTIVE
WAYWARD WILLFUL OBDURATE
PERVERSE STUNKARD THRAWART
STUBBORNNESS STOMACH
ADAMANCY
STUBBY STUB CUTTY SQUAT
STOCKY STUMPY STUBBED
STUCCO ALBARIUM
STUCK FAST MASHED STICKIT
STOODED
STUCK-UP BUG FROSTED
STUD SET BOLT BOSS KNOP KNOT
LNOB NAIL RACE SLUG SPOT BESET
BULLA CLOUT HARAS JOIST WRIST
ASHLAR ENSTAR INSTAR STOOTH
STRING CONTACT POTENCE
QUARTER STUDDLE PUNCHEON
STANDARD STUDDERY
(— FARM) HARAS
(— IN BOOT SOLE) SLUG
(— IN WATCH) POTENCE
(— SHOES) HOBNAIL
(— WITH NAILS) CLOUT
(INTERMEDIATE —) PUNCHEON
(ORNAMENTED —) AGLET AIGLET
STUDDED BOSSY BILLETY STELLED
BILLETTE
STUDDLE POST ROIL
STUDENT BOY DIG WIT COED PLUG
PREP SMUG SOPH AGGIE BAHUR
FUCHS GRIND MEDIC PUPIL SIZAR
SPOON BOCHER BURSAR BURSCH
INTERN JUNIOR JURIST MEDICO
OPTIME PRIMAR PRIMER PUISNE
SCOLOG SENIOR ADVISEE CLASSIC
DANTEAN EDUCAND ETONIAN
FAILURE GOLIARD GRECIAN
INTERNE INTRANT LEARNER
MOOTMAN OPPIDAN PASSMAN
PHARMIC PLUGGER SCHOLAR
STUDIER TEMPLAR THEOLOG
BOTANIST CABALIST COLLEGER
DEMOTIST DISCIPLE EDUCATOR
FEMINIST HOMERIST HOSTELER
ISLAMIST PREMEDIC REPEATER
SECONDAR SUBSIZAR TRANSFER
(— IN TALMUDIC ACADEMY) BAHUR
(— LAST IN CLASS) SPOON
(— OF LOW RANK) TERNAR TERNER
(— WHO LIVES IN TOWN) OPPIDAN
(1ST-YEAR —) FUCHS
(3RD-YEAR —) JUNIOR TERTIAN
(ABNORMALLY ABSORBED —) SAP
(DAY —) EXTERN EXTERNE
(DIVINITY —) STIBBLER
(DRUDGING —) PLUG
(ENGLISH SCHOOL —) BLUE SWOT
ETONIAN SWOTTER

(GRADUATE —) FELLOW
(LAW —) PUNEE JURIST LEGIST
PUISNE TEMPLAR STAGIARY
(MILITARY —) CADET
(NON-COLLEGIATE —) TOSHER
(PLODDING —) DIG SMUG
(WANDERING —) GOLIARD
(PL.) GOWN CLASS HOUSE SEMINAR
STUDIED COOL STUDIOUS
STUDIO LOT SHOT ATELIER
BOTTEGA GALLERY
STUDIOUS BOOKY BOOKISH
CLERKLY DILIGENT SEDULOUS
STUDY CON BEAT BONE BOOK CASE
MUZZ SIFT STUD GRIND ESTUDY
EXAMEN LESSON MUSEUM SCOLEY
SURVEY ABBOZZO ACCOUNT
ANALYZE CANVASS CROQUIS
POCHADE REVOLVE SANCTUM
ANALYSIS BOOKWORK CONSIDER
EXERCISE MEDITATE SCRUTINY
TYPOLOGY
(— HARD) DIG MUG BONE SMUG
STEW SWOT
(— OF PUNISHMENT) PENOLOGY
(— OF SACRED EDIFICES) NAOLOGY
(— OF SNOW AND ICE) CRYOLOGY
(— UNDER PRESSURE) CRAM
(ART —) ABBOZZO CROQUIS
POCHADE
(CLAY —) BOZZETTO
(MUSICAL —) ETUDE
(PRELIMINARY —) SKETCH
(UNINTERESTING —) GRIND
STUFF PAD RAM WAD CRAM GAUM
GEAR PANG STOP TACK TUCK
WHAT CROWD DUROY FARCE
FORCE KEDGE METAL PASTE SQUAB
TRADE FABRIC GRAITH KIBOSH
MATTER PAUNCH STEEVE STODGE
TACKLE TIMBER BOMBARD
BOMBAST DRUGGET ELEMENT
ENFARCE DIAPHANE MARINATE
MATERIAL SPLUTTER WHIPPING
(— AND NONSENSE) HAVERS
PICKLE PIFFLE
(— FILLET OF VEAL) BOMBARD
(— FULL) STODGE
(— OF POOR QUALITY SILK) RASH
(— ONESELF) MAST
(— POULTRY) FARCE MARINATE
(— WITH DRESSING) QUILT
(COTTON —) CALICO
(HOUSEHOLD —) GEAR
(INFERIOR —) MOCKADO
(SILKEN —) TARS TARSE DIAPHANE
(STICKY —) GOOK
(THIN —) CRAPE
(THIN SILK —) LOVE
(WISHY-WASHY —) BLASH
(WOOLEN —) DUROY TWILLY
DRUGGET
(WORTHLESS —) GEAR HOGWASH
STUFFED PANG TRIG BLOAT FARCI
STODGY BLOATED BOMBAST
STUFFING PAD TAR FARCE STECH
STUFF BOMBAST FARCING SAWDUST
STUFFAGE
(— FOR MATTRESS) PULU

STUFFY CLOSE FUBBY FUBSY FUGGY
STIVY WOOLY WOOLLY FROUSTY
STULTIFY SOT PUPPIFY
STUMBLE CHIP FALL HAMP PECK
STOT TRIP HAMEL LURCH SPURN
STOIT STUMP BUMBLE CHANCE
FALTER HALPER HAMBLE HAPPEN
LUMPER OFFEND STEVEL TUMBLE
WAGGER BLUNDER FOUNDER
SCAMBLE SNAPPER STAMMER
STAMPLE STOITER STOTTER
STUMMER FLOUNDER THRUMBLE
STUMBLING HACK HURTING
OFFENCE OFFENSE
STUMP CAG JOB SET BUTT DOCK
GRUB LUMP MORE RUNT SNAG
STAB STAM STOB STUB STUD
CHUNK SCRAB STICK STOCK STOMP
STOOL STOOP STOWL DOTARD
NUBBIN SCRUNT SPRONG STOVEN
WICKET DODDARD RAMPICK
RAMPIKE SLEEPER STUMMEL
BALDHEAD HUSTINGS STUBBLES
(— AND ROOT) MOCK
(— OF TAIL) STRUNT
(CIGAR —) TOPPER
(CRICKET —) STICKS
(DEAD —) RUNT
(TREE —) MOCK STOW STOCK
STOOP ZUCHE DOTARD NUBBIN
STOVEN DODDARD
(WALNUT —) BUTT
STUMPY SNUB BUNTY SNUBBED
STUN DIN BOWL DAZE DAUNT DAVER
DEAVE DOVER DOZEN DROWN
STONY ASTONY BEDAZE BENUMB
DEADEN DEAFEN NOBBLE STOUND
WITHER ASTOUND DAMMISH
SANDBAG SILENCE STUPEFY
STUPEND ASTONISH
(— BY A SHOT) CREASE
STUNNED SILLY STUPENT ASTONIED
STUNNER KNOCKER THUMPER
TRIMMER
STUNNING CRASHING SHOCKING
STUNT GAG KIP BLAST CANOE
CROWL DWARF STINT STOCK
BARANI BARONI CRADDY DOLPHIN
BACKBEND CATALINA CRUCIFIX
PORPOISE SUPPRESS
(SWIMMING —) SHARK SPIRAL
STUNTED URLED GRUBBY RUNTISH
SCROGGY SCRUBBY SCRUFFY
SCRUNTY
STUPA TOPE CHORTEN
STUPEFACTION STOUND STUPOR
STUPEFIED MAD DAMP DAZED
MAZED SILLY BEMAZED DONNERT
DOZENED DOZZLED STUPENT
BESOTTED DATELESS MINDLESS
STUPEFIER OPIUM
STUPEFY FOX BAZE DAMP DAZE
DOZE DRUG DULL GOOF MAZE
STUN BESOT DAUNT DAVER DEAVE
DIZZY DOZEN SHEND SMOKE STONY
ASTONE ASWEVE BENUMB DUDDLE
FUDDLE MUDDLE STOUND ASTOUND
CONFUSE FORDULL SLUMBER
SMNIATE STUPEND ASTONISH

BEFUDDLE BEWILDER CONFOUND
MORPHINE SOPORATE
STUPEFYING STONY
STUPENDOUS GREAT IMMENSE
ENORMOUS
STUPID FAT BETE DOWF DULL DUMB
DUNT FOOL HAZY LEWD NICE NUMB
SLOW BLUNT BRUTE CRASS DENSE
DUNNY GLAKY GOOSY GROSS
HEAVY INERT MOSSY MUZZY SILLY
THICK ASSISH BARREN CUCKOO
DAWKIN DOITED DROWSY DUMMEL
HEBETE LOGGER OBTUSE OPAQUE
SIMPLE STOLID STULTY STURDY
SUMPHY URLUCH WOODEN ASININE
BRUTISH CHUCKLE DOLTISH
DOWFART DUFFING DUMPISH
FATUOUS FOOLISH FOPPISH
GAWKISH GLAIKIT GULLISH INSULSE
LUMPISH LURDANE PEAKISH
PINHEAD PROSAIC SOTTISH TAIVERT
TOMFOOL VACUOUS WITLESS
ANSERINE BAYARDLY BESOTTED
BLOCKISH BOEOTIAN CLODDISH
DONNERED DUNCICAL FOOTLESS
GAUMLESS HEADLESS IMBECILE
STOCKISH
(— PERSON) HOIT JUKES SUMPH
LUMMOX TUMFIE KALLIKAK
STUPIDITY BETISE BOBBERY
DENSITY DUNCERY FATUITY
DULLNESS DUMBNESS HEBETUDE
STUPOR FOG SOG DAMP DOTE
SOPOR SWARF STOUND TRANCE
NARCOMA LETHARGY NARCOSIS
STURDILY BUFF TOUGH
STURDY GID BUFF DUNT RUDE TALL
THRO BURLY CRANK FELON HARDY
HUSKY LUSTY SOLID SOUND STARK
STERN STIFF STOUT VAUDY WALLY
FEERIE PLUGGY ROBUST RUGGED
RUSTIC SQUARE STABLE STEADY
STEEVE STOCKY STRONG STUGGY
VIRILE FECKFUL UPRIGHT VALIANT
STALWART STUBBORN VIGOROUS
YEOMANLY
STURGEON HUSO ELOPS BELUGA
GANOID MAMMOSE STERLET
STUTTER FAM BUFF HACK MANT
STOT STUT GANCH FAMBLE HABBER
HABBLE STAMMER
STUTTERER RATTLER
STUTTERING TRAULISM
STY PEN QUAT STYE WEST FRANK
PIGPEN STITHE HORDEOLUM
STYLE AIR CUT DUB PEN SAY TON
WAY CHIC FACE FORM GARB KIND
MODE MOLD NAME PILE RATE TWIG
VEIN GENRE GETUP GUISE SHAPE
STATE SWANK TASTE FESCUE
FORMAT GNOMON GOTHIC PHRASE
STEELE STYLUS UMBONE COSTUME
DIALECT DICTION FASHION INSTYLE
QUALITY EQUIPAGE LANGUAGE
MARINISM NARRANTE PULLBACK
(— OF ARCHITECTURE) ORDER
DRAVIDA GEORGIAN
(— OF COOKING) CUISINE
(— OF DRESS) GUISE

(— **OF GEM SETTING**) BOX
(— **OF HANDWRITING**) CHANCERY
SCRIPTION
(— **OF HAT**) BLOCK
(— **OF MOUNTING**) SETTING
(— **OF MUSIC**) BOOGIE
(— **OF PAINTING**) GENRE
(— **OF PENMANSHIP**) HAND
(— **OF SPEAKING**) ADDRESS
(**AFFECTED** —) EUPHUISM
(**ARTISTIC** —) GUSTO GOTHIC
ARTIFICE DANDYISM
(**BOOKBINDING** —) ALDINE MAIOLI
MAJOLI FANFARE GROLIER
ETRUSCAN HARLEIAN ROXBURGH
(**CUSTOMARY** —) GATE
(**DISTINCTIVE** —) CLOTHES
(**FAVORED** —) GROOVE
(**HAIR** —) CROP TETE
(**INFLATED** —) FUSTIAN
(**LATEST** —) KICK
(**PRETENTIOUS** —) BOMBAST
(**PROPER** —) WEAR
(**THEATRICAL** —) LYCEUM
STYLET SPEAR STILET STYLUS
TROCAR MANDRIN STILETTE
STYLIDIUM CANDOLEA
STYLISH CHIC DOSS DOGGY NIFTY
NOBBY SASSY SHARP SMART
SWELL TIPPY TOPPY CHEESY
CLASSY DAPPER FLOSSY JAUNTY
SWANKY TONISH DASHING DOGGISH
GENTEEL KNOWING SWAGGER
TOFFISH
STYLOID BELONOID
STYLUS GAD PEN STYLE CUTTER
GREFFE TRACER HARPAGO POINTEL
PYROPEN
STYPTIC ALUM AMADOU MATICO
BAROMETZ STANCHER
STYRENE STYROL CINNAMOL
STYX (**FATHER OF** —) OCEANUS
(**HUSBAND OF** —) PALLAS
(**MOTHER OF** —) TETHYS
SUAEDA DONDIA
SUAN PAN SOROBAN
SUAVE OILY SMUG SOFT BLAND
SOAPY SVELT GLOSSY SILKEN
SMOOTH FULSOME UNCTUOUS
SUAVELY CREAMILY
SUAVITY URBANITY
SUB GRASS
SUBALTERN WART
SUBBASE PLINTH
SUBCINCTORIUM BALTEUS
BALTHEUS
SUBCLASS GENDER BRYALES
CESTODA CYCLIAE DIGENEA
SPECIES AMOEBAEA ANAPSIDA
CESTODES COPEPODA GANOIDEI
SELACHII
SUBCUTANEOUS DEEP
SUBDEACON MINISTER
SUBDIVIDE CARVE MINCE
SUBDIVISION DEN OBE SEX BEAT
CAZA DHER HAPU ITEM TASU
BUNDA CORPS CURIA DEKAN DHERI
FERAE FORTY HSIEN IOWAN NAHIE
OKRUG PHYLE SITIO STAGE TALUK

TARAF TURMA UINTA ALBIAN
ARENIG BANNER BUREAU CERCLE
CIRCLE COHORT COLUMN DAKOTA
DANIAN DOGGER FACIES GUELPH
HEMERA IMBREX LENGTH LUDLOW
MARKAZ NAHIYE OBLAST ONEIDA
SANJAK SECTOR SERIAL SHIRAZ
STRAIN SUBAGE TAHSIL TASSOO
TEHSIL BUKEYEI CENTURY
CHEMUNG CHIRIPA COCHITI
COMARCA ECOTYPE ELEMENT
EPARCHY EPISODE GENESEE
MONTANA PHRATRY RONDOUT
SASTEAN SECTION SEEDBED
SUBAREA SUBLINE SUBPLAT
SUBPLOT SUBRACE SUBZONE
SUPPORT TRENTON TRINITY
WASATCH WASHITA WENLOCK
WICHITA BANOVINA DISTRICT
DIVISION DJAGATAY ENDBRAIN
FLOTILLA GUBERNIA LOCATION
MONTEREY NAUCRARY PRECINCT
STOCKTON SUBCASTE SUBORDER
SUBSTAGE SUBTRIBE TOWNSHIP
(— **OF SCOUTS**) CREW
(**EGYPTIAN** —) KISM
SUBDOMINANT FOURTH
SUBDUE ADAW BEAT BEND QUAY
TAME ACCOY ALLAY AMATE CHARM
CRUSH DAUNT DOMPT QUAIL
QUASH QUELL SOBER STILL
ADAUNT BRIDLE CHASTE DEBELL
DISMAY EVINCE GENTLE MASTER
QUENCH REDUCE SUBACT SUBMIT
UNWILD ABANDON AFFAITE
CAPTURE CHASTEN CONQUER
REPRESS REPRIME SUCCUMB
CONVINCE OVERCOME SUPPEDIT
SUPPRESS SURMOUNT VANQUISH
SUBDUED MAK SOFT TAME SOBER
STILL UNDER BROKEN CHASTE
GENTLE ASHAMED SUBMISS
SOURDINE
SUBFAMILY KHOISAN CUSHITIC
ACRAEINAE
SUBGROUP BAND FAMILY
SUBHEAD BOXHEAD SIDEHEAD
SUBIMAGO DUN
SUBINDEX SUFFIX
SUBIRRIGATE SUB SUBWATER
SUBIRRIGATION SUBBING
SUBJECT DUX PUT ABLE ALLY BODY
BONE ITEM TEXT HOBBY PLACE
STOOP STUDY TESTO THEMA
THEME TOPIC GROUND IMPOSE
LIABLE PATHIC REDUCE SACOPE
SUBDIT SUBMIT THRALL VASSAL
CITIZEN FEODARY FEUDARY
OBVIOUS SERVILE ELECTIVE
INCIDENT INFERIOR OBEDIENT
OCCASION SENTENCE SUBJUGAL
(— **OF DISCOURSE**) NOUN
(— **OF FUGUE**) GUIDA
(— **OF PROPOSITION**) EXTREME
(— **TO ABUSE**) REVILE
(— **TO ARGUMENT**) MOOT
(— **TO BAD TEMPER**) MOODY
(— **TO CHANGE**) MUTABLE FUGITIVE
(— **TO CRITICISM**) SCOURGE

(— **TO FATE**) FIE
(— **TO PERCOLATION**) DISPLACE
(— **TO SOME ACTION**) TREAT
(**CONTROVERTED** —) ISSUE
(**LOYAL** —) LIEGE
(PL.) FOLK
SUBJECTION SLAVERY SERVITUS
THIRLING
SUBJECTIVE IMMANENT INSEEING
INTERNAL PECTORAL EPISTEMIC
SUBJUGATION BONDAGE
SERVITUDE
SUBKINGDOM PHYLUM ANNULOSA
CHORDATA
SUBLEADER HEADMAN
SUBLEASE FARMOUT SUBTACK
SUBLET JOB SUBSET CONACRE
SUBLEASE
SUBLIME FUME GRAND LOFTY
NOBLE REFINE SOLEMN WINGED
ELEVATO EXALTED EMPYREAL
EMPYREAN MAGNIFIC MAJESTIC
SERAPHIC SPLENDID
(— **IN STYLE**) MILTONIC
SUBLIMITY GRANDEUR
SUBLUNARY EARTHLY
SUBMARINE SUB BOAT DIVER FRITZ
GUPPY SUBSEA PIGBOAT TIDDLER
SUBMEDIANT SIXTH
SUBMERGE BOG DIP BURY DIVE
DUNK HIDE SINK SOAK TAKE
DROWN SOUSE SWAMP WHELM
DELUGE DRENCH ENGULF DEMERGE
IMPLUNGE INUNDATE SUBMERSE
SURROUND
SUBMERGENCE ONLAP
SUBMISSION VAIL PATIENCE
SUBMISSIVE MEEK BUXOM DEMISS
DOCILE DUTIFUL PASSIVE SERVILE
SLAVISH SUBJECT SUBMISS
UNERECT OBEDIENT RESIGNED
YIELDING
(— **TO WIFE**) UXORIOUS
SUBMISSIVENESS SLAVERY
SUBMIT BOW EAT ABOW BEND CAVE
LEAN OBEY TAKE VAIL AVALE
DEFER HIELD STAND STOOP YIELD
ASSENT DELATE RESIGN CONSIGN
KNUCKLE SUBJECT SUBMUSE
SUCCUMB TRUCKLE
(— **FOR CONSIDERATION**) REMIT
(— **TAMELY**) EAT
(— **TO**) ABIDE STAND SUFFER
SUBNORMAL SICK ABNORMAL
SUBORDER LARI ALCAE APODA
APODI GALLI GRUES ARDEAE
COHORT CUCULI SAURIA AGLOSSA
ANSERES ARCACEA ASCONES
CORACII COSTATA SARCURA
SYCONES ACRASIDA ADEPHAGA
BATOIDEI COLUMBAE CORACIAE
CURSORIA ENOPLINA EUSUCHIA
FALCONES FREGATAE SELACHII
SUBORDINARY ENDORSE ROUNDEL
SUBORDINATE SUB SINK PETTY
SCRUB UNDER EXEMPT MINION
PUISNE SECOND YEOMAN SERVANT
SERVILE SUBJECT HENCHMAN
INFERIOR MYRMIDON PARERGAL

POSTPONE SERVIENT
SUBORN HAVE BRIBE
SUBOVAL PETALOID
SUBPHYLUM EUCHORDA
SUBPOENA SUMMONS
SUBRACE STOCK
SUBSCRIBE SIGN ASSENT ASCRIBE
CONSIGN SUBSIGN
SUBSCRIBER RAILBIRD
SUBSCRIPT INFERIOR
SUBSEQUENT AFTER LATER
FUTURE PUISNE ENSUING POSTNATE
SUBSEQUENTLY SO LATER SINCE
SUBSERVIENT OILY VASSAL
DUTEOUS SERVILE SLAVISH
OFFICIAL
SUBSHRUB STOCK GUAYULE
COLUMNEA
SUBSIDE DIE EBB LAY LIE CALM
FALL LULL SILE SINK VAIL ABATE
ALLAY LAPSE RESIDE SETTLE
ASSUAGE RELAPSE UNSWELL
WITHDRAW
SUBSIDENCE FALL SETTLING
SUBSIDIARY CHILD DONKEY
SUBSIDY
SUBSIDIZE BONUS
SUBSIDY AID BONUS BOUNTY
POUNDAGE
SUBSILICIC BASIC
SUBSIST BE LIVE RELY
SUBSISTENCE BEING LIVING
SUBSISTENT ENTITY ,
SUBSOIL PAN LECK SOLE SHRAVE
RATCHEL
SUBSTAGE CARY GUNZ IOWAN
MANKATO STADIAL TAZEWELL
SUBSTANCE FAT SUM BODY CORE
GIST GITE TACK WHAT ADROP
AGENT ALLOY ARCHE FOMES
GREAT KEEST METAL MOYEN OUSIA
PROOF SENSE STUFF THING
BOTTOM GADUIN GETTER IMPORT
MATTER STAPLE WEALTH AEROSOL
AGAROID ANTIGEN COLICIN
COLLOID CONTENT ELEIDIN
EMANIUM ERGUSIA ESSENCE
HYALINE MEANING PURPORT
REAGENT SUBJECT SUPTION
ACCEPTOR ADDITIVE ADHESIVE
ALLERGEN AMBEROID ANTIFOAM
BASSORIN HARDNESS MATERIAL
(— CAPABLE OF EXPANSION)
DILATANT
(— FORMED IN VINEGAR) MOTHER
(— FROM CRUSHED APPLES)
POMACE
(— IN BLOOD) ALEXINE ABLASTIN
(— IN LIGHT BULBS) GETTER
(— IN WOODY TISSUE) LIGNIN
(— OF DENTINE) IVORY
(— OF EXTREME HARDNESS)
ADAMANT DIAMOND
**(— PRODUCING POISONOUS
ATMOSPHERE)** GAS
**(— SURROUNDED BY FOREIGN
TISSUE)** ENCLAVE
(— TO ADD STABILITY) BALLAST
(— TRANSPORTING GERMS) FOMES

(— USED AS HYPNOTIC) URAL
(— USED IN DETECTING OTHERS)
REAGENT
(— WITH MOLDY ODOR) CHARACIN
(ADHESIVE —) GLUE GLOEA PASTE
CEMENT STICKER
(AMORPHOUS —) GLASS RESIN
LIGNIN PECTIN FERRITE SAPONIN
(AROMATIC —) BALSAM
(ASTRINGENT —) ALUM CATECHU
(BITTER —) ALOIN LININ ILICIN
(BLACK —) SOOT BLECK
(CLEANSING —) LYE
(COLLOIDAL —) ALGIN EXPANDER
(COMBUSTIBLE —) COAL
(CORROSIVE —) CAUSTIC
(CRYSTALLINE —) LAURIN ALANINE
HELENIN ELATERIN
(DARK —) ATRAMENT
(DISSOLVED —) SOLUTE
(ETERNAL —) DHARMA ADHARMA
(FATLIKE —) DEGRAS LIPOID
ERGUSIA
(FATTY —) SMEAR SUBERIN
(FERMENTATION —) LEAVEN
(FIBROUS —) COTTON
(FILAMENTOUS —) HARL
(FILMY —) GOSSAMER
(FIRST —) YLEM
(GRINDING —) ABRASIVE
(GUMMY —) GUM GURRY AMYLOID
GLACTAN
(HARD ANIMAL —) BONE ENAMEL
(HORNY —) BALEEN CHITIN
CHONDRIN
(HYPOTHETICAL —) FLUID INOGEN
PROTYL
(IDEAL —) CONTINUUM
(INFLAMMABLE —) BITUMEN
(INSOLUBLE —) CARRIER HYALOGEN
(LIVERLIKE —) HEPAR
(NARCOTIC —) DRUG
(NITROGENOUS —) LACTENIN
(POISONOUS —) ARSENIC PHRYNIN
EXOTOXIN
(POWDER OF ANY —) FLOUR
(POWDERY —) STOUR
(PREDOMINATING —) BASE
(RESINOUS —) LAC COPAL
COPALINE COPALITE
(SELF-DEFENSIVE —) ACRAEIN
(SEMISOLID —) GEL
(SOUR —) ACID
(STICKY —) GOO GOOP SIZE STICK
GLUTEN BIRDLIME
(SUBTLE —) SPIRIT
(SWEET —) SUGAR
(SYNTHETIC —) HORMONE
(TRANSLUCENT —) HYALINE
(UNBREAKABLE —) ADAMANT
(UNCREATED —) ADHARMA
(VISCOUS —) GLAIR GREASE
SLUBBER
(VITAL —) KEEST
(WAXY —) CERIN PARAFFIN
SUBERINE
SUBSTANDARD BAD BAUCH
SUBSTANTIAL FAT FIRM MEATY
PUKKA STOUT ACTUAL BODILY

HEARTY SQUARE STABLE STANCH
STUFFY STURDY MASSIVE MATERIAL
SUBSTANT TANGIBLE
SUBSTANTIATE BACK CONFIRM
SUPPORT VALIDATE
SUBSTANTIVE DIRECT
SUBSTITUTE SUB VICE AKORI
EXTRA PROXY VICAR BEWITH
CHANGE DEPUTY DOUBLE ERSATZ
COMMUTE REPLACE RESERVE
STANDBY STOPGAP SUBDEAN
SUFFECT SUPPOSE DISPLACE
EMERGENT
(— FOR TEA) TIA FAHAM
(NOT —) FULL
(POOR —) APOLOGY
SUBSTITUTION SHIFT CHANGE
ERSATZ ENALLAGE EXCHANGE
NOVATION
(— OF SOUNDS) LALLATION
SUBSTRATUM SUB GROUND
SUBBING SUBJECT
SUBSTREAM MATTER
SUBSTRUCTURE PODIUM FOOTING
SUBSUME COVER EXPLAIN INCLUDE
SUBSUMING GENERIC
SUBTENANT VAVASOUR
SUBTERFUGE MASK BLIND CROOK
QUIRK SHIFT TRICK WRINK CHICANE
ARTIFICE PRETENCE TRAVERSE
VOIDANCE
SUBTILE SUBTLE TENUOUS
SUBTITLE TITLE LEADER CAPTION
SUBTLE SLY FINE NICE WILY WISE
ACUTE ARGUTE CRAFTY FRAGILE
SUBTILE CLERGIAL
(TOO —) FINESPUN
SUBTLETY FRAUD DECEIT EXILITY
FINESSE DELICACY FINENESS
QUIDDITY QUOLIBET
SUBTLY FINE SLILY SLYLY
SUBTRACT BATE PULL TAKE SHAVE
DEDUCE DEDUCT DETRACT
SUBDUCE SUBDUCT SUBTRAY
DIMINISH
SUBTRIBE HAPU SENAAH SEMNONES
SUBURB ANNEX BORGO BARRIO
PETTAH BANLIEU ENDSHIP
FAUBOURG
(PL.) SKIRTS ENVIRONS OUTPARTS
SUBURBIA
SUBURBIA VILLADOM
SUBVERSION FALL SABOTAGE
SUBVERSIVE RUINOUS
SUBVERT SAP KILL RAZE RUIN
EVERT UPSET GAINSAY OVERSET
REVERSE RUINATE OVERTURN
SUBVERTED LOST
SUBWAY DIVE METRO
SUCCEED GO FAY HIT FARE RISE
WORK CLICK ENSUE FADGE PROVE
SPEED COTTON FOLLOW SECOND
THRIVE ACHIEVE PROSPER
THROUGH FLOURISH SUPPLANT
(— TO THRONE) ACCEDE ASCEND
SUCCEEDING VICE AFTER CHANGE
ULTERIOR
SUCCESS DO GO HIT MAX WIN WOW
BANG CESS LUCK SMASH SPEED

THRIFT EXPLOIT FORTUNE FURTHER
THEEDOM FELICITY GODSPEED
(— IN A MATCH) GAME
(BRILLIANT —) ECLAT
(SUDDEN —) KILLING
(UNEXPECTED —) JACKPOT
(WORLDLY —) ARTHA
SUCCESSFUL HOT SOCK LUCKY
SPEEDFUL THRIVING
SUCCESSFULLY GREAT HAPPILY
PROUDLY
SUCCESSION RUN SUIT ROUND
SUITE TRACK ASSISE COURSE
SEQUEL SERIES STREAM STRING
HEIRDOM SUCCESS ANCESTRY
DIADOCHE MUTATION SEQUENCE
(— OF CHANGES) FLUX
(— OF CHORDS) CADENCE
(— OF CRUSTS) CALICHE
(— OF STAGES) CASCADE
(— OF WAVES) CRIMP
(— RULERS) DYNASTY
SUCCESSIVELY AROW
SUCCESSOR HEIR CALIF HERES
CALIPH HAERES EPIGONUS
(— OF CHIEFTAIN) TANIST
(— OF MUHAMMAD) CALIF CALIPH
(PL.) DIADOCHI
SUCCINCT BRIEF SHORT TERSE
CONCISE LACONIC SUMMARY
SUCCINIC DIACETIC
SUCCOR AID HELP RESET SERVE
SPEED ASSIST RELIEF RESCUE
SUPPLY UPTAKE COMFORT DELIVER
PRESIDY RELIEVE SECOURS
SUSTAIN BEFRIEND
SUCCULENT FRIM FRUM LUSH
JUICY LUSHY PAPPY PULPY SAPPY
YOUNG CASHIE FLESHY TENDER
WATERISH
SUCCUMB BREAK QUAIL STOOP
TRAIK YIELD
SUCH SIC SICK THAT SWICH
SUCHNESS TATHATA
SUCK SOUK SWIG SWOOP SUCKLE
(— DRY) SOAK
(— UP) DRINK ABSORB TIPPLE
SUCKEN THIRL
SUCKER CHUB FISH GULL SOBOL
THIEF CHUPON CUPULE MULLET
RATOON REDFIN SOBOLE SPROUT
SQUARE SUPPER TILLER CUTLIPS
GONOTYL LOCULUS OSCULUM
SCOURGE BOTHRIUM HUMPBACK
PUSHOVER REDHORSE SURCULUS
SUCKLE FEED MILK SUCK LACTATE
NOURISH
SUCKLING SUCKER LACTANT
SUCKLER TEATLING
SUCTION INTAKE
SUCTORIA ACINETAE

SUDAN
CAPITAL: KHARTOUM
DESERT: NUBIAN
LANGUAGE: GA EWE IBO KRU EFIK
MOLE TSHI YORUBA MANDINGO
MEASURE: UD

MOUNTAIN: KINYETI
NATIVE: DAZA GOLO NUER SERE
DINKA FULAH HAUSA MOSSI
NUBIYIN
REGION: DARFUR KASSALA
KORDOFAN
RIVER: NILE
TOWN: KOSTI MEROE ATBARA
ALUBAYD MALAKAL OMDURMAN
WEIGHT: HABBA

SUDANESE FULA FULAH
SUDAN GRASS GARAVA GARAWI
SUDDEN FERLY HASTY ICTIC SWIFT
ABRUPT FIERCE SNAPPY SPEEDY
PRERUPT HEADLONG SPURTIVE
SUBITANY SUBITOUS
SUDDENLY BOB POP BOLT FLOP
SLAP AMAIN SHORT SKELP SOUSE
ASTART BOUNCE PRESTO SUBITO
ASUDDEN UNAWARES
SUDDENNESS ATTACK SUDDENTY
SUDORIFIC SWEAT SWEATER
HIDROTIC SUDATORY
SUDRA VELLALA
SUDS BUCK FOAM SAPPLES
SOAPSUDS
SUE LAW WOO SUIT IMPLEAD
TROUNCE
SUET TALLOW
SUFFER BYE GET LET BEAR DREE
FIND GAIN HURT PAIN PINE ALLOW
DREIE LABOR PROVE SMART SMOKE
STAND THOLE ABEGGE ENDURE
PERMIT AGONIZE SUPPORT SUSTAIN
UNDERGO TOLERATE
(— AGONY) THROE
(— AT STAKE) SMOKE
(— DEFEAT) BOW
(— FOR) ABY ABYE ABIDE
(— FROM TIME) AGE
(— GREAT AFFLICTION) GROAN
(— HUNGER) CLEM STARVE
AFFAMISH
(— LOSS OF) GIVE
(— PAIN) STOUND ANGUISH
(— PENALTY) SWEAT
(— REMORSE) RUE
(— RUIN) WRECK
(— SYNCOPE) FAINT
(— THROUGH) PASS
(— TO ENTER) ADMIT
SUFFERABLE PATIBLE
SUFFERANCE PAIN MISERY
PATIENCE THOLANCE
SUFFERER MARTYR AMNESIC
DOORMAT PATIENT
SUFFERING BALE COST DREE HURT
PAIN PINE RACK DOLOR GRIEF
SMART WRAKE PATHIC PATHOS
THRALL INVALID LANGUOR PASSION
PASSIVE TRAVAIL DISTRESS
HARDSHIP
(— FROM HANGOVER) CHIPPY
(— FROM ILL HEALTH) DOWN
(— OF MIND) CARE
(—S OF CHRIST) AGONY

SUFFICE DO LAST REACH SERVE
SATISFY
SUFFICIENCY ENOUGH ADEQUACY
SUFFICIENT DUE FAIR GOOD AMPLE
DECENT ENOUGH BASTANT
ADEQUATE RELEVANT COMPETENT
(BARELY —) SCANT SKIMP SCRIMPY
(BE — FOR) COVER
SUFFICIENTLY DULY WELL ENOUGH
SUFFIX POSTFIX
SUFFOCATE CHOKE DROWN SMOOR
STIVE STUFF SWELT SLOKEN STIFLE
OVERLIE QUACKLE SMOLDER
SMOTHER SCUMFISH STRANGLE
THROTTLE
SUFFRAGE VOTE VOICE TONGUE
VERSICLE
SUFFUSE FILL BATHE EMBAY INFUSE
SUFFUSION COLOR
SUGAR CANDY DIOSE IDOSE MELIS
PIECE SUCRE THIRD ACROSE
ALDOSE ALLOSE FUCOSE GULOSE
HEXOSE INVERT KETOSE LYXOSE
OCTOSE PANELA TALOSE TRIOSE
XYLOSE AGAVOSE ALTROSE
BASTARD CHITOSE GLUCOSE
GLUTOSE GLYCOSE LACTOSE
MALTOSE PAPELON PENOCHI
PENTOSE PENUCHE SORBOSE
SUCROSE SWEETEN TETROSE
THREOSE BROWNING CONCRETE
CYMAROSE DEXTROSE FRUCTOSE
FURANOSE LEVULOSE PYRANOSE
RHAMNOSE RHODEOSE SECALOSE
TURANOSE
(BROWN —) CARAIBE JAGGARY
JAGGHERY
(COARSE —) RAAB
(CRUDE —) GUR HEAD MELADA
CONCRETE
(INFERIOR —) BASTARD
SUGARCANE CANE GRAIN GLUMAL
RATOON MATTRESS
(— SAP) LIQUOR
SUGARHOUSE (PART OF —)
PURGERY
SUGARLESS DRY
SUGARPLUM KISS
SUGARY FAT SUGAR SWEET
OVERRIPE
SUGGEST JOG BEAR GIVE HINT MINT
IMPLY OFFER SPEAK ALLUDE INDITE
INFUSE MOTION PROMPT RESENT
SUBMIT CONNOTE DICTATE INSPIRE
INDICATE INTIMATE
(— DRINKING) PROPOSE
(— INSIDIOUSLY) INFUSE
(— STRONGLY) ARGUE
SUGGESTIBLE SOFT
SUGGESTION CUE CAST HINT TANG
GLIFF ADVICE BREATH MOTION
SMATCH INKLING LEADING PROFFER
REMNANT SOUPCON WRINKLE
INNUENDO INSTANCE PROPOSAL
SUGGESTIVE ANICONIC PREGNANT
(— OF MELODY) CANOROUS
SUICIDAL KAMIKAZE
SUIT DO GO APT DOW FIT GEE HIT
SET SIT ACTO LIKE LIST PAIR SORT

ADAPT AGREE APPLY BEFIT BESIT
CLUBS COLOR DRAPE DRESS
FADGE FANCY FRAME HABIT LEVEL
MATCH PLEAD QUEME SAVOR
SERVE SHAPE STAND SUING TALLY
AFFEIR ANSWER BECOME COHERE
COMPLY DITTOS HEARTS PRAYER
SPADES SPEECH SQUARE BEHOOVE
COMPORT COSTUME COULEUR
PURSUIT REQUEST SEERPAW
DIAMONDS INSTANCE QUADRATE
SKELETON STANDARD TAILLEUR
TROPICAL
(— AT LAW) ACTO CASE LAWSUIT
(SWIMMING —) BATHER BIKINI
SUITABILITY (MUTUAL —) DECENCY
IDONEITY SYMPATHY
SUITABLE APT FIT PAT ABLE FEAT
GAIN GOOD JUMP JUST MEET TALL
WELL WEME DIGNE EQUAL FITTY
QUEME RIGHT SUITY COMELY
FITTEN GAINLY GIUSTO HABILE
HONEST LIABLE LIKELY PROPER
SUITLY AVENANT COMMODE
CONDIGN CONGRUE FITTING
IDONEAL PLIABLE SEEMING
BECOMING ELIGIBLE FEASIBLE
HANDSOME IDONEOUS SORTABLE
(— FOR STAGE PERFORMANCE)
ACTING
SUITABLENESS APTNESS HONESTY
APTITUDE PROPERTY
SUITABLY FITLY MEETLY TIDELY
APROPOS GRADELY
SUITCASE BAG CAP GRIP CAPCASE
DORLACH KEESTER
SUITE SET SUIT SWEEP SWEET
SERIES PARTITA RETINUE
ENSEMBLE EQUIPAGE
(— OF MOLDINGS) LEDGMENT
(— OF ROOMS) FLAT CHAMBER
SUITED FIT ADAPT SEEMLY ADAPTED
ASSORTED
(POORLY —) CROOK
SUITING COVERT CHEVIOT
SUITOR MAN SUER SWAIN WOOER
GALLANT SERVANT
SUKU WASUKUMA
SULFIDE GLANCE CUBANITE
SULFURET
SULFUR BRIMSTONE
SULK DOD PET CHAW CRAB DORT
GLUM SULL BOODY FRUMP GLUMP
GROUT GRUMP GROUCH SNUDGE
THURMUS
(PL.) GEE HUMP MUMPS FRUMPS
SULLENS BOUDERIE
SULKER MUMPER
SULKINESS DORT GRUMP
SULKY CART CHUFF DODDY DORTY
GOURY HUFFY HUMPY CHUFFY
GLUMPY GROUTY JINKER SNUFFY
STUFFY SULLEN SUMPHY DOGGISH
HUFFISH MUMPISH
(NOT —) GOOD
SULLEN DOUR FOUL GLUM GRIM
SOUR BLACK CHUFF CROSS DUMPY
FELON GRUFF HARSH MOODY
RUSTY STERN SULKY SURLY

WEMOD CRUSTY DOGGED GLOOMY
GLUMMY GLUMPY GLUNCH GROUTY
MOROSE MULISH SOMBER SOMBRE
STUFFY AUSTERE CRABBED
CYNICAL FRETFUL LOURING
MUMPISH PEEVISH CHUMPISH
CHURLISH LOWERING PETULANT
SPITEFUL STUNKARD
SULLENNESS GEE DORT GLUM
MUMPS STOMACH
SULLIED DIRTY SPOTTED
SULLY BLOT BLUR DASH FOUL SLUR
SMIT SMUT SOIL CLOUD DIRTY
GRIME SMEAR SMOKE STAIN TAINT
DARKEN DEFILE SMIRCH SMUTCH
ATTAINT BEGRIME BESMEAR
BLEMISH CORRUPT DISTAIN ECLIPSE
POLLUTE SLUBBER TARNISH
BESMIRCH
SULPHATE ALUM BARITE ILESITE
LOWEITE SULFATE VITRIOL
KRAUSITE
SULPHIDE HEPAR GLANCE ZARNEC
SULFIDE ZARNICH CUBANITE
(PL.) MATTE
SULPHUR ORE SPIRIT SULFUR
YELLOW QUEBRITH BRIMSTONE
SULPHURIC ACID VITRIOL
SULTAN SOLDAN
SULTANATE SULTANY ZANZIBAR
SULTANESS SOWDONES
SULTRY CLOSE FLUSH FAINTY
SMUDGY POTHERY PUTHERY
SWELTRY FEVERISH
SUM ALL GOB CASH DRAB DUMP
FARM FINE FOOT FUND MASS TALE
DEDIT GROSS KITTY SUMMA TOTAL
WHOLE AMOUNT DEMAND DYADIC
FIGURE NUMBER DECUPLE INGOING
MANBOTE SUBSIDY SUMMARY
SUMMATE ENTIRETY OCTONION
QUANTITY MOUNTANCE
(— AND SUBSTANCE) TOUR SHORT
UPSHOT
(— AS COMPENSATION FOR
KILLING) MANBOTE
(— FOR REENLISTMENT) GRATUITY
(— FOR SCHOLARSHIP) BURSARY
(— IN BASSET) SEPTLEVA
(— OF 25 POUNDS) PONY PONEY
(— OF 3 FARTHINGS) GILL
(— OF 500 POUNDS) MONKEY
(— OF DETERMINANTS) STIRP
(— OF EXPONENTS) DEGREE
(— OF FACTORS) COMPLEX
(— OF GOOD QUALITIES) ARETE
(— OF MONEY) POT BANK COVER
STOCK BUNDLE ACCOUNT STIPEND
(— OF) SIGMA
(— PAYABLE AT FIXED INTERVALS)
FARM
(— RISKED) STAKE
(— UP) ADD TOT FOOT RECKON
SUBSUME SUMMATE COMPRISE
CONCLUDE PERORATE
(ENTIRE —) SOLIDUM
(EXCESS —) BONUS
(FORFEITED —) DEDIT
(GREAT —) PLUNK SIGHT MICKLE

(LARGE —) GOB SCREAMER
(PETTY —) CENT DIME DRAB
(SMALL — OF MONEY) SPILL
DRIBBLE DRIBLET
(TRIFLING —) HAY
(UNEXPENDED —S) SAVINGS
(VECTOR —) GRADIENT
SUMAC KAREE SUMACH ANACARD
BURTREE SCOTINO SHOEMAKE
SUMATRA (LANGUAGE IN —) NIAS
(MEASURE OF —) PAAL
(MOUNTAIN IN —) LEUSER KERINTJI
(RIVER IN —) HARI MUSI ROKAN
DJAMBI
(TOWN IN —) ACHIN KUALA MEDAN
NATAL SOLOK DJAMBI LANGSA
PADANG RENGAT BONKULIN
SUMBUL SAMBUL MUSKROOT
SUMERIAN ACCADIAN AKKADIAN
SUMMARIZE PRECIS RESUME
ABSTRACT
SUMMARY SUM LEAD BRIEF CHART
SCORE SHORT SUMMA TOTAL
PRECIS RESUME SUMMAR CHAPTER
CONCISE EPITOME EXTRACT
MEDULLA VIDIMUS ABSTRACT
ARGUMENT BREVIARY BREVIATE
DRUMHEAD HEADNOTE SUCCINCT
SYNOPSIS
(— OF FAITH) SYMBOL
(— OF PRINCIPLES) CREED
SUMMATION SUM DIGEST SUMMARY
SUMMER SHEMU SOMER AESTAS
SIMMER DORMANT
(OF —) ESTIVAL
SUMMER CYPRESS KOCHIA
SUMMER FLOUNDER PLAICE
SUMMERHOUSE FOLLY KIOSK
MAHAL TUPEK ALCOVE CASINO
GAZEBO PAGODA CABINET
SUMMER HYACINTH GALTONIA
SUMMER TANAGER REDBIRD
SUMMERWOOD LATEWOOD
SUMMIT DOD SUM TIP TOP VAN
ACME APEX BALD CRAP DODD
HELM KNAP KNOT PEAK ROOF
CREST CROWN SPIRE COMBLE
HEIGHT VERTEX ZENITH CALOTTE
SUMMARY SUMMITY PINNACLE
(— OF TUBE) MOUTH
(— WITHOUT FOREST) BALD
(ROCKY —) KNOT
(ROUND —) DOD DODD
(SNOW-CAPPED —) CALOTTE
SUMMON BAN CRY BUZZ CALL CITE
DRUM HAIL SIST BUGLE CHARM
CLEPE EVOKE HIGHT KNELL SOUND
VOUCH ACCITE ADVOKE BECALL
COMPEL DEMAND SOMPNE VOCATE
ACCERSE COMMAND CONJURE
CONVENE CONVENT CONVOKE
PROVOKE SUMMONS WHISTLE
ASSUMMON EXORCISE
(— FOR HIRING) YARD
(— INTO COURT) DEMAND
(— TOGETHER) BAND MUSTER
ASSEMBLE
(— UP) FIND GATHER COLLECT
SUMMONER SUMNER LOCKMAN

SOMPNER OUTRIDER

SUMMONING CALL ARRAY
(— **OF KING'S VASSALS**) BAN
SUMMONS BAN CRY CALL BIDDING
CALLING STICKER WARNING
WARRANT CITATION VOCATION
(**FALCONER'S** —) WO
SUMP SINK STANDAGE
SUMPTUOUS RICH GRAND SHOWY
WLONK COSTLY DELUXE SOLEMN
SUPERB COSTLEW ELEGANT
SPLENDID
SUMPTUOUSNESS DAINTY
SUMPTURE
SUN SOL ATEN ATON INTI LAMP
STAR SENGE SURYA TITAN SUNLET
DAYSTAR IOSKEHA PHOEBUS
SAVITAR JOUSKEHA
(— **MOON AND STARS**) HOST
(**RISING** —) HERAKHTI
SUNAPEE TROUT SAIBLING
SUNBEAM BANANA
SUN BEAR BRUANG
SUNBIRD MAMO CADET
SUN BITTERN CARLE CAURALE
SUNBIRD
SUN BLIND UMRELLA
SUNBONNET TILT UGLY CRESIE
KAPPIE SHAKER
SUNBURN GREENING HELIOSIS
SUNBURNT ADUST TANNED
SUNBURST SUNRAY SUNBREAK
SUNSHINE
SUNDAE GEDUNK
SUNDAY EXAUDI JUDICA GAUDETE
TRINITY
(**THIRD** — **AFTER EASTER**) JUBILATE
SUNDER PART TWIN BREAK SEVER
TWAIN TWINE DEPART DIVIDE
SINDER ASUNDER DISALLY DISJOIN
DIVORCE DISSEVER SEJUGATE
SEPARATE UNSOLDER
SUNDEW DROSERA EYEBRIGHT
SUNDIAL DIAL GHURRY HOROLOGE
SCAPHION SOLARIUM
SUN DISK ATEN ATON CAKRA
CHAKRA
SUNDOG WINDGALL
SUNDOWNER WHALER TUSSOCKER
SUN-DRIED TILED
SUNDROPS SCABISH
SUNDRY DIVERS DIVERSE SEVERAL
SUNFISH SUN HURO MOLA RUFF
BREAM FLIER FLYER ROACH SUNNY
KIVVER MOLOID REDEAR REDEYE
CRAPPIE CROPPIE PERCOID
BLUEGILL FLATFISH FLOUNDER
HEADFISH MOONFISH PONDFISH
WARMOUTH
SUNFLOWER GOLD HELIO CANADA
GOLDEN SUNFOIL GIRASOLE
TURNSOLE
(— **STATE**) KANSAS
SUN-GREBE FINFOOT SUNBIRD
GRUIFORM
SUNK SUNKEN
(— **TO LOW STATE**) ABJECT
SUNKEN SUNK HOLLOW
SUNLESS BLAE

SUNLIGHT GLARE
SUNN SAN SANN DAGGA SANAI
JANAPA MADRAS JANAPAN
SANNHEMP
SUNNITE IHLAT SUNNI SUNNIAH
SUNNY GOOD SUNSHINE
SUN PARLOR SOLARIUM
SUNRISE ARIST SUNUP ORIENT
SUNSET SUNFALL
(— **STATE**) OREGON ARIZONA
SUNSHADE PARASOL ROUNDEL
TIRESOL SOMBRERO
SUNSHINE SUN SHINE SUNLIGHT
(— **STATE**) FLORIDA
SUNSPOT SPOT FACULA MACULA
SUNSPURGE SUNWEED TURNSOLE
WARTWEED WARTWORT
SUNSTROKE HELIOSIS SIRIASIS
SUNTAN MERIDA
SUN TREE HINOKI
SUNWISE DEASIL DESSIL
SUNYATA VOID
SUP EAT DINE SOWP FEAST
CONSUME SWALLOW
SUPAWN MUSH
SUPERABOUND OVERFLOW
SUPERABUNDANCE FLOOD EXCESS
CATARACT PLETHORA PLEURISY
SUPERABUNDANT RANK LAVISH
PROFUSE
SUPERALTAR PREDELLA
SUPERANNUATE OVERYEAR
SUPERB GRAND GOLDEN GORGEOUS
SPLENDID
SUPERCARGO MERCHANT
SUPERCILIOUS GRAND POTTY
PROUD OVERLY SNIFFY SNIPPY
SNOOTY SNOTTY SNUFFY HAUGHTY
ARROGANT CAVALIER SNIFFISH
SUPERIOR
SUPERCLASS AGNATHA
SUPERCONSCIOUSNESS SAMADHI
SUPERCOOL SUBCOOL SURFUSE
SUPERFAMILY APINA APOIDEA
BOVOIDEA
SUPERFICIAL GLIB ECTAL SUPER
FACIAL FACILE FLIMSY FORMAL
FROTHY GLASSY OVERLY SLIGHT
OUTSIDE OUTWARD SHALLOW
SKETCHY SLIGHTY SURFACE
SURFACY EXTERNAL MAGAZINY
SMATTERY DEPTHLESS
SUPERFICIALLY FLEET
SUPERFICIES TERM EXTENT
SUPERFLUITY FAT FRILL LUXUS
EXCESS OVERSET SURFEIT
(**CONFUSING** —) FLUTHER
SUPERFLUOUS SPARE USELESS
NEEDLESS
SUPERFRONTAL FRONTLET
SUPERHEATED GASEOUS
SUPERHUMAN DEMON DAEMON
DIVINE INHUMAN UNHUMAN
SUPERIMPOSE LAY OVERLAY
SURPRINT
SUPERIMPOSING DISSOLVE
SUPERINTEND CON CONN GUIDE
OVERSEE PRESIDE
SUPERINTENDENCE CARE

CONTROL EPISCOPY GUIDANCE
SUPERINTENDENCY EDILITY
AEDILITY
SUPERINTENDENT BOSS SUPE
EPHOR SUPER EDITOR VENEUR
VIEWER CAPTAIN EPHORUS
MANAGER DIRECTOR OVERSEER
SURVEYOR SWINGMAN
SUPERIOR JOE AYNE COOL FINE
MORE OVER TRIE ABBOT ABOVE
CHIEF CREAM EIGNE ELDER ELITE
EXTRA FANCY FRANK GREAT LIEGE
PRIOR UPPER ABBESS BETTER
COCKUP CUSTOS DOMINA FATHER
FORBYE MAHANT SELECT SENIOR
STRONG FORTHBY PALMARY
RANKING ABNORMAL DOMINANT
GUARDIAN SINGULAR SPLENDID
SUPERIAL
(— **OF CONVENT**) HEGUMEN
(— **TO**) BEFORE
SUPERIORITY DROP GREE PRICE
HEIGHT MASTERY PROWESS
EMINENCE PRIORITY
(**MENTAL** —) GENIUS
SUPERLATIVE RAVING CURIOUS
CRASHING OLYMPIAN PEERLESS
SWINGING
(**ABSOLUTE** —) ELATIVE
SUPERLATIVELY CRACKING
SWINGING
SUPERMAN OVERMAN
SUPERNATURAL DIVINE NUMINOUS
SUPERIOR
(— **FORCE**) WAKANDA
SUPERSTITION FREIT IDOLATRY
SUPERORDER GLIRES
SUPERPOSE APPLY
SUPERSCRIBE DIRECT
SUPERSCRIPT SUPERIOR
SUPERSEDE REPLACE OVERRIDE
SUPPLANT
SUPERSTITIOUS FREITY
SUPERTONIC SECOND
SUPERVENE FOLLOW
SUPERVISE GUIDE DIRECT GOVERN
HANDLE SURVEY FOREMAN
OVERSEE ENGINEER OVERLOOK
CHAPERONE
SUPERVISION EYE CARE DUTY
HAND CHECK CHARGE
SUPERVISOR BULL EPHOR GUIDE
SUPER CENSOR GASMAN RUNMAN
SOURER WARDEN DESKMAN
ALYTARCH CHAIRMAN FLOORMAN
FOREHAND KNIFEMAN LEACHMAN
MASHGIAH OVERSEER
SUPINE INERT DROWSY LANGUID
SERVILE UPRIGHT CARELESS
INACTIVE INDOLENT LISTLESS
SLUGGISH
SUPPER MEAL CUDDY HOCKEY
PASCHAL
(**HARVEST-HOME** —) HOCKEY
(**LAST** —) MAUNDY
SUPPING CENATION
SUPPLANT FOLLOW REMOVE
REPLACE DISPLACE DISPLANT
SUPPLE BAIN FLIP OILY SOFT LINGY

LITHE SLAMP SWACK AJOINT
LIMBER LITHER LUTHER SUMPLE
SWANKY WANDLE LISSOME PLIABLE
SPRINGE FLEXIBLE

SUPPLEJACK SOAPWORT

SUPPLEMENT ARM EKE MEND TACK
ANNEX SUPPLY BOLSTER CODICIL
ADDENDUM APPENDIX BOUNTITH
(PL.) FIXINGS

SUPPLEMENTAL SPECIAL

SUPPLEMENTARY ADDED RIPIENO
REMANENT

SUPPLENESS WHIP

SUPPLIANT ASKER PLEADING

SUPPLICATE BEG PRAY CRAVE
PLEAD INVOKE OBTEST SUPPLY
BESEECH ENTREAT IMPLORE
REQUEST SOLICIT PETITION

SUPPLICATION CRY VOW BEAD BILL
LIBEL VENIE LITANY PRAYER
CRAVING SYNAPTE ENTREATY
PETITION PLEADING ROGATION
ROGATIVE SUFFRAGE

SUPPLICATORY EUCTICAL

SUPPLIED (— **WITH FOOD**) THORN
(AMPLY —) ABUNDANT
(SCANTILY —) BARE

SUPPLIER SOURCE

SUPPLIES STOCK STUFF DUFFEL
STORES VICTUAL ESTOVERS
ORDNANCE

SUPPLY FEED FILL FIND FRET FUND
GIVE HEEL LEND LINE ARRAY
CATER ENDUE EQUIP INDUE OFFER
SERVE STOCK STORE STUFF YIELD
BUDGET DONATE EMPLOY FOISON
LAYOUT POCKET SUBMIT ADVANCE
FORTIFY FRAUGHT FURNISH
LISSOME PROVIDE
(— **ABUNDANTLY**) SWILL
(— **ARRANGED BEFOREHAND**)
RELAY
(— **FOR AN OCCASION**) GRIST
(— **OF MONEY**) BANKROLL
(— **OF POTENTIAL JURORS**) TALES
(— **OF TIN**) SERVING
(— **PROVISIONS**) PURVEY
(— **THE NEED**) FOR
(— **WITH CLOTHES**) INFIT
(— **WITH FUEL**) STOKE
(— **WITH MONEY**) GILD
(— **WITH OXYGEN**) AERATE
(— **WITH WATER**) FANG
(CACHED —) CAVE
(CONSTANT —) STREAM
(EXTRA —) RESERVE
(FRESH —) RECRUIT
(HIDDEN —) HOARD
(INADEQUATE —) DEARTH
(OVERABUNDANT —) SURFEIT
(PLENTIFUL —) CHOICE
(RESERVE —) CUSHION
(RICH —) ARGOSY
(SCANTY —) SCANT

SUPPORT AID ARM BAY BED BOW
KAI LEG PEG RIB TIE TOM ABET
ABUT AXIS BACK BASE BEAM BEAR
BUOY CRIB DADE FEND FIND FIRM
FORK FUEL HAVE HELP HOLD KEEP

KILP LIFT POST PROP RACK REST
ROCK SALT SIDE STAY STEM STUD
TRIG ADOPT ANGEL APPUI ATLAS
BIPOD BLOCK BRACE CARRY CHAIR
CHEER CHOCK CLEAT CRANK
FAVOR FLOAT FRAME OXTER PLUNK
RANCE SALVE SHORE SPURN STAFF
STAKE STEAD STELL STIPE STOCK
STRUT STULL TOWER VOUCH WEIGH
ANCHOR ASSERT ASSIST BARROW
BEHALF CHEVAL COLUMN CORSET
CRADLE CRUTCH DEFEND DONKEY
DUOPOD GARTER PATTEN PILLAR
POTENT PULPIT PUTLOG SADDLE
SECOND SHIELD SOCKET SPLINT
STAYER STEADY SUFFER TASSEL
TIMBER TINGLE TORSEL UPHAND
UPHOLD UPKEEP UPTAKE WHIMSY
ARMREST BACKING BOLSTER
COMFORT CONFIRM CRIPPLE
DEADMAN ENDORSE FINDING
FULCRUM GROMMET HOUSING
JACKLEG JUSTIFY KEEPING
KNUCKLE NOURISH NURTURE
PABULUM PROTECT RADICAL
SPIRALE SQUINCH STADDLE
STANDER STIFFEN STIRRUP SUBSIST
SUSTAIN THICKEN TRESTLE
ADJUMENT ADVOCATE BALUSTER
BEFRIEND BESTRIDE BOOKREST
BUTTRESS CAPSHORE FAIRLEAD
FOOTREST FORESTAY FORTRESS
HANDREST HOLDFAST JACKSTAY
KEYSTONE MAINSTAY MAINTAIN
MOUNTING NEEDLING OVERCAST
PEDESTAL PEDIMENT STANDARD
STILLAGE STOCKING STRENGTH
SYMPATHY UNDERLIE UNDERPIN
UNDERSET
(— **FOR ANVIL**) STOCK
(— **FOR BELL CLAPPER**) BALDRIC
(— **FOR CATALYST**) CARRIER
(— **FOR HEAVY MACHINERY**)
BUNTING
(— **FOR LEVER**) BAIT
(— **FOR LIFE-CAR**) BAIL
(— **FOR MILL**) LOWDER
(— **FOR MINE PASSAGE**) OVERCAST
(— **FOR PLATFORM**) STEMPEL
STEMPLE
(— **IN A LATHE**) DOCTOR
(— **IN PAPERMAKING TUB**) DONKEY
(— **OF COPING**) KNEELER
(— **OF MOLD CORE**) ARBOR
ARBOUR
(— **OF RAIL**) CHAIR BALUSTER
(— **THROUGH BIT AND BRIDLE**)
APPUI
(CRUTCHLIKE —) DEADMAN
(ELBOW-SHAPED —) CRANK
(EMBEDDED —) SPURN
(FIREPLACE —) ANDIRON
(GIVE —) FEED
(INCLINED —) RIDER
(MINING —) CAP FRAME
(PORTABLE —) STOOL
(PRINCIPAL —) BACKBONE
(TEMPORARY —) NEEDLING
(UPRIGHT —) POPPET BANISTER

(WHEELED —) CARRIAGE
(PL.) SHIPWAY

SUPPORTED BASED BLOCKED
ACCOSTED SUCCINCT
(— **BY EVIDENCE**) PROBABLE

SUPPORTER ALLY JOCK ATLAS
STOOP COHORT DRAGON SATRAP
BOOSTER DEVOTEE FAVORER
FOUNDER LAUDIAN PATROON
PROPPER SUPPORT ADHERENT
ASSERTER ERASTIAN ESPOUSER
FAVORITE HENCHMAN UPHOLDER
CHURCHITE
(ATHLETIC —) CUP JOCK
(CHIEF —) STOOP
(PL.) SECOND

SUPPORTING BEHIND BEARING

SUPPOSE SAY SEE SET WIS WIT
DEEM POSE READ TAKE TROW
WEEN ALLOW COUNT ETTLE FANCY
GUESS JUDGE OPINE SEPAD THINK
ASSUME DEVISE DIVINE EXPECT
RECKON BELIEVE CONCEIT
DARESAY IMAGINE PRESUME
PROPOSE SUPPONE SURMISE
CONCEIVE CONCLUDE CONSIDER
OPINIATE

SUPPOSED ALLEGED ASSUMED
PUTATIVE

SUPPOSING IF

SUPPOSITION IF IDEA FICTION
SURMISE WEENING

SUPPOSITORY BOUGIE CANDLE
PESSARY

SUPPRESS LAY DOWN GULP HIDE
HUSH SINK SLAY SNUB STOP BLACK
BURKE CHOKE CRUSH ELIDE QUASH
QUELL SHUSH SMORE SPIKE STILL
QUENCH SQUASH STIFLE CONTAIN
CUSHION INHIBIT OPPRESS
REPRESS SILENCE SMOLDER
SMOTHER SQUELCH RESTRAIN
STRANGLE SUPPRIME VANQUISH

SUPPRESSED BLIND CENSORED

SUPPRESSION ABEYANCE AMEIOSIS
BLACKOUT
(— **OF VOWEL**) ELISION
(— **OF WORD SOUNDS**) SYNCOPE
ECLIPSIS

SUPPURATE RUN BEAL WHEAL
DIGEST MATTER QUITTER
MATURATE

SUPPURATION PYOSIS BEALING
COCTION

SUPPURATIVE DIGERENT

SUPRACLAVICLE SCAPULA

SUPREMACY PALM PRIMACY
DOMINION OVERRULE

SUPREME HIGH LAST CHIEF VITAL
SUBLIME SUMMARY TOPLESS
FOREMOST GREATEST PEERLESS

SURA FATIHA FATIHAH

SURCHARGE PACK

SURCINGLE WANTY ROLLER

SURCOAT JUPON CYCLAS KABAYA

SURD SHARP ATONIC FLATED

SURE COLD BOUND SECURE SICKER
STEADY WITTER ASSURED CERTAIN

PERFECT COCKSURE POSITIVE
UNERRING
SURELY WIS FINE SURE PARDY
REDLY ATWEEL PARDIE
SURENESS SURETY SECURITY
SURETY VAS ANDI BAIL BAND
BORROW CAUTION ENGAGER
SOVERTY SPONSOR BAILSMAN
SECURITY
SURETYSHIP SPONSION
SURF BREACH KALEMA
(— NOISE) RUT ROTE
SURFACE DAY AREA FACE ORLO
PLAT RYME SIDE BOSOM FLOOR
STONE SWARF CHROME FINISH
GROUND SCRUFF ASPHALT
BLANKET COUNTER ENVELOP
OUTFACE OUTSIDE STRETCH
ADHEREND CONCRETE EXTERIOR
PLATFORM
(— BETWEEN FLUTES OF SHAFT)
ORLO
(— BETWEEN TRIGLYPH CHANNELS)
MEROS
(— IN BEATER) BACKFALL
(— OF BEAM) BACK
(— OF BODY) FLESH HABIT
(— OF COAL) BUTT
(— OF CRICKET FIELD) CARPET
(— OF DIAMOND) SPREAD
(— OF EARTH) DUST GROUND
TERRENE
(— OF ESCUTCHEON) FIELD
(— OF GROUND OVER MINE) DAY
(— OF PARACHUTE) CANOPY
(— OF RIFLE BARREL) LAND
(— OF SAWED LUMBER) FUR
(— OF TOOTH) TRITOR
(— OF VAULT) GROIN
(— OF WATER) RYME SCRUFF
(— WITHIN EARTH) GEOID
(CONCAVE —) LAP
(CURVED —) BELLY
(DULL —) MAT MATTING
(FLAT —) BED FLAT AEQUOR
PAGINA
(FLOOR —) BOWL
(GEOMETRIC —) TORE CONOID
SPHERE CONICOID CYLINDER
HELICOID
(GLOSSY —) GLAZE
(GROOVED —) DROVE
(HAIRY —) NAP
(HORIZONTAL —) LEVEL
(INCLINED —) CANT DESCENT
(MINERAL —) DRUSE
(PAVED —) FOOTWALK
(PILE —) FRIEZE
(PLANE —) AREA FACET
(PRINCIPAL —) FACE
(PRINTING —) CUT
(PROTECTIVE —) LAGGING
(ROAD —) MACADAM CORDUROY
(ROUGH —) KEY CRIZZLE STUBBLE
(ROUGHENED —) MAT FOOTGRIP
(SLIPPERY —) GLARE
(SLOPING —) SHELVING
(STRIKING —) BLADE
(UNDER — OF SKI) PALM

(UNGLOSSY PAINT —) FLAT
(UPPER —) NOTAEUM
(UPRIGHT —) JAMB
SURFACER SEASONER
SURF DUCK COOT SCOTER
SURFEIT CLOY FILL GLUT SATE
STAW STALL STUFF AGROTE
ENGLUT SICKEN SATIATE SATIETY
SURCLOY SATURATE
SURFEITED SAD SICK BLASE JADED
WEARY REPLETE SATIATED
SURF FISH PERCH ALFIONA
SURF SCOTER COOT SCOTER
SURFER PISHAUG SKUNKTOP
SURF SHINER SPARADA
SURGE GUST TIDE WASH DRIVE
GURGE LUNGE SPURT SWELL
BILLOW BREACH COURSE WALLOW
WALTER ESTUATE REDOUND
AESTUATE UNDULATE
(SHOREWARD —) SUFF
SURGEON (ALSO SEE PHYSICIAN
AND DOCTOR) LEECH ARTIST
INTERN MEDICO OPERATOR
SAWBONES
(TREE —) TREEMAN
SURGEONFISH TANG TANGE
DOCTOR MEDICO BARBERO
SURGEON SAWBONES
SURGERY KNIFE
SURGING WALE ESTURE ESTUOUS
SURICATE ZENICK MEERKAT
SURINAM TOAD PIPA PIPAL
SURINAMINE ANDIRINE ANGELINE
SURLINESS MOROSITY
SURLY BAD ILL GRUM LUNT BLUFF
CHUFF GRUFF GURLY PURDY
ROUGH RUNTY RUSTY CHUFFY
CRUSTY GRUFFY GRUMPY MOROSE
RUGGED SNARLY SULLEN CHURLISH
SURMISE DEEM REDE GUESS INFER
TWANG SURMIT JALOUSE SUSPECT
WEENING MISTRUST
SURMOUNT TOP BEAT TIDE CROWN
ENSIGN HURDLE MASTER OUTTOP
OVERGO SUBDUE CONQUER
SURPASS OVERCOME SUPERATE
(— DIFFICULTIES) SWIM
SURMOUNTING BROCHANT
SURNAME BYNAME SURNOUN
COGNOMEN OVERNAME SURSTYLE
SURPASS CAP COB TOP WAR BANG
BEAT CAMP COTE DING FLOG FOIL
HEAD PASS SHED WHAP EXCEL
OUTDO OUTGO ATREDE BETTER
EXCEED OUTRAY OUTVIE OUTWIT
OVERDO PRECEL ECLIPSE FORPASS
OUTPEER OVERTOP PARAGON
PRECEDE ANTECEDE DISTANCE
DOMINATE OUTCLASS OUTMATCH
OUTRANGE OUTREACH OUTSTRIP
OUTWRITE SURMOUNT
SURPASSING BEST FINE ABOVE
PASSANT PASSING DOMINANT
TOWERING
SURPLICE COTTA EPHOD CHRISOM
(PL.) WHITES
SURPLUS OVER PLUS REST EXCESS
LUMBER VELVET OVERAGE

OVERRUN OVERSUM ARISINGS
LEFTOVER OVERCOME OVERMUCH
OVERPLUS
SURPRISE CAP SHED SWAN YACH
AMAZE SHOCK SNEAK FERLIE
WAYLAY WONDER ASTOUND
GLOPPEN PERPLEX STARTLE
ASTONISH BEWILDER CONFOUND
DUMFOUND
(BY —) ABACK
(EXCLAMATION OF —) QUOTHA
(EXPRESS —) MIRATE
(SUDDEN —) KICK
SURPRISING FERLIE STRIKING
SURRA MBORI
SURREJOINDER TRIPLY
SURRENDER HEM LET PUT CEDE
CESS DING FALL QUIT TAKE REMIT
YIELD ADDICT REMISE RENDER
RESIGN SUBMIT ABANDON CONCEDE
DELIVER FORSAKE KAMERAD
ABDICATE ABNEGATE DEDITION
DELIVERY RENOUNCE UNDERLIE
(— BY DEED) REMISE
SURREPTITIOUS SECRET BOOTLEG
FURTIVE SNEAKING
SURROUND HEM LAP ORB BELT
DIKE DYKE FOLD GIRD GIRT HOOP
WRAP BESET BRACE CLASP EMBAY
EMBED FENCE HEDGE IMBED INARM
ROUND BECLIP BEGIRD BEGIRT
CIRCLE COLLET CORRAL ENFOLD
ENWRAP FORSET GIRDLE IMPALE
INCASE INVEST SPHERE SWATHE
ARROUND BESEIGE BESTAND
COMPASS EMBOSOM ENCLAVE
ENCLOSE ENROUND ENVELOP
ENVIRON INVOLVE WREATHE
CLOISTER ENCIRCLE ENTRENCH
STOCKADE
(— WITH BOOM) CRIB
(— WITH CORD) GIRT
(— WITH MORTAR) GROUT
SURROUNDED AMID AMONG AMIDST
AMONGST BETWEEN
SURROUNDING MIDST ROUND
CIRCUM AMBIENT
(PL.) SCENE HARNESS ENVIRONS
SURVEILLANCE SCRUTINY
STAKEOUT
SURVEY SEE DIAL SCAN VIEW AVIEW
STOCK STUDY PERUSE REGARD
REVIEW SEARCH CANVASS CAPSULE
OVERSEE SURVIEW THEORIC
EPISCOPY LUSTRATE OVERLOOK
OVERVIEW PROSPECT SURVEYAL
TRAVERSE
(— RAPIDLY) GLANCE
(— TIMBER) SKYLOOK
(BRIEF —) APERCU
SURVEYING GEODESY GROMATICS
(MINE —) LATCHING
SURVEYOR BOLO ARTIST DIALER
DIALLER NOTEMAN CHAINMAN
GROMATIC LEVELMAN
SURVIVAL ECHO RELIC RELICT
(ANACHRONISTIC —) LEFTOVER
(USELESS —) SNUFF

SURVIVE LAST BILEVE OUTLAST
OUTLIVE
SURVIVOR RELICT
SUSCEPTIBILITY CAVIL SENSE
EMOTION FEELING FRAILTY
(— **TO ILL-HEALTH**) DELICACY
SUSCEPTIBLE EASY SOFT LIABLE
FEELING PATIENT SENSIBLE
TOLERANT
(— **TO CHANGE**) CASALTY
SUSIAN ELAMITE
SUSLIK SISEL ZIZEL MARMOT
SUSPECT FEAR DOUBT FANCY
GUESS SMOKE THINK BELIEVE
ENDOUTE JALOUSE MISDEEM
SUPPOSE DISTRUST JEALOUSE
MISDOUBT MISTRUST
(**NOT** —) COLD
SUSPECTED SPOTTED SUSPECT
SUSPEND CALL HALT HANG OUST
SHUT SIST STAY BREAK CLOSE
DEBAR DEFER DEMUR EXPEL POISE
REMIT SLING SWING APPEND
DANGLE ADJOURN EXCLUDE
FLUIDIZE INTERMIT OVERHANG
REPRIEVE SCAFFOLD SUSPENSE
(— **ANCHOR**) COCKBILL
SUSPENDED SWING AFLOAT LATENT
HANGING PENDANT PENDENT
PENSILE HOVERING SUSPENSE
SUSPENDER GALLUS GARTER
BRETELLE
(PL.) BRACES GALLOWS GALLUSES
SUSPENSE DEMUR POISE
SUSPENSION FOG BREI FUME SIST
STAY STOP DELAY DOUBT MAGMA
SMOKE BREACH CUTOFF SLURRY
AEROSOL FAILURE RESPITE
ABEYANCE BACTERIN EMULSION
INFUSION SHUTDOWN SUSPENSE
WISHBONE
(— **OF JUDGMENT**) EPOCHE
(— **OF NOISE**) HUSH
(— **OF RESPIRATION**) SYNCOPE
SUSPENSIVENESS DRIVE
SUSPENSORY SUPPORT
SUSPICION HINT DOUBT SOUPCON
SURMISE SUSPECT UMBRAGE
DISTRUST JEALOUSY MISDOUBT
MISTRUST TINCTURE
SUSPICIOUS SHY FISHY LEERY
PEERY QUEER SMOKY JEALOUS
SUSPECT DOUBTFUL WAFFLIKE
SUSPICIOUSLY ASKANCE
SUSQUEHANNA CONESTOGA
SUSTAIN ABET BACK BEAR BUOY
DURE HELP HOLD LAST PROP STAY
ABIDE CARRY FAVOR SPRAG STAND
ASSIST CONVEY ENDURE FOSTER
SECOND SUCCOR SUFFER UPHOLD
UPSTAY CONTAIN NOURISH
OUTBEAR PROLONG SUPPORT
UNDERFO BEFRIEND BUTTRESS
CONTINUE MAINTAIN PRESERVE
SUSTAINED SOUTENU
SUSTENANCE GEAR SALT BREAD
FOISON LIVING RELIEF ALIMENT
PABULUM TABLING
SUSU GERIP SOOSOO DOLPHIN

SUSURRUS WHISPER
SUTLER PROVANT VIVANDIE
SUTTEE SATI
SUTURE SEAM RAPHE SETON
HARMONY PTERION
SVANTOVIT TRIGLAV
SWAB GOB MOP SWOB PATCH
DOSSIL SPONGE EPAULET SWABBER
SQUILGEE
SWADDLE SWEEL SWATHE
SWAG DRUM GAME LOOT BOOTY
LUCRE MONEY BOODLE FESTOON
MATILDA
SWAGE BOSS MOUTH UPSET FULLER
JUMPER SHAPER SWAGER SWEDGE
FLATTER
(PL.) OLIVER
SWAGGER JET ROY BRAG COCK
FACE ROLL BOAST BRAVE NUTTY
STRUT SWANK SWASH BOUNCE
GOSTER HECTOR PARADO PRANCE
RENOWN RUFFLE SPROSE BLUSTER
BRAVADO GAUSTER PANACHE
ROISTER SOLDIER DOMINEER
TIGERISM
SWAGGERER HUFF SWAG FACER
TIGER CUTTLE JETTER PISTOL
BRAVADO HUFFCAP RUFFLER
FANFARON
SWAGGERING HUFFY FACING
GASCON HUFFCAP TEARCAT
BLUSTERY TIGERISH
SWAGMAN WHALER DRUMMER
TRAVELER
SWAIN COLIN CUDDY STREPHON
SWAINSONA INDIGO
SWALE SLASH
SWALLOW OFF SUP BOLT DOWN
GAUP GAWP GLUT GULP SINK TAKE
CLUNK DRINK GORGE GURGE
POUCH QUILT SLOCK SWOOP
ABSORB ENGLUT ENGULF GLUTCH
GOBBET GOBBLE GODOWN GUZZLE
IMBIBE INGEST MARTIN POCKET
PROGNE SWELLY CONSUME
ENGORGE ARUNDELL WITCHUCK
(— **GREEDILY**) BEND SLUP GORGE
GULCH SWILL WORRY INHALE
(— **HASTILY**) SWAP SWOP GLOUP
(— **IN AGAIN**) RESORB
(— **UP**) GULF SWAMP ABSORB
DEVOUR
(— **WITH GREEDINESS**) ENGORGE
(**LOSS OF ABILITY TO** —) APHAGIA
(**NOISY** —) SLURP
(**WOMAN TURNED INTO** —) PROCNE
SWALLOWTAIL TROILUS
SWAMP BOG FEN FLAT FLOW MIRE
MOSS SLEW SLUE SOAK SUMP VLEI
VLEY WHAM WHIN FLUSH LERNA
LETCH MARSH SWALE SWANG
URMAN DELUGE DISMAL ENGULF
MORASS SLOUGH CIENAGA
POCOSIN GREENING INUNDATE
QUAGMIRE
SWAMP COTTONWOOD LIAR
SWAMPER BUSHER GOPHER
SWAMPHEN COOT

SWAMP LOOSESTRIFE PEATWEED
PEATWOOD
SWAMP MAHOGANY GUNNUNG
SWAMP MILKWEED DAGGA
SWAMPY PUXY BOGGY POOLY
CALLOW POACHY QUASHY QUEASY
SLUMPY MOORISH
SWAMPY CREE MASKEGON
SWAN COB ELK PEN OLOR CYGNET
HOOPER SWANNET WHOOPER
(**FLOCK OF** —**S**) GAME MARK
SWANFLOWER SWANWORT
SWANK CHIC
SWANKY SWASH
SWAP CHOP SWOP TRADE TRUCK
DICKER EXCHANGE
SWARD SOD TURF SPINE SWARF
SWATH SWARTH
SWARM FRY SNY BIKE CAST FARE
HOST KNIT NEST SORT SWIM
CLOUD CROWD FLOCK FLUSH
FRACK HORDE SNARL FLIGHT
HOTTER RABBLE SWARVE THRONG
SUBCAST
(— **IN**) FILL
(— **OF BEES**) BIKE HIVE
(— **OF INSECTS**) BAND FLIGHT
(— **OF PEOPLE**) BIKE DRIFT
(**THIRD** — **OF BEES**) COLT
SWARMING ALIVE ASWARM SWARMY
SWARTBACK SWARBIE
SWARTHY DUN DARK BLACK DUSKY
GRIMY MOORY SWART MORIAN
SWARTH BISTRED BISTERED
SWASH SWIG SWILL SWATCH
SWABBLE SWASHWAY
SWASHBUCKLER SWASH GASCON
SLASHER SWASHER
SWASTIKA FYLFOT GAMMADION
SWAT SWOT DEHGAN STRIKE
SWATH SWIPE STADDLE
SWATHE LAP BIND WRAP SWARF
SWADDLE WINDROW
SWATTER FLYSWAT
SWAY NOD WAG BEAR BIAS FLAP
HIKE LILT ROCK ROLL RULE SWAB
SWAG SWIG TILT TOSS WALD WAVE
CARRY CHARM LURCH POWER
REIGN SHAKE SWALE SWING WAVER
WHEEL AFFECT ALLURE CAREEN
DIRECT EMPIRE WAGGLE COMMAND
SHOGGIE STAGGER SWABBLE
SWIGGLE
SWAYBACK WARFA LORDOSIS
RENGUERA
SWAYING ASWAY ROLLING
SWAZILAND (**CAPITAL OF** —)
MBABANE
(**LANGUAGE OF** —) SISWATI
(**RIVER IN** —) USUTU KOMATI
MHLATUZE UMBULUZI
(**TOWN IN** —) MANZINI
SWEAR VOW VUM DAMN SINK SNUM
SWAN SWOW TAKE CURSE ADJURE
AFFIRM BEDAMN DEPONE DEPOSE
OBJURE CONJURE DEJERATE
EXECRATE FORSWEAR
(— **FALSELY**) RAP MOUNT
FORSWEAR MONSWEAR

SWEARING JURATION
(FALSE —) PERJURY
SWEARWORD CUSS
SWEAT DEW WET STEW WASH
BREAN MADOR SUDOR SUDATE
LAUNDER PARBOIL SWELTER
SWIVVET TRANSUDE
(— SKINS) STALE
(DYNAMITE —) LEAK
SWEATBOX HOTBOX
SWEATER FROCK GANSEY JUMPER
WOOLLY CARDIGAN SLIPOVER
SWEATHOUSE TEMESCAL
SWEATING TUB ASWEAT SWELTRY
SUDATION SUDATORY
SWEATY PUGGY ASWEAT PERSPIRY
SUDOROUS SWEATFUL

SWEDEN

CAPITAL: STOCKHOLM
COIN: ORE KRONA SKILLING
DIVISION: AMT LAEN SKANE
OREBRO UPPSALA GOTALAND
JAMTLAND SWEALAND
GULF: BOTHNIA
ISLAND: OLAND GOTALAND
LAKE: SILJAN VANERN MALAREN
VATTERN DALALVEN HJALMREN
STORAVAN
MEASURE: AM ALN FOT MIL REF
TUM FAMN STOP FODER KANNA
KAPPE LINJE NYMIL SPANN
STANG TUNNA FATHOM JUMFRU
KOLLAST OXHUVUD TUNLAND
FJARDING KAPPLAND KOLTUNNA
MOUNTAIN: SARV AMMAR OVIKS
HELAGS SARJEK
PROVINCE: KALMAR OREBRO
GOTLAND HALLAND UPPSALA
ALVSBORG BLEKINGE ELFSBORG
JAMTLAND MALMOHUS
WERMLAND
RIVER: DAL UME GOTA KLAR LULE
KALIX PITEA RANEA LAINIO
LJUSNE TORNEA WINDEL
ANGERMAN
TOWN: UMEA BODEN BORAS
EDANE FALUN GAVLE LULEA
MALMO PITEA VISBY YSTAD
ARVIKA OREBRO LUDVIKA
UPPSALA GOTEBORG NYKOPING
VASTERAS
WEIGHT: ASS LOD ORT MARK
PUND STEN UNTZ NYLAST
LISPUND SKEPPUND

SWEEP BUCK DUST RAFF SOOP
SWAY TILT BESOM BROOM DIGHT
DRIFT FETCH SCOPE SKIRL SWIPE
SWOOP BREADTH CLEANSE
PICOTAH SHADOOF STRICKLE
(— A NET) BEAT
(— MAJESTICALLY) SWAN
(— OF SCYTHE) SWATH SWATHE
(— OFF) SLIPE
(— ON CULTIVATOR) SKIN
(CHIMNEY —) CHUMMY SWEEPY
RAMONEUR

(HAY —) BUCK
SWEEPBOARD STRICKLE
SWEEPER BUNGY SWEEP TOPAZ
BHANGI BHUNGI MEHTAR PRYLER
ROADER SOOPER TOPASS
BROOMER TUBEMAN BHUNGINI
MATRANEE SCRUBBER
SWEEPING SURGE RASANT SWEEPY
(— FOR FISH) DRAFT DRAUGHT
(PL.) DUST FULVIE FULZIE RIFFRAFF
SWEET DOUX DUMP FOOL SOOT
SUCK CREAM DILIS DOUCE DULCE
FRESH HONEY MERRY SOOTH SPICY
SPLIT DULCET FRUITY GENTLE
SILKEN SILVER SIRUPY SUGARY
DARLING FAIRING HONEYED INSIPID
MUSICAL PANDROP SUGARED
SWEETLY WINNING WINSOME
AROMATIC ENGAGING FLUMMERY
LIEBLICH LUSCIOUS NECTARED
PLEASANT
(SLIGHTLY —) SEC
SWEET BAY BREWSTER MAGNOLIA
SWEETBREAD BUR BURR
(— OF DEER) INCHPIN
SWEETBRIER BEDEGUAR EGLANTINE
SWEET CALABASH KURUBA
SWEET CASSAVA AIPI AIPIM
SWEET CICELY MYRRH
SWEET CLOVER LOTUS MELILOT
SWEET COLTSFOOT LAGWORT
SWEETEN CANDY HONEY SUGAR
SWEET PURIFY ADDULCE CLEANSE
DULCIFY FRESHEN MOLLIFY
PERFUME MITIGATE
SWEET FENNEL FINOCHIO
FLORENCE
SWEET FERN FERNGALE
SWEETFISH AYU
SWEET FLAG SEDGE BEEWORT
CALAMUS
SWEET GALE GOLD GAGEL
BAYBUSH FLEAWOOD GALEWORT
GALLBUSH
SWEET GUM AMBER COPALM
STORAX BILSTED
SWEETHEART JO BOY GRA HON
JOE LAD PUG SIS AGRA BABY BEAU
DEAR DOLL DOXY FAIR GILL GIRL
JILL LADY LASS LIEF LOVE MASH
MORT POUT AGRAH BULLY BUSSY
CHERI COOKY DOLLY DONAH
DONEY DRURY FLAME LEMAN
LOVER PUGGY SPARK SWEET
COOKIE EMILIA FELLOW FRIEND
MOPSEY PIGEON STEADY WAHINE
AMOROSA BELOVED PHYLLIS
PIGSNEY QUERIDA SPRUNNY
SWEETIE TOOTSIE DOWSABEL
DULCINEA FOLLOWER LADYBIRD
LADYLOVE LIEBCHEN LOVELASS
MISTRESS SWEETING TRUELOVE
SWEETLEAF DYELEAVES
SYMPLOCOS
SWEET MARJORAM OREGANO
SWEETMEAT DUMP KISS DULCE
GOODY PLATE SPICE TOFFY
BUCAYO COMFIT DRAGEE DREDGE
JUNKET BANQUET CARAWAY

CLAGGUM LOUKOUM PENUCHE
SUCCADE CONSERVE HARDBAKE
MARZIPAN
(PL.) BALUSHAI CONFETTI
SWEETNESS DULCE HONEY SIRUP
SYRUP DULCOR DOUCEUR DULCITY
SUAVITY FLORIMEL WORDNESS
SWEET ORANGE CHINA CHINO
SWEET PEA CATGUT LATHYRUS
SWEET PEPPERBUSH CLETHRA
SOAPBUSH
SWEET POTATO YAM SWEET
BATATA CAMOTE KUMARA
SWEET RUSH SQUINANT
SWEET-SMELLING AROMATIC
SWEETSOP ANON ATES ATIS ATTA
CORAZON SWEETING
SWEET-SOUNDING MERRY
SWEET VIOLET FINELEAF
SWEET WILLIAM DIANTHUS
SWELL BAG NIB NOB BEAL BELL
BLAB BLOW BLUB BOLL BULB BULK
BUMP BUOY DOME FILL GROW
HOVE HUFF HUSH PINK PLIM RISE
TOFF TONY WAVE BELLY BLOAT
BULGE BUNCH FLASH PLUFF SMART
STOCK STRUT SURGE TULIP BILLOW
BOWDEN DILATE EXPAND GROWTH
LOVELY SPRING STROUT TUMEFY
UPRISE AUGMENT BLUBBER
BURGEON DISTEND INFLATE
SWAGGER OVERBLOW TURGESCE
(— OF GUN MUZZLE) TULIP
(— OF WATER) HUSH SURF FLOOD
SURGE
(— OUT) BAG POD BUNT DRAW
POUT BOSOM BILLOW SPONGE
BALLOON BLADDER
(HEAVY —) RUN SEA
SWELLDOODLE EGGFISH
SWELLED BIAS
SWELLFISH BLOWER PUFFER
TAMBOR
SWELLING BIG BUR NOB PAP PIN
BLAB BUBO BUMP BURR CLAP
COWL CURB FROG FULL GALL KNOB
KNOT NODE POKE PONE AMPER
BLAIN BOTCH BOUGE BULGE BUNCH
BUNNY EDEMA JETTY MOUSE
SURGE SWELL TUMOR ANCOME
ASWELL BOSOMY BUNCHY CALLUS
FLATUS GIBBER GROWTH KERNEL
PIMPLE STRUMA SWELTH WARBLE
AMPULLA BOSSING CAPELET
CHAGOMA CUSHION GOUNDOU
HAPTERE PUSTULE SURGENT
TURGENT UREDEMA UROCELE
APOSTEME BULLNECK CHEMOSIS
DACRYOMA FURUNCLE GLANDULE
GOURDING HAPTERON HEMATOMA
MUCOCELE NODOSITY PUMPKNOT
QUELLUNG STYLOPOD VESSICON
(— IN HORSE'S CHEST) ANTICOR
(— OF PLANT TISSUE) GALL
(— OF THE CHEEK) HONE
(— ON ANIMAL'S JOINTS) BUNNY
(— ON HEAD) COWL
(EYE —) STY STYE
SWELTER STEW SWELT

SWELTERING STEWY SULTRY
SWELTRY
SWERVE BOW CUT LUG BIAS FADE
JOUK SKEW VARY WARP SHEER
STRAY DEPART DEVIATE DIGRESS
DIVERGE
SWIDDEN CAINGIN KAINGIN
SWIFT CRAN FAST FLIT MAIN VITE
FLEET HASTY LIGHT QUICK RAPID
SNELL SWITH WIGHT WINDY
ARROWY MARLET NIMBLE RAKING
SOUPLE SPEEDY STRICT SUDDEN
SWIFTY TOTTER WINGED COLLIER
DEVELIN FLIGHTY POSTING
SWALLOW TANTIVY DEVELING
HEPIALID PEGASEAN SCREAMER
SCUTTLER SQUEALER SWIFTLET
SWIFTLY FAST SWAP APACE SNELL
SNELLY LIGHTLY STEEPLY TANTIVY
SWIFTNESS FOOT HASTE SPEED
CELERITY FASTNESS VELOCITY
SWIG SCOUR SWILL SWING SWIGGLE
SWILL SOSS SLOSH SLUICE
HOGWASH PIGWASH SWILLING
SWIM COWD SAIL SOOM SPAN TEEM
BATHE CRAWL FLEET FLOAT GLIDE
SWARM OVERFLOW
(— IN NEW DIRECTION) MILL
(— TOGETHER) SCHOOL
SWIMMER BATHER NATATOR
SWIMMING ASWIM NATANT FLOTANT
NATATION
(— STUNT) MARLIN WALKOVER
SWIMMING POOL POOL THERM
PLUNGE THERME PISCINA
NATATORY
SWINDLE DO CON GIP GYP JOB RIG
BILK FLAP HAVE MACE PULL RAMP
ROOK ROPE SWIZ BUNCO BUNKO
CHEAT FLING FOIST GOUGE LURCH
PLANT ROGUE SHARK SHARP SHAVE
SLANG SPOOF SWIZZ UNCLE
BOODLE BUCKET DIDDLE FIDDLE
HUSTLE INTAKE NOBBLE SUCKER
TREPAN FINAGLE THIMBLE VERNEUK
FLIMFLAM
SWINDLER DO FOB GYP LEG BILK
FYNK HAWK SKIN CHEAT CROOK
FAKER GREEK HARPY KNAVE
MACER ROGUE CHIAUS GOUGER
INTAKE RINGER ROOKER SALTER
SHAVER VERSER MACEMAN
MAGSMAN NOBBLER SHARPER
SLICKER SPIELER BARNACLE
BLACKLEG FINAGLER GILENYER
LUMBERER PIGEONER SHELLMAN
TRAMPOSO
(DECOY —) BARNARD
SWINDLING MACE BUNCO BUNKO
ROOKY SHARK GYPPERY JOUKERY
CHEATERY JOOKERIE
SWINE HOG OIC PIG SOW BOAR
GALT GILT PORK SUID YILT DUROC
ESSEX SWIPE WHITE GUSSIE
POLAND PORKER PORKET BUSHPIG
PECCARY SUFFOLK SUIDIAN
CHESHIRE HYOTHERE LANDRACE
TAMWORTH
(— AND FOOD) PANNAGE

(— AND MAN) OMNIVORA
SWINEHERD GURTH HOGMAN
EUMAEUS HOGHERD HOGWARD
SWINE-LIKE GADARENE
SWING GO HIKE JUMP LILT SCUP
STOT SWAY SWEE TURN SHAKE
SHOWD SLING SWALE TREND
DANGLE GYRATE HANDLE SWINGE
SWITCH SWIVEL TOTTER JUMPING
SHOGGIE SWINGEL WAMPISH
BRANDISH FLOURISH
(— A SHIP) SPRING
(— AROUND) JIB SLEW SLUE
SLOUGH
(— BY BATTER) CUT
(— FROM POSITION) CANT
(— FROM SIDE TO SIDE) JOW
(— FROM THE TIDE) TEND
(— OF PENDULUM) BEAT
(— OF SAIL) GYBE JIBE
(— OF SWORD) MOULINET
(— OUT OF LINE) SWAG
(— THE FOREFEET) DISH
(RHYTHMICAL —) LILT
(WILD —) HAYMAKER
SWINGING BANK ASWING SWINGY
SWINGLE SWORD SCUTCH SWIPPLE
SWING SEAT TRANSOM
SWINISH SOWISH HOGGISH PORCINE
SWIPE COP CHOP GLOM WIPE
SNAKE STEAL VULTURE
SWIRL BOIL GULF HURL PURL WALM
GURGE SWALE SWEEL SWORL
SWOOSH WREATHE
(— OF SALMON) BULGE
SWIRLING VORTICAL
SWISH HISH WHIP SMART SWILL
WHISH
SWISS MUFF SWISSER
(— PINE) MUGHO
SWITCH GAD TAN TWIG WAND
AZOTE BIRCH BREAK SHUNT SWISH
CHANGE CUTOUT DERAIL DIPPER
FERULA FERULE LARRUP RATTAN
SCUTCH SILENT SPRING HICKORY
KIPPEEN SCOURGE SQUITCH
HAIRWORK POSTICHE
(— FOCUS) FADE
(ELECTRIC —) KEY
(RAILROAD —) GATE POINT
SWITCH ENGINE GOAT
SWITCHMAN SHUNTER SWITCHER

SWITZERLAND
BAY: URI
CANTON: URI ZUG BERN VAUD
BASEL AARGAU GENEVA
GLARUS LUZERN SCHWYZ
TICINO VALAIS ZURICH GRISONS
THURGAU FRIBOURG OBWALDEN
CAPITAL: BERN BERNE
COIN: FRANC RAPPE RAPPEN
ANGSTER DUPLONE BLAFFERT
LAKE: URI ZUG THON AGERI
LEMAN MORAT BIENNE BRIENZ
GENEVA LUGANO SARNEN
WALLEN ZURICH HALLWIL
LUCERNE LUNGERN VIERVALD

MEASURE: POT AUNE ELLE FUSS
IMMI MUID PIED SAUM ZOLL
LIEVE LIGNE LINIE MAASS
MOULE POUCE SCHUH STAAB
TOISE PERCHE SETIER STRICH
JUCHART KLAFTER VIERTEL
MOUNTAIN: JURA RIGI ROSA
BLANC CENIS KARPF LINARD
PIZELA BERNINA BEVERIN
GRIMSEL PILATUS ROTONDO
BALMHORN JUNGFRAU
MATTERHORN
MOUNTAIN PASS: CENIS FURKA
ALBERG MALOJA BRENNER
GRIMSEL SIMPLON SPLUGEN
LOTSCHEN
NAME: HELVETIA
RIVER: AAR INN AARE THUR BROYE
DOUBS LINTH REUSS RHINE
RHONE MAGGIA SARINE TICINO
PRATIGAU
TOWN: BALE BERN BIEL BRIG
CHUR SION BASEL VEVEY
GENEVA GLARUS LUZERN
SCHWYZ ZURICH FYZABAD
HERISAU LUCERNE LAUSANNE
MONTREUX
VALLEY: AAR ZERMATT ENGADINE
WEIGHT: PFUND CENTNER
QUINTAL

SWIVEL LOPER SWAPE SWIPE
CASTER FIDDLE TIRRET TOGGLE
TONGUE TRAVERSE TRUNNION
SWOLLEN BLUB FULL PLIM RANK
BLOWN CHUFF GOUTY GREAT
GUMMY POBBY PROUD TUMID
BOLLEN BRAWNY BULLED GOURDY
TURGID BESTRUT BLOATED
BLUBBER BULBOUS GIBBOSE
GIBBOUS GOURDED GOUTISH
TURGENT BEPUFFED BLADDERY
TUMOROUS
SWOON KEEL SWEB SWIM DROWN
DWALM FAINT SLOOM SOUND
SWARF SWELT STOUND SWOUND
TRANCE ECSTASY SWITHER
SYNCOPE SWOONING
SWOONING ASWOON SYNCOPE
SWOOP CHOP JOUK SWAP SWOP
SOUSE STOOP SWOPE POUNCE
SOURCE DESCEND
SWOOPING SOUSE
SWORD FOX SAX BILL DIRK FALX
GRAM IRON PATA SAEX SPIT TOOL
TURK BILBO BLADE BRAND DEGEN
DIEGO ESTOC GULLY KNIFE KUKRI
PRICK RIPON SABER SABRE SHARP
STEEL ANDREW BARONG BILBOA
CATTAN DAMASK DUSACK FLORET
GLAIVE HANGER KHANDA KUKERI
MIMING PARANG PINKER PORKER
RAPIER SMITER SPATHA TILTER
TIZONA TOLEDO WAFTER BALMUNG
BRANDON CURTANA CUTLASH
CUTLASS ESPADON ESTOQUE
FERRARA FLEURET IMPALER
JOYEUSE MALCHUS MORGLAY

SHABBLE SLASHER SNICKER
SPURTLE TOASTER WHIFFLE
WHINGER ACINACES BASELARD
CAMPILAN CLAYMORE DAMASCUS
DURENDAL FALCHION FLAMBERG
SCHLAGER SPADROON SPITFROG
WACADASH WHINYARD
(— OF CHARLEMAGNE) JOYEUSE
(— OF CID) TIZONA
(— OF HERMES) HARPE
(— OF LANCELOT) ARONDIGHT
(— OF ROLAND) DURENDAL
(— OF SIEGFRIED) GRAM BALMUNG
(— OF SIR BEVIS) MORGLAY
(— OF ST. GEORGE) ASCALON
ASKELON
(— USED BY ST. PETER) MALCHUS
(BLUNT —) WAFTER SCHLAGER
(CELTIC —) SAX SAEX
(DOUBLE-EDGED —) KEN PATA
KHANDA SPATHA
(DUELLING —) EPEE SHARP
(DYAK —) PARANG
(FENCING —) EPEE FOIL SABER
SABRE RAPIER
(HALF OF —) FORTE
(JAPANESE —) CATAN CATTAN
KATANA WACADASH
(LONG —) SPATHA WHIFFLE
(MATADOR'S —) ESTOQUE
(MORO —) BARONG CAMPILAN
(NARROW —) TUCK
(NORMAN —) SPATHA
(PERSIAN —) ACINACES
(POINTLESS —) CURTANA
(RUSTY —) SHABBLE
(SHORT —) DIRK ESTOC KUKRI
SKEAN WHINGER WHINYARD
(THRUSTING —) ESTOC STOCK
(TWO-HANDED —) ESPADON
CLAYMORE
(WOODEN —) WASTER STRICKLE
SWORD-BEARER VERGER SELICTAR
PORTGLAVE
(PL.) ENSIFERI
SWORD DANCER MATACHIN
SWORDFISH AU ESPADA ESPADON
XIPHIAS ALBACORA BILLFISH
BOATBILL FORKTAIL XIPHIOID
SCOMBROID
SWORDPLAY SPADROON
SWORD-SHAPED ENSATE ENSIFORM
GLADIATE
SWORDSMAN BLADE BLADER
FENCER SLASHER SWORDER
THRUSTER
SWORDTAIL HELLERI
SWORN AVOWED
SYAGUSH SHARGOSS
SYBARITE EPICURE
SYBARITIC SENSUOUS
SYCAMORE MAY DAROO COTONIER
LACEWOOD PLANTAIN
SYCEE SHOE
SYCOPHANCY FAWNERY
SYCOPHANT TOADY COGGER
FAWNER GNATHO HANGBY TAGTAIL
CLAWBACK PARASITE
SYCOPHANTIC FAWNING SERVILE

SLAVISH OBEDIENT TRENCHER
SYCOSIS MENTAGRA
SYENITE APPINITE TRACHYTE
SYLLABARY KANA IROFA IROHA
SYLLABIC SONANT CENTROID
SONANTIC
SYLLABLE ARSIS BREVE GROUP
SHORT DISEME SYLLAB THESIS
TRISEME ASSONANT
(— DENOTING ASSENT) OM
(BOBIZATION —) BO CE DI GA GE
LO MA NI
(LAST — BUT ONE) PENULT
(LAST —) ULTIMA
(LONG —) LONG
(MUSICAL —) DI DO FA FI LA LE LI
ME MI RA RE RI SE SI SO TA TE TI
TO UT SOL
(REFRAIN —) DILDO
(SHORT —) MORA SHORT
(STRONG —) STRESS
(UNACCENTED —S) THESIS
SYLLABUS PROGRAM VIDIMUS
HEADNOTE SYNOPSIS
SYLLOGISM BARBARA ABDUCTION
ENTHYMEME
(SERIES OF —S) SORITES
SYLPH ARIEL SYLPHID
SYLVAN WOODY FOREST SILVAN
WOODEN WOODISH SYLVATIC
SYLVITE HARDSALT
SYMBIOSIS LICHENISM MUTUALISM
NUTRICISM
SYMBOL KEY CODE FISH FOUR ICON
IDOL IKON MARK NEUM SEAL SIGN
TYPE CREST CROSS EAGLE IMAGE
INDEX CARACT CIPHER EMBLEM
ENSIGN FIGURE LETTER PNEUME
SHADOW SIGNAL FACIEND MANDALA
PALATAL CEREMONY CONSTANT
DIRECTOR EXPONENT GUTTURAL
IDEOGRAM LOGOGRAM OPERATOR
SWASTIKA SYMBOLUM TRISKELE
(— FOR WAVELENGTH) LAMBDA
(— OF DISTINCTION) BELT HONOR
(— OF FAITHFUL DEAD) ORANT
(— OF FRANCE) LILY
(— OF MONK) COWL
(— OF PHYSICIAN) CADUCEUS
(— OF RAILROAD) HERALD
(— OF SPRING) KARPAS
(— OF STRENGTH) HORN
(— OF SUN) DISC DISK
(— ON UNCHANGEABLENESS)
LEOPARD
(— REPRESENTING THE ABSOLUTE)
TAIKIH
(ALGEBRAIC —) EXPONENT
(CRICKET —) ASHES
(CRUSADERS' —) CROSS
(CURVED —) HOOK
(KOREAN —) TAHGOOK
(MAGIC —) CARACT
(MATHEMATICAL —) KNOWN
FACTOR FACIEND OPERAND
(PHALLIC —) LINGA LINGAM
(PICTOGRAPHIC —) ISOTYPE
(PRINTING —) DIAGONAL
(PRONUNCIATION —) ENG

(RELIGIOUS —) LABRYS
(PL.) KATAKANA
SYMBOLIC GRAPHIC SHADOWY
ANICONIC
SYMBOLICAL ALLUSIVE MYSTICAL
SYMBOLISM CONOLOGY
SYMBOLIZE BODY SIGN TOKEN
FIGURE SAMPLE SHADOW SYMBOL
TYPIFY EXPRESS PORTEND SIGNIFY
RESEMBLE
SYMMETRICAL FORMAL DIMERIC
REGULAR SHAPELY SPHERAL
BALANCED
(NOT —) SKEW
SYMMETRY MEASURE
SYMPATHETIC AKIN FERE SOFT
WARM HUMAN FELLOW KINDLY
TENDER PIETOSO SIMPATICO
SYMPATHIZER FABIAN BLACKNEB
SHAYSITE
SYMPATHY PITY RUTH FLESH PHILIA
CONSENT EMPATHY AFFINITY
KINDNESS
SYMPHONY SINFONIA
SYMPOSIUM POTATION
SYMPTOM MARK NOTE SIGN
SHOWER STIGMA INSTANCE
PRODROME
SYNAGOGUE SHUL SCHUL ALJAMA
PROSEUCHA
SYNAPSIS PAIRING
SYNAPTE ECTENE EKTENE
SYNARTHROSIS SUTURE
SYNCHRO SELSYN
SYNCHRONIZER SPEEDGUN
SYNCLINE DOWNFOLD ISOCLINE
SYNCOPATED ZOPPA ABRIDGED
SYNCOPE SWOON COTYPE FAINTING
SYNDICATE HUI GROUP
SYNDICATED CANNED
SYNECDOCHE MERISM
SYNERGIST BOOSTER SESAMIN
SYNOD SOBOR
SYNODAL SENAGE
SYNONYM ANTONYM HOMONYM
EUPHONYM POLYONYM
SYNOPSIS BRIEF TABLE EPITOME
SUMMARY ABSTRACT SCENARIO
SYLLABUS
SYNSACRUM SACRARY
SYNTACTICAL FORMAL
SYNTHESIS SUMMA FUSION
SYSTASIS
SYNTHETIC ERSATZ SYSTATIC
SYPHILIS POX LUES SYPH CRINKUM
GRINCOME

SYRIA

CAPITAL: DAMASCUS
COIN: POUND TALENT PIASTER
DISTRICT: ALEPPO HAVRAN
LAKE: DJEBOID TIBERIAS
MEASURE: MAKUK GARAVA
MOUNTAIN: HERMON LIBANUS
NAME: ARAM
NATIVE: DRUSE ANSARIE
SARACEN ANSARIEH
RIVER: ASI BARADA JORDAN

KNABUR ORONTES EUPHRATES
TOWN: ALEP HAMA HOMS NAWA
BUSRA CALNO DERRA HALAB
HAMAH IDLIB JERUD RAQQA
ALEPPO BALBEL BIERUT
LATAKIA SELEUCIA
WEIGHT: COLA ROTL ARTAL
ARTEL RATEL TALENT

SYRINGE GUN HYPO ENEMA SCOOT DOUCHE FILLER SQUIRT SCOOTER SERRING
SYRINGIN LILACIN
SYRNIUM STRIX
SYRYENIAN SYRYAN ZYRIAN
(PL.) KAMI KOMI
SYRUP DIBS LICK SIRUP ORGEAT ANTIQUE ECLEGMA FALERNUM QUIDDANY
(STARCH —) GLUCOSE
SYRUPY FRUITY
SYSTEM ISM AREA CREDO FRAME ORDER CIRCLE METHOD SCHEME STEREO SYNTAX COMPLEX DUALISM ECONOMY FAGGERY NAVARHO REGIMEN ENSEMBLE GALENISM RELIGION UNIVERSE
(— OF BARS) LATTICE
(— OF BELIEFS) FAITH
(— OF BELL CHANGES) CATERS QUATERS STEDMAN
(— OF CORDS) BRIDLE
(— OF CROSSING THREADS) LEASE
(— OF ETHICS) SELFISM

(— OF EXCHANGE) KULA
(— OF FAITH) CREED
(— OF GEARS) COMPOUND
(— OF JOINTS) CLEAT
(— OF LANGUAGE SIGNS) SIGNARY
(— OF LAW) EQUITY
(— OF LINES IN EYEPIECE) RETICLE RETICULE
(— OF MANUAL TRAINING) SLOJD SLOYD
(— OF MEANING) SEMANTIC
(— OF MEDICINE) AYURVEDA
(— OF NUMERALS) ALGORISM
(— OF OCCULT THEOSOPHY) CABALA
(— OF PHILOSOPHY) HUMISM HOBBISM SAMKHYA SANKHYA STOICISM
(— OF PHONETIC NOTATION) ROMIC
(— OF PRINCIPLES) CODE
(— OF RAYS) ASTER
(— OF ROCKS) CENOZOIC DEVONIAN SILURIAN
(— OF RULE) REGIME
(— OF RULES) ART
(— OF SOLMIZATION) FASOLA
(— OF SPACES) LACUNOME
(— OF SYMBOLS) CODE
(— OF TENANCY) CROFTING
(— OF TRANSPORTATION) AIRLINE AIRMAIL
(— OF TRUSSING) CABANE
(— OF VALUES) ETHOS
(— OF WEIGHTS) TROY

(— OF WIRES) HARNESS
(— OF WORSHIP) CULT CULTUS
(— OF WRITING) KANJI BRAILLE ALPHABET
(ACOUSTICAL —) SODAR
(AGRICULTURAL —) KOLKOZ KOLKHOS
(ALARM —) BUG
(BETTING —) ALEMBERT
(COLLOIDAL —) SOL
(COMMUNICATION —) BLOWER CIRCUIT
(CULTURAL —) ISLAM
(DEFENSE —) SAGE
(DISPERSE —) GEL
(ELECTRICAL —) SELSYN
(GEOLOGICAL —) KEEWATIN TERTIARY
(HAULING —) DILLY
(IRRIGATION —) KAREZ
(LANGUAGE —) LATINXUA
(NAVIGATION —) GEE LANAC SHORAN
(RELIGIOUS —) LAW CULT CULTUS SHIISM SUNNISM DRUIDISM
(RHYTHMIC —) STROPHE GLYCONIC
(SOCIAL —) CASTE
(STAR —) GALAXY
(TECHNOLOGICAL —) FORDISM
(TELEVISION —) SCOPHONY
(TRUCK —) TOMMY
SYSTEMATIC ORDERLY REGULAR METHODIC
SYSTEMATIZE CODIFY ORGANIZE

T TEE TARE TANGO
TAAL AFRIKAANS
TAB JAG PAN TAG BILL COST CHECK
FLASH PRICE TALLY WATCH EARTAB
EARTAG SIGNAL TOEPLATE
TABANID GADFLY
TABERNACLE PIX PYX HOVEL
SACRARY
TABES WASTING
TABETIC MARCID
TABLATURE LYRAWAY PICTURE
PAINTING
TABLE KEY PIE PYE RUN BANK BUCK
DAIS DESK FORM MESS BELLY
BENCH BOARD CANON CHART PINAX
PLANK SCALE STALL STAND STONE
WAGON COMMON SCHEME TABLET
TABULA TARIFF TRIPOD VANNER
CABARET CAMBIST CONSOLE
COUNTER DIAGRAM DIPTYCH
DRESSER PROJECT SHAMBLE
TABLEAU TESSERA TROLLEY
WHIRLER CALENDAR CREDENCE
GUERIDON PEDIGREE PEMBROKE
REGIMENT SPECULUM STILLAGE
TOILETTE VANITORY
(— FOR BOWING HAT-BODY) HURL
(— FOR GLAZING LEATHER) BANK
(— FOR ORNAMENT) CARTOUCH
(— FOR PHOTOGRAPHIC PLATES)
WHIRLER
(— FURNISHED WITH MEAL) SPREAD
(— IN STORE) COUNTER
(— OF ANCESTORS) PEDIGREE
(— OF CONTENTS) INDEX METHOD
(— OF DECLINATIONS) REGIMENT
(— TOP) AMOEBA
(— USED IN FELTING A HAT) BASON
(— WITH BRAZIER BENEATH)
TENDOOR TENDOUR
(ARITHMETIC —) TARIFF
(ASTROLOGICAL —) SPECULUM
(BOTANIC —) KEY
(CIRCULAR —) ROUNDEL
(COMMUNION —) ALTAR
(DINING —) MAHOGANY
(DRESSING —) TOILET VANITY
TOILETTE
(FOLDING —) SERVETTE
(INNER —) HOME
(MASSAGE —) PLINTH
(MUSICAL —) DIAGRAM
(NIGHT —) SOMNO
(PRINCIPAL —) DAIS
(PROFUSELY ORNAMENTED —)
PEMBROKE
(SERVING —) WAGON
(SHAKING —) SLIMER
(SMALL —) KURSI STAND TABORET
TABOURET
(TEA —) TEAPOY
(WRITING —) DESK
TABLEAU LAYOUT PAGEANT
TABLECLOTH CLOTH COVER
TABLE D'HOTE DINNER
TABLELAND PLAT PUNA PUNO
KAROO TABLE KARROO PLATEAU
BALAGHAT
TABLET PAX BRED ALBUM FACIA

PIECE PINAX SLATE TABLE TABULA
TABULE TROCHE ASPIRIN CODICIL
DIPTYCH PALETTE PREFORM
TABLING CARTOUCH CHURINGA
TABULATE TRIPTYCH
(— BEARING SYMBOL OF CHRIST)
PAX
(— FOR PUBLISHING LAWS)
PARAPEGM
(— OVER SHOP FRONT) FACIA
FASCIA
(MEDICATED —) ASPIRIN JELLOID
TABELLA
(MEDICINAL —) DISC DISK TROCHE
(MEMORIAL —) BRASS TABUT
(PAINTER'S —) PALETTE
(SQUARE —) ABACK
(UPRIGHT —) STELA STELE
(VOTIVE —) PINAX
(WRITING —) CODICIL TRIPTYCH
TABLEWARE CHINA FLATWARE
HAVILAND
TABOO KAPU TABU TAPU
FORBIDDEN INEFFABLE
TABOR ATABAL TABRET TIMBRE
TABORIN TIMBREL
TABULATION SCALE SCHEME
TABLING
TABUT TAZIA TAZEEA
TACHOMETER CUTMETER
TACHYGLOSSUS ECHIDNA
TACIT SILENT IMPLICIT
TACITURN DUMB STILL SILENT
RESERVED
TACK LAY BEAT CAST STAY BASTE
BOARD FETCH ENTAIL LAVEER
TACKET TINGLE SADDLERY
(GLAZIERS' —) BRAD
TACKER GUN SPREADER
TACKLE CAT RIG TAW SWIG TACK
YOKE ANGLE FALLS ATTACK
BURTON COLLAR GARNET JIGGER
LEDGER RUNNER STEEVE TAGLIA
TEAGLE DERRICK HALYARD
HARNESS RIGGING FISHFALL
PURCHASE TACKLING
(— FOR RAISING BOAT) FALLS
(— TO HOIST ANCHOR) CAT
(COMBINATION OF —S) JEER JEERS
(FISHING —) TEW LEGER OTTER
LEDGER
TACT TOUCH ADDRESS CONDUCT
DELICACY
TACTFUL DISCREET GRACEFUL
TACTFULLY HAPPILY
TACTLESS BRASH
TACTIC GAME
TADPOLE POWHEAD BULLHEAD
POLEHEAD POLLIWOG PORWIGLE
TAEL LIANG
TAENNIN KOSIN KOUSIN
TAFFETA TABBY FLORENCE
TAFFY GUNDY TOFFY TOFFEE
CLAGGUM
TAG HE EAR TAB TIG TAIL TICK
AGLET DAGGE LABEL TALLY TOUCH
AIGLET EARTAB EARTAG FOLLOW
SWATCH TAGGLE TAGRAG TICKET
TIGTAG HANGTAG

(— OF A LACE) AGLET AIGLET
(ANGLING —) TOUCH
(ORNAMENTED —S) FANCY
TAGALOG PULAHAN
TAGESTES MARIGOLD
TAGRAG SHAGRAG
TAHITI (CAPITAL OF —) PAPEETE
(FORMER NAME OF —) OTAHEITE
(MOUNTAIN IN —) OROHENA
TAHR KRAS JHARAL
TAHSILDAR TALUKDAR
TAI LI AHOM SHAM THAI PORGY
KHAMTI
TAIGA URMAN
TAIL BOB BUN CUE BUNT BUSH CLUB
FLAG POLE SCUT BRUSH CAUDA
SNAKE START STERN TRAIN TWIST
FLIGHT FOLLOW RUMPLE SWITCH
TAILET TAILLE FANTAIL FOXTAIL
RATTAIL
(— OF ARTIFICIAL FLY) TOPPING
(— OF BELL CLAPPER) FLIGHT
(— OF BIRD OR ANIMAL) CUE POLE
START
(— OF BIRD) FAN
(— OF BOAR) WREATH
(— OF CART) ARSE
(— OF COAT) DOCK
(— OF COMET) BEARD STREAM
STREAMER
(— OF DEER) FLAG SINGLE SHINGLE
(— OF DOG) FLAG STERN
(— OF FISH) UROSOME
(— OF FLY) WHISK
(— OF FOX) BUSH BRUSH FOXTAIL
(— OF HARE OR RABBIT) BUN FUD
BUNT SCUT
(— OF HORSE) BOB
(— OF MAN'S TIED HAIR) CLUB
(— OF METEOR) TRAIN
(— OF MUSICAL NOTE) QUEUE
(— OF PUG DOG) TWIST
(— OF SQUIRREL) BUN
(— OF STANZA) CODA
(DRAGON'S —) KETU
(STUMP OF —) STRUNT
(TIP OF —) TAG
TAILBAND FOOTBAND
TAILBOARD ENDGATE ENDBOARD
ENDPIECE
TAILED CAUDATE CAUDATED
TAILING CHAT
(PL.) SAND TAIL GRUFFS
TAILLE TALLY
TAILLESS ACAUDAL ANUROUS
ACAUDATE ECAUDATE
TAILOR SLOP SNIP BUILD DARZI
GORER SHRED DARZEE FULLER
SARTOR SNYDER STITCH BOTCHER
CABBAGE SNIPPER TIREMAN
CLOTHIER SEAMSTER SEMPSTER
SHEPSTER
(ITINERANT —) CARDOOER
TAILORBIRD DARZEE
TAILPIECE QUEUE ANQUERA
TAILRACE AFTERBAY
TAILSPIN FLICKER
TAILSTOCK DEADHEAD
TAINO HAITIAN

(— BELIEFS) ZEMIISM
TAINT HAUL HOGO MOIL SMUT SPOT
VICE CLOUD STAIN TOUCH DARKEN
INFECT REMORD SMIRCH SMUTCH
ATTAINT BLEMISH CORRUPT
DEBAUCH ENVENOM FLYBLOW
FORRUMP POLLUTE TARNISH
VITIATE EMPOISON TAINTURE
TAINTED OFF GAMY HIGH BLOWN
PINDY SAPPY TAINT WEMMY
ROTTEN SINFUL SMUTTY CORRUPT
FLYBLOWN
TAIWAN (CAPITAL OF —) TAIPEI
(ISLAND GROUP OF —) MATSU
PENGHU QUEMOY
(MOUNTAIN IN —) TZUKAO YUSHAN
HSINKAO
(OTHER NAME OF —) FORMOSA
(RIVER IN —) WUCHI TACHIA
CHOSHUI HUALIEN TANSHUI
(TOWN IN —) TAINAN TAIPEI
KEELUNG TAICHUNG
TAJIN TOTONAC
TAJ MAHAL (SITE OF —) AGRA
TAKE COP HIT NIM NOB BEAR BONE
DRAW FANG GLOM HAVE LEAD
TACK TEEM TOLL ADOPT AFONG
BRING CARRY CATCH CREEL FETCH
GRASP GRIPE LATCH SEIZE SNAKE
ACCEPT CLUTCH COTTON DERIVE
EXTEND FERRET FINGER RECIPE
SNATCH TAKING ATTRACT CABBAGE
CAPTURE RECEIVE UNPURSE
UNDERNIM
(— A BATH) TOSH
(— A CERTAIN POSITION) SIT
(— A DIRECTION) STEER
(— A DRINK) SMILE
(— A LITTLE) DELIBATE
(— A NAP) DOSS
(— A STAND) ASSERT
(— ACTION) ACT
(— ADVANTAGE) DO ABUSE BLUDGE
CLUTCH EXPLOIT
(— AFTER) BRAID FOLLOW
(— AIM) BEAD
(— AS ONE'S OWN) ADOPT
(— AWAY) BATE EASE HENT LIFT
TOLL WISP BENIM BLEED HEAVE
REAVE STEAL CONVEY DEDUCE
DEDUCT DEMISE DEPOSE DEVEST
DIVEST ELOIGN EXEMPT REMOVE
UNVEST ABJUDGE BEREAVE
DEPRIVE DETRACT FORTAKE
RETRACT SUBDUCE SUBLATE
ABSTRACT DEROGATE DIMINISH
SUBTRACT
(— BACK TO ONESELF) RESUME
(— BACK) RECALL RECANT REVOKE
RETRACT
(— BY FRAUD) BOB
(— BY LEVY) ESTREAT
(— BY STEALTH) HOOK SNITCH
(— BY STORM) EXPUGN INVADE
SURPRISE
(— CARE) FIX SEE GARE KEEP MIND
TEND WARD YEME NURSE BEWARE
GOVERN INTEND CUIDADO HUSBAND
CHAPERON

(— CENSUS OF) MUSTER
(— CHANCE) DICE RISK
(— CHARGE OF) CURE SOLICIT
(— CHARGE) ATTEND
(— COVER) COOK
(— DAMAGE) BANGE
(— DINNER) DINE
(— DOWN) STOOP STRIKE
(— EXCEPTION) DEMUR STRAIN
(— FOOD) EAT DINE GRUB
(— FOR GRANTED) BEG ASSUME
(— FOR ONESELF) CAB
(— FOR RESALE) FLOG
(— FORM) FORM INFORM
(— FRAUDULENTLY) STEAL STRIKE
(— FRIGHT) BOOGER
(— FROM DEPOSIT) DRAW
(— FROM) DETRACT
(— GOLFING STANCE) ADDRESS
(— GREAT DELIGHT) REVEL
(— HEART) BRACE
(— HEED) RECK TENT
(— HOLD) GET BITE GRAB PINCH
SEIZE ARREST BEGRIPE
(— HOLIDAY) LAKE
(— IN BY LEAKING) LADE
(— IN LIVESTOCK) AGIST
(— IN SAIL) BRAIL
(— IN) IN EAT SUP BITE HOAX KEEP
DOWSE DRINK ABSORB DEVOUR
ENFOLD GATHER HARBOR INCEPT
INGEST INSORB INSUME INTAKE
MUZZLE BEGRIPE EMBRACE
INCLUDE
(— INTO HANDS) TOUCH EMBRACE
(— LEGALLY) ATTACH
(— LEVEL OF) BONE
(— LUNCH) TIFFIN
(— MEALS) BOARD
(— NOTE OF) NB COUNT SMOKE
NOTICE WITNESS
(— OATH) ABJURE
(— OFF) OFF DOFF LIFT VAIL DOUSE
SHUCK STRIP DEDUCT
(— OFFENSE) DORT HUFF
(— ON) MOUNT START
(— ONE'S LEAVE) CONGEE
(— ONESELF) BETAKE
(— OUT OF EARTH) EXTER
(— OUT) DELE KILL EXCERPT
AIRBRUSH
(— PAINS) BOTHER
(— PART) LEAD FIGHT ENGAGE
(— PLACE) BE DO GO COME GIVE
PASS ARISE BEFALL HAPPEN
(— PLEASURE IN) ENJOY ADMIRE
(— PORTION OF) PARTAKE
(— POSSESSION) GRIP ANNEX
BESET SEIZE SPOIL EXTEND
CONQUER INHERIT DISTRAIN
(— REFUGE) HIDE SOIL EVADE
HAVEN WATCH
(— ROOT) MARE MORE ENROOT
STRIKE
(— SHAPE) JELL
(— SHELTER) HOWF NESTLE
SHROUD
(— SUPPER) SUP
(— THE PLACE OF) ENSUE SECOND

SUPPLY DISPLACE SUPPLANT
(— THOUGHT) ADVISE
(— TO BE TRUE WITHOUT PROOF)
PRESUME
(— TO TASK) JACK CARPET
(— TO WING) FLUSH
(— UNAWARE) DECEIVE
(— UP AGAIN) RESUME
(— UP WITH) ALL
(— UP) ENTER MOUNT ADSORB
ASSUME GATHER HANDLE STRIKE
(— WELL OR ILL) RESENT
(— WIND ON OPPOSITE QUARTER)
JIBE
TAKEN TON TAIN
(— ABACK) BLANK
(— AWAY) ADEMPT
TAKEOFF SPOOF SCRAMBLE
TAKEOUT STACK
TAKER PERNOR
TAKING HOT TAKY ADOPTION
PERNANCY
(— EVERYTHING INTO ACCOUNT)
OVERALL
(— OF LIFE) BLOOD
(— PLACE) AGATE
TALAK AHSAN
TALARI PATACA PATACOON
TALAUS (FATHER OF —) BIAS
(MOTHER OF —) PERO
(SON OF —) ADRASTUS
(WIFE OF —) LYSIMACHE
TALC SPAAD TALCUM AGALITE
STEATITE
TALE SAW DIDO JEST LEED REDE
TELL BOURD CRACK FABLE RECIT
SPELL SPOKE STORY WINDY AITION
FABULA LEGEND PISTLE PURANA
FABLIAU FICTION HISTORY
MARCHEN ROMANCE ANECDOTE
FOLKTALE SPELLING
(— OF ACHIEVEMENTS) GEST
GESTE
(— OF GOLD COAST NEGROS)
NANCY
(COMIC COARSE —) FABLIAU
(DEVISED —) AITION
(EPIC —) TAIN
(FALSE —) VANITY SLANDER
(FATEFUL —) WEIRD
(FOLK —) NANCY THRENE
(HUMOROUS —S) FACETIAE
(MERRY —) BOURD
(POETIC NARRATIVE —) SAGA
(SHORT —) LAI CONTE
TALEBEARER BUZZER GOSSIP
TATTLER TALEPYET TELLTALE
TALEBEARING TALEWISE
TALENT GIFT HEAD VEIN DOWER
DOWRY VERVE CICHAR GENIUS
ABILITY CHARISM FACULTY
CAPACITY CHARISMA
TALENTED ABLE CLEVER GIFTED
TALER ORT THALER
TALIPES CLUBFOOT
TALISMAN ANGLE CHARM IMAGE
SAFFI AMULET GRIGRI SAPHIE
SCARAB TELESM ICHTHUS ICHTHYS
GREEGREE

TALK GAB JAW JIB SAW SAY YAP
BUCK BUKH CANT CARP CHAT CHIN
GAFF GIVE GUFF KNAP MEAN TALE
TOVE WORD CRACK FABLE MOUTH
PARLE PITCH SPEAK SPELL SPIEL
SPOKE TUTEL COMMON GAMMON
INDABA KORERO PATTER SERMON
SPEECH STEVEN TOMGUE YABBER
ADDRESS DISCUSS LIPWORK
PALABRA PALAVER PARRALL
PURPOSE WINDJAM CAUSERIE
COLLOQUY CONVERSE LANGUAGE
PARLANCE QUESTION
(— ABOUT) HASH
(— BACK) SASS
(— BIG) BOUNCE
(— BOASTFULLY) GAS
(— BOMBASTICALLY) BEMOUTH
(— CASUALLY) DISH
(— CONFIDENTIALLY) CUTTER
(— CONFUSEDLY) HOTTER
(— DISMALLY) CROAK
(— EMPTILY) BLOW
(— FAMILIARLY) TOVE CONFAB
(— FATUOUSLY) BABBLE
(— FONDLY) COO
(— FOOLISHLY) BLAT FLAP HAVER
BABBLE DRIVEL FOOTER FOOTLE
GABBLE GIBBER SAWNEY TOOTLE
BLATHER BLETHER
(— GLIBLY) PATTER
(— GLIBLY) SCREED
(— IDLY) GAB BLAB CHIN GASH
FABLE GABBLE JANGLE TATTLE
CHATTER GNATTER PRATTLE
(— IMPUDENTLY) SASS
(— INACCURATELY) BLAGUE
(— INARTICULATELY) CHUNNER
CHUNTER
(— INCESSANTLY) YANK BURBLE
CHATTER
(— INCOHERENTLY) BABBLE
HOTTER MITHER MOIDER
(— INCONSIDERATELY) BLAT
(— INFORMALLY) HOBNOB
(— INSOLENTLY) SNASH
(— INTENDED TO DECEIVE)
GAMMON PALAVER
(— IRRATIONALLY) RAVE
(— MONOTONOUSLY) DRONE
(— NEEDLESSLY) PALAVER
(— NOISILY) CLAP BLATTER
BRABBLE
(— NONSENSE) GAS ROT DROOL
FUDGE
(— OFFICIOUSLY) BLEEZE
(— PERTLY) CHELP
(— PRIVATELY) COLLOGUE
(— RAPIDLY) GABBLE JABBER
GNATTER
(— SCANDAL) HORN
(— SNAPPISHLY) KNAP
(— SPORTIVELY) DAFF
(— SUPERFICIALLY) SMATTER
(— TEDIOUSLY) DINGDONG
(— THOUGHTLESSLY) BLAB
(— TOGETHER) DEVISE
(— VAGUELY) WOOZLE
(— VOLUBLY) CHIN PATTER

(— WEAKLY) DRIVEL
(— WITH) CONTACT
(— WITHOUT MEANING) GABBLE
(ABSURD —) BOSH
(ABUSIVE —) HOKER JAWING
(ARROGANT —) GUM BRAG
(BOASTFUL —) BULL GAFF
(BOMBASTIC —) FLASH
(COMMON —) FAME FABLE
HEARSAY
(DECEPTIVE —) GAMMON
(EMPTY —) GAS BOSH GASH FRASE
GLOZE FRAISE BLAFLUM GASSING
PRATTLE BALLYHOO GALBANUM
(ENTHUSIASTIC —) JAZZ
(FALSE —) BALLYHOO
(FAMILIAR —) CONFAB CHITCHAT
(FANTASTIC —) GUYVER
(FOOLISH —) GUP GAFF JIVE BLEAT
CLACK FABLE BLETHERS
(FORMAL —) ADDRESS
(GLIB —) JIVE
(IDLE —) GAB BLAB BUFF CHAT
GAFF GEST GUFF FABLE GESTE
BABBLE CLAVER GOSSIP JANGLE
CHATTER CLATTER PALAVER
TWATTLE BABBLING
(IMPUDENT —) PRATE SLACK
(INCOHERENT —) GABBER JABBER
(INFORMAL —) CAUSERIE
(INSINCERE —) BUNKUM
(JESTING —) CHAFF JAPERY
(LIGHT —) TRIFLING
(MEANINGLESS —) SLIPSLOP
(NONSENSICAL —) BLABBER
BLATHER FOLDEROL
(PIOUS OR SANCTIMONIOUS —) PI
(RAPID —) GABBLE JABBER
CHATTER CLATTER
(SCOLDING —) HARANGUE
(SILLY —) BUFF CLART FOOTLE
TWADDLE
(SMALL —) CHAT BACKCHAT
CHITCHAT
(SMOOTH —) GLOZE BLARNEY
(TRIFLING —) PRATTLE CHITCHAT
(USELESS —) WASTE
(VIOLENT —) BLUSTER
(WEAK —) SLIPSLOP
(WHINING —) BLEAT
TALKATIVE COSY GASH GLIB NAWY
BUZZY TALKY CHATTY CLASHY
CRACKY FLUENT FUTILE VOLUBLE
BIGMOUTH FLIPPANT TELLSOME
TALKATIVENESS FUTILITY
TALKER CAMPER POTGUN CAUSEUR
SPIELER
(IDLE —) WHIFFLER
(PROFESSIONAL —) JAWSMITH
(SENSELESS —) RATTLE
TALKING (LOUD —) NORATION
TALKING-TO EARFUL LECTURE
TALKY GABBY
TALL HIGH LANKY LOFTY STEEP
WANDY CRANEY PROCERE
(— AND FEEBLE) TANGLE
(VERY —) TAUNT
TALLAGE CUTTING
TALLER DOMINANT

TALLOW SUET SEVUM ARMING
TAULCH
TALLY TAB JUMP SUIT AGREE CHECK
COUNT SCORE STICK STOCK
CENSUS STRING SWATCH TAILYE
COMPORT TAILZIE
TALMUD GEMARA
TALON FANG SERE UNCE CLUTCH
POUNCE UNGUIS WEAPON
(— OF TOOTH) HEEL
TALONID HEEL
TALPA TESTUDO
TALTHIB GLAGA GLAGAH
TALUS SCREE RUBBLE ASTRAGAL
TAMANDUA ANTEATER
TAMARACK LARCH LARIX EPINETTE
TAMARIN PINCHE JACCHUS
LEONCITO MARIKINA MARMOSET
TAMARIND SAMPALOC
TAMARISK ATLE JHOW HEATH
TAMASHEK TUAREG
TAMBOURINE RIKK TAAR DAIRA
TAMBO TABOUR TIMBER TABORIN
TIMBREL
TAME MAN DEAD MEEK MILD PACK
ACCOY ATAME BREAK DAUNT MILKY
SPAKE CADISH ENTAME GENTLE
INWARD MEEKEN UNWIFE AFFAITE
CORRECT INSIPID SUBDUED
CICURATE DOMESTIC MANSUETE
(— FALCON) MAN RECLAIM
TAMED BROKE GENTLE
TAMIL VELLALA
TAMMY TAMIS STAMIN
TAMONEA MICONIA
TAM-O-SHANTER TAM TAMMY
TAMP PUG STEM
TAMPER FIX COOK FAKE FOOL GAFF
TOUCH DABBLE FIDDLE MEDDLE
MONKEY POTTER PUDDLE PUTTER
TEMPER FALSIFY TRINKLE
TAMPION TOMKIN TAMPOON
TAM-TAM GONG
TAN FAN ARAB BARK ADUST ASCOT
DRESS TANKA TAWNY ORIOLE
COCONUT EMBROWN LEATHER
SUNBURN
(BEACH —) SEDGE
(TROTTEUR —) BAY
TANACETYL THUJYL
TANAGER YENI LINDO REDBIRD
WARBIRD CARDINAL EUPHONIA
FIREBIRD ORGANIST
TANBARK BARK TAWN AVARAM
TURWAR ALGERIAN ALGERINE
TANDAN EELFISH
TANEKAHA TOATOA
TANG NIP TING VEIN SHANK STRAP
TASTE TWANG RELISH TANGLE
TONGUE SEATANG FAREWELL
TANGELO UGLI
TANGENCY CONTACT
TANGENT SLOPE
TANGERINE NAARTJE MANDARIN
TANGIBLE ACTUAL TACTILE
CONCRETE MATERIAL PALPABLE
TANGLE COT ELF TAT FANK FOUL
HARL SHAG TAUT HARLE KNURL
SNARL SNIRL THRUM TWINE WOPSE

BALTER ENTRAP HANGER JUNGLE
MOMBLE MUCKER RAFFLE SLEEVE
TAFFLE TARDLE TAUGHT TEIHTE
BRANGLE TAISSLE THICKET
FURBELOW SCROBBLE
(PL.) COBWEB

TANGLED AFOUL TOUSY MESHED
SNARLY TAUTED IMPLICIT INTORTED
INVOLVED
(— **UP**) HAYWIRE

TANGLEHEAD PILI

TANGY BRISK

TANHA TRISHNA

TANK DAM DIP TAL BOSH SUMP
BASIN MIXER STANK STEEP TRUNK
BLOWUP BOILER HOPPER PANZER
TROUGH BATTERY BLOWPIT
BREAKER CISTERN FLUSHER
PISCINA PLUNGER POACHER
SETTLER STEEPER BLEACHER
DIGESTOR LANDSHIP SUBSIDER
(— **FOR DYE OR SOAP**) BECK
(— **FOR FISH**) STEW TRUNK
AQUARIUM STEWPOND
(— **IN SHIP**) FOREPEAK
(**ARMORED** —) FLAIL WHIPPET
LANDSHIP
(**PAPER MANUFACTURING** —)
POACHER
(**PHOTOGRAPHIC** —) CUVETTE
(**POTTER'S** —) PLUNGER
(**RECTANGULAR** —) BOWLY
(**SALT MANUFACTURING** —)
GRAINER
(**STORAGE** —) CHEST
(**SUGAR REFINING** —) TIGER
BLOWUP
(**TANNING** —) FLOATER
(PL.) HEAVIES

TANKAGE AMMONATE

TANKARD GUN JACK FACER STOOP
STOUP PEWTER POTTLE TANKER
GODDARD

TANNED BROWN RUDDY TAWNY
BRONZED
(**NOT** —) RAW

TANNER EGGER SAMAR BARKER
STAKER PERCHER

TANNING PASTING
(— **SOLUTION**) PLUMPER

TANSY COSTMARY

TANSY MUSTARD FLIXWEED
FLUXWEED

TANSY RAGWORT RAGWEED

TANTALIZE GRIG JADE TEASE
HARASS

TANTALUS (**DAUGHTER OF** —) NIOBE
(**FATHER OF** —) JUPITER THYESTES
(**MOTHER OF** —) PLUTO
(**SON OF** —) PELOPS
(**WIFE OF** —) DIONE

TANTAMOUNT SAME

TANTRA AGAMA

TANTRUM HISSY TIRRIVEE WINGDING

TANZANIA
CAPITAL: DARESSALAM
LAKE: RUKWA

NATIVE: BANTU SUKUMA
MAKONDE SWAHILI
RIVER: RUVU WAMI RUAHA
KAGERA RUFIJI RUVUMA
PANGANI MBENKURU
TOWN: WETE KILWA MOSHI TANGA
ARUSHA DODOMA KIGOMA
MWANZA TABORA MTAWARA
MOROGORO
WEIGHT: FARSALAH

TAO MAN PEASANT
(— **PRACTICE**) WUWEI

TAP BOB DAB PAT TAT TIP TIT TOP
BEAT COCK DRUB FLIP JOWL PENK
TICK TIRL TUNK APPEL FLIRT QUILL
SNOCK START ALETAP BROACH
CANNEL DABBLE FAUCET NATTLE
TAPLET DRAWOFF HEELTAP
PERCUSS
(— **A CASK**) QUILL STRIKE
(— **A DRUM**) TUCK
(— **FOR A LOAN**) TIG
(— **ON SHOE**) CLUMP UNDERLAY
(— **ON THE SHOULDER**) FOB
(— **REPEATEDLY**) DRUM
(— **THE GROUND**) BEAT
(**FENCING** —) BEAT
(**MASTER** —) HOB HUB
(**SMART** — **OF THE FOOT**) APPEL

TAPA KAPA SIAPO KIKEPA

TAPACOLA TURCO

TAPE LEAR FERRET GARTER SCOTCH
TAPERY YNKELL BINDING MEASURE
TAPELINE TELETAPE
(**FISH** —) SNAKE
(**LAMP** —) WICK
(**LINEN** —) INKLE
(**METALLIC** —) GALLOON
(**NARROW** —) TASTE
(**RED** —) WIGGERY

TAPE GRASS EELGRASS

TAPEMAN CHAINMAN

TAPER DRAW RISE DRAFT GAUDY
SCARF SNAPE SWAGE CIERGE
DRAUGHT LIGHTER PRICKET
TRINDLE DIMINISH
(— **OF A SPRING**) DRAW
(— **OF PATTERN**) STRIP
(— **OFF**) CEASE TONGUE

TAPERED BARRELED BOATTAIL
GRADUATED

TAPERING SHARP SPIRAL SPIRED
TERETE SPIRING FUSIFORM
SUBULATE

TAPER ROD PODGER

TAPESTRY ARRAS TAPET TAPIS
COSTER DORSER DOSSER CEILING
GOBELIN HANGING SUSANEE
VERDURE AUBUSSON MORTLAKE

TAPEWORM TAPE LIGULA TAENIA
COENURE HYDATID PLATODE
BANDWORM COENURUS DAVAINEA
FLATWORM HELMINTH
(PL.) CYSTICA

TAPHOLE TAP FLOSS MOUTH

TAPIR ANTA KUDA DANTA TENNU
TAPIROID

TAPPED ABROACH

TAPPET WIPER

TAPROOM TAP SALOON BARROOM
BUVETTE TAPHOUSE

TAPSTER NICKPOT SKINKER

TAPUYAN GE GES GHES BUGRE
GESAN JUYAS CAYAPO GOYANA
CAMACAN CARAHOS COROADO
TIMBIRA APINAGES BOTOCUDO
CAINGANG CHAVANTE

TAR PAY BREA BINDER ALKITRAN
(**BIRCH** —) DAGGETT
(**MINERAL** —) MALTHA

TARA DOLMA

TARANTULA HUNTER JAYHAWK
MYGALID

TARBOOSH FEZ

TARDIGRADA ARCTISCA

TARDILY SLOWLY

TARDINESS SLOTH TARDITY

TARDY LAG LAX DREE LATE SLOW
SLACK DREIGH LAGGED REMISS
LAGGING DILATORY LATESOME

TARE VETCH LEAKAGE
(PL.) FILTH

TARES ZIZANY

TARGET AIM MOT BUTT MARK WAND
CLOUT LEVEL PRICK ROVER SCOOP
SCOPE TARGE WHITE BANNER
NIVEAU OBJECT SLEEVE COCKSHY
INCOMER OUTGOER SARACEN
POPINJAY
(— **OF KNEELING FIGURE**) SQUAW
(— **OF LEVELING STAFF**) VANE
(— **OF RIDICULE**) GAME
(— **RING**) SOUS
(**EASY** —) SITTER
(**PIECE OF** —) SCAB
(**RAILROAD SWITCH** —) BANNER
(**STRIKE A** —) KEYHOLE
(**THROWN** —) COCKSHY COCKSHUT
(**TOWED** —) DROGUE
(**UNIDENTIFIED** —) SKUNK

TARHEEL STATE NORTHCAROLINA

TARIFF AVERAGE TRIBUTE

TARNISH DIM BLOT SMIT SOIL
CLOUD DIRTY STAIN SULLY TACHE
BREATH DARKEN DEFILE INJURE
SMIRCH ASPERSE BEGRIME
BESMEAR OBSCURE BESMIRCH
DISCOLOR

TARO COCO DALO EDDO GABE KALO
MASI TALO COCCO KAROU TANIA
TANYA COCKER TARROW YAUTIA
DASHEEN MALANGA COCOROOT
EDDYROOT

TAROT NAIB TAROCCO

TARPON SABALO

TARRAGON TARCHON ESTRAGON

TARRY BIDE STAY STOP ABIDE
DALLY DEMUR PAUSE ARREST
LINGER REMAIN SOJOURN

TARSIER LEMUR

TARSOMETATARSUS SHANK

TARSUS HAND ANKLE DIGITAL
(**BIRD'S** —) SHANK

TART ACID FLAN SOUR BOWLA
CUPID EAGER SHARP SNIPPY
SUNKET PIQUANT POLYNEE

PUNGENT SUBACID TARTLET
TURNOVER
TARTAN PLAID
(— **PATTERN**) SETT
TARTAR ARGAL ARGOL CALCULUS
TARTNESS ACRITY ACIDITY
VERDURE ACERBITY ASPERITY
VERJUICE
TASK FAG JOB TAX CHAR DARG TOIL
CHARE CHORE GRIND KNACK
LABOR NULLO STINT CHARGE
DEVOIR NIYOGA PENSUM RAMSCH
TOURNE FATIGUE SWEATER
TRAVAIL BUSINESS EXERCISE
TRAUCHLE
(— **AS PSYCHOLOGICAL TEST**)
AUFGABE
(**ASSIGNED** —) STENT STINT DEVOIR
(**EASY** —) PIPE SNAP SETUP
(**ONEROUS** —) CORVEE
(**ROUTINE** —) DRUDGE
TASKMASTER DRIVER TASKER
RAWHIDER
TASMANIA (**CAPITAL OF** —) HOBART
(**LAKE IN** —) ECHO SORELL
(**MOUNTAIN IN** —) DROME NEVIS
BARRON CRADLE LOMOND
HUMBOLDT
(**RIVER IN** —) ESK HUDN TAMAR
GORDON JORDAN PIEMAN DERWENT
(**TOWN IN** —) BURNIE HOBART
TASMANIAN DEVIL DASYURID
TASMANIAN WOLF HYENA
THYLACINE
TASSEL TAG TUFT LABEL THRUM
TARCEL TARGET TOORIE CORDELLE
(PL.) ZIZITH
TASTABLE GUSTABLE
TASTE EAT GAB GOO LAP SIP CAST
DASH GOUT GUST HINT PREE RASA
SALT TANG TEST TINT WAFT ASSAY
DRINK FANCY GUSTO HEART PROVE
RELES SAVOR SHADE SKILL SMACK
SNACK SPICE TOOTH TOUCH
DEGUST FLAVOR GENIUS LIKING
PALATE RELISH SAMPLE SMATCH
ATTASTE PREGUST SOUPCON
THOUGHT APPETITE JUDGMENT
PENCHANT SAPIDITY
(— **COMBINED WITH APTITUDE**)
FLAIR
(— **IN MATTERS OF ART**) FANCY
(**BAD** —) GOTHISM
(**DECIDED** —) PENCHANT
(**DELICATE** —) BREED
(**DISCRIMINATING** —) SKILL
(**GOOD** —) DECORUM
(**STRONG** —) GOO
(PL.) MERIDIAN
TASTEFUL NEAT ELEGANT GUSTOSO
TASTELESS DEAF FLAT FLASH
MALMY VAPID WERSH WALLON
FATUOUS INSIPID INSULSE WEARISH
UNSAVORY
TASTER TRIER
TASTING ASSAY
(— **OF MALT**) CORNY
TASTY GUSTABLE TASTEFUL
TATAR KIN JUNG KITAN SOYOT

CHAZAR KHAZAR KHITAN KHOZAR
SHORTZY MELETSKI
(PL.) HU
TATOUAY CABASSOU
TATTER JAG RAG TAG SHRED
FITTER LIBBET TAGRAG TARGET
FLITTER TROLLOP
(PL.) DUDS TAVERS FITTERS
RIBBONS TAIVERS FLITTERS
TATTERED DUDDY BEATEN TAGGED
FORWORN TATTERY TOTTERED
TATTLE BLAB GASH CHEEP CLASH
CLYPE PEACH SNEAK TUTEL GOSSIP
QUATCH SNITCH TATTER TITTLE
CLATTER
TATTLER LAB CLASH SNIPE FABLER
GAMBET GOSSIP TUTLER YELPER
TITTLER TELLTALE
TATTLING LEAKY FUTILE
TATTOO TAT MOKO PINK POUNCE
TATTOOED PINKED
(— **MAN**) YUN
TATTOOING MOKO
TAUGHT MAK TEACHED INSTRUCT
(**EASILY** —) DOCIBLE
TAUNT BOB MOB CHIP GIBE JAPE
JEER JEST MOCK PROG SKIT TWIT
CHECK FRUMP GLAIK JAUNT SCOFF
SCORN SLANT SLARE SLART DERIDE
SNEEST UPCAST SARCASM TWITTER
RIDICULE
TAUNTING RAIL
TAUPE MOLESKIN
TAUROTRAGUS OREAS ORIAS
TA-URT THOUERIS
TAUT SNUG TORT STIFF TIGHT
CORDED
TAUTEN SNUB STIFFEN SWIFTER
TENSION
TAUTOG CHUB MOLL LABROID
TAVERN INN BUSH HOWF VENT
MITER MITRE TAMBO BISTRO
CABACK BUVETTE CABARET
OSTERIA TABERNA GASTHAUS
ORDINARY POTHOUSE TAPHOUSE
TAW TER SCORE MARBLE GLASSIE
SHOOTER
TAWDRY CHEAP GAUDY GILDED
TINSEL
TAWNY FUSC BRUSK DUSKY FULVID
TANNED FULVOUS JACINTH
TAW-SUG SULU
TAX LAY LOT CAST CESS DUTY GELD
GELT GILD LEVY POLL RATE SCAT
SCOT SESS TAIL TASK TOLL ABUSE
AGIST DONUM FINTA HANSA HANSE
LEKIN MAILL OBROK QUINT SCATT
STENT TOUST VERGI WATCH ZAKAH
ZAKAT ABKARI ASSESS AVANIA
BURDEN CEDULA DEMAND EXCISE
EXTENT HIDAGE IMPOST JEZIAH
KHARAJ MURAGE OCTROI OCTROY
PAVAGE PURVEY SENSUS STRAIN
SURTAX VINAGE BOOMAGE
BOSCAGE CHANCER CHEVAGE
CHIVAGE CONDUCT FINANCE
GABELLE LASTAGE PATENTE
PENSION POLLAGE PONTAGE
SCUTAGE STIPEND TAILAGE

TERRAGE TRIBUTE ALCABALA
AUXILIUM BONAUGHT CARUCAGE
CORNBOLE DANEGELD EXACTION
EXERCISE KERNETTY MALTOLTE
OBLATION PESHKASH ROMESCOT
ROMESHOT STACKAGE SUPERTAX
TAXATION WHEELAGE
(— **AT HARVESTTIME**) CORNBOLE
(— **FOR STORING LOGS**) BOOMAGE
(— **OF ONE-FIFTH**) QUINT
(— **ON EVERY PLOW**) CARUCAGE
(— **ON HERRING CATCH**) LASTAGE
(— **ON LIQUOR**) ABKARI
(— **ON SALT**) GABELLE
(— **ON UNBELIEVERS**) KHARAJ
(— **ON WALLS**) MURAGE
(— **ON WOOD**) BOSCAGE
(— **ON WOOL**) MALETOTE
MALTOLTE
(— **TO PETTY PRINCES**) KERNETTY
(— **TO SYNAGOGUE**) FINTA
(— **TO TENTH AMOUNT**) TITHE
(— **UNDULY**) STRAIN
(**CAPITATION** —) JIZYA JIZYAH
(**CHINESE** —) LEKIN LIKEN LIKIN
(**EXTRAORDINARY** —) AUXILIUM
(**IRISH** —) BONAGHT
(**MOHAMMEDAN** —) JEZIAH
(**PARISH** —) PURVEY
(**PHILLIPINES** —) CEDULA
(**POLL** —) TOLL CENSUS
(**RUSSIAN** —) OBROK
(**SPANISH** —) ALCABALA ALCAVALA
(**TURKISH** —) VERGI AVANIA
TAXABLE LISTABLE
TAX COLLECTOR TITHER GABELLER
TAXGATHERER POLLER TAXMAN
TAXI JIXIE CRAWLER
TAXICAB CAB HACK CRUISER
MOTORCAB
TAXIDERMY NASSOLOGY
TAXING SEVERE GRUELING
TAXON MONERA
TAXONOMIST LUMPER SPLITTER
TAYASSU PECARI
TAYRA GALERA
TCHAMBULI CHAMBERI
TEA CHA CHIA TCHA THAM TSIA
ASSAM CAPER CHAIS CONGO
FAHAM HYSON MIANG PEKOE STEEP
CONGOU KEEMUN OOLONG PTISAN
SUNGLO REDROOT TWANKAY
AUTUMNAL GOWIDDIE SOUCHONG
WORMSEED
(**AFRICAN** —) CAT KAT QAT KHAT
QUAT
(**BLACK** —) BOHEA CONGO OOPAK
OOPACK SYCHEE
(**COARSE** —) BANCHA
(**HIGH-GRADE** —) GYOKURO
(**INFERIOR** —) BOHEA
(**MEDICINAL** —) TISANE
(**MEXICAN** —) BASOTE APASOTE
(**POOR** —) BLASH
TEA BOWL CHAWAN
TEACAKE LUNN SCONE
TEACH ARAL LEAR READ SHOW
TECH TENT CARRY COACH EDIFY
ENDUE LEARN SPELL TRAIN TUTOR

WISSE INFORM PREACH SCHOOL
BITECHE EDUCATE EXAMPLE
EXPOUND GRAMMAR AMAISTER
DISCIPLE DOCUMENT INSTRUCT
PUPILIZE
(— TO FIGHT) SPAR
TEACHABLE DOCILE DOCIBLE
TEACHABLENESS DOCITY DOSSETY
TEACHER RAB ALIM GURU AKHUN
BIDDY CADET GUIDE MOLLA RABBI
REBBE TUTOR USHER AKHUND
AMAUTA DOCENT DOCTOR DOZENT
FATHER MADRIH MAULVI MENTOR
MULLAH PANDIT PUNDIT RABBAN
READER REGENT RHETOR SUPPLY
ACHARYA ALFAQUI DOMINIE
MAESTRA MAESTRO MUNCHEE
MURSHID PEDAGOG SHASTRI
SOPHIST SPONSOR STARETS
TRAINER ALFAQUIN AYUDANTE
DIRECTOR EDUCATOR EXTENDER
GAMALIEL MAGISTER MELAMMED
MISTRESS MOONSHEE MUJTAHID
(— OF ELOQUENCE) RHETOR
(— OF EMINENCE) MAESTRO
(— OF HIGH LEARNING) SOPHIST
(— OF KORAN) ALFAKI ALFAQUIN
(— OF PAUL) GAMALIEL
(INCA —) AMAUTA
(MOHAMMEDAN —) COJA HODJA
KHOJA KHOJAH
TEACHING LAW DHARMA DOCENT
LESSON LORING ACROAMA TUITION
BUDDHISM DIDACTIC DOCTRINE
DOCUMENT TUTELAGE
(PL.) ACOUSMA BROWNISM
CACODOXY DIDACTICS
TEAK SAJ DJATI EBONY
TEAKETTLE SUKE SUKEY CHAFER
KETTLE POURIE CRESSET
TEAL CRICK BLUEWING GARGANEY
SARCELLE
TEAM SET FIVE PLOW SIDE SPAN
YOKE DRAFT SWING PLOUGH
SEXTET DRAUGHT CARTWARE
(— 2 ABREAST, 1 LEADING) SPIKE
UNICORN
(— HARNESSED ONE BEFORE
ANOTHER) TANDEM
(— OF 3 HORSES ABREAST) TROIKA
(— OF GLASSWORKERS) SHOP
CHAIR
(— THAT FINISHES LAST) DOORMAT
(2-HORSE —) PODANGER
(3-HORSE —) RANDOM
(ATHLETIC —) CLUB
(BASEBALL —) NINE
(BASKETBALL —) FIVE
(FOOTBALL —) ELEVEN
TEAMSTER CARTER TEAMEO
CARTMAN SKINNER TEAMMAN
TEAPOT TRACK TRACKPOT
TEAR RIP RIT RUG TUT CLAW PILL
PULL RACE RASE RAVE REND RIVE
RUGG SKAG SNAG STUN BREAK
CLAUT LARME PEARL SHARK SLENT
SPALT SPLIT TOUSE CLEAVE
HARROW RANCHE RIPPLE SCHISM
SCREED WRENCH CHATTER

CONVELL DISCIND EYEDROP
SCRATCH DISTRAIN FRACTURE
LACERATE LACHRYMA TEARDROP
(— APART) REND TEASE DISCERP
DIVULSE
(— ASUNDER) DIVEL
(— AWAY) AVULSE
(— DOWN) UNPILE DESTROY
DEMOLISH
(— IN NEGATIVE) SLUG
(— INTO PIECES) DRAW TOLE DEVIL
SHRED TEASE LANIATE
(— INTO SHREDS) HOG DEVIL
TATTER
(— INTO) LAMBAST LAMBASTE
(— OFF) STRIP ABRUPT DISCERP
(— OPEN) PROSCIND
(— UP BY THE ROOTS) ARACHE
(PL.) DEW BRINE RHEUM EYEWATER
TEARDROP EYEWATER
TEARFUL SOFT TEARY WEEPY
LIQUID WATERY WEEPLY FLEBILE
MAUDLIN SHOWERY SNIVELY
SNIVELLY
TEARING SCREED
(— AWAY) AVULSION
TEARPIT LARMIER
TEASE COD FUN ROT TAR TRY TUM
BAIT DRAG FASH FRET HARE HOCK
JADE JIVE JOSH LARK NARK RAZZ
TARR TOUT WORK CHAFF CHEEK
CHEVY DEVIL FEEZE TARIE TAUNT
TOOSE WRACK BANTER BOTHER
CADDLE CHIVVY HARASS HOORAY
HURRAH MOLEST MURDER PESTER
PLAGUE HATCHEL TERRIFY
TORMENT WHERRET
TEASEL KING TASSEL TEASLE
MANWEED
TEASELER GIGGER TEASER
TEASELING MOZING
TEASER TIZEUR
TEASING CHAFF MERRY BANTER
DEVILING QUIZZING
TEAT DUG PAP TIT DIDDY SPEAN
NIPPLE SUCKLE
TEA TREE TI MANUKA
TECHNICIAN SWITCHER
TECHNIQUE FEAT GATE WRINKLE
COQUILLE INDUSTRY SPICCATO
(BILLIARD —) FOLLOW
(DANCE —) HEELWORK
(DECORATION —) IKAT
(JUMPING —) SCISSORS
(WRESTLING —) GLIMA
(WRITING —) CUBISM
TECHNOLOGY FISHERY TECHNIC
CERAMICS
TECMESSA (FATHER OF —)
TELEUTAS
(HUSBAND OF —) AJAX
(SON OF —) EURYSACES
TECOMIN LAPACHOL
TECTRIX COVERT
TEDDER KICKER
TEDIOUS DEAD DREE DULL LATE
POKY PROSY ALENGE BORING
DREECH DREIGH ELENGE MORTAL
IRKSOME PREACHY PROSAIC

VERBOSE BORESOME DRAGGING
TIRESOME WEARIFUL
TEDIUM IRK YAWN ENNUI BOREDOM
TEE COCK TIGHT TOZEE WITTER
BULLHEAD
TEEM SNY FLOW SWIM SWARM
ABOUND BUSTLE SCRAWL
TEEMER SHOOTMAN
TEEMING BIG ALIVE TUMID FERTILE
GUSHING TEEMFUL BRAWLING
PREGNANT SWARMING
TEENY SMALL
TEESWATER MUGS MUGGS
TEETER ROCK WAVER JIGGLE
QUIVER SEESAW TREMBLE
TEETH CTENII CHOPPERS CRACKERS
GRINDERS
(HAVING —) IVORIED
(SET OF —) DENTURE
TEETHRIDGE ALVEOLE ALVEOLUS
TEETOTUM TOTUM WHIRLIGIG
TEGETICULA PRONUBA
TEGMENTUM ROOF
TEGULA SQUAMA EPAULET SCAPULA
PATAGIUM SQUAMULA
TEGUMENT COAT TEGMEN
TEHUELCHE PATAGON
TEJU TEIOID JACUARU TEGUEXIN
TELAMON ATLAS
(BROTHER OF —) PELEUS
(FATHER OF —) AEACUS
(MOTHER OF —) ENDEIS
(SON OF —) AJAX TEUCER
(WIFE OF —) GLAUCE HESIONE
TELAMONES ATLANTES
TELEDU BADGER STINKARD
TELEGONUS (FATHER OF —)
ULYSSES
(MOTHER OF —) CIRCE
(SON OF —) ITALUS
(WIFE OF —) PENELOPE
TELEGRAM TAR WIRE FLASH FLIMSY
TELEGRAPH WIRE CABLE BUZZER
TELEGRAM TELOTYPE
TELEMACHUS (FATHER OF —)
ULYSSES
(MOTHER OF —) PENELOPE
(SON OF —) LATINUS
TELENCEPHALON ENDBRAIN
TELEOLOGICAL TELIC FINALIST
TELEOLOGY FINALITY
TELEPHASSA (DAUGHTER OF —)
EUROPA
(HUSBAND OF —) AGENOR
(SON OF —) CADMUS PHOENIX
TELEPHONE PHONE HANDSET
TELEPHOTE DIAPHOTE
TELEPHUS (FATHER OF —)
HERCULES
(MOTHER OF —) AUGE
TELESCOPE TUBE COUDE GLASS
SCOPE TRUNK ALINER FINDER
ALIGNER BINOCLE TRANSIT
PROSPECT SPYGLASS
(SURVEYOR'S —) LEVEL
TELEVISION AIR
TELIOSPORE TELEUTO
TELL SAY DEEM MEAN MOOT READ
SHOW TALE AREAD AREED BREAK

BREVE COUNT NEVEN PITCH SPELL
STORY TEACH UTTER AUTHOR
DEVISE IMPART INFORM MUSTER
QUETHE RECITE RELATE REPEAT
REPORT REVEAL CONFESS DIVULGE
NARRATE PARTAKE RECOUNT
ACQUAINT REHEARSE
(— CONFIDENTIALLY) CONFIDE
(— CONFUSEDLY) SPLATHER
(— EARNESTLY) ASSURE
(— IN ADVANCE) FORESAY
(— LIES) BELY LIGE BELIE
(— OFF) JAR
(— ROMANCES) GEST GESTE
(— SECRETS) CHEEP CLYPE SPILL
(— STRIKINGLY) CRACK
(— TALES) CANT
TELLER SPINNER STORIER TALLIER
FABLEIST FABULIST SENACHIE
TELLING REDE PUNGENT POWERFUL
(— OF SECRETS) BLAB
TELLTALE BLAB CLASH TATTLER
TITTLER REGISTER
TELLURIDE ALTAITE
TELSON PLEON
TELUGU GENTU GENTOO TELINGA
TEM TUM ATMU ATUM
TEMERITY GALL CHEEK AUDACITY
RASHNESS
TEMPER CUE MAD BAIT BATE COOL
DASH DRAW MOOD MULL NEAL
PADD SCOT TONE ALLOY BIRSE
BLOOD CREST DELAY FRAME GRAIN
HUMOR IRISH SAUCE SOBER TRAMP
ADJUST ANIMUS ANNEAL DANDER
MASTER MONKEY SEASON SPLEEN
STRAIN SUBMIT CHASTEN CLIMATE
COURAGE HACKLES QUALIFY
STOMACH EBENEZER GRADUATE
MITIGATE MODERATE MOORBURN
(— CLAY) TAMPER
(— METAL) ALLAY
(— OF MIND) CUE SPIRIT
(CAPRICIOUS —) SPLEEN
TEMPERAMENT GEMUT HEART
HUMOR CRASIS KIDNEY TEMPER
STOMACH SANGUINE
TEMPERAMENTAL FITIFIED
TEMPERANCE MEDIETY SOBRIETY
TEMPERATE CALM COOL MILD SOFT
GREEN SOBER TEMPRE MODERATE
ORDINATE
TEMPERATURE SUN HEAT TEMP
HOTNESS
TEMPERED HARD SOBER SARCENET
TEMPEST GALE THUD WIND ORAGE
STORM TUMULT TORMENT TURMOIL
WEATHER
TEMPESTUOUS WILD GUSTY STERN
WINDY RUGGED STORMY VIOLENT
STALWART
TEMPLATE CURB NORMA TEMPLET
PADSTONE STRICKLE
TEMPLE VAT WAT DEUL FANE NAOS
RATH CANDI GUACA HUACA KIACK
KOVIL MARAE RATHA CHANDI
HAFFET HERION MANDIR SACRUM
SHRINE TEOPAN TJANDI VIHARA
HERAEUM HERAION TEMPLET

TEMPLUM VARELLA OLYMPIUM
PANTHEON RAMESEUM TEOCALLI
VALHALLA
(— AREA) MANDAPA
(CAVE —) SPEOS
(FIJI —) BURE
(HAWAIIAN —) HEIAU
(PART OF —) PRONAOS
(SHINTO —) SHA JINJA JINSHA
YASHIRO
(STUDY OF —S) NAOLOGY
(TOWERLIKE —) ZIGGURAT
TEMPLET FORMER
TEMPO TAKT TIME AGOGE
MOVEMENT
TEMPORAL CARNAL TIMELY
EARTHLY PROFANE SECULAR
TEMPORARY FLYING INTERIM
STOPGAP WHILEND EPISODAL
EPISODIC TEMPORAL
TEMPORIZER DRIFTER POLITIC
TEMPT EGG FAND FOND LURE TEMP
TENT COURT ALLURE ASSAIL
ENTICE INVITE SEDUCE ASSAULT
ATTEMPT SOLICIT SUGGEST
TEMPTATION TRIAL ATTEMPT
TESTING
TEMPTER DEVIL
TEMPTING ALLURING INVITING
TEMPTRESS SIREN DELILAH
TEN ICRE IOTA CHANG DIKER
CHEUNG DECADE DENARY DICKER
ARTICLE BRISQUE
(— OF TRUMPS) GAME
TEN'A KOYUKON
TENACE FORK
TENACIOUS FAST ROPEY TOUGH
CLEDGY DOGGED GRIPPY PLUGGY
STICKY STRONG GRIPPLE ADHESIVE
GRASPING HOLDFAST
TENACIOUSNESS TENACY
FASTNESS
TENACITY LENTOR COURAGE
TENACULUM CLASP
TENANCY CONACRE JOINTURE
TENANT KMET LEUD SAER BARON
CEILE DRENG LAIRD BORDAR
COTTAR COTTER DRENGH GENEAT
HOLDER INMATE LESSEE MOLMAN
RADMAN RENTER SOCMAN VASSAL
CHAKDAR COTTIER FEODARY
FEUDARY GAVELER HOMAGER
SOCAGER SOKEMAN VAVASOR
COLIBERT CUSTOMER SERGEANT
SUCKENER
(LIFE —) LIVIER LIVEYER
(NEW —) INCOME INCOMER
TENCH CYPRINID
TEN COMMANDMENTS DECALOG
TEND HOP NOD RUN SET WRY BABY
BEND DRAW GROW KEEP MAKE
MIND MOVE TENT DRESS GROOM
NURSE OFFER SOUND TREND
VERGE WATCH GOVERN INTEND
CHERISH CONDUCE DECLINE
INCLINE PROPEND
(— A FIRE) STOKE
(— IN A CERTAIN DIRECTION) LEAD
(— TO ONE POINT) CONVERGE

(— TOWARD) AFFECT
(— WHILE AT PASTURE) GRAZE
TENDENCY SET BENT BIAS HAND
TONE VEIN DRAFT DRIFT DRIVE
HABIT KNACK TENOR TREND TWIST
ANIMUS COURSE EONISM GENIUS
MOTION APTNESS CONATUS
DRAUGHT IMPULSE LEANING
NITENCY SAMKARA APTITUDE
INSTINCT STEERING VERGENCY
(— IN NATURE) KIND
(— TO APPROACH) ADIENCE
(— TO STICK TOGETHER) CLANSHIP
(— TO WITHDRAW) ABIENCE
(— TO WRATH) TIDE
TENDER TID BEAR COCK FINE FOND
FRIM FRUM KIND NESH SOFT SORE
TAKE TART TENT WARM CAGER
DEFER FRAIL GREEN OFFER PAPPY
DELATE DRIVER GENTLE GIMPER
GINGER HUMANE LOVELY RAISER
SILKEN ADVANCE AMABILE
AMOROUS CONCHER CRAMPER
FLESHLY MASHMAN OBLATIO
PATACHE PINNACE PITEOUS PITIFUL
PORRECT PROFFER RUTHFUL
STENTER CAMELEER COCKBOAT
EFFETMAN FEMININE HEATSMAN
HERDSMAN LADYLIKE MERCIFUL
MORTISER SPREADER
TENDERFOOT DUDE INNOCENT
TENDERHEARTED HUMAN PITIFUL
TENDERLOIN FILET FILLET
UNDERCUT
TENDERLY FONDLY GENTLY
AMOROSO
TENDERNESS CHERTE TENDER
DELICACY FONDNESS KINDNESS
SYMPATHY TENERITY YEARNING
(— OF FEELING) FLESH
TENDINOUS SINEWY
TENDON CORD TAIL CHORD NERVE
SINEW TENON LEADER STRING
TENDRIL CURL CLASP CROOK TWIST
CIRRUS WINDER CAPREOL CIRRHUS
TENTACLE
TENEMENT LAND RENT CHAWL
DECKER LIVING WARREN HOLDING
LETTING BUILDING PRAEDIUM
TENES (FATHER OF —) CYNCUS
(MOTHER OF —) PHILONOME
(SLAYER OF —) ACHILLES
TENET ADOXY CREDO CREED
DOGMA BELIEF GNOMON HOLDING
MISHNAH PARADOX DOCTRINE
(PL.) FAITH FAMILISM
TENFOLD DENARY DECUPLE
TENNE TAWNY ORANGE HYACINTH

TENNESSEE
CAPITAL: NASHVILLE
COLLEGE: FISK LANE SIENA
BETHEL BELMONT LAMBUTH
LEMOYNE MILLIGAN TUSCULUM
VANDERBILT
COUNTY: DYER KNOX RHEA
COCKE GILES MEIGS OBION
GRUNDY MCMINN SEVIER UNICOI

BLEDSOE FENTRESS
INDIAN: SHAWNEE CHEROKEE CHICKASAW
LAKE: DOUGLAS CHEROKEE REELFOOT WATTSBAR
MOUNTAIN: GUYOT LOOKOUT
MOUNTAIN RANGE: SMOKY
NATIONAL PARK: SHILOH
NATIVE: WHELP
NICKNAME: VOLUNTEER
PRESIDENT: POLK JACKSON
RIVER: ELK DUCK CANEY HOLSTON HIWASSEE CUMBERLAND
STATE BIRD: MOCKINGBIRD
STATE FLOWER: IRIS
STATE TREE: POPLAR
TOWN: ALCOA PARIS CAMDEN SPARTA DICKSON MEMPHIS PULASKI GALLATIN KNOXVILLE

TENNIS (— SHOT) LET LOB DINK
TENON COG PIN COAK STUB TUSK LEWIS TOOTH TABLING DOVETAIL LEWISSON
TENOR PES FECK TONE VEIN COURSE EFFECT TAILLE TENURE CURRENT PURPORT STRENGTH TENDENCY TENORINO
TENOROON FAGOTTINO
TENOR VIOL VIOLET
TENOR VIOLIN ALTO
TENPINS NEWPORT
TENPOUNDER AWA CHIRO MACABI BONEFISH BONYFISH LADYFISH SKIPJACK SPRINGER
TENREC TANGUE CENTETES CENTETID HEDGEHOG HEDGEPIG
TENSE EDGY RAPT TAUT STIFF CORDED FLINCH FUTURE INTENT NARROW STRAIT STRICT BRITTLE INTENSE PRIMARY FRENETIC PRETERIT SYNTONIC
TENSION BENT HEAT DRIVE STEAM SATTVA SPRING STRAIN STRESS TROPPO BALANCE STRAINT TENSURE ISOTONIA
TENT AUL TOP HALE PAWL TAWN TELD TILT CABIN CRAME LODGE TOPEK TUPIK CANNAT CANVAS DOSSIL SEARCH WIGWAM BALAGAN CABINET KIBITKA MARQUEE SPARVER TABERNA TENTLET TENTORY ZDARSKY PAVILION TENTICLE TENTWORK
(— WHERE GOODS ARE SOLD) CRAME
(CIRCULAR —) YURT YOURT YURTA KIBITKA
(INDIAN —) TEPEE WIGWAM
(SAMOYED —) CHUM
(SOUTH AMERICAN —) TOLDO
TENTACLE HORN SAIL PACLE FEELER BRACHIUM
TENTATIVE GINGERLY
TENT CATERPILLAR WEBWORM
TENTERER RACKER RATCHER
TENTH DIME TITHE DECIMA

(— OF CENT) MILL
(— OF LINE) GRY
TENUITY EXILITY DELICACY
TENUOUS FILMY FOGGY FRAIL TENDER FRAGILE GASEOUS SLENDER SUBTILE ETHEREAL GOSSAMER
(TOO —) FINESPUN
TENUOUSNESS FRAILTY
TENURE FEU TAKE TERM GAVEL JAGIR BARONY CAPITE JAGHIR SOCAGE ALMOIGN BONDAGE BORDAGE BURGAGE CENSIVE CURTESY FARMAGE JAGHEER SOCCAGE SOREHON COPYHOLD DRENGAGE FREEHOLD OVERLAND SOCMANRY SUITHOLD VAVASORY VENVILLE
TEPEE CHUM TENT TIPI LODGE TEEPEE WICKIUP
TEPHROSIA CRACCA
TEPID LEW WARM WLACH WLECH LUKEWARM
TEQUISLATEC CHONTAL
TERATOMA EMBRYOMA
TERCET TRISTICH
TEREBINTH TEIL
TEREDO WOODWORM
TERETE CENTRIC
TEREUS (FATHER OF —) MARS
(SON OF —) ITYS
(WIFE OF —) PROCNE
TERGITE TERGUM PYGIDIUM
TERGIVERSATION DECEIT
TERM HALF NAME NOME WORD LEASE RHEMA SPEAK STYLE TRYST ABBACY GNOMON NOTION PARODY EPITHET EXTREME SESSION SUBJECT SUMMAND TERMINE VOCABLE EQUIVOKE HEADWORD MAHALATH POCHISMO SEMESTER TERMTIME
(— IN JAIL) JOLT
(— IN LOGIC) CONSTANT
(— OF ABUSE) CUSSWORD
(— OF ADDRESS) SIRRAH MADONNA
(— OF CONTEMPT) SLIPE PILCHER TITIVIL
(— OF DEFERENCE) AHUNG
(— OF ENDEARMENT) ASTOR CHUCK COCKY HONEY ASTHORE MACHREE STOREEN POSSODIE POWSOWDY
(— OF IMPRISONMENT) LAG LAGGING STRETCH
(— OF PUNISHMENT) JOB
(— OF RATIO) EXTREME
(— OF REPROACH) MINGO
(— OF SYLLOGISM) EXTREME ARGUMENT
(ARITHMETICAL —) NOME GNOMON
(HYPHENED —) COMPOUND
(LITERAL —S) LETTER
(SOCIAL —S) FOOTING
(UNIVERSAL —) CONCEPT
(PL.) LAY MEANS
TERMAGANT JADE SHREW VIXEN VIRAGO
TERMINABLE FINITE

TERMINAL JACK LAST POLE ANODE DEPOT IMPUT INPUT MUCRO CATHODE POTHEAD DESINENT
TERMINATE CUT END ABUT CALL HALT KILL ABORT BLEED CEASE CLOSE ISSUE LAPSE EXPIRE FINISH FOREDO RESULT INCLUDE TERMINE COMPLETE CONCLUDE DISSOLVE
TERMINATED EXPIATE
TERMINATING FINAL
(— ABRUPTLY) BLIND
(SUDDENLY —) ABRUPT
TERMINATION END ISH DATE TERM CLOSE EVENT ISSUE ENDING EXITUS EXPIRY FINALE PERIOD UPSHOT TERMINUS
(— OF CHURCH CHOIR) CHEVET
(— OF FURNITURE LEGS) FOOT
(— OF RIGHT) LAPSE
TERMINATIVE FINITIVE
TERMINOLOGY JARGON
TERMINUS END FLAT
(— IN FINGERPRINT) DELTA
(— OF PERIOD) TIME
TERMITE ANAI ANAY KING NASUTE WORKER POLILLA
TERMITOPHILE SYMPHILE
TERN KIP DARR INCA LARI NOIO PIRL PIRR RIXY LARID NODDY PEARL SCRAY SKEER SKIRR STERN CHIRRE KERMEW PICKET GOELAND MEDRICK PIRRMAW RITTOCK SEAFOWL STRIKER TARRACK TERNLET MANUSINA SPARLING TIRRACKE
TERPENE CARENE PINENE BORNANE SANTENE THUJENE CAMPHENE FENCHENE LIMONENE NOPINENE
TERRA GE GAEA TELLUS
(DAUGHTER OF —) RHEA THEA PHOEBE TETHYS THEMIS MNEMOSYNE
(HUSBAND OF —) URANUS
(SON OF —) OCEANUS
TERRACE POY DAIS PNYX STEP XYST BENCH HEIAU LINCH OFFSET LINCHET CHABUTRA
(LOUNGING —) LANAI
(NATURAL —) MESA
TERRA JAPONICA GAMBIR GAMBIER
TERRAPENE CISTUDO
TERRAPIN EMYD COUNT COODLE POTTER SLIDER TURPIN TURTLE EMYDIAN FEUILLE SKILPOT REDBELLY
(FEMALE —) HEIFER
(MALE —) BULL
TERRARIUM VIVARIUM
TERRELLA EARTHKIN
TERRENE EARTHLY
TERRESTRIAL EARTHY EARTHLY TERRENE PLANETAL SUBLUNAR SUBSOLAR
TERRET CRINGLE
TERRIBLE DIRE UGLY GHAST LURID DEADLY TARBLE TRAGIC TURBLE DIREFUL FEARFUL FERDFUL GHASTLY HIDEOUS ALMIGHTY BHAIRAVA FLEYSOME HORRIBLE

TERRIFIC TIMOROUS TRAGICAL

TERRIBLY FELLY FIERCE GRISLY
CONSARN

TERRIER SKYE LHASA BOSTON
DANDIE RATTER SCOTTY DIEHARD
SCOTTIE ABERDEEN AIREDALE
RATTONER SEALYHAM VERMINER
WIREHAIR

TERRIFIC FINE SWEET GORGON
FEARFUL GORGEOUS

TERRIFIED AFRAID AGHAST
GHASTLY

TERRIFY AWE COW HAG BREE DARE
FEAR FLAY FLEY DREAD GALLY
SCARE ADREAD AFFRAY AGRISE
AWHAPE DISMAY FLIGHT FREEZE
FRIGHTEN

TERRIFYING GHASTLY HIDEOUS
FLEYSOME TERRIBLE

TERRITORIALISM ITOISM

TERRITORY FEE GOA HAN SOC
AREA MARK PALE SOKE BANAT
DUCHY FIELD MARCH STATE TUATH
BORDER COLONY DOMAIN EMPERY
EMPIRE GROUND APANAGE CONFINE
COUNTRY DEMESNE DUKEDOM
EARLDOM ENCLAVE EPARCHY
REGENCY SATRAPY APPANAGE
CASTLERY CONFINES CONQUEST
DISTRICT DOMINION IMPERIUM
LIGEANCE LUCUMONY PARMESAN
PASHALIK REGALITY SEIGNORY

TERROR AWE FEAR FRAY ALARM
APPAL DREAD PANIC AFFRAY
ALARUM APPALL FRIGHT HORROR
DRIDDER DREDDOUR SURPRISE

TERRORISM NIHILISM

TERRORIST GOONDA ALARMIST
SICARIUS

TERRORIZE FRIGHTEN

TERROR-STRICKEN AWFUL

TERSE CURT COMPACT CONCISE
LACONIC POINTED SUMMARY
UNWORDY SUCCINCT

TERSENESS BREVITY LACONISM

TERTIARY NEOZOIC PALAEIC

TESSELLATED MOSAIC

TESSELLATION AREOLE

TESSERA TILETTE ABACULUS
TESSELLA

TEST CON SAY TRY FAND FEEL
FOND TASK TENT ASSAY AVENA
CANON CHECK ESSAY GROPE ISSUE
PROBE PROOF PROVE SENSE
SOUND TASTE TEMPT TESTA TOUCH
TRIAL SAMPLE TIENTA APPROOF
APPROVE AUSSAGE CONTROL
EXAMINE GANTLET PLUMMET
TESTATE BIOASSAY EXERCISE
GAUNTLET SEROLOGY STANDARD
(— **EGGS**) CANDLE
(— **FOR WEIGHT AND FINENESS**)
PYX
(— **GROUND**) BOSE
(— **OF COURAGE**) SCRATCH
(— **OF CRINOID**) CALYX
(— **OF ORE**) VAN
(**SEVERE** —) CRUCIBLE
(**SYPHILIS** —) KOLMER

TESTA TEST LORICA EPISPERM

TESTACEOUS SHELLY

TESTAMENT TEST QUETHE
WITWORD

TESTAR TETARD

TESTATOR LEGATOR

TESTED FIRED TRIED WEIGHED

TESTER TRIER CONNER PROVER
SPARVER DENIERER TESTIERE
(**BUTTER** —) SEARCHER

TESTICLE STONE BALLOCK DIDYMUS
GENITOR

TESTIFY SPEAK SWEAR AFFIRM
DEPONE DEPOSE WITTEN WITNESS
EVIDENCE
(— **FALSELY**) MOUNT
(— **TO**) BESPEAK

TESTIMONIAL SCROLL

TESTIMONY TEST ATTEST PROBATE
TESTATE TESTIFY WITNESS
EVIDENCE

TESTING ASSAY CRUCIAL

TESTIS BALL GONAD STONE
BALLOCK CULLION KNOCKER
SPERMARY
(**PL.**) COBS CODS COJONES
DOWSETS

TEST TUBE PROOF TESTER
PROBATE

TESTUDINATA CHELONIA

TESTUDO SNAIL GALAPAGO
TORTOISE

TESTY DONCY MUSTY TUTTY DONSIE
PATCHY SPUNKY PEEVISH TETTISH
TOUSTIE WASPISH SNAPPISH

TETANIC SPASTIC

TETANUS LOCKJAW HOLOTONY

TETE-A-TETE TWOSOME CAUSEUSE

TETHER BAND STAKE TEDDER
TOGGLE PASTERN CABESTRO
(— **A HAWK**) WEATHER

TETHYS APLYSIA
(**DAUGHTERS OF** —) OCEANIDES
(**FATHER OF** —) URANUS
(**HUSBAND OF** —) OCEANUS
(**MOTHER OF** —) TERRA

TETHYUM CYNTHIA

TETRACHORD GENUS HYPATON
LICHANOS

TETRACTYS TETRAD

TETRAD FOURFOLD

TETRADRACHMA OWL

TETRAGONAL DIMETRIC

TETRAHEDRITE FAHLERZ FAHLORE
PANABASE

TETRAHEXAHEDRON FLUOROID

TETRAHYDRIDE GERMANE
STANNANE

TETRASACCHARIDE LUPEOSE

TETTER DARTRE

TETTIX ACRYDIUM

TEUCER (**FATHER OF** —) TELAMON
SCAMANDER
(**MOTHER OF** —) HESIONE

TEUTON GOTH LOMBARD

TEUTONIC GOTHIC GERMANIC
GOTHONIC

TEXAS

CAPITAL: AUSTIN
COLLEGE: SMU TCU RICE WILEY
BAYLOR
COUNTY: BEXAR ERATH GARZA
FANNIN GOLIAD YOAKUM
ZAPATA ZAVALA HIDALGO
REFUGIO ATASCOSA
FORTRESS: ALAMO
INDIAN: LIPAN BILOXI KICHAI
SHUMAN HASINAI COMANCHE
TONKAWAN
LAKE: FALCON TEXOMA AMISTAD
NATIVE: TEJANO
NICKNAME: LONESTAR
PRESIDENT: JOHNSON
EISENHOWER
RIVER: RED PECOS BRAZOS
NUECES TRINITY
STATE BIRD: MOCKINGBIRD
STATE FLOWER: BLUEBONNET
STATE TREE: PECAN
TOWN: GAIL VEGA WACO BRYAN
MARFA OZONA PAMPA TYLER
BORGER DALLAS DENTON
ELPASO KILEEN LAREDO
ODESSA QUANAH SONORA
ABILENE HOUSTON LUBBOCK
AMARILLO BEAUMONT
FLOYDADA GALVESTON

TEXAS BUCKTHORN LOTEBUSH

TEXAS FEVER TRISTEZA

TEXT BODY MIQRA PLACE SAKHA
TESTO PURANA SCRIPT SHAKHA
TEXTUS TEXTLET ANTETHEM
PERICOPE VARIORUM
(— **OF ADVERTISEMENT**) COPY
(— **OF OPERA**) LIBRETTO
(— **SET TO MUSIC**) ORATORIO
(**SHASTRA** —) SRUTI SHRUTI

TEXTBOOK DUNCE TUTOR GENETICS

TEXTILE (**ALSO SEE FABRIC**) SABA
STUFF GREIGE MOCKADO SAGURAN
SINAMAY TEXTURE TIFFANY
(— **MACHINE**) WILLOW
(**PL.**) DRAPE

TEXTURE WEB BONE HAND KNIT
WALE WOOF GRAIN COBWEB
FABRIC WEFTAGE FRACTURE
(— **OF SOAP**) FIT

THAI LAO SIAMESE

THAILAND

CAPITAL: BANKOK BANGKOK
COIN: AT ATT BAHT FUANG TICAL
PYNUNG SALUNG SATANG
ISLAND: PHUKET
ISTHMUS: KRA
MEASURE: WA KEN NIV NMU RAI
SAT SEN SOK WAH YOT KEUP
NGAN TANG YOTE KWIEN LAANG
SESTI TANAN KABIET KAMMEU
CHAIMEU ROENENG CHANGAWN
MOUNTAIN: KHIEO MAELAMUN
NATIVE: LAO THAI

THAILAND
PLAIN: KHORAT
RIVER: CHI NAN PING MENAM
MEKONG MEPING
TOWN: UBON PUKET RANONG
AYUDHYA AYUTHIA BANGKOK
LOPBURI RAHAENG SINGORA
SONGKLA KHONKAEN KIANGMAI
THONBURI
WEIGHT: HAP PAI SEN SOK BAHT
HAPH KLAM KLOM CATTY
CHANG COYAN PILUL FLUANG
SALUNG SOMPAY TAMLUNG

THALER DALER
THALLOGEN AMPHIGEN
THALLOID FRONDOSE
THALLUS FROND THALAMUS
THAMNIUM
THAMNOPHIS EUTAENIA
THAMYRAS (FATHER OF —)
PHILAMMON
(MOTHER OF —) ARGIOPE
THAN AS NA NE OR TO AND BUT
NOR THEN TILL
THANE THEGN BANQUO GESITH
ABTHAIN MACDUFF
THANK GRACE MERCY REGRACY
REMERCY
THANKFUL GRATEFUL
THANKLESS INGRATE SLOWFUL
THANKS TA GRACE MERCI MERCY
GRAMERCY
THANKSGIVING GLORY DOXOLOGY
THANK-YOU-MA'AM CAHOT
THAT AS AT SE BUT HOW THE THO
WHO YAT LEST THAM THIK THON
WHAT YOND THICK THILK THOUGH
BECAUSE
(— IS TO SAY) NAMELY
(— ONE) ILLE
(— WHICH HAS TO BE PROVED)
IQED
(— YONDER) THON
THATCH NIPA DATCH SIRKI SIRKY
STING THRUM CADJAN
(— OVER BEEHIVE) HOOD
THATCHED THACK REEDED
THATCHER HELER CROWDER
HELLIER THACKER
THAUMAS (DAUGHTER OF —) IRIS
HARPY
(FATHER OF —) NEPTUNE
(MOTHER OF —) TERRA
(WIFE OF —) ELECTRA
THAUMATURGIST(PL.) GOETAE
THAUMATURGY MAGIC
THAW GIVE MELT FRESH UNTHAW
DEFROST
THE LA LE SE TA THI THAM THEY
YARE THERE
THEA CAMELLIA
(FATHER OF —) URANUS
(HUSBAND OF —) HYPERION
(MOTHER OF —) TERRA
THEANO (FATHER OF —) CISSEUS
(HUSBAND OF —) ANTENOR
(SISTER OF —) HECUBA
THEATER CINE GAFF KINO CAVEA

HOUSE LEGIT ODEUM SCENE STAGE
CINEMA OZONER ADELPHI COCKPIT
GUIGNOL ORPHEUM THEATRE
BIOSCOPE COLISEUM PANTHEON
SHOWSHOP SPELLKEN STRAWHAT
THEATRON
THEATRICAL HAMMY STAGY
DRAMATIC SCENICAL SINGSONG
THEATRICALITY HAM
THEBAN LAIUS NIOBE AMPHION
CADMEAN JOCASTA OEDIPUS
PENTHEUS
THECA CUP URN CELL VAGINA
CAPSULE PYXIDIUM VAGINULE
THEELIN ESTRONE FEMININ OESTRIN
THEFT CRIB LIFT HEIST PINCH
SCORE STEAL FURTUM STOUTH
BRIBERY LARCENY MICHERY
PICKING PILFERY ROBBERY
STEALTH BURGLARY STEALAGE
STEALING
(LITERARY —) PIRACY
(PETTY —) CRIB PICKERY
THEIR ARE HER ORE HORE YARE
THEIRS HERN THEIRN
THEM A EM HI UM HEM MUN HEMEN
THEME DUX BASE IDEA TEMA TEXT
DITTY HOBBY MOTIF PLACE SCOPE
TESTO THEMA TOPIC URLAR
MATTER MYTHOS SUBJECT
ANTETHEM
(— OF FUGUE) DUX
(HACKNEYED —) CLICHE
(RECURRING —) BURDEN
THEMIS (DAUGHTER OF —) DICE
IRENE EUNOMIA
(FATHER OF —) URANUS
(HUSBAND OF —) JUPITER
(MOTHER OF —) TERRA
THEMSELVES HEM HEMSELF
THEN SO AND POI THO ANON SYNE
THENCE AWAY THEN THEREFRO
THEOCRACY KHALSA
THEODOLITE TAIPO TRANSIT
TRANSEPT
THEOLOGIAN FAQIH ULEMA DIVINE
MUJTAHID
THEOLOGY KALAM IRENICS DIVINITY
POIMENIC POLEMICS
THEORBO ARCHLUTE
THEOREM DUAL LEMMA CONVERSE
THEORETIC PURE
THEORETICAL BOOK CLOSET
THEORIC ABSTRACT ACADEMIC
ARMCHAIR PLATONIC
THEORIST OPINATOR
THEORIZE SUGGEST
THEORIZING IDEOLOGY
THEORY ISM OVISM EROTIC ETHICS
HOLISM LAXISM SYSTEM AGOGICS
ATOMISM CAMBISM DUALISM
FORMISM HOBBISM PEELISM
PLENISM THEORIC TYCHISM
ACOSMISM AXIOLOGY DITHEISM
DYNAMISM ENERGISM ESTHETIC
ETIOLOGY FEMINISM FINITISM
GHOSTISM GOBINISM HEDONICS
IDEALISM IDEOLOGY MOLINISM
MONADISM PROGRESS SEMANTIC

SEMIOTIC SPERMISM
THEOW SERF THRALL THEWMAN
THERAPEUTICS ACEOLOGY
THERAVADA HINAYANA
THERE ERE YARE ALONG VOILA
WHERE YONDER THEASUM THITHER
THEREABOUTS NEARBY
THEREAFTER UPON THENCE
THEREFORE SO ERGO THEN ARGAL
HENCE FORTHY IGITUR THENCE
THEREON UPON
THEREUPON SO SINCE WITHAL
THEREON THEREUP
THEREWITH MIT WITH
THERIACA GALENA
THERMOMETER GLASS HYDRA
CELSIUS REAUMUR
THERMOPLASTIC SARAN
THERMOSTAT DETECTOR PYROSTAT
THERSANDER (FATHER OF —)
POLYNICES
(MOTHER OF —) ARGIA
(SLAYER OF —) TELEPHUS
THESAURUS TREASURE
THESE THIR THIS THEASUM
THESEUS (FATHER OF —) AEGEUS
(MOTHER OF —) AETHRA
(SON OF —) HIPPOLYTUS
(WIFE OF —) PHAEDRA
THESIS ACT THEMA DOWNBEAT
LOGICISM THESICLE
THESTIUS (DAUGHTER OF —)
ALTHAEA
(FATHER OF —) PARTHAON
(MOTHER OF —) EURYTE
(SON OF —) TOXEUS PLEXIPPUS
THETIS (FATHER OF —) NEREUS
(HUSBAND OF —) PELEUS
(MOTHER OF —) DORIS
(SON OF —) ACHILLES
THEY A HI THO THEI
(— READ) LEG
THIAMINE ANEURIN
THICK FAT SAD HAZY SLAB BLIND
BROAD BURLY BUSHY CLOSE
CRASS DENSE FOGGY GREAT
GROSS MURKY SOLID SQUAB STIFF
STOUT CHUMPY COARSE GREASY
LUBBER SLABBY SPISSY STOCKY
STODGY BLUBBER GRUMOUS
FAMILIAR LUTULENT MOTHERED
(— WITH SMOKE) SMUDGY
(11 POINTS —) HEAVY
(SHORT AND —) SQUAT
THICKEN BODY CLOT FULL BREAK
KEECH LITHE DEEPEN HARDEN
ENGROSS STIFFEN
THICKENED BODIED BULLED
FURRED CALLOUS CLUBBED
THICKENING FALX LEAR ROUX
SWELL CALLUS CLAVATE LIAISON
PLACODE CRASSULA PYCNOSIS
EPHIPPIUM
(— OF COAL SEAM) SWELLY
(— OF LETTER STROKE) STRESS
THICKET COP RONE SHAG SHAW
BLUFF BRAKE CLUMP COPSE DROKE
HEDGE QUICK SHOLA SLICK THICK
BOSKET BUSHET COVERT GREAVE

JUNGLE MALLEE QUEACH SPINNY
BOSCAGE BOSQUET BRUSHET
COPPICE CORYLET SPINNEY
WOODRIS CHAMISAL QUICKSET
SHINNERY THICKSET
THICKHEADED DULL DENSE
THICKHEADED FLY CONOPID
THICK-KNEE CURLEW DIKKOP
BUSTARD
THICKLY STEFLY
THICKNESS PLY BODY LAYER
DIAMETER
(**— OF CHIP**) CUT FEED
(**— OF CLOTH**) LAY
(**— OF METAL**) GRIP
(**— OF PAPER**) BULK CALLIPER
UNDERLAY
(**ONE — OVER ANOTHER**) LAYER
(**SECOND —**) DOUBLING
THICKSET STUB BEEFY PUNCH
SQUAT THICK CHUMPY HUMPTY
PLUGGY STOCKY STUBBY STUGGY
NUGGETY SQUATTY
THIEF GUN NIP CHOR GILT LIFT MILL
PRIG BUDGE CREEP CROOK FAKER
GANEF PIKER SNEAK TAKER TILER
ANGLER CANNON CLOYER DISMAS
GONOPH HOOKER KALLAN LIFTER
MICHER NIMMER NIPPER PICKER
PIRATE RATERO ROBBER SNATCH
TOSHER WASTER BOOSTER
COLLERY FOOTMAN GORILLA
GRIFTER HARRIER HEISTER
LADRONE LURCHER MEECHER
MERCURY PRIGGER PRIGMAN
PROLLER PROWLER SNAPPER
SPOTTER STEALER THIEVER
CLYFAKER CONVEYER CUTPURSE
FINGERER HARROWER PETERMAN
PICAROON PICKLOCK PILFERER
PRIGSTER SNATCHER
(**— AT A MINE**) CAVER
(**CATTLE —**) BLOTTER PLANTER
RUSTLER
(**CLEVER —**) KID CANNON
(**CRUCIFIED —**) DISMAS
(**MOUNTAIN —**) CHOAR
(**NIGHT —**) SCOURER
(**PETTY —**) HOOKER SLOCKER
(**RIVER —**) ACKMAN LUMPER
(**VAGABOND —**) WASTER
(**WHARF —**) TOSHER
THIEVE NIM
THIEVING LAW SHARK PUGGING
PROGGERY STEALING
THIEVISH STEALY FURTIVE KLEPTIC
SCADDLE PRIGGISH
THIEVISHNESS PRIGGISM
THIGH HAM HOCK FEMUR FLANK
GAMMON
(**— PAIN**) MERALGIA
THILL FILL SILL BLADE SHAFT
LIMBER
THIMBLE SKEIN BUSHEL GOBLET
SLEEVE CRINGLE
THIMBLEBERRY MULBERRY
THIN HOE LEW FINE FLUE FUSE
LANK LEAN LIMP PRIN RARE SLIM
WEAK WHEY EXILE FRAIL GAUNT

GAUZY LATHY PEAKY SHEER SLINK
SMALL SPARE SWAMP THIRL WASHY
WIZEN AERIAL BLASHY DILUTE
FLUTED HOLLOW MAUGER MEAGER
MEAGRE PEAKED SCRANK SEROSE
SEROUS SHELLY SKINNY SLIGHT
SPINNY SUBTLE TENDER TWIGGY
WATERY WEAKEN COVERED
FOLIOUS FRAGILE GRACILE
HAGGARD SANIOUS SCRAGGY
SCRAILY SCRANKY SCRAWNY
SHALLOW SHILPIT SLENDER
SPINDLY TENUOUS THREADY
ARANEOUS CACHETIC EGGSHELL
HAIRLINE ICHOROUS MACILENT
SCRAGGED SCRANNEL SKINKING
VAPORISH WATERISH SPINDLING
(**— AND PINCHED**) CHITTY
(**— LEATHER**) DOLE
(**— OUT**) HOE CHOP DISBUD
FEATHER
(**— SEEDLINGS**) SINGLE
(**— THE WALLS**) IRON
THINE TUUM
THING JOB RES BABY ITEM SORT
WHAT CHEAT CHOSE ANIMAL
DINGUS FELLOW GILGUY MATTER
ARTICLE DINGBAT MINIKEN
SHEBANG WHATNOT THINGLET
(**— DONE**) FACT ACTUS
(**— FOUND**) TROVE
(**— OF LITTLE ACCOUNT**) GEWGAW
(**— OF LITTLE VALUE**) NIFLE TRIFLE
TRINKET
(**— OF LITTLE WORTH**) STIVER
(**— TO BE REGRETTED**) DAMAGE
(**— TO EXHIBIT**) BRAVERY
(**—S PROHIBITED**) VETANDA
(**ANOTHER —**) ALIUD
(**CONSECRATED —**) ANATHEMA
(**ENORMOUS —**) MONSTER
(**ENTIRE —**) INTEGRAL
(**EXTRAORDINARY —**) ONER
(**FAIR —**) POTATO
(**FIT —**) CHECKER
(**GOOD —**) WELFARE
(**HOLY —S**) HAGIA KODASHIM
(**IMPORTANT —**) ACE
(**INSIGNIFICANT —**) SCRAT
(**INSIGNIFICANT —S**) SMATTER
(**JEWISH —S**) JUDAICA
(**LITTLE —S**) FEWTRILS
(**LIVING —S**) BIOTA
(**MISSHAPEN —**) ABORTION
(**NEW —**) NEWEL
(**OUTMODED —**) SNUFF
(**PETTY —**) SHABBLE
(**PRECIOUS —**) JEWEL
(**PRECISE —**) POINT
(**RIDICULOUS —**) MONUMENT
(**RIGHT —**) POTATO
(**ROTTEN —**) ROTTOCK
(**SAD —**) RUTH
(**SILLY —**) TRIMTRAM
(**SINGLE —**) UNIT
(**SMALL —**) SNIPPET
(**STRAY —**) WAIF
(**STUNTED —**) SCRUNT SNEESHIN
(**SURE —**) CERT SNIP

(**TERRIFYING —**) BOGEYMAN
(**UNEXPECTED —**) GODSEND
(**UNIQUE —**) ONER UNICUM
(**UNREAL —**) NOMINAL
(**UNSUBSTANTIAL —**) PUFF
(**WORLDLY —S**) EARTH
(**WORNOUT —**) SNUFF HUSHEL
(**PL.**) GEAR REALIA SQUARES
THING-IN-ITSELF THINGY
NOUMENON
THINGUMBOB DODAD DOODAD
JIGGER THINGUM
THINK LET SEE WIS WIT DEEM FEEL
HOLD MAKE MEAN MINT MULL MUSE
READ TROW WEEN ALLOW FANCY
GUESS JUDGE LOUSE OPINE PANSE
SEPAD ESTEEM EXPECT FIGURE
IDEATE RECKON REPUTE BELIEVE
CONCEIT IMAGINE REFLECT
SUPPOSE COGITATE CONSIDER
ENVISAGE
(**— BEST**) SEEM
(**— HARD**) YERK
(**— OF AS**) ACCOUNT
(**— OF**) MIND PURPENSE
(**— OVER**) BETHINK
(**— UP**) INVENT
(**— UPON**) BROOD
(**— WELL OF**) APPROVE
THINKER SOPHIST
(**CHINESE —**) LEGALIST
THINKING CONCEIT THOUGHT
(**CLEVER —**) HEADWORK
THINLY AIRILY SPARSE SPARSELY
THINNESS RARITY EXILITY FINESSE
TENUITY EXIGUITY
THINNING BALK BAULK CLEANING
THIRD FACE GAMMA TERCE THREE
DITONE TERTIA TIERCE
THIRDLY TERTIO
THIRD-RATE C3 HEDGE
THIRD-RATER PIKER
THIRST DRY ADRY DRYTH APOSIA
DROUTH THRIST DROUGHT DIPSOSIS
THIRSTING SITIENT
THIRSTY DRY ADRY ATHIRST
DROUGHTY
THIS HE SO THIK THILK
THISTLE PUHA HOYLE CARDON
DASHEL DINDLE FISTLE TEASEL
CALTROP CARLINA GUTWEED
RAURIKI WARATAH BEDEGUAR
CALTHROP COMPOSIT ECHINOPS
MILKWEED
THITHER TO YON YOND THERE
YONDER ULTERIOR YONDWARD
THOAS (DAUGHTER OF —)
HYPSIPYLE
(**FATHER OF —**) BACCHUS
(**MOTHER OF —**) ARIADNE
(**WIFE OF —**) MYRINE
THOMIST AQUINIST
THOMSONITE MESOLE MESOTYPE
OZARKITE
THONG RIEM BRAIL GIRTH LASSO
LEASH ROMAL STRAP THUNK
WHANG WHANK LACING LINGEL
STRING TWITCH AMENTUM BABICHE

LANIARD LANYARD LATCHET RIEMPIE
(— ON JAVELIN) AMENTUM
(HAWK'S —) BRAIL
THOR THUNAR THUNOR
THORACIC DORSAL
THORAX CHEST TRUNK BREAST PEREION ALITRUNK CORSELET FOREBODY
THORITE ENALITE ORANGITE
THORN BROD BUSH GOAD PIKE STUG BRIAR BRIER DOORN PRICK SPIKE FUSTIC JAGGER PRICKER STICKER COCKSPUR THORNLET
(PL.) SPEAR HAYBOTE
THORN APPLE HAW METEL STAMONY
THORNBACK RAY DORN ROKER
THORNBILL TOMTIT
THORNY HARD SPINY PRICKLY SCROGGY SPINOUS THISTLY THORNED
THORON RADON
THOROUGH RUN DEEP FIRM FULL SOUND ERRANT HOLLOW STRICT HOTSHOT INGOING REGULAR COMPLETE GROUNDLY INTIMATE
THOROUGHBRED HOTBLOOD
THOROUGHFARE BUND DRUM ROAD ALLEY AVENUE STREET HIGHWAY PARKWAY WHITEHALL
THOROUGHGOING PAKKA ARRANT ERRANT HEARTY PROPER PUREDEE RADICAL ABSOLUTE PROFOUND TRUEBRED
THOROUGHLY BUT FULL GOOD INLY CLEAN FULLY PROOF DEEPLY GAINLY KINDLY PROPER RICHLY RIPELY WHOLLY ROUNDLY SOAKING SOBBING SOGGING SOUNDLY DRIPPING GROUNDLY HEARTILY INWARDLY
THOROUGHWORT BONESET
THOSE THEM THEY YOND
THOTH DHOUTI
THOUGH AS AND SET YET ALTHO ALTHOUGH
THOUGHT CARE IDEA MOOD VIEW FANCY TASTE TRACE NOTION PENSEE CONCEIT CONCEPT COUNSEL OPINION SURMISE PEMMICAN RUMINATE
(— OUT) ADVISED
(CAREFUL —) ADVICE ACCOUNT
(HIGHEST —) IDEE
(REASONED —) STUDY
(UNCLEAN —) SEWERAGE
(WELL-EXPRESSED —) STROKE
THOUGHTFUL EARNEST PENSIVE SERIOUS STUDIED THOUGHTY
THOUGHTFULNESS GRACE COUNSEL
THOUGHTLESS RASH DIZZY GLAKY SUPINE GLAIKET RAMSTAM HEEDLESS RECKLESS
THOUSAND CHI MIL GRAND MILLE CHILIAD
(10 —) MYRIAD
(100 —) LAC LAKH

THOUSANDTH (— OF CUBIC CENTIMETER) LAMBDA
(— OF INCH) MIL
(HUNDRED —) SSU
THRACIAN GETE GETAN GETIC THRAX
THRALL SERF GURTH SLAVE CAPTIVE
THRALLDOM BONDAGE SLAVERY THIRLAGE
THRASH DAD LAM PAY TAN BANG BEAT BELT COMB DING DRUB DUST FLAX LACE LICK LOUK MILL PAIL SOLE SOWL SWAP SWOP TOSE WALK WHAP WHIP WHOP YERK BASTE BELAM BLESS CURRY DRASH FLAIL FRAIL LINCH LINGE NOINT SLATE SWACK SWING TABOR TARGE THUMP TOWEL TWINK WHALE WHANG ANOINT BUMFEG CUDGEL FETTLE JACKET MUZZLE RADDLE STOUSH SWINGE TANCEL THREAP THRESH THWACK WALLOP LAMBACK LEATHER SWADDLE TROLLOP TROUNCE BETHWACK BUMBASTE LAMBASTE LAMBSKIN RIBROAST
THRASHER THREAPER THRESHER
THRASHING TOCO BELTING LICKING WARMING WHALING DRUBBING
THRASYMEDES (FATHER OF —) NESTOR
(MOTHER OF —) ANAXIBIA
THREAD BAR END BAVE CHIP CLEW CLUE CORD DOUP FILE FILM GIMP GOLD LACE LINE POIL PURL SILK TRAM WIRE WORM BRIDE CHIVE FIBER FIBRE FLOAT FLOSS HYPHA INKLE REEVE SCREW SETON SHIVE SHOOT SHUTE STEEK TWEER TWIRE TWIST WATAP BOTTOM COBWEB COTTON ENFILE FIBRIL INFILE SINGLE STAMEN STITCH STRAIN STRAND STRING TISSUE BABICHE BASTING DOUPING SLUBBER SPIREME TWITTER WARPING ACONTIUM FILAMENT GOSSAMER LIGATURE PICKOVER RAVELING SPINNING SPIRICLE
(— AROUND BOWSTRING) SERVING
(— IN SEED COATING) SPIRICLE
(— LEGS OF RABBIT) HARL HARLE
(— OF SCREW) WORM
(— OF WAX) SWARF
(— USED FOR COCOON) BAVE
(—S THAT CROSS WARP) WEFT WOOF
(40 —S) BEER BIER
(BADLY TWINED —) SLUBBER
(BALL OF —) CLEW CLUE CLOWE GLOME
(BUTTONHOLE —S) BAR
(COARSE —) GIRD
(COARSEST — IN LACE) GIMP
(COILED —) COP
(FLOATING —) PICKOVER
(HARD —) LISLE
(LINEN —) LINE INCLE INKLE
(LOOSELY TWISTED —S) BUMP

(METAL —) LAME WIRE
(OAKUM —) PLEDGET
(PULLED —) SNAG
(REFUSE —S) BUR BURR
(SHOEMAKER'S —) END LINGEL LINGLE
(SILK —) TRAM TRAME DOUPIONI
(SOFT SHORT —) THRUM
(STRONG —) GOUNAU
(SURGICAL —) SETON
(WARP —) END STAMEN
(WAXED —) TACKER
(WEFT —) SHOT
(PL.) FLOSS
THREADBARE BARE SEAR SERE TRITE PILLED SHABBY NAPLESS
THREADFIN SEER SEIR SULEA BARBUDO KINGFISH SEERFISH
THREADFISH COBBLER SUNFISH
THREADING SCREW STRINGING
THREADLIKE FILATE FILOSE
THREAT ATTACK MENACE THUNDER
(PL.) MINES
THREATEN BRAG FACE BOAST SHORE ATTACK IMPEND MENACE ENDANGER MINATORY
THREATENED FRAUGHT
THREATENING BIG GLUM UGLY ANGRY BOAST SABLE GREASY BANEFUL RAMPANT MINATORY MINITANT
(— TO RAIN) HEAVY
THREE TREY GIMEL LEASH TRIAS TERNARY TERNION
(— CENT PIECE) TRIME
(— IN ONE) TRIUNE
(— MILES) LEAGUE
(— OF A KIND) GLEEK BRELAN TRIPLET
(GROUP OF —) TRIO TRIAD TRIPLE
(SET OF —) PAIRIAL
THREE-DIMENSIONAL CUBIC CUBICAL
THREEFOLD TERN TRINE TERNAL TREBLE TRINAL TRIPLE TERNARY TRIFOLD TRIPLEX THRIBBLE
THREE-FORKED TRISULC
THREEPENCE JOEY TREY THRIP THRUM TICKEY TICKIE
THRENODY HEARSE THRENE
THRESH COB BEAT CAVE LUMP WHIP BERRY FLAIL FRAIL SPELT STAMP THRASH
THRESHEL DRASHEL
THRESHER TASKER
THRESHER SHARK FOX FOXFISH WHIPTAIL
THRESHOLD HEAD SILL SOLE DEARN LIMEN DRASHEL DOORSILL
THRIFT SAVING VIRTUE ECONOMY STATICE THEEDOM
THRIFTILY NEAR
THRIFTLESS WASTEFUL
THRIFTY CANNY FENDY PUIST FRUGAL SAVING CAREFUL SPARING
THRILL JAG BANG DIRL GIRL KICK FLUSH SHOOT THIRL DINDLE STOUND TICKLE TREMOR ENCHANT FRISSON VIBRATE FREMITUS

(SHARP —) ZING
THRILLING VIBRANT TINGLING
THRINTER FRONTER
THRIPID PHYSOPOD
THRIPS BLACKFLY PHYSOPOD
THRIVE DOW GROW LIKE RISE THEE
ADDLE FADGE MOISE PROVE THRAM
BATTEN BATTLE CATTER CHIEVE
PROSPER STORKEN SUCCEED
WELFARE FLOURISH THRODDEN
(— IN) LOVE
THRIVING BIEN GRUSHIE THRIFTY
BLOOMING TOWARDLY
THRIVINGLY GAILY GAYLY BRAVELY
THROAT MAW CRAG CROP GOWL
GULA HALS HASS LANE GORGE
HALSE SWIRE FAUCES GARGET
GULLET GUTTUR GUZZLE RICTUS
CHANNEL JUGULUM STOMACH
SWALLOW WEASAND THRAPPLE
THROPPLE THROTTLE
(— OF ANCHOR) CLUTCH
(— OF COROLLA) FAUCES
(— OF FROG) KNEE
(MOUTH AND —) WHISTLE
(SORE —) HOUSTY
THROATLATCH FIADOR
THROB ACHE BEAT BELK DRUM
DUNT LEAP PANT QUOP WARK
FLACK STANG WARCH STOUND
STRIKE STROKE WALLOP FLACKER
PULSATE VIBRATE FLICHTER
(— IN PAIN) STOUND
(RAPID —S) FRIMITTS
THROBBING DUNT ATHROB THRILL
PITAPAT
THROE PANG PULL STOUR SHOWER
PAROXYSM
(—S OF DEATH) AGONY
THROMBIN PLASMASE
THROMBOPLASTIN COAGULIN
CYTOZYME
THROMBOSIS SHOCK CORONARY
THRONE GADI ASANA GADDI GADHI
SELLE SIEGE STALL STATE STEAD
STOOL SEGGIO SHINZA TRIBUNE
CATHEDRA SEGGIOLA SINHASAN
(BISHOP'S —) SEE APSE CATHEDRA
THRONE ROOM AIWAN
THRONG CREW HEAP HOST ROUT
CHIRT CROWD FLOCK FRACK POSSE
PRESS SHOAL SWARM RESORT
THRAVE THREAT THRIMP THRUST
COMPANY TEMPEST THRUTCH
SURROUND
(— OF SEAFOWL) SAVSSAT
(CONFUSED —) LURRY
THRONGED ALIVE FREQUENT
NUMEROUS
THROTTLE GUN CHOKE STIFLE
GARROTE STRANGLE THROPPLE
THROUGH BY PER DONE THRU WITH
ROUND AROUND
(RIGHT —) TILL
THROUGHOUT ABOUT ABROAD
BEDENE BIDENE DURING ENTIRE
PASSIM SEMPRE OVERALL THRUOUT
THROW GO DAB HIP HIT PAT PEG
PUT SHY ACES BIFF BUCK BUNG

CALE CAST CHIP COOK CUCK DART
DASH DROW HAIL HANK HIPE HULL
HURL HYPE JERK LACE MILL PECK
PICK SEND SKIM SLAT SOSS TOSS
TURF VANG WARP WURP YEND
CHUCK CHUNK DOUSE FLICK FLING
FLIRT FLURR HEAVE PITCH SLING
SPANG DEVEST ELANCE HAUNCH
HURTLE INJECT LAUNCH SLIGHT
THRILL BLUNDER BUTTOCK
COCKSHY MANGANA UPTHROW
VIBRATE CATAPULT JACULATE
(— ABOUT) BOUNCE
(— ASIDE) DEVEST
(— AWAY) DICE DOFF BANDY WAIVE
PROJECT JETTISON SQUANDER
(— BASEBALL) BURN
(— BY KICKING) WINCE
(— CARELESSLY) COB
(— DICE) JEFF
(— DOWN) EVEN PILE LODGE
DETURB THRING FLATTEN
(— FORTH) EJECT
(— FORWARD) LAUNCH
(— HEAVILY) LOB
(— HEEDLESSLY) SLIGHT
(— IN CRAPS) CRAP CRABS
BOXCARS
(— INTO CONFUSION) CLUB
FLUTTER CONFOUND CONVULSE
(— INTO DISORDER) ADDLE BOLLIX
DERANGE DISRANK DISRUPT
EMBROIL DISARRAY
(— INTO PERPLEXITY) FLUMMOX
(— INTO WASTE) BACK
(— JERKILY) FLIRT
(— LIGHT UPON) ILLUME
(— LIQUID) JAW
(— OF A STEER) DOGFALL
(— OF SHUTTLE) SHOT SHOOT
SHUTE
(— OF THREES) COCKEYES
(— OFF COURSE) EMIT SHED
DERAIL
(— OFF) CANT CAST SPILL SLOUGH
CONFUSE UNBURDEN
(— ONESELF) CLAP
(— OPEN) DISPARK
(— OUT) FIRE HOOF LADE BELCH
EJECT ERUPT SPOUT DETURB
IGNORE EXTRUDE
(— QUICKLY) LASH
(— SIDEWISE) SHY
(— SILK) THROWST
(— SMARTLY) SLAT
(— STEER) BUST
(— STICKS) SQUAIL
(— STONES) ROCK
(— TOGETHER) HUDDLE
(— UNDER) SUBJECT
(— UP) CAVE PICK VOMIT
(— VIOLENTLY) BUZZ DING PASH
SOCK SMASH HURTLE WHITHER
SPANGHEW
(— WITH A JERK) JET CANT SQUIRR
FLOUNCE
(— WITH GREAT FORCE) BUZZ
SWACK
(— WITHOUT VIOLENCE) HURL

(CHEATING — OF DICE) KNAP
(FREE —) FOUL
(LARIAT —) HOOLIAN
(LOWEST — AT DICE) AMBSACE
AMESACE
(WRESTLING —) HANK HIPE HYPE
BUTTOCK BACKHEEL
THROWAWAY DODGER
THROWBACK ATAVISM
THROWER TRAMMER THROWSTER
(SPEAR —) ATLATL
THROWING DARTING
THROWING-STICK ATLATL
WOMMERA WOOMERA HORNERAH
TROMBASH TRUMBASH
THROWN (— AWAY) CASTAWAY
(— DOWN) DEJECTED
THROWSTER TWISTER
THRUM FUM STRUM THUMB
THRUSH POP OMAO SOOR APTHA
BREVE FRUSH GRIVE MAVIS OUZEL
PITTA SABIA SHAMA SHIRL SPREW
UZZLE VEERY APHTHA DRAINE
JAYPIE KICKUP MISSEL OLOMAO
PULISH SHRITE JAYPIET REDWING
WAGTAIL BELLBIRD CHERCOCK
FORKTAIL PRUNELLA SHAGBARK
THRASHER THROSTLE THRUSHEL
THRUSTLE URTICATE WOODCHAT
THRUSHLIKE TURDOID
THRUST DAB DEG DIG DUB JAB JAG
JAM JOB POP PUG BANG BEAR BIRR
BOKE BORE BUCK BUTT CANT CHOP
CRAM DART DASH DUSH FOIN HURL
KICK LICK MURE PASS PICK PILT
POKE PORR POSS POTE PROD PUSH
SEND SINK SPAR STAB STOP TILT
VENY WHAP WHOP BREAK DRIFT
DRIVE EXERT HUNCH LUNGE POACH
POINT PROKE PUNCH SHOOT SPANK
STAVE STICK STOKE STUFF THROW
DARTLE PLUNGE POUNCE STITCH
STRAIN STRESS STRIKE STRIPE
BEARING IMPULSE SHOULDER
STOCCADO
(— A LANCE) AVENTRE
(— ASIDE) DAFF SHUFFLE
(— AWAY) DOFF SHOVE DETRUDE
ABSTRUDE
(— DOWN) THRING DEPULSE
DETRUDE
(— IN) INSERT STRIKE INTRUDE
(— OF ARCH) DRIFT
(— OF EXPLOSION) BLOWOUT
(— ONESELF) CHISEL
(— OUT) REACH STRUT EXSERT
DETRUDE EXTRUDE OBTRUDE
PROTRUDE
(— SUDDENLY) STRIKE
(— THROUGH) ENFILED
(— WITH ELBOW) HUNCH
(— WITH GREAT FORCE) BUZZ
(— WITH NOSE) NUDDLE
(— WITH WEAPON) FOIN SHOVE
(DAGGER —) DAG
(FENCING —) PASS VENY VENUE
REPOST TIMING PASSADO RIPOSTE
STOCCADO STOCCATA
(HOME —) HAI HAY

(MATADOR'S —) ESTOCADA
(SARCASTIC —) GIRD
THUD BAFF DUMP PHUT PLOD SWAG
DOYST FLUMP POUND SQUELCH
THUG GOON GOONDA RODMAN
GORILLA HOODLUM GANGSTER
THUJA BIOTA
THUJONE SALVIOL
THULUTH SOOLOOS
THUMB POLLEX THENAR THROOM
(BALL OF —) THENAR
THUMBSTALL POUCER POUSER
THUMP COB DAD DUB BANG BEAT
DING DIRD DRUB DUNT KNUB LUMP
PAKE POLT SOSS THUD TUNK YARK
YERK BLAFF BLIBE BUNCH CLOUR
CLUNK CRUMP KNOCK POUND
TABOR THACK WHELK BOUNCE
HAMMER PUMMEL THUNGE
THUMPING WHAPPING WHOPPING
THUNDER SULFUR FOULDRE
SULPHUR INTONATE
THUNDERBOLT BOLT FIRE VAJRA
FULMEN FOULDRE ARTIFACT
FIREBOLT
THUNDERSQUALL BAYAMO
VENDAVAL
THUNDERSTONE ARTIFACT
THUNDERSTORM HOUVARI
TEMPEST TORNADO
THURIBLE CENSER
THUS AS SIC DYCE THUSLY
THISWISE THUSGATE
THWACK DUNT CRUMP SOUSE
THWART BALK WART BENCH CROOK
CROSS SPITE THROW ZYGON
BAFFLE SCOTCH STYMIE SNOOKER
CONTRAIR CONTRARY TRAVERSE
THWARTING CROSS CROSSING
THYESTES (BROTHER OF —)
ATREUS
(FATHER OF —) PELOPS
(MOTHER OF —) HIPPODAMIA
THYLACINE YABBI
THYINE THUGA THUYA
THYME MARUM PELETRE HILLWORT
SERPOLET
TI KI TOI TITI
TIARA MITER CIDARIS TIARELLA
TIBBU DAZA TEDA

TIBET

CAPITAL: LASSA LHASA
COIN: TANGA
LAKE: ARU BAM BUM NAM MEMA
TOSU JAGOK TABIA DAGTSE
GARHUR KASHUN SELING
TANGRA YAMDOK KYARING
TERIMAN TSARING ZILLING
JIGGITAI
LANGUAGE: BODSKAD
MOUNTAIN: KAMET SAJUM KAILAS
BANDALA
MOUNTAIN RANGE: KAILAS
KUNLUN HIMALAYA
NATIVE: BHOTIA BHOTIYA
RIVER: NAK NAU SAK SONG INDUS
SUTLEJ MATSANG SALWEEN

TOWN: NOH KARAK LHASA
GARTOK TOTLING GYANGTSE
SHIGATSE

TIBETAN BALTI DRUPA BHOTIA
BHUTIA CHAMPA DROKPA KHAMBA
KHAMBU PANAKA SHERPA TANGUT
BHOTIYA BHUTANI GYARUNG
TIBIA SHIN SHANK CNEMIS SHINBONE
TIBOURBOU CORTEZ
TIC FIXATION
(ONE SUBJECT TO —) TIQUEUR
TICK FAG JAR KEB BEAT KADE NICK
PEAK PICK PIKE CHALK CHICK
CRIKE PIQUE STRAP IXODID PALLET
TALAJE TAMPAN ACARIAN ARGASID
BEDTICK IXODIAN PINOLIA
ARACHNID CARAPATO GARAPATA
GARAPATO TURICATA
TICKED MACKEREL
TICKET LOT TAG BLANK CHECK
DUCAT FICHE TOKEN BALLOT
BILLET COUPON DOCKET PIGEON
POLICY RETURN BENEFIT ETIQUET
CONTRACT DEADHEAD STOPOVER
TRANSFER
(COMMISSION —) SPIFF
(FREE —) PASS
(LOTTERY —) BLANK HORSE
BENEFIT
(SALES —) TRAVELER
(SEASON —) IVORY
(PL.) PAPER
TICKET WINDOW GUICHET
TICKING KISS TICK BEDTICK
TICKLE AMUSE TEASE EXCITE KITTLE
PLEASE THRILL TIDDLE CUITTLE
TICKLISH GOOSEY KITTLE KITTLY
QUEASY TENDER TOUCHY TRICKY
KITTLISH
TICKSEED COREOPSIS
TICK TREFOIL BEDSTRAW SAINFOIN
TICKSEED
TIDBIT SAYNETE BEATILLE
KICKSHAW
TIDDLEYWINK SQUAIL
TIDE FLOW NEAP WAVE AGGER
ROUST SPRING OVERTIDE
SEAFLOOD
(— MOVEMENT) LAKIE
TIDINGS NEWS WORD RUMOR
SOUND UNCOW ADVICE MESSAGE
(GLAD —) GOSPEL
TIDY RID COSH MACK NEAT SIDE
SMUG SNOD SNUG TAUT TOSH TRIG
WEME CHART DONCY DONSY
DOUCE NATTY QUEME TIGHT
DONSIE FETTLE POLITE SPOONY
ALLIGATE MACKLIKE MENSEFUL
TIE BOW LAP TYE BAND BIND BOND
CAST DRAW KILT KNOT LACE LOCK
ROOT WISP YOKE ASCOT BRACE
CADGE LEASH NEXUS POINT THRAP
THROW TRUSS ATTACH BUNDLE
CONNEX COUPLE FASTEN LIGATE
SECURE DOGFALL FOULARD
JAZZBOW NECKTIE SHACKLE
SLEEPER SPANCEL TABLEAU

CROSSTIE INTERTIE LIGATURE
STANDOFF STRINGER VINCULUM
(— BENEATH) SUBNECT
(— IN TENNIS) DEUCE
(— IN WRESTLING) DOGFALL
(— KNOT) CAST
(— LEGS) HOBBLE
(— ONIONS) TRACE
(— SCORE) PEELS
(— THE SCORE) EQUALIZE
(— TOGETHER) KNIT LEASH
HARNESS
(— UP SHORT) SNUB
(— UP) SNUB TRAMMEL LIGATURE
TWITCHEL
(LEATHER —) WANTY
(MADE-UP —) TECK
(NEEDLEWORK —) BRIDE
(PL.) GILLIES
TIED FAST KNIT SQUARE
TIEPIN SCARFPIN STICKPIN
TIE PLATE TURTLE
TIER ROW BANK DECK RANK CHESS
STORY WITHE DEGREE PINAFORE
(— OF CASKS) RIDER
(— OF SEATS) CIRCLE
(— OF SHELVES) STAGE
TIERCE LEASH THIRD
TIFF MIFF TIFT
TIFFIN CONDOR
TIGER SHER SHIR TIGRE TIGERKIN
TIGER CAT CHATI
TIGERFOOT IPOMOEA
TIGER SNAKE ELAPID ELAPOID
TIGHT WET FULL HARD SNUG TAUT
TIDY CLOSE DENSE DRUNK STENT
TENSE STINGY STRAIT STRICT
AIRTIGHT
TIGHTEN JAM CALK FIRM FRAP
CAULK CINCH CLOSE FEEZE SCREW
THRAP WRENCH STRAITEN
TIGHTFISTED STINGY
TIGHT-LIPPED SILENT
TIGHTLY FAST HARD SHORT STRAIT
CLOSELY
TIGHTS MAILLOT LEOTARDS
TIGHTWAD FIST PIKER STIFF
TILDE TIL WAVE TITTLE
(HAVING A —) CURLY
TILE LUMP FAVUS KASHI LATER
SLATE IMBREX LAPPET PAMENT
QUARRY SLATER TEGULA AZULEJO
CARREAU CONDUIT PANTILE
QUARREL STARTER MAINTILE
(— USED IN MOSAIC) ABACULUS
(HEXAGONAL —) FAVUS
(HOLLOW —) BACKING
(LARGE —) DALLE QUARL QUARLE
(MAH JONG —) HONOR SEASON
(ONE-HALF —) HEAD
(PERSIAN —) KASHI
(ROUNDED —) CREASE
(SMALL —) TILETTE
(SQUARE —) QUADREL QUARREL
TILER HELER HELLIER
TILL TO EAR FIT LOB CASH FARM
PLOW TEAL TOIL DRESS LABOR
UNTIL WHILE FURROW MANURE
PLOUGH TILLER WHILST HUSBAND

SHUTTLE DUCKFOOT OXHARROW
TILLABLE EARABLE
TILLAGE ARABLE GAINOR MANURE
ARATION CULTURE TILTURE
TILLED GEOM TOILED
TILLER HELM STERN STOOL
HUSBAND KILLIFER
TILLING EARTH FALLOW
TILT DIP TIP TOP BANK CANT CAVE
COCK HEEL LIST SWAG TRAP
BRASH HEELD HIELD JOUST STOOP
TIPUP CASTER TILTER TOPPLE
CURRENT TOURNEY COCKBILL
QUINTAIN
(— BRICK) HACK
(— IN WATER) DABBLE
(— OF BOWSPRIT) STAVE
(— OF NOSE) KIP KIPP
TILTED ACOCK ASTOOP
TILT HAMMER OLIVER
TILTING DIP JOUSTING
TIMBAL DRUM TYMBALON
TIMBER CAP LOG RIB BEAM BIBB
BUNK CLOG DRAM FELL FISH FROG
GIRT PUMP RAFF SKID SPAR SPUR
TREE WOOD CAHUY CAVEL CRUCK
FLOOR GRIPE JOIST KEVEL LEDGE
ORGUE PLATE RIDER SISSU SPALE
STICK BEARER BRIDGE BUMPER
CAMBER CORBEL DAGGER FENDER
FOREST KNIGHT LIZARD ROOFER
SISSOO SUMMER TIMMER BOLSTER
CARLING DEADMAN DIVIDER
FALLAGE FUTCHEL FUTTOCK
GROUSER PARTNER PITWOOD
RIBBAND TRANSOM CORDWOOD
COULISSE DOGSHORE FOREHOOK
STRINGER STUMPAGE TRIPSILL
WOODFALL
(— BETWEEN TRIMMERS) HEADER
(— CUT TO LENGTH) JUGGLE
(— IN MINE) COG STULL LIFTER
DIVIDER JUGGLER
(— KEPT DRY) BRIGHT
(— ON SLED) BUNK
(— PIECE) PUTLOG
(— SAWED AND SPLIT) LUMBER
(— SUPPORTING CAP) LEGPIECE
(— SUSTAINING YARDS) MAST
(— TO PROP COAL) BROB
(CONVEX —) CAMBER
(CURVED —) CRUCK
(CUT —) FELL
(FELLED —) HAG
(FLOOR —) JOIST SUMMER
(FLOORING —) BATTEN
(FRAMING —) PUNCHEON
(HORIZONTAL —) REASON
(NORWEGIAN —) DRAM
(PHILIPPINE —) LAUAN
(PRINCIPAL — OF VESSEL) KEEL
(ROOF —) LEVER RAFTER
(ROOFING —S) SILE
(SHIP'S —) KEEL KNEE RUNG SPUR
LEDGE WRONG DAGGER HARPIN
LACING SCROLL BRACKET FUTTOCK
STEMSON DOGSHORE STANDARD
(SHIPBUILDING —S) STOCKS
DEADWOOD HARPINGS

(SLABBED —) CANT
(SUPPORT —) SILL GIRDER LEDGER
STRINGER
(SYSTEM OF —S) BOND
(UNCUT —) STUMPAGE
(WEATHERBEATEN —) DRIKI
TIMBERLAND STICKS WOODLAND
TIMBERMAN BRACER
TIMBO CUBE AJARI
TIMBRE CLANG COLOR KLANG
COLORING
TIMBREL TABOR TABOUR
TIME DAY ELD BELL BOUT HINT
HOUR SELE TIDE WHET ABYSS
CHARE EPOCH FLASH FRIST KALPA
SITHE SPACE STOUN STOUR TEMPO
TEMPS VOLTA WHACK WHILE
COURSE KAIROS PERIOD SEASON
STOUND TEMPUS CADENCE
DEWFALL SESSION MOVEMENT
(— AFTER) POST
(— ALLOWED FOR PAYMENT)
USANCE
(— FOR PAYING) KIST
(— FOR PAYMENT) CREDIT
(— GRANTED) FRIST
(— IN SERVICE) AGE
(— INTERVENING) INTERIM
MEANTIME
(— LONG SINCE PAST) YORE
(— OF BEAUTY) BLOOM
(— OF CRISIS) EXIGENT
(— OF DYING) LAST
(— OF EXPIRY) ISH
(— OF EXUBERANCE) CARNIVAL
(— OF FEASTING) GUTTIDE
(— OF HIGHEST STRENGTH)
HEYDAY
(— OF LIGHT) DAY
(— OF MATURITY OR DECLINE)
AUTUMN
(— OF NEWS STORY) BREAK
(— OF OLD AGE) SUNSET
(— OF QUIET) DEAD
(— OF REST) BREATH SABBATH
(— OF WOE) WOSITH
(— TO COME) FUTURITY
(ANOTHER —) AGAIN
(AT ANOTHER —) ALIAS
(BRIEF —) TINE FLASH THROW
(BY THE —) AGAINST
(EACH —) ONCE
(EXTENDED —) TRAIN
(FIXED —) HOUR STEVEN
(GAY —) FRISK WHOOPEE
(GOOD —) BALL BASH BEANO
JOLLY BARNEY FROLIC HOLIDAY
(HARD —) GYP BUSINESS
(IMMEASURABLY LONG PERIOD OF
—) EON AEON
(INFINITE —) ABYSS
(LONG —) AGE
(OLD —S) ELD
(PAST —) FORETIME
(POINT OF —) MOMENT
(RIGHT —) TID
(SECOND —) YET EFTSOON
EFTSOONS
(SET —) TRYST

(SHORT —) TIFF SPACE START
MINUTE STOUND
(SPARE —) TOOM
(TRIPLE —) TRIPLA
(UNENGAGED —) LEISURE
(WORKING —) CORE
(PL.) SYSE
TIME CLOCK BUNDY TELLTALE
TIMELESS AGELESS ETERNAL
DATELESS
TIMELESSNESS ETERNITY
TIMELY PAT DULY TIDY COGENT
TIMEFUL TIMEOUS TOWARDLY
TIMEPIECE DIAL CLOCK TIMER
VERGE WATCH GHURRY PENDULE
HOROLOGE HOROLOGY
TIMETABLE SCHEDULE
TIMID SHY ARGH EERY NESH SELY
SHAN BAUCH BLATE EERIE FAINT
PAVID SCARE SCARY AFRAID
COWARD ASHAMED BASHFUL
FEARFUL FRIGHTY NERVOUS
RABBITY SCADDLE STRANGE
TREMBLY COWARDLY FEARSOME
GHASTFUL RETIRING TIMOROSO
TIMOROUS
TIMIDITY SHYNESS TIMERITY
FUNKINESS
TIMIDLY SMALL
TIMOR (CAPITAL OF —) DILI
(COIN OF —) AVO PATACA
(ISLAND OF —) MOA LETI LAKOR
(LANGUAGE OF —) TETUM
(TOWN IN —) KUPANG ATAMBUA
TIMOROUS FAINT MILKY TIMID
AFRAID COWISH TREPID FEARFUL
FERDFUL FEARSOME SHEEPISH
TEMEROUS TIMOROSO
TIN SN DIXY JOVE DIXIE KATIN
SWELL TINNY KHATIN JUPITER
PILLION STANNUM PRILLION
TINGLASS
(MESS —) DIXY DIXIE
(ROOFING —) TERNE
(SHEET —) LATTEN LATTIN
(TIE — CAN TO TAIL) TAILPIPE
TINAMOU YUTU MACUCA YNAMBU
TATAUPA MARTINET
TINCAL ALTINCAR
TINCTURE BUFO DRUG COLOR
IMBUE SMACK STAIN TAINT TENNE
TINCT ARGENT ARNICA ELIXIR
DIAMOND ARAMAIZE INFUSION
LAUDANUM TAINTURE
TINDER SPUNK AMADOU TENDRE
FIREBOX
TINE KNAG SNAG TANG GRAIN
OFFER POINT PRONG RIGHT TOOTH
GRAINING TINEWARE TINEWEED
(ANTLER'S —) RIGHT CROCKET
SURROYAL
TIN FOIL TAIN
TINGE DYE EYE HUE CAST DASH
TINT WOAD COLOR FLUSH IMBUE
PAINT SAVOR SHADE STAIN TAINT
TINCT SEASON SMUTCH BEPAINT
DISTAIN GLIMPSE DISCOLOR
TINCTION TINCTURE
TINGED FLORID GILDED

TINGGIAN ITNEG ITANEG

TINGLE SOO BURN DIRL GELL GIRL THIRL DINDLE SWIDGE TINKLE PRINGLE PRINKLE TRINKLE

TINKER PRIG TINK CAIRD FIDDLE FIDGET MUGGER KETTLER PROJECT TRAVELER

TINKLE TINK DINDLE DINGLE TINGLE TRINKLE TWINKLE

TINNER TINKER

TINSEL GAUDY TINSY TINNET

TINT DYE EYE COLOR ENNUE GRAIN TINCT TINGE SPRAING
(**— IN HORSE'S COAT**) BLOSSOM
(**— WITH COSMETICS**) SURFLE
(**CLANG —**) TIMBRE

TINTED TINCT

TINWORKS STANNARY

TINY TINE BITSY BITTY DEENY SMALL TEENY TIDDY WEENY ATOMIC BITTIE WEESHY MINIKIN ATOMICAL

TIP CAP DIP END FEE NEB TOP APEX CANT CAVE COCK HEEL HELD HORN KEEL LEAD LIST PALM PIKE PILE SWAG TILT TYPE VAIL GRIFF HEELD MUCRO POINT POUCH SPIRE SPURE STEER CAREEN CENTER CENTRE TICKLE TIPLET TIPPLE TOPPLE WHEEZE APICULA CUMSHAW DERTRUM DOUCEUR GRIFFIN POINTER WRINKLE APICULUS BONAMANO ENTOMION FOOTHOLD GRATUITY
(**— OF ANTENNA**) ARISTA
(**— OF BILLIARD CUE**) LEATHER
(**— OF BIRD'S BILL**) DERTRUM
(**— OF FOX'S BRUSH**) CHAPE
(**— OF SKI**) SHOVEL
(**— OF SPIDER**) BULB
(**— OF STAMP**) SHOE
(**— OF TOE**) POINTE
(**— OF TONGUE**) CORONA
(**— OF UMBO**) BEAK
(**— OF WHEAT KERNEL**) BRUSH
(**— OF WHIP**) SNAPPER
(**— ON ORGAN PIPE**) TOE
(**— OVER**) TOP PURL
(**— UP**) CANT
(**ABRUPT —**) MUCRO
(**BOW —**) HORN
(**INWARD —**) BANK
(**LARGE —S**) LARGESS LARGESSE

TIPCART COUPE COCOPAN

TIPCAT CAT PIGGY PUSSY KITCAT PIGGIE

TIPPED BANKED
(**EASILY —**) CRANK

TIPPER DUMPER THROWER TIPPLER

TIPPET FUR AMICE SCARF ALMUCE SINDON LIRIPIPE LIRIPOOP

TIPPLE BIB NIP POT SOT DRAM GILL BIBBER BIBBLE FUDDLE PUDDLE SIPPLE TIPPLER TOOTHFUL

TIPPLER SOUSE TOAST WINER BIBBER BOLLER BUBBER DRAMMER PANURGE POTATOR TUMBLER WHETTER ALESTAKE MALTWORM

TIPPLING POTTING BIBACITY BIBATION

TIPSY CUT BOSKY DRUNK FRESH MUSED TIGHT TOZIE BUMPSY GROGGY SLEWED SPRUNG EBRIOSE EBRIOUS EXALTED ELEVATED MUCKIBUS OVERSEEN PLEASANT

TIP-TOP SWELL TIPPY TOPPING

TIRADE SCREED STOUSH JEREMIAD

TIRE DO FAG HAG LAG BORE CORD FLAT FLOG JADE KILL MOIL SHOE LABOR SPARE WEARY CASING HAGGLE HARASS SICKEN TIRING TUCKER BALLOON EXHAUST FATIGUE FRAZZLE TRACHLE CLINCHER FORSPEND
(**— OUT**) HAG FLOG THEAD BEJADE HARASS
(**WORN —**) CARCASS

TIRED SAD TAM BEAT BOEG DEAD TIRY BLOWN WEARY AWEARY BLEARY BUSHED PLAYED TAVERT FORWORN TAIVERT FATIGATE FORWAKED

TIREDNESS FATIGUE

TIRESOME DRY DREE FAGGY ALANGE BORING DREICH PROLIX IRKSOME PROSAIC TEDIOUS BORESOME BROMIDIC ENNUYANT LONGSOME

TIRING DRUDGING

TIRL RISP

TIRTHANKARA JINA

TISAMENUS (FATHER OF —) ORESTES THERSANDER
(**MOTHER OF —**) HERMIONE

TISANE PTISAN TILLEUL

TISSUE FAT WEB CORK FOIL PITH TELA TEXT FACIA GLEBA GRAFT SUBER TRAMA CALLUS DARTOS DIPLOE FABER FASCIA LIGNUM PANNUS PHLOEM SHEATH TEXTUS ADENOID ALBUMEN BINDWEB CAMBIUM CLYPEUS EPITELA EXPLANT HYDROME KLEENEX MESTOME NEURINE PHLOEM TEXTURE TWITTER ADHESION BLASTEMA DESMOGEN ECTODERM ENDODERM EPIPLOON HISTOGEN HYPODERM ISOGRAFT MERISTEM OSTEOGEN PERIDERM PERIDESM STEREOME
(**— OF FUNGUS**) CENTRUM
(**— SURROUNDING TEETH**) GUM
(**BLACK —**) CLYPEUS
(**CONNECTING —**) STROMA TENDON LIGAMENT
(**CORK —**) SUBER
(**FATTY —**) LARD GREASE
(**HARD —**) BONE
(**HYPOTHETICAL —**) COAGULIN
(**LYMPHOID —**) TONSIL
(**NERVE —**) GANGLION
(**SOFT —**) FLAB
(**VEGETABLE —**) ARMOR
(**WOOD —**) LIGNUM VITRAIN
(**PL.**) CHIRATA CHIRETTA MESODERM

TISWIN TESVINO TEXGUINO

TIT TID MESIA TITTY BLUECAP COLETIT MUFFLIN

TITAN BANA LETO MAIA ASURA ATLAS COEUS CREUS CRIOS DIONE THEIA CRONOS CRONUS PALLAS PHOEBE TETHYS THEMIS IAPETUS OCEANUS HYPERION

TITANIC HUGE GREAT TITAN IMMENSE COLOSSAL GIGANTIC

TITANITE SPHENE GROTHITE LEDERITE LIGURITE

TITANIUM DIOXIDE ANATASE

TITA ROOT MISHMI MISHMEE

TITHE DIME TEIND TENTH DECIMA PREBEND TITHING

TITHING BORGH BORROW DECIME DENARY DECENARY

TITHINGMAN DEAN DECURION TUTTIMAN

TITHONUS (FATHER OF —) LAOMEDON
(**MOTHER OF —**) STRYMO

TITI ORA TEETEE WISTIT SAIMIRI WISTITI IRONWOOD MARMOSET ORABASSU OUISTITI

TITILLATE KITTLE TICKLE

TITILLATING GAMY GAMEY

TITLARK PIPIT TEETING

TITLE AGA AYA BAN BEG BEY DAN DOM DUE FRA JAM LAR MIR PAN SAG SIR ABBA ABBE AGHA AMIR ANBA DAME DEVI EMIR FRAY GAON GRAF HAJI HERR KHAN KNEZ LARS NAME PANI SIDI SLUG ABGAR ABUNA AMEER CCOYA CLAIM CROWN EMEER FRATE GHAZI GOODY GRACE HADJI HAJJI HAKAM HANUM HONOR KNIAZ KNYAZ MIRZA MPRET NAWAB NEGUS NIZAM PANNA RABBI RIGHT SINGH SOPHI SOPHY UNWAN BASHAW BEGANI COUSIN DEGREE DEMAND DESPOT DOMINE EXARCH HANDLE HUZOOR LEGEND MADAME MASTER MEHTAR MISTER PESHWA PREFIX SHERIF SQUIRE SUFFEE TITULE VIDAME ALFEREZ ALTESSE ALTEZZA BAHADUR CANDACE CAPTION CONVITO CRAWLER DIGNITY EFFENDI EPITHET ESQUIRE FIDALGO GAEKWAR GRAVITY HEADING HIDALGO INFANTE KHEDIVE MAHARAO MESSIRE RABBONI SHAREEF TITULUS VOIVODE BANNERET BASILEUS COMMENDA CONVIVIO EMINENCE GOSPODIN HIGHNESS HOLINESS HOSPODAR INTEREST LOKINDRA MAGISTER MAHARAJA MAHARANA MAHARSHI MISTRESS MONSIEUR PADISHAH PRINCIPE RAUGRAVE SUBTITLE TAMBURAN TITULADO
(**— ACQUISITION**) USUCAPT
(**— OF BOOK**) QUARE
(**— OF MEMBER OF PRIMROSE LEAGUE**) KNIGHT
(**— OF RESPECT**) SIR SRI COJA LIEF MIAN SHRI SIDI BURRA HODJA KHAJA KHOJA MADAM SAHIB KHOJAH MADAME MILADY
(**BENEDICTINE —**) DOM
(**MOCK —**) IDLESHIP

TITMOUSE MAG NUN TIT MAGG
OXEYE PARUS SPICK FUFFIT HEFFEL
PUFFER TOMTIT VERDIN BLUECAP
BUSHTIT COLETIT COLMOSE
GOLDTIT GRIGNET HAGMALL
JACKSAW MUFFLIN PINCHEM
PINNOCK TINNOCK TITMALL
TOMNOUP CHICADEE HACKMALL
OVENBIRD REEDLING SHABROON
SHARPSAW
TITTER GIGGLE SNICKER TWITTER
TITTLE JOT TITLE MINUTE
TITULAR LEGAL HONORARY
TITYUS (FATHER OF —) TERRA
JUPITER
(MOTHER OF —) ELARA
TIU ER EAR TIW TYR ZIO ZIU TIWAZ
SAXNOT
TIV MUNCHI
TIZZY PUCKER SWIVET SWIVVET
TLAKLIUT ECHE LOOT WISHRAM
TLEPOLEMUS (FATHER OF —)
HERCULES
(MOTHER OF —) ASTYOCHIA
(SLAYER OF —) SARPEDON
TLINGIT SITKA KOLUSH SUMDUM
CHILCAT CHILKAT STIKINE
TMESIS DIACOPE
TNT TROTYL
TO A AD FOR INTO TILL UNTO UPON
(— A CONCLUSION) OUT
(— BE SURE) EVEN
(— BE) IBE
(— COME) BEHIND
(— COMPLETION) DOWN
(— IT) TOOT SESSA
(— PRESS) DOWN
(— SUCH DEGREE) EVEN
(— THAT TIME) UNTIL
(— THE END) AF
(— THE OPPOSITE SIDE) ACROSS
(— THE REAR) ABAFT ASTERN
(— THIS PLACE) HERE HITHER
(— THIS) HERETO
(— VICTORY) ABU ABOO
(— WHAT) WHERETO
(— WIT) NAMELY INNUENDO
SCILICET
TOAD PAD AGUA BUFO FROG HYLA
PIPA PODE HYLID PADDO PADDY
PIPAL PIPID TOADY ANURAN
CRAPON PEEPER BUFONID CHARLIE
CRAPAUD CRAWLER CREEPER
FROGLET GANGREL HOPTOAD
PADDOCK PODDOCK PUDDOCK
QUILKIN REPTILE SERPENT
GANGEREL
TOADFISH SAPO SARPO GRUBBY
SLIMER CABEZON FROGFISH
LORICATE SCORPION
TOADFLAX FLAX FLAXWEED
FLAXWORT FLUELLEN GALLWEED
GALLWORT RAMSTEAD
TOAD RUSH SALTWEED
TOADSTOOL CANKER FUNGUS
TOADY FAWN SUCK TOAD ZANY
COTTON EARWIG FAWNER FLUNKY
GREASE LACKEY FLUNKEY LACQUEY
PLACEBO SHONEEN TRUCKLE

BOOTLICK LICKSPIT PARASITE
TOADYING GNATHONIC
TOADYISM FLUNKISM
TOAST WET TOSS BREDE ROUSE
SKOAL TRINQ BIRSLE BUMPER
CHEERS HEALTH PLEDGE PROSIT
BRISTLE CAROUSE CHEERIO
FRIZZLE LEHAYIM PROFACE
PROPINE RESPECT SLAINTE
WASSAIL BRINDISI
(— AND ALE) SWIG
(— ONESELF) LEEP
(JACOBITE —) LIMP
TOBACCO CANE CAPA HAND LEAF
LUGS NAVY POAK POKE QUID ROLL
SHAG WEED BACCO BACCY BACKY
BROKE CUBAN DARKS FOGUS
PETUN REGIE SMOKE SNOUT TABAC
TWIST BACKER BRIGHT BURLEY
COLORY COWPEN FILLER HAVANA
RETURN TOMBAC TUMBAK CAPORAL
CRACCUS GAGROOT GORACCO
KNASTER LATAKIA NAILROD NICOTIA
ORONOKO PERIQUE PIGTAIL
SOTWEED UPPOWOC CANASTER
HONEYDEW MAKHORKA MARYLAND
NICOTIAN ORONOOKO SEEDLEAF
VIRGINIA
(— AND PAPER) MAKINGS
(— CAKED IN PIPE BOWL) DOTTEL
DOTTLE TOPPER
(— HAVING OFFENSIVE SMELL)
MUNDUNGO
(— IN ROPES) BOGIE
(— JUICE) AMBEER PRAISS
(— MOISTENED WITH MOLASSES)
HONEYDEW
(— MOSAIC) WALLOON
(— PASTE) GORACCO
(— ROOM) PRIZERY
(— WORKER) LOOPER LEAFBOY
LEAFGIRL
(CAKED —) HEEL
(COARSE —) SHAG SCRAP CAPORAL
(CUT —) PICADURA
(DRIED —) TABACUM
(HARD-PRESSED —) NAILROD
(INDIAN —) GAGROOT PUKEWEED
EYEBRIGHT
(INFERIOR —) LUGS
(LADIES' —) CUDWEED
(LOWER LEAVES OF —) FLYING
(PERSIAN —) SHIRAZ TUMBEK
TUMBEKI
(PERUVIAN —) SANA
(POOR QUALITY —) DOGLEG
(PULVERIZED —) SNUFF
(QUID OF —) CUD
(RAW —) LEAF
(ROLLED —) CARROT
(SMALL PIECE OF —) FIG
(VIRGINIA —) COWPEN VIRGINIA
TOBACCO WORM HORNWORM
TOBOGGAN CARIOLE CARRIOLE
TOCHARIAN A AGNEAN
TOCHARIAN B KUCHEAN
TODAY DAY NOW NOWADAYS
TODDLE TOT FADGE DADDLE DIDDLE
DODDLE PADDLE TOTTLE WADDLE

TODDLER TROT GANGREL TROTTIE
TODDY TOD TUBA TERRY SAGWIRE
TO-DO ADO FUSS STIR WORK STINK
DOMENT HOOPLA FLUSTER
FOOSTER FOOFARAW TRAVALLY
TODY ROBIN
TOE TER DIGIT DACTYL HALLUX
MINIMUS TOENAIL POULAINE
(— OF BIRD) HEEL
(LITTLE —) MINIMUS
(PL.) TUN TAIS TOON
TOEPLATE SHOD
TOFF NOB
TOGA GOWN ROBE TOGUE TRABEA
TOGETHER ONCE SAME YFERE
BEDENE INSAME JOINTLY ENSEMBLE
(— WITH) AND INTO
TOGGLE COTTAR COTTER TOGGEL
NETSUKE
TOGO (CAPITAL OF —) LOME
(LANGUAGE OF —) EWE TWI MINA
HAUSA KABRAIS LOTOCOLI
(NATIVE OF —) EWE MINA CABRAI
KABRAI OUATCHI
(RIVER IN —) OTI ANIE HAHO MONO
(TOWN IN —) ANECHO PALIME
SOKODE ATAKPAME
TOIL FAG TUG DARG GRUB HACK
MOIL MUCK PLOD TASK WORK
LABOR SCRAT SLAVE SWINK TWEIL
BILDER DRUDGE EFFORT HAMMER
MITHER MOIDER STRIVE UNRUFE
FATIGUE TRAVAIL TURMOIL
DRUDGERY INDUSTRY
TOILER SLAVE MOILER WORKER
TOILET CAN LOO HEAD JOHN BIFFY
CRAPPER BASEMENT BATHROOM
LAVATORY PLUMBING
TOILSOME HARD SWEATY ARDUOUS
TOILFUL MOILSOME SWEATFUL
TOJOLABAL CHANABAL
TOKAY TUCKTOO
TOKEN BUCK CENT HARP SIGN TYPE
BADGE CHECK INDEX SCRIP BEAVER
CASTOR COLLAR COPPER COUPON
DOLLAR EMBLEM JETTON MARKER
OSTENT REMARK SIGNAL TICKET
WITTER AUSPICE COUNTER
EARNEST INDICIA MEMENTO
PRESAGE SYMPTOM TESSERA
BUNGTOWN COINTISE EVIDENCE
FOOTSTEP FORBYSEN INSTANCE
KEEPSAKE MONUMENT SHILLING
SIGNACLE
(— OF LUCK) HANSEL HANDSEL
(— OF RESPECT) SALUTE
(— OF SUPERIORITY) PALM
(— OF VICTORY) LAUREL
(CANADIAN —) HARP
(LOVE —) DRURY AMORET
(PORCELAIN —S) PI
TOKHARI KUCHEAN
TOLERABLE GAY SOSO PRETTY
TARBLE PATIBLE BEARABLE
PASSABLE PORTABLE
TOLERABLY GAIN GEYAN FAIRLY
MEETLY MEETERLY
TOLERANCE MERCY SHERE LEEWAY
REMEDY

TOLERANT SOFT BENIGN
TOLERATE GO BEAR BIDE HACK
HAVE ABIDE ALLOW BROOK SPARE
STAND STICK ACCEPT ENDURE
PARDON PERMIT SUFFER COMPORT
SUPPORT SUSTAIN
TOLERATION WITHGANG
TOLL JOW TAX JOWL PIKE RENT
KNELL PEAGE CAPHAR EXCISE
PEDAGE PESAGE BOOMAGE
KEELAGE LASTAGE LOCKAGE
MULTURE PASSAGE PICCAGE
PONTAGE SCAVAGE SUMMAGE
TERRAGE TOLLAGE TRONAGE
BERTHAGE STALLAGE WEIGHAGE
WHEELAGE
(PL.) CUSTOMS RAHDARI RATTAREE
TOLLHOUSE TOLLERY
TOLLIKER DUMMY
TOLSEN FOOTSTEP
TOLUENE DILUENT
TOLYL CRESYL
TOMAHAWK HATCHET NEOLITH
TOMATO TOM BERRY BURBANK
TOMB PIR CIST MOLE GRAVE GUACA
HUACA MAZAR SPEOS TABUT
THOLE TURBE BURIAL CHULPA
DARGAH DURGAH GALGAL HEARSE
SAMADH SHRINE SYRINX THOLOS
TROUGH TURBEH CHULLPA
MASTABA OSSUARY TOMBLET
TRITAPH CENOTAPH CISTVAEN
CUBICULO HALLCIST KISTVAEN
MARABOUT MASTABAH MONUMENT
TREASURY
(— OF MOSLEM SAINT) ZIARA
ZIARAT
(CAVE —) SPEOS
(PREHISTORIC —) KURGAN
TOMBAC ORSEDE ORSEDUE
TOMBOY GAMINE HOYDEN TOMRIG
TOMBSTONE SLAT TITLE THROUGH
TOMCAT GIB TOMMY PODGER
THOMAS
TOMCOD GADE GADID SMELT
GADOID WHITING TOMMYCOD
TOMENTUM WOOL
TOMFOOLERY HELL HORSE
TOMMY FOOL PODGER REQUIN
TOMMYROT WAHOO
TOMMY TALKER KAZOO
TOMORROW MANANA MORROW
TOMORN
TOMTATE CAESAR
TON TUN TOUN STYLE
TONALAMATL TZOLKIN
TONALITY KEY
TONE A F DO FA LA MI RE SI SO TI
DOH KEY SOH SOL CALL FLAT NOTE
COLOR COUAC DRONE FIFTH FORTE
PRIME SHARP SIXTH SOUND STYLE
TONUS ACCENT DEGREE FOURTH
SECOND FORMANT MEDIANT
PARTIAL DEMITINT ELEVENTH
FORENOTE HARMONIC SONORITY
(— A DRAWING) STUMP
(— DOWN) DRAB TAME SOFTEN
SUBDUE
(BROKEN —) CRACK

(COMPLEX —) KLANG
(DEEP —) BASS
(DOMINANT —) ANIMUS
(DRAWLING —) DRANT DRAUNT
(KEY —) KEYNOTE
(LOUD —) FORTE
(LOW —) SEMISOUN
(MONOTONOUS —) DRONE
(SHARP NASAL —) TWANG
(SIGNIFICANT —) ACCENT
(SINGLE UNVARIED —) MONOTONE
(STRIDENT —) COUAC
(WHINING —) GIRN
TONGA (CAPITAL OF —) NUKUALOFA
(COIN OF —) PAANGA
(ISLAND OF —) ONO TOFUA VAVAU
HAAPAI
(TOWN OF —) NEIAFU
TONGS SNAPS SERVER FORCEPS
GRAMPUS TUEIRON SCISSORS
TONGUE COG GAB CHIB CLAP KALI
NEAP PAWL POLE REED CLACK
IDIOM VOICE GADABA GLOSSA
KABYLE KALIKA LANGUE LINGUA
SPEECH CLAPPER DIALECT FEATHER
ILOKANO LANGUET DOVETAIL
LANGUAGE LORRIKER PLECTRUM
(— IN FLOORING) SPLINE
(— OF BELL) CLAPPER
(— OF JEW'S-HARP) TANG
(— OF LAND) REACH LANGUE
LANGUET
(— OF OXCART) COPE
(— OF SHOE) FLAP KILTY KILTIE
(— OF VEHICLE) NEAP SHAFT
(BELLOWS —) GUSSET
(GIVE —) PRATE
(GOSSIPING —) CLACK CLACKER
(PIVOTED —) PAWL
(ROMANY —) ROMANES
(PL.) GAURA
TONGUEFISH SOLE
TONGUE-LASH SCOLD
TONGUE-LASHING RAT TOCO
BUSINESS
TONGUE-TIED SILENT
TONIC DO DOH ALOE KEEP PICJI
BRACER SAMBUL SONANT SUMBUL
BONESET CALAMUS CALOMBO
CHIRATA COLOMBA DAMIANA
FUMARIA GENTIAN KEYNOTE
NERVINE SALICIN TONICAL
ANTHEMIS BARBERRY BERBERRY
HELONIAS ROBORANT TRILLIUM
TONICITY MYOTONIA
TONKA BEAN GAIAC CUMARU
GUAIAC COUMAROU
TONNA DOLIUM
TONNAGE PORTAGE
TONSIL ALMOND KERNEL ADENOID
AMYGDAL AMYGDALA
TONSILITIS QUINSY
TONSURE CROWN SHAVE SHEAR
CORONA DIKSHA RASURE
TONSURED PEELED PILLED SHAVED
TOO SO ALSO OVER TROP LUCKY
OVERLY LIKEWISE
TOOL (ALSO SEE IMPLEMENT AND
INSTRUMENT) AX ADZ AWL AXE BIT

BUR DIE DIG GIN GUN HOB KEY LAP
LOY RIP SAW SAX TAP TIT VOL ZAX
ADZE BORE BRAY BURR CLAW
COMB DADO DISC DISK DUPE EDGE
FILE FLAY FROE FROG FROW GAGE
HACK HAWK HONE LEAF LOOM MILL
PICK ROLL SEAX SLED SNAP SPID
SPUD STOP TAMP TIER VISE AUGER
BLADE BORAL BORER BRAKE
BRAND BREAK BRUSH BURIN DARBY
DOLLY DRIFT DRILL DUMMY EDGER
FLAKE FLOAT FLUTE GAUGE GOUGE
GUIDE HARDY HOBBY HOWEL KNIFE
KNURL LEVEL MAKER MODEL PLANE
POINT PRUNT PUNCH QUIRK SABER
SABRE SCREW SHAVE SHELL SLICE
SLICK SNIPE SPADE SPEAR SPLIT
STAKE STAMP STING STOCK STRIG
STYLE SWAGE TEWEL TOYLE UPSET
VALET WAGON BEADER BEATER
BIFACE BLADER BODKIN BROACH
BUFFER CALKER CHASER CHISEL
CLEAVE COGGLE COLTER CRADLE
CRANNY CUTTER DEVICE DIBBLE
DIGGER DOCTOR DRIVER ENGINE
FASCET FERRET FILLET FLANGE
FLORET FLUTER FORMER FRAISE
FULLER GIMLET GLAZER GOFFER
GRAVER GUMMER HACKER HAMMER
HEMMER HOGGER HOLDER HULLER
JIGGER JUMPER LADKIN LASTER
LIFTER NIBBER PALLET PARTER
PICKAX PICKER PLIERS PROPER
PUPPET REAMER RIPPER ROCKER
RUNNER SAPPER SCRIBE SEATER
SHAPER SHAVER SHEARS SHOVEL
SKIVER SLATER SOCKET SQUARE
STYLET STYLUS SWIVEL TAGGER
TASTER TONGUE TREPAN TURNER
TURREL TWILLY VEINER WAGGON
WIGWAG WIMBLE WORDLE WORMER
YANKEE ABRADER BLOCKER
CALIPER CAULKER CHAMFER
CHIPPER CHOPPER CLEANER
CLEAVER COULTER CREASER
DIAMOND DOLABRA DRESSER
FISTUCA FLANGER FREEZER
FROTTON GRAINER GROOVER
GRUBBER GUDGEON JOINTER
KNOTTER LOGHEAD MITERER
POINTEL POINTER PROFILE RIVETER
ROUGHER ROUNDER SCAUPER
SCORPER SCRIBER SCRIVER
SCURFER SLASHER SLEEKER
SLICKER SPLAYER SPUDDER
STEMMER STRIKER STROKER
TICKLER TREBLET TWIBILL UPRIGHT
WRAITHE BIFACIAL BILLHOOK
BOOTJACK BURGOYNE CALLIPER
CREATURE CRIPPLER CROSSCUT
CROWFOOT DUCKFOOT ELEVATOR
EXPANDER FLOUNDER GRAVETTE
GRIFFAUN POLISHER PRITCHEL
PROPERTY PUNCHEON RAVEHOOK
RECAPPER SCRAPPLE SCULPTOR
SPLITTER STIPPLER STRICKLE
STRINGER SURFACER THWACKER
TOLLIKER WARKLOOM WORKLOOM
SCRATCHER

(— **A BOOK**) FINISH

(PL.) TEW FISH GEAR TRADE CUTLERY GIBBLES PIONERY ENGINERY

TOOLED GOFFERED

(— **WITHOUT GILDING**) BLIND

TOOLHOLDER TURRET MONITOR

TOOLSHED DOGHOUSE

TOON LIM CEDAR TOONWOOD

TOOT BLOW TOWT BLAST SOUND TRUMPET

TOOTH BIT COG GAM JAG PEG DENS DENT FANG LEAF RASP SNAG TIND TINE TUSH TUSK IVORY MOLAR PEARL PRONG RAKER TENON BROACH CANINE CUSPID CUTTER DENTAL INDENT JOGGLE TRIGON TRITOR DENTILE DIVIDER GRINDER INCISOR LATERAL SURDENT UNCINUS ABUTMENT BICUSPID BLEPHARA DENTICLE EYETOOTH GAGTOOTH MARGINAL PREMOLAR SAWTOOTH SPROCKET TOOTHLET TRIGONID

(— **OF A MOSS**) BLEPHARA

(— **OF HORSE**) DIVIDER

(— **OF MOLLUSC**) MARGINAL

(— **OF PINION**) LEAF

(— **OF RADULA**) UNCINUS

(— **ON ROTATING PIECE**) WIPER

(**ARTIFICIAL** —) DUMMY PONTIL

(**CANINE** —) CUSPID HOLDER LANIARY CYNODONT DOGTOOTH EYETOOTH

(**GEAR** —) COG GUB DENT ADDENDUM SPROCKET

(**HARROW** —) TINE

(**MOLAR** —) WANG

(**UPPER SURFACE OF** —) TABLE

TOOTHACHE WORM DENTAGRA

TOOTHED SERRATE VIRGATE SERRATED

TOOTHLESS GUMMY

TOOTHPICK QUILL ARKANSAN

TOOTHWORT CROWTOE COOLWORT

TOP CAP COP GIG TAP TIP ACME APEX BEAT COCK CULM HEAD HELM ROOF SKIM STOP BLOOM CHIEF COVER CREST CROWN FANCY GIGGE RIDGE SPIRE STRIP TOTUM TRUMP UPPER CALASH CAPOTE CULMEN SUMMIT UPWARD VERTEX SPINNER ROUNDTOP SURMOUNT TEETOTUM

(— **FOR CHIMNEY OR PIPE**) COWL HOOD

(— **OF ALTAR**) MENSA

(— **OF AUTOMOBILE**) HEAD HOOD

(— **OF CAPSTAN**) DRUMHEAD

(— **OF FURNACE**) ARCH

(— **OF GLASS**) PRETTY

(— **OF HEAD**) MOLD PATE MOULD SCALP VERTEX

(— **OF HELMET**) SKULL

(— **OF HILL**) KNAG KNAP KNOLL

(— **OF INGOT**) CROPHEAD

(— **OF MOUNTAIN**) MAN

(— **OF PLANT OR TREE**) CROP

(— **OF ROOF**) DECK

(— **OF SPINDLE**) COCKHEAD

(— **OF THUNDERCLOUD**) INCUS

(— **OF WOODEN STAND**) CRISS

(—**S OF CROP**) SHAW

(**BOOT** —) RUFF

(**BOX** —) COUPON

(**CARRIAGE** —) CALASH

TOPAZ PYCNITE PYCNIUM

TOPCOAT OVERCOAT SIPHONIA

TOPE DHER DHERI STUPA SOUPFIN

TOPER BOUSER CUPMAN POTMAN POTTER SIPPER SUPPER TROUGH BOMBARD POTLING SWILLER TOSSPOT BLACKPOT DRUNKARD MALTWORM

TOPI TIANG

TOPIC HARE ITEM TEXT HOBBY THEMA THEME BURDEN GAMBIT GROUND MATTER SUBJECT OCCASION

TOPKNOT ONKOS TOPPING

TOPMAN COB

TOPMINNOW GUPPY LIMIA GULARIS HELLERI SAILFIN GAMBUSIA

TOPOGRAPHIC TERRAIN

TOPPLE TOP TILT LEVEL TOTTLE

TOPSAIL RAFFE RAFFEE

TOPSOIL KELLY

TOPSTONE CAPSTONE

TOPSWARM TOPCAST

TOPSY-TURVY COCKEYED REELRALL

TOQUE ZATI MUNGA MACACO RILAWA MACAQUE

TOQUILLA JIPIJAPA

TORCEL BURN BERNE BORNE

TORCH DUCK JACK LAMP LINK LUNT PINE WASE WISP BLAZE BRAND FLARE MATCH FOCKLE LAMPAD MASHAL MUSSAL BRANDON CRESSET GRIDDLE LUCIGEN ROUGHIE TORCHET FLAMBEAU

TORCHBEARER KERYX LINKBOY LINKMAN DADUCHUS TORCHMAN

TOREADOR TORERO CAPEADOR

TORIL CHIQUERO

TORMENT WO TAW TRY WOE BAIT BALE FRET MOIL PAIN PANG PINE RACK TUCK CHEVY CURSE DEVIL GRILL HARRY SCALD TEASE TWIST WRING CHIVVY HARASS HARROW HECTOR INFEST PLAGUE TRAVEL AFFLICT BEDEVIL CRUCIFY HAGRIDE HATCHEL MALISON PERPLEX PINDING TERRIFY TORTURE TRAVAIL DISTRAIN LACERATE MACERATE

(**EXTREME** —) AGONY

TORMENTED CRUCIATE

TORMENTIL SEPTFOIL

TORMENTING PLAGUY

TORMINA TORSION

TORN RENT BROKEN BLASTED

TORNADO VORTEX CYCLONE TRAVADO TWISTER

TORPEDO FISH SHELL SQUIB BATOID

TORPID FOUL NUMB BROSY INERT SODDEN STUPID TOGGER LANGUID TORPENT COMATOSE COMATOUS SLUGGISH

TORPIFY DAZE ETHERIZE

TORPOR COMA SLEEP SWOON ACEDIA SLUMBER LETHARGY

TORQUE BEE SARPE TWIST

TORRENT FLOW RUSH FLOOD SPATE STREAM NIAGARA

TORREYA SAVIN TUMION

TORRID HOT SULTRY BOILING

TORSALO BERNE

TORSION STRESS DIDROMY

TORT LIBEL WRONG

TORTE DOBOS

TORT-FEASOR ACTOR

TORTICOLLIS WRYNECK

TORTILLA TOSTADO

TORTOISE EMYD BEKKO GAPER COOTER GOPHER TURTLE EMYDIAN HICATEE MUNGOFA TESTUDO GALAPAGO KASHYAPA SHELLPAD SHELLPOT TERRAPIN

TORTOISESHELL CAREY

TORTUOUS CRANKY SCREWY SINUATE WRIGGLY SINUATED

TORTURE TAW BOOT CARD FIRE PAIN PANG PINE RACK AGONY SCREW TWIST ENGINE EXTORT IMPALE MARTYR AFFLICT AGONIZE BOOTING CRUCIFY PERPLEX TORMENT

TORTURER BOURREAU

TORUS CORK TORE BASTON BOLTEL BOUTELL BOWTELL THALAMUS

TORY BANDIT OUTLAW ROBBER PEELITE TANTIVY LOYALIST

TOSS COB LAB SHY BUNG CANT CAST CAVE DOSS FLAP FLIP HIKE PASS SHAG SLAT TOUT CHAFE CHUCK FLICK FLING FLIRT FLURR HEAVE TEAVE THROW BETOSS BOUNCE DANDLE TOTTER WALTER WELTER WENTLE BLANKET TURMOIL WAMPISH WHEMMEL

(— **A COIN**) SKY

(— **A JACK**) LAG

(— **ABOUT**) SWAB TAVE POPPLE THRASH THRESH TORFLE WAMPISH

(— **ASIDE**) BANDY

(— **AWAY**) BLOW

(— **HEAD**) CAVE GECK

(— **OF THE HEAD**) HEEZE

(— **OFF**) SWAP SWOP

(— **ON WAVES**) SURGE

(— **TO AND FRO**) WALK

(— **TOGETHER CONFUSEDLY**) SCRAMBLE

(— **WITH THE HORNS**) DOSS HIKE

TOSSING SURGING

(— **OF BULLFIGHTER**) COGIDA

TOSTAO TESTON

TOTAL SUM TOT DEAD MERE TALE COUNT GROSS MOUNT SUMMA UTTER WHOLE ENTIRE GLOBAL OMNIUM SUMMED TOTTLE EMBRACE FOOTING GENERAL PERFECT ABSOLUTE COMPLETE ENTIRETY SURMOUNT TEETOTAL

TOTALITY ALL BODY HEAP BEING ALLNESS ECOLOGY ETERNITY

HUMANITY INTEGRAL INTERVAL
OMNITUDE
TOTALLY COLD GOOD QUITE
WHOLLY
TOTEM HUACA
TOTTER TOT ROCK TOIT WALT
SHAKE WAVER COGGLE DODDER
DOTTER FALTER JOGGLE STAVER
SWERVE TITTER TOTTLE WAMBLE
WANGLE WAPPER BRANDLE FRIBBLE
STAGGER TREMBLE WHITHER
TITUBATE
TOTTERING SHAKY GROGGY
CRAMBLY PALSIED RICKETY
TOTTERY TITUBANT WAMBLING
TOUCAN TOCO TUCANA ARACARI
TOUCH GET RAP TAG TIG TIP ABUT
BILL DASH FEEL HAND KISS KNEE
MEET PALP PEAL PLAY RAKE RINE
TACT TAKE GLISK GRAZE GROPE
SPICE TAINT TASTE TATTO TINGE
TRAIT TREAT AFFECT ATTAIN
CARESS FINGER GLANCE HANDLE
REGARD SCRUFF SMUTCH STRAIN
TACTUS TWITCH ATTAINT ATTINGE
CONTACT FEELING SOUPCON
TACTION FLOURISH TINCTURE
(— A KEY) STRIKE
(— BRIEFLY) GLANCE
(— CARESSINGLY) FLATTER
(— CLOSELY) IMPINGE
(— GENTLY) DAB TAT TICK BRUSH
(— LIGHTLY) GRAZE SCUFF SKIFF
(— OF BRUSH) HAND
(— OF COLOR) EYE
(— OF PAINT) GLOB
(— OF PLEASURE) GLISK
(— RIGHTLY) NICK
(DELICATE —) STROKE
(FINISHING —) HOODER COPESTONE
(SLIGHT —) SKIFF SMATCH
TOUCHDOWN ROUGE
TOUCHED FEY DOTTY
TOUCHING ABOUT LIBANT TENDER
AGAINST CONTACT TANGENT
ADJACENT POIGNANT
(— LIGHTLY) LAMBENT
TOUCHSTONE TEST TOUCH LYDITE
BASANITE STANDARD
TOUCHWOOD FUNK MONK PUNK
SPUNK PUNKWOOD
TOUCHY HUFFY MIFFY SNAKY
FEISTY KITTLE SNAKEY SNUFFY
SPUNKY TENDER TETCHY GROUCHY
NERVOUS PEEVISH TEMPERY
TICKLISH
TOUGH RUM BHOY HARD TAUT WIRY
CLUNG HARDY STIFF STOUT WITHY
KNOTTY SINEWY STARCH STRONG
HICKORY BULLYBOY LEATHERY
UNTENDER
TOUGHEN TAW ANNEAL ENDURE
HARDEN TEMPER
TOUGHENED CLUNG
TOUGHNESS TUCK FIBER FIBRE
STRENGTH TENACITY
TOUPEE RUG DOILY SCALP
POSTICHE TOPPIECE
TOUR GIRO TURN SWING TOWER

TURUS JUNKET SAFARI JOURNEY
INVASION PROGRESS TOURETTE
(— OF DUTY) HERD STATION
(CANARY —) GLUCK GLUCKE
TOURACO LORY LOURIE TURAKOO
TOURBILLON KARRUSEL
TOUR DE FORCE STUNT
TOURIST TOURER TRIPPER VISITANT
TOURMALINE SHORL SCHORL
DRAVITE ACHROITE SIBERITE
TOURNAMENT TILT JOUSTS
TOURNEY BONSPIEL CAROUSEL
TOURNEUR DEALER
TOURNEY PLAY
TOURNIQUET GARROT STANCH
TWISTER STANCHER TORCULAR
TOUSLE SOOL SOWL RUMPLE
TOOZLE
TOUSLED TOWZIE TUMBLED
UNKEMPT
TOUT SKIV BRUIT PLIER STEERER
TOW CRIB HAUL PULL HURDS STUPE
TRACK TRACT CODILLA CORDELLE
TOWAGE TRACKAGE
TOWAI BIRCH KAMAHI
TOWARD AD INTO TORT ANENT
ANENST AGAINST FORNENT
ADVERSUS GAINWARD
(— CENTER OF EARTH) DOWN
(— CENTER) CENTRAD
(— ONE SIDE) ASLANT
(— THE END) SF
(— THE HEAD) ANTERIOR
(— THE REAR) ABACK DORSAD
BACKWARD
(— THE RIGHT) DEXTRAD
(— THE SIDE) LATERAD
(— THE STERN) AFTER
TOWEL CLOUT WIPER DIAPER
LAVABO RUBBER
TOWER TOR PEEL PIKE REAR RISE
SOAR SPUR TOUR BABEL BROCH
HEAVE MINAR MOUNT PYLON SIKAR
SPIRE STUPA TEXAS ASCEND
ASPIRE BELFRY CASTLE CHULPA
DOKHMA DONJON GOPURA ROLLER
RONDEL SPRING TURRET BASTIDE
CHULLPA DERRICK GIRALDA
LANTERN MIRADOR NURAGHE
SHIKARA SIKHARA STEEPLE
TALAYOT TORREON TOURNEL
TRACKER TURRION BARBICAN
BASTILLE CLOGHEAD DOMINEER
RONDELLE SCRUBBER TOURELLE
TOWERLET
(— CONTAINING COKE) SCRUBBER
(— FOR SENTINEL) GUERITE
(— OF FORT) SPUR
(— OF MOSQUE) MINARET
(— OF SILENCE) DAKHMA
(— ON SUMMIT) PIKE
(— OVER) DROWN BESTRIDE
(ATTACHED —) DETAIL
(BELL —) CARILLON
(CONNING —) SAIL
(FRACTIONATING —) STILL
(PYRAMIDAL —) SIKAR VIMANA
SHIKARA SIKHARA
(SIGNAL —) BANTAYAN

(WIND —) BADGIR
TOWERING EMINENT SUPERNAL
AMBITIOUS
TOWERMAN LEVERMAN
TOWER MUSTARD CRUCIFER
TOWHEE JOREE CHEWINK CHEEWINK
TOWING TRACKAGE
TOWLINE CORDELLE
TOWN BY BYE HAM WON CAMP CITY
STAD WENE WICK BAYAN BOURH
BRUGH BURGH DERBY MACHI
PLACE PLECK SIEGE STAND STEAD
VILLE CIUDAD HAMMON ORANGE
PUEBLO STAPLE BASTIDE BOROUGH
CHESTER OPPIDUM QUIVIRA
TOWNLET BOOMTOWN BOURGADE
ENCEINTE HOMETOWN TOWNSHIP
(DESOLATED —) GUBAT
(FORTIFIED —) BURG BURGH
ENCEINTE
(MYTHICAL —) QUIVIRA
(SMALL —) SHTETL SHTETEL
(UNFORTIFIED —) BOURGADE
(WALLED —) CHESTER
(PL.) PARGANA
TOWN HALL HALL CABILDO
RATHAUS TOLBOOTH STADHOUSE
TOWNSHIP DEME DORP VILL BAYAN
TREEN BOROUGH
TOWNSMAN CAD CIT SNOB TOWNY
TOWNEE BURGHER CITIZEN
COCKNEY OPPIDAN
(PL.) BURGWARE
TOWROPE TOW GUNLINE TOWLINE
CORDELLE
TOXALBUMIN ROBIN PHALLIN
TOXEMIA BLACKLEG ECLAMPSIA
TOXIC VENOMOUS
TOXIN BOTULIN EXOTOXIN
TOY DIE GAY TOP COCK DOLL FOOL
MOVE PLAY BLOCK DALLY FLIRT
HAPPY KNACK LAKIN PLAID SPORT
TRICK WALLY BAUBLE DANDLE
DOODLE FADDLE FINGER FIZGIG
GEWGAW LAKING PRETTY PUPPET
RATTLE SUCKER BLOWOUT CRICKET
DREIDEL PLAYOCK TANGRAM
TRINKET TUMBLER WHIZZER
GIMCRACK KICKSHAW PINWHEEL
SQUAWKER SQUEAKER TEETOTUM
WINDMILL ZOETROPE
(— AMOROUSLY) MIRD
(— WITH) PADDLE
(FLYING —) PIGEON
TOYON TOLLON CHAMISO
TRACE RUN TUG WAD CAST ECHO
HINT LICK MARK RACK SHOW SIGN
STEP TANG TINT TROD BRING
GHOST GLEAM GLIFF GRAIN PRINT
SHADE SPOOR STAMP STEAD THEAT
TINGE TOUCH TRACK TRACT TRAIL
TRAIN TRESS DERIVE ENGRAM
HARBOR LACING RESENT SHADOW
SKETCH SMUTCH STRAIN STREAK
SWATHE COCKEYE GLIMPSE
MENTION REMNANT SOUPCON
SURMISE SYMPTOM THOUGHT
UMBRAGE VESTIGE WHISPER
DESCRIBE ENGRAMMA FOOTSTEP

SKERRICK TINCTURE WAINROPE
(— A BEE) COURSE
(— A CURVE) SWEEP
(— A DESIGN) CALK
(— MATHEMATICALLY) GENERATE
(— OF A HARE) FARE
(— ON CHART) PRICK
(— THE COURSE OF) DEDUCE
(HARNESS —) TUG THEAT TREAT
(MEMORY —) ENGRAM ENGRAMME
(SLIGHT —) GHOST STAIN SMATCH
SPARKLE
(SLIGHTEST —) SCINTIL
(PL.) FEUTE

TRACER SEEKER OUTLINER
SEARCHER

TRACERY FANWORK FROSTING
TRAILERY

TRACHEA ARTERY WINDPIPE
(— OF CRANE) TRUMP

TRACHEID HYDROID

TRACHYANDESITE ARSOITE
VULSINITE

TRACHYTE PIPERNO

TRACING BAROGRAM POLYGRAM
TRAILING

TRACK DOG PUG RAT RUT TAN WAD
WAY CLEW CLUE DRAW FARE FOIL
FOOT HUNT LANE MARK PAGE PATH
PIST RACE RACK RAIK RAIL ROAD
SHOE SLOT SPUR TROD VENT
BLOCK CHUTE DRIFT FEUTE HOUND
LODGE PISTE PLANE SLIDE SPACE
SPOOR STEAD SWATH TRACE
TRACT TRADE TRAIL TRAIN TREAD
BEARER COURSE GROOVE HARBOR
LADDER RETURN RUNWAY SIDING
SLEUTH STRAIN SWATHE CHANNEL
FOILING FOOTING PATHWAY
TANGENT TRAFFIC VESTIGE
BACKBONE FOOTSTEP GUIDEWAY
TRANSFER TRECKPOT TREKPATH
WAGONWAY
(— FOR ROPE) CHANNEL
(— GAME) DRAW
(— OF DEER) SLOT STRAIN
(— OF GAME IN GRASS) FOILING
(— OF HARE) FILE
(— OF WOUNDED BEAST) PERSUE
(— ON PRINTING PRESS) BANK
BEARER
(RAILROAD —) LEAD SPUR STUB
SIDING TANGENT APPROACH
BACKBONE
(RUNNING —) FLAT CINDERS
(SHORT BRANCH —) RETURN
(SIDE —) LIE HOLE
(SKATER'S —) FLAT
(TEMPORARY —) SHOOFLY
(WORM —) NEREITE

TRACKER PUGGI PUGGY TRAILER
TRAILMAN

TRACKLESS INVIOUS PATHLESS

TRACKMAN SPIKER

TRACT AREA BEAT DUAR FLAT ZONE
CAMPO COAST DRIVE ESSAY FIELD
GRABE HORST PATCH SWEEP
TRACK BARONY BUNDLE EXTENT
REGION ENCLAVE EURIPUS

QUARTER ROYALTY TERRAIN
TRACTUS BROCHURE CAMPAGNA
CAMPAIGN CINGULUM DISTRICT
FARMHOLD FORESTRY PAMPHLET
PROVINCE TOWNSITE TREATISE
(— KEPT IN NATURAL STATE) PARK
(— OF BARREN LAND) BARREN
DERELICT
(— OF GRASSLAND) PRAIRIE
(— OF LAND) CRU DOAB DUAB
DUAR GORE MARK BLOCK CHASE
CLAIM EJIDO FRITH GRANT LAINE
SCOPE SWELL EIGHTY ESTATE
FOREST GARDEN ISLAND POLDER
STRATH AIRPORT QUILLET RESERVE
TERRAIN BOUNDARY CLEARING
DERELICT FARMHOLD INTERVAL
SCABLAND SLASHING
(— OF MUDDY GROUND) SLOB
(— OF OPEN UPLAND) DOWN
DOWNS
(— OF UNCOVERED ICE) GLADE
(— OF WASTE LAND) HEATH
(BOGGY —) RUNN MORASS
(CLAYEY —) TAKYR
(CLEARED —) JUM JHUM JOOM
(DRY —) SEARING
(FORESTLESS —) STEPPE
(GENITAL —) BEARING
(IRREGULAR —) GORE
(OPEN —) VEGA SLASH
(SANDY —) DEN DENE
(SWAMPY —) FLOW BAYGALL
(UNOCCUPIED AND UNCULTIVATED
—) DESERT
(WATERLESS —) THIRST

TRACTABLE EASY SOFT BUXOM
TAWIE DOCILE GENTLE TOWARD
DUCTILE FLEXILE AMENABLE
FLEXIBLE GUIDABLE TOWARDLY
YIELDING

TRACTARIANISM PUSEYISM

TRACTION DRAFT DRAUGHT

TRACTOR CAT MULE DRAGON
BOBTAIL CRAWLER PEDRAIL
(TRAILER —) RIG

TRADE CHAP CHOP COUP DEAL SELL
SWAP CHEAP CRAFT GRAFT PRICE
TREAD TROKE TRUCK BAKERY
BARTER CHANGE EMPLOY HANDLE
MISTER NIFFER OCCUPY SCORCE
SCORSE BARGAIN CALLING
CHAFFER FACULTY MYSTERY
SCIENCE BUSINESS CABOTAGE
EXCHANGE

TRADEMARK CHOP MARK BRAND
COUPON

TRADER SART BANYA PLIER BALIJA
CHETTY DEALER MONGER NEPMAN
TROKER CHAPMAN MARWARI
SANGLEY TRUCKER ASTORIAN
CHANDLER KURVEYOR MERCHANT
OPERATOR
(HORSE —) JOCKEY
(INEXPERIENCED —) LAMB

TRADESMAN CIT BAKAL COOPER
EGGLER SELLER TENSOR FRUITER
GOLADAR OCCUPIER UPHOLDER

TRADESWOMAN WINSTER

TRADITION CABAL STORY SUNNA
CABALA SMRITT SUNNAH THREAP
HALACHA HALAKAH HEREDITY
HERITAGE TRANSFER
(PL.) LEGEND

TRADITIONAL CLASSIC

TRADUCE ILL SLUR ABUSE DEFAME
MALIGN VILIFY ASPERSE DETRACT

TRAFFIC COUP DEAL MANG MART
MONG BROKE TRADE BARTER
PALTER TRAVEL CHAFFER DEALING
BUSINESS CHAFFERY COMMERCE
EXCHANGE
(— IN SACRED THINGS) SIMONY
(— IN SLAVES) MAGONIZE

TRAFFICKER COUPER DEALER

TRAGEDY BUSKIN TRAGIC TROIADES

TRAGIC DIRE DREADFUL THESPIAN

TRAGICOMEDY DRAME

TRAGOPAN MONAL

TRAGUS EARLET

TRAIL PAD PUG DRAG FOIL HARL
HUNT NECK PATH PIST SLOT BLAZE
CRAWL DRAIL PISTE ROUTE SPOOR
STOCK SWEEP TRACE TRADE TRAIN
COMING DAGGLE FOLLOW RUNWAY
SHADOW SLEUTH STRAIN TAIGLE
TRAPES DRAGGLE TRAFFIC
OUTTRAIL STRIGGLE TRAILERY
(— ALONG) STREEL TRAPES
(— OF A FISH) LOOM
(— OUT) STREAM
(— THROUGH MUD) DAGGLE
(DESCENDING —) BAHADA BAJADA
(MOUNTAIN —) CLIMB
(WAGON —) RUDLOFF

TRAILBLAZER HARBINGER

TRAILER SEMI COACH BOXCAR
CARAVAN FLATBED FROGGER
GONDOLA

TRAIN SET DRAG GAIT SECT TILL
TURN ZULU BEARD BREED COACH
DRESS DRILL ENTER FOCUS LOCAL
RANGE TRACE TRACT TRADE TRAIL
TRYNE DIRECT GENTLE GROUND
INFORM MANURE NUZZLE RAPIDE
REPAIR SCHOOL SEASON STRING
SUBWAY AFFAITE BRIGADE
CARAVAN EDUCATE FREIGHT
GEARING LIMITED PEDDLER
RATTLER RETINUE SHUTTLE
VARNISH CIVILIZE DISCIPLE
ELECTRIC EQUIPAGE EXERCISE
HIGHBALL INSTRUCT MANIFEST
REHEARSE
(— AN ANIMAL) BREAK
(— FINE) GAUNT
(— FOR FIGHTING) SPAR
(— OF ANIMALS) COFFLE
(— OF ATTENDANTS) CORTEGE
(— OF COMET) TAIL
(— OF EXPLOSIVE) FUSE
(— OF MINING CARS) JAG RUN TRIP
(FUNERAL —) CONVOY
(PACK —) CONDUCTA
(RAILROAD —) DRAG HOOK LOCAL
PICKUP EXPRESS FREIGHT LIMITED
RATTLER

TRAINED GOOD MADE ADEPT BROKE BROKEN
TRAINEE BOOT CADET
TRAINER FEEDER JINETE LANISTA
TRAINING DRILL THEAT ASCESIS ASKESIS CULTURE NURTURE PAIDEIA BREEDING
(— IN HUMANITIES) CIVILITY
(— OF HORSE) DRESSAGE
(RELIGIOUS —) SADHANA
TRAIT ITEM LEAD MARK VEIN ANGLE CHARM KNACK TRACT AMENITY ELEMENT HALLMARK JAPANISM
(CULTURE —) SURVIVAL
(FOREIGN —) EXOTISM
(GOOD —) THEW
(UNDESIRABLE —) DEMON DAEMON
(WELL-DEFINED —) STREAK
(PL.) CORNERS
TRAITOR JUDAS RUSTY WARLOCK ISCARIOT PRODITOR SQUEALER TRADITOR TREACHER
TRAITOROUS FALSE FELON
TRAJECTORY SPORABOLA
TRA-LA-LA TRALIRA
TRAM TUB DRAM TRAMCAR TRAMMEL TRANVIA
(SET OF —S) JOURNEY
TRAMCAR TRAM DUMMY PICKUP
TRAMMEL TRAM HAMPER STIFLE COTTEREL
TRAMMER PUTTER
TRAMONTANE OVERBERG
TRAMP BO BUM PAD BOOM HAKE HIKE HOBO HUMP PUNK SLOG SWAG VAMP WALK YEGG BURLY CAIRD CLAMP JAVEL PIKER SHACK STIFF STRAG TRAIK TRAIL TRASH TROMP TROUT BAGMAN GAYCAT JOCKER PICARO STODGE STRAMP STROLL TINKER TRANCE TRAPES TRUANT TRUDGE DRUMMER FLOATER RUFFLER SWAGGER SWAGMAN TRAIPSE TRAMPLE TROUNCE TROWANE YEGGMAN FOOTSLOG GANGEREL STROLLER TRAVELER VAGABOND SUNDOWNER
(— ABOUT) WAG
(LONG —) HUMP
(PL.) MONKERY
TRAMPING MONKERY
TRAMPLE HOX JAM PUG FARE FOIL FULL HOOF CHAMP SCAUT SPURN TRAMP TRASH TREAD DEFOIL DEFOUL PADDLE SAVAGE STOACH STRAMP WADDLE OPPRESS OVERRUN SCAMBLE FORTREAD OVERRIDE
TRANCE RAPTUS AMENTIA ECSTASY SAMADHI
TRANQUIL CALM COOL EASY LOWN MILD SOFT EQUAL QUIET STILL GENTLE PACATE PIPING SERENE CALMATO EQUABLE PACIFIC RESTFUL PEACEFUL
TRANQUILIZE CALM LULL QUIET STILL BECALM PACIFY SERENE SETTLE SOFTEN SOOTHE APPEASE COMPOSE

TRANQUILIZING SOOTHING
TRANQUILLITY KEF LEE EASE REST PEACE SATTVA SERENE HARMONY QUIETAGE QUIETUDE SERENITY
TRANS ANTI
TRANSACT DO PASS AGITATE CONDUCT PERFORM
TRANSACTION DEAL GAGE GAGER ACTION AFFAIR MARGIN SPREAD BARGAIN MOHABAT PASSAGE CONTRACT KNOCKOUT
(PL.) ACTA BUSINESS
TRANSCEND PASS SOAR EXCEED OVERTOP SURPASS
TRANSCENDENTAL ACOSMIC
TRANSCENDING EXQUISITE
TRANSCRIBE COPY BRAILLE DESCRIBE EXSCRIBE
TRANSCRIBED CANNED
TRANSCRIBER COPIER COPYIST
TRANSCRIPT COPY SCORE TENOR DOUBLE APOGRAPH EXSCRIPT
TRANSCRIPTION(PL.) PAZAND PAZEND
TRANSEPT PLAGE PORCH
TRANSFER CEDE DEED FLIT GIVE SALE SELL TURN CABLE CARRY CROSS DROGH REFER REMIT SHIFT ASSIGN ATTORN CHANGE DECANT DELATE DONATE REMOVE SWITCH CESSION CONNECT CONSIGN DELIVER DEVOLVE DISPONE MIGRATE TRADUCE ALIENATE ANTEDATE CROCKING DELEGATE DELIVERY DONATION EXCHANGE TRANSACT TRANSUME VIREMENT
(— DYE) EXHAUST
(— HEAT) CONVECT
(— HOMAGE) ATTORN
(— MOLTEN GLASS) LADE
(— OF ENERGY) FLOW
(— OF PROPERTY) DEED GIFT GRANT DISPOSAL
(— PIGMENT) FLUSH
TRANSFERENCE DEMISE EMOTION REMOVAL DELATION DISPOSAL TRANSFER
TRANSFIGURE DEIFY CLARIFY
TRANSFIX FIX DART PITCH STAKE STICK SKEWER THRILL
TRANSFORM TURN SHIFT TOUCH CHANGE STRIKE CONVERT FASHION PERMUTE CATALYZE DISGUISE HETERIZE
(— ENERGY) ABSORB
TRANSFORMATION CHANGE HAIRWORK
TRANSFORMER SET DIMMER JIGGER TEASER VARIAC BALANCE BOOSTER HEDGEHOG
TRANSFUSE ENDUE INDUE
TRANSGRESS ERR SIN BREAK OFFEND OVERGO DIGRESS DISOBEY VIOLATE INFRINGE OVERPASS OVERSLIP OVERSTEP
TRANSGRESSION SIN SLIP CRIME FAULT SCAPE BREACH DELICT ESCAPE MISDEED OFFENSE DELICTUM OVERLOUP TRESPASS

TRANSGRESSOR SINNER OFFENDER
TRANSIENCE FUGACITY
TRANSIENT FLIGHTY PASSING FLEETING FUGITIVE
TRANSIENTLY HOVERLY
TRANSIT BINOCLE PASSAGE TRANSEPT
TRANSITION CUT JUMP LEAP SEGUE SHIFT FERMENT PASSAGE
TRANSITORINESS CADUCITY
TRANSITORY FLEET CADUCE FLYING BRITTLE PASSANT PASSING SLIDING VOLATIC WHILEND CADUCOUS FLEETING FLITTING TEMPORAL VOLATILE
TRANSLATE DRAW MAKE TURN WEND RENDER CONVERT ENGLISH EXPOUND TRADUCE CONSTRUE INTERPRET
TRANSLATION CAB KEY CRIB PONY STEP TROT GLOSS HORSE TARGUM UNSEEN BICYCLE CABBAGE ENGLISH THARGUM TRADUCT VERSION SUBTITLE VERBATIM
(— OF THE CLASSICS) JACK
(LOAN —) CALQUE
TRANSLATOR TURNER
TRANSLUCENT CLEAR LUCID LIMPID LUCENT HYALINE
TRANSMIGRATION SAMARA SAMSARA SANSARA
TRANSMISSION ENTAIL DESCENT GEARBOX SENDING TRANSFER
(— OF SOUND) AUDIO
(— TO OFFSPRING) HEREDITY
TRANSMIT AIR EMIT SEND CARRY CONVEY DEMISE DERIVE ENTAIL EXPORT IMPACT IMPART RENDER CONDUCT FORWARD TRADUCE TRADUCT TRAJECT BEQUEATH DESCRIBE
TRANSMITTER TUBA SLAVE SPARK BEACON JAMMER SENDER VEHICLE RADIATOR
TRANSMITTING ALIVE
TRANSMUTE CHEMIC CHEMICK ENNOBLE PERMUTE EXCHANGE TRANSMUE TRANSUME
TRANSOM PATIBLE TRAVERSE
TRANSPARENCY SLIDE
TRANSPARENT THIN CLEAR FILMY LUCID BRIGHT LIMPID LUCENT CRYSTAL FRAGILE HYALINE HYALOID DIOPTRIC LUCULENT LUMINOUS LUSTROUS PELLUCID
TRANSPIRE HAPPEN
TRANSPLANT SPOT SHIFT DEPLANT
TRANSPORT DAK JOY ROB BEAR BOAT BUSS DAWK DRAY HAUL PORT RAPE RAPT RIDE SHIP CANOE CARRY DROGH FERRY FLUTE GILLY BANISH BARREL CONVEY DEPORT GALLOP WAFTER ECSTASY EXPRESS FRAUGHT ONERARY RAPTURE TRADUCE TROOPER CABOTAGE CARRIAGE DAYDREAM ENRAVISH PALANDER
(— FOR CRIME) LAG
(— LOGS) BOB

(— ORE) SLUSH

TRANSPORTATION AIR DAK FARE
AIRLIFT BOATAGE FREIGHT TRAJECT
TRANSPORT

TRANSPORTED RAPT

(— BY GLACIER) ERRATIC

TRANSPOSE CONVERT REVERSE

TRANSPOSITION SHIFT ANSWER
ANAGRAM

TRANSUBSTANTIATION METUSIA

TRANSVAAL DAISY GERBERA

TRANSVAALER TAKHAAR

TRANSVERSE CROSS FACING
THWART OBLIQUE

TRANSVERSELY ATHWART

TRANSVESTISM EONISM

TRANSVESTITE BERDACHE

TRAP COY GET GIN PIT SET FALL
GIRN GRIN HOOK LACE LIME NAIL
PUTT TIPE TOIL WAIT WEEL BRAKE
BRIKE CATCH LEASH PLANT POUND
SNARE SPELL STALE SWICK SWIKE
TRAIN CRUIVE EELPOT ENGINE
KEDDAH POCKET QUILEZ SNATCH
STAYER WILLOW FLYTRAP PITFALL
PITFOLD PUTCHEN PUTCHER
RATTRAP SETTING SPRINGE
TRAMMEL BIRDLIME COALHOLE
DEADFALL DOWNFALL TRAPROCK

(— FOR BIRDS) SCRAPE

(— FOR LARGE GAME) HOPO

(— FOR RABBITS, MICE, ETC) TIPE
TYPE

(— FOR RATS) CLAM

(— FOR SALMON) PUTT

(— FOR SMALL ANIMALS) HATCH

(— FOR THE FEET) CALTROPS

(— IN POKER) SANDBAG

(— INTO SERVICE) CRIMP

(FISH —) FYKE KILL LEAP WEEL
WEIR CREEL WILLY CORRAL
WILLOW

(SAND —) BUNKER

TRAPDOOR DROP SLOT TRAP
SCRUTO VAMPIRE TRAPFALL

TRAPPED CORNERED

TRAPPER WIRER VOYAGEUR

TRAPPINGS GEAR JHOOL ARMORY
TOGGERY BARDINGS EQUIPAGE
HOUSINGS

TRAPSHOOTING SKEET

TRASH ROT BOSH GEAR GOOK JUNK
PELF RAFF TOSH TRAG CLART
DRECK DRUSH STUFF SWASH
THROW TRADE TROKE WASTE
WRACK BUSHWA CULTCH KELTER
PALTRY RAMMEL REFUSE RUBBLE
SCULCH TROUSE BAGGAGE
BEGGARY FULLAGE GARBAGE
PEDLARY RUBBISH TOSHERY
TRAFFIC BLATHERY CLAPTRAP
FLUMMERY MUCKMENT PEDDLERY
SKITTLES SMACHRIE TRASHERY
TRUMPERY

TRASHY CHEAP FLASH TOSHY TRIPY
PALTRY SLUSHY BAGGAGE RUBBISH
RIFFRAFF RUBBISHY SIXPENNY
TRUMPERY

TRAVAIL PAIN TASK TOIL AGONY

LABOR TORMENT

TRAVEL GO BAT BUS FLY GIG WAG
FARE GANG HIKE PASS PATH RIVE
TOTE TRIP VAMP WEND COVER
KNOCK SLOPE THROW TRACK
CRUISE TRANCE VOYAGE EXPRESS
JOURNEY TRAVAIL TRUNDLE
WAYFARE PROGRESS TRAVERSE

(— ACROSS SNOW) MUSH

(— AIMLESSLY) SAUNTER

(— ALONG GROUND) TAXI

(— AROUND) TURN COAST CIRCLE
GIRDLE COMPASS

(— AT GOOD SPEED) CRACK

(— AT HIGH SPEED) HELL BARREL
SCORCH

(— AT RANDOM) DRIFT

(— AT SPEED OF) DO

(— BACK AND FORTH) SHUNT
COMMUTE

(— BY AIRCRAFT) AIR FLY AIRPLANE

(— BY OX WAGON) TREK

(— FAST) STREAK

(— IN A VEHICLE) TOOL

(— ON FOOT) HIKE SHANK
KNAPSACK

(— ON WATER) SAIL

(— OVER) TRANCE TRAVERSE

(— THROUGH WOODS) BUSHWACK

(— THROUGH) GO

(— WITHOUT EQUIPMENT) SIWASH

(DAY'S —) JORNADA JOURNAL
JOURNEY

TRAVELER GOER CRAWL FARER
GUEST HORSE BAGMAN GANGER
KILROY POSTER SAILOR VIATOR
CRUISER DRUMMER FOOTMAN
HOWADJI LEEFANG PILGRIM
SWAGGIE TRAILER TREKKER
WAYGOER ARGONAUT EXPLORER
MAGELLAN OUTRIDER VOYAGEUR
WAYFARER

(COMPANY OF —S) CARAVAN

TRAVELER'S JOY HAGROPE
BINDWITH

TRAVELING ERRANT

TRAVELING SALESMAN RIDER
DRUMMER

TRAVERSE DO GO SEE BURN DENY
KNEE LIFT MAKE PASS SPAN WALK
COAST COVER CROSS SHEAR
SWEEP THIRL TRACE TRACK CIRCLE
COURSE DENIAL OVERGO PERCUR
TRAVEL WANDER CHANNEL
JOURNEY MEASURE OVERRUN
PARADOS PERVADE DESCRIBE
OVERPASS OVERWEND SCRAMBLE
UNTHREAD

TRAVERTINE TOPHUS

TRAVESTY EXODE PARODY SATIRE
EXODIUM TRAVEST

TRAVOIS DRAY TRAVOY ALLIGATOR

TRAWL SEINE BOULTER DRAGNET
STOWNET TRAWLNET

TRAWLER PAREJA BRAGOZZO

TRAY HOD CASE TILL TRUG BATEA
BOARD FLOAT SCALE SLICE SUSAN
GALLEY MONKEY SALVER SERVER
SERVET VOIDER WAITER BALANCE

CABARET COASTER CONSOLE
SHALLOW DEJEUNER

(— FOR CRUMBS) VOIDER

(— FOR DRYING FISH) FLAKE

(— FOR MATCH SPLINTS) CAUL
MONKEY

(— FOR SHELLFISH) FLOAT

(— FOR TYPE) GALLEY

(— TO CATCH OVERFLOW) SAFE

(CIRCULAR —) ROUNDEL

TREACHEROUS FOUL CATTY FALSE
PUNIC SNAKY SWACK FELINE
FICKLE HOLLOW YELLOW SNAKISH
FRAUDFUL IMPOSING PLOTTING
SLIDDERY

TREACHERY GUILE SWICK TRAIN
DECEIT FELONY PERFIDY TREASON
UNTRUTH DASTARDY DISTRUST
TRAHISON TRAITORY

TREACLE DIBS CLAGGUM THERIAC

TREAD FIT PAD BEAT FOOT PATH
POST RUNG STEP VOLT CLAMP
TRACK TRADE DEFOIL DEFOUL
PADDLE CRAWLER FEATHER
FOOTING RETREAD TREADER
FOOTSTEP

(— CLUMSILY) CLUMP BALTER

(— DOWN SHOE HEEL) CAM

(— HEAVILY) SPURN TRAMPLE

(— OF FOWL'S EGG) GRANDO

(— ON) FOIL

(— TO MUSIC) FOOT

(TIRE —) COVER

TREADLE PEDAL CHALAZA

TREASON SEDITION

TREASURE POSE ROON HOARD
PRIZE STORE TROVE VALUE
BURSAR COFFER FINDAL GERSUM
WEALTH ASTHORE FINANCE
THESAUR WARISON GARRISON
TREASURY

(— STATE) MONTANA

(LITTLE —) STOREEN

(PL.) CIMELIA

TREASURE BOX HANAPER

TREASURED DEAR CHARY
PRECIOUS

TREASURER BOWSER BURSAR
FISCAL GABBAI BOUCHER HOARDER
SPENDER BHANDARI COFFERER
HAZNADAR PROVISOR RECEIVER

TREASURY FISC FISK KIST CHEST
HOARD PURSE COFFER CORBAN
FISCAL FISCUS BOWSERY BURSARY
CHAMBER CHECKER CHEQUER
HORDARY AERARIUM THESAURY
TREASURE

TREAT RUN USE DEAL DOSE HOCK
LEAD PLAY BEANO BESEE COVER
DIGHT GUIDE LEECH SERVE SETUP
SHOUT TRACT TRAIT WRITE
DEMEAN DOCTOR GOVERN HANDLE
LIQUOR PADDLE REGALO CONDUCT
ENTREAT GARNISH ACTIVATE
AIRBRUSH

(— A HIDE) DRUM

(— AS EQUAL) EVEN

(— BADLY) ILLGUIDE

(— CARELESSLY) BANG BANDY

(— **CLOUDS**) SEED
(— **CONFIDENTIALLY**) HUSH
(— **CRUELLY**) CRUCIFY
(— **DAINTILY**) PAMPER
(— **DIABOLICALLY**) BEDEVIL
(— **DISCOURTEOUSLY**) DISGRACE
(— **FIBERS**) GILL
(— **FLOUR**) AGENIZE
(— **FONDLY**) DANDLE
(— **FUR**) CARROT
(— **GENTLY**) FAVOR
(— **ILLNESS**) POMSTER
(— **IMPROPERLY**) MISUSE
(— **IMPUDENTLY**) NOSE
(— **LIGHTLY**) SCRUFF
(— **LOVINGLY**) COAX
(— **MALICIOUSLY**) SPITE
(— **MASH**) LAUTER
(— **OF DRINKS**) SETUP
(— **OF**) DISCOURSE
(— **ROUGHLY**) BANG MUMBLE
GRABBLE MALTREAT
(— **SILK TO RUSTLE**) SCROOP
(— **SLIGHTINGLY**) LIGHTLY
(— **STEEL**) HARVEY
(— **UNFAIRLY**) DO
(— **UNSKILLFULLY**) FOOZLE
(— **WITH ACID**) SOUR
(— **WITH CARE**) CODDLE
(— **WITH CONTEMPT**) HUFF SNUB
BLURT FLIRT FLOCK FLOUT FLAUNT
BAUCHLE
(— **WITH HEAT**) FOMENT
(— **WITH HONOR**) RESPECT
(— **WITH INATTENTION**) FORGET
(— **WITH INDULGENCE**) FONDLE
(— **WITH PARTIALITY**) ACCEPT
(— **WITH RESPECT**) HONOR
(— **WITH RIDICULE**) SCOUT
(— **WITH RUDENESS**) FRUMP
(— **WITH TAR**) BLACK
(— **WITH TENDERNESS**) CODDLE
(**NEW YEAR'S EVE** —) HAGMENA
HOGMANAY
TREATISE AGAMA DONET FAUNA
FLORA LIBEL SILVA SUMMA SYLVA
TRACT TREAT BOTANY POETRY
POMONA SERTUM SYSTEM ALGEBRA
ANATOMY BIOLOGY COMMENT
DIETARY GEOLOGY GRAMMAR
HISTORY PANDECT PHYSICS
PINETUM POETICS ZOOLOGY
ALMAGEST BROCHURE CALCULUS
DIDACTIC ECTHESIS EXERCISE
GENETICS GEOMANCY GEOMETRY
GERMANIA HORNBOOK LAPIDARY
MONUMENT PANTHEON PASTORAL
PRACTICE SITOLOGY SPECULUM
TRACTATE
TREATMENT CURE WORK TREAT
USAGE ANIMUS DETAIL FACIAL
QUARTER BEHAVIOR DEMEANOR
ENTREATY
(— **BY MASSAGE**) SEANCE
(— **FOR WOOLLENS**) SPONGING
(**BAD** —) MISUSAGE
(**COLD** —) FREEZE
(**COMPASSIONATE** —) MERCY
(**CONTEMPTUOUS** —) SPURN

(**CRUEL** —) SEVERITY
(**DIRE** —) DOLE
(**HARMFUL** —) ABUSE
(**INHUMAN** —) CRUELTY
(**LUXURIOUS** —) DELICACY
(**SEVERE** —) ROUGH
TREATY MISE ACCORD CARTEL
CONCORD ENTENTE LOCARNO
ALLIANCE TREATISE
TREBLE TRIPLE DESCANT MINIKIN
SOPRANO TRIPLUM
TREBUCHET DONDINE DONDAINE
TREE TI ACH AMA ARN ASH BAY BEL
BEN BUR DAK DAR EBO ELM FIG FIR
GUM HAW KOA KOU LIN OAK SAJ
SAL TAL TUI ULE YEW ACLE AGBA
AKEE ANAM ANAN ANDA ARAR
ASAK ASOK ATIS ATLE AULU AUSU
BAKU BITO BOGO BREA BURI BURR
CADE COLA CRAB DATE DHAK DILO
DITA DOON EBOE IPIL JACK KINO
KOKO LIME MABI MORA OHIA PALA
PINE POLE POON SADR SORB SUPA
TALA TAWA TCHE TEAK TEIL TITI
TOON TREW TUNG TUNO UPAS
VERA WOOD YATE YAYA AALII
ABETO ABURA ACANA ACAPU
ACOMA AFARA AGATI AGOHO AKEKI
ALAMO ALANI ALDER ALGUM ALISO
ALMON ALMUG AMAGA AMAPA
AMBAK ANABO ANJAN APPLE
ARACA ARBOR ARECA ARJAN
ARJUN ARTAR ASOKA ASPEN ATLEE
BABUL BALAO BALSA BALTA BANAK
BEECH BEHEN BETIS BIRCH BONGO
BOREE BOSSE BUMBO CACAO
CARAP CAROB CEBIL CEDAR CEIBO
DADAP DHAVA DHAYA DILLY DURIO
ELDER GABUN GAIAC GENIP GINEP
GINKO HAZEL ICICA IXORA JAMBO
JIQUE JIQUI KAPOR KAPUR KEENA
KOKAN KOKIO KONGU KUSAM
LANSA LARCH LARIX LEHUA LEMON
LICCA LIMBA LINDE LINER LINGO
MAHOE MAHUA MAMIE MAPLE
NARRA NIEPA NURSE OADAL OSAGE
OSIER PACAY PAPAW PECAN PIPER
RAULI ROBLE ROHAN ROWAN SALAI
SAMAN SASSY SCRAG SIMAL SIRIS
SISSU STICK SUMAC TABOG TARFA
TENIO TERAP TIKUR TIMBO TINGI
TOONA TUART ULMUS UMIRI URUCA
URUCU UVITO WAHOO YACAL
YACCA YULAN ZAMAN AHKROT
AKEAKE ALAGAO ALERGE ALERSE
ALFAJE ALMOND ALUPAG AMAMAU
AMBASH AMUGIS AMUYON ANAGAP
ANAGUA ANAQUA ANGICO ANILAO
ARALIA ARANGA ARBUTE AUSUBO
AZALEA BABOEN BACURY BAHERA
BAKULA BALSAM BANABA BANAGO
BANANA BANCAL BANIAN BANYAN
BARBAS BATAAN BIRIBA BOMBAX
BONDUC BONETE BOTONG BRAUNA
BUCARE BUSTIC CALABA CAMARA
CANELA CANELO CAPUMO CARAPA
CASSIA CATIVO CAUCHO CEDRON
CHALTA CHERRY CHICHA CHINAR
CHOGAK CITRON COBOLA COCUYO

CUMBER DATURA DHAMAN DHAURA
DHAURI DRIMYS DURIAN ELCAJA
EMBLIC EMBUIA FEIJOA FILLER
FUSTIC GABOON GINGKO GUAIAC
GURJAN GURJUN IDESIA IDIGBO
ILIAHI ILLIPE ILLUPI JAGUEY JUJUBE
KAMALA KEMPAS KINDAL KITTUL
LANSAT LANSEH LAUREL LIGNUM
LINDEN LITCHI LOCUST LONGAN
MAFURA MALLET MAYTEN MEDLAR
MILKER ORANGE PANAMA PAWPAW
PIQUIA POPLAR RAMBEH ROHUNA
RUNNEL SABICU SABINO SANDAN
SANTOL SAPELE SAPOTA SAPOTE
SATINE SAWYER SERAYA SINTOC
SISSOO SOUARI STYRAX SUMACH
SUNDRI TALUTO TARATA TEETEE
TIKOOR TIMBER TINGUY TOATOA
TOTARA TUPELO URUCUM URUSHI
UVALHA WABAYO WAHAHE WALNUT
WAMARA WAMPEE WANDOO
WATTLE YACHAN YAGHAN YAMBAN
YOHIME ZAMANG ACHIOTE ACHUETE
AILANTO AKEPIRO AMBATCH
AMBOINA AMUGUIS AMUYONG
ANABONG ANNATTO ANONANG
APITONG APRICOT ARARIBA
ARAROBA ARBORET ARBUTUS
AROEIRA ASSAGAI AVOCADO
AVODIRE BANILAD BANKSIA
BECUIBA BENZOIN BILLIAN BOLLING
BUBINGA BUCKEYE BUISSON
CADAMBA CAJAPUT CANELLA
CARAIPE CASTANA CATALPA
CAUTIVO CERILLO CHAMPAC
CHECHEM CHECKER CHENGAL
COCULLO CONIFER COUMARU
CURUPAY CYPRESS DEADMAN
DESCENT DETERMA DHAMNOO
EPACRID FRUITER GONDANG
GRIBBLE GUMIHAN HICKORY
HOLLONG HOPBUSH HORMIGO
KAMASSI KAMBALA KICKXIA
KITTOOL KOKOONA KOOMBAR
KUMQUAT LOGWOOD MADRONA
MANJACK MARGOSA PARAIBA
PEREIRA PIMENTO PULASAN
PYRAMID RATWOOD REDWOOD
SERINGA SERVICE SHITTAH SPINDLE
STOPPER SUNDARI SURETTE
TANGELO TANGHIN TARAIRI
TARATAH TARWOOD TINDALO
TREELET TWISTER URUNDAY
VETERAN WALAHEE WALLABA
WEENONG WONGSHY WONGSKY
YAMANAI YOHIMBI ACEITUNA
ALGAROBA ALLSPICE ALMACIGA
ALMANDER ALMENDRO ALOEWOOD
AMARILLO ARAGUANE ARBOLOCO
ARBUSCLE AVELLANO BAKUPARI
BASSWOOD BAYBERRY BELLWOOD
BINDOREE BITANHOL BLACKBOX
BOARWOOD BORRACHA BREADNUT
CABREUVA CAMELLIA CAMUNING
CARAGANA CARAUNDA CHAMPACA
CHESTNUT CHINCONA CHINOTTO
COPALCHE CRABWOOD CUCUMBOL
DEADFALL DOMINANT DOTTEREL
DOVEWOOD DRACAENA DRUMWOOD

ETABALLI FIREFALL FORESTER
GAMDEBOO GEELHOUT GENISARO
GUACACOA GUAYROTO HALAPEPE
HARDTACK HARDWOOD HOLDOVER
HORNBEAM HOROPITO IRONWOOD
ISHPINGO ITCHWOOD JELOTONG
JELUTONG KAJUGARU KINGWOOD
KNOBWOOD LACEBARK LEADWOOD
LORDWOOD MAHOGANY MANDARIN
MILKWOOD MOKIHANA OLEASTER
ONEBERRY PEDIGREE PINKWOOD
RAMBUTAN RASAMALA SANDARAC
SANDWOOD SAPUCAIA SASSWOOD
SEBESTEN SHAGBARK SHAVINGS
SILKWOOD SLOGWOOD SOAPBARK
STANDARD SUCUPIRA SWEETSOP
SYCAMORE TAMARACK TAMARIND
TANEKAHA TREELING TURMERIC
ZAPATERO
(— CUT BACK) DOTARD POLLARD
(— FURNISHING SUPPORT TO VINE)
HUSBAND
(— IN STREAM) SAWYER
(— LEFT IN CUTTING) HOLDOVER
(— ON WALL) RIDER
(— OVER 2 FT. DIAMETER) VETERAN
(— SYMBOLIZING UNIVERSE)
YGDRASIL
(— WITH BRANCHES TRIMMED) LOP
LOPSTICK
(—S IN FOREST) STAND
(AROMATIC —) CLUSIA LABIATE
(AUSTRALIAN —) ASH GUM TOON
BELAH BELAR BOREE BUNDY BUNYA
GIDIA HAZEL KARRI NONDA PENDA
SALLY WILGA BAOBAB DRIMYS
GIDGEE GIMLET GYMPIE KOWHAI
MARARA PEROBA SALLEE
DOGWOOD GEEBUNG BEEFWOOD
CARABEEN COOLABAH FLINDOSA
GRAVILEA IRONBARK LACEBARK
QUANDONG ROSEBUSH SANDSTAY
SOAPWOOD TILESEED
(BIG —) SEQUOIA
(CEYLON —) HORA
(CITRUS —) SHADDOCK
(CLOTHES —) COSTUMER
(CLUMP OF —S) TOLL TUMP STELL
(CUBAN —) JIQUE JIQUI GUACACOA
(CURSED —) WARYTREE
(DEAD —) RUNT SNAG RAMPIKE
(DEAD —S) DRIKI
(DECAYED —) DOTTEREL
(DWARF —) SCRUB ARBUSCLE
(EVERGREEN —) FIR YEW PINE SUGI
TAWA ABIES ATHEL CAROB CEDAR
CLOVE HOLLY LARCH LEMON OLIVE
THUJA BALSAM BIBIRU COIGUE
COIHUE KANAGI KAPUKA LOQUAT
ORANGE SPRUCE ARDISIA BEBEERU
BILIMBI CONIFER HEMLOCK JUNIPER
MADRONA EUCALYPT EUONYMUS
(FAMILY —) STEMMA DESCENT
PEDIGREE
(GENEALOGICAL —) ARBOR JESSE
(GROWTH OF —S) SYLVAGE
(GUM —) KARI KINO BABUL BALTA
BUMBO ICICA KARRI KIKAR GIMLET
MALLET STORAX TEWART WANDOO

GOMMIER COOLIBAH
(HAWAIIAN —) KOA LEHUA ILIAHI
(INFERNAL —) ZAQQUM
(JAPANESE —) KAYA KIAKI KEYAKI
KADSURA KATSURA
(MANDARIN —) SATSUMA
(MEXICAN —) ULE AMAPA DRAGO
EBANO SERON CAPULI CATENA
CHILTE CAPULIN COPALCHE
(MYTHICAL —) TUBA
(NEW ZEALAND —) AKE KARO KAWA
MIRO PUKA RATA RIMU TAWA TORU
WHAU HINAU KAORI KAURI MAIRE
MANGI MAPAU MATAI TOWAI
AKEAKE KAMAHI KANUKA KAPUKA
KARAKA KARAMU KAWAKA KONINI
MANUKA PURIRI TARATA TITOKI
TOATOA TOTARA WAHAHE AKEPIRO
MANGERO PUKATEA TARAIRI
TARWOOD KAWAKAWA KOHEKOHE
MAKOMAKO
(ORNAMENTAL —) LABURNUM
(PHILIPPINES —) DAO IBA TUA TUI
BOGO DITA IFIL IPIL AGOHO AGOJO
ALMON AMAGA ANABO BAYOG
BAYOK BETIS DANLI GUIJO LAUAN
LIGAS TABOG YACAL ALAGAO
ALUPAG AMUYON ANAGAP ANUBIN
ARANGA BANUYO BATAAN BATETE
BATINO BOTONG DUNGON KATMON
LANETE MABOLO MARANG MOLAVE
SAGING TALUTO AMUGUIS
AMUYONG ANABONG ANOBING
ANONANG APITONG BINUKAU
CAMAGON DANGLIN MANCONO
MAYAPIS TINDALO ALMACIGA
BITANHOL KALIPAYA KALUMPIT
LUMBAYAO MACAASIM MALAPAHO
TANGUILE
(POISONOUS —) GUAO UPAS LIGAS
TANGHIN TANQUEN
(POLYNESIAN —) MACUDA
(SHADE —) ELM DILLY GUAMA
HEVEA CATALPA HALESIA INKWOOD
JOEWOOD SYCAMORE
(SHOWY —) ASAK ASOK ASOKA
(SMALL —) AKE BOX TCHE ALDER
CUMAY DWARF NENAS NGAIO
SERON AKEAKE BLOLLY CHANAR
JOJOBA KOWHAI ARBORET
INKWOOD JOEWOOD KADAMBA
STADDLE TREELET EMAJAGUA
HARDTACK HUISACHE OLEASTER
SNOWBALL SOURWOOD TREELING
(SPINY —) LIME AROMA AROMO
HONEY BOOGUM BUCARE BUMELIA
CATECHU COLORIN LAVANGA
COCKSPUR
(STANDING —) FILLER
(STUNTED —) SCRAB SCRUB
SCRUNT
(THORNY —) BEL BAEL BREA
LEMON AMBACH SAMOHU AMBATCH
(TIMBER —) ASH DAR ENG FIR SAL
ACLE ANDA BAKU COCO CUYA EKKI
IPIL PELU PINE TALA TEAK ACAPU
ALMON AMAPA AMATE AMBAY
ANJAN ARACA BANAK BIRCH CAROB
CEDAR COCOA CULLA EBONY ERIZO

FOTUI HALDU ICICA IROKO KAURI
KHAYA KIAKI KOKAN MANIU MAPLE
NARRA ROBLE TIMBO ALERCE
ALUPAG BABOEN BACURY BANABA
BANCAL CARBON CHUPON CORTEZ
DAGAME DEGAME DUKUMA ESPAVE
FREIJO GAMARI GUMHAR IMBUIA
JACANA LEBBEK MUERMO SANDAN
SATINE AMUGUIS AROEIRA BECUIBA
BILLIAN CARAIPI CYPRESS ESPAVEL
GATEADO GOMAVEL GUARABU
GUAYABI HARPULA HOLLONG
KOOMBAR LAPACHO REDWOOD
AMARILLO BOARWOOD CABREUVA
CARACOLI COCOBOLO CRABWOOD
DONCELLA GUATAMBU GUAYACAN
MAHOGANY SLOGWOOD SUCUPIRA
(TRAINED —) ESPALIER
(TROPICAL —) AKEE AULU DALI
EBOE EKKI GUAO INGA MABA MAHO
MAJO PALM SHEA ACKEE BALSA
BONGO COUMA DALLI FOTUI GUAMA
GUARA ICICA ILAMA JIGUA MARIA
NEPAL NJAVE POOLI TARFA ANUBIN
BAKULA BALATA BANANA CASHEW
CEDRON CHUPON GENIPA HACKIA
ITAUBA LEBBEK LECYTH MAMMEE
PERSEA ANGELIN ANNATTO
CAULOTE COPAIBA DATTOCK
EHRETIA EUGENIA GATEADO
GUACIMO LAPACHO MAJAGUA
MOMBINI SANDBOX SOURSOP
SURETTE BEEFWOOD CALABASA
CAMUNING CORKWOOD FUNTUMIA
MUSKWOOD PATASHTE SWEETSOP
TAMARIND
(UNARMED —) ALBIZZIA
(VARNISH —) DOON THEETSEE
(XEROPHYTIC —) SAXAUL
(YOUNG —) RUNNEL SPRING TILLER
SAPLING SEEDLING SPRINGER
(PL.) BLUFF RINDS SILVA
TREE CREEPER TOMTIT
TREE CYPRESS GILIA
TREE DUCK FIDDLER YAGUAZI
TREE FROG FERREIRO
TREE MOSS USNEA
TREENAIL NOG GUTTA MOOTER
TRUNNEL
TREE PEONY MOUTAN
TREE TOAD HYLA HYLID ANURAN
TREETOP LAP LOP
TREFOIL CANCH LOTUS CLAVER
CROWTOE BEDSTRAW SAINFOIN
TICKSEED
TREHALOSE MYCOSE
TRELLIS TRAIL PERGOLA TARLIES
ESPALIER
TREMATODE FLUKE MARITA
STRIGEID
TREMBLE DARE DIRL RESE BEVER
QUAKE SHAKE SLOWS WIVER
AGRISE DIDDER DINGLE DITHER
DODDER FALTER HOTTLE NITHER
QUAVER QUIVER SHIMMY THRILL
TITTER TOTTER TREMOR TRYMIE
WABBLE WOBBLE FLICKER
SHUDDER STAGGER TWIDDLE
WHITHER THRIMBLE

(PL.) TIRE TIRES

TREMBLER BUZZER HAMMER
VIBRATOR

TREMBLING BEVER SHAKY DITHER
TREMOR TREPID AQUIVER DODDERY
QUAKING QUAVERY QUIVERY
TREMBLY TWITTER

TREMBLY WOOZY

TREMENDOUS BIG AWFUL GIANT
GREAT LARGE TEARING ENORMOUS
HORRIBLE TERRIBLE TERRIFIC
MONSTROUS

TREMOLO HURRY TRILLO

TREMOR RIGOR SHAKE DINDLE
QUIVER THRILL SHUDDER TREMBLE

TREMULOUS ASPEN QUAKY SHAKY
PALSIED SHIVERY TREMBLY
SKIMMERY TINGLING

TRENCH GAW SAP FOSS GRIP GURT
LINE MOAT SICK SIKE TAJO TRIG
BOYAU CHASE DITCH DRAIN DRILL
FLOAT FOSSE GRAFF GRAFT GRAVE
GROOP SEUCH TRINK COFFER
FURROW GUTTER SHEUGH ACEQUIA
CUNETTE OPENCUT SLIDDER
ENCROACH LOCKSPIT SPREADER
THOROUGH TRESPASS
(— BELOW FOREST FIRE) GUTTER
(— FOR BURYING POTATOES) CAMP
(— FOR DRAIN TILES) CHASE
(— FORMED BY BANKING
VEGETABLES) GRAVE
(ARTIFICIAL —) LEAT
(IRRIGATION —) FLOAT SUGSLOOT

TRENCHANT ACID EDGED SHARP
TUANT INCISIVE

TRENCHER PLATTER ROUNDEL

TREND BEND BIAS HAND TONE TURN
BULGE CURVE DRIFT SENSE SLANT
SWING TENOR SQUINT STRIKE
CURRENT DOWNSIDE MOVEMENT
TENDENCY
(LOWERING PRICE —) EASE

TREPANG BALATE SWALLO
SWALLOW TITFISH TEATFISH

TREPIDATION FEAR DISMAY

TRESPASS DEBT GILUT POACH
BREACH FURTUM INVADE INTRUDE
OFFENSE ENCROACH ENTRENCH
INFRINGE INTRENCH OVERLOUP

TRESS CURL LOCK TAIL BRAID
SWITCH RINGLET WIMPLER

TRES-TINE TRAY ROYAL

TRESTLE MARE HORSE INRUN
CHEVALET SAWHORSE

TREVALLY TURRUM

TREWS TROUSERS

TRIACETATE ACETIN EUROBIN

TRIAD TRIAS TRINE TRIUNE TERNARY
TERNION TRILOGY TRINARY TRINITY
TRIMURTI TRIRATNA

TRIAL SHY TRY BOUT DOOM FIRE
HACK OYER STAB TEST TURN
ASSAY CROSS ESSAY GRIEF ISSUE
POINT PROOF TASTE TOUCH WHACK
ASSIZE EFFORT EQUITY TRINAL
APPROOF ATTEMPT CALVARY
DISGUST HEARING PROVING
SCRATCH CRUCIBLE EXERCISE

JUDGMENT QUAESTIO TENTAMEN
(— BY BATTLE) WAGER
(— BY ORDEAL) ORDALIUM
(— FOR HOUNDS) DERBY
(— OF SPEED) DASH
(EXPERIMENTAL —) TENTAMEN
(SEVERE —) ORDEAL CRUCIBLE

TRIANGLE APEX CYMBAL OXYGON
TRIGON ISOCELE PYRAMID SCALENE
TRINITY TRIQUET DINGDONG

TRIANGULAR HEATER CUNEATE
HASTATE
(— AREA) QUIRK
(— CLOTH) GORE
(— INSET) GODET

TRIBAL GENTILE GENTLIC TRIBULAR

TRIBE AO GI ATI AUS BOH EVE EWE
GOG KHA KIN KRA ROD SUK YAO
ADAI AKAN AKHA AKIM AKKA BAYA
BONI CLAN DAGO GUHA PURU
QUNG RACE RAVI REKI SAHO SEID
SHIK SHOR SIOL SOGA SUKU SUSU
TOBA TURI TUSH UBII VEPS VILI
VIRA YANA AEQUI ANGKA APTAL
ARAWA BASSI BATAK BESSI CHANG
CINEL DADJO DEDAN DIERI FIRCA
GIBBI HORDE HOUSE ICENI KAJAR
KANDH KEDAR KHOND KIWAI
KONGO KOTAR KREPI LANGO MARSI
MBUBA MENDE MENDI MOSSI MUTER
NANDI PHYLE PONDO QUADI SERER
SOTIK STAMM SUEVI TAIPI TAULI
TCAWI TEKKE TELEI TUATH VEPSE
VOLOF WAKHI WARRI WASHO
WAYAO YOMUD ADIGHE AGAWAM
ANAMIM ANTEVA APAYAO ARAINS
BANYAI BASOGA BUDUMA BUSAOS
CHAMPA CHAWIA CHORAI DOROBO
FAMILY HERULI KARLUK KEREWA
KHAMTI KONYAK KORANA LOBALE
MANGAR MOLALA NATION NERVII
PAHARI PHYLON POKOMO RAMNES
SHAGIA SICULI SIMEON SUKUMA
TAINUI TAMOYO TCHIAM TELEUT
THUSHI TUSHIN TYPEES VENETI
WABENA WABUMA WAGOMA
WAGUHA WAHEHE WARORI WASOGA
WAVIRA ZARAMO ZEGUHA ZENAGA
ABABDEH ABANTES AIAWONG
AKWAPIM AMAKOSA ANOMURA
ANTAIVA ARVERNI BAGIRMI
BAKATAN BAKONGO BAKUNDA
BAMBARA BASONGO CABINDA
CHAOUIA CHAUWIA CHITALI
CHONTAL CHUKCHI COLLERY
DADAYAG DADSCHO ILLANUN
JAZYGES KABINDA KABONGA
KHOKANI KOLDAJI KONIAGA
KOREISH KUBACHI KURUMBA
LLANERO NAIADES PALAUNG PARISII
PIMENTO RAURACI SAMBALA
SAMBARA SEKHWAN SENONES
SEQUANI SHAMMAR SHERANI
SHUKRIA SILIPAN SUIONES SUKKIIM
TAKELMA TARKANI TURKANA
VIDDHAL WAGWENO WAICURI
WAMBUGU WAREGGA WASANGO
ZONGORA AMAFINGO ANDOROBO
ASHANGOS ASSHURIM AWABAKAL

BARKINJI BATETELA BOANBURA
CHERUSCI GEZRITES JICAQUES
KUKURUKU LANDUMAN NEBAIOTH
ORUNCHUN PALLIVAN PHASIRON
PUPULUCA PURUPURU RAHANWIN
SAKALAVA SHINWARI SINGSING
SINTSINK TCHUKCHI TENGGRIS
USTARANA WANGATTA WAPOGORO
WAPOKOMO
(— OF ISRAEL) DAN GAD ASHER
REUBEN EPHRAIM ISSACHAR
MANASSEH
(CHINESE —S) HU
(PRIVILEGED —) MAGHZEN
MAKHZAN
(SEA GYPSY —) SELUNG

TRIBROMOETHANOL AVERTIN

TRIBULATION AGONY MISERY
SORROW DISTRESS

TRIBUNAL BAR FEME ROTA VEHM
COURT FEHME FORUM JUNTA
VEHME MAJLIS ACUERDO ESGUARD
MEJLISS RIGSRET AREOPAGY

TRIBUNE BEMA VELUTUS

TRIBUTARY ARM BRANCH FEEDER
TYBURN

TRIBUTE AID FEE TAX GELT LEVY
PORT RENT SCAT CANON GAVEL
HANSE MAILL SALVO SCATT
CHAUTH HERIOT HIDAGE HOMAGE
IMPOST CARATCH CHEVAGE
CHIEFRY OVATION PENSION
SYNODAL TREWAGE AUXILIUM
BRENNAGE HEREGELD PESHKASH
ROMESCOT ROMESHOT

TRICE GIRD BLINK THROW INSTANT

TRICHECHUS MANATUS

TRICHINA NEMATODE

TRICHION CRINION

TRICHOME SCALE

TRICHOMONIASIS CANKER
ABORTION

TRICK DO BOB COG CON CUN DAP
DOR FOB FOX FUB FUN GIN GUM
JIG JOB PAW BILK BITE BORE CHAW
CHIP DIDO DIRT DUPE FAKE FIRK
FLAM FLUM FOOL GAFF GAME GAUD
GECK GULL HAVE HOAX JAPE JEST
JINK JOUK JUNT LOCK LURK PASS
PAWK PRAT PULL RORT RUSE SELL
SKIT SLUR TURN WILE WIPE WOOL
BLEAR BLINK CATCH CHEAT CONNU
CRAFT CREEK CROOK CULLY
CURVE DODGE DORRE ELUDE FEINT
FETCH FOURB FRAUD GLEEK GRIFT
GUILE KNACK PAVIE PLANT PRANK
SHIFT SHINE SKITE SLICK STUNT
TRAIN TRUFF TWIST WHEEL WREST
WRINK BAFFLE BANTER BEGUNK
BEJAPE BLENCH BROGUE CAUTEL
CHOUSE CRADDY DECEIT DELUDE
DOUBLE EUCHRE FOURBE HOCKET
HUMBUG JOCKEY JUGGLE MANNER
PLISKY POLICY SCONCE SHAVIE
SPRING TREPAN VAGARY WHEEZE
WINNER CANTRIP CHICANE CONCEIT
FICELLE FINESSE FORWARD
GUILERY KNAVERY MARLOCK
PAGEANT SHUFFLE SLEIGHT

WHIZZER ARTIFICE CHALDESE
CLAPTRAP CLOWNADE CONTOISE
CROTCHET DELUSION DOUBLING
FLAGARIE FLIMFLAM GILENYIE
INTRIGUE JEOPARDY PRACTICE
PRANCOME PRESTIGE QUENTISE
SLAMPAMP TRAVERSE TRICKING
(— OUT) FINIFY
(BEGUILING —) WILE
(CARD —) CLUB HEART SPADE
STICH DIAMOND WEAVING
(FRAUDULENT —) RIG TOP
(JUGGLING —) FOIST
(KNAVISH —) DOGTRICK
(LOVE —) AMORETTO
(MEAN —) TOUCH
(MONKEY —) SINGERIE
(OLD —) CONNU
(PETTY —S) CRANS
(SIX —S) BOOK
(SMART —) LIRIPIPE LIRIPOOP
(STUPID —) SHINE
(VEXING —) CHAW
(WRESTLING —) CHIP CLICK FAULX
FORWARD
(PL.) DAGS
TRICKER TRUMPER
TRICKERY DOLE GAFF SHAM TRAP
TRAY WILE COVIN FRAUD HOCUS
SHARK TRAIN CAUTEL COVINE
DECEIT JAPERY JUGGLE TREGET
DODGERY FALLACY GULLERY
JOUKERY KNAVERY PAWKERY
SLEIGHT ARTIFICE CHEATING
JOOKERIE JUGGLERY PRACTICE
TRICKING TRUMPERY
TRICKILY FOXILY
TRICKINESS PAWKERY
TRICKISH KNAVISH FRAUDFUL
TRICKLE DRIP DRILL STILL TRILL
DISTIL DRIVEL SICKER SIGGER
STRAIN ZIGGER DISTILL DRIBBLE
DRIZZLE TRINTLE
TRICKSTER GULL SHAM TRAPAN
SLICKER TRICKER SLEEVEEN
TRAMPOSO
TRICKSY ELFISH QUIRKSEY
TRICKY SLY DEEP BRAID DODGY
FIKIE GAUDY ROWDY SNIDE ARTFUL
CATCHY LUBRIC QUIRKY SHIFTY
SMARTY TWISTY DEVIOUS SLANTER
TRICKLE WINDING FLIMFLAM
JUGGLING LUBRICAL SHIFTFUL
SKITTISH SLIDDERY SLIPPERY
TORTUOUS TRICKING
TRICLINIC ANORTHIC
TRICOT JERSEY
TRICYCLE VELO CYCLE TRIKE
WHEEL TANDEM TRICAR RANTOON
ROADSTER SOCIABLE
TRIDENT VAJRA TRISUL TRISULA
TRIED TESTED PROBATE WEIGHED
RELIABLE
TRIFLE ACE BOB DAB HAW PIN SOU
TOY BEAN COOT DOIT FICO FOOL
HAIR HOOT JAUK MOCK MOTE PLAY
RUSE DALLY FLIRT FLUKE GLAIK
ITEMY NIFLE PLACK POINT SCRAT
SPORT TRICK TRUFF BAWBEE

BREATH DABBLE DANDLE DAWDLE
DELUDE DIBBLE DOODAD DOODLE
FADDLE FESCUE FIDDLE FOOTER
FOOTLE FRIVOL GEWGAW MONKEY
NIDDLE NIGNAY PADDLE PALTER
PETTLE PICKLE PIDDLE PIGGLE
PINGLE POTTER PUTTER TIFFLE
VANITY WANTON FEATHER FRIBBLE
NOTHING QUIDDLE THOUGHT
TRANEEN TRINKET TRIVIAL WHIFFLE
COQUETTE FALDERAL FLIMFLAM
FOLDEROL GIMCRACK KICKSHAW
MOLEHILL NIHILITY NUGAMENT
RIGMAREE TRANTLUM
(— WITH) JANK DANDLE DELUDE
NIGGLE
(ATTRACTIVE —) CONCEIT
(LITERARY —) TOY
(MERE —) SONG STRAW
(MEREST —) FIG
(PL.) NUGAE TRIVIA GIBLETS
FEWTRILS
TRIFLER DOODLE PLAYER FLANEUR
FOOTLER FRIBBLE NUGATOR
PINGLER TWIDDLER WHIFFLER
TRIFLING AIRY FOND IDLE FUNNY
INANE LIGHT PETTY POTTY SILLY
SMALL FLIMSY FUTILE LEVITY
LIMUTE LITTLE PALTRY SIMPLE
STRAWY TOYISH FOOLISH FRIBBLE
ITEMING TRIVIAL TWATTLE
COQUETRY FIDDLING FLIMFLAM
FRIPPERY IMMOMENT NUGATORY
PIDDLING SNIPPING
TRIFOLIUM CLOVER TREFOIL
TRIG TRIM CHIPPER
TRIGGER VERGE TRICKER
TRIGGERFISH COCUYO TURBOT
OLDWIFE BALISTID FILEFISH
OLDWENCH
TRIGON TRINE SABBEKA SACKBUT
SAMBUCA TRIGONON
TRIGONOMETRY SPHERICS
TRILL BURR FLAP ROLL SHAKE
QUAVER THRILL TRILLO WARBLE
TRILLET
TRILLIUM SARA TRUE SARAH TRUMP
BENJAMIN TRUELOVE
TRILOBITE EODISCID
TRIM AX AXE CUT DUB GIM LIP LOP
NET BARB BEAD BUTT CLIP CROP
DEFT DINK FEAT FUSS GASH GIMP
HACK JIMP LACE NEAT PICK SNAG
SNOD SNUG SPUR STOW TACK
TOSH TRIG BRAID BRUSH CLEAN
COPSE DRESS FITTY GENTY HEDGE
KEMPT KNIFE PREEN PRIME PRUNE
PURGE SAUCY SHAVE SHEAR
SHRAG SHRIP SLEEK SMART SMIRK
SPRIG STUMP TIGHT TRICK VERGE
BARBER DAPPER DONSIE DOUBLE
FETTLE PICKED REFORM SHROUD
SPRUCE SVELTE SWITCH TRIMLY
CHIPPER FEATHER FLOUNCE
SCISSOR MANICURE ORNAMENT
TRIMMING
(— A BOAT) SIT
(— ENDS OF HAIR) SHIRL
(— HEDGE) DUB

(— HIDES) ROUND
(— MEAT) CONDITION
(— SAIL) FILL
(— SEAMS) FETTLE
(— SHOE) FOX
(— TREES) PRIME SWAMP
(— WITH EMBROIDERY) GIMP PANEL
TRIMLY SMARTLY SPRUCELY
TRIMMED PEEKABOO
TRIMMER FINER BRIDLE TACKER
VOLANT ROUNDER SMOCKER
SCRATTER
TRIMMING COQ FUR GIMP LACE
BRAID CHAPE COQUE FRILL GUARD
INKLE JABOT RUCHE ERMINE
LACING OSPREY PURFLE ROBING
BEADING FALBALA FURRING
GALLOON MARABOU PUFFING
BRAIDING EAVESING FALDERAL
FOLDEROL FROSTING FROUFROU
FURBELOW JEWELING PAILETTE
PEARLING PICKADIL PLASTRON
SOUTACHE SPAGHETTI STRAPPING
(PL.) LOP FLOTS SHORTS FIXINGS
LOPPING BRAIDING FRILLIES
TRIMURTI TRINITY
TRINE TRENE TRIGON
TRINIDAD-TOBAGO (CAPITAL OF —)
PORTOFSPAIN
(POINT OF —) GALERA
(RIVER OF —) ORTOIRE
(TOWN OF —) ARIMA LABREA
SIPARIA
TRINITARIAN MATHURIN
TRINITY TRIAD TRIAS TRINE TRIUNE
GODHEAD TERNARY TRIMURTI
TRINUNITY
TRINKET TOY DIDO GAUD BIJOU
HEART KNACK TAHLI BAUBLE
DEVICE DOODAD GEWGAW BIBELOT
TRANGAM TRANKUM GIMCRACK
TRANTLUM TRINKLET WHIMWHAM
(PL.) TRINKUMS
TRINKETRY KNAVERY
TRINITROTOLUENE TOLITE TRITON
TRIO GLEEK TERZET TRIUNE
TERZETTO
TRIOLEFIN TRIENE
TRIONYX AMYDA
TRIOPAS (DAUGHTER OF —)
IPHIMEDIA
(FATHER OF —) NEPTUNE
(MOTHER OF —) CANACE
(SON OF —) ERYSICHTHON
TRIOPS APUS
TRIP HOP JAG JET JOG TIP BOUT
CHIP FOOT GAIT GATE RAKE SKIP
TOUR TROT TURN BROAD DANCE
DRIVE HITCH JAUNT SALLY CRUISE
ERRAND FLIGHT HEGIRA OFFEND
OUTING RAMBLE SAFARI SASHAY
VOYAGE JOURNEY SAILING
SETDOWN STUMBLE TRIPPER
CAMPAIGN PERIPLUS
(— ALONG) CHIP LINK
(— IN WRESTLING) CHIP CLICK
(— INTO COUNTRY) CAMPAIGN
(— UP) SUPPLANT
(HUNTING —) SHOOT

(PLEASURE —) JUNKET
TRIPE PAUNCH ROLPENS TRILLIBUB
TRIPLE TRINE TREBLE TERNARY
TRIFOLD TRIPLEX THRIBBLE
TRIPLET TRIN BRELAN PARIAL
TERCET TRIOLE TRIPLE TERZINA
TRIOLET HEMIOLIA TRILLING
TRIPLING TRISTICH
TRIPLETAIL SAMA CHOBIE FLASHER
GROUPER
TRIPLICITY TRIGON
TRIPOD CAT TRIP SPIDER TEAPOY
TRIPOS TRIVET TRESTLE
TRIPODY HEMIEPES
TRIPOLI SILEX TRIPEL
TRIPPER DECKMAN
TRIPTOLEMUS (FATHER OF —)
CELEUS
(MOTHER OF —) METANIRA
TRISMUS LOCKJAW TETANUS
TRITE FADE HACK WORN BANAL
CONNU CORNY HOARY MUSTY
STALE VAPID BEATEN COMMON
MODERN HACKNEY PERCOCT
TRIVIAL SHOPWORN
TRITENESS BATHOS
TRITERPENOID CERIN
TRITON NEWT TRUMPET
(FATHER OF —) NEPTUNE
(MOTHER OF —) AMPHITRITE
TRITURATE POUND POWDER
TRITURATION TRIPSIS
TRITURUS MOLGE
TRIUMPH WIN PALM INSULT PREVAIL
VICTORY CONQUEST
(— OVER) SCALP
TRIUMPHANT VICTOR JUBILANT
TRIUMPHING OVANT
TRIUNGULIN CRAWLER
TRIVET SPIDER TRIPOD TRESTLE
TRIPPER BRANDISE
TRIVIAL JERK NICE VAIN LEGER
LIGHT PETTY SILLY SMALL TIDDY
FIDFAD FOOTLE SLIGHT TOYISH
COMICAL PIPERLY PUERILE
SHALLOW TIDDLEY DOGGEREL
FEATHERY FOOTLING GIMCRACK
PIDDLING PILULOUS TRIFLING
TRINKETY
(NOT —) SOLID EARNEST
TRIVIALITY FOLLY NIGNAY TRIFLE
INANITY IDLENESS NONSENSE
NUGACITY
TROCHANTER SCAPULA
TROCHE ROTULA TABLET CACHUNDE
PASTILLE
TROCHEE CHOREE CHOREUS
TROCHEUS
TROCHLEA PULLEY
TROCTOLITE GABBRO
TRODDEN TRADED
(MUCH —) BEATEN
TROGLODYTIC SPELEAN
TROGON QUEZAL QUETZAL
TOCORORO
TROILUS (FATHER OF —) PRIAM
(MOTHER OF —) HECUBA
(SLAYER OF —) ACHILLES
TROJAN TROIC DARDAN ANTENOR

(PL.) TEUCRI
TROLL HARL SPIN TROW HARLE
MOOCH TRAWL TROLLOL
TROLLER MOOCHER
TROLLOP CUT DOXY BITCH DOXIE
TROLL TRULL DOLLOP
TROMBONE BONE TRAM BUSINE
POSAUNE SACKBUT SLIPHORN
TRONA URAO
TROOP FARE GING ROUT TURM
ROUTE SOLAK STAND TURMA
WERED CORNET RISALA ROUGHT
SCHOOL THREAT TICHEL TROUPE
COMPANY COMITIVA
(— OF ARMED MEN) CREW
(— OF FOXES) SKULK
(—S ATTACHED TO SOVEREIGN)
GUARDS
(—S IN BATTLE ARRAY) SHELTRON
(—S ON WING OF ARMY) ALARES
(ASSAULTING —S) WAVE
(BOMBAY —S) DUCKS
(CAVALRY —) CORNET
(GIRL SCOUT —) SHIP
(LIGHT-ARMED —S) PSILOI
(SCOTTISH —S) JOCKS
(PL.) PARADE
TROOPER BARGIR RUTTER BARGEER
TROPARION HIRMOS HEIRMOS
TROPARY KATABASIS
TROPE IMAGE EVOVAE
TROPHONEMA VILLUS
TROPHOZOITE CEPHALIN SPORADIN
TROPHY BAG PALM PRIZE SCALP
REWARD LAURELS
TROPIC SOLAR TROPHIC
TROPINE HYOSCINE
TROS (FATHER OF —) ERICTHONIUS
(MOTHER OF —) CALLIRRHOE
(SON OF —) ILUS GANYMEDE
ASSARACUS
TROT JOG SPUD TRIG FADGE HURRY
PIAFFE
TROTH CERTY TROGS TRUTH CERTIE
TROTTER DRIVER CRUBEEN
SPANKER
TROUBADOR MINSTREL SORDELLO
TROUBLE ADO AIL DIK HOE ILL IRK
MAR WOE BEAT BUSY CAIN CARK
EARN FASH FIKE JEEL MASH MOIL
PAIN PINE ROUT SORE STIR TEEN
TINE TRAY UNRO WORK ANNOY
BESET CROSS DROVE DUTCH GRIEF
HAUNT LABOR ROWEL SMITE SPITE
STEER STURT SUSSY THRIE TWEAK
WHILE WORRY BOTHER BURBLE
CADDLE CUMBER DITHER EFFORT
GRIEVE GRUDGE HARASS KIAUGH
MOLEST POTHER RATTLE RUBBER
SORROW TAKING THREAT UNEASE
UNRUFE WORRIT AFFLICT AGITATE
ANXIETY CHAGRIN DISEASE DISTURB
DRUBBLE EMBROIL FASHERY
INFLICT PERTURB PILIKIA SCRUPLE
SPUTTER THOUGHT TRACHLE
TRAVAIL TRIBBLE TURMOIL
BUSINESS DARKNESS DISORDER
DISQUIET DISTRESS NOISANCE
VEXATION WANDRETH

(— ONE'S SELF) PASS
(PL.) CHAGRINS
TROUBLED DRUBLY DRUMLY
GRUMLY QUEASY FRETFUL
HAUNTED HARASSED
TROUBLESOME DIK ILL HARD FIKIE
SHREWD STICKY HARMFUL
TEWSOME UNTOWARD
TROUBLED CAREFUL AGITATED
TROUBLESHOOTER FIXER
TROUBLESOME SAD PLAGUY
UNEASY PESTFUL ANNOYING
FASHIOUS SPITEFUL
TROUBLESOMENESS BOTHER
TROUBLING CHRONIC
TROU-DE-LOUP TRAPHOLE
TROUGH BOX CUP HOD RUN TOM
BACK BOSH BUNK COVE DAIL DALE
DISH DORR SHOE SINK TRAY TROW
BAKIE CHUTE DITCH LAVER SHOOT
SHUTE SLIDE SPOUT STRIP ALVEUS
BACKET BUDDLE GUTTER HARBOR
LAVABO MANGER RUNNER SALTER
SINKER SLUICE STRAKE TROGUE
VALLEY WALLOW CHENEAU
CONDUIT LAUNDER RIFFLER
TRENDLE TROFFER LAVATORY
(— FOR ASHES) BAKIE
(— FOR COOLING INGOTS) BOSH
(— FOR PAPER PULP) RIFFLER
(— FOR WASHING ORE) TOM HUTCH
STRIP BUDDLE STRAKE
(— IN MONASTERY) LAVABO
(— OF A WAVE) SULK
(— OF CIDER MILL) CHASE
(— OF ROCK) SYNCLINE
(— OF THE SEA) ALVEUS
(ANNULAR —) CUP
(EAVES —) CANAL CHENEAU
(GLACIAL —) DORR
(SHEEP-DIPPING —) DUP
(WOODEN —) TRUG BAKIE TROGUE
TROUNCE MOP FLOG TRAMP
WHOMP COURSE CUDGEL CANVASS
TROUNCING LACING WARMING
TROUPE SERVANTS CUADRILLA
TROUSER STROSSER
TROUSERING CASINET
TROUSERS BAGS CORDS DUCKS
JEANS KICKS PANTS SLOPS TONGS
TREWS BRAIES DENIMS SHORTS
SKILTS SLACKS WHITES BOTTOMS
BRACCAE BROGUES KERSEYS
NANKINS SHALWAR SLIVERS
STRIDES BLOOMERS BREECHES
FLANNELS KICKSEYS MOLESKIN
NANKEENS OVERALLS SHINTYAN
TROUT CHAR KELT PEAL POGY
BROOK BROWN CHARR LAKER
LUNGE SEWEN SHARD SQUET SQUIT
TRUFF FINNOC KIPPER MYKISS
QUASKY SALTER TAIMEN TRUCHA
TULADI BOREGAT BROOKIE
BROWNIE COASTER HERLING
OQUASSA POUNDER RAINBOW
SQUETEE AUREOLUS BODIERON
GILLAROO HARDHEAD KAMLOOPS
SAIBLING SALMONID SISCOWET
(SMALL —) SCURLING SKIRLING

(YOUNG —) WHITLING
TROUVERE BLONDEL
TROW DROW TRUE FAITH BELIEF
COVENANT
TROWEL HAWK LEAF PIPE DARBY
DERBY FLOAT TAPER TREWEL
(HEARTSHAPED —) HEART DOGTAIL
(MOLDER'S —) LEAF TAPER
(PLASTERER'S —) FLOAT
TRUANT HOOKY TRONE TROUT
MICHER MEECHER TRIVANT
VAGRANT
TRUCE PAX BARLEY TREAGUE
INDUCIAE
TRUCK DAN UTE BUNK CORF DRAB
DRAG DUCK DUMP GUNK RACK
WYNN BOGIE BUGGY DILLY DOLLY
GILLY LORRY BARTER BUMMER
CAMION DIESEL DROGUE DRUGGE
DUMPER JITNEY SLOVEN TIPPER
TURTLE CARAVAN FOURGON
GONDOLA SKIDDER SLEEPER
TROLLEY TRUCKLE TRUNDLE
DELIVERY HAULAWAY TRANSFER
(COAL —) DAN
(LOGGING —) BUNK BUMMER
(MINING —) CORF BARNEY
(TIMBER —) DRUG WYNN
TRUCKLE FAWN TOADY SLAVER
TRUCKLING SERVILE
TRUCULENCE BRAG
TRUCULENT MEAN CRUEL HARSH
FIERCE SAVAGE SCATHING
TRUDGE JOG PAD HAKE PLOD STOG
JAUNT TRACE TRAMP TRASH
STODGE TRAIPSE
TRUE SO GOOD JUST LEAL PURE
REAL VERY VRAI PLUMB RIGHT
SOOTH SOUND VERAY FIDELE
LAWFUL DEVOTED GENUINE
GERMANE PRECISE SINCERE
STAUNCH FAITHFUL RELIABLE
RIGHTFUL SOOTHFUL UNERRING
(— TO THE FACT) LITERAL
(QUESTIONABLY —) ALLEGED
TRUFFLE TRUB TRUFF EARTHNUT
TRUISM SOOTH
TRULL DELL BLOWZE CALLET
TRULY YEA AWAT EVEN IWIS JUST
QUITE SOOTH SYKER TIGHT ATWEEL
DINKUM INDEED SIMPLY VERILY
INSOOTH SOOTHLY VERAMENT
WITTERLY
TRUMP DIS DIX LOW PAM LILY RUFF
BASTA BASTO DEECE TROMBE
MANILLA MATADOR TRIUMPH
SPADILLE
(2ND HIGHEST —) MANILLE
TRUMPERY MOCKADO GIMCRACK
PEDDLERY
TRUMPET BEME LURE TUBA TRUMP
BOZINE BUCCIN CORNET KERANA
LITUUS TROMBA TULNIC ALCHEMY
BUCCINA CLARINO CLARION
KERRANA SALPINX NARSINGA
SLUGHORN SOURDINE WATERCUP
TRUMPET BELL CODON PAVILON
TRUMPET CALL DIAN DIANA
SENNET

TRUMPET CREEPER TECOMA
COWHAGE CREEPER FOXGLOVE
HELLVINE
TRUMPETER MOKI AGAMI TRUMP
TOOTER JACAMIN TUBICEN YAKAMIK
TRUMPETER FISH MOKI MOKIHI
TRUMPETER PERCH MADO
TRUMPETS WATERCUP
TRUMPETWOOD IMBAUBA
TRUNCATED STUBBED TRUNKED
TRUNCHEON BATON WARDER
SPONTON PARTISAN SPONTOON
TRUNDLE HURL RUNG TROLL
RUNDLE TRUCKLE WALLOWER
TRUNK BOX BODY BOLE BOOT BULK
KIST LICH RUNT STAM STEM STUD
CABER PETER SHAFT STICK STOCK
TORSO ARIGUE BARREL CAUDEX
COFFER LOCKER CARCASS
CORSAGE STOWAGE TRUNCUS
SARATOGA
(ARTERIAL —) AORTA
(ELEPHANT'S —) SNOUT
(FOSSIL —) CYCAD
(SMALL —) HATBOX
**(TREE — OVER 8 INCHES IN
DIAMETER)** MAST
(TREE —) BOLE BUTT STICK
(TRIMMED TREE —) LOG
(WORSHIPPED TREE —S) IRMINSUL
TRUNKFISH CHAPIN BOXFISH
COWFISH
TRUSS SPAN WARREN
(— OF STRAW) WAP
(— UP) KILT
TRUST AFFY HOPE LITE POOL RELY
REST TICK TREW TROW FAITH FRIST
GROUP TRUTH BELIEF CARTEL
CHARGE CORNER CREDIT DEPEND
FIANCE LIPPEN OFFICE TICKET
BELIEVE BETRUST CONFIDE
CREANCE CRIANCE JAWBONE
SECRECY VENTURE AFFIANCE
COMMENDA CREDENCE MONOPOLY
RELIANCE
TRUSTED FIDUCIAL
TRUSTEE FEOFEE SINDICO VISITOR
MUTWALLI
TRUSTWORTHINESS HONOR TRUST
HONESTY CREDENCE AXIOPISTY
TRUSTWORTHY SAFE SURE SOOTH
SOUND SYKER TRIED HONEST
SECRET SECURE SICKER STABLE
TRUSTY COCKSURE CREDIBLE
FIDUCIAL RELIABLE TRUSTFUL
TRUSTY TRIG FECKFUL STAUNCH
FAITHFUL RELIABLE
TRUTH TAO UNA SOOTH TROTH
WHITE SATTVA VERITY VERITAS
VERACITY VERIDITY VERIMENT
(— TABLE) MATRIX
(IDEAL —) CHRIST DHARMA
(IN —) CERTES
(RELATING TO —) ALETHIC
(ULTIMATE —) LIGHT SUNYATA
TRUTHFUL TRUE VERY SOOTH
HONEST VERIDIC
TRUTHFULLY GOSPELLY

TRUTHFULNESS HONESTY
VERACITY
TRY GO SHY BURL HACK PENK PREE
SEEK SLAP TEST TIRL TURN AFOND
ASSAY CRACK ESSAY ETTLE FLING
GROPE JUDGE OFFER PROVE SENSE
SOUND TASTE TEMPT TOUCH
WHACK WHIRL APPOSE ASSAIL
FRAIST GRIEVE STRIVE AFFLICT
AFFORCE APPROVE ATTEMPT
DISCUSS ESPROVE IMITATE
STAGGER ENDEAVOR STRUGGLE
(— DESPERATELY) AGONIZE
(— FOR GOAL) SHOT
(— HARD) STRIVE
(— OUT) SAMPLE AUDITION
(— TO ATTAIN) AFFECT
(CASUAL —) FLING
(QUICK —) SLAP
TRYING ARDUOUS CRUCIAL
GRUELING
TRYSAIL SPENCER
TSETSE FLY KIVU GANDI DIPTERAN
GLOSSINA
T-SHAPED TAU
TSILTADEN CHILION
TSUBO BU
TSWANA CHUANA SECHUANA
TUAREG IMOHAGH IMOSHAGH
TUATARA GUANA GUANO IGUANA
HATTERIA
TUB FAT HOD KID KIT SOE SOW TUN
VAT BACK BOWK COOL CORF COWL
GAWN KNOP MEAL TYND TYNE
BOWIE ESHIN KEEVE KIVER SKEEL
STAND BUCKET KEELER KILLER
KIMNEL TROUGH TURNEL BATHTUB
BREAKER SALTFAT TANKARD
TRUNDLE KOOLIMAN LAVATORY
(— FOR ALEWIVES) HOD
(— FOR AMALGAMATING ORES)
TINA
(— FOR BREAD) BARGE
(— OF BUTTER) COOL
(— OF HOGWASH) SWILLTUB
(— USED AS DIPPER) HANDY PIGGIN
(— WITH SLOPING SIDES) SHAUL
(BREWER'S —) BACK KEEVE
(LAUNDRY —) WASHTRAY
(MESS —) KID KIT
(MINING —) CORF
(TANNING —) LEACH
(WATER —) DAN JAILER
(WOODEN —) KIT SOE KIMNEL
TRINDLE
TUBA BASS HELICON BOMBARDON
TUBE TAG BEAK BODY BOOT CANE
CASE CAST CORE DRUM DUCT
HORN HOSE PIPE REED WORM
BATON CANAL CORER CROOK
CRYPT DRAIN GLAND HEART LINER
QUILL SIGHT SLIDE SPILE SPOUT
THECA THIEF TRUMP TUBAL VALVE
AUDION CALCAR CANNEL CANNON
COLUMN CORNET DEWCAP FILTER
GULLET HEADER NOZZLE OCTODE
SLEEVE SUCKER SYRINX THROAT
TRIODE TUBING TUBULE TUNNEL
UPTAKE VESSEL BLOWGUN

CHIMNEY CONDUIT CUVETTE
DROPPER FERRULE FISTULA
HOUSING OOBLAST OVIDUCT
QUILLET ROSTRUM SALPINX
SHALLOT SNORTER SNUFFER
SOXHLET STOPPLE THIMBLE
TUBULUS VENTURI ADJUTAGE
BOMBILLA CORNICLE DIATREME
DRAWTUBE FAIRLEAD GRADUATE
ORTHICON OVARIOLE PENSTOCK
PIPESTEM SAUCISSE SIPHONET
SLEEVING URCEOLUS ZOOECIUM
(— AT BASE OF PETAL) CALCAR
(— CARRYING BASSOON
MOUTHPIECE) CROOK
(— COVERING TRACE CHAIN) PIPING
(— FOR DEPOSITING CONCRETE)
TREMIE
(— FOR DRINKING MATE) BOMBILLA
(— FOR LINING WELL) WELLRING
(— FOR STIFFENING STRING) TAG
(— FOR TRANSFERRING LIQUID)
SIPHON SYPHON
(— FOR WINDING THREAD) COP
(— FROM SHIP'S PUMP) DALE
(— IN ENGINE CYLINDER) LINER
(— OF BALLOON) APPENDIX
(— OF GUN) BORE BARREL
(— OF RETORT) BEAK ROSTRUM
(— OF SPIRIT LEVEL) BUBBLE
(— OF TOBACCO) CIGARET
(— TO LINE A VENT) BOUCHE
(— TWISTED IN COILS) WORM
(— USED IN WHALING) LULL
(AMPLIFIER —) STAGE
(BONE —) SNUFFER
(DISTILLING —) TOWER
(ELECTRO —) BULB
(ELECTRODE —) AUDION
(ELECTRON —) DIODE DRIVER
KLYSTRON PLIOTRON
(FIREWORKS —) LEADER
(GLANDULAR —) CRYPT
(GLASS —) SIGHT MATRASS
(HONEY —) NECTARY SIPHONET
(KNITTED —) STOCKING
(PAPER —) LEADER PASTILLE
(PASTRY —) CORNET
(POLLEN —) SPERMARY
(RECTIFIER —) IGNITRON
(SILK — OF SPIDER) SPIGOT
(SPEAKING —) GOSPORT
(SUCKING —) STRAW
(SURGICAL —) CANNULA
(THERMOMETER —) STEM
(VACUUM —) DIODE KEYER HEXODE
HEPTODE DYNATRON
TUBELET CIRCLET
TUBER ANU SET ANYU BULB CLOG
ROOT SEED SETT YAMP SALEP
JICAMA PIGNUT POTATO WAPATA
WINDER YAUTIA EARTHNUT
MURRNONG
TUBERCLE PEARL NODULE STEMMA
CUSPULE VERRUCA
TUBERCULAR PHTHISIC
TUBERCULOSIS CON CLYERS
DECLINE SCROFULA
TUBING HOSE TUBAGE

TUBMAN DUCKER
TUBULAR PIPY PIPED TUBATE
CANNULAR
(NOT —) FARCTATE
TUBULE TRACHEA TUBULET
TUBULUS
TUCANO BETOYAN
TUCK TOKE STUFF TRUSS FLANGE
(— IN) TRUSS TROUSS
(— UP) FAKE KILT
TUCKER CORDER KILTER PLEATER
**TUESDAY (SECOND — AFTER
EASTER)** HOCKDAY HOKEDAY
TUFF TRASS PEPERINO PORODITE
SANTORIN
TUFT EAR FAG FOB NOB SOP TOP
COMA DOWN KNOB KNOP MOCK
TUFF TUSK BEARD BUNCH CREST
FLOCK STUPA THRUM WHISK
CIRRUS DOLLOP PAPPUS PENCIL
TASSEL TUFFET CIRRHUS FEATHER
FLOCCUS HOBNAIL PANACHE
SCOPULA TOPKNOT TOPPING
TUSSOCK FLOCCULE
(— OF BRISTLES) BIRSE
(— OF CLOTH) FAG
(— OF DOWN) FRIEZE
(— OF FEATHERS) EAR HORN HULU
EGRET
(— OF FILAMENTS) BYSSUS
(— OF GRASS) FAG SOP MOCK
HASSOCK TUSSOCK
(— OF HAIR ON HORSE'S HOOF)
FETLOCK
(— OF HAIR) TOP TUZZ BRUSH
SWITCH COWLICK FEATHER
FLOCCUS SCOPULA TOPKNOT
IMPERIAL KROBYLOS
(— OF HAY) SOP
(— OF MALE TURKEY) BEARD
(— OF WOOL) FOB TUSK TUZZ
FLOCK
(— ON BIRD'S HEAD) COP CUCK
EGRET
(— ON PINEAPPLE) CROWN
(— ON SEED PLANT) PAPPUS
(— ON SPIDER'S FEET) SCOPULA
(—S OF ROPE YARN) THRUM
(VASCULAR —) GLOMUS
TUFTED COMOSE TAPPET TAPPIT
TUG LUG RUG TIT TOG CHUG DRAG
HALE HAUL PULL TOIL TUCK CHUFF
HITCH PLUCK SHRUG TRACE
RUGGLE TOWBOAT TUGBOAT
TUGBOAT TOW TUG TOWBOAT
TRACKER
TUI POE TUA KOKO TUWI POEBIRD
TUITION CUSTODY
TULIP LILY LILIUM BIZARRE BREEDER
TURNSOLE
TULIP TREE POPLAR BASSWOOD
CUCUMBER
TULIPWOOD AUBURN
TULLE ILLUSION
TUMATAKURU IRISHMAN MATAGORY
TUMBLE TOP COUP WALT LATCH
SPILL THROW TIFLE TRACE COTTON
GROVEL PURLER TIFFLE TOPPLE

WALTER WAMBLE WELTER STUMBLE
WHEMMEL
(— OVER) TIPPLE WALLOP
TUMBLE-DOWN RUINOUS
TUMBLER NUT CLICK GLASS LEVER
WIPER ROLLER ACROBAT DRUMMER
TIPPLER TOPPLER
TUMID TURGID BLOATED BULGING
FUSTIAN TURGENT INFLATED
TUMOROUS
TUMOR PAP WEN BEAL PIAN WART
AMPER BOTCH MYOMA NEVUS
PHYMA SWELL AMBURY ANBURY
EPULIS GLIOMA GYROMA INCOME
KELOID LIPOMA MYXOMA NUROMA
RISING WARBLE ADENOMA ANGIOMA
CYSTOMA DERMOID DESMOID
FIBROID FIBROMA LUTEOMA
MYELOMA OSTEOMA OSTEOME
SARCOMA TESTUDO THYMOMA
ULONCUS ATHEROMA BLASTOMA
CHLOROMA CHORIOMA EMBRYOMA
GLANDULE HEMATOMA HEPATOMA
HOLDFAST LYMPHOMA MELANOMA
MELICERA ODONTOMA PHLEGMON
PLASMOMA PSAMMOMA SCIRRHUS
SEMINOMA TERATOID TERATOMA
WINDGALL
(— OF EYELID) GRANDO
(— ON HORSES'S LEGS) JARDE
(PUSTULAR —) BLAIN
(SKIN —) OUCH
(STUDY OF —S) ONCOLOGY
TUMULT DIN COIL FARE FLAW FRAY
FUSS HURL MUSS REEL RIOT ROUT
VISE BRAWL BROIL HURLY HURRY
LURRY NOISE ROUST STOOR STOUR
WHIRL BUSTLE CLAMOR DIRDUM
EMEUTE FRACAS HUBBUB MUTINY
RABBLE RIPPET RUFFLE STEERY
UPROAR UPSTIR BLUSTER BOBBERY
FACTION FERMENT GARBOIL
TEMPEST TURMOIL DISORDER
SEDITION STIRRING
TUMULTUOUS HIGH LOUD RUDE
NOISY ROUGH STORMY FURIOUS
HURRIED LAWLESS RIOTOUS
VIOLENT AGITATED CONFUSED
DRAWLING HURTLING
TUMULUS MOTE TUMP MOUND
BARROW BURIAN COTERELL
TUN CASK HAAB
(20 —S) KATUN
(ONE-THIRD —) TERTIAN
TUNA AHI ATUN TUNNY BLUEFIN
PELAMYD ALBACORE KAWAKAWA
TUNE AIR ARIA DUMP FADO LEED
NOTE PORT RANT SONG CHARM
CHORD DRANT POINT ATTUNE
GROUND MAGGOT STRAIN STRING
GUAJIRA HALLING MEASURE
MELISMA SONANCE ANGLAISE
FANDANGO GUARACHA HABANERA
(— A HARP) WREST
(— AN INSTRUMENT) STRING
(DANCE —) FURIANT ANGLAISE
GALLIARD
(FOLK —) FADO
(HILLBILLY —) HOEDOWN

(LIGHT —) TOY
(LITTLE —) CATCH
(LIVELY —) LILT SPRING HORNPIPE
(MELANCHOLY —) DUMP
(SACRED —) CHORAL CHORALE
(TRADITIONAL —) TONE
TUNEBO TAME GUACICO
TUNEFUL TUNY CHANTANT
TUNESOME
TUNEFULNESS MELODY
TUNGSTEN W WOLFRAM SCHEELIN
TUNGUS EVENK LAMUT
TUNIC COAT JAMA JUPE VEST
COTTE FROCK GIPPO JAMAH JUPON
PALLA ACHKAN BLIAUT CAMISE
CHITON CYCLAS FECKET HARDIE
KABAYA KIRTLE TABARD ARISARD
BLEAUNT CAMISIA PALTOCK
SURCOAT TUNICLE COLOBIUM
GANDOURA SUBTUNIC SUBUCULA
SUKKENYE
(— OF MAIL) HAUBERK
(HOODED FUR —) SOVIK
TUNICATE SALP SALPA SALPID
ASCIDIAN TUNICARY UROCHORD
TUNICLE SACCOS
TUNING ANESIS
TUNING FORK EVEL EVIL FORK
TUNER DIAPASE DIAPASON
MODULANT
TUNING HAMMER KEY

TUNISIA
CAPE: BON BLANC
CAPITAL: TUNIS
COIN: DINAR
GULF: GABES TUNIS HAMMAMET
ISLAND: DJERBA
LAKE: ACHKEL DJERID BIZERTE
MEASURE: SAA SAH SAAH CAFIZ
WHIBA METTAR
PORT: SFAX GABES TUNIS SOUSSE
BIZERTE
RIVER: MEDJERDA
TOWN: BEJA SFAX SUSA GABES
GAFSA MATEUR NABEUL
SOUSSE BIZERTE JENDOUBA
TEBOURBA ZAGHOUAN
WEIGHT: SAA ROTL ARTAL ARTEL
RATEL UCKIA KANTAR

TUNNEL ADIT BORE CAVE PUKA
SINK TUBE DRIFT DRIVE KAREZ
STALL BURROW PIERCE
(— INTO AN IGLOO) TOSSUT
TUNNY TUNA ALBACORE SCOMBRID
(YOUNG —) PELAMYD
TUP TIP TRIP MONKEY BLISSOM
TURBAN PAT MOAB PATA SASH
TUFT LUNGI MITER MITRE PATTI
TOWEL TUFFE MANDIL WRAPPER
KAFFIYEH PUGGAREE SEERBAND
TOLIPANE TULIPANT TURBANTO
TURBELLARIA APROCTA
TURBELLARIAN FLATWORM
TURBID FAT RILY DROVY GUMLY
MUDDY ROILY DRUMLY GRUMLY
QUALLY FECULENT LUTULENT

TURBIDITY RILE
TURBOT BRET BRILL WHIFF
FLATFISH
TURBULENCE FURY UPROAR
FERMENT RIOTING
TURBULENT GURL HIGH LOUD RUDE
WILD ROUGH WROTH RUGGED
STORMY UNRULY YEASTY FURIOUS
RABBISH RACKETY TROUBLE
VIOLENT MUTINOUS
TURDUS MERULA
TUREEN DISH TERRINE
TURF SOD VAG CESS DELF FAIL
FALE FEAL FLAG FLAT FLAW PONE
SUNK DELFT SCRAW SPINE SWARD
TRUFF FLAUGHT SHIRREL SODDING
(— CUT BY GOLF STROKE) DIVOT
(— FOR LINING PARAPET) GAZON
(DRIED — FOR FUEL) VAG
(PARED —) BEAT
(ROUGH —) GOR
(SMALL PIECE OF —) TAB
(THIN LAYER OF —) FLAW
TURF SPADE SLANE
TURGID TUMID INFLATED
TURGIDNESS TYMPANY
TURK TURCO TURKO SELJUK
CORSAIR OSMANLI OTTOMAN
TURQUET KONARIOT
TURKANA ELKUMA

TURKEY
CAPE: INCE BAFRA ANAMUR
HINZIR KARATAS KEREMPE
CAPITAL: ANKARA
COIN: PARA AKCHA ASPER ATTUN
REBIA AKCHEH SEQUIN ZEQUIN
ALTILIK BESHLIK PATAQUE
PIASTER MEDJIDIE ZECCHINO
DISTRICT: PERA BEYOGLU CILICIA
GULF: COS ANTALYA
LAKE: TUZ VAN EGRIDIR BEYSEHIR
MEASURE: DRA OKA OKE PIK
DRAA HATT KHAT KILE ZIRA
ALMUD BERRI DONUM KILEH
ZIRAI ARSHIN CHINIK DJERIB
FORTIN HALEBI PARMAK
NOCKTAT
MOUNTAIN: AK ALA KARA HASAN
HINIS HONAZ MURAT MURIT
ARARAT BINGOL BOLGAR
SUPHAN ERCIYAS KARACALI
PROVINCE: SERT SIIRT ANGORA
EYALET
RIVER: DICLE FIRAT GEDIZ HALYS
IRMAK KIZIL MESTA SARUS
SEIHUN SEYHAN SEYLAN TIGRIS
SAKARYA MAEANDER
SEAPORT: ENOS IZMIR MERSIN
SAMSUN TRABZON ISTANBUL
TOWN: URFA ADANA BURSA IZMIR
KONYA MARAS SIIRT SIVAS
AINTAB EDESSA EDIRNE ELAZIZ
MARASH SAMSUN ERZURUM
KAYSERI SCUTARI USKUDAR
ISTANBUL STAMBOUL
WEIGHT: OKA OKE DRAM KILE
ROTL ARTAL ARTEL CEQUI

CHEKE KERAT MAUND OBOLU
RATEL BATMAN DIRHEM KANTAR
MISKAL DRACHMA QUINTAL
YUSDRUM

TURKEY STAG STEG BUSTARD
ERECTER ERECTOR GOBBLER
ALDERMAN
(MALE —) TOM
(YOUNG —) POULT
TURKEY BUZZARD AURA
BROMVOEL BROMVOGEL GALLINAZO
TURKEY-COCK STAG
TURKEY OAK CERRIS
TURKI KAZAK QAZAQ KAZAKH
TURKISH TURK TURCIC OSMANLI
OTTOMAN
TURKISH DELIGHT LOUKOUM
TURKOMAN SEID ERSAR
TURK'S CAP LILY MARTAGON
TURMERIC REA ANGO HALDI OLENA
HULDEE AZAFRAN CURCUMA
TURMIT TURNIP
TURMOIL ADO DIN COIL DUST MOIL
TOIL TOSS BURLE HURLY HURRY
STROW TOUSE WHIRL HASSLE
JABBLE UPROAR WELTER CLUTTER
EMOTION FERMENT GARBOIL
HURLING MAKADOO RUMMAGE
TEMPEST DISPEACE DISQUIET
TURN GO BOW CUT GEE JAR RUN
TON WIN AIRT BEND BOUT BOWL
CALE CAST CHAR CHOP COCK EDDY
GIRO HACK HEAD HINT HURL JAMB
KINK PULL QUIP ROLL ROVE SLEW
TOUR VEER VERT VICE WAFT WELT
WIND AIRTH ANGLE BLANK CHARE
CRANK CRASH CREEK CRICK
CROOK ELBOW FEEZE GLINT PIVOT
PLUCK PRICK QUIRK SHIFT SPELL
SWING SWIRL TARVE TERVE TREND
TRILL TROLL TWINE TWIST VERSE
VOLTI WHEEL WREST ATTURN
BOUGHT CIRCLE COURSE DEPEND
DIRECT DOUBLE GRUPPO GYRATE
INDENT INTEND INTURN POSSET
QUEEVE RESORT RETURN ROTATE
SPIRAL STRAIN SWIVEL TOURNE
TURKEN VOLUME VOLUTE WIMPLE
CONVERT CRANKLE CRINKLE
DEFLECT DISTURB FLEXION
FLEXURE FLOUNCE INCLINE INFLECT
PASSADE REVERSE REVOLVE
SERPENT TWINGLE TWISTER
VERSATE WREATHE CLINAMEN
DOUBLING FLECTION TOURNURE
VOLUTION
(— ABOUT) SLEW SLUE SLOUGH
WINDLASS
(— AGAINST) CROSS
(— AROUND) GYRE WELT WEND
RATCH BEWEND SPHERE
(— ASIDE) ERR WRY DAFF SKEW
WARD ABHOR AVERT BLENK DETER
EVADE FENCE GLENT SHEER WAIVE
BLENCH DEPART DETURN DIVERT
SWERVE SWITCH CRINKLE DECLINE
DEFLECT DEVIATE DIGRESS

DIVERGE PERVERT SCRITHE
(— AT DRINKING) TIRL
(— ATTENTION) ADVERT ADDRESS
(— AWAY) DOFF AVERT CHARE
HIELD REPEL AVERSE DESERT
DETURN DIVERT REVOLT ABANDON
DECLINE REVERSE OVERTURN
WITHTURN
(— AWRY) CONTORT
(— BACK ON) RUMP
(— BACK) KEP ABORT FLIPE FLYPE
RETORT RETURN REVERT REFLECT
UNTWIST RENVERSE
(— BROWN) AUGUST
(— BY TOSSING) FLAP
(— CARD FACE UP) BURN
(— DOWN) DIP DENY
(— FOR BETTER) CRISIS
(— IN ARCHERY) END
(— IN CROQUET) BISK BISQUE
(— IN ROPE) NIP RIDER
(— INSIDE OUT) EVERT INVERT
(— INTO ICE) CONGEAL
(— INTO VINEGAR) ACETIFY
(— LEAVES OF BOOK) LEAF TOSS
(— OF AFFAIRS) GO JOB KICK
(— OF CABLE) BITTER
(— OF DUTY) TOUR SHIFT TRICK
(— OF EVENTS) WENT
(— OF FANCY) GUST
(— OF MIND) FREAK
(— OF TIDE) PINCH
(— OF WIT) FLIRT
(— OF YARN) MOUSING
(— OFF) SHUNT DIVERT
(— ON LATHE) THROW
(— ON) HIT
(— OUT TO BE) PROVE EXFLECT
(— OUT) GO USH BEAR FALL FARE
OUST SORT TAKE CHIVE FUDGE
OUTPUT SUCCEED
(— OUTWARD) EVERT SPLAY
(— OVER) CANT FLAP FLIP KEEL
VETTE VOLVE CLINCH DESIGN
AGITATE CAPSIZE
(— POINT OF) ABATE
(— RAPIDLY) SPIN TIRL GIDDY
(— RIGHT) HAP HUP
(— SAIL YARD) BRACE
(— SKIS) STEM
(— SOUR) FOX BLINK PRILL BLEEZE
CHANGE SOUREN
(— SUDDENLY) FLOP
(— TO NEAR SIDE) HAW
(— TO OFF SIDE) GEE
(— TO ONE SIDE) CORNER GOGGLE
(— TO THE LEFT) HAW PORT WIND
WYND
(— UP NOSE) FLIRT SNURL
(— UP) FACE HAPPEN
(— UPSIDE DOWN) CANT COUP
WHELM INVERT QUELME WHELVE
(— VESSEL IN CIRCLE) CHAPEL
(— WHEELS) CRAMP
(— YELLOW) FIRE
(COMPLETE —) LAP
(DOWNWARD —) SLIDE
(ECCENTRIC —) CRANKUM
(FORTUNATE —) BREAK

(HALF —) CARACOLE
(IN —) AROUND
(SHARP —) DOUBLE WRENCH
ZIGZAG HAIRPIN
(SKI —) SWING CHRISTIE TELEMARK
(SUDDEN —) CURL
(PL.) ALLEGRO
TURNBUCKLE TURNEL TURNBOUT
TURNCOAT APOSTATE RENEGADE
TURNED SOUR VERSED COCKEYED
INFLEXED
(— ABOUT) CONVERSE
(— BACK) EVOLUTE
(— DOWNWARD) ABASED DEFLEXED
(— EDGEWISE) BLIND
(— INWARD) VARUS
(— TOWARD ONE SIDE) AWRY
(— TOWARD) ANODIC
(— UP) ACOCK URVED
(— WRONG WAY) AWK
TURNER SLICE BODGER SLIDER
TWIRLER
TURNING HEAD TWIST VOLTA WRINK
DETOUR ROTARY FLEXION FLEXURE
VOLVENT FLECTION STREPSIS
WHEELERY
(— OF EYE) CAST
(— SOUR) ACESCENT
(— TO RIGHT) DEXTRO
(— TOWARD STEM) ADVERSE
(METAL —S) SWARF
(PL.) SCULL
TURNIP BAGA NAPE NEEP RAPE
NAVEW SWEDE RAPEYE TURMUT
CRUCIFER RUTABAGA
(PL.) KRAUT RAPPINI
TURNIP-SHAPED NAPIFORM
RAPACEUS
TURNIX QUAIL HEMIPOD ORTYGAN
HEMIPODE
TURNKEY SCREW LOCKSMAN
TURNOUT RIG SETOUT EQUIPAGE
TRANSFER
TURNOVER BRAMBLE EMPANADA
FLAPJACK
(PL.) PIROJKI PIROSHKI
TURNPIN TAMPION
TURNSOLE HELIO
TURNSPIT HASTLER
TURNSTILE TIRL STILE TURNGATE
TURNPIKE
TURNSTONE PLOVER REDLEG
CHICARIC CREDDOCK
TURNTABLE RACER ROTARY
NONSYNC PLAYBACK
TURNUS (FATHER OF —) DAUNUS
(MOTHER OF —) VENILIA
(SLAYER OF —) AENEAS
TURPENTINE THUS TURPS SCRAPE
THINNER
(BORDEAUX —) GALIPOT
TURPITUDE FEDITY
TURQUOISE TURKEY TURKIS
CALAITE CALLAIS
TURRET BELFRY CUPOLA GARRET
GAZEBO LOUVER TOURET GUERITE
MIRADOR MONITOR BARTIZAN
GUNHOUSE TURRICLE PEPPERBOX
TURTLE EMYD ARRAU CARET CAREY

TORUP COODLE COOTER JURARA
SLIDER THURGI TURKLE CRAWLER
CREEPER EMYDIAN JUNIATA
LOGHEAD SNAPPER TORTUGA
CHELONID FLAPJACK HAWKBILL
MATAMATA SHAGTAIL STINKPOT
TERRAPIN TORTOISE
(— HAVING COMMERCIAL SHELL)
CHICKEN
(OLD —) MOSSBACK
TURTLEHEAD BALMONY CHELONE
CODHEAD
TUSCANY COLCOTHAR
TUSK CUSK HORN IVORY TOOTH
ELEPHANT
(— OF WILD BOAR) RAZOR
(ELEPHANT'S —) SCRIVELLO
TUSSLE TUG BICKER TASSEL
TOUSLE WARSLE
TUXEDO TUX TUCK
TUSSOCK HASSOCK
TUT HOOT TOOT HOOTS
TUTELAGE TUTELE YEMSEL
NURTURE TEACHING
TUTELARY GENIUS
TUTOR DON TUTE COACH TRACH
DOCENT FEEDER GROUND MASTER
PEDANT SCHOOL GRINDER TEACHER
CRANSIER CREANCER GOVERNOR
PANGLOSS PUPILIZE
TUTTI RIPIENO
TUTU TOOT TUPAKIHI
TWADDLE ROT FUDGE HAVER
BABBLE DRIVEL FOOTLE PIFFLE
TOOTLE TWATTLE NONSENSE
SLIPSLOP
TWANA COLCINE
TWANG TANG PLUCK SNUFFLE
TWANGLE TWANKLE
TWAYBLADE DUFOIL TWIFOIL
(PL.) LISTERA
TWEAK FEAK TWIG
TWEED PATTU PATTOO
TWEEZERS TIT TWIRK TWINGE
TWITCH MULLETS PINCERS
PINCETTE VOLSELLA
TWELFTH TWALT DOZENTH
(— OF INCH) SECOND
(— OF LIGHT PERIOD) INCH
(— PART) UNCIA
TWELVE TWAL DOZEN DICKER
DODECADE
TWELVEMONTH TOWMONT
TWELVER IMAMI
TWELVE-TONE SERIAL
TWELVE-TONE-ROW SET
TWENTIETH VIGESIMAL VINGTIEME
TWENTY KAPH CORGE KAPPA
SCORE COOREE
TWENTY-FIVE QUARTERN
TWENTY-FOURTH CARAT
TWENTY-ONE VANJOHN BLACKJACK
TWICE BIS DOPPIO
(— A DAY) BID
TWIDDLE TWEEDLE TWITTER
TWIG COW CHAT RICE RISP SLIP
WAND YARD BIRCH BRIAR BRIER
SHRAG SHRED SPRAY SPRIG STICK
TWIST VIRGA WAVER WITHE BALEYS

FESCUE GREAVE SALLOW SPRING
SWITCH WATTLE WICKER SCOLLOP
TWIGLET ANAPHYTE
(— FOR SNUFF) DIP
(— GROWING FROM STUMP) WAVER
(— IN BIRD SNARE) SWEEK
(— WORN AT SACRIFICES)
INARCULUM
(—S FOR BURNING) CHATWOOD
(—S FOR WATTLING) FRITLES
(—S MADE INTO BROOM) BESOM
(BARE —) COW
(DRIED —) CHAD
(LITTLE —) SURCLE
(THATCHING —) SCOLLOP
(WILLOW —) SALLOW ANAPHYTE
TWIGGED VIRGATE
TWIGGY SPRAYEY
TWILIGHT DIMPS DUMPS GLOAM
TWALE DIMMET DIMMIT UGHTEN
DUCKISH COCKSHUT EVENGLOW
GLOAMING GRISPING CREPUSCLE
(— OF THE GODS) RAGNAROK
(DARKER PART OF —) DUSK
(MORNING —) DAWN
TWILL WALE CHINO CADDIS RUSSEL
CADDICE DUNGAREE
TWILLED CORDED
TWIN DUAL GEMEL SOSIE DIDYMUS
JUMELLE SIAMESE TWINDLE
DIDYMATE DIDYMOID DIDYMOUS
PARASITE TWINLING
(PL.) GEMEL COUPLET
TWINE MAT COIL DUNE LACE PIRL
WIND WRAP TWIRL TWIST INFOLD
INTORT ANAMITE ENTWINE
SKEENYIE
(HANK OF —) RAN
(PITCHED —) WHIPPING
TWINEBUSH PINBUSH
TWINFLOWER LINNAEA
TWINGE GIRD PANG PULL SHOOT
TOUCH TWANG STOUND
(— OF CONSCIENCE) SCRUPLE
(— OF PAIN) GLISK
TWINKLE WINK BLINK TWEER TWINK
TWIRE SIMPER WINKLE SPARKLE
TWINKLING MOMENT TWINKLY
TWINLEAF HELMETPOD
TWIRL SPIN TIRL DRILL QUERL TRILL
TWIRK TWIST WHIRL TRUNDLE
TWIDDLE TWIZZLE
(— OF BAGPIPE) WARBLER
TWIST BOB CUE MAT PLY WIN WIP
CAST COIL CURL DRAW HURL KICK
KINK PIRL RICK SKEW SLEW SLUB
SLUE TURN WARP WIND WISP WORK
CHINK CRANK CRICK CRINK CROOK
CURVE FEEZE GNARL KINCH PLAIT
QUIRK QUIRL REEVE SCREW SKELL
SNAKE SNIRL SNURL SPIRE SWIRL
THROW TWEAK TWIND TWINE TWIRE
TWIRL WINCE WITHE WREST
BOUGHT DETORT EXTORT HANKLE
INTORT QUEEVE SLOUGH SPRAIN
SQUIRL SQUIRM STRAND TWEEZE
WAMBLE WARPLE WASHIN WICKER
WIMBLE WRABBE WRITHE CHIGNON
CONTORT CRANKLE CROOKLE

CRUMPLE DISTORT ENTWINE
ENTWIST FLOUNCE GIMMICK
SQUINCH TORTURE TWISTER
TWISTLE TWIZZLE WREATHE
WRIGGLE CLINAMEN CONVOLVE
ENTANGLE FOREHARD FORETURN
SPRINKLE SQUIGGLE VOLUTION
(— A ROPE) DALLY
(— AWAY) WAIVE
(— BACK) RETORT
(— FORCIBLY) WRING
(— IN A ROPE) GRIND SQUIRM
(— IN GRAIN OF A BOW) BOUGHT
(— IN ONE'S NATURE) KINK
(— OF FACE) STITCH
(— OF HAY) HAYBRAND
(— OF PAPER) SPILL
(— OF PEN IN WRITING) QUIRK
(— OF SPEECH) CRANK
(— OF THE MOUTH) DRAD
(— OF TOBACCO) ROLL
(— OF YARNS) FORETURN
(— OUT OF SHAPE) CONTORT
(— SHARPLY) FEAK
(— TOGETHER) CABLE RADDLE
TWISTED CAM KAM WRY AWRY
TORT KINKY SCREW TORSE WRONG
ATWIST GAUCHE HURLED KNOTTY
SCREWY SKEWED SWIRLY THROWN
TURKEN TWISTY WARPED WRITHE
CRISPED CROOKED GNARLED
KNOTTED SCREWED TORQUED
TORTILE TORTIVE WHELKED
WREATHY COCKEYED IMPLICIT
INTORTED INVOLVED NONPLANE
THRAWART WREATHEN
TWISTING DALLY KNECK AJOINT
TWIRLY TWIDDLY SQUIGGLY
STREPSIS
TWIT TIT CHECK TAUNT ETWITE
TWITTER RIDICULE
TWITCH TIC TIT FEAK FIRK JERK
JUMP PIRN TWIG WINK YANK PLUCK
START THRIP TWEAK TWICK TWIRK
QUATCH QUETCH QUITCH TWINGE
TWITCHEL
TWITCHING TIC JERKS PALMUS
WORKING SACCADIC
TWITTER TWIT CHIRM GARRE TWINK
JARGON WARBLE CHIPPER CHITTER
QUITTER TWITTLE WHITTER
TWO TWA BOTH TWAY TWIN TWAIN
BINARY COUPLE DOUBLE
(— LINES) LONGWAYS
(— OF A KIND) BRACE
(IN —) ATWO
(US —) UNC
TWO-COLORED BICHROME
TWO-FACED JANUS JANIFORM
TWO-FIFTEEN PM TIME
TWOFOLD DUAL DUPLE BACKED
BIFOLD DOUBLE DUPLEX DIGONAL
DIPLOID TWIFOLD DIDYMATE
DIDYMOID DIDYMOUS DIPLASIC
TWEYFOLD
TWO-FOOTED BIPED
TWO-FORKED BIFURCAL
TWO-HANDED BIMANAL BIMANOUS
TWO-HORNED BICORN BICORNED

TWOPENCE TUPPENCE
TWOS POT DEUCE
TWO-UP SWY
TYCOON SHOGUN TAIKUN
TYDEUS (FATHER OF —) OENEUS
(MOTHER OF —) PERIBOEA
(SON OF —) DIOMEDES
TYMPANUM DRUM TYMPAN
EARDRUM EPIPHRAGM
TYNDAREUS (FATHER OF —)
OEBALUS
(WIFE OF —) LEDA
TYPE CUT ILK CAST KIND MAKE
MOLD NORM SORT TAKE BOGUS
IMAGE MOULD STAMP EMBLEM
KICKER LETTER NATURE SHADOW
STRIPE SYMBOL TAKING TIMBER
BATARDE FASHION PARABLE
ANTETYPE EXEMPLAR
(— BLOCK) QUAD
(— OF EXCELLENCE) PARAGON
(— PLACED BOTTOM UP) TURN
(— SET UP) MATTER
(ASSORTMENT OF —) FONT
(DANCE —) LASYA
(DISARRANGED —) PI PIE
(GERMAN —) FRAKTUR
(HEAVY-FACED —) IONIC
(HIGHEST —) PINK
(IDEAL —) CHRIST
(OPPOSITE —) ANTITYPE
(PHYSICAL —) HABIT
(RACIAL —) DEHWAR
(REPRESENTATIVE —) GENIUS
(SET —) STICK
(STYLE OF —) DORIC ELITE GOUDY
GREEK IONIC KABEL ROMAN
BODONI CASLON GOTHIC HEBREW
ITALIC JENSON MODERN BOOKMAN
CENTURY ELZEVIR EMERALD
FULLFACE GARAMOND
TYPEBAR(PL.) BASKET
TYPEFACE FACE BOLDFACE
SANSERIF
TYPEHOLDER PALLET
TYPESETTER MONO
TYPESETTING FAT PHAT
TYPEWRITER MILL TYPER TYPIST
PORTABLE
TYPHON (FATHER OF —) TARTARUS
(MOTHER OF —) TERRA
TYPHOON WIND CYCLONE TUFFOON
TYPICAL FAIR TYPAL TYPIC USUAL
AVERAGE CLASSIC PATTERN
PERFECT REGULAR
TYPIFY TYPE IMAGE SHADOW
EPITOMIZE REPRESENT SYMBOLIZE
TYPIFYING GENERIC
TYR ER EAR TIU TYRR
TYRANNICAL LORDLY SLAVISH
ABSOLUTE DESPOTIC
TYRANNIZE DOMINEER OVERLORD
TYRANNOUS ABSOLUTE
TYRANNY ROD DESPOTISM
TYRANT ANARCH DESPOT NIMROD
FUEHRER PHARAOH PHALARIS
TYRANT FLYCATCHER PEWEE
TYRO HAM COLT PUPIL NOVICE

RABBIT TYRONE BEGINNER
NEOPHYTE
(FATHER OF —) SALMONEUS

(HUSBAND OF —) CRETHEUS
(MOTHER OF —) ALCIDICE
(SON OF —) AESON NELEUS PELIAS

PHERES AMYTHAON
TYRRHENIAN ETRUSCAN
TYTO ALUCO STRIX

U UNCLE UNION
UDDER BAG DUG TID EWER ELDER
SUMEN VESSEL

UGANDA
CAPITAL: KAMPALA
COLLEGE: MAKERERE
FORMER CAPITAL: ENTEBBE
LAKE: KYOGA ALBERT EDWARD
GEORGE VICTORIA
LANGUAGE: ATESO GANDA
LUGANDA SWAHILI
MOUNTAIN: ELGON
NATIVE: ATESO BANTU LANGO
ACHOLI ANKOLE BAGISU BAKIGA
BASOGA BATORO BAGANDA
BUNYORO LUGBARA NILOTIC
SUDANIC
PLATEAU: ANKOLE
PROVINCE: BUGANDA
RIVER: ASWA KAFU PAGER
KATONGA
SEAPORT: MOMBASA
TOWN: JINJA MBALE ENTEBBE
MOMBASA

UGLY FOUL AWFUL OUGLE SNIVY
UNKED CRANKY DREEPY GORGON
HOMELY LAIDLY CRABBED GRIZZLY
HIDEOUS HOUGHLY VICIOUS
GRUESOME UGLISOME UNLOVELY
UGLY-TEMPERED SNARLISH
UGNI BLANC TREBBIANO
UIGHUR JAGATAI
UITOTAN KAIMO WITOTAN
UKE JARANA
UKULELE UKE TAROPATCH
ULCER FRET KYLE SORE WOLF
BOTCH ULCUS MORMAL TETTER
CHANCRE EGILOPS ENCAUMA
AEGILOPS FONTANEL FOSSETTE
ULCUSCLE
(ARTIFICIAL —) ISSUE
ULCERATING EXEDENT
ULCERATION CARIES BEDSORE
HELCOSIS
ULEX LING
ULEXITE TIZA
ULNA CUBIT CUBITAL CUBITUS
ULTIMATE IT DIRE LAST FINAL
ULTIME SUPREME ABSOLUTE
EVENTUAL FARTHEST ULTIMITY
ULTIMATELY FINALLY
ULTIMO PAST
ULTRA EXTREME FANATIC FORWARD
ULTRACONSERVATISM TORYISM
ULTRACONSERVATIVE WHITE
ULTRAFASHIONABLE RITZY SWELL
SWAGGER
ULTRAMONTANISM CURIALISM
ULUA PAPIO PAPIOPIO
ULYSSES (FATHER OF —) LAERTES
(MOTHER OF —) ANTICLEA
(SLAYER OF —) TELEGONUS
(SON OF —) TELEMACHUS
(WIFE OF —) PENELOPE
UMBEL RAY RADIUS SERTULE
UMBELLA SERTULUM UMBELLET

UMBELLIFERONE CUMARIN
COUMARIN
UMBER OMER OMBER PARTRIDGE
UMBILICUS NAVEL
UMBO BEAK UMBONULE
UMBONES NATES
UMBRA DOGFISH MUDFISH NUCLEUS
UMBRINE
UMBRAGE PIQUE SNUFF OFFENSE
UMBRELLA BELL GAMP MUSH
BROLLY CHATTA PAYONG PILEUS
CHATTAH GINGHAM ROUNDEL
FITTISOL KITTYSOL MUSHROOM
TYRASOLE
UMBRELLA BIRD COTINGA
COTINGID
UMBRELLA BUSH MILJEE
UMBRELLA PALM KENTIA
UMBRELLA PLANT SEDGE GLUMAL
UMBRELLA TREE WAHOO
ELKWOOD MAGNOLIA
UMBRETTE UMBRE HOMBRE
UMBRET CICONIID
UMBRIAN IGUVINE
UMBURANA ROBLE
UMLAUT MUTATION METAPHONY
UMPIRE UMP JUDGE TRIER ARBITER
DAYSMAN ODDSMAN STICKLER
UNABASHED BROWLESS
UNABBREVIATED FULL
UNABLE UNHABILE
UNACCENTED GRAVE LIGHT ATONIC
UNACCEPTABLE DREADFUL
UNACCOMPANIED BARE SOLO
ALONE SINGLE
UNACCOUNTABLE STRANGE
UNACCUSTOMED UNUSED
STRANGE INSOLITE WONTLESS
UNACQUAINTED STRANGE
UNCOUTH
UNADORNED DRY BALD STARK
RUSTIC SIMPLE AUSTERE INORNATE
UNADULTERATED NET FRANK
HONEST VIRGIN GENUINE SINCERE
UNADVANTAGEOUSLY ILL
UNAFFECTED EASY REAL PLAIN
HOMELY NATIVE RUSTIC SIMPLE
ARTLESS BUCOLIC SINCERE
SEMPLICE
UNAFRAID BOLD BRAVE DEFIANT
UNAGGRESSIVE AMIABLE
UNALERT SUPINE
UNALLOYED DEEP SOLID VIRGIN
GENUINE
UNALTERABLE IMMUTABLE
UNAMBIGUOUS EXPLICIT
UNANIMATED FLAT VAPID INSIPID
UNANIMITY ATTACK CONSENT
UNANIMOUS SOLID WHOLE
UNANIME UNIVOCAL
UNAPPROACHABLE STATELY
UNARMED BARE INERM UNBARBED
UNASSAILABLE SECURE
UNASSUMED NATURAL
UNASSUMING SHY HUMBLE MODEST
SIMPLE NATURAL RETIRING
UNATTACHED FREE LOOSE SINGLE
UNATTENDED SINGLE
UNATTRACTIVE BLAH UGLY WORSE

HOMELY FRUMPISH UNLIKELY
UNAVAILING VAIN FUTILE GAINLESS
UNAVOIDABLE SHUNLESS
UNAVOWED SECRET
UNAWARE UNWARE WITLESS
HEEDLESS INNOCENT UNBEWARE
WARELESS
UNAWARES ABACK SHORT
UNBALANCED HITE DOTTY NUTTY
FRUITY UNEVEN FANATIC
DERANGED LOPSIDED
UNBAR UNSLOT
UNBARRED UNSTOKEN
UNBECOMING RUDE INEPT INDIGN
UNMEET BENEATH IMPROPER
INDECENT UNSEEMLY UNWORTHY
UNBELIEF UNFAITH
UNBELIEVABLE HOT THIN
UNBELIEVER PAGAN GIAOUR
ATHEIST DOUBTER INFIDEL
SCOFFER SKEPTIC
UNBEND REST THAW FRESE RELAX
UNTIE EXTEND DISBEND UNCROOK
UNBENDING RIGID STARK STERN
STIFF THARF OBDURATE RAMRODDY
RESOLUTE
UNBIASED FAIR JUST DETACHED
UNBIND FREE UNDO UNTIE UNGIRD
UNDRESS
UNBLAMABLE INNOCENT
UNBLEACHED BLAE BLAY ECRU
BEIGE BROWN
UNBLEMISHED FAIR PURE SOUND
ENTIRE SPOTLESS
UNBLOCK REDD
UNBLOODY INCRUENT
UNBOLT OPEN UNBAR UNPIN
UNBOSOM OPEN
UNBOUGHT UNCOFT
UNBOUND FREE LOOSE
UNBOUNDED HUGE
UNBRANDED SLICK NATIVE
UNBROKEN DEAD FLAT FERAL
FLUSH SOLID SINGLE CERRERO
UNRACED STRAIGHT UNBACKED
WAKELESS
UNBUILD DESTROY
UNBUILT UNBIGGED
UNBURDEN EMPTY UNLOAD UNSHIP
UNBURNISHED WHITE MATTED
UNCANNY EERY UNCO EERIE SCARY
UNCOW UNKID WEIRD WISHT
CREEPY SPOOKY UNCOUTH
ELDRITCH POKERISH
UNCASTRATED INTACT
UNCAUGHT UNHENT
UNCEASING ENDLESS ETERNAL
EASELESS MINUTELY
UNCEREMONIOUS CURT BLUFF
BLUNT SHORT ABRUPT FAMILIAR
INFORMAL
UNCERTAIN WAW DARK HAZY WILD
FLUKY SHADY SHAKY WAUGH
CASUAL CLOUDY CRANKY FITFUL
FLUKEY GLEAMY QUEASY CASALTY
CHANCEY COMICAL DUBIOUS
TRICKSY VARIOUS WILSOME
CATCHING DELICATE FLICKERY
FUGITIVE HOVERING INSECURE

SLIPPERY TECHNOUS TICKLISH
UNCERTAINTY MIST WERE DEMUR
DOUBT MAYBE BAFFLE BALANCE
DUBIETY CASUALTY SUSPENSE
UNSURETY
UNCHALLENGED ACCEPTED
UNCHANGEABLE FAST STABLE
DURABLE ETERNAL
UNCHANGING STATIC ETERNAL
UNIFORM STATICAL
UNCHASTE LEWD FRAIL LIGHT
IMPURE WANTON FORLAIN
HAGGARD SCARLET IMMODEST
UNCHASTITY BAWDRY STUPRUM
ADULTERY
UNCHECKED LIBERAL RAMPANT
UNCIFORM HAMATUM
UNCINARIA NECATOR
UNCIVIL RUDE BLUFF ROUGH RUSTY
CRUSTY RUGGED UNFEEL IMPOLITE
UNCIVILIZED RUDE WILD MYALL
INCULT SAVAGE UNCIVIL IGNORANT
SYLVATIC
UNCLAD LOOSE UNDRESSED
UNCLE EME OOM YEME BUNKS
NUNKY NUNCLE
UNCLEAN FOUL TREF VILE BLACK
TARRY TERFA TREFA COMMON
FILTHY IMMUND IMPURE DEFILED
UNCLEANNESS DIRT FOULNESS
UNCLEAR DIM HAZY SHAGGY
UNCLEARLY DIMLY
UNCLENCH UNDOUBLE
UNCLOSE OPE OPEN UNHASP
DISCLOSE
UNCLOTHE TIRL SPOIL UNRIG
DEVEST DESPOIL
UNCLOUDED CLEAR
UNCOIL UNLINK
UNCOLORED FAIR
UNCOMBED UNKAMED UNTEWED
UNCOMBINED FREE FRANK
UNCOMELY INDECENT
UNCOMFORTABLE HOT EVIL POOR
HARSH UNKET UNKID QUEASY
STICKY UNFELE
UNCOMMON MUCH NICE RARE SELD
UNCO BYOUS FORBY UNCOW
VAUDY DAINTY FORBYE SCARCE
SPECIAL STRANGE UNUSUAL
SINGULAR UNWONTED
UNCOMMONLY UNCO BYOUS EXTRA
UNCOW UNCOLY
UNCOMMONNESS SCARCITY
UNCOMMUNICATIVE DUMB SILENT
PRIVATE RESERVED
UNCOMPLICATED RURAL HONEST
SIMPLE
UNCOMPOUNDED SIMPLE SIMPLEX
UNCOMPROMISING ACID FIRM
GRIM RIGID STERN STOUT ULTRA
SEVERE STRICT STRONG EXTREME
UNCONCEALED BARE OPEN
OUVERT APPARENT
UNCONCERN APATHY EASINESS
UNCONCERNED COOL EASY BLAND
CASUAL CARELESS
UNCONCERNEDLY LIGHTLY
UNCONDITIONAL FREE FRANK

UTTER SIMPLE ABSOLUTE EXPLICIT
TERMLESS
UNCONFINED LAX FREE LOOSE
UNCONGENIAL HATEFUL INGRATE
KINDLESS
UNCONNECTED GAPPY DETACHED
UNCONQUERED INVICT INVICTED
UNCONSCIOUS OUT COLD BRUTE
ASLEEP BLOTTO CUCKOO TORPID
UNAWARE COMATOSE IGNORANT
UNCONSTRAINED FREE UNNET
SIMPLE FAMILIAR
UNCONTROLLABLE WILD
UNCONTROLLED FREE LIBERAL
UNBITTED
UNCONVENTIONAL LOOSE CASUAL
DEVIOUS BOHEMIAN INFORMAL
UNCONVINCING FALSE FISHY
UNCOOKED RAW
UNCOUNTABLE SUMLESS
UNCOUPLE CUT DISLINK
UNCOUTH RUDE CRUDE DORIC
GURLY UNKED UNKIT GOTHIC
JUNGLY QUAINT RENISH AWKWARD
BOORISH CUBBISH HIRSUTE
LOUTISH UNGAINLY YOKELISH
(— **PERSON**) TUG
UNCOVER BARE DOFF HUNT ROUT
TIRL TIRR BREAK STRIP TIRVE
UNLAP UNLID UNWRY DETECT
EXHUME SEARCH UNBARE UNCASE
UNHALE UNVEIL UNDRAPE UNEARTH
DISCLOSE DISCOVER UNMANTLE
UNMUFFLE
UNCOVERED BARE OVERT
UNCTION CHRISM OINTMENT
UNCTUOUS FAT OILY SALVY SLEEK
SOAPY SUAVE GREASY COURTLY
PINGUID
UNCULTIVATED RAW BRUT FERAL
DESERT FALLOW INCULT SAVAGE
SLOVEN WILDERN
UNCULTURED RUDE INCULT
ARTLESS
UNCUT RASPED
UNDAMAGED WHOLE
UNDARKENED CLEAR
UNDAUNTED BOLD BRAVE MANLY
SPARTAN FEARLESS INTREPID
UNDE WAVY UNDEE
UNDECAYED GREEN
UNDECEIVE DISABUSE
UNDECIDED MOOT DUBIOUS
PENDING DOUBTFUL WAVERING
UNDECIDEDLY HUMDRUM
UNDECLARED SECRET
UNDEFENDED UNKEPT
UNDEFILED PURE CHASTE INTACT
VIRGIN
UNDEFINED OBSCURE
UNDELIVERABLE DEAD
UNDEMONSTRATIVE COLD ASEPTIC
LACONIC RESERVED
UNDENIABLE BRUTAL
UNDENIABLY INDEED
UNDEPENDABLE CASUAL FLUFFY
UNDER SUB BAJO BELOW INFRA
NEATH SOTTO ANEATH ANUNDER
BENEATH

(— **ORDERS**) SUPPOSED
(— **THE WORD**) IV
(— **THE YEAR**) SA
(— **THIS TITLE**) HT
(— **THIS WORD**) SV SHV
(— **WAY**) AFOOT
UNDERBODICE JUMP BASQUINE
UNDERBRUSH FILTH COVERT
GARSIL MAQUIS RAMMEL ABATURE
UNDERBURNED SOFT
UNDERBUTLER WASHPOT
UNDERCARRIAGE BOGY BOGEY
BOGIE
UNDERCLAY WARRANT
UNDERCLOTHES LININGS
UNDERCOAT PILE ALPACA
SURFACER
UNDERCOVER SECRET
UNDERCRUST ABAISSE
UNDERCURRENT UNDERLAY
UNDERRUN UNDERSET
UNDERCUT JAD HOLE LAME POOL
SUMP KIRVE NOTCH
UNDERDONE RARE
UNDERDRAWERS FLANNELS
UNDERESTIMATE DISPRIZE
MINIMIZE
UNDERFRAME SOLE
UNDERGARMENT BAND SLIP
CYMAR SIMAR SKIRT SMOCK TUNIC
WAIST BODICE CAMISE CILICE
CORSET GIRDLE STAMIN CHEMISE
DOUBLET DRAWERS STAMMEL
TALLITH KNICKERS
(PL.) SMALLS FLANNELS FLIMSIES
SNUGGIES
UNDERGO SERVE ENDURE SUFFER
SUSTAIN
UNDERGRADUATE MAN TASSEL
SERVITOR
UNDERGROWTH RUSH RAMMEL
SPRING BUSHWOOD
UNDERHAND SLY DERN SHADY
BYHAND SECRET OBLIQUE
INVOLVED SINISTER SNEAKING
UNDERHANDED DERN FUNNY
FILTHY SECRET SINISTER
UNDERIVED ORIGINAL
UNDERLAYER SLASHING
UNDERLIE SUBTEND
UNDERLING MENIAL SEQUEL
UNDERER INFERIOR
UNDERLYING COVERT IMPLICIT
UNDERMINE SAP CAVE HOLE POOL
ERODE KNIFE WEAKEN FOUNDER
SUBVERT ENFEEBLE SUPPLANT
UNDERMINED ROTTEN
UNDERNEATH BELOW BENEATH
UNNEATH
UNDERNSONG TIERCE
UNDERPANTS BRIEFS BLOOMERS
KNICKERS
UNDERPART BELLY
UNDERPASS DIVE SUBWAY
UNDERRATE DECRY DISCOUNT
UNDERRUN BOTTOM
UNDERSACRISTAN CUSTOS
UNDERSHIRT VEST SHIFT SHIRT
CAMISA JERSEY LINDER SEMMIT

SINGLET WRAPPER
UNDERSHRUB HEATH PINKEYE
SEEPWEED SUBSHRUB
UNDERSIDE BOTTOM BREAST
(— OF CLOUD) BASE
(— OF FINGER) BALL
(— OF FLOOR) CEILING
UNDERSIZED DEENY SCRUB STUNT
UNDERSKIRT QUILT CRINOLINE
UNDERSTAND CAN CON GET KEN
SEE GAUM HAVE MAKE TAKE TWIG
BRAIN ENTER GRASP REACH SAVVY
SEIZE, SENSE SKILL SPELL ACCEPT
COTTON FIGURE FOLLOW INTAKE
INTEND SUBAUD UPTAKE CONCEIT
DISCERN COMPRISE CONCEIVE
CONSTRUE CONTRIVE FORSTAND
PERCEIVE PERSTAND UNDERNIM
UNDERSTANDING KEN WIT GAUM
HEAD CLASP HEART INWIT SENSE
SKILL ACCORD INTENT NOTION
REASON TREATY UPTAKE COMPACT
CONCEPT ENTENTE INSIGHT
MEANING WITNESS DAYLIGHT
(IMPERFECT —) DARKNESS
UNDERSTATEMENT LITOTES
UNDERSTOOD LUCID SUPPOSED
(— ONLY BY SPECIALLY INITIATED)
ESOTERIC
(EASILY —) EASY CLEAR EXTANT
(NOT —) DARKSOME
UNDERSTUDY DOUBLE
UNDERSURFACE SOLE
UNDERTAKE GO TRY DARE FANG
FOND GRANT OFFER ASSUME
INCEPT PLEDGE ATTEMPT EMBRACE
EMPRISE PRETEND UNDERFO
CONTRACT PRESTATE
(— RESPONSIBILITY) ACCEPT
ANSWER
UNDERTAKER UPHOLDER
UNDERTAKING JOB AVAL TASK
CAUTIO EFFORT SCHEME VOYAGE
ATTEMPT CALLING PROJECT
VENTURE COVENANT
(— IN CARDS) CONTRACT
(UNPROFITABLE —) FOLLY
UNDERTEACHER USHER
UNDERTONE INKLING SUBTONE
UNDERTOW SEAPOOSE
UNDERVALUE DECRY DISPRIZE
DISVALUE
UNDERWAIST CAMISOLE
UNDERWATER (— DEVICE) OTTER
PARAVANE
UNDERWEAR BRIEFS SHORTS
SKIVVY UNDIES DESSOUS HEAVIES
LINGERIE PRETTIES
UNDERWING CATOCALA
UNDERWOOD FRITH BOSCAGE
COPPICE
UNDERWORLD DUAT DEWAT HADES
ORCUS SHEOL MICTLAN XIBALBA
GANGLAND
UNDERWRITE SIGN INSURE
ENDORSE
UNDERWRITER INSURER
UNDESERVED INDIGN
UNDETERMINED UNSET DUBIOUS

AORISTIC DOUBTFUL INFINITE
UNDEVELOPED CRUDE SLOVEN
GERMING IMMATURE JUVENILE
UNDEVIATINGLY SMACK
UNDIFFERENCED ENTIRE
UNDIFFERENTIATED GLOBAL
AMERISTIC
UNDIGESTED CRUDE
UNDIGNIFIED DOGGREL DOGGEREL
UNDILUTED MERE NEAT PURE
NAKED SHEER SHORT STRAIGHT
UNDIMINISHED ENTIRE
UNDIMMED CLEAR
UNDINE NIX
UNDISCIPLINED WANTON COLTISH
UNDISCLOSED HIDDEN SEALED
UNDISCRIMINATING GROSS
UNDISGUISED BALD PLAIN
UNDISMAYED ONFLEMED
UNDISPUTED LIQUID
UNDISTINGUISHED GROSS
COMMON UNNOBLE FAMELESS
NOTELESS
UNDISTORTED CLEAR
UNDISTURBED SOUND VIRGIN
TRANQUIL
UNDIVIDED WHOLE ENTIRE SINGLE
UNDO COOK SLIP FORDO SPEED
UNPAY DEFEAT DIDDLE FOREDO
UNBIND UNKNIT UNLOCK UNTUCK
UNWORK DEFEISE DESTROY
UNRAVEL UNRIVET UNTWIRL
UNWEAVE UNWREST DECIPHER
DISSOLVE DISTRUSS UNFASTEN
UNDOER ACHAN
UNDOGMATIC AGNOSTIC
UNDOING DEFEAT DOWNFALL
UNDOMESTICATED WILD FERAL
FERINE
UNDOUBTEDLY SURELY FRANKLY
UNDRESS MOB DOFF FLAY TIRR
STRIP UNRAY UNRIG DEVEST
DIVEST UNBUSK UNCASE UNLACE
UNRIND UNROBE UNTIRE DISCASE
UNARRAY UNREADY UNSPOIL
UNTRUSS NEGLIGEE UNATTIRE
UNDRESSED UNDIGHT
UNDUE EXTREME
UNDULATE WAVE WAVY FLOAT
SWING BILLOW GYROSE KELTER
UNDATE UNDOSE FLICKER UNDATED
UNDULATING SURGING FLEXUOUS
INDENTED
UNDULATION FOLD ROLL WAVE
CRIMP TEETER WAVING CRIMPING
UNDULATORY WAVY
UNDUTIFULNESS IMPIETY
UNDYED CORAH
UNDYING IMMORTAL
UNEARTH DIG MOOT EXPOSE
UNCOVER DISCOVER
UNEARTHLY EERY EERIE WEIRD
AWESOME UNCANNY UNGODLY
UNEASINESS ENVY GENE FIDGET
NETTLE SORROW UNEASE AILMENT
ANXIETY DISEASE MISEASE
TROUBLE DISQUIET DISTASTE
UNEASY SICKLY FIDGETY INQUIET

RESTIVE UNQUIET WORRIED
RESTLESS
UNEDUCATED SIMPLE IGNORANT
UNEMBELLISHED DRY PROSE
AUSTERE
UNEMOTIONAL DRY COLD COOL
STOIC STONY STOICAL
UNEMOTIONALLY EVENLY
UNEMPLOYED IDLE ORRA VOID
OTIANT OTIOSE VACANT IDLESET
LEISURE UNBUSIED
UNEMPLOYMENT IDLENESS
UNENCUMBERED VACANT
EXPEDITE
UNENDING ABYSMAL AGELONG
CHRONIC ENDLESS UNDYING
TERMLESS TIMELESS
UNENJOYABLE JOYLESS
UNENLIGHTENED MISTY HEATHEN
IGNORANT
UNENTHUSIASTIC COLD
UNEQUAL IMPAR DISPAR UNEGAL
UNEVEN INEQUAL INFERIOR
(— TO STRAIN) FEEBLE
UNEQUALED UNIQUE NONESUCH
UNEQUIVOCAL DIRECT SQUARE
DEFINITE DISTINCT EXPLICIT
UNERRING DEAD TRUE DEADLY
INERRANT
UNERRINGLY CLEAN
UNEVEN EROSE GOBBY HAGGY
JAGGY MEALY ROUGH HOBBLY
PLATTY RAGGED RUGGED SPOTTY
TWITTY UNFAIR UNLIKE DIURNAL
ERRATIC HOTTERY INEQUAL
STREAKY UNEQUAL HUMMOCKY
SCRATCHY SNAGGLED
(— IN COLOR) CLOUDY
UNEVENNESS BUMP WAVE FRAZE
ANOMALY ASPERITY
UNEVENTFUL STILL UNDATED
UNEXCITED LEVEL
UNEXCITING DEAD DULL TAME
BORING PROSAIC
UNEXPECTED EERY EERIE ABRUPT
SUDDEN UNWARY INOPINE
UNLOOKED
UNEXPECTEDLY UNWARES
UNAWARES
UNEXPIRED ALIVE
UNEXPLAINED HIDDEN
UNEXPOSED RAW
UNFADABLE FAST
UNFADED FRESH BRIGHT
UNFAILING SURE DEADLY INFALLID
UNERRING
UNFAIR FOUL WRONG BIASED
SHABBY UNEVEN UNJUST DEVIOUS
PARTIAL SLANTER UNEQUAL
UNSEEMLY WRONGFUL
UNFAIRLY HARDLY
UNFAIRNESS INEQUITY
UNFAITHFUL INFIDEL TRAITOR
DISLOYAL RECREANT
UNFALTERING SURE TRUE STEADY
UNERRING
UNFAMILIAR NEW FREMD HEATHER
STRANGE UNKNOWN
UNFASTEN FREE OPEN UNDO

LOOSE UNPIN UNBIND UNHASP
UNLIME UNLINK UNLOCK UNMAKE
UNTINE UNDIGHT UNHITCH UNSTECK
UNTRUSS
UNFATHOMABLE ABYSSAL
PROFOUND
UNFATHOMED COSMIC
UNFAVORABLE BAD ILL FOUL HARD
POOR SHREWD UNFAIR UNKIND
ADVERSE AWKWARD FROWARD
HOSTILE UNHAPPY BACKWARD
CONTRARY INIMICAL SINISTER
UNKINDLY
UNFAVORABLY BADLY CROSS
UNFEELING COLD DULL HARD
CRASS CRUEL HARSH ROCKY
STERN STONY BRUTAL LEADEN
MARBLE STOLID CALLOUS
OBDURATE
UNFEELINGLY HARSHLY
UNFEELINGNESS APATHY
UNFEIGNED OPEN TRUE HEARTY
CORDIAL NATURAL SINCERE
UNFETTERED FREE UNGYVED
UNFILLED BLANK EMPTY VACANT
VACUOUS
UNFINISHED RAW GRAY GREY
KACHA KUTCHA RAGGED KACHCHA
STICKIT IMMATURE
UNFIRED GREEN
UNFIRM UNFAST
UNFIT BAD SICK UNAPT WISHT
WRONG COMMON FAULTY NOUGHT
UNTIDY DISABLE UNFITTY IMPROPER
UNFITTEN UNLIKELY UNLIKING
UNFITTING UNMEETLY
UNFLEDGED SQUAB CALLOW
UNFLINCHING LEVEL STAUNCH
UNFOLD OPEN BREAK BURST SOLVE
UNLAP UNTIE DEPLOY EVOLVE
EXPAND EXPLAT FLOWER SPREAD
UNFURL UNPLAT UNROLL UNTUCK
BLOSSOM DEVELOP DISPLAY
DIVULGE EXPLAIN UNPLAIT
UNRAVEL UNWEAVE UNDOUBLE
UNPLIGHT
UNFOLDED EVOLUTE EXPANDED
UNFOLDING DISPLAY
(— OF EVENTS) ACTION
(— TO VIEW) BURST
UNFORCED EASY GLIB WILLING
UNFORESEEN SUDDEN IMPREVU
UNAWARE
UNFORMED CALLOW INFORM
UNFORTUNATE ILL EVIL POOR
DONCY WEARY SHREWD HAPLESS
UNHAPPY UNLUCKY LUCKLESS
UNTOWARD WANHAPPY
UNFREQUENTED EMPTY UNCOUTH
SOLITARY
UNFRIENDLY ILL COLD FOUL CHILL
BITTER CHILLY FIERCE FROSTY
UNSOME HOSTILE INGRATE
STRANGE INIMICAL
UNFROCK DEFROCK DEGRADE
DISFROCK UNPRIEST
UNFRUITFUL BLUNT BARREN
EFFETE WASTED STERILE USELESS
INFECUND

UNFULFILLMENT BREACH
UNFURL SPREAD UNFOLD DEVELOP
OUTROOL
UNFURNISHED BARE VACANT
UNGAINLY LANKY SPLAY WEEDY
CLUMSY UNGAIN AWKWARD
BOORISH NUNTING UNHEPPEN
UNLICKED UNWIELDY
UNGENEROUS MEAN SHABBY
STINGY GRUDGING
UNGIRDED DISCINCT
UNGODLINESS ATHEISM IMPIETY
UNGODLY SINFUL WICKED GODLESS
IMPIOUS PROFANE
UNGOVERNABLE WILD UNRULY
FROWARD IMPOTENT
UNGRACEFUL HARD CLUMSY
ANGULAR AWKWARD HALTING
UNTOWARD
UNGRACEFULLY HARSHLY
UNGRACIOUS GRUFF UNFEEL
UNFELE SNAPPISH
UNGRATEFUL UNKIND INGRATE
UNGROOMED UNDRESSED
UNGUARDED STIFF
UNGUENT CEROMA CHRISM PIMENT
POMADE POMATUM UNCTION
OINTMENT
UNGULATE HOG PIG DEER HORSE
TAPIR HOOFED AMBLYPOD
ELEPHANT
UNGUMMED BRIGHT
UNHALLOWED IMPURE UNHOLY
PROFANE
UNHAMPERED FREE DIRECT
EXPEDITE
UNHAPPINESS MISERY SORROW
ILLFARE SADNESS UNBLISS
UNHAPPY SAD DISMAL UNLUCKY
UNLUSTY WANSOME DEJECTED
DOWNBEAT DOWNGONE WOBEGONE
WRETCHED
UNHARMED SAFE UNSHENT
UNHARNESS UNGEAR OUTSHUT
UNHORSE UNTACKLE
UNHEALED GREEN
UNHEALTHY BAD MORBID QUEASY
SICKLY UNHALE NAUGHTY PECCANT
MALADIVE
UNHEATED COLD
UNHEEDED IGNORED UNTENTED
UNHEEDING DEAF CARELESS
UNHESITATING READY UNPOISED
UNHITCH OUTSPAN
UNHOLY IMPURE WICKED IMPIOUS
PROFANE
UNHORSE PURL THROW UNCOLT
DISMOUNT UNSADDLE
UNHURRIED EASY SLOW SOFT
SOBER
UNHURT SAFE HARMLESS HURTLESS
UNHARMED
UNIAT MALKITE MELCHITE
UNICORN LIN REEM KILIN LICORN
LICORNE NARWHAL HOWITZER
UNICORN FISH LIJA UNIE
UNICORN PLANT MARTINOE
UNICUM UNION

UNIDENTIFIED FACELESS
INCOGNITO
UNIFICATION SYSTEM ENSEMBLE
UNIFIED GLOBAL
UNIFIER UMBRELLA
UNIFORM KIT DEAD EVEN FLAT JUST
LIKE SELF SUIT BLUES CLOTH
KHAKI SOLID SUITY GLOBAL
GREENS LIVERY SINGLE STEADY
EQUABLE REGULAR SIMILAR
SUNTANS CONSTANT EQUIFORM
EQUIPAGE MEASURED STANDARD
UNIVOCAL
(— IN HUE) FLAT
(LEATHER —) BUFF
(NOT —) SQUALLY
(PRISONER'S —) STRIPES
UNIFORMITY ONENESS EQUALITY
EVENNESS MONOTONY SAMENESS
UNIFORMLY EVENLY EQUALLY
UNIFY MERGE UNITE CEMENT
COMPACT UNITIZE COALESCE
UNILATERAL SECUND
UNIMAGINATIVE DULL SODDEN
STUPID LIMITED LITERAL PROSAIC
UNIDEAL PEDANTIC
UNIMPAIRED FRESH SOUND ENTIRE
INTACT
(— BY) DEVOID
UNIMPASSIONED SOBER WHOLE
STEADY
UNIMPEDED FREE EXPEDITE
UNIMPORTANT VAIN PETTY CASUAL
SIMPLE TRIVIAL IMMOMENT
TRINKETY
UNINFORMED GREEN UNTOLD
IGNORANT
UNINHABITED WILD EMPTY DESERT
VACANT DESOLATE WASTEFUL
UNINHIBITED LARGE
UNINJURED INTACT SINCERE
UNINSPIRED HACK STODGY
DRYASDUST
UNINSTRUCTED IGNORANT
UNINTELLIGENT DUMB OBTUSE
STUPID ASININE FOOLISH VACUOUS
UNINTELLIGIBLE BLIND MISTY
OPAQUE MYSTICAL
UNINTENTIONAL UNMEANT
UNINTERESTING DRY ARID COLD
DRAB DREE DULL FADE FLAT
DREAR SANDY STALE BORING
DREICH JEJUNE INSIPID BROMIDIC
FRUMPISH
UNINTERMITTENT ITHAND
UNINTERRUPTED SMOOTH STEADY
ENDLESS ETERNAL STRAIGHT
UNINTERRUPTEDLY AWAY
UNIO MUSSEL
UNION ZYG BLOC DUAD ALLOY
GROUP JOINT NONOP UNITY ENOSIS
FUSION GREMIO TAWHID CONCERT
CONTACT MEETING ONENESS
SOCIETY ADHESION ALLIANCE
COHESION ESPOUSAL JOINTURE
JUNCTION JUNCTURE SODALITY
SYSTASIS TRIALISM VINCULUM
(MARITAL —) BED
(SEXUAL —) COPULA COUPLING

(TURKISH —) JETTRU
UNIONIST REFUGEE
UNIQUE ODD SOLE UNIC ALONE
UNION SINGLE SULLEN UNICUM
ALONELY SOLEYNE SPECIAL
STRANGE ISOLATED SINGULAR
UNIQUENESS SOLITUDE
UNISON FIRST HOMOPHONY
UNIT (ALSO SEE MEASURE) ONE
ATOM KLAN FLOOR HUMIT MONAD
NEPER ADDRESS DIOPTER ELEMENT
ENERGID KLAVERN
(— IN COUNTING FISH) MEASE
(— IN EARTHWORK) FLOAT FLOOR
(— OF 100 MEN) CENTURY
(— OF ABSORPTION) SABIN
(— OF ACCELERATION) GAL
(— OF ACTION) EPISODE
(— OF ANGULAR MEASURE)
CENTRAD
(— OF ARCHEOLOGICAL
CLASSIFICATION) ASPECT
(— OF BRIGHTNESS) STILB
LAMBERT
(— OF CAPACITANCE) JAR
(— OF CAPACITY) LAST ARDAB
ARDEB AMPHORA
(— OF COMIC STRIP) BOX
(— OF COUNTING) POINT
(— OF DESIGN) LARME
(— OF DISTANCE) DAY
(— OF ELASTANCE) DARAF
(— OF ELECTRIC CAPACITY) FARAD
(— OF ELECTRIC CONDUCTANCE)
MHO
(— OF ELECTRIC FORCE) VOLT
KILOVOLT STATVOLT
(— OF ELECTRIC INDUCTANCE)
HENRY
(— OF ELECTRIC INTENSITY)
AMPERE OERSTED
(— OF ELECTRIC RELUCTANCE) REL
STATOHM
(— OF ELECTRIC RESISTANCE) OHM
BEGOHM
(— OF ELECTRICITY) ES COULOMB
(— OF ENERGY) ERG JOULE
ATOMERG QUANTUM
(— OF FINENESS) CARAT KARAT
(— OF FLOW) CUSEC
(— OF FLUIDITY) RHE
(— OF FLUX DENSITY) GAUSS
(— OF FORCE) G DYNE STAPP
STHENE POUNDEL
(— OF FREQUENCY) HERTZ
FRESNEL
(— OF GOVERNMENT) DEME LAND
KREIS GEMEINDE
(— OF ILLUMINANCE) LUX
(— OF INTERSTELLAR SPACE)
PARSEC
(— OF LAND AREA) ARE SULUNG
(— OF LANGUAGE) SYLLABLE
(— OF LIGHT INTENSITY) PYR
(— OF LIGHT) LUMEN
(— OF LOUDNESS) SONE DECIBEL
(— OF MACHINERY) STAND
(— OF MAGNETIC FLUX) WEBER

(— OF MAGNETIC FORCE) KAPP
GILBERT
(— OF MAGNETIC INTENSITY)
GAMMA
(— OF MAGNIFICATION) DIAMETER
(— OF MASS) SLUG DALTON
AVOGRAM
(— OF MEMORY) BIT
(— OF METRICAL QUANTITY) MATRA
(— OF MOMENT) DEBYE
(— OF MOMENTUM) BOLE
(— OF NARCOTIC) JOLT
(— OF NYLON FINENESS) DENIER
(— OF ONE INCH) BUTTON
(— OF PAIN INTENSITY) DOL
(— OF PERMEABILITY) DARCY
(— OF PIPE) FOURBLE
(— OF POWER) WATT DYNAM
KILOWATT PONCELET
(— OF PRESSURE) BAR BARAD
BARIE BARYE GWELY CENTIBAR
(— OF PRESSWORK) TOKEN
(— OF RADIATION) LANGLEY
(— OF RADIOACTIVITY) CURIE
(— OF ROCKET) STAGE
(— OF SATURATION) SATRON
(— OF SOCIETY) CLAN HORDE
CHAPTER
(— OF SPEECH) WORD
(— OF SPEED) BAUD KNOT
(— OF THICKNESS) POINT
(— OF TIME) BEAT SVEDBERG
(— OF TRADING) CONTRACT
(— OF VELOCITY) VELO
(— OF VISCOSITY) POISE STOKE
SECONDS
(— OF WAVELENGTH) ANGSTROM
(— OF WEIGHT) SSU TON GRAM
CARAT GRAIN OUNCE POUND STEIN
ARROBA GRAMME
(— OF WIRE MEASUREMENT) MIL
(— OF WORK) ERG CROP HOUR
ERGON JOULE KILERG DINAMODE
(— OF YARN SIZE) CUT
(— OF ZO) CORGE
(ADMINISTRATIVE —) HSIEN AGENCY
BUREAU DISTRICT
(ARBITRARY —) OLFACTY
(ARCHERY —) END
(ARMY —) LEGION BRIGADE
COMPANY MAHALLA
(ARTILLERY —) BATTERY
(AVAILABLE AS —) MARRIED
(BOWLING —) ALLEY
(BOY SCOUT —) SHIP
(BUILDER'S —) SQUARE
(CIGAR-MANUFACTURING —)
BUCKEYE
(COLLECTIVE —) COMMUNE
(COMBAT —) ARMAMENT
(DISCRETE —) FRACTION
(EDUCATIONAL —) COURSE
(ELECTROMAGNETIC —) ABFARAD
ABHENRY MAXWELL ABAMPERE
(FUNDAMENTAL —) BASE
(GRAMMATICAL —) JUNCTION
(HARMONIC —) CELL
(HOUSING —) HUTMENT
(HYPOTHETICAL —) ID IDANT

(LIFE —) BIOPHORE
(LIVING —) BIONT BIOGEN
(LOGARITHMIC —) BEL
(LOGGING —) CHANCE
(MILITARY —) ARMY GOUM CORPS
GROUP LANCE SQUAD BRIGADE
PLATOON SECTION COMMANDO
DIVISION REGIMENT SQUADRON
(NAZI —) FEHME
(ORGANIZATIONAL —) CELL
ACTIVITY
(PHOTOMETRIC —) VIOLLE
(POLITICAL —) SOVIET
(RHYTHMIC —) BASIS COLON
(SELF-PERPETUATING —) BIOSOME
(SOCIAL —) SEPT GROUP KRAAL
SOCIUS
(STORAGE —) BUFFER
(TERRITORIAL —) STAKE STATE
COMMOT CANTRED CANTREF
KINGDOM
(THERMAL —) THERM CALORY
CALORIE
(TRIBAL —) TOWNSHIP
(VOTING —) CENTURY
UNITE ADD MIX ONE OOP PAN SAM
SEW UNE UNY ALLY BAND BIND
CLUB COAK FUSE HASP JOIN KNIT
KNOT LINK SAMM SEAM SOUD UNIT
BANDY CLOSE GRADE GRAFT INONE
JACOB JOINT MERGE NITCH UNIFY
WHOLE ATTACH CEMENT CONCUR
COUPLE EMBODY ENTIRE GATHER
LAUREL LEAGUE SOLDER SPLICE
STRIKE SUTURE ACCRETE AMALGAM
CLUSTER COALITE COMBINE
CONJOIN CONNECT CONSORT
JACOBUS SIAMESE ALLIGATE
ANCYLOSE ANKYLOSE ASSEMBLE
COALESCE COMPOUND CONCRETE
CONSPIRE COPULATE FEDERATE
LAMINATE COLLIGATE
(— BY INTERWEAVING) PLEACH
SPLICE
(— BY THREADS) SEW STITCH
(— CLOSELY) FAY YOT WELD
CEMENT COTTON
(— FOR INTRIGUE) CABAL
(— HOSE) COLLECT
(— IN MARRIAGE) WED SACRE
SACRI SPLICE SPOUSE
(— METALS) WELD SWEAT
UNITED ONE TIED ADDED FUSED
JOINT ALLIED CONNATE ENDLESS
UNIONED COMBINED CONCRETE
CONJOINT CONJUNCT FEDERATE
UNITING SUTURE
UNITY UNION SYSTEM ONENESS
UNITUDE IDENTITY SODALITY
SYMPATHY TOTALITY
(— OF SPIRIT AND NATURE)
ABSOLUTE
UNIVERSAL ALL LOCAL TOTAL
WHOLE WORLD COMMON GLOBAL
PUBLIC VERSAL GENERAL GENERIC
CATHOLIC ECUMENIC
(TRANSCENDENT —) IDEA
UNIVERSALITY ALLNESS OMNITUDE
UNIVERSE ALL LOKA MASS OLAM

WORLD COSMOS SYSTEM
CREATURE EXEMPLAR
(SIDEREAL —) SPACE
UNIVERSITY STUDY CAMPUS
SCHOOL ACADEMY COLLEGE
MADRASA STUDIUM VARSITY
MADRASAH
UNJUST HARD UNFAIR WICKED
UNEQUAL UNRICHT UNRIGHT
WRONGFUL
UNJUSTIFIED INVALID
UNJUSTLY UNDULY FALSELY
UNKEELED RATITE
UNKEMPT FROWZY RUGGED
SHAGGY INCOMPT RAFFISH
RUFFLED SHAGRAG TOUSLED
DRAGGLED SCRAGGLY SLIPSHOD
STRUBBLY UNCOMBED
UNKIND BAD ILL MEAN VILE CRUEL
HARSH STERN SEVERE UNMEEK
UNKINDNESS DISFAVOR
UNKNOWABLE SEALED
UNKNOWN IGN UNCO UNKET UNKID
IGNOTE MUNKAR SEALED SECRET
UNWARE UNWIST FARAWAY
OBSCURE UNCOUTH UNHEARD
IGNORANT UNAWARES UNKENNED
UNWITTING
UNLADEN LEAR LEER
UNLATCH UNSNECK
UNLAWFUL ILLEGAL ILLICIT
NONLICET UNLEEFUL UNLEISUM
UNLEARNED LEWD GROSS
BOOKLESS IGNORANT UNLEARED
UNLESS BUT NIF LESS NISI SAVE
BINNA NOBUT LESSEN ONLESS
WITHOUT
(— BEFORE) NIPR NIPRI
(— OTHERWISE NOTED) NAN
UNLETTERED LEWD BORREL
IGNORANT
UNLIGHTED BLIND LAMPLESS
UNLIKE DIFFORM DISLIKE DIVERSE
(MOST —) OTHEREST
UNLIKELY DUBIOUS
(MOST —) LAST
UNLIMITED VAST SOVRAN
UNTERMED
(— IN POWER) ALMIGHTY
UNLINED SINGLE
UNLOAD TIP DROP DUMP HOVEL
DECANT STRIKE UNLADE UNSHIP
UNSTOW DELIVER DEPLETE
DETRUCK DISLOAD UNTRUSS
DISCHARGE
UNLOCK UNMAKE RESERATE
UNLOUKEN
UNLOOSE OUTWIND UNRIVET
UNLUCKY FAY ILL EVIL FOUL DONSY
DISMAL DONSIE HOODOO HAPLESS
INFAUST UNHAPPY UNCHANCY
UNTOWARD
(— THING) AMBSACE
UNMAN UNDO CRUSH UNNERVE
UNMANAGEABLE ROID DONSY
RANDY RESTIVE CHURLISH
STAFFISH
UNMANLY SOFT MANLESS UNLUSTY
UNMANNERLY RUDE BOORISH

UNCIVIL IMPOLITE UNGENTLE
UNMARKED MAVERICK NOTELESS
UNMARRIED ONE LONE SOLE OLEPI
YOUNG ONLEPY SINGLE
UNMASK EXPOSE UNFACE DISMASK
UNCLOAK
UNMASKING EXPOSURE
UNMEASURED UNMEET MODELESS
UNMELODIOUS SCRANNEL
UNMERCHANTABLE SALABLE
SALEABLE
UNMERCIFUL CRUEL PITILESS
RUTHLESS
UNMETHODICAL CURSORY
UNMINDFUL SLOWFUL CARELESS
HEEDLESS MINDLESS
UNMISTAKABLE FLAT OPEN BROAD
CLEAR FRANK PLAIN PATENT
EXPRESS APPARENT DECISIVE
MANIFEST UNIVOCAL
UNMISTAKABLY SIGNALLY
UNMITIGATED GROSS ARRANT
DAMNED SOVRAN PERFECT
PUREDEE REGULAR ABSOLUTE
UNMIX EXSOLVE
UNMIXED DEEP MERE PURE SELF
SOLE BLANK SHEER UTTER IMMIXT
SIMPLE STRAIGHT
UNMODIFIED BRUTE STRAIGHT
UNMOLESTED SACKLESS
UNMOVED CALM COOL FIRM STONY
TIGHT IMMOTE SERENE ADAMANT
IMMOVED
UNMOVING INERT IMMOBILE
IMMOTIVE
UNMUSICAL NOTELESS SCABROUS
UNNATURAL EERY EERIE CLAMMY
CREEPY UNKIND STRANGE
UNCANNY VIOLENT ABNORMAL
FARCICAL KINDLESS UNKINDLY
UNNECESSARY USELESS NEEDLESS
UNNEEDED WASTE
UNNERVE UNMAN UNMAKE WEAKEN
ENERVATE PARALYZE
UNNERVED SHOOK
UNNOTICED SILENT
UNOBJECTIONABLE VENIAL
UNOBSERVANT HEEDLESS
UNOBSTRUCTED FAIR FREE OPEN
APPARENT
UNOBTRUSIVE SHY MODEST
SEDATE DISCREET RETIRING
UNOCCUPIED IDLE VOID BLANK
EMPTY WASTE VACANT LEISURE
UNSEATED WASTEFUL
UNORGANIZED ACOSMIC INCHOATE
UNORTHODOX HERETIC
UNOSTENTATIOUS SHY QUIET
LENTEN MODEST
UNPACK UNFARDLE
UNPAID DUE UNQUIT UNWAGED
HONORARY WAGELESS
UNPAIRED IMPAR
UNPALATABLE SOD HARD BITTER
BRACKISH
UNPARALLELED ALONE UNIQUE
EPOCHAL PEERLESS SINGULAR
UNPEERED
UNPERTURBED BLAND STILL

UNPLEASANT BAD ACID EVIL HARD
NICE SOUR UGLY AWFUL CRUDE
GRIMY GUMMY HAIRY HARSH
MUCKY ROUGH BRUTAL CRIMPY
RANCID STICKY THRAWN UNFELE
UNGAIN UNLIEF BEASTLY BILIOUS
GHASTLY INGRATE SPINOUS
UNLUSTY UNQUEME UNSONCY
CHISELLY DREADFUL HORRIBLE
INDECENT SCABROUS UNLOVELY
UNPLEASANTLY QUEER HARDLY
UNWINLY
UNPLEASANTNESS ILLNESS
UNPLOWED LEA
UNPOETICAL MUSELESS
UNPOLISHED ILL RUDE BLIND
CRUDE ROUGH COARSE INCULT
RUGGED RUSTIC SAVAGE SHAGGY
UPLAND INCOMPT UNKEMPT
AGRESTIC
UNPOPULARITY ENVY
UNPRACTICED RAW FRESH
UNTRADED
UNPREDICTABLE CHANCY CRANKY
ERRATIC
UNPREJUDICED FAIR
UNPREMEDITATED CASUAL
UNPREPARED TARDY
UNPREPOSSESSING SEEDY
UNPRETENDING LOWLY HOMELY
HUMBLE
UNPRETENTIOUS HOMY HOMEY
PLAIN SOBER COMMON HOMELY
HUMBLE MODEST SIMPLE DISCREET
HOMESPUN
UNPRINCIPLED LIMMER
UNPRODUCTIVE DRY SHY ARID
DEAD DEAF LEAN ADDLE DUSTY
WASTE BARREN GEASON SAPLESS
STERILE WOODSERE
UNPRODUCTIVENESS BORASCO
BORASQUE BORRASCA
UNPROFESSIONAL LAY LAICAL
UNPROFITABLE BAD DRY DEAD
SECK BARREN BOOTLESS GAINLESS
UNGAINLY
UNPROGRESSIVE SLOW DORMANT
BACKWARD
UNPROMISING BLUE DUBIOUS
UNPRONOUNCED MUTE
UNPROPITIOUS ILL EVIL FOUL
THRAW MALIGN SULLEN ADVERSE
AVERTED INFAUST OMINOUS
THRAWART
UNPROTECTED NAKED EXPOSED
HELPLESS
UNPUBLISHED INED INEDITED
UNQUALIFIED NET BARE FULL MERE
PURE BLACK PLUMP SHEER UNFIT
DIRECT ENTIRE UNABLE CLOTTED
PLENARY IMPLICIT INHABILE
UNQUESTIONABLE ASSURED
CERTAIN DECIDED ABSOLUTE
DECISIVE DISTINCT
UNQUESTIONED CLEAR
UNQUESTIONING IMPLICIT
UNRAVEL REDD UNDO BREAK
ENODE FEAZE RAVEL SOLVE TIFFLE

UNFOLD UNKNIT UNLACE ENODATE
RESOLVE
UNREAL GOTHIC CHEMICK FANCIED
SHADOWY AERIFORM CHIMERIC
FARCICAL ILLUSORY NOTIONAL
SCENICAL VISIONAL
UNREALISTIC CHIMERIC
UNREALIZED BEHIND
UNREASONABLE ABSURD FANATIC
ABSONANT
UNREASONABLENESS ALOGY
INSANITY
UNREASONABLY SINFULLY
UNREASONING BRUTE
UNRECOGNIZED UNSUNG CRYPTIC
UNWITTED
UNRECOVERABLE DEAD
UNRECTIFIED IMPURE
UNREDEEMED CHEAP
UNREFINED RAW DARK LOUD
BRUTE CRUDE DORIC GROSS
COARSE COMMON EARTHY JUNGLY
VULGAR BOORISH UNCOUTH
UNKEMPT DREADFUL SWAINISH
UNREFLECTING GLIB
UNREGENERACY ADAM
UNREGENERATELY MANLY
UNREHEARSED IMPROMPTU
UNRELATED FREMD STRAY UNAKIN
UNTOLD EXTREME FRAMMIT
POSITIVE
UNRELAXED UNSLAKED
UNRELENTING GRIM HARD IRON
CRUEL STERN SEVERE RIGOROUS
UNRELIABLE FISHY SHADY FICKLE
GREASY UNSAFE CASALTY STREAKY
WILDCAT FECKLESS GLIBBERY
SLIPPERY TICKLISH
UNRELIEVED DEAD BRUTE ABJECT
EXQUISITE
UNREMITTING BUSY FAST HARD
DOGGED
UNREMUNERATIVE HONORARY
UNRESERVED FREE CLEAN FRANK
ROUND COMMON UNCLOSE EXPLICIT
UNRESERVEDNESS FREEDOM
UNRESISTING BUXOM
UNRESPONSIVE DEAD DUMB
BARREN SILENT STUBBORN
UNREST MOTION AILMENT DISREST
WANREST DISQUIET CHEMISTRY
PSYCHOSIS
UNRESTRAINED LAX FREE WILD
BROAD FANTI FRANK LARGE LOOSE
FACILE FANTEE LAVISH UNTIED
WANTON FLYAWAY RAMPANT
RIOTOUS FAMILIAR FREEHAND
LAXATIVE PINDARIC
UNRESTRAINT LICENSE IMMUNITY
UNRESTRICTED FREE GLOBAL
SOVRAN UNZONED
UNRETURNED UNYOLDEN
UNREVEALED UNTOLD
UNRIG STRIP
UNRIGHTEOUSNESS ADHARMA
UNRIPE RAW CRUDE GREEN CALLOW
UNCURED IMMATURE
UNROBE DISROBE UNDRESS
DISARRAY

UNROLL EVOLVE UNCURL DEVELOP
OUTROLL TRINDLE UNTREND
UNROOF TIRL TIRR TIRVE DISROOF
UNRUFFLE SMOOTH SOOTHE
MOLLIFY
UNRUFFLED CALM COOL EASY EVEN
QUIET SOBER STILL ASLEEP PLACID
SEDATE SERENE SMOOTH
DECOROUS
UNRULY HIGH RAMP ROYT TOUGH
HAUNTY WANTON LAWLESS
RAMMAGE ROPABLE UNRULED
VICIOUS WANRULY WAYWARD
INDOCILE MUTINOUS
UNSADDLE UNPANEL
UNSAFE HOT EXPOSED INSECURE
PERILOUS
UNSATISFACTORY BAD ILL EVIL
CROOK SHREWD WRETCHED
UNSATISFYING DUSTY HOLLOW
UNSAVORY WERSH INSIPID WEARISH
UNSAY WITHDRAW
UNSCHOLARLY BOOKLESS
UNSCRUPULOUS SKIN BRAZEN
DEVIOUS DEXTROUS RASCALLY
UNSEASONABLE LAT UNRIPE
UNTIDY UNCHANCY UNTIMELY
UNSEASONED RAW GREEN
UNSEAT ADDRESS DISSEAT
UNSEEING BLIND GAZELESS
UNSEEMLY HOIDEN UNFAIR
IMPROPER INDECENT SEEMLESS
UNMEETLY UNWORTHY
UNSEEN SECRET UNEYED VIEWLESS
UNSERRIED LOOSE
UNSETTLE JAR TURN UNFIX UNSET
UPSET COMMOVE DERANGE
DISTURB STAGGER UNHINGE
UNQUEME DISORDER DISQUIET
DISTRACT
UNSETTLED MOOT LIGHT SHAKY
UNSAD VAGUE BROKEN FICKLE
QUEASY VAGOUS DUBIOUS SHUTTLE
UNSTAID RESTLESS UNSTABLE
UNSHAKABLE DOGGED ADAMANT
IRONCLAD
UNSHAKEN FIRM STEADY UNMOVED
UNSHOOK RESOLUTE
UNSHAPELY DEFORMED UNMACKLY
UNSHARED SOLE
UNSHEATH DISCASE
UNSHEATHED BARE
UNSHOD BAREFOOT DISCALCED
UNSHORN UNPOLLED
UNSIGHTLY UGLY MESSY HOMELY
INDECENT
UNSKILLED JAY PUNY GREEN
PUISNE UNGAIN UNSEEN STRANGE
FECKLESS
UNSKILLFUL ILL EVIL RUDE
ARTLESS UNFEATY BUNGLING
TINKERLY UNHEPPEN
UNSMILING GLUM AUSTERE
UNSOCIABLE SULLEN INSOCIAL
UNSOILED CLEAN
UNSOPHISTICATE SQUARE
UNSOPHISTICATED JAY NAIF PURE
FRANK GREEN NAIVE SILLY CALLOW
SIMPLE BUCOLIC VERDANT

HOMEBRED HOMESPUN INNOCENT
UNSOUND BAD ILL EVIL SICK ADDLE
CRAZY CRONK DICKY DOTTY DOZED
SANDY SHAKY ABSURD FAULTY
FLAWED HOLLOW INFIRM INSANE
ROTTEN UNHALE INVALID RICKETY
UNWHOLE
UNSOUNDNESS CRACK INSANITY
UNSPIRITUAL CARNAL
UNSPOILED RACY UNSHENT
UNSPOKEN TACIT SILENT
UNSPORTSMANLIKE DIRTY
UNSPOTTED CLEAR SPOTLESS
UNSTABLE FLUX BATTY LOOSE
SANDY BROTEL CHOPPY FICKLE
FITFUL FLITTY LABILE LUBRIC
ROTTEN SHIFTY TICKLE UNFIRM
WANKLE WANKLY DWAIBLE
DWAIBLY DWEEBLE RICKETY
SLIDDER SLIDDRY VOLUBLE
FEVERISH FIRMLESS FUGITIVE
INSECURE LUBRICAL REMUABLE
SKITTISH SLIPPERY TICKLISH
TOTTLISH VARIABLE
(MENTALLY —) BRAINISH
UNSTEADILY GROGGILY
UNSTEADINESS FALTER
UNSTEADY WALT CRANK CRONK
DOTTY FLUKY LIGHT NERVY SLACK
TIPPY TIPSY TOTTY UNSAD WALTY
WONKY COGGLY FICKLE FLICKY
FLUFFY GROGGY JIGGLY JOGGLY
SWIMMY TOTTIE WAFFLY WAGGLY
WAMBLY WANKLE WEEWAW
WEEWOW DODDERY GLAIKIT
JIGGETY QUAVERY TITTUPY
TOTTERY WAYWARD STAGGERY
TICKLISH TITUBANT UNSTABLE
VARIABLE
UNSTINTED LAVISH ENDLESS
UNSTRESS SLACK
UNSTRESSED SHORT
UNSTRING DISSOLVE
UNSTUDIED GLIB CASUAL CARELESS
GLANCING
UNSUBDUED VIRGIN UNBOWED
UNSUBSTANTIAL TOY LIMP THIN
WINDY AERIAL CHAFFY FLIMSY
SLEAZY SLEEZY SLIGHT UNREAL
FOLIOUS FRAGILE INSOLID
SHADOWY TENUOUS FILIGREE
FINESPUN FOOTLESS GIMCRACK
VAPOROUS
UNSUCCESSFUL BAD MANQUE
UNSPED STICKIT UNHAPPY
ABORTIVE
UNSUITABLE INEPT UNAPT UNDUE
UNFIT UNKIND UNMETE UNCOMELY
UNGAINLY UNLIKELY
UNSUITABLENESS IMPOLICY
UNSUITED BAD
UNSULLIED FAIR PURE CLEAR
VIRGIN INNOCENT SPOTLESS
VIRGINAL
UNSUPPLIED HELPLESS
UNSUPPORTED BLIND NAKED
BACKWARD STAYLESS
UNSURE TIMID INFIRM DOUBTFUL
INSECURE UNSICKER

UNSURPASSED CHAMPION
UNSUSPECTING INNOCENT
UNSWEET UNSOOT
UNSWERVING FIXED FLUSH LOYAL
DIRECT STEADY STRICT STURDY
STAUNCH
UNSWERVINGLY HEADLONG
UNSYMMETRICAL LOPSIDED
UNSYMPATHETIC HARD STONY
FROZEN GLASSY HOSTILE KINDLESS
UNTAINTED FREE GOOD PURE
INNOCENT
UNTAMED WILD FERAL RAMAGE
SAVAGE HAGGARD RAMMISH
WARRAGAL
UNTANGLE FREE SLEAVE UNLACE
UNTAUGHT WASTE UNLERED
IGNORANT
UNTHINKABLE PUERILE
UNTHINKING GLIB BRUTE CASUAL
FECKLESS HEEDLESS
UNTHINKINGLY STUPID
UNTIDINESS JAKES LITTER
UNTIDY DOWDY GAUMY MESSY
ROOKY BUNTING DRAGGLY LITTERY
RUMMAGY UNSIDED DRAGGLED
SLOVENLY STRUBBLY UNHEPPEN
UNTIE UNDO UNBIND UNLASH
UNLATCH UNTRUSS UNTWINE
UNFASTEN
UNTIL AD OR TO GIN HENT INTO
UNTO FORTO TWELL WHILE WHILES
WHILST PENDING
(— THEN) BEFORE
UNTILLED INCULT UNEARED
UNTIMELY UNTIDY IMMATURE
PREVIOUS TIMELESS
UNTIRING BUSY SEDULOUS
TIRELESS
UNTITLED (— MEN) AUMAGA
UNTOLD VAST UNQUOD
UNTOUCHABLE DOM HARIJAN
CHANDALA
(PL.) PANCHAMA
UNTOUCHED FREE INTACT
UNTOWARD ILL UNRULY FROWARD
WAYWARD
UNTRAINED RAW RUDE GREEN
HAGGARD
UNTRAMMELED FREE
UNTRIED MAIDEN UNSOUGHT
UNTRIMMED UNTEWED
UNTRODDEN PATHLESS UNFOOTED
UNTROUBLED CHEERY
UNTRUE FLAM FALSE LEASE WRONG
UNFAST DISLOYAL
UNTRUSTWORTHINESS FALSITY
UNTRUSTWORTHY SHAKY LIMBER
TRICKY UNSURE SLIDDERY
SLIPPERY
UNTRUTH LIE FABLE LEASE SKLENT
FALSITY UNTROTH
UNTRUTHFUL SLANTER
UNTUTORED IGNORANT
UNTWILLED PLAIN
UNTWINE FRESE UNTWIST
UNTWIST FAG FEAZE UNLAY UNSPIN
UNTWIRL
UNTWISTED SLEIDED

UNUSABLE WASTE INUTILE
UNUSED IDLE FRESH WASTE INURED
MAIDEN DERELICT INITIATE
UNWONTED
UNUSUAL ODD EERY RARE SELD
TALL CRAZY EERIE FORBY NOVEL
UTTER WEIRD EXEMPT FORBYE
SCREWY SINGLE UNIQUE STRANGE
ABNORMAL DISTINCT ESPECIAL
INSOLENT KNOCKOUT SELCOUTH
SINGULAR SPANKING UNCOMMON
UNTRADED UNWONTED
UNUSUALLY EXTRA
UNVARIED SAMELY
UNVARNISHED EVERYDAY
UNVARYING FLAT FRANK LEVEL
STABLE UNIFORM
UNVEIL REVEAL UNCOVER UNCROWN
UNDRAPE UNSCREEN UNWIMPLE
UNVERSED STRANGE
UNWANTED STRAY TRAMP FAULTY
UNWARRANTED UNDUE
UNWARY RASH UNAWARE CARELESS
HEEDLESS WARELESS
UNWASHED SOAPLESS
UNWASTEFUL FRUGAL
UNWAVERING FIRM CLEAN LEVEL
SOLID GLASSY STABLE EXPRESS
STAUNCH
UNWAVERINGLY FAST
UNWEAKENED CLEAR
UNWELL ILL EVIL SICK BADLY
CROOK AILING CHIPPY WICKED
COMICAL
UNWHOLESOME ILL EVIL SICK
CAGMAG IMPURE MORBID SICKLY
CORRUPT NOISOME NOXIOUS
UNCLEAN DISEASED
UNWIELDY BULKY CLUMSY UNRIDE
AWKWARD HULKING CUMBROUS
UNGAINLY
UNWILLING CHARY LOATH SWEER
WERSE AVERSE ESCHEW
BACKWARD GRUDGING
UNWILLINGLY MAUGER MAUGRE
UNWILLINGNESS GRUDGE NOLITION
UNWIND UNCLEW UNREEL UNREAVE
UNTWINE
UNWISE FALSE INANE SIMPLE
FOOLISH WITLESS
UNWITTING UNWIST WEETLESS
UNWOMANLY MANKIND
UNWORLDLY WEIRD ASTRAL
UNWORTHY BASE INDIGN BENEATH
UNDIGNE WANWORDY
UNWOUNDED COLD
UNWREATHE UNPLAT
UNWRINKLED BRANT BRENT
UNWROUGHT RAW LIVE
UNYIELDING SET ACID DOUR FAST
FIRM GRIM HARD RIGID STARK
STIFF STITH STONY TOUGH FLINTY
FROZEN GLASSY KNOBBY STEELY
STURDY ADAMANT AUSTERE
COSTIVE FROWARD CHURLISH
OBDURATE OBEDIENT STUBBORN
UNYOKE UNTEAM OUTSHUT
OUTSPAN
UP ON ONE OOP ABOUT ASTIR

DORMY DORMIE
(— AND ABOUT) AFOOT
(— TO THE TIME) UNTIL
(— TO) INTO
(— YONDER) UPBY UPBYE
(FARTHER —) ABOVE
(HIGH —) ALOFT
UPANISHAD ISHA KATHA
UPAS DITA CHETTIK
UPBEAT ARSIS AUFTAKT ANACRUSIS
UP-BOW POUSSE
UPBRAID CHEW RAIL SNUB TUCK
TWIT ABUSE ROUSE SCOLD TAUNT
UPBRAY EMBRAID REPROVE
DISGRACE OUTBRAID
UPCARD STARTER
UPFOLD SADDLE ANTICLINE
UPHEAVAL BOIL UPLIFT RUMMAGE
UPTHROW
UPHILL UPBANK UPWITH
UPHOLD AID TOM ABET BACK FAVOR
AFFIRM ASSERT DEFEND SOOTHE
BOLSTER SUPPORT SUSTAIN
CHAMPION MAINTAIN PRESERVE
UPHOLDER DEFENDER ERASTIAN
FEUDALIST
UPHOLDING BEHIND
UPHOLSTER SQUAB
UPHOLSTERER TAPISER UPHOLDER
UPLAND DOWN DOWNS MAUKA
COTEAU FASTLAND
(PL.) BRAES DOWNS
UPLAND PLOVER QUAILY HILLBIRD
PAPABOTE
UPLIFT TOSS BOOST TOWER
UPTHRUST
UPLIFTED ERECT EXALTEE
UPON ON PON SUR INTO OVER
ABOVE AGAINST
(— THAT) THEREAT
UPPER VAMP SKIVE VAMPEY
SUPERIOR
(PL.) FINISH
UPPERCUT BOLO
UPPER HURONIAN LAWSON
UPPERMOST UMEST UPMOST
OVEREST BUNEMOST OVERMOST
UPPER VOLTA (CAPITAL OF —)
OUAGADOUGOU
(LANGUAGE OF —) BOBO LOBI
SAMO MANDE MOSSI
(MOUNTAIN IN —) TEMA
(NATIVE OF —) BOBO LOBI SAMO
BISSA HAUSA MANDE MARKA MOSSI
PUEHL TUAREG SENOUFO VOLTAIC
YATENGA MANDINGO
(RIVER IN —) VOLTA SOUROU
UPRAISED SUBLIME
UPRIGHT FAIR GOOD HARR JUST
PROP STUD TIDY TRUE ANEND
CHEEK ERECT GUIDE JELLY MORAL
RIGHT ROMAN SETUP STALE STALK
STILE DIRECT ENTIRE HONEST
SQUARE FRIZZEN HOUSING
JANNOCK PITPROP SINCERE
INNOCENT RIGHTFUL STANDARD
STANDING STRAIGHT VERTICAL
VIRTUOUS
(NOT —) BEVEL

(PL.) STUDDING
UPRIGHTNESS HONOR TRUTH
EQUITY HONESTY PROBITY
JUSTNESS
UPRISING RIOT EMEUTE MUTINY
PUTSCH REVOLT TUMULT UPRISE
UPRISAL
UPROAR DIN RUT CAIN GILD MOIL
RIOT ROUT BURLE CHANG FUROR
HURLY RUMOR STOUN STOUR
CLAMOR DIRDUM FRACAS HABBLE
HUBBLE HUBBUB RANDAN RATTLE
RIPPET RUCKUS RUMBLE SHINDY
STEVEN STOUND TUMULT CATOUSE
FERMENT GAUSTER ORATION
OUTROAR RUCTION STASHIE
TURMOIL BROUHAHA SCOUTHER
STIRRING TINTAMAR
UPROARIOUS FURIOUS ROUTOUS
UPROOT HACK LOUK MORE UNROUT
UNPLANT DISPLANT ROOTWALT
SUPPLANT
UPROOTED LUMPEN
UPSET ILL TIP TOP TUP CAVE COUP
COWP FUSS JUMP PURL TILT TURN
WELT EVERT KNOCK ROUSE SHAKE
SKELL WHELM BOTHER DISMAY
QUELME TIPPLE TOPPLE UPCAST
WALTER CAPSIZE DERANGE
DISTURB FRAZZLE HAYWIRE
OVERSET PERVERT REVERSE
SLATTER SUBVERT TEMPEST
TURMOIL CAPSIZAL DISTRAIT
OVERTILT OVERTURN STREAKED
SUPPLANT TURNOVER
(**EASILY** —) FUSSY
UPSHOT ISSUE SHORT UPSET
EFFECT SEQUEL UPPING OUTCOME
UPSHOOT UPSTROKE
UPSIDE-DOWN CRAZY OVERHAND
UPSEDOUN
UPSTAIRS ABOVE
UPSTANDING GRADELY
UPSTART KIP QUAT SNIP SQUIRT
UPSKIP DALTEEN PARVENU
ARRIVIST MUSHROOM SKIPJACK
UPSPRING
UP-TO-DATE ABREAST TODAYISH
UPWARD ALOFT UPLONG UPWAYS
UPWITH SKYWARD UPALONG
UPWARDS
UPWARD-MOVING ANABATIC
URAEUS ASP
URAMIL MUREXAN
URANUS OURANOS HERSCHEL
(**WIFE OF** —) GAEA
URAO TRONA
URARTAEAN KHALDIAN
URARTU VAN
URATE LITHATE
URBAN TOWN URBIC URBANE
BURGHAL
URBANE CIVIL SUAVE POLITE
SVELTE AMIABLE GRACIOUS
URBANITY SUAVITY ELEGANCE
URCHIN IMP ELFIN GAMIN KEELIE
NIPPER HURCHEON
URD MUNGO
URDEE MATELEY

URDU REKHTA REKHTI MOORISH
URGE ART DUN EGG HIE PLY PUT
SIC SUE TAR YEN BROD COAX
CRAM EDGE FIRK GOAD MOVE PING
SICK SPUR WHIP CROWD DRIVE
FILIP FORCE HOOSH IMPEL LABOR
PRICK SPANK TREAT COMPEL
DEHORT DESIRE ENGAGE EXCITE
FILLIP HARDEN HOICKS HUSTLE
INCITE INDUCE INVITE MOTION
PROPEL STRAIN THREAP THREAT
ANIMATE COMMOVE ENFORCE
INSTANT OPPRESS PERSIST SOLICIT
SUGGEST URGENCY INSTANCE
PERSUADE
(— **IMPORTUNATELY**) DUN PRESS
(— **ON A HORSE**) HUP CRAM CHUCK
(— **ON**) EGG ERT HAG SOOL ALARM
CHIRK CROWD DRIVE FILIP HASTE
HURRY IMPEL YOICK ALARUM FILLIP
HARDEN HASTEN INCITE
(— **STRONGLY**) EXHORT SOLICIT
(— **WITH VEHEMENCE**) DING
URGENCY NEED PRESS STRESS
URGENCE EXIGENCY INSTANCE
INSTANCY
URGENT HOT DIRE RASH ACUTE
HASTY STRONG BURNING CLAMANT
EXIGENT INSTANT URGEFUL
CRITICAL PRESSING PRESSIVE
URGING QUEST
URIAL SHA OORIAL
URINAL DUCK SANITARY
URINATE WET LEAK EMPTY STALE
PIDDLE EVACUATE
URINATION MICTION NOCTURIA
URINE MIG SIG LAGE LANT WASH
STALE WATER NETTING EMICTION
(— **USED AS COSMETIC**) LOTIUM
URN JAR EWER KIST URNA VASE
CAPANNA
(— **FOR MAKING TEA**) KITCHEN
SAMOVAR
(— **IN KENO**) GOOSE
(**BURIAL** —) OSSUARY
(**CINERARY** —) DINOS DEINOS
(**STONE** —) STEEN
URN-SHAPED URCEOLAR
UROCHORDA ASCIDIA TUNICATA
UROSTYLE COCCYX
URSA MAJOR OKNARI CHARIOT
WAGONER WAGGONER
URSINE ARCTOID
URTICARIA HIVES UREDO CNIDOSIS
URTICASTRUM LAPORTEA

URUGUAY
CAPITAL: MONTEVIDEO
DEPARTMENT: ROCHA SALTO
FLORES ARTIGAS SORIANO
ESTUARY: PLATA
LAKE: MERIN MIRIM DIFUNTOS
MEASURE: VARA LEGUA CUADRA
SUERTE
RIVER: MALO MIRIM NEGRO
ULIMAR CUAREIM QUEGUAY
YAGUARON CEBOLLATI
TOWN: MELO MINAS ROCHA

SALTO RIVERA DURAZNO
FLORIDA PAYSANDU
WEIGHT: QUINTAL

URUGUAYAN ORIENTAL
URUS TUR URE AUROCHS
US S HIS HIZ HUZ
USABLE FIT UTIBLE SERVABLE
USAGE USE ASAL FORM WONE
HABIT HAUNT SUNNA USURE
CUSTOM MANNER FASHION
HALACHA HALAKAH USATION
PRACTICE
(**BAD** —) ABUSAGE
(**HARD** —) GRIEF
(**RELIGIOUS** —) RITUS
(PL.) CEREMONY
USE URE BOOT CALL DUTY HAVE
NAIT NOTE USUS WISE APPLY AVAIL
GUIDE HABIT SPEND TREAT USAGE
WASTE BEHOOF EMPLOY FINISH
HANDLE OCCUPY USANCE ACCOUNT
ADHIBIT ENTREAT IMPROVE SERVICE
UTILITY ACCUSTOM EXERCISE
FUNCTION PRACTICE
(— **AS WONTED**) ADOPT
(— **EXPERIMENTALLY**) TRY
(— **FIGURE OF SPEECH**) TROPE
(— **IMPROPERLY**) ABUSE
(— **INDISCRIMINATELY**) HACK
(— **OF MORE WORDS THAN**
NECESSARY) PLEONASM
(— **OF NEW WORD**) NEOLOGY
(— **OF SUBTERFUGE**) CHICANE
(— **UP**) EAT TIRE WEAR SHOOT
ABSORB DEVOUR EXPEND GUZZLE
PERUSE CONSUME EXHAUST
OVERWEAR
(— **WASTEFULLY**) SPILL
(— **WITH FULL COMMAND**) WIELD
(**EXCESSIVE** — **OF FACE AND**
HANDS) ABHINAYA
(**FOR TEMPORARY** —) JURY
(**FRUGAL** —) SPARE
(**GENERAL** —) CURRENCY
(**LITURGICAL** —) RITE
(**MUCH IN** —) GREAT
(**UNRESTRICTED** —) FREEDOM
USED WONT
(— **CONTINUOUSLY**) HOT
(— **IN FLIGHT**) VOLAR
(— **UP**) ALL BEAT SHOT SPENT
FOREWORN
(**MUCH** —) GREAT HACKNEY
USEFUL GAIN GOOD UTILE UTIBLE
HELPFUL THRIFTY BEHOVELY
UTENSILE
(— **FOR LONG TIME**) HARD
USEFULNESS USE AVAIL VALUE
WORTH PROFIT MILEAGE UTILITY
USELESS IDLE LEWD VAIN VOID
WIDE EMPTY DOLESS NOUGHT
OTIOSE SCREWY TRASHY INUTILE
STERILE VAINFUL BOOTLESS
FOOTLESS FOOTLING WASTEFUL
USELESSNESS FUTILITY IDLENESS
USER USUS
USHABTI SHAWABTI

USHER BOW USH SHOW HERALD
ISCHAR SEATER CHOBDAR HUISHER
JANITOR MARSHAL STEWARD
USSR (SEE RUSSIA)
USUAL RIFE COMMON FAMOUS
NORMAL SOLEMN VULGAR WONTED
AVERAGE GENERAL NATURAL
REGULAR TYPICAL USITATE
EVERYDAY FREQUENT HABITUAL
ORDINARY ORTHODOX
USURER SHARK GAVELER
HARPAGON
USURP ASSUME INVADE PRESUME
ACCROACH ARROGATE
USURY GAVEL OCKER USURE
USANCE GOMBEEN

UTAH

CAPITAL: SALTLAKECITY
COLLEGE: WEBER
COUNTY: JUAB CACHE PIUTE
SEVIER TOOELE UINTAH
SANPETE
INDIAN: UTE
LAKE: SALT SWAN SEVIER
MOTTO: INDUSTRY
MOUNTAIN: LENA LION WAAS
KINGS PEALE TRAIL FRISCO
NAVAJO SWASEY GRANITE
GRIFFIN HAWKINS PENNELL
LINNAEUS
MOUNTAIN RANGE: CEDAR HENRY
HOGUP UINTA WAHWAH
TERRACE CONFUSION
NATIONAL PARK: ZION
NICKNAME: MORMON BEEHIVE
RIVER: WEBER JORDAN SEVIER
STATE BIRD: SEAGULL
STATE FLOWER: SEGOLILY
STATE TREE: SPRUCE
TOWN: MOAB OREM DELTA HEBER
KANAB LOGAN MAGNA MANTI
NEPHI OGDEN PRICE PROVO
KEARNS TOOELE VERNAL

UTENSIL (ALSO SEE IMPLEMENT AND
TOOL) HOD BOAT IRON MOLD PECK
STEW BAKER FRIER FRYER GRILL
KNIFE MOULD RICER SCOOP SHEET
SHELL SIEVE SLICE ULLER BEATER
BREWER COOKER DABBER FUNNEL
GRATER GRILLE KETTLE LINGEL

MASKER POPPER PUSHER SHAKER
SIFTER BRAZIER BROILER DUSTPAN
FLIPPER GLUEPOT MUDDLER
SCUMMER SKIMMER STEAMER
STIRRER TOASTER CALABASH
GRIDIRON SAUCEPAN SAUCEPOT
SHREDDER SPOUCHER STRAINER
(**— FOR COVERING FIRE**) CURFEW
(**LITURGICAL —**) ASTERISK
(**PL.**) BATTERY COOKWARE
IRONWARE
UTERUS WOMB BELLY METRA
MATRIX BEARING
UTILITARIAN USEFUL ECONOMIC
UTILITY USE AVAIL USAGE PROFIT
BENEFIT SERVICE
UTILIZE USE EMPLOY ENLIST
CONSUME EXPLOIT HARNESS
HUSBAND
UTMOST END BEST LAST MOST
FINAL EXTREME OUTMOST SUPREME
DAMNDEST POSSIBLE UTTEREST
UTOPIA ZION
UTOPIAN IDEAL
UTOPIANISM FUTURISM
UTRAQUIST CALIXTIN
UTRICULUS ALVEUS
UTTER ASK OUT SAY BARK BLOW
BOOM DRIB FAIR GASP GIVE HURL
MAIN MOOT MOVE PASS PURE RANK
SEND VENT VERY BLACK COUGH
CRUDE FETCH FRAME FRANK
GROSS ISSUE MOUTH RAISE SHEER
SOUND SPEAK SPELL STARK THICK
TOTAL VOICE ACCENT BROACH
DAMNED DIRECT INTONE PARLEY
PROFER TONGUE BLUSTER
BREATHE DELIVER ENOUNCE
EXCLAIM EXPRESS OUTMOST
OUTTELL PERFECT PROLATE
UPBRAID ABSOLUTE BLINKING
COMPLETE CRASHING INTONATE
(**— ABRUPTLY**) BLURT
(**— AFFECTEDLY**) KNAP MINCE
(**— ARGUMENTS**) BLAZE
(**— CASUALLY**) DROP
(**— EXPLOSIVELY**) BOLT
(**— FALSEHOODS**) FABLE
(**— FOOLISHLY**) BLABBER
(**— HALTINGLY**) BLUBBER
(**— HURRIEDLY**) CHOP
(**— IN HARSH VOICE**) GRIT GRATE

(**— INADVERTENTLY**) SLIP
(**— INDISTINCTLY**) CHEW
(**— LOUD CRY**) BRAY BLARE
(**— LOUDLY**) CRY BLAT CALL HALLO
HALLOO HULLOO PRABBLE
(**— LOW SOUNDS**) MURMUR
WHISPER
(**— MEANINGLESS SOUNDS**) BABBLE
(**— RAPIDLY**) FIRE CHATTER
(**— RAUCOUSLY**) BLAT
(**— REPETITIVELY**) CHIME
(**— RHETORICALLY**) DECLAIM
(**— SOLEMNLY**) SWEAR
(**— STUPIDLY**) BLUNDER
(**— SUDDENLY**) CRACK
(**— UNCTUOUSLY**) DROOL
(**— VIGOROUSLY**) FLING
(**— WITH EFFORT**) HEAVE
UTTERANCE CRY GAB CALL OSSE
DITTY PAROL VOICE ACCENT
ACTION BREATH CHORUS DRIVEL
GIBBER ORACLE PAROLE EXPRESS
INKLING LALLING STATUTE
DELIVERY FOOTNOTE HOMESPUN
JUDGMENT LOCUTION SYLLABIC
(**— FROM A DIVINITY**) ORACLE
(**— OF VOCAL SOUNDS**) PHONESIS
(**CONDEMNATORY —**) INFAMY
(**DEFECTIVE —**) STAMMER
(**FAINT —**) INKLING
(**FOOLISH —**) DRIVEL
(**FOOLISH —S**) GUFF
(**GUSHING —**) EFFUSION
(**IMPULSIVE —**) BLURT
(**MALICIOUS —**) SLANDER
(**OFFENSIVE —**) AFFRONT
(**PROPHETIC —**) OSSE
(**PUBLIC —**) AIR
(**SHORT —**) DITTY
(**SOLEMN —**) EFFATE EFFATUM
(**VAPID —**) CUCKOO
(**PL.**) BYRONICS
UTTERED SPOKEN
UTTERLY DOG BONE DEAD BLACK
OUTLY PROOF HOLLOW MERELY
BLANKLY OUTERLY SHEERLY
PROPERLY
UVULA CION UVULE PLECTRUM
STAPHYLE
UVULARIA OAKESIA
UZBEK JAGATAI

V VEE FIVE VICTOR
  (INVERTED —) CARET
VACANCY HOLE WANT VACUIT
  VACUITY VACATION
VACANT IDLE VOID BLANK EMPTY
  FISHY INANE WASTE DEVOID
  HOLLOW DORMANT UNFILLED
  (BECOME —) FALL
VACATE QUIT TOLL VOID AVOID
  EMPTY WAIVE VACANT ABANDON
  RESCIND ABROGATE EVACUATE
VACATION OUT REST LEAVE OUTING
  RECESS HOLIDAY NONTERM
  VACANCY
  (SUMMER —) LONG
VACCINE BACTERIN BIOLOGIC
VACCINIA COWPOX
VACILLATE SWAG WAVE DACKER
  DITHER HALPER WABBLE WOBBLE
  SHAFFLE STICKLE WHIFFLE
  HESITATE
VACILLATING INFIRM HALTING
VACILLATION WAVERING
VACUITY BLOW VACANCY FONTANEL
VACUOUS DULL BLANK EMPTY SILLY
  VACANT
VACUUM GAPE VOID VACANCY
  VACUITY VACATION
VAGABOND BUM VAG HOBO KERN
  JAVEL ROGUE SHACK STIFF BRIBER
  CANTER HARLOT JOCKEY PICARA
  PICARO RODNEY RUNNER TAGRAG
  TRUANT WAFFIE ERRATIC FAITOUR
  GADLING GANGREL OUTCAST
  SCOURER SWAGMAN SWINGER
  TINKLER TRUCKER VAGRANT
  VAURIEN WASTREL BOHEMIAN
  BRODYAGA CURSITOR CUSTROUN
  FUGITIVE GLASSMAN PALLIARD
  RAPPAREE RUNABOUT RUNAGATE
  WHIPJACK
VAGARY WHIM FANCY FREAK VAGUE
  CAPRICE CONCEIT CRANKUM
  FLAGARIE VAGRANCY
  (PL.) HUMORS
VAGINATE SHEATHED
VAGRANCY MOPERY ROGUING
VAGRANT BUM WAFF WAIF CAIRD
  PIKER PIKEY ROGUE SKELB STRAG
  TRAMP ARRANT CASUAL SHAKER
  SHULER TINKER TRUANT VAGROM
  VAGUER WAFFIE DEVIOUS DRIFTER
  ERRATIC FLOATER GANGREL
  ROGUISH SKILDER SWAGMAN
  TINKLER TRAMPER TROGGER
  BRODYAGA PLANETIC STROLLER
  VAGABOND SHACKLING
VAGUE LAX DARK HAZY FOGGY
  FUZZY GROSS LOOSE MISTY
  CLOUDY DREAMY MYSTIC SHAGGY
  BLURRED EVASIVE OBSCURE
  SHADOWY UNFIXED CONFUSED
  INFINITE NUBILOUS
VAGUELY DIMLY DARKLY DUMBLY
  DREAMILY
VAIN MAD IDLE NULL PUFF VOID
  WANE EMPTY FLORY PROUD SAUCY
  VOGIE WASTE FLIMSY FUTILE
  HOLLOW VAUNTY BIGGITY CARRIED

TRIVIAL VAINFUL CONCEITY
  NUGATORY PEACOCKY VAPOROUS
  WASTEFUL
  (NOT —) SOLID
VAINGLORY RUFF GLORY VANITY
  ELATION
VAINLY IDLY TOOMLY
VAIR POTENT
VAISRAVANA BISHAMON
VAISYA BAIS BICE
VAJRA DORJE
VALANCE PELMET FRONTLET
  PALMETTE
VALE DALE DEAN DELL BACHE
  BATCH ENNIS
VALEDICTORY FAREWELL
VALENCE ADICITY ATOMISM
VALERIAN HELIO BENNET SUMBUL
  ALLHEAL CUTHEAL SETWALL
  CETEWALL
VALERIC PENTOIC
VALET MAN ANDREW SIRDAR
  TARTAR WALLIE CRISPIN TIREMAN
VALIANT SAD BRAG PREU PROW
  WILD BRAVE LUSTY ORPED PROUD
  STOUT WIGHT FIERCE HEROIC
  DOUGHTY GAILLARD GALLIARD
  INTREPID STALWART VIRTUOUS
VALID FAIR GOOD JUST LEGAL
  SOUND COGENT LAWFUL BINDING
  ETERNAL WEIGHTY FORCIBLE
  VAILABLE VALIDOUS VALUABLE
VALIDATE FIRM SEAL VALID AFFIRM
  CONFIRM
VALIDITY FORCE VIGOR STRENGTH
VALISE BAG GRIP MAIL DORLACH
  SATCHEL VALLIES SUITCASE
VALKYRIE SHIELDMAY
VALLECULA VALLEY
VALLEY DIB GUT COMB COOM COVE
  DALE DELL DENE GILL HOLE HOPE
  HOWE HOYA PARK VALE WADI
  WADY ATRIO BACHE BREAK CHASM
  COMBE COOMB DHOON GHYLL
  GLACK GOYAL GOYLE SLACK SLADE
  SWALE TEMPE YUNGA BOLSON
  BOTTOM CANADA CLOUGH COULEE
  DINGLE HOLLOW LAAGTE LEEGTE
  RINCON STRATH AIJALON BLOWOUT
  GEHENNA VAALITE
  (— BETWEEN CONES OF VOLCANO)
  ATRIO
  (— IN THESSALY) TEMPE
  (— ON MOON'S SURFACE) RILL
  CLEFT RILLE
  (— ON MT BLANC) NANT
  (CIRCULAR —) RINCON
  (DEEP —) CANON CANYON
  (FLAT-FLOORED DESERT —)
  BOLSON
  (GRASSY MOUNTAIN —) HOLE
  (LOWEST PART OF —) SOLE
  (MINIATURE —) GULLY GULLEY
  (NARROW —) DEAN DENE GLEN
  GLACK GOYLE KLOOF CLOUGH
  (SECLUDED —) GLEN DINGLE
  (TRENCHLIKE —) COULEE
VALOR ARETE MERIT VALUE BOUNTY
  VALOUR BRAVERY COURAGE

PROWESS STOMACH CHIVALRY
  VALIANCY
VALOROUS BRAVE VIRTUOUS
VALUABLE DEAR COSTLY PRIZED
  WORTHY EMINENT WEALTHY
  PRECIOUS PRIZABLE SINGULAR
VALUATION PRIZE VALOR VALUE
  ESTEEM EXTENT ESTIMATE
  TAXATION
VALUE SET COST FECK FOOT HOLD
  RATE TELL AVAIL CARAT CHEAP
  COUNT FORCE PRICE PRIZE STAMP
  STENT STOCK VALOR WORTH
  ASSESS ASSIZE EQUITY ESTEEM
  EXTENT FIGURE HIDAGE MATTER
  MOMENT PRAISE REGARD VALURE
  VALUTA VIRTUE ACCOUNT ADVANCE
  APPRIZE CAPITAL CHERISH
  COMPUTE PRETIUM RESPECT
  VALENCY WERGILD ESTIMATE
  EVALUATE GOODWILL SPLENDOR
  TREASURE VALIDITY VALLIDOM
  (— HIGHLY) PRIZE ENDEAR
  (— OF ANGLE) EPOCH
  (— OF COW) SET
  (— OF TIMBER) STUMPAGE
  (ABSOLUTE —) MODULUS
  (AESTHETIC —) AMENITY
  (ESTABLISHED —) PAR
  (GOOD —) SNIP
  (MATHEMATICAL —) EXTREMUM
  (NEGATIVE —) DISVALUE
  (STUDY OF —) AXIOLOGY
  (TESTED —) ASSAY
VALUED DEAR
VALUELESS BAFF STRAWY
  NAUGHTY
VALVE TAP COCK DISC DISK GATE
  ORAL STOP CHOKE CLACK MIXER
  VALVA WAFER CUTOUT DAMPER
  KICKER PALLET POPPET POTLID
  SCUTUM SLUICE SUCKER VENTIL
  WASHER CLICKET DRAWOFF
  PETCOCK REDUCER SCALLOP
  SCOLLOP SHUTOFF VALVULA
  VALVULE DRAWGATE EPITHECA
  EPIVALVE STOPCOCK THROTTLE
  (— OF BARNACLE) SCUTUM
  (— OF MUSICAL INSTRUMENT)
  PISTON VENTIL
  (— OF PUMP BOX) FANG
  (THIN —) WAFER
  (TRIPLE —) KICKER
VAMBRACE BRACELET
VAMOOSE SCRAM CHEESE DECAMP
  SKIDDOO
VAMPIRE LAMIA ALUKAH
VAN WAN FORE LEAD SAIL FRONT
  TRUCK VAUNT WAGON VAWARD
  CARAVAN FOURGON FOREWARD
  KHALDIAN
VANADATE UVANITE TURANITE
VANDAL HUN HUNLIKE SARACEN
  HOOLIGAN
VANE FAN TEE WEB COCK TAIL WING
  FAINE BUCKET TARGET DOGVANE
  FLIGHTER VEXILLUM
  (— OF ARROW) FEATHER
  (— OF CONVEYOR BELT) FLIGHT

(— OF FEATHER) WEB FLUE
VEXILLUM
(— OF SURVEYING STAFF)
TRANSOM
(— OF WINDMILL) FAN FANE TAIL
FAINE
(COOLING — IN BREWING)
FLIGHTER
VANESSA PYRAMEIS
VANGUARD FORLORN
VANISH DIE FLY DROP FADE FLEE
MELT PASS SANT WEDE WEND
CLEAR FLEET SAUNT SLIDE EXHALE
EVANISH SCATTER CONQUEST
DISSOLVE EVANESCE
(— BY DEGREES) DRILL
VANISHED LAPSED EXTINCT
VANITY ABEL POMP VAIN FOLLY
PRIDE EGOISM FEATHER FOPPERY
INANITY SANDUST IDLENESS
IDLESHIP
VANNER SLIMER
VANNIC KHALDIAN
VANQUISH GET WIN BEAT LICK MILL
UTTER EXPUGN MASTER OUTRAY
SUBDUE THRASH CONQUER
OVERWIN SMOTHER CONQUEST
OVERCOME SURMOUNT VENKISEN
VANQUISHED CRAVEN
VAPID DRY DULL FADE FLAT STALE
TRITE JEJUNE INSIPID WATERISH
VAPOR FOG FUME REEK ROKE STEW
BOAST BRUME EWDER HUMOR
SMOKE STEAM STIFE BREATH
VAPOUR EXHAUST HALITUS
(HOT —) LUNT
(NOXIOUS —) DAMP
(PL.) BRUME
VAPORIZATION BURNUP
VAPORIZE DRIVE FLASH STEAM
AERATE AERIFY VAPORATE
VAPOROUS FUMY FUMID HUMID
FUMISH FUMOSE STEAMY VOLATILE
VARANGIAN VARIAG WARING
(PL.) ROS
VARIABILITY HETERISM
VARIABLE FLUX FREE CHOPPY
FICKLE FITFUL KITTLE WRAIST
CEPHEID FACIENT FLUXILE MUTABLE
ROLLING STREAKY UNEQUAL
VARIANT VARIOUS ARGUMENT
FLOATING FLUXIBLE SHIFTING
SKITTISH UNSTABLE VEERABLE
(EXCEEDINGLY —) PROTEAN
VARIANCE ODDS DISCORD DISPUTE
VARIANT STATE
(— IN WHEAT) SPELTOID
(PL.) DIAPHONE
VARIATION REX TURN ERROR
ROGUE SHADE CHANGE DOUBLE
JITTER SWITCH CYCLING DESCANT
EXTREME SHADING VARIETY
WINDING DIVISION DYNAMICS
HETERISM MUTATION
(— IN AIR PRESSURE) ROBBING
(— IN CURRENT) SURGE
(— IN FREQUENCY) SWINGING
(— IN SPEED) HUNTING
(— OF COLOR) ABRASH

(— OF PUPIL OF EYE) HIPPUS
(— OF SHOE) SPRING
(— OF VOWELS) ABLAUT
(ALLOWABLE —) LEEWAY
(BALLET —) ATTITUDE
(TOPOGRAPHICAL —) BREAK
(PL.) PIBROCH
VARICOCELE RAMEX
VARIED SORTY DAEDAL SEVERAL
VARIANT VARIOUS MANIFOLD
VARIED BUNTING PRUSIANO
VARIEGATE DROP FRET FLECK
FREAK SHOOT DAPPLE STRIPE
VARIFY CHECKER
VARIEGATED FAW PIED SHOT JASPE
LYART SHELD DAEDAL MARLED
MENALD MOSAIC SKEWED CHECKED
DAPPLED FREAKED FRETTED
PECKLED SPARKED VARIOUS
DISCOLOR FRECKLED OVERSHOT
PANACHED SKEWBALD
VARIEGATION COLOR
VARIETY FORM KIND MODE SORT
BRAND BREED CLASS SPICE
CHANGE STIRPS STRAIN STRIPE
SPECIES VARIENS
VARIOLA HORSEPOX
VARIOUS MANY SERE DIVERS
SUNDER SUNDRY VARIED DIVERSE
SEVERAL VARIANT MANIFOLD
VARISCITE UTAHITE
VARLET BOY LAD GIPPO JIPPO
PAVISER COISTREL VARLETTO
VARNISH DOPE JAPAN LACKER
MEDIUM PUNDUM FIXATIF LACQUER
VEHICLE VERMEIL FIXATIVE
OVERGILD THEETSEE
VARY HUNT ALTER BREAK DRIFT
SHIFT SPORT CHANGE DIFFER
RECEDE VARIFY CHECKER DEVIATE
DISSENT DIVERGE VARIATE
DISAGREE
VARYING CURRENT
VASE PYX URN OLLA VASA VASO
ASKOS CYLIX DINOS DIOTA KYLIX
PYXIS BASKET BOWPOT COTULA
COTYLA CRATER DEINOS DOLIUM
FILLER HYDRIA KALPIS KOTYLE
KRATER LEKANE SITULA AMPHORA
AMPULLA CANOPUS PATELLA
POTICHE PSYKTER SCYPHUS
SKYPHOS STAMNOS URCEOLE
BOUGHPOT LECYTHUS LEKYTHOS
MURRHINE PROCHOOS
(— FOR PERFUME) CONCH
(— ON PEDESTAL) TAZZA
(—S UNDER THEATER SEATS)
SCHEA
VASODILATOR KELLIN KHELLIN
VASSAL MAN WER BOND LEUD CEILE
LIEGE SLAVE CLIENT GENEAT
SACOPE BONDMAN FEEDMAN
FEODARY HOMAGER RUDIGER
SAMURAI SERVANT SUBJECT
PALATINE
(PL.) MANRED
VASSALAGE MANRED MANRENT
VAST HUGE BROAD ENORM GREAT
LARGE STOUR VASTY COSMIC

IMMANE MIGHTY UNTOLD IMMENSE
VASTITY ENORMOUS INFINITE
MOUNTAIN SPACIOUS
VASTNESS IMMANE GRANDEUR
WIDENESS
VAT ARK BAC DIP FAT PIT TAP TUN
BACK BECK COOM FATE GAAL GAIL
GYLE KEEL KIER TINE APRON
COOMB FETTE FLOAT KEEVE KIEVE
ROUND STAND STEEP KIMNEL
MOTHER BLUNGER DRAINER
GRAINER KEELVAT STEEPER
PRESSFAT
(— USED IN MEASURING SLIPS) ARK
(BREWER'S —) BACK FLOAT KEEVE
UNION CUMMING
(CHEESE —) CHESSEL CHESSET
CHESSART
(COOLING —) KELDER
(DYER'S —) JIG LEAD DYEBECK
(EVAPORATING —) APRON GRAINER
(FERMENTING —) TUN COMB COOM
GYLE KEEL COOMB FLOAT
(TANNER'S —) TAP HANGER
SPENDER
(TEXTILE —) KIER
(WINE —) LAKE
VAUDEVILLE ZARZUELA
VAULT BOUT COPE JUMP LEAP PEND
SKIP TOMB VOLT WOWT AZURE
CROFT CRYPT EMBOW VOLTO
CUPOLA FORNIX SHROUD DUNGEON
TESTUDO VALTAGE CATACOMB
LEAPFROG MONUMENT
(— IN CEILING) LACUNAR
(— OF HEAVEN) WELKIN
(— OF SKY) CONVEX ZENITH
CONCAVE
VAULTED CONCAVE CRYPTED
EMBOWED
VAULTING POMADA POMMADO
VAUNT GAB BRAG BOAST ROOSE
VOUST AVAUNT INSULT GLORIFY
FLOURISH
(— ONESELF) WIND
VAUNTMURE MANURE
VEAL VEAU SLINK FRICANDO
(LIKE —) VITULINE
VECTOR I K PHASOR GRADIENT
VEDDOID PANYAN
VEDIC (— PRINCIPLE) RTA RITA
VEER CUT DIP FLY CAST CHOP SLEW
SLUE SWAY WYRE FETCH SHIFT
SWOOP BROACH CHANGE SLOUGH
SWERVE TUMBLE DEVIATE WHIFFLE
VEERING DRIFT CHOPPY
VEGETABLE PEA YAM BEAN BEET
CORN KALE LEEK OKRA CHARD
GRASS ONION SABZI SALAD
CARROT CELERY LEGUME LENTIL
POTATO RADISH SQUASH TOMATO
TOPEPO TURNIP BLOATER CABBAGE
CELTUCE LETTUCE PARSNIP
PEASCOD RHUBARB SPINACH
VEGETAL BROCCOLI EGGPLANT
RUTABAGA
(— MATTER) SUDD
(—S FOR MARKET) TRUCK
(EARLY —) PRIMEUR

(EARLY —S) HASTINGS
(GARDEN —S) SASS SAUCE
(HYBRID —) GARLION
VEGETATION HERB COVER GREEN
SCRUB GROWTH HERBAGE
COVERAGE PLANTAGE PLEUSTON
SMELLAGE
(DECOMPOSED —) STAPLE
(SCRUB —) BRUSH
(UNWANTED —) FILTH
VEGETATIVE PLANTAL
VEHEMENCE FURY GLOW HEAT
RAGE WARMTH STRENGTH
VIOLENCE
VEHEMENT HOT HIGH KEEN LOUD
ANGRY EAGER FIERY HEFTY YEDER
ARDENT BITTER FERVID FIERCE
FLASHY HEARTY HEATED RAGING
STRONG ANIMOSE ANIMOUS
FURIOSO INTENSE JEALOUS
VIOLENT
VEHEMENTLY PELLMELL
VEHICLE BUS CAB CAR FLY VAN
ARBA AUTO CART DUKE FLAT GOER
JEEP SLED TAXI TEAM WAIN ARABA
BRAKE BREAK BUGGY CARRY DILLY
FLAIL GUIDE HANSA NODDY STAGE
WAGON BLADER CHARET CISIUM
DIESEL HEARSE JITNEY MEDIUM
PEDRAL RANDEM SLEDGE SLEIGH
SURREY TRISHA TROIKA CARRIER
CHARIOT CRUISER HOTSHOT
ICEBOAT KIBITKA MACHINE MINIBUS
OMNIBUS PEDICAB PEDRAIL
SHUTTLE SPEEDER SPRAYER
STEAMER STEERER TARTANA
TAXICAB TRAVOIS TURNOUT UTILITY
AUTORAIL AUTOSLED CARRIAGE
CHARETTE CYCLECAR DEADHEAD
DELIVERY ELECTRIC FILMOGEN
SHOWCASE SOCIABLE UNICYCLE
(— DRAWN BY BULLOCK) EKKA
(— FOR COLORS) MEGILP
(— FOR HAULING) TRACTOR
(— ON RUNNERS) SLED CARRO
SLEDGE SLEIGH ICEBOAT AUTOSLED
(— PULLED BY MAN) BROUETTE
RICKSHAW
(— RUNNING ON RAILS) LORRY
TRAIN
(— WITH 3 HORSES ABREAST)
TROIKA
**(— WITH 3 HORSES BEHIND EACH
OTHER)** RANDEM
(2-WHEELED —) GIG CART SULKY
TONGA CISIUM JINGLE LIMBER
BICYCLE CALECHE CROYDON
RICKSHAW
(AMMUNITION —) CAISSON
(AMPHIBIOUS —) BUFFALO
(AWKWARD —) ARK
(CHILD'S —) PRAM WALKER
SCOOTER STROLLER
(COVERED —) SEDAN LANDAU
CARAVAN KIBITKA
(EARTH-MOVING —) SCOOP
(LITTLE —) HINAYANA
(LUMBERING —) TUG TODE
(OBSOLETE —) CRATE

(POOR-QUALITY —) DOG
(RUDE —) KIBITKA
(SLEDGE-LIKE —) GAMBO
(WHEELLESS —) DRAY
(PL.) PARK
VEIL WRY FALL FILM HIDE MASK
WRAP COVER GLOSS SHADE VELUM
VIMPA VOLET WREIL BUMBLE FAILLE
SHADOW SHROUD VEILER WEEPER
WIMPLE CORTINA CURTAIN
ENDOTYS PARANJA VEILING
ENDOTHYS HEADRAIL MAHARMAH
MANTILLA TELEBLEM
(— IN CHURCH) AER ENDOTYS
ENDOTHYS
(— ON FUNGI) CORTINA
(DOUBLE —) YASHMAK
(HUMERAL —) SUDARY
(WIDOW'S —) WEEPER
VEILED COVERT VELATED
SHROUDED
VEILING PURDAH GOSSAMER
VEIN BAR LOB RIB CAVA LODE MOOD
RAKE REEF VENA AMPER CLOUD
COMES COSTA LEDGE MEDIA NERVE
RIDER SCRIN VARIX LEADER MEDIAL
STRAIN STREAK VENULA VENULE
AXILLAR AZYGOUS CUBITAL
DROPPER JUGULAR NERVURE
PRECAVA PRESTER SAPHENA
VEINLET AXILLARY EMULGENT
PREMEDIA PROFUNDA SUBCOSTA
(— OF LEAF) RIB COSTA MIDRIB
(— OF MINERAL) STREAK STRINGER
(— OF ORE) LODE ROKE LEDGE
RIDER SCRIN LEADER STRING
DROPPER UNDERSET
(— OF WING) CUBIT CUBITAL
CUBITUS SUBCOSTA SUBCOSTAL
(GRANITIC —) ELVAN
(QUARTZ —) SADDLE
(VARICOSE —) AMPER
VEINED MARBLED NERVOSE
VELA SAILS
VELAR GUTTURAL
VELD BUSHVELD SOURVELD
VELELLA SALLYMAN
VELLEITY WOULDING
VELLINCH FLINCHER
VELLUM ORIHON
VELOCIPEDE HOBBY STEED TRICAR
BICYCLE DICYCLE RANTOON
SPEEDER DRAISINE TRICYCLE
VELOCITY DRIFT CELERITY RAPIDITY
STRENGTH
(— OF 1 FOOT PER SECOND) VELO
(— OF FLOW) CURRENT
VELOUR SOLEIL
VELOUTE POULETTE
VELUM VEIL VELAMEN VELARIUM
VELVET PILE YUZEN BIRODO VELURE
FRAYING VELLUTE
VELVETEEN TRIPE
VELVET GRASS FOG
VELVETLEAF DAGGA PAREIRA
VENAL CORRUPT SALABLE HIRELING
SALEABLE VENDIBLE
VEND HAWK SELL UTTER MARKET
PEDDLE

VENDIBLE VENAL SALABLE
SALEABLE
VENDOR FAKER SELLER VENDER
BUTCHER HUSTLER PITCHER
PURLMAN VIANDER PITCHMAN
SAUCEMAN VENDITOR
VENEER BURL BURR JAPAN SHOOK
SKILLET
VENEERER DUSTER
VENERABLE OLD HOAR SAGE
HOARY AUGUST SACRED VETUST
ANCIENT VENERAL VINTAGE
VENERATE FEAR DREAD HALLOW
REVERE VENERE RESPECT WORSHIP
VENERATED HOLY SACRED
HALLOWED
VENERATION AWE CULT DULIA
CULTISM RESPECT DEVOTION
VENETIAN RED SIENA SIERRA
VENETIAN SUMAC SCOTINO

VENEZUELA

CAPITAL: CARACAS
COIN: REAL MEDIO FUERTE
BOLIVAR CENTIMO MOROCOTA
GULF: PARIA
MEASURE: GALON MILLA FANEGA
ESTADEL
MOUNTAIN: PAVA YAVI DUIDA
ICUTU CONCHA CUNEVA PARIMA
IMUTACA MASAITI RORAIMA
NATIVE: CARIB TIMOTE TIMOTEX
GUARAUNO
RIVER: META APURE CAURA
ARAUCA CARONI CUYUNI
GUANARE ORINOCO ORITUEO
PARAGUA SUAPURE VICHADA
GUAVIARE VENTUARI
STATE: LARA APURE SUCRE ZULIA
ARAGUA FALCON MERIDA
BOLIVAR COJEDES GUARICO
MONAGAS TACHIRA YARACUY
CARABOBO TRUJILLO
TOWN: AROA CORO ATURES
CUMANA MERIDA BARINAS
CABELLO GUAWARE MARACAY
MATURIN CARUPANO TACUPITA
VALENCIA
WEIGHT: BAG LIBRA

VENGEANCE WREAK WRECK
AVENGE ULTION WANION ALASTOR
REVENGE VINDICT REQUITAL
VINDICTA
VENILIA (HUSBAND OF —) DAUNUS
(SISTER OF —) AMATA
(SON OF —) TURNUS
VENISON BILTONG
VENOM GALL ATTER VIRUS POISON
SWELTER CROTALIN CROTALUS
VENOMOUS TOXIC ATTERN DEADLY
SNAKEY VENOMY BANEFUL NOXIOUS
SMITTLE SNAKISH POISONED
VIPERINE VIRULENT
VENT EMIT HOLE REEK BELCH DRAIN
FROTH ISSUE TEWEL OUTAGE
OUTLET CHIMNEY EXPRESS
OPENING ORIFICE OUTCAST

OUTFALL OUTTAKE RELEASE
VENTAGE APERTURE BREATHER
DIATREME FONTANEL MOFFETTE
SESPERAL SPIRACLE SUSPIRAL
VENTHOLE VOMITORY
(— IN EARTH'S CRUST) VOLCANO
(VOLCANIC —) BOCCA DIATREME
SOLFATARA
VENTILATE AIR WIND AERATE
EXPRESS
VENTILATION AERAGE AIRING
VENTILATOR BADGIR LOUVER
FEMERELL
VENTING GUST
VENTRAL HEMAL STERNAL
ANTERIOR INFERIOR
VENTRICLE HEART TRICORN
DIACOELE
VENTURE HAB RUN SET CAST DARE
JUMP KITE LUCK MINT REST RISK
WAGE ETTLE FLIER FLYER FROST
RISCO SALLY STAKE TEMPT WAGER
CHANCE DANGER HAZARD SASHAY
FLUTTER IMPERIL JEOPARD
PRESUME ENDANGER GETPENNY
(— AT DICE) THROW
(— TO SAY) DARESAY
VENTURESOME BOLD RASH RISKY
DARING TEMEROUS
VENTURESOMELY CHANCILY
VENUS LOVE VESPER LUCIFER
HESPERUS PHOSPHOR
(FATHER OF —) JUPITER
(HUSBAND OF —) VULCAN
(MOTHER OF —) DIONE
(SON OF —) CUPID AENEAS
VENUSEAN VENEREAN
VERACIOUS TRUE VERY TRUTHY
SINCERE VERIDIC FAITHFUL
TRUTHFUL
VERACITY HSIN TROTH TRUTH
VERITY FIDELITY
VERANDA PYAL LANAI PORCH
STOOP PIAZZA BALCONY GALERIE
GALLERY
VERB RHEMA ACTIVE NOMINAL
DEPONENT
(AUXILIARY —) BE DO CAN MAY
HAVE MUST WILL SHALL
VERBAL ORAL WORDY
VERBATIM DIRECT VERBAL
DIRECTLY
VERBENA ALOYSIA VERVAIN
VERBENALIN CORNIN
VERBIAGE TALK
VERBOSE WINDY WORDY PROLIX
VERBAL DIFFUSE WORDISH
(NOT —) LEAN
VERDANT BOSKY GREEN VIRID
VERDICT WORD VARDI ASSIZE
FINDING OPINION DECISION
JUDGMENT VEREDICT
VERDIGRIS AERUGO CANKER
VERDET
VERDIN GOLDTIT
VERDURE GREENTH GREENERY
VIRIDITY
VERGE TOP EDGE WAND YARD
TOUCH BORDER TRENCH TRIGGER

VERGER WANDSMAN
VERGILIAN MARONIAN MARONIST
VERIFICATION AUDIT AVERRAL
CHECKUP AVERMENT
VERIFY AVER TRUE AUDIT CHECK
PROVE ATTEST RATIFY COLLATE
CONFIRM CONTROL JUSTIFY
SUPPORT
VERILY AMEN FAITH PARDY CERTES
INDEED PARDIE FAITHLY
VERITABLE REAL TRUE VERY
ACTUAL HONEST PROPER GENUINE
VERIMENT
VERITY TROTH TRUTH VERIDITY
VERJUICE VARGE
VERMICULE VAALITE
VERMICULITE KERRITE MACONITE
VERMIFUGE KOSIN HARMAL HARMEL
KAMALA KAMELA KOOSIN HELONIAS
VERMILION RED GOYA MINIUM
PAPRIKA PIMENTO VERMEIL
ZINOBER CARMETTA CINNABAR
TOREADOR
VERMIN FILTH CARRION VARMINT
VERMIS WORM

VERMONT

CAPITAL: MONTPELIER
COLLEGE: BENNINGTON
MIDDLEBURY
COUNTY: ESSEX ORANGE
ORLEANS LAMOILLE
LAKE: CASPIAN DUNMORE
SEYMOUR CHAMPLAIN
MOUNTAIN: BROMLEY HOGBACK
PROSPECT MANSFIELD
MOUNTAIN RANGE: GREEN
TACONIC
PRESIDENT: ARTHUR COOLIDGE
RIVER: SAXTONS NULHEGAN
WINOOSKI
STATE BIRD: THRUSH
STATE FLOWER: CLOVER
STATE TREE: MAPLE
TOWN: BARRE STOWE GRAFTON
NEWFANE RUTLAND
UNIVERSITY: NORWICH

VERMOUTH CINZANO CHAMBERY
VERNACULAR LINGO COMMON
JARGON PATOIS ROMAIC VULGAR
CHALDEE DIALECT SCOTTISH
VERNALIZE IAROVIZE JAROVIZE
YAROVIZE
VERONICA HEBE SUDARIUM
VERNICLE
VERRUCOSE WARTY WARTED
VERSATILE HANDY FICKLE MOBILE
FLEXILE
VERSE FIT EPIC LINE POSE RANN
RICH RIME SONG BLANK IONIC
METER METRE RHYME STAVE STICH
TANKA ADONIC ALCAIC BURDEN
CHIAVE CYWYDD DIPODY HEROIC
JINGLE PANTUN SCAZON STANZA
VERSET ANAPEST DICOLON
DOGGREL ELEGIAC PAEONIC
PENNILL SAPPHIC SAVITRI SOTADIC

STICHOS TRIPODY TROILUS
CHOLIAMB DACTYLIC DINGDONG
DOGGEREL GLYCONIC LEONINES
PRIAPEAN RESPONSE SENTENCE
SINGSONG TERETISM TRIMETER
VERSICLE
(— FORM) VIRELAY KYRIELLE
(— OF 14 LINES) SONNET
(— OF 2 FEET) DIPODY DIMETER
(— OF 6 FEET) CHOLIAMB SENARIAN
SENARIUS
(— WITH LIMPING MOVEMENT)
SCAZON
(DEVOTIONAL —) ANTIPHON
(HINDU —) SLOKA
(JAPANESE —) HAIKAI
(UNMELODIOUS —) TERETISM
(PL.) TRIPOS PINDARICS
VERSED SEEN WITTY BESEEN
TRADED STUDIED FREQUENT
OVERSEEN SCIENCED
(WELL —) SKILLFUL
VERSICLE VERSE VERSET STICHOS
SUFFRAGE
VERSIFIER BARD POET RHYMER
VERSER METERER
VERSIFY METER
VERSION DRAM DRAUGHT EDITION
READING TURNING
(SHORT —) BRIEF
(SIMPLIFIED —) KEY
(TRANSLATED —) CONSTRUE
VERSO REVERSE
VERT VERD POMME VENUS PRASINE
SINOPLE GREENHEW
VERTEBRA AXIS ATLAS DORSAL
LUMBAR SACRAL ACANTHA
CENTRUM CERVICAL METAMERE
PROATLAS RACKBONE SPONDYLE
VERTEBRATA CRANIATA CRANIOTA
VERTEBRATE CRANIATE SAUROPSID
VERTEX APEX COPE POLE CROWN
PITCH SUMMIT VERTICAL
VERTICAL ERECT PLUMB SHEER
WHIRL ORTHAL UPRIGHT COLUMNAR
SHEERING STRAIGHT
VERTICALLY PLUMP ENDLONG
SHEERLY DIRECTLY PALEWISE
VERTICIL WHORL
VERTIGINOUS DIZZY
VERTIGO DINUS TIEGO MEGRIM
MIRLIGO SWIMMING WHIRLING
VERUMONTANUM COLLICLE
VERVAIN GERVAO FROGFOOT
IRONWEED
VERVE DARE DASH BOUNCE ENERGY
PANACHE VITALITY VIVACITY
VERY SO ALL BIG DOG GAY GEY
MUY BRAW DEAD FELL FULL JUST
MAIN MUCH PURE RARE REAL SAME
SELF SUCH TRES UNCO WELL ASSAI
AWFUL BLAME BULLY CRAZY
DOOMS JOLLY MOLTO PESKY RIGHT
SOWAN SUPER SWITH UNCOW
VERRA BITTER BLAMED DAMNED
DEUCED FREELY GAINLY LIVING
MAINLY MASTER MIGHTY NATION
POISON PROPER STRONG VERRAY
WONDER AWFULLY BOILING

GALLOWS GREATLY PASSING
SOPPING STRANGE DEUCEDLY
DREADFUL ENORMOUS FAMOUSLY
POWERFUL PRECIOUS SPANKING
SWINGING WHACKING
VESICANT LEWISITE
VESICA PISCIS MANDORLA
VESICATORY BLISTER
VESICLE BLEB CYST APTHA BULLA
BURSE FLOAT APHTHA AMPULLA
BLADDER HYDATID POMPHUS
UTRICLE VACUOLE AEROCYST
MIDBRAIN VESICULA
VESICULAR BULLOSE BULLOUS
VESPERAL TOWEL
VESPERS LYCHNIC PLACEBO
EVENSONG
VESSEL (ALSO SEE BOAT AND SHIP)
GO CAN CAT COG CUP FAT GUM
HOY NEF PIG POT TUB VAS VAT VIA
BARK BOAT BODY BOMB BOOT
BOSS BOWL BRIG BUSH BUSS CASK
CELL COWL DISH DRIP DUCT GAWN
GRAB HORN HULK JACK JUNK LOTA
PINK PINT POST PROW SAIL SHIP
SNOW TING YAWL AMULA BAKIE
BARGE BASIN BIDET BIKIE BOCAL
BOYER CADUS CANNE CHURN
COGUE CRACK CRAER CRAFT
CRARE CRUET CRUSE DIOTA DUBBA
FLASK GLOBE GUIDE JUBBE KETCH
LADLE LAKER LAVER LINER PIECE
PYKAR SCOOP SMACK STEAM STILL
XEBEC YANKY ZABRA BANKER
BARQUE BARREL BILALO BOILER
BOTTLE BOUTRE BUCKET BURNER
CAIQUE CANNER CAPPIE CHARGE
CODMAN COFFIN CONCHA COOLER
COPPER CRATER CRAYER CRUISE
CUTTER DECKER DEINOS DOGGER
DUBBAH ELUTOR FESSEL FIRKIN
FLAGON HOLCAD HOOKER JAGGER
KERNOS KETTLE KRATER LANCHA
LATEEN LEKANE LORCHA MASLIN
MONKEY MULLER PACKET PANKIN
PATERA PICARD PITHOS POURIE
ROLLER SALTER SATTIE SEALER
SERVER SETTEE SHIBAR SITULA
SMOKER TARTAN TENDER TOPMAN
VESICA WHALER BAGGALA BALLOEN
BALLOON BLICKEY BLICKIE
BUGGALO CARAVEL CARRIER
CISTERN CLIPPER CORSAIR
COUGNAR CRAGGAN CRESSET
CRISSET CRUISER CUVETTE
DRIFTER DRINKER DROGHER
FELUCCA FLYBOAT FRIGATE
GABBARD GABBART GAIASSA
GALASSA GUNBOAT ORANGER
PATAMAR PINNACE POACHER
POLACRE PSYKTER REDUCER
SALTFAT SCALDER SEEDLIP
SETTLER SPARGER SPOUTER
STEAMER STEEPER TRACHEA
TRENDLE UTENSIL BELANDER
BENITIER BILANDER BILLYBOY
BIRDBATH BLEACHER CORVETTE
CRUCIBLE CRUISKEN CUCURBIT
DECANTER DIGESTER DUTCHMAN

EFFERENT EMISSARY FIREBOAT
FLESHPOT GALLIPOT GALLIVAT
GAROOKUH GAYDIANG HELLSHIP
HONEYPOT INKSTAND INRIGGER
IRONCLAD IRONSIDE KEELBOAT
LATEENER LAVATORY NITRATOR
PICAROON SCHOONER SMUGGLER
SPITTOON WATERPOT
(— FOR COAL) GEORDIE
(— FOR DYE) TOBY
(— FOR HEATING LIQUIDS) ETNA
(— FOR HOLY WATER) FAT FONT
STOCK STOOP STOUP
(— FOR HYPODERMIC USE) AMPUL
AMPULE AMPOULE
(— FOR LIQUID WASTE) DRIP
(— FOR MEASURING ORE) HOPPET
(— FOR MOLTEN METAL) LADLE
(— FOR ORE WASHINGS) LOOL
(— FOR PERFUMES) CENSER
(— FOR SOLDIER'S FOOD) MESSTIN
(— FOR WINE SAMPLING) TASTER
(— HOLDING CONDIMENTS) CRUET
CASTER
(— IN MINE) CORB
(— MADE OF HOLLOW LOG) GUM
(— OF BARK) COOLAMAN
COOLAMON COOLIMAN
(— OF HORN) BUGLE
(— ON TRIPOD) HOLMOS
(— ROWED BY OARS) CATUR
GALLEY
**(— STATIONED IN ENGLISH
CHANNEL)** GROPER
(— USED IN MAKING GLAZE) HILLER
(ABANDONED —) DERELICT
(ARMORED —) CRUISER IRONCLAD
IRONSIDE
(BAPTISMAL —) FONT
(BARGELIKE —) PANGARA
(BLOOD —) AORTA ARTERY
BLEEDER EFFERENT
(BREWER'S —) ROUND
(CANDLEMAKING —) JACK
(CHEMIST'S —) BATH FLASK STILL
BEAKER RETORT
(CHINESE —) JUNK SAMPAN
(CIRCULAR —) KIT
(CLUMSY —) CRAY CRARE
HAGBOAT
(COASTING —) DHOW DONI GRAB
PONTIN SHEBAR SHIBAR TRADER
COASTER GRIBANE
(CODFISHING —) BANKER CODMAN
(DECORATIVE —) AIGUIERE
(DISTILLING —) BODY STILL RETORT
CUCURBIT
(DRINKING —) CAP CUP TIN BOOT
PECE FOUNT GLASS GOURD JORUM
SCALE BICKER CAPPIE CHOPIN
COOPER COOTIE DIPPER DUBBER
FIRLOT GOBLET KITTIE QUAICH
QUAIGH RABBIT RUMKIN BIBERON
CANAKIN CANIKIN GALLIOT
SCYPHUS SKINKER SKYPHOS
TANKARD CANNIKIN CYLINDER
(DUTCH —) KOFF YANKY HOOKER
SCHUIT SCHUYT
(EARTHEN —) PIG BAYAN PANKIN

TINAGE CRAGGAN
(ELECTROPLATING —) TROUGH
(EUCHARISTIC —) AMA PYX AMULA
PYXIS FLAGON COLUMBA CHRISMAL
CIBORIUM
(GLASS —) VERRE UNDINE BALLOON
(HERRING-FISHING —) BUSS
(HOLLOW METALLIC —) BELL
(INVERTED —) BELL
(LADLING —) GAUN
(LARGE-NECKED —) JORDAN
(LATEEN-RIGGED —) DHOW LATEEN
LATEENER
(LEATHER —) BOOT JACK OLPE
GIRBA DUBBER
(LEVANTINE —) JERM SAIC
(LONG-NECKED —) GOGLET GUGLET
(LYMPHATIC —) LACTEAL
(MALAYAN —) PROA COUGNAR
(MELTING —) GRISSET
(OPEN —) LOOM
(PERFORATED —) LEACH
(PINECONE-SHAPED —) THYRSE
(PORTUGUESE —) MULET
(RARE —) SNOW
(SEED —) POD BUTTON
(SERVING —) ARGYLE ARGYLL
SERVER
(SHALLOW —) KIVER SKEEL BEDPAN
PANCHION
(SMALL —) CAG HOY VIAL PHIAL
VEDET JIGGER LIEPOT PICARD
TINLET YETLIN FLIVVER VEDETTE
YETLING GALLIPOT
(TOP-HEAVY —) CRANK
(TURKISH —) MAHONE
(WHALING —) WHALER SPOUTER
(WICKER —) POT
(WINE —) AMA AMULA TINAGE
(WOODEN —) COG KIT BOSS BAKIE
KIVER BICKER CAPPIE COOTIE
DUDDIE FIRKIN STOUND
(PL.) CRAFT WAFTAGE
VEST GARB GOWN ROBE GILET
ACCRUE ATTACH FECKET INVEST
JACKET JELICK LINDER WESKIT
ENFEOFF CLOTHING
(— IN) STATE
VESTA WAX
(FATHER OF —) SATURN
(MOTHER OF —) RHEA
(SISTER OF —) JUNO CERES
VESTED BESTEAD DONATIVE
VESTIBULE HALL ENTRY FOYER
PORCH ATRIUM EPINAOS NARTHEX
PASSAGE ANTEROOM VESTIARY
VESTIGE TAG DREG MARK RACK
SIGN PRINT RELIC SPARK TRACE
TRACK TRACT UMBRA SHADOW
MENTION LEFTOVER TINCTURE
VESTIGIAL REDUCED
VESTING ADITIO
VESTITURE TIRE RAIMENT TUNICLE
VESTMENT ALB CAP ALBE COPE
PALL VEST AMICE COTTA EPHOD
FANON RABAT RASON STOLE
RHASON ROCHET SACCOS SAKKOS
VAKASS MANIPLE ORARION PALLIUM
PILLION PLUVIAL TUNICLE VESTURE

CHASUBLE DALMATIC PHRYGIUM RATIONAL SCAPULAR SURPLICE VESTIARY
(PL.) GARB GEAR DRESS CLOTHING

VESTRY SACRISTY VESTIARY

VESUVIANITE EGERAN CYPRINE IDOCRASE VESUVIAN XANTHITE

VETCH DAL ERS AKRA LUCK TARE TINE ERVIL FITCH AXSEED FECCHE THETCH ARVEJON TINETARE TINEWEED

VETERAN VET CHAUVIN EMERITUS HARDENED SEASONED

VETERINARIAN VET LEECH FARRIER

VETERINARY VET FARRIERY

VETIVER BEN KHUS CUSCUS KUSKUS KHASGHAS KHUSKHUS

VETO KILL DISALLOW NEGATIVE

VEUGLAIRE FOWLER

VEX FRY TEW CARK CHAW FASH FAZE FRET FYKE GALL HALE ITCH RILE ROIL RUCK TEEN TOUT YOKE ANGER ANNOY CHAFE FRUMP GRAME GRILL GRIND GRIPE HARRY SCALD SPITE STURT TARRY TEASE WORRY WRACK WRATH YEARN BOTHER BURDEN CORSIE COTTER CUMBER GRIEVE GRUDGE HARASS HARROW INFEST NETTLE OFFEND PLAGUE POTHER RUFFLE THREAT WORRIT BEDEVIL CHAGRIN DESPITE PERPLEX PROVOKE TORMENT BULLYRAG EXERCISE IRRITATE MACERATE

VEXATION VEX CHAW FASH MOIL TEEN TRAY CHAFE CROSS ERROR GRIEF HARRY PIQUE SPITE STEAM WORRY BOTHER REPINE CHAGRIN DISGUST NOISANCE SORENESS

VEXATIOUS SORE TEEN PESKY ACHING FIERCE SHREWD VEXFUL IRKSOME PRICKLY TARSOME ANNOYING CUMBROUS FRAMPOLD PHRAMPEL UNTOWARD VEXATORY WEARIFUL

VEXED DIK MAD RILY SORE TEEN WAXY WILD WRAW ANGRY NARKY RAGGY ROILY MIFFED MUFFED SHIRTY SNUFFY FRABOUS GRIEVED IRKSOME OUTDONE
(EASILY —) CROSS

VEXILLUM WEB VEXIL BANNER STANDARD

VEXING CHRONIC TECHING WAYWARD ANNOYING NETTLING TEACHING

V-GOUGE VEINER

VIABLE VITAL HEALTHY

VIAL AMPUL CRUET PHIAL AMPULE CASTER CASTOR AMPOULE

VIANDS CATE DIET FOOD CHEER VIANDRY VICTUALS

VIBRANT RINGY BRAWLING RESONANT SONOROUS VIGOROUS

VIBRATE JAR WAG BEAT CAST DIRL PLAY ROCK TIRL WHIR PULSE QUAKE SWING THIRL THROB TRILL WAVER DINDLE JUDDER QUAVER QUIVER SHIVER THRILL WARBLE

CHATTER FLUTTER LIBRATE STAGGER TREMBLE TWIDDLE EVIBRATE FLICHTER RESONATE
(— ABNORMALLY) SHIMMY

VIBRATING (— OF AIRPLANE) BUFFET

VIBRATION BUZZ DIRL FLIP TIRL SWING DINDLE QUAVER QUIVER THRILL TREMOR DANCING FLUTTER TEMBLOR DIADROME FREMITUS VIBRANCY
(— OF SAW) CUPPING
(RATTLING —) JAR

VIBRATO TRILL WHINE

VIBRATOR TREMBLER

VIBRISSA FEELER SMELLER

VIBURNUM MAE MAY SNOWBALL

VICAR PROXY DEPUTY STALLAR ALTARIST STALLARY

VICE SIN EVIL CRIME FAULT TAINT ULCER DEFECT DEPUTY INIQUITY

VICE-GERENT EPHOR

VICE-PRESIDENT (— OF SANHEDRIN) ABBETDIN

VICEREGENT VICAR SUBPRIOR

VICEROY EARL VALI NABOB NAWAB NAZIM SUBAH EXARCH KEHAYA PROREX PROVES SATRAP WARDEN PROVOST TSUNGTU SUBAHDAR

VICIA FABA

VICINITY HERE SHADOW ENVIRONS
(— OF MINE SHAFT) COLLAR
(NEAR —) SUBURBS

VICIOUS BAD ILL EVIL LAZY LEWD MEAN UGLY VILE ROWDY TOUGH SINFUL STRONG VITIAL WICKED CORRUPT IMMORAL SKAITHY DEPRAVED DEVILISH FRATCHED INFAMOUS THEWLESS

VICIOUSNESS VICE

VICISSITUDE CHANGE MUTATION
(— OF FORTUNE) WEATHER

VICTIM BUTT DUPE GOAT GULL PREY PATHIC CASUALTY
(— FOR SHARPERS) JAY
(INTENDED —) CHUMP
(SACRIFICIAL —) HOST MERIAH
(UNFORTUNATE —) BASTARD

VICTIMIZATION RIDE

VICTIMIZE HOAX BUNCO BUNKO COZEN

VICTOR COCK CAPTOR MASTER WINNER BANGSTER

VICTORFISH AKU

VICTORIA (FATHER OF —) PALLAS
(MOTHER OF —) STYX

VICTORIAN GENTEEL

VICTORIOUS VICTOR WINNING

VICTORY WIN PALM PRICE BETTER SUBDUE VICTOR SACKING TRIUMPH WINNING CONQUEST DECISION WALKOVER
(EASY —) BREEZE
(OVERWHELMING —) SWEEP

VICTUAL BIT VITE VITTLE
(BROKEN —S) SCRAN
(PL.) KAI BITE CHOW FOOD GRUB PROG SAND VIVERS

VICTUALER PURVEYOR

VIDELICET NAMELY SILICET

VIE ENVY JOSTLE STRIVE COMPETE CONTEND CONTEST EMULATE

VIETNAM (SEE NORTH VIETNAM AND SOUTH VIETNAM)

VIETNAMESE ANNAMESE

VIEW EYE KEN FACE GLOM MAKE VISE AVIEW BLUSH CATCH MOUTH SCAPE SCENE SIGHT VISTA VIZZY ADVICE ADVISE ASPECT DEVICE GLANCE REGARD SURVEY ALOGISM CONCEIT FEELING GLIMPSE KENNING LOOKOUT OFFLOOK OPINION RESPECT SCENERY SURVIEW THOUGHT AIRSCAPE CONSPECT EYESIGHT OFFSCAPE SEASCAPE SENTENCE
(— ATTENTIVELY) GAZE
(— CLOSELY) INSPECT
(— FROM AFAR) DESCRY
(— FROM ANGLE) SLANT
(— OF MAN) DUALISM
(— WITH SURPRISE) ADMIRE
(BRIEF —) SNAPSHOT
(COMPREHENSIVE —) PANORAMA
(GENERAL —) LANDSKIP
(OPEN —) LIGHT
(PHYSICAL —) INSIGHT
(SATISFYING —) EYEFUL

VIEWPOINT SIGHT LAXISM

VIGIL WAKE WATCH WAKING AGRYPNIA

VIGILANCE WATCH JEALOUSY

VIGILANT AGOG WAKE WARY ALERT AWAKE AWARE CHARY SHARP JEALOUS WAKEFUL CAUTIOUS WATCHFUL

VIGOR GO SAP VIM VIR VIS BIRR DASH EDGE ELAN LUST PITH SEVE SNAP TUCK ARDOR DRIVE FLUSH FORCE GREEN JUICE NERVE POWER ENERGY ESPRIT FOISON GINGER SPRAWL SPRING STARCH VIGOUR VIRTUS FREEDOM SMEDDUM STAMINA STHENIA FLOURISH STRENGTH TONICITY VITALITY
(FULL OF —) LIFESOME
(MENTAL —) DOCITY SPIRIT
(RENEWED —) REST

VIGOROUS YEP ABLE CANT FRIM HALE LIVE RUDE SPRY YEPE CRANK EAGER FRACK FRANK JUICY LUSTY NIPPY PITHY SASSY SOLID STARK STIFF STOUT TOUGH VIVID FLORID GOLDEN HEARTY LIVELY POTENT ROBUST RUGGED SINEWY SQUARE STRONG BUCKISH CHIPPER CORDIAL DRASTIC FECKFUL FURIOUS HEALTHY NERVOSE NERVOUS VALIANT VIBRANT ZEALOUS ATHLETIC BOUNCING CHOPPING FORCEFUL MUSCULAR SLAMBANG SLASHING STUBBORN VEHEMENT VIGOROSO YOUTHFUL
(NOT —) GENTEEL

VIGOROUSLY DOWN FELL HARD VERN CRANK SNELL TIGHT VERNE HARDLY SNELLY FRESHLY SMARTLY STOUTLY WIGHTLY HEARTILY

VIGOROUSNESS ENERGY FREEDOM
VIKING DANE WIKING NORSEMAN
VIKRAMADITYA BIKRAM
VILE BAD BASE CLAM FOUL CHEAP
MUCKY POCKY RUSTY SLIMY WILLE
ABJECT CRUSTY DRAFTY DRASTY
FILTHY LECHER NOUGHT PALTRY
SORDID TURPID UNKIND BENEATH
CAITIFF CORRUPT DEBASED
HATEFUL IGNOBLE SLAVISH VICIOUS
BASEBORN DEPRAVED UNKINDLY
VILENESS FEDITY VILITY
VILIFICATION REPROACH
VILIFY ILL VILE ABUSE LIBEL STAIN
DEFAME MALIGN REVILE SLIGHT
ASPERSE BLACKEN DEBAUCH
DETRACT TRADUCE REPROACH
STRUMPET
VILIPEND BELITTLE
VILL HAM TOWN TOWNSHIP
VILLA ALDEA DACHA DATCHA
QUINTA TRIANON
VILLAGE BY AUL BYE GAV HAM KOM
PAH REW BURG DORP HOME MURA
TOWN VILL WICK ALDEA BOURG
CASAL PLACE THORP VICUS ALDEIA
BARRIO BUSTEE CASTLE GOTHAM
HAMLET HAMMON MOUZAH PETTAH
PUEBLO AMBALAM BOROUGH
CAMPODY CASERIO ENDSHIP
MAABARA MISSION OUTPOST
BEREWICK BOURGADE CAMPOODY
CRANFORD TOLDERIA VILLACHE
VILLAGET VILLAKIN
(— IN WHICH BARLEY IS GROWN)
BEREWICK
(— OUTSIDE OF FORT) PETTAH
(AFRICAN —) STAD KRAAL
(ARABIAN —) DOUAR
(ARGENTINE —) TOLDERIA
(FRENCH —) BASTIDE
(IMAGINARY —) CRANFORD
(INDIAN —) CASTLE PUEBLO
CAMPODY CAMPOODY
(JAPANESE —) MURA BUSTI BUSTEE
(JAVANESE —) DESSA
(MALAY —) CAMPONG KAMPONG
(MAORI —) KAIK KAIKA KAINGA
(MEXICAN —) EJIDO
(NEW ZEALAND FORTIFIED —) PA
PAH
(RUSSIAN —) MIR STANITSA
STANITZA
VILLAIN IAGO LOUT SERF BADDY
BRAVO CHURL DEMON DEVIL FAGIN
FELON HEAVY KNAVE ROGUE
SCAMP SHREW BADDIE VILIACO
SCELERAT
VILLAINOUS BAD EVIL GALLUS
GALLOWS KNAVISH VILEYNS
FLAGRANT RASCALLY
VILLAINY CRIME KNAVERY
VILLEIN SERF CHURL COTTER
VILLAR BONDMAN TOWNMAN
VILLAIN COTARIUS
VILLI (HAVING —) ZONARY
VILLOUS SHAGGY
VIM ZIP GIMP ZING FORCE VIGOR

ENERGY GINGER SPIRIT STARCH
VINEGAR
VINA BEN BIN BINA
VINCENTIAN LAZARIST
VINDICATE FREE CLEAR RIGHT
WREAK ACQUIT ASSERT AVENGE
EXCUSE UPHOLD ABSOLVE DERAIGN
JUSTIFY PROPUGN REVENGE
SUSTAIN
VINDICATION APOLOGY THEODICY
VINDICATOR VINDEX ASSERTER
DEFENDER
VINDICTIVE HOSTILE PUNITIVE
SPITEFUL VENGEFUL
VINE AKA FIG HOP IVY IYO BINE
CARO GOGO ODAL SOMA TINE
AKEBI BUAZE BWAZI CAAPI CACUR
GUACO KAIWI KUDZU LIANA PALAY
PRIVY TACSO TIMBO TRAIL TWINE
WITHE WONGA BEJUCO CISSUS
COBAEA COWAGE DERRIS DODDER
ECANDA GERKIN IPOMEA JICAMA
LABLAB RUNNER TURURI TWINER
ULLUCO WINDER APRICOT BIGROOT
BONESET BRAMBLE CALAMUS
CATVINE CERIMAN CLIMBER
COWHAGE COWITCH CUPSEED
EPACRID GHERKIN IPOMOEA
LAVANGA PAREIRA PUMPKIN
TRAILER VINELET YANGTAO
ATRAGENE BINDWEED BOXTHORN
CLEMATIS COMEBACK CUCUMBER
CUCURBIT DECUMARY DOLICHOS
EARDROPS EARTHPEA EVONYMUS
GULANCHA HEARTPEA HEMPWEED
MUSCATEL REDWITHE TINETARE
TINEWEED TRAILERY TRAILING
TREEBINE VINIFERA WINETREE
WISTARIA WISTERIA
VINEGAR EISEL ESILL ACETUM
ALEGAR ASCILL SOURING
BEEREGAR VINAIGRE
VINEGAR EEL EELWORM
VINEGARY ACETOSE ACETOUS
VINEGROWER VINITOR
VINEYARD CRU CLOS COTE VINER
VINERY WINEYARD
VINGT-ET-UN MACAO MACCO
VINOUS WINY
VINTAGE OLD VINT WINE CUVEE
ARCHAIC CLASSIC VENDAGE
OUTMODED
VIOL GUE GIGA LIRA TURR GIGUE
GUDOK TARAU VOYAL VOYOL
CHELYS FIDDLE VIELLE VIOLET
MINIKIN QUINTON SARINDA SULTANA
VIHUELA VIOLONE BARBITON
BASSETTE SERINGHI VIOLETTE
VIOLA ALTO QUINT TENOR TENORE
VIOLET
VIOLA BASTARDA BARITONE
BARYTONE
VIOLA DA BRACCIO QUINT
VIOLA D'AMORE VIOLET
VIOLA DA GAMBA GAMBA
VIOLATE ERR SIN FLAW ABUSE
BREAK CRACK FORCE HARRY
LOOSE VIOLE WRONG BREACH
BROACH DEFILE INVADE OFFEND

RAVISH DEBAUCH DISOBEY FALSIFY
INFRACT OUTRAGE POLLUTE
DEFLOWER DISHONOR FORSWEAR
FRACTURE INFRINGE MISTREAT
STUPRATE SURPRISE TEMERATE
TRESPASS VIOLENCE
VIOLATED FRACTED INFRACT
VIOLATION SIN DEBT ABUSE CRIME
ERROR FAULT SALLY BREACH
INJURY
(HOCKEY —) STICKS
VIOLATOR WRONGER
VIOLENCE FURY NEED RAGE RUFF
BRUNT FORCE RIGOR STORM
BENSIL ESTURE HUBRIS RANDOM
RAPINE STOUSH BENSAIL BENSALL
OUTRAGE FEROCITY SEVERITY
SORENESS
(LETHAL —) DEATH
VIOLENT BIG HOT TEZ DERF HARD
HIGH MAIN RANK RUDE WILD WOOD
ACUTE FIERY HEADY HEAVY HEFTY
RABID SHARP SMART STARK STERN
STIFF STOOR STOUR STOUT WROTH
BROTHE FIERCE HEARTY MANIAC
MIGHTY SAVAGE SEVERE STORMY
STRONG STURDY SUDDEN CRIMSON
FURIOUS HOTSPUR RAMMISH
RAPEFUL RUFFIAN TEARING
VIOLOUS WILSOME CHURLISH
DIABOLIC FLAGRANT FORCEFUL
IMPOTENT MANIACAL RIGOROUS
SEETHING SLAMBANG STALWART
VEHEMENT
VIOLENTLY HARD AMAIN HOTLY
HARDLY SORELY HOPPING SOUNDLY
VIOLET CANON GRAPE MAUVE VIOLA
BLAVER CANYON DAHLIA DAMSON
EVEQUE JOHNNY HOOKERS LOBELIA
OPHELIA PRELATE PRIMULA
PUREAYN CLEMATIS DAMEWORT
FINELEAF IANTHINE ROOSTERS
WISTERIA
VIOLIN GUE KIT ALTO GIGA AMATI
CROWD GEIGE GIGUE REBAB REBEC
STRAD TARAU VIOLA CATGUT
CHORUS CROUTH FIDDLE FITHEL
REBECK TAILLE VIOLON CATLING
CHROTTA CREMONA THEYAOU
VIOLAND VIOLINO GUARNERI
KEMANCHA VIOLOTTA
VIPER ASP HABU ADDER ASPIC
ATHER URUTU WYVER ASPIDE
DABOIA DABOYA JESSUR KATUKA
KUPPER HAGWORM MAMUSHI
VIPERID AMMODYTE CERASTES
JARARACA VIPERINE
VIRAGO RANDY AMAZON BELDAM
CALLET BELDAME TRIMMER VIRAGIN
RIXATRIX
VIREO REDEYE GRASSET TEACHER
GREENLET PREACHER
VIRGATE YOKE VERGE YARDLAND
(HALF —) MANTAL
VIRGIN NEW LIVE MAID PURE FRESH
CHASTE MAIDEN VESTAL INITIAL
PUCELLE DOROTHEA PARAMOUR
(— OF PARADISE) HURI HOURI

VIRGINAL CHERRY INTACT SYMPHONY TRIANGLE

VIRGINIA

CAPITAL: RICHMOND
COLLEGE: AVERETT HOLLINS MADISON RADFORD LONGWOOD
COUNTY: BATH PAGE BLAND FLOYD SMYTH SURRY WYTHE AMELIA LOUISA ACCOMAC HENRICO PULASKI ROANOKE CULPEPER FLUVANNA TAZEWELL
INDIAN: SAPONI TUTELO MONACAN MANAHOAC MEHERRIN NOTTAWAY POWHATAN
LAKE: KERR SMITH
MOUNTAIN: CEDAR ELLIOT ROGERS BALDKNOB
MOUNTAIN RANGE: CLINCH ALLEGHENY BLUERIDGE
PRESIDENT: TYLER MONROE TAYLOR WILSON MADISON HARRISON JEFFERSON WASHINGTON
RIVER: DAN JAMES POTOMAC RAPIDAN
STATE BIRD: CARDINAL
STATE FLOWER: DOGWOOD
STATE TREE: DOGWOOD
TOWN: GALAX LURAY SALEM MARION BEDFORD BRISTOL EMPORIA NORFOLK PULASKI ROANOKE DANVILLE HOPEWELL MANASSAS STAUNTON TAZEWELL

VIRGINIA COWSLIP LUNGWORT
VIRGINIA CREEPER CREEPER WOODBIND WOODBINE
VIRGINIA KNOTWEED JUMPSEED
VIRGINIAN BEAGLE COOHEE CAVALIER TUCKAHOE
VIRGINIA SNAKEROOT SANGREL SNAGREL
VIRGINIA STICKSEED SOLDIERS
VIRGINIA WATERLEAF SHAWNY
VIRGINIA WILLOW ITEA
VIRGINITY HONOR PUCELAGE
VIRGIN MARY DESPOINA THEOTOCOS
VIRGIN'S-BOWER LOVE HONESTY MOONWORT
VIRGULE VIRGULA DIAGONAL
VIRIDIAN EMERAUDE
VIRILE MALE MANLY
VIRILITY LUST GREEN MANHEAD MANHOOD
VIRTUAL IMPLICIT
VIRTUALLY BUT NEARLY MORALLY
VIRTUE JEN HSIN THEW ARETE FAITH GRACE POWER VALOR VERTU WORTH BOUNTY DHARMA CHARISM CHARITY JUSTICE PROBITY QUALITY CHARISMA CHASTITY EFFICACY GOODNESS MORALITY PARAMITA
(CONFUCIAN —) LI
(PL.) CIVISM

VIRTUOSO EXPERT SAVANT ESTHETE LAPIDARY
VIRTUOUS GOOD PURE BRAVE CIVIL MORAL CHASTE HONEST MODEST GODDARD SAINTED SINCERE UPRIGHT VIRTUAL STRAIGHT
VIRULENCE VIRUS
VIRULENT ACRID RABID DEADLY MALIGN VIROSE NOXIOUS VIRIFIC VENOMOUS
(LESS THAN —) MITIS
VIRUS VENOM POISON PATHOGEN SPECIFIC
VIS PEIKTHA
VISAGE FACE CHEER IMAGE VISOR ASPECT FASHION
VISCERA GUTS HASLET INSIDE UMBLES GARBAGE GIBLETS HASSLET INMEATS INNARDS INSIDES NUMBLES ENTRAILS
VISCID SLAB WAXY GOOEY GLAIRY STICKY LENTOUS STRINGY VISCOUS MOTHERED
VISCIDITY LENTOR
VISCOSITY BODY
(— UNIT) POISE
VISCOUS LIMY ROPY SIZY SLAB GOBBY GUMMY ROPEY SLIMY STIFF TARRY SIRUPY SLABBY SMEARY SNOTTY STICKY THONGY VISCID LENTOUS SQUISHY VISCOSE MUCULENT
VISE GEE CHAP JACK SHOP VICE CHEEK CLAMP CRAMP WINCH
VISHNU RAMA VASU KALKI KRISHNA BALARAMA BHAGAVAT
VISIBLE OUT FAIR SEEN CLEAR GROSS EXTANT SIGHTY EVIDENT GLARING OBVIOUS SIGHTLY APPARENT DIOPTRIC EXPLICIT EXTERNAL MANIFEST PROSPECT
(BARELY —) DARK
(SCARCELY —) DIM
VISION EYE RAY DREAM FANCY SIGHT FANTAD SEEING SWEVEN AISLING SHOWING SPECTER SPECTRE EYESIGHT PHOTOPIA
(— IN DIM LIGHT) SCOTOPIA
(BLURRED —) SWIMMING
(DEFECTIVE —) ANOPIA
(IMAGINARY —) SHADOW
(IMPERFECT —) DARKNESS
(MULTIPLE —) POLYOPIA
VISIONARY FEY AERY AIRY WILD IDEAL VIEWY ASTRAL INSANE SHANDY UNREAL DREAMER FANTAST LAPUTAN UTOPIAN ACADEMIC DELUSIVE FANCIFUL FINESPUN IDEALIST NOTIONAL PHANTAST QUIXOTIC ROMANTIC UTOPIAST VISIONER
VISIT DO GAM SEE VIS CALL CHAT STAY APPLY HAUNT TRYST VIZZY COSHER RESORT RETURN CEILIDH CEILIDHE FREQUENT INVASION
(— BETWEEN WHALERS) GAM
(— PERSISTENTLY) INFEST
(— PROFESSIONALLY) ATTEND
(— RELATIVES) COUSIN

(— WRETCHED NEIGHBORHOODS) SLUM
(CEREMONIAL —) SELAMLIK
VISITATION SENE VISIT SENDING
VISITING ACTIVE SOCIAL
VISITOR GUEST LAKER CALLER VISITANT
(MEALTIME —) SCAMBLER
(PL.) COMPANY
VISOR BILL SIGHT UMBER UMBRE VIZOR BEAVER MESAIL UMBRIL VIZARD EYESHADE
VISTA VIEW SCENE OUTLOOK
VISUAL OPTIC OCULAR SCOPIC VISORY VISIBLE
VISUALIZE SEE FANCY IDEATE SYMBOL IMAGINE PICTURE CONCEIVE ENVISAGE
VITAL LIVE BASIC CHIEF FRESH SAPPY LIVELY MOVING VIABLE ZOETIC ANIMATE CAPITAL CORDIAL EXIGENT NEEDFUL ESSENTIAL
VITALITY SAP VIM LIFE COLOR GUSTO JUICE BIOSIS BREATH ENERGY FOISON HEALTH STARCH VIVENCY STRENGTH
(DEFICIENT —) ASTHENIA
(LACKING —) STUFFY TURNIPY
VITALIZE ACTIVATE ENERGIZE
VITAMIN BIOTIN CITRIN NIACIN ADERMIN ANEURIN CHOLINE THIAMIN TORULIN ADVITANT INOSITOL NUTRAMIN ORYZANIN VITAMINE
VITIATE BEAT SPOIL TAINT CANCEL DEBASE POISON CORRUPT DEPRAVE
VITIATED PICAL CORRUPT
VITICULTURIST VIGNERON
VITREOUS GLASSY GLAIZIE VITREAN VITROUS
VITRIFY GLAZE
VITRIOL BLUEJACK COPPERAS
(PL.) SORY
VITRIOLIC SHARP BITING BITTER CAUSTIC MORDANT SCATHING
VITUPERATE RAIL ABUSE CURSE SCOLD BERATE REVILE
VITUPERATION ABUSE VITUPER
VITUPERATIVE ABUSIVE REVILING SHAMEFUL
VIVACE VIVO LEBHAFT
VIVACIOUS GAY AIRY BRISK CRISP MERRY SUNNY ACTIVE LIVELY LIVING SPARKY VIVACE ANIMATE JOCULAR ANIMATED SPIRITED SPORTIVE
VIVACITY BRIO FIRE LIFE ZEAL ARDOR VERVE VIGOR ESPRIT GAIETY GAYETY SPIRIT SPRAWL SPARKLE
VIVARIUM STEW VIVARY STEWPOND
VIVAT HOCH
VIVERRINE CIVET GENET FOUSSA MUSANG LINSANG FALANAKA MONGOOSE SURICATE
VIVID DEEP HARD KEEN LIVE RICH VIVE BRISK FRESH GREEN LURID QUICK RUDDY SHARP GARISH LIVELY LIVING STRONG VISUAL

EIDETIC FLAMING FREAKED
GLARING GLOWING GRAPHIC
INTENSE VIOLENT COLORFUL
DISTINCT DRAMATIC SLASHING
STRIKING VIGOROUS
VIVIDNESS COLOR EMPHASIS
VIVIFY LIFE FOMENT ANIMATE
QUICKEN SPARKLE
VIVIPARUS PALUDINA
VIXEN BARD FURY SCOLD SHREW
VIRAGO TAGSTER TRIMMER
VIZIER WAZIR ATABEG ATABEK
VISIER
VLACH WALLACH
V-MAIL AIRGRAPH
VOCABULARY CANT SLANG JARGON
DICTION LEXICON POCHISMO
WORDBOOK
(UNDERWORLD —) ARGOT
VOCAL GLIB ORAL VOWEL FLUENT
TONGUED VOCULAR ELOQUENT
VOCALIST BOPPER SINGER BOPPIST
BOPSTER SONGSTER VOCALLER
VOCATION CALL HOBBY METIER
CALLING SCIENCE
VOCATIONAL BANAUSIC
VOCIFERATION CLAMOR OUTCRY
VOCIFEROUS LOUD NOISY BAWLING
BLATANT BRAWLING STRIDENT
VODKA SAMOGON SAMOGONKA
VOGUE CUT TON CHIC MODE TURN
STYLE CUSTOM FASHION RECLAME
PRACTICE
VOGUL MANSI
VOICE SAY VOX EMIT GIVE HARP
PIPE TONE TURN WISH FROTH
LEDEN RAISE RUMOR SOUND UTTER
ACTIVE CHOICE STEVEN TAISCH
THROAT TONGUE EXPRESS OPINION
SONORIZE DIATHESIS
(— PRAISE) SLAVER
(ARTIFICIAL —) FALSETTO
(FIFTH —) QUINTUS
(HOARSE —) FOGHORN
(LOWEST —) BASS BASSO
(MIDDLE —) MOTETUS
(PRINCIPAL —) CANTUS
(PUBLIC —) CRY
(SINGING —) ALTO BASS TENOR
BREAST SOPRANO BARITONE
FALSETTO
(TENOR —) TAILLE
(UPPER —) DESCANT DISCANT
VOICED SOFT WEAK TONIC MEDIAL
SONANT PHTHONGAL
VOICELESS MUM DUMB HARD MUTE
SURD SHARP ATONIC FLATED
SILENT ANAUDIA APHONIC SPIRATE
APHONOUS BREATHED NOTELESS
VOID NO BAD FREE KORE LEAR LEER
MUTE NULL PASS ABYSS AVOID
BLANK EGEST EJECT EMPTY INEPT
LAPSE PURGE SLICE SPACE WASTE
DEVOID HOLLOW VACANT VACUUM
CONCAVE INVALID VACANCY
VACUITY EVACUATE INDIGENT
NONBEING
(— OF FEELING) BLATE
(— OF SENSE) INANE

(— OF SUBSTANCE) JEJUNE
VOIDED FALSE CLECHE CLECHY
CLECHEE
VOILE NINON
VOLATILE LIGHT FIGENT LIVELY
VOLAGE BUOYANT DARTING
ELASTIC FLIGHTY FLYAWAY
GASEOUS FUGITIVE SKITTISH
VAPOROSE VAPOROUS FUGACIOUS
VOLATILITY LEVITY
VOLCANO APO DOME ETNA ASKJA
PELEE SHASTA VULCAN FURNACE
VULCANO FUMAROLE KRAKATOA
SPITFIRE VESUVIUS
(MUD —) SALSE SALINELLE
VOLE CRABER CRICETID
VOLITATION FLIGHT VOLATION
VOLITION WILL CHOICE INTENT
VOLENCY
VOLLEY CROWD DRIFT VOLEE
FLIGHT BARRAGE PLATOON
BLIZZARD
VOLPLANE GLIDE
VOLSUNG WAELS
VOLT VOLTA REPOLON
(— AMPERE UNIT) VAR
VOLTAGE KICKBACK
VOLTAIC GUR GALVANIC
VOLTE-FACE BACKFLIP
VOLUBILITY FLUENCY
VOLUBLE GLIB WORDY FLUENT
VOLUME MO PEN BAND BOOK BULK
SIZE TOME SPACE CUBAGE
CONTENT DIURNAL MENAION
VOLUMEN CAPACITY CUBATURE
SOLIDITY STRENGTH
(— OF SOUND) STRESS
(— OF WORT) LENGTH
(PATTERN —) DUMMY
VOLUMINOUS FULL AMPLE BULKY
LARGE BOUFFANT
VOLUNTARILY WILLES WILLICHE
VOLUNTARY FREE WILLY SORTIE
WILFUL PRELUDE SORTITA WILLFUL
WILLING ELECTIVE FREEWILL
HONORARY OPTIONAL POSTLUDE
UNFORCED
VOLUNTEER OFFER ENLIST
PROFFER STRANGER
(— STATE) TENNESSEE
VOLUPTUARY SYBARITE
VOLUPTUOUS ADIN LUXIVE LYDIAN
SULTRY WANTON SENSUAL
DELICATE LUSCIOUS SENSUOUS
VOLUPTUOUSNESS DELICE LUXURY
VOLUTE TURN HELIX SCROLL
VOLUTA CILLERY VOLUTION
VOLUTION COIL TWIST WHORL
VOLVA CUP WRAPPER
VOMIT CAT PUT BALK BOCK BOKE
CACK CAST PICK PUKE SICK SPEW
SPUE VOME WOOM BRAKE EVOME
HEAVE REACH RETCH SHOOT
POSSET REJECT VOMITO CASCADE
CASTING REGORGE DISGORGE
PARBREAK SICKNESS VOMITING
VOMITING BOKE EMESIS PYEMESIS
VOMITUS SPEW SPUE
VOODOO HEX OBI CHARM OBEAH

HOODOO SORCERER
(— DESIGN) VERVER
(— SPELL) MOJO
VOODOOISM VODUN WANGA
VORACIOUS GORB GREEDY BULIMIC
ESURINE GLUTTON THROATY
EDACIOUS ESURIENT RAVENING
RAVENOUS
VORACITY EDACITY
VORTEX APEX EDDY GYRE SWIRL
WHIRL
VOTARESS NUN
VOTARY PALMER ZEALOT DEVOTEE
SECTARY ADHERENT DEVOTARY
FOLLOWER
VOTE AYE CON NAY PRO ELECT
FAGOT GRACE VOICE BALLOT
DIVIDE FAGGOT TONGUE APPROVE
PLUMPER SUFFRAGE
(— AGAINST) NAY KNIFE
(— APPROVAL) CONFIRM
(— FOR) AY AYE PRO SUPPORT
(— OF ASSENT) PLACET
VOTER BOLTER POLLER CHOOSER
ELECTOR FLOATER ASSENTOR
VOTIVE VOWED
VOTYAK UDMURT
VOUCH ABLE ASSURE ATTEST
AVOUCH ENDORSE ACCREDIT
VOUCHER CHIT CHALAN POLICY
TICKET WARRANT
VOUCHSAFE GIVE SEND DEIGN
GRANT VOUCH BETEEM PLEASE
WITSAFE
VOUSSOIR QUOIN WEDGE
KEYSTONE SPRINGER
VOW LAY VUM AVOW OATH SNUM
VOTE SWEAR VOUCH BEHEST
PLEDGE BEHIGHT PROMISE
PROTEST
VOWEL SHWA WIDE GLIDE SCHWA
VOCOID AUGMENT GEMINATE
(— POINT) SERE
(CHANGE OF —) UMLAUT
(GROUP OF 2 —S) BROAD DIGRAM
DIGRAPH
(PREFIXED —) AUGMENT
(SHORT —) MATRA
VOYAGE SAIL TRIP VIAGE CRUISE
FLIGHT TRAVEL CARAVAN JOURNEY
PASSAGE SAILING STEAMER
PERIPLUS SHIPPING
VOYAGING SEA NAVIGANT
VULCANITE EBONITE
VULCANIZATION BURNING
VULCANIZE BURN CURE METALIZE
VULCANIZER CEMENTER
VULGAR LOW LEWD LOUD RUDE
FLASH GROSS SLANG SLIMY
COARSE COMMON PORTER RABBLE
VULGUS WOOLEN BOORISH
GENERAL KNAVISH LOWBRED
MOBBISH OBSCENE POPULAR
SECULAR TABLOID VILLAIN
WOOLLEN CHURLISH MECHANIC
PANDEMIC PLEBEIAN PORTERLY
POTHOUSE SOUTERLY
VULGARIAN SLOB RAFFISH

VULGARITY SHODDY FOULNESS
  HARLOTRY
VULGARIZE PLEBIFY PROFANE
VULGARIZED DEGRADED
VULGARLY CHEAPLY
VULNERABILITY GAP EXPOSURE

VULNERABLE LIABLE EXPOSED
VULPINE FOXY ALOPECOID
VULTURE AURA GEIR PAPA AREND
  GRAAP GRAPE GRIPE SWIPE URUBU
  CONDOR CORBIE FALCON GRIPHE
  RAPTOR SNATCH TORGOS GRIFFIN

  GRIFFON GRYPHON NEKHEBT
  AASVOGEL DIRTBIRD GEREAGLE
  NEKHEBET ZOPILOTE GALLINAZO
VULVA DOCK PUDENDUM
VUM SNUM

W WAW WHISKEY WILLIAM
WA VU KAWA LAWA
WABBLE COCKLE COGGLE HOBBLE WAGGLE WARBLE WAUBLE WOBBLE
WABBLY COGGLE WAGGLY WOBBLY
WABBY LOON WHABBY
WABRON WAYBERRY
WACKY CRAZY INSANE MENTAL ERRATIC
WAD BAT BET BOB PAD COLF LINE POKE SWAB SWOB WISP WAGER PLEDGE SCOURER GRAPHITE
WADDLE WAG HODDLE PODDLE TODDLE WALLOP WIDDLE WAUCHLE
WADDY PEG STICK COWBOY RUSTLER WHADDIE
WADE FORD WYDE SLOSH PLODGE PLOUTER PLUTTER
(— IN MUD) LAIR
WADI OUED WASH GULLY RAVINE
WADSET PAWN PLEDGE MORTGAGE
WAFER HOST ABRET OBLEY CACHET GAUFRE LAVASH MATZOH OFLETE POPADAM FLATBROD
WAFF WAG FLAP GUST ODOR PUFF WAVE WHIFF PALTRY FLUTTER GLIMPSE LOWBORN
WAFFIE VAGRANT VAGABOND
WAFFLE GOFER WAFER GAUFRE BLATHER
WAFT PUFF WHEFT WHIFF BECKON
WAG LUG NOD WIG WIT WOG CARD CHAP FLAG WAFF WALK DROLL JOKER SHAKE TROLL FARCER JESTER NICKUM WADDLE WAGGLE WAGWIT WIGWAG HUMORIST SLYBOOTS
WAGE FEE PAY WAR HIRE LEVY FIGHT WADGE WEDGE EMPLOY ENGAGE PACKET
(— BATTLE) STRIKE
WAGER GO BET LAY SET VIE WED GAGE HOLD PAWN TOSS WOID BOUND PRIZE RAISE REVIE SPORT STAKE STOOP WADGE DEPONE GAMBLE IMPONE LEVANT WEDFEE STOATER QUINELLA
WAGES FEE PAY UTU GAGE HIRE MEED GAGES TUNCA REWARD SALARY PENSION SERVICE STIPEND GRATUITY LABORAGE PAYCHECK REQUITAL
WAGGISH DROLL JOKEY JOCOSE JESTING JOCULAR ROGUISH WAGSOME HUMOROUS SPORTIVE
WAGGLE WAG WIGGLE WOBBLE WOGGLE
WAGON CAR FLY VAN CART CHAR DRAY PLOW RACK TEAM TRAM WAIN WANE BUGGY DILLY JERKY RULLY TRUCK CAMION ROLLEY SPIDER TELEGA CAISSON CHARIOT COASTER FOURGON TUMBREL TUMBRIL DEMOCRAT LANDSHIP RUNABOUT WHITETOP
(— WITHOUT SPRINGS) JERKY TELEGA
(BAGGAGE —) FOURGON
(COVERED —) VAN CARAVAN

LANDSHIP CONESTOGA
(LUMBER —) GILLY
(MINING —) TRAM RULLY ROLLEY
(ROUNDUP —) HOODLUM
(RUSSIAN —) TELEGA
(STATION —) SUBURBAN
(TEA —) SERVER
WAGONER AURIGA TREKKER WAINMAN
WAGONLOAD FODDER FOTHER
WAGONMAN FOOTMAN
WAGTAIL MOLLY OATEAR WAGGIE WASHER WATERIE SEEDBIRD WASHDISH WASHTAIL
WAHINE WIFE WOMAN FEMALE VAHINE FEMININE MISTRESS
WAHOO ONO PETO BASSWOOD EUONYMUS GUARAPUCU
WAIF WEFT STRAY FEEBLE PALTRY STRAFE CURRENT IGNOBLE WASTREL
WAIL CRY WOW BAWL GURL HOWL KEEN MOAN RAME YARM CROON MOURN ULULU LAMENT YAMMER EJULATE PLANGOR ULULATE ULLAGONE
WAILING WO WOE LAMENT ULULANT
WAIN CART WAGON WEYNE CHARIOT
WAINSCOT CEIL
WAINSCOTING CEILING PANELING
WAIST JOSIE BASQUE BLOUSE BODICE HALTER MIDDLE TAILLE CORSAGE PIERROT
WAISTCOAT VEST BENJY GILET FECKET JERKIN VESKIT WESKIT SINGLET CAMISOLE
WAISTER TROUNCER
WAIT BIDE HOLD KEEP LITE PARK STAY TEND WHET ABIDE DEFER HOVER TARRY WATCH ATTEND DEPEND EXPECT HARKEN LAYOUT LINGER
(— A WHILE) TAIHOA
(— FOR) KEEP ABIDE AWAIT ATTEND EXPECT
(— ON) HOP SEE SERVE INTEND LACKEY
(— TABLE) HASH SERVE
WAITER MOZO CARHOP DRAWER FLUNKY GARCON HASHER KIDNEY SALVER TENDER THOMAS DAPIFER FLUNKEY KELLNER PANNIER PICCOLO SERVITOR KITMUDGAR
WAITING DORMANT
WAITRESS HASHER PHYLLIS
WAIVE ABEY DEFER EVADE FORGO ABANDON DECLINE FORSAKE POSTPONE RENOUNCE
WAKA CANOE
WAKE WAK CROW NECK PLAY STIR ALERT REVEL ROUSE TANGI TRAIL VIGIL WATCH AROUSE AWAKEN EXCITE FEATHER
WAKEFUL ALERT WACKER RESTLESS VIGILANT WAKERIPE WALKRIFE WATCHFUL
WAKEFULNESS VIGIL WATCH INSOMNIA
WAKE-ROBIN SARA SARAH TRILLIUM

WAKF WAQF VAKUF VACOUF
WALACHIAN RUMAN VLACH ROMANESE
WALAHEE ALAHEE
WALAPAI HUALPAI
WALDENSIAN LEONIST PATARIN SABOTIER
WALE RIB PICK WEAL WELT RIDGE WHELP CHOICE HARPIN STROKE **(PL.)** BEND HARPINS
WALES CYMRU CAMBRIA

WALES

BAY: SWANSEA CARDIGAN TREMADOC
COUNTY: FLINT RADNOR DENBIGH ANGLESEY CARDIGAN MONMOUTH PEMBROKE
HILLS: MALVERN
LAKE: VYRNWY
LANGUAGE: CYMRAEG
MEASURE: COVER CANTRED CANTREF LESTRAD LISTRED CRANNOCK
MOUNTAIN: SNOWDEN
MOUNTAIN RANGE: BERWYN CAMBRIAN
PEOPLE: CYMRY KYMRY WELSH
PORT: CARDIFF
RIVER: DEE USK WYE TAFF TEME TOWY TEIFI SEVERN VYRNWY
TOWN: RHYL ROSS FLINT TOWYN AMLWCH BANGOR BRECON CARDIFF NEWPORT SWANSEA HEREFORD HOLYHEAD PEMBROKE

WALK GO JET MOG FOOT GAIT GANG HIKE HOOF LAMP PACE PAUT REEL STEP TROD ALLEE ALLEY ARBOR LEAVE MARCH PORCH SHANK SLOPE SPACE STALK TRACE TRACK TRADE TRAMP TREAD TROOP ATTEND AVENUE BEHAVE BOUNCE BRIDGE BROGUE DANDER PASEAR SASHAY STROKE TODDLE TRAVEL TRUDGE BERCEAU CRAMBLE FOOTING GALLERY SHUFFLE STRETCH TRACHLE TRAIPSE TURNOUT AMBULATE ARBORWAY FLAGGING FRESCADE NAVIGATE TRAVERSE
(— ABOUT) SLOSH
(— AFFECTEDLY) PRINK
(— AIMLESSLY) PAUP POAP
(— AWKWARDLY) STAUP SHAMBLE
(— BEFORE) PREAMBLE
(— BRISKLY) LEG SKELP
(— CAUTIOUSLY) STALK
(— CLUMSILY) JOLL STUMP LOPPET
(— FOR CATTLE) GANG
(— FOR EXAMINING ENGINE) GALLERY
(— FOR EXERCISE) HIKE GRIND
(— HEAVILY) PLOD STUMP TRAMP LAMPER PLODGE
(— IDLY) DANDER POTTER SAUNTER
(— IN AFFECTED MANNER) MINCE

(— LAME) LIMP HIRPLE HOBBLE CRIPPLE
(— LEISURELY) AMBLE DANDER STROLL
(— ON) BEAT TREAD
(— OUT) FLOUNCE
(— RAPIDLY) LAMP STAVE
(— SHAKILY) DOTTER
(— SLOWLY) JET LAG
(— SMARTLY) LINK
(— STEADILY) SNOVE SNOOVE
(— UNSTEADILY) REEL FALTER STAVER STAGGER STUMBLE
(— WAVERINGLY) SHEVEL WARPLE
(— WITH DIFFICULTY) CRAMBLE CRAMMEL LOUTHER
(— WITH JERK) HIRCH
(— WITH LOFTY GAIT) JET
(— WITH OSTENTATION) PRANCE
(— WITH SHUFFLE) COONJINE
(— WITH STRIDES) STAG
(— WITH TREES) XYST XYSTUS ALAMEDA
(— WITHOUT LIFTING FEET) SCUFF
(BACKSTAGE —) BRIDGE
(COOL —) FRESCADE
(COVERED —) CLOISTER
(COVERED —) PORCH
(FOLIAGE-COVERED —) BERCEAU
(HARD —) STRAM SWINGE
(LIMPING —) GIMP
(LONG —) STRAM
(POMPOUS —) STRUT
(PUBLIC —) XYST XYSTUS ALAMEDA
(RAISED —) GALLERY
(SHADED —) MALL ARBOR
(TEDIOUS —) TRAIL
WALKER GOER FOOTER FULLER GANGER FOOTMAN TODDLER
(PL.) FEET
WALKING HOTFOOT PASSANT AMBULANT GRADIENT TRIPPING
WALKING STICK BAT CANE GIBBY KEBBY STICK WADDY KEBBIE SPECTER ASHPLANT GIBSTAFF WOODHORSE
WALKOUT STRIKE
WALKWAY CATWALK SIDEWALK
WALL WA DAM FIN MUR WAW BAIL BELT CELL CORE CRIB CURB DICK DIKE DRUM DYKE FACE HEAD MURE PACK SKIN SPUR WING WOGE ATTIC BOARD CHEEK CRUST DIGUE EMURE FENCE HEDGE MEURE MURAL PIRCA SHOJI WOGHE WOUGH BAFFLE BAILEY BATTER CUTOFF DOKHMA IMMURE LEADER PARIES PRETIL REBOTE RIPRAP SCREEN SEPTUM SHIELD VALLUM CHEMISE CURTAIN ENCLOSE MIZRACH PARAPET PERPEND PLUTEUS REREDOS TAMBOUR FIREBACK SPANDREL TRAVERSE
(— ABOVE FACADE) ATTIC
(— AROUND) IMMURE
(— BEHIND ALTAR) REREDOS
(— BETWEEN TWO OPENINGS) PIER
(— CARRYING CUPOLA) DRUM
(— CARRYING ROOF) BAHUT

(— CROSSING RAMPART) SPUR
(— IN ROMAN ARENA) SPINA
(— IN TRUCK) HEADER
(— OF BLAST FURNACE) DAM INWALL FIREBACK
(— OF CLAY) COTTLE
(— OF HOOF) CRUST
(— OF MINE) FACE
(— OF MOUTH) CHEEK
(— OF TENT) KANAT CANAUT
(BODY —) MANTLE
(CIRCULAR —) CASHEL
(CORE —) HEARTING
(CURVED —) SWEEP
(DIVIDING —) SEPTUM
(END — OF BUILDING) GABLE
(FISH —) LEADER
(HIGHEST PART OF —) CRAPWA
(INNER SLOPE OF —) BATTER
(LOG —) CRIB
(LOW —) BAHUT PODIUM PLUTEUS
(LOWER PART OF —) DADO
(OUTER — OF CASTLE) BAIL BAILEY
(PEAT —) COP
(PUDDLE —) HEARTING
(RETAINING —) CRIB BULKHEAD
(SCARPED —) GHAT
(SECONDARY —) CHEMISE
(SUSTAINING —) RIPRAP
(THINNED PART OF —) ALLEGE
(VENTRAL —) STERNUM
(WING —) AILERON
(PL.) PERICARP
WALLABA APA
WALLABY WURRUP TOOLACH WURRUNG BOONGARY KANGAROO PADMELON WHIPTAIL
WALLACHIAN RUMAN
WALLAROO EURO
WALLBOARD GOBO
WALLET JAG JAGG MAIL POKE BOGET BOUGE BULCH BULGE SCRIP BUDGET READER SACKET ALFARGA ALFORJA LEATHER BILLFOLD NOTECASE
WALLEYE WHALL SAUGER LEUCOMA WATCHEYE EXOTROPIA
WALLEYED PIKE DORE DORY JACK PERCID SALMON WALLEYE PICKEREL
WALLFLOWER CUBA CHEIR GILLY JACKS KEIRI GELOFER WARRIOR GILLIVER
WALL HAWKWEED LUNGWORT
WALLOP BEAT BEER FLOP SLUG SOCK PASTE POUND VALOP GALLOP IMPACT WALLOW FLUTTER TROUNCE FLOUNDER LAMBASTE
WALLOW FADE LAIR ROLL SOIL SLOSH WALWE GROVEL MUDDLE WALTER WELTER WITHER SLUDDER SWELTER FLOUNDER KOMMETJE VOLUTATE
WALLOWISH FLAT WELSH INSIPID
WALLPAPER GROUND SCENIC HANGING TENTURE TAPESTRY
WALL PEPPER SEDUM STONECROP
WALL PLATE PAN RASEN
WALL RUE TENTWORT

WALLY TOY FINE SPOIL PAMPER ROBUST STRONG STURDY SPLENDID VIGOROUS
WALNUT ACAPU NOGAL TRYMA AKHROT BANNUT HEARTNUT
(BRAZILIAN —) EMBOYA IMBUIA
(PL.) JUGLANS
WALNUT SHELL BOLSTER
WALPI HUALPI
WALRUS MORSE WALTRON PELAGIAN PINNIPED ROSMARINE
WALT CRANK UNSTEADY
WALTZ LUG CARRY MARCH VALSE BOSTON BREEZE FLOUNCE
WAMARA CLUBWOOD IRONWOOD PANOCOCO
WAMBLE ROLL SPIN WAMEL NAUSEA REVOLVE
WAMBLY FAINT SHAKY
WAME WEM WAMB WYME BELLY
WAMPUM PEAG FADME HAWOK MONEY PAAGE SEWAN FATHOM SEAWAN ROANOKE
WAMUS JACKET WAMPUS WARMUS
WAN DIM HAW FADE PALE PALY SICK BLAKE FAINT WHITE FEEBLE PALLID SALLOW GHASTLY LANGUID
WANAPUM SOKULK
WAND ROD VARE YARD BATON STAFF STICK VERGE VIRGA FERULA THYRSE WATTLE RHABDOS THYRSUS CADUCEUS
WANDER BAT BUM ERR GAD WAG HAAK HAIK HAKE MAZE MUCK RAVE ROAM ROIL ROLL ROVE WALK WILL WORE DAVER DRIFT GLAIK KNOCK RANGE ROGUE SHACK SLOSH STRAY TAVER TRAIK VAGUE WAIVE WAVER CANDER DANDER DAUNER FORAGE LOITER MITHER MOIDER MUCKER PALMER PERUSE RAMBLE RANGLE STRAKE STROLL SWERVE WILDER MEANDER TRAFFIC TRAIPSE VAGRATE VANDYKE CUTICULA SQUANDER STRAGGLE STRAVAGE
(— ABOUT) DIVAGATE
(— ABSTRACTEDLY) MOON
(— AIMLESSLY) SWAN SLOSH TRACE MEANDER
(— AS A VAGABOND) SHACK
(— AS A VAGRANT) LOITER
(— AT RANDOM) SQUANDER
(— ERRATICALLY) SWASH
(— FROM DIRECT COURSE) STRAGGLE
(— FROM PLACE TO PLACE) WAG
(— IDLY) HAKE LOUT MAUNDER SHACKLE
(— IN DELIRIUM) DWALE DWALL
(— IN MIND) DAVER DANDER DELIRE
(— LEISURELY) BUMMEL
(— RESTLESSLY) FEEK
WANDERER WAIF ROVER VAGUE RANGER PILGRIM RAMBLER FUGITIVE RUNAGATE TRAVELER VAGABOND
WANDERING GAD ROAM ERROR STRAY VAGUE ARRANT ASTRAY

ERRANT MOBILE ROVING VAGANT
VAGOUS DEVIOUS NOMADIC
ODYSSEY VAGANCY WINDING
ABERRANT FLOATING FUGITIVE
PELAGIC PLANETAL PLANETIC
RAMBLING RESTLESS TRAILING
VAGABOND WINDRING
WANDFLOWER GALAX SPARAXIS
WANDOROBO WAASI
WAND-SHAPED VIRGATE
WANE GO EBB SET WELK WILK
DECAY UNWAX WANZE REPINE
DECLINE DWINDLE DECREASE
(— **OF MOON**) WADDLE
WANGA CHARM SPELL OUANGA
WONGAH SORCERY
WANGLE FAKE SHAKE WIGGLE
FINAGLE
WANIGAN ARK CHEST COFFER
WANGUN
WANT HURT LACK LIKE MISS NEED
OONT PINE VOID WANE WONT
CRAVE FAULT FORGO BESOIN
CHOOSE DEARTH DEFECT DESIRE
MISTER PENURY PLIGHT ABSENCE
BEGGARY BLEMISH BORASCA
DEFAULT MISEASE NEEDHAM
POVERTY REQUIRE VACANCY
MISCHIEF WANTROKE
(— **EXCEEDINGLY**) DIE
(— **OF ENERGY**) ATONY
(— **OF GOOD SENSE**) FOLLY
(— **OF REST**) UNRO
(— **OF SUCCESS**) FAILURE
(— **OF VIGOR**) DELICACY
WANTAGE ULLAGE
WANTING LACK VOID WANE ALACK
MINUS ABSENT LACKING MISSING
INDIGENT
(— **ORIGINALITY**) BANAL
WANTON JAY NAG DAFT GOLE IDLE
LEWD NICE RAGE SKIT CADGY
DALLY LIGHT SAUCY GIGLET
GIGLOT HARLOT HAUNTY LACHES
LUBRIC RAKISH RIGSBY TICKLE
TOYING TOYISH UNRULY COLTISH
FULSOME GIGGISH HAGGARD
IMMORAL KITTOCK LUSTFUL
PAPHIAN RIGGISH RIOTOUS
SMICKER WAYWARD FLAGRANT
LUSCIOUS MISTRESS PETULANT
PLAYSOME RUMBELOW SLIPPERY
SPITEFUL SPORTIVE UNCHASTE
WANTONNESS FOLLY PRIDE SPORT
RAGERY SUCCUDRY SURQUIDY
WAP BIND BLOW WHOP WRAP BLAST
FIGHT KNOCK STORM TRUSS
BUNDLE STRIKE
WAPITI ELK ALCE DEER LOSH LUSH
STAG MARAL MOOSE CERVID
WAMPOOSE
WAR WIN CAMP FEUD MART FIGHT
SWORD WORSE WORST BATTLE
CONTEND CRUSADE CONFLICT
GUERILLA OVERCOME
(**RELIGIOUS** —) JEHAD JIHAD
WARBLE SING CAROL CHANT CHIRL
CHIRM SHAKE TRILL YODEL JARGON
RALISH WARNEL WORMIL DESCANT

VIBRATE WOURNIL
WARBLE FLY OXFLY BOTFLY
GADFLY OESTRID OESTRIAN
WARBLER CUT KIT CHAT SMEU
WREN FITTE CANARY EYSOGE
SMEUTH SYLVIA TITIEN CREEPER
CROMBEC FANTAIL HAYBIRD
HAYSUCK PITBIRD REDPOLL SYLVIID
TROCHIL BEAMBIRD BLACKCAP
FAUVETTE MALURINE MOCKBIRD
OVENBIRD PINCPINC REDSTART
REEDBIRD RIRORIRO
WAR CLUB MAR MER MERE MERAI
MARREE
WAR CRY ALALA SLOGAN
WARD CARE GUARD MAHAL VICUS
WAIRD WATCH ALUMNA BARRIO
CALPUL DEFEND ROWENA KEEPING
NATUARY CALPOLLI CONTRADA
(— **OFF**) FEND WEAR WERE AVERT
AWARD FENCE PARRY REPEL
SHIELD BUCKLER EXPIATE FORFEND
WARDAGE WARTH
WARDEN ALCADE DIZDAR PORTER
RANGER REGENT ROLAND WARNER
ALCAIDE HOGMACE LEATMAN
ROWLAND CLAVIGER
WARDER PORTER GUARDER
HEIMDAL TURNKEY WATCHMAN
BEEFEATER
WARDROBE KAS CLOSET VESTRY
ALMIRAH ARMOIRE VESTUARY
WARE CLOTH GOODS SPEND
FABRICS SEAWEED SQUANDER
(**CERAMIC** —) SPODE
(**ENAMELED** —) BILSTON COALPORT
(**INFERIOR** —S) SLUM
(**KIND OF** —) RAKU MINTON
WHIELDON
(**MAJOLICA** —) DERUTA
(**PORCELAIN** —) CHINA BERLIN
(**UNGLAZED** —) BISQUE
(**PL.**) TROKE CHAFFER TROGGIN
WAREHOUSE GOLA GOLAH STORE
BODEGA FONDUK GODOWN STAITH
ALMACEN FUNDUCK SPICERY
STOWAGE ENTREPOT MAGAZINE
SERAGLIO
WARFARE WAR ARMS IRON ARMOR
BATTLE PSYWAR MILITIA CONFLICT
WAR-HORSE CHARGER COURSER
DESTRER TROOPER DESTRIER
WARILY TIPTOE GINGERLY
WARINESS CAUTEL CAUTION
DISTRUST WARESHIP WARIMENT
WARKLOOM TOOL WARKLUME
WARLIKE WARLY MARTIAL FIGHTING
MILITARY BELLICOSE
(**NOT** —) IMBELLIC
WARLOCK IMP WITCH SPRITE
WARLOW WIZARD CONJUROR
SORCERER
WARLORD TUCHUN
WARM HOT LEW LUO LOO RUG BASK
BEEK KEEN LEWD MILD CALID
CHAFE EAGER FRESH MALMY
MUNGY SLACK TEPID TOAST
ACHAFE ARDENT DEVOUT DIGEST
FOSTER GENIAL HEARTY HEATED

RIZZLE TENDER CHERISH CLEMENT
CORDIAL GLOWING THERMAL
ZEALOUS FRIENDLY SANGUINE
(**MODERATELY** —) LEW SLACK
TEPID
(— **UP**) SCORE
WARMHEARTED KIND TENDER
FRIENDLY GENEROUS
WARMING FOVENT
WARMOUTH BIGMOUTH FLATFISH
SACALAIT
WARMTH GLOW HEAT LIFE ZEAL
ARDOR LEWTH ENERGY FERVOR
ARDENCY PASSION CALIDITY
FERVENCY
(**INNER** —) JUICE
WARN REDE WARD WERN ALERT
AREAD WEIRD ADVERT ADVISE
EXHORT INFORM CAUTION
COMMAND GARNISH PREVISE
ADMONISH THREATEN
(— **OFF**) FORBID
WARNING AHEM ITEM ALARM CHECK
KNELL CAVEAT LESSON NOTICE
OFFICE SAMPLE SIGNAL AVISION
CALLING CAUTION JIGGERS
MEMENTO MONITOR SUMMONS
DOCUMENT GARDYLOO MONITION
(— **OF DISASTER**) DIRE
(**ARCHERY** —) FAST
WARP CUP WEB BIAS CANE CAST
LIFT WARF WERP WIND ANGLE
CHAIN CHOKE CROOK GEYZE
KEDGE PORRY THRAW TWINE
WEAVE BUCKLE CHEESE DEFORM
WASHIN DEFLECT DISTORT SKELLER
(— **IN WEAVING**) CRAM
WARPED WRY BUCKLED GNARLED
HOUSING
WARPER BALLER
WARPING BOW PANDATION
WARRAGAL WILD DINGO HORSE
OUTLAW
WARRANT ABLE AMRIT BERAT FIANT
SANAD VOUCH AMRITA ASSERT
BRANCH BREVET DOCKET ENSURE
INSURE PARDON PERMIT PLEVIN
POLICY POTENT SUNNUD TICKET
BEHIGHT JUSTIFY PRECEPT
GUARANTY MITTIMUS
WARRAU GUARANO
WARREN CONYGER WARRANT
WARRIOR TOA WER EARL HERO
KEMP RINK WEER BERNE FREIK
FREKE HAGEN LLUDD SINGH THANE
THEGN OSSIAN WARMAN WEAPON
FIGHTER SOLDIER STARKAD
WARWOLF ZERBINO CHAMPION
RODOMONT SHARDANA STARKATH
SWORDMAN WARFARER
(— **CLASS**) MAGANI
(— **OF NOBLE RANK**) EARL
(**AMERICAN INDIAN** —) BRAVE
SANNUP
(**BOASTFUL** —) RODOMONT
(**BRYTHONIC** —) LLUDD
(**BURGUNDIAN** —) HAGEN
(**FEMALE** —) AMAZON SHIELDMAY
(**IRISH** —) FENIAN

(KAFFIR —S) IMPI
(MUSLIM —) GAZI GHAZI
(NOTED —) THANE THEGN
(SCANDINAVIAN —) BERSERK
(SCOTTISH —) ZERBINO
(TROJAN —) AGENOR
(VALIANT —) TOA
(VIRGIN —) CAMILLA
(PL.) CHIVALRY GAMMADIM
WARSHIP GUIDE WAFTER CRUISER
MONITOR SULTANA SULTANE
CORVETTE
WART RAT WRAT AMBURY ANBURY
PUSTULE VERRUCA VERRUGA
EPIDERMA PAPILOMA
(POTATO —) CANKER
WART HOG EMGALLA
WARTLIKE PYRENOID
WART SNAKE XENODERM
WARY SHY CAGY WISE CAGEY
CANNY DOWNY HOOLY LEERY
TENDER CAREFUL GUARDED
PRUDENT WAREFUL CAUTIOUS
SKITTISH VIGILANT WATCHFUL
WAS VAS WIS WUZ WYS PAST
WISSHE
(— ABLE) COULD
(— NOT) NAS
(I —) CHWAS
WASH DO BOG FEN LAG LAP NET
TUB BEER BUCK EDDY HOSE HUSH
LAVE SILT SUDS WADI BATHE
CLEAN CLEAR DOLLY DRAFF ERODE
MARSH RINSE SCRUB SLOSH SOUSE
SWILL BUDDLE CRADLE DOLLIE
LOTION PURIFY SLOOSH SLUICE
SOZZLE STREAM ALLUVIO CLEANSE
LAUNDER SHAMPOO ALLUVIUM
EYEWATER LAVAMENT LAVATORY
(— A GAS) SCRUB
(— AWAY) GULL
(— BY TREADING IN WATER) TRAMP
(— DOWN) SIND SOOGEE
(— FOR GOLD) PAN
(— GIVEN TO SWINE) DRAFF
(— GRAVEL) ROCK
(— IN LYE) BUCK
(— LIGHTLY) RINSE
(— OFF) DETERGE
(— ORE) TYE HUTCH BUDDLE
CRADLE STRAKE
(— OUT) SIND ELUTE FLUSH
LAVAGE
(— ROUGHLY) SLUSH
(— THOROUGHLY) SCOUR
(— VIGOROUSLY) SLOSH
(— WITH BROOM) TYE
(— WITH COSMETIC) SURFLE
SURPHUL
(DRY —) ARROYA ARROYO
WASHBASIN LAVER LAVABO
LAVATORY ALJOFAINA
WASHCLOTH FLANNEL
WASHED (— UP) SHOT THROUGH
WASHER BUR BURR DRUM ROVE
CLOUT BUTTON RONDEL SOURER
GROMMET LEATHER RACCOON
COTTEREL LAVENDER RONDELLE
SCRUBBER

WASHERMAN DHOBI DHOBIE
LAVANDERO
WASHERWOMAN LAUNDER
WASHING LAG BATH LAVAGE
SLOOSH LAUNDRY ABLUTION
LAVAMENT LAVATION
(PL.) ELUATE
WASHING MACHINE DASHWHEEL

WASHINGTON
CAPITAL: OLYMPIA
COLLEGE: WHITMAN
COUNTY: ASOTIN KITSAP SKAGIT
YAKIMA CLALLAM KITTITAS
DAM: COULEE
INDIAN: LUMMI MAKAH TWANA
SAMISH SKAGIT YAKIMA
CHINOOK CLALLAM COWLITZ
SANPOIL CHIMAKUM OKANAGON
LAKE: CHELAN
MOUNTAIN: JACK TUNK ADAMS
LEMEI LOGAN MOSES SLOAN
QUARTZ SIMCOE STUART
OLYMPUS RAINIER SHUKSAN
MOUNTAIN RANGE: KETTLE
CASCADE OLYMPIC
NICKNAME: EVERGREEN
RIVER: SNAKE YAKIMA COLUMBIA
SOUND: PUGET
STATE BIRD: GOLDFINCH
STATE FLOWER: RHODODENDRON
STATE TREE: HEMLOCK
TOWN: OMAK PASCO TACOMA
YAKIMA EPHRATA EVERETT
OTHELLO SEATTLE SPOKANE
LONGVIEW

WASHOUT FLOP STUMOR FAILURE
WASHROOM BASEMENT LAVATORY
WASHSTAND COMMODE
WASHTUB FLASKET
WASHY SOFT WEAK LOOSE MOIST
FEEBLE PALLID WATERY DILUTED
WASP MASON SPHEX WHAMP WOPSE
BEMBEX DAUBER DIGGER HORNET
TIPHIA TREMEX VESPID CYNIPID
DRYINID EUMENID MASARID SCOLIID
SERPHID SIRICID SPHECID STINGER
ACULEATE MUTILLID POMPILID
WASPISH TESTY FRETFUL PEEVISH
CHOLERIC SNAPPISH
WASSAIL TOAST PLEDGE CAROUSE
REVELRY CAROUSAL
WASTE EAT FUD GOB TED BURN
GNAW JUNK LOSS PASS ROSS SACK
TEAR TINE WEAR WILD DROSS
EXILE HAVOC SCRAP SLOOM SLOTH
SLOUM SPILL TABID THRUM BANGLE
BEZZLE COMMON DEBRIS DESERT
DEVOUR DIDDLE DRAFFY DRIVEL
ELAPSE EXPEND FOREST GARBLE
GOUSTY LAVISH MOLDER MUDDLE
PADDLE PERISH RAVAGE REFUSE
SPILTH WESTEN CONNACH
CONSUME EXHAUST FRITTER
GARBAGE MULLOCK RUBBISH
SLATTER CONFOUND DEMOLISH
SLATTERN SQUANDER

(— AWAY) BATE MELT DECAY
DWINE SWAIN SWEAL TRAIK TABEFY
WINDLE DWINDLE FORPINE MISLIKE
DISSOLVE EMACIATE FORSPEND
MACERATE
(— GRADUALLY) WEAR ABSUME
(— IN DRUNKENNESS) SOT
(— IN RIOT) BEZZLE
(— OF INK) INKSHED
(— OF SILK COCOONS) KNUB
(— TIME) FOOL FRIG IDLE DALLY
DEFER DRILL DAWDLE DIDDLE
FOOTER FOOTLE LOITER DRINGLE
FOOSTER GAUSTER
(COAL —) SLUDGE
(COTTON —) FLUKE SLASHER
SPOOLER
(FOOD —) SLOP
(LIQUID —) DRIPPING EFFLUENT
(MINING —) GOB GOAF
(WOOL —) FUD GARNETT
(YARN —) THRUM EYEBROW
WASTEBASKET HELL HELLBOX
WASTED IDLE FORWORN RAVAGED
DECREPIT
WASTEFUL LAVISH PROFUSE
DESOLATE PRODIGAL SPENDFUL
WASTEFULNESS WAIT UNTHRIFT
WASTELAND CURAGH CURRACH
WASTER THIEF LEISTER WASTREL
PRODIGAL
WASTING FRET DECAY LIGHT
AWASTE ATROPHY CACHEXY
EXEDENT MISLIKE PREYING TABIFIC
CACHEXIA PHTHISIS SYNTEXIS
(— AWAY) SYNTECTIC
WASTREL WAIF REFUSE WASTER
VAGABOND STROYGOOD
WATCH EYE FOB NIT SEE SPY TAB
DIAL ESPY GLIM GLOM HACK HEED
KEEP LOOK MARK MIND PIPE TOUT
TWIG VACH WAIK WAKE WARD
YARD CLOCK GUARD SCOUT SPIAL
SUPER TIMER VERGE VIGIL VIRGE
WAKEN WHEEL BEHOLD DEFEND
DIACLE FOLLOW HUNTER PERDUE
SENTRY SHADOW TICKER TICTIC
TURNIP WAKING YEMING OBSERVE
OVERSEE STRIKER THIMBLE
TOMPION HOROLOGE MEDITATE
SENTINEL SPECTATE TICKTICK
(— FOR) TENT ABIDE AWAIT
(— OF ARMY) BIVOUAC
(— ON THE SLY) FOX
(— OVER) HOLD KEEP TEND TENT
GUARD ATTEND OVERLOOK
(— PEOPLE EATING) GROAK
(— QUIETLY) HINT
(— THAT STRIKES) STRIKER
REPEATER
(— UNIT) LIGNE
(— WITH HINGED COVER) HUNTER
(ALARM —) TATLER TATTLER
(CLOSE —) SCRUTINY
(NAUTICAL —) HACK DOGWATCH
(NIGHT —) LICHWAKE LYKEWAKE
WATCHBAND WRISTER WRISTLET
WATCH CRYSTAL LUNET LUNETTE
WATCHDOG CUR GARM GARMR

MATIN BANDOG KRATIM CERBERUS

WATCHER VEIL WAKER VIEWER
WAITER MUSAHAR SPOTTER
WATCHMAN

WATCHFUL IRA ALERT AWARE
CANNY CHARY ERECT TENTY
WAKER TENTIE WACKER ANXIOUS
GUARDED JEALOUS LIDLESS
WAKEFUL VIGILANT WAKERIFE
WAUKRIFE

WATCHFULNESS OUTLOOK
JEALOUSY

WATCHMAN FLAG MINA WAIT
GUARD SCOOT VIGIL WATCH ASKARI
BANTAY GHAFIR SERENO SHOMER
TOOTER WAITER WARDEN WARDER
BELLMAN CHARLEY GUARDER
TALLIAR WAKEMAN CHOKIDAR
SENTINEL

(NIGHT —) SERENO CHARLIE

WATCHTOWER WARD BEACON
GARRET MIZPAH SENTRY ATALAYA
LOOKOUT MIRADOR SENTINEL
SPECCHIE

WATCHWORD CRY MAXIM ALERTA
ENSIGN PAROLE SIGNAL NAYWORD
PASSWORD

WATCH WORKS MOVEABLE

WATER EAU TJI AGUA AQUA BATH
BRIM BROO BURN LAGE LAKE POND
POOL TIDE WAVE ABYSS BILGE
FLUME LOUGH LYMPH RIVER TABBY
TEARS TUBIG BALLOW BAREGE
CAMLET CONGEE CONJEE PAWNEE
PHLEGM SALIVA STREAM VADOSE
WATHER AQUATIC CRYSTAL
JAVELLE IRRIGATE SNOWMELT

(— AFTER BOILING RICE) CONGEE
CONJEE

(— AS REFUGE FOR GAME) SOIL

(— AT THE MOUTH) DROOL

(— BY CALENDERING) TABBY

(— FOR BREWING) BURN

(— IN SOIL) HOLARD

(— IN WEIR) LASHER

(— REDDISH WITH IRON) RIDDAM

**(— RUNNING AGAINST MAIN
CURRENT)** EDDY

(— SPIRIT) KELPIE

(— SURROUNDED BY ICE) WAKE

(— UNDER PRESSURE) HUSH

(BAPTISMAL —) LAVER

(BOTTOM — OF SEA) ABYSS

(BUBBLING —) SPRUDEL

(DEEP —) BALLOW

(DIRTY —) SAUR PUDDLE

(FEN —) SUDS

(FROZEN —) ICE FROST

(HOLY —) HYSSOP

(HOT —) SOUP

(LIVING —) RASA

(MINERAL —) VICHY SELTER
SELTZER

(OPEN —) POLYNYA

(RED —) RESP RIDDAM

(ROUGH —) SEA

(SALT —) BRACK BRINE SEAWATER

(SOAPY —) SUDS GRAITH

(SPLASH OF —) FLASH

(STILL —) KELD LOGIN

(SULPHUR —) BAREGE

(SURFACE OF —) RYME

(SWEETENED —) AMRIT AMRITA

(WASHING —) LAVATION

(PL.) APSU

WATER ARUM DRAGON

WATER BAG CHAGUL MATARA
MUSSUK

WATERBIRD ALCATRAS

WATERBRAIN GID

WATERBUCK COB CHUZWI DEFASSA
WATERDOE

WATER BUFFALO KERBAU

WATER CARRIER BHISTI AGUADOR
BHEESTY

WATER CART DILLY

WATER CASK WINGER

WATER CHESTNUT LING CALTROP
SALIGOT

WATER CHINQUAPIN BONNET
NELUMBO WANKAPIN YONCOPIN
RATTLENUT

WATER CLOCK GHURRY
CLEPSYDRA

WATER CLOSET PETTY PRIVY
STOOL SANITARY NECESSARY

WATER COCK KORA

WATERCOLOR GRAPHIC

WATERCOURSE (ALSO SEE STREAM
AND RIVER) RUN URN AGOS DIKE
DYKE GOTE HAHR KHOR LADE LEAT
WADI WADY YORA AUWAI BAYOU
BROOK CANAL CANEL COWAL
DITCH DRAIN ARROYO CANNEL
COURSE FURROW GUTTER KENNEL
NULLAH TRINKET

WATERCRESS EKER KERS CARSE
KERSE BILDERS NOSESMART

WATER DOG OTTER WATERRUG

WATER DRINKER HYDROPOT

WATERED MOIRE

WATERFALL LIN LYN FALL FOSS
LINN SALT FORCE SAULT SPOUT
CATADUPE CATARACT OVERFALL

(FROZEN —) ICEFALL

WATER FENNEL EDGEWEED

WATER FLEA CYCLOPS DAPHNID

WATERFOWL WADER SWIMMER

WATERFRONT PRAYA

WATERGALL WINDDOG WINDGALL
JELLYFISH

WATER GERMANDER SCORDIUM

WATER HEMLOCK CICUTA DEATHIN
JELLICA

WATER HOG BUSHPIG CAPYBARA

WATER HOLE DUB CHARCO TINAJA
ALBERCA

WATER ICE SHERBET

WATERINESS AQUEITY AQUOSITY

WATERING EPIPHORA

WATER JUG GAMLA GOMLAH
GOOLAH

WATERLEAF SHAWNY

WATER LETTUCE QUIAPO

WATER LILY DUCK LOTOS LOTUS
WOCAS WOKAS BOBBIN CANDOCK
NELUMBO CAMALOTE NENUPHAR

WATERLOGGED SOGGY SWAMPY
EDEMATOUS

WATERMAN MERMAN QUENCH
OARSMAN

WATERMARK CROWN TIDEMARK

WATERMARKED LAID

WATERMELON PEPO GOURD MELON
TSAMA CITRUL SANDIA ANGURIA
MILLION CUCURBIT PEPONIDA
PEPONIUM SKIPJACK

WATER MOCCASIN CONGO

WATER NEWT ASK TRITON

WATER OPOSSUM YAPOK YAPOCK

WATER OUZEL PIET OOZEL OWZEL
DIPPER DUCKER

WATER PEPPER LAKEWEED

WATER PLANT LIMU AQUATIC

WATER PLANTAIN ALISMA
THRUMWORT

WATERPOT FONTAL

WATERPROOF RAINCOAT

(— MATERIAL) KERATOL

WATER RAIL RUNNER BILCOCK
MOORHEN OARCOCK

WATER RAT VOLE CRABER
MUSKRAT WATERRUG

WATER SCORPION NEPID

WATERSHED BROW DIVIDE DIVORT
SNOWSHED

WATER SHIELD FANWORT
DEERFOOD FROGLEAF

WATERSKIN MASHAK MATARA
MUSSUK MUSSACK MUSSICK

WATER SOLDIER PONDWORT

WATER SPIRIT ARIEL KELPY KELPIE
UNDINE

WATERSPOUT RONE CANAL SPATE
SPOUT VORTEX PRESTER TWISTER
CATARACT GARGOYLE

WATER STRIDER SKATER SKIMMER
SKIPPER SKETCHER

WATER THRUSH KICKUP WAGTAIL

WATER TIGER DYTISCID

WATERTIGHT THEAT THEET TIGHT
STANCH THIGHT STAUNCH

WATER WALLY BATAMOTE

WATERWAY GUT CASH DOCK HOLE
LODE DITCH INLET ARTERY SEAWAY
CULVERT FAIRWAY HIGHWAY
IGARAPE

(ARTIFICIAL —) LEAD CANAL

(PL.) SCUPPERS

WATERWHEEL NORIA SAGEER
SAKIEH DANAIDE SAKIYEH
TYMPANUM

WATERY WET LASH PALE SICK
WHEY BOGGY MOIST SAMMY
WASHY BLASHY FLASHY LIQUID
PALLID SEROSE SEROUS SWASHY
AQUATIC AQUEOUS CHOROUS
HYDROUS PHLEGMY HUMOROUS
ICHOROUS SKINKING

WATTLE GILL JOWL PLAT SALY TWIG
WAND BOREE COOBA FRITH MULGA
SALLY SALWE STAVE STICK HURDLE
JEWING JOLLOP LAPPET SALLOW
BLUEBUSH CARUNCLE

WATTLEBIRD IAO MOHO MINER
MANUAO MAOMAO GILLBIRD

WATTLE CROW KOKAKO
WAVE FAN FLY JAW SEA WAW BECK
FLAG FLAP GUST LUMP SUFF SULK
SWAY WAFF WAFT WAWE YTHE
BLESS CRIMP FLASH FLOAT PULSE
SHAKE SURGE SWELL SWING
BILLOW COMBER FLAUNT MARCEL
RIPPLE ROLLER WINNOW BREAKER
BRIMMER CRIMPLE FLICKER
FLUTTER TSUNAMI WHIFFLE
ARTEFACT BRANDISH FLOURISH
GRAYBACK UNDULATE UNIPULSE
WHISTLER WHITECAP
(— OF EXCITATION) IMPULSE
(— OF FLAG) DOT DASH
(— OF SHIP) BONE
(ELECTRIC —) STRAY CARRIER
(TIDAL —) EAGER
(PL.) SURF
WAVER HALT REEL SWAG SWAY
VARY CHECK DAKER DOUBT FLOAT
SWALE SWING WIVER DACKER
DAIKER DITHER FALTER MAMMER
QUIVER SWERVE TEETER TOTTER
WABBLE WOBBLE BALANCE FLICKER
FLITTER FLUTTER STAGGER
SWITHER VIBRATE HESITATE
WAVERING WAW WAVY WEAK
WAUCH WAUGH FICKLE GROGGY
WAVERY WIGGLY DUBIOUS
LAMBENT SHUTTLE DOUBTFUL
FLEXUOSE FLEXUOUS FLICKERY
HOVERING WAVEROUS
WAVINESS CRIMP
WAVING UNDE WAFT AWAVE OUNDY
UNDEE WAFTURE FLOURISH
WAVY ONDE UNDE UNDY CRISP
MOIRE SNAKY UNDEE FLECKY
SNAKEY UNDATE WIGGLY BUCKLED
CRINKLY CURVING ENDATED
ROLLING SINUATE UNDULAR
ENRIDGED FLEXUOUS ONDOYANT
SQUIGGLY UNDULATE
(PEOPLE WITH — HAIR) VEDDOID
WAWL HOWL WAIL WOWL SQUALL
WAX WOX CERE CODE GROW RAGE
WACE WOXE SCALE BECOME
CAPPING CERESIN KLISTER
CARNAUBA CERESINE CEROXYLE
COCCERIN EPILATOR INCREASE
(— IN HONEYCOMB) CAPPING
(— STRONG) PREVAIL
(CHINESE —) PELA
(COBBLER'S —) CODE
(KIND OF —) PINSANG
(SKI —) KLISTER
WAXBILL ASTRILD REDBILL
WAXEN WAX PALLID CEREOUS
WAXER GLAZER WAXMAN
WAXFLOWER EPIPHYTE
WAX MYRTLE ARRAYAN
WAX PLANT HOYA
WAXWING WAXBIRD RECOLLET
SILKTAIL
WAXY ANGRY VEXED PLIABLE
YIELDING
WAY LAW PAD TAO VIA WON WYE
FARE FORE FORM GAIT GANG GATE
KIND LANE LARK PACE PATH PAWK

RAKE ROAD SORT TOBY WISE
ALLEY CHANT FORTH GOING GUISE
HABIT MOYEN ROUTE SHEAR STEPS
STYLE TRACT TRADE ACCESS
AVENUE CAREER CHEMIN COURSE
MANNER METHOD STREET TRAJET
CHANNEL FASHION HIGHWAY
PASSAGE SKIDWAY APPROACH
CONTRADA DISTRICT FOOTPATH
THOROUGH VICINITY LAUNCHING
(— OF DEPARTURE) EXIT
(— OF LIFE) LARK TRACE
HEDONISM
(— OF SPEAKING) AMBAGE
(— OF THINKING) DIET
(— OF WALKING) JET
(— OUT) IT EXIT SALVO
(— THROUGH MINEFIELD) BREACH
(CLEVER —) KNACK
(INDIRECT —) AMBAGES
(LONG —) FAR
(MAJOR —) STEM
(NARROW —) DRANG
(ODD —S) JIMJAMS
(PLANK —) BRIDGE
(ROUNDABOUT —) DETOUR CIRCUIT
(SETTLED —) BIAS
(SIDE —) BRANCH
(SLOPING —) RAMP
(UNDEVIATING —) GROOVE
(PL.) DAPS
WAYBILL WILLIE
WAYFARER SHULER VIATOR PILGRIM
SHUILER TRAVELER
WAYFARING TREE WHITTEN
COTTONER VIBURNUM
WAYLAY BELAY BESET BLOCK
BRACE AMBUSH FORLAY FORSET
FORELAY OBSTRUCT SURPRISE
WAYLAYER WAIT
WAYMARK AHU
WEAK DIM LEW COOL DOWY FOND
LAME NESH NICE PALE PUNY SELI
SELY SOFT THIN WASH WAUF WOKE
BAUCH BAUGH CRIMP DICKY FAINT
FLASH FRAIL JERKY LIGHT NAISH
REEDY ROCKY SEELY SILLY SLACK
STANK WASHY WAUGH WEARY
WERSH YOUNG CADUKE DEBILE
DILUTE DOTISH FEEBLE FLABBY
FLAGGY FLIMSY FOIBLE GROGGY
INFIRM LIMBER LITTLE MARCID
SEMMIT SICKLY SINGLE SWASHY
TENDER UNSURE UNWISE WAIRCH
WATERY DWAIBLY DWEEBLE
FLACCID FOOLISH FRAGILE INSIPID
INVALID LANGUID PIMPING PUERILE
REGULAR RICKETY SAUGHEN
SHALLOW SHILPIT SLENDER
SPINDLY TOTTERY UNHARDY
UNLUSTY WEARISH ASTHENIC
CHILDISH DECREPIT DEFINITE
FECKLESS FEMININE FLAGGING
GRIPLESS HELPLESS IMBECILE
IMPOTENT LADYLIKE LANGUENT
PHTHISIC RESOLUTE RUSHLIKE
SACKLESS SCRANNEL UNMIGHTY
UNWIELDY
(— FROM FATIGUE) TANGLE

(— FROM HUNGER) LEER
(— IN RESOLUTION) FRAIL
(MENTALLY —) TOTTY
WEAKEN GO LAG SAP DAMP FAIL
HURT MELT SINK THIN ALLAY
BLUNT BREAK CRAZE DELAY QUAIL
SHAKE SPEND WATER APPALL
DEACON DEADEN DEFEAT DEJECT
DENUDE DILUTE FALTER IMPAIR
INFIRM LABEFY LESSEN REBATE
REDUCE SICKEN SOFTEN CORRODE
CORRUPT CRIPPLE DECLINE
DEPRESS DISABLE MOLLIFY
QUALIFY RESOLVE UNBRACE
UNNERVE CASTRATE DIMINISH
EMBEZZLE ENERVATE ENFEEBLE
ETIOLATE INFRINGE LABEFACT
UNSTRENG
WEAKENED GROGGY ANODYNE
INVALID SHOTTEN DECREPIT
LABEFACT STRAINED
WEAKENING CHRONIC FAILURE
FLAGGING
WEAKEST RECKLING
WEAKFISH DRUM TROUT ACOUPA
SALMON CORBINA CORVINA
DRUMMER SQUETEE TOTOABA
TOTUAVA BLUEFISH CHICKWIT
WEAKLY FEEBLY FEMALE SIMPLY
WEAKLING TOY WRIG DUGON
PULER SLINK SOFTIE RECKLING
SOFTLING
WEAK-MINDED DAFT DOTY DOTED
FOOLISH
WEAKNESS ATONY CRACK CRAZE
FAULT FOLLY TOUCH ATONIA
DEFECT FOIBLE ACRATIA FAILING
FISSURE FRAILTY DEBILITY
DELICACY FONDNESS
(CARNAL —) FLESH
WEAL WHEAL RICHES STRIPE
WEALTH WELFARE
WEALTH WAD WON DHAN GEAR
GOLD GOOD MUCK WONE THING
WORTH GRAITH MAMMON POCKET
PURPLE RICHES TALENT CASHBOX
FORTUNE RICHDOM WARISON
WELFARE CATALLUM OPULENCE
OPULENCY PROPERTY TREASURE
(— OF NATION) STOCK
(PATRON OF —) YAKSHA
WEALTHY FAT FULL OOFY RICH
WELI AMPLE PURSY TINNY OOFIER
COUTHIE MONEYED PURSIVE
ABUNDANT AFFLUENT
WEAN CHILD SPAIN SPANE WAYNE
INFANT ESTRANGE
WEAPON (ALSO SEE SPECIFIC TYPE
OF WEAPON) ARM BOW GUN BILL
BOLA BOLO CLUB COSH DART EDGE
EPEE FALX FOIL IRON MACE PATU
PIKE TOOL WIWI ADAGA ARROW
BILLY CAKRA DEATH FLAIL KNIFE
LANCE ONCIN SHARP SPEAR SQUID
STEEL SWORD VOUGE WAPIN
CANNON CHAKRA DAGGER GLAIVE
MACANA ARCHERY BAZOOKA
FIREARM GISARME HALBERD
HARPOON HURLBAT JAVELIN

LIANGLE POUNAMU SHOTGUN
SLASHER STICKER TICKLER
WHIFFLE ARBALEST BLOWBACK
BLUDGEON CROSSBOW FAUCHARD
HEDGEHOG LEEANGLE PARTISAN
TROMBASH
(DEADLY —) DEATH
(LINE OF —S) RIDGE
(PREHISTORIC —) CELT
(PL.) WAR TACKLE ARCHERY
WEAPONRY

WEAR KIT BEAR FRAY FRET GROW
HAVE PASS CHAFE GUARD SPEND
VOGUE WEARY ABRADE BATTER
BECOME BETHUMB CONSUME
DEFENSE DEGRADE FASHION
FATIGUE FRAZZLE PROCEED
WEATHER PROGRESS
(— AN OPENING) BREACH
(— AND TEAR) GAFF SLITE
GRUELING
(— AWAY) EAT FADE FRET GALL
GNAW GULL PINE ERODE GULLY
SCOUR SPEND ABRADE CORRADE
CORRODE CONTRIVE
(— CLOTHES) DRESS
(— DOWN) BRAY GRIND ABRASE
GRAVEL
(— FURROWS) GUTTER
(— IN PUBLIC) SPORT
(— OFF) FRAY ABRADE
(— OUT) DO BURN COOK FLOG
JADE TIRE TUCK BREAK SLAVE
SLITE SPEND BUGGER HATTER
MAGGLE PERUSE EXHAUST
FORWEAR FORWORK HACKNEY
INVALID SHACHLE OVERFRET
OVERWEAR
(— SHIP) CAST
(— SHOES OUT OF SHAPE)
SHACHLE SHACKLE
(— TIGHT CORSETS) LACE
WEARIED AWEARY FORGONE
FATIGUED WEARIFUL
WEARINESS TIRE FATIGUE
BRAINFAG SICKNESS VEXATION
WEARING DECAY SCUFF BURNING
CLOTHES ABRASION GARMENTS
GRINDING
WEARISOME DRY DULL HARD
WEARY MORTAL PROLIX SODDEN
IRKSOME TEDIOUS SAWDUSTY
TIRESOME TOILSOME
WEARISOMENESS TEDIUM
WEARY FAG IRK SAD BOEG BORE
MOIL PALL PUNY SADE TIRE TIRY
WEAK WORE WORN BORED BREAK
CURSE SPENT HARASS PLAGUE
SICKLY SQUEAL EXHAUST FATIGUE
IRKSOME FATIGATE FORCHASE
GRIEVOUS TIRESOME WRETCHED
FORJASKIT
(BECOME —) JADE
WEARY WILLIE TRAMP
WEASAND WISEN GULLET THROAT
WIZZEN TRACHEA WINDPIPE
WEASEL CANE VAIR VARE WARE
HULDA HURON SNEAK STOAT TAIRA
TAYRA ERMINE FERRET HULDAH

VERMIN ARCTOID VORMELA
FUTTERET MUISHOND MUSTELIN
WHITRACK
WEASEL CAT LINSANG
WEATHER SKY DIRT RAIN TIME
COLLA STORM WINDWARD
(— CONDITION) WHITEOUT
(FAIR —) SHINE
(HOT AND HUMID —) SIZZARD
(INCLEMENT —) SEASON
(INTERVAL OF FAIR —) SLATCH
(UNDER THE —) SEEDY
(VIOLENT —) ELEMENTS
WEATHERBEATEN SEAGOING
WEATHERCOCK COCK FANE VANE
FAINE FANACLE
WEAVE CANE HABI HUCK JOIN LACE
LENO LOOM REED ROCK SPIN WALE
WARP WIND WOOF DOBBY DRAPE
PLAIT TWINE UNITE BROCHE
DAMASK DEVISE DIAPER DOBBIE
FABRIC CANILLE ENTWINE FASHION
INDRAPE SATINET SHUTTLE
VANDYKE DIAGONAL DUCHESSE
OVERSHOT
(— PATTERNS INTO) BROCADE
(BASKET —) BARLEYCORN
(CARPET —) FLOSSA
(HERRINGBONE —) SUMAK SOUMAK
SHEMAKA
(LATTICE —) TEE
(OPEN —) LENO BAREGE
WEAVER KORI TANTI WEBBE
DRAWBOY WEBSTER WOBSTER
PENELOPE TAPESTER
WEAVERBIRD NUN BAYA MAYA
TAHA FINCH MUNIA VIDUA WEBBE
BISHOP CANARY OXBIRD WHIDAH
WHYDAH BENGALI AMADAVAT
AVADAVAT CARDINAL MANNIKIN
WEAVING TANIKO TEXTURE
WEBBING
(— OF WORDS) CONTEXT
(— TOGETHER) PLEXURE
WEAZEN WIZEN SHRINK WIZENED
WEB PLY WOB CAUL FELT MAZE
TENT TOIL VANE WARP WEFT
SNARE THROW TWIST FLEECE
TISSUE ENSNARE FEATHER LAYETTE
TEXTURE SNOWSHOE VEXILLUM
(— IN EYE) HAW
(CRANK —) THROW
WEBBED RINGED PALMATE
WEBBING MAT WEB PALAMA
WEB-FOOTED PALAMATE PALMIPED
WEB SPINNER EMBIID WEBWORM
WED GET BEWED BRIDE MARRY
STAKE WAGER ENGAGE PLEDGE
SPOUSE ESPOUSE WEDLOCK
WEDDING SPLICE NUPTIAL
WEDLOCK ESPOUSAL MARRIAGE
WEDGE KEY COIN FROE FROW GLUT
HORN KYLE PLUG STOB TRIP WAGE
CHOCK CHUCK CLEAT COIGN HACEK
HORSE QUINE SCOTE SLICE THROW
COTTER CUNEUS QUINET SCOTCH
EMBOLUS QUINNET SCHOCHE
VOUSSOIR
(— BETWEEN TWO FEATHERS) KEY

(— IN) JAM JAMB
(— OF OATMEAL) FARL FARLE
(— TO PREVENT MOTION) CHOCK
(CURVED —) CAM
(WOODEN —) COW GLUT JACK
WEDGER SPRINGER
WEDGE-SHAPED CUNEAL SPHENIC
CUNEATED SPHENOID
WEDLOCK WIFE SPOUSAL MARRIAGE
SPOUSAGE
WEDNESDAY MIDWEEK
WEE TINY EARLY SMALL TEENY
YOUNG LITTLE
WEED BUR HOE BURR CHOP CULL
DOCK FORB LOUK SHIM SIDA TARE
WEID CIGAR DRANK DRAWK DRESS
DROKE FLESH DARNEL JIMSON
KNAWEL RIPGUT SARCLE SPURGE
SPURRY STROIL ASHWORT COHITRE
CUCKOLD EGILOPS GARMENT
GOSMORE HOGWORT SANDBUR
TOBACCO VERVAIN VERVINE
CHADLOCK COCKSPUR COWWHEAT
PIRIPIRI PLANTAIN PURSLANE
TOADFLAX ALFILERIA MARIJUANA
(MEXICAN —) BIRDEYE
(TROUBLESOME —) KEX TITTER
(PL.) FILTH WRACK DISMAL SPRING
WEEDAGE TRUMPERY
WEEDER SARCLER
WEEDY FOUL LANKY
WEEK OOK WOK OULK WOKE
SENNET STANZA HEBDOMAD
SENNIGHT
(TWO —S) FORTNIGHT
WEEKDAY FERIA WARDAY
WEEKLY AWEEK
WEEL LEAP POOL TRAP RIGHT
WHIRLPOOL
WEEN MEAN VENE WEND FANCY
GUESS EXPECT BELIEVE IMAGINE
SUPPOSE CONCEIVE
WEENY TINY SMALL WEESHY
WEEP CRY ORP SOB BAWL BEND
GIVE LEAK OOZE PIPE TEAR WAIL
GREET BEWAIL BEWEEP BOOHOO
LAMENT SHOWER BLUBBER
LAPWING SQUINNY COMPLAIN
WEEPER GREETER MOURNER
CAPUCHIN
(PL.) FLENTES
WEEPING WOP GREET MILCH RAINY
LAMENT OOZING PIPING MAUDLIN
TEARFUL DRIPPING LACRIMAL
MADIDANS PLORATION
WEEPING SINEW GANGLION
WEEVER JUGULAR STINGBULL
WEEVIL MAX BOUD POPE WHULE
PICUDO WEEBLE BILLBUG BRUCHUS
VAQUITA CURCULIO WOODWORM
(PLUM —) TURK
WEFT WEB PICK WOOF BLAST
FABRIC FILLING
WEIGH GO SIT HEFT PEIS TARE TELL
COUNT HEAVE HOIST PEIZE POISE
RAISE SCALE BURDEN PONDER
ANALYZE BALANCE DEPRESS
LIBRATE CONSIDER EVALUATE
MEDITATE MILITATE

(— DOWN) LADE SWAY SWEE
BESET HEAVY PEISE CADDLE
CHARGE CUMBER PESTER DEPRESS
FREIGHT INGRATE OPPRESS
OVERLAY ENCUMBER
(— UPON) SIT GRIEVE
WEIGHER BOXMAN PEISER SCALER
WEIGHING (— MACHINE) TRON
SCALE TRONE
WEIGHT (ALSO SEE MEASURE AND
UNIT) BOB FEN FOB MAN NET RAM
SER SIR TOM TUP ABAS ATOM BEEF
CLOG DROP GRAM HEFT IRON KITE
LEAD LOAD MACE MEAL NAIL ONUS
PEIS POND PORT ROTL SEAM SINK
WAIT ABBAS CLOVE CRITH GARCE
MAUND PEASE PEISE POISE POIZE
PRESS RIDER SCALE STAMP
AUNCEL BURDEN CHARGE HAMMER
IMPORT MOMENT MONKEY PASSIR
PONDER PONDUS SINKER STRESS
BALLAST DOLPHIN GRAVITY MILLIER
PLATINE PLUMMET POSIURE
CHALDRON DEMIMARK DUMBBELL
ENCUMBER FARASULA PRESSURE
QUINCUNX STANDARD STRENGTH
(— AFTER TARE DEDUCTION)
SUTTLE
(— CARRIED BY HORSE) IMPOST
(— CLOTH) FLOCK
(— FOR HURLING) HAMMER
(— FOR LEAD) FOTMAL
(— FOR PRECIOUS STONE) CARAT
(— FOR WOOL) TOD SARPLER
(— FOR WOOL, CHEESE, ETC.)
CLOVE
(— OF 100 LBS.) CENTAL CENTENA
CENTNER
(— OF 1000 LIVRES) MILLIER
(— OF 20 OR 21 LBS.) SCORE
(— OF 40 BUSHELS) WEY
(— OF 5 UNCIAE) QUINCUNX
(— OF BROADSIDE) GUNPOWER
(— OF COAL) KEEL
(— OF COFFEE) MAT
(— OF HYDROGEN) CRITH
(— OF METAL) JOURNEY
(— OF ONE 100TH TAEL) FEN
(— OF ONE 10TH TAEL) MACE
(— OF PENDULUM) BOB
(— OF PILE DRIVER) TUP
(— OF RAW SILK) PARI
(— OF SILK OR RAYON) DRAMMAGE
(— ON MINE SWEEPER) KITE
(— ON STEELYARD) PEA
(— ON WATCH CHAIN) FOB
(— TO BEND HOT METAL) DUMPER
(— TO DETECT FALSE COINS)
PASSIR
(— TO HINDER MOTION) CLOG
(— WHICH VESSEL CAN CARRY)
TONNAGE
(ABYSSINIAN —) FARASULA
(CARAT —) SILIQUA
(CLOCK —) PEISE
(FALSE —) SLANG
(GREATLY VARYING —) MAN MAUND
(HEAVY —) MONKEY
(LIGHT —) SUTTLE

(MONEYER'S —) DROIT
(ORIENTAL —) CATTY
(SASHCORD —) MOUSE
(SHUFFLEBOARD —) SHIP
(SMALL —) MITE GERAH RIDER
(SPLINE —) DOLPHIN
(UNIT OF —) SER VIS WEY LAST
ROTL SEER LIANG LIBRA LINGO
MINAL PECUL PERIT PIKOL KANTAR
LINGOE MISKAL POCKET LISPUND
PRICKLE QUINTAL ZOLOTNIK
WEIGHTED BIAS LOADED
WEIGHTER FULLER
WEIGHT-PRODUCING GRAVIFIC
WEIGHTY GRAVE GREAT HEAVY
HEFTY MASSY VALID COGENT
SOLEMN EARNEST MASSIVE
ONEROUS PEISANT SERIOUS
TELLING GRIEVOUS MATERIAL
POWERFUL PREGNANT
WEIR DAM CRIB KEEP LEAP STOP
CAULD DOACH GARTH GORCE
HATCH HEDGE STANK LASHER
WEIRD ODD EERY UNCO UNKO EERIE
UNCOW UNKID CREEPY ELDRICH
ELRITCH UNCANNY UNUSUAL
WIZARDLY
(— SISTERS) FATES
WEITSPEKAN YUROK
WEKA RAIL WOODHEN RAILBIRD
WELCOME SEE FAIN GOOD HAIL
ADOPT CHEER GREET RESET TREAT
ACCOIL INVITE SALUTE ACCLAIM
ACCUEIL AMBRACE GRATIFY
BIENVENU GREETING HAEREMAI
PLEASANT
WELD SHUT WELL SWAGE UNITE
WOALD ACACIA
WELDED SHOT
WELDING FUSION SHUTTING
WELFARE SEL GOOD HALE HEAL
SELE WEALTH BENISON BLESSING
WELKIN SKY HEAVENS WALKENE
WELL AIN EYE GAY PIT WEL BENE
FINE FLOW GOOD PANT PUIT PURE
RITE SAFE SINK WINK AWEEL
BOOLY BOWLY GREAT MUSHA
OILER QUELL WISHA BUCKET
CENOTE ENOUGH FAIRLY GASSER
NICELY OFFSET PUMPER TUNNEL
FALLWAY GRADELY HEALTHY
WILDCAT BOREHOLE FOUNTAIN
GRAITHLY POSTHOLE WATERPIT
WEALSOME
(— AND STRONG) BUNKUM
(— THROUGH FLOORS OF
WAREHOUSE) FALLWAY
(— UP) WALL WALM DIGHT
(AS —) ALSO
(NONPRODUCTIVE —) DUSTER
(NOT —) DONNY SOBER INVALID
(OIL —) OILER GASSER GUSHER
SPOUTER WILDCAT STRIPPER
(RECTANGULAR —) BOOLY BOWLY
(SACRED — AT MECCA) ZEMZEM
(TOLERABLY —) GAYLIES GEYLIES
(VERY —) BRAWLY CLEVER
WELL-BALANCED SOBER
WELL-BEHAVED GOOD NICE

MODEST MANNERED
WELL-BEING HEAL SKIN WEAL
HEALTH WEALTH COMFORT
EUCRASY WELFARE EUCRASIA
WELLBORN GENTLE EUGENIC
WELL-BRED GENTIL POLITE
GENTEEL REFINED CULTURED
LADYLIKE
WELL CASING STEANING
WELL-CHOSEN CHOICE
WELL-CONSIDERED THRIFTY
WELL CURB PUTEAL
WELL-DEFINED STRICT
WELL-DISPOSED SIB FAIN GOOD
VAIN
WELL DONE SHABASH
WELL-DRESSED BRAW GASH
BRAWLY
WELL-FED BLOWSY BLOWZY
CHUBBY GAWCEY GAWSIE
WELL-FORMED TIGHT DECENT
PROPER SEEMLY SHAPELY
WELL-FOUNDED FIRM GOOD JUST
SOUND WORTHY
WELL-GROOMED SMUG CRISP
SOIGNE SOIGNEE
WELL-GROUNDED VALID
WELL-GROWN THRODDY
WELL-HUSBANDED THRIFTY
WELL-INFORMED KNOWING
PERFECT
WELL-INTENTIONED AMIABLE
WELL-KEPT SMUG POLITE
WELL-KNIT WIRY
WELL-KNOWN BREEM BREME
BEATEN FAMOUS KENNED FAMILIAR
WELL-LIKED FANCIED POPULAR
WELL-MADE CLEVER
WELL-MANNERED POLITE
COURTEOUS
WELL-NIGH WELLY ALMOST NEARLY
WELLMOST
WELL-ORGANIZED SNOD
WELL-PLEASED FAIN VAIN
WELL-PROPORTIONED SUING
TRETIS HANDSOME
WELL-READ STUDIED LITERARY
WELL-ROUNDED CHUBBY
WELL-SHAPED CLEVER FEATOUS
WELL-TILLED NOT NOTT
WELL-TO-DO ABLE BEIN BIEN EASY
WARM PODDED
WELL-WISHER FRIEND FAVORER
WELS WALLER SHEATFISH
WELSH (ALSO SEE WALES) CYMRY
FUDGE TAFFY CYMRIC KYMRIC
CAMBRIAN
WELSHER QUITTER
WELSHMAN CELT KELT TAFFY
BRYTHON CAMBRIAN
WELSH ONION CIBOL CIBOULE
CHESBOLL
WELT RIDGE STRIP WHELP WELTING
BANDELET TURNOVER
(SHOE —S) WATTIS
WELTANSCHAUUNG FAITH
IDEOLOGY
WELTER REEL RIOT TOSS WILT
GROVEL TUMBLE WALLOW WRITHE

SMOTHER STAGGER SWELTER
(— **OF SOUNDS**) DIN
WELWITSCHIA TUMBOA
WEM FLAW SCAR SPOT STAIN
WEN CYST WYNN CLIER CLYER
TALPA TUMOR GOITER
WENCH DELL DILL DOXY DRAB GILL
GIRL JADE MAID MOLL PRIM TRUG
GOUGE KITTY MADAM QUEAN TRULL
WHORE AUDREY BLOUSE BLOWEN
BLOWZE DRAZEL JILLET KITTIE
MOTHER POPLET WOTLINK
POPLOLLY
(**CLUMSY** —) MODER MODDER
MOTHER MAUTHER
WENCHER DRABBER STRIKER
WEND BOW END SORB VEND STEER
BETAKE DEPART DIRECT TRAVEL
PROCEED SORBIAN LUSATIAN
(— **ONE'S WAY**) MARK
WENT GODE LANE ROAD YEDE
ALLEY PASSAGE
(— **ABOUT**) WOLK
WENTLETRAP SCALA
WENZEL JACK
WERE (— **IT NOT**) SAVE
WEREWOLF TURNSKIN VERSIPEL
WEST STY BEWEST PONENT
OCCIDENT
WESTERN PONENT SCAEAN
HESPERIC SANDWICH
WEST HIGHLAND KYLOE

WEST VIRGINIA

CAPITAL: CHARLESTON
COLLEGE: SALEM BETHANY
CONCORD MARSHALL
BLUEFIELD
COUNTY: MINGO ROANE UPSHUR
BARBOUR KANAWHA
INDIAN: MONETON
LAKE: LYNN
NICKNAME: MOUNTAIN
RIVER: ELK OHIO KANAWA
POTOMAC GUYANDOT
STATE BIRD: CARDINAL
STATE FLOWER: RHODODENDRON
STATE TREE: MAPLE
TOWN: ELKINS KEYSER RIPLEY
VIENNA WESTON BECKLEY
GRAFTON SPENCER WEIRTON
FAIRMONT WHEELING

WESTWARD WESSEL OCCASIVE
WESTLINS
WET DEW DIP SOP WAT DAMP DANK
LASH MOIL SLOW SOAK SOFT UVID
BATHE DABBY DROOK DRUNK
HUMID JUICE JUICY LEACH MADID
MOIST MOOTH RAINY SLAKE SNAPY
SOBBY SOPPY SPEWY STEEP TIGHT
WEAKY CLASHY DABBLE DAGGLE
DAMPEN HUMECT IMBRUE JARBLE
LABBER MADEFY MARSHY MOISTY
QUASHY SHOWER SLABBY SOBBED
SPONGY SPOUTY SWASHY WATERY
ARROUSE BLUBBER DRABBLE
FLOTTER MOISTEN SLOPPED
SOBBING SPEWING SPRINGY

IRRIGATE SATURATE SLATTERY
SLOBBERY SLOTTERY WATERISH
(— **AND STORMY**) FOUL
(— **LIGHTLY**) SPRINKLE
(— **THOROUGHLY**) SOUSE DRENCH
(**SOFTLY** —) SQUASHY
(**VERY** —) SOPPY
WETHER PUR RAM HAMEL DINMAN
DINMONT
WETNESS DANK
WETTING SOUCE SOUSE SOWSE
MOILING
WHACK DAD LAM TRY BANG BELT
BIFF DEAL HACK SWAK TIME DRIVE
SHARE STATE SWACK WHANG
CHANCE DEFEAT STROKE THWACK
BARGAIN LAMBACK PORTION
WHACKING VERY WHALING
WHOPPING EXTREMELY
WHALE SEI CETE HUEL HULL LASH
ORCA WALL KOGIA POGGY SCRAG
SPERM STUNT BALEEN BELUGA
BLOWER FINNER GIBBAR KILLER
THRASH BOWHEAD DOLPHIN
FINBACK FINFISH GIBBERT
GRAMPUS RIPSACK RORQUAL
SPOUTER ZIPHIAN BALAENID
CACHALOT CETACEAN DOEGLING
GREYBACK HARDHEAD HUMPBACK
JUBARTES MUTILATE THRASHER
ZIPHIOID
(— **BUTCHER**) LEMMER
(— **REFUSE**) GURRY
(**FINBACK** —) GRASO
(**SCHOOL OF** —**S**) GAM POD
WHALEBONE BALEEN
WHALER HEADER BUSHMAN
SPOUTER SWAGMAN WHACKER
WHOPPER CETIDIDE
WHALESKIN MUKTUK
WHANG BEAT BLOW FLOG CHUNK
THONG WHACK THRASH RAWHIDE
WHARF KEY POW DOCK GARE PIER
QUAY SLIP BERTH JETTY STADE
STAITH STRAND LANDING PANTALAN
STELLING
WHARVE WARVE WHIRL WHORL
WHAT FAT HOT HOW WET WHO
HOOT HOTE WHEN STUFF WHICH
MATTER PARTLY
WHATA FUTTAH FUTTER
WHATNOT OMNIUM ETAGERE
WHATSOEVER MORTAL
WHEAL HIVE HUEL WALE WELT
URTICA POMPHUS
WHEAT WIT CORN CONES EMMER
FULTZ GRAIN SPELT SPICA TRIGO
BULGAR BURGUL CEREAL KANRED
STAPLE TURKEY EINKORN FORMITY
FRUMETY KUBANKA MARQUIS
POLLARD FRUMENTY SPELTOID
(— **BOILED IN MILK**) FURMITY
(— **MEASURE**) TRUG
(**BEARDED** —) RIVETS
(**CRACKED** —) GROATS
(**GRANULATED** —) SUJI SUJEE
(**HARD** —) DURUM
(**PARCHED** —) BULGUR
WHEATCAKE PURI

WHEATEAR CHACK ARLING WITTOL
CHACKER ORTOLAN SNORTER
WITTALL CHICKELL
WHEATGRASS BLUESTEM
WHEATLIKE VULGARE
WHEEDLE COG CANT CLAW COAX
CARNY FLUFF GLOSE GLOZE INGLE
JOLLY BANTER CAJOLE FLEECH
GLAVER RADDLE SMOOGE WHILLY
BLARNEY CUITTLE PALAVER
SMOODGE TWEEDLE COLLOGUE
SCROUNGE
WHEEDLING BUTTERY
WHEEL BOB BUR COG FAN NUT ORB
BEAD BUFF GEAR HELM HURL PURL
ROLL RULL STAR TIRL WYLE ATHEY
FLIER FLUFF FLYER IDLER NORIA
REWET RHOMB ROWEL SWING
TRUCK BILOBE CASTER CASTOR
CIRCLE DRIVEN DRIVER FANNER
HORRAL JAGGER KURUMA LEADER
PINION ROLLER ROTATE RUNDLE
RUNNER TRACER BALANCE BICYCLE
CHUKKER GUDGEON LANTERN
PEDRAIL PRICKER REVOLVE
STEPNEY TRAILER TRILOBE TRINDLE
TRUCKLE TRUNDLE UNILOBE
WILDCAT FOLLOWER ODOMETER
SPROCKET
(— **A SKIN**) FLUFF
(— **CHARGED WITH DIAMOND DUST**)
SLITTER
(— **CONTROLLING RUDDER**) HELM
(— **FOR EXECUTIONS**) RAT
(— **IN KNITTING MACHINE**) BUR
BURR
(— **IN TIMEPIECE**) BALANCE
(**BUCKET** —) LIFTER
(**DIAMOND** —) SKIVE
(**GEAR** —) DRIVEN HELICAL
(**GRINDING** —) SHELL
(**GROOVED** —) PULLEY SHEAVE
SHIVER
(**INTERRUPTER** —) TICKER TIKKER
(**LOCOMOTIVE** —) DRIVER
(**METAL** —) FILET FILLET
(**MILL** —) PIRN
(**PAIR OF LOGGING** —**S**) CATYDID
KATYDID
(**POINTED** —) TRACER
(**POLISHING** —) BOB BUFF SKAIF
SKEIF BUFFER SCAIFE
(**POTTER'S** —) LATHE THROW
(**SPINNING** —) TURN CHARKA
CHARKHA
(**SPUR** —) ROWEL
(**TANK** —) BOGY BOGEY BOGIE
(**TOOTHED** —) GEAR PINION
ROULETTE
(**TURBINE** —) ROTOR
(**TWO PAIRS OF** —**S**) CUTS CUTTS
(**VANED** —) FLIER FLYER
(**WATER** —) NORIA SAKIA SAKIEH
SAKIYEH TYMPANUM
(PL.) KATYDID
WHEELBARROW GURRY BARROW
CARRIAGE
WHEELER POLER PUSHER
WHEEL-SHAPED ROTATE ROTIFORM

WHEELWORK MOTION

WHEELWRIGHT WHEELER
WOODMAN WHEELMAN

WHEEZE JOKE HOOSE HOOZE TRICK
COGHLE

WHELK FILK GRUB WELT BUCKIE
MAGGOT PAPULE PIMPLE WINKLE
PUSTULE

WHELP CUB PUP SON CHIT FAWN
PUPPY YELPER KITLING SPROCKET

WHEMMEL UPSET FUMMEL FUMMLE
WHAMBLE OVERTURN

WHEN AS BUT FAN FRO GIN THO
WON THAN THEN THOA TILL SINCE
UNTIL ENOUGH ALTHOUGH

WHENEVER ONCE

WHERE AS FAR FUR FAUR FEAR
FERRE PLACE QUAIR THERE
WHITHER LOCATION

(— **ABOVE MENTIONED**) US

WHEREFORE WHY CAUSE FORWHY
REASON

WHERENESS UBIETY

WHEREVER THERE

WHEREWITHAL MEANS MONEY
RESOURCES

WHERRET BOX CUFF SLAP HURRY
TEASE WORRY TROUBLE WHIRRICK

WHERRY BARGE ROWBOAT WHIRREY

WHET WET GOAD HONE TIME TURN
GRIND POINT RIFLE ROUSE SLITE
WHILE EXCITE INCITE STROKE
QUICKEN SHARPEN APERITIF
EXACUATE

WHETHER IF GIF GIN WHAR WHERE
EITHER

WHETSTONE BUR RIP RUB BUHR
BURR SLIP STONE RUBBER STRAIK
SHARPER WASHITA WHITTLE
RUBSTONE STRICKLE

WHEY PALE QUAY WHIG SERUM
THRUST WATERY

WHIBA UEBA

WHICH AS THE WHO THAT QUILK
WHILK

(— **SEE**) QV QQV

WHICKER NEIGH WHINNY WIGHER

WHIDAH BIRD VEUVE WEAVER
WHYDAH REDBILL

WHIFF FAN GUF BLOW GUFF GUST
HINT PUFF TIFT WAFT WIFT FLUFF
QUIFF SMOKE EXHALE MAGRIM
MEGRIM WHIFFET

WHIFFLE FIFE SWAY FLICKER
FLUTTER

WHIFFLETREE HEELTREE
SWINGLEBAR

WHIG JOG QUIG WHEY

WHILE AS BIT GAM THO YET FILE
FYLE TIDE TILL WHEN WHET WOLE
FILIE PIECE SPACE STEAD STOUN
THROW UNTIL STOUND WHENAS
WHILOM BEGUILE TROUBLE
EXERTION OCCASION

(— **AWAY**) AMUSE FLEET DIVERT
DECEIVE

(**LITTLE** —) AWEE DRASS WHILEY
WHILEEN WHILOCK

WHILES UNTIL SOMETIMES

WHILLY GULL CAJOLE WHEEDLE

WHILST TILL UNTIL

WHIM BEE FAD GIG GIN TOY FIKE
FLAM KINK CRANK FANCY FLISK
FOLLY FREAK HUMOR QUIRK THRUM
FEGARY FITTEN MAGGOT MEGRIM
SPLEEN VAGARY WHIMSY BOUTADE
CAPRICE CONCEIT WRINKLE
CROTCHET

WHIMBREL JACK SPOW SPOWE
CURLEW MAYBIRD MAYFOWL
TITTEREL

WHIMPER GIRN MEWL PULE WAIL
WEAK BLEAT WHINE SIMPER
WHINGE YAMMER GRIZZLE SNIFFLE
SNUFFLE WHINDLE WHINNEL
WHITTER WHINNOCK

WHIMSICAL FANCY COCKLE FLISJY
NOTION QUAINT BIZARRE GIGGISH
BIZZARRO FANCIFUL FREAKISH
HUMOROUS NOTIONAL SINGULAR

WHIMSY WHIM FREAK VAGARY
CAPRICE WHIMWHAM

WHIN FUN ULEX FURZE WHINCOW
WOODWAX

WHINCHAT TICK UTICK WHEATEAR

WHINE WOW GIRN GOWL MEWL
PULE TIRM TOOT YARM YIRN BLEAT
CROON MEECH QUINE TWINE
WHAUP WHEWT SNIVEL TREBLE
WHINGE WINNEL YAMMER WHIMPER
WHINDLE

WHINNY HINNY NEIGH PLAIN
SNICKER WHICKER

WHINSTONE TRAP WHIN SCURDY

WHINYARD SWORD HANGER
POCHARD WHINGER SHOVELER

WHIP CAT EEL FAN GAD ROD TAW
BEAT CAST COIL DICK DUST FLOG
FOAM GOAD HIDE JERK LASH LICK
LOUK PLET TAWS URGE WHUP
ABUSE AZOTE BIRCH CRACK FLAIL
FLICK FLISK IMPEL KNOUT LEASH
PLETE QUILT ROMAL SLASH STRAP
SWEPE SWING SWISH TAWSE
THONG THUMP AROUSE BREECH
CHABUK DEFEAT FEAGUE INCITE
LAINER LARRUP LICKER MAIDEN
NETTLE PIZZLE QUIPPE SCUTCH
SNATCH SWITCH TICKLE CHABOUK
CHICOTE COWHIDE COWSKIN
CURBASH KURBASH LAMBAST
LAYOVER NAGAIKA RAWHIDE
SCOURGE SHINGLE SJAMBOK
SLASHER TICKLER CHAWBUCK
COACHMAN CONFOUND FLAGELLA
KOURBASH PEPPERER

(— **EGGS**) CAST

(— **HANDLE**) CROP

(— **IN PIANO ACTION**) WIPPEN

(— **WITH 3 LASHES**) PLET PLETE

(**HORSE** —) WAND

(**JOCKEY'S** —) BAT

(**RIDING** —) CROP DICK QUIRT

(**RUSSIAN** —) KNOUT

WHIPLASH COSAQUE CRACKER

WHIPPED BEATEN BROKEN
DEFEATED FOUETTEE CHANTILLY

WHIPPER TICKLER THONGMAN

THRASHER THREAPER

WHIPPER-IN PRICKER

WHIPPERSNAPPER SQUIRT
WHIFFET WHIPSTER

WHIPPING LICK TOCO TOKO HIDING
CLANKER FANNING SERVING
BIRCHING BROWSING SKELPING

WHIPPING POST FORK PILLAR

WHIP SCORPION GRAMPUS
PHRYNID PEDIPALP WHIPTAIL

WHIPSOCKET SNEAD

WHIPSTITCH MINUTE INSTANT
OVERCAST

WHIR BIRR ZIZZ WHIRRY

WHIRL BIRL EDDY FURL GYRE HURL
PURL RUSH SPIN TIRL DRILL GIDDY
SKIRL SQUIR SWIRL THIRL THROW
TWIRL TWIST WALTZ WHORL
BUSTLE CIRCLE GYRATE HURTLE
SWINGE VORTEX WHORLE WINDLE
WIRBLE MIZMAZE REVOLVE
TRUNDLE TURMOIL VERTICIL

(— **ABOUT**) DOZE GURGE

(— **IN THE AIR**) WARP

WHIRLIGIG GIG SPIN TURN WHEEL
FIZGIG FISHGIG

WHIRLING GIDDY WHEELY
GYRATION GYRATORY VORTICAL

WHIRLPOOL EDDY GULF SUCK WELL
WIEL GORCE GOURD BULLER
GORGES SWELTH VORTEX GURGLET
SWALLOW SWILKIE SUCKHOLE
MAELSTROM

WHIRLWIND OE DEVIL VORTEX
PRESTER TORNADO

WHISHT HUSH SILENCE

WHISK ZIP FISK TUFT WHID WHIP
WISP CAURI FLICK FLISK HURRY
SPEED SWISH CHAURI CHOWRY
SWITCH COWTAIL WHISKER

WHISKER HAIRLINE VIBRISSA
(PL.) BEARD ZIFFS WEEPER
GALWAYS VIBRISSA MOUSTACHE
SIDEBURNS

WHISKY RYE BOND CORN CIDER
IRISH USQUE POTEEN REDEYE
SCOTCH BOURBON BLOCKADE
BUSTHEAD CREATURE POPSKULL
USQUABAE

(**GLASS OF** —) RUBDOWN

(**RAW** —) DRUDGE

WHISPER BUZZ HARK HINT ROUN
RUNE ROUND RUMOR TRACE TUTEL
BREATH BREEZE HARKEN MURMUR
SUSURR TITTLE WHISHT HEARKEN
SUSURRUS

WHIST MORT VINT QUIET BOSTON
SILENT WHEESHT

WHISTLE BLOW CALL FUTE PIPE
WHEW QUILL WHAUP WHEEP WHUTE
BUZZER CUCKOO FUSSLE HOOTER
SIFFLE SISTLE SQUEAL YELPER
TWEEDLE BIRDCALL

WHISTLE FLUTE SIFFLOT

WHISTLER PIPER MARMOT ROARER
FLUTIST LAPWING SIFFLEUR

WHISTLING PIPY PIPEY ROARING
SIFFLET RHONCHUS

WHIT BIT JOT ATOM DOIT HATE

HOOT IOTA QUAT QUIT BODLE GROAT POINT QUITE SPECK CIVITE PARTICLE TWOPENNY

WHITE CUT WAN BAWN FITE HOAR LILY PALE QUAT QUIT ASHEN BLOND HOARY LABAN LINEN SNOWY ALBINO ARGENT BLANCH BRIGHT BUCKRA CANDID CIVITE ERMINE SILVER WINTRY CANDENT LEUCOUS NIVEOUS WHITTLE FAVORITE INNOCENT LACTEOUS
(**— AND SMOOTH**) IVORINE
(**— OF EGG**) GLAIR ALBUMEN
(**— PERSON**) OFAY
(**POOR —**) YAHOO CRACKER

WHITE ALDER CLETHRA

WHITE ANT ANAY NASUTE TERMITE

WHITEBAIT SMELT ICEFISH SALANGID SALMONID

WHITEBEAM ARIA SERVICE MULBERRY

WHITEBOY PET LEVELER

WHITE BRYONY COWBIND

WHITE CEDAR JUNIPER

WHITE CLOVER SHAMROCK

WHITEFISH BLOAT CISCO PILOT POWAN BELUGA CHIVEY POLLAN TULIPI VENDIS BLOATER BOWBACK LAVARET VENDACE BLACKFIN GREYBACK HUMPBACK MENOMINI SALMONID SCHNABEL TULLIBEE

WHITEFLY HOMOPTER MEALYWING

WHITE GUM TUART

WHITE-HEADED GOLDEN FAVORED FORTUNATE

WHITE HELLEBORE ITCHREED ITCHWEED

WHITE IPECAC ITOUBOU

WHITE LEAD CERUSE

WHITE MAPAU PIROPIRI

WHITE MUSTARD KEDLOCK SINAPIS CRUCIFER

WHITEN SCURF ALBIFY BLANCH BLANCO BLEACH BLENCH DEALBATE EMBLANCH ETIOLATE

WHITENESS IVORY ALBEDO ARGENT CANDOR PURITY CANITIES PALENESS

WHITE OAK ROBLE

WHITE POPLAR ABELE ABELTREE

WHITE SNAKEROOT STEVIA POOLWORT RICHWEED WHITETOP

WHITE STURGEON BELUGA

WHITETHROAT JACK MUFF MUFTY MUGGY PEGGY EYSOGE MILLER MUFFET WHISKY WINNEL HAYSUCK WHEYBIRD

WHITEWASH LIME GLASS BLANCH PARGET CHICAGO LIMEWASH PALLIATE

WHITEWEED DAISY

WHITE WHALE BELUGA

WHITHER GUST HURL RUSH WHIZ HURRY SHAKE WHERE FLURRY BLUSTER WHERETO

WHITING BARB HAKE CORBINA CORVINA KINGFISH MOONFISH

WHITING-POUT BIB KLEG BLENS

WHITISH BAWN PALE DILUTE SUBALBID

WHITLOW FELON ANCOME FETLOW BREEDER PANARIS RUNROUND

WHITLOW GRASS DRABA

WHITRACK WEASEL FUTTERET WHITTRET

WHITSUNDAY TERM

WHITSUNTIDE PINXTER PINGSTER PINKSTER

WHITTLE CUT PARE CARVE KNIFE STEEL TWITE EXCITE MANTLE THWITE BLANKET

WHIZ BUZZ DEAL GIRL PIRR QUIZ SING WHIR ZIZZ SOUGH WHISH WHIZZ WIZARD BARGAIN SWITHER WHINNER

WHIZ-BANG EXPERT NOTABLE

WHO AS HOW THE WHA WHAT WHICH

WHOA WO WAY WHO STOP

WHOEVER WHATSO EVERWHO

WHOLE ALL HOW SUM BODY COOL EVEN HALE HALF HOLY HULL BLOCK GREAT GROSS HAILL SOUND TOTAL TOTUM TUTTA UNCUT CORPSE ENTIRE HEALED INTACT GENERAL INFRACT INTEGER PERFECT SINCERE SOLIDUM COMPLETE ENSEMBLE ENTIRETY GLOBULAR INTEGRAL LIVELONG OUTRIGHT UNBROKEN
(**— OF ANY ORGANISM**) SOMA
(**— OF REALITY**) ABSOLUTE
(**ORGANIC —**) SYSTEM

WHOLEHEARTED HEARTY SINCERE ZESTFUL COMPLETE IMPLICIT

WHOLESALE MASSIVE SWEEPING

WHOLESALER JOBBER EXPORTER

WHOLESOME GOOD CLEAN SOUND SWEET BENIGN SAVORY HEALTHY PRUDENT CURATIVE HALESOME HEALSOME HOMELIKE REMEDIAL SALUTARY HEALTHFUL

WHOLE-SOULED SINCERE

WHOLLY ALL FAIR FLAT HALE ONLY BLACK CLEAR FULLY QUITE STARK ALGATE BODILY FLATLY HOLLOW PURELY SOLELY ALGATES ROUNDLY SOLIDLY TOTALLY DIRECTLY ENTIRELY

WHOOP BOOM HOOP HOOT BOOST RAISE SHOUT EXCITE HALLOO HOOPOE

WHOOPING COUGH KINKHOST CHINCOUGH PERTUSSIS

WHOP WAP BEAT THUD THUMP STRIKE THRASH

WHOPPER LIE SIZER BOUNCER CRUMPER SLAPPER SNAPPER SWAPPER SWINGER STRAPPER WALLOPER

WHOPPING VERY LARGE BANGING RAPPING WAPPING WHALING SWINGING WHACKING

WHORE DRAB JILT FILTH WENCH HARLOT PUTAIN DEBAUCH STRUMPET SUCCUBUS

WHOREMONGER HOLOUR

WHORL TURN CYCLE SPIRE SWIRL WHIRL THWORL VOLUTE WHARVE WREATH ANNULUS GYRATION VERTICIL VOLUTION

WHORTLEBERRY HOT HURT FRAWN HOOTE FRAGHAN BILBERRY

WHY HOW QUI ENIGMA FORWHY

WICK BAD EVIL FARM TOWN ANGLE CREEK DAIRY MATCH QUICK SNAST CORNER LIVING WICKED VILLAGE FARMSTEAD
(**— CLOGGED WITH TALLOW**) ROUGHIE
(**LONG WAXED —**) TAPER

WICKED BAD SAD DARK EVIL FAST FOUL IRON LAZY LEWD MEAN PIKY VILE BLACK CURST FELON SHREW SORRY WRONG WROTH CURSED GUILTY LITHER LUTHER NEFAST PERDIT PITCHY SEVERE SHREWD SINFUL UNHOLY UNJUST UNLEAD UNLEDE UNWELL CAITIFF DARKSUM GODLESS HEINOUS HELLISH IMMORAL NAUGHTY NINETED NOXIOUS PRAVOUS PROFANE ROGUISH UNGODLY UNSEELY UNSOUND UNWREST VICIOUS VILLAIN CRIMINAL DARKSOME DEPRAVED DEVILISH DIABOLIC ENORMOUS FELONOUS FIENDISH FLAGRANT MESCHANT OBDURATE TERRIBLE UNKINDLY

WICKEDNESS ILL SIN EVIL HARM VICE CRIME FOLLY GUILT BELIAL FELONY NOUGHT UNGOOD ATHEISM DEVILRY ILLNESS DARKNESS DEVILTRY INIQUITY MISCHIEF SATANISM WANGRACE

WICKERWORK WEB WEEL TWIGGEN BASKETRY

WICKET GATE HOOP HATCH PITCH STUMP GUICHET
(**FALLING OF —S**) ROT

WICKETKEEPER STUMP STUMPER

WICKIUP HUT WAKIUP SHELTER

WIDDRIM FIT FURY

WIDDY NOOSE WIDOW WITHY HALTER

WIDE FAR LAX DEEP ROOM SIDE AMPLE BROAD LARGE ROOMY SHARP SLACK WRONG ASTRAY ROOMWARD SPACEFUL SPACIOUS
(**— OF THE MARK**) AWRY ABROAD
(**— OF**) BESIDE
(**LONG AND —**) SIDE

WIDE-AWAKE FLY FOXY KEEN LIVE ALERT FLASH LEERY SLIPPY KNOWING WAKEFUL WATCHFUL

WIDELY FAR BROAD ABROAD GREATLY LARGELY

WIDEN FLAN REAM DILATE EXPAND EXTEND FLANGE FUNNEL BROADEN

WIDENESS WIDTH BREADTH

WIDESPREAD RIFE DIFFUSE GENERAL CATHOLIC EXTENDED SWEEPING

WIDGEON SMEE WHIM GOOSE WHEWER ZUIZIN POACHER

POTCHER BALDPATE BLUEBILL WHISTLER

WIDOW VID BALO DAME SKAT BLIND KITTY VEUVE WEEDA WIDDY MATRON RELICT TERCER DOWAGER EMPRESS BARONESS DOWERESS (PL.) VIDUAGE

WIDOWHOOD VIDUAGE VIDUITY

WIDTH GAPE SIDE RANGE SCOPE BREADTH OPENING FRONTAGE FULLNESS LARGEOUR LATITUDE WIDENESS
(— OF CUT) KERF
(— OF HORSESHOE) COVER
(— OF PALM) HAND
(— OF PAPER) FILL
(— OF PULLEY) FACE
(— OF SHIP'S BAND) STRAKE ·
(— OF SHIP) BEAM
(— OF TYPE) SET
(— OF WEB) DECKLE

WIELD PLY RUN BEAR WALT WIND EXERT SWING VELDE EMPLOY GOVERN HANDLE MANAGE STRAIN CONTROL

WIFE UX FEM HEN MRS RIB WYF BABY BIBI DAME DORA ENID FEME FERE FRAU FROW JAEL LADY MAKE MATE RANI UXOR DIRCE DONNA DUTCH FEMME LUCKY MATCH MUJER SQUAW WOMAN ELMIRE EMILIA GAMMER KEEPER MATRON MISSIS MULIER SPOUSE VENDER WAHINE BEDMATE DIONYZA EMPRESS PARTNER WEDLOCK DEIANIRA DEIDAMIA ERIPHYLE HELPMATE HELPMEET MISTRESS PECULIAR
(— OF COTTER) COTQUEAN
(— OF KNIGHT OR BARONET) DAME
(— OF MOHAMMEDAN) KHADIJA
(AFFIANCED —) FUTURE
(INDIAN'S —) WEBB
(OLD —) GAMMER
(PL.) PUNALUA

WIG BOB JIZ RUG TIE FRIZ GIZZ JANE JIZZ LOCK TETE TOUR BUSBY CAXON FLASH JASEY MAJOR SCALP SCOLD ADONIS BRUTUS FROWZE PERUKE REBUKE TOUPEE TOUPET COMBING RAMILIE SCRATCH SHEITEL SPENCER BOBJEROM CHEDREUX CHEWELER NIGHTCAP PERUKERY POSTICHE ROGERIAN VALLANCY
(— WITH ROUGHLY CROPPED HAIR) BRUTUS
(18TH CENTURY —) ADONIS GEORGE
(BUSHY —) BUSBY
(GRAY —) GRIZZLE
(WORSTED —) JASEY

WIGGLE JET HOTCH JIGGLE WABBLE WANGLE

WIGGLER PUPA LARVA WRYER

WIGHT MAN SWIFT STRONG VALIANT CREATURE STALWART

WIGMAKER WIGGER PERUKER PERUKIER

WIGWAG SIGNAL

WIGWAM LODGE WEEKWAM WICKIUP

WIKENO NIKENO HEILTSUK

WILD REE SHY FAST RUDE SCAR WOWF CRAZY FANTI FELON FERAL GIDDY MYALL RANDY RANTY ROUGH ROYET SKEER WASTE DESERT FANTEE FERINE FIERCE LAVISH MADCAP NATIVE RAMAGE RANDOM RENISH SAVAGE SHANDY STORMY UNRULY BERSERK BREACHY ERRATIC FRANTIC GALLOUS GALLOWS HAGGARD HOWLING MADDING OUTWARD RIOTOUS SKADDLE SKEERED WILDING ABERRANT AGRESTAL BARBARIC DESOLATE FAROUCHE FRENETIC HALUCKET HELLICAT RECKLESS UNTILLED WARRAGAL WILLYARD
(— CARD) FREAK

WILD ASS GOUR KIANG KULAN COTULA KOULAN ONAGER QUAGGA CHIGETAI

WILD BALSAM APPLE CREEPER

WILD BEE KARBI

WILD BOAR APER SUID TUSKER SOUNDER SUIDIAN WILRONE SANGLIER

WILD BUFFALO ARNA ARNEE

WILD BUSH BEAN PHASEMY

WILD CABBAGE YELLOWS

WILD CARDAMOM RUEWORT KNOBWOOD

WILD CARROT DILL ELTROT FIDDLE BIRDNEST HILLTROT

WILDCAT CAT BALU EYRA CHATI CHAUS MANUL TIGER MARGAY SERVAL WAGATI COLOCOLA

WILD CELERY ACHE ECHE EELGRASS SMALLAGE

WILD CHERRY GEAN

WILD CHERVIL KECK COWWEED HONEWORT MILKWEED

WILD CYCLAMEN SOWBREAD

WILD DOG ADJAG DHOLE DINGO GUARA AGUARA AGOUARA CIMARRON WARRAGAL

WILDEBEEST GNU

WILDERNESS BUSH WILD WASTE DESERT FOREST WESTERN SOLITUDE

WILD-EYED HAGGARD RADICAL

WILDFOWL VOLATILE

WILD GARLIC MOLY

WILD GERANIUM ALUMROOT DOVEFOOT FLUXWEED

WILD GOAT TUR IBEX TAHR EVECK PASAN MAZAME MARKHOR AEGAGRUS MARKHOOR

WILD HORSE BRUMBY KUMRAH TARPAN BRUMBIE WARRAGAL WARRIGAL

WILD HYACINTH CUCKOO CROWTOE GREGGLE BRODIAEA CROWFOOT

WILD INDIGO SHOOFLY

WILD LETTUCE FIREWEED

WILD MAN SAVAGE WOODMAN WOODSMAN

WILD MANGOSTEEN SANTOL

WILD MARJORAM ORGAN ORGAMY ORGANY ORIGAN ORGAMENT

WILD MULBERRY YAWWEED

WILD MUSTARD CHARLOCK

WILDNESS FERITY HEYDAY HEYDEY FEROCITY SAVAGERY SAVAGISM

WILD OAT DRANK DRAWK DROKE HAVER HEVER EGILOPS

WILD ONION UMBEL UMBELLA

WILD OX BUF YAK ANOA BUFF REEM UNICORN

WILD PARSLEY ELTROT HILLTROT

WILD PEAR DOGBERRY

WILD PLUM SLOE ISLAY

WILD POTATO MANROOT WAPATOO

WILD RADISH RUNCH

WILD RICE MANOMIN

WILD SAGE EYESEED

WILD SARSAPARILLA SHOTBUSH

WILD SERVICE TREE SORB SORBUS

WILD SHEEP SHA URIAL AOUDAD ARGALI BHARAL NAYAUR BIGHORN MOUFLON

WILD SWAN ELK

WILD THYME HILLWORT SERPOLET

WILD TOBACCO GAGROOT SOURBUSH MARIJUANA SALVADORA

WILD TURNIP NAVEW

WILD VANILLA LIATRIS

WILE PAUK PAWK RUSE FRAUD GUILE TRICK ALLURE BLENCH DECEIT ENGINE ENTICE BEGUILE ARTIFICE TRICKERY

WILGA WILLOW

WILL EGO MAY ULL FATE LIST TEST WISH LEAVE OUGHT SHALL WORST ANIMUS CHOICE DESIRE DEVICE DEVISE LEGATE LIKING QUETHE SCRIPT APETITE CODICIL PASSION WITWORD AMBITION BEQUEATH PLEASING PLEASURE VOLITION
(— NOT) WONT WINNA WONNA WUNNA WONNOT
(— OF DEITY) DECREE
(— OF GOD) LAW
(— OF LEGISLATURE) ACT
(— TO LIVE) TANGHA
(FREE —) ACCORD
(GOOD —) GREE
(I —) CHILL
(ILL —) ARR ENVY HEST ANIMUS ENMITY UNTHANK AMBITION

WILLET TATLER TATTLER

WILLFUL HEADY WILLY FEISTY UNRULY HAGGARD WAYWARD WILSOME CAMSTRARY

WILLFULLY WOLDES SCIENTER

WILLIES JUMPS CREEPS

WILLING BAIN FAIN FREE GLAD LIEF RATH PRONE READY MINDED TOWARD CONTENT UNFORCED

WILLINGLY LIEF SOON FREELY GLADLY LIEFLY FRANKLY READILY

WILLINGNESS HEART FREEDOM FAINNESS

(— **TO FIGHT**) DEFIANCE
WILLIWAW STORM WOOLLY
TEMPEST
WILLOW DULY ITEA SALE WYLW
OSIER SALEW SALIX WIDDY WITHY
WOODY DUSTER SALLOW TEASER
TWILLY WITHEN WUDDIE
(— **FOR THATCHING**) SPRAYS
(— **IN TEXTILES**) WOLF
(**NATIVE** —) COOBA COOBAH
(**SIMPLE** —) WHIPPER
WILLOWER DULER DUSTER TEASER
WILLIER
WILLOW HERB WICOPY EPILOBE
FIRETOP PIGWEED ROSEBAY
BURNWEED FIREWEED
WILLOW WARBLER SMEU SMEUTH
MUDDLER TROCHIL OVENBIRD
WILLOW WREN PEGGY
WILLOWY SUPPLE SLIPPER
DELICATE
WILLY-NILLY PERFORCE
WILSON'S PLOVER COLLIER
WILSON'S SNIPE JACK SHADBIRD
WILSON'S TERN MEDRICK
WILSON'S THRUSH VEERY
WILT EBB SAG DROP FADE FLAG
WELK DROOP SUCCUMB COLLAPSE
WILTED EMARCID
WILY SLY FOXY CANNY SLICK
ARTFUL ASTUTE CLEVER CRAFTY
QUAINT SHREWD STALKY SUBTLE
CUNNING POLITIC VERSUTE
WINDING
WIMBLE BORE BRISK ACTIVE GIMLET
LIVELY NIMBLE WIBBLE WUMMEL
WIMPLE BEND WIND CURVE TWIST
GORGET RIPPLE MEANDER
WIMLUNGE
WIN BAG COP HIT DRAW GAIN HAVE
LAND LICK FORCE SCORE ATTACH
CLINCH OBTAIN ACHIEVE CONQUER
DESERVE HARVEST POSSESS
TRIUMPH DECISION OVERCOME
STRAIGHT
(— **AGAINST**) BREAK SCOOP
(— **AWAY**) STEAL DEBAUCH
(— **BACK**) RECOVER
(— **BY GUILE**) GET POT BEAR
CARRY RAISE TRAIN GATHER
CAPTURE INVEIGLE PROMERIT
(— **NARROWLY**) SQUEEZE
(— **OVER**) DEFEAT DISARM
(— **OVERWHELMINGLY**) SWEEP
WINCE KICK CHECK QUECH CRINGE
FLINCH QUATCH QUINCH QUITCH
RECOIL SHRINK
WINCH CRAB JACK REEL WINK
GIPSY WINZE ROLLER WHIMSY
WINDLE CATHEAD TRAVELER
VARIABLE WINDLASS
WIND AIR COP LAP BALL BIRR BISE
BIZE COIL CONE CURL EAST FIST
FLAW FOHN GALE GUST KINK PUFF
PUNO ROLL WEST WRAP BATCH
BLAST BLORE CRANK CREEK
CROOK FOEHN QUILL SPOOL
STORM TRADE TREND TWINE TWIST
WEAVE WITHE BOTTOM BOUGHT

BREEZE BUSTER CAURUS COLLAR
KECKLE SANSAR SHAMAL SPIRAL
SPIRIT SQUALL WAMPLE WESTER
ZEPHYR BREATHE CRANKLE
CRINKLE CYCLONE ENTWINE
EQUINOX ETESIAN GREGALE
INVOLVE MEANDER MISTRAL
SERPENT SINUATE TEMPEST
TWINGLE TWISTER WEATHER
WHIRLER WINDILL ARGESTES
DOWNWARD EASTERLY FAVONIUS
(— **ABEAM**) LASK
(— **ABOUT**) WIRE SNAKE
(— **AFTER DYEING**) BATCH
(— **FROM THE ANDES**) PAMPERO
(— **IN AND OUT**) INDENT WINGLE
(— **MAGNETS**) COMPOUND
(— **OF ARGENTINA**) ZONDA
PAMPERO
(— **OF HAWAII**) KONA
(— **OF OREGON AND WASHINGTON**)
CHINOOK
(— **OF TUNISIA**) CHILE CHILI CHILLI
(— **ROPE**) WORM WOOLD
(— **THREAD OR YARN**) QUILL
CHEESE
(— **TO PREVENT CHAFING**) KECKLE
(— **WOOL**) TREND
(— **YARN**) BEAM SERVE WINDLE
(—**S OF CHILE AND PERU**) SURES
(**ADRIATIC** —) BORA
(**BREAKING** —) FIST
(**BROKEN** —) HEAVES
(**COLD** —) BISE BIZE BORA SARSAR
BLIZZARD
(**COOLING** —) IMBAT
(**DEAD** —) NOSER
(**DESERT** —) SAMUM GIBLEH SAMIEL
SIMOOM SIMOON SIROCCO
(**DRYING** —) TRADE
(**EASTERLY** —) LEVANT LEVANTER
(**FIERCE** —) BUSTER
(**GUST OF** —) FLAN FLAW
(**HIGH** —) RIG
(**HOT** —) GIBLEH SOLANO CHAMSIN
KHAMSIN SIROCCO
(**LIGHT GENTLE** —) BREEZE
(**MOUNTAIN** —) PUNA
(**NORTH** —) BISE AQUILO BOREAS
AQUILON MISTRAL
(**NORTHEAST** —) BURAN GREGALE
(**NORTHWEST** —) CAURUS
(**PERIODICAL** —) ETESIAN MONSOON
(**PERSIAN GULF** —) SHAMAL SHARKI
SHIMAL
(**PERUVIAN** —) PUNO
(**ROARING** —) BLORE
(**SEVERE** —) SNIFTER
(**SOUTH** —) NOTUS AUSTER
(**SOUTHEAST** —) EURUS SOLANO
(**SOUTHEASTERLY** —) SHARKI
SHURGEE
(**SOUTHWEST** —) CHINOOK LIBECCIO
(**STRONG** —) BIRR
(**VIOLENT** —) BUSTER SQUALL
SNORTER
(**WARM** —) FOHN FOEHN CHINOOK
SANTANA

(**WEST** —) ZEPHYR FAVONIUS
ZEPHYRUS
WINDAGE DRIFT
WINDER REEL WINCH DRUMMER
PLUGGER SKEINER SPOOLER
TENDRIL
WINDFALL VAIL GRAVY MANNA
FALLING BLOWDOWN BUCKSHEE
WINDGALL PUFF WINDDOG
WINDING LINK MAZY CRANK LACET
SPIRE GYRATE SCREWY SPIRAL
TWISTY WANLAS CRINKLE DEVIOUS
MEANDER SINUOUS SNAKING
WRIGGLY WRINKLE
(**PL.**) RADDLINGS
WINDING-SHEET SHROUD SUDARY
CEREMENT
WINDING STAIR COCKLE COCLEA
WINDER COCHLEA
WINDLASS CRAB WINK FEARN
WINCH STOWCE STOWSE TACKLE
TURNEL WINDLE TWISTER WILDCAT
ARTIFICE DRAWBEAM MANEUVER
WINDMILL JUMBO MOTOR COPTER
PINWHEEL
(— **BAR**) UPLONG
(— **SAIL**) AWE EIE EIGHE FLIER
FLYER SWEEP SWIFT
WINDOW BAY EYE ROSE SASH SLIT
SLOT CHAFF GLAZE GRILL INLET
LIGHT SIGHT THURL AWNING
DORMER GRILLE LANCET PEEPER
SPLITE THURLE WICKET BALCONE
COUPLET DORMANT FENSTER
GUICHET LUTHERN MIRADOR
ORIFICE TRANSOM VENTANA
WINNOCK CASEMENT FANLIGHT
FENESTER FENESTRA JALOUSIE
VENETIAN
(— **OF TWO LIGHTS**) COUPLET
(**BAY** —) ORIEL MIRADOR
(**BLANK** —) ORB
(**DORMER** —) DORMANT LUCARNE
LUTHERN
(**HIGH NARROW** —) LANCET
(**OVAL** —) OXEYE
(**ROUND** —) OXEYE OCULUS
ROUNDEL
(**SEMICIRCULAR** —) FANLIGHT
(**TICKET** —) GRILLE GUICHET
(**TWIN** —) AJIMEZ
(**PL.**) STORMS
WINDOW DRESSING TRIM FRONT
FACADE
WINDOW FRAME SASH REVEAL
WINDOW OYSTER COPIS
WINDOWPANE LIGHT LOZEN QUIRK
LOZENGE
WINDOWSILL SOLE
WINDPIPE HALS ARBER ARBOR
ERBER HALSE WIZEN ARTERY
GUGGLE STROUP WEEZLE KEACORN
THACHEA WEASAND THRAPPLE
THROPPLE THROTTLE
WINDROW BANK HEAP RIDGE
SWATH SWATHE
WINDSOR CHAIR FANBACK
WINDSTORM BLOW BURA THUD
BURAN BOURRAN

WINDWARD ALOOF WEATHER
(— **SIDE**) KOOLAU
WINDY BLOWY EMPTY GASSY GUSTY
HUFFY PROUD STARK SWALE
FLIMSY STORMY WONDIE BREATHY
FEARFUL GUSTFUL NERVOUS
VENTOSE VIOLENT
(— **CITY**) CHICAGO
WINE CUP VIN BOIS BUAL CUIT CUTE
DEAL PALM PORT RAPE ROSE ROSY
TENT TYRE CAPRI GRAPE KRAMA
LUNEL PETER PORTO SCIAN SHRAB
TINTO VINUM WHITE BARSAC
CORTON COUTET GRAVES KIJAFA
LISBON MASDEU PIMENT ROCHET
SAUMUR SHIRAZ SOLERA TIVOLI
ALICANT AMBONNA BACCHUS
BANYULS BARBERA BASTARD
CATAWBA CHACOLI CHATEAU
DEZALEY FALERNO MARSALA
MISSION MOSELLE ORVIETO
PALERMO PIGMENT RHENISH
ROSOLIO SERCIAL SILLERY
VERNAGE VIDONIA VINTAGE
APERITIF BORDEAUX BURGUNDY
CHARNECO DELAWARE LACHRYMA
LIBATION MALVASIA MARSALLA
RIESLING ROCHELLE RULANDER
RUMBOOZE SPARKLER
(— **BOILED WITH HONEY**) MULSE
(— **CHEST**) TANTALUS
(— **FROM VINEGAR**) ESILL
(— **MIXED WITH WATER**) KRASIS
(— **OF EXCELLENT QUALITY**)
VINTAGE
(— **OF SACRAMENT**) BLOOD
(— **SELLER**) ABKAR BISTRO WINARE
(— **SERVING**) VOIDEE
(**AROMATIZED** —) DUBONNET
(**BULK** —) CUVEE
(**CONSECRATED** —) CUP
(**FIRST-GROWTH** —) LAFITE LAFITTE
(**FRANCONIAN** —) STEIN LEISTEN
(**GREEK** —) RUMNEY
(**HEATED** —) WHITEPOT
(**JAPANESE** —) SAKI
(**LIGHT** —) BUAL CAPRI BAROLO
CANARY
(**MULLED** —) GLUHWEIN
(**NEW — BOILED DOWN**) CUIT CUTE
(**NEW** —) MUST
(**PALM** —) SAGWIRE
(**RED** —) MACON TINTA BEAUNE
CLARET CHIANTI HOLLOCK
ALICANTE BURGUNDY CABERNET
FLORENCE
(**REVIVED** —) STUM
(**RHINE** —) HOCK SYLVANER
(**SPANISH** —) SACK TENT DULCE
OPORTO SHERRY ALIKANT BASTARD
(**STILL** —) PONTAC PONTACQ
(**SWEET** —) TYRE DULCE CANARY
BASTARD MALMSEY CHARNECO
MUSCATEL
(**TENT** —) TINTO
(**TOKAY** —) ESSENCE
(**TUSCAN** —) VERDEA CHIANTI
FLORENCE
(**WHITE** —) HOCK SACK CAPRI

CASEL FORST BARSAC MALAGA
BROMIAN CATAWBA CHABLIS
CONTHEY LANGOON BUCELLAS
RIESLING SAUTERNE VERMOUTH
(PL.) PALUS
WINEBERRY MAKO MAKOMAKO
WINEGLASS FLUTE
WINEGROWER WINER VIGNERON
WINESHOP BISTRO BODEGA
WINE-VAULT SHADE
WING ALA ARM ELL FAN FLY OAR
RIB VAN FORE JAMB SAIL TAIL
ALULA BLOCK FLANK JAMBE PINNA
POINT SHEAR VOLET BRANCH
FLETCH FLIGHT HALTER PENNON
PINION POISER DEMIVOL ELYTRON
ELYTRUM BALANCER DISPATCH
(— **OF ARMY**) HORN
(— **OF BUILDING**) ELL JAMB JAMBE
ALETTE FLANKER
(— **OF SHELL**) AURICLE
(— **OF THEATER**) COULISSE
TORMENTOR
(— **OF TRIPTYCH**) VOLET
(—**S DISPLAYED**) VOL
(**BASTARD** —) ALULA
(**BIRD'S** —) FLAG
(PL.) PENS FEATHERS
WINGED AILE ALATE LOFTY RAPID
SWIFT ALATED PENNED PENNATE
ELEVATED
WINGED DISK FEROHER
WING-FOOTED FLEET SWIFT ALIPED
WINGLESS APTERAL
WING-LIKE ALARY ALIFORM
PTEROID
WING SHELL STROMB ELYTRON
STROMBUS
WINK BAT NAP PINK BLINK DEATH
FLASH PRINK SLEEP TWINK
CONNIVE FLICKER INSTANT NICTATE
SPARKLE TWINKLE
WINKER EYE BLINKER EYELASH
WINKING BLINK
WINKLE PERIWIG TWINKLE
WINNER VICTOR FACEMAN
BANGSTER
WINNING GAIN SWEET PROFIT
GAINING VICTORY WINSOME
CHARMING
(— **OF ALL TRICKS**) CAPOT
SCHWARZ
(PL.) WIN VELVET
WINNOW FAN WIM CHAR SIFT WIND
DIGHT SIEVE DELETE REMOVE
SELECT WINDER SEPARATE
WINNOWER VAN WINDER DIGHTER
WINSOME GAY SWEET CHARMING
CHEERFUL PLEASANT
WINTER BISE SNOW YEAR HIEMS
DECEMBER HIBERNATE
(— **OVER**) HOG
WINTERBERRY PRINOS HOOPWOOD
WINTERBLOOM AZALEA
WINTERGREEN JINKS CHINKS
PYROLA DRUNKER BOXBERRY
DRUNKARD EYEBERRY GAYWINGS
IVYBERRY LIMONIUM RATSBANE
SHINLEAF TEABERRY

WINTERLIKE BRUMAL
WINTRY AGED COLD WHITE BOREAL
HIEMAL STORMY CHILLING
HIBERNAL
WINTUN COPEHAN
WINY VINOUS DRUNKEN
WIPE BEAT BLOW DRUB DUST GIBE
DIGHT SWIPE CANCEL SPONGE
SPUNGE STRIKE ABOLISH CLEANSE
SQUEEGEE
(— **BEAK OF HAWK**) FEAK
(— **NOSE**) SNITE
(— **OFF**) SCUFF
(— **OUT**) ERASE SCRUB SWEEP
EFFACE DESTROY
(— **UP**) SWAB SWOB
WIPER DUSTER TRIPPET
WIRE GUY TAP BINE CORE DENT
DRAG FILE FUSE PURL CABLE
OUTER RISER SNAKE SWEEP TAPER
BRIDGE FESCUE FINGER HEATER
JUMPER NEEDLE STAPLE STOLON
STRAND DROPPER HAYWIRE
LAMETTA LASHING PRICKER
SHIFTER SNUFFER FILAMENT
LIGATURE PALISADE PULLDOWN
STRINGER TELEGRAM
(— **BETWEEN TWO VESSELS**) SWEEP
(— **FOR CUTTING CLAY**) SLING
(— **FOR SUSTAINING HAIR**)
PALISADE
(— **IN BLASTING CAP**) BRIDGE
(— **IN CATHETER**) STYLET
(— **IN WEAVING LOOM**) DENT
(— **OF GOLD,SILVER OR BRASS**)
LAMETTA
(— **TO ADJUST WICK**) SNUFFER
(— **TO CLOSE A BREAK**) JUMPER
(— **TO REMOVE TUMORS**) LIGATURE
(— **USED AS POINTER**) FESCUE
(— **USED IN SPLICING CABLES**)
TAPER
(—**S BOUND TOGETHER**) SELVAGE
(4 —**S TWISTED TOGETHER**) QUAD
(**ENAMELED** —) LITZ
(**FENCE** —) DROPPER
(**FRAYED** —) JAGGER
(**GOLD** —) KINSEN
(**PALLET** —) PULLDOWN
(**PRIMING** —) PICKER EPINGLETTE
(**SURGICAL** —) STYLET
(**TWISTED** —) HEADLE HEDDLE
(**VENT** —) PRICKER
WIRE CUTTER SECATEUR
WIREDRAW WREST OUTWIT
DEFRAUD DISTORT ELONGATE
WIREGLASS FLUTE
WIRE GRASS POA
WIRELESS RADIO
WIRE ROPE JACKSTAY
WIRETAP BUG
WIREWORM ELATER ELATRID
MILLIPEDE
WIRY THIN HARDY STIFF WITHY
FEEBLE KNOTTY SINEWY STRINGY
THREADY
WIS KNOW THINK SURELY SUPPOSE

WISCONSIN

CAPITAL: MADISON
COLLEGE: RIPON BELOIT ALVERNO CARROLL VITERBO CARTHAGE
COUNTY: DOOR VILAS JUNEAU CALUMET SHAWANO WAUSHARA
INDIAN: FOX SAUK KICKAPOO WINNEBAGO
LAKE: POYGAN MENDOTA WISSOTA
MOUNTAIN: TIMSHILL SUGARBUSH
NATIVE: BADGER
NICKNAME: BADGER
RIVER: FOX CHIPEWA STCROIX
STATE BIRD: ROBIN
STATE FLOWER: VIOLET
STATE TREE: MAPLE
TOWN: ANTIGO BELOIT RACINE WAUSAU ASHLAND BARABOO KENOSHA MADISON OSHKOSH PORTAGE SHAWANO LACROSSE SUPERIOR WAUKESHA MILWAUKEE

WISDOM WIT LORE SABE SABBY SAVEY SENSE SOPHY ADVICE GNOSIS HOKMAH POLICY SATTVA SOPHIA WISURE CUNNING MINERVA SAGESSE SLEIGHT AFTERWIT JUDGMENT PRUDENCE SAPIENCE
(DIVINE —) WORD THEOMAGY
(ESOTERIC —) GNOSIS
(SUPREME —) PRAJNA
WISE HEP SLY DEEP GASH GOOD KIND SAGE SANE SEND TURN CANNY FRESH GUIDE SMART SOUND WITTY ADVISE CRAFTY DIRECT QUAINT WITFUL WITTER ANCIENT ERUDITE GNOSTIC KNOWING LEARNED POLITIC PRUDENT SAPIENT THRIVEN PERSUADE PROFOUND SENSIBLE SPACIOUS
(— MAN) AMAUTA
WISEACRE SAGE DUNCE GOTHAM SOLONIST WISEHEAD WISELING
WISECRACK JOKE QUIP
WISENT BISON AUROCH UROCHS BONASUS
WISH CARE GIVE GOAL HOPE LIST LUST MIND VOTE WANT WILL BOSOM COVET CRAVE DREAM HEART TASTE VOICE DESIRE UTINAM FAREWELL GODSPEED PLEASURE
(DEATH —) DESTRUDO
(SLIGHT —) VELLEITY
WISHBONE FURCULA FOURCHET FURCULUM
WISHFUL EAGER HOPEFUL LONGING ALLURING
WISHING ANXIOUS DESIROUS
WISHY-WASHY PALE THIN WEAK BLAND VAPID FEEBLE DILUTED INSIPID SLIPSLOP
WISKET BASKET WHISKET
WISP WUSP SCRAP SHRED SKIFF

SKIFT TWIST RUMPLE CRUMPLE MASSAGE
(— OF HAY) RISP
(— OF STRAW) WAP WASE DOSSIL
(— OF THATCH) TIPPET
WISPY FRAIL NEBULOUS
WISTERIA FUJI KRAUNHIA
WISTFUL INTENT PENSIVE WISHFUL MOURNFUL YEARNING
WISTITI WISTIT MARMOSET
WIT VAT VYT WAG KNOW NOUS SALT BRAIN HUMOR IRONY SENSE THINK WHITE WOTTE ACUMEN ESPRIT POLICY SANITY SATIRE WISDOM CUNNING PICADOR SARCASM SUPPOSE THINKER WITWORM BADINAGE REPARTEE
(BITING —) DICACITY
(PL.) BUTTONS
WITCH ALP ANI HAG HEG HEX MARE SAGA TRAT WYCH BRUJA BUTCH GREBE LAMIA WIGHT ASUANG CARLEY CARLIN CUMMER DOWSER DUESSA HECATE KIMMER PILWIZ WIZARD AGANICE CANIDIA HAGGARD HELLCAT SYCORAX BABAJAGA CAROLINE ERICHTHO SORCERER SPAEWIFE VERSIERA WALKYRIE
(PL.) COVEN
WITCHCRAFT CHARM GOETY CUNNING HEXEREI SORCERY BRUJERIA DEVILTRY PISHOGUE WIZARDRY
WITCH DOCTOR BOCOR BOKOR GOOFER GUFFER
WITCHERY CHARM SPELL SORCERY SORTIARY
WITCHES'-BROOM STAGHEAD
WITCHGRASS COUCH PANIC PANICLE
WITE WAT BLAME FAULT WAYTE CENSURE REPROACH HAMESOKEN
WITH BY CUM MID MIT WUD AVEC CHEZ DOWN AMONG ANENT WIGHT AGAINST
(— HAND ON HIP) AKIMBO
(— REGARD TO) ABOUT
(— SPEED) TIVY
WITHDRAW GO COY DROP TAKE AVOID DEMIT LOOSE REVEL SHIFT START UNSAY CHANGE DECEDE DESERT DETACH DETRAY DEVOID EFFACE FLINCH MINISH RECALL RECANT RECEDE RETIRE REVOKE ROGATE SECEDE SHRINK SINGLE SYPHON ABSCOND CONCEAL DESCEND DETRACT FORSAKE INVEIGH RETRACT RETREAT SCRATCH SCUTTLE SECLUDE SUBDUCE SUBDUCT UNSCREW SEPARATE SUBTRACT
(— FROM POKER POT) DROP
(— FROM) VAIK
(— SUPPORT) ABANDON
WITHDRAWAL DRAIN FLIGHT HIDING OFFLAP RETIRE SHRINK ABSENCE PULLOUT REGRESS RETIRAL RETREAT SCUTTLE

(— OF BUILDING FACE) SETBACK
WITHDRAWN SHY ASOCIAL INGROWN SECLUSE DISTRAIT ISOLATED SECLUDED
WITHE HANK ROPE TIER TWIG WITHY WATTLE WICKER CRINGLE
WITHER BURN DAZE FADE MIFF PINE RUST SEAR STUN WARP WELK BLAST CLING DAVER DECAY QUAIL WIZEN COTTER SHRINK WALLOW WELTER WILTER WINDER AREFACT DECLINE FORWELK SENESCE SHRIVEL LANGUISH PARALYZE
WITHERED DRY ARID SEAR SERE CORKY SCRAM MARCID BLASTED UNGREEN WIZENED
WITHHELD DEFERRED SUSPENSE
WITHHOLD CURB DENY HIDE KEEP STOP CHECK SCANT ABSENT DEPORT DETAIN REFUSE ABSTAIN BOYCOTT DEFORCE FORBEAR OUTHOLD REPRESS RESERVE SUSPEND RESTRAIN SUBTRACT
(— CONSENT) DECLINE
WITHHOLDING DETAINER
(— OF DUES) CHECKOFF
WITHIN IN ON BEN BIN INBY INLY INTRA HEREIN INSIDE INWITH INDOORS ENCLOSED INCLUDED INWARDLY
WITHOUT EX BUT OUT SEN BOUT FREE OHNE SANS SINE MINUS SENZA FAILING OUTSIDE WANTING INNOCENT OUTDOORS
(— A FLANGE) BALD
(— A MATE) ODD
(— ACTION) DEEDLESS
(— BEGINNING OR END) ETERNAL
(— BLEMISH) CHOICE
(— CONTENTS) INANE
(— DELAY) AWAY FOOTHOT SUMMARY
(— DELIBERATION) HEADLONG
(— EMOTION) DRYLY DULLY
(— EXCEPTION) ALWAYS
(— FEET) APOD
(— FUNDS) CLEAN
(— HORNS) ACEROUS
(— INTEREST) BARREN
(— LIGHT) APHOTIC
(— LIMITS OF DURATION) AGELESS
(— ORDER) ANYHOW
(— POWER) ADRIFT
(— QUESTION) EASILY SECURELY
(— REALITY) AIRY
(— REASON) BLINDLY
(— REMEDY) BOOTLESS
(— ROADS) INVIOUS
(— RULE OR LAW) ANARCHIC
(— SADDLES) ASELLATE
(— TEETH, TONGUE OR CLAWS) MORNE
(— WINGS) APTEROUS
WITHSTAND BIDE DEFY TAKE ABIDE OPPOSE OPPUGN RESIST CONTAIN CONTEST FORBEAR SUSTAIN CONFRONT WITHSTAY
WITHY WIRY AGILE OSIER WOODY WILLOW WOODIE WINDING

WITLESS MAD GROSS INSANE STUPID FATUOUS FOOLISH UNWITTY HEEDLESS SLAPHAPPY
WITLOOF ENDIVE CHICORY
WITNESS SEE TAKE TEST PROOF ATTEST BEHOLD MARTYR RECORD TESTIS TESTOR CURATOR TESTATE TESTIFY EVIDENCE RECORDER SUFFRAGE
(FALSE —) JUROR
(PL.) SECTA
WITNESS-BOX STAND
WITOTO HUITOTE
WITTICISM WIT JEER JEST JOKE SLENT WHEEZE
WITTING NEWS TIDINGS
WITTOL FOOL CUCKOLD WITTALL
WITTY GASH WILY WISE DROLL LEPID SHARP SMART CLEVER FACETE JOCOSE JOCULAR KNOWING CONCEITY HUMOROUS
(NOT —) INFICETE
WIVERN DRAGON WYVERN
WIZARD SEER SHIZ FIEND DOCTOR EXPERT PELLAR WARLOW CHARMED MAGICAL SPAEMAN WARLOCK WISEMAN CONJUROR MAGICIAN SORCERER TROLLMAN WITCHMAN
(PL.) GOETAE
WIZARDRY SORCERY
WIZEN DRY WITHER SHRIVEL
WIZENED GIZZEN WEAZEN
WOAD DYE NIL ODE ANIL KERS NILL OADE CRESS ANILLA INDICO INDIGO PASTEL
WOADWAXEN ALLELUIA ALLELUJA
WOBBLE COCKLE COGGLE HOBBLE QUAVER TITTER WABBLE WIGGLE TREMBLE
WOBBLY LOOSE SHAKY COGGLY DRUNKEN DOUBTFUL
WOE WA WEI BALE BANE PAIN PINE WAWE GRIEF MISERY SORROW TROUBLE WILLAWA CALAMITY DISTRESS WELLADAY WELLAWAY
WOEBEGONE WAFF UNHAPPY DEJECTED DESOLATE DOWNCAST
WOEFUL MEAN DISMAL PALTRY RUEFUL DIREFUL DOLEFUL RUTHFUL DOLOROUS PITIABLE WRETCHED
WOLF GLUT LOBO CANID FREKI YABBI CHANCO COYOTE FAMINE FENRIR ISGRIN KABERU LOAFER MASHER SIGRIM THOOID POVERTY ISENGRIM
(FOX —) ZORRO
WOLFBERRY BUCKBUSH
WOLFHOUND ALAN BORZOI PSOVIE
WOLFISH LUPINE RAVENOUS
WOLFLIKE THOOID
WOLFRAMITE CAL TUNGSTEN
WOLFSBANE ACONITE DOGBANE FOXBANE
WOLF SPIDER HUNT JAGER HUNTER JAEGER JAYHAWK LYCOSID TARANTULA
WOLVERINE PIG GLUT GORB MIKER GLOTUM HELLUO GLUTTON GUTLING LURCHER MOOCHER RAVENER SWILLER CARCAJOU DRAFFMAN GOURMAND GULLYGUT
(— STATE) MICHIGAN
WOMAN BIM DAM EVE HEN HER JUG MEG SHE TEG TIT BABE BABY BINT BOSS CONY DAME FAIR FEME FLAG FROW JADE JANE LADY MARY MORT PERI SLUT WIFE BIDDY BIMBO BLADE BROAD CHINA DONAH FEMME JATNI LUBRA LUCKY MUJER QUEAN SKIRT SMOCK SQUAW TAGGE TWIST UMMAN VROUW BURDIE CALICO CARLIN CUMMER FEMALE GIMMER HEIFER KIMMER LUCKIE MANESS SISTER TOMATO VIRAGO WAHINE CARLING CHANGAR DISTAFF PARTLET PINNACE PLACKET QUAEDAM MISTRESS
(— DESERTED BY HUSBAND) AGUNAH
(— OF CONSEQUENCE) HERSELF
(— OF LOW CASTE) DASI
(— OF RANK) DOMINA
(— OF UNSTEADY CHARACTER) FLAP
(— OF WEALTH) FORTUNE
(— WHO ACTS AS ADVISER) EGERIA
(— WITH 3 CHILDREN) TRIPARA
(— WITH ONE CHILD) UNIPARA
(ABORIGINAL —) GIN LUBRA
(ABUSIVE —) FISHWIFE
(ALLURING —) DISH
(ATHENIAN — OF HIGH RANK) GERARA GERAERA
(ATTRACTIVE —) DOLLY SHEBA DOLLIE CHARMER
(AUSTRALIAN —) BINT
(AWKWARD —) ROIL
(BEAUTIFUL —) HURI PERI BELLE HOURI SIREN SPARK CHERUB EYEFUL MUSIDORA
(BOISTEROUS —) HOYDEN
(BOLD —) RAMP
(CLEANING —) CHAR
(COARSE —) BEAST BLOWZE RULLION
(COOLIE —) CHANGAR
(COY —) HAGGARD
(CREMATED —) SATI SUTTEE
(DEAR —) PEAT
(DUTCH OR GERMAN —) FRAU FROW FROKIN FRAULEIN
(ENGAGED —) BONDAGER
(ENTICING —) SIREN
(EVIL OLD —) HAG HELLHAG
(FASHIONABLE —) MILADY GALLANT ELEGANTE
(FAT —) BOSS FUSTILUGS
(FINE —) SCREAMER
(FIRST —) EMBLA
(FLIRTING —) FIZGIG
(FORWARD —) STRAP
(GAUDY —) JAY
(GENTLE —) DOVE
(GOSSIPY —) HAIK HAKE BIDDY TABBY
(GROSS —) SOW
(GYPSY —) ROMI ROMNI GITANA
(ILL-TEMPERED —) VIXEN
(IMMORAL —) RIG GITCH FLAPPER HARLOTRY
(INDIAN —) SQUAW WENCH KLOOCH BUCKEEN
(INSPIRED —) PHOEBAD
(ITALIAN —) DONNA
(LASCIVIOUS —) GIGLET
(LEARNED —) PUNDITA CLERGESS
(LEWD —) REP SLUT BITCH HUSSY HUZZY BROTHEL
(LOOSE —) BAG BIM KIT TIB DRAB FLAP BIMBO TROLL GILLOT HARLOT LIMMER BAGGAGE FRANION TROLLOP
(LOUD-SPOKEN —) RANDY
(LOW OR WORTHLESS —) JADE JURR SLINGDUST
(MARRIED — OF LOWLY STATION) GOODY
(MASCULINE —) AMAZON RULLION CORQUEAN
(MEEK —) GRIZEL
(MYTHOLOGICAL —) HEROINE
(OLD —) GIB HEN BABA TROT CRONE FAGOT FRUMP TROUT BELDAM CARLIN GAMMER GEEZER GRANNY GRANDAM HARRIDAN
(OLD SHRIVELED —) FAGOT FAGGOT
(PEDANTIC —) BLUE
(PERT —) CHIT
(PORTUGESE —) SENHORA
(PREGNANT —) GRAVIDA
(PRIGGISH —) PRUDE
(RUSTIC —) JOAN
(SCOLDING —) SHREW
(SHORT OR STUMPY —) CUTTY
(SHREWISH —) JADE HARPY SKELLAT
(SLATTERNLY —) DRAB FLEABAG
(SLENDER GRACEFUL —) SYLPH
(SLIPSHOD —) MAUX CLATCH TROLLIMOG
(SLOVENLY —) BAG DAW SOW SLUT BESOM TAWPY TROLL TROLLOP SLATTERN
(SPANISH —) DONA GITANA
(SPANISH-INDIAN —) CHOLA
(SPITEFUL —) CAT FURY BITCH
(SQUAT —) TRUB
(SQUEAMISH —) COCKNEY
(STAID —) MATRON
(STATELY —) JUNO
(STORMY VIOLENT —) FURY
(TRACTABLE —) SHEEP
(UGLY —) HAG GORGON
(UNCHASTE —) JILT
(UNMARRIED —) DAME GIRL SPINSTER
(VIXENISH —) HARRIDAN
(WANTON —) MINX TRUB PARNEL
(WICKED —) JEZEBEL
(WISE —) VOLVA ALRUNA ALRUNE
(WITHERED —) CRONE
(YOUNG —) BIT BIRD BURD CHIT DAME DELL DOLL GIRL LASS PUSS BEAST CHICK FILLY FLUFF TOAST DAMSEL HEIFER PIGEON SHEILA SUBDEB BAGGAGE CHICKEN

DAMOZEL FLAPPER WINKLOT
BRISETTE DAUGHTER GRISETTE
WOMAN HATER MISOGYNIST
WOMANISH FEMALE FEMININE
LADYLIKE PETTICOAT
WOMANKIND WOMEN CALICO
MUSLIN FEMINIE
WOMAN'S TONGUE LEBBEK
WOMB BELLY CRADLE UTERUS
WOMBAT KOALA BADGER DIDELPH
VOMBATID
WOMEN DISTAFF
(— OF EARLY CHURCH) SETTERS
AGAPETAE
WON CITY LIVE ROOM ABIDE DWELL
REGION
WONDER AWE MUSE SELI SIGN
TROW UNCO UNKO VERY FARLY
FERLY SELLE SELLY UNCOW
ADMIRE MARVEL MIRATE MAGNALE
MIRABLE MIRACLE PORTENT
PRODIGY STRANGE UNCOUTH
AMERVEIL SELCOUTH SURPRISE
WONDERFUL KEEN SELI FERLY
GRAND GREAT SELLE SWELL
WAKON MIGHTY AMAZING GALLANT
MIRABLE MIRIFIC STRANGE
GLORIOUS MIRABILE WONDROUS
WONDERFULLY AMAZING
WONDER-WORKER THEURGIC
THEURGIST
WONG FIELD GROVE PLAIN MEADOW
WONKY AWRY SHAKY WRONG
UNSTEADY
WONT APT USE FAIN USED VAIN
HABIT USAGE CUSTOM INCLINED
WONTED USUAL HAUNTED
WOO SUE LOVE SEEK SUIT WALE
COURT SPARK SPOON ASSAIL
SPLUNT SUITOR ADDRESS
WOOD (ALSO SEE TREE AND TIMBER)
HAG KIP BOIS BOSK BOWL EKKI
HOLT KIRI MASS MOCK PALO SUPA
TREE WOLE CAHUY CHARK CROWD
EDDER FLOUR GROVE HURST
HYRST RESAK STICK STUFF WEALD
ALMOND ANGILI AUSUBO BRAZIL
EKHIMI FOREST ITAUBA JARANA
LUMBER PALING SPINNY TIMBER
APITONG AVODIRE COPPICE
DADDOCK DUDGEON HAYBOTE
SATINAY VENESIA BAGTIKAN
CRANTARA FIREBOOT
(— BURNT AS PERFUME) AGALLOCH
(— FOR CARPENTRY) STUFF
(— FOR REPAIRING HEDGE) TINING
HAYBOTE
(— OF SMALL EXTENT) GROVE
(— OF THE VERA) VENESIA
(— ON RAFTER) FUR
(— ROTATED ON STRING) ROMBOS
RHOMBOS
(— USEFUL FOR TINDER) PUNK
SPONK TOUCHWOOD
(— YIELDING PERFUME) LINALOA
(BABUL —) SUNT
(BLACK —) EBONY
(CONE-SHAPED PIECE OF —) ACORN
(DARK RED —) RATA

(DENSIFIED —) STAYPAK
(ELASTIC —) SYCAMORE
(FLAT ROUND PIECE OF —)
TRENCHER
(FLEXIBLE —) EDDER
(FOSSIL —) PINITE PEUCITES
(FRAGRANT —) CEDAR
(FUEL —) ESTOVERS
(HARD —) ASH DAO SAL BAKU IPIL
KARI LANA POON ANJAN EBONY
GIDYA KARRI KOKRA MAPLE ZANTE
BANUYO CAMARA FREIJO GIDGEE
KEMPAS SABICU WALNUT CURUPAY
DATTOCK HICKORY GUAIACUM
IRONBARK MAHOGANY
(HEAVY —) DAO EBON EBONY
CHENGAL GUAYABI SUCUPIRA
(LIGHT —) POON BALSA HEMLOCK
(LIMBA —) KORINA
(LOGGED —) CHIP
(LOST —) CHIPPAGE
(LUSTROUS —) LEZA BOARWOOD
(MATCHBOX —) SKILLET
(MOTTLED —) AMBOINA
(NARROW BAR OF —) SLAT
(NUMBER 1 —) DRIVER
(NUMBER 2 —) BRASSIE
(NUMBER 3 —) SPOON
(NUMBER 4 —) CLEEK
(OILY —) BATETE
(OLIVE —) COLLIE
(PETRIFIED —) LITHOXYL
ROCKWOOD
(PINKISH —) BOSSE
(POINTED PIECE OF —) TRIPPET
(REDDISH —) KOA KARI KARRI
ARANGA BANABA CHERRY DUNGON
SATINE KAMBALA
(REDDISH-YELLOW —) GUYO
(ROTTEN —) DADDOCK
(SANDARAC —) ALERCE
(SOFT —) KIRI GABUN GABOON
ELKWOOD AGALLOCH GUATAMBU
(SQUARE LOG OF —) NOG
(STICK OF —) BILLET
(STRIP OF —) LATH STAVE BATTEN
REEPER REGLET
(WATER RESISTING —) AMUBIS
(YELLOWISH —) HALDU FUSTIC
IDIGBO KADAMBA KAMASSI
GUATAMBU
WOOD ANEMONE CYME EMONY
BOWBELLA SNOWDROP
WOODBARK SABLE BLONDINE
WOODBINE BIND WIDBIN EGLATERE
WOODCARVER BODGER
WOODCHUCK CHUG CHUCK MONAX
MARMOT SUSLIK WEJACK MOONACK
GROUNDHOG
WOODCOCK QUIS PEWEE PEWIT
SNIPE SNITE SHRUPS BECASSE
SIMPLETON
WOODCUT BLOCK
WOODCUTTER AXEMAN LOGGER
WOODMAN WOODSMAN
WOOD DUCK SQUEALER BRANCHIER
WOODED BOSKY TREEY HYLEAN
SYLVAN FORESTED
WOODEN DRY DULL STIFF TREEN

CLUMSY STICKY STOLID TIMBER
AWKWARD DEADPAN TIMBERN
LIFELESS
WOOD GUM XYLAN
WOOD HEN WEKA
WOODHEWER PICUCULE
WOOD HOOPOE WHOOP WHOOPE
IRRISOR DUNGBIRD PICARIAN
WOOD HYACINTH SCILLA
CROWTOE GREGGLE HAREBELL
WOOD IBIS STORK GANNET JABIRU
IRONHEAD
WOODLAND DESERT MIOMBO
SPRING
(WASTE —) WEALD
WOODPECKER AWL CHAB JYNX
KATE PEEK ECCLE HECCO HEWEL
ICKLE SPEKT HECKLE NICKLE
PECKER PIANET PICULE SPRITE
TAPPER YAFFLE YUKKEL CLIMBER
CREEPER FLICKER HEWHOLE
HICKWAY LOGCOCK REDHEAD
SAPSUCK SNAPPER SPEIGHT
WHETILE WITWALL WRYNECK
DIRTBIRD KICKWALL PICARIAN
PICUCULE POPINJAY RAINBIRD
RAINFOWL WALLHICK
(LIKE A —) PICIFORM
WOODPILE STRAN STRAND
WOODRICK
WOOD ROBIN MIRO TOMTIT
WOODRUFF HAIROF MUGGET
MUGWET WOODROW HAIRHOOF
WOODS BOSK BUSH BOSQUE
WOODSMAN BUSHY SILVAN SYLVAN
BUSHMAN BUSHWACK
WOOD SORREL OCA COCKOO
HEARTS LUJULA OXALIS TREFOIL
ALLELUIA ALLELUJA SHAMROCK
STABWORT
WOOD THRUSH MAYBIRD
WOODTURNER BODGER
WOODWIND OBOE FLUTE CORNET
BASSOON PIBGORN PICCOLO
CLARINET
WOODWORK CEILING
WOODWORKER JOINER TURNER
MILLMAN
WOODWORM GRIBBLE
WOODY WITHY FRITHY STICKY
SYLVAN XYLOID LIGNOSE LIGNEOUS
WOOER BEAU LOVER WOWER
SUITOR COURTER WOOSTER
COURTIER PARAMOUR
WOOF WEFT WOUGH FILLING
TEXTURE
WOOING SUIT WOHLAC
WOOL OO COT DAG HOG VOL WOW
BEAT BLUE FRIB PULU ROCK FADGE
LAINE MUNGO STUFF TIPPY ALPACA
ARGALI BOTANY BREECH FLEECE
GREASE JACKET JERSEY KERSEY
LUSTER SLIVER WETHER COMBING
HASLOCK KASHMIR MORLING
STUBBLE WIGGING CASHMERE
CLOTHING COMEBACK MORTLING
PICKLOCK TOMENTUM
(— AS IT COMES FROM SHEEP)
GREASE

(**— FROM DEAD SHEEP**) MORLING
MORTLING
(**— FROM LEOMINSTER**) ORE
(**— ON SHEEP'S LEG**) GARE BREECH
(**— ON SHEEP'S THROAT**) HASLOCK
(**— WEIGHT**) TOD
(**COARSE —**) ABB SHAG BRAID
COWTAIL
(**COTTON —**) CADDIS CADDICE
(**DUNGY BIT OF —**) FRIB
(**FINE GRADE OF —**) PICKLOCK
SPINNERS
(**GREASY —**) TIPPY
(**INFERIOR GRADE OF —**) HEAD
(**KNOT OF —**) NOIL
(**LAMB'S —**) WASSAIL
(**LOCK OF —**) FLOCK STAPLE
(**LONG —**) BLUE
(**LOW GRADE OF —**) LIVERY
(**MATTED —**) DAG SHAG
(**PULLED —**) SLIPE
(**RECLAIMED —**) MUNGO SHODDY
(**REFUSE —**) COT COTT FLOCK
PINION
(**ROLL OF —**) CARDING
(**RUSSIAN —**) DONSKY
(**SMALL PIECE OF —**) TATE
(**SPUN —**) YARN
(**WOUND —**) TREND
WOOLCLOTH HODDEN
WOOLEN (ALSO SEE FABRIC) CADDIS
CAMLET SUCLAT CADDICE
PASHMINA
(PL.) LAINAGE
WOOL FAT LANOLIN
WOOLLY SHEEP LANATE LANOSE
COTTONY FLOCCOSE PERONATE
WOOLLY BEAR WOUBIT
WOOLLY CROTON HOGWORT
WOOZY SICK DRUNK TIGHT VAGUE
BLURRY WOOLLY
WORD GIG MOT EZEL GULE HAIT
NEWS RAFF TERM VERB WHID
WHUD ADNEX CHEEP COUCH DERRY
DILLY FITCH GLOSS HAPAX HOKEY
HYNDE LEMMA MAXIM ORDER
PAROL RHEMA RUMOR SPELL
ACCENT ADVERB AVOWAL BREATH
ETYMON KIBBER LATIVE ONEYER
PAROLE PLEDGE QUATCH REMARK
REPORT SAYING ACCOUNT ADJUNCT
BICCHED COMMAND COMMENT
DICTION DUCDAME GENTILE GITTITH
HOMONYM INCIPIT MESSAGE
PALABRA PRAYFUL PRENZIE
PROMISE PROVERB SYNONYM
VOCABLE ACROSTIC CATCHCRY
CHEVILLE COMPOUND ENCLITIC
EQUIVOKE FRABJOUS FRINGENT
IDEOGRAM ILLATIVE LATINISM
SYLLABLE SYNTAGMA
(**— AS CALL TO DUCK**) DILLY
(**— EXPRESSING COMMAND**)
JUSSIVE
(**— FORMED FROM VOWELS**)
EUOUAE
(**— FROM INITIAL LETTERS**)
ACRONYM
(**— IN A PUZZLE**) LIGHT

(**— MISPRONOUNCED**) BEARD
(**— OF CONCLUSION**) AMEN
EXPLICIT
(**— OF HONOR**) PAROLE
(**— OF MOUTH**) FIDELITY
(**— OF OPPOSITE MEANING**)
ANTONYM
(**— OF SECONDARY RANK**) ADNEX
(**— OF UNCERTAIN MEANING**)
FRINGENT
(**— OF UNKNOWN MEANING**) KIBBER
ONEYER PRAYFUL PRENZIE
(**—S IN LOW TONE**) ASIDE
(**—S OF OPERA**) LIBRETTO
(**BIBLICAL — OF DOUBTFUL
MEANING**) EZEL FITCH GITTITH
(**CALL —**) JINGO
(**CHARACTERIZING —**) EPITHET
(**CODE —**) DOG FOX JIG ABLE EASY
ECHO GOLF ITEM KING BRAVO
DELTA HOTEL INDIA SUGAR
GEORGE CHARLIE
(**GATHERING —**) SLOGAN
(**HONEYED —S**) MANNA
(**HYPHENATED —**) SOLID
(**IDENTIFYING —**) LABEL
(**LAST — OF SPEECH**) CUE
(**MEANINGLESS —**) DERRY
(**METAPHORICAL —**) KENNING
(**MNEMONIC —**) VIBGYOR
(**NONSENSE —**) RAFF RAFFE
FRABJOUS
(**ORIGINAL —**) STEM
(**PARTING —**) ENVOI
(**QUOTED —**) CITATION
(**REDUNDANT —**) CHEVILLE
(**ROOT —**) ETYMON
(**SIGNAL —**) NAYWORD SECURITY
(**SINGLE —**) PHRASE
(**SOURCE —**) ETYMON
(**THIEVES' SLANG —**) TWAG WHID
(**UNEXPLAINED —**) DUCDAME
(**UTTERED —S**) SPEECH
(PL.) LIP TALK SPEECH LANGUAGE
DISCOURSE
WORDBOOK LEXICON SPELLER
LIBRETTO
WORDINESS VERBIAGE
WORDING LEGEND DICTION
PHRASING
WORDLESS DUMB TACIT SILENT
TACITURN
WORDPLAY EQUIVOKE
WORDY PROLIX VERBAL DIFFUSE
VERBOSE WORDISH
WORK DO GO ACT FAG JOB DIKE
DYKE FEND FRET NOTE OPUS TASK
TEND TOIL GRAFT GRIND KARMA
KNEAD LABOR PRESS YAKKA
ARBEIT EFFECT HUSTLE OE1VRE
REDUIT RESULT STRIVE THRIFT
CALLING EXECUTE EXPLOIT
FERMENT HEXAPLA LOUSTER
MISSION OPERATE OPIFICE
OPUSCLE OUVRAGE OVERAGE
PICHERY PURSUIT TRAVAIL
ADVOCACY AGENTING BUSINESS
CAPONIER DEMILUNE DRUDGERY
ENDEAVOR FUNCTION INDUSTRY

LABORAGE OPUSCULE PARERGON
RETRENCH EXECUTION
(**— ACROSS GRAIN**) THURM
(**— ACTIVELY**) LOUSTER
(**— AGAINST**) KNIFE ATTACK
COMBAT
(**— AIMLESSLY**) FIDDLE
(**— AS REPORTER**) HEEL
(**— BEYOND ONE'S POWERS**)
OVERDO
(**— CARELESSLY**) RABBLE
(**— DILIGENTLY**) PEG STRIKE
BELABOR
(**— DONE**) WRIHTE
(**— FOR**) LABOR SERVE BESWINK
(**— FREE**) START
(**— HARD**) TEW MOIL SLOG SWOT
BULLOCK LEATHER
(**— HIDES**) BEAM
(**— INSIDUOUSLY**) WORM
(**— INTO A MASS**) KNEAD
(**— LAND**) FLOAT
(**— LEISURELY**) DAKER DAIKER
(**— OCCASIONALLY**) SMOOT SMOUT
(**— OF ACKNOWLEDGED
EXCELLENCE**) CLASSIC
(**— OF ART**) GEM CRAFT ANTIQUE
CAPRICE CREATION EPIPHANY
EXERCISE
(**— OF FICTION**) SHOCKER
(**— OF HISTORY**) STORY
(**— OF MENIAL KIND**) DRUDGE
(**— ONE'S WAY**) WISE
(**— OUT IN ADVANCE**) FOREPLOT
(**— OUT**) FUDGE SOLVE DESIGN
EVOLVE
(**— OVER**) DIGEST
(**— PAID FOR IN ADVANCE**) HORSE
(**— PERSISTENTLY**) HAMMER
(**— RESEMBLING PATCHWORK**)
CENTO
(**— SLIPSHOD**) MULLOCK
(**— STEADILY**) PLY
(**— TO EXHAUSTION**) FAG
(**— TO WINDWARD**) CLAW
(**— TOGETHER**) COACT
(**— TRIFLINGLY**) PIDDLE
(**— UNDER ANOTHER NAME**)
ALLONYM
(**— UNFAIRLY OR CRUELLY**) HORSE
(**— UP**) SPUNK
(**— UPON**) TILL LABOR
(**— UPWARD**) HIKE
(**— VIGOROUSLY**) BEND
(**ALLEGORICAL —**) BESTIARY
(**CANVAS —**) POINT
(**CLEANING —**) CHAR
(**CLUMSY —**) BOTCH
(**COMPLETED —**) TRAVAIL
(**CONTRACT —**) GYPPO
(**DAMASCENE —**) KOFTGARI
(**DAY'S —**) DARG DARGUE
(**DECORATIVE —**) FLOCKING
(**DIVINE —**) THEURGY
(**DULL —**) DRUDGERY
(**EMBOSSED —**) CELATURE
(**FRAUDULENT —**) JERRY
(**HAND —**) CAMAY
(**HARD —**) TEW MOIL MUCK SWOT

TWIG YERK SWEAT EFFORT LEATHER SLAVERY SLOGGING
(JOINER —) FINISH
(LITERARY —) STUDY CHASER SEQUEL SERIAL CLASSIC DIPTYCH
(LURID —) BLOOD
(MANUAL —) FATIGUE
(METAL —) NIELLO
(MOSAIC —) EMBLEM
(ORNAMENTAL —) BEADWORK FILIGREE LEAFWORK
(PIECE OF —) JOB
(REFERENCE —) BIBLE SOURCE
(SACRED —) HIERURGY
(SCHOLASTIC —) SUMMA
(SKILLED MECHANICAL —) SLOJD SLOYD
(SOCIAL —) ALMONING
(WOMAN'S —) DISTAFF
(PL.) CANON PLANT STODGE FACTORY BUSINESS
WORKABLE YOUNG PLIANT FEASIBLE
(EASILY —) SWEET
WORKADAY HUMDRUM PROSAIC ORDINARY
WORKBASKET CABA
WORKBENCH SIEGE DONKEY TEMPLATE
WORKED INWROUGHT
(— OUT) DEAD
(— UP) ANGRY EXCITED
WORKER (ALSO SEE WORKMAN AND LABORER) AGER CARL DOER HAND HIND ICER SCAB AXMAN BOXER BUTTY DEMAS DRIER EDGER ENDER FILER FIRER FIXER FLYER FOXER GLUER GORER HOLER INKER JERRY LINER LURER MAXIM MINIM NURSE TAPER TOWER ASHMAN BACKER BAILER BALLER BANDER BEADER BENDER BINDER BINMAN BLADER BLOWER BOILER BONDER BOOKER BOSHER BRACER BUFFER BUMPER BURNER BURRER CAPPER CARMAN CASTER CASUAL CHASER COMBER COOKER DAYMAN DIPPER DOCKER DOGGER DOTTER DUMPER ETCHER FACTOR FAGGER FANMAN FASHER FEEDER FELLER FILLER FITTER FLAKER FLAMER FLUTER FLUXER FOILER FOLDER FORCER FORMER FRAMER GASSER GOFFER GRADER GUMMER GUTTER HASHER HEADER HEELER HELPER HEMMER HOLDER HOOKER HOOPER HOPPER HUNKIE INKMAN JOGGER JOINER LEAFER LEASER LEGGER NOILER PUGGER READER REEDER SCORER SEAMAN SEAMER SHAKER SKIVER SLAKER SLICER SLIDER SLOPER STAVER STAYER TOILER TOPPER BUILDER CREATOR EMPLOYE FIELDER LABORER
(— IN LEATHER) BEAMER CHUMAR JACKER BLACKER CHUCKLER
(— IN METALS) SMITH FLAPPER
(ADDITIONAL —) EXTRA
(AGRICULTURAL —) ARKIE KISAN

(AIRCRAFT —) BOOTMAN
(ANT —) MAXIM ERGATES REPLETE
(ASBESTOS —) COBBER
(AUTO —) DISKER
(BAKERY —) BRAKER COOLER DIVIDER BENCHMAN SPREADER
(BLUE-COLLAR —) STIFF
(BREWERY —) HOPPER STEEPER STILLMAN
(BRICK —) DAUBER CROWDER
(CANNERY —) SLIMER SCALDER SHEDMAN
(CLOCK —) STAKER
(COAL —) SUMPER GEORDIE SPRAGGER
(DOCK —) BUNGS HOLDMAN SHENANGO
(DOMESTIC —) HELP
(FELLOW —) CONFRERE
(FOUNDRY —) FLOGGER SNAGGER
(GARMENT —) FACER SLEEVER ASSORTER INSEAMER
(GUN —) BLUER
(HARD —) SLOGGER
(HAT —) CURLER BRIMMER
(HIDE —) HEFTER COLORER
(HOSPITAL —) ALMONER
(HOTEL —) SCRUB
(ICEHOUSE —) AIRMAN
(JEWELRY —) ARBORER
(LOGGING —) SNIPER SKIDDER
(MATTRESS —) BEATER
(MIGRATORY —) HOBO
(MILL —) BILLER SPOUTER
(MINE —) BYEMAN FOOTER GOPHER LANDER DROPPER FACEMAN SLEDGER SWAMPER DRIFTMAN
(ORCHARD —) SMUDGER
(PACKINGHOUSE —) COOK
(PAPERMILL —) SIZER SIZEMAN
(PIANO —) BELLYMAN
(PLODDING —) GRUBBER
(POTTERY —) CASER BATTER BEDDER FETTLER JOLLIER JUSTLER
(PRINTING —) FLY FLYBOY
(PUERTO RICAN —) GIBARO JIBARO
(QUARRY —) BREAKER
(RAILROAD —) JERRY HERDER BRAKEMAN
(SAWMILL —) BOLTER SETTER BOATMAN DECKMAN CHAINMAN
(SHOE —) CASER FOXER ARCHER FUDGER HEELER CHALKER BOTTOMER
(SKILLED —) ARTISTE
(SLAUGHTERHOUSE —) FATTER SHOVER SINGER SLIMER CHEEKER CHOPPER KNOCKER LIMEMAN SCALPER SCRIBER STICKER SNATCHER
(TANNERY —) GATER STONER CROPPER CURRIER DELIMER BEAMSMAN SEASONER
(TEXTILE —) DOFFER DOUPER DRAWER GIGGER LAPPER LEASER SINGER CREELER DOUBLER JACKMAN KETTLER SKEINER SPINNER SHUTTLER SOFTENER SPLITTER TEASELER

(THEATER —) FLYMAN STAGEMAN
(TOBACCO —) BULKER SIFTER STEMMER SCRAPMAN SPRIGGER STICKMAN STRIPPER
(UNSKILLED —) HELPER DILUTEE GREENER
(USELESS —) TOOL
(WHITE-COLLAR —) EFFENDI
(YARN —) SOURER CHAINER
(PL.) LABOR
WORKHORSE AVER AIVER TRESTLE SAWHORSE
WORKHOUSE UNION FACTORY WORKSHOP
WORKING PLAY GOING OPENCUT FUNCTION LABORAGE OPENCAST OPENWORK OPERATIC
(— ALONE) HATTING
(— HARD) HOPPING
(— OF MINE) GWAG CROSSCUT
(— ON) PRACTICE
(MINE —S) SPLIT
WORKMAN (ALSO SEE WORKER AND LABORER) BOSS HAND MATE ROTO CAGER CONER EXTRA FINER FLINT FLUER FROCK LAYER MAJOR MIXER POLER TONER TRIER TUBER BLOUSE BOOMER BOWLER BUCKER BUMMER COATER DIPPER DRIVER FORKER GAGGER HANGER LASTER LATHER MASTER NIPPER OILMAN PUFFER RUNNER SAMMER SCORER SHAKER SKIVER SLICER SLIDER SOAKER SPIKER STAGER STAVER TAPPER TARRER TEEMER TILTER TIPMAN TIPPER TOPMAN WARMER WASHER WETTER WRIGHT ARTISAN DRUMMER HOTSHOT LUDDITE SHOPMAN
(CHIEF —) BOSS
(CLUMSY —) BUNGLER
(FELLOW —) BULLY BUTTY
(PROFICIENT —) DEACON
(UNSKILLFUL —) BUTCHER
(PL.) VOLK
WORKMANLIKE DEFT ADEPT SKILLFUL
WORKMANSHIP HAND FABRIC OVERAGE ARTISANRY
WORKROOM DEN STUDY ATELIER
WORKS HACIENDA
(— OF CLOCK) WATCH
(SALT —) SALINA
WORKSHOP LAB SHED SHOP FORGE LODGE SMITHY ATELIER BOTTEGA HOSPITAL OFFICINA PLUMBERY SKINNERY
WORKTABLE BENCH
WORLD ORB LOKA VALE WARD EARTH WADRU WARDE CAREER PUBLIC KINGDOM MONDIAL CREATION CREATURE UNIVERSE
(— OF BOXING) FISTIANA
(— OF DARKNESS) SHEOL
(— OF DOGS) DOGDOM
(— OF FASHION) STYLEDOM SWELLDOM
(— OF GODS) DEVALOKA
(— OF THE DEAD) DEEP

(— OF WOMEN) FEMINIE
(ACADEMIC —) CAMPUS
(EXTERNAL —) NONEGO
(LOWER —) ORCUS
(PRIVATE —) AUTOCOSM
(THE —) FOLD
(TWO-DIMENSIONAL —) FLATLAND
WORLDLING DIVES
WORLDLY LAY WARLY CARNAL
EARTHY MUNDAL EARTHLY FLESHLY
MUNDANE PROFANE SECULAR
SENSUAL TERRENE
(NOT —) INTERIOR
WORLD-WEARY BLASE
WORLDWIDE GLOBAL ECUMENIC
GLOBULAR PLANETAL
WORLD-WISE KNOWING
WORM BOB EEL ESS LOA MAD LURG
NAIS NEMA ARTER CADEW FLUKE
LYTTA PIPER SCREW SNAKE
DRAGON NEREID NEREIS PALMER
PALOLO SHAMIR SYLLID SYLLIS
TEREDO VERMIS WRETCH ANNELID
ASCARID CARBORA ENOPLAN
SABELLA SAGITTA SERPENT
SERPULA SETARID SHUFFLE SPIONID
TAGTAIL TRICLAD WRIGGLE
BRANDLIN CEPHALOB CERCARIA
CHETAPOD CHETOPOD GILTTAIL
HELMINTH LEODICID MEASURER
POLYCLAD STRONGYL TRICHINA
VERMICLE TOOTHACHE
(— USED FOR BAIT) TAGTAIL
(BLOODSUCKING —) LEECH
(CADDIS —) CADEW PIPER CADBAIT
(FLUKE —) PLAICE
(MEASURING —) LOOPER
(MUD —) IPO LOA
(SHIP —) BROMA COBRA
(PL.) APODA ENTOZOA
WORM-EATEN PITTED DECAYED
VERMOULU WERMETHE
WORMER JAG
WORMHOLE PIQURE
WORMLIKE VERMIAN
WORMSEED AMBROSIA
WORMWOOD MOXA ABSINTH
CUDWEED COMPOSIT MINGWORT
WORMY EARTHY
WORN SEAR SERE USED PASSE
TRITE MAGGED MIZPAH SHABBY
CONTRITE
(— NEXT TO SKIN) INTIMATE
(— OUT) SHOT BANAL JADED SEELY
SPENT STALE STANK BEATEN
BEDRID BLEARY EFFETE SCREWY
SHABBY CRIPPLE FORWORN
DECREPID FOUGHTEN HARASSED
OBSOLETE STRICKEN
(— SMOOTH) BEATEN
WORRICOW DEVIL BUGABOO
BUGBEAR HOBGOBLIN
WORRIED TOEY UNEASY ANXIOUS
FRETTED STREAKED
WORRIT VEX WORRY DISTRESS
WORRY DOG HOE HOW HOX LUG
NAG RUX TEW VEX BAIT BITE CARE
CARK FAZE FIKE FRAB FRET FUSS
HARE MOIL STEW ANNOY CHEVY

CHOKE FEEZE GALLY HARRY HURRY
LURRY PHASE SCALD SHAKE TEASE
TOUSE TOWSE BOTHER CADDLE
COTTER CUMBER FERRET FIDGET
GALLOW HARASS HATTER HECTOR
INFEST MOIDER PESTER PLAGUE
POTHER ANXIETY CHAGRIN
HATCHEL TROUBLE TURMOIL
WHERRET FASHERIE STRANGLE
WORRYING ANXIOUS
WORSE VER WAR SEAMY
WORSEN DESCEND
WORSHIP GOD CULT HERY RANK
ADORE DULIA HONOR NAMAZ
WURTH YAJNA CREDIT PRAISE
REPUTE REVERE BAALISM ELOHISM
ICONISM IDOLISM IDOLIZE IMAGERY
OBSERVE BLESSING HIERURGY
VENERATE
(— OF SHAKESPEARE) BARDOLATRY
(FORM OF —) RITUAL
(HIGHEST KIND OF —) LATRIA
(INFERIOR KIND OF —) DULIA
(SERPENT —) OPHISM
(STAR —) SABAISM
WORSHIPER ISIAC BHAKTA PRAISER
IDOLATER
(— OF STARS) AKKUM SABIAN
(FIRE —) PARSI GHEBER GUEBER
PARSEE
(SERPENT —) SETHIAN SETHITE
WORSHIPFUL GOOD PROUD
NOTABLE
WORST ACE GET BEST LAST OUTDO
SHEND WREST DEFEAT
WORSTED GARN JERRY SERGE
VESSES WHIPCORD
WORT GAIL GYLE SWAT PLANT
LENGTH TUTSAN FILLING KRAUSEN
POTHERB
(FERMENTED —) FEED WASH
(UNFERMENTED —) GROUT
WORTH FECK MEED CARAT MERIT
PRICE VALOR VALUE BECOME
BOUNTY DESERT ESTEEM REGARD
RICHES VALENT VIRTUE WEALTH
DIGNITY PRETIUM VALIANT WORSHIP
SPLENDOR TREASURE VALIDITY
VALLIDOM
(NET —) CAPITAL
WORTHINESS DESERT WORSHIP
WORTHLESS BAD LOW WAF BAFF
BALD BARE BASE EVIL IDLE LEWD
RACA SLIM VAIN VILE WAFF BLANK
BLOWN DUSTY FLASH FOUTY LOSEL
PUTID SLINK SORRY STRAW WASHY
CHAFFY CHEESY CRUMMY DRAFFY
DRASTY DROSSY HOLLOW LIMMER
LITHER LUTHER NAUGHT PALTRY
TRASHY WOODEN BAGGAGE
FUSTIAN NAUGHTY PIPERLY
RAFFISH RUBBISH SCABBED SHILPIT
USELESS FECKLESS HARLOTRY
NUGATORY PRECIOUS RASCALLY
RUBBISHY TRUMPERY VAGABOND
WANWORDY WRETCHED
(— THING) AMBSACE
WORTHLESSNESS BELIAL UNTHRIFT
WORTHWHILE TANTI

WORTHY BIG DEAR FAIR GOOD
HOLY TIDY AUGHT CANNY DIGNE
EXALT HONOR JELLY NOBLE PIOUS
GENTLE CONDIGN GRADELY
PAREGAL THRIFTY ELIGIBLE
VALUABLE WAUREGAN
(— OF BELIEF) CREDIBLE
(— OF DEVOTION) HOLY
(— OF PRAISE) LAUDABLE
WOULD WAD WID WANT WISH
COULD SHOULD
(— NOT) NOLD WADNA WADDENT
(I —) CHUD CHOLD
WOUND ARR CUT HEW WIN BITE
CALK CLAW DUNT FAKE FOIN GALL
GORE HARM HURT MAIM PAIN PINK
RASE RAZE RIST SCAR SKAG SORE
STAB TEAR VULN WING BLESS
BROKE GANCH GRIEF KNIFE KNOCK
SHOOT STICK STING SUGAT THIRL
TOUCH BREACH BRUISE CREASE
ENTAME GRIEVE HARROW INJURE
LAUNCH LESION MARTYR OFFEND
PIERCE PLAGUE SCOTCH TRAUMA
AFFLICT ATTAINT BLIGHTY DIACOPE
GUNSHOT SCRATCH DISTRESS
FLANKARD FLEABITE INCISION
LACERATE SPURGALL
(— FROM BOAR'S TUSK) GANCH
GAUNCH
(— FROM BULL'S HORN) CORNADA
(— FROM RUBBING) GALL
(— IN DEER'S SIDE) FLANKARD
(— MADE BY THRUST) FOIN
(— ON FOOT) FIKE
(— WITH POINTED WEAPON) STAB
SWORD
(DEEP —) DIACOPE
(MINUTE —) PRICK
(TRIFLING —) FLEABITE
(PL.) NOUNS
WOUNDED HURT WUND VULNED
WINGED VULNOSE STRICKEN
WOUNDWORT BETONY ALLHEAL
HERCULES
WOU-WOU WAWA WAWAH CAMPER
GIBBON
WOVEN BROCHE BROWDEN
DAMASSE
(— FULL WIDTH) SEAMLESS
(— WIDE) BROAD
(— WITH RIB) SOLEIL
WOW HIT MEW BARK HOWL RAVE
WAIL WHINE SUCCESS
WRACK KELP RACK RUIN CUTWEED
DESTROY DOWNFALL EELGRASS
WRECKAGE
WRAITH WAFT FETCH GHOST SPOOK
DOUBLE SHADOW SWARTH
SPECTRE
WRANGLE RAG YED CAMP MOIL
SPAR TIFT ARGLE ARGUE BRAWL
CHIDE DAFER FLITE JOWER PLEAD
STRUT ARGUFY BICKER CAFFLE
CAMPLE CANGLE DACKER FRAPLE
FRATCH HAGGLE HASSLE JANGLE
RAGGLE THREAP BRABBLE
BRANGLE DISPUTE PICKEER

QUARREL SCRAFFLE SQUABBLE TIRRWIRR

WRANGLER CAMPER COWBOY GRATER HAFTER WRAGER DEBATER DEFENDER OPPONENT

WRANGLING JANGLE

WRAP HAP LAP LOT WAP BIND FURL ROLL WHIP CLASP CLOAK LAMBA MANTA NUBIA SERVE TWINE WOOLD AFGHAN BURLAP CLOTHE COCOON COOLER DOLMAN EMBALE MOIDER MUFFLE PATTOO SWATHE WRIXLE ENVELOP INVOLVE SWADDLE UMBELAP BARRACAN
(— **DEAD BODY**) CERE
(— **ONESELF**) HUDDLE
(— **UP HEAD**) MOB MOP MOBLE
(— **UP**) HAP MAIL ENROL IMPLY
(— **WIRE AROUND FISHING LINE**) GANGE
(— **WITH BANDAGE**) SWATHE
(PL.) SECRECY RESTRAINT

WRAPPER APRON COVER MOTTO PILCH SHAWL SMOCK COUPON FARDEL JACKET ENVELOP OVERALL SARPLER COVERING MAHARMAH WOOLPACK
(— **FOR BOOK**) JACKET
(— **FOR CUTLET**) PAPILLOTE
(— **WORN IN EGYPT**) GALABIA GALABEAH

WRAPPING WAP PACK GELILAH LAPPING COVERING MANTLING
(— **FOR DEAD**) CEREMENT
(— **OF HEBREW SCROLL**) GELILAH
(— **OF ROPE**) SERVICE

WRASSE COOK BALLAN CONNER CUNNER LABRID HOGFISH PIGFISH SEAWIFE CORKWING DONCELLA JANIZARY LADYFISH SENORITA

WRATH IRE FURY GRIM ANGER WROTH FELONY PASSION VIOLENCE

WRATHFUL IRY EVIL HIGH ANGRY IRATE WROTH IREFUL RAGING FURIOUS JEALOUS CHOLERIC

WREAK CAUSE AVENGE EXPEND GRATIFY INDULGE INFLICT REVENGE
(— **DESTRUCTION**) ESTREPE

WREATH LEI ORLE PLAY CROWN GREEN LAURE LORRE OLIVE TORSE WHORL WRASE ANADEM CRANTS CREASE LAUREL POTONG TORTIL CHAPLET CORONET CROWNAL DOLPHIN FESTOON GARLAND WRINKLE KELYPHYTE
(**SPIRAL** —) VOLUTION

WREATHE BIND WIND CRISP TWINE TWIST INTORT WRITHE CONTORT ENTWINE INTWIST INVOLVE

WREATHED SPIRY TORTIVE WRITHED INTORTED TORTILLE

WRECK HULK RUIN BLAST CRACK SHOOT SMASH WRACK DESPOIL DESTROY FOUNDER GODSEND SHATTER TORPEDO DEMOLISH SABOTAGE SHAMBLES
(**HUMAN** —) DERELICT

WRECKAGE FINDAL FLOTSAM GODSEND WAVESON SHAMBLES

WRECKED NOUGHT

WREN GIRL STAG TOPE CUTTY JENNY KITTY PEGGY SALLY STAID TYDIE SCUTTY TIDIFE TIDLEY TINTIE TOMTIT WRANNY BLUECAP MALURINE WRANNOCK

WRENCH KEY PIN RUG PULL RACK RICK RUGG TEAR CRICK CRINK FORCE THRAW THROW TWIST WRAMP WREST BEDKEY SPRAIN STRAIN TWEEZE DISTORT SPANNER SPANULE SQUINCH TORTURE TWISTLE

WREST REAR REND EXACT FORCE TWIST ARREST EXTORT WRENCH WRITHE ABSTORT WIREDRAW
(— **AWAY**) STRIP DESPOIL

WRESTLE PRAY RASSLE SQUIRM TUSSLE WRAXLE WRITHE GRAPPLE SCUFFLE THRIMBLE THRUMBLE

WRESTLER MATMAN WELTER CLICKER MATSTER GRAPPLER

WRESTLING SUMO PALESTRA WRAXLING
(— **TECHNIQUE**) GLIMA

WRETCH DOG MIX FILE WARY MISER SLAVE THING BUGGER PERSON SQUALL BRETHEL CAITIFF CAMOOCH CHINCHE GLUTTON HILDING SCROYLE CREATURE MESCHANT POLTROON RECREANT SCULLION

WRETCHED EVIL FOUL MEAN DAWNY DEENY GAUNT WISHT WOFUL YEMER CAITIF DISMAL MEAGER PALTRY SHABBY SICKLY UNLEAD UNLEDE WOEFUL ABYSMAL BENEATH FORLORN OUTWORN SQUALID UNSEELY MESCHANT
(— **PERSON OR ANIMAL**) MISERY

WRIGGLE REG RIG FRIG WIND WRIG SLIDE WRELE WRING SQUIRM WAMBLE WANGLE WARPLE WIDDLE WIMPLE WINTLE WRITHE EYEBROW SNIGGLE TWIDDLE TWINGLE WRABILL WRESTLE SCRIGGLE SQUIGGLE

WRIGGLING EELY SCRIGGLE SQUIGGLY

WRIGGLY SNAKY SNAKISH SQUIRMING

WRING RACK DRAIN EXACT SCREW TWIST WREST EXTORT OPPRESS SQUEEZE TORMENT TORTURE
(— **THE NECK**) SCRAG

WRINGER RUNG WRUNG SQUEEZER

WRINKLE RUT DRAW FOLD FURL HINT KNIT LIRK RUCK RUGA SEAM BREAK CRIMP CRISP DELVE FAULT FRILL REEVE RIVEL SNIRL BUCKLE COCKLE CRAVAT CREASE FURROW METHOD PUCKER RIMPLE RUMPLE RUNKLE SCRIMP WREATH BLEMISH CRINKLE CRUMPLE CRUNKLE FROUNCE FRUMPLE CONTRACT IRRUGATE RUGOSITY
(— **OF FLESH**) CRAVAT

WRINKLED PURFLY RUGATE RUGGED RUGOSE RUGOUS SEAMED

COCKLED SAVOYED CRUMPLED FURROWED PUCKERED WRIZZLED

WRINKLING KNIT KNOT FROWN

WRIST CARPUS SHACKLE

WRISTER MUFFETEE

WRISTLET WRISTER MUFFETEE

WRISTWATCH BAGUET BAGUETTE

WRIT AIEL CAPE MISE PONE TOLT ALIAS BREVE BRIEF ERROR RECTO UTRUM BRIEVE CAPIAS ELEGIT EXTENT VENIRE ACCOUNT DEDIMUS DETINUE EXIGENT LATITAT PLURIES PRECEPT PROCESS SUMMONS WARRANT CESSAVIT COSINAGE DETAINER DOCUMENT FORMEDON MANDAMUS MITTIMUS NOVERINT PRAECIPE QUOMINUS REPLEVIN SUBPOENA TESTATUM WARRANTY
(— **FOR SUMMONING EXTRA JURORS**) TALES

WRITE INK PEN BACK BOOK DITE DRAW READ CLERK DRAFT STYLE AUTHOR ENFACE INDITE SCRIBE SCRIVE ADDRESS COMPILE COMPOSE DICTATE EMPAPER EXARATE BIOGRAPH INSCRIBE
(— **ADDRESS**) BACK
(— **BRIEFLY**) JOT
(— **CARELESSLY**) DASH SCRAWL SCRIBBLE
(— **DOWN**) SIGN BREVE DENOTE RECORD AMORTIZE DESCRIBE
(— **FURTHER**) ADD
(— **HASTILY**) SCRATCH SCRIBBLE SQUIGGLE
(— **IN A LARGE HAND**) ENGROSS
(— **IN LARGE CHARACTERS**) TEXT
(— **ON FRONT OF BILL**) ENFACE
(— **PASTORAL POEMS**) ENFACE
(— **WHAT IS NOT TRUE**) FABLE

WRITER PEN BARD HACK PUFF ALVAR GHOST ODIST SQUIB AUTHOR FATHER GLOZER HEROIC LAWYER LETTER MUNSHI NOTARY PENMAN PRABHU PROSER PURVOE SCRIBE TRAGIC YEOMAN ADAPTER ADSMITH ANALYST DIARIST ELOHIST ESSAYER GLOSSER GNOMIST HYMNIST IAMBIST JUVENAL LAUDIST MUNCHEE PENSTER PROPHET PROSAIC REVUIST SCRIVER STYLIST SUMMIST TEXTMAN AUGUSTAN BLURBIST COMEDIAN COMPOSER DECADENT DECADIST DIDACTIC EMBOSSER EPISTLER ESSAYIST FABLEIST FABULIST GROMATIC HUMORIST IDYLLIST MONODIST MOONSHEE NOVELIST PARODIST PENWOMAN PREFACER PRESSMAN PROSAIST PROSEMAN PSALMIST REVIEWER SCRIPTER VERSEMAN
(— **OF BURLESQUE**) GABBER
(**FREE-LANCE** —) CREEPER
(**HACK** —) PENSTER
(**INCOMPETENT** —) BOTCHER

WRITHE WRY WIND THROW TWIRL TWIST WRING SQUIRM TERVEE WAMBLE WRABBE WRENCH AGONIZE WRESTLE WRIGGLE

WRINGLE CONVOLVE
WRITHING EELY WRING WRITHY
WRITING BOOK FAIT PAGE POEM
KANJI LIBEL CADJAN GOSSIP
LEGEND LETTER PAGINE SCRIPT
SCRITE SCRIVE UNCIAL ARTICLE
DIPLOMA ESCRIPT SCREEVE
/.POCRYPH CONTRAÇT DOCUMENT
GRAVAMEN HARANGUE KAKEMONO
LETTRURE LIPOGRAM PAMPHLET
SCRIBING SONNETRY
(— **OF LITTLE VALUE**) STUFF
SCRIBBLE
(— **ON PAPER SCROLL**) MAKIMONO
(— **ON SILK**) KAKEMONO
(— **UNDER SEAL**) BOND
(**BITTER** —) DIATRIBE
(**CARELESS** —) SCRAWL
(**CRAMPED** —) NIGGLE
(**CURSIVE** —) JOINHAND
(**HUMOROUS** —S) FACETIAE
(**ILLUMINATED** —) FRACTUR
(**MUSICAL** —) GIMEL GYMEL
(**PRETENTIOUS** —) FUSTIAN
(**SACRED** —) ARANYAKA BRAHMANA
SCRIPTURE
(**SHORT** —) SCRIP
(**SYLLABIC** —) KANA
(**VAPID** —) WASH
(**VERBOSE** —) TOOTLE
(PL.) LEGENDA ARANYAKA
POSTHUMA
WRITING CASE STANDISH
WRITTEN KETIB KETHIB KTHIBH
GRAPHIC LITERAL

(— **ABOVE**) SS
(— **AFTER**) ADSCRIPT
(— **HASTILY**) STRAY
WROCLAW BRESLAU
WRONG BAD CAR ILL MIS OUT WET
AWRY HARM HURT SORE SOUR
TORT WITE AGATE AGLEE AGLEY
AMISS CRIME DUTCH FALSE GLEED
GRIEF MALUM UNFIT WATHE WOUGH
AGUILT ASTRAY BLOOEY FAULTY
INJURE INJURY NOUGHT OFFEND
SARAAD SINFUL UNTRUE WICKED
WONDER ABUSION DAMNIFY
DEFRAUD IMMORAL INJURIA
MISBEDE NAUGHTY UNRIGHT
VIOLATE AGGRIEVE COCKEYED
MISTAKEN PERVERSE UNLEEFUL
(**CIVIL** —) TORT
(**IMAGINARY** —) WINDMILL
WRONGDOER ACTOR SINNER
FAULTER MISDOER OFFENDER
WRONGDOING MISS CRIME FAULT
DEFAULT
WRONGHEADED WRY PERVERSE
WRONGFUL UNFAIR UNJUST
TORTIOUS TORTUOUS UNLAWFUL
WRONGLY AMISS BADLY FALSE
NOUGHT UNRICHT UNRIGHT
OVERWART
WROTH ANGRY IRATE IREFUL
WROUGHT BEATEN CARVEN
FORMED SHAPED VROCHT CREATED
HAMMERED
(**ELABORATELY** —) LABORED

WRY ASKEW AVERT TWIST WRING
WRONG WRITHE DEFLECT DISTORT
TWISTED WRITHEN SATURNINE
WRYNECK IYNX JYNX SLAB WEET
LOXIA PEABIRD WEETBIRD
WYCH ELM WITCH WITCHEN
WYLIECOAT WALYCOAT NIGHTGOWN
PETTICOAT
WYND HAW ALLEY CLOSE

WYOMING

CAPITAL: CHEYENNE
COUNTY: TETON UINTA GOSHEN
BIGHORN LARAMIE NIOBRARA
INDIAN: ARAPAHO
LAKE: JACKSON
MOUNTAIN: ELK CLOUD GANNET
HOBACK FREMONT ATLANTIC
SHERIDAN
MOUNTAIN RANGE: TETON
ABSARO BIGHORN LARAMIE
RATTLESNAKE
NICKNAME: EQUALITY
RIVER: GREEN SNAKE PLATTE
POWDER BIGHORN
STATE BIRD: MEADOWLARK
STATE FLOWER: PAINTBRUSH
STATE TREE: COTTONWOOD
TOWN: CODY LUSK CASPER
BUFFALO LARAMIE RAWLINS
WORLAND GREYBULL
KEMMERER SHERIDAN
SUNDANCE

X EX XRAY ERROR MISTAKE
XANTHIC YELLOW
XANTHIPPE (HUSBAND OF —)
  SOCRATES
XANTHIPPUS (SON OF —) PERICLES
XEBEC SHIP CHEBEC CHEBECK
  SHABEQUE
XENIUM GIFT DAINTY DELICACY
XERES JEREZ SHERRY

XHOSA KAFIR KAFFIR
  (PL.) AMAKOSA AMAXOSA
XIPHISTERNUM XIFOID
XIPHOSURUS LIMULUS
X-RAY UROGRAM
XUREL SCAD SAUREL
XUTHUS (ADOPTED SON OF —) ION
  (BROTHER OF —) DORUS AEOLUS
  (FATHER OF —) HELLEN

(WIFE OF —) CREUSA
XYLEM HADROM HADROME XYLOGEN
XYLOID WOODY LIGNEOUS
XYLOPHONE REGAL SARON BALAFO
  GAMBANG GAMELAN MARIMBA
  BALAPHON GAMELANG GIGELIRA
  STICCADO
XYSTUS WALK XYST PORTICO
  TERRACE

Y WY YA WYE YOD YOKE YANKEE
(— **CONNECTION**) SIAMESE
(— **COORDINATE**) SINE
YABBER TALK JABBER LANGUAGE
YABBY CRAWLIE
YACARE CAIMAN CAYMAN JACARE
YACHT SAIL SCOW BRUTE YATCH
DINGHY SONDER YEAGHE KEELBOAT
YAFF YAP BARK YELP
YAFFLE ARMFUL YAFFIL
YAHOO BRUTE CLOWN ROWDY
BUMPKIN
YAHWEH GOD JAVE JAHVAH
YAHWIST JEHOVIST
YAK GAG JOKE LAUGH BULBUL
SARLAK SARLYK YAMMER CHATTER
YAKALA JAGA
YAKKA WORK LABOR
YAKUT SAKHA
YAM HOI UBE UBI UVE JAMB LIMA
RAIL TUGUI IGNAME INAMIA INHAME
POTATO BONIATA
(**TARO** —) KOKO
YAM BEAN KAMAS JICAMA WAYAKA
SINCAMAS
YAMEN COURT YAMUN OFFICE
YAMEO LLAMEO
YAMMER CRY WAIL SCOLD WHINE
YEARN YOMER GRUMBLE WHIMPER
YAMP YAMPA SQUAWROOT
YANAN NOZI
YANG HONK GURJUN
YANK FLOG JERK SLAP HOICK
SNAKE BUFFET
YAP BARK YAWP YELP MOUTH
SCOLD WAFFLE BUMPKIN CHATTER
KYOODLE
YAPOK YAPOCK OPOSSUM OYAPOCK
YAQUI YAKI HIAQUI
YARD HAW YED CREW CROW DUMP
FOLD SKID SPAR TILT COURT
GARTH PATIO STICK CANCHA
HOPPET LOANIN CURTAIN GARSTON
KNACKERY OUTGARTH
(— **OF SAWMILL**) DUMP
(— **WHERE COWS ARE MILKED**)
LOANIN LOANING
(1-16TH OF A —) NAIL
(1-3RD OF CUBIC —) CARTLOAD
(20 —S) SCORE
(5 AND A HALF —S) ROD
(FINAL —) FELL
(GRASSY —) GARSTON
(PAVED —) CAUSEY
(POULTRY —) BARTON
(SAIL —) RAE
YARD GRASS ELEUSINE MANGRASS
YARDLAND VERGE VIRGATE
YARDMASTER DINGER
YARDSTICK VERGE YAIRD METRIC
MEASURE METWAND METEWAND
STANDARD
YARE YAR AYRE YORE BRISK READY
LIVELY NIMBLE PROMPT
YARETA LLARETA
YARM WAIL NOISE OUTCRY SHRIEK
YARN ABB END FOX CORD GARN
GIMP PIRN SILK SLIP WEFT WHIP
DYNEL FLOSS GRAIN INKLE PITCH

ALASKA ANGORA BERLIN BROACH
CADDIS COTTON CREWEL CUFFER
DACRON ESTRON FLORET FRIEZE
MERINO MOTTLE PEELER RATINE
SAXONY SINGLE STRAND THREAD
VINYON WOOLEN ZEPHYR ACETATE
CADDICE FILLING GENAPPE INGRAIN
MELANGE RACKING SCHAPPE
VIGOGNE WORSTED ASBESTOS
BOURETTE CHENILLE FORTISAN
ROUNDING SPINNING VIGOREUX
WHEELING
(— **FOR WARP**) ABB
(— **FROM FLOSS SILK**) FLORET
(— **SIZE**) TYPP
(BALL OF —) CLEW CLUE
(BITS OF ROPE —) THRUMS
(BUNDLE OF —) PAD
(CONICAL MASS OF —) COP
(ELASTIC —) LASTEX
(EXAGGERATED —) STRETCHER
(FINE SOFT —) ZEPHYR KASHMIR
CASHMERE
(LINEN —) SPINEL
(ROLL OF —) PRICK CHEESE
(ROPE —S) SOOGEE
(SMALL PIECE OF SPUN —) RABAND
ROBBIN ROPEBAND
(UNEVEN —) BOUCLE
(PL.) FOX MENDINGS
YARRAN GIDYA MYALL GIDGEA
GIDGEE
YARROW ALLHEAL CAMMOCK
MAUDLIN MILFOIL
YASHIRO SHA
YASHMAK VEIL ASMACK YAKMAK
YATAGHAN SABER ATAGHAN
SIMITAR
YATTER CHATTER PRATTLE
YAUD MARE YADE
YAUPON ASSI HOLLY YUPON CASINA
CASSINE
YAUTIA COCO TARO TANIA COCKER
TANIER MALANGA
YAW GAPE YAWN LURCH SHEER
BROACH SWERVE
YAWL HOWL DANDY MIZZEN SCREAM
SCHOKKER
YAWN GAP GALP GANE GANT GAPE
YANE ABYSM CHAUM CAVITY
TEDIUM DULLNESS
YAWNING HIANT CHASMA GAPING
OSCITANT
YAWP BAWL GAPE STARE SQUAWK
YAMMER COMPLAIN
YAWS TUBBA TUBBOE
YAWWEED RHUBARB
YAYA COPA
YEA YA YES YOY YIGH TRULY
ASSENT REALLY VERILY
YEAN EAN LAMB
YEANLING KID LAMB EANLING
YEAR EAR SUN AYRE HAAB TIME
ANNUS VAGUE WINTER ZODIAC
TOWMOND TZOLKIN BIRTHDAY
(— **OF EMANCIPATION**) JUBILEE
(ACADEMIC —) SESSION
(IN THIS —) HA
(LAST —) FERNYEAR

(MANY —S) AGE
(MAYAN —) TUN HAAB
(SABBATICAL —) JUBILE JUBILEE
(PL.) SEASONS
YEARBOOK ANNUAL SERIAL
ANNUARY
YEARLING COLT HORNOTINE
YEARLY ANNUAL SOLEMN
YEARN HO YEN ACHE BURN EARN
GAPE HONE IRNE LONG PANT PINE
SIGH CRAVE GREEN GRIEN ASPIRE
CURDLE GRIEVE HANKER YAMMER
YEARNING EROS DESIRE HANKER
RENNET CRAVING EARNFUL
HOMESICK
YEAST BEE EST BARM BEES EAST
KOJI SOTS FROTH SPUME LEAVEN
NEWING RISING SIZING TORULA
FERMENT SIZZING EMPTINGS
(FILM —) FLOR
YEASTY LIGHT FROTHY TRIVIAL
RESTLESS
YEGG ROBBER BURGLAR
YELL CRY CALL GOWL HOWL ROAR
YARM YAUP YOWL YOWT GOLLY
SHOUT TIGER BELLOW GOLLAR
HOLLER SCREAM YAMMER YELLOCH
SCRONACH
YELLOW (ALSO SEE COLOR) OR
GULL AMBER BLAKE BLOND FAVEL
FLAVE JAUNE PALEW SHELL YELWE
ALMOND BANANA FLAVID MELINE
MIMOSA NUGGET OXGALL BISCUIT
JASMINE JONQUIL LEGHORN
MEXICAN MUSTARD NANKEEN
OATMEAL POPCORN SAFFRON
TILLEUL WHEATEN YUCATAN
AUREOLIN GENERALL ICTEROID
LUMINOUS MARIGOLD ORPIMENT
PRIMROSE
(— **AS BUTTER**) BLAKE
(BROWNISH —) FULVID FULVOUS
(GOLDEN —) FLAVID
(GREENISH —) ACACIA
(INDIAN —) PURI PURREE
(LEMON —) GENERALL
YELLOW ALDER SAGEROSE
YELLOW BEDSTRAW CRUDWORT
CURDWORT FLEAWEED
YELLOW BUGLE IVA IVE IVY
YELLOW CLINTONIA DOGBERRY
YELLOW FOXTAIL STICKERS
YELLOW GENTIAN FELWORT
YELLOWHAMMER SKYT YITE
AMMER GOWDY SKITE GLADDY
GOLDIE VERDIN YORLIN FLICKER
GLADEYE YELDRIN YOLDRING
(— **STATE**) ALABAMA
YELLOW IRIS SEDGE LEVERS
DAGGERS
YELLOWISH SALLOW ICTERINE
SAFFRONY
(— **GREEN**) GLAUCOUS
(— **RED**) FALLOW
YELLOW JACKET VESPA VESPID
YELLOW JASMINE WOODBINE
YELLOWLEGS KILLCU TATLER
WINTER YELPER TATTLER
YELLOW MACKEREL CREVALLE

YELLOWNESS FLAVEDO
YELLOW POND LILY DUCK CLOTE
  CLOTS NUPHAR
YELLOW PRICKLE RUBIA
YELLOW RATTLE RATEL
  COCKSCOMB LOUSEWORT
YELLOW TOADFLAX RAMSTEAD
YELLOW WAGTAIL OATEAR
YELLOW WATER LILY KELP WOKAS
YELLOWWOOD FUSTIC FUSTOC
  MANGWE VIRGILIA
YELP CRY YAP YIP BAFF BARK KIYI
  WAFF YAFF YAUP YAWP BOAST
  YAMPH AVOCET SQUEAL YAFFLE
  YELLOW
YELPING CRY

YEMEN

ANCIENT KINGDOM: SABA SHEBA
CAPITAL: SANA SANAA
COIN: RIYAL
MUSLIM SECT: SHIA SUNNI
PEOPLE: ZAIDI SHAFAI
PORT: MOKA MOCHA
REGION: TIHAMA
RULER: IMAM
TOWN: MOKA DAMAR MOCHA
  TAIZZ HODEIDA

YEN EYES LONG URGE YEARN
  DESIRE SUCKER LONGING
YEOMAN CHURL CLERK WRITER
  GOODMAN GUIDMAN GRAYCOAT
  RETAINER BEEFEATER
YERBA SANTA TARBUSH
YERK BEAT GOAD HURL JERK KICK
  STAB YARK THUMP EXCITE THRASH
  LASHING
YES AY DA IS JA OC SI YA AYE ISS
  YAS YAW YEA YEP YIS YUH YUS
  YEAH TRULY
YESTERDAY YESTER YESTREEN
  (OF —) PRIDIAN
YET AND BUT YIT EVEN STILL
  ALGATE HOWEER THOUGH FINALLY
  HOWEVER HITHERTO
YETT GATE
YEUK EWK YUK ITCH YUCK ITCHING
YEW YO HEW UGH YOE YOW VIEW
  TAXUS TOPIARY CHINWOOD
YEX YOLK
YIDDISH JEWISH
YIELD GO BOW CUT ILD PLY BEAR
  BEND CAST CEDE CESS COME CROP
  DRAG FOLD GIVE HEAR HELD LOUT
  QUIT SELL VAIL WAGE AGREE
  ALLOW AMAIN AVALE AWALE BRING
  BUDGE CARRY CAUSE DEFER
  GRANT HEALD HIELD LEAVE OFFER
  SLAKE STOOP ACCEDE AFFORD
  BOUNTY BUCKLE COMPLY CONFER
  FOLLOW IMPART OUTPUT RELENT
  RENDER RETURN SUBMIT SUPPLY
  SWERVE UNGIVE UPGIVE ABANDON
  ANALYZE CONCEDE DELIVER
  FURNISH HARVEST KNUCKLE
  OUTTURN PRODUCE PROVIDE
  REDOUND RUCKSEY SUCCUMB

BEGRUDGE FRUITAGE OVERGIVE
  UNDERLIE
(— FRUIT) ADDLE GRAIN
(— GRASS) GRAZE
(— OF FIELD) BURDEN
(— OF MINE) BONANZA
(— ON BOND) BASIS
(— TO TEMPTATION) FALL
(— TO) INDULGE
(— UP) LET FORLET FORLEIT
(— WELL) HIT BLEED
YIELDING ABLE MEEK NESH SOFT
  TALL WAXY NAISH WAXEN BONAIR
  FACILE FEEBLE FLABBY LIMBER
  OUTPUT PLIANT QUAGGY SUPPLE
  BEARING CESSION FINGENT FLACCID
  DEDITION LADYLIKE RECREANT
(— IRREGULARLY) BUNCHY
(— OF HORSE) FLEXION
(— STAGE) SEAR
(— TO IMPULSES) ABANDON
YIN SHANG
YIRMILIK METALLIK
YODEL SONG JODEL WARBLE
  REFRAIN
YODH IOD JOD
YOGA JOG
YOGI JOGI FAKIR FAKEER
YOKE BOW YOK BAIL CROW DRAG
  FORK HOOP PAIR POKE SOLE
  BANGY FURCA SHEBA SPANG
  BANGHY COUPLE INSPAN DRAGBAR
  HARNESS OPPRESS ADJUGATE
(— BAR) SKEY
(— TO HOLD DRILL) CROW
(— TO RAISE CANNON) BAIL
YOKEFELLOW MATE FELLOW
  PARTNER YOKEMATE
YOKEL YOB BOOR CLUB FARMER
  HAYSEED WAYBACK ABDERITE
  CHAWBACON
YOKING BOUT CONTEST MUGGING
YOLDRING YOWLEY
YOLK CENTER YELLOW ESSENCE
  LATEBRA VITELLUS
(HAVING A —) LECITHAL
YON YONDER THITHER BACKWARD
YONDER THAT THERE THOSE
  THITHER
YORE PAST YARE YEARS
(OF —) OLDEN
YORKER TICE
YORKSHIREMAN TIKE TYKE
  LEAROYD
YORUBA NAGO
YOU DU HE IT OW TA TU WE YA YO
  ONE OWE SHE SIE YOW YUH THOU
  YOUSE YOURSELF
YOUNG FRY JUV BIRD CALF DROP
  BIRTH BROOD FETUS FRUIT GREEN
  SMALL UNOLD JUNIOR KINDLE
  JUVENAL IMMATURE YEANLING
  YOUTHFUL
(— OF ANY ANIMAL) FRY BABY
  CALF FOAL JOEY LAMB TOTO
(— OF BEAST) SLINK
(— OF BIRD) CHICK
(— OF CAMEL) COLT
(— OF DOG) WHELP

(— OF FISH) FRY
(— OF SEA TROOT) HERLING
(VERY —) SUCKING NEPHIONIC
  SHIRTTAIL
YOUNGER KID LESS PUNEE JUNIOR
  PUISNE OFFSPRING
YOUNGEST (— OF BROOD)
  WALLYDRAG
YOUNGSTER KID BIRD COLT CHILD
  YOUTH BUTTON SHAVER URCHIN
  YONKER YOUNKER SPALPEEN
YOUNKER DUPE CHILD KNIGHT
  NOVICE SQUIRE YUNKER
YOUR OR YO THY YAR YER OURE
  OWRE YOURN
YOURSELF ITSELF HERSELF HIMSELF
  ONESELF
YOUTH BOY BUD IMP LAD CHAP
  PAGE BAHUR CHABO GROOM HYLAS
  POULT PRIME SPRIG SWAIN WHELP
  BOCHUR BURSCH EPHEBE HOYDEN
  INFANT JUVENT KOUROS MASTER
  SPRING SQUIRT YONKER CALLANT
  EPHEBOS GOSSOON JUVENAL
  PUBERTY SAPLING YOUDITH
  YOUNGTH ENDYMION JUVENILE
  SPRINGAL
(— WHO SERVES LIQUORS)
  GANYMEDE
(GODDESS OF —) HEBE
(IMPUDENT —) SQUIRT
(NON-JEWISH —) SHEGETZ
(PERT —) PRINCOX
(RUDE —) HOYDEN
(RUSSIAN — ORGANIZATION)
  KOMSOMOL
(SILLY —) CALF SLENDER
(WELLBORN —) CHILD
YOUTHFUL RATH FRESH GREEN
  YOUNG BOYISH GOLDEN JUNIOR
  MAIDEN NEANIC VIRGIN YOUTHY
  LADDISH PUERILE YOUNGLY
  IMMATURE JUVENILE SPRINGAL
  VIGOROUS
YOUTHFULNESS JEUNESSE
YOWL GOWL HOWL WAIL YELL YELP
YUAN DOLLAR
YUAPIN YARURA
YUCCA LILY PITA YUCA DATIL IZOTE
  PALMA JOSHUA LILIAL LILIUM
  PALMITO SOAPWEED
YUGA KALI

YUGOSLAVIA

CAPITAL: BEOGRAD BELGRADE
COIN: PARA DINAR
GULF: KVARNER
LAKE: SCUTARI
MEASURE: RIF AKOV RALO DONUM
  KHVAT LANAZ STOPA MOTYKA
  PALAZE RALICO
MOUNTAIN: TRIGLAV DURMITOR
MOUNTAIN RANGE: DINARIC
PEOPLE: SERB CROAT SLOVENE
PORT: KOTOR SPLIT RIJEKA
  NOVISAD BELGRADE DUBROVNIK
REGION: BANAT BOSINA SRBIJA
RIVER: DRIM IBAR KRKA SAVA

TISA BOSNA CAZMA DRAVA
DRINA RASKA TAMIS VRBAS
DANUBE MORAVA VARDER
VELIKA NERETVA
TOWN: NIS AGRAM BUDVA RTANJ
SPLIT USKUB BITOLA MORAVA
MOSTAR OSIJEK PRILEP

RAGUSA RIJEKA SKOPJE
VARDAR ZAGREB CATTARO
NOVISAD PRIZREN MONASTIR
SARAJEVO SUBOTICA
WEIGHT: OKA OKE DRAMM TOVAR
WAGON SATLIJK

YULE NOEL CHRISTMAS
YUMA CUCHAN
YUMAN PATAYAN
YUNX WRYNECK
YURT TENT

Z ZAD ZED ZEE ZETA ZULU IZARD
ZEBRA IZZARD
(SHAPED LIKE A —) OPENBAND
ZABAGLIONE SABAYON
ZAFFER SMALT SAFFIOR ZAPHARA
ZAGREUS (FATHER OF —) JUPITER
(MOTHER OF —) PROSERPINE

ZAIRE
CAPITAL: KINSHASA
LAKE: KIVU MWERU
LANGUAGE: KIKONGO LINGALA
SWAHILI TSHILUBA
MONEY: ZAIRE
MOUNTAIN RANGE: MITUMBA
VIRUNGA RUWENZORI
PROVINCE: KIVU KASAI EQUATOR
KATANGA ORIENTAL
RIVER: RUKI CONGO DENGU IBINA
KASAI LINDI ZAIRE LIKATI
LOMAMI LUKUGA UBANGI
ARUWIMI LUALABA LULONGA
TOWN: BAYA BOMA LEBO AKETI
KAMINA KIKWIT BUTEMBO
KOLWEZI BAKWANGA YANGAMBI

ZAMBIA
CAPITAL: LUSAKA
COIN: KWACHA
CONGO: KINSHASA
FALLS: VICTORIA
LAKE: MWERU BANGWEULU
TANGANYIKA
LANGUAGE: LOZI BEMBA TONGA
LUVALE NYANJA AFRIKAANS
MOUNTAIN RANGE: MUCHINGA
RIVER: KAFUE LUANGWA LUAPULA
ZAMBEZI
TOWN: KITWE NDOLA LUAPULA
LUANSHYA MUFULIRA

ZAMBO CHINO SAMBO CAFUSO
CURIBOCA
ZAMIA BANGA CICAD CYCAD
COONTIE
ZAMINDAR MALIK
ZAMOUSE GAMOUS
ZAMPOGNA BAGPIPE PANPIPE
ZANDER ZANT PERCID SANDER
SANDRA
ZANTHOXYLUM FAGARA
ZANY FOOL CRAZY TOADY SAWNEY
BUFFOON IDIOTIC CLOWNISH
SCREWBALL
ZANZIBAR (SEE TANZANIA)
ZAPARO IQUITO
ZAPATEROL LIMA BOXWOOD
CERILLO
ZARAH KAZOO
ZEAL FIRE MOOD ARDOR FLAME
HEART FERVOR WARMTH DEVOTION
GOODWILL JEALOUSY
(WITH —) DINGDONG
ZEALOT BIGOT VOTARY VOTEEN

ZELANT DEVOTEE FANATIC
CANANEAN SERAPHIC SICARIUS
VOTARESS VOTARIST
ZEALOUS HOT HIGH ARDENT FERVID
STRING CORDIAL DEVOTED
EARNEST EMULOUS FERVENT
FORWARD JEALOUS PUSHFUL
VIGOROUS
(— ABOUT BEAUTY) ESTHETIC
ZEALOUSLY FAST INNERLY
HEARTILY
ZEBRA DAUW EQUID HORSE QUAGGA
SOLIPED
ZEBRAWOOD ARAROBA ZINGANA
ZEBU BRAMIN BRAGMAN BRAHMIN
(HYBRID OF — AND CATTLE)
CATTABU
(HYBRID OF — AND YAK) ZOBO
ZECCHINO SEQUIN
ZEN (— PARADOX) KOAN
(— QUESTIONS) MONDO
ZENANA HAREM HARIM SERAGLIO
ZENICK SURICATE
ZENITH ACME PEAK HIGHT HEIGHT
SUMMIT VERTEX
ZEOLITE ANALCIME ANALCITE
ZEPHYRUS FAVONIUS
(SON OF —) CARPOS
(WIFE OF —) CHLORIS
ZEPPELIN ZEP ZEPP AIRSHIP
ZERO OH NIL NUL BLOB DUCK NULL
AUGHT CLOSE EMPTY OUGHT TRAIN
ABSENT CIPHER NAUGHT LACKING
NOTHING NULLITY SCRATCH
NINETEEN
ZEST EDGE ELAN JASM GUSTO
FLAVOR RELISH STINGO PIQUANCY
ZESTFUL RACY SPICY BREEZY
ZETES (BROTHER OF —) CALAIS
(FATHER OF —) BOREAS
(MOTHER OF —) ORITHYIA
ZETHUS (BROTHER OF —) AMPHION
(FATHER OF —) JUPITER
(SE)(MOTHER OF —) ANTIOPE
ZEUS ZAN SOTER ALASTOR CRONION
KRONION POLIEUS CRONIDES
(BROTHER OF —) HADES POSEIDON
(FATHER OF —) KRONOS
(MOTHER OF —) RHEA
(SISTER OF —) HERA HESTIA
DEMETER
(SON OF —) ARES
(WIFE OF —) HERA JUNO METIS
THEMIS EURYNOME
ZEUXIS UNDERLAY
ZIGZAG BOYAU CRANK BROKEN
INDENT CRANKLE CHEVONRY
FLEXUOSE TRAVERSE
ZIMARRA CYMAR SIMAR CASSOCK
ZIMB FLY ZEBUB
ZINC FAR SPELT ZINCUM SPELTER
TUTENAG EXCLUDER
ZING PEP VIM ZIP DASH SNAP
ENERGY SPIRIT
ZINGEL PERCID
ZINKE CORNET

ZINNIA CRASSINA
ZION SION ISRAEL UTOPIA
ZIONIST IRGUNIST
ZIOSITE THULITE
ZIP VIM DASH SNAP FORCE WHISK
BUTTON ENERGY STINGO
ZIPPER FASTENER
ZIRCON JARGON AZORITE MALACON
HYACINTH STARLITE
ZITHER KIN CANON CANUN GUSLI
KANOON CITHARA GITERNE GITTERN
AUTOHARP GALEMPONG
(JAPANESE —) KOTO
ZITHER HARP KOTO
ZIZITH SISITH FRINGES TASSELS
TSITSITH
ZO DZO ZOH ZOBO
ZOARITE BIMMELER
ZOBO ZO DZO ZOH ZOBU
ZODIAC GIRDLE BALDRIC BAWDRICK
SIGNIFIER
(SIGN OF —) LEO RAM BULL CRAB
FISH GOAT LION ARIES LIBRA SCALE
TWINS VIRGO ARCHER CANCER
GEMINI PISCES TAURUS SCORPIO
AQUARIUS CAPRICORN
ZONA ZOSTER
ZONE BED AREA BAND BEAM BELT
HALO PLAGE TRACT CIRCLE REGION
ZODIAC CLIMATE HORIZON
ZOMULET CINGULUM FRONTIER
HABENULA HISTOGEN STRINGER
(— OF CONFLICT) FRONT
(— OF FLAME) MANTLE
(— OF MINERALS) CORONA
(— OF VENUS) CEST CESTUS
(ABYSSAL —) BASSALIA
(PALEONTOLOGIC —S) ASSISE
(SAFETY —) ISLET ISLAND REFUGE
(STRATOGRAPHIC —) HEMERA
(WELDING —) ROOT
ZOOECIUM AUTOPORE
ZOOID PERSON SIPHON BRYOZOAN
HYDRANTH POLYPIDE ZOOTHOME
ZOOPHYTE CORAL SPONGE
HYDROID
ZOOSPORE MONAD SWARMER
ZOOCARP
ZORIL SKUNK POWCAT CHINCHE
POLECAT MUISHOND
ZOROASTRIAN GABAR PARSI
PARSEE
ZOROASTRIANISM MAZDAISM
ZOUAVE ZUZU SCALER ZOUZOU
ZOUNDS OONS WAUNS ZOONS
ZUCCETO CALOTTE SOLIDEO
SKULLCAP
ZUNI CIBOLAN SHALAKO
ZWINGLIAN TIGURINE
ZYGOMATIC JUGAL
ZYGOSPORE COPULA
ZYGOTE OOSPERM OOSPORE
SPORONT OOKINETE
ZYME YEAST ZYMIN ENZYME
FERMENT
ZYRIAN KOMI SYRYAN